Contributors

All Music Guide

Vladimir Bogdanov, President
Chris Woodstra, Vice President
of Content Development,
Editor-in-Chief

AMG Popular Music Department

John Bush, Senior Editor
Stephen Thomas Erlewine,
Senior Editor
Joslyn Layne, Associate Editor

Assistant Editors

Al Campbell
Andy Kellman
Greg McIntosh
Sean Westergaard
Tim Sendra
Stacia Proefrock
Heather Phares
Mackenzie Wilson

Staff Writers

Thom Jurek
Wade Kergan

Copy Editing

Jason Birchmeier
Amy Cloud
Aaron Warshaw
Dave Lynch

Data Processing

Mark Donkers, Manager
Jonathan Ball
Matt Collar
Jack "Lee" Isles
Zac Johnson
Aaron Latham
Corwin Moore
David Serra
Donn Stroud
Rob Theakston
Dan Trenz
Chris True

Contributors

Iván Adaime
Aric Laurence Allen
Jason Anderson
Rick Anderson
Jason Ankeny
Glenn Astarita

Jon Azpiri
Jason Birchmeier
Roxanne Blanford
Drago Bonacich
Mario Mesquita Borges
Matt Borghi
Adam Bregman
Brandon Burke
John Bush
Nathan Bush
Blake Butler
Becky Byrkit
Al Campbell
Dean Carlson
Matt Carlson
Bil Carpenter
Daphne G.A. Carr
Sean Carruthers
Garth Cartwright
Bill Cassel
David M. Childers
Paul Clifford
Matt Conaway
Dave Connolly
Stephen Cook
Sean Cooper
François Couture
Rosalind Cummings-Yeates
Peter J. D'Angelo
Mike DaRonco
Michael Di Bella
Tim DiGravina
Charlotte Dillon
Eleanor Ditzel
John Dougan
Travis Drageset
John Duffy
Kurt Edwards
Jason Elias
Stephen Thomas Erlewine
Keith Farley
Kathleen C. Fennessy
Trent Fitzgerald
John Floyd
Luke Forrest
Christina Fuoco
Robert Gabriel
Michael Gallucci
Chris Genzel
Daniel Gioffre
Dan Gizzi
Joshua Glazer
David Gonzales
Nicholas Gordon
Rev. Keith A. Gordon
Michael Gowan
David Gozales

Thom Granger
Adam Greenberg
JT Griffith
Tim Griggs
Erik Hage
Andrew Hamilton
Amy Hanson
Craig Harris
Ralph Heibutzki
Alex Henderson
John Hinrichsen
Ed Hogan
Kenyon Hopkin
Hal Horowitz
Steve Huey
Eddie Huffman
Ken Hunt
Jack LV Isles
Qa'id Jacobs
Jesse Jarnow
David Jehnzen
Zac Johnson
Liana Jonas
Thom Jurek
Matthew Kantor
Irene Kao
Jason Kaufman
Andy Kellman
Wade Kergan
Nic Kincaid
Ashleigh Kittle
Brad Kohlenstein
Todd Kristel
Steve Kurutz
Lynda Lane
Theresa E. LaVeck
Joslyn Layne
Dan LeRoy
Emilie Litzell
Steven Loewy
Johnny Loftus
Steven Losey
Bret Love
Lars Lovén
Craig Lytle
Jason MacNeil
Kingsley Marshall
Stewart Mason
Burgin Mathews
Derrick Mathis
Kieran McCarthy
Steven McDonald
Kembrew McLeod
Lee Meyer
Brad Mills
Ted Mills
Brian Musich

Alvaro Neder
Chris Nickson
Ed Nimmervoll
Alex Ogg
Brian O'Neill
Nick Pfeiffer
Heather Phares
Richard Pierson
Diana Potts
Greg Prato
Stacia Proefrock
Jose F. Promis
Mark Pytlik
Nathan Rabin
Brian Raftery
Ned Raggett
Darren Ratner
Mark Richardson
Vince Ripol
William Ruhlmann
Jim St. James
Mtume Salaam
Quibian 'Q' Salazar-Moreno
Tom Schulte
Linda Seida
Tom Semioli
Tim Sendra
Alan Severa
Joshua David Shanker
JoE Silva
Douglas Siwek
Chris Slawecki
Craig Robert Smith
David Ross Smith
Kerry L. Smith
Don Snowden
Charles Spano
Leo Stanley
Stanton Swihart
Jason D. Taylor
Ken Taylor
Rob Theakston
Scott Thill
Bradley Torreano
Blue Gene Tyranny
Richie Unterberger
Victor W. Valdivia
Joe Viglione
David Peter Wesolowski
Sean Westergaard
Brian Whitener
MacKenzie Wilson
Christopher Witt
Martin Woodside
Ron Wynn
John Young
Curtis Zimmermann

Introduction

Rap music. Even at the beginning of a new millennium, some cultural critics were still calling the phrase an anachronism. But anyone surprised by the ascendance of hip-hop as a commercial and artistic force need only look to the dawn of two other music revolutions, jazz and rock, to find the same types of dismissals and criticisms: "This isn't music, it's just noise"; "There's no melody"; and, best of all, "This music will never be popular." Even Kurtis Blow, the first rapper on a major label, didn't think the music had many prospects when he began recording back in the early '80s. Twenty years later, rap was dominating the pop charts, with well over half of the entries on the Top 100 coming from hip-hop artists or R&B singers with a heavy rap influence. And while, initially, most chart-bound artists needed to dilute their sound to really cross over, by the late '90s, it was hardly necessary at all; hardcore rappers like DMX and Jay-Z were selling millions of records with few concessions to mainstream audiences.

For those who didn't understand it or never investigated its origins, hip-hop seemed to have come from nowhere. Still, the MCs blasting out of teenagers' ghetto blasters during the late '80s relied on decades of formative influences: black power performers from Gil Scott-Heron to the Last Poets, jive bandleaders as far back as Cab Calloway, rhyming comedians like Pigmeat Markham, Jamaican deejays U-Roy and Dennis Alcapone as well as the dub poetry of Mutabaruka and Linton Kwesi Johnson, poetry from the African griots, even rapping radio DJs like Frankie Crocker. Hip-hop producers looked mostly to soul and funk, pumping up the power of the backbeat with drum machines, samplers, as well as the kinetic power of turntable techniques like beat-matching and scratching.

When it all began, however, back in the early '70s, it was merely DJs repeating the drumbreaks from funk or disco records for the benefit of their dancers (aka B-boys). By the end of the decade, innovators like Kool DJ Herc and Grandmaster Flash commanded a following in the Bronx and all over greater New York City. Rappers, who'd arrived on the scene merely to lead the crowds and hype the DJs, began turning the tide in 1979 when R&B hit-maker and entrepreneur Sylvia Robinson roped in a quartet of second-rank rhymers and recorded a massive dance hit, "Rapper's Delight," billed to the Sugarhill Gang.

Though DJs like Grandmaster Flash and Afrika Bambaataa remained a potent force in hip-hop, MC-led artists like the former B-boy Kurtis Blow and Treacherous Three came to rule the roost during the early '80s. Still mostly party music, hip-hop became known for simple, party-pleasing choruses and tons of novelty songs. The old-school era came to a close when Run-D.M.C. began crossing over in a big way during the mid-'80s. A generation of teenagers reared on rap finally came of age, inspiring some of the most artistic, uncompromising rap music ever produced: Eric B. & Rakim, Public Enemy, Boogie Down Productions, and dozens of other New York crews. The West Coast scene, active on a regional basis since the dawn of the '80s, finally broke through with success from N.W.A and (later) Ice Cube and Dr. Dre.

It was the end of the '80s when hip-hop finally broke through to the mainstream; even Run-D.M.C. had seemed like a lone success-maker, but with multi-million sales awards granted to MC Hammer and Vanilla Ice, it was clear that the major labels had finally found a way to consumers' hearts. The rap scene began fragmenting into many different styles: rough East Coast hardcore, an alternative rap scene also centered in New York (and initially championed by old school hero Afrika Bambaataa), smooth but ominous West Coast G-funk, the Southern sound of bounce and bass, a return-to-the-DJ movement dubbed turntablism, and countless regional styles who took elements of many different styles. Dr. Dre's immense success during 1993 with *The Chronic* proved that rap could be artistic *and* commercial, while more and more rappers found themselves scaling the charts without resorting to crossover moves.

By the beginning of the new millennium, the pop charts were, increasingly, a mirror of the rap charts. Also, hip-hop had permeated every continent with a youth culture, and dedicated scenes flourished in Japan, Sweden, Britain, France, and the Philippines, among others. Critics argued that, even while rappers professed allegiance to the streets that made them, their focus on a celebrity lifestyle had removed them from great music-making, while a burgeoning underground was left to push the music forward (Ironically, these artists were heard more by fans of alternative of music than by most rap fans.) Most importantly, though, millions of hip-hop fans ignored such petty disputes.

Just as happens with every other style of music, the best in rap and hip-hop will remain relevant for decades to come, and the best tool for wading through the large (and ever-increasing) pool of recordings is the one you have in your hands, *The All Music Guide to Hip-Hop*. Spanning recordings from four decades, this guide lays it all out, from Kool DJ Herc to Eminem, covering every artist in dozens of subgenres and pointing the way to their best recordings. Also, *The All Music Guide to Hip-Hop* is geared to listeners at every level, from those just beginning to investigate rap's golden age (roughly 1986 to 1992) to those wanting to check out the latest rappers in the underground hip-hop scene. Equal emphasis is given to the latest rappers hitting the charts, and nearly forgotten hip-hop crews from the birth of rap in the late '70s.

Separate sections at the back cover the best in various-artist compilations and mixtapes, style and scene essays (including recommended recordings), a list of the best songs and albums in each style, and a separate section with biographies and reviews on non-rap artists who've influenced rap—everyone from Jamaican deejays to proto-rappers from soul and jazz, contemporary R&B singers, and the best of the rap-rock groups. Few people who know music well would dispute the idea that hip-hop is the most distinctive and dynamic music developed since the advent of rock & roll, and with *The All Music Guide to Hip-Hop*, readers finally have a source to find the music that proves it.
—*John Bush*

All Music Guide to

hip-hop

THE DEFINITIVE GUIDE

TO RAP & HIP HOP

Edited by

Vladimir Bogdanov

Chris Woodstra

Stephen Thomas Erlewine

John Bush

AMG
All Media Guide

Backbeat
Books

All Media Guide has created the world's largest and most comprehensive information databases for music, videos, DVDs, and video games. With coverage of both in-print and out-of-print titles, the massive AMG archive includes reviews, plot synopses, biographies, ratings, images, titles, credits, essays, and thousands of descriptive categories. All content is original, written expressly for AMG by a worldwide network of professional staff and freelance writers specializing in music, movies, and games. The AMG databases—**All Music Guide**®, **All Movie Guide**®, **and All Game Guide**™— are licensed by major retailers and Internet content sites and are available to the public through its websites (www.allmusic.com, www.allmovie.com, www.allgame.com) and through its series of books: *All Music Guide, All Music Guide to Rock, All Music Guide to Country, All Music Guide to Jazz, All Music Guide to Blues, All Music Guide to Soul, All Music Guide to Hip-Hop*, and *All Music Guide to Electronica*.

All Media Guide 301 E. Liberty Street, Suite 400, Ann Arbor, MI 48104
T: 734/887-5600 F: 734/827-2492
www.allmediaguide.com email: feedback@allmediaguide.com

Published by **Backbeat Books**
600 Harrison Street, San Francisco, CA 94105
www.backbeatbooks.com
Email: books@musicplayer.com
An imprint of the Music Player Group
Publishers of *Guitar Player, Bass Player, Keyboard,* and other magazines
United Entertainment Media, Inc.
A CMP Information company

CMP
United Business Media

All Media Guide

Distributed to the book trade in the U.S. and Canada by
Publishers Group West, 1700 Fourth Street, Berkeley, CA 94710

Distributed to the music trade in the U.S. and Canada by
Hal Leonard Publishing, PO Box 13819, Milwaukee, WI 53213

Cover Design: Wagner Design, Ann Arbor, MI
Text Composition: Interactive Composition Corporation

Library of Congress Cataloging-in-Publication Data

All music guide to hip-hop: the definitive guide to rap & hip-hop/edited by Vladimir
  Bogdanov . . . et al.].
     p. cm.—(All music guide)
  Includes index.
  ISBN 0-87930-759-5 (alk. paper)
  1. Rap (Music)—Discography. 2. Hip hop—Encyclopedias. 3. Sound
  recordings—Reviews. I. Bogdanov, Vladimir, 1965- II. AMG all music guide series.

ML156.4.R27A45 2003
782.421649–dc22   2003057799

Printed in the United States of America
03 04 05 06 07   5 4 3 2 1

Contents

How to Use This Book

ARTIST NAME

VITAL STATISTICS: For groups, **f.** indicates date and place of formation; **db.** indicated date disbanded. For individual performers, date and place of birth (**b.**) and death (**d.**), if known, are given.

INSTRUMENT(S) / STYLE(S): Indicates the instruments played if the artist is an individual, followed by the styles of music associated with the performer or group.

BIOGRAPHY: A quick view of the artist's life and musical career. For major performers, proportionately longer biographies are provided.

ALBUM REVIEWS: These are the albums selected by our editors and contributors.

KEY TO SYMBOLS: ● ☆ ★

☆ **ESSENTIAL RECORDINGS:** Albums marked with a star should be part of any good collection of the genre. Often, these are also a good first purchase (filled star). By hearing these albums, you can get a good overview of the entire genre. These are must-hear and must-have recordings. You can't go wrong with them.

●★ **FIRST PURCHASE:** Albums marked with either a filled circle or a filled star should be your first purchase. This is where to begin to find out if you like this particular artist. These albums are representative of the best this artist has to offer. If you don't like these picks, chances are this artist is not for you. In the case of an artist who has a number of distinct periods, you will find an essential pick marked for each period. Albums are listed chronologically when possible.

ALBUM TITLE: The name of the album is listed in bold as it appears on the original when possible. Very long titles have been abbreviated, or repeated in full as part of the comment, where needed.

DATE: The year of an album's first recording or release, if known.

RECORD LABEL: Record labels indicate the current (or most recent) release of this recording. Label numbers are not included because they change frequently.

ALBUM RATINGS: ✦ TO ✦✦✦✦✦ In addition to the stars and circles used to distinguish exceptional noteworthy albums, as explained above, all albums are rated on a scale from one to five diamonds.

REVIEWERS: The name of each review's author is given at the end of the review.

Run-D.M.C.

f. 1982, Queens, NY **db.** Nov. 6, 2002
Group / Golden Age, Hip-Hop, East Coast Rap, Hardcore Rap

More than any other hip-hop group, Run-D.M.C. are responsible for the sound and style of the music. As the first hardcore rap outfit, the trio set the sound and style for the next decade of rap. With their spare beats and excursions into heavy metal samples, the trio were tougher and more menacing than their predecessors Grandmaster Flash and Whodini. In the process, they opened the door for both the politicized rap of Public Enemy and Boogie Down Productions, as well as the hedonistic gangsta fantasies of N.W.A. At the same time, Run-D.M.C. helped move rap from a singles-oriented genre to an album-oriented one—they were the first hip-hop artist to construct full-fledged albums, not just collections with two singles and a bunch of filler. By the end of the '80s, Run-D.M.C. had been overtaken by the groups they had spawned, but they continued to perform to a dedicated following well into the '90s.
—Stephen Thomas Erlewine

☆ **King of Rock** / 1985 / Profile ✦✦✦✦
Take the title of Run-D.M.C.'s *King of Rock* somewhat literally. True, the trailblazing rap crew hardly abandoned hip-hop on their second album, but they did follow through on the blueprint of their debut, emphasizing the rock leanings that formed the subtext of *Run-D.M.C.* Nearly every cut surges forward on thundering drum machines and simple power chords, with the tempos picked up a notch and the production hitting like a punch to the stomach. If the debut suggested hard rock, this *feels* like hard rock—over-amplified, brutal, and intoxicating in its sheer sonic force. What really makes *King of Rock* work is that it sounds tougher and is smarter than almost all of the rock and metal records of its time. *—Stephen Thomas Erlewine*

★ **Raising Hell** / 1986 / Profile ✦✦✦✦✦
By their third album, Run-D.M.C. were primed for a breakthrough into the mainstream, but nobody was prepared for a blockbuster on the level of *Raising Hell*. Run-D.M.C. and *King of Rock* had established the crew's fusion of hip-hop and hard rock, but that sound didn't blossom until *Raising Hell*, partially due to the presence of Rick Rubin as producer. Rubin loved metal and rap in equal measures and he knew how to play to the strengths of both, while slipping in commercial concessions that seemed sly even when they borrowed from songs as familiar as "My Sharona" (heard on "It's Tricky"). Along with longtime Run-D.M.C. producer Russell Simmons, Rubin blew down the doors of what hip-hop could do with *Raising Hell* because it reached beyond rap/rock and found all sorts of sounds outside of it.
—Stephen Thomas Erlewine

Tougher than Leather / 1988 / Profile ✦✦✦✦
At the end of 1986, *Raising Hell* was rap's best-selling album up to that point, though it would soon be outsold by the Beastie Boys' *Licensed to Ill*. Profile Records hoped that Run-D.M.C.'s fourth album, *Tougher than Leather*, would exceed the Beastie Boys' quintuple-platinum status, but unfortunately the group's popularity had decreased by 1988. One of Run-D.M.C.'s strong points—its love of rock & roll—was also its undoing in hip-hop circles. Any type of crossover success tends to be viewed suspiciously in the 'hood, and hardcore hip-hoppers weren't overly receptive to "Miss Elaine," "Papa Crazy," "Mary, Mary," and other rap/rock delights found on the album. Thanks largely to rock fans, this album did go platinum for sales exceeding one million copies—which, ironically, Profile considered a disappointment. But the fact is that while *Tougher than Leather* isn't quite as strong as Run-D.M.C.'s first three albums, it was one of 1988's best rap releases. *—Alex Henderson*

Down With the King / May 4, 1993 / Profile ✦✦✦
After 1990's lackluster *Back From Hell*, most hip-hop fans thought that Run-D.M.C. was no longer capable of delivering a solid record. *Down With the King* proved those doubters wrong. Although it didn't burn up the charts like *Raising Hell* and wasn't as innovative as their first album, *Down With the King* showed that they remained strong and talented; it also didn't hurt that the production was provided by several of the 1990s' most talented artists, including Public Enemy, Pete Rock, Naughty By Nature, and Q-Tip.
—Stephen Thomas Erlewine

Style Descriptions

ACID JAZZ

The music played by a generation raised on jazz as well as funk and hip-hop, Acid Jazz used elements of all three; its existence as a percussion-heavy, primarily live music placed it closer to jazz and Afro-Cuban than any other dance style, but its insistence on keeping the groove allied it with funk, hip-hop, and dance music. The term itself first appeared in 1988 as both an American record label and the title of an English compilation series that reissued jazz-funk music from the '70s, called "rare groove" by the Brits during a major mid-'80s resurgence. A variety of acid jazz artists emerged during the late '80s and early '90s: live bands such as Stereo MC's, James Taylor Quartet, the Brand New Heavies, Groove Collective, Galliano, and Jamiroquai, as well as studio projects like Palm Skin Productions, Mondo Grosso, Outside, and United Future Organization.

ALTERNATIVE RAP

Alternative Rap refers to hip-hop groups that refuse to conform to any of the traditional stereotypes of rap, such as gangsta, funk, bass, hardcore, and party rap. Instead, they blur genres, drawing equally from funk and pop/rock, as well as jazz, soul, reggae, and even folk. Though Arrested Development and the Fugees managed to cross over into the mainstream, most alternative rap groups are embraced primarily by alternative rock fans, not hip-hop or pop audiences.

BASS MUSIC

Springing from the fertile dance scenes in Miami (freestyle) and Detroit (electro) during the mid-'80s, Bass Music brought the funky-breaks aesthetic of the '70s into the digital age with drum-machine frequencies capable of pulverizing the vast majority of unsuspecting car or club speakers. Early Miami pioneers like 2 Live Crew and DJ Magic Mike pushed the style into its distinctive booty obsession, and Detroit figures like DJ Assault, DJ Godfather, and DJ Bone melded it with techno to create an increasingly fast-paced music. Bass music even flirted with the charts during the early '90s, as 95 South's "Whoot (There It Is)" and 69 Boyz' "Tootsee Roll" both hit the charts and went multi-platinum.

BRITISH RAP

Although it is rarely heard outside of the U.K. and Europe, British Rap has its own traditions and is a style onto itself. Though it doesn't have quite the heritage of American hip-hop, many British rappers grew up within the fertile Caribbean raggae tradition and introduced patois into hip-hop styles. British rap began in the late '80s, and it used the sonic collage of Public Enemy as a launching pad. Soon, many U.K. rappers were adding acid-house flourishes to their sound, resulting in a music style that was darker than its American counterpart. There were poor facsimiles of American rappers, but the best British hip-hop fell into three different camps. Groups like Prodigy fused hip-hop with rave. Groups like Leftfield went for a dance-club style of hip-hop. Massive Attack slowed hip-hop beats down and added acid jazz textures, resulting in trip-hop. By the end of the '90s, a generation of rap fans had assumed control of the scene, resulting in excellent work from the Herbaliser, Roots Manuva, New Flesh, and many others.

CHRISTIAN RAP

Christian Rap is hip-hop with religious and inspirational themes. Most Christian rap doesn't show the sonic innovation of secular rap, simply because the groups don't have such strong competition. Frequently, Christian rap falls somewhere between old school hip-hop and the rap of the late '80s. Though it was unusual for Christian rap to be as hard as gangsta rap or as groove-oriented as G-funk, variations on both styles—led, respectively, by Gospel Gangstas and Kirk Franklin—began to appear during the late '90s.

COMEDY RAP

Comedy Rap is hip-hop that is designed to amuse and entertain. Frequently, it is the raps themselves that are humorous, but the music itself—particularly in the case of Biz Markie, arguably the greatest comedy rapper to date—can be clever and funny, as well. Comedy rap flourished in the '80s, when hip-hop itself was lighter than it was in the '90s (when gangsta rap kept the music somber). There have been a few rap parodies, such as Arsenio Hall's Chunky A, but most comedy rap is a combination of real hip-hop and street humor.

CONTEMPORARY R&B

Contemporary R&B developed after years of urban R&B. Like urban, contemporary R&B is slickly produced, but many of the musicians—Maxwell, D'Angelo, Terence Trent D'Arby—are obsessed with bringing the grit, spirit, and ambitiousness of classic soul (Marvin Gaye, Stevie Wonder, Otis Redding) back to contemporary soul and R&B.

DIRTY RAP

Dirty Rap is hip-hop that is focused solely on sex. The fathers of the genre, 2 Live Crew, were one of the leading groups of the groove-heavy Miami bass sound, and that bass-driven groove remained at the foundation of dirty rap. Most dirty rap was simply blue party rap, designed to keep the party rolling, and it rarely had much musical or lyrical depth.

DIRTY SOUTH

Dirty South popped up in the latter half of the '90s, after gangsta rap became the standard currency of hip-hop. Dirty South drew from *The Chronic* and 2 Live Crew's filthy traditions in equal measure, arriving at a stoned, violent, sex-obsessed and (naturally) profane brand of modern hip-hop. The style drew its name from Goodie Mob's 1995 song of the same name and they, along with Outkast, were the best the genre had to offer, since both their lyrics and music were sharper than such contemporaries as the No Limit posse.

EAST COAST RAP

At the dawn of the hip-hop era, all rap was East Coast Rap. All of rap's most important early artists were based in the New York City area—old school legends like DJ Kool Herc, Grandmaster Flash, Afrika Bambaataa, the Sugarhill Gang, Kurtis Blow, and Run-D.M.C. As rap grew and became more diverse over the course of the '80s, productive scenes began to spring up in other locations around the country; nonetheless, East Coast rap dominated through most of the '80s. Although the sound of East Coast rap wasn't completely uniform, from the mid- to late '80s it tended to gravitate to more aggressive beats and sample collages, and many MCs prided themselves on their technical dexterity in crafting lyrics. In other words, with some exceptions, East Coast rap became a music intended more for intense listening than for the dancefloor, helping develop the genre into a respected art form as it grew more elaborate and complex. Typifying this golden era of the East Coast sound were artists like Eric B. & Rakim, Boogie Down Productions, and Slick Rick, all of whom boasted immense lyrical skill rooted in old school style, as well as the harder-hitting sounds of EPMD and Public Enemy. Also based on the East Coast were the Native Tongues, a collective of positive, Afro-centric artists assembled by Afrika Bambaataa; while De La Soul, A Tribe Called Quest, the Jungle Brothers, and other, mostly New York-based groups had a major impact on hip-hop in the late '80s, they were more readily identified with their musical eclecticism than any specific geographic location. N.W.A's 1989 album *Straight Outta Compton* served notice that the West Coast had toughened its sound to go along with its already gritty, street-level subject matter; combined with West Coast rap's ability to retain its primary function as party music, this helped make it the dominant force in hip-hop during the '90s. The rise of Southern rap further ensured that East Coast rap could no longer dominate as it once had, but the '90s were hardly a wash for the region. In addition to Puff Daddy's hugely lucrative, pop-accessible Bad Boy label, the East Coast produced its share of varied, highly acclaimed artists, including lyrical virtuoso Nas, the eclectic Fugees and Roots, and the hugely influential hardcore unit Wu-Tang Clan.

ELECTRO

Blending '70s funk with the emerging hip-hop culture and synthesizer technology of the early '80s produced the style known alternately as Electro. But what seemed to be a brief fad for the public—no more than two or three hits, including Afrikaa Bambaataa's "Planet Rock" and Grandmaster Flash's "The Message," neither of which made the pop Top 40—was in fact a fertile testing ground for innovators who later diverged into radically different territory, including Dr. Dre (who worked with the World Class Wreckin' Cru) and techno godfather Juan Atkins (with Cybotron). Electro also provided an intriguing new direction for one of the style's prime influences: Herbie Hancock, whose 1973 *Headhunters* album proved a large fusion hit, came storming back in 1983 with the electro single "Rockit." Despite its successes (documented in full on Rhino's four-disc *Electric Funk* set), the style was quickly eclipsed by the mid-'80s rise of hip-hop music built around samples (often from rock records) rather than musical synthesizers. Nevertheless, many techno and dance artists continued harking back to the sound, and a full-fledged electro revival emerged in Detroit and Britain during the mid-'90s.

FOREIGN RAP

Foreign Rap is hip-hop rapped in a language that is not English or Spanish. Generally, foreign rap is European in origin and the music resembles Euro dance as much as it does American hip-hop. It isn't as hard as American or British hip-hop and often follows trends instead of blazing new paths. The notable exception to that rule is jazz-rap, as European hip-hop acts were heavily influenced by England's acid house and acid jazz, and these ideas later spilled over to the hip-hop that was made in Europe.

FREESTYLE

Often growing in tandem with contemporary styles like electro and house, Freestyle emerged in the twin Latin capitals of New York City and Miami during the early '80s. Freestyle classics like "I Wonder If I Take You Home" by Lisa Lisa & Cult Jam, "Let the Music Play" by Shannon, and "Party Your Body" by Stevie B relied on angular, synthesized beats similar to electro and early house, but also emphasized the romantic themes of classic R&B and disco. The fusion of mechanical and sensual proved ready for crossover during the period, and both Shannon and Lisa Lisa hit the Top 40 during 1984-1985. Freestyle also dovetailed nicely with the rise of dance pop during the mid-'80s—Madonna's early producer and remixer, John Benitez (aka Jellybean), was also active in the freestyle community. By the end of the decade, a number of artists—Exposé, Brenda K. Starr, Trinere, the Cover Girls, India, and Stevie B—followed them into the pop or R&B charts. Even after popular success waned in the late '80s, though, freestyle moved to the underground as a vital stream of modern dance music alongside house, techno, and bass music. Similar to mainstream house, freestyle artists are usually (though by no means exclusively) either female vocalists or male producers. Newer figures like Lil Suzy, George Lamond, Angelique, Johnny O, and others became big stars in the freestyle community.

G-FUNK

G-Funk is the laid-back, Parliament/Funkadelic-inspired variation of gangsta rap developed by Dr. Dre in the early '90s. Distinguished by its whiny, cheap synthesizers, slow grooves, deep bass, and, occasionally, faceless female backing vocals, G-funk became the most popular genre of hip-hop in the early '90s. After the success of Dr. Dre's 1992 album *The Chronic*—the album where he invented and named the genre—many new rap artists and producers followed his musical techniques, making it the most recognizable sound in rap for most of the early '90s.

GANGSTA RAP

Gangsta Rap developed in the late '80s. Evolving out of hardcore rap, gangsta rap had an edgy, noisy sound. Lyrically, it was just as abrasive, as the rappers spun profane, gritty tales about urban crime. Sometimes the lyrics were an accurate reflection of reality; other times they were exaggerated comic book stories. Either way, it became the most commercially successful form of hip-hop in the late '80s and early '90s. In the process, gangsta rap caused considerable con-

troversy, as conservative organizations tried to get the albums banned. Even when the activist groups forced certain bands off major labels, the groups continued to make their music uncensored.

GO-GO

Go-Go was a bass-heavy, funky variation of hip-hop that was designed for house parties. Lyrically, there was little of substance in go-go, but the main message was the beat, not the words. During the mid-'80s, go-go was quite popular within the rap and R&B underground, particularly around the D.C. area where it originated. It never became a pop success, however; the closest it came to a crossover hit was in 1988, when EU—along with Trouble Funk, the definitive go-go band—had a moderate hit with "Da Butt," taken from Spike Lee's *School Daze*. During the late '80s and early '90s, go-go was supplanted by Miami bass music, which took the groove-oriented aesthetic of go-go, turned up the bass, and de-emphasized the already-slim lyrics.

GOLDEN AGE

Hip-hop's Golden Age is bookended by the commercial breakthrough of Run-D.M.C. in 1986 and the explosion of gangsta rap with 1993's *The Chronic* by Dr. Dre. Those six years witnessed the best recordings from some of the biggest rappers—LL Cool J, Public Enemy, EPMD, Big Daddy Kane, Eric B. & Rakim, N.W.A, Boogie Down Productions, Biz Markie—in the genre's history. Overwhelmingly based in New York City, golden-age rap is characterized by skeletal beats, samples cribbed from hard-rock or soul tracks, and tough dis raps. Rhymers like PE's Chuck D, Big Daddy Kane, KRS-One, and Rakim basically invented the complex wordplay and lyrical kung-fu of later hip-hop. The Def Jam label became the first big independent in hip-hop, while Cold Chillin', Jive and Tommy Boy also made strides.

HARDCORE RAP

While the term can refer to several different musical sensibilities, Hardcore Rap is marked by confrontation and aggression, whether in the lyrical subject matter, the hard, driving beats, the noisy sampling and production, or any combination thereof. Hardcore rap is tough, streetwise, intense, and often menacing (although the latter isn't always the case; there is room for humor and exuberance as well). Gangsta rap is the style most commonly associated with hardcore rap, but not all hardcore rap revolves around gangsta themes, even though there is a great deal of overlap, especially among hardcore rappers of the '90s. The first hardcore rap came from the East Coast during the late '80s, when artists began to move away from party rhymes and bragging about their microphone skills; their music and language began to reflect the gritty, often harsh urban surroundings in which it was usually created and enjoyed. Before any specific formula for gangsta rap had been invented, artists like New York's Boogie Down Productions and L.A.'s Ice-T were committing detailed observations of street life to tape; plus, Public Enemy's chaotic sound collages were setting new standards for production power, and N.W.A celebrated the bleakness of the ghetto and the gangsta lifestyle with an over-the-top machismo. In the early '90s, hardcore rap was essentially synonymous with West Coast gangsta rap until the 1993 emergence of the Wu-Tang Clan, whose spare, minimalistic beats and haunting string and piano samples became a widely imitated style. With its slamming, hard-hitting grooves and street-tough urban grit, hardcore rap became hip-hop's most popular crossover style during the latter half of the '90s, its subject matter now a mix of party anthems, gangsta's money/sex/violence obsessions, and occasional social commentary. Artists like the Notorious B.I.G., DMX, and Jay-Z became platinum-selling superstars, and Master P's brand of gangsta-oriented Southern hardcore also became a lucrative commercial force, even if it didn't produce crossover hit singles on the same level.

HIP-HOP

In the terminology of rap music, Hip-Hop usually refers to the culture—graffiti spraying, breakdancing, and turntablism in addition to rapping itself—surrounding the music. As a style, however, hip-hop refers to music created with those values in mind. Once rap had been around long enough to actually have a history, hip-hop groups began looking back to old school figures including MCs like Kurtis Blow and Whodini, and DJs like Grandmaster Flash and Afrika Bambaataa. In fact, the latter's Zulu Nation collective sprang up in the late '80s around two of the most notable hip-hop artists, De La Soul and A Tribe Called Quest. With rap music's mainstream breakout during the '90s, dozens of hip-hop artists pointed the way back to the old school, including underground rappers like Mos Def and Pharoahe Monch.

JAZZ-RAP

Jazz-Rap was an attempt to fuse African-American music of the past with a newly dominant form of the present, paying tribute to and reinvigorating the former while expanding the horizons of the latter. While the rhythms of jazz-rap came entirely from hip-hop, the samples and sonic textures were drawn mainly from cool jazz, soul-jazz, and hard bop. It was cooler and more cerebral than other styles of hip-hop, and many of its artists displayed an Afro-centric political consciousness, complementing the style's historical awareness. Given its more intellectual bent, it's not surprising that jazz-rap never really caught on as a street favorite, but then it wasn't meant to. Jazz-rap styled itself as a more positive alternative to the hardcore/gangsta movement taking over rap's mainstream at the dawn of the '90s, and concerned itself with spreading hip-hop to listeners unable to embrace or identify with the music's increasing inner-city aggression. As such, jazz-rap found its main audiences in places like college campuses, and was also embraced by a number of critics and white alternative rock fans. Afrika Bambaataa's Native Tongues posse—a loose collective of New York–based, Afro-centric rap groups—was the most important force in jazz-rap, including groups like A Tribe Called Quest, De La Soul and the Jungle Brothers; Digable Planets and Gang Starr were other notable early artists. During the mid-to late '90s, as alternative rap moved into a wider-ranging eclecticism, jazz-rap was not often pursued as an exclusive end, although the Roots frequently incorporated it in their live-instrumentation hip-hop.

LATIN RAP

Latin Rap refers to hip-hop and rap performed by Latino performers. They may rap in either English or Spanish, and the music often demonstrates the influence of percolating Latin rhythms.

OLD SCHOOL RAP

Old School Rap is the style of the very first rap artists who emerged from New York City in the late '70s and early '80s. Old school is easily identified by its relatively simple raps—most lines take up approximately equal amounts of time, and the rhythms of the language rarely twisted around the beats of the song. The cadences usually fell squarely on the beat, and when they didn't, they wouldn't stray for long, returning to the original pattern for quick resolution. The emphasis was not on lyrical technique, but simply on good times—aside from the socially conscious material of Grandmaster Flash, which greatly expanded rap's horizons, most old school rap had the fun, playful flavor of the block parties and dances at which it was born. In keeping with the laid-back, communal good vibes, old school rap seemed to have more room and appreciation for female MCs, although none achieved the higher profile of Grandmaster Flash & the Furious Five or Sugarhill Gang. Some old school songs were performed over disco or funk-style tracks, while others featured synthesized backing (this latter type of music, either with or without raps, was known as electro). Old school rap's recorded history begins with two 1979 singles, Fatback's "King Tim III" and Sugarhill Gang's "Rapper's Delight," although the movement had been taking shape for almost a decade prior. Sugarhill Records quickly became the center for old school rap, dominating the market until Run-D.M.C. upped the ante for technique and hardcore urban toughness in 1983-1984. Their sound and style soon took over the rap world, making old school's party orientation and '70s funk influences seem outdated. When compared with the more complex rhythms and rhyme schemes of modern-day rap—or even the hip-hop that was being produced less than ten years after "Rapper's Delight"—old school rap can sound dated and a little unadventurous. However, the best old school tracks retain their liveliness as great party music no matter what the era, holding up surprisingly well considering all that's happened since.

PARTY RAP

Party Rap is bass-driven, block-rockin' hip-hop that only has one thing on its mind—to keep the groove going. The lyrics are all inconsequential, with none of the political overtones of hardcore rap and only a fraction of the cleverness of old school rap. Instead, it's all about the music, with the bass and drums taking precedence. It's closely related to Miami bass music, but there is usually one vocal hook—such as "Da Dip" or the chorus of "Rump Shaker"—that makes the record memorable.

POLITICAL RAP

Looking to move on from the block-party atmosphere of old school rap and eager to vent their frustrations with the '80s version of the inner-city blues, a select few hip-hop groups merged deft rhymes with political philosophy to create

a new style of rap. Inspired by '70s political preachers from the Last Poets to Gil Scott-Heron, Public Enemy was the first and best of the political rap groups. Frontman Chuck D twisted rhymes better than any other rapper to date, all the while taking to task the government ("Black Steel in the Hour of Chaos," "Fight the Power"), the culture of white America ("Rebel Without a Pause," "Burn Hollywood Burn"), and all sorts of specific sociopolitical issues ("911 Is a Joke," "Night of the Living Baseheads") over the sonic terrorism of PE's production crew, the Bomb Squad. KRS-One and his group Boogie Down Productions began speaking out as well, with brutal broadsides like "Illegal Business" and "Stop the Violence" that spoke to the black community as well as the leaders of the free world. What looked to be a fertile new ground for exploration, however, proved remarkably short-lived. Public Enemy trailed off after 1991, and despite great recordings from a new generation of political rappers (Poor Righteous Teachers, Paris, X-Clan, Disposable Heroes of Hiphoprisy), the commercial explosion of a new hip-hop sound—gangsta rap or G-funk—made record labels less adventurous about nonestablishment messages.

POP-RAP

Pop-Rap is a marriage of hip-hop beats and raps with strong melodic hooks, which are usually featured as part of the chorus section in a standard pop-song structure. Pop-rap tends to be less aggressive and lyrically complex than most street-level hip-hop, although during the mid- to late '90s, some artists infused the style with a more hardcore attitude in an attempt to defuse backlash over their accessibility. Pop-rap got its start in the late '80s, when artists like Run-D.M.C., LL Cool J, and the Beastie Boys began to cross over into the mainstream. Shortly thereafter, rappers like Tone-Loc, Young MC, and DJ Jazzy Jeff and the Fresh Prince recorded singles emphasizing their good-humored storytelling abilities, to massive chart success; a number of other, mostly singles-oriented acts followed in their wake with similarly good-natured party tunes and novelties. With the possibility of popular acceptance very real, other artists—around the same time—began to play up rap's connection to R&B and dance music. This latter group often relied on samples to supply their melodies, and with the 1990 explosion of MC Hammer and Vanilla Ice, pop-rap was often derided (and, occasionally, taken to court) for its willingness to borrow hooks from well-known hit songs without altering those appropriations very much, if at all. This gave the style a not entirely deserved bad reputation, since many '90s artists continued to score big pop hits while developing their own distinctive sounds (PM Dawn, Naughty By Nature, House of Pain, Arrested Development, Coolio, Salt-N-Pepa, Sir Mix-a-Lot, etc.). Meanwhile, Dr. Dre's catchy G-funk and Puff Daddy's Hammer-esque plundering of '80s pop hits helped bring gangsta and hardcore themes to the top of the charts; by the end of the '90s, pop-rap was dominated by artists they had influenced and/or mentored, as well as artists who blended rap with urban soul.

RAP-ROCK

Rap-Rock was a continuation of rap-metal, a hybrid of hip-hop and heavy metal pioneered by such bands as Anthrax. Rap-metal had big, lurching beats and heavy, heavy riffs—occasionally, it sounded as if the riffs were merely overdubbed over scratching and beatbox beats. Rap-rock was a little more organic, often because it was a rock song where the vocalist rapped instead of sang. Nevertheless, there were certainly elements of hip-hop in the rhythms, too, since there was more funk to rap-rock than to normal hard rock. At times, the difference between rap-metal and rap-rock may be minute, since they both favor loud guitars and beats, but the main difference is that organic, integrated sound, best heard on Kid Rock's 1998 rap-rock masterpiece, *Devil Without a Cause*.

SOUTHERN RAP

Long a third wheel to the East Coast and West Coast hip-hop scenes, Southern Rap emerged in the '90s as a fertile scene unto itself, particularly in Miami, New Orleans, and Atlanta. In the late '80s, Southern rap was primarily associated with Miami bass music, also popularly known as "booty rap" both for its rump-shaking grooves and the central preoccupation of its lyrics. Chief among its artists was Luther Campbell's 2 Live Crew, which took sexual lyric content to a hard-partying extreme, provoking outcries from pro-censorship forces across the country. The sound of Miami bass spread through the rest of the South and remained a national dancefloor staple through the '90s, with artists like Tag Team, 95 South, the 69 Boyz, Quad City DJ's, and Freak Nasty all scoring huge hit singles (albeit with lyrics far less explicit than Campbell's). Atlanta had its share of bass-heavy party rap artists, but also offered a quirkier, more distinctive (and critically acclaimed) style incorporating the funk of classic Southern soul. The cerebral Arrested Development was the first to hit the national scene in 1992, and they were followed a few years later by protégés of the harder-edged

Organized Noize production squad, most notably OutKast and Goodie Mob. If Atlanta was the creative center of Southern rap, New Orleans was surely its commercial center. Master P built a lucrative empire with No Limit record label, and even if he and his roster didn't really push the envelope artistically—most No Limit albums stuck to West Coast G-funk, Wu-Tang-style hardcore, and nothing but straight-up gangsta lyrics—No Limit pumped out product with assembly-line efficiency and became a constant presence on the national album charts during the late '90s. Toward the end of the decade, fellow New Orleans label Cash Money and its house producer Mannie Fresh—whose distinctive approach reworked the Southern bass sound—scored a national breakout with Juvenile, establishing them as a legitimate rival force.

TRIP-HOP

Yet another in a long line of plastic placeholders to attach itself to one arm or another of the U.K. post-acid house dance scene's rapidly mutating experimental underground, Trip-Hop was coined by the English music press in an attempt to characterize a new style of down-tempo, jazz-, funk-, and soul-inflected experimental breakbeat music which began to emerge around in 1993 in association with labels such as Mo'Wax, Ninja Tune, Cup of Tea, and Wall of Sound. Similar to (though largely vocal-less) American hip-hop in its use of sampled drum breaks, typically more experimental, and infused with a high index of ambient-leaning and apparently psychotropic atmospherics (hence "trip"), the term quickly caught on to describe everything from Portishead and Tricky, to DJ Shadow and U.N.K.L.E., to Coldcut, Wagon Christ, and Depth Charge—much to the chagrin of many of these musicians, who saw their music largely as an extension of hip-hop proper, not a gimmicky offshoot. One of the first commercially significant hybrids of dance-based listening music to crossover to a more mainstream audience, trip-hop full-length releases routinely topped indie charts in the U.K. and, in artists such as Shadow, Tricky, Morcheeba, the Sneaker Pimps, and Massive Attack, account for a substantial portion of the first wave of "electronica" acts to reach stateside audiences.

TURNTABLISM

Even though DJs like Grandmaster Flash, Afrika Bambaataa, and Grand Wizard Theodore were the leading figures of hip-hop during the 1970s, by the time rap hit the mainstream in the mid-'80s, the MC had begun taking over the stage. After all, to have any chance at radio airplay and commercial crossover, tracks obviously needed a vocal focus. Inevitably, the mixers responsible for the first hip-hop street jams were inevitably pushed to the back. Though the balance will probably never be righted, the increasing focus on all aspects of rap culture during the mid-'90s resulted in the emergence of Turntablism as a separate style. The stars here were the DJs, and instead of tight rhymes and smooth flow in their repertoire, they had scratching, spinbacks, phasing, and two-turntable acrobatics (or beat juggling). Some of the most popular mixers (DJ Shadow, most notably) constructed their mixes with literally thousands of records at their disposal, and the more obscure the better. Most were either drum breaks from rare jazz, soul, or funk records (instructional and educational records were also popular, given the nonsensical vocal samples). The avant-garde figure Christian Marclay began constructing turntable symphonies in the early '80s, using material from a variety of musical sources. In 1987, a relic of the disco era named *the Disco Mix Club* (later just *DMC*) held its first mixing championship. The

contest soon became the stage for turntablists to flaunt their talents and earn the respect of their peers. Excellent second-generation DJs like Q-Bert, Mixmaster Mike, DJ Apollo, and Rob Swift became leading figures of the emerging turntablism, some as individuals and some as part of new turntablist collectives like Invisibl Skratch Piklz, the X-Men (later the X-Ecutioners), and the Beat Junkies. Though albums by turntablists never quite crossed over to rock audiences, a new breed of mixer—exemplified by DJ Shadow—earned acclaim in critical quarters by downplaying the role of live performance and physical skills in favor of full-length studio works of art.

UNDERGROUND RAP

Underground Rap falls into two categories. It is either hardcore hip-hop that pushes musical boundaries and has lyrics that are more inventive than gangsta clichés, or it is hardcore gangsta rap that wallows in all of the musical and lyrical clichés of the genre. What the two styles have in common is that they have little regard for mainstream conventions, and they celebrate their independent status. Underground rap also tends to be produced for less than hip-hop on major labels, and it often sounds like it.

WEST COAST RAP

West Coast Rap dominated the hip-hop scene for the middle of the '90s, making gangsta rap into a popular phenomenon and establishing Dr. Dre as one of the most influential figures in rap history. Still, even if Dre's patented G-funk defined the West Coast sound and style for many, California's rap scene was a great deal more diverse. Up until the mid- to late '80s, West Coast rap mostly imitated East Coast party rap, already considered old school in its place of origin; however, both Los Angeles and the Bay Area soon proved to be fertile pastures. The former produced the landmark proto-gangsta recordings of Ice-T, the hugely influential, Latino-tinged stoner funk of Cypress Hill, and the warped comedy of the Pharcyde; the Bay Area countered with the pimp-obsessed rhymes of Too Short, the P-Funk-inspired, good-humored Digital Underground, and the pop breakthrough of MC Hammer. In short, West Coast rap became as eclectic and difficult to pigeonhole as East Coast rap. However, N.W.A's 1989 gangsta rap landmark *Straight Outta Compton* set the stage for a more identifiable West Coast style—its sound was hard hitting and minimalistic, its lyrics alternating between violent hedonism and righteously angry social commentary. Upon leaving N.W.A, Ice Cube made solo records that maintained this lyrical tone while employing noisy, Public Enemy-style production; his bandmate Dr. Dre discovered Snoop Doggy Dogg, signed to Death Row Records, and at the end of 1992 released *The Chronic*, the album that defined G-funk and spawned legions of imitators. *The Chronic*'s gangsta hedonism and production style—whiny synthesizers, rolling P-Funk beats, and deep, slow grooves—provided the blueprint that made Death Row the biggest hip-hop label of the early '90s, scoring hits by Snoop, Warren G, tha Dogg Pound, and more. Controversial gangsta star Tupac joined the label in late 1995 and became a crossover superstar with the Dre duet "California Love," and Coolio had taken a more pop-oriented version of the West Coast sound to the top of the charts earlier in the year with "Gangsta's Paradise." However, West Coast dominance soon crumbled—Tupac was murdered in 1996, Dre jumped ship, and Death Row CEO Suge Knight was jailed over business practices. By the end of the '90s, hip-hop's focus had turned back to the East Coast and to the emerging South.

A+

Hip-Hop, Pop-Rap

A+ came into the rap game with a lot going for him. He was one of the youngest rappers to be taken seriously by their older peers, and was thought to be one of the more promising future prospects. After his first album, his verse with the Lost Boyz, Canibus, and Redman on "Beasts From the East" helped to firmly establish him as a talented rapper. His second album, *Hempstead High*, was more mainstream and may have diminished some of his street credit. —*Brad Mills*

● **Latch-Key Child** / Aug. 27, 1996 / Kedar ♦♦♦
A little kid with a lot to say, A+ seems very mature for his age. He isn't exactly talking about school dances and his grades on this album, even if his name is A+. You'd think he was 25 if it weren't for his voice and his photo on the cover of the album. Not the only one tooting his horn, industry veterans like Mobb Deep and Q-Tip show up for appearances, and—particularly on the Mobb Deep track—A+ delivers a few memorable verses to complement Prodigy's always-present microphone dominance. Not the longest album in the world at just 13 tracks, it leaves you wondering why they didn't fill it up with a few more songs. But all in all, this is a good album; it will be interesting to see if A+ will truly develop into the prodigy he seems to be. —*Brad Mills*

Hempstead High / Feb. 23, 1999 / Kedar ♦♦♦
A+ exhibited enough potential on his debut album, *Latch Key Kid*, for many to consider him one of hip-hop's most promising future lyrical assassins. After all, you do not hear many 14-year-old shorties rocking the mic as profusely as he did on his debut. However, after a two-year layoff in between LPs, A+ has moved on to more adult topic matter and seems eager to present himself as hip-hop's version of Usher. But not only has A+ lost his innocence, he has also lost any sense of originality. One of A+'s major drawbacks is he tends to mimic the flow of whomever he is teamed up with, whether it be Canibus, or Psycho Drama. He waters down this recording with blatant crossover reaches like "Don't Make Me Wait" and "Price of Fame." "What Da Deal" Cardan is especially disheartening, as both MCs trade woeful verses and Cardan sounds like a carbon copy of Mase or Cam'ron. The few gems on this album stick out like a sore thumb, since they're few and far between. A+ brings guaranteed action with cuts like the heavily mix-tape circulated "Boy II Men" featuring Lost Boyz & Canibus, and a surprisingly tight collaboration "Watcha Weigh Me" featuring MJG. When A+ sticks to simple yet effective beats and rhymes, he reaps the benefits, as on "Parkside Garden." A+ desperately needs to find his own unique identity and style. "Hempstead High" is aptly titled, as it is a high schoolish effort at best; hopefully, with his next LP A+ will mature mentally, instead of physically, and come into his own. —*Matt Conaway*

Aaliyah (Aaliyah Haughton)

b. Jan. 16, 1979, Brooklyn, NY, d. Aug. 25, 2001, Abaco, The Bahamas
Vocals / Urban, Contemporary R&B, Hip-Hop, Dance-Pop
A star in the R&B world before she was even out of her teens, Aaliyah's promising career was tragically cut short by her death in a plane crash at age 22. Even with only three albums under her belt, she'd already earned a place as a talented trendsetter among the R&B elite. Following a successful transition to a more mature image, Aaliyah played a major role in popularizing the stuttering, futuristic production style that consumed hip-hop and urban soul in the late '90s. Her work with Timbaland, especially, was some of the most forward-looking R&B of its time, even while the competing neo-soul movement was gaining prominence. Aaliyah's death came on the heels of her third and

most accomplished album, making it especially unfortunate that she was robbed of a chance to continue her creative development. Aaliyah Dana Haughton was born January 16, 1979, in Brooklyn, and named after a Swahili word meaning "most exalted one." Her uncle, Barry Hankerson, was a manager and entertainment lawyer who was married to Gladys Knight for a time, and her mother, also a singer, enrolled Aaliyah in voice lessons before she'd even started school. Still very young, she moved with her family to Detroit, where she sang in several school plays. At age nine, she successfully auditioned for the TV show *Star Search*, where she performed "My Funny Valentine" (and lost). Two years later, thanks to her uncle Hankerson's connections, she spent five nights in Las Vegas performing as part of Gladys Knight's revue. In addition to his niece, Hankerson was also managing a rising R&B star named R. Kelly, and introduced the two in 1992. Kelly soon took Aaliyah under his wing and began writing and producing songs for her.

Aaliyah's debut album, *Age Ain't Nothing but a Number*, was released in the summer of 1994 and quickly became a platinum-selling hit on the strength of two smash singles, "Back & Forth" and "At Your Best (You Are Love)" (the latter an Isley Brothers cover). Both songs hit the pop Top Ten and went gold, and "Back & Forth" went all the way to number one on the R&B charts, while "At Your Best" fell one spot short. Late in the year, Aaliyah found herself at the center of controversy when rumors spread that the 15-year-old singer had married Kelly, who was more than ten years her senior. Although both camps were resolutely tight lipped, documents later confirmed that the two had wed in the state of Illinois that August and gotten an annulment shortly thereafter. By the time the media buzz died down, the two had parted ways both personally and creatively.

In 1996, Aaliyah released her follow-up album, *One in a Million*, which signaled a newly emerging maturity. She worked with several different producers, most notably Timbaland, who cowrote several tracks with his songwriting partner, Missy Elliott (soon to become a solo star in her own right). Several of these—"If Your Girl Only Knew," "One in a Million," "4 Page Letter"—became hits, with "If Your Girl Only Knew" going all the way to the top of the R&B charts. The Diane Warren-penned ballad "The One I Gave My Heart To" was also a Top Ten R&B hit, and *One in a Million* wound up going double platinum. In the meantime, Aaliyah graduated from high school (in 1997) and contributed several songs to film soundtracks. "Journey to the Past," from *Anastasia*, was nominated for an Oscar, and in early 1998 she had a major hit with "Are You That Somebody?" from Eddie Murphy's *Dr. Dolittle* (in which she also made a cameo appearance).

Aaliyah took her time recording a follow-up, and put the process completely on hold to start an acting career. She co-starred with martial arts master Jet Li and rapper DMX in 2000's urban Shakespeare adaptation *Romeo Must Die*, and her accompanying soundtrack single, "Try Again," became her first number-one hit on the pop charts that summer. Aaliyah subsequently completed filming on the Anne Rice vampire flick *Queen of the Damned*, playing the title role as a vampire queen, and was cast in a prominent role in the two sequels to *The Matrix*. Plus, she finally finished her long-awaited third album, with Timbaland again handling the most prominent tracks. Released in the summer of 2001, *Aaliyah* completed the singer's image overhaul into a sensual yet sensitive adult. The record received excellent reviews, and the first single, "We Need a Resolution," was a Top 20 R&B hit.

About a month after the album's release, Aaliyah traveled to the Bahamas to film a video for its second single, "Rock the Boat." On August 25, she and several members of the crew boarded a small twin-engine Cessna plane returning to the mainland. The plane crashed shortly after takeoff, exploding on impact; Aaliyah and seven other passengers were killed instantly, and the ninth later died at a Nassau hospital. Investigations into the crash showed that the plane had been loaded far past its weight capacity, and that pilot Luis Morales had recently been arrested for crack cocaine possession (traces of which, along with alcohol, were found in his system); furthermore, the charter company, Blackhawk International Airways, had not authorized him to pilot the craft in question. Naturally, the R&B community reacted with an outpouring of shock and sorrow, and *Aaliyah* became the singer's only chart-topping album, eventually going double platinum. "Rock the Boat" and "More Than a Woman" were both posthumous Top Ten hits on the R&B chart, and *Queen of the Damned* was a commercial success upon its release in early 2002, topping the box office in its first week. As details continued to emerge from the plane crash investigation, Aaliyah's parents filed suit against Blackhawk Airways, Virgin Records, and several other companies. At the end of 2002, the posthumous album *I Care 4 U* entered the charts at number three; it mixed some of the singer's biggest hits with a selection of unreleased material. The title track was a Top 20 pop hit, and "Miss You" topped the R&B charts early the next year. —*Steve Huey*

Age Ain't Nothing But a Number / 1994 / Blackground ♦♦♦♦
Aaliyah has a pleasant voice, but the real reason the teenager's debut album, *Age Ain't Nothing But a Number*, was a hit is the radio-ready production courtesy of R. Kelly, her husband. Kelly wraps Aaliyah's voice in layers of lush synths and deep grooves, while adding songs that are frequently better than the ones on his own album, *12 Play*. *Age* may have its share of filler, but its singles are slyly seductive. —*Stephen Thomas Erlewine*

One in a Million / Aug. 27, 1996 / Blackground ♦♦♦♦♦
Aaliyah's second album doesn't necessarily prove that she is indeed *One In A Million*, but it does showcase more depth and talent than her acclaimed debut. That's due not only to the greater variety of material on *One in a Million*, or to the way that her producers (Vincent Herbert, Jermaine Dupri, and many others) immaculately produce each track, but also to the fact that Aaliyah's singing is smoother, more seductive, and stronger than before. It might not be the commercial juggernaut of *Age Ain't Nothin' But a Number*, but *One in a Million* is a more consistently satisfying album. —*Leo Stanley*

● **Aaliyah** / Jul. 17, 2001 / Blackground ♦♦♦♦♦
Aaliyah waited nearly five years to deliver her third album, but considering that she was essentially growing up—it was the equivalent of spending time in college—when she came back with an eponymous record in the summer of 2001, she came back strong. *Aaliyah* isn't just a statement of maturity and a stunning artistic leap forward; it is one of the strongest urban soul records of its time. Where such peers as Macy Gray and Jill Scott work too hard to establish their ties with classic soul, Aaliyah revels in the present, turning out a pan-cultural array of sounds, styles, and emotions. This sound is entirely unfamiliar—part of the pleasure is how contemporary it sounds—but she sounds just as comfortable within the sonicscapes of Timbaland as Missy Elliott and, possibly, less self-conscious. Aaliyah never oversings, never oversells the songs—this comes on easy and sultry, and there's a lot of substance here, in terms of the songwriting and the songs themselves. Urban albums rarely come any better than this, and there haven't been many records better than this in 2001, period. —*Stephen Thomas Erlewine*

I Care 4 U / Dec. 10, 2002 / Blackground ♦♦♦♦♦
Respecting the legacy of one of R&B's most important artists during the '90s, Universal and Blackground waited more than a year after her death to deliver a new Aaliyah release. Considering all the time that had gone by, however, fans could be forgiven for expecting an album of all-new material to compensate for the long drought. *I Care 4 U* actually balances a brief hits collection with a half-dozen new songs, most of the fresh material appearing only after a run-through of the hits from her three proper albums. There isn't too much to complain about concerning the hits selection; *I Care 4 U* touches on most of the highlights from her seven-year career: "Back & Forth" and "At Your Best (You Are Love)" from her first album, "One in a Million" and "Got to Give It Up" from 1996's *One in a Million*, and three tracks from 2001's *Aaliyah*. (Surely though, the compilers could've found room on this 14-track collection for a pair of her Top Ten greats, "If Your Girl Only Knew" and "The One I Gave My Heart To," or the *Romeo Must Die* hit "I Don't Wanna.") Of the new tracks, four of the six feature composer credits from Johnta Austin ("I Don't Wanna"), and his affectionate, smoky ballads are perfectly suited to Aaliyah's vocals. "Miss You," the presciently titled single, and "All I Need" don't have the edge of her classic Timbaland productions, but they stand up well—even when they're slotted next to the best songs of her

career. Aaliyah was well ahead of her time during her brief career, and *I Care 4 U* hangs together well, the hits showing the power of her voice and the strength of her accompanying productions, while the new songs provide an intriguing look at where Aaliyah may have taken her career had she lived. —*John Bush*

Above the Law

f. 1997, Los Angeles, CA, **db.** 2000
Group / Gangsta Rap, G-Funk, West Coast Rap
Part of the post-N.W.A explosion of California gangsta rap, Above the Law came out of the Eastern Los Angeles suburb of Pomona; leader Cold 187um, aka Big Hutch (born Gregory Hutchinson), was joined by KMG the Illustrator (born Kevin Dulley), Go Mack (born Arthur Goodman), and DJ Total K-Oss (born Anthony Stewart). Mixing '70s vintage-funk and soul samples with live instrumentation (Hutchinson had studied jazz while in school), the group signed with Eazy-E's Ruthless Records and issued their debut album, *Livin' Like Hustlers*, in 1990; split into violence- and sex-themed sides, it was coproduced by Dr. Dre (prior to N.W.A's rancorous breakup) and received well in gangsta circles. The *Vocally Pimpin'* EP appeared in 1991, and the full-length follow-up *Black Mafia Life* was released in 1993. Go Mack left the group shortly thereafter, and Above the Law stuck with the trio format for their last Ruthless album, 1994's *Uncle Sam's Curse*, which featured greater contributions from KMG. Following Eazy-E's tragically sudden death, Above the Law left Ruthless for Tommy Boy, debuting in 1996 with *Time Will Reveal*; although the lyrics stuck with the group's well-worn gangsta themes, it demonstrated that Big Hutch's skills as a G-funk producer were becoming ever more polished. 1998's *Legends* kept the West Coast gangsta flame burning, but proved to be their last release on Tommy Boy; they formed their own label, West World, and struck a distribution deal with Street Solid for 1999's *Forever: Rich Thugs*. The same year, Big Hutch released his solo debut, *Executive Decisions*. In 2000 Big Hutch was recruited by Suge Knight to become the new house producer and musical director at Death Row Records, making it the new home of Above the Law as well. They recorded a new album called *Diary of a Drug Dealer*, but the release dates were continually pushed back while Big Hutch worked on production assignments, including the debut album by Crooked I; amid all the album delays, rumors began to circulate about the group's breakup. —*Steve Huey*

Livin' Like Hustlers / 1990 / Ruthless ♦♦♦♦
With albums by Ice-T, N.W.A, the Geto Boys, and Eazy-E having popularized gangsta rap in the late 1980s, the stage was set for the success of Above the Law. The members of this South Central L.A. group had close ties to members of N.W.A—Above the Law produced their own debut album, *Livin' Like Hustlers*, with Dr. Dre, and recorded it for Eazy's Ruthless label (which was going through Epic as well as Priority and Atlantic). Though not in a class with Ice-T or N.W.A's work, *Hustlers* is a sobering depiction of ghetto life in L.A. Violent, profane and graphic, songs like "Another Execution," "Menace to Society," and "Murder Rap" let listeners know exactly what life in South Central was like. The imaginative Dre's input as a producer is consistently beneficial, and he sees to it that the CD comes alive musically. ATL's lyrics would sound increasingly clichéd as the 1990s progressed, but *Hustlers* shows that at the dawn of the decade, the Angelenos had some freshness. —*Alex Henderson*

● **Black Mafia Life** / 1993 / Warner Brothers ♦♦♦♦
Above the Law's second album had three things working against it. One: Over two years had passed since their debut (unless you factor 1991's *Vocally Pimpin'* EP), which certainly left many with the impression that they were no longer. Two: They had to follow up a strong Dr. Dre-produced debut with in-house production. Three: It was nearly half an hour longer than the debut, leaving it wide open for filler issues. Despite these factors, the members of Above the Law proved with *Black Mafia Life* that they were more than a one-album wonder. They returned with a record that was both more laid-back and assured, yet the sound was tougher all the same. The tales spun by Cold 187um, KMG, Big Hutch, and Go Mack are as unrelentingly grim as ever, yet this is—if anything—a party record, full of grooves and licks swiped from Bootsy Collins, the Fatback Band, and Curtis Mayfield. Cold 187um's slick sampling work—almost as accomplished as Dre's on the debut—combined with live instrumentation more than make up for the fact that none of the thoroughly convincing MCs are lyrical masters. Lop off a few substandard

moments, replace them with one or two big singles (admittedly, nothing here is as hot as the debut's "Untouchable"), and you'd have a West Coast classic. —*Andy Kellman*

Uncle Sam's Curse / 1994 / Ruthless ✦✦✦
Above the Law's third album, *Uncle Sam's Curse*, shows the Los Angeles rap crew incorporating some of Dr. Dre's sonic innovations into their basic gangsta rap sound. The group remains fine rappers and several of the tracks rank among their finest work, but the album is little more than a holding pattern—instead of moving forward, they're just keeping up with their contemporaries. —*Stephen Thomas Erlewine*

Time Will Reveal / 1996 / Tommy Boy ✦✦✦
In 1996, the debate over gangsta rap raged on. Anti-gangster rap activist C. Delores Tucker made headlines by railing against the form's violent imagery, while gangsta rappers insisted that they were simply telling it like it was and "keeping it real." What Tucker didn't realize was that gangsta at its best (Ice-T, Ice Cube) wasn't simply cheap exploitation, but a cry for help and an informative audio documentary on ghetto life. Unfortunately, gangsta on the whole had long since lost its freshness and become extremely predictable. While Above the Law's lyrics sounded fresh on its first album, *Livin' Like Hustlers*, the L.A. gangsta outfit was sounding pretty clichéd lyrically when it joined Tommy Boy with *Time Will Reveal*. Before playing the CD, one could guess that it consisted of more first-person accounts of "pimpin' and hustlin'"—and sure enough, that's exactly what it consists of. But as predictable as ATL's lyrics are, Cold 187um's sleek production is something to admire. 187's very musical, Dr. Dre-influenced production style keeps things fresh, although the lyrics show little or no growth. —*Alex Henderson*

Legends / Feb. 16, 1998 / Tommy Boy ✦✦✦
By album number five, fans knew what to expect from Above the Law. *Legends* didn't throw any curveballs; instead, it stuck to the group's regular attack with little apparent desire to expand or progress. While few West Coast gangsta groups were as skilled as Above the Law, the passage of time only shows more how *Legends* wasn't much more than just another album from the group. As ever, the group's production is its top asset, and the MCs, though hardly masters, remain vivid and convincing storytellers. Had this been the first or second record released by a newer group a few years earlier, it wouldn't have gone nearly as ignored—so this is definitely a record for the devoted. —*Andy Kellman*

Forever Rich Thugs / Oct. 26, 1999 / Street Solid ✦✦✦
Recording for Street Solid in the late 1990s, Gregory Hutchinson—who also went by Cold 187um as well as Big Hutch—had two careers. The South Central L.A. gangsta rapper launched a solo career with 1999's *Executive Decisions*, but he was still a member of Above the Law, whose *Forever Rich Thugs* is among the group's more memorable releases. Lyrically, this CD breaks no new ground for ATL, who still rap in the first person about players, pimps, and hustlers and don't offer any insights that they weren't offering nine years earlier. But while *Forever Rich Thugs* isn't groundbreaking, the CD commands attention thanks to its infectious beats, above-average hooks, and melodic grooves. Whether Hutch, Big Mil, or D.J. Silk is doing the producing, Dr. Dre's sleek production style is an influence throughout the album. Without question, *Forever Rich Thugs* is among ATL's best-sounding CDs. To be sure, ATL's lyrics can be quite predictable, but musically, *Forever Rich Thugs* has no problem grabbing one's attention and keeping it. —*Alex Henderson*

Abstract Mindstate

Group / Underground Rap, Hip-Hop
Abstract Mindstate the M.O.D. (Misfitz of Dialogue) comprised MCs Ice Gre and Ebony Poetess the Hellcat. Mindstate formed at Jackson State in Mississippi, where Gre and EP helped form the Stewpot Stowaways, a hip-hop crew of "outcasts," or individuals who were originally from the Jackson area. The Stewpot Stowaways collective also featured David Banner and Kamikaze, who would go on to form Crooked Lettaz. In 2001, Kamikaze appeared on *We Paid Let Us In!*, Abstract Mindstate's debut album for 404 Entertainment. With songs like "Equiponderance," "Taoism," and "The Art of Speaking," Abstract Mindstate aligned itself with the consciousness of the underground hip-hop movement. But despite its independent release, *We Paid* featured innovative production that reached beyond the nebulous boundaries of the underground movement. In late 2002, Ice Gre contributed to Gravel Records' *Chicago Project: 100% Chicago Hip Hop.* —*Johnny Loftus*

● **We Paid Let Us In!** / Jun. 12, 2001 / Cream ✦✦✦✦
Even if this Chicago duo's moniker doesn't clue you into the fact that they're coming on the conscious hip-hop tip, it should at least make it clear that this is *not* your typical bling-bling, bitches, and gangsta crap. Instead, you get progressive, positive songs like "Equiponderance," which blends jazzy beats and slinky string samples with clever lyrics that present the duo as "the underground masters of twisted wordplay and delivery." Even when the group takes a more tough, street-minded approach on songs like "Wonder Twins," it's just to take on wack MCs and "ten hoes with no flows, all rockin' Timbos." For an underground hip-hop group, the production on *We Paid Let Us In!* is both impressively tight and diverse, ranging from the soulful groove of "The Storm" to the stripped-down minimalist funk of "Taoism." And though the group needs to master the art of crafting memorable vocal hooks, their crafty blend of intelligent rhymes and colorful samples places Abstract Mindstate the M.O.D., alongside artists like Common, among the best Chicago's urban scene has to offer. —*Bret Love*

Abstract Rude

Underground Rap, Alternative Rap, Hip-Hop
As a product of the legendary Goodlife open mic sessions who wished to highlight the nuances of the Los Angeles underground rap scene, Abstract Rude first made a name for himself in 1994 as an executive producer of the *Project Blowed* compilation. The groundbreaking album also pinpointed Abstract Rude as a skillful MC, capable of expressing extremely soulful sentiments with his mystical themes and deeply pronounced voice. As a longtime collaborator with Aceyalone and as a founding member of Abstract Tribe Unique, Abstract Rude carved out a niche for himself as hip-hop's most accessible healer. Most comfortable fronting the atmospheric production provided by Fat Jack on albums such as *Mood Pieces* and *South Central Thynk Tank*, Abstract Rude proves that clarity in rap is just as impressive as complexity. His work on the Haiku d'Etat project in 1997, which aimed to merge hip-hop with jazz, only further illustrated his interest in placing his music within a historical context. All in all, Abstract Rude is an artist that both your grandmother and your little brother could appreciate. Having run the gamut of label affiliations, from being completely independent to being signed to Capitol's Grand Royal to being independent again by way of Ocean Floor, Abstract Rude seems to have found an appropriate home for himself at Battle Axe; his 2001 album, titled *P.A.I.N.T.*, is further proof that Abstract Rude is a true lyrical heavyweight. —*Robert Gabriel*

● **P.A.I.N.T.** / Sep. 18, 2001 / Battle Axe ✦✦✦
Following the release of *Code Name: Scorpion*, a collaboration with fellow Battle Axe artist Moka Only, Abstract Rude's first legitimate solo LP gathers other prominent underground MCs for this solid autumn 2001 release. After singles for Grand Royal and Big Dada, much anticipation has built for a showing of what the deep-voiced rapper can do over an entire record, and the results prove mixed. With a baritone voice most similar to Chali 2Na and lyrical content ranging from the hip-hop game to the spirit of industry independence, AR's vocal delivery is laid-back and seems most comfortable bouncing off syncopated beats from the mid-bpm funk palette. Highlights include "Birds of a Feather," with its kinky beat and clean production; "Dawning of the A.G.E.," on which AR flows over down-home B3 organ samples and features Grouch and Eligh; and most notably, a standout collaboration with Atmosphere's Slug and Eyedea along with Busdriver and LMNO on "Frisbee," a blue-collar salute to musical liberation. Conclusively, Abstract Rude illustrates his voice's niche in hip-hop, though whether or not it can stand alone without a strong supporting cast is yet to be seen. —*Nic Kincaid*

Abstract Tribe Unique

f. Los Angeles, CA
Group / Hip-Hop, Underground Rap
Based out of the South Central L.A. hip-hop community, the Abstract Tribe Unique's lyrical theme has always revolved around their surroundings of growing up in the projects. First featured on their 1997 self-released *Underground Fossils* album, the urban storytelling continued two years later on their followup *South Central Thynk Tank* on Ocean Floor Records. —*Mike DaRonco*

● **South Central Thynk Taynk** / Sep. 5, 2000 / Massmen ✦✦✦✦
In an attempt to lend emotional credibility to the genre of rap, much in the same way that Curtis Mayfield or Marvin Gaye did for '70s soul music,

Abstract Tribe Unique not only goes out on a limb but also proves it to be a beautiful place to perch. With the beats provided by Fat Jack bordering on the ethereal and the lyrics provided by Abstract Rude lingering among the esoteric, *South Central Thynk Tank* is an album made especially for mature hip-hop aficionados. Whether it be the guiding nature of "No Regrets," the brutal truth of "Why Oh Why," the opulent projections of "Just Like Akira," or the hopefulness of "Through These Streets," Abstract Tribe Unique is certainly not afraid to let it all hang out as they deal with delicate issues. Neo-soul before there was ever such a thing as neo-soul, *South Central Thynk Tank* naturally bridges the gap between musical generations. Yet not to be confused as soft, the heart of the lion pumps strong throughout the album and especially on tracks such as "LA Styles Back" and "Showgun." —*Robert Gabriel*

Aceyalone

Hip-Hop, West Coast Rap, Alternative Rap
A founding member of Freestyle Fellowship, Aceyalone played an important role in the evolution of literate hip-hop on the West Coast during an era when hardcore gangsta rap reigned. Following the dissolution of the group, Aceyalone embarked on a solo career that never resulted in enormous success but did allow him to maintain his revered status within the West Coast underground hip-hop scene. He debuted solo on *All Balls Don't Bounce* (1995) and followed up with *A Book of Human Language* (1998). After a three-year absence from the hip-hop scene, Aceyalone returned in 2001 with *Accepted Eclectic*, an album released by the Ground Control label, which also proceeded to re-release his debut album. —*Jason Birchmeier*

★ **All Balls Don't Bounce** / Oct. 24, 1995 / Capitol ✦✦✦✦✦
The breakout MC from the woefully underappreciated Freestyle Fellowship, Aceyalone emerged as the godfather of the L.A. underground scene with his 1995 solo debut, *All Balls Don't Bounce*. A spectacular lyrical milestone, *All Balls* was overlooked at the time, and later slipped quietly out of print. This is extremely unfortunate, since Aceyalone is one of the greatest lyricists the West Coast has ever produced, twisting his fluid rhymes around and off the beat with the improvisational assurance of Rakim. What's more, his subject matter goes beyond the battle rhymes that most mike virtuosos hone their technique with. He's cerebral and philosophical, yet bursting with confidence at the same time, which lends a definite sense of excitement to his literate wordplay. His lyrics aren't just long strings of ten-cent words—they're an important part of the songs' rhythmic drive, and he knows when to leave empty space in his lines to keep the groove flowing smoothly. The production on *All Balls Don't Bounce* is solid if unspectacular, usually spare and jazzy, with lots of piano/keyboard samples and some fitting nods to the abstract side of hard bop. If it's occasionally geared to spotlight the lyrics, that's only logical, especially when the results are as daring as "Arythamaticulas." Lead single "Mic Check" and "All Balls" are textbook MC showcases, as is "Knownots," a tag-team track with future Haiku d'Etat cohorts Mikah 9 and Abstract Rude. On the vibraphone-driven jazz-rap cuts "The Greatest Show on Earth" and "Headaches & Woes," Acey lays down some of the most rhythmically sophisticated, complex rhymes since the Native Tongues. His positive attitude toward women is more than just political correctness; he's nothing less than enraptured by them. In "Annalillia," he can't resist being shot down repeatedly by a fascinating and independent woman, and in "Makeba," he tries to win back a favorite ex-girlfriend who left without warning. It all adds up to a singular debut from a major talent. —*Steve Huey*

A Book of Human Language / Apr. 14, 1998 / Project Blowed ✦✦✦✦
A hip-hop concept album with a rather broad concept: the main thread seems to be that the song titles all begin with "The" ("The March," "The Vision," "The Hunt," etc.). If *A Book of Human Language*'s 20 tracks drag somewhat at times—and are weighed down by a bit too much THC-induced profundity—this is easily forgiven, since it is a relief to hear a rapper rap about something other than his own greatness. Aceyalone wins major points for even trying to tackle weighty topics like life, death, time, and language. The production is organic and rich, but just ragged enough to sound honest. Add in a spoken-word excerpt from "Jabberwocky," exceedingly deft rhyming and a hip-hop answer to Pink Floyd's "Time" ("The Grandfather Clock"), and you have a quite ambitious and pleasing package. —*Bill Cassel*

Accepted Eclectic / Mar. 6, 2001 / Ground Control ✦✦✦✦✦
By the time Aceyalone recorded his third solo album, he was recognized as a founding father of the L.A. underground. In an era dominated by gangsta rap,

he'd posited an alternative based on intellectual lyrics and virtuosic microphone technique, and his work—both solo and with Freestyle Fellowship—helped inspire future crews to return to hip-hop's basic elements. Acey stuck around via a series of independent side projects and underground supergroup collaborations, and finally returned to his solo career with 2001's excellent *Accepted Eclectic*. For all his lyrical talent, Aceyalone has sometimes been plagued by erratic production, and *Accepted Eclectic*—despite a few cheap-sounding drum machines in spots—takes steps to remedy that situation with a stronger, funkier set of beats. It also backs off the overambitious concept of *A Book of Human Language*, instead simply letting Aceyalone's winning personality shine through. He's his usual reflective self on the excellent "I Never Knew," about how you have to experience the bad to appreciate the good, and "I Can't Complain," where he's grateful just to have his basic needs met. But there are plenty of exciting moments as well. "Rappers Rappers Rappers" and "Golden Mic" are showcases for his tremendous wordplay and rapid-fire rhyming skills, respectively, and the shifting classical samples of the title track make it one of the best productions in his catalog. "Master Your High" samples Slick Rick's "Hey Young World" as the basis for a witty riff on overindulgent kids who haven't learned to hold their liquor or drugs. Those are just the top highlights on a strikingly consistent album that's packed with imaginative, smooth-flowing rhymes, and a simple joy in creating them. —*Steve Huey*

A.D.O.R. (Eddie Castellanos)

b. Manhattan, NY
Vocals / Hip-Hop, Pop-Rap, Gangsta Rap, Hardcore Rap
A.D.O.R. (born Eddie Castellanos) burst on the rap scene seemingly out of nowhere when he dropped, in the summer of 1992, the infectious Pete Rock-produced single "Let It All Hang Out," an unexpected Top Ten *Billboard* hit and instant classic. In fact, the rapper did not emerge out of an artistic vacuum, nor was the Pete Rock connection a fortuitous one. Castellanos was born in the Washington Heights section of Manhattan to a professional musician father who would often take his young son along with him during late or all-night jam and recording sessions around New York City. When he was six, his family moved to Mt. Vernon, NY—later known to hip-hop aficionados as "money-earnin'" Mt. Vernon—where Castellanos grew up alongside some of rap's and R&B's most gifted burgeoning talents. In high school he rubbed shoulders with, among others, classmates Sean "Puffy" Combs, Heavy D, Al B. Sure, and, of course, Pete Rock, and began to earn a reputation around the neighborhood as an MC. Demo recordings of the newly christened A.D.O.R. (short for, variously, "Another Dimension of Rhythm" or "A Declaration of Revolution") eventually made their way to Uptown Records, and Combs became one of Castellanos' early supporters, personally shopping his music around the industry. Soon thereafter, DJ Eddie F of Heavy D & the Boyz signed him to a production and management deal with Untouchables Entertainment, and he found himself in the studio recording "Let It All Hang Out" for Atlantic Records.

A well-received live performance on Fox's popular sketch-comedy show *In Living Color* and a second single, and the underground hit "One for the Trouble" (produced by Marley Marl and Kevin "K-Def" Hanson, and later the vocal hook for Fatboy Slim's "Old Skool Mix" of Wildchild's 1995 club anthem "Renegade Master"), soon followed, as did live performances supporting Tupac and the Notorious B.I.G. A.D.O.R. was supposed to back up those successes with the completed full-length *The Concrete*; unfortunately, adversity soon struck. His production and management deals collapsed, and Atlantic decided to shelve the record. Castellanos rebounded by forming Tru Reign Records and inaugurated his new label with another Rock-produced single, "Enter the Center," in 1996. It sold remarkably well for an indie record and earned strong radio support, leading to the release of his official debut album, *Shock Frequency*, in 1998. The next year, Tru Reign signed a national deal with Nile Rodgers' Sumthing Distribution, which put out the second A.D.O.R. album, *Animal 2000*. In 2003 a pair of additional albums arrived, the compilation of hits and exclusive tracks, *Classic Bangerz, Vol. 1*, and an all-new studio album, *Signature of the Ill*. —*Stanton Swihart*

● **Shock Frequency** / Aug. 25, 1998 / Tru Reign ✦✦✦
In 1992 A.D.O.R. came out of nowhere with the tasty Pete Rock-produced "Let It All Hang Out" with its irresistible horn loop and tight flow, giving the artist one of the surprise hits of the summer. He then set out to record an album,

The Concrete, that was to make good on the early promise, but several years passed with nary another peep from the artist, before Atlantic Records announced in 1995 that they were dropping A.D.O.R. from the label, and with him his proposed album. Disheartened, he formed his own Tru Reign Records in 1996 and a full-length debut, *Shock Frequency*, finally came out on the label in 1998. It received only mixed (though generally positive) critical notices. A primary reason for the lack of enthusiasm among some critics was a legitimate flaw that gradually surfaces upon listening to the work: namely that, for a record appearing in 1998, *Shock Frequency* was, well, very 1992. While this alone is not enough to sink the music or invalidate its numerous pleasures, it does have the effect of sapping some of the album's vibrancy and rendering it irrelevant to an industry that had already passed it by. Duly noted. But it is apparent why A.D.O.R. would have wanted hip-hop fans to hear these songs: not only were they tracked by such heavyweights as Rock, Diamond D., and Clark Kent, but they are also superb by any standard of measurement. Chief among the outstanding tracks is, of course, "Let It All Hang Out," which retains every ounce of its original force, as well as an added sense of staying power that it couldn't possibly have conveyed in 1992. The other Rock songs are nearly its equals, as are the Rock facsimiles "Shock to Bliss" and "Shock Frequency," and Kent's "From the Concrete" is excellent. The rest sags a bit under the weight of those cuts, but *Shock Frequency* still would have rated higher were it not for its history of bad luck. —*Stanton Swihart*

Aesop Rock (Ian Bavitz)

Alternative Rap, Underground Rap

New York City-based hip-hop artist Aesop Rock possesses a rapping style similar to such eccentric artists as Kool Keith and Del tha Funkee Homosapien, while building a following with a series of releases on the Def Jux label. After the release of his debut full-length, *Mush*, Aesop Rock issued a pair of singles for Def Jux, *Coma* and *Boom Box*, before issuing his second full-length overall, *Labor Days*, in September of 2001, an album which surprisingly featured numerous references to history and mythology (not your usual hip-hop subject matter). —*Greg Prato*

Float / 2000 / Mush ◆◆◆◆

Words to describe this work would be surprising, analytical, darkness, mystery, lyricism, and jealous. Jealous because it's likely that every person who has ever tried to rap would wish he could rhyme like this guy, and every poet would wish to dream with such imagery. If you're into booty shakin' and dancing, and that's the reason you listen to hip-hop, do not buy this album. But if you like hip-hop for rhymes that make you think, this guy just can't be slept on. For example, "6B Panorama" discusses the view from his NYC apartment and starts like this: "I was sitting on my fire escape and I saaaaaaw … Sturdy bridges, decorated with dirty pigeons, a vagabond beggin' for three pennies and a princess, a junky tourniquet surgeon urgin' the needle in, a batty senior citizen flashin' that awful teethless grin." Artists such as Aesop Rock paint intricate abstract pictures with their music, and it's simply too much information to handle in a single sitting. This album is so complex that it may never be fully comprehended by the listener, but you may find yourself walking along listening one day and finally figure out one of the metaphors—a great feeling. This is one of a few albums definitely worth any import pricing. One more quote: "(I see) a challenge, a chance to add real colors to my favorite palette, raise my mighty mallet toward the gods and swing my talents!" —*Brad Mills*

● **Labor Days** / Sep. 18, 2001 / Def Jux ◆◆◆◆◆

After finding an eager online audience for his dense soundscapes and even more complex rhymes, New York MC Aesop Rock released his most potent combination of words and music on his Def Jux debut. Crammed with references to history and mythology, as well as the usual pop-culture name checks, Aesop's lyrics remain unusually verbose and intelligent here, but he's also able to spin them into compelling stories. The best example is the bittersweet, follow-your-dreams saga of "No Regrets," which chronicles a woman's sacrifices for art from childhood to old age. Besides the wealth of detail, the song doesn't sugarcoat the loneliness of its subject, even as it shows her at ease with her choices. And on "9-5ers Anthem," Aesop—who still works a day job himself—allays any concerns about him being a hip-hop elitist, offering a shout out to the blue-collar masses. There are still instances where he gives his listeners simply too much information to process for a pop song ("The

Tugboat Complex, Pt. 3"), but overall he does his best job yet at balancing smarts and accessibility. Of course, with such a focus on lyrics, it's easy to ignore the beats behind them—but while the sampled backing is sometimes on the plain side, *Labor Days* contains some inventive bites from classical music, and more than a few tunes will grow on you, if given the chance. —*Dan LeRoy*

Daylight EP / Feb. 5, 2002 / Def Jux ◆◆◆

Cannibal Ox and Company Flow may have played a more visible role in the Def Jux label's rise to critically acclaimed status in the early 2000s, but Aesop Rock also garnered a considerable amount of attention for the alternative rap label. He collaborates with producer Blockhead here, though Cannibal Ox fans will be happy to know that El-P produces one of this EP's tracks, "Nickel Plated Pockets." But for the most part, this EP is a showcase for Blockhead and Aesop. The two lay down quite a few tracks that are on a par with those found on Aesop's preceding full-length *Labor Days*, making this EP a wonderful follow-up that should interest fans of the Def Jux establishment. —*Jason Birchmeier*

Afrika Islam

b. Jun. 19, 1962
Producer, DJ / Pop-Rap, Old School Rap

Best known for his production work with hardcore rapper Ice-T, Afrika Islam is a virtuoso DJ, able to spin four turntables at one time. Beginning his career as an apprentice to Afrika Bambaataa, in the late '70s Islam met Earl Chin at radio station WHBI, who offered the young DJ a show. Calling his show Zulu Beats, Islam teamed up with the group Supreme Team and began gaining a substantial following at the station. After a short period as a DJ for the Rock Steady Crew in the early '80s, Islam moved to L.A. where he appeared in films such as *Breakin' II* and *Pump up the Volume*. Islam also began doing production work for Ice-T, producing four gold albums for the hardcore rapper, including the *Colors* and *New Jack Hustler* soundtracks. Through his work with Ice-T, Islam also began remixing for other artists, including Michael Jackson, New Order, and the Eurythmics. Afrika Islam exported his successful Zulu Beats show to Japan in 1992. —*Steve Kurutz*

● **Afrika Jam** / 1997 / East West ◆◆◆

Afroman (Joseph Foreman)

Comedy Rap, Dirty Rap, Alternative Rap

Born Joseph Foreman, Afroman may be the first artist to achieve a worldwide hit with the assistance of the Internet. Citing his influences as Too Short, Big Daddy Kane, and 2 Live Crew, he began his rap career in the eighth grade when he started making homemade tapes of his own songs and passing them out to his classmates. He got his start as a performer at church where he played drums and eventually moved on to playing guitar. For a while, he used to work as a baggage handler at an airport while trying to make an impression with his songs.

He was still living in East Palmdale, L.A., when in November 1999 Afroman released his first album, *Sell Your Dope*, and played parties, sidewalks, and contests. Not finding L.A. to his liking, he moved to Hattiesburg, MS, where he teamed up with drummer Jody Stallone and keyboardist/bassist Daryl Havard. In the spring of 2000 he concocted his second LP, *Because I Got High*, with producer Tim Ramenofsky. He distributed it at shows and with the help of T-Bone Records in Hattiesburg. The more people he performed for, the more word of mouth spread, with not just a little help from the Internet's controversial music file swapping service, Napster. Someone who got their hands on his music at a show posted the track "Because I Got High" to Napster, and suddenly everything changed for Afroman. Then Howard Stern's radio show boosted its popularity by playing the song on his show. "Because I Got High," based on Afroman's inability to clean up his room, lists a number of activities—cleaning his room, going to court, attending class—that get derailed because of "reefer madness."

Afroman eventually also gained the attention of Universal Records, who signed him to a six-album deal. His first Universal album, *The Good Times*, was a compilation of his first two LPs and a few new ones. "Because I Got High" was also included on the soundtrack to Kevin Smith's film *Jay and Silent Bob Strike Back*, starring Matt Damon and Ben Affleck. "Because I Got High" became a huge hit around the world in the last quarter of 2001. —*Ed Nimmervoll*

Because I Got High / Jun. 20, 2000 / T-Bone ✦✦✦
Released roughly a year before Afroman received worldwide notoriety for the title track, the dirty Southerner released this record to an underground that welcomed him with open arms. Aside from the Grammy-nominated obvious hit, there are some songs here that give "Because I Got High" a run for its money. Make no mistake, Afroman is primarily into two things: getting high and scoring with the ladies. And while the concept is nothing new to rap, he does it with a certain swagger that is seldom seen in the genre. However, that is not to say that *Because I Got High* isn't without fault. There are some songs that definitely go on a bit too long, and there are times when he tries a bit too hard to become the next Blowfly. But that's part of the charm of this record. It's a look deep into the recording studio with guys that just want to make music and have fun doing it. —*Rob Theakston*

● **The Good Times** / Aug. 28, 2001 / Uptown/Universal ✦✦✦
"Because I Got High" is one of those genius, perfectly conceived and executed singles that seem to arise from the ether as if they've always been there. Sparsely instrumented, recorded so nonchalantly it's hard to believe that anybody believed that the tape was rolling, it's a riot—it's not just a frat rock anthem, it's a logical, brilliant record, escalating from verse to verse, with its consciously offhanded comments still capable of eliciting extreme laughter on the 20th spin. It's so good, in fact, that it's easy to expect the rest of Afroman's *The Good Times* to be of similar caliber, but it's not, even if "The American Dream" borrows the backing track wholesale. Problem is, Afroman doesn't rely on the cleverness that informs "Because I Got High," but he trades it for vulgarity that could have been acceptable if it had a spark of wit—instead, it just lays there. It's not necessarily a bad listen, since it is in the same vein as the hit, and is fairly well produced, but it just doesn't have the spark that makes "Because I Got High" such an intoxicating, irresistible single. So, if you're looking just for that song, you're better off with the *Jay & Silent Bob Strike Back* soundtrack, because at least with that you get Jason Mewes' brilliant updating of "Jay's Rap." —*Stephen Thomas Erlewine*

Afros

Group / Golden Age
A trio with a penchant for sight gags linked to huge bushy hairstyles from the same decade (two members, Hurricane and Koot Tee, were clean shaven, while DJ Kippy-O had an extensive afro). The group also has a good pedigree, with Hurricane being a DJ for the Beastie Boys and a rapper for Davy D. Their material is more in a mode of parody/satire than confrontation, with a couple of political-consciousness and cultural-awareness cuts added to spice the menu. —*Ron Wynn*

● **Kickin' Afrolistics** / 1990 / Ral ✦✦✦✦✦
A side project of Run-D.M.C.'s Jam Master Jay, *Kickin' Afrolistics* was a satirical look at '70s blaxploitation films and the ever popular afro. Filled with Jay's signature production and Beastie Boy DJ Hurricane helping to supply the rhymes and beats, it's a solid album that doesn't fail to deliver musically. However, while the satirical concept was original at the time, it seems a bit dated at present and wears thin after a while—especially when bordering on Digital Underground territory. For serious heads only. —*Rob Theakston*

Afu-Ra (Aaron Phillip)

Vocals / Hip-Hop, East Coast Rap
From his 1994 breakout on Jeru the Damaja's "Mental Stamina," Afu-Ra has fused classic East Coast hardcore with the sensitive, intelligent wordplay expected from a committed Rastafarian. He started out much like any other young New York rapper, though his rhymes impressed Jeru the Damaja enough to include him on his debut. Becoming a Jeru protégé (just as Jeru had come up with Gang Starr), Afu-Ra appeared on the second Jeru album (*Wrath of the Math*) as well, but moved out on his own for the 1998 single "Whirlwind Thru Cities," an underground favorite. *Body of the Life Force*, his debut album, appeared in 2000, boasting features for GZA and Cocoa Brovaz. Afu-Ra hooked back up with Gang Starr's DJ Premier (who'd helmed quite a few Jeru tracks) for 2002's *Life Force Radio*. —*John Bush*

Defeat/Mortal Kombat [Single] / Aug. 17, 1999 / Gee Street ✦✦
"Defeat" is produced by DJ Premier and he did a great job. By the time Afu-Ra starts rapping, you're hooked. "Mortal Kombat" is produced by DJ Roach and is a slower song with an Asian influence to it. Wu-Tang's Masta Killa joins Afu Ra on "Mortal Kombat." —*Dan Gizzi*

Body of the Life Force / Oct. 10, 2000 / Koch International ✦✦✦
Five years after debuting with a few rhymes on Jeru's *The Sun Rises in the East*, Afu-Ra released his full-length debut, *Body of the Life Force*. Though his first single, 1998's "Whirlwind Thru Cities" (also included here), shows the influence of Jeru, elsewhere he's definitely his own man. Optimistic and spiritual where Jeru was aggressive and metaphysical, Afu-Ra has dozens of good lyrical ideas, though he often phrases the same way, with a heavy focus on multiple internal rhymes à la Rakim. Fortunately, there's a parade of solid productions lending variety, led by Muggs on "Soul Assassination" and DJ Premier on "Mic Stance" and "Defeat." Afu-Ra also invited a few guests, and the collaborations are welcome: GZA matches wits on "Bigacts Littleacts," Cocoa Brovaz and Jahdan show up on "D&D Soundclash" (Afu-Ra's salute to his roots at the legendary D&D Studios), and Wu-Tang's Masta Killa leads him into hardcore territory for "Mortal Kombat." —*John Bush*

● **Life Force Radio** / May 21, 2002 / Koch International ✦✦✦✦
Afu-Ra's sophomore effort, the aptly titled *Life Force Radio*, is an album that manages to cover every form of hip-hop in a collection of 17 impressive tracks. This Rastafarian doesn't bother to busy himself with the overdone ghetto glamour that crews such as No Limit and Cash Money dispense, and instead steers toward a more intelligent form of rap. "Stick Up" does have themes common to the gangsta style, yet Afu-Ra's flows are far from generic, which helps add weight to the cut and lets this song aspire to a whole different plane than the overproduced, faceless clones plaguing the rap scene. Throughout the album, Afu-Ra's talent prevails as a dominating new force in a scene that foolishly overlooked his debut, and this hip-hop prodigy could be given the same respect as Nas, the Roots, and Jurassic 5. Undeniable skill and prowess invade every crevice on *Life Force Radio*, whether on the spunky love tune "Open" or the straight-up club smash "Hip Hop," and not once does Afu-Ra disappoint. The album also features heavyweight performances from such notable MCs as RZA from the Wu-Tang Clan, M.O.P., and Guru, as well as additional production by Easy Mo Bee and True Master. Over all of this, DJ Premier's spectacular production gives the album a life of its own. Enjoyable, moving, and remarkably clever, *Life Force Radio* should finally bring recognition to one of hip-hop's freshest and most entertaining new faces. —*Jason D. Taylor*

AG (Andre Barnes)

Hardcore Rap
A founding member of New York's D.I.T.C. (Diggin' in the Crates Crew), AG made his first appearance on Lord Finesse's debut album, *Funky Technician*, in 1990. Teaming up with partner Showbiz in 1991, the duo released their first EP, *Party Groove/Soul Clap*, and were subsequently signed to Payday Records. AG stuck with Showbiz, releasing three albums in the early to mid-'90s, and appeared on plenty of D.I.T.C.-related albums, among others. His first solo effort, *The Dirty Version*, was released on Silvadom Records in 1999. —*Brad Mills*

● **The Dirty Version** / Sep. 21, 1999 / Silva Dom ✦✦✦
Though billed as AG's first solo effort, *The Dirty Version* is actually a collaborative effort between AG and his Ghetto Dwellaz (D-Flow and Party Arty) affiliates. Wherever AG emerges, beats are sure to follow, and the production (Showbiz, Premier, Buckwild, Diamond D, and Lord Finesse) is the LP's backbone. Even though AG's frequent collaborations with the Ghetto Dwellaz create disconcerting gaps in continuity, there's no disputing the groupings between AG and his esteemed D.I.T.C. cohorts, "Drop It Heavy" featuring KRS-One and Big Pun, "Weed Scented" featuring Guru and OC, and "Underground Life" featuring Fat Joe and GD. While AG runs the risk of overexposing himself before the highly anticipated D.I.T.C. project, this serves as an adequate appetizer before the impending feast. —*Matt Conaway*

Ahmad (Ahmad Ali Lewis)

b. Los Angeles, CA
West Coast Rap
Los Angeles rapper Ahmad Ali Lewis was only 18 when he burst onto the scene in 1994 with the laid-back groove of "Back in the Day," based around a sample of the Staple Singers' "Let's Do It Again" and produced by Berry Gordy's son Kendal. With its images of playground foolery and junior-high discovery, "Back in the Day" depicted Ahmad's South Central neighborhood in an idyllic, wistful light—a Norman Rockwell painting in rap. In the years

after Dr. Dre's G-funk masterpiece *The Chronic*, West Coast hip-hop found other voices in Ahmad, Montell Jordan, and MC Hammer. Songs like "Back in the Day" or Jordan's "This Is How We Do It" were G-funk lite. They were more about the partying than the thugging, and in doing so tapped into what's always made California pop music successful nationwide—everyone knows the party's always better out there in the sunshine. Ahmad rode "Back in the Day"'s sunlit vibe to the top of the charts, and saw Giant release his self-titled debut in May of 1994. Unfortunately, Ahmad learned of hip-hop's fleeting celebrity the hard way, and soon dropped off the radar, relegating the one-hit wonder of "Back in the Day" to mix-tape gem status forevermore. —*Johnny Loftus*

Ahmad / 1994 / Giant ✦✦✦✦
Ahmad's 1994 self-titled debut was G-funk lite. It avoided the gangsta violence and cultural criticism that defined much of the music from his South Central neighborhood, and followed instead in the laid-back footsteps of Dr. Dre's epochal 1992 release *The Chronic*. While it lacked Dre's midas production and wasn't quite as solid as stylistic contemporary Montell Jordan's *This Is How We Do It*, Ahmad was still full of great songs. With its images of playground foolery and junior-high discovery, "Back in the Day" depicted Ahmad's boyhood days in an idyllic, wistful light—a hip-hop Norman Rockwell painting. It was the only significant single from Ahmad's debut, but by no means was it the only thing worth hearing. "Touch the Ceiling," "Can I Party?," and the self-explanatory "We Want the Funk" were all charming, Parliament/Funkadelic-style jams. "Homeboys First," while a bit clichéd, was rumbling and jocular, with a debt to *Low End Theory*-era Tribe Called Quest. Ahmad wasn't able to capitalize on his success, and eventually faded from sight. But his debut is a memorable ride, with a youthful, effervescent vibe as warm as the California sun. —*Johnny Loftus*

Aim (Andy Turner)

Producer / Trip-Hop, Club/Dance
Aim's Andy Turner is a cinematic British trip-hop producer who retains close ties to the rap influences of his youth. The son of a jazz musician, Turner began his music career in 1989 as a rap DJ. He began recording as well and signed to the Grand Central label after meeting label head Mark Rae at a record store. Turner made his Aim debut with 1995's *Pacific Northwest EP* and followed with tracks from a few Grand Central compilations as well as another EP, *Soul Dive*. In 1999 he released his album debut, *Cold Water Music*. Turner has also remixed Ian Brown, St. Etienne, the Charlatans UK, Raissa, and Mucho Macho. —*John Bush*

● **Cold Water Music** / Oct. 11, 1999 / Grand Central ✦✦✦✦
From the traditionalist artwork on the cover to the intro (a hazy, spoken-word track reminiscent of Lee Hazlewood), listeners can easily be forgiven for expecting an electronica/rock crossover album on the order of Air or Groove Armada. Instead, Aim's *Cold Water Music* is a jazzy, beat-heavy project that's just a few steps removed from straight-ahead hip-hop. Producer Andy Turner, a self-confessed beathead, cycles between jazz-rap and alternative wall-of-sound influences to bedrock his productions. Turner also gets props for drafting three excellent rappers—Q'n'C, YZ, and AG—to add vocals, resulting in several tracks that evoke the heyday of rap's golden age, but are also tough enough to survive even on modern mainstream rap radio. Though half of the standard songs are vocal tracks, Turner also shines on the instrumentals, constructing a paranoid beat symphony on "Demonique" with shrieking strings and an extended vocal sample from some forgotten B-movie. —*John Bush*

Hinterland / Feb. 26, 2002 / Grand Central ✦✦✦✦
Hinterland not only proves that *Cold Water Music*, the first Aim record, was no fluke, but arguably betters it with a broader palette and a finer production touch. Andy Turner lays *way* back on the groove, coming on like Sade on the skeletal "Good Disease," then inviting veteran producer Diamond D. to take his sweet time with some diss rhymes for "The Omen." Elsewhere, "A Twilight Zone" has an appealing pastoral quality not heard in dance circles since Beth Orton's *Central Reservation*. There's nothing revolutionary here, just a few downtempo beats and breaks with atmospheric overlays reminiscent of soundtracks from the '60s and '70s. Still, Turner's gotten even better at his pacing; he balances the vocal features (only five) among excellent instrumentals like "Guimar" and "Linctus," the highlights here. Though it's so laid-back as to be nearly horizontal, *Hinterland* is still an entertaining listen,

an excellent album from one of the best producers in the post-trip-hop brigade. —*John Bush*

Akinyele (Akinyele Adams)

Dirty Rap, Hardcore Rap
Gangsta-funk rapper Akinyele (aka Akinyele Adams) followed the obscenity-laced recordings of 2 Live Crew with his own homage to sex on his 1993 debut, *Vagina Diner*. Recorded for Interscope, it was followed a year later by *Bomb*. After moving to Zoo Records, Akinyele found an underground radio hit with the title track from his 1996 EP, *Put It in Your Mouth*. *Aktapuss: The Soundtrack* followed in 1999. —*John Bush*

● **Put It in Your Mouth EP** / Aug. 13, 1996 / Volcano ✦✦✦
Don't ignore the title—*Put it In Your Mouth* sounds exactly like what the title suggests. Akinyele has crafted a sexist and unbearbly hedonistic bass-heavy slice of gangsta funk with *Put It In Your Mouth*, one that isn't notable for anything but the single entendres that permeate its lyrics. Its sheer, blatant vulgarity made the song an underground hit, but the rest of the EP is populated with lesser-rans that'll ensure the group's winning streak stops at one. —*Leo Stanley*

Aktapuss: The Soundtrack / Oct. 26, 1999 / Volcano ✦✦
A modern blaxploitation flick with an updated boost to the gangsta poses and misogynistic attitudes, *Aktapuss* was directed by Lionel C. Martin (a noted music-video director) and the soundtrack was performed by Akinyele. As on almost every piece of material recorded by the rapper since his 1993 debut *Vagina Diner*, *Aktapuss* is completely sex obsessed and frequently misogynistic, as track titles like "P***y Makes the World Go Round," "I'm a Ho," "Eat P***y," and "I'd Rather F**k U!" can attest. —*Keith Farley*

Anakonda / Jul. 10, 2001 / Koch International ✦✦✦
A resident of the Lefrak area of Queens, NY, Akinyele makes rhymes that always seem to revolve around women and sex, and it's been working for years now. *Anakonda* is more of the same, with some thugs and guns thrown in, but he generally sticks to the game plan and delivers a strong yet somewhat short album. Fans of this kind of stuff (2 Live Crew, Too Short) will undoubtedly appreciate *Anakonda*, but for the average rap fan there just isn't much new here. Adding to that, a might-be opera singer pops up on a few hooks throughout the album, making for some of the most annoying choruses yet to be heard. Fortunately, there are some catchy and creative beat productions to savor, but there just isn't a "Put It in Your Mouth" or "Take a Lick," like his last albums had, that would propel this album to purchase status. —*Brad Mills*

Aleem

f. 1980, New York, NY
Group / Electro
Comprised of two brothers who can trace their music business roots back to the late-'60s Greenwich Village scene (where they shared an apartment with Jimi Hendrix), the Aleems are most noted for forming Nia Records in the early '80s. The label became home to such notable rappers as Marley Marl and MC Shan and helped develop the careers of MCs such as Sparky D. After Nia folded, the Aleems recorded an album for Atlantic Records, *Casually Formal*, before opening up their own recording studio in the late '80s. —*Steve Kurutz*

Casually Formal / 1986 / Atlantic ✦✦✦
The Aleems' brand of electro-techno funk/rock gained a small cult following in New York, NY, and with scattered fans worldwide. They managed small hits on their own Nia label with "Release Yourself," "Get Loose," and "Confusion," which resulted in the Atlantic deal. Leroy Burgess (ex-leader of Black Ivory and identical twins Tunde-Ra and Taharqa Aleem goes for the brass ring with fine examples of what they do: "Love's on Fire," "Two Faces," and "Dance to the Groove"; the album mixes upbeat dancefloor jams with mid-tempo romps and ballads. They added "Confusion," originally released on Nia, for this set. The Aleems, with Burgess and Sonny Davenport, wrote and produced all the material. Burgess also recorded with the Aleems as Calebur. —*Andrew Hamilton*

Shock! / Atlantic ✦✦
If you're not familiar with Leroy Burgess' final Black Ivory albums where the New York trio ventured from the love ballads that made them a cult item, you

won't recognize him with the Aleem Brothers on this or their first Atlantic LP. If you're looking for the searing falsetto-singing Burgess, look elsewhere. With Tunde-Ra and Taharqa Aleem, Burgess serves up another platter of electric soul that's far less compelling than their Atlantic debut. "Love Shock" is true Aleem and "Searchin'" is interesting, but the rest merely redo, to a lesser degree, what made them an underground interest. This was the Aleems' final album as artists, though they still run a recording company in the Big Apple and produce others. —*Andrew Hamilton*

Ali (Ali Jones)

Southern Rap, Pop-Rap

Following Nelly's breakthrough in 2001, one of his fellow group members in the St. Lunatics, Ali, signed with Nelly's label Universal. That same year, Ali introduced himself to the masses on the debut St. Lunatics album, *Free City* (also released by Universal), and returned shortly after with his debut album in early 2002. The album featured contributions from Nelly and the other St. Lunatics as well as production work by Jason "Jay E" Epperson and Waiel "Wally" Yaghnam. —*Jason Birchmeier*

Heavy Starch / Apr. 30, 2002 / Universal ✦✦✦
Throughout his debut album, *Heavy Starch*, Ali offers much of the same singsong rap style that fellow St. Lunatic Nelly popularized. Anyone who enjoyed the first Nelly album, *Country Grammar*, and the subsequent St. Lunatic album, *Free City*, should enjoy this album as well, given the similarity. However, Ali brings a slightly different agenda to the proceedings. You can tell that he wants to be just as much fun and carefree as Nelly, but he's a much more insightful artist. Unfortunately, these two sides of his character often clash in subtle ways during particular moments during *Heavy Starch*. For instance, just a mere glance at the cover photo—no girls, no jewelry, no fancy cars, no cocky posturing—contrasts what you'd expect from Ali given his Nelly affiliation. This sense of dissonance (does Ali want to be himself or who everyone expects him to be?) too often weighs down *Heavy Starch*. Granted, there are plenty of fun songs here—most of them produced by either Jason "Jay E" Epperson or Waiel "Wally" Yaghnam—yet they don't always seem sincere. Too often Ali seems conflicted, and you can't help wishing he'd drop the act and be himself rather than the flossed-out playboy he's expected to be. —*Jason Birchmeier*

Ali Dee (Ali Theodore)

Producer / Hip-Hop

The son of an Egyptian dancer and a Russian Jewish dancer and choreographer (as well as the nephew of Cyd Charisse), Ali Dee (aka Ali Theodore) studied jazz dance between the ages of 9 and 12 but began to breakdance after watching Swipe from Rock Steady Crew. He moved to rapping by the year of his high school graduation in 1988 and began to produce in 1990, starting with Kid Panic's "Baby, We Can Do This." That single caught Hank Shocklee's eye, so the legendary producer recruited Ali Dee for his Bomb Squad production team. He worked on the *Juice* soundtrack and Aaron Hall's "Don't Be Afraid," which reached the top of *Billboard*'s R&B chart. His first single as a rapper, "Who's da Flava/Bring It On," was followed by *Bring It On.* —*John Bush*

● **Bring It On** / Mar. 9, 1993 / EMI ✦✦✦✦
Add Ali Dee to the list of rappers successfully exploiting rap/jazz fusion. His cut "Dee Swings Jazz" expertly demonstrates the genres' shared qualities, and his whole release has both a loose, improvisational air and an edgy, combative street vibe. The single "Who's Da Flava" attracted the most attention, but there are other, equally sharp tunes like "Styles Upon Styles" and "Got 2 B Real." Sometimes he does overdo it on the violence and distasteful language, but even then he doesn't just depend on predictable obscenities, injecting some clever retort or taking another direction. —*Ron Wynn*

Tha Alkaholiks

f. 1991, Los Angeles, CA
Group / Hip-Hop

Party rappers from the West Coast, tha Alkaholiks entered the hip-hop field by working with King Tee on his 1993 *Tha Triflin' Album*; after touring with KRS-One, Ice Cube, and Too Short, they found a major-label contract with Loud/RCA. The group came together in the early '90s, after DJ E-Swift (born Eric Brooks) and Tash (born Rico Smith)—both raised in Cincinnati—had

worked together in Disturbers of the Peace (D.O.P.). The two settled permanently in Los Angeles and met J-Ro (born James Robinson), who had worked in Total Control with rapper Suavee D and King Tee (opening for the Real Roxanne and Dana Dane, among others), but was looking to move on. Named tha Alkaholiks, the trio worked with King Tee on his single "I Got It Bad Y'All," and signed to Loud/RCA for the 1993 single "Likwit/Only When I'm Drunk." Debut album *21 & Over* followed later that year, while their second, *Coast II Coast*, saw the trio working with East Coast heavyweight Q-Tip even while they maintained a West Coast party vibe throughout. Tha Alkaholiks released their third album, *Likwidation*, in August 1997, and became the Liks for 2001's *X.O. Experience*. —*John Bush*

● **21 & Over** / Apr. 1993 / Loud ✦✦✦✦
Ohio natives turned West Coast underground kings, tha Alkaholiks have long been one of hip-hop's best-kept secrets; hilarious lyrical acrobats who have never received the critical or commercial support they deserve. Assembled by gangsta rapper King Tee, they offer a witty, anarchic, and party-friendly alternative to the stone-faced, largely humorless gangsta rap that ruled the West Coast throughout much of the early '90s. With the punch lines and comic timing of comedians and undeniable skills and killer delivery of topnotch MCs, rappers J-Ro and Tash have more than enough talent and energy to back up their endlessly clever boasting. Producer, DJ, and occasional MC, E-Swift is the group's secret weapon, an unjustly underrated beatsmith whose rubbery grooves and infectious production help make tha Alkaholiks perhaps the greatest party group in hip-hop history. With titles like "Last Call," "Mary Jane," and "Only When I'm Drunk," tha Alkaholiks will never be mistaken for members of some sort of latter-day temperance movement, but their music, rhymes, and beats are so irreverent, infectious, and just plain fun that their booze-loving shtick never gets old. Brief (only ten songs) and filler free, *21 & Over* is perhaps the quintessential West Coast party album, as well as one of the most promising debut albums of the '90s, regardless of genre. —*Nathan Rabin*

Coast II Coast / Feb. 28, 1995 / Loud ✦✦✦✦
Tha Alkaholiks' wonderfully assured 1993 debut, *21 & Over*, established the group as the closest thing hip-hop has to the Marx Brothers—a trio of inspired comic anarchists devoted to, in their own immortal words, "hoes, flows, and 40 oz." But while *21 & Over* won tha Alkaholiks (who eventually changed their name to Tha Liks) a sizable cult following, it failed to win the group the sort of attention and sales that Likwit Crew affiliate protégé Xzibit eventually snagged by hooking up with super-producer Dr. Dre. Undeterred, Tha Liks released *Coast II Coast* in 1995, a solid, consistent, and hilarious follow-up that sticks to the group's winning formula while offering enough variation, stylistically and sonically, to keep things interesting. Alkaholik DJ E-Swift still handles the bulk of the production, but he's joined behind the boards by Lootpack's Madlib (also known as Quasimoto) and East Coast heavyweight Diamond D, who provides the hypnotic *Enter the Dragon* sample that propels "Let It Out." Then-newcomer Xzibit makes his presence felt throughout, ripping snidely misogynistic rhymes on "Hit And Run" and getting in touch with his inner Big Bank Hank on the hilarious old school parody "Flashback." The rest of *Coast II Coast* nicely balances J-Ro and Tash's lyrical acrobatics with E-Swift's rubbery grooves, resulting in an album that's jazzier and more laid-back than Tha Liks' debut—Q-Tip of A Tribe Called Quest even pops up on "All the Way Live"—but no less winning. *Coast II Coast* failed to net Tha Liks gold or platinum sales, but it otherwise succeeds smashingly, effortlessly satisfying Liks diehards while still leaving them thirsty for more. —*Nathan Rabin*

Likwidation / Aug. 12, 1997 / Loud ✦✦✦✦
Tha Alkaholiks' blend of gangsta rap, metal, and alternative rap is beginning to show signs of wear on their third album, *Likwidation*, but there are enough strong cuts to make the record another solid addition to their catalog. —*Leo Stanley*

X.O. Experience / Jul. 3, 2001 / Loud ✦✦✦✦
Tha Alkaholiks return minus a few syllables (please now refer to them as tha Liks). The trio's first LP in four years, *X.O. Experience*, has a very familiar theme, which J-Ro elegantly reiterates on "Bullyfoot": "Keep it pouring motherf*cker till it hurts to swallow." Though Tash and J-Ro's frat-boy exuberance still runs rampant, the group's return is marked by a noticeable change in direction. With *X.O. Experience*, tha Liks are hunting for the one thing that has previously eluded them—commercial success. In doing so, E-Swift revamps

tha Liks' sound, eschewing their largely drunken, funk-based upbringing and leading the group into the now very fashionable computerized domain. The trio's breakout, the Neptunes-produced lead single "Best U Can," best exemplifies their flossier outlook. Tha Liks' unabashed attempt to finally break through commercially does lead to a few missteps. The jubilant low-end production found throughout adds a fresh dimension to tha Liks' lyrical guzzling, exemplified by Rockwilder's vibrant electronic effects on "Run Wild" and DJ Scratch's boombastic drum bursts on "Bullyfoot," featuring the eternally amped Busta Rhymes. With *X.O. Experience*, tha Liks have accomplished their goal. They have crafted a party LP that any hip-hop fan can enjoy. —*Matt Conaway*

All City

f. 1993

Group / Hip-Hop, Freestyle, East Coast Rap

The Brooklyn-based hip-hop duo All City comprised rappers J. Mega and Greg Valentine. The duo came together in 1993 after back-to-back solo performances at a Lyricists' Lounge open mic session; both performers so impressed the crowd and each other that they decided to team up. Signing with Onyx's label Armee, All City issued their debut LP, *Metropolis God*, in 1998. —*Jason Ankeny*

● **Metropolis Gold** / Oct. 20, 1998 / MCA ✦✦

All City's debut album, *Metropolis Gold*, is a good example of a rap release that has the same problem as some hard bop and jazz fusion recordings: though you admire the artists' technique, you often feel you're getting too much technique and not enough storytelling. The CD leaves no doubt that Brooklyn MCs J. Mega and Valentine (collectively All City) have strong rhyming technique, but technique alone isn't enough to make it a great album. Most of the time, they're simply content to show off their chops, and even though that can be exhilarating, it can also wear thin. The rappers are at their best when they tell some type of meaningful story instead of just boasting. Reflecting on the harsh realities of life in Brooklyn's ghettos, "Afta Hours" and "Timez Iz Hard" are among the album's more memorable cuts. But on the whole, *Metropolis Gold* is an unfocused and erratic example of chops for the sake of chops. —*Alex Henderson*

All Natural

f. 1996

Group / Underground Rap

Chicago's underground hip-hop group All Natural features Capital D and Tone B. Nimble, the leaders of the city's Family Tree Crew. They self-released their 1997 single *Writers Block* and their 1998 debut album *No Additives, No Preservatives*, which sold over 5,000 copies. All Natural switched to Thrill Jockey for their 2001 follow-up *Second Nature*, which featured contributions from likeminded artists such as the Molemen, Dug Infinite and No I.D., Lone Catalysts, and Mr. Greenweedz. —*Heather Phares*

No Additives, No Preservatives / Feb. 16, 1998 / All Natural ✦✦✦✦

● **Second Nature** / Apr. 24, 2001 / Thrill Jockey ✦✦✦✦

All Natural's first full-length release in several years is another example of a rap album that should have been shorter. But it's still a satisfying effort despite its excessive length. Capital D delivers fast-paced, intelligent, complex rhymes and seems comfortable with both social consciousness and braggadocio; he's not perfect, however, so sometimes his delivery sounds rushed or his rhymes seem uninspired (e.g., "Mayor Daly" and "On the Daily"). Of course, the album also features several guest MCs, including J.U.I.C.E. (on "Ill Advisory," where his style contrasts effectively with Capital D, Daily Planet's Spotlight (on "Queens Get the Money," whose anti-gold-digger message contrasts with the positivity of most of this album), and Atmosphere's Slug (who shines on "Uncle Sam"). Meanwhile, DJ Tone B. Nimble shows off his turntablist skills and shares production chores with Capital D, Molemen's Memo (who handles the decks on the percussion-heavy "Chatham" and two other tracks) and His-Panik (who layers strings over the heavy bass line of "The Stick Up" and piano over the sloomy drums of "Queens Get the Money"), Lone Catalysts' Jason Rawls (who adds a piano loop that blends perfectly with MC Jason Sands' delivery on "Renaissance"), and G(riot) (whose tracks include the affecting instrumental "The Next Mile"). The production is somewhat uneven, but overall this is a solid, understated, jazz-inflected

album that will definitely reward listeners' attention, even though it won't send the future of music in any unexpected directions. —*Todd Kristel*

Allfrumtha i

Group / Hip-Hop, Hardcore Rap

Signed to Mack 10's production company, Allfrumtha was formed by Squeek-Ru and Binky. The duo released their self-titled debut album in April 1998. —*John Bush*

● **Allfrumtha i** / Apr. 21, 1998 / Priority ✦✦✦

At first, Allfrumtha i's eponymous debut appears to fulfill the potential of their cameos on the celebrated Westside Connection and Mack 10 albums. The duo has an intense vocal interplay and Squeek-Ru, in particular, has a flair for imaginative, hard-edged rhymes. The only problem with the record is that the duo can't keep the beats and rhymes coming with the same intensity that begins the record. By the end of the record, they've aired most of their ideas twice, and the beats have lost their originality. Still, the best moments on the first half of the record prove Allfrumtha i is a West Coast duo with enormous potential. —*Leo Stanley*

The Almighty RSO

f. 1993, Boston, MA

Group / Hip-Hop, East Coast Rap

Hailing from Boston, the mid-'90s rap group The Almighty RSO (which stands for "Rock Solid Organization") is comprised of Deff Jeff, E-Devious, Tony Rhome, and Ray Dog. After releasing an EP, *Revenge of da Badd Boyz*, in 1994, they delivered their full-length debut, *Doomsday: Forever RSO*, in the fall of 1996. The album became a success on the strength of the hit single "You Could Be My Boo," which featured guest vocals by hip-hop diva Faith Evans. —*Stephen Thomas Erlewine*

● **Doomsday: Forever RSO** / Nov. 19, 1996 / Virgin ✦✦✦

Dooms Day Forever RSO is a promising debut album from The Almighty RSO that balances wit and social commentary with excellent party jams, like the Faith Evans duet "You Could Be My Boo." While the album runs a little too long and is bogged down by a few too many pedestrian rhythm tracks, the group has terrific rhyming skills and at their very best, they demonstrate how hardcore rap can move beyond its gangsta origins. —*Leo Stanley*

AMG

Vocals / Hardcore Rap, Gangsta Rap, West Coast Rap

Select recording artist AMG hasn't made much hip-hop impact. His toughtalking, prototype gangsta rap was featured on two discs for Select in 1991. *Bitch Betta Have My Money* charted, peaking at 63 on the pop album charts. *Ballin' Out of Control* followed in 1995, trailed two years later by *Pimp's Anthem*. *Bitch Betta Have My Money 2001* appeared at the turn of the millennium. —*Ron Wynn*

Give a Dog Bone / 1991 / Select ✦✦✦

Sullen, cold, and occasionally provocative commentary from AMG doesn't shed much light on any situation—social, political, or romantic. The production is acceptable, and the rapping and rhymes are mildly amusing, but there's little here that's inspirational, compelling, or worth hearing more than once. —*Ron Wynn*

● **Bitch Betta Have My Money** / 1992 / Select ✦✦✦✦✦

Men are from Pluto and women from Jupiter. Fine. But after listening to *Bitch Betta Have My Money*, one wonders if AMG had ever actually experienced up-close and personal contact with any genuine members of the female species prior to recording his second effort. The music is—not to put more of a fine a point on it than it deserves—misogyny raised to the nth power. As sophomoric potty talk, offensive (tongue-in-cheek?) sexism, and blatant female bashing goes, though, the album is fitfully amusing and more than mildly entertaining. Or rather, to be more precise, if you can bring yourself to swallow or overlook the more insulting vulgarities and self-styled roll pimping—not, it should be noted, an easy task at times, considering the extent of some of the nastiness?*Bitch Betta Have My Money* is a far sight more diverting than the average 2 Live Crew horn-fest, partly because AMG seems to include himself in the joke more often than not, and because P-Funk-laced tunes like "The Vertical Joyride," "Mai Sista Izza Bitch" (on which Boss delivers a decidedly nondainty pimp slap of her own), and the DJ Quik-produced "Nu Exasize" are undeniably fonkay ear-candy. The album, on the other hand, is nowhere near as jocular or sociopolitically hard hitting as either N.W.A or Ice-T—or even Sir Mix-A-Lot—and it would be difficult to envision the impulse that would lead to selecting an AMG album off the shelf before one of his musical superiors. That being said, the title track, in particular, is a classic bit of disrespectful smack-talk, and so obviously the artistic apex of AMG's career that the rapper tried to bottle the magic once again a decade later with the far less memorable or successful *Bitch Betta Have My Money 2001*. It is cautiously recommended, then, if you collect locker-room gangsta rap, and so long as you also have access to a shower nearby. —*Stanton Swihart*

Bitch Betta Have My Money 2001 / Dec. 5, 2000 / Lightyear ✦✦✦

Amil

b. New York, NY
Hip-Hop, Urban, Gangsta Rap, Hardcore Rap
Amil is a female rapper from New York whose vocals were featured on the popular rap singles "Can I Get A…" and "Jigga What?" by Jay-Z. She is the child of a black father and a European/Cherokee mother, raised in all five boroughs of New York. Her earliest influences were classic rap groups, such as Run-D.M.C., who she would mimic and practice rapping over when she was young. When she was 12, Amil started rapping at talent shows, beginning her local popularity as a female rap artist. In 1997, she became part of the group Major Coins, through which she met rapper Jay-Z. At the time Jay-Z was recording his third album, *Vol. 2 Hard Knock Life*, and wanted one of the women in Major Coins to do vocals on the album. By chance, Amil accompanied the group member to the studio, and Jay-Z asked her to freestyle on the album. Soon after Major Coins broke up, Amil decided to follow a solo career. She became a part of the group associated with Jay-Z's label, Roc-A-Fella, joining the 1999 Hard Knock Life Tour. After the tour she appeared as a guest on albums for Mariah Carey, Jermaine Dupri, and Funkmaster Flex. Amil released her first solo project through Roc-A-Fella, *All Money Is Legal*, in late 2000. —*Diana Potts*

● **All Money Is Legal** / Aug. 29, 2000 / Roc-A-Fella ✦✦✦
Female rapper Amil maintains her sultry sassiness on debut album *All Money Is Legal*. She picks up where things left off, rapping with Jay-Z, and delves back into her New York childhood street smarts to deliver a decent first introduction. *All Money Is Legal* is a personal album with ups and downs, and Amil aims to appeal to all audiences. She is brash and explicit on tracks such as "Heard It All" and "That's Right" (which features Jay-Z), but she also plays one for her own people on "4 Da Fam." She's passionate, but mysterious. She doesn't have to be the pretty face in Jay-Z's entourage. She's bold enough to make it solo. *All Money Is Legal* also features guest spots from Destiny Child's Beyonce, Beanie Siegal, and Carl Thomas. —*MacKenzie Wilson*

Another Bad Creation

f. Atlanta, GA
Group / Urban, New Jack Swing
Michael Bivins, a founding member of New Edition and part of the trio Bell Biv Devoe, struck commercial gold as the manager/producer of this Atlanta preteen quintet. Chris Sellers, Dave Shelton, Romell Chapman, and brothers Marliss and Demetrius Pugh landed a platinum release with *Coolin' at the Playground Ya' Know!* for Motown in 1991. Both "Iesha" and "Playground" were Top Ten pop and R&B singles. —*Ron Wynn*

● **Coolin' at the Playground Ya Know!** / 1991 / Motown ✦✦✦✦✦
This bit of kiddie R&B did well with its intended audience. Motown has revived itself in the 1990s through more concentrated marketing strategies and smarter, streetwise production. While they haven't been able to do as well with this group as Boyz II Men, Motown scored some points by recycling some Jackson 5 material and aiming at the audience forfeited by Bell Biv Devoe's move into adult territory. —*Ron Wynn*

It Ain't What U Wear It's How U Play It / Sep. 21, 1993 / Motown ✦✦✦

Anquette

Vocals / Hip-Hop
Rap fans who think there's just one thing on Luther Campbell's mind would get a far different impression by listening to female rapper Anquette. Though she recorded for his Luke Skyywalker Records (later just Luke), she took on political and social issues as well as recording bass-heavy party tracks. Her 1986 single, "Throw the P," was a biting female answer record to 2 Live

Crew's "Throw the D," and a follow-up named "Janet Reno" from 1988 congratulated the Florida district attorney for locking up deadbeat dads. The single may even have helped garner support among urban audiences for Reno, then locked in a tough reelection bid with her GOP challenger, Jack Thompson, the Miami lawyer who led the crusade to convict Campbell for obscenity. (Thompson also attempted to make a campaign issue of Reno as an alleged lesbian and alcoholic.) Reno cruised to an easy victory, and one year later, Anquette was rewarded with a moderate R&B hit, "I Will Always Be There for You." Her only LP, *Respect*, followed later that year. —*John Bush*

Respect / 1989 / Luke ✦✦
Long before Janet Reno became the U.S. Attorney General under Bill Clinton, she was the heroine of rapper Anquette, who draws on Reno's crusading efforts as inspiration for her 1989 debut LP *Respect*; on the song "Janet Reno," Anquette celebrates the attorney's prosecution of men charged with delinquent alimony payments. The cut is one of *Respect's* few inspired moments, however; by and large, the homespun beats are repetitive and Anquette's rhymes, though earnest, lack pizzazz. —*Jason Ankeny*

Anticon

f. 1997, San Francisco, CA
Group / Underground Rap, Hip-Hop, Alternative Rap
Believing that rap needs a healthy alternative underground to counter mainstream hip-hop, Anticon is a collective loosely modeled after the American indie rock movement. Made up of eight MCs and producers—Alias, Dose One, Jel, Odd Nosdam, Passage, Sole, the Pedestrian, and Why?—the collective pioneered a sound that matches obscure, near-beat poetry lyrics to beats that incorporated abrasive noise samples and unusual time signatures. Their origins started with the Live Poets, a crew based in Maine in the early '90s that was led by Sole. After releasing their own records and trying to create a buzz in the industry, he became disenchanted with the East Coast scene and began seeking other areas of the country with a similar offbeat attitude. He decided to move to San Francisco's Bay Area with fellow Live Poet Alias, where a number of MCs from Minneapolis and Canada were working with local rappers on new and experimental projects. They first met Minnesota native Slug, who was a fan of the Live Poets, and these three decided to work together with California MC Dose One on Deep Puddle Dynamics, an embryonic Anticon project. Although the four MCs had only briefly known one another, they shared a common vision, so they began to look for others who might be interested in starting a label with them.

The core group of eight came together over the next year, and by the end of 1997 they had started Anticon, with Sole and Dose One acting as the unofficial "leaders." The ground rules were simple: Their artists were encouraged to record as much as they wanted and to work for other labels if they liked, but they would make 50 percent profit from anything they released through Anticon. Sole worked out a deal with Caroline Records, and soon they were distributing Anticon's first singles and compilations in limited release. A number of New York underground MCs, including El-P and members of Company Flow, criticized their records and had a brief press war with Sole, but they were otherwise winning over new listeners with their offbeat approach. Tortoise's John Herndon became one of their biggest supporters in the press, so he brought them to the attention of his publicist, who in turn hooked up with the label and marketed the collective as the hip-hop equivalent of post-rock. The mainstream music press began to cover their releases, and soon they were making enough money to support a weekly showcase in San Francisco, as well as a website and a newsletter. The Internet became a key part of their growth, as fans from around the world could now download tracks from Sole and Themselves, as well as directly speak to the artists through e-mail and their site's message board. Their growing fan base led to a relationship with acid jazz label Mush, who began exclusively distributing Anticon albums by the turn of the century. Between the increased publicity, better distribution, and—most importantly—a gifted lineup of what Sole referred to as "avant-garde hip-hop," Anticon had found their niche as one of the most distinct and creative rap labels of their time. —*Bradley Torreano*

● **Music for the Advancement of Hip Hop** / Jul. 30, 1999 / Massmen ✦✦✦✦
From the title you should know this isn't your average hip-hop record. *Anticon's* sound is an acquired taste. The various MCs that make up *Anticon* almost seem like they want to be different. They revel in it. They want to push boundaries of hip-hop. They may not, but they try. On the beat of "It's Them"

you hear it repeat a few times, then it gets cut up and slowed down and Dose flows with the choppy beat. But with lyrics like "It doesn't look like an ice sculpture!... or does it?" it doesn't really do much for the listener. One bright spot on this album is "Nothing but Sunshine" by Slug, where he talks about what he went through as a kid over a nice piano beat done by Moodswing9. Another nice track is "Simulated Snow" by Sixtoo, who also did the beat. The beat at first starts off with just a piano loop, then the drums slowly creep in and out, and they change enough to keep the listener entertained. Sixtoo's lyrics are nice, but there is no passion behind them and his delivery is dry. So if you want to hear some abstract hip-hop from a variety of different artists, this may be the album for you. —*Dan Gizzi*

We Ain't Fessin' [Single] / Feb. 25, 2002 / Anticon ♦♦♦
This three-track single of Anticon affiliates includes one track from Deep Puddle Dynamics and two from Anticon, though the rapper roster for each track is roughly the same: Slug, Alias, Eyedea, and Dose One. The first track (and the highlight), Deep Puddle's "More From June," is the usual stoner hip-hop, rambling and caustic, surprisingly produced by Chicago post-rock hand John Herndon. —*John Bush*

Antipop Consortium

f. 1997, New York, NY, **db.** Aug. 2002
Group / Underground Rap, Hardcore Rap, East Coast Rap
Antipop Consortium emerged in the early 2000s as one of the underground hip-hop scene's most inventive groups, bridging the gap between New York hip-hop and glitchy IDM. Group members Priest, Beans, and M. Sayyid joined forces in 1997, along with producer E. Blaize, who would become the group's most celebrated member. After some underground singles that didn't reach far beyond New York's boroughs, the Ark 75 label released *Tragic Epilogue*, the group's debut full-length, in 2000. Though the album wasn't quite as daring as Antipop Consortium's successive releases, it nonetheless garnered substantial acclaim, placing the group among similarly edgy New York underground rap artists such as Company Flow.

In fact, *Tragic Epilogue*'s acclaim even crossed the Atlantic. Warp Records—the legendary IDM label based in England best known for releasing artists such as Aphex Twin, Boards of Canada, and Autechre—decided to sign the group, quite a noteworthy move for both parties: Warp was known for IDM, not hip-hop, and Antipop Consortium was potentially distancing itself from the finicky underground hip-hop scene. Regardless of the risks involved, Warp released Antipop Consortium's *The Ends Against the Middle* EP in late 2001, followed shortly after in 2002 by a full-length effort, *Arrhythmia*. Both releases incorporated an obvious IDM influence, particularly from a production standpoint. Producer E. Blaize moved away from straight hip-hop breakbeats, going instead with glitchy beats and angular rhythms. As a result, Antipop Consortium crossed over from the stateside underground hip-hop scene to the more international IDM scene, which was becoming increasingly interested in rap during the early 2000s. After wrapping up DJ Shadow's North American tour in late July 2002, Antipop Consortium disbanded. It was expected that High Priest, Beans, and M. Sayyid would release solo material by the end of the year. —*Jason Birchmeier*

Tragic Epilogue / Feb. 22, 2000 / 75 Ark ♦♦♦♦
The tongue-tripping raps, obtuse science-fiction metaphors, and excellent minor-key productions on *Tragic Epilogue* immediately recall Kool Keith's *Doctor Octagon*, the 1996 LP that energized the rap underground. Still, Antipop Consortium never come across as derivative; the raps (mostly by Beans, High Priest, and Sayyid) are steadily inventive and on a similar high plane as the best non-mainstream rappers out there (Kool Keith, Jurassic 5, Mos Def). Though all of the best tracks ("Nude Paper," "Laundry," "9.99," "Your World Is Flat") come on the first side, and the second doesn't really compete, Antipop Consortium's debut is well produced and well performed. —*John Bush*

Shopping Carts Crashing / 2001 / Japanese Import ♦♦♦
Shopping Carts Crashing, the first Japanese-only original rap album, was the usual for Antipop Consortium, an appealingly skewed collection of productions. If these tracks barely come together on a first listen, they make more sense after a few times through, either dense ("Starring Me as Me") or skeletal ("M"), but always imaginatively obtuse. The trio gets in some good rhymes while indulging in baffling mayhem—whether it's quoting from *The Mary Tyler Moore Show* theme (with their raps, no less) or sampling an opera singer. —*John Bush*

The Ends Against the Middle EP / Nov. 13, 2001 / Warp ♦♦♦♦
Following in the footsteps of the superb *Tragic Epilogue* and the Japan-only *Shopping Carts Crashing, The Ends Against the Middle* EP is seven more songs of genius raps and murky, demented hip-hop electronica. Where too many collectives try too hard to sound like DJ Shadow and match their samples with subpar scratching, Antipop Consortium concentrate on their melodies as much as, if not more than, their raps. Sinister and aggressive, yet wholly accessible due to the mind-numbing vocal skills on display, these seven smart sonic creations blend into one long treat. Glitchy, twinkling electronics and insanely entertaining puns and word associations make for a fun, spooky listening experience. Standouts include the weird textured beats of "3903" and the echoing head funk of "Splinter." Longtime fans of Warp might balk at the release of a rap album, but *The Ends Against the Middle* defies genre labeling. With its twisted, thrilling IDM undertones and its intense atmosphere, *The Ends Against the Middle* makes perfect sense as a Warp release. As on other releases, Antipop Consortium stand above many of their hip-hop and electronica peers here, because they're as talented at blending their influences as they are at molding innovative, inspiring songs. —*Tim DiGravina*

● **Arrhythmia** / Apr. 2, 2002 / Warp ♦♦♦♦
Returning to the deft, cerebral sound invented on *Tragic Epilogue*, Antipop Consortium's first full-length for Warp Records is by far the group's best work to date and takes a strong stride in the fusion of "out" hip-hop and electronic music. Released only six months following the somewhat understated *The Ends Against the Middle* EP, this completely new group of songs pushes the boundaries of musical structure while still basking in hip-hop authenticity. While the easy comparison would reference Antipop as the Sun Ra of rap, the group's musical sophistication manifests itself as a genuine expression of the limitless possibilities within its composition—without seeming like an attempt to outsmart the commercial rap competition. So dropping a beat over a ping-pong ball on "Ping Pong" and then rhyming on top comes off as par for the course rather than contrived abstraction, while ironically, the improvement in production and skill here might lead the group into a higher hip-hop strata. Using voices like soloing instruments and orchestrating more chorus-like samples and loops than on previous works, Antipop's sound reverberates quality with each listen to *Arrhythmia*, a feat of clever artistic strength. —*Nic Kincaid*

Antipop Consortium vs. Matthew Shipp / Feb. 18, 2003 / Thirsty Ear ♦♦♦♦
He grooves, he dances (figuratively) on his keys, he delights with phantasmagorical wonders: He is none other than the wondrous Matthew Shipp, who invites you into his den of magical juxtapositions. Step right up, ladies and gentlemen, right this way, and open the doorway to new sounds, or at least combinations you never expected. This one matches the hip-hop conundrums of Antipop Consortium, who will wow you with its revolutionary discombobulations, with the cerebral machinations of free jazz wizard Matthew Shipp, who lays it down low with stretched fingers that scratch the pavement. The pianist brings with him old friends—bassist William Parker, trumpeter Daniel Carter, drummer Guillermo E. Brown, and vibist Khan Jamal—but when they confront the cool sounds of Antipop, they defer with respectful submission. The fireworks do not ignite the way they might have, but that is the nature of experimentation. Nevertheless, this is all great fun, a function of Shipp's slippery mind, and the results are not only danceable but disconcertingly so. Shipp is downright melodic for the most part, and even the hip hip-hoppers seem barely radical. And yet the outcome is not liable to be quite anything you've heard before. Sure, it crosses over and you have to suspend critical analysis, at least sometimes, but kudos to Antipop and Shipp for expanding their horizons, for dreaming, and for trying something new and keeping it fresh. —*Steven Loewy*

Apache

Vocals / Hip-Hop
Building his New Jersey street credibility in the late '80s by fronting the hip-hop group the Flavor Unit, Apache eventually broke solo to show off his own microphone skills and won the recognition of Tommy Boy Records in the process. After the release of his self-titled debut in 1991, Apache scored the underground hit "Gangsta Bitch" without the use of radio or video airplay in 1993. Upon his minor success, Apache followed through with "Apache Ain't Shit" that same year. —*Mike DaRonco*

● **Apache Ain't Shit** / 1991 / Tommy Boy ✦✦✦
It's impossible to examine *Apache Ain't Shit* without some discussion of political and social issues. Parts of Apache's album indulge in what comes across as racist, anti-white humor—most notably, "A Fight" and "Kill D'White People." Some have argued that because the tunes are exactly that—humor—listeners shouldn't take everything the New Jersey rapper says seriously. Humor is, to be sure, a big part of *Apache Ain't Shit*, and the CD's title lets listeners know that some of that humor is quite self-deprecating. How many people in rap—a genre that can be very ego driven—would have an album title telling listeners they "aren't shit?" And the sexually explicit "Who Freaked Who" finds female rapper Nikki D telling Apache how disappointing he was in bed. So listeners certainly can't say that Apache doesn't have a lot of laughs at his own expense. And because *Apache Ain't Shit* contains so much self-deprecating humor, some hip-hop writers argued that his more questionable lyrics weren't to be taken seriously. In 1989 the same type of arguments were used to defend Axl Rose's use of offensive language on Guns N' Roses' controversial "One in a Million"; Rose insisted that he wasn't a racist and that the tune wasn't meant to be taken seriously. Some blacks who knew Rose personally agreed that he wasn't really a racist, and even though they were probably right, "One in a Million" is still guilty of insensitivity. Similarly, even if "A Fight" is only meant to be a tasteless joke, it doesn't exactly go out of its way to promote healthy race relations. But as questionable as some of Apache's lyrics are, he isn't without talent. For those who have a taste for raunchy humor, explicit tunes like "Woodchuck" and the single "Gangsta Bitch" are genuinely funny. Questionable lyrics and all, this is an often entertaining, if uneven, debut that managed to stimulate a fair amount of discussion among hip-hoppers in 1993. —*Alex Henderson*

Apache Indian (Steven Kapur)

Dance-Pop, Ragga, Bhangra
British vocalist Apache Indian (born Steven Kapur) performs a highly eclectic form of raggae informed by the bhangra style of his East Indian heritage. After cutting his teeth toasting in U.K. dance halls, Apache Indian began to release singles in the early '90s. Many of these singles would appear on his 1993 major-label debut, *No Reservations*, including "Don Raja," a song that exemplifies Apache Indian's cross-cultural fusion and earned him a new nickname as well.

By the mid-'90s, raggae production often included elements of hip-hop, and Apache Indian's next record was no exception. Featuring guest appearances from Jamaican reggae stars Frankie Paul, Yami Bolo, and American MC Tim Dog, 1995's *Make Way for the Indian* included sampled tabla beats and spawned a U.S. club hit with the shuffling R&B of "Boom Shak-a-Lak." The "Don Raja" of British ragga began to increase his international exposure, appearing in Hindi films like *Love Birds* and a feature role in *Love Story '98*. He continued to record as well, releasing *Real People* in 1998 and *Karma* in 2001. —*Wade Kergan*

No Reservations / May 4, 1993 / Mango ✦✦✦
While his music is not bhangra in any accepted sense, he grew out of the bhangra scene. His is a remarkable bhangra-related dance music often carrying a social message in a mixed Punjabi, English, and West Indian patois. Tracks such as "Chok There" (slang for "Tear the house down"), "Move over India," "Don Rajae," and "Arranged Marriage" made it a remarkable debut. (With one qualification: several tracks had previously appeared on *Apachi Indian by Don Raja*, a mini-album for Jet Star (SDCD46) which spelled his name in a nonstandard way.) —*Ken Hunt*

● **Make Way for the Indian** / Apr. 11, 1995 / Mango ✦✦✦✦✦
Steve Kapur is of East Indian descent, but he grew up in Birmingham, England, an industrial town burdened with economic hardship but blessed with a large immigrant population of various ethnicities, notable among them West Indians from Jamaica and actual Indians from India. Under the stage name Apache Indian, Kapur was one of the first artists to successfully fuse dancehall reggae with bhangra (the rock-influenced dance music favored by the Anglo-Indian youth), and he achieved significant chart success with his early singles and debut album. *Make Way for the Indian* was his sophomore effort and failed to achieve the same success, but it's an eminently worthwhile album nevertheless. Here he covers the Willie Williams tune "Armagideon Time" with the help of dancehall superstar Yami Bolo and "Raggamuffin Girl" with Frankie Paul. "Boba" is one of the most explicitly

bhangra-based songs he has recorded, and it's one of the best things on the album, which also includes his huge hit "Boom Shak a Lak." Song for song, it's difficult to see why this disc didn't perform as well in the marketplace as his debut. —*Rick Anderson*

The Arabian Prince

b. Compton, CA
Producer, Vocals / Old School Rap, Hip-Hop, West Coast Rap, Gangsta Rap
Though he's known mostly (if at all) for his early membership in N.W.A, the Arabian Prince had been a producer and DJ since the early '80s, which undoubtedly helped him sustain his career after leaving N.W.AHe began in the music business while still in middle school, recording mix-tapes after hours at KACE radio (where his father worked) and DJing school dances as well as the occasional club date. The Arabian Prince began recording his own tracks during 1982-1983, and coproduced Bobby Jimmy & the Critters as well as doing live dates with the Egyptian Lover, World Class Wreckin' Cru, and the L.A. Dream Team. Early singles like "Innovator" and "Situation Hot" got much respect on the Los Angeles club scene, and his consistent studio experimentation led to some work with Dr. Dre and N.W.A for 1988's *Straight Outta Compton*. One year later saw the release of his own first full-length, *Brother Arab*, for Orpeus. The single "She's Got a Big Posse" found some chart action, and *Tha Underworld* followed in 1992. *Where's My Bytches*, released in 1995, was his last LP of the '90s, though he pursued several musical projects as well as ownership in a special-effects company and animation studio. —*John Bush*

Brother Arab / Sep. 1989 / Orpheus ✦✦✦
This album is hard-hitting hip-hop with an unrepentant gangsta tone. Arabian Prince angered some in the middle-class community with this unrelenting condemnation of inner city life. It was vicious and vulgar, but delivered with the kind of cold, harsh slant that made it convincing. —*Ron Wynn*

● **Tha Underworld** / 1992 / EMI ✦✦✦✦✦
Arabian Prince doesn't discuss anything that hasn't been talked about numerous times by other gangsta types. But his commentaries on drugs, violence, sex, and such are done in such a deadpan yet defiant and angry manner that you're hooked even while being disgusted by a litany of hopelessness and injustice. —*Ron Wynn*

India.Arie

b. Denver, CO
Vocals, Guitar (Acoustic) / Neo-Soul, Contemporary R&B, Urban
One of a handful of neoclassic soul artists to emerge following the late '90s success of artists like D'Angelo and Lauren Hill, Atlanta's India.Arie stood poised at the beginning of 2001 to make a major impact. A studied songwriter and guitar player rooted in the R&B, soul, Motown, and blues of the past, but grounded in the post-hip-hop urban world of today, Arie's debut, *Acoustic Soul*, was rich with textured songs, kooks, and impressively mature lyrics considering the artist had only been writing songs for five years.

Born in Denver, CO, to parents from Memphis and Detroit, music was always in Arie's life. The family moved to Atlanta when India was 13 and after high school she began playing guitar at the encouragement of her mother. Involvement in the fertile Atlanta urban music scene led to the formation of an artist's collective called Groovement and an independent label, EarthShare, which released a compilation CD featuring Arie's first songs. A second-stage slot on the 1998 Lilith Fair tour garnered major-label interest, but Arie eventually signed with Motown after being assured of having full artistic control. Work on *Acoustic Soul* dragged out nearly two years, but Arie's relentless pursuit of perfection and musical integrity yielded very pleasing results: as successful a graft of classic soul and modern hip-hop style productions yet attempted. The album's first single, "Video," received strong radio and club play early in the year, and the full-length followed in March. Just over a year later, India.Arie had completed her second record, *Voyage to India*, and it appeared in September 2002. —*John Duffy*

● **Acoustic Soul** / Mar. 27, 2001 / Motown ✦✦✦✦✦
As one of the most promising neoclassic soul artists yet to emerge in the past few years, India.Arie casts her lot with the best artist of her label's storied history, playing deeply introspective songs laced with glistening acoustic guitar, churchy organ, and smooth, supple beats. When she name-checks those artists no longer with us she claims as influences (Ma Rainey, Miles Davis,

Karen Carpenter, Charlie Patton, Stevie Ray Vaughan, Donny Hathaway, etc.) in three separate interludes, you have no doubt she is looking back as well as forward, even going so far as to invoke Sam Cooke's "A Change Is Gonna Come." But *Acoustic Soul* is at its best when the arrangements are deliberately modern. And despite the uniqueness of being a guitar-based R&B album, it is Arie's thick, sandy voice that shares star billing with her exceptional lyrics. Betraying youthful vulnerability while at the same time projecting strength, confidence, and uncanny insight for a 25-year-old singer/songwriter, Arie wraps herself effortlessly around the deep, funky sensuality of "Brown Skin," and stands tall in defiance of pop-fashion expectations on the irresistibly catchy "Video." The uplifting "Faith, Courage, Wisdom" rides along on a euphoric chorus, and the plainly autobiographical "Back to the Middle" recounts an emotional and spiritual coming of age. Without the many concrete references to the great R&B music of the past, *Acoustic Soul* would be a purely modern gem, but as Arie is determined to pay her debts up front, it is much more, and that is admirable. —*John Duffy*

Voyage to India / Sep. 24, 2002 / Motown ✦✦✦✦
Despite an excellent debut, India.Arie still had much to prove with her second record. Several of her neo-soul compatriots, from D'Angelo to Erykah Badu to Macy Gray, had faltered with sophomore albums, and it appeared she may have already said everything she had to say on *Acoustic Soul*. That anticipation, and trepidation, is exactly what makes *Voyage to India* such a beautiful surprise; it's a record that easily equals her debut, boasting better vocal performances but also better songwriting and accompanying production. As on her debut, there is a marked balance of organic and artificial: an acoustic guitar paces many tracks, though the edges are shorn off for a digital feel; the beats are often sampled, but there are still plenty of handclaps and fingersnaps; and the arrangements are simple yet obviously very polished. The improvement in her songwriting is most obvious from the first three tracks (after the short intro). The themes driving "Little Things" (keeping it simple), "Talk to Her" (the importance of honesty, warmth, and communication in relationships), and "Slow Down" (taking life one day at a time) certainly have been covered already, many times even, but India.Arie writes with a fresh perspective that makes it sound as though she's the first to broach the topic. And, finally, her delivery is the best of any neo-soul vocalist, barring only the incomparable Jill Scott, alternately earnest and playful and sexy and questing. It all adds up to one of the most glowing comebacks of the year (if she ever left), an important record whose stamp—the Motown logo—isn't the only thing it has in similarity with a classic LP by Marvin Gaye or Stevie Wonder. —*John Bush*

Stretch Armstrong

Producer / East Coast Rap, Hip-Hop, Underground Rap
A hip-hop fixture since the dawn of the '90s, DJ Stretch Armstrong has been instrumental in presenting up-and-coming MCs through his media barrage of radio programs, mix-tapes, and even video games. The New York native's first notoriety came as half of the Stretch Armstrong and Bobbito Show, which quickly became one of the premier forums for the city's emerging hip-hop talent to be heard. Several of the '90s' biggest names in rap received early notice on the Columbia University radio program, including the debut of the Notorious B.I.G., or just Biggie Smalls as he was known in 1991. His appearance on the show was widely circulated, as were many of the show's legendary freestyle sessions, and led to Biggie's mention in a magazine column, which led to his introduction to Sean "Puffy" Combs. Biggie wasn't the only artist to freestyle on the show and subsequently blow up: Nas, Wu-Tang Clan, Mobb Deep, and countless others all appeared on the show. By 1998, the show had run its course, but not before *The Village Voice* declared the Stretch Armstrong and Bobbito Show "the best hip-hop show in New York" and *Source* magazine voted it "the best hip-hop show of all time." The demise of the show was not the end of Armstrong's radio career, however, and it was on Hot 97—the only commercial radio station in New York dedicated to hip-hop at the time—that he continued with XL Radio.

The mid-'90s also saw the first of Armstrong's forays into record production with Dolo, which released singles from MF Grimm, the Korp, Dutchmin, and Powerule. Dolo was also the outlet for Stretch's Lesson mix-tapes that always featured exclusive tracks and freestyles. Dolo was retired at the end of the '90s while Armstrong worked briefly with Game Records. The short

association lasted long enough for the busy DJ to make it into over seven million homes as one of the radio personalities on Game Radio, one of the fictitious stations featured in the popular Grand Theft Auto III video game. Spit Inc., a new label helmed by the enterprising DJ, appeared in 2001 with a compilation featuring 50 Cent and Royce da 5'9". —*Wade Kergan*

Spit / May 8, 2001 / Landspeed ✦✦✦
Mix tape DJs rely upon their connections and contacts among MCs and DJs, and Stretch Armstrong is flush with both of these. Even though *Spit* isn't a proper mix tape and is more of a label compilation for Spit Inc., Armstrong comes through with a solid list of exclusive contributions. The MC contingent is strong: Royce da 5'9", Pretty Ugly, and the real king of New York, 50 Cent (forget the Jay-Z/Nas melodrama, 50 stole the crown before they even started kicking up dust), all deliver. And while the A-Team isn't in the same tongue-twisting league, they breath some new life into Mister Cee's ubiquitous "Where Brooklyn At?" chant. And with Rush, Clark Kent, and Mobb Deep's Havoc helming some of the production, the beats are good, too. But as well-rounded a collection as it is, it still feels like everyone here is holding back. Which doesn't detract from *Spit* as a compilation, but does not bode well for Spit Inc. as a label. —*Wade Kergan*

Arrested Development

f. 1988, Atlanta, GA, **db.** 1996
Group / Political Rap, Hip-Hop, Urban, Alternative Rap, Southern Rap
One of the major success stories of 1992, Arrested Development was a progressive rap collective fusing soul, blues, hip-hop, and Sly and the Family Stone-influenced funk with political, socially conscious lyrics. The group was founded in the late '80s by rapper Speech and DJ Headliner, who decided to make the transition to a more positive, Afro-centric viewpoint after hearing Public Enemy. Arrested Development's debut album took its title from the amount of time it took the group to secure a record contract; *3 Years, 5 Months and 2 Days in the Life Of...* included the hit single "Tennessee," a strongly spiritual track that hit the Top Ten and sparked the album to sell over four million copies. Its two follow-ups, "People Everyday" (a rewrite of Sly's "Everyday People") and "Mr. Wendal" did likewise. Accolades poured in; Arrested Development won Grammys for Best Rap Album and Best New Artist, and were named *Rolling Stone's* Band of the Year. The group returned one year later with *Zingalamaduni*, which some reviews hailed as a major work, though overall response was more ambivalent. In 1996, contrary to Speech's earlier assertion that the group would be around for ten or 12 years, Arrested Development officially broke up. Speech went solo, though his debut album failed to make an impact. —*Steve Huey*

● **3 Years, 5 Months & 2 Days in the Life Of . . .** / Mar. 24, 1992 / Chrysalis ✦✦✦✦✦
Widely adored when it appeared in 1992, Arrested Development's debut album, *3 Years, 5 Months & 2 Days in the Life Of...* seemed to herald a shining new era in alternative rap, when audiences and critics of all colors could agree on the music's importance. Of course, that didn't happen, as Dr. Dre instead took gangsta rap to the top of the charts with *The Chronic*. In retrospect, *3 Years...* isn't quite as revolutionary as it first seemed, though it's still a fine record that often crosses the line into excellence. Its positive messages were the chief selling point for many rock critics, and it's filled with pleas for black unity and brotherly compassion, as well as a devotion to the struggle for equality. All of that is grounded in a simple, upbeat spirituality that also results in tributes to the homeless (the hit "Mr. Wendal"), black women of all shapes and sizes, and the natural world. It's determinedly down to earth, and that aesthetic informs the group's music as well. Their sound is a laid-back, southern-fried groove informed by rural blues, African percussion, funk, and melodic R&B. All of it comes together on the classic single "Tennessee," which takes lead rapper Speech on a spiritual quest to reclaim his heritage in a South still haunted by its history. It helped Arrested Development become the first rap group to win a Grammy for Best New Artist, and to top numerous year-end critical polls. In hindsight, there's a distinct political correctness—even naïveté—in the lyrics, which places the record firmly in the early '90s; it's also a bit self-consciously profound at times, lacking the playfulness of peers like the Native Tongues. Nonetheless, *3 Years...* was a major influence on a new breed of alternative Southern hip-hop, including Goodie Mob, OutKast, and Nappy Roots, and it still stands as one of the better albums of its kind. —*Steve Huey*

Unplugged / Mar. 1993 / Chrysalis ✦✦
Basically a live re-recording of *3 Years, 5 Months & 2 Days in the Life Of...* (minus their breakthrough hit, "Tennessee"), *Unplugged* breaks no new ground for Arrested Development. Eight of the 11 songs on the album are from their debut, and the three new tracks are slight. The album is filled out with remixes of seven tracks, which are the instrumental tracks with the vocals turned down (they are still slightly audible). Despite the fact that it doesn't offer anything not on *3 Years*, the album is an enjoyable listen. — *Stephen Thomas Erlewine*

Zingalamaduni / Jun. 14, 1994 / Chrysalis ✦✦✦
The follow-up to Arrested Development's hugely acclaimed debut, *Zingalamaduni* was something of a letdown, and not just because conscious rap's moment in the sun was over for the time being. The record is simply less exciting, falling prey to too many aimless grooves that don't always capture the effortless earthiness of the debut's best moments. That's a shame, because there are subtle progressions on the group's signature sound. There's more frequent and explicit use of African musical elements, especially chanting; that reflects a slightly more Afro-centric viewpoint in the lyrics (not to mention the album's title, which is Swahili for "beehive of culture"), which tones down the sunny positivity of the debut somewhat. A few cuts are jazzier than anything on the debut, yet the overall lack of focus produces too many lackluster-to-average moments. The best tracks are a match for their counterparts on *3 Years*...(save for "Tennessee"); songs like "Mr. Landlord," "Ache'n for Acres," "Praisin' U," and the catchy "In the Sunshine" illustrate why some critics found reasons to like *Zingalamaduni* that weren't purely intellectual. But overall, it failed to captivate Arrested Development's audience the way its predecessor had. Not until the ascendance of the Fugees would another group command the level of critical and commercial respect that Arrested Development had in its prime. — *Steve Huey*

The Best of Arrested Development / Jun. 2, 1998 / EMI ✦✦✦✦
The Best of Arrested Development is part of EMI-Capitol Special Markets' excellent *Ten Best Series*, a budget-line series that features an artist's ten biggest hits in their original recorded versions. All of the group's seven charting R&B hits—"Tennessee," "People Everyday," "Revolution," "Mr. Wendal," "Natural," "Ease My Mind," and "United Front"—along with three album tracks, like "Fishin' 4 Religion" and "Give a Man a Fish" are here. Although the CD is not sequenced in chronological order, the very fact that all these hits are on one disc at such an affordable price makes *The Best of Arrested Development* a terrific choice for budget-minded casual fans. — *Stephen Thomas Erlewine*

Greatest Hits / Jul. 31, 2001 / Disky ✦✦✦✦
Released only in England/Europe, *Greatest Hits* rounds up pretty much anything that most Arrested Development fans could want from the band—which means that it leans pretty heavily on the first album, containing such hits as "Mr. Wendal" and "Tennessee," plus album cuts like "Fishin' 4 Religion" and the non-LP single "Revolution." There are also two unplugged cuts, which are OK, but the main problem with the collection is that the original version—or even the original single version—of "People Everyday" is not here, only the "Metamorphosis Radio Edit." This isn't enough to sink the collection, but it may be enough for some listeners to wait for a definitive anthology that contains all the original versions of the big hits. — *Stephen Thomas Erlewine*

● **Classic Masters** / Jan. 29, 2002 / Capitol ✦✦✦✦✦
For a brief, shining moment at the dawn of the '90s, it seemed that Arrested Development's debut *3 Years, 5 Months & 2 Days in the Life Of...* would have as lasting an impact as Nirvana's *Nevermind*, which also ruled the charts in 1992. As it turns out, *Nevermind* ushered in years of grunge, indie rock, and, sadly, terrible hard rock, but *3 Years* wound up as the last big gasp of alternative rap before it was subsumed by gangsta after *The Chronic*. As such, Arrested Development's music has dated slightly, sounding like its time rather than transcending it, as this edition of *Classic Masters* illustrates. As a collection, it's quite good, containing not just every one of the group's hits and singles but also a B side ("Southern Fried Funk"), a few album tracks, and Speech's 1995 solo single, "Like Marvin Said (What's Goin' On)." Several singles stand the test of time and emerge as classics, particularly "Tennessee," while several sound a little too closely tied to their time, but overall this is an excellent overview of the last great Daisy-Age era alternative rap crew. *3 Years* remains definitive, but if you want a sampler, containing bits of *Zingalamundi* plus *Revolution*, this is the one to get. — *Stephen Thomas Erlewine*

Arsonists

f. 1993
Group / Hip-Hop, Alternative Rap
Originally going under the name Bushwick Bomb Squad since their formation in 1993, members Q-Unique, D-Stroy, Freestyle, Swel Boogie, and Jise One played around in the underground hip-hop field for a short duration before signing to the independent Fondle 'Em Records and changing their moniker to the Arsonists. With three 12" singles that followed—one of which was released on a division of Geffen Records—a deal on Matador followed in 1999. Their debut full-length, *As the World Burns*, was released later that year. — *Mike DaRonco*

● **As the World Burns** / Aug. 24, 1999 / Matador ✦✦✦✦
Rising from the ashes of New York's dog-eat-dog underground scene were the five spontaneously combustible members making up Arsonists: Q-Unique, D-Story, Freestyle, Swel Boogie, and Jise One. Fundamentally sound and immersed in hip-hop's old school heritage, Arsonists amiably keep everything in-house for their debut (which is nearly unheard of nowadays), as there are no outside production or industry-related collaborations. A sumptuously diverse group, each of Arsonists brings differentiating lyrical styles, yet together they manage to mesh into a group setting. Arsonists burn the competition with the expedited cadences of "Blaze," while upholding their vowel to preserve hip-hop's four essential elements with "Flashback." Dispensing a plethora of spit-boxing exhibitions, they give a consummate New York verbal flogging to "Shaboing," the flame-broiled "Venom," and the slow-burning "Worlds Collide." Arsonists have not arrived—they have emerged, and hip-hop is undeniably a purer place because of it. — *Matt Conaway*

Date of Birth / Sep. 11, 2001 / Matador ✦✦✦✦
On the sophomore release from this Brooklyn underground trio (surfacing here as Jise, Q-Unique, and Swel 79), the Arsonists continue to swim away from the mainstream, not in a calculated manner as some backpackers do to try to make a name, but because for these self-proclaimed hip-hop pyromaniacs, this is the only way to make their music. As a result, many hip-hop luminaries have taken notice, including the legendary Chuck D, who at one time quipped: "When you see a group like the Arsonists out there, they're better than what any major label has got." Living by KRS-One's immortal credo—"Rap is something you do, hip-hop is something you live"—the Arsonists set fire to many a microphone and drum machine on *Date of Birth*. Again sticking to their largely in-house production protocol (though the Beatnuts' Psycho Les drops a burner on "Self Righteous Spics"), flaming arrows are fired on the rollicking "Space Junk" and the classical piano-infused "Alive." But these are mere warm-up acts for two of the more memorable underground tracks in recent memory: the hilariously sharp "Millionaire," a slick, hip-hop parody of Regis Philbin's *Who Wants to Be a Millionaire* game show, and "Language Arts," a blazing combination of kabuki theater strings and Akira Kurosawa film aesthetic. While the album lapses occasionally with a couple of patches of redundant production, *Date of Birth* is a strong follow-up from a crew who keep it real by nature. — *M.F. Di Bella*

Articolo 31

f. Italy
Group / Foreign Rap
One of the most popular names in Italian hip-hop, the duo known as Articolo 31 debuted with *Strade di Citta* in 1993. Four more albums followed during the mid- to late '90s: *Messa di Vespiri, Così Com'è, Nessuno,* and *Xché Si!* — *John Bush*

● **Best of Articolo 31** / Jan. 9, 2001 / Best Sound ✦✦✦✦

Artifacts

f. Newark, NJ, **db.** 1997
Group / Hip-Hop, East Coast Rap, Club/Dance
The Artifacts are a throwback hip-hop duo from Newark, NJ. Their music reflects and emphasizes three of the four elements of true hip-hop culture: MCing, DJing, and their specialty, graffiti writing or "bombing"; both Tame One and El the Sensai are proficient at all three. With unique styles that play off each other well, Tame and El's graf-rap was well received by underground audiences and continued in the Jersey rap tradition of Redman and Lords of the Underground. The crew scored an underground classic with their debut

single in 1994, "Wrong Side of The Tracks," serving notice to their graffiti bombing missions and their Jersey heritage. The debut album, *Between a Rock & a Hard Place*, followed soon afterward. Tight, funky production provided the duo's B-boy stance the chance to take shape. Although it contained more of the same, the 1996 follow-up album, *The Art of Facts*, was not nearly as successful critically, getting lost amid the burgeoning kingpin gangster attitude of Jay-Z and Nas. The Artifacts were hard-nosed backpack hip-hoppers in the halcyon days of hip-hop's golden age revisited, before hip-hop's mainstream explosion and the elevating gangster hardcore style that led to the violent deaths of Tupac Shakir and Notorious B.I.G. The duo split in 1997 and now release singles as solo artists. —*Michael Di Bella*

● **Between a Rock & a Hard Place** / 1994 / Big Beat ✦✦✦✦
This is a strong mid-nineties hip-hop album from two Jersey-ites with a fairly unique style, b-boyism mixed with EPMD-esque funk flavor. Hard-edged but not gangster, the Artifacts stress the true elements of hip-hop culture in their music with an accent on their forte, graffitti writing. Calling their debut album the "the first and last showing of grafitti rock," the Artifacts rap about typical subjects like marijuana and skirt chasing but their cleverness and wit are singular. Tracks like "Wrong Side of the Tracks," "Flexi Wit Da Tech," and "C'mon With Da Git Down" are arguable nineties underground classics while other tracks like the Redman-produced "Comin' Through Your F****n' Block" and "Wassup Now Muthaf****" also hit hard. The synoptic track "Whayback" is a shout to rap's forefathers and a longing for hip-hop's glory days of old. Although slack in a few places, overall, this a stellar album and a sincere attempt to keep the essence of hip-hop alive. —*Michael Di Bella*

That's Them / Apr. 15, 1997 / Big Beat ✦✦✦
Artifacts don't run the gauntlet too much, but their take on tough beats'n'production with straight-ahead raps proves effective on their second album. The feature, "Collaboration of Mics," also includes Jamar and Finesse. —*John Bush*

Ashanti (Ashanti S. Douglas)

b. Glen Cove, NY
Vocals / Urban, Contemporary R&B
With hitmaker Irv Gotti at the helm, Ashanti blasted into the urban music scene in 2002, topping the charts with multiple singles at once. She quickly became a sensation, gracing the covers of magazines and dominating urban radio. Ashanti built her reputation with duets, where she would complement already popular rappers—Ja Rule ("Always on Time"), Fat Joe ("What's Luv?"), the Notorious B.I.G. ("Unfoolish")—contrasting the tough-guy male perspective with her own. It didn't take the young vocalist long to make a name for herself, though; her debut album topped the *Billboard* album chart just as her debut solo single, the album's title track, was topping the Hot 100 chart. Her presence was inescapable.

Ashanti's overnight jump to superstardom followed that of Ja Rule, a similar urban music sensation helmed by Gotti. The New York producer took notice of Ashanti initially because of her beauty, dancing, and acting. She trained as a dancer at the Bernice Johnson Cultural Arts Center, learning a number of dance styles. She danced most notably in Disney's *Polly*, which starred Phylicia Rashad, and also appeared in a number of big-name music videos, in addition to other dance work. As an actress, she made a name for herself with roles in Spike Lee's *Malcolm X* and ·*Who's da Man* before that. The multitalented vocalist was causing quite a stir, and Gotti did what he could to bring her into his Murder Inc. fold. After showcasing her swooning voice on Big Pun's "How We Roll" and the *Fast and Furious* soundtrack—both in 2001—Gotti put Ashanti to work on her debut album, which he produced.

Success came quickly. A duet with Ja Rule, "Always on Time," hit number one on *Billboard*'s Hot 100 chart in early 2002 just as a duet with Fat Joe, "What's Luv?" was creeping toward the same number-one position. These two airplay-heavy singles, of course, set the stage perfectly for Ashanti's self-titled debut release. The album's lead single, "Foolish," raced up the Hot 100 chart, entering the Top Ten in March alongside "Always on Time" and "What's Luv?" giving her three Top Ten songs in the same week, including the number one and two positions, a quite spectacular feat. And then Ashanti's album debuted at number one on the album chart, selling an astounding 500,000-plus copies in its first week. With all this chart topping, Ashanti set some sales records and her success continued. Gotti readied a remix of "Foolish," titled "Unfoolish," that featured the Notorious B.I.G. and again overtook

urban radio, where no artist was more omnipresent throughout 2002 than Ashanti. —*Jason Birchmeier*

● **Ashanti** / Apr. 2, 2002 / Murder Inc. ✦✦✦
Young, pretty, sexy, stylish, and hip, Ashanti is everything a modern, post-hip-hop soul crooner should be. She looks the part, trucks with hitmakers—at the time her eponymous debut was released, she was featured on a hit single by Fat Joe—and even approximates Alicia Keys's visuals on the back cover. She can sing, but she's not showy; she never hyperventilates, she croons. Her first album sounds modern, with fairly fresh beats and lightly insistent hooks, and is just naughty enough to warrant a parental advisory sticker (though if you're just listening to this record, it's nigh on impossible to figure out where the objectionable lines are). So why doesn't *Ashanti* play as greater than the sum of its parts? Largely because it lacks distinctive material, in either terms of the actual songs or the production—and when that's combined with a singer who is good, yet not distinctive herself, the entire production sounds as if its treading water or providing nifty aural wallpaper. It's not bad by any means, and it has its moments, but at 17 tracks, including skits, it all becomes a blur. A pleasing blur, one that shows promise, but a blur all the same. —*Stephen Thomas Erlewine*

Asheru (Gabriel Benn)

b. Maryland
Hip-Hop
It took several years after its formation in 1996 before the Unspoken Heard began to make waves in the East Coast hip-hop underground; but the rapper/producer collective, based in the nation's capital, certainly did just that as the new millennium turned, and Asheru and Blue Black had a lot to do with the success. Asheru (born Gabriel Benn), a Maryland native, and Blue Black (born Robert Jackson), who originally hailed from the Bronx, met and became friends while each was a student at the University of Virginia (majoring and eventually taking degrees in anthropology and sociology, respectively). Both men were long interested in rapping; they soon formed a duo and fell in with a group of similarly inclined students: the nucleus of what would ultimately become the "Home of the New Age B-boy," Charlottesville indie label Seven Heads Entertainment (J-Live, Mr. Complex, Richy Pitch, Djinji Brown). Alternately setting up shop in Washington, D.C., and New York City after graduation, Benn took a full-time job as a middle-school teacher and Jackson became involved in e-commerce, all the while working on music in their spare time. Blue Black was the first to represent the Heard in 1996 with the solo 12", "Sun Up From Sun Down." He was joined by Asheru on the classic 1999 single *Better/Smiley*, which was bookended by a pair of Unspoken Heard EPs, *Cosmology* and *Jamboree*, all released on Seven Heads. Asheru and Blue Black both gave up their day jobs in 1999 to dedicate more time to recording and touring. (Benn additionally became an educational consultant, developing original curricula and conducting workshops; Jackson became a business consultant.) The result of their increased efforts in the studio was a literate, conscientious 2001 debut effort, *Soon Come?* Heavily indebted to the New York "new school" sound of the early '90s, especially the Native Tongues vibe, the album developed a steady buzz, landing it on a number of year-end best-of lists. —*Stanton Swihart*

● **Soon Come?** / Sep. 4, 2001 / Seven Heads ✦✦✦✦
This is a perfect example of post-millennial hip-hop for purists who prefer their albums in a decidedly erudite, East Coast/Native Tongues mold, but without having to experience the guilty feelings that afflict those snagged in a musical time loop. This D.C. duo has the same sort of complex singing deliveries, engage in the same sort of sinewy rhyme tradeoffs, and are just as cerebral, optimistic, and liltingly uplifting as A Tribe Called Quest and De La Soul (or to strike a nearer chronological note, simpatico peers like Black Star and Jurassic 5). The only quality *Soon Come?* cannot communicate to quite the same degree is the wonderment that accompanies ingenuity and stylistic freshness. By 2001 this sort of buoyant, loose hip-hop had become a part of the genre's history; nevertheless, the duo proved here that they were no mere relic and that they still had plenty of corners in which to root around. The album taps a bubbling reserve of energy and vitality, and Asheru and Blue Black stir in just enough of the new with a whole lot of old school style to make an irresistible blend. Snatches of very cool jazz saunter into the backgrounds of great cuts like "Dear You," "Elevator Music," "Live at Home," "Jamboree," and "This Is Me," the latter of which lays a particularly brilliant

electric guitar tag-down as backdrop to some equally fetching linguistics, and the rest of the album maintains an extremely relaxed, laid-back vibe, like a small gathering of friends trading rhymes over a couple bottles of wine and a few Lee Morgan, Wes Montgomery, and Thelonious Monk albums. Of such a quality that it should have been for 2001 what *Quality Control* was to the previous year, *Soon Come?* unfortunately didn't have a similar, deserved commercial impact. It does have all the attributes, however, that keep heads across the hip-hop spectrum nodding, and it raised the level of anticipation for future joints from the Unspoken Heard crew. — *Stanton Swihart*

Atmosphere

f. Minneapolis, MN

Group / Underground Rap, Hip-Hop

Atmosphere is a hip-hop group from Minneapolis that centers around rapper Slug (aka Sean Daley). The son of a black father and a white mother who divorced when he was a teenager, Slug became entranced with hip-hop, graffiti, and breakdancing, and formed the Rhyme Sayers Collective with two high school friends—Siddiq Ali (Stress) and Derek Turner (Spawn). After some early gigs as Urban Atmosphere, where Slug DJed behind Spawn's rhyming, the pair hooked up with producer Ant (Anthony Davis), as well as likeminded locals such as MC Musab, Mr. Gene Poole, and the Abstract Pack, forming an underground hip-hop clique dedicated to freestyling, clever and complex lyrics, and anti-gangsta positivity. In 1998 Atmosphere released its debut album, *Overcast!*, which quickly became regarded as an underground hip-hop classic thanks to Slug's deeply personal, poetic musings, as well as Ant's bare bones—but inventive—production. The next Atmosphere album was titled *Sad Clown Bad Dub II*, a 2000 set originally sold while the group was on tour. (Now out-of-print, it's a highly sought-after collector's item.) A year later, the group released *Lucy Ford: The Atmosphere EPs*, a collection of three EPs built around the theme of Slug's complicated relationship with his ex-girlfriend, the lost love of his life. The group has toured consistently, both at home and overseas; while Ant usually doesn't accompany the group on the road, Mr. Dibbs of the group 1200 Hobos often joins in behind the turntables and Slug is usually assisted on the mic by young rappers like the teenaged Eyedea. In June 2002 the group—down to the duo of Slug and Ant—unleashed *God Loves Ugly*, an 18-track effort that returned to previous themes ("F*@k You Lucy"), but also contained the group's most pop-friendly single to date, "Modern Man's Hustle." — *Dan LeRoy*

Overcast! EP / 1998 / Rhymesayers ✦✦✦

Atmosphere is a two-man group made up of MCs Slug and Spawn. There are a few pieces of filler on *Overcast!*, but it does have its share of good songs too, such as "1597," "Sound Is Vibration," "Scapegoat," and "Cuando Limpia El Humo." "Sound Is Vibration" has a heavenly feel due to the harp used in the beat, and Slug and Spawn bring a lot of energy to the song. "Scapegoat" is a creative song done by Slug, in which he talks about all the excuses people use for their mistakes without considering their own faults. The only guest on the album is Beyond, who appears on "Current Status" and "Adjust." All songs are produced by Ant. — *Dan Gizzi*

● **Lucy Ford: The Atmosphere EPs** / 2000 / Rhymesayers ✦✦✦✦

The opening track on *Lucy Ford*, "Between the Lines," burrows into the heads of a frustrated policeman, an oblivious young girl who watches movies perpetually to get away from her own life, and an indie rapper who descends into self-abnegation instead of self-aggrandizement—hardly typical subject matter for a rap song. In fact, with Slug's singsong delivery, it hardly seems like a rap song at all, and is tugged back toward the genre only by Ant's steady beat making. But then Atmosphere proves not to be typical in most every respect on this debut full-length, which is much the better for the duo's, and particularly its MC's, peculiarities. *Lucy Ford* actually collects the bulk of a pair of early Fat Beats-distributed vinyl EPs from the Minneapolis-based group on a single long-playing disc. It makes for a sterling introductory display. Like Eminem, Atmosphere is a joy to hear when caricaturing old school trash talking ("Guns and Cigarettes," with a truly inspired, bluesy Ant track) and even more so when Slug is lampooning his own penchant for indulgent egotism ("It Goes") with hilarious, self-deprecating one-liners. At other times, however, Atmosphere bogs down in a more earnest self-involvement, as on the romance ballad "Don't Ever Fucking Question That," where the duo reaches for heartfelt with less-than-convincing results. Slug excels when he allows his obvious passion to settle on subjects outside himself, as when he tries to coax

the hip-hop community toward a higher calling on "Tears for Sheep," or, more breathtakingly, mixes autobiographical details with flights of pure imagination. The best tracks tend to occur when he plums the psychological depths of complex characters through brainy, abstract, and freewheeling narratives that exist somewhere in a surreal netherworld ("If I Was Santa Claus," "Aspiring Sociopath," "Party for the Fight to Write," "The Woman With the Tattooed Hands," the aforementioned "Between the Lines"). On these songs the duo approaches dazzling heights that Eminem could never approach. Despite its few flaws, including a bit of merely serviceable filler, *Lucy Ford* offered one of the freshest voices in rap in 2000; in fact, its stronger moments are among the most forward-thinking hip-hop ever made. — *Stanton Swihart*

God Loves Ugly / Jun. 11, 2002 / Fat Beats ✦✦✦

Coming straight outta the rough'n'tumble surroundings of Minneapolis/ St. Paul, the Rhymesayers clique is slowly but surely putting Minnesota on the hip-hop map. OK, so the frozen lands that gave listeners Prince and Morris Day & the Time may seem like a fairly unlikely setting for the next hip-hop hotbed, but you can't deny the talent the area's been bringing to the table. First, Eyedea won the country's biggest MC battle with a brilliant display of freestyle ability, now Atmosphere's latest album states the case that there are some serious skills in the Great White North. The group is fronted by Slug, whose densely packed rhymes on the opening "Onemosphere" and "The Bass & the Movement" showcase a clever lyrical flow that recalls early De La Soul if they'd been produced by El-P. On "Hair" and the title track, the MC exposes a refreshing sense of self-deprecating realism all too often lacking among the current hip-hop scene's posturing poseurs. Though the lo-fi D.I.Y. production slows the momentum on a handful of tracks, when Slug's rhymes and producer Ant's beats click, the results are as good as underground hip-hop gets. — *Bret Love*

Audio Two

f. Brooklyn, NY

Group / East Coast Rap, Golden Age

Siblings of MC Lyte and a pair of the most notorious gay-bashers in hip-hop, Audio Two—Gizmo Dee and Milk—released a trio of albums during the late '80s and early '90s, each of which had good moments drizzled throughout patches of filler. The Brooklyn brothers were signed to First Priority by the label's president, their father. "Top Billin'," "What More Can I Say," and "Hickeys Around My Neck" won the duo some fans, but it wasn't enough to make the album worthy of classic status. *I Don't Care: The Album* followed in 1990 and featured "Whatcha Lookin' At?," the most homophobic track in their catalog. Despite an appearance from their sister, the album flopped. *The First Dead Indian* closed out their run in 1992. — *Andy Kellman*

● **What More Can I Say?** / 1988 / First Priority ✦✦✦

Aided by Stetsasonic's Daddy O on a pair of cuts ("Make It Funky" and "Top Billin'"), Audio Two's full-length debut is a patchy affair, just like the albums that would follow from the Brooklyn duo. Neither Gizmo Dee nor his brother Milk are proficient rappers with above-average lyrical capabilities, but the way they play off each other is occasionally enough to cause some excitement. "Top Billin'" stands easily as the best track here, thanks in no small part to Daddy O's sparse yet infectious work—the beat would later reappear in Mary J. Blige's "Real Love." Other entertaining moments include "Hickeys Around My Neck" and "Make It Funky." — *Andy Kellman*

I Don't Care: The Album / 1990 / First Priority ✦✦

Best known for producing MC Lyte, Audio Two sold the most albums along the northeastern corridor. The Brooklyn group's late-'80s and early-'90s albums weren't remarkable, but they had their moments. *I Don't Care: The Album* has a few decent tracks, including the catchy "Start it Up, Y'all" (which features guest Lyte) and the obnoxious "Get Your Mother Off the Crack." But on the whole, the album is quite forgettable. The New York-sounding production, full of soul samples, is very predictable, and most of the lyrics are routine, run-of-the-mill boasting. Audio is at its lowest on "When Milk's On the Mic" and "Whatcha Lookin' At?," both of which are repugnant, hateful examples of overt gay-bashing. It's best to pass on this CD. — *Alex Henderson*

The First Dead Indian / 1992 / First Priority ✦✦

Awesome 2

Group / Hip-Hop

With the distinction of hosting the longest-running rap show (*The Awesome 2 Radio Show*, c. 1982), Awesome 2 became the wise men of rap, offering consultation and advice to many of its biggest names, including Big Daddy Kane, EPMD, and Nice & Smooth. The duo, Special K and DJ Teddy Tedd, are cousins who originally replaced Afrika Islam's Wednesday afternoon slot at WHBI in New York. The show became so popular, and the demo-tape pile so large, that the duo decided to host a successful Rap Talent Night that lasted two years. In 1990, Special K and Teddy Tedd branched out into production, compiling the *History of Rap* series for Select Records. —*Steve Kurutz*

● **The Awesome 2 Present: The History of Rap, Vol. 1** / 1990 / Select ✦✦✦✦
Presented by Awesome 2, Special K and DJ Teddy Tedd, *The History of Rap, Vol. 1* is a devastating collection of classic old school tracks, compiling both the familiar ("The Message" by Grandmaster Flash, "The Breaks" by Kurtis Blow, "Planet Rock" by Afrika Bambaataa) and a few of those more familiar to DJs ("That's the Joint" by the Funky 4+1, "Feel the Heartbeat" by the Treacherous Three). —*Keith Farley*

Ayeesha

Christian Rap

Christian hip-hop artist Ayeesha grew up in a neighborhood touched by gang violence, but turned to church and school activities as a means of escape. The California native began performing at an early age, starting as a rapper at eight and participating in her school's theater and sports programs until graduation. After receiving a bachelor's degree in liberal studies from a San Bernardino college, Ayeesha pursued her music career and released *Listen Closely* on Grapetree Records in 1999. —*Heather Phares*

● **Listen Closely** / Aug. 10, 1999 / Grapetree ✦✦✦
Halfway between smooth vocal R&B and the rowdier sound of No Limit, Ayeesha's *Listen Closely* trades in her accomplished vocals for sullen rhymes and occasional diva theatrics. Though it's an interesting fusion of soft and hard, a few of the tracks seem forced. Highlights include "Edge of Life," "Don't Wanna Die," and "Hold On." —*Keith Farley*

AZ (Anthony Cruz)

b. Brooklyn, NY

East Coast Rap, Gangsta Rap, Hip-Hop

One of the numerous thoughtful, literate gangsta rappers to emerge from New York during the mid-'90s, AZ never garnered the attention of peers like Nas and Jay-Z. Instead, he saw his debut album, *Doe or Die*, become a critical favorite in late 1995 before his career suddenly went downhill after such modest and short-lived success. Critics and b-boys alike celebrated AZ and his debut album for a literate approach to the gangsta lifestyle. Like his aforementioned peers Nas and Jay-Z, AZ brought not only intelligence to his rhymes but also an impressive flow and delivery that further set him apart from the flood of New York MCs fighting for survival in the crowded rap game. Unfortunately, despite *Doe or Die*'s quiet success, AZ stumbled in successive years, finally scoring a new major-label relationship with Motown in the early 2000s.

Born in Brooklyn as Anthony Cruz, AZ first came to the greater rap community's attention in a big way after his stellar performance on Nas' "Life's a Bitch" in 1994. Given AZ's similarity to Nas and the overwhelming response to Nas' *Illmatic* album, it was just a matter of time before AZ would score a record deal, a feat he accomplished in 1995. The resulting debut album, *Doe or Die*, shook the New York hip-hop scene as Nas' *Illmatic* and Mobb Deep's *Infamous* had done shortly before it. Like those albums, *Doe or Die* reveled in the street life—hustling for cash, peddling drugs, violent encounters, mandatory boasting, struggling daily just to maintain—but took a literate and thoughtful approach to the often exploitative gangsta motifs. Furthermore, like Nas, AZ had Pete Rock crafting the beats, which won the young rapper instant credibility among the hip-hop community.

When word hit the street that AZ was an official member of the supergroup known as the Firm, his status only rose higher. Anchored by Nas, Foxy Brown, Nature, and AZ on the mics, with Dr. Dre and the Trackmasters on the beats, it would seem as if the group could do no wrong. The group's 1997 album ended up being a surprise failure, though, buried under ridiculous expectations and too much hype. But AZ's bad fortune didn't stop there. He returned a year later with his sophomore album, *Pieces of a Man*, an album that came and went relatively unnoticed and uncelebrated. For the next few years, AZ became a forgotten name. No longer with a major-label contract, he managed to release the little-heard *S.O.S.A.* record in 2000. It didn't sell

many copies or resurrect his career but rather reaffirmed the fact that he was indeed a talented rapper whether the public and the industry wanted to acknowledge it or not.

Within a year's time, AZ secured a new major-label relationship with Motown, a label that had never had much, if any, success with rap artists. Still, the Brooklyn rapper wouldn't let the label's reputation hold him back, as he illustrated on *9 Lives*, unofficially hailed as his comeback album. Though lacking big-name production and employing a skimpy roster of guest rappers, the album did showcase AZ's lyrical prowess and his endurance, anchored by the sample-laced lead single "Problems." —*Jason Birchmeier*

● **Doe or Die** / Oct. 10, 1995 / EMI ✦✦✦✦✦
In 1995 it was easy to confuse comrades and collaborators Nas and AZ, so similar in style were their street-schooled lyrical concerns and their austere, lazy-eyed rhyming styles. AZ, in fact, first came to the attention of the rap scene by contributing a verse to the former's classic 1994 single "Life's a Bitch." To compound the resemblance, he called on Pete Rock to produce a couple tracks ("Gimme Your's" and "Rather Unique," both stellar) on this introductory recording, just as Nas had on his classic debut. The two albums are very much the twin sides of the same double-headed coin. They are so closely connected, in fact, that it's difficult to pinpoint where *Doe or Die*'s points of departure are located. Many of its character sketches (the Buckwild-produced "Ho Happy Jack"), urban-caked admonitions ("Mo Money Mo Murder," on which Nas, in fact, turns up to return the favor, the equally hard-hitting title track), and gritty expressions of love ("I Feel for You," a pumped-up "One Love") are every bit as meditative and literate, peppered with authentic, incisive documentary detail. Ultimately, AZ's album is not quite as compact and consistent, and, unlike its mirror image, its focus lapses right toward the end. But while *Doe or Die* is not quite on an artistic par with, or as free flowing a masterpiece as, the landmark *Illmatic*, it is not far behind in terms of quality, either. Certainly it was one of the strongest, most promising debut efforts of 1995, and probably one of the year's strongest rap albums, period. As with Nas, he would have a difficult time following up on this early juggernaut. —*Stanton Swihart*

Pieces of a Man / May 19, 1998 / Virgin ✦✦✦✦
AZ had a lot to prove with his second album, *Pieces of a Man*. Not only did he have to prove that the success of his debut *Doe or Die* was not a fluke, he had to live up to his success with the Firm and as a guest artist with Monifah, D'Angelo and Nas. For the most part, he lives up to these expectations on *Pieces of a Man*. There are certainly some slow spots on the record, but the production from the Trackmasterz and Dr. Dre is appealing, funky, and seamless, blending street rhythms with radio-ready hooks. Furthermore, AZ's lyrical skills are increasing, as the best moments (including the single "What's the Deal") prove. The moments that work on *Pieces of a Man* are so strong that they make the lesser, lazier moments forgivable. —*Stephen Thomas Erlewine*

S.O.S.A. (Save Our Streets AZ) / 2000 / ✦✦✦✦
After bursting onto the scene with a cameo in Nas' classic "Life's a Bitch," Brooklyn native AZ has struggled to find a place in the hip-hop landscape. Often mired by poor production and a lack of support from record companies, AZ's substantial lyrical gifts have been relegated to the dustbin of hip-hop history. His 2000 album, *S.O.S.A. (Save Our Streets AZ)*, is his third attempt at acceptance, a lean ten-track effort that should turn a few heads. AZ is at the top of his game on tracks like "Platinum Bars" and the low-riding funk of "Bodies Gotta Get Caught." Similarly, the lead single "I Don't Give a Fuck Now" along with "Problems" and "Let's Toast" demonstrate the power of AZ's lyrical wizardry. More than just saving the streets, *S.O.S.A.* may be what it takes to save AZ's career. —*Jon Azpiri*

9 Lives / Jun. 12, 2001 / Motown ✦✦✦
Five years after the critical celebration surrounding his debut release, *Doe or Die*, AZ's name suddenly didn't seem all that familiar. Sure, *Doe or Die* had indeed been a quiet classic of sorts, but it never shook the cash register, and his subsequent efforts were even less successful from a commercial standpoint. Perhaps it was no surprise then that he encountered problems with his label after the indifferent response to his sophomore album in 1998. But three years later, AZ returned with a new label, Motown, and what he obviously feels is a comeback of sorts, *9 Lives*. There are some problems with this comeback, though. First of all, Motown has never been known as a fostering environment for rap artists. Second, perhaps related to the first problem,

there is a serious lack of big-money talent on *9 Lives*—no Pete Rocks or Jay-Zs for this album. Granted, these problems are purely commercial, but they're bad omens for any contemporary, commercial rap effort. Whether or not AZ actually succeeds with his unofficial comeback from a commercial standpoint, he's done an admirable job when judged purely on artistic merit—his rhymes are obviously well written, he delivers them with enthusiasm, and his low-profile production team turns in some good second-rate DJ Premier/Pete Rock-style sample-laden beats. But "admirable performance" is about the best you can say about the album. It's been over five years since *Doe or Die*, and AZ has never blossomed in the way that Nas and Jay-Z did—*Doe or Die* was his pinnacle and sadly remains so. He's not quite as wordy as Nas, not as grimy as Mobb Deep, and not as jiggy as Jigga. With a little more charisma or wit, he'd be a noteworthy talent, or with beats by Pete Rock he'd at least rival his performance on *Doe or Die*. But as things stand on *9 Lives*, AZ remains second tier, lacking a unique identity in a game with few unclaimed niches and little patience. —*Jason Birchmeier*

Aziatic / Jun. 11, 2002 / Motown ♦♦♦♦♦
Since teaming up with Nas on *Illmatic*, widely considered one of the greatest albums in hip-hop, AZ has been looked upon to do amazing things with his music. Has he lived up to those high expectations? On this album he has. From start to finish, the beats on this album are complex, inventive, and almost perfectly suited for AZ's style of rhyming. He's carefully crafted this album rather than slapped it together overnight to meet his quota, and it shows. It helps immensely that he's brought along people like DR Period,

Az Izz, Nas, and Buckwild, but they don't outshine the younger AZ and he holds his own well. One problem that AZ has always had is that he lives in the shadow of his work in the mid-'90s. There's a new era of hip-hop fans who may not know him as well as the rest, but he's done well to reach out and offer the new generation something as well. There aren't just the thuggish tracks, but also some tracks suitable for the club and the ladies, such as "Take It Off." Lyrically, musically, and historically, AZ has come up with his best work in a long time on this album. The biggest complaint is the length of the LP, with only three songs going over four minutes. Why he would make such a great album and end it short is beyond comprehension. —*Brad Mills*

Az Yet

f. 1995

Group / Hip-Hop, Urban

Not long after securing a contract with the LaFace label and releasing their self-titled debut album in late 1996, hip-hop group Az Yet reached the R&B Top 20 with their "Last Night" single. The track hit gold by early 1997. —*John Bush*

● **Az Yet** / Oct. 29, 1996 / LaFace ♦♦♦

Az Yet's eponymous debut is an engaging collection of straight-ahead party hip-hop highlighted by the single "Last Night." Although the remainder of the album isn't quite as memorable as "Last Night," there are enough strong moments to make it a worthwhile listen. —*Leo Stanley*

B

B-Legit

Hip-Hop, Gangsta Rap, Hardcore Rap, West Coast Rap

B-Legit (aka the Savage) had previously performed with the Click before striking out on his own with 1995's *Tryin' to Get a Buck*. For his second release, 1996's *Hemp Museum*, he moved to Jive Records and worked with E-40 and Kurupt (the Dogg Pound); *Ghetto Smile* followed in 1997, and two years later B-Legit resurfaced with *Hempin' Ain't Easy* and then *Hempin'* in mid-2000. —*John Bush*

● **Tryin' to Get a Buck** / Feb. 28, 1995 / Jive ✦✦✦✦
B-Legit is probably a rapper because he's E-40's cousin. That said, he does a formidable job, with smooth lyrics and flow. You know what to expect after seeing the cover of this CD, with a couple of guys with masks on their faces reloading a handgun in a store while robbing it. It's more of a gangsta rap album than anything, but B-Legit took some extra steps to make it original. Half the album is devoted to weed, while the other half is about drinking. He talks a lot about his childhood and what it was like growing up in the 'hood. While this album has its strong points, B-Legit's simple rhymes may leave some listeners bored very quickly. He isn't really known as a lyricist, but still his rhymes are interesting and usually follow a story line. Overall a pretty good album if you like this kind of gangsta rap. —*Brad Mills*

Hemp Museum / Nov. 26, 1996 / Jive ✦✦✦✦
B-Legit's *Hemp Museum* works the standard West Coast gangsta territory without much distinction for most of its overlong running time, but when the thick-tongued rapper cuts "Check It Out" with E-40 and tha Dogg Pound's Kurupt, he demonstrates his true skills. Unfortunately, those very skills are buried by predictable beats and rhymes for much of *Hemp Museum*. —*Leo Stanley*

Hempin' Ain't Easy / Nov. 9, 1999 / SWI ✦✦✦
Former Sick Wid It affiliate B-Legit spends the majority of *Hempin' Ain't Easy* boasting about blazing bud the way fellow Cali Bay Area rapper Too Short boasts pimpin'-ain't-easily about exploiting women. Beyond his drug-game fixation, B-Legit is as witty as ever and hosts some notable guests: rappers Snoop Dogg, Kurupt, Mack 10, Lil' Keke, Mac Shawn, and E-40 as well as producers Ant Banks, Studio Ton, Daz Dillinger, Meech Wells, Tone Capone, and Bosko. *Hempin' Ain't Easy* is thus a solid West Coast release with an all-star lineup, not quite as inspired as his *Hemp Museum* album from a year earlier but solid nonetheless and certainly worthwhile for fans of Bay Area rap. —*Jason Birchmeier*

Hard 2 B-Legit / Aug. 27, 2002 / Koch International ✦✦✦
On his fifth album, B-Legit seems to be moving slightly out of the underground and edging toward the mainstream. The feints toward mass acceptance are pretty minor—he's not trying to be Nelly or anything—and basically consist of making only every third or fourth song about the power and glory of weed instead of every other verse. Of course, the weed songs are still what he does best; "Luv 2 Get High" and "Bag Habit" feature the loosest, slyest rhymes on the album. Elsewhere, as on "I'm Singlin'" and "Whatcha Talkin'," B-Legit sounds like he's making a conscious attempt to clean up his sound, but as a result, these tracks lack the personality and sparkle of earlier albums like *Hempin' Ain't Easy*. The knockout punch is "Straight Fool," a duet with E-40 set to a wiggy sample that sounds like it could come off a Missy Elliot or Timbaland record and featuring the toughest delivery and sharpest rhymes on the entire album. —*Stewart Mason*

Heather B.

Hip-Hop, Gangsta Rap, Party Rap, Club/Dance

Best known as a member of the original MTV *Real World* cast, rapper Heather B. began as a part-time performer with KRS-One's Boogie Down

Productions when she added vocals to the group's *Sex and Violence* album. After appearing on *Real World*, Heather recorded a single for Elektra Records, "I Get Wreck," and pressed her own copies of another single, "All Glocks Down," that was eventually released by Pendulum Records. —*Steve Kurutz*

Takin' Mine / Jun. 11, 1996 / Pendulum ✦✦✦
Heather B. started her career as a member of the 1992 cast of MTV's reality soap opera, *The Real World*. As if to silence critics that would claim such a starting point is proof that her music is weak and lame, she simply rages throughout her debut album, *Takin' Mine*. Heather B. plays by the gangsta rules, spitting out her lyrics over a spare, funky beat. Although her conviction, as well as her sense of style and timing, is impressive, there's nothing on *Takin' Mine* that hasn't been heard before—these are hardcore clichés, from the hedonistic lyrics to the G-funk production. For connoisseurs and aficionados, *Takin' Mine* has something to offer—particularly in the way Heather B.'s lyrical observations suggest that she could develop a style more personal and, therefore, impressive—but for anyone else, the album will sound a bit rote. —*Leo Stanley*

● **Eternal Affairs** / Feb. 12, 2002 / Sai ✦✦✦✦
Heather B. flows like a veteran on *Eternal Affairs*, never short on knowledge or stamina. Moreover, an impressive cast of New York's finest joins her for the album, in particular legendary producers DJ Premier and Pete Rock. She opens the album with lyrical guns blazing on "Live MC," which then goes into "Steady Rockin'," Premier's contribution to the album. On most of *Eternal Affairs'* dozen songs, B. holds her own; on the few songs with guest MCs, however, she matches her guests rhyme for rhyme, the most noteworthy contributors being Queen MCs Nature and Horse, the latter a member of Nas Bravehearts' posse. Perhaps because she's a female competing in a man's world—the rap world, that is—she spits her rhymes with force and a bit of aggression. No matter the reason, her rhymes never go unheard, particularly with the excellent productions she has backing her. —*Jason Birchmeier*

Mark B

Producer / Ambient Breakbeat, Underground Rap, Hip-Hop

Mark B is just one of the excellent DJ/producers on Jazz Fudge Recordings, the label most closely associated with Britain by way of Russia's DJ Vadim. Compared to the usual run of scratch-happy turntablists in underground rap, Mark's much more reliant on drum-machine dinosaurs and samplers. He began recording for Jazz Fudge in 1995, and produced a couple of tracks for Vadim's 1996 debut *U.S.S.R. Repertoire (The Theory of Verticality)*. Mark B released his own first album, *Underworld Connection*, the following year and collaborated with rapper Blade for 1998's excellent *Hitmen for Hire* LP. In 1999, he teamed up with Taskforce for the album *New Mic Order*. Mark B also contributed to the Om compilation *Deeper Concentration, Vol. 2*. —*John Bush*

Underworld Connection / Jul. 21, 1997 / Jazz Fudge ✦✦✦
Recorded for DJ Vadim's stellar label Jazz Fudge, *Underworld Connection* contains all the usual abstract hip-hop clichés: shrieking '50s strings, '60s spy music, and '70s funk with incredibly obscure spoken-word bits. Fortunately, Mark B has a way with his studio gear, and he tweaks the mix until it becomes quite a unique work. —*John Bush*

● **Hitmen for Hire** / Apr. 13, 1998 / Jazz Fudge ✦✦✦✦
Instead of delving further into abstract hip-hop, Mark B teamed up with the rapper Blade for his second album. The collaboration works quite well, as Blade and B (plus Mr. Thing from Scratch Perverts on scratching) construct

a dense underground rap album that fortunately never moves too far into beat headspace. From the scratchy old samples on "Intense Preparations" (featuring Lewis Parker) to the 808 bump of "Use Your Head," Mark B displays his considerable production skills, and Blade matches him with verbal dexterity. As could be expected, there are a couple of instrumentals that get a bit bland, and (for better or worse) there are many sophomoric samples. Any way you dice it, though, *Hitmen for Hire* is an excellent hip-hop album. —*John Bush*

Tairrie B.

Hip-Hop, Hardcore Rap
Californian Tairrie B. recorded one hip-hop album in 1990 with the help of N.W.A's Eazy-E and additional production assistance from Schoolly D. In spite of her novel appearance and persona—Tairrie was a blonde hip-hop feminist able to meet males on their own level while remaining distinctly feminine—the album failed to make much of an impact, and Tairrie B. disappeared from the scene. —*Steve Huey*

● **The Power of a Woman** / 1990 / MCA ♦♦♦
Tairrie B. certainly gets points for effort on her debut release—her swaggering toughness and secure femininity make for an intriguing contrast, and Tairrie sounds like she can hold her own with anyone. However, her thin voice doesn't give her music the weight of her rhymes or persona, even though Schoolly D contributes stellar production work on two tracks. Still, songs like "Murder She Wrote" and "Ruthless Bitch" are almost enough to make the album successful. —*Steve Huey*

Baba

b. Manhattan, NY
Alternative Rap, Hip-Hop
Baba is a New York-based MC and hip-hop philosopher. Born and raised in Manhattan, Baba's Russian/Jewish parents were members of the Living Theater, an avant-garde performance collective that used to stage theater events in places as disparate or unlikely as a farm, street corner, or prison. The young Baba even lived for a time in Australia, where his mother was born. Baba channeled the cross-cultural sights and sounds of his youth into his art, and began to make a name for himself in New York City as a "conscious" rapper. Velour Records took notice, and in 2001 released *Mind Music*, Baba's full-length debut. A bouillabaisse of downtown jazz, didgeridoo, and straight-up New York City hip-hop textures, *Mind Music* was anchored by Baba's deep, singsongy flow, and suggested influences like A Tribe Called Quest and KRS-One. Velour released "Big Up" and "Let It Shine" as singles, and in summer of that same year, *Mind Music* was picked up for wider release. Baba has kept busy, performing with likeminded artists such as Black Eyed Peas and Jurassic 5. True to his roots in activism and awareness, Baba is also involved with New York City's DOOR youth development agency, where he coordinates a music and poetry program for children. —*Johnny Loftus*

● **Mind Music** / Jun. 19, 2001 / Velour ♦♦♦
If Mystikal's credo is "Shake your ass, watch yourself," then Baba's comes from the track "Bounce": "Bounce to the rhythm, verbalize your vision." Baba's debut album, *Mind Music*, is the embodiment of its title. This is not gangsta rap or hip-hop-hurray rap; this is philosopher rap. Similar to the styles of De La Soul and Black Eyed Peas, Baba is more likely to wax poetic about the promise of the examined life than glorify misogyny or drug pushing. The NYC-based rapper shows how exposure and openness to a wide range of musical influences can meld into one complex style. You'll hear elements of dancehall, soul, and old school rap—all in the same song, in the case of "Blues Man." Along with genre blending, Baba likes to layer the music to add the intricacy. While he repeats a simple chorus on "X-perience," he lays down another track of elaborate rhymes behind that. The clash of words requires you to use your brain instead of just groove; you can decide for yourself if that's a good thing. With many intellectual endeavors, passion can take a backseat to rationality. Baba generally overcomes this, although it'd be a stretch to say the beats are infectious. The best rump shaker of the bunch is definitely his collaboration with DJ Logic on "Beatbox Logic," which combines Logic's great funk sense with Baba's didgeridoo and beatbox technique—an interesting world music twist on an old school rap technique. —*Michael Gowan*

DJ Babu (Chris Oroc)

DJ / Turntablism, Hip-Hop, Underground Rap, West Coast Rap
Born Chris Oroc, DJ Babu is a member of Dilated Peoples and the on-again/off-again DJ crew Beat Junkies. The California-based DJ began making mix tapes in the early '90s and joined the Beat Junkies in 1994. Babu has won multiple competition titles including the DMC Championship in 1997 and multiple ITF titles. As a revered battle DJ, he has appeared in and hosted numerable videos and—under the name Turntablist—produced perhaps the genre's most popular battle record, 1996's *Super Duck Breaks*, which sold over 10,000 copies, and its inevitable follow-up, *Super Duper Duck Breaks*, in 2000. —*Wade Kergan*

● **Duck Season, Vol. 1** / 2002 / Sequence/Ultra ♦♦♦
The second release for the Sequence Records imprint under the Virgin/Ultra canopy, DJ Babu, acclaimed DJ for the Beat Junkies and Dilated Peoples, steps out solo with his own mix CD. Featuring new tracks and mixes of De La Soul, Pete Rock, the Visionaries, Quasimoto, Jurassic 5, Dilated Peoples, and Big Daddy Kane just for starters, this collection exceeds the expectations of most mixes and comes through with a listenable compilation packaged with a loose but lovable duck theme. Though lacking the scratching that is part of the Babu repertoire, *Duck Season* is still an outstanding representation of one turntablist's greatest ears and wrists. —*Nic Kincaid*

Baby Beesh

West Coast Rap, Hardcore Rap
Emerging from the Bay Area in 1994, rapper Baby Beesh was part of Potna Deuce, whose album *Welcome to da Tilt* appeared briefly on Profile before disappearing. Beesh and the rest of the Potna Deuce crew would release 1996's *Heron Soup* independently before disbanding altogether. Beesh next formed Latino Velvet with N2Deep's Jay Tee, releasing *The Golden State* in 1996. *The Rumble* followed three years later, at which point Beesh parted ways with Latino Velvet and the Bay Area scene. He headed south to Houston, TX, where Dope House signed him as a solo artist. *Savage Dreams*, his 2001 debut for the label, was heavily influenced by the Dirty South, complete with gaudy cover art. But by 2002's *On tha Cool*, Beesh seemed to have mellowed in sound and attitude. The album's trippy stoner vibes intersected with Beesh's West Coast chest thumping to suggest War's "Low Rider" performed by Tupac Shakur. *On tha Cool* was produced by Mario Ayala and Happy Perez and featured contributions from Dope House artists South Park Mexican and Russell Lee, as well as a Latino Velvet reunion on "They Don't Even Know." —*Johnny Loftus*

Savage Dreams / Jun. 19, 2001 / Dope House ♦♦♦
Baby Beesh's first album for the Houston-based Dope House imprint finds him mixing his Latin-inflected West Coast flow with dirty South beats and flavor, courtesy of his new Texan friends. The result is quite effective. Originally from the Bay Area, Beesh was a protégé of legendary Hispanic MC Kid Frost (aka Frost). The influence is apparent in his smooth style, but Beesh doesn't let his heritage dominate *Savage Dreams*. Rather than make his solo debut a "Latino rap album," it is mostly a dirty South record, full of the leering boasts and skittering beats that typify the genre. "Whodoo" is a fabulous introduction, giving Beesh space to boast about his ability to party with anyone in a car with beats you can hear 14 blocks away. "Watch How Quick" is straight-up West Coast, but "Nana Tonight" is more typical of the album's dirty South vibe. "Nice ta Meet Ya" and "Cool Tonight," with their soulful choruses, are likely intended to have crossover potential. But it's "Too Many Things"' flirtation with pop structure that will likely appeal to a wider audience. *Savage Dreams* is not necessarily intended as a crossover record; indeed, the majority of its 19 tracks are delightfully raunchy tributes to Beesh and his crew's lovemaking prowess and insatiable appetite for marijuana. But the album's lighter moments illustrate well the MC's multigenre appeal and suggest that, while Dope House and dirty South are the current names in his game, Baby Beesh has the talent to take his flow anywhere he wants it go. —*Johnny Loftus*

● **On tha Cool** / Jun. 11, 2002 / Dope House ♦♦♦
Those who know Baby Beesh look forward to what he's going to do next. It seems like every time around something has changed; he's working with new people, in a new group, on a new label—pick and choose from the above. This album is a funky and eclectic adventure with songs as distinct as Beesh's

music career itself. He's got party tracks, danceable tracks, deep and bassy beats, a reggae-inspired track, and mellow relaxing tunes, too. While the beats draw you in, the lyrics may lose you. He's not a bad lyricist by any means, but with so many great rappers releasing music nowadays, Baby Beesh is floating somewhere in the middle as far as wording goes. Still, if you're looking for something that's more good music than a gift from lyrical heaven, this is a good listen. *—Brad Mills*

Baby Bugsy

Gangsta Rap, Hardcore Rap

Cleveland rapper Baby Bugsy began representing Gettin Paid Records in 1998, several years before he unleashed his debut, *Being Bad Beat Good.* He returned in 2002 with *Blow: Based on a True Story* (2002), an album that took inspiration from the film of the same name about becoming rich after dealing cocaine. Becoming rich definitely figures into Bugsy's lyrical themes as the rapper explores the gangsta side of the genre, unafraid to showcase a hardcore style. Bugsy worked closely with producer Mac D and joined fellow Gettin Paid artists To tha Left, Cheree Deck, Manish Squad, and C-Dell on the label's roster. *—Jason Birchmeier*

● **Blow: Based on a True Story** / May 28, 2002 / Gettin Paid ✦✦✦
For *Blow: Based on a True Story,* Baby Bugsy takes much inspiration from the film of the same name. Like that film, Bugsy's lyrics are about getting paid—doing whatever you need to do, be it selling coke or making rap music. His gangsta tendencies don't stop there, though. Bugsy raps about Cleveland, the northern Ohio industrial city he represents, and the hardships involved with living there. Mac D offers lots of thumping beats, and Bugsy raps with a style quite similar to that of Bone, Cleveland's most recognized rap act. *—Jason Birchmeier*

Baby DC (Derek Coleman)

b. Jan. 7, 1986, Oakland, CA
Vocals / Hip-Hop
Rapper Baby DC was born Derek Coleman in Oakland, CA, on January 7, 1986; weaned on the music of N.W.A, Too Short, and Kool Moe Dee, he began rapping as a toddler, and entered a professional career at age five. After Too Short invited Baby DC to perform at a San Jose barbecue attended by a crowd of 3,000 people, the youngster began making live appearances across the country; the first artist to appear on Too Short's Bay Leaf imprint, the 12-year-old issued his debut album, *School Dayz,* in 1998. *—Jason Ankeny*

School Dayz / Sep. 29, 1998 / Jive ✦✦
Too Short's growing label empire continued with *School Dayz,* the first release from Baby DC, a 12-year-old rapper who worked with Ant Banks. Hip-hop fans familiar with Master P.'s Lil' Soldiers will know about what to expect here—namely, a surprisingly squeaky-voiced kid trying to act as hard as his grown-up heroes in the hip-hop world. Whereas Master P. felt free to include almost as many obscenities as the rest of his No Limit releases, Too Short and Ant Banks designed *School Dayz* so all content would be safe for kids of all ages. As such, the rhyme topics look back to early pop-rappers like Kid 'N Play or Kriss Kross instead of the thug-life tactics to which many producers resorted to move products. Baby DC does a good job; he's not only a solid rapper for his age, he's a solid rapper period, and the single "Candy Girl" is a fun update of the Jackson 5-type infatuations for the hip-hop age. Though he can't quite keep it up for the entire LP, Baby DC has a lot of time to improve. *—John Bush*

Baby S

West Coast Rap

Raised on the West Side of Los Angeles, Baby S is a gangsta rapper whose primary influences include DJ Quik, Snoop Doggy Dogg and late N.W.A member Eazy-E. Baby has a rapping style that is unmistakably California—the minute he starts to flow, one can easily tell that he is from the West Coast. The L.A. resident started rapping when he was in grammar school; that was in the '80s, and his desire to rap was inspired by popular hip-hop films like *Krush Groove* and *Beat Street.* Those movies were released at a time when New York still dominated rap, but in the late '80s, the Big Apple's position as hip-hop's capital was seriously challenged by the West Coast—and Baby, like many Southern Californians, came under the influence of the gangsta rappers who were coming out of South Central L.A. and Compton, CA. He was

a major fan of N.W.A's seminal, ultra-influential *Straight Outta Compton* album of 1989, and after that, he was influenced by Compton's DJ Quik and Long Beach's Snoop Doggy Dogg. Those gangsta rappers not only influenced his twangy flow, but also his lyrics (which are full of gangsta/thug life imagery). Along the way, Baby met various West Coast hip-hoppers who helped him out, including producer Battlecat (known for his work with Snoop and tha Eastsidaz) and veteran L.A. rapper King T (who was among Southern California's first hardcore rappers and used to go by King Tee). In 1998, T featured Baby on "Squeeze Yo Balls," one of the tunes on his *Thy Kingdom Come* album. Later that year, Baby appeared on rapper Kurupt's hit single "We Can Freak It," which Battlecat produced. In 2001 Baby recorded his debut album, *Street Fractions,* for Blast Entertainment/Ruthless Records (distributed by Epic/Sony). *—Alex Henderson*

Street Fractions / Feb. 26, 2002 / Blast ✦✦✦
Before the rise of Death Row Records in 1993, Eazy-E's Ruthless Records was the premiere label for Southern California gangsta rap. Not every artist who recorded for Ruthless was on the gangsta tip; the D.O.C. wasn't really a gangsta rapper and J.J. Fad specialized in bubblegum pop-rap. But thanks to N.W.A's albums and Eazy's solo projects, Ruthless went down in history as a gangsta rap powerhouse. When Eazy died of AIDS in 1995, Ruthless wasn't discontinued—and Eazy's widow, Tomica Wright, became the executive producer on albums by MC Ren and Bone Thugs N Harmony (among others) in the late '90s. Recorded for Blast Entertainment/Ruthless (distributed by Epic/Sony) in 2001 and released in 2002, this debut album by Los Angeles resident Baby S is quite faithful to Ruthless' history. *Street Fractions* is typical Southern California gangsta rap; Baby, like so many of his homies in greater Los Angeles, spends much of his time rapping about players, ballers, hustlers, and, of course, "bitches and hoes" (not necessarily in that order). Baby has an unmistakably L.A.-sounding flow along the lines of Eazy-E, Snoop Doggy Dogg, and DJ Quik, and his material (most of it produced by Step) is generally quite derivative. But while *Street Fractions* is hardly groundbreaking by early-2000s standards, the CD does have its moments. Some of the tunes aren't terribly memorable, but some are catchy enough—Baby is at his best on slick, well-produced items that include "Didn't Ask 2 Be a Gangsta," "Hitz 4 Days," and the single "I'm Ghetto." And "So S," one of the album's best tracks, offers an interesting fusion of West Coast gangsta rap and dirty South sensibilities. The uneven *Street Fractions* won't go down in history as a masterpiece, but again, the CD does have its moments. *—Alex Henderson*

Backbone

Dirty South, Urban
Affiliated with the Atlanta-based Dungeon Family collective—led by Organized Noize, OutKast, and Goodie Mob—Backbone emerged with his solo debut in the wake of OutKast's *Stankonia*-fueled crossover success. The album, *Concrete Law,* hit the streets in 2001, led by the single "5 Deuce, 4 Tre," and featured numerous appearances by the extended Dungeon Family. *—Jason Birchmeier*

Concrete Law / Jun. 19, 2001 / Universal ✦✦
While Backbone is a member of the Dungeon Family crew that also includes Southern rap heavyweights such as Outkast and Goodie Mob, the Atlanta rapper takes a decidedly different approach to hip-hop. While those groups have a broader perspective, Backbone's music is drenched with images of street life and drug dealing. Tracks like the lead single, "5-Deuce-4 Tre," and "Under Streetlights" offer blow-by-blow accounts of life as a drug dealer. Musically, Backbone offers some typical Southern bounce although he does throw in a pleasant surprise with "Like This" which has an old school Run-D.M.C. feel to it. Although the ten-year vet has plenty of lyrical prowess, he wastes most of it on tired, old ghetto clichés. Instead of relying on the same tired imagery and taking the easy way out, it seems Backbone should probably try and grow one. *—Jon Azpiri*

Bad Azz

Vocals / Hip-Hop, Gangsta Rap, Hardcore Rap, West Coast Rap
West Coast rapper Bad Azz is far from well-known, yet he has worked with some of the best-selling hip-hop artists of all time, including Snoop Dogg, Warren G, and Tupac Shakur. Bad Azz first got into the rap game in his hometown of Long Beach, playing at house parties and eventually joining the

LBC Crew. After deciding to go solo, he had a brief stint on Snoop Doggy Dogg's label, Doggy Style Records. That relationship quickly fell apart and Bad Azz found himself without a label, doing guest appearances on various projects to keep busy. Eventually he landed at Priority Records and at the age of 23, he released his first solo album *Word on Tha Street*. Three years later, he followed up with 2001's *Personal Business*. *—Jon Azpiri*

● **Word on Tha Street** / Sep. 29, 1998 / Priority ◆◆◆

Personal Business / Jul. 17, 2001 / Priority ◆◆◆

Erykah Badu (Erica Wright)
....

b. Feb. 26, 1972, Dallas, TX

Vocals / Neo-Soul, Hip-Hop, Alternative Rap, Contemporary R&B, Urban, Adult Alternative Pop/Rock

She grew up listening to '70s soul and '80s hip-hop, but Erykah Badu drew more comparisons to Billie Holiday upon her breakout in 1997, after the release of her first album, *Baduizm*. The grooves and production on the album are bass-heavy R&B, but Badu's languorous, occasionally tortured vocals and delicate phrasing immediately removed her from the legion of cookie-cutter female R&B singers. A singer/songwriter responsible for all but one of the songs on *Baduizm*, she found a number-12 hit with her first single "On & On," which pushed the album to number two on the charts.

Born Erica Wright in Dallas in 1972, Badu attended a school of the arts and was working as a teacher and part-time singer in her hometown when she opened for D'Angelo at a 1994 show. D'Angelo's manager, Kedar Massenburg, was impressed with the performance and hooked her up with the singer to record a cover of the Marvin Gaye/Tammi Terrell duet "Precious Love." He also signed Badu to his recently formed Kedar Entertainment label and served as producer for *Baduizm*, which also starred bassist Ron Carter and members of hip-hop avatars the Roots on several tracks. The first single, "On & On," became a number-one R&B hit in early 1997, and *Baduizm* followed it to the top of the R&B album charts by March. Opening for R&B acts as well as rap's Wu-Tang Clan, Erykah Badu stopped just short of number one on the pop album charts in April. Her *Live* album followed later in the year. In 2000 she returned with her highly anticipated second studio album, *Mama's Gun*, which was coproduced by Badu, James Poyser, Bilal, and Jay Dee and contained the hit single, "Bag Lady." *—John Bush*

● **Baduizm** / Feb. 11, 1997 / Kedar ◆◆◆◆◆

Two years after D'Angelo brought the organic sound and emotional passion of R&B to the hip-hop world with 1995's *Brown Sugar*, Erykah Badu's debut performed a similar feat. While D'Angelo looked back to the peak of smooth '70s soul, though, Badu sang with a grit and bluesiness reminiscent of her heroes, Nina Simone and Billie Holiday. "On & On" and "Appletree," the first two songs on *Baduizm*, illustrated her talent at singing soul with the qualities of jazz. With a nimble, melodic voice owing little to R&B from the past 30 years, she phrased at odds with the beat and often took chances with her notes. Like many in the contemporary rap world, though, she also had considerable talents at taking on different personas; "Otherside of the Game" is a poetic lament from a soon-to-be single mother who just can't forget the father of her child. Erykah Badu's revolution in sound—heavier hip-hop beats over organic, conscientious soul music—was responsible for her breakout, but many of the songs on *Baduizm* don't hold up to increased examination. For every intriguing track like "Next Lifetime," there's at least one rote R&B jam like "4 Leaf Clover." Jazz fans certainly weren't confusing her with Cassandra Wilson—Badu had a bewitching voice, and she treasured her notes like the best jazz vocalists, but she often made the same choices, the hallmark of a singer rooted in soul, not jazz. Though many fans would dislike (and probably misinterpret) the comparison, she's closer to Diana Ross *playing* Billie Holiday—as she did in the 1972 film *Lady Sings the Blues*—than Holiday herself. *—John Bush*

Live / Nov. 18, 1997 / Kedar ◆◆◆

Conventional wisdom dictates that an artist should not release a live album as their second record, especially if it follows the debut by a matter of months. However, Erykah Badu is not a conventional artist and *Live* is not a conventional live album. While her debut, *Baduizm*, earned strong reviews and healthy sales, her concerts became equally popular and she became known as a powerhouse live performer. *Live* solidifies that reputation, delivering soulful, gritty versions of cuts from *Baduizm*, a few covers, and the spectacular

new single, "Tyrone." Not only does it illustrate the depths of Badu's talents, but *Live* is as strong and captivating as *Baduizm*. *—Leo Stanley*

Mama's Gun / Oct. 31, 2000 / Kedar ◆◆◆◆

Since the arrival of Erykah Badu onto the neo-soul scene back in 1997 with *Baduizm*, commercial music has stood up and taken notice with an onslaught of similar artists reaching comparable peaks of mainstream success. After taking some time off for introspection and to raise her son, Badu returns with *Mama's Gun*, which is a turning point for her in many ways. Gone are the cryptic "Baduizms" that glossed all over her first release, replaced with a more honestly raw Badu singing directly from her heart rather than her head. Sonically, Badu wades out into adventurous territories as well. From the Jimi Hendrix-inspired opening number to the closing ten-minute song suite, she develops fresh aspects of her sound, employing artists such as legendary jazz vibraphonist Roy Ayers, jazz trumpeter Roy Hargrove, Stephen Marley, and Roots drummer ?uestlove; she sought after producer Jay Dee as well. The results are consistently tasteful, which only helps to prove once again that Badu is miles ahead of the rest. *—Rob Theakston*

Bahamadia (Antonia Reed)
....

b. Philadelphia, PA

Underground Rap, Hip-Hop, Club/Dance

Bahamadia rose to prominence on the hip-hop scene as the female protégée of Gang Starr's Guru, and lent her smooth-flowing raps to a variety of projects during the late '90s, including several electronica and acid jazz artists. Born Antonia Reed in Philadelphia, Bahamadia started out DJing at local house parties in the early to mid-'80s, and soon stepped out front to prove her skill on the mic as well. She remained a presence on the Philly hip-hop scene, but didn't make her first recordings until hooking up with producer/radio personality DJ Ran, who helmed her independent 1993 single "Funk Vibe." "Funk Vibe" caught the attention of Gang Starr MC Guru, who took an interest in Bahamadia's career and helped her get a record deal with Chrysalis. Her first singles, 1994's "Total Wreck" and 1995's "Uknowhowwedu," were well received in the underground for their jazzy flavor and laid-back raps. She also appeared on the second volume of Guru's acclaimed *Jazzmatazz* project. The full-length LP *Kollage* followed in 1996, and featured production by both Guru and DJ Premier of Gang Starr, as well as fellow Philly natives the Roots. Unfortunately, Chrysalis folded a year later, and Bahamadia chose to wait out her contract before resuming her solo career. In the meantime, she made a string of musically adventurous guest appearances that solidified her underground reputation: the Roots (*Illadelph Halflife*'s "Push up Ya Lighter"), Sweetback (Sade's backing band), drum'n'bass auteur Roni Size (the title track of the landmark *New Forms*), Towa Tei, acid jazzers the Brand New Heavies, the Herbaliser, trip-hoppers Morcheeba ("Good Girl Down"), Rah Digga, Slum Village, and Talib Kweli's Reflection Eternal (their collaboration, "Chaos," appeared on the seminal Rawkus compilation *Soundbombing, Vol. 2*). She also hosted a hip-hop radio show in Philadelphia from 1997 to 1999. In 2000 she signed with the L.A.-based indie Goodvibe and released the chilled-out seven-track EP *BB Queen* (as in "beautiful black"), which received excellent reviews. *—Steve Huey*

● **Kollage** / Mar. 19, 1996 / Chrysalis ◆◆◆◆

Bahamadia's debut album, *Kollage*, is an underrated, jazzy affair paced by some nifty production and the MC's own dryly gentle delivery. Despite her laid-back, even deliberate flow, she has a confident, upfront presence on the mic, with strong rhyming skills and a fondness for old school wordplay (as demonstrated on, naturally, "Wordplay"). Being a protégée of Gang Starr and a native of Philadelphia, she gets production help from the former's DJ Premier *and* Guru, as well as the latter's Roots. The music often recalls both of those artists, as well as the unassuming, low-key ambience of Digable Planets. But there's also often a dreamier quality than any of those groups, thanks to some spacy keyboards and fusion samples, and some R&B elements as well, most notably on the excellent single "I Confess." Other highlights include her two early singles, "Total Wreck" and "Uknowhowwedu," and the quietly shimmering "Spontaneity." *Kollage* isn't hugely varied, but it is fairly consistent, and fans of intellectual bohemian hip-hop will find this album very good at what it does. *—Steve Huey*

BB Queen EP / Jul. 25, 2000 / Goodvibe ◆◆◆◆

After a four-year exodus, Bahamadia couldn't have picked a more opportune time to reintroduce herself to the hip-hop masses. After all, the female MC arena changed considerably after the Philly native dropped her 1996 debut, *Kollage*. Injecting some much-needed class back into the female ranks, Bahamadia transcends the common denominator (sexuality and gold digging) of her scantily clad colleagues. Though she returns without the aid of DJ Premier, the hypnotic lounge music of Jay Dee's soulful apprentices Kwele and EQ enables Bahmadia's subtle flow more of an opportunity to truly flourish. Her eternal optimism is defined by the sublime "Beautiful Things," a wonderfully crafted track that reminds us to appreciate the simple things we often take for granted. Just as refreshing is the red-tag anthem, "Commonwealth (Cheap Chicks)," a track dedicated to the thrift-store honeys that try to stay with it while rocking discounted gear. —*Matt Conaway*

Arthur Baker

b. Apr. 22, 1955, Boston, MA
Producer, Remixing, Drums / Club/Dance, Electro, Hip-Hop
Arthur Baker was among the most visible and widely imitated of the early hip-hop producers, masterminding breakthrough experiments with tape edits and synthetic beats before crossing over to introduce the art of remixing into the pop mainstream. He began his career as a club DJ in Boston and landed his first production work at Emergency Records, debuting with Northend's "Happy Days." After relocating to New York in 1979, Baker quickly immersed himself in the nascent hip-hop scene; there he was recruited by the Salsoul label to helm a session for Joe Bataan that yielded the rap novelty "Rap-O-Clap-O." His stay in the Big Apple largely unsuccessful, he then returned to Boston, producing a handful of singles that went nowhere, among them Glory's "Can You Guess What Groove This Is?"

A move back to New York followed, at which time Baker joined the staff of Tommy Boy Records, where he teamed with coproducer Shep Pettibone to record Afrika Bambaataa's groundbreaking 1982 single "Jazzy Sensation," a remake of Gwen McCrae's "Funky Sensation." Assuming sole production control, Baker next reunited with Bambaataa for the classic "Planet Rock," a watershed in hip-hop's early evolution—a wholly synthesized record inspired by Kraftwerk's "Trans-Europe Express," its programmed beats left an indelible imprint on the music released in its wake. Baker's success at Tommy Boy led to the formation of his own label, Streetwise Records; after helming underground club hits for Rockers Revenge, Nairobi, and Citispeak, he signed a then-unknown New Edition, issuing the teen vocal group's debut single, "Candy Girl," in 1982.

Baker's gradual absorption into the pop mainstream continued in 1983, when the cutting-edge British dance group New Order contacted him to produce their single "Confusion"; the record became an immediate club classic, even scraping into the American R&B charts. Remixes of the track also helped pioneer the remix aesthetic throughout the rock mainstream, and soon Baker was producing material for Naked Eyes, Face to Face, Diana Ross, Jeff Beck, and others. In 1989, he also assembled artists including Al Green, ABC, and Jimmy Somerville to record the all-star LP *Merge*, credited to Arthur Baker & the Backbeat Disciples. After a follow-up, 1991's *Give in to the Rhythm*, he returned to production, albeit no longer exerting the same kind of influence as in the decade prior. —*Jason Ankeny*

Merge / Sep. 1989 / A&M ✦✦✦✦
By the time Arthur Baker got around to making an album under his own name in 1989 (or as "Arthur Baker and the Backbeat Disciples," at any rate), he had a lot of favors to call in, having spent most of the '80s remixing music for half of the pop music community. But even on his own tracks, he remained a remixer and producer, creating sparkling dance grooves and having such guests as Al Green, Martin Fry of ABC, Jimmy Somerville, and Andy McClosky of Orchestral Manoeuvres in the Dark, among others, sing over them. The result set the toes tapping (although the album was surprisingly eclectic, not all hardcore dance music by any means), but it was hard to identify as the work of a particular artist. Nevertheless, individual cuts stood out: Green's "The Message Is Love" got into the R&B charts, and it and "It's Your Time" were U.K. hits. The album, however, failed to take off, and Baker left A&M. —*William Ruhlmann*

Give in to the Rhythm / Oct. 8, 1991 / RCA ✦✦✦
Once again Arthur Baker creates a state-of-the-art dance album that comes off, with its six different vocalists (including Al Green, Lee John, Adele Bertei, and Tata Vega), sounding like a various artists compilation. The tracks are constructed for maximum dance floor efficiency (plus a few concessions to

rap), and the singers are suitably emphatic. The clubs were impressed, and individual songs—"IOU," featuring Nikeeta (a remake of an early Baker production), and the soulful "Leave the Guns at Home," with Green—slipped into the pop and R&B charts. But Baker still doesn't add up as a name recording artist and may be better off back behind the mixing desk. —*William Ruhlmann*

● **Breakin'** / Oct. 16, 2001 / Perfecto ✦✦✦✦
Electro and hip-hop pioneer Arthur Baker's productions in the '90s exerted nowhere near the influence they did during the previous decade. That said, *Breakin'* is probably the closest thing to a proper anthology of Baker's earlier works on the market—which is quite surprising, given the prolific string of groundbreaking hits Baker produced for various artists during that period of time. It also makes this record somewhat of a befuddlement. The only drawback to *Breakin'* is that it's a two-disc affair, and the first half is definitely something that hinders the potency of this release. Consisting of remixes and collaborations that are up-tempo numbers bordering on progressive house, the songs are simply average at best, with absolutely no trace of the innovative nature or creative ambition Baker once so brilliantly displayed. But while the first CD consists of predominately new productions, the second CD is where the true gold and watershed moments of Baker's career are compiled. Starting off with the painfully brilliant remix of New Order's "Confusion," the disc moves at a breakneck pace through some of the most brilliant moments of hip-hop and electro. His productions of "Looking for the Perfect Beat" and several others sound just as fresh now as when they were debuted on the dancefloors around the world. Capping out the second disc with the anthem "Planet Rock" leaves you with a feeling of elation that one man could produce this many hits and so many more, but then also a feeling of bewilderment—as to what exactly happened from then until now. Enjoy the second disc, but leave the first one in the case. —*Rob Theakston*

Charli Baltimore (Tiffany Lane)

b. Philadelphia, PA
Hip-Hop, Gangsta Rap
Rapper Charli Baltimore was born Tiffany Lane in Philadelphia; her music career blossomed after she began a relationship with the Notorious B.I.G., and she adopted her stage alias from the name of Geena Davis' character in the film *The Long Kiss Goodnight*. In the wake of the Biggie's murder, Baltimore teamed with producer Lance "Un" Rivera to release a handful of singles and soundtrack appearances before issuing her oft-delayed debut LP, *Cold as Ice*, in 1999. —*Jason Ankeny*

Cold as Ice / Aug. 3, 1999 / Epic ✦✦
Some people get their start in the music industry the strangest ways. More times than not in hip-hop, it's *who* you know rather than *what* you know, and such is the case with Charli Baltimore. After saying that, she has developed into a somewhat talented rap artist, but certainly nothing worthy of the attention she gets and guest appearances she draws. There are plenty of great MCs who will never get to grace a DJ Premier beat, or have Ghostface Killah on a track with them. It's a bit of a shame that an unknown rapper gets this kind of attention just because she's, well, a she. This album is riddled with guest appearances, and most of the time Charli is there as a shoe-in while the others rap. It seems like a lot of the rappers even had to step down their game so as not to embarrass Charli lyrically. Still, there are a lot of people who don't listen to hip-hop just for groundbreaking lyrics, and the musical side of the album is pretty good, with some good producers creating the beats. Overall, you really need to like Charli Baltimore to appreciate this album and put it in your rotation. —*Brad Mills*

Afrika Bambaataa (Kevin Donovan)

b. Apr. 10, 1960, South Bronx, NY
DJ, Producer, Vocals / Hip-Hop, Club/Dance, Electro, Old School Rap, Urban
A seminal Bronx DJ during the 1970s, Afrika Bambaataa ascended to godfather status with *Planet Rock*, the 1982 hip-hop classic that blended the beats of hip-hop with techno-pop futurism inspired by German pioneer Kraftwerk. Even before he began recording in 1980, Bambaataa was hip-hop's foremost DJ, an organizer and promoter of the large block parties during the mid- to late '70s which presaged the rise of rap. After the success of *Planet Rock*, he recorded electro-oriented rap only sparingly, concentrating instead on fusion—exemplified by his singles with ex-Sex Pistol John Lydon

and fellow godfather James Brown. Bambaataa had moved to the background by the late '80s (as far as hip-hop was concerned), but the rise of his Zulu Nation collective—including De La Soul, Queen Latifah, A Tribe Called Quest, and the Jungle Brothers—found him once more being tipped as one of rap's founding fathers.

Born Kevin Donovan in the Bronx on April 10, 1960, Afrika Bambaataa Aasim took his name from a 19th-century Zulu chief. Beginning in 1977, Bambaataa began organizing block parties and breakdancing competitions around the Bronx. His excellent turntable techniques led many to proclaim him the best DJ in the business (though Grandmaster Flash and DJ Kool Herc were more innovative), and his record debut—as a producer—came in 1980 with Soul Sonic Force's "Zulu Nation Throwdown." The single was a rallying cry for the Zulu Nation, a group of likeminded Afro-centric musicians that only gained fame in the late '80s but had influenced the rise of hip-hop crews throughout the decade.

Aside from more production credits on several later singles during 1980-1981, Afrika Bambaataa didn't become an actual recording artist until 1982. He signed with Tommy Boy records and released his first single, "Jazzy Sensation," early that year. "Planet Rock" followed in June and quickly exploded. Recorded with the help of producer/dancefloor authority Arthur Baker and assimilating the melody of Kraftwerk's "Trans-Europe Express," the single hit number four on the R&B charts (but missed the pop Top 40) and joined the Sugarhill Gang's "Rapper's Delight" as one of the early classics of hip-hop. (Grandmaster Flash's "The Message" followed just three months later.) In the single's wake came dozens of electro groups and recordings, though none touched the quality of *"Planet Rock"*—except, perhaps, Bambaataa's own follow-up, "Looking for the Perfect Beat." Out of those electro groups came several predominant dance styles of the '80s and '90s: Detroit techno, Miami bass, and, to a more limited extent, Chicago house.

Freed somewhat by his newfound popularity, Afrika Bambaataa began branching out in 1984, recording "Unity" with help from James Brown and "World Destruction" with John Lydon (as Time Zone). That same year, Bambaataa delivered an album debut of sorts, *Shango Funk Theology*, recorded as Shango with Material personnel Bill Laswell and Michael Beinhorn. A virtually LP-length single titled "Funk You!" appeared in 1985, after which Bambaataa recorded his proper album debut, *Beware (The Funk Is Everywhere)*. He left Tommy Boy in 1986 after an album compilation of "Planet Rock" mixes, and signed with Capitol. The first album release for the label was 1988's *The Light*, recorded as Afrika Bambaataa & the Family, which included contributions from George Clinton, UB40, Bootsy Collins, and Boy George. Three years later, Bambaataa's third album, *1990-2000: Decade of Darkness*, was released on Capitol, coinciding with his career retrospective *Time Zone*, released on his own Planet Rock Records. Bambaataa recorded erratically during the '90s, but returned in 1997 with Zulu Groove.

The new millennium brought the release of *Hydraulic Funk* on Strictly Hype. *Electro Funk Breakdown* followed in early 2001. —*John Bush*

Looking for the Perfect Beat / Dec. 1982 / Tommy Boy ✦✦✦✦✦
Producer Arthur Baker proved the real star on this seminal 1982 mini-album, adding what were then state-of-the art studio effects and mixing gimmicks to balance often repetitive rhythms. This was a milestone record, despite what sound like limited rap skills by 1990s standards. —*Ron Wynn*

Planet Rock—The Album / 1986 / Tommy Boy ✦✦✦✦✦
All the important early 12"s from 1982 to 1984 are here, including "Planet Rock" and "Looking for the Perfect Beat," plus three previously unreleased tracks. (Recorded with Soulsonic Force.) —*John Floyd*

Beware (The Funk Is Everywhere) / 1986 / Tommy Boy ✦✦✦✦
A semi-remarkable album from Afrika Bambaataa, following up on the success of *Planet Rock*. This one has fewer full-fledged anthems, but what's here isn't bad at all. "Bambaataa's Theme" uses his trademark mix of electronic backings and heavier beats. "Tension" slows down and softens with female vocal leads. "Rock America" and the cover of MC5's "Kick out the Jams" are closer stylistically to *Planet Rock*, with added guitar riffs throughout. On side B, he moves into more straightforward old school rap and beat-laden grooves immersed completely in the funk tradition, including "Bionic Kats," a knock-off of "Atomic Dog." For Bambaataa fans, this album is certainly a worthwhile addition. For those wishing for a basic introduction or a more comprehensive look at the ridiculously wide breadth of Bambaataa's music, the *Planet Rock*

album or Tommy Boy's greatest-hits compilation (*Looking for the Perfect Beat*) would probably be in order. —*Adam Greenberg*

The Light / 1988 / EMI ✦✦
Diverse personalities and styles are the hook for this 1988 album, which isn't an Afrika Bambaataa project, but a group effort with some Bambaataa involvement. The guest list ranges from Boy George to George Clinton, Yellowman, UB40, and Bootsy Collins, with Bambaataa offering a brief, rather formulaic rap on UB40's "Reckless" and "Shout It Out." This was a mildly entertaining effort, but so varied that there was no cohesion or unified focus. —*Ron Wynn*

1990-2000: The Decade of Darkness / Jun. 1991 / EMI ✦✦✦
After several lackluster albums, Afrika Bambaataa came back with a record that explored modern-day dance trends without losing his signature sound. Fueled by righteous social commentary throughout the songs, the record showed that he wasn't creatively spent. It wasn't as innovative as his groundbreaking singles from the early '80s, but it was far from being an embarrassment. —*Stephen Thomas Erlewine*

Don't Stop . . . Planet Rock (The Remix EP) / 1992 / Tommy Boy ✦✦
An updated EP takes the by now ancient "Planet Rock" beat and runs it through the 1990s hip-hop production machine. The results aren't all that successful, even though the sound is now contemporary. But its hook was old school, as was its charm. The newer version lacks bite. —*Ron Wynn*

Zulu Groove / Nov. 18, 1997 / Hudson Vandam ✦✦✦
Something of a collection of various styles and genres crossed over by Bambaataa on his musical journeys. The album begins (and ends) with "World Destruction," a single originally cut in 1984 with John Lydon of Sex Pistols fame. Following the opening is "Shango Message," with a stunningly Parliament-esque hook, and an old favorite, "Zulu Groove." Before the album ends, Bambaataa shows off a little of his diversity with "Soca Fever," which as the title implies, involves some measure of soca within it (although there may not be all that much that survives by the time the dense overlaying beats are added). The main drawback of this album is that the liner notes are less than thorough. Despite this minor shortcoming, for a fan of Bambaataa, the album might not be that bad of a choice at all. For newcomers to his work, something a little more traditional might be in order—Tommy Boy compilations, perhaps, for "Looking for the Perfect Beat" and "Planet Rock." —*Adam Greenberg*

Electro Funk Breakdown / Mar. 6, 2001 / DMC ✦✦✦
Few artists have been more influential on the current electronic music scene than the legendary Afrika Bambaataa, whose groundbreaking blending of Kraftwerk's "Trans-Europe Express" with hip-hop beats for Soulsonic Force's breakthrough hit, "Planet Rock," set the stage for countless genre-blending fusionists that followed. Now one of the nation's most in demand DJs, it seems appropriate that Bambaataa should mix the last *United DJs of America* disc of the 20th century. And what a mix it is, flowing seamlessly from Shiraz' maddeningly addictive "Cinder Blocks" into S*H*A*C*K's ultra-funky "Dish Cuts 2" and his own "Bambaataa's Theme" (which sounds like New Order covering Midnite Starr, or vice versa) without missing a beat. Strange selections like DJ Boo's "Rock & Roll Part 2 (Raise the Roof)" and 12 Gauge's Dirty South romp "Dawg Call (Who Let the Dogs Out)" seem like head-scratchers at first, but make sense in the greater context of Bambaataa's eclectic mix. —*Bret Love*

★ **Looking for the Perfect Beat: 1980-1985** / Mar. 20, 2001 / Tommy Boy ✦✦✦✦✦
As a major architect of early hip-hop, Afrika Bambaataa is perhaps more deserving of a respectable compilation treatment than anyone. And while his considerable influence has largely been brushed aside by a rap world that sadly ignores far too many of its innovators, *Looking for the Perfect Beat* may help to change that. Whatever your opinion on the shelf life of his music, Bambaataa was an innovator of the highest order. While many rappers would be content to sample and name check James Brown ad nauseam, Bambaataa collaborated with the Godfather of Soul himself on the sharp "Unity Part 1 (The Third Coming)." The amazing double punch of "Planet Rock" and "Looking for the Perfect Beat" serve as the centerpiece of this disc, while "Zulu Nation Throwdown" sits as a perfect opening track, in its time initiating a back-to-roots aesthetic that was years ahead of the Afro-centric rap explosion of the late '80s. *Looking for the Perfect Beat* also nicely augments

the resumé of producer Arthur Baker, a trailblazing dance remixer of the early '80s. Sadly missing are any significant liner notes or photographs. Also available as a limited edition, two-LP set. —*John Duffy*

Ant Banks

b. Oakland, CA

Producer / Gangsta Rap, West Coast Rap

Ant Banks, a Bay Area producer who began working behind the scenes with local legend Too Short, first appeared on two 1992 hip-hop soundtracks, *Juice* and *Menace II Society*. That same year, he was on production with Too Short (*Shorty the Pimp*) as well as associates Spice 1 and Pooh-Man. Through his connections, Banks signed a contract with Jive Records and released his debut album, *Sittin' on Something Phat*, in 1993. The record featured live instrumentation, including guitar by notable former Parliament mainstay Michael Hampton. *The Big Badass* and *Do or Die* followed during 1994-1995, showing Banks' capable techniques behind the microphone as well as the mixing board. For 1997's *Big Thangs*, however, he recruited some of the West Coast's best rappers to assist him, including Ice Cube, 2Pac, Too Short, and Ice-T. The strategy paid off, as the album hit the Top 20. In April of 1999, Banks released his T.W.D.Y. project, experiencing a substantial hit with the track "Players Holiday." A little over a year later, he followed with the second T.W.D.Y. album, *Lead the Way*. —*John Bush*

The Big Badass / May 10, 1994 / Jive ✦✦✦

With *Big Badass*, Ant Banks turns in another album of his standard-issue gangsta rap. By this time, Ant Banks has very little new to offer—not only does the music sound tired, but he no longer has unique perspective; he has already said everything he has to say. There are a couple of tracks that would keep the interest of his dedicated fans, but most of the album is too repetitive to warrant anything more than a cursory listen from most hip-hop afficionados. —*David Jehnzen*

Big Thangs / Jul. 8, 1997 / Priority ✦✦✦✦

Ant Banks may not have a terrific or distinctive rhyming style, but he has an ear for thick, funky grooves. That alone makes his records enjoyable, even if he has trouble sustaining momentum over the course of a full-length album. Still, *Big Thangs* is a more consistently pleasurable listen than many of his records, and that's due to his ear. Much like his recent work with E40 and Dru Down, Ant's *Big Thangs* resonates with deep bass and party rhythms. There isn't much to think about here—the lyrics are primarily cartoonish gangsta or party anthems—but it does keep the good times rolling. —*Leo Stanley*

● **The Best of Ant Banks** / Mar. 10, 1998 / Jive ✦✦✦✦

Since Ant Banks' albums are always uneven, the release of *The Best of Ant Banks* was welcome indeed. Boasting 16 tracks, including such Banks hits as "2 Kill a G," "Roll 'Em Phat," "Money Don't Make a Man," and "Spice 1 Wit Da Banksta," the album distills all of his best moments onto one disc, making it the most consistent and entertaining record in his catalog. —*Stephen Thomas Erlewine*

MC Paul Barman

b. New Jersey

Underground Rap, Hip-Hop, Alternative Rap

It's almost an understatement to say that New Jersey-native MC Paul Barman defies hip-hop convention. Rail thin and lilly white with a mop of curly hair hanging off his head, Barman plays the geek image to the hilt. His off-kilter verses and painful delivery almost seem like a put-on, but the Brown graduate has a disarming charm and comes with serious credentials. With only one EP under his belt, Barman attracted critical attention from heavyweights like *The New York Times* and *Rolling Stone* and found the opportunity to work with a number of respected artists. The legendary Prince Paul produced Barman's debut EP, *It's Very Stimulating*, which was released in early 2000 by prestigious underground label WordSound. Barman's unconventional rapping was bolstered by his aptitude for storytelling and the album's hilarious, self-deprecating anecdotes. Barman switched to Matador for the release of *How Hard is That?* later that year. Though Barman's act smacks of novelty to some, *How Hard Is That* was another winner. Definitely one of a kind, Barman has earned the respect of his peers, appearing on projects like *Deltron 3030* and albums by the likes of Mr. Dead and Masta Ace. —*Martin Woodside*

It's Very Strange / 1999 / WordSound ✦✦

MC Paul Barman is the epitome of white-boy rap. Featuring his questionable rhyming skills and nasally vocals, *It's Very Strange* is meant to be taken in a very tongue-in-cheek manner. Unfortunately, Barman's joke of parodied white-bread hip-hop is about as funny as his physical appearance (which bears a frightening resemblance to the comedian Carrot Top). Even with his personal rants of low self-esteem and high school trauma, Barman completely oversteps the fine line between humor and embarrassment. Even the introduction provided by Prince Paul fails to save this sinking punch line. —*Mike DaRonco*

● **It's Very Stimulating** / Jan. 4, 2000 / WordSound ✦✦✦

Supersmart hip-hop maverick or self-consciously wacky novelty act? Brown graduate and Prince Paul protégé MC Paul Barman suggests a little of both on his much-buzzed 2000 debut EP *It's Very Stimulating*. Self-deprecating, whip-smart, and adventurous, Barman is a true hip-hop original, a brainy clown with a demented flow that suggests equally the scatological obsessions of Kool Keith and the anything-goes raunchiness of a borscht-belt comic. Whether proposing tongue-in-cheek school reform on "School Anthem" or dissing frat boys on "MTV Get Off the Air, Part 2," Barman's brainy, geeky sensibility, self-deprecating sense of humor, and off-the-wall pop culture references are undeniably original and singularly refreshing. But Barman also has a dispiriting tendency to lay on the shtick a little too heavy, relying on the novelty of his subject matter to compensate for hip-hop skills (breath control, timing, delivery) that are sometimes downright amateurish. And for every pop-culture reference that's genuinely funny ("I don't have to be in a Ken Kesey state/To create something you can appreciate" is a particular highlight), there are several that seem to exist solely to illustrate that Barman's Ivy League education didn't go to waste. Legendary producer Prince Paul's production is stellar throughout, however, full of the irreverent humor and inventive sampling that has become his trademark. Ultimately, *It's Very Stimulating* is little more than a simultaneously tempting and frustrating appetizer for Barman's first album, a work that will go a long way toward determining whether Barman is indeed a forward-thinking hip-hop genius or just an overeducated novelty act with a good vocabulary and too much time on his hands. —*Nathan Rabin*

Paullelujah! / Oct. 15, 2002 / Coup d'Etat ✦✦✦

As a rapper, MC Paul Barman makes a pretty good humorist, though he's actually more clever than he is funny. Like Gonzalez and others on the fringes of even the rap underground, his flow has more in common with the oldest of old school rap, pre-Rakim "stylists" like Kurtis Blow or Spoonie Gee. To this Barman adds a layer of postmodern irony that wears much less well than Gonzalez, since he lacks both delivery and good ideas for rhymes. He does get in a few biting lines on the abortion-activist nightmare "N.O.W." (sample: "If you all are so destitute, why do you dress so cute?"). He's much less intelligent, though, during "Burping & Farting," which describes in exacting detail the scientific process necessary for both acts. "Cock Mobster" is Fred Schneider meets the Native Tongues, with some of the most embarrassing raps to emerge from a noncommercial hip-hop artist in some time. A Dylanesque talking blues on time travel is only interesting the first time, and unlike many alternative rappers, the production isn't enough to make this one good on its own. —*John Bush*

Bas-1

b. Oakland, CA

Hip-Hop, Underground Rap

From his first work in the mid-'80s, Oakland rapper Bas-1 has years of experience in every element of hip-hop (DJing, MCing, breaking, tagging). Though he's kept mostly to the underground, he finally began getting his own releases—for Heratik and Bomb Hip Hop—just after the end of the millennium. He began breaking in the late '80s, found his true love, MCing, several years later, and added tagging and scratching to his repertoire by the end of the '80s. During 1989-1990, he recorded tracks with producer Dion Evans (who would later work with 2Pac), but also spent time touring the world with Rock Steady Crew, and joined his own crew, Style Elements, during the late '90s. His full-length debut, 2001's *For the Mentally Astute: Theory of a Throw Up*, was a collaboration with producer Fanatik, and he recorded a single named "Instant Rap Star" for Bomb Hip Hop later that year. He also had a few tracks on Living Legends' 1999 LP *The Underworld*. —*John Bush*

● **For the Mentally Astute: Theory of a Throw Up** / Jan. 1, 2001 / Heratik ✦✦✦
A full-length, triple-vinyl/CD collaboration between lyricist Bas-1 (pronounced Boss-swan) and beatmaker/producer Fanatik, *For the Mentally Astute: Theory of a Throw Up* (released on Fanatik's own Heratik Productions label) follows two introductory singles taken from this recording. Representing a self-proclaimed new style in hip-hop, "Elemental" is comprised of the four core elements of the genre, MCing, DJing, b-boying, and graffiti writing, all key components to the culture noted within their music and packaged throughout the product. An intellectual recording both in its broken, cerebral beats as well as in Bas' inquisitive subject manner, Fanatik's work with Planet Asia, Rasco, and as a Stones Throw solo artist comes through in the overall maturity of the production, with the aesthetic rocking an old school comportment. For the amount of scratching and twisting beats, *For the Mentally Astute* emits an essence of improvisation that retains tremendous sturdiness. Though while the narrative abilities Bas demonstrates are outstanding and his viewpoints are worthy of a focused ear, the victorious artistic achievement performed on this record is hands-down the instrumental beneath. *— Nic Kincaid*

Highly Effective People [Single] / Feb. 6, 2001 / Heratik ✦✦
The apt Bay Area MC/freestyle impresario Bas-1 pairs up with beatmaker Fanatik on this 12" single, "Highly Effective People" b/w "It's a Klassic," on mandarin orange vinyl for Heretik/Insiduous Urban Records. The A side makes an early case for quality hip-hop with a palatable beat underneath a "Light Another"-type doobie-reflection session. Bas-1's playful rhyme style and attitude toward getting the mind's attention is well stated without being intrusive—bouncing off the beats with ease and positive flow. Side B's "It's a Klassik" is much more active musically, with a crisp break and some nice scratching. All in all a good musical introduction to *For the Mentally Astute* LP. *— Glenn Astarita*

Toy Story/Mentally Astute [Single] / Aug. 21, 2001 / Heratik ✦✦✦
The second single released off the *For the Mentally Astute* LP, "Toy Story" b/w the title track takes a giant leap from "Highly Effective People," with a marvelous old school groove swinging over a Saturday afternoon beat. Bas-1's gift is quickly establishing itself with each new song released: his ability to make his rhymes sound like freestyles while shaping his words with a saucy drawl. As a duo, their stripped-down schoolyard hip-hop style is aesthetically charming, reminiscing with a sound that lends itself more to the '80s than to the early 2000s, capturing a fresher-era feel. The bonus "Mentally Astute Remix Instrumental" is particularly inspired and adequately illustrates the impetus behind Fanatik's ramping career in Bay Area beat mining. The cerebrally exploratory and musically exceptional B side expands on the premise, turning out Bas-1's best performance on record with self-proclaimed lyrical *savoir faire* that's hard to totally disagree with. *— Nic Kincaid*

Rob Base (Robert Ginyard)

b. May 18, 1967, Harlem, NY
Hip-Hop, East Coast Rap, Club/Dance
Best known for his 1988 platinum hip-hop classic "It Takes Two," Rob Base (with DJ E-Z Rock) rode his hit onto R&B radio stations as well as dance clubs, providing a touchstone for the style known as hip-house. After leaping several hurdles—vicious rumors about his personal life plus the legal action of Maze's Frankie Beverly after Base sampled Maze on his hit "Joy and Pain"—he responded in 1989 with *The Incredible Base*. None of the singles on his second album had the force of "It Takes Two," however, and Rob Base was largely forgotten several years later.

Born Robert Ginyard in Harlem, Rob Base began performing with a group called the Sureshot Seven while in fifth grade. By the time of high school graduation, the only members left were him and DJ E-Z Rock (born Rodney Bryce, Harlem, NY), so the duo began recording. Their first single, "DJ Interview," appeared on the World to World label, and they gained a distribution deal with Profile by 1987. The first Profile release, the title-track single from their debut album, *It Takes Two*, became a street sensation upon its release in mid-1988. Though the single just barely reached the R&B Top 20 and Pop Top 40, massive club airplay enhanced its impact considerably. Both the single and album eventually went platinum, and Rob Base and DJ E-Z Rock gained Single of the Year honors both in *Spin* and *The Village Voice*. The second single, "Get on the Dance Floor," continued Base's dance appeal, though his excellent rapping helped him retain his street credentials.

By the end of 1989, however, Rob Base was on his own; his only explanation for the disappearance of DJ E-Z Rock was "personal problems." The release of *The Incredible Base* in 1989 was a bit of a comedown; despite several interesting tracks—including a reworking of Edwin Starr's "War"—neither the album nor any singles connected with listeners. *— John Bush*

● **It Takes Two** / 1988 / Profile ✦✦✦✦✦
Without question, Rob Base & DJ E-Z Rock had the party anthem of 1988 in "It Takes Two"—an insanely infectious rap/dance gem using a James Brown/Lynn Collins classic of the same name as a reference point. While the song was a major hit in dance music and club circles, Base won over hip-hop's hardcore with his strong technique as a rapper. Though most of this debut album falls short of that megahit's excellence, it's a generally decent effort that has both hip-hop and R&B appeal. A reflection on societal breakdown, the sobering "Times Are Gettin' Ill" is atypical of this album—which favors soul-flavored party music over social and political commentary. From Maze's "Joy & Pain" (which the duo used without Frankie Beverly's permission, inspiring him to threaten legal action) to the house-influenced "Get on the Dance Floor," *It Takes Two* thrives on strong hooks and unapologetic escapism. *— Alex Henderson*

The Incredible Base / Nov. 1989 / Profile ✦✦✦
Rob Base had parted company with DJ E-Z Rock by the time he recorded his second album, *The Incredible Base*, but his approach didn't change significantly. The New Yorker still favored party music over social or political commentary, and managed to appeal to both hardcore hip-hoppers and R&B fans who weren't necessarily big rap supporters. Though nothing here is in a class with the first album's unforgettable title song, this CD definitely has its strong points. On "War," Base samples Edwin Starr's Motown classic, not to make a political statement, but to question the feuds that were so prevalent in rap in the late '80s and early '90s. "If You Really Want to Party," "Turn It Out (Go Base)," and "Get Up and Have a Good Time" won't win any awards for profound lyrics, but they function quite well on the dancefloor. Like so many rappers, Base couldn't count on longevity—by the mid-'90s, his popularity had faded considerably. *— Alex Henderson*

Break of Dawn / Sep. 13, 1994 / Funky Base ✦✦

Basehead

f. 1991
Group / Political Rap, Alternative Pop/Rock, Alternative Rap
Basehead is the creation of Michael Ivey, a middle-class suburban kid from Maryland. Ivey recorded the bulk of Basehead's 1992 debut, *Plays With Toys*, on a four-track at home with various friends. Combining laid-back, stoned hip-hop rhythm tracks, pop hooks, drawled raps, and pseudo-folky guitar, the record received glowing reviews in alternative publications and was played frequently on college radio. Ivey assembled a touring band and used them on parts of Basehead's 1993 follow-up, *Not in Kansas Anymore*. The critical reception was mixed and the record didn't receive much airplay or sales. The following year Ivey assembled the alternative hip-hop collection *B.Y.O.B.*, which featured several of his own contributions; Basehead's *Faith* followed in 1996. *— Stephen Thomas Erlewine*

● **Play With Toys** / 1992 / Imago ✦✦✦✦
Basehead mastermind Michael Ivey's debut album, almost literally a bedroom music project with a friend or two helping out here and there, plays like one long, stoned recording session where songs and subjects seemed to be inspired by the clutter around him (one of the best cuts here is called "Ode to My Favorite Beer"). Ivey worked the slacker lifestyle (and all the nothingness that accompanies it) into *Play With Toys'* 11 songs a little before it became an alt-rock cliché (it was originally released in 1991 on the indie Emigre label), making this album both a milestone and a sadly neglected piece of loose-grooved invention that was lost in the modern-rock shuffle. Combining hip-hop beats, sluggish folk styles and a pop acumen that coalesced into a generational statement of sorts, *Play With Toys* is an ambitious undertaking, despite its attempts to be otherwise. *— Michael Gallucci*

Not in Kansas Anymore / 1993 / Imago ✦✦✦
Although it retains many of the same qualities of their critically acclaimed debut, Basehead's second album, *Not In Kansas Anymore*, is missing a key ingredient—charm. Where *Play With Toys* was a unique record, creating its own world with stoned, hazy funk and psychedelic, lo-fi hip-hop, *Not In*

Kansas Anymore sounds lazy. Musically, it is a continuation of the debut—in fact, its a replica of the debut, offering the same tricks without any new flourishes. That doesn't mean it's a bad record. There are several tracks that rank with the best songs on the debut, but there's nothing that has the same sense of discovery that made *Play With Toys* an interesting record. *—Stephen Thomas Erlewine*

Faith / May 1996 / Imago ✦✦✦

In a bizarre turn of events, Basehead's Michael Ivey abandoned slacker suburban life for mystical, spiritual territory on his third album, *Faith*. He didn't leave behind his trademark amalgam of funk, hip-hop, and kitschy pop but he has become more focused. Unfortunately, you don't listen to Basehead to hear direction—Ivey's charm has always been in his fragmented, hazy cut-and-paste approach. Though he comes up with some fine results on *Faith*—and it has to be seen as a comeback after the rote *Not in Kansas Anymore*—the album doesn't quite reach its lofty goals. *—Stephen Thomas Erlewine*

Bass Junkie (Phil Klein)

Producer / Bass Music, Party Rap

U.K.-based producer Phil Klein releases Miami bass-inflected new school electro under his Bass Junkie aegis. Appearing most recently on the Breakin' Records label and on his own Parallax imprint, Klein's Bass Junkie material draws liberally from classics of electro-funk and bass music—from Freestyle's "It's Automatic" and Unknown DJ's "808 Beats" to Maggotron's "Planet of Bass"—combining truckloads of samples with crisp, up-tempo rhythms and, naturally, the deepest of bone-rattling bass. Although his discography includes a number of tracks released as Battle Systems, I.B.M., and Cybernet Systems, Klein's most popular work to date has been his Bass Junkie material, most likely via its association with the Breakin' Records label (associated with Rephlex Records recording artist DMX Krew). Following a pair of Bass Junkie releases for his own Parallax label, Klein began releasing records through Breakin' in 1997 with the *Unknown Funk EP*. An additional EP (*In Bass No One Can Hear You Scream*) and an LP (*Bass Junkie*) appeared through Breakin' in 1998. Klein's affection for bass music has also stretched into a long-running collaboration with one of the genre's most acclaimed early innovators Scott Weiser, aka Miami-based Dynamix II. Bass Junkie and Cybernet Systems tracks have appeared on a number of Dynamix compilations, with the label also issuing a full-length CD of Klein's Bass Junkie material in 1996. *Bass Time Continuum* followed three years later. Additionally, Klein and Weiser share a writing credit on the title track to Klein's *Borg EP* (1996, Panic Trax), and on several releases as I.B.M. *—Sean Cooper*

A Bass Odyssey EP / 1996 / Parallax ✦✦✦

As the title implies, these four tracks have at least one thing in common: deep and rumbling bass. The influence of Miami freestyle and bass music producers such as Tony Butler and Maggotron on Klein's hybrid electro-funk comes closest to the surface on tracks such as "Energy Flow," but as with his other Bass Junkie material, he doesn't simply let it rest there, combining old school sample collage with heavier, new-breed syncopation and subtle acid lines. Good stuff. *—Sean Cooper*

Bass, Below & Beyond EP / 1997 / Parallax ✦✦✦✦

Klein's most equitable pairing of old school electro bass with a new school sensibility to date, with each track a snapshot on the music's current legacy. From the megamix-y "Program the 808" (with shards of the Unknown DJ's "808 Beats" and "Sweat") to the digital mash-up of Kraftwerk and Uncle Jamm's Army on "Computer Control" and "Automatic Bass," this four-tracker has one for each occasion. Less of a novelty record than the previous *A Bass Odyssey EP. —Sean Cooper*

I, Borg EP / 1997 / Battle Trax ✦✦✦✦

Four hardcore-leaning remixes of Klein's stonkin' Dynamix II collaboration, "We Are Borg" (from his '95 Panic Trax twelve, "The Borg EP"). The mixes are pretty samey and none of them hit with quite the intensity of the original, but Klein's shifting focus from version to version on the various rhythmic elements of the original (the brittle, sprangy snares; the deep, Miami-style bass) is competent and inventive. *—Sean Cooper*

● **Bass Junkie** / 1998 / Breakin' ✦✦✦✦✦

A mixture of material old and new, some previously available only through Klein's limited-run Parallax imprint, this LP offers kinetic, speaker-melting electro-bass, as expected. *—Sean Cooper*

Bass Mekanik (Neil Case)

b. Jamaica

Producer, Mixing / Bass Music, Party Rap, Southern Rap

Bass Mekanik is a pseudonym of producer Neil Case, one of the premier forces in bass music. He got his start as a DJ in his native Jamaica, where he first became fascinated with the low frequencies in the records he was spinning. Moving on to a job as an assistant engineer in Kingston's Dynamic Sound Studios, he worked with reggae legends like Jimmy Cliff and Peter Tosh while learning the technical aspects of a recording career. After years behind the boards at Dynamic, he moved to Miami and started releasing homemade bass mixes consisting of his own material. Going under the alias of Beat Dominator for the first two years, he decided to switch to the more relevant Bass Mekanik moniker in 1994. Releasing a series of albums, compilations, singles, and collaborations, he became one of the biggest names in the field of bass music, with CDs like *Audio Toolbox* and *Best of Food for Woofers* becoming staples of the stereo competition scene. He did this with virtually no promotion, relying on the ultra-low frequencies in his music to appeal to aficionados of car stereos. Word of mouth became his most important advertising tool, and he reciprocated by talking with his fans about what his music could do to further compliment their stereos. Case became such a key figure in the scene that he had a line of car audio components named after him, inspiring him to move further into the business aspect of his art. He started his own label and website, http://www.BassMekanik.com, in 2001. *—Bradley Torreano*

Quad Maximus / Aug. 14, 1994 / Pandisc ✦✦✦

V 5.0 / Jun. 29, 1999 / Pandisc ✦✦✦

End-of-the-millennium Bass Mekanik includes another vicious set of deep-bass jams guaranteed to rattle your speakers and, just maybe, entertain your mind as well. *—Keith Farley*

● **Powerbox: The Bassest Hits** / Jun. 20, 2000 / Pandisc ✦✦✦

Beastie Boys

f. 1979, New York, NY

Group / Golden Age, Hip-Hop, Alternative Pop/Rock, Alternative Rap, Old School Rap, Hardcore Punk

As the first white rap group of any importance, the Beastie Boys received the scorn of critics and strident hip-hop musicians, who accused them of cultural pirating, especially since they began as a hardcore punk group in 1981. But the Beasties weren't pirating—they treated rap as part of a post-punk musical underground, where the do-it-yourself aesthetics of hip-hop and punk weren't that far apart. Of course, the exaggerated b-boy and frat-boy parodies of their unexpected hit debut album, *Licensed to Ill*, didn't help their cause. For much of the mid-'80s, the Beastie Boys were considered as macho clowns, and while their ambitious, Dust Brothers-produced second album, *Paul's Boutique*, dismissed that theory, it was ignored by both the public and the press at the time. In retrospect, it was one of the first albums to predict the genre-bending, self-referential pop kaleidoscope of '90s pop. The Beasties refined their eclectic approach with 1992's *Check Your Head*, where they played their own instruments. *Check Your Head* brought the Beasties back to the top of the charts, and within a few years, they were considered one of the most influential and ambitious groups of the '90s, cultivating a musical community not only through their music but also with their record label, Grand Royal, and their magazine of the same name.

It was a remarkable turn of events for a group that demonstrated no significant musical talent on their first records. All three members of the Beastie Boys—Mike D (born Mike Diamond, November 20, 1966), MCA (born Adam Yauch, August 5, 1965), and Ad-Rock (born Adam Horovitz, October 31, 1967)—came from wealthy middle-class Jewish families in New York and had become involved in the city's punk underground when they were teenagers in the early '80s. Diamond and Yauch formed the Beastie Boys with drummer Kate Schellenbach and guitarist John Berry in 1981, and the group began playing around clubs around New York. The following year, the Beasties released the 7" EP *Pollywog Stew* on the indie Rat Cage to little attention. That year, the band met Horovitz, who had formed the hardcore group the Young and the Useless. By early 1983, Schellenbach and Berry had left the group—they would later join Luscious Jackson and Thwig, respectively—and Horovitz had joined the Beasties. The revamped group released the rap record "Cookie Puss" as a 12" single later in 1983. Based on a prank phone call the group made to Carvel Ice Cream, the single became an underground hit in New York. By early 1984, however, they had abandoned punk and turned their attention to rap.

In 1984, the Beasties joined forces with producer Rick Rubin, a heavy metal and hip-hop fan who had recently founded Def Jam Records with fellow New York University student Russell Simmons. Def Jam officially signed the Beastie Boys in 1985, and that year they had a hit single from the soundtrack to *Krush Groove* with "She's on It," a rap track that sampled AC/DC's "Back in Black" and suggested the approach of the group's forthcoming debut album. The Beasties received their first significant national exposure later in 1985, when they opened for Madonna on her Virgin Tour. The trio taunted the audience with profanity and were generally poorly received. One other major tour, as the openers for Run-D.M.C.'s ill-fated Raisin' Hell trek, followed before *Licensed to Ill* was released late in 1986. An amalgam of street beats, metal riffs, b-boy jokes, and satire, *Licensed to Ill* was interpreted as a mindless, obnoxious party record by many critics and conservative action groups, but that didn't stop the album from becoming the fastest-selling debut in Columbia Records' history, moving over 750,000 copies in its first six weeks. Much of that success was due to the single "Fight for Your Right (To Party)," which became a massive crossover success. In fact, *Licensed to Ill* became the biggest-selling rap album of the '80s, which generated much criticism from certain hip-hop fans who believed that the Beasties were merely cultural pirates. On the other side of the coin, the group was being attacked from the right, who claimed their lyrics were violent and sexist and that their concerts—which featured female audience members dancing in go-go cages and a giant inflatable penis, similar to what the Stones used in their mid-'70s concerts—caused even more outrage. Throughout their 1987 tour, they were plagued with arrests and lawsuits, and were accused of inciting crime.

While much of the Beasties' exaggeratedly obnoxious behavior started out as a joke, it became a self-parody by the end of 1987, so it wasn't a surprise that the group decided to revamp their sound and image during the next two years. During 1988 they became involved in a bitter lawsuit with Def Jam and Rick Rubin, who claimed he was responsible for the group's success and threatened to release outtakes as their second album. The group finally broke away by the end of the year and relocated to California, where they signed with Capitol Records. While in California, they met the production team the Dust Brothers, and they convinced the duo to use their prospective debut album as the basis for the Beasties' second album, *Paul's Boutique*. Densely layered with interweaving samples and pop culture references, the retro-funk-psychedelia of *Paul's Boutique* was entirely different than *Licensed to Ill*, and many observers weren't quite sure what to make of it. Several publications gave it rave reviews, but when it failed to produce a single bigger than the number 36 "Hey Ladies," it was quickly forgotten about.

Despite its poor commercial performance, *Paul's Boutique* gained a cult following, and its cut-and-paste sample techniques would later be hailed as visionary, especially after the Dust Brothers altered the approach for Beck's acclaimed 1996 album, *Odelay*. Still, the record was declared a disaster in the early '90s, but that didn't prevent the Beasties from building their own studio and founding their own record label, Grand Royal, for their next record, *Check Your Head*. Alternating between old school hip-hop, raw amateurish funk, and hardcore punk, *Check Your Head* was a less accomplished than *Paul's Boutique*, yet it was just as diverse. Furthermore, the burgeoning cult around the Beasties made the album a surprise Top Ten hit upon its spring 1992 release. "Jimmy James," "Pass the Mic," and "So Whatcha Want" were bigger hits on college and alternative rock radio than they were on rap radio, and the group suddenly became hip again. Early in 1994, they collected their early punk recordings on the compilation *Some Old Bullshit*, which was followed in June by their fourth album, *Ill Communication*. Essentially an extension of *Check Your Head*, the record debuted at number one upon its release, and the singles "Sabotage" and "Sure Shot" helped send it to double-platinum status. During the summer of 1994, they coheadlined the fourth Lollapalooza festival with the Smashing Pumpkins. That same year, Grand Royal became a full-fledged record label as it released Luscious Jackson's acclaimed debut album, *Natural Ingredients*. The Beasties' *Grand Royal* magazine was also launched that year.

Over the next few years, the Beasties remained quiet as they concentrated on political causes and their record label. In 1996 they released the hardcore

EP *Aglio e Olio* and the instrumental soul-jazz and funk collection, *The In Sound From Way Out!* Also that year, Adam Yauch organized a two-day festival to raise awareness and money about Tibet's plight against the Chinese government; the festival went on to become an annual event. The Beastie Boys' long-awaited fifth LP, *Hello Nasty*, finally appeared during the summer of 1998. —*Stephen Thomas Erlewine*

☆ **Licensed to Ill** / 1986 / Def Jam ✦✦✦✦✦

Perhaps *Licensed to Ill* was inevitable—a white group blending rock and rap, giving them the first number-one album in hip-hop history. But that reading of the album's history gives short shrift to the Beastie Boys; producer Rick Rubin and his label, Def Jam; and this remarkable record, since mixing metal and hip-hop isn't necessarily an easy thing to do. Just sampling and scratching Sabbath and Zeppelin to hip-hop beats does not make for an automatically good record, though there is a visceral thrill to hearing those muscular riffs put into overdrive with scratching. But, much of that is due to the producing skills of Rick Rubin, a metalhead who formed Def Jam Records with Russell Simmons and had previously flirted with this sound on Run-D.M.C.'s *Raising Hell*, not to mention a few singles and one-offs with the Beasties prior to this record. He made rap-rock, but to give him lone credit for *Licensed to Ill* (as some have) is misleading, since that very same combination would not have been as powerful, nor would it have aged so well—aged into a rock classic—if it weren't for the Beastie Boys, who fuel this record through their passion for subcultures, pop culture, jokes, and the intoxicating power of wordplay. At the time, it wasn't immediately apparent that their obnoxious patter was part of a persona (a fate that would later plague Eminem), but the years have clarified that this was a joke—although, listening to the cajoling rhymes, filled with clear parodies and absurdities, it's hard to imagine the offense that some took at the time. Which, naturally, is the credit of not just the music—they don't call it the devil's music for nothing—but the wild imagination of the Beasties, whose rhymes sear into consciousness through their gonzo humor and gleeful delivery. There hasn't been a funnier, more infectious record in pop music than this, and it's not because the group is mocking rappers (in all honesty, the truly twisted barbs are hurled at frat boys and lager lads), but because they've already created their own universe and points of reference, where it's as funny to spit out absurdist rhymes and pound out "Fight for Your Right (To Party)" as it is to send up street-corner doo wop with "Girls." Then, there is the overpowering *loudness* of the record—operating from the axis of where metal, punk, and rap meet, there never has been a record this heavy and nimble, drunk on its own power yet giddy with what they're getting away with. There is a sense of genuine discovery, of creating new music, that remains years later, after countless plays, countless misinterpretations, countless rip-off acts, even countless apologies from the Beasties, who seemed guilty by how intoxicating the sound of it is, how it makes beer-soaked hedonism sound like the apogee of human experience. Maybe it is, maybe it isn't, but in either case, *Licensed to Ill* reigns tall among the greatest records of its time. —*Stephen Thomas Erlewine*

★ **Paul's Boutique** / Jul. 1989 / Capitol ✦✦✦✦✦

Such was the power of *Licensed to Ill* that everybody, from fans to critics, thought that not only could the Beastie Boys not top the record but also they were destined to be a one-shot wonder. These feelings were only amplified by their messy, litigious departure from Def Jam and their flight from their beloved New York to Los Angeles, since it appeared that the Beasties had completely lost the plot. Many critics in fact thought that *Paul's Boutique* was a muddled mess upon its summer release in 1989, but that's the nature of the record—it's so dense, it's bewildering at first, revealing its considerable charms with each play. To put it mildly, it's a considerable change from the hard rock of *Licensed to Ill*, shifting to layers of samples and beats so intertwined they move beyond psychedelic; it's a painting with sound. *Paul's Boutique* is a record that only could have been made in a specific time and place. Like the Rolling Stones in 1972, the Beastie Boys were in exile and pining for their home, so they made a love letter to downtown New York—which they could not have done without the Dust Brothers, a Los Angeles-based production duo who helped redefine what sampling could be with this record. Sadly, after *Paul's Boutique* sampling on the level of what's heard here would disappear; due to a series of lawsuits, most notably Gilbert O'Sullivan's suit against Biz Markie, the entire enterprise too cost prohibitive and risky to perform on such a grand scale. Which is really a shame, because if ever a record could be used as incontrovertible proof that sampling is its own art form, it's

Paul's Boutique. Snatches of familiar music are scattered throughout the record—anything from Curtis Mayfield's "Superfly" and Sly Stone's "Loose Booty" to Loggins & Messina's "Your Mama Don't Dance" and the Ramones' "Suzy Is a Headbanger"—but never once are they presented in lazy, predictable ways. The Dust Brothers and Beasties weave a crazy quilt of samples, beats, loops, and tricks, which creates a hyper-surreal alternate reality—a romanticized, funhouse reflection of New York where all pop music and culture exist on the same strata, feeding off each other, mocking each other, evolving into a wholly unique record, unlike anything that came before or after. It very well could be that its density is what alienated listeners and critics at the time; there is so much information in the music and words that it can seem impenetrable at first, but upon repeated spins it opens up slowly, assuredly, revealing more every listen. Musically, few hip-hop records have ever been so rich; it's not just the recontextulations of familiar music via samples, it's the flow of each song and the album as a whole, culminating in the widescreen suite that closes the record. Lyrically, the Beasties have never been better—not just because their jokes are razor sharp, but because they construct full-bodied narratives and evocative portraits of characters and places. Few pop records offer this much to savor, and if *Paul's Boutique* only made a modest impact upon its initial release, over time its influence could be heard through pop and rap, yet no matter how its influence was felt, it stands alone as a record of stunning vision, maturity, and accomplishment. Plus, it's a hell of a lot of fun, no matter how many times you've heard it. —*Stephen Thomas Erlewine*

☆ **Check Your Head** / Apr. 21, 1992 / Grand Royal ♦♦♦♦♦

Check Your Head brought the Beastie Boys crashing back into the charts and into public consciousness, but that was only partially due to the album itself—much of its initial success was due to the cult audience that *Paul's Boutique* cultivated in the years since its initial flop release, a group of fans whose minds were so thoroughly blown by that record, they couldn't wait to see what came next, and this helped the record debut in the Top Ten upon its April 1992 release. This audience, perhaps somewhat unsurprisingly, was a collegiate Gen-X audience raised on *Licensed to Ill* and ready for the Beastie Boys to guide them through college. As it happened, the Beasties had repositioned themselves as a lo-fi, alt-rock groove band. They had not abandoned rap, but it was no longer the foundation of their music; it was simply the most prominent in a thick pop-culture gumbo where old school rap sat comfortably with soul-jazz, hardcore punk, white-trash metal, arena rock, Bob Dylan, bossa nova, spacy pop, and hard, dirty funk. What they did abandon was the psychedelic samples of *Paul's Boutique*, turning toward primitive grooves they played themselves, augmented by keyboardist Money Mark and coproducer Mario Caldato Jr. This all means that music was the message and the rhymes, which had been pushed toward the forefront on both *Licensed to Ill* and *Paul's Boutique*, have been considerably de-emphasized (only four songs—"Jimmy James," "Pass the Mic," "Finger Lickin' Good," and "So What'cha Want"—could hold their own lyrically among their previous work). This is not a detriment, because the focus is not on the words, it's on the music, mood, and even the newfound neo-hippie political consciousness. And *Check Your Head* is certainly a record that's greater than the sum of its parts—individually, nearly all the tracks are good (the instrumentals sound good on their subsequent soul-jazz collection, *The In Sound From Way Out!*), but it's the context and variety of styles that give *Check Your Head* its identity. It's how the old school raps give way to fuzz-toned rockers, furious punk, and cheerfully gritty, jazzy jams. As much as *Paul's Boutique*, this is a whirlwind tour through the Beasties' pop-culture obsessions, but instead of spinning into Technicolor fantasies, it's earth-bound D.I.Y. that makes it all seem equally accessible—which is a big reason why it turned out to be an alt-rock touchstone of the '90s, something that both set trends and predicted them. —*Stephen Thomas Erlewine*

Some Old Bullshit / Feb. 8, 1994 / Grand Royal ♦♦

In the hilarious liner note/photo package with the disc is an indignant letter from a punk fan in about 1982 or so complaining bitterly about the Beastie Boys as being little more than "a pathetic, feeble imitation of Minor Threat." The thing is, that's fairly accurate. Collecting some of the long out-of-print/hard-to-find early releases by the band—the *Polly Wog Stew* EP and the *Cookie Puss* single, mainly—*Some Old Bullshit* is mostly that, if an entertaining enough variety. The eight *Polly Wog Stew* tracks are brattish hardcore and not much more, mainly interesting to hear Mike D's lead snotty whine

and sometimes amusing lyrics ("Egg Raid on Mojo" is about carrying out such an assault on the doorman of a Manhattan club). "Jimi" is the best of the bunch because it isn't anything like hardcore, but more an attempt at noisy psychedelia that sounds like a sweeter, younger version of the Butthole Surfers. There's one other reason to at least give the album an initial ear: the drummer at this point was Kate Schellenbach, eventual founding member of Luscious Jackson a decade later. The *Cookie Puss* tracks signal the initial transmogrification of the Beasties into the hip-hop monsters of the later '80s, if a bit hamhandedly. There's old school synth beats and bass, some minimal scratching, and vocals that in retrospect sound like Ween, but not much else—the mock reggae anthem "Beastie Revolution" is pretty funny, though. As an amusing bonus, two radio tracks from the hardcore days are included: rough takes on "Egg Raid on Mojo" and "Transit Cop." —*Ned Raggett*

Ill Communication / May 23, 1994 / Grand Royal ♦♦♦♦

Ill Communication follows the blueprint of *Check Your Head*, accentuating it at some points, deepening it in others, but never *expanding* it beyond the boundaries of that record. As such, it's the first Beastie Boys album not to delve into new territory, but it's not fair to say that it finds the band coasting, since much of the album finds the group turning in muscular, vigorous music that fills out the black-and-white sketches that comprised *Check Your Head*. Much of the credit has to go to the group's renewed confidence in—or at least renewed emphasis on—their rhyming; there are still instrumentals (arguably, there are too many instrumentals), but the Beasties do push their words to the forefront, even on dense rockers like the album's signature tune, "Sabotage." But even those rhymes illustrate that the group is in the process of a great settling, relying more on old school-styled rhyme schemes and word battles than the narratives and surreal fantasies that marked the high points on their first two albums. With this record, the Beasties confirm that there is indeed a signature Beastie Boys aesthetic (it's too far-ranging and restless to be pegged as a signature sound), with the group sticking to a blend of old school rap, pop culture, lo-fi funk, soulful jazz instrumentals, Latin rhythms, and punk, often seamlessly integrated into a rolling, pan-cultural, multicultural groove. The best moments of *Ill Communication* rank with the best music the Beasties have ever made, as well as the best pop music of the '90s, but unfortunately, it's uneven and rather front loaded. The first half overflows with brilliant, imaginative variations on their aesthetic: the assured groove of "Sure Shot," the warped rap of "B-Boys Makin' With the Freak Freak," the relentless dirty funk of "Root Down," the monumental "Sabotage," and the sly "Get It Together," highlighted by a cameo from Q-Tip of A Tribe Called Quest. After that, the album seems to lose its sense of direction and momentum, even if individual moments are very good. Any record that can claim jams as funky and inventive as "Flute Loop" and "Do It," or instrumentals as breezy as "Ricky's Theme," is certainly better than its competition, but there are just enough moments that rank as obvious filler to slow its flow, and to keep it from standing proudly next to *Check Your Head* as a wholly successful record. Even if it is a little uneven, it still boasts more than its fair share of splendid, transcendent music, and it really only pales in comparison to the Beasties' trio of classic records. By any other measure, this is a near-masterpiece, and it is surely a highlight of '90s alternative pop/rock. —*Stephen Thomas Erlewine*

The In Sound From Way Out! / Apr. 2, 1996 / Grand Royal ♦♦♦

Originally released through the Beasties' French fan club, *The In Sound From Way Out!* is a collection of the group's funky instrumentals from *Check Your Head* and *Ill Communication*, with a couple of new tracks thrown in. The Beasties have a flair for loose, gritty funk and soul-jazz, and the stuttering, greasy keyboards of Money Mark give the music an extra edge—he helps make the music sound as authentic as anything from the early '70s. Fans of the band's dynamic wordplay might find *The In Sound From Way Out!* a disappointment, but anyone that grooved on the wildly eclectic fusions of *Check Your Head* and *Ill Communication* will find the album endlessly enjoyable. —*Stephen Thomas Erlewine*

Hello Nasty / Jul. 14, 1998 / Grand Royal/Capitol ♦♦♦♦♦

Hello Nasty, the Beastie Boys' fifth album, is a head-spinning listen loaded with analog synthesizers, old drum machines, call-and-response vocals, freestyle rhyming, futuristic sound effects, and virtuoso turntable scratching. The Beasties have long been notorious for their dense, multi-layered explosions, but *Hello Nasty* is their first record to build on the multi-ethnic junk culture breakthrough of *Check Your Head*, instead of merely replicating it.

Moving from electro-funk breakdowns to Latin-soul jams to spacey pop, *Hello Nasty* covers as much ground as *Check Your Head* or *Ill Communication*, but the flow is natural, like *Paul's Boutique*, even if the finish is retro-stylized. Hiring DJ Mixmaster Mike (one of the Invisibl Skratch Piklz) turned out to be a masterstroke; he and the Beasties created a sound that strongly recalls the spare electronic funk of the early '80s, but spiked with the samples and postmodern absurdist wit that have become their trademarks. On the surface, the sonic collages of *Hello Nasty* don't appear as dense as *Paul's Boutique*, nor is there a single as grabbing as "Sabotage," but given time, little details emerge, and each song forms its own identity. A few stray from the course, and the ending is a little anticlimactic, but that doesn't erase the riches of *Hello Nasty*—the old school kick of "Super Disco Breakin'" and "The Move"; Adam Yauch's crooning on "I Don't Know"; Lee "Scratch" Perry's cameo; and the recurring video game samples, to name just a few. The sonic adventures alone make the album noteworthy, but what makes it remarkable is how it looks to the future by looking to the past. There's no question that *Hello Nasty* is saturated with old school sounds and styles, but by reviving the future-shock rock of the early '80s, the Beasties have shrewdly set themselves up for the new millennium. — *Stephen Thomas Erlewine*

The Sounds of Science / Nov. 23, 1999 / Grand Royal ✦✦✦✦
At the close of the '90s, the Beastie Boys had only released five albums, which may not seem like enough music to provide the foundation for a double-disc retrospective. But between 1981 and 1999, they released countless B sides, non-LP singles, and EPs, resulting in a sprawling discography ripe for a compilation. So, in 1999 the Beasties released the two-disc compilation *The Sounds of Science*, which covers every incarnation of the band from *Polly Wog Stew* to *Hello Nasty*. Inevitably, some well-known songs are missing—only three cuts from *Licensed to Ill* are here, and their breakthrough single "Rock Hard" had to be pulled when AC/DC refused permission for a sample. Ultimately, that doesn't matter, since the set captures the spirit of the Beasties so well. Usually, compilations that don't follow chronological order are a little muddled, but *The Sounds of Science* benefits from its jumbled sequencing, since it emphasizes the band's astonishing musical reach and consistency. After all, every album since *Paul's Boutique* has followed a similarly unpredictable pattern, as the group moved from hip-hop to punk to funk to jazz. What's remarkable about *The Sounds of Science* is that it has all the obvious suspects, but since they're rubbing singles with album tracks and B sides like "Skills to Pay the Bills," two outtakes from the abandoned country album, alternate versions of "Jimmy James" and "Three MC's and One DJ," Fatboy Slim's brilliant remix of "Body Movin'," goofs like the Biz Markie-sung cover of "Benny and the Jets," and the excellent new single "Alive," it all sounds fresh. There's much more than hits here, but *The Sounds of Science* achieves something most anthologies don't: it summarizes the attitude and spirit of the band, while offering some new revelations even for dedicated fans. — *Stephen Thomas Erlewine*

● **Video Anthology** / Oct. 10, 2000 / Voyager ✦✦✦✦✦
Beastie Boys fans should prepare for a feast with this two-DVD collection from the Criterion collection (Capitol Records had planned a regular collection, but seem to have abandoned it along the way). The collection is not by any means completely comprehensive (there are 18 videos included), but it does manage to be exhaustive in terms of what it does cover (and offer). Each disc includes nine videos, with each group presented twice—the first is a sequential presentation that offers a choice of Dolby 2.0, Dolby 5.1, band commentary track, or directors commentary track. While the Beastie Boys tracks are more or less continuous, with pauses, the directors' commentary tracks are built up from sessions with various directors, including some conducted by telephone by Criterion producer Ralph Spaulding (these have a tendency to wander off in oddball directions; it's surprising how willing people are to give bizarre answers to freaky questions). The directors tend to be more to the point than the band, who keep running out of things to talk about in regard to the video. The second presentation sets up the access track by track. This allows for the incorporation of a great deal of supplementary material, from basic data on each shoot to photographs (a goldmine for fans of Spike Jonze, who is nigh-unto obsessive about photodocumenting whatever he works on) to video proposals, designs, and background materials. What fans will want to get at, however, is the impressive number of remixes that the set sports—more than 40 remixes are included as alternate audio tracks. Many of the tracks also include alternate

video angles—usually consisting of assemblies of footage from stages prior to the editing process. An excellent set, certainly good for the hardcore element of Beasties fandom and a treat for serious video geeks. Working through this set, be warned, is an effort that will consume hour after hour. — *Steven McDonald*

The Beat Junkies

f. 1992, Orange County, CA
Group / Turntablism, Hip-Hop, Underground Rap
Along with the Invisibl Skratch Piklz and the X-Ecutioners, the Beat Junkies were one of the seminal DJ crews that revived the art of turntablism (i.e., using turntables as musical instruments in and of themselves) during the '90s. Distinguished by their multicultural membership and trademark Green Lantern rings, the Beat Junkies were formed in Orange County (outside Los Angeles) in 1992 by J-Rocc (born Jason Jackson). Fellow core DJs Rhettmatic (born Nazareth Nizra) and Melo-D (born David Mendoza) were joined by charter members Curse, Icy Ice, Symphony, and DJ What?! Other crew members came onboard within the next year, including core DJ Babu (born Chris Oroc) and two future members of the Invisibl Skratch Piklz, Shortkut and D-Styles, plus Havikk and Tommy Gun. Mr. Choc completed the crew upon his arrival in 1995. That year, the Beat Junkies got their own radio show in the suburb of Santa Ana, and began testing their skill regularly on the DJ battle circuit around southern California. The core quartet of J-Rocc, Babu, Rhettmatic, and Melo-D all won individual titles at various levels of competition, and as a team, the Beat Junkies won the ITF (International Turntable Federation) world team championships in both 1997 and 1998, after which they collectively retired from competition. Also in 1997, the Beat Junkies released their first widely available (i.e., nonmixtape) album, *The World Famous Beat Junkies, Vol. 1*, on PR Records. It was followed by further volumes on Blackberry in 1998 and 1999, with the former including their ITF championship-winning routine from that year. J-Rocc and Babu teamed up to form the Bumrush Bros., who appeared on the 1999 Rawkus compilation *Soundbombing, Vol. 2*, and also opened the Fat Beats record shop in Los Angeles, which later spawned an acclaimed compilation series of its own. Babu became the third member of the L.A. underground rap crew Dilated Peoples, serving as DJ on their acclaimed albums *The Platform* and *Expansion Team*; meanwhile, Rhettmatic landed a similar post in the Visionaries, and Melo-D served as the in-house DJ for *Vibe* magazine's late-night television spin-off. Several crew members past and present also worked in radio or other aspects of the industry. In 2001 J-Rocc launched the group's own Beat Junkie Sound label with *Classic Material*, a collection of Beat Junkie-related items spanning 1995-2000. — *Steve Huey*

● **The World Famous Beat Junkies, Vol. 1** / Jun. 3, 1997 / PR ✦✦✦✦
Turntablism: at times, extraordinary. At others, kind of like watching a musical circus act. Luckily, the first mix album put out by the Beat Junkies collective gives the reigns to ITF world-champion (and Dilated Peoples member) DJ Babu with very few moments of stylistic silliness. This turntablist mix simply knows when to let the actual tunes take center stage. So, while there is more than enough deck trickery, Babu lets songs such as Kool Keith's "Lovely Lady" or the De La Soul, A Tribe Called Quest, and Jungle Brothers collaboration "How Ya Want It" play out with little overbearing technical wizardry. Which isn't to say the mix is lacking in skills. He also consistently adds unobtrusive layers of background scratches and beats as he lets Beat Junkies founder J-Rocc chime in every once awhile to praise the laid-back party. Babu even takes a segment in the middle of the mix to show off a drunken, sultry flurry of fantastic beat juggling that should impress even the most trainspottery of turntablism fans. If his style could be described, it would include the fact that he uses a much more soulful and collaborative effort with the original recordings instead of a reliance on lightning deck-blaze aesthetics, which can only be good. Because this first volume in the *World Famous Beat Junkies* series proudly shows off skills that adhere just to the grooves themselves. Even the biggest opponents to "style over substance" would have to applaud that. — *Dean Carlson*

The World Famous Beat Junkies, Vol. 2 / Oct. 17, 1998 / Blackberry ✦✦✦✦
The World Famous Beat Junkies, Vol. 2 is another double-disc mix album, this time spotlighting the skills of Beat Junkie DJ Rhettmatic instead of Babu. Naturally, there are appearances from other key members as well, and a couple of archival pieces of interest: Rhettmatic's award-winning routine at the

1996 DMC competition, and the four-man routine featuring Rhettmatic, J-Rocc, Melo-D, and Babu that won the 1997 ITF team championship. Disc one is mostly a collection of underground favorites, with work by Dilated Peoples, Mos Def, Jurassic 5, the Lootpack, Defari, Slum Village, and Rasco, among others. Disc two features a few more freestyles and exclusive tracks, all enlivened by excellent scratching and mixing. Die-hard turntable aficionados will find all of the Beat Junkies' compilations necessary, but thanks to strong track selection, this one might just be the pick of the litter. —*Steve Huey*

The World Famous Beat Junkies, Vol. 3 / Nov. 9, 1999 / Blackberry ◆◆◆
Volume three in the *World Famous Beat Junkies* series throws the spotlight onto Melo-D, who handles the majority of the mixing and scratching work here. It's only a single-disc collection this time out, featuring a healthy blend of underground favorites (mostly from the West Coast) and lesser-known up-and-comers. Quasimoto, Defari, Rasco, Xzibit, Dilated Peoples, the Lootpack, and Saukrates are all present, and there are some exclusives and freestyle cuts as well. True to the Beat Junkies' name, though, the real focus is on the DJ's rhythm tracks, and Melo-D shows that he's more than up to snuff with the rest of his mates. —*Steve Huey*

Da Beatminerz
f. 1993, Brooklyn, NY
Group / Hip-Hop, East Coast Rap
The production team known as da Beatminerz came together in the late '90s to rejuvenate hip-hop with their purist aesthetics, which looked back to the genre's pioneering New York-based producers rather than the contemporary synthesizer-based sounds that were suddenly becoming the norm. The five group members, led by brothers DJ Evil Dee and Mr. Walt, honed their beatmaking skills individually before joining forces and crafting the collective's trademark "boom bap" sound: an emphasis on the bottom end, the bass lines, the hard kicks, and the snares. The collective's breakthrough came on their debut album for the prestigious Rawkus label in 2001, *Brace 4 Impak*, making them one of the few production-based acts in hip-hop to release an album under their own name. Like their contemporaries—Hi-Tek, Jay Dee, and Pete Rock—they left the rapping to a disparate, yet impressive, roster of their hometown's finest.

As mentioned, the five group members—the aforementioned Dee and Walt, along with Baby Paul, Chocolate Ty, and Rich Black—began their production careers as individuals. Walt worked at the Music Factory in Jamaica, Queens, where he first met Paul, and associated with superstar patrons such as Q-Tip. At the same time, Walt's brother, Dee, became friends with two other beatmaking DJs in his neighborhood, Ty and Black—the former part of the Shadez of Brooklyn crew, the latter part of the Pitch Black crew. It was Dee, though, who had the most success as part of the group Black Moon, who garnered substantial recognition with their *Enter da Stage* album.

The success of Black Moon led to the official formation of da Beatminerz around the time of Smif-n-Wessun's similarly praised *Dah Shinin'* album, which featured production work by the group. Next came various productions for rappers such as Rah Digga, Mark Morrison, the Roots, and Eminem, among others. It wasn't long before Rawkus came calling and asked the group to record a debut album. The resulting album featured an array of guest rappers, most notably Busta Rhymes, Pete Rock, Naughty By Nature, Talib Kweli, Total, and Cocoa Brovaz. —*Jason Birchmeier*

Brace 4 Impak / Jul. 31, 2001 / Priority ◆◆◆
Da Beatminerz, one of the premier production teams of '90s underground hip-hop, provided much of the sonic framework for such Boot Camp Clik classics as *Enta Da Stage* by Black Moon in 1992 and *Dah Shinin'* by Smif-n-Wessun in 1994. The five-member team consists of Mr. Walt, Rich Blak, Baby Paul, Chocolate Ty, and resident Black Moon and New York Hot 97 DJ Evil Dee. Though they continued to work with other Boot Camp artists such as Heltah Skeltah and O.G.C., the crew mostly took a back seat in the late '90s, until Black Moon's long-awaited sophomore release, *War Zone*, dropped in early 1999. As previously evidenced on *War Zone*, on *Brace* their signature sound of heavy drum kick drops and sparse, crackling snares seems to have been transformed into a more muddy-sounding style. Once trendsetters themselves, Da Minerz take a couple of cues from others in the production field, including Ruff Ryders' producers Swizz Beats and Irv Gotti and Dirty South producers like Timbaland and the Neptunes. However, the beats on the album do have a decidedly East Coast spin, and many top-name Atlantic Coast artists come along for the ride. The Flip Mode Squad, complete with Busta Rhymes and Rah Digga in tow, get down-and-dirty on the streaky "Take That," and rap veterans Naughty By Nature weigh in on "Thug Love." But the more subtle cuts are the strength of this project, Talib Kweli and Total's "Anti-Love Movement" and "Open" by Pete Rock and former Soul II Soul lead singer Caron Wheeler are definitely on the mark. The final two cuts bring in some theme with "Let's Talk About It," a memorial to fallen rappers, and the scintillating "Ghetto 2 Ghetto," with a sample from the intro to Nas' *Illmatic* album. The album employs some gifted MCs and all in all demonstrates this production team still has a few stunners in the old trick bag. —*M.F. Di Bella*

The Beatnuts
f. 1989, Queens, NY
Group / Hip-Hop, East Coast Rap, Latin Rap
An underground Latino crew who moved from being strictly producers to make some action on the other side of the mixing board as well, the Beatnuts first hooked up in the late '80s, with Junkyard Ju-Ju (aka JuJu, born Jerry Tineo) and Psycho Les (born Lester Fernandez) being joined by Fashion (aka Kool Fashion, born Berntony Smalls). After working with the Jungle Brothers, the trio connected with Monie Love on a production job for "Pups Lickin Bone" from her 1990 debut album, *Down to Earth*. They also worked on remixes for Cypress Hill, Naughty By Nature, Da Lench Mob, and Prime Minister Pete Nice, earning their own contract with Combat Records for the 1993 mini-LP *Intoxicated Demons*. The album's release was held up when Kool Fashion was arrested and jailed for six months on a drug conviction, but the Beatnuts released a self-titled album the following year, on Violator/Relativity. After a hiatus verging on three years, Fashion became a Muslim and left the Beatnuts, releasing his debut solo album, *God Connections*, with production help from his old bandmates. JuJu and Psycho Les finally returned to release the Beatnuts' third album, *Stone Crazy*, in 1997. *Musical Massacre* followed two years later. *Take It or Squeeze It*, issued in spring 2001, captured the Beatnuts' danceable funk as well as collaborations with Method Man and Fat Man Scoop. The next year, *The Originators* brought back Al Tariq (that is, Kool Fashion) and delivered another round of bionic beats. —*John Bush*

Intoxicated Demons / Apr. 6, 1993 / Relativity ◆◆◆
Flashy, booty-slapping Latino hip-hop created by horny substance abusers—what's not to like? This mini-LP debut by Colombian/Dominican producers the Beatnuts passes the booze and spliffs in such a high-volume block-party quake of ungainly rhymes that one instantly remembers why careless hip-hop used to be so fun. Imagine a lewd and sentient wife beater and you have "World's Famous." Picture some good luvin' take on Public Enemy and you have "Reign of the Tec." Squint real hard and one can see a winking jab at A Tribe Called Quest's "Butter" strutting around until it gets the attention it wants ("Third of the Trio"). This is an intentionally offensive group just begging to be let out of their underground cages. Don't let anybody tell you otherwise: *Intoxicated Demons* is a fine debut, no matter its raunchy hubris. Because the more hardcore rap fans the Beatnuts annoy, the better they sound. —*Dean Carlson*

Street Level / Jun. 21, 1994 / Relativity ◆◆◆◆

Stone Crazy / Jun. 24, 1997 / Relativity ◆◆◆
The Beatnuts' third album, *Stone Crazy*, is a clever combination of jazz-inflected rhythms and hardcore rhyming, highlighted by dense, provocative production. It's lacking some of the energy of the group's first two records, yet *Stone Crazy* proves that the Beatnuts continue to push the envelope. —*Leo Stanley*

● **A Musical Massacre** / Aug. 10, 1999 / Relativity ◆◆◆◆◆
The fourth offering from the rambunctious hip-hop junkies the Beatnuts is an all-out assault on the eardrums. This is crack-open-a-party music, with beats that have been chiseled with a Latin feel. Lyrics are rough, rugged, and raunchy. Songs like "Watch Out Now" and "Turn It Out" (featuring Greg Nice) are just plain fun, as close to feel-good music as hardcore hip-hop gets. Other tracks that will satisfy include "Puffin' on a Cloud," "You're a Clown" (featuring Biz Markie), "Buddah in the Air," and the Spanglish headsplitter "Se Acabo." Even the thematic "Look Around," a departure from the Beatnuts' usual hedonistic content, is a pleasant surprise. The true core of the Beatnuts' sound is their fleshy, textured beats, which are dense and dipped in

cannabis—flutes, synthesizers, and various percussion instruments seem to float over and around deep drum-machine kicks and snares. Swelling with an eclectic assortment of hypnotic sounds, *A Musical Massacre* is among 1999's most entertaining hip-hop albums. —*Michael Di Bella*

Take It or Squeeze It / Mar. 20, 2001 / Loud ✦✦✦
Once again, *Take It or Squeeze It* proves just how inventive the Beatnuts can get behind the production boards; the beats, samples, and found sounds they employ result in their most colorful tracks to date, furthering their deep-rooted East Coast hip-hop influences with a subtle Latin influence. Unfortunately, their rhymes and songwriting don't quite measure up to their soundscapes. Far too often they recycle classic hip-hop clichés—smoking, boasting, partying—and while these sort of rhymes no doubt keep the energy level high and the vibes carefree, their playful, freewheeling attitude becomes tiring with multiple listens, particularly for anyone who already owns their past albums. Furthermore, they can't flow as well as they like to think they can here—when they invite Method Man to join the party on "Se Acabo Remix," this becomes quite evident as their average mic skills pale in comparison. Smartly, they don't invite many top-caliber rappers to guest on their album, which keeps them from getting too overshadowed. In terms of songwriting, they let their production dominate their songs, often letting samples stand as choruses rather than coming up with witty or catchy vocal hooks—and if they don't do that, they usually just come up with a simple chant such as in "Prendelo (Light It Up)." These criticisms aren't anything new, though. The Beatnuts began their career not as MCs but as producers, and obviously it remains their strength. If you don't mind the simple-minded, playful rhymes and the lack of strong songwriting, then you'll find much to savor here; the Beatnuts lay down some of the best East Coast hip-hop beats in New York, beats that retain the true spirit of the genre's fun and innocent late-'80s golden era. —*Jason Birchmeier*

Classic Nuts, Vol. 1 / Feb. 19, 2002 / Relativity ✦✦✦✦

Present: The Originators / Jul. 23, 2002 / Landspeed ✦✦✦
From the roaring crowd of the intro through to the "$5 million cribs, and all we do is make hits" chorus call of the closing "Back 2 Back", the sixth half-length broadcast from Junkyard Ju Ju and Psycho Les is a lesson in braggadocio. In the finest tradition of New York hip-hop, the Queen's duo utilise minimal grooves to maximum effect, flexing an enviable line in sampled hooks and some irresistible basslines which insist that listeners nod their heads as if some kind of aural hypnotism. "Yae Yo" is typical, opening with a slice of Debbie Harry before winding down the turntable to make room for a funky as you like flute loop, while the hand claps and Bootsy-inspired low-end theory of "Routine" are dirtier than the 2 Live Crew in full lyrical flow. On the downside, as with much of their previous material, most of the lyrics don't stand up to close scrutiny but even the uninspired—not to mention geographically challenged crew/city/state/country shouts of "Ya Better Believe"—fail to dent the Beatnuts ability to bend a sing-a-long hook around a groove so infectious it clamps to the subconscious with the tenacity of a pit-bull. —*Kingsley Marshall*

Bell Biv DeVoe

f. 1988

Group / Urban, New Jack Swing, Hip-Hop
Bell Biv DeVoe was hatched in the minds of its members, New Edition's Ricky Bell, Michael Bivins, and Ronnie DeVoe, upon the departure of lead singer Bobby Brown in 1986. But it wasn't until after New Edition completed its supporting tour for the album *Heart Break* in 1988 that the trio gave in to the urgings of *Heart Break* producers Jimmy Jam and Terry Lewis and decided to chart its own course. Bell Biv DeVoe enlisted a variety of producers for its debut album, including Jam and Lewis and Public Enemy producers Hank and Keith Shocklee. The results were quite unlike anything in New Edition's repertoire: The beats were funkier, the lyrics and vocals were sexier, and the overall sound had a harder, hip-hop-tinged edge. The album's title track, "Poison," became a number-three smash, and it was followed by the equally successful "Do Me!" and the R&B hits "BBD (I Thought it Was Me)," "When Will I See You Smile Again?," and "Dope!" The album itself went on to sell over three million copies and was followed by a remix album the next year. Meanwhile, Bivins took some time off to assemble the so-called East Coast Family, discovering and producing debut albums for Another Bad Creation and Boyz II Men. *Hootie Mack*, Bell Biv DeVoe's

second proper album, was released in 1993 but didn't make as much of an impact. In 1996, all three members of Bell Biv DeVoe participated in a reunion of New Edition. —*Steve Huey*

Poison / Mar. 1990 / MCA ✦✦✦✦
With so many faceless, soundalike albums having come out of the "new jack swing" hybrid in the late '80s and early to mid-'90s, it's important to give credit to the form's more creative and imaginative figures. Along with Guy and Bobby Brown, Bell Biv DeVoe (a New Edition spinoff trio comprised of Ricky Bell, Michael Bivens, and Ronnie DeVoe) delivered some of new jack swing's most worthwhile material. A hard-edged, tough-minded blend of R&B/funk and hip-hop, *Poison* was (like Brown's *Don't Be Cruel*) a radical departure from the Jackson 5-influenced "bubblegum soul" New Edition was originally known for. Defined by their urgency, rawness, and vitality, "Poison," "BBD (I Thought It Was Me)?," "She's Dope!," and "Do Me!" are considered new jack swing classics and are indeed among the best the style has to offer. Taking a break from the CD's overall aggression, BBD moves closer to New Edition's sound with the decent, though far from outstanding, ballads "When Will I See You Again" and "I Do Need You." While other "new jacks" were content to simply emulate Guy, the distinctive BBD deserves applause for daring to stake out its own territory. —*Alex Henderson*

WBBD-Bootcity! [Remix Album] / 1991 / MCA ✦✦✦
Bell Biv DeVoe was all over "urban contemporary" radio in 1991, when MCA Records set out to milk the trio's tremendous popularity for all it was worth with this generally decent and likeable, though far from outstanding, collection of remixes. The best remixes surprise us by adding something different and fresh to familar songs—and *WBBD Bootcity!* (which is presented in the form of an "urban contemporary" radio program, and even includes an interview with BBD) doesn't add anything particularly memorable or interesting to "BBD (I Thought It Was Me)?," "She's Dope!," and other major hits from the triple-platinum *Poison*. There are a few surprises, including a jazz-influenced version of "Do Me" that is decidedly less forceful than the original version. But on the whole, *WBBD* takes a predictable, play-it-safe approach that fails to demonstrate how inventive remixes can be. This is a CD that only the most hardcore BBD fanatics should check out. —*Alex Henderson*

Hootie Mack / Jun. 1993 / MCA ✦✦✦
Hootie Mack not only keeps the same energetic vibe that made *Poison* a hit but also expands upon that base, adding a more street-oriented production that, at its best, is more sexy and funky than their debut. Unfortunately, the high points on this album aren't as numerous as those on *Poison*; not only that, but the good songs didn't receive much airplay, causing the album to drop off the charts quickly. —*Stephen Thomas Erlewine*

● **The Best of Bell Biv DeVoe** / Sep. 26, 2000 / MCA ✦✦✦✦
On the one hand, Bell Biv DeVoe deserves a good best-of compilation—they were one of the freshest-sounding new jack swing acts to hit the charts during the style's early-'90s heyday. On the other hand, they only recorded two albums during that heyday (not counting a remix album), and their third wasn't released until after this 2000 compilation, *The Best of Bell Biv DeVoe*. Thus, listeners get five tracks from the group's blockbuster debut, *Poison*; six from their decent but less-inventive follow-up, *Hootie Mack*; the non-LP single "Gangsta"; and four tracks from the aforementioned remix album, *WBBD-Bootcity!*, including the otherwise-unavailable single "Word to the Mutha." Aside from *Hootie Mack*'s "Something in Your Eyes" (an R&B Top Ten), all of the group's biggest hits came from *Poison*—the crossover smashes "Poison" and "Do Me!," the R&B chart-topper "BBD (I Thought It Was Me)?," and the R&B Top Tens "When Will I See You Smile Again?" and "She's Dope." As such, casual fans might be just as happy with the mid-priced compilation *20th Century Masters—The Millennium Collection*, which—even though it features fewer songs—still has all their major hits, and costs a few dollars less. But for more devoted fans who want a generous BBD compilation, *The Best of Bell Biv DeVoe* does have all their best moments in one place, and makes for an excellent summary of why they were important to the development of '90s R&B. —*Steve Huey*

BBD / Dec. 18, 2001 / Big Ten ✦✦✦
Bell Biv DeVoe's first album of new material in eight years, *BBD*, attempts to reclaim the popular success of the trio's first album. It's sexier than anything BBD had done before, every song being not about love but instead sex—straight-up freaky sex with no apologies and little passion. In addition, the

former New Edition singers also do a lot of flossing here, rapping about champagne, cars, and money. This is a very brash and unapologetic album, an album that turns seduction into sport. These three guys, of course, popularized this style of urban music a decade earlier, a time when songs like "Do Me!" seemed quite steamy. Well, time certainly hasn't cooled them a bit. BBD is just as frank about its intentions as it ever was, if not more so. What has changed, however, is the production style. BBD goes with a long list of producers, among them Rockwilder, the big-money rap producer who crafts "Da Hot S*** (Aight)," this album's standout moment. But its Rockwilder's only production, and the other producers aren't quite as noteworthy. This is a minor issue, though, in the end. Ricky, Michael, and Ronnie dominate this album, and they're as determined as they've ever been. If anything, their determination pushes them too far, to the point where they force the songs. Yet after nearly a decade of inactivity, the hunger is understandable, and fans of the trio should certainly rejoice its return. Among an industry of teenage sensations who come and go with each passing year, these three guys refuse to quit. Thankfully, with every successive comeback they adapt their style to the moment and never sound like the aging adults they've become. BBD has somehow managed to sound eternally young and consistently contemporary, two often overlooked accomplishments that are more impressive than mere chart success. —*Jason Birchmeier*

Benzino (Ray Scott)

Vocals / East Coast Rap

Perhaps better known for his shady reputation than for his accomplishments, Benzino worked in the rap industry for a decade before going solo in 2001 with much hoopla. During the final months of 2001, he became a regular fixture in *The Source* magazine, even appearing on the cover despite being relatively unaccomplished relative to the usual cover features. Moreover, his album featured a spectacular array of big-name guests, everyone from P. Diddy to producer Teddy Riley. But his album flopped, selling less than 75,000 copies. Worse, his label, Motown, dropped him less than four months after releasing his album. Benzino bounced back, but not without a tarnished reputation. Shortly after the circus-ring hoopla surrounding his debut died down, it came out that Benzino secretly co-owned *The Source*. This news explained why the magazine endorsed him so much and perhaps why so many rappers were quick to grant him favors (presumably in exchange for favorable coverage in the influential publication).

Originally known as Raydog, the Boston rapper/producer (born Ray Scott) joined the rap group Almighty RSO in the early '90s. The group didn't attain much success, debuting on Virgin Records in 1996 with *Doomsday: Forever RSO* then quickly disappearing. But Benzino remained busy as part of the production team Hangmen 3. He also busied himself with Made Men, a trio that debuted in 1999 on Restless. In addition to his work with Hangmen 3 and Made Men, Benzino also befriended David Mays, CEO of *The Source*, the rap industry's leading magazine. The specifics are sketchy at best, but somehow Benzino managed to secretly become co-owner of *The Source*. Keeping this in mind, it's no coincidence that Benzino embarked on his solo career in 2001 with much support from his magazine: among other endorsements for his debut album, *The Benzino Project*, he appeared on the cover as well as a fold-out centerfold. Even with the endorsements, however, *The Benzino Project* flopped. Motown dropped the rapper after less than four months of his album's release, citing poor sales (under 75,000 Soundscans) and requesting that the unrecouped balance (773,000 dollars) be compensated with advertising space in *The Source*.

Note, though, that an article published in the December 2001 issue of *GQ* by Maximillian Potter may have had something to do with Motown's decision. In the article, titled "Getting to the Source," Potter detailed the magazine's lack of editorial integrity, drawing from accounts of former *Source* executives such as former music editor Reginald Dennis and cofounder/CEO Mays' original partner, John Shecter. In particular, Potter details Mays' longtime relationship with Benzino, including brushes with the law. The article presented an unfavorable view of both *The Source* and Benzino, perhaps giving Motown yet more incentive beyond sales to drop the troubled rapper. The master tapes to *The Benzino Project* went to Surrender Records, who re-released the album as *The Benzino Remix Project* in 2002. Though tagged as a "remix" album, it differed only slightly from the original Motown release: most notably, different versions of "Bang ta Dis," "Figadoh," and "Boottee" that featured different guests but the same beats.

Benzino decided shortly afterward to launch a press assault on Eminem, eventually releasing the "Pull Your Skirt Up" single, which spouted off several insults toward the white rapper. Targeting Eminem because of his skin color, Benzino's attack was met with an indifferent media, although Eminem offered two strong rebuttals in the form of underground singles. Not to be outdone, Benzino began claiming that the track was a response to racism in America, and started claiming it was the machine he was railing against, not Eminem. But mere weeks after stepping away from these claims, he released another single entitled "Die Another Day," where he called D-12 "house niggas," compared Eminem to David Duke and Hitler, compared himself to Malcolm X, warned Eminem's daughter that she might end up dead, and then chastised other rappers for battling with one another. —*Jason Birchmeier*

The Benzino Project / Oct. 30, 2001 / Motown ✦✦✦

Though this is his debut album, Benzino is no stranger to the rap industry. He began his career as a member of the Almighty RSO and at the time of this album's release was a member of both Made Men and Hangmen 3, the latter one of the rap industry's prominent East Coast production teams. Don't expect *The Benzino Project* to resemble either the previously released Made Men or Hangmen 3 albums too much, however. Here Benzino takes center stage and establishes himself as a charismatic rapper, not afraid to gloat with unexpected eccentricity. He does so with an impressive list of guests: P. Diddy, Outlawz, Scarface, Snoop Dogg, Pink, Foxy Brown, Black Rob, Prodigy, Bobby Brown, Cormega, and Raekwon. The Made Men and Hangmen 3 albums similarly featured an ensemble of guests, but not like this: Benzino brings in the best the industry has to offer here, not a bunch of no-names. You can't help feeling that he's showcasing his industry clout. And he probably is. As part of Hangmen 3, Benzino has worked with many of these artists, and now it's their time to assist him. One unexpected guest who particularly delivers two vital assists is Teddy Riley, the veteran producer who here offers two standout tracks: "Bootiee" and "Figadoh." It's not just these two tracks, though, that offer stunning beats. Actually, every production here is quite stunning. Hangmen 3 clearly can craft beats. Everyone knew that. What everyone didn't know, however, was that Benzino could launch his own solo career with such charisma, something which thankfully compensates for his average-at-best rapping. —*Jason Birchmeier*

The Benzino Remix Project / Jun. 18, 2002 / Red Urban ✦✦✦

After Motown dropped Benzino when his debut album flopped—also partly because of his shady affiliation with *The Source*—they assigned the album's masters to Surrender Records, who then re-released the album as *The Benzino Remix Project*. The idea was to repackage the album and try to give it a second life. The problem, though, is that this "remix" album is essentially the same as the original with only a few exceptions: most notably a different version of "Figadoh" featuring Busta Rhymes and M.O.P., a different version of "Boottee" featuring G. Dep and Fabolous, and an added remix of "Bang ta Dis" featuring Prodigy and Bars & Hooks. Besides these three exceptions, *The Benzino Remix Project* differs very little from *The Benzino Project*. So, as a result, it's best to view this as a re-release rather than a remix album. Anyone who buys both will be quite upset at the almost unnoticable differences. You can't help but feel a bit resentful about the deceptive nature of this re-release. It's intended to be viewed as a remix album, for sure—particularly since it arrived around the same time that the "this is the remix!" phenomenon was sweeping through the rap industry in summer 2002. No, this isn't a remix album. It's simply a revised edition of Benzino's disappointing debut album. It makes few, if any, improvements to remedy what made *The Benzino Project* so disappointing in the first place. —*Jason Birchmeier*

Redemption / Sep. 24, 2002 / Elektra ✦✦

No one exemplifies the term "rap game" quite like Ray Benzino, whose bizarre journey to hip-hop relevancy hits a speed bump nearly every time he releases a record. Circa late 2001, it was the controversy bubbling up around his *Source*-hyped record *The Benzino Project* (all that promotion stemmed from his co-ownership of the magazine). One year later, it was his single "Pull Your Skirt Up," a dis track focused on Eminem, an easy target; Benzino's puerile race baiting fooled no one and, fittingly, sparked a pair of far superior answer tracks from Eminem himself. *Redemption*, Benzino's third straight record on a different label, is supposed to make it all better for hip-hop fans (he helpfully includes the definition of the word on the cover just to make sure they get the point), but it illustrates only that self-promotion is about all this rapper/producer has going for him. He's got moderate skills, but he's no match for 90 percent of the rappers making records for major labels, and his productions hop on nearly every bandwagon he can flag down. Four of the tracks are Hangmen 3 productions, and they're the best here. "Rock the Party," a Mario Winans production (and feature), is far superior to anything else, though guests Jadakiss, Scarface, and Daz Dillinger each get in good rhymes on their tracks. —*John Bush*

B.G.

Southern Rap, Dirty South
Long before the Cash Money camp became known as Cash Money Million-aires, the label got its start hustling albums by a young teen known as B.G., who eventually scored a national anthem with his track "Bling-Bling." Orig-inally known as the Baby Gangsta, B.G. grew up in the dangerous uptown section of New Orleans, among some of the most poverty-ridden areas of America. There he struggled to stay out of trouble and stay in school, yet thrived as a talented young rapper. Two ambitious entrepreneurs, Ronald "Slim" Williams and his brother Bryan "Baby" Williams, heard about the infamous Baby Gangsta and soon signed him to their infantile Cash Money label.

At the alarming age of only 11, B.G. recorded his first album, *True Story* (1993, re-released in 1999), and quickly made a name for himself in the South. The Cash Money brothers rushed the prodigy back into the studio to record yet another album, *Chopper City* (1997), which again captivated the region with its teen gangsta firing off rhymes with the poise of a seasoned veteran. Realizing this was no mere novelty act, the Williams brothers kept shuttling B.G. back into the studio, resulting in two successive follow-ups: *It's All on U, Vol. 1* and *It's All on U, Vol. 2* (both 1997). Around this same time, with the money they had made off the B.G. albums, Cash Money signed a few other local rap artists and created the Hot Boys, a group featuring B.G., Juvenile, Lil' Wayne, and Young Turk. The first Hot Boys album, *Get It How U Live!* (1997), further established B.G. as an up-and-coming rapper.

Following the uncanny success of the Hot Boys' debut in the South and in the Midwest with little to no commercial airplay, the Williams brothers signed a deal with Universal Records in summer 1998 that provided distri-bution, marketing, and promotion support for future Cash Money releases. Now, with this deal signed, B.G.'s next album, *Chopper City in the Ghetto* (1999), surprised many by debuting at number nine on the *Billboard* charts. The album's lead single, "Cash Money Is an Army," supplied some push, but it was the anthemic "Bling-Bling" that hit big. Another Hot Boys album, *Guerrilla Warfare* (1999), followed soon after, driven by the successful single "I Need a Hot Girl," and next, B.G.'s catalog was re-released in the wake of Cash Money's sudden rise to success. In late 2000, long after the Cash Money camp had become a household name, B.G. dropped his sixth solo album, *Checkmate*, led by the single "I Know," only weeks after the release of *Baller Blockin'*, a soundtrack and straight-to-video film also featuring the ever-busy B.G. The rapper then surprisingly parted ways with Cash Money as rumors circulated. He resurfaced a few years later with *Livin' Legend* (2003), which Koch released. —*Jason Birchmeier*

Chopper City / Feb. 26, 1997 / Cash Money ♦♦
Besides the street-level gangsta clichés inherent in tracks like "Niggas N Trouble," "Play'n & Laugh'n," and "All on U," B.G.'s smooth flow and laid-back raps make *Chopper City* a solid album, even packed in the middle of his hec-tic release schedule. The productions on highlights like "Uptown Thang: Wait'n on Your Picture," and "All on U" stick to mid-tempo G-funk, but are inventive and solid nevertheless. —*Keith Farley*

Chopper City in the Ghetto / Apr. 20, 1999 / Uptown/Universal ♦♦♦
B.G.'s *Chopper City in the Ghetto* stands as one of the Cash Money label's greatest accomplishments, notably popularizing the phrase "bling-bling" in the featured hit single of the same name. Here, as well as on other Cash Money albums of the time like Juvenile's *400 Degreez* (1998) and Lil' Wayne's *Tha Block Is Hot* (1999), the Cash Money Millionaires truly are on fire: B.G. and his fellow Hot Boys are blossoming as MCs, and producer Mannie Fresh is perfecting his patented style. In addition to the anthemic single "Bling-Bling," the album also includes "Cash Money Is an Army." As always with golden age Cash Money albums like *Chopper City in the Ghetto*, Fresh produces every track and the other Cash Money Millionaires often guest. —*Jason Birchmeier*

True Story / Jun. 29, 1999 / Uptown/Universal ♦♦
An artifact of Cash Money's earliest era, *True Story* represents the label's humble beginnings in addition to B.G.'s. Cash Money originally released this album in 1995, years before breakthrough hits like "Bling-Bling" and "Back That Azz Up," and later revived it in the wake of B.G.'s breakthrough *Chop-per City in the Ghetto* album in 1999. Unlike the older B.G. of that album, the Baby Gangsta of *True Story* is indeed a baby—barely a teen he is. It's under-standable, then, that the rapper is a little undeveloped. Moreover, producer Mannie Fresh hadn't yet entered his prime either, so the album as a whole seems formative relative to what Cash Money would deliver a few years later, when they re-released *True Story*. —*Jason Birchmeier*

● **Checkmate** / Oct. 31, 2000 / Uptown/Universal ♦♦♦♦
At the time of this album's release in late 2000, a Cash Money backlash had already crept across America among critical rap listeners. Those critics had accused the Cash Money Millionaires of churning out generic rap driven by floss-themed lyrics, a bling-bling mentality, club-style bounce beats, and little imagination. A few songs into *Checkmate*, it seems obvious that this criticism had perhaps crept into the Cash Money camp's consciousness; producer Mannie Fresh takes a much more experimental approach on this album, as B.G. presents a darkened palette of lyrics filled less with blatant hooks than literate rhymes—in sum, this isn't your ordinary Cash Money album. At first, these changes seem welcome. After all, Cash Money's output had begun to get a bit generic, particularly with Juvenile's *Tha G Code* and Big Tymers' *I Got That Work*, albums of singles and recycled filler. But after an initial lis-ten to *Checkmate*, fans of Cash Money's previous output may long for a re-turn to form; this album's conscious aspiration to bring a new sound is often awkward. First of all, Fresh's beats are much more cluttered, filled with lay-ers of synths. Second, B.G. abandons simplicity and hooks, emphasizing his storytelling lyrics instead. In the end, it sounds as if both Fresh and B.G. are truly motivated to step up their game, a motivation that takes the duo away from their original strength: writing simple, radio-friendly, hook-laden club tracks. There aren't "Back That Azz Up"'s here. Even "I Know," the album's lead single, isn't especially catchy. As a result of this album's aspirations to be an out of the ordinary Cash Money release, it demands the listener to be open minded and accept the fact that this isn't a very catchy album, quite the op-posite of Lil' Wayne's simple yet catchy *Lights Out* album released almost si-multaneously. If you want creativity (granted, it's often ill-conceived creativ-ity) rather than sugar-coated hooks, try this album, and make sure to give it a few listens to digest. It definitely has awkward moments, but it also has some rewarding moments such as "Bounce With Me" (truly uncanny beats) and "Hennessey & XTC" (truly comical lyrics), along with other songs such as "U Know How We Do" and "Get in Line" that manage to merge inventive beats with engaging lyrics without resorting to force-fed hooks. —*Jason Birchmeier*

Big Daddy Kane (Antonio Hardy)

b. Sep. 10, 1968, Brooklyn, NY
Golden Age, Hip-Hop, Hardcore Rap, Pop-Rap
Emerging during hip-hop's massive creative expansion of the late '80s, Big Daddy Kane was the ultimate lover man of rap's first decade, yet there was more to him than the stylish wardrobe, gold jewelry, and sophisticated charisma. Kane possessed a prodigious rhyming technique honed from nu-merous b-boy battles; he could also be an Afro-centric consciousness-raiser versed in the philosophy of the Nation of Islam's Five Percent school, or a smooth urban soul crooner whose singing was no match for his talents as an MC. While he never scored much pop-crossover success, his best material ranks among the finest hip-hop of its era, and his sex-drenched persona was enormously influential on countless future would-be players.

Big Daddy Kane was born Antonio Hardy in Brooklyn on September 10, 1968; the stage name "Kane" was an acronym for King Asiatic Nobody's Equal. In 1984, he met Biz Markie, and the two struck up a friendship. Kane would go on to cowrite some of the Biz's best-known raps, and both eventu-ally became important members of the Queens-based Juice Crew, a collective headed by renowned producer Marley Marl. Kane signed with Marl's Cold Chillin' label in 1987 and debuted the following year with the 12" single "Raw," which became an underground sensation. His first album, *Long Live the Kane*, followed not long after and was equally well-received, producing another underground classic in "Ain't No Half-Steppin'." Kane consolidated his success with 1989's *It's a Big Daddy Thing*, which spawned arguably his most effective love-man song in "Smooth Operator" (and also found him working with new-jack producer Teddy Riley on "I Get the Job Done"). 1990's *Taste of Chocolate* was a wide-ranging effort, highlighted by Kane's duets with Barry White and comedian Rudy Ray Moore, aka Dolemite.

Kane's first major misstep came with the 1991 album *Prince of Darkness*, a mellower, more R&B-based collection that failed to play to the rapper's strong suits; however, he maintained his sex-symbol status by posing for Madonna's notorious 1992 photo book *Sex*, as well as *Playgirl* magazine. 1993's *Looks Like a Job For...* was something of an artistic comeback, but it failed to re-establish his status in the hip-hop community, which was in the midst of a Dr. Dre-inspired love affair with gangsta rap. Kane moved to the MCA label for 1994's *Daddy's Home*, and dabbled in an acting career with appearances in Mario Van Peebles' 1993 black Western *Posse* and 1994's *Gunmen*. However, he largely retired from the scene over the next few years. Kane resurfaced in 1998 on Blackheart Records, releasing what was ostensibly his farewell album, *Veteranz Day*. —*Steve Huey*

Long Live the Kane / Jun. 21, 1988 / Cold Chillin' ✦✦✦✦✦
Even though he spends a good 90 percent of the album boasting about his skills and abilities on the microphone, and cutting those of other MCs, Big Daddy Kane consistently proves himself a thrilling artist on his debut album, *Long Live the Kane*, one of the most appealing creations from the original new school of rap. This debut captures the Big Daddy Kane who rocked the house at hip-hop clubs and verbally cut up any and all comers in the late '80s with his articulate precision and locomotive power—the Big Daddy Kane who became an underground legend, the Big Daddy Kane who had the sheer verbal facility and razor-clean dexterity to ambush any MC and exhilarate anyone who witnessed or heard him perform. There are missteps here, to be sure—especially "The Day You're Mine," on which Kane casts himself as a loverman over a stilted drum machine and lackluster, cheesily seductive singing (offering a glimpse of the particular corner into which he would eventually paint himself). But there are also plenty of legitimate early hip-hop classics, none of which have lost an ounce of their power, and all of which serve as reminders of a time and era when hip-hop felt immediate, exciting, fresh, and a little bit dangerous (in the figurative, rather than literal, sense), and when hip-hop spawned commercial tastes of the moment rather than surrendering to them. Although his next album would be nearly the artistic equal of the debut—and, in many ways, even bettered it—Big Daddy Kane would never sound as compelling or as fresh as on this first effort. —*Stanton Swihart*

It's a Big Daddy Thing / Sep. 15, 1989 / Cold Chillin' ✦✦✦✦✦
If Big Daddy Kane's debut album painted him as an enormously talented battle MC, his follow-up, *It's a Big Daddy Thing*, finds him aggressively expanding into new territory and gunning for a wider audience outside the hip-hop faithful. Unlike later efforts, most of it is rousingly successful, making for an album that's arguably just as strong as his near-classic debut. This is where Kane starts to take his place as one of hip-hop's first sex symbols, thanks to the gliding "Smooth Operator," the somewhat dated ballad "To Be Your Man," and the Teddy Riley-produced, new jack swing track "I Get the Job Done." If the latter is a blatant attempt at crossing over, with a vastly different sound than anything else on the album, it's also a player's statement of purpose. Elsewhere, Kane plays the anti-drug, pro-education social commentator, bringing his Nation of Islam beliefs further into the spotlight on tracks like "Another Victory," "Children R the Future," "Calling Mr. Welfare," and "Rap Summary (Lean on Me)." "Pimpin' Ain't Easy" sits a little uneasily alongside that progressive-minded material, not just for its obvious subject matter but for the line where Kane declares himself "anti-faggot"; nonetheless, it remains something of a favorite among fans who look past that slip. And of course, there are plenty of showcases for Kane's near-peerless technique, including "Mortal Combat," a live version of the rare B side "Wrath of Kane," and "Warm It Up, Kane." There's some filler in the second half, like the amusing, blaxploitation-styled "Big Daddy's Theme," but overall *It's a Big Daddy Thing* is a strong, varied album that captures every important side of one of rap's major talents. —*Steve Huey*

Taste of Chocolate / Oct. 30, 1990 / Cold Chillin' ✦✦✦✦
Big Daddy Kane gave one of his most consistent efforts with *Taste of Chocolate*, his third album. Kane not only had first-rate technique and rhyming skills working to this CD's advantage, he also had quite a bit of excellent and varied material to choose from. Though he still spends too much

time bragging about his microphone skills, such hard-hitting numbers as "Mr. Pitiful" and the sobering "Dance With the Devil" show just how substantial he can be. This time, Kane is joined by a number of distinguished guests, including Barry White (who is typically charismatic on the rap ballad "All of Me"), Malcolm X's daughter Gamilah Shabazz (with whom he duets on "Who Am I"), and the raunchy comedian Rudy Ray Moore. When Kane and Moore exchange insults on "Big Daddy Vs. Dolemite" things get outrageously entertaining. —*Alex Henderson*

Prince of Darkness / Oct. 29, 1991 / Cold Chillin' ✦✦
More soul based than his previous records, Kane not only has a slightly changed musical style on *Prince of Darkness* but also changes his rapping style to suit the sound, bringing a faster, twisting wordplay to his rhymes. When the change in style works—as in "I'm Not Ashamed"—the record is deadly, but when it doesn't, it's deadly boring; unfortunately, most of the record doesn't work. —*Stephen Thomas Erlewine*

Looks Like a Job For . . . / May 25, 1993 / Cold Chillin' ✦✦✦✦
After the stylistic missteps and weak self-productions of *Prince of Darkness*, Big Daddy Kane returned to the rhyme with 1993's excellent *Looks Like a Job For...*, an album that updated his sound for the early '90s but left plenty of room for the greatest to freestyle. And led by a pair of TrakMasterz productions, the title track and the casually, hilariously dismissive "How U Get a Record Deal?," it started off incredibly strong. Nearly all of these were the usual battle raps, but Kane also had much to say with tracks like "Rest in Peace" and "Brother Man, Brother Man," the latter featuring him smoothly trading rhymes with his protégé, Lil' Daddy Shane. —*John Bush*

Daddy's Home / Sep. 13, 1994 / MCA ✦✦✦✦
It looks like the return of the loverman on the cover of Big Daddy Kane's sixth LP, *Daddy's Home*, though hardcore fans who bought it anyway were treated to a tight, tough record that alternated classic Kane with a few surprisingly successful detours and enough space to salute the next generation of East Coast hardcore. He set it off on an excellent opener, breaking up his usually quick flow for a few gems of carefully phrased, lyrically lurching rap that make him sound like the return of the drunken master. "Brooklyn Style . . . Laid Out" and the hands-in-the-air jam "In the PJ's" are great double features for Big Daddy Kane and Big Scoob. For the irresistible "Show and Prove," Big Daddy Kane invited a pair of young rappers, Jay-Z and Ol' Dirty Bastard, well before they would appear on their own records (both MCs' styles are definitely in place, and Jay-Z gets in a few zany speed raps). One detour that didn't work was "Don't Do It to Yourself," an attempt at duplicating West Coast G-funk that doesn't come across. Despite a few choruses that sounded a little tired, *Daddy's Home* proved that Kane was still in prime form. —*John Bush*

Veteranz Day / Apr. 28, 1998 / Blackheart ✦✦✦
The Big Daddy Kane who righteously catapulted atop hip-hop's hierarchy with certified classic albums *Long Live the Kane*, and *It's a Big Daddy Thing* unfortunately quickly diminished his impeccable reputation by attempting to become hip-hop's version of Barry White/Dolemite. BDK began to spiral out of control with the release of 1990's *Taste of Chocolate* and he has fought desperately, yet unsuccessfully ever since to recapture his crown. D-Day has finally arrived for Kane, as his seventh and supposedly last (we all know how long MCs stay retired) very appropriately entitled LP *Veteranz Day* is finally ready for mass consumption. Thankfully, Kane seems to have listened to those who clamored for him to bring it back to the streets. Another unexpected twist was that Kane choose almost exclusively to keep things in house, producing all but four of its 13 full-length endeavors. Big Daddy shows his versatility flexing lyrical muscle over "Terra N Ya Era." With "Entraprizin" Kane makes sure to reiterate that the wrath of Kane has yet to cease. The end to end burner here is "Unda Presha," as Daddy spits rhymes galore, going straight for the jugular displaying the killer instincts which were so prevalent in his earlier days. However, all is not well for Kane, as previous shortcomings do eventually creep their way into the setting. Not ready to give up on his prince of darkness alter ego, "Change This Game Around" is a lazy ode to his favorite pastime of hitting skins. Giving it up for the old school he thanks everyone for "2 Da Good Tymz" a clumsy attempt at a club track, which is hampered by unoriginal production. Expectations were low for this project, but this is most definitely Kane's best body of work since *Looks Like a Job For...*, and much more of a cohesive effort then the last debacle he brought forth. Although not breaking any new ground, Kane

does deliver enough quality cuts to keep fans from writing out his death certificate prematurely. —*Matt Conaway*

★ **The Very Best of Big Daddy Kane** / Mar. 6, 2001 / Rhino ✦✦✦✦✦
How do you become a hip-hop legend and still remain somewhat underappreciated? If you're Big Daddy Kane, you hit the scene right after one of the greatest MCs ever to pick up a mic (Rakim), record lots of battle rhymes when your peers (KRS-One, Chuck D) are getting political, and cross over to R&B listeners before hip-hop figured out that it didn't have to compromise to do so. Kane was one of the prime movers behind the quantum leap in lyrical technique that took place during the late '80s, rapping with excellent diction at a more frantic pace than the smooth, effortless-sounding Rakim. Time has been kind to his work, as Rhino's *The Very Best of Big Daddy Kane* demonstrates. Its selections concentrate mostly on Kane's first (and best) two albums, pulling six tracks from *Long Live the Kane* and seven from *It's a Big Daddy Thing.* The opening trio of classics—"Raw," "Set It Off," and "Ain't No Half-Steppin'"—are flawless bids for immortality all by themselves, and haven't lost an ounce of energy, nor has the storming live cut "Wrath of Kane." Despite his reputation as a battle MC, Kane's Nation of Islam beliefs did pop up in the occasional message cut, represented here by "Word to the Mother (Land)" and "Another Victory." And even if they made purists uneasy at the time, Kane's crossover efforts were where his image as hip-hop's leading loverman came together. "Smooth Operator" and "Cause I Can Do It Right" hold up just fine, and while the Teddy Riley-produced "I Get the Job Done" has a jarringly different new-jack sound, the spirit behind it is pretty infectious all the same. (The ballad "Very Special," on the other hand…well, it made the charts.) Even so, there's no better place than this to get acquainted with one of the golden age's greatest rappers. —*Steve Huey*

Big Ed the Assassin

Gangsta Rap, Hardcore Rap, Southern Rap
Starting off his career with TRU (Master P, C-Murder, Silkk), Big Ed—as he was known then—appeared on many tracks throughout No Limit's first commercially successful album, entitled *True*, in 1995. From there, he went on to appear on many singles within the No Limit family, plus his debut album, *The Assassin*, in 1998. With a name change to Big Ed the Assassin and his time away from No Limit under his own label Special Forces Records, he dropped his 2000 effort in the appropriately titled album *Special Forces*. —*Brad Mills*

● **Special Forces** / May 9, 2000 / Special Forces ✦✦✦✦
This is a lengthy effort including appearances by Fiend, C-Murder, Mr. Serv On, and several others. Big Ed brings a bit more lyrical ability than most of the No Limit artists, but with the same hardcore, in-your-face, fast-paced delivery that's become their trademark. Although leaving No Limit for this album, it's pretty hard to tell. The same production style, rapping delivery, guest artists, and overall sound all add up to much of the same thing. This is a solid album, with differing sounds and stories throughout. If you're a fan of No Limit, this album won't disappoint. If you were expecting a change in Big Ed with his new label, you're not going to find it here. —*Brad Mills*

Big Hutch (Gregory Hutchinson)

Vocals, Producer / Hardcore Rap
Gregory Hutchinson, who also goes by Cold 187um and Big Hutch, is among the many gangsta rappers who came out of South Central Los Angeles in the late '80s. Lyrically, the rapper/producer has never been known for his subtlety—many of Hutch's lyrics are graphic, violent, and disturbing accounts of thug life in L.A.'s inner-city neighborhoods. The Southern Californian is best-known for his association with Above the Law, one of South Central L.A.'s most famous (or infamous) gangsta rap groups. Heavily influenced by N.W.A and the seminal Ice-T, Hutch formed Above the Law with fellow L.A. residents Go Mack (Authur Goodman), KMG the Illustrator (Kevin Dulley), and Total K-oss (Anthony Stewart) in 1989. That year, the group caught the attention of late N.W.A member Eazy-E (Eric Wright), who signed ATL to his Ruthless label. Different labels were distributing Ruthless at the time; for N.W.A and Eazy, Ruthless went through Priority, although Ruthless went through Atlantic for the D.O.C. and J.J. Fad. And in the case of ATL, Ruthless was distributed by Epic. Produced with N.W.A's Dr. Dre, ATL's debut album, *Livin' Like Hustlers*, was released by Ruthless/Epic in early 1990. The strong influence of N.W.A and Ice-T was evident throughout the album; rapping in the

first person, Hutch and his colleagues held nothing back and told listeners just how violent and dangerous the ghetto streets of South Central L.A. could be. Hutch, Ice-T, N.W.A, Houston's Geto Boys, Philadelphia's Schoolly D, and other gangsta rappers who emerged in the '80s weren't the first to rap about thug life and the social problems of the inner city. But because they rapped in the first person and took listeners inside the minds of thugs, felons, gang members, drug dealers, pimps, players, and hustlers, many listeners found gangsta rap to be more troubling than the third-person message raps that had been coming from New York since the early '80s. When Grandmaster Flash & the Furious Five, Run-D.M.C., the Fat Boys, and other New York MCs rapped about the problems of the inner city, they stuck to the third person and didn't portray the thugs they were rhyming about; Hutch and other gangsta rappers, however, actually gave listeners a thug's perspective. Hutch, like many other gangsta rappers, has been accused of glorifying and promoting black-on-black crime and he has often countered that he is merely drawing attention to the inner city's problems, not encouraging them. *Livin' Like Hustlers* was a hit, and in 1993, ATL's second album, *Black Mafia Life*, was released by Warner Bros. After providing a third album, *Uncle Sam's Curse*, for Ruthless in 1993, ATL signed with Tommy Boy in 1996 and recorded two albums for that New York label: 1996's *Time Will Reveal* and 1998's *Legends*. Then, in 1999, the group moved to Street Solid, the hip-hop/urban division of producer James Warsinske's L.A.-based Solid Entertainment (formerly AVC Entertainment). At Street Solid, Hutch had two careers, he was still a member of ATL but launched a solo career on the side. ATL's *Forever Rich Thugs* came out on Street Solid in 1999, and Warsinske's label released Hutch's first solo album, *Executive Decisions*, that same year. Along the way, Hutch has done his share of producing; the rappers he produced in the '90s or early 2000s range from Snoop Doggy Dogg, Eazy-E, MC Ren (formerly of N.W.A), and South Gate to Kokane and E-40. Most of the rappers Hutch has produced are West Coast gangsta rappers, although he has also worked with the female group H.W.A. (whose X-rated, sexually explicit lyrics have more in common with Lil' Kim or Luther Campbell and 2 Live Crew than gangsta rap). —*Alex Henderson*

● **Executive Decisions** / Jun. 29, 1999 / Street Solid ✦✦✦
In the late 1990s, Big Hutch, aka Cold 187um, had two careers in music: he was still a member of Above The Law, and with *Executive Decisions*, the L.A.-based gangsta rapper delivered his first album as a solo artist. Although not quite as violent as some of ATL's albums, this CD covers much of the same territory lyrically—after ten years with ATL, Hutch was still rapping about the lives of pimps, players, hustlers, gangsters and high rollers and reflecting on how rough life in South Central L.A. can be. So Hutch's solo debut isn't groundbreaking, but even so, the MC is clever and entertaining enough to hold our attention. Dark, twisted humor was always one of Hutch's strong points, and there's no shortage of it on *Executive Decisions*—much like Martin Scorsese's *Goodfellas* or Quentin Tarantino's *Pulp Fiction*, this CD is amusing and disturbing at the same time. And musically, *Executive Decisions* is easy to admire. Hutch, Chill, DJ Silk, and others who help with the producing all take a cue from Dr. Dre and do their part to give this CD a clean, melodic, sleek type of sound. —*Alex Henderson*

Big L (Lamont Coleman)

b. May 30, 1974, New York, NY, **d.** Feb. 15, 1999
Producer, Vocals / Hip-Hop, East Coast Rap, Club/Dance
A member of Fat Joe's D.I.T.C. crew, rapper Big L was born Lamont Coleman on May 30, 1974. He made his solo debut with 1995's *Lifestylez Ov Da Poor and Dangerous*, scoring a series of underground hits including "No Endz, No Skinz," "Street Struck," and "Da Graveyard"; Big L's best-known effort, the single "Ebonics," followed on his own Flamboyant label in the summer of 1998. Around the same time, he joined the Bronx-based hip-hop supergroup D.I.T.C. (Diggin' in the Crates), appearing on their single, "Dignified Soldiers." On the evening of February 15, 1999, Big L was shot and killed just blocks away from his Harlem home; he was just 24 at the time of his death. Both the D.I.T.C. album *Worldwide* and the second Big L solo effort, *The Big Picture*, followed in 2000. —*Jason Ankeny*

● **Lifestylez Ov Da Poor and Dangerous** / 1995 / Columbia ✦✦✦
Having made a name for himself as a guest MC on D.I.T.C. (Diggin' in the Crates) projects such as Diamond D's *Stunts, Blunts & Hip-Hop* and Showbiz & AG's *Runaway Slave*, the flamboyantly gifted Lamont Coleman (aka Big L)

dropped his debut in early 1995. A product of the mean streets of Harlem, L made his bones in the rap game with his rapid fire freestyle delivery and clever punchline-peppered rhymes. A patchwork album with a few outstanding cuts, *Lifestylez* fails to package the lightning-in-a-bottle talent of this cut-above MC. The album showcases L as a master of the lyrical stickup undressing his competition with kinetic metaphors and a brash comedic repertoire. The lead track, "Put It On," produced by Kid Capri, is a party cut with a criminal attitude. "M.V.P." snatches a brief segment from DeBarge's "Stay With Me" (later aggrandized on the Notorious B.I.G.'s popular remix of "One More Chance"). "Da Graveyard" features a young Cam'ron (here Killa Kam) and most notably a superb verse from a pre-Jigga Jay-Z (at the outset of his solo career). With better production and marketing, Big L might have found himself with a platinum album but instead he settled for platinum respect. This album captures the dynamic potential of a street legend, a legend who would later be gunned down in his prime. —*Micheal Di Bella*

The Big Picture / Jul. 11, 2000 / Priority ✦✦✦
The second and final album from the late Big L showcases the Harlem MC as a master of the punchline and a vicious storyteller with a razor-blade-under-the-tongue flow. Unfortunately, despite a well-meant effort from Rawkus Records, *The Big Picture* fails to capture Big L's underground legacy. A member of the New York underground collective's Diggin' in the Crates crew, L's 1995 debut on Columbia Records, *Lifestylez Ov Da Poor and Dangerous*, was met with a lukewarm response despite his rugged talents. As a result, Big L was dropped from Columbia primarily because *Lifestylez* lacked the supersonic production to match his rough, witty style. On *The Big Picture*, even with a few production heavyweights in on the project, the production is again suspect. The album billed as a classic has merely the makings of one, all-star producers like Pete Rock and Premier and heavyweight guest appearances including a duet with another fallen rap star, Tupac Shakur. There are about five good tracks on the album, two of which are spectacular: "Flamboyant" over a soulful bump provided by Mike Heron is the heavy-hitter on the album followed closely in quality by the flute-laced "Holdin' It Down" produced by Pete Rock and featuring AG "Ebonics" is L's clever slang dictionary and the two DJ Premier-produced tracks, "Platinum Plus" featuring Big Daddy Kane and "The Enemy" featuring Fat Joe, are also worthy of note. Here is an underground king that finds only slight aboveground success posthumously. Rawkus' scramble to compile new and old tracks into a cohesive product proved too difficult a task. In the end, there is too much gloss on this undergrounder's parting project; *The Big Picture* does not do justice to Big L. Big L may be remembered as a gifted MC who put out mediocre albums, but he will not be forgotten by hip-hop fans on the strength of his underground legacy and respect. Big L (1974-1999) was gunned down in his own Harlem neighborhood in early 1999. —*Michael Di Bella*

Big Mike (Michael Banks)

Vocals, Producer / Hip-Hop, Gangsta Rap, Southern Rap
A member of the divergent Rap-A-Lot Records family, based in Houston, Big Mike (aka Michael Banks) first made his name with the Geto Boys. Members Scarface and Bushwick Bill hired him to take the place of Willie D. after a fallout within the group. Mike appeared on the 1993 album *Uncut Dope*, and began his solo career one year later with *Somethin' Serious*, recorded for Rap-A-Lot. When the label signed a deal with Virgin, Big Mike moved as well. His second album, *Still Serious*, hit the Top 20 upon release in April 1997. —*John Bush*

Somethin' Serious / 1994 / Rap-A-Lot ✦✦✦

● **Still Serious** / Apr. 8, 1997 / Noo Trybe ✦✦✦✦
From the outset, Big Mike's delayed second album *Still Serious* signals that it isn't that much different from his debut, *Somethin' Serious*. Big Mike is still working the same Southern rap territory as before—it's simple, straight-ahead funk and hip-hop that occasionally dips into gangstaland. The production is as simple as the music, and its smooth, funky grooves let Mike's rhymes move to the foreground. This time around, he has a more measured and reasoned attitude toward gangstas and guns, and his preaching helps balance the party raps that form the bulk of the album. *Still Serious* doesn't offer anything new or unique, but what it does offer is good indeed. —*Leo Stanley*

Hard to Hit / May 25, 1999 / Priority ✦✦✦

Big Moe

Dirty South, Underground Rap, Southern Rap
Houston bred a growing scene of homegrown rap artists throughout the mid-to late '90s, and Big Moe became one of the first to break out of Texas and go national. Unlike most of the Houston rappers, who tended to offer a hardcore style, Moe offered a much more accessible one. He both rapped and sang, and his producers crafted smooth, melodic tracks that bounced along at a leisurely pace. Plus, he precisely balanced the fine line between the underground and mainstream. Moe's songs were often street themed, with intoxicants being a prime theme; yet they were simultaneously radio friendly and hook laden, with his breakthrough single, "Purple Stuff," being a perfect example.

Like many of his Houston peers, Moe began his career freestyling on DJ Screw's mix tapes before graduating to Wreckshop Records. The label released the big man's debut album, *City of Syrup* (2000), the title nodding to Houston's reputation for drinking codeine-laced syrup, which Moe pours from a Styrofoam cup on the album's cover. *City of Syrup* featured a noteworthy hit, "Mann!," that Moe intended to be the dirty South's answer to Black Rob's East Coast hit "Whoa!" His intentions proved successful, and listeners rewarded him with a reputation-establishing hit. A year and half later, Moe returned with his second album, *Purple World* (2002), the album that would introduce him to the world. It offered a who's who ensemble of Houston vocalists, excellent production by Blue and Salih Williams, and two versions of Moe's breakthrough single, "Purple Stuff." Plus, Priority Records distributed the album, ensuring that it would be everywhere, from the street corners of Houston to the Wal-Marts of suburban America. Even MTV gave Moe's *Willy Wonka and the Chocolate Factory*-themed video a few rotations. —*Jason Birchmeier*

City of Syrup / Jul. 18, 2000 / Wreckshop ✦✦✦
Before anyone knew who Big Moe was following the release of his debut, *City of Syrup*, they knew the cover to his album. It catches your eye: Moe—they call him "big" for a reason, by the way—standing over an outline of Houston's skyline, pouring out a large Styrofoam cup of purple stuff. If you were down with the dirty South, you knew what the purple stuff was. If not, you were baffled. Either way, the cover art caught your eye. But that's just the album cover. The real surprise came when you listened to the album and realized that Moe wasn't just another of the seemingly myriad Screwed Up Click members. No, he was much more than that. He can rap, he can sing, and he can do both very well. Plus, Moe wasn't afraid to exploit Houston's syrup-sippin' reputation to his benefit. Doing so worked for Three 6 Mafia, and the big man made it work for himself. Plus, Moe had another noteworthy feature that made *City of Syrup* worth investigating: "Mann!," a song that he intended as the dirty South's answer to Black Rob's East Coast anthem, "Whoa." It all worked: the syrup-pouring cover, Moe's sing-rapping, and "Mann!" In the end, *City of Syrup* became the surprise album of 2000—at least down South, that is. But this album never spread too far from Houston like Moe's later recordings would. It's an underground album. It may have plenty of hooks and much to offer overall, but it's also awfully lo-fi. Still, even if *City of Syrup* doesn't have the studio polish of *Purple World*, it's a successful album, an album so successful it surprised nearly everyone who heard it. —*Jason Birchmeier*

● **Purple World** / Apr. 23, 2002 / Priority ✦✦✦✦
To most urban/rap listeners, the Houston rap scene seemed more of a curious oddity than a serious breeding ground for great music. *Purple World* convincingly argues otherwise. It's a great album, plain and simple, on a par with the best albums that came out of New York, Atlanta, and Los Angeles in 2002. The real beauty of *Purple World*, though, is how Big Moe sticks with his Houston peers. No, the Neptunes and Dr. Dre don't produce any tracks here, nor will you find P. Diddy or Snoop Dogg on *Purple World*. Instead, Moe teams up with Houston's finest: Lil' Keke, Lil' Flip, Hawk, D-Gotti, Big Pokey, Ronnie Spencer, and more. Plus, he works exclusively with producers Blue and Salih Williams, one of the keys to why *Purple World* is so amazing. These two may not be well known, but they're incredibly talented. They have their own style—smooth, melodic tracks that bounce along at a leisurely pace—yet they're also not afraid to replay elements of popular songs like "Just the Two of Us" and "I Just Wanna Love U (Give It 2 Me)." The resulting beats are incredibly unique, much like Moe's sing-rapping. The big guy sings on every song, but his hooks never overwhelm the rapping. It's truly the best of both

worlds. *Purple World*, and particularly the hit "Purple Stuff," cross the boundary between hardcore rap and pop-rap, offering you both at once. This, more than anything, is why it crossed over when so many other Houston artists failed to do so in the early 2000s. It appeals to everyone, from thugs to your little sister. —*Jason Birchmeier*

Big Noyd

Hip-Hop, Hardcore Rap

Big Noyd first made his name as an MC on the Mobb Deep albums *The Infamous* and *Hell on Earth*. After the release of the latter in 1996, Big Noyd released his own album, *Episodes of a Hustla*, for Tommy Boy Records. The album gained a spot on the R&B charts later that year. —*John Bush*

● **Episodes of a Hustla** / Sep. 16, 1996 / Tommy Boy ◆◆◆
At the dawn of the 1990s, most New York rappers weren't nearly as threatening as the gangsta rappers who were coming from the West Coast. But Queens took a more threatening turn later in the decade, when the borough gave us such hardcore rappers as Capone-N-Noreaga and Mobb Deep. These guys were all of the things that California's gangsta rappers had been criticized for being—violent, profane, crude and menacing. Another MC who came out of that scene was Big Noyd, who was featured on some of Mobb Deep's albums before recording his first solo project, *Episodes of a Hustla*. Most of the CD was produced by Mobb Deep's Havoc, whose partner Prodigy is featured on some of the material. As hardcore as this decent, though uneven, effort is, tunes like "Infamous Mobb," "It's On You," and "Recognize and Realize" really aren't gangsta rap (even though some consider Noyd a gangsta rapper). While Ice-T, the Geto Boys and N.W.A offered first-person narratives about crime in the ghetto, Noyd's approach is more rhetorical than anything. Noyd uses violent, disturbing imagery to create an atmosphere, but unlike Ice-T or Ice Cube, he's more interested in showing off his rhyming skills than making an overall statement about inner-city life. The end result is an album that, unlike N.W.A's *Straight Outta Compton* or Ice Cube's *Death Certificate*, isn't saying very much, but isn't without entertainment value. —*Alex Henderson*

Big Pokey

b. Houston, TX

Southern Rap, Dirty South, Gangsta Rap, Underground Rap

One of the more accomplished members of the Screwed Up Click, Big Pokey hooked up with DJ Screw in the early '90s and started dropping rhymes on the DJ's many mix tapes. His first full-length album finally appeared in 1999, *Hardest Pit in the Litter*, which ended up being one of the better underground albums to come out of the South that year. A year later, Pokey returned with *D-Game 2000*, another album of mid-tempo 808-driven beats featuring several of his Houston peers as guests. In 2001 he collaborated with the Wreckshop Wolfpack for *Collabo* and then returned in 2002 with another solo album, *Da Sky's da Limit*. Blessed with a Notorious B.I.G.-like rap style, Pokey had spent a few years playing football and studying kinesiology at Abilene Christian College before finally deciding to dedicate himself to rapping. —*Jason Birchmeier*

● **Hardest Pit in the Litter** / May 18, 1999 / Uptown/Universal ◆◆◆
Big Pokey's major-label debut, *Hardest Pit in the Litter*, is firmly entrenched in dirty South tradition, borrowing from such hardcore Texas rappers as the Geto Boys. The music itself doesn't show much imagination—it's basically lean, spare, hard hitting, and heavy on the bass—but Big Pokey is a strong rapper. True, he doesn't show much range as far as his topics go, but his rhymes have energy, which elevates *Hardest Pit in the Litter* to slightly above average status, even though the material is a little too uneven. —*Stephen Thomas Erlewine*

D-Game 2000 / Aug. 22, 2000 / Chevis ◆◆

Big Punisher (Christopher Rios)

b. Nov. 10, 1971, Bronx, NY, **d.** Feb. 7, 2000, White Plains, NY

Gangsta Rap, East Coast Rap, Hardcore Rap, Latin Rap

The first solo Latino rapper to go platinum, Big Punisher was also yet another member of the hip-hop community to fall victim to an early death—though in his case, it was due to health problems, not violence. In contrast to his large frame, Big Pun was a surprisingly graceful and nimble rapper, delivering his often clever, tongue-twisting rhymes at a torrential pace. Big Pun was born

Christopher Rios on November 10, 1971, and grew up in the South Bronx's Puerto Rican community. He endured a rough childhood in an unstable home, and moved out when he was 15, dropping out of high school around the same time. Still, he continued his education on his own, and became interested in rapping and breakdancing (he was a solid athlete during his teen years). In 1989, under the name Big Moon Dog, he and several friends formed a street-corner rap group called the Full a Clips Crew. He later changed his name to Big Punisher, after the Marvel Comics superhero, and caught his big break when he met and impressed fellow Bronx rapper Fat Joe in 1995. He guested on a couple of Fat Joe tracks, "Fire Water" (which also featured Raekwon) and "Watch Out," and following an appearance on Funkmaster Flex's *The Mix Tape, Vol. 1*, quickly made a name for himself in the underground community. He guested prominently on the Beatnuts' "Off the Books" in 1997, and also worked with B Real and Flesh-N-Bone. Pun scored an underground hit of his own with "I'm Not a Player" in 1997, and also contributed "You Ain't a Killer" to the *Soul in the Hole* basketball documentary. With Fat Joe's help, he secured a deal with Loud Records. Big Pun's solo debut, *Capital Punishment*, was released in 1998 and debuted in the Top Five thanks to "Still Not a Player," a club-ready remix of "I'm Not a Player" that proved massively popular. Earning credibility in the hardcore rap world as well, *Capital Punishment* went on to sell over two million copies.

The following year, Pun teamed up with his mentor, Fat Joe, and several up-and-coming MCs to form the Terror Squad, which released a self-titled debut album. Pun stayed in the public eye with guest work on records by Noreaga and Jennifer Lopez (the hit "Feelin' So Good," which also featured Fat Joe) while working on his second album. Unfortunately, his longtime struggles with overeating and obesity were beginning to get the better of him. At Fat Joe's urging, he checked into a weight-loss clinic in North Carolina, where he lost 80 pounds. However, he returned to the Bronx before finishing the program and gained back everything he'd lost, plus some extra; reports had his weight fluctuating between 450 and 700 pounds during his last few years. Tragically, but perhaps not unpredictably, Big Punisher suffered a fatal heart attack on February 7, 2000; he was only 28 years old, and left behind a wife and three children. His completed second album, *Yeeeah Baby*, was released two months later to positive reviews and entered the charts at number three. 2001's *Endangered Species* was a compilation mixing hits, guest appearances, and unreleased material; it, too, was a Top Ten seller. Big Pun's life was the subject of the 2002 documentary film *Still Not a Player*. —*Steve Huey*

● **Capital Punishment** / Apr. 28, 1998 / Relativity ◆◆◆◆
Big Punisher's debut album, *Capital Punishment*, established him as one of the stronger New York natives working hardcore rap territory toward the end of the '90s. He's a terrific lyricist with microphone technique to spare, and actually rhymes faster than his clear influence, the Notorious B.I.G.. He's also quite versatile, aiming for the dance clubs, the ladies, the hip-hop purists, and the mean streets at varying points on the album, and connecting with all of them pretty well. Similarly, the production—by a cast of many—is tough and funky, paced by deep street beats, but remains accessible to audiences outside the hardcore faithful. The close cousins "I'm Not a Player" and "Still Not a Player," the latter Big Pun's breakthrough hit, manage to be cocky and self-deprecating at the same time, and the other widely exposed track, "You Ain't a Killer," is Big Pun at his grittiest. There are numerous guest appearances, the best of which include mentor Fat Joe (on several tracks), the Roots' Black Thought on the MC showcase "Super Lyrical," Prodigy and Inspectah Deck on "Tres Leches (Triboro Trilogy)," and an extra-insane Busta Rhymes on "Parental Discretion." *Capital Punishment* isn't quite a classic—for one thing, it's too long, and for another, it doesn't really break much new ground stylistically—but it's very well executed, and demonstrates just how much talent and potential Big Punisher had. —*Steve Huey*

Yeeeah Baby / Apr. 11, 2000 / Loud ◆◆◆◆
Arriving just two months after his death from a heart attack, Big Pun's second album *Yeeeah Baby* proves the rapper's demise was doubly tragic. Of course, the death of anyone at a young age is a tragedy in itself, but *Yeeeah Baby* displays an artist evolving beyond his previous work with remarkable ease. On the highlights "Watch Those," "Off Wit His Head," and "New York Giants," Pun spits out inventive rhymes and paces his delivery with excellence, more than proving that he should be considered in the Top Ten list for late-'90s MCs—among considerable competition (DMX, Jay-Z, Method Man). He also salutes his Latin heritage all over the album, switching from street

slang to Latin lingo without batting an eye, and working a flute *charanga* sample on "100%." Despite a variety of track masters throughout the album, *Yeeeah Baby* is quite seamless, thanks no doubt to friend and partner Fat Joe (the executive producer) as well as Pun himself. He would've been proud. —*John Bush*

Endangered Species / Mar. 27, 2001 / Relativity ✦✦✦✦
At the age of 28, Big Pun joined a long list of deceased rappers who left fans too early. *Endangered Species* is a compilation of much of Pun's best work. All of Pun's hits are included here, including "It's So Hard" and the infectious dancefloor filler "Still Not a Player." Also included are several of Pun's most memorable guest appearances, such as his cameo on the Beatnuts classic "Off the Books," as well as some of his work with Terror Squad. Most of Big Pun's fans will buy the album for unreleased material such as "Mama" and "Wishful Thinking," a collaboration with Kool G Rap and Cypress Hill's B Real. While the unreleased material may not be Big Pun's best work, it will not disappoint his fans. The album includes some of Pun's remixes of pop hits like Ricky Martin's "Livin' la Vida Loca" and Brandy's "Sittin' on Top of the World." Taken as a whole, the album is an impressive document of an artist that truly was a force to be reckoned with. —*Jon Azpiri*

Big Tiger

b. Houston, TX
Southern Rap
Representing Houston, TX, Big Tiger is one of the first artists out of the Swisha House International record label. His big break came with the track "Big Ballin', Shot Callin'" from Swisha House's debut *The Day Hell Broke Loose* in 1999. The song was a hometown hit in Texas and neighboring Louisiana, and set the stage for his own debut album, *I Came to Wreck*, in 2001. —*Brad Mills*

I Came to Wreck / Aug. 7, 2001 / Swisha House International ✦✦✦
The highly anticipated album from Big Tiger will be a welcome addition for many Southern gangsta rap fans. Compared with some of the stuff coming out of the South in 2001, he's a lyrical genius. The beats fit his rhyming style, with smooth bass lines and interesting sampling. There have been a lot of expectations given to the Swisha House label to put out some quality music, and this is a decent beginning for one of its headlining acts. There are plenty of guest appearances here, with Mista Masta, Archie Lee, AD, Al Bolden, and Big Pic each surfacing several times. Highlight tracks are "Tiger Is His Name," "Grippin Grain," and two of Tiger's solo tracks, "Ex-Girlfriend" and "Steal Off," work really well. —*Brad Mills*

Big Tymers

f. 1998, New Orleans, LA
Group / Dirty South, Gangsta Rap
Comprised of Bryan "Baby" Williams, Cash Money Records' cofounder, and Mannie Fresh, the label's in-house producer, Big Tymers incorporated substantial outside talent into their ranks and scored some huge hits in the process. Beginning with the duo's first release in 1998, *How You Luv That?* (re-released as *How You Luv That?, Vol. 2* later that year), Big Tymers featured all of the rappers on Cash Money's roster: initially Lil' Wayne, B.G., Juvenile, and Turk; later T.Q., Boo, and Gotti; and others as well. This plethora of outside assistance served many purposes, among them promoting the label's solo artists and also taking some of the spotlight off from Williams and Fresh, who admittedly weren't two of the label's better rappers, recognized instead for their overly brash style of ghetto haughtiness. The two drastically improved their rapping, and more importantly their songwriting, for *I Got That Work* (2000) and *Hood Rich* (2002), their second and third albums, respectively. These albums spawned two sizable hits a piece—"Get Your Roll On" and "#1 Stunna" on the former, "Still Fly" and "Oh Yeah!" on the latter—and made Big Tymers the most consistent Cash Money act following the departure of Juvenile from the label. —*Jason Birchmeier*

How You Luv That? / Mar. 17, 1998 / Cash Money ✦✦
Putting aside their production roles for a bit, Brian "Baby" Williams and Mannie Fresh pick up the microphone for *How You Luv That?* and with much outside assistance deliver an album highlighted by a few standout songs early in the proceedings. As with most Cash Money releases, the highlights come immediately—"Playboy (Don't Hate Me)," "Stun'n," "Tear It Up," and "How U Luv That?"—followed by a sizable drop-off, which signals the

turn toward guest-laden semipromotional filler. These latter tracks, featuring performances by Hot Boys Lil' Wayne, B.G., and Juvenile among others, are somewhat hit-and-miss, often dependent upon whether or not the hooks catch you. Despite its sometimes weak moments, *How You Luv That?* remains one of the best early releases by Cash Money and will give you a great taste of how the successful label began. (Cash Money re-released *How You Luv That?* as *How You Luv That?, Vol. 2* in late 1998 after signing its distribution deal with Universal Records. This re-release substitutes a remix of "Stun'n" for the original version and adds "Big Ballin'," "Money & Power," and "Drop It Like It's Hot.") —*Jason Birchmeier*

I Got That Work / May 16, 2000 / Cash Money ✦✦✦
Big Tymers Brian "Baby" Williams and Mannie Fresh step up their game a bit for *I Got That Work*, improving both as rappers and songwriters and delivering two big hits in the process, "Get Your Roll On" and "#1 Stunna." *How You Luv That?*, the duo's debut release two years earlier, had set the Big Tymers apart from the other, and considerably younger, Cash Money Records group, the Hot Boys. Unlike like them, the Big Tymers are full-fledged adults; in fact, Williams and Fresh produce the Hot Boys and thus play father-figure roles within the Cash Money family to a certain extent. Yet, for as much game as they can spit, the Big Tymers proved to be so-so rappers on *How You Luv That?*, often overshadowed by their Hot Boy protégés. However, during the two-year interim leading up to *I Got That Work*, Williams and Fresh considerably improved as rappers. Here, they're as good as any of the Hot Boys, whether it be Lil' Wayne, B.G., Turk, or Juvenile, and they certainly boast and brag better, whether about money making ("10 Wayz," "We Hustle"), bling-blinging ("#1 Stunna," "Stuntastic"), women mastering ("Snake," "Rocky"), or themselves ("Big Tymers," "Hard Life"). Moreover, the Big Tymers deliver a rambunctious club-banger with the album-opening "Get Your Roll On." Following this rowdy beginning, the album moves toward its other highlights—"Nigga Couldn't Know," "#1 Stunna," and "No, No"—before descending into guest-laden complacency. As usual, Fresh's beats remain affecting until the album's end, but the songwriting grows progressively less so, often seeming unlabored, as if the Big Tymers are content to ride out the remainder of their 18-track album after delivering the early-album highlights. Regardless of this common grievance, the Big Tymers impressively step up their game for *I Got That Work* and deliver enough highlights to surely appease their fans. —*Jason Birchmeier*

● **Hood Rich** / Apr. 30, 2002 / Cash Money ✦✦✦✦
Hood Rich showcases many of the changes that occurred within the Cash Money camp during the two years since the Big Tymers' previous album, *I Got That Work* (2000). Most notably among these changes, the Hot Boys—Lil' Wayne, B.G., Turk, and Juvenile—make no appearances here after being prominently featured on past releases, replaced by several newcomers: Tateeze, Boo, Gotti, T.Q., and Mikkey. Moreover, for the first time ever, the Big Tymers bring in an outside producer, Jazze Pha, to complement the tireless Mannie Fresh. As you may presume given the Big Tymers' past reliance on the Hot Boys's rapping and Fresh's beats, this shuffling of personnel consequently broadens the duo's style. The Big Tymers embrace different styles of songwriting and incorporate more harmonious hooks after having taken somewhat of an assembly-line approach on past releases. The album-opening singles, "Oh Yeah" and "Still Fly," stand out as clear evidence, both songs going with sang rather than chanted hooks. The remainder of the album generally continues on in this mode, offering a significant scope of variety in the process. Even so, *Hood Rich* really doesn't move too far away from what the duo had been doing previously. Baby and Fresh boast more than ever, mostly about cars, money, and women as always, and the two are just as street as ever despite the omnipresent singalong hooks. Longtime Cash Money fans, however, will surely miss the Hot Boys and perhaps the less-polished sound of past releases, but the Big Tymers have made changes for the better. *Hood Rich* is by far their most accomplished album yet and also their most mature. It's an increasingly artistic step toward mainstream acceptance that's importantly subtle—not so big of a step that it will turn away longtime fans but big enough to draw in more listeners than ever. —*Jason Birchmeier*

Bigg Nastee (Nebraska Franklin)

Hip-Hop, Hardcore Rap
Based out of Chicago, IL, Nebraska Franklin—aka Bigg Nastee—worked his way up in the local hip-hop scene throughout the mid-'90s and would have released a full-length in 1996 if it wasn't for his conflicts with the label Island

Black Music. For the next three years, Nastee would eventually land gigs across the country—notably in Los Angeles, Detroit, New York, and Miami— and a chance to perform with such acts as the Wu-Tang Clan, Too Short, Goodie Mob, Outkast, and Da Brat, among others. With all this experience under his belt, another deal came about through a division of Mercury Records in 1999, resulting in the release of *My Life, Dreams and Feelings*. —*Mike DaRonco*

My Life, Dreams and Feelings / Aug. 10, 1999 / Crash ♦♦♦
The brainchild of Chicago's Nebraska Franklin, *My Life, Dreams and Feelings*, showcases his talents at rapping, crooning, writing songs, and even playing an instrument or two. The single "It Done Been One" is a highlight, fusing rhymes and romance with a special flair rarely seen in contemporary R&B. —*Keith Farley*

Biz Markie (Marcel Hall)

b. Apr. 8, 1964, Harlem, NY
Golden Age, East Coast Rap, Comedy Rap, Pop-Rap
Biz Markie's inclination toward juvenile humor and his fondness for goofy, tuneless, half-sung choruses camouflaged his true talents as a freestyle rhymer. Biz may not have been able to translate his wild rhyming talents to tape, but what he did record was worthwhile in its own way. With his silly humor and inventive, sample-laden productions, he proved that hip-hop could be funny and melodic, without sacrificing its street credibility. His distinctive style made his second album, *The Biz Never Sleeps*, a gold hit and its single "Just a Friend" into a Top Ten pop single. While its success made Biz a semistar, it also cursed him. Not only was he consigned as a novelty act, but it brought enough attention to him that Gilbert O'Sullivan sued him over the unauthorized sample of "Alone Again (Naturally)" on Biz's 1991 album, *I Need a Haircut*. The lawsuit severely cut into his career, and 1993's *All Samples Cleared!* was the last record he released during the '90s. However, Biz's reputation was restored somewhat in the mid-'90s, as the Beastie Boys championed him, and other alternative rap groups showed some debt to his wild, careening music.

A native of New York, Biz (born Marcel Hall) first came to prominence in the early '80s, when he began rapping at Manhattan nightclubs like the Funhouse and the Roxy. Biz met producer Marley Marl in 1985, and began working as a human beatbox for Marl-connected acts MC Shan and, later, Roxanne Shanté. He also recorded his first set of demos, and by 1988, had signed with Cold Chillin'. Later that year, he released his debut, *Goin' Off*, which became a word-of-mouth hit based on the underground hit singles "Vapors," "Pickin' Boogers," and "Make the Music With Your Mouth, Biz." A year later, he broke into the mainstream when "Just a Friend," a single featuring rapped verses and out-of-tune sang choruses, reached the pop Top Ten, and its accompanying album, *The Biz Never Sleeps*, went gold.

The Biz Never Sleeps put him near the top of the hip-hop world, but he fell from grace as quickly as he achieved it. Biz's third album, *I Need a Haircut*, was already shaping up to be a considerable sales disappointment when he was served a lawsuit from Gilbert O'Sullivan, who claimed that the album's "Alone Again" featured an unauthorized sample of his hit "Alone Again (Naturally)." O'Sullivan won the case in a ruling that drastically changed the rules of hip-hop. According to the ruling, Warner Bros., the parent company of Cold Chillin', had to pull *I Need a Haircut* from circulation, and all companies had to clear samples fully before releasing a hip-hop record. Biz countered with his 1993 album, *All Samples Cleared!*, but his career had already been hurt by the lawsuit, and the record bombed. For the remainder of the decade, he kept a low profile, occasionally guesting on records by the Beastie Boys and filming a freestyle television commercial for MTV2 in 1996. The alliance with the Beasties raised his profile considerably, but Biz didn't record any further solo albums and instead began DJing. —*Stephen Thomas Erlewine*

Goin' Off / Feb. 23, 1988 / Cold Chillin' ♦♦♦♦♦
The Cold Chillin' class clown, Biz Markie debuted with *Goin' Off*, one of the most unrelentingly amusing sets of productions and performances of anyone during hip-hop's golden age. Markie was an oversized teenager with lyrical talents (if not finesse) far beyond his years, and material opposed to most every rapper around—trading in nightclubs for the mall and striking a pose for picking your nose. Yes, the rhymes were often rudimentary or obvious (and many of the best were actually written by Big Daddy Kane), but his infectious optimism and winning flair (plus the masterful production of Marley

Marl) carried Biz Markie far beyond the status of a novelty act. His first single, "Make the Music With Your Mouth, Biz," introduced him as a human beatbox, but he went on from there to encompass a straight-ahead but hilarious game of the dozens ("Nobody Beats the Biz"), a tribute to his favorite haunts around Brooklyn ("Albee Square Mall"), and a track with some wry cynicism about the price of fame ("Vapors"). The rangy Marley Marl cued up some classic backing tracks for these songs, with any hint of braggadocio counteracted by his carnival-esque production sense. Since a 1995 reissue on Cold Chillin' substituted new Marley Marl remixes for a few of the originals, it's best to spring for the 2001 two-fer *Goin' Off/The Biz Never Sleeps*. —*John Bush*

The Biz Never Sleeps / Oct. 10, 1989 / Cold Chillin' ♦♦♦♦
On the cover to *The Biz Never Sleeps*, Biz Markie's in the lab with his chemistry set, cooking up a concoction of colorful liquids that's bound to explode sooner or later. Inside, however, the music wasn't quite as dynamic; Markie decided to produce and write this record entirely by himself, instead of relying on help from Cold Chillin' beatmaster Marley Marl (who'd produced his excellent debut). The results veered dangerously close to the standard indulgent sophomore album, though Markie's natural charm and a blockbuster hit ended up carrying the proceedings. It certainly didn't start out very well, the opener being a long-winded "Dedications" that was little more than the title indicated, and "The Dragon," a one-joke track about odd smells. Rap fans with a sense of humor, however, were willing to forgive nearly anything after hearing "Just a Friend," the result of an intriguing story rap interspersed with a bizarre bout of crooning that, once again, ably demonstrated how far Biz's charm could take him (in this case, all the way to the Top Ten). "Spring Again" and "I Hear Music" were yet more loopy productions with a universal theme, while Markie even sounded intoxicating while freestyling about a nonexistent dance over a simple loop ("Mudd Foot"). It was obvious the (teenage) lunatics had been released from the asylum; the wonders of technology allowed the Biz and T.J. Swan to have their thank-you lists superimposed, inside the credits, on their bared boxer shorts. —*John Bush*

I Need a Haircut / Aug. 27, 1991 / Cold Chillin' ♦♦♦
Biz Markie, rap's clown prince, can usually be counted on to deliver goofy humor, and *I Need a Haircut* is as wildly entertaining as anything he's ever done. Biz isn't one to rap about his sexual prowess, drive-by shootings near the projects, or Louis Farrakhan's ideology. In contrast to the sobering gangster rap of N.W.A and Ice-T, the angry political protests of Public Enemy and Boogie Down Productions, and the machismo of LL Cool J, Biz Markie seeks only to amuse, entertain, and have fun. Indeed, rap doesn't get much sillier than "T.S.R. (Toilet Stool Rap)" and "Kung Fu." The Brooklyn native's third album also contains "Alone Again," the song that incorporated Gilbert O'Sullivan's pop hit "Alone Again Naturally" (allegedly without the pop singer's permission) and inspired a major lawsuit. —*Alex Henderson*

All Samples Cleared! / Jun. 22, 1993 / Cold Chillin' ♦♦♦
Chastened by his court battle over a sample from pop crooner Gilbert O'Sullivan, Biz Markie returned with *All Samples Cleared!*, a safe record, both legally and artistically. Sampling conservatively, Markie nevertheless opened with a forceful statement of purpose ("I'm the Biz Markie"), but elsewhere hoped for another hit with the same blend of great storytelling and artless balladeering that had made "Just a Friend" his only Top Ten hit. "Young Girl Bluez," one of the few outside productions, was a solid return to form, but his reinvention as a disco diva for "Let Me Turn You On" was a step too far. *All Samples Cleared!* had a few amusing songs, including "I'm a Ugly Nigga (So What)" and "The Gator (Dance)," as well as an interesting blend of humor with social topic ("Hooker Got a Boyfriend"), but for the most part Biz Markie was keeping his head down, and it showed. —*John Bush*

Biz's Baddest Beats / Jul. 1, 1994 / Cold Chillin' ♦♦♦♦

★ **The Best of Cold Chillin'** / Oct. 17, 2000 / Landspeed ♦♦♦♦♦
Much more than just the clown prince of hip-hop during the late '80s and early '90s, Biz Markie was one of the golden age's most talented, distinctive, and inventive rappers whether he was talking about his skills on the mic ("Nobody Beats the Biz") or his favorite brand of spaghetti sauce ("Biz Is Goin' Off"). And like the other acts on the Cold Chillin' label, he benefited from one of the era's greatest producers, Marley Marl. Led by Marl's raw, drum-heavy tracks and great scratching, *The Best of Cold Chillin'* is a definitive look back for rap fans, gathering 17 tracks from the Biz's four LPs for

the label and wisely balancing trademark hits like "Just a Friend" and "Vapors" with rare, early material like the solo human-beatbox number "One Two." The compilation also focuses heavily on his first two albums, with tracks from 1988's seminal *Goin' Off* and the following year's breakout *The Biz Never Sleeps. —John Bush*

Goin' Off/The Biz Never Sleeps / Jun. 26, 2001 / Landspeed ✦✦✦✦✦
Following on from the 2000 release *The Best of Cold Chillin',* Landspeed packaged Biz Markie's first two LPs, 1988's *Goin' Off* and 1989's *The Biz Never Sleeps,* into this two-fer package. Just like the best-of, this one has almost all of his favorite tracks—"Pickin Boogers," "Vapors," "Make the Music With Your Mouth Biz," "Nobody Beats the Biz," "Just a Friend," and "Biz in Harmony." Yes, it does add a few that the best-of didn't have, but there are a few great tracks missing to recommend it to any but the most committed fans. If *The Best of Cold Chillin'* wasn't enough for you, this is the logical next step. —*John Bush*

Greatest Hits / May 7, 2002 / Landspeed ✦✦✦
In mid-2002, for reasons unclear, Landspeed Records supplanted their own excellent *The Best of Cold Chillin'* volume covering Biz Markie with the shorter *Greatest Hits.* It, too, covers all of the Biz's seminal hits—"Nobody Beats the Biz," "Make the Music With Your Mouth, Biz," "Vapors," "Just a Friend"—but misses out on some great early material. The only reason to recommend *Greatest Hits* over *The Best of Cold Chillin'* is the tacking of Biz Markie's 2001 comeback single, "Turn tha Party Out"—though it's also on the turn-back-the-clock, various-artists compilation *Superrappin', Vol. 2. —John Bush*

Black Dave

Hip-Hop
After appearing on releases by Kilo and Da Organization, rapper Black Dave released his debut album, *Next Stop the Ghetto,* on Triad in 1998; the first single, "This Is Not 4 Free," appeared on the *Dollar* soundtrack, while the second, "Big Mama (Go Big Girl)," became a Top Ten hit on *Billboard*'s rap singles chart in 1999. —*Steve Huey*

Next Stop the Ghetto / Sep. 15, 1998 / Triad ✦✦✦
Led by the largely positive anthem "Big Mama (Go Big Girl)" as well as by mildly pleasant sex tracks like "1-900-Got No Love" and "Grind Grind," Big Dave's *Next Stop the Ghetto* rolls along on a low-riding G-funk cushion. —*Keith Farley*

Black Dynasty

f. Oakland, CA
Group / West Coast Rap
Although not a huge name in hip-hop, Oakland, CA, gangsta rap outfit Black Dynasty had a regional Bay Area hit when they recorded their 1995 single "Deep East Oakland." Locally, the song became an anthem; just as Boogie Down Productions' "South Bronx" was a favorite in the Big Apple (especially the Bronx) and N.W.A represented Compton, CA, "Deep East Oakland" celebrated the eastern part of the city that offered everyone from Too Short and Digital Underground to MC Hammer and Oaktown's 357. But Black Dynasty was active in the Bay Area several years before "Deep East Oakland" was recorded. The group actually goes back to the late '80s, when Kariem Abdullah and his brother Dion Stewart started performing together. By the end of the '80s, Oakland had come to be recognized as a major player in the hip-hop field; the X-rated Too Short and pop-rapper Hammer had exploded commercially, and Black Dynasty launched their recording career with a 1990 EP titled *8-Ball in the Corner Pocket* (which was released by a small local label called Flammy Flam Records). In 1993, Black Dynasty provided their first full-length album, *Asphalt Jungle,* which sold about 10,000 copies (mostly in the Bay Area). In 1995, they put out their second album, *Deep East Oakland,* which sold over 20,000 copies thanks to the title song. It was also in 1995 that Black Dynasty went on tour with Too Short and Compton gangsta rapper DJ Quik, but after that, things went downhill for the group. Stewart was shot and killed by an Oakland convenience store owner during a failed robbery attempt, and Black Dynasty ended up going on hiatus. After Stewart's death, some fans assumed that Black Dynasty was history, but in 2002, Abdullah decided to resurrect Black Dynasty and recorded *Reality Check: Deep East,* the group's first album in seven years. Released on the independent Community Musician label, *Reality Check* opens with "Deep East Oakland,

Part II (Reality Check)"—a sequel to the original "Deep East Oakland"—and is dedicated to Stewart. —*Alex Henderson*

Reality Check: Deep East / Oct. 8, 2002 / Community Musician ✦✦✦
Some rappers become internationally famous by representing the 'hood; thanks to N.W.A, rap fans in Stockholm, Sweden, and Milan, Italy, have learned a lot about Compton, CA, and its social problems even if they have never visited North America. For other MCs, however, representing the 'hood can mean more local than national or international success—and the 'hood could be anywhere from Memphis to São Paulo, Brazil, to Warsaw, Poland. For Black Dynasty, the 'hood is East Oakland. That's the area that the West Coast group celebrated on its 1995 single "Deep East Oakland," which became a big local anthem in the Bay Area even though it wasn't a huge seller in other regions of the United States. After the death of group member Dion Stewart—who was shot and killed by an Oakland convenience store owner during a failed robbery attempt—Black Dynasty went on hiatus. *Reality Check,* a 2002 effort, is their first release in seven years. This CD opens with "Deep East Oakland, Pt. II (Reality Check)," which is a sequel to the original "Deep East Oakland" and sets the tone for the rest of the album. *Reality Check* is typical West Coast gangsta rap, and the material employs the usual playa/baller/pimpin' imagery that one expects from this type of group. Lyrically, there's nothing groundbreaking about the album; Black Dynasty's Kariem Abdullah doesn't say anything that Dr. Dre, Above the Law, DJ Quik, and Compton's Most Wanted weren't saying ten years earlier. Nonetheless, most of the tunes are enjoyably funky, and Abdullah does have a likable way of riding a P-funk-influenced groove. *Reality Check* won't go down in history as one of rap's all-time masterpieces, but it's a decent, if derivative, comeback for the Oakland outfit. —*Alex Henderson*

Black Eyed Peas

f. Los Angeles, CA
Group / Hip-Hop, Alternative Rap
Positive messages and breakdancing are integral parts of hip-hop culture, but by 1990 those elements had been temporarily eclipsed by the tough gangster image and bleak but compelling lyrics of West Coast groups like N.W.A. However, despite sharing a zip code, Black Eyed Peas' vision goes beyond the cracked-sidewalk vignettes and sampled gunfire of Los Angeles' gangster style. The socially conscious group's earliest connections go back to high school, when Will I Am and Apl de Ap were part of Tribal Nation, a breakdancing crew. Eventually the pair focused more on music—hip-hop, specifically—and split off into their own as Atban Klann, their esoteric name an acronym for A Tribe Beyond A Nation. Eazy-E's Ruthless Records signed the group in 1992, but many in the Ruthless camp were puzzled by the group and the enthusiasm of Eazy, who had no problem reconciling his own gangster style with the peace-minded breakdancing of Atban. Although an album was recorded, Ruthless shelved it, unsure how to market a group whose style wasn't dependent on violent braggadocio like N.W.A.

The death of Eazy-E in 1995 signaled the end of any further deals with Ruthless. Undaunted by the experience, Will and Apl recruited another dancer/MC, Taboo, and reappeared as Black Eyed Peas. BEP began playing shows around L.A., impressing hip-hop fans with their mic skills and dazzling them with their footwork as well. In 1998 their debut, *Behind the Front,* was released to critical acclaim—not only for the trio of MCs, but for their live band and backing vocalist Kim Hill as well. Featuring guest appearances from Jurassic 5's Chali 2na, De La Soul, and Macy Gray, BEP's sophomore effort, *Bridging the Gap,* was released in 2000. —*Wade Kergan*

● **Behind the Front** / Jun. 30, 1998 / Interscope ✦✦✦✦
Black Eyed Peas bring some positivity and fun back into hip-hop. Musically there is almost no realm this group does not touch—right from the jump, the stylistic innocence of "Fallen Up," complete with striking guitar licks, sums up what BEP is all about. They attack the so-called hardcore MCs playing the role of dress-up: "I see you try to dis our function by stating that we can't rap/Is it cuz we don't wear Tommy Hilfiger or baseball caps?/We don't use dollars to represent/We just use our innocence and talent." The wonderfully crafted, old school-influenced first single, "Joints and Jam," is perfect for the summertime frame of mind. With "Karma" they explore the notion of reaping what you sow. "Love Won't Wait" is a simultaneous infusion of R&B and hip-hop, as the group deals with a deteriorating romance. But the undisputed champ of this recording is "Positivity"—you can't help but reminisce about

yesteryear's MCs kicking conscious lyrics to educate the hip-hop masses. "Nowadays it's hard to make a living/But easy to make a killing/Cuz people walk around with just one inch of feeling/I feeling nauseated from your evil drug dealing/Blood spilling, the definition of top billing." In all honesty, the MCs who make up BEP—Taboo, Will, and A8—are not going to be confused as being superlyrical by any means. But their chemistry and insightful, original topic matter is used with enough efficiency to mask that slight blemish. —*Matt Conaway*

Bridging the Gap / Sep. 2000 / Interscope ◆◆◆◆
Is this the real thing or a substitute? In 1998, Black Eyed Peas released their debut, *Behind the Front*, and by most accounts, it snugly filled a hole left behind by the absent, optimistic talents of A Tribe Called Quest and De La Soul. So in the same year that Jurassic 5 complete their first proper release and De La Soul finally return, is there any room for a group like BEP anymore? Well, maybe. While the album fails in its titular intention of bringing together the two exclusionary worlds of rap and rock, it still diligently follows in the footsteps of its predecessor's highs. Maybe one might have to look toward Kim Hill—the group's backing vocalist—who seems to have a larger impact this time. Hill hovers over terrific sun-streaked ditties like "Tell Your Mama Come" and the irrepressible "Hot" without a hitch. The other collaborations follow her lead too. From Macy Gray to Les Nubians to Mos Def to, yes, even Jurassic 5 and De La Soul, none of these guest artists feel out of place or contrived. Undoubtedly, this second release finally proves that BEP get to mark their own territory in the history of old school, soulful—and playful—hip-hop. Because *Bridging the Gap* is a terrific follow-up full of warmth. Unlike what the advertisements might say, this is a multiethnic, multifaceted substitute that should be accepted immediately. —*Dean Carlson*

Black Jesus

Underground Rap
Indiana rapper Black Jesus first gained national exposure with his song "What That Thing Smell Like"—and its accompanying video—which was popular enough to maintain a nine-month reign on BET's late-night program *Un-Cut*. The Midwest MC began as a concert promoter in the mid-'90s with his own production company, Scrilla Entertainment. In 2000 he helped form Before and After Records, and the following year Black Jesus became the label's breakout artist with "What That Thing Smell Like." —*Wade Kergan*

Black Moon

Group / Hip-Hop, Underground Rap
They didn't gain as much critical hype as other acts in the independent rap scene (perhaps due to a laid-back release schedule), but Black Moon have been one of its better acts. Buckshot, 5ft., and DJ Evil Dee debuted in 1993 with *Enta da Stage*, an excellent album with plenty of old school vibes on singles like "How Many MCs" and "Who Got the Props." The remix album *Diggin' in dah Vaults* followed in 1996, and second album *War Zone* finally appeared in early 1999. —*John Bush*

● **Enta da Stage** / Nov. 15, 1993 / Nervous ◆◆◆◆◆
Released in 1993, Black Moon's debut *Enta da Stage* was a real departure from the high-energy extroverted hip-hop of the time. MCs Buckshot and 5ft. Accelerator (though Buckshot dominates) attack their verses with an aggressive nihilism not heard since Kool G Rap's peak. Theirs is a grim reality, filled with guns, weed, and violence. Buckshot displays none of the usual ganster remorse; he is a willful public menace. The Beatminerz production crew craft subtereanean beats to match Buckshot's mayhem. The tracks are dark, layered with muted jazz samples, and seemingly bottomless. *Enta da Stage* is hip-hop made for headphones and basements rather than for the clubs. It set the tone for much of the hip-hop to follow. Biggie Smalls suicidal thoughts and Noreaga's boisterous thuggery both have their roots here. The album marked a turning point in hip-hop. —*Christopher Witt*

Diggin' in dah Vaults / Oct. 29, 1996 / Wreck/Nervous ◆◆◆
With its first single, "Who Got the Props," Black Moon earned instant underground status. The cut eventually led to the equally outstanding *Enta da Stage*, which continued to mine the hazed-out jazzy vibe of "Props" as well as its street-savvy, quintessentially New York vocal style. It took longer than expected, however, for that album to appear. During the recording process, the trio produced a wealth of material that didn't make the album's final cut, and in the wake of the critical praise lavished on the debut as well as the fan

demand created by it, Nervous Records decided to round up some of those unreleased tracks and couple them with remixes and previously uncollected single sides for the compilation *Diggin' in dah Vaults*. It is understandably not as consistent in sound as the group's debut, but Black Moon managed to turn that into an attribute. Specifically, the group split the album almost right down the middle and imbued each side with its own general tone and atmosphere. The first half is markedly unlike the mellow production values of the debut. The updated "Act Like U Want It," for instance, dispenses with the playful bass line and steady beat of the original album in favor of a funky piano figure and chaotic, siren-filled atmosphere. The other remixes go through more or less similar metamorphoses, while the new tracks follow in turn, ranging from the straight-up street corner exercise of "Buckshots Freestyle Joint" to the exuberant afternoon jam "F*ck It Up." The mood then shifts back to the viscous souled-out, after-hours sound that characterized *Enta da Stage*, as if following the trio through a city day and then on into the urban night, from a sweatier, more in-your-face feel—all concrete and traffic and metallic sounds and swagger—in the former half to cool, shadow-filled, chill-out tracks in the latter. Both styles suit Black Moon—and the listener—just fine. —*Stanton Swihart*

War Zone / Feb. 23, 1999 / Priority ◆◆◆◆
Returning with their sophomore record almost six years after their debut, Black Moon recruited Busta Rhymes, Q-Tip, Cocoa Brovaz, and Da Beatminerz (for production). *War Zone* has a lush, old school flavor (especially on the single "Two Turntables and a Mic") and giving one of the tracks ("Evil Dee Is on the Mix") makes *War Zone* better than the average rap album circa 1999. —*Keith Farley*

Black Rob (Robert Ross)

East Coast Rap, Hip-Hop, Gangsta Rap
Bad Boy Records rapper Black Rob began his recording career appearing on albums like the Cru's *Da Dirty 30* and collaborating with artists like L.O.X., Busta Rhymes, Lil' Kim, and Total before releasing his first album, *Life Story*, in 1999. The debut featured the hit single "Whoa!" and appearances from L.O.X., Cheryl Riley, the Goodie Mob's Cee-Lo, and Carl Thomas. —*Heather Phares*

Life Story / Sep. 28, 1999 / Bad Boy ◆◆◆
After the Notorious B.I.G. was killed, Puffy Combs spent a lot of time trying to fill the big man's shoes. To this end, the Bad Boy label chief has enlisted a slew of substitutes, creating a catalog of dance-friendly, thug-life chronicles of high-life fantasies and gritty realities. Enter Harlem native Black Rob. A competent MC with a guttural delivery that recalls the smooth, reserved style of the late B.I.G., Black Rob constructs explicit tales with hooks you can feel and lyrics that stick. On a disc that includes support from Mase, Jennifer Lopez, Puff Daddy, and the Lox, Black Rob details hard street life replete with pain, death, and stark honesty. With 20 thoroughly bruising cuts, Black Rob's debut may just succeed in helping Puff Daddy regain the street credibility lost when Combs achieved mainstream/crossover status. —*Roxanne Blanford*

Black Sheep

f. 1990, Bronx, NY
Group / Golden Age, Hip-Hop, Alternative Rap, East Coast Rap
Remembered for a couple of striking singles and their membership in the Native Tongues family of groups, Black Sheep also recorded one of rap music's most entertaining debuts, *A Wolf in Sheep's Clothing*. Handling both production and delivery, Dres and Mista Lawnge appeared headed for a long, rewarding career, but unfortunately faded after the release of their long-delayed sophomore set.

Both members, Andre Titus (Dres) and William McLean (Mista Lawnge), were natives of New York who grew up in North Carolina. Titus the son of a military man. Both were also hip-hop fans during the mid-'80s, Dres as an MC and Mista Lawnge as a DJ. Looking for a record contract, Lawnge moved to New York—where he'd spent time as a child—and played a gig with DJ Red Alert, who introduced him to Mike Gee of the Jungle Brothers. Gee's connection to the newly christened Native Tongues family (headed by Afrika Bambaataa along with Queen Latifah) inspired Lawnge to form Black Sheep and recruit Dres as the group's MC. The duo's first release, "Flavor of the Month," was one of the hottest rap singles of 1991, and the ascendancy of Native Tongues groups De La Soul and A Tribe Called Quest only improved

Black Sheep's fortunes. Their debut album, *A Wolf in Sheep's Clothing*, released on Mercury late that year, hit number 30 on the album charts and the next single, "The Choice Is Yours," was an MTV hit (thanks to director Chuck Stone's video) and a surprising success at college radio (aside from specialty shows, rap rarely appeared on college play lists). The album eventually moved close to one million copies, and the pair appeared on the Brand New Heavies' *Heavy Rhyme Experience, Vol. 1* next to the era's hottest rappers: Main Source, Gang Starr, Kool G Rap, and the Pharcyde.

Black Sheep's follow-up, *Non-Fiction*, was doomed from the start. Released in 1994, the record received close to zero promotion and lacked the imagination of *A Wolf in Sheep's Clothing.* The single "Without a Doubt" got a little airplay, but the duo split soon after. Both worked on varying projects, and Dres released his solo debut, *Sure Shot Redemption*, in 1999. (One year later, he appeared in the film *Once in the Life*, Laurence Fishburne's debut as a director, playing a bagman for a drug kingpin.) Black Sheep reunited to produce a track for the film's soundtrack, toured with Das EFX, and announced the recording of a new album. —*John Bush*

★ **A Wolf in Sheep's Clothing** / Oct. 22, 1991 / Mercury ✦✦✦✦✦
Playfully satirical, witty, and incredibly imaginative, *A Wolf in Sheep's Clothing* introduced one of the freshest talents in early-'90s rap, a self-produced duo who caught the tail end of the Native Tongues family. Though Dres and Mista Lawnge didn't match the brilliant wordplay of A Tribe Called Quest or De La Soul, their topics were well-chosen, presented in a hilarious context, and backed up by strong productions and great rapping. *A Wolf in Sheep's Clothing* wasn't a comedy record, but it was difficult to tell the difference between half-serious or half-joking, especially since they were often the objects of their jokes. They poked fun at many aspects of black music and culture of the early '90s, everything from the persuasive gangster mentality ("U Mean I'm Not") to groups obsessed with the Afro-centric viewpoint ("Are You Mad?"), and sex raps ("La Menage"), as well as a amusingly incorrect response to feminism ("L.A.S.M."). They also dropped a few of the best hip-hop club tracks of the era, including insanely catchy items like "The Choice Is Yours (Revisited)," "Try Counting Sheep," and "Flavor of the Month." (Another smooth dance tune, "Strobelite Honey," was dreadfully honest about girls who look better under the lights than on closer inspection.) Polar opposites to the ranks of somber political rappers, and deftly counteracting the indulgence and self-seriousness of many alternative groups, Black Sheep hit a height with their debut that few hip-hop acts ever would. —*John Bush*

Non-Fiction / Dec. 6, 1994 / Mercury ✦✦
Three years isn't an especially long time between albums, but in hip-hop an epoch separated 1991 from 1994. That made it especially difficult for Black Sheep to follow up their prescient debut, and unfortunately, it appeared they'd run out of significant ideas after just one LP. *Non-Fiction* is bland where *A Wolf in Sheep's Clothing* was exciting, stiff, and rigid instead of dexterous, and most astonishing of all, unreflective and self-serious where their debut had been imaginative and playful. "Autobiographical" is an interesting opener, telling the story of Black Sheep's transition from New York to Carolina and back, but despite some smooth raps and interesting wordplay, nothing else here says anything. The smooth club single "Without a Doubt" is the only track catchy enough to rank with the first record, and Black Sheep's sharp social critiques were entirely missing. Similar to the Pharcyde, their stylistic brothers from the West Coast, the sophomore slump hit Black Sheep particularly hard, and practically destroyed them as creative artists. —*John Bush*

Quint Black (Quinton Banks)

Hardcore Rap, West Coast Rap
A onetime hip-hop producer whose list of credits includes work with Too Short, MC Breed, E-40, and Daz Dillinger, rapper Quint Black (born Quinton Banks) made his solo debut with *Dirty Rice*, released on Short Records in 1999. —*Jason Ankeny*

Dirty Rice / Aug. 24, 1999 / Jive ✦✦✦
Quint Black got his big break through Too Short, the all-time king of rhymes about pimping, which makes Black's musical background in gospel rather amusing in this context. Too Short makes a guest appearance on Black's debut disc, *Dirty Rice*, which mixes gospel-influenced soul and R&B sounds (although definitely not subject matter) with typical Southern rap grooves and well-done production touches. The subject matter is nothing all that

different from legions of other late-'90s rap releases, but Black's rhyming is competent, and there's no reason this shouldn't appeal to fans of that now-standard hip-hop fare, even if the philosophizing sometimes seems knee-jerk and poorly thought through. —*Steve Huey*

Blackalicious

f. 1992, Davis, California
Group / West Coast Rap, Underground Rap, Hip-Hop
Like a few other West Coast rap acts, including the Pharcyde and Jurassic 5, Blackalicious has generally favored what hip-hoppers call the "positive tip"; in other words, its lyrics have often been spiritual and uplifting rather than violent or misogynous. Like a lot of experimental alternative rappers, Blackalicious can be quirky and eccentric; nonetheless, spirituality is a big part of the group's music. Although Blackalicious wasn't formed until the early '90s, some of its members had known each other since the late '80s. Founding members Gift of Gab (T.J. Parker) and Chief Xcel (Xavier Mosley) first met in Sacramento, CA, in 1987 when they were students at John F. Kennedy High School. Neither of them was originally from Sacramento; DJ/producer Xcel (who was going by DJ IceSki at the time) was a native of the San Francisco Bay Area, while rapper Gift of Gab was from Los Angeles' suburban San Fernando Valley. They went their separate ways after the Gift of Gab (also known as Gabby T) graduated from Kennedy High in 1989, but were reunited in Davis, CA, in 1992. By that time, Xcel had become a student at the University of California at Davis and the Gift of Gab moved to Davis to form Blackalicious with him. U.C. Davis was where Xcel had started working with a hip-hop outfit called the SoleSides Crew, whose members included DJ Shadow, Lateef the Truth Speaker, and Lyrics Born, and in 1992, the SoleSides Crew became part of Blackalicious. SoleSides Records was the name of the SoleSides Crew's Northern California record company and in 1994, that label released Blackalicious' debut single "Swan Lake." Although not a triple-platinum smash, the single was a small underground hit that fared well among alternative rap audiences. The following year, SoleSides Records released a Blackalicious EP titled *Melodica*. By late 1997, SoleSides Records had gone out of business; however, it soon re-emerged as Quannum Records. In 1999, Quannum put out a Blackalicious EP, titled *A2G*, and in 2000, Quannum released the group's full-length album *NIA* (whose title is the Swahili word for purpose). After being together eight years, Blackalicious finally signed with a major label when, in late 2000, the Californians were signed by MCA. In April 2002, MCA released Blackalicious' full-length album *Blazing Arrow*, which boasts guest appearances by artists who range from vocalist Zack de la Rocha (of Rage Against the Machine fame) to the Roots' ?uestlove to veteran soul singer Gil Scott-Heron. —*Alex Henderson*

Melodica EP / Jul. 31, 1995 / SoleSides ✦✦✦
As only the second release from the underground Bay Area hip-hop label then known as SoleSides, Blackalicious' *Melodica* is an admirable effort that gives a glimpse of the group's potential. Unlike the more funky and aggressive sounds that populate their later releases, *Melodica* leans more toward a smoky and groovy vibe that is reminiscent of early-'90s hip-hop like Digable Planets and A Tribe Called Quest. When they truly click on tracks like "Lyric Fathom" and "Rhymes for the Deaf, Dumb & Blind," producer Chief Xcel and MC the Gift of Gab prove to be an engaging duo. Most of the other songs, including the successful single "Swan Lake," feature more sparse and laid-back beats that sometimes overstay their welcome and lead to gratuitously long tracks. Despite more references to getting high and drunk than the social and musical discourse of *NIA*, the Gift of Gab shines brightest on *Melodica*, firmly asserting on almost every song that he is just as dexterous and gifted as any other underground or mainstream MC. Because it is not easy to find, this album is probably best suited for the true fan who is rounding out their Blackalicious collection. For everyone else, most of its best tracks are featured on *SoleSides Greatest Bumps*, which also features labelmates and *Melodica* contributors DJ Shadow, Lateef the Truth Speaker, and Lyrics Born. —*Lee Meyer*

A2G EP / Jun. 22, 1999 / Quannum ✦✦✦✦
An EP meant to hold fans' attention between the exceptional *Melodica* and its full-length follow-up, *NIA*, *A2G* definitely didn't find the duo in a holding pattern. In fact, the album contains some mind-blowing moments, especially the highly original, Cut Chemist-produced album closer, "Alphabet Aerobics," a riveting overhaul and reinvention of "A to G" that went on to become an impressive concert staple and showcase for the constantly brilliant Gift of

Gab, one of the very finest MCs to ever pick up a microphone. While Chemist's track alone—building from a spare mid-tempo thump into a blazing electronic maelstrom by progressively piling on the samples and ratcheting up the bpms—is as innovative as hip-hop gets, he is trumped by Gift of Gab, who goes through the alphabet letter by letter, two lines apiece. By the time he hits x, y, and z, he is spitting out lyrics with astonishing verbal virtuosity. But he barely outshines Chief Xcel, who, par for the course with the entire Quannum Projects crew, loads the music with clever samples and newfangled beats (especially on the funk-laced "Clockwork") to keep things ever inventive. —*Stanton Swihart*

NIA / Feb. 8, 2000 / Quannum Projects ✦✦✦✦✦
After recording a string of singles and EPs stretching back to 1994, the Blackalicious duo finally released their full-length debut, *NIA*, in early 2000. It's an album that stakes the claim of Chief Xcel and Gift of Gab as not only the best pair of rappers in the underground but also the best pair of producers. As could be expected from an urban-underground crew, Blackalicious look back to earthy jazz-funk, rare-groove, and sampladelic old school rap for their sound. Still, the productions on tracks like the great opening bout "The Fabulous Ones," "Do This My Way," and the tongue-twisting alphabet song "A to G" are much rawer and deeper—and just plain better—than most any underground rap crew could manage. And as good as these tracks are, the raps are even better. Chief Xcel and Gift of Gab stay deep in the groove, switching between straight-ahead solo rhyming, sing-speak vocals, and one-two choruses with almost as many rapping styles as there are tracks. There's just a little too much material here—19 tracks spread across 74 minutes—but *NIA* is an excellent tribute to the growing vitality of the rap underground. —*John Bush*

● Blazing Arrow / Apr. 30, 2002 / MCA ✦✦✦✦✦
The late '90s ushered in a second golden age of progressive hip-hop, as a group of ambitious young lions rose from the underground to redefine the art of lyrical technique and revive the idea that hip-hop had relevant statements to make. With their 2000 debut album, Blackalicious established themselves as one of the West Coast's top outfits in this vein, and while it was very good, their follow-up, *Blazing Arrow*, is simply fantastic, vaulting the duo to the forefront of the progressive hip-hop pack. Much of *Blazing Arrow* retains *NIA*'s airy, laconic feel, but the group's sense of craft has improved to a startling degree; the hooks are sharper and more plentiful, Gift of Gab's rhymes are denser, Chief Xcel's production is more breathtakingly lush, and his arrangements more sophisticated. What's more, the tracks draw from a rich sonic palette—not just the expected jazz-funk and old school influences, but straight pop (check the Nilsson sample on the title track) and smooth soul (particularly the Philly variety, but also the contemporary neo-soul revival) in particular. In spite of the duo's intellectual bent, the grooves on *Blazing Arrow* exude a tremendous warmth that's only complemented by the positivity of their messages. And if Gift of Gab wasn't recognized among hip-hop's premier lyricists before, he certainly ought to be now; his raps are jampacked with internal rhymes, allusions, metaphors, ten-cent words, and amazing tongue-twisting feats of skill. Guests include members of Jurassic 5, Dilated Peoples, and Latyrx (all worthy company), not to mention singer/songwriter Ben Harper, Zack de la Rocha (Rage Against the Machine), and the legendary Gil Scott-Heron. All the pieces add up to not just one of the best rap albums of 2002, but one of the richest, most captivating albums to emerge from hip-hop's artsy new underground. —*Steve Huey*

Blackstreet

f. 1994, db. 1999
Group / Hip-Hop, Urban, Club/Dance, New Jack Swing
One of the top R&B vocal groups of the '90s, Blackstreet was founded by singer, producer, and new jack swing pioneer Teddy Riley after the breakup of his seminal trio Guy. Riley had taken a few years to concentrate on his booming production career, which saw him working with Wreckx-N-Effect, Bobby Brown, Michael Jackson, and SWV, among others. His itch to get back in the performing arena resulted in the formation of Blackstreet in 1994, which included singers Chauncey "Black" Hannibal, Levi Little, and Joe Stonestreet in addition to Riley. Stonestreet was replaced by Dave Hollister prior to the recording of the group's self-titled debut album, which appeared in the spring of 1994. On the strength of "Before I Let You Go," a Top Five hit on the R&B charts, *Blackstreet* was a platinum-selling hit even without much

crossover exposure. Two more singles from the album, "Booti Call" and "Joy," were minor hits as well. Hollister subsequently left for a solo career and Little exited as well; their replacements were Mark Middleton and Eric Williams. The new additions helped set the stage for Blackstreet's pop breakthrough with 1996's *Another Level*. More specifically, it was the inescapable smash single "No Diggity," which featured special guest Dr. Dre, that put them over the top. "No Diggity" reigned for four weeks on top of the pop charts and won a Grammy for Best R&B Vocal by a Duo or Group; it also pushed sales of *Another Level* past the four million mark. The follow-up single, "Don't Leave Me," was a decent-sized hit in 1997, and the group later made a guest appearance on Jay-Z's "The City Is Mine" and teamed with Mya and Mase for the hit "Take Me There" from the *Rugrats* soundtrack.

More personnel shifts had ensued following their blockbuster success, however: Middleton left for his own solo career and was replaced by Terrell Phillips. Blackstreet's third album, *Finally*, was released in early 1999, and though it contained "Take Me There" (and a bevy of guest cameos), it spent only one week in the Top Ten. The group's commercial momentum had slowed in the intervening years, and *Finally* struggled to go gold. Tensions within the group and with their label, Interscope, ran high, and a rift between Hannibal and Riley spelled the end of the road for Blackstreet before the year was even out. Reports surfaced in early 2000 that Hannibal had sued Riley for $2 million, but after Riley filed a countersuit, Hannibal denied that he had ever taken legal action and the matter was dropped. Riley recorded a reunion album with Guy in 2000, and subsequently began working on material for his first solo record. However, he had second thoughts about disbanding Blackstreet, and patched things up with Hannibal; Middleton and Williams returned to restore the *Another Level* lineup, and Riley's solo project became a Blackstreet reunion. The resulting album, *Level II*, was released in early 2003. —*Steve Huey*

Blackstreet / 1994 / Interscope ✦✦✦
Teddy Riley is an impeccable craftsman and genius of sorts, not to mention a trendsetter. In releasing so much product, however, his music can also occasionally descend into a pedestrian, formulaic version of new jack swing, the production style he himself invented, fine-tuned, and perfected. That pitfall plays out intermittently on Blackstreet's debut album. Some of the music and vocal harmonies blend together or sound like new-jack retreads, and a handful of the songs are so commercially savvy and obviously directed toward the mainstream public that it is hard to wholly enjoy them. Some of the songs, too, are less than fully formed, consisting of just a single melody or groove that exists for the sole purpose of moving feet and/or giving the quartet an excuse to harmonize. More often, however, Blackstreet hits the spot with a sleek and inventive progression on the new-jack template, sharpening and filling out the sound that Guy made famous. Riley makes sure the beats are hip-hop savvy and the bass is booming, and then slathers squealing synthesizer lines all over them. Frankly, he is not technically a fantastic singer, at least in comparison to his three harmonizing mates, but his voice has such a distinctive character that it has always been entirely ingratiating, making up in expressiveness for any lack in range or virtuosity. The songs on which he takes lead invariably stand out and tend to be the most appealing cuts. The glue on the album, though, is the tight four-part harmony singing of Blackstreet, and it leads to some brilliantly catchy R&B tracks, songs that easily stood out in the mid-'90s urban soul crowd. —*Stanton Swihart*

● Another Level / Sep. 9, 1996 / Interscope ✦✦✦✦
Powered by the massive hit single "No Diggity," *Another Level* is arguably the finest album created by Teddy Riley, the leader of Blackstreet. Riley has masterminded an album that blends street-level rhythms with urban soul and pop crossover potential, adding two new members—Eric Williams and Mark Middleton—to the lineup in order to position Blackstreet as an heir to the classic R&B vocal group tradition. The realignment works, since the group sounds fuller and more eclectic with the two added voices. But the key to the success of *Another Level* is Riley's songwriting, which is by and large catchy and inventive, whether he is writing ballads or party jams. *Another Level* sags a bit halfway through—it's hard to sustain interest for a nearly 70-minute album—but it has enough strong moments to make it an enjoyable listen. —*Stephen Thomas Erlewine*

Finally / Mar. 23, 1999 / Interscope ✦✦✦
The title is a not-so-subtle admission that it took a little longer than expected for Blackstreet's third album to hit the shelves. Delays are commonplace in

pop music, but they're not welcome, since part of the game is capitalizing on recent successes—in this case, that would have been "No Diggity," a Teddy Riley masterpiece that broke Blackstreet big. *Finally* didn't arrive quickly enough to expand on that success, but it feels as if it could have followed shortly after *Another Level*, since Riley doesn't really expand his sound that much on the third record. That's not to say it isn't enjoyable, since Riley knows how to make infectious funk and seductive ballads. He also knows that cameos sell a record, and he's loaded this disc with appearances from celebrities like Stevie Wonder and Janet Jackson. It's fun to hear the guests appear, but it takes away from Blackstreet somewhat, especially since the guests are the only noteworthy things on a few cuts. Nevertheless, there's no discounting Riley's skills, and he delivers some dynamic grooves and soothing slow jams throughout the record. They're not radically different from those on *Another Level*, but in a way, they don't need to be. At their best, Riley and Blackstreet are among the best '90s new-jack soul has to offer, and there's just enough of the group at their best on *Finally* to make it worth the wait. —*Stephen Thomas Erlewine*

Bavu Blakes

Hip-Hop, Southern Rap
Bavu Blakes is originally from Dallas, but after attending the University of Texas in Austin, he stayed in the "live music capital of the world" to leave his own musical mark. A conversational MC capable of both pointed criticism and witty lyricisms, Blakes' unique style is intellectual without being boring. In other words, his beats are still tight. Blakes was instrumental in the further establishment of Austin's nascent hip-hop scene with the formation of Hip Hop Humpday. A loose collective of DJs, MCs, musicians, and artists, Humpday was built around Blakes, Tee Double, and Tray God. Each Wednesday at Club Mercury on Austin's 6th Street, the Humpday crew would present freestyle battles, live music, performances, and the best tracks from around the globe. It was a hodgepodge of unpredictability, but one that supported the city's burgeoning scene. In 2002, Word4Word released *Create & Hustle*, Blakes' full-length debut. A concept album of sorts, the album presented the daily life of Blakes as a struggling artist grappling with a difficult world. Critiques of hip-hop culture and more personal moments intersected with downtempo grooves and live jazz instrumentation, making for a solid debut. In February of 2003, Blakes appeared as a guest MC on Hydroponic Sound System's *Synthesis* EP. —*Johnny Loftus*

● **Create & Hustle** / 2002 / Word4Word ✦✦✦
Bavu Blakes makes hip-hop sensible once again for those who have become disillusioned by music made by marketing gimmick. His conversational style of MCing presents the modern black American experience in succinct and honest fashion. Opening the album by stating that "I'm not down with being inferior to nobody," Bavu goes on to prove why he has become known as both a community leader and a freestyle champion in his home of Austin, TX. Throughout the album his orientation toward improvisational jazz is enhanced by the presence of Dwayne "D-Madness" Jackson on bass and Scott Levy on drums, as well as DJ Logic and Baby G on turntables. Produced by a full stable of Austin up-and-comers including Nick Nack, Arson Optics, DJ Massive, aQ, Pea Dee, DJ Phyfteen, and Obadele Thompson, *Create & Hustle* is as diverse as it is focused. Tackling difficult topics such as misogyny and classism as unfortunate components of hip-hop culture, Bavu makes his mark as an outspoken cultural critic on Sarcasm and Overnight. Meanwhile deep personal issues recur on introspective excursions including Only Your Life, I, and See You. Succeeding in its quest "to make rap music raw again," *Create & Hustle* is a pleasant surprise in a sea of cliché. —*Robert Gabriel*

Mary J. Blige

b. Jan. 11, 1971, Bronx, NY
Vocals / Hip-Hop, Urban, Club/Dance, Contemporary R&B
When her debut album, *What's the 411?*, hit the street in 1992, critics and fans alike were floored by its powerful combination of modern R&B with an edgy rap sound that glanced off of the pain and grit of Mary J. Blige's Yonkers, NY, childhood. Called alternately the new Chaka Khan or new Aretha Franklin, Blige had little in common stylistically with either of those artists, but like them helped adorn soul music with new textures and flavors that inspired a whole generation of musicians. With her blonde hair, self-preserving slouch and combat boots, Blige was street tough and beautiful all at once, and

the record company execs who profited off of her early releases did little to dispel the bad-girl image that she earned as she stumbled through the dizzying first days of her career. As she exorcised her personal demons and softened her style to include sleek designer clothes, she remained a hero to thousands of girls growing up in the same kinds of rough places she came from. Blige reinvented her career again and again by shedding the bad habits and bad influences that kept her down; by the time her fourth album, *Mary*, was released in 1999, she had matured into an expressive singer able to put the full power of her voice behind her music, while still reflecting a strong urban style. With her fifth album, *No More Drama*, it wasn't just Blige's style that shone through the structures set up for her by songwriters and producers, it was her own vision—spiritual, emotional, personal, and full of wisdom, and reflected an artist who was comfortable with who she was and how far she had come.

Born in the Bronx on January 11, 1971, Blige spent the first few years of her life in Savannah, GA, before moving with her mother and older sister to the Schlobam housing projects in Yonkers, NY. Her rough life there produced more than a few scars, physical and otherwise, and Blige dropped out of high school her junior year, instead spending time doing her friends' hair in her mother's apartment and hanging out. When she was at a local mall in White Plains, NY, she recorded herself singing Anita Baker's "Caught Up in the Rapture," into a karaoke machine. The resulting tape was passed by Blige's stepfather to Uptown Records' CEO Andre Harrell. Harrell was impressed with Blige's voice and signed her to sing backup for local acts like Father MC. In 1991, however, Sean "Puffy" Combs took Blige under his wing and began working with her on *What's the 411?*, her debut album. Combs had a heavy hand in *What's the 411?*, along with producers Dave Hall, Mark Morales, and Mark Rooney, and the stylish touches that they added to Blige's unique vocal style created a stunning album that bridged the gap between R&B and rap in a way that no female singer had before. Uptown tried to capitalize on the success of *What's the 411?* by issuing a remixed version of it a year later, but it was only a modest success creatively and commercially.

Her 1994 follow-up, *My Life*, again featured Combs' handiwork, and if it stepped back stylistically from its urban roots by featuring less of a rap sound, it made up for it with its subject matter. *My Life* was full of ghetto pathos and Blige's own personal pain shone through like a beacon. Her rocky relationship with fellow Uptown artist K-Ci Hailey likely contributed to the raw emotions on the album. The period following the recording of *My Life* was also a difficult time professionally for Blige as she severed her ties with Combs and Uptown, hired Suge Knight as a financial advisor and signed with MCA.

Share My World in 1997 marked the beginning of Blige's creative partnerships with Jimmy Jam and Terry Lewis. The album was another hit for Blige and debuted at number one on the *Billboard* charts. Critics soured somewhat on its more conventional soul sound, but Blige's fans seemed undaunted. By the time her next studio album, *Mary*, came out in 1999, the fullness and elegance of her new sound seemed more developed, as Blige exuded a classic soul style aided by material from Elton John and Bernie Taupin, Stevie Wonder, and Lauryn Hill. *Mary* made it obvious that the ghetto fabulous style and more confrontational aspects of her music were gone, while the emotive power still remained.

That power also helped carry the more modern-sounding 2001 release, *No More Drama*, a deeply personal album that remained a collective effort musically yet reflected more of Blige's songwriting than any of her previous efforts. The Mary J. Blige on *No More Drama* seemed miles away from the flashy kid on *What's the 411?*, yet it was still possible to see the path through her music that produced an older, wiser, but still expressive artist. —*Stacia Proefrock*

● **What's the 411?** / Jul. 1992 / MCA ✦✦✦✦✦
With this cutting-edge debut, Mary J. Blige became the reigning queen of her own hybrid category: hip-hop soul. In retrospect, it is easier to place the album into the context of her career and, as such, to pinpoint the occasions when it runs wide of the rails. For instance, the synthesizer-heavy backdrops ("Reminisce," "Love No Limit") are sometimes flatter or more plastic than either the songs or Blige's passionate performances deserve, while the answering-machine skits, much copied in the wake of *What's the 411?*, haven't worn well as either stand-alone tracks or conceptual segues. Despite the minor flaws, the music is indeed revelatory on a frequent basis. "Real Love" and the gospel-thrusted "Sweet Thing" (the primary reason for the Chaka Kahn

comparisons) are and likely will remain timeless slices of soul even after their trendiness has worn off. "You Remind Me" and the duet with Jodeci's K-Ci ("I Don't Want to Do Anything") are nearly as effecting in their own right. It is nevertheless unclear how much of the hip-hop swagger in her soul was a genuine expression of Blige's own vision or that of her admittedly fine collaborators (Svengali Sean "Puffy" Combs, R&B producers Dave Hall and Devante Swing, rap beatsmith Tony Dofat, rapper Grand Puba). Certainly the singer comes across as street-savvy and tough—"real," in the lingo of the day—and even tries her hand at rhyming on the title track, but never again would her records lean this heavily on the sonic tricks of the rap trade. The eloquence and evocativeness that comes through in her voice, on the other hand, could be neither borrowed nor fabricated, making *What's the 411?* one of the decade's most explosive, coming-out displays of pure singing prowess. A momentous album, it is not Blige's finest. In fact, those who prefer their soul more stirring, heart on sleeve, or close to the bone would likely find her fluid, powerfully vulnerable next recording (*My Life*) or one of the consistently strong subsequent efforts that followed it more to their liking. For broad appeal and historical importance, though, *What's the 411?* is an inarguably paramount and trailblazing achievement. —*Stanton Swihart*

What's the 411? (Remix) / 1992 / MCA ✦✦✦

Mary J. Blige's debut album is an uneven affair, but amid some of the more pedestrian and formulaic R&B, it contains some sensational urban soul music. Songs such as "Real Love" and "Sweet Thing" heralded the arrival of a true and distinctive talent. As was *de riguer* in early-'90s R&B, MCA/Uptown followed up Blige's debut with an identically titled remix album. The idealistic view is that her record company chose to release such an album because it wanted to elevate the less successful moments on her debut to the heights reached by its hits. The cynical view is that the record company wanted to economically (as opposed to artistically) capitalize on the success of the hit singles. Whatever the motivation behind it, *What's the 411? Remix* plays like a combination of both reasons. What this means is that it's a wildly uneven record, like the album which it attempts to illuminate and recontextualize, maintaining both highlights and low points. It takes the same general thematic form as its predecessor, opening with a series of phone messages that serve to punctuate how many famous friends and admirers Mary J. Blige has before launching into the remixed versions of her songs. The production credits also punctuate the scope of her admirers, while inadvertently contributing to the album's primary problem: inconsistency. The main change the production work accomplishes is realigning Blige much more firmly with the hip-hop side of her hip-hop/soul blend. Sharp, repetitive beats and rumbling bass roll out and there's the frequent presence of rap stalwarts such as Sean "Puffy" Combs, Craig Mack, Kid Capri, Greg Nice, and Biggie Smalls on various tracks, all of whom either rap or, in Puff Daddy's case, leave fingerprints all over the production (given his fondness for recasting the songs by interspersing unmistakable vintage licks from classic rap songs from the past and present). Sometimes the bevy of different sounds works wonderfully, at least on a song-by-song basis ("Sweet Thang," "Love No Limit," and Puffy and Jesse West's "Reminisce" remix, which sonically references Pete Rock & C.L. Smooth's "T.R.O.Y." and includes a cameo from the latter), improving on the original in the process. Other times, the production just seems to make a song drag or sound overly generic in comparison to the original (the Teddy Riley-remixed "My Love"). On the whole, there is not much on this album that outshines *What's the 411?*, and the step back into hip-hop doesn't seem to suit Blige as much as it did the first time around. By her next proper studio album, she would make it apparent that she planned to delve far more deeply into her soul half than her hip-hop one. —*Stanton Swihart*

My Life / Nov. 29, 1994 / MCA ✦✦✦✦

Perhaps the single finest moment in Sean "Puffy" Combs' musical career has been the production on this, Mary J. Blige's second proper album. The production is not exactly original, and there is evidence here of him borrowing wholesale from other songs. The melodic sources this time around, though, are so expertly incorporated into the music that they never seem to be intrusions, instead playing like inspired dialogues with soulsters from the past, connecting past legacies with a new one. This certainly isn't your parents' (or grandparents') soul. But it is some of the finest modern soul of the '90s, backing away to a certain extent from the hip-hop/soul consolidation that Blige introduced on her debut album. The hip-hop part of the combination takes a few steps into the background, allowing Blige's tortured soul to carry the

album completely, and it does so with heartwrenching authority. *My Life* is, from beginning to end, a brilliant, wistful individual plea of desire. Blige took a huge leap in artistry by penning almost everything herself (the major exception being Norman Whitfield's "I'm Going Down") in collaboration with coproducers Combs and multi-instrumentalist Chucky Thompson, and everything seems to leap directly from her gut. Blige's strain is sleekly modern and urban, and the grit in it comes from being streetwise and thoroughly realistic about the travails of life. *My Life*, nevertheless, emanates from some deep, dark place where both sadness and happiness cohabitate and turn into one single, beautiful sorrow. —*Stanton Swihart*

Share My World / Apr. 22, 1997 / MCA ✦✦✦✦

The hype that surrounded Mary J. Blige in the beginning was simply ridiculous. When *What's the 411?* was released in 1992, she was exalted as "the new Chaka Khan"— a definite exaggeration, considering how uneven that debut album was. But Blige did show promise, and by the time she recorded her third album, *Share My World*, she had developed into a fairly convincing soul/urban singer. Her strongest and most confident effort up to that point, *Share* had much more character, personality, and honesty than most of the assembly line fare dominating urban radio in 1997. For all their slickness, emotive cuts like "Get to Know You Better," "Love Is All We Need," and "Keep Your Head" left no doubt that Blige was indeed a singer of depth and substance. Although high tech, the production of everyone from R. Kelly (with whom she duets on the inviting "It's On") and Babyface to Jimmy Jam and Terry Lewis doesn't come across as forced or robotic but, in fact, is impressively organic. With *Share My World*, Blige definitely arrived. —*Alex Henderson*

The Tour / Jul. 28, 1998 / MCA ✦✦✦

The hype that surrounded Mary J. Blige in 1992 was definitely excessive, and those who exalted her as the "new Chaka Khan" did both Khan and Blige an unforgivable disservice (few could live up to such a title). But as the 1990s progressed, Blige really did evolve into one of the decade's most appealing R&B vocalists, and she's in good to excellent form on *The Tour*, which was recorded on her *Share My World* Tour of 1997-1998. The very fact that a live urban contemporary album came out in the late 1990s was quite surprising; after all, R&B had become so technology driven and studio oriented that few R&B artists even bothered to make live albums anymore. But Blige was an exception, and she proves herself capable of taking it to the stage on passionate versions of such hits as "My Life," "Mary Jane (All Night Long)," "Reminisce," and "Mary's Joint." Blige could have done without the male band member who tries to function as her onstage cheerleader, but even so, this is an impressive release that her followers will want. —*Alex Henderson*

Mary / Aug. 17, 1999 / MCA ✦✦✦✦

Perhaps it was inevitable that Mary J. Blige would mature, toning down the raunchier elements of her persona that have been evident since her debut, while repositioning herself as a classicist soul singer. Even so, the sheer classiness of *Mary*, her fourth album, may come as a bit of a surprise. Blige made a conscious effort to create an album that recalled the classic dawning days of quiet storm yet worked as a unified, cohesive album. That meant that the more overt hip-hop elements have been subdued in favor of '70s soul. There's still grit in the music, but it's been glossed over with a polished production, and she now favors sophisticated songs, including material from such writers as Stevie Wonder, Bacharach & David, Lauryn Hill, and Elton John & Bernie Taupin. Some of these writers were collaborators and others contributed songs outright, but the amazing thing about the end result belongs to nobody else but Blige. It's different, to be sure, but still her—and it's a rewarding, engaging way to mature. Blige's voice is richer and her skills have deepened, and her new songs, while not as streetwise, are worthy of her talents. Consequently, *Mary* is a thoroughly winning album. —*Stephen Thomas Erlewine*

No More Drama / Aug. 28, 2001 / MCA ✦✦✦✦

Listeners of Mary J. Blige's seasoned and confident fifth studio release will have zero problems remembering the album's title, *No More Drama*. An urban-sounding vocal sample that sings, "Mary J. Blige, no more drama," plays throughout the length of the 17-track disc. This very well may be the first time such a tactic has been used in contemporary music; generally a vocal sample repeats throughout the course of only one song, but because the fare on *No More Drama* is so good, this recurring vocal sample is as subtle and congruent as a consistent drum hit. Blige has come a long way since 1992's breakthrough, *What's the 411?*, and that's made very clear on this solid disc. The singer/songwriter has blossomed into an all-out R&B diva—with a hip-hop edge—full of soul and command. Her songs on this recording exude the wisdom of a woman who's seen it all and has found her center. And she will no longer tolerate drama, pettiness, and overall crap. In 2001's crop of R&B singers, Blige's voice was truly inimitable. It's husky, strong, soulful, and full of maturity. Make no mistake, though, this lady can still flow like no one's business; just check out the bouncy album opener "Love." In fact, many of the record's cuts are standout moments. For instance, only Blige has the guts to write and pull off a song called "PMS," a soulful and bluesy number that describes, in detail, this condition inherent to the female experience. And while she also explores themes of love, Blige's disc is essentially a journey through her personal evolution and spirituality. The final cut, "Testimony," best summarizes the album's theme: finding what's real in life. And for Blige, that's self-love and God. To her credit, Blige has a killer instinct for penning lyrics that people can relate to and creating gritty, thick, and soul-infused R&B fare. (She does get some help on this disc from such R&B and hip-hop heavyweights as Missy Elliot, Jimmy Jam, and Terry Lewis, among others.) Her music is more than heard; it is felt, and audiences would be hard pressed to not surrender to her groove. Interestingly, many of Blige's peers sing about drama, but not this artist—not anymore. (*No More Drama* was re-released in early 2002 with a handful of different tracks.) —*Liana Jonas*

Dance for Me / Jul. 22, 2002 / MCA ✦✦✦
Yes, *Dance for Me* is another remix album from a hip-hop/urban artist, following hot on the heels of high-profile remix releases from P. Diddy and others. But unlike any other mainstream artist, Mary J. Blige has the range and energy of the best disco divas, plus the exquisite taste of any dance scenester—both of which combine to make *Dance for Me* one of the best, most innovative remix albums of recent vintage. Included are remixes from producers like Junior Vasquez, Hex Hector, and Barry Harris (from Thunderpuss), who've done dozens of remixes for artists like Blige in the past, and easily display a flair for giving her songs the natural settings they deserve. "No More Drama," the title track from her full-length of 2001, particularly shines after getting treated by Thunderpuss. Tweaked out to nearly ten minutes with no sign of stretch marks, the song becomes a multipart epic in the hands of Blige, freestyling like the best dance vocalists of *any* era, from Loleatta Holloway to La India. "Family Affair," the Dr. Dre production (originally) with the lyric that spawned this album's title, boasts a chunky, classic-disco rework from Spanish Fly, while Vasquez and Hector give their inclusions the high-energy synthetics of hard house. Al B. Rich offers some variety (and a nod to dance taste-makers) with a two-step groove for "Never Been," and the last track—Blige's 1999 cover of the seminal disco anthem "Let No Man Put Asunder" by First Choice—ends it on a high note, proving to anyone who's curious that, no matter who invented the remix, Mary J. Blige is her generation's most artistic diva. —*John Bush*

Blind Craftsmen

f. Maryland
Group / Alternative Rap, Hip-Hop
Based out of Maryland, Matt Fiero and Keith Anderson met in high school and began refining what would turn out to be the Blind Craftsmen. They're a rap group with imaginative lyrics and songs that strive to have relevance and meaning to a specific topic. Their first album is entitled *Through the Eye's of We*. —*Brad Mills*

● **Through the Eye's of We** / Sep. 26, 2000 / Da Hill ✦✦✦✦
This LP is a pleasant surprise from start to finish. The Blind Craftsmen are a duo made up of MCs Matt and Keith. They're a couple of kids from Baltimore, MD, put on CD by Da Hill Records, a local label. They bring an experienced lyrical ability to the microphone that's definitely unexpected, and really put together what can easily be called a complete album. There have been many epic storytelling efforts in hip-hop, and this is that kind of album. Although it doesn't follow a strict path or storyline, it flows well from the intros to the tracks and vice versa, keeping the listener interested even after it's been played out. Standout tracks are "Don't Dance," "Altered Reality," and "Insanity," and the beats are well produced. All in all, a great first effort for a young group with hopefully a lot ahead of them. —*Brad Mills*

Blood of Abraham

Group / Hip-Hop
Blood of Abraham, an Afro-centric Jewish rap duo mentored by the late Eazy-E, emerged in the early '90s. At the time, the group stood as a testament to hip-hop's ever-burgeoning ability to defy cultural boundaries. The combo consists of MCs Benyad and Mazik. Benyad was born Ben Mor in Israel to Moroccan-Jewish parents and raised in Nigeria until the age of ten, when his family moved to L.A. Mazik was born David Saevitz in Santa Monica, CA, to a part-Irish father and a Jewish mother and raised in Las Vegas. The duo's first big move toward public recognition came when they convinced Compton gangsta rap icon Eazy-E to let them perform during a gang-truce event he was hosting on Sunset Strip in 1992. Eazy, impressed with Blood of Abraham, convinced them to reject another label offer in favor of signing to Ruthless Records (the home of N.W.A). Eazy also offered Mazik, who had recently come to L.A. from Las Vegas and was homeless at the time, living quarters in a huge house he owned down the street from Dr. Dre.

The group recorded *Future Profits* in 1993 and even shot a video at the Wailing Wall in Jerusalem. The album was released in 1994 and contained the provocative, epithet-heavy track "Niggaz and Jewz (Some Say Kikes)," which tore into racism and anti-Semitism. The notorious track featured Eazy and contained the sampled voice of a Klansman. (The track also featured the recorded debut of rapper Will.I.Am, who would later to rise to prominence with Black Eyed Peas.) The album received generally a positive response; however, when Eazy fell terminally ill with AIDS, Ruthless Records began to deteriorate. With no promotion behind it, *Future Profits* sank out of site. Blood of Abraham re-emerged with *Eyedollartree* (a pun on "idolatry") in 2000. The album condemned greedy consumerism and featured a ten-minute experimental film that mixed stock footage and noirish photography. The effort featured appearances by Divine Styler, Kool Keith, and Will.I.Am. —*Erik Hage*

Future Profits / Nov. 16, 1993 / Relativity ✦✦✦
On *Future Profits*, their debut and final release, Los Angeles-based rappers Benyad and Mazik deliver a confused but engaging effort that deals with an odd subject in the world of rap—Jewish identity. Although Jews have made prominent contributions in hip-hop (see the Beastie Boys and MC Serch of 3rd Bass), it is rare to actually hear Jewish religious beliefs end up in lyrical form. Doing exactly that, Blood of Abraham create 14 songs which all include references to their religion. Beginning with the bouncy, reggae-flavored "This Great Land Devours," the duo take shots at so-called rednecks ("Southern Comfort"), bigots ("Stick to Your Own Kind"), and past and future missionaries ("Stabbed by the Steeple"). The varied and unique music behind the raps from producer Brett "Epic" Mazur relies heavily on jazz samples, but hard rock and spoken-word snippets are also utilized. The album's fatal flaw is revealed when Blood of Abraham team up with labelmate and pioneering gangsta rapper Eazy-E for a song examining discrimination faced by African-Americans and Jews (they use much harsher terminology). While progressive throughout their only full-length release, Blood of Abraham are considered by most to be no more than a hip-hop identity crisis. —*Craig Robert Smith*

● **Eyedollartree** / May 2, 2000 / Atomic Pop ✦✦✦
These two Jewish rappers are better known for the high-profile artists with whom they've been associated (they were discovered and signed by N.W.A's Eazy-E, while Crazy Town's Brett "Epic" Mazur was once their DJ and producer) than for their music. But their 1993 debut, *Future Profits*, made a minor splash thanks to "Niggas and Jewz (Some Say Kikes)," a controversial collaboration with Eazy. Unfortunately, their mentor's death left them without a label, and nobody heard a peep from Blood of Abraham for the next seven years. *Eyedollartree* is, thankfully, a more mature effort, with a well-developed sociopolitical consciousness that gives them a progressive sort of appeal. Songs like "Know the Half" and "Only the Wise" show a knack for crafting memorable hooks, while "99¢ Lighter" features WILL.I.Am of Black Eyed Peas and "Omegatron" features Divine Styler and Kool Keith, placing their sound squarely in the alternative rap scene. Unfortunately, the album was released just as the duo's new label, Atomic Pop, began experiencing financial difficulties, so few fans even knew *Eyedollartree* existed. Hopefully they won't have to wait another seven years for the next one. —*Bret Love*

Bloods & Crips

f. Los Angeles, CA

Group / Gangsta Rap, Hardcore Rap, West Coast Rap

Given the infamous violent reputation of rival Los Angeles gangs the Bloods and the Crips, it seems impossible that the two could collaborate on a music project, but that's exactly what the Bloods & Crips did on *Bangin on Wax* in 1993, organized by Los Angeles area producer Ron "Ronnie Ron" Phillips and rapper Tweedy Bird Loc. The success of N.W.A had frustrated many in the gang community, who saw the group capitalizing on the gang lifestyle. Actual gang members and local rappers auditioned in an open try-out, with the best talents from both gangs being chosen to record. Some of the names to make the cut were Red-Rum-781, Sin Loc, Blue Ragg, Red Rag, Bloody Mary, and Lil' Stretch. *Bangin on Wax* was recorded in only two weeks and became an underground hit, selling over 400,000 copies and producing the popular single "Piru Love." A second Bloods & Crips album, *The Saga Continues*, came out in 1994, but was the last time the two gangs would collaborate. However, it was not the last of either the Bloods or Crips as artists. Ronnie Ron continues to issue albums from gang members on his Dangerous Records imprint under the names Nationwide Rip Ridaz (Crips) and Damu Ridaz (Bloods). Some of the MCs on *Bangin on Wax* went on to record as the Young Soldierz, and Domino, who went under the name Genuine Draft, had a hit pop-rap single in 1994 with *Sweet Potatoe Pie.*
— *Wade Kergan*

● **Bangin' on Wax: Greatest Hits** / Aug. 27, 1996 / Dangerous ◆◆◆◆

Like the People and the Folks in Chicago, the Crips and the Bloods are rival Los Angeles gangs whose bloody battles were the subject of many West Coast rap songs in the 1980s and 1990s, including Ice-T's "Colors." The Crips and the Bloods started out in L.A., but as their membership grew, they formed factions in cities ranging from Seattle and Portland to Oakland, Phoenix, and Houston. Gangsta rappers often rapped in the first person about gang violence and portrayed gang members on their recordings, but as a rule, they were careful to avoid mentioning any particular gang by name; giving the impression that they were active gang members could get them killed by members of the rival gang. *Bangin' on Wax* is unique in that it finds various gangsta rappers from South Central L.A. rapping in the first person about their experiences as either Crips or Bloods. Half of the CD is devoted to Crips, the other half to Bloods, and the end result is a jolting audio documentary on the horrors of gang life. Crip rappers angrily voice their hatred of Bloods (whom they call slobs) on tunes like "Another Slob Bites the Dust" and "Mackin' to Slob Bitches," while Blood rappers are equally vehement in their denunciation of Crips (whom they call crabs) on such numbers as "Rip a Crab in Half" and "I Killed Ya Dead Homies." If listeners don't already know how passionately the two groups hate each other, they will after hearing this CD. To be sure, this project was controversial, and Dangerous/Pump was criticized for giving gang members a platform. The label could hardly be accused of taking sides, however; its goal was to be informative, and *Bangin' on Wax* is definitely informative—not to mention disturbing.
— *Alex Henderson*

Kurtis Blow (Kurtis Walker)

b. Aug. 9, 1959, New York, NY

Vocals, Keyboards, Producer / Hip-Hop, Old School Rap

As the first commercially successful rap artist, Kurtis Blow is a towering figure in hip-hop history. His popularity and charisma helped prove that rap music was something more than a flash-in-the-pan novelty, paving the way for the even greater advances of Grandmaster Flash and Run-D.M.C. Blow was the first rapper to sign with (and release an album for) a major label; the first to have a single certified gold (1980's landmark "The Breaks"); the first to embark on a national (and international) concert tour; and the first to cement rap's mainstream marketability by signing an endorsement deal. For that matter, he was really the first significant solo rapper on record, and as such he was a natural focal point for many aspiring young MCs in the early days of hip-hop. For all his immense importance and influence, many of Blow's records haven't dated all that well; his rapping technique, limber for its time, simply wasn't as evolved as the more advanced MCs who built upon his style and followed him up the charts. But at his very best, Blow epitomizes the virtues of the old school: ingratiating, strutting party music that captures the exuberance of an art form still in its youth.

Kurtis Blow was born Kurtis Walker in Harlem in 1959. He was in on the earliest stages of hip-hop culture in the '70s—first as a breakdancer, then as a block-party and club DJ performing under the name Kool DJ Kurt; after enrolling at CCNY in 1976, he also served as program director for the college radio station. He became an MC in his own right around 1977, and changed his name to Kurtis Blow (as in a body blow) at the suggestion of his manager, future Def Jam founder and rap mogul Russell Simmons. Blow performed with legendary DJs like Grandmaster Flash, and for a time his regular DJ was Simmons' teenage brother Joseph—who, after changing his stage name from "Son of Kurtis Blow," would go on to become the first half of Run-D.M.C. Over 1977-1978, Blow's club gigs around Harlem and the Bronx made him an underground sensation, and *Billboard* magazine writer Robert Ford approached Simmons about making a record. Blow cut a song cowritten by Ford and financier J.B. Moore called "Christmas Rappin'," and it helped him get a deal with Mercury once the Sugarhill Gang's "Rapper's Delight" had climbed into the R&B Top Five.

Blow's second single, "The Breaks," was an out-of-the-box smash, following "Rapper's Delight" into the Top Five of the R&B charts in 1980 and eventually going gold; it still ranks as one of old school rap's greatest and most enduring moments. The full-length album *Kurtis Blow* was also released in 1980, and made the R&B Top Ten in spite of many assumptions that the Sugarhill Gang's success was a onetime fluke. Although the album's attempts at soul crooning and rock covers haven't dated well, the poverty-themed "Hard Times" marked perhaps the first instance of hip-hop's social consciousness, and was later covered by Run-D.M.C. Blow initially found it hard to follow up "The Breaks," despite releasing nearly an album a year for most of the '80s. 1981's *Deuce* and 1982's *Tough* weren't huge sellers, and 1983's *Party Time* EP brought D.C. go-go funksters E.U. on board for a stylistic update. Around this time, Blow was also making his mark as a producer, working with a variety of hip-hop and R&B artists; most notably, he helmed most of the Fat Boys' records after helping them get a record deal. 1984's *Ego Trip* sold respectably well on the strength of cuts like the DJ tribute "AJ Scratch," the agreeably lightweight "Basketball," and the Run-D.M.C. duet "8 Million Stories." Blow followed it with an appearance in the cult hip-hop film *Krush Groove*, in which he performed "If I Ruled the World," his biggest hit since "The Breaks."

"If I Ruled the World" proved to be the last gasp of Blow's popularity, as hip-hop's rapid growth made his style seem increasingly outdated. 1985's *America* was largely ignored, and 1986's *Kingdom Blow* was afforded an icy reception despite producing a final shout in "I'm Chillin'." Critics savaged his final comeback attempt, 1988's *Back By Popular Demand*, almost invariably pointing out that the title, at that point, was not true. In its wake, Blow gave up the ghost of his recording career, but found other ways to keep the spirit of the old school alive. In the early '90s, he contributed rap material to the TV soap opera *One Life to Live*, and later spent several years hosting an old school hip-hop show on Los Angeles radio station Power 106. In 1997 Rhino Records took advantage of his status as a hip-hop elder statesmen by hiring him to produce, compile, and write liner notes for the three-volume series *Kurtis Blow Presents the History of Rap.* The same year, he was a significant presence in the rap documentary *Rhyme and Reason.* Blow's music has also been revived by younger artists seeking to pay tribute: Nas covered "If I Rule the World" on 1996's *It Was Written*, and R&B group Next sampled "Christmas Rappin'" for their 1998 smash "Too Close." — *Steve Huey*

Kurtis Blow / 1980 / Mercury ◆◆◆◆◆

Back in hip-hop's old school era—roughly 1978-1982—albums were the exception and not the rule. Hip-hop became a lot more album minded with the rise of its second generation (Run-D.M.C., Whodini, the Fat Boys, among others) around 1983-1984, but in the beginning, many MCs recorded nothing but singles. Two exceptions were the Sugarhill Gang and Kurtis Blow, whose self-titled debut album of 1980 was among hip-hop's first LPs and the first rap album to come out on a major label. Thus, *Kurtis Blow* has serious historic value, although it is mildly uneven. Some of the tracks are superb, including "The Breaks" (a Top Five R&B smash in 1980) and "Rappin' Blow, Part Two," which is the second half of Blow's 1979 debut single, "Christmas Rappin'." And "Hard Times" is a forceful gem that finds Blow addressing social issues two years before Grandmaster Flash & the Furious Five popularized sociopolitical rapping with 1982's sobering "The Message." Some of the other tracks, however, are decent but not remarkable. Switching from rapping to singing, Blow detours into Northern soul on the Chi-Lites-influenced ballad "All I Want in This World (Is to Find That Girl)" and arena rock on an unexpected cover of Bachman-Turner Overdrive's "Takin' Care of Business." While those selections are likable and kind of interesting—how many other old school rappers attempted to sing soul, let alone arena rock?—the fact remains that rapping, not singing, is Blow's strong point. And Mercury really screwed up by providing only the second half of "Christmas Rappin'"; that landmark single should have been heard in its entirety. But despite its flaws and shortcomings, *Kurtis Blow* is an important album that hip-hop historians should make a point of hearing. —*Alex Henderson*

Deuce / 1981 / Mercury ✦✦✦✦
Things cooled quickly for Kurtis Blow following the success of "The Breaks" in 1980. He was unable to get any single from this record on the charts, even though "Rockin'" and "It's Gettin' Hot" were well produced and competently delivered. But rap was still far from being a mainstream phenomenon, and this album did very poorly commercially. —*Ron Wynn*

Tough / 1982 / Mercury ✦✦

Ego Trip / 1984 / Mercury ✦✦✦
By the time Kurtis Blow recorded 1984's *Ego Trip*, the Harlem MC was no longer considered cutting edge in hip-hop circles. Blow, who was at the height of his popularity around 1979-1981, had come to be regarded as old school—and in 1984, cutting edge meant Run-D.M.C., LL Cool J, the Fat Boys, the Beastie Boys, and Whodini. But even if Blow's rapping style was sounding somewhat dated in 1984, he still had impressive technique. Although uneven, *Ego Trip* has a lot going for it. Some of the material is excellent, especially the hit "Basketball" (which salutes the sport's big names), the skeletal "AJ Scratch," and the sociopolitical offerings "I Can't Take It No More" and "8 Million Stories" (which features Run-D.M.C. and puts a 1980s spin on the old TV series *The Naked City*). Other tracks, meanwhile, are decent but not great—like Blow's previous LPs, *Ego Trip* isn't without filler. Hip-hop was becoming increasingly album minded in 1984, but Blow had come out of an era in which singles dominated hip-hop and albums were the exception instead of the rule—which may explain why his albums tended to be inconsistent. But *Ego Trip* has more plusses than minuses, and its best tracks are first-rate. —*Alex Henderson*

America / 1985 / Mercury ✦✦✦

Kingdom Blow / 1986 / Mercury ✦✦
Kurtis Blow's sixth Mercury LP wasn't a pretty thing to behold. He tried everything from autobiographical material ("The Bronx") to b-boy narratives ("I'm Chillin'") and novelty cuts ("Magilla Gorilla"), but nothing clicked, either commercially or aesthetically. —*Ron Wynn*

Back By Popular Demand / 1988 / Mercury ✦✦
In the early '80s Blow successfully brought rap to the middle of R&B radio with 1980's "The Breaks." Other hits include "Party Time," "If I Ruled the World," and the prime go-go of "I'm Chillin'"; Blow also produced the Fat Boys and effervescent tracks like "Can You Feel It" and "Fat Boys Are Back," and the suave "Pump It Up." But by 1988 Blow's hitmaking streak turned stone cold. In many respects, *Back By Popular Demand* provides a blueprint for what not to do on a late-'80s rap album. The first track and initial single has Blow putting himself on the ropes and the defensive as he proclaims his return, but he never really went anywhere. The song, like the majority of this effort, employs a harder, James Brown sample-laden sound. The best interpolation and rhyme, "I'm True to This," attains the edge Blow desired with good use of a loop from Lyn Collins' kinetic "Think." The too-brief "Get on Up" and "Suckers in the Place" almost work as well. Despite the few bright spots, this is one of those albums that just seemed to be doomed from the start. Blow tacks a doggerel rap on "Stay on the Scene," which manages to squander loops from "Funky President" and "Strawberry Letter 23." "I Feel Good," "Express Yourself," and "Only the Strong Survive" are ghastly and would have stalled even the most charmed of careers. Despite the promise, *Back By Popular Demand* was left in the dust by more challenging and better-executed albums. —*Jason Elias*

★ **The Best of Kurtis Blow** / Jun. 7, 1994 / Mercury ✦✦✦✦✦
While he made many groundbreaking singles, Kurtis Blow was never a consistent album artist, making this best-of collection his definitive artistic statement. Throughout the early '80s, Blow helped define what rap could do, and these tracks confirm his status as one of hip-hop's legendary acts. —*Stephen Thomas Erlewine*

Body Count

f. 1989
Group / Rap-Metal, Heavy Metal, Rap-Rock
Maybe no one saw the humor, or maybe they were distracted by the barely competent heavy metal of the album, but rapper Ice-T's heavy metal group launched a hurricane of publicity with their self-titled debut album, *Body Count*. Ice-T's music had been hard as heavy metal for a number of years, and on 1991's landmark *OG Original Gangster*, he recorded the speed metal/hip-hop fusion "Body Count" with his band of the same name. Body Count's lineup included Ernie-C (guitar), D-Roc (guitar), Mooseman (bass), and Beatmaster V (drums), all of whom attended Crenshaw High School in South Central Los Angeles. On the 1991 Lollapalooza tour, Ice-T performed with Body Count and earned a substantial amount of fans and praise. "Body Count" was a highlight of *OG* and, not coincidentally, it was the most serious and best song on their 1992 album. For the rest of *Body Count*, the band engaged in heavy metal clichés and lyrics that were either humorously over the top or cringe inducing.

After it was out for a couple of months, fury over the song "Cop Killer" made the album a symbol for everything that was wrong with popular culture. After several months of constant bad publicity, Warner Brothers and Ice-T pulled the song from the album; several months later, he parted ways with the record company.

Body Count released their second album, *Born Dead*, on Ice-T's new record label, Priority, in 1994. The record failed to generate either controversy or sales and disappeared shortly after its fall release, after which Mooseman left the band. Despite declining interest in Body Count, Ice-T stuck with the band, recording the group's third album, *Violent Demise: Last Days*, in 1997; sadly, Beatmaster V fell victim to leukemia early that year. Upon the release of *Violent Demise*, most critics suddenly got Body Count's sense of humor and, consequently, the album received fairly good reviews, yet failed to sell. —*Stephen Thomas Erlewine*

● **Body Count** / Mar. 30, 1992 / Sire ✦✦✦
Divorced from the controversy that surrounded its release, Body Count's self-titled debut is a surprisingly tepid affair. Apart from the previously released "Body Count" (which appeared on Ice-T's 1991 album *O.G. Original Gangster*), the record is devoid of serious commentary, trading intelligence for a lurid comicbook depiction of sex, violence, and "Voodoo." All of Ice-T's half-sung/half-shouted lyrics fall far short of the standard he established on his hip-hop albums. The controversial "Cop Killer," which is nothing more than a standard thrash-metal chant, stands out because it is one of the few tracks that doesn't rely on garish, cartoonish imagery. There's the saga of "Evil Dick," which tells Ice-T to not "sleep alone." There's "KKK Bitch," where he crashes a Ku Klux Klan meeting and screws the grand dragon's daughter. There's "Voodoo," where a witch doctor cripples our hero with a voodoo doll. There's "Mama's Gotta Die Tonight," where Ice-T offs his mother because she's a racist. By the time the band works around to the power ballad "The Winner Loses" and Ice-T is crooning "My friend's addicted to cocaine," it's unclear whether the record is a parody or a horribly flawed stab at arena metal. It would help if the band wrote riffs that were memorable or if they conveyed a sense of kinetic energy instead of tossing out their riffs in a workmen-like fashion. Perhaps *Body Count* was intentionally humorous—although the group's follow-up, *Born Dead*, suggests that it wasn't—but in any case, the record was simply embarrassing. After "Cop Killer" was pulled from the album, it was replaced with a bland version of Ice-T's rap classic "The Iceberg" recorded with Jello Biafra. —*Stephen Thomas Erlewine*

Born Dead / 1994 / Virgin ✦✦
All of the controversy over "Cop Killer" and Body Count's debut obscured one important fact—they're not a very good band. *Born Dead* makes that clear by replicating all of *Body Count*—all of the plodding riffs, embarrassing singing, obvious attempts at social commentary, and the relentless "Body Count, Body Count, Body Count, BC, BC, BC" chants. All that's missing is humor. Not even the worst material on *Body Count* is unintentionally funny; it's just embarrassing. Ice-T can pull this material off live; on record, his band just sounds like a heavy metal relic from the late '80s. —*Stephen Thomas Erlewine*

Violent Demise: Last Days / Mar. 11, 1997 / Virgin ✦✦✦
A significant improvement over the stilted *Born Dead*, *Violent Demise: Last Days* is, in many ways, the best record Body Count has made to date. Where

the band's speed-metal has seemed dated in the past, the group sounds fiery throughout *Violent Demise*, giving the music a visceral punch it had clearly been lacking in the past. Ice-T's lyrics fall halfway between outrage and outrageous, especially on the anti-O.J. Simpson "I Used to Love Her," "Dead Man Walking," and "You're F**kin' with BC," which pushes their self-promoting chants to ludicrous extremes. Even though the music has more punch than before, it doesn't have the ridiculous sense of humor that made *Body Count* a gonzo classic of sorts, but the sheer force of the record is a welcome change of pace from a band that seemed incapable of true sonic power. —*Stephen Thomas Erlewine*

Bomb the Bass (Tim Simenon)

b. 1968, London, England

Producer / House, Acid House, Club/Dance, Electronica, Hip-Hop

Bomb the Bass' Tim Simenon is a sampladelic British hip-hop producer who also coproduced a pair of massive international hits: Neneh Cherry's "Buffalo Stance" and Seal's "Crazy." Born in Brixton of Malaysian and Scottish parentage, Simenon grew interested in dance production after studying studio engineering and DJing at London's Wag Club, a Mecca for fellow breakbeat mavens like S-Express' Mark Moore and Coldcut's Jonathan More and Matt Black. In 1987, Simenon constructed a pastiche of a DJ record titled "Beat Dis," which incorporated samples from Public Enemy to Ennio Morricone to classic television shows *Dragnet* and *The Thunderbirds*. Packaged to resemble a white-label import from America, the track became an underground hit and, after its reissue on Rhythm King, a surprising number-two smash on the British charts in early 1988. (Coldcut's "Doctorin' the House" and S-Express' "Theme From S-Express" both followed "Beat Dis" into the Top Ten.)

Later that year, Simenon followed with an LP (*Into the Dragon*) featuring an expanded Bomb the Bass lineup: producer Jonathan Saul Kane (who later recorded as Depth Charge) and vocalists Maureen Walsh and Lauraine Macintosh. Two singles from the album, "Megablast" and an inventive cover of the Burt Bacharach-Dionne Warwick classic "Say a Little Prayer," hit the British Top Ten as well. Also in 1988, Simenon coproduced two tracks for the debut of Neneh Cherry, step-daughter of free jazz trumpeter Don Cherry. Both singles, "Buffalo Stance" and "Manchild," became British Top Ten hits. After completing work on his own studio, he also produced a track for Adamski ("Killer") and mixed a single named "Crazy" for an Adamski protégé, Seal.

With all the outside recording commissions, it took nearly three years for Simenon to ready a follow-up to the first Bomb the Bass LP. *Unknown Territory* finally dropped in 1991, led by another Top Ten single, "Winter in July," and sporting a mid-tempo hip-hop aesthetic that would only earn critical attention several years later after being dubbed trip-hop. He also produced a range of acts, from Eternal to Sinead O'Connor during the early '90s, and more fruits of his collaborative nature arrived in 1995 with the third Bomb the Bass album, *Clear*. The album featured vocal tracks featuring O'Connor, Justin Warfield, Bernard Fowler, Bim Sherman, and Leslie Winer, as well as the instrumental input of Tackhead/On-U Sound compatriots Keith LeBlanc, Doug Wimbish, and Skip McDonald. Simenon again turned to outside work during the late '90s, remixing and producing for David Bowie, Depeche Mode, U2, Gavin Friday, Curve, *Booth & The Bad Angel*, and Hardfloor. —*John Bush*

Into the Dragon / Oct. 1988 / Rhythm King ++++

Though Simenon's breakout hit "Beat Dis" isn't quite as frenetic as contemporary material by Coldcut (or even M.A.R.R.S.), the debut Bomb the Bass LP is an intriguing trip through sampledelic hip-hop, electro, acid house, and even dance-pop (as on his other hits, "Don't Make Me Wait" and the Burt Bacharach cover "Say a Little Prayer"). Much of the album mines territory similar to "Beat Dis"—that is, inventive hip-hop tracks like "On the Cut," "Megablast (Hip Hop on Precinct 13)," and "Dynamite Beats," which are somewhat indebted to Mantronix. —*Keith Farley*

● **Clear** / 1995 / 4th & Broadway +++++

Though Bomb the Bass' third album, *Clear*, was originally a scattershot, kinetic dance record, Tim Simenon restructured the record for its American release. The American version of *Clear* demonstrates a distinct trip-hop, techno, jazz, and dub influence, as well as the literary lyical pretentions that were present on the original English release. Simenon created a subdued,

multi-layered album, where instruments float in and out of the mix over a deep, laid-back groove. All of the rappers on the record are guest stars, including Sinead O'Connor and Justin Warfield. Although their contributions are impressive, the true star of the album is Simenon, who has made an album that proves he isn't stuck in the late-'80s house/techno rut and can compete with '90s artists like Tricky and Portishead. Still, the album highlight comes with a La Funk Mob reworking. —*Stephen Thomas Erlewine*

Beat Dis: The Very Best Of / 2002 / BMG ++++

Tim Simenon's Bomb the Bass pet project pumped some of the best acid house straight into late-'80s dance clubs. Best known stateside for the seminal "Beat Dis," similarly groundbreaking slow-beat club groove, and the Burt Bacharach cover "Say a Little Prayer," Simenon's brand of acid-laced rap and snappy sampling kept sweat flowing coast to coast. Unfortunately, by the time the band's second album appeared in 1991, Bomb the Bass was all but forgotten in the beginnings of the grunge backlash. However, the sonics have continued to percolate, hence the welcome appearance of the U.K. compilation *Beat Dis: The Very Best Of*, which serves up a healthy hodgepodge of hits and a neat tweak for aging ravers' long-lost brain cells. In no particular order, *Beat Dis* unravels 1988 through 1991, commencing with the 12" version of "Beat Dis" and ending with the absurdly short "Megamix," while hitting all the important points in between. First-wave favorites include the aforementioned "Say a Little Prayer" and "Shake It," while the 1991 incarnation weighs in mightily with "Dune Buggy Attack" and the British hit "Winter in July." An extra welcome bonus is the inclusion of the nearly metaphysical and ever so slightly menacing "The Air You Breathe," which emerges remarkably undated in comparison to some of the servings on offer. And, while it's true that heavy house and its culture are now tossed off as just another shallow moment in the increasingly angst-ridden musical scape, *Beat Dis: The Very Best Of* remains a potent portent of where the climate is probably headed in the endless turning of reinvention anyway. Besides, there's nothing fallow in a few great grooves. —*Amy Hanson*

Bone Thugs-N-Harmony

f. 1993, Cleveland, OH

Group / Hardcore Rap, Gangsta Rap, G-Funk

Graced with a quick, sometimes sung delivery, Bone Thugs-N-Harmony burst out of the Midwest in the mid-'90s with a pair of massive hits ("Thuggish Ruggish Bone" and "Tha Crossroads") along with a great album (*E 1999 Eternal*) and then quickly unraveled. Eazy-E signed the group—initially comprised of Krayzie Bone, Wish Bone, Flesh-N-Bone, Layzie Bone, and Bizzy Bone—to Ruthless Records and released a debut EP, *Creepin on ah Come Up* (1994). The EP boasted "Thuggish Ruggish Bone," a conventional G-funk song with an unconventional array of Bone Thug rappers that became an overnight summer anthem, especially throughout the Midwest. Amid the fervor, the Cleveland rap group entered the studio immediately and emerged with a remarkable album, *E 1999 Eternal* (1995). The album topped the charts and spawned a pair of popular singles, "1st of tha Month" and "Tha Crossroads," the latter a Grammy Award recipient. It was all downhill from here for Bone, though. As was in vogue at the time, the group members pursued respective solo careers and also a Mo Thugs Family spin-off group, none of these ventures fruitful. At this point, the onetime cohesive group, who specialized in interwoven, harmonious singing as well as rapping, became conflicted and failed to collaborate well, particularly after their ambitious *The Art of War* album (1997) sold poorly. A second round of solo albums sold even more poorly, and Bone became somewhat of a has-been. Occasional reunions such as *BTNHResurrection* (2000) produced moments of glory, but these were brief and few and far between. —*Jason Birchmeier*

E 1999 Eternal / Jul. 25, 1995 / Ruthless ++++

Following the surprising success of Bone Thugs-N-Harmony's summer 1994 anthem "Thuggish Ruggish Bone," the group returned a year later with *E 1999 Eternal*, an impressive full-length debut that dismisses any notion that the group was merely a one-hit wonder. From beginning to end, the album maintains a consistent tone, one that's menacing and somber, produced largely by DJ U-Neek, who frames the songs with dark, smoked-out G-funk beats and synth melodies. The Bone Thugs interweave their voices well, trading off verses and harmonizing on the choruses; plus, they sound more enthused and collaborative here than they ever again would, as they would later splinter and grow apart. There are a few standout moments, most notably the

Grammy Award-winning ballad "Tha Crossroads" and the feel-good welfare ode "1st of tha Month," as well as, of course, some obligatory blaze-some-to-this tracks, "Budsmokers Only" and "Buddah Lovaz." The intermittent tracks are good old-fashioned gangsta rap about murder, drugs, and money, though Bone's harmonious delivery makes them exceptionally interesting. In the end, the consistent tone that makes *E 1999 Eternal* such a beginning-to-end listen is unique among Bone's subsequent albums, which tend to be jumbled, as is the remarkable group cohesiveness, which is central to the appeal of standout songs like "Tha Crossroads" and "1st of tha Month." Putting aside the disappointments that laid ahead for Bone, *E 1999 Eternal* stands as one of the most accomplished, unique hardcore rap albums of the '90s, one that's often unfairly overlooked, if not dismissed entirely. (The original release featured a different version of "Tha Crossroads" titled simply "Crossroad" that was quickly replaced by a radio-aired, Grammy-winning remix.) —*Jason Birchmeier*

The Art of War / Aug. 5, 1997 / Ruthless ✦✦✦
The double-disc album was the bane of mid-'90s hip-hop. Single-disc albums tended to be overly long in the first place, but double discs were even worse, since it required artists incapable of successfully filling out a 70-minute disc to produce *twice* as much music. And it wasn't a question of the two-disc set being an artistic statement—as if the rappers had so much to say they couldn't contain themselves to one disc—it was purely a commercial decision, so they could take home more royalties. It could be argued the first two double-disc rap albums by 2Pac and the Notorious B.I.G. justified their length, since they were hip-hop giants, and the Wu-Tang Clan's *Wu-Tang Forever* more than justified its length with vision, depth and variety. However, Bone Thugs-N-Harmony's double-disc *The Art of War* can only qualify as an exercise in pure indulgence. Unlike the aforementioned artists, Bone doesn't possess either a lyrical or musical vision; their most distinctive trademark, whiny "soulfully" sung vocals alternating with raggae-inflected raps, was lifted from Snoop Dogg and Dre productions. While the group is capable of producing a catchy single, they don't have the personality to sustain an album, much less a double-disc set. By the end of the second disc, they have repeated all of their ideas at least five times apiece, and only a few of those ideas resulted in actual songs in the first place. Even hardcore fans will find *Art of War* to be an endurance test. As the cliché says, it's a double album that would have made an excellent single disc—and in this case, that means a standard 45-minute record, not a 70-minute CD. —*Stephen Thomas Erlewine*

● **The Collection, Vol. 1** / Nov. 17, 1998 / Ruthless ✦✦✦✦
Bone Thugs-N-Harmony had only released two albums and an EP, plus a handful of side projects, when they released *The Collection, Vol. 1* in the fall of 1998. Usually, that would be the sign of a rip-off, but since their albums have been notoriously uneven, this functions as a useful summary for both casual and hardcore fans alike, since it contains all of their best songs, from "Thuggish Ruggish Bone" and "For tha Love of Money" to "1st of tha Month" and "Tha Crossroads." It also contains their cover of N.W.A's "Fuck tha Police," previously only available on a tribute album. It may be of interest to collectors, but it's a weak cover and is the only thing marring this otherwise fine compilation. —*Stephen Thomas Erlewine*

BTNHResurrection / Feb. 29, 2000 / Ruthless ✦✦
Almost three years after the epic-length *The Art of War* album and following solo albums by group members Krayzie Bone (*Thug Mentality 1999*) and Bizzy Bone (*Heaven'z Movie*), Bone Thugs-N-Harmony returned with a comeback album fittingly named *BTNHResurrection*. Much has changed in the rap game in just a few short years, however. Bone Thugs were on top of the world between 1995 and 1996, though now they're merely trying to fit in during an era when weed-smoking gangsters have been replaced by champagne-sipping players, and any hint of vocal harmony will get you labeled an R&B act. Over the course of the 16 tracks here, the core trio work to their strengths, constructing dense rhymes and trading off with a smooth flow. It's difficult to escape the feeling that time has passed them by, however, and *BTNHResurrection* isn't quite the return to old glories that fans must wish it could have been. —*John Bush*

The Collection, Vol. 2 / Nov. 14, 2000 / Ruthless ✦✦✦
More of an odds-and-ends collection than a best-of, Bone Thugs-N-Harmony's *The Collection, Vol. 2* compiles various non-album songs by the group, among them a few remixes. As such, the gap-filling release is mainly for completists and shouldn't be mistaken for a best-of, since it's far, far from that. —*Jason Birchmeier*

Thug World Order / Oct. 29, 2002 / Ruthless ✦✦✦
Bone Thugs-N-Harmony is a good example of a group that has become little more than a brand name as its various members devote more of their time to solo projects. *Thug World Order* is only their fourth proper album in seven years, although many solo albums and recordings by other configurations have emerged during the period. By now, however, every album by the group seems like a reunion effort, their last one being dubbed *BTNHResurrection*, while, on this album, one of the members mutters unconvincingly, "I ain't gonna say we back, 'cause we never left...." The group's musical approach hasn't changed much, its raps offset by vocal harmonies and its musical beds anchored by samples as surprising as Phil Collins' "Take Me Home." Lyrically, their concerns are also much the same, extending from boasting and reflections on life in the 'hood to complaints about low-quality drugs ("Bad Weed Blues") and the duplicitousness of women with whom they have had sex ("Not My Baby"). But their attention seems distracted, especially when they interrupt the proceedings with commercials for their upcoming solo projects, and the album's disappointing initial commercial reception suggested that their audience wasn't paying close attention, either. —*William Ruhlmann*

Boo-Yaa T.R.I.B.E.

f. 1990, Los Angeles, CA
Group / Gangsta Rap
The six sons of a Samoan-descended Baptist minister comprising Los Angeles' Boo-Yaa T.R.I.B.E. have never had their brand of gangsta rap criticized as a commercial pose, as all members have been in prison at one time or another for producing and selling drugs and/or gun running. Brother Robert Devoux's death in a shooting provided the impetus for the formation of the Boo-Yaa T.R.I.B.E., which takes its name from a slang term for discharging a shotgun, by lead rapper Ganxsta Ridd, Ganxsta OMB, EKA, Rosco, Don-L, and the Godfather. The sextet moved to Tokyo to live with a sumo wrestler cousin and escape L.A.'s gang warfare; they performed as a dance-oriented rap outfit in Japan during the late '80s. Encouraged by their success, they returned to Los Angeles to pursue a record contract and were signed by Island. The aggressive, slamming *New Funky Nation* was released in 1990. After a four-year layoff, the T.R.I.B.E. returned with *Doomsday*, an album in similar style which contained rebukes of rappers posing as genuine gangstas for profit. Five years later, *Mafia Lifestyle* was released in fall 2000. —*Steve Huey*

● **New Funky Nation** / 1990 / 4th & Broadway ✦✦✦✦
While most rappers have been very reliant on technology, L.A.'s Boo-Yaa T.R.I.B.E. insisted on using "real instruments" both on stage and in the studio. On stage, they definitely strived for the type of spontaneity that funk bands generated in the 1970s. The Samoan-American gangster rappers and their associates use plenty of actual horns, bass, guitar, drums and percussion on *New Funky Nation*—an enjoyable debut album clearly influenced by WAR, Parliament/Funkadelic, Tower of Power and other '70s bands. Their reflections on gang violence in L.A. aren't all that memorable, but the T.R.I.B.E.'s knack for strong hooks and a blend of rap and old school soul/funk instrumentation make this CD well worth hearing. —*Alex Henderson*

Doomsday / 1995 / Bullet Proof/Music For Nations ✦✦✦✦

Mafia Lifestyle / Oct. 31, 2000 / S.m. Records ✦✦✦

Boogie Boys

f. Harlem, NY
Group / Hip-Hop, Old School Rap
A Harlem rap ensemble, the Boogie Boys scored one big hit in 1985 with "A Fly Girl," for Capitol, that peaked at number six on the R&B charts. William "Boogie Knight" Stroman, Joe "Romeo J.D." Malloy, and Rudy "Lil' Rahiem" Sheriff comprised the group. But things went downhill after that promising start, and by 1988 Sheriff had left the group. They soon disbanded. —*Ron Wynn*

City Life / 1985 / Capitol ✦✦

Survival of the Freshest / 1986 / Capitol ✦✦

Boogie Down Productions

f. 1986, Brooklyn, NY, **db.** 1993

Group / Golden Age, Political Rap, Hip-Hop, Hardcore Rap, East Coast Rap, Gangsta Rap

Boogie Down Productions was one of the most important and influential hip-hop groups of the latter half of the '80s. Led by the often brilliant and incendiary MC KRS-One, BDP were pioneers of both hardcore and political (or "conscious") rap—and if that seems contradictory, it also illustrates the scope of KRS-One's talent for chronicling and even shaping his culture. Musically, BDP usually employed spare, minimal backdrops that accentuated KRS-One's booming delivery, and they were also among the very first hip-hop artists to incorporate elements of Jamaican raggae and dancehall into their style. Early on, BDP devoted itself to brash but realistic narratives of ghetto life, which made them a street-level sensation; however, after the murder of original DJ Scott La Rock, KRS-One—who now essentially *was* BDP—devoted himself to socially and politically conscious material that earned him the nickname the Teacher. In the process, he helped pave the way for both gangsta rap *and* the positive, Afro-centric Native Tongues movement—a legacy no other rapper can claim. KRS-One retired the Boogie Down Productions moniker in the early '90s to release records under his own name; to this day, he remains one of hip-hop's most outspoken and respected intellectuals.

KRS-One's real name is Laurence Krisna Parker, or simply Kris Parker; some accounts hold that he was born with the "Krisna" moniker, while others suggest it was a nickname given to him during his youth for his interest in spirituality. Born in Brooklyn's Park Slope area in 1965, his Trinidad-born father was deported not long after his birth, and he later adopted his stepfather's last name of Parker. Early in his teens, he dropped out of high school and left home, migrating to the South Bronx; although he survived mostly on the streets and in homeless shelters, he continued his education by studying extensively in public libraries. During this period, he became interested in hip-hop culture, writing his own raps and tagging graffiti under the name KRS-One (originally an abbreviation for "Kris Number One" but later turned into the acronym "Knowledge Reigns Supreme Over Nearly Everyone"). At 19, he spent a brief time in jail for selling marijuana; after his release, he met social worker Scott Sterling at a Bronx shelter in 1985. Sterling was also a DJ who performed under the name Scott La Rock, and when the two became friends, they decided to form a rap group, which they called Boogie Down Productions.

BDP's first independently released single was 1986's "Crack Attack," and they soon completed a full-length album for the small indie label B Boy Records (which was rumored to be a front for a pornography operation). The record, *Criminal Minded*, earned them a rabid cult following on the streets when it appeared in 1987, and today is considered an early classic of hardcore rap. KRS-One's detailed depictions of urban realities—drugs, survival through violence, promiscuity, hip-hop turf wars—were sometimes harsh and sometimes gleefully celebratory. He hadn't yet developed a unified message, but his was the voice of a rebellious, intelligent young street poet, and it connected mightily with his audience. Meanwhile, La Rock's bare-bones production sometimes interpolated pop and rock samples, and the raggae inflections of the classic "9mm Goes Bang" produced a groundbreaking early fusion of hip-hop and reggae. The record's strong street buzz attracted the attention of RCA affiliate Jive, which signed the duo to a record contract. Unfortunately, not long afterward, La Rock was shot dead trying to break up an argument at a party in the Bronx.

Shattered by the loss of his best friend, KRS-One picked himself up and decided to continue Boogie Down Productions as a tribute to La Rock's memory. He recruited his younger brother Kenny Parker as a regular DJ, and also employed side members like D-Nice and Ms. Melodie (the latter, born Ramona Scott, was also his wife for a time). Convincing Jive to stick with his new crew, KRS-One completed *By All Means Necessary* in 1988, which marked the first time he took on the role of the Teacher. Also considered a landmark, *By All Means Necessary* was one of the first rap albums devoted primarily to social commentary, and contained militant, deeply personal message tracks like "My Philosophy" and "Stop the Violence." The same year, during a BDP/Public Enemy concert, a young fan was killed in a fight; galvanized into action, KRS-One founded the Stop the Violence Movement and organized the all-star charity single "Self-Destruction," which raised half a million dollars for the National Urban League in 1989.

Also in 1989, Boogie Down Productions returned with an even more politicized, intellectual album, *Ghetto Music: The Blueprint of Hip Hop*. BDP's auxiliary personnel expanded to include several more members, like Scottie Morris and Ms. Melodie's sister Harmony, but the sound wasn't any more fleshed out; in fact, it was resolutely skeletal, the antithesis of what KRS-One perceived as a new, unhealthy pop-crossover mentality overtaking hip-hop. Taking on issues like black-on-black crime, police brutality, education, and spirituality, KRS-One found his audience growing and the mainstream paying attention to his message. *The New York Times* invited him to write editorials, and he found intense demand for his views on the college lecture circuit. However, many critics found that his intellectual credibility got the better of him on the next BDP album, 1990's *Edutainment*. Despite a minor hit single in "Love's Gonna Get'cha (Material Love)," *Edutainment* was roundly criticized as being full of preachy, didactic lecturing, which also came at the expense of compelling musical backing. KRS-One further alienated his audience via a 1992 altercation with hippie-fied pop-rappers P.M. Dawn. After the group jabbed at him as "a teacher of what?" during a magazine interview, KRS-One and part of BDP stormed P.M. Dawn's New York concert, physically throwing frontman Prince Be off the stage and launching into their own set. KRS-One later explained that he was opposed to hip-hop taking such a soft, crossover-oriented direction, although P.M. Dawn had never claimed street credibility, and it seemed an odd approach from the founder of the Stop the Violence Movement. Amid negative reaction from his own fans, he later apologized publicly.

In the meantime, BDP kept recording. 1991 saw the release of *Live Hardcore Worldwide*, one of the first live hip-hop LPs. It was basically a way to get the material from *Criminal Minded* back in print, in a format where royalties could be collected (an ongoing dispute with B Boy Records was tying up the original recordings). The same year, he made a high-profile guest appearance on R.E.M.'s "Radio Song," and recorded the album *Civilization vs. Technology* with the education-oriented side project H.E.A.L. Bowing to requests from fans, BDP returned to the harder-hitting beats of its earlier material on 1992's *Sex and Violence*, which some critics hailed as a return to form, but failed to recapture his former audience. By this time, KRS-One was divorced from Ms. Melodie, and had pared down his supporting cast to Kenny Parker and Willie D. For his next project, KRS-One decided to simply put Boogie Down Productions to rest and record under his own name; his solo debut, *Return of the Boom Bap*, was released in 1993. Since then, he's released several more solo albums, and maintained an active presence in the media and on the lecture circuit. —*Steve Huey*

★ **Criminal Minded** / 1987 / Sugar Hill ✦✦✦✦✦

Criminal Minded is widely considered the foundation of hardcore rap, announcing its intentions with a cover photo of KRS-One and Scott La Rock (on his only album with Boogie Down Productions) posing with weapons—an unheard-of gesture in 1987. BDP weren't the first to rap about inner-city violence and drugs, and there's no explicit mention of gangs on *Criminal Minded*, but it greatly expanded the range of subject matter that could be put on a rap record, and its grittiest moments are still unsettling today. Actually, that part of its reputation rests on just a handful of songs. Overall, the record made its impact through sheer force—not only KRS-One's unvarnished depictions of his harsh urban environment, but also his booming delivery and La Rock's lean, hard backing tracks (which sound a little skeletal today, but were excellent for the time). It's important to note that KRS-One hadn't yet adopted his role as the Teacher, and while there are a few hints of an emerging social consciousness, *Criminal Minded* doesn't try to deliver messages, make judgments, or offer solutions. That's clear on "South Bronx" and "The Bridge Is Over," two of the most cutting—even threatening—dis records of the '80s, which were products of a beef with Queens-based MC Shan. They set the tone for the album, which reaches its apex on the influential, oft-sampled "9mm Goes Bang." It's startlingly violent, even if KRS-One's gunplay is all in self-defense, and it's made all the more unsettling by his singsong raggae delivery. Another seminal hardcore moment is "P Is Free," which details an encounter with a crack whore for perhaps the first time on record. Elsewhere there are a few showcases for KRS-One's pure rhyming skill, most notably "Poetry" and the title track. Overall it's very consistent, so even if the meat of *Criminal Minded* is the material that lives up to the title, the raw talent on display is what cements the album's status as an all-time classic. —*Steve Huey*

☆ **By All Means Necessary** / 1988 / Jive/Novus ✦✦✦✦✦
The murder of DJ Scott La Rock had a profound effect on KRS-One, resulting in a drastic rethinking of his on-record persona. He re-emerged the following year with *By All Means Necessary*, calling himself the Teacher and rapping mostly about issues facing the black community. His reality rhymes were no longer morally ambiguous, and this time when he posed on the cover with a gun, he was mimicking a photo of Malcolm X. As a social commentator, this is arguably KRS-One's finest moment. His observations are sharp, lucid, and confident, yet he doesn't fall prey to the preachiness that would mar some of his later work, and he isn't afraid to be playful or personal. The latter is especially true on the subject of La Rock, whose memory hangs over *By All Means Necessary*—not just in the frequent name-checks, but in the minimalist production and hard-hitting 808 drum beats that were his stock in trade on *Criminal Minded*. La Rock figures heavily in the album opener, "My Philosophy," which explains BDP's transition and serves as a manifesto for socially conscious hip-hop. The high point is the impassioned "Stop the Violence," a plea for peace on the hip-hop scene that still hasn't been heeded. Even as KRS-One denounces black-on-black crime, he refuses to allow the community to be stereotyped, criticizing the system that scoffs at that violence on the spoken recitation "Necessary." "Illegal Business" is a startlingly perceptive look at how the drug trade corrupts the police and government, appearing not long before the CIA's drug-running activities in the Iran-Contra Affair came to light. There are also some lighter moments in the battle-rhyme tracks, and a witty safe-sex rap in "Jimmy," a close cousin to the Jungle Brothers' "Jimbrowski." Lyrics from this album have been sampled by everyone from Prince Paul to N.W.A, and it ranks not only as KRS-One's most cohesive, fully realized statement, but a landmark of political rap that's unfairly lost in the shadow of Public Enemy's *It Takes a Nation of Millions*. —*Steve Huey*

Ghetto Music: The Blueprint of Hip Hop / Jun. 1989 / Jive ✦✦✦✦✦
The second Boogie Down Productions album devoted mostly to consciousness raising, *Ghetto Music: The Blueprint of Hip Hop* finds KRS-One evolving into a fierce advocate for both his community and his chosen art form. He's particularly concerned about the direction of the latter: He's wary of hip-hop being coopted by the pop mainstream, and the album's title comes from his conviction that real hip-hop is built on the vitality and rebelliousness of the streets. Accordingly, *Ghetto Music* contains a few more battle rhymes than usual, plus some showcases for pure MC technique, in keeping with the most basic elements of the music. The production, too, is still resolutely minimalist, and even if it's a little more fleshed out than in the past, it consciously makes no concessions to pop or R&B accessibility. There are more reggae inflections in KRS-One's delivery than ever before, audible in about half the tracks here, and the production starts to echo dancehall more explicitly on a few. Meanwhile, as the Teacher, he's actually put together lesson plans for a couple tracks: "Why Is That?" and "You Must Learn" are basically lectures about biblical and African-American history, respectively. This is where KRS-One starts to fall prey to didacticism, but he has relevant points to make, and the rapping is surprisingly nimble given all the information he's trying to pack in. Elsewhere, "Who Protects Us from You?" is a bouncy anti-police-brutality rap, and KRS closes the album with the point that "World Peace" can only be achieved through a pragmatic, aggressive struggle for equality. Although *Ghetto Music* has a few signs that KRS is starting to take himself a little too seriously (he dubs himself a metaphysician in the liner notes), overall it's another excellent effort and the last truly great BDP album. —*Steve Huey*

Edutainment / Jul. 1990 / Jive ✦✦✦
KRS-One's artistic winning streak continued with *Edutainment*, Boogie Down Productions' fourth album. True to form, he focuses on black history and speaks out on homelessness, racism, police excesses, and materialism with clarity and insight. KRS was often compared to Public Enemy leader Chuck D because of his consistently sociopolitical focus, but there's no mistaking the fact that his unique mixture of black nationalism, Eastern religion (both Hinduism and Buddhism), and Rastafarian philosophy is very much his own. From a commercial standpoint, he had become a little too intellectual and wasn't selling as many albums as many in rap's gangster school. But from an artistic perspective, *Edutainment* is as commendable as it is riveting. —*Alex Henderson*

Live Hardcore Worldwide / Mar. 12, 1991 / Jive ✦✦✦
Live albums are a rarity in rap—and understandably so. In contrast to funk and soul bands of the 1960s and '70s—many of whom couldn't wait to "take

it to the stage" and were thrilling live—hip-hoppers have been so reliant on technology that their live performances usually leave much to be desired. Many rappers have excelled in the studio only to be frightfully awkward and forgettable live. It came as a major surprise when Boogie Down Productions released this live album. While KRS-One's performances of such gems as "Jimmy," "The Bridge Is Over," "My Philosphy," and "South Bronx" are enjoyable, a lot is clearly lost in the transition from the studio to the stage. Like so many rappers—or for that matter, '90s urban contemporary artists—KRS is simply too studio oriented to generate the kind of excitement that bands like Parliament and the Ohio Players did on stage. —*Alex Henderson*

Sex and Violence / Feb. 25, 1992 / Jive/Novus ✦✦✦
The final album released under the Boogie Down Productions name, *Sex and Violence* is a partial return to form after the overly preachy ego trip of *Edutainment*. Specifically, it's a return to the aggressive beats of KRS-One's earlier work, except with a more contemporary sound—this is the first BDP album to rely on multiple outside producers, which supplies a much-needed sonic update. As a result, some BDP fans feel that *Sex and Violence* is an underrated effort—it packs more of a punch, and KRS-One is refocusing on the art of MCing, not to mention his dancehall reggae influence. That said, it isn't a complete success, since his usual consistency of vision isn't quite there. There are a number of good moments: the single "Duck Down," "Like a Throttle" (which fears that Islamic spirituality has become nothing but a hip-hop fad), and "Poisonous Products." But elsewhere, some of his observations are more provocative than immediately insightful. He urges the "Drug Dealer" to invest his profits in the black community, and on "Build and Destroy" he brands high-ranking black officials like Clarence Thomas and Colin Powell nothing short of devils for their assimilation. Plus, "13 and Good" and "Say Gal" both have a discomforting undercurrent of misogyny unbecoming a teacher. There's enough vitality on *Sex and Violence* to make it worthwhile for fans, but overall it doesn't rank with the best of KRS-One's work. —*Steve Huey*

Man & His Music (Remixes from Around the World) / Sep. 23, 1997 / M.I.L. ✦✦
Man & His Music (Remixes from Around the World) compiles a number of remixes of classic BDP tracks from the late '80s and early '90s. While some of these cuts will be of interest to hardcore fans and dance collectors, none are particularly revelatory or inventive, and most fans of KRS-One's incendiary hip-hop won't need to bother with this disc. —*Stephen Thomas Erlewine*

Best of B-Boy Records / May 8, 2001 / Landspeed ✦✦✦
This is a collection of old school classics from KRS-One's BDP crew, including "Dope Beat," "P Is Free," "Poetry," and "The Bridge Is Over," among others. This is the material that has KRS-One declaring himself the god of hip-hop, and he definitely pushed the envelope in a day when rap music was a lot more political and introspective. This is a good introductory compilation for a new generation of listeners interested in learning about the roots of rap music, and equally valuable to those who were around in the BDP days but for one reason or another no longer have all those old records. —*Brad Mills*

Boogiemonsters

f. Virginia
Group / Hip-Hop, Underground Rap, Trip-Hop, Turntablism
New Yorkers Vex and Mondo met Jamaica-born brothers Yodared and Myntric at Virginia State University. Boogiemonsters began rapping at shows around campus and, after winning first place at Howard University's famous Hip-Hop Convention, they recorded a demo and began shopping it around New York. Pendulum/EMI signed the four MCs and, in 1994, released *Riders of the Storm: The Underwater Album*. —*John Bush*

Riders of the Storm: The Underwater Album / Aug. 9, 1994 / Pendulum/EMI ✦✦
Soulful, funky, and R&Bish, the Boogiemonsters' raps have a sense of spirituality that gives songs such as "Mark of the Beast" and "Recognized Thresholds of Negative Stress" a reflective air. If it has one problem, albeit a small one, *Riders of the Storm* is too laid-back—only two later songs break into the mid-tempo range. —*John Bush*

Boom Bip (Bryan Hollon)

Beatbox, Producer / Underground Rap, Hip-Hop
Boom Bip is a Cincinnati-based hip-hop artist whose command of the human beatbox and sample salvage has few equals beside Rahzel the Godfather of

Noise. After playing in several bands during high school, he became a DJ in 1993 while attending college in Cincinnati. Offbeat turntablist methods gradually raised his profile, and he began recording for the Lex label. During 2001, Boom Bip collaborated on an LP with rapper Doseone, and provided remixes for Four Tet and Jamie Lidell. He also began a series of breaks records (*Doo-Doo Breaks*) for the Mush label, and in 2002, released his solo debut, *Seed to Sun*, as part of a contract between Lex and Britain's prestigious Warp. —*John Bush*

Circle / May 27, 2002 / Leaf ✦✦✦✦✦
Before Clouddead hopped the Atlantic to hit Will Ashton's respected Big Dada imprint, Cloud's Dose and DJ/producer Boom reached critical mass at San Francisco's Mush in 2000, with this re-release through the influential Leaf label receiving a rapturous response two years later. Loaded with 29 tracks, each containing literally reams of thoughts, there is an awful lot to take in, but the experience proves well worth the investment, with *Circle*'s renunciation of traditional hip-hop in favor of a collation of loose conceptual movements that ultimately add up to one of the most progressive albums to have ever graced the genre. Boom's otherworldly production and sense of the epic match the rapid-fire delivery of Dose blow for blow—though occasionally the lyrics come so quickly that lines have to be spun simultaneously through different speakers. Fans of DJ Shadow will go wild for the apocalyptic beats, while the wordplay will have even the most ardent anti-hip-hopper turning the corner, and even those more used to Aphex Twin will tune into the obtuse theatrics. Check your preconceptions at the door and fast-forward to some spine-shivering hip-not futurism. —*Kingsley Marshall*

● **Seed to Sun** / Sep. 17, 2002 / Lex ✦✦✦✦✦
Boom Bip, a Cincinnati producer/DJ (roughly in that order), comes from a long line of twisted hip-hop mentalists, stretching from Biz Markie to Company Flow to Kid Koala. And listeners expecting something special from an unknown granted a licensing to the quality-control experts at Warp won't be disappointed by *Seed to Sun*; it's experimental hip-hop being done on a level reached by few producers out there. More experimental, rangier, and lighter than any Co-Flow material, but more producer driven than Kid Koala's records, the album encompasses analog electronics, beat-heavy experimental techno, turntablist scratching, and dozens of mostly unrecognizable samples (one strain that briefly emerges from the soup: B.J. Thomas' "Everybody's Out of Town"). Surprisingly, *Seed to Sun* is also very melodic, audible even when Boom Bip layers dense beats and samples over his tracks, as on "Closed Shoulders." For "The Unthinkable," one of the few vocal tracks, guest Buck 65 comes off like a countrified rapper produced by El-P. The other top-notch vocal comes from Dose One (from Anticon), prefacing a Cypress Hill-goes-pop chorus on "Mannequin Hand Trapdoor I Reminder" with some paranoid musings. Nothing against El-P; he's a great producer, and deserves most of the hype he's gotten. It's just that *Seed to Sun* does what he does so much better. —*John Bush*

Boot Camp Clik

Group / Gangsta Rap, Hardcore Rap, Southern Rap
Boot Camp Clik is a loose congregation featuring similar-minded underground hardcore rappers like Originoo Gunn Clapaz, Cocoa Brovaz, Buckshot, Heltah Skeltah, Bucktown Juveniles, Jahdan, and Illa Noyz, all of whom are concerned about keeping the music real and on a street level. That meant much of the music on their debut, *For the People*, sounded a little similar; still, this is the very thing that makes Boot Camp Clik appealing to a certain audience. Their second record, *The Chosen Few*, appeared in 2002. —*Stephen Thomas Erlewine*

For the People / May 20, 1997 / Priority ✦✦✦
The Boot Camp Clik is a bit like a low-rent Wu-Tang Clan. Instead of establishing themselves as a crew before recording an album together, the rappers—including Heltah Skeltah, Smif-n-Wessun, and OGC—each made solo albums and reunited in 1997 to make *For the People*. Happily, the group used the opportunity wisely, deciding to forge ahead to new sonic territory. Leaving gangsta rap and standard funk behind as the group abandons their production crew Da Beatminerz, the Boot Camp Clik has created an appealingly off-kilter sound that relies equally on wobbly rhythms, old school synths, and acoustic instruments. There are times that the mix is too dense, particularly when the group tries to get slow and soulful, but *For the People* is the best thing anyone in the Boot Camp Clik has yet produced. —*Leo Stanley*

● **Boot Camp Clik's Greatest Hits: Basic Training** / Mar. 14, 2000 / Priority ✦✦✦✦✦
This compilation from the Crooklyn warrior b-boy crew known as Boot Camp Clik contains a cross-section of the posse's hits. BCC brought a military attitude and a rough, rumbling sound to the hip-hop table. The sound and feel is the essence of the Boot Camp, largely provided by the production team, the Beatminerz. Two members of the production squad, DJ Evil Dee and Mr. Walt, deployed missile-type beats with a signature bone-snapping snare. On the microphone, Boot Camp soldiers possess the kamikaze philosophy of infantrymen and the skills and wit of generals. Beats and flows are fashioned by the notion of Brooklyn as a treacherous abyss of warfare and gunplay, a proving ground for mental and physical toughness. Black Moon was the first out the gate with the 1993 release of *Enta da Stage*, an underground favorite that found mild commercial success with the remix of "I Gotcha Opin," which lifted Barry White's "Playing Your Game, Baby" effortlessly. *Enta da Stage* introduced the focal member and mastermind of the crew, Buckshot the B.D.I. In late 1993, the next battalion, Smif-n-Wessun (later incarnated as the Cocoa Brovaz), dropped "Bucktown," the anthem for the Camp, and their blistering debut, *Dah Shining*, followed shortly thereafter in 1994. Heltah Skeltah and O.G.C. teamed up as the Fab Five in 1995 with "Lefleur Leflah" to take BCC into a newer, funkier direction. These two platoons followed in the footsteps of their Boot Camp predecessors laying further claim to the Brooklyn battlefield. Heltah Skeltah's debut *Nocturnal* and O.G.C.'s debut *Da Storm* took the Boot Camp back to the basement. With the heartbeat of Brooklyn beating within them, BCC is a unified collective that invented a rugged sound. —*Michael Di Bella*

The Chosen Few / Oct. 8, 2002 / Duckdown ✦✦✦✦
Five years after their first full-length, Boot Camp Clik again came together with an LP that finally delivered on the promise that'd kept hip-hop fans hoping for an album to rank with incredible singles from the collective like Black Moon's "How Many MCs" and Smif-n-Wessun's boot-camp anthem "Bucktown." Featuring the combined talents of members of Black Moon and Cocoa Brovaz (the reincarnated Smif-n-Wessun), plus Originoo Gun Clappaz, *The Chosen Few* is one of the tightest rap albums of the year. Better yet, it succeeds by keeping it simple: the production, the beats, and the themes—nearly everything except the rapping. The productions come from a parade of family members (da Beatminerz, Hi-Tek, Coptic) with nothing to prove on their own, instead simply concentrating on constructing tough beats and kinetic tracks. The crew set it off with a pair of openers, "And So" and "Let's Get Down 2 Bizness," that top anything heard on 1997's *For the People*. From there, Boot Camp Clik cycle through everything that fans could've asked for; a crazy party track ("That's Tough [Little Bit]"), a classic beatdown on "Whoop His Ass," and a rough-and-rugged "Bucktown" sequel ("Welcome to Bucktown U.S.A."). Considering nearly all of them have their own projects on the front burner, it may be awhile for another full LP from Boot Camp Clik, but the collective has left listeners with plenty to keep them happy. —*John Bush*

Bootleg (Ira Dorsey)

b. Flint, MI
Hardcore Rap, Gangsta Rap
Dayton Family founder Bootleg made a name for himself in the Midwest hardcore rap underground not only as a member of the infamous Flint, MI, group but also as a solo artist. While many MCs rap about crime and the gangsta lifestyle, few can actually back up their talk. No stranger to crime or prison, Bootleg is one of the few hardcore rappers who speaks directly from experience. It's this sincerity and experience that sets him apart from his wannabe peers, making him one of the Midwest's most notorious hardcore rappers.

After joining forces with fellow Flint MCs Shoestring and Matt Finkle, Bootleg tagged the trio the Dayton Family in commemoration of the shady, crime-ridden street they called home. By 1995 the trio had released their first album, *What's on My Mind?*, followed a year later by the gold-selling *F.B.I.* While both albums generated a substantial amount of attention and hype in the underground hardcore rap scene, the law unfortunately intervened, and the group members soon found themselves behind bars for various crimes. Of course, prison wasn't a new experience for Bootleg. In fact, he'd spent the greater part of the '90s behind bars, accumulating priceless experiences that fueled his criminal-minded rhymes.

Once Bootleg finally got out of prison, he used every free moment to work on his solo debut, 1999's *Death Before Dishonesty*. Unfortunately, partly because of the three-year interval since *F.B.I.*, Bootleg's debut didn't sell as well as hoped for, and Relativity Records quickly parted ways with the troubled rapper. In 2001 Bootleg returned to the rap game, though, joining forces with the Detroit-based Overcore label (Esham, Natas). That year he released his second album, *Hated By Many, Loved By Few*, as did the other Dayton Family members. —*Jason Birchmeier*

Death Before Dishonesty / Mar. 23, 1999 / Relativity ✦✦✦
Three years after the Dayton Family entered their unofficial prison-related sabbatical, Bootleg appeared with his first solo album, *Death Before Dishonesty*. In those three years since the Dayton Family's *F.B.I.* album, a lot had happened. Thankfully, despite all the personal drama, Bootleg and his producer, Steve Pitts, had managed to hone their craft, resulting in the most polished Dayton Family-related release of the 1990s. The inclusion of female vocalists on some of the song's hooks was a major change from the nothing-but-hardcore rap sound of *F.B.I.*; furthermore, a wide range of guest rappers appear here, with the most notable exception being Bootleg's longtime partner, fellow Dayton Family founder Shoestring. So the album ends up sounding like quite a departure from the Dayton Family albums, thanks mostly to the revolving ensemble of guests and Shoestring's absence. The increased variety from song to song is welcome, but die-hard fans will probably long for the classic Dayton Family sound—posse cuts driven by hard beats. Granted, *Death Before Dishonesty* is a respectable album, but it's not exactly what Dayton Family fans are probably looking for. —*Jason Birchmeier*

● **Hated By Many, Loved By Few** / Jul. 10, 2001 / Overcore ✦✦✦✦
The return of the Dayton Family in 2001 brought with it a trio of solo albums by group members Ghetto E, Shoestring, and Bootleg. All had signed to the Detroit-based Overcore label (Esham, Natas, Mastamind) and seemed renewed after some unsuccessful debut albums on major labels. Of those three albums, Bootleg's stands out as the best in terms of not only the production but also in terms of rhymes. In fact, *Hated By Many, Loved By Few* is so impressive relative to those other two albums that it's almost a disservice to associate Bootleg with his peers. Sure, Ghetto E's *Ghetto Theater* and Shoestring's *Cross Addicted* have their merits, but those albums reflect an admittedly lo-fi aesthetic and are a little short on creativity. Bootleg's album succeeds where those albums faltered. The beats are potent, fueled by live instruments and dirty South-style drum machine beats and synths; in fact, their unique sound helps set this album apart from the numerous underground hardcore rap albums released in 2001. But it are Bootleg's efforts that make this album so impressive. His MCing style is reminiscent of 2Pac—fast paced, aggressive, and unapologetic. In addition, he brings in a number of other vocalists to give the album additional depth and a sense of variety. Furthermore, where *Death Before Dishonesty* was wounded by its crossover ambitions, *Hated By Many* returns to the hardcore gangsta style that the Dayton Family is known for, and thanks to its impressive execution, it's the better album. Overall one of the best underground hardcore rap albums of 2001, Bootleg's second album proves that he's the most talented member of the Dayton Family. —*Jason Birchmeier*

Born Jamericans

Group / Hip-Hop, Dancehall, Ragga, Club/Dance
Fusing hip-hop and dancehall reggae, Born Jamericans earned a cult following with their pair of mid-'90s albums. The duo was comprised of Mr. Notch, who favored smooth vocals, and Edley Shine, who delivered rough raggae raps. Born Jamericans' debut album, *Kids From Foreign*, became a reggae hit upon its 1994 release, and they became a favorite of the reggae circuit, opening for Buju Banton, Shabba Ranks, Zhané, and Shai, among many others. Mad Lion, Shinehead, and Johnny Osbourne all were featured on the group's second album, *Yardcore*, which was released in the spring of 1997. —*Stephen Thomas Erlewine*

Kids From Foreign / Jun. 7, 1994 / Delicious Vinyl ✦✦✦✦
Although the duo occasionally falls prey to style over substance, Born Jamericans' debut, *Kids From Foreign*, is an impressive collection of street-oriented hip-hop and dancehall reggae, highlighted by the singles "Boom Shak-A-Tack" and "Cease & Seckle." —*Leo Stanley*

Yardcore / May 27, 1997 / Delicious Vinyl ✦✦✦
While most hip-hop/reggae hybrids feature endless streams of lyrics indistinguishable to those not familiar with the dialect, Born Jamericans slow up the beat and infuse the style with lover's rock. The result is a rather seductive album of mellow grooves and sensual lyrics that leans much closer to the sounds of Jimmy Cliff than to that of Buju Banton. High points include "State of Shock," which features Johnny Osbourne, and the cover of Frankie Avalon's "Venus." Even though the style gets a bit long winded and the tracks tend to blur, there is still enough strong material on this album to make it worth listening to, and perhaps slow dancing to as well. —*Curtis Zimmermann*

● **The Best of the Born Jamericans** / Feb. 19, 2002 / Rhino ✦✦✦✦
Rhino's 2002 collection *The Best of the Born Jamericans* is an excellent summary of the duo's recordings for Delicious Vinyl, containing five songs a piece from *Kids From Foreign* and *Yardcore*, plus two previously unreleased tracks and a dancehall remix of their biggest hit, "Boom Shak-A-Tack." Although they never got much bigger than that song, they did mix hip-hop and reggae quite nimbly, and this is the best place for the curious to check it out. —*Stephen Thomas Erlewine*

Boss (Lichelle Laws)

b. Detroit, MI
Vocals / East Coast Rap, Hardcore Rap, Gangsta Rap
Born Lichelle Laws, Boss is a female gangster rapper who, along with her partner, Dee, became the first female rap act to be signed to Russell Simmons' Def Jam West label. Originally the two hailed from Detroit, but after a brief stint in New York, the pair headed west to L.A. where they lived in near poverty for three years before gaining the attention of DJ Quik and receiving a record deal, eventually releasing *Born Gangstaz* in 1992. —*Steve Kurutz*

● **Born Gangstaz** / 1992 / Def Jam ✦✦✦✦
Just as fantastic and less forced than plenty of other gangsta rap records released in 1992, Boss' *Born Gangstaz* is a remarkable album that has gone underappreciated in the hip-hop world. Abetted by a laundry list of reputable producers—Jam Master Jay, T Ray, MC Serch, Def Jef, AMG, Erick Sermon—MC Lichelle Laws and DJ Irene Moore shrug at a cruel world, claim not to care, drink like fishes, smoke like Cypress Hill, live like thieves, and accord the opposite sex no respect whatsoever. In fact, no one and nothing is given any degree of respect, and it's clear that they've got a death wish. All of this would be met with a shrug if Laws had less-than-remarkable vocal and lyrical skills, but she's just as adept at painting vivid scenarios while riding the rhythms as any of her producers. She doesn't simply flip the gender roles of the average gangsta record; "tricks" expecting to get some end up getting some in the form of bullets. Her delivery consistently sounds collected but set to blast, and the productions almost always complement her detached, matter-of-fact viewpoint. Too bad the answering-machine messages left by Laws' parents soften the blunt impact of this cold, cold record. —*Andy Kellman*

Brand Nubian

f. 1989, New Rochelle, NY
Group / Golden Age, Alternative Rap, Jazz-Rap
The Five Percent Nation of Islam was a popular inspiration for numerous thinking-man's rap groups during the early '90s, and Brand Nubian was arguably the finest of the more militant crop. Although they were strongly related to the Native Tongues posse in style and sound, they weren't technically members, and were less reserved about spotlighting their politics and religion. Their outspokenness led to controversy, on an even larger scale than similarly minded groups like the X-Clan or Poor Righteous Teachers, in part because Brand Nubian's sheer musicality made them so listenable regardless of what their messages were. The hoopla surrounding their aggressive Afrocentrism sometimes overshadowed the playful and positive sides of their work, as well as the undeniable virtuosity of lead MC Grand Puba's rhymes—all showcased to best effect on their highly acclaimed debut, *One for All*. Brand Nubian was formed in 1989 in the New York suburb of New Rochelle. Grand Puba (born Maxwell Dixon) had previously recorded with a group called Masters of Ceremony, and was joined by Sadat X (born Derek Murphy, originally dubbed Derek X), Lord Jamar (born Lorenzo DeChalus), and DJ Alamo (Murphy's cousin). The group signed with Elektra and released their debut album, *All for One*, in 1990. Most reviews were glowing, but the stronger rhetoric on the album—especially the track "Drop the Bomb"—drew fire from some quarters, including some white Elektra employees reluctant

to promote what they saw as reverse racism. Ultimately, the uproar didn't really hurt Brand Nubian's career, but neither did it produce a wider hit with pop or R&B audiences, despite the high regard in which the singles "All for One," "Slow Down," and "Wake Up" are held. A far more serious blow was Grand Puba's departure from the group in late 1991, owing to tensions that had arisen over his handling the lion's share of the rapping. Not only did Brand Nubian lose their clear focal point and chief producer, they also lost DJ Alamo, who elected to continue working with Puba. Puba released his solo debut, *Reel to Reel*, in 1992; meanwhile, Lord Jamar and Sadat X regrouped with DJ Sincere (born Terrence Perry) and issued *In God We Trust* in 1993. It sold fairly well, just missing the Top Ten on the R&B chart, and the single "Punks Jump up to Get Beat Down" was something of a hit, though it also drew fire for its anti-gay slurs. In Puba's absence, the pro-Islam rhetoric grew stronger, with more explicit support for the controversial Minister Louis Farrakhan. By the time of 1994's *Everything Is Everything*, they'd gotten downright dogmatic, and critics who'd previously defended the group now found them difficult to stomach, both lyrically and musically.

In the wake of the icy reception afforded *Everything Is Everything*, the remaining members of Brand Nubian drifted apart. Sadat X reunited with Grand Puba for "Play It Cool," a track on the latter's second solo album; Sadat also released his solo debut, *Wild Cowboys*, in 1996, and subsequently guested on records by a new wave of underground hip-hoppers. Lord Jamar, meanwhile, moved into production, and also landed a recurring role on HBO's prison drama *Oz*. In 1998, with a new alternative rap movement gaining prominence, the original four members of Brand Nubian reunited for the Arista album *Foundation*, which received highly positive reviews. Grand Puba and Sadat X both subsequently returned to their solo careers. —*Steve Huey*

● **One for All** / 1990 / Elektra ✦✦✦✦✦
Brand Nubian never sold as many albums as the many West Coast rappers burning up the charts in the early 1990s, but the New York group commanded great respect in East Coast rap circles. In black neighborhoods of New York and Philadelphia, Nubian's debut album, *One for All*, was actually a bigger seller than many of the platinum gangsta rap releases outselling it on a national level. Influenced by De La Soul and the Jungle Brothers, Nubian favored an abstract rapping style, and East Coast rap fans were drawn to the complexity of jams like "Dance To My Ministry," "Ragtime" and "All for One." Grand Puba, Lord Jammer, and Saddat X had a lot of technique, which was what hip-hoppers favored in the east. On the whole, Nubian's Nation of Islam rhetoric isn't as overbearing as some of the recordings that other Five Percenters were delivering at the time. The CD is a bit uneven, but on the whole is likable and exhilarating. —*Alex Henderson*

In God We Trust / Feb. 2, 1993 / Elektra ✦✦✦✦
Their first album after losing talented MC Grand Puba, Sadat X and Lord Jamar were joined by DJ Sincere for this 1993 effort, which earned some notoriety for the homophobic taunts included in "Punks Jump Up to Get Beat Down." Elsewhere the record is a rallying call for Louis Farrakhan's Nation of Islam—notably on "Allah and Justice" and "Meaning of the 5%." If you can get past the religious dogma, the musical platform is tough and compelling, and the rhymes are delivered with surprising dexterity and poise in the absence of Puba. —*Alex Ogg*

Everything Is Everything / Nov. 1, 1994 / Elektra ✦✦✦
Brand Nubian cover a wide variety of styles and issues on this album. Their message is positive, but they come down hard on stereotypes and blacks killing other blacks. Sampling from rock and jazz alike, the group's scratchy rhythms are a good complement to the lyrics. —*John Bush*

Foundation / Sep. 29, 1998 / Arista ✦✦✦✦
Foundation, the first album since Brand Nubian's 1990 debut that featured all four original members, is an incredible return to form. The rhymes by Grand Puba, Sadat X, and Lord Jamar are as striking as they were on the group's breakout, and the focus on message tracks is a refreshing turn from the rap world's played-out tales of thug life. "Don't Let It Go to Your Head" is a cautionary tale for arrogant one-hit rappers, while "Probable Cause" is a scathing attack on the notorious tactics of the New Jersey state police and "I'm Black and I'm Proud" is an enjoyable roots epic. There are plenty of simple feel-good tracks as well, although those omnipresent Wu-Tang strings appear on several songs (just as on every other major rap album released in 1998). The group ably manage to sidestep another late-'90s rap cliché, enlisting a different outside producer for each track. Though *Foundation* is no different—featuring DJ Premiere, Lord Finesse, and Chris "C.L." Liggio, among others—most of the best tracks were helmed by Nubian members Grand Puba or DJ Alamo. Of the few NYC rap acts still left a decade after rap's golden age, Brand Nubian sounded the freshest. —*John Bush*

★ **The Very Best of Brand Nubian** / Sep. 18, 2001 / Rhino ✦✦✦✦
Politically controversial in their time, Brand Nubian doesn't sound like the dangerous, Afro-centric militants they were originally made out to be in some quarters. Maybe it's because their jazzy, post-Native Tongues music is so ingratiating; maybe it's because Grand Puba has such a playful, easygoing presence on the mic; maybe it's just that, in the new millennium, politics are no longer the way rap groups ruffle feathers. Whatever the case, Rhino's *The Very Best of Brand Nubian* is an essential summation of the uncompromisingly pro-black, often very positive group's career. Grand Puba, clearly their most inventive lyricist, departed after their excellent debut, *One for All*, and was definitely missed on subsequent albums. So instead of trying to balance the picture, the compilation wisely leans heavily on *One for All*, from whence come seven of the 16 tracks (eight if you count the Pete Rock remix of "Slow Down"). We also get two Grand Puba solo singles and one track from the group's latter-day reunion with Puba, "Don't Let It Go to Your Head." That leaves three tracks from *In God We Trust*, just one from the coolly received *Everything Is Everything*, and another hard-to-find remix (of "Punks Jump Up to Get Beat Down"). One could make the case that "Step to the Rear" and "Who Can Get Busy Like This Man" should also have made the cut from the debut, instead of the two remixes, but then again, there had to be a decent reason to buy this comp, even if all the post-*One for All* material included here is worth rescuing. As for the group's politics, the "white devil" fixation on "Drop the Bomb" and "Wake Up (Reprise in the Sunshine)" *can* sound paranoid to nonbelievers. But really, it shouldn't detract from the group's numerous strengths, which make *The Very Best of Brand Nubian* an extremely high-quality listen. —*Steve Huey*

Breakestra

f. 1996, Los Angeles, CA
Group / Hip-Hop, Deep Funk Revival
Formed by breaks fanatic Miles Tackett, Breakestra is a ten-piece, hip-hop orchestra based in Los Angeles. The group came together in 1997 around Tackett's DJ gigs at a coffeehouse. A multi-instrumentalist whose work on upright cello has appeared on recordings by B.B. King, Macy Gray, and Black Eyed Peas, Tackett was a funk fan who got into hip-hop during the late '80s—courtesy of the Ultramagnetic classic *Critical Beatdown*—when he realized it was keeping the funk flame alive. A wish to play instrumental hip-hop in a band context brought the group together, with Tackett alongside drummer Josh "Wallet" Cohen, reed player Geoff "Double G" Gallegos, trumpeters Todd Simon and Paul Vargas, trombone player Dan Osterman, keyboard player Carlos Guaico, percussionist Davy Chegwidden, guitarist Dan Ubick, and vocalists Sol Sista DeMya and Mixmaster Wolf (aka Stones Throw honcho Peanut Butter Wolf). Their club night Root Down brought in crowds, along with the cream of the rap underground (Jurassic 5, Dilated Peoples, Company Flow, DJ Shadow, Freestyle Fellowship), and their first single, "Getcho Soul Togetha," appeared on Stones Throw in 1999. That year also brought an intriguing demo called *The Live Mix Tape*—including Breakestra covers of a host of deep funk classics—but an official release (as *The Live Mix, Pt. 1*) waited until 2001 and only appeared in Japan. The second volume followed later that year, and was released on Stones Throw. —*John Bush*

Deuces Up, Double Down EP / 2001 / Stones Throw ✦✦✦
The follow-up to their 2000 LP, the *Deuces Up, Double Down* EP expands upon Breakestra's old school funk mastery. While their debut displayed the band's proficiency in performing the classic breaks of the genre, these extraordinarily funky five tracks, along with their discography of underground 45s, lay deep into their stark ability to contribute to the movement. Featuring the Miles Tackett (This Kid Named Miles) original single "Deuces Up, Double Down," a wild, old school Hot Pie and Candy-sounding deep funk groove, the EP also presents great renditions of the "Humpty Dump" and a "Funky Soul"/"16 Corners" medley. With the corroboration of their Stones Throw brethren, the funk genre is as strong and popular as it has been in decades, and Breakestra is one of its finest pupils. —*Nic Kincaid*

- **The Live Mix, Pt. 2** / Feb. 20, 2001 / Stones Throw ♦♦♦♦

A year or so before there was an actual band called Breakestra, there existed a first Breakestra recording. An explanation is required. In 1996 Miles Tackett gathered together a group of friends for an extended jam session. The object: take vintage soul, funk, and jazz breaks and replay them as a live "mix," sort of funk with a hip-hop ethos. That session was recorded and became the cassette-only collector's item *Live Mix, Pt. 1*. The group, under Tackett's direction, would eventually evolve into Breakestra, and it sold the cassette in the Los Angeles nightclubs where it held a showcase fittingly called "The Breaks." By 2000, Breakestra had finally emerged on the international music scene, and after word had gotten out about *Live Mix, Pt. 1* (particularly in Europe), Tackett and manager Charles Raggio decided to make it available for the first time on CD as a limited run of 1,000 copies, sold exclusively through online retailer Giant Peach. (It was also later made available in Japan by Stones Throw with initial sales of Breakestra's *Live Mix, Pt. 2*.) A complicated backstory that still doesn't answer the important question: is it worth going to the trouble of tracking down? Indeed, it is. And it sounds just like you might expect from the above explanation: a Tower of Power for the rap generation. The set that takes up the opening two-thirds of the album is the aforementioned continuous mix of breakbeats (Jimmy Smith's "Root Down," Herbie Hancock's "Open Your Eyes," Bobby Byrd's "I Know You Got Soul") as sampled by artists like De La Soul and A Tribe Called Quest and then translated back into the live vernacular. Breakestra's versions pass the blindfold test and then some. That leaves a trio of songs: the band's initial 1999 single, "Getcho Soul Together," a funky howl of a song that channels the spirit of the J.B.'s at their juicy best; a facsimile cover of the rare Sly & the Family Stone track "Remember Who You Are"; and "Sexy Popcorn Pot," which might just as well be an original as a hybrid of James Brown's "Mother Popcorn" and Tony Alvon & the Belairs' crate-digger classic "Sexy Coffee Pot" (the obvious prototype), even if you can never quite make the distinction of which it is. A bit rough in spots, but no matter—funk is supposed to be messy. And this album is funk to the bone. *—Stanton Swihart*

Brotha Lynch Hung (Kevin Mann)

b. Sacramento, CA
Producer, Vocals, Engineer / Gangsta Rap, Hardcore Rap, Underground Rap, Hip-Hop

A versatile producer as well as an excellent solo rapper in his own right, Brotha Lynch Hung was born Kevin Mann in Sacramento. He hooked up with Master P for a 1993 EP named *24 Deep* and followed it up with his 1995 debut solo album, *Season of da Siccness*. Mann worked on production for Master P's *I'm Bout It*, E-40's *Southwest Riders*, and Mr. Serv-On's *Life Insurance* before turning back to his own career. Given a big push by Master P's breakout success in the middle of 1997, Brotha Lynch Hung's sophomore album, *Loaded*, followed in 1997. *EBK4* followed in 2000 and both *Blocc Movement* and *Virus* appeared the next summer. The year 2002 was less busy, with *Appearances: Book 1* being released in the spring and the *Plague* DVD following it that summer. *—John Bush*

- **Season of da Siccness** / Feb. 28, 1995 / Black Market ♦♦♦♦♦

After the Geto Boys, it seemed that rap couldn't get any more extreme or hardcore. But in 1995, *Season of da Siccness* proved that in fact it could. Thriving on shock value and outrageousness, Brother Lynch Hung is to rap what grindcore bands like Cannibal Corpse and Carcass are to metal. On this very twisted CD, the obscure and underground Sacramento MC calls himself "The Ripgut Cannibal" and portrays a psycho who's part Jeffrey Dahmer, part Hannibal Lecter, and part ghetto gangbanger. Lynch's accounts of cannibalism and dismemberment must be taken for exactly what they are: outrageous entertainment, pure and simple. Obviously, *Siccness* isn't for everyone. But those interested in the hip-hop equivalent of a slasher movie may find Lynch (whose rapid-fire delivery brings to mind Spice 1) quite entertaining. *—Alex Henderson*

Loaded / 1997 / Black Market ♦♦♦♦

Full of references to cannibalism, 1995's controversial and unique *Season of da Siccness* sent shock waves through hip-hop's underground and gave Brotha Lynch Hung a small cult following. But when the controversial Sacramento rapper's third album, *Loaded*, soared to the top of the urban charts, it was clear that he had become a major star in rap, much more than a cult figure. Some hip-hoppers wondered if Lynch would continue to portray "The

Ripgut Cannibal" on CD, but *Loaded* isn't nearly as gruesome or as shocking as its predecessor. Gone were the references to cannibalism, and the album's sexually explicit lyrics and references to inner-city violence and marijuana smoking aren't anything out of the ordinary by gangsta-rap standards. What really makes this enjoyable, if uneven, CD noteworthy is Lynch's impressive technique—the Spice 1-influenced rapper delivers one tricky, difficult tongue-twister after another. *Season of da Siccness* remains Lynch's best album, but *Loaded* definitely has its pleasures. *—Alex Henderson*

EBK4 / Jun. 27, 2000 / Black Market ♦♦

Underground gangsta rappers such as Brotha Lynch Hung seem to struggle with their attempts to gain recognition in an increasingly crowded rap game. On past albums—particularly the infamous *Season of da Siccness* album— the Sacramento rapper used shock tactics to get attention, taking the generic gangsta motifs of violence, drugs, and misogyny to their furthest limits. With *EBK4*, Brotha Lynch Hung stays true to his style, again turning to these same motifs: romanticized urban tales of grotesque murder ("Blood on da Rug"), blazing up insane amounts of chronic with Snoop Dogg ("Dogg Market"), and speaking of women as though they are mere commodities waited to be exploited ("Every Single B*%#$"). Of course, by the year 2000 these topics have become very tired. Sure, N.W.A and the Geto Boys rose to fame using this same formula, but by the end of the '90s, any seasoned rap listener had heard these same stories countless times. If only Brotha Lynch Hung had some striking beats or a smooth delivery, this could be decent record; unfortunately though, the lumbering, dark soundscapes aren't going to make anyone bounce, the Sacramento rapper doesn't come close to any proven rapper in terms of skills, and, ultimately, none of his guest rappers—with the exception of an incredibly sedate Snoop Dogg—elevate this album beyond its amateur sound. Most probably don't expect *EBK4* to compare to the work of Mobb Deep or Master P, but one must see this album for what it is: yet another poorly produced record of second-rate rappers trying to come off as hardcore gangsta to the point that it seems just far too contrived for an experienced listener to take seriously. *—Jason Birchmeier*

Blocc Movement / Aug. 28, 2001 / JCOR ♦♦

The Broun Fellinis

f. 1993
Group / Jazz-Funk, Jazz-Rap

The Broun Fellinis are a jazz/hip-hop trio hailing from the Bay Area whose members include percussionist Professor Boris Karnaz (born Kevin Carnes), bassist Kirk the Redeemer, and woodwind player Black Edgar Kenyatta. Their debut, *Aphrokubist Improvisations, Vol. 9*, was released in 1995. The group has created their own mythology explaining their origins—they claim to be from the mythical land of Boohaabia, which floats off the coast of Madagascar and is surrounded by the Phat Temple, the Ministry of Imagination, and the Oasis of Surprise, which are all at equal distances from Boohaabia. Further, Karnaz claims that Boohaabia may be reached through the group's music, or perhaps through Kirk the Redeemer's bass cabinet if the pilgrim has brought him some cashews; Karnaz promises that the listener's chair will then sink six inches into the sand and giraffes will appear, ready to take the listener wherever he may want to go. *—Steve Huey*

Aphrokubist Improvisations, Vol. 9 / May 16, 1995 / Moonshine ♦♦♦♦

Don't let the album title, silly concepts, or the fact that this promising debut is on an ambient/dance label fool you. If you are into the more populist directions that the new school of jam-friendly jazz (see Medeski Martin & Wood, Charlie Hunter, etc.) is taking, this CD is sure to please. The group is essentially a trio, with David Boyce (aka Black Edgar Kenyatta) on sax, keyboards, and vocals; Kevin Carnes (aka Borris Karnaz) on drums, percussion, and vocals; and Ayman Mobarek (aka Ayman Rastabebish) on bass. But they also get by with a little help from their friends, serving up a heady mixture of jazz, psychedelia, funk, and spoken word poetry that has a little something for everyone. *—Bret Love*

- **Out Through the "N" Door** / Sep. 26, 2000 / Weed ♦♦♦♦

Let's just say that it's likely no accident that the Broun Fellinis' record label is called Weed. A bass-drums-sax trio (reedsman David Boyce doubles on raps of a type not seen in jazz since Sun Ra was piloting the Arkestra through the interstellar void) from San Francisco, the Broun Fellinis mix AACM-style free jazz; funk rhythms; a post-hip-hop, pan-global sensibility; and a trippy, Lord Buckley-esque sense of whimsical wordplay. Boyce's raps are also among the most optimistic and inclusive since the heyday of the Native Tongues movement in the early '90s, making *Out Through the "N" Door* equally impressive for old school hip-hop heads disillusioned by the relentlessly grim gangsta scene. Utterly fearless both musically and lyrically, the trio barrels through these 13 tracks at an often-manic pace, pausing only for Kirk Peterson's lyrical "Bass Interlude" (yes, this album even has a worthwhile bass solo—will wonders ever cease?) and the moody ballad "Rahel," a pacific respite in the center of an otherwise turbulent but rarely less-than-fascinating album. —*Stewart Mason*

Foxy Brown (Inga Marchand)

b. Sep. 6, 1979
Hip-Hop, East Coast Rap, Hardcore Rap
Before she had released any material at all, Foxy Brown appeared on several 1995-1996 platinum singles, including her first credit, LL Cool J's "I Shot Ya," as well as Total's "No One Else" remix of Jay-Z's "Ain't No …," Toni Braxton's "You're Makin' Me High" remix, and Case's "Touch Me, Tease Me." The incredible success led to a major-label bidding war at the beginning of 1996, and by March, Brown had signed with the Def Jam label as another in the ranks of young and hard female rappers.

The Brooklyn native—separate from a similarly named reggae artist—was born in 1979; in 1994, while still a teenager, she won a talent contest in Brooklyn and was invited to freestyle on stage. At that time, Trackmasters were working on LL Cool J's *Mr. Smith* album, and they decided to let her rap over "I Shot Ya." The single became a hit, prompting Brown's work with Total, Braxton, and Case, as well as her induction into the Firm posse (led by Nas and also including AZ and Cormega). Brown's debut album, *Ill Na Na*, was produced by Trackmasters and featured appearances from Blackstreet, Method Man, and Kid Capri. It hit number seven its first week on the album charts. *Chyna Doll* followed in late 1998 and the provacativity continued on 2001's *Broken Silence.* —*John Bush*

- **Ill Na Na** / Nov. 19, 1996 / Def Jam ✦✦✦✦
After appearing as a guest on a number of albums, most notably LL Cool J's, Foxy Brown finally delivered her debut album *Ill Na Na* in late 1996. On her cameos, the teenage rapper rhapsodized about her three obsessions—fashion, sex, and the mafia—and all three dominate the discourse on *Ill Na Na*. Taken on their own terms, any of those lyrics could get rather tedious, but Foxy Brown has a sexy, assured delivery that makes her superficial preoccupations seductive. Furthermore, the album benefits greatly from the production efforts of the TrackMasters, who give the music a sleek, contemporary edge which makes even the weaker tracks quite listenable. Foxy Brown is also assisted by cameos by Mobb Deep's Prodigy, Nas, Snoop Doggy Dog and Az, among others, which gives the album star power, but it doesn't necessarily need it—she has enough charisma to steal the show. —*Stephen Thomas Erlewine*

Chyna Doll / Nov. 17, 1998 / Def Jam ✦✦✦
Foxy Brown's sophomore outing, *Chyna Doll*, entered the U.S. album charts at number one, then quickly plummeted, largely due to its lack of imaginative beats, insightful rhymes, and a real hit single. The album opens with an introduction consisting of Brown's mama giving birth to li'l Foxy, all the while yelling obscenities and "I own the hookers, I own the pimps," then giving what she owns to her baby. Lovely indeed. Brown's reputation as a 'hoodish sex kitten, played to the hilt on this album, comes off as more pornographic than sexy, evident on the track "Dog and a Fox" (with DMX). Other tracks, such as "Job," which features Mya and samples Gwen Guthrie's "Ain't Nothin' Goin' on But the Rent," and "I Can't," which features Total and samples Wham!'s "Everything She Wants," are completely lackluster, despite the presence of well-known hooks and R&B singers. There are a couple of interesting tracks, such as lead single "Hot Spot," "Can U Feel Me Baby," and the early rap retro-sounding "Tramp," but for the most part, this album is full of unappealing, pornographic raps, lame beats, and pathetic gangster posturing. The sophomore slump is evident here, but the charismatic Brown fortunately redeemed herself in 2001 with *Broken Silence.* —*Jose F. Promis*

Broken Silence / Jun. 5, 2001 / Uptown/Universal ✦✦✦
Foxy Brown is up to her old tricks on her third album, *Broken Silence.* She is still the undisputed queen of materialism, evident on "Fallin'," where she drops names of countless designer brands, rapping about Range Rovers, Gucci, Prada, etc. She is still taking aim at legions of triflin' ex-friends,

including other rappers, ex-boyfriends, etc., etc. Brown is as 'hood and street as ever, but on this album, she extends her musical wings and embraces other styles to fine effect, making this her most entertaining and musically adventurous album to date. Reggae and dancehall influences abound, most notably on the terrific singles "Oh Yeah" and "Tables Will Turn." The most interesting song, however, is "Hood Scriptures," which, like Jay-Z's "Big Pimpin'," incorporates eastern influences, adding a whole new dimension to hip-hop possibilities. "The Letter" is a sparse, mini-masterpiece, where Brown apologizes to her mother (in what could be interpreted as a thinly veiled suicide note) for the hell she's put her through, accompanied by a tinkling piano and Ron Isley's angelic vocals. Brown gets as sensitive and introspective as is possible, while still remaining as explicit as ever, as she reminisces over her defunct relationship with rapper Kurupt on "Saddest Day." Yes, Foxy Brown is street and she is the center of her world's rumor mill, but this album, ripe with tasteless materialism, explicit sexual references, and violent raps, can honestly be called a musical step forward, and is a compelling testament to the life of a girl from the 'hood. —*Jose F. Promis*

Bubba Sparxxx

Dirty South
No doubt the first of his kind, Bubba Sparxxx dumbfounded the hip-hop community—and soon after, the mass market—when he emerged out of nowhere with Timbaland in late 2001. When his debut single, "Ugly," hit urban radio, it was unmistakably a Timbaland production—the "Get Ur Freak On" samples being a sort of trademark stamp. This drew initial attention to Sparxxx, who many initially thought of as yet another dirty South rapper, albeit one lucky enough to be the flagship for Timbaland's start-up Beat Club label. But when the video for "Ugly" hit MTV and Sparxxx's face subsequently began appearing in the press, the dumbfoundment truly set in: Sparxxx was not only from the South but was very large—and white. In other words, he seemed the antithesis of what a rapper was suppose to be, and similar to the overnight success previous white rappers experienced—Beastie Boys, Vanilla Ice, Eminem—Sparxxx was suddenly more than just an anomaly; he was a bona fide superstar.

While Sparxxx's rhymes initially drew attention to the rapper—and rightfully so—you can't help but marvel at his story. Yes, he was white and large. But he was also from the backwoods of the South—about as far from the streets as you could get. Born Warren Anderson Mathis on March 6, 1977, Sparxxx grew up in the country on a dirt road 15 minutes north of LaGrange, GA, a rural town itself 65 miles southwest of Georgia. As you can imagine, he lived a sheltered youth, with his closest neighbor over a half mile away. Yet it was that neighbor, a black kid, who turned him onto rap via mix mailed tapes from New York.

Sparxxx's introduction to rap music was through 2 Live Crew—a far stretch from Rakim or Grandmaster Flash. It caught his attention, though, and soon Sparxxx began broadening his taste for rap music, taking a particular liking for early-'90s West Coast gangsta rap: N.W.A, Too Short, and Eazy-E. Later, when he discovered Altanta rappers OutKast, Sparxxx knew his interests were moving into the forefront of his mind. He began writing rhymes at age 15 and would battle with fellow rap-minded students at school. His rapping was more of a hobby than a possible profession for Sparxxx at the time, though. Throughout high school, football took precedence over everything else for the young Sparxxx; he played tight end and linebacker, earning All-Region honors as a senior.

When a football career never happened for Sparxxx and a brief stab at college didn't hold his interest, he turned to rap. His break came when he met Shannon Houchins, a staff producer for Jermaine Dupri's So So Def label in Atlanta. In late 1996, Houchins paired Sparxxx with then-So So Def rapper Lil' Devil for a group called One Card Shi. Though the duo did record some material together, it never saw the light of day and Sparxxx began pursuing a solo career, working with Houchins again in 1999 on some songs. These recordings resulted in the 12-song *Dark Days, Bright Nights* indie release on Sparxxx's own Nocents Records. After moving a surprising number of units after getting radio play in the surrounding Georgia area, Nocents became 11th Hour Entertainment, and the album fell into the lap of Interscope Records head honcho Jimmy Iovine.

Iovine liked what he heard and flew Sparxxx out to California to discuss a label deal. Offers soon came in from a number of labels, and suddenly Sparxxx's breakthrough seemed just on the horizon. He decided to stick with

Iovine's Interscope empire and soon found himself working with Timbaland. Over the course of two weeks, the two recorded six songs and Sparxxx also worked with other producers like Organized Noize and Houchins. "Ugly" became the lead single; an all-important video communicating Sparxxx's rural, white, country-boy background hit MTV; the evidence of his breakthrough came when the Interscope version of *Dark Days, Bright Nights* debuted at number three on the *Billboard* chart, making him the next in a short list of overnight-superstar white rappers. —*Jason Birchmeier*

● **Dark Days, Bright Nights** / Sep. 18, 2001 / Interscope ✦✦✦✦

Bubba Sparxxx is a great idea executed pretty damn well. He's the redneck version of Eminem, a talented bubba sponsored by a great producer (in this case, Timbaland), given a lively soundscape as a background for his semi-autobiographical humorous sketches of life as who he is. Sparxxx is neither as nimble a rapper as Eminem, nor is he as imaginative, so this doesn't have the impact of either the *Slim Shady* LP or *Marshall Mathers* LP, but Timbaland is an exceptional producer who can give a gifted, but limited, MC like Bubba Sparxxx a huge boost by simply giving him music that sounds good. And that's the case on *Dark Days, Bright Nights*, since it has a dexterous, adventurous production that gives the album a real boost. Sparxxx himself is pretty good—his voice tends to blend into the mix a little too much and he's not as imaginative as, say, Pete Nice, MC Serch, or, yes, Eminem, but he never stumbles, either. So, the album winds up as a solid debut—nothing is as good as "Ugly" (it'd be hard to top those ethereal wordless backing vocals, regardless of how good the rest of the album was), and it ultimately runs a little too long, but it still is better than most rap debuts of 2001, not just because of the mastermind of Timbaland but also because Bubba Sparxxx is still a strong focal point, even when he tends to repeat himself. —*Stephen Thomas Erlewine*

Buck 65 (Richard Terfry)

b. Sackville, Nova Scotia, Canada
Vocals / Underground Rap, Alternative Rap
Born in Lower Sackville, Nova Scotia, Richard Terfry (aka Buck 65, Stinkin' Rich) spent the majority of his adolescence as a self-described b-boy. He eventually moved to Halifax in 1989, where he founded a seminal hip-hop show on local college radio. The program (dubbed "The Bassment") helped Terfry cement his status as Halifax's premier hip-hop head; inch by inch, artist collaborations, production duties, and club residencies soon followed. During this time, Terfry dabbled with mic duty, often to acclaimed results. 1992's *Chin Music* helped him win a deal with local label Murderecords; 1996's *Psoriasis* (recorded with friend Sixtoo under the moniker Sebutones) garnered underground plaudits; 1997's 12" trilogy *The Wild Life* raised eyebrows overseas. Later that year, Terfry's first well-circulated full-length followed; *Language Arts* was hailed by everyone who heard it as hip-hop triumph. Fusing Terfry's hard-luck grumble with a decidedly lo-fi (but immaculately produced) instrumentation, it trumpeted his (and Halifax's) entry onto the hip-hop circuit. In spite of (or perhaps, as a result of) his tendency to veer toward more opaque territories Terfry's albums rarely come with any tangible track listing) the big guns soon came calling; revered turntablist Mr. Dibbs was reportedly so enamoured with Terfry's records that he inducted Buck 65 into seminal underground collective 1200 Hobos. Now fraternizing with the likes of heroes such as Biz Markie, Peanut Butter Wolf, and Cut Chemist, Terfry's follow-up was even more inspired. 1999's *Vertex* was hailed by critics as a progressive, brilliantly conceived concept album; a regulated mix of measured neuroses and marble-mouthed charm. 2001's *Man Overboard* followed on that note, pitting Terfry's numerous personalities against each other, often to brilliant effect. —*Mark Pytlik*

● **Vertex** / Dec. 1999 / Four Ways to Rock ✦✦✦✦

In spite of sounding like it was recorded in some poorly lit cellar, *Vertex* is rife with bright flashes of Buck 65's subdued brilliance. Although the overall aesthetic of the record is of a decidedly D.I.Y. flavor (with 65 handling everything from the decks to production duties), it never feels anything less than wholly authentic. Chalk that up to 65's seemingly boundless spectrum of ideas; where other MCs might self-reflexively limit themselves (and their subject matter) to the confines of some predetermined blueprint, 65 gives listeners every neuron in his muddled brainwaves. One minute he's playing the part of a contemplative, well-endowed centaur ("I'm a man but I'm built like a horse from the waist down"), the next he's documenting his real-life baseball team's victory in the 1993 Nova Scotia Provincial Championships.

Equally remarkable is Buck 65's adroit turntablism. Here he eschews letter-perfect technique in favor of his own hard-won, tricked-up minimalism; the result is an album that somehow sounds outside (but not ahead) of hip-hop. No doubt, then, *Vertex* is an inadvertent paean to the possibilities of imagination and innovation. —*Mark Pytlik*

Bullfrog

f. Jul. ??, 1994, Montreal, Quebec, Canada
Group / Acid Jazz, Club/Dance
Forming in 1994, in Montreal, Canada, Bullfrog started conquering the North American dance-club scene shortly after their first performances. Consisting of Mark Robertson (guitar, vocals), Eric San aka Kid Koala (turntables), James Sobers, Peter Santiago (bass), Massimo Sansalone (drums), and Joanna Peters (percussion, vocals), Bullfrog chose to blend a series of styles and influences for their tunes. Combining pop influences with danceable rhythms and achieving multiple and visionary melodies, the crew relied mostly on their common musical experience as inspiration, namely Koala, also a collaborator for Gorillaz and Deltron 3030. The group's energizing rhythms brought them an ever-growing power at their restless shows and at the same time secured them a considerable following. Performing on the same stage as Maceo Paker and Medeski Marin & Wood, Bullfrog steadily increased its loyal fan base and confirmed its respectable praise during the following years. After releasing two self-titled EPs and playing countless live performances, it was only in 2001 that the team ultimately decided to release their self-titled debut album, *Bullfrog*. —*Mario Mesquita Borges*

● **Bullfrog** / Oct. 16, 2001 / Ropeadope ✦✦✦

Fresh off his tour opening for Radiohead, turntablist Kid Koala (aka Eric San) appears with Bullfrog on the Canadian group's full-length debut. The band previously issued two EPs, and much of the material on this Ropeadope release consists of new versions of songs from the EPs. The quintet, here supplemented by Koala as well as MC Blu Rum 13 (aka James Sobers), is basically a groove outfit, anchored by bassist Peter Santiago and drummer Massimo Sansalone. While it is Koala and Rum who separate the unit from the pack, the music itself isn't especially outstanding—nor for that matter is Koala's scratching. However, the two complement each other nicely, creating a nice textural bed. A highlight of the disc, if only for its potential energy, is the cut "Live, Somewhere Else," where Rum freestyles along with Koala as the DJ throws out a sample. Unlike his expansively melodic sets opening for Radiohead, Koala's work is limited almost exclusively to rhythmic scratching, which certainly diminishes his impact as a DJ. —*Jesse Jarnow*

The B.U.M.S (Brothas Unda Madness)

Group / Hip-Hop, Gangsta Rap, G-Funk, Hardcore Rap
Taking a cue from fellow Los Angeles alternative-to-gangster rappers the Pharcyde, the duo known as Brothas Unda Madness stirred things up on the stagnant West Coast platform in the mid-'90s. With some help from well-known California wake-up show hosts such as the Bay Area's Baka Boyz and L.A.'s King Tech, E-Vocalist and D-Wyze were able to gain a foothold in the West Coast underground scene. Their first single, "Elevation," borrowed freely from Teddy Pendergrass' bedroom anthem, "Close the Door," and paved the way for their critically acclaimed debut, *Lyfe 'N' Tyme*, released in May of 1995. On the album, the B.U.M.S exercised an intellectual hoodlum point of view combining street philosophy with b-boy posturing. The crew's straight-ahead delivery and multisyllabic rhymes belied the relaxed flows of most West Coast artists of the era. *Lyfe 'N' Tyme* also featured the underground hits "Take a Look Around" and "6 Figures & Up." The duo also worked with Oakland's Saafir on the slamming B-side cut "Rain." —*Michael Di Bella*

● **Lyfe 'N' Tyme** / May 11, 1995 / Priority ✦✦✦✦✦

The B.U.M.S debut album *Lyfe 'N' Tyme* is a rough, vicious collection of West Coast gangsta hip-hop, following the G-funk tradition of Dr. Dre. It has its weak spots—the production isn't imaginative and many of the tracks fall flat—but the crew shows great promise; they are charimatic and talented enough to not make the album's flaws noticeable. —*David Jehnzen*

Busdriver (Regan Farquhar)

Underground Rap, Alternative Rap
Possessing a hyper-literate, intellectual style of rapping augmented with dizzying elocution that would tongue-tie even the fiercest auctioneer,

Busdriver is eclectic and eccentric enough to cite vocalese jazz singer Jon Hendricks as a primary influence. Born Regan Farquhar, the Los Angeles MC was introduced to hip-hop culture early—his father wrote the screenplay to one of the earliest films focusing on hip-hop, *Krush Groove*. He began rapping at age nine, releasing his first record at age 13 with his group, 4/29, named after the 1992 L.A. riots. By the mid-'90s, Busdriver was a regular at the Project Blowed open mic, where he would meet future collaborators and underground luminaries like Aceyalone, Abstract Rude, and Freestyle Fellowship. Busdriver guested on upwards of 20 singles, and by 2001 he could no longer be contained by guest spots, releasing his first full-length, *Memoirs of the Elephant Man*. There were just as many detractors as supporters for his singular style, which was so densely packed it made his chosen name seem a reference for multiple-personality disorder, and the lo-fi production also left more listeners scratching heads than nodding them. His next album, *This Machine Kills Fashion Tips* (2002), continued in a similar manner before being trumped by better production and more focused rhymes on *Temporary Forever* the same year. Joined by another West Coast avant-garde MC, Radioinactive, and the breezy, fractured pop of electronic producer Daedelus, Busdriver released yet another odd puzzle piece in 2003, *The Weather*. —*Wade Kergan*

● **Temporary Forever** / 2002 / Temporary Whatever ✦✦✦✦
It's clear Busdriver loves the sound of his own voice; his ego is sprayed all over the 18 wildly diverse tracks on *Temporary Forever*. It's just as clear, however, that his talents are at least as massive as his ego, since the album has so many incredible ideas and catchy riffs that it trumps entire careers by some rappers out there. A bit of a human beatbox, Busdriver is actually closer to an actor or mimic, putting on so many different personas that the album sounds like it features half-a-dozen Wu-Tang Clans. He races a flute loop across "Imaginary Places," scatting his lines along with the melody virtually every time a sample breaks through. He's even playful and humorous on the message tracks, agonizing over his own death in "Gun Control" like Bugs Bunny play-acting in front of Elmer Fudd (which makes sense, since he has at least as many different voices as Mel Blanc). His constant faux-theatrical riffs can wear on subsequent listens, but *Temporary Forever* introduces one of the most imaginative talents to ever grace the rap world. (Sample lyric: "Go back to Compton you dirty n***ger, we don't sell watermelons here, is what I yell at the white folks on the way to the gun show once a year.") —*John Bush*

The Weather / Feb. 18, 2003 / Mush ✦✦

Da Bush Babees

f. 1992
Group / Hip-Hop, Ragga, Hardcore Rap
MCs Babe-Face Kaos, Y-Tee, and Mister Man grew up in the West Indies (Y-Tee in Jamaica, Mister Man and Kaos in Trinidad), so reggae was a strong inspiration to their early years; hip-hop also figures in, however. All transplanted New Yorkers, they formed in 1992 when Mister Man saw Kaos perform. The two began collaborating, and after Mister Man suggested adding a reggae toaster, Y-Tee joined Da Bush Babees. When their concert dates sparked major-label interest, the trio performed a few live office auditions and signed with Reprise, within three months of launching the band. Their debut, *Ambushed* (1994), featured production from Jermaine Dupri, Nikke Nikole, J. Prins Matteus, Mark Batson, Salaam Gibbs, and the group itself. Other releases included 1995's *Remember We* and 1996's *Gravity*. —*John Bush*

Ambushed / Dec. 6, 1994 / Reprise ✦✦✦

● **Gravity** / Oct. 15, 1996 / Warner Brothers ✦✦✦✦
After releasing a debut album, *Ambushed*, that went virtually nowhere in 1994, Da Bush Babees (consisting of Mr. Man, Lee Majors, and Y-Tee) from Flatbush came correct on this hugely improved second effort. There is not a single wrong note struck throughout *Gravity*, and it is just as artistically successful as albums from sonically similar groups such as A Tribe Called Quest (Q-Tip rhymes on "3 MCs" and associate the Ummah contributes production) and the Roots (human beatbox Rahzel is featured on "The Beat Down"), if not commercially so. The production is expertly minimalistic, and it creates a completely mellow, jazzy, shimmering recording that taps deeply into the hallucinatory, stoned, late-night vibe of both hip-hop and jazz. The primary touchstone, though, is dub reggae, and dub's characteristic rubbery bass gives the recording a bottomless, gummy, echoey resonance. The raggae-fied trio

is just as lyrically intelligent as their sonic influences suggest. On "S.O.S.," one of two songs to feature a contribution from Mos Def, Lee Majors raps that "it's hard to be a prophet/and still make a profit," and the line inadvertently spotlights why *Gravity* is paradoxically more aesthetically but less commercially successful than any number of MTV-ready peers of the trio. Implied in the couplet is an understanding apology and built-in excuse for fellow rap groups that sacrificed their creativity and watered down their edge for financial gain. Also inherent in the line, however, is the reason Da Bush Babees stood out from those peers with this album: They chose to maintain their artistic integrity. —*Stanton Swihart*

Bushwick Bill

b. Jamaica
Hip-Hop, Gangsta Rap, Southern Rap
A onetime member of Houston's Geto Boys, Bushwick Bill created a stir with his 1992 release *Little Big Man*. It was an unvarnished, sometimes frightening release, with details about the shooting incident that cost him an eye, along with the customary sexism, violent imagery, and outlandish inner-city narratives that have long been the group's stock-in-trade. He issued two more albums during the latter part of the decade: *Phantom of the Rapra* in 1995 and *No Surrender...No Retreat* in 1998. *Universal Small Souljah* followed in early 2001. —*Ron Wynn*

Little Big Man / Sep. 8, 1992 / Priority ✦✦✦
Bushwick Bill went solo and made an effective debut album, chronicling the shooting incident which cost him an eye in graphic detail. While the Geto Boys were more disgusting than incisive, he actually turned in some coherent message tracks, notably "Letter From KKK" and "Stop Lying." Of course, it wouldn't have been a Bushwick Bill disc without some disgusting tracks, and "Ever So Clear" and "Call Me Crazy" certainly fit that description. —*Ron Wynn*

● **Phantom of the Rapra** / Jul. 11, 1995 / Rap-A-Lot ✦✦✦✦✦
Although Bushwick Bill changed his name before the release of *Phantom of the Rapra* (to the absurd Dr. Wolfgang Von Bushwickin The Barbarian Mother-Funky Stay High Dollar Billstir), he hasn't changed his musical style at all for his second solo album. Throughout the record, Bushwick runs through his standard lyrical targets over his standard musical backdrops. That doesn't mean *Phantom of the Rapra* is a tedious listen. By now, Bushwick Bill is a skilled, accomplished professional and he knows how to entertain. And that's what the record is, even if he does bring politics into the fray every once in a while. Bushwick's taste for comic book violence and horror films overshadows his social commentary, as well as his latent misogynist tendencies. But that affection for the theatrical and the bizzare is what makes *Phantom of the Rapra* such enjoyable, volatile entertainment. Unlike his imitators, Bushwick knows exactly how to satisfy fans of ridiculously violent hardcore rap. —*Stephen Thomas Erlewine*

No Surrender . . . No Retreat / Oct. 27, 1998 / Wrap ✦✦✦
No Surrender...No Retreat kicks off with the kind of incendiary gangsta rap that you'd expect from Bushwick Bill (aka Dr. Wolfgang or the Game Warden). Using improbably tight beats with backing tracks that sound like a video game gone mad, Bill and his posse hit the beach ready for battle: "5 Element Combat," "2 Hard 2 Test," and "In My Hood." However, that's about as far as the revolution gets (except for "Tragedy" and "3 Hard Headz"). *No Surrender...*retreats from its political posturing with "My Bitch," a song so graphic it makes Salt-N-Pepa's "Shoop" sound like Mary Wells' "My Guy." (Female rapper Kaos also takes the lead on "Kaos Cidity," sounding every bit bad enough to eat Eve for breakfast, although you sure wouldn't want her to rap about it.) Most of the 19 tracks on this disc hearken back to the classic soul/funk music of the '70s, a sweet setting for Bill's often-gruff vocals (read "totally wasted"). However, Bill takes a backseat much of the time, employing a slew of guest rappers (Nate G., Kyhil, Ken Crossley) to do what they do better. On this effort, Bill seems happy in the role of the wise commentator, exhorting listeners to mind their dollars and sense. Although it's questionable whether anyone is buying Bushwick Bill's discs looking for catchy soul/rap songs, *No Surrender* gives 'em a few: "Hood Rat," "Gangsta Funk," "Don't Be Afraid." It's the mix of militant rap and soulful slices of life in the 'hood that makes the disc appealing. The misogyny, the foul mouth, the revolving-door rappers, and the lame R&B love songs (what are "P. Funk" and "Let's Give Love Another Try" even doing on the same disc?) are baggage, but producer

Tim Hill keeps the disc afloat with tasteful accompaniment. This is far from a revolutionary manifesto, but with a lot of tracks and a little of everything, *No Surrender...No Retreat* is no rip-off. —*Dave Connolly*

Universal Small Souljah / Mar. 13, 2001 / Nu Wave ✦✦
It looks as though Bushwick Bill's well has run dry on this album, as he tries but mostly fails to reclaim the respect of Southern rap fans. He's been around for many years now with the Geto Boys, and then through a slew of good solo albums. Unfortunately, *Universal Small Souljah* just doesn't rank with his previous works. A lack of originality really hurts the effect, along with terror that just doesn't seem so terrifying anymore. Hopefully, this isn't the last of Bushwick Bill; only his next album will tell. —*Brad Mills*

Busta Rhymes

b. 1972, Brooklyn, NY
Hip-Hop, Alternative Rap, East Coast Rap, Hardcore Rap
The most idiosyncratic personality in rap and possessor of its most recognizable delivery, a halting, raggae-inspired style with incredible complexity, inventiveness, and humor, Busta Rhymes formed Leaders of the New School in 1990 and released two albums with the group before breaking out with a 1996 solo hit single, "Woo-Hah!! Got You All in Check."

Born in East Flatbush, Brooklyn, in 1972 of Jamaican heritage (a definite influence on his rapping style), Busta moved to Long Island in 1983 and, at Uniondale High School, met up with MCs Charlie Brown, Dinco D., and Cut Monitor Milo. Inspired by fellow Long Islanders Public Enemy and Eric B. & Rakim, the foursome united as Leaders of the New School and signed a deal with Elektra Records right out of the gate, when Busta was only 17 years old. Much respected in the hip-hop underground for their Afro-centric philosophy and tough rapping styles, Leaders of the New School debuted in 1991 with *Future Without a Past* but released only one more album, 1993's *T.I.M.E.*, before breaking up the following year.

Out on his own for the first time, Busta called on some friends, appearing on A Tribe Called Quest's "Scenario," the incredible remix of Craig Mack's "Flava in Ya Ear" (also featuring Notorious B.I.G. and LL Cool J), as well as other projects with Boyz II Men, Mary J. Blige, and TLC. He also appeared in the 1995 John Singleton film *Higher Learning* and earned a solo contract with Elektra. Busta's first album, *The Coming*, proved a huge hit; the single "Woo-Hah!! Got You All in Check" hit the Top Ten and pushed the album into gold-record territory. His second album, *When Disaster Strikes*, debuted at number three in September 1997. *Extinction Level Event* followed a year later, and in mid-2000, Busta released *Anarchy* while appearing on the silver screen in a remake of the blaxploitation classic *Shaft*. —*John Bush*

● **The Coming** / Mar. 26, 1996 / Elektra ✦✦✦✦✦
Busta Rhymes delivered his debut album, *The Coming*, three years after the Leaders of the New School unofficially disbanded, and it reflects the change in hip-hop between 1993 and 1996. *The Coming* is indebted to the slow, spare, and quietly menacing funk and soundscapes of the Wu-Tang Clan—in fact, Ol' Dirty Bastard appears on one of the album's most infectious tracks, the single "Woo-hah!! Got You All in Check." Busta Rhymes, like Ol' Dirty, is a surreal, inspired rapper, but his skills are on a whole different level. Though his talents were evident on the Leaders of the New School records, Busta Rhymes has never had such an impressive showcase for his rhymes as he does on *The Coming*. Busta doesn't have a deep message in his raps, but he twists words and phrases around with an insane, invigorating flair. Like many hip-hop albums of the mid-'90s, *The Coming* is padded with too much material, but Busta Rhymes' brilliant raps keep the record from sinking during its monotonous passages. —*Stephen Thomas Erlewine*

When Disaster Strikes / Sep. 23, 1997 / Elektra ✦✦✦✦✦
Busta Rhymes' second album, *When Disaster Strikes*, is a sprawling, often brilliant mess that confirmed his status as one of hip-hop's most singular characters. Restraint isn't Rhymes' strong suit, and thus the album careens from sheer genius to repetitive indulgence and right back again. When Rhymes is on, there's no one like him, and when he isn't, it's like the calm before the storm. Fortunately, he's on most of the time on *When Disaster Strikes*, helped out by what would become his favorite theme for the next several years: the coming apocalypse. Even if the concept doesn't carry through the entire album, *When Disaster Strikes* is framed as a premillennium party spinning out of control, sort of like the dark side of Prince's "1999." Rhymes presides over the chaos like a mad master of ceremonies, running amok with

his posse at his back (there are countless shout-outs to the Flipmode Squad). It's a hugely effective persona when paired with Rhymes' caffeinated, herky-jerky flow, and helped prove he was more than just a novelty. The album's two big hit singles, "Dangerous" and the creepy "Put Your Hands Where My Eyes Could See," are terrific, but there are more than a few moments that are just as inspired. The second half of the album slows down the momentum somewhat, with a bevy of guests, collaborations, and posse cuts; a few offer some welcome variety, but often they don't replace Rhymes' manic energy with anything quite as exciting. Still, nearly every rap album from this era has its share of filler, and it doesn't prevent *When Disaster Strikes* from ranking as arguably Rhymes' definitive original album. —*Steve Huey*

Extinction Level Event (The Final World Front) / Dec. 8, 1998 / Elektra ✦✦✦✦
Busta Rhymes rocketed to superstardom in an alarmingly short time, simply because there was no other rapper quite like him. Nobody else in his position had his wild sense of humor, reckless fashion sense and, most importantly, willingness to take risks. Yes, underground rappers like the Jurassic 5 and the entire Wu clan relentlessly pushed the boundaries of hip-hop, but they operated at the fringes of pop culture. Busta placed himself smack in the middle of middle America, gleefully taking cameos on *Cosby* and recruiting both Janet Jackson and Ozzy Osbourne to appear on his third album, *Extinction Level Event (The Final World Front)*. Where this could seem like pandering by some artists, there's no condescension or crass commercialism in his approach. Busta's party is careening out of control because he doesn't see a reason to exclude anybody. That's the reason why *E.L.E.* is a richer listen than most contemporary hip-hop records—it has hard beats, weird samples, unpredictable musical juxtapositions and collaborations, and sharp, intelligent rhymes. Like any artist who attempts so much, Busta occasionally falls flat (the rewrite of "Iron Man" wasn't a great idea), but there's so much happening on *E.L.E.* that the missteps don't really matter—especially since Busta has come up with a party record that doesn't just sound like the end of the millennium, it *feels* like it. —*Stephen Thomas Erlewine*

Anarchy / Jun. 20, 2000 / Elektra ✦✦✦
Busta Rhymes is undoubtedly one of the best and most distinctive rappers of the '90s. He's also one of the most prolific; *Anarchy*, released in the summer of 2000, is his fourth album since 1996. Each one has been jammed full of material and also a little erratic, packed not only with great singles and tongue-twisting performances but also filler that gets by mostly on Busta's personality. Clocking in at around 78 minutes, *Anarchy* is no exception to the rule. Its best moments are as brilliant as ever, but there are also signs that Busta's winning formula is starting to show a little wear and tear. "C'Mon All My Niggaz, C'Mon All My Bitches" has the insanely rapid-fire delivery of *Extinction Level Event*'s "Gimme Some More," which sums up the difficulty of *Anarchy* in a nutshell: no matter how incredible it is, we've heard much of this from Busta before. Of course, the converse is also true: a lot of it is still incredible, no matter how familiar, and there are a few intriguing production touches. But, perhaps for the first time, Busta's singular yet now familiar style isn't quite enough to carry the weaker material, which often feels too tossed off. It doesn't help, either, that *Anarchy* follows the same sort of millennial-apocalypse concept that enlivened *E.L.E.* (and, to a certain extent, *When Disaster Strikes*); it's a little disappointing to hear such an inventive rapper retreading familiar territory. It seems almost impossible that Busta could produce a true failure, but by this point, a growing number of fans may not salivate over a new album nearly as much as the inevitable best-of collection. —*Steve Huey*

★ **Total Devastation: The Best of Busta Rhymes** / Oct. 2, 2001 / Rhino ✦✦✦✦✦
One of the most gifted and instantly recognizable rappers of the '90s, Busta Rhymes parlayed a madcap personality and seemingly inexhaustible energy into stardom during an era when hip-hop was dominated by gangstas and materialism. Busta's music sounded fairly distinctive—herky-jerky funk laced with offbeat samples and eerie, apocalyptic production touches—but the star of the show was his wildly off-kilter, dancehall-influenced flow, which was really like nothing else in rap. Still, despite many astounding individual moments, his albums were so sprawling that none really maintained their momentum from start to finish, making him an excellent candidate for a best-of. The 18 cuts collected on Rhino's chronologically arranged *The Best of Busta Rhymes* are chosen as well as one could hope, spanning all the singles

and vitally necessary cuts from his four platinum solo albums (although diehards might find a personal favorite missing). There's also the hit non-LP reworking of "Turn It Up" (with new lyrics and a "Knight Rider" sample), plus two singles from the classic Leaders of the New School debut *Future Without a Past*. The leap in his technique from the Leaders cuts to the brilliant "Woo-Hah!! Got You All in Check" is startling, but the collection's true revelation is the way it brings Busta's versatility into its sharpest focus yet. There's plenty of his trademark mania, of course, but there are also softer collaborations with female singers, dance-oriented club tracks, and creepy, more subdued mood pieces. Since this is only Busta's best, things never fly off in too many different directions, and fans who might miss the out-of-control feel of his albums may also find it easier to realize that whatever Busta tries, his rhymes remain as dizzyingly intricate and witty as ever. *The Best of Busta Rhymes* paints as definitive a portrait as possible of one of rap's most electrifying talents, but, more than that, it's simply an irresistible listen. —*Steve Huey*

Genesis / Nov. 13, 2001 / J-Records ✦✦✦✦

Busta Rhymes takes his charismatic style of rapping and applies it to a new production style on *Genesis*, his fourth solo album. This time around the beats seem darker and more synth-oriented, giving it an edge reminiscent of the bass-heavy G-funk sound. "As I Come Back" is a good example, featuring a sustained keyboard note droning on throughout the chorus with Busta rapping in his raspy style. On the other hand, Rhymes can still make a good dance song, like the hypnotic "What It Is," a fractured funk anthem that features robotic female vocals from Kelis and a slow beat consisting of clicks and snaps. Other guest appearances include P. Diddy's turn on the dramatic "Pass the Courvoisier," Mary J. Blidge on "There's Only One," and the occasional appearances by the Flipmode Squad, as well as production work from Pete Rock and Dr. Dre, among others. The only questionable track is a remake of Public Enemy's classic "Shut 'Em Down" that may leave some fans cold due to its different feel and message. But outside of the one track, this is another solid release from a consistent hip hop artist who can still make relevant, interesting albums long after his days with the Leaders of the New School. —*Bradley Torreano*

It Ain't Safe No More / Nov. 26, 2002 / J-Records ✦✦✦✦

No matter whether the title's a reference to the increased risk of terrorism in Busta's hometown circa 2002 ("shit is crazy!") or to the fact that rap's most volatile and unpredictable personality is back and bigger than ever, *It Ain't Safe No More* continues in the vein of loose-cannon classics like 1997's *When Disaster Strikes* and 2001's *Genesis*. And when he's on, he's better than ever too; the title track features a P-funk singalong and a vivid synth-heavy production over some of the tightest spitfire raps heard on any hip-hop LP of the new millennium. After a half-hearted melodrama called "What Do You Do When You're Branded," Busta returns to what he does best on "Call the Ambulance"—incapacitating all comers with rhymes as hardcore as they are hilarious. "What Up" is half-Neptunes and half-Raymond Scott, and the single "Make It Clap" is just the latest classic Flipmode anthem. Except for a few overblown performances and quasi-epic productions, *It Ain't Safe*

No More finds Busta Rhymes with the same sure grip on his distinctive personality. —*John Bush*

Busy Bee

Vocals / Old School Rap, Hip-Hop

First coming on the scene in 1977, New York-based MC Busy Bee has worked with many of hip-hop's founding fathers, including Melle Mel, Afrika Bambaataa, and Kool DJ AJ, to name a few. Mostly known for his comedic rhymes, Busy originally gained a large following through MC battles in Staten Island, Brooklyn, and New Jersey (he won the New Music Seminar's MC World Supremacy Belt in 1986). In the early '80s Afrika Bambaataa asked Busy to join his Zulu Nation, where the young MC would DJ for Bambaataa's Zulu Nation parties. In 1982 Busy also appeared in the classic hip-hop film *Wild Style*, playing none other than an MC. In addition to his DJ work with other artists, Busy has also released his own albums on the Brass, Sugar Hill, and Strong City labels. —*Steve Kurutz*

Thank God for Busy Bee / 1992 / Pandisc ✦✦

Known for his charismatic and humorous approach to rhyming, MC Busy Bee did things properly and brought together some of the best production talent in the world for this record. World-class producer Diamond D produced four of the 16 tracks on the album, from the slow smooth bass lines of "Get With Me" to the more upbeat "I Got Things Sewed" to the almost G-funk-sounding "My Personality." Other influential artists featured here include Grandmaster Melle Mel, Kid Capri, and Jazzy Jay. —*Brad Mills*

BWP

f. 1990

Group / Southern Rap, Dirty Rap, Party Rap, Hip-Hop

The female trio Bytches With Problems (BWP) debuted in 1991 to a mix of outrage and indifference with *The Bytches* on No Face. They were subsequently signed by RAl-Chaos, a label distributed by Columbia, and issued *Life's a Bitch* in 1993. But they've shown little beyond the ability to match vulgarities with their male counterparts. Rather than being shocking, both CDs have demonstrated the trio's minimal creativity and competence, particularly in rhyming ability. Neither album has unveiled any particularly imaginative production, either. —*Ron Wynn*

● **The Bytches** / Feb. 19, 1991 / Ral ✦✦✦✦✦

Like Hoes with Attitude, Bytches With Problems was often called a female 2 Live Crew because of its X-rated, rude, and crude lyrics. And like the Crew, the Bytches were a guilty pleasure one would enjoy only after his girlfriend had left the room. This CD isn't breathtaking or revolutionary by any means, but it's enjoyable and often amusing. Say what you will about such obnoxious fare as "Cotex" and "Two Minute Brother"—this CD is highly entertaining. Critics of the Bytches argued that this CD promoted a stereotypical image of African-American women—the problem with that argument is that someone would have to be quite a racist to think that all black women are like what this CD portrays. Not for the politically correct crowd, *The Bytches* should be enjoyed only by those who aren't offended by sexually explicit lyrics. —*Alex Henderson*

C-Bank

Group / Electro, Club/Dance

C-Bank, an electro studio project by production and remix legend John Robie (Afrika Bambaataa, New Order, Cabaret Voltaire), was led by vocalist Jenny Burton (born Nov. 18, 1957). Robie and Burton took the group into the R&B charts in 1983 with the synth-heavy barnstormer "One More Shot." Later that year, however, Burton went out on her own with the Top 20 single "Remember What You Like" on Atlantic. C-Bank's label, Next Plateau, scrounged enough material for a *Greatest Hits* compilation almost 15 years later. —*John Bush*

● **Greatest Hits** / Mar. 11, 1997 / Next Plateau ◆◆◆

C-BO

b. California

Vocals, Producer / Hardcore Rap, West Coast Rap, Gangsta Rap

Beginning with his 1993 debut, *Gas Chamber*, C-BO made it clear that he planned on surprising rap listeners with his controversial lyrics, which would eventually land him in jail. Of course, the hardcore Californian's steady rise toward continued popularity increased year by year, with an album being released nearly every year following his jaw-dropping debut. With album titles such as *The Autopsy* and *Tales From the Crypt*, C-BO quickly attained a cult following, similar to the small legions of listeners swarming perverse rappers such as Esham, Brotha Lynch Hung, and Three Six Mafia. Yet as C-BO began to mature as an artist, he moved away from exploitative themes, though he still ranked among the West Coast's most extreme hardcore rappers. By the time his 1998 album, *'Til My Casket Drops*, the Cali rapper found himself debuting at number 41 on *Billboard*'s Top 200 album chart, an amazing feat for such an underground rapper. In 2000—oddly after being jailed in 1998 for his lyrical content—he released *Enemy of the State* on Warlock, continuing his climb to recognition. —*Jason Birchmeier*

The Autopsy / 1994 / Awol ◆◆

C-BO's album debut is a harder-than-thou trip through gangsta funk, heavy on the syrupy grooves and blaxploitation samples. The title track, "Murder Man," and "America's Nightmare" reveal few subtleties, and even what could possibly be a laid-back track ("Groovin' on a Sunday") has the same old played-out street nightmares. C-BO is a deft rapper though, indebted to Ice Cube and undeniably West Coast in his flow and sneer. A bare half-hour (and only six tracks) long, *The Autopsy* does what it does well, but never really reaches out for anything more than straight G-funk. —*Keith Farley*

Tales From the Crypt / Jun. 15, 1995 / Awol ◆◆◆

Completely of its time, *Tales From the Crypt* is a low-rider nightmare derivative of Dr. Dre's horrorcore production on *"Murder Was the Case"* and the laid-back G-funk of Warren G. C-BO still sounds like an Ice Cube clone, and though the production is a bit more fleshed out than on *The Autopsy*, there's just not much going on here. —*Keith Farley*

One Life 2 Live / Feb. 4, 1997 / Awol ◆◆◆

One Life 2 Live is a funky gangsta rap record in the vein of *The Chronic*, *Doggystyle* and *All Eyez On Me*. Namely, it's the kind of record where the nominal lead rapper, in this case C-BO, acts more like a ringleader than a rapper, coordinating all of his fellow rappers through a number of party jams and rarely taking the spotlight himself. Generally, this doesn't make the music weaker—especially in the case of the aforementioned albums—but it makes them stylistically indistinct, which is the problem with *One Life 2 Live*. Since there is a revolving cast of generic rappers, the album never develops a personality of its own. It's good for parties, but that's about it. —*Leo Stanley*

'Til My Casket Drops / Feb. 24, 1998 / Awol ◆◆◆◆

C-BO doesn't show many signs of diversity on *'Til My Casket Drops*, preferring to stick to the bass-heavy, hardcore gangsta funk that has defined '90s hip-hop instead of breaking new ground. The lack of new sounds, in conjunction with his fondness for cartoonish violence and self-mythologizing doom and gloom, can make *'Til My Casket Drops* a little tiresome to some ears, bu the record remains C-BO's most consistently entertaining collection of rhymes, rhythms, and beats since *Tales From the Crypt*. —*Leo Stanley*

Enemy of the State / Jul. 11, 2000 / Warlock ◆◆◆

Since making his debut on the late Tupac Shakur's 1996 album, *All Eyez on Me*, Sacramento-based rapper C-BO is probably known more for his brushes with the law than his work in the studio. Despite spending time in jail, C-BO managed to release six albums in quick succession. *Enemy of the State* ranks among his best efforts. The title track is a dramatic song filled with pianos and strings that seems to come out of a horror-movie soundtrack. "Nothin' Over My G's" and "Spray Yourself" are also impressive gangster rants. While most will be repelled by C-BO's dark, violent worldview, there is no question that he has a voice that should be heard. C-BO is a talent who belongs behind a mic, not behind bars. —*Jon Azpiri*

Life As a Rider / Sep. 25, 2001 / Warlock ◆◆◆

C-BO continues to smooth out the darker elements of his music on *Life As a Rider*. He's still one of the most hardcore rappers on the West Coast, but the death obsessions that characterized his early albums for Awol—*The Autopsy* (1994) and *Tales From the Crypt* (1995)—have been displaced by more of a big-baller mentality. C-BO's "rider" persona is much more accessible than his former "American nightmare" persona, and it also helps that he works primarily with producer Mike Mosley on *Life As a Rider*, who lays down beats that sound obviously influenced by Dr. Dre's early-2000s sound. You could argue that C-BO is compromising his former hardcore-as-hardcore-gets approach for a more commercially viable gangsta approach that's not too far removed from what you'd expect from latter-day 2Pac or Snoop Dogg and his Eastsidaz posse; however, the change is actually quite welcome. C-BO had exhausted his "American nightmare" style by the end of the '90s. So, even if he's merely following the trends in West Coast gangsta rap, it's a new direction for him to head in, something that longtime C-BO fans will either complain about or, more likely, accept as part of the rapper's growth—artistically as well as commercially. —*Jason Birchmeier*

West Coast Mafia / Jul. 23, 2002 / West Coast Mafia ◆◆◆

Debuting on a new label, West Coast Mafia, with an album of the same name, C-BO continues his dark vision of left-coast gangster politics, with the apocalyptic chords and lyrical menace to match. C-BO starts right from the beginning, reassuring listeners that the West Coast is still selling records with "Milk & Honey" and reminding everyone who's really gangsta with "We Did It." "Can U Deal Wit This?" finds him trading some great rhymes with Killa Tay and Big Lurch, while Roger Troutman Jr. makes up for the absence of his father on talkbox guitar. Though C-BO raps prove he's still at the top of his game, the productions are a bit samey, with dark chords and trebly percussion rollers on most every track. —*John Bush*

C-Murder

Dirty South, Hardcore Rap

C-Murder is the younger brother of Master P, the founder and president of No Limit Records. That explains his membership in the No Limit family, the label where nepotism rules, but he's actually one of the stronger rappers on the label. He may stick to the predictable gangsta musical blueprint, but as a rapper, he had an original style and interesting wordplay that separated him from the No Limit pack.

C-Murder made his first recorded appearance as a member of Tru, a trio that also featured his brothers Master P and Silkk the Shocker. Their first album, *True*, was released in 1995 and was followed by *Tru 2 Da Game* in 1997. During that year, C-Murder appeared on a number of No Limit releases, including Master P's *Ghetto D* and the *I'm Bout It* soundtrack. In the spring of 1998, he released his solo debut, *Life or Death*; *Bossalinie* followed a year later. In 2000 he reached superstar status, first with his appearance in the 504 Boyz smash hit "Wobble Wobble," then with his third and most successful album yet, *Trapped in Crime*, propelled by the commercial success of its C-Murder/Snoop Dogg/Magic collaboration, "Down for My N's." This album also signaled the launch of Tru Records, C-Murder's new label, which promised to be accompanied by a clothing line and successive releases. His 2002 release, *Tru Dawgs*, was a test for the label but was preceded by tragedy when C-Murder was arrested for shooting someone in a nightclub. He went to jail right after the album was finished, and was there during the release of the CD. Master P has been a vocal supporter of C-Money since the incident, claiming that he wasn't involved and it is a case of mistaken identity. —*Stephen Thomas Erlewine*

● **Life or Death** / Mar. 17, 1998 / No Limit ✦✦✦✦
C-Murder is one of the big boys in the No Limit posse, which may raise your expectations for his debut album, *Life or Death*. After all, so many members of the No Limit team survive entirely on marketing, not on the music, which often seems like an afterthought. There are times on *Life or Death* that the music is simply tedious and pedestrian, but those are often saved by C-Murder, who is one of the most charismatic rappers on No Limit. He's not necessarily original—you can certainly hear elements of Snoop Dogg in his delivery—but he has the conviction and charm to sell his tales of sex, violence, drugs, all the things that make the gangsta's world go 'round. —*Stephen Thomas Erlewine*

Bossalinie / Mar. 9, 1999 / Priority ✦✦
No Limit never apologized for making albums on an assembly line—and really, considering that nearly every record they released went gold at a minimum, they probably felt no apologies were necessary. Because of this crass practice, it was difficult to differentiate between records and artists, meaning that the subtle pleasures of, say, Silkk the Shocker were lost to most ears. That wasn't the case with C-Murder, however. The youngest brother of Master P and Silkk, C-Murder shares portions of his siblings' talents, and his debut *Life or Death* illustrated that he was poised to take his Snoop/2Pac delivery to another level. His sequel, *Bossalinie*, unfortunately doesn't follow through on the success of his opening salvo. C-Murder has gotten lazy, choosing to spin out predictable gangsta tales without honing his craft. Before, it seemed as if he was developing a signature style, but here he falls back on clichés. Combine the flat delivery with the flat production on *Bossalinie* and the result is a by-the-books No Limit record, the kind of which will please the devoted but nobody else. —*Stephen Thomas Erlewine*

Trapped in Crime / Aug. 22, 2000 / No Limit ✦✦✦✦
Upon an initial listen, it's very easy to dismiss this album as yet another shoddy collection of second-rate tracks carried by one catchy single, "Down for My N's." Upon a closer listen, however, the No Limit crew seems to have risen their standards here. The 24 tracks feature some fairly solid beats by the more competent producers on No Limit—XL, Ke-Noe, Carlos Stephens—staying true to the patented drum-machine bounce beats and synth that propelled some of the label's better past tracks. Furthermore, C-Murder manages to integrate some moderately effective choruses into his songs, particularly the anthem chant of "Down for My N's." As good as this album is relative to the many lackluster albums released by No Limit in the late '90s, though, it still seems that C-Murder and his crew will never grow out of the clichés they have defined for themselves. In fact, the album's title is fitting, when you consider how C-Murder seems forever confined to thuggishness, or so it seems judging by his rhetoric: "I'm forever tru 'til I'm dead," "How a thug nigga like it girl?" "What you bout boy?," "You need a thug in yo life," "F*ck them other niggas 'cuz I'm down for my niggas," and so on. Yes, this is pretty much standard No Limit fare, but it's one of the better late-'90s releases the label churned out and thus worthwhile for fans. —*Jason Birchmeier*

C-P-3.Com / Oct. 23, 2001 / Priority ✦✦✦
C-Murder never really had much success relative to his brothers, Master P and Silkk the Shocker. His albums sold, but not nearly as well as the other

No Limit releases. And there's a reason for that—he never really had much going for him besides nepotism. He proved this album after album. So, given his consistent inability to impress even those within the ardent No Limit cult, you can't help but marvel at the idea of C-Murder trying to start his own sub-label, Tru Records. He pitched the idea on *Trapped in Crime* yet never really made much of it. On *C-P-3.Com*, though, C-Murder puts quite a push behind his new label and his modest stable of affiliates: T-Bo, New-9, Wango, Bass Heavy, XL, and a few others. You really have to admire his efforts and commend his ambition. C-Murder seems to have learned quite a bit about the rap game from his older brother when it comes to filling out an album with promotional cameos and pitching his product. Unfortunately, much like his brother, his business instincts heavily outweigh his musical talents. More than anything—the rapping, the beats, the skits, the marketing-savvy booklet—it's C-Murder's downright lack of creativity that makes *C-P-3.Com* such a disappointment. There's nothing on this album that C-Murder hasn't offered before on previous releases, not to mention the myriad other No Limit albums. And worse, the beats and rapping on *C-P-3.Com* make past albums like *Life or Death* sound like masterpieces. The beats are stiffer than ever and the rhymes are more staged than ever. If you couldn't stomach prime-era No Limit, there's little chance you'll make it more than a few songs into this album—and even that may be a stretch. All you can really do is hope that C-Murder will eventually realize that he's better off saving his money than investing in ill-fated ventures like Tru Records and albums like this. —*Jason Birchmeier*

Tru Dawgs / Apr. 30, 2002 / Riviera ✦✦
Shortly before C-Murder's arrest in 2002, he had been busy at work on *Tru Dawgs*. Intended as a showcase for the No Limit rapper's many affiliates, the album features a long list of guests, among them Snoop Dogg, Master P, Silkk the Shocker, Keith Murray, Mia X, Bizzy Bone, da Brat, and Jermaine Dupri. In addition, C-Murder also features many lesser-known rap artists on *Tru Dawgs*. Anyone familiar with the late-'90s era of No Limit, when the label regularly featured innumerable guests on every release, should find a certain amount of comfort in this format. C-Murder himself is more of a presenter here than a performer, only appearing on five of the songs. Yet with so many different guests, some of them seasoned veterans, others hungry rookies, you don't really mind that C-Murder is for the most part missing in action. His guests are just as talented as him, if not sometimes more so, and each no doubt represents the "tru" spirit that C-Murder so ardently embraces. —*Jason Birchmeier*

Slimm Calhoun

Dirty South, Southern Rap
Hailing from College Park, GA, rapper Slimm Calhoun grew up listening to the groundbreaking hip-hop sounds of Run-D.M.C., Kurtis Blow, and Grandmaster Flash. In 1994 he hooked up with Outkast and the Dungeon Family crew, who took Calhoun under their wing. Signed to Outkast's own label, Aquemini (via Elektra), in the late '90s, Calhoun's debut, *The Skinny*, was originally supposed to be issued in mid-2000, but its release date kept getting pushed back until finally seeing the light of day in April 2001. Despite the delay, Calhoun kept himself busy by guesting on Outkast's breakthrough album *Stankonia* (the track "Gangsta Shit") and toured with Outkast as part of the rapper's Stank Love tour, joining in on a medley of three songs from *The Skinny* each night. —*Greg Prato*

● **The Skinny** / Apr. 2001 / Elektra ✦✦✦
An artist affiliated with mega hip-hop heavyweights Outkast will certainly arouse a raised eyebrow in the hip-hop community, but it won't necessarily translate to a gold plaque for that artist's debut. Released on Outkast's Aquemini label, Outkast protégé Slimm Cutta Calhoun's debut album is unpolished but contains some evidence that the young Atlien will be heard from in the future. Slimm's energetic, concise delivery and Georgia drawl tear up tracks, but the overall presentation is still too immature. The Outkast massive's production team, Organized Noise, lends their swampy dirty South sound for a majority of the album. Some of the tracks have high-caliber quality, most notably "Time Lock," powered by a grimy, effect-ridden guitar riff, and the heartfelt "Lil Buddy." However, there are not enough of these inspired production efforts to aid young Slimm's developing talents. Big Boi and Andre of Outkast chip in for a couple of tracks, but their assists are unable to truly pick this album up off the mat. Those

looking for the much more dynamic sounds of other Outkast affiliates such as Goodie Mob, Cool Breeze, and Witchdoctor will be mostly disappointed. —*M.F. Di Bella*

Cali Agents

Group / Hip-Hop, West Coast Rap, Underground Rap

Bringing together the talents of respected West Coast solo rappers Rasco and Planet Asia, both of whom had piled up music awards and critical praise within the hip-hop community, Cali Agents issued their debut album in 2000, *How the West Was Won.* The recording, which reflected influences from both coasts, combined the strength of Rasco's powerful delivery with the fluid lyrics of Planet Asia. —*Stacia Proefrock*

● **How the West Was One** / Jun. 13, 2000 / Ground Control ◆◆◆◆

Rasco and Planet Asia, two West Coast MCs who had enjoyed mildly successful and well-respected solo careers, joined forces in 2000 to produce a group much stronger than the sum of its parts. Their individual releases, although technically sound, had been a bit monotonous at times, but as a tag team duo they complemented each other perfectly. Rasco played the part of the grumpy, serious old veteran, scolding those he didn't approve of, while Planet Asia personified the younger, wilder side, playing off his partner to include some fun in the mix. Together with a diverse lineup of producers, they created an incredibly simple yet effective sound, combining hard drumbeats with a violin, piano, or guitar sample in a formula heavily influenced by Gang Starr's DJ Premier. Lyrically, the duo tiptoed between pleasing an underground audience highly suspicious of the mainstream and attempting to make a living and enjoy success. Planet Asia summed up the group's approach on "This Is My Life," rhyming "Not only do we rock fresh gear, but when it comes to hip-hop we're like a breath of fresh air, like yeah!/And just to let y'all side busters know, we rep the underground but still we're out to make dough." Cali Agents crafted a surprising debut that struck a balance between different hip-hop crowds, East and West Coast, underground and above, but managed to maintain their artistic integrity. —*Luke Forrest*

Cam'ron (Cameron Giles)

b. Harlem, NY

East Coast Rap, Gangsta Rap, Pop-Rap

Rapper Cam'ron was born and raised in Harlem, attending Manhattan Center High School, where one of his basketball teammates was Mason "Mase" Betha, who also became a successful rapper. Though his playing earned him scholarship offers from top colleges, Cam'ron was unable to take advantage of them because of his poor academic record, and he enrolled at a small college in Texas instead. He quickly dropped out and returned to Harlem, where he became a drug dealer before turning to rap. Hooking up with the Bad Boy posse, he developed a pop-rap style similar to chief Bad Boy Puff Daddy. But Cam'ron didn't sign with Bad Boy; Mase introduced him to the Notorious B.I.G., who in turn brought in his partner Lance "Un" Rivera. Un signed Cam'ron to his Untertainment label, distributed by Epic Records. Cam'ron first attracted attention with "Pull It," which earned airplay in May 1998. "357" was featured in the movie *Woo* and became his first R&B chart entry in June. Then in July came "Horse & Carriage," featuring Mase. It made the R&B Top Ten and just missed hitting the pop Top 40, setting up Cam'ron's debut album, *Confessions of Fire,* which went gold and made the Top Ten of both the pop and R&B charts. "Feels Good" featuring Usher was another R&B chart entry in December. "Let Me Know" made the pop and R&B charts in June 1999. A year later, "What Means the World to You" heralded the release of Cam'ron's biographical sophomore album, *S.D.E.* (the initials standing for Sports, Drugs, and Entertainment). Cam'ron worked with Ol' Dirty Bastard, Mobb Deep's Prodigy, and producer Digga to complete the album, which was released in September 2000. After moving to Jay-Z's Roc-A-Fella label, his single "Oh Boy" became a big hit on urban radio in 2002, and the album *Come Home With Me* performed well too. Early the following year, his protégés the Diplomats debuted with the two-disc set *Diplomatic Immunity.* —*Stephen Thomas Erlewine*

Confessions of Fire / Jul. 14, 1998 / Epic ◆◆◆

Following in the footsteps of Sean "Puffy" Combs, Cam'ron has created an accessible fusion of rap and pop that manages to keep some sort of street edge. Of course, that doesn't mean Cam'ron is hardcore—he may come off as an East Coast gangsta, but his music is polished and melodic…much like that of Puff, his mentor. He happens to be a better rapper than Puffy, but he doesn't have the pop flair that makes Combs' productions big hits. Still, he shows promise on his debut, *Confessions of Fire.* Although it has too many songs and some tracks blend together, he shows potential as a charismatic rapper and there are enough strong singles, including "357" and "Horse & Carriage," to make it worth a listen for fans of East Coast popcore. —*Stephen Thomas Erlewine*

S.D.E. / Sep. 19, 2000 / Epic ◆◆◆

Cam'ron, who scored a gold album and a string of chart singles with his first album, *Confessions of Fire,* begins his second with the uncompromising "F*** You," which establishes immediately that he is turning to a more aggressive gangsta style. Thereafter, the rapper covers the usual subjects for the genre, cursing freely in depictions of sexual and physical violence against women, drug usage, and gunplay. Producer Darrell "Digga" Branch provides rudimentary backing tracks that sample such familiar tunes as Edwin Starr's "War" and the Police's "Roxanne," while Cam'ron expresses rage in slow raps that often devolve into little more than complaining. In "Do It Again," the 22-year-old reflects back on his life, pondering whether he would change anything. "I live my life for thugs, I live my life for drugs, f*** everybody else," he says. Haunted by his own chance of violent death, he follows "Come Kill Me" with "What I Gotta Live For." As the album goes on, guest rappers make more frequent appearances, and several of them, notably Freaky Zeeky and Jimmy Jones, turn out to be faster and more vocally adept than Cam'ron. They provide the only moments when *S.D.E.* (the initials stand for Sports, Drugs, and Entertainment) rises above the pedestrian, though they prove no respite from the onslaught of vulgarities. (Oddly enough, though, the final track, "My Hood," does give some relief, since it is a so-called clean edit, which is to say that offensive words simply have been wiped out of the rap, leaving awkward silences and rendering it largely incomprehensible. There is no notation about the edit, and it may be a simple mistake, since the entire album was also released in a "clean" version.) —*William Ruhlmann*

● **Harlem's Greatest** / Mar. 26, 2002 / Epic ◆◆◆◆◆

Epic only released two Cam'ron albums before letting the rapper slip to Roc-A-Fella in 2002, but that didn't prevent the label from compiling the *Harlem's Greatest* best-of compilation. The best songs from Cam'ron's very successful debut, *Confessions of Fire* (1998)—"357," "Horse & Carriage," "Glory"—and his quickly forgotten follow-up, *S.D.E.* (2000)—"That's Me," "What Means the World to You," "Let Me Know"—are here, making it a perfect album to pick up for anyone curious about the rapper's pre-"Oh Boy" recordings, back when he found success as a pop-rapper alongside Puff Daddy and Mase. —*Jason Birchmeier*

Come Home With Me / May 14, 2002 / Roc-A-Fella ◆◆◆◆

Just when it seemed as if everyone had forgotten about Cam'ron, he returned in 2002 as part of Jay-Z's industry-dominating Roc-A-Fella collective. If that wasn't reason enough to inspire curiosity, Cam'ron's lead single, "Oh Boy," blew up urban radio all summer. His rugged rapping and Just Blaze's soulful production made "Oh Boy" the huge success that it was, yet the joy of hearing Cam'ron on the radio again also had a bit to do with the revival. The Harlem rapper had fallen off the map after *S.D.E.* (2000), his poorly recieved album from two years earlier. Just two years before that, Cam'ron was one of the industry's most promising pop-rappers. His first album, *Confessions of Fire* (1998), produced several singles, including his collaboration with Mase, "Horse & Carriage." However, 1998 felt like the distant past in 2002, and Cam'ron needed a big comeback after falling into obscurity during the interim. *Come Home With Me* is indeed that big comeback. Even though the Roc-A-Fella roster appears on only two songs—"Welcome to New York City," featuring Jay-Z, and "The Roc (Just Fire)," featuring Memphis Bleek and Beanie Sigel—Cam'ron doesn't really need the assistance here. He comes hard on most tracks, yet his muscle is complemented by producer Just Blaze and his trademark sampling style. Just Blaze doesn't produce every track on this album, but he does provide the key moments: "Oh Boy" and "The Roc (Just Fire)." Overall, Cam'ron couldn't return with a stonger comeback album than this: He's affiliated with one of the industry's most successful labels, helmed by a hot producer, and armed with a dynamite lead single. Cam'ron may not record the style of pop-rap you once associated with him, but when the resulting album is this solid from top to bottom, you really can't argue. Instead, you should be thankful. —*Jason Birchmeier*

Diplomatic Immunity / Mar. 11, 2003 / Def Jam ✦✦
On his third record, *Come Home With Me*, Cam'ron began paving the way for a few of his protégés (Juelz Santana, Jimmy Jones [aka the Ghetto's Advocate], Freekey Zekey), and the foursome came together as the Diplomats for a massive two-disc extravaganza, *Diplomatic Immunity*. With three of the four due for *another* full Roc-A-Fella release later in 2003—plus a film release for *Come Home With Me*—the big question became quantity control, so it's no wonder that their combined talents can't keep this two-hour release together. As on *Come Home With Me*, the combination of Cam'ron with producer Just Blaze provides the highlights, "I Really Mean It" and the Starship-sampling "Built This City." Both of them appear on the second disc, and there really isn't much to recommend on the first. There's a pointless remix of the Cam'ron/Juelz Santana/Freekey Zekey feature "Hey Ma" (originally on *Come Home With Me*), with Toya providing some R&B vocals, and the bizarre inclusion of "Bout It Bout It, Pt. III" featuring Master P himself. Aside from Cam'ron, the Diplomats aren't good enough to carry these tracks themselves, and the lack of quality productions (or producers) makes this an easy one to skip, even for fans of Cam'ron. —*John Bush*

Camp Lo

f. 1995, Bronx, NY
Group / Jazz-Rap, Pop-Rap, Hip-Hop, Club/Dance
Camp Lo is a rap group from the Bronx who melds hip-hop with jazz sensibilities and funk. After having a hit single, "Coolie High," from *The Great White Hype* soundtrack in early 1996, they released their debut album, *Uptown Saturday Night*, in February of 1997. The album was reissued two years later on Arista Records, and a second album (*Let's Do It Again*) finally appeared in 2002. —*Stephen Thomas Erlewine*

● **Uptown Saturday Night** / Jan. 28, 1997 / Profile ✦✦✦✦
Camp Lo's debut album is a refreshing fusion of hip-hop, soul, and jazz that manages to avoid most jazz-rap clichés while retaining street credibility. *Uptown Saturday Night* doesn't really break any new ground, yet it doesn't sound tired either, primarily because the rappers of Camp Lo have a deft, graceful rhythmic touch and their producers (including Ski and Trugoy Tha Dove) are skilled musicians, capable of weaving funky sonic layers that never sound too spare or overloaded. In short, *Uptown Saturday Night*, even with its occasional dull patches, is a worthwhile debut. —*Leo Stanley*

Let's Do It Again / May 21, 2002 / Dymond Crook ✦✦✦
Five long years after a refreshing debut, Camp Lo returned with a sophomore record which (unfortunately) found them fitting into the tight hip-hop mainstream much better than previously. There's little here that hints at 1997's *Uptown Saturday Night* or "Luchini (aka This Is It)," one of the best hip-hop singles of all time. Yes, the production is much more inventive than most commercial rap, but the rhythms and even occasionally the delivery recall the rolling tracks of Jay-Z or Eightball & MJG, without the flair or confidence. —*John Bush*

Candyman

b. Jun. 25, 1968
Hip-Hop, Pop-Rap
Los Angeles rapper Candyman was featured backing Tone-Loc before he earned his own solo stint. His 1990 debut, *Ain't No Shame in My Game*, scored a Top Ten pop hit with "Knockin' Boots." The following year, he released another less successful LP for Epic, *Playtime Is Over*. He released *I Thought U Knew* for IRS in 1993, which also failed to click. The year 2000 saw the release of Candyman's *Knockin' Boots 2001: A Sex Odyssey*, an album featuring his 1990 hit single remixed and new cuts as well. —*Ron Wynn*

● **Ain't No Shame in My Game** / Sep. 24, 1990 / Epic ✦✦✦✦✦
When a rapper does well in the R&B or pop markets, hip-hop's hardcore tends to view the artist with suspicion, however strong his or her rapping skills might be. That was exactly what happened to Candyman when "Knockin' Boots" (a catchy single that sampled Betty Wright's "Tonight Is the Night") enjoyed considerable crossover action. Some hardcore rappers questioned Candyman's legitimacy, but make no mistake—*Ain't No Shame in My Game* proves that the Angeleno's rapping skills were solid. While this decent debut album has its share of lighthearted R&B-flavored fare (including "Playin' on Me," "Melt in Your Mouth," and of course "Knockin' Boots"), more aggressive, in-your-face tunes like "Today's Topic," "5 Verses of Def," and "The Mack Is

Back" demonstrated that Candyman had no problem handling hardcore b-boy rap. The overall result is a generally likable, if a bit uneven, CD. —*Alex Henderson*

Playtime Is Over / Jul. 1991 / Epic ✦✦✦

I Thought U Knew / Jun. 29, 1993 / IRS ✦✦

Canibus (Germaine Williams)

b. 1974, Jamaica
East Coast Rap, Hardcore Rap
Though heralded as a prospective talent at the time of his major-label debut in 1998, Canibus nonetheless became little more than a momentary phenomenon as his subsequent work failed to match the hype surrounding him. Following some underground work and cameo appearances, most notably on Wyclef Jean's "Gone Till November" remix in 1997, Canibus feuded famously with LL Cool J. The resulting exchanges—Canibus' "Second Round K.O." and LL's "The Ripper Strikes Back," both spirited battle tracks—garnered significant attention and, of course, promotion as well. Expectations were therefore high when Canibus unleashed his Wyclef-produced full-length debut, *Can-I-Bus* (1998), shortly afterward on Universal. Critics unfortunately panned the album and listeners did so as well, so Canibus receded from the spotlight quickly. He returned two years later with his follow-up for Universal, *2000 B.C.*, but it too found little embrace, and Canibus soon found himself returning to the underground circuit from which he came. He interestingly sought to battle his way back into the spotlight as he originally had, ultimately confronting Eminem, of all rappers. The tactic proved fruitless, though, and alienated Canibus even further from the mass market. Even so, he retained a cultish following and continued to release albums independently of the majors, occasionally firing off more of the battle raps he remains most known for.

Born Germaine Williams in 1974 in Jamaica, Canibus moved to the United States with his mother at a young age. Because his mother's career required constant relocation, the family moved frequently and the soon-to-be rapper found solace within himself. His rhetorical abilities blossomed later, once hip-hop became the guiding force in his life. He began rhyming and in the mid-'90s joined a group called T.H.E.M. (The Heralds of Extreme Metaphors), which consisted also of his partner Webb. Following a fallout with his partner, Canibus pursued a solo career and began infiltrating the mix-tape circuit. By 1997, he had approached the brink of the major-label rap game, guesting regularly on high-profile releases: He contributed to "Uni-4-orm," an inclusion on the *Rhyme & Reason* soundtrack also featuring Heltah Skeltah and Rass Kass; "Love, Peace & Nappiness," an inclusion on the Lost Boyz's *Love, Peace & Nappiness* also featuring Redman and A+; "Making a Name for Ourselves," an inclusion on Common's *One Day It'll All Make Sense*; the non-album remix of Wyclef Jean's "Gone Till November"; and most famously, "4, 3, 2, 1," an inclusion on LL Cool J's *Phenomenon* also featuring Redman, DMX, and Method Man.

Of the several guest appearances, "4, 3, 2, 1" certainly meant the most, as it brought together many of New York's preeminent hardcore rappers and thus ushered Canibus into that same elite class. At the same time, however, Canibus lashed out shortly afterward with the Mike Tyson-featuring "Second Round K.O.," where he rhymed, "So I'm a let the world know the truth, you don't want me to shine/You studied my rhyme, then you laid your vocals after mine." In fact, the entirety of the song directed barbed rhymes at LL: "You walk around showin' off your body cause it sells/Plus to avoid the fact that you ain't got skills/Mad at me 'cause I kick that shit real niggaz feel/While 99 percent of your fans wear high heels," and so on. Shortly thereafter, LL sought his revenge, releasing "The Ripper Strikes Back" on the *Survival of the Illest* soundtrack (1998) and thus channeling even more attention toward Canibus. From the track's chorus ("Can-I-bus? Yes you can!") to practically every line of the verses ("You soft as a newborn baby takin' a nap/Make my dick hard with that bitch-ass track/Where you at? Smokin' in some one-room flat/Suckin' on Clef's dick hopin' to come back"), LL unleashed a fury of insults and threats. The media, of course, elevated the battle to grand heights, as even MTV gave the story headlines. In the aftermath of 2Pac's and Biggie's deaths, such confrontations fascinated the rap community, and Canibus certainly capitalized on his newfound publicity.

As for his debut full-length, *Can-I-Bus* (1998), though, the response was sobering. Critics expressed little support, and sales quickly dropped as listeners also felt genuinely disappointed. Executive produced by Wyclef, the album suffered on many levels, both production-wise and rhetorically (critics targeting Canibus' delivery more than his lyrics or themes). The momentum that "Second Round K.O." had generated simmered almost immediately, and it didn't help that LL's "Ripper Strikes Back" found substantial acceptance at the time as well. In the two years following the release of *Can-I-Bus*, the rapper maintained an extremely low profile, much in contrast to the regular guest appearances he had made leading up to his debut. As a result, when he finally did return with his follow-up album, *2000 B.C.* (2000), few noticed; it came and went generally unheard, and Canibus returned to the underground after parting ways with Universal. He continued to record albums and release them on the independent circuit; furthermore, he retained a small base of fans as well, yet his days as the next big thing had clearly come and gone, as they similarly had for so many other talented rappers. —*Jason Birchmeier*

Can-I-Bus / Sep. 8, 1998 / Uptown/Universal ◆◆◆
Prior to the release of his debut album, Canibus had a hit with "Second Round K.O.," a single that attacked L L Cool J in a style reminiscent of classic '80s cutting contests. It was an audacious beginning to what appeared to be a promising career, but the full-length album *Can-I-Bus* doesn't quite live up to the potential indicated in that hard-hitting single. Part of the problem is that Canibus is a monotonous rapper, sticking to the same delivery no matter what the subject of the lyrics or the tone of the music. He also shows surprising misogynist, violent, and homophobic streaks, especially for a protégé of the Fugees' Wyclef Jean. Even with all these faults, Canibus does have his strengths—in particular, his intense delivery is intoxicating in its power (which is part of the problem, too, since its very intensity can be too much)—and when he's on his game, he comes up with some clever, unexpected turns of phrase. Unfortunately, those moments only occur sporadically over the course of this overlong debut, but when they do happen, it's easy to see what all the hype is about. —*Stephen Thomas Erlewine*

● **2000 B.C.** / Jul. 18, 2000 / Uptown/Universal ◆◆◆
Thanks to a legendary feud with LL Cool J, Canibus was thrust on the hip-hop scene with so much hoopla you would have sworn he was being promoted by Don King. But after being labeled the next Rakim, Canibus' enigmatic debut, *Can-I-Bus*, was such a major disappointment it left the masses chanting a slogan Public Enemy made famous over a decade ago—"Don't Believe The Hype." With his sophomore effort, *2000 B.C.*, Canibus remains a lightning rod for controversy, as he continues to chastise his arch nemesis LL. But Canibus also adds a new name to his hit list, as the LP's blazing title track contains a scornful dis of Wyclef: "You mad at the last album I apologize for it, I can't call it m*********** Wyclef spoiled it." Though there is some validity to that claim, airing beefs like the one directed at his former mentor reek of irony. While the rugged drum tracks provided by a largely unknown squad of producers are more conducive to Canibus' cold and calculated flow then the melodic palette of Wyclef's, it is virtually a wash in terms of quality. Yet, there is no disputing that Canibus is an MC's MC. His authoritative vocals demand immediate attention and his brutal array of battle rhymes are utterly breathtaking: "100 Bars" and "Lyrical Modulation." While the pugilistic MC shows growth as an artist, Canibus' vast potential remains largely unrealized thanks to bland production. —*Matt Conaway*

"C" True Hollywood Stories / Oct. 30, 2001 / Archives ◆◆◆
Canibus is always doing something different. It seems like most of the better rappers and groups nowadays don't do many albums the same as one another, but adapt their style to keep people intrigued. Canibus does this here, with an almost mellow, laid-back offering. This album is really relaxed; the MC from "100 Bars" or "Poet Laureate" isn't found here. The beginning of the LP starts with a few intros and some tracks where Canibus takes on the form of Stan from the Eminem song. It's interesting, but not necessarily effective. The video game samples used throughout are a really weird thing about this album. Some of them are just plain annoying, but still Canibus proves that he can rock over anything. This is a long album, something that Canibus obviously worked pretty hard on. If you're a die-hard fan, don't expect the MC murderer listeners have grown used to, but don't completely write it off either. An introspective effort. —*Brad Mills*

Mic Club: The Curriculum / Nov. 19, 2002 / Mic Club ◆◆◆
Four years removed from the flash-in-the-pan success of "Second Round K.O.," Canibus seems to have finally come to terms with his has-been status

on *Mic Club: The Curriculum*, where he emphasizes heady rhyming rather than his pointed dis tracks of the past. The first two hard-hitting tracks, "Poet Laureate" and "Master Thesis," illustrate this well. Canibus had always been a thoughtful rapper with a gift for bookish wordplay, even if he'd garnered much more attention for his battling skills as displayed previously on "Second Round K.O." (pointed at LL Cool J) and "Stan Lives!" (at Eminem). Other tracks here like "Cenoir Studies 02" and "Dr. C Ph.D" similarly boast an educated demeanor, and Canibus teams up with fellow street intellectual Kool G Rap on "Allied Meta Forces." Given the shortage of hardcore yet scholarly rappers out there, Canibus offers a refreshing alternative to his bestial hardcore peers as well as his boringly behaved scholarly ones and presents himself as a proud, true anomaly. —*Jason Birchmeier*

Cannibal Ox
f. Harlem, NY
Group / Underground Rap, Hip-Hop, East Coast Rap
As hip-hop became increasingly commercial and calculated in the late '90s, a thriving indie scene began developing in response, one of the more significant artists in that underground scene being Cannibal Ox. The Harlem duo—Vast Aire and Vordul Megilah—eschewed the trademark late-'90s "Cash, Money, Hoes"/"Bling-Bling" style in favor of an edgier approach that confronted commercial hip-hop, acting almost as a foil to everything popular at the time in hip-hop—namely, the mentality valuing materialism over creativity and ultimately craft. Of course, one cannot mention Cannibal Ox without bringing attention to the duo's producer, El P, one of the more inventive beatmakers of his time. *The Cold Vein*, Cannibal Ox's 2001 LP, broke through to the mainstream on a small level, initially drawing nothing but praise from such noteworthy publications as *The Wire* and *CMJ*, in addition to the expected hip-hop press. Countless comparisons to *36 Chambers*-era Wu-Tang somewhat pigeonholed the group, even though the tag was no doubt flattering and drew the attention of many curious heads. —*Jason Birchmeier*

● **The Cold Vein** / May 15, 2001 / Def Jux ◆◆◆◆
While it can be said that many underground crews have been floundering in the gray matter of indie hip-hop, Cannibal Ox filled that area in with 2001's *The Cold Vein* for El P's Def Jux imprint. The music press had been quick to point out that Vast Aire and Vordul Megilah's attack is at times highly derivative of the Wu-Tang Clan, and the point is valid. Thankfully, El P (a serious candidate for producer of the year) lays out some of the most lushingly intriguing sounds and beats that feel as herky-jerky as they sound gilded with silk. It's a bit misleading to harp on the Wu factor that *The Cold Vein* contains since this record's content is immensely original and the Wu references that seem present are in the enlightened gloomy flow and psychedelic backdrops—not (with all due respect) in the kitschy hooks and unfocused rhymes that Wu-Tang are also known for. Aire and Megilah swirl around in b-boy posturing and obtuse nonsense as their innovation rears its head at every corner with scatter-shot lines like: "And I ain't dealin' with no minimum wage/I'd rather construct rhymes on a minimum page," and "You were a still-born baby, your mother didn't want you but you were still-born." While there's not a throwaway track per se, the album's length does run a bit long (at least they didn't make it into a double CD as a lot of rap acts have been known to do). To their immense credit, Cannibal Ox and El P have assembled one of the most listenable hip-hop albums in far too long. Headz be aware: Independent hip-hop has a new voice and this is your beat fix for 2001. —*Jack LV Isles*

Caparezza (Michele Salvemini)
b. Italy
Foreign Rap
Before he reemerged in 2001 as Caparezza, Italy's Michele Salvemini was a clean-cut, b-boy-style pop singer named Mikimix. His 1999 full-length, *La Mia Buona Stella*, produced the Italian hit single "E La Notte Se Ne Va," a slice of Europop closer to Color Me Badd or Enrique Iglesias than anything resembling American hip-hop. But it was the fluid style of Dr. Dre protégé Xzibit that Caparezza most closely resembled on *Tutto Cio Che C'E*, the 2001 debut of his new moniker. Caparezza made clear the distinction between past and present personas with furious raps about personal honesty and music business hypocrisy, painting a picture of himself as a pawn who knew he could be king. *Tutto Cio Che C'E*'s kitchen-sink production drew on elements

of both West and East Coast American hip-hop, as well as breakbeats, acoustic guitars, piano, and European influences suggesting Salvemini's Europop past, albeit with much better beats and basslines. Caparezza went on to contribute raps to likeminded projects by Speaker Cenzou and DJ Honey. — *Johnny Loftus*

● **Tutto Cio Che C'E** / Feb. 13, 2001 / EMI ✦✦✦✦

Caparezza's *Tutto Cio Che C'E* showcases just how solid international rapping had become by the end of the '90s. The Italian rapper drops his rhymes with just as much fluency and dexterity as his American peers throughout the album. He rhymes at a quick pace, partly because the Italian dialect works well within the context of hip-hop rhyming, rolling off the tongue with a liquid-like flow because of its heavy use of vowels at the end of most words. Linguistic analysis aside, Caparezza obviously has a mastery of the Italian dialect and how to shape it into highly alliterate rhymes that fly out of his mouth at a dizzying speed. It also helps that he has great beats to drop his rhymes over—not so much the sampled breakbeats that characterize New York hip-hop, the synthesized funk that characterizes California gangsta rap, or the drum machine beats that characterize the dirty South, but an uncanny style of beats that defy much of the precedent established by American rap. The beats on *Tutto Cio Che C'E* draw their sounds from everywhere, for example, the heavy metal guitar crunch of "Mea Culpa." It's this experimental approach to beatmaking, as well as Caparezza's mastery of the Italian dialect, that make this album so stunning. — *Jason Birchmeier*

Capone

b. Los Angeles, CA
Vocals / Gangsta Rap, Hardcore Rap, Latin Rap
Latin rapper Capone was born and raised in Los Angeles, forming his own label, Latino Jam, in 1998 to issue his debut single, "Kick It 4 la Raza." The full-length *Chicano World* was released in 1999; both *Raza Rolls Deep* and *Mis Carnales, Vol. 1* appeared the following spring. *Second to None* was issued in fall 2000; *Barrio Dope* surfaced in spring 2001. — *Jason Ankeny*

● **Chicano World** / Aug. 24, 1999 / On My Hustle ✦✦

Capone, the Texas rapper (not the Noreaga compatriot still in lockdown), salutes his Latino heritage all through *Chicano World*. With a few productions by the man himself and a D.I.Y. eithic learned from Master P., Capone trades Spanglish raps and "Don't Mess with Tex-Mex" themes on "Chicano Life," "Tejas Gangster Style," and "Don't F**k with Mexicans." While the raps are occasionally mediocre and repetitive, the productions are even worse from that standpoint and sound like they were all recorded with the same synthesizer. — *Keith Farley*

Barrio Dope / Mar. 27, 2001 / Latino Jam ✦✦

Capone-N-Noreaga

f. Queens, NY
Group / Gangsta Rap, East Coast Rap, Hardcore Rap
Queens rap duo Capone-N-Noreaga enjoyed massive street credibility with the release of their debut album, *The War Report*, which earned them a devoted following in the hardcore rap world. Capone (born Kiam Holley) and Noreaga (born Victor Santiago) grew up in the projects of Queensbridge and LeFrak City, respectively, and endured rough childhoods and multiple run-ins with the law. They met in 1992 while serving kitchen duty together at Collins Correctional Facility in New York, and became friends; upon their release, they decided to team up as rappers, taking their performing names from two legendary gangsters. In 1996, they signed with Penalty Records; their first release was the single "Illegal Life," and they next teamed up with Mobb Deep for "L.A., L.A.," another salvo in the East Coast/West Coast feud. Before their debut album was completed, Capone was sent back to prison for violating his parole on a weapons possession charge. Noreaga finished *The War Report* on his own, and it was a substantial underground success upon its release in 1997, making the R&B Top Five and going gold. With Capone incarcerated, the duo's thugged-out image rang true, and the singles "Closer" and "T.O.N.Y. (Top of New York)" saw some action on the rap charts. Noreaga capitalized on the album by starting a solo career, but remained loyal to Capone, visiting his friend often and giving Capone executive producer credits on the two popular solo albums (*N.O.R.E.* and *Melvin Flynt—Da Hustler*) he recorded over 1998-1999.

Capone was released from prison in early 1999, and the two immediately reteamed for the much-anticipated *The Reunion*, which was released in 2000

on Tommy Boy. Dissatisfied with the promotion, Capone-N-Noreaga asked to be released from their contract, and signed with Def Jam in 2001. Later that year, Capone ran into further trouble with the law; he was charged with assault following a nightclub brawl involving gunfire in Queens, but the charge was dropped due to lack of evidence. Not long after the incident, he was arrested at a Greensboro, NC, airport for possession of marijuana, but avoided jail time. Noreaga released his third solo album, *God's Favorite*, in 2002, and Capone was reportedly working on his own solo debut at the same time. — *Steve Huey*

● **The War Report** / Jun. 17, 1997 / Penalty ✦✦✦✦

As Capone-N-Noreaga—which naturally translates into the clever initials CNN—were recording their debut album, Capone was sent to jail, leaving Noreaga to handle the majority of *The War Report* himself, with the occasional help of such stars as Nas. It's a testament to the talents of both Capone and Noreaga that C's absence is barely felt and *The War Report* turns into a stellar debut. Both rappers have a distinctive rhythmic style and aren't afraid to deviate from traditional hardcore rap themes. Nor are they constrained by musical stereotypes, since *The War Report* explodes with impressionistic samples, gritty and evocative loops, and funky rhythms. The only thing that makes *The War Report* a disappointment is the knowledge that it would have been an even better album if Capone had been able to participate in the entire recording. As it stands, it's merely superb. — *Leo Stanley*

The Reunion / Nov. 21, 2000 / Tommy Boy ✦✦✦

For an example of how dramatically hip-hop's tectonic plates shift, look no further than Capone-N-Noreaga. Just a mere three years prior to the release of *The Reunion*, the group's debut, *The War Report*, had Capone and Noreaga poised to become one of New York's most promising hip outfits. However, their wings were clipped by the lengthy prison stay Capone began serving shortly before the release of their debut, an artistic death sentence that prohibited the crew from being able to release a follow-up until *Reunion*. Aided by two commercially successful solo endeavors, Noreaga has attempted to keep the embers warm for Capone-N-Noreaga's aptly titled *The Reunion*. Yet, for a crew that should be chomping at the bit to regain their previous stature, that hunger does not correlate here. However, *The Reunion* does have an upside, exemplified by the frenetic "Bang Bang" featuring Foxy Brown and the essential DJ Premier-laced "Invincible." But these tracks merely quell the monotony for brief stretches. Contributions from close-knit associates—Nas ("B EZ") and production from Mobb Deep's Havoc ("Gunz in da Air")—do little to lighten the load, and their contributions are more detrimental than beneficial. Eager to quickly capitalize on Capone's release, *The Reunion* sounds like a hurried project, one where the material has been compromised just to get product on the streets. With *The Reunion*, Capone-N-Noreaga take a step backward. — *Matt Conaway*

Cappadonna (Darryl Hill)

East Coast Rap, Hardcore Rap, Hip-Hop
Cappadonna (born circa 1969) was one of the last members to join the Wu-Tang Clan. He had known the members since grade school in Staten Island, and he had even decided at the age of 15 that he could write and perform lyrics. It wasn't until 1995, however, that he made his recorded debut, appearing on Raekwon's *Only Built 4 Cuban Linx* album. With that album, he became an official member of the Wu-Tang Clan, and from there on out, he frequently appeared on Wu records. In 1996, he played a large role on Ghostface Killah's *Ironman*. During 1997, his Wu apprenticeship continued, as he rapped on the Clan's second album, *Wu-Tang Forever*.

Cappadonna's solo debut, *The Pillage*, finally appeared in March 1998. Like any Wu project, the record featured RZA as the executive producer and cameos from a number of other Wu members, including Method Man, U-Cool, and Raekwon. As the sixth Wu solo project, the album was an instant success upon its release, debuting at number three on the charts. A sophomore effort, *The Yin and the Yang*, followed in 2001. — *Stephen Thomas Erlewine*

● **The Pillage** / Mar. 24, 1998 / Columbia ✦✦✦✦

By the time Cappadonna released his solo debut album *The Pillage* in the spring of 1998, the Wu-Tang sound as masterminded by the RZA had become familiar. That's not to say that it was played out, however. The RZA's skeletal, menacing production is bracing even after it's become familiar, which is to Cappadonna's benefit, since *The Pillage* doesn't really expand the Wu sound any further. With producer cohorts Goldfinghaz and Tru Master, the RZA has re-created his signature sound; while it sounds terrific, it nevertheless will be a little frustrating, since not only does it lack the thrill of the new, but the album isn't as focused as such previous RZA/Wu masterpieces as Raekwon's *Only Built 4 Cuban Lynx* and Genius' *Liquid Swords*, which both found individual voices within RZA's sound. Cappadonna, in contrast, is a foot soldier, capable of turning out great songs ("The Pillage," "Splish Splash," "Dart Throwing"), but also capable of just going through the motions. Consequently, *The Pillage* packs more punch than the average late-'90s hip-hop record, but it doesn't reach the dazzling standards of past Wu classics. —*Stephen Thomas Erlewine*

The Yin and the Yang / Nov. 2001 / Sony ✦✦✦
A year after the breath of fresh air that was Wu-Tang Clan's *The W*, major members RZA and Ghostface Killah both deflated the balloon with mostly disappointing solo albums. At the tail end of 2001, Wu associate Cappadonna dropped his own sophomore joint, and though he does fulfill the promise in the intro that "you gonna hear a lot of different things," *The Yin and the Yang* can't break the increasing curse on Wu-Tang solo albums. Cappadonna starts off with a few string-heavy, soul-sampling productions by his usual partners (8-Off the Assassin, True Master, Neonek), spitting solid mush-mouthed rhymes, trying (and usually failing) to capture the obtuse metaphysics of Method Man and Ol' Dirty Bastard. Of course, it's difficult to take the apocalyptic philosophizing on "Bread of Life" at face value, especially coming after a degrading track like "Super Model." The flip side of *The Yin and the Yang* is more promising; "Love Is the Message" is a distinct detour, sampling the hit of the same name by M.F.S.B. for an intriguing, swinging track. Cappadonna also joins forces with the So So Def crew (specifically, Jermaine Dupri and Da Brat) for another highlight, "We Know." Though his rapping ranks above the norm, *The Yin and the Yang* doesn't live up to expectations for Wu-Tang fans. —*John Bush*

Cappadonna Hits / Nov. 20, 2001 / Sony ✦✦✦
Cappadonna's rare hits collection appears *before* close to half of the material it comprises was even released—due to a pushed-back release date for his sophomore record. For the only casually obsessive Wu-Tang fan, this two-album distillation is a better choice than either of his first two solo records, though it's a baffler why this was even released. (The one quality that would've made it worthwhile, the inclusion of his Wu-Tang Clan features, is a missed opportunity.) For what it's worth, *Cappadonna Hits* does the job, grabbing a handful of highlights ("Splish Splash," "Black Boy," and "Slang Editorial") from *The Pillage*, along with the best from *The Yin and the Yang* ("Love Is the Message," "The Grits," and "Super Model"). —*John Bush*

Captain Rapp

Vocals, Producer / Old School Rap, West Coast Rap
Although Captain Rapp was never an international superstar, he was one of the pioneers of rap on the West Coast and enjoyed a small cult following in that part of the United States. The Los Angeles resident first made his mark in the early '80s, recording a 1981 single, "Gigolo Rapp," as half of the duo Disco Daddy & Captain Rapp. At the time, rap was dominated by the East Coast—most of the hip-hoppers who were well known in 1981 (Kurtis Blow, Grandmaster Flash & the Furious Five, the Treacherous Three, to name a few) were from New York or, in the case of the Sugarhill Gang, nearby New Jersey. But Captain Rapp realized that hip-hop could be big on the West Coast, and he wasn't alone. The people who gave Disco Daddy & Captain Rapp the chance to record "Gigolo Rapp" were Duffy and Jerry Hooks, who had a small indie label called the Rappers Rapp Disco Record Company. The father-son team along with Sylvia Robinson had been doing on the East Coast with Sugar Hill Records—which was considered the Motown of hip-hop in the early '80s—and envisioned their label as a West Coast counterpart. While "Gigolo Rapp" received very little attention on the East Coast, it was a minor hit in L.A. and enjoyed some airplay on a few local urban stations.

After parting company with Disco Daddy, Captain Rapp went solo and in 1983 recorded the sociopolitical cult classic "Bad Times (I Can't Stand It)," which Jimmy Jam & Terry Lewis produced with electro-hopper Rich Cason. A major departure from the lighthearted, feel-good escapism of "Gigolo Rapp," the sobering "Bad Times (I Can't Stand It)" addressed such topics as AIDS, child abuse, abortion, poverty, homelessness, and U.S. foreign policy in El Salvador. Lyrically, the single (which came out on the Saturn label) is every bit as gutsy and hard hitting as any of the sociopolitical gems that Run-D.M.C. and Grandmaster Flash & the Furious Five provided on the East Coast in 1983.

After "Bad Times (I Can't Stand It)," Captain Rapp didn't do a lot of recording. But the MC did return to the studio in 1992, when he provided a sociopolitical sequel to "Bad Times," titled "Bad Times, Part 2: The Continuance." —*Alex Henderson*

DJ Cash Money & MC Marvelous (Jerome Hewlett)

Group / Turntablism, Hip-Hop
An oft-cited influence among DJs, Philadelphia's Cash Money (born Jerome Hewlett) is credited with creating one of the crucial scratches of the turntable art form—the transformer scratch. The ever-self-effacing Cash Money credits another DJ, Spinbad, with the invention, but historians/trainspotters of the form say that Cash Money was the one to perfect it. His mixes graced many of Sleeping Bag Records' releases and his record with MC Marvelous (Marvin Berryman), *Where's the Party At?*, came out on the label in 1988. Since then he has competed internationally, winning the prestigious DJ World Championship in the late '80s and being named Greatest DJ in the World. If that wasn't honor enough, turntable manufacturer Technics made Cash Money the first inductee into the DJ Hall of Fame in 1998. —*Wade Kergan*

● **Where's the Party At?** / 1988 / Sleeping Bag ✦✦✦
Undernoticed and undervalued, this album boasts a nice mix of juvenile humor, funk-tinged hip-hop, and excellent production. —*Ron Wynn*

Cash Money Millionaires

Group / Southern Rap, Dirty South
The Cash Money Millionaires included whatever rappers happened to rap for Cash Money Records at the given moment. During the label's initial breakthrough and golden era, the group included Baby, Mannie Fresh, Juvenile, B.G., Turk, and Lil' Wayne. The group issued the *Baller Blockin'* collection (2000), which also included contributions from some of the group's inspirations, namely Eightball & MJG, E-40, Nas, and Rappin' 4-Tay. The album accompanied the straight-to-video film of the same name. —*Jason Birchmeier*

● **Baller Blockin'** / Sep. 12, 2000 / Uptown/Universal ✦✦✦
The *Baller Blockin'* soundtrack features the Cash Money crew—Juvenile, B.G., Turk, Lil' Wayne, Big Tymers—along with a cast of other well-known rappers that specialize in the same sort of affluent gangsta ballin'—E-40, UGK, Eightball & MJG, Nas, Mack 10, Rappin' 4-Tay. Though it would be wonderful to hear all these non-Cash Money rappers spewing their rhymes over Mannie Fresh's bounce beats, it doesn't happen. But at least half of the album features some of Fresh's best production work yet, with the other tracks being crafted by an adequate stable of other producers. This integration of non-Cash Money rapping and production actually works in the album's favor. Where past albums such as *Tha G Code* and *I Got That Work* became a bit oversaturated with Fresh's trademark beats and the Cash Money crew's excessive "bling-bling," "ice," and "stunna" talk, the non-Cash Money tracks here bring the much-needed sense of variety that these aforementioned albums lacked. Though Nas and Mack 10 do seem like the East and West Coast's Cash Money equivalent, their distinct rapping style, stance, and production motifs function as nice sabbaticals, providing the sort of perspective that makes one realize how unique the Cash Money aesthetic really is. As always, there is the obvious single on this album, "Baller Blockin'," along with a few other songs that could just as easily be seen as hit singles—Juvenile's "Rover Truck," Big Tymers' "Let Us Stunt," Eightball & MJG's "Ballin' Gs"—as well as a few songs that are worth repeated listens—B.G.'s "Thugged Out," Nas' "What You Gonna Do." What really seems out of place here are the two Unplugged contributions, which are essentially Cash Money's take on R&B as produced by Stormy Day. Of course, with such a broad palette of styles, there are going to be a few tracks worth skipping, but this album's variety seems preferable to Cash Money's usual gluttonous dose of overabundance. —*Jason Birchmeier*

Ca$hflow

f. 1984, Atlanta, GA
Group / Urban
When Cameo's Larry Blackmon relocated to Atlanta in the '80s, one of the groups he signed to his Atlanta Artists label was Ca$hflow. They blended funk, rap, and urban contemporary stylings, and featured lead vocalist Kary Hubbert, backed by drummer Gaylord Parson, keyboardist James Duffie, and keyboardist Regis Ferguson. Their debut LP, *Ca$hflow*, yielded one

moderate hit, "Mine All Mine," in 1986, which did respectably well internationally and in clubs, but didn't excite R&B fans. They issued a follow-up LP, *Big Money*, in 1988. — *Ron Wynn*

Ca$hflow / 1986 / Atlanta Artists ◆◆

● **Big Money** / 1988 / Atlanta Artists ◆◆
Run-of-the-mill ballads and funk permeate this Atlanta-based quartet's second album, produced by Larry Blackmon of Cameo fame. Some of the songs sound Cameo-ish, but there's nothing as sweet as Candy here. *Big Money* has eight tracks that clock in at barely 35 minutes. Hopefully, the record company didn't waste *big money* on this release. — *Tim Griggs*

Casual
Vocals / Underground Rap, Hip-Hop
Casual was third out the gate (following Del tha Funkee Homosapien and Souls of Mischief) from the Hieroglyphics crew, the undisputed kings of the Oakland underground scene. Casual's stature suggests that he may be the crew's bodyguard, until the mic is in his hand and the MC commences his verbal onslaught. Anything but casual in the sound booth, the gifted freestyler, known for his fierce battle tactics, dropped the moody *Fear Itself* in 1994 to a chorus of cheers from the underground set. Cas scored underground hits with "Didn't Mean To" and "That's How It Is," but overall, the Hiero sound takes an edgy, soulful turn on *Fear*. The album goes from playful to hyper-psychedelic with tracks like the brawling "Chained Minds." Casual mostly chilled on the low for a couple of years, despite his well-publicized vicious freestyle wars with onetime Hiero affiliate Saafir in 1994-1995. Cas returned with the limited-edition albums *Meanwhile* and *VIP* in 1997 and 1999. Cas also put in work on the heralded Hiero compilation *Third Eye Vision* in 1998. — *Michael Di Bella*

● **Fear Itself** / Feb. 1, 1994 / Jive ◆◆◆◆
Casual's 1994 debut *Fear Itself* was the Oakland, CA, rhyme crew Hieroglyphic's third attempt to seize the listening public's attention with their unique brand of hip-hop. Whereas fellow Hieroglyphic Del the Funky Homosapien plays the part of the sly ghetto wise guy sliding in and out of trouble, Casual is the burly troublemaker. He'll punch you in the face, sex your girl up, and generally flout good manners. The deep-voiced MC produces an unending and seemingly unstoppable flow of boasts and taunts, mercilessly skewering the wack rappers and fools he sees about him. The simplicity of his message belies the complexity of his vicious wordplay. The beats mirror Casual's rhyme flow with break after break filling each song. The production doesn't differ much from the organic funk on the other Hieroglyphics albums of the same period (*No Need for Alarm* and *93 'Til Infinity*), except perhaps that the aggressiveness is turned up a notch. The tracks gallop along with a brutal funkiness to match the muscle of Casual's rhymes. Like other Hieroglyphics releases, *Fear Itself* is a family affair with Souls of Mischief, Extra Prolific, and Del making guest appearances. The album will already be part of Hieroglyphics fan's collection, but others will find much here to like as well. — *Chris Witt*

Meanwhile . . . / 1997 / Hiero Imperium ◆◆◆◆
Casual's major-label debut album came and went without making much of a dent commercially, or really even in the hip-hop community, for that matter. But that has always seemed to be the case with the Hieroglyphics crew, perhaps because they are too artistic, too tuned in to their own lyrical and musical impulses rather than those that move huge units on hype and trendiness alone. With his cassette-only second album, *Meanwhile...*, released on Hieroglyphics' own Hiero Imperium label, Casual didn't stand much of a chance at expanding his fan base, and that is unfortunate, because it is a breath of fresh air in the same way that spiritual cousins the Roots, Common, and the Native Tongues collective are. Casual's delivery and outlook is less overtly loopy than crewmates Souls of Mischief and Del, and his music is mostly less trippy, more reliant on deep, West Coast bass grooves and loping funk instrumentation than witty samples, but that does not mean it is devoid of the same abundant lyrical skill and robust exuberance, because it has those qualities in spades. In fact, the same sense of pleasure that is evident in the rest of the Hieroglyphic camp permeates Casual's rhymes, though he is a bit more straightforward, and the gluey bass-led tracks and bare-bones beats are a perfect fit for Casual's expressive, singsong vocals, which, other than recalling Del's deep delivery, has its closest kinship with old schoolers such as Sugarhill Gang and Furious Five as well as fellow West Coasters the Alkaholiks. Whether

it be turning the same noir sample that Portishead used as the basis for "Sour Times" on its head or simply kicking freestyles with his mates, Casual never drops the ball. It's too bad the public probably will. — *Stanton Swihart*

He Think He Raw / Aug. 7, 2001 / Red Urban ◆◆◆
After listening to some of the tracks on *He Think He Raw*, fans of Casual's work with the Hieroglyphics may think they bought the wrong album. After all, rudimentary hip-hop tales of sexual conquests like "Windows" and "New Wave Freak" seem a far cry from his innovative work with Del tha Funkee Homosapien and the Hieroglyphics collective. There is plenty of material, however, for listeners who want to hear about more than booze and broads. Casual is on point on "I Gotta (Get Down)," an Alchemist-produced track that doesn't sacrifice lyrical content in favor of a catchy beat. Unfortunately, there are too few of these tracks on *He Think He Raw*. While it is hardly a bad album, it's impossible for anyone familiar with his earlier work to not think that Casual could have done better. — *Jon Azpiri*

Cee-Lo (Thomas Burton)
Southern Rap, Neo-Soul, Dirty South
The first member of Goodie Mob to go solo, Cee-Lo adopted a much more charismatic and flamboyant style for his 2002 debut album than his group had in the late '90s. The singer/rapper aligned himself more with eccentric alternative rappers like Andre 3000 of OutKast and Q-Tip of A Tribe Called Quest. Like those two, Cee-Lo wasn't scared to go against the norms, dressing flamboyantly rather than conservatively and performing sincerely rather than brashly. Perhaps not coincidentally, Artista—the label backing OutKast and the Dungeon Family—supported Cee-Lo's ambitions just as the early-2000s neo-soul movement approached its commercial zenith. The single "Closet Freak" led the album, which was titled *Cee-Lo Green and His Perfect Imperfections*, and followed Arista's late 2001 Dungeon Family release, which had featured prominent contributions from Cee-Lo. — *Jason Birchmeier*

● **Cee-Lo Green and His Perfect Imperfections** / Mar. 19, 2002 / Arista ◆◆◆◆
Following the success of OutKast in 2001, Arista Records followed up with several affiliated releases, one of them being Cee-Lo's debut album, *Cee-Lo Green and His Perfect Imperfections*. The most well-known member of Atlanta rap group Goodie Mob, Cee-Lo had contributed heavily to the debut Dungeon Family release, *Even in Darkness* (2001), and Arista used the momentum of that album—as well as the concurrent neo-soul movement—to market Cee-Lo's debut. For the album, the rapper/singer emphasized his singing more than his rapping. First of all, he worked with no big-name producers or guests, placing himself prominently in the spotlight. Second of all, he incorporates quite a bit of live instrumentation, evoking a sense of '70s soul and funk rather than '90s rap by doing so. Like another album released around the same time in early 2002, Q-Tip's *Kamaal: The Abstract*, Cee-Lo's debut finds a recognized rap artist delving into neo-soul and baring his soul in the process. Whether or not his fans choose to delve in as well doesn't seem too important to Cee-Lo, since he makes few commercial pleas, instead pleasing his own muse. — *Jason Birchmeier*

Cella Dwellas
Group / Hardcore Rap, Hip-Hop
The Cella Dwellas first created a buzz with the single "Land of the Lost," which originally appeared on *Nudder Budders*, a Loud Records sampler in 1994. The duo was originally thought to be a part of the burgeoning mid-'90s horrorcore sound popularized by groups like the Gravediggaz. However, the horrorcore-esque "Land of the Lost" was just the tip of the iceberg for the Flatbush, Brooklyn, duo. In early 1996, Ug and Phantasm dropped their debut LP *Realms N' Reality*, a swooping phantasmagoric album that wove hardcore New York hip-hop seamlessly with a Saturday morning adventure cartoon feel. The CDs' style combines Dungeons and Dragons-style role-playing games, horror flicks, slick, rugged beats, and imaginative, often humorous lyrics. *Realms and Reality* was an exciting and bizarre ride through two warped intellects. The tandem then vanished for almost four years, returning as simply the Dwellas in 2000 with *Last Shall Be First*. — *Michael Di Bella*

● **Realms and Reality** / Mar. 26, 1996 / RCA ◆◆◆◆
Before the 1996 release of the full-length album *Realms and Reality*, Flatbush, Brooklyn artists the Cella Dwellas toiled underground surfacing in early 1995 on a Masta Ace B side titled "For the Mind." The Dwellas' underground respect created enough of a stir to get them signed to Loud Records;

a sneak preview single, "Land of The Lost," showed up soon after on a Loud Records sampler. *Realms and Reality* is replete with the CDs' unique mix of sorcery and gangsta-ism. The Dwellas consist of Phantasm the Tall Man, an esoteric, edgy MC; and Ug the Imagination, a rough and rugged lyricist who is also unpredictably clever. The opening cut on the album "Advance to Boardwalk," a conceptual trip around the Monopoly game board, introduces the listener to the Dwellas' wizardry. There are two different styles that the duo employ on the album: fantasia bordering on horrorcore and straight-up hardcore hip-hop. Tracks like "Mystic Freestyle," "Realm Three," and "Cella Dwellas" sound straight out of a fantasy role-playing game while cuts like "Hold U Down," "Good Dwellas," and "Medina Style" are devastatingly banging. "Medina Style" may best represent the core of the Dwellas: a melodic yet rough groove with the CD's dropping vicious call-and-response rhymes over it. Cella Dwellas' music is hypnotic and other-worldly. Production, mainly by Nick Wiz, DJ Slice, and Megahurtz, is eclectic and gritty but also slick. *Realms and Reality* is a bizarre trip through the minds of Ug and Phantasm. The duo's lyrical content may be based on hallucinations and magic but their precision and articulation on the mic make this album accessible and exciting. —*Michael Di Bella*

● **The Last Shall Be First** / Sep. 26, 2000 / Loud ✦✦✦✦
Originally known as the Cella Dwellas, the Dwellas, as their original name suggests, consider themselves to be strictly underground. Their debut album, 1996's *Realms and Reality*, was filled with dank imagery and beats. *The Last Shall Be First* is in the same vein; however, the group seems to have taken their lyrical flow up a notch. Their improved flow can best be heard on "On the Run," a densely packed, well-told narrative. Also impressive is "Main Aim," a banging horn-filled track first featured on the soundtrack to the film *Soul in the Hole*. With outstanding cameos from the likes of Large Professor and Inspectah Deck, this shows that they can more than hold their own among hip-hop heavyweights. After listening to *The Last Shall Be First*, it's clear that the Dwellas have risen to another level. —*Jon Azpiri*

Celly Cel (Marcellus McCarver)

Gangsta Rap, West Coast Rap, Hardcore Rap, G-Funk
Born Marcellus McCarver, Celly Cel grew up in Vallejo, CA, just north of San Francisco and the surrounding Bay Area. His drawling hardcore gangster lyrics and G-funk productions first appeared in 1994 on *Heat 4 Yo Azz*, but Celly had been making demos and honing his skills as far back as 1990. Released on E-40's Sick Wid' It label, *Heat 4 Yo Azz* was well received and the following year his best-selling album to date, *Killa Kali*, was unleashed. Celly didn't have another release of his own until 1998's *G Filez*; in the interim, however, he managed to show up on records by E-40, Mossie, B-Legit Jay Tee, D-Shot, Young Dre, Latino Velvet, and Messy Marv. Sick Wid It and Celly Cel parted ways after *The G Filez* and a best-of was released the next year. Celly didn't miss a beat, though, and in 2000 he started his own label, Realside Records, and released a new album, *Deep Conversation*. His next project was a hardcore rap supergroup, the Criminalz with Spice 1 and Jayo Felony. Their Realside album, *Criminal Activity*, was released in 2001. —*Wade Kergan*

Heat 4 Yo Azz / Oct. 11, 1994 / Jive ✦✦✦

The G Filez / Jul. 14, 1998 / Jive ✦✦✦

The Best of Celly Cel / May 18, 1999 / Jive ✦✦✦✦
On his first few albums, Celly Cel often came off as a G-funk journeyman, fully informed of what he spoke but relaying it in clichéd terms heard elsewhere and done better by others. However, each of his records *Heat 4 Yo Azz, Killa Kali*, and *The G Filez* had hits among the misses, and this best-of does a fine job of collecting those moments. "Heat 4 Yo Azz," from the album of the same name is worth the price of admission alone, as is his classic remix of "It's Goin' Down" featuring B-Legit, Mack 10, and Rappin' 4-Tay. —*Wade Kergan*

● **Deep Conversation** / Jun. 20, 2000 / Realside ✦✦✦✦
Deep Conversation finds West Coast rapper Celly Cel improving his lyrical delivery overtop equally improved accompanying beats to the point where he has evolved into one of the coast's best MCs. On past albums Celly Cel has struggled to separate himself from the countless other West Coast gangsta rappers following in the footsteps of Too Short, Ice-T, and N.W.A. During his stint with the Sick Wid' It label, Celly Cel fell into the common pitfall of conformity, and then on his Jive album, *The G Filez*, he broke out of generic gangsta trappings and came into his own. The rapper's evolution from

gangsta to a well-rounded artist with a unique style continues on *Deep Conversation*. On two of the album's best songs, "Return of the Real Niggaz" and "Which One Is U?," Celly Cel definitely flexes his ego a bit, but he also ironically comments on the practice of ego flexing, calling out his fellow hustlas and playas while making a conscious effort not to fall victim to the same stereotypes he critiques. Other songs such as "Make Um Bounce," "The Dog in Me," and "What You Need" also stand out with their entertaining subject matter involving some of the more cheery aspects of a G-lifestyle. Of course, lyrics do not carry a rap album by themselves and *Deep Conversation* definitely benefits from the rapper's lucid delivery and the album's pristine West Coast G-funk sound. Until Celly Cel scores some major-label distribution, don't expect him to gain too much national recognition, but among his West Coast peers—Too Short, E-40, Ice Cube, Kurupt, Spice 1—his performance on *Deep Conversation* furthers his position as one of the most talented rappers in California. —*Jason Birchmeier*

Channel Live

Group / Hip-Hop, Gangsta Rap, East Coast Rap, Hardcore Rap, Club/Dance
The rap duo Channel Live debuted in 1994 with the platinum single "Mad Izm," which they followed with the gold-status album *Station Identification* in 1995. That year also saw the release of singles such as "Sex for Sport" and "Reprogram," which weren't quite as successful as their previous efforts. The group returned a few years later on the *One Million Strong* compilation, and 2000 saw the release of the single "Wild Out 2K" and the album *Armaghetto*. —*Heather Phares*

● **Station Identification** / 1995 / Capitol ✦✦✦
On their album debut *Station Identification*, Hakim and Tuffy cover social problems such as sex and violence over KRS-One's lean production grooves. The previous singles "Mad Izm" and "Reprogram" are definitely the highlights here, but the duo get in plenty of great raps on the album tracks as well. —*John Bush*

Armaghetto / Jul. 18, 2000 / Flavor Unit ✦✦✦
Since dropping the classic single "Mad Izm" in 1994, Channel Live hasn't been overly active. Linking up with Flavor Unit Records in 2000, they've put together a lackluster effort in *Armaghetto*. With uninspiring production, flawed delivery, and lyrics consisting mainly of gangster plots and street drama, the group fails to convince. A guest appearance by Method Man on "Ghetto BI" has a triumphant sound to it and is about the only track worth checking out. —*Brad Mills*

Joey Chavez

b. Los Angeles, CA
Producer / Underground Rap, Hip-Hop
One of the West Coast's more renowned underground hip-hop producers, Joey Chavez made a name working with artists such as Defari, Aceyalone, Phil da Agony, and Encore, along with more recognized rappers such as the Beastie Boys, Dilated Peoples, and Kool Keith. He released the instrumental album *Music From the Connection* in 2001, a wonderful summary of his aesthetic. —*Jason Birchmeier*

● **Music From the Connection: An Instrumental Album** / Jul. 24, 2001 / Battle Axe ✦✦✦✦
If you didn't associate the word "funky" with Joey Chavez's production skills before this album, your attitude is likely about to change. Some of the grooviest, deepest, most intricate hip-hop beats are featured here, with Chavez responsible for all of them. What makes this album different from most instrumental albums is that these beats are completely finished with all the right elements in all the right places. From the start of each tune the track kindly introduces you to the beat and then rides with you through a musical journey. These are the kind of beats where you almost don't miss the MC because of the varied elements that keep your attention coming back for more. It wouldn't be a bad idea to get out your headphones for this one. —*Brad Mills*

Chi-Ali (Chi Ali Griffith)

East Coast Rap, Hip-Hop
At 14, Chi-Ali was the youngest member of the Native Tongues coalition. On the strength of a few verses on Black Sheep's first album, he released his solo debut, *The Fabulous Chi-Ali*, on Relativity Records in 1992. "Age Ain't Nothin'

But a #" and "Roadrunner" became Top Ten rap hits that year, but he never released another full-length. —*Christopher Witt*

● **The Fabulous Chi-Ali** / Mar. 24, 1992 / Relativity ◆◆◆
While Chi-Ali isn't completely lacking in talent, his youth certainly shows. The contrast between his still-boyishly high voice and his rhymes about drinking, sexing up girls, and gun toting are sometimes unnerving, but more often it's just absurd. Chi-Ali makes his case on "Age Ain't Nothin' but a #" when he states that he has no time for younger women (13-year-olds); he wants an older woman (a 17-year-old). Unfortunately, Chi-Ali, with his high voice and at times uneven flow, just can't carry an entire album. Tellingly, on the best song on the album, "Let the Horns Blow," Chi-Ali is shunted aside by guest rappers and fellow Native Tonguers, Dres (Black Sheep), Phife (A Tribe Called Quest), and Dove (De La Soul). He's a boy among men. The album's only saving grace is the hot, sample-crazy production from the Beatnuts. The Queens duo make *The Fabulous Chi-Ali* bearable but of little interest except perhaps to Native Tongue completists. —*Christopher Witt*

Chill Rob G. (Robert Frazier)

b. Queens, NY
East Coast Rap
Born Robert Frazier, Chill Rob G is a gruff Queens, NY, MC who was part of Wild Pitch producer the 45 King's Flavor Unit MCs in the early '90s. He released one album, *Ride the Rhythm*, but is best known for an unlikely association with techno-pop group Snap. Snap had an international hit with "The Power," based around samples of Rob G's "Let the Words Flow." A different version was recorded for *Ride the Rhythm*, but the damage to Chill's credibility—a tough New York MC with a dance-pop hit—was already done. Little was heard from the talented rapper until he appeared on two tracks on British producers DSP's 2002 album, *In the Red*. —*Wade Kergan*

● **Ride the Rhythm** / 1990 / Wild Pitch ◆◆
Ride the Rhythm doesn't look like other rap records from the early '90s—in fact it looks sort of like a techno-pop record. The title rides along in a heavily stylized font across the bottom while in the foreground an image of a city-steppin' Chill Rob G presides as cool as his name, which hangs above riddled with bullet holes; meanwhile, in the background an op-art pattern dominates to the right of Chill, while cops and street-prestige symbols of cars and women compete on the left. The dichotomy is puzzling but understandable. Chill Rob G is a tough East Coast rapper, but the song he's best known for is an international pop hit, "The Power," by Snap! Granted Chill was only sampled by the Europop group, but, perhaps in an attempt to grab some of the cash, he covers Snap!'s version of "The Power" on *Ride the Rhythm*. Even though the song would sound perfectly normal on one of Snap!'s albums, here it nearly derails an otherwise solid album. The other songs represent classic early-'90s chopped-funk production, courtesy of Flavor Unit producer the 45 King. The pinnacle of their collaboration is the classic "Let the Words Flow," which manages to maintain its bulldog stance and be danceable at the same time. And that is the attempt of the rest of *Ride the Rhythm* as well, only in the hands of Chill it sounds more like a command than an invitation. —*Wade Kergan*

Chino XL

Vocals / Hip-Hop, Hardcore Rap, Underground Rap
Hailing from East Orange, NJ, Chino released his debut album, *Here to Save You All*, in 1996 and has since had plenty of now famous appearances on DJ Sway and Tech's morning radio show "The Wakeup Show." He's been called the king of metaphors and for good reason, everyone that likes their rhymes laden with punchlines should definitely check him out. —*Brad Mills*

● **Here to Save You All** / Apr. 1996 / American ◆◆◆◆
Years before Eminem began outraging parents and pop stars alike with his brutally funny lyrics, New Jersey's Chino XL was already making the musical world safe for brainy, tasteless battle rappers with his enormously promising but little-remembered debut, 1996's *Here to Save You All*. As might be expected from a rapper who boasts about his SAT scores, Chino is both smart and eccentric, and like Eminem, he uses his razor-sharp wit to lyrically dismember everyone from Will Smith to Magic Johnson to Chubb Rock. Considering the similarities between Detroit's most notorious native son and Chino XL, it's no wonder Eminem basher Evidence of Dilated Peoples has decried the sometimes Slim Shady as a "fake Chino XL." It's not an entirely fair criticism, but it does contain a grain of truth, particularly since, like Eminem, Chino has a tendency to alternate between gleefully mean-spirited black comedy with tortured, self-deprecating introspection. "It's All Bad" is undoubtedly the album's most elaborate, ambitious, and unusual song, beginning like a typical rags-to-riches narrative but taking a detour into a surreal theoretical universe where Chino's a huge, coke-addled megastar whose career and life are both falling apart before his eyes. "Who Am I" smartly and sensitively addresses the complexities, frustrations, and ambiguities of Chino's mixed-race heritage, while "Kreep" borrows the chorus of Radiohead's breakthrough hit in dramatizing the ins and outs of a dysfunctional relationship. The same overbearing force of personality that makes Chino a hero to some will undoubtedly turn off others, but for the most part, *Here to Save You All* is one of the most distinctive and underrated debuts in hip-hop history. —*Nathan Rabin*

Chocolate Bandit

Southern Rap, Dirty South
After a stint as a professional football player, Southern rap artist Chocolate Bandit signed to Death Row Records. His "What's the Deal" single was featured on Death Row's *Gang Related* soundtrack. However, that was the culmination of his Death Row stint since the label entered a dormant period following 2Pac's death. Chocolate Bandit returned in 2001 with *Lyrical Warfare*, an album he recorded for Countryboy Records. The album features production by Reggie Moore. —*Jason Birchmeier*

● **Lyrical Warfare** / Nov. 20, 2001 / Countryboy Records ◆◆
Lyrical Warfare shows that country boys can rap, too—something Chocolate Bandit goes out of his way to let you know. In fact, Chocolate's record label is actually called Countryboy Records, and nearly every song on the album features a rapper from the Countryboy roster. However, there's a difference between rapping and rapping well. And, unfortunately, this album showcases the former but not the latter—Chocolate can drop rhymes but not incredibly well, and it doesn't help that this album's production is horrid. It's not just the beats that prove near inlistenable but rather the vocals, which sound like they've been treated with effects for the worse. Nonetheless, even if *Lyrical Warfare* sounds budget, those who enjoy hearing the country represented should find something here of worth. It's perhaps most interesting to hear the smooth R&B vocals that occasionally appear in an attempt to instill more "soul" into the album. —*Jason Birchmeier*

Chubb Rock (Richard Simpson)

b. May 28, 1968, Jamaica
Urban, Hip-Hop
Weighing in at 250 pounds, Chubb Rock (born Richard Simpson) often evokes images of a hip-hop Barry White (whom he dueted with on *And the Winner Is…*). Chubb Rock had a group while he was a teenager in New York but started his career in earnest after he dropped out of college. After three singles from his first album went nowhere, his second album, *And the Winner Is…*, was released to greater commercial and critical acclaim, thanks to a remixed single version of "Caught Up" that was released prior to the album. After 1991's *The One* and 1992's *I Gotta Get Mine Yo*, Chubb Rock's career again faltered, and five years passed prior to the release of *The Mind*. —*Stephen Thomas Erlewine*

Chubb Rock Featuring Hitman Howie Tee / 1988 / Select ◆◆◆
Chubb Rock's entertaining debut featured tracks by Hitman Howie Tee over interesting raps, witty quips, and good samples from disco and funk works. Though it didn't generate any hits, "Daddy's Home" and "Momma Was a Rolling Stone" were definitely worthy of the charts. —*Ron Wynn*

● **And the Winner Is . . .** / 1989 / Select ◆◆◆◆◆
His follow-up, *And the Winner Is…*, was much more clever and entertaining than his debut, with a couple of hits ("Ya Bad Chubbs," "Stop That Train," the title track) to boot. Chubb Rock featured sharp humor with first-rate samples and production, plus insightful commentary on ghetto violence and the ignorance of the NARAS (National Academy of Recording Arts and Sciences). —*Ron Wynn*

The One / 1991 / Select ◆◆◆
If you'd asked leading hip-hop experts what the main difference between East Coast and West Coast rappers was in the early 1990s, he would have explained that the West was more interested in beats and grooves, while the

Northeast was concerned with rapping technique. Well respected in New York rap circles, Chubb Rock had plenty of technique—something there's no shortage of on *The One*. The album leaves no doubt that his rapping skills were first-rate, but technique only carries Rock so far. Although decent and at times exhilarating, *The One* isn't a great album. Rock (who often incorporates dancehall reggae) is at his best on excellent message songs like "What's the Word" and "The Night Scene," an arresting description of the horrors that surround drugs. But his boasting raps wear thin after a while. Rock has the chops; it's his lyrics that aren't always memorable. —*Alex Henderson*

I Gotta Get Mine Yo / 1992 / Select ✦✦
Chubb Rock's fourth effort, released in 1992, features thoughtful racial meditations such as "The Hatred," and sappy ballads like "I Don't Want to Be Lonely," and spare, stripped-down rhythms including "Black Trek IV—The Voyage Home." —*Jason Ankeny*

The Mind / May 27, 1997 / Select ✦✦✦
Chubb Rock's comeback effort *The Mind* finds the heavyweight rapper returning hard, balancing his cartoonish gangsta rap with fun, funky party tunes. The problem is, *The Mind* sounds like it would have been a great record in 1990, not 1997. Chubb is in fine form, but the music is often predictable and occasionally dated. At its best, Chubb overcomes such limitations by concentrating on hot beats and crisp, clear production, but it's clear from the record that Chubb hasn't quite assimilated all the innovations of the '90s. —*Leo Stanley*

Chunky A (Arsenio Hall)

Pop-Rap, Song Parody, Comedy Rap
Once upon a time in the early '90s, Arsenio Hall was an important supporter of rap. He had a hit talk show that featured live performances from some of hip-hop's finest, including De La Soul, Leaders of the New School, and, of course, MC Hammer. All of which was inspiration for Chunky A, Hall's portly rapping alterego. Chunky A released one album, *Large & In Charge*, in 1991. Met with the painful silence that every comedian fears, Chunky A quickly faded, followed shortly thereafter by the career of Arsenio Hall. —*Wade Kergan*

Large & In Charge / 1991 / MCA ✦
When he was riding high, talk-show host/comedian Arsenio Hall got a vanity deal from MCA for a CD featuring his "alternate" personality, rapper Chunky A. This was his foray into hip-hop/novelty humor; it wasn't very funny except for the cut "Owww!," which scraped the pop charts' lower end, and "Dope, The Big Lie," a good anti-drug track. Even "Stank Breath" wasn't nearly as outrageous as it would have been if done by Biz Markie. —*Ron Wynn*

Cilvaringz (Tarik Azzougarh)

b. Tilburg, Holland
Hip-Hop
Cilvaringz is a Wu family member from Tilburg, Holland. He is the very first international Wu-Tang member, gaining entrance after several unsuccessful trips to New York attempting to speak with RZA, the head of the Wu-Tang Clan. He eventually succeeded by meeting RZA's sister and convinced her to set up a meeting. After hearing his work, RZA decided to sign Cilvaringz to Wu-Tang Records. Cilvaringz has also released an instrumental album entitled *The Mental Chamberz*. —*Brad Mills*

● **The Mental Chamberz** / Jun. 1, 2001 / Wu-Tang ✦✦✦
As a completely instrumental album, this isn't the sort of thing you'd be expecting for the first release of a new Wu-Tang Clansman, but it sets the stage for what may be a devilishly good first album. The beats on this release have that simple complexity that Wu-Tang beats are known for, with a simple repetitive head-nodding beat, plus a complex melodic background behind the bass. Lyric lovers may find themselves a touch bored listening to an instrumental album, but the fact that it was created with those intentions has given the producers many advantages, allowing them to expand the melodies properly. In summation, this is a collection of Wu breakbeats at their finest, melded into a journey of abstractness with a hip-hop beat, and definitely worth a listen. —*Brad Mills*

Don Cisco

Producer / Latin Rap, West Coast Rap, Underground Rap, Hardcore Rap
San Franciscan Latino hip-hop artist Don Cisco has been a part of the city's scene since the mid-'90s, working as a songwriter, producer, and a member of Latino Velvet. His solo debut *Oh Boy* arrived in 2000 and featured guest appearances from Kurupt and B-Legit. —*Heather Phares*

● **Oh Boy** / Aug. 29, 2000 / Thump Street ✦✦✦
Showcasing plenty of welcomed brown pride, California Bay Area rapper Don Cisco proves himself to be truly talented on his debut, *Oh Boy*. Balancing a smooth flow with charismatic lyrics, the Latin rapper moves through a stunning number of tracks without exhausting thematic material. In fact, he seems never short of lyrics, and his heavy use of interludes brings a cinematic element of theatrics to the album which furthers his sense of character. In sum, for underground rap circa 2000, this album features an artist capable of going head to head with most major label MCs, along with slick, funk-influenced production. Furthermore, the straight-up Latin moments, such as the chorus to "Mamacita"—featuring the superstar lineup of Cisco, Frost, Soopafly, and Kurupt—bring a new aesthetic to hip-hop. —*Jason Birchmeier*

West Coast Locos / Jan. 15, 2002 / Thump Street ✦✦✦
West Coast Locos compiles songs produced primarily by Don Cisco that feature the West Coast Chicano rapper and many of his affiliates. The album includes a remix of his breakthrough hit, "Oh Boy," which had appeared on his previous release of the same name for Thump Street Records. Unfortunately, due to the numerous guest appearances, *West Coast Locos* often seems as if it's a compilation album. Though this practice had somewhat become the norm in rap music circa 2001, the myriad guests take away from the album since they aren't as impressive as Cisco himself. —*Jason Birchmeier*

The Click

f. Vallejo, CA
Group / West Coast Rap, Gangsta Rap, Hardcore Rap
A Bay Area family affair, The Click is a four-member hip-hop posse from Vallejo, CA, headed up by rapper E-40 (Earl Stevens) and including his brother D-Shot, sister Suga T, and cousin B-Legit, who grew up in the same household. Though he first achieved solo success, E-40 actually began his career with the group, which was formed in 1986 as the Most Valuable Players and performed at a Grambling State University talent show. The response encouraged the group to rename itself and get down to business, and they released a single called "The King's Men." Meanwhile, E-40—earning his nickname of Charlie Hustle—followed the path of many other successful entrepreneurs, selling tapes from the trunk of his car in the late '80s. (He did so, however, while also managing a family run clothing store and working a day job at an oil refinery.) E-40 started his own label, Sick Wid' It Records, that put out a couple of Click cassettes and the group's official debut, *Down & Dirty*. In 1993, the perseverance paid off as E-40 landed a guest spot on Spice 1's *187 He Wrote* and got the attention of Jive Records, which signed a distribution deal with Sick Wid' It. After the 1994 success of *The Mail Man*, E-40's first album for the label, Jive released Click's major-label debut, *Game Related*, the following year. But thanks to E-40's solo career, plus the solo outings of Click's three other members, it was six years before a follow-up saw the light of day. *Money & Muscle*, which was finally released in 2001, saw the group once again serving up heavy-bottomed, West Coast G-funk with occasionally lighthearted lyrics, such as "Hector da Ho Protector," a direct descendant of E-40's 1994 hit "Captain Save a Ho." —*Dan LeRoy*

● **Game Related** / Nov. 7, 1995 / Jive ✦✦✦
In addition to being solo stars in their own right, the members of The Click are all family; the group is comprised of Suga T, brothers E-40 and D-Shot, and cousin B-Legit. The Click's *Game Related* isn't markedly different than any of the group's solo work, nor does the team effort result in a stronger, more consistent record than their solo albums. Instead, The Click's record is a competent collection of hard-edged Californian hip-hop that has the occasional highlight, but more often than not it's simply average. —*Stephen Thomas Erlewine*

Money & Muscle / Sep. 25, 2001 / Jive ✦✦✦

Clipse

f. 1992, Virginia
Group / Hip-Hop, Alternative Rap
Hailing from Virginia, the duo known as Clipse were actually one of the rare first artists to work with the Neptunes. Meeting Pharrell Williams in the early '90s, he was very impressed by their talents and decided to help them get a gig. Hooking them up with East/West Records, an early single flopped and

the group seemed done with. Williams was not discouraged, and continued to hype the group until Star Trak/Arista picked up the group in 2001. The Neptunes stepped behind the boards and the end result was *Lord Willin'*, their 2002 full-length debut. —*Bradley Torreano*

● **Lord Willin'** / Aug. 20, 2002 / Arista ✦✦✦
Rap and drugs—the somewhat unholy marriage is now decades deep. Not surprisingly, the conjunction has produced some dynamic musical results that have been readily smoked, ingested, and snorted by the mainstream music listening public. Back in the late '80s, Ice-T was one of the first rappers to blur the lines between the rap world and the underworld. On his single "I'm Your Pusher," which tastefully sampled Curtis Mayfield's "Pusherman," Ice-T compared his whole album (*Power*, 1988) to drug weight, proposing that his music would be something rap fans would fiend for the same way a smoker fiends for nicotine. In the early part of the 21st century, after the Virginia-based production team the Neptunes' had splashed their electro-synth beats everywhere, from songs with hardcore rapper N.O.R.E. to pop sensation Britney Spears. Pharrell Williams and partner Chad Hugo created their own label, Star Trak Entertainment. The first act signed to the Star Trak label was a pair of Neptunes cohorts known as the Clipse, a sibling duo of highly skilled VA transplants (by way of the Bronx) with some obvious nefarious connections to the world of drug hustling. Pusha T and Malice rocked the rap world in the summer of 2002 with their first single, "Grindin'," a dark and gritty tale of the street pharmacist's everyday strive to make ends meet. Over a thunderous throwback knock from the Neptunes, "Grindin'" was one of the summer of 2002's most prolific anthems and transported Clipse to the realm of overnight rap success. *Lord Willin'* is an oft-scary trip down the backstreets of Tobacco Road as Malice and Pusha T recount the trials and tribulations of the drug trafficker turned MC. Following in the footsteps of such rap criminologists as Kool G Rap, Nas, Jay-Z, and Mobb Deep, the Clipse offer the Virginia hustler's viewpoint with clever, hard-hitting lyrics like: "…I'm from Virginia where ain't s***t to do but cook/pack it up, sell it triple price/f***k the books…" and "Virginia's for lovers but trust there's hate here.…" While the two MCs' presence is invariably formidable on virtually all of the tracks, the Neptunes' pop-ish turn in their beatwork doesn't always do justice to the depths that Clipse MCs wish to plunder. The Neptunes' synth-gloss production style, while generally soulful and rarely without edge, misses the mark in case of the crossoverish "Ma, I Don't Love Her" featuring Faith Evans, as the MCs seem thoroughly out of their element. The album also has a slapped-together, noncohesive feel that detracts from its more enjoyable aspects. On the flip side, the follow-up club banger "When the Last Time" is a catchier alternative to the crew's lead single and tracks like "Comedy Central" featuring Fabolous and "I'm Not You" featuring Jadakiss and Styles of the L.O.X. are also a cut above run of the mill. —*M.F. DiBella*

Clouddead

Group / Underground Rap, Alternative Rap, Experimental, Ambient
The mysterious Clouddead combines such underground hip-hop artists as Doseone, Why?, and Odd Nosdam together for the first time. Their music is unlike anything you'd expect from a group of rap connoisseurs—it's both experimental and ambient, not unlike Brian Eno's 1978 classic, *Music for Airports*, with chanted vocals that recall Tibetan monks. Instead of writing traditional songs, the band opted for their 2001 self-titled release to be released as a series of 10" singles, comprised of six separate movements. Each release focused on a different musical theme, and included a different guest artist for each segment—Illogic, DJ Signify, Sole, the Wolf Bros, Mr. Dibbs, and the Bay Area Animals. Each of the six singles are meant to be played back to back, to create one single full-length work. —*Greg Prato*

● **Clouddead** / Apr. 24, 2001 / Mush ✦✦✦✦
Culled from a series of limited 10" releases, Clouddead's eponymous debut isn't so much a fully formed album as it is a well-executed exercise in seasick, proggist psychedelia. With background textures that rival Boards of Canada in pastoral, tree-lined opacity and an obvious predilection for boggy atmospherics, Clouddead handily distances themselves from the rest of their hip-hop brethren. Indeed, this is something more considered and sinister—less about wayward braggadocio than it is about keeping your doors deadbolted at all hours of the night. Even their less-is-more approach to vocalism eventually starts playing tricks on your mind; when lyricists Dose and Why? emerge, it's usually to puncture the pleasant fog of some dulcet, wavering

sample. The whole album reads like that; the sonic equivalent of your first legitimate drug trip as narrated by two jittery but triumphant kids who can't bear to keep their choice hiding place a secret any longer. While it's perhaps a tad overlong, *Clouddead* doesn't suffer from any shortage of great ideas. It's menacing, it's enthralling, and it's one of few modern-day records (hip-hop or otherwise) that honestly doesn't sound like anything—or anyone—else. —*Mark Pytlik*

Cocoa Brovaz

f. 1997, Brooklyn, NY
Group / Hip-Hop, East Coast Rap
The hardcore rap duo Cocoa Brovaz paired Tek and Steele, who together emerged from Brooklyn in 1993 under the name Smif-n-Wessun. Debuting two years later with *Dah Shinin'*, they immediately ran into interference from Smith & Wesson firearms, resulting in a three-year legal battle that ended with the adoption of the name Cocoa Brovaz; under that moniker, they issued *The Rude Awakening* in 1998. —*Jason Ankeny*

● **The Rude Awakening** / Mar. 31, 1998 / Priority ✦✦✦
Once the Smith & Wesson gun company realized there was a pair of rappers performing under the name Smif-n-Wessun, the duo had to change their name. They chose Cocoa Brovaz and released their second album, *The Rude Awakening* (possibly a reference to their legal troubles), under that moniker in the spring of 1998. All things considered, the legal mishap was little more than a speed bump for the duo; the end result is every bit as good as their first effort, if not better. The pair of hardcore gangstas are still hurt by their reliance on clichés—when it comes right down to it, they aren't offering any new insights, they're simply respinning the standard dope-money-guns-'n'-hoes line—but they're saved by their energy and hard-hitting delivery. Usually, that makes the standard-issue music fairly compelling; there are moments that drag on *Rude Awakening*, but not as many as on Smif-n-Wessun's *Dah Shinin'.* In other words, it's an improvement and a step forward in Cocoa Brovaz developing their own identity. —*Leo Stanley*

Cold Crush Brothers

f. 1978, Bronx, NY, **db.** 1986
Group / Hip-Hop, Old School Rap
The Cold Crush Brothers were one of the first rap crews to emerge from the Bronx soon after hip-hop's birth in the mid-'70s. Along with Grandmaster Flash & the Furious Five, Grand Wizard Theodore & the Fantastic 5 MCs, and the Funky Four Plus One, these four NYC natives were already well established long before the Sugarhill Gang made rap a household word with their multiplatinum-selling 12" "Rapper's Delight." In fact, as legend has it, it was a Cold Crush Brothers tape that a pizza-shop worker (and soon-to-be Sugarhill Gang member Big Hank) was rapping to when Sugar Hill Records owner Sylvia Robinson heard him in 1979. Instead of telling Robinson who the real artists on the tape were, he gathered some friends who soon became part of the much more successful and well-known Sugarhill Gang.

Founding members Grandmaster Caz, the Almighty KG, Tony Tone, JDL, Easy AD, and DJ Charlie Chase were showmen as well as a skilled tag team of rappers. They practiced and perfected their routines for over a year beginning in 1978 and began performing live, especially at numerous "MC battles" that took place at that time. One of these battles was caught on tape in 1981 and released in 1991 on a CD titled *Afrika Bambaataa Presents Hip-Hop Funk Dance Classics, Vol. 1.* It, along with the Cold Crush Brothers' *Live in 82* album, epitomized hip-hop before it became the commercial monster it was in the 1990s. The simple party-flavored rhymes hark back to a more innocent time when MC stood for Master of Ceremonies, DJs actually did something other than scratch over a DAT tape, and the only references to killing were metaphors. In 1982 they appeared in the legendary hip-hop film *Wild Style* as well as put out the excellent 12" "The Weekend." The Cold Crush Brothers never released a proper full-length album but did release a number of influential singles on the Tuff City label, including "Fresh, Wild, Fly and Bold." Most of these singles are collected on 1996's *Fresh, Wild, Fly & Bold.* They broke up in 1986, but reappeared on Terminator X's second solo album, *Super Bad.* —*Kembrew McLeod*

Live in 82 / 1994 / Tuff City ✦✦✦✦
This live album is low quality by most sonic standards, but it is one of the only ways one can hear hip-hop as it was originally performed before DAT

machines rendered the DJ a mere ornament who occasionally "scratched" over prerecorded tapes during live performances. Further, it captures a moment in time when hip-hop was party music, before Grandmaster Flash's "The Message" opened up the possibilities for more reality-based raps. One can feel the energy in the interaction between the MCs and the audience who chanted to the looped beat created by the DJ spinning two of the same records, alternately returning each record to the beginning of the breakbeat in a seamless fashion. —*Kembrew McLeod*

Fresh, Wild, Fly & Bold / 1996 / Tuff City ✦✦✦✦✦

This collects the Cold Crush Brothers' major 12" singles, and serves as sort of a greatest hits that never were. Sure, these songs are now considered classics, but none of them ever garnered the commercial success of other rap artists such as Kurtis Blow. The songs "Fresh, Wild, Fly and Bold," "Weekend," "Punk Rock Rap," and the brilliantly titled (and previously unreleased) "We Reserve the Right to Rock" serve as the core of this essential collection. —*Kembrew McLeod*

● **Cold Crush Brothers vs. Fantastic Romantic 5** / Jul. 28, 1998 / Slammin ✦✦✦✦✦

The second (official) live Cold Crush tape to surface, this one earns classic status, not because it's the best that's ever been heard, but because it's the best-sounding—and the only one coming straight from one of the sources: DJ Charlie Chase. He offered it as a way to beat the bootleggers (and finally earn some proceeds himself), also explaining in the intro, "I cleaned up the vocals and recut the beats." As dangerous as the word "recut" sounds, this battle tap really *is* a classic (and if parts were redone, they certainly don't reveal any artificial sources). Chase gives plenty of time to the Cold Crush (it's possible he didn't even have the Fantastic Five section on tape), who take up nearly all of the 45-minute disc. Though a few tracks are crammed front to back with line after line of dizzying, single-cadence old school rapping, it's clear that the Cold Crush were masters of keeping the beat going at their frequent club dates. —*John Bush*

Coldcut

f. 1986, London, England

Group / House, Acid House, Club/Dance, Trip-Hop, Electronica, Mixed Media, Hip-Hop

DJs Jonathan More and Matt Black, aka Coldcut, rose to acclaim in the mid-'80s through production and remix work for a number of modern rock, hip-hop, and dance outfits, including Yaz, Lisa Stansfield, Junior Reid, Blondie, Eric B. & Rakim, and Queen Latifah. While that connection has pegged them as a product of the U.K. acid house and rave scenes, the pair's larger commitment has been to urban breakbeat styles such as hip-hop, ambient dub, and jungle; the three of which have constituted the bulk of their recorded output since their first mid-'80s white-label EP, *Hey Kids, What Time Is It?* Comprising project titles like Hedfunk, Hex, DJ Food, and Coldcut, More and Black have assembled an empire of U.K. breakbeat and experimental hip-hop through their Ninja Tune/Ntone labels and been a unifying force in underground experimental electronic music through their eclectic radio show, Solid Steel, and club and tour dates.

More and Black got their start, not surprisingly, as radio DJs, working at the pirate station Network 21 during the first half of the '80s, and latching onto the snowballing club scene mid to late decade. Their claim to early fame, *Hey Kids, What Time Is It?*, was modeled on the cut'n'scratch turntable aesthetic of underground deck heroes like Grandmaster Flash and Double D & Steinski. Widely regarded as the U.K.'s first breaks record and an influential force in bringing identity to London's nascent club culture, the record—released as a U.S. import billed to DJ Coldcut to avoid sample litigation—opened as many doors for More and Black as it did for DJs, bringing scads of production and remix work their way. The attention (and sales royalties) also allowed them to launch their Ninja Tune and Ntone labels, which together have been home to some of the most acclaimed and influential artists of London's post-rave underground scene, including DJ Food, Drome, Journeyman, 9 Lazy 9, Up, Bustle & Out, and the Herbaliser.

Although Coldcut was their earliest nom de plume, following a befuddled contract with Arista, the name remained in legal channels for the following few years. The intervening period found the pair no less active, releasing a flood of material under different names and continuing to work with young groups. The year 1996 brought the Coldcut name back to More and Black,

and the pair celebrated with a mix CD as part of the *Journeys By DJ* series dubbed *70 Minutes of Madness*. The release was credited with bringing to wider attention the sort of freestyle mixing the pair were always known for through their radio show on KISS FM, Solid Steel, and their steady club dates, a style that has since taken off through clubs like Blech and the Heavenly Sunday Social. In 1997, Coldcut finally released another full-length, *Let Us Play!* Two years later, the pair followed up with the remix album *Let Us Replay!*—*Sean Cooper*

Hey Kids, What Time is It? EP / 1987 / White Label ✦✦✦

With only 500 pressed, Coldcut's "bootie" debut has been known to fetch upwards of a c-note in U.K. shops. It features Pretty standard James Brown and Jimmy Smith meet the Bomb Squad on frappé, with scratches and left-field references compiled with tight, dizzying precision. —*Sean Cooper*

What's That Noise? / Sep. 1989 / Tommy Boy ✦✦✦

English DJs Matt Black and Jonathan More came up in the mid-'80s by way of a good deal of remix work for the likes of Yaz, Eric B. and Rakim, Blondie, and Queen Latifah. They struck out on their own with the monumental *Hey Kids, What Time Is It?* EP, which showcased their heady blend of hip-hop production aesthetics and proto-acid house grooves. This 1989 long player finds the duo ranging far and wide with their smart, yet fluid mix and features such heavyweight guests as Latifah, reggae singer Junior Reid of Black Uhuru fame, the Fall's Mark E. Smith, and singer Lisa Stansfield. A fine starting point for the curious. —*Stephen Cook*

● **Journeys By DJ: 70 Minutes of Madness** / 1996 / Music Unites/Sony ✦✦✦✦✦

Although this mixed CD is a compilation of material by numerous different artists (from Harold Budd to Dillinja, Joanna Law to the Jedi Knights), only some of which is the pair's own, it's an ample illustration of the sort of freestyle approach to composition the pair helped popularize. The group jump from style to style at will, drawing out the connections between hip-hop, jungle, techno, electro, ambient, and beyond, with first-rate mixing and turntable work. —*Sean Cooper*

Coldcut & DJ Food Fight / Jan. 1997 / Ninja Tune ✦✦✦

The second mix album released by the preeminent DJing team in trip-hop, *Coldcut & DJ Food Fight* is limited by the inclusion of only Ninja Tune artists (including Luke Vibert, Funki Porcini, Up Bustle & Out, DJ Vadim, the Herbaliser and Drome, plus Coldcut and DJ Food themselves). As such, it suffers from a lack of variety, with only several breakbeat tracks to leaven the decidedly trip-hoppish affair. Though Coldcut's mixing and scratching skills are stellar, and the various samples provide sustained interest, the album just doesn't measure up to 1995's classic *Journeys By DJ*. While the previous album moved from Boogie Down Productions to Jhelisa Anderson and Mantronix to Photek with grace, the inherent limitations of a Ninja Tunes-only mix LP sinks the whole affair before it begins. (*Coldcut & DJ Food Fight* was released as half of a double-disc compilation called *Cold Krush Cuts*, which also includes DJ Krush's *Back in the Base* mix LP.) —*John Bush*

Let Us Play! / Sep. 8, 1997 / Ninja Tune ✦✦✦✦

Decade-long veterans of the electronica scene, label heads of the respected Ninja Tune records, owners of their own mix show on Radio 1, and Coldcut still haven't learned to make a good long player. While Jonathan More and Matt Black were responsible for one of the highlights of electronic music history with their 1996 *Journeys By DJ* compilation, *Let Us Play!* shows the duo weighed down by a long cast of collaborators (much as their last proper album, 1989's *What's That Noise?*). While the presence of funk drummer Bernard "Pretty" Purdie, old school rap impresario Steinski, post-punk and spoken-word firebrand Jello Biafra, tabla specialist Talvin Singh (plus sympathizers like the Herbaliser and Jimpster on production) does provide several highlights—and also testifies to Coldcut's philosophy of throwing hip-hop, electronica, funk, and a little bit of a whole lot more into the ring and enjoying the free-for-all—the album moves much slower than Coldcut's mix material (which usually averages two minutes per track, as opposed to six or seven on *Let Us Play!*). Besides the syrupy feel of the LP, the abundance of message tracks ("Noah's Toilet," Biafra's "Every Home a Prison," "Cloned Again") subvert the message of the title, indicative of Coldcut's playful qualities over the years. The lone highlight is the single "More Beats + Pieces," a remake of the 1988 original, which was constructed from samples in homage to pioneering hip-hop DJs who manned two turntables with little opportunity to fall back on samplers and expensive keyboards. —*John Bush*

Let Us Replay! / Jan. 26, 1999 / Ninja Tune ◆◆◆
Let Us Replay! is a double-disc remix album that also includes a few live tracks from Coldcut's innovative world tour. The reworkings benefit from the recruitment of a variety of wide-ranging but very sympathetic figures including Cornelius, Grandmaster Flash, Shut Up and Dance, Carl Craig and Mixmaster Morris. The live tracks are a bit less entertaining and are quite similar to their album versions. —*John Bush*

Common (Lonnie Rashied Lynn)

b. Chicago, IL
Political Rap, Hip-Hop, Jazz-Rap, Alternative Rap
Common (originally Common Sense) was a highly influential figure in rap's underground during the '90s, keeping the sophisticated lyrical technique and flowing syncopations of jazz-rap alive in an era when commercial gangsta rap was threatening to obliterate everything in its path. His literate, intelligent, nimbly performed rhymes and political consciousness certainly didn't fit the fashions of the moment, but he was able to win a devoted cult audience. By the late '90s, a substantial underground movement had set about reviving the bohemian sensibility of alternative rap, and Common finally started to receive wider recognition as a creative force. Not only were his albums praised by critics, but he was able to sign with a major label that guaranteed him more exposure than ever before.

Common was born Lonnie Rashied Lynn on the South Side of Chicago, an area not exactly noted for its fertile hip-hop scene. Nonetheless, he honed his skills to the point where—performing as Common Sense—he was able to catch his first break winning *The Source* magazine's Unsigned Hype contest. He debuted in 1992 with the single "Take It EZ," which appeared on his Combat-released debut album *Can I Borrow a Dollar?* Further singles "Breaker 1/9" and "Soul by the Pound" helped establish his reputation in the hip-hop underground, although some critics complained about the record's occasional misogynistic undertones. Common Sense subsequently wound up on Ruthless Records for his 1994 follow-up *Resurrection*, which crystallized his reputation as one of the underground's best (and wordiest) lyricists. The track "I Used to Love H.E.R." attracted substantial notice for its clever allegory about rap's descent into commercially exploitative sex-and-violence subject matter, and even provoked a short-lived feud with Ice Cube. Subsequently, Common Sense was sued by a ska band of the same name, and was forced to shorten his own moniker to Common; he also relocated from Chicago to Brooklyn.

Bumped up to parent label Relativity, Common issued the first album under his new name in 1997. *One Day It'll All Make Sense* capitalized on the fledgling resurgence of intelligent hip-hop with several prominent guests, including Lauryn Hill, Q-Tip, De La Soul, Erykah Badu, Cee-Lo, and the Roots' Black Thought. The album was well received in the press, and Common raised his profile with several notable guest spots over the next couple of years; he appeared on Pete Rock's *Soul Survivor*, plus two watermark albums of the new progressive hip-hop movement, Mos Def and Talib Kweli's *Black Star* and the Roots' *Things Fall Apart*. Common also hooked up with indie-rap kingpins Rawkus for a one-off collaboration with Sadat X, "1-9-9-9," which appeared on the label's seminal *Soundbombing, Vol. 2* compilation.

With his name popping up in all the right places, Common landed a major-label deal with MCA, and brought on Roots drummer ?uestlove as producer for his next project. *Like Water for Chocolate* was released in early 2000 and turned into something of a breakthrough success, attracting more attention than any Common album to date (partly because of MCA's greater promotional resources). Guests this time around included Macy Gray, MC Lyte, Cee-Lo, Mos Def, D'Angelo, jazz trumpeter Roy Hargrove, and Afro-beat star Femi Kuti (on a tribute to his legendary father Fela). Plus, the singles "The 6th Sense" and "The Light" (the latter of which earned a Grammy nomination for Best Rap Solo Performance) earned considerable airplay. Following that success, Common set the stage for his next record with an appearance on Mary J. Blige's *No More Drama* in early 2002. He issued his most personal work to date with *Electric Circus* in December 2002. —*Steve Huey*

Can I Borrow a Dollar? / 1992 / Relativity ◆◆◆
A former *Source* magazine "Unsigned Hype" winner, Common Sense almost singlehandedly put Chicago hip-hop on the map in the early '90s with this excellent debut, which displayed a truly unique sound that, nevertheless,

situated the rapper somewhere between the ground staked out by A Tribe Called Quest and Gang Starr. *Can I Borrow a Dollar?* features the fabulous, oddly muted production of 2 pc. Drk Productions (Immenslope and Twilite Tone). They opt for a spare, minimalist production that prominently features understated keyboard loops over simple drum tracks, occasionally augmented by saxophone or flute for an overall jazzy, laid-back feel. The production perfectly complements Common Sense's hiccuping/singsongy vocal style and involved rhymes. His lyrics are packed with allusions and references to pop and street culture nearly as eclectic as those of the Beastie Boys. Though sometimes lighthearted to the point of aimlessness and occasionally veering into harder-hitting (vaguely misogynistic) sentiments, *Can I Borrow a Dollar?* acted, for the most part, as an antidote to the exaggeratedly hard-core rhymes of a lot of early '90s hip-hop. Standout tracks such as "Charms Alarm," "Take It EZ," and the only outside production, the Beatnuts' characteristically bell-driven "Heidi Hoe," are calls to arms to all hangers-on and fakers in the hip-hop community. This is one of the most underrated hip-hop debuts in the '90s. —*Stanton Swihart*

Resurrection / Oct. 25, 1994 / Ruthless ◆◆◆◆
Although Chicago is often praised for its blues, jazz, and house music, the city has failed to be successful when it comes to rap. One of the few Chicago MCs who has enjoyed any type of national attention is Common Sense, whose complex style of rapping and jazz-flavored tracks inspires comparisons to De La Soul, Digable Planets, A Tribe Called Quest, and the Pharcyde. On his sophomore effort, *Resurrection*, the South Sider doesn't hesitate to let us know that he has considerable technique, and in fact, he sometimes displays too much of it for his own good. Nonetheless, his intelligence, wit, and originality make this CD impressive. *Resurrection's* standout track is "I Used to Love H.E.R.," which seems to describe a lover's moral and spiritual decline, but is actually addressing what Common views as hip-hop's decline (in particular, gangsta rap's exploitation of sex and violence). Also quite noteworthy are "Nuthin' to Do" (which speaks out on the deterioration of Chicago's neighborhoods) and the introspective "Book of Life," a commentary on trying to keep it together in a society that has lost all traces of sanity. —*Alex Henderson*

One Day It'll All Make Sense / Sep. 30, 1997 / Relativity ◆◆◆◆
With his previous records (released under the name Common Sense), Common demonstrated that he was one of the few Midwestern rappers to have a unique vision, but *One Day It'll All Make Sense* is where his talents come into focus. Blending hip-hop with jazz is a '90s cliché, but Common relies on bebop rhythms and street poetry, resulting in an album that has a loose, organic flow. The grooves have deep roots and the rhymes have humor, heart, and intelligence—few of contemporaries could achieve the emotional impact of "Retrospect for Life" or the gospel-tinged "G.O.D. (Gaining One's Definition)." And that extra layer of emotional involvment give *One Day It'll All Make Sense* a weight and spituality that makes the record special. Certianly few of his peers have made an album as musically and lyrically rich as this, and it's about time others follow his lead. —*Leo Stanley*

● **Like Water for Chocolate** / Mar. 28, 2000 / MCA ◆◆◆◆◆
Common spent the '90s carrying the Native Tongues torch through an era dominated by gangsta rap, earning a sizable underground following. Positive-minded alternative rap came back into vogue by the new millennium, and Common managed to land with major label MCA for 2000's *Like Water for Chocolate*. The album established him as a leading figure of alternative rap's second generation, not just because of the best promotion he'd ever had, but also because it was his great musical leap forward, building on the strides of *One Day It'll All Make Sense*. There's production work by the Roots' ?uestlove, neo-soul auteur D'Angelo, the Soulquarians, and DJ Premier. But the vast majority of the album was handled by Slum Village's Jay Dee, and his thick, mellow, soul- and jazz-inflected sonics make *Like Water for Chocolate* one of the richest-sounding albums of the new underground movement. Common isn't always a master technician on the mic, but it hardly matters when the music serves his deeply spiritual vision and smooth-flowing raps so effectively. The singles "The Light" and "The 6th Sense" are quintessential Common, uplifting and thoughtful, and helped bring him a whole new audience. They're well complemented by the slinky, jazzy funk and lush neo-soul ballads that make up the record. Not everything is sweetness and utopia, either; Common sends up his own progressive image on "A Film Called (Pimp)," which features a hilarious guest appearance by MC Lyte, and spins a gripping first-person tale of revenge on the streets on "Payback Is a Grandmother"

(though the tougher "Dooinit" feels a bit forced). The album could have been trimmed a bit to keep its momentum going, but on the whole, *Like Water for Chocolate* is a major statement from an artist whose true importance was just coming into focus. *—Steve Huey*

Electric Circus / Dec. 10, 2002 / MCA ✦✦✦✦

Firmly out of the underground by the time *Electric Circus* came out in late 2002, Common takes the vision to the next level, employing high-profile producers ?uestlove, Dilla (Jay Dee), and the Neptunes. It's no surprise that the ?uestlove tracks push the most unclaimed territory. The Roots' *Phrenology* record, which appeared concurrent with *Electric Circus*, also flips the script on preconceived notions of beats and rhymes. Frequently the new sound on both records is pushed into a strange, sometimes aggressive, blunted rock/soul hybrid that still pulls the line for able-bodied MCs. Then there's also the Neptunes' tracks here, which are perfectly suited for MTV and urban radio. The Mary J. Blige duet, "Come Close," is a slow-paced dialogue between Common and Blige that borders on typical, but will still find a great number of fans. "Electric Wire Hustler Flower" is the true centerpiece of the record, though—another ?uestlove jam, the song is tough but sensitive enough to maintain the layers of rhythm, rhyme, and abstraction. *Electric Circus* does suffer from that which ails many contemporary hip-hop albums—too many guests (including a strange appearance by Laetitia Sadier [Stereolab]) and a generally lengthy program drag this one down a tad. Nonetheless, *Electric Circus* is a brave and ruthless statement wrapped in sincerity. *—Jack LV Isles*

Company Flow

f. 1992, Queens, NY, **db.** 2000
Group / Underground Rap, Hip-Hop

One of the most influential rap groups of the late '90s, Company Flow laid the groundwork for nearly all the experimental hip-hop that followed. They were an instrumental force in revitalizing underground hip-hop as a whole, and in making Rawkus Records the new movement's most prominent indie label. Company Flow's sound—dense, abstract lyrics underpinned by irregular beats and spacy, basement-level production—was like nothing else in hip-hop at the time, and their uncompromising attitude and willingness to push the envelope became hallmarks of the independent hip-hop scene. Although they managed only one proper album, the classic *Funcrusher Plus*, the full extent of their legacy is just beginning to be felt.

Company Flow was founded in 1992 in Queens by MC/producer El-Producto (El-P for short; born Jaime Meline), along with Bigg Jus and DJ Mr. Len. Highly intelligent but kicked out of several schools for problems with authority, El-P had previously signed a restrictive solo deal that kept him from recording for years; he even served an internship with an entertainment lawyer in hopes of resolving his difficulties. After getting his GED at age 16, he studied sound engineering, and formed Company Flow after meeting DJ Mr. Len at his 18th birthday party. The two put out a single, "Juvenile Techniques," on the small Libra label in 1993, and Libra employee Bigg Jus soon befriended the group and became its third member. Company Flow set up its own label, Official Recordings, and released the single "8 Steps to Perfection," which began to create an underground buzz. The group worked day jobs to fund their first EP, 1995's *Funcrusher*, which sold over 30,000 copies despite being available only in double-vinyl format. Now with an even stronger buzz, Company Flow was courted by several labels, but held out for an extremely artist-friendly deal that would allow them to maintain ownership of their masters and publishing rights, receive 50 percent of the net profits from their recordings, and not commit them to multiple album releases. The only label to accept their terms was Rawkus Records, a financially struggling indie with no clear musical identity at the time. Company Flow's signing gave them instant street credibility, and paved the way for the label to spearhead the resurgence of underground hip-hop with a roster including Mos Def, Talib Kweli, Pharoahe Monch, and others.

Company Flow, meanwhile, added a spate of new tracks to *Funcrusher* to create their debut full-length, *Funcrusher Plus*. Acclaimed by many and misunderstood by some, *Funcrusher Plus* is considered a landmark. Heavy touring and promotion ensued, after which Bigg Jus struck out on his own (as the group had planned for some time). El-P and Mr. Len followed up with *Little Johnny From the Hospitul: Breaks End Instrumentuls, Vol. 1*, an album of dark instrumental hip-hop that disappointed some fans but pleased others. Also that year, they contributed the topical "Patriotism" to Rawkus' *Sound-*

bombing, Vol. 2 compilation (which was titled after a phrase they'd coined in the early days). By 2000, Rawkus was pushing to break itself into the mainstream, and their relationship with Company Flow began to break down. They officially parted ways by the end of the year, and not long after the group decided to disband amicably. El-P set up his own Def Jux label and assembled a roster of progressive rap artists, including Cannibal Ox, Aesop Rock, Mr. Lif, and RJD2, not to mention his own solo recordings, which began with 2002's abrasive and acclaimed *Fantastic Damage*. *—Steve Huey*

★ Funcrusher Plus / Jul. 28, 1997 / Rawkus ✦✦✦✦✦

Featuring material recorded over 1994-1997, Company Flow's official full-length debut, *Funcrusher Plus*, had a galvanizing effect on the underground hip-hop scene. It was one of the artiest, most abstract hip-hop albums ever recorded, paving the way for a new brand of avant-garde experimentalism that blatantly defied commercial considerations. Musically and lyrically, *Funcrusher Plus* is abrasive and confrontational, informed by left-wing politics and the punked-out battle cry "independent as f*ck." It's intentionally not funky and certainly not danceable; the beats are tense and jagged, and often spaced far apart to leave room for the MCs' complex rhymes. Bigg Jus' and El-P's lyrical technique is so good it's sometimes nearly impenetrable, assaulting the listener with dense barrages of words that take a few listens to decipher. Even if this is all highly off-kilter, it's also a conscious return to hip-hop on its most basic, beats-and-rhymes level; hooks or jazz and funk samples aren't even considerations here. The production is spacy and atmospheric, often employing weird ambient noises and futuristic synths that clash with the defiantly low-budget production values. It's also quite minimalist, particularly on tracks like "Vital Nerve," which is basically just a three-note synth line over a beat, and the classic Indelible MC's single "The Fire in Which You Burn," where Co-Flow trades rhymes with the Juggaknots over a skittering beat and sitar drone. Other tracks have sci-fi and conspiracy theory undertones; some are set in an Orwellian dystopia, while some pointedly satirize corporate and capitalist greed. Yet there's also some straightforward realism, as on "Last Good Sleep," a frightening domestic abuse drama. *Funcrusher Plus* demands intense concentration, but also rewards it, and its advancement of hip-hop as an art form is still being felt. It's difficult, challenging music, to be sure, and it's equally far ahead of its time. *—Steve Huey*

Little Johnny From the Hospitul: Breaks End Instrumentuls, Vol. 1 / Jun. 15, 1999 / Rawkus ✦✦✦

Little Johnny From the Hospitul is an instrumental album and a dark affair with slowish textured beats. These aren't your average hip-hop beats, with basic drum loops and DJ scratches thrown in; it's obvious that El-P and DJ Mr. Len spent considerable time constructing the songs. On "Suzy Pulled a Pistol on Henry," the kid from "Bad Touch Example" (on the *Funcrusher Plus* album) gets revenge on the person that molested her. Other standout songs on the album are "Gigapet Ephany," "Wurker Ant Uprise," and the always addicting "Shadows Drown," which features the distant sounds of water to distorted voices to the sounds of electronic locusts. *—Dan Gizzi*

D.P.A (As Seen on TV)/Iron Galaxy EP / 2000 / Def Jux ✦✦✦

The first release on Company Flow frontman El-P's label Def Jux also marks the last from the seminal New York duo, who announced their breakup in the fall of 2000. Sharing the bill with labelmates Cannibal Ox as a double 12", Company Flow continues to further push the boundaries of quality underground hip-hop. "D.P.A. (As Seen on T.V.)" is suitelike, with beats and production that are apocalyptic in scope. El-P's lyrics are rapid fire, packing in cinematic imagery without resorting to the hip-hop cliché of a catchy chorus or hook. Momentum is not lost as the duo serves up the pounding "Simple," and a cameo from Ill Bill adds extra venom to "Simian D (Feelin' Ignorant)" on the B side. Newcomers Cannibal Ox benefit from the violently murky production techniques exhibited by El-P on the second 12", which features the ominous "Iron Galaxy" and the spooky synthesizer-driven "Straight Off the D.I.C." Even the instrumentals of all the tracks presented stand strong on their own merits, a signature trademark of classic hip-hop 12" singles. *—Douglas Siwek*

Compton's Most Wanted

f. 1989, Compton, CA
Group / Gangsta Rap, West Coast Rap, G-Funk

Though N.W.A got most of the recognition, Compton's Most Wanted also did much to popularize and proliferate early-'90s West Coast gangsta rap. Led by future solo artist MC Eiht and legendary West Coast electro producer the Unknown DJ, this Compton, CA, group (also known as CMW) reveled in themes involving primarily guns, women, gangs, and drugs, setting the precedent for what would eventually become clichéd. More importantly, the group possessed a knack for writing laid-back gangsta ballads characterized not so much by aggression but rather by languid production laced with '70s soul motifs and reflective lyrics. CMW scored its breakthrough hit in 1991 with "Growin' Up in the 'Hood," which had been included on the popular *Boyz n the 'Hood* soundtrack. The song hit number one on *Billboard*'s Hot Rap Singles chart the same week the soundtrack topped the R&B album charts. Shortly afterward, Eiht embarked on a solo career. Once his debut album, *We Come Strapped* (1994), debuted at number five on *Billboard*'s charts, the rapper didn't look back, leaving his group behind for nearly a decade until they briefly reunited in the early 2000s for a comeback album and best-of collection.

Comprised of rappers Eiht and Chill MC, turntablist DJ Mike T, and producers DJ Slip and the Unknown DJ, CMW came together in 1989 and recorded a debut album, *It's a Compton Thang* (1990). The album was a landmark for its time, standing beside N.W.A's *Straight Outta Compton* (1988) as a genre-defining work. The following year they toured with fellow gangsta rappers the Geto Boys and recorded a follow-up album, *Straight Checkn'em* (1991), around the same time they were climbing the charts with "Growin' Up in the 'Hood," the lead single from their album that also had been included on the *Boyz n the 'Hood* soundtrack (1991). Riding atop the single's success, *Straight Checkn'em* peaked at number 26 on *Billboard*'s R&B chart in September, signaling the group's closest brush yet with commercial success. The following year came *Music to Driveby* (1992), a fine album that, unfortunately, would signal the group's dissolution.

By this point, the rap community had elevated Eiht to superstar status, and his role as an actor in the film *Menace II Society* (1993) only solidified his status, along with his solo contribution to the chart-topping soundtrack. And once his solo album, *We Come Strapped* (1994), debuted in *Billboard*'s Top Five, he didn't look back for several years, as he continued to release one album after another. By the end of the decade, though, West Coast gangsta rap had lost much of its popularity, and Eiht's solo career reflected this. Not surprisingly, he reunited with the former members of CMW (sans the Unknown DJ) to record their first album in years, *Represent* (2000), an album met with little fanfare. A retrospect best-of album, *When We Wuz Bangin'* (2001) followed, commemorating the group's ten-year anniversary. Eiht resumed his solo career thereafter. —*Jason Birchmeier*

It's a Compton Thang / Feb. 1990 / Orpheus ♦♦♦
Rudimentary yet undoubtedly cornerstone, *It's a Compton Thang* brings together for the first time a talented group of rap artists highlighted by future and former West Coast legends—MC Eiht and the Unknown DJ, respectively—that would build upon the prototype N.W.A had established two years earlier on *Straight Outta Compton*. Compton's Most Wanted follow that prototype very closely here, even going so far as sampling N.W.A on the album opener, "One Time Gaffled 'Em Up." *It's a Compton Thang* is more than simply a second-rate *Straight Outta Compton*, though. In fact, it expands upon that prototype, specifically with late-album highlight "Late Night Hype," a laid-back G-funk ballad that set the stage for a million others in the coming years. Beyond historical significance, *It's a Compton Thang* doesn't quite measure up to what CMW would do in subsequent years. The Unknown DJ and DJ Slip piece together some memorable productions from classic samples, among them James Brown's "Payback" on "Final Chapter," and the rappers similarly deliver some uniquely old school style, yet all of this is more novel than anything, particularly to contemporary listeners—more reminiscent of the much-treasured golden age than the much-criticized gangsta age. And while that golden age sense is precisely what's so much fun about this album, it's not what CMW would embody thereafter, as they hardened both their production and their rapping, which are anything but hard here. All of that aside, the true beauty of *It's a Compton Thang* is the initial synthesis of former electro legend the Unknown DJ with future gangsta icon MC Eiht as well as the pleasant reminder that West Coast gangsta rap was once more about old-fashioned fun than cheap thrills. —*Jason Birchmeier*

Straight Checkn'em / Jul. 16, 1991 / Orpheus ♦♦♦
Compton's Most Wanted's second CD got more sullen, combative, and sexist in its language and themes than the debut. Where "Duck Sick" and "It's a Compton Thang" at least had some swagger and a taste of humor to offset the posturing, "Can I Kill It?" and "Compton's Lynchin'" were more surly, while "Gangsta Shot Out" and "Growin' Up in the 'Hood" were fatalistic and "Raised in Compton" despairing rather than informative. Only "Mike T's Funky Scratch" sounded a lighter note, and that was due to its being a declaration of rap prowess rather than street superiority. —*Ron Wynn*

Music to Driveby / Jun. 1992 / Orpheus ♦♦♦♦
The third and commercially most successful album by Los Angeles rappers Compton's Most Wanted contained such terse narratives as "Dead Men Tell No Lies" and "Hit the Floor." If there hadn't been such an abundance of similar material in the early '90s, these tales might have triggered intense scrutiny and analysis. Instead, the most common response is that M.C. Eiht's raps aren't quite as loose or expressive as those of Spice 1, Ice Cube, Nas, or many others telling identical stories. —*Ron Wynn*

Represent / Oct. 24, 2000 / Half Ounce ♦♦♦
A decade after Compton's Most Wanted released their 1990 landmark debut, *It's a Compton Thang*, the group reunited for a solid, albeit by-the-numbers, comeback album, *Represent*. Much had changed over the course of that decade, namely the popular rise and fall of West Coast gangsta rap. Group leader MC Eiht had never left the game during that time, recording a series of solo albums, so he's still in prime condition here. As for the other members of CMW, though, you have to wonder. Producer DJ Slip had stayed relatively busy during the decade, producing MC Eiht at times, but the other members had dropped out of the game. And perhaps most importantly, the Unknown DJ, the legendary electro producer who had borne the group initially, is notably absent here. Even so, *Represent* certainly sounds like a CMW album, just as thuggish and threatening as *Music to Driveby*, the group's most recent release, from eight years earlier. Yet that's precisely what's a little disappointing about *Represent*—ten years later, CMW is content doing essentially what they were doing before. Longtime fans will undoubtedly welcome this, but anyone who felt indifferent to CMW in the first place will likely feel similarly here. It's nonetheless always a pleasure to pick apart DJ Slip's productions and call out the samples, perhaps the most famous one here being the chilled-out synth ambience from Rick James' "Hollywood" serving as the backdrop to "Then U Gone," one of *Represent*'s standout moments. As they say, sometimes the more things change, the more they stay the same, and as far as CMW is concerned here, that indeed seems to be the case. —*Jason Birchmeier*

● **When We Wuz Bangin' 1989-1999: The Hitz** / Jan. 23, 2001 / The Right Stuff ♦♦♦♦♦
The 1989-1999 time span cited in the title of *When We Wuz Bangin'* is a little misleading. Compton's Most Wanted did in fact span a decade, forming in 1989 and debuting a year later, but the group spent most of the ensuing decade inactive, releasing only three albums during a three-year span (1990-1992). Throughout most of the '90s, group leader MC Eiht trudged on with his up-and-down solo career and took producer DJ Slip along for part of the ride. The remaining members of CMW meanwhile remained mostly confined to old school obscurity. As short lived as the talented group had been, though, they did release a wealth of blueprint West Coast gangsta rap during their three-album span, each album—*It's a Compton Thang* (1990), *Music to Driveby* (1992), and *Straight Checkn'em* (1991)—offering a few standout singles. Many of those singles are compiled here ("One Time Gaffled 'Em Up," "Late Night Hype," "Growin' Up in the 'Hood") as are several of Eiht's bigger solo hits ("All for the Money," "Streiht Up Menace," "Days of '89") and even some rare recordings (DJ Premier's remix of "Def Wish II"). The inclusion of Eiht's solo work is key, since he did have a few great gangsta ballads, but you could argue that those songs had little to do with Compton's Most Wanted and occupy precious disc space that could have instead featured gang-bangin' songs like "Hood Took Me Under" or "Straight Checkn'em." Yet because the group had only three albums to pick from, and near-synchronous ones at that, the sequencing here works better and makes for a more interesting, chronological listen, even if it makes *When We Wuz Bangin'* more of an Eiht best-of than a CMW one. Whatever way you look at it, though, here is where you'll find some of the best laid-back gangsta ballads ever, as that was Eiht's specialty. —*Jason Birchmeier*

The Comrads

Group / Hip-Hop, Gangsta Rap, Alternative Rap, Hardcore Rap, West Coast Rap, Pop-Rap

Longtime protégés of West Coast heavyweight Mack 10, The Comrads is made up of Kmac and Gangsta, a pair of Lynnwood rappers that try to carry the torch of West Coast gangsta rap. The pair made a major splash in the L.A. area in the summer of 1997 with *Homeboyz*. After struggling to find a home, Comrads set up camp with Mack 10's private label, Hoo Bangin'. In 2000, Comrads released their first album for a major label, *Wake Up & Ball. —Jon Azpiri*

Wake Up & Ball / Jun. 27, 2000 / Priority ♦♦
This L.A. duo, protégés of Mack 10, have had regional hits in the past, but broke out nationally with *Wake Up & Ball. Wake Up & Ball* stays safe within the confines of West Coast hip-hop styles, with its time-tested blend of George Clinton and Roger Troutman-inspired G-funk. Comrads do mix the formula a bit in tracks like the dancehall-tinged "Bom Bom" and the R&B-laced track "Wanna B Gangstas." Those pleasant diversions, unfortunately, are few and far between. Too often, the album wastes its time on filler like "Murder Murder" and "Thug Niggaz." Mediocrity tends to dominate throughout *Wake Up & Ball*, an average effort that does little to raise the status of West Coast hip-hop. —*Jon Azpiri*

Confrontation Camp

Group / Hardcore Rap, Hip-Hop, Rap-Rock

Stemming from his strong political roots, Public Enemy's Chuck D comes together with Confrontation Camp. It's about hip-hop and the raw aggression behind riveting rap rhyming, and frontman Kyle Ice Jason is immersed in classic East Coast rap. Chuck D (who goes by Mistachuck) joins P.E. alum Professor Griff to deliver hard-hitting societal issues through poetic beatboxing and vocalic disarray. Confrontation Camp was signed to Artemis and released *Objects in the Mirror Are Closer Than They Appear* in July 2000. —*MacKenzie Wilson*

Objects in Mirror Are Closer Than They Appear / Jul. 25, 2000 / Artemis ♦♦

If you've ever listened to Body Count, Kid Rock, or any of the dozens of other bands milking the rap-rock sound for all it's worth, you already know the formula behind this side project featuring Public Enemy's Chuck D and Professor Griff: loud, screeching guitars + bombastic beats + in-your-face rap vocals = one big headache for all but the most die-hard fans of the genre. But the blame can't all fall on Chuck D's head, as the greatest voice in hip-hop remains its most effective, with powerful lyrics and a booming tone that would make E.F. Hutton sit up and listen. Instead, the finger must be pointed at frontman Kyle Jason, whose vocals don't stand out from the cacophonous racket, and Chaingang, the four-piece band whose workmanlike funk/metal grooves sound like every other band who's ever tried this sound on for size. To be fair, songs like "Brake the Law" and "Carry My Load" show more than enough promise to suggest the band would be far more potent in a live setting. But Confrontation Camp is ultimately the victim of poor timing—a decent band whose sound is a thing of the past. —*Bret Love*

Conscious Daughters

f. Oakland, CA
Group / Hip-Hop, Gangsta Rap, Hardcore Rap

The Conscious Daughters, who emerged in the socially aware, Afro-centric milieu of early-'90s Bay Area hip-hop, were a female rap duo from Oakland consisting of Carla Green and Karryl Smith. Ultrapolitical, militant hiphopper Paris championed the pair early on and helmed their 1993 debut, *Ear to the Street*, producing and writing all of the tracks and (along with engineer Eric Valentine) playing on them as well. The themes echoed the "thug-life" sentiments of much of the West Coast hip-hop at the time, employing a distinctly women's perspective (particularly on tracks such as "Princess of Poetry," "Wife of a Gangsta," and "Crazybitchmadness"). The Conscious Daughters next appeared on their mentor Paris' 1994 album, *Guerilla Funk*, adding raps to tracks such as "Bring It to Ya." The duo finally dropped their sophomore effort, *Gamers*, in 1996. The Daughters pitched in on production this time around, with help from such able hands as Studio Ton, Tone Capone, and omnipresent ally Paris. *Gamers* featured a host of guest artists, among them Nate Fox, Harm, Suga T, Mystic, Lil Kristen, Rose, Sandy Griffith (da Old

Skool), Saafir, Father Dom, Money B, and C-Funk (many of which cropped up on the final track, "All-Star Freestyle"). —*Erik Hage*

Ear to the Street / Nov. 30, 1993 / Priority ♦♦♦
An obscure female rap duo from East Oakland, the Conscious Daughters were among the acts that the militant sociopolitical rapper Paris signed to his Scarface label, which was being distributed by Priority when *Ears to the Street* came out in 1993. Although produced by Paris, the CD falls short of the excellence of Paris' own albums. But it's a generally decent, if uneven, hardcore rap effort, and like Paris, the Conscious Daughters have a lot on their minds. The album's most memorable songs are also its most sociopolitical. "Shitty Situation" angrily describes the plight of a young single mother who gets no support from the baby's father, while "Wife of a Gangster" paints a sobering picture of the violent world that a criminal's wife faces on a daily basis. "We Roll Deep," however, is memorable not because of its lyrics but because of its effective sampling of a Lonnie Liston Smith jazz-pop instrumental from the early 1980s. The Smith sample brings a taste of acid jazz to the CD, but make no mistake: *Ears to the Street* is a hardcore rap album first and foremost. —*Alex Henderson*

● **Gamers** / Mar. 5, 1996 / Priority ♦♦♦

Control Machete

Group / Latin Rap, Tropical, Rock en Español

Mexican Latin rap threesome Control Machete burst into the local rock scene in the mid-'80s, making its debut with the release of *Mucho Barato* in July of 1997. Led by Fermín IV, Pato, and Toy Kenobi, the band returned in March of 1999 with *Artilleria Pesada*, produced by Antonio Hernández and Jason Roberts. In addition, Fermín IV recorded a song alongside Cypress Hill called "Siempre Peligroso," which was featured on the album *Grandes Exitos en Español*. He also participated in Chris Vrenna's project Tweaker and played with Los Angeles-based hip-hop act OMD. Control Machete joined similar Latin rock groups on a compilation called *Spanglish 101*, released by Kool Arrow Records. —*Drago Bonacich*

Mucho Barato / Jul. 1, 1997 / Polygram ♦♦♦♦

Artilleria Pesada: Presenta / Mar. 30, 1999 / Universal Latino ♦♦♦♦♦

● **Solo Para Fanaticos** / Mar. 19, 2002 / Universal Latino ♦♦♦♦♦
Control Machete's third full-length record became their first greatest-hits compilation, opening with the urban "Si Señor" and including their 1997 smash "¿Comprendes Mendes?," and a remix of "Asi Son Mis Dias." *Solo Para Fanaticos* is composed of Fermín IV's, Pato's, and Tony Kenobi's most popular and experimental songs, such as the hip-hop and alternative pop/rock "Presente," the tropical meets Latin rap "Grita," and the powerful metal-rap "Mexican Curios." In addition, this collection delivers "La Lupita," from Control Machete's debut *Mucho Barato* and "Desde La Tierra (El Tercer Planeta)," from their 1999 album called *Artilleria Pesada. —Drago Bonacich*

Coo Coo Cal

Gangsta Rap, Hardcore Rap

Milwaukee rapper Coo Coo Cal mixes Midwestern slang with the unmistakable sound of South-inspired beats, resulting in a style that mixes a number of hip-hop influences together as one, as evidenced by 1999's *Walkin' Dead* and 2001's *Disturbed*, the latter of which was his first for the Tommy Boy label and featured a trade-off with Chicago rapper Twista on the track "We Ride." Coo Coo Cal deals with the expected hip-hop subject matter (everyday life and struggles within the inner city), but injects his own personality into the proceedings to create his own hip-hop style. —*Greg Prato*

Disturbed / Sep. 18, 2001 / Tommy Boy ♦♦
Cal's second album, and his major debut, is saved by the hit single "My Projects." It pushes the rapper's gruff style to the forefront, and the rinky-dink beats (monotonous and tedious by album's end) aptly serve the song. The rest of *Disturbed*, however, is basically standard-issue hip-hop, buoyed occasionally by street authenticity. —*Michael Gallucci*

Cool Breeze

Southern Rap, Dirty South

A product of the same Georgia-based Dungeon Family crew which also gave rise to hip-hop acts including the Goodie Mob and OutKast, rapper Cool

Breeze first surfaced during the mid-'90s, appearing on a series of soundtracks including *Set It Off* and *Hoodlum*. After scoring a hit with the infectious "Watch for the Hook," he released his debut solo LP, *East Point's Greatest Hits*, on Interscope in 1999. —*Jason Ankeny*

● **East Point's Greatest Hits** / Mar. 23, 1999 / Interscope ✦✦✦✦

Another offering from the Organized Noize camp (Goodie Mob, Outkast), Cool Breeze's debut doesn't measure up to that of his Southern neighbors, but remains solid throughout. Breeze's storytelling prowess is on display with "Black Gangster," and the syncopated drumming on "Hit Man" lures you in to Breeze's "Dirty South." The album's undisputed highlight is "Watch for the Hook," where a pounding posse cut, featuring rapid fire rhymes from Goodie Mob and Outkast, make for one of 1999's most memorable rap tracks. —*Craig Robert Smith*

Coolio (Artis Leon Ivey Jr.)

b. Aug. 1, 1963

Hip-Hop, West Coast Rap, Pop-Rap

Coolio was one of the first rappers to balance pop accessibility with gritty, street-level subject matter and language. Yet despite his nods to hardcore, his music was clearly more happy-go-lucky at heart; he shared the West Coast scene's love of laid-back '70s funk, and that attitude translated to his music far more often than Dr. Dre's Death Row/G-funk axis. Most of Coolio's hits were exuberant, good-time party anthems (save for his moody signature song "Gangsta's Paradise"), and he created a goofy, ingratiating persona in the videos that supported them. He was also popular with younger audiences and became a favorite on Nickelodeon comedy shows thanks to the thin, spidery dreadlocks that stuck straight out of his head in all directions. In the process, Coolio took the sound of West Coast hip-hop to wider audiences than ever before, including those put off by—or too young for—the rougher aspects of G-funk. A combination of inactivity, legal troubles, and newly emerging rap stars stole Coolio's thunder in the late '90s, but by that point he'd helped lay the groundwork for an explosion of hardcore-themed pop-rap (most notably Puff Daddy's Bad Boy empire), and played an underappreciated role in making hip-hop the mainstream pop music of choice for a new generation.

Coolio was born on August 1, 1963, in the South Central L.A. area of Compton. As a young boy, he was small, asthmatic, highly intelligent, and a bookworm, which often made life outside the home difficult. His parents divorced when he was 11, and searching for a way to fit in at school, he started running with the Baby Crips and getting into trouble. Even so, he still wasn't really accepted and was never formally inducted into the gang; he tried to make up for it by creating a menacing, unstable persona and carrying weapons to school, and his once-promising scholastic career wound up falling victim to his violent, poverty-stricken environment. At 17, he spent several months in jail for larceny (apparently after trying to cash a money order that had actually been stolen by one of his friends). After high school, he studied at Compton Community College; he also began taking his high school interest in rap to the stage and took his performing name from a dozen contests in which someone called him "Coolio Iglesias." He became a regular on Los Angeles rap radio station KDAY and cut one of the earlier SoCal rap singles, "Watcha Gonna Do." Unfortunately, he also fell prey to crack cocaine addiction, which derailed his music career. Coolio entered rehab and straightened himself out by taking a job as a firefighter in the forests of northern California. Upon returning to L.A. a year later, he worked various odd jobs—including security at Los Angeles International Airport—while getting his rap career back on track.

Coolio cut another single, "You're Gonna Miss Me," that went nowhere. However, he began making connections in the L.A. hip-hop scene, meeting up with WC and the Maad Circle and guesting on their 1991 debut album *Ain't a Damn Thang Changed.* He then joined a collective dubbed the 40 Thevz and wound up landing a deal with Tommy Boy. Accompanied by DJ Brian "Wino" Dobbs, Coolio recorded his debut album, *It Takes a Thief,* which was released in 1994. The lead single, "County Line," was a humorous recounting of the indignities of welfare, but the record really took off when "Fantastic Voyage," a rap remake of the funk classic by Lakeside, was released as a single. Accompanied by a typically playful video, "Fantastic Voyage" rocketed to number three on the pop charts, pushing *It Takes a Thief* into the Top Ten and past the platinum sales mark. Many critics and listeners welcomed his friendlier, gentler approach to the gangsta-dominated

West Coast sound, in spite of the fact that some of his album cuts tackled hardcore themes in a similarly profane manner.

Following up his breakthrough success, Coolio teamed up with gospel-trained singer L.V. on a tune based on Stevie Wonder's *Songs in the Key of Life* cut "Pastime Paradise." "Gangsta's Paradise" was a social statement about ghetto life, and the music was dark, haunting, and spellbindingly atmospheric. In other words, it was nothing like what the public had come to expect from Coolio, and a less than enthusiastic Tommy Boy discouraged him from putting it on an album, instead placing it on the soundtrack to the film *Dangerous Minds,* which starred Michelle Pfeiffer as a tough inner-city teacher. Released as a single, "Gangsta's Paradise" was a staggeringly huge hit; it became Coolio's first number-one pop single and also the first ghetto-centric rap song to hit number one in the U.K. Its chart longevity was such that, even with the Mariah Carey/Boyz II Men duet "One Sweet Day" setting a new record for most weeks at number one that year, "Gangsta's Paradise" still managed to beat it out as the number one single of 1995. It was such a phenomenon that when Weird Al Yankovic recorded the parody "Amish Paradise" (authorized by Tommy Boy but not Coolio, leading to much discord), the accompanying album *Bad Hair Day* became his biggest-selling record *ever.* Naturally, "Gangsta's Paradise" was featured on Coolio's next album, released toward the end of 1995, and naturally, it was the title track. It later won a Grammy for Best Solo Rap Performance.

The triple-platinum *Gangsta's Paradise* album kept the hits coming: the bright party anthem "1, 2, 3, 4 (Sumpin' New)" hit the Top Ten in 1996, and the safe-sex anthem "Too Hot" was fairly popular as well. Meanwhile, Coolio toured the world, contributed the theme song to the Nickelodeon comedy series *Kenan & Kel,* and began pursuing an acting career, making his screen debut with a cameo in the 1996 comedy *Phat Beach*; he would also land a small role in the following year's *Batman and Robin.* Coolio's third album, *My Soul,* could well have been expected to be a major event, given his massive success last time out. However, things had changed drastically by the summer of 1997: the specter of the 2Pac/Biggie murders still hung heavily over the hip-hop landscape, and Puff Daddy was rapidly becoming a breakout star with the young audience that had previously belonged to Coolio. *My Soul*'s lead single, the elegiac "C U When U Get There" (which sampled Pachelbel's "Canon in D"), seemed to fit the mood of the times, but the album barely scraped the Top 40 and became one of the lowest-profile platinum hits of the year.

The disappointing performance of *My Soul* was complicated by various legal difficulties. In late 1997, Coolio and seven members of his entourage were arrested for allegedly shoplifting from a German clothing store and assaulting the owner; he was later convicted on accessory charges and fined. Not long after that incident, German police threatened to charge Coolio with inciting crime after missing the humor behind his in-concert suggestion that listeners steal his album if they couldn't afford it. In the summer of 1998, Coolio was arrested again, this time in Lawndale, CA; he was pulled over and cited for driving on the wrong side of the road with an expired license and was also charged with carrying a concealed weapon (despite having alerted the officer to the presence of the unloaded semi-automatic pistol in the vehicle) and possessing a small amount of marijuana. Things weren't all bad, though; he appeared regularly on the revived *Hollywood Squares* and set up his own label, Crowbar. In 1999, he played triplets in the film *Tyrone,* but had to postpone a Crowbar promotional tour after an auto accident. He continued to take a number of small film roles, but his much-delayed fourth album remained only a rumor (though it was confirmed that he had recorded "The Hustler," a rap update of Kenny Rogers' "The Gambler" with Rogers himself on vocals, back in 1998). Finally, five years after his last album, *El Cool Magnifico* appeared on the Riviera label. —*Steve Huey*

It Takes a Thief / Jul. 19, 1994 / Tommy Boy ✦✦✦✦

Just when it looked like rap would completely succumb to the violent hyperbole and mean-spirited "realness" of gangsta rap, new blood entered the scene in 1994 to nudge the genre back toward friendlier turf. That new blood included Nas, Craig Mack, and Coolio, whose *It Takes a Thief* starts with the easy-rolling funk of Lakeside's "Fantastic Voyage" and goes from there, infusing rap with a much-needed sense of humor and the promise of good times. While Coolio is no simp—"County Line" playfully explores the hassles of welfare, while some tracks dip into gangsta territory—he manages to make rap a cool, inclusive journey. —*Eddie Huffman*

Gangsta's Paradise / Nov. 21, 1995 / Tommy Boy ✦✦✦✦✦
Most of Coolio's hit debut *It Takes a Thief* was fairly upbeat material, but the appearance of the stark single "Gangsta's Paradise" in the summer of 1995 signaled a change in the rapper's music. Driven by an ominously deep bass line and slashing strings, the creeping, threatening funk of "Gangsta's Paradise" was the most chilling thing Coolio had recorded to date, but the menace didn't come at the expense of his considerable talent for immediate, catchy hooks. Consequently, the single shot to the top of the charts and hovered in the Top Ten for many weeks. The album followed shortly afterward, and it didn't fail to deliver on the promise of the single. Not only did Coolio expand his sound, but his songwriting skills improved, as *Gangsta's Paradise* has very few weak moments. Alternating between slow, funky grooves and elastic, party-ready anthems, *Gangsta's Paradise* is proof that Coolio is one of the most exciting and interesting hip-hop artists of the mid-'90s. —*Stephen Thomas Erlewine*

My Soul / Aug. 26, 1997 / Tommy Boy ✦✦✦✦
Coolio's third album, *My Soul*, follows the same formula as its two predecessors, which isn't necessarily a bad thing. Where others have failed as pop-rappers, Coolio succeeds because of his love of melody, message, and funky beats. *My Soul* lacks anything as monolithic as "Gangsta's Paradise," yet it has a more elaborate production, boasting obscure samples, violins, sound bites, and guitars. It also is remarkably consistent, delivering very few subpar cuts over the course of the album. That would be enough to distinguish it from the ranks of overstuffed gangsta rappers, but what makes *My Soul* another winner is how Coolio is unafraid to be both serious and funny, catchy and funky. It's a small, subtle difference, but it's what makes *My Soul* a thoroughly enjoyable record, no matter if you're going out or staying in. —*Stephen Thomas Erlewine*

● **Fantastic Voyage: The Greatest Hits** / Jul. 17, 2001 / Tommy Boy ✦✦✦✦✦
Over the course of three albums in the 1990s, Coolio took West Coast hip-hop even farther into the mainstream than Dr. Dre. Even though he nearly succumbed to the perils of the streets in his youth, Coolio's take on the '70s funk-obsessed L.A. sound was usually far more good-humored than the menacing Death Row crew. His gangsta roots could play to the hardcore faithful, but he also snagged plenty of younger listeners with his fun-loving party music and genial (if profane) comic persona. (In fact, it's difficult to imagine Puff Daddy becoming an across-the-board pop star without Coolio first sparking that younger audience's interest in hip-hop.) Coolio's broad appeal, combined with a knack for finding (often borrowing) memorable hooks, helped make him one of the best pop-rap artists of the '90s, as demonstrated by *Fantastic Voyage: The Greatest Hits*. It's a straightforward 13-track collection centered around Coolio's signature party anthems—"Fantastic Voyage," "Too Hot," "1, 2, 3, 4 (Sumpin' New)"—plus his moody masterpiece, "Gangsta's Paradise," and one previously unissued track, "Aw Here It Goes" (a theme for the Nickelodeon comedy series *Kenan & Kel*). Yet the lesser-known tracks are often pretty catchy themselves, proving that Coolio's talents extend beyond the handful of irresistible singles for which he's primarily known. Even if nothing else quite matches the heights of those few classics, *Fantastic Voyage: The Greatest Hits* is still an infectious, consistently entertaining listen. —*Steve Huey*

El Cool Magnifico / Oct. 15, 2002 / Riviera ✦✦✦
With all manner of party and sex jams exploding on rap radio during 2002, Coolio's return to the record bins, properly handled, could've brought him back into the mainstream. Well, it's clear he knew exactly what he needed to get back to the charts, but most of these tracks just aren't handled well enough to float next to contemporary rap. The few party tracks on tap suffer from an amateur sound that's just enough to keep them from getting any airplay; "I Like Girls" has a retro-electro feel that probably could've done it, and one of Coolio's best performances in a few years, but it's the only one here with any promise. "What Is an MC?," "Cadillac Vogues," and "Ghetto Square Dance" (the latter a "Fantastic Voyage" remake) smack of small ideas—not to mention small studios. Coolio's still a pretty solid party rapper, but it's clear the rap world passed him by more than five years before the appearance of *El Cool Magnifico*. —*John Bush*

Cormega

b. Queensbridge, NY
Hip-Hop, East Coast Rap
Though an undeniably articulate and thoughtful rapper, Cormega's reputation in the hip-hop underground resulted more from his longtime adversarial

relationship with Nas than from his own music. This seemingly endless verbal bout between the two kept Cormega's career afloat while he struggled to release an album in the late '90s. In fact, he didn't release an album until 2001, five years after debuting on Nas' "Affirmative Action." During those five years, Cormega rapped in the New York underground scene as a mix-tape favorite. He took a thug/hustler approach, rapping about the violent and tragic side of street life; however, he did so in a tremendously lucid manner, commanding a liquid-smooth flow and clear articulation. As a result, though it took him years of struggle to release a debut album, when he finally released *The Realness* in 2001, he thoroughly impressed many, earning many end-of-the-year nods from critics.

Nas and Cormega, who both represent Queensbridge, met at the dawn of the '90s and became companions. Cormega unfortunately went away to prison, though, as his companion's rap career began to take flight in a big way. Nas subsequently dedicated the song "One Love" from his debut album, *Illmatic* (1994), to Cormega, who soon after left prison. Together again, the two collaborated on Nas' second album, *It Was Written* (1996), with Foxy Brown and AZ on the song "Affirmative Action." The foursome called themselves the Firm and planned to record a group album. But Cormega ended up being replaced by yet another Queens rapper, Nature, reportedly because of Nas' manager at the time, Steve Stout. The Firm album flopped, but Cormega still resented being ousted from the group. As a result, he released the song "Fuck Nas and Nature" and spoke venomously of the two.

Of course, these sort of battles are a longtime staple of East Coast hip-hop and often promote all involved. It perhaps wasn't a surprise, then, when Cormega found himself being offered a contract with Def Jam Records. A double-sided 12" resulted from the pairing—"Angel Dust" b/w "Killaz Theme II"—but that was unfortunately all. The album that Cormega had readied for Def Jam to release, *The Testament*, continually got pushed back, never surfacing. The reasons vary, depending on who you ask—most likely because the Nas-Cormega heat cooled—but whatever the reason, Cormega parted ways with Def Jam and took the independent route. He created his own label, Legal Hustle, and signed a distribution deal with Landspeed Records. Finally, in 2001, after much bootlegging, Cormega's debut album, *The Realness*, finally appeared on the market. Many were quick to declare it one of the year's best hip-hop releases, and it seemed that Cormega's legacy had proven accurate. He indeed proved to be an incredible rapper: articulate and passionate, uncompromising and uncommercial.

Given all the fanfare surrounding Cormega's long-awaited splashing debut, it came as a bit of a surprise when Nas dissed him on the song "Destroy & Rebuild" from his comeback album, *Stillmatic* (2001). Just as he had done before with "Fuck Nas and Nature," Cormega readied a comeback track, "The Slick Response," which featured the beat from Mtume's "Juicy Fruit." Another Nas-related song, "Love in Love Out," would appear on Cormega's forthcoming second album, *The True Meaning* (2002). A few months prior to the release of *The True Meaning*, Body Shop Records released *Hustler/Rapper*, a collection of mix-tape recordings that featured Cormega. Though a shoddy collection, *Hustler/Rapper* includes a few key tracks such as "Angel Dust" and "Realmatic," the latter yet another Nas dis. Upon its release in summer 2002, *The True Meaning* demanded much attention despite being an indie release, like *The Realness* had, and featured production from such luminaries as Large Professor and the Alchemist. —*Jason Birchmeier*

● **The Realness** / Jul. 24, 2001 / Landspeed ✦✦✦✦
With a fresh batch of new material, Cormega's "official" debut, *The Realness*, manifests under stealth-like conditions. Yet, it successfully conveys what his aborted Def Jam debut, *The Testament*, implied three years previously—that Mega is one of the most promising thug poets to emerge in quite sometime. Though the usual live-guy repertoire and topic matter is recycled, Cormega paints with a broader lyrical brush then most hood aficionados, as his articulate verses far surpass the limitations of what the typical halfway crook is capable of expressing. Displaying a gripping range of vocal gifts, "The Saga" and "Fallen Soldiers" offer vivid street mathematics with Kool G Rap-like narrative abilities. Likewise, Mega's ode to hip-hop, "American Beauty," is a continuation of Common's "I Used to Love Her," where his love for the art is evident: "Primo treated her good, made her the queen of my hood." Though the sonic landscape of *The Realness* is headlined by the Infamous Family members Havoc and Alchemist, it is a

handful of upstarts (Jay Love, Big Ty, Sha Self) who carve out the LP's sound identity. This cast of rising and unknown names turns in a yeoman's job behind the boards, meshing a diverse assortment of ominous synth and keyboard arrangements around Mega's deep lyricism. While Mega has had to weather Def Jam's businessman ways, and his own inner demons (jail time) to get here, he may never taste redemption this sweet again. —*Matt Conaway*

Hustler/Rapper / Feb. 26, 2002 / Body Shop ♦♦

Shortly after the release of Cormega's long-awaited debut album, *The Realness*, Body Shop Records released this mishmash of previously released recordings by the Queensbridge rapper. If you don't mind wading through this hodgepodge of brief snippets and freestyle rhymes, there are a few fully formed tracks here. Unfortunately, there aren't nearly enough to make this album worth your time unless you're an ardent fan. Overall, *Hustler/Rapper* seems like an insincere cash-in attempt by Body Shop Records. —*Jason Birchmeier*

The True Meaning / Jun. 11, 2002 / Legal Hustle ♦♦♦♦

Cormega continues to do on *The True Meaning* what he began on his previous album, *The Realness*—prove that he deserves his much-hyped reputation. After all, how many rappers would dare throw barbs at Nas? Jay-Z did and you saw what happened. Well, with the exception of "Love in Love Out"— where Cormega answers Nas' "Destroy & Rebuild" over a crackling sample of the beat from Isaac Hayes' "Your Love Is So Doggone Good"—he saves most of his barbs for the streets: the much-circulated Nas disses "A Slick Response" and "Realmatic" aren't here, if you're wondering. Still, he stands as a fearless, confident rapper on *The True Meaning*, calling himself "Queensbridge's most respected rapper" on "Ain't Gone Change," a brief testament where he declares his dedication to the underground rather than commerce. He may not care much for Nas, but Cormega definitely cares about hip-hop. Every track here bleeds with passion. Cormega has much to say about hip-hop culture (and street culture, in turn) and says it lucidly and articulately. You really want to hear what he has to say, and that's perhaps why the brevity of *The True Meaning*, which clocks in at under 40 minutes, is a bit disappointing. You want more. You really do. But Cormega doesn't waste any time, dropping two or three verses per song and then moving on to the next— giving you three minutes, at most, per track. There are a few songs that break from this formula: the big hooks of the title track and the Large Professor verse on "The Come Up," for instance. Yet for the most part, Cormega sticks to lyric spitting and not much else—no big-name guests, no skits, no girl-boy duets, no frills anywhere—precisely the reason why hip-hop purists have championed him. —*Jason Birchmeier*

Cosmic Slop Shop

Group / G-Funk, West Coast Rap, Gangsta Rap

After controversies over their label head and the horrific actions of group member Big Lurch, Cosmic Slop Shop's brief musical career will probably be better remembered for the strange situations that resulted from it. Composed of rappers Doonie Baby, Lurch, and producer Rick Rock, the group came together in the San Francisco Bay Area's Slop Shop Studios, the inspiration for their name along with the Funkadelic single "Cosmic Slop." Rock had worked on a number of indie releases, as well as a disc from Compton's Most Wanted, but found Lurch and Doonie took to his beats easier than most rappers he worked with. Meanwhile, James Mtume was looking at acts for his record label, and was turned onto the group by a rep for MCA Records. This was a curious situation, since his reputation in hip-hop circles was blemished, stemming from a feud with Stetsasonic over his outspoken condemnation of sampling. In 1997, the signing of Cosmic Slop Shop was met with raised eyebrows from his critics, who thought he was just smoothing over his perception in the hip-hop community. Still, the group released *Da Family* on Mtume's label in the summer of 1998. Despite the group's attempts to promote the "Sinful" single throughout the fall, it went nowhere on the charts. By 1999 they decided to go their separate ways instead of recording a second disc, leaving Rock to become a successful producer for Xibit and Busta Rhymes, among others. Doonie Baby became a freelance rapper in the California area, while Big Lurch became one of rap's most gruesome figures only three years later. In the summer of 2002, he was found by a friend roaming the streets of Los Angeles, naked and bloody. When investigated, police discovered that he had murdered and partially ate

his girlfriend after smoking PCP, and he was arrested and sent to prison soon after. —*Bradley Torreano*

● **Da Family** / Jun. 2, 1998 / MCA ♦♦♦

In 1988, producer/songwriter James Mtume generated some controversy with his stand against excessive sampling in hip-hop. Rap group Stetsasonic responded by attacking Mtume and defending sampling on "Talkin' All That Jazz," and others accused him of having an anti-rap attitude. But Mtume insisted that he wasn't against rap—he simply felt that too much sampling wasn't healthy for black music. And when Mtume launched his MCA-distributed Mtume Music Group label ten years later, it turned out that its first release was a rap album: *Da Family*. Cosmic Slop Shop took its name from Funkadelic's 1973 classic "Cosmic Slop," and George Clinton's influence is noticeable on such cuts as "Twizms," "Butterscotch," and "My World," although the group isn't as consistently Clinton-esque as Digital Underground. Based in the Bay Area, the hardcore rappers originally came from the South; but their rapid-fire tongue-twisters have a lot more in common with Spice 1 and Brotha Lynch Hung than the "booty music" that southern MCs were known for. While some of the lyrics are fairly clever, and some of the melodic tracks are infectious, the main problem with *Da Family* is the bigoted lyrics that pop up here and there. Gays and lesbians are called "faggots and dykes," while White women are labeled "bony-ass white bimbos." Insulting gays, lesbians, and white females isn't about "keeping it real"—it's about being divisive and hateful. —*Alex Henderson*

Count Bass D

Hip-Hop, Bass Music

Count Bass D is a rapper and multi-instrumentalist based in the country music capital of Nashville, unique in that he eschews sampling techniques in favor of recording his own keyboard/bass/drum grooves completely live in the studio. He grew up in the Bronx, London, and Canton, OH, and learned to play drums at age four through his father, a West Indian minister who encouraged him to perform music at his church. The Count quickly learned piano and organ, and added bass to his repertoire later on. Meanwhile, he fell in love with hip-hop and honed his rapping skills while hanging out with friends. After attending a music school in Pennsylvania and pursuing an interest in R&B and jazz, he enrolled at Middle Tennessee State University in Nashville for the sole purpose of using the school's equipment to finish a demo tape. While there, he also hosted his own rap video show on the campus television station. His demo tape wound up getting him a record deal, and his debut album, *Pre-Life Crisis*, was released in 1995. —*Steve Huey*

● **Pre-Life Crisis** / Sep. 26, 1995 / Sony ♦♦♦

The Coup

Group / Political Rap, Alternative Rap, Hardcore Rap, Underground Rap, Hip-Hop

The Coup were one of the most overtly political bands in rap history. Formed in the early '90s, The Coup were obviously influenced by the black power rhetoric of "conscious" rappers like Public Enemy and KRS-One, but they were perhaps even more inspired by a heavy-duty, leftist reading list that included Marx and Mao. Lead rapper/producer Boots (born Raymond Riley) was involved in political activism long before he was a musician; his fervent dedication to social change was the overriding influence on every Coup album. Second rapper E-Roc and DJ Pam the Funkstress rounded out the trio. Released in 1993, The Coup's debut album, *Kill My Landlord*, was a highly charged blend of leftist resistance and '70s funk. If it had been released a mere four or five years earlier, the highly politicized *Kill My Landlord* might have gained The Coup nationwide notoriety and platinum album sales. As it was, gangsta rap was all the rage, and *Kill My Landlord* achieved only moderate sales but nearly unanimous critical acclaim.

A year later, the Coup's follow-up, *Genocide & Juice*, continued their agenda of sociopolitical insubordination. Not surprisingly, the Coup again received more support from critics than the record buying public. The next several years saw the Coup go through career-threatening changes. They ended their association with their label, Wild Pitch, and suspended their activity as a band. With the band dormant, Boots went to work for a shipping company but continued his political activism. Among other endeavors, he headed the Young Comrades, a group of social activists whose activities included storming the Oakland City Council. Boots' rap partner, E-Roc, left the group, and Pam continued her DJing. In 1998, the Coup, now a duo of Boots and Pam, resurfaced on the Bay Area independent label Dogday. The result: *Steal This Album. Party Music*, The Coup's fourth studio effort, was issued in November 2001. —*Mtume Salaam*

Kill My Landlord / May 4, 1993 / Wild Pitch ✦✦✦
The heyday of Public Enemy and Boogie Down Productions was over by the time The Coup released their incendiary debut album *Kill My Landlord*. Gangsta hedonism had replaced black-power politics as the hip-hop menace *du jour*, and that's perhaps the only reason this revolution-minded outfit failed to become the controversial boogeymen they seem tailor-made to be. Unabashedly Marxist (the first line on the album is "Presto, read the Communist Manifesto…"), The Coup takes political rap to a whole new level of intelligence, attacking not only racism but also the economic and class factors that keep African Americans oppressed. Much of *Kill My Landlord* is fiercely polemical, but to the group's credit, it sounds too invigorating to resemble the hour-long lecture it could easily have been. There's a palpable sense of glee at some of the more transgressive statements: the album-opening one-two punch of "Dig It!" and "Not Yet Free," the pro-L.A. riot "The Coup," the anti-police brutality "I Know You." *Kill My Landlord* doesn't have as much of the wry humor or storytelling that would enrich later releases, but it is in evidence: "Last Blunt" is told from the perspective of a stoner who wants to quit but can't face the pressure of a tough everyday life. Lead rapper Boots Riley sprinkles his rhetoric with clever wordplay, declaiming in a deadpan baritone that resembles an eerily calm Chuck D. He's supported by a bed of thick, loping Oakland funk that blends vintage soul samples (courtesy of DJ Pam the Funkstress) with live instrumentation. Parts of the album are somewhat underdeveloped musically (especially over the second half), which means that it isn't quite as consistent as its successors. But the high points are brilliant, making *Kill My Landlord* well worth the hunt for Coup fans. —*Steve Huey*

Genocide & Juice / 1994 / Wild Pitch ✦✦✦✦
A subtler and more fully realized effort than the debut, *Genocide & Juice* finds The Coup truly coming into their own, refining their mix of revolutionary politics and easy-rolling funk into some of the best political hip-hop ever put to wax. The main difference here is a richly developed cast of characters, as Boots and E-Roc put human faces on their beliefs and paint sympathetic portraits of working-class African Americans, struggling to make ends meet any way they can, often stuck with little education and fewer options. Socialist ideology is rarely far from the surface, but because of the way it's presented, it seems just as logical in context as opposing racism. The opening three songs are intertwined together, and mark a quantum leap in the group's sophistication. "Fat Cats, Bigga Fish" introduces a small-time hustler scraping together a living; together with his cousin, he infiltrates a party for corporate fat cats, who happen to enjoy imitating rappers, and drop freestyles about their abuses of power on the screamingly funny "Pimps." Finally, on "Takin' These," the two hustlers rob the party blind, Robin Hood style, chanting a chorus lifted from *Lady and the Tramp*'s "The Siamese Cat Song." Just in itself, that trio is a tour de force, displaying a sharp satirical instinct that's rare in any form. Although there are a few missteps, the remainder of the album is more consistent than *Kill My Landlord*, which fell prey to some sleepy beats at times. "The Name Game" makes the point that a few famous rappers don't amount to much when there's no broad economic base to help average African Americans improve their lives. Another highlight is "Repo Man," a bitter yet catchy complaint that's about not just the villainous title character but also the circumstances that make him necessary. All in all, *Genocide & Juice* is an enormously sophisticated work that The Coup would only go on to better the next time out. —*Steve Huey*

● **Steal This Album** / Nov. 10, 1998 / Dogday ✦✦✦✦✦
Steal This Album is The Coup's masterstroke, taking the advances of *Genocide & Juice* to the next level and coming up with one of the most underappreciated hip-hop albums of the '90s. Down to a duo, The Coup officially becomes a vehicle for Boots Riley's observations, which it mostly was already; still, there's a greater focus simply from the fact that it's a product of one ambitious vision. Boots' impassioned political rhetoric is still in full force, but the main strengths of *Steal This Album* are its fleshed-out characters and witty, detailed, image-rich storytelling that would do Slick Rick proud. Its intellectual and emotional depth comes from Boots finding the humanity not only in his ideology but also in a much-maligned class of people, articulating their

frustrations and analyzing the world they live in from both the inside and outside. His flair for the dramatic reaches its apex on the seven-minute saga "Me and Jesus the Pimp in a '79 Granada Last Night." It's a complex, cinematic story about a young man who loathes his father—an abusive pimp who eventually beats his mother to death—but can't help internalizing some of the same behavior. Equally touching is "Underdogs," a heartbreaking account of the everyday reality of poverty. Boots' ironic wit is all over the rest of the record. The dark-humored "Breathing Apparatus" finds a gunshot victim with no health insurance pleading with his friend not to let doctors pull the plug. Elsewhere, the previous album's Repo Man returns (in the person of Del tha Funkee Homosapien) on "The Repo Man Sings for You"; and Boots acts out a gleefully provocative fantasy (on record, anyway) with "Piss on Your Grave," which concerns slave owner George Washington. The whole album is strikingly consistent, managing to be smart, funny, touching, and funky all at once; it's nothing short of brilliant. —*Steve Huey*

Party Music / Nov. 6, 2001 / 75 Ark ✦✦✦✦
The Coup finally attracted some publicity with their fourth album, *Party Music*, though it was for unfortunate reasons. The original cover, completed in June 2001, depicted Boots and Pam in front of an exploding World Trade Center, with Boots pushing the button on a detonator. Luckily, the album wasn't scheduled for release until after September 11, and the artwork was hastily withdrawn; nonetheless, it made the rounds on the Internet, and even briefly drew the attention of the FBI. Even if the image is now too provocative and emotionally charged, its anti-capitalist symbolism is appropriate for the album's contents, which mark a return to the often militant tone of The Coup's early work. Album openers "Everythang," "Ghetto Manifesto," and "Ride the Fence" are all rousing calls to action, and fellow left-wing populists Dead Prez make a guest appearance on "Get Up." There's also some of the pointed satire of *Genocide & Juice*—Boots makes "5 Million Ways to Kill a C.E.O." sound like a new dance craze, and there are some broad, "Pimps"-like stereotypes of rich folks on "Lazymuthafucka" (though they're intended as an antidote to even broader stereotypes of poor people). But Boots doesn't abandon the sensitive storytelling of *Steal This Album* either. "Wear Clean Draws" advises his young daughter on how to grow up strong in a harsh world, and "Nowalaters" is another stunning, emotionally complex story-song about a young man nearly duped into taking responsibility for a child that isn't his. Musically, Boots' production is the fullest The Coup has ever had on record, making heavy use of live instruments in creating a warm, organic re-creation of late-'70s synth funk. Other than that, *Party Music* doesn't really break much new ground for The Coup; it's more a consolidation of their strengths, touching on a little bit of everything they've done well in the past. Hopefully, it will stay in print longer than their first three records. —*Steve Huey*

Steal This Double Album / 2002 / Polemic ✦✦✦✦✦

Crash Crew

f. 1977, Harlem, NY
Group / Old School Rap
The six-man Crash Crew recorded a few old school anthems, one of which ("High Powered Rap") was released before Grandmaster Flash found a hit with the same jam (as "Freedom"). Based in Harlem's Lincoln Projects, the collective was formed by high school friends E.K. Mike C, Reggie Reg (Reginald Payne), La Shubee, Barry Bistro, G-Man, and DJ Darryl C (Darryl Calloway). Beginning around 1977, gigs at block parties and Harlem's Club 197 gave them experience, and E.K. Mike C's studio connection gave them a chance to record much earlier than most other rappers. Borrowing from the funk track "Get up and Dance" by Freedom, Crash Crew recorded a short demo named "High Powered Rap" and sold the self-released single to fans at shows. Time hasn't recorded whether Sugar Hill got the idea for a new recording based on the song from Crash Crew or some other source, but regardless, the first national hit for Grandmaster Flash & the Furious Five was 1980's "Freedom," based on the same song. The group's first release on Sugar Hill, the single reached the R&B charts—it was indeed far superior to Crash Crew's version—and caused some enmity between the two acts.

Ironically, Crash Crew soon made their own appearance on Sugar Hill, with quite a few tracks, including old school classics "We Are Known as MC's (We Turn Parties Out)" and "Breakin' Bells (Take Me to the Mardi Gras)." Even with five rappers, Crash Crew wasn't a very talented rap group; they excelled at party jams with a lot of repeat choruses instead of rapping. The group disappeared soon after, and none of the members continued in the music industry. In 2000, Sequel compiled their work for the collection *We Are Emcees*. —*John Bush*

● **We Are Emcees** / Jun. 12, 2001 / Sequel ◆◆◆◆

Credit to the Nation

Group / British Rap, Hip-Hop, Political Rap

A platform for the sensitive yet political lyrics of MC Fusion, chart rappers Credit to the Nation managed modest hits in Britain with 1993's "Call It What You Want" and 1994's "Teenage Sensation." The group comprised MC Fusion (born Matty Hanson in 1971, Wednesbury, West Midlands) along with a pair of dancers, T-Swing and Mista-G. Encouraged by agit-poppers Chumbawamba, Credit to the Nation signed to One Little Indian and debuted with a single that featured Chumbawamba, "Enough Is Enough." During mid-1993, "Call It What You Want" spent a few weeks on the charts, thanks in large part to its obvious hook—stolen from Nirvana's "Smells Like Teen Spirit." Debut album *Take Dis* followed by the end of the year, and an early 1994 single, "Teenage Sensation," reached number 24 on the charts. Doing little to dispel the notions of British rap as distinctly inferior to its American counterpart (at least, circa 1994), Fusion's lyrics were simplistic and his rapping style rather straightforward. Still, his lyrical themes were unabashedly important, and his tracks took on racism ("Rising Tide") and sexism ("Lady Needs Respect"), nearly every one a direct commentary on issues of the day. Credit to the Nation's second album, *Daddy Always Wanted Me to Grow a Pair of Wings*, fared badly with fans and record buyers, and a brief 1998 comeback with a track ("Tacky Love Song") sampling Radiohead's "High and Dry" failed to keep the group from disappearing. —*John Bush*

● **Take Dis** / 1993 / One Little Indian ◆◆◆

Daddy Always Wanted Me to Grow a Pair of Wings / 1996 / One Little Indian ◆◆◆

Keep Your Mouth Shut / Nov. 3, 1998 / EMI ◆◆

Crimewave

f. New York, NY

Group / East Coast Rap, Hardcore Rap

New York rapper Shamus started Crimewave in 1996, and six years later, in 2002, he actualized his dream, releasing the debut Crimewave album on his label of the same name. In addition to Shamus, Crimewave also includes Karachi-Raw, Fluid, Skar, and Maximillan. The group's debut album, *Scripture Won: The Definition Of...*, showcased the various members, giving them all a chance to shine. Each of the members come with a rather hardcore style, rapping about life as a rapper in New York: the hustle, the envy, the battles, the glory, and so on. —*Jason Birchmeier*

● **Scripture Won: The Beginning Of ...** / Mar. 26, 2002 / Crimewave ◆◆◆◆
*Scripture Won: The Beginning Of...*introduces the five-member rap group Crimewave. Shamus leads the group, both executive producing the album and writing the liner notes. All five members embody the same sort of ideals that characterize most New York rap collectives: rise from the ghetto, struggle to survive, strive for a dream, lose close friends, do some dirt, hustle for money, start a label, and finally, rise to the top of the rap game. Though Crimewave doesn't necessarily accomplish much more than their hardcore rap peers from New York (everyone from Biggie and Jigga to Mobb Deep and the Wu-Tang Clan), they preach these standard ideals with heart. These guys really have struggled to reach the position they're in on *Scripture Won*, and they tell you throughout the album how they did it and how they plan to continue doing it. Plus, they get some help from producers Psycho Les, Precision, and Alchemist, among others. —*Jason Birchmeier*

Crooked Lettaz

f. Mississippi

Group / Hip-Hop

With their own style of hip-hop observation through growing up on the wrong side of Mississippi, David Banner and Kamikaze wanted to let the world know of their ghetto upbringing when they formed Crooked Lettaz. With Penalty Records backing them up for the release of their 1999 debut *Grey Skies*, Banner and Kamikaze also spent a big chunk of their time lecturing at colleges for the sake of their Book Bank Project; a non-profit

organization that collects books for underprivileged kids in underprivileged neighborhoods. —*Mike DaRonco*

● **Grey Skies** / Apr. 20, 1999 / Penalty ◆◆◆
While the profile of Southern hip-hop had risen in the few years preceding this album's release, relatively little had come out of the state of Mississippi. That is until Crooked Lettaz released their debut album, *Grey Skies*. MCs David Banner and Kamikaze have contrasting styles that work well together as both spit out thoughtful lyrics on tracks like "Chicken & Swine," "Trill," and "I Know." Production-wise, the album is a fresh take on Southern hip-hop. "A Girl Named Cim" features live instrumentation, something rarely heard on hip-hop records from down South. "Firewater" cleverly blends blasting horns and popping snares along with, of all things, a Japanese koto, while "Get Crunk" cleverly reworks Run-D.M.C.'s classic "Rock Box." Overall, *Grey Skies* is an impressive effort, showing that there is more to the state of Mississippi than the blues. —*Jon Azpiri*

Cru

Group / Hip-Hop, Gangsta Rap, Hardcore Rap, Club/Dance

Cru's dark and explosive debut album in 1997, *Da Dirty 30*, was embraced by the hardcore set. The entirely in-house-produced album named after an investigation into New York City's corrupt 30th police precinct, is fiercely stark and eclectic, lifting samples from Portishead, Sade, and Stevie Wonder. Cru's lyrical content deals with the perils of life in the South Bronx and the hip-hop game. While much of their storytelling gratuitously glorifies the hip-hop gangsta lifestyle, their music is not without morals and messages as well. The various rhyme styles range from Onyx-like howling to b-boy notepad recitations. —*Michael Di Bella*

● **Da Dirty 30** / Jul. 15, 1997 / Def Jam ◆◆◆◆◆
Although it runs a little long and is lacking in imagination, Cru's *Da Dirty 30* is a solid debut from the hardcore rappers. Musically, *Da Dirty 30* works the standard post-gangsta, hardcore territory—there are deep bass grooves, but also menacing, skeletal soundscapes in the vein of the Wu-Tang Clan. Lyrically, Cru can be a little weak, but there are times when the crew pulls it all together, and at those moments, *Da Dirty 30* is strong, invigorating hardcore hip-hop. —*Leo Stanley*

Crucial Conflict

f. 1995, Chicago, IL

Group / Hip-Hop, Hardcore Rap, Urban

Blending Cypress Hill's weed philosophy with a self-styled hopalong hip-hop sound based on the Old West, Chicago's Crucial Conflict hit the airwaves in 1996 with the marijuana ode "Hay." Members Wildstyle, Kilo, Coldhard, and Never grew up on Chicago's west side and began rapping as a way to pass time on the mean streets. Signed to Universal in 1996, the foursome hit the R&B Top Five with the June release of *The Final Tic*, which went gold later that year. *Good Side, Bad Side* followed in 1998. —*John Bush*

● **The Final Tic** / Jul. 2, 1996 / Pallas/Universal ◆◆◆◆◆
Crucial Conflict is a hip-hop collective featuring Coldhard, Wildstyle, Kilo, and Never. On their debut album, *The Final Tic*, the group has created a distinctive musical style, which they've dubbed "Rodeo," as well as "Snappin," a term they use to refer to their own brand of rhyme. Of course, the group aren't quite the trailblazers they would like to be—this is still funky, hardcore rap at its most basic. However, it sounds damn good, particularly when they work a deep groove and catchy hook like they do on the hit single "Hay." The rest of *The Final Tic* isn't quite up to that standard, but it provides enough thrills to satisfy most fans of their sound. —*Leo Stanley*

Good Side, Bad Side / Oct. 20, 1998 / Pallas/Universal ◆◆
On their second album, these Bone Thugs-N-Harmony wannabes unleash some mighty rolls of the tongue in their collective quest to be among the fastest rappers in hip-hop, but their stale sound and even weaker rhymes all but render them useless in the global music community. There's a consistent Southern vibe and some competent verbal flexing on the 18 cuts that make up *Good Side, Bad Side*, but Crucial Conflict have neither the staying power nor the brains to make it more than another fleeting gust of wind in the hip-hop air. The muscle that gives them their power—again, their mile-a-minute rap style that swings between singsongy R&B and gangsta toughness—has been done before; there's no denying the beef that the Bone boys have with the Crucial crew. One OK track: "Scummy." —*Michael Gallucci*

Crusaders for Real Hip Hop

Group / Alternative Rap

Looking back to hip-hop's glory days as early as 1990, Crusaders for Real Hip-Hop recorded one album—*Deja Vu, It's '82*—for Profile. Founded by producer Tony D, the group also included rappers Don Nots, Mr. Law, and Rahzii. —*John Bush*

● **Deja Vu, It's '82** / 1992 / Profile ◆◆◆

The title *Deja Vu, It's '82* implies that this CD is an exercise in hip-hop nostalgia—that in 1992, the interracial rap group was nostalgic for the hip-hop of the early '80s. But truth be told, *Deja Vu, It's '82* isn't nearly as retro as its name implies. Producer Tony D is hardly oblivious to the hip-hop production styles of the early '90s, and his extensive use of samples will prevent anyone from mistaking this album for a 1982 recording. Further, the rapping of group members Don Nots, Rahzii, and Mr. Law is quite mindful of early-'90s rapping styles and will not be mistaken for the early-'80s rapping of Dr. Jeckyll & Mr. Hyde, the Treacherous Three, or Grandmaster Flash and the Furious Five. The pro-marijuana anthem "Higher" owes a creative debt to Cypress Hill, although Crusaders for Real Hip Hop are far from gangsta rap—the thing they get from Cypress is an appreciation of marijuana, not a knack for violent lyrics. Most of their lyrics are standard New York boasting fare, and like so many East Coast MCs of the early '90s, the Crusaders make a point of emphasizing their flows. Though tunes like "We Love the Hotties" and "That's How It Is" aren't brilliant or distinctive, they're catchy, likable items that make ample use of the MCs' strong techniques. This decent, if unremarkable, CD wasn't a big seller, and it turned out to be the little-known group's only album for Profile. —*Alex Henderson*

Cuban Link (Felix Delgado)

b. Havana, Cuba

Vocals / Latin Rap

Born Felix Delgado, Cuban Link is best known as a member of the Latino hip-hop group the Terror Squad, which consists of Big Punisher, Fat Joe, Prospect, Armageddon, and Triple Seis. As his name would suggest, Cuban Link was born in Havana, Cuba, and his family immigrated to the U.S. in 1980, eventually settling in the South Bronx. Cuban Link first garnered national attention with his appearance on the Beatnuts' classic, "Off the Books," along with fellow Latino rapper Big Pun. Cuban Link got even more acclaim as a member of the Terror Squad, where the young rapper was mentored by Fat Joe and Big Punisher. While often overshadowed by the large presence of Joe and Pun, Cuban Link more than held his own with his charisma and stage presence. In 2000 Cuban Link released *24-K*, his first solo album. —*Jon Azpiri*

● **24-K** / 2000 / ◆◆◆

With Big Pun's unfortunate passing, Cuban Link's debut, *24-K*, shoulders a considerable burden, as it will play a major role in determining how future Terror Squad endeavors unfold. Dependant on its level of success, Link's solo bow will either lead to a renewed anticipation in the Latino based crew or a retreated interest; the enigmatic album does a little of both. As expected, the commercial formula that came so easily to the charismatic Pun is emulated here, as Link's infectiously naughty "Project Party," featuring Sunkiss, and the sweat-inducing drum patterns of the Neptune produced "Still Telling Lies" beg for heavy rotation. While a slew of less redeeming crossover reaches exemplify the carefree existence Link frequently portrays. Frivolous collaborations of this sort stand in stark contrast to the depth he exudes on touching odes to his mom ("Hey Mama"), and Pun ("Flowers for the Dead"). On "90 Miles and Running" he laments "don't let the pretty face fool ya" and, true to his words, the fortunes of *24-K* evolve dramatically when Link places a premium on the facets he is most adept in; taking it to the streets. A more focused artist surfaces on "Murda Murda," which features Ja Rule, and the high-impact "Men of Business," with Noreaga, Kool G Rap, Lord Tarik, and M.O.P. Yet, the LP's most essential cuts are highlighted by the obvious chemistry between Link and his T-Squad brethren: Fat Joe on the paranoid "Why Me" and a posthumous appearance from Pun on "Toe to Toe," where both MCs trade powerful verses over the Roots' "Clones" and Mobb Deep's "G.O.D. Pt 3." *24-K* is a diverse debut, but it is one that settles rather then stirs. Clocking in at a laborious 73 minutes, this long-winded effort, much like Link himself, harbors overambitious tendencies, as the artist's appeasing nature prevents *24-K* from achieving a lasting identity. —*Matt Conaway*

Cut Chemist (Lucas Macfadden)

DJ, Producer, Turntables, Engineer / Hip-Hop, Underground Rap, Turntablism

As well as being one of the ablest solo turntablists on the globe, Cut Chemist is also a member of two highly rated crews: underground rap kings Jurassic 5 and the Latin-funk band Ozomatli. He came up with the L.A. rap group Unity Committee, and debuted on wax with the B side of UC's 1993 single "Unified Rebelution." The track, "Lesson 4: The Radio," was a tribute to and continuation of Double D and Steinski's seminal hip-hop collage masterpiece "Lessons 1-3," and included nods to Indeep, Bob James, Spoonie Gee, and Dan Ackroyd.

Soon after the record's release, Unity Committee came together with another group, Rebels of Rhythm, to form Jurassic 5. Cut Chemist kept quite busy with the group, contributing "Lesson 6" to the group's eponymous EP and producing the entire record. He also delved into remixing (DJ Shadow, Liquid Liquid) and outside work (scratching for Less Than Jake; appearing with another Los Angeles group, Ozomatli). In mid-1997, Cut Chemist recorded his album debut, *Live at the Future Primitive Sound Session*, with Shortkut of Invisibl Skratch Piklz. His tracks have also appeared on two seminal turntablist compilations, *Return of the DJ, Vol. 1* and *Deep Concentration*. —*John Bush*

● **Live at the Future Primitive Sound Session** / Apr. 7, 1998 / Ubiquity ◆◆◆◆◆

Working interchangeably, Cut Chemist and Shortkut handled a total of five turntables on this album, recorded live in San Francisco. Unlike the vast majority of turntablist albums, *Live at the Future Primitive Sound Session* ably approximates the incredible excitement of actually *watching* a world-class DJ team in action. Old school fans will recognize much of the material (from Eric B. & Rakim, Ultramagnetic MC's, Newcleus, Afrika Bambaataa, even a dramatically reworked version of the Beastie Boys' "Egg Man"), but there are quite a few rare grooves in the mix as well—including what could be the first use of Homer & Jethro in a hip-hop context. Continually inventive and entertaining, *Live at the Future Primitive Sound Session* is one of the early turntablist classics. —*John Bush*

Brainfreeze / 1999 / Sixty 7 ◆◆◆◆◆

The hip-hop mix tape has come so far. As passed down through DJs such as Kid Capri and Funkmaster Flex, it has served essentially the same purpose—as a compilation of segued-together cuts rather than a stand-alone work itself and, therefore, an archetypal soundtrack to house parties or underground gatherings. But taking its cue instead from Grandmaster Flash, who pioneered the form commercially on his landmark cut classic "The Adventures of Grand Master Flash on the Wheels of Steel," *Brainfreeze* transforms the mix tape into a genuine piece of musical art, a sampladelic, turntablist collage that may be the apotheosis of—or at least a turning point for—the genre. Even prior to the release of the album, the collaboration between Cut Chemist and DJ Shadow had developed an almost legendary buzz. In the fall of 1999 the two kicked off a series of live performances sponsored by San Francisco art collective and record label Future Primitive Sound. *Brainfreeze* captures for posterity, in two uninterrupted takes, the live DAT rehearsal tapes from the duo's premiere show together, and it is an amazing display of spontaneous music making. The music splits the difference between the groundbreaking, Brian Eno-worthy soundscapes that have characterized DJ Shadow's solo career and the ebullient, breakbeat-savvy, street-corner jive of old school-style rap, as exemplified by Chemist's crew Jurassic 5. Some of the snippets cut and pasted here will be readily familiar to longtime fans of rap music, and some formed the basis for tracks on Shadow's first two albums, but the majority are from extremely rare and generally forgotten 45s absent from the crates of even the most ardent beatdiggers. The project itself signifies a duality of sacrifice and resurrection. Sacrifice applies because in the act of spinning these premium records the DJs were literally destroying or damaging their rare vinyl. Also, due to the music's improvisational nature, the set could never possibly be repeated in quite the same way. On the other hand, it is a resurrection in that it synthesizes a half-century of soul and funk music that has fallen through mainstream cracks, thereby revealing an entire alternate history of principally black urban music. Unfortunately, the album stops short of being the actual history lesson it might have been, as it fails to list the artists and song credits. Some of the value in uncovering them in the first place is, as a result, nullified. It is a minor blemish, however, when measured against the visionary, forward-looking aura of *Brainfreeze*. It is a dizzyingly brilliant, virtuoso work of two exceedingly fecund imaginations. —*Stanton Swihart*

Bunky's Pick [Single] / Aug. 7, 2001 / Stones Throw ✦✦✦
The triple-split single *Bunky's Pick* offers a track each from Stones Throw heroes Cut Chemist and Madlib, plus Billy Wooten's "In the Rain" (all but the Madlib cut also appear on the brilliant Stones Throw compilation *The Funky 16 Corners*). Cut Chemist's track is eight minutes of hard-driving funk turntablism, while Madlib's "6 Variations of In the Rain" is a typically imaginative yet rambling after-hours jam. —*John Bush*

Product Placement EP / Nov. 1, 2001 / One29 ✦✦✦✦
Despite its extremely limited release, *Brainfreeze* quickly garnered a wellspring of underground attention that soon turned into ever-growing adulation, in part based upon the almost mythic stature accorded the original live shows from which it arose, oftentimes by mere word of mouth. The plaudits were well deserved but, as a result, the album soon became one of the most rabidly sought after collectibles of the newly minted millennium, with bootlegged copies selling for upwards of $50 on eBay. Because of this unforeseen demand, DJ Shadow and Cut Chemist were ultimately forced to pull the album from circulation. (It eventually saw a limited re-release.) That same demand, however, might well have been the impetus that led to a second collaboration. Whatever the catalyst behind it, *Product Placement* makes for an equally sensational recording. The format remains in place. Two extended, uninterrupted tracks are built from scratch out of rare vinyl. The resulting music makes use of some of the same samples as its predecessor, but a large portion of the album is given over to fresh 45s, and even the holdovers find new contexts in which to fit. Again, most of these are extremely rare slabs of filthy great soul and funk, spun and segued in such a seamless manner that you can't help occasionally catching your breath at the effect. Shadow and Chemist could clearly claim master status on their instruments by this point but, more importantly, each had such a profound knowledge and love of the obscure music used here that the collages sound instantly classic. But *Product Placement* is also a different animal from *Brainfreeze* in several respects, one of them implied by the album title. Interspersed throughout the two mixes is a wealth of vintage jingles and commercial advertisements for everything from gas to milk to motocross. The impact is recognizable from the first notes, turning the music whimsical and tongue-in-cheek, a tangible playfulness further enhanced by a wealth of borrowed old school rap samples. *Product Placement* even dips into rock and psychedelic music. The duo's liberal use of the Outcasts' "Loving You Sometimes" during the album's second track works to particularly brilliant effect, transforming what was already a wizardly DJ display into a heady, tripped-out delight. —*Stanton Swihart*

Cut 'N' Move

f. Copenhagen, Denmark
Group / Urban, Acid Jazz, Club/Dance
Formed in Copenhagen, Denmark, in the early '90s, Cut 'N' Move was a club-oriented group specializing in dance-rap, urban contemporary, and acid jazz. Hip-hop was a major influence on the group, but Cut 'N' Move's recordings weren't made with rap's hardcore in mind—it was in European dance-music circles that Cut 'N' Move received some attention. Members included rapper MC Zipp (who rapped with only a very slight trace of a Scandinavian accent), female singer Thera, and producers/mixers Jorn K and Per Holm. In 1991 Epic released the group's debut album, *Get Serious*, and chose the title song (a rap-dance number) as the first single. 2000's *The Sound of Now* followed after a long absence. —*Alex Henderson*

Get Serious / Jul. 30, 1991 / Soulpower ✦✦
Ranging from dance-rap to sleek R&B/pop and acid jazz (which isn't really jazz—it's dance music with jazz overtones), *Get Serious* sounds a lot like the type of club-oriented album that could have come out of England in the early 1990s. But Cut 'N' Move wasn't British; the group was based in Copenhagen, Denmark. Like much of the pop that was recorded in neighboring Sweden, *Get Serious* contains nothing but English lyrics. The CD's most impressive track is the haunting "No Connection"; most of its other selections fall under the heading of likable, but not mindblowing. Opting for variety, Cut 'N' Move provides funky dance-rap tunes like "Say It Loud," "Cyclone Zone," and "Girl, You Got Me Working," along with decent R&B offerings such as "Message of Love" and "How to Allow It." Although not a huge seller in the U.S., *Get Serious* received some attention in European club circles. —*Alex Henderson*

Frankie Cutlass

b. Puerto Rico
Producer / Freestyle, Club/Dance
Much like his idol Marley Marl, Frankie Cutlass gathered MCs and vocalists under the umbrella of projects—which he spearheaded as producer and mixer—while still maintaining an edge as a DJ by playing consistently in clubs, both dance and hip-hop oriented. Originally from Puerto Rico, he moved to Spanish Harlem in New York with his family while still a child, and began to grasp America's culture firsthand through the influence of hip-hop. His brother, a member of the Zulu Nation, taught him to DJ, and Cutlass first hit the decks in the '80s at the age of 12. He joined his own crew later on, working with DJ Funkmaster Flex's Flip Squad. By the early '90s he had moved into production as well, working with TKA, K7, and the Cover Girls. The recording sphere beckoned, and by 1994 he had produced his first record, "Puerto Rico Ho." It and the later single, "Boriquas on the Set," became underground hits, spurring Frankie Cutlass to sign with Relativity Records. His first album with the label, 1997's *Politics & Bullshit*, showed his enthusiasm for the old school rap he had grown up with. The album's single, "The Cypher, Pt. 3," reunited several veterans of Marley Marl productions, including Biz Markie, Roxanne Shanté, Big Daddy Kane, and Craig G. Also lending their talents were Mobb Deep, Redman, Method Man, and Smif-n-Wessun. —*John Bush*

The Frankie Cutlass Show / Jan. 14, 1994 / Moonroof ✦✦✦
● **Politics & Bullshit** / Feb. 11, 1997 / Relativity ✦✦✦✦
Frankie Cutlass has done the same thing with this, his second album, as he did with his first—produce a bunch of beats and invite some famous MCs to rock over them, package it up, and ship it out. Though a few of the pairings are a bit questionable, the artists are great; unfortunately, the album is on the short side. What's here is very good indeed. It's hard to go wrong when you have Redman, Sadat X, Biz Markie, Craig G, Kool G Rap, M.O.P., Fat Joe, Keith Murray, Heltah Skeltah, the Lost Boyz, and more to fill up your album with music for you. Most surprisingly, there's a comeback track by one of the all-time greatest female MCs, Roxanne Shanté. —*Brad Mills*

Cutthroat

b. Ypsilanti, MI
Vocals / Underground Rap, Hip-Hop
A young lyricist from Ypsilanti, MI, Cutthroat started practicing the lyrical craft at the tender age of 14. Serious about his mission to master the art of MCing, Cutthroat reached out to the ever-thriving eastern Michigan hip-hop underground and found common ground with a number of MCs, DJs, and producers. Though the immense skills of Detroit artists like Eminem, D-12, Slum Village, and Royce 5'9 might make any MI rapper think twice about the MC field, Cutthroat persisted, forming his own record label, Golden Glair Records. With a little help from Detroit area rap pioneer Mark Kempf (the man who helped Eminem and Bizarre get their start) and his Silent Records staff, Cutthroat was able to release his debut full-length album, *Analyze & Interpret*, in late 2000. —*M.F. Di Bella*

● **Analyze & Interpret** / 2000 / Golden Glair ✦✦✦
There is a tangible sense of urgency throughout the debut release from Ypsilanti, MI, native Cutthroat. Attempting to carve out a niche in the Detroit area rap scene, Cutthroat comes across as a talented, raw lyricist of the underground variety. A veteran of basement tapes and painstaking years of building his craft, the Midwest MC spits with a rapid-fire, flaming tongue. His deliberate style is complemented by equally tailored production schemes of guttural bass drums and low-register piano tones provided by O.P.M. The underground mantra of tearing down artists who stress gloss over substance at times gets repetitive on this effort, but the sentiment is well taken nonetheless. Detroit-area underground rap has always had the benefit of influences from both coasts, and *Analyze & Interpret* is no exception. The tri-metropolitan styles of Eastern Michigan's Ypsilanti/Ann Arbor/Detroit underground railroad are reflected most potently on the top-notch crew love track "The Cypha"; the MCs featured could certainly give Eminem's D-12 crew a run for their money. While some of the tracks come off better than others, none of the 17 offerings is wasted or without some pith or heartfelt

emotion. The most sincere composition is the irresistible "From My Eyes to Your Ears," a didactic ode to life's daily struggles. While the style employed does not always engage and occasionally tries to cram too many words into rhymes, Cutthroat's fierce lyrical energy rarely misses the mark. —*M.F. Di Bella*

Cybotron

f. 1980, Detroit, MI

Group / Techno, Electro, Detroit Techno, Club/Dance

The seminal electro group Cybotron provided the first home for the recordings of techno godfather Juan Atkins. With partner Rick Davis (aka 3070), Atkins recorded several of electro's best moments; the singles "Alleys of Your Mind," "Enter," and "Clear," were dark dystopias of the post-industrial steel city within tight Kraftwerk-inspired funk. Their success prompted Fantasy Records to sign the group, and release 1983's *Enter* LP. Atkins left soon after due to artistic differences (specifically, Davis' defined pop slant), and later defined early Detroit techno with his recordings as Model 500. Davis continued to release albums as Cybotron into the mid-'90s, though the mystical R&B direction of efforts like *Empathy* and *Cyber Ghetto* were quite a turn from the group's beginnings. For fans of electro and techno, Cybotron ended when Juan Atkins left. —*John Bush*

Enter / 1983 / Fantasy ◆◆◆◆

Later reissued in 1990 as *Clear*, the original incarnation of Cybotron's debut had a considerably different track listing than the one later generations were accustomed to, a slower, less-aggressive progression of funk-washed proto-techno that many have argued kept the spirit of the album alive the best. From the deadeye synth pop of "Enter" and "Alleys of Your Mind" to the obligingly experimental flip of "Cosmic Cars," "Cosmic Radiance," and "El Salvador," *Enter*'s fusion of Kraftwerk and Public Image Ltd. was never lost or frustratingly inaccessible, a superior sequence of electronic optimism and increasingly common concerns of a megasterile future. —*Dean Carlson*

★ **Clear** / 1990 / Fantasy ◆◆◆◆◆

The only old school electro LP with any amount of staying power (thanks in part to its release on Fantasy), this CD release of the Cybotron album previously known as *Enter* includes crucial early singles like "Alleys of Your Mind," "Cosmic Cars," and techno's first defining moment, "Clear." The collision of Atkins' vision for cosmic funk and the arena-rock instincts of Rick Davis result in a surprisingly cohesive album, dated for all the right reasons and quite pop minded. Ecological and political statements even crop up with the final tracks, "Cosmic Raindance" and "El Salvador." —*John Bush*

Cypress Hill

f. 1988, Los Angeles, CA, **db.** 1993

Group / West Coast Rap, Latin Rap, Rap-Rock, Alternative Rap, Hardcore Rap

Cypress Hill were notable for being the first Latino hip-hop superstars, but they became notorious for their endorsement of marijuana, which actually isn't a trivial thing. Not only did the group campaign for its legalization, but their slow, rolling bass-and-drum loops pioneered a new, stoned funk that became extraordinary influential in '90s hip-hop—it could be heard in everything from Dr. Dre's G-funk to the chilly layers of English trip-hop. DJ Muggs crafted the sound, and B Real, with his pinched, nasal voice, was responsible for the rhetoric that made them famous. The pro-pot position became a little ridiculous over time, but there was no denying that the actual music had a strange, eerie power, particularly on the band's first two albums. Although B Real remained an effective lyricist and Muggs' musical skills did not diminish, the group's third album, *Temples of Boom*, was perceived by many critics as self-parodic, and the group appeared to disintegrate shortly afterward, though Muggs and B Real regrouped toward the end of the '90s to issue more material.

DVX, the original incarnation of Cypress Hill, formed in 1986 when Cuban-born brothers Sen Dog (born Senen Reyes, November 20, 1965) and Mellow Man Ace hooked up with fellow Los Angeles residents Muggs (born Lawrence Muggerud, January 28, 1968) and B Real (born Louis Freese, June 2, 1970). The group began pioneering a fusion of Latin and hip-hop slang, developing their own style by the time Mellow Man Ace left the group in 1988. Renaming themselves Cypress Hill after a local street, the group continued to perform around L.A., eventually signing with Ruffhouse/Columbia in 1991.

With its stoned beats, B Real's exaggerated nasal whine and cartoonish violence, the group's eponymous debut became a sensation in early 1992, several months after its initial release. The singles "How I Could Just Kill a Man" and "The Phuncky Feel One" became underground hits, and the group's public pro-marijuana stance earned them many fans among the alternative rock community. Cypress Hill followed the album with *Black Sunday* in the summer of 1993, and while it sounded remarkably similar to the debut, it nevertheless became a hit, entering the album charts at number one and spawning the crossover hit "Insane in the Brain." With *Black Sunday*, Cypress Hill's audience became predominantly white collegiate suburbanites, which caused them to lose some support in the hip-hop community. The group didn't help matters much in 1995, when they added a new member, drummer Bobo, and toured with the fifth Lollapalooza prior to the release of their third album, *Temples of Boom*. A darker, gloomier affair than their first two records, *Temples of Boom* was greeted with mixed reviews upon its fall 1995 release, and while it initially sold well, it failed to generate a genuine hit single. However, it did perform better on the R&B charts than it did on the pop charts.

Instead of capitalizing on their regained hip-hop credibility, Cypress Hill slowly fell apart. Sen Dog left in early 1996 and Muggs spent most of the year working on his solo album. *Muggs Presents the Soul Assassins* was released to overwhelmingly positive reviews in early 1997, leaving Cypress Hill's future in much doubt until the release of *IV* in 1998. Sen Dog had come back for the record. He had left because he felt he did not get enough mic time, but after a few years with a rock band he was more than happy to return. Two years later, the group released the double-disc set *Skull & Bones*, which featured a disc of hip-hop and a disc of their more rock-inspired material. Appropriately, the album also included rock and rap versions of the single "Superstar," bringing Cypress Hill's quest for credibility and crossover hits full circle. The ensuing videos for both versions featured many famous rap and rock musicians talking about their profession, and the song was a smash on MTV because of it. In the winter of 2001, the group came back with *Stoned Raiders*, another album to heavily incorporate rock music. —*Stephen Thomas Erlewine*

★ **Cypress Hill** / Aug. 13, 1991 / Ruffhouse ◆◆◆◆◆

It's hard enough to transform an entire musical genre—Cypress Hill's eponymous debut album revolutionized hip-hop in several respects. Although they weren't the first Latino rappers, nor the first to mix Spanish and English, they were the first to achieve a substantial following, thanks to their highly distinctive sound. Along with the Beastie Boys and Public Enemy, Cypress Hill was also one of the first rap groups to bridge the gap with fans of both hard rock *and* alternative rock. And, most importantly, they created a sonic blueprint that would become one of the most widely copied in hip-hop. In keeping with their pro-marijuana stance, Cypress Hill intentionally crafted its music to sound stoned—lots of slow, lazy beats, fat bass, weird noises, and creepily distant-sounding samples. The surreal lyrical narratives were almost exclusively spun by B Real in a nasal, singsong, instantly recognizable delivery that only added to the music's hazy, evocative atmosphere; as a frontman, he could be funny, frightening, or just plain bizarre (again, kind of like the experience of being stoned). Whether he's taunting cops or singing nursery rhyme-like choruses about blasting holes in people with shotguns, B Real's blunted-gangsta posture is nearly always underpinned by a cartoonish sense of humor. It's never clear how serious the threats are, but that actually makes them all the more menacing. The sound and style of *Cypress Hill* was hugely influential, particularly on Dr. Dre's boundary-shattering 1992 blockbuster *The Chronic*; yet despite its legions of imitators, *Cypress Hill* still sounds fresh and original today, simply because few hip-hop artists can put its sound across with such force of personality or imagination. —*Steve Huey*

Black Sunday / Jul. 20, 1993 / Ruffhouse ◆◆◆◆

Black Sunday made Cypress Hill's connection to rock & roll more explicit, with its heavy metal-like artwork and noisier, more dissonant samples (including, naturally, stoner icons Black Sabbath). It's a slightly darker affair than its groundbreaking predecessor, with the threats of violence more urgent and the pot obsession played to the hilt (after all, it was a crucial part of their widespread appeal). Apart from those subtle distinctions, the sound of *Black Sunday* is pretty much the same as *Cypress Hill*, refining the group's innovations into an accessible bid for crossover success. In fact, it's a little startling how often *Black Sunday* recycles musical ideas and even lyrical catchphrases from the endlessly inventive debut. And the rock-derived, verse-chorus song structures start to sound a little formulaic by the end of the record (how many choruses feature Sen Dog repeating part of whatever B Real just said?). But in spite of that, *Black Sunday* still sounds vital and lively, since the group has a surer sense of craft. Most of the tracks are fleshed out into structured songs, in contrast to the brief sketches that punctuated *Cypress Hill*. The album benefits immensely from the resulting clutch of excellent singles (and songs that could have been), and while a couple of tracks feel redundant and underdeveloped, *Black Sunday* is overall a consistent, engaging listen, especially the flawless first half or so. Unfortunately, it's also the group's last great album, thanks to the musical recycling operation that began here and would handicap much of their subsequent work. —*Steve Huey*

Cypress Hill III: Temples of Boom / Oct. 31, 1995 / Ruffhouse ✦✦
On Cypress Hill's third album it seems as if all the blunts and bong hits finally began to catch up with the group. Where *Black Sunday* had been a rousing album perfect for moshing crowds, *Temples of Boom* shows few signs of energy, instead feeling tranquil, sedate, and downright lazy. Muggs' beats are more evocative than ever here, but rather than sounding invigorating they sound disorientating, even a bit lulling. Given Cypress Hill's affinity for blazing up the bud, trippy beats aren't necessarily a bad thing by any means, but without any inspired rhymes to accompany his beats, Muggs' efforts feel empty. B Real can't manage to muster much energy on any of these tracks, and Sen Dog comes off sounding like a farce; furthermore, the fact that neither of the MCs manage to come up with anything inventive in terms of lyrics only further hurts the album. Overall, this is a lackluster album with only the smoked-out beats being its engaging feature, and even the beats will more likely put listeners to sleep than inspire them. Here it became clear that the inventive spirit of Cypress Hill's debut had been long exhausted, and the large audience garnered by the commercial success of *Black Sunday* began receding. —*Jason Birchmeier*

Unreleased & Revamped EP / Aug. 1996 / Ruffhouse ✦✦
On *Cypress Hill III: Temples of Boom*, Cypress Hill sounded a little tired, clinging to their slow, druggy beat a bit too much. The *Unreleased & Revamped* EP was released a few months after the album, which signals that the EP is an attempt to salvage their reputation. That suspicion is confirmed by the list of remixers and collaborators. None of the guest musicians—from the Fugees and A Tribe Called Quest to Redman, MC Eiht, and Erick Sermon—are traditional West Coast rappers, they are musicians that are pushing the boundaries of hip-hop in 1996. In another attempt to restore their street credibility, Cypress Hill have distanced themselves from the alternative rock audience they cultivated through an appearance at Lollapalooza and with *Temples of Boom*. So, the group has clearly tried to make a break from their trademark sound and their attempts are marginally successful. "Boom Biddy Bye Bye," which features a remix from the Fugees, is particularly successful, but most of the EP contains the germs of an idea, not the fruition of one. Still, the EP is encouraging to long-term fans who may have thought that Cypress Hill had lost the plot with *Temples of Boom*. *Unreleased & Revamped* suggests they are about to get back on track. —*Stephen Thomas Erlewine*

IV / Oct. 6, 1998 / Ruffhouse ✦✦
And the bongloads just keep getting packed deeper and deeper...even if no one really cares. On their fourth album of herb-induced hip-hop, the once-interesting, now-derivative trio turns itself over to the world of played-out beats and rhymes. Tired tales of guns, gangs and, of course, weed fire up *IV*, making it sound more like a lame attempt at a reunion gig than the next chapter in the revitalization of their career, which it should be. Worse, they've added stupid sex raps to their repertoire, dulling their edge and throwing Cypress Hill into the discard pile with countless other once-relevant hip-hoppers. Still, the sonic landscape that they trudge across here is occasionally sprinkled with some wild scenes. The Godzilla-like screams of their debut have been replaced by slinkier, more bass-driven beats, but there's also a lot of aural action going on in the background. Which, alas, doesn't quite compensate for the overriding flaws. —*Michael Gallucci*

Los Grandes Exitos en Espanol / Oct. 19, 1999 / Ruffhouse ✦✦
Cypress Hill has always been one of the most popular hip-hop groups in Latino circles (most of the group has a Hispanic background), so an album of *Grandes Exitos en Espanol* makes much more sense than it would for Method Man or Jay Z. For anyone who doesn't understand Spanish (especially fans who have heard all of these productions, but one, before), the album is occasionally diverting just to hear the group rhyming in Spanish.

"Insane in the Brain" becomes "Loco en el Coco," "How I Could Just Kill a Man" becomes "No Entiendes la Onda," and "I Wanna Get High" becomes "Yo Quiero Fumar." The bonus track is "Siempre Peligroso," recorded with Fermin IV Caballero of Control Machete. —*Keith Farley*

Skull & Bones / Apr. 25, 2000 / Columbia ✦✦✦✦
Despite the best efforts of DJ Muggs, Cypress Hill ran out of gas fairly quickly, entering a tailspin as soon as their third album. Back at full strength with the return of Sen Dog, Cypress Hill devised a full-scale comeback with their fifth album, *Skull & Bones*. The idea behind the album was to divide it into two—a hip-hop disc (*Skull*) and a rock disc (*Bones*). This would guarantee some publicity, at the very least, and, hopefully, it would win over the new generation of adolescents who flipped for rap-metal acts like Kid Rock and Limp Bizkit. On paper, it's a sound theory, but there was a slight flaw—the group is kind of lame when they rock. Their band is competent enough, and B Real's voice does sound good with overdriven guitars, but their rock songs utterly fall apart, since they have no hooks, no catchy riffs, and no character. If rap-rock was all there was to *Skull & Bones*, it would be a bit of an embarrassment. Fortunately, the *Skulls* disc is their finest effort since *Black Sunday*. Muggs is in prime form, creating funky, ominous, evocative soundscapes, which B Real makes the most of with fluid rhymes. At times, B Real does descend into tastelessness ("Stank Ass Hoe"), and neither he nor Sen Dog really find any new lyrical ground, but sonically, *Skulls* is a blast; B Real's whine and Sen Dog's gruff, blunt style are the perfect match for Muggs' darkly cinematic soundscapes, and, on a purely sonic level, it's quite intoxicating. At their best, Cypress Hill is a hip-hop experience unlike any other, and, ignoring the *Bones*, this is the best they've been in a long, long time. —*Stephen Thomas Erlewine*

Live at the Fillmore / Dec. 12, 2000 / Sony ✦✦✦✦
While Cypress Hill's *Skull & Bones* album showcased its sudden interest in merging hard rock with rap, *Live at the Fillmore* stands as a better testament to the group's newfound ability to synthesize the two styles into an invigorating formula. The album gets off to a fiery start with some rowdy renditions of the group's early-'90s material—"Hand on the Pump," "How I Could Just Kill a Man," "Insane in the Membrane"—before the sound of heavy metal guitars appears midset. Besides integrating guitar riffs into Muggs' already adrenalized beats, the group reinterprets older songs such as "A to the K," making them sound new. Of course, Cypress Hill wouldn't be Cypress Hill without its adamant smoking advocacy, and starting with the trippy siren intro to "I Wanna Get High," the group moves through a medley of bud-smoking songs before the mosh-inciting conclusion of "Riot Starter" and "(Rock) Superstar." Long before the album comes to a close, Cypress Hill makes a strong argument for the rousing characteristics of its live show, quickly dismissing any claims that hip-hop isn't potent when performed live. In fact, the group manages to bring to its older material a sense of enthusiasm that was never there before—with or without guitars, Cypress Hill has never sounded this inspired on any of its '90s albums. By delivering one Cypress Hill classic after another with ferocity, MCs B Real and Sen Dog whip the crowd into a frenzy, further adding to the music's energy. Finally, the fact that this was a one-shot performance recorded without any post-production makes *Live at the Fillmore* even more impressive. —*Jason Birchmeier*

Stoned Raiders / Dec. 4, 2001 / Sony ✦✦✦
Ten years after the release of their first album, Cypress Hill has maintained a distinctive personality that has stuck around through several different musical directions. Never a band that has been afraid to experiment, the rock/rap sound they attempted on *Skull & Bones* is again one of the driving forces of the album. Where on that release they attempted to separate the tracks into the rap and rock sides, they just keep it all in the same mix here. Another huge difference between the two records is the quality of their rock/raps compared to their regular hip-hop sound. The biggest problem with *Skull & Bones* was that the rock songs were missing strong hooks, keeping them from being a successful blend of the two genres. But on *Stoned Raiders*, the rock songs are some of the strongest tracks. The best song on the entire album might be "Bitter," a brooding slow-burner that shows B Real laying down disjointed rhymes over shuffling jazz drums and strummed surf guitar. Other notable rock tracks include "Amplified," a Rage Against the Machine knockoff that features some subpar rhyming from Sen Dog but a catchy chorus, and the opener "Trouble," which utilizes Roni Size-esque percussion with trippy guitar courtesy of Fear Factory's Christian Olde Wolbers. The

percussion is actually one of the standouts of the record; DJ Muggs and live drummer Bobo do a meticulous job of finding unique beats for the record. Unfortunately, many of the hip-hop tracks do not come near to the rock songs. There are a few exceptions, especially toward the beginning of the album. "Southland Killers" is a great duet between B Real and MC Ren; in fact, Ren contributes his best rhymes since N.W.A's *Niggaz4life*. And "Kronologik" is a spellbinding retelling of Cypress Hill's history that adds some clever insight into some of the notable events in their career. But many of the other rap songs simply do not have the beats or the choruses to keep them interesting, a problem that would seem unthinkable considering how incredibly unique and catchy their first two albums are. The biggest disappointment is "Red, Meth & B," a collaboration between Redman, Method Man, and B Real that has a fairly interesting beat but reveals a surprising lack of chemistry between the three. Overall, *Stoned Raiders* is a good album despite its varying quality, and should appeal to those who enjoyed their previous album's experiments with rock. —*Bradley Torreano*

Stash: This Is the Remix EP / Jul. 2, 2002 / Columbia ◆◆◆
Though brief, *Stash* offers an incredible array of Cypress Hill recordings, half of which are remixed by in-house producer DJ Muggs, half by outside producers Fredwreck, Tony Morello, and the Alchemist. The Muggs remixes—the "Harpsichord Mix" of "Illusions," the "Blackout Mix" of "Latin Lingo," and the "Slow Roll Remix" of "Throw Your Set in the Air"—are mostly straightforward, never departing too far from the originals, often slowing down the tempo. Conversely, the outside producers do depart from the originals quite considerably: Fredwreck gives "Amplified" his patented Snoop Dogg-esque G-funk sound, Morello infuses "Checkmate" with violent guitars, and the Alchemist delivers a serene yet incredibly paranoid version of "(Rap) Superstar." The resulting six-track collection of these previously released remixes offers much variety in a brief amount of time. Considering this, *Stash* shouldn't be written off as a throwaway B sides collection but rather should be viewed as an always-interesting variation of the standard Cypress Hill sound. —*Jason Birchmeier*

D-Don

Hip-Hop, Gangsta Rap, Hardcore Rap

Hardcore rapper D-Don is one of many 2000-era hip-hop artists to concentrate mostly on gangsta/hustler themes in his lyrics, but he comes with a higher pedigree than most; friend and mentor Redman appears on D-Don's 2000 debut *Bonafide: Portrait of a Hustler*, as well as in the first video, "And You Know That." Noreaga (formerly of Capone-N-Noreaga) also collaborates on the album, which was coproduced by D-Don himself. — *Steve Huey*

Bonafide: Portait of a Hustler / Sep. 19, 2000 / Lightyear ✦

A stumbling attempt at East Coast gangsta rap with a hardcore attitude, *Bonafide: Portrait of a Hustler* never gets even moderately impressive, except for the fact that D-Don produced as well as rapped almost the entire album. Despite his remarkable work ethic, the rapper unfortunately stumbles through his attempt at smooth lyrical flow, interesting lyrical topics, and solid beats; in fact, everything seems shoddy. The guest appearances by Redman and Noreaga may interest some. — *Jason Birchmeier*

D-Nice (Derrick Jones)

b. Jun. 19, 1970, Bronx, NY
Vocals, Producer / Golden Age, East Coast Rap

D-Nice became Boogie Down Productions' DJ after the death of Scott LaRock (the man who discovered him), prior to group's second album, *By All Means Necessary*. However, his first production was actually "Self Destruction," the single released by the Stop the Violence Movement; the project, put together by KRS-One and the DJ, featured Big Daddy Kane, Doug E. Fresh, and MC Lyte. Born Derrick Jones, D-Nice left BDP in 1990, after the *Edutainment* album, to go solo. *Call Me D-Nice*, released in 1990 on Jive, featured a pair of *Billboard* rap-chart hits in "Call Me D-Nice" (number one) and "Crumbs off the Table" (number 17). Unlike KRS-One, his lyrical content was rarely politically charged, but "Glory" took a look at the black man's role in the Civil War. The less-successful *To tha Rescue* followed the next year. After that, he took on occasional production duties for the likes of LeShaun, Nuttin' Nyce, and Hi-Five. — *Andy Kellman*

● **Call Me D-Nice** / 1990 / Jive ✦✦✦✦

D-Nice had two albums as a DJ with Boogie Down Productions under his belt when he went solo with *Call Me D-Nice*, and he was still a youngster at the time. Though hardly a masterpiece, his debut album proved that he didn't go out on his own for the sake of ego. Anyone expecting something on the level of BDP's best work was clearly asking for too much; that's a big cloud that many put over D-Nice's head. After all, there are few MCs you can compare to KRS-One, so why compare an MC whose primary talents are as a DJ and beatboxer? The album delivered a bona fide classic with the title track, full of boastful rhymes and instantly memorable swollen organs and buzzing bass lines. Only once does he attempt edutainment, and that's on "Glory," a school report in the form of a song that summarizes the Civil War film of the same name. Otherwise, he keeps it to bragging, throwing requisite bones to the R&B lovers ("It's Over") and the fellas who stood poised to label him a softie ("Pimp of the Year"). The production is spare and basic for most of the duration, and it complements the remainder of the BDP-related releases just fine. — *Andy Kellman*

To tha Rescue / Nov. 26, 1991 / Jive ✦✦✦

One strange thing about D-Nice's second solo album is how, in "25 ta Life," he claims not to be into treating women like hookers, when a song from his debut—"Pimp of the Year"—painted a very different picture. And no disrespect to Too Short (at least everyone knows where *he* stands), but you can't give him a guest spot on your record and expect to be considered

anti-womanizer. Whether or not "Pimp of the Year" was intended as a spoof, it's all but impossible to not see a contradiction. At any rate, *To tha Rescue* is a slight dip from *Call Me D-Nice*; even with a revolving door of a supporting cast that includes Too Short, Naughty By Nature, and KRS-One, D-Nice wasn't able to put together an album that progressed from his debut. The album isn't without its winning spots, however. In "Time to Flow," he sounds tougher than ever; he steps up and swaps verses with Treach without sounding any less intense than his sparring partner. On "No No No," a track produced with Skeff Anselm, he delivers some lines worthy of KRS: "But don't talk about thieves/'Cause on the whole, America's the greatest country that was ever stole." D-Nice's own productions aren't as strong as ones from his brethren. This places the album a notch below the debut. — *Andy Kellman*

D-Shot

Group / Hip-Hop, Gangsta Rap, Hardcore Rap, West Coast Rap

The brother of West Coast rapper E-40, D-Shot first surfaced alongside his sibling as a member of the Click; he made his solo debut in 1994 with *Shot Calla*, followed three years later by *Six Figures. Money, Sex, & Thugs* marked his first for the new millennium, released in summer 2001. — *Jason Ankeny*

Shot Calla / Sep. 27, 1994 / Jive ✦✦✦

● **Six Figures** / Jul. 29, 1997 / Jive ✦✦✦

It runs a little long and spends a little too much time with gangsta clichés, but D-Shot's second album, *Six Figures*, offers enough straight hardcore dope to make it worthwhile for any gangsta aficionado. D-Shot's rhyming is deft, and even if he simply recycles gangsta themes, he does it well. If the production was a little more varied, *Six Figures* would have been a better album, but as it stands, it's still a strong listen, filled with hard grooves and harder rhyming. — *Leo Stanley*

D-12

f. Detroit, MI
Group / Hardcore Rap

Wherever rapper Eminem goes, controversy and headlines are sure to follow. With so many people unsure about whether to love him or hate him, five young rappers have decided to join him on his latest project, D-12. Also known as the Dirty Dozen, D-12 is a sextet of Detroit-based rappers—all between the ages of 23 and 25. Members Bizarre, Swift, Kon Artis, Proof, and Kuniva claim they are "here to bring the sick, the obscene, the disgusting." With this agenda in tow, D-12 could prove to be the sequel to the controversial parade that Eminem started with the explicit lyrics on his solo albums *Slim Shady* (UNI/Interscope Records, 1999) and the in-your-face single "Way I Am" (2000, UNI/Interscope Records).

D-12's 2001 debut album, *Devil's Night* (Interscope/Shady Records), had potential to cause some waves, with the inclusion of their raucous 2000 single, "Shit on You." D-12 was originally founded by members Bizarre and Proof around 1990, but the size and scope of the group expanded when Proof brought in childhood friend Eminem (it turns out that the pair grew up near each other, but went to different high schools) and the rest of the gang. Along their quest to stir the already controversy-infested waters of rap, all five members come complete with aliases, while each of them bears a tattoo of the name of former D-12 member, Bugz, who was gunned down at a picnic party. D-12 is (listed in no particular order by real name and alias/alter ego) Rufus Johnson, aka Peter S. Bizarre (Bizarre is also a member of the group the Outsidaz which includes Rah Digga and Eminem; he has appeared in magazines such as *The Source* and is the winner of *Inner City Entertainment*'s Flava of the Year award for September 1998), Mr. Denine Porter, aka Kon Artis (Kon

Artis is a producer for D-12), O. Moore, aka Swifty McVay (Swifty joined D-12 in 1998 after Bugz died), Von Carlisle or Hannz G., aka Kuniva (Kuniva was a part of Da Brigade along with Kon Artis), and DeShaun Holton, aka Proof or Dirty Harry (Proof is known for his freestyle talents; he won *The Source* Magazine Freestyling Competition back in 1999). D-12 requests that concerned fans contact the organizations that are focusing their "hateful attention" on Eminem (contact numbers for GLAAD and the Family Violence Prevention Fund are listed on the D-12 website www.d12net.com). —*Kerry Smith.*

● **Devil's Night** / Jun. 19, 2001 / Interscope ◆◆◆◆
Many will be tempted to dismiss D-12's debut album as exploitative juvenilia, similar to how fellow Detroit hardcore rap acts such as ICP and Esham had been treated in the past. In fact, it's hard *not* to dismiss this album as shock rap because that's exactly what it is—there's no denying it. As witty as Eminem may be—and he's by far the most creative member of the group— the countless forays into theatrical perversity far outnumber his more literate moments. For this reason, *Devils' Night* should alienate a large percentage of the millions of people who purchased Eminem's *Marshall Mathers* a year earlier, leaving mostly a core audience of young wanna-be-insane teenage boys who can appreciate this sort of juvenilia. But to dismiss the album strictly because of its themes would be unfortunate. As challenging as it may be for many to stomach the constant and incredibly explicit sex, violence, and drug references, there is a stunning album lurking beneath that deserves recognition. Functioning as the album's executive producer and as the producer for most of the album's beats, Eminem has done a wonderful job crafting this album and its foreboding feel. Immensely influenced by the style of sparse beats Dr. Dre employed on Eminem's past solo hits, the troublemaking MC's beats steal the show here, particularly on the album's standout moment, "Purple Pills." In fact, Eminem's beats often contest the few equally impressive tracks that Dre contributes. Besides the remarkable production, Eminem also showcases his blossoming genius on several of the song's hooks, bringing a pop-rap approach to hardcore lyrics. Yet no matter how accomplished this album is from a production and songwriting angle, it's impossible to look past the disturbing lyrics, especially those of Bizarre, and also Eminem's moments of unnecessary instigation. This album is obviously targeting those with a taste for perversity. If that means you, then you'll love this; if that doesn't mean you, then the album is still worth investigating, if only for Eminem's show-stealing performance as not only an MC but also a surprisingly adept producer and songwriter. —*Jason Birchmeier*

D&D Project

Group / Hip-Hop, Club/Dance
D&D Studios is a small, one-room, eight-track studio started in the Bronx by David Lotwin and Doug Grama after they met each other in high school. Originally doing mainly freestyle and dance music, DJ Premier began producing all his work at the studio and coincidentally has brought just about everyone who's important in New York hip-hop through the studio at one time or another, including KRS-One, the Beatminerz, Nas, Jay-Z, Blackmoon, Funkmaster Flex, and the Notorious B.I.G., among others. By the late '90s, it had become one of the most famous studios in all of hip-hop. —*Brad Mills*

The D&D Project / 1995 / Arista ◆◆
This is a CD put out by the infamous D&D Studios in New York City. Although the studio has been the home of some of the most influential hip-hop productions in history, this album is passable at best, with nothing close to the quality of the first track on the CD, "1, 2 Pass It." The anthem includes work from Mad Lion, Doug E. Fresh, KRS-One, Fat Joe, Smif-n-Wessun, and Jeru the Damaja. Il Unorthodox delivers a comical flow and lyrics on "Just a Little Flava," but the album as a whole just doesn't offer anything new or even succeed at doing the old very well. —*Brad Mills*

D'Angelo (Michael Eugene Archer)

b. Feb. 11, 1974, Richmond, VA
Vocals, Producer, Keyboards / Neo-Soul, Urban, Contemporary R&B
D'Angelo was one of the founding fathers and leading lights of the neo-soul movement of the mid- to late '90s, which aimed to bring the organic flavor of classic R&B back to the hip-hop age. Modeling himself on the likes of Marvin Gaye, Stevie Wonder, Prince, Curtis Mayfield, and Al Green, D'Angelo's influences didn't just come across in his vocal style—like most of those artists, he wrote his own material (and frequently produced it as well), helping to

revive the concept of the R&B auteur. His debut album, *Brown Sugar*, gradually earned him an audience so devoted that the follow-up, *Voodoo*, debuted at number one despite a five-year wait in between.

Michael D'Angelo Archer was born February 11, 1974, in Richmond, VA, the son of a Pentecostal minister. He began teaching himself piano as a very young child, and at age 18, he won the amateur talent competition at Harlem's Apollo Theater three weeks in a row. He was briefly a member of a hip-hop group called I.D.U. and signed a publishing deal with EMI in 1991. His first major success came in 1994 as a writer/producer, helming the single "U Will Know" on the *Jason's Lyric* soundtrack; it featured a onetime, all-star R&B aggregate dubbed Black Men United. That helped lead to his debut solo album, 1995's *Brown Sugar*. Helped by the title track and "Lady," *Brown Sugar* slowly caught on with R&B fans looking for an alternative to the hip-hop soul dominating the urban contemporary landscape; along with artists like Erykah Badu, Lauryn Hill, and Maxwell, D'Angelo became part of a retro-leaning, neo-soul revivalist movement. *Brown Sugar* received enormously complimentary reviews and sold over two million copies, and D'Angelo supported it with extensive touring over the next two years.

Then, not much of anything happened. D'Angelo took some time off to rest and split acrimoniously with his management; meanwhile, EMI went under, leaving his 1998 stopgap release *Live at the Jazz Cafe* out of print. On occasion, D'Angelo contributed a cover tune to a movie soundtrack, including Eddie Kendricks' "Girl You Need a Change of Mind" (*Get on the Bus*), the Ohio Players' "Heaven Must Be Like This" (*Down in the Delta*), and Prince's "She's Always in My Hair" (*Scream 2*). He also duetted with Lauryn Hill on "Nothing Really Matters," a cut from her Grammy-winning blockbuster *The Miseducation of Lauryn Hill*. Still, fans awaiting a proper follow-up to *Brown Sugar* remained frustrated—at first by no news at all, and then by frequent delays in the recording process and the scheduled release date. Finally, the special-guest-laden *Voodoo* was released in early 2000 and debuted at number one, an indication of just how large—and devoted—D'Angelo's fan base was. The extremely Prince-like lead single, "Untitled (How Does It Feel)," was a smash on the R&B charts and won a Grammy for Best Male R&B Vocal; likewise, *Voodoo* won for Best R&B Album. Reviews of *Voodoo* were once again highly positive, although a few critics objected to the looser, more atmospheric, more jam-oriented feel of the record, preferring the tighter songcraft of *Brown Sugar*. —*Steve Huey*

● **Brown Sugar** / Jul. 3, 1995 / EMI ◆◆◆◆◆
By the mid-'90s, most urban R&B had become rather predictable, working on similar combinations of soul and hip-hop, or relying on vocal theatrics on slow seductive numbers. With his debut album, *Brown Sugar*, the 21-year-old D'Angelo crashed down some of those barriers. D'Angelo concentrates on classic versions of soul and R&B, but unlike most of his contemporaries, he doesn't cut and paste older songs with hip-hop beats; instead, he attacks the forms with a hip-hop attitude, breathing new life into traditional forms. Not all of his music works—there are several songs that sound incomplete, relying more on sound than structure. But when he does have a good song—like the hit "Brown Sugar," Smokey Robinson's "Cruisin'," or the bluesy "Shit, Damn, Motherf*ker," among several others—D'Angelo's wild talents are evident. *Brown Sugar* might not be consistently brilliant, but it is one of the most exciting debuts of 1995, giving a good sense of how deep D'Angelo's talents run. —*Stephen Thomas Erlewine*

Voodoo / Jan. 11, 2000 / Virgin ◆◆◆◆
Five years after his *Brown Sugar* album helped launch contemporary R&B, D'Angelo finally returned with his sophomore effort, *Voodoo*. His soulful voice is just as sweet as it was on *Brown Sugar*, though D'Angelo stretches out with a varied cast of collaborators, including trumpeter Roy Hargrove and guitarist Charlie Hunter, fellow neo-soul stars Lauryn Hill and Raphael Saadiq, and hip-hop heads like DJ Premier, Method Man & Redman, and Q-Tip. It must have been difficult to match his debut (and the frequent delays prove it was on his mind), but *Voodoo* is just as rewarding a soul album as D'Angelo's first. —*John Bush*

Chuck D (Carlton Douglas Ridenhour)

b. Aug. 1, 1960, Roosevelt, Long Island, NY
Vocals, Producer / East Coast Rap, Hip-Hop, Hardcore Rap
As the founder of Public Enemy, Chuck D is one of the most colossal figures in the history of hip-hop, not to mention its most respected intellectual.

He redefined hip-hop as music with a message, and his strident radicalism ushered in an era when rap was closely scrutinized for its content; although rap's primary concerns have changed over the years, its status as America's most controversial art form has only gotten stronger since Public Enemy hit the scene. Chuck D was born Carlton Douglas Ridenhour in Roosevelt, Long Island, on August 1, 1960. His parents were both political activists, and he was a highly intelligent student, turning down an architecture scholarship to study graphic design at Long Island's Adelphi University. While in school, he put his talents to use making promotional flyers for hip-hop events, and went on to cohost a hip-hop mix show on the campus radio station with two future Public Enemy cohorts, Bill Stephney and Hank Shocklee.

Under the name Chuckie D, he rapped on Shocklee's demo recording, "Public Enemy No. 1," which caught the interest of Rick Rubin at Def Jam. In response, the now simply named Chuck D assembled Public Enemy, a group designed to support the force of his rhetoric with noisy, nearly avant-garde soundscapes. Public Enemy debuted in 1987 with *Yo! Bum Rush the Show*, a dry run for one of the greatest three-album spans in hip-hop history. Released in 1988, *It Takes a Nation of Millions to Hold Us Back* was acclaimed by many critics as the greatest hip-hop album of all time, and was instrumental in breaking rap music to white, alternative rock audiences. *Fear of a Black Planet* (1990) and its follow-up, *Apocalypse '91... The Enemy Strikes Black*, consolidated Public Enemy's position as the most important rap group of its time. There were storms of controversy along the way, most notably Chuck D's endorsement of the polarizing Muslim minister Louis Farrakhan, and group member Professor Griff's highly publicized anti-Semitic slurs. But on the whole, Public Enemy's groundbreaking body of work established Chuck D as one of the most intelligent, articulate spokesmen for the black community. He became an in-demand speaker on the college lecture circuit (much like his peer KRS-One), and was frequently invited to provide commentary on TV news programs.

Muse Sick-N-Hour Mess Age (1994) found the group's status slipping, and the following year Chuck put PE on hiatus while planning its next move. In the meantime, he released his first solo album, *The Autobiography of Mistachuck*, in 1996, and published the book version of his autobiography the following year. He reconvened Public Enemy for the soundtrack to Spike Lee's 1998 film, *He Got Game*, and the following year left Def Jam over the label's refusal to allow him to distribute Public Enemy music via free Internet downloads. Signing with the web-based Atomic Pop label, Chuck became an outspoken advocate of MP3 technology, and made 1999's *There's a Poison Goin' On... the first full-length album by a major artist to be made available over the Internet (it was later released on CD as well). He continued his lecturing into the new millennium and made regular appearances on the Fox News Channel as a commentator. Even if Public Enemy never recaptures the popularity or vitality of its glory years, Chuck D's legacy is secure enough to keep him a respected voice on the American cultural landscape. *—Steve Huey*

The Autobiography of Mistachuck / Oct. 22, 1996 / Mercury ✦✦✦
Chuck D was always the driving force behind Public Enemy, so perhaps it should come to no great surprise that his solo debut, *The Autobiography of Mistachuck*, sounds like it is a Public Enemy album. However, there are subtle differences. *The Autobiography of Mistachuck* isn't as noisy as PE, and it has more overt soul, funk, and R&B influences. Similarly, Chuck's lyrics have become more nuanced, which doesn't mean they're softer—it just means that he has a richer template to draw from. While the album is a little too long and it contains a few weak patches, it's an excellent effort that follows through on the promise of *Music for our Mess Age*, while correcting its problems. *—Stephen Thomas Erlewine*

Davy D.

Producer, Guitar / Old School Rap, Hip-Hop
Davy D., also known as Davy DMX (named after the Oberheim drum machine), got involved with hip-hop by DJing around neighborhoods in Queens. In the early '80s, as a guitarist, he joined with bassist Larry Smith and drummer Trevor Gale to form Orange Krush, a group who recorded a handful of singles, in addition to several backing tracks for Run-D.M.C., Sweet G, and Lovebug Starski. After the group separated, he worked with Kurtis Blow as a DJ and guitarist, providing significant contributions

to "If I Ruled the World" and "The Breaks." Scattered singles like 1984's "One for the Treble" and 1985's "The DMX Will Rock" put him on the map as a solo artist; in 1987, a full-length album called *Davy's Ride* followed for Def Jam. Apart from occasional behind-the-scenes work on records, Davy DMX also appeared as a member of the Afros, a comical group who sprouted from another group called Solo Sounds. Tuff City released a collection of four-track recordings called *FFFresh*, albeit without his knowledge. *—Andy Kellman*

Davy's Ride / 1987 / Def Jam ✦✦✦

Tony D.

b. Trenton, NJ
Producer, Vocals / Hip-Hop
New Jersey rap artist Tony D. made a promising debut in 1991 with his *Droppin' Funky Verses* album for 4th & Broadway, an album he both produced and rapped on; however, it was several years before he returned to the rap game, primarily as a producer. From Trenton, NJ, and white, Tony D. surely wasn't your typical rapper in the early '90s. His debut release was impressive, particularly for its time, featuring the two singles "E.F.F.E.C.T." and "Check the Elevation." Unfortunately, 4th & Broadway underwent challenging times, eventually meeting its demise, and Tony D. never got the chance to record a follow-up album for the label. It also didn't help that he was white and from Jersey rather than New York; in the early '90s, rap was still evolving as a genre, and whoever didn't fit the prototypical mold was often refused opportunities. Nonetheless, Tony D. made a low-key return several years later, in 1995, with an album for Contract Records, *Flav (Beats) From the Cave*. During this mid-'90s era, he also began producing tracks for other rappers such as WC, Wise Intelligent, and Kwest tha Madd Ladd. In 1997 he recorded the *Pound for Pound* album for Grand Central and then moved to Rufflife, where he recorded *Master of the Moaning Beats* (2001). *—Jason Birchmeier*

● **Droppin' Funky Verses** / 1991 / 4th & Broadway ✦✦✦✦
In the early '90s, Vanilla Ice was the whipping boy of hip-hop's hardcore, which resented the fact that someone with such limited rapping skills was selling millions of CDs. Some of Vanilla's most blistering critics were fellow Anglos; as they saw it, he was making white rappers look bad and making it even more difficult for them to be accepted by African-American listeners. But one theory has it that Vanilla inadvertently did other white rappers a favor—he made them work extra hard to prove that they weren't anything like him and that other white guys could, in fact, rap. And to be sure, there are many white MCs who have excellent rapping skills, including Everlast, House of Pain, Beastie Boys, 3rd Bass, Eminem, and Tony D. The latter showed a lot of promise on *Droppin' Funky Verses*, his debut album of 1991. Anyone who doubts that a white MC can rap his funky head off need only listen to forceful numbers like "Birdie Disease," "Tony Don't Play That," and "Harvey Wallbanger," all of which are pure, unadulterated hardcore rap with a strong East Coast flavor. It's impossible to miss the fact that Tony D. is from the Northeastern corridor; no one will mistake *Droppin' Funky Verses* for either West Coast gangsta rap or Southern bass. The Trenton, NJ, native's sample-heavy production is quite typical of Northeastern hip-hoppers of the early '90s; as a producer, he reminds one of Marley Marl or DJ Mark the 45 King rather than a West Coast heavyweight like the influential Dr. Dre. *Droppin' Funky Verses* falls short of superb, but it's definitely solid—and it leaves no doubt whatsoever that an Anglo MC can have impressive rapping skills. *—Alex Henderson*

Pound for Pound / Sep. 15, 1997 / Grand Central ✦✦✦
Tony D's first full-length for Grand Central (though he had been producing singles for the label for several years) is that rare work of instrumental hip-hop—an album of unvaried midtempo beats and stoned grooves which actually succeeds despite the lack of rapping. The addition of beatmeisters Spikey T, Mr. Scruff, and Buffy Brox make *Pound for Pound* a satisfying success. *—John Bush*

Willie D. (William Dennis)

Gangsta Rap, Hardcore Rap, Southern Rap, Hip-Hop
Originally a member of Houston horror-rappers the Geto Boys, Willie D (born William Dennis) released his first solo album, *Controversy*, in 1989. Willie parted ways with the Geto Boys in 1992, but shock tactics of his

former group are in full force on "F—- Rodney King" from his second album, *I'm Goin Out Lika Soldier*. Willie's next album, 1994's *Play Witcha Mama*, featured a guest spot from Ice Cube on the title track. A Geto Boys reunion in 1996 titled *The Resurrection* resuscitated the career of the group, but Willie D wasn't heard from again until 2000 with *Loved by Few, Hated by Many*—which may have referred to the disproportionate slant against Willie among rap fans. The suggestive title was changed in 2001 when it was re-released as *Relentless*. Despite near-universal disregard for his talents, Willie D returned with yet another album in 2003, *Unbreakable*. —*Wade Kergan*

Controversy / 1992 / Priority ♦♦

Former Geto Boy Willie Dee started his own controversy when he lit into Rodney King on this album. "F—- Rodney King" was a blistering indictment and denunciation depicting King as a sellout, traitor, and collaborator for asking his now-famous "Can't we all just get along" question during the L.A. riots. Unfortunately, the rage D felt toward King or America in general wasn't effectively communicated, either on that cut or the rest of the album. The raps were unfocused, the beats predictable, and the rhymes seldom catchy or inventive. —*Ron Wynn*

● **I'm Goin' Out Lika Soldier** / 1992 / Priority ♦♦♦

If anger, a righteous cause and intensity were all that were necessary to make a great hip-hop (or any other kind of) record, this would have been a masterpiece. Unfortunately, little things like creativity, vision, and focus also count, and Willie D's second release came up woefully short in all these categories. He also issued one of the ugliest, most vindictive songs cut by anyone on the hip-hop tip the entire year. No matter what he felt about Rodney King's call for racial unity during the L.A. riots, it didn't merit the venom spewed on "F—- Rodney King." —*Ron Wynn*

Play Witcha Mama / Oct. 25, 1994 / Wrap ♦♦♦

Following the controversial *I'm Goin' Out Lika Soldier* and driven by the popularity of the title track as a single, *Play Witcha Mama* furthered Willie D's career, establishing the confrontational rapper as a solo artist as well as a member of the proven group the Geto Boys, alongside the more sincere Scarface and the more comical Bushwack Bill. And like Willie D's other albums such as *Loved By Few, Hated By Many*, the rapper heads into paradoxical territory: on the one hand, he seems overly theatrical and outrageous, yet on the other hand, he seems overly personal and confessional. It's often difficult to know when the Southern rapper is playing and when he's being sincere. For example, it certainly seems like he's joking around when he talks about "playing witcha mama," but after making it through this album and realizing how crazed this rapper is, it doesn't exactly seem like such a joke anymore—this is the sort of guy that's being earnest when he says such things. Still, Willie D just goes to such lengths, trying to sound confrontational, that much of this album comes off as being contrived. Furthermore, in terms of production, this album is similar to the rapper's other 1990s albums in that it suffers from shoddy beats and poor sound quality. Though it's evident that he's grown since *I'm Goin' Out Lika Soldier*, Willie D still can't be taken too seriously on this album, which tends to dilute its potency. —*Jason Birchmeier*

Loved By Few, Hated By Many / Oct. 24, 2000 / Virgin ♦♦

Loved By Few, Hated By Many won't help Willie D move out of fellow Geto Boy-turned-successful solo artist Scarface's shadow, making it fairly evident who the group's true superstar is. In fact, this album makes it all too evident where Willie D suffers. Before even commenting on his rapping, the album's shoddy production isn't going to do anything but take away from his rapping; even the best rapper needs good beats, and this album's budget production and sound quality aren't nowhere near where they need to be. Still, even if one looks past the poor production, he doesn't do much to improve upon this sour spot, as he lays down inspired (and occasionally heartfelt) yet clumsy rhymes. He wants to come off hard, and to a certain extent does so, posing with guns in the liner notes. Yet posing is one thing, and rapping is another. When Willie D tries to come hard in his rhymes, he just isn't very menacing, sounding like a desperate rapper trying to sound hard for credibility reasons. He would be better off dropping the hard gangsta pose and focusing his efforts on wit, creativity, or confession instead. If anything, this album should help you understand why Scarface did his best to establish himself as a solo artist. —*Jason Birchmeier*

Da Brat (Shawntae Harris)

b. Apr. 14, 1974, Chicago
West Coast Rap, Urban, Hip-Hop

Da Brat was one of the first of a new breed of hard-edged female MCs to hit the hip-hop scene during the '90s. Although sexuality was certainly part of her image, it wasn't as important to her as it was to Lil' Kim or Foxy Brown; instead, Da Brat made her name as a tough, profane rhymer whose hardcore attitude and lyrical skills were never in doubt. Da Brat was born in 1974, and started rapping at age 11. Still a teenager, she was discovered by producer Jermaine Dupri in 1992, when she won an amateur rap contest and got a chance to meet Dupri's protégé Kris Kross. With their endorsement, Dupri signed her to his So So Def label and produced her debut album, *Funkdafied*, which was released in 1994. The title track was an enormous hit, going to number two on the R&B charts and spending nearly three months on top of the rap singles chart. Its success—as well as that of the follow-up singles "Fa All Y'All" and "Give It 2 You"—helped Da Brat become the first female rapper ever to have a platinum-selling album. *Funkdafied* also hit number one on the R&B album chart, a staggering achievement for a debut release by a female rapper.

For her 1996 follow-up, *Anuthatantrum*, Da Brat took greater control of her music and persona, scoring hits with "Sittin' on Top of the World" and "Ghetto Love." The album was another commercial success, returning her to the R&B Top Five and the pop Top 20. In its wake, Da Brat made high-profile cameo appearances on records by the likes of Mariah Carey, Missy Elliott, Total, Dru Hill, and Lil' Kim, among others. She also made her film debut in 1996 in the Shaquille O'Neal comedy *Kazaam*. Just prior to the release of her third album in 2000, Da Brat was arrested on assault charges after allegedly pistol-whipping another woman during an altercation at an Atlanta nightclub. She later pled guilty to a lesser charge of reckless conduct, and was let off with a fine, probation, and community service. Meanwhile, her album *Unrestricted* appeared in the spring of 2000, and found her sporting a somewhat sexier image. It became not only her second R&B chart-topper but also her biggest album on the pop charts to date, climbing into the Top Five. She also enjoyed hits with the singles "That's What I'm Looking For" and "What'Chu Like." In 2001 Da Brat returned to the big screen in Mariah Carey's ill-fated film *Glitter*. —*Steve Huey*

● **Funkdafied** / 1994 / So So Def/Chaos ♦♦♦♦

The first album by a female rapper ever to sell one million copies, *Funkdafied* is a promising debut effort that finds Da Brat still solidifying her style. She's a very good rapper without a strong identity of her own yet, and despite her own obvious intensity, she seems infatuated with the offhanded drawl of Snoop Doggy Dogg on much of the album. She's not just influenced by him, but cops recognizable inflections, phrasing, and vocal riffs, and producer Jermaine Dupri sometimes supports her with Dr. Dre-style G-funk tracks, most obviously on the single "Fa All Y'All." But even at its most derivative, *Funkdafied* has spirit. Repeatedly announcing, "I ain't no muthafuckin' joke," Da Brat paints herself as a cussin', weed-smokin' badass bitch who can hang with the boys and beat them at their own game. Cuts like "Da Shit Ya Can't Fuc Wit," "Fire It Up," and "Give It 2 You" effectively establish her tough-talking persona, and the smash title cut is a breezy, laid-back party jam. On quite a few tracks, Da Brat augments her Snoop fixation by referencing lines from '80s classics, almost as though she feels compelled to prove she knows her history; she can also rely a little too heavily on her catch phrase, "Brat-tat-tat-tat." But even if she isn't quite there yet, Da Brat knows who she wants to be, and she has the talent and production to make the journey entertaining. —*Steve Huey*

Anuthatantrum / Oct. 29, 1996 / Columbia ♦♦♦♦

Da Brat's second album, *Anuthatantrum*, is a slight improvement over her debut, even if it lacks an instantly obvious single on the order of "Funkdafied." Her persona is pretty much the same (she doesn't take crap and likes to swear and smoke pot), and so is her flow. The main difference is that this time around, her rhymes are much more her own, without all the old school quotes and obvious Snoop Dogg bites that sometimes pulled the focus away from her strengths on *Funkdafied*. Similarly, Jermaine Dupri's production is less indebted to Dr. Dre's G-funk sound, instead following the early-'80s urban funk direction he also hinted at on the debut. The two excellent singles, "Sittin' on Top of the World" and "Ghetto Love," sample Rick James and El Debarge, respectively, and there are some more laid-back moments with live keyboards and acoustic guitar work. (The "Stayin' Alive" cop on

"Keepin' It Live" is far less inspired, however.) Of course, there's another ode to marijuana on "Let's All Get High," which features special guest Krayzie Bone; there are also a few songs where Da Brat prides herself on being more spoiled than ever, thanks to her success. It's another brief album, but *Anuthatantrum* does show Da Brat making subtle progress, and Dupri's production is inviting once again. —*Steve Huey*

Unrestricted / Apr. 11, 2000 / Columbia ✦✦✦
Poising herself halfway between knowing sexual object and vengeful love goddess, Da Brat rages through her third album, constructing wonderfully dense raps and delivering them with skill and panache. There is a bit more R&B on *Unrestricted* than Da Brat fans will expect, but given the rapper's uncompromising stance, it never feels like a sellout. Check her hometown salute "Chi-Town" and "Pink Lemonade," and her double team (with R&B singer Kelly Price) on the spurned-love story "Runnin' Out of Time." Producer Jermaine Dupri spreads the synthesizer strings a bit too thick but shows his beats are among the best of the major super-producers on the block. —*John Bush*

Daddy Freddy (S. Frederick Small)

b. 1965, Kingston, Jamaica
Dancehall, Ragga, Hip-Hop
The world's fastest rapper according to the *Guinness Book of World Records*, Jamaican-born Daddy Freddy was also one of the first artists to fuse ragga and dancehall with hip-hop, helping establish a style that would become highly influential during the '90s. Freddy (born S. Frederick Small, 1965, Kingston) grew up in the Trenchtown area and began performing for his uncle's sound system, eventually moving on to join Lieutenant Stitchie and, most importantly, Sugar Minott. His gig with Minott's sound system helped make his name in Jamaica (and, following an overseas tour, the U.K.); in 1985, he made his first recording for Clement "Coxsone" Dodd's Studio One label, a single titled "Zoo Party," that was built on the rhythm of the early ragga smash "Under Mi Sleng Teng." Aided by his hit debut album *Body Lasher*, Freddy scored a remarkable six Top Ten hits in Jamaica during 1986, including a collaboration with Pinchers called "Joker Lover," which topped the charts.

In 1987 Freddy returned to the U.K., where he signed with the Music of Life label and began working with producer Asher D. The resulting album, *Raggamuffin Hip-Hop*, was one of the first fusions of dancehall toasting with hip-hop rhythms, breaking a great deal of new ground. Freddy continued to record dancehall reggae singles for the Jamaican audience while making guest appearances with pop and dance artists like Go West, Meli'sa Morgan, and Beats International (the pre-Fatboy Slim project of Norman Cook). In 1988 Freddy entered the *Guinness Book of World Records* with a rap that topped 500 syllables per minute. Despite success in the U.K. and Jamaica, Freddy hadn't made as much of an impression in the States, and he aimed to change that by signing with Chrysalis for the 1991 album *Stress* and the accompanying single "Daddy Freddy's in Town." Both enjoyed modest success, and the follow-up album, *Raggamuffin Soldier*, scored positive reviews, but Freddy never quite became a breakout star in America even with his tremendous technical skill. Freddy soon elected to take a break from his frenetic late-'80s recording schedule, releasing his last Music of Life album, *The Big One*. However, he staged a comeback in 2000 with the acclaimed *Old School, New School*, a collaboration with new U.K. dub wizard the Rootsman. Freddy subsequently returned to Jamaica to begin recording some new dancehall material. —*Steve Huey*

Stress / 1991 / Chrysalis ✦✦✦
● **Raggamuffin Soldier** / 1992 / Chrysalis ✦✦✦✦✦
Daddy Freddy juggles idiomatic influences nicely on *Raggamuffin Soldier*. There are hip-hop-influenced production touches, songs designed to appeal to more traditional reggae fans ("Jah Jah Give Me Vibes"), tunes using both American and Caribbean rap techniques, and even dance, R&B, and soul touches incorporated into some selections. The result is a 15-track disc that should have something for everyone, and one of the few that actually manage to combine things from all styles rather than just throw them together. —*Ron Wynn*

Old School, New School / Jun. 6, 2000 / BSI ✦✦✦✦
Connoisseurs of modern reggae will have high expectations for this collaboration between speed-rap legend Daddy Freddy and experimental U.K. dubmeister the Rootsman, and those expectations will, for the most part, be met.

While Daddy Freddy is famous for his place in *the Guinness Book of World Records* as the world's fastest rapper (clocked, reportedly, at a tongue-numbing 508 syllables per minute), he is less widely recognized as simply one of the best dancehall DJs of the late 1980s and early 1990s. The Rootsman has more of a cult following amongst aficionados of rootswise progressive dub. On *Old School, New School* the Rootsman delivers up a batch of solid rhythms that vary from classic raggae ("Keeping a Session") to ominous modern one-drop ("No Carbon") and steppers ("Where Were You"). Freddy himself is in fine form for the most part—he occasionally loses track of the music's harmonic center, but he never fails to ride the rhythm with utter confidence and poise. Particular highlights include the dark and funky "Worldwide Revolution" and an apparent Eek-A-Mouse tribute, "Wa Do Dem." The program concludes with three excellent remixes. —*Rick Anderson*

Dälek

Vocals, Producer / Underground Rap
Newark, NJ's Dälek undermines the simplistic gloss of mainstream hip-hop with gritty, complex underground hip-hop that at once clicks and whirs like some electronica head trip; layers on environmental ambience; and assaults the listener with aggressive, intelligent rhymes.

Dälek and Oktopus met at William Patterson University in the mid-'90s and began collaborating. Soon, Dälek dropped out of school, cashed in his loans, and put his money into his home studio. The duo's first album, *Negro, Necro, Nekros*, was released on Gern Blandsten in 1998 to critical acclaim. The record combined elements of Faust, the rock grit of the Velvet Underground, shoegazer density, and IDM beats with insightful lyrics, and Dälek were named on *Urb*'s Next 100 list. During their relentless tour schedule, at a college show, the duo met DJ Still and asked him to join the group. Dälek spent the next few years on the road, opening for acts like De La Soul, Prince Paul, DJ Spooky, the Rye Coalition, the Dillinger Escape Plan, the Pharcyde, and the Roots. Dälek's second album, *From Filthy Tongue of Gods and Griots*, was released on Ipecac Recordings in August of 2002. The record expanded their already broad sound and fully realized the group's position beside hip-hop innovators like Antipop Consortium and Clouddead. —*Charles Spano*

● **Negro Necro Nekros EP** / Oct. 13, 1998 / Gern Blandsten ✦✦✦✦
The debut record from Newark, NJ's Dälek is an exercise in experimental hip-hop that focuses as much on beats as it does on the heavy-handed lyrics that carry the group's message. With equally spacious and dark backgrounds created by Oktopus, aka noted indie rock producer Alap Momin, the setting is fittingly sinister for the incensed rhymes of Dälek the MC who leads their attack. Momin also provides plenty of fitting samples over his beats, which contain everything from Indian drums and strings to crazed DJ Shadow-esque breakbeats. Hammering the twisted soundtrack home are the occasionally political and often enraged lyrics, the artist raps with enough control to often hold back until it really matters. His at times whispered musings add to the musical buildups, and when he does finally break on tracks like "Swollen Tongue Bums" his combination of heart and fury carries his poetry across with force. Dälek is the rare hip-hop crew that focuses on the entire package, and the fact that they have enough faith, all of which is merited, in their beats to allow for lengthy musical interludes on tracks like "Images of 44. Casings" makes this all too short record a legitimate force to be reckoned with. Too many crews seem to focus on the trends of the past, but Dälek are looking boldly ahead and their ability to create an abstract new approach is their greatest strength. —*Peter J. D'Angelo*

From Filthy Tongue of Gods and Griots / Aug. 6, 2002 / Ipecac ✦✦✦
If you're the type of hip-hop fan who finds a group like OutKast a tad too experimental for your tastes, you might wanna back away from this album slowly and try not to make any sudden moves. With a cacophonous sound that falls somewhere between the Bomb Squad, Disposable Heroes of Hiphoprisy, and that annoying guy with the jackhammer who *just…won't…stop*, this is music for those people who think Antipop Consortium just isn't quite weird enough. The jarring industrial noise that drives the opening "Spiritual Healing" is your first clue that Dälek is coming from a whole 'nother frame of reference, with producer Oktopus' grinding grooves providing a dense, dark backdrop for some furiously inventive mike work. Thankfully, not every track here is quite so chaotic: The haunting instrumental "Antichristo" wouldn't sound out of place on a DJ Shadow album, while the exotic Indian

drones and tabla beats of "Trampled Brethren" almost border on accessible. But even a noise-loving freak like DJ Spooky would be put off by the dissonant, 12-minute spoken word epic "Black Smoke Rises." Warning: Easy listening this is not. —*Bret Love*

Ruin It / Oct. 1, 2002 / Tigerbeat6 ♦♦♦
Glitch-techno's child genius Kid 606 and Jersey indie hip-hop crew Dälek take six tracks to remix one another's material in what amounts to an above-average attempt to re-create the complexity of Def Jux artists like Cannibal Ox. Opener "Ruin It, Ruin Them, Ruin Yourself Then Ruin Me" is Dälek's sometimes righteous flow laid over a metallic-treated horn solo from the Kid's *Down With the Scene* album. The "Revenge of the Circuit Burners" remix starts with a "Warm Leatherette" electro beat and warps into an amazing track with Dälek finding space between surging electronic sheets to paint an apocalyptic landscape. The two "distressed electronics" tracks, "Vague Recollections" and "Satan's Hard Drive," seem out of place here, as neither appears to feature Dälek nor fit the mood of the otherwise dark, well-planned EP. "Now I'm Completely Ruined," with an almost danceable 4/4 beat, only gives way to Dälek in a breakbeat finale, a halfhearted attempt by Dälek to toast the ills of American culture in its final special-guest moments. —*Daphne G.A. Carr*

Dame Grease

Southern Rap
Growing up on the streets of Harlem, Dame Grease never took to the sounds of rap music until his late teens when he first heard the nocturnal nihilism of N.W.A and Ice-T. This hardcore sound and its affiliated gangsta attitude connected with Grease, who then found himself immersed in the culture after forming a neighborhood group called N.I.B. It wasn't long before he found himself producing beats, looking to the aggressive sounds of the Bomb Squad and Dr. Dre for influence. By the end of the 1990s, Grease had collaborated with such prominent New York rap artists as DMX, the LOX, and Nas. He even took a chance producing the enigmatic Tricky, primarily recognized as a trip-hop producer. Following this courageous project, he formed his own label, Vacant Lot, and began work on his debut release, *Live on Lenox Ave.*, which featured himself producing superstar rappers such as Silkk tha Shocker and Scarface in addition to his roster of Vacant Lot rappers: Meeno, H.O.T. Ones, and N.I.B. Untouchables, among others. —*Jason Birchmeier*

● **Live on Lenox Ave.** / Jul. 18, 2000 / Priority ♦♦
Dame Grease is most renowned for his behind-the-scene work with DMX, Nas, the LOX, and Cam'ron. He is also one of the main participants responsible for devising the highly coveted syncopated template that currently defines mainstream hip-hop. Dame's sample-free, keyboard-friendly creations offer the main source of competition to fellow syncopated lords Swizz Beatz and Mannie Fresh, and his emergence has prevented Swizz and Mannie from exclusively monopolizing this arena. With *Live on Lenox Ave.*, Dame proves to be a full-service beat technician, as he effortlessly tailors his computerized tracks to fit any genre; from the dirty South bounce of "Vacant Lot Gone No Limit" featuring Silkk tha Shocker to the R&B hue of "Harlem Niggas" featuring Mase's Harlem World cronies Loon and Huddy. While Dame's sound is often indistinguishable from that of Swizz's, he does exhibit a soulful side, implementing melodious guitar riffs to Noreaga's "La Da Di La La La." Yet, times are hard on the Ave., as Dame's freshman class of rhyme associates (H.O.T. Ones, Mad.Is.On, Bigga Threat, etc.) are underwhelming throughout, and this nondescript cast of MCs could use more time developing their own identities. In truth, *Live on Lenox Ave.* is so stricken with insufficient lyricism that it turns ordinary tracks from Noreaga, the catchy "La Da Di La La La," and Nas' "Wanna Play Rough" (a track resurrected from the *Nastradamus* sessions) into the LP's main highlights. —*Matt Conaway*

Dan the Automator (Dan Nakamura)

Producer, DJ / Hip-Hop, Alternative Rap, Underground Rap, Alternative Dance, Electronica
Dan "the Automator" Nakamura is a San Francisco-based hip-hop producer whose work with "Kool" Keith Thornton on the latter's Dr. Octagon project shot him to unlikely acclaim in 1996. With a series of ever more elaborate conceptual projects since then, Nakamura's wildly imaginative productions and offbeat sense of humor made him one of the leading figures in the underground renaissance of alternative rap in the late '90s.

A classically trained violinist in his younger days, Nakamura instead fell in love with Kraftwerk and old school hip-hop, as well as R&B and rock & roll. He began DJing as a teenager, but was discouraged by the advanced skills of some younger Bay Area DJs (i.e., the ones who would go on to form the legendary Invisibl Skratch Piklz collective). Nakamura instead turned his attention to crafting his own productions, accepting gigs around the Bay Area through the early '90s, which eventually culminated in the Dr. Octagon project in 1995. A lo-fi fusion of hip-hop beats and bizarre atmospherics on par with some of the weirder exports from the U.K. trip-hop scene, Dr. Octagon was released by the tiny Bulk Recordings label in 1995; and achieved a level of overground success increasingly rare in hip-hop's pop-monopolized marketplace when it was reissued by DreamWorks a year later. Propelled by Thornton's pornographic rhymes and mind-bending meter, the record owed its success in equal measure to Nakamura's inventive production, which wed loping, downtempo rhythms with, by turns, weeping violins, space-born bleeps and wiggles, and heavy metal guitar riffs. Not Nakamura's freshman effort by a long shot, the two had actually worked together (with Thornton appearing as Sinister 6000) on Nakamura's debut Automator release, *A Better Tomorrow* EP, appearing on SF's Ubiquity label in early 1996. Nakamura's studio, the Glue Factory, also served as the workshop for recordings by Mo'Wax's DJ Shadow and for various artists on the latter's SoleSides label (most notably on Latyrx's *The Debut*).

When Thornton decided not to tour behind his Dr. Octagon alias, Nakamura racked up a host of other mix and production credits, including Primal Scream, the Eels, DJ Krush, a collaboration with Dust Brother Mike Simpson for Cornershop (several tracks on 1997's acclaimed *When I Was Born for the 7th Time*), and the Jon Spencer Blues Explosion (1998's *Acme*). Nakamura then teamed up with former De La Soul producer Prince Paul as Handsome Boy Modeling School, a reference to an episode of the Chris Elliott sitcom *Get a Life*. In 1999 the duo released an album titled *So…How's Your Girl?*, a freewheeling hodgepodge of old school hip-hop, new school trip-hop, crazed sampling (including plenty of Elliott dialogue), and all-star cameos. The record marked Nakamura as a figure to watch, and that reputation was confirmed with 2000's Deltron 3030 project, a collaboration with rapper Del tha Funkee Homosapien and DJ Kid Koala. The trio's self-titled debut was an elaborate science-fiction concept album set in a bleak and distant future, and Nakamura's detailed, cinematic production offered a rich and believable soundtrack. That same year, Nakamura issued a retooled version of his debut EP (with several extra tracks) under the title *A Much Better Tomorrow* on the hip-hop-oriented label 75 Ark.

In 2001 Nakamura snared his widest audience yet with the cartoon band Gorillaz, an eclectic collaboration with Blur's Damon Albarn, artist Jamie Hewlett, Cibo Matto's Miho Hatori, and former Talking Heads Chris Frantz and Tina Weymouth. Their barely classifiable, self-titled debut was a hit on both sides of the Atlantic, going platinum in the U.S. and spawning Nakamura's first major hit single, "Clint Eastwood." Next, Nakamura returned to his Nathaniel Merriweather alias (from the Handsome Boy Modeling School album) for Lovage, a lounge-flavored, Serge Gainsbourg-influenced project that featured vocalists Jennifer Charles (Elysian Fields) and Mike Patton (Faith No More). The Lovage album *Music to Make Love to Your Old Lady By* was released before the end of 2001. Nakamura kicked off 2002 by releasing his first-ever mix album, the well-received *Wanna Buy a Monkey?: A Mixtape Session.* —*Sean Cooper & Steve Huey*

A Better Tomorrow EP / Apr. 15, 1996 / Ubiquity ♦♦♦♦
Producer Dan "the Automator" Nakamura's solo debut for San Francisco acid jazz imprint Ubiquity is not quite as notable a deviation from standard-fare hip-hop/acid jazz production as the just-released Dr. Octagon album, which would eventually earn Nakamura his rep. Still a few notches above the typical, however, with several of the tracks featuring Octagon collaborator "Kool" Keith Thornton (under the name Sinister 6000). —*Sean Cooper*

A Much Better Tomorrow / Jul. 18, 2000 / 75 Ark ♦♦♦♦
Even more optimistic for the future after the passage of three years, Dan Nakamura expanded his *Better Tomorrow* EP out to a full-length with the addition of a host of tracks recorded around the same time. Sinister 6000 (aka Kool Keith) freestyles over half of the tracks, rehearsing for the duo's collaboration later that year on the *Dr. Octagon* LP. Except for the occasional eerie cinema sample, though, the sound is decidedly different from *Dr. Octagon*.

Suitably, these tracks are drum heavy and more reliant on the Automator's production/DJ skills, with Keith spending much less time on the mic. The straight-out instrumentals and studio project tracks don't compare quite as well, though, sounding a bit aimless without at least an occasional rap in front of them. Two other rappers make appearances, Neph the Madman on "Wiling" and Poet on the solid "Buck Buck," while Kool Keith's "King of NY" fondly recalls the Beasties' *Paul's Boutique*. —*John Bush*

● **Wanna Buy a Monkey?: A Mixtape Session** / Feb. 19, 2002 / Ultra ◆◆◆◆◆
Not just a production genius and the birthname behind a handful of indie/rap masked marvels (Handsome Boy Modeling School, Deltron 3030, Gorillaz), Dan "the Automator" Nakamura is also an excellent DJ. But even after ten years in the hip-hop game (and scores of credits), he'd still never released a mix album until 2002's *Wanna Buy a Monkey?*. Nakamura proves the wait was worth it, bookending twin sets of hardcore hip-hop with a middle section comprised of downtempo material like his remix of Air's early classic "Le Soleil Est Pres de Moi" and his own productions of Lovage's "Stroker Ace" and Gorillaz's "Latin Simone." Also including his first credit from 1992 (a single recorded by Black Rob many years before he hooked up with Bad Boy), *Wanna Buy a Monkey?* shows off Nakamura's ear for a great track as well as his deft turntablist skills. Granted, about half of these were Automator productions or remixes to begin with, but *Wanna Buy a Monkey?* doesn't just collect a few of his rarer credits; it fits them into one of the best mix albums of the year. —*John Bush*

Dana Dane

b. Brooklyn, NY
Old School Rap
New York-born rap singer Dana Dane combined light-hearted rap with a love of fashion. While his recordings, including "Cinderfella Dana Dane," "A Little Bit of Dane Tonight," and "Tales From the Dane Side," established him as a powerful rapper, his tastes in clothing inspired him to open IV Plai Boutique. Although the shop has since closed, Dane continued to attract attention with his unique outfits.
    Raised in the Walt Whitman housing project in Fort Greene, Brooklyn, Dane first displayed his talents as a member of a rap group, Kongol Crew, which he formed with High School of Music and Arts classmate Slick Rick. Launching his solo career after graduating from high school, Dane signed with the Profile record label in 1985. While his debut single, "Nightmare," offered hints of his talents, Dane broke through commercially with his first full-length album, *Dana Dane With Fame*, in 1987. The success of the album, which achieved gold-record status, was matched by subsequent albums *Dana Dane 4 Ever* in 1990 and *Rollin' Wit Dane* in 1995. During a late-'90s interview, Dane described his musical approach as "writing stories that have chronological depth as well as moral values." —*Craig Harris*

● **Dana Dane With Fame** / 1987 / Profile ◆◆◆◆◆
Rap was many things in the '80s: sociopolitical, cutting edge, innovative, in your face, insightful, angry, thought provoking, intellectual, entertaining, funny, crude, and so on. Eighties rap could describe tragic social conditions (Ice-T's "Colors," Grandmaster Flash's "The Message") or it could be unapologetically silly (Biz Markie's "Pickin' Boogers"). Rapping with a fake British accent, Dana Dane represented the goofier side of '80s rap. *Dana Dane With Fame*, the New Yorker's debut album, is a classic of its kind. Occasionally this 1987 release touches on social issues, but for the most part, *Dana Dane With Fame* (which was produced by Hurby Luv Bug) doesn't take itself too seriously. Dane's greatest asset is his sense of humor, and the East Coast MC is wildly entertaining on goofy, nutty items like "Nightmares," "Love at First Sight," and the hit single "Cinderfella Dana Dane." But while social commentary isn't the CD's main focus, Dane isn't oblivious to the social problems that plague a major city like New York. On "Delancey Street" (another major hit), Dane raps about three women trying to rob him at gunpoint on Manhattan's Lower East Side. The dark-humored tune manages to be funny and disturbing at the same time; even when he's rapping about urban crime, Dane maintains the silliness that made him so endearing. "Delancey Street" was a song that New Yorkers had no problem relating to in the '80s; back then, the area of Delancey Street near the Williamsburg Bridge was infamous for its high crime rate (although much of Manhattan's Lower East Side became a lot safer in the '90s, thanks to Mayor Rudy Giuliani's war on crime). *Dana Dane With Fame* isn't the MC's

only worthwhile album, but it is definitely his best and most essential. —*Alex Henderson*

Dana Dane 4 Ever / 1990 / Profile ◆◆◆
Quite popular in the mid-1980s, Dana Dane was one of hip-hop's greatest humorists. When other MCs were trying to show how tough and hardcore they could be, Dane usually went for more of a lighthearted approach. Though *Dana Dane 4 Ever* isn't quite as strong as the New Yorker's first album, the CD offers many examples of his witty storytelling. Especially amusing are the sexual escapades described on "Bedie Boo," "Tales From the Dane Side," and "What Dirty Minds You Have." Dane occasionally turns to more serious subject matter and takes a look at the dangers of urban life. "Johnny the Dipper," for example, examines the deadly consequences of a youth's life of crime. But on the whole, *Dana Dane 4 Ever's* tone is anything but serious. —*Alex Henderson*

Rollin' Wit Dane / Mar. 28, 1995 / Maverick ◆◆◆

The Dangerous Crew

Group / Comedy Rap
The Dangerous Crew was comprised of Oakland/Bay Area MCs Too Short, Goldy, Anthony "Ant" Banks, and Father Dom. Banks mixed and coproduced *Don't Try This at Home*, the collective's sole release. Full of goofy R-rated rhymes and plenty of Oaktown boasting, the record was enjoyable, not for its hooks or production trickery, but for its embrace of the quirky personalities involved. Each MC left his own indelible mark on the microphone, even if the album was a throwaway between each member's respective solo projects. *Don't Try This at Home* also featured guest shots from Erick Sermon, as well as Digital Underground's Shock-G. —*Johnny Loftus*

● **Don't Try This at Home** / Nov. 21, 1995 / Dangerous ◆◆◆
The Dangerous Crew's *Don't Try This at Home* doesn't break any new ground, but it is a thoroughly enjoyable collection of West Coast hip-hop. Led by Too Short and featuring Ant Banks, Goldy, and Father Dom, the Dangerous Crew has a stellar lineup of MCs and they all contribute their fair share of first-rate rhymes. The production doesn't show much imagination, yet the personalities manage to make *Don't Try This at Home* an entertaining record. —*Stephen Thomas Erlewine*

Darkleaf

Group / Underground Rap, Alternative Rap
Darkleaf emerged from the Los Angeles underground in the early '90s, after the legendary Unity Committee split in two. One faction became Jurassic 5; the other, Darkleaf. From the beginning, MCs Kemit and Metalogik, producers and MCs Longjevity and Jahli, and DJ Mixmaster Wolf wanted to be the darkest bees in the hive. Refusing to submit to the too-easy clichés and vapidity of mainstream hip-hop, Darkleaf developed a style that referenced Sun Ra, Chick Corea, and Jimi Hendrix, among others. Home recording, studio trickery, spoken word, complicated vocal interplay—Darkleaf's palette was full. In 2002, *F— the People* appeared on the California imprint Ubiquity. A dark, swirling album of disorienting rhythms and unsettling rhymes, *F— the People* established Darkleaf's uncompromising sound outside the depths of the L.A. underground. —*Johnny Loftus*

● **F— the People** / Mar. 19, 2002 / Ubiquity ◆◆◆◆
Grown out of the legendary Unity Committee, Darkleaf has deep roots in the L.A. underground. The Unity Committee eventually split in two, one faction going on to form the Jurassic 5 while the others mined considerably different territory, creating the diverse, dystopian sound that characterizes *F— the People*. As the title implies, this is a dark, often angry album. All five members take a turn at the mike, lending a wide range of perspectives—from the philosophical to the paranoid—to seething songs like "Sounds of Armageddon" and "Commercial." While the lyrics are intense, the music behind them is even more challenging. Producers Jahli and Longevity, along with sterling DJ Mixmaster Wolf, combine to give *F— the People* its dense, surprisingly intricate sound. Scratches, spoken words, skewered breakbeats, snatches of horns, and disjointed guitar riffs are all in the mix here, blended together and set into a deep and murky low end. Anchored in the clutter of thick bass and hypnotic beats, the complicated soundscapes of *F— the People* reveal themselves slowly, becoming more and more engaging with each listen. —*Martin Woodside*

DarkRoom Familia

f. Hayward, CA

Group / Gangsta Rap, Hardcore Rap, Latin Rap

Latin gangster rappers DarkRoom Familia hail from Hayward, CA (a town close to Oakland), and were originally formed in 1988. Like other burgeoning gangster rappers of the era, major labels weren't quick to sign such bands, so the bandmembers had to sell their tapes by taking them personally to record stores in the area as word of mouth quickly began to spread. Dark-Room Familia became one of rap's most prolific bands, issuing albums (whether it be by the band or solo releases by its members) at an extremely brisk rate. Eight albums were issued between 1999 and 2001 alone, including such titles as *Traficantes*, *Veteranos*, *Felony Consequences*, *From the Barrio With Love*, *Gang Stories: The Darkroom Uncensored*, *Homicide Kings*, *Smile Now Cry Later*, and *Men of Honor*, as well as the compilation *Barrio Classics: 1988-1998*. — *Greg Prato*

● **Barrio Classics: 1988-1998** / Sep. 25, 2001 / Brown Power ◆◆◆

Das EFX

f. 1991, Petersburg, VA

Group / Golden Age, East Coast Rap, Hip-Hop

Das EFX's wildly playful, rapid-fire stuttering—dense with rhymes and nonsense words—was one of the most distinctive and influential lyrical styles in early-'90s hip-hop. While the duo completely rewrote the MC rule book, they themselves were increasingly pegged as a one-dimensional novelty the longer their career progressed, despite watching elements of their style creep into countless rappers' bags of tricks. Krazy Drayz (born Andre Weston; Teaneck, NJ) and Skoob (born Willie Hines) were both raised in Brooklyn, but didn't begin performing together until they met at Virginia State University in 1988. Removed from an active music scene, the two were free to develop their most idiosyncratic tendencies; they started making up gibberish words (anything ending in "-iggity" was a favorite) that added loads of extra syllables to their lines, and wove plenty of pop-cultural references into the tongue-twisting lyrical gymnastics that resulted. Das EFX caught their big break when they performed at a talent show judged by EPMD; though they didn't win, EPMD was impressed enough to offer them a deal, and the duo became part of the Def Squad crew of protégés.

Signing to the East West label, Das EFX began work on their debut album, commuting between Virginia and New York and mailing tapes to EPMD (then touring the country) for guidance. Upon its release in 1992, *Dead Serious* caused an immediate sensation, and is still considered something of a landmark in hip-hop circles. The first single, the instantly memorable signature song "They Want EFX," was a Top 40 pop hit and a Top Ten R&B hit, and helped push sales of *Dead Serious* past the platinum mark. Wary of being pigeonholed by repeating themselves, the duo slowed down their lyrical flow and downplayed the surrealistic side of their interplay on the follow-up album, 1993's *Straight Up Sewaside*, which went gold. Around the time of 1995's disappointing *Hold It Down*, Das EFX found themselves caught in the middle of EPMD's ugly breakup; it led to a three-year absence from recording. By the time they returned in 1998 with *Generation EFX*, the group was playing more to a devoted but narrower cult audience; they have remained largely silent since. — *Steve Huey*

★ **Dead Serious** / Apr. 7, 1992 / East West ◆◆◆◆◆

Das EFX—part of EPMD's Def Squad crew, which also included K-Solo and Redman, among others—made such a wide breakthrough in 1992 with their debut album that their hit "They Want EFX" was even referenced in the lily-white teen serial *Beverly Hills 90210*. That *Dead Serious* could have that sort of broad impact and still retain its credibility within the underground hip-hop community says something about its appeal, which was considerable. But the album wasn't just appealing; it was also enormously influential, ushering in an entirely unique rhyming flow that influenced any number of rappers, established and novice alike. What exactly the duo is rapping about is anyone's guess. One thing is for sure: Their lyrics are about as far removed from hardcore realism as they could possibly be, and although there are certain elements of boasting, it is so cut up and contorted that it never sounds like there's even a hint of the humdrum here. None of the lyrical clichés that can occasionally bog down even the finest hip-hop artist are present. Members Dre and Skoob (tellingly, "books" spelled backwards) instead engage in lightning-fast, tongue-twisted word association and stream-of-consciousness

rants rich in pop-cultural references and allusions. It was a completely original rhyming style in 1992—one of the reasons it had such an impact both in the insular world of hip-hop and on the wider public—but it also had an invigorating looseness that lent itself to commercial radio. "They Want EFX" is clearly the creative highlight of the album; the other songs work the same basic template, and each one is nearly equal in execution and charm, particularly the jaunty "Mic Checka" and "Jussummen." — *Stanton Swihart*

Straight Up Sewaside / Nov. 16, 1993 / East West ◆◆◆◆

By the time *Sewaside* saw the light of day, the public hadn't fully absorbed Das EFX's innovative debut, *Dead Serious*. The hardcore rap game had barely caught up with the brilliance of their rapid-fire vocal delivery and sample-laden beats. But then again, another crew from Staten Island emerged in 1993 and took the rap game by total storm, leaving the genius of *Sewaside* somewhat overshadowed by their dominance. However, this change in climate shouldn't overshadow *Sewaside* as a crucial record in the Das EFX canon. While the duo's methods of madness were slowly emulated by a plethora of MCs, Das EFX stayed with the same effective blueprint laid down in *Dead Serious*. By maintaining this consistency, *Sewaside* lacks the punch in the gut that *Dead Serious* delivered, but it's still a solid record that completists and newfound fans will equally enjoy. — *Rob Theakston*

Hold It Down / Oct. 1995 / East West ◆◆

Although the duo tries very hard, there isn't much on *Hold It Down*, Das EFX's third album, that makes it very different from their previous records. The production is a bit leaner and their delivery is a bit harder, yet that doesn't disguise the fact that the beats aren't as strong as their earlier albums, nor are their raps as exciting and inventive. Nevertheless, there are some strong moments on *Hold It Down*, and it should please fans of the duo, even if it doesn't appeal to the same large audience that embraced their debut. — *Stephen Thomas Erlewine*

Generation EFX / Mar. 24, 1998 / Elektra ◆◆◆

Das EFX never quite recovered from the perception that their hyperspeed rhyming style was little more than a novelty. Not only were they written off in some quarters, but their hard-edged, rhyme-centric style was overshadowed by the moked-out gangsta funk coming from the West Coast. *Hold It Down*, their third album, suffered from not only these problems but also the fact that it wasn't very good. On the other hand, its follow-up, *Generation EFX*, is a hard-hitting return to form. Enlisting a number of guest artists and producers—including EPMD, Tumblin' Dice Productions, Angel "8-Off" Aguilar, Nocturnal, Miss Jones, and Redman—the group revamps their trademark sound; it's still recognizably EFX, but it's harder and hipper than before. Like all their albums, *Generation EFX* relies more on style than substance—not all of the hooks hold, some of the grooves just lie there—but on the whole, it's their best album since *Straight Up Sewaside*. — *Stephen Thomas Erlewine*

The Very Best of Das EFX / Jul. 3, 2001 / Rhino ◆◆◆◆◆

Rhino/Elektra Traditions' 2001 release *The Very Best of Das EFX* is an excellent summary of the duo's seminal recordings for Elektra. When they came crashing out in 1992 with *Dead Serious*, the group was a bold change, thanks to their revolutionary quick-fire, stuttering delivery. The record was hailed as a mini-masterpiece, but like a lot of rap crews, what was praised upon the debut became ignored by the third, often because the once-fresh style now seemed stale, even if it was their signature sound. And, while the quality of their recordings did dip somewhat after the first album, they still turned out fine recordings, as this collection proves. True, it does tilt toward the debut, with no less than seven selections from *Dead Serious*, but it also contains three cuts from *Straight Up Sewaside* and four from 1995's *Hold It Down*, ending with two tracks from their final Elektra album, 1998's *Generation EFX*. This winds up as an excellent summary, providing a huge portion of their greatest album, with cuts from the other albums that prove they hadn't lost their talents after the debut. And while *Dead Serious* remains a landmark, this may be the best choice for anybody indeed wanting to hear *The Very Best of Das EFX*. — *Stephen Thomas Erlewine*

Dayton Family

f. Flint, MI

Group / Gangsta Rap, Hardcore Rap, Underground Rap

Though the Dayton Family never extended their reach to either the West or East Coast, the little-known rap group garnered a substantial cult following in the Midwest during the mid-'90s with their potent hardcore rap. Their unlikely home base of Flint, MI, immediately gave them an idiosyncratic identity; a relatively uneventful, far-from-glitzy postindustrial city an hour outside of Detroit, Flint hosts some of the most depressed ghettos in America. It was from these hopeless streets that the Dayton Family arose, naming themselves after one of the city's most infamous hustling streets, Dayton Avenue. Like Detroit's Esham and Memphis' Three 6 Mafia, the Dayton Family sincerely emulated their Midwestern mentality: a dark, grim mentality focused on modest survival rather than riches or fame. Unfortunately, the group's members all endured problems with the law throughout the late '90s; their numerous indictments prevented them from ever capitalizing on their modest success. As a result, years passed with only the occasional solo album to retain any interest in the cult group.

Back in the early '90s, Shoestring and Bootleg met via their younger brothers (one of them being future group member Ghetto E), and immediately began writing rhymes together, resulting in their first song "Dope Dayton Ave." It wasn't long before another aspiring rapper named Steve Hinkle joined the duo and then, after teaming up with a local producer named Steve Pitts, the Dayton Family officially became a group. Together they recorded a 12" and got signed by the small Atlanta indie label PO Broke, who then released the group's debut album, *What's on My Mind?*, in 1995. In addition to this debut album, the Dayton Family also managed to score a slot on No Limit's *Down South Hustlers* compilation, where they opened the double album with their "Stick N Move" track—a magnificent break, the Dayton Family now had recognition not only in Flint but also throughout the South.

After substantial touring and word-of-mouth promotion, the Dayton Family returned to the studio to record their follow-up album, *F.B.I.* As a testament to their quick ascension to the position of being one of the underground's most up-and-coming hardcore rap groups, *F.B.I.* ended up going gold and even managed to inch into the R&B Top Ten chart at one point in late 1996. Unfortunately, just as the Dayton Family were on their way to mass recognition in the hardcore rap underground, the law intervened. Between *What's on My Mind?* and *F.B.I.*, group member Steve Hinkle had gone to jail, being replaced by Bootleg's younger brother, Ghetto E. But if that wasn't enough, Bootleg ended up being indicted after the release of *F.B.I.*, soon followed by other group members over the course of the successive years. Throughout the late '90s, while the Dayton Family dealt with their legal problems, both Bootleg and Shoestring managed to record and release solo albums in 1999. Unfortunately, neither of the albums managed to sell many copies outside of Flint and suddenly the group was bordering on the brink of calling it quits. Yet in early 2001, Ghetto E and Shoestring both signed to Detroit rapper Esham's Overcore label, a testament of the group's continuing persistence in the face of constant adversity. —*Jason Birchmeier*

What's on My Mind? / Jun. 20, 1995 / PO Broke ✦✦✦
Originating from the unlikely locale of Flint, MI, the Dayton Family scored a distribution deal with Relavity and saw their debut album, *What's on My Mind*, spreading outside their hometown to become an unlikely mid-'90s underground favorite. It was the unique ideology of the group's primarily members, Shoestring and Bootleg, that made this album so intriguing. Nothing like New York or Los Angeles, Flint presented a different sort of ghetto lifestyle that the Dayton Family exploited perfectly, a lifestyle more akin to other postindustrial ghetto environments such as Gary, IN, or Detroit, MI, than L.A. or NYC. In sum, these guys don't rap about getting rich or riding around in expensive cars—they rap about getting by and surviving. It's a rather grim portrait, to be quite honest. And this decadence is exactly what made this album so appealing. The production isn't that noteworthy, as it rather liberally co-opts the early-'90s West Coast gangsta sound, but on "Flint Town," in particular, the beats elevate the already impressive rapping to wonderful heights. Anyone unaccustomed to the Midwestern sounds of acts such as Esham or Three 6 Mafia are in for a surprise with this album—this isn't even close to being your standard East or West Coast rap. Their subsequent album, *F.B.I.*, and their solo albums are much more polished, but this album's grit and the album-concluding "Flint Town" makes this an album that still sounds unlike any others. —*Jason Birchmeier*

● **F.B.I.** / Sep. 24, 1996 / Relativity ✦✦✦✦
With their second album *F.B.I.*, the Dayton Family stick to the gangsta clichés that made their debut *What's On My Mind?* a buzz band in underground hip-hop circles. Borrowing from the slow G-funk of West Coast rap and the mafia imagery of the East coast, the Dayton Family concocts a strong set of

hardcore rap. What makes *F.B.I.* a better album than their debut is the clean but powerful production from Steve Pitts, who keeps the music uncluttered so the crew's lyrical skills can shine through. *F.B.I.* sags a bit in the middle, like most of its overlong contemporaries, but the best moments illustrate what a gifted group the Dayton Family is. —*Leo Stanley*

Welcome to the Dopehouse / May 21, 2002 / Koch International ✦✦✦
One of the most underrated crews in commercial hip-hop, Flint's Dayton Family returned in 2002 with a solid third album, especially so considering there'd been no less than five solo albums since the last Dayton Family LP, 1996's *F.B.I.* Again, producer Steve Pitts plays a big role, laying down a variety of deep tracks over the hard-hitting flow of rappers Shoestring, Bootleg, and Ghetto E, and dropping the beats out entirely for a section of "Do You Remember." "Big Mac 11" and the hardly welcoming "Welcome to Flint" are strong tracks too; unlike most hour-long hip-hop production LPs, *Welcome to the Dopehouse* stays solid throughout, thanks to Pitts' production as well as the rapping. —*John Bush*

dc Talk

f. Washington, D.C.
Group / Alternative CCM, CCM, Christian Rap
The first gospel act to incorporate hip-hop influences (though the trio rarely departs from standard pop/rock), dc Talk became one of the most popular groups in Christian contemporary music during the mid-'90s, when their fourth album, *Jesus Freak*, made the highest debut for a gospel act on *Billboard*'s album charts. Formed in Washington, D.C., during the late '80s, the group first comprised Toby McKeehan and Michael Tait. Adding Kevin Max Smith to the lineup soon after, the group added elements of hip-hop to their self-titled debut album, which appeared in 1988 on the ForeFront label. Neither McKeehan, Tait, nor Smith were comfortable playing instruments on their recordings, so each recorded only vocals by the time of 1991's *Nu Thang*. After the release of *Free at Last* just one year later, dc Talk concentrated on touring for several years, during which a change of image resulted in the group's resemblance to a grunge band. Indeed, 1995's *Jesus Freak* featured more raging guitars, though within the medium of harmonic pop/rock. Upon its release, *Jesus Freak* sold more copies than any gospel album in history and eventually moved over one million copies. *Supernatural* followed in 1998. —*John Bush*

DC Talk / 1988 / ForeFront ✦✦

Nu Thang / 1991 / ForeFront ✦✦✦

Free at Last / 1992 / ForeFront ✦✦✦✦✦
Their breakthrough album, *Nu Thang* expands the group's musical boundaries and appeal, with impressive covers of "Jesus Is Just Alright" and "Lean on Me, " and the trio's best original compositions to date. —*Thom Granger*

Jesus Freak / 1995 / Chordant ✦✦✦
After building a dedicated following with three albums of Christian hip-hop, dc Talk makes a play for crossover success with *Jesus Freak*. As the title indicates, the group members haven't abandoned their religious base. What they have done, is expand their musical pallete. Keeping a solid hip-hop foundation, the trio adds elements of soul, psychedelic rock, and pop, making *Jesus Freak* their most ambitious album to date. It also happens to be their best. dc Talk fuses their diverse influences together with style and grace, making the music sound seamless. The lyrics frequently avoid standard clichés, managing to celebrate Christianity without sounding preachy. With its musical diversity and well-crafted lyrics, *Jesus Freak* is the album that will convince secular listeners that dc Talk is worth a listen. —*Stephen Thomas Erlewine*

Supernatural / Sep. 22, 1998 / Virgin ✦✦✦
You have to dig pretty deep on *Supernatural* to find dc Talk's Christian roots. Adopting an even more mainstream approach to making records, Jesus-pop's onetime favorite poster-boys are all over the Top 40 map on their fifth album. Listen, don't they sound a little alternative here? Is that a hip-hop beat there? And isn't that ballad pretty? Also tossing in some new age musical mysticism, classic-rock guitar crunches, and even jazzy interludes along with the usual contemporary pop conventions, dc Talk have just about every format covered here. Maybe if they stuck with just one, they could perfect it rather than projecting the desperately airplay-hungry image that's all over *Supernatural*. Big G and His Son do make a few appearances here and there, but the references are so thin, the band could just as well be praising a girlfriend, or spouting

cryptic *X-Files*-type messages for the paranoid, and possibly spiritually devoid, masses. —*Michael Gallucci*

● **Intermission: The Greatest Hits** / Nov. 21, 2000 / ForeFront ✦✦✦✦
For a Christian band to sell over five million records is a lofty statement; throw in numerous Grammy, Dove, and *Billboard* awards as well as 14 number-one hits and the reason why it was time for a greatest-hits package from dc Talk becomes clear. Concerning collections, *Intermission* is a gem, drawing from four studio albums and one compilation, with room for two previously unreleased tracks. Highlights from 1994's *Free at Last* include the rap-laced Doobie Brothers cover "Jesus Is Just Alright" and "Luv Is a Verb." From the multiplatinum *Jesus Freak*, dc Talk includes the title track, "Just Between You and Me," and "Minds Eye," among others. Also included on *Intermission* is the cut "My Will" from the Michael W. Smith *Exodus* project. The song is one that highlights the incredible spiritual fortitude and vocal harmonies that the band is known for. dc Talk's latest studio venture *Supernatural* is represented by only two cuts, the title track and "Consume Me." One tasty tidbit is the Larry Norman gospel classic "I Wish We'd All Been Ready" from the 1991 disc entitled *One Way*. This rendition is powerful—as the lyrics ooze with heartfelt passion—and a nice inclusion in the collection. Of the two new cuts on the disc, "Sugar Coat It" is the better one. The song moves with an energetic pulse; the harmonies are tight and the raps are modern. Notably lacking from *Intermission* is the band's latest number-one single "Dive" and the popular "What Have We Become." dc Talk has always shined as a live band, so something from its live release *Welcome to the Freakshow* would have been fitting. Still, *Intermission* is a bold statement of where the band has been and where it's going. —*Steven Losey*

Solo EP / Apr. 24, 2001 / Forefront ✦✦✦
When the trio dc Talk released their best-of album *Intermission* in 2000, many thought it was the end of the group's collaboration. However, members Toby McKeehan, Michael Tait, and Kmax assured listeners that the project and one-year break they were taking were merely the beginning of more to come, not only from dc Talk as a whole but from the three as individual artists. *Solo*, the 2001 EP from dc Talk, is a preview of McKeehan, Tait, and Kmax's solo projects, all released in 2001. The album opens with a live recording of "40 Live" from dc Talk, followed by two songs from Tait's album *Empty*. "Alibi" is rock influenced, with strong adult contemporary/alternative stylings. It is definitely one of the EP's strongest offerings, speaking of continual excuses in a relationship and the pain it incurs. "All You Got" builds on "Alibi," but is musically more mellow. Tait provides driving rhythms, stirring vocals, and a sound that leaves the listener longing for more. The songs "Return of the Singer" and "Be" come from Kmax's album *Stereotype Be*. Musically, he leans toward alternative, at times techno-influenced, rock in "Return of the Singer" and a slightly subdued alternative rock sound in "Be," a song encouraging individuals to be true to who they are. Toby McKeehan's tracks, "Somebody's Watching" and "Extreme Days," round out the release. A combination of rock, alternative, and rap, McKeehan also employs R&B flavoring on "Somebody's Watching," giving the song a sound comparable to that of Out of Eden. In the end, the EP only serves to remind listeners that McKeehan, Tait, and Kmax continue to grow and stretch their artistic abilities with time, resulting in cutting-edge and extremely well-crafted contributions not only to Christian music but to music in general. —*Ashleigh Kittle*

De La Soul

f. 1987, Amityville, Long Island, NY
Group / Hip-Hop, Alternative Rap, Golden Age
At the time of its 1989 release, De La Soul's debut album, *3 Feet High and Rising*, was hailed as the future of hip-hop. With its colorful, neo-psychedelic collage of samples and styles, plus the Long Island trio's low-key, clever rhymes and goofy humor, the album sounded like nothing else in hip-hop. Where most of their contemporaries drew directly from old school rap, funk, or Public Enemy's dense sonic barrage, De La Soul were gentler and more eclectic, taking in not only funk and soul, but also pop, jazz, reggae, and psychedelia. Though their style initially earned both critical raves and strong sales, De La Soul found it hard to sustain their commercial momentum in the '90s as their alternative rap was sidetracked by the popularity of considerably harder-edged gangsta rap.

De La Soul formed while the trio—Posdnuos (born Kelvin Mercer, August 17, 1969), Trugoy the Dove (born David Jude Jolicoeur, September 21, 1968), and

Pasemaster Mase (born Vincent Mason, March 27, 1970)—were attending high school in the late '80s. The stage names of all of the members derived from in-jokes: Posdnuos was an inversion of Mercer's DJ name, Sound-Sop; Trugoy was an inversion of Jolicoeur's favorite food, yogurt. De La Soul's demo tape, "Plug Tunin'," came to the attention of Prince Paul, the leader and producer of the New York rap outfit Stetsasonic. Prince Paul played the tape to several colleagues and helped the trio land a contract with Tommy Boy Records.

Prince Paul produced De La Soul's debut album, *3 Feet High and Rising*, which was released in the spring of 1989. Several critics and observers labeled the group as a neo-hippie band because the record praised peace and love as well as proclaiming the dawning of "the D.A.I.S.Y. age" (Da Inner Sound, Y'all). Though the trio was uncomfortable with the hippie label, there was no denying that the humor and eclecticism presented an alternative to the hardcore rap that dominated hip-hop. De La Soul quickly were perceived as the leaders of a contingent of New York-based alternative rappers which also included A Tribe Called Quest, Queen Latifah, the Jungle Brothers, and Monie Love; all of these artists dubbed themselves the Native Tongues posse.

For a while, it looked as if De La Soul and the Native Tongues posse would eclipse hardcore hip-hop in terms of popularity. "Me, Myself and I" became a Top 40 pop hit in the U.S. (number one R&B), while the album reached number 24 (number one R&B) and went gold. At the end of the year, *3 Feet High and Rising* topped many best-of-the-year lists, including *The Village Voice*'s. With all of the acclaim came some unwanted attention, most notably in the form of a lawsuit by the Turtles. De La Soul had sampled the Turtles' "You Showed Me" and layered it with a French lesson on a track on *3 Feet High* called "Transmitting Live From Mars," without getting the permission of the '60s pop group. The Turtles won the case, and the decision had substantial impact not only on De La Soul but also on rap in general. Following the suit, all samples had to be legally cleared before an album could be released. Not only did this have the end result of rap reverting back to instrumentation, thereby altering how the artists worked, it also meant that several albums in the pipeline had to be delayed in order for samples to clear. One of those was De La Soul's second album, *De La Soul Is Dead*.

When *De La Soul Is Dead* was finally released in the spring of 1991, it received decidedly mixed reviews, and its darker, more introspective tone didn't attract as big an audience as its lighter predecessor. The album peaked at number 26 pop on the U.S. charts, number 24 R&B, and spawned only one minor hit, the number-22 R&B single "Ring Ring Ring (Ha Ha Hey)." De La Soul worked hard on their third album, finally releasing the record in late 1993. The result, entitled *Buhloone Mindstate*, was harder and funkier than either of its predecessors, yet it didn't succumb to gangsta rap. Though it received strong reviews, the album quickly fell off the charts after peaking at number 40, and only "Breakadawn" broke the R&B Top 40. The same fate greeted the trio's fourth album, *Stakes Is High*. Released in the summer of 1996, the record was well reviewed, yet it didn't find a large audience and quickly disappeared from the charts. Four years later, De La Soul initiated what promised to be a three-album series with the release of *Art Official Intelligence: Mosaic Thump*, though reviews were mixed, it was greeted warmly by record buyers, debuting in the Top Ten. —*Stephen Thomas Erlewine*

★ **3 Feet High and Rising** / 1989 / Tommy Boy ✦✦✦✦✦
The most inventive, assured, and playful debut in hip-hop history, *3 Feet High and Rising* not only proved that rappers didn't have to talk about the streets to succeed, but also expanded the palette of sampling material with a kaleidoscope of sounds and references culled from pop, soul, disco, and even country music. Weaving clever wordplay and deft rhymes across two dozen tracks loosely organized around a game-show theme, De La Soul broke down boundaries all over the LP, moving easily from the groovy my-philosophy intro "The Magic Number" to an intelligent, caring inner-city vignette named "Ghetto Thang" to the freewheeling end-of-innocence tale "Jenifa Taught Me (Derwin's Revenge)." Rappers Posdnuos and Trugoy the Dove talked about anything they wanted (up to and including body odor), playing fast and loose on the mic like Biz Markie. Thinly disguised under a layer of humor, their lyrical themes ranged from true love ("Eye Know") to the destructive power of drugs ("Say No Go") to Daisy Age philosophy ("Tread Water") to sex ("Buddy"). Prince Paul (from Stetsasonic) and DJ Pasemaster Mase led the way on the production end, with dozens of samples from all sorts of left-field

artists—including Johnny Cash, the Mad Lads, Steely Dan, Public Enemy, Hall & Oates, and the Turtles. The pair didn't just use those samples as hooks or drumbreaks—like most hip-hop producers had in the past—but as split-second fills and in-jokes that made some tracks sound more like DJ records. Even "Potholes on My Lawn," which samples a mouth harp and yodeling (for the chorus, no less), became a big R&B hit. If it was easy to believe the revolution was here from listening to the rapping and production on Public Enemy's *It Takes a Nation of Millions to Hold Us Back*, with De La Soul the "D.A.I.S.Y. age" seemed to promise a new era of positivity in hip-hop. —*John Bush*

De La Soul Is Dead / May 13, 1991 / Tommy Boy ✦✦✦✦
On their notorious second album, De La Soul went to great lengths to debunk the "D.A.I.S.Y. age" hippie image they'd been pigeonholed with, titling the record *De La Soul Is Dead* and putting a picture of wilting daisies in a broken flowerpot on the cover. Critics and fans alike were puzzled as to why the group was seemingly rejecting what had been hailed as the future of hip-hop, and neither the reviews nor the charts were kind to the album. It isn't that De La tries to remake their sound here—*Dead* keeps the skit-heavy structure of the debut, and the surreal tone and inventive sampling techniques are still very much in evidence. But, despite a few lighthearted moments ("Bitties in the BK Lounge," the disco-flavored "A Roller Skating Jam Named 'Saturdays'"), a distinct note of bitterness has crept into De La's once-sunny outlook. On the one hand, they're willing to take on more serious subject matter; two of the album's most powerful moments are the unsettling incest tale "Millie Pulled a Pistol on Santa" and Posdnuos' drug-addiction chronicle "My Brother's a Basehead," both true-life occurrences. Yet other tracks betray a brittle, insular state of mind; one running skit features a group of street thugs who ultimately throw the album in the trash for not having enough pimps, guns, or curse words. There are vicious parodies of hip-house and hardcore rap, and the single "Ring Ring Ring (Ha Ha Hey)" complains about being harassed into listening to lousy demo tapes. Plus, the negativity of the bizarre, half-sung "Johnny's Dead" and the hostile narrator on "Who Do U Worship?" seemingly comes out of nowhere. *Dead* is clearly the product of a group staggering under the weight of expectations, yet even if it's less cohesive and engaging, it's still often fascinating in spite of its flaws. —*Steve Huey*

Buhloone Mindstate / Sep. 21, 1993 / Tommy Boy ✦✦✦
The last album of De la Soul's creative prime, *Buhloone Mindstate* was also their last with producer Prince Paul. After the claustrophobic *De La Soul Is Dead*, *Mindstate* is a partial return to the upbeat positivity of *3 Feet High and Rising*, though not its wildly colorful invention. Instead, *Buhloone Mindstate* takes a calmer, more laid-back approach—the music is often more introspective, and the between-song skits have been jettisoned in favor of a tighter focus. The surrealism of *Buhloone Mindstate*'s predecessors has largely evaporated, and the production, while still imaginative, doesn't quite dazzle the way it used to. Then again, it's admirable that the group is trying to mature and progress musically, and they would never experiment quite this ambitiously again. There's quite a bit more live instrumentation here, with extensive, jazzy guest work by the JB Horns. In fact, the guests threaten to overpower the first half of the album; "Patti Dooke" and "I Be Blowin'" are both extended showcases for the horns, and the latter is a full-fledged instrumental led by Maceo Parker. They're followed by a group of Japanese rappers on "Long Island Wildin'," and it isn't until the terrific single "Ego Trippin', Pt. 2" that De La really takes over. Many of the record's best raps follow: the reflective old school tribute "Breakadawn," the jazzy "I Am I Be" and "In the Woods," and the Biz Markie collaboration "Stone Age." If *Buhloone Mindstate* is a great deal more straightforward than De La's earlier work, its high points are still excellent and well worth the time of any fan. In fact, many De La diehards feel that this album is hugely underrated. —*Steve Huey*

Stakes Is High / Jul. 2, 1996 / Tommy Boy ✦✦✦
Seven years after its debut album, De La Soul was still one of the most unpredictable and risk-taking groups in rap. On the excellent *Stakes Is High*, the Long Island natives continue to thrive on the abstract and the cerebral. Instead of the lightheartedness that characterized *3 Feet High and Rising*, they favor a harder, tougher approach that's closer to their second album, *De La Soul Is Dead*. Jazz remains a strong influence for the group, who sample the improvised works of Milt Jackson, Lou Donaldson, and Chico Hamilton, as well as classic soul by the likes of the Commodores and Sly & the Family Stone. This eclectic approach certainly didn't hurt the group's popularity in

alternative rock and acid jazz circles, but in 1996 rap's hardcore seemed much more interested in gangster rap. —*Alex Henderson*

Art Official Intelligence: Mosaic Thump / Aug. 8, 2000 / Tommy Boy ✦✦
De La Soul came storming back after four years of recording inactivity—and practically a decade out of the hip-hop limelight—with a promise to release three full albums in a series they dubbed *Art Official Intelligence*. From the first volume, *Mosaic Thump*, it's clear that despite laudable ambitions, comeback albums should be focused and lean, not as flabby as this one. Unfortunately, the trio of Posdnuos, PA Mase, and Dave (formerly Trugoy the Dove) fall into the same trap they did on 1991's *De La Soul Is Dead*: an inventive, intelligent group attempts to prove themselves flexible enough to survive in a changing music world, and subsequently loses most of their appeal in the process. *Mosaic Thump* begins with "U Can Do (Life)," a surprisingly weak attempt at hip-hop soul. Posdnuos' raps are occasionally thoughtful and clever, but he seems obsessed with being as hardcore as DMX or Jay-Z. Aside from a few solid productions by outsiders (Ad Lib's "My Writes," Jaydee's "Thru Ya City," Rockwilder's "I.C. Y'All." with Busta Rhymes), most of *Mosaic Thump* was produced by De La Soul themselves, and the music is just as limpid and flat as the rapping. —*John Bush*

AOI: Bionix / Dec. 4, 2001 / Tommy Boy ✦✦✦✦
Ever since their 1989 debut with *3 Feet High and Rising*, De La Soul has puzzled fans by continually resisting the laid-back grooves and intelligent message tracks of hip-hop's best first album ever. From their sophomore rebuke *De La Soul Is Dead* to the harder-than-thou *Mosaic Thump*, the trio has often sacrificed happiness for hardcore, even when it's clear they do positivity better than any other rap group. *Bionix*, the second volume in De La Soul's comeback trilogy *Art Official Intelligence* presents the trio in astronaut gear on the cover, while inside a female-vocal intro proclaims the new De La Soul: "Better, stronger, faster." Listeners a bit doubtful after the rapid disappearance of first installment *Mosaic Thump* can rest easy; the trio sounds positively refreshed here, finally content to concentrate on their specialties: wrapping groovy, sparkling productions around smart, sympathetic themes with rapping that doesn't scrimp just because they're not gangsta. "Baby Phat" is first, a wickedly wonderful tribute to the beautiful black woman in all of her various shapes and figures. Producer Dave West spins a beautiful sample (from Wings' "Wonderful Christmas Time") for the highlight, a midtempo hand-waver named "Simply." Though this is by no means a hardcore album, the trio also spit a few bars, criticizing the easy answers of organized religion on "Held Down" (as well as on the three "Rev. Do Good" interludes scattered during the rest of the LP). De La Soul handed virtually all of the production duties over to the talented West, and it pays off doubly, not only giving *Bionix* a great sense of album flow, but freeing up the trio to concentrate on their excellent rapping (probably the best since their debut). It hardly seemed possible that De La Soul was capable of such incredible work after being lapped by most of the hip-hop world, but *Bionix* ranks right up there with *3 Feet High and Rising*. —*John Bush*

Dead Prez

Group / Hardcore Rap, Underground Rap, Alternative Rap, Southern Rap
The Florida-based political rap duo Dead Prez consists of Sticman and M-1, a pair of rappers inspired by revolutionaries from Malcom X to Public Enemy. They immersed themselves in political and social studies as they forged their own style of hip-hop, which debuted on the Loud '97 *Set Up* tape "Food, Clothes and Shelter." They went on to work with Big Punisher on his 1998 album *Capital Punishment* and released singles like 1998's "Police State With Chairman Omali" and 1999's "It's Bigger Than Hip-Hop." Their debut album, *Lets Get Free*, followed in early 2000. —*Heather Phares*

● **Lets Get Free** / Feb. 8, 2000 / Relativity ✦✦✦✦✦
Signed to a label (Loud) notorious for its astute thug philosophers (Wu-Tang, Mobb Deep, and Big Pun), the Dead Prez's empowering debut, *Lets Get Free*, seems like a misplaced oddity. Yet, the disputatious duo of Sticman and M-1 would be an oddity on any label, as they shoulder the burden of revitalizing a genre (pro-black) which has been seemingly erased from the collective consciousness. Taking social activism to new heights, the Dead Prez are the most revolutionary hip-hop group to emerge since Public Enemy lost its audience and N.W.A disbanded. Sticman and M-1 chronicle a broad range of politically pressing issues which pertain to the black community—from the inadequacies of inner-city public schooling ("They Schools") to socially repressive bureaucracies ("Police State"). But the Dead Prez are more then just agenda

and rhetoric; the group's topical diversity is equally inspiring, seamlessly shifting from the mind-pillaging "Psychology" into the conversational foreplay of "Mind Sex." Yet it is "Animals in Us" that best illustrates just how innovative this group can be. —*Matt Conaway*

Turn off the Radio: The Mixtape, Vol. 1 / Nov. 19, 2002 / Full Clip ✦✦✦
Despite a dispute with their previous home at Loud that has temporarily stripped M-1 and Sticman of their Dead Prez moniker, the pair continues to run with the same politically aware baton first witnessed in their 2000 debut, *Lets Get Free*, with the whole messy experience only strengthening their militant resolve. The music itself makes like a sonic freight train, with orchestral rises and inventive percussive patterns pushing things along with considerable power, while the lyrical subject matter is dominated by fighting the dark forces of oppression. Whether concerned with George Bush, club dress codes, or hip-hop's ongoing predilection with bling, DPZ's informed words echo the thoughts of predecessors Chuck D and KRS-One, with the only weak links coming in their occasional misguided foray into R&B—the soul keys of "B.I.G. Respect" most notably out of place amongst the incitement excitement of "We Need a Revolution" and the pleas of "Hit Me, Hit Me." These blips are few and far between, however, and do little damage to an otherwise superbly executed LP, where contributions from the Beatnuts, Peoples Army, and the Coup and an inspired spoken cameo from Cameo's Larry Blackmon only broaden the appeal of an already impressive body of work. —*Kingsley Marshall*

The Deadly Venoms

Group / Hip-Hop
Although not as well known as other contemporary female rappers, the women who make up the Deadly Venoms are no strangers to the rap world. Each member has had a history in the business with varying degrees of achievement. Finesse, N-Tyce, Champ MC, and newcomer J-Boo were brought together under the tutelage of rap producers Norman "Storm" Bell and Russell "Russ Prez" Pressley in response to the lackluster respect paid to women rappers. Finesse, whose tough pretty-lady persona was one-half of the pioneer female rap duo Finesse & Synquis, had been rapping since 1987 when she and Synquis unleashed a pair of singles, "Soul Sisters" and "Kickin' It." N-Tyce had recorded since 1990, but the Greensboro, NC, native didn't make an impact until the 1994 release of "Hush Hush Tip." Champ MC had been rapping professionally since the age of 19 and was considered a female Rakim in style and delivery. She performed on a couple of singles for Elektra Records but never attained much individual recognition. J-Boo hails from Queensbridge, NY, a neighborhood best known for producing fellow East Coast rapper Nas. This stint with the Deadly Venoms represented J-Boo's professional debut as an MC. Due to legal issues and a corporate merger, the release of the Deadly Venoms' debut was delayed, and they were dropped from the A&M record label. —*Roxanne Blanford*

● **The Antidote** / Oct. 20, 1998 / A&M ✦✦✦
In the early '90s, the idea of female rappers was still a novelty. There was Queen Latifah, MC Lyte, Salt 'n Pepa and Roxanne Shante', but nothing compared to male heavy hitters like Run-D.M.C., LL Cool J, Heavy D and later, Sean "Puffy" Combs, Tupac and Biggie Smalls. The Deadly Venoms banded together in 1998 to break that mold. Representing the "fairer, but not weaker" branch of the Wu-Tang Clan tree, the Venoms combined their collective expertise and individual styles for their debut, *The Antidote*, and proved that an all-female posse can lay down a devastating rhyme with the best of them. Their rap themes, emboldened with lyrical and poetic skill, are laced over flavorful loops and explosive hooks. The ladies give it their best shot, most notably N-Tyce on the cutting track "Slice Like Swords," where her North Carolina drawl spews unapologetically as she boasts about her power to attract the opposite sex. Wu-Tang Clan's RZA, Inspectah Deck, Method Man, and Ol' Dirty Bastard are all on hand to lend their hard-edged touch to the mix and, in so doing, succeed in outshining their protégés. Not to worry. The Deadly Venoms couldn't have asked for better teachers and partners. While *The Antidote* may not cure your hunger for rap, it will certainly ease the pangs. It's not really filling, but it tastes alright. —*Roxanne Blanford*

The Deckwrecka

Vocals / Hip-Hop
The Deckwrecka, also known as London DJ Agzilla, is part of the small but passionate U.K. hip-hop scene. He began DJing in 1986, but it wasn't until

1990, when he met industrial funk pioneers 23 Skidoo, that he began to play and record in earnest. Along with members of 23 Skidoo, he formed Ronin Records in 1989 and began to release records from the U.K. hip-hop underground. Deckwrecka spent the first half of the '90s doing production for Ronin and eventually he began to release his own records. The *Deckwrecka* series began in 1995, and by 2003 six volumes had been released. Productions with Skitz and Roots Manuva also found their way onto his resumé and his first full-length, *V for Vengance*, dropped in 2000. Shortly thereafter, Deckwrecka's productions began making their way onto big-name alternative hip-hop mixes by the likes of DJ Spooky, Nightmares on Wax, and his sometimes-collaborator Roots Manuva. His second solo album, *A Better Tomorrow?*, came out in 2002. —*Wade Kergan*

● **A Better Tomorrow?** / Apr. 22, 2002 / Ronin ✦✦✦
The 'wrecka—aka London DJ Agzilla—returns to Skidoo's respected rap imprint with his sophomore outing. His often cumbersome 28-track solo debut behemoth *V for Vengeance* proved something of a testing ground for this majestic second album, which keeps the angst-riddled tales from the city from grinding to a halt through deft flicks of production that retain a common thread throughout the wealth of contributors, including notable U.K. lyric spitters Rodney P, Titan Sounds, and the Extremists. While the air-horn-punctuated guitar power chords that reinforce the gruff growling of Scare Electric in "Vibekiller" or the almost-pop, spoken-word vocals of Lee Hudson that embellish the title track stand as highlights, it's the silken R&B tones of Rosita Lynch that steal the show; however, the funk nodder of "Who's That Girl" and the Silent Eclipse feature "Linguistix" are by far the most cohesive use of Agzilla's line in soul-jazz samples, thumping percussion, and grinding bass lines. —*Kingsley Marshall*

DeeJay Punk-Roc

b. 1971, Brooklyn, NY
Producer, Remixing / Trip-Hop, Big Beat
DeeJay Punk-Roc was born in Brooklyn, NY, back in 1971. The youngest of six children, Punk-Roc cut his teeth on the funky sounds of such 1970s and '80s stars as Parliament, Barry White, the Isley Brothers, Sugarhill Gang, and Grandmaster Flash; he also began DJing at parties. A troubled teen, he dropped out of high school at 16 years of age, but soon enlisted in the military to put his life back on track. Being stationed in Japan, Germany, and England helped broaden Punk-Roc's mind, and it was after his stint with the military that a friend turned him onto the wonders of writing and recording music. After DJing at a series of parties in a neighborhood school park, he recorded the original track "My Beatbox" for Airdog Recordings (Punk-Roc's U.K. label). His debut full-length, *ChickenEye*, was released in Britain in mid-1998, and picked up for U.S. distribution through Epic by autumn; it was praised as "the *OK Computer* you can breakdance to" by *Vox* magazine. The mix album *Anarchy in the USA* followed in 1999. —*Greg Prato*

● **ChickenEye** / May 18, 1998 / Epic ✦✦✦✦
On his debut full-length, *ChickenEye*, DeeJay Punk-Roc introduces his original dance-rich sound. The songs reflect Punk-Roc's specialties—dance/ electronic, funk, jazz, and hip-hop, with a production that jumps from retro to current in the blink of an eye. While it was meant to be played on the dancefloor, *ChickenEye* succeeds on the strength of its songwriting; you don't have to be a dance guru to appreciate the irresistible beats and electro sounds. Featuring Punk-Roc's first-ever single, "My Beatbox," and the other tracks are often just as enjoyable—"Far Out," "No Meaning," and "The World Is My Ashtray" are all tasty dance ditties. By touching upon so many musical styles, DeeJay Punk-Roc turns in an impressive debut. —*Greg Prato*

Anarchy in the USA / Jun. 15, 1999 / Moonshine ✦✦✦
Deejay Punk-Roc's very own mix album from Moonshine Music presents a series of big-beat anthems in waiting from Lo-Fidelity Allstars ("Lazer Sheep Dip Funk"), Trinity Hi-Fi ("TV Dinner for One"), Liquitek ("Pheelin' Phased"), Expansion Union ("Worldwide Funk"), and a remix of Roc's own "I Hate Everybody." He only reaches into the back of the crates for one genuine old school jewel—the 45 King's "1-900 Number"—and the preponderance of big-beat material does weigh the collection down in spots. —*John Bush*

Spoiling It for Everyone / Sep. 4, 2000 / Independiente ✦✦✦
Such is the precariousness of the graffiti-spraying, breakdancing world of b-boys and b-girls that its champions can either look like underground

heroes swilling gallons of good vibes or outdated fools twirling on their asses. Certainly DeeJay Punk-Roc often flipped back and forth from both fates throughout his career. Which makes *Spoiling It for Everyone* just as mighty and diverse as his work in the past, but also just as dubious. Early bird "The Living Sound of Reality" is probably the most promising. It offers frenetic scratching, educational samples, and booming beatboxing that would cause even Bentley Rhythm Ace's retinas to turn green. Not to be outdone, songs like "Hi-Fi Wrecker" quickly follow up by cutting huge slabs of electro breakbeats that not only showcase a bass line miles ahead of the drum'n'bass elite but also mate nicely with 2000's previous jungle-inspired hip-hop gem, Bahamadia's "Pep Talk." With the album's old school adoration and ADD rapidity, it's eclecticism done right. The pseudo-corner, slap-bass, R&B harmonies of "Blow My Mind," conversely, only taint these highs. Instead of flashing new b-boy stances, it cringes on its own bloated weight and makes the album look like one of those repugnant "desert island" lists trying too hard. It was a close call too. For a musician who tries so hard to show off his worldly record collection, DeeJay Punk-Roc seems to have once again only gotten it about half right. So take heed: you can get drunk off of Roc's funkladen, big beat-a-delic hip-hop, but you'd feel a hangover only minutes later. —*Dean Carlson*

Deepspace 5

Group / Underground Rap
The Deepspace 5 collective features a number of underground hip-hop artists, most notably members of Pride and Labklik. These two crews hooked up at the 1998 Cruvention with Sev Statik, and the collective began working on what would ultimately result in an independently released five-song EP, followed by the *Night We Called It a Day* album for Uprok Records. Besides the aforementioned Pride crew—Soul Heir the manCHILD, DJ Dust, Sintax the Terrific, and the Recon—and Statik, Deepspace 5 also features Fred Bruno, Playdough, Listener, DJ Beat, Illtripp 1, the Beat Rabbi, and Stu Dent. —*Jason Birchmeier*

● **The Night We Called It a Day** / Jan. 8, 2002 / Uprok ✦✦✦
Following an independently released five-song EP, the Deepspace 5 collective returns with their full-length debut for Uprok Records, *The Night We Called It a Day*. The 15-song album features a host of underground rap artists—Soul Heir the manCHILD, DJ Dust, Sintax the Terrific, the Recon, Sev Statik, Fred Bruno, Playdough, Listener, Illtripp 1, the Beat Rabbi, and more—who all drop literate and often humorous rhymes on this anticommercial affair. The album's standout track is the seven-minute-plus title track. —*Jason Birchmeier*

Def Jef (Jeffrey Forston)

Producer, Vocals / Alternative Rap, Political Rap
One of the better sociopolitical rappers of the late '80s and early '90s, Def Jef (born Jeffrey Forston) released an excellent debut (1989's *Just a Poet With Soul*) and a mildly disappointing follow-up (1991's *Soul Food*) before going into production. When he left the MC spotlight, he worked on records by a number of artists—as a producer and remixer—including Nas, 2Pac, Snoop Dogg, Nadanuf, Boss, Bone, and Shaquille O'Neal. He made short appearances in the films *Downtown* (1990) and *Deep Cover* (1992), and he also remained active as the music supervisor for MTV's *Lyricist Lounge* program. In 2002, he and his Kontrol Freaks production unit put together Kontrol Ya'self, a piece of audio software with beats, samples, and tracks. —*Andy Kellman*

● **Just a Poet With Soul** / 1989 / Delicious ✦✦✦✦✦
Raised in Harlem and the Bronx, Def Jef is a talented rapper who hung out in the same neighborhoods that gave us Grandmaster Flash & the Furious Five, Kurtis Blow, and the Treacherous Three and was exposed to their music at an early age. When he moved to Los Angeles and signed with Delicious Vinyl in the late 1980s, the influence of hip-hop's old school remained. Jef's debut album, *Just a Poet With Soul*, wasn't as big a seller as the albums Young MC and Tone-Loc had recorded for Delicious, but jams like "Droppin' Rhymes on Drums" (which employs Etta James as a background singer), "God Made Me Funky," and "Give It Here" made it clear that his rapping skills were first-rate. Jef is at his most interesting on the excellent sociopolitical offerings "Black to the Future" and "Downtown," both of which make us wish he devoted more time to message songs and less time to boasting

lyrics. But even so, *Just a Poet With Soul* is exhilarating and relentlessly funky. —*Alex Henderson*

Soul Food / 1991 / Delicious ✦✦✦
Def Jef followed up *Just a Poet With Soul* with the equally likable *Soul Food*, which regrettably didn't bring the underexposed L.A.-based rapper the commercial success he deserved. The CD's more sociopolitical songs are also its best, including "Get Up 4 the Get Down," "Don't Sleep (Open Your Eyes)," and the reggae-influenced "Voice of a New Generation." But Jef is also quite enjoyable on more escapist tunes like "Cali's All That" (a duet with Tone-Loc), "Fa Sho Shot" (which samples L.T.D.'s 1977 hit "Back In Love Again"), and the single "Here We Go Again." Jef may have been "coolin' in Cali," but *Soul Food* is a very East Coast-sounding disc illustrating the fact that the MC never forgot his New York upbringing. —*Alex Henderson*

Def Squad

Group / Hip-Hop, Hardcore Rap, Gangsta Rap, Pop-Rap, Underground Rap
Rap supergroup the Def Squad comprised Redman, Keith Murray, and Erick Sermon. After scoring a hit with their cover of the classic "Rapper's Delite," the trio issued their debut LP, *El Niño*, on Def Jam in 1998. DreamWorks released their second album, *Def Squad Presents Erick Onasis*, two years later. —*Jason Ankeny*

● **El Niño** / Jun. 30, 1998 / Def Jam ✦✦✦
As the first album from a genuine hip-hop supergroup, the Def Squad's *El Niño* has all the makings of a classic release. After all, Erick Sermon, Redman, and Keith Murray have all appeared on each other's albums before, but this is the first time they've had the opportunity to tear it loose for the length of a full album. Unfortunately, *El Niño* doesn't have the power of a full-force storm and, given the combined talents of the crew, it should. Instead of hitting hard and moving into new territory, the group plays it safe, keeping the productions spare and simple, relying on old school breaks and beats. At times, they pull it all together, as on the propulsive "Can You Dig It," but considering the Def Squad's pedigree, *El Niño* should have been better. —*Stephen Thomas Erlewine*

Def Squad Presents Erick Onasis / May 16, 2000 / DreamWorks ✦✦✦
Erick Sermon, "the Green Eyed Bandit," the premier East Coast funketeer, and one-half of one of hip-hop's pillar groups, EPMD, returned as Erick Onasis alongside the Def Squad in the summer of 2000. Featuring a host of guests from the four corners of hip-hop, the E-Double took his funky experimentation into the next millennium with *Erick Onassis*. Claiming millionaire status and taking on the moniker of one of America's old-money clans (similar to Jay-Z's Roc-A-Fella title), E lays his brand of brash and bouncy beats as the background for a slick gangsta-player persona trading in his trademark lisped, laid-back flow. Erick Onassis and his cohorts for the album are in your face, claiming cash money as king. There is precious little else on this album but bragging over funk tracks. But to the E, the funk is all that matters and the musical and emotional range consists only of how deep into the river of funk he wants to take the listener. He teams up with an eclectic and well-chosen mix of artists, all of whom play off of his down-bottom grooves expertly. "Why Not" features "the Ruler" Slick Rick in a rehash of the hook from Rick's classic "Mona Lisa." Def Squad heavy-hitters Redman and Keith Murray throw their hats in the ring for "Hostility." The West Coast-inspired "Focus" features Cali's Xzibit and DJ Quik. Eazy-E appears posthumously on "So Sweet." Def Squad crooner Dave Hollister adds his vocal styling to "Can't Stop." But the best cut is arguably "Van Gundy," a posse joint in which E's old tag-team partner Parish Smith bats clean-up. While musically this album drives along in basically one gear, overall the ride is pretty smooth and enjoyable. —*Michael Di Bella*

Defari (Duane Johnson Jr.)

b. Santa Monica, CA
West Coast Rap, Hip-Hop
A member of the Likwit Crew alongside King T, tha Alkaholiks, and Xzibit, rapper Defari was born Duane Johnson Jr. in Santa Monica, CA. He began DJing in 1982, moving on to MCing five years later; music remained only a hobby, however, and after earning a sociology degree at the University of California at Berkeley he went on to receive a master's degree in history and education at Columbia, accepting a high school teaching position upon graduating. In 1994 Defari recorded his first demo, soon after meeting Alkholiks

producer E-Swift; together they recorded the track "Big Up," which appeared on the 1995 compilation *Next Chapter: Strictly Underground*. A single, "Bionic," followed a year later before Defari signed with Tommy Boy Records to issue his full-length debut *Focused Daily* in 1999. —*Jason Ankeny*

● **Focused Daily** / Feb. 9, 1999 / Tommy Boy ✦✦✦
With a day job as an Inglewood, CA, high school teacher, and with a master's degree from Columbia University, Defari Herut (aka Duane Johnson) defines the term "hip-hop scholar." His straightforward rhyming style emphasizes positivity, and on "Never Lose Touch," he even gives thanks to his mother in the chorus. Although overly employing braggadocio tactics in dissing lesser rappers, his clever verses ("lyrics shine time after time, brighter than briquettes") on tunes like "Likwit Connection" make up for the shortfall. —*Craig Robert Smith*

Definition of Sound

f. 1989, London, England
Group / Acid House, Club/Dance
The London-based duo known as Definition of Sound created an appealing and exciting blend of post-acid house hip-hop that merged freestyle, reggae, rap, funk, rock, and R&B. One minute the group sounded like Al Green, the next Van Morrison, the next the Ombres. Kevin Clark and Don Weekes met at a mutual friend's house while they were listening to new and rare records and freestyling raps. Weekes, who had recorded with Coldcut's Matt Black and was briefly a member of X Posse, was impressed with Clark's skills and soon the two were working together on material. The two recorded a demo tape and under the name Top Billin' released two underground hits, "Naturally" and "Straight From the Soul" on the Dance Yard label. The interest generated by the singles led to a deal with Circa Records—and a U.K. following that grew as they opened shows for such visiting acts as KRS-One and Kid 'N Play. The Virgin Records-financed dance label Cardiac signed the group to a U.S. deal after hearing them at an industry conference.

Their first Cardiac album, *Love and Life: A Journey With the Chameleons*, was an adventurous, impressive collection of hip-hop. The first single, "Now Is Tomorrow," was an uptempo jam that featured jangling lead guitar, whooshing flanging effects, soulful vocals by guest singer Elaine Vassell, and an inspirational message. It was a hit on dance and rap charts in the middle of 1991. The second single, "Wear Your Love Like Heaven"—a Top Ten U.K. hit in early 1992—merged streetwise b-boy feel with Donovan's bubblegum '60s sensibility. The third single, "Moira Jane's Cafe," sounded like it was cut in Memphis with a spoken intro that sounds like Elvis, prominent rock guitar, and thick, fatback drums. "Love and Life" was named Rap Album of the Year by Britain's *Record Mirror* and had glowing reviews in *Billboard*, *Rockpool*, *The Source*, and other stateside publications. Just as it seemed that Definition of Sound was about to be heard around the world, Cardiac Records folded as a result of EMI's takeover of Virgin.

Their new label, Charisma, took enthusiastic delivery of their sophomore album, *The Lick*, only to fold in turn into West Coast Virgin a week before it was due to ship. As the corporate dust settled, one of the things buried beneath it was the new Definition of Sound record. Hard times, no money, no record deal, and a yearning to redefine themselves led Definition of Sound into the streets of London to drink in the bittersweet tastes of life, love, and despair. After more than a year in which they wrote and recorded nearly 30 new songs, Clark and Weeks signed a deal with Mercury and started making their third album, *Experience*. The clever, finely crafted songs were exuberant and introspective, from those two self-described "chameleons" of 1991—a little older and a lot wiser. The duo collaborated with famed '80s producer Chris Hughes (Adam & the Ants, Tears for Fears, Robert Plant). The result of that unlikely alliance was, according to *NME*, "like the delayed hit of a powerful drug"—an indefinable cocktail of '60s pop, psychedelic soul, R&B, and various shades or rock, all set in a lush, multilayered ambient soundscape. —*Ed Hogan*

● **Love and Life: A Journey With the Chameleons** / 1991 / Cardiac ✦✦✦
Along with the Dream Warriors, Definition of Sound released albums that tried to capitalize on the native tongue sound pioneered a year or two before by De La Soul and A Tribe Called Quest. The typically long-winded album title, sounding like undergrad essay titles; flowery quasi-mysticism; a taste for sampling that rifled through white beat groups of the '60s looking for hooks: all these factors make Definition of Sound followers, not trendsetters.

However, it's not a bad album, and has less filler than Dream Warriors' debut. The standout track, and the album's single, "Now Is Tomorrow" mixes rapped verses with soul diva choruses from Elaine Vassel—it's a joyous explosion of noise that unfortunately demands the rest of the album match it in energy and verve. Only a few are up to the challenge: "Dream Girl," which sounds like a caffeinated P.M. Dawn with a great deal of "Strawberry Fields Forever" blended in—if rap was going to get psychedelic, this would have been the way through; and "City Lights," based around "Smiling Faces Sometimes" by the Undisputed Truth. Maybe the weakest part of the album are the lead rappers Kevwon and the Don, one of which sounds like Q-Tip. In the face of some brilliant production work by the Red King and Donwon (possibly the two rappers?), they have little really to say, or little personality to stand out. Worth looking for in the discount bin. —*Ted Mills*

The Lick / 1992 / Charisma ✦✦
Experience / Feb. 1996 / Fontana ✦✦✦
Experience is an inventive, sample-adelic album bursting with nods to all sorts of styles from swinging pop to classic soul. Even though the two best tracks ("Boom Boom" and "Pass the Vibes") come first, later songs "Feels Like Heaven" and "Mama's Not Coming Home" display the Definition duo's continual wish to try out new ideas in sound and expand their repertoire. —*Keith Farley*

Del tha Funkee Homosapien (Teren Delvon Jones)

b. Aug. 12, 1972, Oakland, CA
Hip-Hop, Alternative Rap, West Coast Rap
Cousin of renowned gangster rapper Ice Cube, Del tha Funkee Homosapien (real name Teren Delvon Jones) was born in Oakland, CA, on August 12, 1972, and got his start with Ice Cube's backing band, Da Lench Mob. But Del's rap isn't as grim or violent as Ice Cube's is, in fact, he's been known to include something in his music that's far too uncommon in most rap: humor. Signed to Elektra/Asylum, Del's debut release, *I Wish My Brother George Was Here*, was issued in 1991 and produced by Cube. Like most rap at the time, it featured numerous samples of Parliament/Funkadelic classics from the '70s. Del's follow-up, 1994's *No Need for Alarm*, was a departure musically, as Ice Cube was no longer in the production seat and the P-funk sounds were dropped in favor of a more sophisticated, almost jazzy sound. Despite his noble experimentation, Del's sophomore effort failed commercially, as it would take four years for the rapper to plot his next move and issue another recording. Having left Elektra, Del aligned himself closely to a few fellow rapper friends, Casual and Souls of Mischief, and issued his third release overall, 1998's *Future Development*, for the same label as his friends, Hieroglyphics Records. The year 2000 saw the release of an all-new Del solo release, *Both Sides of the Brain*, as well as a self-titled debut release by a side project, Deltron 3030, which saw Del join forces with both the Automator and Kid Koala. —*Greg Prato*

● **I Wish My Brother George Was Here** / 1991 / Asylum ✦✦✦✦✦
Del tha Funkee Homosapien may be the cousin of gangsta rap icon Ice Cube, who was the executive producer on this debut, but it would be hard to imagine two more dissimilar artists. Yet, just as Ice Cube helped popularize and legitimize West Coast gangsta rap with N.W.A, Del helped lay the foundation for what would become California's thriving underground scene with his seminal debut, *I Wish My Brother George Was Here*. Predating similarly seminal debuts from likeminded artists like the Alkaholiks, Souls of Mischief, Freestyle Fellowship, and Pharcyde, *Brother George* takes the Parliament/Funkadelic-derived G-funk sound popularized by N.W.A and spins it into exciting new directions, replacing gangsta rap's nihilism with a healthy sense of the absurd. Released while Del was still a teen, *Brother George* offers a take on city life that's wry and bemused rather than tense and violent, addressing such crucial issues as having to ride the bus ("The Wacky World of Rapid Transit") and shiftless friends ("Sleepin' on My Couch") with a refreshingly assured comic sensibility. Bolstered by a pair of terrific, typically irreverent singles, ("Dr. Bombay" and "Mr. Dobalina"), *Brother George* imbued the otherwise grim West Coast hip-hop scene with a welcome dose of irreverence, proving that you didn't have to conform to any single image to be taken seriously as a rapper. Although for the most part an endearingly lightweight effort, *Brother George* does address serious topics on occasion, with "Dark Skin Girls" attacking media and personal perceptions of African-American beauty with a viciousness that borders on blatant sexism. Del has accomplished

much since the release of *Brother George*—the *Deltron 3030* album completed his evolution from smart-ass b-boy prodigy to indie rap superhero—but nothing he's done since has quite matched the charm, fun, and sheer exuberance of his stellar debut. —*Nathan Rabin*

No Need for Alarm / 1994 / Elektra ✦✦✦
After helping create the West Coast underground scene with his 1991 debut, Del tha Funkee Homosapien made a radical departure with 1994's *No Need for Alarm*, eschewing the familiar G-funk of his debut for a jazzier, more sophisticated sound more akin to East Coast acts like Black Moon and Main Source. The thematic and lyrical content of Del's work underwent a considerable change as well, with *No Need for Alarm* largely avoiding the endearing comic vignettes and blunted utopian vision of his debut for a never-ending string of battle raps. Del's loopy sense of humor remained intact, but without the structure and pop savvy of *I Wish My Brother George Was Here, No Need for Alarm* felt a bit aimless, even if it did contain some of Del's best work to date. "Catch a Bad One" showcases Del's new direction to the best effect, driven by Casual's sinister, hypnotic, string-laced production and some of the fiercest and most potent battle raps of Del's career. When *No Need for Alarm* works, it's terrific—funny, skillfully produced and wonderfully propulsive. Unfortunately, it only works about a third of the time. Critics have taken Del's debut to task for having a fairly generic P-funk-dominated sound more in line with executive producer Ice Cube's work than Del's unique sensibility, but Del has always functioned better when paired with strong collaborators. Sure, it could be argued that *I Wish My Brother George Was Here* and *Deltron 3030* reflect the sensibilities of producers and coproducers Ice Cube and DJ Pooh and Dan the Automator as much as they do Del, but working with strong-willed peers has a tendency to temper the artist's tendency toward self-indulgence and bring out the best in him. Without a strong sense of direction, *No Need for Alarm* is frustratingly uneven, rich, and transcendent one moment and aimless and repetitive the next. Still, it's a challenging, unique, and uncompromising follow-up, one well worth picking up for anyone interested in either the evolution of West Coast hip-hop or just the evolution of one of its most talented, eccentric, and gifted artists. —*Nathan Rabin*

Future Development / 1998 / Hieroglyphics Imperium ✦✦✦
Sort of a stop-gap cassette-only release (available exclusively on the Hieroglyphics web site) between Del's two original major-label albums and his first independent release on Hieroglyphics' own Imperium label, the optimistically titled *Future Development* (which also acts like a promise) doesn't show any signs of negligence. Nothing here is tossed off or given inattention. What does seem different about the album is that its themes are less serious, more rock-a-party, in the old school sense: hanging out, scoping girls, making rhymes, telling stories. Instead of the observational seriocomedy of his debut and the acid-psychedelia of the follow-up, Del has lightened the load on his space-holding unofficial third release. Elements of urban commentary and acid dementia (especially the former) are still present, but they seem less front-and-center. As such, the album is less coherent than his previous two albums and less immediate sounding without being immaterial. The characteristic Funkee Homosapien presence is still apparent, and it is impossible not to find something inviting about it. Del's voice really does recall his cousin Ice Cube's deep Southern drawl, but instead of an audible chip on the shoulder, Del is buoyant and fun and, not least of all, lyrically dexterous. He brings the West Coast funk, too-loping, low-end heavy, Saturday-afternoon summer funk—and, as with all things Del, it comes out mutated, alien, and just plain different than anyone else's hip-hop production, but in this case, far less manic than usual. The affect is a smiling sort of somnolence, almost to the point of jazzy, chill-out hip-hop. Instead of internalizing the stress of the world, Del chooses to "Stress The World" this time around, taking a quick break before he proceeds to his future development. —*Stanton Swihart*

Both Sides of the Brain / Apr. 11, 2000 / Red Urban ✦✦✦✦
Both Sides of the Brain is Del tha Funkee Homosapien's fourth album, on which Del makes an effort to show both sides of his personality. For example, on "Proto Culture," Del is joined by Khaos Unique, and the two rap about one of their favorite things—video games. The listener also gets to see another side of Del on "Jaw Gymnastics," on which Del and Casual team up for a fierce battle rhyme. Throughout the album, Del does the same thing, covering topics from drunk driving and crack addicts to the importance of good hygiene. Besides Casual on "Jaw Gymnastics" and Khaos Unique on "Proto

Culture," Del is also joined by El-P on "Offspring" and A+ on "Stay on Your Toes." Del produced the majority of the album, and even though he hasn't produced much in the past, most of his beats are good. The listener can also hear Del's video game obsession in a lot of the songs he produced, as many contain samples from video games. —*Dan Gizzi*

Delinquent Habits

f. 1991, Los Angeles, CA
Group / Latin Rap, Hip-Hop, West Coast Rap
Delinquent Habits formed in Los Angeles in 1991. The group was one of the first Latino hip-hop acts, mixing English, Spanish, and Spanglish lyrics together. Delinquent Habits consists of rappers Kemo (David L.K. Thomas), Ives (Ivan S. Martin), and O.G. Style (Alejandro R. Martinez). Upstart record label PMP released the group's self-titled debut *Delinquent Habits* in 1996. The album, executive produced by Cypress Hill's Sen Dog, combined obscure funk with traditional Latin rhythms and sold an amazing 350,000 copies in the U.S. and over one million worldwide. The single, "Tres Delinquents," moving 450,000 copies, charted in hip-hop as well as pop and R&B. Their second album, *Here Come the Horns*, was ready for release when PMP went out of business in 1998. This album may be one of the undiscovered gems of the rap genre as it features an appearance by the late rapper Big Punisher. *Merry Go Round*, their third album, was picked up by Miles Copeland's Ark 21 label after initially being released by the band. Delinquent Habits has performed on national TV including appearances on NBC's *Late Night With Conan O'Brien, Yo! MTV Raps*, and *La Hora Lunatica With Huberto Luna*. The group toured with rap artists like the Fugees, metal acts like Korn, and rockers like Beck, rapping as far away from home as Europe, South America, and Asia. —*JT Griffith*

Merry Go Round / Jun. 20, 2000 / Ark 21 ✦✦✦
From the moment the polished *Merry Go Round* kicks in, it's DJ O.G. Style dominating the proceedings with his squiggly sounding scratches, Spanish guitar loops, and tinkling piano samples, which overshadow rappers Ives and Kimo's decent but undistinguished rhyming. The album's other rising star is Michelle, a Latin siren who appears on three songs singing mostly in Spanish. There are no shortage of strictly West Coast, cruising-with-the-top-down-passing-a-fatty-type tunes like "Boulevard Star" and "Return of the Tres." Thankfully, Delinquent Habits don't overdo it with the pot references, which is about as tired a subject in Latin rap as shootin' and killin' folks is in mainstream rap. The Habits' lyrics are also extremely laid-back and free of any reference to gangs and violence, except when they occasionally dis that whole scene. In fact, the majority of *Merry Go Round* sounds very phat indeed. Perhaps there is a radio programmer out there willing to take a chance and reach out to rap radio's huge Latino audience, but, regardless, Delinquent Habits have fashioned the finest melding of hip-hop and Latin grooves to date. —*Adam Bregman*

Deltron 3030

Group / Hip-Hop, Alternative Rap, Underground Rap
The underground hip-hop supergroup Deltron 3030 features Deltron Zero (Del tha Funkee Homosapien), the Cantankerous Captain Aptos (producer/remixer Dan "the Automator" Nakamura), and Skiznod The Boy Wonder (turntablist Kid Koala). Much like Nakamura's previous conceptual projects, Dr. Octagon and Handsome Boy Modeling School, Deltron 3030's self-titled album and single sends the hip-hop triumvirate into the year 3030, where—as the sole survivors of earth—they travel through the galaxy. Both the album and single were released in 2000 on 75 Ark Records. An album of instrumentals tracks from *Tron 3030* followed a year later. —*Heather Phares*

● **Deltron 3030** / May 23, 2000 / 75 Ark ✦✦✦✦✦
The heir apparent to eccentric production wizard Prince Paul, Dan "the Automator's" left-field conceptual brilliance rapidly made him a hero to underground hip-hop fans. For the Deltron 3030 project, he teamed up with likeminded MC Del tha Funkee Homosapien and turntablist Kid Koala, both cult favorites with a similarly goofy sense of humor. Deltron 3030's self-titled debut is exactly what you might expect from such a teaming: a wildly imaginative, unabashedly geeky concept album about interplanetary rap warriors battling to restore humanity's hip-hop supremacy in a corporate-dominated dystopia (or something like that). It's difficult to follow the concept all the way through, but it hardly matters, because *Deltron 3030* is some of the best

work both Del and Dan have ever done. In fact, it's the Automator's most fully realized production effort to date, filled with sumptuous, densely layered soundscapes that draw on his classical background and, appropriately, often resemble a film score. For his part, Del's performance here revitalized his reputation, thanks to some of his best, most focused work in years. Long known for his abstract, dictionary-busting lyrics, Del proves he can even rhyme in sci-fi technospeak, and the overarching theme keeps his more indulgent impulses in check. Plus, there's actually some relevant commentary to be unearthed from all the oddball conceptual trappings; in fact, *Deltron 3030* is probably the closest hip-hop will ever come to an equivalent of Terry Gilliam's *Brazil*. The album boasts cameos by Damon Albarn (on the proto-Gorillaz "Time Keeps On Slipping"), Prince Paul, MC Paul Barman, and Sean Lennon, among others, but the stellar turns by its two main creators are the focus. It's not only one of the best albums in either of their catalogs, but one of the best to come out of the new underground, period. —*Steve Huey*

Tron 3030: The Instrumentals / Mar. 6, 2001 / 75 Ark ✦✦✦
In much the same way that *The Instrumentalyst* was Dr. Octagon's *Dr. Octagonecologyst* album stripped of its weird, paranoid rap vocals, *Tron 3030: The Instrumentals* is the instrumental sibling of Deltron 3030's self-titled album. In both cases, with Dr. Octagon and with Deltron 3030, the music comes from the mind and mixing desk of genius producer Dan "the Automator" Nakamura. The trade-off of turntablist DJ Q-Bert for Kid Koala doesn't seem to make much of a difference, as Nakamura's music is as epic, creepy, and outright blessed as ever. Where *Instrumentalyst* excised Kool Keith, *The Instrumentals* loses the vocal work of Sean Lennon, Damon Albarn, Del tha Funkee Homosapien, Money Mark, and other indie stars of the rock and hip-hop genres. But there's no indication here that any pulse or life was taken from the 12 tracks. Instead, the album comes across like a zany, cut-and-paste film score. Trumpets twist and morph into otherworldly sound elements, vintage piano notes mingle with Kid Koala's warped scratches, and snippets of vocals from Del tha Funkee Homosapien and various other Deltron 3030 cohorts appear just frequently enough to make one salivate at the thought of the cousin album. There's no denying that *The Instrumentals* is a moody album, but its mood is always engaging and frequently quite touching. The sampled vocals that repeat as if stuck on a skipping loop on "Madness," "I'm caught in the grips of this city madness," are somehow hopelessly romantic. It's astonishing that the album works on so many levels; it's a comedy hip-hop album similar to Nakamura's Handsome Boy Modeling School project, a collection of lush, jazzy soundscapes, an instrumental cousin to an indie all-star album, and a series of songs that would make for an incredible film score. Like every project Dan Nakamura has been associated with, Deltron 3030 makes for immensely entertaining listening, and *Tron 3030: The Instrumentals* is simply another amazing addition to Nakamura's already stellar accomplishments. It's every bit as essential as *Deltron 3030*, if not more so. —*Tim DiGravina*

The Demigodz

Group / Underground Rap
During 2002, the Ill Boogie label called on the Demigodz (producer/MC Celph Titled plus producer/MC Apathy) for two volumes in their *Earplug* series: *Don't You Even Go There* and *The Godz Must Be Crazy*. Apathy has also released a couple of singles on his own, while Celph Titled has also worked in several crews (A.P.E.X., Equilibrium) and rhymed on tracks by Lexicon and Lord Digga. —*John Bush*

● **The Godz Must Be Crazy** / Apr. 16, 2002 / Ill Boogie ✦✦✦
This extended EP, the second entry in Ill Boogie's *Earplug* series, makes one yearn for something lengthier from the New York/Connecticut-based Demigodz, because it is a compressed *tour de force* that is top-to-bottom dynamite. Apathy and Celph Titled, the duo who spearheads the loose collective, must have paid close attention (as far as vocal and production style is concerned) to Jay-Z and Wu-Tang Clan's records, because they possess the furtive sense of humor and peerless lyrical skill of the former and the almost archaic, labyrinthine, and self-invented language of the latter. The Demigodz, though, obviously haunt the underground instead of the mainstream; yet unlike a large portion of the undie rap crowd, this music is accessible. *The Godz Must Be Crazy* tempers an eye-opening brashness with a penchant for side-splitting self-deprecation (sometimes featuring both at once, as on the

boisterous freestyle triumph "Off the Chrome"), as well as a tendency to deflate typical hip-hop facades (check "The Demigodz" or the homage to and parody of Dr. Dre's *The Chronic* on "Intro"). And the group goes well beyond its pair of catalysts; they are a near-supergroup of up-and-coming luminaries like 7L & Esoteric, Louis Logic, and L-Fudge, all of whom come out slamming here, particularly on the great title posse cut. Slightly overshadowed by all the incomparable rhyme flow is some outstanding, cinematic production work, mostly from Celph Titled. —*Stanton Swihart*

Detroit's Most Wanted

f. Detroit, MI
Group / Gangsta Rap, Hardcore Rap
Detroit's Most Wanted (DMW) surfaced during the early-'90s gangsta rap phenomenon and faded away in the mid- to late '90s once the hoopla simmered. Similar to the countless other niche market-orientated gangsta rap start-ups of the time, the group was essentially a Detroit-style N.W.A: The members rapped about violence, drugs, sex, and anything else with shock value over West Coast-style beats. DMW released a number of LPs throughout the '90s, averaging around one release every year. Bryant Records released the albums, going through a number of small distributors. Despite the group's productivity, DMW never attained much commercial success, and the little success the group had was confined to the Midwest, for the most part. It's perhaps no surprise DMW struggled for sales given the myriad other gangsta rap groups flooding the streets during the early to mid-'90s. DMW didn't have anything particularly novel to offer listeners, and the group's name automatically inspired comparisons to Compton's Most Wanted and Philly's Most Wanted. The group's lack of creativity when it came to choosing a name is fairly synonymous with the group's artistic approach—DMW were better at emulating than creating. And they weren't very good at that, either. While other Detroit gangsta rappers from the time like Natas and ICP traded gangsta rap for horror rap and rap-metal once the style went out of style in the late '90s, DMW didn't. Consequently, the group's career came to an end. Few remember the group—except perhaps for "Money Is Made" and "Pop the Trunk"—and DMW's many albums quickly went out of print and remained so. —*Jason Birchmeier*

Money Is Made / Dec. 26, 1991 / Bryant ✦
Tricks of the Trades, Vol. 2: The Money Is Made / Apr. 6, 1992 / Bryant ✦✦
Early Days / Nov. 15, 1994 / Push Play ✦✦

Devin (Devin Copeland)

b. St. Petersburg, FL
Vocals / Hip-Hop, Southern Rap
Devin Copeland aka Devin the Dude was born in St. Petersburg, FL, and later moved to Texas while in the fourth grade. As a child he went back and forth from New Boston and Houston and finally settled in the latter after he graduated high school. In the late '80s, Devin met Rob Quest, a blind rapper and producer who was part of a Houston crew called the Coughee Brothas. Later on, the duo formed a group named the Odd Squad and recruited Devin's long-time friend Jugg Mugg and a local DJ named DJ Screw. Screw (who was later replaced by DJ Styles) took the group's demo tape to Rap-A-Lot Records CEO James Smith, who quickly signed the group in 1992. Their debut album, *Fadanuf fa Erybody!!*, was released in 1994 with "I Can't See It" as the lead single and video.

Although hip-hop fans praised the effort put out by the Odd Squad, their album was not as commercially successful as they hoped. While the group went back to the drawing board, Rap-A-Lot franchise artist Scarface approached Devin to be a part of his new group, Facemob. Facemob released one album in 1996, *The Other Side of the Law*, and then broke up due to internal problems. At this time, Devin decided to work on his debut solo album, *The Dude*, with the help of Smith and Scarface.

The Dude was released in 1998 with virtually no video and little radio play. *The Dude* was a smoothed-out, funk-laden album and an ode to wine, women, and weed. Regardless, the album built a large underground following and even caught the attention of veteran hip-hop producer Dr. Dre. He contacted Devin in 1999 and asked him to be a part of the *2001* album on the track "Fuck You." This single appearance made Devin a hot commodity, earning him appearances on songs with De La Soul, Raphael Saadiq, veteran rap group UGK, and a solo track on the *Oz* soundtrack.

His anticipated sophomore LP, *Just Tryin' ta Live*, was released in 2002 and featured appearances from Nas, Xzibit, and Raphael Saadiq with production from Dre, DJ Premier, and his Coughee Brothas. —*Quibian 'Q' Salazar-Moreno*

The Dude / Jun. 16, 1998 / Virgin ✦✦✦

On the basis of *The Dude*, Devin was labeled by some the new Too Short. In this case, it is actually a pretty on-target characterization. There are, of course, important differences. For one, he is a far sight funnier than Oakland's finest. To be deadly accurate, he's hysterically funny. And Too Short never attempted the smooth crooning into which Devin frequently and ably slides during his choruses. But in a more fundamental way, the Houston rapper is more like an updated and melodious hip-hop Dolemite, because the whole tone of *The Dude* is waka-waka blaxploitation smutty and smoove. The album title, in fact, is a reference and tribute to the 1974 Quincy Jones album of the same name, and as the rapper himself once pointed out, the main themes of his music are "weed, wine, and women," with little deviation. The music complements the mood in every regard. Pimp-sleek bass is mixed with heavy-lidded Southern rhythms, while Devin floats through the libertine backdrops with a rather severe case of laid-back nonchalance. It is a winning combination devoid of all the typical playa politics—violence and drama don't come within a country mile of these songs. If it is not exactly world-beater stuff, it definitely is an extremely randy good time. *The Dude* didn't sell too well with the general public; the album, however, did score some major points and found an admiring, devoted fan base in one place where it counted for extra: among Devin's fellow rappers. —*Stanton Swihart*

● **Just Tryin' ta Live** / Jan. 29, 2002 / Virgin ✦✦✦✦

Reminiscent of other great storytellers like Slick Rick, Devin the Dude is a true gift to laid-back Southern rap. This is his first real solo LP, and he didn't do it alone, given the presence of Raphael Saadiq, Xzibit, Nas, and Pooh Bear, and a couple of appearances by the Odd Squad. It's obvious that Devin put a lot of soul into this album, and it shows through in deep and reflective stories that evolve slowly through the album. Most of the songs are rather humorous, such as "R & B," which would seem to be about rhythm & blues, but it's really about Devin's need for reefer and beer. "Lacville '79" follows, one of the smoothest tracks on the LP. Again hitting some comedy notes ("I'm rollin', car not stolen, prolly never will be, it's much too olden"), Devin continues to tell a story about how he's happy with his girlfriend since she didn't mind pushing the car when it stopped working. The track titled "Who's That Man, Moma" is equally as amusing. The beats on the disc are smooth and funky, perfect slow-driving music. Devin's style is a mix somewhere between Too Short and Warren G; he almost sings as he raps and it works wonderfully on this album. —*Brad Mills*

DFC

Group / Hardcore Rap, Political Rap

What DFC actually stands for has changed a few times during this Flint, MI, group's existence. Dope Flint Connection was how they started, Da Flint Crew and Da Funk Crew are a few of the permutations, but the hardcore sound of the group has remained intact. One of the first Midwest rap breakouts, "Ain't No Future in Yo' Frontin'" introduced the world to MC Breed & DFC in 1991. The self-titled album that spawned the hit would be the only time DFC would share billing with MC Breed, but the group—Al "Alpha" Breed (cousin of MC Breed) and T-Trouble E—have remained close to their former partner. Their first release on their own, *Things in tha Hood*, featured production from MC Breed and Warren G and included the minor hit "Caps Get Peeled" featuring MC Eiht. They released a second effort in 1997, *Whole World's Rotten*, but have not been heard from since. —*Wade Kergan*

● **Things in tha Hood** / Mar. 22, 1994 / Big Beat ✦✦✦

When Ice-T, N.W.A, and Eazy-E first became popular in the late '80s, West Coast gangsta rap wasn't just about exploitation—those Los Angeles rappers were making a serious sociopolitical statement and did their part to bring attention to the social problems of the inner city. But in the 1990s, a lot of the gangsta rap that came from California *was* exploitive—not to mention cliché ridden and predictable. On 1994's *Things in tha Hood*, DFC pours on the usual gangsta rap clichés, and the L.A. group doesn't have anything new or different to say when it comes to gang violence, drugs, or sex. But while DFC's lyrics are hardly innovative or groundbreaking by 1994 standards, the beats ultimately prove to be the saving grace of this enjoyable, if derivative,

CD. Dr. Dre didn't produce any of the material on *Things in tha Hood*; nonetheless, his influence is all over this album. The producers include Warren G, MC Eiht (of Compton's Most Wanted fame), and the D.O.C., and every one of them is heavily influenced by Dre's production style. DFC wins no awards for originality, but when you're grooving to G-funk jams like "You Can Get the Dick" and "2-2 the Chest," you have to acknowledge that the L.A. residents do have a way with a hook. —*Alex Henderson*

Diamond D

Producer, Vocals / Hip-Hop, Alternative Rap, Jazz-Rap, Underground Rap

Veteran hip-hop producer Diamond D has helped out with several of rap music's most acclaimed LPs, including A Tribe Called Quest's *The Low End Theory* and the Fugees' *The Score*. In 1992 he recorded his first solo album, the underground classic *Stunts, Blunts & Hip-Hop* (which was released by Diamond & the Psychotic Neurotics). Although it never sold very many copies, it increased his status, and he worked with Illegal, House of Pain, KRS-One, and the Pharcyde during the mid-'90s. A host of top-flight rappers returned the favor for his sophomore album, *Hatred, Passion & Infidelity*, including Busta Rhymes, Phife Dawg (A Tribe Called Quest), and Pete Rock. —*John Bush*

● **Stunts, Blunts & Hip-Hop** / Jul. 1992 / Chemistry ✦✦✦

Diamond D had quietly provided some exciting production work and made strides within the rap music industry and community throughout the early '90s, but his name didn't become immediately recognizable until his classic guest appearance rapping on A Tribe Called Quest's "Show Business" ("Take it from Diamond/ It's like mountain climbing/ When it comes to rhyming/ You gotta put your time in"), off their masterful second album, *The Low End Theory*. Even amid vintage verses by such lauded hip-hop company as Tribe's Q-Tip and Phife and Brand Nubian's Lord Jamar and Sadat X, something about Diamond D's forthright and rock-solid, but totally laid-back, style stood out. Hip-hop heads waiting to hear more from him were rewarded with a veritable wealth of treasures when *Stunts, Blunts & Hip-Hop*, Diamond D's debut album, was released the following year. The album instantly became—and remains—something of an underground masterpiece. *Stunts* is a hugely sprawling, amorphous thing. Nearly 70 minutes would generally seem far too long for a hip-hop album to sustain any degree of good taste, especially one that is mostly song based and keeps the *de rigueur* between-song skits to a minimum. There is, in fact, a fair amount of filler here; but even that filler, after several listens, is so ingratiating that the album would seem incomplete without it, and it helps the album to actually be listenable in its entirety, as a single, long, whole statement. Part of the reason even the filler works is because the production—most of it by Diamond D himself—is uniformly excellent. The music he comes up with is just as steady as his rhyming. As for his simile-heavy lyrics, they can occasionally seem stilted or awkward, and aren't exactly complex, but Diamond spins a long yarn—sometimes autobiographical, sometimes fantastical, sometimes a projected scenario—with the best of them, although he can also delve too often into blanket boasting, and sometimes his words lack any particular direction. It's the everyone-in-the-studio ambience, though, rather than any particular standout aspect, that propels the album. Certain songs do stand out from the overall tapestry of the album: the woeful girl-gone-wrong tale "Sally Got a One Track Mind"; "What U Heard," with its bouncy bass line; the insistent "Red Light, Green Light"; the Jazzy Jay-produced "I Went for Mine"; the loping "Check One, Two"; the groovy "Freestyle," coproduced by Large Professor; "K.I.S.S.," coproduced by Q-Tip; and the jazz-tinged "Feel the Vibe." But they make far more sense as part of the album's cycle. The most enjoyable way to listen to the album's individual parts is to also listen to the stuff that surrounds it. —*Stanton Swihart*

Hatred, Passion & Infidelity / Aug. 26, 1997 / Mercury ✦✦✦

Bronx-born artist Diamond D is both lyricist and producer, and happens to be proficient at both tasks. *Hatred, Passion & Infidelity*, the second solo album from Diamond D, doesn't reach the extreme heights of creativity and originality attained by his first album, *Stunts, Blunts & Hip-Hop*. Diamond produced 13 of the 16 tracks on this album, and as could be expected, his sense of melody and motivational rhythm makes each of them instrumentally interesting and enjoyable. His lyrical dexterity exhibited is exciting, providing a swift narrative which carries the listener willingly from song to song. However, this album suffers from thematic inconsistency; two spots, "Can't

Keep My Grands to Myself" and "Cream 'N Sunshine," seem like forced attempts to attract a crossover, pop audience. The hybridization of R&B/pop and hip-hop instrumentation are unnatural, unsuccessful, and uncharacteristic of Diamond D. The rest of the tracks on this album excel and provide for an entertaining listen. Sideman John Dough adds strong lyrics to "Flowin'," "J.D.'s Revenge," and "On Stage." Reggae style chanter Don Barron (on Masters of Ceremony fame) gives an interesting touch to "MC IZ My Ambition." Phife (of A Tribe Called Quest) and lyricist/producer extraordinaire Pete Rock are both featured on "Painz and Strife." Diggin' in the Crates family members Fat Joe, Big L, Lord Finesse, and AG join Diamond on "5 Fingas of Death" for a dark and ominous posse cut. Legendary MC Sadat X (of Brand Nubians) and K. Terroribul join Diamond on "Never." K. Terroribul also appears on "K.T." and "On Stage." Aside from the two blemishes on this release, *Hatred, Passion & Infidelity* is a fair representation of Diamond D's skills on the microphone and behind the mixing board; an album a serious fan should have. —*Qa'id Jacobs*

Dice Raw

Gangsta Rap, Hardcore Rap
Despite his relatively young age, Philadelphia rapper Dice Raw is steeped in hip-hop history. A longtime protégé of Philadelphia group the Roots, he hooked up with the band while still in high school after Kelo, a member of the group's production team, spotted him in a local talent show. The group quickly took the young rapper under their collective wings and decided to bring his talent along slowly. He made his debut in "The Lesson, Pt. 1." Soon after, he made a name for himself with distinct cameos on "Adrenaline" and "Lockdown," where his hard-hitting style worked perfectly alongside the heady rhymes of Roots leader Black Thought. In 2000 Dice Raw released his first solo album, *Reclaiming the Dead*, for MCA. —*Jon Azpiri*

● **Reclaiming the Dead** / Oct. 24, 2000 / MCA ♦♦♦
With his debut, *Reclaiming the Dead*, the Roots' unofficial member, Dice Raw, makes it clear that his mission centers predominantly on reinstating the old school aesthetics Y2K hip-hop fans have become so disenfranchised from; Dice reiterates this predication by enlisting forgotten Philly pioneer EST from Three Times Dope to drop a few choice words on his "Intro." Yet, EST is not preaching to the choir. Reason being, Dice is neither assertive nor convincing in the pursuit of this ideology, as *Reclaiming the Dead* is swayed by myriad outdated concepts and contradictory sentiments. Though Dice flashes the lyrical prowess he exhibited on early Roots bangers with "Lava" and the spacy "Kamal Beat," where he boasts, "If Jesus could rap/He couldn't f*ck with me," even Dice's repertoire of braggadocios cannot make amends for a host of blatant crossover attempts, such as "Raw Sex" and "If I Only Had Words," which interpolates Cleveland's "Last Night a DJ Saved My Life" for the zillionth time. If *Reclaiming the Dead* proves anything, it proves that Dice is most comfortable in his original surroundings. Malik B and Black Thought's inclusion on "Lockdown" and "Thin Line (Between Raw and Jiggy)" provides the necessary checks and balance that force Dice to spit at a higher level of efficiency. —*Matt Conaway*

Digable Planets

f. 1991
Group / Alternative Rap, Jazz-Rap, Urban
Though they were not the first to synthesize jazz and hip-hop, Digable Planets epitomized the laid-back charm of jazz hipsters better than any group before or since. The trio's 1993 debut album, *Reachin' (A New Refutation of Time and Space)*, was a mellow ride packed with samples from Art Blakey, Sonny Rollins, and Curtis Mayfield, and the single "Rebirth of Slick (Cool Like Dat)" became a Top 20 pop hit. After embarking on an ambitious tour, which included several live musicians, the Planets returned in late 1994 with their best album yet. *Blowout Comb* continued the group's jazz-rap fusion, but also saw them branching out to embrace the old school sound of the street as well.

Digable Planets formed in the early '90s, when Butterfly (born Ishmael Butler, Brooklyn, NY) met Ladybug (born Mary Ann Vieira, Silver Springs, MD) while attending college in Massachusetts. The two later hooked up with Doodlebug (born Craig Irving, Philadelphia, PA) in Washington, D.C., and began recording. Their first single, "Rebirth of Slick (Cool Like Dat)," released on the Pendulum subsidiary of Warner, hit the R&B Top Ten while their

debut, *Reachin' (A New Refutation of Time and Space)*, and was a critical and commercial success. Digable Planets' resulting tour had a laid-back vibe more in keeping with a jazz show than any hip-hop concert, though the live musicians were criticized for doing little more than re-creating samples from the album. The trio solved that problem with the release of their second album, *Blowout Comb*, in late 1994. Much stronger than its predecessor, it used fewer samples and even included several solos; with no strong single to carry it, however, *Blowout Comb*'s sales performance was not up to that of *Reachin'*. After *Blowout Comb*, Digable Planets basically dissolved due to the dreaded "creative differences". —*John Bush*

● **Reachin' (A New Refutation of Time and Space)** / Sep. 27, 1993 / Pendulum ♦♦♦♦♦
Landing in 1993, Digable Planets' *Reachin' (A New Refutation of Time and Space)*, settled in on the consciousness of a large cross-section of listeners ranging from alt-rockers, metal freaks, and headz worldwide. A surprise hit with the press and the general populace alike, *Reachin'* was released at the most opportune time of the nineties. The so-called alternative scene had just blown up in '91/'92, so commercial radio was actually playing something close to variety and major labels were signing acts and developing them at an unprecedented level. Played on rock and urban stations, Digable Planets' debut represented an actual alternative to the masses that had grown up on Van Halen and Whitney Houston and as a result, Digable Planets found themselves with a Top 20 single in "Rebirth of Slick (Cool Like Dat)." In a lot of ways the song paints the picture for the rest of the album with samples that are drenched in cool jazz and interlaced with smart catchy rhymes that move across the hip hop spectrum of self-aggrandization and political awareness. The widespread appeal of *Reachin'* lies in the smooth delivery of Doodle, Ladybug and Butterfly. Never too excited but always passionate, they keep it going with seemingly lighthearted pieces like "Where I'm From." Here Butterfly almost falls into hip-hop stereotype by tripping on the theme of geographical location (see *Paul's Boutique*); but instead of really letting the listener know where they're from, they go into a chorus of "everywhere, everywhere," thus really pointing out this record's underlying theme. Under the 'hood of inventive beats, and well-placed layered samples are the ideas and attitudes of universal and cosmic spirituality combined with personal consciousness expansion that crosses geographical and ethnic boundaries. This is easily one of the most successful hip-hop records ever made and a must-have selection in most *any* collection. —*Jack LV Isles*

Blowout Comb / Oct. 18, 1994 / Pendulum ♦♦♦♦♦
Media darlings after the commercial success of their debut, Digable Planets attempted to prove their artistic merit with this second album, and succeeded wildly. A worthy, underrated successor, *Blowout Comb* was just as catchy and memorable as their first, and also offered the perfect response to critics and hip-hop fans who complained they weren't "real" enough. Except for a dark, indecipherable single named "Dial 7 (Axioms of Creamy Spies)," *Blowout Comb* excelled at pushing great grooves over sunny-day party jams, even when the crew was providing deft social commentary—as on "Black Ego" and "Dial 7 (Axioms of Creamy Spies)." The trio used their greater clout to invite instrumentalists instead of relying completely on samples, and the music took on more aspects of the live jam than before. Though *Blowout Comb* still borrowed a host of riffs from great jazz anthems (from Bob James to Bobbi Humphrey), Digable Planets used them well, as beds for their back-and-forth freestyling and solos from guests. The Digables remade Roy Ayers' "We Live in Brooklyn, Baby" into "Borough Check," and invited Guru from Gang Starr to salute Brooklyn's block parties and barbershops. (The focus on the neighborhood even carried over to the liner notes, laid out like a community newspaper.) The closer, a brassy, seven-minute "For Corners," also captured that fleeting feeling of neighborhood peace. Though *Blowout Comb* lacked the commercial punch of *Reachin'*, Digable Planets made great strides in the two areas they'd previously been criticized: beats and rhymes. The beats were incredible, some of the best *ever* heard on a rap record, a hip-hop version of the classic, off-kilter, New Orleans second-line funk. The productions, all crafted by the group themselves, were laid-back and clearly superior to much hip-hop of the time. The raps, though certainly not hardcore, were just as intelligent as on the debut, and flowed much better. While *Reachin'* came to sound like a moment in time for the jazz-rap crowd, *Blowout Comb* has remained a timeless classic. —*John Bush*

Digital Underground

f. 1987, Oakland, CA, **db.** 1996
Group / Alternative Rap, West Coast Rap, Hip-Hop

While hip-hop was consumed by the hardcore, noisy political rap of Public Enemy and the gangsta rap of N.W.A, Digital Underground sneaked out of Oakland with their bizarre, funky homage to Parliament/Funkadelic. Digital Underground built most of their music from P-funk samples and developed a similarly weird sense of style and humor, highlighted by Shock G's outrageous costumes and the whole band's parade of alter egos. Of all these alter egos, Shock G's Humpty Hump—a ridiculous comical figure with a Groucho Marx nose and glasses and a goofy, stuttering voice—was the most famous, especially since he was immortalized on their breakthrough single, "The Humpty Dance." Over the course of their career, Digital Underground have featured numerous members, but throughout it all, Shock G has remained at their core, developing the band's sound and style, which they had from the outset, as their 1990 debut, *Sex Packets*, proved. *Sex Packets* was an instant hit, thanks to the loopy single "The Humpty Dance," and while they never scaled such commercial heights ever again, their role in popularizing George Clinton's elastic funk made them one of the most important hip-hop groups of their era.

Shock G (born Gregory E. Jacobs, August 25, 1963) spent most of his childhood moving around the East Coast with his family, eventually settling in the Bay Area of California. He dropped out of high school in the late '70s and spent several years pursuing a life of crime before eventually finishing his degree and going to college to study music. Along with Chopmaster J, Shock G formed Digital Underground in 1987, and the duo released the single "Underwater Rimes" that year, which went to number one in the Netherlands. In 1989 the group signed with Tommy Boy, and that summer "Doowutchyalike" became an underground hit. By that time, Digital Underground had expanded significantly, featuring DJ Fuze, Money B (born Ron Brooks), and Schmoovy-Schmoov (born Earl Cook). *Sex Packets*, the group's debut album, was released in the spring of 1990, and "The Humpty Dance," which was rapped by Shock G's alterego Humpty Hump, climbed all the way to number 11 on the pop charts, peaking at number seven on the R&B charts. With its P-funk samples, jazzy interludes, and innovative amalgam of samples and live instrumentation, *Sex Packets* received positive reviews and went platinum by the end of the year.

Digital Underground followed *Sex Packets* in early 1991 with *This Is an EP Release*, their first recording to feature rapper Tupac Shakur. The EP went gold and set the stage for their second album, *Sons of the P*, which was released that fall. On the strength of the gold single "Kiss You Back," *Sons of the P* also went gold, but it received criticism for its similarity to *Sex Packets*. By the time Digital Underground delivered their third album, *The Body-Hat Syndrome* in late 1993, hip-hop had become dominated by gangsta rap, particularly the drawling G-funk of Dr. Dre, which ironically was heavily indebted to Clinton. Consequently, their fan base diminished significantly, and *The Body-Hat Syndrome* disappeared shortly after its release. Nearly three years later, Digital Underground returned with *Future Rhythm*, which spent a mere three weeks on the charts. *Who Got the Gravy?* followed in 1998. —*Stephen Thomas Erlewine*

★ **Sex Packets** / Jan. 1990 / Tommy Boy ◆◆◆◆◆
Sex Packets is a vibrant, wildly funny record that transcends any attempt to dismiss it as mere novelty. Novelty records are throwaways—cheap gags that are funny once, but never pay off with repeat plays, something that *Sex Packets* certainly does. *Sex Packets* is layered like any good story. Corny jokes, gross-out tales, flights of fancy, and sheer absurdist humor coexist comfortably, usually within the course of one song. Take "The Humpty Dance," their breakthrough single and timeless party anthem. Within that one song, Humpty Hump spills out countless jokes, spinning between inspired allusions and thuddingly obvious cut-ups, which are equally funny because of the irrepressible, infectious nature of his rap. And he's so confident in his skills, he's sexy, which is kind of what the album is about—it shows that sex is funny, and sexier because of it. But the very name of the album should be a clear indication that Digital Underground doesn't take any of this stuff all that seriously while creating elaborate, fantastical settings that reveal boundless imagination. The showiest number, of course, is the "Sex Packets" suite that concludes the album, built around their idea for a drug that creates full-blown sexual fantasies (virtual reality before it was in vogue), but their skill

at creating distinctive worlds is just as apparent on the endless party of "Doowutchyalike." These are the things that are buried beneath the band's jokes and an enormous amount of George Clinton samples. Much of the music on *Sex Packets* uses the P-funk canon as their foundation (a notable exception being a swinging interpolation of a Jimi Hendrix *Band of Gypsys* cut on "The New Jazz (One)," a cracking showcase for their team vocal skills). It's so strong an influence, it may seem easy to reduce Digital Underground to the status of mere Clinton imitators, but they take his blueprint, expand it, and personalize it, creating a record that is as loose and funny as anything in the P-funk empire, and in some ways, easier to access, since the party feels wide open. Few hip-hop albums sound as much like a constant party as this, and years later, it's still impossible to resist. —*Stephen Thomas Erlewine*

This Is an EP Release / 1991 / Tommy Boy ◆◆◆◆
Released in the same era of expansive and humorous hip-hop debuts by De La Soul, Digable Planets, Gang Starr, and A Tribe Called Quest, Digital Underground's similarly disposed first album and follow-up EP offered a party-friendly alternative to gangsta rap with a heavy dose of P-funk, jazz, and Prince's electro-funk aesthetic. The Oakland-based crew, featuring Shock G as alterego and frontman Humpty Hump, would continue to ride high with *Sons of the P*, but never really captured the inspired mix of their first forays into the hip-hop arena. That said, curious fans should first check out the group's maiden *Sex Packets* release before diving into this six-song collection; while solid in its own right, the EP does contain two nonessential remixes of tracks off of *Sex Packets*. And even though new cuts like the extended funk jam "Same Song" (featuring a nasty Bernie Worrell-meets-Jimmy Smith synth-organ solo), "Nuttin' Nis Funky," "Arguin' on the Funk," and "Tie the Knot" are all impressive, *This Is an EP Release* does not expand on the sound of *Sex Packets*. Still, a very enjoyable selection of cuts full of top-notch rapping, samples, scratches, and elastically funky bass and beats. —*Stephen Cook*

Sons of the P / Oct. 15, 1991 / Tommy Boy ◆◆◆◆◆
If it ain't broke, don't fix it: *Sons of the P* offers more of the loopy humor and P-funk fixations that made Digital Underground's debut album *Sex Packets* an instant classic. And if *Sons of the P* doesn't quite hit the absurd heights of its predecessor's best tracks, it's still a strong, engaging listen and an entirely worthy follow-up. The group doesn't take the title *Sons of the P* lightly; their George Clinton obsession isn't just manifested in samples; it's everywhere from the extended, chorus-heavy song structures right down to the back-cover art, a P-funk-style comic strip recasting DU as part of the *Clones of Dr. Funkenstein* concept. Once again, there are two great singles in the affectionate "Kiss You Back" and the Humpty Hump feature "No Nose Job," which rips black celebrities who surgically alter themselves to look less ethnic. In fact, the group goes in for some overt social commentary on several other tracks as well: "Heartbeat Props" are directed at still-living heroes in the struggle for equality, and "The Higher Heights of Spirituality" is a brief utopian dream. On the other hand, the album closes with "Good Thing We're Rappin'," a full-on pimp rhyme courtesy of Humpty Hump that's a little less genial and a little more Too $hort than you might expect from DU. A few tracks don't make much of an impression, but on the whole, *Sons of the P* makes a convincing case for DU as the rightful spiritual heirs to the P-funk legacy—and George Clinton himself even endorses that idea on the title track. —*Steve Huey*

The Body-Hat Syndrome / Oct. 5, 1993 / Tommy Boy ◆◆◆
Rebounding, in the charts anyway, from the relative downturn of 1991's *Sons of the P* LP, Digital Underground continued cultivating its own brand of P-funk culture on *The Body-Hat Syndrome* two years later, stuffing what had been the group's first year of silence with a fresh batch of funk-infused rap. Digital Underground's last effort for longtime label Tommy Boy, *The Body-Hat Syndrome* lacked some of the bright spark and humor that informed the band's first two albums. With the edgy grind of the leading single, "The Return of the Crazy One," and its accompanying X-rated video (reworked for public consumption) boosting the band back into the spotlight, the rest of the album unfurled to less than outstanding crossover commercial acclaim—the album's second single, the slightly melancholy and anti-racism cultural awareness politico "Whassup Wit the Love," barely cracked the R&B Top 100. But that's not to say that this set doesn't represent another brilliant feather in the group's cap—it does. Smooth grooves, understated humor, and gentle remonstrations of peace, love, and manifesto continue to

drive the Digital Underground style, here sampled across a chunky 20-track set. "Holly Wanstaho" is a fantastic jazz-tripped reinvention of Parliament's "Holly Wants to Go to California," while the completely original big bass beat "Brand Nu Swetta" is the perfect dance groove. The three-part "Body-Hats" breaks up the action. Two bonus tracks, "The Humpty Dance Awards" and "Wheee!," are included on *The Body-Hat Syndrome*'s CD issue. With a smart balance between old school, new school, and their own school sonics, Digital Underground has once again brought funk history to life, passing the torch to the next generation and, above all, having one hell of a good time doing it. —*Amy Hanson*

Future Rhythm / Jun. 1996 / Radikal ✦✦

With each new album, Digital Underground develop and deepen their homage to George Clinton's P-funk, coming up with new, inventive ways to carry on the tradition. Unlike the G-funk-inspired crews down in Southern California, the Underground plays fast and loose with their inspiration, keeping true to the wild-ass eclecticism of Parliament/Funkadelic's best moments. On *Future Rhythm*, DU have added a concept of their own—namely, the record is a concept album about moving the funk and hip-hop into the next century. Unfortunately, the music never sounds any different than the group's previous releases, with the notable exception of the exclusion of the good-time party raps that always ranked among the crew's finer moments. So, the concept never quite takes hold, and the music is similar to the group's other recordings, but so what? Digital Underground has found a way to infuse hip-hop with not only the sound but also the spirit of George Clinton in a way no other rapper (with the exception of Dr. Dre, who took the sound but ignored the spirt) has ever done. And that means that even their lesser efforts, such as *Future Rhythm*, have some fine cuts to offer. —*Leo Stanley*

Who Got the Gravy? / Sep. 8, 1998 / Interscope ✦✦✦✦

When Digital Underground recorded *Who Got the Gravy?* in 1998, its challenge was to acknowledge late-1990s rap tastes without being unfaithful to its history. And the Bay Area group pulls it off nicely on this album. Though not quite in a class with *Sex Packets*, *Gravy* was among the strongest rap releases of 1998. Underground was still greatly influenced by George Clinton's P-funk, and the quirky rapping of Shock G and Humpty Hump leaves no doubt that this is a Digital Underground release. But this time, the group brings a strong East Coast element to the mix. Blastmaster KRS-One has lively cameos on "Cyber Teeth Tigers" and the opener "I Shall Return," while Humpty's and Brooklyn's equally goofy Biz Markie prove quite compatible on "The Odd Couple." Given how senselessly violent the East Coast/West Coast rap rivalries had become in the 1990s, one can't help but see the CD's New-York-meets-Oakland flavor as a call for East/West unity. Of course, there were numerous rappers who refused to get caught up in that type of silly regionalism, and the Oaktown and New York MCs heard on *Gravy* are a prime example. *Gravy* demonstrated that in 1998, the Underground still had some highly entertaining tricks up its sleeve. —*Alex Henderson*

Lost Files / Oct. 26, 1999 / Lil Butta ✦✦✦

No Nose Job: The Legend of Digital Underground / Jun. 19, 2001 / Tommy Boy ✦✦✦✦

A major part of hip-hop's explosion of creativity during the late '80s and early '90s, Digital Underground was the first major rap group to draw their inspiration from Parliament-funkadelic. They followed that blueprint even more closely than the legions of West Coasters who walked the trail they blazed; the Underground didn't just draw from George Clinton's loose, funky beats and crazed party atmosphere, but also replicated P-funk's extended jams (albeit without the instrumental solos). Shock G's numerous alteregos and goofy sense of humor fit perfectly into the playful vibe of post-De La Soul, pre-Chronic hip-hop, and the group recorded more than a few terrific singles. All of those singles are present in some form on *No Nose Job: The Legend of Digital Underground*, which mixes full-length album versions (including the full 6:30 of the group's signature smash "The Humpty Dance") with briefer radio edits. Those shorter versions don't quite capture the way Digital Underground sounded on album (and, for a group able to craft such excellent singles, they were surprisingly consistent and engaging on their best albums). But that actually works as a better introduction for newcomers, who get most of the group's best songs in pure concentrated form. *Sex Packets* is still an essential classic, but *No Nose Job* will likely end up a necessary purchase for many. —*Steve Huey*

Dilated Peoples

f. 1992

Group / West Coast Rap, Underground Rap, Alternative Rap, Hip-Hop, Turntablism

With just a few (mostly underground) releases, Dilated Peoples have energized the rap underground in similar fashion to fellow West Coast crew Jurassic 5. The duo of Evidence and Akaa came together in the mid-'90s, when they met at many of the same hip-hop shows; after deciding to start making tracks together, they formed Dilated Peoples. Once they added to the fold an excellent turntablist, DJ Babu of the Beat Junkies, the group recorded the singles "Third Degree" and "Work the Angles" for ABB Records. The latter became an underground hit via hip-hop radio and clubplay, prompting Dilated Peoples' signing to Capitol. *The Platform* followed in May 2000. The group's follow-up for Capitol, *Expansion Team*, was released in late 2001 to positive reviews, and the group hit the road the following March, touring with the film *Scratch*, a documentary about hip-hop DJs and turntablists. —*John Bush*

● The Platform / May 23, 2000 / Capitol ✦✦✦✦✦

Dilated Peoples' debut album was hugely anticipated in the hip-hop underground, thanks to a handful of excellent singles and guest appearances that began several years prior. When it was finally released in 2000, *The Platform* thrilled some and mildly disappointed others. Dilated is very much a part of the back-to-basics, old school-worshiping wing of the underground, most often compared to fellow Southern Californians the Jurassic 5. They've got DJ Babu of the Beat Junkies working turntables, adding an extra dimension of authenticity to Iriscience and Evidence's well-honed microphone technique. Therein lies the rub: The trio's skills are all beyond question, but sometimes the album can feel like a formalist exercise. That's largely due to the lack of variety in lyrical content, which generally consists of one purist-friendly battle rhyme after another. It's all well executed, but considering how far hip-hop has come, it's hard not to want a more personal statement, or a few topics other than wack MCs and keeping the culture real. But other than that, *The Platform* is an excellent debut. The production (chiefly by Alchemist) is lean and inventive throughout, supporting the two MCs' abstract poetics with a subtle flair. Plus, their single-minded love of hip-hop brings a tremendous enthusiasm to the best tracks. The title track, "Triple Optics," and the underground classic "Work the Angles" are particular highlights, and guests B Real, tha Alkaholiks, Planet Asia, and Aceyalone all put in memorable appearances (especially tha Alkaholiks, on "Right On"). If it's occasionally uneven, *The Platform* is still better than the vast majority of its competition, and whether or not they ultimately prove to be the saviors of hip-hop (as some would have it), their promise is undeniable. —*Steve Huey*

Expansion Team / Oct. 23, 2001 / Capitol ✦✦✦✦✦

A mostly successful refinement of their debut, *Expansion Team* finds Dilated Peoples attempting to broaden their lyrical outlook somewhat, while taking advantage of a bigger budget to experiment with a varied cast of producers. Thanks to the latter, *Expansion Team* is arguably an even better-sounding album than its accomplished predecessor, boasting endless subtleties and imaginative touches in its backing tracks. And if the record is still heavy on the battle rhymes, Evidence and Iriscience are turning their attention elsewhere, particularly to the perils of fame and success (or of being just on the verge of both). "Trade Money" and "Proper Propaganda" take on money and the media, respectively, and there's also a brewing social consciousness on the brief "War," which is set to a rattling snare-drum march beat. Plus, there are plenty of lyrical assurances that Dilated will stay true to its underground, purist approach; the group even takes pride in the fact that that's what's gotten them where they are now. There's a turntablist showcase for members of the Beat Junkies on "Dilated Junkies," and guest spots from tha Liks and the Roots' Black Thought; meanwhile, the array of production talent includes DJ Premier, Da Beatminerz, the Roots' ?uestlove, and DJ Babu himself. The Alchemist, however, shines just as brightly as on the debut, helming the excellent lead single "Worst Comes to Worst." Dilated Peoples still don't sound as transcendent as some would have—they're never quite as unstudied or breezy as Jurassic 5—but *Expansion Team* indicates that they're continuing to grow, which means the fundamentals of hip-hop are in good hands. —*Steve Huey*

Daz Dillinger (Delmar Arnaud)

b. Long Beach, CA

Producer, Vocals / G-Funk, West Coast Rap, Gangsta Rap

One of the most important members of the mid-'90s Death Row Records empire, producer/rapper Daz Dillinger worked alongside some of the West Coast's best rappers. Along with Kurupt, Nate Dogg, and Snoop Dogg, Dillinger (at time known as Dat Nigga Daz) was one of the Long Beach, CA, clique that had been introduced to Dr. Dre through Warren G during the preliminary stages of the legendary *Chronic* album. Though Dillinger played only a minor role in the success of that album as a rapper, his subsequent contributions to Snoop Dogg's *Doggystyle* album as a rapper quickly established him as an up-and-coming West Coast talent. And when his production helped make 2Pac's *All Eyez on Me* such a success, he was chosen to be Dr. Dre's successor for the production of Snoop's *Tha Doggfather* album.

Around the same time, he was part of a duo also including Kurupt known as tha Dogg Pound that released a somewhat overlooked album, *Dogg Food*. Of course, following the departure of Dr. Dre, the death of 2Pac, and the imprisonment of Suge Knight, Death Row suddenly lost its momentum—and Dillinger's career with it. During the late '90s, he continued his efforts as a prolific producer but saw his long-finished solo album for Death Row, *Retaliation, Revenge & Get Back*, get continually pushed back until it was finally released in 1998 to an indifferent audience; the album did feature "In California," though, which proved to be a minor hit. In 2000 Dillinger released his second album, *R.A.W.*, on his Dogg Pound Records label. The record found Dillinger dissing Suge Knight, Death Row, and even his cousin Snoop Dogg. Yet without major-label push, the album was greeted quietly. *—Jason Birchmeier*

● **Retaliation, Revenge & Get Back** / Mar. 17, 1998 / Death Row ✦✦✦
Come the spring of 1998, Death Row was a mighty lonely place. Dre had been gone for nearly two years, Snoop enlisted in the No Limit army, Tupac was dead, Suge was in jail. Only Dat Nigga Daz—now known as Daz Dillinger—remained, and he was determined to keep the Death Row torch burning with his first solo album, *Retaliation, Revenge & Get Back*. It's a bit better than tha Dogg Pound's disappointing 1995 effort *Dogg Food*, but it finds Daz in an awkward position. He does what he does—namely, G-funk—well, but in 1998 G-funk is an anachronism. True, Master P builds on the G-funk sound (no matter how much he would like to deny it), but his stripped-down, cheap productions are the sound of the late '90s—the loping beats and whiny synths of G-funk belong to the early '90s. And that's where Daz is stuck, no matter how you look at it. If you look past that, however, *Retaliation, Revenge & Get Back* is a solid record that delivers exactly what it promises—straight-up gangsta rap, nothing more and nothing less. There are no surprises, but few albums since *Doggystyle* have given the G-funk audience exactly what they want as *Retaliation* does. By that standard, Daz's debut is a success. *—Leo Stanley*

R.A.W. / Aug. 29, 2000 / D.P.G. ✦✦
After Daz Dillinger's Death Row debut, *Retaliation, Revenge & Get Back*, was greeted by an indifferent audience despite being a quality West Coast release, the rapper/producer returned in mid-2000 with *R.A.W.* on his own Dogg Pound Records label. Aesthetically similar to his days with Death Row, *R.A.W.* should please anyone who misses the mid-'90s G-funk sound, particularly Dillinger's more acclaimed work: tha Dogg Pound's *Dogg Food*, Snoop Dogg's *Tha Doggfather*, and 2Pac's *All Eyez on Me*. Kurupt plays a big role here, as does Soopafly, another of Dillinger's peers from the Death Row days; other guests include Mac-Shawn, Tray Deee, and Lil' C-Style. "What It Is" stands out on the album, mostly because Daz speaks up about his bitter feelings toward Death Row and, surprisingly, his cousin Snoop Dogg. "Who's Knocking at My Door" also stands out with a great beat, and "I'd Rather Lie to You" finds the rapper tackling some serious issues. Overall, this album is hurt by its lack of major label polish and also from its compiled feel. Mostly because of these reasons, and also because Daz isn't one of the West Coast's best rappers, this album isn't as great as it could be. As might be expected, the production is the album's most notable feature, making *R.A.W.* worth seeking out if you are a fan of Dillinger's trademark West Coast beats. And finally, though the album isn't as well crafted as *Retaliation, Revenge & Get Back*, it does find a more mature Daz, which is a welcome change over the theatrical Death Row posing that hampers his mid-'90s work. *—Jason Birchmeier*

Longbeach 2 Fillmoe / Jan. 16, 2001 / Black Market ✦✦✦
The infamous Daz Dillinger, one part of tha Dogg Pound, is back at it again but without Kurupt this time. Instead, he's given J.T. the Bigga Figga a chance to shine on what's more of a compilation of cameo appearances than a succinct album. Dillinger skipped production duties on this and let Sean-T take a stab at the mixing board. The result is a fresh new album that's sure to please a lot of his fans. Still, the album isn't without its slow spots. They drag their feet a bit on the tracks with a few too many guest appearances; there are even a few songs with neither of the headlining rappers. Fortunately, the addition of Sean-T as a producer really shook it up and gave them that extra bit of creativity to work with. Perhaps if Dillinger had done the beats himself, *Longbeach 2 Fillmoe* would be a bit more of the same again. While a fairly strong album, this is still nowhere near the potential of these two artists. If they'd made it more of a duo effort rather than a group project, it would have resulted in a better LP. *—Brad Mills*

This Is the Life I Lead / Jun. 11, 2002 / DPG ✦✦
Following 2001's *Longbeach 2 Fillmoe*, his double-team turn with J.T. the Bigga Figga, Daz Dillinger returned with an album that's clearly his own. He not only released it on his own DPG Recordz, but produced every track by himself (with help from Mike Dean) and kept the guest rappers to a minimum. The easy-rolling party anthem "Keep It Gangsta" finds him turning in a deep, lazy-day G-funk cut with no problems, and pushing against the tide of the post-gangster rap mainstream in the process. On "I Live Every Day Like I Could Die Every Day," Dillinger hits out against major labels, as well as ghetto life, though the light chorus keeps it all upbeat. The party joints here sound a lot better than hardcore tracks like "Drama" and "Run tha Street." Another disappointment: "B*tch B*tch B*tch Make Me Rich," with Too Short, despite some fine live bass from Shorty B. *—John Bush*

Dimples D. (Crystal Smith)

Vocals / Old School Rap

"Sucker DJ's (I Will Survive)" by Dimples D. was one of Marley Marl's first successes, a hip-hop one-shot that made little noise upon release in 1983 but charted across Europe when a remix was released seven years later. Born Crystal Smith, she was selected to voice the track by Marl, a New York DJ and aspiring producer. It was released on the Party Time label in 1983, one year before Marley Marl's breakthrough on Roxanne Shanté's "Roxanne's Revenge," one of many answer records on U.T.F.O.'s "Roxanne, Roxanne." The track was often sampled by Marl himself, and radically reworked in 1990, with the addition of a sprightly sample lifted from the *I Dream of Jeannie* theme song that earned it chart success in Europe. *—John Bush*

● **Sucker DJ [Single]** / Jul. 1, 1991 / Warlock ✦✦✦

Dirty

f. 1999, Montgomery, AL

Group / Dirty South, Southern Rap

The highly touted Southern rap duo Dirty signed with Universal Records in late 2000 in the wake of the South's late-'90s emergence as a major force in the rap game, becoming the first major rap act to arise from Alabama. Originating from Montgomery, group members Big Pimp and Mr. G' Stacka fused quick-firing styles in the tradition of Southern pioneers Outkast with a unique Alabama-style pimp-meets-gangsta disposition and some refreshingly inventive production. With an elegant delivery, they stood above their legions of Dirty South peers, experiencing remarkable popularity in their hometown thanks to their *The Pimp & da Gangsta* album, which became a regional smash hit when originally released independently by Nfinity Music. Though preceded by their 1999 release, *Countryversatile*, it was this second album which inspired the hype that led to their signing with Universal. In February 2001 *The Pimp & da Gangsta* saw national release in a more polished state with new tracks. *—Jason Birchmeier*

● **The Pimp & da Gangsta** / Feb. 27, 2001 / Universal ✦✦✦✦
A regional phenomenon before being re-released nationally, *The Pimp & da Gangsta* stands as a second-generation dirty South album, a well-crafted album that harks back to Outkast's style-defining landmark debut, *Southernplayalisticadillacmuzik*. The fact that group members Big Pimp and Mr. G' Stacka sound so similar to early Outkast is both inviting and frustrating. On the one hand, their quick delivery comes across amazingly lucid, and their "pimp & gangsta" personas make for a well-balanced duo; furthermore, they

handle similar subject matter elegantly, covering all the staples of the dirty South lifestyle, staples first explored on *Southernplayalisticadillacmuzik*—smokin' on "wood," "bending corners" in their Cadillac, being "all about that bread," "pulling tricks," etc. This is where the slight problem arises—Dirty recycles *Southernplayalisticadillacmuzik* almost *too* well, from the ornament cosmic synths lacing their beats to the emphasis on catchy, tongue-twisting choruses to the duo's knack for dropping their own lingo. Yet as derivative as this album is, Dirty shamelessly wears their influences on their sleeve and have enough talent and confidence to make their second-generation rehashing respectable rather than rudimental. The album's first track, "Rollin' Vogues," serves as a perfect introduction, with Big Pimp and Mr. G'stacka forming a catchy hook about "rollin' in vogues/with triple gold/on Cadillacs/getting blowed up/chillin' in the back/smokin' on that wood/feeling so pimp tight." The album's title track is also a fitting portrait of their dual roles as pimp and gangsta, while another of the album's numerous highlights, "Hit Da Floe," is a tailor-made club anthem, with a midtempo, stuttering rhythm perfect for head nodding and ass shaking. In fact, there really isn't much filler here at all. Dirty is able to stretch out their pimp and gangsta personas well across the album's 15 tracks, interspersing a healthy dose of humor ever so often to keep things entertaining as well as crunk. In the end, it's probably most stunning to think about how dirty is still honing their craft here; Big Pimp and Mr. G' Stacka must have spent plenty of time studying their mid-'90s Eightball & MJG and Outkast because they execute their dirty South motifs with near perfection. Few artists have such a grasp of their influences, foreshadowing a healthy future for the dirty South rap game. (This album was originally released independently by Nfinity Music before being re-released nationally by Universal. The latter version features a few new tracks.) —*Jason Birchmeier*

Keep It Pimp and Gangsta / Feb. 25, 2003 / Universal ✦✦✦✦
The similarity between the title of this album and the title of its predecessor is telling, since Big Pimp and Mr. G' Stacka hardly change their pitch, and as a result, the duo's ties to the Southern rap blueprint drawn by Outkast and Eightball & MJG remain tight. Just as the title implies, *Keep It Pimp and Gangsta* has little to do with a shift or progression, which actually suits them fine—they're far from original, but they do what they do so well that it simply doesn't matter. Most priceless moment: the falsetto Prince-style delivery of "Keep It," in which the cautionary chorus warns "Your b*tch ass about to die." —*Andy Kellman*

Disco D (Dave Shayman)

Group / Hip-Hop, Techno Bass
Dave Shayman, better known as Disco D, was just 18 years old when he emerged as a fresh face to the Detroit/Ann Arbor ghetto-tech and turntablist scene. From February to December of 1998, he was the resident at a club night sponsored by Ann Arbor's Intuit-Solar Records. The night gave Shayman the opportunity to spin with Derrick May, Amon Tobin, and Terrence Parker. In 1998 he released his first 12" EP, *D-Down*, on Intuit-Solar. In August of 1998, he signed on with Chicago-based Mixconnection Multimedia. That year, he released his second 12" record, *Cannot Stop This*, on MCM's sublabel, Contaminated Muzik. The ghetto-tech release received mixes by jungle producers, Danny the Wildchild and Phantom 45. In 1999 Disco D released *Incomprehensible Representation of Self.* —*Diana Potts*

● **Straight out tha Trunk** / Oct. 23, 2001 / Gti Recordings ✦✦✦
The first CD release from Ann Arbor playboy Disco D outlines what's expected from any booty techno DJ: at least an hour of nonstop sonic terrorism, simply packed with renegade scratching, pitched-up vocal tags, and speedy electro-bass, heavy on the 2-step lurch. Blazing through almost 50 tracks in under an hour, Disco D drags in dozens of superb samples, raps, productions, callouts, and remixes; anything capable of moving the typical no-attention-span dancefloor crowd. Despite the booty bump of most tracks, he does give the females equal time, working deftly from the thug shout-out "Where They At" directly into its "Ladies Night Remix." Disco D also provides a glimpse at Detroit future/past techno on "Time Space Scrilla," and gets some great rapping on the cuts " "Tekno 4X4/Detroit Zoo" and the official Disco D remix of Eightball & MJG's "Buck Bounce." —*John Bush*

Disco Four

Group / Hip-Hop
Disco Four was one of the prime party-jam producers in rap's old school, recording classics like "Move With the Groove" and "Do It, Do It" for Enjoy

during the early '80s. Based in Harlem, the group formed around Ronnie D, DJ Al Bee, Greg G, Mr. Troy, Country, Kool Gee, and DJ Al Bee. A fraternal connection with Bobby Robinson—one of the members was his son—got them signed up to the Enjoy label (then the hottest place for hip-hop), but nepotism had nothing to do with their classic debut, 1980's "Move With the Groove." A smooth, quick-paced party track, it was followed by "Do It, Do It" in 1981 and "Country Rock and Rap" in 1982. That same year, they also appeared on Profile (then in its infancy) with another club track, "We're at the Party." Disco Four didn't do much more in the way of recording, except for a 1986 single on Danya ("Get Busy") and a Profile Christmas record one year later. —*John Bush*

The Disposable Heroes of Hiphoprisy

f. 1990, San Fransisco, CA, **db.** 1993
Group / Political Rap, Hip-Hop, Alternative Rap
An outgrowth, both musically and ideologically, of the San Francisco-based avant-garde industrial jazz collective the Beatnigs, the Disposable Heroes of Hiphoprisy formed in 1990. Comprised of former Beatnigs Michael Franti and Rono Tse, the duo quickly established themselves among rap's foremost proponents of multiculturalism and liberalism; pointedly attacking hip-hop tenets like homophobia, misogyny, and racism, Franti's narratives addressed issues ranging from "Television: The Drug of the Nation" to "Socio-Genetic Experience" (about his childhood raised by white parents) with clarity and depth.

Opening slots for everyone from Public Enemy and Arrested Development to Nirvana and U2 attested to the nerve hit by the Heroes' 1992 debut, *Hypocrisy Is the Greatest Luxury*, although some members of the rap community dismissed the duo as an attempt to quell white America's apprehensions over the violent worldview depicted in the grooves of gangsta rap records. Consequently, the Disposable Heroes of Hiphoprisy never attracted the African-American audiences their music actively sought, and after joining beat legend William S. Burroughs on his 1993 release *Spare Ass Annie and Other Tales*, the duo disbanded; while Tse later worked with the Bay Area rap unit Mystik Journeymen, Franti formed Spearhead, a more roots-oriented concern. —*Jason Ankeny*

● **Hypocrisy Is the Greatest Luxury** / 1992 / 4th & Broadway ✦✦✦✦
The Disposable Heroes tackled every last big issue possible with one of 1992's most underrated efforts. Dr Dre and G-funk became all the rage by the end of the year and beyond, but for those looking for at least a little more from hip-hop than that soon-to-be-clichéd style, *Hypocrisy Is the Greatest Luxury* did the business. The group's origins in the Beatnigs aren't hidden at all—besides a stunning, menacing revision of that band's "Television, the Drug of the Nation," the Heroes' first single, the combination of Bomb Squad and industrial music approaches is apparent throughout. Consolidated's Mark Pistel coproduced the album while Meat Beat Manifesto's Jack Dangers helped mix it with the band, creating a stew of deep beats and bass and a constantly busy sonic collage that hits as hard as could be wanted, but not without weirdly tender moments as well. On its own it would be a more than attractive effort, but it's Michael Franti's compelling, rich voice and his chosen subject matter that really make the band something special. Nothing is left unexamined, an analysis of the American community as a whole that embraces questions of African-American identity and commitment ("Famous and Dandy (Like Amos 'n' Andy)") to overall economic and political insanity ("The Winter of the Long Hot Summer," a gripping, quietly threatening flow of a track). There's even a great jazz-funk number, "Music and Politics," with nothing but a guitar and Franti's fine singing voice, ruminating on emotional expression in music and elsewhere with wit and sly anger. Top it off with a brilliant reworking of the Dead Kennedys' anthem "California Uber Alles," lyrics targeting the then-governor of the state, Pete Wilson, and his questionable stances, and revolutions in thought and attitude rarely sounded so good. —*Ned Raggett*

D.I.T.C.

Group / Hip-Hop, East Coast Rap, Hardcore Rap, Underground Rap
One of the most beloved hip-hop crews in rap music, D.I.T.C. (an acronym for Diggin' in the Crates) consists of veteran rappers, DJs, and producers dedicated to the true essence of rap music: original lyrics and strong beat-savvy productions. With their dedication to hip-hop purity, members Showbiz & AG (Andre the Giant), Diamond D, Lord Finesse, Fat Joe, O.C., Buckwild, and

the late Big L have at least one classic album under their belts. Although they never reached the success of their multiplatinum peers, individually they became successful by maintaining their integrity and earning major respect within the rap community.

Lord Finesse (born Robert Hall) is a legendary MC-turned-producer who has produced tracks for Notorious B.I.G. (1997's *Ready to Die*) and Dr. Dre (1999's *Chronic*). As a young cocky MC, he would travel to any borough in New York to battle their best rapper and win. He shopped his demo to various record labels and eventually dropped the first of several records, his 1990 classic *Funky Technician*. The record had a few tracks produced by his good friend Diamond (formerly Diamond D), a former member of the rap group Ultimate Force. One of the oldest members in the D.I.T.C. crew, Diamond got his first whiff of hip-hop DJing for Jazzy Jay of the Zulu Nation in 1979. In the mid-'80s, he was turntable scratching at late-night park parties, often competing with area top DJs (Showbiz was once his nemesis). In 1992 this DJ, then a producer, showcased New York City's underground talent and his rap skills on his classic debut *Stunts, Blunts & Hip-Hop*.

Bronx native Fat Joe became the first Latino rapper in New York to secure a solo deal with a major label with his 1993 debut *Representin'*. In 1998 his *Don Cartagena* release went gold (500,000 copies sold). Showbiz and AG were the first to adopt the do-it-yourself attitude by releasing their 1992 debut EP, *Can I Get a Soul Clap*, practically out of the trunk of their cars. Showbiz, a name he stole from an old Richard Pryor record, pioneered taking an instrumental and looping voices over it. His partner AG was known as the Bronx's "punchline" rapper. Through the mid-'90s, he was a prolific producer, producing tracks for primarily underground rap acts. In 1999 AG restarted his rap career with his solo CD *Dirty Version*.

Meanwhile, another Bronx native named Buckwild, who once started out as Lord Finesse's apprentice in his production company, started producing tracks around 1994. He later delivered melodic beats for rap heavyweights like Fat Joe, Notorious B.I.G., Big L, Mic Geronimo, and Big Pun. But it was his first at-bat, producing tracks for O.C.'s *Word Life* in 1994, that established him as a vital producer in the underground rap scene. O.C., one of hip-hop's most energetic lyricists, was an up-and-coming MC before *Word Life*. After the album's release, he made numerous guest appearances on other D.I.T.C. members' records while maintaining a low profile.

The final member of D.I.T.C. was Big L, a lyrically ferocious MC with raps deadlier than a snakebite and mannerisms cooler than the uptown pimp he claimed to be on records. Calling himself the flamboyant (meaning "rich") MC, he dropped his classic 1994 record *Lifestylez ov da Poor and Dangerous* on Columbia. He was gearing up for a comeback, with a second CD due for release on Rawkus, when he was slain on February 15, 1999. The crew came together later that year for a memorial concert at Trammps in New York (anthologized by a series of CD releases), and recorded a self-titled group record in 2000. — *Trent Fitzgerald*

Live at Trammps New York, Vol. 1: In the Memory of Big L / 1999 / P-Vine ♦♦♦

● **D.I.T.C.** / Feb. 22, 2000 / Tommy Boy ♦♦♦♦
Hip-hop has not witnessed an assemblage of talent like the Diggin' in the Crates crew since the Shaolin invasion (Wu-Tang Clan). This eight-man conglomerate contains some of New York's biggest underground luminaries (O.C., AG, Big L, Fat Joe, Showbiz, Lord Finesse, and Buckwild). This unit's talent pool runs so deep that finding time for each artist proves to be troublesome, as Fat Joe and Buckwild (one production credit) seem to be the odd men out here. If anything, this project reiterates what a tragic loss Big L was to the hip-hop community, as he establishes dominance on every track he appears on. Most notable was the flamboyant MC's solo cut "Ebonics," an essential street-lingo dictionary for those who are still slang handicapped. While "Day One" is the group's most cohesive team effort, their collaborations are often overshadowed by individual contributions; AG's "Weekend Nights" and O.C.'s "Champagne Thoughts." While D.I.T.C.'s in-house producers handle things admirably, the LP's best production comes courtesy of honorary member DJ Premier on "Thick." D.I.T.C. pays homage to Big L on the heartfelt "Tribute," but now the crew is forced to deal with another loss to their family, Big Pun, whose two appearances only add to the LP's somber ambience.

While D.I.T.C.'s debut has been highly anticipated, it has also been oft-delayed, and some of the tracks included here have been widely accessible

for quite some time. All of which makes one wonder if the delays may have contributed to the Dignified Soldiers missing their window of opportunity. — *Matt Conaway*

Divine Styler

Hip-Hop
An Islamic/Afro-centric rapper, Divine Styler began his commercial career with Ice-T's Rhyme Syndicate label; he recorded two albums, 1989's *Word Power* and 1991's *Spiral Walls Containing Autumns of Light*, that strongly favored lyrical development over musical complexity. After several years off record, he hooked up with the SoleSides family of artists and made features for Styles of Beyond, Everlast, the Beat Junkies, and Quannum. He also recorded his third album, *Wordpower, Vol. 2: Directrix*, for a 1999 re-release. — *Steve Huey*

Word Power / 1989 / Epic ♦♦♦♦

● **Spiral Walls Containing Autumns of Light** / Apr. 1991 / Giant ♦♦♦♦♦
Arguably the most undeservedly ignored hip-hop release of the early '90s, *Spiral Walls* is a mind-blowing, astonishing album that glitters like a dark jewel, equally nightmarish and astonishingly beautiful. Regardless of the work Styler did before or since, here he completely resisted categorization throughout—and even more amazingly, he did so on a disc released via a major label, thanks to über-manager Irving Azoff's Giant Records. Quite what Azoff thought he was going to get is a mystery for the ages, but what he got can't be summed up easily at all. The best description ever given is "Parliament/Funkadelic meets the Residents," and even this doesn't hint at the sheer range and ability on display. Though he works with a great band—guitarist Jeff Phillips, bassist Tony Guarderas, and drummer Kendu Jenkins—none of them slouches—Styler is the undisputed center of the album. He produces and arranges everything, feeding his voice through any number of production tricks, able to sweetly sing, MC like nobody's business, and essaying spoken word pieces with unsettling, dramatic power. Funky rock jams, delicate acoustic folk, industrial noise beats, freeform electronic weirdness, and more collide and recombine throughout—one can never accurately predict what will be around the corner. As for what Styler has to say, it can be everything from over-the-top raging alienation, as on the harrowing "Love, Lies and Lifetimes' Cries," to evocative, heartfelt praise and love for Allah. "Walk of Exodus" is one fine instance of the latter, as is the simply lovely "Width in My Depth," his voice, gentle percussion and Phillips' ringing guitar as pure and wonderful as it gets. *Spiral Walls* in the end is the album Prince could only wish to make in the '90s—all-encompassing, spiritual, disturbing, and never, ever boring, a true lost classic. — *Ned Raggett*

Wordpower, Vol. 2: Directrix / Feb. 9, 1999 / Dope Trax ♦♦♦♦
In a virtually unloving industry, Divine Styler's second solo album is a truly inspiring love piece, focusing on the self-empowerment aspects of life, over acid infused breakbeats. The Pharaoh Divine Styler divulges potent doses of uplifting abstract lyrics, however the true genius of this recording lays in his work behind the boards. Coming exquisitely original in the house of God, "Hajji" attacks from the jump with its voice manipulated supernova distortion, and DJ Rhettmatic's scratches on the 1's and 2's. With "Time Fold 79" Divine puts his breath control on full display, over a plush piano arrangement, a true dedication to hip-hop's glory days. Creating nothing but time-bomb's waiting to explode, "Directrix" is guaranteed head-nodding material. DS spits his lyrics in a robotic talking mode, fluctuating in and out of this hazy futuristic track. Joining forces for the first of two collabo's with his labelmates Styles Of Beyond, "Nova" has a definite "Hot Sex" vibe permeating from its every orifice. SOB's combine wonderfully with DS, as Takbir's performance is especially invigorating. "Microphenia" continues assaulting your eardrums, befuddling you with its seemingly out of nowhere soundscapes, and the SOB's 1nce again aid DS lovely with their spies are us espionage steez. The old school breakbeat and quick thrusting bursts of energy propel "Before Mecca," as it has lost no luster off its original shine. DS outdoes himself with "Make It Plain," as he implements sonic explosions that hit them from every possible angle, making it an unparalleled listening experience. There is a huge discrepancy in terms of quality from the first side of this LP, to the second (where most of the tracks mentioned above are located). DS finds a nice groove on the B side, whereas side A is much less cohesive and uneventful. Divine Styler's style is unlike anything you've ever heard, and it takes more then a few listens to fully decipher what's going on. His elevated intellectually stimulating wordpower is a nice change of pace, and far from

the usual m.o. hip-hop LP's contain nowadays. While, DS does a nice job of using hip-hop as a medium for getting his message out to the masses, his lyricism takes a backseat to his uncompromising underground production. Enticing, informative, and done with nothing but the upliftment of man and woman at heart, that alone is enough to be applauded for. —*Matt Conaway*

DJ Assault

b. 1996, Detroit, MI

DJ, Producer / Techno Bass, Electro-Techno, Dirty Rap

DJ Assault has had a large hand in bringing ghetto-tech, aka booty music, from the urban streets of Detroit to the suburban club circuit. The incorporation of electro beats with hardcore, sometimes pornographic lyrics, is what makes ghetto-tech highly distinguishable from its other techno cousins. (Though DJ Assault actually formed as a duo—with Craig Adams and Ade' Mainor, aka Mr. De—the latter left in 2000.) Two self-run record labels, Assault Rifle and Electrofunk, have released Assault's signature tracks, "Crank This Mutha," "Sex on the Beach," and "Ass N Titties."

At the tender age of 12, Craig Adams began his DJ career spinning at local parties and events in his hometown of Detroit. He took a three-year hiatus to study at the Univerity of Atlanta, but soon moved back to Michigan to start producing music in his own studio. Adams finished his studio by adding a local producer, Mr. De. After ill relations with a prior label, the two formed Electrofunk in 1996. Shortly thereafter, they released their first EP, *Terrortech EP*, with the singles "Crank This Mutha" and "Technofreak." The album was a good introduction of the new brand of techno that incorporated heavy bass beats, techno samples, and simple, catchy vocal hooks. During the summer of 1996, Assault released the first *Straight Up Detroit Sh*t (SUDS)* mix CD. Due to the first CD's popularity, Assault released the second volume that September. More popularity would follow the production team with the ghetto-tech anthems "Ass N Titties" and "Sex on the Beach." After only a year of being in business, Adams and De were able to say that they had sold more records than any other techno artist in the region at that time.

In 1997, due to the amount of production and popularity, Electrofunk split in two—Assault Rifle Records and Electrofunk Records Distribution. This allowed the two to produce and distribute their own material. In April of 1997 *SUDS, Vol. 3* was released along with *Belle Isle Tech*. The latter contained two CDs, one completely rap and the other a compilation of Assault Rifle and Electrofunk releases. The CD offered both sounds of the urban streets to suburban and urban fans. At the end of 1997, DJ Assault released *SUDS, Vol. 4*, which featured 99 tracks and served as an example of the fast style of DJing that developed around ghetto-tech. Unfortunately, Adams and Mainor dissolved their partnership in mid-2000, due to private reasons, and went their separate ways. Adams immediately started his own label, Jefferson Ave., named for a major street in Detroit that runs from the east to the west side. Adams released an album of the same name in 2001 with local label Intuit-Solar. The album introduced Assault as a solo artist along with his rapping alterego, Craig Diamonds, the Street Narrator. —*Diana Potts*

Belle Isle Tech / 1997 / Assault Rifle ✦✦✦

Representing some of the most nonsocially redeeming "straight-up ghetto sh*t" to ever come out of Detroit, the sounds of DJ Assault and his partner, Mr. De, are well represented on this release. The first album of this two-record set features the duo's brand of potent gangster rap, which merges the violent egomania of N.W.A with the pornographic sexism of 2 Live Crew. The second album features a 38-track mix consisting exclusively of the booty/ghetto-tech anthems produced by the popular Detroit duo. After experiencing the two very different albums it becomes apparent that Assault and De should stick to producing beats and their booty anthems or else continue to sharpen their rapping skills. Though the ghetto duo do an admirable job of laying rhymes over their hip-hop beats on this, their first attempt at rap, their lack of noteworthy lyrical content becomes stale after the jokes and attitude get old. On the other hand, the accompanying mix CD illustrates exactly why this duo rose to such prominence so quickly. Flying through one pitched-up booty-shakin' track after the next, Assault moves through his most revered classics—"Ass N Titties," "Sex on the Beach," "Dick By the Pound"—while still managing to make the mix flow smoothly. The second disc of this album is a perfect place for new-comers to get a quick education in not only Assault's late-'90s canon but also in his quick mixing style. Look for the Mo Wax re-release, which conveniently removes the rap disc, leaving only the mix disc. —*Jason Birchmeier*

Straight Up Detroit Shit, Vol. 4 / 1997 / Electrofunk ✦✦✦

By the fourth installment in the *Straight Up Detroit Shit* series, DJ Assault has truly found his niche, with enough self-produced anthems to highlight his mix and a large enough crate of obscure electro, booty, techno, bass, and hip-hop records to fill out the album. This mix is about as good as Assault gets technically, though with time he thankfully furthers his canon of records to choose from when mixing, as here there are a few moments within the mix when the tracks become both lackluster and generic. —*Jason Birchmeier*

● **Off the Chain for the Y2K** / Oct. 31, 2000 / Intuit-Solar ✦✦✦✦

Sit down and listen to lots and lots of ghetto-tech. Then put on Assault and the reason why he's light years ahead will be readily apparent. There's the effortless complexity, the seamless, brilliant transitions, the sheer musical virtuosity—and that's not even getting into Assault's personae, the tough player routine that shields the nerdy knob twister interior. Like Assault's other Detroit mixpolations, this album compresses several albums' worth of material onto a single disc, except this one ups the ante, jamming eight six-tracks into an hour, for an average of 30 seconds a song. *Off the Chain* also ratchets up the pace, with bpms charting in gabba territory. Stylistically, the album picks up where the more insane parts of *Belle Island Tech* left off and runs screaming into the distance, inventing new regions of noise and rhythm. The album's breakthrough track, however, is "Sometimes," which sets Assault apart aesthetically with its honest and, in its way, beautiful treatment of sexual relations that accepts both sexual vulnerability and aggressivity. The running joke of the rest of the album is that people keep calling him, interrupting his work on the album, so Assault just puts it into the mix. It's a perfect example of what makes ghetto-tech formally interesting—the ability to absorb any influence and subsume it into the mix, much like Public Enemy's collage style enabled them to incorporate and deflate criticism in a single move. It's truly unlike anything else and it's not even his best album. —*Brian Whitener*

Jefferson Ave. / Jul. 24, 2001 / Intuit-Solar ✦✦✦

When *Jefferson Ave.* hit the streets in summer 2001, most people knew DJ Assault strictly as a DJ. His *Off the Chain for the Y2K* album had surprised many in 2000, as did his relentless touring. Anyone who wasn't from Detroit had probably never heard anyone spin records the way Assault does—not just his frenzied mixing style but also his patented style of superfast porno bass music. If that's what you're expecting with *Jefferson Ave.*, though, you're in for a surprise. In short, this is a studio album, not a mix album. And it features not so much DJ-oriented tracks as it does listener-oriented songs—songs with singalong choruses and, more importantly, rapping. Yes, Assault isn't a DJ but rather an MC here. The three songs that were at the beginning of *Off the Chain for the Y2K* should give you a good idea of what to expect: a fast booty-bass rhythm, a sleazy singalong hook, and just as sleazy rapping during the verses. Sure, it doesn't take long to deduce that Assault is no Rakim, but at least he never claims to be. His rhymes should appeal to the same crowd that finds 2 Live Crew engaging, and his beats should get booties in motion at any club. And beyond that, these songs are undeniably catchy and will have you singing along to the hooks while you shake your ass. Unfortunately, Assault's songs don't hold up so well when they're not within the context of a DJ set. Most will find that within a studio album context, these songs get boring after the first minute and seem relatively lifeless without the kinetic force of a track-a-minute DJ set to drive them. Still, you get the sense that Assault isn't about to give up his DJing profession and is merely taking a vain stab at crossover success here. —*Jason Birchmeier*

DJ Baby Anne

DJ / Bass Music, Club/Dance

Club impresario DJ Baby Anne introduced herself as one of the defining mixers of the latter '90s, not to mention becoming one of the few female bass DJs matching the vibrance of her fellow counterparts such as Alice Deejay and Debbie Deb. Inspired by friend and dance guru DJ Icey, Baby Anne bought her first set of Technics in 1992 and heavily absorbed the skills of her mentor. Early on, the two played gigs together and Baby Anne quickly shared her passion of breakbeats and electro-bass in and around the Miami club circuit. She's released six singles on DJ Icey's imprint Zone Records as well as issuing tracks to the Phattraxx compilation *Bass Queen: In Mix (A Bass and Breaks Continuous Mix)* in 1999. In July 2000 Baby Anne became a house-hold mixer for Phattraxx, holding a residency at Icon in Orlando. During this time, she also released *Bass Queen: In the Mix, Vol. 2.* —*MacKenzie Wilson*

● **Bass Queen: In Mix (A Bass and Breaks Continuous Mix)** / Jul. 13, 1999 / Pandisc ✦✦✦✦

DJ Baby Anne is a Florida-based DJ whose mixing skills are demonstrated on this album by a continuous mix of tracks by artists as celebrated as DJ Icey and as obscure as Isle Natividad. Bass fans will not be disappointed: that Florida sound shudders through loud and clear, especially on Sharaz's "Jam the Box '99" and on "Go Round-n-Round" by Victor Victorious (presented here in an Atmospherix remix). DJ Baby Anne's own "The Bass Queen" and "Abercrombie" are also both quite good, but pride of place probably goes to the extremely heavy and nicely titled "Pepper Spray" by DJ 43. Honorable mention goes to Isle Natividad, whose "Isle's Tribal Disco" manages to subtly embed a soca beat and samba whistle into its four-on-the-floor club groove. —*Rick Anderson*

DJ Cam (Laurent Daumail)

b. Paris, France

DJ, Producer / Downbeat, Ambient Breakbeat, Trip-Hop, Electronica, Hip-Hop

Parisian hip-hop devotee Laurent Daumail is one of a few but growing number of French artists updating hip-hop for the chill-out crowd, drawing on the beats'n'samples groundwork of producers such as Rakim, DJ Premier, and Prince Paul and combining it with broad, impressionistic strokes of dub, jazz, and soundtrack-y ambience. Like countrymen the Mighty Bop and la Funk Mob, Cam is stylistically closest to Mo'Wax artists such as DJ Shadow and DJ Krush; minimalist, downbeat instrumental hip-hop built from obscure samples and stompbox turntable accompaniment, bent and twisted into new, artfully arranged compositions. His debut, 1994's *Underground Vibes*, was released on the tiny French label Street Jazz and was followed by a live recording for the Inflammable imprint (one of only a few "live" recordings in a genre so reliant on the temporal concessions of the recording studio). Dubbed *9 Underground Live*, the album featured performed extrapolations of many of the tracks from his debut, as well as a few new and improvised tracks. Now nearly impossible to find, those first two albums were reissued in America by Shadow Records, packaged together as the single-CD priced *Mad Blunted Jazz* (particularly useful since acquiring both on import could run more than $50!).

Although Cam's music has found little acceptance in his home country, where racial tension has stratified the hip-hop community into rigid definitions of what the music is—and who should be making it (Cam himself is white)—audiences in the U.K., Japan, and America have begun picking up on his style. In 1996 Cam was featured on, among many others, the sprawling Mo'Wax compilation *Headz 2*, remixed tracks for such artists as Tek 9 and la Funk Mob, and most recently collaborated on live and in-studio projects with Snooze and DJ Krush (he cowrote a few tracks on the latter's 1997 Mo'Wax release, *Mi Sound*). Cam released *Substances* on Inflammable in 1997. The next year, his major-label debut, *The Beat Assassinated*, appeared on Columbia Records. In 2000 he released a three-volume series named *The Loa Project*. Cam dropped *HoneyMoon*, a smooth mix album that combined jazz and underground hip hop, at the close of 2001. —*Sean Cooper*

Underground Vibes / 1994 / Street Jazz ✦✦✦✦

Cam's debut collection of "abstract hip-hop" finds similar company in artists such as DJ Krush, Howie B., and the Solid Doctor, with pitched down, echo-chamber beats, sparse jazz and funk quotes, and turntable atmospherics combining into a smooth, impressionistic affair. The album was reissued by Shadow records—together with his live Inflammable follow-up, *9 Underground Live*—as *Mad Blunted Jazz* in 1996. —*Sean Cooper*

9 Underground Live / Jun. 11, 1996 / Inflammable ✦✦✦✦

Live hip-hop albums are hardly common, but then neither is Cam's approach here, seamlessly blending loping, downtempo breaks with thick, dubby basslines, deft, heavily treated scratching, and instrumental samples and vocal drop-ins which make for a solid, tight flow. Cam presents live, tricked-up improvisations of tracks from his debut album, *Underground Vibes*, as well as a few new ones. The album was reissued as disc two of the domestic Shadow label's double Cam release, *Mad Blunted Jazz*. —*Sean Cooper*

● **Mad Blunted Jazz** / Nov. 12, 1996 / Shadow ✦✦✦✦✦

Electronica producers like the Orb had been mining the ideas of minimalist and house producers for years, and DJ Cam's fusion of jazz and hip-hop

was creative and artistically successful in much the same way—instead of Tangerine Dream or Steve Reich, substitute Ahmad Jamal or Bobby Hutcherson and Gang Starr. Cam's vision of the late-night creep encompassed lots of oddly tuneful piano or vibes samples and the type of simple East Coast beats favored by DJ Premier and the like. The American Shadow label combined his first two records, the studio *Underground Vibes* and the live *9 Underground Live*, to create a two-fer that's very necessary for those interested in early trip-hop. DJ Cam wasn't a crate digger like DJ Shadow; he much preferred creating a reflective atmosphere around a chosen few samples, usually familiar. While simplistic (especially early in his career), it was often very effective, as the best tracks here illustrate. "Sang-Lien" has only vibes, a fragment of a flute line, and muted trumpet, but Cam still creates something very special with the addition of a French chanteuse. "Mad Blunted Jazz" switches it up a bit, moving between multiple drum tracks and samples. Most of these are little more than background hip-hop tracks that the average rapper wouldn't even consider rhyming over, but in the grand tradition of ambient music (from Satie to Eno), DJ Cam's productions ranked near the top. —*John Bush*

Substances / 1996 / Inflammable ✦✦✦

This release is a far more diverse set of relaxed (and occasionally not so) deviations from clubland, with bits of jungle, electro, and even house creeping into the mix. Cam has broadened the scope of his sound, here; where previous releases tended to focus on sonic depth rather than breadth, atmosphere occupying first chair, *Substances'* sample arrangements are in places almost epic, and the beatwork is far more complex and inventive. —*Sean Cooper*

The Beat Assassinated / May 11, 1998 / Inflamable ✦✦✦

While *Substances* moved DJ Cam closer to the minimalist beat camp headed up by DJ Krush, *The Beat Assassinated* is a bit more tied to upfront hip-hop. True, the concrete beats and basement-style productions heard here are far removed from any rap on the charts in America, but the addition of rappers like Channel Live, Silvah Bullet, and DJ Djam results in a comfortable balance between underground and mainstream. —*John Bush*

The French Connection / 2000 / Shadow ✦✦✦

Borrowing the wider name recognition of mixer DJ Cam, its compadre in the French rap scene, the Parisian avant hip-hop imprint Artefact Records released this 2000 label retrospective, with tracks from ten different producers. Though none of these artists are well known in the international electronic community, they acquit themselves quite well, each taking the template of downbeat hip-hop and adjusting it thanks to influences from jazz and sound-track work ("Hide & Seek" by Shinju Gumi, "Spook" by O'Neill), fusion or quiet storm R&B ("Garance" by Art Ensemble, "One of These Days" by Zend Avesta), sample-driven American rap (the DJ Cam remix of "More" by Baron Samedi, "Underwater Rhymes" by Doctor L.), and true avant-garde ("Fog Plants" by Naruhisa Matsuoka). DJ Cam's mixing is smooth; it spotlights the diversity of the label, quite underrated considering the quality on display here. —*John Bush*

The Loa Project, Vol. 2 / Jul. 11, 2000 / Six Degrees ✦✦✦✦

For *The Loa Project, Vol. 2*, DJ Cam expanded his emphasis on cellar-dwelling hip-hop to embrace the legacies of disco and dub, two styles whose roots lie quite close to the beginnings of rap in the early '70s. For "Ganja Man," Cam reprises the bass line from a seminal Augustus Pablo dub version ("King Tubby Meets the Rockers Uptown") to create an intriguing jump-up drum'n'bass track. The French producer also salutes the disco/house axis with several tracks, including the jazzy house jam "Juliet" and the breakbeat filter-disco number "DJ Cam Sound System." Of course, ranging from genre to genre is nothing new for the vast majority of electronic producers, so the risk here becomes losing the distinctive DJ Cam sound to a wash of bland stylistic exercises. Fortunately, his production and beat-mining skills rescue any possible impression of look-what-I-can-do studio theatrics. And Cam also works through plenty of hip-hop territory. The scratchy hardcore musings of "Mental Invasion" are reminiscent of DJ Premier, one of hip-hop's best, and Cam even tips his hat to Timbaland with the hyper-breakbeat R&B of "You Do Something to Me" (featuring China). "Ghetto Love" isn't quite the G-funk jam listeners might expect, instead comprising some quintessentially cinematic dark trip-hop. Despite the diversity, *The Loa Project, Vol. 2* hangs together well since DJ Cam only enlarged his focus to include styles with much kinship to his first love. Note to indie rock fans: the Franck Black who features on "Candyman" is apparently *not* the former Pixies frontman, though it's unclear from the track and the liner notes just who he is or what he does. —*John Bush*

HoneyMoon / Oct. 2, 2001 / Chronowax ◆◆◆◆

HoneyMoon, a downtempo mix date for Chronowax, finds Parisian DJ Cam on what he calls "a journey through the beauty of music." He certainly starts in the right place, with the groovy, downtempo, horn-driven "Loran's Dance" from Grover Washington Jr.'s 1979 LP *Reed Seed*. From there, Cam concentrates on smooth underground rap by a few obscure names: 3582, with the jazzy "Early Morning"; Que-D, on the minimal, stuttered-piano-sampling "Cash Flow"; and Phat Kat, a harder rapper who looks back to G-funk with "Microphone Master." Cam deftly breaks up the set with Coldcut's classic deep-groove version of "Autumn Leaves," then returns to the hip-hop underground with great tracks from Londoner TY ("The Tale"), Lil Dap ("Brooklyn Zone"), and Bahamadia ("Philadelphia"). With one more trick up his sleeve, Cam breaks from Mr. Scruff's "So Long" into the final track, a lush Henry Mancini instrumental named "Lujon." It's a clever, understated mix that works equally well for relaxation or concentrated listening. —*John Bush*

Soulshine / May 21, 2002 / Inflamable ◆◆◆

While DJ Vadim—another European hip-hop mixer whose career began on the same trajectory—pursued breakbeat hip-hop into the realm of heavily American/underground rap, the production work of Frenchman DJ Cam has become much smoother and closer in sound and execution to the British acid jazz scene. *Soulshine* is his smoothest record yet, opening with a breezy jazz dancer ("Summer in Paris") with a live band sporting a crossover groove while vocalist Anggun enthuses about the unique Parisian vibes. Cam also cultivates his American R&B connection, drafting Cameo's Larry Blackmon and Nathan Leftenant for a serviceable Roy Ayers impression, while "Condor (Espionage)" features Guru (aka Baldhead Slick) relaxing over a live cut. For DJ Cam, musical maturity seems to mean arrangements utilizing a live band, and though *Soulshine* has them throughout, there's much less of innovation happening here than on his early work. Two tracks that work are the pair of *real* hip-hop tracks: "Bounce" and "Voodoo Child," the latter a tough remix by DJ Premier with Afu Ra on vocals. —*John Bush*

DJ Cash Money

Bass Music, Party Rap

DJ Cash Money, not to be confused with the better-known DJ of the same name from Philadelphia, spins Miami bass and booty music. He has spun at such clubs as Club Zanzibar in South Beach, where he recorded his *Booty Mix Live* CD (2000) for Pandisc. The mix featured local favorites by such producers as Crazy L'eggs, Splack Pack, the Puppies, DJ Laz, Clay D, the Low End Boys, Bass Mekanik, and others. —*Jason Birchmeier*

● **The Booty Mix Live: Music for Your A$$** / Sep. 26, 2000 / Pandisc ◆◆◆

Miami booty maestro DJ Cash Money lays down 33 tracks on this set, focusing primarily on artists affiliated with the Pandisc label: Low End Boys, Bass Mekanik, Get It Boyz, DJ Laz, Crazy L'eggs, and others. Unfortunately, he never breaks away from this specific sound, characterized by high-speed rapping and booty bass. Where his many of his peers go out of their way to diversify their track selection, Cash Money drops nothing but Miami tracks, resulting in a homogeneous mix. —*Jason Birchmeier*

DJ Chuck Chillout (Charles Turner)

b. Oct. 22, 1962, Bronx, NY

DJ / East Coast Rap, Hip-Hop, Golden Age

DJ Chuck Chillout has been one of the more valuable behind-the-scenes figures in the rap community since the early '80s, most notably as a DJ, producer, and radio host. He was one-third of the B-Boyz, a Bronx-based group that released the oft-sampled "Rock the House" on Vintertainment in 1983. From there, his stature grew through his shows on KISS and WBLS; he also worked sporadically with a number of groups, including Run-D.M.C. and Public Enemy (a mixing credit on "Night of the Living Baseheads" being the most significant). In 1989 Chillout joined up with Kool Chip for *The Masters of the Rhythm*, an album released on Polygram. After that, he continued to work with underground groups and host radio programs. —*Andy Kellman*

● **Masters of the Rhythm** / 1989 / Mercury ◆◆◆

DJ Clue?

b. Queens, NY

DJ, Producer / Hip-Hop, East Coast Rap

One of the handful of DJs to make the jump from mix tapes to the major labels, DJ Clue? hooked up with Jay-Z's Roc-A-Fella Records camp for a bit in the late '90s, then moved on to his own camp, Desert Storm Records. The Queens native built his reputation with street-level mix tapes, as most DJs tend to do in New York, and he quickly became one of the city's leading DJs, graced with the latest tracks by the biggest names. Popular New York hip-hop station Hot 97 brought him aboard for a while in the late '90s alongside fellow DJ heavyweight Funkmaster Flex. The air time furthered his reputation, and Jay-Z in turn invited him to join forces with Roc-A-Fella, who released Clue?'s major-label debut, *The Professional* (1998). The album featured primarily exclusive tracks, each boasting one of New York's top rappers, everyone from Nas and Mobb Deep to DMX and Ja Rule. A second volume followed in 2000, and in the meantime Clue? toured with Roc-A-Fella in support of Jay-Z's *Hard Knock Life* album as documented on *Backstage* (2000). He then parted ways with Roc-A-Fella and embarked on his own path, establishing Desert Storm Records and debuting Fabolous in 2001. —*Jason Birchmeier*

The Professional / Dec. 8, 1998 / Def Jam ◆◆

Now rolling with Roc-A-Fella y'all, Clue?'s days of slinging tapes on your neighborhood corner are all but over. Recognized worldwide for reinventing the art of the mix tape, Clue? enlisted some of hip-hop's biggest guns for his major-label debut. Aiding Clue? in his quest for the Clueminati, Nas revisits his *Illmatic* roots with "Queensfinest." The pairing of Cam'ron, Big Pun, Noreaga, and Canibus on "Fantastic Four" is worth mentioning solely for the hypnotic verse Canibus delivers. Jayhovah touches down lending his labelmate a hand, combining forces with Ja Rule for some "Gangsta Shit." Mobb Deep and Big Noyd are at it once again on "The Professional," as they are merciless on a fiery violin-laced number from Vic. Meanwhile, EPMD and the Def Squad play hot potato on "It's My Thang '99" and Raekwon lends his lyrical swordmanship to "Brown Paper Bag Thoughts." Like any mix tape or soundtrack, you have to accept the good and bad with a grain of salt. Clue? makes feeble attempts to refresh cuts like "That's the Way" featuring Mase, Foxy, and Fabolous Sport, and "I Like Control" featuring Missy, Mocha, and Nicole Wray, leaving them virtually untouched. Clue? definitely knows how to move the crowd and does serve up another installment of exclusive material, but he implements little of the turntable manipulation that makes DJs so vital to the art of hip-hop. As Pete Rock stated ever so eloquently, "This I dedicate to those mix tapes I hate/exclusive shit/it holds no weight/put your skills on the plate/backspin to '88." —*Matt Conaway*

The Perfect Desert Storm / 2000 / ◆◆◆

A spirited, if innocuous collection of high-profile chest-thumping gangsta rap hits all put together by the beloved mixtape defender DJ Clue. *The Perfect Desert Storm* is Clue's second real effort out of the underground and shows that the world of official CD releases still leaves him a bit lost. Surely, anybody craving the glamour-stricken top rung of the hardcore rap ladder will have a blast. Jay-Z, DMX, Lil' Kim, Method Man, and the like all appear here. It's the sudden jolts, invasive segue shouts, and very little (if any) DJ tricks that will put off most plugged in hip-hop fans. While Clue's tricks in his word-of-mouth mix tape past hinted at a maverick talent championing his favorite tunes, efforts like this show little progression other than a glorified and clumsy collection status. To be fair, the level of enthusiasm in Clue remains strong. The party feel jolts up in the midst of a simple parade of hits (Sheik's "Two Tears in a Bucket" or QB's Finest's "Oochie Wally"), which make it far more than some awful "Greatest Gangsta Rap Hits!" television compilation. It's just not something that will prevent any oversaturated fans in either the hardcore or Rawkus vein from shaking their heads in simple irritation. —*Dean Carlson*

● **Backstage** / Aug. 29, 2000 / Roc-A-Fella/Def Jam ◆◆◆

Recognized as the rotten apple's most prominent mix tape slinger, DJ Clue's second major-label compilation, *Backstage*, is another installment of exclusive material that promotes the impending theatrical release of Jay-Z's Hard Knock Life Tour. Though classifying Clue as a "DJ" is certainly a stretch (check out Revolution, Babu, and X-Ecutioners among many for confirmation), he is undeniably a keen entrepreneur, as his star-powered projects are habitually saturated with the biggest names in hip-hop. While Jigga, and Damon Dash's brainchild provided hope that hip-hop's floundering major-arena tour marketability could be resurrected, Clue's accompanying score fails too make the same impact. Like most compilations, or soundtracks, *Backstage* contains a slew of filler material, and a fair amount of crooning from Jay-Z's R&B stable. While the old (Redman), and new (Lady Luck) school of New Jeruz combine forces on the delectably rugged "Come and Get It," as the crews headlining MCs prove, *Backstage* is ultimately the Roc's show. Although his star-pupils, Beanie Sigel and Memphis Bleek, rise to the occasion. Jay-Z contributions keep the spotlight directly centered on him with the sexually suggestive verses of "Best of Me Part 2" f/Mya. But the true burner here is a lost cut from Jigga's *Vol.2* studio sessions, "People's Court," as Jay continues too push all the right sampling buttons, this time by devouring Judge Wapner's theme music. —*Matt Conaway*

The Professional, Pt. 2 / Dec. 19, 2000 / Roc-A-Fella ♦♦♦
Mixtape DJs have sure come a long way over the years, and no one knows that better than DJ Clue? The NY-based spinner got his start peddling mixtapes on the streets. A few years later, his album *The Professional, Pt. 2* hit the *Billboard* Top Ten album chart. Looking at the list of artists on Clue?'s play list, it's easy to see why the album has had such success. This time out, Clue? enlisted the likes of Jay-Z, DMX, Beanie Sigel, Redman, Nas, Foxy Brown, Trick Daddy, and Eminem among many others. What is likely to draw the attention of hip-hop fans are the exclusive tracks on the album, including "Change the Game (Remix)," which mixes artists from both coasts such as tha Dogg Pound, Jay-Z, Beanie Sigel, and Memphis Bleek. Another exclusive track is "What the Beat" with Method Man, Eminem, and Royce da 5'9". Also impressive are "Live From the Bridge" by Nas and "The Best of Queens" by Mobb Deep. While there aren't any dead spots on the album, *The Professional, Pt. 2* suffers in comparison to some of Clue?'s other mix tapes because he plays it safe, relying too heavily on big-name rappers. One of the joys of a good mix tape is discovering new artists alongside more established ones, but Clue? offers too few opportunities to check out something new. Also annoying is Clue?'s habit of shouting over all of the tracks. While it's common for mix tape DJs to shout and give shoutouts over tracks, Clue? takes it to an extreme. There is a lot to like about *The Professional, Pt. 2.* He should let the music speak for itself. —*Jon Azpiri*

DJ Craze (Aristh Delgado)

b. Nov. 19, 1977, Managua, Nicaragua
DJ / Turntablism
Although born in Nicaragua, Aristh Delgado—better known as DJ Craze—grew up in Miami, where bass rules hip-hop and scratching is its most eloquent expression. Craze is one of the most accomplished of turntablists, with over a dozen competition titles to his name, including a record three consecutive World DMC Championship titles. His first album, *Crazee Musick*, was released on San Francisco's Bomb Hip Hop in 1999. A second solo album, *Scratch Nerds*, was released in 2002, but solo scratch sagas aren't Craze's only credits. He's also a member of turntable crew the Allies, who released *D-Day* in 2000. —*Wade Kergan*

United DJs of America, Vol. 16: The Nexxsound / Oct. 24, 2000 / Razor & Tie ♦♦♦
On the follow-up to his debut album, three-time DMC World Champion DJ Craze takes a break from the original music heard on his first album (although he includes his own "Nothing" in the set) to release the 16th mix compilation in Mixer's *United DJs of America* series. It is also the first time Craze showcases his drum'n'bass over his hip-hop side, although both are key elements in his makeup, alongside the Miami bass boom of his native city. The album works as both a dance floor-ready mix tape and a compilation of exclusive underground junglist tracks from revered British labels like V Recordings, Undiluted, and Virus. It is also a magnificent exhibition of Craze's way around the decks, particularly the mixer. Both his battling savvy and dance floor wizardry come into play. He expertly moves through paranoid tech-step funk (Trace & Optical, the Pedge) and hard-edged darkside dub (Decoder/Substance's "Rubbery"), to more repetitive and hypnotic breakbeat stylists (Distorted Minds) and ambient sounds (J. Malik's "Solarized"), and finally to almost soulful strains of drum'n'bass (Total Science's "Peacemaker," Supply & Demand's refracted "Show Me") in a virtually vocal-free set that emphasizes the movement quotient over the introspective, easy-listening

one. There is nothing easy about the set, but it is sweaty and neon encrusted, a post-midnight urban cyberscape. It rocks a party hard but also carries an emotional weight. Craze doesn't display his turntablist skills as readily or prevalently as he might during a hip-hop showcase (the only real hint of hip-hop comes during the "Intro" with Mic Rippa and during his single-deck demonstration, "Craze's Tablist Outro"), although his subtle scratching throughout cuts like a precise blade and turns his transitions into minor works of art themselves. He mostly allows his selections to speak for themselves and tell their own stories—and they speak to the feet most of all. —*Stanton Swihart*

DJ Dirty Money

DJ / Gangsta Rap, Hardcore Rap, Dirty South
One of the dirty South's leading semilegal mix CD purveyors, DJ Dirty Money churned out a series of albums for Dirty Harry Productions beginning in the late '90s that were highlighted by well-known hits. Dirty Money spun mostly dirty South favorites (Missy, OutKast, Three 6 Mafia, Cash Money Millionaires) but would throw in a few East and West Coast ones here and there (Biggie, Nas, Ice Cube, Eric B. & Rakim). Though his track selection was generally excellent and trendy, Dirty Money's mixes suffered from poor quality and limited distribution. —*Jason Birchmeier*

● **Dirty Azz South "Gangsta Mix"** / Mar. 23, 1999 / Dirty O.G. ♦♦♦
Throughout his *Dirty Azz South "Gangsta Mix,"* DJ Dirty Money generally mixes Southern rap a cappella over various instrumental tracks, most of which are well known and either East or West Coast. The leading Southern rappers circa 1999, particularly Eightball, Master P, and the Cash Money Millionaires, get plenty of spins, though Dirty Money does showcase a fair share of lesser-known rappers like Lil' Keke. Some of his instrumentals are unlikely choices, like Snoop Dogg's "Vapors," the Notorious B.I.G.'s "Sky's the Limit," and Eazy-E's "Real Muthaphuckkin G's." These sometimes odd combinations lead to interesting results, and it helps that Dirty Money mixes fairly smoothly. The track listing is off, though, as is the sequencing, so you're somewhat at the mercy of Dirty Money's lead. —*Jason Birchmeier*

Mixin' 4 da Chewin / Jun. 27, 2000 / Dirty Harry ♦♦♦
DJ Dirty Money works through mainly dirth South tracks over the course of *Mixin' 4 da Chewin.* He drops quite a few Cash Money tracks, including "We on Fire," "Tha Block Is Hot," "True Story," and "Juvenile on Fire," though interperses them throughout the mix. The album's track listing is a little misleading, as Dirty Money mixes rather freely from one track to the next. He unfortunately does so rather sloppily at times, but the emphasis here seems to be more on track selection than mixing skills, for better or worse. —*Jason Birchmeier*

DJ Eddie Def

DJ / Club/Dance, Turntablism
DJ Eddie Def (The Last Kreep) can easily be considered a pioneer of turntablism, creating his art through scratching and quick mixing. He began his career in San Francisco's Mission district where he met DJ Quest and DJ 2 Fresh. Def and Quest hooked up in 1988 and were joined by DJ Cue in 1991, thereby forming a trio called the Bullet Proof Scratch Hamsters (now called the Bullet Proof Space Travelers). On his own, DJ Eddie Def has produced several solo LPs featuring some of the craziest breakbeats and drum-loop combinations ever heard. —*Brad Mills*

Wax People / 1999 / Hip Hop Slam ♦♦♦
This compilation put out by DJ Eddie Def is a collection of beats cut and mixed by Eddie himself, with hundreds of various voice samples and sound bites from movie, television, and other records mixed in. From the opening song "A Very Furious Mixture of Noise," which is just that, to "Cry Baby," which is a rock track with a baby crying in synch with an electric guitar, this compilation bleeds energy. Absolutely crazy throughout, this kind of thing is helping Eddie solidify himself as one of the most experimental forerunners of turntablism as an art. Additionally, DJ Quest and DJ Flare make cameo scratch appearances on their own respective tracks. —*Brad Mills*

Open Your Mind / Dec. 12, 2000 / Hip Hop Slam ♦♦♦

● **Stuff** / Jan. 16, 2001 / Stray ♦♦♦♦
Eddie Def has been doing strange things with his turntables for a long time now. Thankfully he's very good at it, and always provides the breakbeat

community with a new twist on things. With *Stuff,* Eddie has brought out the drum machine and has created some interesting pieces for a niche market to savor. Instrumental throughout, there are some well-used voice samples and catchy breaks. Overall, this album is good if you're into that crazy electronic experimental stuff with a beat, and with tracks like "Bad Trip," "12 Step Program," and "Boombap Must Die!" it's an enjoyable mix. —*Brad Mills*

Inner Scratch Demons / Mar. 20, 2001 / Ipecac ✦✦✦✦
DJ Eddie Def is one of the new faces in a growing stable of artists on Mike Patton's neophyte Ipecac label. For those unfamiliar with Patton's past, the Ipecac name tag is a serious warning sign that the musician in question possesses some outlandish quality that separates them from the herd. DJ Eddie Def, who has spun live with the likes of Buckethead, Brain, and Patton himself, is no exception to this rule. *Inner Scratch Demons* presents the fierce turntablist in his full glory, tossing around records with a fury that makes conventional DJs look plain silly. The Beastie Boys, crying infants, killer jazz grooves, John Cougar Mellencamp riffs, *Star Wars* humor—they all find solace within DJ Eddie Def's forty-something-minute sampling rant. It's extreme, but also completely listenable, which isn't something you can say of all Ipecac Recordings. "I Like It You Like It," featuring Z-Man's wild lyrics and groovy beat, make it perfect fodder for mixed tapes. Some of it takes a few listens to digest, but if you take the time to let it sink in, your patience will be rewarded. This is one of the best three releases in Ipecac's history to date. —*Kieran McCarthy*

DJ Faust

b. North Carolina
Producer, DJ / Underground Rap, Turntablism
DJ Faust is a turntablist with an incredibly dense style of cut-and-paste mixing that leaves little room for pause and entertains shades of original musique concrète producers like Pierre Schaeffer and Pierre Henry. Born in North Carolina but based in Atlanta around the Third World Citizens collective (including DJ Shotgun from Goodie Mob), Faust released his debut *Man or Myth?* in 1998. The *Fathomless* EP followed later that year, trailed in 1999 by *Inward Journeys.* —*John Bush*

● **Man or Myth?** / Jul. 28, 1998 / Bomb Hip Hop ✦✦✦✦✦
One of the best turntablist debuts on record (or CD for that matter), *Man or Myth?* references dozens of groove classics—from Zapp to Public Enemy to Coldcut to the Steve Miller Band to Mantronix—but crosscuts through them with such speed and accuracy that Faust remains the focus throughout. While too many turntablists use their albums more for scratching workouts, Faust lets the beats speak for themselves, working in short bursts of scratching only occasionally. Sequenced as one track (although it lists 27 on the back cover), *Man or Myth?* is an essential piece of the instrumental hip-hop puzzle. DJs Shotgun, Craze and Shortee—from Faust's Third World Citizens collective—feature on a couple of tracks. —*John Bush*

Inward Journeys / Aug. 17, 1999 / Bomb Hip Hop ✦✦✦✦
Faust's second album in just over a year is yet another trip through the mind (and turntables) of one of the best DJs out there. It's just as dense as *Man or Myth?* but takes Faust's beatboxing skills even further. There's a certain amount of "been there done that" to the proceedings, but Faust's deft turntable skills rescues any case of the musical blah's. —*Keith Farley*

DJ Food

f. 1992
Group / Jungle/Drum 'N' Bass, Trip-Hop, Club/Dance
DJ Food is a collaborative project between Coldcut/Ninja Tune duo Matt Black and Jonathan More, and second-half PC (born Patrick Carpenter) and Strictly (Kevin Foakes). Although the moniker originally referred only to Black and More's several-volumed series of stripped-down breaks records designed for deck use (i.e., "food" for DJs), club booking demands for the assumedly proper-named DJ Food dictated the pair make an ongoing project of it. Adding PC and Strictly to spice things up (and differentiate DJ Food from Coldcut when they played the same bill), the quartet released a series of 12" singles in various combinations starting in 1994 (including "Freedom"/"Consciousness"), with their proper full-length debut, *A Recipe for Disaster*, appearing the following year. The quartet also toured Europe, Canada, and America as DJ Food (mainly DJing) and regularly mashed it up side by side on Coldcut's weekly KISS FM show Solid Steel. PC and Strictly were also

hired on by Warp Records to compile and mix a series of releases entitled *Blech* drawing from the influential experimental techno label's back catalog. More and Black continued to split their time between DJ Food and Coldcut, as well as the day-to-day operation of their immensely popular Ninja Tune and Ntone labels. DJ Food's second production album, *Kaleidoscope,* appeared in April of 2000 to warm reviews. A year later, the pair inaugurated a Solid Steel CD series with the mix album *Now, Listen!* —*Sean Cooper*

Jazz Brakes, Vol. 1 / 1992 / Ninja Tune ✦✦

Jazz Brakes, Vol. 2 / 1992 / Ninja Tune ✦✦
Available on CD as well as vinyl (though for unknown reasons, since these are mostly tools for DJs), DJ Food's second volume of *Jazz Brakes* includes 23 tracks of two- to three-minute samples and loops, all guaranteed to not upset the mood between tracks in a usual DJ's set. Titles such as "Last Coltrane to Skaville," "Cosmic Jam, Part 1," "Funky Emergency," and "Deadly Serious Bass Party" tell most of the story here. —*John Bush*

A Recipe for Disaster / 1995 / Ninja Tune ✦✦✦✦✦
Although More and Black's best works are scattered over endless singles, EP, and compilation tracks, *A Recipe for Disaster* proves they can pull an album off when they feel like it. Together with a handful of collaborators, the pair split their resources between funky instrumental hip-hop, drum'n'bass, turntable experiments, and armchair trip-hop, providing a good cross-section of the group's various styles. —*Sean Cooper*

Kaleidoscope / Apr. 4, 2000 / Ninja Tune ✦✦✦✦✦
Apparently comprising recordings from 1996 right up to the year of its release, *Kaleidoscope* continues on from the proper DJ Food debut *A Recipe for Disaster* with a collection of beat-heavy turntablist productions that often hit the high peaks of their close friends Coldcut. Since PC and Strictly *are* DJs first and foremost, *Kaleidoscope* has an atmosphere of cut'n'paste schizophrenia, experimental risk taking, and rampant comedy reminiscent of their previous mix-album assignments (the Warp compilation *Blech* and Coldcut's *Journeys By DJ*). As on *A Recipe for Disaster* however, the production is *much* better than listeners should expect from a pair of turntable twisters. Jazz is undeniably the backbone of this album, straight from the opener "Full Bleed" where a raw drumkit pounds out stuttered breakbeats with plenty of high-maintenance cymbal work. There are references to all sorts of jazzcats from the cool era, including the fiery Quincy Jones sample that drives "The Riff" and the collaboration with jazz poet Ken Nordine on "The Ageing Young Rebel." The most inventive track is undoubtedly "Break," which turns a spoken-word piece by Lightnin' Rod dealing with billiards (pun definitely intended) into a turntablist high-wire act by repeatedly cutting off the audio between syllables. Even when you've put aside the high-profile musical references and silly sense of humor, though, *Kaleidoscope* remains a great album. Even "Nocturne" and "The Crow," a pair of downtempo tracks with little (on the surface) to recommend them, are still very compelling. With productions these strong, perhaps it's time for PC and Strictly to strip the DJ from their albums just to make sure no one confuses them with part-time producers. —*John Bush*

● **Now, Listen!** / Sep. 18, 2001 / Ninja Tune ✦✦✦✦✦
For those lucky few able to tune it in or dig up the session CD-R's passed from fan to fan, Coldcut and DJ Food's *Solid Steel* program has been, bar none, the leading light of the turntablist underground since its 1988 inception. As freewheeling as American crews like Invisibl Skratch Piklz or Beat Junkies but able to cast a much wider net over the font of musical knowledge on record, the Ninja Tune collective have blown up London's airwaves—first on the pirate station Kiss FM and later on BBC—with mix after invincible mix of the broadest beats in the world. Finally, in 2001, Ninja Tune inaugurated a (hopefully long) series of *Solid Steel* mixes with *Now, Listen!,* the results of a 60-minutes-of-madness session featuring DJ Food (aka PC and Strictly) plus DK. Though it wasn't recorded entirely live, the results are far too thrilling to bother quibbling over technicalities. The musical mind-melds include ska-revivalists the Beat over an early Roni Size production, the Commodores' "Assembly Line" mixed up with educational records, a Mr. Scruff track over a Motion Man rap, and Cut Chemist's ironically Coldcut-referencing "2.5 Minute Workout" of Blackalicious' "Alphabet Aerobics," plus snippets of everyone from Ray Bradbury to Herbie Hancock to Perrey-Kingsley to *Man from U.N.K.L.E.* star David McCallum to Innerzone Orchestra to Four Tet to David Shire's score to the 1974 heist film *The Taking of*

Pelham One-Two-Three. No surprise—it's also one of the best-paced mixes heard on an official release since Coldcut & PC's *60 Minutes of Madness* tape from 1996. Showcasing the best in dance and groove no matter which historical or musical boundaries they obliterate in the process, *Now, Listen!* is one of the best mix albums released to date, and the best since Coldcut's own *Journeys By DJ: 60 Minutes of Madness* from 1996. —*John Bush*

DJ Fury (Brian Graham)

b. Sanford, FL
Arranger, Producer, DJ / Bass Music
Amid the many artists contributing to the largely undocumented Miami bass scene centered on Joey Boy Records in the 1990s, DJ Fury certainly stands out as a major talent, as part of Bass Patrol and also as a solo artist. Born Brian Graham in Sanford, a small town in central Florida, Fury began his music career as a breakdancer and soon after moved to house party throwing. He spent some time in the U.S. Air Force soon afterward and earned enough money to buy production equipment. He then began collaborating with rapper RX-Lord (Robert Lewis) as Bass Patrol and signed to Miami's preeminent bass label, Joey Boy. In addition to annual Bass Patrol releases (later compiled on a series of best-of collections), Fury also released solo albums: *Bass Man* (1992), *This Is the Way It's Done, Not the Way It Should Be Done* (1994), *Back 2 da Bassics* (1996), and a *Greatest Hits* collection (1996). After a few low-profile years, Fury resurfaced in the early 2000s with a comeback album, *Still Blowin' Speakers* (2000), and his own label, Full Moon Records. —*Jason Birchmeier*

Furious Bass / 1992 / On Top ✦✦
Furious Bass singles out this prolific underground hip-hop producer as a capable cartoonist of Miami bass music. "Undercover Lover" is porn-fixated Afrika Bambaataa, while "Boom Contest" and "Games of the Lame" sweat and grind on electro beats and periodic digital rhymes. The end result pumps like an old school rap DJ slowing down drum'n'bass syncopation to an amateurish and persuasive crawl. —*Dean Carlson*

DJ Godfather (Brian Jeffries)

Producer, DJ / Electro-Techno, Hip-Hop, Bass Music, Detroit Techno
A DJ recognized equally for his ability to drop a set of either electro, hip-hop, or booty, DJ Godfather eventually reached the point in the late '90s where he could integrate each of these often clashing sounds into the same set, a quickly mixed collage of bass-heavy beats. In addition to his role as a mind-blowing DJ unwilling to stick with conventional techniques, Godfather also managed to release a substantial canon of work on the Twilight 76 label and its spin-off, Databass, which also illustrated his diverse taste in bass music. Of course, it took several years for him to merge these styles together in a seamless manner, as he often paraded as either a hip-hop, electro, or booty DJ, depending on his audience. His first mix CD, *Da Bomb, Vol. 1*, stands as a perfect example of how he suddenly shifts from bass music to hip-hop near the conclusion of the mix as if he were two different DJs. Yet this ability to morph into whatever rocked the given crowd earned him a cult following in Detroit, where he would often cater to both the hip-hop and rave communities.

As the '90s came to a close, Godfather began to evolve into his signature style as a producer of what was then known as booty music—bass-heavy electro tainted with sleazy ideology and hip-hop accessibility—scoring a huge anthem with "Player Haters in This House," which he stretched out into a booty-themed album of the same name. Yet at the same time that he began churning out booty tracks on Databass he was also releasing purist electro records on Twilight 76. During this same time, another Detroit DJ/producer, DJ Assault, was doing similar work, marrying techno with booty music and releasing numerous records similar to Godfather's "Player Haters in This House." By the time Godfather released *Da Bomb, Vol. 3*, he finally had a healthy palette of techno-flavored booty tracks to work with thanks to Assault and was able to navigate his way through numerous musical styles seamlessly—electro, bass, booty, hip-hop, and jungle—creating a collage of sounds referred to by many as ghetto-tech. As the '90s drew to a close he continued this synthesis, releasing additional EPs on Twilight 76 and Databass while further perfecting his unparalleled DJing techniques. —*Jason Birchmeier*

Da Bomb, Vol. 1 / 1998 / Databass ✦✦✦
On DJ Godfather's first volume in his *Da Bomb* series, he still seems to be realizing his style and skills, resulting in a somewhat tentative mix. As he

would continue do on the improved successive volumes, Godfather focuses primarily on his patented style of booty music: the bass-heavy sounds with a sexually provocative tone created exclusively for the means of dancing, freaky style. Unfortunately, there are some problems with this particular volume. First of all, this volume predates Detroit's ghettotech boom, leaving Godfather a little hard up for good booty tracks. Second, he tends to force his mixes, making this far from a seamless mix. Similarly, he spends too much time scratching his records rather than mixing them, perhaps impressing a few but frustrating most who could care less about how fast he can scratch. Finally, the tracks tend to be a mix of hip-hop and booty bass music, as if he isn't sure what sort of DJ he wants to be at this point. Thankfully, the successive volumes are drastic improvements. —*Jason Birchmeier*

Da Bomb, Vol. 2 / 1999 / Databass ✦✦✦
On the second volume in his series of mix CDs, DJ Godfather makes great strides over his mediocre first volume. Essentially, this is practically the same mix—even with the same sort of mini hip-hop set at the end—but this time Godfather mixes are much cleaner, and he has a better arsenal of tracks to choose from. Of the 60 tracks that precede the hip-hop section of the mix, he alternates between Detroit electro such as Drexciya's "Aquatic Beta Particles," bass tracks with catchy vocal chants such as "Get Yo Jit On," and the occasional raunchy booty track such as "Dick-N-Balls." It's a potent mix that has become his signature style, though it tends to be a bit less pornographic than his succeeding volume. The hip-hop mix that begins with Puff Daddy's "Mo Money, Mo Problems" is the only questionable part of the mix. First of all, the trendiness of hip-hop means that even while the aforementioned Puff Daddy track may have been hot at the time of the mix, it has since become the butt of jokes. Furthermore, when he works tracks such as this into his set, they fit rather well; yet when he goes through an extended series of these records, it sounds too contrived. Finally, the accessible, simple tempo and beats of hip-hop seems far too anticlimatic relative to the craziness of his booty bass and electro tracks. —*Jason Birchmeier*

● **Da Bomb, Vol. 3** / 1999 / Databass ✦✦✦✦
DJ Godfather improves slightly on the third volume of this mix series, to the point of near perfection. Gone are the out of place hip-hop sets that concluded the two preceding volumes, and he manages to present a wider variety of tracks here, with a fun emphasis on booty tracks. The inclusion of tracks by his closest competitor in Detroit's ghetto-tech scene, DJ Assault, only strengths the mix. Tracks such as "Ass N Titties" and "Shake It Baby," along with a few other Assault classics, fit in perfectly with Godfather's style. Furthermore, Godfather doesn't let his peer steal the show and concludes the set with a great track of his own, "Player Haters in Dis House." The inclusion of Detroit electro classics such as Model 500's "No UFOs"—sounding like it's being spun at 45 rpm rather than 33—only brings more interesting moments to the set. So rather than functioning as strictly a great uptempo dance mix—which it no doubt is—this volume also has more than a few noteworthy moments for trainspotters as well, making it one of the best-recorded testaments of Detroit's postmodern style of ghetto-tech DJing. —*Jason Birchmeier*

DJ Graffiti

DJ / Underground Rap, Hip-Hop
Based in Ann Arbor, DJ Graffiti was one of Michigan's top hip-hop DJs, even while studying law at the University of Michigan. With a background in jazz percussion, Graffiti moved smoothly into mixing and founded his own Bling Free label as well as working for 7 Heads (J-Live, Asheru, El Da Sensei). His series of *Bling Free* mix tapes earned him the tag "underground mix tape king of Michigan." —*John Bush*

● **Bling Free, Vol. 2: Wake Up!** / Oct. 15, 2002 / Bling Free ✦✦✦✦
Spinning through almost three dozen crack underground tracks in less than an hour, DJ Graffiti displays deft hands on the decks as well as an eye to the acts and tracks that alternative hip-hop fans want to hear. Amidst shout-outs from Dilated Peoples and Slum Village (among others), Graffiti drops Jurassic 5's so-new-it's-shrink-wrapped, old school anthem "What's Golden," the solid Blackalicious/Latyrx joint "It's Going Down," and selected excellence from J-Live, Mr. Lif, Talib Kweli, DJ Jazzy Jeff, and KRS-One. And next to his selection skills, his scratching and spinbacks show plenty of flair as well. Graffiti even keeps it real, Michigan style, choosing a track from Ann Arborite Dabrye to play over a short spoken-word from Eminem. This one is recommended. —*John Bush*

DJ Hollywood

b. Dec. 10, 1954

DJ, Vocals / Hip-Hop, Old School Rap

One of the earliest MCs on the scene, DJ Hollywood originated the practice of delivering extensive rhymes over recorded music, the essence of hip-hop. Yet because of his location (Manhattan), the types of records that he spun (disco), and the crowd he played to (downtown hustler types), DJ Hollywood remains an underrated figure in the development of hip-hop (a term that he originally coined).

    Forming his own singing group at the age of 14, by 1971 Hollywood had moved on to DJing in Harlem clubs such as the Charles Gallery. As the disco movement began growing momentum, DJ Hollywood implemented record mixing, a technique he learned from a club owner, to isolate the funkiest or most danceable parts of the records. This gained him a wide following and, by the mid-'70s, Hollywood's performances at the Apollo Theatre influenced many younger artists such as Kurtis Blow and the Fatback Band. Reigning as one of the top DJs until the mid-'80s, DJ Hollywood faded out of the rap world for a time while fighting drug addiction. He returned in the early '90s to work with Lovebug Starski, performing shows in the New York and New Jersey areas. — *Steve Kurutz*

● **Hollywood's World** / Jun. 13, 1995 / Tuff City ✦✦✦

   Rarities / Oct. 27, 1995 / Ol Skool Flava ✦✦✦

DJ Honda

DJ, Producer / Hip-Hop, Club/Dance, Foreign Rap, Underground Rap

Japanese dance innovator DJ Honda has been crafting his funkadelic hip-hop slicing and dicing since his late teens, yearning to play up to American stylings of rock music. Such motivation led him to play guitar with the band Clique, but they didn't achieve the sort of stardom that DJ Honda was looking for. Instead, DJ Honda headed to the mixing booth, which lead him to make friends with Afrika Bambaata and Universal Zulu Nation and earn major airplay on Tokyo radio stations. In the mid-'90s, he released a slew of singles while making international headway in the club/dance circuit, and made his debut with *Out for the Cash* in 1995. *HII* followed three years later, showcasing collaborations with De La Soul and KRS-One. That same year brought a split between he and Sony Music, leaving DJ Honda to create his own label DJ Honda Recordings. — *MacKenzie Wilson*

   DJ Honda / Jul. 2, 1996 / Relativity ✦✦✦

DJ Honda's eponymous album is a mix album, featuring the DJ's seamless remixes of cuts by tha Alkaholiks, Grand Puba & Sadat X, Tariq, Redman, and Biz Markie, among several others. It's an excellent mix album—not only are the beats and grooves continually danceable, it's possible to hear how inventive and talented DJ Honda is. — *Leo Stanley*

● **HII** / Mar. 24, 1998 / Relativity ✦✦✦✦

DJ Honda's second album *HII* is a quantum leap over his debut, largely because he's given himself freedom to cut and paste his own backgrounds and he's enlisted a number of collaborators (X-ecutioners, KRS-One, Mos Def) to spice up the mix. He's not a postmodernist like DJ Shadow—he's a modern hip-hop DJ, reviving the musical adventure of early hip-hop. Occasionally, the tracks collapse under their own ambitions, but much of *HII* simply tears along, pushing acid jazz and street-level beats together. It's a fascinating, invigorating listen that more than makes the case that in the late '90s international hip-hop can be more exciting than the homegrown kind. — *Stephen Thomas Erlewine*

DJ Hurricane (Wendell Fite)

b. Queens, NY

DJ, Producer / Hip-Hop, East Coast Rap, Turntablism

One of New York's premier hip-hop artists on the turntables, DJ Hurricane fostered his skills alongside Run-D.M.C. in the Hollis, Queens area of New York City before eventually hooking up with the Beastie Boys, where he made a name for himself as the group's DJ before going on to release his own albums. Back during the infantile era of hip-hop, Hurricane began rhyming at the tender age of 11, eventually forming a group called the Solo Sounds and later the Afros. While serving as one of Run-D.M.C.'s body guards on the 1986 Raising Hell tour, he became friends with the Beastie Boys, who were the tour's opening act. It wasn't long before the Beasties offered Hurricane an opportunity to be their exclusive DJ. As the Beasties rose to fame with each successive album in the 1990s, Hurricane simultaneously reveled in the spotlight, releasing his first solo album in 1995 on Grand Royal, titled *The Hurra*. Five years later in late 2000, after having parted ways with the Beasties following their *Ill Communication* album in 1998, Hurricane released the album *Don't Sleep*, which found him much more conceptually collected and with a broad scope of guest artists. — *Jason Birchmeier*

● **Severe Damage** / 1997 / Wiija ✦✦✦

Hurricane's second album, *Severe Damage*, impoves on is debut *The Hurra* by offering harder, more imaginative beats that are based on old school rhythms, yet are grittier and funkier. The rapping remains a bit of a problem—Hurricane might be a hell of a DJ, but he's a little awkward rapping and his lyrics often are clichéd—but the sheer musical force of the album makes it a worthwhile listen. — *Stephen Thomas Erlewine*

Don't Sleep / Oct. 10, 2000 / TVT ✦✦✦

In a year where the producer grew to a level of prominence increasingly closer to that of the MC, with Dr. Dre, Mannie Fresh, and Swizz Beatz getting substantial acclaim and other producers such as Muggs and Dame Grease crafting their own full-length albums, it's not surprising to see a DJ as prominent as DJ Hurricane getting the chance to release a full-length album. Like Muggs and Grease, DJ Hurricane recruits a large roster of MCs to bring some personality to his beats, and, again like Muggs and Grease, his album ultimately falls short with its number of lackluster MC performances despite the excellent beats. It's been said before: not even the best production can overcome dull rapping. There are a few shining moments here, such as "Freeze the Frame" featuring a charged Public Enemy, "Make Things Better" featuring Talib Kweli, "Connect" featuring the near-but-not-quite gangsta charisma of Xzibit, and "Blow It Up" featuring the West Coast stance of Hittman. With 18 tracks, there are quite a few solid beats spoiled by mediocre rapping, and the inclusion of "We Will Rock You," a cover of the Queen classic featuring Scott Weiland, is a looming mistake. In the end, if you can look beyond the oft-poor rapping, there are some great East Coast neo-old school beats here; note though that De Roc and Swift C assist Hurricane with production on every track. — *Jason Birchmeier*

DJ Icey

b. Florida

DJ, Producer / Trip-Hop, Funky Breaks, Big Beat, Club/Dance

DJ Icey's breakbeat funk helped jumpstart the increasingly fertile dance scene in and around Orlando, FL, during the '90s. Born and raised in the Sunshine State, Icey first got into music via early-'80s synth pop, industrial, and hip-hop. The boom in club music during the late '80s hooked him as well, and when he began DJing early in the '90s, he usually played out acid house and funky breaks. He gained a residency at the Edge, one of Orlando's seminal clubs, and soon began playing farther afield thanks to the burgeoning U.S. dance underground. (The club later went under, though not before hosting the Chemical Brothers' first American appearance, an invite extended by Icey himself.) When British DJ and long-time A&R kingpin Pete Tong heard an early single produced for Icey's own Zone Records in 1996, he signed the big-beat precursor *Galaxy Breaks* to his ffrr label. Even while spinning in several cities per week, DJ Icey managed to produce a good dozen singles per year for Zone, usually out of his studio in Orlando. His first major mix set, 1997's *The Funky Breaks*, was followed a year later by his full-length production debut *Generate*. Following in the footsteps of notable DJs from Tong to Fatboy Slim, DJ Icey released a volume in the *Essential Mix* series in 2000. Three years later, DJ Icey returned with his slickest breakbeat effort to date. *Different Day* appeared on System in March 2003. — *John Bush*

The Funky Breaks / Aug. 11, 1997 / ffrr ✦✦✦✦

Icey's first major mix album verges from a remix of PM Dawn's "Watcher's Point of View" to Armand Van Helden's reworking of Genaside II's "Narramine" with breakbeat regulars like Headrillaz and Richard F., as well as two tracks ("Grand Canyon Suite" and "Beats-A-Rockin") from Icey himself. — *John Bush*

Generate / Jun. 30, 1998 / ffrr ✦✦✦✦

DJ Icey has been a top breakbeat DJ for so long, it's a bit of a surprise that his own full-length reveals that he's got some great productions up his sleeve. Though *Generate* includes predictable nods to electro ("Ease the Beat Back Up") and big beat ("Can't Stop This Track"), each are well done and lead to other interesting tracks, like the straight-ahead acid-techno of "Take the Time" and even beatless leanings on "The Air Is Full of Sound." It's not quite up to the quality of Chemical Brothers/Prodigy territory, but *Generate* is a solid album. —*John Bush*

● **Essential Mix** / Aug. 22, 2000 / Sire ✦✦✦✦✦
The breaks aren't quite as funky as they used to be, but with his *Essential Mix*, DJ Icey moves the earthy big-beat style forward to embrace futuristic breakbeat trance and electro. Icey also keeps the energy level peaking throughout, even while he ropes in a cast of musically varied producers and remixers, from big-beat rawkers Freestylers to trance maestros Novy Vs. Eniac to Detroit electro mainstay DJ Godfather to symphonic techno forebears Orbital (plus four of his own productions). In an era when the heavily commercial side of progressive trance is usually a DJ's easiest way out, Icey's *Essential Mix* warps the style until it meets his own ends. —*John Bush*

DJ Jazzy Jeff (Jeff Townes)

b. Jan. 22, 1965
Producer, DJ / Hip-Hop, Pop-Rap
DJ Jazzy Jeff's accomplishments extend well beyond his status as one-half of a multiplatinum rap duo. Regarded as a pioneering turntable tactician for his well-honed skills and for his development of the transformer scratch, the Philadelphian (born Jeff Townes) founded a production house—called A Touch of Jazz—a few years into his alliance with Will Smith as DJ Jazzy Jeff & the Fresh Prince. Since parting ways with his partner, the DJ has worked on records by KRS-One, Kenny Lattimore, Jill Scott, J-Live, and King Britt's Sylk 130. In 2002 he put together a stylistically diverse solo album for BBE; *The Magnificent*, like a Quincy Jones record, found Jeff supported by a number of costars, most of whom were also Philadelphians. —*Andy Kellman*

● **The Magnificent** / Aug. 13, 2002 / Rapster ✦✦✦✦
It's easy to consider DJ Jazzy Jeff an old school head, by simple virtue of his not being very active in the rap mainstream during the past ten years—unlike the former Fresh Prince. Granted his first solo shot by BBE (the British beat ambassadors responsible for great hip-hop mixes by Pete Rock and Kenny Dope, among others), Jeff keeps is hometown, inviting a wealth of Philly names, including Shawn Stockman (from Boyz II Men), Jill Scott, and, for four tracks, Pauly Yamz and Baby Blak. And just like some of his classic hits with Will Smith, *The Magnificent* comes very correct with beatbox breaks, jazzy guitar and keys, lots of vocal harmonies on the choruses, and the sub-frequency, almost percussive bass lines often heard on later A Tribe Called Quest LPs. For the most part, Jeff keeps to the background—every track here has a featured vocalist—though Pauly Yamz and Baby Blak sing his praises on the title-track opener, and J-Live gives him plenty of room for scratching on the spectacular "Break It Down." It's hard to say how long DJ Jazzy Jeff took making these tracks, though *The Magnificent* has an incredible range; Jeff does it *all* well, even when moving from soulful R&B ("Rock Wit U" with Eric Roberson) to basement hip-hop on the very next track ("Scram" with Freddie Foxxx). Those who can make it to the end—admittedly, 17 tracks are a lot to deal with—get treated to a fun Roy Ayers redo, "We Live in Philly," with Jill Scott playfully stretching out on a dream-time vocal performance that references plenty of Philadelphia landmarks, along with a range of Philly celebrities: Dr. J, Pooh Richardson, Maurice Cheeks, Schoolly D., Frankie Beverly, and Patti LaBelle, among others. —*John Bush*

DJ Jazzy Jeff & the Fresh Prince

f. 1986, Philadelphia, PA, **db.** 1993
Group / Hip-Hop, Urban, Pop-Rap
To many present-day listeners, DJ Jazzy Jeff & the Fresh Prince are best remembered for launching the superstar music/acting career of the latter, now known by his real name of Will Smith. In their heyday, however, the Philadelphia duo played a major role in making rap music accessible to pop audiences, as well as younger listeners. Smith's raps were never anything more than PG-rated, and his genial, winning personality came through in the good-humored stories that many of his best raps wove. His partner, Jeff Townes, was one of Philadelphia's best DJs, an inventive scratcher who provided appropriately playful backdrops. At a time when rap wanted to establish itself as the authentic voice of the streets, DJ Jazzy Jeff & the Fresh Prince were often ridiculed as bubblegum kiddie rap—they weren't aggressive,

outraged, gritty, or urban enough to fit the prevailing hip-hop fashion of the time. However, in hindsight, it's clear that the duo's appeal was a natural result of simply being themselves, not from pandering to middle-class youth or posing as something they weren't. That's why the best of their work still sounds lively, full of youthful energy and breezy wit, and ranks as some of the most infectious pop-rap of its time.

DJ Jazzy Jeff (born Jeffrey Townes, January 22, 1965) and the Fresh Prince (born Willard Smith, September 25, 1968) got together in 1986, when they performed together at a house party after years of separately pursuing hip-hop around the Philadelphia area. Later that year, they performed at the New Music Seminar, where Jeff placed first in the DJ competition; the attention helped them land a record deal with Jive and the Fresh Prince turned down his acceptance into M.I.T. Their first single, "Girls Ain't Nothing But Trouble," was built around a sample of the theme from "I Dream of Jeannie," and the humorous video began to build the duo an audience through MTV. It helped their 1987-released debut album, *Rock the House*, go gold and set the stage for their breakthrough success with the 1988 follow-up *He's the DJ, I'm the Rapper*. One of the first double-LP sets in rap history (thanks to a number of tracks showcasing Jeff's turntable artistry), it also became one of the genre's biggest sellers up to that point, moving more than 2.5 million copies after the comic video for "Parents Just Don't Understand" became a runaway hit on MTV. A playful riff on the generation gap, "Parents Just Don't Understand" hit number 12 on the singles charts, went gold, and won the first-ever rap Grammy; the duo toured extensively behind it, aided in their dealings with concert promoters by their nonthreatening image.

Hip-hop, however, was an extraordinarily difficult field in which to sustain career momentum. Even though it was released only a year later, *And in This Corner...* failed to generate nearly as much attention—despite going gold—partly because the lead single, "I Think I Can Beat Mike Tyson," failed to catch fire. The album was also hurt by a rapidly changing hip-hop climate; De La Soul's rapturously received debut, *3 Feet High and Rising*, had succeeded in bringing positivity and humor to hip-hop with less of a comic-novelty flavor and seemingly countless new pop-rap fads were springing up by the minute. Fortunately, Smith's performances in the duo's videos had attracted notice in the television world. Convinced of Smith's potential to become a warm, charismatic, clean-cut star in the acting world, NBC gave him a starring role in a sitcom named after his rap persona, *The Fresh Prince of Bel Air*, which followed a young Philadelphian sent to live with his rich relatives in California to keep out of trouble. Although Smith wasn't yet a seasoned actor, executives were correct about his comic appeal and the show became a hit, running for six seasons; Townes was given a recurring role as Smith's character's streetwise friend (aptly dubbed Jazz).

Although Smith had taken a hiatus from DJ Jazzy Jeff & the Fresh Prince to concentrate on getting his sitcom off the ground, the duo reconvened in 1991, buoyed by their increased visibility. Featuring more outside productions, *Homebase* returned Townes and Smith to the platinum sales mark and produced their biggest hit ever in the warm, laid-back party tune "Summertime," where Smith nostalgically reminisced about summers growing up in Philadelphia in a way that appealed to listeners of all ages. "Summertime" became their first and only Top Five pop hit, peaking at number four. A follow-up LP, *Code Red*, was released in 1993, but didn't sell very well in the U.S.; oddly, the single "Boom! Shake the Room" became their first number-one hit in the U.K. Nonetheless, Smith decided to focus full-time on his acting career, appearing in the critically acclaimed *Six Degrees of Separation* (also in 1993). Proving he could cut it on the big screen, Smith went on to star in numerous big-budget Hollywood blockbusters, including *Independence Day*, *Men in Black*, *Enemy of the State*, *Wild Wild West*, and *Ali* (the latter of which earned him an Oscar nomination); he also returned to music as a solo artist, selling millions more albums than he did with DJ Jazzy Jeff thanks to his enormous exposure. Townes, meanwhile, formed a production company called A Touch of Jazz, and worked as a producer and mixer for several hip-hop and R&B artists (including a few of Smith's solo cuts). —*Steve Huey*

Rock the House / 1987 / Jive ✦✦✦✦
In the 1980s, Philadelphia's hip-hop scene was diverse. At one extreme was the controversial Schoolly D, who was among the founders of gangsta rap even though he wasn't as big as West Coast agitators like N.W.A and Ice-T. And at the other extreme was DJ Jazzy Jeff & the Fresh Prince, whose fun,

lighthearted, often goofy tales were great for comic relief. *Rock the House*, the duo's debut album of 1987, demonstrated that Will Smith, aka the Fresh Prince, was as entertaining and amusing a storyteller as Dana Dane or Slick Rick. But unlike those New York MCs, DJ Jazzy Jeff & the Fresh Prince weren't off-color or controversial—in fact, their unthreatening, clean-cut image led some journalists to dub them "the Cosby kids of rap." And the Philadelphians had no problem with that; in a 1989 interview, Smith asserted that he was proud to be compared to the Cosby kids. You won't find a lot of hard-hitting social commentary on *Rock the House*; Smith and his partner keep things lighthearted on tunes like "Girls Ain't Nothing But Trouble" (the hit single that sampled the *I Dream of Jeannie* theme and put them on the map) and "Just One of Those Days." Equally strong is "Guys Ain't Nothing But Trouble," a sequel to "Girls Ain't Nothing But Trouble" that features female rapper Ice Cream Tee (who had a lot of potential but didn't get very far as a solo artist). Is *Rock the House* pop-rap? Absolutely. But for DJ Jazzy Jeff & the Fresh Prince, lighthearted doesn't mean lightweight. In terms of rapping technique, Smith could hold his own against any of the more hardcore rappers who came out of Philly in the 1980s. This excellent LP is a classic of its kind. —*Alex Henderson*

☆ **He's the DJ, I'm the Rapper** / 1988 / Jive ✦✦✦✦✦
This is the album on which DJ Jazzy Jeff & the Fresh Prince hit commercial pay dirt, the album that introduced the duo's jokey, benign, and somewhat goofball demeanor to a wide audience. Without *He's the DJ, I'm the Rapper*, in fact, it could be argued that you never would have had Will Smith, movie star, as the album afforded him a level and type of exposure he would never thereafter relinquish. Oddly enough, it is DJ Jazzy Jeff who generally was cited as the musical star of the duo, at least in the rap community, on account of his groundbreaking and always-wizardly work on the turntables. That skill is evident ("D.J. on the Wheels"), but often takes a backseat here in deference to the Fresh Prince's whimsical story-songs. To be frank, Smith's rhymes and antics can become rather, well, hokey, like Slick Rick with an antiseptic tongue, but they are always good natured and good fun, admirable qualities in themselves considering rap's growing inclination at the time to drift toward the hardcore and polemical sides of the street. *He's the DJ* is almost cartoon-like by comparison. Painfully corny music videos for the hit singles "Parents Just Don't Understand" and "Nightmare on My Street" underscored the impression to an even greater extent. The reality, though, is slightly more interesting than the caricature. There are songs here ("Brand New Funk," "Pump Up the Bass," the title track) that go straight to the heart of hip-hop's traditional role as sweaty house-party soundtrack and which highlight a more "street" facet of the duo. Still, this is not a consequential album. It is an extremely likable one, however, with a youthful vigor, animateness, and a spirited sense of humor undiminished by the ensuing decades. Compared with some of the strains of rap that were to follow, which often mistook sarcasm or irony for drollery, *He's the DJ* seems a quaint, practically naïve artifact of an era before bling-bling and Benzes became the norm. —*Stanton Swihart*

And in This Corner . . . / Oct. 1989 / Jive ✦✦✦
This CD offers more wit and whim from Jeff and the Prince, this time with assistance from saxes, flutes, and trumpets. Though not as commercially successful as its predecessors, it's actually a more faithful rap work. —*Ron Wynn*

Homebase / Jul. 23, 1991 / Jive ✦✦✦✦✦
After the disappointingly uneven *And in This Corner...*, DJ Jazzy Jeff & the Fresh Prince restarted their commercial momentum with *Homebase*, which fitted Will Smith's rhymes with up-to-date, radio-friendly production and a much richer overall sound. For the first time, the album's key single wasn't a comic narrative: "Summertime" was a warm, breezy reminiscence about growing up in Philadelphia and attending barbecues where the whole community showed up to see and be seen. It had all the good vibes of a typical Fresh Prince number, but it was clearly a more mature effort, and that's *Homebase* in a nutshell. The smoothed-out R&B background of "Summertime" provides a template for the record's poppier moments, and there's a thumping new club influence on the dancefloor cuts. Lyrically, when he's not trying to move your butt, Smith paints himself as more of a ladies' man, in keeping with his new young-adult persona. If he's still more innocent than LL Cool J, he's throwing out all his best lines on the single "Ring My Bell" and trying to play the field on "A Dog Is a Dog." And there are a few story-

songs, like "Who Stole the DJ" and "You Saw My Blinker," that benefit from the fresher-sounding beats. While it doesn't have the youthful, old school charm of *He's the DJ, I'm the Rapper*, *Homebase* is a successful reinvention that laid the groundwork for Smith's multimedia stardom as an adult. —*Steve Huey*

Code Red / Oct. 12, 1993 / Jive ✦✦✦
After years of proclaiming that he wouldn't do gangsta rap, the Fresh Prince finally succumbs to a harder-edged style on *Code Red*. And, surprisingly, he pulls it off well, thanks to sharp production and his endearing personality. —*Stephen Thomas Erlewine*

● **Greatest Hits** / Apr. 28, 1998 / Jive ✦✦✦✦✦
DJ Jazzy Jeff & the Fresh Prince actually turned out better albums than many of their pop-rap contemporaries, but like their peers, they excelled at singles, not albums. That's what makes the appearance of *Greatest Hits* welcome. Although it has its flaws—the sublime "Summertime" is here twice, but only as an "Extended Club Mix" and a "'98 remix"—it remains an excellent summation of their career, boasting such hits as "Girls Ain't Nothing But Trouble," "I Think I Can Beat Mike Tyson," "Parents Just Don't Understand," "Boom! Shake the Room," "Ring My Bell," "A Nightmare On My Street," and, as a bonus, Will Smith's 1997 solo hit "Men in Black." —*Stephen Thomas Erlewine*

DJ Kool (John W. Bowman Jr.)
....
b. 1959, Washington, D.C.
DJ, Producer / Club/Dance, Go-Go, Old School Rap, Hip-Hop
A fusion of feel-good go-go music with hip-hop's original block-party aesthetic led DJ Kool to the fore in rap's return to the old school during the late '90s. A veteran of D.C.'s go-go circuit who worked as a warm-up DJ for Rare Essence during the early- to mid-'80s, Kool began recording in 1988 and early on tried to inform the studio art of hip-hop with a live feel in keeping with his experience. His first album, *The Music Ain't Loud Enuff*, used call and response much like early hip-hop and go-go (and also included the hip-house track "House Your Body" prefaced by a remarkably accurate monologue on the history of house music).
   Kool took it to the stage in 1992 with the mini-LP *20 Minute Workout*, recorded live in Richmond, VA, and released on Steve Janis' CLR Records. By the time of 1996's *Let Me Clear My Throat*, mostly recorded live in Philadelphia, the East Coast underground was buzzing about Kool's way with a crowd. American Records won a five-way bidding war and reissued *Let Me Clear My Throat* early the following year; providing remixes of the title track were Funkmaster Flex and Mark the 45 King (whose funky underground hit "The 900 Number" was the basis for the title track in the first place), helping it climb into the Top Five on the rap charts. In mid-2000, he and Fatman Scoop released the remixed Rob Base classic "It Takes Two." —*John Bush*

The Music Ain't Loud Enuff / 1990 / Creative Funk ✦✦✦✦
DJ Kool's album debut was an incredibly wide-ranging LP with few similarities to any contemporary hip-hop act, except possibly Mantronix. Including the dancehall raggae track "Raggae Dance," the hip-house track "House Your Body," several crucial sample productions (the title track, "What the Hell You Come in Here For," "How Low Can You Go") and even the touching R&B production "Pressed Against the Glass," Kool proves himself a master of just about every type of party music then circulating. —*John Bush*

20 Minute Workout EP / 1992 / CLR ✦✦✦
Given he's the hardest-working man in the rap business, it shouldn't be a surprise that DJ Kool's *20 Minute Workout* EP actually lasts twice that long. Of course, "20 Minute Workout" is the title track and not a reference to the CD's length, but it's still a perfect summation of DJ Kool's tremendous energy and determination. The first track is, indeed, "20 Minute Workout," recorded live in Richmond, and it shows Kool getting a crowd into it like few rappers are able. The other inclusions are solid as well, featuring sampladelic hardcore tracks like "Bass N the Truck" and "4 the Brothas N the Ghetto," plus a few remixes and bonus beats. —*John Bush*

● **Let Me Clear My Throat** / Apr. 1996 / American ✦✦✦✦✦
DJ Kool's *Let Me Clear My Throat* was one of the most invigorating hip-hop records of the mid-'90s, simply because it didn't follow conventional hardcore, alternative, or gangsta rap patterns. Instead, DJ Kool returned to the wild, careening atmosphere of freestyle, old school hip-hop, anchoring the

rhymes with spare scratching and elastic reggae grooves. The result was one hell of a party album, filled with terrific beats and infectious, humorous rhymes. —*Leo Stanley*

DJ Krush (Hideaki Ishii)

b. 1962

Producer, DJ / Hip-Hop, Trip-Hop, Ambient Breakbeat, Electronica

Japanese turntablist and producer DJ Krush is one of the few island-nation throw-ups to be embraced by the global hip-hop world. Releasing material through Sony in Japan, Mo'Wax and Virgin in the U.K., and Axiom, Shadow, and A&M in America, Krush's heady brand of experimental, (largely) instrumental hip-hop has been praised by everyone from hardcore underground hip-hop 'zines like *The Bomb* to the speckless offices of *Rolling Stone* and *Spin*. Beginning as a bedroom DJ in the mid-'80s following the Japanese leg of the Wildstyle tour, Krush moved into mobile DJing, backing up rappers, and eventually solo production. Although his Japan-only debut freely mixed elements of R&B and acid jazz with the beefy breakbeat backbone of midtempo hip-hop, Krush's work has since tended more toward the abstract, applying heavy effects and sample manipulation to thick, smart breaks, layered, almost ambient textures, and subtle, inventive scratching. Krush came to larger acclaim in the mid-'90s through his association with the London-based Mo'Wax label, which released his *Strictly Turntablized* in 1994 and *Meiso* in 1996, both reissued stateside by A&M. While *Turntablized* is closer to a collection of DJ tools, *Meiso* is a return of sorts to his earlier work, including rappers such as Guru and C.L. Smooth on a few tracks and incorporating a wider variety of instrumental sounds and atmospheres. In addition to 1997's *Milight*, Krush also featured on a number of various-artists collections, including Mo'Wax's celebrated *Headz*, as well as *Altered Beats* and *Axiom Dub* (both out on Bill Laswell's Axiom label). *Kakusei* appeared on Mo'Wax/Columbia in 1999, followed by the mix albums *Code 4109* and *Tragicomic* the next year. —*Sean Cooper*

Strictly Turntablized / 1994 / Mo'Wax ✦✦✦✦

Poised halfway between a late-night downbeat record and a nearly anonymous beats-and-breaks volume, *Strictly Turntablized* was one of the first trip-hop records out of the gate, and the subtitle says it better than any review could: "Excursions into the hip-hop avant-garde." DJ Krush's productions were deeper than Cam's and darker than Shadow's, and if they seldom averaged more than one or two ideas per track, most of them made up for it with a heavy dose of atmospheric menace. "Kemuri" paved the way with a break to make Premier himself proud, and just enough scratching to preserve the vibes. "Fucked-Up Pendulum" was interesting as well, earning its title with an offbeat (literally) sample that was more musique concrèté than hip-hop. A few other tracks were solid examples of instrumental hip-hop, but several others sounded in dire need of vocals to break them up. Krush would later learn how to give his productions voice, but with *Strictly Turntablized* he built the foundation for trip-hop to come. —*John Bush*

Krush / 1995 / Shadow ✦✦✦✦

DJ Krush's first stateside release is a fine affair; if *Strictly Turntablized* is the one most often raved about in the hip-hop underground with regard to his early work, that's not for this release's lack of trying. Working with a variety of his countrymen throughout, who tackle everything from guest vocals to a variety of instruments, *Krush* sets the late-night, smoky urban mood from the start and doesn't let up throughout. Funky beats are spare but effective, launching grooves that unfold just enough over the course of his tracks, edgy and slightly unnerving. Many of his best efforts come on brief link tracks, like "Underneath the System," with a queasy, drugged-out feeling that any number of trip-hop wannabes would have killed to create. While he has a definite sound and style, he also knows how to create any number of variations or twists with it, with fine results. His collaborations with vocalists and rappers show him holding back just a touch to allow them full room to breathe; it's more like he's the backing musician for them, an unexpected twist given that this is his album. "Keeping the Motion" features sweet R&B singing and reasonably OK MC work from Monday Michiru, adding some fine sass to the affair, while Carla Vallet's multilingual spoken word breaks and softly crooned chorus on "Murder of Soul" also has a nice bite. On the instrumental tip, his affinities to jazz are clear. The edgy, electronic burn of "Roll and Tumble" is broken up in a neat way by Kim Shima's piano and Takeharu Hayakawa's bass. Meanwhile, both Kazufumi Kodama's calmer trumpet on

the lovely, echo-heavy "On the Dub-Bue" and Kobutaka Kuwabara's more aggressive work on "Edge of Blue" bring to mind what Miles Davis might have done had he lived well into the '90s. —*Ned Raggett*

Meiso / 1996 / Mo'Wax ✦✦✦✦

Having won a deserved underground reputation, DJ Krush was able to take things to a higher plane with his excellent *Meiso* album, featuring another range of strong collaborations to help him carry out his mission of creativity with the turntables. Kicking off with the excellent "Only the Strong Survive," featuring C.L. Smooth, *Meiso* resembles *Krush* in that shorter bridge tracks crop up between longer songs, all flowing together just so. His overall approach remains unchanged: low, mid- to slow-tempo grooves and breaks, with varying low bass tones, touching on everything from jazz and funk to experimental ambient production. The album's mood is at once reflective and edgy, always threatening to get vicious just around the corner. Highlights of his strictly solo tracks include "What's Behind Darkness?" and the deceptively gentle "Blank." Most of Krush's collaborators this time around are on the vocal tip; musically, the real winner comes with the astonishing "Duality." This track is a full partnership with the equally well-ranked DJ Shadow; one can easily tell when the latter takes over the drum programming for the tune, with a shimmering darkness cascading down. Vocally, both Black Thought and Malik B. of the Roots take a spin with the tight grooving title track, getting in some wonderfully playful rhymes playing off Krush's Japanese background while the man himself shows some smart scratching flash. Deflon Sallahr of Hedrush kicks down with a confrontational effort on "Ground," while a more than logical fellow traveler in jazz and hip-hop, the legendary Guru, works out the music with Krush as Big Shug delivers a bold gangsta rap on "Most Wanted Man." —*Ned Raggett*

Cold Krush Cuts/Back in the Base / Feb. 4, 1997 / Ninja Tune ✦✦

DJ Krush'w full-length works have always been a bit hard to swallow given the unyielding predomination of midtempo hip-hop, and his contribution to *Cold Krush Cuts*, the double-disc Ninja Tunes mix compilation (one disc of Krush, one of Coldcut) is no different. Restricted to using only Ninja Tune artists (DJ Vadim makes eight appearances!), the material is similar sounding and repetitious—even more so than DJ Krush's albums. Aside from the chosen records, Krush's mixing skills are okay but overshadowed by Coldcut and DJ Food on the other disc. —*John Bush*

Milight / Aug. 18, 1997 / Mo'Wax/FFRR ✦✦✦✦

The follow-up to Krush's excellent *Meiso* was a slightly more unusual affair, consisting of a series of collaborative pieces throughout, with only one or two exceptions, and with each particular guest bookending their respective track with a brief reflection on what the future of the world will hold. The results are a touch mixed but still a fairly good effort, as always with Krush's brand of jazz-tinged, heavy, druggy breakbeats and scratches at the center of things. His style remains pure and fierce, if anything becoming even more effectively unnerving and atmospheric with time, as the lovely blend of nature sounds and keyboards on "Jugoya" shows. The first collaboration, "Shin-Sekai," also demonstrates this perfectly; fellow Japanese musician Rino lays down a pretty fierce rap while Krush's blend of shuffling but hard-hitting drums and mysterious tones—pianos, sighing electric guitar, and other strange moans in the mix—carry everything before it. Producer Shawn J. Period throws in a lot of additional music, subtly but with great effect, like a strange haunted house, on "Listen," while DJ Cam, in an echo of *Meiso*'s DJ Shadow trade-off "Duality," jams with Krush to create the slamming mini-duel "Le Temps." Guest MCs this time out include Tragedy and partner Stash, laying down a harrowing and saddening tale of crime and its consequences on the hard-hitting "Real," while cult figure Mos Def spins his usual magic on the quietly chaotic salute to Japanese hip-hoppers, "Shinjiro." One of the most inspired moves comes at the end: a cover of John Lennon's "Mind Games" with guest singer Eri Ohno giving it a good soul revamp over the steady, big-impact rhythms. —*Ned Raggett*

Ki-Oku / Jan. 26, 1998 / Instinct ✦✦✦✦

Anyone who remembers trumpeter Toshinori Kondo's work with such thorny avant-gardists as John Zorn, Derek Bailey, Fred Frith, and Peter Brotzmann's Die Like a Dog Quartet may be a bit taken aback by the extreme accessibility of his collaboration with pioneering turntablist DJ Krush. Much of the music on *Ki-Oku* flirts with smooth-groove jazz—Kondo's muted trumpet line on "Mu-Getsu" sounds an awful lot like something Chris Botti would play, while the duo's instrumental take on the Bob Marley classic "Sun Is Shining" comes off just a little bit muzak-y. On the other hand, "Ki-Gen" and "Ko-Ku" both find Kondo using synthesized treatments in a way that evokes Jon Hassell's work with Brian Eno, while on the latter DJ Krush layers slightly menacing keyboard washes beneath Kondo's unassuming trumpet lines. This is one of those albums that reveals more with repeated listens; if it sounds too easy at first, listen again—there's lots of interesting stuff going on beneath what sometimes sounds like a merely pleasant surface. —*Rick Anderson*

Holonic: The Self Megamix / Feb. 2, 1998 / Mo' Wax ◆◆◆◆
Megamixes are almost never very interesting, as they mostly consist of DJs placing their own interpretive tastes and ideas over those of the artists being mixed, but as the subtitle indicates, DJ Krush's *Holonic: The Self Megamix* is actually more of a greatest-hits collection than a traditional megamix. Taking tracks (or bits and pieces thereof) from all of his previous albums, from 1994's *Strictly Turntablized* through 1997's *Milight*, DJ Krush turns these fragments into a cohesive, free-flowing whole. The album is heaviest on tracks and samples from *Milight*, even including some of the spoken-word segments from that album, but *Holonic* has a much brighter and less-heavy vibe than that doomy, almost-apocalyptic album. DJ Krush's music could never be called cheerful—his jazzy, minor-key grooves and atmospheric use of found sound and unidentifiable samples is just too dark and moody—but *Holonic* has a playful quality that's largely been missing from his work since the days of *Strictly Turntablized*. Neither a traditional greatest hits nor the average megamix, *Holonic* is nevertheless an excellent introduction to DJ Krush's work. —*Stewart Mason*

● **Kakusei** / Mar. 8, 1999 / Mo'Wax / Columbia ◆◆◆◆◆
Continuing his series of solo albums as collaborative efforts, DJ Krush touched down after a slight absence with *Kakusei*, another invigorating, moody, and powerful release. Steering away from the overall concept of *Milight* but working with another slew of musical partners, Krush once again lets his abilities at both musical creation and turntablism work together for great results. "Escapee," a track worked on with fellow beatmaster A.S.A., is almost stereotypically Krush, but it sounds so great, the crackle of vinyl and acoustic bass moan steering the course. Other musical collaborations abound, unsurprisingly: "Parallel Distortion" with DJ Sak features odd video game noises and a quirky synth bass rhythm echoing through the flow, while "Krushed Wall" has the Rhythm Troops having a blast with the usual Krush sound and tons of unexpected stops, scratches, and cuts. Some returnees from *Milight* surface, including members of Kemuri Productions, who appear on the quietly head-nodding "Inorganizm" and "No More," and Shawn J. Period, who on "The Dawn" works with Krush on a great series of orchestrations to flesh out the track. Plenty of strictly solo efforts crop up as well, including the abrasive electronics of "85 Loop" and the smooth-going "Final Home." Vocally, there's not as much going on this time around; aside from brief shout-outs here and there, it's strictly an instrumental affair. —*Ned Raggett*

Code 4109 / Apr. 25, 2000 / Red Ink ◆◆◆◆
Code 4109 is the first "proper" mix album from one of trip-hop's reigning DJ masters—his two previous efforts, *Back in the Base* and *Holonic*, were restricted to, respectively, material from the Ninja Tune label and his own work. It's also an excellent compilation, never sacrificing the trademarked earthy grooves on the altar of experimentalism. None of the tracks are obvious inclusions—except for a few of Krush's own productions—and the material that is here has obviously been worked on heavily while on the turntables; Krush transforms, tweak scratches, and attempts all manner of effects on the tracks. From the vicious detuned monster "Back to the Essence" (by Gravity) near the beginning, he spins material from those with similar aesthetics (DJ Cam, the 45 King, Jazzanova) and uses more eccentric inclusions (John Klemmer, Beats International, a Bulgarian choir, Japanese jazz artist Minuro Muraoka) as layering for the stoned beats and haunted basslines on the primary tracks. More so than most of DJ Krush's material, *Code 4109* progresses through different sounds and styles with panache and dexterity. —*John Bush*

Zen / Aug. 7, 2001 / Red Ink ◆◆◆◆
For *Zen*, Japanese producer/mixer DJ Krush works his way into a vision of sublime, downbeat hip-hop that's a snug fit with the title. The opening "Song 1" is an irresistible slice of trance-state trip-hop, with the cascading notes of a vibraphone and flute perfectly complementing the atmospheric grooves. Krush also continues the collaborational bent of previous LPs, with hip-hop heads Black Thought and ?uestlove from the Roots (appearing on separate tracks), Company Flow, and DJ Disk alongside left-field choices Zap Mama,

N'Dea Davenport, and trumpeter Kazufumi Kodama. On these tracks the beats and effects are more pointed than on the opener and, as in the past, DJ Krush proves he's a stellar jack-of-all-trades trackmaster. The tuneless bass line and production gloom surrounding "Vision of Art" are the perfect bedrock for hardcore paranoiacs Company Flow, while the frenetic, quasi-jungle programming on "Sonic Traveler" only highlights the incredible flair of guest Tunde Ayanyemi (on kudi and bata drums). And while any other hip-hop producer would burn out on at least a *few* collaborations, Krush just keeps turning out excellent song beds: for DJ Disk on "Duck Chase," for Zap Mama on "Danger of Love," and for Kazufumi Kodama on "Day's End." All these great appearances make any disappointment caused by the lack of solo jaunts after "Song 1" practically nil. —*John Bush*

The Message at the Depth / Feb. 11, 2003 / Red Ink ◆◆◆◆
In the world of independent hip-hop, artists either trailblaze like Quasimoto and El-P or salute their forebears like Blackalicious and Jurassic 5. Japanese breaks maestro DJ Krush is a curious exception to the rule; he seems virtually unaffected by trends yet encompasses many of them in his productions, and offers something different with virtually each release. Similar to lauded underground labels from Def Jux to Big Dada, *The Message at the Depth* is underground rap for the digital age, far removed from the moldy crates and dusty beats of Krush's Mo'Wax classic *Strictly Turntablized*. His beats are digital, heavily resampled, and quantized, splintering off like drum'n'bass patterns but possessing a depth and clarity not seen since the heyday of Massive Attack. And with far fewer collaborations here than on his last record, *Zen*, there's more room to hear Krush at his best. A pair of instrumentals, the dark breaks symphonies "Sanity Requiem" and "The Blackhole," fare much better than the high-profile vocal features for Antipop Consortium and Anticon, which add surprisingly little to the proceedings. Anticon's collaboration, the stoner nightmare "Song for John Walker," is a sub-Cannibal Ox performance; even DJ Krush can't put together a production to make them sound relevant. The best rapping comes from Japanese MC Inden, who gets his point across on "Toki No Tabiji (Journey of Time)" without needing to resort to English. "But the World Moves On" is the only track to look back to the same grooves heard on *Zen*, with bassist D-Madness and alto Masato Nakamura helping Krush conjure a dark Asiatic vibe. —*John Bush*

DJ Laz (Lazaro Mendez)

Producer, DJ, Bass / Hip-Hop, Club/Dance, Bass Music
A prominent name in Latin bass music, rapper/producer DJ Laz (aka Lazaro Mendez) started his musical career at age 15, spinning, mixing, and scratching at local clubs in South Florida. This led to jobs as a DJ at WHQT FM and WPOW 96.5 FM, where he is one of the station's most popular on-air personalities. DJ Laz signed with the respected bass music label Pandisc and released his debut album, *DJ Laz Featuring Mami El Negro*, in 1991; the single "Mami El Negro" debuted in the Top 100. His other albums, which include 1993's *Journey Into Bass*, 1996's *King of Bass*, 1998's *Cruzin'*, and 2000's *Pimpin'*, were also released by Pandisc and featured rappers like Trick Dog, Celo, Hallucination, and Daddy C. In addition to his duties as a rapper and DJ, Laz also promotes shows and performs at Ft. Lauderdale clubs such as Zippers and Roxy, and has remixed tracks for Luther Campbell, 2 Live Crew, Will Smith, and Gloria Estefan. —*Heather Phares*

● **Journey Into Bass** / Nov. 30, 1993 / Pandisc ◆◆◆◆
Greatest Hits / Aug. 21, 2001 / Pandisc ◆◆◆◆

DJ Logic (Jason Kibler)

DJ / Jazz-Funk, Turntablism, Hip-Hop
Turntable maestro DJ Logic (real name Jason Kibler) is widely credited for helping to bring jazz into hip-hop's sphere of influence. Hailing from the Bronx, he kicked off his adventures on the decks in the 1980s by playing at local community events. The next decade, however, saw him growing rapidly in stature as a pro musician. First he joined the group Eye & I, performing with such bands as Living Color and Body Count. He then hooked up with talented jazz trio MMW (keyboardist John Medeski, drummer Billy Martin, and bassist Chris Wood), touring heavily and working on the celebrated *Combustication* record. He released his debut album, the aptly titled *Project Logic*, to wide critical acclaim in 1999. Two years later, he was again collecting plaudits en masse after putting out the cutting-edge *The Anomaly* album. Logic surfaced alongside guitarist Vernon Reid in 2002 for *Front End Lifter*,

a fun, adventurous album the two recorded as Yohimbe Brothers and then toured behind late in the year. —*David Peter Wesolowski*

Project Logic / Oct. 12, 1999 / Ropeadope ◆◆◆◆

A lot of DJs have stepped to the front, recording as leaders, to varying degrees of success. While many of these efforts have been entertaining, very rarely do they succeed on a truly musical level. With the release of *Project Logic*, DJ Logic (aka Jason Kibler) changes all that. Playing in Vernon Reid's band, and several years with Medeski, Martin & Wood, has not only given DJ Logic valuable training as an improvising musician, but has also left him incredibly well connected to boot. This album was recorded in a series of sessions in New York, where DJ Logic, bassist Melvin Gibbs (Decoding Society, Rollins Band), and drummer Skoota Warner let the tapes roll with a myriad of invited guests. These improvised sessions were then edited and sometimes overdubbed to create the album. This gives the tracks the feeling (rightfully so) that actual musicians recorded this in real time, while listening to each other; that it's not just a studio creation. The only exception is "Spider Dance," where vocalist Jennifer Charles (Elysian Fields) joins on a track that could have come off the Golden Palominos' *Pure*. The other tunes explore various funky jazz settings, except for "Eyes Open (But Dead)," a straight-up hip-hop piece, and "Una Cosa Buena," a Latin number. Another highlight, "Mnemonics," has Logic mixing records from an Indian vocalist, while also utilizing a live tabla player and cornetist Graham Haynes. Besides the usual suspects (MMW, Vernon Reid), a host of New York's finest appear: Marc Ribot, Steven Bernstein & Briggan Krauss of Sex Mob, and even legendary producer Teo Macero dusts off his horn to play on a track. The result is a fine musical offering that breathes the air of jazz improvisation; unprecedented by a DJ. —*Sean Westergaard*

● **The Anomaly** / May 22, 2001 / Ropeadope ◆◆◆◆◆

On his second solo album, DJ Logic creates a true anomaly in the electronic jazz genre: a set that remains true to the improvisational spirit of jazz *and* makes you want to shake your ass. Unlike recent techno jazz albums by artists such as St. Germain, the songs on *The Anomaly* never drift into dull repetition—each tune constantly surprises with unexpected turns. *The Anomaly* is a bit fresher and funkier than his equally excellent debut *Project Logic*, which tended toward the dense and industrial. Logic earned his pedigree working with latter-day jazz saints such as Vernon Reid and Medeski Martin and Wood, and both Reid and Medeski lend a hand to their disciple on this album. In particular, Medeski's funk organ gospel adds an extra kick to "French Quarter," a nasty jam replete with a Tower of Power-like horn refrain. He and his excellent band Project Logic dip into trip-hop with "Black Buddha," layering velvety sax and flute melodies and ambient accompaniment. "Soul Kissing" finds Logic delving into Eastern rhythms with a violin playing the main melody and tablas filling out the sound. He even pulls off a deft hip-hop tune on "The Project," thanks to Subconscious' heady rap. Logic experiments on several tracks to varying success, including a bizarre meld of industrial and aria on "Hip-Hopera," which sounds like an eerie ghost haunting a sheet metal factory. But no matter what concoctions he tries, Logic keeps it lively and intense. *The Anomaly* works well whether you're on the dancefloor or sitting on the living room floor. —*Michael Gowan*

DJ Magic Mike (Michael Hampton)

b. 1967, Orlando, FL

DJ, Producer, Mixing / Bass Music, Party Rap, Southern Rap

DJ Magic Mike, the breakthrough bass producer after 2 Live Crew, was the music's most crucial recording artist. An underground label impresario on the order of Master P, Mike's productions were much rougher than the slick Miami bass sound and pursued a gritty old school vibe—more akin to Ultramagnetic MC's than Luther Campbell—long after most hip-hop producers had gone pop in the late '90s.

The former Michael Hampton began his mixing career before he was even a teenager, spinning at a roller rink and selling mix tapes. By the age of 14, he was hosting a drive-time radio show in his native Orlando. He began concentrating on club work after finishing high school, and debuted on wax with 1987's "Boot the Booty" for Vision Records.

One year later, local promoter Tom Reich offered DJ Magic Mike a chance at a half-share in his own Cheetah Records if Mike's releases sold well. His first singles under the agreement, "Magic Mike Cutz the Record" and "Drop the Bass," both became big regional hits, sparking the release of his debut

album, *DJ Magic Mike and the Royal Posse* in 1989. He took more of a guiding hand over his own instrumental productions for the follow-up, 1990's *Bass Is the Name of the Game*, and the album went gold despite its low vocal content. Mike's breakthrough LP, *Ain't No Doubt About It*, appeared in 1992, followed by the release of two LPs on the same day; both *Bass: The Final Frontier* and *This Is How It Should Be Done* charted, and the former went gold. Although his recording schedule continued apace during the mid-'90s (and the number of his full-length releases climbed into the double digits), fewer of his LPs charted. Mike picked up the commercial slack with advertising appearances for Coca-Cola and Pioneer, and has also worked with Sir Mix-A-Lot, 2 Live Crew, MC Shy D, and Poison Clan. The new millennium saw Mike issue *Magic's Kingdom* and continue his output of mix albums. —*John Bush*

Bass Is the Name of the Game / 1990 / Cheetah ◆◆◆◆

Magic Mike's first major LP included at least a half-dozen bass classics like "Drop the Bass," "House of Magic," "Feel the Beat," and "Yo." Proof positive of its classic status came in 1998 when it was digitally remastered and reissued by Cheetah. —*John Bush*

● **Cheetah's Bassest Hit** / 1993 / Cheetah ◆◆◆◆◆

All of DJ Magic Mike's classic early productions (except for "Magic Mike Cutz the Record") appear on this 1993 Cheetah collection, including the furious scratching and Beastie Boys-sampling of "Drop the Bass," the rolling, laid-back "Def and Direct," a rough-and-smooth East Coast cut called "Class Is in Session," and the sexed-up "Are You Ready." Mike's scratches, drum programming, and sample work are all excellent, though a bit restrained by the frequent raps. There is a bit of overlap with *Foundations of Bass*, but this is the more crucial collection. —*John Bush*

This Is How It Should Be Done / Nov. 2, 1993 / Magic ◆◆◆◆

In the late 1980s and early to mid-1990s, DJ Magic Mike enjoyed what you could call "quiet success"—he had his share of million sellers and was hardly obscure, but he didn't receive nearly as much hype and publicity as Luther Campbell. Although *This Is How It Should Be Done* wasn't hyped to death by the media, it was a major hit among bass lovers. The most important element of this CD isn't the rapping—in fact, many of the tunes don't contain any rapping at all—it's Mike's talents as a producer/mixmaster. "Magic's Cuttin' Up!," "Keep It Goin' Now," "Magic's Funky Jeep Beats," and other exhilarating tunes on this album are essentially vehicles for his cutting, mixing, and producing. On *This Is How It Should Be Done*, the most valuable tools in Mike's arsenal aren't his rappers—samples, soundbites, beats, and turntables are the things that do the most to make this album come alive. —*Alex Henderson*

Represent / May 10, 1994 / Magic ◆◆◆

Uniting DJ Magic Mike with the Royal Posse, *Represent* differs from some of Mike's other albums in that it emphasizes rapping, flowing, and lyrics. The CD isn't devoid of instrumentals, and it isn't without abundant proof of Mike's impressive skills as a mixmaster/producer. But this time, rapping isn't just an afterthought and doesn't take a back seat to cutting, mixing, scratching, and producing—from the fast, hyper, danceable booty rhyming of "Move Them Butts" to slower, more serious tunes like "Down Through the Years," "(O.K. Nigga) Here We Go" and the title song, rapping is *Represent's* main thrust. Some of the Royal Posse members that Mike prominently features include Infinite J., Daddy Rae, and K. Dog, all of whom contributed to the lyric writing. Bass enthusiasts will definitely want *Represent*, which is among Mike's most memorable releases. —*Alex Henderson*

Bass Bowl / Oct. 25, 1994 / Magic ◆◆◆

Although DJ Magic Mike's CDs were placed in the rap bins, the main reason to acquire *Bass Bowl* isn't the rapping—it is Mike's skills that as a mixmaster/producer that take center stage on this good-to-excellent CD. "Get On It Dog Gone it" and "Mo Booty" are infectious examples of fast, hyper, Southern-style booty rap, but many of the tunes contain no rapping at all—rather, they consist of instrumental tracks combined with various samples, soundbites, cuts, or scratches. Mike is fairly unpredictable, and he keeps things interesting by sampling and mixing a variety of soul, hip-hop, and funk, as well as reggae and jazz. You can see the parallels between Orlando, FL, resident Mike and the bass DJs of Miami, and his eclectic approach also inspires comparisons to Northeastern mixmasters like Grandmaster Flash and Public Enemy's Terminator X. But make no mistake, *Bass Bowl* is the work of an innovator whose style is very much his own. —*Alex Henderson*

Foundations of Bass, Vol. 1 / Apr. 29, 1997 / Cheetah ✦✦✦✦✦
A balanced collection from DJ Magic Mike's entire career pre-1996, *Foundations of Bass* borrows half of its tracks from Mike's first two LPs, focusing more on bass music and light, rolling jams than the hip-hop slant of the other major Mike collection. As usual, Mike doesn't range very far for his samples, but he usually finds something special to say with each of them, often over only a skeletal beat plus rims and a hi-hat. Lowrider experiments like "Feel the Bass" and "For the Easy Listeners" gradually give way to an example of classic rap-and-scratch hip-hop ("Abracadabra"), with room for an energizing live version of Mike's classic "Drop the Bass" "showing what Orlando's all about." Meanwhile he shows why he deserves the "DJ" and the "Magic" in his title with "This DJ Cuts Different Ways" and "M&M Getting Off," both putting to shame most of the overly intellectual turntablists out there. —*John Bush*

More Bootyz in Motion / Jan. 11, 2000 / K-Tel ✦✦✦✦
Because this collection was mixed, compiled, and edited by DJ Magic Mike, some might think it contains nothing but Florida-style bass music. But while bass dominates *More Bootyz in Motion*, not everything on the CD is bass music per se. Released in 2000, this compilation spans 1983-1998 and focuses on 1980s electro-hop as well as Florida-style bass. Of course, the two styles are similar—both are fast and hyper and both are aimed at the dancefloor. So not surprisingly, Mike has no problem making everything flow. 1980s electro-hop hits like Debbie Deb's "When I Hear Music" and Twilight 22's "Electric Kingdom" work as well as bass favorites such as the Quad City DJs' "C'mon 'N' Ride It (The Train)," Luke's "Raise the Roof," the Get Funky Crew's "Shake Them Titties," 12 Gauge's "Dunkie Butt '96," and 95 South's "Rodeo." One can easily guess who will and won't buy this collection—Southern bass enthusiasts are more likely to pick it up than Northeastern corridor hip-hoppers, who tend to dismiss bass and electro-beat as lowest-common-denominator music, seeing both styles as a bastardization of New York hip-hop. But bass' detractors can say what they will—this collection is a lot of fun, and there's no law stating that rapping has to be intellectual 100 percent of the time. Plus, when it comes to the art of mixing, few can compete with DJ Magic Mike. —*Alex Henderson*

Magic's Kingdom / Aug. 22, 2000 / Restless ✦✦✦
DJ Magic Mike breaks out of his mold as primarily a bass music producer with *Magic's Kingdom*, a daring album featuring a wide array of guest rappers and just as many different stylistic approaches. Taking on a Dr. Dre-like role as a craftsman directing a roster of artists, Mike manages to produce his most interesting album in years, as he explores everything from Southern-flavored rap to fairly straightforward R&B, in addition to a handful of instrumental tracks featuring his turntable skills. Yet just because it's an interesting album doesn't necessarily mean that it's a remarkable effort; granted, it's one of Mike's most realized and ambitious efforts, but it's just far too diverse, too indecisive, and too short on stellar talent to ever make a lasting impression. —*Jason Birchmeier*

DJ Melo-Mix

DJ / Dirty South, Hardcore Rap
Hailing from Indiana, DJ Melo-Mix stood as one of the few Midwestern rap DJs with mix CDs on the national market during the late '90s and early 2000s. During his stint of activity, he independently released an album every year or so, generally mixing the latest hits (usually hardcore and dirty South ones) with a handful of old school classics. He never broke out of the Midwest but maintained a strong presence in his home state, where he would often DJ at college parties and other high-profile local events. —*Jason Birchmeier*

The Best of DJ Melo-Mix, Pt. 1: Ride or Die / Mar. 9, 1999 / Melo-Mix ✦✦✦
The Best of DJ Melo-Mix, Pt. 1: Ride or Die isn't really a best-of album in the traditional sense but rather a particularly focused mix. Melo-Mix draws from all coasts—East (the Notorious B.I.G.), West (Too Short), and South (Master P)—as well as from all ages—old school (Run-D.M.C.), golden (EPMD), and contemporary (Eightball & MJG)—and he often mixes them together, a cappella over instrumentals. Furthermore, he tends to pitch his records down, not to the point of "screwing" them, but enough to alter the feel of them. He doesn't cut up the tracks much, instead generally cross-fading them into one another and letting them play out. This mixing style emphasizes the track selection and pitching, though unfortunately the track sequencing is confusing to

navigate. The overall effect is a relatively laid-back mix that's full of surprises, as old meets new school and East meets West Coast. —*Jason Birchmeier*

● **Best of DJ Melo-Mix, Pt. 2: The Blunt Burner** / Mar. 14, 2000 / Melo-Mix ✦✦✦✦
Like his first best-of, *Best of DJ Melo-Mix, Pt. 1: Ride or Die*, his second, *The Blunt Burner*, isn't really a best-of but rather a particularly considered mix. Melo-Mix again lays a cappella over instrumentals, often transitioning mid-track, and again pitches most tracks down, giving them a mellow feel. For instance, he mixes the vocal to Dr. Dre's "The Watcher" over the beat to Busta Rhymes' "Put Your Hands Where My Eyes Could See," then Q-Tip's "Vibrant Thing" over the Notorious B.I.G.'s "Hypnotize," and so on. Some of the transitions are a little more abrupt than you'd expect, but it's the creative combinations that stand out most here, as Melo-Mix shows love for all coasts, often simultaneously. As with the first volume, the confusing track sequencing is frustrating; however, because *The Blunt Burner* is an album that flows best from beginning to end, it's not that big of an issue, particularly when practically every track is a recognizable hit. —*Jason Birchmeier*

DJ Murdermixx

DJ / Dirty South, Hardcore Rap
Along with DJ Dirty Money, DJ Murdermixx represents the dirty South style of hip-hop spinning as a member of the Dirty Harry Productions camp. His *Phat Azz Mixes!!* album showcases his skills on the turntables along with some of the more prominent freestyle sessions he has participated in with various rappers including the Hot Boys. Somewhat similar to East Coast DJs such as Funkmaster Flex and Detroit DJs such as DJ Godfather, DJ Murdamixx sticks primarily to the hardcore/gangster/booty blend of hip-hop, incorporating tracks from mostly down South but also from some of the bigger East and West coast anthems. A sophomore effort, *Mixin' on Some Syzurp!!*, appeared in summer 2001. —*Jason Birchmeier*

Phat Azz Mixes!! / Aug. 29, 2000 / Dirty Harry ✦✦
Phat Azz Mixes!! features half a CD of DJ Murdermixx's style of spinning and half a CD of his freestyle sessions with various MCs. The first half of mixing features some shining moments such as the opening segment featuring Trick Daddy's "Shut Up." Besides other dirty South anthems such as this, Murdermixx does manage to integrate some East Coast records such as Raekwon's "Live From New York" and a bit of West Coast flavor with Tha Eastsidaz's "Got Beef." It's refreshing to hear him bring some of these other styles to his blend of Southern hip-hop records, which tend to be characterized by bass-heavy beats and sleazy attitude; unfortunately, his mixing is less than stellar relative to the better-known hip-hop DJs such as Funkmaster Flex and DJ Cash Money or ghettotech DJs such as DJ Godfather and DJ Assault. When the freestyle segment begins, the album goes even further downhill. Sure, there are some great moments such as when the Hot Boys step up and lay down some great rapping, but this part of the CD just doesn't flow well at all, disrupting the sense of continuity established by the opening mix. There are some good moments on this album, but overall Murdermixx isn't much better than a generic hip-hop DJ, making this a disappointing listen. —*Jason Birchmeier*

DJ Paul (Paul Beauregard)

b. Memphis, TN
Producer, Vocals, Keyboards, Engineer / Hardcore Rap, Southern Rap
Together with production partner Juicy J, DJ Paul played an important role in the South's rise to prominence within the once East and West Coast-dominated rap industry. Behind the duo's leadership, Three 6 Mafia rose from an underground phenomenon in Memphis to a nationally recognized rap empire, spinning off numerous solo albums for the collective's many members in the mid- to late '90s. Like his production partner, DJ Paul specialized in dark, eerie tracks driven by bass-heavy beats and haunting sounds. He also raps as a member of Three 6 Mafia and contributes rhymes to most of the albums he produces for such artists as Project Pat, Gangsta Boo, La Chat, and Tear da Club Up Thugs. Moreover, DJ Paul ventured into filmmaking with *Choices* (2001), a straight-to-video film starring most of the Three 6 Mafia collective.

Juicy J (born Jordan Houston) and DJ Paul (Paul Beauregard) first came together at the dawn of the '90s, when they worked as DJs in the Memphis area. The two soon began producing their own tracks and invited numerous

Memphis rappers to rap over the beats. They released the resulting tracks locally as Triple 6 Mafia; years later these recordings would resurface as re-releases. In 1995, the loose collective changed its name to Three 6 Mafia and self-released its debut album, *Mystic Stylez*. The album became an underground success, and Three 6 Mafia, in turn, signed a distribution deal with Relativity for its Hypnotized Minds imprint. Throughout the late '90s, Juicy J and DJ Paul produced numerous albums a year for Hypnotized Minds and capitalized on the lucrative distribution deal. By the end of the decade, the two producers were at the helm of an empire, having extended their brand to alarming lengths, culminating with their commercial breakthrough album, *When the Smoke Clears* (2000), which debuted at number six on *Billboard*'s album chart. —*Jason Birchmeier*

Underground 16: For da Summa / May 21, 2002 / D.evil ♦♦♦
During a rare lull in the Three 6 Mafia camp's usually relentless release schedule, the Memphis collective re-released some of their underground recordings from the early '90s, including DJ Paul's *Underground 16: For da Summa*. Originally released locally in 1994, a few years before Three 6 went national, *For da Summa* isn't nearly as polished or commercial as their later output, sounding precisely as it's billed: underground. Paul didn't simply repackage the original tape from 1994, though. Since Paul had produced *For da Summa* as well as rapped on it, he returned to the studio and made some edits before re-releasing it in 2002. Most notably, he's given the production a new gloss and replaced some of the original vocals. On the re-release, Paul raps on most of the songs, though he spotlights fellow Three 6 members Lord Infamous, Crunchy Black, La' Chat, and Frayser Boy at times. Some of the highlights include the album opener, "Back da Fuck Back," where Paul samples the famous piano line from 2Pac's *All Eyez on Me* album opener, "Ambitionz az a Ridah." Another highlight is "Cyoazzndalot," which features a rap by Project Pat, who happened to be incarcerated at the time of *For da Summa*'s re-release, and also two versions of long-time Three 6 anthems: "Break da Law," which features newcomer Frayser Boy here, and "Where Is da Bud, Pt. II," which features Lord Infamous on his own. *For da Summa* overall isn't on a par with Three 6's best work, but fans of the camp's early underground recordings should especially savor this, as it's about as buck as Three 6 has ever been. Plus, if you particularly like Paul, you'll love *For da Summa*, as Juicy J is nowhere to be found here, either as a producer or rapper. Lastly, Three 6 enthusiasts should find *For da Summa* quite curious, as it sheds light on the camp's much-storied yet seldom-heard underground years in Memphis. —*Jason Birchmeier*

DJ Pooh (Mark Jordan)

Producer, DJ / Hip-Hop, Gangsta Rap, Hardcore Rap
DJ Pooh (born Mark Jordan) began his musical career in the mid-'80s, when he produced LL Cool J's *Bigger and Deffer*. For the next 10 years, he continued to produce other hip-hop artists, and he also made cameos in films and videos, where he usually accompanied Ice Cube. In 1992 Pooh founded Da Bomb label. Three years later, he became an in-demand producer following his work on tha Dogg Pound's *Dogg Food* and 2Pac's double album *All Eyez on Me*. In 1997 he launched a solo career with *Bad Newz Travels Fast*, which was released on Atlantic Records. —*Stephen Thomas Erlewine*

Bad Newz Travels Fast / Jul. 15, 1997 / Atlantic ♦♦♦
DJ Pooh had been working as a producer for almost ten years before releasing his debut album, *Bad Newz Travels Fast*. That time certainly helped him hone his skills as a producer and a musician, yet that doesn't necessarily make him a rapper. Although the sound of the record is superb, there are only a handful of fully realized songs on the albums. Pooh's production means the record is listenable, but the lack of consistent material means there's little reason to play anything but the singles on this overly long album. —*Leo Stanley*

DJ Premier (Chris Martin)

Producer, DJ, Mixing / East Coast Rap, Jazz-Rap, Hip-Hop
No more than three producers (Dr. Dre, RZA, and Prince Paul) can test DJ Premier's status as the most important trackmaster of the '90s, and no style is more distinctive. Aggressive and raw, a Premier track was an instantly recognizable sound clash of battling loops and heavy scratching—all of them perfectly timed—that evoked the sound of Brooklyn better than anyone. Besides helming tracks for his main concern, Gang Starr, since their 1989 debut, Premier's productions appeared on many of the East Coast's most

important records: Nas' *Illmatic*, the Notorious B.I.G.'s *Ready to Die* Jay-Z's *Reasonable Doubt*, Jeru the Damaja's *The Sun Rises in the East*, and Mos Def's *Black on Both Sides*.

Premier, born Chris Martin, spent time in Brooklyn and Houston while growing up, and studied computer science at Prairie View A&M outside Houston. Known as Waxmaster C, he'd already learned to play a variety of instruments and also managed a record store. After moving back to Brooklyn, around 1987-1988 he came into contact with Guru, a Boston native. Guru had already formed a group named Gang Starr two years earlier (and recorded with the 45 King), but his former partner, Mike Dee, had returned to Boston. DJ Premier and Guru signed to Wild Pitch and released a debut single ("Manifest") and album (*No More Mr. Nice Guy*). Gang Starr's interest in melding hip-hop with jazz informed the record, and they were invited to add to the soundtrack for Spike Lee's 1990 film *Mo' Better Blues*. Their subsequent work was much more mature and unified, with a pair of instant East Coast classics (1991's *Step in the Arena* and 1992's *Daily Operation*) arriving in short order. DJ Premier had been working with other vocalists for years, and his productions for the 1990 landmark *Funky Technician* by Lord Finesse and DJ Mike Smooth cemented his status as one of the best producers around. He soon began recording exclusively at D&D Studios, a spot soon to become a shrine for hip-hop fans (thanks in large part to his own work).

The year 1994 was a huge one for Premier, probably the best year for any rap producer ever; in addition to dropping another Gang Starr classic, *Hard to Earn*, his productions appeared on five-star, all-time classics by Nas (*Illmatic*), the Notorious B.I.G. (*Ready to Die*), and Jeru the Damaja (*The Sun Rises in the East*), as well as Big Daddy Kane and Branford Marsalis' Buckshot LeFonque project. Though his workload dropped off considerably during the late '90s, he still managed to place tracks on three of the first four Jay-Z albums, and returned in force with the new millennium, including shots with Common, D.I.T.C., D'Angelo, Jadakiss, and Snoop Dogg. —*John Bush*

• **New York Reality Check 101** / Jan. 5, 1998 / Payday ♦♦♦♦
New York Reality Check 101 mixed by DJ Premier is a solid example of '90s underground hip-hop of New York; if DJ Premier is behind something it must be good. The album is a compilation of 14 singles that DJ Premier adeptly cuts back and fourth accompanied with an ongoing narration by Primo himself. Songs to check for include but are not limited to ED O.G.'s "Off Balance," Company Flow's "8 Steps to Perfection," and the resonating piano-laced Shades of Brooklyn's "Change." The only two cuts to really avoid are Brainsick Mob's "Mixmaster" and Finsta Bundy's "Feel the High Pt. 2," not because they are terrible, but rather because they just lack the soul and creativity the other 12 songs are steeped with. In other words, the aforementioned cuts seem weak because the rest of the album is so solid. DJ Premier is associated with another project that proliferates quality hip-hop; just consider it a bonus that he helps expose good music otherwise not readily available in mainstream markets. —*Nick Pfeiffer*

DJ Q-Bert (Richard Quitevis)

b. 1969
DJ, Producer / Hip-Hop, Turntablism
DJ Q-Bert (born Richard Quitevis) first emerged in the underground turntablist scene as a member of San Francisco's Invisibl Skratch Piklz (with D-Styles, Yogafrog, MixMaster Mike, and Shortkut). Along with other Bay Area groups like the X-Men and the world-famous Beat Junkies, the Piklz were determined to reestablish the DJ's place in rap music. Looking backward into rap's past and forward into its future, Q-Bert and the Skratch Piklz championed a move away from the empty showmanship DJing that had become toward the essential elements of technique and musicianship. Q-Bert in particular embarked on a mission outside the rap community, to dispel misconceptions about the DJ's art through teaching and preaching the gospel of the turntable. Q-Bert's DJ skills were recognized as early as 1985. In 1994 he released his mix tape *Demolition Pumpkin Squeeze Musik*, a 60-minute nonstop scratch and breakbeat extravaganza which increased his profile (the tape made *The Wire* magazine's essential Turntablism Primer list in January 1999). Wider recognition came with the birth of the Invisibl Skratch Piklz in 1995. The all-DJ group quickly established itself as an unstoppable live force at underground shows and DJ competitions. They reigned supreme at the Disco Mixing Club (DMC) World Championship, taking its title three years in a

row. They were so dominant at the event that they were asked to abstain from future competitions. Q-Bert then took a spot on the judge's panel. The Invisibl Skratch Piklz toured the globe throughout the latter part of the 1990s. Various members took their craft outside of the live arena and into middle schools, high schools, and universities (and onto the Turntable TV videos) where they gave seminars and tutorials on DJ history and technique.

In 1996 Q-Bert leant his deft scratchwork to Dr. Octagon's classic *Dr. Octagonecologyst* album. As a Skratch Pikl, he contributed to *The Invisibl Skratch Piklz Vs. The Klamz Uv Deth* (an enhanced CD released in 1997), Bomb Hip Hop's *Return of the DJ, Vol. 1* (the menacing Invasion of the Octopus People), numerous breakbeat compilations (Dirtstyle), and the *Shiggar Fraggar Show* series. Q-Bert's conventional solo debut came in 1998 with the (first?) turntable concept album *Wave Twisters*.

Q-Bert has become a sort of ambassador for the turntable. He has gained great respect both for his spectacular skills (including numerous scratch inventions) and for his work to help the turntable community. Along with Mix Master Mike, he was inducted into the DMC DJ Hall of Fame in 1998. As a group, the Invisibl Skratch Piklz made *A. Magazine*'s 100 Most Influential Asian Americans list in 1999. That same year, the group called it quits in an amicable breakup. Q-Bert kept busy, lecturing at Scratchcon 2000 and launching *Wave Twisters* the movie (an animated feature film based on the album). —*Nathan Bush*

● **Wave Twisters, Episode 7 Million: Sonic Wars Within the Protons** / Nov. 2, 1998 / Galactic Butt Hair ✦✦✦✦✦
Dubbed the first "scratch concept album," *Wave Twisters* is the first full-length from the man considered to be the world's greatest turntablist—DJ Q-Bert. As a member of the Northern California DJ collective Invisibl Skratch Piklz, innovation has always been the norm for Q-Bert, aka Richard Quitevis. Continuing to break new ground, his debut gives further evidence that the most talented record spinners have evolved into complete musicians. Song by song, the record explains a tale of an entire civilization that communicates only through the sounds of scratching. Q-Bert's legendary hand graces 17 tracks, and fellow Piklz Mix Master Mike, Shortkut, and other guests come along for a wild ride where nothing is off limits. From standard breaks being sliced and diced to oblivion, to methodically cutting up a female orgasm at the album's metaphorical climax, it never gets boring. —*Craig Robert Smith*

Demolition Pumpkin Squeeze Music / 1994 / Preschool Breaks ✦✦✦✦✦
The format of choice for a hip-hop DJ wanting to establish a reputation has long been the mix tape. Production cost is minimal, and while distribution may be limited, it's sufficient for creating a local following. Many well-known rappers and DJs began their careers with this medium. While they may seem like relics these days, cassette tapes continued to thrive in the underground rap world long after the advent of the CD. Along with Invisibl Skratch Piklz performances and *The Shiggar Fraggar Show* releases, the *Demolition Pumpkin Squeeze Music* tape established Q-Bert's reputation on the wheels of steel. A continuous mix of cobwebbed breakbeats, highly inventive scratches, and an endless array of hilarious samples, it begins on page one of a fantastical Buck Rogers/Spiderman serial, followed by extended use of Rush's "Tom Sawyer." Before you can check to make sure you put the right tape in your deck, however, the mayhem begins. A chattering beat starts up, which Q-Bert repeats (looping manually on turntables) and rearranges. Just when you begin to settle in, he drops a sweet slice of funk and you can feel the party vibe. Only moments later, however, he's off again on another tangent. The results can be daunting at first. He never heads too far into any one direction before bringing out another rhythm, but of course, that's the idea, and after a while the tape's internal logic begins to make perfect sense. It's a valuable look into an often ignored and maligned subculture. Included are lessons on graffiti art, a seminar on the tonal possibilities of the turntable, and a veritable breakbeat primer. All of this is merely a byproduct of a highly entertaining, nonstop mix. —*Nathan Bush*

DJ Quik (David Blake)

b. Compton, CA
Producer, DJ, Vocals / West Coast Rap, Gangsta Rap
Like many of his West Coast gangsta peers in the early '90s, DJ Quik's career began wonderfully then slowly descended with each passing year. In 1991, when a 20-year-old Quik debuted on Profile Records, West Coast gangsta rap reigned and his label controlled the rap industry. These factors, coupled with

Quik's production abilities, resulted in a very successful debut album, *Quik Is the Name*. The album did well on the charts and won favor on the streets. Quik had become one of the rap industry's most promising talents. Like Dr. Dre, he embodied everything that characterized West Coast gangsta rap and he could both write, rap, and produce his own albums. By the late '90s though, when gangsta rap fell out of favor and Quik's albums began to sound increasingly predictable, many tagged the artist as a has-been, something that had happened to most early-'90s gangsta rappers. Rather than retire, Quik turned to production and reclaimed some of the glory he had experienced in the early '90s. He produced songs for such artists as Kurupt ("Can't Go Wrong"), Xzibit ("Sorry I'm Away So Much"), Eightball & MJG ("Buck Bounce"), and Truth Hurts ("Addictive"), with several songs being sizable hits.

While practically still a teenager, Quik began his rap career at the dawn of the '90s in Compton, CA, where he was born and raised alongside Dr. Dre, Ice Cube, Eazy-E, MC Eiht, Above the Law, and numerous other Los Angeles rap artists. Like many of these peers, he recorded for Profile Records. His debut, *Quik Is the Name* (1991), launched his career well, spawning two sizable hit singles: "Born and Raised in Compton" and "Tonight." The two songs charted Top 20 on *Billboard*'s R&B chart, the latter even charting pop. The hits drove his album into the Top Ten on the album chart and Quik suddenly rose to the top of the rap industry at a very young age.

Unfortunately, his success went downhill from there. Quik released several successive albums throughout the '90s, but none of them came close to matching the success of his debut. By the early 2000s, most of his initial fans had long abandoned him and his releases became increasingly rare. Many criticized him for being formulaic, while others for lightening his style. Arista finally dropped him following the lukewarm reception given to his *Balance & Options* album (2000).

Despite these struggles, Quik excelled as a producer. Songs like "Buck Bounce" (Eightball & MJG, 2001) and "Addictive" (Truth Hurts featuring Rakim, 2002) became huge hits and Quik reclaimed some of the success that had long evaded him in the late '90s. He readied a comeback album, *Under tha Influence*, and began working with a variety of collaborators, most notably Dr. Dre. Furthermore, he abandoned his long-time West Coast style for a more unique sound that was very much his own. —*Jason Birchmeier*

Quik Is the Name / 1991 / Profile ✦✦✦✦✦
The release of DJ Quik's debut album, *Quik Is the Name*, in 1991 begged the question: does rap really need yet another gangster rapper? Indeed, by that time, rap had become satured with numerous soundalike gangster rappers—most of whom weren't even a fraction as interesting as such pioneers of the style as Ice-T, N.W.A, and Schoolly D. Nonetheless, rapper/producer Quik turned out to be more noteworthy than most of the gangster rappers who debuted that year. Lyrically, the former gangmember (who grew up in the same L.A. ghetto as N.W.A, Compton) doesn't provide any major insights. His sex/malt liquor/gangbanging imagery was hardly groundbreaking in 1991. But his hooks, beats, and grooves (many of which owe a debt to '70s soul and funk) are likeable enough. —*Alex Henderson*

Way 2 Fonky / 1992 / Profile ✦✦✦✦✦
DJ Quik proved his mettle with "Jus Lyke Compton," a definitive bit of regional touting that proclaimed West Coast rap the style setter and all others followers. Whether or not you bought the line, you were hooked by the rap. Nothing else on the disc matched this single's intensity and wit, but it helped him earn a second straight gold LP. —*Ron Wynn*

Safe & Sound / Feb. 21, 1995 / Profile ✦✦✦

Rhythm-Al-Ism / Nov. 10, 1998 / Arista ✦✦✦
Considering its guest list—packed with enough star power (El DeBarge, Snoop Dogg, Nate Dogg, Peter Gunz, Hi-C, AMG, and 2 II None) to fill a "Wrestlemania" card—rhythmalism promises more than it actually delivers. Its most clever moments ("Medley For a 'V' [The Pu**y Medley]") address colloquialisms for genitalia and all the wonderful things it's good for. "Down, Down, Down," "I Useta Know Her," and "No Doubt" (rhymes with: "I got something for your mouth") are plain nasty. Just what rap needs: One more guy boasting about his majestic penis and how good he is at treating women like gutter trash. —*Chris Slawecki*

Balance & Options / May 16, 2000 / Arista ✦✦✦
Like 1998's *Rhythm-Al-Ism*, *Balance & Options* is yet another star-filled joint for DJ Quik. Featuring appearances from AMD, Erick Sermon, Skaboobie,

James DeBarge, the long-lost Digital Underground, and Raphael, Quik comes correct with tracks like "U Ain't Fresh" and "Do Watcha Want." —*John Bush*

Under tha Influence / Jun. 4, 2002 / Ark 21 ✦✦✦✦

During DJ Quik's decade-long descent from superstar status to near obscurity, he lost much of his fan base mostly because he failed to change his style. Ever since he became an overnight sensation back in 1991 with *Quik Is the Name*, the producer/rapper continued to mine the G-funk style for all it was worth, interpolating Zapp, Cameo, and P-funk to no end. Thankfully, the end finally arrives with *Under tha Influence*, a welcomed comeback album for Quik. Rather than stick with the G-funk, he presents an array of beats that sound just as much dirty South as they do West Coast. Like Dr. Dre, a similar producer/rapper from Compton, Quik obviously found much inspiration in the early-2000s dirty South style of beatmaking—big, sparse, bass-heavy beats offset by subtle, rattling, high-end percussion—and replaces the "crunk" element with a slowed-down, smoked-out West Coast sense of groove. The formula worked well on the coast-to-coast hit song he produced for Eightball & MJG in 2001, "Buck Bounce," and it works well here, especially on songs like "Trouble," "Come 2Nyte," and "Ev'ryday," where he features vocalists on the hook—AMG, Truth Hurts, and James DeBarge, respectively. Granted, Quik still sounds a bit ordinary as a rapper, but his production work here is nothing short of amazing and amazingly varied. The result is his best work in years—perhaps even his most accomplished work to date. —*Jason Birchmeier*

● The Best of DJ Quik: Da Finale / Nov. 19, 2002 / Arista ✦✦✦✦

Supposedly, DJ Quik's last solo album, *The Best of DJ Quik: Da Finale*, is an awesome collection from an excellent rapper who is much better known for his production skills. Quik has worked with an incredible amount of superstars including Janet Jackson, 2Pac, Snoop Dogg, Talib Kweli, Whitney Houston, and Dr. Dre, but his rapping is a whole other universe. Coming straight outta Compton's mean streets in 1991, Quik had a style not so different than Eazy-E, though Quik is a more accomplished rapper with better vocal skills. Though Quik rapped about the 'hood and didn't shy away from telling it like it was, he generally concentrated more on party-oriented jams, rather than the gangsta raps which ruled the hip-hop scene in the early '90s. That's not to say that Quik didn't rap about gangs, but he didn't overglamorize that scene the way many others did. Quik released six albums and they are well represented in these 19 tracks. "Tonite," "Born and Raised in Compton," and "Loked Out Hood" are classic tunes from his debut album, *Quik Is the Name*, that feature some of the best hip-hop grooves from that period. Other songs like "Jus Lyke Compton" from *Way 2 Fonky* and "Pitch in ona Party" from *Balance & Options* couldn't be any catchier. The two new tracks, "Streetz Is Callin'" and "Quik's Groove VII" are not essential, but for folks who don't have many or any of Quik's solo albums, this collection is recommended. —*Adam Bregman*

DJ Rectangle

Producer, DJ / Turntablism, Underground Rap, Hip-Hop

DJ Rectangle is known as a battle DJ—he won the U.S. DMC championship in 1993—as well as a producer and prolific mix DJ. Since the mid-'90s, Rectangle has produced a seemingly endless series of schizophrenic battle records and party-friendly mix tapes. The Los Angeles-based DJ's mixes favor West Coast artists, often with exclusive tracks from well-known artists like Dr. Dre and Warren G, who has employed Rectangle as his live DJ since 2000. He has occasionally stepped into the role of producer, helming tracks for major-label acts like Funkdoobiest and Whoridas. —*Wade Kergan*

Ultimate Ultimate Battle Weapon, Vol. 1 / 1998 / Ground Control ✦✦

● Ill Rated / Oct. 26, 1999 / Down Low ✦✦✦

DJ Rectangle's second mix album for Down Low includes a couple of freestyles by Warren G and Twinz, plus an introduction by Ice Cube and hip-hop favorites from Ol' Dirty Bastard ("Shimmy Shimmy Ya"), Redman & Method Man ("How High"), Mobb Deep ("Eye for an Eye"), Grand Puba ("A Little of This"), Coolio ("Gangsta's Paradise"), Notorious B.I.G. ("One More Chance"), and many others. More of a party DJ than a true turntablist (that's a compliment, by the way), Rectangle keeps the mix going consistently throughout the album, working his way around the tracks and keeping just the right amount of improvisation to display his impressive skills. —*Keith Farley*

DJ Red Alert

DJ / Hip-Hop, Old School Rap

A popular radio personality and rap archivist, Red Alert is known for breaking the careers of many in hip-hop's elite, including Boogie Down Productions, Black Sheep, A Tribe Called Quest, and the Jungle Brothers. Red Alert began his career by working for Afrika Bambaataa and the Zulu Nation. After working his way through the ranks and becoming a top DJ, Red Alert's equipment was stolen, setting him back several months. The DJ's comeback in the early '80s coincided with the move of Bambaataa and his DJ crew to the downtown clubs in Manhattan. Left to his own devices in Harlem, Red Alert began gaining a large following at local clubs. When New York's KISS-FM approached Bambaataa to do a late-night rap show, he instead deferred the show to his DJs (of which Red Alert was the third chosen). He used the opportunity to his advantage, building a large following at the station and releasing "Hip-Hop Wax, Vol. 2," a series of scratch records by various DJs around New York.

Through his radio show Red Alert made several contributions to the hip-hop community, including breaking new acts as well as introducing various slang terms into the vernacular. Red Alert also became the head of a group of like-minded hip-hop artists known as the Native Tongues, which included De La Soul, the Jungle Brothers, and A Tribe Called Quest. The influential DJ has also executive produced albums by the latter two acts. —*Steve Kurutz*

● Beats, Rhymes & Battles, Vol. 1 / Aug. 7, 2001 / Relativity ✦✦✦✦

On *Beats, Rhymes & Battles, Vol. 1*, long-time New York icon DJ Red Alert compiles the most famous MC battles of the '80s and importantly narrates the album, revealing the stories behind the rhymes. He begins in 1984 with the Roxanne episode that began with U.T.F.O.'s "Roxanne, Roxanne" and was eventually followed by innumerable answer records, most notably Roxanne Shanté's "Roxanne's Revenge" and the Real Roxanne's "The Real Roxanne," which are both compiled here. He then moves on to the back-and-forth Queensbridge-South Bronx rivalry between Marley Marl's Juice Crew ("The Bridge," "Kill That Noise") and KRS-One's Boogie Down Productions ("South Bronx," "The Bridge Is Over"). Next comes LL Cool J's pair of late-'80s answer records ("Jack the Ripper," "To da Break of Dawn") in particular response to Kool Moe Dee, whom he surprised on stage mid-performance in Dallas in 1988, according to Red Alert. The two concluding battles (Doug E. Fresh and Slick Rick versus Salt-N-Pepa; Antoinette versus MC Lyte) aren't quite as spirited, though the stories are curious to hear. You've likely heard many of the tracks on *Beats, Rhymes & Battles, Vol. 1* before if you're a hip-hop enthusiast; however, Red Alert's stories are worthwhile by themselves, as he speaks communally with much flair and shares many little-known anecdotes. —*Jason Birchmeier*

DJ Revolution

b. Los Angeles, CA

DJ, Producer / Club/Dance, Alternative Rap, Turntablism

DJ Revolution is a Los Angeles native mostly known for his DJ residency with Sway & King Tech on their nationally syndicated hip-hop radio exhibition called *The Wakeup Show*. He had a hand in the production and scratching on Styles of Beyond's debut album, while releasing his own, entitled *R2K Version 1.0*, in 1999. A year later saw him release his next full-length effort, *In 12's We Trust*. —*Brad Mills*

● R2K Version 1.0 / Sep. 28, 1999 / Blackberry ✦✦✦✦

After hearing *The Wakeup Show*, one should clearly understand if they like hip-hop or not, because that's about as real as it gets. Over the years, the show has brought almost every legendary MC the world knows at one point or another through their studios. It is therefore comforting that DJ Revolution has not forgotten that method for success in the mixed-album market, again bringing some of the tastiest records in hip-hop to his turntables for a little cutting and mixing. A few of the standard people appear, including Planet Asia, Big L, Rasco, Kool Keith, and Eminem, but more notably there are some rappers that a lot of listeners may have yet to hear from that appear as well. Guys like Lootpack, Buc Fifty, Droop Capone, Insane Poetry, and Royce da 5'9" round it out nicely and bring a bit more credibility to what's going on in the underground of hip-hop. With so many DJs making mixed compilations, it can be hard to single out winners, but this album's quality is hard to overlook. —*Brad Mills*

In 12's We Trust / Aug. 22, 2000 / Ground Control ✦✦✦

World-renowned radio turntablist DJ Revolution is known for putting together solid mix tapes, but finally fans get to enjoy an album of his comprised of entirely original material. *In 12's We Trust* is the name of DJ Revolution's freshman attempt at producing a full album, and while it is obvious he is a competent DJ, his production skills have yet to reach his skills on the turntables. The album has mostly turntable-inspired tracks, but DJ Revolution includes a handful of songs featuring up-and-coming underground MCs. Hands down, the best cut on the album is "Evolution" featuring Evidence of the Dilated Peoples; the beats and the rhymes are on point. In the end, while the album does an excellent job of exposing turntablism as an art form to the masses, it only does an adequate job of elevating hip-hop production as a whole. —*Nick Pfeiffer*

DJ Screw (Robert Earl Davis)

d. Nov. 16, 2000, Houston, TX

DJ, Producer / Hip-Hop, Southern Rap, Gangsta Rap, Hardcore Rap, Dirty South, Underground Rap

After spending most of the 1990s as an infamous local phenomenon in Houston, TX, DJ Screw suddenly found himself gaining sudden notoriety before his unfortunate death in late 2000. The Houston DJ made a name for himself primarily because of his uncanny mixing style, which found him pitching *down* his records to a lumbering and quite eerie pace. Over the course of the '90s, what began as novelty actually became a rather lucrative venture for Screw, who produced hundreds of mix tapes, with some estimates projecting his total number of tapes topping over a thousand; furthermore, he sold the tapes at his Houston-based record store, Screwed Up Records and Tapes. Oddly enough, he preferred to release his mixes almost exclusively on cassette, though fans often recorded the mixes and traded them via the Internet; in addition, countless "screwed" remixes of popular rap anthems were widely available on Napster thanks to his cultish following.

Yet it's hard to imagine Screw's legacy being what it is if not for his role as an adamant advocate of "syrup sippin'," a Southern rap phenomenon involving codeine-infused cough syrup—the resulting intoxication induces a hallucinatory state where everything slows down and becomes the senses swirl. As marijuana was to early-'90s gangsta rap, LSD was to late-'60s psychedelic rock, ecstasy was to late-'80s rave—and so on—the syrup sippin' advocated by Screw's trippy hip-hop mixes led to a small drug movement within the late-'90s dirty South genre, reaching its zenith with Three 6 Mafia's hit "Sippin' on Some Syrup" in 2000. It's hard to deny that this phenomenon wasn't as important to Screw's popularity as his music was (especially considering some of his tape titles: Syrup & Soda, Syrup Sippers, Sippin' Codeine, etc.). Still, Screw did serve as a leader for Houston's burgeoning rap scene; his home studio, the Screw Shop, functioned as the home base for what was loosely referred to as the Screwed Up Click, including semisuccessful rappers such as Big Pokey and Lil' Keke, along with about 30 others were known locally.

Ironically, when Screw was found dead in his studio of a fatal heart attack at the tender age of 30 on the morning of November 16, 2000, *The Houston Chronicle* published a story stating that police suspected Screw of overdosing on the same syrup he so adamantly advocated. Weeks later the theory proved valid, making the artist the victim of his own self-promoted phenomenon. More unfortunate, though, was the loss of Screw to Houston's fledgling scene, which seemed on the verge of being nationally recognized as a Southern rap mecca. His legacy lived on, though, since his trademark mixing style was by no means exclusive, as countless imitators had arisen in the South by the time of his death, the most noteworthy being the Swisha House and Beltway 8 record labels. —*Jason Birchmeier*

3 'n the Mornin', Pt. 1 / Sep. 26, 1995 / Big Tyme ✦✦✦

One of the few DJ Screw mixes to ever get released on CD, the first entry in the two-volume *3 'n the Mornin'* series finds the infamous Houston syrupsippin' DJ screwing and chopping tracks by Dr. Dre ("Dre Day") and LL Cool J ("Rock tha Bells") along with Laid-Back's old school classic "White Horse." As usual, the tracks are slowed down to the point where you can barely recognize them, resulting in a highly disorienting listen. —*Jason Birchmeier*

3 'n the Mornin', Pt. 2 / Apr. 1996 / Big Tyme ✦✦✦

The second volume in this series concentrates almost exclusively on Texas rappers, as DJ Screw brings tracks by artists including Lil' Keke, Botany Boys,

and ESG to a near standstill. In addition, he throws in Mack 10's "Fo Life," a rather well-known track among the other underground tracks. The choice to concentrate on music from the artists comprising Houston's Screwed Up Click instantly differentiates this mix from the first volume, which was comprised of primarily well-known tracks; therefore, this volume is a bit more representative of Screw's traditional Southern style. —*Jason Birchmeier*

● **All Work, No Play** / Jan. 26, 1999 / Jam Down ✦✦✦✦

Like DJ Screw's *3 'n the Mornin'* series of CDs from the mid-'90s, which illustrates his unique method of slowing down his records to a hallucinatory blur, *All Work, No Play* operates similarly. The mix focuses on Screw's Houston camp of rappers (the Screwed Up Click), including tracks by Mobb Figgas, Hardheadz, and Lil' Keke, who proves to be the album's obvious superstar. Overall, a better album than the two *3 'n the Mornin'* albums in terms of mixing, though the fact that *3 'n the Mornin', Vol. 1* featured major hits by nationally recognized artists may appeal to some listeners more, depending on how much you enjoy Southern rap. —*Jason Birchmeier*

DJ Shadow (Josh Davis)

b. 1973, Hayward, CA

Producer, DJ / Hip-Hop, Trip-Hop, Ambient Breakbeat, Turntablism, Electronica

DJ Shadow's Josh Davis is widely credited as a key figure in developing the experimental instrumental hip-hop style associated with the London-based Mo'Wax label. His early singles for the label, including "In/Flux" and "Lost and Found (S.F.L.)," were all-over-the-map mini-masterpieces combining elements of funk, rock, hip-hop, ambient, jazz, soul, and used-bin incidentalia. Although he'd already done a scattering of original and production work (during 1991-1992 for Hollywood Records) by the time Mo'Wax's James Lavelle contacted him about releasing "In/Flux" on the fledgling imprint, it wasn't until his association with Mo'Wax that his sound began to mature and cohere. Mo'Wax released a longer work in 1995—the 40-minute single in four movements, "What Does Your Soul Look Like," which topped the British indie charts—and Davis went on to cowrite, remix, and produce tracks for labelmates DJ Krush and Doctor Octagon plus the Mo' trip-hop supergroup U.N.K.L.E.

Josh Davis grew up in Hayward, CA, a predominantly lower-middle-class suburb of San Francisco. The odd White suburban hip-hop fan in the hard-rock-dominated early '80s, Davis gravitated toward the turntable/mixer setup of the hip-hop DJ over the guitars, bass, and drums of his peers. He worked his way through hip-hop's early years into the heyday of crews like Eric B. & Rakim, Ultramagnetic, and Public Enemy; groups which prominently featured DJs in their ranks. Davis had already been fiddling around with making beats and breaks on a four-track while he was in high school, but it was his move to the NorCal cow town of Davis to attend university that led to the establishment of his own SoleSides label as an outlet for his original tracks. Hooking up with Davis' few b-boys (including eventual SoleSides artists Blackalicious and Lyrics Born) through the college radio station, Shadow began releasing the *Reconstructed From the Ground Up* mix tapes in 1991 and pressed his 17-minute hip-hop symphony "Entropy" in 1993. His tracks spread widely through the DJ-strong hip-hop underground, eventually catching the attention of Mo'Wax. Shadow's first full-length, *Endtroducing . . .*, was released in late 1996 to immense critical acclaim in Britain and America. *Preemptive Strike*, a compilation of early singles, followed in early 1998. Later that year, Shadow produced tracks for the debut album by U.N.K.L.E., a long-time Mo'Wax production team that gained superstar guests including Thom Yorke (of Radiohead), Richard Ashcroft (of the Verve), Mike D (of the Beastie Boys), and others. His next project came in 1999, with the transformation of SoleSides into a new label, Quannum Projects. Nearly six years after his debut production album, the proper follow-up, *The Private Press*, was released in June 2002. —*Sean Cooper*

Entropy [Single] / 1993 / SoleSides ✦✦✦

Shadow's first full-blown blast of heady, groove-heavy instrumental experiments, released on his own SoleSides label. One continuous track moving from upbeat deck-work and bin-shuddering beats through thick, downtempo head music. The flip is a forgettable vehicle for rapper and labelmate Asia Born (now Lyrics Born). —*Sean Cooper*

In/Flux [Single] / Oct. 1993 / Mo'Wax ✦✦✦✦✦

Somewhat sloppy, it almost doesn't matter given the scope and originality of the result. Moving from a kinetic, signature Shadow opening through uptempo funky breakbeats and stoney, textured, downbeat hip-hop, it's easy to see how influential "In/Flux" was on a generation of musicians looking for somewhere to take hip-hop. —*Sean Cooper*

Lost and Found (S.F.L.) [Single] / 1994 / Mo'Wax ◆◆◆
A split with DJ Krush, Shadow's side kipes the opening drum break from U2's "Sunday Bloody Sunday," cutting and layering it over chilling guitar and organ samples. The vocal break was lifted, according to Davis, from a late-'60s prison record. —*Sean Cooper*

What Does Your Soul Look Like? EP / Feb. 1995 / Mo'Wax ◆◆◆◆◆
"Soul"'s four parts are united in name only, with Shadow moving from solemn breakbeat-noir through alternately light, uptempo and slower, more questioning moods. Like past releases, his needlework is inspired, with textured, musical scratches that do more than simply accentuate. Shadow's best, most unified work. —*Sean Cooper*

★ **Endtroducing** . . . / Nov. 19, 1996 / Mo'Wax ◆◆◆◆◆
As a suburban Californian kid, DJ Shadow tended to treat hip-hop as a musical innovation, not as an explicit social protest, which goes a long way toward explaining why his debut album *Endtroducing* . . . sounded like nothing else at the time of its release. Using hip-hop, not only its rhythms but its cut-and-paste techniques, as a foundation, Shadow created a deep, endlessly intriguing world on *Endtroducing*, one where there are no musical genres, only shifting sonic textures and styles. Shadow created the entire album from samples, almost all pulled from obscure, forgotten vinyl, and the effect is that of a hazy, half-familiar dream—parts of the record sound familiar, yet it's clear that it only suggests music you've heard before, and that the multilayered samples and genres create something new. And that's one of the keys to the success of *Endtroducing*—it's innovative, but it builds on a solid historical foundation, giving it a rich, multifaceted sound. It's a major breakthrough not only for hip-hop and electronica but also for pop music. —*Stephen Thomas Erlewine*

Camel Bobsled Race (Q-Bert Mega Mix) EP / 1998 / Mo'Wax ◆◆◆
Camel Bobsled Race, Q-Bert's megamix of DJ Shadow music, isn't quite the masterpiece it could have been, but it's hardly a disaster. Recorded live, with both DJs scratching, the mix essentially reconfigures the bulk of *Endtroducing*, adding a couple of singles to the mix. There are layers of new samples and scratches, taken from everything from spoken-word records to jazz. The end result is intriguing and often entertaining, even if it doesn't offer any new revelations. *Camel Bobsled Race* was released as a bonus disc on the U.S.-only singles and B-sides compilation *Preemptive Strike*. —*Stephen Thomas Erlewine*

Preemptive Strike / Jan. 13, 1998 / Mo'Wax ◆◆◆◆
DJ Shadow assembled the singles collection *Preemptive Strike* as a way for American audiences to catch up on his career prior to his debut album, *Endtroducing*. The 11-track album contains three new interludes and three complete singles that he released on Mo'Wax—"In/Flux," "What Does Your Soul Look Like," and "High Noon"—and a bonus disc, "Camel Bobsled Race," which is a megamix of DJ Shadow material by DJ Q-Bert. Given that *Endtroducing* was a masterpiece of subtly shifting texture, *Preemptive Strike* almost seems purposely incoherent, even though the tracks are sequenced chronologically. The jerky flow can make the album a little difficult to assimilate on first listen, but it soon begins to make sense, even if it never achieves the graceful flow of the album. Several of the selections on *Preemptive Strike* were available in different forms on *Endtroducing*—parts four and one of "What Does Your Soul Look Like" are in their original forms here, presented along with one and three, and there's the "extended overhaul" of "Organ Donor." All of these are significantly different from the LP versions, and "What Does Your Soul Look Like" is necessary in its original, half-hour, four-part incarnation. But the key moments are the seminal "In/Flux," which arguably created trip-hop, and "High Noon," the dynamic, fuzz-drenched single that was his first single release since *Endtroducing*. Those three A sides are reason enough for any serious fan of the debut to pick up *Preemptive Strike*, but the B sides and "Camel Bobsled Race" are equally intriguing, making the package a nice summation of DJ Shadow's most important singles through the end of 1997. —*Stephen Thomas Erlewine*

The Private Press / Jun. 4, 2002 / MCA ◆◆◆◆◆
More than five years on from his breakout *Endtroducing* . . . , hip-hop's reigning recluse showed he still had plenty of tricks up his sleeve—as well as many more rare grooves left for sampling. Shadow had kept a low recording profile during past years, putting out only a few mix sets alongside a pair of collaborations (*Psyence Fiction* by U.N.K.L.E. and *Quannum Spectrum*). That lack of product actually *helps The Private Press* display just how good a producer he is; the depth of his production sense and the breadth of his stylistic palette prove just as astonishing the second time out. His style is definitely still recognizable, right from the start; "Fixed Income" and "Giving Up the Ghost" carefully layer wistful-sounding string arrangements overtop cavernous David Axelrod breaks (the latter a bit reminiscent of "Midnight in a Perfect World" from *Endtroducing* . . .). From there, though, DJ Shadow seldom treads the same path twice, switching from strutting disco breaks ("Walkie Talkie") to melancholy '60s pop that sounds like the second coming of Procol Harum ("Six Days"). "Right Thing/GDMFSOB" is pure breakers revenge, boasting accelerating, echoey electro breakbeats and enough confidence to recycle Leonard Nimoy's "pure energy" sample and make it work. Later, Shadow turns to pure aggro for the hilarious road-rage comedy of "Mashin' on the Motorway" (with Lateef the Truth Speaker behind the wheel), then summons the conceptual calm of a David Axelrod classic on the very next track with solo piano and a vocal repeating Bible text. Fans may have grown impatient waiting almost six years for the second DJ Shadow LP, but a classic like *The Private Press* could last at least that long, and maybe longer. (Initially, most copies of *The Private Press* on sale in America included a track available for download as a bonus.) —*John Bush*

DJ Skribble (Scott Ialacci)

DJ, Producer / Club/Dance, Hip-Hop
DJ Skribble formed Young Black Teenagers in the early '90s with rappers Kamron, ATA, Firstborn, and Tommy Never. After the release of two YBT albums, the group broke up, but Skribble kept going. In 1996 he added theater to his resumé when he worked with Bill Irwin for the musical *Hip Hop Wonderland*. He also worked on the debut album by the Fugees' Wyclef Jean, then released his own debut mix set, *Traffic Jams, Vol. 1*, in November 1997. *MDMA, Vol. 1* followed a year later, trailed in 1999 by a second volume of *Traffic Jams*. In September of 2000, Skribble was added to the roster of Essential Mix DJs with the release of *Essential Dance 2000*. Making appearances on networks like MTV (*The Grind, Yo! MTV Raps, Global Groove*) and being involved with New York radio station WKTU, Skribble (or "Skribs") is also involved with Cindy Margolis, cohosting her self-titled beach-party theme show. Skribble turned to an even more commercial dance/mix sound with the release of *Essential Spring Break* in mid-2001, and invited listeners into his own pad for 2001's *Skribble's House*. —*John Bush*

MDMA, Vol. 1 / Jun. 23, 1998 / Warlock ◆◆◆◆
MDMA stands for "Music 4 Dance, Music 4 Attitude" and that credo perfectly sums up this continuous mix album by DJ Skribble and Anthony Acid. The two DJs/mixers link together 16 tracks, ranging from original pieces to songs by Marina, Ell is D, J. Cee, Kenlou 6, the Jungle Brothers, Razor & Go, Fire Island, and Junior Vasquez. It's a continually inventive, entertaining house record that offers ample proof of Skribble's skills. —*Stephen Thomas Erlewine*

MDMA, Vol. 2 / Jul. 20, 1999 / Warlock ◆◆
DJ Skribble and Anthony Acid returned in 1999 for the second volume in the *MDMA* series of mix albums. There isn't anything particularly novel about this volume. In fact, it's probably the most lackluster and faceless mix in the series. Few of these tracks ever became more than novelties, with the exception of a Pete Rauhofer production ("Aura Tribe"), and even that sounds of its time. This was Skribble's last entry into the series before he left for bigger and better things as a commercial-as-commercial-gets DJ in the early 2000s. Acid returns for the next volume by himself, moving the series more toward a trance sound. —*Jason Birchmeier*

Traffic Jams 2000 / Oct. 19, 1999 / Warlock ◆◆◆
It's not the most hands-on DJ record ever released, but *Traffic Jams 2000*— produced by DJ Skribble with his partner DJ Slynke—balances a few tracks of turntable acrobatics ("Skribtro & Slynktro," "We Represent Queens," "You Know Our Names") with recent hip-hop hits from Sporty Thievz ("Can't F*** Wit' Me"), Trick Daddy ("Walking Like A"), the Beatnuts ("Party"), Kurupt ("Don't You . . ."), and Common ("No Competition"). Skribble and Slynke mess with the mix on a few tracks, including a hilarious backdrop to Juvenile's "187" consisting of razor-edge symphonic strings. For the most

part, though, *Traffic Jams 2000* just keeps on rolling with the hits, no small feat at that. *—John Bush*

Essential Dance 2000 / Sep. 12, 2000 / Atlantic ✦✦✦
This is a nicely assembled party set, to say the least, with some interesting choices: remixes of Bob Marley, Cher, and Paula Cole are worked in with Filter, Moby, and Vengaboys. DJ Skribble's mixing is precise, matching tone as well as bpm, something that adds to the experience of an album like this. For what it is, it's good. *—Steven McDonald*

Essential Spring Break / Apr. 10, 2001 / Sire ✦✦✦
Essential Spring Break isn't quite as overtly commercial as DJ Skribble's preceding *Essential Dance 2000* mix. Where the MTV-sponsored DJ sought to incorporate as many dance "hits" as possible on that mix—"Kernkraft 400," "9PM (Till I Come)," "Sexual (Li Da Di)," "Sun Is Shining," and so on—he instead tries to incorporate a selection of tracks on *Essential Spring Break* that may not necessarily be well known stateside but at least allow him to work toward a consistent mood. Of course, this may limit the album's crossover possibilities, but it's a welcome change for anyone who appreciates a well-crafted DJ mix. By concentrating on tracks that segue well into one another, Skribble ends up piecing together a respectable mix album that moves from the sort of lighthearted garage/house tracks popular in the U.K. circa 2001 ("Salsoul Nugget [If U Wanna]," for example) to more trance-rooted tracks during the latter half of his 17-track mix ("Sandstorm"). Despite this album's promising start, the mass-appealing tendencies of Skribble again detract from his ability to offer a well-mixed album; the last few tracks may be anthems—particularly the ubiquitous DJ Tiesto remix of Delirium's "Silence"—but they can't help feeling undeniably superfluous. Granted, seasoned electronic dance music listeners probably won't even give this album a chance given its commercial tendencies. Still, those who consider themselves fans of the *Ministry of Sound* or *Gatecrasher* mix albums will find this mix remarkably similar in approach and almost on par, and those who consider themselves no more than casual fans of dance music may find this album more accessible than most DJ mix albums. *—Jason Birchmeier*

Skribble's House / Dec. 11, 2001 / Sire ✦✦
It's a sure bet the party never ends at DJ Skribble's house, though his third set for the *Essential* series runs into a rut of driving, nondescript dance music with few lows and, surprisingly, few highs to balance it out. After beginning with a club remix of the club crossover of the year (Missy Elliott's "Get Ur Freak On"), Skribble ventures into dubbed-out trance with Danny Tenaglia's smoothed-out mix of "I Feel Loved" by Depeche Mode and a dreadful Underworld pastiche, "Brand New Day" by Mike Macaluso. Midway through the mix, he finally picks up the tempo with tracks from Trisco ("Musak"), Max Linen ("The Soulshaker"), and his own "My Man" (featuring Alexis), but the energy doesn't last long. *—John Bush*

DJ Smurf

Producer, DJ / Dirty Rap, Party Rap, Bass Music, Club/Dance
Old school DJ and producer DJ Smurf came out of Atlanta's massive bass music scene, releasing his first major album, *Versastyles*, for Wrap Records in 1995. Two years later, *Collipark Music* appeared on the Benz label, with appearances by MC Shy D and tha Rhythum. *Dead Crunk* followed in 1998, with *NonStop Booty Shake* appearing a year later. *—John Bush*

Versastyles / Feb. 7, 1995 / Wrap ✦✦
NonStop Booty Shake / Nov. 16, 1999 / Fortune Entertainment ✦✦✦
Bass superproducer DJ Smurf returned with *NonStop Booty Shake*, as usual a family affair with long-time friends MC Shy D and DJ Kizzy Rock plus his sister tha Rhythum. Smurf's far from sly on cuts like "Cum on Me," "It's Dat Ass You Shakin'," and "Make That Ass Clap," but his productions are as solid and groove laden as ever. *—Keith Farley*

DJ Spinna

Producer, DJ, Programming, Engineer, Remixing / Hip-Hop, Turntablism, Underground Rap, East Coast Rap
DJ Spinna's accomplishments surpass those of most DJs, yet he remained strictly an underground artist despite his astonishing talent. Though primarily known for his hip-hop work, Spinna also expanded his reach to include downtempo house music as well. The New York DJ remixed tracks for many artists such as Soulstice and Nightmares on Wax. He also produced a number

of artists such as rappers Guru and J-Live and his own rap group, Jigmastas. Along with his partner, MC Kriminul, the duo debuted as Jigmastas in 1996 with the single "Beyond Real," which they released on their own independently operated label of the same name. Besides his Jigmastas albums and his occasional productions, Spinna mixed several albums for various labels. For instance, *Raiding the Crates* (2002) compiles tracks from the Chicago deep house label Guidance, and *The Beyond Real Experience, Vol. 2* (2002) compiles tracks from his own label. In addition, Spinna mixed an album for BBE, *Strange Games and Things* (2001), that creatively compiles an eccentric blend of old school tracks such as Eddie Kendricks' "Girl You Need a Change of Mind," Rick James' "Mary Jane," and Donald Byrd's "Wind Parade." *—Jason Birchmeier*

● **Heavy Beats, Vol. 1** / Jun. 14, 1999 / Rawkus ✦✦✦✦✦
As hip-hop prepares itself for the dawn of a new era, a modernistic class of distinguished beat constructors are anxious to apply their signature on the Y2K sound. One producer who will surely help define the millennial sound is DJ Spinna, the newest gem unveiled from NY's underground hip-hop scene. Chock full of scintillating grooves, Spinna's debut is a treat old school purists will surely sink their teeth into. It's obvious Spinna spent many nights burning the midnight oil digging through dusty 12-inches, as he provides innovative production and ungodly breakbeats. But Spinna's debut is not all intergalactic warfare, as he recruited many familiar faces—Eminem and Thirstin Howell on "Who Dees," Talib Kweli and Apani B on "Time Zone"—to augment his mind-expanding creations. *—Matt Conaway*

Strange Games and Things / Mar. 27, 2001 / BBE ✦✦✦✦
English label BBE started the *Strange Games and Things* series, and it became their most popular sets. The mixed portions of this set were previously sold separately. This three-CD set compiles one mix CD with a generous two full CDs of the tracks in their original form. At the time of this release, no American company would ever think to offer something so substantial without tons of filler and the same tracks making an uncalled-for appearance. While the songs here are great, the star of the show is Brooklyn, NY, producer/remixer DJ Spinna. This set not only shows off his turntable prowess, but the Rain Man-like recall of the rare mostly '70s to '80s R&B/jazz songs that are mostly midtempo and sensual. The best remixing comes when the integrity of the original is not tampered with. It also helps to keep the changes daring while retaining the essence of what made a song special. These are lessons DJ Spinna has no trouble with on *Strange Games and Things*. What makes DJ Spinna stick out is his quirkiness and great ear. Dee Dee Sharp's "Easy Money" leads into Johnny Bristol's "If I Can't Stop You" so well it's humorous. What he does to Eddie Kendricks' "Girl You Need a Change of Mind" and Donald Byrd's "Wind Parade" is nothing short of amazing. *Strange Games and Things* is an all but perfect set featuring classic, hard-to-find tracks and DJ Spinna's deft and definitive skills. *—Jason Elias*

All Mixed Up / May 8, 2001 / Urban Theory ✦✦✦

Raiding the Crates / Feb. 12, 2002 / Shadow ✦✦✦
If you're a deep house aficionado, you're sure to love this generous continuous mix from Brooklyn-born DJ Spinna, who has raided the Guidance records catalog to bring you an hour and a quarter of trance-inducing, dubbed-up club grooves for your hand-waving, hip-shaking, glow-sticking pleasure. The disc starts off with jazzy, faintly Latin grooves courtesy of Brace, Butti49, and Chuck Perkins, but then quickly sinks into four-on-the-floor house beats and stays there for most of the 21 tracks that remain. There are occasional detours, such as Paul Hunter's jazz-flavored "Reflection" and the explicitly reggae-inflected "Righteous Dub" by Uptight Productions (and don't miss the Mutabaruka cameo). But otherwise, this is a long exercise in trancey club grooves, and as such it's mostly attractive in a purely functional way. Highlights include the cool Jazzanova remix of Ursula Rucker's "Circe" and a very pretty number called "Baghdad Cafe" by A:Xus (featuring vocals from Naomi Nsombi). This one is recommended. *—Rick Anderson*

Mix the Vibe: Eclectic Mindset / Apr. 15, 2002 / King Street ✦✦✦
With less of an accent on turntablist credentials, DJ Spinna's *Mix the Vibe: Eclectic Mindset* focuses on consistency and tone. Starting off with doe-eyed hip-hop and ending with the luminous vibes of the Ananda Project and What's Happenin', there's a lot to say for DJ Spinna's world of soulful, R&B-influenced, pretension-phobic rhythm mixing. There's a small section midway through where Spinna does a simple spin-back cross-fade from Mondo

Grosso's after-club jazz cut "MG4BB" to the scattered Ron Trent mix of Eri Ito's "Sona Mi Areru Ec Sancitu," and it sounds not only natural but also smart and quietly exciting. It's a symbolic moment for the album and corroboration that Spinna was discovering that there was more on his mind than record-collector chic. —*Dean Carlson*

The Beyond Real Experience, Vol. 2 / Jul. 9, 2002 / Beyond Real ◆◆◆◆
DJ Spinna adds another gem to his impressive array of mix albums with *The Beyond Real Experience, Vol. 2.* The New York turntablist throws down tracks from his own hip-hop label, Beyond Real. Many of the same rappers show up continually in the mix: Old World Disorder, Shadowman, Guru, Skam, Mr. Akil, and Sadat X, all of whom make multiple appearances. Plus, Spinna throws in several tracks by his own rap group, Jigmastas. Most of the featured rappers are up-and-comers at this point in time, 2002, though it's great to see Guru and Sadat X here, two veterans from the early '90s. The mixing, of course, is unbelievable. Spinna showcases not only some of the best releases from his label but also some of his best turntablist techniques. —*Jason Birchmeier*

Here to There / Feb. 4, 2003 / Rapster ◆◆◆◆
DJ Spinna does it like most can only talk it. Coming from the ethnically diverse streets of Brooklyn and learning the art of DJing in the eclectic atmosphere of college radio, Spinna effortlessly moves from hip-hop to house to funk and groove without causing the typically rigid music industry to bat an eye. He is a rare talent who can mix CDs for both underground hip-hop giant Rawkus and revered New York house label King Street. BBE's "Beat Generation" series was custom made for Spinna, encouraging well-known producers to make an album without any of the usual restrictions of genre or commerciality. And while spectacular releases by Jaydee and Pete Rock remained mostly in the realm of hip-hop, Spinna follows the lead of DJ Jazzy Jeff by turning in a recording that plays out like a music collector's ideal urban radio station. The opening carnival of "Alfonso's Thang" announces the album's intentions with the sort of old school hip-hop funk that everyone loves. From there, Spinna runs through R&B, broken beat, hip-hop, and house with equal ease. No matter what the style, the production remains lush and musical. Spinna's production is so strong that every cut maintains a central vibe, even with a different vocalist appearing on each track. Such an accomplishment places Spinna next to fellow modern visionaries 4Hero, King Britt, and Carl Craig, all of whom wait their turn to be written into history next to legendary producers such as Quincy Jones and Gil Evans. Listeners can only hope that contemporary ears will become more attuned to musical statements that transcend easy genre compartments. —*Joshua Glazer*

DJ Spooky (Paul D. Miller)

b. 1970, Washington, D.C.

DJ, Producer / Electronica, Experimental Techno, Turntablism, Illbient, Trip-Hop, Post-Rock/Experimental

DJ Spooky (Tha' Subliminal Kid) is the most noted (and notorious) proponent of turntablism, an approach to hip-hop and DJing whose philosophy merges avant-garde theories of musique concrèté with the increased devotion paid to mixing techniques during the 1990s. Though he's overly intellectual at times (to the detriment of his recordings, interviews, and mixing dates), Spooky was a critical figure in spotlighting the DJ as a postmodern poet in his own right. Influenced equally by John Cage and Sun Ra as well as Kool Herc and Grandmaster Flash, few artists did more to mainstream the DJ-as-artist concept than he.

Spooky was born Paul Miller in Washington, D.C. His father was a lawyer and member of the faculty at Howard University but died when Miller was only three. He inherited his father's record collection, which, along with frequent trips around the world (thanks to his mother's international fabric store), opened his eyes to a wide range of music. Growing up in the '80s saw Miller interested in D.C.'s hardcore punk scene and British ska-punk as well as go-go music. While attending college in Maine, Spooky began mixing on his own radio show and attempted to introduce his KRS-One tapes into classroom discussions on deconstruction (an idea made quite conceivable just ten years later). After graduating with degrees in French literature and philosophy, he moved to New York, where he wrote science fiction alongside advertising copy and pursued visual art as well. He was still into hip-hop, however,

and formed the underground Soundlab collective (with We, Byzar, Sub Dub, and others), a scene that later morphed into the illbient movement.

After an assortment of singles and EPs during 1994-1995, Spooky gained a record contract from Asphodel in 1996 and released his debut album, *Songs of a Dead Dreamer*. The single "Galactic Funk" became a hit on the club scene, leading to recording appearances with Arto Lindsay and remixing spots for Metallica, Sublime, Nick Cave, and Spookey Ruben; Spooky also began writing regular journalist columns, for *The Village Voice* and *Vibe*. As if that didn't keep him busy, he also released the mix album *Necropolis: The Dialogic Project*, recorded a Paul D. Miller solo LP titled *Viral Sonata*, and performed in a new digital version of the Iannis Xenakis composition *Kraanerg*. His second proper album, 1998's *Riddim Warfare*, saw Spooky with a cast including disparate indie-world figures from Dr. Octagon to Thurston Moore. He has also mounted visual exhibits at the Whitney Museum in New York and scored the award-winning 1998 film *Slam*. One year later he released *File Under Futurism*, a coproduction with the Freight Elevator Quartet. The year 2000 saw the release of a collaborative effort with Scanner entitled *The Quick and the Dead*. The highly praised mix CD *Under the Influence* appeared the following year, but the next real album to appear from the DJ was 2002's *Modern Mantra*. That same year, as part of its Blue Series Continuum, Thirsty Ear released *Optometry*, a collaboration featuring Spooky with numerous progressive jazz artists such as William Parker and Matthew Shipp. Its remix companion *Dubtometry*, appeared early in 2003. —*John Bush*

● **Songs of a Dead Dreamer** / Mar. 26, 1996 / Asphodel ◆◆◆◆◆
Arguably but understandably, the amount of hype and academic discussion surrounding DJ Spooky's work has often obscured his gifts and abilities. Strip away everything, even his own detailed essays and reflections on his work that form this disc's liner notes, and what's left is creative and mysterious work that stands up well on its own merits. Not as *sui generis* as some would have him be—his roots in everything from avant-garde classical music to the groundbreaking work of Jamaican dub are clear—he's a marvelous synthesizer of varying trends, as *Songs of a Dead Dreamer* demonstrates throughout. The illbient tag is one of the more facile labels applied to his work; the intent is there (uneasy hip-hop rhythms in ambient space), but not the true range of what he is capable of. Instead, *Songs of a Dead Dreamer* is more a consistent and total exploration of sound and atmosphere, as much indebted to the effect of film soundtracks as it is to getting a good groove and beat on, and more. "Juba," with its haunting string sample floating through the hissing, low mix, or the distinctly dub-tinged "Anansi Abstrakt," one of many such tracks on the album showing that touch, are but two highlights of many. His DJing skills themselves aren't as prominent as are his abilities to arrange and create overall pieces, but when he lets the former through more, as with the key central scratch on "Galactic Funk (Tau Ceti Mix)," it's all for the service of further improving the song. Said song also has some righteous synclavier action, confirming that it's not just music to relax to. —*Ned Raggett*

Necropolis: The Dialogic Project / May 21, 1995 / Knitting Factory ◆◆◆
When this album was released in 1995, DJ Spooky (That Subliminal Kid) was not yet the legend of abstract electronica that he would later become. Here he presents an overlong program of remixes by unknown (Byzar, Ben Neill) and relatively famous (Sub Dub, DJ Soulslinger) electronic dance artists, with some tracks lasting as long as 12 minutes and each featuring a prologue than runs as much as five. The length of these tracks is not a problem in itself, but the random shapelessness of them is. DJ Spooky has an autodidact's love of big words and impatience with coherent syntax ("The anomalies in this mix are coordinate points marking an invisible terrain"), and that combination of intellectual attributes finds direct expression in his music, which is filled with fascinating sounds and textures but is frustratingly bereft of discipline or organization. Hence his remix of Ben Neill's "Grapheme," in which sonic effluvia bob around in a dark sea of noise, and his own "Journey (Paraspace Mix)," a shapeless sound pastiche that mutters and grumbles without ever generating the slightest interest. Those who endure the first half-hour of this 75-minute program will be rewarded by Sub Dub's skanking "SoundCheck" and DJ Soulslinger's excellent "Abducted (U.F.O. Mix)," but it's hard going until then. There's no excuse for music this potentially interesting to be this boring. —*Rick Anderson*

Synthetic Fury EP / Feb. 10, 1998 / Asphodel ◆◆◆◆
This EP, which is actually nearly 30 minutes long, shows why DJ Spooky was the first turntablist signed to a major label. The opening track, "You Are

About to Witness," sets syncopated scratching against a Bomb Squad-like backdrop of wailing sirens, screeching *Psycho* samples, and a classic N.W.A line before morphing into "Dumb Mutha Fucka," a furiously funky descent into hell that matches thunderous drums and sheets of psychedelic samples against a maddeningly infectious string melody. On "Sum Ill Shit (Clinton Street Dub)," Spooky deconstructs his whacked-out sound even further, tweaking a bass line straight outta the Jack Bruce songbook and taking it into the deepest, darkest recesses of psychedelic dub. But the EP's high point is the supremely bizarre title track, a seven-minute epic of insane samples, distorted voices, and schizophrenic style changes that will leave "normal" listeners dizzy, disoriented, and completely discombobulated. In a subgenre where originality and creativity are held in the highest esteem, DJ Spooky proves himself to be truly one of a kind. —*Bret Love*

Haunted Breaks, Vol. 1 EP / Aug. 18, 1998 / Home Entertainment ✦✦✦
Haunted Breaks, Vol. 1 is an approximately 40-minute, limited-edition breakbeat EP; it finds Spooky harking back to old school rave sounds. —*Steve Huey*

Riddim Warfare / Sep. 21, 1998 / Outpost ✦✦✦✦
Though he has his fingers in just about every beat-oriented pot of the late '90s (from hip-hop to trip-hop to drum'n'bass to illbient to turntablism), DJ Spooky managed to control his various inspirations for *Riddim Warfare*, instead of falling prey to the musical-eclecticism-for-its-own-sake concept that often derails similar producers. On the album's half-dozen or so hip-hop tracks, the production is appropriately dense and paranoid for abstract-philosopher rappers like Kool Keith, Sir Menelik, Organized Konfusion, and Killah Priest of Wu-Tang Clan. Elsewhere, Spooky sandwiches the tech-step drum'n'bass stormer "Post-Human Sophistry" right next to a track recorded live in Brazil with Arto Lindsay (which resembles a fusion of hip-hop with early Weather Report). Only one man could conceive of an album including turntable battles, a workout for Sonic Youth guitarist Thurston Moore, and a spoken-word piece on the same album. Through it all, DJ Spooky makes it work in fine fashion. —*John Bush*

File Under Futurism / Sep. 21, 1999 / Caipirinha ✦✦✦✦✦
DJ Spooky's *File Under Futurism* is the result of a six-month collaboration with the Freight Elevator Quartet, an avant-garde electronic and acoustic group dedicated to pioneering new musical sounds and techniques. *File Under Futurism* features variations on compositions by DJ Spooky that were then reworked and remixed by both Spooky and the Freight Elevator Quartet. Each of the album's pieces reflects society's increasing speed and reliance on technology while exploring different subgenres of electronic music, from the breakbeat-inflected "File Under Futurism (Groove Protocol Mix)" to the minimalist, cello-driven "Downtempo Manifesto," to the heavily processed digital hardcore of "Experimental Asynchronicity" to the gentler, ambient "Chromatic Aberration." *File Under Futurism* also includes DJ Spooky turntablisms "Interstitial A" and "Interstitial B," as well as Freight Elevator Quartet compositions like "Bring Me My Mental Health" and "The RCA Mark II Synthesizer," which was composed on the first synthesizer ever built. An ambitious and fascinating album, *File Under Futurism* is a rare, successful combination of academics and kinetics. —*Heather Phares*

Under the Influence / Sep. 18, 2001 / Six Degrees ✦✦✦✦
One never knows what to expect with a recording from DJ Spooky. He's an artist who has been all over the map, and this is something that he continues to do as his catalog of excellent recordings grows. With DJ Spooky's 2001 release, *Under the Influence*, out on the Six Degrees Records label, he has created a long-running seamless sonic tapestry. Rather than create yet another mix CD based on dancefloor hits and trends, Six Degrees created the *Under the Influence* series, which allows the artist or DJ to mix their own favorites—recordings that are especially profound, inspirational, and significant to them. DJ Spooky's contribution is the first disc in this series. This mix is excellent with a capital "e." It's profoundly accessible, danceable, and even listenable, but DJ Spooky has maintained his wholly experimental edge with this release and from the moment his turntables power up to the end of the recording, just under 74 minutes later, it's pure magic. Enough good things can't be said about DJ Spooky's critically profound *Under the Influence*. —*Matt Borghi*

Modern Mantra / May 21, 2002 / Shadow ✦✦✦✦
DJ Spooky's mix-album trawl through the deep, varied back catalog of Shadow Records is a great mix of laid-back breaks and hip-hop, populated by long-buried tracks from several scenes all over the world. (Granted, Shadow is as much a domestic distributor as it is a record label.) Spooky's mixing is excellent; with deft transitions and great scratching (plus just a bit of post-production), he injects energy into blunted hip-hop from Sharpshooters and DJ Cam, then ups the tempo with a great mini-set of drum'n'bass with highlights from Jack Dangers (the Meat Beat Manifesto main man) and Cujo (aka Amon Tobin). *Modern Mantra* finally touches down with jazzy, experimental selections from Goo ("The OG") and Spaceways ("Requiem for Ra") and ends by stretching back to early-'90s ambient with Prototype 909 and a closer from Moby's *Ambient* album of 1993. DJ Spooky compensates for the lack of vocals by dropping a pair of ace Aesop Rock tracks (the album's only outside licensing) and makes a smooth transition from post-millennium sound sculptor Russell Mills to the genesis of Shadow in the early-'90s ambient techno scene. —*John Bush*

Optometry / Jul. 2002 / Thirsty Ear ✦✦✦✦
Thirsty Ear's Blue Series has already been host to many progressive jazz projects, among them albums by William Parker, Matthew Shipp, Craig Taborn, Guillaume Brown, Mat Maneri, Tim Berne, and others. The label also did a project with British DJ drum'n'bass duo Spring Heel Jack that was neither a jazz album nor a DJ record, but some strange amalgam unto itself. DJ Spooky's *Optometry* is the next installment in the Blue Series' DJ experiments, and it's one that succeeds on every level. For starters, *Optometry* is fully a DJ outing and fully a jazz record. The band playing with Spooky is comprised of Parker; Shipp; Brown; Medeski , Martin & Wood's Billy Martin; Joe McPhee; Carl Hancock Rux; and others. Spooky plays bass and kalimba besides his turntables and mixing board. He illustrates, collages, paints, spindles, cuts, and mixes a live performance by the rest of the band. On "Reactive Switching Strategies for the Control of Uninhabited Air," Billy Martin cascades snares and toms in counterpoint to his ride cymbal, setting up a rhythm that is followed by Parker and Shipp. Shipp's playing fleshes out the motif and makes it a modal stretch, and the time signatures fluctuate between four and eight, as Spooky dovetails–à la Brian Eno–various timbres and harmonics emitted by the individual musicians, as well as the quartet sound. Slipping keyboard washes in between Shipp's repetitive lines that are big enough for Parker to vamp crazily on, and putting distance in between various segments is the DJ's art here. The title track moves from abstract arpeggiattic saxophone striations by McPhee to phat, dirty, nasty, synth lines from Shipp, playing some combination of the funk in Sun Ra's *Lanquidity* and Herbie Hancock's *Head Hunters*. While this is happening, Parker pops and bows his bass to stay alongside the bottom end of the groove for a particularly disorienting effect, as it almost falls apart at the beginning of each chorus. Spooky samples all the proceedings and mirrors them back slightly altered while adding loops and found sounds to break down even the most innate structure in the tune so it has to be built according to memory. Whew! When the scratch attempts to do that, Shipp moves to his acoustic piano, and McPhee comes inside to refract Shipp's lines back to the rhythm section—which includes Spooky at this point. And this goes on for almost 12 minutes. There is no let-up in the creative vibe here; each member attempts to express for the collective. Spooky included. Riff, vamp, timbral fractures, lyrical tension, splintered harmonics, and a constant, seductive sense of groove permeate this jazz album, opening up a door onto a brave new future for a free jazz with soul—Spooky has exceeded all expectations here. —*Thom Jurek*

Dubtometry / Mar. 18, 2003 / Thirsty Ear ✦✦✦✦
It's the obvious next step for DJ Spooky. Take the tracks he worked over on his groundbreaking *Optometry* album and give them to various remixers so they can create their own vision of his sound—a refraction of it, if you will. For the most part, the overworked "dub" tag doesn't really apply, even when he brings in a couple of dub masters like Lee "Scratch" Perry and Mad Professor. But it's a hook to hang it all on. And certainly some of the people here have clear ideas. Karsh Kale, for example, makes a percussive vehicle of "Variation Cybernetique," with tablas unsurprisingly to the fore. It's interesting to compare with Twilight Circus' take on the same piece, which heads toward dreamier realms altogether. Blend offers an almost gamelan sensibility to "Kollage," with plenty of delay creating something quite otherworldly. Negativland's trademark cut-up sensibility comes to "Asphalt," hitting high on the disorientation factor. If you're expecting dub in the Jamaican way—a remix that's aimed at both feet and head, you won't find it here; this is strictly cerebral. But it's a very successful brain warp that often

pushes all the way to the edge (stand up DJ Goo). It makes you wonder if remixes of the remixes might come next, like ripples moving out across a pool. It'd certainly be an interesting idea. In the meantime, be happy with this, a fabulous idea made flesh. —*Chris Nickson*

DJ T-Rock

DJ / Turntablism, Party Rap

Hailing from Atlanta, DJ T-Rock has been a hip-hop DJ since the late '80s and is a member of the Third World Citizens crew along with DJ Faust and Shortee. His first album, *Who's Your Daddy*, was released on Bomb Hip Hop in 1999, and balanced turntable tricks and an old school party atmosphere. A second release, *Sikinthehed*, came out in 2001. —*Wade Kergan*

● **Who's Your Daddy** / Jul. 27, 1999 / Bomb Hip Hop ◆◆◆◆
Just the latest in a line of excellent turntablists making their album debut on Bomb Hip-Hop, DJ T-Rock is a bit more old school than DJ Faust, and much more focused on keeping things going than creating the hip-hop equivalent of musique concrète. He keeps the beats steady for the most part, and spends much of his time scratching in vocal samples lifted from old school R&B, educational records, and all sorts of used-bin rejects. It's not quite as energetic and propulsive as brilliant turntablist full-lengths by Cut Chemist (*Live at Future Primitive Sound Session*) and Mix Master Mike (*Anti-Theft Device*), but *Who's Your Daddy* makes for an hour of fun and funk for hip-hop fans of all ages. —*John Bush*

DJ U-Neek

Producer, DJ / Club/Dance, Bass Music

The producer behind the success of Bone Thugs-N-Harmony, DJ U-Neek earned a Grammy for his work on the group's smash hit "The Crossroads." He released the solo album *Ghetto Street Pharmacist* in the fall of 1999. —*Jason Ankeny*

● **Ghetto Street Pharmacist** / Oct. 5, 1999 / Thump ◆◆◆
As the producer of Bone Thugs-N-Harmony, DJ U-Neek established himself as a savvy hip-hop mastermind, able to balance commercial sensibilities with a street attitude. This was most evident on Bone Thugs' 1995 album, *E. 1999 Eternal*, which boasted "Crossroads." It took DJ U-Neek four years to break out on his own with *Ghetto Street Pharmacist*, a record that confirms his producing skills yet sounds a little dated. Like many albums by producers, it showcases style over content, trying a few too many things at once. Since U-Neek doesn't rap, he has an ever-rotating cast of guest artists taking the mic, concentrating on artists he's developing. He doesn't really give these rappers their own sound, so thankfully they distinguish themselves with their rhyming styles, most of which are pretty good. At its best, *Ghetto Street Pharmacist* plays like a good mix tape, one where the music flows naturally from one song to the next. Still, it's curiously underwhelming as a whole. If anything, U-Neek doesn't try enough different styles, sticking a little too close to the pop-flavored hardcore of Bone Thugs, which sounds outdated in 1999. When he shake things up, though, his true skills shine through. He does shake things up often enough on *Ghetto Street Pharmacist* to keep it interesting, but not quite enough to keep it constantly compelling. —*Stephen Thomas Erlewine*

DJ Uncle Al (Albert Moss)

DJ / Hip-Hop, Club/Dance, Bass Music

DJ Uncle Al (born Albert Moss), an incredibly prolific Miami producer, uses the sound of bass music plus Latino rap, standard hip-hop, and reggae on his parade of releases for On Top Records. Since 1994, Uncle Al has averaged almost two albums per year, with the help of his many protégés, including the Zoe Pound and Cloud Nine. —*John Bush*

What's My Name / Feb. 15, 1994 / On Top ◆◆◆

DJ Vadim (Vadim Peare)

b. Russia

Producer, DJ / Trip-Hop, Ambient Breakbeat, Underground Rap, Hip-Hop, Electronica

Hip-hop's influence spread far and wide during the '80s, as witnessed by the growth of the international scene during the following decade. Standing beside brilliant DJs from Japan (Krush) and France (Cam), Russia's DJ Vadim has proved to be the most popular advocate of hip-hop to come out of the

former Soviet bloc, triggered mostly by the fact that he moved to Britain early in life. Upon arrival, he set up his own Jazz Fudge Records later that year to issue a demo he called *Derelicts of Conformity* (by Son of Seth). He finally released the recordings early in 1995, as DJ Vadim's *Abstract Hallucinating Gasses* EP.

Britain's top hip-hop and acid jazz DJs began playing the record and, after being scouted by several labels, Vadim signed a contract with Ninja Tune. Several EPs released during 1995-1996 showed him to be quite an experimentalist, working heavily with static and noise, never content to let his ideas meander past the two- or three-minute point. His first LP, *U.S.S.R. Repertoire (The Theory of Verticality)*, was released in late 1996. The following year, Vadim began working on acts for Jazz Fudge; he issued the compilation *Sculpture & Broken Sound*, then debuted his own Andre Gurov project with the album *A New Rap Language*. His next project, the highly touted remix album *U.S.S.R. Reconstruction*, appeared in 1998, and was followed a year later by *U.S.S.R.: Life From the Other Side*. His third U.S.S.R. record, *The Art of Listening*, dropped in 2002. Vadim has also worked as the Bug, with Kevin Martin, Dave Cochran, and Alex Buess. —*John Bush*

U.S.S.R. Repertoire (The Theory of Verticality) / Oct. 14, 1996 / Ninja Tune ◆◆◆◆
Of the countless abstract hip-hop LPs released during 1996-1997 (with Ninja Tune bearing much of the load), *U.S.S.R. Repertoire* could be one of the best. Vadim's attention to detail when structuring beats, samples, and noise is impeccable over the course of the album's 26 tracks. With just the right blend of forbidding atmosphere and subtle funkiness, Vadim created an excellent album his first time out. —*John Bush*

U.S.S.R. Reconstruction / Jan. 26, 1998 / Ninja Tune ◆◆◆◆
DJ Vadim selected a baker's dozen of the best producers in the field for work on *U.S.S.R. Reconstruction*. From nu-school electro producers (Reflection, Clatterbox) to more likeminded beatmeisters (DJ Krush, Silent Poets, Kid Koala) to freeform experimenters (Oval, Techno Animal), the album flows without a hitch through the darkest hip-hop and beat exploration, though the material never becomes as abstract as on Vadim's debut. —*John Bush*

● **U.S.S.R.: Life From the Other Side** / Sep. 14, 1999 / Ninja Tune ◆◆◆◆◆
DJ Vadim's debut introduced one of the world's best producers in abstract underground rap, a minimalist hip-hopper able to weave a funky break around the slightest piece of noise detritus. After recording a solid remix album (*U.S.S.R. Reconstruction*), Vadim returned in late 1999 with the sophomore-slump-breaking *U.S.S.R.: Life From the Other Side*. Whereas with his first album Vadim worked on a miniature scale, constructing breaks and beats out of abstract noise, here the sound is more upfront and swaggering, much closer to the commercial rap world than before. (Of course, thanks to producers like Timbaland and Swizz Beatz, the commercial rap world had moved much closer to Vadim, as well.) Since he's working with rappers on more than half of the tracks here, Vadim transforms himself from a solo turntablist into a genuine rap trackmaster with catchier riffs and tighter beats than most in Britain's instrumental hip-hop underground. Two tracks, "Viagra" (with El-P from Company Flow) and "English Breakfast" (with Swollen Members), display this excellent fusion by blending the hard-hitting, stutter-stepped style of production perfected by DJ Premier with just a few of the paranoid breaks and hostile atmospheres of Vadim's debut. On a similarly high level as landmarks like Dr. Octagon and Company Flow's *Funcrusher Plus*, *U.S.S.R.: Life From the Other Side* proves Vadim is not only one of the most creative turntablist/producers but also one of the most talented trackmasters in the healthy rap underground. —*John Bush*

U.S.S.R.: Life From the Other Side (Instrumentals) / Nov. 23, 1999 / Caroline ◆◆◆

U.S.S.R.: The Art of Listening / Oct. 2002 / Ninja Tune ◆◆◆◆
U.S.S.R.: The Art of Listening, even more than its predecessor, represents a large leap toward the rapping side of hip-hop, with guests on every track but one and virtually no space for the exquisite ambient breakbeat of previous DJ Vadim productions. It's difficult to mourn the loss of Vadim the solo artist, though, when the tracks *and* productions found here are so refreshing and totally distinct. All but one of the rappers are fresh faces (for a Vadim LP), which paves the way for talented newcomers (Yarah Bravo, Phi-Life Cypher, Vakill, TTC), some of whom have their own releases but all of whom will benefit from more attention. Vadim continues to strip his productions down,

so far in fact that occasionally there's more space *between* the sounds than there are sounds themselves. One of the best tracks, "It's On" features the excellent Vakill freestyling over some standard jazz keys but also a few blink-and-miss-it samples: Jew's harp, the distinctive sound of Japanese noh music, and a precious few grunts and moans from an earthy blues vocalist. Yarah Bravo is easily the most distinctive rapper here; she plays with her rhymes, drawling like a sloshed debutante and practically tripping over her own vocals like the hip-hop equivalent of Jackie Chan's drunken master. Gift of Gab from Blackalicious brings it back to the earthier side of alternative (read: American) rap with the deep groove "Combustible," but great features for Phi-Life Cypher and Demolition Man return to the up-and-coming British sound of raggae flow over heavily distorted analogue synth. While his sizable generosity—inviting an assortment of voices to appear on his own album—initially appears to be a fault, it quickly becomes clear this is a blessed virtue instead. —*John Bush*

U.S.S.R.: The Art of Listening (Instrumentals) / Dec. 10, 2002 / Ninja Tune ✦✦✦

DJ Z-Trip (Zach Sciacca)
....
DJ, Producer / Underground Rap, Turntablism, Alternative Rap
DJ Z-Trip already had a few mixes out—including one in the prestigious *Future Primitive Soundsession* series—when his collaboration with DJ P, *Uneasylistening, Vol. 1*, showed up in 2001. The unorthodox mix made many music fans take notice, if only to puzzle over unlikely pairings like Del tha Funkee Homosapien with Phil Collins and Bruce Hornsby with Run-D.M.C. A native of Queens, NY, Z-Trip (born Zach Sciacca) spends much of his time touring and traveling, but has roots in Phoenix, AZ, where he's part of the Bombshelter Crew with DJ Radar. —*Wade Kergan*

Monkey Breaks, Vol. 1 / May 5, 1998 / Ubiquity ✦✦✦

● **Live at the Future Primitive Soundsession, Vol. 2** / Dec. 21, 1999 / Future Primitive ✦✦✦✦✦
The first volume of *Live at the Future Primitive Soundsession* helped popularize turntablism (instrumental hip-hop composed exclusively on turntables) with the inspired pairing of Cut Chemist on beats and Shortkut on "lead" scratching. The second volume, while failing to achieve the notoriety of its predecessor, is in the end the more engaging and accessible record. Phoenix DJs Radar and Z-Trip worked together regularly as part of the Bombshelter DJs crew, so their live collaboration was seamless and carefully planned. The foundation of the record is superbly mixed hip-hop classics like LL Cool J's "Rock the Bells," Eric B. & Rakim's "I Know You Got Soul" (an a cappella version mixed with the instrumental from Whodini's "Friends"), and Doug E. Fresh & the Get Fresh Crew's "The Show," but these ingredients are tweaked, chopped, and blended with all manner of sound effects, brief vocal snippets, and breaks from classic rock staples like Pink Floyd's "Is There Anybody Out There?" and Aerosmith's "Sweet Emotion." To their credit, Radar and Z-Trip never sound like they are showing off or performing for other DJs. The focus from the first needle drop is rocking the appreciative crowd, and the record is closer to a killer mix tape than the abstract needle thrashing of the Invisibl Skratch Piklz. Without question, this is one of the best records of its kind. —*Mark Richardson*

Uneasy Listening, Vol. 1 / 2001 / ZTRIP ✦✦✦
Public Enemy, Cyndi Lauper, the Police, Pink Floyd, Del tha Funkee Homosapien, and "The Imperial March" all were present on DJ Z-Trip and DJ P's initial addition to the world of genre-less turntablist hip-hop mix albums. Fortunately, this wasn't just a clever sequence of songs, but rather a massive mélange of credibility-baiting combinations, such as Depeche Mode being smothered over Bruce Hornsby or, indescribably, making a searing marriage of Metallica's "For Whom the Bell Tolls" and Midnight Oil's "Beds are Burning." Soulwax, the Avalanches, and innumerable bedroom bootleggers might have done similar tricks with considerably more emotional participation, but luckily there was enough going on here to back up the obvious niche appeal. —*Dean Carlson*

DMX (Earl Simmons)
....
b. Dec. 18, 1970
East Coast Rap, Hardcore Rap
Following the deaths of Tupac Shakur and the Notorious B.I.G., DMX took over as the reigning, undisputed king of hardcore rap. He was that rare

commodity: a commercial powerhouse with artistic and street credibility to spare. His rapid ascent to stardom was actually almost a decade in the making, which gave him a chance to develop the theatrical image that made him one of rap's most distinctive personalities during his heyday. Everything about DMX was unremittingly intense, from his muscular, tattooed physique to his gruff, barking delivery, which made a perfect match for his trademark lyrical obsession with dogs. Plus, there was substance behind the style; much of his work was tied together by a fascination with the split between the sacred and the profane. He could move from spiritual anguish one minute to a narrative about the sins of the streets the next, yet keep it all part of the same complex character; sort of like a hip-hop Johnny Cash. The results were compelling enough to make DMX the first artist ever to have his first four albums enter the charts at number one.

DMX was born Earl Simmons in Baltimore, MD, on December 18, 1970. He moved with part of his family to the New York City suburb of Yonkers while still a young child. A troubled and abusive childhood turned him violent, and he spent a great deal of time living in group homes and surviving on the streets via robbery, which led to several run-ins with the law. He found his saving grace in hip-hop, starting out as a DJ and human beatbox, and later moved into rapping for a greater share of the spotlight, taking his name from the DMX digital drum machine (though it's also been reinterpreted to mean "Dark Man X"). He made a name for himself on the freestyle battle scene, and was written up in *The Source* magazine's Unsigned Hype column in 1991. Columbia subsidiary Ruffhouse signed him to a deal the following year, and released his debut single "Born Loser." However, a surplus of talent on the Ruffhouse roster left DMX underpromoted, and the label agreed to release him from his contract. He issued one further single in 1994, "Make a Move," but was convicted of drug possession that same year, the biggest offense of several on his record.

DMX began to rebuild his career with an appearance on one of DJ Clue?'s underground mix tapes. In 1997 he earned a second major-label shot with Def Jam, and made a galvanizing guest appearance on LL Cool J's "4, 3, 2, 1." Further guest spots on Mase's "24 Hours to Live" and fellow Yonkers MCs the LOX's "Money, Power & Respect" created an even stronger buzz, and in early 1998 he released his debut Def Jam single, "Get at Me Dog." The song was a gold-selling smash on the rap and dance charts, and paved the way for DMX's full-length debut, *It's Dark and Hell Is Hot*, to debut at number one on the pop charts. Produced mostly by Swizz Beatz, who rode the album's success to a lucrative career of his own, *It's Dark and Hell Is Hot* earned DMX numerous comparisons to 2Pac for his booming, aggressive presence on the mic, and went on to sell over four million copies. Not long after the album's release in May 1998, DMX was accused of raping a stripper in the Bronx, but was later cleared by DNA evidence. He went on to make his feature film debut costarring in Hype Williams' ambitious but unsuccessful *Belly*.

Before the end of 1998, DMX completed his second album, and a pending buyout of Def Jam pushed the record into stores that December. Featuring a controversial cover photo of the rapper covered in blood, *Flesh of My Flesh, Blood of My Blood* entered the charts at number one and eventually went triple platinum. The following year, DMX hit the road with Jay-Z and the Method Man/Redman team on the blockbuster Hard Knock Life tour. During a tour stop in Denver, a warrant for his arrest was issued in connection with a stabbing, of which he was later cleared; another incident occurred in May, when he was accused of assaulting a Yonkers man who'd allegedly harassed his wife (the charges were once again dropped). More serious charges were brought that summer, when DMX's uncle/manager was accidentally shot in the foot at a New Jersey hotel. Police later raided DMX's home, and filed animal cruelty, weapons, and drug possession charges against the rapper and his wife; he eventually plea-bargained down to fines, probation, and community service. In the midst of those difficulties, the Ruff Ryders posse—of which DMX was a core, founding member—released a showcase compilation, *Ryde or Die, Vol. 1*. With contributions from DMX, as well as Eve, the LOX, and multiple guests, *Ryde or Die, Vol. 1* debuted at number one in the spring of 1999, further cementing DMX's Midas touch.

Toward the end of 1999, DMX released his third album, *... And Then There Was X*, which became his third straight to debut at number one. It also produced his biggest hit single since "Get at Me Dog" with "Party Up (Up in Here)," which became his first Top Ten hit on the R&B charts. The follow-ups "What You Want" and "What's My Name" were also quite popular, and their success helped make … *And Then There Was X* the rapper's best-selling album to date, moving over five million copies. During its run, DMX returned to the big screen with a major supporting role in the Jet Li action flick *Romeo Must Die*. In the meantime, he was indicted by a Westchester County, NY, grand jury on weapons and drug charges in June of 2000. He also entangled himself in a lengthy legal battle with police in Cheektowaga, NY (near Buffalo), when he was arrested in March for driving without a license and possession of marijuana. He missed one court date, and when he turned himself in that May, police discovered more marijuana in a pack of cigarettes the rapper had brought with him. He pled guilty and was sentenced to 15 days in jail, and his appeal to have the sentence reduced was finally denied in early 2001. After stalling for several weeks, he turned himself in and was charged with contempt of court. He was further charged with assault when, upon learning he would not be let out early for good behavior, allegedly threw a food tray at a group of prison officers. He later bargained the charges down to reckless assault and paid a fine, and accused guards of roughing him up and causing a minor leg injury.

Not long after DMX's release from jail, his latest movie, the Steven Seagal action film *Exit Wounds*, opened at number one in the box office. DMX also contributed the hit single "No Sunshine" to the soundtrack, and signed a multipicture deal with Warner Bros. in the wake of *Exit Wounds'* success. With his legal problems finally resolved, he returned to the studio and completed his fourth album, the more introspective *The Great Depression*. It was released in the fall of 2001 and became his fourth straight album to debut at number one. Although it went platinum quickly, it didn't have the same shelf life as his previous releases. In late 2002, DMX published his memoirs as *E.A.R.L.: The Autobiography of DMX*, and also recorded several tracks with Audioslave (i.e., the former Rage Against the Machine). One of their collaborations, "Here I Come," was featured on the soundtrack of DMX's next film, a reunion with Jet Li called *Cradle 2 the Grave*. The film opened at number one upon its release in March 2003, and its DMX-heavy soundtrack debuted in the Top Ten. —*Steve Huey*

● **It's Dark and Hell Is Hot** / May 12, 1998 / Def Jam ✦✦✦✦
Just as rap music was reaching its toughest, darkest, grimmest period yet following the assassinations of 2Pac and Biggie in the late '90s, along came DMX and his fellow Ruff Ryders, who embodied the essence of inner-city machismo to a tee, as showcased throughout the tellingly titled *It's Dark and Hell Is Hot*. Unlike so many other hardcore rappers who were more rhetorical than physical, DMX commanded an aggressive aura without even speaking a word. He showcased his chiseled physique on the arresting album cover and trumpeted his animalistic nature with frequent barking, growling, and snarling throughout the album. He furthermore collaborated with muscular producers Swizz Beatz and Dame Grease, who specialized in slamming synth-driven beats rather than sample-driven ones. Yet further unlike so many other hardcore rappers from the time, DMX was meaningful as well as symbolic. He professed an ideology that stressed the inner world—characterized by such qualities as survival, wisdom, strength, respect, and faith—rather than the material one that infatuated most rappers. It helped, of course, that his album includes a few mammoth highlights ("Ruff Ryder Anthem," "Get at Me Dog," "Let Me Fly," and "I Can Feel It") as well as a light, mid-album diversion ("How's It Goin' Down"). The long running length of *It's Dark and Hell Is Hot* does wear you down after a while, since nearly every song here sans "How's It Goin' Down" hits hard and maintains the album's deadly serious attitude. Even so, it's perhaps DMX's most essential album. *It's Dark and Hell Is Hot* may not be his best, nor an outright classic, but it lays out DMX's complex persona with candor, from his faith in God to his fixation with canine motifs, and does so with an engaging sense of dramatic flair. —*Jason Birchmeier*

Flesh of My Flesh, Blood of My Blood / Dec. 15, 1998 / Def Jam ✦✦✦✦
On the heels of his multiplatinum debut *It's Dark and Hell Is Hot*, DMX unleashed his dogs again on an album overflowing with raw energy and spiritual catharsis. The irascible Yonkers MC, 27 at the time of this recording, continues the Ruff Ryder legacy on this follow-up release. DMX's canine split-personality flow is like none other, not only rhyming over tracks but also barking expression over explosive beats. Production here—by Swizz Beatz, PK, DJ Shok, Dame Grease—is mostly stripped-down, pure high-tech drum machine and synthesizer combinations that are sure to inspire emotional and adrenal responses in listeners. Although DMX is no new-jack, he is a part of a no-frills new breed of MCs that hold nothing back on the

microphone; emphasis is on emotion rather than on wordbending. Standout cuts include "Blackout," with guest appearances from fellow hip-hop heavyweights the Lox and Jay-Z; "Coming From," a duet with the queen of hip-hop/R&B, Mary J. Blige, which stuns the ears with a haunting piano loop; "The Omen," a bout with the devil featuring the demonic Marilyn Manson on the hook; and the opening cut on side B, "Slippin,'" an introspective look inside DMX's struggle to stay on top of his art while dealing with the perils of his reality. This is a very spiritual album, a testimony to one artist's struggle with the manifestations of good and evil. The final cut, "Ready to Meet Him," a conversation between DMX and his god, punctuates this realness. —*Michael Di Bella*

… And Then There Was X / Dec. 21, 1999 / Def Jam ✦✦✦✦
Though it's DMX's third album in two years, *… And Then There Was X* doesn't show much sign of burnout. True, it's similar to his last, which balanced new school gangsta tracks ("The Professional," "Make a Move") with a couple that question the inevitable trappings that come with success ("Fame," "One More Road to Cross"). And the productions by Swizz Beats, P. Killer Trackz, and Shok—all part of Ruff Ryder Productions, Inc.—are heavily synthesized and occasionally melodramatic, just like both of his previous albums. Even when Swizz Beats' usually reliable productions fall through, DMX brings it all back with his tough rhymes and inventive wordplay. He's still torn between the thug life and spiritual concerns (even including a long prayer in the liner notes), but the most exciting tracks on *… And Then There Was X* are good-time joints like "Party Up" and "What's My Name?" —*John Bush*

The Great Depression / Sep. 2001 / Uptown/Universal ✦✦✦
Four albums into this career, DMX begins to show signs of exhaustion on *The Great Depression*, where he sometimes seems to approach his songs as routinely as he would one of his films. The rapper-turned-actor has always been dramatic, perhaps never more so than on his impressive debut, where he embodied late-'90s inner-city machismo to a tee. He's just as dramatic here, though much less effective, exploring a number of sympathetic themes such as his grandmother's sad passing away ("I Miss You"), his thinning fan base ("When I'm Nothing"), his perennial adversaries ("I'm a Bang"), his conflicted relationship with God ("A Minute for Your Son"), and, as always, his partly imaginary legion of critics, rivals, and haters (pretty much every other song). Not much of this is new territory for DMX, who tends to repeat himself on every album, as if he'd said everything he's possible of saying on his explosive debut. While this repetition gets tiresome for those who've heard a few of his albums, it's not so unfavorable when it comes to trademark anthems like "Who We Be" and "We Right Here." Very much modeled after previous DMX rallying cries like "Ruff Ryder Anthem" and "What's My Name?," this pair of hard-hitting Black Key productions features DMX at his spirited best. Elsewhere, though, not even an impressive lineup of producers (Swizz Beatz, Dame Grease, Just Blaze, Bink, and P.K.) nor a few unusual ventures (the near-literal interpolation of Stephanie Mills' "What Cha Gonna Do With My Lovin'" and the wounded emoting of "I Miss You") can liven the by-the-script sense of *The Great Depression*, the first omen of DMX's inevitable descent. —*Jason Birchmeier*

Do or Die

f. 1995, Chicago, IL
Group / Hip-Hop, Gangsta Rap, Hardcore Rap
Chicago's Do or Die gained a hit with their first single, "Po Pimp." Released on a tiny Chicago label, the track became a local hit and sparked the group's signing by Houston's Rap-A-Lot Records. Given a wide release in the summer of 1996, the single hit number 22, increasing the buzz for a full-length from the group. In September of that year, *Picture This* was released on Rap-A-Lot. Do or Die returned to action in the spring of 1998, releasing their second album, *Headz or Tailz. Victory* followed two years later. —*John Bush*

● **Picture This** / Sep. 3, 1996 / Neighborhood Watch/R-A-L/Noo Trybe ✦✦✦✦
Do or Die's 1996 full-length debut *Picture This* followed the success of their single "Po Pimp" with more bass-heavy gangsta grooves and more of Tung Twista's smooth, rapid-fire rapping. Along with "Po Pimp," "Money Flow," "Kill or Be Killed," "Shut 'Em Down," and "Paperchase" are some of the album's best examples of the group's soul-inflected gangsta rap. —*Heather Phares*

Headz or Tailz / Apr. 7, 1998 / Rap-A-Lot ✦✦✦
Even though they're from the Midwest, traditionally not one of the strongholds of gangsta rap, Do or Die isn't one of the most distinctive gangsta

outfits. They fall prey to the same pimp-money-blunts-'n'-hoes formula that plagues gangsta rap, which might make the disc a little frustrating even to aficionados of the style. However, this time they have managed to come up with a triad of fine singles with "Still Pop Pimpin'," "Who Am I," and "Nobody's Home." They're not quite enough to make the filler excusable, but they might be enough to make *Headz or Tailz* worth purchasing by hardcore gangsta fanatics. — *Stephen Thomas Erlewine*

Victory / Mar. 14, 2000 / Rap-A-Lot ♦♦♦
A sense of soul doesn't often find its way into the often thuggish sound of gangsta rap, with the one notable exception of Bone Thugs-N-Harmony. And much like that unique Cleveland group, Do or Die approach gangsta rap ideology with a quick-paced rapping style, an upliftingly soulful feel, and plenty of harmony. For example, on *Victory*'s lead single, "Can U Make It Hot," the bounce beats feature some uplifting strings, and the trio spew a rather melodic style of rapping, with Mo Unique laying down a nice R&B chorus—it's a quite uncanny mix. Some of the songs on the album make this mix work wonderfully, such as the anthem-worthy "Bounce for Me," even if they sound a bit too contrived. So don't be intimidated by the trio's name, though they may pose as gangstas, naming their songs "Thuggin It Out" and "If U Scared," for example. This isn't the sort of ugly grime or sleazy pimping that one finds on the usual gangsta album; instead, most should find Do or Die's sound surprisingly accessible and unintimidating. They can pose all they want, but when they make such harmonious and soulful music, they come off a bit too refined for their own good. Yet in the end, when one looks past their near-paradoxical stance, their music does feature some nice melodic hooks that should score them substantial appeal. — *Jason Birchmeier*

The D.O.C.

b. Texas
Vocals / Gangsta Rap, West Coast Rap
After the release of his debut album, the career of Texas-born rapper the D.O.C. was shattered by a car crash that almost took his life. Although he could no longer rap like he used to, his former producer Dr. Dre featured the rapper on his groundbreaking album *The Chronic*, which built on the foundation laid by the D.O.C.'s *No One Can Do It Better*. He was also featured on Snoop Doggy Dogg's *Doggystyle*. The D.O.C. returned in early 1996 with *Helter Skelter*, his first album in nearly seven years. The album received mixed reviews and failed to earn a large audience, leaving the charts a few months after its release. — *Stephen Thomas Erlewine*

★ **No One Can Do It Better** / 1989 / Ruthless ♦♦♦♦♦
An early landmark of West Coast rap, the D.O.C.'s debut album *No One Can Do It Better* remains sorely underheard today, largely because the car crash that destroyed the rapper's voice also cut short his time in the spotlight before he'd had a chance to really cement his reputation among the general public. When *No One Can Do It Better* was released, the West Coast had just started to break nationally, thanks to the gangsta movement, and wasn't known for much outside of N.W.A and Ice-T. In the D.O.C., however, the scene found a new level of credibility: a highly skilled battle rhymer who could hold his own with any East Coast lyrical virtuoso. Though his chops are rarely mentioned in the same breath, the D.O.C. clearly ranks up near the master technicians of the era, Rakim and Big Daddy Kane; while he may not be as smooth as the former or as spectacularly wordy as the latter, he has a distinctively rough, commanding voice and an aggressive, hard-hitting flow all his own. There's another important reason to hear *No One Can Do It Better*: it's where Dr. Dre's legend as a producer really begins. *Straight Outta Compton* notwithstanding, Dre truly comes into his own here, crafting funky, varied tracks that blend synths, drum machines, samples, and live instrumentation. You won't hear anything that resembles a blueprint for *The Chronic*, but sonically they're as rich as anything around at the time. Both Dre and the D.O.C. are remarkably consistent throughout, so special mention has to go to the rousing N.W.A posse cut "The Grand Finale," which even features DJ Yella on live drums. It's a shame that the D.O.C. never got the chance for a proper follow-up, but in *No One Can Do It Better*, he at least has one undeniable masterpiece. — *Steve Huey*

Helter Skelter / Jan. 23, 1996 / Giant ♦♦♦
After releasing his debut album *No One Can Do It Better*, the D.O.C. suffered a severe car accident which did irreparable damage to his vocal chords. It left

him with a thin, raspy voice that was simply unusable for several years. In 1996 he made his comeback with *Helter Skelter*, an album that illustrated how ragged his voice was. While the backing tracks to *Helter Skelter* are solid, if generic, gangsta rap recorded by a live band, the D.O.C. simply doesn't have enough power to make the songs interesting. Sometimes the harsh growl of his voice sounds threatening, giving the tracks a menacing power. Too often, the D.O.C. simply sounds tired and worn. It's admirable that he attempted the comeback, but the musical results don't justify the effort. — *Stephen Thomas Erlewine*

Dr. Dooom

Vocals, Producer / Underground Rap
Projected to be the successor for Kool Keith's Dr. Octagon project, Dr. Dooom actually released just one record, 1999's *First Come, First Served*, on the Funky Ass label. Subsequently Keith released records as Kool Keith. —*John Bush*

● **First Come, First Served** / May 4, 1999 / Funky Ass ♦♦♦♦
One of the better albums in the Kool Keith catalog, *First Come, First Served* is further evidence that the volatile MC works best with an alterego—in this case Dr. Dooom, a serial killer with a fondness for cannibalism, pet rats, and Flintstones vitamins. During the album's opening skit, Dr. Dooom symbolically kills off Keith's best-known persona, Dr. Octagon, signaling Keith's desire to move away from the alternative audience who embraced that album and back to his roots in street-level hip-hop (as he makes clear on "Mental Case"). Dr. Dooom is accordingly darker and more violent, but way too far out to fulfill Keith's aspirations; he simply doesn't fit into hip-hop's obsession with realism. Of course, that hardly means the album is a failure. *First Come, First Served* is one of his strongest outings as a pure MC; it's full of complex, idiosyncratic flows that sometimes sound like he's ignoring the beat, yet come together in the end anyway ("No Chorus" and "Dr. Dooom's in the Room" are two terrific examples). At least half the album seems to be set in the ghetto housing project Dr. Dooom calls home, and even if it isn't as bleak as the inside of his "Body Bag"-filled "Apartment 223," it's still a chaotic place to live. Guests Jacky Jasper and Motion Man partner with Keith as the nightmarish "Neighbors Next Door" and the brothers from the "Housing Authority," respectively; the left-field disses of "You Live at Home With Your Mom" are another highlight. The second half loses a bit of focus as it gets away from the concept, but overall it's pretty consistent, thanks to returning producer KutMasta Kurt—who, ironically, cribs from the horror-flick style of Dr. Octagon on several cuts. The album may not be on that level, but it is quite good and deserves bonus points just for the bizarre No Limit cover-art parody. — *Steve Huey*

Dr. Dre (Andre Young)

b. Feb. 18, 1965, Los Angeles, CA
Producer, Vocals, Keyboards / Gangsta Rap, G-Funk, West Coast Rap
More than any other rapper, Dr. Dre was responsible for moving away from the avant-noise and political stance of Public Enemy and Boogie Down Productions as well as the party vibes of old school rap. Instead, Dre pioneered gangsta rap and his own variation of the sound, G-funk. BDP's early albums were hardcore but cautionary tales of the criminal mind, but Dre's records with N.W.A celebrated the hedonistic, amoralistic side of gang life. Dre was never much of a rapper—his rhymes were simple and his delivery was slow and clumsy—but as a producer, he was extraordinary. With N.W.A he melded the noise collages of the Bomb Squad with funky rhythms. On his own, he reworked George Clinton's elastic funk into the self-styled G-funk, a slow-rolling variation that relied more on sound than content. When he left N.W.A in 1992, he founded Death Row Records with Suge Knight, and the label quickly became the dominant force in mid-'90s hip-hop thanks to his debut, *The Chronic*. Soon, most rap records imitated its sound, and his productions for Snoop Doggy Dogg and Blackstreet were massive hits. For nearly four years, G-funk dominated hip-hop, and Dre had enough sense to abandon it and Death Row just before the whole empire collapsed in late 1996. Dre retaliated by forming a new company, Aftermath, and while it was initially slow getting started, his bold moves forward earned critical respect.

Dre (born Andre Young, February 18, 1965) became involved in hip-hop during the early '80s, performing at house parties and clubs with the World Class Wreckin' Cru around South Central Los Angeles and making a handful of recordings along the way. In 1986, he met Ice Cube, and the two rappers began writing songs for Ruthless Records, a label started by former drug pusher Eazy-E. Eazy tried to give one of the duo's songs, "Boyz-n-the 'Hood," to HBO, a group signed to Ruthless. When the group refused, Eazy formed N.W.A—an acronym for Niggaz With Attitude—with Dre and Cube, releasing their first album in 1987. A year later, N.W.A delivered *Straight Outta Compton*, a vicious hardcore record that became an underground hit with virtually no support from radio, the press, or MTV. N.W.A became notorious for their hardcore lyrics, especially those of "Fuck tha Police," which resulted in the FBI sending a warning letter to Ruthless and its parent company, Priority, suggesting that the group should watch their step.

Most of the group's political threat left with Cube when he departed in late 1989 amid many financial disagreements. While Eazy appeared to be the undisputed leader following Cube's departure—and he was certainly responsible for the group approaching near-parodic levels with their final pair of records—the music was in Dre's hands. On both the 1990 EP *100 Miles and Runnin'* and the 1991 album *Efil4zaggin* ("Niggaz4life" spelled backward), he created dense, funky sonic landscapes that were as responsible for keeping N.W.A at the top of the charts as Eazy's comic-book lyrics. While the group was at the peak of their popularity in 1991, Dre began to make efforts to leave the crew, especially after he was charged with assaulting the host of a televised rap show in 1991. The following year, Dre left the group to form Death Row Records with Suge Knight. According to legend, Knight held N.W.A's manager at gunpoint and threatened to kill him if he refused to let Dre out of his contract.

Dre released his first solo single, "Deep Cover," in the spring of 1992. Not only was the record the debut of his elastic G-funk sound, it also was the beginning of his collaboration with rapper Snoop Doggy Dogg. Dre discovered Snoop through his stepbrother Warren G, and he immediately began working with the rapper—Snoop was on Dre's 1992 debut, *The Chronic*, as much as Dre himself. Thanks to the singles "Nuthin' but a 'G' Thang," "Dre Day," and "Let Me Ride," *The Chronic* was a multiplatinum, Top Ten smash, and the entire world of hip-hop changed with it. For the next four years, it was virtually impossible to hear mainstream hip-hop that wasn't affected in some way by Dre and his patented G-funk. Not only did he produce Snoop's 1993 debut, *Doggystyle*, but he orchestrated several soundtracks, including *Above the Rim* and *Murder Was the Case* (both 1994), which functioned as samplers for his new artists and production techniques, and he helmed hit records such as Blackstreet's "No Diggity," among others, including a hit reunion with Ice Cube, "Natural Born Killaz." During this entire time, Dre released no new records, but he didn't need to—all of Death Row was under his control, and most of his peers mimicked his techniques.

The Death Row dynasty held strong until the spring of 1996, when Dre grew frustrated with Knight's strong-arm techniques. At the time, Death Row was devoting itself to 2Pac's label debut, *All Eyez on Me* (which featured Dre on the breakthrough hit, "California Love"), and Snoop was busy recovering from his draining murder trial. Dre left the label in the summer of 1996 to form Aftermath, declaring gangsta rap dead. While he was subjected to endless taunts from his former Death Row colleagues, their sales slipped by 1997 and Knight was imprisoned on racketeering charges by the end of the year. Dre's first album for Aftermath, the various-artists collection *Dr. Dre Presents . . . The Aftermath* received considerable media attention, but the record didn't become a hit, despite the presence of his hit single, "Been There Done That." Even though the album wasn't a success, the implosion of Death Row in 1997 proved that Dre's inclinations were correct at the time. Both *2001* and its companion instrumental version followed in 1999. —*Stephen Thomas Erlewine*

★ **The Chronic** / Dec. 15, 1992 / Death Row ✦✦✦✦✦
With its stylish, sonically detailed production, Dr. Dre's 1992 solo debut *The Chronic* transformed the entire sound of West Coast rap. Here Dre established his patented G-funk sound: fat, blunted Parliament/Funkadelic beats, soulful backing vocals, and live instruments in the rolling bass lines and whiny synths. What's impressive is that Dre crafts tighter singles than his inspiration George Clinton—he's just as effortlessly funky, and he has a better feel for a hook, a knack that improbably landed gangsta rap on the pop charts. But none of *The Chronic's* legions of imitators were as rich in personality, and that's due in large part to Dre's monumental discovery, Snoop Doggy Dogg. Snoop livens up every track he touches, sometimes just

by joining in the chorus—and if *The Chronic* has a flaw, it's that his relative absence from the second half slows the momentum. There was nothing in rap quite like Snoop's singsong, lazy drawl (as it's invariably described), and since Dre's true forte is the producer's chair, Snoop is the signature voice. He sounds utterly unaffected by anything, no matter how extreme, which sets the tone for the album's misogyny, homophobia, and violence. The Rodney King riots are unequivocally celebrated, but the war wasn't just on the streets; Dre enlists his numerous guests in feuds with rivals and ex-bandmates. Yet *The Chronic* is first and foremost a party album, rooted not only in '70s funk and soul, but also that era's blue party comedy, particularly Dolemite. Its comic song intros and skits became prerequisites for rap albums seeking to duplicate its cinematic flow; plus, Snoop and Dre's terrific chemistry ensures that even their foulest insults are cleverly turned. That framework makes *The Chronic* both unreal and all too real, a cartoon and a snapshot. No matter how controversial, it remains one of the greatest and most influential hip-hop albums of all time. —*Steve Huey*

Concrete Roots / Sep. 20, 1994 / Triple X ✦✦
Released after Dr. Dre became the most popular rapper of the '90s, *Concrete Roots* offers a selection of his earliest material which is strictly pedestrian old school material. It would be several years before Dre developed a distinctive style, so most of this music is surprisingly generic and unengaging—the album is for dedicated fans only. —*Stephen Thomas Erlewine*

First Round Knock Out / May 21, 1996 / Triple X ✦
Containing a variety of rap and R&B that Dr. Dre produced in the 1980s and '90s—both before and after N.W.A—*First Round Knock Out* reminds us just how musical a producer he has been, whether working with Rose Royce or Snoop Doggy Dogg. Most of the songs themselves are decent but not remarkable; however, Dre is so imaginative in the studio that even average material comes alive. The pre-N.W.A Dre is represented by World Class Wreckin' Cru tracks like "Juice" and "The Fly," both examples of the high-tech sound L.A. rappers were known for in the early to mid-1980s. That style (which was indebted to both Kraftwerk's innovations and Afrika Bambaataa's "Planet Rock") is a long way from the hardcore gangster rap of Kokane's "Nickel Slick Nigga," the D.O.C.'s previously unreleased "Bridgette" (a sexually explicit song Atlantic wouldn't release when it was recorded in 1989), and Dre's duet with Snoop, "Deep Cover." These tunes aren't in a class with Dre's work with N.W.A, but his studio skills never fail to impress. —*Alex Henderson*

Back N Tha Day / Sep. 24, 1996 / Blue Dolphin ✦
Back N Tha Day is one of many budget-priced compilations of Dr. Dre's early, pre-N.W.A material but it *is* different than the rest. Instead of relying on Dre's occasionally awkward old school material, the compilation consists entirely of mid-'90s remixes of his old school recordings, adding two previously unreleased tracks as enticement for hardcore fans, who probably gave up following these scatter-shot releases long ago. Since Dre's old school, early-'80s recordings are primarily of historical interest anyway, *Back N Tha Day* qualifies as the most exploitive release among legions of exploitive records. —*Stephen Thomas Erlewine*

Dr. Dre Presents . . . The Aftermath / Nov. 26, 1996 / Aftermath/Interscope ✦✦✦
Dr. Dre shifted directions drastically halfway through 1996, leaving Death Row Records and abandoning gangsta rap, claiming that he had "Been There, Done That." So, Dre founded a new record label, Aftermath, and built an artist roster consisting entirely of new, unproven talent. He also decided not to concentrate on rap, signing urban R&B acts as well as hip-hop. Aftermath's initial release was the various-artists compilation *Dr. Dre Presents . . . The Aftermath* and one listen proves that Dre wasn't kidding when he said he wasn't interested in gangsta rap anymore. There are a number of rappers on *The Aftermath*, even a handful of hardcore rappers, but nothing fits into the standard G-funk template. The true revelation of the album is Dre's skill for urban R&B and soul, all of which sounds fresh and exciting compared to several of the fairly pedestrian hip-hop tracks. Despite the success of these urban productions, none of the actual performers make much of an impact—the tracks are impressive only because it demonstrates Dre's musical versatility and skill. In fact, the two tracks that really stand out—Dre's stately, sexy "Been There, Done That" and the powerful "East Coast / West Coast Killas," which features cameos by B Real, KRS-One, Nas, and RBX—are a combination of terrific production and personality, which is usually what results in great singles. But that doesn't mean that *The Aftermath* is a washout. Instead,

it's a promising fresh start for Dr. Dre that is full of potential and enough great music to make it a vital listen. —*Stephen Thomas Erlewine*

2001 / Nov. 16, 1999 / Aftermath ✦✦✦✦

The *Slim Shady* LP announced not only Eminem's arrival, but it established that his producer Dr. Dre was anything but passé, thereby raising expectations for *2001*, the long-anticipated sequel to *The Chronic*. It suggested that *2001* wouldn't simply be recycled *Chronic*, and, musically speaking, that's more or less true. He's pushed himself hard, finding new variations in the formula by adding ominous strings, soulful vocals, and reggae, resulting in fairly interesting recontextualizations. Padded out to 22 tracks, *2001* isn't as consistent or striking as *Slim Shady*, but the music is always brimming with character. If only the same could be said about the rappers! Why does a producer as original as Dre work with such pedestrian rappers? Perhaps it's to ensure his control over the project, or to mask his own shortcomings as an MC, but the album suffers considerably as a result. Out of all the other rappers on *2001*, only Snoop and Eminem—Dre's two great protégés—have character and while Eminem's jokiness still is unpredictable, Snoop sounds nearly as tired as the second-rate rappers. The only difference is, there's pleasure in hearing Snoop's style, while the rest sound staid. That's the major problem with *2001*: lyrically and thematically, it's nothing but gangsta clichés. Scratch that, it's über-gangsta, blown up so large that it feels like a parody. Song after song, there's a never-ending litany of violence, drugs, pussy, bitches, dope, guns, and gangsters. After a full decade of this, it takes real effort to get outraged at this stuff, so chances are, you'll shut out the words and groove along since, sonically, this is first-rate, straight-up gangsta. Still, no matter how much fun you may have, it's hard not to shake the feeling that this is cheap, not lasting, fun. —*Stephen Thomas Erlewine*

Doctor Dre (Andre Brown)

b. Dec. 5, 1963, Westbury, Long Island, NY
East Coast Rap, Hip-Hop, Party Rap

Not to be confused with the N.W.A member and multiplatinum producer of the same name, the jovial Doctor Dre (born Andre Brown) was one of the most visible members of the hip-hop community throughout the late '80s and early '90s. A former DJ at Adelphi's radio station, an ex-member of Def Jam's Original Concept ("Knowledge Me"/"Can You Feel It"), and a temporary live DJ for the Beastie Boys, Dre, along with Ed Lover, hosted the *Yo! MTV Raps* program for several years and became a hip-hop icon in the process. For thousands upon thousands of young viewers across the States, Dre and Lover were *the* faces of rap music. The duo starred together in 1993's *Who's the Man*, a hip-hop comedy about two Harlem barbers turned cops (it was the first feature directed by Ted Demme, one of *Yo! MTV Raps*' creators). The duo decided to step out on its own as a recording entity the following year, with the release of 1994's *Back Up Off Me!* Two years after that, the duo put out a book called *Naked Under Our Clothes*. Once Dre's profile waned, he went into radio broadcasting. —*Andy Kellman*

Back Up Off Me! / Nov. 8, 1994 / Relativity ✦✦

Doctor Dre and Ed Lover were always more entertaining as television personalities than rappers, and that is what makes *Back Up Off Me!* such a frustrating listen. It's evident that the two personalities work off of each other well, but their charisma is buried underneath uninspired backing tracks and lame rhymes. The simple fact is, neither of them are particularly good rappers, so they can't save the weak music. —*Stephen Thomas Erlewine*

Dr. Jeckyll & Mr. Hyde

f. 1981, Harlem, NY **db.** 1987
Group / Old School Rap

Andre Harrell (Dr. Jeckyll) and Alonzo Brown (Mr. Hyde) first joined up in 1980 with Harlem World Crew, but they eventually broke from the group to form Dr. Jeckyll & Mr. Hyde, adding DJ George Llado (Scratch on Galaxy). The group became known most for their first single, "Genius Rap," which incorporated the Tom Tom Club's "Genius of Love" and hit number 31 on the black singles chart. Scattered singles—"The Challenge," "Fast Life," "Gettin' Money"—were released between 1982-1984, leading up to the group's lone album, 1985's *Champagne of Rap*. Though the duo split in 1987, Brown briefly continued to record as a solo artist. "Genius of Rap" has made appearances on old school compilations throughout the years, including the second volume of Thump's *Lowrider Jams* series, as well as the second volume of Rhino's

Street Jams series. Harrell became a major executive producer and led the successful Uptown label. —*Andy Kellman*

Dr. Octagon (Keith Thornton)

Vocals, Producer / Hip-Hop, Trip-Hop, Electronica, Underground Rap

After single-handedly redefining "warped" as the mind and mouth behind the Bronx-based Ultramagnetic MC's, "Kool" Keith Thornton—aka Rhythm X, aka Dr. Octagon, aka Dr. Dooom, aka Mr. Gerbik—headed for the outer reaches of the stratosphere with a variety of solo projects. A onetime psychiatric patient at Bellevue, Keith's lyrical thematics remained as freeflowing here as they ever were with the NY trio, connecting up complex meters with fierce, layers-deep metaphors and veiled criticisms of those who "water down the sound that comes from the ghetto." His own debut single, "Earth People" by Dr. Octagon, was quietly released in late 1995 on the San Francisco-based Bulk Recordings, and the track spread like wildfire through the hip-hop underground, as did the subsequent self-titled full-length released the following year. Featuring internationally renowned DJ Q-Bert (also of the Invisibl Skratch Piklz) on turntables, as well as the Automator and DJ Shadow behind the boards, *Dr. Octagonecologyst*'s left-field fusion of sound collage, fierce turntable work, and bizarre, impressionistic rapping found audiences in the most unlikely of places, from hardcore hip-hop heads to jaded rock critics. Although a somewhat sophomoric preoccupation with body parts and scatology tended to dominate the album, Keith's complex weave of associations and shifting references is quite often amazing in its intricacy.

The record found its way to the U.K.-based abstract hip-hop imprint Mo'Wax (for whom Shadow also recorded) in mid-1996 and was licensed by the label for European release (Mo'Wax also released a DJ-friendly instrumental version of the album titled, appropriately, *The Instrumentalyst: Octagon Beats*). The widespread popularity of the album eventually landed Keith at Geffen splinter Dreamworks in 1997; the label gave *Dr. Octagonecologyst* its third release mid-year, adding a number of bonus cuts. In early 1999, however, Keith's alterego Dr. Dooom unfortunately "killed off" Dr. Octagon on the opening track of the 1999 album *First Come, First Served* (released on Thornton's own Funky Ass label). Kool Keith signed to Ruffhouse/MCA for his second album under *that* alias, 1999's *Black Elvis/Lost in Space*. Records released as Kool Keith followed in 2000 (*Matthew*) and 2001 (*Spankmaster*), while the 2002 collaboration *Gene* appeared as KHM (Kool Keith plus H-Bomb and Marc Live). —*Sean Cooper*

★ **Dr. Octagonecologyst [Dr. Octagon]** / May 6, 1996 / DreamWorks ✦✦✦✦✦

It's hard to exaggerate the role that Kool Keith's debut solo album as Dr. Octagon played in revitalizing underground hip-hop. It certainly didn't bring the scene back to life single-handedly, but it attracted more attention than any nonmainstream rap album in quite a while, thanks to its inventive production and Keith's bizarre, free-associative rhymes. *Dr. Octagonecologyst* represented the first truly new, genuine alternative to commercial hip-hop since the Native Tongues' heyday. It appealed strongly to alternative audiences who'd grown up with rap music, but simply hadn't related to it since the rise of gangsta. Moreover, it predated seminal releases by Company Flow, Black Star, and the Jurassic 5, helping those groups get the attention they deserved, and reinvented Keith as a leader of the new subterranean movement. As if that weren't enough, the album launched the career of Dan the Automator, one of the new underground's brightest producers, and shed some light on the burgeoning turntablist revival via the scratching fireworks of DJ Q-Bert. The Automator's futuristic, horror-soundtrack production seemed to bridge the gap between hip-hop and the more electronic-oriented trip-hop (which has since narrowed even more), and it's creepily effective support for Keith's crazed alterego. Dr. Octagon is an incompetent, time-traveling, possibly extraterrestrial surgeon who pretends to be a female gynecologist and molests his patients and nurses. The concept makes for some undeniably juvenile (and, arguably, hilarious) moments, but the real focus is Keith's astounding wordplay; it often seems based on sound alone, not literal meaning, and even his skit dialogue is full of non sequiturs. Keith has since lost his taste for the album, tiring of hearing it compared favorably to his subsequent work, and complaining that the only new audience he gained was white. However, it's the best musical backing he's ever had (especially the brilliant singles "Earth People" and "Blue Flowers"), and even if he's since explored some of these themes ad nauseam, *Dr. Octagonecologyst* remains as startling and original as the day it was released. —*Steve Huey*

The Instrumentalyst: Octagon Beats / Dec. 9, 1996 / DreamWorks ✦✦✦
This is essentially the entire *Dr. Octagon* album sans vocals and slightly remixed. If any other artist released an album such as this it would be considered throwaway trash...something for the hardcore fans. But Dan the Automator's backing tracks are so fresh and original, it's actually nice to just hear the beats minus the rhymes. —*Kembrew McLeod*

tha Dogg Pound

Group / G-Funk, West Coast Rap, Gangsta Rap

Though Dr. Dre, Snoop Dogg, and 2Pac may have stolen the spotlight, tha Dogg Pound played an important role in the success of Suge Knight's Death Row empire before the duo moved on to solo careers. Dogg Pound members Daz Dillinger and Kurupt aided in the success of the both Dr. Dre's *The Chronic* (1992) and Snoop Dogg's *Doggystyle* (1993) before finally getting the chance to work on their own album, *Dogg Food* (1995). Following their solo release, tha Dogg Pound remained prolific as both Daz and Kurupt went on to record solo albums, the former also producing a number of tracks for 2Pac's *All Eyez on Me* (1996) and Snoop's *Tha Doggfather* (1996). Unfortunately, the duo's lack of substantial commercial success and the subsequent downfall of Death Row brought about tha Dogg Pound's demise at the end of the '90s, and Daz and Kurupt decided to concentrate on their respective solo careers.

In the beginning, Daz and Kurupt were two of several artists on the Death Row roster. Both made minor contributions to Dre's *The Chronic* (1992) before making substantially larger contributions to Snoop's *Doggystyle* (1993). In fact, their omnipresence on Snoop's album spawned the opportunity to capitalize on that album's success; it was no surprise, then, when Death Row tagged Daz and Kurupt as Snoop protégés, tagging them tha Dogg Pound for promotional reasons. Granted, Snoop played a large role in tha Dogg Pound, as did Nate Dogg, but with the release of *Dogg Food* (1995), it was undeniably clear that Daz and Kurupt needed no mentoring. Unfortunately, *Dogg Food* didn't match the success of preceding Death Row releases; it spawned two minor hits—"Let's Play House" and "New York, New York," featuring Nate Dogg and Snoop, respectively—yet for the most part, the album was considered a slight disappointment. Following *Dogg Food*, Daz and Kurupt both went on to work on solo albums—*Retaliation, Revenge & Get Back* (1998) and *Kuruption!* (1998), respectively—that were even less successful than *Dogg Food* in terms of record sales.

By 1998, Death Row's reign had long ended, and few saw the post-2Pac remnants as being relevant, partly explaining the loss of interest in tha Dogg Pound during the mid- to late '90s. The duo were also criticized for being second-rate relative to the other Death Row artists, a perhaps unfair comparison. Either way, it wasn't long before Daz and Kurupt embarked on full-fledged solo careers. Kurupt had modest success with his *Tha Streetz Iz a Mutha* (1999) while Daz dropped off the radar and released *R.A.W.* (1999). Yet after Dre's return in 2000 and the steady West Coast rap renaissance that began as a result, Death Row dug through their vaults—as they had done for similar Snoop and 2Pac releases—assembling what would eventually surface as tha Dogg Pound's *2002* (2001). The album featured appearances by the likes of 2Pac, Xzibit, Nate Dogg, a remix of Jay-Z's "Change the Game" featuring the Roc-A-Fella clique, and a Dr. Dre-produced lead single, "Just Doggin." —*Jason Birchmeier*

● **Dogg Food** / Oct. 31, 1995 / Death Row ✦✦✦
Before the release of tha Dogg Pound's debut album, *Dogg Food*, various conservative organizations attacked the record for being exceedingly violent and vulgar, pressuring Warner Brothers not to release the album. Not only did the company agree, it also sold off all of its interests in Interscope Records. Of course, that didn't stop the album from being released—Interscope signed a distribution deal with Priority Records. It's ironic that *Dogg Food* caused so much controversy, because, musically, the album is a very conservative piece of gangsta rap. Essentially, *Dogg Food* is the third rewrite of Dr. Dre's *The Chronic*, following Snoop Doggy Dogg's *Doggystyle* and the *Murder Was the Case* soundtrack. Even though Dr. Dre is only listed as an executive producer, his influence is all over the album, as Dat Nigga Daz faithfully reproduces all of the elements of Dre's trademark G-funk style—slow, loping beats, deep, elastic rhythms, the occasional wail from a female singer, and layers of cheap, whiny synthesizers. Not only is the music numbingly familiar, the lyrics are pedestrian as well, chronicling the typical complaints and fantasies of

gangsta rap, which would have been fine if Dat Nigga Daz and Kurupt were compelling rappers with a distinctive style of their own. But they're not—they're monotonous and predictable, never once breathing life into the material. Three years after *The Chronic*, neither Dr. Dre nor his protégés have found a way to expand on his groundbreaking work. —*Stephen Thomas Erlewine*

Dillinger & Young Gotti / May 1, 2001 / DPG ✦✦✦
In the wake of all that has transpired in the saga of Death Row Records, Daz Dillinger and Kurupt are two of the only artists to come out unscathed. While Suge Knight was sentenced to jail time and 2Pac was murdered, Daz and Kurupt laid low for several years after the release of their 1995 album *Dogg Food*. In 2001, with a new name and a new label, the artists formerly known as tha Dogg Pound are back with more of that West Coast G-funk that made Death Row famous in the first place. Daz openly flaunts his gang affiliation on "DPG" while Xzibit makes a cameo on the stellar track "Gangsta-Like." For the most part, DPG has put together a winning package of G-funk that is far from fresh but still entertaining. A lot has happened since Daz' and Kurupt's heyday with Death Row, but this album proves that the more things change, the more they stay the same. —*Jon Azpiri*

2002 / Jul. 31, 2001 / Death Row ✦✦✦
Yet another of Death Row's vault releases, tha Dogg Pound's *2002* follows the precedent set by Snoop Dogg's *Dead Man Walkin'* and 2Pac's *Until the End of Time*, both of which were released a few months before this album. Like those albums, *2002* compiles a disparate collection of leftover tracks, in this case culled from Daz Dillinger and Kurupt's never-finished sophomore release. As tempting as it is, though, to dismiss this album as the yet another exploitative attempt by Suge Knight to make it seem as if Death Row was somehow still relevant in the 21st century, *2002* actually deserves some recognition. Leftover vault recordings or not, there are a few wonderful moments on *2002*. In fact, there are enough standout moments that this album actually challenges the duo's mediocre *Dogg Food* for the status of being a better album. In particular, the Dr. Dre-produced "Just Doggin" just may be tha Dogg Pound's career pinnacle—a straightforward song featuring Nate Dogg on the hook and a slightly out-of-the-ordinary pre-*2001* Dre beat that carries the song for almost five wonderful minutes. Besides this impressive song, *2002* also offers "Every Single Day," noteworthy for its wild wah-wah guitar-driven beat, in addition to a better than average performance by Snoop on not one but two verses. Then there's an out-of-place yet no doubt welcome collaboration with Jay-Z, Beanie Sigel, and Memphis Bleek on a remix of "Change the Game," and there's also the standout album-opening "Roll Wit Us" and notable yet uninspired appearances by Xzibit and 2Pac. Besides these numerous highlights, there are a number of unmemorable songs that are at best on par with much of what's found on *Dogg Food*. In the end, *2002* is worth picking up for the aforementioned highlights if you're a West Coast G-funk fan, especially if you enjoyed *Dogg Food*, even if much of the remaining album is admittedly disparate. —*Jason Birchmeier*

Nate Dogg (Nathaniel Dawayne Hale)

b. Los Angeles, CA

Vocals, Producer / G-Funk, Neo-Soul, West Coast Rap

He's known as the soul man of G-funk, and before his first album had ever been released, Nate Dogg made appearances on several huge hits: "Regulate" with Warren G, 2Pac's *All Eyez on Me*, and the soundtrack to *Murder Was the Case*. The cousin of Snoop Dogg, Nate was born in Los Angeles and began working with Warren early in the '90s. By 1994, the duo hit number two on the pop charts with "Regulate," from the soundtrack to *Above the Rim*. The two later severed their relationship, with Warren going on to multiplatinum success. Nate scored again in 1996 with "Never Leave Me Alone," featuring Snoop, and released his debut album, *G-Funk Classics, Vols. 1 & 2*, early the following year on Breakaway. —*John Bush*

G-Funk Classics, Vols. 1 & 2 / Jul. 21, 1998 / Breakaway ✦✦✦
Two years is an eternity in hip-hop, especially for rappers arriving at the tail end of a trend. Such is the case with Nate Dogg, a talented rapper who first made waves on Warren G's seminal "Regulate" in 1993, and then signed a solo contract shortly afterward. If he had been able to deliver his debut album, *G-Funk Classics, Vol. 1*, in 1995/early 1996 like he intended, he may have been a major star. Instead, the album was shelved due to legal problems at Death Row Records, and he wasn't able to release the album until the

summer of 1998. By that time, the record had become a double-disc set named *G-Funk Classics, Vols. 1 & 2*, and perhaps more importantly, gangsta rap, particularly West Coast G-funk, had diminished in popularity. It was a case of bad timing, pure and simple—*G-Funk Classics* sounded dated, and its bloated running length made it seem even more of a dinosaur than it actually was. And that's all too bad, because Nate Dogg has a wonderful, jazzy vocal style that's terrific to hear. If he had fresh productions, his raps would have sounded kinetic and alive; instead, they sound like canned gangsta rap. The album would have been helped immeasurably by a little editing—there are a handful of great cuts scattered across these two discs, but it takes too much effort to track them down. That, combined with the delay, prevented *G-Funk Classics* from being the explosive debut it could have been. —*Stephen Thomas Erlewine*

The Prodigal Son / Sep. 19, 2000 / KTR ✦✦✦
Released six years after Nate Dogg's breakthrough success with Warren G on "Regulate," the follow-up to his *G-Funk Classics, Vols. 1 & 2* album, *The Prodigal Son*, suffers mostly from a lack of major-label polish. Sure, it features some talented collaborators, including Daz Dillinger, Warren G, Snoop Dogg, and Kurupt contributing some rhymes. However, the contributions seem rather unfocused and a bit lackadaisical; in fact, it sounds like the sort of album that was put together modestly on weekends or over the course of a session or two. Yet even if *The Prodigal Son* doesn't have the flair of a Snoop album or the meticulousness of a Dr. Dre production, it's still a fine album, full of wonderfully soulful and harmonious Nate Dogg vocals and some well-crafted G-funk grooves. Furthermore, the producers on this album—Nate, Warren G, Daz, Soopafly, Teddy Riley—all deserve a substantial amount of acclaim for their by-the-books G-funk, even if it sounds unpolished and a bit quickly thrown together. Unfortunately, without a glossy video, a blatant radio single, or a major label marketing budget, this album stands as a possible cult favorite for G-funk fanatics who already own all the Dre-, Snoop-, and Dogg Pound-affiliated albums and want to dig a little deeper. —*Jason Birchmeier*

● **Music & Me** / Dec. 4, 2001 / Elektra ✦✦✦✦
Despite being a true clutch player throughout the '90s and into the early 2000s, it took Nate Dogg nearly a decade to record an impressive album. It's hard to believe. After all, nearly everything Nate touched turned to gold, whether it was G-funk classics like Warren G's "Regulate" and tha Dogg Pound's "Let's Play House" or latter-day West Coast anthems like Snoop Dogg's "Lay Low" and Dr. Dre's "The Next Episode." Nate even expanded his Midas touch beyond Cali, scoring hits down South with Ludacris ("Area Codes") and out East with Fabolous ("Can't Deny It"). If rap had a true clutch player in 2001, it was Nate: if you needed a hit, you put Nate on the hook and it became a surefire hit. However, clutch player or not, Nate still hadn't recorded a successful album of his own. His previous efforts were haphazard and underfinanced. *Music & Me* is his first great album, an album on a par with his undeniable talent as a vocalist—nothing less than impressive; perhaps even peerless. Before bestowing all the praise on Nate though, it's important to recognize the contributions made by producers Megahertz, Bink, and Mel-Man—three of rap's most promising producers at the time of this album's release in late 2001. They don't craft your typical hip-hop tracks because Nate isn't your typical rapper. He doesn't rap; he sings. Therefore, he needs songs that are actually songs and not just beats to drop rhymes over. And these producers deliver just that: developed songs. The many guest rappers—Snoop, Kurupt, Dre, Ludacris, Xzibit, Fabolous, and more—no doubt help the album, though. They keep the album from getting too smooth and too smoked out; they "keep it G.A.N.G.S.T.A.," as Nate would say. And, yeah, he surely represents the gangsta rather than the silky ladies' man on this album. Every song Nate sings is about females to some extent, but he's not whispering sweet poesy into their ears. To quote the Dogg himself, "Your wife/My bitch/Your love/My trick." No apologies. That's what's great about Nate—he's got love but he's also a gangsta; he's radio friendly but he's also blunt. Rarely can you have it both ways—elegance that's not pandering. —*Jason Birchmeier*

Domino

Producer, Vocals / Urban, Hip-Hop

Domino's "Sweet Potatoe Pie" was a pop and R&B hit from his self-titled debut LP. The album was issued in December of 1993. Three years later, Domino delivered his second album, *Physical Funk*, which failed to become

as successful as its predecessor; *Dominology* followed in 1997. *D-Freaked It* marked his long-awaited follow-up in summer 2001.—*Ron Wynn*

● **Domino** / Dec. 7, 1993 / OutBurst ✦✦✦✦
Rapper Domino's scattershot/stuttering rhyming (a near-flawless imitation of early Das EFX) yielded a big hit with "Getto Jam," and is the hook for his self-titled CD. "Do You Qualify" offers a comic (if not comical) spin on a tale of mistaken identity and consensual sex, while "Money Is Everything" and "Sweet Potato Pie" provide Domino's insights into materialism and sexual conquest, and "Raincoat" is his safe sex lecture. He's not really a gangsta, satirist, or protester; Domino's songs are delivered in a deadpan, half-sung, half-spoken fashion, and he's aided by tight production from DJ Battlecat and smart samples. —*Ron Wynn*

Physical Funk / Jun. 11, 1996 / OutBurst ✦✦✦

Dorasel

Gangsta Rap, Hardcore Rap, Southern Rap

Dorasel is a convict turned rapper, signed to Rap-A-Lot Records in 2001 directly from jail. His first album, *Unleash the Beast*, is his attempt at staying clean, concentrating his efforts on something more productive. He joins fellow Rap-A-Lot artists such as Scarface, Yuk Mouth, Devin the Dude, the 5th Ward Boyz, and the Geto Boys. —*Brad Mills*

● **Unleash the Beast** / Jul. 31, 2001 / Rap-A-Lot ✦✦
At the start of hearing this album, it quickly became evident that Dorasel sounds strikingly similar to fellow labelmate Scarface. It's not so much his delivery, but more in his deep voice. After hearing the rest of the album, it became even more evident that he's just not on Scarface's level of lyricism. What really ruins this release is Dorasel's basic and overly simplistic rhymes. He puts his words together with a reckless abandon that spoils any chance of creating an interesting album. There are a few good tracks here, including the rugged "War" and the posse cut, "Shame on It," with two members of the Outlawz. The rest of the album mainly consists of danceable nightclub filler tunes. —*Brad Mills*

Double Helix

Group / Underground Rap

Fast and furious in their delivery, this underground rap duo composed of MCs Spontaneous and JON?DOE met on the Internet. One of them is from Ohio, while the other hailed from California. They now both live in California and released their first full-length album, *DNA-lysis*, in 1999. —*Brad Mills*

● **DNA-lysis** / 1999 / Indie Pennant ✦✦✦✦
Part of the novelty of Double Helix arises as a result of the odd cultural intersection that they represent—originally from Toledo, OH, the duo eventually moved to California to make their way in the recording world. Partly, it arises from their enigmatic stance and obvious, impressive lyrical innovation. For those who like their wordplay eccentric and smoldering, Spontaneous and JON?DOE provide some astounding flashes of pure verbal invention, derived from straight-up battle rhyming, but a few hyperdrive light years beyond it. If there is anything that jumps out about *DNA-lysis*, it is the fresh sense of boundlessness here: punchlines by the dozen, more references than a shelf full of encyclopedias, verses that are whole lexicons, rhapsodic flares that are impossible to catch up with. Spon, specifically, rhymes not only over the beat, but around it and through it, keeping his flow so irregular and interesting that you can't help but be drawn into its mazes, but JON?DOE, slightly more conventional, has plenty of dazzling moments as well. The tracks are kept gritty and grounded in the underground aesthetic, with dark, bottom-stubborn street beats that, on the whole, seem far more east of the Mississippi than sunny California. To be perfectly frank, it is difficult to grasp even half of what is being said. *DNA-lysis* requires several listens just to get used to the mismatched dialogue, a couple to soak in the outpouring of words, and another few to start picking out phrases and buried ideas. This is certainly something new under the sun, but it also has the occasional lapse, mainly when the pair return to well-trodden underground rap turf or flame more commercial-minded (and, it bears noting, successful) peers. Nevertheless, Double Helix is always fascinating. A real treat for dedicated hip-hop heads, the album will take some exertion on the part of the general listener. It is well worth the effort. —*Stanton Swihart*

The Down South Players

f. Florida

Group / Dirty South, Hip-Hop, Gangsta Rap

This is a rap crew from Florida made up of K-Lo, Rahming, and Six-1. Their debut album, *Now What?*, was released in 1998 on Restless Records. Their music is typical thug stuff, with quite a bit of R&B thrown in for the choruses. —*Brad Mills*

Now What? / Nov. 10, 1998 / Restless ✦
The Down South Players' first album doesn't really live up to any expectations. *Now What?* starts off all right, but it quickly becomes evident that these guys don't have much to offer lyrically, at least over a full-length album. Most of the time they have trouble staying focused on much of anything, and can't really piece together a story like some of the more skilled rappers around. With so many rappers releasing music, it's important to stand above the rest, and the Down South Players don't achieve that here. —*Brad Mills*

Downtown Science

Group / Alternative Rap, Golden Age, East Coast Rap

Downtown Science was a brief collaboration between Sam Sever (born Sam Citrin) and Bosco Money (born Kenneth Carabello) that produced one neglected album that was released on Def Jam in 1991. Apart from some light rotation enjoyed by the supporting single "If I Was," the self-titled album all but disappeared shortly after release—an unfortunate thing, since Sever's production work was just as stellar as it was on 3rd Bass' *Cactus Album*. Sever continued to do sporadic remix and production work (including a solo single for Mo'Wax and his Raiders of the Lost Art project). —*Andy Kellman*

● **Downtown Science** / 1991 / Def Jam ✦✦✦✦✦
Downtown Science is not merely an important hip-hop footnote on account of its biracial makeup, which was at the time virtually unprecedented in the rap community, nor is it merely a worthy one-shot wonder from one of genre's most fecund eras; rather, it is a shamefully neglected masterwork as forceful and hard hitting as the albums Public Enemy was making during the same period. In fact, Bosco Money, Downtown Science's wordsmith, is every bit as conscientious and commanding, if not quite as steely and polemical, as Chuck D. (And, as if in homage, the duo does a fine job absorbing the chaotic, kitchen-sink production style of the Bomb Squad on the tensile "Delta Sigma.") His rhyming style is extremely cerebral and exists on a cutting edge off of which few rappers have had the daring to dangle since, and always with a disarming stoicism that injects his words with even more authority, in both a moral and aesthetic regard. Sam Sever, fresh off acclaimed work with 3rd Bass, displayed here the reason that his production skills were in such demand at the time. Even with several nods to rap's past, he steers clear of overused samples and beats, and each track, in addition to providing a backdrop for Bosco Money's meticulous rhymes, is quite forward looking in its own right. Years before RZA or El-P carved out distinctive sonic niches with their claustrophobic, bloodshot, alien atmospheres, Sam Sever laid down jittery, paranoid sci-fi landscapes on brilliant songs like "This Is a Visit," "Radioactive," and "Room to Breathe." But the duo also broke it down old school style on "Somethin' Spankin' New," and they spin off some sweaty urban funk with "Down to a Science" and the Big Daddy Kane-like "Keep It On." The roleplaying single "If I Was" made a brief appearance on urban play lists; otherwise, *Downtown Science* somehow failed to make much of a dent, and was promptly forgotten. But fans of visionary rap would do themselves a favor in tracking down this gem. —*Stanton Swihart*

Drag-On

Vocals / East Coast Rap, Hardcore Rap

East Coast rapper Drag-On had a long and profitable history in the background of hardcore rap albums; contributing to projects like DMX's two multiplatinum albums, Ruff Ryders' *Ryde or Die, Vol. 1*, DJ Clue?'s *The Professional*, and several compilations and soundtracks. In early 2000 he released his first solo album, *Opposite of H2O*, which brought him up to the forefront and showcased his talent for laid-back, slippery grooves and thug rhymes. —*Stacia Proefrock*

● **Opposite of H2O** / Feb. 15, 2000 / Interscope ✦✦✦
While DMX remains top dog of the Ruff Ryder family hierarchy, the emergence Eve, the Lox, and in-house producer Swizz Beatz has expedited the label's transformation from a once-emerging force into a hip-hop powerhouse of the late '90s and early 2000s. The next wave of the double R movement is Drag-On, and title of his debut, *The Opposite of H2O*, refers to his self-acclaimed lyrical zest. Drag's high voltage persona but juvenile rhyme schemes are most pressing when aligned with his Ruff Ryders cohorts: "Here We Go" featuring Eve, "Niggas Die 4 Me" featuring DMX, and "Ready for War" featuring the Lox. But in a most unenviable catch-22, Drag's lyrical deficiencies are also magnified by these groupings, as inept solo tracks "Ladies 2000" and "Groundhog's Day" reveal an MC who is still very codependent on his crew. Overall, *Opposite of H2O* crashes and burns. —*Matt Conaway*

Dream Warriors

f. 1988, Toronto, Ontario, Canada

Group / Political Rap, Jazz-Rap

A pair of deft, intelligent rappers based in Toronto, King Lou and Capital Q formed Dream Warriors and released one of the finest alternative rap records of the era, 1991's *And Now, the Legacy Begins*. The pair began working together in 1989, organizing their own Beat Factory Productions with Rupert Gayle and signing to 4th & Broadway. The single "Wash Your Face in My Sink" prefaced the release of *And Now, the Legacy Begins*, and another track, "My Definition of a Boombastic Jazz Style," became an early touchstone in the jazz-rap movement. Both singles hit the Top 20 in Britain, while in their own country the LP went gold and collected a Juno award. Unfortunately, the LP title proved ironic; four long years after their debut, the duo finally returned with *Subliminal Simulation*. It was barely received at all, especially in America, and the band's final album, *The Master Plan*, wasn't even released in America. —*John Bush*

And Now, the Legacy Begins / 1991 / 4th & Broadway ✦✦✦✦✦
Part of the slew of grand early-'90s hip-hop releases that avoided tough criminal posing for inventive, witty lyrics and arrangements, *And Now the Legacy Begins* is a hilarious, entertaining rollercoaster of a record. That the Warriors themselves were Canadian shows that north of the U.S. border isn't all Rush tribute bands, as the duo plays around with any number of inspired samples and grooves, from jazz to harder-edged beats, with style and skill. The most well-known track, "My Definition of a Boombastic Jazz Style," predicts a particular pop trend well in advance, using Quincy Jones' brilliant "Soul Bossa Nova" as its base long before fellow Canuck Mike Myers made the original the Austin Powers theme song. The flow of King Lou and Capital Q, mostly the former, fits the stuttering, dramatic pace of the arrangement to a T, bringing an instant smile to the face and dance to the feet. The lead-off single, "Wash Your Face in My Sink," is an equal winner, a nutty warning to a friend who doesn't have it all together about cleanliness set to an equally playful arrangement. Things aren't always pretty, though—"U Could Get Arrested" is a slamming attack on police racism delivered with belligerent panáche. Throughout the album the Warriors show that they know their pop culture cold. As jazz-inspired producers and arrangers, the Warriors and their various studio assistants may not always be as perfectly smooth as A Tribe Called Quest or Guru, but the results are rarely anything but a joy to hear. —*Ned Raggett*

Subliminal Simulation / 1995 / EMI ✦✦
On *Subliminal Simulation*, the band tries to spread out a few ideas over the course of an album. Except for some interesting forays into spoken word and three standout tracks ("Day in Day Out," "Tricycles and Kittens," and "California Dreamin'"), Dream Warriors' jazz-rap formula has run out of steam. —*John Bush*

● **Anthology: A Decade of Hits 1988-1998** / Jun. 22, 1999 / Priority ✦✦✦✦
Though often neglected within the jazz-rap community during their brief, three-album run, Dream Warriors recorded a legion of interesting tracks, and *Anthology* does a better job than either of those albums in summarizing what made them so great. Featuring two versions of their nearest thing to a hit, "My Definition of a Boombastic Jazz Style," the album also scores with a few collaboration tracks including others in the jazz-rap royalty—"It's a Project Thing" with DJ Premier, "I've Lost My Ignorance" with Premier and Guru (i.e., Gang Starr), and "Tricycles and Kittens" with Digable Planets. Elsewhere, Dream Warriors salute their Caribbean influences with tracks like "Sound Clash" with Beenie Man and "Dem No Ready" with General Degree. It's a great look at one of the better hip-hop groups of the '90s. —*Keith Farley*

D.R.E.S. tha Beatnik (Andre Lett)

Beatbox, Vocals / Hip-Hop

Andre Lett, aka D.R.E.S. tha Beatnik (or Divine Real Essence of Sound), grew up in Philadelphia, but made a name for himself in Atlanta, GA, as a human beatbox of phenomenal talent. In the tradition of Doug E. Fresh, Biz Markie, and Rahzel, the Godfather of Noize, D.R.E.S. created with his mouth sounds that emulated those of drum machines, turntables, and samplers—the tools of hip-hop. It was a lost art, dating from an age when instantaneous, perfect home recording was a fable. But D.R.E.S. set out to prove that ability—not technology—was the real talent. In 2000 he won the Amateur World Beatbox Championships, where the judges included hip-hop legends like Rahzel and Grandmaster Flash. D.R.E.S. continued to take his adopted hometown of Atlanta by storm, and in early 2001 released the *Have Mic… Will Travel* EP on the 4 Kings label. The project was the first 100-percent beatbox album of its kind, and established D.R.E.S. tha Beatnik not only as a formidable beatboxer but also as a talented MC. In July of 2002, 4 Kings released *Have Mic… Will Travel: The Live Experience*, a recording of a D.R.E.S. show from April of that year at Atlanta's Midtown Café. It showcased the rapper's studio material while spotlighting his beatbox skills in a live setting. *—Johnny Loftus*

● **Have Mic … Will Travel** / 2001 / 4 Kings Entertainment ◆◆◆
In the grand human beatbox tradition of Doug E. Fresh, Biz Markie, and the Roots' Rahzel, Atlanta favorite D.R.E.S. tha Beatnik makes the music with his mouth, matching a knack for old school infectiousness with a formidable new school rhyme flow. The sound works best on the folk-hop groove of "Microphone Fitness Session," which finds him nimbly trading rhymes with Anthony David, whose acoustic guitar gives the song an original, rootsy vibe. The underground approach to production gets a but muddy at times, but overall this is a solid hip-hop debut. *—Bret Love*

Dru Down

Vocals / West Coast Rap, Gangsta Rap

Oakland rapper Dru Down debuted in 1994 with *Explicit Game*, scoring a hit with the single "Mack of the Year"; the record also served as a launching pad for his Bay Area cronies the Luniz. Down returned in 1996 with *Can You Feel Me*; that same year, he also made his film debut in *Original Gangstas*. *—Jason Ankeny*

Explicit Game / Sep. 6, 1994 / Relativity ◆◆◆
When *Explicit Game* came out in 1994, numerous West Coast rappers were jumping on the G-funk bandwagon and emulating the recordings that Dr. Dre and Snoop Doggy Dogg were providing for Death Row Records. There is no shortage of Dre/Snoop influence on this CD but, while other Californians were content to be clones of Death Row artists, Oakland's Dru Down was his own man. Definitely a cut above most of the G-funk efforts that came from the West Coast in 1994, *Explicit Game* draws on a variety of gangsta rap influences. In addition to the Dre/Snoop influence, one hears elements of DJ Quik, Eazy-E, and Ice Cube in his rapping style and, at times, Down hints at Cypress Hill, which was a rare example of an L.A. gangsta rap group favoring the sort of complex flow you would have expected from an East Coast group. Down's rapping isn't as consistently complex as Cypress Hill's, but the Cypress Hill influence is still one of the effective tools in his arsenal. By 1994 standards, *Explicit Game* isn't groundbreaking—Down was hardly the first person to rap about inner-city thug life on the West Coast, and this certainly isn't the first gangsta rap CD to be influenced by Dr. Dre's production style. But while Down isn't an innovator, he isn't faceless either. *Explicit Game* doesn't have the historic importance of N.W.A's *Straight Outta Compton*, Dre's *The Chronic*, or Ice-T's *Rhyme Pays*, but it's still among 1994's more memorable G-funk/gangsta rap efforts. *—Alex Henderson*

● **Can You Feel Me** / Aug. 20, 1996 / Relativity ◆◆◆◆
Can You Feel Me is a revelation, proving that Dru Down has rhyming skills far superior to most of his West Coast gangsta rap brethren. While the music isn't stylistically different from G-funk, it is catchier and more memorable than many sub-Dre productions. More importantly, Dru Down is a terrific rapper, capable of laconic phrasing like Snoop Dogg or wild, freestyle stream-of-conscious bursts of energy. Combined with the first-rate music, the lyrical skills make *Can You Feel Me* one of the finest hip-hop records of 1996. *—Leo Stanley*

Gangsta Pimpin' / Feb. 26, 2002 / C-Note ◆◆◆◆
California Bay Area gangsta rapper Dru Down takes his pimpin'-themed rhymes to another level on *Gangsta Pimpin'*, no doubt a suitable name for

this album. Much like fellow Bay Area rappers E-40 and Too Short, as well as his group, the Luniz, Dru has his mind on a few things in particular: women, money, partying, and more women—in that order. You can't help but find this album quite fun and somewhat humorous; Dru doesn't take himself too seriously, exemplified best on songs such as "Bloodsucker." Much like post-Death Row Snoop Dogg, Dru is a rather peaceful gangsta, interested in getting his pimp on and livin' large like a real hustler—in other words, the Cali dream for a G like himself. His previous albums have explored similar "gangsta pimpin'" themes, but here Dru seems a bit more amusing than usual—perhaps even cartoonish—thanks to his lighthearted attitude toward the gangsta lifestyle. *—Jason Birchmeier*

Dru Hill

f. 1995

Group / Hip-Hop, Urban, Club/Dance

High school friends Jazz, Sisqó, Nokio, and Woody formed Dru Hill in 1995; named in honor of their Baltimore neighborhood, Druid Hill Park. The rappers performed at the music-industry convention Impact '96 and were signed by Island not long after. By late 1996, Dru Hill had released its self-titled debut album, produced by Keith Sweat, Stanley Brown, and Tim "Dawg" Patterson. The single "Tell Me"—culled from the soundtrack to the film *Eddie*—became a Top Five R&B hit and later went gold; *Enter the Dru* followed in 1998. *—John Bush*

● **Dru Hill** / Nov. 19, 1996 / Island ◆◆◆◆
Rich harmonies and sleek R&B production with an abundance of vocal acrobatics are all key elements of Dru Hill's eponymous debut. Immediate comparisons to Jodeci and Boyz II Men come to mind, but what makes Dru Hill stand out from the pack is the rawness of Keith Sweat's productions. Other songs on here are of noteworthy interest only to diehard Dru Hill fanatics, but it was the monster "Tell Me" that effectively put Dru Hill near the head of R&B's class of 1996—a year that featured stellar releases by Aaliyah, Jay-Z, and several others at the peak of their games. An impressive debut and a razor-sharp clue of the great things to come. *—Rob Theakston*

Enter the Dru / Oct. 27, 1998 / Island ◆◆◆
The best of the late-'90s R&B crooning quartets ups the musical ante on their sophomore album, lacing the silky-smooth grooves with splashes of street-tough shouts that are meant to antagonize as much as they are to seduce. And for a good deal of *Enter the Dru*, the formula works. There's a gutsy edge to the songs here (especially the hard-knocking "How Deep Is Your Love") that make onetime peers like Boyz II Men sound like the soulless R&B robots they are. Even when they get all warm and cozy with Babyface on the potentially mushy "These Are the Times" (in spite the absurdity of the straight-faced line "Tear you up in little pieces/Swallow you like Reese's Pieces"), Dru Hill slice into the section of '90s soul music that crosses bedroom come-ons with classic street savvy (and nervy beats) without sounding at all whipped. *—Michael Gallucci*

Dru World Order / Nov. 26, 2002 / Def Soul ◆◆◆
After Sisqó's solo debut pushed two big hits ("Thong Song," "Incomplete") to the top of the charts, it appeared Dru Hill was going to have to recruit a replacement for its best-known name. When the group finally returned in 2002, though, it not only welcomed Sisqó back to the fold but added a member (Skola) to make the group a quintet. The third album, *Dru World Order*, proves the group possesses as much talent as any of their contemporaries in the R&B world. First of all, it's largely self-contained; Nokio produced over half the album, and much of the songwriting was kept in-house as well. And with the gospel fervor of new addition Skola, Dru Hill sounds stronger and smoother than it has in the past. The single "I Should Be…" is solid, if a little in the line of standard material for them, but "On Me" (featuring N.O.R.E.) and "Old Love" are two of the most inspired songs they've ever recorded. The songwriting tends to similar themes, as do the songs themselves, but having the most polished harmonies on the R&B block makes Dru Hill capable of smoothing over any of the rough spots on *Dru World Order*. *—John Bush*

DSP

f. London, England

Group / Underground Rap, Hip-Hop

Hip-hop producers Jonny Cuba and the Loop Professor are among the best in the steadily growing rap scene based in south London (much less greater

Britain). A few years of producing underground tapes and tracks preceded the release of their first LP, after which the duo toured with British beat kings from the Herbaliser to Nightmares on Wax. They also licensed music to a few video games before Ninja Tune released their higher-profile second LP, *In the Red*, in 2002. —*John Bush*

● **In the Red** / Jun. 25, 2002 / Ninja Tune ✦✦✦✦
The name and title evokes glitchy, distorted techno, but DSP, or Dynamic Syncopation, is a hip-hop production duo crafting tracks from the detritus of brassy late-'60s soul (think DJ Premier or a darker Jurassic 5). Their guest rappers keep up with the great productions, spraying lyrics like Apathy (on "Trife-A-Saurus Rex") or arguing over Brit-inflected speed rapping like the Phi-Life Cypher team ("My Verse 1st"). Musically, "Systematic" (with Mass Influence) and "Outtaplace" (with Dell Wells) are the big highlights, a pair of tough-minded tracks with a hint of menacing synth and chunky, three- or four-note bass lines. Back-in-the-day rapper Chill Rob G also gets a great features. Like the best of hip-hop's old school—and unlike a lot of underground rap crews—DSP understand the virtue of keeping it simple. —*John Bush*

Dungeon Family

f. 2001, Atlanta, GA
Group / Southern Rap, Alternative Rap, Dirty South
Following the remarkable success of Outkast's *Stankonia* and its subsequent touring, L.A. Reid at Arista Records gave the Atlanta duo the go-ahead to record as Dungeon Family, a rap supergroup featuring other Atlanta-based rap artists affiliated with Outkast, in hopes of capitalizing on *Stankonia's* momentum. Dungeon Family also includes members of Goodie Mob and Organized Noize, along with several other lesser-known affiliates like Cool Breeze and Backbone. The supergroup's first album, *Even in Darkness* (2001), featured production by Organized Noize and Earthtone III, in addition to rapping by the group's numerous members. —*Jason Birchmeier*

● **Even in Darkness** / Nov. 6, 2001 / Arista ✦✦✦
Truly a supergroup, Dungeon Family includes members of Outkast and Goodie Mob along with production by Organized Noize and Earthtone III (ET3)—some of the most creative rap artists the South has to offer. And since this album follows Outkast's extremely celebrated *Stankonia* album and the subsequent year of nonstop touring, it arrived with plenty of enthusiasm. However, despite the wealth of talent on *Even in Darkness*, you can't help feeling a little disappointed—the end result isn't quite equal to the sum of its parts. Don't blame the producers, though. Organized Noize and ET3 offer some of their most creative tracks to date, taking dirty South flourishes light years into the future. In particular, ET3's "Crooked Booty" and Organized Noize's "Trans DF Express" stand out, with both production teams going out of their way to bring a sci-fi, electronica-style sound to hip-hop with plenty of synth flourishes. But as wonderful as this album's production is, the songwriting is lacking. Everyone wants to rap on this album—over a dozen Family members, to be precise—but no one seems interested in writing songs. Potential hit singles like "Trans DF Express" and "6 Minutes (Dungeon Family It's On)" feature hooks, as do most of the other songs, yet the hooks don't hook you—they're simply there because the song needs one. They're added-on ornament rather than the foundation of the song, and, worse, they're gimmicky retreads of endlessly recycled motifs (interpolations of "Trans Europe Express" and "The Show"). And that's really what makes *Even in Darkness* a slightly disappointing album—there's creative production and some impressive rhyming but no "Ms. Jackson"-quality songwriting. It's as if everyone's too busy fighting over the microphone for anyone to sit down and write some well-crafted songs. Still, even if this album feels like a disappointment in the aftermath of *Stankonia's* brilliance, it's still one of the most creative rap albums of 2001. Even when these guys are giving halfhearted efforts, they're still years ahead of their peers. —*Jason Birchmeier*

Jermaine Dupri

b. Sep. 23, 1973, Atlanta, GA
Producer, Mixing, Executive Producer / Urban, Pop-Rap, Hip-Hop
Beginning with breakout success in 1992 upon the discovery of teenage rappers Kris Kross, Jermaine Dupri became one of the most consistent and all-persuasive producers of the 1990s, producing practically the entire careers of many artists on his label, So So Def Recordings (including platinum entries like Xscape and Da Brat as well as Kris Kross). In addition, Dupri provided a

steady hand to many of the most high profile R&B albums of the decade, such as TLC's *CrazySexyCool* (ten times platinum) and Mariah Carey's *Daydream* (eight times platinum).

His promising musical career began before he was even ten years old. His father, Atlanta manager Michael Mauldin, had coordinated a Diana Ross show in 1982; to the delight of concert-goers, Dupri managed to get on stage and dance along with Ross. He began performing around the country, appearing with Herbie Hancock and Cameo before he opened the New York Fresh Fest, with Run-D.M.C., Whodini, and Grandmaster Flash. Dupri's production career began in 1987, when at the age of 14 he produced and secured a record contract for the trio Silk Tymes Leather. Two years later, he formed So So Def Productions in Atlanta; by 1991 Dupri had found his first platinum act.

After seeing the pint-size rap duo Kris Kross performing in a local mall, he signed them and prepared their debut album. *Totally Krossed Out* spent two weeks at number one, and quickly sold four million copies. The pair's lack of staying power was somewhat obvious, and Dupri kept working, producing tracks on TLC's first two albums, which sold over 15 million copies between the two of them.

During 1993-1994, Dupri debuted two of his new So So Def acts, Xscape and Da Brat. Both debut albums hit platinum, thanks in large part to Dupri, and by the end of 1994, he had become one of the most respected R&B producers in the business. He worked with superstar Mariah Carey and old school rap acts like Run-D.M.C. and Whodini. Dupri's next major success came in 1997, when he took over the production for a sophomore album by a suave teenage R&B singer named Usher. The album, *My Way*, became one of the biggest of the year, selling over two million copies in its first three months of release.

Taking a page from the book of fellow superproducer Sean "Puffy" Combs (who debuted a solo project in mid-1997), Dupri returned to performing in early 1998 with a single, "The Party Continues." After collaborating with Snoop Doggy Dogg, fellow Atlanta residents Outkast, Slick Rick, Nas, and Master P, he released his debut solo album (as JD), *Life in 1472*, in July 1998. —*John Bush*

● **Jermaine Dupri Presents: Life in 1472** / Jul. 21, 1998 / So So Def ✦✦✦✦
Long before he released his first solo album, Jermaine Dupri established himself as a hip-hop hitmaker to be reckoned with. He sent Kriss Kross, Da Brat and Xscape to the top of the charts, provided hit remixes for the likes of Dru Hill and ran the So So Def label—all before he decided to launch a career with *Jermaine Dupri Presents: Life in 1472* in 1998. Like many producers, Dupri has surrounded himself with an all-star cast of guest performers, all to make the spotlight a little less harsh. As it turns out, he needn't worry about his own skills—he's a fine rapper, putting such peers as Puff Daddy to shame—but all the other rappers and singers help make *Life in 1472* feel like a real party. It's one of the few star-studded records to actually work, precisely because JD is such a talented producer—he crafts slamming tracks with real bass grooves and catchy hooks. *Life in 1472* drags a little in the middle, like almost any party, but the vibes are good throughout, and it creates some nice memories, which is enough to make it a top-notch debut. —*Stephen Thomas Erlewine*

Instructions / Oct. 2, 2001 / So So Def ✦✦✦
For his second solo album, Atlanta producer/entrepreneur Jermaine Dupri goes out of his way to yet again show just how much of a self-described "baller" he is. This mentality partly informs this album's title, *Instructions*, with JD telling what it's like at the top and how you'll never get there. As you can probably imagine, there's little modesty here and JD could care less—he seems to revel in his own vanity. Even if you wanted to, you'd have a hard time arguing with him: His So So Def label delivered popular albums and artists throughout the '90s—Kris Kross, Jagged Edge, Usher, Da Brat, Lil' Bow Wow—and he hires a star-studded roster of big-money guests for this album. Unfortunately, despite his big reputation and even bigger bank account, JD doesn't live up to his own hype on *Instructions*. His rhymes flow well but are overflowing with clichés and constant boasting. He's better at coopting rhymes than coming up with his own. Moreover, sans the standout Neptunes production ("Let's Talk About It" featuring the Clipse), it also doesn't help that JD produces nearly the entire album—he's clearly no Dr. Dre. And you can't help but wonder who's coming up with the beats, JD or coproducer Bryan-Michael Cox. Like JD himself, *Instructions* seems to rely more on its surface gloss than its substance. Even so, there are several highlights, mostly courtesy of the

guests, some of the more noteworthy moments being "Ballin' Out of Control" with Nate Dogg, "Welcome to Atlanta" with Ludacris, and "Money, Hoes & Power" with UGK. —*Jason Birchmeier*

The Dust Brothers

f. 1983, Los Angeles, CA
Group / Hip-Hop, Club/Dance, Alternative Dance
The Dust Brothers were among the preeminent producers of the 1990s, helming records for everyone from Tone-Loc to Beck to Hanson while influencing countless others with their signature cut-and-paste marriage of hip-hop and rock. Not to be confused with the British production duo the Chemical Brothers, who began their career under the same name before receiving a cease-and-desist order, the Los Angeles-based Dust Brothers were Mike Simpson and John King, who met in 1983 while working at the Pomona College radio station. They originally teamed to DJ at parties, and by the end of the decade scored a production deal with the Delicious Vinyl label. In 1989 they scored chart success producing debuts from rappers Tone-Loc (the monster hit "Wild Thing") and Young MC, but their most distinctive early work was on the Beastie Boys' groundbreaking *Paul's Boutique*, widely acclaimed among the most innovative and influential albums of the period for its pioneering use of digital sampling. In the years to follow, the Dust Brothers emerged among the most sought-after remixers and producers in the industry, working on projects for everyone from White Zombie to Technotronic to Shonen Knife; they also founded their own label, Nickel Bag (later changed to Ideal), and in 1996 helmed Beck's extraordinary *Odelay*. Branching out even further, in 1997 they produced Hanson's chart-topping "MMMBop," as well as a handful of tracks from the Rolling Stones' *Bridges to Babylon* LP. Their first full-length solo record was the score for the 1999 film *Fight Club*. —*Jason Ankeny*

● **Fight Club** / Jul. 27, 1999 / Restless ◆◆◆◆
The score to David Fincher's controversial, subversive film *Fight Club* was composed and performed by the Dust Brothers, whose production and remixing work with artists like the Beastie Boys, Beck, and the Chemical Brothers helped shape the sound of the '90s. Their music for *Fight Club* reflects their own hip-hop and dance roots, as well as the film's edgy, underground tone in its blend of trip-hop, drum'n'bass, and electro elements. —*Heather Phares*

Dynamix II

f. 1985, Miami, FL
Group / Club/Dance, Electro, Bass Music
Miami's David Noller and Scott Weiser, aka Dynamix II, are among a very few of the first wave of American electro and bass music artists to have successfully translated their old school credentials into new school relevance. The producers behind classic roof raisers "Bass Generator," "Ignition," and "Just Give the DJ a Break," Noller and Weiser carved out a signature niche in early electro with a kitchen-sink-style megamix approach, amplifying electro's energy level, deepening the low end, and playing up its robotic themes with ample vocoded vocals and squirty electronics. The group formed in 1985 after Noller, a local DJ who had recently started making tracks, met Weiser and the two began building a studio together. Noller was signed to Bass Station records at the time, and Dynamix appeared through a handful of other Miami labels before the pair set up their eponymous imprint in 1988. Although mostly of only local interest beginning in the late '80s, when electro died out in favor of rap, the group got a big boost nearly a decade later, when U.K.-based label Rephlex—owned by Richard James, aka Aphex Twin—reissued *Electro Bass Megamix: 1985 to Present*, an all-in-one-place collection of their biggest tunes from over the years, and originally released on the Joey Boy label in 1997. A stream of new material has appeared since then, including "We Are Your Future" and "The Plastic Men," both through Joey Boy. A collaboration with British producer Ian Loveday, aka Eon, also appeared through Wax Trax/TVT in 1999. Additionally, Dynamix II have remixed fellow Florida group Rabbit in the Moon and Expansion Union. Most of their LPs and singles from throughout the years remained in print. —*Sean Cooper*

● **Electro Bass Megamix: 1985 to Present** / Nov. 11, 1997 / Joey Boy ◆◆◆◆◆
An excellent Dynamix II collection and a great pointer to how exciting electro really can be, *Electro Bass Megamix* runs through every feted Dynamix II single in the mix format they were created to serve. It just wouldn't be a proper compilation without "Just Give the DJ a Break," "Feel the Bass," and "Bass Generator," though the album hits other high points with "Hypnotic 808" and "DJ's Go Berzerk." The collection was reissued in 1998 by Rephlex with the title *Electro Megamix*. —*John Bush*

E-40 (Earl Stevens)

West Coast Rap, G-Funk, Gangsta Rap

Throughout the '90s and into the next decade, E-40 led a generation of Cali Bay Area rappers and attracted a large cult following of listeners that spread from the West Coast to the South. Forty's uncanny rhyme delivery set him apart from the mainstream, as he coined a plethora of slang terms and experimented with overdubbed vocals. Moreover, his longevity and sincerity earned him many alliances, first among his Bay Area colleagues, then with Jive Records and numerous Dirty South camps, among them No Limit and Cash Money Records. Forty never did completely cross over to mainstream success, remaining mainly a regional sensation, yet influenced many over the years with his unique style and stayed true to his principles throughout. Born Earl Stevens and later host to numerous nicknames—"Charlie Hustle," "Forty Fonzarelli," "40-Watter," and more—40 grew up in the Cali Bay Area and aspired to follow in the footsteps of Too Short. Like that Oakland legend, 40 built a street presence with mix tapes long before he released his first album. After years of mix-tape hustling, he decided to start his own label, Sick Wid' It, and began extending his reach beyond the streets of Vallejo, the Bay Area city he called home. Forty entered the national rap game forcibly in 1994 with an EP (*The Mail Man*), a single ("Captain Save a Hoe"), and an album (*Federal*); he also released an album by his group, the Click (*Down and Dirty*).

These recordings made their way to the office of Jive Records, who offered to distribute the Sick Wid' It catalog. As part of the deal, in 1995 Jive rereleased the aforementioned releases as well as new albums by 40 (*In a Major Way*) and the Click (*Game Related*), and attracted substantial interest toward the Sick Wid' It camp. For 40's next album, *Tha Hall of Game* (1996), he again worked with longtime producer Mike Mosley but also collaborated with Bay Area heavyweight Ant Banks, who produced "Rappers' Ball," a successful single that featured Too Short and K-Ci.

After *Tha Hall of Game* put 40 on the brink of a mainstream breakthrough, the rapper took a year off and returned with a massive double album, *The Element of Surprise* (1998), and then another album shortly afterward, *Charlie Hustle* (1999). These two albums, unfortunately, did little to expand 40's fan base; nor did subsequent albums such as *Loyalty and Betrayal* (2000) and *Grit & Grind* (2002), though they did spawn a few popular singles ("Nah Nah," "Rep Yo City"). By this point, ten years or so after 40 had established Sick Wid' It, the rapper seemed perennially poised for breakthrough success yet, at the same time, was perfectly content with his strong following amid the West Coast and Dirty South scenes. —*Jason Birchmeier*

Federal / Jun. 28, 1994 / Jive ♦♦

E-40 began as a money-hungry gangsta rapper, as showcased here on *Federal*, with its respective Mob and Gangsta sides. Studio Ton handles the production duties, and guests including B-Legit are few and far between. The music itself is stark and definitely underground, a bit dated as well, characteristic of the early-'90s West Coast gangsta rap movement. Forty certainly improved his game in later years, thus making *Federal* somewhat of a curiosity, where it's most interesting to juxapose the youthful hustler here with the towering don of subsequent albums. —*Jason Birchmeier*

In a Major Way / Mar. 14, 1995 / Jive ♦♦♦

On *In a Major Way*, E-40 establishes himself as a West Coast kingpin after some formative previous ventures. He most notably teams up with three of the Cali Bay Area's leading rappers of the time—2Pac, Mac Mall, and Spice 1—for the posse track "Dusted 'n' Disgusted." Elsewhere he trades verses with fellow Click members B-Legit and Suga T and also Funk Mobb leader Mac Shawn. The Suga T collaboration, "Sprinkle Me," particularly stands out and would help spawn the female rapper's own solo career hereafter. Yet even

with productions by longtime 40 standbys Mike Mosely and Studio Ton, *In a Major Way* suffers from relatively poor production, more a consequence of the low budget than the artists themselves. —*Jason Birchmeier*

● **Tha Hall of Game** / Oct. 29, 1996 / Jive ♦♦♦♦

Following a few underground-quality efforts by E-40, Jive Records finally delivered its promise and bankrolled their new, unconventional signee's first hallmark album, *Tha Hall of Game*. Until this point 40 had shown enormous potential, but no matter how exceptional the rapper's style was, his recordings sounded a bit too lo-fi for universal acceptance. That's certainly not the case though with *Tha Hall of Game*, which features a long list of contributers, including several A-list producers and rappers. The standout track, and the one that introduced 40 to a legion of new fans, "Rappers' Ball" teams up the rapper with fellow Bay Area vet Too Short, hook-singer K-Ci, and an explosive Ant Banks production. Elsewhere 40 reprises his classic hit "Captain Save a Hoe" with the Click on "Captain Save Them Thoe" for all his new fans who hadn't yet heard his signature anthem, and 2Pac steals the show on "Million Dollar Spot." The full lineup of producers—Banks, Mike Mosely, Rick Rock, Tone Capone, and Studio Ton—offer some of their best, and the overall style is more G-funk than gangsta rap, a wonderful transition that suits 40's increasingly tongue-twisting style well. —*Jason Birchmeier*

The Element of Surprise / Aug. 11, 1998 / Jive ♦♦♦

It can be argued that the worst hip-hop trend in the late '90s was, not the incessant recycling of *The Chronic* (although that did grow rather tiresome), but the proliferation of double disc sets. Even if an artist has a lot to say, it's hard to fill two hours with compelling music. Out of all the rappers who released double discs, only the two that inaugurated the trend—2Pac and the Notorious B.I.G.—produced records that came close to being continually interesting. The others were bloated and overwrought, and E-40's *The Element of Surprise* is simply the latest contender in this sweepstakes. It's too long and doesn't progress musically from the typical Bay Area bumpin' that is his trademark. That doesn't mean that *The Element of Surprise* is worthless. Quite the contrary; E-40 is such a gifted rapper, with impeccably smooth delivery and startling images, that it's a pleasure to hear him—it's just that the length of the album has the effect of diluting his power, since the music gets monotonous and he doesn't find enough new topics to keep the songs engaging. If it was trimmed by nearly two-thirds, *The Element of Surprise* would be truly compelling. As its stands, only the dedicated could search through all these songs to find the good stuff. —*Stephen Thomas Erlewine*

Charlie Hustle: The Blueprint of a Self-Made Millionaire / Oct. 26, 1999 / Jive ♦♦♦♦

With the 1999 release of his fifth solo effort, E-40 commemorated ten years in the rap music business. Undoubtedly, more than a flash in the pan, E-40's staying power as one of the tried and true superstars in the rap game is validated by the workmanship in *Charlie Hustle: The Blueprint of a Self-Made Millionaire*, a display of guttural growls and speed rap techniques that takes listeners along a journey through the harsh realities of surviving in inner city ghettos. This 17-track recording artfully delivers funky backbeats, melodic hooks, and a flurry of synthesizer-enhanced rhythms to complement the unique stutter-stop patois of E- 40's flowing rap lyrics. This is best evidenced on "Big Ballin' with My Homies" and "Rules and Regulations," where the masterful MC adopts various styles of cadence and vocal texture to hype the overall effect. Fellow West Coast rappers C-Bo, Yukmouth, Fat Joe, and Jayo Felony guest star on what amounts to a semi-autobiographical accounting of E-40's own ascent from the ghetto to the California suburbs. All in all, this is a furious and energetic release of truths, guts, and the triumph of the American Dream. —*Roxanne Blanford*

Loyalty and Betrayal / Oct. 10, 2000 / Jive ✦✦✦
Never one to repeat himself, E-40 has always pushed the boundaries, and *Loyalty and Betrayal* exemplifies that well. The unconventional Bay Area game spitter comes with a different style on every track, and sometimes it's consequently questionable whether he's pushing the boundaries of rap itself or those of good taste. The album-opening intro and title track definitely start *Loyalty and Betrayal* off rather oddly, as it seems like 40 is more interested in showing off all his latest slang, delivery styles, and studio tricks than delivering a good old-fashioned rhyme that gets the party started properly. Not every track here is questionable, though. The Eightball and Jazze Pha collaboration, "Ya Blind," ranks among 40's best, as does the laid-back Nate Dogg and Battlecat collabo, "Nah Nah," and the above-average Click collabo, "Pop Ya Collar." There are a few other notable collaborations here, though they're not always the best songs. As with practically every 40 album, *Loyalty and Betrayal* is spotty—at times downright brilliant but at other times plodding. And if anything, following his prolific and celebrated late-'90s run, 40 seems intent on trying new styles, as if he doesn't want to repeat himself. That makes for a surprising, unique listen, but it also means *Loyalty and Betrayal* isn't going to be a hallmark release like *Tha Hall of Game* was four years earlier, when 40 was first establishing the style he inches away from here. —*Jason Birchmeier*

Grit & Grind / Jun. 25, 2002 / Jive ✦✦✦✦
In a rap world increasingly populated by monotoned players and smoother-than-smooth R&B crooners, E-40's deft delivery and playful wordplay remain a real breath of fresh air. As usual for him (as well as most rappers), *Grit & Grind* has a few too many tracks; still, it's definitely front loaded with talent, from the opener, "Why They Don't F**k Wit Us" (punctuated by organ lines and a female chorus), to the second track, "The Slap," with a barrage of rhyming riffs that finds him worrying a batch of suffixes like a dog with a bone. The productions, most by Rick Rock, are fleshed out and never reliant on the usual West Coast clichés. The metro-mentioning "Rep Yo City," with Petey Pablo, Eightball, Bun B, Lil Jon & the Eastside Boyz, is another highlight. —*John Bush*

Andrew E.

Foreign Rap
Philippine rapper/comedian Andrew E. was a DJ in a disco when, in the late '80s, he heard hip-hop for the first time. While he didn't quite know what it was, the fast-talking fellow was sure he could make a few dollars doing it. Source material for the erstwhile DJ was simple—Andrew simply looked at the nightlife and youth culture that surrounded him. In 1990 he struck gold with the single "Humanap Ka Ng Panget," and never looked back. His next single, "Andrew Ford Medina," was a harmless ditty about Andrew's adventures with two randy sisters; the song was as controversial as it was successful, and it established Andrew as the Tone-Loc of the Philippine rap game. Originated by Francis Magalona, whose music was more patriotic than erotic, Andrew's blue rhymes and boisterous personality were a bit of a shock for the nation's older generation. But that didn't stop Andrew from releasing numerous albums featuring songs like "Mahirap Maging Pogi," which explained how difficult life was for Andrew—his good looks made all the girls crazy. After five albums, a greatest-hits package from Viva Records, and over 25 films (mostly slapstick comedies), it was time for a break. Andrew took a break for most of the mid-'90s, but returned in 1999 with *Wholesome*, an album with lyrics that definitely weren't. *Much More Wholesome* followed in 2000, and another greatest-hits collection appeared in 2002. The comeback resolidified his stature as a giant in the scene; Andrew E. found another career as a mentor for young Philippine rappers like Carlos Agassi. —*Johnny Loftus*

● **The Best of Andrew E.** / 1992 / Viva ✦✦✦✦
After Andrew E. recorded a number of popular albums for Viva Records, the label came out with *The Best of Andrew E.* in 1992. Andrew E. is often credited, along with Francis M., with introducing rap in the Philippines and helping to make it popular. Many songs on *The Best of Andrew E.* received wide airplay at the time of their initial release, including "Andrew Ford Medina," a high-spirited rap on which Andrew E. tells of meeting a girl and going to her house, where he massages her "front and back." The girl says she wants to make love with him and her older sister says she wants to "join in." Andrew E. became typecast as someone who makes dirty songs because of "Andrew

Ford Medina," but most songs on *The Best of Andrew E.* aren't dirty, but in fact are innocuous and even entertaining, if not particularly deep or meaningful. In the Philippines, audiences aren't much interested in serious songs that discuss important Philippine issues, such as poverty and corruption, and mostly want to be entertained and have fun. "Ganyon" concerns the joys of dancing with Andrew E., while "Mahirap Maging Pogi" tells how difficult life can be for Andrew E. because he is so handsome that girls don't leave him alone. "Dahil Sa Iyo/Lahat Ng Araw" and "Mas Gusto Mo Sya" feature straightforward raps about love. Raising the level of enjoyment for a listener is the excellent and often exciting instrumentation, even on the slow raps. Andrew E.'s style of rapping is distinctive and displays originality as well. This is a very good rap album. —*David Gonzales*

Wholesome / 1999 / Epic ✦✦✦
The title of Philippine rapper Andrew E.'s 1999 album, *Wholesome*, is just the opposite of the album's material, which contains many double entendres that can easily be interpreted as sexual in nature, as well as some content that is just plain sexual. The album's last three songs, however, are "clean." The album marks a comeback for Andrew E., widely regarded, along with Francis M., as one of the founding fathers of Philippine rap. He was absent from the recording/rapping scene for a while, as he notes here, and is back to reclaim his title. He got his wish, as *Wholesome* was a top-selling album. "Fax Me" is representative of the album's double-entendre element, and is about a girl who likes to "fax" a lot. The melody from the chorus of Diana Ross' "Touch Me in the Morning," is used for the lyrics "Fax me in the morning/Then just walk away/We will fax tomorrow/'Cuz we faxed yesterday." "Picnic" tells about, among other things, licking a lollipop from "top to bottom." Other lyrics on the album are more explicit. Andrew E. also spends much time decrying his critics, who thought he was gone for good. Andrew E. is an excellent, fluid rapper, and the musicianship throughout the album is also excellent. —*David Gonzales*

Much More Wholesome / 2000 / Epic ✦✦✦
In 2000 Philippine rapper Andrew E. followed up 1999's best-selling *Wholesome* with *Much More Wholesome*. On "Ang Bastos Daw" (They Said It's Gross), he notes the criticism he received for *Wholesome* (which contained many double entendres with sexual connotations), pointing out that the album remained a top seller despite attempts to ban the music in such cities as Baguio, Dagupan, and Cebu. He says that the lyrics only became obscene when people thought of them as such. Not many people will be convinced, though, and he neglects mentioning "Mahal Kita" (I Love You), which contained explicit sexual lyrics. On *Much More Wholesome*, he greatly tones down the double entendres and sexual content. "Text," for example, is a commentary on the popularity of phone texting in the Philippines. Still, "OU812" contains explicit lyrics of a sexual nature. As on *Wholesome*, he decries his critics, and often boasts about his talents, aptly pointing out that he still makes albums while other local rap groups have disappeared. —*David Gonzales*

Andrew E. Greatest Hits: The Very Best of Wholesome / 2002 / Sony Philippines ✦✦✦
After an absence from the Philippine music scene, rapper Andrew E. returned in 1999 to score massive commercial success with *Wholesome*, his first album for Epic. The album's contents, however, were the opposite of wholesome, as the songs were centered on double entendre of a sexual nature, and also contained some straightforward raunchiness. *Much More Wholesome* (2000) was also successful, after which Andrew E. left the label and returned to local independent Viva Records, for which he had recorded a number of albums years earlier. Hence, the appearance of *Andrew E. Greatest Hits: The Very Best of Wholesome*. As noted earlier, many songs are saturated with double entendre, including "Rubber Dickey," which tells how much fun a girl can have with a "rubber dickey," so much fun that she won't need her boyfriend anymore. Andrew E. had one of 1999's biggest hits with "Banyo Queen" (Queen of the Bathroom), about a guy and a girl who go to a hotel room. The song samples from Ben E. King's "Stand By Me." On "Ang Bastos Daw" (Very Disgusting), from *Much More Wholesome*, Andrew E. answers his critics who complain of his raunchiness that the "dirtiness" is only in their minds, as the lyrics themselves are not explicit. This explanation, however, is weak, as most anyone would think his songs are dirty, and he neglects to mention the songs that are out-and-out raunchy, such as "Malupit" (Cruel), also included here. The songs on *Much More Wholesome*

did not contain nearly as much double entendre as did *Wholesome*, and perhaps he toned down the contents in response to all the criticism. —*David Gonzales*

Tha Eastsidaz

f. 1999, Los Angeles, CA
Group / West Coast Rap, Gangsta Rap
Protégés of Snoop Doggy Dogg, Long Beach, CA-based duo tha Eastsidaz teamed rappers Big Tray Deee and Goldie Loc, whose partnership was forged in 1999. Their debut album, *Snoop Dogg Presents Tha Eastsidaz*, appeared early the following year on the newly formed Dogghouse label. —*Jason Ankeny*

Tha Eastsidaz / Jan. 18, 2000 / TVT ✦✦✦✦
Snoop Dogg has always been remarkably intuitive when it comes to selecting his business associates. After all, he has had the good fortune of being mentored by arguably the industry's best producer (Dr. Dre) and its shrewdest businessman (Master P). Now that Snoop's name has become synonymous with platinum plaques, the next logical step in his evolution was to do some mentoring of his own. Snoop's first entrepreneurial undertaking is the debut from fellow LBC mashers tha Eastsidaz (Tray Deee and Goldie Loc). While the group's chemistry flourishes on the spirited lead single "G'd Up," Snoop often overshadows his protégés by being predominantly featured on most of the LP's cuts. Also, the overwhelming abundance of guests (Dr. Dre, Xzibit, Kurupt, Warren G, and Nate Dogg) precludes tha Eastsidaz from achieving any lasting unit cohesion, often making the duo seem like visitors on their own debut. —*Matt Conaway*

● **Duces n' Trays: The Old Fashioned Way** / Jul. 31, 2001 / TVT ✦✦✦
Dogghouse records and its flagship act, tha Eastsidaz, at first admittedly seemed like a questionable venture on the part of Snoop Dogg back in 1999. After all, his reputation wasn't exactly on solid ground at the time, and his timing wasn't exactly ideal either—West Coast rap in general had faltered ever since 2Pac's death. Yet despite the odds, everything worked out for Snoop. The debut Eastsidaz album didn't exactly set the charts on fire, but it did garner some respectable sales, and more importantly, it set the precedent for Snoop's post-No Limit sound: Battlecat and Meech Wells laid down the beats; Kokane, Nate Dogg, and Butch Cassidy sang the hooks; Snoop loomed above with his sticky-icky adlibbing; and Goldie Loc and Tray Deee dropped the gangsta rhymes. *Duces n' Trays* finds this sure-fire team of Cali crips returning a year and a half later, far more experienced and with a noticeably greater sense of camaraderie. In practically every way, *Duces* is a noticeably stronger album than its predecessor—beats, rhymes, hooks, songwriting—and it features even more talent with unlikely contributions from Mobb Deep, Hi-Tek, Lil' Mo, and Swizz Beatz. But it's the in-house talent that steals the show on *Duces*, in particular newcomer LaToiya Williams and the ubiquitous Kokane, two vocalists who offset the gruff rapping in nearly every one of the album's 20 songs with their singing. Furthermore, for every straight-ahead gangsta rap song here, there's an unexpected venture into rap-soul such as "So Low," where there's more singing than rapping. This balance between brash posturing and laid-back crooning seems to be Snoop's new sound, and you can't help but feel that it's an inevitable evolution for the '70s funk/soul-influenced West Coast sound. So even if *Duces* could use a few more hooks, it shows that Snoop is headed in the right direction. If Dogghouse can avoid inner strife and continue to blossom, it could realistically change the sound of West Coast rap just as Death Row did a decade earlier when Snoop was just a pup. —*Jason Birchmeier*

Eazy-E (Eric Wright)

b. Sep. 7, 1964, Compton, CA, **d.** Mar. 26, 1995, Los Angeles, CA
Vocals, Executive Producer / Gangsta Rap, West Coast Rap, Hardcore Rap, Dirty Rap
Whether as a member of N.W.A, a solo act, or a label head, Eazy-E was one of the most controversial figures in gangsta rap. While his technical skills as a rapper were never the greatest, his distinctive delivery (invariably described as a high-pitched whine), over-the-top lyrics, and undeniable charisma made him a star. Following N.W.A's breakup, E's street credibility took a major beating, though his recordings continued to sell well when they appeared; unfortunately, he was diagnosed with AIDS in 1995, and died not long after.

Eric "Eazy-E" Wright was born September 7, 1964, in Compton, CA, a rough part of the Los Angeles metro area that N.W.A would later make notorious. A high school dropout, Wright turned to drug dealing to support himself, and eventually used the profits to start his own rap label, Ruthless Records, with partner and music-business veteran Jerry Heller. E discovered a major performing talent in the D.O.C., and recruited Ice Cube and Dr. Dre to write songs for his stable of artists. When their composition "Boyz-N-the-'Hood" was rejected by Ruthless signee HBO, Cube, Dre, and E formed the first version of N.W.A to record it themselves. Their first album, *N.W.A and the Posse*, was released in 1987 and largely ignored; after a few tweaks of the lineup and the rough-edged subject matter, 1988's *Straight Outta Compton* made N.W.A into superstars. E seized the opportunity to release a solo project later in the year, titled *Eazy-Duz-It*, which would be the only full-length album he would complete; it would sell well over two-million copies.

After Ice Cube's bitter departure from N.W.A toward the end of 1989 (precipitated in part by Heller's business tactics), Eazy-E took over his not inconsiderable share of the rapping and songwriting duties, becoming the group's dominant voice on 1991's *Efil4zaggin*. His taste for cartoonish vulgarity began to undermine the claims of realistic inner-city reporting that the group had used to defend themselves. Disputes between the members led to N.W.A's breakup that summer, and a court battle between Ruthless and Dre's new label Death Row soon followed, with Eazy alleging that Death Row head Suge Knight had coerced Ruthless into releasing Dre from his contract. The case was eventually thrown out, but a bitter feud between Dre and Eazy raged for the next several years; Dre's seminal solo debut *The Chronic* made merciless fun of Eazy. E's 1992 solo EP *5150: Home 4 tha Sick* sold well, but did little to dispel his increasingly cartoonish image; he found more success running the Ruthless label, with a roster that included Above the Law, N.W.A bandmate MC Ren, the poorly received all-female group H.W.A. (Hoez With Attitude), and, eventually, the lucrative Bone Thugs-N-Harmony. Eazy addressed his feud with Dre on the 1993 EP *It's On (Dr. Dre) 187um Killa*, which famously included an actual photo of Dre wearing makeup and sequins during his World Class Wreckin' Cru days. Still, save for dissing Dre, Eazy didn't seem to have much to say, and despite healthy record sales, his artistic credibility was declining at an alarming rate. Eazy didn't help matters much when, in early 1993, he spoke out in support of Theodore Briseno, the only LAPD officer involved in the Rodney King beating to express displeasure; later in the year, he paid $2,500 to attend a Republican fundraiser, which his detractors saw as a further betrayal of his roots.

In early 1995, Eazy entered the hospital with respiratory difficulties, believing he had developed asthma. The diagnosis was far more serious: he had contracted AIDS. Eazy announced his plight to the public shortly thereafter, winning admiration for his straightforward attitude. Sadly, just a few weeks later, on March 26, 1995, the disease claimed his life. The record he had been working on, *Str8 Off tha Streetz of Muthaphu**in Compton*, was released posthumously (in unfinished form) later in the year. In 2002, on the seventh anniversary of his death, some previously unreleased material from the Ruthless vaults was released as the EP *The Impact of a Legend*, which was accompanied by a DVD. —*Steve Huey*

Eazy-Duz-It / 1988 / Ruthless ✦✦✦
Eazy-E's solo debut, *Eazy-Duz-It*, isn't far removed from his work with N.W.A, essentially functioning as a compliment to the group's groundbreaking *Straight Outta Compton* album from the same year. Like *Straight Outta Compton*, *Eazy-Duz-It* features Dr. Dre's then-trendsetting production work, and it also features appearances by Eazy's other groupmates in N.W.A: Ice Cube and MC Ren. So, taking this into consideration, *Eazy-Duz-It* plays very much like a spin-off sequel to *Straight Outta Compton*; however, like most spin-off sequels, this one seems a bit hasty—thrown together quickly to capitalize on the success of its predecessor. Above all, the songwriting seems disappointingly unlabored. The topics aren't nearly as gripping as those found on *Straight Outta Compton*. For instance, you won't find anything here as outspoken as "Fuck the Police," as riotous as "Straight Outta Compton," as epochal as "Gangsta Gangsta," as heedful as "Dopeman," or as feel-good as "Express Yourself." Rather, you'll find Eazy-E taking a predictable traditional hip-hop stance—he's mostly either egotistical (on the two album highlights, "We Want Eazy" and "Eazy-Er Said Than Dunn") or thuggish (most of the remaining album). Granted, it's easy to attack Eazy as an MC, particularly because his rapping isn't any more impressive than his songs, but doing so

diverts you from what's most important here. All songwriting and rapping aside, what elevates *Eazy-Duz-It* above and beyond almost every other West Coast rap album of this formative era are Dre's trademark production and Eazy's gangsta posturing. These two qualities alone make this album fascinatingly influential—the seed from which myriad gangstas sprouted during the early-'90s West Coast rap explosion. Following *Eazy-Duz-It*, Eazy would return as a better rapper with more to say, but he would never again seem as iconic as he does here. —*Jason Birchmeier*

5150: Home 4 tha Sick EP / Dec. 28, 1992 / Priority ◆◆

Distanced from Ice Cube and Dr. Dre, the two artists most responsible for his own success, Eazy-E doesn't have a lot going for him on *5150: Home 4 tha Sick*. Released in late 1992, two weeks after Dre reinvented himself on *The Chronic*, this brief EP finds Eazy in a desperate scenario. He hadn't released any solo material since his 1988 debut album, *Eazy-Duz-It*, and the runaway success of his former groupmates, Ice Cube and Dre, had quickly made everyone forget about Eazy. The five songs on *5150* unfortunately don't do much to reclaim Eazy's once-towering stature among the gangsta rap scene. The only song really worth noting is "Only If You Want It," clearly the EP's centerpiece and certainly a career highlight for Eazy. Elsewhere, "Neighborhood Sniper" and "Niggaz My Height Don't Fight" are unwittingly asinine attempts to seem dangerous, just as "Merry Mutha******* Xmas" is an unwittingly asinine attempt to seem humorous. In the end, Eazy's efforts here on *5150* fall flat, functioning as little more than the gap filler his quickly fading career so badly needed at the time. You'd think he'd have more to offer—after all, it'd been four years since his last solo release—but this only goes to show how essential Ice Cube and Dre were to Eazy's initial success. With an odd twist of fate, though, Dre's pointed dis on "Dre Day" would give Eazy the chance he needed to rejuvenate his career following his misstep here on *5150*. A year later, in late 1993, Eazy would return with another EP, this one much more impressive: *It's On (Dr. Dre) 187um Killa*, easily the most accomplished work of the late rapper's short-lived career. [The 2002 reissue of Eazy's debut album, *Eazy-Duz-It*, appended the long-out-of-print *5150: Home 4 tha Sick* EP as bonus tracks.] —*Jason Birchmeier*

It's On (Dr. Dre) 187um Killa EP / Nov. 5, 1993 / Ruthless ◆◆◆◆

Though not necessarily one of rap's most shining moments by any means, *It's On (Dr. Dre) 187um Killa* does stand as Eazy-E's best moment outside of N.W.A, showcasing his amazingly sarcastic and downright ruthless sense of wit. More than anything else, this EP was thrown together as a quick answer to Dr. Dre's *The Chronic*, an album ridden with lyrical shots at Eazy. Songs here such as "Real Muthaphu**in G's" and "It's On" are pointed directly at Dre and Snoop Dogg, with Eazy showing no remorse whatsoever. The irony of this is the fact that Eazy coopts Dre's style for this EP, rapping over production that is obviously modeled after Dre's signature flute- and synth-laden G-funk melodies of the time (produced, in part, by Dre's old partner, Yella). Sure, this release is definitely lacking in quantity (being forced to yet again resurrect "Boyz-N-the-'Hood"), and Eazy doesn't have much to say outside of his relentless Dre-aimed disses and his odes to sex and drugs. But despite these complaints, "Real Muthaphu**in G's" and "It's On" remain some of Eazy's best solo songs ever, and "Gimmie That Nutt" remains a timeless nasty club anthem. Though it's a bit odd to consider a quickly thrown-together EP such as this to be the highlight of Eazy-E's brief solo career, it's hard to say that it isn't. It seems Dre's disses were the best motivation for Eazy's often halfhearted rap career. —*Jason Birchmeier*

Str8 Off tha Streetz of Muthaphu**in Compton / 1995 / Relativity ◆◆◆

At the time of his death, Eazy-E was completing a comeback album that was intended to restore his street credibility, which had taken a savage beating in the early '90s. *Str8 Off tha Streetz of Muthaphu**in Compton*, the album he left unfinished, does show more ambition than his previous *It's On*, but it's unlikely that it would have made him a star again. Collaborating with his former N.W.A partners Ren and Yella, Eazy-E sounds revitalized, but the music simply isn't imaginative. Instead of pushing forward and creating a distinctive style, it treads over familiar gangsta territory, complete with bottomless bass, whining synthesizers, and meaningless boasts. The occasional track, like the surrealistic "The Muthaphu**in Real" and the menacing "Ole School Shit," illustrate what Eazy-E could have done if hadn't been tied to his pedestrian production, but the majority of *Str8 Off the Streez* is depressingly by the books. Sadly, the album is the farthest thing from a graceful departure. —*Stephen Thomas Erlewine*

● **Eternal E** / Dec. 1995 / Ruthless ◆◆◆◆

During his short career, Eazy-E only released one full-length album but managed to release a number of tracks on EPs and with N.W.A; most of the notorious rapper's best moments from these releases are included here on *Eternal E*, which is essentially a greatest-hits collection. Unfortunately, as great as it is to hear some of Eazy-E's best moments—"Boyz-N-the-'Hood," "8 Ball," "Eazy-Duz-It," "Only If You Want It"—there are several unacceptable exceptions. Most notably, the material from his most realized moment, *It's On (Dr. Dre) 187um Killa*, is nowhere to be found. Furthermore, the majority of his solo material pales in comparison to his work with N.W.A on tracks such as "Fuck the Police" and "100 Miles and Runnin'," and this collection sadly only features four N.W.A songs. So it's almost ironic that this greatest-hits collection ignores his greatest hits (most likely for the licensing costs required to secure the absent material). It would also be nice to have some of Eazy-E's posthumously released material from the *Str8 Off tha Streetz of Muthaphu**in Compton* sessions included here. So even though this album is still the best introduction to his canon of work for novices, it functions poorly as a comprehensive representation of Eazy-E's short career, as it ignores much of his best work. —*Jason Birchmeier*

The Impact of a Legend / Mar. 26, 2002 / Ruthless ◆◆◆

Eazy-E died of AIDS—a tragic, ironic ending for an artist who pioneered the gangsta mentality with his recordings with N.W.A and as a solo artist. This collection purports to pay tribute to him, or celebrate his legacy, but the end result is bizarre. This is not an album—it's a CD, enhanced with a video game, with a bonus DVD, containing music videos, plus karaoke, topped off with a comic book in the liner notes. Basically, if you're a fan of *some* kind of media, you'll find it here, albeit presented in cut-rate fashion. And since this is a disc that tries to sell Eazy to a modern audience, who allegedly doesn't know about him, you get music that's hopped up in strange, counter-intuitive ways, plus the odd instance of apologizing for what Eazy was. This is especially true of the comic book, which is an apologetic rant attempting to mythologize Eazy as a martyr—portraying him as a savvy businessman, suggesting that those who alleged paternity in the wake of his death were just gold diggers (as Tom Laikous would say, "Ohhh, Really???"), whitewashing his end ("Mom, I have something like Magic Johnson… IDS"), suggesting he worked until the end, and, best of all, brushing off the celebrated incident of Eazy attending a fundraiser for Bush Mach I with "I Ain't No F*ckin' Republican; I got $1 million worth of publicity for $1,500" (yeah, that's right!; just like how John Lennon voted Tory not to keep his millions, but to generate copy). Perhaps there are some good cuts scattered on the CD, but no matter how you look at it, this is a startling piece of pure product—and one that's not even that well assembled. —*Stephen Thomas Erlewine*

Ed O.G. & Da Bulldogs

f. Boston, MA

Group / Hip-Hop, East Coast Rap, Hardcore Rap, Gangsta Rap

Ed O.G. (born Edward Anderson) penned a poignant and brilliant message track on his 1991 CD *Life of a Kid in the Ghetto*. "Be a Father to Your Child" was a much more effective plea for parental responsibility than scores of political rhetoric spewed by left- and right-wing types. The entire disc was a disturbing, evocative, and wonderfully produced and performed look at inner-city life that neither glorified nor minimized the tragedy nor understated the triumphs inherent in surviving the madness. The follow-up, *Roxbury 02119*, wasn't quite as captivating, but was still miles ahead of many more heavily hyped and promoted hip-hop releases in 1994. —*Ron Wynn*

● **Life of a Kid in the Ghetto** / 1991 / PWL America ◆◆◆◆◆

Ed O.G. made a signature song with "Be a Father to Your Child." It was arguably 1991's finest message song, a no-nonsense plea to men to support their children regardless of circumstance. It was the finest cut on an above-average concept album, which contained several searing, insightful tunes that presented dilemmas, but neither glorified them nor made them seem unsolvable. "Gotta Have Money (If You Ain't Got Money You Ain't Got Jack)" sounded a rather pessimistic note, but is balanced by "Stop (Think for a Moment)." "Dedicated to the Right Wingers" was a smartly conceived challenge to conservatives to address problems in a real rather than rhetorical or symbolic manner. —*Ron Wynn*

Roxbury 02119 / Jan. 18, 1994 / Chemistry ✦✦✦
The second Ed O.G. album wasn't quite as ambitious or satisfying as his debut. There were no standout singles, and Ed O.G.'s rapping lacked the power, conviction, and satirical clout he had previously displayed. The production wasn't as varied, nor were the rhymes and stories as gripping. But it was still much better than much of the prototype "gangsta" material flooding the marketplace. —*Ron Wynn*

Edan (Edan Portnoy)

Vocals, Producer / Underground Rap, Hip-Hop, Old School Rap
There was a small but vital hip-hop genesis in Boston at the tail end of the 1990s led by a motley group of artists (Porn Theatre Ushers, Skitzofreniks, 7L & Esoteric, Mr. Lif, Insight) who shared a number of musical attributes—a love of block rockin' retro beats and veneration for the hip-hop "new school" of the late '80s and early '90s, and a proclivity for irreverent, tongue-in-cheek lyrical styles, to name the most significant. Bedroom geek Edan (aka the Humble Magnificent) was the most block rockin' and irreverent of all Boston's underground scientists. A triple threat on the microphone, as a producer, and behind the wheels of steel, his music—a willfully oddball and eccentric blend of rap's past and future—caught on first among the progressive cognoscenti of London, but had such exuberance and appeal that it was only a matter of time before it staked out territory on its home turf as well.

Edan Portnoy grew up a musically inclined loner in the suburbs of Baltimore, MD. Inspired from an early age by the Beatles, Jimi Hendrix, and psychedelic rock, he picked up the guitar and bass during his adolescent years, but when N.W.A dropped *Straight Outta Compton* in 1988, it instantly captured the ten-year-old's imagination and altered his musical path. By the time he was a teenager, Edan had begun to dig up and collect rare LPs and try his hand at making elementary beats inspired by the likes of Main Source, Pete Rock & C.L. Smooth, and the Native Tongues family, as well as old school heroes both famous (Slick Rick, Big Daddy Kane, Ultramagnetic MC's) and obscure (DJ Cash Money, Percee P). After graduation from high school, he moved to Boston to study guitar at the Berklee College of Music, ultimately dropping out before taking a degree but not before delving into production and engineering. His newfound technical facility helped as he began creating his own tracks and, due to lack of an MC, rhyming on them as well. It resulted in a series of CDRs (including an unofficial debut album called *Architecture* and an early EP version of *Primitive Plus*), sold mostly at live gigs around Boston, and now-classic 12" singles, culminating with the much-sought-after "Sing It, Shitface," released by Boston indie Biscuithead Records in 1999.

Very much an acquired taste, Edan's popularity began to spread slowly throughout England. Due to its built-in fan base of vintage hip-hop, the rapper was given a measure of respect in England that was difficult to come by in his rap-saturated home country, and British promoters took the opportunity to fly him over for well-received live shows. In early 2002 the artist prepared a proper full-length edition of *Primitive Plus* (adding six new songs to the original EP) for release on British label Lewis Recordings. The album received rapturous reviews both in America and overseas. He followed it several months later with an EP, *Sprain Your Tape Deck*, also on Lewis, as well as outside production for and collaborations with Count Bass D ("How We Met") and Mr. Lif ("Live From the Plantation"), among others. —*Stanton Swihart*

Edan the DJ: Fast Rap / 2001 / Lewis ✦✦✦✦
Edan went above and beyond the call with this extremely limited-edition record, the release of which closely coincided with the appearance of his astonishing *Primitive Plus*, a debut album that was marinated in an overriding romance with old school rap. An impeccably chosen mix set, *Fast Rap* peels away several more layers from that romance, in the process revealing Edan to be as rapacious as he is eccentric when it comes to collecting rare vinyl. Mostly cherry-picked from one of hip-hop's premium eras (1988-1992), the song list includes a handful of classic material, opening with the landmark "Raw" from Big Daddy Kane (who appears twice), then bleeding into Melle Mel's awesome "Freestyle." Eric B. & Rakim, EPMD, LL Cool J, the DJ's beloved Ultramagnetic MC's, and Pete Rock & C.L. Smooth also make appearances, and each of their tracks sound as good as the day they were hatched. Bolstering those classics are cuts by lesser-known but still esteemed underground crews like Organized Konfusion, Main Source, K Solo, and Lord Finesse, all of which longtime fans of the genre will recognize, if not already know. But interspersed among such venerated company are idiosyncratic

songs by a number of off-the-wall rappers (Sir Ibu of Divine Force?) that not even the most rabid of hip-hop heads may have previously heard. Of these, several deserve special mention. Unique's "Axe-Maniac" is as manic and edgy as anything by Kool G Rap & DJ Polo, while MC Jewel does a sensational Kool Keith impression on "Reflection of Perfection." Freshco & Miz and Percee P. & Ekim both rattle off some vicious battle rhymes, and the Dismasters get not one but two cuts, for good reason. But in Black, Rock & Ron's "Stop the World," the album unearths an honest-to-goodness lost rap classic. Edan does very little in the way of manipulation (the occasional shout-out aside), mostly concerning himself with segueing from song to song. But that is enough when the set burns this white hot. —*Stanton Swihart*

Sprain Your Tape Deck / 2002 / Lewis ✦✦✦
Two steps forward for every one step back is the basic pattern of this fine follow-up EP to Edan's brilliant full-length debut. But the album backpedals only in the respect that it repeats a pair of songs from *Primitive Plus*, "Run That Shit" and the instant classic "MCs Smoke Crack," so it is not a retreat at all, especially when you consider the great leap into the deep end of rap oddness that his previous effort represented. In fact, *Sprain Your Tape Deck* is essentially a continuation of the Edan aesthetic, part wild-style throwback and part future Dada, where old school 808 drum loops mingle with the rapper's one-of-a-kind b-boy worldview. The four new songs are all clean winners, the humor ratcheted up yet another notch. Only Edan, the aluminum smoker, would have the shamelessness to plead with other MCs to hang out at the park and arcade with him, to buy each other ice cream and work on metaphors together ("Let's Be Friends"). And only Edan could make the recitation of a menu or cookbook ("Beautiful Food") not merely funny but dazzlingly so. The best comes last—a late-night homage to spiritual mentor Schoolly D that is a pitch-perfect trip back to 1986, when, if you think about it, hip-hop's future seemed much more unpredictable, full of possibilities, and enticing than it did circa 2002. —*Stanton Swihart*

● **Primitive Plus** / Mar. 19, 2002 / Solid ✦✦✦✦✦
"There can be no future without a past." Never before has an album exemplified that hip-hop credo with more maverick boldness than *Primitive Plus*. It is a wild, weird, instantly left-field rap masterpiece from one seriously bugged-out, innovative loner. Edan, a Boston suburbanite, plays the bedroom-geek wunderkind on "One Man Arsenal" who does triple time on production, behind the turntables, and rocking the microphone and also gives a throwback to b-boy partying like it's 1989. The result is an unholy amalgam of decidedly far-out nonconformity, the acute verbal lacerations of Rakim, and Kool Keith's untamable flights of fantasy ("Ultra '88" is, in fact, a tribute to the Ultramagnetic MC's). Like the latter legend, Edan packs a wicked sense of humor and brandishes it often with a sometimes barbed but always hilariously nutso outcome (on "MCs Smoke Crack," for instance, he characteristically cops to smoking not crack but aluminum). It allows him to facetiously lampoon conventional rap pretenses and attitudes even as he wallows in them with obviously reverent glee, effectively honoring the genre as a true devotee while managing to stand outside it as a commentator. It is a line that *Primitive Plus* expertly straddles throughout. Electro and '80s street beats knock about with old school audio snippets, vintage samples, and video-game sci-fi backdrops, then collide headlong with eclectic pop and rock production techniques, resulting in a rich, layered, complex musical undergirding that is electric boogaloo fresh on the one hand and extremely forward looking and path clearing on the other. The album blasts the cobwebs from hip-hop's rusted infrastructure, gives it a wax and polish to make in presentable in the present, then promptly rides it into the space age. In other words, it simultaneously blazes a trail backward and ahead. Not surprisingly, it took an English label to release the album. This is psychedelic hip-hop that can make you dizzy with its embarrassment of delights. A message to Beck: here are your real two turntables and a microphone. [*Primitive Plus* was also issued in the U.K. on Lewis Recordings.] —*Stanton Swihart*

The Egyptian Lover (Greg Broussard)

Producer, Vocals / Electro, Club/Dance, Old School Rap, Urban, West Coast Rap
One of the most innovative producers of the old school/electro era, Egyptian Lover's Greg Broussard recorded a parade of singles during the mid-'80s that proved influential for decades. Influenced himself by Kraftwerk/hip-hop soundclashes like Afrika Bambaataa's "Planet Rock" and Man Parrish's

"Hip-Hop Be Bop (Don't Stop)," as well as the extroverted black-lover soul of Prince and Zapp, Broussard began recording from his Los Angeles base in 1983. One year later, he emerged with the breakdancing anthem "Egypt, Egypt," released on the Freak Beat label. Similar to excellent tracks being produced all over America—from Detroit (Cybotron) to New York (Mantronix)— "Egypt, Egypt" and successors "What Is a DJ If He Can't Scratch," "And My Beat Goes Boom," and "Computer Love (Sweet Dreams)" spent much time in DJ crates during the '80s and '90s. Broussard also released several LPs during the mid-'80s, including 1984's *On the Nile* (practically a greatest-hits compilation), 1986's *One Track Mind*, and 1988's *Filthy*; the first two appeared on his own Egyptian Empire label. After several years away from music, he returned in 1994 with *Back From the Tomb* and the following year's *Pyramix.* —*John Bush*

● **On the Nile** / 1984 / Egyptian Empire ✦✦✦✦✦
Before Ice-T, N.W.A, and the late Eazy-E made Los Angeles famous (or infamous) for gangsta rap in the late '80s, the city's rap community was best known for a high-tech, futuristic approach that owed a lot to Afrika Bambaataa's 1982 classic, "Planet Rock." In the early to mid-'80s, L.A.-based electro-hoppers like the Egyptian Lover, the World Class Wreckin' Cru (the group that Dr. Dre belonged to before N.W.A), the Arabian Prince, and Uncle Jam's Army didn't get much respect from East Coast hip-hoppers, who insisted that their music wasn't gritty enough. But those artists did enjoy a cult following in Southern California. Besides, the Egyptian Lover never claimed to be a hardcore rapper; *On the Nile*, his debut album of 1984, doesn't pretend to be a Run-D.M.C., LL Cool J, or Fat Boys release any more than Grover Washington Jr. claimed to be a jazz purist. The closest this LP comes to an East Coast hip-hop vibe is the single "What Is a DJ If He Can't Scratch"; all of the other tracks offer a synthesizer-driven blend of rap, dance music, and electro-funk. Though "Planet Rock" is a strong influence on this release, it is hardly the Egyptian Lover's only influence—his sound also owes a debt to Germany's seminal Kraftwerk (whose innovations greatly influenced "Planet Rock"), Prince, Man Parrish, and Giorgio Moroder, as well as Middle Eastern and North African music. The Egyptian Lover never had great rapping skills, but he was definitely an original and imaginative producer/writer—and his risk-taking spirit serves him well on definitive, high-tech tunes like "Egypt, Egypt," "My House (on the Nile)," and "Girls." *On the Nile* isn't the only Egyptian Lover LP that is worth owning, but most fans insist that it is his most essential and consistent album—and they're absolutely right. —*Alex Henderson*

One Track Mind / 1986 / Egyptian Empire ✦✦✦
When the Egyptian Lover's second album, *One Track Mind*, came out in 1986, gangsta rap had yet to become huge. Ice-T's *Rhyme Pays* and N.W.A's *N.W.A & the Posse*—two landmarks in West Coast gangsta rap—didn't come out until 1987, and East Coast hip-hoppers still associated Southern California with the electro-hop style that the Egyptian Lover is best known for. Anyone who expects to find hardcore rap on *One Track Mind* is bound to be disappointed; this LP isn't for rap purists. But those who appreciated his first album, *On the Nile*, will find this to be a respectable, if imperfect, sophomore effort. Egyptian's influences remain the same; the quirky rapper/producer still combines his appreciation of Afrika Bambaataa's "Planet Rock," Prince, Man Parrish, and Kraftwerk with elements of North African music and Egyptian imagery. It's a strange mixture—Egyptian inhabits a place in which rap, Prince's Minneapolis sound, European synth pop, and North African music come together. But it's a mixture that works well on infectious electro-hop jams like "Livin' on the Nile," the single "Freak-A-Holic," and "A Stranger Place (The Alezby Inn)," which bears a bit of a resemblance to Prince's "Erotic City." As the title *One Track Mind* indicates, the Egyptian Lover shares Prince's love of all things erotic. But this LP is never X-rated; the lyrics are suggestive rather than explicit, which is why some of the tunes on *One Track Mind* had urban radio potential. Egyptian, however, was never a superstar, although he did enjoy an enthusiastic cult following. While *One Track Mind* isn't as essential as *On the Nile*, it's a likable release that fans of the electro-hop sound will enjoy. —*Alex Henderson*

Filthy / 1988 / Priority ✦✦✦
It's ironic that many East Coast hip-hoppers of the 1980s had such a low opinion of the Egyptian Lover and other Los Angeles residents who specialized in the electro-hop style—ironic because Egyptian and his colleagues were heavily influenced by Afrika Bambaataa's "Planet Rock," which is considered one of 1982's definitive New York hip-hop singles. Of course, Egyptian was never

the hardcore hip-hopper that Bambaataa is; his forte is a club-friendly mixture of rap, dance music, and synth funk. When *Filthy* came out in 1988, electro-hop was starting to decline in popularity in Southern California—thanks to the success of Ice-T, N.W.A, and Eazy-E, Los Angeles rappers were becoming known for gangsta rap instead of electro-hop. But Egyptian carried on, avoiding hardcore rap and sticking to material that had a lot of dance and urban appeal. Parts of *Filthy* find him singing instead of rapping, including the addictive synth funk single "D.S.L.'s"; the Cameo-minded "Overdose"; and the eerie, Europop-influenced "Whisper in Your Ear." Meanwhile, Egyptian sticks to rapping on futuristic, "Planet Rock"-influenced electro-hop items such as "Baddest Beats Around" and "I Want Cha." Egyptian isn't a great singer any more than he is a great rapper—his strong points are producing and writing—but he still manages to be effective. The most surprising thing on the LP is a cover of Booker T. & the M.G.'s' early-'60s instrumental "Green Onions," which gets an almost Doors-like makeover—not the sort of thing one expected from Egyptian, but then, he always did have eclectic tastes. A fairly diverse effort, *Filthy* falls short of essential but will appeal to Egyptian's die-hard fans. —*Alex Henderson*

Eightball (Premro Smith)
b. Memphis, TN
Producer / Southern Rap, Dirty South
As a member of the popular Eightball & MJG duo, this large rapper labored for years in the Southern rap underground before making the jump from cult success to coast-to-coast stardom. His career began as part of the Memphis, TN, duo Eightball & MJG back in the early '90s, when you had to be from either New York or Cali to get a major-label deal. The two took the indie route, garnering a cult following in the South long before anyone in New York or Cali even knew who Eightball & MJG even were. By the end of the '90s, the two rappers were legends in the South, seen by most as pioneers of the dirty South movement. In addition to his work with MJG, Eightball guested on countless songs and released solo albums, his debut being the triple-disc *Lost* (1998). By the time he released his second solo album in late 2001, *Almost Famous*, Eightball had never been more recognized yet still hadn't totally crossed over to mainstream success, hence the album title. —*Jason Birchmeier*

Lost / May 19, 1998 / Uptown/Universal ✦✦✦
In the late '90s, bigger meant better in hip-hop. Ever since 2Pac raised the stakes with his double-disc opus *All Eyez on Me*, rappers were racing to keep pace, issuing double-disc albums at the drop of a hat. And that's why it didn't really come as a surprise when Eightball released *Lost* as a triple-disc set in the summer of 1998. Upon close inspection, the third disc is revealed to be a sampler of the Suave House record label. Unfortunately—for Eightball's sake, at least—that sampler turns out to be more interesting than *Lost*. Even though it's his first album without MJG, Eightball sounds no different on *Lost* than he did on any of its predecessors—he's simply turning out the same Southern gangsta riffs he has for years. The law of averages guarantees that there's a fair share of strong material here, but it's a shame that none of it sounds as inspired as the best moments of the third disc. The Suave House sampler showcases Southern rap at its best—it's raunchy, lyrically deft and, above all, funky. Master P, the Goodie Mobb, Mystikal, Silkk the Shocker, Psycho Drama, and many other rappers are featured on the sampler, which provides an excellent introduction to Southern hip-hop. That alone makes *Lost* worth picking up, and in that context, the averageness of Eightball's double-disc effort isn't so bad. —*Stephen Thomas Erlewine*

8 Ball Presents: The Slab / Apr. 24, 2001 / 8 Ways ✦✦✦
Still riding off the success of his *Space Age 4 Eva* album with MJG, 8 Ball returned with this impressive compilation in spring 2001. Functioning as the debut for his new 8 Ways label, *8 Ball Presents: The Slab* features several familiar names from the South, such as MJG, Lil' Keke, DJ Squeeky, and Project Playaz, along with two other big-money artists from the Bay Area, including E-40 and Too Short. But for the most part, *The Slab* serves to introduce a number of talented rappers from the South—in particular, Texas and Memphis, TN—that only the most die-hard dirty South fans will probably be familiar with. As such, this compilation will surely satisfy anyone intrigued by the style of rap associated with 8 Ball or Lil' Keke. Not only do most of the featured artists sound similar to these two obvious touchstones, but this compilation also features some top-notch production that is heavy on the synth

and the bass. Granted, there are some songs here that aren't quite up to par with the album's better moments—"Creeses & Pieces" being a true highlight—yet with nearly 20 songs total and around a dozen rappers dropping rhymes, there's plenty of diversity. Recommended to even the most casual 8 Ball and MJG fans, and also recommended to anyone willing to dig deeper than the first tier of well-known dirty South artists in search of some of the style's more underground talents. —*Jason Birchmeier*

Lay It Down / Oct. 23, 2001 / Draper Inc. ♦♦
Lay It Down gathers up the leftovers from Eightball's late-'90s stint with Tony Draper's Suave House label. Most of these tracks were several years old by the time they were released. They're still potent, however, albeit somewhat haphazardly produced, and showcase Eightball during his underground years, shortly before he became more well known. Though *Lay It Down* doesn't quite compare to Eightball's other solo albums, it's nonetheless a quality collection of vault recordings that completists should savor. —*Jason Birchmeier*

• **Almost Famous** / Nov. 20, 2001 / JCOR ♦♦♦
Having already established himself as a living legend in the dirty South scene back when the movement was strictly underground, Eightball set his sights on crossover success with *Almost Famous*. At the time of the album's release in late 2001, the self-proclaimed fat mack had almost made it there, as the album title confidently points out. Unlike his sprawling triple-disc debut album, *Lost* (1998), this follow-up features only a few guests (Carl Thomas, P Diddy, and Ludacris, most notably) and virtually no outside producers, emphasizing solely Eightball himself instead. Indeed, *Almost Famous* centers distinctly on the rapper, exploring his personal life in depth, both past and present. It's undoubtedly nice to hear Eightball flow unaccompanied here, though you do miss longtime partner MJG at times. Even so, Eightball could use a little bit more help, not from outside rappers but rather from his producers, who don't provide anything particularly exceptional to work with here, beat or song wise. Eightball thus carries *Almost Famous* largely alone, and while the big man is more than capable of doing so, he sure could use some of the stellar production (courtesy of Swizz Beatz, DJ Quik, and Jazze Pha) that had characterized his previous album with MJG, *Space Age 4 Eva* (2000). —*Jason Birchmeier*

Eightball & MJG

f. Memphis, TN
Group / Southern Rap, Dirty South
Eightball & MJG may have never made a significant impact nationally during their rise to fame in the 1990s, yet they indeed made an incredible impact throughout the South, where the Memphis-bred duo pioneered what countless dirty South rappers would emulate years later. The two began on the Southern underground circuit, where they peddled their tapes in such major markets as Memphis, Houston, and Atlanta. After a few years of this, Eightball & MJG helped launch Suave House Records in 1993 and attract a pair of national distribution deals soon afterward. By the end of the '90s, just as the dirty South movement broke nationally, the duo issued their final Suave House album, the classic *In Our Lifetime, Vol. 1* (1999), and declared themselves Southern rap pioneers. Few argued, as the two and particularly Eightball made countless cameo appearances for an array of fellow Southern rappers, earning the duo respect for their work ethic and diplomacy as well as their mature perspective and street-smart wits. In later years, Eightball & MJG finally began flirting with crossover success, ultimately signing to P Diddy's Bad Boy label in 2002.

Eightball (Premro Smith) and MJG (Marlon Jermaine Goodwin) grew up in the rough Orange Mound area of Memphis and met at Ridgeway Junior High in 1984. They shared a passion for hip-hop, which hadn't yet made a strong impact in the South, and soon formed a partnership. After years of mix-tape work, later re-released on *Lyrics of a Pimp* (1997) and *Memphis Under World* (2000) compilations, the two started Suave House Records with savvy 20-year-old CEO Tony Draper. The label released Eightball & MJG's debut full-length, *Comin' Out Hard* (1993), a cult classic produced entirely by the duo and popularized by the song "Armed Robbery."

Each successive year brought with it a new album: *On the Outside Looking In* (1994) and *On Top of the World* (1995), the latter distributed nationally by Relativity. These releases continued to expand the duo's reach throughout the South, so much so that Universal Records offered Draper a lucrative distribution deal in 1997 for Suave House. Eightball & MJG afterward released a pair of solo albums—*Lost* (1997) and *No More Glory* (1998),

respectively—and went on to record their crowning achievement, *In Our Lifetime, Vol. 1* (1999). The album elevated the duo to nationally recognized status and earned universal acclaim, ultimately standing as one of the definitive dirty South albums of the era, alongside Goodie Mob's *Soul Food* (1995) and OutKast's late-'90s work.

Eightball & MJG parted ways with Suave House in 1999 and maintained a relatively low profile for a few years until they notably signed with P Diddy's Bad Bay label in 2002, recording an album for JCOR (*Space Age 4 Eva* [2000]) and scoring a widespread club hit ("Buck Bounce") in the meantime. —*Jason Birchmeier*

Comin' Out Hard / Aug. 1, 1993 / Suave House ♦♦♦
Though this 1993 album may sound a bit lo-fi to modern ears, it's considered one of the most influential Southern rap albums ever alongside Outkast's *Southernplayalisticadillacmuzik* (1994) and Goodie Mob's *Soul Food* (1995) as precedent-setting works. Of course, *Comin' out Hard* isn't nearly as polished as these two other albums; produced entirely by the duo, it was recorded on a shoestring budget and released on their own Suave House indie label to an audience that didn't yet exist. If you can get past the muddled production aesthetic, it's a rather potent album. Eightball is at his most furious here, spitting rhymes with plenty of aggression; conversely, MJG is confidently posed in his pimp stance here, a bit laid-back and chilled out. Furthermore, succinct at only nine tracks, the album doesn't come across bloated and effectively communicates the duo's patented pimp ideology. Subsequent 1990s albums by the duo would possess better production values, but none of them are as trendsetting and innovative as this effort; as a result, it has garnered a substantial cult following and is revered by those who remember its initial impact. —*Jason Birchmeier*

On the Outside Looking In / 1994 / Suave House ♦♦♦
Eightball & MJG made some significant strides forward on their second collection *On the Outside Looking In*. Featuring improved production skills and tighter rapping, the album suggested that the duo had the Southern potential to break nationally. —*Stephen Thomas Erlewine*

On Top of the World / Nov. 1995 / Suave House/Relativity ♦♦♦
Eightball & MJG's breakthrough album *On Top of the World* improves on their previous two albums. The duo builds on the G-funk stylings of Dr. Dre, making the music rougher and rawer. The album includes the single "Break 'Em Off" and "Friend or Foe," which features guest appearances from Mac Mall, E-40, and Big Mike. —*Stephen Thomas Erlewine*

Lyrics of a Pimp / Dec. 23, 1997 / OTS ♦♦
Before Eightball & MJG debuted nationally with *Comin' Out Hard* on Suave House in 1993, the duo released a number of underground recordings, many of which were later compiled on *Lyrics of a Pimp* in 1997. Of particular note here is Eightball & MJG's first big hit, "Listen to the Lyrics," as well as the early version of "Armed Robbery," their later hit. The sound quality here is obviously lo-fi, as independent recordings were still a rare occurrence at the time, particularly in the South, yet the historical nature of these recordings should interest die-hard fans curious about the duo's humble beginnings. —*Jason Birchmeier*

• **In Our Lifetime, Vol. 1** / May 18, 1999 / Suave House ♦♦♦♦♦
Aging does not become most hip-hop artists, nor do reunions. However, there are always exceptions that prove the rule and, apparently, *In Our Lifetime, Vol. 1* is one of those cases. Eightball & MJG went on hiatus in 1998, and they both released solo albums that weren't bad, but weren't particularly noteworthy, either. Their reunion on *In Our Lifetime, Vol. 1* is another story altogether. Working with producers Organized Noise, T-Mix, and Black, the duo have found an appealing variation on the dirty South sound—a smooth groove that recalls classic late-'70s/early-'80s funk, while taking chances with its drum machine rhythms and the overall sonic texture. Even the hardest-hitting cuts, "Get It Crunk" and "We Started This," have a spacey feel to their production. It all holds together, and none of the guest artists—including Cee-Lo, Big Duke, Nina Creque, and Outkast—detracts from Eightball & MJG, who have written some of their finest lyrics yet. The entire album is designed as an oral history of their past, and since they have a loose narrative to follow, they've wound up creating their most coherent—and arguably best—album yet. Very few rappers could claim to get better with age, but it seems like Eightball & MJG may be doing just that. —*Stephen Thomas Erlewine*

Memphis Under World / Feb. 22, 2000 / OTS ♦♦

Like *Lyrics of a Pimp*, *Memphis Under World* compiles previously unavailable Eightball & MJG material from the duo's underground days. The key tracks are indeed here—"Listen to the Lyrics," "Armed Robbery," and "Pimp N My Own Rhymes"—as are some collaborations with fellow Memphis rappers, most notably Three 6 Mafia on "Break da Law." There isn't as much material here as on *Lyrics of a Pimp*, yet *Memphis Under World* should nonetheless similarly interest die-hard fans curious about Eightball & MJG's humble beginnings amid the small-scale Memphis underground scene. —*Jason Birchmeier*

Space Age 4 Eva / Nov. 21, 2000 / JCOR ♦♦♦

After the thoughtful reflection of *In Our Lifetime, Vol. 1* (1999), which had cast Eightball & MJG as been-there, done-that Southern rap sages and earned widespread acclaim in the process, the duo responded with the lighthearted *Space Age 4 Eva*. This album, Eightball & MJG's first non-Suave House release, returns to the space-age pimping that had been the duo's stock in trade for years. The club-orientated tracks stand out, particularly the Swizz Beatz-produced "At the Club" and the DJ Quik-produced "Buck Bounce," both of which paired Eightball & MJG with non-Southern big-name producers for the first time. Elsewhere, a pair of Jazze Pha productions also stand out, the meditative "Thingz" and the aggressive "Pimp Hard," as do the celebratory title track and the surprisingly intense album closer, "Thank God." While these individual moments feature some of the best production work Eightball & MJG had ever rapped over, the album itself as a whole plays like a mishmash, more a collection of big-name producer collaborations than a cohesive whole, which many of the duo's previous albums had been. —*Jason Birchmeier*

El Da Sensei

Underground Rap, East Coast Rap

El Da Sensei stepped onto the hip-hop scene as one half of the Newark, NJ, duo, the Artifacts. The Artifacts first rose to fame with the hit "Wrong Side of the Tracks." After El Da Sensei and his partner Tame-One sent a rough demo to Bobbito the Barber at WKCR in New York, the group was signed to Big Beat/Atlantic Records. They released their debut album, *Between a Rock & a Hard Place*, in 1994 with "Wrong Side of the Tracks" as the lead single and video. After that initial hit, the Artifacts splashed the world with joints like "Come on With the Come On" and "Dynamite Soul," and went onto tour the U.S. as well as Europe and Japan. They had developed a fan base of hardcore hip-hoppers, being graffiti artists and hip-hop purists themselves; they sparked a new subculture in hip-hop called "backpackers." In 1996 the group followed up their debut with their sophomore album, *That's Them*. Although not nearly successful as the first album, many hip-hop fans claim the album is an "underground classic," spawning the underground hits "The Art of Facts" and "The Ultimate." Shortly after the release of the second album, El and Tame decided on an amicable breakup. After the split, El Da Sensei went on his own traveling around the world and appeared on numerous compilations from Japan to Norway to Germany. During this time, he dropped the singles "Frontline" and "Got That" to let fans know he was still working. In the fall of 2002, El finally dropped his debut solo album, *Relax, Relate, Release*, through 7 Heads Entertainment. The album featured guest appearances from Sadat X (of Brand Nubian), J-Live, Organized Konfusion (Pharoah Monch and Prince Po), Mike Zoot & F.T., Asheru, and others. —*Quibian 'Q' Salazar-Moreno*

● **Relax, Relate, Release** / Oct. 1, 2002 / 7 Heads ♦♦♦

EL-P (Jaime Meline)

Producer / Underground Rap, Hip-Hop, Alternative Rap

EL-P, aka El Producto, is one of hip-hop's most obstinate and adventurous pioneers, combining a mid-'80s lo-fi old school aesthetic with a progressive rock musician's inclination to push boundaries. He has never succumbed to the whims of corporate hip-hop, instead choosing to pursue his own decidedly uncommercial leanings. In the mid-'90s, he developed a strong reputation with the groundbreaking trio Company Flow, a band whose achievements include the first LP, *Funcrusher Plus*, on Rawkus Records, a label that is considered by many the best label for intelligent hip-hop. Over the group's auspicious stint together, he proved he was himself capable of intense lyricism and sonic production so powerful it could stand on its own. In the latter

part of the '90s, El-P was also a collaborator with Blackalicious, Mos Def, and Dilated Peoples. In 2001, after releasing one last album with Harlem rappers Cannibal OX, the group chose to amicably pursue their own directions. El-P had started his own label, Definitive Jux, and was also selected to work on former Rage Against the Machine frontman Zack de la Rocha's first solo album. Somehow he found the time to work on his own solo release during all of this, *Fantastic Damage*, which saw the light of day in May of 2002. —*Kieran McCarthy*

El-P Presents Cannibal Oxtrumentals / Mar. 19, 2002 / Definitive Jux ♦♦♦♦

Usually, instrumental hip-hop albums are of limited appeal to most consumers. Without the skillful rhyming of a charismatic MC, even the most artfully constructed beats simply are not especially intriguing to anyone except aspiring rappers looking for beats to rhyme over, and DJs looking for beats to use as segues. But with a handful of producers, instrumental rap LPs can be as compelling as the originals. *El-P Presents Cannibal Oxtrumentals* compiles the backing tracks from Cannibal Ox's 2001 release, *The Cold Vein*, and the album's main producer, Definitive Jux's formidable founder El-P (formerly of Company Flow) reveals himself to be as skillful a producer as the Automator or RZA, and even without Cannibal Ox's vocals, the instrumentals are still worth listening to. Mainly the album sounds as if it were the soundtrack from an unmade film, much as the work Eno made in the 1970s, since the tracks have a distinct cinematic quality that allows them to cohere and flow beautifully. Furthermore, plenty of little touches emerge that would otherwise be obscured by vocals, such as the electric guitar riffs in "Pigeon," or the cathedral-like organ in "A B-Boy's Alpha." *Oxtrumentals* serves not only as a worthy companion piece to *The Cold Vein* but also as a fascinating album in its own right. —*Victor W. Valdivia*

● **Fantastic Damage** / May 14, 2002 / Definitive Jux ♦♦♦♦♦

Of all the boundary-pushing underground hip-hop acts who emerged in the late '90s, Company Flow was easily among the hardest and least compromising, spinning highly technical rhymes over buzzing, lo-fi beats with virtually no concessions to melody or polish. It comes as no surprise that one-time Company Flow leader El-P's solo debut, *Fantastic Damage*, takes a similar approach—yet it's a logical and distinct progression from the sound that made Company Flow such seminal figures in underground rap. *Fantastic Damage* is even more aggressive and confrontational in its approach, and this time out, El-P himself is solely responsible for the sonic backdrop, producing the entire record by himself. If the production sounds a little fuller than Company Flow's essential *Funcrusher Plus*, it's likely because in many places El-P has fleshed out his scuzzy, banging, stop-start percussion tracks with abrasive, distorted noise, which sounds like nothing so much as the furies unleashed. There are also plenty of tinny, blooping vintage synths that lend the music a cold, inhuman air—and that's no doubt intentional, because *Fantastic Damage* paints a chilling portrait of contemporary society that's so bleak it often crosses into the apocalyptic. The music makes El-P's paranoid totalitarian nightmares totally convincing, not just because of its sheer wallop, but also in the subtler details that emerge with repeated listens—the bizarre sound snippets and ghostly washes that seem to teeter on the edge of madness. Throughout the record, El-P proves he's one of the most technically gifted MCs of his time, spitting out near-impossible phrases and rhythmic variations that simply leave the listener's head spinning. Accessible it isn't, but *Fantastic Damage* constitutes some of the most challenging, lyrically dense hip-hop around, assembled by one of the genre's true independent mavericks. —*Steve Huey*

Fandam Plus: Instrumentals, Remixes, Lyrics & Video / Oct. 1, 2002 / Definitive Jux ♦♦♦♦

Much as his work with Cannibal Ox proved before, El-P is truly one of music's most innovative, idiosyncratic producers, fusing the blunt crudeness of early-'80s hip-hop with the futuristic sweep and experimentation of progressive pioneers like Brian Eno and Can. *Fandam Plus*, a two-disc set that compiles instrumentals from his solo debut, *Fantastic Damage*, as well as remixes, demonstrates El-P's truly unusual talents. The instrumentals are especially powerful. Stripped of their vocals, they reveal new dimensions to what were previously only backing tracks. "Deep Space 9mm" and "Truancy" sound truly creepy and unnerving here, while "Dead Disnee" becomes even funnier with only the chirpy chorus vocals left. The second disc, which contains some remixes and enhanced content, is not quite as interesting. The remixes are enjoyable enough, but don't really add to or radically alter the music, so they really only prove how impressive El-P's original work was to begin with. (The second disc also contains enhanced content, mainly videos and lyrics.) It may seem strange to consider an instrumental hip-hop album as essential listening, but *Fandam Plus* is so experimental and inventive that it should appeal to more than just El-P fans. — *Victor W. Valdivia*

Elementz

Group / British Rap, Underground Rap

Based in Birmingham, U.K., the Elementz were comprised of Lickal Vain, Torsion, Noir Star, Decision, and DJ Rhize. As concerned with changing states of mind as much as states of dancefloors, the Elementz MCs brought socially conscious raps over beats that morphed from downtempo to jazzy to banging in the blink of an eye or the twist of a phrase. Formed in early 2000, the Elementz crew quickly made a name for itself in the U.K.'s underground hip-hop community with the *Neon Verses* EP, issued by Different Drummer that same year. Featuring three tracks with vocals and three without, the collection established the Elementz as competitors alongside Birmingham hip-hop heavyweights like MSI & Asylum. In February of 2001, the Elementz released an album version of *Neon Verses*, this time with 20 tracks. It further solidified the crew's reputation for uniquely formed beats (incorporating such disparate elements as oboe and homemade samples) behind socially informed raps. — *Johnny Loftus*

● **Neon Verses** / Feb. 6, 2001 / Different Drummer ✦✦✦

"Birmingham's a city, a small world of darkness," the Elementz recount on the leadoff track "Speech Therapy," from their album *Neon Verses*. It's a statement uttered by many of England's new artists as they attempt to reconcile the dark and dreary environments of many of the country's industrialized cities with problems of their own. The Elementz, a collective of hip-hoppers that rhyme in the vein of A Tribe Called Quest, Digable Planets, and Mos Def, are intent on changing things for the better while remaining true to their roots. And being a part of this consciousness raising style of hip-hop sometimes assumes a great deal of responsibility. With that in mind, Elementz never miss a beat. The entire record, so stylized yet sensible, is packed with strong beats, clever delivery, even more clever lyrics, and scaled-down production that never oversteps its boundaries. They also employ vibes, oboe, and other instruments quite nicely to weave some gorgeous melodies into their message-filled lyrics. These are men with strong voices, thick rhythms, and a definite vision that screams out above any mainstream hip-hop today. Brimming with tracks, 20 in total, *Neon Verses* is a brilliant debut for these young MCs. Forget Britain, the Elementz have their eyes on the prize, and it's got nothing to do with money. — *Ken Taylor*

11/5

Group / Hip-Hop, Gangsta Rap, G-Funk

11/5 was one of the first gangsta rap groups to surface in the California Bay Area. The trio featuring Taydatay, Hennessy, and Maine-O debuted in 1995 with their *Fiendin' 4 tha Funk* album on Dogday Records, which featured the hit song "Brousin'," followed a year later by the *A-1 Yola* album; both albums were produced by T.C., best known for his work with RBL Posse. *Bootlegs & G-Sides* followed, compiling the trio's appearances on non-11/5 albums. Despite being one of the Bay Area's pioneering hardcore rap groups, 11/5 never experienced the widespread success that peers such as Spice 1 and E-40 found in the late '90s. — *Jason Birchmeier*

Collections: Bootlegs & G-Sides / Aug. 5, 1997 / Dogday ✦✦✦

● **Hits and More, Vol. 1** / May 7, 2002 / Five Star ✦✦✦

Missy Elliott (Melissa Elliott)

b. Portsmouth, VA

Vocals, Producer / Hip-Hop, Urban, Alternative Rap

No female rap artist paralleled the success of Missy Elliott, neither during her reign nor before, and none was more deserving. Unlike most of urban music's female superstars, Missy writes her own songs as well as performs them, and her creative wit in on a par with her stylish demeanor. In addition to her talent and showmanship, though, she established herself as a genuine hitmaker alongside her longtime producer, Timbaland. She initially scored hits for others, namely Aaliyah ("One in a Million," "If Your Girl Only Knew") and to a lesser extent 702 ("Steelo") before moving on to score a dazzling run for herself. Her debut album, *Supa Dupa Fly* (1997), spawned a number of

hits such as "The Rain" that were more trendsetting than they were chart topping. The chart toppers, of course, came soon after: "She's a Bitch" and "Hot Boyz" (1999); "Get Ur Freak On" and "One Minute Man" (2001); and "Work It" and "Gossip Folks" (2002). In each of these, Missy proved that, with both dignity and joviality, women could be sexual as well as forceful. As a result, she defied every stereotype imaginable without forsaking her broad fan base. Born in Portsmouth, VA, in 1971 as Melissa Elliott, Missy's professional music career began when Jodeci member/producer Devante Swing signed her and her group, Sista, to his Swing Mob record label. Unfortunately, Swing Mob Records fell through and along with it the plans for Sista's debut album. Determined to move forward, Missy turned to longtime acquaintance Timbaland, who happened to be producing some tracks for Aaliyah's *One in a Million* (1996) album. It proved to be a key move for Missy, as the album racked up enormous sales. Soon record execs were knocking on her door. Missy began working with a number of artists as either a songwriter or a vocalist/rapper before finally signing herself a deal with Elektra in 1996. A year later, *Supa Dupa Fly* hit the streets and soon after went platinum, thanks to "The Rain." Besides the sales numbers, the album also proved critically successful, impressing nearly everyone who heard it. It had not only radio-ready singles ("Sock It 2 Me," "Beep Me 911," "Hit 'Em Wit da Hee") but also an astounding array of album tracks that showcases just how multitalented Missy indeed was, singing on some, rapping on others.

In 1999 she returned with her much-awaited follow-up album, *Da Real World*, an even more ambitious album that featured two mammoth hits—"She's a Bitch" and "Hot Boyz"—along with an array of often daring collaborations with such unlikely candidates as Eminem. Around this same time, she began appearing in TV ads for the Gap and Sprite, proving that she was not only she a musical talent but also an important icon for the era. The cycle repeated itself in 2001 when she released *Miss E...So Addictive*, again powered by two huge hits: "Get Ur Freak On" and "One Minute Man." Her remarkable popularity continued a year later with her next album, *Under Construction*, and its leadoff single, "Work It." — *Jason Birchmeier*

★ **Supa Dupa Fly** / Jul. 15, 1997 / Goldmind/Elektra ✦✦✦✦✦

Arguably the most influential album ever released by a female hip-hop artist, Missy "Misdemeanor" Elliott's debut album, *Supa Dupa Fly*, is a boundary-shattering postmodern masterpiece. It had a tremendous impact on hip-hop, and an even bigger one on R&B, as its futuristic, nearly experimental style became the de facto sound of urban radio at the close of the millennium. A substantial share of the credit has to go to producer Timbaland, whose lean, digital grooves are packed with unpredictable arrangements and stuttering rhythms that often resemble slowed-down drum'n'bass breakbeats. The results are not only unique, they're nothing short of revolutionary, making Timbaland a hip name to drop in electronica circles as well. For her part, Elliott impresses with her versatility—she's a singer, a rapper, and an equal songwriting partner, and it's clear from the album's accompanying videos that the space-age aesthetic of the music doesn't just belong to her producer. She's no technical master on the mic; her raps are fairly simple, delivered in the slow purr of a heavy-lidded stoner. Yet they're also full of hilariously surreal free associations that fit the off-kilter sensibility of the music to a tee. Actually, Elliott sings more on *Supa Dupa Fly* than she does on her subsequent albums, making it her most R&B-oriented effort; she's more unique as a rapper than she is as a singer, but she has a smooth voice and harmonizes well. Guest rappers Busta Rhymes, Lil' Kim, and da Brat all appear on the first three tracks, which almost pull focus away from Elliott until she unequivocally takes over with the brilliant single "The Rain (Supa Dupa Fly)"; elsewhere, "Sock It 2 Me," "Beep Me 911," and the weeded-out "Izzy Izzy Ahh" nearly match its genius. Elliott and Timbaland would continue to refine and expand this blueprint, sometimes with even greater success, but *Supa Dupa Fly* contains the roots of everything that followed. — *Steve Huey*

Da Real World / Jun. 22, 1999 / Goldmind/Elektra ✦✦✦✦

It's really not that difficult to hurdle the sophomore blues provided you're an excellent songwriter and performer, that you have the same, equally excellent producer behind the scenes who contributed to the first album, and most importantly, that you haven't tampered with the hitmaking formula from the first. Thankfully, *Da Real World* is clearly a Missy Elliott album in most respects, with Timbaland's previously trademarked, futuristic-breakbeat production smarts laced throughout. The churchgoing Elliott has often remarked that she wishes she didn't need profanity to get attention, and the album accordingly includes satirical nods to other clichéd notions of hip-hop—the single "She's a Bitch" is the best example, wherein Elliott reappropriates the insult to refer to strong females. She also takes on the cartoonish Eminem for "Bus a Rhyme," a track that turns out to be one of the best on the album. Da Brat and Aaliyah make repeat appearances, and Redman and Outkast's Big Boi also contribute to this excellent follow-up. —*Keith Farley*

Miss E . . . So Addictive / May 15, 2001 / Goldmind/Elektra ◆◆◆◆◆
Sounding more assured of her various strengths than at any time since her startling debut, Missy "Misdemeanor" Elliott broke in several directions for 2001's *Miss E…So Addictive*. At the same time, she's a sexed-up rapper demanding respect from men, a loved-up club diva leading the charge of rappers into the brave new world of dance culture, and a sensitive female spreading syrup over a few great ballads. It's a tribute to her incredible song-writing skills and Timbaland's continuing production excellence that she can have it any way she wants it and still come away with a full-length that hangs together brilliantly. She definitely starts out hardcore, with a pair of self-explanatory titles ("Dog in Heat," "One Minute Man") featuring Elliott cooling down on a trio of rappers (Redman, Method Man, Ludacris) and definitely getting the best of them. By "Get Ur Freak On," the lead single, she's changed angles and become a new-millennium diva straddling the worlds of hip-hop and commercial dance with bumping club tracks like "Scream aka Itch" and "4 My People." But before listeners can reconcile Elliott the club kid, special guest Ginuwine takes the album into love-ballad territory with "Take Away," a half-step ballad with an irresistible plucked-string production from Timbaland. Though *Miss E…So Addictive* is undeniably Elliott's affair, Timbaland's production really stretches out and pulls the album together. He's less reliant on his oft-copied trademarks, and more willing to experiment with left-field samples and seemingly odd bridges that always work despite the audio high-wire act. Though it fails to come up with anything to top her big singles hit, "The Rain (Supa Dupa Fly)," *Miss E…So Addictive* is her best album so far. —*John Bush*

Under Construction / Nov. 12, 2002 / Elektra ◆◆◆◆◆
The fact that Missy Elliott still considers her work to be "under construction" should, justifiably, send everyone else in the rap world scurrying back to the drawing board. No other commercial rapper sounded more in command of her production and flow than Elliott during 2002, and it's no surprise that *Under Construction* ranks as one of the best rap LPs of the year (granted, it came against relatively weak competition). While Timbaland's stark digital soul girds these tracks, Missy herself continues her artistic progression, trying to push hip-hop forward with an almost pleading intro and neatly emphasizing her differences from other rappers by writing tracks for nearly every facet of the female side of relationships. The hit single "Work It" turns the tables on male rappers, taking charge of the sex game, matching their lewdest, rudest rhymes, and also featuring the most notorious backmasked vocal of the year. Elliott more than keeps up with a dirty-minded Method Man as well on "Bring the Pain," strikes back at haters on the self-explanatory "Gossip Folks," and produced her own duet with Beyoncé Knowles, "Nothing Out There for Me," a track that finds her trying to lure Knowles out to a party (using her best Timbaland impression) over the wishes of the diva's homebound man. She also recognizes the constantly changing aspects of sexuality, admitting how dependent she is on a man during "Play That Beat" but ruminating on the curious power of the female persuasion on "P**ussy**cat." Elliott goes on a refreshing old school tear with "Back in the Day," featuring Jay-Z having more fun than he's had in a while and Missy crooning, "What happened to those good old days, when hip-hop was so much fun/Those parties in the summer y'all, and no one came through with a gun." The disc closes with the TLC duet "Can You Hear Me," a tribute to Aaliyah and Lisa "Left Eye" Lopes. Missy Elliott obviously understands how important hip-hop can be when rappers concentrate on the music instead of the violent lifestyle; fortunately, her talents are just as strong as her vision. —*John Bush*

Eminem (Marshall Mathers III)

b. Oct. 17, 1972, St. Joseph, MO
Hardcore Rap, Hip-Hop
A protégé of Dr. Dre, rapper Eminem emerged in 1999 as one of the most controversial rappers to ever grace the genre. Using his biting wit and incredible skills to vent on everything from his unhappy childhood to his contempt for the mainstream media, his success became the biggest crossover

success the genre had seen since Dre's solo debut seven years earlier. The controversy over his lyrics was the best publicity any musician could afford, and being the first Caucasian rapper to make a significant impact in years may have given him a platform not afforded to equally talented African-American rappers. A gifted producer as well, his talents always seemed overshadowed by his media presence, which was a mix between misunderstood genius and misogynistic homophobe. Both may be true, but his message spoke to legions of disaffected youth who had few role models in the rap world who could relate to the white lower-class experience.

He was born Marshall Mathers III in St. Joseph, MO (near Kansas City), spending the better part of his impoverished childhood shuttling back and forth between his hometown and the city of Detroit. Initially attracted to rap as a teen, Eminem began performing at age 14, performing raps in the basement of his high school friend's home. The two went under the names Manix and M&M (soon changed to Eminem), which Mathers took from his own initials. Due to the unavoidable racial boundaries that came with being a white rapper, he decided the easiest way to win over underground hip-hop audiences was to become a battle rapper and improv against other MCs in clubs. Although he wasn't immediately accepted, through time he became such a popular attraction that people would challenge him just to make a name for themselves. His uncle's suicide prompted a brief exodus from the world of rap, but he returned and found himself courted by several other rappers to start groups. He first joined the New Jacks, and then moved on to Soul Intent, who released Eminem's first recorded single in 1995. A rapper named Proof performed the B side on the single and enjoyed working with Eminem so much that he asked him to start yet another group. Drafting in a few other friends, the group became known as D-12, a six-member crew that supported one another as solo artists more than they collaborated. The birth of Eminem's first child put his career on hold again as he started working in order to care for his family. This also instilled a bitterness that started to creep into his lyrics as he began to drag personal experiences into the open and make them the topic of his raps.

A debut record, 1996's *Infinite*, broke his artistic rut but received few good reviews, as comparisons to Nas and AZ came unfavorably. Undaunted, he downplayed many of the positive messages he had been including in his raps and created Slim Shady, an alterego that was not afraid to say whatever he felt. Tapping into his innermost feelings, he had a bounty of material to work with when his mother was accused of mentally and physically abusing his younger brother the same year. The next year his girlfriend left him and barred him from visiting their child, so he was forced to move back in with his mother, an experience that fueled his hatred toward her and made him even more sympathetic toward his brother. The material he was writing was uncharacteristically dark as he began to abuse drugs and alcohol at a more frequent rate. An unsuccessful suicide attempt was the last straw, as he realized his musical ambitions were the only way to escape his unhappy life. He released the brutal *Slim Shady EP*, a mean-spirited, funny, and thought-provoking record that was light years ahead of the material he had been writing beforehand. Making quite the impression in the underground not only for his exaggerated, nasal-voiced rapping style but also for his skin color, many quarters dubbed him the music's next "great white hope."

According to legend, Dr. Dre discovered his demo tape on the floor of Interscope label chief Jimmy Iovine's garage, but the reality was that Eminem took second place in the freestyle category at 1997's Rap Olympics MC Battle in Los Angeles and Iovine approached the rapper for a tape afterward. It wasn't until a month or two later that he played the tape for an enthusiastic Dre, who eagerly contacted Eminem. Upon meeting, Dre was taken back by his skin color more than his skill, but within the first hour they had already started recording "My Name Is." Dre agreed to produce his first album and the two released "Just Don't Give a Fuck" as a single to preview the new album. A reconciliation with his girlfriend led to the two getting married in the fall of 1998, and Interscope signed the rapper and prepared to give him a massive push on Dre's advice. An appearance on Kid Rock's *Devil Without a Cause* only helped the buzz that was slowly surrounding him.

The best-selling *Slim Shady LP* followed in early 1999, scoring a massive hit with the single and video "My Name Is," plus a popular follow-up in "Guilty Conscience"; over the next year, the album went triple platinum. With such wide exposure, controversy ensued over the album's content, with some harshly criticizing its cartoonish, graphic violence; others praised its edginess and surreal humor, as well as Eminem's own undeniable lyrical skills and Dre's inventive production. In between albums, Eminem appeared on Dre's *Dr. Dre 2001*, with his contributions providing some of the record's liveliest moments.

The Marshall Mathers LP appeared in the summer of 2000, moving close to two million copies in its first week of release on its way to becoming the fastest-selling rap album of all time. Unfortunately, this success also bred more controversy, and no other musician was better suited for it than Eminem. Among the incidents that occurred included a scuffle with the Insane Clown Posse's employees in a car stereo shop, a bitter battle with pop star Christina Aguilera over a lyric about her fictional sexual exploits, a lawsuit from his mother over defamation of character, and an attack on a Detroit clubgoer after Eminem allegedly witnessed the man kissing his wife. Fans ate it up as his album stood strong at the top of the charts. But the mainstream media was not so enamored, as accusations of homophobia and sexism sprang from the inflammatory lyrics in the songs "Kill You" and "Kim." It was this last song that ended his marriage, as the song's chosen topic (violently murdering his real-life wife Kim Mathers) drove his spouse to a suicide attempt before they divorced. Eminem toured throughout most of this, settling several of his court cases and engaging a mini-feud with rapper Everlast.

The annual Grammy Awards nominated the album for several awards, and to silence his critics the rapper called on Elton John to duet with him at the ceremony. In 2001 he teamed with several of his old Detroit running buddies and reformed D-12. Releasing an album with the group, Eminem hit the road with them that summer and tried to ignore the efforts of his mother, who released an album in retaliation to his comments. After getting off of the road, he stepped in front of the camera and filmed *8 Mile*, a film loosely based on his life directed by the unlikely fan Curtis Hanson (*Wonder Boys*). His constant media exposure died out as well, leaving him time to work on new music.

When he re-emerged in 2002, he splashed onto the scene with "Without Me," a single that attacked Moby and Limp Bizkit and celebrated his return to music. Surprisingly, the following album, *The Eminem Show*, inspired little controversy. Instead, the popular second single "Cleanin' Out My Closet" told of his dysfunctional childhood and explained his hatred toward his mother in a mannered, poignant fashion. And being Eminem, he followed this up with an appearance at MTV's Video Music Awards that inspired boos when he verbally assaulted Moby for no apparent reason. —*Jason Ankeny and Bradley Torreano*

☆ **The Slim Shady LP** / Feb. 23, 1999 / Interscope ✦✦✦✦✦
Given his subsequent superstardom, culminating in no less than an Academy Award, it may be easy to overlook exactly how demonized Eminem was once his mainstream debut album, *The Slim Shady LP*, grabbed the attention of pop music upon its release in 1999. Then, it wasn't clear to every listener that Eminem was, as they say, an unreliable narrator, somebody who slung satire, lies, uncomfortable truths, and lacerating insights with vigor and venom, blurring the line between reality and parody, all seemingly without effort. *The Slim Shady LP* bristles with this tension, since it's not always clear when Marshall Mathers is joking and when he's dead serious. This was unsettling in 1999, when nobody knew his backstory, and years later, when his personal turmoil is public knowledge, it *still* can be unsettling, because his words and delivery are that powerful. Of course, nowhere is this more true than on "97 Bonnie and Clyde," a notorious track where he imagines killing his wife and then disposing of the body with his baby daughter in tow. There have been more violent songs in rap, but few more disturbing, and it's not because of what it describes, it's *how* he describes it—how the perfectly modulated phrasing enhances the horror and black humor of his words. Eminem's supreme gifts are an expansive vocabulary and vivid imagination, which he unleashes with wicked humor and unsparing anger in equal measure. The production—masterminded by Dr. Dre but also helmed in large doses by Marky and Jeff Bass, along with Marshall himself—mirrors his rhymes, with their spare, intricately layered arrangements enhancing his narratives, which are always at the forefront. As well they should be—there are few rappers as wildly gifted verbally as Eminem. At a time when many rappers were stuck in the stultifying swamp of gangsta clichés, Eminem broke through the hardcore murk by abandoning the genre's familiar themes and flaunting a style with more verbal muscle and imagination than any of his contemporaries. Years later, as the shock has faded, it's those lyrical skills and the subtle mastery of the music that still resonate, and they're what make *The Slim Shady LP* one of the great debuts in both hip-hop and modern pop music. —*Stephen Thomas Erlewine*

★ **The Marshall Mathers LP** / May 23, 2000 / Interscope ✦✦✦✦✦
It's hard to know what to make of Eminem, even if you know that half of what he says is sincere and half is a put-on; the trick is realizing that there's truth in the joke, and vice versa. Many dismissed his considerable skills as a rapper and social satirist because the vulgarity and gross-out humor on *The Slim Shady LP* were too detailed for some to believe that it was anything *but* real. To Eminem's credit, he decided to exploit that confusion on his masterful second record, *The Marshall Mathers LP*. Eminem is all about blurring the distinction between reality and fiction, humor and horror, satire and documentary, so it makes perfect sense that *The Marshall Mathers LP* is no more or no less "real" than *The Slim Shady LP*. It is, however, a fairly brilliant expansion of his debut, turning his spare, menacing hip-hop into a hyper-surreal, wittily disturbing thrill ride. It's both funnier and darker than his debut, and Eminem's writing is so sharp and clever that the jokes cut as deeply as the explorations of his ruptured psyche. The production is nearly as evocative as the raps, with liquid bass lines, stuttering rhythms, slight sound effects, and spacious soundscapes. There may not be overpowering hooks on every track, but the album works as a whole, always drawing the listener in. But, once you're in, Eminem doesn't care if you understand exactly where he's at, and he doesn't offer any apologies if you can't sort the fact from the fiction. As an artist, he's supposed to create his own world, and with this terrific second effort, he certainly has. It may be a world that is as infuriating as it is intriguing, but it is without question his own, which is far more than most of his peers are able to accomplish at the dawn of a new millennium. —*Stephen Thomas Erlewine*

The Eminem Show / May 26, 2002 / Interscope ✦✦✦✦
It's all about the title. First time around, Eminem established his alterego, Slim Shady—the character who deliberately shocked and offended millions, turning Eminem into a star. Second time at bat, he turned out *The Marshall Mathers LP*, delving deeper into his past while revealing complexity as an artist and a personality that helped bring him an even greater audience and much, much more controversy. Third time around, it's *The Eminem Show*—a title that signals that Eminem's public persona is front and center, for the very first time. And it is, as he spends much of the album commenting on the media circus that dominated his life ever since the release of *Marshall Mathers*. This, of course, encompasses many, many familiar subjects—his troubled childhood; his hatred of his parents; his turbulent relationship with his ex-wife, Kim (including the notorious incident when he assaulted a guy who allegedly kissed her—the event that led to their divorce); his love of his daughter, Hailie; and, of course, all the controversy he generated, notably the furor over his alleged homophobia and his scolding from Lynne Cheney, which leads to furious criticism about the hypocrisy of America and its government. All this is married to a production very similar to that of its predecessor—spare, funky, fluid, and vibrant, punctuated with a couple of ballads along the way. So, that means *The Eminem Show* is essentially a holding pattern, but it's a glorious one—one that proves Eminem is the gold standard in pop music in 2002, delivering stylish, catchy, dense, funny, political music that rarely panders (apart from a power ballad "Dream On" rewrite on "Sing for the Moment" and maybe the sex rap "Drips," that is). Even if there is little new ground broken, the presentation is exceptional—Dre never sounds better as a producer than when Eminem pushes him forward (witness the stunning oddity "Square Dance," a left-field classic with an ominous waltz beat)—and, with three albums under his belt, Eminem has proven himself to be one of the all-time classic MCs, surprising as much with his delivery as with what he says. Plus, the undercurrent of political anger—not just attacking Lynne Cheney but also raising questions about the Bush administration—gives depth to his typical topics, adding a new, spirited dimension to his shock tactics as notable as the deep sentimental streak he reveals on his odes to his daughter. Perhaps the album runs a little too long at 20 songs and 80 minutes, and would have flowed better if trimmed by 25 minutes, but that's a typical complaint about modern hip-hop records. Fact is, it still delivers more great music than most of its peers in rock or rap, and is further proof that Eminem is an artist of considerable range and dimension. —*Stephen Thomas Erlewine*

Encore (Shaya Bekele)

Hip-Hop, Gangsta Rap, Alternative Rap, Hardcore Rap, Underground Rap
Milpitas, CA's underground rapper Encore discovered hip-hop at an early age

and tried his hand at many of the style's aspects, including DJing, breaking and popping, and graffing, but found rhyming to be the least expensive—and most expressive—way to become involved in the hip-hop scene.

After he finished high school and left the army, Encore formed the Vinyl Miners with two old friends, DJ/producer Architect and MC 50 Grand, who soon departed for L.A. Architect and Encore continued to collaborate on tracks, which blended the DJ's inspired beats and samples with Encore's intelligent rhymes, often influenced by Islam and ancient African and Egyptian studies. Encore recorded singles for Certified Records and Stones Throw Records before appearing on Dan "The Automator" Nakamura and Prince Paul's Handsome Boy Modeling School album, *So…How's Your Girl?* The West Coast rapper's debut album, *Self-Preservation*, arrived in 2000 on 75 Ark Records. —*Heather Phares*

● **Self-Preservation** / Mar. 7, 2000 / 75 Ark ✦✦✦✦
Without any major-label hype, or crew affiliation, Encore has still managed to create quite a buzz for himself (no small feat these days). The ripples that his handful of underground singles generated were significantly intensified by his Rakim-like verbal explosion, "Waterworld," on Prince Paul and the Automator's critically acclaimed Handsome Boy Modeling School project. Encore's sheer lyrical dexterity is engraved into every verse of his debut, *Self-Preservation*, on which he effortlessly conjures up images of a time when MCing was in its purest form. The man behind the music, Architect, follows suit, as his crisp drum loops and pristine samples show very little evidence of contemporary influence. The contentious "Love and Hate" reiterates Encore's traditionalist convictions, as he paints an alternately affectionate and condemning mural of hip-hop, while ".084" reveals how an arrest for DUI compelled Encore to reevaluate his lifestyle and, in turn, led him to embrace the Islamic faith. His debut record proves that he is one of the most promising MCs to emerge from the flourishing Bay Area hip-hop scene. —*Matt Conaway*

EPMD

f. 1987
Group / Golden Age, East Coast Rap, Hardcore Rap
On the surface, the sample-reliant productions and monotone rapping styles of Erick Sermon and Parrish Smith had little to recommend them, but the duo's recordings as EPMD were among the best in hip-hop's underground during the late '80s and early '90s. Over the course of four albums (from the 1988 classic *Strictly Business* to 1992's *Business Never Personal*), they rarely varied from two themes: dissing sucker MCs and recounting sexual exploits. But a closer look reveals that the duo's rhymes were nothing less than incredible, simply undervalued because of their lack of intonation during delivery. EPMD also had a feel for a good groove, and created numerous hip-hop classics, including "It's My Thing," "You Gots to Chill," "Get the Bozack," "Strictly Business," and "Rampage."

Though EPMD's hardcore style influenced the urban-oriented gangsta '90s, Erick Sermon (aka E Double E; b. Nov. 25, 1968) and Parrish Smith (aka Pee MD; b. May 13, 1968) were both raised in the Long Island suburb of Brentwood. They moved into rap separately, with Smith DJing for Rock Squad on a single for Tommy Boy. After coming together in 1987—naming themselves EPMD, short for "Erick and Parrish Making Dollars"—the duo recorded their debut "It's My Thing" in three hours. The single was later licensed to Chrysalis, and EPMD signed to Sleeping Bag/Fresh Records for debut album *Strictly Business*. Propelled by several strong singles ("You Gots to Chill," the title track), the album eventually went gold, as did 1989's follow-up, *Unfinished Business*. Signed to Def Jam by the beginning of the '90s, EPMD returned in 1990 with *Business As Usual* and *Business Never Personal* two years later. By 1992, they presided over an extended family dubbed the Hit Squad, including Redman, K-Solo, and Das EFX. The duo split later that year, however, prompting solo careers for each; Sermon debuted in 1993 with *No Pressure*, and Smith made his statement on 1994's *Shade Business*. The duo re-formed EPMD in 1997, recording a strong comeback LP, *Back in Business*. *Out of Business* followed in 1999. —*John Bush*

★ **Strictly Business** / 1988 / Priority ✦✦✦✦✦
EPMD's blueprint for East Coast rap wasn't startlingly different from many others in rap's golden age, but the results were simply amazing, a killer blend of good groove and laid-back flow, plus a populist sense of sampling that had

heads nodding from the first listen (and revealed tastes that, like Prince Paul's, tended toward AOR as much as classic soul and funk). A pair from Long Island, EPMD weren't real-life hardcore rappers—it's hard to believe the same voice who talks of spraying a crowd on one track could be name checking the Hardy Boys later on—but their no-nonsense, monotoned delivery brooked no arguments. With their album debut, *Strictly Business*, Erick Sermon and Parrish Smith really turned rapping on its head; instead of simple lyrics delivered with a hyped, theatrical tone, they dropped the dopest rhymes as though they spoke them all the time. Their debut single, "You Gots to Chill," was a perfect example of the EPMD revolution; two obvious samples, Zapp's "More Bounce to the Ounce" and Kool & the Gang's "Jungle Boogie," doing battle over a high-rolling beat, with the fluid, collaborative raps of Sermon and Smith tying everything together with a mastery that made it all seem deceptively simple. There was really only one theme at work here— the brilliance of EPMD, or the worthlessness of sucker MCs—but every note of *Strictly Business* proved their claims. —*John Bush*

Unfinished Business / 1989 / Priority ✦✦✦✦✦
EPMD avoided the dreaded sophomore curse and kept its artistic momentum going on its second album, *Unfinished Business*. Once again, the duo triumphed by going against the flow—when MCs ranging from Public Enemy to Sir Mix-A-Lot to N.W.A weren't hesitating to be abrasive and hyper, EPMD still had a sound that was decidedly relaxed by rap standards. For the most part, EPMD's lyrics aren't exactly profound—boasting and attacking sucker MCs is still their favorite activity. However, Erick and Parrish do challenge themselves a bit lyrically on "You Had Too Much to Drink" (a warning against drunk driving) and "Please Listen to My Demo," which recalls the days when they were struggling. But regardless of subject matter, they keep things exciting by having such an appealing, captivating sound. —*Alex Henderson*

Business as Usual / 1990 / Def Jam ✦✦✦
Business as Usual is an ironic title for EPMD's third album—for in terms of production, it was anything but business as usual for the Strong Island rappers. While *Strictly Business* and *Unfinished Business* favored a very simple and basic approach to production consisting primarily of samples (many of them clever) and drum machines, the production is busier and more involved this time—and even suggests Marley Marl. Unfortunately, the sampling isn't as clever as before. What didn't change was EPMD's relatively laid-back approach to rapping and a preoccupation with sucker MCs. Though not as inspired as its two predecessors, the album does have its moments—including "Rampage" (which unites EPMD with LL Cool J), "Give the People," and "Gold Digger," a candid denunciation of "material girls" who exploit and victimize men financially after a divorce. —*Alex Henderson*

Business Never Personal / Jul. 28, 1992 / Def Jam ✦✦✦✦✦
Having recorded two undeniable hip-hop classics right out the box, EPMD met with a modicum of disapproval for the first time ever upon the release of its third album, which was graded down by some fans and critics because it seemed to be, yes, more business as usual rather than any sort of musical maturation or progression. Unbowed, Erick and Parrish returned with what, at the time, was rumored even before it hit shelves to be their final album together. Indeed, the duo broke up not long after *Business Never Personal* came out. It was a perfect way to go out together. The album proved to be both a commercial and artistic triumph at the time, and with each passing year, it sounds more and more like their finest—if not their most historically important—recording. Unapologetically underground throughout its career up to this point, the duo was savvy enough to throw a bone to an ever-growing rap-listening public in a supposed bid for crossover appeal even as it was taking its concluding bow, thereby negating any cries of "sell-out" that otherwise might have been tossed at the group's reputation for independence from any commercial concerns. Frankly, though, it would have been a difficult claim to make stick against EPMD anyway. Despite its appealing Zapp sample and hook, "Crossover" is every bit as coated in street soot as the rest of its music. Nevertheless, it is undoubtedly the catchiest thing the pair had ever created. The rest of the album is harder hitting but in every respect as captivating, running from the abrasively metallic "Boon Dox" to the crowd-moving Hit Squad posse cut "Head Banger," and returning the group more often than not to the scowling (though often tongue-in-cheek) intensity and minimalistic aesthetic of its first two records. And if Erick and Parrish hadn't yet made the impending end of their partnership explicit enough, they do so on the final

track, where they finally, figuratively kill off Jane, the transvestite prostitute who had hawked them through each of their albums. —*Stanton Swihart*

Back in Business / Sep. 16, 1997 / Def Jam ✦✦✦

EPMD's reunion album *Back in Business* may not be entirely successful, but it's far from being an embarrassment. Erick Sermon and Parrish Smith remain strong, if unexceptional rappers, but the true news is in the music. Much of *Back in Business* captures the wild spirit of EPMD's classic late-'80s albums, complete with dense layers of sounds, samples, and funky beats. There's enough skill and invention in the production—and just enough energy in the rapping—to make *Back in Business* a welcome comeback. —*Leo Stanley*

Out of Business / Jun. 29, 1999 / Def Jam ✦✦✦✦

After the popular, praised 1997 comeback album *Back in Business*, Erick Sermon and Parrish Smith returned with another solid effort that proved they remained one of the best combos in hip-hop, as relevant and tight in 1999 as they were ten years earlier. Most of the tracks are in-house productions (either Sermon or Smith), a true rarity in the '90s hip-hop world, and they lend the album a continuity sorely lacking considering the legion of rap albums that feature a different producer for each track. And as the duo has done for ages, EPMD does more than just trade in familiar riffs to drive the tracks on *Out of Business*. The only familiar sample is on the "Intro," and even there, Sermon and Smith turn "Fanfare for Rocky" into something over and above the original. The pair's raps have definitely progressed in the past ten years, as "Pioneers," "U Got Shot," "Right Now," and "Hold Me Down" more than prove. One of the album highlights is the anti-crossover diatribe "Rap Is Still Outta Control," featuring Busta Rhymes (another rapper who's been around long enough to know) and including great lines like, "They took our music and our beat and tried to make it street/And then got in the magazine to try to sound all sweet." Still, EPMD occasionally falls prey to current trends, with obligatory string-sample productions on "Symphony" and "Symphony 2000" (the latter with Redman, Method Man, and Lady Luck) that serve only to obscure the great guest raps. Despite the title, in the liner notes EPMD dispels any rumors that this could be the duo's last album. —*John Bush*

Greatest Hits / Nov. 23, 1999 / Def Jam ✦✦✦✦✦

Greatest Hits is a 13-track overview of EPMD's first five albums, culling many of the group's best moments into a fantastic set of loose, flowing grooves. There's a major problem with the compilation, though, and it isn't the fact that a few classics are missing (where are "Let the Funk Flow" and "The Steve Martin"?), though that could be a problem for some. No, the problem is that *Greatest Hits* was released only as a bonus disc that was packaged in a limited-edition issue of the 1999 album *Out of Business*. Which was one of the better albums in the EPMD catalog, but it's doubtful that anyone looking for an overview of the group's career will want to spring for it. As an introduction to the group and an indicator of their accomplishments, *Strictly Business* still can't be beat. —*Steve Huey*

Eric B. & Rakim

f. 1985 **db.** 1992

Group / Golden Age, Hip-Hop, East Coast Rap

They never had a mainstream hit of their own, but during rap's so-called golden age in the late '80s, Eric B. & Rakim were almost universally recognized as *the* premier DJ/MC team in all of hip-hop. Not only was their chemistry superb, but individually, each represented the absolute state of the art in their respective skills. Eric B. was a hugely influential DJ and beatmaker whose taste for hard-hitting James Brown samples touched off a stampede through the Godfather of Soul's back catalog that continues up to the present day. Rakim, meanwhile, still tops fan polls as the greatest MC of all time. He crafted his rhymes like poetry, filling his lines with elaborate metaphors and complex internal rhymes, and he played with the beat like a jazzman, earning a reputation as the smoothest-flowing MC ever to pick up a mic. His articulation was clear, his delivery seemingly effortless, and his influence on subsequent MCs incalculable. Together, their peerless technique on the microphone and turntables upped the ante for all who followed them, and their advancement of hip-hop as an art form has been acknowledged by everyone from Gang Starr to the Wu-Tang Clan to Eminem. While certain elements of their sound might come off as slightly dated today, it's also immediately clear how much of a hand Eric B. & Rakim had in leading hip-hop into the modern age.

Eric B. was born Eric Barrier in 1965 in Elmhurst, Queens; his future partner, William Griffin Jr., was born in 1968 and also hailed from the suburbs of New York, specifically Wyandanch, Long Island. At age 16, Griffin converted to Islam and adopted the name Rakim Allah. Barrier played trumpet and guitar early on, but switched to the turntables in high school, and eventually landed a job as the mobile DJ for radio station WBLS. It was there that he met Rakim, and the two officially formed a partnership in 1985. Their first single—"Eric B. Is President" (an ode to Barrier's DJ skills) b/w "My Melody"—was released on the tiny Harlem-based indie label Zakia. It was a street-level sensation during the summer of 1986, and the duo was picked up by the larger 4th & Broadway imprint. The equally monumental singles "I Ain't No Joke" and "I Know You Got Soul" sampled James Brown and his cohort Bobby Byrd, respectively, and their utter funkiness began to revolutionize the sound of hip-hop. Moreover, Rakim's line "pump up the volume" on the latter track was in turn sampled itself, becoming the basis for M/A/R/R/S' hit of the same name.

In 1987, 4th & Broadway issued the duo's full-length debut, *Paid in Full*; accompanied by a mighty underground buzz, the record climbed into the Top Ten on the R&B LP charts (as would all of their subsequent albums). Additionally, the British DJ duo Coldcut remixed the title cut into a bona fide U.K. smash. The exposure helped make "Paid in Full"'s drum track one of the most sampled beats this side of James Brown's "Funky Drummer"; it provided the foundation for Milli Vanilli's "Girl You Know It's True," among many other, more credible hits. On the heels of *Paid in Full*, Eric B. & Rakim signed with MCA subsidiary UNI and consolidated their reputation with another landmark hip-hop album, 1988's *Follow the Leader*. The title cut took its place among the classic singles already in their canon, and Jody Watley soon tapped the duo for a guest spot on her 1989 single "Friends," which brought them into the pop Top Ten for the first and only time.

The 1990 follow-up *Let the Rhythm Hit 'Em* proved relatively disappointing from a creative standpoint, although 1992's slightly jazzier *Don't Sweat the Technique* was a more consistent affair that bolstered their legacy. As it turned out, the record also completed that legacy. The duo's contract with MCA was almost up, and they had discussed the possibility of each recording a solo album. Unfortunately, the resulting tension over the future of their partnership ultimately destroyed it. In the aftermath of the breakup, various legal issues prevented both parties from starting their solo careers for quite some time. The only recording to appear was Rakim's first solo cut, "Heat It Up," which was featured on the soundtrack of the 1993 film *Gunmen*. Finally, in 1995, Eric B. issued his self-titled solo debut on his own 95th Street label. Rakim, meanwhile, signed with Universal and delivered a pair of acclaimed comeback albums, 1997's *The 18th Letter* and 1999's *The Master*. —*Steve Huey*

★ **Paid in Full** / 1987 / 4th & Broadway ✦✦✦✦✦

One of the most influential rap albums of all time, *Paid in Full* only continues to grow in stature as the record that ushered in hip-hop's modern era. The stripped-down production might seem a little bare to modern ears, but Rakim's technique on the mic still sounds utterly contemporary, even state of the art—and that from a record released in 1987, just one year after Run-D.M.C.'s hit the mainstream. Rakim basically invents modern lyrical technique over the course of *Paid in Full*, with his complex internal rhymes, literate imagery, velvet-smooth flow, and unpredictable, off-the-beat rhythms. The key cuts here are some of the most legendary rap singles ever released, starting with their debut sides, "Eric B. Is President" and "My Melody." "I Know You Got Soul" singlehandedly kicked off hip-hop's infatuation with James Brown samples, and the duo topped it with the similarly inclined "I Ain't No Joke," a stunning display of lyrical virtuosity. The title cut, meanwhile, planted the seeds of hip-hop's material obsessions over a monumental beat. There are also three DJ showcases for Eric B., who like Rakim was among the technical leaders in his field. If sampling is the sincerest form of admiration in hip-hop, *Paid in Full* is positively worshipped. Just to name a few: Rakim's tossed-off "pump up the volume," from "I Know You Got Soul," became the basis for M/A/R/R/S' groundbreaking dance track; Eminem, a devoted Rakim student, lifted lines from "As the Rhyme Goes On" for the chorus of his own "The Way I Am"; and the percussion track of "Paid in Full" has been sampled so many times, it's almost impossible to believe it had a point of origin. *Paid in Full* is essential listening for anyone even remotely interested in the basic musical foundations of hip-hop—this is the form in its purest essence. —*Steve Huey*

☆ **Follow the Leader** / 1988 / UNI ✦✦✦✦✦
Having already revolutionized hip-hop, Eric B. & Rakim came up with a second straight classic in their sophomore album *Follow the Leader*, which basically follows the same blueprint for greatness, albeit with subtle refinements. Most noticeably, Eric B.'s production is already moving beyond the minimalism of *Paid in Full*. *Follow the Leader* finds him changing things more often: dropping in more samples, adding instruments from musician Stevie Blass Griffin, and generally creating a fuller sound over his rock-solid beats. It's still relatively spare, but the extra sonic weight helps keep things fresh. For his part, Rakim wasn't crowned the greatest MC of all time for the variety of his lyrical content, and *Follow the Leader* is no different. Yet even if he rarely deviates from boasting about his microphone prowess (and frankly, he's entitled), he employs uncommonly vivid and elaborate metaphors in doing so. A case in point is "Microphone Fiend," which weaves references to substance addiction throughout in explaining why Rakim can't keep away from the mic. The album-opening title cut is one of his most agile, up-tempo lyrical showcases, demonstrating why he's such a poetic inspiration for so many MCs even today. "Lyrics of Fury" manages to top it in terms of sheer force, using the break from James Brown's "Funky Drummer" before it saturated the airwaves. And, of course, there are several more turntable features for Eric B. *Follow the Leader* may not have broken much new ground, but it captures one of the greatest pure hip-hop acts at the top of their form, and that's enough to make it a classic. *—Steve Huey*

Let the Rhythm Hit 'Em / May 1990 / MCA ✦✦✦
One thing the rap audience will never be accused of is having the world's longest attention span. Even some of the most celebrated hip-hoppers can fade in popularity after only a few albums. Eric B. & Rakim were extremely popular in the mid- to late 1980s, but by 1990, rap buyers were starting to lose interest in them. Not much different from *Paid in Full* or *Follow the Leader*, *Let the Rhythm Hit 'Em* makes rapping technique its number-one priority. At time when West Coast MCs like Ice-T and Ice Cube were mainly interested in getting a political message across, Rakim's goal was showing us how much technique he had. Rakim may rap in a deadpan tone, but "Step Back," "No Omega," and other tunes leave no doubt that he had sizable chops. There are a few message raps (including "In the Ghetto"), although Rakim spends most of his time finding tongue-twisting ways to boast and brag about his microphone skills. The overall result is a CD that is enjoyable, yet limited. *—Alex Henderson*

Don't Sweat the Technique / 1992 / MCA ✦✦✦✦
Starting with their 1987 debut, *Paid in Full*, Eric B. & Rakim earned raves for Eric B.'s often flawless, judicious productions and Rakim's serious yet relentlessly rhythmic rhyming style. This 1992 album finds the duo picking up from where they left off of 1990's *Let the Rhythm Hit 'Em*. "What's on Your Mind" has Rakim with intents to woo under a bubbling track with an adroit interpolation of D Train's 1983 hit of the same name. That track aside, *Don't Sweat the Technique* has Rakim in bleak spirits as thoughts of combat, revenge, and unfortunate "accidents" are not far from his mind. "Casualties of War" has Rakim as an all-purpose psycho with the unsettling hook, "I get a rush when I see blood and dead bodies on the floor." Although it's supposed to be gripping, the thought of a war-ravaged Rakim with his pistols blazing after hearing a truck backfiring is hilarious. All of *Don't Sweat the Technique* would be more disturbing if it wasn't for the brilliant ear of Eric B. who can cut the tension and exact magic out of a going-nowhere track. Although the lyrics and premise of "What's Going On" aren't extremely sharp, the cracking snare drums and low bass riffs are a perfect complement to Rakim's delivery. The title track is also jazz influenced, but not as potent as the Simon Law and Mr. Lee's Funky Ginger remixes that don't appear here. Like many albums of this type, *Don't Sweat the Technique* ends on tracks of little distinction but it is another strong effort from one of rap's most respected acts. *—Jason Elias*

20th Century Masters—The Millennium Collection: The Best of Eric B. & Rakim / Jun. 19, 2001 / Hip-O ✦✦✦✦✦
Eric B. & Rakim really didn't have crossover hits, but anybody that paid any attention to hip-hop in the late '80s didn't just know of them, they considered them one of the greatest outfits working. Even in the '90s, Rakim was considered one of the greatest MCs ever to hit the mic, and it's easy to see why—great voice, unbelievable flow, cutting lyrics. Both *Paid in Full* and *Follow the Leader* are widely considered to be pinnacles of hip-hop's golden age, but they never had a full-fledged hits collection until 2001's *20th Century*

Masters—The Millennium Collection. Actually, that's not entirely true, since Rakim's solo debut, *The 18th Letter*, was initially released with a bonus disc containing the group's greatest hits. That collection is more comprehensive than this 11-track overview, but this still gets the job done effectively. Some might complain that "Paid in Full" is included in the British hit Coldcut remix instead of the original, but the basic lay of the land remains the same—all the major songs (minus "My Melody") are here, and the results are pretty stunning. Both Eric B. and Rakim were visionaries, and while some of the productions may now sound a little dated, years after their initial release the urgency of the performances and freshness of the ideas have not been diluted. This record, as much as any other they released, vividly captures their brilliance. *—Stephen Thomas Erlewine*

ESG

f. 1978, South Bronx, NY
Group / Club/Dance, Electro, Old School Rap
It certainly wasn't by design that the South Bronx-based group ESG affected post-punk, no wave, hip-hop, and house music. They opened for Public Image Ltd. and A Certain Ratio, they released records on the same label as Liquid Liquid, they had their music sampled countless times, and they became a play-list staple at '70s dance clubs like the Paradise Garage and the Music Box. The group's only aspiration was to play their music—simplistic in structure and heavy on rhythm—and sell lots of records.

The four Scroggins sisters—Deborah (bass, vocals), Marie (congas, vocals), Renee (vocals, guitar), and Valerie (drums)—formed a group with the support of their mother, who bought instruments to keep her daughters busy and away from trouble; at the time, each sibling was teenaged. Basing their sound on a mutual love for James Brown, Motown, and Latin music, the sisters went through a number of name changes before finally settling on ESG. "E" stood for emerald; Valerie's birthstone; "S" stood for sapphire, Renee's birthstone; and as for "G," well, neither Deborah nor Marie had a birthstone beginning with that letter, but they did want their records to go gold. After permanently adding nonrelative Tito Libran to the lineup as a conga player (some male members came and went prior to this), ESG was officially born. The group began by learning and playing songs by the likes of Rufus and the Rolling Stones; they also learned from watching music programs like *Don Kirschner's Rock Concert and Soul*. The Scroggins' mother had barely scraped up enough cash to buy those instruments, so she didn't have enough left to get them music lessons. The group entered talent contests and even won a few of them. After performing at one particular New York show that they did not win, a judge named Ed Bahlman, the owner of 99 Records (a record shop and a label that included Y Pants, Liquid Liquid, Bush Tetras, and Konk on its roster) was impressed enough to take them under his wing as a manager and producer. At this point, ESG had a few of their own songs. Figuring people would know when they screwed up a cover, the group decided to write their own songs in order to sidestep audience knowledge of when mistakes were being made.

Bahlman booked ESG at punk clubs. The group's sparse, heavily rhythmic, and unpolished sound fit right into the New York scene that Bahlman's label was a significant factor in. They debuted in 1979 at a place called the Mechanical Hall. A four-song repertoire was all they had to work with, and after those songs were over, the crowd asked for more. The same four songs were played over again. At another early gig, ESG opened for the Factory label's A Certain Ratio. ESG didn't know A Certain Ratio from *A Tramp Shining*, but Factory head Tony Wilson asked the openers if they'd like to record something for his label. This resulted in *You're No Good*, a three-song single produced by Martin Hannett. The songs—"You're No Good," "UFO," and "Moody"—remain the group's best-known material. These three songs are among the best to have come from New York's no wave scene, a scene that ESG had little business being part of. ESG wasn't self-consciously arty and they didn't come from a punk background; they simply wrote and played their music without conceptualization. None of this matched with the no wave bands, but the sound the group made certainly did.

The three songs from the *Moody* 7" were issued in the States on 99 with three live songs from a Hurrah's appearance added. A year later, 99 issued another three-song single in the form of *ESG Says Dance to the Beat of Moody*. This proved to people too dear to Factory and Hannett that the group had their own sound down and didn't need any outside influence or manipulation. A good debut LP, *Come Away With ESG*, came in 1983 and continued in the vein of the previous releases. After that, the group went dormant for several years. One major factor was Dahlman's decision to shut down 99. A legal battle with Sugar Hill over Grandmaster Flash's sampling of Liquid Liquid's "Optimo" caused him financial and mental stress, with Sugar Hill's fall into receivership—and inability to award 99 their due settlement—acting as the final straw.

ESG would soon become victims of uncleared samples as well. In fact, there was a period during the early '90s when rap singles using the siren sound from "UFO" seemed more common than ones that sampled James Brown. ESG resurfaced for a number of small-label releases during this period, and a 1993 release was pointedly titled "Sample Credits Don't Pay Our Bills." Throughout the '90s, ESG's stature as an influential group began to rise, with groups like the Beastie Boys and Luscious Jackson citing them as a profound discovery. The value of the group's rare early releases responded in kind, which was remedied somewhat by the U.K.'s Soul Jazz label. *A South Bronx Story*, a compilation that included all the group's best material, was released in 2000. The renewed interest helped lead to another resurfacing that culminated in a 2002 album, *Step Off*, for Soul Jazz. With a revamped lineup that included Renee Scroggins' daughters, Nicole and Chistelle, *Step Off* was met with the consensus that the group had picked up exactly where it left off. —*Andy Kellman*

- **A South Bronx Story** / May 8, 2000 / Universal Sound ✦✦✦✦✦
With their limited resources, the Scroggins sisters put the boogie down in the Boogie Down Bronx. Major kudos to Universal Sound for compiling ESG's best works for *A South Bronx Story*, a crucial document of sparse, old school funk. Until 2000, the group's scant material had been nearly impossible to find. The most legendary inclusion is the Martin Hannett-produced 7" EP that was originally released on Factory (later released as a 12" in the U.S. by 99 with live tracks backing it). This release featured their trademark "Moody," which ended up being listed as a Top 50 classic by nearly all of New York's dance clubs; it was also immortalized on a volume of Tommy Boy's excellent *Perfect Beats* series, lodged between Liquid Liquid and Strafe. Like the remainder of their recorded output, it featured the three "R"s: rhythm, rhythm, and more rhythm. Also on the debut EP was their most sampled "UFO"; the nauseous siren trills at the beginning found sped-up use in at least half a dozen rap tracks in the late '80s and early '90s. Big Daddy Kane and LL Cool J used it, and the Bomb Squad slyly swiped it for Public Enemy's "Night of the Living Baseheads." But arguably their best moment was "Dance" with its jumpy Motown rhythm, post-punk bass, and narrative/old school vocals. It sounds like a wild mix of the Supremes and *Metal Box*-era Public Image Limited. Deborah's bass, though not as musicianly, captures the spirit of PiL's Jah Wobble copping Motown session bassist James Jamerson. It's that sort of sprited, unconscious hybrid that made ESG so unique. After all, they played the opening night of Manchester's Factory club and the closing night of Larry Levan's Paradise Garage. —*Andy Kellman*

E.S.G. (Cedric Hill)

Southern Rap, Underground Rap, Dirty South

Dirty South pioneer E.S.G. trailblazed through the late-'90s movement and helped to popularize the "chopped and screwed" style associated with his one-time home, Wreckshop Records. The "Everyday Street Gangsta" (born Cedric Hill) made his first major move in 1995 when Perrion Entertainment released *Ocean of Funk* (1995), which featured his breakthrough single, "Swangin' and Bangin'," and its accompanying "Chopped and Screwed" mix. Though commonplace a few years later, the chopped and screwed style of remixing hadn't yet become trendy. Thus the mix became just as popular as the song itself, if not more so. This success inspired Perrion to reissue the most impressive songs from *Ocean of Funk* ("Swangin' and Bangin'," "Crooked Streets," and "Smoke On") on *Sailin' da South* (1995), this album distributed widely by Priority. Following these related 1995 albums by Perrion, E.S.G. maintained a low profile while imprisoned yet continued to reap the continuing success of *Sailin' da South* as its reach spread beyond Texas. He returned from prison in 1998 with a dark album for Blackhearted (*Return of the Living Dead*). Around this time, E.S.G. took on an increasingly hardcore stance, presumably in response to the rising competition throughout the dirty South movement. He next joined forces with Wreckshop Records, an up-and-coming Houston label driven by the reputation of the immortalized DJ Screw, and recorded a pair of albums, *Shinin' & Grindin'* (1999) and *City Under Siege* (2000), as well

as a chopped and screwed remix of the latter. By this point considered one of the eminent rappers in Texas alongside Lil' Keke, Fat Pat, U.G.K., and Lil' Troy, E.S.G. capitalized on his reputation by coestablishing his own label, S.E.S. Records. The label's first release, *Boss Hoggs Outlaws* (2001), paired the rapper with newcomer Slim Thug and sought to initiate S.E.S. among the increasingly crowded dirty South market. —*Jason Birchmeier*

Return of the Living Dead / Feb. 24, 1998 / Blackhearted ✦✦✦
E.S.G. returned from prison in 1998 a very different rapper than he had been in 1995 when he scored himself a big hit with "Swangin' and Bangin'." As evidenced on *Return of the Living Dead*, the change isn't necessarily a bad one, as E.S.G.'s rapping has actually improved and he's certainly more thoughtful than before. His worldview had been tainted, though, during his time in prison, for better or worse. The glints of hardcore characteristics that had characterized his 1995 work have been compounded here. It's somewhat a sign of the times, since rap took a general turn toward the dark side in the wake of 2Pac's and Biggie's deaths and had shown omens of doing so even before, but it's also E.S.G. himself who seems to have darkened. He flows a bit more rugged than before, and he raps mostly about the dark side of urban life—crime, drugs, violence, dirty money, and so on—rather than good times. The distinctly Houston production style certainly helps the end result. The rhythms lope more than they hit or boom, and the emphasis is on lo-fi home-brewed funk with a syrupy pace rather than hip-hop à la New York, G-funk à la Cali, or bass à la Atlanta. —*Jason Birchmeier*

- **Boss Hogg Outlaws** / Nov. 6, 2001 / S.E.S. ✦✦✦✦
Following several solo albums for Wreckshop and Perrion during the mid- to late '90s, E.S.G. teamed up with Slim Thug for *Boss Hogg Outlaws*, the first release on S.E.S. Records. Along with producer SIN, the Houston duo began S.E.S. in 2002, hoping to capitalize on the suddenly lucrative dirty South scene and, in particular, the burgeoning Houston scene. E.S.G. & Slim Thug operate much like Eightball & MJG, complementing one another. It also helps that they can trade off verses, helping the songs flow better from verse to verse; furthermore, the songs flow even better when they invite guests such as Lil' Keke, Daz Dillinger, and Bun B to drop a verse. A large step forward for E.S.G. and an impressive first step for Slim Thug, *Boss Hogg Outlaws* shows much promise for the duo's S.E.S. label. —*Jason Birchmeier*

Esham (Rashaam Smith)

b. Long Island, NY

Vocals, Producer / Hardcore Rap, Underground Rap

As an underappreciated cult artist, Esham's harsh hardcore rap thrived in this hometown of Detroit, MI, for years before an ensemble of artists with a similar style began crossing over into the mainstream in the late '90s. Long before rock acts such as Limp Bizkit began rapping, long before rappers such as Kid Rock began rocking, Esham was integrating a rock influence into his rap in the early '90s, crafting a unique style of self-declared "acid rap." In fact, this term is rather fitting, given Esham's taste for hallucinogenic rhymes revolving around paranoia, death, drugs, sex, and downright evil—an extremely decadent synthesis of all things nightmarish. Beyond his knack for rock-influence beats and exploitatively themed rhymes, Esham also proved himself to be a prolific artist, releasing over an album a year after debuting with his first album in 1990 at the tender age of 13. Yet despite his impressive credentials, by the end of the '90s, the Detroit rapper still hadn't extended his reach beyond his cult following, unlike other Detroit artists such as Eminem, Kid Rock, and ICP, and other similar rap groups such as Three 6 Mafia and Brotha Lynch Hung.

As a youth, Esham (born Rashaam Smith) divided his time between New York and Detroit, spending summers with his grandmother in the hip-hop mecca participating in that culture's mid- to late-'80s boom, while spending the remainder of the year with his mother in the depressed, postindustrial, musical melting pot of East Detroit. Given his participation in New York's burgeoning late-'80s rap movement during his summers, it wasn't that out of the ordinary that he was writing his own rhymes by the time he was ten. Yet the fact that he self-released his debut album, *Boomin' Words From Hell*, three years later in 1990 while a high school freshman was *definitely* out of the ordinary. With his older brother handling the business side of the music, including the birth of Esham's own label, Reel Life Productions, the rapper concentrated on his rhymes. Furthermore, he also happened to produce every beat on his first album in addition to busting every rhyme, a truly remarkable accomplishment given his young age, especially considering the album's still-impressive quality.

After *Boomin' Words From Hell*, Esham churned out two quick four-song EPs, *Homey Don't Play That* and *Erotic Poetry*, before returning in 1992 with an ambitious double album that found him furthering his descent into decadence. Titled *Judgement Day* and released in two separately sold volumes, the album showed the artist having evolved also in terms of rapping and production (using a broad palette of rock samples ranging from Black Sabbath's "War Pigs" to Black Flag's "Rise Above"), in addition to his more horrifying subject matter. Furthermore, Esham also debuted his group project, Natas (supposedly an acronym for Nation Ahead of Time and Space, rather than "Satan" spelled backwards as many presume). Also featuring fellow Detroit rappers Mastamind and TNT, Natas' debut album, *Life After Death*, was nearly as hardcore as Esham's solo material, though a bit more pornographic. In late 1992 came the *Hellterskkkellter* EP, which foreshadowed Esham's next album, 1993's *KKKill the Fetus*. That year also saw the release of the second Natas album, *Blaz4me*, followed by the *Maggot Brain Theory* EP and *Closed Casket*, both released in 1994, and another Natas album in 1995, *Doubelievengod*.

With each album following the *Judgement Day* series, Esham's work had continued to evolve in terms of craft, with increasingly meticulous production and better rapping. More significant, though, were the changes that took place in the beats and in the subject matter. Where Esham's early albums were soundscapes pieced together from rock samples and some lo-fi drum machines and bass guitar, his albums began to take on a more conventional production feel, using fewer samples and more polished beats. In addition, his rhymes didn't get any less wicked—still obsessed with decadence—but they did become less juvenile and more creative. By the time *Dead Flowerz* was released in 1996, Esham did show a move away from exploitative subject matter, though—a change that divided his cult audience. On the one hand, it made his music more accessible, and many acknowledged the fact that his lyrics relied less on exploitative themes and more on creativity. Yet on the other hand, his die-hard fans loathed the fact that Esham was slowly drifting toward conventional themes, even if his music was improving. The two 1997 releases—*Bruce Wayne: Gotham City 1987* and Natas' *Multikillionaire*—confirmed the trend, even if the albums had their share of disturbing moments.

When *Mail Dominance* came out in 1999, Esham was clearly a much different rapper than he had been years earlier when he championed everything controversial. This album found him tackling conventional themes and laying down fairly conventional beats (coproduced by Jade Scott [aka Santos]); yet it's important to keep in mind that Esham still gave his music a trademark twist and instilled his dark, angry attitude into music, proving that he didn't need to rely on exploitation any longer to impress listeners. His longtime friends had a hard time accepting this, but when he returned with Natas' *WWW.Com* in 2000, it was clear that Esham's career was indeed moving to the next level. On this album, he emphasized live instrumentation in his beats, including a heavy use of bass guitars, which of course alluded to the rap-metal of acts such as Korn and a reinvigorated Kid Rock. It's also important to note that Esham signed a distribution deal with TVT for his Overcore label (formerly Reel Life) before releasing *WWW.Com*, a good business move that assured quality distribution of his albums across America. To commemorate this new deal, Esham put together *Bootleg: From the Lost Vault, Vol. 1*, a compilation released in 2000 including a wide array of his early material along with a few new tracks for old fans. That same year, TVT distributed rereleased versions of *Detroit Dog Shit* (another compilation originally released in 1997) and his other major solo albums.

Following Eminem's major breakthrough in 2000 and the successive hype surrounding D-12, Esham's profile suddenly rose, and he positioned himself for a breakthrough of his own in 2001. Just before releasing his long-awaited *Tongues* album, Overcore released Kool Keith's *Spankmaster* album, which featured considerable contributions by Esham. And with Keith also featured on *Tongues*, a new audience suddenly discovered the cultish Detroit rapper. Released in summer 2001, *Tongues* no doubt stood as Esham's most labored album to date, a 24-track epic featuring a broad range of production styles and quick segues from one song to the next, with few songs clocking over four minutes. In an effort to promote the album, the rapper embarked on the Warped tour that summer with Keith and made sure to stir up a feud with Eminem. —*Jason Birchmeier*

Boomin' Words From Hell / 1990 / Reel Life ✦✦

First released in 1990, a few years before gangsta rap took over the rap genre and nearly a decade before heavy-metal-influenced rap rose from the underground, Esham's debut deserves recognition merely for its aims if not also for its accomplishments. It's a rather primitive album, composed with nothing more than a bass guitar, drum machine, sampler, mic, and tiny budget, yet it transcends its lo-fi trappings with its unique character. Esham isn't making gangsta rap here, even if his music shares that style's anger, and he obviously isn't making conventional East Coast hip-hop; instead, he crafts his own style—later dubbed "acid rap"—that coopted hardcore rap's aggression, gangsta rap's angst, East Coast hip-hop's emphasis on MCing, and added a dark aura of murky beats and truly horrifying lyrics about exploitative topics such as murder, sex, drugs, evil, and the devil. The prototype for the musical style that he would develop and arguably wear out by the end of the 1990s is here—just the tip of the iceberg, though. Many of the songs here are fairly mediocre relative to Esham's later work, but there are a few gems here that foreshadow his subsequent work. In particular, "Red Rum," "4 All the Suicidalist," and "Devil's Groove" stand out and flirt with the sample-based production that would dominate the following *Judgement Day* albums. Besides these three tracks, there aren't too many highlights here, though a few songs such as "Esham's Boomin'" and "Some Old Wicket Shit!!!" are important lyrically, as the artist first begins to define his theatrical persona. —*Jason Birchmeier*

Judgement Day, Vol. 1 / 1992 / Reel Life ✦✦✦✦

Esham's ambitious *Judgement Day* double album may not be his most well-crafted work, but it certainly stands as his most inspired work of the '90s, surpassing any of his solo albums or his Natas albums in sheer scope. Released in 1992, years before the double album became an accepted practice in rap, *Judgement Day* finds the Detroit rapper at his most demented, rapping almost exclusively about horrifying topics such as death, Hell, drugs, ghetto, and straight-up nihilism. While most may not find such disturbing subject matter difficult to enjoy or even stomach, it is hard to deny that Esham's work on this album is precedent setting and to a certain degree influential on subsequent underground rap artists. Besides his nightmarish lyrics, Esham also produces the sample-ridden beats on this album, an accomplishment that rivals his rapping. The production is admittedly lo-fi, yet this is an important element of its appeal; with his taste for fuzzy Funkadelic-styled rock samples, the bedroom studio-sounding production's griminess that results as much from its sampled roots as its quality feels somewhat consistent with Esham's rapping—this is the definition of underground rap. There aren't any of the glossy commercial elements of hip-hop production anywhere to be found here, and also thanks to the album's downright disturbing rapping, this album became and remains an underground cult classic. With this album being as raw as Esham could ever get in terms of both production and rapping, it's no surprise that subsequent releases found him steadily cleaning up both his production and rapping. (Note that *Judgement Day, Vol. 1* and *Judgement Day, Vol. 2* were released separately, though intended as companions.) —*Jason Birchmeier*

Judgement Day, Vol. 2 / 1992 / TVT ✦✦✦

The companion to *Judgement Day, Vol. 1*, this album isn't quite as strong as the first volume, suffering mostly from a number of weak tracks. Granted, "Judgement Day," "Wake the Dead," and "Devil Gets Funky" are rather impressive moments, but this album feels a bit like a collection of leftovers relative to the more consistent first volume. Still, the production is ridden with plenty of grit, and Esham pushes the limits on how disturbing he can be, particularly on "Living in Incest" and "Crib Death," which are much more distasteful than his traditionally morbid lyrics on the first volume. In fact, there are moments on this album when Esham simply goes too far. Of course, this album's challenging and disturbing attributes stand as part of its perverse allure. Still, the first volume doesn't rely quite so much on cheap shock, instead focusing on evocative horror motifs, making *Judgement Day, Vol. 2* the less important of the two. (Note that *Judgement Day, Vol. 1* and *Judgement Day, Vol. 2* were released separately, though intended as companions.) —*Jason Birchmeier*

KKKill the Fetus / Jun. 16, 1993 / TVT ✦✦✦✦✦

As the follow-up to his as-disturbing-as-possible *Judgement Day* double album, *KKKill the Fetus* isn't too much of a divergence, still finding Esham practicing his morbid rapping and his grimey production. Here, he manages to cram 23 songs onto the album by keeping the songs short; it ends up being an effective strategy. First of all, it allows him to cover more subject matter, with each song introducing new themes (whether you enjoy his lyrics or not, you can't deny his strengths as a storyteller here). Second, his songs function better short rather than long, given his knack for using samples and gimmicky lyrics. So, in the end, Esham covers a lot of ground here, both in terms of rapping and in terms of production. Again, it's debatable which of the two is his strength. At this point in his career, his rapping has already reached near-peak levels, and his production shows a continued path toward an inventiveness. *Kill the Fetus* simply repeats what Esham had done on *Judgement Day*, trimming it down to one album and tightening his songwriting; following this release, he would begin to experiment a bit rather than again repeat himself. Never again would Esham be so gritty. —*Jason Birchmeier*

Closed Casket / Nov. 22, 1994 / Warlock ✦✦✦

Closed Casket finds Esham indulging in his arguably theatrical, undoubtedly harsh fascination with morbidity one last time before moving away from blatant death themes on his following albums: *Dead Flowerz, Bruce Wayne: Gotham City 1987*, and *Mail Dominance*. Since this album follows some rather outrageous efforts, including the visually disturbing cover to the *Maggot Brain Theory* EP and the evil themes of *Judgement Day*, most fans taking a chronological approach to his catalog should be fairly numb to Esham's exploitative shock attempts. Yet if this is one of your first experiences with Esham the Unholy, this album should pack a punch with its dark nature. Either way, the production improves upon past albums, not as reliant on samples and obviously more crafted, but, unfortunately, not much else has changed. At this point in his career, after the cult success of his double-disc album *Judgement Day*, Esham seemed a little of unsure where to head creatively, recycling himself in an effort to deliver what fans wanted: more malicious fascinations with perverse themes. In the end, he delivers on his promise with *Closed Casket*, even if it seems a bit derived. —*Jason Birchmeier*

Dead Flowerz / May 1996 / TVT ✦✦✦

Dead Flowerz finds the prolific Detroit rapper Esham honing his self-described "acid rap" style, leaving behind many of his more disturbing lyrical themes in favor of more traditional themes. Many who have come to expect the usual shocks will loathe his maturation, just as those once turned off by his outrageous need to be overtly perverse may finally manage to stomach his music. Either way, look at this album as the turning point. Assuming this, it should come as no surprise that his production sound has evolved beyond gritty, lo-fi, sample-based beats in favor of a polished sound. Still, there is enough sleaze on this album to distance this album from any other late-'90s rappers, so even if Esham does clean up his act here, it's still far too outrageous for mainstream audiences. As he continued to evolve his cultist fan base, certain compromises had to be made involving how far he could take his exploitation, and this album is proof of what compromises were made. —*Jason Birchmeier*

Detroit Dog Shit / 1997 / Reel Life ✦✦✦✦

Alongside *Bootleg, Detroit Dog Shit* serves as an excellent introduction to Esham's deep catalog and perverse sound, compiling many of his best songs from the 1990s while adding a few previously unreleased tracks. There are reasons why beginning with one of Esham's compilations is probably the best idea for newcomers. First of all, he takes rap to exploitative extremes, rapping about morbid and sexually perverse topics while also venturing into bleak nihilism on nearly every song—his view of the world is tainted with horror. Second, besides being hard to stomach, Esham is also a prolific artist, churning out 11 albums during the 1990s in addition to several albums as a trio with Natas. In sum, getting a diverse representation of his canon can be a rather daunting task. Thankfully, *Detroit Dog Shit's* 20 tracks summarize his 1990s accomplishments before he ultimately showed signs of mellowing out by the decade's end. Songs such as "Acid" and "Momma Was a Junkie" showcase his urge to revel in decadence, while songs such as "Rockz Off" and "Pussy Ain't Got No Face" portray his misogynistic side, and songs such as "Wake Up Dead" and "Losin' My Religion" find him acting morbid and evil. Looking past his primary subject matter—death, horror, drugs, sex, evil—he's a surprisingly fluid rapper capable of funneling his angst into his voice. Furthermore, his self-produced tracks are rather stunning sample-loaded soundscapes that brought Black Sabbath-meets-Funkadelic guitar sounds to nocturnal hip-hop beats long before anyone ever heard of Kid Rock or Insane Clown Posse. It's arguable whether this album captures his best moments

better than 2000's *Bootleg*—both are great and far surpass his individual albums in terms of quality—just make sure you get the TVT re-release of this album. —*Jason Birchmeier*

Bruce Wayne: Gotham City 1987 / Jun. 1997 / TVT ✦✦✦

Five years after his double-disc ode to morbidity, *Judgement Day*, Esham's *Bruce Wayne: Gotham City 1987* album finds him distancing himself fairly far from the death-obsessed themes of his early work. Instead, Esham takes a stab at conceptualization, casting himself as Bruce Wayne. It's a refreshing change for the prolific Detroit rapper, and it's no doubt an intriguing venture; however, the album doesn't fully realize its potential. Instead of indulging in the theatrics that made *Judgement Day*—even with its sincerely perverse themes and admittedly juvenile slant—so utterly fascinating, Esham spends too much time here posing in traditional rap clichés, rapping about "how it's time to make another million" on the opening track, "Comerica." It's sad to see Esham, a truly uncompromising underground rapper, turn into what he presented an alternative to. Luckily, his production is still signature, and his role playing does make for an interesting album, particularly on the second half of the album. This is definitely one of Esham's better albums, but it's hard to get over the fact that it never realizes its potential as a wonderful play on Detroit as Gotham City and himself as Bruce Wayne. —*Jason Birchmeier*

Mail Dominance / Feb. 26, 1999 / TVT ✦✦

As his final solo album of the 1990s, Esham's *Mail Dominance* finds few traces of the morbid themes that populated the rapper's early-'90s work. At this point in his career, the Detroit artist opted for a more respectable route, rapping more about himself and why he's so great than the trademark horror tales that made albums such as *Judgement Day* and *KKKill the Fetus* such cult favorites. So, in a way, it's sad to see Esham trade in his once inaccessible qualities for a much more palatable approach (it's debatable whether or not this constitutes "selling out"). Yet it's also nice, in a way, to see him rely on his rhyming skills and production rather than his often novelty tactics of the past. On songs such as "Oucha Atmosphere" and "Twerk Yo Body," Esham's skills are blatantly apparent; though he may not be nearly as commercially successful as the majority of 1990s rappers, he's unquestionably one of the best in terms of delivery and flow. Unfortunately, on *Mail Dominance* it's not his delivery or flow that seems questionable but rather his lyrics and the production. When not rapping about nihilistic themes, Esham struggles to find engaging lyrics; here he's best when he raps indecipherably. In terms of production, Santos collaborates with Esham for this album, bringing plenty of new ideas, some of which work and many that don't; similarly, the beats are a far departure from the grimy samples of his early-'90s work. Yet for as much as this album distinctively feels like Esham consciously not trying to make an Esham album, it's hard not to favor his more perverse moments, even if he's at the top of his skills here—it sounds as if he's changing styles just to change. Because of this, *Mail Dominance* comes off sounding quite experimental, a sort of test to see if Esham's ventures into respectability seem pragmatic. —*Jason Birchmeier*

● Bootleg: From the Lost Vault, Vol. 1 / Mar. 28, 2000 / TVT ✦✦✦✦✦

The infamous Detroit rapper Esham has become a legend in the rap underground. Since 1990, when he was a teenager, Esham has been releasing album after album of hardcore rhymes with a harsh, self-produced style of beats that often takes on the feel of hard rock. Though many outside of the Detroit area probably aren't familiar with the artist, he deserves recognition for innovating the rap-meets-heavy-metal sound that became a trend. Though it parades itself as a collection of previously unreleased tracks, only three of the 16 tracks can not be found on previous albums. Instead of a collection of rarities, *Bootleg* functions more as a sampler of the rapper's past work, drawing from his deep back catalog of nine full-length albums and several EPs. Much of Esham's early work on *Bootleg* will no doubt shock those unfamiliar with his ferocity. Songs such as "Redrum" from 1990's *Boomin' Words From Hell* are about as hardcore as rap can get. This particular song samples the bass line from Funkadelic's "You and Your Folks" to give itself a funky yet rocking beat. The fact that most of these songs are comprised of samples and were recorded on low-budget equipment in the early to mid-'90s also gives them a very rough and gritty feel quite unlike today's polished hip-hop. Another early Esham track, "KKKill the Fetus" samples a distorted electric guitar for its beats and George Clinton's monologue from "Maggot Brain" to lend it a very creepy feel. Lyrics such as "My suicide solution is a

38 revolver/I'm your problem solver/Your life if full of horror/Some are born today and some will die tomorrow," are downright gruesome and will instantly alienate many, but Esham seems a bit less naughty on more recent songs like "Outcha Atmosphere" and "Twerk Your Body" from 1999's *Mail Dominance*. The bottom line is that he is just far too insane and dark for the masses. His style of music—self-described as "acid rap"—makes N.W.A sound weak and Limp Bizkit like the Backstreet Boys. For anyone out there looking for some hardcore rap with a deranged sense of reality, Esham's *Bootleg* functions as a perfect introduction to a sound quite unlike anything on the market at the time of its release. Though not nearly as fresh as his latest album under the name Natas, *Www.com*—an amazing rap album produced with real basses and guitars—*Bootleg* should earn the Detroit rapper the respect and album sales he deserves after producing some totally unique music in the shadowy ghettos of the city's east side for a decade. —*Jason Birchmeier*

Tongues / Jun. 19, 2001 / TVT ♦♦♦
If there was ever a moment in time when Esham seemed positioned to break out of the Midwest and expand his small cult audience, the summer of 2001 stood as that golden moment. Primarily thanks to Eminem's enormous success the year before and the substantial hype surrounding D-12, many were suddenly eyeing the Motor City as a potential hotspot for dysfunctional rap artists. And if the public wanted dysfunctional artists, Esham certainly fit the bill. Furthermore, Overcore—Esham's label, led by producer Santos—beefed up its reputation by releasing albums by the infamous Kool Keith and the Dayton Family before dropping *Tongues*, in hopes of building up as much anticipation as possible. Yet if everyone was looking at *Tongues* as the album that would enable Esham to cross over to mainstream success, they were foolish. *Tongues* is too far out of the ordinary to cross over—creative, yes, but also odd. First of all, it's filled to the brim with 24 songs and no interludes, meaning that few songs could clock over three minutes. The countless songs segue into one another with surprising ease, making the album seem like an extended medley. Second, the production style varies considerably from song to song. Esham and Santos' beats are dense, lo-fi, and often characterized by an unfamiliar combination of synthesizers, guitars, and drum programming. In terms of songwriting, few of the songs, given their brevity, follow a linear verse-chorus-verse template. There are a handful of standout songs with hooks, but a good majority of the songs are experiments that are often awkward. Finally, Esham's rhymes find him returning to his psychotic early-'90s roots, the sort of insane behavior that scares most people. In the end, while *Tongues* is no doubt Esham's most labored and ambitious album to date, it's also a challenging album that is accessible only in spots. There are career highlights such as his collaborations with Keith on "All Night Everyday" and the Dayton Family on "Fuck a Lover"—along with "God," "Everyone," and "So Selfish," three other great moments. Unfortunately, there are a number of rough areas on the album as well, particularly the first few songs. But at least, even if Esham is forever damned to underground status, he's incorporating an impressive degree of creativity and courage; very few rap artists are capable of crafting an album this dense and this labored, even if it is purposefully inaccessible. —*Jason Birchmeier*

esQuire (Kevin Herron)

Alternative Rap, Comedy Rap
The self-styled "boy who invented rap," esQuire was a striking and much-appreciated alternative to his contemporaries within the Detroit hip-hop scene—favoring colorful, tongue-in-cheek lyrics and funky, swaggering beats over the ridiculously grim-and-gritty approach of Eminem and his ilk, his music evoked the halcyon days of old school rap while infusing the genre with a glitz and showmanship all his own. esQuire was born Kevin Herron in Detroit in 1976—the child of a musician father and dancer mother, he later recalled that his first exposure to rap was Blondie's classic "Rapture." As a teen Herron briefly studied cello, but did not begin rapping until a student at the University of Michigan, making his public debut at a 1999 show headlined by rapper Princess Superstar.

The following year, while attending a ballroom dancing class, he befriended fledgling DJ/producer Craig LeRoQ (born Craig Badynee), and they began recording together—in mid-2000, Herron adopted the larger-than-life esQuire persona in advance of an opening slot for rapper Peaches, and a legend was born. Complete with vintage track suits and a pudding-bowl haircut

that would have made Brian Jones swoon with envy, esQuire immediately set new standards for hip-hop fashion—even better, his live shows featured a group of sexpot go-go dancers to guarantee maximum entertainment value. Q made his recorded debut in December 2000, issuing "The Boy Who Invented Rap" on the Japanese label Escalator; a year later, he returned with "Let's Get Right Down to the Real Nitty Gritty," one side of a split single with Losfeld. By now a near-mythological figure among Motor City concertgoers, in May 2002 esQuire issued the 12" "Brandy and Xanax"; the four-song *Viva Detroit!* dropped around the same time, but was made available exclusively to the hipsters in attendance at his headline show at Southfield's Buddha Lounge. In February 2003, U.K. label Rex Records issued a 10" version of "Brandy and Xanax," with the accompanying video clip earning airplay on Britain's MTV2. —*Jason Ankeny*

● **Viva Detroit! EP** / May 17, 2002 / ♦♦♦♦
EsQuire almost single-handedly makes reparations for the sins inflicted by other white Detroit rappers like Eminem, Kid Rock, and Insane Clown Posse—owing more to *Rushmore*'s Max Fischer than any of his Motown antecedents, Q's witty lyrics, nasal raps, and terribly clever production boast a style and flair sadly lacking from the homophobic white-trash bullshit clogging the marketplace. *Viva Detroit!*, a four-song EP supposedly available only to guests of a May 2002 show at the Buddah Lounge in Southfield, MI, deserves far wider exposure—with a genial goofiness harking back to the glory days of De La Soul and Biz Markie, cuts like "The Boy Who Invented Rap" and "Party in Detroit" are deliriously fun, complete with MC5 samples and big, funky beats. Some video content of those go-go dancers would have been a nice addition, but hey, nobody's perfect. —*Jason Ankeny*

Esso (Curt Swain)

Hardcore Rap, Underground Rap
While it's easy to draw multiple comparisons between Esso and Eminem—both from the Detroit area; both white; both with "E" names; both with similar idioms, dialects, and attitudes; and so on—it doesn't discount the former's abilities. In fact, it should come as a flattering comparison, though perhaps a bit too obvious. After all, love him or hate him, Eminem brought something new to the rap game, and Esso offers much of the same. Perhaps thankfully, however, he's not nearly as controversial or baiting as Eminem—he keeps it real, for the most part. The Flint-based independent label Slum Nation released Esso's debut album, *The Product*, in late 2001. The album featured the lead single "What Yall Want." —*Jason Birchmeier*

● **The Product** / 2001 / Slum Nation ♦♦♦
Esso's full-length debut, *The Product*, showcases the young MC's impressive talents. Since he's from the less-than-major city of Flint, MI, and not signed to a major label—and, in addition, white—Esso has the cards stacked against him in the rap game. However, that doesn't limit his ambitions, as *The Product* illustrates. It's easy to make comparisons between Esso and Eminem, but more than his witty rhymes, his quick delivery, his liquid flow, and his creative yet budget beats (for the most part, courtesy of Exodus), Esso's attempt to be himself rather than a 2Pac wannabe is most rewarding. Overall, this is a promising start for Esso. It makes one hope he can continue moving forward. —*Jason Birchmeier*

Faith Evans

b. Jun. 10, 1973, Newark, NJ
Vocals / Hip-Hop, Urban
In spite of the fact that Faith Evans carved out a recording career in her own right, her name will forever remain linked in the minds of many to her late husband the Notorious B.I.G. Evans was an active session singer and songwriter before signing her own solo deal and marrying Biggie, and while she never matched the level of his stardom, she continued to come into her own as a vocalist in the years after his untimely death.

Faith Evans was born on June 10, 1973, and grew up in Newark, NJ, where she began singing in church at the mere age of two. A high school honor student, she sang in her school's musical productions before winning a full scholarship to Fordham University. After just one year, though, she left college to put her jazz and classical training to use in the field of contemporary R&B. It didn't take her long to find work and over the next few years, she sang backup and wrote songs for artists like Hi-Five, Mary J. Blige, Pebbles, Al B. Sure!, Usher, Tony Thompson, and Christopher Williams. Thanks to her work on Blige's 1994 sophomore effort, *My Life*, Evans met producer/impresario Sean "Puffy" Combs, who signed her to his Bad Boy label. In 1995 Evans released her debut album, *Faith*, which went platinum on the strength of the hit R&B singles "You Used to Love Me" and "Soon As I Get Home." The same year, she met fellow Bad Boy artist the Notorious B.I.G. (some accounts say at a photo shoot, others a phone conversation) and married him after a courtship of just nine days; shortly thereafter, she guested on a remix of his smash single "One More Chance."

Over the next couple of years, Evans continued her behind-the-scenes work, performing and writing for records by the likes of Color Me Badd and LSG. She and Biggie also had a son, Christopher Wallace Jr., in late 1996; however, by that point, their marriage had already become strained. Biggie had publicly taken up with rapper Lil' Kim and rumors had been spreading about an Evans liaison with Biggie's rival 2Pac (alluded to on 2Pac's venomous "Hit Me Off"). The couple had unofficially separated when Biggie was shot and killed in March 1997. A grief-stricken Evans was prominently featured on the Puff Daddy tribute single "I'll Be Missing You," which with its cribbed Police hook zoomed to the top of the charts and became one of the year's biggest hits.

Evans' sophomore effort *Keep the Faith* followed in 1998 and it spun off several R&B hits over the next year, including "Love Like This," "All Night Long," and the Babyface-produced R&B number-one "Never Gonna Let You Go." In the meantime, she worked with Aaron Hall, Tevin Campbell, and DMX, among others, and also made high-profile guest appearances on 1999 hits, Whitney Houston's "Heartbreak Hotel" and Eric Benet's "Georgy Porgy." She began dating and eventually married record executive Todd Russaw, who took an active role in helping manage her career. In 2001 Evans released her third album, *Faithfully*, a more up-tempo record that received her strongest reviews to date; it also produced hit singles in "You Gets No Love" and "I Love You," and her duet with Carl Thomas on "Can't Believe" was nominated for a Grammy. *—Steve Huey*

Faith / 1995 / Bad Boy ✦✦✦

Faith Evans had written songs for a variety of new jack and hip-hop artists (including Mary J. Blige, Al B. Sure!, Pebbles, and Christopher Williams) before releasing her first album, *Faith*. The record proves that she is as powerful in the spotlight as she is behind the scenes. Evans builds on a basic, hip-hop-influenced funk, alternating between simmering grooves and sultry ballads. *Faith* does have a couple of dull spots, but the album is a first-class debut. *—Stephen Thomas Erlewine*

Keep the Faith / Oct. 27, 1998 / Bad Boy ✦✦✦✦

Faith Evans' second album *Keep the Faith* was met with quite a bit of anticipation. The album was released three years after her acclaimed, soulful, and raw debut *Faith*, and in that time she had witnessed the murder of her husband the Notorious B.I.G., which led to the biggest hit of her career (and one of the biggest of the 1990s), the tribute "I'll Be Missing You" (in collaboration with Puff Daddy). *Keep the Faith* proved to be a success, and she happily avoided the curse of the sophomore slump. The album scored two Top Ten singles with the irresistible dance/R&B cut "Love Like This" and its follow-up, the equally intoxicating "All Night Long." Aside from those two dance numbers, the rest of the album falls somewhere between heavy ballads and mid-tempo grooves. Ms. Evans shines when she sings fast or mid-tempo songs, such as the slick "Life Will Pass You By," but the ballads weigh too heavily on this otherwise fine album. Some of the ballads stand tall, such as the gorgeous "My First Love" and the inspiration-tinged "Keep the Faith," while others are about as entertaining and inspired as tree sap ("Anything You Need" and the yawn-inducing interludes). Unfortunately, these ballads are all lumped together on this album, to the point where they almost blend into one long drip of molasses. However, the classy Ms. Evans possesses a beautiful voice, is a gifted songwriter, and happily steers clear of the tacky clichés that burden so much contemporary R&B. So despite the heavy reliance on ballads, this is actually a fine album, and is without a doubt a highlight of 1990s soul-pop music. Other notable tunes include the beautiful "Never Gonna Let You Go," which could be classified as the last great Babyface hit song of the 1990s (that song, incidentally, topped the R&B charts and hit the Top 20 on the pop charts), and the Dianne Warren-penned "Lately I," which never became the hit it should have been. *—Jose Promis*

● **Faithfully** / Nov. 6, 2001 / Bad Boy ✦✦✦✦✦

Given Faith Evans' somewhat spotty track record and Puff Daddy/P. Diddy's slippage since his name change, it might have made some sense to greet

Evans' third album, *Faithfully*, with a bit of skepticism. As it turns out, such doubts were unwarranted, since this is her grittiest, funkiest, best record to date. There are so many collaborators on each track and so many producers—usually around five songwriters for each track (but if a song is sampled, as many as 14 writers are credited)—that it seems a minor miracle that it holds together at all, but *Faithfully* gels better than any previous Faith Evans record, in large part because so much of it is devoted to hard-edged, funky dance numbers, whether it's hip-hop-influenced cuts like "Alone in This World" or the wonderful neo-disco "Back to Love." This switch from her previous album, which emphasized ballads and mid-tempo grooves, gives the album more character, since the dance numbers mix well with the sultrier numbers and they both work equally well. If the album is hurt by anything, it's its length—like most modern hip-hop-related albums, it runs too long—but it is rich with vibrant songs, lively production, and Evans' best singing to date on what ultimately is not just her best album, but another excellent female urban R&B album in a year overflowing with them. *—Stephen Thomas Erlewine*

Eve (Eve Jihan Jeffers)

b. Nov. 10, 1978, Philadelphia, PA
East Coast Rap, Hardcore Rap

Eve was one of a new breed of tough, talented, commercially viable female MCs to hit the rap scene during the late '90s. Though she could be sexy when she chose, she wasn't as over-the-top as Lil' Kim or Foxy Brown, and as part of the Ruff Ryders posse, her production was harder than Da Brat's early work with Jermaine Dupri. In the end, Eve came off as her own person; a strong, no-nonsense street MC who could hold her own with most anyone on the mic; and was finding success on her own terms. She was born Eve Jihan Jeffers in Philadelphia on November 10, 1978, and started out as a singer in her early teens, performing with an all-female vocal quintet. She was also honing her skills as a rapper in impromptu battles with friends, and before she left high school, she formed a female rap duo called EDGP (pronounced "Egypt"), adopting the name Gangsta. EDGP performed at local talent shows and club gigs, often to the detriment of Eve's dedication to school. When the group broke up, she went solo and changed her name to Eve of Destruction; she also moved to the Bronx in the wake of her mother's remarriage, and worked for a time as a table dancer at a strip club. Unhappy with this direction, she decided to give rap another shot after being encouraged by Mase.

Through some of her friends, Eve scored a meeting with Dr. Dre in Los Angeles, and surprised him by turning it into an audition. Dre liked what he heard and signed her to a one-year deal with his new label Aftermath. Eve recorded a few tracks, including one, "Eve of Destruction," that ended up on the *Bulworth* soundtrack in 1998. However, Aftermath was searching for a direction at the time, and Eve wound up lost in the shuffle. Her contract expired without an album even in the works, but fortunately, she'd met DMX when the rising new star was in Los Angeles promoting his smash debut, *It's Dark and Hell Is Hot*. Eve passed a battle-rap audition to join DMX's Ruff Ryders posse, and in 1999 she contributed to their label's *Ryde or Die, Vol. 1* compilation. Thanks to DMX's star power, it entered the charts at number one, and Eve's track "What Ya Want" was released as a single. It hit the R&B Top Ten, and Eve built more anticipation for her debut album with high-profile guest spots on the Roots' "You Got Me" and the Blackstreet/Janet Jackson duet "Girlfriend/Boyfriend."

Eve's first full-length was titled *Let There Be Eve... Ruff Ryders First Lady* and released in September 1999. With Ruff Ryders the biggest name in rap, the album was an instant smash; it entered the charts at number one—the first time a female rapper had ever accomplished that feat—and went on to sell over two million copies. Eve also scored hits with the R&B Top Ten "Gotta Man" and the anti-domestic violence track "Love Is Blind," and guested on Missy Elliott's hit "Hot Boyz." After touring in support of the record, Eve returned to the studio and delivered her follow-up, *Scorpion*, in early 2001. The album received strong reviews and topped the R&B charts, while debuting at number four on the pop side. The lead single "Who's That Girl?" had some chart success, but it was the follow-up, a duet with No Doubt's Gwen Stefani called "Let Me Blow Ya Mind," that really broke Eve on the pop charts. The song rocketed to number two and went on to win a Grammy in the newly created category of Best Rap/Sung Collaboration; it also helped *Scorpion* go platinum.

Eve next set about establishing a movie career; she made her box-office debut in the Vin Diesel action blockbuster *XXX*, which was released in the summer of 2002. Not long after, she was also seen in a prominent supporting role in the Ice Cube comedy *Barbershop*. Amidst all this activity, Eve released her third album, *Eve-Olution*, in August 2002. It debuted in the Top Ten, and found Eve returning to the soul singing of her youth on a surprising number of tracks. The single "Gangsta Lovin'," which featured guest vocals from Alicia Keys, was a number-two smash on both the pop and R&B charts, and the follow-up "Satisfaction" was nominated for a Grammy. In early 2003 Eve signed with the UPN network to produce and star in a multiracial sitcom about a fashion designer. —*Steve Huey*

Let There Be Eve . . . Ruff Ryder's First Lady / Sep. 14, 1999 / Interscope
    ◆◆◆◆

The full title of Eve's full-length debut is *Let There Be Eve . . . Ruff Ryders' First Lady* for a reason. The Philadelphia rapper sets out to prove she's earned her place in the Ruff Ryders crew, matching rhymes, raunch, and rounds with the hardest hardass. Minimal beats laced with synthesized strings and keyboards back traditional hip-hop brag fests like "Let's Talk About." Eve shows up guests Drag-on, DMX, and others with boasts of sexual prowess, withering insults to inadequately endowed brothers, and violent sister-centered anthems like "My B(*****)." A few short skits offer snapshots of Eve's beloved hometown. The irresistible party anthem "We on That S(***)," reminiscent of Coolio's "Fantastic Voyage," chronicles a night of clubbing and rounds out the street picture. "Ain't Got No Dough," a fabulous collaboration with Missy Elliot, is a fiery bridge between street-centered raps and the more interesting tracks. Purring and pissed, it's an edgier alternative to TLC's hit "No Scrubs." Eve's conviction and passion make her noticeable no matter what the subject, but she truly stands out when the stories become personal, examining the cost of the hard life she champions in other songs. "Love Is Blind" is a painful look at domestic violence. Self-respect and positivity are the moral of "Heaven Only Knows." Both tracks are backed by beautiful arrangements with acoustic guitar and lush vocals. Eve maintains her hardcore image in these tracks, but with a subtle vulnerability that promise lots of interesting things to come from this Philly prodigy. —*Theresa E. LaVeck*

● **Scorpion** / Mar. 6, 2001 / Interscope ◆◆◆◆

When Eve debuted in 1999, she surprised many as one of the few female rappers capable of attaining both popularity and respect without having to take on a sleazy role or sacrifice any of her muscle. In fact, her muscle seemed to be what impressed the rap community most. If anything, Eve brings even more muscle to her follow-up album, *Scorpion*. Her rhymes flow just as lucidly here as they did on her debut, and she sounds even more confident than before. Given her ensemble cast of producers and guest rappers, she probably should sound confident. When you have Swizz Beatz and Dr. Dre handling the better part of your album, along with a few other tracks handled by Ruff Ryder producers Teflon and DJ Shok, there isn't need to worry—you know the beats are going to be cutting edge. In terms of guests, the Ruff Ryders (DMX, Drag-On, and LOX) make their expected cameos. On paper, everything looks great—more muscle, top producers, and top rappers. And the results are just that—great. A few songs really stand out here: the leadoff single "Who's That Girl?," a Teflon track with a quick tempo and an extremely catchy chorus; "Let Me Blow Ya Mind," a Dr. Dre/Scott Storch track with an unmistakable *2001* sound and a smooth R&B chorus featuring Gwen Stefani on backup vocals; and "Life Is Hard," a unique soulful moment late in the album with Teena Marie contributing a diva chorus and Eve dropping some heartfelt lyrics. At 16 tracks, this album doesn't overreach and really doesn't have too many surprises. There are a few flawed moments where the choruses aren't as catchy as they intend to be, but for the most part Eve plays it safe. If you liked her first album, you'll like this one even better. —*Jason Birchmeier*

Eve-Olution / Aug. 27, 2002 / Interscope ◆◆◆

Having proved herself with 2001's rough and tough *Scorpion*, Eve changed direction slightly for *Eve-Olution*. The focus here is less hip-hop and more contemporary R&B, with fewer rappers invited as guests—only two tracks, "Hey Y'All" featuring Snoop Dogg and Nate Dogg and the *Scorpion* sequel "Double R What" featuring Jadakiss and Styles. After the intro, Eve focuses squarely on neo-soul, but doesn't contribute much to the style; "What" (with Truth Hurts) and "Gangsta Lovin'" (with Alicia Keys), are surprisingly mediocre, with the guests vamping over bland choruses and Eve contributing only a few good rhymes. Elsewhere, the productions keep the groove going, but not much else: definitely a surprise, considering the beatheads

behind the boards (Irv Gotti, Dr. Dre, Swizz Beatz, Poke & Tone) don't get much hotter. ("Irresistible Chick," one of the few keepers, features a smooth Irv Gotti production that's moving almost as fast as Eve's fluid raps.) There are a few OK tough-love tracks along the lines of *Scorpion*'s "You Had Me, You Lost Me" and "You Ain't Gettin' None," and a nod to her Ruff Ryders past with "Ryde Away," but *Eve-Olution* can't offer as much as either of her first two solid LPs. —*John Bush*

Everlast (Erik Schrody)

Vocals, Producer / Alternative Rap, Hardcore Rap, Rap-Rock
Once best known for his tenure in the rap unit House of Pain, Everlast successfully reinvented himself in 1998 with the best-selling *Whitey Ford Sings the Blues*, a largely acoustic, hip-hop-flavored effort in the genre-crossing mold of Beck. Born Erik Schrody, Everlast first surfaced in Los Angeles as a member of Ice-T's Rhyme Syndicate Cartel, issuing his debut album, *Forever Everlasting*, in 1990. When the album failed to find an audience, he formed House of Pain with Danny Boy and DJ Lethal; carving out an image which drew heavily on Everlast and Danny Boy's shared Irish heritage, the trio managed to overcome the stereotypes facing white rappers and scored a massive hit with their 1992 single "Jump Around." Their self-titled debut LP also went platinum, but when follow-ups including 1994's *Same as It Ever Was* and 1996's *Truth Crushed to Earth Shall Rise Again* failed to repeat House of Pain's early success, the group disbanded. Everlast then returned to his solo career, but while recording *Whitey Ford Sings the Blues* he suffered a massive cardiac arrest stemming from a congenital defect, resulting in heart bypass surgery and an artificial valve implant. Following his recovery, he completed the album, which appeared in the fall of 1998 to strong commercial notices: hitting the Top Ten, going platinum, and launching the Top 40 single "What It's Like." After appearing on Santana's vaunted comeback album *Supernatural*, Everlast began work on a follow-up with an eclectic group of guest artists. Titled *Eat at Whitey's*, the album was released in late 2000. —*Jason Ankeny*

Forever Everlasting / Mar. 27, 1990 / Warner Brothers ◆◆◆

Here's a little-known fact of rap history: before Everlast enjoyed recognition as a member of House of Pain, he pursued a career as a solo artist. *Forever Everlasting*, his first and only pre-Pain solo album, is a decent, though not outstanding release proving that he had strong rapping skills long before becoming well known. Ice-T, who serves as this CD's executive producer, once said of Everlast, "Hearing him rap, you'd never know he was white"—and to be sure, the L.A.-based MC is far from a pop rapper. Though most of his lyrics aren't remarkable, this CD definitely has its moments—most notably, "Speak No Evil" (a reflection on injustice in America) and the angry "Fuck Everyone." —*Alex Henderson*

● **Whitey Ford Sings the Blues** / Sep. 8, 1998 / Tommy Boy ◆◆◆◆◆

Saying that Everlast showed a great deal of artistic growth between his first and second solo albums would be a understatement. While 1990's *Forever Everlasting* was a decent, if uneven, debut, Everlast's second solo album, *Whitey Ford Sings the Blues* is an amazingly eclectic gem that finds him really pushing himself creatively. Between those two albums, Everlast joined and left House of Pain, which evolved into one of the most distinctive rap groups of the 1990s. While Pain's albums thrived on wildness for its own sake, *Whitey Ford* has a much more introspective and serious tone. Everlast, who was born with a heart defect, was in the process of recording the album when he needed life-saving open-heart surgery; in fact, he was lucky that he was around to see *Whitey Ford* completed and released. Though not without its share of hardcore b-boy rap, *Whitey Ford* also finds Everlast playing acoustic guitar, doing some singing and exploring folk-rock, Memphis soul and heavy metal. As a singer, Everlast has a relaxed style that sounds a bit like Gil Scott-Heron. "Today (Watch Me Shine)," "Ends," and "What It's Like" venture into Neil Young/Bob Dylan territory, while "Hot to Death" is blistering metal with industrial touches. And the plot thickens—on "The Letter" he raps over a jazz-influenced piano. Given how rap's hardcore tends to frown on rappers crossing over to rock, it took guts for Everlast to be so diverse. But it's a good thing that he did, for his risk taking pays off handsomely on this outstanding release. —*Alex Henderson*

Eat at Whitey's / Oct. 17, 2000 / Tommy Boy ◆◆◆◆

Nobody ever would have guessed that the leader of House of Pain would come back after a bout of obscurity and a serious heart attack to reinvent himself as a hip-hop troubadour, rasping out bluesy folk-rock to a steady-rolling beat. The fact that Everlast had the vision to change his tune was surprising enough, but the fact that it worked *and* found a wide audience was stunning. When it came time to deliver *Eat at Whitey's*, the follow-up to *Whitey Ford Sings the Blues*, in 2000, Everlast was smart enough to expand on a good thing, turning out a sequel that built on the folk-rap-rock that rejuvenated his career, while adding slight new twists. The problem is, the new twists, particularly in the guise of cameos from rockers like Carlos Santana and Warren Haynes, don't work particularly well. Also, whenever he veers toward straight rap, such as on the B Real duet "Deadly Assassins," the music falls a little flat—just like it did on the predecessor. Still, these not-quite-successful moments don't detract from an album that delivers on the promise of *Whitey Ford*. Whenever Everlast lays back and spins stories and tall tales on his own, his blend of folk, rock, blues, rap, and pop culture clicks. It can be a little silly—his rhymes are occasionally goofy, his growl a little too raspy—but at its best, it's evocative, catchy, and ingratiating. If he can't sustain the quality of the first three songs throughout the record, at least it connects several more times, enough to make *Eat at Whitey's* satisfying for listeners that want a little more of "What It's Like." —*Stephen Thomas Erlewine*

Archie Eversole

b. Jul. 26, 1984, Germany
Dirty South
A product of rap's dirty South school, Atlanta, GA, resident Archie Eversole is a hardcore rapper who thrives on thug-life imagery and specializes in lyrics that are violent and/or sexually explicit. Eversole's style of rapping is distinctly Southern, but not all of his influences are from the Deep South; Eversole's rhymes also owe a creative debt (either direct or indirect) to the late Tupac Shakur and West Coast gangsta rappers like Dr. Dre, N.W.A, and Above the Law.

Anyone who still thinks of rap as the new kid on the block should consider the following: although Eversole was almost an adult when he recorded his debut album, *Ride Wit Me Dirty South Style*, in the early 2000s, he is young enough to be LL Cool J's son. The members (or ex-members) of the Fat Boys, Run-D.M.C., U.T.F.O., and Whodini are old enough to be the father of Eversole, who was born on a military base in Germany on July 26, 1984. But Eversole's parents weren't professional rappers. Both of them were in the United States military—his father was in the navy, while his mother was in the army—and both of them were stationed in Germany (which explains why Eversole was born in that country even though he isn't of German descent). But, when Eversole's parents returned to the U.S., he ended up being raised in the College Park section of Atlanta. Sadly, Eversole has been quoted as saying that he has never gotten along with his parents. But he did seem to get along with his brothers, and they were the ones who encouraged him to rap.

As a teenager, Eversole decided to enter an Atlanta studio and record a demo. Producer Mason "Phat Boy" Hall, aka Big Mace, happened to be in the studio that day; Mace (the CEO of Phat Boy Records and a fellow Atlanta resident) came across Eversole by accident and decided that he was interested in working with the aspiring rapper. Before long, Mace arranged for Eversole to be featured on "Tig Ole Bitties With the Ass to Match," a tune from Phat Boy artist MGD's debut album, *Everlasting Yay*. But Eversole's own album was delayed when he ended up being incarcerated for eight months on a charge of simple assault. While he was locked up, Eversole did a lot of writing; and as soon as he got out, the rapper (who was 17 at the time) started recording his first album. Produced by Break Bread Productions (which is Phat Boy's in-house production team), the album was released by MCA in May 2002. —*Alex Henderson*

● **Ride Wit Me Dirty South Style** / Jun. 18, 2002 / MCA ✦✦✦
Some veteran hip-hop heads have expressed their concerns over the direction of hardcore rap in the late '90s and early 2000s. Their generalization is as follows: hardcore rap had more of a conscience in the '80s, and too much late-'90s/early-2000s rap just talks about bling-bling, fast cars, player haters, gats, thugs, blunts, bitches, hoes, and hotties with big booties. But truth be told, rap has room for positive, uplifting MCs (the Roots, Common, Blackalicious) as well as rhymers who specialize in raunchy, explicit, over-the-top entertainment (Eminem, Too Short). Archie Eversole's debut album, *Ride Wit Me Dirty South Style*, usually falls into the latter category. The Atlanta-based rapper, who was only 17 when he recorded this CD, occasionally addresses

sociopolitical concerns in a serious manner—on the disturbing "Why Me," Eversole expresses the desperation of a ghetto teenager who wonders why he has to grow up in such a dangerous, unsafe environment. But most of the time, *Ride Wit Me Dirty South Style* isn't an album that is trying to save the world—this disc isn't trying to be Public Enemy's *It Takes a Nation of Millions to Hold Us Back*, Boogie Down Productions' *By All Means Necessary*, or even Ice-T's *Power* (which used thug life imagery to warn ghetto kids that crime is a dead end). Most of the time, Eversole's album is a stereotypical dirty South effort that inundates listeners with the usual gangsta clichés and sex-and-violence themes. This is hardly the most original or innovative release in the world—there are countless dirty South rappers doing this type of thing—but the beats are generally infectious and Eversole comes up with some catchy hooks here and there. Although not a masterpiece, *Ride Wit Me Dirty South Style* is an entertaining, if uneven and derivative, example of Southern hardcore rap. —*Alex Henderson*

Extended F@mm

Group / Comedy Rap, Alternative Rap, West Coast Rap
Decrying the lack of solid rap groups, Extended F@mm came together around a foursome of New York-based battle MCs—Tonedeff, Session, PackFM, and Substantial. Each member of the quartet spent much time trying to make their own way in the rap underground; Tonedeff released a few solo singles and backed KRS-One on his Nelly dis track "Clear 'Em Out," while Session spent time with EPMD's Hit Squad, PackFM came in second at *The Source*'s *Unsigned Hype Live* show, and Substantial had a few releases of his own. As Extended F@mm, they debuted with a single ("The Evil That Pens Do") and released their full-length debut *Happy F*ck You Songs* in 2002. —*John Bush*

● **Happy F*ck You Songs** / Nov. 26, 2002 / QN5 ✦✦✦
The quartet Extended F@mm came together on this EP project with a throwback approach and a uniquely humorous posture. Mixing acerbic wit and playful rhyme treatments with traditional b-boy swagger, the crew calls to mind such underground forerunners as De La Soul, Souls of Mischief, and Leaders of the New School. But while the against-the-grain/satirical angle was appreciated in an era where carbon-copy hip-hop had been pervasively proliferated, EF's sound was simply not compelling enough to truly wake up the ears of dormant hip-hop heads. At its best, this release mimics the blueprint of De La's classic debut (*3 Feet High and Rising*), but the problem here is the crew seemingly can't make up its mind if it wants to be taken seriously or if it simply wants to farcically send up the rap game. Skills-wise, EF's lineup can hold their own against many of the 21st-century rap's top sellers (a legion that EF quite obviously despises), but unfortunately the beats (Tonedeff, Elite, Deacon the Villain) tend toward the tinny and gimmicky (for example, sampling the theme from Tetris on "Line Drop"). This is not to say that the piece is not without memorable moments, including the outrageously comical (albeit in poor taste) "Pebble Jam," featuring a faux freestyle battle between an American militarist ("I.W.") and a Middle Eastern caricature ("Osama Gin Laden"). A number of incredibly funny skits ("Intro," "Pause," and "Fin"), the aptly titled "Obligatory Posse Cut," and a show-stopping hidden track also make this joint worth a listen. —*M.F. DiBella*

Extra Prolific (Duane Lee)

b. Sep. 18, 1973
Underground Rap, West Coast Rap, Hip-Hop
The Hieroglyphics-related Extra Prolific was basically a solo act, the creation of Duane "Snupe" Lee along with studio cohorts like Domino and A+. His LP debut, *Like It Should Be*, was released on Jive in 1994. Despite the single "Brown Sugar" briefly creeping into the rap charts, Extra Prolific was dropped from the label. In 1996, he returned with a record (*2 for 15*) recorded for his own label, Security. —*John Bush*

● **Like It Should Be** / Oct. 25, 1994 / Jive ✦✦✦
By 1994, the Hieroglyphics crew had been on a scorching hot streak (in terms of album quality if not necessarily sales) that extended back to Del's *I Wish My Brother George Was Here* and included Souls of Mischief's *'93 'Til Infinity*, the sophomore Funkee Homosapien album *No Need for Alarm*, and Casual's *Fear Itself*. Extra Prolific concluded this winning run with yet another highly satisfying, if meager-selling, effort. Unsurprisingly, *Like It Should Be* shares many of the characteristic qualities of the other Hieroglyphics efforts,

not least the brilliantly flaky production. Chiefly courtesy of a pair of the collective's in-house producers (Domino, A+) as well as Extra Prolific's own resident beatsmith, DJ, MC, and mastermind Duane "Snupe" Lee (Mike G. rounds out the duo, though only nominally a presence), the album is full of clever, unusual, and flat-out playful samples that twist molasses-thick soul and smooth jazz into strangely compelling mutations. Besides Snupe's ability behind the boards, he is a solid, imaginative rhymer. His syrupy, lackadaisical way with a lyric is very much owing to the rapper's original Houston home. This separates his style from the eccentric flows of his compatriots; unfortunately, the comparison doesn't always stand Snupe in the most beneficial light. He doesn't have the sort of idiosyncratic delivery that sets apart MCs like Del and Opio (who gets the best of his guest spot on "Now What"). For instance, Casual positively steals the brief "Cash Money" with his featured verse. The album, as a result, is perhaps not quite of a piece with efforts by Extra Prolific's crewmates. Regardless, even if second-level Hieroglyphics, *Like It Should Be* is quite strong and possesses a plethora of exceptional tracks—"Sweet Potato Pie," "One Motion," "In 20 Minutes," "First Sermon"—that belong in every collection of alternative West Coast rap. —*Stanton Swihart*

Fab 5 Freddy (Fred Braithwaite)

b. 1959
Vocals / Hip-Hop, Old School Rap

One of rap's most colorful and recognizable characters, at various points in his life Fab 5 Freddy has been a nationally exhibited painter, an actor, a screenwriter, a rapper, a graffiti artist, a producer, and a host for MTV, each endeavor carrying Freddy's trademark zeal and charisma.

Growing up in the Bedford-Stuyvesant section of New York, Freddy first entered the underground culture as a popular graffiti artist. Using the tags "Bull 99" and "Fred Fab 5," Freddy's work became a fixture on subway cars and walls throughout the city. Graduating from high school in the late '70s, the young artist studied painting at Medgar Evans College where he emulated the pop art of Andy Warhol. After fostering a friendship with music columnist Glenn O'Brien, Freddy became a cameraman and regular guest on his public-access show. It was through this friendship that Fab 5 was introduced to the downtown hipster scene which included Debbie Harry of the group Blondie, Warhol, Keith Haring, and Jean-Michel Basquiat (Harry even mentioned Freddy in the lyrics of Blondie's 1981 hit "Rapture"). Though he pursued painting throughout the early '80s, Freddy gradually became more interested in other aspects of black culture including breakdancing and hip-hop. This interest led to his production of the soundtrack album and a lead role in the 1982 film *Wild Style*.

During the late '80s Freddy began directing videos for rappers such as KRS-One, Shabba Ranks, Queen Latifah, EPMD, and others. At around the same time Fab 5 was also approached by MTV producer Ted Demme to host a new show, *Yo! MTV Raps*. Through his exposure on MTV, Freddy was widely acknowledged as a champion and founding father of hip-hop culture. In 1992 the multimedia star compiled a dictionary of hip-hop slang titled *Fresh Fly Flavor.* —*Steve Kurutz*

Fabolous (John Jackson)

b. Brooklyn, NY
East Coast Rap, Pop-Rap, Gangsta Rap

By being the right person in the right place at the right time, Fabolous became an overnight superstar in late summer 2001 with his debut single, "I Can't Deny It." Though the young rapper represents Brooklyn and is no doubt representative of the East Coast rap style, he also happens to embody a large dose of the bling-bling mentality often associated with the dirty South style as well as the "gangsta" mentality associated with the West Coast—the makings of a true crossover artist. And the fact that he's young with poster-boy looks doesn't hurt either. So, in sum, Fabolous followed in the footsteps of other early-2000s overnight sensations like Nelly by representing his hood while also making subtle concessions to the masses. At the time, New York didn't have any ice-sportin', Cristal-poppin', 'hood-representin' rappers—at least not since the death of the Notorious B.I.G. and the simultaneous popular demise of Puff Daddy. Fabolous filled this gaping niche perfectly.

DJ Clue certainly knew what he was doing when he made the young rapper the flagship of his start-up label, Desert Storm. Though a no-name at the time, Clue's calculation proved genius. He hired a handful of producers, rappers, and vocalists for Fabolous' debut album, *Ghetto Fabolous*: Ja Rule, the Neptunes, Lil' Mo, and Timbaland, to name a few. And by teaming Fabolous with Nate Dogg—who had become a hot commodity in the rap community that summer, virtually omnipresent on the radio with hits like "Area Codes" and "Lay Low"—Clue had an undeniable hit song to drive the album's initial sales. This song was the perfect crossover hit, merging Fabolous' East Coast image and rhymes with Nate Dogg and producer Rick Rock's West Coast

sound—and interpolating a trademark 2Pac lyric for the hook obviously didn't hurt. As expected, the song became a huge hit, storming up the *Billboard* Hot 100 chart, and built up ample anticipation for the album *Ghetto Fabolous.* —*Jason Birchmeier*

● **Ghetto Fabolous** / Sep. 11, 2001 / Elektra ✦✦✦
From out of nowhere, Fabolous swooped onto the hip-hop scene in summer 2001 with this big-money debut album and a sure-fire hit ("I Can't Deny It"). It also didn't hurt that Fabolous' rhymes happen to fit right in the with the Zeitgeist of the moment, being somewhat of an East Coast Cash Money Millionaire-style, bling-blingin' gangsta rapper. Besides Jay-Z's occasional departure into materialism and/or hedonism à la "I Just Wanna Love U," the East Coast didn't really have a young, ice-sportin' player—at least not since the popular downfall of Bad Boy following the Notorious B.I.G.'s death. So if all this sounds a bit calculated, it's probably because it is. The flagship for DJ Clue's Desert Storm label, Fabolous is targeted at a specific niche, and he's a well-positioned product for sure. You know this before even hearing the music just by glancing over the credits: big-money, of-the-moment producers like the Neptunes, Rockwilder, and Timbaland drop some beats, and big-name, all-over-the-airwaves rappers/vocalists like Ja Rule, Lil' Mo, Jagged Edge, and Nate Dogg contribute some hooks—these are can't-miss artists capable of propelling a no-name like Fabolous to overnight stardom. And that's exactly how it worked, thanks to the Rick Rock-produced, Nate Dogg-graced "I Can't Deny It," a song that conveniently steals a trademark 2Pac line for its hook ("I can't deny it I'm a f*ckin' ridah," from "Ambitionz as a Ridah"). As calculated as it may be, it's an irresistible hook, but the remainder of the album unfortunately isn't nearly as alluring. Fabolous can rap, no doubt, and he's fairly witty in addition, but after a few songs you begin to tire of his juvenile mentality that seems to revolve around girls, money, partying, and materialism—that is, unless you share this same mentality. Quite simply, Fabolous has more than enough style but not much substance, and you can only employ so many Timbalands and Nate Doggs over the course of an album. —*Jason Birchmeier*

Street Dreams / Mar. 25, 2003 / Elektra ✦✦✦
His first record was the hottest rap debut of 2001 (despite an ominous release date: 9/11), and Fabolous consolidated his commercial clout, if not his artistic importance, with a safe sophomore record called *Street Dreams*. There's little doubt that Fabolous has rapping talents to match his name, with the smoothest flow of any East Coaster and dozens of great ideas. To capitalize on what made *Ghetto Fabolous* such a big hit, *Street Dreams* has plenty of club tracks ("Not Give a F✦✦✦✦," "Can't Let You Go," and "Trade It All, Pt. 2" featuring P. Diddy) and a few that advertise his hardcore credentials ("Not Give a F✦✦✦✦," "Up on Things" featuring Snoop Dogg, "Keepin It Gangsta" with Styles and Jadakiss). Elsewhere he dismisses a raft of female admirers ("Call Me," "Into You" featuring Ashanti) and shows a level of general disinterest to rival anyone with a major-label deal. One of the singles, "This Is My Party," is one of the worst tracks on the album, a lame mid-tempo grind with a one-note chorus featuring Fabolous intoning "This is my party, so get fly if you like to" over and over. The productions are much better than the songs, with good work coming from Tone & Poke, Timbaland, and executive producers DJ Clue and DURO. —*John Bush*

Facemob

Group / Gangsta Rap, Hardcore Rap, West Coast Rap

Protégés of Scarface, Facemob formed around the talents of five rappers from five different states, with no connections that *didn't* involve the former Geto Boy. Florida native Devin originally performed with Rap-A-Lot's Odd Squad;

Houston's Smit-D was a childhood friend of Scarface's; 350, the only female member, was invited after passing him a tape at a show in Cleveland; from St. Paul, DMG originally impressed Scarface so much he gained his own solo album (1993's *Rigormortiz*) for RAL; and Chicago native Chi-Ray, who the group formed around, wasn't so much a rapper as a veteran of area talent shows. The group released a heavily hyped 1996 debut, *The Other Side of the Law*, on Rap-A-Lot, and returned (surprisingly) in 2002 with *Silence*. —*John Bush*

● **The Other Side of the Law** / Aug. 7, 1996 / Interface/Rap-A-Lot/Noo Trybe ✦✦✦

Facemob are the protégés of Scarface and it shows—throughout their debut album, *The Other Side of the Law*, Facemob deals in the hard-edged psuedo-reality tales that have always distinguished the work of the Geto Boys. However, the group has yet to find a voice of their own. Although the Mob can occasionally craft an insightful, cutting lyric, they tend to rely on both musical and lyrical gangsta clichés, which makes the record a chore to listen to for anyone but afficanados. —*Leo Stanley*

Silence / Nov. 19, 2002 / Rap-A-Lot ✦✦

The Fam

Group / Hardcore Rap, Underground Rap
Chicago-based hardcore rap collective the Fam not only reps its city but also Think Big Entertainment, the label run by group member K-Ill. In addition to K-Ill (aka B.K.R.), the Fam also includes Redbone (aka Chella), 704 (aka the Nice MC), and Snake (aka G.S.). The group debuted in 2002 with *Big Businezz*, which set the stage for successive solo albums by each of the group members pending the financial well-being of Think Big Entertainment. —*Jason Birchmeier*

● **Big Businezz** / Mar. 12, 2002 / Think Big ✦✦✦
Big Businezz features each of the Fam's four members—K-Ill, Redbone, 704, and Snake—along with guest appearances by Traneroc and Ski. The Chicago collective reps its city and its label, Think Big Entertainment, with a rather hardcore style. In addition to an aggressive and sometimes harsh delivery, the rappers also tackle some uncomfortable subject matter: killing, kidnapping, crack smoking, being a hoodrat, being broke, finding a constant weed fix, and the nature of love in the 'hood. Anyone who finds such subject matter fascinating should no doubt marvel at the Fam since they discuss these issues from the standpoint of Chicago's hoodlife rather than that of Los Angeles, New York, or the dirty South. —*Jason Birchmeier*

The Fat Boys

f. 1982, Brooklyn, NY
Group / Hip-Hop, Old School Rap, Comedy Rap
One of early rap's most successful acts, the Fat Boys parlayed a combined weight of over 750 pounds into a comic novelty act that sustained them through several albums and hit singles. Originally known as the Disco 3, Brooklynites Mark "Prince Markie Dee" Morales, Damon "Kool Rock-Ski" Wimbley, and Darren "Buff the Human Beatbox" Robinson won a talent contest at Radio City Music Hall in 1983, thanks in part to Robinson's talent for using his mouth to improvise hip-hop rhythms and a variety of sound effects. The trio changed their name and recorded a series of good-time party anthems and songs humorously exploiting their weight; their first few records were produced by Kurtis Blow and feature fusions of hip-hop with reggae and rock. The Fat Boys hit their commercial peak with 1987's platinum LP *Crushin'*, a collection of entertaining party tunes that included a hit collaboration with the Beach Boys, "Wipeout." The group took the opportunity to star in the comedy film *Disorderlies* that year. *Coming Back Hard Again* essentially repeated the formula of *Crushin'*; the cover this time was "The Twist (Yo' Twist)," which featured backing from Chubby Checker. However, audience tastes were changing, and the Fat Boys' gimmicky novelty act was quickly becoming passé. The group tried to expand their artistic and street credibility with the ill-advised "rap opera" *On and On*, which promptly stiffed and prefaced the group's breakup. Prince Markie Dee recorded a solo album in 1992 and went on to a successful R&B songwriting/producing career. Robinson died of a heart attack in December 1995. —*Steve Huey*

The Fat Boys / 1984 / Sutra ✦✦✦✦✦
Because of their comic image, some hip-hoppers dismissed the Fat Boys as a novelty act—some, but not many. The fact is that they were among the best

and most popular rappers of the mid-1980s. Along with Run-D.M.C., LL Cool J, and Whodini, the Fat Boys were the finest that hip-hop's "Second Generation" (as it was called) had to offer. After making some noise as the Disco Three, the rotund Brooklynites changed their name to the Fat Boys in 1984 and hit big with this excellent debut album, which is humorous, wildly entertaining, and unapologetically funky. Everything from "Fat Boys" to the amusing "Jailhouse Rap" proves that their rapping skills were first rate. One of the group's strongest assets was Darren Robinson, aka the Human Beat Box, who was known for making percussive sounds with his voice. A celebration of his talent, "Human Beat Box" uses no actual instruments—only Robinson emulating them. This album is a true hip-hop classic. —*Alex Henderson*

The Fat Boys Are Back / 1985 / WEA ✦✦✦
One of the things that people in the music world have come to fear is the infamous sophomore slump. But there were no signs of a sophomore slump on the Fat Boys' second album, *The Fat Boys Are Back*. The Brooklyn trio showed a great deal of promise on its self-titled debut album of 1984, and this LP is also excellent. Because the Fat Boys acted like buffoons, some people dismissed them as a mere novelty act. But for all their clowning, the Fat Boys had impeccable rapping technique—the skills that they bring to "Yes, Yes Y'all," the title song, and other wildly infectious offerings are first rate. Much to their credit, this album is fairly unpredictable; *The Fat Boys Are Back* finds them rapping to everything from sleek urban contemporary ("Pump It Up") to hard rock ("Rock-N-Roll") and reggae ("Hard Core Reggae"). The latter, in fact, is one of the most impressive examples of hip-hop/reggae fusion to come from rap's second generation. But the Fat Boys don't need real instruments to bust a rhyme; on the a cappella "Human Beat Box, Part II," their only "instrument" is the voice of the late Darren Robinson, aka the Human Beat Box, who used his voice to simulate instruments. Arguably, Robinson and Doug E. Fresh were the closest thing that 1980s hip-hop had to Bobby McFerrin. As time passed, the Fat Boys started sounding like a caricature of themselves. But when *The Fat Boys Are Back* came out in 1985, they were still among the most exciting groups in hip-hop. —*Alex Henderson*

Big & Beautiful / 1986 / Sutra ✦✦
The train began derailing for the Fat Boys with their third album. It was their first that failed to go gold, and such songs as "Beat Box Is Rockin'," "Breakdown," and "Go For It" were indications that their novelty tunes and party rapping were becoming passé. They would make a brief comeback the next year fueled by the film *Disorderlies*, but the end was nearing for the trio. —*Ron Wynn*

Crushin' / 1987 / Mercury ✦✦✦✦✦
The Fat Boys enjoyed their biggest year in 1987. Their film *Disorderlies* proved much more commercially resilient than anticipated, and this LP earned their only platinum certification, while becoming the lone Fat Boys album to make the pop Top 10 (peaking at number 8). They also landed a Top 20 single with an updated version of "Wipeout." —*Ron Wynn*

Coming Back Hard Again / 1988 / Tin Pan Apple ✦✦✦
The last Fat Boys LP to make any noise, *Coming Back Hard Again* proved their second most successful album, peaking at 33 and earning them their last gold record. It piggybacked on the success of "Louie Louie," their last chart single. They did try to adjust to changing audience demands, cutting "Rock the House, Y'All" and "Powerlord," but the Fat Boys' strength remained novelty numbers and weight-based raps like "Big Daddy" and "Pig Feet," which had lost almost all their popularity. —*Ron Wynn*

Mack Daddy / 1991 / Emperor ✦✦✦
The Fat Boys were past their prime both creatively and commercially when *Mack Daddy* was recorded in 1991. Down to a duo consisting of Kool Rock-ski and Buff Daddy, the group significantly changes its style to appeal to early-'90s hip-hop tastes. The result is an album that isn't in a class with 1984's *The Fat Boys* or 1985's *The Fat Boys Are Back*, but isn't anything to be ashamed of either. Gone are the comic elements that had characterized them in the past, and none of the material is very pop influenced. Numbers like "Fly Car," "You're Da Man," and "Mack Daddy" sound like the work of a group that had been listening to a lot of Public Enemy (along with some Ice Cube), although none of the lyrics are sociopolitical. And the influence of new jack swing is hard to miss on "Tonight" and "Whip It on Me." But as likable as the CD is, this new version of the Fat Boys failed to take off commercially. —*Alex Henderson*

● **All Meat No Filler: The Best of the Fat Boys** / Mar. 18, 1997 / Rhino ◆◆◆◆◆
All Meat No Filler: The Best of the Fat Boys is an excellent 18-track compilation of all of the Fat Boys' biggest hits, including "Fat Boys," "Human Beat Box," "Jail House Rap," "Can You Feel It," "The Fat Boys Are Back," "Hard Core Reggae," "Falling in Love," "Wipeout" (with the Beach Boys), and "The Twist (Yo, Twist!)" (with Chubby Checker). Although some of the latter-day cuts have aged poorly, the Fat Boys' earliest singles are groundbreaking and timeless records, proving that they weren't merely a novelty act. —*Stephen Thomas Erlewine*

Fat Joe (Joseph Cartagena)

b. Bronx, NY
Producer, Vocals / East Coast Rap, Gangsta Rap, Pop-Rap, Latin Rap, Hardcore Rap
Latino rapper Fat Joe (aka Fat Joe da Gangsta, Joey Crack, and his real name Joe Cartagena) was raised in the South Bronx area of New York. It was through an older brother that Cartagena learned the ways of the street, as well as discovering rap music via the sounds of such groundbreaking artists as Theodore, Funky Four Plus One, and the Furious Five. Eventually going by the name of Fat Joe, the rapper secured a recording contract with the Relativity label in the early '90s, resulting in the release of his full-length debut, *Represent*, in 1993 (which spawned the single "Flow Joe," peaking at the number-one spot on *Billboard*'s Hot Rap Singles chart). Two years later, Fat Joe issued his sophomore effort, *Jealous One's Envy*, which included a cameo appearance by KRS-One as well as production contributions by the likes of DJ Premier, LES, and Domingo. Around the same time, Fat Joe appeared on LL Cool J's big hit "I Shot Ya" (along with Foxy Brown and Keith Murray) and collaborated with the Wu-Tang Clan's Raekwon on a track from the "Envy" single, called "Firewater." By the late '90s, Fat Joe had switched record labels (signing on with Atlantic) and tried his hand at other nonmusical career ventures such as opening a clothing store called Fat Joe's Halftime, a barber shop, and a fashion line, FJ560. In addition, he signed a production and distribution deal with Atlantic Records and Mystic Entertainment (which he runs along with a partner named Big Greg). The year 1998 saw the release of Fat Joe's debut for Atlantic, *Don Cartagena*, which featured cameo appearances by the likes of Puff Daddy, Nas, Raekwon, Big Pun, and Jadakiss (L.O.X.), following it up in 2001 with *Jealous Ones Still Envy (J.O.S.E.)*, which included contributions from Ludacris, Petey Pablo, M.O.P., R. Kelly, and Remy. —*Greg Prato*

Represent / Jul. 27, 1993 / Relativity ◆◆◆
When Fat Joe debuted in 1993, few would have guessed that he'd be topping the charts years later—both the album charts as a gangsta (*Don Cartagena*) and the pop charts as a charmer ("What's Luv?," his duet with Ashanti). After all, when he released *Represent* in 1993, Fat Joe was known as Fat Joe da Gangsta and had no qualms about being hardcore. And that's precisely how he flows on this album—gangsta and hardcore. It helps, though, that Diamond D, one of New York's finest producers from the early '90s, keeps the beats flowing throughout *Represent*. Moreover, it helps that Fat Joe had a catchy single here, "Flow Joe," to market the album with as well. Granted, *Represent* finds Fat Joe dropping rather juvenile rhymes relative to his later work, but you can hear on this album what all the fuss would be about later. —*Jason Birchmeier*

● **Jealous One's Envy** / Nov. 1995 / Relativity ◆◆◆
The infamous Fat Joe (aka Joey Crack), a heavyset bully of a rapper out of the South Bronx, dropped this noisy jackhammer of an album in late 1995. The follow-up to his street-acclaimed *Represent* from 1993 is bloated with vivid tales of violence and fortified claims to street credibility. Joe has an old-world sense of the criminally minded and displays a Cosa Nostra-like romanticism in his hearty boasts to rap supremacy. An interlude of Spanish braggadocio over the melodic *Godfather* theme and a Frank White (Christopher Walken) monologue from *King of New York* are proof of Joe's self-professed kingpin status. The healthy dose of inspired production from heavyweights Diamond D, Premier, and Domingo provide an amply pugilistic background for Joe's nitroglycerin-fueled verbal warfare. Joe makes no bones about his affiliations with drug trafficking and thievery either: "I'm the realer MC/the drug dealer MC." The legendary KRS-One climbs aboard on "Bronx Tale" and the Wu-Tang's Raekwon helps out on "Respect Mine." Even the shamelessly purloined sample of Marvin Gaye's "Sexual Healing" on "Envy" cannot slow down this driving record. Few rap albums of the modern era have the pure testicular quality of *Jealous One's Envy*, and the lyrical content, while tending to be repetitive, is always clever and never nauseating. A solid second effort from a true Bronx Bomber. —*Micheal Di Bella*

Don Cartagena / Jul. 14, 1998 / Atlantic ◆◆◆
The third album from power-Bronx Latino rapper Fat Joe tones down his once-prevalent gangsta leans—they're still there, though, from the album's title to rhythmic gunshot bursts guiding the cuts—and builds up his 'hood and familial loyalties through a series of melodically enticing (and vaguely Wu-Tangish) songs. Like he did on Big Punisher's album from the same year, *Capital Punishment*, Fat Joe works *Don Cartagena*'s slinky street beats into a semi-sublime hip-hopera that's more than a sum of its parts. Only the between-song skits (which are juvenile and mood dropping) and the overloaded guest list (cameos from Puff Daddy, Nas, Big Punisher, Raekwon and The Terror Squad merely skim the surface of the overwhelming uselessness of this overplayed genre trend) wear down *Don Cartagena*'s often mesmerizing and noble attempt at a late-'90s rap resuscitation. —*Michael Gallucci*

Jealous Ones Still Envy (J.O.S.E.) / Dec. 4, 2001 / Atlantic ◆◆◆
Fat Joe's *Jealous Ones Still Envy* follows the precedent set by his preceding albums, not offering anything particularly novel but rather carrying on in the great "Big Poppa" tradition of Notorious B.I.G.-influenced rap. Joe's still putting it down for NYC, repping himself as part thug, part player. It's the age-old scenario—if Joe's not keepin' it real on the streets the grimy way, he's loungin' like a pimp and livin' large. A few albums into his career, Joe has this approach down to a science. In fact, much of this album resembles his past work in terms of lyrics. It's only the production and guest appearances that set *Jealous Ones Still Envy* apart from previous Fat Joe albums like *Don Cartagena* (1998) and *Jealous Ones Envy* (1995). Some of this album's featured producers include Irv Gotti, Rocwilder, Bink Dog, Buckwild, and Alchemist; featured rappers include Ludacris, Petey Pablo, M.O.P., R. Kelly, and Remy. Since this is Joe's first album in three years—not counting the Terror Squad album—fans were no doubt hungry upon its release, evidenced by the eager embrace of the album's lead single (the R. Kelly collabo, "We Thuggin'"), even if the Puerto Rican rapper is serving up more of the same. —*Jason Birchmeier*

Loyalty / Nov. 12, 2002 / Atlantic ◆◆◆
Loyalty is the name of the game for Fat Joe this time out, as it relates to fans still true to the Bronx's hardest rapper despite chart success with Ashanti, his own loyalty to his hardcore past considering there's a spate of joints for the ladies this time out, and having his loyalty to deceased partner Big Pun questioned by Pun's widow in a highly publicized radio bout just before the album's release. Driven by the breakout of his Ashanti duet "What's Luv?," *Loyalty* comes with hardcore-but-hot joints like the sleek single "Crush Tonight" (with Ginuwine), "Bust at You," the Irv Gotti production "Turn Me On," and "TS Piece" (the latter with Terror Squad's Remy holding on the female end). Fat Joe proves he's still got a lot of hardcore in him, though, with "Gangsta" and "Born in the Ghetto," plus another volume in the "Sh*t Is Real" saga and a new Terror Squad anthem, "Prove Something." —*John Bush*

Father MC (Timothy Brown)

Pop-Rap, Hip-Hop
Father MC straddled the line between hip-hop and new jack swing, which resulted in a number-20 hit, "I'll Do 4 U," from his debut album *Father's Day*. Nearly two years after his debut, Father MC followed with *Close to You*. Its success was almost guaranteed by Father MC's appearance on the CD *Uptown MTV Unplugged*. Father MC was formerly a dancehall reggae performer, and there was some reggae influence interspersed with the sentimental love lyrics and hip-hop production. After a four-year studio hiatus, he returned in 1999 with *No Secrets*, and another lengthy pause preceded 2003's *My*. —*Ron Wynn*

● **Father's Day** / 1990 / Uptown ◆◆◆◆
Before Puffy, Mary J., and the rest of the blingers went off to successful chart domination, there was Father MC. Perfecting the marriage of soul, R&B, and rap into a successful formula, *Father's Day* was not only important, it was a litmus test that launched the careers of both aforementioned artists—as Combs was head producer and Blige made her musical debut as a background singer. Leading off with the new jack classic "I'll Do 4 U," it's immediately apparent that the trio was onto something big. Unfortunately, the rest of the album becomes somewhat formulaic after this point, but the impact of *Father's Day*'s tone and textures would be felt for years to come. —*Rob Theakston*

Close to You / 1992 / Uptown ✦✦✦
Bronx rapper Father MC faked folks out on both sides of the style line when
he released his second album in 1992. Those expecting 100-percent hardcore
blanched at hearing sentimental love themes and straight R&B; others who
thought he was strictly a new jack swinger were caught sleeping when the
booming beats of the title track were cranked up on the box, or when Father
MC matched one-liners with Lady Kazan on "I've Been Watching You."
—*Ron Wynn*

My / Mar. 18, 2003 / Empire Musicwerks ✦✦✦
In a genre where the average shelf life of an MC is less than two records (three
at most), Father MC deserves special recognition for his longevity and commitment to the game. But after a three-year hiatus and yet another jump to
a different label, *My* isn't exactly the stuff strong comebacks are made of.
Aside from the title track, there isn't anything necessarily outstanding or anything that jumps out during the hour-long jaunt through Father's testimony
to his city. The usual wide range of topics—including partying, hustling, and
lust for women—is covered, and once again the ever-special obligatory dedication track to mama is present. It's not a bad record by any stretch, but
longevity does not equate with quality and one can't help but wonder what
would have happened if he would have taken a little more time and crafted
My with a little more attention to overall production. —*Rob Theakston*

Fatlip (Derrick Stewart)

Producer, MC / Hip-Hop, Alternative Rap, West Coast Rap, Underground Rap
Born Derrick Stewart, Fatlip was a member of the influential underground
hip-hop group the Pharcyde and has also settled into a solo career. In the early
'90s, Stewart was working at local clubs around L.A. when he formed the
Pharcyde with Romye "Booty Brown" Robinson, Imani Wilcox, and Tre
"Slimkid" Hardson, who were members of a dance troupe known as "242."
By the time they were all 21, the Pharcyde had signed a record deal with Delicious Vinyl and produced three albums filled with sharp lyrics and tight
tracks that managed to achieve commercial success while still maintaining a
distinct underground flavor.
    Fatlip left the Pharcyde shortly after the release of their 1995 album,
Labcabincalifornia, due to creative differences, personal problems, and the
desire to start a solo career. As a solo artist, Fatlip continued his innovative
work with his solo first single "What's up Fatlip?" from *Prime Cuts, Vol. 1*,
a collection of new songs and artists on the Delicious Vinyl label. A projected
full-length, to be titled *Revenge of the Nerd*, failed to appear. —*Jon Azpiri*

What's up Fatlips? [Single] / Feb. 29, 2000 / Delicious Vinyl ✦✦✦
The single "What's up Fatlip?" has a carnival-esque groove that complements
Fatlip's unique brand of self-deprecating hip-hop. In a genre where self-
assurance and bravado are at a premium, it stands out as a three-and-a-half-
minute tribute to his endless shortcomings and insecurities. The B side,
"Goldmine," is also excellent, a leering sex rap reminiscent of Ol' Dirty
Bastard. —*Jon Azpiri*

Fermin IV (Morelos Fermin IV)

Latin Rap
Owner of one of the most peculiar voices in the Latin rap scene, Fermin IV
began getting involved in hip-hop music after listening to American rap
groups from the 1980s. In 1994, his first band, called Prófuga de Metate,
debuted with an independently produced demo. A year later, ex-Pasto Pato
and ex-La Ultima de Lucas' keyboardist Toy joined him to assemble Control
Machete. Soon, the Mexican threesome became a worldwide top-selling Latin
rap outfit with two chart-topping albums, 1997's *Mucho Barato* and 1999's
Artillería Pesada Presenta.
    After moving from Monterrey to Cuernavaca, Morelos Fermin IV started
working on his first solo album. In February 2001, Universal Music Mexico
signed him up to release *Boomerang*, including "004," featured on the *XXX*
movie soundtrack. —*Drago Bonacich*

Boomerang / Jul. 30, 2002 / Universal Latino ✦✦✦

Field Mob

f. Albany, GA
Group / Dirty South, Southern Rap
While hip-hop prides itself on being the soundtrack to the streets, Field Mob
does their best to represent the country. The duo of Boondox and Kalage hail

from Albany, GA, a small town outside of Atlanta that is best known as the
birthplace of soul legend Ray Charles. The pair chose the name Field Mob to
represent The Field, a small area of Albany where they grew up. The two met
in high school after Boondox saw Kalage freestyling in the school courtyard.
Boondox challenged him to a battle the next day, and afterward they decided
to become partners. The Mob landed a deal with a small independent record
label and recorded their first single which caught the attention of MCA
Records. MCA quickly signed them to a deal, and in 2000, they released their
first album, *613: Ashy to Classy*. Despite their age and lack of experience,
613: Ashy to Classy is a polished effort that features clever lyrics and solid
production. The same can be said for *From tha Roota to tha Toota*, the 2002
follow-up that showed the Georgia natives collaborating with Trick Daddy
and moving closer to the Outkast-esque production work they hinted at on
their debut. The pair of youngsters has shown they can compete with the best
hip-hop has to offer, and they'll do it while wearing their country roots with
pride. —*Jon Azpiri*

613: Ashy to Classy / Dec. 12, 2000 / MCA ✦✦✦✦
The downhome rappers from Albany, GA, have put together a debut that
demonstrates that they should be mentioned alongside other great Georgia
rappers such as Goodie Mob and Outkast. Like their predecessors, Field Mob
has put together a mix of social commentary and Southern bounce that would
appeal to listeners on both sides of the Mason-Dixon line. While too many
Southern hip-hop artists resort to formulaic tracks, the album's production
feels fresh. "Dead in Yo Chevy," with it's pounding 808 drum beats and catchy
hook, seems to be designed to be boomed out of car stereos. The same can be
said for "Crutch," a smooth mid-tempo song about friendship. Rappers
Boondox and Kalage complement the solid production with clever rhymes.
Check out "Channel 6:13, Part I," a clever song that incorporates several TV
characters into a humorous narrative, sort of like a modern version of Slick
Rick's "Bedtime Story." Similarly, "My Man Roni" is a playful battle of the sexes
that steers clear of the usual he said she said banter. There are some small
miscues—a track like "Dimez" lacks the shine of other songs—but, as a whole,
613: Ashy to Classy provides a big helping of Southern comfort. —*Jon Azpiri*

• **From tha Roota to tha Toota** / Oct. 22, 2002 / MCA ✦✦✦✦
Some music critics have observed that if rap is "the CNN of the streets" (to
borrow a phrase coined by Public Enemy leader Chuck D), country is "the
CNN of the suburbs." Historically, hip-hoppers have tended to address urban
inner-city concerns, whereas country singers have often focused on things
that people in suburbia and small towns can relate to. But here's the thing:
plenty of people in large cities listen to Patty Loveless and Randy Travis, and
plenty of hip-hop heads live in small and medium-sized towns. So it was inevitable that a Southern rap group like Field Mob would end up bringing
a more rural perspective to hip-hop—well, rural up to a point. Field Mob's
Boondox Blax has described Albany as being "like a metropolitan area, but
it's rural at the same time"—and that rural/metropolitan blend makes for
many interesting moments on the duo's second album, *From tha Roota to
tha Toota*. Hip-hop heads from the Boogie Down Bronx or West Philadelphia
will no doubt find this CD to be extremely Southern sounding, which is a
good thing because Southern sounding is exactly what Field Mob is going for.
At the same time, Boondox and his partner, Kalage, rap about many of the
same social problems that northern MCs rap about—poverty, drugs, and incarceration are among the topics that they address. But even though the subject matter isn't radically different from what you might hear on a Northern
(or West Coast) rap project, Field Mob's beats and flows give their work a certain freshness. Field Mob's beats never sound generic, and the Southerners
don't go out of their way to emulate popular MCs from other parts of Georgia.
All things considered, *From tha Roota to tha Toota* is among the more
memorable dirty South efforts of 2002. —*Alex Henderson*

Fiend (Ricky Jones)

Vocals / Dirty South, Southern Rap, Hardcore Rap
One of Master P's many No Limit soldiers during the label's peak, Fiend never
experienced much solo success though he contributed heavily to the work of
his colleagues, most notably P's crossover hit, "Make Em Say Ugh." Born
Ricky Jones and raised in the 17th ward of New Orleans, Fiend lost his
brother at a young age; the loss made a strong mark on the eventual rapper
and darkly tainted his worldview. He later embraced rap music and signed to
Big Boy Records, also home to Mystikal at the time. The label released Fiend's

first hit single, "Baddest Muthafucka Alive," and also *Won't Be Denied* (1995), which featured another hit, "All I See." These singles inspired Master P to sign the blossoming rapper to his No Limit label and debut him on the *I'm Bout It* soundtrack ("Don't Mess Around") (1997). That same year Fiend most notably contributed to Master P's crossover hit "Make Em Say Ugh" as well as its heavily MTV-rotated video. The rapper remained a loyal soldier thereafter, contributing to numerous other No Limit releases and preparing his own, *There's One in Every Family* (1998). The album sold exceptionally well but didn't spawn any major hits, nor did its follow-up, *Street Life* (1999). Regardless, Fiend made preparations to join a promising new No Limit supergroup, Tank Dawgs, which also consisted of C-Murder, Mac, and Snoop Dogg. By this point, though, Master P's tank began to run out of fuel as a commercial backlash mounted. Fiend soon found himself out of work and dropped out of the game after a short yet incredibly productive stint as a No Limit soldier. —*Jason Birchmeier*

● **There's One in Every Family** / May 5, 1998 / No Limit ✦✦✦✦

Street Life / Jul. 6, 1999 / No Limit ✦✦✦
On his second album for No Limit, Fiend again worked with the in-house production team Beats By the Pound. They provide the backing for his hard-hitting urban war stories. There's no mistaking this for anything but a No Limit release (especially with all the guest rappers), but *Street Life* fares much better than average for hip-hop's most notorious label. —*Keith Farley*

5th Ward Boyz

Group / Hip-Hop, Gangsta Rap, Hardcore Rap, Southern Rap
The first artists brought to Rap-A-Lot Records after the infamous Geto Boys, 5th Ward Boyz originally comprised Andre "007" Barnes and Eric "E-Rock" Taylor. The trio originally recorded for Dewey Forker's Underground Records, but moved through a deal between Forker and Rap-A-Lot chief James Smith. The two executives helped produce the debut 5th Ward Boyz album, 1991's *Ghetto Dope*, which was distributed through Priority. The 5th Ward Boyz released *Gangsta Funk* the following year, then added third member Richard "Lo-Life" Nash for 1995's *Rated G. Usual Suspects* followed in 1997, and two years later the group returned with *P.W.A. The Album: Keep It Poppin'*. A fifth album, *Recognize the Real*, was released in fall 2000. —*John Bush*

● **Rated G** / Nov. 28, 1995 / Rap-A-Lot ✦✦✦✦✦
As the title indicates, 5th Ward Boyz's second album *Rated G* is nothing but straight-up G-funk. The group works the standard booming bass and slinky keyboards for all they're worth, and they occasionally come up with first-class tracks like "Concrete Hell," which comes through with a subdued, muscular force. However, the group can't sustain that power throughout the course of the album. Frequently, *Rated G* is simply competent—it's well done but delivered without much style or originality. None of the members are particularly distinctive rappers, nor is the music exceptionally produced and arranged. Even with these drawbacks, *Rated G* remains enjoyable. It is the work of talented, but not inspired, imitators and it will do if *The Chronic* and *Doggystyle* are sounding stale. —*Stephen Thomas Erlewine*

Usual Suspects / Nov. 18, 1997 / Rap-A-Lot ✦✦
The 5th Ward Boyz took their name from the same infamous Houston ghetto that gave us the Geto Boys, one of the first groups to embrace gangsta rap in the 1980s. Like the Geto Boys, 5th Ward Boyz specialized in gangsta rap and offered violent, profane depictions of life in the Fifth Ward. But while the early gangsta rap of the Geto Boys, Ice-T, N.W.A, and Schoolly D had a definite freshness and was quite cutting edge, there's nothing fresh about *Usual Suspects.* "Got II Be Down II Die," "Heat," "Pussy, Weed and Alcohol," and other tunes on this routine, unoriginal effort don't say anything that older gangsta rappers weren't saying eight years earlier. A few of the songs are memorable—most notably, "Live Your Life" and "Mama's Praying," which describes a mother's prayer that her son won't get caught up in the criminality that surrounds her in the ghetto. But on the whole, *Usual Suspects* demonstrated that in 1997 there were still many rappers who were content to offer one tired, worn-out, gangsta-rap cliché after another. —*Alex Henderson*

50 Cent (Curtis Jackson)

b. Queens, NY
East Coast Rap, Hardcore Rap
In many ways the ideal East Coast hardcore rapper, 50 Cent endured substantial obstacles throughout his young yet remarkably dramatic life before

becoming in early 2003 the most-discussed figure in rap, if not pop music in general. Following an unsuccessful late-'90s run at mainstream success (foiled by an attempt on his life in 2000) and a successful run on the New York mix-tape circuit (driven by his early-2000s bout with Ja Rule), Eminem signed 50 to a seven-figure contract in 2002 and helmed his quick rise toward crossover success in 2003. The product of a broken home in the rough Jamaica neighborhood of Queens and, in turn, the storied 'hood's hustling streets themselves, 50 lived everything most rappers write rhymes about but never actually experience: drugs, crimes, imprisonments, stabbings, and, most infamously of all, shootings; all of this before he even released his debut album. Of course, such experiences became 50's rhetorical stock in trade. He reveled in his oft-told past, he called out wanna-be gangstas, and he made headlines. He even *looked* like the ideal East Coast hardcore rapper: big framed with oft-showcased biceps, abs, and tattoos as well as his trademark bulletproof vest, pistol, and iced crucifix. Furthermore, his distaste for flossing stunner rappers and materialistic women—yet somewhat paradoxically coupled with his appetite for guns, drugs, and wealth—made him a welcome alternative to the bling-bling sect in the early 2000s.

Born Curtis Jackson and raised in Southside Jamaica, Queens, 50 grew up in a broken home. His hustler mother passed away when he was only eight, and his father departed soon after, leaving his grandmother to parent him. As a teen, he followed the lead of his mother and began hustling. The crack trade proved lucrative for 50; until he eventually encountered the law, that is, and began making visits to prison. It's around this point in the mid-'90s that he turned toward rap and away from crime. His break came in 1996 when he met Run-D.M.C.'s Jam Master Jay, who gave him a tape of beats and asked him to rap over it. Impressed by what he heard, Jay signed the aspiring rapper to his JMJ Records label. Not much resulted from the deal, though, and 50 affiliated himself with Trackmasters, a commercially successful New York-based production duo (comprised of Poke and Tone) known for their work with such artists as Nas and Jay-Z. Trackmasters signed the rapper to their Columbia sublabel and began work on his debut album, *Power of the Dollar*. A trio of singles preceded the album's proposed release: "Your Life's on the Line," "Thug Love" (featuring Destiny's Child), and "How to Rob."

The latter track became a sizable hit, attracting a lot of attention for its baiting lyrics that detail how 50 would rob particular big-name rappers. This willingness to rap openly and brashly and the attention it attracted came back to haunt him, however. His first post-success brush with death came shortly after the release of "How to Rob," when he was stabbed at the Hit Factory studio on West 54th Street in Manhattan. Shortly afterward came his most storied incident: on May 24, 2000, just before Columbia was set to release *Power of the Dollar*, an assassin attempted to take 50's life on 161st Street in Jamaica, Queens (near where Jam Master Jay would later be fatally shot two and half years later), shooting him nine times with a 9mm pistol while the rapper sat helpless in the passenger seat of a car. One shot pierced his cheek, another his hand, and the seven others his legs and thighs; yet he survived, barely. Even so, Columbia wanted nothing to do with 50 when they heard the news, shelving *Power of the Dollar* and parting ways with the now-controversial rapper.

During the next two years, 50 returned to the rap underground where he began. He formed a collective (G Unit, which also featured Lloyd Banks and Tony Yayo), worked closely with producer Sha Money XL (who had also been signed to JMJ around the same time that 50 had), and began churning out mix-tape tracks (many of which were later compiled on *Guess Who's Back?* in 2002). These mix-tape recordings (many of which were hosted by DJ Whoo Kid on CDs such as *No Mercy, No Fear* and *Automatic Gunfire*), earned the rapper an esteemed reputation on the streets of New York. Some of them featured 50 and his G Unit companions rapping over popular beats (Raphael Saadiq's "Be Here," Wu-Tang Clan's "Ya'll Been Warned"), others mocked popular rappers (namely Ja Rule, who quickly became an arch-rival), and a few discussed his shooting ("F*ck You," among others). This constant mix-tape presence throughout 2000-2002 garnered industry attention as well as street esteem, particularly when Eminem declared on a radio show his admiration for 50. A bidding war ensued, as Em had to fend off numerous other industry figures, all of whom hoped to sign 50, driving up the signing price into the million-plus figures in the process and slowly moving the rapper into the up-and-coming spotlight once again as word spread.

Despite the bidding war, Eminem indeed got his man, signing 50 to a joint deal with Shady/Aftermath; the former label Em's, the latter Dr. Dre's.

During the successive months, 50 worked closely with Em and Dre, who would coexecutive produce his upcoming debut, *Get Rich or Die Tryin'*, each of them producing a few tracks for the highly awaited album. Before *Get Rich* dropped, though, Em debuted 50 on the *8 Mile* soundtrack. The previously released (via the underground, that is) "Wanksta" became a runaway hit in late 2002, setting the stage for "In da Club," the Dre-produced lead single from *Get Rich*. The two singles became sizable crossover hits—the former peaking at number 13 on *Billboard*'s Hot 100 chart, the latter at number one—and Interscope (Shady/Aftermath's parent company) had to move up *Get Rich*'s release date to combat bootlegging as a result.

Amid all this, 50 made headlines everywhere. Most notably, he was tied to Jam Master Jay's shooting in October 2002, the F.B.I.'s investigation of Murder Inc.'s relationship to former drug dealer Kenneth "Supreme" McGriff, and the shooting incident at the offices of Violator Management. Furthermore, he made more headlines when he was jailed on New Year's Eve 2002 for gun possession. The media relished his life story, particularly his storied brush with death—and not just the expected media outlets like MTV—even such unlikely mainstream publications as *The New York Times* ran feature stories ("Amid Much Anticipation, a Rapper Makes a Debut"). By the time *Get Rich* finally streeted on February 6, 2003, he had become the most discussed figure in the music industry, and, bootlegging or not, his initial sales figures reflected this (a record breaking 872,000 units moved in five days; the best-selling debut album since SoundScan started its tracking system in May 1991), as did his omnipresence in the media. *—Jason Birchmeier*

Power of the Dollar [Unreleased] / Jul. 4, 2000 / Trackmasters/Columbia/ Sony ✦✦✦

You can say this much for 50 Cent: the man knows how to make an entrance. Before he released the uproariously cunning single "How to Rob," few knew this Queens, NY, native even existed. But by naming names and placing his own persona deep in the middle of a nonexistent battle (specifically, casting hip-hop stars as targets for 50 Cent's hardcore, comedic robbing spree), he assured himself a place among the industry's most illustrious performers. After all, a challenge rarely goes unanswered in hip-hop circles and when that gauntlet is raised, the best retaliation is a lyrical one. Thus setting the stage for his own legend to emerge, 50 Cent recorded a powerful debut CD to prove he was no one-hit wonder. Tracks on *Power of the Dollar* utilize penetrating wit and funk-infused beats, accompanied by grand orchestrations of commanding horns, pronounced percussion, and various string elements. "Slow Doe" features Latin guitar grooves and "Your Life's on the Line" conveys street life through hard, violent rhythms. Using a New York "double-time" rap style, 50 Cent presents his verbal art as a visceral and bold experience. But when he was shot two months before the album's projected release, Columbia shelved the entire project and released 50 Cent from his contract. *—Roxanne Blanford*

Guess Who's Back? / Apr. 26, 2002 / Full Clip ✦✦✦✦

Months before 50 Cent burst into the mainstream with *Get Rich or Die Tryin'*, his "In da Club"-highlighted debut for Shady/Aftermath, the highly touted rapper cleaned out his closet with *Guess Who's Back?* The skimpily packaged album, released by the indie label Full Clip and documented by no credits whatsoever, compiles what it terms as "underground classics and freestyles." Unless you're connected to the New York mix-tape circuit or happen to own a bootlegged version of 50's unreleased 2000 debut album for Columbia, the Trackmasters-produced *Power of the Dollar*, none of the 18 songs here are going to be familiar—they're all previously unreleased, legally that is. However, if you're indeed down with the underground, either via the streets of NYC or the bandwidth of cyberspace, many of these songs will be familiar. About half come from *Power of the Dollar*, including such highlights as "Life's on the Line," "Ghetto Qua Ran," and "As the World Turns," while the others, such as "That's What's Up" (a G Unit posse track over the beat to Wu-Tang's "Ya'll Been Warned"), "Too Hot," and "Who U Rep With" (the latter two featuring Nas, who is sampled for the hook to "F*ck You" also), come mostly from mix-tapes. A few of the inclusions suffer from shoddy sound quality, particularly the trio of freestyles that close the album, while a few others *sound* like mix-tape tracks, lacking commercially orientated production and verse-chorus-verse structures. It's this occasional underground sense, though, that makes *Guess Who's Back?* such a worthwhile listen for fans. Granted, this album isn't an authentic NYC-style mix tape, but it's awfully close, definitely modeled after one and therefore representative of precisely why 50

went on to become the most talked-about upcoming rapper in a decade. There's a reason a million-dollar bidding war broke out for 50 in 2002, and *Guess Who's Back?* showcases that reason better than any other legal release out there. Before 50 was "In da Club" with Eminem and Dr. Dre, he was here, releasing a plethora of mix-tape tracks for the underground with hopes of one day getting rich or dying trying. *—Jason Birchmeier*

● Get Rich or Die Tryin' / Feb. 6, 2003 / Interscope ✦✦✦✦

Probably the most hyped debut album by a rap artist in about a decade, most likely since Snoop's *Doggystyle* (1993) or perhaps Nas' *Illmatic* (1994), 50 Cent's *Get Rich or Die Tryin'* certainly arrived amid massive expectations. In fact, the expectations were so massive that they overshadowed the music itself—50 becoming more of a phenomenon than simply a rapper—so massive that you had to be skeptical, particularly given the marketing-savvy nature of the rap world. Even so, *Get Rich* is indeed an impressive debut, not quite on the level of such landmark debuts as the aforementioned ones by Snoop or Nas—or those by Biggie, Wu-Tang, or DMX either—but impressive nonetheless, definitely ushering in 50 as one of the truly eminent rappers of his era. The thing, though, is that 50 isn't exactly a rookie, and it's debatable as to whether or not *Get Rich* can be considered a true debut (see the unreleased *Power of the Dollar* [2000] and the *Guess Who's Back?* compilation [2002]). That debate aside, however, *Get Rich* plays like a blueprint rap debut should: there's a tense, suspenseful intro ("What Up Gangsta"), an ethos-establishing tag-team spar with Eminem ("Patiently Waiting"), a street-cred appeal ("Many Men [Wish Death]"), a tailor-made mass-market good-time single ("In da Club"), a multifaceted tread through somber ghetto drama (from "High All the Time" to "Gotta Make It to Heaven"), and finally three bonus tracks that reprise 50's previously released hits ("Wanksta," "U Not Like Me," "Life's on the Line")—in that precise order. In sum, *Get Rich* is an incredibly calculated album, albeit an amazing one. After all, when coexecutive producer Eminem raps, "Take some Big and some Pac/And you mix them up in a pot/Sprinkle a little Big L on top/What the fuck do you got?" you know the answer. Give Em (who produces two tracks) and Dr. Dre (who does four) credit for laying out the red carpet here, and also give 50 credit for reveling brilliantly in his much-documented mystique—from his gun fetish to his witty swagger, 50 has the makings of a street legend, and it's no secret. And though he very well could be the rightful successor to the Biggie-Jigga-Nas triptych, *Get Rich* isn't quite the masterpiece 50 seems capable of, impressive or not. But until he drops that truly jaw-dropping album—which you know he will—this will certainly do. *—Jason Birchmeier*

Fingathing

Group / Alternative Rap, Turntablism, British Rap, Underground Rap

The instrumental hip-hop duo of DJ Peter Parker and bassist Sneaky started performing as Fingathing in 1999. Peter Parker was a bedroom DJ discovered by Mark Rae of trip-hoppers Rae & Christian at a DMC competition in 1997; Sneaky—a classically trained bassist—was working in a popular Manchester club when the pair met. Their first full-length, *The Main Event*, was issued in 2000 on Rae's Grand Central label. Live dates, including a stint opening for DJ Shadow, followed the release of their sophomore effort, *Superhero Music*, in 2002. *— Wade Kergan*

The Main Event / Nov. 28, 2000 / Grand Central ✦✦✦

The duo of Peter Parker and Sneaky, aka Fingathing, know a thing or two about records. Every textured break on *The Main Event* is so perfectly mixed that you'd swear it was done digitally. Not for these guys, though. Truly, the Fingathing duo is a pair of extremely talented turntablists working in a similar vein as Kid Koala or Rob Swift. Admittedly, they share more with Kid Koala, as their canvas is flecked with childlike humor and wickedly quick scratches. Needless to say, these need lists are big fans of outrageously obscure samples, and they use them at every chance. Their use of Classics IV's "Spooky" on "Come on Girls" stands out immediately as the most poignant and groovy homage on the record. From time to time, the use of samples overshadows Fingathing's incredible skill, but listeners will undoubtedly recognize these two musicians as skilled purveyors of the genre. It's rare that discs released by scratch or battle DJs ever hold a candle to their respective live performances, but here Fingathing definitely defy convention. The production value of *The Main Event* is higher than a lot of digitally produced electronic records and is also assembled with much more care. It is likely that too much care takes the happy sting out of a couple tracks on this disc, but that is definitely the exception and hardly the standard. British audiences have been raving over Fingathing for ages. It's only a matter of time before the U.S. does, too. —*Ken Taylor*

● **Superhero Music** / Jun. 25, 2002 / Grand Central ✦✦✦
The second album from the dynamic duo comes with a suitably apt title from a pairing that counts a certain Peter Parker among its number. The cutups have grown up in the two years since their debut, *The Main Event*, with inspiration coming more from the somber material of DJ Shadow than the crazed comic book shenanigans of fellow turntablist Kid Koala. As such, the classically trained Sneak is given much more room to demonstrate his skills with a double bass, while Parker's Technics trickery is kept from the comics in favor of a role that is best described as slick sample manipulation. Though the album has a sense of the cinematic running throughout its 22 tracks, "Spacecrumbs" and "Once Upon a Time in the East" act as memorable highlights with strings shivering down the spine of thoughtful beats and widescreen arrangements. —*Kingsley Marshall*

The Firm

Group / Hip-Hop, East Coast Rap, Hardcore Rap
The East Coast gangsta rap supergroup the Firm never lived up to its excessive hype and instead became a brief footnote in the careers of its main participants. The foursome included four New York rappers—Nas, Foxy Brown, AZ, and Nature—but was actually the pet project of its producers: Nas Escobar (as he referred to himself at the time), Steve "Commissioner" Stoute, Dr. Dre, and the Trackmasters. On paper, the group seemed nothing short of spectacular: on the vocals Nas and Foxy Brown, two of New York's favorite rappers at the time; on the beats Dre and the Trackmasters, two of the industry's most accomplished producers of the time; and signing the checks Stoute, the man standing alongside Puff Daddy as New York's biggest career booster. On paper this looked like an invincible team for sure; however, the overconfident, overreaching attitudes of all involved ironically became the group's downfall.

An early form of the Firm appeared on "Affirmative Action," a standout song from Nas' second album, *It Was Written*. Foxy Brown, AZ, and Cormega joined Nas for the song—each taking a verse—and it became an album highlight as well as a much-talked-about song on the streets. Of course, Cormega got the boot in favor of Nature for reasons that vary depending on who you ask (reportedly because either Stoute or Nas—or both—preferred Nature). Up until this incident, Cormega and Nas had been comrades. Following the incident, however, Cormega took his beef to the streets, penning the inflammatory track "Fuck Nas and Nature" and letting it circulate through the mix-tape market. Things would never be the same between the two former comrades.

But the Cormega incident had little to do with why the Firm flopped. Rather, it became an instance of overconfidence and overreaching. All involved with the project hyped it heavily, creating a huge buzz on the streets. Dre and the Trackmasters split the production duties, and Stoute brought in a number of guests to pad the album, most likely hoping to spin off successful careers for several of the newcomers. It didn't work that way, though. Instead, listeners rejected the overhyped album, unhappy with the excessive guests and skits; they wanted to hear Nas and Foxy Brown, not a bunch of no-names (keep in mind that the outside packaging listed no guests besides the primary participants, though actually there are guests on nearly every song). It, of course, didn't help that none of the singles hit big and that the primary draws—Nas and Foxy Brown—seemed like guests themselves on their own album. The album quickly collected dust on record store shelves, and all involved returned to their solo careers, happy to put the embarrassment behind them. The only person to really mention the fiasco years later was Cormega, who continued to resent being ousted from the group. —*Jason Birchmeier*

● **The Firm: The Album** / Oct. 21, 1997 / Interscope ✦✦✦
With a cast list lengthy enough to compete with that of a small movie, *The Firm: The Album* is an auditory trip into the lives of a handful of nefarious individuals living a gangster lifestyle, however unconvincing. Major players on this project include Nas "Escobar," Foxy Brown, AZ "Sosa,"and Nature, although tracks are peppered with additional and less popular MCs such as Pretty-Boy ("Firm All Stars"), Wizard ("Untouchable"), Canibus ("Desperados"), Noriega ("I'm Leaving"), and Half-A-Mil ("Throw Your Guns"). Dr. Dre

and the Trackmasters share equal billing as supervising producers. Dr. Dre's production is atypically diverse from track to track and lacks any samples or arrangements reminiscent of his work with N.W.A, Snoop Doggy Dogg, or his own solo projects. This diversity may be the result of the collaboration with Chris "Glove" Taylor on the production tasks for five of the six tracks for which Dre is responsible. The teamwork production of the Trackmasters is orchestrated by Poke, Tone, Curt Gowdy, L.E.S., and provides the instrumentation for the remaining seven of 13 songs. Overshadowed by lewd profanity, violence, and limited scope of content, *The Firm: The Album* fails to make a favorable or unique impression amongst contemporary releases. —*Qa'id Jacobs*

Five Deez

f. Cincinnati, OH
Group / Hip-Hop, Underground Rap
Just one of the acts making Cincinnati one of the seminal cities for underground rap, Five Deez formed around area producer/MC extraordinaire Fat Jon the Ample Soul Physician and MC/producer Pase Rock. The pair debuted with EPs in 1999 and 2000, then released their first full-length, *Koolmotor*, in 2001. Both are also heavily involved in the Cincinnati-based Wanna Battle crew, also including DJ Hi-Tek, Talib Kweli, Lone Catalysts, and Rubix. —*John Bush*

Blue Light Special/Wow/The Rock Rule/The Rock Rehab [EP] / 1999 / BUKA ✦✦✦
Despite their name, Five Deez are made up of two men: MC/producer Fat Jon and MC/DJ Pase Rock. "Blue Light Special" has a nice, mellow feel most of the time. Unfortunately, the song is periodically interrupted by a sound that resembles a cross between a drum sample and squealing tires; this disrupts the mellow vibe and hurts the song. Mr. Dibbs of the 1200 Hobos helps out on the beat to "Wow." It's solid, but nothing special lyrically or production-wise. "The Rock Rule" has a basic drum pattern with a few nice guitar sounds, but not much else. "The Rock Rehab" features no real beat, just some nice beatboxing. Five Deez do a good job flowing over the beatbox beat, and have a lot of energy on this track. Too bad they didn't bring that same energy to the rest of this 12". —*Dan Gizzi*

Secret Agent Number EP / Oct. 3, 2000 / Dimensia ✦✦✦
With the '90s rush of high-profile shiny rappers glamorizing ghettos and gangster life, the days of soulful words and funky beats from the likes of De La Soul and A Tribe Called Quest were washed away. Though Five Deez is not quite on the par of either De La or Tribe, with the *Secret Agent Number* EP they combine real instruments, deep beats, and turntablism while demonstrating heavy rhyming skills and techniques. With this release there is also some obvious and welcome growth on the part of the duo's production team. Given the ill state of the rap world in 2000, Five Deez is definitely not rap's savior—but the duo is refreshing nonetheless. —*Diana Potts*

● **Koolmotor** / Nov. 27, 2001 / Counterflow ✦✦✦✦
The highly anticipated full-length debut from Cincinnati-based Five Deez brings an expected display of kingly beats from Fat Jon "the Ample Soul Physician" and fledgling vocal chops from Kyle David, Pase, and Fat Jon himself. With 14 tracks as musically challenging as these, it is no wonder why the vocal/lyrical output comes up short of that level, however still quite outstanding for their first official full-length. Using live bass, guitar, and saxophones to complement turntables and the plethora of rhythmic roles held down by Fat Jon, this Midwestern crew has a tangible energy and enthusiasm that comes off as sincere and well nurtured. With an instrumentals album and various side-project records forthcoming on the young, prolific Counterflow label, this is a crew to watch very closely. —*Nic Kincaid*

Flavor Flav (William Drayton)

b. Mar. 16, 1959, Roosevelt, Long Island, NY
Hip-Hop, East Coast Rap, Hardcore Rap
Chuck D's comic foil in the pioneering rap group Public Enemy, Flavor Flav was born William Drayton on March 16, 1959. A classically trained pianist, he was rapping under the alias MC DJ Flavor when he first met graphic design student Carlton Ridenhour, who under the name Chuck D formed Public Enemy in 1982; following the release of their 1987 debut LP *Yo! Bum Rush the Show*, the group emerged as the most important act in hip-hop if not all of contemporary music, brilliantly fusing socially conscious, politically

charged rhymes with chaotic cut-and-paste productions to forever reshape the direction of not merely rap but rock as well. As the cartoonish counterpoint to Chuck's authoritarian presence, Flavor Flav essentially invented the role of the rap sidekick, innovating the absurdist delivery later borrowed by everyone from Busta Rhymes to Ol' Dirty Bastard; with his gold teeth, clownish sunglasses, and omnipresent clock dangling from his neck, Flavor also became PE's visual focus, taking lead vocal duties on hits including the classic "911 Is a Joke." Even as Public Enemy's influence waned in the mid-'90s, Flavor Flav continued to make headlines for his frequent run-ins with the law; he also worked on his long-awaited solo album, reportedly delivering two completed records to Def Jam which the label rejected on both occasions. A full-length titled *It's About Time* was set to be released on the Lightyear imprint in late 1999, but it never surfaced. —*Jason Ankeny*

It's About Time [Unreleased] / Nov. 23, 1999 / Lightyear

Flesh-N-Bone (Stanly Howse)

Gangsta Rap, Hardcore Rap

Undoubtedly the most troubled member of the volatile Cleveland rap group Bone Thugs-N-Harmony, Flesh-N-Bone struggled to release some spotty solo albums amid a series of legal problems. The brother of Layzie Bone—the group's guiding force—Flesh experienced instant celebrity status alongside his fellow Bone Thugs with the success of 1994's *Creepin on Ah Come Up* and 1995's *E 1999 Eternal*. The multiplatinum success of these albums and the resulting Grammy provided Flesh with the opportunity to record his debut solo album, *T.H.U.G.S.: Trues Humbly United Gatherin' Souls*, on the mammoth rap label Def Jam; unfortunately, the album didn't live up to expectations, selling poorly and receiving less than favorable reviews. Then in July 1997, around the time Bone Thugs-N-Harmony—minus Flesh—released their double album, *Art of War*, he was charged with assault and battery as well as with possession of an explosive after police raided his home, finding a stolen gun and explosives; Flesh also went into drug rehab in Los Angeles. A year later he served some time in jail for the previous year's probation violations. Though there was plenty of talk about Flesh-N-Bone's sophomore album (tentatively titled Book of Thugs) in mid-1998, the album didn't appear on shelves until October 2000 with a new title, *5th Dog Let Loose*, and a new label, Koch. In September, weeks before the release of his album, Flesh was sentenced to ten years in jail for threatening a friend with an AK-47 in December 1999, his latest run-in with authorities. —*Jason Birchmeier*

● **T.H.U.G.S.: Trues Humbly United Gatherin' Souls** / Nov. 19, 1996 / Def Jam ✦✦✦

Flesh-N-Bone's solo release is a continuation of the rapid-fire delivery of lyrics patented by Bone Thugs-N-Harmony. The words come so fast you're forced to listen intently to identify them. Lots of preaching and sermonizing here; the first cut uses lines from the "Lord's Prayer," while "Reverend Run Sermon" features Run (of Run-D.M.C.) preaching a short message. A message ballad, "World So Cruel" samples Kenny Gamble and Bunny Sigler's "Love, Need and Want You," originally done by Patti Labelle. The lazy, floating "NorthCoast" is a charming incorporation of rap and jazz that would be equally at home on a contemporary jazz CD. The chorus is sung sweetly by Tiarra and Damon Elliot, while the lyrics speak of different streets on the Northside of Cleveland; Jimmy Z plays some nice sax and Layzie Bone leads the smoothie. As for hardcore, "Nothin' But Da Bone in Me" represents: the chorus smacks, and the bass line is too cool, while an eerie synthesizer accents the barrage of lyrics—it's the obvious single. There's a message in the plodding "The Silence Isn't Over," but it takes a few repeat plays for it to sink in. Where are the lyrics when you need them? "Coming 2 Serve You" is blatant gangsta rap, as the lyrics tell a chilling story involving murder. To get the best, you've got to hear the redundant too, and there are many among the 17 selections. Even lyrics spewed out like machine-gun rounds get boring after a few spins, regardless of how ingenious and unique the technique. —*Andrew Hamilton*

5th Dog Let Loose / Oct. 10, 2000 / Koch International ✦✦

Rumored for release back in 1999 on Def Jam as Book of Thugs, Flesh-N-Bone's second album, *5th Dog Let Loose*, mysteriously appeared a year later on Koch with a new title and a disjointed feel. If Def Jam had dropped Flesh from its roster after hearing the demos from this record, it wouldn't be surprising. *5th Dog Let Loose* does little to dismiss the critics who labeled Flesh the least talented member of Bone Thugs-N-Harmony after his disappointing

first album. Like on his debut, Flesh can't seem to make up his mind about whether he's a hard-rapping ghetto thug or a melodic gospel rapper. Perhaps if he could find a smooth balance between the two styles as Bone Thugs-N-Harmony did on their breakthrough album, *E 1999 Eternal*, his juxtaposing natures could be forgiven, yet he never really comes close on *5th Dog Let Loose*. Songs such as "Amen" and "Way Back" stand out with their harmonious use of vocals, while other songs such as "Kurupted Flesh" and "Armegeddon" weigh down the album with their hard edge. The fact that Flesh struggled with jail sentences while working on the album probably didn't help. Producer Damon Elliott was left to piece it all together pretty much on his own, perhaps explaining the unpolished feel of the album. If anything, *5th Dog Let Loose* reaffirms the popular theory that Bone Thugs-N-Harmony works well as a group with their collage of harmonious voices but suffers as solo artists without the vocal harmonies and juxtapositions or the charisma offered by a group. —*Jason Birchmeier*

Flipmode Squad

Group / East Coast Rap, Hardcore Rap, Hip-Hop

Baby Sham, Lord Have Mercy, Rampage, Rah Digga, and Spliff Star first appeared alongside Busta Rhymes as Flipmode Squad in 1996 on his album *The Coming*. The Brooklyn crew released their debut, *The Imperial Album*, in 1998 and members kept busy guesting on albums by Busta and others—as well as releasing the occasional solo album. Rampage's *Scouts Honor… by Way of Blood* was released in 1997 and featured the Flipmode loyal cut "Flipmode Iz da Squad." Rah Digga also stepped out of the Squad to release Dirty Harriet in 1999 with her crew appearing on "Just for You." A second Flipmode Squad release, *Rulership Movement*, was set for release in 2003. —*Wade Kergan*

● **The Imperial Album** / Sep. 1, 1998 / Elektra ✦✦✦

Busta Rhymes' rap posse (which includes newcomers Rampage, Lord Have Mercy, Spliff Star, Rah Digga, and Baby Sham, as well as Busta himself) bust out the jams on this audacious debut, which mixes Busta's typically tight beats and surrealistic words with a wise-ass street savvy usually reserved for his best singles. But *The Imperial* drags on a bit too long, filling its 73 minutes with partial track ideas (including the prerequisite, and ineffective, between-song skits) and lyric and melodic fragments that seem to have no beginning or end—unsurprisingly, not unlike Busta's solo work. Still, Busta has always dropped a couple of decent cuts per album, and *The Imperial* is no exception: "Everybody on the Line Outside" (a sort-of sequel to Busta's own "Put Your Hands Where My Eyes Could See"), "Cha Cha Cha" and "Everything" are lightning-quick attacks of hip-hop aptitude. —*Michael Gallucci*

Fog

Group / Lo-Fi, Turntablism, Experimental Rock, Trip-Hop

Multi-instrumentalist Andrew Broder began making eccentric turntablist music as Fog and hooked up with the British label Ninja Tune. Born in Minneapolis, MN, where he continued to reside, Broder turned to music as an escape from the outside world. He confined himself to his basement and learned several instruments while simultaneously taking an interest in the escapist aspects of hip-hop. Eventually, after growing ill and dropping out of school, Broder dedicated himself to music, crafting eccentric tracks that were rooted in hip-hop but integrated numerous other elements and instruments. His recordings attracted the interest of prominent British trip-hop label Ninja Tune, who released a self-titled collection of his work in 2002, followed by the *Check Fraud* 12". At this point, Broder began collaborating with a few fellow Minneapolis musicians—guitarist Jeremy Ylvisaker, bassist Baer Erickson, drummer Martin Dosh—and turned his solo project into a full-fledged group capable of performing live. —*Jason Birchmeier*

● **Fog** / Feb. 19, 2002 / Ninja Tune ✦✦✦

Fog starts out as a spoken word and synthesizer mélange, then segues to "Smell of Failure" ("I get this whiff in my nose sometimes," says Andrew Broder aka Fog, "Like a burning smell/It's the smell of failure"), which is a feedback-ensconced series of vocoder reps. At "Pneumonia" the album slows to a Neil Young-inspired dirge, then switches to scratches and samples. Surprises are around every turn. "Check Fraud" features rudimentary Japanese flute, sound effects, and lilting flamenco guitar. Broder was 23 at the time of this recording, and with it he pulls the listener into his single-minded diversions so that all can witness spurts of revelation within his quest for musical footing. —*Travis Drageset*

Force M.D.'s

f. 1983, Staten Island, NY
Group / Urban, New Jack Swing, Quiet Storm
Although not as well-known as other New York hip-hop acts of the early '80s, Staten Island's Force M.D.'s were a vital crew in the early history of street hip-hop and one of the first vocal groups to fuse doo wop-influenced harmonies with hip-hop beats. Originally a street troupe known as the LD's, the group sang and danced on Greenwich Village street corners and the Staten Island ferry. Its members included brothers Stevie D and Antoine "TCD" Lundy, their uncle Jesse Lee Daniels, and friends Trisco Pearson and Charles "Mercury" Nelson. The group hooked up with DJ Dr. Rock and, billing themselves as Dr. Rock and the MC's, began playing in local hip-hop venues. However, by the time the group signed to Tommy Boy in 1984 as the Force M.D.'s (M.D. standing for "musical diversity"), they had evolved into a more straightforward R&B vocal group, distinguished mostly by their street attitude. The M.D.'s had a string of R&B hits through the '80s, but their only pop hit was the Top Ten Jimmy Jam/Terry Lewis-penned ballad "Tender Love," which was featured in the movie *Krush Groove*. In 1987 the group produced their first R&B number one, "Love Is a House," but their popular appeal began to ebb the following year. Mercury and Trisco left in 1990 and were replaced by Rodney "Khalil" Lundy and Shawn Waters. The group released the album *Get Ready* in 1994 as several members worked with other artists as producers. Though Nelson, Lundy, and DJ Dr. Rock each died an early death (Nelson of a heart attack, Lundy of Lou Gehrig's disease), the group returned in 1998, signed to a contract thanks to fellow Staten Island-natives Wu-Tang Clan. *—Steve Huey*

Love Letters / 1984 / Tommy Boy ✦✦✦
The debut album from this quintet offered a mix of R&B, hip-hop, dance and an excellent vocal presentation. "Let Me Love You" and "Forgive Me Girl" were two of the four singles released from this album. Both singles peaked at number 49 after ten weeks on the *Billboard* R&B charts. The latter is an up-tempo track with a hip-hop backbeat featuring the whistling falsetto of the late Antoine Lundy. But the big hit off this album was "Tears," a doo-wop-flavored ballad also featuring Lundy, but with a more apologetic tone. The single peaked at number nine after a 21-week run. This album set the stage for the success that the group would later enjoy. *—Craig Lytle*

Chillin' / 1986 / Tommy Boy ✦✦✦✦✦
Chillin' is a mid-'80s album featuring the Staten Island hip-hop/doo-wop group Force M.D.'s. They predated the current hot trend featuring singing groups blending classic R&B and soul harmonies with hip-hop productions. While their sound now seems dated, it was quite revolutionary in its time. This album had three chart hits, and the group was then at its peak. *—Ron Wynn*

Touch and Go / 1987 / Tommy Boy ✦✦✦
The title track was a Top 10 R&B hit, and Force M.D.'s were at their best on this album. The leads, harmonies, songs, production, and arrangements never sounded better, and they certainly paved the way for the many new jack vocal groups of the '90s. *—Ron Wynn*

Step to Me / Sep. 4, 1990 / Tommy Boy ✦✦✦
Force M.D.'s were a dominant ensemble in the mid- and late '80s. They struck just the right chord between classicism and modernism with their hip-hop/doo-wop blend, and although this wasn't their biggest album, it still did quite well among both old and young black music fans. *—Ron Wynn*

For Lovers and Others: Force M.D.'s Greatest Hits / Feb. 18, 1992 / Tommy Boy ✦✦✦✦
This is a solid collection of captivating love songs, featuring singles taken from the quartet's previous albums. However, of the 12 selections presented, four never charted, the most notable being "Sweet Dreams." Groomed around the smooth-sailing falsetto of the late Antoine "TCD" Lundy, the single is augmented by the group's faintly audible background vocals. With this album's debut, the label seized the opportunity to release "Your Love Drives Me Crazy"; previously appearing on the quartet's gold-selling album *Touch and Go*, Antoine Lundy humbly steps into the intro with a juvenile vocal expression, which does not discredit his delivery. As the melody develops, Lundy's voice graciously amplifies with maturity and emotion. The featured single on this compilation release, "Your Love Drives Me Crazy" peaked at 78 after only six weeks on the *Billboard* R&B charts. This is a classic R&B cut among many. *—Craig Lytle*

● **Let Me Love You: The Greatest Hits** / Mar. 20, 2001 / Tommy Boy ✦✦✦✦
Force M.D.'s predated the explosion of new-jack swing in the late '80s, but they definitely helped lay the groundwork, fusing R&B vocal harmonies with street-level hip-hop beats. Their most popular material, however, tended to concentrate more on the urban R&B end of that spectrum, as displayed on *Let Me Love You: The Greatest Hits*. The collection gathers a generous 17 cuts, making it the definitive overview of the group's achievements. *—Steve Huey*

Foreign Legion

Group / Alternative Rap, Underground Rap
Foreign Legion began in the late '80s in San Jose, CA, where layabouts Prozack and DJ Design would amuse themselves by stealing bicycles and making rhymes. Years later, after meeting and collaborating with Marc Stretch, the duo became a trio, and Foreign Legion's cynical, lyrical take on underground hip-hop was born. *Full Time B-Boy*, the group's debut 12" single, was issued by ABB Records in 1999; the *Nowhere to Hide* 12" followed a year later on Insidious Urban. With Marc Stretch's and Prozack's call-and-response choruses and the quirky beats of DJ Design, the songs were an instant success. By now, Foreign Legion had established its headquarters in San Francisco, the home of likeminded artists such as Del tha Funkee Homosapien and DJ Shadow. In September of 2000, the group's full-length debut, *Kidnapper Van: Beats to Rock While Bike-Stealin'*, was released on Insidious Urban. The album presented Foreign Legion as a rap crew that wasn't afraid to poke fun over dope beats; favorite targets included themselves and the state of hip-hop music in general. After a brief hiatus, the trio returned in late 2002 with the *Happy Drunk* and *Voodoo Star* 12"s, which led up to *Playtight*, Foreign Legion's second sophomore full-length effort for Insidious Urban. The group embarked on a European tour in March of 2003. *—Johnny Loftus*

● **Kidnapper Van: Beats to Rock While Bike-Stealin'** / Sep. 19, 2000 / Insiduous Urban ✦✦✦
On their website, Foreign Legion seems like a group with a great sense of humor often not found in hip-hop, and Prozack (aptly named as his real name is Zach) is even a standup comedian. What's found on the album is a collection of great beats, good content, and excellent scratching. Unfortunately, the three MCs do little to impress with their lyrical abilities and word delivery. Undoubtedly there are some good moments in songs like "Overnight Success," where the group talks about the hard work they've put in to get where they are now, and "Full Time B-Boy," which speaks of the differences between "real" rap artists and others who are only in it for the fortune and fame. One thing that's rather disappointing is that the two songs that stand out the most are from an EP the group released in 1999. If you're a fan of underground hip-hop, this is more polished than most records floating around in that area and is worth some attention, but the album just doesn't have the repeated listening lasting appeal that can be found elsewhere in this genre. *—Brad Mills*

John Forté

Producer, Vocals / Hip-Hop, Urban, Alternative Rap
The first non-Fugee signed to the trio's Refugee Camp label, John Forté met the group through vocalist Lauryn Hill early in the '90s, before the Fugees had even signed a recording contract. Also of Haitian descent, Forté worked on production for their breakout album, 1996's *The Score*, and also toured as part of Wyclef Jean's solo project, the Refugee Camp Allstars.
Forté debuted with the 1998 album *Poly Sci* and the single "Ninety Nine," before disappearing from the music scene for approximately four years. He returned with an introspective album titled *I, John* on a new record label. Unlike his debut album, which had featured assistance from the Fugees, this follow-up featured not a single Fugee. Instead, Forté worked with cowriter Joel Kipnis and such accomplished artists as Tricky, Esthero, and Herbie Hancock. *—John Bush*

● **Poly Sci** / Jun. 23, 1998 / RuffHouse ✦✦✦
As a protégé of hip-hop supergroup the Fugees, and a member of adjunct group the Refugee All Stars, John Forté exhibits the same intriguing mix of street and mainstream culture that helped the band rise above all prescribed boundaries. *Poly Sci* displays the same pumpin' beats blended with pop elements and articulate lyrics, that made groundbreaking hits out of *The Score* and *Wyclef Jean Presents the Carnival*, both of which Forté wrote, produced

and performed on. Filled with all the swagger and attitude essential to hip-hop, yet tempered with softer pop sensibilities, as on the quirky "Ninety Nine (Flash the Message)," and the slightly psychedelic "Madina Passage," and the easygoing title tune, this debut promises a flourishing solo career for Forté. —*Rosalind Cummings-Yeates*

I, John / Apr. 23, 2002 / Transparent ✦✦✦
Four years after his debut release, *Poly Sci*, John Forté returned with a substantially different album titled *I, John*. Unlike his fun debut, this album takes a more serious approach to music making. Anyone who heard *Poly Sci* will find the high level of introspection quite surprising. No longer is Forté partying with the Fugees and rap superstars such as DMX and Fat Joe. Rather, Forté works with cowriter Joel Kipnis and accomplished low-profile artists such as Tricky, Esthero, and Herbie Hancock on *I, John*. Furthermore, he throws the rules out the window, making his own style of music rather than the hot sound of the moment. —*Jason Birchmeier*

Devino Fortunato

West Coast Rap, G-Funk, Hardcore Rap
Devino Fortunato was an Oakland-area rapper who burst onto the scene with 2002's *Cognac Loungin'* for the upstart Bay Area label Real Smooth. While his work as an EMT kept him busy by day, by night it was the G-funk world of liquor, cars, women, and hustling. It was the latter that informed the content of his debut, an independent album that nevertheless boasted high-quality West Coast-style production and Fortunato's own boast-filled flow, which at times suggested the unadorned honesty of 2Pac. After his spectacular debut, Fortunato appeared at numerous Real Smooth events with labelmates Xeno and Tazz. —*Johnny Loftus*

● **Cognac Loungin'** / May 28, 2002 / Real Smooth ✦✦✦✦
Though it's just his first album, Devino Fortunato is already celebrating the high life with a set of player tracks and unapologetic hip-hop, from the alcohol serenade "Licqa Sto" to the booty anthem "Dance for Me" to the no-explanation-necessary "Ghetto Soliloquoy." No matter that it's not the freshest style, *Cognac Loungin* is full of great productions, with the West Coast blueprint of syrupy G-funk given a good airbrushing of synths and samples. The rapping is just as solid, especially from Fortunato, but his guests too: Xeno, Ebony Black, Tazz. A great independent production that puts to shame most major-label rap product. —*John Bush*

The 45 King (Mark James)

b. Oct. 16, 1961
Producer, Mixer / Hip-Hop, Party Rap, East Coast Rap
Producer DJ Mark "the 45 King" burst onto the rap scene during the late '80s with his bona fide breakbeat classic "The 900 Number." However, following successful productions for Queen Latifah and his own crew, the Flavor Unit, the 45 King's resistance to changing trends and hip-hop's own fleeting loyalty combined to ensure his eventual obscurity. Continually respected by the hip-hop underground, he remained a prolific producer throughout his career, lending his remixing and engineering skills to nearly 40 releases from 1987 to 2000.

Born Mark James, the 45 King (as he prefers, simply, to be known) got his first taste of rap music in the late '70s as the "record boy" for Bronx-based rap pioneers the Funky Four (pre-Plus One). Learning the ropes of the hip-hop trade, James received an invaluable insider's look at the coveted breakbeat records that were the very battle tools of DJ competitions. Departing from the Funky Four circle, the 45 King spent the mid-'80s as a DJ on the New Jersey scene. In 1983, at the age of 22, his first production for MC Marky Fresh caught the attention of KISS-FM's Kool DJ Red Alert. It wasn't until 1987 that James' career really got underway however, with his work for Wild Pitch artist Latee on "This Cut's Got Flavor." That same year, the 45 King slowed down the sax solo from a record he'd received from Tuff City's Aaron Fuchs, and dropped the results over an irresistibly funky break. The resulting track, "The 900 Number," exploded, its horn line (sampled from Marva Whitney's James Brown-produced "Unwind Yourself") forever ingrained in the collective hip-hop psyche. The 45 King was awarded a production deal and a long-term contract. He proceeded to showcase the members the Flavor Unit on a series of Tuff City releases. Debuts from Lakim Shabazz (*Pure Righteousness*) and Chill Rob G ("Court Is in Session") were released in 1988. The following year, new Tommy Boy recording artist Queen Latifah selected the 45 King to contribute tracks to her debut *All Hail the Queen*. The collaboration produced Latifah hits "Wrath of My Madness" and "Ladies First."

However, Tuff City failed to get behind Shabazz's sophomore, 45 King-produced *Lost Tribe of Shabazz* (1989), and the album drifted into obscurity. Eventually dropped from Tommy Boy, Latifah relocated to Motown, and the new label's efforts to polish the rapper's sound meant the 45 King's services were not requested. Suddenly, the confines of a long-term contract failed to appeal. James spent the early '90s remixing, producing, and constructing his own phenomenal solo recordings under titles like Lost Breakbeats, Breaka-palooza, and The 45 Kingdom. In 1996, DJ Kool's recycling of the 45 King's classic "900 Number" took off, climbing to number five on the rap charts. Acknowledging the song's source, the MC released a new 45 King remix of the track. James' resurgence coincided with the growing interest in hip-hop's old school stylings. In 1997 England's Ultimate Dilemma paid tribute, reissuing the producer's Lost Break Beat series as *Universal Beat Generation*. One year later, the 45 King's production of Jay-Z's "Hard Knock Life (Ghetto Anthem)" (complete with *Annie* sample) scaled the charts, proving the producers lasting viability. —*Nathan Bush*

The 900 Number EP / 1987 / Tuff City ✦✦✦
Master of the Game / 1989 / Tuff City ✦✦
Like, say, Grandmaster Flash before him, DJ Mark the 45 King is a turntable wizard whose gift for manipulating the wheels of steel have made him a bigger name than many of the rappers who work with him. On the first half of *Master of the Game*, he is joined by Markey Fresh and Lakim Shabazz, both of whom spend most of their energy rapping about the greatness of DJ Mark, who samples from obscure soul, disco and funk records. On the second half, the 45 King goes solo, allowing his slicing and dicing of swing, house and disco records to exist without verbal accompaniment. —*Jason Ankeny*

Breakmania, Vol. 1 / Aug. 22, 1995 / Real Tuff Breaks ✦✦
Breakmania, Vol. 2 / Aug. 22, 1995 / Real Tuff Breaks ✦✦
The second volume in Mark the 45 King's series of killer breaks offers just that: a baker's dozen set of beats-minus-rhymes for aspiring producers—or those who like to keep their hip-hop *real* simple. Produced in conjunction with the Tuff City Squad, *Breakmania, Vol. 2* keeps it heavily East Coast and jazzy on occasion but does offer a few tracks of Zapp-inspired G-funk. —*John Bush*

Freddie Foxxx (James Campbell)

b. Westbury, NY
Producer, Vocals / Hardcore Rap, East Coast Rap
Born James Campbell in Westbury, NY, in 1969, veteran rapper Freddie Foxxx was in a group by the age of ten and made his recorded debut as Freddie C. in 1986 on a 12" by Supreme Force. He landed a deal with MCA and released *Freddie Foxxx Is Here* in 1989. After making noted appearances on records by Kool G Rap & DJ Polo, Boogie Down Productions, and Naughty By Nature, he recorded *Crazy Like a Foxxx* for Epic, which never saw the light of day—only a few promotional copies were leaked prior to the label's decision to keep it on the shelf.

Foxxx spent a couple years underground and reappeared with contributions to records by Gang Starr and M.O.P. Frustrated by the "sink or swim" practices of the common major label, he also started his own label, Kjac, and received distribution from Landspeed for his second official solo record, 2000's *Industry Shakedown*. Billed as Bumpy Knuckles, he developed the alterego after hearing a comment from someone who witnessed a display of his pugilist skills. With production work from DJ Premier, Diamond D, and Pete Rock, the record took aim at the evils of the record industry—evils that Foxxx/Knuckles knows plenty about. —*Andy Kellman*

Freddie Foxxx Is Here / 1989 / MCA ✦✦
● **Industry Shakedown** / Jun. 20, 2000 / Landspeed ✦✦✦✦
Bumpy Knuckles has been doing cameos in the hip-hop game for years; finally, with his debut album, *Industry Shakedown*, he truly gets to shine. The title of the album conjures up the notion of music business deconstruction and many of the songs are dedicated to or touch upon this very subject. Bumpy Knuckles (aka Freddie Foxxx) has a blunt delivery, to say the least, and this album is replete with vulgarities and slurs, but don't let that turn you away, roughness is inherent of a "Bumpy" style. That's how the self-proclaimed "thug" gets his point across. In fact, if there were a "clean" version

of the album, more than half the lyrics would be edited out. *Industry Shakedown* stands above many contemporary hip-hop albums in the production arena. The album features the production of the one and only DJ Premier, the ever-consistent Pete Rock, the slept-on Diamond D, and the up-and-coming beatsmith, the Alchemist. Check the sure-shot tracks, "Bumpy Knuckles Baby," "Stock in the Game," and "Part of My Life." Bumpy himself even tries his hand at production, but his exploits tend to be the weakest tracks on the album; they are avoidable. All in all, the beats elevate *Industry Shakedown* to the upper echelons of turn-of-the-century hip-hop. —*Nick Pfeiffer*

Michael Franti

Vocals, Producer / Political Rap, Alternative Rap

Since his days as a member of the Beatnigs while in his early twenties, Franti has grown from angry young hip-hopper with a political, socially conscious bent (the Disposable Heroes of Hiphoprisy, Spearhead), to a man who has channeled his seriousness, his social unease, and his desire for change and merged them with his love for music, particularly old school R&B, soul, and hip-hop. What he has left behind in brash, make-some-noise aesthetic he has gained in compassion. And through his use of his own raw power—charisma, sex appeal, sense of social injustice—he has carried out in his music a community-generated passion in much the same way as Gil Scott-Heron or Marvin Gaye. Franti was adopted at birth by white parents in the predominantly black community of Oakland, CA. That set of contradictory circumstances instilled in him a hyperawareness of his own cultural identity, as did the sobering fact that his more thoughtful, less provocative style of expression was not accepted by the African-American audience that had embraced a harsher, more combative faction of the hip-hop movement.

In 1986 Franti formed the drum'n'bass/industrial duo the Beatnigs with turntablist Rono Tse which disbanded after releasing one album. He then formed the Disposable Heroes of Hiphoprisy, whose combination of jazz-influenced heavy rap set out to challenge the materialism and misogyny of what had become mainstream rap. His next project, Spearhead produced the critically acclaimed *Home* in 1990, which contained his biggest single "Hole in the Bucket," a thoughtful lament on the plight of the homeless, and "Positive" which addressed the growing AIDS epidemic. The album boasted adept funk samplings, sinuous guitar vamps, and soulful, melodic tracks about family and social injustice. 1997's *Chocolate Supa Highway* was not as pop-friendly as *Home* but neither did its themes of kidnappings and police brutality lend themselves to such overt accessability. Its mixture of harsher musical styles—techno, rock, and funk—was a step forward for Franti as his worldview broadened and deepened. In 2001 Franti released *Stay Human*. In it he expresses his anger at the system, his advocacy of love, and his belief in freedom through individuality and self-expression through a set of songs that revolve around a fictitious death penalty case. In it his embrace of the genres that inspired him is achieved with a musical eloquence. —*Travis Drageset*

The Dawning: Rock the Nation / Nov. 21, 2000 / Boo Boo Wax ◆◆◆

● **Stay Human** / May 15, 2001 / Six Degrees ◆◆◆◆
This is an album of two levels: the level that makes the first impression is the radio phone-in show that Michael Franti chose to use as a conceptual framework in which these 13 new songs are embedded. The drama that unfolds during that radio show (supported by liner notes at the front of the CD booklet) centers on a death penalty case. The events documented in those segments sound all too familiar in their gruesomeness, so it becomes compelling to check the booklet to see if these are indeed authentic recordings of a broadcast or staged ones as part of the album's two-level concept (and only a short remark near the end of the booklet gives the answer to that). The impressive impact of that scenario is rounded off by quotes in the booklet from various activists and musicians who oppose the death penalty (with names ranging from Bono to Jello Biafra). The second level of the album provides a contrast to all that on a musical level—the actual songs being predominantly based in the elegance of early-'70s soul music—although Franti makes sure to get a resolute message across in the lyrics, and there are plenty of contemporary sound elements in the arrangements to keep this from becoming a purely "retro" album. However, both the styles and the lyrics do hark back to 30 years ago, when black music regularly sounded this elegant and lyrically aware. As it often was then, this album's message is essentially one of tolerance as the key to all kinds of solutions (as the title track, "Stay Human," puts it: "All the freaky people make the beauty of the world"), paired

with militant resolve to spread that message, especially on songs like "Rock the Nation" and "Listener Supported." Most of the songs are actually pretty laid-back (underlining the anti-violence stance of the lyrics). That in itself would be nothing new for a Spearhead album, but the crisp production this time around (the best yet on a Spearhead album) steers clear of a certain dull monotony that weighed down the previous albums. The elegance and lightness of touch results in highlights such as "We Don't Mind" and "Do Ya Love." As usual with Spearhead, rapping remains just one of the parts of the musical picture, and indeed, after all the heavy-duty militancy that hip-hop brought to bear on black music in the past 20 years, hearing this album raises the question of how much has actually been achieved, when in 2001 a new album can feel contemporary although the sound and feelings expressed are very close to what they were like 30 years back. That possibly gives Franti a kind of outsider position, and some people might well deride this album's "hippy ideals," but it is a valid and entertaining attempt at furthering social awareness on the strength of the most satisfying Spearhead songs yet. —*Alan Severa*

Freak Nasty

Hip-Hop, Southern Rap, Party Rap

Freak Nasty was hardly a talented rapper—he was clumsy and often tripped over his rhymes—but he did manage to write an incessantly catchy song with "Da Dip." After his first album, *Freak Nasty*, failed to make an impact in 1994, the Southern-based rapper seemed destined to fade away. Instead, he and his production team concocted the ridiculously simple and naggingly catchy "Da Dip," driven mostly by a bass-driven groove and lyrical hook. The single was featured on Freak Nasty's second album, *Controversee...That's Life...And That's the Way It Is*, which was released in the fall of 1996. Over the winter and spring of 1997, "Da Dip" became an underground hit, eventually crossing over into the mainstream in the summer of 1997. It stayed on the charts for weeks, but the album itself never took off. *Dowhatchafeel* appeared the following year, and in the spring of 2000 Freak Nasty resurfaced with *Which Way Is Up*. —*Stephen Thomas Erlewine*

● **Controversee...That's Life...And That's the Way It Is** / Oct. 29, 1996 / Triad ◆◆◆
Freak Nasty's name might lead you to believe that he's far "nastier" than he actually is. He is neither gangsta nor prankster—he's just a party rapper, ready to do da dip at a moment's notice. Which is to say that *Controversee... That's Life...And That's the Way It Is* isn't that deep—unless you're talking about the grooves, that is. *Controversee* is a phat, phunky party record, with enough strong songs to keep it rolling along. And it does have one unforgettably infectious song with "Da Dip," a relentlessly stupid singalong destined to be a party classic. Nothing is as naggingly catchy as that, and his attempts to rewrite "Da Dip" (not to mention the song's remixes) can be a little grating, but *Controversee* remains a good party album. —*Leo Stanley*

Freestyle (Tony Butler)

Producer / Techno, Electro, Electro-Techno, Hip-Hop

One of the most prolific and influential of the '80s electro artists, Miami-based producer Tony Butler recorded a string of popular club tracks on Power/Jam Packed and his own Music Specialist label in the mid-'80s, helping to build the electro legacy that would give birth to Miami-style bass music and freestyle (named after Butler's primary pseudonym), as well as influence '90s post-techno artists such as Autechre and Biochip C. Butler's earlier tracks under his own name are all electro classics, with singles such as "Fix It in the Mix," "Jam the Box," and "Get Some" exploring a thinner, more stripped-down sound similar to Man Parrish and Cybotron. Butler's tracks with Freestyle are perhaps the more well known, and include such club staples as "It's Automatic," "Don't Stop the Rock," and "The Party Has Begun." His more commercial, pop-oriented writing and production work with Trinere, Debbie Deb, and Shannon, however, remain his claim to fame. Butler continued to live and record in Miami thereafter. —*Sean Cooper*

● **Freestyle** / Aug. 1, 1990 / Pandisc ◆◆◆◆◆
One of the few (occasionally) available Freestyle collections from Pandisc, this self-titled disc includes just eight tracks, though it has most of the best: "Don't Stop the Rock," "It's Automatic," "The Party's Just Begun," and "Come to My House," plus a wild "Freestyle Mega Mix." —*John Bush*

Freestyle Fellowship

f. 1991, Los Angeles, CA

Group / Political Rap, Hip-Hop, West Coast Rap, Alternative Rap

Los Angeles-based alternative rappers Freestyle Fellowship (Aceyalone, Mikah 9, P.E.A.C.E., and Self Jupiter) first began slapping together their crazy word salads in the early '90s, resulting in their first record, *To Whom It May Concern*, which was issued in a limited run (only 300 vinyl copies and 500 tapes) yet managed to produce the seeds of their loyal following. Rising out of the jazz and granola environment of Leimert Park, they remained on the edge of the rap scene that paid more attention to West Coast-style gangsta rap—a style that was almost the direct opposite of the sound collages and free, creative lyrics Fellowship was putting together. The group released only one more album, 1993's *Inner City Griots*, before breaking up due to Self-Jupiter's incarceration. The band reunited briefly for one show in 1998 and then sporadically in 1999 to produce a few benefit concerts and participate in a "We Are the World"-style single called "Mumia 911," designed to raise awareness and funds for deathrow inmate Mumia Abu-Jamal. Their first album was also re-released on CD in 1999, as well as a new 12" with rap producer O.D. ("Can You Find the Level of Difficulty in This?"), put out by Celestial Records. —*Stacia Proefrock*

To Whom It May Concern . . . / 1991 / Beats & Rhymes ◆◆◆◆◆

Freestyle Fellowship's first album is a potent glimpse into the subcultural, conscientious side of Los Angeles hip-hop, one that would later be eclipsed by gangsta boogie from the likes of Dr. Dre, Snoop Dogg, and all the pretenders who followed in their wake. As such, the joint—like much of the work from De La Soul, Pharcyde, A Tribe Called Quest, and other equally diverse artists of the period—is a snapshot of a burgeoning art form's purity before it capitulated to the market and rolled out its gripload of Kristal and Bentley worshipers. Not that Freestyle Fellowship ever wandered down that path: They were too busy twisting tongues with blissed-out, stream-of-consciousness rhymes—which is more or less what you'll find, without the hard-hitting beats, on *To Whom It May Concern*. For example, songs like "Jupiter's Journey" and "Sunshine Men" showcase Self-Jupiter and J. Sumbi's respective rhyme flows, but ignore song structure altogether; basically, you're getting the MC without the DJ, which can get boring after a while. But when they pull it all together and work as a collective (as their name implies), things heat up quickly, like on "Convolutions," a breakneck bebop session that is over all too quickly, or "We Will Not Tolerate" and "Dedications," shout sessions that are truncated versions of songs found on their later (and better) album, *Inner City Griots*. Which is not to say that *To Whom It May Concern* is a snoozer when each rapper works alone. Most of the woefully underrated Aceyalone's tunes are bracing exercises in skill and speed, and Mikah 9 and Self-Jupiter are stellar wordsmiths. But a fellowship functions best when everyone is working together, and there's more evidence of this particular group's promise in its ensuing work. —*Scott Thill*

★ **Inner City Griots** / 1993 / 4th & Broadway ◆◆◆◆◆

Freestyle Fellowship emerged on the L.A. rap scene during the early '90s. Given the chance to hone its skills at a health food store's open-mike nights, the group quickly earned the attention and respect of the city's hip-hop underground. Their second album, 1993's *Inner City Griots*, is the only completely collaborative album released during the group's career. Surprisingly, each MC (Mikah Nine, Jupiter, Peace, and Aceyalone) seems fully matured at this early stage. On *Inner City Griots*, the production is improved to match the group's vibrant, dexterous wordplay. Swapping rhymes with agility and grace, the Fellowship is a rap tag team par excellence. At times, the lyrics are so dense and the delivery so quick that the words are practically indecipherable. Yet the rappers are just as adept at slowing down the pace without losing a bit of their lyrical energy or creativity. Unrestricted by tired rap themes, the Fellowship strikes at a range of subjects. The abrasive opening one-two of "Blood" and "Bullies of the Block" might throw listeners off guard but as "Everything's Everything" opens, they provide assurances that "It's all right y'all." The guns are dropped and microphones prevail. *Inner City Griots* (a griot is an African storyteller) takes on Aceyalone's twisted nursery rhyme "Cornbread," the positive vibes of "Inner City Boundaries," the locker-room machismo of "Shammy's" (an inevitable ode to the ladies), and "Way Cool," a tale of serial killing horror. On "Park Bench People," Freestyle Fellowship even asks whether rap music is big enough to take in a sung rumination on homelessness. With live instrumentation provided by the Underground

Railroad (whose members appear throughout the album), the song stretches into a section reminiscent of '70s Stevie Wonder. Like all great groups that preceded it, the Fellowship was simply testing the limits of hip-hop and its own capabilities on this multifaceted collection. —*Nathan Bush*

Temptations / Oct. 16, 2001 / Ground Control ◆◆

Though they've become legendary figures in the West Coast hip-hop underground through their appearances at clubs like L.A.'s renowned Good Life, *Temptations* is only the third album that MCs Aceyalone, Mikah Nine, Self-Jupiter, and P.E.A.C.E. (who actually sits most of this one out) have released as Freestyle Fellowship. It certainly qualifies as long awaited—it's Fellowship's first outing together since 1993's *Inner City Griots*—and it finds the group's mike skills as hot as ever. But the uncompromising attitude spelled out in the song "No Hooks No Chorus" ends up hurting the album, as too many tracks focus almost exclusively on the lyrical end of the hip-hop equation, backing the group's rhymes with raw, repetitive grooves. It's an approach that probably works well live, but it makes seemingly endless songs like the title cut tough to fight through at home. And while it's difficult to argue with any of the group's MCs—particularly the dexterous, fleet-tongued Aceyalone—when they make their case on "Best Rapper in the World," it's also hard to avoid imagining how many more converts Fellowship might have attracted with just a little more imagination musically. —*Dan LeRoy*

Fresh Kid Ice (Chris Wong Won)

Bass Music, Dirty Rap, Party Rap, Hip-Hop

Fresh Kid Ice (aka Chris Wong Won) was a founding member of 2 Live Crew. While the famously explicit Crew would go on to make history in Florida, it actually began in California, when Ice, DJ Mr. Mixx, and Amazing V released the "Revelation" single in 1985. The single became quite popular in Miami, so Ice and Mixx moved across the country to capitalize on it (leaving Amazing V behind in the process). The duo quickly issued the "What I Like" single, on which Ice took Amazing V's place as lead rapper. They also secured a record deal with Miami kingpin Luke Skyywalker (later known simply as Luke, or Luther Campbell), who would eventually join 2 Live Crew as its infamous mouthpiece. Brother Marquis, a pal from California, also joined the 2 Live fold. As a fellow MC in the group, Ice was an integral part of the absurd series of events in Florida after 1989's *As Nasty as They Wanna Be* was released to the horror of the American Family Association. The notoriety gained from the controversy garnered Ice and 2 Live Crew a distribution deal with Atlantic, which released the hit single and album *Banned in the USA* in 1990. But despite the group's popularity, a 1991 live album and the tepid *Nasty* follow-up, *Sports Weekend*, failed to sell. Ice, Luke, and the rest of 2 Live Crew parted ways.

In 1992, Ice released a solo album, *The Chinaman*, a name the Trinidad-born rapper sometimes went by. He also reteamed with the Crew's Mr. Mixx as the Rock on Crew to record *Deal With This*. The year 1994 found Ice regrouping with Luke for the set *Back at Your Ass for the Nin-4*, recorded as the New 2 Live Crew with Miami rapper Verb. The new album was made up in part with songs that had originally appeared on *Deal With This*. The New 2 Live Crew didn't last long; it broke down when Campbell left again for a solo career. In 1996, Ice and Mr. Mixx reformed 2 Live Crew without Campbell and released the album *Shake a Lil' Somethin'*. It was followed in 1998 by *The Real One*, again without Campbell. In 2001, Ice issued *Some Nasty Shit* on his own CMR (China Man Records) imprint. —*Johnny Loftus*

The Chinaman / 1992 / Eff ◆◆

Doug E. Fresh (Doug E. Davis)

b. Sep. 17, 1966, Barbados

Vocals, Beat Box / Old School Rap, Hip-Hop, Golden Age

The first human beatbox in the rap world, and still the best of all time, Doug E. Fresh amazed audiences with his note-perfect imitations of drum machines, effects, and often large samples of hip-hop classics. Fresh was born Doug E. Davis in Barbados, and his first appearance came in 1983 on a single for Spotlight called "Pass the Budda," with Spoonie Gee and DJ Spivey. His introduction to most hip-hop fans, though, came one year later with his astonishing performance in *Beat Street* behind the Treacherous Three. His first solo features also came in 1984, with "Just Having Fun," waxed for Enjoy, and "Original Human Beatbox" for Vinententertainment.

By 1985, Fresh was one of the biggest names in rap music, and his first single for Reality, "The Show/La Di Da Di," became a hip-hop classic. It was recorded with his Get Fresh Crew, including MC Ricky D (only later to gain fame as Slick Rick), along with Barry Bee and Chill Will. His first LP, 1987's *Oh, My God!*, featured most of his showpieces, like "Play This Only at Night" and "All the Way to Heaven," along with nods to reggae and even gospel. His second album, 1988's *The World's Greatest Entertainer*, broke into the *Billboard* charts thanks to another hot single, "Keep Risin' to the Top," but Slick Rick had already broken from the pack and his LP of the same year, *The Great Adventures of Slick Rick*, did much better than Doug E. Fresh. Fresh took a break and wasn't able to regain momentum with 1992's *Doin' What I Gotta Do*, released through MC Hammer's Bust It label. He did reunite on a Slick Rick LP, and recorded again in 1995 for Gee Street. —*John Bush*

Oh, My God! / 1987 / Reality ✦✦✦
This CD features zany rhymes, slashing beats, with bits and pieces of everything from reggae to gospel to funk. —*Ron Wynn*

The World's Greatest Entertainer / 1988 / Reality ✦✦✦
With the exception of the monster hit "Keep Rising to the Top," Fresh trimmed the religious zealotry and increased the lyrical and rhythmic potency. —*Ron Wynn*

Doin' What I Gotta Do / Apr. 27, 1992 / Bust It ✦✦✦

Play / Nov. 1995 / Gee Street ✦✦✦
In an effort to bring the old school sound back in full effect, MC/human beatbox king Doug E. Fresh returned in the mid-'90s with a comeback album that called for a return to the traditions that originally made hip-hop great. Classic funk breakbeats, party-over-here vocals, catchy call-and-response choruses that get the crowd involved, and that inimitable Doug E. Fresh beatbox: it's all there on *Play*, one of the best party-friendly rap records since Run found religion. With the exception of a brief but glaring misstep on "Freak It Out!," a misogynistic rap featuring Luke, *Play* is a welcome flashback to the days when guns, drugs, sex, and violence were not the genre's primary lyrical focus. For the most part, Doug E. and his new crew prove you can be positive and original, yet still have slammin' beats that will appeal to the modern hip-hop crowd. —*Bret Love*

● **Greatest Hits, Vol. 1** / Aug. 1996 / Bust It ✦✦✦✦✦
Greatest Hits, Vol. 1 collects all of Doug E. Fresh's biggest hit singles—including "La Di Da Di," "Keep Risin' to the Top," and "The Show," adding a couple of new tracks produced by Sean "Puffy" Combs for good measure. It's a concise and entertaining retrospective that sums up his career very well. —*Stephen Thomas Erlewine*

Frontline

Group / Underground Rap, Alternative Rap
A Windy City consortium with a backpacker sensibility, this umbrella crew is actually a record label disguised as a group. Consisting centrally of four MCs/producers—jDoubleu, Atlas, Banner, and Chauncie Gardner (whose moniker is taken from the Adamic Peter Sellers character in the movie *Being There*)—Frontline's goal was to challenge the status quo of the rap game. Their music sounds like the end result of living, breathing, and sleeping hip-hop for weeks on end in a basement studio. Psychological catharsis bleeds from their edgy tracks, concepts, and lyrics; their music is experimental with an emphasis on the mental. While the Detroit sound of Eminem/D-12 is darkly humorous, clever, and over the top, Frontline's sound is emblematic of Chicago's deep underground: starkly serious (with some hints at humor) and primal without sacrificing complexity. Frontline seems to be more concerned with moving hip-hop back toward its essence than going platinum. The debut project from the Frontline camp, *Overlooked*, found an audience mostly in the Midwest in early 2001 and served as a precursor for solo albums from each of its members à la the Wu-Tang Clan. —*M.F. Di Bella*

● **Overlooked** / 2001 / Frontline Entertainment ✦✦✦
A classic example of nouveau basement hip-hop, Chicago-based quartet Frontline's full-length debut is a nocturnal foray into the dark side of creativity coupled with a scathing indictment of the current state of hip-hop. In the tradition of Chicago underground artists such as Rubberoom and B Movie Fiends, Frontline offers electro-shock rap therapy in the form of cloistered, basement-studio tracks combined with mind-twisting rhymes with touches of dark humor. The ambidextrous foursome consisting of jDoubleu, Atlas, Banner, and Chauncie Gardener (yes the intellectually

challenged Peter Sellers character in the film *Being There*) scan heavy lyrical topics mixed with standard hip-hop posturing. The spiny production is mostly handled by Gardner and jDoubleu. This album is less abstract than the twisted psychologics of, say, Kool Keith, but are no less visceral or disturbing. While not always the most listenable brand of hip-hop, this deep underground effort creates a contemplatively chaotic mood. A good demonstration of the ever-thriving Midwest underground scene. —*M.F. Di Bella*

Frost (Arturo Molina Jr.)

b. May 31, 1964, East Los Angeles, CA
Old School Rap, Latin Rap, West Coast Rap, Gangsta Rap
Frost—originally known as Kid Frost—was a pioneer in the field of Latin hip-hop, cutting some of its very first records and helping to bring exposure to other bilingual MCs. Frost was born Arturo Molina Jr. on May 31, 1964; while he spent some time with his family on military bases in Guam and Germany, he was raised primarily in East L.A. He started rapping in 1982, and became an accomplished breakdancer as well, joining the top-notch Uncle Jamm's Army crew. He adopted the name Kid Frost in tribute to Ice-T, whom he often battled at parties and clubs as the West Coast hip-hop scene was first taking shape. During this era, he released several 12" singles, including "Rough Cut" (with N.W.A's DJ Yella) and "Terminator." He subsequently left rap for a time, but returned in the late '80s, when he hooked up with producer/DJ Tony G (born Gonzales). Their collaboration on the 1990 single "La Raza" broke Kid Frost to a wide audience, and became a much-loved anthem for Chicano hip-hop fans. Paced by his smooth, laid-back flow, his good-time debut album *Hispanic Causing Panic* was released on Virgin that year, and was one of the first full-lengths in Latin hip-hop history, along with Mellow Man Ace's *Escape From Havana* the preceding year.

In the wake of "La Raza," Kid Frost assembled a collective of bilingual rappers dubbed Latin Alliance, which also featured A.L.T., Lyrical Engineer, and Markski; the group released its lone album in 1991. The following year, Kid Frost issued his second album, *East Side Story*, a loose concept record that spun off the singles "No Sunshine" and "Thin Line." Virgin subsequently dropped him, however, and after shortening his name to the more mature Frost, he signed with Eazy-E's Ruthless label shortly before the rapper's untimely death from AIDS. *Smile Now, Die Later* (1995) reinvented Frost as a hardcore urban rapper rhyming over Latin-inflected G-funk beats. It became his first album to reach the Top 40 of the R&B charts, and the single "East Side Rendezvous" was a minor success. Frost followed it up in 1997 with *When HELL.A. Freezes Over*, but subsequently parted ways with Ruthless. He resurfaced on the smaller independent label Celeb, where he released two albums, *That Was Then, This Is Now, Vols. 1-2*, over 1999-2000. Still active over a decade after his debut album, Frost released the aptly titled *Still Up in This $#*+!* on the indie label Hit-A-Lick in 2002; it was later picked up by Koch for distribution. The same year, he masterminded a compilation of Latino rappers for 40 Ounce Records titled *Raza Radio*. —*Steve Huey*

Hispanic Causing Panic / 1990 / Virgin ✦✦✦✦
Hispanic Causing Panic was an early landmark of Latin hip-hop, simply by virtue of the fact that Kid Frost was one of the first Latino MCs to release an album. Of course, it also doesn't hurt to have a groundbreaking lead single on the order of "La Raza," a smoky, laid-back Latin funk groove with anthemic Spanglish lyrics about being brown and proud. It's an utterly distinctive, original sound (and miles better than anything Gerardo ever tried). Unfortunately, it isn't explored very much over the rest of *Hispanic Causing Panic*. Kid Frost spends most of his time rhyming in English, which isn't necessarily a bad thing, but he doesn't make as strong a musical statement as he might have if he'd played with the Latin foundations of "La Raza" on more of his additional material. Instead, he sticks with a fairly typical golden age production style for much of the album, which is accessible without being overly pop-friendly. What's more, his rapping style largely abandons the sly purr of "La Raza," sounding more like your average East Coast MC of the time (with Big Daddy Kane a particular influence). It's as though he wants to prove he can make it on others' terms as well as his own. There are exceptions, of course: "Ya Estuvo (That's It)" puts on a bilingual clinic in MC skills, and the chilling street narratives "Come Together" and "Homicide" return to the ice-cool delivery that marks Frost at his most distinctive. They're good enough to make the remainder of *Hispanic Causing Panic* frustrating—it's good, but it doesn't have enough of what makes Kid Frost so unique. —*Steve Huey*

Smile Now, Die Later / Oct. 24, 1995 / Relativity ✦✦✦
Between his first solo album, *Hispanic Causing Panic*, and his second record, *Smile Now, Die Later*, Frost dropped the "Kid" prefix from his name, which is only appropriate—he matured quite a bit between the two records. Where *Hispanic Causing Panic* was a party record infused with the occasional self-aware/socially conscious vibe, *Smile Now, Die Later* is a politically charged album, a warning to all of his fellow Latino ghetto denizens to protect themselves. Since Frost's lyrical outlook has grown, it's only appropriate that his music has become richer—now it draws from a variety of sources, from hardcore hip-hop and Latin beats, to deep funk and soul ballads. Like any mid-'90s hip-hop album, *Smile Now, Die Later* runs a bit too long, but if it's boiled down to its essential items, it is one fine listen. —*Leo Stanley*

That Was Then, This Is Now, Vol. 1 / Aug. 31, 1999 / Celeb ✦✦✦

That Was Then, This Is Now, Vol. 2 / Sep. 26, 2000 / Celeb ✦✦✦✦
The follow-up to Frost's original *That Was Then, This Is Now* finds the Latino gangsta from Los Angeles polishing up his sound, resulting in a refined effort that elevates him to acknowledged status within the overcrowded gangsta rap genre. Despite not being affiliated with a major label, Frost's sound is remarkably pristine, both in terms of lyrical flow, talented guest rappers, and a smooth West Coast funk sound. Frost may not ever reach the recognized level of his peers, but with this album, he definitely deserves recognition as one of the best gangsta rappers in the game circa 2000. He not only showcases an elaborate gangsta lifestyle with his lyrics but also keeps his beats far funkier than what you would probably expect from an indie gangsta rapper. —*Jason Birchmeier*

● **Frost's Greatest Joints** / Feb. 27, 2001 / Thump ✦✦✦✦✦
Released just over a decade after his solo career began, *Frost's Greatest Joints* showcases exactly why the MC leads the West Coast Latin rap scene. This compilation goes all the way back to his debut album, *Hispanic Causing Panic* (1990), to start things off with "La Raza," his breakthrough song. From there *Greatest Joints* moves chronologically, culling "No Sunshine," "Thin Line," and "Mi Vida Loca" from *East Side Story* (1992) before skipping around to collect a few of the better songs from Frost's mid- and late-'90s albums. In short, Frost endured for over a decade for a reason, and this compilation showcases his skills better than anything else in his canon. It also proves insightful, illustrating how the carefree, party-orientated Kid Frost evolved into the wiser, more earnest Frost. —*Jason Birchmeier*

Still up in This $#*T / Apr. 23, 2002 / Koch International ✦✦✦
Frost looks tired on the cover of his *Still up in This $#*T*, and you can imagine why. In the liner notes, he discusses all the "ish" he went through since his previous album, *That Was Then, This Is Now, Vol. 2* (2000). During that two-year span, some of Frost's family passed away and some of his acquaintances took advantage of him. Rather than come out vengeful, however, Frost comes out wise and reserved, thankful for what he has and trying his best to be tolerant of the "ish" rather than angry about it. Anyone who has followed Frost throughout his prolific run as a West Coast Chicano rapper will appreciate his mature stance on *Still up in This $#*T*. Unfortunately, anyone not familiar with much of Frost's past recordings may not see the significance of this album's change in tone. You need a bit of context to comprehend this significance, and once you have that context, you'll no doubt appreciate Frost's growth. —*Jason Birchmeier*

Fu-Schnickens

f. 1991, Brooklyn, NY
Group / Hip-Hop, Comedy Rap, Alternative Rap
One of the oddest groups in hip-hop history, Fu-Schnickens' manic, wildly playful raps were more than just pop-culture-obsessed novelties: they were often marvels of technical achievement on the mike as well. Spiritually speaking, Moc Fu (born J. Jones), Poc Fu (born Lennox Maturine), and group focal point Chip Fu (born Roderick Roachford) were descendents of De La Soul and cousins of Das EFX. They wove dense, tongue-twisting, absurdist lyrics that were filled with references to cartoons, karate flicks (even before the Wu-Tang Clan), and assorted TV and junk culture trivia. Not only that, their raps were distinctly influenced by dancehall reggae, peppered with comic vocal impressions, and occasionally even recited backward—at the same high velocity. Their personas were just as colorful; they sometimes wore kung fu-style costumes, and their name was a combination of "For

Unity" and a completely made-up word that meant "coalition," according to the group.

Fu-Schnickens was formed in the East Flatbush section of Brooklyn, where all three members had grown up, and made a strong impression around New York with a series of club dates showcasing their amazing technique and bizarre sense of humor. In 1991 the group performed at a rap conference at Howard University, and Jive Records promptly signed them up. Their dance-hall-inflected debut single, "Ring the Alarm," appeared in 1992 and proved quite popular among hip-hop fans, making the Top Ten on the rap singles chart. The group's full-length debut album, *F.U.: Don't Take It Personal*, followed close behind, and made the R&B Top 20 on the strength of the cult classic singles "La Schmoove" and "True Fuschnick." However, it wasn't until 1993 that Fu-Schnickens truly caught the mainstream's ear, thanks to the one-off team-up with NBA star Shaquille O'Neal on "What's Up Doc? (Can We Rock)." It was the only Fu-Schnickens single to reach the pop Top 40, and spawned a national catchphrase. The group's second album, *Nervous Breakdown*, followed in 1994, but didn't cause quite the same stir as its predecessor, and Fu-Schnickens quietly faded away from the hip-hop scene. —*Steve Huey*

F.U. Don't Take It Personal / Feb. 25, 1992 / Jive ✦✦✦✦✦
Even before they made it to the record bins, three-man New York crew Fu-Schnickens created quite a buzz in the hip-hop community with the oddity of their group name. Once they dropped their debut album, *F.U. Don't Take It Personal*, their music turned out to be every bit as curious and intriguing. The music is inundated with kung fu movie dialogue snippets and all manner of lyrical references to pop culture, both obscure and otherwise; this provides the album with a joyous, tongue-in-cheek, almost cartoonish flair. That sense is countered by the machine-gun-rapid toasting and almost military-like shouts of the three MCs (Poc, Chip, and Moc Fu), who trade off rhymes so telepathically that they seem to finish each other's sentences half the time. In this regard, they fit in perfectly with peers such as Leaders of the New School and Brand Nubian, as part of the early-'90s new wave of rap crews that catapulted hip-hop into the future partially by playing up the camaraderie of old school rap groups. All the peer crews, however, were so progressive because they grew up fully in a hip-hop culture and lifestyle, and knew where they wanted to take it, thereby developing unique styles and, occasionally, novelties to help them stand out. Fu-Schnickens were no different in this respect, and although their fashion sense (kung fu outfits on the cover) and taste in influences may have initially painted them as a novelty, their approach to music was straight serious on this debut album, and it shows. With production help from A Tribe Called Quest, they create spare, tension-filled, intense soundscapes, and twist reggae and vintage soul samples into unrecognizable, bass-heavy tracks. Even better is the trio's ear for vocal hooks, which stamp each song with an instant appeal. —*Stanton Swihart*

Nervous Breakdown / Oct. 25, 1994 / Jive ✦✦✦✦
When this Brooklyn trio emerged in 1992 with a unique style that combined high-speed rapping, dancehall chatting, and backward rhymes with *Looney Tunes*-inspired voice impressions and craftily arranged hip-hop grooves, the rap world had never heard anything like it. It took the group several years to follow up its gold debut, *F.U.: Don't Take It Personal*, but *Nervous Breakdown* proved that the Fu-Schnickens could deliver the goods. The album shows an improved lyrical maturity among all three members, but most noticeably Chip Fu, whose hyperactive, onomatopoeic flow has more hilarious, colorful cartoon imagery than anyone this side of the late, great Mel Blanc. While Poc Fu and Moc Fu are both better than average MCs with their own unique styles, it is Chip Fu's innovative approach that provides the distinctive personality that sets the group apart from other rap groups of the era. From the opening track, "Breakdown," on, this is a frenzied, fast-paced rollercoaster ride of originality that doesn't let up until the last song ends. —*Bret Love*

● **Greatest Hits** / Dec. 1995 / Jive ✦✦✦✦✦
A 12-track summation of the group's two albums, *Greatest Hits* boils down the Fu-Schnickens' output to the absolute cream of the cream. Except maybe for Das EFX, there are very, very few rappers who sound quite like the Fu-Schnickens; some might match the wild, referential lyrics, some the blazing speed of their delivery, but not both. All three MCs are terrific in their own right, and developed a near-telepathic interplay. But Chip Fu is clearly the genius of the group, shifting voices, tossing in weird noises, and enunciating barrages of words that are nearly impossible to keep up with. Similarly, the high points on *Greatest Hits* are so dizzying that some other excellent tracks

pale in comparison. "La Schmoove" and "What's Up Doc? (Can We Rock)," which feature A Tribe Called Quest and Shaquille O'Neal, respectively, are jaw-dropping hip-hop classics, and "True Fuschnick" isn't far behind. Tracks like "Ring the Alarm," "Cray-Z," and "Original Rude Boy" point up the group's dancehall reggae influence, and feature the sort of hyperspeed chatting that could give Daddy Freddy a run for his money. The production, meanwhile, is quietly inventive in its own way, leaving room for the lyrics but adding just enough to the off-kilter atmosphere. Aficionados will likely want everything the group recorded, but if you just want the general idea, *Greatest Hits* will demonstrate that there's way too much talent on display for this music to be a mere comic novelty. —*Steve Huey*

The Fugees

f. 1987

Group / Hip-Hop, Alternative Rap, East Coast Rap

The Fugees translated an intriguing blend of jazz-rap, R&B, and reggae into huge success during the mid-'90s, when the trio's sophomore album *The Score* hit number one on the pop charts and sold over five million copies. The trio formed in the late '80s in the New Jersey area, where Lauryn Hill and Prakazrel Michel ("Pras") attended a local high school and began working together. Michel's cousin Wyclef Jean ("Clef") joined the group (then called the Tranzlator Crew), and the trio signed to Ruffhouse/Columbia in 1993 after renaming themselves the Fugees (a term of derision, short for refugees, which was usually used to describe Haitian immigrants). Though the group's debut album, *Blunted on Reality*, was quite solid, it reflected a prevailing gangsta stance that may have been forced by the record label.

No matter how pigeonholed the Fugees may have sounded on their debut, the group had obviously asserted their control by the time of their second album, *The Score*. With just as much intelligence as their jazz-rap forebears, the trio also worked with surprisingly straight-ahead R&B on the soulful "Killing Me Softly With His Song," sung by Lauryn Hill. Elsewhere, Clef and Pras sampled doo wop and covered Bob Marley's "No Woman No Cry," giving the record familiarity for the commercial mainstream, but keeping it real with insightful commentary on their urban surroundings. *The Score* became one of the surprise hits of 1996, reaching number one on the pop charts and making the Fugees one of the most visible rap groups around the world. During 1997, the crew played on the Smokin' Grooves tour, and took time out while Hill gave birth to a child and Clef issued a solo album, *The Carnival Featuring the Refugee Allstars*. In 1998 Hill released her smash record *The Miseducation of Lauryn Hill* and in 2000 Clef released his second solo disc, *The Ecleftic: 2 Sides II a Book*. In turn, their solo success cast further doubt on another Fugees release. —*John Bush*

Blunted on Reality / Feb. 1, 1994 / Ruffhouse ✦✦✦

Given the brilliance of *The Score* and the shortage of Fugees albums in the '90s, many fans probably sought out *Blunted on Reality*. After all, though the album pretty much disappeared as soon as it appeared back in early 1994, it *was* still the Fugees, and that was reason enough for many to seek it out. Those fans no doubt were a little shocked, though, by what they found. Yes, *Blunted* features Wyclef, Lauryn Hill, and Pras, but it's not quite the same trio that fans of *The Score* have come to know. Here they offer their take on rap circa 1993. However, rather than use rap as a starting point and depart from there into myriad other directions as they did on *The Score*, they used rap as a starting point and never depart, instead emulating the popular style of the era. In that sense, it comes across as a bit derived and undoubtedly confined by its stifled creative ambitions. If you think back, you'll probably remember 1993 as being the pinnacle of gangsta rap—Dr. Dre's *The Chronic* was ubiquitous with not only its reach but also its influence, and Death Row was literally changing the game. If you keep this context in mind, it's a little easier to understand why *Blunted on Reality* sounds nothing like *The Score*. It's essentially the Fugees trying to earn respect in an era of gangstas, chronic, bitches, and guns by trying to come across as being hardcore. And, unfortunately, as hard as the Fugees portray themselves here, it can't help but seem a little silly in retrospect. That's kind of what this album is—silly. It doesn't intend to be, but, in the post-*Score* world, it's hard to imagine Wyclef, not to mention Hill, fronting like a gangsta. Besides the fronting, there just aren't that many impressive moments here, perhaps an even better reason to avoid this album. It's the sort of album that is best seen as novelty. Devoted fans may wish to seek it out for curiosity's sake, and that's understandable,

but no one should approach this album expecting the prequel to *The Score*. —*Jason Birchmeier*

★ **The Score** / Feb. 1996 / Ruffhouse ✦✦✦✦✦

A breath of fresh air in the gangsta-dominated mid-'90s, the Fugees' breakthrough album, *The Score*, marked the beginning of a resurgence in alternative hip-hop. Its left-field, multiplatinum success proved there was a substantial untapped audience with an appreciation for rap music but little interest in thug life. *The Score*'s eclecticism, social consciousness, and pop smarts drew millions of latent hip-hop listeners back into the fold, showing just how much the music had grown up. It not only catapulted the Fugees into stardom, but also launched the productive solo careers of Wyclef Jean and Lauryn Hill, the latter of whom already ranks as one of the top female MCs of all time based on her work here. Not just a collection of individual talents, the Fugees' three MCs all share a crackling chemistry and a wide-ranging taste in music. Their strong fondness for smooth soul and reggae is underscored by the two hit covers given slight hip-hop makeovers (Roberta Flack's "Killing Me Softly With His Song" and Bob Marley's "No Woman, No Cry"). Even when they're not relying on easily recognizable tunes, their original material is powered by a raft of indelible hooks, especially the great "Fu-Gee-La"; there are also touches of blues and gospel, and the recognizable samples range from doo wop to Enya. Their protest tracks are often biting, yet tempered with pathos and humanity, whether they're attacking racial profiling among police ("The Beast"), the insecurity behind violent posturing ("Cowboys"), or the inability of many black people in the Western Hemisphere to trace their familial roots ("Family Business"). Yeah, the Chinese restaurant skit is a little dicey, but on the whole, *The Score* balances intelligence and accessibility with an easy assurance, and ranks as one of the most distinctive hip-hop albums of its era. —*Steve Huey*

The Score: Bootleg Versions EP / Nov. 26, 1996 / Ruffhouse ✦✦✦

Released several months after the Fugees became stars, *Bootleg Versions* is an EP of remixes from the Fugees' two albums, *Blunted on Reality* and *The Score*. None of the new mixes have the spark or fire of the originals, yet some of the reworking will be of interest to hardcore fans. By and large, however, it doesn't add any new dimension the Fugees' music. —*Leo Stanley*

Greatest Hits / Mar. 25, 2003 / Columbia ✦✦✦

As wonderful and compelling as the Fugees were during their brief moment in the sun (circa 1996), it's difficult to make the case for a Fugees *Greatest Hits*. The trio only put out two records, the first a muddled attempt at weed-soaked hardcore, the second an excellent fusion of hip-hop and soul, so the obvious choice for record buyers is that final full-length, *The Score*. This compilation includes seven tracks from *The Score*, prefacing it with two selections from the 1994 debut (*Blunted on Reality*) and tacking on Lauryn Hill's first solo recording, "The Sweetest Thing"—originally on the *Love Jones* soundtrack and later included on her first album, *The Miseducation of Lauryn Hill*. Anyone interested in hearing what the Fugees sounded like before *The Score* is subjected to *Blunted on Reality*'s pair of substandard singles ("Vocab," "Nappy Heads"), though wiser compilers would've chosen early songs that paved the way for *The Score*, like the graceful Hill feature "Some Seek Stardom." Brief and perfunctory, *Greatest Hits* is basically a budget compilation with a more artful cover. —*John Bush*

Full Force

f. Brooklyn, NY

Group / Hip-Hop, Old School Rap, Electro

Full Force rose to prominence in the mid-'80s, writing and producing popular R&B hits for Lisa Lisa and Cult Jam before embarking on a moderately successful solo career that ultimately led them back to production work in the late '90s. The six-man collective—featuring Paul Anthony, Bowlegged Lou, B-Fine, Baby Gerry, Shy Shy, and Curt-t-t—originated in Brooklyn, NY, where they originally met up in the late '70s with Steve Salem, a business-savvy individual who functioned as their manager. With a manager in place and plenty of talent between the various group members, Full Force struggled throughout the early '80s to find a label willing to sign them. Eventually they got a break when they wrote and produced fellow Brooklyn group U.T.F.O.'s "Roxanne Roxanne," a rap song that would attain a certain level of fame thanks to a series of answer records. In early 1985, the single peaked at number ten on *Billboard*'s R&B charts, proving a substantial hit for both the rap group and the production team. From there, Full Force moved onto their next major success with Lisa Lisa and Cult Jam, a pop group led by a 16-year-old singer named Lisa Velez. Originally Velez had auditioned for the production team, who then went ahead and recorded "I Wonder if I Take You Home" with her, releasing the single under the moniker Lisa Lisa and Cult Jam With Full Force on an indie New York label, Personal. The song initially scored success overseas before eventually being released by Columbia in the U.S. after getting immense play in New York clubs as an import single. Almost overnight, the song topped *Billboard*'s dance chart and went on to peak at number six on the R&B chart by summer 1985. Thanks to the momentum surrounding the hit single, Full Force signed a deal with Columbia to release solo material. Though they scored some minor R&B hits on their own ("Temporary Love Thing," "Unfaithful So Much," "All in My Mind"), their biggest success continued to be as a production team for Lisa Lisa and Cult Jam ("All Cried Out," "Head To Toe," "Lost In Emotion"). In 1988 Full Force produced James Brown's *I'm Real*, scoring a substantial hit for the struggling legend with the album's title track, and worked with a number of late-'80s pop stars: Jasmine Guy, Cheryl Pepsii Riley, and Samantha Fox, among others. Throughout the early and mid-'90s, the production team remained relatively quiet before again churning out a number of late-'90s R&B-flavored pop hits with Selena, Backstreet Boys, and LFO, among others. *—Jason Birchmeier*

Full Force / 1985 / Columbia ✦✦✦
Although they were among the hottest production and performance combos on the scene in the mid- and late '80s, Full Force was never able to translate that magic to their own albums. This 1986 debut included the mildly entertaining "Alice, I Want You Just For Me!," but was mostly either uneventful love tunes, haphazard novelty pieces, or unfocused and formulaic quasi-raps. *—Ron Wynn*

● **Full Force Get Ready 1 Time** / 1986 / Columbia ✦✦✦✦✦
The second Full Force release was a little better than the first, but still far from the levels they were scoring with Lisa Lisa & Cult Jam. Once more, they were unable to get any breakout or chart singles, and while songs like "Body Heavenly" and "Old Flames Never Die" may have contained potentially catchy lyrics, they lacked defined vocals, attractive arrangements, or interesting production. *—Ron Wynn*

Guess Who's Comin' to the Crib? / 1987 / Columbia ✦✦✦✦✦
Full Force's third album did only marginally better than the first two; it peaked a little higher on the low end of the pop albums chart. They tried everything in their creative arsenal, from the bittersweet sentiments of "Love Is For Suckers (Like Me And You)" to the naughty double-entendre notions expressed on "Low Blow Brenda" and even a traditional soul number, "Take Care of Homework." Nothing clicked, and it probably didn't help matters that the album included the justifiable but shrill diatribe "Black Radio." *—Ron Wynn*

Don't Sleep! / Aug. 31, 1992 / Capitol ✦✦
Despite the success Full Force enjoyed producing Lisa Lisa & Cult Jam, Samantha Fox, and U.T.F.O. in the 1980s, the band's own albums weren't big hits. When Force switched from Columbia to Capitol with *Don't Sleep!*, things didn't improve at all. Despite the input of James Brown ally Bobby Byrd, this CD is a disappointment. Force had often failed to live up to its great potential at Columbia, and the same things happen on *Don't Sleep!* There are a few bright spots, including "Wait Till I Get Home" and the silky "Your Place or Mine," but most of the material is pedestrian and contrived. On such new-jack-swing-oriented product as "Quickie" and "Nice N' Sleazy," the Brooklynites sound like they're making one last desperate attempt to appeal to urban contemporary radio. But radio proved unreceptive, and the album died a quick death. *—Alex Henderson*

Still Standing / Jun. 26, 2001 / TVT ✦✦✦
The album title *Still Standing* may be a reference to Full Force being written off by the record industry to a large degree after their gold and platinum '80s heyday. After writing and producing hits for the Backstreet Boys, Britney Spears, *NSync, 3LW, and others, the Brooklyn-born group recorded this album, which includes new material as well as their own previous hits (most of which are on *Ahead of Their Time: Greatest Hits*) and the ones they produced on Lisa Lisa & Cult Jam, James Brown, and others. All of which makes *Still Standing* part greatest hits, part comeback, and part tribute, with some current performers appearing (reportedly for free) on some new tracks. Still, it's on the more old school-oriented cuts that the album succeeds. The smooth

cover of the Floaters' "Float On," titled "Float on With Us," features Kevon Edmonds and Gerald Levert. Full Force is said to have traveled back to the Detroit studio where the original was recorded to pick up on the song's vibe. Of all the tracks, the soul-fired ballad "Kiss It Where It Hurts," the raw "The Good, the Bad, the Thuggly," and "Born to Love Only You" come closest to the tone of their best stuff. On their next album, cuts like these would be the way to go. *—Ed Hogan*

Fun-Da-Mental

f. 1991, London, England
Group / Club/Dance, British Rap, Hip-Hop
In 1991, Aki Qureshi ("Propa-Gandhi") saw a need in his homeland of Great Britain for a music group devoted to publicizing the social injustice directed at members of its Asian and Afro-Caribbean communities, and the collective Fun-Da-Mental was born. Qureshi built a following by releasing singles on his own independent label, Nation Records, and integrating multimedia spectacles into the group's concerts. Dave "Impi-D" Watts joined the group in 1993, and together the two formed the musical core of Fun-Da-Mental, writing most of the worldbeat-influenced music, integrating tapes of recorded speeches into the songs and taking their turns rapping. Their 1995 debut, *Seize the Time*, features eight lyricists and five rappers altogether; *Erotic Terrorism* followed in 1998. *—Steve Huey*

● **Seize the Time** / 1995 / Mammoth ✦✦✦✦
It's a severe pity the original lineup of the group didn't stick around long enough to record a full debut album, but one listen to the horrific phone message from a pissed-off bigot at the start of the album explains why it is any version of the band existed in the first place. Compared to the thrilling audacity of admitted inspirations Public Enemy at its finest, *Seize the Time* doesn't quite measure up—Aki Nawaz and engineer Graeme Holdaway aren't the Bomb Squad, and though Nawaz sure wants to sound like Chuck D, he just doesn't quite have the sheer heft and charisma. As a solid listen to conscious and wide-ranging hip-hop action from a different cultural context than America, though, it's more than successful. The use of an array of classical Indian musical samples, as well as Bollywood soundtracks and live contributions on tablas and flutes, acts as both statement of purpose and the basis of attractive new fusions that would gain more popularity throughout the '90s. Strong examples include "Dollars or Sense," riding over a deep, pounding beat and swirling string, vocal, and flutes, and the immediately following "Mother India," a shimmering, sitar- and orchestra-infused number with guest vocals from Subi Shah celebrating famous Hindi heroines. Meanwhile, the open celebration of Allah and Islam throughout the album—"Mera Mezab" makes for a defiant, proud statement of belief over a weird, attractively minimal throb that turns into a full-on jam—works other familiar hip-hop tropes and lyrical sentiments into a new lather. Compared to where later Anglo-Asian groups like Asian Dub Foundation would take Fun-Da-Mental and many other sources of inspiration, *Seize the Time* sounds like a product of its time, but it's still an inspired collection with much to recommend it. *—Ned Raggett*

Erotic Terrorism / May 5, 1998 / Beggars Banquet ✦✦✦✦
By the time Fun-Da-Mental reappeared with a second album proper, things were surprisingly different for Nawaz and company. Instead of Public Enemy, the touchstones were the Chemical Brothers and the Prodigy, aiming for a largely instrumental industrial/metal/hip-hop/techno sound that's not always as distinct or unique as the *Seize the Time* mélange. Perhaps the goal was to aim at a different audience, but it's not quite the result perhaps intended. That said, everyone's still righteously pissed off, though music rather than the often-distorted vocals really is *Erotic Terrorism*'s focus, and when the beats get really frenetic or creative, as on the blunt charge of "Demonised Soul" or the echoed rage and rave of "Furious," it's a treat. Nawaz seems to be a one-man band throughout, with only a bassist and banjo player otherwise credited, though he again works with Graeme Pickering as engineer. Various samples of Indian music again appear with regularity throughout *Erotic Terrorism*, but equally prominent are huge slabs of feedback and massive drumming and percussion loops. Where chanting and tablas have more of the focus, as on the soaring, inspirational stomp of "Ja Sha Taan," there's still a rough, low electronic undercurrent. Given Nawaz's own rock drumming background via groups like the Southern Death Cult, it's not too surprising to hear in context, just a bit of a jarring leap. Nawaz and

Pickering actually do show a greater sense of drama and dynamics than before—sudden cuts between loud and soft passages create some effective moments throughout, while the grunts and children's cries on "Blood in Transit" are disturbing. Above all else, there's the overriding message of the fight against bigotry and oppression—as the horribly tasteless and racist old song that's sampled to start things off makes all too clear. —*Ned Raggett*

La Funk Mob

f. 1991, Paris, France
Group / Hip-Hop, Club/Dance, Trip-Hop, Electronica
Although MC Solaar was the only French rapper of note during the '90s, several hip-hop production crews made inroads in the quintessentially American style, including DJ Cam, the Mighty Bop, and La Funk Mob. The latter team was formed by Boom Bass and Philippe Zdar in the early '90s, though Boom Bass had worked with Solaar on his first two solo albums, weaving samples from Black Sheep to Serge Gainsbourg. The act debuted with a track on the 1993 compilation album *Jimmy Jay Présente 'Les Cool Sessions'* and signed to Britain's seminal Mo'Wax for two 1994 EPs, *Tribulations Extra Sensorielles* and *Casse les Frontieres, Fou les Têtes en L'air* ("Breaking Boundaries, Messing Up Heads"). Little was heard from the duo during 1997-1998, though two side projects (Motorbass and L'homme Qui Valait 3 Milliard) saw release, and Boom Bass again provided production work for MC Solaar on his third album, *Paradisiaque*. The duo resurfaced as Cassius in 1999 for the purpose of French progressive house. —*John Bush*

Breaking Boundaries, Messing Up Heads EP / Apr. 1994 / Mo'Wax ♦♦♦
A double 10" set, La Funk Mob's second release for Mo'Wax includes a "Techno Disc" (with a great Carl Craig remix) and a "Hip-Hop Disc." —*John Bush*

● **Tribulations Extra Sensorielles EP** / Aug. 1994 / Mo'Wax ♦♦♦♦
An extended EP of clean trip-hop and electro minimalism, *Tribulations Extra Sensorielles* is a Mo'Wax highlight, sparked by "Ravers Suck Our Sound." —*John Bush*

Funk Mobb

Group / West Coast Rap, Gangsta Rap, Hardcore Rap
Cali Bay Area rapper Mac Shawn led the Sick Wid It signees Funk Mobb, a short-lived group that released just one album, *It Ain't 4 Play* (1996). Sick Wid It was a noteworthy rap label at the time, distributed by Priority and also home to E-40 and the Click. Despite the Sick Wid It association and the Priority distribution, Funk Mobb (comprised also of G-Note and K-1) unfortunately enjoyed little success. Shawn thus embarked on a solo career beginning with *Music fo the Mobb* (1997) and signed to the soon-to-collapse Death Row Records soon after, while his group mates fell into obscurity. —*Jason Birchmeie*

● **It Ain't 4 Play** / Jul. 15, 1996 / Sick Wid It ♦♦♦♦
It Ain't 4 Play is an entertaining but workmanlike set of Californian gangsta rap. While the production isn't particularly impressive, the rhyming skills of the Funk Mobb are first rate, making even the weaker moments on this overlong album entertaining. —*Leo Stanley*

Funkdoobiest

f. 1992
Group / Hip-Hop, Alternative Rap, West Coast Rap
Protégés of Cypress Hill superproducer DJ Muggs, Funkdoobiest—as their name made clear—specialized in a stonerfriendly brand of Latin hip-hop that often recalled their mentors. The group was formed in Los Angeles in 1992 by Puerto Rican MC Son Doobie (born Jason Vasquez), Sioux MC Tomahawk Funk (born Tyrone Pachenco), and DJ Ralph M. (born Ralph Medrano, who'd previously worked with Kid Frost). The trio became part of the Soul Assassins crew, along with Cypress Hill and House of Pain, and landed a deal with Epic in 1993. DJ Muggs produced their debut album, *Which Doobie U B?*, which appeared later that year and went gold on the strength of singles like "Bow Wow Wow," "The Funkiest," and "Freak Mode." Now established as cult favorites, Funkdoobiest returned in 1995 with *Brothas Doobie*, which was somewhat less successful but did produce a couple more underground hits in "Rock On" and "Dedicated." Following *Brothas Doobie*, Tomahawk Funk left the group to raise his family. Funkdoobiest reconvened as a duo, switched to RCA subsidiary Buzz Tone, and recorded their third album, 1998's *The Troubleshooters*, without Muggs behind the boards. Their newly revised

sound incorporated soul and stronger Latin influences, and resulted in the underground hit "Papi Chulo." By 2002, Son Doobie was reportedly working on a solo album. —*Steve Huey*

● **Which Doobie U B?** / May 4, 1993 / Epic ♦♦♦♦
Funkdoobiest's debut album, *Which Doobie U B?*, sounds a lot like their mentors in Cypress Hill—a *lot*. Not only is DJ Muggs' production very similar, but lead MC Son Doobie's flow often resembles a more robotic version of B Real (that's a compliment, by the way). But it all works anyway—Muggs is in his absolute prime as a producer here, and Son Doobie's rhymes are fittingly surreal and stoner friendly, albeit more cartoonish than menacing like his Cypress counterpart. The record is front loaded with its best songs—"The Funkiest," "Bow Wow Wow," and "Freak Mode" were the underground hits, and they're also the first three cuts here. Most of the rest of the album keeps their vibe going with pretty admirable consistency, and stays engaging the whole way through. B Real drops in for a guest spot on the Little Richard-sampling "Wobbabalubop," and there are some nifty echoing drums on "Here I Am." It may not break any new ground, but frankly, *Which Doobie U B?* is better than any latter-day Cypress Hill album. —*Steve Huey*

Brothas Doobie / 1995 / Epic ♦♦♦
A more laid-back album than their first, *Brothas Doobie* also deals with a few social problems, an improvement over the debut's continuous self-praising. —*John Bush*

The Troubleshooters / Jan. 13, 1998 / Buzz Tone ♦♦♦
With their third album, *The Troubleshooters*, Funkdoobiest broke away from the stoned, rolling Muggs beat that characterized their first two records. With the assistence of several production teams—including Da Beatminerz, Ski, and Rectangle—the duo has developed a stylish fusion of contemporary urban soul, G-funk, and Latin rhythms. Occasionally, the collision of cultures feels a little forced—with its Squirrel Nut Zippers sample, the single "Papi Chulo" (Spanish for "Big Papa") sounds a little awkward, even though it works—but on the whole, the record is a solid leap forward for a duo that once seemed lost in the shadow of Cypress Hill. —*Leo Stanley*

Funkmaster Flex (Aston Taylor)

b. Bronx, NY
DJ, Producer / East Coast Rap, Hip-Hop
Not since the early '80s when DJs such as Grandmaster Flash and Afrika Bambaataa were acknowledged as two of rap's most popular figures had a hip-hop DJ attained such prominent status among the masses as New York's Funkmaster Flex. Throughout the 1990s he reigned over New York's mammoth rap scene, capable of making or breaking artists with his high-profile position at the top-rated radio station in America's top radio market, Hot 97. By the mid-'90s, he was also the weekly DJ at one of New York's top clubs, the Tunnel, and also had his radio show broadcasting on Los Angeles' Power 106, America's second-largest radio market. Furthermore, Flex began releasing commercially successful mix albums in the mid-'90s, beginning with the first volume of the long-running *60 Minutes of Funk* series. At the end of the decade, his popularity only continued to rise, landing him a coveted position on MTV with his own daily show, *Direct Effect*. Though hip-hop DJs such as Eric B and Terminator X had been recognizable names in the '80s and '90s, Funkmaster Flex was the first pure DJ without any affiliated MCs to match the popular success that early-'80s artists such as Grandmaster Flash had attained, harking back to the early days of hip-hop when the DJ overshadowed the MC.

The son of a Jamaican DJ, Flex was born in the Bronx as Aston Taylor and bought his first set of turntables at age 16, influenced by early New York hip-hop DJs such as DJ Red Alert. His radio career began at KISS-FM as an assistant to Chuck Chillout in the late '80s. When Chillout transferred to WBLS, Flex accompanied him and soon began spinning at clubs and parties, where people began to take note of his skills. Among those fascinated with his talents were the programming chiefs at Hot 97, who offered him a prominent role as one of the city's top hip-hop DJs. In 1995 he released his first major-label mix album, *The Mix Tape, Vol. 1: 60 Minutes of Funk*, and followed this album with two more volumes on Loud Records by the end of the '90s, along with an album on Def Jam, *The Tunnel*. In 2000 he mixed a collection of that year's biggest rap anthems for Arista, *Vibe Hits, Vol. 1*, and continued the *60 Minutes of Funk* series. In addition to his duties as a radio DJ, an MTV host, and as a successful album artist, Funkmaster Flex has also served as a remixer. —*Jason Birchmeier*

- **The Mix Tape, Vol. 1: 60 Minutes of Funk** / Nov. 21, 1995 / Loud ✦✦✦✦
Funkmaster Flex's *The Mix Tape, Vol. 1* recalls hip-hop's past while pointing toward its future. Featuring a wide array of hip-hop styles graced by amazing freestyle raps by some of the '90s' top MCs, the album sounds like a mix-tape compiled from the radio and 7" singles—there's simply nothing but first-rate music, with no filler whatsoever. Although there are elements of old school rap as well as modern funk, the daring production and stunning rhymes make *The Mix Tape* a rarity of mid-'90s hip-hop—it's a record that sounds like none of its competition. It announces itself as an instant classic. —*Stephen Thomas Erlewine*

The Mix Tape, Vol. 2: 60 Minutes of Funk / Feb. 11, 1997 / Relativity ✦✦✦
The Mix Tape, Vol. 2: 60 Minutes of Funk is every bit as engaging its predecessor, capturing Funkmaster Flex as he spins through a stack of modern and classic hip-hop and R&B, with various guest rappers freestyling while he does so. The energy is equal to *Vol. 1*, and while some listeners might find the relentless but seamless mixing to be a little amelodic and irritating, any true hip-hop fan will consider the album a treasure. —*Leo Stanley*

The Mix Tape, Vol. 3: 60 Minutes of Funk, The Final Chapter / Aug. 11, 1998 / Loud ✦✦✦
The third (and final, according to the album's subtitle) chapter of New York DJ Funkmaster Flex's mix albums is the best of the bunch, a gritty combination of old (A Tribe Called Quest, House of Pain, Naughty By Nature) and new school rappers (Missy Elliott, Wu-Tang Clan, Busta Rhymes). Flex's deft skill at remixing some familiar tunes—he often takes a minute or two of a cut and works brand-new beats, as well as some exclusive freestyling courtesy of top-name artists themselves, into the grooves—makes *The Mix Tape* more than just a lazy compilation of radio hits. Still, when you get down to it, it really doesn't amount to much more than 75 minutes (despite the title's claim of only 60) of a guy spinning some of his favorite records, albeit with style. —*Michael Gallucci*

The Tunnel / Dec. 7, 1999 / Def Jam ✦✦✦✦✦
It takes a pretty connected man to assemble the most star-studded rap album ever released. *The Tunnel* features all of the biggest and best MCs in hip-hop—DMX, Jay-Z, Nas, Method Man, Eminem, LL Cool J, Snoop Dogg, Capone-N-Noreaga, Mary J. Blige, Raekwon, and Redman and Erick Sermon—freestyling over tracks, most of them produced by Rockwilder or Funkmaster Flex himself. The affair is somewhat similar to his popular mixtape series, which alternated hip-hop classics with guest appearances from MCs inserted between standard productions. The mere presence of all these incredible rappers is more than enough to push *The Tunnel* over the top, and the addition of a live freestyle between 2Pac and the Notorious B.I.G. recorded in 1993 makes it worthwhile for that track alone. Among many highlights, "True" with Method Man, "For My Thugs" with Jay-Z, "We in Here" with the Ruff Ryders, and "Ill Bomb" with LL Cool J are the best here. —*Keith Farley*

Vibe Hits, Vol. 1 / Nov. 7, 2000 / Arista ✦✦✦
Compiled in conjunction with *Vibe* magazine, this nothing-but-the-hits set pretty much settles into formula. It does adhere itself to a single urban pop format, so the shifts aren't as jarring as the ones found on, say, the *Totally Hits* compilations (where Matchbox Twenty, Pink, and John Michael Montgomery all share space). But it also sticks pretty close to home, offering tracks

mostly from its label home. The best cuts—Next's "Wifey," Donell Jones' "U Know What's Up," Deborah Cox's "We Can't Be Friends"—aren't quite A-list material, and the album's best song, TLC's "Unpretty," is a hollow remix that doesn't do justice to its subtle beauty. —*Michael Gallucci*

The Mix Tape, Vol. 4: 60 Minutes of Funk / Dec. 5, 2000 / Loud ✦✦
Funkmaster Flex keeps his *Mix Tape: 60 Minute of Funk* going with *Volume 4*, which features mainly freestyles. Performers include some of the industry's top rappers—primarily New Yorkers like DMX and Ja Rule but also a few out-of-town surprises like Eminem and Ludacris—most of whom freestyle over Flex's own productions. The plethora of exclusive productions sets *Volume 4* apart from its predecessors, which were more straightforward mix albums comprised of previously released hits. As such, *Volume 4* offers a lot of performances that cannot be found elsewhere, so fans of the featured rappers should take note. Newcomers are probably better served by earlier volumes, though, as the inclusions here aren't quite as astounding as the proven hits of before; nor is Flex's mixing, since he's more interested in showcasing his beatmaking than his turntablism. —*Jason Birchmeier*

Funky Four Plus One

f. 1979 **db.** 1983
Group / Hip-Hop, Old School Rap, Electro
The Funky Four Plus One were one of the first hip-hop groups that contained a female MC and were certainly the first group of their kind that released records commercially. Further, the group were the among the first wave of Bronx crews to release records after the initial success of the Sugarhill Gang in 1979. The Funky Four consisted of DJ Breakout, K.K. Rockwell, Keith Keith, Lil' Rodney Cee, Jazzy Jeff, and the "plus one"—Sha Rock. Among DJ Breakout's peers in the early to mid-'70s were such hip-hop pioneers as DJ Kool Herc, Afrika Bambaataa, and Grandmaster Flash. In fact, one of the earlier members of the Funky Four—Raheim—left to join Grandmaster Flash & the Furious Five, who was replaced by Lil' Rodney Cee. A unique aspect of the group was that Sha Rock wasn't portrayed as a sex object but was more or less considered equal among the male members of the group. Aside from the minor success of the all-female Sugar Hill Records rap crew Sequence, the Funky Four Plus One signified the last moderate success of a woman in the rap industry until Roxanne Shanté and Salt-N-Pepa came along in the mid-'80s.

Aside from the novelty of having a woman in their ranks, they are one of the most influential but overlooked old school hip-hop groups—having been sampled by a wide assortment of later hip-hop artists including the Beastie Boys (on their *Paul's Boutique* record). Along with Grandmaster Flash, they began recording 12" singles for Enjoy Records—releasing what is considered the longest rap song ever: "Rappin' and Rockin' the House" (at over 15 minutes, it outlasts the lengthy "Rapper's Delight"). After they grew displeased with what they considered to be Enjoy's poor distribution, they followed Grandmaster Flash to the Sugar Hill Records label. There they cut the all-time classic "That's the Joint" but never went on to release a full-length record. After only moderate success, the group went their separate ways in the early '80s with Lil' Rodney Cee and K.K. Rockwell forming Double Trouble and Sha Rock joining Lisa Lee and Debbie Dee as part of US Girls (who appeared in the 1984 film *Beat Street*). While no full-length ever was released by the Funky Four Plus One, many of their singles can be found scattered on old school hip-hop compilations. —*Kembrew McLeod*

- **That's the Joint [Single]** / 1981 / Sugar Hill ✦✦✦

G. Dep

b. Harlem, NY
East Coast Rap

G. Dep joined the Bad Boy family during the rebuilding years following the Notorious B.I.G.'s death in the late '90s. Hailing from the same Harlem streets of fellow Bad Boy rapper Black Rob, Dep, aka the Deputy, first appeared on Rob's 1999 debut album and subsequently continued to make cameos with other Bad Boy artists. Following Combs' conversion to P. Diddy, Bad Boy entered its *Saga Continues* era, beginning with Combs' album of the same name. Dep played an important role in this Bad Boy era, being second only to Black Rob as Combs' right-hand man. Dep's debut album, *Child of the Ghetto*, appeared in late 2001, featuring "Let's Get It," one of the better songs on the previously released *Saga Continues*, along with the lead single "Special Delivery." —*Jason Birchmeier*

● **Child of the Ghetto** / Nov. 20, 2001 / Bad Boy ✦✦✦
Another in Sean "P. Diddy" Combs' line of successors to the departed Notorious B.I.G., G. Dep joined fellow Harlem rapper Black Rob during Bad Boy's early-2000s rebuilding era. Unfortunately, like the others who followed in Biggie's large shoes—also including the somewhat martyred Shyne, in addition to Black Rob—the "Deputy" doesn't live up to his promise. However, just because Dep is no Biggie doesn't mean Combs doesn't go out of his way to propel his protégé to stardom. In fact, Combs does nearly everything he can on *Child of the Ghetto* as an executive producer to make it a strong debut: the guest appearances (Rakim, Kool G Rap, most of the Bad Boy roster), the multitude of amazing productions (courtesy of the low-profile yet impressive in-house producers), the obvious radio-ready singles ("Special Delivery," "Let's Get It"), a few character-developing skits, and plenty of glossy photos in the CD booklet. In sum, Combs does a great job with this album—he does what a rap producer should. And he doesn't let guests steal the show from Dep—for the most part, Dep does all the rhyming. However, just because Combs puts together a proper debut doesn't mean it's worth listening to. And, in the case of *Child of the Ghetto*, you're probably alright just hearing the singles and not bothering with the album. Granted, there are some stunning productions here—the beat on "Special Delivery," in particular—and Dep is no doubt skilled. However, these attributes don't compensate for the lack of engaging songwriting. In sum, this album needs some hooks—desperately. There aren't any "Big Poppas" or "It's All About the Benjaminses" here—not even something as forced as "Bad Boy for Life." This presents a dilemma. There aren't enough pop hooks here for this to be a pop-rap record, like the most successful Bad Boy albums have been in the past, but it's also not ghetto enough to be a street record. While he may indeed be a "child of the ghetto," Dep certainly isn't ghetto any longer, even if he tries to convince you otherwise with all his drug talk—he's Combs' well-fed, nicely groomed protégé. And it's not difficult to see through the unintended irony of Dep's pampered-thug façade. This doesn't help the album—either you're ghetto or you're pop; you can't be both, and pathos only goes so far. It's unintentional ironies like this that make it difficult to take P. Diddy (or is it Puffy?) seriously or as anything more than a manipulator. —*Jason Birchmeier*

Warren G (Warren Griffin III)

b. Nov. 10, 1971
G-Funk, West Coast Rap

Born Warren Griffin III, Warren G exploded out of the burgeoning Long Beach rap scene in 1994 with the smash single "Regulate," a duet with longtime friend Nate Dogg, and its accompanying album, *Regulate...G Funk Era*. G grew up in Long Beach listening to his parents' extensive collection of

jazz, soul, and funk records, also frequently hanging out at the local V.I.P. record store. As a teenager, he and his friends Nate Dogg and future superstar Snoop Dogg formed a rap group called 213, after their area code. Unfortunately, all three had brushes with the law and spent time in jail, which motivated them to get jobs, also working on their music on the side. Eventually, the V.I.P. record store allowed the trio to practice and record in a back room. It was here that Snoop cut the demo "Super Duper Snooper," which G played for his half-brother Dr. Dre at a party. Dre invited all three to his studio and wound up collaborating with Snoop on *The Chronic*. While G also made several contributions, he opted to develop his talents mostly outside of Dre's shadow. He honed his musical skills while producing such artists as MC Breed and 2Pac. A break came when his vocal collaboration with Mista Grimm, "Indo Smoke," appeared on the *Poetic Justice* soundtrack. Soon after that, G recorded his debut album for Death Row. "Regulate" appeared on the *Above the Rim* soundtrack and was released as a single. It quickly became a massive hit, peaking at number 2 on the *Billboard* charts and pushing the album up to the same position. The album eventually went triple platinum, with "This D.J." becoming his second Top 10 hit.

Warren G took nearly three years to complete his second album, returning in the spring of 1997 with *Take a Look Over Your Shoulder*, which was greeted with decidedly mixed reviews and weak sales. *I Want It All* followed in 1999. —*Steve Huey*

● **Regulate...G Funk Era** / Jun. 7, 1994 / Def Jam ✦✦✦✦
Anchored by the laid-back G-funk anthem "Regulate," Warren G's appropriately titled *Regulate...G Funk Era* embodies the mid-'90s era of Cali sunshine, endless blunts, and switch-hittin' lowriders with a welcome and somewhat surprising sense of kindheartedness. Unlike most of his West Coast G-funk peers, Warren doesn't celebrate drive-by gang-bangin', dirty-money stackin', nor G's-up, hoes-down pimpin'. Sure, he says the *f* word once in a while and puffs on the cheeba-cheeba when it's passed his way, but he's essentially a good-natured, all-ages rapper, interested in nothing more than good ol'-fashioned hip-hop. He professes his demeanor succinctly on the catchy hook to "This DJ," the other era-defining highlight here: "It's kinda easy when you're listening to the G-ed-up sound/Pioneer speakers bumpin' as I smoke on a pound/I got the sound fo yo' ass and it's easy to see/That this DJ be Warren G." Like his step-brother, Dr. Dre, Warren is a more talented producer than rapper, and it's his by-the-book G-funk beatmaking that truly shines here. For instance, another album highlight, "Do You See," boasts an elastic bass line and whistling synth hook, capturing the essence of G-funk as only Dre himself could. Warren further compensates for his middling rapping with a couple of guests, a few skits, and a brief running time. Even if "Regulate" and "This DJ" tower far above everything else here, *Regulate...G Funk Era* is nonetheless a minor gem among the myriad G-funk albums of the mid-'90s, and Warren embodies the style itself here with a precision perhaps second only to his older brother and does so with a refreshing air of harmlessness. —*Jason Birchmeier*

Take a Look Over Your Shoulder / Mar. 25, 1997 / Def Jam ✦✦
Warren G's debut album was a refreshing, soulful variation on G-funk, but his second album, *Take a Look Over Your Shoulder*, is one of the most predictable and tired entries in the G-funk canon. As always, the record is impeccably produced, filled with deep grooves and slow, funky beats, but the music never does anything adventurous. Even if the music is predictable, it can be fitfully enjoyable, which can't be said about Warren G's lazy rhyming. None of his lyrics raise above the perfunctory level, and occasionally they sink so low as to be embarrassing, as on the completely misguided cover of Bob Marley's "I Shot the Sheriff." From an artist that once seemed so promising, it's a disheartening turn of events. —*Leo Stanley*

I Want It All / Oct. 12, 1999 / Restless ✦✦✦✦

After a disappointing sophomore album that failed to cement his superstar status, Warren G returned to what made him famous—his production skills—and for the most part, left the rapping to his many guests. For listeners who haven't kept up with the rapper/producer since his 1994 chart run, *I Want It All* will sound completely familiar. It's an album of impeccably produced deep-groove G-funk, with tight harmonies anchoring the choruses of highlights like "Gangsta Love" (featuring Kurupt, Nate Dogg, and RBX), "I Want It All" (featuring Mack 10), "You Never Know" (featuring Snoop Dogg, Phats Bossi, and Reel Tight), and "We Got That" (featuring Eve, Drag-On, and Shadow). While scads of guest shots are the norm on hip-hop albums and often grow tiresome, most all of them work on *I Want It All* simply because Warren G is, above all, a great producer. He knows how to team rappers together and he knows which types of productions best emphasize their delivery talents. Though *I Want It All* occasionally skirts the borders of hip-hop lite, it's chocked with quality mid-tempo productions and excellent rapping. —*John Bush*

Return of the Regulator / Dec. 11, 2001 / Uptown/Universal ✦✦✦

Return of the Regulator is Warren G's go-for-broke comeback attempt, one that looks good both on paper and in concept as well as in title. Warren has returned here to the basics and reunited with many of those who he initially began his career with, namely Dr. Dre, Nate Dogg, and Snoop Dogg. His concerted efforts, as both a rapper/vocalist and a producer/songwriter, are clearly evident. If anything, *Return of the Regulator* is certainly a considered album. It begins on a high note with a radio-ready Dre production, "Lookin' at You," that finds Warren dueting with Ms. Toi. The next few songs feature collaborations with many of the West Coast's most talented hired hands: Nate Dogg, Soopafly, and Butch Cassidy. George Clinton makes an appearance on "Speed Dreamin'," and Warren reunites with his old school homies Nate Dogg and Snoop (originally a trio known as 213) on one of the album's highlights, "Yo' Sassy Ways." Elsewhere, "Ghetto Village" shamelessly interpolates Stevie Wonder's "Village Ghetto Land" quite notably. From beginning to end, you can sense Warren's sense of purpose here—he knows a rapper's shelf life is brief, and his is running out. He gives you everything he's capable of, from a radio-ready duet to a pop-rap interpolation. Warren wants this to be a strong comeback album. That's obvious. And that's also partly what feels so uneasy about *Return of the Regulator*—you can sense the desperation as well as the calculation. The album is too self-conscious for its own good at times, and as much as he tries, Warren still struggles to rap as eloquently as his colleagues. The end sum of *Return of the Regulator*, then, isn't quite equal to its many parts. Its assembly is nonetheless still a feat, making this Warren's most labored effort to date, even if it isn't quite the red-carpeted return he'd like it to be. —*Jason Birchmeier*

Craig G

East Coast Rap, Hip-Hop, Golden Age

Craig G's two-phased career began in the late '80s when he ran with legendary producer Marley Marl and his Juice Crew posse, and resumed in the early 2000s when he became one of New York's more influential DJs. The Queensbridge rapper teamed with Marley early on, back in 1985, when the two recorded "Shout" and "Transformer," both released by Pop Art Records. Though definitely not as treasured as other Marley classics from the era such as MC Shan's "The Bridge" or Kool G Rap & DJ Polo's "Poison," the recordings were some of the producer's first and remain noteworthy, albeit hard to find, as a result. G's key recordings came shortly afterward, namely the solo "Droppin' Science" and the Juice Crew collaboration "The Symphony" (both 1988). The latter track in particular stands out as a landmark moment in the evolution of hardcore rap, establishing the blueprint that endless East Coast posses like the Wu-Tang Clan would emulate a generation later, yet the former remains probably G's most lasting solo performance; both classics later compiled on Marley's *House of Hits* best-of (1995).

In the wake of "The Symphony," G signed to Atlantic while most of his Juice Crew colleagues remained with Cold Chillin', the label that had long supported the collective; yet, according to G in "The Blues," the label also withheld the rapper's royalty payments. The move from Cold Chillin' to Atlantic proved fatal, as neither of G's albums, *The Kingpin* (1990) and *Now, That's More Like It* (1991), made any impact, even with Marley's production. So, as Juice Crew peers Big Daddy Kane, Biz Markie, Masta Ace, and Kool G

Rap & DJ Polo rose to prominent, long-winded careers, G's simmered quickly. He maintained a low profile for years before finally re-emerging in the late '90s as a moonlighting underground MC, and then in the early 2000s as one of the leading DJs amid New York's competitive field. He more notably contributed to the April 2002 edition of the *Cornerstone Mixtape* series and spun for one of the city's leading rap stations, WZMX Hot 93.7, at the time. —*Jason Birchmeier*

The Kingpin / 1990 / Atlantic ✦

It's not that Craig G and more notably, Marley Marl, didn't make good music and shouldn't be included when looking at old school hip-hop. They did make some good stuff, but not on this album. This is easily the worst work put out by both of these guys. There are ugly and commercial beats, unthoughtful lyrics, and absolutely no vibe to carry this through. It's almost like Craig G forgot how to rap and was trying to improvise his way through or trying to get all the lyrics written in one day. With so many other rappers making good records, this surely isn't going to cut it. —*Brad Mills*

Now, That's More Like It / 1991 / Atlantic ✦✦

● **Cornerstone Mixtape, No. 38** / Apr. 2002 / Cornerstone ✦✦✦

Craig G and DJ Buck throw down for the April 2002 edition of the *Cornerstone Mixtape*. Craig G, the onetime Juice Crew member back in the late '80s/early '90s, represents WZMX Hot 93.7, while Buck represents WWKX Hot 106. Both DJs drop mostly East Coast tracks: Some of the artists Craig G features include Jay-Z ("Guess Who's Back"), GZA ("Fame"), and Mobb Deep ("Get Away"); some of those Buck features include Flipmode ("Here We Go"), Nature ("Nas Is Not"), and Tweet ("Call Me"). Located between the two sets, the "Cornerstone Inter-Mix-Sion" includes Tweet and Jade's "Sexual Healing (Oops, Pt. 2)." In addition, a second disc features more tracks, mostly urban ones with an R&B slant in unmixed, radio-edit format: Angie Stone's "Wish I Didn't Miss You," Nappy Roots' "Po' Folks," and Truth Hurts' "Addictive." The second disc also features a few videos, including Nas' "One Mic." The array of music here is extensive and vast, making *Cornerstone Mixtape, No. 38* a wonderful snapshot of its momentary era. The promotional nature of the double-disc album prevents Craig G and Buck from letting loose as much as they'd probably like, but the resulting listen is nonetheless worthwhile, particularly if you would like to revisit urban music circa mid-2002 for an hour or two. —*Jason Birchmeier*

Gambino Family

Group / Hip-Hop, Gangsta Rap, Southern Rap

The rap group Gambino Family comprised Gotti, Regginelli, P'heno, and Melchior. Their No Limit label debut *Ghetto Organized* was released in 1998. —*Jason Ankeny*

● **Ghetto Organized** / Oct. 20, 1998 / No Limit ✦✦

Anyone familiar with No Limit Records will know what to expect from the Gambino Family's debut album *Ghetto Organized*. They'll even know the cover, thanks to the months and months of advertising in the liner notes of various No Limit releases. That's the Master P game plan—familiarity breeds cash. Such consistent plugging guarantees that the core No Limit audience will try the new albums, which is about the only way to sell an album as stultifying as the Gambino Family's *Ghetto Organized*. Like any release on No Limit, *Ghetto Organized* is filled with cheaply made, bass-heavy jams, and each track features a plethora of guest artists. This time around, however, all the guests feel like camouflage, an effort to disguise the truly unremarkable Gambino Family. There's little or no imagination to the lyrical ideas on the record, nor does the crew flash much verbal dexterity—all of which only emphasizes the lameness of the music. No Limit records are formulaic, but when the formula works, they're effective. When the formula fails, the results are mind-numbingly dull. That's the case here. —*Stephen Thomas Erlewine*

Gamma

f. London, England

Group / British Rap, Underground Rap

British rap trio Gamma formed around a pair of Birmingham MCs, Juice Aleem and Blackitude (aka Ebu). The two were down in London for a rap battle when they met Lord Redeem, a native of the capital who had also spent time in Texas while growing up. The trio began rapping together, though Gamma's debut (on the flip of a 1999 Roots Manuva single on Big Dada) featured just Juice and Ebu. As a trio, their debut was the 2000 single *Black*

Atlantian, also on Big Dada. They followed later that year with a full-length, *Permanament*, featuring production by their loose collective known as Shadowless Productions and Mister Mitchell. Juice Aleem has also worked closely with fellow Big Dada act New Flesh. —*John Bush*

● **Permanament** / Oct. 31, 2000 / Big Dada ✦✦✦
Although British electronic music has long given nods to American hip-hop culture via the gangsta posturing of jungle or the head-nodding tempos of trip-hop, it took an absurdly long time for an island with such a large population of hip-hop consumers to come up with a true hip-hop export worth mentioning. Fortunately, when the Brit-hop scene did finally take hold, it possessed its own cultural subtleties that can be more fresh and invigorating than its overplayed American counterparts. *Permanament* is an album that would never find favor with American audiences, and it is better for it. Because while the production work by Shadowless has the easily recognizable RZA tendency for minor chords, it is dirtied up to a gritty mishmash of sounds that is proudly part of parent label Ninja Tune's Wall of Sound approach to hip-hop music. MCs Blacktude, Aleem Juice, and Lord Redeem all rhyme with a British-accent-meets-Caribbean-patois, courtesy of their island heritage. This makes for a cadence that is more musical than the straight ebonics of U.S. rappers. And as a unit, the trio shadowboxes like the best moments of Jurassic 5 before coming together for the chanting choruses. So street they don't have to proclaim it, Gamma is the overseas alternative in a country that is equally as saturated by P. Diddy as the U.S. is. —*Joshua Glazer*

Gang Starr

f. 1988

Group / Hip-Hop, East Coast Rap, Golden Age, Jazz-Rap
Never overly prolific nor overly popular, Gang Starr nonetheless became and remains one of hip-hop's most admired acts ever, the duo's legacy nothing short of legendary in terms of influence. DJ Premier and Guru, the duo's respective producer/DJ and lyricist/MC, set standards for early-'90s hip-hop with their two touchstone releases: *Step in the Arena* (1991) and *Daily Operation* (1992). Beginning with these releases, both listeners and critics heaped mounds of praise on Premier and Guru—the former because of his DJ-style beatmaking and jazzy sound, the latter because of his socially conscious lyrics and no-nonsense stance. Following these two undisputed classics, Premier became one of New York's most demanded producers and crafted hits for the city's finest MCs: the Notorious B.I.G., Nas, Jay-Z, KRS-One, and more. Guru likewise collaborated with plenty of famous artists—Roy Ayers, Donald Byrd, N'Dea Davenport, and more—on his solo debut, *Jazzmatazz, Vol. 1*. After this point, however, Gang Starr became somewhat of a side project for Premier and Guru, who both forged on with their respective solo careers. More albums came—each impressive, beginning with the tough *Hard to Earn* album in 1994—yet Gang Starr had already attained their summit of popularity and acclaim in the early '90s and, as a result, continually battled their own growing legacy, as fans billed every successive album as a comeback.

Premier and Guru began humbly enough, releasing *No More Mr. Nice Guy* (1989), an ambitious debut album seeking to heavily incorporate a jazz aesthetic into hip-hop. Ambitious or not, the formative album didn't impress too many (though there were promising moments like "Manifest" and "DJ Premier in Deep Concentration"), and Gang Starr took two years to reconsider their approach. The duo then returned with a new record label and a fresh approach. It worked marvelously as *Step in the Arena* (1991) set new standards with not only its beats but also its lyrics. Premier had blossomed into one of New York's most savvy producer/DJs, capable of using samples in ways never before imagined and garnered much acclaim for his subtle use of jazz. Similarly, Guru's literate, thoughtful, and, most of all, earnest lyrics stood out among the brash materialism increasingly plaguing the genre, and his trademark monotone delivery didn't hurt either. A year later came *Daily Operation* (1992). If *Step in the Arena* had been and remains a masterpiece, this album is nothing short of that mark; in fact, it's generally viewed as Gang Starr's crowning achievement.

While both *Step in the Arena* and *Daily Operation* astounded critics and street-level listeners, the albums never inspired any big breakthrough hits, and Gang Starr remained somewhat of a cult favorite. Songs like "Just to Get a Rep," "Step in the Arena," "Take It Personal," and "Soliloquy of Chaos" became underground classics but never crossed over to the mainstream.

Despite Premier's reputation as a hitmaker, Gang Starr openly spurned "mass appeal" and refused to adjust their style to any sort of trend. *Hard to Earn* (1994) strongly confirmed this anticommercial stance, especially the "Mass Appeal" single, and the duo didn't return until four years later with *Moment of Truth* (1998) and *Full Clip* (1999) shortly after. The former album and its big single, "You Know My Steez," proved that, despite Gang Starr's long absence, Premier and Guru could still make excellent hip-hop—an entire album of it, in fact. The latter album, a double-disc retrospective commemorating Gang Starr's ten-year anniversary, showcased some of the duo's best moments and added some bonuses for longtime fans.

Following the best-of collection, Premier and Guru quietly rested the Gang Starr moniker. Even so, they remained active over the years: Guru continued releasing star-studded solo albums, and Premier continued producing countless tracks for New York's finest. While it's somewhat ironic that Premier produced so many across-the-board hits for others but not himself, Gang Starr never attained Nas- or Jay-Z-level stardom *because* of their uncompromising, somewhat highbrow style, something which the two refused to dilute with mass appeal, precisely the reason why their influence has proven so timeless. —*Jason Birchmeier*

No More Mr. Nice Guy / 1989 / Wild Pitch ✦✦✦
You don't hear much of *Step in the Arena* on Gang Starr's first album. In fact, aside from some scrupulous lyrical stances by Guru ("Manifest," "Positivity") and some of DJ Premier's hallmark brilliance behind the turntables, this Gang Starr isn't instantly recognizable as the duo that would soon become one of the most respected rap groups of the 1990s. The Gang Starr of *No More Mr. Nice Guy* still has a leg knee-deep in the old school aesthetic. As a result, Premier's beats are quite a bit simpler and sometimes cruder than we would come to expect from him (though still several cuts above the rest of the class), and Guru spends considerable energy talking up his own microphone skills and tearing down the next MC's (sometimes electrifyingly, as on "Gotch U"). That is not the same thing, however, as saying that *No More Mr. Nice Guy* is a subpar album. It is not, by any means. In fact, it is quite good in its way, but it is also safe to say that the recording is not representative of the Chrysalis-era Gang Starr devotees would eventually come to revere. Approach the album on its own terms, though, and it has a lot to offer, namely its early, tentative steps into the sampling of jazz. The most conspicuous attempt in this direction is the fine "Jazz Music," which was, nevertheless, reworked to much better effect a few years later for the soundtrack to Spike Lee's *Mo' Better Blues* as "Jazz Thing." The scratching showcase "DJ Premier in Deep Concentration" is an antiquated delight that dips into jazz as well, while the conscientious "Cause and Effect," steely "2 Steps Ahead," and uncharacteristic guest production from DJ Mark the 45 King, "Gusto," are all classics waiting to be rediscovered. Indicative or not, fans of the group will want this album, as will those with a jones for the original new school revolution. More casual fans can probably start their collections with *Step in the Arena*, which *is* a required purchase. [The 2001 Wild Pitch Classics reissue adds three bonus tracks, the strongest of which is "Here's the Proof."] —*Stanton Swihart*

☆ **Step in the Arena** / 1991 / Chrysalis ✦✦✦✦✦
The album on which DJ Premier and Guru perfected the template that would launch them into underground stardom and a modicum of mainstream success. Guru's deadpan monotone delivery was shockingly different from other early-'90s MCs, many of who were either substituting charisma for substance or engaging in hardcore "realism" without really commenting on black inner-city life or offering ways to alter the situation for the better. But it is Guru who sounded like the real clarion call of and to the street on *Step in the Arena* ("Why bring ignorance/where we're inviting you to get advancement," he intones on "Form of Intellect"). *Step in the Arena* was the first real mature flowering of his streetwise sagacity. His voice would grow more assured by the next album, but here Guru imparts urban wisdom of a strikingly visible variety. It's easy to allow yourself to get caught up in the fantasy of hardcore rap, but it is somewhat more involving and disorienting to hear truth that avoids exaggeration or glorification. Guru is not easy on any aspect of the inner city, from the "snakes" that exploit the community ("Execution of a Chump") to those that are a product of it ("Just to Get a Rep"), and the result is a surprising but hard-fought compassion ("Who's Gonna Take the Weight?" pleads for the acceptance of responsibility, for not taking the easy path). He seems to have somehow developed a hopefulness out of the bleak

surroundings. DJ Premier was already near the top of his game at this early point. His production seems less jazz fueled on *Step in the Arena*, opting more for spare guitar lines and tight beats, as well as his unmistakable vocal cut-up style of scratching for a slightly warped and out-of-phase soundscape. —*Stanton Swihart*

★ **Daily Operation** / May 5, 1992 / Chrysalis ✦✦✦✦✦
On *Step in the Arena*, DJ Premier and Guru hit upon their mature sound, characterized by sparse, live jazz samples, Premier's cut-up scratching, and Guru's direct, unwavering streetwise monotone; but with *Daily Operation* the duo made their first masterpiece. From beginning to end, Gang Starr's third full-length album cuts with the force and precision of a machete and serves as an ode to and representation of New York and hip-hop underground culture. The genius of *Daily Operation* is that Guru's microphone skills are perfectly married to the best batch of tracks Premier had ever come up with. Guru has more of a presence than he has ever had, slinking and pacing through each song like a man with things on his mind, ready to go off at any second. Premier's production has an unparalleled edge here. He created the minimalist opening track, "The Place Where We Dwell," out of a two-second drum-solo sample and some scratching, but is also able to turn around and create something as lush and melodic as the jazz-tinged "No Shame in My Game" without ever seeming to be out of his element, making every track of the same sonic mind. For an underground crew, Gang Starr has always had a knack for crafting memorable vocal hooks to go with the expert production, and they multiply both aspects on *Daily Operation*. Every song has some attribute that stamps it indelibly into the listener's head, and it marks the album as one of the finest of the decade, rap or otherwise. —*Stanton Swihart*

Hard to Earn / Mar. 8, 1994 / Chrysalis ✦✦✦✦
Gang Starr came out hard on their 1994 album, *Hard to Earn*, an album notably different from its two predecessors: *Step in the Arena* (1991) and *Daily Operation* (1992). While those two classic albums garnered tremendous praise for their thoughtful lyrics and jazzy beats, *Hard to Earn* seems much more reactionary, especially its lyrics. Guru opens the album with a tough, dismissive spoken-word intro: "Yo, all you kids want to get on and sh*t/Just remember this/This sh*t ain't easy/If you ain't got it, you ain't got it, motherf*cker." While this sense of superiority is undoubtedly a long-running convention of not just East Coast rap but rap in general, you don't expect to hear it coming from Gang Starr, particularly with such a bitter tone. Yet this attitude pervades throughout *Hard to Earn*. Songs such as "Suckas Need Bodyguards" and "Mass Appeal" take aim at unnamed peers, and other songs such as "ALONGWAYTOGO" similarly center on "whack crews." The best moments on *Hard to Earn* aren't these songs but instead "Code of the Streets" and "Tonz 'O' Gunz," two songs where Guru offers the type of social commentary that made Gang Starr so admirable in the first place. Yet, even though *Hard to Earn* is a bit short on such thoughtful moments, instead weighed down a bit with harsh attitude, it does offer some of DJ Premier's best productions ever. He's clearly at—or, at least, near—his best here. There isn't a song on the album that's a throwaway, and even the interludes are stunning. Given the subtly bitter tone of this album, it perhaps wasn't surprising that Guru and Premier took some time to pursue solo opportunities after *Hard to Earn*. You can sense the duo's frustration with the rap scene circa 1994. The two didn't return with another Gang Starr album until four years later when they dropped *Moment of Truth*, a succinct comeback album that reaffirmed their status as one of New York's most thoughtful and artistic rap acts. —*Jason Birchmeier*

Moment of Truth / Mar. 31, 1998 / Noo Trybe ✦✦✦
By the release of *Moment of Truth* in the spring of 1998, Gang Starr were rap veterans, having spent nearly ten years as professionals. That elapsed time meant that the album was positioned as something of a comeback, since the duo had been inactive for four years, and it had been even longer since they had a hit. They knew they had to come back hard, and *Moment of Truth* almost accomplishes their goals. Retaining the swing of their jazz-rap fusions, Gang Starr nevertheless have their rhythms hit at a street level, and Guru's rhymes are his best in years. It may not have the thrill of discovery that made their first albums so exciting, and it does suffer from a few slow spots, but on the whole it's a successful return. —*Stephen Thomas Erlewine*

Full Clip: A Decade of Gang Starr / Mar. 23, 1999 / Cooltempo ✦✦✦✦✦
Considering that the only previous hip-hop hits collection to stretch two full CDs came from 2Pac (and that only after his death), Gang Starr's *Full Clip* is

a surprising release, though it's incredibly welcome. The duo of DJ Premier and Guru has been one of the longest continuous acts on the rap scene, beginning with 1989's *No More Mr. Nice Guy* and a spot on the soundtrack to Spike Lee's 1990 film *Mo' Better Blues*. And as demonstrated by Premier's stunning productions on classic early tracks like "Who's Gonna Take the Weight," "Words I Manifest," and "Just to Get a Rep," Gang Starr hit its stride early, and just kept on hitting peak after peak during the '90s with "Speak Ya Clout," "Code of the Streets," "Tonz 'O' Gunz," and "You Know My Steez." And new tracks, usually the bane of any best-of collection, provide quite a few highlights here—including "Full Clip," "Discipline" (featuring Total), and "All 4 Tha Ca$h." Also, the set compiles several notable B sides—"The ? Remainz," "Credit Is Due," and "You Know My Steez (Remix)"—as well as soundtrack works like "1/2 & 1/2" (from *Blade*), "Gotta Get Over" (from *Trespass*), and "The Militia II (Remix)" (from *Belly*). Though Guru's monotone raps can grate over the course of two hours, *Full Clip* documents one of the best, most underrated hip-hop groups ever, from their jazzy beginnings into Premier's harder productions from the mid-'90s and beyond. —*John Bush*

Gangsta Blac

b. Memphis, TN
Dirty South, Hardcore Rap
Long recognized as one of Memphis' top MCs, Gangsta Blac remained strictly an underground phenomenon before breaking out of the South in the early 2000s. His career began as a member of the Memphis-based Three 6 Mafia clique before going solo in the mid-'90s. Influenced by the harsh ghetto rap of Eightball & MJG and the Geto Boys, Gangsta Blac's music incorporates the bleak ideology of gangsta rap with a Southern attitude and rowdy dirty South beats. His hit single "Southern Parkway" extended the artist's reach beyond Memphis, getting substantial airplay in other Southern rap hotspots such as Atlanta, Birmingham, and Houston. In 2001 his *Down South Flava* positioned Gangsta Blac on the verge of spreading his reach even further out of the South thanks to the rising levels of attention being focused on Southern rappers. —*Jason Birchmeier*

● **I Am Da Gangsta** / Dec. 15, 1998 / Super Sigg ✦✦✦
Although it still falls prey to some tired gangsterisms, Gangsta Blac's second album *I Am Da Gangsta* is a marked improvement from his debut, in particular with his rapping—both his style and his lyrics are more forceful and incisive. Similarly, the music itself is more authoratative, even if it is at times a tad staid and predictable. What counts is that Gangsta Blac frequently fulfills the potential he illustrated on *Can It Be* with *I Am Da Gangsta*. He might not be the definitive gangsta, but he is on his way to being worthy of the title. —*Leo Stanley*

Gangsta Boo (Lola Mitchell)

b. Memphis, TN
Hardcore Rap, Southern Rap, Gangsta Rap, Dirty South, Dirty Rap
An anomaly within the generally misogynist late-'90s dirty South rap scene, Gangsta Boo won substantial acclaim among audiences without sacrificing her pride. As a member of Memphis, TN, hardcore rap group Three 6 Mafia, she had held her own; it wasn't until her debut album, though, that she really started garnering an unprecedented amount of attention. Under the wings of Three 6 Mafia leaders Juicy "J" and DJ Paul's production, *Enquiring Minds* found Gangsta Boo confronting the lyrical issues that hardcore female rappers such as Lil' Kim have to address: sexual politics, money-hungry stereotypes, proving that a female can be hardcore, and so on. Then after the success of this album, she played an important role in the success of Three 6 Mafia's *When the Smoke Clears* in 2000. She has also appeared as a member of Tear da Club Up Thugs and Hypnotize Camp Posse. —*Jason Birchmeier*

● **Enquiring Minds** / Sep. 29, 1998 / Relativity ✦✦✦
The first proper Three 6 Mafia solo album, Gangsta Boo's *Enquiring Minds* quickly elevated her to celebrity status among Three 6 Mafia's cult audience of fanatics, and also garnered her substantial respect from both her broader set of fans and from the Southern rap scene as well. In all honesty, it's a fairly standard affair for producers Juicy "J" and DJ Paul, who had their duties down to assembly line efficiency at this point in late 1998, churning out multiple records a year. Yet the fact that Gangsta Boo is a female MC in a genre that tends to hold a rather misogynist stance against women and also tends to be overly lacking in female MCs is indeed notable. This anomaly actually works

in Gangsta Boo's favor here, though, as she is able to toy with such intriguing topics as sexual politics and being hardcore from the female point of view. Sure, this album isn't a masterpiece, but it is a bit of landmark given Gangsta Boo's gender and her respect-demanding performance. —*Jason Birchmeier*

Both Worlds *69 / Jun. 26, 2001 / Relativity ✦✦✦
Gangsta Boo first came on the scene in 1998 with her successful and superficial single "Where Dem Dollars At?" *Both Worlds: *69*, produced by hip-hop heavyweights DJ Paul and Juicy "J," is more of the same. Like "Where Dem Dollars At?," tracks like "Can I Get Paid" are drenched in shallow materialism. When not obsessing over dollars, Gangsta Boo focuses on raw sexuality with tracks like "I Faked It." Gangsta Boo shows some signs of growth, particularly on the song "You Gonna Be a Victim" and "Hard Not to Kill," but too often she relies on previous successes, rather than look toward the future. —*Jon Azpiri*

Gangsta Pat (Patrick Hall)

Gangsta Rap, Hardcore Rap, Dirty South
One of the first Memphis rappers to make the major-label jump, Gangsta Pat never attained the acclaim or success of fellow Memphis pioneers Three 6 Mafia and Eightball & MJG, yet he still remains noteworthy for his trailblazing. Pat's career began promisingly when Atlantic signed him at the dawn of the gangsta rap era and released *#1 Suspect* (1991) as well as two accompanying singles, "I'm tha Gangsta" and "Gangsta's Need Love 2." Like most of Atlantic's other rap releases from the time, Pat's debut made little impact, quickly going out of print and leaving the rapper without a recording contract soon after. Pat returned to the underground the next year with Wrap Records, a short-lived indie label distributed by Ichiban. Wrap released two Pat albums, *All About Comin' Up* (1992) and *Sex, Money & Murder* (1994), as well as two respective singles, "Gangsta Boogie" and "That Type of Gangsta." Once again, Pat found little success beyond the Atlanta-Memphis axis and thus packed his bags, moving to Power Records for *Deadly Verses* (1995) and *Homicidal Lifestyle* (1997). These two albums showcased a more introspective and mature style, as Pat sped up his flow à la Bone and darkened his themes à la Three 6 Mafia. Regardless, despite the cult following he began to garner with these two highly regarded albums, he couldn't translate the support into national sales, and he moved on to yet another label, Redrum. He remained there for quite a while, releasing a string of albums beginning with *The Story of My Life* (1997) that tended to emulate the trends of their respective eras. Perhaps as a plea for much-needed publicity, Pat targeted Three 6 Mafia on his 1999 album, *Tear Yo Club Down*, with a pointed dis track. —*Jason Birchmeier*

#1 Suspect / 1991 / Atlantic ✦
Popularized by Ice-T, N.W.A, and Eazy-E in the late '80s, gangsta rap was at first a riveting depiction of the horrors of ghetto life. But the music industry—true to form—reduced it to a shallow formula and milked it for all it was worth. Countless clone artists, one just as faceless as the next, flooded the market in the early 1990s. One of them was Gangsta Pat, who hails from Memphis but sounds like he could be from Compton, CA, or South Central L.A. Offering very little originality, *#1 Suspect* is a perfect example of the unimaginative nature of so much of the gangsta rap that labels were quick to record at the time. The rap ballad "Gangster's Need Love 2" is a fairly entertaining bit of dark humor, but tracks like "Legion of Doom," "Project Pimps," and "Gangster Shit" are cliché ridden and painfully generic. Hip-hop aficionados should be sure to avoid this CD. —*Alex Henderson*

Homicidal Lifestyle / Jan. 14, 1997 / Power ✦✦
As the kingpin of Memphis, Gangsta Pat tends to get overlooked in the gangsta rap wars, and for good reason—there's no competition in Memphis. Sure, there are a few other rappers, but for the most part, Gangsta Pat works in a vacuum, and that's the reason why *Homicidal Lifestyle* is so predictable, featuring the same beats and rhymes as his previous albums, which are not all that dissimilar from N.W.A and Dr. Dre records. Granted, *Homicidal Lifestyle* has a couple of good grooves and rhymes scattered throughout the album, but it's hard to take any record whose highlight is a by-the-books party number called "I Wanna Smoke" all that seriously. —*Leo Stanley*

The Story of My Life / May 13, 1997 / Redrum ✦✦
After a few shoddy efforts that were notable mostly because they came out of the South at a time when rap was primarily a West and East Coast phenomenon, Gangsta Pat released *The Story of My Life*, the inaugural release

on the Redrum label. It's fairly ambitious relative to his preceding albums, often drifting into contemporary R&B with a gangsta rap edge—best exemplified on "G's Ain't Suppose to Cry" and "Sittin on tha Porch"—while still keeping its focus on a hardcore gangsta sound. —*Jason Birchmeier*

● **Tear Yo Club Down** / Nov. 9, 1999 / Redrum ✦✦✦
One of Gangsta Pat's more notable releases, *Tear Yo Club Down* features the fiery title track, which is a pointed dis toward fellow Memphis rappers Three 6 Mafia, who also happen to be substantially more popular. The track is clearly a plea for publicity, but it's nonetheless one of Gangsta Pat's most spirited performances ever and highlights an otherwise OK batch of material that's generally on a par with the bulk of the rapper's prolific 1990s output. —*Jason Birchmeier*

Show Ya Grill / Nov. 7, 2000 / Redrum ✦✦
On his third solo album for Redrum Records (and fourth overall if you count the first Die Hard Organization album), talented Memphis, TN, dirty South auteur Gangsta Pat again proves his talents by doing virtually everything: rapping, producing, keyboards, guitar, bass, mixing, and anything else he can imagine to credit himself for in the liner notes. His ability to handle this broad scope of duties effectively proves to be even more impressive, although it's debatable whether he's a better producer than he is a rapper. Unfortunately, talent doesn't necessarily imply originality, and Gangsta Pat struggles to do anything particularly inventive here. Both the production and rapping on *Show Ya Grill* emulate popular dirty South motifs at the time of its release in late 2000, though his inclusion of guitar into the sporadic drum machine beats is admittedly engaging. During the many self-serving moments such as "Interview #1" and "Commercial #2" it starts to become increasingly apparent that Gangsta Pat's strengths lie more in his ability to create a commercial product than creative music. He's essentially making trendy music and doing it in an efficient manner, just as he'd been doing annually for nearly a decade (reprising two of his classic tracks, "I'm tha Gangsta" and "Shootin' on Narks," just in case you forgot how long he'd been in the game). —*Jason Birchmeier*

Ganksta N-I-P

Gangsta Rap, Hardcore Rap, Southern Rap
While growing up in Houston's South Park—also the home of the Geto Boys, Scarface, and 5th Ward Boyz—Ganksta N-I-P was influenced by the rhyming skills of Ice-T and the Nation of Islam knowledge of Rakim. The former Rowdy Jones named himself Ganksta N-I-P—NIP stands for "Nation of Islam is powerful"—and began rapping himself, releasing his first album, *South Park Psycho*, early in the '90s. It sold almost 100,000 copies around the area, and sparked a contract with Priority. Second album *Psychic Thoughts* did even better, and N-I-P worked with an assortment of producers (411, N.O. Joe, Mic B, Information Booth, Swift, and Johnny Cage) to record his third, 1996's *Psychic Thoughts*. *Interview With a Killa* was released in June 1998. —*John Bush*

● **Interview With a Killa** / Jun. 30, 1998 / Rap-A-Lot ✦✦✦✦
Ganksta N-I-P's fourth album, *Interview With a Killa*, doesn't find the Houston-based rapper trying anything new, but it's the best collection of Southern-fried, funky hardcore hip-hop that he's yet assembled. His lyrics are focused, blistering with anger and intelligence, while his music is similarly clear eyed, with hard-hitting rhythms balanced by funky grooves and real instrumentation. It's a dynamic blend that illustrates exactly why N-I-P is one of Houston's best rappers. —*Leo Stanley*

G.A.T.

Group / West Coast Rap, Contemporary R&B, Hip-Hop, Gangsta Rap, Hardcore Rap
A most unusual R&B quartet that came out of Los Angeles in the early '90s, G.A.T. combined 1970s-influenced soul singing with the imagery and themes of gangsta rap. G.A.T. (Gangstas and Thugs) was hardly the only R&B act that was heavily influenced by hip-hop, but it was certainly among the few that embraced the type of thug-life lyrics associated with N.W.A, Ice-T, the Geto Boys, and 2Pac. Reviewers gave G.A.T.'s music such unlikely descriptions as "N.W.A meets the Chi-Lites" and "Ice-T meets the Dramatics," and the quartet really was that unorthodox. Dressing like gangsta rappers, singers Wesley Johnson III, Kenneth Blue, Tyrone Butterfield, and Andrew Sanders gave gritty, troubling, first-person accounts of such things as gang warfare and serving hard time in prison. But G.A.T. was equally convincing when it came

to delivering a silky, 1970s-influenced soul ballad or interpreting the Persuaders' classic "Thin Love Between Love and Hate." The quartet signed with MCA in 1994, and its debut album, *Just Another Day*, came out in 1995. Regrettably, the album didn't sell, and after being dropped by MCA, G.A.T. didn't resurface on another label. —*Alex Henderson*

● **Just Another Day** / Apr. 25, 1995 / MCA ✦✦
One of the most amazingly unorthodox releases of 1995, *Just Another Day* successfully unites West Coast gangsta rap with classic 1970s soul. It may seem an unlikely combination, but in fact, G.A.T. (whose name stands for Gangstas & Thugs) really does bridge the gap between N.W.A and groups like the Dramatics, the O'Jays and the Chi-Lites on this dynamic CD. One minute, this L.A. group is delivering the silkiest, smoothest, and most romantic of soul singing, and the next are rapping about the horrors of gang warfare, black-on-black crime, and incarceration. And the whole thing sounds organic and natural, never forced or contrived. A similar approach had been taken by the group DRI in 1993, but G.A.T. clearly has a vision and style of its own. —*Alex Henderson*

Genelic (Evan Gatica)

Underground Rap
Genelic (aka Evan Gatica) and fellow MC Memphis Reigns released their debut, *Scorpion Circles*, in late 2002 to considerable acclaim in the underground hip-hop community. With dark, moody production from Genelic himself (on his computer, no less), the debut shed light on the promising MC from Santa Cruz, CA. —*Johnny Loftus*

● **Scorpion Circles** / 2002 / ✦✦✦
Santa Cruz MCs Genelic and Memphis Reigns come off as smooth, and admirably assured, on their full-length debut, *Scorpion Circles*. The duo passes the mic back and forth seamlessly, trading fast-paced flows with an infectious exuberance. While pointedly verbose, the lyrics manage to avoid, for the most part, needless grandiloquence. The subject matter tends toward the abstract, which is where these talented MCs occasionally get off track. While the contemplative nature of the vocals is refreshing—musing about transformation, (psychic) movement, and the power of language—there are moments when it all gets a bit too meandering and vague. The competent, varied production here helps to minimize that, and mixes things up nicely. Complementary but never obtrusive, the low end ranges from soft, sleepy drums to greasy beats and rumbling bass lines. Relying heavily on moody symphonics—snatches of drifting horns, melancholy guitars, baroque horns, stark Chinese harps—the music both drives and matches the deeply reflective, yearning quality of the vocals: bolstering the imagistic, strongly poetic moments that stand out the most here. —*Martin Woodside*

Genius (Gary Grice)

b. Staten Island, NY, **db.** Aug. 22, 1966
Hip-Hop, East Coast Rap, Hardcore Rap
The Genius, aka the GZA, was the most cerebral MC in the Wu-Tang Clan, as well as perhaps the most acclaimed. His cool, precise flow and intricate, literate rhymes weren't as theatrical as Method Man or Ol' Dirty Bastard, the two biggest commercial stars to spring from the collective. But among hip-hop aficionados, the Genius was revered for his flawless technique and lyrical dexterity, and was considered by many to be the best pure rapper in the entire Clan. The Genius was born Gary Grice on August 22, 1966, in Staten Island, NY, and shuttled between several other New York boroughs with various relatives during his childhood. He started learning rhymes by the earliest hip-hop MCs while spending time in the Bronx, and returned to Staten Island to share them with his cousins, who later became Ol' Dirty Bastard and the RZA. In fact, the three of them first teamed up in the early '80s as part of an obscure group called All in Together Now.

Time passed, and the Genius landed a recording contract with Cold Chillin', which, unfortunately, was nearing the end of its brilliant run. In 1991 he became the only future Wu-Tang member to release a solo album prior to the Clan's formation, with *Words From the Genius*. Produced mostly by Easy Mo Bee, the album flopped badly and, creatively, did little to hint at the Genius' future standing. Conflicts with the label sent the Genius packing, and he reteamed with a similarly disenchanted RZA (fresh off a failed stint with Tommy Boy) and Ol' Dirty Bastard to cofound the Wu-Tang Clan. Adding six other friends and associates, the group became an underground sensation

and took the rap world by storm with its 1993 debut *Enter the Wu-Tang (36 Chambers)*. Their innovative contract allowed each member to sign a solo deal with whatever label they chose, and the Genius wound up on Geffen. In 1994 his first post-Wu solo track, "I Gotcha Back," appeared on the soundtrack of the film *Fresh*. His second solo album, *Liquid Swords*, followed in 1995 and was hailed as a hip-hop classic thanks to its coolly understated menace. While it didn't make him a star on the level of Method Man, the album did sell well, reaching the pop Top Ten and falling one spot short of the top of the R&B charts. There were no big mainstream hits, but the title cut, "Cold World," and "Shadowboxin'" all did well on the rap charts.

Following the Clan's 1997 sophomore set *Wu-Tang Forever*, the Genius returned to the solo arena with 1999's *Beneath the Surface*. While critics didn't praise it quite as lavishly as *Liquid Swords*, it was another well-received effort (especially compared to some of the lackluster follow-ups elsewhere in the Wu-Tang camp), and it topped the R&B album charts. After reconvening with the Wu for 2000's *The W* and 2001's *Iron Flag*, the Genius dropped his fourth solo effort, *Legend of the Liquid Sword*, in late 2002, consolidating his reputation as one of the most skillful rappers around. —*Steve Huey*

Words From the Genius / 1991 / Cold Chillin' ✦✦
When the Wu-Tang Clan came out of the gate in late 1993, they brought with them a new style, a style that literally changed the rap game just as Dr. Dre had done a year earlier. But even though it seemed like the Wu came from nowhere, they actually had a rather modest beginning. *Words From the Genius* is that beginning. Released in 1991 on the once-mighty Cold Chillin' label, the album features the Genius, and to a lesser degree RZA (here known as Prince Rakeem), in rather pedestrian form (sorry, no Marley Marl beats here). When you consider Cold Chillin's roster in 1991—most notably Big Daddy Kane and Kool G Rap—*Words From the Genius* seems to be a perfect fit. Like those two rappers, the Genius merged bravado with the darkside of street life and delivered his street-smart rhymes with muscle. The Genius unfortunately sounds kind of flat here; not just because you've come to know him as GZA, the most insightful and lyrically dexterous member of the Wu, but mostly because he hasn't yet honed those qualities, instead emulating his Cold Chillin' peers. Wu devotees should nonetheless find *Words From the Genius* at least somewhat of a novelty, and Cold Chillin' fans will find that it's a decent, though often dismissed, entry in the label's canon. —*Jason Birchmeier*

★ **Liquid Swords** / Nov. 1995 / Geffen ✦✦✦✦✦
Often acclaimed as the best Wu-Tang solo project of all, *Liquid Swords* cemented the Genius/GZA's reputation as the best pure lyricist in the group—and one of the best of the '90s. Rich in allusions and images, his cerebral, easy-flowing rhymes are perhaps the subtlest and most nuanced of any Wu MC, as underscored by his smooth, low-key delivery. The Genius' eerie calm is a great match for RZA's atmospheric production, which is tremendously effective in this context; the kung fu dialogue here is among the creepiest he's put on record, and he experiments quite a bit with stranger sounds and more layered tracks. Not only is RZA in top form, but every Clan member makes at least one appearance on the album, making it all the more impressive that *Liquid Swords* clearly remains the Genius' showcase throughout. All of his collaborators shape themselves to his quietly intimidating style, giving *Liquid Swords* a strongly consistent tone and making it an album that gradually slithers its way under your skin. Mixing gritty story songs and battle rhymes built on elaborate metaphors (martial arts and chess are two favorites), the Genius brings his lyrical prowess to the forefront of every track, leaving no doubt about how he earned his nickname. Creepily understated tracks like "Liquid Swords," "Cold World," "Investigative Reports," and "I Gotcha Back" are the album's bread and butter, but there's the occasional lighter moment ("Labels" incorporates the names of as many record companies as possible) and spiritual digression ("Basic Instructions Before Leaving Earth"). Overall, though, *Liquid Swords* is possibly the most unsettling album in the Wu canon (even ahead of Ol' Dirty Bastard), and it ranks with *Enter the Wu-Tang (36 Chambers)* and Raekwon's *Only Built 4 Cuban Linx* as one of the group's undisputed classics. —*Steve Huey*

Beneath the Surface / Jun. 29, 1999 / MCA ✦✦✦✦✦
There were so many Wu-Tang-related projects released during 1998 and 1999 that listeners—and even fans—could be forgiven for a bit of apathy regarding the second solo effort by Wu-Tang's Genius/GZA. The collective's trademark detuned strings had gone from *de rigueur* to downright dated by mid-1999, and except for a well-received RZA solo album earlier in the year, the lead in

hip-hop's hype game appeared to have been taken over by Timbaland's brand of future funk. It may not have proved the commercial smash of a proper Wu-Tang LP, but Genius/GZA's *Beneath the Surface* is a worthy continuation and development of the Wu-Tang Clan conglomeration. The best tracks here, "Amplified Sample" and "Crash Your Crew," are quintessentially Wu-Tang, but with important tweaks to the trademark sound. The crisp, clean production—by Wu associates Inspectah Deck, Mathematics, and Arabian Priest—sounds much better than any project that had been recently issued (even RZA's *Bobby Digital*), and GZA's raps prove he's the most innovative and talented vocalist Wu-Tang had to offer. The only failure (at least in terms of sound) is "Victim," a cloying track with a bit of scratched acoustic guitar and some *X Files*-styled strings. Other than a few "skits" that disturb the flow, *Beneath the Surface* is arguably the best thing to come out of the Wu camp since their second proper album, *Forever*. —*John Bush*

Legend of the Liquid Sword / Dec. 10, 2002 / MCA ✦✦✦
Released at the end of a quiet year for the Wu-Tang family, GZA's *Legend of the Liquid Sword* proves Gary Grice is easily the most underrated rapper in the fold, and definitely the most consistent as a solo artist. The album gains power as it progresses; after a compelling "Auto Bio" that's chained down by a bland production, and "Did Ya Say That," wherein the Genius sounds downright confused (or worse, resigned) about the game of label politics, *Legend of the Liquid Sword* locks into a great groove with the single "Knock, Knock" and rarely misses after that. Unsurprisingly, the Wu-Tang features "Fam (Members Only)," featuring RZA and Masta Killa, and "Silent," featuring Ghostface Killah, are big highlights, with a sound similar to 2001's *Iron Flag*. Surprisingly, though, his track with low-profile Wu-Tang member Inspectah Deck bests the other two. "Fame" finds the Genius weaving some clever word games around celebrity names, and guest Allen Anthony makes the title track into a grand funk jam akin to OutKast. The productions on *Legend of the Liquid Sword* are below average for a talent like his, but chances are good that's by design; since GZA is a rapper's rapper, his smooth flow and excellent imagination are all that's necessary to propel any of these tracks. —*John Bush*

Gerardo (Gerardo Mejía)

b. Apr. 16, 1965, Guayaquil, Ecuador
Pop-Rap
Ecuadorian-born Gerardo became a chart topper after issuing a single called "Rico Suave," which was featured in his 1991 debut album, *Mo' Ritmo*; in addition, the album contains a cover of George Clinton's "We Want the Funk." Chuck Reed produced his following album, *Dos*, in 1992. Gerardo established himself as one of the first breakthrough Latin dance performers singing in the English/Spanish mixture known as Spanglish. After releasing 1994's *Asi Es* and 1995's *Derrumbe*, the Latin rap artist returned in 2001 with *Gerardo: Fame, Sex y Dinero*, which features the hit single "Sigo Siendo Rico." —*Drago Bonacich*

● **Mo' Ritmo** / 1991 / Interscope ✦✦✦
It's hard to imagine a rap album produced by pop singer Michael Sembello (best known for his 1983 hit "Maniac" from the film *Flashdance*) being terribly hardcore, and hardcore is one thing *Mo' Ritmo* definitely isn't. A pop-rap effort with Latin touches, *Mo' Ritmo* was dismissed by hip-hop's hardcore, but did well among pop audiences. Gerardo isn't a great rapper any more than this is a great album, but some of the songs are catchy enough—most notably, "Fandango," "Latin Till I Die" (which employs the groove to Tito Puente's salsa classic "Oye Como Va"), and the hits "Rico Suave" and "We Want the Funk." Most of the lyrics are in English, though Gerardo also does a fair amount of rapping in Spanish. Though the CD has its moments, Gerardo's limitations are obvious. After enjoying his 15 minutes of fame with *Mo Ritmo*, Gerardo was quickly forgotten by the fickle teen audience. —*Alex Henderson*

Dos / 1992 / Interscope ✦✦
Dance-pop and teen pop audiences can be incredibly fickle, and no one knows that better than Gerardo. In 1991 the Ecuadorian pop-rapper's debut album, *Mo' Ritmo*, was a major hit in the dance-pop and teen markets. Hip-hop's hardcore gave Gerardo little or no respect, but the teenagers and young adults who listened to Exposé, Debbie Gibson, the Cover Girls, and Kylie Minogue loved him—for about a year, that is. When Gerardo followed up *Mo' Ritmo* with 1992's *Dos*, he got a rude awakening. Commercially,

this sophomore effort was a disappointment; many of the teens who bought *Mo' Ritmo* ignored *Dos*, which is quite similar to its predecessor. The albums take the same approach—slick, commercial pop-rap with Latin touches and lyrics in both English and Spanish—but *Dos* didn't have a smash single like "Rico Suave." For the most part, this CD is forgettable, but there are some decent tracks here and there—most notably, "It's a Latin Thing" and "Hollywood." But even if *Dos* had been more consistent and memorable, it probably would have been a poor seller. In 1992 there was a backlash against Gerardo in the dance-pop and teen pop markets—again, those audiences can be extremely fickle, and the word "loyalty" is not in their vocabulary. Loyalty is what you receive if you're José José or Celia Cruz; it doesn't come with the territory when you're catering to fickle teens who are looking for the flavor of the month. But all was not lost for the pop-rapper; 2001's *Gerardo: Fame, Sex y Dinero* (originally called Fame, Sex y Dinero) was surprisingly good and is edgier than any of his early-'90s output. Arguably, that CD is Gerardo's best release. Hardly essential, *Dos* is only recommended to those who are into collecting as much pop-rap as possible. —*Alex Henderson*

Gerardo: Fame, Sex y Dinero / Oct. 9, 2001 / Thump ✦✦✦
Not all commercial pop-rap is created equal. Some of it is respectable—Salt-N-Pepa's "Push It" and Ton Loc's "Wild Thing" immediately come to mind—and some of it is very lightweight (Vanilla Ice, Icy Blu). In the early '90s, hip-hop's hardcore dismissed Gerardo as the Latino equivalent of Vanilla Ice—and the Ecuadorian-born rapper did record his share of teen-oriented drivel. But this self-titled CD (which was originally called *Fame, Sex y Dinero*) is surprisingly good. While *Gerardo* is far from hardcore rap, it isn't vacuous teen pop either. A definite improvement over his early-'90s albums, this bilingual CD finds Gerardo (who turned 36 in 2001) providing a fairly interesting and edgy blend of rap, dance-pop, and Latin music. Of course, the term "Latin music" can mean different things to different people—Latin music is everything from the nuevo flamenco that is incredibly popular in Spain to Argentinean tango to the ranchero, mariachi, and Tejano that Mexicans enjoy. On this CD, he blends rap and dance-pop with tropical grooves—he is salsa minded on "Latin Playas Anthem" and "Tu Galan," but employs a Dominican merengue beat on "My House (Mi Casa)," "Las Manos Arriba," and the infectious single "Sigo Siendo Rico." "Infectious," in fact, is a word that describes most of the tunes on this club-friendly, dance-oriented CD, which won't win over hip-hop's hardcore but is certainly superior to early-'90s releases like *Mo' Ritmo* and *Dos*. *Gerardo* is not only a fun party album, it is arguably the pop-rapper's best and most substantial release. —*Alex Henderson*

Geto Boys

f. 1986
Group / Gangsta Rap, Hardcore Rap, Southern Rap
Though the controversial subject matter of gangsta rap wasn't much of a barrier to popular success during the '90s, the Geto Boys' recordings proved almost too extreme for widespread exposure. Blocked from distributing their 1990 major-label debut by Geffen—who insisted that a track dealing with necrophilia as well as murder was a step too far—the group was saved by producer Rick Rubin, who arranged another distributor for the album, released on his own Def American label. The controversy, which occurred two years earlier than similar censorship incidents involving Ice-T and 2 Live Crew, gave the Geto Boys a large amount of publicity. Their follow-up, *We Can't Be Stopped*, eventually hit platinum, though the trio of Scarface, Willie D., and Bushwick Bill began to fracture by 1993. After releasing solo albums during the mid-'90s, the Geto Boys reunited in 1996 for their most praised album yet, *The Resurrection*.

When the Geto Boys came together in 1986, though, it was with a completely different lineup. Formed as the Ghetto Boys in Houston by rap entrepreneur James "Lil' J" Smith (and signed to his Rap-A-Lot label), the group originally consisted of Prince Johnny C., the Slim Jukebox, and DJ Reddy Red. During 1987-1988, both Johnny C. and the Jukebox quit, forcing Smith to add a dwarf-dancer-turned-rapper named Bushwick Bill (born Richard Shaw, Jamaica) and two Rap-A-Lot solo acts: Ackshen (aka Scarface born Brad Jordan, Houston) and Willie D. Dennis (born Houston).

After the Geto Boys' *Grip It! On That Other Level* caught the ear of hip-hop impresario Rick Rubin (LL Cool J, Beastie Boys), Rubin remixed and re-recorded tracks from the album. He was ready to release it on his Def American label in 1990 when distributor Geffen balked at "Mind of a

Lunatic," a track which described necrophilia with a murder victim. By late 1990, Rubin had found another distributor, Giant Records, and the album was released—as *The Geto Boys*—that same year.

The Geto Boys' association with controversy was far from over, though; rap groups were a hot topic for moral-minded politicians during the early '90s, and several leaders used the Geto Boys as an example to decry the state of modern music. The fires were fanned in 1991 with the release of the group's second proper LP, *We Can't Be Stopped*. Before the release of the album, Bushwick Bill had lost an eye in a shooting incident with his girlfriend, and the cover featured Willie D. and Scarface wheeling Bill into an emergency room, with a prominent shot of the damaged eye. Inside the album, proceedings were among the most extreme in the history of recorded music. Obviously, radio airplay was nonexistent, but *We Can't Be Stopped* still went platinum in early 1992—thanks to the underground hit "Mind Playing Tricks on Me," one of the most effective inner-city vignettes in hip-hop history.

By 1993, all three members had begun solo careers, though Willie D. was the only one completely separated from the band, citing artistic differences. Scarface and Bill continued with new member Big Mike, releasing *Uncut Dope* in 1992 and *Till Death Do Us Part* the following year, but split late in 1994. Just one year later, Willie D. returned to the fold for another Geto Boys release, *The Resurrection*, which showed the group in fine form. *Da Good, Da Bad & Da Ugly* followed in 1998. —*John Bush*

Making Trouble / 1988 / Rap-A-Lot ✦

As the seldom-heard, mostly unknown original Geto Boys album—back when they were still the "Ghetto" Boys—*Making Trouble* should interest strictly enthusiasts of the Houston group, if that, and probably only to a slight extent. At this point, back in 1988, around the time when James Smith (then known as Lil' J) first launched his Rap-A-Lot label, the group had an entirely different lineup comprised of DJ Ready Red, Prince Johnny C. and the Slim Jukebox. Scarface and Willie D. hadn't yet joined the group, and Bushwick Bill was just the hypeman/dancer. Furthermore, the group hadn't yet found a novel identity for themselves, as they essentially emulate Run-D.M.C. here—two MCs/one DJ, heavy metal guitar riffs, fat gold chains, top hats, and everything. The most interesting moment here comes in "My Balls and My Word," where samples from Brian De Palma's film *Scarface* are worked into the beats, unknowingly foreshadowing the group's future under the leadership of Mr. Scarface himself. Of the original Ghetto Boys, DJ Ready Red stands out most as the group's Jam Master Jay, cutting up the wax with quite astonishing ability while Prince Johnny C. and the Slim Jukebox trade off "we will rock you"-style rhymes. By all means, avoid this album if you're a newcomer and start with the later Geto Boys albums, particularly the self-titled one (1990) and *We Can't Be Stopped* (1991), as *Making Trouble* is merely a novelty that even the most die-hard fans may find of little value. (Rap-A-Lot re-released *Making Trouble* at various points over the years, including in 1991 [with Priority distribution] and 1995 [Virgin], and repackaged the album to reflect the group's later name change to "the Geto Boys.") —*Jason Birchmeier*

The Geto Boys / 1990 / Rap-A-Lot ✦✦✦✦

This is a revamped version of *Grip It! On That Other Level*, an album released earlier in the year on Rap-A-Lot. Rick Rubin stepped in, signed the group to Def American, and proceeded to tweak some of the tracks; some other tracks were simply lifted from *Grip It!*, while a couple went so far as to have new vocals recorded. This works like a charm—the album is expertly sequenced, and some songs seem to have twice the impact of their original incarnations. "Mind of a Lunatic" is one such song, and it's one of the primary tracks that caused the Def American-affiliated Geffen to pull the plug on distribution. A horror fantasy of grim, graphic proportions, it's a gangster flick and a psychological thriller rolled into the form of a song. One of its cleanest lines is as follows: "She begged me not to kill her, I gave her a rose—then slit her throat and watched her shake 'til her eyes closed." The rest of the album helped draw the lyrical blueprint that countless groups either mimicked or borrowed from, from the yuks served up by Bushwick in "Size Ain't Shit" to the ridiculously misogynistic rhymes in "Gangster of Love," which are delivered over the guitar lick from Lynyrd Skynyrd's "Sweet Home Alabama." You can also either blame them or thank them for the endless flurry of *Scarface* samples that have littered/adorned so many hip-hop records. —*Andy Kellman*

Grip It! On That Other Level / 1990 / Rap-A-Lot ✦✦✦

A major leap from 1988's clunky and derivative *Making Trouble*, it was this record that gained the attention of Rick Rubin, who would swiftly sign the group to Def American and re-release slightly altered versions of many of these songs for the group's self-titled album. Since ten of the 12 tracks found here would be improved or simply lifted for *The Geto Boys*, there isn't much of a reason why anyone would need this, even though Rap-A-Lot continued to keep it in print. "Seek and Destroy" and "No Sellout" are the only two songs that aren't available elsewhere; the former is a decent, speedy Scarface track, while the latter is a pro-black cut headed by Willie D. The most significant difference between this and the self-titled album can be heard in the versions of "Mind of a Lunatic." The actual backing track was hardly adjusted—if at all—for the self-titled album, but the deliveries from Bushwick Bill, Scarface, and Willie D. are much more horrifying and claustrophobic on that later version. Plus, it also sounds much more gut kicking coming after "Size Ain't Shit." On this disc, it's the final track and seems sequentially out of place. —*Andy Kellman*

We Can't Be Stopped / Jul. 1, 1991 / Rap-A-Lot ✦✦✦✦

The cover of the Geto Boys' *We Can't Be Stopped* shows a member with his eye poked out. It's grotesque, but realistic—a realistic cover for an album whose violent, profane lyrics paint a vivid and accurate picture of life as the Geto Boys knew it growing up in Houston's tough ghetto known as the 5th Ward. This CD isn't as thought provoking as Ice-T, N.W.A, or Ice Cube can be—nor is it the Geto Boys' best offering. But it's an engaging, disturbing effort that comes across as much more heartfelt than the numerous gangster rap albums by the N.W.A and Cube clones and wannabes who jumped on the gangster bandwagon in the early '90s. *We Can't Be Stopped* serves as an unsettling reminder of the type of ugly social conditions that were allowed to fester in poor inner-city neighborhoods. —*Alex Henderson*

Uncut Dope: Geto Boys' Best / 1992 / Rap-A-Lot ✦✦✦✦

When *Uncut Dope* was released in 1992, the Geto Boys had four records behind them, and they were riding high on the success of *We Can't Be Stopped*. This was thanks in large part to the touching "Mind Playing Tricks on Me," a song clean enough to be played on mainstream radio that managed to be almost as psychologically grim as the horrifying "Mind of a Lunatic." This is a lean collection of a dozen tracks, most of which are pulled from *The Geto Boys* and *We Can't Be Stopped*, which makes perfect sense. *Making Trouble* was a debut that barely hinted at the group's potential, and 10/12ths of *Grip It! On That Other Level* was altered and/or resequenced for release as *The Geto Boys*. With the addition of a few at-the-time new tracks—including "Damn It Feels Good to Be a Gangsta"—this provided a decent look at a group that hadn't released a full-blown masterpiece. However, the two albums that immediately predated this disc had plenty of strong material to make for a called-for overview, including "My Mind Playing Tricks on Me," "Assassins," "Mind of a Lunatic," and "Do It Like It G.O." Though 2002's *Greatest Hits* covers the group's last three albums of the '90s, it has its career-spanning scope going for it, but none of the material from those albums stack up to the scattered greatness that came before it. —*Andy Kellman*

● **Greatest Hits** / Dec. 9, 1992 / Priority ✦✦✦✦

This is a second and more inclusive package of the Geto Boys' best moments. The first, *Uncut Dope*, covered the group through 1991's *We Can't Be Stopped*; this opens it up to include tracks from 1993's *Till Death Do Us Part*, 1996's *The Resurrection*, and 1998's *Da Good Da Bad & Da Ugly*. Those three albums were more patchy than the ones that came before them—with the exception of *Making Trouble*—and none of the highlights from them are of the caliber of earlier tracks like "Mind of a Lunatic," "My Mind Playing Tricks on Me," and "Trigga Happy Nigga." So, going strictly by pound-for-pound quality, *Uncut Dope* is the better of the two, but it's not as if later tracks like "Six Feet Deep," "The World Is a Geto," and "Gangsta (Put Me Down)" are entirely undeserving of anthology status. Furthermore, this disc has five more tracks and has better sound quality—naturally so since it was released ten years after *Uncut Dope*. Choosing where to go first with this group is a tough call: *The Geto Boys* is the group's best album, but going with that leaves one without some of the group's best material. And neither *Uncut Dope* nor *Greatest Hits* are clear-cut first stops. Regardless of the choice, some of the most brutally descriptive and alternately funny Southern hip-hop is in well-stocked supply. —*Andy Kellman*

Till Death Do Us Part / Mar. 19, 1993 / Rap-A-Lot ✦✦✦
The Geto Boys' last album finds them expanding on the success of "Mind Playing Tricks on Me" with "Six Feet Deep," but more frequently, it keeps to their standard, grotesque gangsta rap with "Murder Ave." and "This Dick's for You." On these tracks, the whole shock formula seems like a worn-out trick and points the way to their eventual disbanding. *—Stephen Thomas Erlewine*

The Resurrection / Apr. 2, 1996 / Rap-A-Lot ✦✦✦✦
After spending nearly five years apart, the Geto Boys reunited in 1996 and released *The Resurrection*. Since they were more notorious for their lyrical violence than their music—only 1991's *We Can't Be Stopped*, with its stunning single "Mind Playing Tricks on Me," showed the band experimenting musically—it comes as a surprise that *The Resurrection* is such a strong album. Although the band never deviates from their standard blood-guts-sex lyrical routine, they have a greater sense of humor throughout the album. More importantly, they perform with energy and their backing tracks are vigorous and funky. As a result, *The Resurrection* outstrips every other Geto Boys record in every sense—it is the leanest, meanest, and funkiest thing they've ever recorded. *—Stephen Thomas Erlewine*

Da Good Da Bad & Da Ugly / Nov. 17, 1998 / Rap-A-Lot ✦✦✦
The Resurrection was short lived. After the Geto Boys reunited for a final go-around in 1996, the group fell apart, with Bushwick Bill leaving the band. Willie D. and Scarface soldiered on, recruiting DMG to fill the diminutive Bill's large shoes. It doesn't quite work. There are flashes of inspiration throughout *Da Good Da Bad & Da Ugly*, but musically and lyrically, it neither has the Geto Boys' signature sound nor an interesting variation on it. Instead, it feels (and looks) like a poor attempt to keep pace with No Limit. Since Scarface and Willie D. are better MCs than the average No Limit rapper—so is DMG, for that matter—the record works better than the average No Limit album, but feels distressingly anonymous. A few cuts are successful, but the record never gels as a whole, leaving it as a low point in the group's catalog. *—Stephen Thomas Erlewine*

Ghetto Concept

Group / Underground Rap
Kwajo Boateng and partner L "Dolo" Frazer came from Rexdale, Ontario, a ward community deep in the heart of Toronto. Together, they formed the rap duo Ghetto Concept and produced a slew of independently distributed recordings on vinyl and cassette. They won their very first Juno Award in 1994 for the independently released single "Certified Dope." The following year they released "E-Z on tha Motion," winning the 1995 Juno Award. With no major-label backing, these independent rappers released a self-titled, full-length in late 1998 on their own 7 Bills Entertainment label. *—Roxanne Blanford*

● **Ghetto Concept** / 1998 / 7 Bills ✦✦✦✦
Hip-hop was still growing as an established music form in Canada when Ontario's Ghetto Concept released their definitive self-titled debut in late 1998. This 20-track disc was obviously labored over conscientiously, as evidenced by its insightful and varied content. From the opening strains of the Bee Gees' "More than a Woman" sampled on the polemic "Annodomini" to the gentle soul rhythms on "Ol Skool Games" and the hypnotic "Heat of the Night," this collection is more expansive and reflective than other similar releases. Ghetto Concept's economical beat scheme and confrontational, yet cogent street sensibility is overlayed with an appreciation for dancehall/reggae-styled hooks. The narrative flow is smooth and the expletive heavy language on some tracks ("Die 4 Me," "State of Crisis," "Dark Skies," "Soak Da Set," and "Primetime Saturday Night") is startlingly real and jarring, but essential. The language in "Mother's Love" is just as real, but harmoniously bittersweet ("welfare recipient, low income, emotionally numb, painfully young, single-handedly provided for a fatherless son"). Ghetto Concept deserves exceptional mad props for creating a record where the message matters just as much as the beat. *—Roxanne Blanford*

Ghetto E (Ira Dorsey)

b. Flint, MI
Hardcore Rap, Gangsta Rap
When Dayton Family rapper Steve Hinkle was indicted, Ghetto E stepped into his place for the recording of the infamous Flint, MI, rap group's second

album, *F.B.I.* Unfortunately, despite that album's success in the hardcore rap underground and Ghetto E's newfound status alongside his older brother, Bootleg, as a member of the widely respected group, other run-ins with the law prevented the Dayton Family from recording a follow-up album. After finally putting his legal problems behind him, Ghetto E followed in the footsteps of other Dayton Family members Bootleg and Shoestring by recording his debut solo album, *Ghetto Theater*. He released the album on Detroit rapper Esham's Overcore label in early 2001. *—Jason Birchmeier*

● **Ghetto Theater** / Feb. 6, 2001 / Overcore/TVT ✦✦
The third and final member of the Dayton Family to release a solo album, Ghetto E spends the majority of his *Ghetto Theater* album reprising the same themes fans of the infamous Flint, MI, hardcore rap trio have come to expect. In other words, this an extremely decadent album, full of references to violence, drugs, sex, and anything else shocking. In terms of production, things have changed a bit since the last Dayton Family album, 1996's *F.B.I.*; where that album coopted a West Coast gangsta rap sound, this album instead looks to the synth- and drum machine-heavy sounds of Southern rap, particularly that of Three 6 Mafia and Master P. Though Ghetto E is fairly successful in his efforts to create a horrifying portrait of ghetto life, he isn't a very impressive rapper in terms of either lyrics or delivery and, even worse, the album's production is sloppy. Compared to the solo albums of Dayton Family members Shoestring and Bootleg, this album is a slight disappointment. The occasional cameos by Bootleg and Esham (who released the album on his Overcore label) bring some bright spots to the album with their impressive mike skills, and certain tracks have some quality moments, but for the most part this is not much more than another generic hardcore/gangsta rap album with little to get excited about. Granted, Ghetto E's rapping shows potential here, but he needs to polish his delivery, come up with more cinematic lyrics, and, more than anything, hire some creative producers. As is, this album is merely average. It's unfortunate that he couldn't get Esham to play a bigger role in the album—he could have used it. *—Jason Birchmeier*

Ghetto Twiinz

Group / Hardcore Rap, Southern Rap
Based in Houston's notorious 5th Ward and given support by the equally notorious Rap-A-Lot/Noo Trybe stable (Geto Boys, Facemob, Do or Die), the duo of Tonya and Trementhia Jupiter formed Ghetto Twiinz and released their debut album, *Surrounded by Criminals*, in 1996. *In That Water* followed one year later, and in 1998 the duo returned with *No Pain No Gain*. *Got It on My Mind* appeared in early 2001. *—John Bush*

In That Water / Jul. 1, 1997 / Rap-A-Lot ✦✦✦
The Ghetto Twiinz' second album, *In That Water*, finds the group repeating the hardcore formula of their debut, *Surrounded by Criminals*. The group rhymes about crime, sex, dope, and money over funky drum loops and bass grooves. Much of *In That Water* is simply gangsta cliché, yet there are moments where the Ghetto Twiinz make it work, either because they have a clever rhyme or a solid hook. For gangsta junkies, it's worth digging through *In That Water* to find those moments, but casual fans will find the album a little too long and repetitive to be worth the effort. *—Leo Stanley*

Ghostface Killah (Dennis Coles)

Hip-Hop, East Coast Rap, Hardcore Rap
As one of the original members of the seminal '90s rap crew the Wu-Tang Clan, Ghostface Killah (aka Tony Starks) made an impact before he released his debut album, *Ironman*, late in 1996. Like all members of the Wu-Tang Clan, the rapper used the group as a launching pad for a solo career, which was assisted greatly by other members of the Clan, particularly producer RZA. Ghostface Killah had rapped on Wu-Tang's 1993 debut, *Enter the Wu-Tang*, but he didn't distinguish himself until 1995, when he was showcased on fellow Wu member Raekwon's *Only Built 4 Cuban Linx*. Ghostface received good reviews for his appearance on the record, and his contribution to the soundtracks for *Sunset Park* and *Don't Be a Menace to South Central While You're Drinking Your Juice in the 'Hood* also were well received. All of these guest appearances and soundtrack contributions set the stage for Ghostface Killah's solo debut, *Ironman*. Like all Wu-Tang projects, it was produced by RZA and was quite successful in the large hip-hop/rap underground, debuting at number two on the pop charts upon its release. *Ironman*

was also the first album to be released on Razor Sharp Records, RZA's record label on Epic Records. —*Stephen Thomas Erlewine*

● **Ironman** / Oct. 29, 1996 / Razor Sharp/Epic Street ◆◆◆◆◆
Every Wu-Tang Clan solo project has a different flavor, and Ghostface Killah's *Ironman* is no exception. Though it boasts cameos from nearly every other Wu-Tang member—notably Raekwon and Cappadonna—*Ironman* is unlike any other record in RZA's catalog of productions, particularly because it is signficantly lighter in tone. There are still touches of the Wu's signature urban claustrophobia throughout the record, but the music is largely built on samples of early '70s soul, from Al Green to the Delfonics, who make a guest appearance on "After the Smoke Is Clear." Consequently, the mood of the album can switch tones at the drop of the hat, moving from hard funk like "Daytona 500" to seductive soul with the Mary J. Blige duet "All That I Got Is You." *Ironman* bogs down slightly in the middle, yet the record is filled with inventive production and rhymes, and ranks as another solid entry in the Wu-Tang legacy. —*Stephen Thomas Erlewine*

Supreme Clientele / Jan. 25, 2000 / Razor Sharp/Epic Street ◆◆◆◆
Most of the members of rap's Roman Empire, the Wu-Tang Clan, experienced sophomore slumps with their second solo releases, whether artistically or commercially (usually both). The second offerings from Method Man, Ol' Dirty Bastard, GZA, and Raekwon featured some of the old Wu magic, but not enough to warrant a claim to their once total mastery of the rap game. Just as the Wu empire appeared to be crumbling, along came the second installment from the Clan's spitfire element, Ghostface Killah (aka Tony Starks, aka Ironman). Every bit as good as his first release, *Supreme Clientele* proves Ghost's worthiness of the Ironman moniker by deftly overcoming trendiness to produce an authentic sound in hip-hop's age of bland parity. Some of the Wu's slump could be contributed to Wu-Abbott's (aka RZA) relative sabbatical. This album has RZA's stamp all over it, but the guru himself only provides three tracks. On this effort, the Wu-Pupil producers at times seem to outdo their teacher. RZA's best composition is the piano-driven, double-entendre-laced childhood retrospective "Child's Play." But of the many standout cuts, it's the slew of disciple producers paying homage to the Wu legacy that truly makes this album fresh sounding: "Apollo Kids" (Hassan), "Malcolm" (Choo the Specialist), "Saturday Nite" (Carlos "Six July" Broady), "One" (JuJu of the Beatnuts), "Cherchez la Ghost" (Carlos Bess), "Wu Banga 101" (Allah Mathematics). While the album is complete and characteristically Wu sounding, each track is distinctive lyrically, thematically, and sonically. Ghostface's *Supreme Clientele* is a step toward the Wu-Tang Clan's ascent from the ashes of their fallen kingdom. The once-slumbering Wu-Tang strikes again. —*Michael Di Bella*

Bulletproof Wallets / Nov. 13, 2001 / Epic ◆◆◆
Sprucing up the scratchy soul samples of his sophomore *Supreme Clientele* into a relatively pristine mainstream gloss, Ghostface Killah also, unfortunately, removed much of the flair from the most distinctive sound in the Wu-Tang camp. And fans looking for the genuine pain and emotion of his standout, "Hollow Bones" (from Wu-Tang's *The W*), won't be rewarded, either. *Bulletproof Wallets* is basically a party album, at least compared to the usual Wu-Tang gloom and doom, featuring smooth, romantic R&B tracks like the single "Never Be the Same Again" (with Carl Thomas & Raekwon) and "Love Session." One of the few highlights is the opener, "Maxine," an inner-city nightmare given heavy menace by Ghostface's tight rapping and an excellent one-note-horns production. From there, *Bulletproof Wallets* heads south, with a few oddball interludes (usually nursery rhymes substituting weed references) and smooth or stale productions from Wu associates RZA (five songs total), Al Chemist, Allah Mathematics, and Ghostface himself. (Listeners should also beware of the back-cover track listing, which is completely wrong.) —*John Bush*

Ginuwine (Elgin Baylor Lumpkin)

b. Oct. 15, 1975, Washington, D.C.
Vocals, Producer / Contemporary R&B, Hip-Hop, Club/Dance, Urban
Ginuwine was one of R&B's preeminent love men during the '90s heyday of hip-hop soul. Initially teamed with Timbaland, the most innovative producer of the late '90s, Ginuwine's sultry, seductive crooning earned him a substantial female following and made him a regular presence on the R&B charts, even after the futuristic production he favored was eclipsed by the more organic, retro-leaning neo-soul movement.

Ginuwine was born in Washington, D.C., on October 15, 1975, with the unlikely name of Elgin Baylor Lumpkin (after D.C.-born Basketball Hall of Famer Elgin Baylor). As a youngster, Lumpkin's interest in music was ignited by Prince and Michael Jackson, especially the latter's legendary moonwalking performance on the Motown 25th-anniversary special. At the mere age of 12, he began performing at parties and bars with the local hip-hop group the Finesse Five. He later worked as a Michael Jackson impressionist and sang with another local outfit, Physical Wonder; in the meantime, he earned a paralegal degree from a local community college, in case music didn't work out. In 1996 he adopted the name Ginuwine and was discovered by Jodeci. In New York, he met up with young producer Timbaland and cut the track "Pony," whose slow, halting groove and impassioned vocals helped Ginuwine land a deal with Sony's 550 Music imprint.

With the strikingly inventive Timbaland behind the boards, Ginuwine cut his debut album, *Ginuwine…The Bachelor*, and released it later in 1996. "Pony" became a number-one R&B smash, also reaching number six on the pop charts, and the album became an eventual double-platinum hit. It spun off several more R&B hits over the next year, including "Tell Me Do U Wanna," "I'll Do Anything/I'm Sorry," "Holler," and "Only When Ur Lonely"; it also featured an homage to one of Ginuwine's main influences on the cover of Prince's "When Doves Cry." In the wake of the album's success, demand for Timbaland's production services exploded, and Ginuwine became a bona fide sex symbol. He toured heavily in support of *The Bachelor*, and kept his name in the public eye in 1998 with his hit "Same Ol' G," which was featured on the soundtrack to Eddie Murphy's *Dr. Doolittle*. Late that year, he also made his acting debut on an episode of the CBS series *Martial Law*.

Ginuwine returned with his second album, *100% Ginuwine*, in early 1999. Again produced by Timbaland, it entered the pop charts at number five and gave rise to another significant crossover hit in "So Anxious." "What's So Different?" and "None of Ur Friends Business" were also successful on R&B radio, and there was another cover of a Ginuwine hero, this time Michael Jackson's "She's Out of My Life." *100% Ginuwine* became the singer's second straight platinum album. He followed it in the spring of 2001 with *The Life*, his first album to be helmed by producers not named Timbaland. Nonetheless, it was another success, debuting at number three on the charts and once again going platinum. Moreover, the ballad "Differences"—the second single released from the album, after "There It Is"—became Ginuwine's biggest pop hit yet, climbing to number four later that year. In 2002 Ginuwine made his feature-film debut in the gender-bending basketball comedy *Juwanna Mann*, playing (what else?) a slick R&B singer. That summer, Ginuwine returned to the Top Ten courtesy of his duet with P. Diddy on "I Need a Girl (Part Two)." Around the same time, in a somewhat bizarre incident, police captured a Minnesota man who'd been impersonating the singer for the past few years and bilking money from business contacts. His fourth album *The Senior* appeared in early 2003. —*Steve Huey*

● **Ginuwine … The Bachelor** / Oct. 8, 1996 / 550 Music/Epic ◆◆◆◆
By the time *Ginuwine…The Bachelor* was released, Ginuwine was already well on his way to becoming R&B's next big thing—thanks mainly to the ferocious word of mouth perpetuated by his lead single, a cover of Prince's "When Doves Cry." Make no mistake, this was the album that indeed started it all for the young R&B sensation, catapulting him from relative obscurity to the limelight in less time than most of his contemporaries. Led by the ferocious chart-topping opener "Pony," Ginuwine not only became a staple for commercial R&B radio, but he upped the sexual reference ante for many up-and-coming male singers such as Dru Hill, Blackstreet, and such established producers as R. Kelly. Combining the influences of funk, quiet storm, soul, and even a tad bit of electro, Ginuwine effortlessly displays not only a powerful voice but also sharp songwriting and production skills. *Ginuwine… The Bachelor* was a promising debut and only a slight notion of great things to come. —*Rob Theakston*

100% Ginuwine / Mar. 16, 1999 / 550 Music/Epic ◆◆◆◆
Ginuwine's debut album certainly sounded like little else in the modern soul front. Thanks to Timbaland's inventive production, it blended classic soul songwriting with inventive sonic textures, borrowed equally from hip-hop, trip-hop, and electro-funk. For the follow-up, Ginuwine and Timbaland decided that if it ain't broke, just spiffy it up a little bit—which means *100% Ginuwine* uses *The Bachelor* as a blueprint but goes further, boasting more inventive productions and a stronger set of songs. If nothing grabs the ear like

"Pony," most of the songs slowly work their way underneath the skin, revealing themselves as either seductive ballads or ingratiating dancefloor numbers. Timbaland continues to prove that he's one of the savviest producers in modern hip-hop and soul, but Ginuwine remains the star of the show, thanks to his rich, inviting voice. —*Stephen Thomas Erlewine*

The Life / Apr. 3, 2001 / Epic ♦♦♦
On his third album, Ginuwine is even more of a practiced R&B loverman than he was on his first two releases. Big Dog Productions and the team of Troy Oliver and Cory Rooney produce the bulk of the beats here, which, as usual, mostly range from slow to very slow tempos with such trendy touches as acoustic guitar passages. But all that just serves as a bed for Ginuwine's elastic tenor and his message to the women in his audience. The singer sounds like he's been reading women's magazines and tried to construct a persona that's as appealing as possible. "Baby," he croons in "Why Did You Go," "I'm sorry for whatever I've done and I want you to be my wife." In "Differences," he talks about how much he has improved since meeting the woman he's addressing, concluding, "I'm so responsible." Even when he's criticizing a woman, as he does in the album's first single, "There It Is," it's because she's not contributing to the relationship, while he's holding down a steady job and paying the bills. It's only in the album's eighth cut, "How Deep Is Your Love" (an original, not the Bee Gees song), that he begins to apply pressure for sex, ungallantly suggesting that if the woman doesn't come across he'll start cheating on her. "Show After the Show" is a come-on to a post-concert groupie, which seems to negate what's gone before, and "Role Play" moves on to kinky sex, but in the album-closing "Just Because," Ginuwine acknowledges the temptations of his occupation and pleads, "I'm trying to learn to be committed." It's hard to believe that anyone who's swallowed his line before is going to become skeptical now, so *The Life* looks like another winner for him. —*William Ruhlmann*

Goats
Group / Alternative Rap, Alternative Pop/Rock
One of the more overlooked groups in the early-'90s alternative rap movement, the Goats were an interracial Philadelphia trio who featured a live backing band before fellow hometowners the Roots shot to acclaim with a similar format. The Goats sounded a bit different, though, mixing intelligent, Public Enemy-influenced political raps with good-humored Native Tongues positivity, plus a bit of aggressive, hard-partying funk-rock. Oatie Kato (born Maxx Stoyanoff-Williams), Madd, and Swayzack first got together in 1991, and became the first signing for the Philly-based hip-hop label Ruffhouse (which would soon land a distribution deal with Sony). The group released its debut album, 1992's *Tricks of the Shade*, to strongly positive reviews, and shortly thereafter put together an in-concert backing band which took their sound in a rap-rock direction. However, Oatie soon left the group, dissatisfied with the behind-the-scenes excess; he went on to form Incognegro, and took much of the Goats' political perceptiveness with him. The remaining duo debuted the live band on the Goats' second album, 1994's *No Goats No Glory*, which was viewed by many critics as a disappointing follow-up. By 1996, the group had disbanded, but Incognegro would release their debut album by the end of the decade, with Oatie performing under the name MC Uh-Oh. —*Steve Huey*

● **Tricks of the Shade** / Nov. 3, 1992 / Ruffhouse ♦♦♦♦
The Goats' quirky 25-track 1992 debut bears the stylistic influence of hip-hoppers like De La Soul and A Tribe Called Quest; their juxtaposition of rock, funk, and rap rhythms also recalls the heady eclecticism of the Beastie Boys. —*Jason Ankeny*

No Goats No Glory / 1994 / Columbia ♦♦♦
For the follow-up to their promising debut *Tricks of the Shade*, the Goats decided to toughen up both their image and sound. Musically, the plan worked: the beats on this record easily surpass those on *Shade*, incorporating metal and funk seamlessly into a hard, funky swagger that rivals any beats in hip-hop. Lyrically, however, the results are disastrous. The album is bloated with some six or seven songs that seem calculated to cash in on the popularity of Dr. Dre's *The Chronic* (which had been released a year before), complete with rhymes about gunplay, boasts of thuggish behavior, and endless references to smoking pot. The one-dimensional lyrics don't even work as parodies of gangsta rap—they are simply dull and monotonous. The turnabout is especially unjustified coming from a group that had previously condemned

such cheap gimmickry. Their one artistic gamble, "Revolution 94," an eight-minute sound collage á la the Beatles' "Revolution #9," isn't clever—it's interminable. Only "Rumblefish" and "Times Running Up" retain the smart, quirky attitude of their debut. For a perfect example of the hip-hop slide—the notion that an artist's sophomore effort is vastly inferior to the debut—start here. —*Victor Valdivia*

God's Original Gangstaz
Group / Christian Rap
The L.A. Christian rap group God's Original Gangstaz consists of Preach D.O.G. and Mr. Reg N.I.C.E., who were both involved in gangs and drugs as young teens. After they discovered their faith, the duo decided to spread the message through rap, and released *True 2 Tha Game* in 1996 on Grapetree Records. *Resurrected Gangstaz* appeared the next year, followed by *Pawns in a Chess Game* in 1999. —*Heather Phares*

● **Tha G Filez** / Aug. 10, 1999 / Grapetree ♦♦♦
It's difficult to see how gospel and gangsta rap could coexist in the same record store rack, much less in the same group. God's Original Gangstaz deserve credit for taking back the night and capitalizing on the best armor-of-God themes in the Bible to come up with an interesting album that may hold promise for parents wary of buying the latest C-Murder album for their young children. The production is a bit lacking, as derivative as could be expected, but *Tha G Filez* is an interesting ride through contemporary gospel. —*Keith Farley*

Godfather Don
Producer / East Coast Rap, Hardcore Rap
A creative force within New York City's underground hip-hop scene, Godfather Don first appeared in 1991 with *Hazardous*, released on the Select imprint. The album established the Godfather as an MC influenced by the blatant, hard-hitting style of Chuck D. A few years later, the Don appeared on and produced the Ultramagnetic MC's' *Four Horsemen*, which led to a collaboration with that group's standout, Kool Keith. *The Cenobites EP* was issued on Fondle 'Em Records, which was started by New York b-boy, DJ, and man about town Bobbito Garcia. The material on the EP had originally been recorded as gags or promos for Garcia's underground hip-hop radio show on New York's WKCR. *The Cenobites EP* was then reissued by Fondle 'Em as a full-length LP. Throughout the 1990s, Godfather Don continued to work as a producer, working on tracks from Kool Keith, Hostyle, and Ayatollah, among others. In 1999 he released his second album, *Diabolique*, on which his flow was very similar to the bludgeoning raps of his 1991 debut. The album included cameo appearances from Kool Keith and Sir Menelik, and appeared on the Hydra Entertainment imprint, for which Godfather Don continued to record, releasing several 12" singles in 1999, 2000, and 2001. —*Johnny Loftus*

Godfather Don / 1991 / Select ♦♦

● **Diabolique** / 1999 / Hydra ♦♦♦
On Godfather Don's second album, *Diabolique*, the battered New York underground hip-hop veteran breaks no new ground. He sticks to steady, dark beats and confrontational rhymes. Over the course of a song or two this isn't so bad, but the sameness of the production and Godfather Don's not so nimble rhyme flow makes *Diabolique* monotonous. Cameos from Kool Keith and Sir Menelik enliven the proceedings momentarily, but even their weirdness can't save the album. —*Christopher Witt*

Gold Chains (Topher Lafata)
Vocals, Producer / Underground Rap, Techno Bass
A hip-hop hooligan for the indie rock crowd, Gold Chains has recorded for Orthlorng Musork and Tigerbeat6, hardly the equals of Def Jam or Rawkus. Still, he's a talented rapper and producer, closer to seriously humorous rappers like Gonzales than the hip-hop satire of MC Paul Barman. He was born Topher Lafata and grew up in Reading, PA, parlaying an early interest in skateboarding and hardcore punk into a band influenced by post-punk and industrial. He kept on performing while at college in Connecticut, and broadened his interests to include playing with a live hip-hop act. Lafata also bought a four-track, along with sampler and drum machine, and began recording his own tracks. One of his first productions was a tape called *Gold Chains: Music for a Higher Society*, which contributed his performing name

by the time he started doing shows in San Francisco. Support gigs for Kit Clayton and Kid 606 paid major dividends; his first wide release, *Gold Chains EP*, appeared on Clayton's Orthlorng Musork label in late 2001, and his second, *Straight From Your Radio* (another EP), was issued by Kid 606's Tigerbeat6. —*John Bush*

● **Gold Chains EP** / 2001 / Orthlorng Musork ✦✦✦

Gold Chains is actually the alterego of musician Topher Lafata, a San Francisco-based, self-professed "art punk" who creates dense sound collages incorporating large slices of electronica and techno beats along with hip-hop-styled vocals that sound a lot like rapper Ja Rule. The self-titled *Gold Chains* EP provides a fine introduction to Lafata's talents, the erstwhile MC delivering five songs with machine-gun precision and complex electronic instrumentation. On "I Come From San Francisco," he'll steal your girlfriend but would gladly sell her for new studio equipment, and with "No. 1 Face in Hip Hop" Gold Chains declares his dominance of the genre (and his enormous prowess in the bedroom). "Back in the Day" offers some old school turntable gymnastics and MC braggadocio, while "The Wonderful Girls of Hypno" tells of sexual adventures. "Rock the Parti" is a globetrotting tale of danger and excitement punctuated by blazing guitars and wall-of-noise rhythms. Beneath all the sex and party-oriented lyrics, however, Gold Chains kicks out a wicked groove, fat slabs of technological rhythm matched with noisy guitars, found sounds, odd noises, and nightmarish visions that sound like an alien abduction caught on tape. He's either a genius or a fool, creating a fresh new style of dance music that reassembles elements of the familiar with the inspiration of Lafata's colorful imagination and immense talent. The *Gold Chains* EP also includes an entertaining and inventive low-budget video for "I Come From San Francisco" that is viewable on a computer. —*Rev. Keith A. Gordon*

Straight From Your Radio / Sep. 24, 2002 / Tigerbeat6 ✦✦✦

On *Straight From Your Radio*, Topher Lafata raps of his lyrical and sexual prowess over powerful jagged-edge electro; if he lacks the rapping talent of fellow indie-electronic MCs Gonzales and Cex, at least the productions are far better than anyone else doing similar material. His second EP, this one recorded for Tigerbeat6, isn't quite as extreme and inventive as the productions of label boss Kid 606, but it does represent an exciting middle ground between trad dance-pop/hip-hop and the twitchy hardcore gabba preferred by the Kid. Despite a few deft rhymes (sample: "musique concrèté, MCs at my feet"), Gold Chains' rapping is less Rakim and more Fred Durst, and he has trouble bringing across the sexed-up booty techno of "I Treat Your Coochie Like a Maze" or the equally self-explanatory "Mountains of Coke" (both of which are unintentionally hilarious). —*John Bush*

Gonervill

Group / Turntablism

Crafting what they call "organitronic instro hip-hop," Gonervill mixes alternately spooky and soulful melodies with the deft skills of turntablist DJ Eddie Def (also of the Space Travelers and El Stew). The trio also includes drummer Brain, formerly of Primus and Praxis, and the current drummer for Guns N' Roses, and bassist Extrakd, also of El Stew. The trio's self-titled 2001 debut also featured the Limbomaniacs' M.I.R.V. on guitar, as well as contributions from Bill Laswell and Buckethead. —*Heather Phares*

● **Gonervill** / Aug. 7, 2001 / Innerhythmic Foundat ✦✦✦✦✦

Here's an unusual lineup for you. Gonervill is a trio consisting of a drummer (Brain of the Limbomaniacs, Praxis, and Primus) and two turntablists (Extrakd and Eddie Def). Of course, they do get a little help from guitarists Buckethead and M.I.R.V. (and that sure does sound like Bill Laswell on bass on a couple of tracks). But the focus is on Brain's sturdy, funky beats and the mind-blowing turntable skills of Eddie Def and Extrakd. The album hits a high point early on with the densely constructed "Infiltrating Assassin," but maintains a surprisingly consistent level of quality throughout; the psychedelic guitar work on "Unseen Worlds" blends nicely with a welter of manic cuts and scratches from the turntable crew, while the moderately creepy "Fear Is the Killer" takes a breakbeat that sounds as if it was recorded at the Black Ark and combines it with Bernie Worrell-flavored organ parts and a nasty, shuddering bass line. The album closes with "Muad' Dib," a slow and funky Buckethead showcase that draws equally on North African flavors and old school hip-hop. Fans of breakbeat and turntable artistry will ignore this one at their peril. —*Rick Anderson*

Gonzales (Sasha Baron Cohen)

Electronic, Club/Dance, Trip-Hop, Underground Rap

Kooky Canadian Gonzales (also known as "Chilly Gonzales") is a mixed bag of MC meets keyboarding producer meets singer. Though born to the maple leaf, the Kitty-Yo label artist resides in Europe, mainly in Germany. At a young age Gonzales was introduced to the piano by his parents and over-achieving brother. Using the instrument as an avenue of self-expression, he quickly advanced into the production realm. Through his Hollywood-based older brother, Gonzales has done music for soundtracks under various aliases. Known for his often comical live shows, complete with MCing, Gonzales branched off to singing with labelmate Peaches in 2000 for the single "Red Leather." His debut full-length, 2000's *Gonzales Uber Alles*, was followed later that year by *The Entertainist*. Touring and collaborating with Peaches brought both artists more noteriety, with the press nicknaming the duo the "Bonnie and Clyde of prankster rap." Gonzales stepped back into the studio in the spring of 2002 to record *Presidential Suite*, which featured Peaches among many other guest musicians. —*Diana Potts*

Gonzales Uber Alles / Mar. 7, 2000 / Kitty-Yo ✦✦✦

Gonzales Uber Alles is a scattered, frequently engaging album of postmodern synth pop and jazzy, slightly experimental hip-hop heavy on the samples and drum machines. Gonzales is nowhere near as extroverted or obnoxious as on *The Entertainist*, instead playing up his solid production talents, just on the left-field side of commercial hip-hop. Highlights include "Past Your Bedtime" and "The Worst MC." —*John Bush*

● **The Entertainist** / Oct. 31, 2000 / Kitty-Yo ✦✦✦✦

He looks like Jon Spencer but sounds more like Eminem, with a lo-fi 808 nightmare pushing Dr. Dre out of the producer's chair. Still, Gonzales is definitely not the worst MC, as he styles himself on a track heard on his first pure rap LP, *The Entertainist*. He's actually a great rapper, as iconoclastic and inscrutable a figure as Kool Keith or Ol' Dirty Bastard, with an irresistible sense of rhythm, hilarious lyrics, and a raw, kinetic production approach that benefits on several skeletal tracks from Digital Hardcore colleagues Patric Catani and Bomb20. One of the best productions, though, was actually recorded by Gonzales' associate Peaches. The track, "Futuristic Ain't Shit to Me," appears to set out the Chilly Gonzales agenda ("Being futuristic these days means being futuristic on your own terms") though subsequent lyrics ("Being futuristic means loving worms/Saving your sperm/Wearing your pubes in a perm") resist any attempt at analysis. Besides rapping white-boy nonsense like Beck or MC Paul Barman ("Jimmy Carter in the place to be!/Hangin' with Chilly G!"), Gonzales also pokes fun at the legion of sex-crazed rappers out there, with amusing parodies (we're assuming) like "Candy" and "Cum on You." It's unclear whether he's attempting to save rap from the mainstream blahs or ridicule it out of existence, but *The Entertainist* is a brilliant left-field hit for fans of oddball hip-hop production and zany lyrics. —*John Bush*

Presidential Suite / Apr. 30, 2002 / Kitty-Yo ✦✦✦✦

As a white rapper, Gonzales is less like Eminem and more like MC Paul Barman, which is to say that this Canadian-born cut-up and his frequent duet partner, Peaches, are less concerned with being the next hip-hop chart-toppers than with making the genre fun again. And as long as you don't take it too seriously or expect too much artistic depth, his third full-length LP does just that. Chilly G may not be the freshest MC ever to rock the mike, but light-hearted songs like "So Called Party Over There" and "Salieri Serenade" match lo-fi drum machine beats with nerdy rhymes to great effect. But it's in his role as a producer on collaborations with labelmates Feist, Louis Austen, and (of course) Peaches that Gonzales shines brightest, coming off like some sort of mad, retro synth-loving scientist toiling in his lab to concoct freaky backing tracks that could give the Neptunes a run for their money. Now, if only he could refine those mike skills.... —*Bret Love*

Kenny "Dope" Gonzalez

b. Jun. 7, 1970, Brooklyn, NY

Producer, Remixing, DJ / Hip-Hop, Bass Music, Party Rap

Along with Masters at Work partner "Little" Louie Vega, Kenny "Dope" Gonzalez was one of the biggest figures in house music, and one of the prime connections between the underground and the mainstream—together, they produced and remixed an endless list of tracks that made an indelible impact on dance music. With salsa, disco, and house acting as the primary common specialities shared between the two, Gonzalez brought his immersion in rap music to the table, while Vega came from a freestyle angle. The duo helmed full-length albums, including some under the Masters at Work name, in addition to one with their Nuyorican Soul project.

Like Vega, the Brooklyn-born Gonzalez was prolific on his own before and during the partnership, starting out as a DJ. In the '80s, he founded the Dope Wax label while doing production for several New York dance labels, including Big Beat, Cutting, Nervous, and Strictly Rhythm (home to his releases as the Untouchables). Masters at Work actually began around this time, originating as a partnership between Gonzalez and Mike Delgado; the two organized parties under the name. A few years after he aligned himself with Vega, he established the Bucketheads, a studio project that released a string of extremely successful singles and a pair of full-lengths (both "The Bomb" and "Got Myself Together" topped the dance singles chart). Gonzalez released several solo productions under his own name throughout the early 2000s, through the Tu Chicks, Freeze, and TNT labels. His skills as a DJ were demonstrated with a pair of impressive releases for the U.K.'s BBE label, too: 1998's *Hip Hop Forever* was a triple-disc set, including an early-'90s-centric mix on one disc and the selections in full on the other two. The similarly formatted *Disco Heat* came four years later, which focused on underground disco and house classics from the late '70s. —*Andy Kellman*

Hip Hop Forever / Nov. 3, 1998 / BBE ◆◆◆◆

The first of the three discs in this set from BBE is an ace set of mostly golden age hip-hop tracks mixed by Kenny "Dope" Gonzalez, who rolls through classics like Kool G Rap & DJ Polo's "Ill Street Blues," Jeru the Damaja's "Come Clean," Ed O.G. & da Bulldogs' "I Got to Have It," EPMD's "You Gots to Chill," and Method Man's "Bring the Pain." With 19 cuts presented in just over an hour, Gonzalez can allow the bulk of each track to play out before switching to the next one. The mixing, the selections, and the sequencing leave little to be desired. Apart from an pseudo-ominous voice that comes in every now and then to announce "Kenny 'Dope' Gonzalez," it's a smooth, uninterrupted ride. Just as remarkable, discs two and three allow each track from the mix to be presented in full, free of mixing. As a bonus on top of that, a handful of tracks that aren't on the mix are also present, including the Basement Khemists' "Everybody," Sunz of Man's "Shining Star," Common's "Resurrection '95," and Xzibit's "Los Angeles Times." Just like Gonzalez' similarly formatted *Disco Heat* set (also on BBE), *Hip Hop Forever* can be either nostalgic or educational to the listener, and it's undeniably fun regardless. —*Andy Kellman*

Goo

Ambient Breakbeat, Trip-Hop

Also known as "Le Gooster" and "DJ Goo," Goo was born Nguxi de Carvalho in Geneva at the end of the '60s. With Angolan ancestry and heavily influenced by music at a young age, by 11 Goo was spinning vinyl. In 1987 he purchased a Technics 1200 for his first turntable. After moving to the United States to study architecture, Goo became a household name in San Diego's dance circles in 1991. The following year, he returned to Switzerland and created a group called Tribe Vibes. Mixing dance with touches of jazz and hip-hop, Goo joined Silent Majority in 1993. The group released three albums as well as an EP while fostering a devoted fan base. In 1994 Goo performed at New York's New Music Seminar and the Montreaux Jazz Festival. Goo's first important creation was establishing the Five Star Galaxy, a collective of artists who released albums on its own label. In 1996 he released his debut effort, *Zig Zag Zen*. He also appeared on various dance album compilations in Europe and North America. In 1999 Goo formed his own label, Synchrovision. In 2000 Goo released *Fractal Abstraction* while opening for groups like the Roots, Gang Starr, and De La Soul. In 2001 he released *Elements*. He has performed at various DJ events and has been a regular host at the famed Blue Note in England. His sound has been compared to the likes of DJ Krush. —*Jason MacNeil*

Fractal Abstraction / Sep. 12, 2000 / Shadow ◆◆◆◆

Switzerland isn't usually considered one of the world's centers of experimental hip-hop and turntable artistry. But give Goo (aka Le Gooster) some time, and maybe it will be. *Fractal Abstraction* is certainly at least as impressive as anything being produced by better-known artists from areas more generally associated with those genres. Opening with the hilarious samples ("This is a turntable/Do not confuse it with a sewing machine") and expert turntable work of "Synchrovision," the program proceeds through dancehall-inflected

trip-hop ("Offishall Chamberlain," big beat-inflected trip-hop "B.B.M.Q."), a bit of straight-up abstract groove with French movie samples ("L'Interrociteur"), and even some modified dub reggae (Minded). There are some very fine singers on this album, although none are credited (unless they're all Goo, which seems unlikely), as well as more bone-deep grooves and mind-expanding textures than you can shake a stick at. *Fractal Abstraction* is very impressive, and highly recommended. —*Rick Anderson*

● Elements / May 22, 2001 / Shadow ◆◆◆◆

This is the second Shadow release by Goo, a European turntablist who also runs his own label, Synchrovision, out of Switzerland. As with his previous effort, the mood is dark and funky, slightly down-tempo, but never afraid to kick things up a notch when the spirit directs. One might not normally associate Switzerland with experimental hip-hop, but after listening to *Elements* you'd swear there was a thriving scene. Goo has certainly absorbed a ton of influences somewhere along the way—on "Bomboclat Elements" he draws on jungle, reggae, and jazz to produce a piece of atmospheric and dub-inflected funk; "The Greatest" (here in a version remixed by DJ Cam) is a breakbeat tribute to Muhammad Ali; "Amour Bleu" takes lazy, jazzy beats and marries them to a rag bag of samples and virtuosic turntablism. The end result, a constantly fascinating album that dances lightly on the boundaries between acid jazz, breakbeat funk, and abstraction, is highly recommended. —*Rick Anderson*

Goodie Mob

f. 1991, Atlanta, GA
Group / Southern Rap, Dirty South

Goodie Mob's earnest and reverent approach made them one of the more admired groups of their era, and undeniably one of the most respected groups in the often irreverent and scoffed-at dirty South scene, if not *the* most respected. The Atlanta group's first album, *Soul Food* (1995), stands as one of the earliest Southern rap albums to emerge on a major label and, along with OutKast's debut, essentially proved that rap was no longer a West and East Coast phenomenon. Besides being pioneering, *Soul Food* also stood out for its quality—the album dealt with serious themes and featured an undeniably unique aesthetic, attributed as much to producers Organized Noize as group members Cee-Lo, Khujo, T-Mo, and Big Gipp. Goodie Mob's sincerity continued with *Still Standing*, their 1998 sophomore album, as did their still-unique sound. By this time, the dirty South movement had been put in motion and the group suddenly found themselves with a considerable following, most newcomers astounded by Goodie Mob's thoughtfulness relative to their Southern peers. As the '90s came to a close, Goodie Mob's close allegiance to fellow Atlanta rappers OutKast proved noteworthy in the wake of that group's breakthrough with *Stankonia*. No longer was Goodie Mob a cult phenomenon but rather a mass phenomenon. This commercial consciousness that had first surface on 1999's *World Party* had now become a more glaring issue for Goodie Mob, a group that had always prided themselves on sincerity rather than calculation. The pioneering yet increasingly conflicted group sadly broke up at this point, and the members embarked independently, beginning with Cee-Lo, who debuted in 2002 with *Cee-Lo Green and His Perfect Imperfections*. —*Jason Birchmeier*

★ Soul Food / Nov. 21, 1995 / La Face ◆◆◆◆◆

Over the years, Southern rap has come to be associated mostly with hit-factory labels like No Limit and Cash Money, or in its early days Miami bass music. In general, it's never been afforded much critical respect, but that started to change in the '90s, when Atlanta established itself as the home of intelligent, progressive Southern hip-hop. Despite some excellent predecessors, Goodie Mob's debut album, *Soul Food*, is arguably the city's first true classic, building on the social conscience of Arrested Development and the street smarts and distinctive production of OutKast. In fact, the production team behind the latter's *Southernplayalisticadillacmuzik*, Organized Noize, is also present here, and really hit their stride with a groundbreaking signature sound that reimagines a multitude of Southern musical traditions. *Soul Food* is built on spare, funky drum programs, Southern-fried guitar picking in the Stax/Volt vein, occasional stabs of blues harmonica, and strong gospel overtones in the piano licks and meditative keyboards. There's an even stronger spiritual flavor in the group's lyrics, based on a conviction that religion has been the saving grace of African-American culture as it's endured centuries of oppression. The album even opens with lead rapper Cee-Lo singing an original spiritual called "Free." Goodie Mob is firmly grounded in reality, though—they rail against a system stacked against poverty-stricken blacks, and are more than willing to defend themselves in a harsh environment, as on the gritty street tales "Dirty South," the eerie single "Cell Therapy," and "The Coming." The meat of the album, however, lies in its more reflective moments: the philosophical "Thought Process"; "Sesame Street," a reminiscence on growing up poor and black; "Guess Who," one of hip-hop's greatest mama tributes ever; and the warm title track, which is about exactly what it says. If soul food was aptly named for its spiritual nourishment, the same is true of this underappreciated gem. —*Steve Huey*

Still Standing / Apr. 7, 1998 / La Face ◆◆◆◆
Goodie Mob's debut album was a production masterpiece that ranks as perhaps the most Southern-sounding Southern rap album ever recorded; similarly, lead rapper Cee-Lo is one of the most Southern MCs on record, with a raspy, nasal, rural-sounding drawl that's utterly distinctive. The follow-up album, *Still Standing*, is mostly more of the same great stuff, with producers Organized Noize refining the soulful, organic blueprint laid out on *Soul Food*. There are some more up-tempo percussion tracks here, with a few detours into more typical Southern bounce tracks; it's mildly disappointing to hear Goodie Mob following trends instead of setting them, but they're well executed all the same. When the results are more imaginative, as on the hit single "They Don't Dance No Mo'" and "Ghetto-ology," it's a terrific expansion of the group's sound; so is the heavy, guitar-driven rocker "Just About Over." The hardcore themes that occasionally popped up on *Soul Food* are a smaller presence on *Still Standing*; even so, while the group may be progressive in sentiment, they still aren't gentle in language. And their trademark social and spiritual awareness is very much in evidence. "The Experience" is a nimble meditation on the word "nigga"; "Black Ice," "Fly Away," and "Inshallah" have the deep gospel feel that makes Goodie Mob so unique; "Beautiful Skin" professes deep respect for women who respect themselves; and "Gutta Butta" and "Greeny Green" are reflections on neighborhood pride (by way of not littering) and materialism, respectively. Cee-Lo is even more of a breakout individual presence on *Still Standing*, and his unique style can sometimes overshadow his bandmates; plus, a few tracks just aren't that engaging. But overall, *Still Standing* is an excellent follow-up to a major artistic statement. —*Steve Huey*

World Party / Dec. 21, 1999 / La Face ◆◆◆
Fresh for the end of the millennium, Goodie Mob cut loose and put the bounce back into Southern rap with their third album. As listeners might gather from the title, *World Party* is just that—a party record, with fewer message tracks than were found on Goodie Mob's first two albums. In their place are hands-in-the-air party songs like the title track, "Get Rich to This," "Chain Swang," and the great TLC collaboration "What It Ain't (Ghetto Enuff)." The production, mostly by Organized Noize or Deric "D-Dot" Angelettie (aka the Madd Rapper), isn't quite as strong as it has been in the past, but Goodie Mob's laid-back rhymes and vocal choruses make up for the deficit. —*John Bush*

Gorillaz

f. 2000
Group / Hip-Hop, Alternative Pop/Rock, Alternative Rap
Conceived as the first virtual hip-hop group, Gorillaz blends the musical talents of Dan "the Automator" Nakamura, Blur's Damon Albarn, Cibo Matto's Miho Hatori, and the Tom Tom Club's Tina Weymouth and Chris Frantz with the arresting visuals of Jamie Hewlett, best known as the creator of the cult comic *Tank Girl*. Nakamura's Deltron 3030 cohorts Kid Koala and Del tha Funkee Homosapien round out the creative team behind the Gorillaz quartet, which includes 2-D, the cute but spacy singer/keyboardist; Murdoc, the spooky, possibly Satanic bassist who is the brains behind the group; drummer Russel, who is equally inspired by "Farrakhan and Chaka Khan" and is possessed by "funkyphantoms" that occasionally rise up and provide some zombie-style rapping; and last but not least, Noodle, a ten-year-old Japanese guitar virtuosa and martial arts master. The group's website, www.gorillaz.com, showcases Hewlett's visuals and the group's music in eye- and ear-catching detail. Gorillaz debuted in late 2000 with the *Tomorrow Comes Today* EP, which they followed early the next year with the "Clint Eastwood" single; their self-titled full-length debut arrived in spring 2001 in the U.K. —*Heather Phares*

● **Gorillaz** / Apr. 24, 2001 / Virgin ◆◆◆◆◆
It's tempting to judge Gorillaz—Damon Albarn, Tank Girl creator Jamie Hewlett, and Dan "the Automator" Nakamura's virtual band—just by their brilliantly animated videos and write the project off as another triumph of style over substance. Admittedly, Hewlett's edgy-cute characterizations of 2-D, Gorillaz' pretty-boy singer (who looks a cross between the Charlatans' Tim Burgess and Sonic the Hedgehog), sinister bassist Murdoc, whiz-kid guitarist Noodle, and b-boy drummer Russel are so arresting that they almost detract from Gorillaz' music. The amazing "Thriller"-meets-*Planet of the Apes* clip for "Clint Eastwood" is so visually clever that it's easy to take the song's equally clever, hip-hop-tinged update of the Specials' "Ghost Town" for granted. And initially, Gorillaz' self-titled debut feels incomplete when Hewlett's imagery is removed; the concept of Gorillaz as a virtual band doesn't hold up as well when you can't see the virtual bandmembers. It's too bad that there isn't a DVD version of *Gorillaz*, with videos for every song, à la the DVD version of Super Furry Animals' *Rings Around the World*. Musically, however, *Gorillaz* is a cutely caricatured blend of Albarn's eclectic Brit-pop and Nakamura's equally wide-ranging hip-hop, and it sounds almost as good as the band looks. Albarn has fun sending up Blur's cheeky pop on songs like "5/4" and "Re-Hash," their trip-hop experiments on "New Genious" and "Sound Check," and "Song 2"-like thrash-pop on "Punk" and "M1 A1." Despite the similarities between Albarn's main gig and his contributions here, *Gorillaz* isn't an Albarn solo album in disguise; Nakamura's bass- and beat-oriented production gives the album an authentically dub and hip-hop-inspired feel, particularly on "Rock the House" and "Tomorrow Comes Today." Likewise, Del tha Funkee Homosapien, Miho Hatori, and Ibrahim Ferrer's vocals ensure that it sounds like a diverse collaboration rather than an insular side project. Instead, it feels like a musical vacation for all parties involved—a little self-indulgent, but filled with enough fun ideas and good songs to make this virtual band's debut a genuinely enjoyable album. —*Heather Phares*

B-Side Collection / Jan. 1, 2002 / EMI ◆◆◆◆
The good part about being a fictional cartoon band that has their music supplied by popular cult musicians is that even the B sides need to be carefully calculated. Instead of getting the lowbrow toss-aways that haunt most collections like this, Gorillaz supply listeners with some high-quality toss-aways instead. The most ear-pleasing tracks come from teaming with rapper Phi Life Cypher, who adds a bizarre hardcore rap to the remix of "Clint Eastwood," which also benefits from a well-rounded breakdown. "The Sounder," their other collaboration, is a hip-hop/blues mix featuring Damon Albarn squeaking out the lyrics to a clever Automator beat. "Faust" is an interesting elevator music experiment, while the poppy "12D3" is the closest this project has ever come to sounding like Albarn's Blur. "Hip Albatross" is a disturbing sound collage featuring Albarn's weak voice rambling beneath the creepiness, while the awesome "Ghost Train" is like Prince filtered through Kraftwerk. Some very good remixes of "Left Hand Suzuki Method" and "19-2000" are included, and the two other tracks are just revisiting from the first album under the guise of an "edit." This is a pretty good album that does not often take the easy way out. A few tracks are questionable (and leaving off the "9 11" single is a big mistake), but fans should be happy with the rare material found here. —*Bradley Torreano*

G-Sides / Feb. 26, 2002 / Virgin ◆◆◆
Though it seems a bit soon for a virtual group with only one album to its name to be releasing a B-sides collection, Gorillaz' *G-Sides* more or less justifies its existence by gathering some of the best extra tracks from the band's singles, most of which are only available as imports. As with Gorillaz, which surrounded catchy songs like "Clint Eastwood" and "19-2000" with quirkier, more experimental tracks, the band uses its B sides as a chance to stretch out even further musically, either with remixes or with unconventional musical sketches. *G-Sides* features some of each, ranging from the even bouncier, more upbeat remix of "19-2000" by Soulchild to the rather eerie "Hip Albatross," which mixes samples of moaning zombies from *Dawn of the Dead* with trip-hoppy beats and moody guitars. Rapper Phi Life Cyber reinforces Gorillaz' hip-hop roots by joining them on two tracks, a reworking of "Clint Eastwood" and "The Sounder." The appealingly simple "12D3," with its strummy guitar and playful Damon Albarn vocals, recalls some of Blur's later work, and the funky, quirky "Ghost Train" and the English version of "Latin Simone" also are as enjoyable as anything that appeared on *Gorillaz*. Aside

from the Wiseguys' rather limp reworking of "19-2000," the only problem with *G-Sides* is its brevity; the U.S. version only includes ten of their B sides, none of which are from their biggest single, "Clint Eastwood." And while most of the import singles featured CD-ROM tracks of the group's amazing animated videos, none of them appear here. Though the enhanced version of *G-Sides* and the Japanese *B-Side Collection* feature more of Gorillaz' B sides, and they'll probably have a video collection sooner rather than later, these kinds of omissions make *G-Sides* a slightly frustrating collection. Gorillaz completists will no doubt have all of the import singles already, but *G-Sides* is the logical next step for anyone intrigued by the group's debut. —*Heather Phares*

Laika Come Home / Jul. 16, 2002 / Astralwerks ◆◆◆
The enormous success of Gorillaz' self-titled debut spawned a couple of collections from the animated hip-hop group as a way of satisfying their public until their Svengalis, Dan "the Automator" Nakamura and Damon Albarn, could reconvene to deliver new material. *G-Sides* was a more or less straightforward B sides collection, while *Laika Come Home* offered a unique twist on the remix album. Instead of hiring several DJs and artists to remix the group's songs, Albarn and Nakamura had Space Monkeyz, who did a dub version of "Clint Eastwood" as a B side for that single, rework all of Gorillaz' songs as dub excursions. While the actual identities of the Space Monkeyz are questionable—gorillaz.com says they are "mutant offspring of the monkey cosmonauts sent into space during the Cold War"—their remixing skills and dedication to authentic-sounding dub are undeniable. An appropriately laid-back, playful feel permeates *Laika Come Home*; the album's best moments, such as "19-2000 (Jungle Fresh)," "New Genius (Brother) (Mutant Genius)," and "M1A1 (Lil' Dub Chefin')" explore the dub influences at the root of Gorillaz' sound and offer a fun, fresh take on the songs. In all, while it's not as exciting—or, arguably, necessary —as a new Gorillaz album, *Laika Come Home* is still a more satisfying work than the usual boring or unpredictable remix album. Fans awaiting the Gorillaz' next move will be sufficiently entertained by this summery, spacy collection. —*Heather Phares*

Gospel Gangstaz

Group / Contemporary Gospel, Christian Rap
The Gospel Gangstaz comprised DJ Dove, Chilly Chill, Tic Toc, and Mr. Solo, all onetime Los Angeles gangbangers who later spread the Lord's message via the hard beats and gritty rhymes of the West Coast rap sound. Debuting in 1994 with *Gang Affiliated*, the group returned two years later with *Do or Die; I Can See Clearly Now* followed in 1999. —*Jason Ankeny*

● **I Can See Clearly Now** / May 18, 1999 / B-Rite ◆◆◆◆
After years of mediocre, overly rock-oriented crossovers between gospel and the rap scene, Kirk Franklin & the Family led a resurgence in the field with albums that did equally well in both areas. *I Can See Clearly Now* by Gospel Gangstaz is the next step in the evolution, with all aspects of the album—production, rapping, lyrics—up to the level of (if not superior to) secular hip-hop. The tight grooves and excellent gospel background singers make the title track a highlight, and though a few other tracks are somewhat derivative of contemporary rappers like Busta Rhymes and Master P, *I Can See Clearly Now* works just as well with secular listeners as praise music. —*John Bush*

Irv Gotti (Irving Lorenzo)

b. 1971, Queens, NY

Producer, Executive Producer / East Coast Rap, Pop-Rap, Hardcore Rap, Urban
Hitmaker Irv Gotti produced a flurry of hits for such artists as Ja Rule, Ashanti, and DMX beginning in the late '90s, in the process building his Murder Inc. boutique label into a small empire. Like other superstar producers Dr. Dre and Timbaland, Gotti's name often carried more clout than that of his artists, and the major labels came to him often in search of hit productions for their own artists. When he wasn't busy in the studio, Gotti also managed to stir up controversy, whether with his arch-rival 50 Cent or his alleged criminal background.

Born Irving Lorenzo in Hollis, Queens, in 1971, Gotti's career in the rap industry as a producer began in the mid-'90s when he aligned himself with Mic Geronimo, a New York MC whose debut album, *The Natural* (1995), featured Gotti's production (as DJ Irv, his onetime moniker). Gotti's big break

came when he contributed production to *Reasonable Doubt* (1996), Jay-Z's debut album. The album became an overnight classic, and soon Gotti's beats were in demand. He next began working with DMX, whose debut album, *It's Dark and Hell Is Hot* (1998), similarly became a very influential album within the trendy rap industry. Then came Ja's debut album, *Venni Vetti Vecci* (1999). This album wasn't quite as successful as Jay-Z's or DMX's debuts, but it further established Gotti's hitmaking ability with unknown artists. The hits only increased with each passing year. Following Gotti's success executive producing DMX and Ja, Def Jam—the label responsible for both artists—granted the producer his own boutique label, Murder Inc., which Def Jam would market and distribute.

Murder Inc.'s flagship release, *Irv Gotti Presents: The Murderers* (2000), didn't quite scale the charts like Gotti's work for Jay-Z or DMX had, though. Nonetheless, he continued producing hits, most notably for Ja, whose second album, *Rule 3:36* (2000), racked up a number of chart-topping Gotti productions, as did his next album, *Pain Is Love* (2001). Thanks to Gotti's success with Ja, Def Jam gave the producer more room to establish Murder Inc. as a franchise on a par with other boutique labels such as Roc-A-Fella and Bad Boy. Gotti then delivered the superstar Def Jam had hoped for: Ashanti. Gotti and the young female vocalist collaborated on a series of chart-topping hits in early 2000s, among them Ja's "Always on Time," Fat Joe's "What's Luv?," and Ashanti's own "Foolish," all three Top Ten hits—simultaneously!

By this point, Gotti had risen to Dr. Dre-like proportions in the rap industry. He was more than a producer; he was a hitmaker, and for a while, he made headlines regularly. He spoke the media about his plans to work with Michael Jackson and sign Nas to Murder Inc. Just before the 2002 holiday season he banked on his marketable name yet again by releasing a remix album, *Irv Gotti Presents: The Remixes*, comprised mainly of reworked tracks featuring Ashanti, Ja, and a stable of others. Then controversy struck. Throughout all of his hitmaking and headlines, Gotti had long fostered a shady persona. He initially presented himself as a self-made don, particularly when he was on the rise during the late '90s. For instance, he named his SoHo studio the Crack House. He furthermore allegedly had ties to Kenneth "Supreme" McGriff, a legendary drug dealer also from Queens. These ties were well documented in various songs, among them a particularly revealing one, "Ghetto Qua Ran," by popular rapper 50 Cent. The young, loud-mouthed fellow Queens native had a long, adversarial relationship with Gotti and the Murder Inc. camp, a storied one that involves shootings, stabbing, and orders of protection.

Amid all of this controversy, the FBI decided to investigate. They raided the Murder Inc. office on January 3, 2003, and the investigation made headlines everywhere, from MTV News ("Drugs, Friends & Allegations: Inside the Murder Inc. Raid") to *The New York Times* ("Inquiry Into Rap Label Asks if 'Gangsta' Is More Than Genre"). More shootings followed throughout New York: The office of 50 Cent's management company, Violator, was shot up multiple times, and Gotti's brother, Chris, was subsequently shot in the leg outside of the Def Jam office. —*Jason Birchmeier*

● **Irv Gotti Presents: The Inc.** / Jul. 2, 2002 / Def Jam ◆◆◆◆
Two years after the lukewarm reception given to his *Murderers* various-artists album, Irv Gotti unleashed his second, *Irv Gotti Presents: The Inc.* During the two-year intermission, Gotti's label, Murder Inc, grew enormously. In particular, Ja Rule and Ashanti scored huge hits, and Gotti himself moved further toward Dr. Dre-size proportions as a producer. Given all the success for Gotti and his label, it's understandable that he'd return with a hard-hitting follow-up to his *Murderers* collection. Gotti first diversified his roster, adding Charli Baltimore in hopes of duplicating the success of Ashanti. Similarly, he integrated more R&B into his songs, often juxtaposing his male gangstas with his hook-singing females just as he'd done on so many hits for Ja. Besides the vocals, he changed his production style a bit—actually, to be more accurate, that of his coproducers—moving closer toward the sound Dre and the Neptunes popularized in the early 2000s: real instruments and tight rhythms. Finally, he expanded his roster, bringing in yet more thugs to complement Ja, Caddillac Tah, and Black Child. The result seems great in concept and works well on songs like "Down 4 U" and "Ain't It Funny." The non-singles aren't quite as memorable, often weighed down by excessive thuggishness. Still, there's a wealth of music here, everything from girly melodies ("No One Does It Better") to brute swaggering ("We Still Don't Give a F**k"). It's important to keep in mind, however, that Gotti didn't intend this album to play seamlessly but rather more like a sampler. And as a label sampler,

The Inc. surely succeeds, giving you a taste of everything from the girly stuff to the brute swaggering. —*Jason Birchmeier*

Irv Gotti Presents: The Remixes / Oct. 29, 2002 / Universal ♦♦♦
Irv Gotti's *The Remixes* functions as much more than just a cash-in effort; it's a chance for one of hip-hop's most respected trackmasters to revamp tracks from his solid 2002 LP, *The Inc.* Gotti disses P. Diddy's *We Invented the Remix* with a spoken intro, then launches with "Unfoolish," his production hit for protégé Ashanti also heard on P. Diddy's record. Ashanti does well on mixes of "I'm So Happy" and "The Pledge," while Gotti detours into hardcore with a tough remix of "O.G." with Caddillac Tah. The new tracks "Poverlous" and "Me & My Boyfriend" also shine, showing Gotti's way with a production—smoking tracks that borrow from hardcore, funk, and old school but always sound original. It's obviously not as necessary as the original *Irv Gotti Presents: The Inc.,* but much fun for the already converted. —*John Bush*

GP Wu

f. 1996, Staten Island, NY
Group / East Coast Rap, Hardcore Rap
Relatively minor stars in the Wu-Tang constellation, GP Wu released their debut, *Don't Go Against the Grain,* in 1998. That album was produced by Daddy O from Stetsasonic and Hank Shocklee of Bomb Squad and Public Enemy fame, making the Wu-Tang connection even more tenuous. However, as Wu-Tang Clan historians will undoubtedly know, the four GP Wu members—Rubberbands, June Luva, Pop da Brown Hornet, and Down Low Recka—all made appearances on Shyheim's first two albums, *Shyheim a/k/a the Rugged Child* (1994) and *Lost Generation* (1996). The connection was made indelible on Shyheim's *Manchild* album cover from 1999, featuring the shirtless MC with a GP Wu tattoo on his bicep. —*Wade Kergan*

● **Don't Go Against the Grain** / Jan. 27, 1998 / MCA ♦♦♦
Yet another offshoot of the wildly successful Wu-Tang Clan, the four members of GP Wu (Rubberbands, June Luva, Down Low Recka, and Pop da Brown Hornet) do a good job of replicating the Wu-Tang sound, but fail to live up to the somewhat lofty standards the rap conglomerate has established. *Don't Go Against the Grain* is a very consistent effort, overflowing with the style that is so distinct to hardcore East Coast rap. Consistency, however, is not necessarily genius. While the album is not completely forgettable, it fails to be particularly memorable either. —*David M. Childers*

Grand Puba (Maxwell Dixon)

b. New Rochelle, NY
Golden Age, Hip-Hop, East Coast Rap, Jazz-Rap
Maxwell Dixon, better known as Grand Puba, is best known for fronting Brand Nubian for the group's first album—and the excellent full-blown reunion album, 1998's *Foundation*—but he actually made his commercial debut with the Masters of Ceremony, a group who released a 1988 album (*Dynamite*) on 4th & Broadway. Puba went solo with 1992's *Reel to Reel,* which featured the excellent singles "360 Degrees (What Goes Around)" and "Check It Out" (with Mary J. Blige). Never the most prolific rap artist, it took three years for a sophomore release (1995's *2000*), and his third album (the lackluster *Understand This*) didn't come until 2001. Throughout his career, his lyrical schemes have been drizzled with the influence of his Nation of Islam beliefs. —*Andy Kellman*

● **Reel to Reel** / 1992 / Elektra ♦♦♦♦
In a sense, Grand Puba really never was a genuine member of Brand Nubian. He was several years older than Lord Jamar and Sadat X and had already recorded with the old school crew Masters of Ceremony several years before finally hooking up with his younger mates. And even the mostly collective-minded *One for All* featured a couple Puba solo joints. Based on the sophomore Brand Nubian outing, it is pretty clear that Grand Puba's carefree verbal play, completely unencumbered by ideology, tempered the more in-your-face manifestation of Jamar and Sadat X's radical politics since *In God We Trust,* as thrillingly polemical as it could be, was also rather severe and uncompromising, even apocalyptic, in its outlook, and therefore off-putting at times. Likewise, based on this debut solo album, it's clear that Brand Nubian created precisely the right context in which Puba's self-reflexive braggadocio could flourish without wearing thin because *Reel to Reel,* as much fun as it is, has little in the way of substance. As a result, the record never becomes more than a pleasing divertissement. Minus any counterweights who can "drop the

science," Puba, like some sort of hip-hop Dolemite, proved to be interested mostly in self-puffery, partying, and playing the ladies. While the persona is entertaining as far as it goes, it doesn't have a lot of mileage in it unless you have a high tolerance for tall tales about stunts and blunts. The artist himself had a good time satirizing this penchant at the beginning of the classic "Wake Up" from *One for All,* but he seems to have lost sight of some of the possibilities for self-parody here. Having said that, the album really does have a lot to offer, including the irresistible one-two punch of "Check Tha Resume" and "360 Degrees," the deep-fried "Honey Don't Front," and the delightfully lazy "Who Makes the Loot?," whipped off with Brand New Heavies when they were at their funkiest. The production (most of it by the artist himself) is universally excellent, and Puba is, without a doubt, one of the most clever, most cheekily complex MCs to ever pick up a microphone. Just bring your incredulity and sense of humor—the lower the brow, the better—and *Reel to Reel* is a real hoot. —*Stanton Swihart*

2000 / Jun. 20, 1995 / Elektra ♦♦♦
Grand Puba's second solo album continues his groundbreaking fusion of jazz and hip-hop, adding a harder, street-oriented edge for *2000.* The production saves the album, even when the songs are weak. —*Stephen Thomas Erlewine*

Understand This / Oct. 23, 2001 / Koch International ♦♦
After being hailed as a promising talent following his debut with Brand Nubian in 1990, Grand Puba struggled through a rocky decade. His 1992 solo debut, *Reel to Reel,* and a 1998 reunion album with Brand Nubian, *Reunited,* ended up being the only other highlights in an otherwise quiet decade for Puba. In 2001, however, he made an ambitious return to the rap game with *Understand This,* his first solo album in over five years and the first album on his Rising Son label (distributed and marketed by Koch). Furthermore, Puba produces every track on this comeback album. But, despite his ambition, Puba's return feels awkward and ultimately a bit embarrassing. Rap has always been a culture by and for youth, and particularly in the early 2000s more than ever. Therefore, a veteran like Puba seems more than a little out of place among other East Coast rappers of the era like Jay-Z and DMX. Ultimately, Puba's just too old for the rap game. He's out of touch with the times and sounds ridiculous trying to coopt early-2000s lingo like "ice." And it doesn't help that his productions, though adequate, are less than engaging. In the end, like the many other comebacks rappers trying to make comebacks in the early 2000s, Grand Puba ultimately embarrasses himself with *Understand This.* Sure, you have to commend his efforts and his courage, but, even if you're a longtime fan, you kind of wish he'd thrown in the towel when he was still on top of the game. It'd be different if Puba would have stuck with his old style. However, that's sadly not the case. He's an old man unsuccessfully trying to sound young. —*Jason Birchmeier*

Grand Wizard Theodore (Theodore Livingstone)

DJ / Hip-Hop, Old School Rap
One of early hip-hop's most skilled DJs, Grand Wizard Theodore is universally acknowledged as the inventor of the scratch. Grandmaster Flash pioneered many early turntable techniques, including "cutting" records (manually cueing up duplicate copies of the same record in order to play the same passage, cutting back and forth between them), but it was the young Theodore who built on Flash's work by taking the scratching sound, made when the records were cued, and adding a rhythm that made the turntable into a percussion instrument the DJ could "play." Theodore is also credited with pioneering the needle drop, a technique where instead of cueing up the record silently, the DJ simply drops the needle onto the exact start of the passage to be played.

Grand Wizard Theodore was born Theodore Livingstone and grew up in the Bronx. His older brothers Gene and Claudio were an early hip-hop duo called the L-Brothers, and they frequently collaborated with Grandmaster Flash. Flash discovered that young Theodore (not even a teenager yet) had a natural affinity for the turntables, and when Flash spun records in public parks, he would sometimes set up a milk crate to let Theodore DJ. According to legend, Theodore invented scratching largely by accident, circa 1977 (when he was about 13 or 14); holed up in his bedroom playing records, Theodore had to pause to hear his mother scold him about the volume, and happened to move one of the records back and forth. He liked the sound and played with it often, developing the technique until it was ready for public performance. Flash picked up on it quickly, and Theodore in turn began copying Flash's acrobatic record-spinning tricks (using his elbows, feet, etc.).

By the time the '80s rolled around, Grand Wizard Theodore was one of the top DJs in New York. He hooked up with a crew that was most often billed as Grand Wizard Theodore and the Fantastic Five MCs, which released the cult classic single "Can I Get a Soul Clap" in 1980 on the Tuff City label. The group never recorded a proper album, but they did appear in the 1983 old school hip-hop film *Wild Style* (which later became a cult classic); they recorded several songs on the soundtrack and appeared in an MC battle sequence with their chief rivals the Cold Crush Brothers. While Grand Wizard Theodore never received the same wide acclaim as Grandmaster Flash during his career, he was eventually rediscovered by hip-hop historians, which helped him land some international DJ gigs in the '90s. He also appeared at the Rock and Roll Hall of Fame's 1999 hip-hop conference, and teaches advanced classes in the art of DJing. — *Steve Huey*

Grandmaster Caz (Curtis Fisher)

Old School Rap, Hip-Hop, Party Rap
The first simultaneous DJ and MC in hip-hop history, Grandmaster Caz is perhaps best known for rhymes he didn't even perform—namely, the uncredited verses that Big Bank Hank borrowed for the groundbreaking Sugarhill Gang single "Rapper's Delight." The fact that neither Caz nor his group the Cold Crush Brothers ever recorded an official full-length album also doesn't help shed much light on his legacy—an unfortunate injustice, considering he was one of the most important and influential pioneers of old school rap.

Grandmaster Caz was born Curtis Fisher and grew up in the Bronx, where DJ Kool Herc began playing block parties in the early '70s. Caz attended his first Herc party in 1974, and was amazed by the huge, booming sound system and the way Herc worked the crowd. Inspired to try doing the same thing, he immediately purchased some equipment and adopted the DJ name Casanova Fly (which later morphed into Grandmaster Caz). After honing his skills, Caz teamed up with JDL (aka Jerry Dee Lewis) to form the Notorious Two, and during this period became the first DJ to rap while handling records on the turntables. Both Caz and JDL joined the Cold Crush Brothers circa 1978-1979, with Caz becoming a full-time MC. In 1979, former R&B singer and label head Sylvia Robinson discovered Caz's friend Big Bank Hank rapping along with one of Caz's practice tapes. Impressed, she invited him to become the third member of a studio rap group called the Sugarhill Gang, which was set to record the first rap single. Without revealing the true author, Hank went to Caz and asked to borrow the rhymes for the record; Caz agreed, hoping for an eventual favor in return—which never materialized, and neither did songwriting credit or royalties.

Despite that mishap, Caz did find a measure of underground success with the Cold Crush Brothers. They recorded several singles for the Tuff City label during the early '80s (compiled in 1996 on *Fresh Wild Fly & Bold*), and became one of the most popular live rap groups in New York during the pre-Run-D.M.C. era. Most prominently, the Cold Crush Brothers appeared in the 1983 old school hip-hop film *Wild Style*, which has since become a cult classic; they recorded the theme song and engaged in an MC battle with their chief rivals, Grand Wizard Theodore and the Fantastic Five.

Like most other old school artists, the Cold Crush Brothers didn't survive the advent of Run-D.M.C., and Caz launched a brief solo career in the late '80s. Again recording for Tuff City, his singles included "Mr. Bill," "Yvette," "Count Basie," "I'm Caz," "Casanova's Rap," and "Get Down Grandmaster." None of them made much of an impact, and Caz faded from the music scene for a time. With more attention being paid to the roots of hip-hop in the late '90s, Caz's name resurfaced as an early pioneer, and he began making appearances at historical conferences like the one staged in 1999 by the Rock and Roll Hall of Fame. In 2000 he released a new single titled "MC Delight," which addressed the "Rapper's Delight" controversy. — *Steve Huey*

● **The Grandest of Them All** / 1992 / Tuff City ✦✦✦
When an artist has an album titled *The Grandest of Them All* and one of its tracks is titled "I'm a Legend," he is likely to be accused of having a swollen, excessively large ego. But in the case of Grandmaster Caz, saying "I'm a Legend" isn't empty boasting—it's a statement of fact. One of the pioneers of old school hip-hop, Caz really is a legend. The New Yorker is a veteran of the late-'70s South Bronx/Harlem scene that also gave us Kool DJ Herc,

Grandmaster Flash & the Furious Five, Kurtis Blow, the Cold Crush Brothers, and the Treacherous Three—in other words, the MCs and DJs who paved the way for everyone from Run-D.M.C. to Public Enemy to Ice-T. When *The Grandest of Them All* came out in 1992, Caz was no longer considered cutting edge; hip-hoppers identified him with rap's old school era of the late '70s and early '80s. But this album doesn't sound quite as dated as some might assume; tunes like "Star Search," "Ducksauce," and "I'm a Legend" aren't oblivious to early-'90s rap tastes. Nonetheless, Caz doesn't try to hide his old school heritage. The album is full of references to hip-hop's early years, and even though Caz tries to update his rapping style somewhat, he still sounds like a product of rap's old school era. And why shouldn't he? If it wasn't for Caz and his pioneering hip-hop colleagues in Harlem and the South Bronx, many of the rappers who emerged in the 1980s wouldn't have been so successful. *The Grandest of Them All* doesn't contain the veteran MC's most essential work, but it's a decent, respectable effort that showed Caz still had some tricks up his sleeve in 1992. — *Alex Henderson*

Grandmaster Flash (Joseph Saddler)

b. Jan. 1, 1958, Barbados, West Indies
DJ, Producer / Hip-Hop, Club/Dance, Electro, Old School Rap
DJ Grandmaster Flash and his group the Furious Five were hip-hop's greatest innovators, transcending the genre's party-music origins to explore the full scope of its lyrical and sonic horizons. Flash was born Joseph Saddler in Barbados on January 1, 1958; he began spinning records as a teen growing up in the Bronx, performing live at area dances and block parties. By age 19, while attending technical school courses in electronics during the day, he was also spinning on the local disco circuit; over time, he developed a series of groundbreaking techniques including "cutting" (moving between tracks exactly on the beat), "backspinning" (manually turning records to repeat brief snippets of sound), and "phasing" (manipulating turntable speeds)—in short, creating the basic vocabulary which DJs continue to follow even today.

Flash did not begin collaborating with rappers until around 1977, first teaming with the legendary Kurtis Blow. He then began working with the Furious Five—rappers Melle Mel (Melvin Glover), Cowboy (Keith Wiggins), Kid Creole (Nathaniel Glover), Mr. Ness aka Scorpio (Eddie Morris), and Rahiem (Guy Williams); the group quickly became legendary throughout New York City, attracting notice not only for Flash's unrivaled skills as a DJ but also for the Five's masterful rapping, most notably for their signature trading and blending of lyrics. Despite their local popularity, they did not record until after the Sugarhill Gang's smash "Rapper's Delight" proved the existence of a market for hip-hop releases; after releasing "We Rap More Mellow" as the Younger Generation, Flash and the Five recorded "Superappin'" for the Enjoy label owned by R&B legend Bobby Robinson. They then switched to Sugar Hill, owned by Sylvia Robinson (no relation), after she promised them an opportunity to rap over a current DJ favorite, "Get Up and Dance" by Freedom (the idea had probably been originally conceived by Crash Crew for their single "High Powered Rap").

That record, 1980's "Freedom," the group's Sugar Hill debut, reached the Top 20 on national R&B charts on its way to selling over 50,000 copies; its follow-up, "Birthday Party," was also a hit. "The Adventures of Grandmaster Flash on the Wheels of Steel" (1981) was the group's first truly landmark recording, introducing Flash's "cutting" techniques to create a stunning sound collage from snippets of songs by Chic, Blondie, and Queen. Flash and the Five's next effort, 1982's "The Message," was even more revelatory—for the first time, hip-hop became a vehicle not merely for bragging and boasting but also for trenchant social commentary, with Melle Mel delivering a blistering rap detailing the grim realities of life in the ghetto. The record was a major critical hit, and it was an enormous step in solidifying rap as an important and enduring form of musical expression.

Following 1983's anti-cocaine polemic "White Lines," relations between Flash and Melle Mel turned ugly, and the rapper soon left the group, forming a new unit also dubbed the Furious Five. After a series of Grandmaster Flash solo albums including 1985's *They Said It Couldn't Be Done*, 1986's *The Source*, and 1987's *Da Bop Boom Bang*, he reformed the original Furious Five lineup for a charity concert at Madison Square Garden; soon after, the reconstituted group recorded a new LP, 1988's *On the Strength*, which earned a lukewarm reception from fans and critics alike. Another reunion followed in 1994, when Flash and the Five joined a rap package tour also including

Kurtis Blow and Run-D.M.C. A year later, Flash and Melle Mel also appeared on Duran Duran's cover of "White Lines." Except for a few compilations during the late '90s, Flash was relatively quiet until 2002, when a pair of mix albums appeared: *The Official Adventures of Grandmaster Flash* on Strut and *Essential Mix: Classic Edition* on ffrr. —*Jason Ankeny*

The Message / 1982 / Sugar Hill ✦✦✦✦✦
Grandmaster Flash and the Furious Five merged the Afro-centric consciousness expressed by such early rappers as Gil Scott-Heron and the Last Poets with b-boy production to create "The Message," an all-time rap anthem. It was the focal point of *The Message*, which also included "It's Nasty" and "Scorpio," two other strong cuts that might have been winners on their own. Unfortunately, rather than a starting point, this album proved to be their ultimate peak. —*Ron Wynn*

The Source / 1986 / Elektra ✦✦✦
Grandmaster Flash's follow-up to *The Message* was his first without the Furious Five. Things weren't the same from a compositional or performance standpoint, as his raps seemed weaker and his rhymes almost devoid of crispness, humor, or insight. Only "Ms. Thang" and "Street Scene" offered any hint of the incisiveness or vision depicted in "The Message." —*Ron Wynn*

Da Bop Boom Bang / 1987 / Elektra ✦✦
The fire was gone and the imagination and flair diminished on this 1987 album. Grandmaster Flash sounded too tired on such cuts as "Big Black Caddy," "Get Yours," and "U Know What Time It Is" to recapture the spirit and bristling intensity that made "The Message" an anthem. He was sadly more effective doing nonsense like "Them Jeans." —*Ron Wynn*

On the Strength / 1988 / Elektra ✦
Grandmaster Flash and The Furious Five tried to regroup on this 1988 release, but old school hip-hop had been lapped by the charge of the new school. There was little interest or response to such cuts as "Tear The Roof Off" and "Boy Is Dope," while "Fly Girl" and "Magic Carpet Ride" sounded dated and weary. —*Ron Wynn*

★ **Message From Beat Street: The Best of Grandmaster Flash, Melle Mel & the Furious Five** / Apr. 19, 1994 / Rhino ✦✦✦✦✦
A diplomatically titled Rhino compilation, *Message From Beat Street: The Best of Grandmaster Flash, Melle Mel & the Furious Five* is a no-brainer collection featuring the absolute best of the group's four years on Sugar Hill—from the national breakout with 1980's "Freedom" to the beginning of the end, Melle Mel and the Furious Five's rap-on-film classic, "Beat Street." Backed by the party-pleasing productions of Joey and Sylvia Robinson plus gorgeous grooves courtesy of the Sugar Hill house band (guitarist Skip McDonald, bassist Doug Wimbish, drummer Keith LeBlanc), Grandmaster Flash and company recorded most of rap's popular classics from the early '80s, providing a crucial bridge from the street-party aesthetic of the late '70s to Run-D.M.C.'s mid-'80s breakout. Rappers Melle Mel, Scorpio, Cowboy, Kid Creole, and Raheem were tied to old school delivery (carefully and slowly phrased), but they did it better than all the others and had the DJ as well as the tracks to match. Flash and the Five also had the most diversity of any other early rap group, encompassing the refreshing Furious Five/Sugarhill Gang collaboration "Showdown" (more a posse track than a battle), a gritty street-level snapshot of modern life (rap's all-time classic "The Message"), and the vocoder paranoia of "Scorpio." Rhino could've done a better job without too much trouble (simply swapping an ineffective new megamix with the DJ landmark "Adventures on the Wheels of Steel" would go a long way), but *Message From Beat Street* is still the best introduction to the authors of old school's greatest hits. —*John Bush*

Adventures of Grandmaster Flash, Melle Mel & The Furious Five: More of the Best / Jul. 1996 / Rhino ✦✦✦✦✦
Although much of Grandmaster Flash's best, biggest, and most groundbreaking work was compiled on *Message From Beat Street: The Best of Grandmaster Flash, Adventures of Grandmaster Flash . . . : More of the Best* is necessary for any comprehensive rap collection. The rest of Grandmaster Flash's most important singles, many of which have not appeared on compact disc before, are corralled onto this single disc. On the whole, the album concentrates on the group's latter-day efforts for Elektra Records, but the cream of the album is the handful of singles for Sugar Hill, including the pioneering "The Adventures of Grandmaster Flash on the Wheels of Steel," which presents the group at its freshest and most innovative. Some of the

Elektra recordings are a little rote and by the book, but the Sugarhill songs help make this an essential purchase. —*Stephen Thomas Erlewine*

Greatest Mixes / Jan. 27, 1998 / Deepbeats ✦✦✦
As Rhino did two compilations in the '90s, this one appeared in 1997 and was released on the English label Deepbeats. *Greatest Mixes* adds a new wrinkle in the tried-and-true greatest-hits sets by including some new mixes of Grandmaster Flash favorites, rare original extended mixes, and some unreleased tracks. Despite all of the offerings, not surprisingly the best songs here are the original extended mixes released in the early to mid-'80s. The brilliant "The Adventures of Grandmaster Flash on the Wheels of Steel" more than sustains its lasting properties and introduces the first instances of sampling and scratching. The overdone "New York New York" from 1983 seems to gain strength from the better stuff before and after it. 1984's "Step Off" and the go-go-fused "Pump Me Up" find the group sliding off the charts, yet continuing to imbue a flashiness and caustic style that set them apart from the increasing competition. Remaining true to its title, *Greatest Mixes* has new mixes from DJs and in doing so makes this careen toward sacrilege. The worst of two negligible takes on "White Lines (Don't Do It)" is the hideous "Jazzy" mix by Cutmaster Swift and Pogo. The classic "The Message" has gauche, old school-styled arrangement from Cutting Edge. While Grandmaster Flash certainly has enough tracks to "tamper" with, *Greatest Mixes* also has unreleased tracks, most notably 1989's great, testy, and spare "Freestyle." This is one of those sets where a single disc is too concise, and without the original version of "The Message," *Greatest Mixes* ends up being much less than it could have been. —*Jason Elias*

Adventures on the Wheels of Steel / 1999 / Sugar Hill/Sequel ✦✦✦✦✦
For old school fanatics who need still more Sugar Hill material, even after Rhino's massive five-disc set *The Sugar Hill Records Story*, Sequel packaged a three-disc box of material recorded by Grandmaster Flash and the Furious Five (plus a few cuts headed by Grandmaster Melle Mel). *Adventures on the Wheels of Steel* spans all the way from their earliest, pre-Sugar Hill recordings (the great singles "Super Rappin' No. 1" and "Flash to the Beat") to the mid-'80s material recorded after Grandmaster Flash split from Sugar Hill (both he and Melle Mel headed collectives composed of former members of the Furious Five). Of course, anyone even vaguely interested in this set is already going to own quite a few of these tracks, from the big Furious Five hits "The Message" and "White Lines" to much-anthologized classics like "Birthday Party," "New York New York," "The Showdown," "Scorpio," and "Message II (Survival)." Where this collection really begins to excel, and attract collectors, is the large number of rarities included. Sure, most old school fans have "The Adventures of Grandmaster Flash on the Wheels of Steel," but how many have even heard Melle Mel's 1984 update "The New Adventures of Melle Mel"? The Furious Five were well known for their social critiques, but after Grandmaster Flash left the fold the group continued to record solid message tracks like "Jesse" (for Jesse Jackson's 1984 presidential campaign), the con-man game "Hustlers Convention," and "Vice." Truth to tell, there are only a pair of unreleased tracks on *Adventures on the Wheels of Steel*, but at least half of these 34 tracks have never been seen on compact disc. —*John Bush*

The Official Adventures of Grandmaster Flash / Jan. 29, 2002 / Strut ✦✦✦✦✦
Leave it to the archivists at Strut to uncover another facet of the near-legendary New York dance scene of the '70s and '80s. After releases from Larry Levan and Danny Krivit shedding light on what it meant to go clubbing in the late '70s, the label moved to hip-hop—that other musical phenomenon of the era—with *The Official Adventures of Grandmaster Flash*. Half mix album and half history lesson, the compilation cuts back and forth between interviews, vintage or newly recorded turntable sessions, and a few old school stand-alones—Babe Ruth's "The Mexican," Kraftwerk's "Trans Europe Express," Yellow Magic Orchestra's "Computer Games"—to get listeners in the mood. Only two of the seven mix sessions are old, though the new mixes were apparently done the same way they would've if he'd been allowed his own mix album in 1982 instead of 2002. (It's a fact obviously hard to prove, but the closest he got at the time, 1981's seven-minutes-of-madness single "The Adventures of Grandmaster Flash on the Wheels of Steel," is still breathtaking.) The new mixes sound just as good, with the Master flashing across the spectrum of '70s dance—from Parliament to Thin Lizzy to Cerrone to Spoonie Gee to the Eagles—with deft flicks of the wrist serving as all the transition he

needs. The 20-page color liners, produced with Frank Broughton and Bill Brewster (of the mixing history lesson *Last Night a DJ Saved My Life*), are the next best thing to a full video documentary. It's just slightly less revelatory than Strut's crown jewel, Larry Levan's *Live at the Paradise Garage* (mostly because few knew that one existed), but *The Official Adventures of Grandmaster Flash* is still the best look at the best DJ in history. —*John Bush*

Essential Mix: Classic Edition / May 7, 2002 / ffrr ✦✦✦

During the '90s, it seemed nearly every year brought yet another Grandmaster Flash compilation—so much so that classic productions like "White Lines (Don't Do It)" and "The Message" began sounding played out. Finally, in 2002, two labels started paying attention to Grandmaster Flash the seminal DJ, instead of Grandmaster Flash the chart hero. Hot on the heels of Strut's fantastic *The Official Adventures of…*, ffrr released *Essential Mix: Classic Edition*, similarly a contemporary look at the classic sound of the wildly diverse old school rap scene. Surprisingly, though, there's little overlap between the two; instead of '70s funk mastermixes, here Flash focuses on mostly straight run-throughs of synth-heavy, early-'80s R&B nuggets from Nu Shooz, Fatback, Maze, Rockers Revenge, D Train, and Weeks & Co. *Essential Mix: Classic Edition* doesn't have the restless creativity and energy that sparks *The Official Adventures*, but there *is* a lot of great material; highlights come with the transition from Blondie's Flash-dropping "Rapture" into "Last Night a DJ Saved My Life" and on to Liquid Liquid's "Cavern" (whose bass line powered Grandmaster Flash's own "White Lines"). —*John Bush*

Grandmaster Melle Mel (Melvin Glover)

b. New York, NY

Vocals, Producer / Old School Rap, Electro, Club/Dance

Lyrical leader of the original Furious Five and founder of a splinter version of the group during the mid-'80s, Melle Mel wrote many of the legendary raps featured on Grandmaster Flash tracks. Born Melvin Glover, he and his brother Nate (aka Kidd Creole) (not the Caribbean dance-popster of the same name) joined up with Cowboy (Keith Wiggins) in 1978 to form the Three MC's, with production handled by Grandmaster Flash (Joseph Saddler). After Scorpio (originally Mr. Ness, aka Ed Morris) and Raheim (Guy Williams) joined up as well, the group recorded two singles (one as the Younger Generation, and Flash and the Five) before they became Grandmaster Flash and the Furious Five and recorded the magnificent "Superappin'" for Enjoy, owned by R&B legend Bobby Robinson.

One year later, the group began recording for Sugar Hill and scored on the R&B charts with the wild party jams "Freedom" and "Birthday Party." In 1982 "The Message" became an instant rap classic, one of the first glimmers of social consciousness in hip-hop, and Melle Mel was responsible for many of the cutting lyrics. The record's enormous success ended up fracturing the group, however, despite subsequent successes like "New York New York" and "The Message II (Survival)." Melle Mel wasn't happy about sharing composer credits for "The Message" (especially with Sylvia Robinson), and Flash sued Sugar Hill, citing Robinson's conflict of interest (she not only coowned the label but also produced and managed the group). Though most of their beefs were directed at Sugar Hill and not inwards, Grandmaster Flash and the Furious Five split down the middle, with Flash departing for Elektra with Kidd Creole (Mel's brother) and Raheim while Melle Mel stayed put and formed his own version of the group with Cowboy and Scorpio. (After a court battle regarding rights to the name, Melle Mel was allowed the use of "Grandmaster" as well.) Late in 1983, Sugar Hill released Melle Mel's "White Lines (Don't Don't Do It)," variously described as anti-drugs or pro-drugs, though the death of one of Mel's friends, a drug dealer, a few weeks before release caused him to add the parentheses.

Mel's best year came in 1984, when he rapped over Chaka Khan's platinum, Grammy-winning "I Feel for You" (the first exposure to rapping for mainstream audiences). He was also drafted for the rap film *Beat Street*, where Grandmaster Melle Mel and the Furious Five performed their new hit "Beat Street" (aka "Beat Street Breakdown") and appeared next to Afrika Bambaataa, the Treacherous Three, Doug E. Fresh, and Rock Steady Crew. Mel recorded a pair of LPs for Sugar Hill during the mid-'80s, then reunited with Flash and the rest of the original Furious Five for a 1988 LP titled *On the Strength*. It failed miserably in an atmosphere that was decidedly anti-old school, and neither of them recorded for almost ten years. A 1997 record, *Right Now*, paired Melle Mel with Scorpio, but also failed to sell. His new project, Die Hard, debuted in 2001 with *On Lock*. —*John Bush*

● **The Best of Old School Rappers** / Oct. 4, 1994 / Sugar Hill ✦✦✦

Right Now / Apr. 8, 1997 / Straight Game ✦✦

Right Now is an admirable but ultimately uninvolving comeback album from Grandmaster Melle Mel and Scorpio. Although they rap with a surprising amount of strength and skill for veteran rappers, the rhymes aren't particularly intriguing and the production is stiff, making the music unfortunately unengaging. Even with such significant flaws, it's hard to deny that there's some thrill in hearing the pair reunited and rhyming—it's just too bad they didn't have more things to say. —*Leo Stanley*

Grandmaster Slice

Vocals, Producer / Hip-Hop, Pop-Rap, Club/Dance

An LL Cool J disciple, Grandmaster Slice recorded a pair of hits, the slick club tune "Shall We Dance (Electric Slide)" and the commercial R&B track "Thinking of You" (an even tamer takeoff on "I Need Love"). Born and raised in small-town southern Virginia, Slice hit the rap game as a pre-teenager and DJed for a local group named Ebony Express. He later hooked up with a former rival, Scratchmaster Chuck T, and in 1989 the duo produced a dance record named "Shall We Dance (Electric Slide)," for the indie Select-O-Hits. It became a hit on the rap charts and was picked up by Creative Funk, who released an LP as well (*Shall We Dance*). After moving once again, to Jive, Slice reached the singles charts with the crossover-heavy "Thinking of You." A follow-up was not in the wings, though; nine years passed before Grandmaster Slice reached the charts again, with "Strokin' 2000" on the Wingspan label. —*John Bush*

Shall We Dance / 1990 / Creative Funk ✦✦✦

● **Electric Slide (Shall We Dance)** / 1991 / Jive ✦✦✦

Grandmixer D.ST (Derek Howells)

DJ / Turntablism, Old School Rap, Electro

A true showman, Grandmixer D.ST (aka D.ST and D.XT) was not only one of the most precise DJs and record scratchers of the '80s but also one of the most entertaining to watch. Reinventing the normally static stage approach DJs took to their occupation (the job doesn't allow much movement anyway), D.ST transformed the medium with a bag of tricks that included jumping out onto the dancefloor, breakdancing, and even mixing records with his foot. All this caught the attention of the influential Afrika Bambaataa, who employed D.ST as a DJ for his famous parties in the late '70s. D.ST also showed he was skilled at production as well when, in 1983, he worked with Herbie Hancock on the hit "Rockit." D.ST is also known for his work with the Infinity Rappers, an MC troupe that he organized and recorded with on Celluloid Records. In later years he moved into production work, most notably on King Tee's *IV Life* album. —*Steve Kurutz*

Gravediggaz

f. 1993

Group / Hardcore Rap, East Coast Rap, Hip-Hop

Gravediggaz's violent mixture of hardcore gangsta rap and heavy metal was labeled "horrorcore" by some in the press. The whole incident is somewhat ironic, considering the heritage of the group. The mastermind of the group, the Undertaker, is better known as Stetsasonic's Prince Paul (born Paul Huston), who has produced De La Soul among other alternative hip-hop groups. The other members include the Rzarector (RZA of Wu-Tang Clan), the Grym Reaper (Poetic), and the Gatekeeper (Frukwan; born Arnold Hamilton). Gravediggaz's 1994 debut album, *Six Feet Deep*, was a minor hit, breaking the Top 40 of the pop album charts and containing the single "Diary of a Madman." *The Pick, the Sickle & the Shovel* followed in 1997, and a year later the group returned with *Scenes From the Graveyard*. In July 2001, just one month before the release of their next album, group member Poetic passed away due to complications from colon cancer, but keeping with his wishes, the band continued on. —*Stephen Thomas Erlewine*

● **Six Feet Deep** / Aug. 9, 1994 / V2 ✦✦✦✦

Six Feet Deep is a sick joke. A lethally great and a ghoulishly comical one, but a deranged and sadistic prank nonetheless. Eschatological, gruesome, paranoid, and obsessed with death (both imposing and experiencing it), the debut from eeeeevil supergroup Gravediggaz lands somewhere in the nexus at which the bizarre universe of legendary producer Prince Paul—who oversees the whole project while wearing the mask and wielding the shovel of the Undertaker for the occasion—crashes headlong into RZA's dingy, farcical New York City, a haunted, inverse Oz where graffiti meets science fiction meets splatter flick in an unholy alliance that finds Freddy Krueger fiendishly pursuing the turf gangs out of Walter Hill's *The Warriors* down 125th and Elm Streets. Throw in a few crazed variations on medieval torture techniques, a few too many midnight kung-fu screenings, and a few fantasies of bodily damage so giddily, demonically cartoonish that they would make Wile E. Coyote lick his lips with mischievous envy, and you have this brilliantly strange, whimsically jagged horror film in song (critics unofficially dubbed the style horrorcore) with its maimed and gnawed tongue firmly planted in cheek. If you can stomach the buckets of lyrical blood spilled herein, there is no end to the gory highlights, from the running-in-place nightmare of "Nowhere to Run, Nowhere to Hide" to the psychotically nauseous angel-dust high of "Defective Trip (Trippin')" to the willfully objectionable "1-800 Suicide" and self-destructive "Bang Your Head," all of them terribly catchy. As a bonus, *Six Feet Deep* is sure to offend the sensibilities of all middle-aged family-values crusaders and conservative-type politicians—vampires of a different sort—who aren't in on the joke. Overseas, the album was titled *Niggamortis*. With its combined allusion to mortality and example of wicked wordplay, it would have been even more apropos. Whatever it goes by, though, the album can be resurrected again and again without losing any of its devilishly good potency. —*Stanton Swihart*

The Pick, the Sickle & the Shovel / Sep. 16, 1997 / Gee Street ◆◆◆◆
Between the Gravediggaz' first album, *Six Feet Deep*, and the second, *The Pick, the Sickle & the Shovel*, RZA became the most influential producer in hip-hop, as his productions for the various Wu-Tang Clan side projects established his distinctive, skeletal style as rap's cutting edge. So, it's a little surprising that *The Pick* doesn't showcase RZA, even though there are several tangental Wu members on the disc. Instead, the production team of Poetic, True Master, Fourth Disciple, Goldfinghaz, and Darkim mastermind the sound of the album, which is lightyears away from the violent horrorcore of *Six Feet Deep*. *The Pick* has a layered, textured surface, filled with inventive, unpredictable samples that create a hypnotic web. Appropriately, RZA, Prince Paul, Poetic, and Frukwan have smarter rhymes this time around, exploring social problems instead of wallowing in comic book gore. At times, the album's momentum sags, but overall, *The Pick* is a quantum leap forward for the Gravediggaz—unlike its predecessor, it's an album that reflects its creators' intelligence. —*Stephen Thomas Erlewine*

Nightmare in A-Minor / Apr. 9, 2002 / Empire Musicwerks ◆◆◆
After several years of inactivity, the Gravediggaz returned with *Nightmare in A-Minor*. Unfortunately, this is the group's last album, first of all, because the more well-known half—RZA and Prince Paul—had left and second of all because Poetic, one of the two remaining group members, passed away in 2001 after fighting colon cancer for two years. Though *Nightmare in A-Minor* showcases Poetic and Frukwan no doubt trying their best to make the album on a par with the group's first two albums—*Six Feet Deep* (1995) and *The Pick, the Sickle & the Shovel* (1997)—it falls short of the mark. More than anything, the departure of RZA and Prince Paul leaves the Gravediggaz sounding a little weaker than you'd expect. Poetic and Frukwan carry all of this album's weight, and with 19 tracks filling this album to the brim, that's a lot of weight to carry. Thankfully, the duo have producers LG, Diamond J, and True Master to help out with the beats, but even that's not quite enough. Still, even if *Nightmare in A-Minor* doesn't measure up to the group's earlier albums, Poetic's unfortunate passing does make it somewhat of a novelty, particularly for longtime fans of the artist. —*Jason Birchmeier*

Brian Austin Green

db. Jul. 15, 1973
Vocals, Keyboards, Producer / Pop-Rap
Actor, rapper, and has-been Brian Austin Green is truly a renaissance man for our times. The son of country session drummer George Green, he was born July 15, 1973, telling *Playgirl*, "I'm part Scottish, but I've got a whole lot of shit mixed in. I'm like A-1 sauce." Green made his TV debut at the age of 13, guest starring on syndicated series including *Small Wonder* (about a wisecracking child robot, much like Green himself) and *Still the Beaver* (about a retarded 40-year-old named Theodore Cleaver). That same year, he also appeared on *Growing Pains* with that girl who was always vomiting. From 1986-1989, Green co-starred on the long-running CBS prime-time sudser *Knots Landing,* playing

the role of Brian Cunningham. Then, in 1990, his big break came: he was cast as nerdlinger David Silver on the new Fox teen drama *Beverly Hills 90210.* Introduced as a young outsider to the circle of cool kids that included Jason Priestley's Brandon; Shannen Doherty's Brenda; and Luke Perry's mad, bad, and dangerous-to-know Dylan, Silver eventually winnowed his way into the inner sanctum by DJing on the high school radio station, skipping a grade, dating Tori Spelling's Donna Martin, helping Donna Martin graduate, and looking on stupidly while his onetime best friend, Scott Scanlon, blew his brains out while playing with a handgun. David also battled drug, alcohol, and gambling problems, and got an accidental eyeful of stepsister Kelly Taylor's naked goodness. Influenced by A Tribe Called Quest, KRS-One, and no doubt Vanilla Ice, Green began rapping—and as art must imitate life, so did David Silver. The character started kicking some hardcore gangsta shit that brought him to the attention of Icon Records, but evil music mogul Serge Menkin soon forced David to forsake his vision for a mawkish ballad called "Precious"; the fledgling superstar balked, and the deal went sour. Silver pursued various showbiz careers throughout *90210*'s ten-season run, among them club owner, music video director (helming a clip for Powerman 5000), manager for racist hatemonger grunge-wannabes Cain Was Able, music critic for the Beverly Beat, and—most notably—one-hit wonder as a member of the group Jasper's Law, which scored a payola-funded chart smash with the Silver-penned "Keep It Together."

Meanwhile, in real life, Green began work on his Yab Yum label solo debut, produced by the Pharcyde's Tre. "People will trip, but I tell you, Brian's dope," Tre told *URB* magazine. Indeed, Tre, indeed. When Green dropped his debut, *One Stop Carnival*, in 1996, he also dropped his middle name—sadly, some early promos mistakenly credited the disc to "Brain Green." No matter. "[The album] is kinda like dem little carnivals that come to town with the dog-faced boy—it's just a jumble of shit," Green reportedly told *INsider* upon the album's release. "It's not like going to Disneyland where there's a theme. There's no real direction to the album." No doubt this radical lack of focus contributed mightily to *The Onion* naming *One Stop Carnival* one of the least-essential albums of the 1990s. Luckily, Green didn't quit his day job: in the 1996 TV movie *Stolen Youth*, he starred as a young man seduced by his best friend's mother, and in 1997's *Unwed Father*, he played an unwed father. *Beverly Hills 90210* ended production in 2000, and Green has no doubt been totally busy with stuff since. —*Jason Ankeny*

One Stop Carnival / 1996 / Yab Yum ◆◆
Vanilla Ice, come back—all is forgiven! A mortal lock for the short list of worst rap records ever made, Brian (Austin) Green's *One Stop Carnival* is the quintessential misguided celebrity record—it's pallid, uninspired, and insufferably arrogant, with no acknowledgement that its very existence rests solely on Green's limited success as a secondary actor on a fading prime-time drama. It doesn't even translate as a so-bad-it's-good celeb disc because there's no hint Green grasps the project's monumental absurdity—what the hell does a privileged white kid whose paychecks are signed by Aaron Spelling and whose bed is shared by Tiffani-Amber Thiessen know about hip-hop anyway? Wigga please! (It would have been better if Green had rapped in character as *90210*'s David Silver, dropping science on why that bitch Donna Martin won't put out and shit.) Fortunately, like the titular carnival itself, it's mercifully over with one stop—or at least a push of the pause button. —*Jason Ankeny*

Grits

Group / Christian Rap
Nashville-based Christian rap group Grits (an acronym for "Grammatical Revolution in the Spirit") consists of Teron "Bonafide" Carter and Stacey "Coffee" Jones, who debuted in 1995 with *Mental Releases. Factors of Seven* followed in 1997 (on the dc Talk-associated label Gotee), and *Grammatical Revolution* appeared in 1999. —*Steve Huey*

Factors of Seven / 1997 / Gotee ◆◆◆

Grammatical Revolution / May 18, 1999 / Gotee ◆◆◆
With each successive album, Grits continue to improve their production, arranging, and rhyming skills; *Grammatical Revolution* is their most accomplished recording yet, and does the most effective job of getting the duo's spiritual message across. —*Steve Huey*

● **The Art of Translation** / Aug. 27, 2002 / Gotee ◆◆◆◆
On their fourth outing, Grammatical Revolution in the Spirit not only comes up with the best Christian hip-hop album ever, but the Nashville duo delivers a dirty South *tour de force* that only OutKast has matched. The difference

between the two groups is that Coffee (Stacy Jones) and Bonafide (Teron Carter) ignore their Atlanta brethren's exotic P-funk fancies (both lyrical and musical) in favor of plainspoken rhymes, driving bounce, and sledgehammer hooks. But that certainly doesn't imply that Grits lacks innovation, as *The Art of Translation* has a sense of adventure that hip-hop's mainstream lacks. More importantly, the group's style hopping is universally successful, seamlessly incorporating Afro-Cuban sizzle ("Here We Go"), metallic guitar ("Seriously"), and even angsty alt-rock ("Believe," featuring labelmate Jennifer Knapp on the hook) into big-bottomed beats with the help of mixer Serban Ghenea, who adds the hit-bound sheen he brought to albums from Jay-Z, N.E.R.D., and Musiq. Yet, great as the album sounds, nothing on it is more remarkable than the sound of two conscious and gifted MCs responding to hip-hop thuggery with marriage and Jesus, instead of a hopeless "reality" or revolutionary tripe. "When Grits is hot they bubble," they note on "Get It." They're hot here, on the most potent antidote to hip-hop's parade of pathologies in some time. *—Dan LeRoy*

Groove B Chill

Group / Pop-Rap, Alternative Rap, Hip-Hop
Groove B Chill was inspired by the goofy, good-time eclecticism of daisy-age posses like the Jungle Brothers and De La Soul, whose Prince Paul produced their only album, 1990's *Starting From Zero*. Unfortunately, the album failed to quite capture the daisy-age movement's freewheeling style, and the opportunity for a follow-up was never afforded. *—Steve Huey*

● **Starting From Zero** / 1990 / A&M ✦✦✦
In and around 1990, records like these were the order of the day. Carefree and often downright silly rhymes about girls and high school-dominated releases by De La Soul, the Jungle Brothers, and A Tribe Called Quest. Fortunately, each of these groups as well as Groove B Chill were blessed with great production and ultimately that's what makes *Starting From Zero* even comparable to the classic debuts by the groups listed above. When rhyming over either the Prince Paul or Pete Rock-produced tracks, Groove B Chill give the impression that they can hang with the best of them but on their self-produced numbers it becomes clear that they simply weren't up to the task. To their defense, though, comparing this LP to *3 Feet High and Rising*, *Straight Out the Jungle*, *Done by the Forces of Nature*, or *People's Instinctive Travels and the Paths of Rhythm* isn't entirely fair. Not everyone, after all, is capable of making an undisputed hip-hop classic. Inconsistent as it might be, though, with Pete Rock at the controls on "Starting From Zero" and "There It Is," and Prince Paul on "Let It Roll" and "Top of the Hill," one can be assured that at least a handful of jams here could turn a party out. These tracks alone are worth the price of admission while "Let It Roll" in particular is reminiscent of the style Prince Paul employed on De La Soul's stellar debut. *—Brandon Burke*

Groove Theory

f. 1991, New York, NY
Group / Hip-Hop, House, Urban, Soul, Club/Dance
Groove Theory is a duo consisting of former songwriter and session vocalist Amel Larrieux, a New York native, and former Mantronix rapper Bryce Wilson. When they met in 1991 through a mutual friend, both were dissatisfied with their musical careers: Larrieux's voice wasn't capable of the Whitney Houston/Mariah Carey vocal gymnastics expected of black female vocalists, and Wilson wanted a chance to put his unused production talents to work. The two each recognized in the other a chance to express themselves musically in ways they had been looking for, and Groove Theory was born. The group's music is calmer than most hip-hop, concerning itself with romance and sensuality. Their self-titled debut album appeared in 1995. *—Steve Huey*

Tell Me EP / Oct. 3, 1993 / Epic ✦✦✦

● **Groove Theory** / Oct. 24, 1995 / Epic ✦✦✦✦
Groove Theory's debut effort is an exquisite, even innovative album. Not only did it (in retrospect) help to herald the progressive neo-soul movement, but its melding of decidedly hip-hop production techniques—steady drum patterns, plentiful loops and samples (though mixed with live instrumentation), even a modicum of turntable scratching—with the emotional impulses and themes of soul was still a novel approach to making R&B at the time. Just a year later, in fact, Aaliyah hit commercial and artistic pay dirt with her second

album, *One in a Million*, which plays precisely as if Timbaland had heard and then used Groove Theory as its sonic blueprint, right down to the cool, pre-possessing vocals, which are demure rather than ostentatious, unlike the flashy singers then dominating the genre. But *Groove Theory* need not live in the shadow of any other record, since it has an abundance of its own virtues. Its main attribute may be that it introduced the world to Amel Larrieux, whose alluring vocal stylings enliven the proceedings considerably, giving them a certain laid-back radiance. Even without her in the mix, however, the musical valentines created by former Mantronix rapper Bryce Wilson are so butter slick and slide down so easily that the album would have been worth the time regardless. The delicious trip-pop singles "Baby Luv" and "Tell Me" are two of the most seductive, romantic songs of 1995, energetic enough to adapt to the dancefloor or win over the normally R&B-averse heads on the street, but also perfect mood music to play behind those sweet nothings during pillow time. And they aren't the only treasures tucked away on *Groove Theory*. Groove is not, in fact, merely a hypothesis but a reality throughout, particularly on expansive gems like the drive-time chill-out of "Ride," or "Angel" and "You're Not the 1," which beautifully whisk through jazz-flavored atmospheres. *Groove Theory* is highly recommended to a wide range of music fans. *—Stanton Swihart*

The Grouch

b. Oakland, CA
Producer, Vocals / Underground Rap
The Grouch was a founding member of the Living Legends crew, a loose collective of MCs and DJs from the Bay Area, Japan, and Europe. The Living Legends eschewed the gangsta posing that dominated the hip-hop community, especially on the West Coast, in favor of clear-eyed raps about real-life issues. They coupled this with a grassroots approach to the music business, choosing to self-release and market their prodigious output. After forming the Legends crew with Oakland's Mystik Journeymen, Grouch released *Don't Talk to Me*, his first album, on the Living Legends label. It would mark the beginning of an incredibly prolific recording schedule that would also find the Grouch doing his own production work. In 1996 he released *Nothing Changes* on cassette only; it was later remastered and issued on CD. *Success Is Destiny* and *Fuck the Dumb* appeared in 1997 and 1998; various singles and EP releases rounded out the decade. It was also around this time that the Legends crew moved its base of operations from Oakland to Los Angeles, where a portion of its membership—Murs, Scarub, and Eligh—had originally resided before moving to the Bay Area. In 2000 the Grouch and Eligh issued *G & E Music*; that same year *Making Perfect Sense* arrived, which was widely regarded as the best work of the Grouch's career. *Crusader for Justice* followed in 2002. It featured instrumental contributions from the Grouch's father, Stu Blank, who played organ and guitar. (Blank, a renowned Bay Area musician, passed away soon after the recording sessions after a battle with skin cancer.) In February of 2003, the Servin' Justice DVD was released, featuring music videos, live footage, and interviews with the Grouch and members of the Living Legends crew. *—Johnny Loftus*

● **Making Perfect Sense** / Oct. 3, 2000 / G & E Music ✦✦✦✦✦
Making Perfect Sense is a low-key affair that seems resigned, almost satisfied to sneak in under the radar. Nevertheless, the fifth album from prolific rapper/producer the Grouch easily ranks as his finest, and stands among the best of the solo projects from San Francisco/Los Angeles' Living Legends collective. The Grouch produced the majority of the tracks here himself, mixing slender beats with stripped-down funk and soul—along with the occasional off-kilter effect—to create a minimalist yet surprisingly diverse sound. A number of guests take the mike here—most familiar to Living Legends fans—but the Grouch handles most of the lyrics as well, and his vocal style is equally low key, if not quite as arresting. Sounding off on overhyped artists and disingenuous industry types, dismissing his critics, and chronicling his struggles as an independent artist, the Grouch often sounds more than a little bitter. In other moments, praising his friends and those who have stood by him, or preaching the value of self-reliance, he sounds thankful, even hopeful. In either case, the producer/MC isn't finding much to laugh about. *Making Perfect Sense* is clearly no party record. The music is excellent, though, and this is as thoughtful and sincere a hip-hop record as you're likely to hear. *—Martin Woodside*

Group Home

Group / Alternative Rap, Club/Dance

Hip-hop duo Lil' Dap and Melachi—collectively known as Group Home—surfaced in 1995 on a compilation called *Guru Presents Ill Kids Records*, which was released around the same time as their debut album, *Livin' Proof*. In spite of Guru's championing the duo, Group Home remained silent for a few years, finally reappearing in 1999 with the album *A Tear for the Ghetto*, which featured cameos from Guru, Steph Lova, and the Jerky Boys. —*Steve Huey*

● **Livin' Proof** / Nov. 21, 1995 / Payday ✦✦✦✦
The debut album from tried and true members of the Gang Starr Foundation, Lil' Dap and Melachi the Nutcracker, illustrates the benefits of loyalty in the rap game. After paying their dues and appearing on prior Gang Starr projects such as *Daily Operation* and *Hard to Earn*, they earned the right to record their own LP, proudly waving the Gang Starr flag. As a registered battalion under the command of executive producers Guru and DJ Premier (founders of Gang Starr), the talented duo reaped the benefits of membership. The virtuoso DJ Premier provides a rugged and rich musical canvas for the gravel-throated lisp of Lil' Dap and the straight-razor-sharp flow of Melachi. Both MCs pull no punches; their lyrics and deliveries are clear, concise, and to the point. While their lyrical content is profound in its simplicity, the Group Home is never simple. *Livin' Proof* exemplifies the harsh realities of coming up in the concrete jungle and in the rap industry. Tracks like "Suspended in Time," "Serious Rap Shit," and the title cut portray the perilous struggle that faces every MC trying to rhyme and reason his way out of his constrictions. Track after track, Premier astounds with his unpredictable drum sequences embellished by entrancing hints of piano, strings, and horns that seem to dance in and out of the compositions. The results are nothing short of rhythmic masterpieces. Many cuts are preceded or interrupted by short instrumental interludes that leave the listener longing for more. *Livin' Proof* should not be reduced to a pure showcase for Premier; however, the deadpan lyrics of Lil' Dap and Melachi rise to the level of their maestro to create a fairly fantastic debut. —*Michael Di Bella*

A Tear for the Ghetto / Jun. 1, 1999 / Replay ✦✦✦
Group Home's second album, *A Tear for the Ghetto*, may not break much new ground in terms of style or subject matter, but it's solidly constructed, and the guest appearances from Guru, the Jerky Boys, and Steph Lova help enliven the proceedings. —*Steve Huey*

Gucci Crew

f. Miami, FL

Group / Party Rap, Bass Music

Gucci Crew was one of the most prolific and crucial Miami booty-bass groups during the '80s and early '90s; when all was said and done, they had released five studio albums and one compilation. Each studio album was released on the group's own label. They debuted with a self-titled album in 1983 and followed it with 1987's *So Def, So Fresh, So Stupid*, 1988's *What Time Is It? It's Gucci Time*, 1989's *Everybody Wants Some*, and 1990's *G4*. (From the second album on, the group was officially referred to as Gucci Crew II.) Throughout the years, the group stayed true to Miami's legacy of booming 808 drums and party themes, but they were never quite as raunchy (or dynamic) as 2 Live Crew. —*Andy Kellman*

Gucci Crew / 1983 / Gucci Crew ✦✦✦

So Def, So Fresh, So Stupid / 1987 / Gucci Crew ✦✦
The best thing Gucci Crew's *So Def, So Fresh, So Stupid* has going for it is "Sally (That Girl)," which sounds like a continuation of *What Time Is It*'s "Shirley." "Sally (That Girl)" is more efficiently produced and takes the raunchy nursery rhymes a few steps further. Other than that, it's another Gucci Crew album that relies on a couple highlights to carry it. It's decent party music, it sounds good in the car, but nothing much about it is remarkable. Since the same can be said for each of Gucci Crew's records, *The Best of Gucci Crew II*, released by Hot Productions in 1994, is the best place to go—it has all their best-known tracks in one spot. —*Andy Kellman*

What Time Is It? It's Gucci Time / 1988 / Gucci Crew ✦✦✦
Like all the other Gucci Crew records, *What Time Is It?* has a couple great tracks surrounded by a whole bunch of putting around. None of it has aged all too well, but every now and then there's a reminder of the effect this group had on 69 Boyz, Tag Team, 95 South, Freak Nasty, and the like. "Truz 'n'

Vogues" and "Shirley" have all the characteristics of the best bass music—endearingly sloppy singalong choruses, goofy lyrics, and productions that are tailor-made for boomin' vehicles. As fun as most of these songs are, the funniest of them all is the closing "It's So Hard (To Say Goodbye)," a noble, heartfelt attempt at proving to everyone that they weren't one-dimensional. —*Andy Kellman*

Everybody Wants Some / 1989 / Gucci Crew ✦✦✦
Oddly enough, *Everybody Wants Some* brought Gucci Crew its most successful single. "Five Dollar High," a Top 20 rap hit, differed from most of the group's previous material. Rather than being based on booming bass and group choruses, the song is rather cacophonic and jumbled, with a big swipe from Grandmaster Flash's "White Lines." "Everybody Wants Some" and "Can We Get Funky?" return the group to its old formula, with good results. It's just another Gucci Crew record, with mediocre tracks surrounding the highlights. Several bonus tracks (e.g., "Sally [That Girl]," "Shirley," "The Cabbage Patch") were added to the CD edition of the album, which acts as a miniature greatest-hits package. —*Andy Kellman*

G4 / 1990 / Gucci Crew ✦✦✦
Gucci Crew's albums hit the same way almost every time. With one or two great tracks produced, just enough filler was stitched together to fill out each album. *G4* (1990) actually has three highlights—"Booty Shake" (one of their catchiest booty tracks), "Project Girl" (ditto), and "Never Seen You Cry" (a rare tender ballad). None of the filler is downright bad, but since *The Best of Gucci Crew II* contains each of this album's bright spots, there is no need to seek it out. Nonetheless, this album helped establish the group as one of the more prominent members of Miami's thriving early-'90s bass scene. —*Andy Kellman*

● **The Best of Gucci Crew II** / Aug. 3, 1994 / Hot Productions ✦✦✦✦
Perhaps more than any other strain of rap, bass music is a singles game, since very few groups and producers—save for 2 Live Crew and DJ Magic Mike—have been able to deliver albums that are solid from front to back. Gucci Crew exemplifies this notion, since they released plenty of studio albums with scattered highlights and plenty of fluff. That's why compilations like this one come in very handy—*The Best of Gucci Crew II* pulls from *So Def, So Fresh, So Stupid* (1987), *What Time Is It? It's Gucci Time* (1988), *Everybody Wants Some* (1989), and *G4* (1990). Both "Shirley" and its raunchier successor/update "Sally (That Girl)" are on this disc, as are "Truz 'n' Vogues," "The Cabbage Patch," and "Five Dollar High" (a surprising Top 20 rap hit). Since this contains every noteworthy moment from Gucci Crew's history, there is no need to deal with any of the group's proper albums. —*Andy Kellman*

Gunshot

f. 1989, London, England

Group / Hardcore Rap, British Rap, Hip-Hop

One of London's first hardcore rap groups, Gunshot came out of the East End in 1989, formed around the talents of MC Alkaline, MC Mercury, Barry Blue, and DJ White Child Rix. Early singles like "Battle Street Brawl" (for Vinyl Solution) sold surprisingly well, and their debut album, *Patriot Games*, appeared in 1993. A U.K. chart placement for the album and a tour of Europe cemented their status as the leading British hardcore act. Gunshot moved to the Bristol-based Words of Warning label, and earned the highest critical praise of their career in 1997 for *Twilights Last Gleaming*. Three years followed before the release of their third full-length, *International Rescue*. —*John Bush*

Patriot Games / 1993 / Vinyl Solution ✦✦✦

● **Twilights Last Gleaming** / Jun. 2, 1997 / Words of Warning ✦✦✦✦
The London speed rappers slowed down their flow for second album *Twilights Last Gleaming*, shifting focus to the lyrics instead of the delivery. Backed by dense productions influenced by the Bomb Squad, the change works to their advantage on highlights like "Ghetto Heartbeat." Although the rhymes are still incredibly dexterous by anyone's standard (and the beats are as heavy as ever), it's what the group's saying that's really important on the album. —*John Bush*

Guru (Keith Elam)

Jazz-Rap, Acid Jazz, Alternative Rap

Rapper/composer Guru (real name Keith Elam) first rose to prominence as the "lyrical half" of the hip-hop duo Gang Starr, one of the first outfits that attempted to fuse jazz with rap. After three albums by Gang Starr hit record store shelves (1989's *No More Mr. Nice Guy*, 1991's *Step in the Arena*, and 1992's *Daily Operation*), Guru launched his own solo career, issuing *Jazzmatazz, Vol. 1* in 1993. The album featured guest appearances by the likes of Roy Ayers, Donald Byrd, and N'Dea Davenport of the Brand New Heavies, and was followed up two years later by a sophomore solo outing, *Jazzmatazz, Vol. 2: The New Reality*, which again featured a variety of special guests (including Ramsey Lewis, Branford Marsalis, and members of Jamiroquai). Despite his solo career, Guru has remained true to Gang Starr all along, continuing to contribute to such further albums as 1994's *Hard to Earn* and 1998's *Moment of Truth*. Five years after his second solo outing appeared, *Streetsoul* was issued in 2000, which again featured a stellar cast of supporting characters: Herbie Hancock, Isaac Hayes, the Roots, Erykah Badu, and Macy Gray. Wasting little time, Guru returned directly back to the recording studio, issuing a follow-up one year later, *Baldhead Slick & da Click*. In addition to the aforementioned artists, Guru has collaborated with some of rap music's best-known producers, including fellow Gang Starr member DJ Premier, Pete Rock, Alchemist, Ayatollah, and DJ Spinna, as well as Ice-T, Naughty By Nature's Treach, Killah Priest, and Ed O.G. —*Greg Prato*

- **Jazzmatazz, Vol. 1** / 1993 / Chrysalis ◆◆◆◆
One of the first hip-hop records to successfully integrate jazz, *Jazzmatazz, Vol. 1* is a surprising success for Guru. The rapper's warm grooves and laid-back rhymes fit in perfectly with the instrumental tracks provided by a cadre of jazz musicians. The way that the live playing is integrated on this album is different than the way it is done on, say, an Us3 record. On a few occasions, the instrumentalists provide the melodic hook of the song, but more often than not, they are relegated to noodling in the background while Guru raps. Needless to say, this meets with mixed results throughout. The Lonnie Liston Smith collaboration "Down the Backstreets" is a fine track, but the Donald Byrd and Roy Ayers partnerships sound busy and forced. Standout tracks include the two collaborations with Brand New Heavies singer N'Dea Davenport. The jazz connection on these songs is minimal at best, but the well-produced tracks and Davenport's sultry voice are compelling on their own merits. As for Guru himself, some of his raps can only be described as awkward, and it is at these moments when the record is weakest. However, the overall vibe of the album is strong, and inane comments from the leader aside ("Jazz is real, and based on reality," Guru says in his introduction), *Jazzmatazz, Vol. 1* is entertaining, almost despite itself. —*Daniel Gioffre*

Jazzmatazz, Vol. 2: The New Reality / Jul. 18, 1995 / Chrysalis ◆◆◆
The follow-up to the heavily acclaimed *Jazzmatazz, Vol. 1*, this album might not have quite as much jazz-rap power as the first volume did, but it's still quite good. Some of the big guns of jazz found their way onto the album, including Branford Marsalis (who, of course, had already experimented with urban beats a bit with his Buckshot Lefonque project), Freddie Hubbard, Ramsey Lewis, and Kenny Garrett. Underground rapper Kool Keith (at this

point still a member of the Ultramagnetics) also makes an appearance. Dancehall reggae princess Patra is included on a track, as are Chaka Khan and Me'Shell N'Degeocello; Jamiroquai helps out in another. In some ways, the personnel on this album may be slightly superior to the first outing, but the music also seems a tiny bit blander. Still, what makes the *Jazzmatazz* albums special is the live synthesis of jazz and rap. With Guru's vocals over the top of live jazz performers (as opposed the usual samples), interplay is facilitated between the two, and thus a whole new dimension is added to the fusion. For someone interested in jazz-rap in general, the first album is a higher priority (as would be Us3's albums, with extensive Blue Note sampling), but this album is still high on the list. —*Adam Greenberg*

Streetsoul / Sep. 26, 2000 / Virgin ◆◆◆
Give Keith Elam credit for knowing how to surround himself with great talent. It's a fact that has guided his career from the early days of Gang Starr—the group he formed with one of the greatest hip-hop producers of all time, DJ Premier—to his solo *Jazzmatazz* albums, recorded with a host of jazz legends including Roy Ayers, Donald Byrd, Freddie Hubbard, and Branford Marsalis. This third volume in Guru's *Jazzmatazz* series came not only after a five-year break but also at a time when the notion of jazz-rap was almost as antiquated as the '70s jazz-funk sound it helped resurrect back in the late '80s. Guru undoubtedly realized this, so instead of focusing strictly on jazz this time out, he made *Streetsoul* more of a roots album. With all the great contemporary R&B talent on display, though, any jazz-rap fans still left could hardly be annoyed with Guru's shift in focus from jazz to soul. A trinity of late-'90s soul divas—Macy Gray, Erykah Badu, and Kelis—each have features, and the swing-to-urban production behind Badu's contribution frames her vocals excellently. DJ Premier also shows up, contributing his usual excellent trackmaster skills to "Hustlin' Daze," with vocals by Donell Jones. Fellow rap-centrics the Roots make an appearance on the fight-for-your-right anthem "Lift Your Fist," and Guru inserts two pioneer tracks, Herbie Hancock's "Timeless" and Isaac Hayes' "Night Vision" near the end. Unfortunately, the one caveat to *Streetsoul*—Guru's rapping talent hasn't improved at all—is practically unavoidable considering he pops up for a verse or two smack-dab in the middle of almost every track here. —*John Bush*

Baldhead Slick & da Click / Sep. 25, 2001 / Landspeed ◆◆
Guru is a model of understated consistency—from "Manifest" to "Just to Get a Rep" to "You Know My Steez," he can always be depended on for thoughtful and innovative material, if not outright classics. But *Baldhead Slick & da Click*, his first non-*Jazzmatazz* solo effort, veers from this course, with just about nothing notable on the entire disc. Guru sounds obsessed with fake thugs and gangsters, and at 21 tracks without an updated flow or much variation in theme, the record becomes a struggle early on. His usual insight, storytelling, and clever swagger are replaced by a punchless braggadocio, and his guest artists only offer the same. For longtime fans who counted on the monotone to never become monotonous, *Baldhead Slick & da Click* is nothing short of a disappointment. —*Matthew Isaac Kantor*

H-Bom

Pop-Rap, Foreign Rap

Philippine pop-rapper H-Bom first appeared in 1997 with the album *Buhay*. Despite his ominous moniker, H-Bom was rather tame. Rapping predominantly in English, his music recalled such American pop-rap crossovers as Will Smith, Young MC, or Shaggy without the reggae influence. H-Bom's sophomore release, *Pwede Ba?*, appeared in 1998; *D' Real Side* followed in 1999. The album continued in the same vein established by H-Bom's earlier material, with the rapper spinning nonthreatening rhymes and occasionally singing. Like many Philippine pop stars, H-Bom avoided any hard edges on his material in order to cater to the largest audience possible. —*Johnny Loftus*

● **D' Real Side** / 1999 / OctoArts/EMI ✦✦✦

In 1999, Philippine rapper H-Bom released *D' Real Side*. H-Bom raps entirely in English, and his music can be compared to the nonthreatening, entertaining rapping of Will Smith. H-Bom isn't mean or thuggish, though his testosterone makes itself known at times. He raps in a low, sensual voice, and also sings on many of the songs. His rapping is confident, as heard on the opening "I'm Fallen," which also features a guest female singer singing a tender, soulful line. "Why" has a flashy horn section playing the instrumental line from the film *The Pink Panther*, which weaves around the exuberant rapping of H-Bom. Another imaginative arrangement is heard on "Will I–C–U?," which contains a string section playing a beautiful Baroque-style movement, blending majestically with the female backing vocals. "The Unknown" has the hardest edge of any song on the album. H-Bom's rapping here is grittier, and the searing guitar solo adds a tough edge. Mostly, though, the music is accessible and nonthreatening. *D' Real Side* is a well-conceived, enjoyable project. —*David Gonzales*

Haiku D'Etat

Group / Alternative Rap, Underground Rap, Hip-Hop

Haiku D'Etat was more a makeshift hip-hop revolution, or perhaps a temporary force of nature, than a genuine rap group; although "supergroup" is certainly a decent enough beginning, as far as descriptions go, for this magnificent if entirely too-short-lived project. An explosive one-off, *Haiku D'Etat* came to fruition as a result of the teaming up of three of the most gifted West Coast MCs ever to trade tongue-twisting similes and extended metaphors: Mikah 9 and the legendary Aceyalone of the fabled and much lamented Freestyle Fellowship, and Abstract Rude of fellow Angelino mavericks Abstract Tribe Unique. Matching their superior microphone skills to a lush bed of live instrumentation, the trio recorded a sole, practically undistributed self-titled album in 1999 (reissued the next year on tiny indie label Pure Hip-Hop, Inc.) that played to rapturous reviews (including a spot on Robert Christgau's "Dean's List" for the *Village Voice*'s famed year-end "Pazz & Jop" poll) but next to nil in sales. As deserving of being called a particularly melodious poetry outing—with its penchant for labyrinthine wordplay and bohemian effortlessness—as a rap album, its three creators returned to their own solo and group projects soon after its release, leaving *Haiku D'Etat* as one of those albums destined to go undeservedly neglected but deservedly revered. —*Stanton Swihart*

● **Haiku D'Etat** / 1999 / Pure Hip-Hop ✦✦✦✦✦

Though certainly a contentious hypothesis, the claim has been made by some that hip-hop represents the greatest work in the vernacular since James Joyce channeled *Finnegans Wake* through his pen. If that claim has any validity at all, it is because of a group like Haiku D'Etat, the L.A. trio consisting of longtime compatriots Aceyalone and Mikah 9 of the semilegendary Freestyle Fellowship and Abstract Rude of Abstract Tribe Unique, legitimate poets if ever

rap has spawned them. Any nonbeliever need only listen to the brilliant "Non Compos Mentis"—surely one of the singles of 1999, regardless of genre—to see the light, then head on to the rest of the album to revivify one's faith entirely. The trio is not, as Abstract Rude points out on the opening title track, an assemblage of "punchline type" lyricists, but rather top-of-the-line wordsmiths with an astonishing range that, nevertheless, remains nondidactic, easygoing, and whimsical. *Haiku D'Etat* is as strong as, if not stronger than, any previous effort from the Freestyle Fellowship diaspora, hopping from heady, psychotropic high to hallucinogenic higher, from 'shroomed-up cuts ("Studio Street Stage") to dub-heavy, smoked-out ambience ("Los Dangerous," "Pro Tool Robots"). It is both interdimensional and outer space age, all the while keeping a conscientious grip on reality ("Wants Vs. Needs" confronts the rap community's biggest Achilles heel, materialism). There are battle-style bouts of braggadocio ("Firecracker," "Other MC's") as well, though Haiku D'Etat takes the traditional form far beyond the norm as to seem unconnected to the convention at all, and there are paeans to hip-hop ("Still Rappin") so melodious and mellow they might as well be floating. The musical backdrop actually maintains the same high standard as the rhyming, something that had occasionally plagued past efforts from the Project Blowed crew. *Haiku D'Etat* isn't merely advanced-placement rapping, it is the master class. Abstract Rude at one point breaks it down thus: "MCs sound like we sounded last year." But really he's being far too modest. —*Stanton Swihart*

Half-A-Mill (Jasun Ward)

East Coast Rap, Gangsta Rap, Hardcore Rap

Brooklyn-based rapper Half-A-Mill climbed his way up from the underground in the late '90s and nearly broke into the mainstream. His initial breakthrough came in 1997 with an appearance on the one and only album by the Firm, a highly touted supergroup featuring Nas, AZ, Nature, and Foxy Brown alongside producers Dr. Dre and the Trackmasters. Following this high-profile appearance, Half-A-Mill then contributed "Some Niggaz" to the Def Jam-released *Belly* soundtrack in 1998, setting the stage for his solo debut. "Thug Ones." The momentous track, which featured Noreaga, Kool G Rap, and Musolini, sent ripples through the New York hardcore rap scene in 1999 and became the leadoff single for Half-A-Mill's debut album, *Million*. Unfortunately, the album, released in 2000, didn't do as well as many had expected, moving only about 40,000 units—a respectable number yet not quite on a par with the big boys—and the Brooklyn rapper lost much of his momentum. He returned two years later in 2002 with his second effort, *Da Hustle Don't Stop*, which Warlock Records had preceded with the release of "Still." With its defiant hook, this radio-serviced single took aim at those who claim Half-A-Mill had fallen off: "Still gangsta/Still ghetto/Still street." —*Jason Birchmeier*

● **Million** / Apr. 25, 2000 / Warlock ✦✦✦✦

Da Hustle Don't Stop / Jun. 18, 2002 / Warlock ✦✦✦

Handsome Boy Modeling School

Group / Hip-Hop, Alternative Rap, Underground Rap, Alternative Dance

Handsome Boy Modeling School was a teaming of quirky superproducers Prince Paul (best known for his work with De La Soul and Stetsasonic) and Dan "the Automator" Nakamura (fresh off his underground success with Kool Keith's Dr. Octagon album). Taking their name from an episode of the cult Chris Elliott sitcom *Get a Life* (which was sampled several times on their album), Paul and Dan adopted the über-stylish alteregos of Chest Rockwell and Nathaniel Merriweather, respectively. Their debut album, *So...How's Your Girl?*, was a loose concept record packed with guest stars: rappers Del tha Funkee Homosapien, J-Live, and El-P; members of Cibo Matto, Brand

Nubian, and the Beastie Boys; star turntablists like DJ Shadow, DJ Quest, and Kid Koala; electronica artists like Moloko's Roisin Murphy and Atari Teenage Riot's Alec Empire; and even *Saturday Night Live*'s Father Guido Sarducci. *So…How's Your Girl?* was released on Tommy Boy in the fall of 1999 to mostly favorable reviews, and the opening track, "Rock n' Roll (Could Never Be Hip-Hop Like This)," was licensed for a TV ad campaign. Nakamura subsequently moved on to a host of other highly conceptual projects, including Deltron 3030, Gorillaz, and Lovage. — *Steve Huey*

● **So . . . How's Your Girl?** / Oct. 19, 1999 / Tommy Boy ✦✦✦✦✦
The concept behind Handsome Boy Modeling School—if you separate it from its origins in a Chris Elliott sitcom—can be taken as a subtle parody of hip-hop's player affectations: two geeky producers masquerading as jetset male models. Given that framework, and the fact that those two producers are eccentric geniuses Prince Paul and Dan the Automator, you might expect *So…How's Your Girl?* to be a goof from top to bottom. That isn't the case. The album ends up as more of a showcase for their eclecticism, tailoring productions to their collaborators and creating a colorful universe where classicist rap, turntablism, trip-hop, and electronica all get along comfortably. Parts of the album are surprisingly atmospheric, and rely more on the texture of the sound than the star power of the guest—which makes sense for a producer's album. The finished product does lack some of the sheer craziness one might have anticipated, but the meatiness of the best music also keeps the Elliott-centered comedic interludes from turning the project into a mere novelty. The DJ cuts—the duo's own "Rock n' Roll (Could Never Hip-Hop Like This)" and the DJ Shadow/DJ Quest team "Holy Calamity (Bear Witness II)"—are some of the most exciting tracks on the album, and of the rappers, Del tha Funkee Homosapien and Brand Nubian's Grand Puba and Sadat X turn in the most memorable performances. The electronic collaborations range the farthest afield, and provide some of the most intriguing highlights—especially the bluesy trip-hop of "The Truth," featuring Moloko crooner Roisin Murphy. Meanwhile, Alec Empire and El-P—each arguably the most abrasive experimentalist in their field—live up to their billing on the massively distorted "Megaton B-Boy 2000." It's true that a few of the quirkier experiments never quite get off the ground, but by and large, *So…How's Your Girl?* is packed with imaginative, intriguing music. — *Steve Huey*

Hangmen 3

Group / Hardcore Rap, East Coast Rap
Hangmen 3, a production team hailing from Boston, consists of Ray Benzino, Jeff Two Times, and Johnny Bananas. Having worked with Prodigy (Mobb Deep), Kurupt, and The Outlawz, this hip-hop trio focus on their surrounding street life and use this ammunition to power their funkadelic breakbeats and the hardcore rhyming of the Wiseguys (WG). What was once a group of a dozen opposing street thugs, the Wiseguys started in 1995 and signed to Def Jam two years following, resulting in the gangsta-driven debut album *Destiny and Immaturity*. In mid-2000, Hangmen 3 released *No Skits Vol. 1*, a bombastic compilation featuring material from the Wiseguys—Mann Terror, Masta Criminal, Big Roscoe, M3, and Tangg da Juice. — *MacKenzie Wilson*

● **No Skits, Vol. 1** / Jun. 27, 2000 / Surrender ✦✦✦
As rap becomes increasingly regionalized, each city tries its best to present its own trademark sound and style. You can add Boston to your list of cities with thriving rap scenes. The collective of rappers known as the Wiseguys (WG)—Tangg da Juice, Big Roscoe, M3, Masta Criminal, and Mann Terror—supply a strong sense of personality to the production efforts of the Hangmen 3 trio—Ray Benzino, Jeff Two Times, and Johnny Bananas. Of course, this concept of an artistic camp isn't anything new for the rap game; after all, the most monumental innovations within the still-evolving genre came courtesy of rappers/producers collectives: Grandmaster Flash and the Furious Five, Run-D.M.C., Public Enemy, N.W.A, Wu-Tang Clan, and, arguably, even Master P's Southern camp of No Limit soldiers. The Boston crew featured on *No Skits, Vol. 1* do their best to remain innovative and put the New England city more known for its prestigious universities than its ghettos on the map, but they ultimately don't succeed at this noble feat. For, as inventive as their beats are with their funky beats and emotive sample-based ambient soundscapes, the music just doesn't incite the sort of emotion or feeling that it wants to. Similarly, for as literate as the rhymes of the Wiseguys are with their post-gangsta tales and tendencies to favor positive messages despite the ghetto motifs, the rappers just don't have the sort of charisma or character that it

takes to captivate pedestrian listeners. In sum, this Boston crew isn't going to change the rap game like the aforementioned camps, but their ambition does deserve some attention from anyone that has a strong taste for intelligent rap with a strong dose of creativity. In all honesty, this album refreshingly strays from the generic tendencies necessary for commercial success in its effort to come off as groundbreaking. It almost works and at times, during songs such as "Don't Want No Drama," the album should impress anyone with a taste for quality rap, making it an album that may live on as an influential work, even if it isn't in the same category as *Enter the 36 Chambers* or *It Takes a Nation of Millions to Hold Us Back*. Yet in the end, it's not quite inventive enough to win critical opinion, and it's not quite accessible enough to win popular opinion. — *Jason Birchmeier*

Har Mar Superstar (Sean Tillman)

Group / Indie Rock, Contemporary R&B, Hip-Hop
To put it bluntly, Har Mar Superstar (aka Sean Tillman) is a balding, out-of-shape white man with a pencil-thin moustache who croons sex-laden R&B tunes while breakdancing. His live shows, sung to the backing of a small boom box, usually culminate in Har Mar stripping down to his underwear (often of the tighty whitey variety). That's only part of the story, though, for he also happens to sing well and write some fine tunes. In fact, he has penned songs for Jennifer Lopez and Kelly Osbourne; the latter was also his date for the 2002 MTV Video Music Awards. He was picked up by the major label Warner Bros. for his sophomore effort, *You Can Feel Me*, and tapped to open shows for the Strokes and Incubus in sizeable venues.

In another incarnation, St. Paul, MN, native Sean Tillman is known as the cult indie rocker Sean Na Na. He first emerged as a recording artist in the St. Paul, MN, band Calvin Krime in the late '90s; his self-titled debut as Har Mar Superstar emerged in 2000, launching his libidinous, sometimes b-boy prone, R&B persona. The 2002 follow-up, while still dabbling in irony, turned out to be a more fully realized, well-produced, and downright funky release. The project forced many to recognize that trapped inside this chubby white man (who looks like a cross between porn legend Ron Jeremy and comic actor Jack Black) is a first-class soul crooner. In fact, *Rolling Stone* magazine featured Har Mar Superstar as one of its "new faces" of 2002. — *Erik Hage*

● **Insound Tour Support #9 EP** / 2000 / Insound ✦✦✦✦
Worldwide and pound for pound, St. Paul's Har Mar Superstar is the king of modern R&B. Two of this single's tracks appear on his Kill Rock Stars debut, but the exclusive "I'm Your New Babydaddy" is worth listeners' six bucks, if only for guest MC Dirty Preston's flow. Perfect for anyone's next dip to the mall, even if they don't roll on Snelling Ave. — *Jim St. James*

● **Har Mar Superstar** / Jul. 18, 2000 / Kill Rock Stars ✦✦✦✦
Har Mar Superstar is a nasty, filthy, mean-spirited little man. He is Stevie Wonder's dark twin. He is the muddy sludge under Grandmaster Flash's turntable. He is absolutely delightful. Who else but a man with a well-developed sense of irony would include pictures of his nude, Stay-Puf soft torso in the liner notes for his album? From dissing his girlfriend's Tommy Gear to selling her ring on eBay, Har Mar uses that sense of irony, pushing tired, misongynist rap conventions further and further until they snap under the weight of too much excess and become just plain silly. His self-titled debut for the nearly always excellent Kill Rock Stars label shows off this style and more, and even the humorless and easily offended may find themselves irrevocably attracted to this recording, singing along to "Girl, You're Stupid" and more. — *Stacia Proefrock*

You Can Feel Me / Oct. 22, 2002 / Warner Brothers ✦✦✦
Har Mar Superstar is an enigma. The St. Paul-based singer is one part performance artist, one part ironist, and one part darn fine R&B singer. Even more compellingly, his live performances (he has opened for the likes of Incubus and the Strokes, playing to huge audiences, including arenas) consist of Har Mar, aka Sean Tillmann, singing his über-sexed tunes to a tiny disc player while dancing provocatively and slowly stripping down to his tighty whities. The kicker is that Har Mar is a diminutive, profoundly out-of-shape, balding white guy. (His appearance has been quite accurately described as a cross between the actor Jack Black and '70s porn star Ron Jeremy.) Adding to the inwardly tightening circles of confusion: *You Can Feel Me*, his sophomore effort, is a darn fine R&B album. It certainly helps that the listening experience is stripped of Har Mar's visual presentation (the point of which may be to spoof the ludicrously soft-porn tendencies of modern R&B, à la Christina

Aguilera). But *You Can Feel Me* is a genuinely funky, finely produced album that often bypasses white b-boy cheekiness. The slinky groove of "Power Lunch," which features an outstanding vocal performance by Har Mar, is as strong as anything on the urban charts in recent years. At other times, however, the tongue goes back in the cheek, or at least somewhere near it, as with Dirty Preston's obtuse white-boy rap on "One Dirty Minute," which boasts such goofy platitudes as "I'm putting ladies on layaway/ I'm making very sexy installments" atop a gulping, funky bass line. Nevertheless, one thing is undeniable: cosmic joke or not, Har Mar Superstar has put out a great record. —*Erik Hage*

The Hard Boys

Group / Hardcore Rap, Southern Rap, Gangsta Rap
Short-lived hardcore-gangsta rappers the Hard Boys followed the lead of the Geto Boys and N.W.A in the process distancing themselves from their more party-orientated Atlanta peers. The trio released its sole album, *A-Town Hard Heads*, at the dawn of the gangsta rap boom (1992) and did so on the Ichiban-distributed AEI label. Though noteworthy as trailblazers, the Hard Boys couldn't translate their shocking-for-the-time novelty into national sales and fell into obscurity soon thereafter. —*Jason Birchmeier*

● **A-Town Hard Heads** / 1992 / AEI/Ichiban ◆◆◆
Though a lot of MCs were based in Atlanta in the 1980s and 1990s, not many of them were gangsta rappers. A rare example of an Atlanta group embracing straight-up gangsta rap in the early 1990s was the Hard Boys, who recorded the little known *A-Town Hard Heads* in 1991. Heavily influenced by agitators like N.W.A, Ice-T and the Geto Boys, the Hard Boys rap in the first person about thug life in the ghetto. None of the material is distinctive or adds anything new to gangsta rap—except for the references to Atlanta (which the rappers call A-Town), there isn't much to distinguish the Hard Boys from similar artists who have provided graphic, bloody, first-person narratives about the inner city's harsh realities. Be that as it may, the Hard Boys come up with some catchy beats and memorable rhymes here and there. "Death Row," for example, is a poignant commentary on the high mortality rate among young blacks in parts of Atlanta, but the disturbing scenarios it describes could just as easily apply to the South Bronx or New Orleans. *A-Town Hard Heads* won't win any awards for innovation, but it has its moments. —*Alex Henderson*

Hard 2 Obtain

Group / Hip-Hop, East Coast Rap
The Long Island rap trio consisting of MCs Taste and DL and DJ Six Seven, followed in the storied Strong Isle rap tradition of EPMD, Rakim, De La Soul, and Leaders of the New School. In 1994, the three-man group effected a smoothed-out East Coast timbre in stark contrast to the hardcore gangster rap blossoming on both coasts. Their initial single, "LI Groove," found a niche with basement hip-hop heads, and their debut album, *Ism and Blues*, followed on its strength. Production on *Ism*, from the SD50s (onetime beat-makers for Grand Puba) and Roc Raida, was way above garden variety. The album combined laid-back grooves with the work of some talented musicians, providing the album with a quiet cool. MCs Taste and DL brought skills to the table but inevitably fell victim to "blunts and bitches" content a bit much. The album rooted in jazz, R&B, and an old school hip-hop aesthetic caught a ripple of popularity with the nonmainstream hip-hop audience but, rather unfortunately, the threesome were never heard from again. —*Michael Di Bella*

● **Ism and Blues** / 1994 / Big Beat ◆◆◆◆
In early 1994, H2O caught fire with its smash backpacker single "LI Groove," a tune that affirmed through a Rakim sample that the trio represented "New York, from Long Island." On the strength of H2O's newfound respect among hip-hop's cypher legions, H2O dropped *Ism and Blues* to explore three true loves: weed, women, and hip-hop. The album reflects this triple love affair, combining hazy funk and jazz echoes with a rapper's delight format. MCs Taste and DL are b-boys in the traditional sense, playing off each other nicely with call and response rhymes. "LI Groove" may be H2O's only real claim-to-fame track but *Ism and Blues* does contain a few other hidden highlights. The horn-heavy "Ghetto Diamond" is a fortified ode to beautiful women of a hip-hop persuasion and "Heels Without Souls" fuses hip-hop and the R&B-styled vocals of Vinia Mojica with some flair. A propensity toward repetitive rhymes

bogs this album down slightly and, despite worthy efforts, in the end H2O is found to be overmatched in the hip-hop game. This largely slept-on album also features a guest appearance from New Jersey underground stalwarts the Artifacts. —*Michael Di Bella*

Scotty Hard (Scott Harding)

Producer / Hip-Hop, Alternative Rap, Underground Rap, Illbient
Engineer/producer/remixer Scott Harding, aka Scotty Hard, was a Canadian native (from Vancouver, British Columbia) who made his name in New York as part of the burgeoning hip-hop scene. Working in the background on a number of projects with the stars of hip hop, including Kool Keith, Cypress Hill, Boogie Down Productions, Wu-Tang Clan, and Biz Markie, he made the connections necessary to get an all-star cast of supporters when he was ready to do his own solo projects. His first album, *Return of Kill Dog E*, came out in 1999 and was released by WordSound Recordings, a label dedicated to the hip-hop underground. The album featured a unique, sludgy mix of bass, beats, and noise that recalled other white-boy metal rappers like Kid Rock. Hard was also featured on several WordSound compilations, including *Crooklyn Dub, Vol. 2* and *Subterranean Hitz*. —*Stacia Proefrock*

Tré Hardson

Alternative Rap, Contemporary R&B, Hip-Hop
Tré Hardson (aka Slim Kid 3) was one of the rappers who made the Pharcyde the most refreshing alternative rap group on the West Coast. He also spent time producing likely acts such as the Roots and at least one terribly unlikely one, Brian Austin Green (best known for his role on *Beverly Hills 90210*). His solo debut, 2002's *Liberation*, appeared under his given name. —*John Bush*

● **Liberation** / Sep. 10, 2002 / Flying Baboon/i Music ◆◆◆
Liberation is the solo debut for Tré Hardson, formerly one of the leaders for one of hip-hop's most underrated groups, the Pharcyde. The record is full of groove-laden, contemporary R&B singalongs, most recorded with a full band—heavy on the fretless bass, keys, and female backing vocals—and no reliance on sampling. Hardson offers plenty of rhyming space to guests including MC Lyte ("Roots, Love & Culture"), Saul Williams ("Playing House"), Jurassic 5's all-timer Chali 2na ("Follow I'll Lead"), and, best of all (surprisingly), N'Dea Davenport on a nice feature, "Life Is Love." Much of *Liberation* focuses a bit too much on the groove, without enough attention paid to either songwriting or delivery, but it's a great one-man effort. —*John Bush*

Harlem World

Group / Pop-Rap, East Coast Rap
His moment in the spotlight may have been brief, but Mase certainly scored a number of hits during the late '90s alongside his mentor, Puff Daddy, and attempted to capitalize on that success with Harlem World, his spin-off group. On paper, the group seemed incredibly promising: Mase had first scaled the charts with his debut album of the same name, *Harlem World* (1997); he then remained omnipresent throughout the two years leading up to the debut of his group; and most importantly, he had two leading pop-rap producers, Puff Daddy and Jermaine Dupri, supporting him. However, this didn't translate into the sales Dupri had surely hoped for when he signed Harlem World to his So So Def label, as the Kelly Price-featuring lead single, "I Really Like It," didn't cross over as much as expected and the album itself, *Movement* (1999), tanked quickly. This disappointment proved to be a fatal omen when Mase's long-awaited second album, *Double Up*, also tanked and signaled the end of the rapper's brief moment atop the often whimsical rap game. In retrospect, *Movement* remains somewhat noteworthy for its Neptunes productions, "One Big Fiesta" and "Not the Kids" that preceded the duo's remarkable rise to prominence, which came shortly thereafter. —*Jason Birchmeier*

● **The Movement** / Mar. 9, 1999 / Sony ◆◆◆◆
After Mase's debut album *Harlem World* became a huge hit, he decided to confirm his status as a hitmaker and protégé of Puff Daddy by becoming a mogul himself. Working with his producer Jermaine Dupri, he developed a new group confusingly called Harlem World. To the surprise of absolutely no one, Harlem World's debut album *The Movement* sounds like Puffy, Mase, and Dupri—blends of hip-hop, soul and pop, crafted for parties and crossover radio alike. The problem is, none of the six members of Harlem World are particularly distinctive rappers, which ultimately makes *The Movement* feel like a pale shadow of their mentors. Not to say that it doesn't have its

moments. When you have two of the leading lights of contemporary pop-rap masterminding your record, you damn well better deliver a couple of good singles, and they do in the form of "One Big Fiesta" and "You Made Me." The rest of the album is well crafted, but not remarkable. While that may not be a problem for some fans of this style, since it does provide good background music for parties, it doesn't bode well for Harlem World's future movements. —*Stephen Thomas Erlewine*

Harmony (Pamela Scott)

Alternative Rap, East Coast Rap

Harmony's brief career as a solo artist was aided by Boogie Down Productions' KRS-One. In 1990, she released her lone album, *Let There Be Harmony*, on Jive. Produced by KRS-One and frequent BDP associate Sidney Mills (D-Nice, Ms. Melodie, Steel Pulse, Shinehead), the album displayed Harmony's knack for switching between singing and rapping. Much like anyone else remotely connected to BDP, Harmony's subject matter stuck to societal concerns within her community. The album peaked at number 77 on the R&B/hip-hop chart. —*Andy Kellman*

● **Let There Be Harmony** / 1990 / Virgin ✦✦✦
Rappers usually make don't make very good singers, but Harmony was an exception to the rule. An associate of KRS-One and Boogie Down Productions, Harmony switched back and forth between socially aware rapper and gospel-influenced neo-soul singer on her debut album, *Let There Be Harmony*. KRS produced this promising CD with Sidney Mills, and it's hard to miss the BDP leader's influence (both lyrical and musical) on "Art of War," "Tear It Up," "What You Need," and other rap numbers. Meanwhile, Harmony wears her other hat—R&B songstress—convincingly on "Mother Africa," "Your Love Ain't Right," the ballad "Take My Breath Away," and a likable remake of Alicia Myers' 1981 hit "I Want to Thank You." Regrettably, this CD wasn't a big hit among either hip-hop or R&B audiences. As talented and unusual as she is, Harmony remained obscure. —*Alex Henderson*

Hashim (Jerry Calliste Jr.)

Producer / Electro, Club/Dance

If someone in the middle of a group of people discussing classic electro tracks suddenly blurted out, "It's tiiiiiiiiime!" or "Just feel it!" in a quasi-cyborg voice, odds are everyone in that group would instantly know what that person was going on about. They might not know the title of the song or the artist behind it, however; "Al Naafiysh (The Soul)" is the title, and Hashim is the artist. Like Man Parrish's "Hip-Hop Be Bop," Afrika Bambaataa's "Planet Rock," Cybotron's "Clear," and Newcleus' "Jam on It," "Al Naafiysh (The Soul)" is an exemplary slice of early-'80s electro-funk. Had it been titled "It's Time," there's no denying that it would be wider recognized as such.

Hashim was the work of Jerry Calliste Jr.. He became involved with music as a teenager; he was DJing at the age of 12, and in the early '80s, while still a teenager, he promoted parties. Just a little later on, his graffiti work on a banner for Tommy Boy helped him attain a part-time gig doing custodial work at that label's offices. Having taught himself how to play keyboard on a cheap Casio, he produced "Al Naafiysh (The Soul)" and released it with the help of Aldo and Amado Marin. 99's Ed Bahlman initially wanted to release the single, but Calliste negotiated a deal with Aldo Marin, who was starting a label called Cutting. "Al Naafiysh (The Soul)" became Cutting's first release in November of 1983, and Calliste became the label's vice president. Thanks in great part to Hashim's popularity and his in-house production work, the label became one of the most prominent dance independents in the U.S., with releases from 2 in a Room ("Wiggle It"), Nitro Deluxe, and Masters at Work sustaining its heft. Calliste eventually left Cutting and continued working as a promoter. He also went on to start Bassmint Music, an online label and shop based in Ohio. Sporadically he continued to work on his own music. Throughout the years, his tracks have been sampled many times over. Tommy Boy, the same label that said no to releasing "Al Naafiysh (The Soul)" originally, included the song on their definitive *Perfect Beats* series in 1995. —*Andy Kellman*

Al Naayfish (The Soul) [Single] / 1983 / Cutting ✦✦✦
With its robust beat programming and a quasi-cyborg voice that repeatedly barks, "It's tiiiiime!" and "Just feel it!," Hashim's "Al Naayfish (The Soul)" has remained one of the most enduring electro singles since its 1983 Cutting release. The swift, powerful electronic funk rhythm and the eerily drawn-out synth notes help make it as instantly recognizable as anything from Afrika

Bambaataa, Egyptian Lover, or Mantronix. The song has spread on dozens of compilations, including the third volume of Tommy Boy's *Perfect Beats* series. Ironically, Tommy Boy rejected the song when Jerry Calliste Jr., the man behind Hashim, shopped it to them. —*Andy Kellman*

Haystak (Jason Winfree)

b. Nashville, TN
Southern Rap, Underground Rap, Hardcore Rap

Initially known best for being a huge white-boy rapper from Tennessee, Haystak overcame his anomalous status with time as listeners learned to cherish his sincerity. Unlike many of his Southern peers, Haystak didn't embrace materialism and greed; he rapped about his life as so-called white trash, exploring the social dimensions of being white and underprivileged in the South. Following the success of fellow white-boy rappers Eminem and Bubba Sparxxx, Haystak found it easier to earn respect in an industry that had long frowned upon white rappers, particularly those from the country.

Born Jason Winfree in Nashville, TN, to teenage parents and raised by his grandparents, Haystak grew up among impoverished surroundings. He turned to crime as he came of age, ultimately getting busted for bringing Valium and cocaine to school at age 15. After serving a two-year sentence, Haystak turned to rap music as his salvation. Few gave the mammoth country boy a chance to succeed, however. In the late '90s he defied the odds by aligning himself with a local rap label, Street Flavor, and producers Kevin Grisham and Sonny Paradise. The partnership resulted in *Mak Million*, Haystak's 1998 debut album, followed two years later by *Car Fulla White Boys*. By this point Haystak had garnered a substantial regional following, and underground hardcore rap publication *Murder Dog* especially championed the blossoming rapper. The ensuing buzz attracted Koch Records, who signed Haystak and re-released *Car Fulla White Boys* in late summer 2000. Two years later, Koch released Haystak's third album, *The Natural*. —*Jason Birchmeier*

Car Fulla White Boys / Sep. 11, 2000 / Koch ✦✦
It would be easy to dismiss Haystak as just another in a long line of white-boy rappers trying to cash in on the success of Eminem. The husky Memphis rapper comes off as a "Southern Cracker" with mic skills, a pose that would later serve Bubba Sparxxx well with his 2001 hit "Ugly." Musically, Haystak's country-fried Southern rap is indistinguishable from the dozens of other Southern artists who have gotten deals after the success of No Limit and Cash Money Records. "Love You Like" and "Need It Get It" do show some signs of creativity, as does "Brother Like Me," a song that is part heartfelt apology and part sexual braggadocio. Haystak sounds like a host of other B-list Southern rappers and, depending on your perspective, that could be a good thing or a bad thing. *Car Fulla White Boys* shows that Haystak can hold his own with other Southern rappers, but he can't do anything original enough to break away from the pack. (Street Flavor, a Memphis indie label, originally released *Car Fulla White Boys* before Koch signed Haystak and released its own identical version of the album.) —*Jon Azpiri*

● **The Natural** / Jul. 23, 2002 / In the Paint ✦✦✦✦
Eminem jokingly predicted in his 2002 summer smash "Without Me" that "20 million other white rappers" would emerge in the wake of his multiplatinum success. Though that was a bit of an exaggeration, Haystak is one of a growing number of white MCs signed in the years since Slim Shady's breakthrough. Which isn't to say that this Nashville-based rapper and his Crazy White Boys clique are newcomers to the hip-hop scene—on the contrary, the artist formerly known as Jason Winfree has been kicking around the underground scene for more than half a decade, releasing two albums locally before getting signed to Koch. Ultimately, the problems that prevent *The Natural* from being one of the year's most promising hip-hop albums stem less from this plus-sized MC's racial novelty than from a fairly universal failure plaguing the genre: with 18 tracks clocking in at over an hour, there are three or four tracks here that slow the album's momentum halfway through. "White Boy" gets things off to a riveting start, with lyrics that proudly proclaim Haystak's status as a card-carrying member of the white-trash nation, reclaiming slanderous terms like "cracker" as a term of endearment the same way black rappers redefined the n-word. The club-worthy anthem "In Here" bounces along on an infectiously funky dirty South groove, while "Different Kind of Lady" pays tender tribute to the women in the artist's life while recounting scenes from his hardscrabble background. Sadly, the lamentable

"Pit Bull Skit" comes along ten tracks in, followed by two weak tracks—"Killa Man Crew" and "Fucked Up"—that dull the promise of the preceding eight songs. "Oh My God," featuring a guest appearance from extended CWB family member Bubba Sparxxx, closes the album with an in-your-face bang, showcasing a crew packed with a diverse range of microphone talents and perfectly matched by Sonny Paradise and Kevin "DJ Dev" Grisham's sizzling production. But while Haystak's soulful flow, which falls somewhere between Big Pun and Wolfman Jack, is a nice change of pace from the materialistic pretense of the bling-bling contingent, you'll find yourself wishing there was a little less of him to love on *The Natural*. —*Bret Love*

Heavy D & the Boyz

f. 1986, Mt. Vernon, NY
Group / Hip-Hop, Urban, Club/Dance, Pop-Rap

Hip-hop's original overweight lover, Heavy D parlayed an eminently likable persona and strong MC skills into a surprisingly lengthy career, in tandem with his backing group the Boyz. Weighing in at over 250 pounds, his girth could easily have become a one-note premise, but he varied his lyrical concerns to include positive message tracks and fun-loving party jams, and exuded a genuine warmth and respect for women without getting too graphic or sentimental. Musically, his appeal was just as broad—he was able to mix elements of R&B, reggae, dance, and pop into his music, but his raps were quick tongued enough that he avoided the accusations of selling out that dogged many other crossover successes of his era. Moreover, he was an all-around talent—an agile dancer, a naturalistic actor, and an astute businessman who eventually became a label executive. Even after his tenure as a pop hitmaker had effectively ended, he maintained a solid, steady level of popularity all the way through the '90s, and his albums kept on going gold.

Heavy D was born Dwight Errington Myers in Jamaica in 1967 and moved with his family to Mt. Vernon, NY, as a young child. He discovered rap music at age eight and by junior high was making his own demo tapes. He later formed the Boyz with high school friends DJ Eddie F (born Eddie Ferrell), Trouble T-Roy (born Troy Dixon), and G-Wiz (born Glen Parrish). Their demo tape found its way to Def Jam executive Andre Harrell, who was in the process of forming his own label, Uptown. Harrell made Heavy D & the Boyz the first artists signed to Uptown in 1986, and they released their debut album, *Living Large*, in 1987. The singles "Mr. Big Stuff" and "The Overweight Lover's in the House" established Heavy D's image among rap fans, and "Don't You Know" was a crossover hit on the R&B charts, narrowly missing the Top Ten. All told, *Living Large* was a gold-selling hit.

The follow-up album, 1989's *Big Tyme*, was the group's real breakthrough, however. Like its predecessor, it featured production from both Marley Marl and new jack swing guru Teddy Riley. By this time, though, there was a bit more depth to Heavy D's persona, and he was also hitting a peak of consistency as a songwriter. "Somebody for Me," "We Got Our Own Thang," and "Gyrlz, They Love Me" were all significant R&B hits, with the former two reaching the Top Ten; plus, "We Got Our Own Thang" attracted some attention from MTV. *Big Tyme* went all the way to number one on the R&B album charts and made the Top 20 on the pop side; it was also certified platinum. Unfortunately, tragedy struck on the supporting tour: Trouble T-Roy was killed in an accident on July 15, 1990. He became the subject of Pete Rock & C.L. Smooth's elegiac hit "They Reminisce Over You (T.R.O.Y.)" as well as a tribute cut on the next Heavy D & the Boyz album, 1991's *Peaceful Journey*.

Peaceful Journey was another platinum-selling hit, thanks to the single "Now That We Found Love," which made Heavy D a full-fledged mainstream success; it reached the R&B Top Five and just missed the pop Top Ten. "Is It Good to You" and the posse cut "Don't Curse" were also popular with hip-hop fans, and he was also a weekly television presence via his theme song for the sketch comedy series *In Living Color*. *Blue Funk* (1992) was a tougher effort that broke somewhat with Heavy D's well-established image, and perhaps as a result it suffered from underexposure; nonetheless, it managed to go gold, and the singles "Truthful" and "Who's the Man?" scored with rap audiences. In the meantime, Heavy D had been working on establishing a concurrent acting career and landed his biggest role yet as a recurring supporting character on the Fox sitcom *Roc* in 1993; around the same time, he became the vice president of A&R at Uptown. Over the next few years, he would also appear as a recurring character on another Fox sitcom, *Living Single*.

Heavy D & the Boyz returned to platinum status with 1994's *Nuttin' but Love*, which spawned hits in "Black Coffee," the R&B Top Five "Got Me

Waiting," and the title track; it also became their second album to top the R&B charts. 1996 was a big nonmusical year for Heavy D; he briefly served as president of Uptown Records and made his off-Broadway theatrical debut starring in the one-act play *Riff Raff*, which was written and directed by Laurence Fishburne. In 1997 he returned to music as a solo act, releasing *Waterbed Hev* to surprising commercial response; it made the Top Ten on both the pop and R&B charts and produced a Top Five R&B hit in "Big Daddy." His seventh album, 1999's *Heavy*, became his seventh straight to reach the R&B Top Ten. In the meantime, he appeared in the 1999 Eddie Murphy/Martin Lawrence comedy *Life* and landed a prominent supporting role in the Oscar-nominated drama *The Cider House Rules*. In 2000 he landed a recurring role as a counselor on the Fox high school drama *Boston Public*, which lasted for the next several years. —*Steve Huey*

Living Large / 1987 / Uptown ✦✦✦
Heavy D & the Boyz' debut album, *Living Large*, finds the group still in a formative stage, but they're already engaging enough to make the record entertaining, if nothing earth shattering. This being 1987, the production is spare and heavy on the beatbox, with some samples of James Brown and other well-known vintage soul records. As an MC, Heavy D strongly favors swingbeat rhythms at this stage (even saying so at the start of "Here We Go"), and he hasn't yet developed the smooth, resonant delivery that would make his most complex rhymes sound deceptively easy. There isn't as much variety in his subject matter, either—"The Overweight Lover's in the House," "Chunky but Funky," "Overweighter," and "Mr. Big Stuff" represent a major concentration on the most obvious part of his image, charmingly confident though they are. There are some other cuts geared for the dancefloor, and some freestyle-type lyrics that are well executed but rather generic. The excitement of landing a recording contract spills over into "Moneyearnin' Mount Vernon" and "I'm Getting Paid," and there's some pleasant filler elsewhere. But overall, Heavy D hadn't yet hit his stride; that would happen the next time out. —*Steve Huey*

Big Tyme / Jun. 1989 / Uptown ✦✦✦✦✦
Like Whodini, Heavy D. has managed to appeal to both R&B audiences and rap's hardcore. Indeed, Heavy shows strong R&B leanings on *Big Tyme*, his second album, which is definitely softer and more congenial than what one would have expected from Ice-T or Public Enemy that year. But the Long Island MC has a lot of technique—a fact that hardcore hip-hoppers couldn't overlook when hearing him let loose on such numbers as "Here We Go Again, Y'all," "More Bounce," and "You Ain't Heard Nuttin' Yet." Residents of the 'hood may have viewed the commercial appeal that "Somebody for Me" had suspiciously, but they couldn't ignore Heavy's obvious technique. Although not remarkable, *Big Tyme* is an enjoyable effort that works well as escapist party music. —*Alex Henderson*

Peaceful Journey / Jul. 2, 1991 / Uptown/Universal ✦✦✦✦✦
Heavy D maintained his high visibility in both the R&B and rap markets with his third album, *Peaceful Journey*. The title says a lot about Heavy's outlook—he was never an inflammatory, confrontational rapper, and generally sought to entertain rather than challenge. While most of this melodic, very R&B-ish album (which includes his remake of the Gamble & Huff classic "Now That We've Found Love") is fun and escapist in nature, the self-proclaimed Overweight Lover shows himself to be a noteworthy and effective social commentator on the title song, "Letter to the Future" (which urges a teenage criminal to change his ways), and "Sister Sister"—a salute to black women clearly written in response to misogyny in rap. Whether being socio-political or simply aiming to entertain, Heavy still makes it clear that he has a lot of technique. —*Alex Henderson*

Blue Funk / 1992 / Uptown ✦✦✦✦
On his fourth release, Heavy D handed over the production duties to three of the hottest underground producers in the business at the time—Tony Dofat, DJ Premier, and his younger cousin Pete Rock—as well as excellent newcomer Jesse West, and the results are outstanding, if completely unlike any previous or subsequent Heavy D & the Boyz recording. Whereas the Heavster's style had always been positive and accessible before, careful not to come across as too confrontational or provocative, he came entirely streetwise on *Blue Funk*, altering (if only for the moment) his straight-laced reputation. Whether it was a deliberate attempt to shift creative gears and explore different headspace—between each track there is a brief pseudo-therapeutic session—or merely a natural outgrowth of the circles in which the rapper

was traveling at the time, the result is one of his least orthodox but most thoroughly satisfying efforts. It takes a moment to register that it is the Overweight Lover who is spitting out lyrics on "Who's the Man?," a song that even liberally quotes the nonupstanding Cypress Hill. He almost could have passed for Notorious B.I.G. (who, indeed, later shows up on the album) in a blind taste test. Of course, he didn't abandon his sensitivity entirely, as "Truthful," with its R&B hook, immediately makes clear, and still tossed several lovey-dovey cuts to the around-the-way girls. But the album decidedly hits with more force, from the smack-talking "Talk Is Cheap" right down to the final "A Buncha Niggas," on which D successfully orchestrates another top-notch posse cut along the lines of *Peaceful Journey*'s uncharacteristic "Don't Curse." Perhaps sonically the album veered too far from the commercial-ready sound that he had successfully mined up to that point, but *Blue Funk* managed only a lackluster reception from critics. (It was a slightly different story with the public, reaching certified gold status.) In any event, it remains a stellar, wholly underrated entry in his discography. —*Stanton Swihart*

Nuttin' but Love / May 24, 1994 / Uptown ◆◆◆◆
Heavy D continued his '90s resurgence with the release of the multigenre *Nuttin' but Love* in 1994. Calling on the likes of heavyweight producers Erick Sermon, the Trackmasters, Marley Marl, Teddy Riley, Kid Capri, Easy Mo Bee, and fellow money earnin' Mount Vernon native Pete Rock, Hev ventures into slow-jam R&B as well as his usual catchy hip-hop offerings on this funky album. The first single, "Got Me Waiting," fueled by a sample from Luther Vandross' "Don't You Know That?," registered some success as did the follow-up "Nuttin' but Love," which featured an MTV video with a number of up-and-coming supermodels at the time, testimony to the Overweight Lover's Casanova persona. Pete Rock's production is particularly tight including the up-tempo "Black Coffee." While the heavy-handed quiet storm stuff is trite and repetitive, it does not damage the overall pleasurability of the album. Heavy D's respect among the hip-hop community is evidenced by guest appearances (some simply spoken intros) from the likes of LL Cool J, KRS-One, Queen Latifah, and Q-Tip, to name a few. This is a solid release from a slick hip-hop king. —*Michael Di Bella*

Waterbed Hev / Apr. 22, 1997 / Uptown/Universal ◆◆◆
By the mid-1990s, Heavy D wasn't considered as cutting edge as he was in the 1980s, but the MC was still recording worthwhile and satisfying albums that appealed to both R&B/urban audiences (who liked his "nice guy" image and groove-oriented tendencies) and rap's hardcore (which couldn't deny the fact that he could flow with the best of them). Though *Waterbed Hev* (a disc that soared to the top of *Billboard*'s R&B albums chart) is at times a bit harder than he'd been on his early albums, there's no mistaking the fact that this is a Heavy D album through and through. The Overweight Lover's smooth R&B leanings and melodic inclinations had remained strong, and he continued to favor a slick production style. Cuts like "Can You Handle It" (which features tha Dogg Pound) and "Wanna Be a Player" are definitely harder-edged than one expects Heavy to be, but he's still a long way from being as hardcore as Ice-T or Too Short. Not extraordinary but always entertaining, *Waterbed* is a nice example of an artist evolving without being untrue to himself. —*Alex Henderson*

Heavy / Jun. 15, 1999 / Uptown/Universal ◆◆◆
Heavy D always favored laid-back grooves, championing their easy flow during the days when the Bomb Squad ruled. Ten years later, when gangstas all roll to moked-out beats, Hev sounds as fresh as he ever has with his seventh album, *Heavy*. There really isn't anything new here, apart from the occasional production flourish (such as "You Know," with its glorious skittering rap and rhythm), but the legions of producers (including Heavy himself, the Ummah, and Erick Sermon) have given the album an appealing modern sheen, which guarantees that it sounds like 1999 instead of 1989. On top of it all, Heavy D continues to prove that he has an original, graceful delivery—he makes it all seem easy, and that's why his music is still appealing. True, *Heavy* isn't a startling record, but it is a solid, entertaining listen from one of the most reliable artists in hip-hop. —*Stephen Thomas Erlewine*

● **Heavy Hitz** / Sep. 12, 2000 / MCA ◆◆◆◆◆
Heavy Hitz is a near-definitive overview of Heavy D & the Boyz' pop-friendly dance-rap style, featuring not only the group's two big hits—"We Got Our Own Thang" and the Top Ten "Now That We Found Love"—but 13 more of their best tracks as well. And that's not as excessive as it might sound to

casual observers; Heavy D had not only a good-natured persona and sense of humor but also a deceptively nimble delivery on the mic, which helps enliven these already infectious party tunes. Heavy D also had a socially conscious side, recording the occasional ode to harmony between genders and races, but that isn't explored very much here; nonetheless, *Heavy Hitz* will likely be perfectly satisfactory for most listeners. —*Steve Huey*

20th Century Masters—The Millennium Collection: The Best of Heavy D / Sep. 10, 2002 / MCA ◆◆◆
The Heavy D & the Boyz entry in Universal's discount-priced *20th Century Masters—The Millennium Collection* series follows the first seven years of the group's career, from the late-1986 release of their rap remake of Jean Knight's "Mr. Big Stuff" (heard here in a remix) to the early-1994 release of the Top Five R&B single "Got Me Waiting." From that period, all of their Top 40 R&B hits are included, plus the self-defining tracks from their debut album, *Living Large*: "The Overweight Lover's in the House" and "Chunky but Funky" (the latter in a remix), and the tribute to African-American womankind "Sister, Sister." At a time when rap could be brutally hard edged, Heavy D was a good-natured presence, sending himself up and maintaining a positive attitude. This is a good survey of the highlights of the early part of his career—not as complete as the 2000 compilation *Heavy Hitz*, but not as expensive, either. —*William Ruhlmann*

Heltah Skeltah

Group / East Coast Rap, Hip-Hop, Underground Rap, Hardcore Rap
Boot Camp Clik affiliates Heltah Skeltah delivered a celebrated debut album, *Nocturnal* (1996) but struggled to follow through with subsequent output as their reputation simmered despite a fine follow-up, *Magnum Force* (1998). The Brooklyn duo of Ruck and Rock began as two-thirds of the Fab Five along with OGC (the Originoo Gunn Clappaz) and together scored an underground hit with "Leflaur Leflah Eshkoshka." The group split in 1996 to record solo albums for Duck Down Records, Heltah Skeltah's *Nocturnal* and OGC's *Da Storm*. Of the two, Heltah Skeltah's garnered the most acclaim, and the duo thus became a small underground sensation, appreciated largely for their vocally inventive yet strictly hardcore style. Their contributions to the Boot Camp Clik's *For the People* (1997) furthered the acclaim, but by the time Heltah Skeltah returned with their follow-up, *Magnum Force* (1998), the hype had died down, and the album unfortunately met a mediocre acceptance, partly because the duo toned down their hardcore posturing. Following this minor disappointment, Heltah Skeltah maintained a low profile and were not invited to join the long-awaited Boot Camp Clik follow-up, *The Chosen Few* (2002). —*Jason Birchmeier*

● **Nocturnal** / Jul. 1996 / Priority ◆◆◆◆
Heltah Skeltah is Ruck and Rock, two members of the loose-knit East Coast congregation Boot Camp Clik. The duo's debut establishes the crew as one of the most powerful members of the Clik, both in terms of techinque and prodcution. Most of *Nocturnal* is straightahead East Coast gangsta rap, with layered soundscapes and even if they are seamlessly crafted, they are only there as a backdrop—the main intent of the entire album is to showcase the talents of Ruck and Rock, and do they ever display their talents. Throughout the album, Ruck and Rock create a series of intertwining rhymes that are lyrical, hard, and insightful. Naturally, there are some moments that are little too predictable for comfort, but by and large, *Nocturnal* is first-rate, mid-'90s hip-hop. —*Leo Stanley*

Magnum Force / Oct. 13, 1998 / Priority ◆◆
Heltah Skeltah, the duo of Duck Down family members Rock and Ruck, released their second album *Magnum Force*, a declaration of the prowess of their clique of the same name. The first song, "Worldwide" (produced by Self), sets the tone with a refrain that lets the listener know: "We gonna rock the world…if not mutherRuck the world!" The following selection, "Call of the Wild," is also produced by Self and again uses an altered string sample that makes the song feel threatening and dangerous. Featured on "Call of the Wild" are Starang Wonder (from OGC), The Representativz, the young Hardcore, and Doc Holiday. Method Man joins Heltah Skeltah for a thug anthem, "Gunz 'N Ones," produced by Smoke. Starang Wonder comes back with Doc Holiday to spit lyrics with Rock and Ruck on the up-tempo "I Ain't Havin' That," which uses a Redman vocal sample plus the bass line and sounds from A Tribe Called Quest's "Hot Sex." More collaboration occurs on "Brownsville II Long Beach," where tha Dogg Pound lend their West Coast lyrics and

production (by Daz Dillinger) to make a respectable track. "Magnum Force," the album's title song, was produced by GrandDaddy IU and features The Representativz' added rhymes and Rustee Jux's vocals on the chorus. The theme of the album switches with "Hold Your Head Up," produced by NOD and featuring Anthony Hamilton's vocals. The uplifting message in this selection and optimistic plea for all downtrodden to endure is an effective break in the violence and gun talk that predominates on this album. The album ends with one of its stronger selections, "Gang's All Here," which features the production of Smoke and nine minutes of lyrics from members of the Magnum Force Crew and the Boot Camp Clik. (Buck Shot delivers the most notable lyrics in this song.) This album offers only one major sore point: for those who dislike poorly executed efforts to mix R&B and rap music, they will find "Chica Woo" a skippable tune. The skits are mildly amusing and it appear as though there are 19 songs on this album, while there are actually only 14 songs and five skits or interludes. This is a strong album, but hardly more advanced than their last effort, *Nocturnal*. —*Qa'id Jacobs*

Hemisphere

Group / Underground Rap, East Coast Rap
Hemisphere is an Atlanta-based hip-hop duo comprised of MC U-George and DJ/producer Tariq L. They began to collaborate in 1998, after each had established a separate career, George with a solo album (*Just Say Uncle*) and Tariq as a producer for such notables as Da Bush Babees and De La Soul. The Hemisphere handle came from the notion of one sphere with two halves. That unifying theory found its way into each moment of the Hemisphere's debut album, *Performing Artz*, released in spring of 2001. A confluence of jazz, soul, and traditional hip-hop elements, Tariq's beats intersected with U-George's unique flow (he was raised in the Virgin Islands) to create a supremely comfortable-sounding album—the hip-hop equivalent of a warm day in the sun. That same year, the Hemisphere contributed a track—"It's Time"—to *Underground Airplay Version 1.0* from the Lyricist Lounge collective, aligning the duo with such underground hip-hop notables as Mos Def and the X-Ecutioners. —*Johnny Loftus*

● **Performing Artz** / May 8, 2001 / 404 Music Group ✦✦✦✦
Though not nearly as well known as some of its peers on the Lyricist Lounge tour, this Atlanta duo has a similar positive outlook and progressive, sociopolitically conscious hip-hop sound. Although the music provided by DJ/producer Tariq L at times gives *Performing Artz* the underdeveloped, underground hip-hop sound of a really good demo, the songs where his tracks do click with U-George's intricate, intelligent lyrics are as powerful as anything MCs like Talib Kweli and Common have done. "Storm Worldwide" matches a retro organ groove with rapid-fire rhymes that establish the Hemisphere's lyrical prowess, while "Stella!" uses Eugene the 4th's jazzy saxophone fills for a potent number that points out how the root of problems in black families often start with the parents. "Consciousness" sets forth the group's ideological manifesto, and "Time" is a flute-laden flashback featuring an island-flavored melody and guest rhymes from female MC Anjanae. At 19 songs and nearly 70 minutes, you might wish the group had trimmed its debut album down a tad, but the high points are frequent enough to showcase the Hemisphere's massive potential. —*Bret Love*

The Herbaliser

f. 1992, London, England
Group / Hip-Hop, Ambient Techno, Ambient Breakbeat, Trip-Hop, Electronica
The Herbaliser are one of the more purely hip-hop oriented acts on Ninja Tune's roster of sample-based pocket-funk. Combining deft, mid-tempo beats, well-chosen jazz and funk figures, sparse scratching, and even the odd rap, Herbaliser bridge the gap between dusty B-side instrumental hip-hop and London's new school of psychotropic beat scientists. Formed by Ollie Teeba and Jake Wherry in the early '90s, Herbaliser, unlike many of London's abstract beat scene's acid house-steeped big-name artists, trace their roots to American jazz and funk (Roy Ayers, Johnny Pate, Ramsey Lewis) as well as old school hip-hop (particularly of the New York variety—Grandmixer D.ST, Sugarhill, Jungle Brothers). A bass player in acid jazz/funk group the Propheteers, Wherry met local DJ Teeba in South London, where they both lived. The pair assembled a few tracks in Wherry's tiny studio, which they subsequently passed to Ninja Tune bosses Matt Black and Jonathan More (aka Coldcut) in a club. The group were signed to the label shortly after.

Herbaliser released a few warmly received EPs on Ninja Tune in 1994 and 1995 (the hard-to-find *Real Killer* is the best of these) before dropping their debut LP, *Remedies*, which brought both the group and the then up-and-coming Ninja label much attention. While that album capitalized more directly on London's burgeoning underground breakbeat scene, freely mixing styles into a funky, sample-heavy amalgam closer to beat-heavy acid jazz, subsequent singles ("Flawed Hip-Hop," "New & Improved") subtracted the schmaltzier bits from the mix, focusing in and expanding on the group's hip-hop foundation. *Blow Your Headphones*, their second LP, presented a solid hour-plus of the same, simultaneously taking aim at U.K. "trip-hop"'s tendency toward gimmick and noodle over depth and kick. *Very Mercenary* followed in 1999.

Remixes by the group have included DJ Food, Raw Stylus, and label foremen Coldcut's "Atomic Moog," the last of which went to number one on the U.K. singles chart. A touring act as well, Herbaliser assemble a full-blown band for live performances, with Wherry's bass and Teeba's turntable tricks supported by a three-piece horn section and live drums and percussion. Wherry has also released solo material through the Parisian Big Cheese label (under the name the Meateaters) and continued to work with the Propheteers. —*Sean Cooper*

Remedies / 1995 / Ninja Tune ✦✦✦
The Herbaliser's DJ-friendly jazz/funk/hip-hop fusion is well stated on this debut. Although later releases trim back the album's occasional excess of instrumental samples, a few standout tracks and solid production throughout makes *Remedies* a pleasing, if limited, listen. —*Sean Cooper*

● **Blow Your Headphones** / Mar. 11, 1997 / Ninja Tune ✦✦✦✦
The Herbaliser is the most hip-hop of the Ninja Tune lot, and previous releases (such as *Remedies* and the *New and Improved* EP) have illustrated a knack for filling out the jazz and funk roots of hip-hop while remaining both deep and kicking. *Blow Your Headphones* ups the ante considerably, with a nonstop soul drop that pushes the beats even further forward and thins the extraneous samples and genre references. The result is less differentiable from straightahead hip-hop (save for the fact the album's mostly instrumental) but is also less derivative of acid and soul jazz, a connection that tended to mar their previous work. —*Sean Cooper*

Very Mercenary / Apr. 20, 1999 / Ninja Tune ✦✦✦✦
A bit more Carnaby Street than South Bronx (compared to 1997's *Blow Your Headphones*), the Herbaliser's third album works in '60s spy-funk territory to a degree unseen in the group's discography. Though the emphasis on uptempo trip-hop with an old school edge is carried throughout, *Very Mercenary* also hits instrumental tracks like "Missing Suitcase" and "Goldrush" that include a full band. It's a bit less necessary than their previous, but it's a solid record indeed. —*Keith Farley*

Something Wicked This Way Comes / Mar. 19, 2002 / Ninja Tune ✦✦✦✦
Colossal and cinematic, the fourth record from the Herbaliser is a timely achievement in music, a genre-bending statement of creative poignancy. *Something Wicked This Way Comes* is a quiet masterpiece, bringing together a tremendous cast of hip-hop elite and employing more of their own samples and live instrumentation than on their previous releases. The overwhelming credit throughout is how intentional the placement of samples, lyrics, and dynamics are, with the flow of the recording taking precedence over any one particular performance or section. This makes the appearances of Iriscience on "Verbal Anime," Wildflower on "Good Girl Gone Bad," Phi Life Cypher on "Distinguished Jamaican English," and MF Doom on "It Ain't Nuttin'" even more coveted. The instrumental tracks and their trip-hop meadows, acid jazz vamps, and spacy psychedelia make the ride rich and expansive, expounding on some of the same spy-theme sounds introduced on *Very Mercenary*. The result is once again a declaration of the Herbaliser as innovators in the beat genre, and another pioneering feather in Ninja Tune's astonishing hat. —*Nic Kincaid*

Hexstatic

f. 1990, London, England
Group / Ambient Breakbeat, Club/Dance, Trip-Hop, Funky Breaks
Though they're best known in the music world as the award-winning visual arm of audio cut-and-paste experts Coldcut, Hexstatic (previously Hex) has broken down the barriers between music, multimedia, and computers ever since they created the first computer-generated pop video (Coldcut's Christmas Break) in 1990. Graphic design artists Robert Pepperell and Miles Visman

formed Hex along with Coldcut's Matt Black and Jonathan More. While working on videos for artists including Kevin Saunderson, Queen Latifah, and Spiritualized, Hex programmed a video game (High Banana) in 1991 and inaugurated a series of multimedia CD-ROMs just one year later with Global Chaos CDTV, which united music, graphics, and video games into one product. A series of successors (Escape, Global Chaos, and Digital Love) preceded the release of 1994's AntiStatic, another CD-ROM simultaneously released on CD and vinyl by Coldcut's NTone Records.

Throughout the '90s, Hex accompanied Black and More's live performances with visuals, and Pepperell also developed the CD-ROM portion of Coldcut's 1997 LP, *Let Us Play*, plus the software used during the world tour. Though Pepperell and Visman later left Hex, fresh blood came in the form of Stuart Warren Hill and Robin Brunson. Their first work for Coldcut, the Timber video, won awards for its innovative use of repetitive video clips synced to the music. In 2000 they released *Rewind*, their own album for NTone. Obviously a digital-edge release, the two-disc set combined CD-ROM and DVD capabilities to a fully synchronized music video release. In 2003 Hexstatic contributed a second volume to Coldcut's turntablist mix series *Solid Steel, Listen & Learn. —John Bush*

Rewind / Aug. 22, 2000 / NTone ✦✦✦
Multimedia experts Hexstatic undoubtedly have a special interest in communication, so it's no surprise the duo uses its first LP (recorded for their pals at Ninja Tune) to poke fun at the continually confusing digital age. After an intro wherein celebrity announcer Don Pardo reassures audiences that technical difficulties are being attended to for nigh on a full minute, the group launches into "Communication Break-Down," with scattered samples—modem-connect noise, wrong numbers, answering machine messages, and various interference—serving as a bed for Coldcut-style turntablist trip-hop. On the next track, "Deadly Media," a parade of random Japanese vocal snippets gradually organize themselves around rigid 808 breakbeats for a fascinating, hilarious track. Like their award-winning "Timber" video for Coldcut, which chopped and spliced visuals in a similar manner that turntablism does to music, *Rewind* makes complete sense; on these tracks, the percussion lines and beats aren't the only elements serving the rhythm. Though the production is solid, many of the other tracks here use some overly familiar blueprints—especially for Ninja Tune artists—from kung-fu samples (on a track actually *named* "Ninja Tune,") to video game electro ("Vector,") and even the age-old favorite: porn-film samples ("The Horn"). Good music abounds, but Hexstatic proves much more pioneering in the visual realm than the musical. (One place they *really* shine is on the second multimedia disc, which offers an excellent video for each track and a style of choosing videos that will warm the hearts of *Battletech* fans.) —*John Bush*

● **Listen & Learn** / Jan. 27, 2003 / Ninja Tune ✦✦✦✦✦
Audiovisual shaolin savants Stuart Warren Hill and Robin Brunson don't step from behind the shadows of their phenomenally successful multimedia operation very often, and considering they are rare contributors to Coldcut's *Solid Steel* radio show, they proved something of a surprise choice for this sophomore outing in Ninja Tune's mix series. The pair's album, however, proves to be more than on a par with DJ Food's antecedent effort, peppered with vocal samples and technical trickery and aided and abetted by some gadget-laden CD turntables. Indeed, *Listen & Learn* proves an apt title for an album that is a lesson in selection—skipping from their own hazy "Telemetron" through original block-rockers from Dawn Penn, Grandmaster Flash, and Ike & Tina Turner's much-sampled "Funky Mule" before skipping to a more modern fandango by way of Boards of Canada. The three-track electro beatdown and subsequent segue from Michael Viner to Young MC's "Apache"-borrowing "Know How" is inspired, with Hill and Brunson mixing and matching their formidable reputation in the video suite with layer upon layer of record as far as can be, from the Protools-assisted 4/4 nonsense which has become the common weapon of choice for the mixed compilation. Another astonishing addition to what is becoming a wonderful series. —*Kingsley Marshall*

Hi-Tek (Tony Cottrell)

b. Cincinnati, OH
Producer / Hip-Hop, Alternative Rap, East Coast Rap
Hi-Tek played a major role in the highly admired golden age revivalist sound affiliated with the Rawkus Records collective, crafting many of the label's

initial breakthrough releases. While Hi-Tek's production style owes a debt to New York's finest beat makers from the early '90s—DJ Premier, Pete Rock, Large Professor—the producer actually arose from Cincinnati's low-key hip-hop scene rather than the streets of Brooklyn. Local mentors such as Ravi T, J-Fresh, and Sen Sai showed the aspiring youth how to craft beats, and by 1992 he had crossed paths with Mood, one of the Midwest city's premier hip-hop groups. Hi-Tek collaborated on the song "Hustle on the Side" and helped the group score a record deal. Years later the producer befriended Talib Kweli, who was in town working with Mood. This affiliation eventually spawned the Reflection Eternal duo, one of the first acts to put the Rawkus label on the map. But it was Hi-Tek's work with Kweli and Mos Def on the milestone *Black Star* album in 1998 that first made the producer a hot commodity. He next collaborated exclusively with Kweli for *Reflection Eternal* (2000), an album that crossed over from the b-boy camp to the mass market and became a critically championed coast-to-coast success. Then came Hi-Tek's solo spotlight on Rawkus, *Hi-Teknology* (2001), which featured a broad range of up-and-coming MCs, including some of his Cincinnati peers. Between releases he produced tracks for a broad array of rappers, including such notables as Snoop Dogg, Blackalicious, and Raphael Saadiq. —*Jason Birchmeier*

● **Hi-Teknology** / May 8, 2001 / Priority ✦✦✦
Since breaking in quietly with fellow Cincinnati residents Mood in the mid-'90s, DJ Hi-Tek's climb up the crate-digging ranks has been a slow one. While Hi-Tek garnished some well-overdue exposure for his work on Black Star's debut, and running mate Talib Kweli on their critically acclaimed *Reflection Eternal* endeavor, his name is still rarely mentioned when discussing hip-hop's new class of promising beatsmiths. However, Hi-Tek's debut, *Hi-Teknology*, should change that. While Tek collaborates mostly with many familiar faces, he adds a few new wrinkles to his organic compositions, roughing up his trusted MPC-3000 on Cormega's "All I Need Is You" and for the sinister "The Illest It Gets," which features Black Moon's Buckshot. Yet, the heart and soul of *Hi-Teknology* resides with those with whom Tek has already developed a solid working relationship. Talib Kweli and Tek resolidify their chemistry with "Get Back, Pt. 2," and Common enters the fold, with the lyrically enriched "Sun God," as his introspective lyrics emanate with a Marvin Gaye-like quality. Similarly, just as enticing is "Git to Steppin," as Mos Def and Vinia Mojica body rock in perfect unison to Tek's sensuous organ arrangement. Though *Hi-Teknology* follows no discernible path, it is a grab bag of aural treats that enables Tek to display the full range of his production prowess. While Hi-Tek has yet to generate a mainstream buzz, *Hi-Teknology* is just the latest step he has taken to claim his rightful spot among hip-hop's elite soundboys. —*Matt Conaway*

Hi-Town DJ's

Group / Hip-Hop, Club/Dance, Bass Music
The Hi-Town DJ's are comprised of six individuals (rappers Derrick Rahming, Matt Young, and Teeze; record spinner DJ JP; singer Kalo; and stage dancer Chyna Doll) who reject the gangsta approach to hip-hop and embrace the party-hearty vibe instead. All of the band's members originally hailed from either Florida or Hawaii, and were originally assembled by Matt "xsdb" Young of the Icon Entertainment production company, who was looking to put together a band to introduce bass music to the rest of the world. After a demo was completed, the group was soon signed by Restless Soul Records, and recorded their debut album, *We Came 2 Groove*, a sweaty mix of dance and often risqué lyrics. Although many saw the band as bass music purveyors, the group was adamant that they were really just an honest-to-goodness hip-hop act. —*Greg Prato*

● **We Came 2 Groove** / Mar. 24, 1998 / Restless ✦✦✦
The first thing you'll notice after putting on the Hi-Town DJ's debut album, *We Came 2 Groove*, is their awesome bottom-heavy sound, which sometimes unfortunately gets overshadowed by their sophomoric, sexual wordplay. Still, the beats laid down on the album are often irresistible dance rhythms, so it makes up for the lyrical inconsistencies. "It's On" is a strong opener, which would sound perfect being blasted in a dance club, while "Ding-A-Ling" somehow combines Funkadelic sounds with early MC Hammer-style rapping. Rap legend Kurtis Blow makes a cameo appearance on "We Came 2 Groove," which (as the title says) is one of grooviest rhythm-popping tracks on the record. Another bass band, Afro-Rican, adds their raps to four tracks ("Stand By Me," "Thank U Ma'am," "Down Low," and "I Got Money"), which

fits the festive atmosphere perfectly. Other highlights include "Junk in the Trunk" and a special CD-only bonus mix of "Stand By Me" (listed as a Young Lord Remix). —*Greg Prato*

Hieroglyphics

f. Oakland, CA
Group / Underground Rap
The Oakland-based Hieroglyphics are an underground rap collective who, at their best, combine an offbeat sensibility with a strong grounding in battle rhyming, freestyling, and other hip-hop traditions. All the members enjoy their own separate careers—founder Del tha Funkee Homosapien, Casual, the Souls of Mischief, Extra Prolific, producer/manager Domino, Pep Love, and producer Jay Biz (the latter two of which have also worked together as the Prose). Most of the members had known each other since high school (or earlier), and after Del scored a record deal with the help of his cousin, Ice Cube, much of the Hieroglyphics crew wound up with major-label contracts of their own. Del, Souls of Mischief, and Casual, in particular, earned strong cult followings, but Hieroglyphics never produced a breakout mainstream star, and all the members wound up dropped from their respective labels by the mid-'90s despite their generally high-quality work. The crew regrouped with their own label, Hieroglyphics Imperium, which provided not only a platform for their future releases but also total creative control. In addition, the entire collective teamed up for the first album under the Hieroglyphics name, *Third Eye Vision*, in 1998. —*Steve Huey*

Hiero Oldies / 1997 / Hiero Imperium ✦✦✦✦✦
This is a cassette-only, online-only collection of oldies from before Hieroglyphics were famous. Hieroglyphics have never been famous? They should be. Made up of a loose aggregation of Bay Area friends including the crew, Souls of Mischief, and various solo acts, the most successful and idiosyncratic being Del the Funkee Homosapien, Hieroglyphics have consistently cranked out hip-hop that is alternately mellow funky and kaleidoscopically loopy, eschewing hardcore posturing and street-tough poetics for something much sunnier and lyrically intricate, but still hard hitting. Such optimism does not necessarily arise out of a more suburban as opposed to urban-environment, it seems far more likely to be a conscious attempt to stretch possibilities, like a trippy hip-hop version of psychedelia that spins a brightly hued, luminous urbanity out of the ashen surroundings of the city (even a Californian one). So what results is thick, gurgling bass lines and clever samples that would never show up on, say, a Wu-Tang Clan record. Instead there are inspired interpolations of theme music (from *Taxi* on the Souls' opening "Cab Fare," remixed by Domino, and from *Mr. Rogers* on Del's, you guessed it, "Neighborhood"), burping electric keyboards, and blaxploitation guitar, all done with a buoyancy that is infectious. And all done without devolving into out-and-out goofiness; instead the various lyrical approaches, even at this early stake in the game (most of the songs are from the 1991-1992 era when only a few group members were just beginning to hit wax), were compelling and intensely fun, but that sense of enjoyment does not prohibit the Hieroglyphics crew from being insightful, sometimes etching a cutting portrait of urban life, recounting psychological stress (Del's "Crazy Del Song," which, even with its serious theme, comes with a wink), or tearing into stagnant MC's, which, more than most, it has a right to. Mostly, however, the crew is both playful and soulful, neither characteristic as prevalent in hip-hop as testosterone. Not every song is equally strong, but nearly every song shines in some way, and each member (the aforementioned chaps as well as Casual, Extra Prolific, Pep Love, Jaybiz, Opio, Reckless, Hush) steps up to the plate and delivers lyrically or production-wise. The Hiero crew would grow more incisive as the decade progressed (and even on the second side here), but *Hiero Oldies* proves that even before they had established their vision, Hieroglyphics were something special. —*Stanton Swihart*

Hiero B Sides / 1997 / Hiero Imperium ✦✦✦
Another entry in the Hieroglyphics crew's series of cassette- and online-only releases, *Hiero B Sides* is exactly what it says it is, the backsides of various singles garnered from albums by Del tha Funkee Homosapien, Souls of Mischief, Casual, and Extra Prolific, most of which inexplicably gained little commercial success outside of small pockets of the hip-hop community. Unlike many artists, Hieroglyphics are creative enough to put songs as strong as or stronger than the A sides on their singles, full of the same dirty '70s electric pianos, waka-waka guitars, and pulsating rhythmic bottom, and so *Hiero B Sides* would seem to be a perfect introduction to Hieroglyphics artists. But

rather than compiling the B sides as a proper collection, Hieroglyphics have assembled the songs in a seamless fashion so that the cassette plays the role of mix tape. The songs are not sequenced according to linearity or source, they are sequenced logically according to their rhythmic pulse and their compatability with the surrounding songs, into and out of which they roll. On the one hand, because of its relentless nature, *Hiero B Sides* is not likely to inspire sustained listening. On the other hand, it is a perfect party soundtrack. But while it serves that function nicely, it also has the flavor of a missed opportunity. Many of the original versions of these songs are on the individual artists' albums; those albums are mostly out of print, and a couple are even difficult to track down. In addition, some of the songs are remixes or alternate versions even unavailable on the original albums. Couple that with the fact that these B sides are so uniformly strong, and a collection of the songs in their proper forms would be welcome. —*Stanton Swihart*

Hiero Oldies II / 1998 / Hiero Imperium ✦✦✦✦
The second installment of Hieroglyphics oldies (also cassette- and online-only) mines roughly the same plush beginnings ('91 and '92, mostly) of the crew's recorded history and hits with the same force. If anything, the Hiero crew saved the slightly tougher cuts for this collection of early archival recordings, even drawing lyrical blood on occasion, beginning right off with Del tha Funkee Homosapien's "Pistol Whippers" and the Souls of Mischief's "Break a Leg," both of whose sentiments sound sincere. It is also a much more bare-bones collection, including no less than ten 4-track recordings by various members. In that sense, it is less overtly trippy, though there are still plenty of syrupy, sly basslines, chirping keyboards, horns, and vibraphones, but those play themselves out in a much jazzier fashion in these songs. They are only vaguely psychedelic this time around. And it does not matter, because the production is just as accomplished. It is lyrical dexterity, anyway, that makes the Hieroglyphics crew special, and that is abundant on *Hiero Oldies II*. Besides the always phenomenal Del and the grossly underrated Souls (the pointed "Cab Fare"), Casual shines on grittier cuts such as "Fear No Evil," and Pep Love & Jaybiz are revelatory on the mellow "Everyday of the Week." Not everything clicks on the collection; a few songs fall flat or never get off the ground, especially on the second side. But the musical soundscapes and lyrical flights of fancy on a Hieroglyphics album are so varied that the dull spots are barely noticeable. —*Stanton Swihart*

● **Third Eye Vision** / Mar. 24, 1998 / Hiero Imperium ✦✦✦✦
Consisting of Del tha Funkee Homosapien, A+, Opio, Tajai, Phesto, Casual, Domino, Pep Love, and Jaybiz, Hieroglyphics has an all-star lineup of underground talent. One might expect Hieroglyphics to have a gangsta rap or West Coast rap sound since Del tha Funkee Homosapien is related to the infamous Ice Cube; however, *Third Eye Vision* has a traditional underground rap feel reminiscent of albums by Common and Black Star. The 22-track album features strong, clever lyrics accompanied by creative, catchy background beats. Fortunately, Hieroglyphics manages to avoid the common error of over sampling beats, which detracts from the lyrics. The hip-hop group also amazingly uses its large size as an advantage with memorable choruses, unique background voices and raps, and great interplay between lyricists. This synergy is future illustrated by the variety of songwriters and tracks like "You Never Know" and "Miles to the Sun" that are a collaboration by six of the group members. The album's standout track is "You Never Know," which was made into a video and single. —*John Hinrichsen*

The High & Mighty

Group / Hip-Hop, Underground Rap, East Coast Rap
The High & Mighty's momentary affiliation with Rawkus Entertainment in 1999 brought them national acclaim, and the duo returned to the underground thereafter and used the newfound clout to promote their Eastern Conference label. Comprised of Mr. Eon (Eric Meltzer) and DJ Mighty Mi (Milo Berger), the High & Mighty came together in the mid-'90s and decided to form their own label, Eastern Conference. After a few singles, the duo began to earn notice, particularly for the "Open Mic Night" b/w "The Meaning" release in 1997. A year later came another big release, "B-Boy Document" (1998), this one featuring several prominent underground figures: El-P, Mike Zoot, and Mos Def. By this point Rawkus had become very interested in the High & Mighty and released their full-length debut, *Home Field Advantage* (1999) and a reworking of "B-Boy Document" featuring Mos Def and Mad Skillz ("B-Boy Document '99") as well. Following the well-received album,

the High & Mighty returned to the underground and brought many new fans with them. In subsequent years, the duo focused on its label (compiling a number of Eastern Conference All-Stars compilations) and returned with their second album, *Air Force 1*, in 2002. —*Jason Birchmeier*

● **Home Field Advantage** / Aug. 24, 1999 / Rawkus ✦✦✦✦
Home Field Advantage is Mr. Eon's and DJ Mighty Mi's first full-length album, and it's solid. Songs like "Top Prospects" and "B-Boy Document '99" will please many fans of East Coast hip-hop. Unfortunately, other songs like "Hot Spittable," "Weed," and "The Meaning" are kind of boring and seem to be missing something. One thing this album isn't missing is guests. The High & Mighty are joined by Pharoahe Monch, Evidence, Defari, Mos Def, Mad Skillz, Eminem, Cage, Kool Keith, and more. Most tracks have one or two guests helping the High & Mighty out. While the people that they get are good, it would be nice to hear more songs with just Eon. Also, after hearing the intro, "Tip Off Time," it makes you want another track just of Mighty Mi rocking the turntables. —*Dan Gizzi*

Air Force 1 / Feb. 26, 2002 / Landspeed ✦✦✦✦
The High & Mighty's debut album for Rawkus, *Home Field Advantage* (1999), put the duo on the hip-hop map in a big way. At the time, Rawkus was arguably the most esteemed label in underground hip-hop, mostly because of the critical success releases such as Mos Def and Talib Kweli's Black Star had garnered for the New York label. The High & Mighty thus became an overnight sensation with the release of *Home Field Advantage*, thanks to the affiliation. However, the affiliation ended there. The duo left Rawkus after its debut and used its newfound clout to boost the profile of its own label, Eastern Conference, beginning with the Eastern Conference All-Stars collection in 1999, which compiled many of the underground label's 12"-only releases. Three years later, in 2002, the High & Mighty returned with its second album, *Air Force 1*, released on Eastern Conference rather than Rawkus. Granted, not much had changed for High & Mighty members Mr. Eon and DJ Mighty Mi in the interim. They still represented underground hip-hop at its best: lots of scratching and sampling, a quirky and witty rather than tough and glamorous ethos, and no pandering crossover efforts. There were other changes, though: the most obvious being the missing Rawkus affiliation, which is invaluable in underground hip-hop where integrity is all important. And with the missing affiliation comes the missing guests—Mos Def, Pharoahe Monch, Eminem, Kool Keith, etc.—that helped make *Home Field Advantage* such a momentous debut for the High & Mighty. So, the question remains: without the Rawkus brand equity and the who's who of underground hip-hop guest list, is *Air Force 1* a step backward for the Philly duo? There's no easy answer. On the one hand, without the branding and without guests like Eminem, *Air Force 1* obviously isn't going to appeal to as large of an audience as the duo's debut. On the other hand, however, Mr. Eon and DJ Mighty Mi are able to follow their muse here; this is very much their album without any outside influences or voices forcing them to compromise their vision. Therefore, if what you enjoyed best about *Home Field Advantage* was the High & Mighty rather than the Rawkus "sound" or the myriad guests, there's a good chance you may actually prefer this follow-up, even if it's a little rough around the edges (which, of course, is part of its beauty, being an underground hip-hop album). —*Jason Birchmeier*

Lauryn Hill

b. May 26, 1975
Vocals, Producer, Arranger / Hip-Hop, Urban, Alternative Rap, Contemporary R&B, Neo-Soul

Call Lauryn Hill the mother of hip-hop invention; with her 1998 solo debut *The Miseducation of Lauryn Hill*, the Fugees' most vocal member not only established herself as creative force on her own but also broke new ground by successfully integrating rap, soul, reggae, and R&B into her own sound.

Raised in South Orange, NJ, Hill spent her youth listening to her parents' multigenre, multigenerational record collection. She began singing at an early age, and was soon snagging minor roles on television (*As the World Turns*) and in film (*Sister Act II: Back in the Habit*). Her on-again, off-again stint in the Fugees began at the age of 13, but was often interrupted by both the acting gigs and her enrollment at Columbia University. After developing a following in the tri-state area, the group's first release—the much-hyped but uneven *Blunted on Reality*—bombed, almost causing a breakup. But with the multiplatinum *The Score*, the Fugees (and especially the camera-friendly

Hill) achieved international success, though some pundits took shots at their penchant for cover songs.

That criticism made *Miseducation* even more of a surprise. Hill wrote, arranged, or produced just about every track on the album, which is steeped in her old school background, both musically (the Motown-esque singalong of "Doo Wop [That Thing]") and lyrically (the nostalgic "Every Ghetto, Every City"). As *Miseducation* began a long reign on the charts through most of the fall and winter of 1998—initially thanks to heavy buzz and overwhelming radio support for "Doo Wop (That Thing)"—Hill became a national media icon, as magazines ranging from *Time* to *Esquire* to *Teen People* vied to put her on the cover. By the end of the year, as the album topped virtually every major music critic's best-of list, she was being credited for helping fully assimilate hip-hop into mainstream music. (Such an analysis, however, is lightweight at best: hip-hop had been a huge force on the sales and radio fronts for most of the decade, and rappers Jay-Z, DMX, and Outkast had dropped similarly lauded LPs prior to or just after *Miseducation*'s release, adding to the genre's dominant sales for the year.) The momentum finally culminated at the February 1999 Grammy awards, during which Hill took home five trophies from her 11 nominations, including Album of the Year, Best New Artist, Best Female R&B Vocal Performance, Best R&B Song, and Best R&B Album; the most ever for a woman. Shortly after, she launched a highly praised national tour with Atlanta rappers Outkast.

Hill also faced a lawsuit from two musicians who claim they were denied full credit for their work on the album. In an interesting twist, Hill's album proved to be such a commercial and critical success that it shed doubt on the Fugees' future. Their infighting became common knowledge, and matters were complicated when many fans interpreted *Miseducation*'s various anti-stardom rants as a public dissing of co-Fugee Wyclef Jean.

She did continue shaping her solo career. The double-disc *MTV Unplugged No. 2.0* appeared in spring 2002, showcasing a deeply personal performance from Hill. —*Brian Raftery*

★ **The Miseducation of Lauryn Hill** / Aug. 25, 1998 / Ruffhouse ✦✦✦✦✦
Though the Fugees had been wildly successful, and Lauryn Hill had been widely recognized as a key to their popularity, few were prepared for her stunning debut. The social heart of the group *and* its most talented performer, she tailored *The Miseducation of Lauryn Hill*, not as a crossover record, but as a collection of overtly personal and political statements; nevertheless, it rocketed to the top of the album charts and made her a superstar. Also, and most importantly, it introduced to the wider pop world an astonishingly broad talent. Hill's verses were intelligent *and* hardcore, with the talent to rank up there with Method Man. And for the choruses she could move from tough to smooth in a flash, with a vocal prowess that allowed her to be her own chanteuse (à la Mariah Carey). Hill, of Haitian heritage, rhymed in a tough Caribbean patois on the opener, "Lost Ones," wasting little time to excoriate her former bandmates or record-label executives for caving in to commercial success. She used a feature for Carlos Santana ("To Zion") to explain how her child comes before her career and found a hit single with "Doo Wop (That Thing)," an intelligent dissection of the sex game that saw it from both angles. "Superstar" took to task musicians with more emphasis on the bottom line than making great music (perhaps another Fugees nod), while her collaborations with a pair of sympathetic R&B superstars (D'Angelo and Mary J. Blige) also paid major dividends. And if her performing talents, vocal range, and songwriting smarts weren't enough, Hill also produced much of the record, ranging from stun-gun hip-hop to smoother R&B with little trouble. Though it certainly didn't sound like a crossover record, *The Miseducation of Lauryn Hill* affected so many widely varying audiences that it's no surprise the record became a commercial hit as well as a musical epoch maker. —*John Bush*

MTV Unplugged No. 2.0 / May 7, 2002 / Ruffhouse ✦✦✦✦
Lauryn Hill's debut album, *The Miseducation of Lauryn Hill*, became a critical and commercial blockbuster, which the artist herself, always distrustful of the music business, seems to have found a disorienting experience. She has therefore waited nearly four years to make another album, and the album she has made deliberately flies in the face of the previous one and its reception. Resurrecting the MTV *Unplugged* program, she has gone before an audience with an acoustic guitar in her hands to sing a new group of songs. But that unadorned approach is only the beginning. Everything about the performance is unpolished. One suspects that she would resist even

calling it a performance; "I used to be a performer," she notes at the outset. What she is after, in her life and her music, she explains, is "reality," which means everything from being willing to sing the entire set with a raspy voice because that's the state her voice is in on that day to stopping and starting, going up on the lyrics, and even breaking down in tears. The style naturally places an emphasis on the words to the songs, which reinforce Hill's unvarnished approach, attacking the music business and anyone who wants her to be what's she's not, and witheringly criticizing institutions such as the judicial system ("Mystery of Iniquity"). The songs themselves would not require two discs to contain, but they are alternated by lengthy remarks, one spoken interlude running more than 12 minutes, in which Hill elaborates on the importance of being honest and confronting falsehood. She's usually full of herself, and she's often full of it. But that's okay. The point is the unfinished, unflinching presentation of ideas and of a person. It may not be a proper follow-up to her first album, but it is fascinating. — *William Ruhlmann*

Hobo Junction

f. 1990, Oakland, CA
Group / Underground Rap, Hip-Hop, Alternative Rap, West Coast Rap
Hobo Junction formed in 1990, based out of Oakland, California. As an active part of the West Coast hip-hop movement, they released their first effort "Whoriden." The underground success of the song resulted in the group forming Hobo Records in 1994. For the next couple of years, the label produced several albums, singles, and EPs for the group. In 2000 Hobo Junction departed from their label to release *The Cleaners* on Baraka Records. Their single, "Rock the Show" was also used for DJ Serg's debut mix album, *Golden State of Mind.* —*Diana Potts*

- **The Cleaners** / Nov. 21, 2000 / Baraka ✦✦✦
With the release of their first collective full-length album, *The Cleaners*, Hobo Junction in no uncertain terms displays the difference between cheesy corporate hip-hop and reality rap. While many major-label MCs seem stuck on boasting about their newfound wealth, Saafir, Eyecue, Poke Martian, Bignous, Mahasin, Third Rail Vic, and the D.A. are more concerned with delivering gritty narratives born straight from the streets of their hometown Oakland. When Saafir informs listeners that "I always utilize the stealth moves that I'm blessed with/So my spirit won't be looking at the wound where the bullet exits," the urgency of his words are even better felt than heard. Consistent with the urban-industrial orientation of their surroundings, the percussion-heavy production provided by Protest, J Groove, Bignous, C. Broady, and Poke Martian sounds as if it was created in a train yard. Indeed, *The Cleaners* makes for a perfect example of hip-hop fit for warriors. —*Robert Gabriel*

Hoodlum Priest (Derek Thompson)

Hip-Hop, Hardcore Rap
Derek Thompson, of Irish background but born and raised in London, is for all intents and purposes the Hoodlum Priest, his self-chosen moniker for his work as a producer and engineer, using hip-hop, industrial, and techno influences as the source of material for his sounds. While Thompson had done a brief stint with the Cure, his major musical background through the late '70s and '80s was with avant-garde industrialists SPK, which he cofounded in 1978. He continued with the band through the end of the '80s, departing after newer member Graeme Revell took the group to what Thompson felt was too commercial a direction.
His initial goal with Hoodlum Priest, one of several musical projects he explored during the '90s and beyond, was to draw in both film influences on his work—primarily via dialogue but also musically—and hip-hop with a specific goal of recruiting a London-based MC. He was introduced to one, Sevier, at a club performance in 1989, and the two worked together for awhile, but Sevier's strong Christian background and Thompson's more free-thinking philosophy and darker musical approach eventually led to the MC's departure. Thompson continued on his own, interspersing his background work (notably with Apollo 440) with occasional album releases such as 1994's *Beneath the Pavement* and 1998's *Hoodlum Priest.* —*Ned Raggett*

- **Beneath the Pavement** / 1994 / Concrete ✦✦✦✦
Released only in a limited edition of 1,200, *Beneath the Pavement* is a fierce, creative, and thrilling slice of U.K. instrumental electronic music, but one that

values the spoken word in its own way. Rather than rapping himself or using guest performers, Thompson splices in pointed samples of speeches from rallies and film dialogue to make his points, mixing wry irony with darkly critical stabs at the establishment as broadly defined. Thompson's not making philosophy, admittedly, but that's not the point—the attacks on cops, a culture of violence, and more as well as the concurrent need to rise up against idiocy both work here on the immediate level and linger a bit. His musical material can be as warmly beautiful and mysterious as the contemporaneous Bristol trip-hop explosion—check the swooping, haunting strings on both versions of "Rev."—but there's an upfront energy and anger that make the material more than just, say, head-nodding stuff for stoners. "Capital of Pain," with its coruscating guitar samples and horror-movie theatrics, is almost cartoonishly metal but all the better for being wound up so tightly. Where things are more stripped down, as on the obsessive funk of "Radio K.I.L.L.," everything is suffused with threat, the bass lines ominous and burring, the guitar tweaked and nervous. His ear for the combination of word and music results in many fine moments—for instance, the cold, electronically distorted voice introducing "Semtex Revolution" on a bed of organ before the beats brusquely kick in, leading to a high-speed combination of noise. The "Roxy Mix" of "Rev.," meanwhile, makes the track a touch more conventionally dancefloor friendly without being any less fierce, thanks to his use of the core vocal samples from the earlier take. No points for "The Hammer Speaks" though, being nothing more than a motorcycle engine revving up and down. —*Ned Raggett*

The Hot Boys

f. 1997
Group / Southern Rap, Dirty South
Formed in 1997, the Hot Boys consisted of four youthful rappers from the same neighborhood of New Orleans, LA. Two of the four, B.G. and Juvenile, were already regionally successful, each having spent several years making a name for themselves in the local rap scene. The two newcomers, Lil' Wayne and Young Turk, rapped with a polished style that belied their age and inexperience. The Hot Boys' output was significantly similar, in personnel as well as musical direction, to the group members' solo albums. This, coupled with the fact that all four rappers were signed to the same label, made the Hot Boys as much a marketing ploy as an actual group. In 1997 the foursome released their debut album, *Get It How U Live!*, on the then-independent Cash Money Records. The Hot Boys limited themselves to typical gangsta topics: guns, sex, and money. However, the four rappers' entertaining and varied deliveries and original backing tracks (provided by in-house producer Mannie Fresh) separated their release from numerous similarly themed releases. Despite little or no commercial exposure, *Get It How U Live!* quickly sold over 400,000 copies, primarily in the mid-South; following B.G.'s national success, the album was reissued nationally in 1999, followed later that year by *Guerrilla Warfare.* —*Mtume Salaam*

Get It How U Live! / Oct. 28, 1997 / Cash Money ✦✦
Despite containing little else but typical gangsta fare, *Get It How U Live!* managed to parlay the four Hot Boys' catchy, varied styles into an amusing, if incorrigible, collection of hardcore rap. The production skills of multi-instrumentalist Mannie Fresh were responsible for the album's success as were the rappers. Mannie's diverse enjoyable rhythm tracks were virtually unique in 90s-era rap in that they contained no samples or interpolations. Though ultimately lacking substance, the Hot Boys' tales will please fans of well-done gangsta rap. —*Mtume Salaam*

- **Guerrilla Warfare** / Jul. 27, 1999 / Uptown/Universal ✦✦✦✦
Guerrilla Warfare presents Cash Money Records at its finest. Hot Boy$ featured Juvenile, B.G., Lil' Wayne, and Turk rhyming over phenomenal bounce beats provided by Mannie Fresh. Following the success of Juvenile's *400 Degreez* and B.G.'s *Chopper City in the Ghetto, Guerrilla Warfare* highlighted a fully realized regional sound, indigenous to New Orleans. While Mannie Fresh effectively puts a gangsta lean on electro booty bass, the MCs' sport accents dipped deep in a Cajun frying pan. As "I Need a Hot Girl" (featuring Big Tymers) and "We on Fire" made their mark on the airwaves, album tracks such as "Get Out of the Way," "Ridin'," and "Clear the Set" decorated the streets. With something for everyone not dissuaded by a parental advisory, *Guerrilla Warfare* has rap classic written all over it. —*Robert Gabriel*

House of Pain

f. 1990

Group / Hip-Hop, East Coast Rap, Hardcore Rap, Pop-Rap

"Jump Around," an impossibly infectious and catchy single, instantly elevated House of Pain from an unknown white hip-hop group to near stars when it became a massive crossover hit in 1992. It made the band and it also broke the band, consigning them to the level of one-hit wonders. House of Pain continued to release records after their eponymous 1992 debut and "Jump Around," yet none of them gained much attention, partially because of the band's self-consciously loutish behavior. Led by rapper Everlast, the group celebrated their Irish-American heritage by wearing green, drinking prodigious amounts of beer, and swearing constantly. It certainly earned them attention at the outset, particularly when it was tied to a single like "Jump Around," but the bottom quickly fell out of their career. The group's second album, 1994's *Same as It Ever Was*, went gold, but it failed to generate a hit single, and by the time of 1996's *Truth Crushed to Earth Shall Rise Again*, the band had been forgotten.

Everlast (born Erik Schrody, August 18, 1969) became fascinated by hip-hop while he was in high school, eventually becoming part of Ice-T's Rhyme Syndicate. His association with Ice-T led to a contract with Warner Bros., who released his debut album, *Forever Everlasting*, in 1990. After the record bombed, Everlast formed House of Pain with his high school friend Danny Boy (born Daniel O'Connor) and DJ Lethal (born Leor DiMant), a Latvian immigrant. Released on Tommy Boy Records, the group's eponymous 1992 debut was coproduced by Muggs, who masterminded Cypress Hill's groundbreaking debut. Muggs gave "Jump Around" its distinctive, incessant beat, which merged a deep bass groove with drum loops and Public Enemy-styled sirens. On the back of Kris Kross' spring hit "Jump," "Jump Around" became a huge hit in the summer of 1992, peaking at number three on the pop charts. Both the single's video and the remainder of *House of Pain* celebrated the group's Irish heritage in a tongue-in-cheek fashion that quickly became shtick. Throughout their 1993 tour, the group ran into trouble with promoters and the law, culminating in Everlast's March arrest for possessing an unregistered, unloaded pistol at Kennedy Airport. He was sentenced to community service, and later that year, the group began work on their second album.

Like its predecessor, 1994's *Same as It Ever Was* was produced by Muggs. Upon its summer release, the record was greeted with surprisingly strong reviews and sales, debuting at number 12 on the charts. However, the sales quickly slowed as "On Point" failed to become a hit. Most of the next two years were spent in seclusion, and the group returned in the fall of 1996 with *Truth Crushed to Earth Shall Rise Again*, a record that was ignored by both the press and the public. Everlast returned in 1998 as a solo act and gained critical acclaim for his debut, *Whitey Ford Sings the Blues*. *—Stephen Thomas Erlewine*

● **House of Pain** / Jul. 21, 1992 / Tommy Boy ✦✦✦✦

It's an album that ushered in an era of a thousand suburbanites drinking malt liquor, wearing U.S. Postal Service caps, and reawakening their Irish (or in some cases pseudo-Irish) heritage. And it's also the debut album that ushered House of Pain into the forefront of rap culture for a brief period of time. While it's unfair to expect a whole album's worth of quality material like the dynamite classic "Jump Around," there are some strong points on their eponymous debut that emulate the single's strength. Admittedly, there is a significant amount of filler and the topics du jour aren't exactly the most original in hip-hop, but the impact of such songs as "Jump Around," "Shamrocks and Shenanigans," and "Put on Your Shit Kickers" more than makes up for the filler. This debut for a group showed immense promise, but sadly it wasn't fully realized. *—Rob Theakston*

Same as It Ever Was / Jun. 28, 1994 / Tommy Boy ✦✦✦✦

House of Pain's self-titled album had its moments, but on the whole wasn't very memorable. However, the Irish-American group really blossomed on its far superior and much more hardcore second album, *Same as It Ever Was*. With this album, Everlast changed his style of rapping considerably and unveiled a much more distinctive and recognizable approach. Sounding twisted, damaged, and maniacal, Everlast grabs the listener's attention and refuses to let go on such wildly entertaining fare as "Back From the Dead," "Over There Shit," and "Runnin' Up on Ya." House of Pain's subject matter—namely, their superior rapping skills and the threat they pose to sucker MCs—is far from groundbreaking. But an abundance of strong, clever hooks and Everlast's

psycho-like rapping make *Same as It Ever Was* consistently appealing. *—Alex Henderson*

Truth Crushed to Earth Shall Rise Again / Oct. 22, 1996 / Tommy Boy ✦✦✦

Having found its voice on *Same as It Ever Was*, House of Pain delivered an equally captivating effort with its third album, *Truth Crushed to Earth Shall Rise Again*. Being Anglo rappers in a genre that had grown increasingly hostile toward whites, Everlast and Danny Boy encountered their share of racism and bigotry. And they responded by being unapologetically street and hardcore, while bragging about their Irish heritage. On the whole, the album's subject matter isn't very substantial—the group still spends too much time boasting. But as was also the case with *Same as It Ever Was*, the LP is impossible to resist thanks to House of Pain's insanely captivating hooks and Everlast's twisted style of rapping. *—Alex Henderson*

Alfonzo Hunter

b. 1973, Chicago

Vocals / Hip-Hop, Soul, Urban

Part of the rise of mid-'90s soul singers who proved quite proficient at rapping as well, Alfonzo Hunter debuted in 1996 with the first release on Def Squad Records—the label formed by Def Squad and Erick Sermon. Hunter, born in Chicago in 1973, released *Blacka da Berry* in October of 1996. *—John Bush*

● **Blacka da Berry** / Oct. 29, 1996 / Def Squad ✦✦✦

Alfonzo Hunter's debut album *Blacka da Berry* finds the twentysomething singer working the same ground as his contemporaries Maxwell and D'Angelo—namely, classic early-'70s soul. Hunter tries to bring the music up to date more than either Maxwell or D'Angelo, particularly in terms of lyrics—the first single "Just the Way (Playas Play)" sums up the difference in attitude. Also, producers Erick Sermon and the Def Squad bring a hip-hop sensibility to the music, which is often intriguing, if not always very successful. Even with its missteps, *Blacka da Berry* is a promising debut, demonstrating that Hunter is flush with potential and talent. *—Leo Stanley*

Hurricane G (Gloria Rodriguez)

Latin Rap, East Coast Rap, Underground Rap

Born and raised in Brooklyn, female rapper Hurricane G is among the Puerto Rican MCs who came out of New York in the '90s. Hurricane, whose real name is Gloria Rodriguez, took a bilingual approach; most of her lyrics are in English, although she has no problem flowing in Spanish. And when Hurricane provides Spanish-language lyrics, she raps in the Newyorican dialect; a type of Spanish (or "Spanglish") that is spoken by Puerto Ricans in and around the Big Apple. (Other Puerto Rican MCs who have rapped in New Yorican-style Spanish have ranged from Mesanjarz of Funk to the Mean Machine, whose 1981 hit "Disco Dreams" was the first rap single to include Spanish lyrics.) Those who speak Spanish would have no problem identifying Hurricane as a Puerto Rican New Yorker; her use of Spanish is different from the Cuban-American rapping one hears in Miami or the Mexican-American "vato loco" rhymes one associates with West Coast MCs like Kid Frost, Cypress Hill, Lighter Shade of Brown, and tha Mexakinz.

In the '90s, Hurricane became the first female member of the Def Squad, an East Coast hip-hop clique whose other members have included Erick Sermon (of EPMD fame), Keith Murray (best known for his 1994 hit "The Most Beautifullest Thing in This World,"), and Redman. EPMD, in fact, is among Hurricane's influences; like EPMD, Hurricane favors a deadpan, very direct, and straightforward rapping style and doesn't inundate listeners with technique for the sake of technique. Around 1994, the Brooklyn native signed with Capitol, but she didn't get far with that label; when Capitol did a lot of downsizing, Hurricane was among the victims and found herself without a record deal.

It was in early 1997 that she resurfaced on producer Jellybean Benitez' New York-based H.O.L.A. Recordings, whose name is an acronym for "Home of Latino Artists." (Benitez is best known for being among Madonna's early supporters.) H.O.L.A. released *All Woman*, Hurricane's debut album, in September 1997; Benitez was listed as the executive producer. Regrettably, the album wasn't a big seller, and when the 21st century arrived, Hurricane had yet to provide a second album. *—Alex Henderson*

● **All Woman** / Sep. 16, 1997 / H.O.L.A. ✦✦✦

Known for his association with Madonna and his work in dance music, Jellybean Benitez isn't someone you'd expect to serve as executive producer on a hardcore rap effort. But that's exactly what he does on *All Woman*, the debut album by Puerto Rican female rapper Hurricane G. This isn't a rap CD with lots of pop or dance-music influence, and in fact, underproduced jams like "Boriqua Mami," "Underground Locdown," and "El Barrio" are characterized by a definite lack of slickness. The Brooklyn native, who raps in both English and Spanish, goes for simplicity and favors a deadpan, very informal delivery comparable to EPMD. Unlike many New York rappers who were popular in 1997, she doesn't inundate listeners with technique. As much of an in-your-face, tough-girl attitude as she often projects, the hip-hopper shows a lot of vulnerability on "Mama," a touching and poigant ode to her mother. Hurricane does tend to spend too much time boasting (a problem with quite a few MCs), but even so, *All Woman* was one of the more enjoyable rap releases of late 1997. —*Alex Henderson*

H.W.A.

Group / Dirty Rap, West Coast Rap

If BWP (Bytches With Problems) weren't hip-hop's most controversial female group of the early '90s, then H.W.A. (Hoez With Attitudes) certainly qualified. Openly flaunting a loose (to put it mildly) sexual attitude and standing vulgarity to vulgarity with any male rapper, H.W.A. failed to generate much sales action, but certainly got plenty of publicity, including a lengthy article in *The Source* and condemnation from sources as diverse as Rev. Calvin Butts and filmmaker Spike Lee. —*Ron Wynn*

● **Livin' in a Hoe House** / 1990 / Drive-By ✦✦✦

In 1996, Lil' Kim's *Hardcore* demonstrated that a female rapper could be every bit as X-rated as 2 Live Crew or Too Short. But she wasn't the first. In the early '90s, female rap groups H.W.A. (Hoez With Attitude) and BWP (Bytches With Problems) went out of their way to be as offensive and sexually explicit as possible. Released in 1990, *Livin' in a Hoe House* is hardly the first example of women talking dirty. Vanity and other Prince disciples did it in the '80s, and Lucille Bogan's '30s blues classic "Shave 'Em Dry" is as X-rated as anything that H.W.A, BWP, or Lil' Kim ever recorded. But while this album isn't revolutionary, it's entertaining—that is, if you have a taste for crude humor. If you find Rudy Ray Moore, 2 Live Crew, and Too Short entertaining and amusing, you should have no problem getting into "Tight," "Little Dick," "Eat This," and other sexually explicit rhymes. But if you are offended by X-rated humor, it's best to pass on this album. Musically, *Livin' in a Hoe House* is closer to Oakland native Too Short than Luther Campbell's Miami-based 2 Live Crew; the beats and production are very West Coast, although H.W.A. members Kim "Baby Girl" Kenner, Tanya "Jazzy" Kenner, and Dion "Diva" Devoux lived in Chicago before they moved to Los Angeles. This album doesn't have the sort of fast, hyper grooves that 2 Live Crew and other Southeastern bass artists are known for, but lyrically H.W.A. and 2 Live Crew have a lot in common, which explains why this album fared well in what hip-hoppers call the dirty South. *Livin' in a Hoe House* didn't go down in history as one of rap's all-time masterpieces, but it's a guilty pleasure that is good for some cheap thrills. —*Alex Henderson*

Ice

f. 1992
Group / Hip-Hop, Ambient Dub, Underground Rap
The darker visions of industrial-strength trip-hop plus death-metal raging equals the intense dub-hop of Ice. A side project of sorts formed around Godflesh's Justin K. Broadrick and God's Kevin Martin (the same lineup comprising Techno Animal), Ice formed in the early '90s with additional bandmembers Dave Cochrane and Alex Buess. The quartet released *Under the Skin*, their debut LP, in 1993. Broadrick and Martin both kept quite busy with other work—for Techno Animal, Final, Godflesh, God, and others—and released the 1995 remix EP *Quarantine*. Finally, in 1998, Ice returned with their second album, *Bad Blood*, and new drummer Lou Ciccotelli, plus collaborators like Sebastian Laws and Scott Harding of New Kingdom, Blixa Bargeld, DJ Vadim, and El-P from Company Flow. —*John Bush*

Under the Skin / 1993 / Pathological ✦✦✦
Right from the opening notes, it's pretty clear who's in Ice and what they're up to. The music has the same combination of aggressive guitar, dry, steady beats, cryptic vocals, and more that made up so much of Martin and Broadrick's music in the early '90s. Even the artwork—fetuses, guns, and mirror images—and the length of the album (nearly a full CD's worth) all make it clear who is involved. But if there are no outright surprises on *Under the Skin* for those well steeped in Martin and Broadrick and company's anticommercial aesthetic, it's still a treat for said listeners, if not something many who weren't already fans would tolerate. God's *Consumed* is the best immediate comparison for *Under the Skin*, though certainly Godflesh at their most distanced but vicious, as on "Pure II," also has an understandable influence. Martin's inimitable singing approach—howled vocals then heavily and totally echoed into the oblivion—defines the songs as much as Broadrick's blasting feedback, but credit goes as well to the Cochrane/Jobbagy rhythm section, who pound and grind with equally obsessive focus. Martin's sax work crops up on a number of tracks as well, his free jazz love finding some truly extreme places to hang out. There are some moments where the band lives up to its name and chills down dramatically: "Out of Focus," which emphasizes the silence between the beats and sometimes soft (!) guitar chimes as much as the music itself, and, to a lesser extent, "Implosion," with moaning electronic howls and drones chasing more tenor sax parts around the mix. Otherwise, it's pretty much one massive grind and bash after another, manna from heaven for believers and pure torture for most everyone else. —*Ned Raggett*

● **Bad Blood** / Oct. 20, 1998 / Morpheus ✦✦✦
By the time Ice had reconstituted, Martin and Broadrick's ear had taken in hip-hop as a key influence, resulting in a slew of guest MCs taking a bow throughout *Bad Blood*. Not every vocalist comes from that particular background, it should be noted; indeed, on half the tracks none other than Einsturzende Neubaten's Blixa Bargeld participates! Martin's expected roaring isn't present much here—there's little distortion or stretched-out syllables, while a spoken/sung style often takes the fore, cutting in, out, and around the guest turns. Tricky if anything is the role model for Martin, at least to an extent. DJ Vadim crops up on two tracks as well, while Scott Harding contributes beats and loops throughout, but for all the various cameos the core of Ice remains remarkably stable. If there's a musical change, though, it's stripping back Broadrick's punishing guitars in favor of the rasped and whispered singing and MC work. Rather than blare like a monster, Broadrick keeps the same slow drone pace on his chosen instrument but buries and echoes it heavily, lurking like a threat rather than just plain rampaging. The end result sounds a bit like Ice goes trip-hop, for better or worse, specifically in the Massive Attack vein of looming, unsettled doom, though without the

weirdly pretty and human edge that leavens the Bristol collective's work. The downside is that there's not really much variety on *Bad Blood*; distorted crunches and beats mixed with slightly cleaner percussion, interwoven vocals calling for any number of potential apocalypses, random off-kilter samples from who knows where treated with dub echo. However, the lack of variety on *Under the Skin* wasn't a real problem, and, to their credit, Martin and Broadrick aren't simply repeating that album here. —*Ned Raggett*

Ice Cream Tee

b. Philadelphia, PA
Hip-Hop
Not to be confused with Ice-T or Ice Cube, Ice Cream Tee was an obscure female rapper who came out of the Philadelphia rap scene of the 1980s. The MC was born and raised in Philly, where she met DJ Jazzy Jeff and the Fresh Prince before they became well known. In 1987 they featured Ice Cream prominently on "Guys Ain't Nothing but Trouble," the sequel to their hit "Girls Ain't Nothing but Trouble." Ice Cream soon pursued a solo career, and in the late '80s she was being managed by Lady B—a DJ and ex-rapper who was known for her show on Philly's urban contemporary station Power 99 FM and had, in 1979, recorded the single "To the Beat, Y'all" for Tec Records, later reissued by Sugar Hill. Lady B, in fact, was the first female rapper to record as a solo artist. Ice Cream was being managed by Lady B when, in 1989, she recorded her first solo album, *Can't Hold Back*, for Strong City. In contrast to the lighthearted pop leanings of "Guys Ain't Nothing but Trouble," *Can't Hold Back* was a tougher, harder, more aggressive effort along the lines of MC Lyte, Roxanne Shanté, and Queen Latifah. *Can't Hold Back* wasn't a big seller nationally, and Ice Cream never recorded a second album. —*Alex Henderson*

Can't Hold Back / 1989 / Strong City ✦✦

Ice Cube (O'Shea Jackson)

b. Jun. 15, 1969
Vocals, Producer / Golden Age, Gangsta Rap, West Coast Rap, G-Funk, Hardcore Rap
Ice Cube was the first member of the seminal Californian rap group N.W.A to leave, and he quickly established himself as one of hip-hop's best and most controversial artists. From the outset of his career, he courted controversy, since his rhymes were profane and political. As a solo artist, his politics and social commentary sharpened substantially, and his first two records, *AmeriKKKa's Most Wanted* and *Death Certificate*, were equally praised and reviled for their lyrical stance, which happened to be considerably more articulate than many of his gangsta peers. As his career progressed, Cube's influence began to decline, particularly as he tried to incorporate elements of contemporary groups like Cypress Hill into his sound, but his stature never diminished, and he remained one of the biggest rap stars throughout the '90s.

For such a revolutionary figure, Cube (born O'Shea Jackson) came from a surprisingly straight background. Raised in South Central Los Angles, where both of his parents had jobs at UCLA, Cube didn't become involved with b-boy culture until his late teens. He began writing raps while in high school, including "Boyz-n-the 'Hood." With his partner Sir Jinx, Cube began rapping in a duo called CIA at parties hosted by Dr. Dre, and he eventually met Eazy-E, then leading a group called HBO, through Dre. Eazy asked Cube to write a rap, and he presented them with "Boyz-n-the 'Hood," which was rejected. Eazy decided to leave CIA, and he, Cube, and Dre formed the first incarnation of N.W.A. Cube left to study architectural drafting at Phoenix, AZ, in 1987, returning the following year after he obtained a one-year degree. He arrived just in time for N.W.A's breakthrough album, *Straight Outta Compton*. Released late in 1988, *Straight Outta Compton* became an underground hit over the course of 1989, and its extreme lyrical content—which was over the top both lyrically and politically—attracted criticism, most notably from the FBI.

N.W.A may have been rivaling Public Enemy as the most notorious group in hip-hop, but Cube was having deep conflicts with their management, resulting in him leaving the band in late 1989. He went to New York with his new posse, Da Lench Mob, and recorded his first solo album with Public Enemy's production team, the Bomb Squad. Released in the spring of 1990, his debut *AmeriKKKa's Most Wanted* was an instant hit, going gold within its first two weeks of release. While the record's production and Cube's rhythmic skills were praised, his often violent, homophobic, and misogynist lyrics were criticized, particularly by the rock press and moral watchdogs. Even amid such controversy, the album was hailed as a groundbreaking classic within hip-hop, and it established Cube as an individual force. He began his own corporation, which was run by a woman, and he produced the debut album from his female protégée, Yo-Yo. At the end of 1990, he released the EP *Kill at Will*, which was followed in the spring by Yo-Yo's debut, *Make Way for the Motherlode*. That summer, his acting debut in John Singleton's acclaimed urban drama *Boyz 'n the 'Hood* was widely praised.

AmeriKKKa's Most Wanted may have been controversial, but it paled next the furor surrounding Cube's second album, *Death Certificate*. Released late in 1991, *Death Certificate* was simultaneously more political and vulgar than its predecessor, causing more outrage. In particular, "No Vaseline," a vicious attack on N.W.A manager Jerry Heller, was perceived as anti-Semitic, and "Black Korea" was taken as a racist invocation to burn down all Korean-owned grocery stores. The songs provoked public condemnation from the trade publication *Billboard*. It was the first time an artist had been singled out by the magazine. The furor over *Death Certificate* didn't prevent it from reaching number two and going platinum. During 1992 he toured with the second Lollapalooza tour in a successful attempt to consolidate his white rock audience. He also converted to the Nation of Islam during 1992 which was evident on his next album, *The Predator*. Upon its release in November of 1992, *The Predator* became the first album to debut at number one on both the pop and R&B charts. The steady-rolling single "It Was a Good Day" and the Das EFX collaboration "Check Yo Self" made the album Cube's most popular.

However, Cube's hold on the mass rap audience was beginning to slip. His former colleague, Dre, was dominating hip-hop with his stoned G-funk, and Cube tried to keep pace with 1993's *Lethal Injection*. While the album debuted at number five and went platinum, its funkier sound wasn't well received. *Lethal Injection* was Cube's last official album for several years. In 1994 he wrote and produced Da Lench Mob's debut, *Guerillas in tha Mist*, and produced Kam's debut, *Neva Again*, releasing a remix and rarities collection *Bootlegs & B-Sides* at the end of the year. In 1995 he kept quiet, appearing in Singleton's film *Higher Learning* and making amends with Dre on their duet "Natural Born Killaz." The following year, he acted in the comedy *Friday*, which he wrote himself. He also formed Westside Connection with Mack 10 and WC, releasing their debut album, *Bow Down*, at the end of the year. It went gold within its first month of release. In the spring of 1997, Cube starred in the surprise hit horror film *Anaconda*. *War & Peace, Vol. 1 (The War Disc)* followed in 1998; its sequel, *The Peace Disc*, followed two years later. —*Stephen Thomas Erlewine*

Kill at Will EP / 1990 / Priority ✦✦✦✦

Ice Cube's riveting debut album, *AmeriKKKa's Most Wanted* was still burning up the charts when Priority Records released this EP, which lacks that album's overall excellence but has its moments. With *Kill at Will*, Cube unveiled his engaging "The Product" and "Dead Homiez," a poignant lament for the victims of black-on-black crime that is among the best songs he's ever written. Enjoyable but not essential are remixes of "Endangered Species (Tales From the Darkside)" and the outrageous "Get Off My D⁕⁕⁕" and Tell Yo B⁕⁕⁕⁕" to Come Here." Clearly, *Kill at Will* was intended for hardcore fans rather than casual listeners. (The EP was later added to a 2003 expanded edition of *AmeriKKKa's Most Wanted*.) —*Alex Henderson*

☆ AmeriKKKa's Most Wanted / May 16, 1990 / Priority ✦✦✦✦✦

After leaving N.W.A on anything but good terms with Dr. Dre and Eazy-E, Ice Cube launched his solo career with the hard-hitting and impressive

AmeriKKKa's Most Wanted. While the Angelino continued to embrace gangster rap—a style in which MCs provide violent, graphic, first-person portrayals of thugs, gang members, drug dealers, etc.—there's a lot more to this riveting CD than that controversial approach. As much as Cube thrives on the shocking and the profane, it's clear that he isn't glamorizing the harsh urban realities he raps about, but rather, protesting them. "Once Upon a Time in the Projects" is about being arrested for being in the wrong place (a crack house) at the wrong time (during a drug bust), while "Endangered Species" (a duet with Public Enemy leader Chuck D) is a sobering reflection on the high mortality rate among young African-American males. On some of his subsequent recordings, Cube would, artistically speaking, become a victim of his own anger. But on *AmeriKKKa's Most Wanted*, a more lucid Cube quite effectively articulates just how bad things are in the America's inner cities—and how badly things need to change. —*Alex Henderson*

★ Death Certificate / Oct. 31, 1991 / Priority ✦✦✦✦✦

Death Certificate is even harder and angrier than *AmeriKKKa's Most Wanted*, which is both a good and a bad thing, depending on your politics. If you're inclined to see Ice Cube as a spokesman and social commentator, *Death Certificate* will support your claims—it continues the sharp insights and unflinching looks at contemporary urban lifestyles that his solo debut only hinted at; in short, its hardcore without any gangsta posturing. If you're inclined to see Ice Cube as a bigoted, misogynistic rabble-rouser, *Death Certificate* will also support your claims—"No Vaseline" contains explicit anti-Semetic taunts directed at his former manager, there are homophobic slurs scattered throughout the album and women are frequently either bitches or whores. However, if you look beyond the surface—no matter what political viewpoint you happen to have—you will find that Cube's rhymes do promote self-awareness and education. In short, they are some of the most incisive raps about life as a young black man since the advent of Public Enemy. Considering this, it's not surprising that *Death Certificate* bears the mark of Public Enemy's dense, abrasive soundscapes—it's a funkier, noisier, and more musically effective album than *AmeriKKKa's Most Wanted*. Ice Cube had never before created a statement of purpose as coherent and incendiary as *Death Certificate* and, sadly, he never did again. —*Leo Stanley*

The Predator / Nov. 17, 1992 / Priority ✦✦✦

Released in the aftermath of the 1991 L.A. riots, *The Predator* radiates tension. Ice Cube infuses nearly every song, and certainly every interlude, with the hostile mood of the era. Even the album's most laid-back moment, "It Was a Good Day," emits a quiet sense of violent anxiety. Granted, Ice Cube's previous albums had been far from gentle, but they were filled with a different kind of rage. On both *AmeriKKKa's Most Wanted* (1990) and *Death Certificate* (1991), he took aim at society in general: women, whites, Koreans, even his former group members in N.W.A Here, Ice Cube is more focused. He found a relevant episode to magnify with the riots, and he doesn't hold back, beginning with the absolutely crushing "When Will They Shoot?" The song's wall of stomping sound sets the dire tone of *The Predator* and is immediately followed by "I'm Scared," one of the many disturbing interludes comprised of news commentary related to the riots. It's only during the aforementioned "It Was a Good Day" that Ice Cube somewhat alleviates this album's smothering tension. It's a truly beautiful moment, a career highlight for sure. However, the next song, "We Had to Tear This Motha——— Up," eclipses the relief with yet more calamity. By the time you get to the album-concluding "Say Hi to the Bad Guy" and its mockery of policeman, hopelessness prevails. *The Predator* is a grim album, for sure, more so than anything Ice Cube would ever again record. In fact, the darkness is so pervasive that the wit of previous albums is absolutely gone. Besides the halfhearted wit of "Gangsta's Fairytale, Pt. 2," you won't find any humor here, just tension. Given this, it's not one of Ice Cube's more accessible albums despite ironically boasting a few of his biggest hits. It is his most serious album, though, as well as his last important album of the '90s. —*Jason Birchmeier*

Lethal Injection / Dec. 7, 1993 / Priority ✦✦

Following the relentless intensity of his early-'90s albums, particularly his post-Rodney King statement, *The Predator* (1992), Ice Cube reclined a bit and put his rap career on autopilot beginning with *Lethal Injection*, the last album he would record for five years. Yes, it's a disappointing album, but it's not a terrible album by any means, of course. Even if Ice Cube is a little devoid of substance here relative to his rabble-rousing past, he's still a talented rapper, and he has one of the West Coast's premier producers, QDIII, joining him for almost half the album. Unfortunately, much of what made Ice Cube's early-'90s albums so electric—his thoughtfulness, wit, hostility, energy, and social consciousness—is sadly in short supply. For compensation, Ice Cube offers a few standout singles, namely "You Know How We Do It" and "Bop Gun (One Nation)." The former follows the successful template that worked a year earlier with "It Was a Good Day"—a laid-back G-funk ballad laced with an old school funk vibe; the latter clocks over 11 minutes, an epic ode to George Clinton's P-funk legacy. These two songs undoubtedly rank alongside Ice Cube's best work ever. There are a few other songs like "Really Doe" and "Ghetto Bird" that also stand out, but even these songs sound rather lackluster relative to Ice Cube's previous work. He's obviously not interested in making an album as daring and ambitious as *The Predator* again, and you can't really blame him. After all, Ice Cube had delivered three brilliant albums, and a similarly brilliant EP as well, *Kill at Will* (1990), in just three years, not to mention his then-burgeoning role as an actor. He deserved a break. But at least he took the time to craft two standout singles that alone make this album worthy. —*Jason Birchmeier*

Bootlegs & B-Sides / Nov. 22, 1994 / Priority ♦♦
As Ice Cube albums became few and far between once the rapper turned actor, Priority Records started gathering up a few compilations, one less interesting one being *Bootlegs & B-Sides*. The 13 tracks are mostly throwaways, not necessarily bad but not necessarily good either. The few gems buried here are remixes of Cube's biggest hits: "Check Yo Self," "It Was a Good Day," and "You Know How We Do It." The others will interest mainly completists. —*Jason Birchmeier*

Featuring . . . Ice Cube / Dec. 16, 1997 / Priority ♦♦♦
Featuring…Ice Cube gathers up an excellent collection of team-ups indeed featuring Ice Cube. It's a simple idea for a compilation, and it works well for Priority Records, who had a lot of Cube material to draw from and a lot of hungry fans at the time. The majority of the inclusions come from Cube's pre-*War & Peace* albums ("Bop Gun [One Nation]" with George Clinton; "Check Yo Self," Das EFX; "Endangered Species," Chuck D; "It's a Man's World," Yo-Yo), a few from soundtracks ("Natural Born Killaz," Dr. Dre; "Trespass," Ice-T), and a few from the albums of others ("Game Over," Scarface; "West Up!," WC). Everything here is available elsewhere yet in very scattered fashion. Odds are you've heard many of these songs before but not all of them, so *Featuring…Ice Cube* is a welcome inclusion in the rapper's catalog. Not essential but certainly welcome, as essentially every team-up here is a classic from Cube's prime years. —*Jason Birchmeier*

War & Peace, Vol. 1 (The War Disc) / Nov. 17, 1998 / Priority ♦♦♦
Considering that he hadn't delivered a full-fledged solo album since 1993's disappointing *Lethal Injection*, maybe it shouldn't have been a surprise that Ice Cube returned hard in 1998 with *War & Peace, Vol. 1 (The War Disc)*, since five years is a long, long time to stay quiet. What was a surprise was how ambitious the album was. The first installment in a proposed double-disc set, *The War Disc* is a cacophonic, cluttered, impassioned record that nearly qualifies as a return to form. Designed as a hard-hitting record, it certainly takes no prisoners, as it moves from intense street-oriented jams to rap-metal fusions, such as the Korn-blessed "Fuck Dying," with its seething, distorted guitars. It's a head-spinning listen and, at first, it seems to be a forceful comeback. Upon closer inspection, *The War Disc* falters a bit. Not only does the relentless nature of the music wear a little thin, but Cube spends too much time trying to beat newcomers at their own game. His lyrical skills are still intact, but he spends way too much time boasting, particularly about material possessions, and his attempt to rechristen himself Don Mega, in a Wu-like move, simply seems awkward. Even so, the quality of the music—and the moments when he pulls it all together, such as "3 Strikes You In"—sustains *War* and makes it feel more cohesive than it actually is. The key is purpose—even if Cube doesn't always say exactly what he wants, he does have something to say. That alone makes *War & Peace*, with just one album completed, a more successful and rewarding listen than the typical double-disc hip-hop set of the late '90s. —*Stephen Thomas Erlewine*

War & Peace, Vol. 2 (The Peace Disc) / Feb. 29, 2000 / Priority ♦♦♦
Ice Cube's initial *War & Peace* album left a lot of fans feeling disappointed, after having waited five years for it, and the concluding volume isn't any more satisfying. A lot changed in those five years, and Cube does adjust well here to the changing times. Besides, it's simply great to hear him so revived. Yet there's also an undercurrent of stubbornness here that's unsettling. The

opening track, "Hello," is the first omen of what's to come. The tailor-made N.W.A reunion anthem produced by Dr. Dre brings together the surviving members of the legendary gangsta rap pioneers and hits hard, Cube proclaiming on the hook, "I started this gangsta sh*t/And this the muthaf*ckin' thanks I get?" It's a striking beginning—hard hitting, yes, but also openly bitter and haughty. If Cube could keep heavy-hitters like this coming, it'd be easy to accept the attitude, but he doesn't. The album drops off from here. There's a lot of steam and a lot of tension, yet not much artistry. That golden touch Cube had back in the days of *AmeriKKKa's Most Wanted* and *Death Certificate* is sadly missing. There's a nice good-time diversion halfway through "You Can Do It," but that's about it. You're then back to the tension, and it lasts for a straining 17 tracks. In the end, the net total of Cube's two-album creative burst doesn't amount to much. Amid the two-plus hours, there's a small handful of gems buried beneath a lot of tracks you'll find yourself skipping. Here on the *War & Peace* series the aging legend is clearly a changed man, an older, wiser one who's trying hard but who's ultimately incapable of grasping the brilliance of his past. But it's nothing to mourn, as Cube certainly had his moments of glory and continued to have them, albeit in Hollywood rather than Compton. —*Jason Birchmeier*

Greatest Hits / Dec. 4, 2001 / Priority ♦♦♦♦
Although the 17-track *Greatest Hits* covers all phases of Ice Cube's solo career in an extremely balanced fashion, it isn't quite the last word on one of the most seminal figures in hardcore and gangsta rap. It *is* definitely a worthwhile purchase, since it collects all the best singles from Cube's more uneven latter-day efforts; there are also two new cuts (although "In the Late Night Hour" has a lot of rewritten N.W.A rhymes) and a couple that have never appeared on an Ice Cube album: the soundtrack contribution "We Be Clubbin'" and the Westside Connection single "Bow Down" (which are nice for collectors but not all that essential). That occasional filler makes it all the more frustrating that the classic "Dead Homiez" is inexcusably nowhere to be found, and that it apparently wasn't possible to license Cube's duet with Dr. Dre on "Natural Born Killaz." Selection issues aside, the singles from the post-*Predator* era prove that in his best moments, Cube could be a credible radio-crossover artist and keep up with contemporary production trends. As a storyteller (a facet of his work that's underrepresented here), Cube had a knack for keenly observed detail, as evidenced on "Once Upon a Time in the Projects" and his laid-back masterpiece "It Was a Good Day." Still, it doesn't quite add up to a truly classic compilation. Perhaps the problem is that while *Greatest Hits* is a fine, listenable portrait of Ice Cube the sometime hitmaker and full-time hip-hop celebrity, it doesn't completely capture the provocative, incendiary qualities that made him an icon in the first place (for that, listeners will have to go back to *AmeriKKKa's Most Wanted* and *Death Certificate*). For a fully fleshed-out picture of Cube's career, though, *Greatest Hits* is a very good place to go. —*Steve Huey*

Ice-T (Tracy Morrow)

b. Feb. 14, 1959, Newark, NJ
Vocals, Producer / Golden Age, Gangsta Rap, West Coast Rap, Hardcore Rap
Ice-T (born Tracy Morrow) has proven to be one of hip-hop's most articulate and intelligent stars, as well as one of its most frustrating. At his best, the rapper has written some of the best portraits of ghetto life and gangsters, as well as some of the best social commentary hip-hop has produced. Just as often, he can slip into sexism and gratuitous violence, and even then his rhymes are clever and biting. Ice-T's best recordings have always been made in conjunction with strong collaborators, whether it's the Bomb Squad or Jello Biafra. With his music, Ice-T has made a conscious effort to win the vast audience of white male adolescents, as his frequent excursions with his heavy metal band Body Count show. All the while, he has withstood a constant barrage of criticism and controversy to become a respected figure not only in the music press, but the mainstream media as well.

Although he was one of the leading figures of Californian hip-hop in the '80s, Ice-T was born in Newark, NJ. When he was a child, he moved from his native Newark to California after his parents died in an auto accident. While he was in high school, he became obsessed with rap while he went to Crenshaw High School in South Central Los Angeles. Ice-T took his name from Iceberg Slim, a pimp who wrote novels and poetry. Ice-T used to memorize lines of Iceberg Slim's poetry, reciting them for friends and classmates. After he left high school, he recorded several undistinguished 12" singles in the early '80s. He also appeared in the low-budget hip-hop films *Rappin'*, *Breakin'*, and *Breakin' II: Electric Boogaloo* as he was trying to establish a career.

Ice-T finally landed a major-label record deal with Sire Records in 1987, releasing his debut album, *Rhyme Pays*. On the record, he is supported by DJ Aladdin and producer Afrika Islam, who helped create the rolling, spare beats and samples that provided a backdrop for the rapper's charismatic rhymes, which were mainly party oriented; the record wound up going gold. That same year, he recorded the theme song for Dennis Hopper's *Colors*, a film about inner-city life in Los Angeles. The song—also called "Colors"—was stronger, both lyrically and musically, with more incisive lyrics, than anything he had previously released. Ice-T formed his own record label, Rhyme Syndicate (which was distributed through Sire/Warner) in 1988, and released *Power*. *Power* was a more assured and impressive record, earning him strong reviews and his second gold record. Released in 1989, *The Iceberg/Freedom of Speech...Just Watch What You Say* established him as a true hip-hop superstar by matching excellent abrasive music with fierce, intelligent narratives, and political commentaries, especially about hip-hop censorship.

Two years later, Ice-T began an acting career, starring in the updated blaxploitation film *New Jack City*; he also recorded "New Jack Hustler" for the film. "New Jack Hustler" became one of the centerpieces of 1991's *O.G.: Original Gangster*, which became his most successful album to date. *O.G.* also featured a metal track called "Body Count" recorded with Ice-T's band of the same name. Ice-T took the band out on tour that summer, as he performed on the first Lollapalooza tour. The tour set-up increased his appeal with both alternative-music fans and middle-class teenagers. The following year, the rapper decided to released an entire album with the band, also called *Body Count*.

Body Count proved to be a major turning point in Ice-T's career. On the basis of the track "Cop Killer"—where he sang from the point of view of a police murderer—the record ignited a national controversy; it was protested by the NRA and police activist groups. Time Warner Records initially supported Ice-T, yet they refused to release his new rap album, *Home Invasion*, on the basis of the record cover. Ice-T and the label parted ways by the end of the year. *Home Invasion* was released on Priority Records in the spring of 1993 to lukewarm reviews and sales. Somewhere along the way, Ice-T had begun to lose most of his original hip-hop audience; now he appealed primarily to suburban white teens. In 1994 he wrote a book and released the second Body Count album, *Born Dead*, which failed to stir up the same controversy as the first record—indeed, it failed to gain much attention of any sort. Nevertheless, Body Count was successful in clubs and Ice-T continued to tour with the band.

In the summer of 1996, Ice-T released his first rap album since 1993, *VI: Return of the Real*. The album was greeted by mixed reviews and it failed to live up to commercial expectations. *7th Deadly Sin* followed in 1999. Ice-T then returned to acting, taking a role on NBC's *Law & Order: Special Victims Unit* playing, ironically, a police officer. —*Stephen Thomas Erlewine*

Rhyme Pays / 1987 / Sire ✦✦✦
Before Ice-T's ascension, L.A. rappers were known primarily for a synthesizer-dominated sound indebted to Kraftwerk's innovations as well as Africa Bambaataa's 1982 hit, "Planet Rock." While L.A. did have its share of hardcore rappers in the mid-1980s (including Toddy Tee, King Tee, and of course, Ice-T), hardcore rap was dominated by the East Coast. That begin to change in 1987, when Ice-T's debut album, *Rhyme Pays*, was released and sold several hundred thousand copies. Hard-hitting offerings like "409," "Make It Funky," and the title song (which samples Black Sabbath's "War Pigs" and underscores the L.A. resident's love of heavy metal) left no doubt that Ice had very little in common with the Egyptian Lover, the World Class Wreckin' Cru, or the L.A. Dream Team. The album doesn't contain as much gangsta rap as some of his subsequent releases, but it did have enough to stir some controversy. On "Squeeze the Trigger," "Pain," and a new version of "6 'N the Mornin'" (which had been the B side of Ice's 1986 single "Doggin' the Wax" on Techno-Hop), Ice portrays ruthless felons and raps candidly about the horrors of the urban ghetto he'd been only too familiar with. With the release of *Rhyme Pays*, the West Coast was well on its way to becoming a crucial part of hip-hop. —*Alex Henderson*

Power / 1988 / Sire ✦✦✦✦✦
As riveting as *Rhyme Pays* was, Ice-T did hold back a little and avoided being too consistently sociopolitical. But with the outstanding *Power*, the gloves

came all the way off, and Ice didn't hesitate to speak his mind about the harsh realities of inner-city life. On "Drama," "Soul on Ice" (an homage to his idol Iceberg Slim), "High Rollers," and other gangsta rap gems, Ice embraces a first-person format and raps with brutal honesty about the lives of gang members, players, and hustlers. Ice's detractors took the songs out of context, arguing that he was glorifying crime. But he countered that, in fact, he was sending out an anti-crime message in a subliminal fashion and stressed that the criminals he portrayed ended up dead or behind bars. Another track that some misconstrued was "I'm Your Pusher," an interpretation of Curtis Mayfield's "Pusherman" that doesn't promoting the use of drugs, but uses double entendres to make an anti-drug statement. (Ice has always been vehemently outspoken in his opposition to drugs.) In the next few years, gangsta rap would degenerate into nothing more than cheap exploitation and empty clichés, but in Ice's hands, it was as informative as it was captivating. —*Alex Henderson*

☆ **The Iceberg/Freedom of Speech ... Just Watch What You Say** / Oct. 1989 / Sire ✦✦✦✦
Ice-T threw listeners quite a curve ball with his riveting third album, *The Iceberg/Freedom of Speech...Just Watch What You Say*—arguably the closest hip-hop has come to George Orwell's *1984*. Instead of focusing heavily on gangsta rap, Ice-T made First Amendment issues the CD's dominant theme. Setting the album's tone is the opener "Shut Up, Be Happy," which finds guest Jello Biafra (former leader of punk band Dead Kennedys) envisioning an Orwellian America in which the goverment controls and dominates every aspect of its citizens' lives. Though there are a few examples of first-rate gangster rap here—including "The Hunted Child" and the chilling "Peel Their Caps Back"—Ice's main concern this time is censorship and what he views as a widespread attack on free speech in the U.S. As angry and lyrically intense as most of *The Iceberg* is, Ice enjoys fun for its own sake on "My Word Is Bond" and "The Girl Tried to Kill Me"—an insanely funny rap/rock account of an encounter with a dominatrix. —*Alex Henderson*

★ **O.G.: Original Gangster** / May 14, 1991 / Sire ✦✦✦✦✦
One of gangsta rap's defining albums, *O.G.: Original Gangster* is a sprawling masterpiece that stands far and away as Ice-T's finest hour. Taken track by track, *O.G.* might not seem at first like the product of a unified vision; perspective-wise, it's all over the map. There's perceptive social analysis, chilling violence, psychological storytelling, hair-trigger rage, pleas for solutions to ghetto misery, cautionary morality tales, and cheerfully crude humor in the depictions of sex and defenses of street language. But with a few listens, it's possible to assimilate everything into a complex, detailed portrait of Ice-T's South Central L.A. roots—the album's contradictions reflect the complexities of real life. That's why the more intelligent, nuanced material isn't negated by the violence and sexism—both of which, incidentally, are held relatively in check, with the former having been reshaped into a terrifying but inescapable fact of life. That isn't to say that *O.G.: Original Gangster* is designed to appeal to delicate intellectual sensibilities; it's still full of raw, street-level aggression that makes no apologies or concessions. That goes for the music as well as the lyrics. The beats are a little too hard driving and jittery to really breathe like funk, which only adds to the dark, claustrophobic feel of the production. Ice smoothly keeps up with the music's furious pace and also debuts his soon-to-be-notorious metal band Body Count on one track. That kind of artistic ambition is all over the album, whether in the lean musical attack or the urgent rhymes. *O.G.: Original Gangster* is a certifiable gangsta rap classic, and arguably the most realistic, unvarnished representation of a world Ice-T was the first to chronicle on record. —*Steve Huey*

Body Count / 1992 / Sire ✦✦✦
Ice-T's excursion into heavy metal brought him a firestorm of controversy, but the album is actually a tepid collection of '80s-style arena metal that never sounds dangerous. Frequently, it's hard to tell if Ice takes this stuff seriously; tracks like "Body Count" and "Cop Killer" are invigorating stabs at social criticism, but most of the album is filled with stupid attempts at being threatening, like "KKK Bitch" and "Mama's Gotta Die Tonight." Maybe the humor was intentional, but too frequently the record sounded embarrassing. After "Cop Killer" was pulled from the album, it was replaced with a version of "The Iceberg" recorded with Jello Biafra. —*Stephen Thomas Erlewine*

Home Invasion / Mar. 23, 1993 / Priority ✦✦✦
Given the fact that most of *Home Invasion* was recorded during and after the "Cop Killer" media firestorm, it comes as no surprise that the album is an

uneven, muddled affair, not the clean, focused attack of *O.G.: Original Gang-ster*. Instead of producing an album that illustrates his confusion through the music (like Public Enemy's claustrophobic "Welcome to the Terrordome"), Ice-T made a confused album, unsure in its musical and lyrical direction. *Home Invasion* does have some flashes of brilliance (about a third of the album, particularly the tribute to the gang truce, "Gotta Lotta Love"), but it takes a little digging to find the best material. — *Stephen Thomas Erlewine*

The Classic Collection / May 4, 1993 / Rhino ♦♦♦
From N.W.A to Snoop Dogg to Above the Law, any West Coast rapper who has embraced gangsta rap—or hardcore rap period—owes a major debt of gratitude to Ice-T. *Rhyme Pays*, his debut album of 1987, made hip-hoppers all over the world realize that hardcore rap could, in fact, come from Los Angeles. *The Classic Collection* focuses on Ice's formative years and takes a look at the innovator's pre-1987, pre-Sire/Warner Bros. output. Recorded from 1983 to 1986 for various indie labels, Ice's early singles rejected the futuristic, dance-oriented electro-hop style that was prevalent in Southern California at the time. Ice didn't identify with the Egyptian Lover, the World Class Wreckin' Cru, or any of the other L.A. rappers who epitomized electro-hop; his influences were hardcore rappers from New York. Ice's very first single, "The Coldest Rap" (released in 1983), has the type of old school hip-hop flavor that Kurtis Blow and his colleagues were known for, and subsequent singles such as "Killers," "Ya Don't Quit," and "Dog 'N the Wax" are as hard hitting as anything that was coming out of New York at the time. However, only one tune on this CD is full-fledged gangsta rap. The disturbing "Six 'N the Mornin'" (which he re-recorded for *Rhyme Pays*) is a gangsta classic; rapping in the first person, Ice gives listeners some disturbing accounts of thug life in South Central Los Angeles. Rhino concludes this disc with 1992's "Ice-O-Tek," a techno mix that samples the rapper's early singles; the mix is fun, but not essential. *The Classic Collection* isn't for casual listeners, who would be better off sticking to essential albums like *Rhyme Pays*, *Power*, and *O.G.: Original Gangster*. But Ice's die-hard fans will find a lot to admire about this CD, which is easily recommended to serious rap historians. — *Alex Henderson*

VI: Return of the Real / Jun. 1996 / Priority ♦♦♦
As the title says, Ice-T returns to the street and the hardcore beats with his sixth album, *Return of the Real*. In fact, the return isn't just to hardcore—it's to hardcore that happened before gangsta rap, before the message and the music became diluted with endless b-boy posturing and loping P-funk beats. In concept, the album is brilliant—Ice-T has always had an eye for lyrical detail and has always been a vocal supporter of hardcore, street-oriented hip-hop; at the very least, his rejection of G-funk/post-N.W.A gangsta rap is a bold political move. However, *Return of the Real* doesn't quite reestablish Ice-T as a force, mainly because the production sounds a bit dated. Sure, there are the occasional contemporary flourishes—usually in the guise of a Wu-Tang-style soundscape—but for the most part, Ice sounds like he's in his own world. Unfortunately, that doesn't mean that he has created a unique sonic world; it just means that he hasn't progressed far since 1991. Of course, there are a number of tracks that sound vibrant and alive, but *Return of the Real* can't help escape a creeping sense of stagnation that permeates through the entire album. — *Stephen Thomas Erlewine*

The Ice Opinion / Oct. 21, 1997 / Audio Select ♦♦♦
The Ice Opinion, originally a book written by Ice-T, was also released as an audio book in a three-disc set—titled "Who Gives a F°○°k," "A Pimp's Guide to Sex, Rap and God," and "Ya Shoulda Killed Me Last Year." Each volume easily lasts an hour, with Ice talking about his opinions on subjects including sex, violence, music, and religion. Though the set is interesting the entire way, it is a bit much to wade through for all but the most fanatical of listeners. —*John Bush*

7th Deadly Sin / Oct. 12, 1999 / Coroner/Atomic Pop ♦♦♦
With artwork straight out of David Fincher's seminal 1995 serial killer flick *Seven*, Ice-T's seventh album *7th Deadly Sin* looks curiously out of place in 1999, and it has a sound to match. Ice-T doesn't really return to his classic sound of the late '80s/early '90s when he was a key player in the golden age of hip-hop, but he doesn't seem entirely concerned with staying current, either. The end result is a record that occasionally recalls *O.G.* or *Iceberg* while still having elements of everything from RZA's ominous, skeletal productions to the stripped-back Cali-rap of the late '90s. As a result, it straddles two extremes, which can actually be intriguing at times, especially since it is the sonic equivalent of Ice-T's place in hip-hop in 1999—a veteran that isn't washed up,

but isn't quite in step with the times. Unfortunately, his lyrics don't really match the feel of the album, since he's decided to pretty much run through his traditional list of gangsta topics, even adding the now-clichéd slow-jam tribute to Tupac and Biggie with "Valuable Game," a song based around En Vogue's "Don't Let Go" and easily the most embarrassing thing on the album. When he breaks from gangsta tradition or offers a twist on it, as he does on the title track or "Don't Hate the Playa," the songs have the opportunity to really take off, but they just highlight how most of the songs have lyrics that are simply too generic. But if *7th Deadly Sin* is taken on a purely musical level, it can be intriguing. Not always successful, but it at least offers a welcome change after a couple of undistinguished releases. — *Stephen Thomas Erlewine*

Greatest Hits: The Evidence / Aug. 8, 2000 / Atomic Pop ♦♦♦♦
Ice-T, the self-proclaimed "original gangster" of rap, is one of the few hip-hop artists who truly deserves a greatest-hits compilation. In a genre marked by overnight sensations, rapidly changing trends, and fans with short memories, he put together a long career marked by both consistency and innovation. This 16-track compilation, put together by Ice-T himself, covers 14 years, seven albums, and the title themes for two films (*Colors* and *New Jack City*), but fortunately concentrates primarily on the first five years of his career, when he was at his productive peak. Two more recent songs on this release were not previously domestically available, a U.K. remix of "The Lane," which doesn't add anything to the original, and the unreleased track "Money, Power, Women." Both are decent but should have been left off in favor of older, better classics. Fairly informative liner notes describe the creative process behind each song and each album from Ice-T's perspective. Most of the singles and recognizable songs are included here, with the mysterious exception of "Lifestyles of the Rich and Infamous" and "Gotta Lotta Love," which honored the gang truce in the wake of the L.A. riots. Also excluded are memorably risqué songs, such as "Girls L.G.B.N.A.F." and "Girl Tried to Kill Me," and some of Ice-T's more adventurous collaborations, including Body Count, the forerunner to Limp Bizkit and other rap-metal groups. These exceptions are peripheral, however, and the meat of his career is included here. —*Luke Forrest*

Ill Al Skratch

f. Brooklyn
Group / East Coast Rap, Urban, Party Rap, Hip-Hop
Ill Al Skratch had some short-lived mainstream success in the mid-'90s with *Creep Wit' Me*, the duo's 1994 debut album. Two singles from *Creep Wit' Me*— "Where My Homiez?" and "I'll Take Her"—made some ground on the R&B charts, the latter being the bigger hit thanks to Brian McKnight's vocal contributions. Unfortunately, while "I'll Take Her" became a substantial hit, it was more representative of McKnight's style of music than Ill Al Skratch's style of East Coast party rap. Consequently, listeners were confused, and when the Brooklyn duo returned in 1997 with its follow-up album, few noticed. The album fell off the charts quickly and soon Ill and Al Skratch were has-beens.

While the Brooklyn duo's name makes it seem as if Ill Al Skratch is one person rather than two, that isn't the case: There is Ill (acronym for I Lyrical Lord), who is the MC, and then there is Al Skratch, who is the DJ. The two debuted with the "Where My Homiez?" 12" released by Mercury and produced by LG, better known as Easy Mo Bee's brother. The song peaked at number 34 on *Billboard*'s R&B charts and came close to breaking the Top 100 pop singles in summer 1994. Next came "I'll Take Her," which featured McKnight. The song crossed over well, reaching number 62 pop and number 16 R&B in late 1994. When the two returned in 1997 with *Keep It Movin'*, which didn't do nearly as well as *Creep Wit' Me*, it brought the duo's career to a quick halt. —*Jason Birchmeier*

● **Creep Wit' Me** / Aug. 2, 1994 / Mercury ♦♦♦♦
Keep It Movin' / Apr. 22, 1997 / Mercury ♦♦♦
Keep It Movin', Ill Al Skratch's second album, isn't quite as consistent as their debut, but there are enough streetwise, phat beats and strong rhymes to make it a worthy follow-up. —*Leo Stanley*

Illogic

f. Ohio
Group / Underground Rap, Hip-Hop
Illogic has almost single-handedly put Ohio on the map in the world of hip-hop. He's also put himself on the top of many a fan's hopes to take the mic crown and run with it. His debut release, *Unforeseen Shadows*, created

earthquakes in the underground hip-hop community in 1999, with its conscious lyrics, wise and intelligent metaphors, and Illogic's verbal dominance on the beat. His follow-up album, *Got Lyrics?*, was released in 2001, also on the Weightless label. —*Brad Mills*

● **Unforeseen Shadows** / 1999 / Weightless ✦✦✦✦
Illogic is an MC from Columbus, OH, and *Unforeseen Shadows* is his debut album. All the production is done by Blueprint of Greenhouse Effect. Although all the beats are done by one man, the beats don't sound the same. "My Favorite Things" is their take on the song of the same name from the movie *The Sound of Music.* It features a great beat, and while it used the original song as a model it went its own imaginative direction and sounds great. "Illogistics" features a funky guitar sample, and the beat on "Tales of a Griot" has an orchestral feel to it that works really well. Illogic is impressive on the mic; he has a creative flow and good lyrics. On "Check It Out," Blueprint tells Illogic the true test of an MC is his versatility. Illogic shows his versatility throughout *Unforeseen Shadows.* From the personal "Angel" to the battle rhymes of "Me Vs. Myself," he is even able to change his flow to follow the beat at the end of "Illogistics," which speeds up and gets more choppy. *Unforeseen Shadows* is an impressive debut album. —*Dan Gizzi*

Got Lyrics? / Nov. 20, 2001 / Weightless ✦✦
Illogic comes straight outta Cowtown, the nickname that Columbus dwellers have long given their city. He and his Weightless Crew are trying valiantly and passionately to put the area on the hip-hop map; unfortunately, the results are decidedly mixed. Illogic bills himself as a spoken word artist as much as a rapper, and that influence shows on *Got Lyrics?*, his rhymes flow fast and in a monotone, reminiscent of a fellow cerebral talent, the underappreciated Del tha Funkee Homosapien. However, the production is not very innovative or invigorating. The jazzy loops remain far in the background, not complementing the rapping at all, and certainly lacking the charisma to stand on their own should he choose to do instrumental remixes. Get Illogic an innovative producer who's unafraid to take chances and the MC could make some noise, because he certainly has more than enough prowess behind the mic. The DJ-friendly double-vinyl version of the record includes a bonus track featuring a guest appearance from New York's Aesop Rock. —*Brian O'Neill*

Immature
f. 1990, Los Angeles, CA
Group / Pop-Rap, Club/Dance, Hip-Hop, Urban, New Jack Swing
Pre-teenage R&B sensations in the early '90s, Immature were formed in Los Angeles by producer/mentor Chris Stokes around barely ten-year-olds Marques "Batman" Houston, Jerome "Romeo" Jones, and Kelton "LDB" Kessee. The trio recorded their debut album, *On Our Worst Behavior*, for Virgin in 1992 and scored a modest R&B hit with "Tear It Up" (from the animated film *Bebe's Kids*). After moving to MCA for 1994's *Playtyme Is Over*, Immature scored with the pop hits "Never Lie" and "Constantly," pushing the album into gold territory. The trio then appeared in the Kid 'n Play film *House Party 3.* Third album *We Got It* also did well, though no single cracked the Top 40; "Feel the Funk," from the movie *Dangerous Minds*, came the closest, at number 46. For their fourth LP *The Journey*, Immature flirted with changing their name—the obvious choice was Mature—but decided to focus the change in direction on the music. *The Journey* did well on the R&B charts, but failed to translate to a pop success. The new millennium saw the release of a greatest-hits package, issued in February 2001. —*John Bush*

On Our Worst Behavior / 1992 / Virgin ✦✦

Playtyme Is Over / 1994 / MCA ✦
Enjoying a largely teenage and preteen following, Immature moved from Virgin to MCA with its sophomore effort, *Playtyme Is Over*. The label switch didn't mean a change in focus—the group (whose members were 11 or 12 at the time) still offered an abundance of hip-hop-influenced, medium-tempo, new-jack R&B grooves. And the same comparisons were being made; if you believed the hype, Immature was to the 1990s what Frankie Lymon and the Teenagers were to the 1950s, the Jackson 5 was to the 1970s, and New Edition was to the 1980s. But those groups had the chops and excellent songs to back up their hype; none of the tunes on *Playtyme Is Over* are memorable, let alone excellent. Cuts like "Walk You Home" and "Never Lie" have a generic, cookie-cutter quality, and they sound like the product of a marketing meeting rather than artistic inspiration. When Lymon, Michael Jackson and Bobby Brown were teenagers and sang about adolescent love, the sincerity

jumped right out at you—put on Lymon's "Why Do Fools Fall in Love," New Edition's "Mr. Telephone Man," or the Jackson 5's "I Want You Back," and you find yourself thinking about what a bittersweet time adolescence could be. Put on *Playtyme Is Over*, and all you're thinking about is how contrived and formulaic Immature sounds. —*Alex Henderson*

● **The Journey** / Sep. 23, 1997 / MCA ✦✦✦✦
When Immature debuted in 1992 with *On Our Worst Behavior*, there were those who compared the preteen urban contemporary trio to the Jackson 5 and early New Edition. The problem with that comparison was that the members of those groups were better singers and had far superior material to work with. By the time *The Journey* came out in 1997, the members of Immature were 15 and had improved somewhat. Lead vocalist Marques "Batman" Houston hadn't turned into a great singer by any means, but some of the material on this CD is decent, including the Keith Sweat-produced "Extra Extra," the moody, flamenco-influenced "Tamika," and the haunting "24/7," which was produced by Marc Gordon of Levert fame. *The Journey* also has its share of throwaways, and on the whole, the album isn't all that memorable. It's best to pass. —*Alex Henderson*

Incognegro
Group / Hip-Hop, Underground Rap
Considering that everyone who's a part of this Philadelphia hip-hop four-piece was in the Goats, it's hard not to make comparisons of their previous project. Fronted by Maxx Stoyanoff-Williams, one-half of the Goats main lyricists, he's backed with the production styles of Sean Tyson, Mark Boyce, and the drummings of former Bad Brains/Urge Overkill drummer Chuck Treece. Having their own unique flavor of intelligent lyrics, laid-back beats, and slick Hammond organs, their first self-titled full-length was released by Chord Recordings in 1999. —*Mike DaRonco*

● **Incognegro** / May 18, 1999 / Chord ✦✦✦
It'd be easy to compare Incognegro to that other organic hip-hop crew from Philly, the Roots, but differences do reveal themselves. Basically just a three-piece of MC Uh-Oh, DJ Smoove, and keyboardist Gungi Brain, Incognegro aren't quite a hip-hop band like Stetsasonic or the Roots, though Smoove's well-chosen scratches and samples beef up the sound considerably. And Gungi Brain's cascade of shimmering keyboards almost bests one of the current masters—the Roots' Scott Storch—at the jazz-funk-lite treatment, especially on the leadoff track, "Keepin' It Lovely." Much of the rest of *Incognegro* focuses on paranoid bass lines and grungy sampling from Smoove (case in point: the detuned heavy-metal guitar on "Shotgun Shack," and the excellent choice of the Clash's "Brand New Cadillac" to provide a focus to the song of almost the same name)—to anchor MC Uh-Oh's raps. Though Incognegro seem to function at only two speeds, either fusion-lite or dark Wu-Tang-style melodrama, there are few disappointments here. —*John Bush*

Indo G
b. Memphis, TN
Hardcore Rap, Southern Rap
A member of the mid-'90s cluster of Memphis, TN, rappers affiliated with the extended Three 6 Mafia collective—Hypnotize Camp Posse, Prophet Posse, Tear da Club up Thugs—Indo G quickly established himself as one of the city's most talented MCs, examplified with the Juicy J/DJ Paul-produced *Angel Dust* (1998). Yet just as quickly, he found himself ostrocized from the Three 6 camp; without the aid of the Three 6 members and their major-label affiliation with Relativity, his second album, featuring the efforts of the Ghetto Troopers, *Live & Learn*, appeared to an indifferent audience. Before hooking up with Juicy J and DJ Paul, Indo G had recorded with Lil' Blunt as part of a duo in the mid-'90s. —*Jason Birchmeier*

● **Angel Dust** / Aug. 11, 1998 / Relativity ✦✦✦✦
Once Three 6 Mafia gained a measure of respect and popularity, Indo G broke from the ranks and released a solo album, *Angel Dust*. Musically, as well as lyrically, it's not far removed from his main group. It's a familiar mix of low-riding gangsta rap, party-ready grooves, hardcore rhymes, funky beats and bass—with the bass being emphasized, since Indo G and Three 6 Mafia are from the South. The difference is, *Angel Dust* stands out because producers Juicy J and DJ Paul are sonic masters and Indo G is a sharp-minded rapper. These factors are enough to make *Angel Dust* feel fresh, even if the ingredients are familiar. —*Leo Stanley*

Infamous Mobb

f. Queensbridge, NY

Group / Hardcore Rap, East Coast Rap

Infamous Mobb followed the precedent established by fellow Queensbridge rappers Nas and Mobb Deep. The latter introduced the trio—Ty Nitty, Gambino, and Godfather, Pt. 3—on its *Hell on Earth* (1996) and *Murda Muzik* (1998) albums; however, Infamous Mobb didn't release its debut album until 2002, after guest appearances on DJ Muggs' second *Soul Assassins* album and Nas' *QB Finest* collection. The trio's debut album, *Special Edition*, featured extensive production work by Alchemist and was released by Landspeed Records, a small label with little industry push. —*Jason Birchmeier*

● **Special Edition** / Mar. 26, 2002 / Landspeed ◆◆◆
Six years after making its debut appearance on Mobb Deep's *Hell on Earth* album, Infamous Mobb finally delivered its debut album. Though the album wasn't released by a major label, it features prominent collaborators, including Mobb Deep and producers Alchemist and DJ Muggs. Mobb Deep member Prodigy raps on three of the album's songs, and Alchemist produces the majority of the album. However, even with top-notch collaborators like Prodigy and Alchemist, Infamous Mobb fails to impress. Thematically, the trio recycles the New York thug rap of mid-'90s Nas and Mobb Deep and, stylistically, is not on a par with either. Overall, this is second-rate Queensbridge thug rap—nowhere near Nas or Mobb Deep and a tier below other peers such as Cormega and Nature. Nonetheless, Infamous Mobb still reps Queensbridge and its legacy on *Special Edition*, and Alchemist lays down some great beats. Thus, Queensbridge devotees should take note. —*Jason Birchmeier*

Infamous Syndicate

f. Chicago, IL

Group / G-Funk, East Coast Rap

Chicago native and self-styled street poet Lateefa celebrated her 17th birthday in 1997, unaware that a guest at her party, Rashawnna Guy, would soon become her tightest partner in friendship as well as in a mutual pursuit for hip-hop stardom. Rashawnna, or Shawnna, as she's known, is the daughter of blues impresario Buddy Guy and was inspired by rappers Nas, Ice Cube, and the Wu-Tang Clan as she honed her skills in the subways and underground clubs of Chicago. Lateefa, or Teefa, used her writing skills to conceive raps that she worked on over beats her cousin supplied. As a duo, Shawnna and Teefa met with overwhelming homegrown support, and when their demo made waves on local radio, they inked a deal with Relativity Records. In 1998 Infamous Syndicate toured as part of the Lyricist Lounge, receiving critical acclaim as the premiere female duo representing hip-hop from Chicago. —*Roxanne Blanford*

Here I Go [Single] / Jan. 26, 1999 / Relativity ◆◆
● **Changing the Game** / Mar. 16, 1999 / Relativity ◆◆◆
This 1999 release from Infamous Syndicate set itself apart from the sometimes verbally and sexually abrasive female rap pack of its time by crafting creative harmonies around refreshingly sincere lyrics. Although the well-worn topics of love, lust, struggles, and self-discovery are all covered here, Shawnna and Teefa offer an eclectic music base and rap style that is both unique and appealing. To their credit, Infamous Syndicate incorporates contributions from a pool of Chicago's most talented hip-hop producers, adding an element of instrumental versatility and depth to this exceptionally well-produced debut. —*Roxanne Blanford*

Infesticons (Mike Ladd)

Group / Club/Dance, Trip-Hop, Underground Rap

Underground rap impresario Mike Ladd has recorded several LPs of sewer-level hip-hop, both under his own name and as the Infesticons. A big funk fan as a kid, he played drums in a punk band while living around New York during the early '80s and got into hip-hop in 1985. After years of freestyle rhyming (closer to urban poetry than straight-out rapping) and producing, Ladd released his first solo album *Easy Listening 4 Armageddon* in 1997 for Scratchie/Mercury. One year later, the "Blah Blah" single followed on Big Dada, and in 2000 his second LP *Welcome to the Afterfuture* appeared on his own Like Madd Music. Later that year, Ladd signed his new alias the Infesticons to Big Dada/Ninja Tune and released *Gun Hill Road*. Ladd also released a single for the Beastie Boys' Grand Royal label, in their *Blow Up Factor*

series. He returned in 2003, as Majesticons, to release the *Beauty Party* LP. —*John Bush*

Gun Hill Road / May 30, 2000 / Big Dada ◆◆
The cream of the underground hip-hop crop—a gaggle of lost gangstas and a Beastie Boy collaborator—constitutes the wild and should-be-wonderful mob collectively know as the Infesticons, spearheaded by the inimitable Mike Ladd. It should be wonderful, but it isn't: *Gun Hill Road* suffers mightily from blurred vision, splintered beats, tuneless loops, too much noise, and a low rap standard. The sound is pure NYC underground and stellar moments abound, but the overall impact is scattershot. A stunning wealth and breadth of talent, anti-playa attitude, and derangement are on display here, but the feeling is showy and spotty. Highlights have to be Saul Williams' reassuringly nut-case "Monkey Theme," Rob Smith's waveless proto-rap "Chase Theme," and Dana & Majesticon 69's transsexual/freak/funk show "Shampoo Theme." There are some reverential moments to funkadelia and many of Smith and Majesticon's movements are often sheer labyrinths of voicescapes in the most ambitious of the rap traditions. —*Becky Byrkit*

Infinite Mass

f. Sweden

Group / Hip-Hop, Gangsta Rap, Hardcore Rap, Club/Dance

Infinite Mass was the only Swedish hip-hop group that managed to break commercially with West Coast rap and G-funk. Their time in the spotlights in the mid-'90s was brief, but the work they and Latin Kings did in paving way for the wave of Swedish hip-hop in the late '90s should not be underestimated. Infinite Mass was formed in 1991 by Rodrigo Pencheff, Amir Chamdim, and Bechir Eklund, and soon swelled out to become a big collective of rappers, dancers, and musicians. Pencheff was also a member of Latin Kings and in 1992 the two groups participated in a rap contest where Latin Kings were discovered and offered their first record deal. Infinite Mass won the competition, but the international contest that was to follow was canceled. The band was offered to record an EP as compensation and the result was *Infinite Mass*, released later the same year and sold by the band members themselves. At this time, Infinite Mass played political and angry music with clear influences from Public Enemy and N.W.A, as can be heard on the singles and EPs released the following two years, including "Shoot the Racist," which reached some fame through the action movie *Sökarna* in 1993.

With the release of their debut album *The Infinite Patio* in 1995, Infinite Mass had shifted over to G-funk and West Coast rap. The album meant a major breakthrough for the group, though the gangsta image brought them some scorn, and had them answering for the violent lyrics of the whole genre on national television. The album got a Swedish Grammy award for best dance album and the tour that followed was the first ever where Swedish hip-hop drew big crowds. Leila K. had been close a few years earlier, but had quit her tour after only a few concerts. Back from the road, Eklund left the band to start a solo career under the stage name Bashir, while the remaining duo traveled to Los Angeles to find inspiration at the source. There they were introduced to Melle Mel and MC Eith, and managed to get both to participate on *Alwayz Somethang*, released in 1997. But in spite of the star factor these two gave the album, and a gangsta image now even more dependent on classic gangster movies, the album was a commercial failure. The following years saw the members of Infinite Mass working with various other artists as well as setting up their own label, Topaz. In 2000, the single "Enter the Dragon" got much airplay, and being built around a heavy guitar riff, it showed that Infinite Mass had left G-funk behind. The album *The Face*, released in 2001, kept on the same track and was equally discarded as rap-metal and admired for its mix of styles and genres. —*Lars Lovén*

● **Alwayz Somethang** / Jul. 1, 1997 / Warlock ◆◆◆
Live in Sweden / 1999 / Murlyn ◆◆

Infinity tha Ghetto Child (Antwon Buie)

b. 1980, Charleston, SC

Vocals, Producer / Dirty South, Hardcore Rap

South Carolina native Infinity tha Ghetto Child is among the many hardcore rappers who has come out of hip-hop's dirty South school, and many of his rhymes—although not really gangsta rap in the conventional sense—angrily describe the harsh realities of ghetto life and inner-city thug life. His rapping style is not subtle, understated, or laid-back; he has a rough, abrasive, jagged delivery to go with his sobering lyrics (which is quite a contrast to someone like West Coast gangsta rapper Snoop Doggy Dogg, who combines sobering lyrics with a relaxed, lazy rapping style). Ghetto life is something that Infinity tha Ghetto Child has firsthand knowledge of; born Antwon Buie in Charleston, SC, in 1980, he grew up in that south city's infamous Johnson Street Housing Projects where he was surrounded by poverty, black-on-black crime, high unemployment, and drugs. In fact, Infinity's mother was addicted to crack cocaine; his father, meanwhile, was nowhere to be found. Infinity's single mother was not the only crack addict in his life; in the '90s, a teenage Infinity was romantically involved with a female crack addict from his neighborhood. Infinity impregnated that teenage girl, and she had a son by him. Because of the girl's drug problem, the Department of Human Services took their son away from them and placed the child in foster care. But eventually, the courts decided that Infinity could be a responsible parent and awarded him full custody—the girl, meanwhile, entered a drug rehab program and, according to Infinity's publicist, was recovering from her addiction in 2001.

Despite all the misery and dysfunction that surrounded Infinity in the poorest, most depressed, and crime-ridden area of Charleston, he aggressively pursued a career as a rapper. In the late '90s, Infinity recorded various singles and EPs and put them out himself. One of those singles was "Carolina Love," which became a small regional hit and sold more than 20,000 units in that part of the U.S. It was around 1997 that Infinity started working with DJ Bless, a South Carolina hip-hop producer who should not be confused with the alternative rocker Bless. One of the singles that DJ Bless produced for Infinity was "Throw Ya Fingaz Up," which, like "Carolina Love," was a regional hit in parts of the deep South. In the early 2000s, Infinity's work with DJ Bless caught the attention of MCA, which signed the Charleston rapper. *Pain*, Infinity's first full-length album for Never So Deep/MCA, was produced by DJ Bless in 2001 and came out in March 2002; the hard-hitting "In tha Ghetto" was released as the CD's lead single. —*Alex Henderson*

● **Pain** / Mar. 26, 2002 / MCA ♦♦♦
No one will mistake Infinity tha Ghetto Child for Too Short, DJ Quik, or Snoop Dogg. While those West Coast rappers have combined explicit lyrics with a laid-back, easygoing type of flow, Infinity is anything but laid-back when he raps. The Charleston, SC, native barks when he's on the mic, and his rapping is rough and abrasive—he has a harsh rapping style to go with the harsh lyrics that define *Pain*, his first full-length album for Never So Deep/MCA. *Pain* is an appropriate title for this CD because pain is exactly what this CD talks about—the pain of growing up in the projects, the pain of being poor, and the pain of being surrounded by drugs and violent crime. The environment that Infinity vividly (and angrily) describes on *Pain* isn't pretty, and between the harsh sound of his voice and his dark, troubling lyrics, this album doesn't give the listener much room to breathe. Infinity is hardly the first hardcore rapper to talk about ghetto life—the Southerner was only a baby when, in 1982, Grandmaster Flash & the Furious Five's seminal "The Message" gave listeners a no-nonsense account of the types of problems that plagued the inner city. And sadly, *Pain* reminds listeners that 20 years later, those poverty-ridden, high-crime areas (which could be in the South Bronx, South Central L.A., or Infinity's native Charleston) had not improved. But rapping and production styles have evolved considerably since "The Message," and while Infinity's subject matter isn't groundbreaking, the best parts of this album manage to be fairly fresh sounding. Even if *Pain* meanders at times, its best tracks (which include "Streets Claim Me," "Being a Nigga," and "Picture My Plan") are compelling. All things considered, *Pain* is among the more memorable CDs to come from rap's dirty South school in the early 2000s. —*Alex Henderson*

Insane Clown Posse

f. 1990, Detroit, MI

Group / Rap-Metal, Rap-Rock

Insane Clown Posse are a cartoonish metal/rap band with a vaunted live show that features open fires, chainsaws, liters of soda dousing the audience (Faygo being the group's favorite brand), and more emphasis on performance art than the performance of music. In the world of the late '90s, that was more than enough to get them a recording contract with a major label, though the release of their 1997 album *The Great Milenko* came with a bit of controversy. Now just a duo, ICP were originally formed in 1989 as a hardcore Detroit rap group called Inner City Posse. After combusting in 1991, the only

members left, Violent J (born Joseph Bruce) and Shaggy 2 Dope (born Joseph Utsler), slightly altered the name to reflect the fact that they had been visited by the Carnival Spirit, which ordered them to carry word of the impending apocalypse by touring the nation and releasing six "Joker Cards" (popularly known as LPs) with successive revelations of the final judgment. The first, *Carnival of Carnage*, appeared in 1992 on their own Psychopathic Records label. The group became notorious in Detroit's underground scene, but several tours around the region failed to ignite much more than the rage of area leaders.

After the release of 1994's *The Ringmaster*, ICP began to get a bit of attention as a possible follower of cartoon metal bands like Gwar and Green Jelly. Jive Records signed the group and released *The Riddle Box* in 1995, but the record bombed and ICP returned to the ranks of the indies. Just one year later, Hollywood Records gambled on the band and spent more than one million dollars while ICP recorded their new album, *The Great Milenko*. On the day of release in 1997, however, Hollywood pulled the record, citing obscene lyrics and gruesome content—possibly a move by its owner, Disney, to deflect criticism of its practices by the Southern Baptist Federation. In a bizarre twist, yet another major label, Island Records, stepped in to release the album and capitalize on the notoriety ICP had garnered. That notoriety only increased thanks to several incidents that kept them in the headlines: J was arrested after clubbing an audience member with his microphone in late 1997, and shortly thereafter, the group's tour bus ran off the road, leaving J with a concussion. Next, the group and their entourage were involved in a brawl at a Waffle House in Indiana, and both members verbally pleaded guilty to disorderly conduct charges. All the chaos took its toll, as J suffered a panic attack in April 1998 while on stage in Minnesota. However, all of the publicity helped expand the group's cult following to the point where their next album, the 1999 concept record *The Amazing Jeckel Brothers*, debuted in the Top Five. As evidenced by the numerous different collectible covers for *The Amazing Jeckel Brothers*, ICP had become a virtual merchandising machine, complete with comic books to flesh out their elaborate "Dark Carnival" mythology; they also wrote and starred in their own straight-to-video movie, *Big Money Hustlas*, and made guest appearances at wrestling events.

The group spent the summer of 1999 bickering with various tourmates (Coal Chamber in particular), and played at the ill-fated Woodstock '99. Early in 2000, Shaggy collapsed on stage, but the cause was deemed to be nothing more than a combination of the flu and low blood sugar; however, while staging a wrestling event several months later, Shaggy fell off of a steel cage, breaking his nose and cheekbone. Still, ICP managed to make it into the studio to record a follow-up album, and *Big Money Hustlas* was finally released that summer. On Halloween 2000, the group issued their sixth album, which apparently did not count (as all the other albums had) as a "joker card" (in the ICP fantasy world, the sixth joker card was supposed to signal the apocalypse). Similar to Guns N' Roses' *Use Your Illusion*, the album was released in two completely different, separate versions, titled *Bizzar* and *Bizaar*. Finally needing to live up to the years of hype, 2002's *The Wraith: Shangri-La* revealed that the hidden message of their music was always to follow God and make it to heaven. Considering the murder fantasies of "Beverly Kills 50187" and the necrophilic overtones of "Cemetary Girl," this may have been a shock to longtime fans. —*John Bush*

Carnival of Carnage / 1992 / Island ♦♦♦
The Insane Clown Posse introduced themselves to the world (well, at least Detroit) with their debut album, *Carnival of Carnage*. It pretty much spelled out their ludicrous sex'n'drugs'n'crime'n'murder'n'Faygo'n'racism manifesto in no uncertain terms, since subtlety was never part of their agenda. All ICP wants to do is rock the house as if they were a third-rate Beastie Boys supported by a cut-rate Faith No More, all tempered by the sensibility that made GWAR cult heroes—only with, you know, more sexism and jokes that are supposed to be street, but wind up sounding racist. So, *Carnival of Carnage* delivers exactly what it promises. If you're down with the ICP—if you're a juggalo (funny how close that is to "jigaboo," isn't it?)—you'll find that this album got them off on the right track. If you're not with them, this will certainly give you reasons to hate them. —*Stephen Thomas Erlewine*

The Ringmaster / Mar. 8, 1994 / Island ♦♦♦
Ringmaster, the second album from those urban pranksters the Insane Clown Posse, isn't as much a step forward as it is an improvement from their

debut, *Carnival of Carnage*. Not that the group has really gotten any better— they can barely rap, the beats are clumsy, the hard-rock guitars are pandering—but there is more focus on *Ringmaster*, which means that the album hits harder and makes a bigger impression. Of course, that means their overt sexism, inadvertent racism, and rampant juvenilia is right out there in the open, but that's really not going to offend anyone who climbed aboard the bandwagon with *Carnival of Carnage*. It will offend the casual observer, of course, but that's just what they're looking for. Besides, anyone who takes umbrage with the lyrics will miss what's really offensive—the fact that ICP believes this flatulent rap-metal is remotely dangerous. — *Stephen Thomas Erlewine*

● **The Riddle Box** / Oct. 10, 1995 / Battery ◆◆◆

Insane Clown Posse's first national release, *The Riddle Box*, failed to expand the Detroit shock rock/rap duo's audience, which probably came as no surprise to anyone, especially ICP. Success never came easy to Violent J and Shaggy Two Dope, so the tenuous marketing commitment from Jive Records did nothing to dampen the act's spirits. Setting off a series of record-label conflicts, ICP soon left Jive, and due mostly to their own marketing and touring campaigns, there were other labels willing to literally risk millions in an attempt to tap the rappers' commercial potential. Later decisions to follow a Kiss-like publicity and merchandising program proved fruitful, but at the time, music was all ICP had to promote. "Unconvincing" is the first word that comes to mind when attempting to describe the stiff, humorless rhymes and bland beats that fill *Riddle Box*. The gangsta put-ons and misogynistic boasting are impossible to take seriously, and unlike even mediocre hip-hop, this music offers little insight into urban existence. Perhaps ICP's more dynamic delivery and second-rate Cypress Hill aesthetic elevates *Riddle Box* just above its predecessors, but all of the group's musical work is so far below any reasonable rap/rock standard that it hardly matters. This 1995 effort shouldn't disappoint fans of the group, but serious hip-hop and metal listeners— unimpressed with ICP's extra-musical theatrics—should avoid *Riddle Box* like every other episode in the "dark carnival." Kiss had more than a few legitimate pop/rock hooks, Gwar and Green Jelly can be creative and humorous in their delivery, but the appeal of Insane Clown Posse is based solely on marketing savvy and prurient appeal. That ICP has managed to build a multiplatinum empire on a house of joker cards says as much (or more) about the scatological decline of American pop culture as it does about the duo's business acumen. — *Vincent Jeffries*

The Great Milenko / Jun. 24, 1997 / Island ◆◆◆

The Insane Clown Posse had a cult following around their hometown of Detroit in the mid-'90s, eventually winning a major-label contract with Jive. Their deal with Jive was short lived, since *Riddle Box* bombed on the national market—after all, not many people are interested in overweight, dreadlocked jackasses in clown makeup, spewing "naughty" lyrics and spraying their audience with cheap soda. Still, they retained a devoted local following, which led to Hollywood Records signing the group in 1996. Hollywood spent a million dollars on the recording of ICP's label debut, *The Great Milenko*, which let the group work with name producers and guest artists like Slash. As a result, it was a better record than their predecessors, boasting a tougher sound and some actual hooks, without losing the juvenile vulgarity that pleased their following. So, everything should have worked out—ICP had a commercial album that would have brought them a big audience, if the marketplace could overlook the fact that the duo were dressed like evil clowns. But things didn't work out as planned. On the day of the release of *The Great Milenko*, Hollywood pulled the album from the market, claiming that they were unaware of the offensive content of the record. That seems a little unlikely, since a company wouldn't really sink a million dollars into a project being "unaware" of what it was about. Still, the resulting furor meant that the Insane Clown Posse—a group that would never have been famous or infamous— became national figures, and *The Great Milenko* had some sort of hip status. And although it is better than the rest of ICP's work, it's a little ridiculous to think that its mixture of heavy metal and gangsta satire is hip in the late '90s, and it's even more ridiculous to think that it is worth listening to, even if it has vulgar lyrics. It's the sort of record you wish they would take off the stereo at excruciating frat parties. — *Stephen Thomas Erlewine*

Forgotten Freshness, Vol. 1-2 / Aug. 18, 1998 / Island ◆◆

As they gathered strength to write the follow-up to their popular breakthrough *The Great Milenko*, the Insane Clown Posse busied themselves with panic attacks, assaults, bus accidents, restaurant brawls, cameos in porn films,

and assembling *Forgotten Freshness, Vol. 1-2*. A double-disc set of B sides, rarities, non-LP singles, unreleased tracks and remixes, it's the motherlode for the hardcore juggalos. Of course, ICP is the kind of band that winds up only with hardcore fans, but even fans of *The Great Milenko* and *The Riddle Box* may find that sorting through the 23 tracks is a bit of a chore, since there's a reason why many of these songs never made the album—they're simply not very good. Ironically, amidst all this filler, there's Jason Nevins' clever remix of "Hocus Pocus," which only highlights just how pedestrian the rest of the material actually is, and it suggests that ICP would benefit from shaking up their rap-metal formula just a little bit. — *Stephen Thomas Erlewine*

The Amazing Jeckel Brothers / May 25, 1999 / Island ◆◆◆◆

Within every man there is a fight, a struggle between good and evil. Within each man is the ability to create much good or much destruction—it is up to the individual to decide which path to take. An angel, perhaps named Jake, urges each man to follow the path of righteousness; a devil, perhaps named Jack, urges everyone to walk the path of darkness. Sadly, Jack and Jake are fat guys in clown makeup. Yes, it's true that the Insane Clown Posse are back with their fifth proper album (or, in juggalo parlance, the fifth joker card)—and this time, they have alteregos! And a morality tale to tell! For *The Amazing Jeckel Brothers* is a full-fledged concept album about the 19 circles of hell and how each man is torn between the juggling balls of goodness and spraying evil soda on paying patrons. Or something. Certainly, the very fact that ICP is writing a concept album illustrates their growing ambition, and the cast of cameos illustrates their changing audience and stature. Where *The Great Milenko*, the legendarily botched major-label debut, was targeted at white-boy, adolescent metalheads—really, how could any album that contained guest spots from Alice Cooper, Slash, Steve Jones, and Legs Diamond be anything else?—*The Amazing Jeckel Brothers* contains cameos from Snoop Dogg and Ol' Dirty Bastard, plus a cover of a Geto Boys song, which brings ICP to street level . . . or at least the street level that gangsta-loving suburban high schoolers love. Still, the harder beats and the slight removal of metallic tendencies give the album a fresher feel, and the concept, however muddled it may be, does give the album real structure and momentum. So, if *The Amazing Jeckel Brothers* does prove to give the Insane Clown Posse a large audience—the kind fellow Detroit jesters Eminem and Kid Rock earned in early 1999—it won't be just because they've hung around long enough or that their peers have paved the way. It will be because they've actually delivered an album that comes close to fulfilling whatever promise their ridiculous, carnivalesque blend of hardcore hip-hop and shock metal had in the first place. True, *The Amazing Jeckel Brothers* will still annoy anyone who believes ICP are, for lack of a better word, jackasses, but it will satisfy the juggalos, and the music is clever enough to expand their audience. Which is a triumph of some sort, I guess. — *Stephen Thomas Erlewine*

Stranglemania, Vol. 1 / Nov. 1999 / Psychopathic ◆◆◆◆

Insane Clown Posse missed their true calling, as *Stranglemania, Vol. 1* reveals. It may look like nothing more than some goofy independent wrestling matches from the outside, but it's actually several bloody and unbelievably violent matches from Japan as hosted by Violent J and Shaggy Two Dope. Going under fake names, the duo's blustery delivery, wrestling in-jokes, and sardonic approach are the ultimate way to enjoy their sense of humor. Although still filthy and gross, it leaves out the music and focuses on their gimmick, which is far more entertaining than their primary career. Although no wrestling league would touch these guys with a ten-foot pole after getting kicked out of every major promotion in America, Insane Clown Posse missed their calling as wrestling announcers. It may only appeal to juggalos and wrestling fans, but it's the best thing they've released to video. — *Bradley Torreano*

Psychopathic Rydas Dumpin' / Apr. 18, 2000 / Joe & Joey ◆◆◆

Billing themselves as Psychopathic Rydas, Insane Clown Posse and their protégés Twiztid, Blaze, and Mystery released *Dumpin'* as a limited-edition CD of only 5,000 copies that was only available to fans who won a trivia contest. But *Dumpin'* is something more than a mere collectible. Essentially, it's ICP's response to critics who accuse them of being little more than a minstrel parody of gangsta rap. By intentionally using the exact beats used by some of the biggest gangsta artists of the '90s (such as Ice Cube and Cypress Hill) and writing scathing graphic mockeries of gangsta rhymes (right down to stealing Master P's trademark "Uhhhh!"), ICP try to demonstrate that they're more than a novelty. And, as it turns out, with some of the best beats they've ever used, ICP actually pull off their stint as gangsta rappers. "Back 2 Crack," in particular, is simultaneously tasteless and funny, the tale of a gangsta rapper who is tired of trying to keep up with trends and decides to hit the pipe. Others, such as "Plug Dat Puss," are simply tedious sex rhymes, but the quality of the beats seems to bring out the best in ICP and Twiztid, who contribute some of the most skillful rhyming of their career. Unfortunately, ICP's refusal to get permission to sample the beats means that this will always remain an obscure, underground release, but ICP fans should definitely track it down, as it's arguably the most consistent release of their career. — *Victor W. Valdivia*

Bizaar / Oct. 31, 2000 / Island ✦✦

Released simultaneously with another disc called *Bizzar* that had similar cover art but completely different tracks, *Bizaar* is the Insane Clown Posse's attempt to prove that they are not the one-note novelty act they've been labeled. The music, by longtime producer Mike Clark, is actually the best of the band's career, seamlessly fusing metal guitars and shuffling beats. Lyrically, though, the band is still up to the same tricks. Though the ICP make some rather astute lyrical observations from time to time, they still rely too much on sophomoric jokes and shock value. In "Fearless," they rap about various dangerous stunts they can perform to prove their manhood, including asking Michael Jackson's plastic surgeon to do some work on them. "Rainbows and Stuff" is a mean joke, but the singsong verses and deliberately corny lyrics will appeal to the adolescent boy in every listener. Only "The Pendulum's Promise" and "Take Me Away" avoid the wannabe gangsta bluster and misogyny of the other tracks. Of the two albums, *Bizaar* is the weaker although of course fans will want to have both anyway. — *Victor W. Valdivia*

Bizzar / Oct. 31, 2000 / Island ✦✦✦

The companion piece to the simultaneously released *Bizaar*, *Bizzar* contains some of the best backing tracks of the ICP's career, courtesy of producer Mike Clark, as well as some of their most ambitious attempts at lyrical profundity. The ICP's reach still exceeds their grasp, but on the likes of the bluesy, almost ambient "Crystal Ball," they actually have lyrics that don't wallow in macho teenage rebellion. Their flow has improved greatly (though they are still miles away from master rappers such as Chuck D) and they have lessened their need to yell constantly. In fact, the band members truly live up to the clown part of their personas in such moments as their hilarious, dead-on DMX and Lit parodies in "Radio Star." The album's weakest track, however, is their most blatant attempt at radio play: a cover of the 1986 Slyfox hit "Let's Go All the Way" with slightly rewritten lyrics. It's even more irritating than such standard fare as "Let a Killa," which, for all its torrid sexual hostility, seems less contrived. *Bizzar* is the stronger of the two albums the band released together, but fans may feel they are missing part of the story by not getting both. — *Victor W. Valdivia*

Forgotten Freshness, Vol. 3 / Dec. 18, 2001 / Psychopathic ✦✦✦

Insane Clown Posse's *Forgotten Freshness, Vol. 3* isn't an official joker card—that's ICP-speak for a full-length offering of new material. Instead, this 2001 outing, like its predecessor, *Forgotten Freshness, Vol. 1-2*, is a collection of B sides, remixes, and specialty releases. This disc should satisfy listeners interested in hearing new rhymes over old ICP beats ("Posse on Vernor," "It"), professional wrestlers working their freestyle flow ("When Vampiro Gets High"), and Violent J's attempt at new age rap ("Fly Away"). However, rock and hip-hop fans uninterested in such sophomoric musings, comic gangsta stories, and Vanilla Ice guest spots should avoid *Forgotten Freshness, Vol. 3*. There is nothing offered on this collection that will cause ICP detractors or supporters to rethink whether or not the Detroit duo is making a mockery of hard-hop. But those who consider themselves juggalos—that's ICP-speak for consumer, or sucker, depending on one's perspective—might enjoy *Forgotten Freshness, Vol. 3* and its loose and relatively dynamic presentation. — *Vincent Jeffries*

The Wraith: Shangri-La / Nov. 5, 2002 / D3 Entertainment ✦✦

After a decade of proudly releasing offensive, obnoxious, and immature music that has sold like gangbusters to kids around the Midwest, the Insane Clown Posse have finally reached their much-prophesized "sixth Joker card," the last album in a conceptual journey that started with 1992's *Carnival of Carnage*. Claiming that everything up to this point had led to *The Wraith: Shangri-La*, they announce at the beginning that the meaning to their career will become evident by the end. And they wait until the very end of this ambitious album to reveal what it is, despite the occasional reference to

Shangri-La (their bland metaphor for the afterlife). Waxing philosophical about ending the world's pains, ICP seem willing to spread some good vibes this time around. "Homies" might even be the most positive song of their career; it actually has a great message about loyalty and friendship matched to a pleasantly laid-back rock track. Of course, the usual murder fantasies and sex anthems are in abundance, filled with the immature humor that has become their tired trademark. Oddly enough, they almost seem to apologize for repeating their usual hate raps on "The Staleness," which ends with the repetition of, "I'm so sorry I'm stale," in a chanted singalong. A stab at a thuggish street anthem, "Ain't Yo Bidness," is a blatant Eminem rip-off, but that twisted lyrical focus robs the song of any of the self-reflective cleverness that he would have brought to it. But the second half of the song is a definite highlight, as guest rapper Esham helps the Motor City clowns deliver a high-energy ending to an otherwise pedestrian track. In their attempts to change things around, their trademark circus music sound mixes well with rap-rock, and several songs (especially the double punch of "Crossing the Bridge" and "The Raven's Mirror") offer a very original twist on the genre that is distinctly their own. Finally, the album reaches its grandiose ending and reveals that the secret behind the carnival was really…God? Sure enough, their rape fantasies and necrophilia tributes were all orchestrated by the creator of humanity, or at least that's what the clowns say. To say that this is a disappointing way to end their first six records is an understatement, as their evil image and downright hateful early years clash harshly with their sudden new age attitude. Even if it is a joke, it isn't a funny one, or even a clever one. *The Wraith* does reveal a growth both lyrically and musically, but the lofty, feel-good ending is jarringly out of place considering all the hype about the deeper meaning of their message. It's impossible to believe they could have had any religious intentions, kidding or not, planned during the *Carnival of Carnage* years, but this is the kind of skewed logic that has fueled their career. And if you don't agree with them, they've already anticipated that reaction with the last lyrics of the record: "We're not sorry if we tricked you." — *Bradley Torreano*

Inspectah Deck (Jason Hunter)

b. Brooklyn, NY

Producer, Vocals / Hip-Hop, East Coast Rap, Hardcore Rap

Inspectah Deck was one of the Wu-Tang Clan's lesser-known members, despite his talent as both an MC and producer. Born Jason Hunter, Deck earned the first part of his nickname as the quiet, watchful eye in the corner; his other aliases included Rollie Fingers, Fifth Brother, and Rebel INS, the latter a graffiti name tag he used as a youngster. Deck was born in Brooklyn but grew up on Staten Island, attending school with several future Wu members. He was heard on most of the key tracks from the group's classic 1993 debut, *Enter the Wu-Tang (36 Chambers)*, including the singles "C.R.E.A.M." and "Protect Ya Neck." He made guest appearances on most of the ensuing Wu-Tang solo projects, with particularly attention-grabbing work on Raekwon's *Only Built 4 Cuban Linx* and Genius' *Liquid Swords*. However, the release of his own solo debut—which was rumored to be completed in 1995—was postponed indefinitely. Meanwhile, "Let Me at Them," effectively a Deck solo track that was credited to the Clan, appeared on the *Tales From the 'Hood* soundtrack in 1995. Deck was an overlooked presence on the Clan's sprawling second album, *Wu-Tang Forever* (1997); among other appearances, he produced the track "Visionz" and contributed the essentially solo "The City." In 1999, he finally released his debut solo album, *Uncontrolled Substance*, which featured a number of less-exposed Wu-Tang affiliates as guests, not to mention more of Deck's own production. The record sold pretty well, climbing into the Top Five of the R&B charts. Deck subsequently returned to the Wu-Tang fold for the albums *The W* and *Iron Flag*. — *Steve Huey*

● **Uncontrolled Substance** / Sep. 7, 1999 / Relativity ✦✦✦✦✦

While Deck has always been overshadowed by the more personable bees in his Wu-Tang hive, there is no disputing his messiah-like flow and delivery pure as artesian water. Wu-Tang's diehard fans have always demanded more and Deck gives them just that, as he routinely leaves microphones grotesquely disfigured on his stellar debut. Besides the usual assortment of high-powered street jams ("Nightshift" and "Word on the Street") usually found on Wu-Tang endeavors, what separates Deck from the next bodega philosopher lays in his disposition, as he also employs his verbal gifts as a tool of enlightenment. He lays out a path to righteousness with "Elevation" and "Show and Prove," while the warm piano chords of "Longevity" detail his plans for global domination. Although the man behind Wu's music, RZA, only furnishes one track, Deck shows versatility behind the boards as well, handling a majority of the production chores. There is truly no anti-venom on record capable of diluting the Inspecktah's fatal sting once inflicted. —*Matt Conaway*

Intelligent Hoodlum (Percy Chapman)

b. New York, NY
Political Rap
New York rapper Intelligent Hoodlum (born Percy Chapman) served 20 months at Riker's Island for robbery in 1988, using the experience to immerse himself in works on African-American culture and the theology of the Nation of Islam. That combination underscores all of his work and makes his songs radiate with righteousness, anger, indignation, and frustration. It doesn't hurt that ace producer Marley Marl supplies the undergirding as well. —*Ron Wynn*

Intelligent Hoodlum / 1990 / A&M ✦✦✦✦✦
Intelligent Hoodlum's 1990 debut, on the onetime Riker's Island inmate raps of black politics and culture, while finding plenty of room for whimsical observations and some fine vocal flow. Producer Marley Marl of Biz Markie and Big Daddy Kane fame provides the beats and production in fine style: layered, lean, and dope. If you like you old school cuts in the sophisticated Gang Starr and Markie mode, then this collection of hip-hop gold will no doubt be welcome. Add a little De La Soul humor, and you have a solid album. —*Stephen Cook*

● **Tragedy: Saga of a Hoodlum** / Jun. 22, 1993 / A&M ✦✦✦✦
Onetime Riker's Island prisoner Intelligent Hoodlum speaks with genuine insight about inner city hell and chaos. His second album wasn't laden with posturing rhetoric or presented in an ambitiously produced package. Instead, it was a chilling, unapologetic chronicle of brutal, ugly, negative experiences relayed by someone neither celebrating nor regretting what he's seen and heard. There was no attempt to entertain, impress, or amuse in his rapping or rhymes; this was just the straight dope. —*Ron Wynn*

Intricate Dialect

b. Ann Arbor, MI
Underground Rap, Alternative Rap
The Deuce's own Intricate Dialect is an MC that you probably haven't heard of. Not to worry, the man likes it like that. Born and raised in Ann Arbor, MI, ID first embraced the message and medium hip hop offered at the tender age of 12. The first local recognition he received was through the biweekly freestyle sessions he and his friends held at Community High School. It was through these very sessions that he first met Nick the Ferenheight 2040 who quickly became a coconspirator in the quest for laying the perfect beat. Scraping together their money to purchase two turntables and a four-track recorder, the pair devoted themselves to writing, rhyming, mixing, and recording hip-hop they wanted to hear. Three years' worth of these bedroom recordings were sifted through and finally taken in for professional mastering yielding *The Life of Id: Basement Up*, Intricate's first full-length album release. Two years later, the streamlined *Solomon's Treasure* showed the MC moving toward a more original sound that floated on stuttering beats and lush synth lines. While his work earns critical praise from Michigan-area hip-hop heads, radio has been characteristcstically cold to his fresh approach. The almighty underground birthed this verbalist and the underground is where he intends to stay. —*Emilie Litzell*

● **The Life of Id: Basement Up** / 2000 / ✦✦✦✦✦
Coming up from the somewhat sorted collection of *Waterworld* hip-hop, MC Intricate Dialect and producer Farenheight 2040 joined forces to put together *Life of Id: Basement Up*. As the title suggests, there are some unquestionable hints of basement-style production values. Avant-garde jazz samples are countered with gritty, analog loops. ID credits the inspirations of the "underground flavor" with Grandmaster Flash and other pioneers of rap. Whether or not this album preserves a long-standing tradition of underground sensibilities remains to be seen. What is apparent, however, is that this 2000 release is a refreshing change from the overly synthesized, pop-friendly beats that seem to be flooding the market. While a little rough around the edges at certain points, the entire joint maintains a lyrical consistency that's rarely

present in today's rap albums. Not one element of this album constitutes commercial posturing. "Cold Ran Over the World Today" is a smooth, free-flowing promise of elevation, while "Mic in Hand" is a personal manifesto addressing matters of alienation and the release rhyming provides. In all of ID's incarnations, never has he shown any inclination toward mainstream rapping. *Life of Id: Basement Up* comes off as an honest, bare expression of fundamental hip-hop values and personal beliefs. Some of the more obscure references to ancient Egyptian gods could potentially alienate a listener trying to be in on the joke, but the unabashed spiritual beliefs give a deep look into Intricate Dialect's psyche. If the end goal is honest self-expression at whatever cost, ID comes off in spades. The only possible deterrent is the occasional snap, pop, crackle of the "underground" production. All in all, it is a courageous effort. —*Emilie Litzell*

Solomon's Treasure / 2002 / Abolitionists ✦✦✦✦✦
The underground rap scene got a major shot in the arm in the late '90s, and the effect led to several MCs popping up all over the country with fresh and original sounds. One of these talents is Intricate Dialect, a Michigan MC with a silver tongue and a boatload of original rhyming schemes. Floating over a bed of eerie samples and gritty, understated funk bass lines, Intricate Dialect tells detailed stories with a sharp precision, shooting off into weird and engaging tangents while never straying too far from his vision. Tracks take interesting twists, like the way he takes on the persona of a radio DJ while answering on-air phone calls in the infectious "Radio Show/Explore the Universe," just to switch modes and slowly turn the song into a high-concept jam that layers snippets of jazz records into an ever-evolving sonic stew. The production work is first-rate, dropping chilly samples and reverb-drenched passages over stuttered beats with a confidence rarely displayed by indie rappers. But none of it would pull together without Intricate Dialect himself, a dynamic vocalist who has a voice that proves to be as flexible as his unpredictable backing tracks. A gifted storyteller as well as an abstract lyricist, he never fails to grip the listener's attention, even when he gets heady and experimental with his words. Proving that the mind is the most effective tool in hip-hop, Intricate Dialect scores a massive winner on the surprisingly tight *Solomon's Treasure*. With only his sophomore effort, Intricate Dialect displays an incredible understanding of what makes the genre work, and fans of underground rap would do themselves a favor by hunting down this talented MC's efforts. (Copies bought in concert at the time of the release also included a DVD with a endearingly ramshackle video for "Radio Show.") —*Bradley Torreano*

Invisibl Skratch Piklz

f. 1995, San Francisco, CA, **db.** 2000
Group / Underground Rap, Turntablism
The Invisibl Skratch Piklz were a rotating crew of hip-hop DJs whose tactile acrobatics were more accurately served by the term (coined by Piklz founder DJ Q-Bert) "turntablist." A quintet (although their lineup shifted constantly), the group's core consisted of Q-Bert (Rich Quitevis), "Mixmaster Mike" Schwartz, and Shortkut (J. Cruz), with newcomers D-Styles and Yoga Frog replacing founding member DJ Disk (Lou Quintanilla) in 1996. Individually and as a group, the Piklz's reputation in the hip-hop underground is undisputed, and journos get a kick out of describing how they were asked by the world's most prestigious international DJ association (DMC) to stop competing since they were discouraging other DJs from even bothering to enter. But it's the leaps the group have made since they retired from competition that have proved most impressive; dragging turntable tricknology into new and wholly autonomous territories of musicianship being developed by a new generation of bedroom virtuosi, with turntable groups such as the X-Men, the Beat Junkies, and the Skratch Piklz at the forefront.

Although the members had known each other and practiced and played together for years (most notably under the names FM20, Dirt Style Productions, and the Turntable Dragons), the Invisibl Skratch Piklz officially formed in 1995. Citing the underground vitality of turntablism and its distance from the comparatively stale commercial rap scene, the Piklz's stated intent was to focus on the art of DJing (defined by skills such as cutting, scratching, and beat juggling) in order to develop and expand its musical potential. Beginning with a five-part series of mix tapes called the *Shiggar Fraggar Show* (recorded for Oakland-based hip-hop writer/promoter Billy Jam's pirate radio show, Hip Hop Slam), the group quickly evolved from a hybrid of more traditional cutting, scratching, and trick DJing into an autonomous "turntable orchestra"; scratching out by hand (on as many as five turntables at once) a unified montage of beats (i.e., manually scratched kick, snare, hi-hat, etc.), bass lines (i.e., continuous bass tones manipulated by hand and with the turntable's speed and pitch controls), wah-wah pedal effects, and extremely intricate and controlled scratch textures. The first fully formed examples of this emerging aesthetic, "Invasion of the Octopus People," appeared on the underground turntablist compendium *Return of the DJ*, and was later included on Bill Laswell's similarly styled *Altered Beats* (released on Axiom in 1996). Additional international tours, guest appearances, videotapes, and compilation tracks brought these innovations to a wider audience, often to people previously unaware of the music's potential and sophistication.

Although an awareness of the mechanics of scratching is helpful in understanding the group's innovations, the music's logic (as well as its stylistic moorings, from hip-hop to jazz and beyond) is pretty self-evident, a fact which led to a recording deal with the Asphodel label in 1997. Their first release, *Invisibl Skratch Piklz Vs. Da Klamz Uv Deth EP*, is a 12"/CD+ best-of compiling bits of the group's various routines from the past few years. A dozen or so other mix-tape snapshots of the members' ever-evolving sound also exist, as well as a handful of breaks records (among them *Battle Breaks*, *Booger Breaks*, *Toasted Marshmallow Feet Breaks*, and *Eardrum Medicine*), which are also standards of the scene, continually selling out pressing after pressing within weeks. Additionally, Q-Bert contributed turntable work on Kool Keith's immensely popular *Dr. Octagon* LP, and members of the Piklz also appeared on recordings by Saafir, Ras Kass, MCM & the Monster, and Praxis. In 1998, the Beastie Boys invited Mix Master Mike to cut it up on their *Hello Nasty* album and subsequent tour. As Mix Master and Shortkut (who joined the Beat Junkies) focused on their solo work and side projects, the remaining DJs found it impossible to carry on as crew and formally announced their demise as a collective in 2000. — *Sean Cooper*

● **Invisibl Skratch Piklz Vs. Da Klamz Uv Deth EP** / Jul. 28, 1997 / Asphodel ◆◆◆
The ISP's debut vinyl release under their own name is a long-form EP collaging bits and pieces of their live routines from over the previous year or so. Pared back to the trio of Q-Bert, Shortkut, and Mixmaster Mike, the 12" features the group's trademark abstract turntable deviations, wrapping thinly sliced references from soul, rock, jazz, funk, and old school hip-hop (Doug E. Fresh, Too Short, Soulsonic Force, Cybotron) around hand-scratched beats, bass lines, and constantly shifting rhythmic textures. Not as minimal and controlled as similar passages from the group's earlier cassette-only releases and compilation tracks (and therefore suffering a little from sloppiness), but also a bit more fun. Blast 1's gorgeous cover art is also worth noting. — *Sean Cooper*

The Shiggar Fraggar Show!, Vol. 1 / Aug. 1998 / Hip Hop Slam ◆◆◆
Not exactly the Piklz' proper long-form debut, *The Shiggar Fraggar Show!, Vol. 1* is a live album including segments from a Bay Area pirate-radio show done with ISP-members Mixmaster Mike, Q-Bert, Shortkut, Apollo, and DJ Disk. It's just a bit slow out of the gate and doesn't move with the same grace as other fine turntablist moments (like Cut Chemist and Shortkut's *Live at the Future Primitive Sound Session*), but the volatile scratchwork and entertaining samples keep things interesting. Once the tempo picks up, the album steams ahead with bucketfuls of old school flavor. — *John Bush*

The Shiggar Fraggar Show!, Vol. 2 / 1999 / Hip Hop Slam ◆◆◆
Toiret for Godzirra [Video] / ISP Vision ◆◆◆◆

Isis (Lin Que Ayoung)

East Coast Rap, Hardcore Rap, Political Rap, Golden Age
Terrifically skilled MC Lin Que Ayoung recorded as Isis for a brief spate during the early '90s. Her 1990 album, *Rebel Soul*, was produced by the members of X-Clan. And since that group's Professor X took the mic after almost every verse, it was an X-Clan album in every sense but the name. Later in the '90s, Ayoung switched her performing name to Lin Que and released a couple of singles for Sony and Elektra. She eventually went into A&R work and graphic design, and she appeared briefly in Spike Lee's *He Got Game*. — *Andy Kellman*

● **Rebel Soul** / 1990 / 4th & Broadway ◆◆◆◆
Sometimes compared to Queen Latifah, though not nearly as well known, female rapper Isis was an associate of Professor X, the colorful Islamic MC

and black nationalist who founded X-Clan. Isis showed a lot of potential on *Rebel Soul*, which proves that her rapping skills were strong and that her technique was excellent. On such uplifting selections as "State of Mind," "In the Mind of One," and "The Power of Myself Is Moving," Isis preaches a message of black pride and self-awareness without embracing the type of divisive separatist rhetoric that has characterized some Islamic rappers. A colorful character, the Professor is all over this CD and adds a lot to it. Though Isis received favorable reviews from the hip-hop press (especially on the East Coast), *Rebel Soul* was far from a big seller. And regrettably, a commercial breakthrough would continue to elude her. — *Alex Henderson*

The Isolationist

Group / Trip-Hop, Underground Rap, Turntablism
The first international hip-hop supergroup(?) Russian producer DJ Vadim and British turntablist DJ Prime Cuts of the Scratch Perverts joined New York's Anti-Pop Consortium for recordings as the Isolationist. A self-titled album was released in 1999 on DJ Vadim's Jazz Fudge label. — *Wade Kergan*

● **The Isolationist** / Apr. 5, 1999 / Jazz Fudge ◆◆◆
One of the first breakthrough projects released on DJ Vadim's Jazz Fudge label, *The Isolationist* is a collaboration between abstract intellectual hip-hop innovators Anti-Pop Consortium, DJ Vadim, and DJ Primecuts. A masterful use of space-aged production and space in general, this record compliments all contributors and emphasizes each of their strengths while creating one of 1999's most underrated albums. A characteristic Vadim-produced and arranged record, the sound emerges undoubtedly underground, with wide-open organic beats and minimalist tracks that leave most of the room for intelligent lyrics and other-worldly scratching. Specifically, dub-leaning kick-snare combinations with trippy, floating keyboard samples and futuristic factory noises make up a style that the Russian-born producer has perfected before and doesn't stray from. DJ Primecuts of the U.K.'s Scratch Perverts brings his kinky DMC Championship style and cuts raw sonic syncopation on nine of the 19 tracks. The unifying thematic accomplishment that takes place on this venture of underground all-stars is the flow of the entire set as a whole work. Fans of the Ninja Tune Vadim discography all need this record, as do fans of Anti-Pop's *Tragic Epilogue* record on 75 Ark. — *Nicholas Gordon*

The Instrumentalist / Nov. 29, 1999 / Jazz Fudge ◆◆◆

Iswhat?!

f. Cincinnati, OH
Group / Underground Rap
A freewheeling hip-hop trio, Iswhat?! focuses on live performance like the Roots, but instead of saluting rap forebears, seeks a connection with jazz sources. Based in Cincinnati, the group was formed by vocalist Napoleon Maddox, saxophonist Jack Walter, and bassist Matthew Anderson. The group has shared the stage with performers ranging from Mr. Dibbs to Big Daddy Kane to Kwame Turé, and released its first album, *Landmines*, in 1999. *You Figure It Out*... followed in 2003. — *John Bush*

● **You Figure It Out . . .** / 2003 / Iswhat ◆◆◆◆
Forsaking the usual hip-hop standbys (drum programming, samples, constant mic checks), the Cincinnati hip-hop trio Iswhat?! debuted with a challenging record—beginning with the title but extending to the entire set. A complex, difficult album, *You Figure It Out*... is much more musical than lyrical, a fiery fusion of Matthew Anderson's strong, dexterous work on upright bass; Jack Walker's fluid explosiveness on reeds; and the human beat-boxing of Napoleon. Napoleon's speedy rapping, closer in effect to a live poetry slam than usual in hip-hop, is difficult to decipher but offers much to listeners willing to devote the time to message tracks like "Parachutes" and "Can't Get In." Anderson's prime influence comes out in a pair of late-period reworkings of Charles Mingus' material: "Fables of Faubus" and "Trust." Surprisingly, for a first record Iswhat?! was able to get some outstanding collaborations, including Cincinnati's own John Doe (from 1200 Hobos) on scratches, avant-garde jazz luminary Hamid Drake on drums for three tracks, and rap theorist DJ Spooky on a remix of "Parachutes" (also found on his own remix album, *Dubtometry*). A bold and refreshing first effort, *You Figure It Out*... is often frustrating but often stunning. — *John Bush*

J-Dubb

Gangsta Rap, West Coast Rap, G-Funk
Coming from East Oakland, J-Dubb's style of rapping tends to feature the traditional gangsta subject matter—money, sex, drugs, power, ghetto life, and staying true to the streets—much in the spirit of his West Coast peers, particularly the Bay Area camp surrounding Ant Banks, Too Short, and E-40. In 1995, J-Dubb released *Game Related*, which didn't do well nationally but established his presence on the West Coast. Five years later, he followed up this debut with *Money, Trees & Real Estate* on Desperado Records, featuring the single "Life" with Too Short. —*Jason Birchmeier*

● **Money, Trees & Real Estate** / Oct. 3, 2000 / Desperado ✦✦
Not much of a departure from any of J-Dubb's Bay Area peers—Spice 1, Too Short, E-40, Rappin' 4-Tay, T.W.D.Y.—the tracks on *Money, Trees & Real Estate* pretty much fall into the assumed clichés alluded to in the title—not many surprises here. In fact, this album does an admirable job of fitting itself into its assigned niche, from the rather blatant album title to the star-studded list of guest rappers: Spice 1, Too Short, Eightball, and others. What really holds back the album, though, is J-Dubb's lackluster flow and the second-rate G-funk production. Still, when looking for more songs about getting high, getting paid, and being a G, J-Dubb's persona should do the trick—even if this is second-rate, relative to his aforementioned peers. —*Jason Birchmeier*

J-88

f. 2000, Detroit, MI
Group / Alternative Rap, Hip-Hop
In July 2000, shortly after Slum Village released its long-awaited *Fantastic, Vol. 2* album, the Detroit-based hip-hop trio released some of their older material on the brief album *Best Kept Secret*. Clocking in at less than 30 minutes, filled out with some remixes, and attributed to the one-off moniker J-88, *Best Kept Secret* features leftover material from Slum Village's storied and heavily bootlegged, yet never released, *Fantastic, Vol. 1* album. Fans of early Slum Village and particularly then-producer Jay Dee should find the J-88 material enlightening, as it sheds light on precisely why the Detroit trio (then also including Baatin and T3) garnered such hype leading up to their summer 2000 official debut. —*Jason Birchmeier*

● **Best Kept Secret** / Jul. 31, 2000 / Groove Attack ✦✦✦
For those into Slum Village's *Fantastic, Vol. 2* who wondered where the first volume was, this short album provides a missing link. Masquerading under the moniker J-88, the members of Slum Village—James Yancey, RL Altman III, and Titus Glover (also known as Jay Dee, Baatin, and T3, respectively)—released *Best Kept Secret* in July of 2000. This album contains songs from the rare and highly bootlegged *Fantastic, Vol. 1* that weren't on *Vol. 2*, as well as a few new songs and remixes. It's just too bad that the album's ten tracks total less than half an hour. But if it's quality, not quantity, that counts, *Best Kept Secret* is a worthy effort by Slum Village's alterego. Jay Dee showcases his trademark production and arrangement in the laid-back beats and melodies that carry the album. His unique and refreshing style make every second worth listening to, especially "Look of Love, Pt. 1" and "Pt. 2" and "The Things You Do." In addition, the remixes of some of the originals by Madlib and I.G. Culture add different sounds to the album, while still maintaining Jay Dee's musical standards. Unfortunately, the lyrics of MCs Baatin and T3 don't live up to the originality of the music. Although they use clever phrasing and have good delivery, their rhymes are full of the usual misogynistic clichés about women (of course, referred to in a different way) and sex. For that reason, this album is better suited to background listening, when you can appreciate the music without having to listen to the words. —*Irene Kao*

J-Live

Hip-Hop, East Coast Rap, Underground Rap
Brooklyn MC J-Live first garnered notice with the release of his 1995 single "Bragging Writes." Delivering his thoughtful lyrics with confidence and ease, J-Live's rapping was strong and his soul-inflected grooves immediately appealed to fans of underground hip-hop. A year later he followed up with another hit, "Hush the Crowd," and had started to generate a palpable buzz. With tracks produced by luminaries such as Prince Paul, DJ Premier, and Pete Rock, the release of J-Live's full-length debut *The Best Part* was hotly anticipated and the future looked promising for the ascendant MC. At this point, though, J-Live was beset by a host of troubles. Amidst constant label shuffling and plagued by a series of illegal bootlegs, the release of *The Best Part* was delayed for five years. There was some talk that J-Live was behind some of the bootlegs—a few of which were of extremely high quality—and the ongoing saga became something of an underground legend. In the interim, J-Live worked as an eighth-grade teacher in Brunswick and continued to embellish and refine his debut. He kept good company, making cameo appearances on strong album's like Handsome Boy Modeling School's *So How's Your Girl?* and J Rawls' *The Essence of J Rawls*. *The Best Part* finally enjoyed its official release in the fall of 2001. —*Martin Woodside*

● **The Best Part** / 2001 / Triple Threat / 7 Heads ✦✦✦✦✦
The Best Part is, simply put, classic New York hip-hop, or, as J-Live himself labels it, "true school" that can trace its roots in a direct line back to such icons as KRS-One and Big Daddy Kane. Granted, J-Live didn't reach that level of name recognition with this debut album, and even if it doesn't quite attain the heights of the landmark recordings from those artists, it does threaten to scale them. It is a truly cataclysmic tour de force, especially when you consider the hoops through which the music was forced to jump before it finally appeared, long overdue, in 2001. *The Best Part* was near completion as early as 1997, and was once set for official release in 1999 (most of the songs were written between 1995 and 1998). Unfortunately, the album, according to J-Live's own liner notes, was "built, robbed, destroyed, rebuilt, held up, postponed, canceled, shelved, bootlegged, analyzed, exploited, slept on, supported, patiently awaited, and appreciated" long before it ultimately came to commercial fruition for everyone else to appreciate. No wonder, then, that it is such a confident, assured record. No wonder also that the music is very reminiscent of the sounds that were coming out of the alternative New York scene of the fertile early '90s (Pete Rock, DJ Premier, and Prince Paul all lent a hand in the production booth), although, reworked as it frequently was, it sounded just as timely at the outset of the 21st century. So uniformly excellent are the songs that it plays almost like a best-of compilation, but particular highlights include the brilliant call-and-response anthem "YES!," the cool-cat jazz of "Them That's Not," a cerebral stream-of-consciousness head trip, the classic old school pastiche "Kick It to the Beat" (featuring labelmates Asheru and Blue Black, with whom J-Live shares an artistic sensibility), the new wave groove of "Get the Third," and the autobiographical title track. This is one of the *sine qua non* hip-hop joints of the year. —*Stanton Swihart*

All of the Above / Apr. 2, 2002 / Coup d'Etat ✦✦✦✦
Beginning in the mid-'90s, J-Live remained one of the most hyped MCs in New York, where his music circulated more on the streets than in the shops. Despite his talent and street popularity, he unfortunately found himself caught in industry red tape. Anyone outside of New York was out of luck. His music never made it to stores. Finally, with the release of *All of the Above* in 2002, his music made it into the shops and it quickly became apparent that the wait had been worthwhile. Few MCs can match J-Live when it comes to lyrics. He's one of the most literate MCs in the industry, even if few listeners

outside of the New York underground scene have even heard of him. However, he's not catering to the masses on *All of the Above*. The album is strictly for the underground, at times berating the ideology of popular rap—whether it be the backpackers, gangstas, b-boys and girls, Brooklynites, or thugs—particularly during "Interlude 1 (I'm a Rapper)." Actually, most of J-Live's rhymes generally frown upon his "paid in full" peers, so anyone who shares his view—that contemporary MCs in 2002 give rap a bad name—should savor *All of the Above*. From the cover art, which alludes to John Coltrane's *Blue Train* album, to the thorough liner notes, which showcase J-Live's literary values, *All of the Above* is an album for the underground from the underground, one for the students from the teacher. *—Jason Birchmeier*

J-Rocc (Jason Jackson)

Turntablism, Underground Rap, Hip-Hop
One of the original turntablists, J-Rocc founded the Beat Junkies in 1992 with Melo-D and Rhettmatic, but has done just as much on his own as in a group setting. Born Jason Jackson, he began DJing in the mid-'80s with a California group named PSK. Soon after forming, the Beat Junkies became a seminal force in the rise of instrumental hip-hop, including core member Babu plus future stars Shortkut and D-Styles. The group won federation championships in 1997 and 1998, after which they collectively retired from competition. Beat Junkies mixes and studio material continued to pour out. J-Rocc's first widely issued mix album, *Walkman Rotation*, appeared in 1998 on Conception, and he also worked with Babu on the turntablist compilation *Soundbombing, Vol. 2*, plus as the Bumrush Brothers. *—John Bush*

● **Walkman Rotation** / Jun. 23, 1998 / Conception ✦✦✦
Mixed by the Beat Junkies' DJ J-Rocc, *Walkman Rotation* compiles a series of vinyl-only 12" singles issued on the hip-hop label Conception. Among the highlights: Jake One's "No Introduction/No Introdeezy," Eclipse's "My Position," Mr. Supreme's "Any Last Words," and the Diamond Mercenaries' "Living to Die." *—Jason Ankeny*

J-Shin

Group / Urban, Contemporary R&B
Singer/rapper J-Shin combined hip-hop and classic R&B sounds on his debut album, *My Soul, My Life*, which was released in early 2000 by Atlantic Records. *—Heather Phares*

● **My Soul, My Life** / Feb. 29, 2000 / Slip N Slide ✦✦✦✦
With J-Shin, the ranks of artists trying to put the soul back into the R&B field grew by one. Not only does he have the immaculate voice and innate sense of rhythm to stand next to D'Angelo and Maxwell, he also writes lyrics that put the lie to more superficial forms of romance often found on hardcore rappers' LPs. From "Givin' U Luv" to "Sex Is Not" to the best track here, "One Night Stand" (with special guest LaTosha Scott from Xscape), J-Shin shows that love consists of relationships that are both mental and emotional as well as physical, and he does so with a sultry swing that makes *My Soul, My Life* one of the better R&B debuts of the past decade. *—John Bush*

Ja Rule (Jeff Atkins)

b. Queens, NY
Vocals, Producer / East Coast Rap, Hardcore Rap, Gangsta Rap
As the flagship artist for producer Irv Gotti's Def Jam-affiliated Murder Inc. label, Ja Rule became the rap industry's most commercially successful artist during the early 2000s, working closely with the hitmaker and his stable of talent. Ja initially won over a sizable following with *Venni Vetti Vecci* (1999), his rather hardcore debut album modeled largely after the style of rugged thug rap then popularized by DMX and the Ruff Ryder collective. In particular, "Holla Holla" became a breakout hit, but in retrospect it was a minor success relative to what Ja accomplished a year later with his follow-up album, *Rule 3:36* (2000). On this album, Gotti juxtaposed the rapper's thuggish style with a trio of radio-friendly vixens—Christina Milian, Lil' Mo, and Vita—and produced three enormous hit singles: "Between Me and You," "I Cry," and "Put It on Me." These duets established the template for Ja's following album, *Pain Is Love* (2001), which featured yet more chorus-singing divas, this time Jennifer Lopez ("I'm Real") and Ashanti ("Always on Time"), as well as a similarly styled interpolation of Stevie Wonder's "Do I Do" ("Livin' It Up") featuring Case on the hook. By 2002, Ja alone had brought Gotti's Murder Inc. label into the national spotlight and helped break successive artists from the

label; most notably Ashanti, who collaborated with him on "Down 4 U," yet another chart-topping hit. Roughly around this same time, Ja used his fame to launch a minor acting career for himself, beginning with *The Fast and the Furious* (2001), and he began to attract attention from his peers, uniting with Nas on the 2002 MTV Video Music Awards and squabbling with DMX in the press. Later that year he released *The Last Temptation* (2002), which again paired him with urban vocalists for a few singles, this time with Bobby Brown ("Thug Lovin'") and Ashanti ("Mesmerize"). A backlash mounted around this time, as upstart rapper 50 Cent began hurling numerous disses at Ja. *—Jason Birchmeier*

Venni Vetti Vecci / Jun. 1, 1999 / Def Jam ✦✦✦
Before even releasing his debut album *Venni Vetti Vecci*, Ja Rule had made a name for himself appearing on cuts by Mic Geronimo, DMX, and Jay-Z, which naturally increased expectations for his first effort. Perhaps the expectations were raised a little bit too much, since *Venni* isn't the stunner some may have expected, but it nevertheless is a strong opening salvo. Ja Rule doesn't bend the rules of East Coast hardcore hip-hop enough to truly distinguish himself, but he does deliver a solid record, filled with tough party jams and good straight-ahead gangsta. If the record runs a little long, it nevertheless has enough fine moments to make this a promising debut. *—Stephen Thomas Erlewine*

Rule 3:36 / Oct. 3, 2000 / Def Jam ✦✦✦
On his second album, *Rule 3:36*, Ja Rule makes only slight modifications to his style, yet they're nonetheless notable. His debut album, *Venni Vetti Vecci* (1999), had been harsh. Modeling himself to a certain extent after DMX, Ja represented the East Coast thug life, best exemplified by his "it's murda!" trademark holler. What set him apart from your average thug rapper, though, was his self-consciousness—he was a spiritually tormented thug. Still, tormented or not, he was a thug and was not the sort of character that radio or general audiences were willing to grasp. For the most part, Ja remains that way on *Rule 3:36*. But there are a few moments here when he drops his tough-guy facade and becomes vulnerable—even if it's only the slightest sense. It's these moments nonetheless that make *Rule 3:36* an improvement over *Venni Vetti Vecci*. Furthermore, these same moments are what transformed him from just another wannabe DMX into a potential crossover artist and, even better, a rapper with a unique sense of character. To be more specific, the aforementioned moments are the duets: "Between You and Me," "Put It on Me," and "I Cry." Sure, these songs are obvious commercial efforts, calculated perfectly for crossover radio play, but they also bring a welcome sense of variety to *Rule 3:36*. *Venni Vetti Vecci* didn't have lighter moments like these and catered to a niche audience as a result; on the contrary, this album has both lighter moments for radio and tougher moments for the thug crowd, and caters to a crossover audience as a result. *—Jason Birchmeier*

● **Pain Is Love** / Sep. 2001 / Def Jam ✦✦✦✦
By throwing in some thug ballads for the radio, Ja Rule suddenly found himself catapulted to superstar status in 2001 following the unexpected success of "Between Me and You" and its subsequent string of follow-up hits. A string of hits so long, in fact, it set up his third album, *Pain Is Love*, perfectly—a day didn't pass between releases when Ja wasn't a ubiquitous presence on urban radio, or pop radio for that matter. So when *Pain Is Love* hit the streets, it had enormous momentum, with not one but two singles—"Livin' It Up" and "I'm Real"—all over radio. Furthermore, the commercial brilliance carrying the album applies to not only Ja's sales numbers but also his music. Like he had done with *Rule 3:36* in 2000, Ja and producer Irv Gotti only made slight modifications on *Pain Is Love*, and as before, those modifications are more commercial minded than artistic. The thug-meets-diva duets are here again, including some great collaborations with Jennifer Lopez and Missy Elliott, and the thug anthems are still here, including "So Much Pain," a truly stunning collaboration with 2Pac that works better than it should. What makes this a slightly better album than *Rule 3:36*, though, is the album's consistency. There's no longer an obvious distinction between the love songs and the thug songs, and much of that credit goes to Gotti's production. And to top that off, the thug songs here top anything off *Rule 3:36*, somewhat refuting the assumption that Ja had turned into a sissy. What keeps this album from being a true work of art, though, is the lack of artistry. Sure, Ja and Gotti have the commercial side of the music figured out, and prove with "Livin' It Up" that they are practically shameless when it comes to crafting a sure-fire radio hit (this time interpolating Stevie Wonder's "Do I Do"). Such calculated

concessions to the masses, however, make you wonder whether Ja is following his muse or the paper trail. —*Jason Birchmeier*

The Last Temptation / Nov. 19, 2002 / Def Jam ✦✦✦✦

Ja Rule's self-proclaimed return to the streets isn't that rough compared to most hardcore rap; after all, Irv Gotti, Chink Santana, and the rest of Murder Inc. have a formula that's worked well in the past, and they're not about to desert it with artists like Ja and Ashanti hitting the charts every time they release a single. The first up, "Thug Lovin'," sets it off in style, with Ja Rule turning in one of his best raps yet and guest Bobby Brown adding flair to a pop-heavy production. Ashanti shines on the first of her two tracks, "Mesmerize," a smooth and sexed-up duet with a polished, honey-smooth production framing Ja Rule's gravelly hip-hop soul. Her other feature, a remix of "The Pledge" (the latter originally on *Irv Gotti Presents: The Inc.*), boasts great mic features from Nas and Ja Rule, plus a few odd, disembodied lines heard from 2Pac before the fade-out. Stepping in for Ashanti elsewhere with solid vamps are Charli Baltimore ("Last Temptation") and Alexi ("Murder Me"), though Ja does fit in a few real hardcore tracks too: "Pop N****s" and "The Warning." *The Last Temptation* isn't going to surprise anyone familiar with what Murder Inc. is all about, but their trademarked balance of the rough (Ja Rule) and smooth (Irv Gotti) has rarely sounded better than it does here. —*John Bush*

Jadakiss (Jason Phillips)

Vocals, Producer / East Coast Rap, Hardcore Rap, Hip-Hop

Rapper Jadakiss (born Jason Phillips) became a member of the Ruff Ryders in 1999. Five years earlier, he joined the Lox (who started their saga as a group called the Warlocks) and has remained a member of both groups since. The Lox gained national exposure in 1997 with their multiplatinum tribute to the Notorious B.I.G., "We'll Always Love Big Poppa." Jadakiss released his debut solo album, *Kiss tha Game Goodbye*, in August of 2001 on the Ruff Ryders/Interscope label. The guest stars who joined him for his solo project are Naz, Snoop Dogg, Eminem, DMX, Eve, and the entire Ruff Ryders crew. The Ruff Ryders MCs, Eminem, Dr. Dre, the Neptunes, and Swizz Beats worked as producers for the album. The first single from the album is "Put Your Hands Up." Jadakiss released the 12" single "Got It All" in 2000 on Interscope Records. He is featured on the single "WWIII," which also features Snoop Dogg. Jadakiss appears on rapper Angie Martinez's 2001 debut album, *Up Close and Personal* and on Mary J. Blige's 1999 release, *Mary.* —*Kerry L. Smith*

● Kiss tha Game Goodbye / Mar. 27, 2001 / Ruff Ryders ✦✦✦

In terms of sheer anticipation, Jadakiss' buzz was at an apex at the time of this album's release. While fellow L.O.X. members Sheek and Styles flashed improved flows and lyrics on L.O.X.'s sophomore strike *Take It to the Streets*, Jadakiss remained the group's undisputed frontman. And with the streets virtually foaming at the mouth, Jadakiss returned from the lab to birth his solo debut, *Kiss tha Game Goodbye*. As the last bars of *Kiss tha Game Goodbye* ring out, you can't help but be left with one lingering impression: Kiss tha buzz goodbye. Sure, there are some bangers here; the celebratory, Alchemist-produced "We Gonna Make It," featuring Styles bubbles; the DJ Premier-blessed "None of Y'all Betta," featuring Styles and Sheek; and the gully "Un-Hunh," featuring DMX. Yet, these harder-hitting efforts are leavened out by uncharacteristically smooth production, a lack of direction, and, gasp, Jadakiss' yearning for commercial love. With self-explanatory titles like "Nasty Girl," featuring Carl Thomas; "I'm a Gangsta," featuring Parle; and "Cruisin'," featuring Snoop Dogg, it becomes abundantly clear that Jadakiss is trying too hard to please everyone, with little success. But he is not the only one peeling wheels here, as the interchangeable production supplied by Swizz Beatz, Timbaland, and a host of others offers very little assistance. After jumping ship from one former label of the moment (Bad Boy) to another (Ruff Ryders), what did Jadakiss' change of address really accomplish? After all, if he wanted to go the commercial route, who better then P. Diddy to lead him there? Somewhere in the midst of all this you can be sure the shiny-suit man is smiling. —*Matt Conaway*

Jagged Edge

f. Atlanta, GA

Group / Urban, Contemporary R&B

This rough but smooth male vocal quartet Jagged Edge formed in Atlanta, consisting of identical twin brothers Brandon "Case Dinero" Casey and Brian

"Brasco" Casey, who had moved from their native Hartford, CT; Kyle Norman (aka "Quick"), whom they'd met through church activities; and Richard Wingo (aka "Wingo Dollar"), a late addition to the group suggested by Xscape's Kandi Burress, who took their demo to superproducer Jermaine Dupri. Jagged Edge signed to Dupri's So So Def label and in the summer of 1997 released their debut single, "The Way That You Talk," featuring appearances by Dupri and Da Brat; it reached the Top 40 of the R&B chart and was also a pop chart entry. In late 1997, Jagged Edge released their first album, *A Jagged Era*, which went gold and spawned the Top 20 R&B, Top 40 pop hit "Gotta Be." Their next single, "He Can't Love U," appeared in the fall of 1998 and reached the Top Five of the R&B chart and the Top 20 of the pop chart, going gold in the process. It prefaced the group's second album, *J.E. Heartbreak*, which topped the R&B chart and hit the Top Ten of the pop chart, selling over 2,000,000 copies and spawning the number-one R&B hits "Let's Get Married" (also Top 20 pop) and "Promise" (also Top Ten pop). By the time of the release of Jagged Edge's third album, *Jagged Little Thrill*, in late June 2001, its leadoff single, "Where the Party At" (featuring Nelly), was nearing the R&B Top Ten and was in the pop Top 40. —*John Bush and William Ruhlmann*

● A Jagged Era / Oct. 14, 1997 / So So Def ✦✦✦✦

A Bone Thugs-N-Harmony with more polish to their harmonies and fewer rough edges image-wise, Jagged Edge perform well on their debut album, getting into the groove on singles "The Way That You Talk" and "Gotta Be," each of which is impeccably produced by Jermaine Dupri. There are a few songs which don't work at all on *A Jagged Era*, but for the most part, the quartet sounds interesting. —*John Bush*

J.E. Heartbreak / Oct. 19, 1999 / So So Def ✦✦✦

So So Def wisely held back the release of Jagged Edge's second album, *J.E. Heartbreak*, originally scheduled for the fall of 1999, into early 2000, by which time advance single "He Can't Love U" had become a major hit, thus setting the album up to best the gold-selling success of their debut album, *A Jagged Edge*. That said, the group's slavish obeisance to current R&B conventions continued to be its aesthetic stumbling block. As producer/writer Jermaine Dupri's answer to Boyz II Men, Jagged Edge turned out another set full of slow jams indistinguishable from what was already all over urban radio. Their one attempt at something actually edgy came with "Girl Is Mine," but it was marred by one of those drop-out-laden clean edits of what was no doubt a vulgarity-laced rap by Ja Rule (why even bother to bring in a rapper if you are only going to cut his rap to ribbons?). Mostly, the group was much more tasteful, with twin brothers Brian and Brandon Casey contributing lyrics of romantic devotion culminating with "Let's Get Married." It could only be hoped that, having made their commercial breakthrough, Jagged Edge would aim for an artistic breakthrough next time. —*William Ruhlmann*

Jagged Little Thrill / Jun. 26, 2001 / So So Def ✦✦✦✦

Jagged Edge broke through from modest commercial success to star status with their second album, *J.E. Heartbreak*, which threw off three major hits and sold in the millions. The task for the follow-up, of course, is to keep the momentum going. The group and producer Jermaine Dupri deliberately previewed the album with a mid-tempo dance track, "Where the Party At," featuring rapper Nelly, which was bulleting up the charts when the album was released. It effectively countered the group's image, based on its massive hit "Let's Get Married," as a ballad-heavy, domestically minded outfit, the sort of people not much interested in finding out where the party is at. But the album reaffirms that image, with only a few exceptions. All of Jagged Edge's lyrics are written by twin brothers Brendan and Brian Casey, despite the inclusion of guest rappers on four tracks. (As on the previous album, the more edgy raps have had their vulgarities clipped; wouldn't it have made more sense to ask the rappers to curb their language upfront?) And the Casey brothers are very concerned with promoting responsible behavior among their male peers. Dupri has pushed their more prescriptive sentiments to the end of the album (while making sure the few mid-tempo and up-tempo tracks are near the start), but it is these songs that really define Jagged Edge's viewpoint. On "This Goes Out," the Caseys proclaim tolerance for dodgy actions taken to make ends meet and support children, but they draw the line on "Respect," which preaches against domestic violence. Then, on "Hero of Household," they make clear that it's the man who's supposed to wear the pants in the family: "There's gotta be a leader, and that's me." Such sentiments may not please the women otherwise attracted by the group's call for "Responsibility." —*William Ruhlmann*

Don Jagwarr

Hip-Hop, Gangsta Rap, Hardcore Rap
Don Jagwarr, a native of Trinidad, combines hardcore rap, raggamuffin, and West Coast G-funk grooves into what he calls ragga-funk. He first appeared on Ice Cube's "Wicked" and was subsequently signed to Street Knowledge/ Priority. His debut, *Faded*, appeared in 1994. —*John Bush*

● **Faded** / Nov. 8, 1994 / Priority ◆◆◆
You could say that rap and dancehall reggae had something of a mutual appreciation society in the 1980s and 1990s—dancehall was a major influence on rappers ranging from KRS-One and Queen Latifah to Just-Ice, and hip-hop greatly influenced such dancehall artists as Shabba Ranks, Lieutenant Stitchie, and Bounty Killer. The thing that sets *Faded* apart from so much of the dancehall/hip-hop fusion that was going on the 1990s is Don Jagwarr's variety of influences. Jagwarr was born in Trinidad and lived in Brooklyn before moving to Los Angeles, and on this CD, the influence of Jamaican dancehall, East Coast hardcore rap and West Coast gangsta rap (especially Dr. Dre and his associates) come together to create an unorthodox style. Dancehall albums can be limited and one-dimensional, but Jagwarr opts for variety and makes *Faded* fairly unpredictable. Boasting cameos by Ice Cube and the late Tupac Shakur, *Faded* is a decent, if uneven, outing that will appeal to those who are seeking something fresh from dancehall. —*Alex Henderson*

Jaheim (Jaheim Hoagland)

b. New Brunswick, NJ
Contemporary R&B, Urban
Hip-hop balladeer Jaheim Hoagland hails from New Brunswick, NJ, where he grew up in the 176 Memorial Parkway Homes public housing project. Misfortune hit early: his father died in 1981, when he was only two years old. Coming from a musical family helped him overcome the tragedy and the many pitfalls of his environment. His grandfather, Victor Hoagland, sung with many top groups, including the Drifters, and their family reunions were big songfests. Singing at family reunions and local talent shows preceded a successful tryout at the Apollo Theater's notoriously tough talent show. The smooth crooner who sounded like a hybrid of Teddy Pendergrass and Luther Vandross won the contest three times when he was 15.

Two years later, he experienced more tragedy when his mom died. But Hoagland kept the faith and became a sensation in New Jersey at talent shows. He made a tape which led to a deal with Divine Mill Records (a division of Warner Brothers) four years later. Hoagland received good reactions from two singles: "Could It Be" and "Lil Nigga Ain't Mine," on *BET* and other video shows. Appearing with Hoagland on his first album was an all-star crew of RL (from Next), Blackstreet, and Darren and Cliff Lightly. The multi-talented singer also raps, models, and acts and has appeared in *The Source* and other hip-hop publications. Prior to getting his own deal, he worked with Mag supplying backing vocals on the rappers' *Hustlaz Heaven* CD. His second album, *Still Ghetto*, was released at the tail end of 2002. —*Andrew Hamilton*

Ghetto Love / Feb. 13, 2001 / Warner Bros. ◆◆◆
On his debut album *Ghetto Love*, soulful crooner Jaheim runs the gamut of a wide variety of R&B styles, showcasing himself as a multifaceted artist. Despite the ghetto posturing, one listen to the album reveals the baritone-voiced singer to have more in common with the likes of Will Downing or even a more street version of Luther Vandross, with song styles reminiscent of Keith Sweat, especially with his ample use of female vocalists. The album is something of a musical journey. It begins with mid- to up-tempo material, from the '70s sounding "Let It Go" (complete with a horn section) to the album's smoldering first single, "Could It Be," arguably one of the best R&B songs in years. Other breezy tunes follow, such as "Happiness," the Jeep-flavored "Lil Nigga Ain't Mine" (almost comically tacking an obviously sensitive issue), "Finders Keepers," and "Just In Case," which resonates as a perfect summer jam. The album is unfortunately weighted down by some unremarkable material, but thankfully is salvaged at its close, when Jaheim sings more traditional fare, allowing his gorgeous voice to truly shine. Most memorable among these tunes are "Love Is Still Here," which, unfortunately, is more of an interlude than anything else; "Ready, Willing & Able"; and the church-organ lullaby "For Moms."

As a final and remarkable note, Jaheim never stoops to use foul language. The music is just as effective the way it is, without the need to degenerate itself with obscenities. Despite some dull moments, this is a first-rate debut from a very promising artist. —*Jose Promis*

● **Still Ghetto** / Nov. 5, 2002 / Warner Bros. ◆◆◆◆
Jaheim's considerable vocal talents only increased during the recording of his second album, and a stronger set of songs made *Still Ghetto* a definite improvement over the debut. As before, it all begins with his voice: a deep, throaty croon that makes him sound at least ten years older than he actually is (basically, about as old as the soul samples dotted over the record) and marks him as one of the few R&B artists active who can summon the spirit of a Teddy Pendergrass. Better yet, Jaheim takes the loverman persona to another level, devoting more songs here to relationships than love itself; one of the best is "Put That Woman First," his remake of the Stax nugget William Bell's "I Forgot to Be Your Lover," a great performance that's a natural fit with his persona. The single "Fabulous" is simply beautiful, balancing a back-in-the-day feel with self-esteem issues and riding out with a chorus of children's voices. For "Everywhere I Am," Jaheim recorded a postcard to his mother, who died before he gained fame; it's another testament to his power as an artist that *Still Ghetto* never descends into maudlin sentiments. Just like his soul forefathers, everything about Jaheim is honest and heartfelt. —*John Bush*

Jamal

Hip-Hop, Club/Dance
Formerly one half of the East Coast/West Coast adolescent rap duo Illegal, along with Snoop Dogg's young cousin Lil Malik, this Philadelphia native got his start with Atlanta rap mogul Dallas Austin's side project. The duo drew comparisons to another child rap duo from Atlanta, Kriss Kross, but Illegal's focus was on hardcore rap and they never hesitated to dis the Kross boys on wax. Illegal's debut album, *The Untold Truth*, dropped in the fall of 1993 to a lukewarm reception. After disbanding in 1994, Mally G, clearly the more talented member of the duo, got down with Erick Sermon and the Def Squad soon thereafter. In late 1995, Jamal released his debut album *Last Chance, No Breaks* with the elastic support of heavily funky production from the Green Eyed Bandit. Jamal's pistol-whipping lyrics brought him from boyhood to manhood on the microphone and, despite his relative youthfulness, brought him respect as a hardcore lyricist. The singles "Fades 'Em All" and "Unfukwittable" were memorable, as was the inspired polished funk of producers like E-Double, Redman, and Easy Mo Bee. The album also featured guest appearances from fellow funketeers Redman, Keith Murray, and Sir Nose himself, George Clinton. Jamal continued his work on Def Squad projects including *El Nino* in 1998. —*Michael Di Bella*

● **Last Chance, No Breaks** / Oct. 10, 1995 / Rowdy ◆◆◆
Having distanced himself from the unprofitable venture that was his membership in the teen rap group Illegal, Jamal put his career in the capable hands of rap veteran and superproducer Erick Sermon. As the youngest member of the Def Squad (Keith Murray, Redman), Jamal was able to explore and enrich his natural lyrical gift with the benefit of E-Double's uncanny ear for funky beats. *Last Chance* showcases the fiery young MC's tremendous gift of gab and surprisingly mature musical presence. The plethora of funkdafied beats laid down by Sermon, Redman, Rockwilder, and Easy Mo Bee is fertile ground for the young phenom's assertive vocal capacity. The slow undulating bass of "Fades 'Em All" complements the brash MC's attacking style while the raw and rowdy "Unfukwittable" is just pure hormonal rage. A funk-filled feast of an album that also features a track from the lord of the funk, George Clinton. —*Michael Di Bella*

Jay Dee (James Yancey)

b. Detroit, MI
Producer, Vocals / Hip-Hop
After quietly serving as a member of A Tribe Called Quest's production team, the Ummah, Detroit producer Jay Dee quickly became known as a major hip-hop prospect at the beginning of the early 2000s. The hip-hop community took notice of his no-frills, breakbeat-laden classic hip-hop style after he helped craft albums for Common (*Like Water for Chocolate*), D'Angelo (*Voodoo*), and Q Tip (*Amplified*), in addition to other projects of lesser profile. When *Fantastic, Vol. 2*—the long-awaited major-label debut album by

Jay Dee's group, the trio Slum Village—finally appeared in 2000, Jay Dee was no longer a secret, suddenly having become one of hip-hop's most admired and desired producers. His growing reputation and impressive resume presented him with the opportunity to release a solo album in early 2001, *Welcome 2 Detroit*, an album featuring a number of underground Detroit rappers. —*Jason Birchmeier*

● **Welcome 2 Detroit** / Feb. 27, 2001 / BBE ✦✦✦✦

Jay Dee made a name for himself as one-third of A Tribe Called Quest's beatmaking faction (the Ummah). Thanks to his work on Common's critically acclaimed *Like Water for Chocolate* and Q-Tip's post-Quest endeavor Amplified, Dee has also established himself as a hip-hop superproducer. While Dee's stock continues to rise (working with Janet Jackson, Erykah Badu, and Macy Gray), his underground projects have been less fruitful. Reason being, when it comes to enlisting new MCs to collaborate with, Dee has yet to locate a lyricist capable of augmenting his sublime production. This fact became apparent during Dee's short-lived stint as a member of Slum Village, and the trend continues with his first solo outing, *Welcome 2 Detroit*. Here, Dee continues to showcase a diverse assortment of sensuous melodies and booming funk samples. The Detroit breed MCs who Dee chooses to highlight— Phat Kat on "Rico Suave Bossa Nova" and Beej on "Beej-N-Dem Pt. 2" prove to be very mediocre lyricists. Yet Dee did manage to round up a few hometown prospects, as Frank N Dank liven up "Pause" and Elzhi rips a few furious verses on "Come Get It." Though Dee flips a few clumsy bars as well, *Welcome 2 Detroit* really takes off when he sticks solely to an instrumental script, retouching trumpeter Donald Byrd's "Think Twice" and transforming Kraftwerk's indelible "Trans-Europe Express" into the strippers' anthem in waiting "B.B.E." (Big Booty Express). —*Matt Conaway*

Unreleased: Official Jay Dee Instrumentals Series, Vol. 1 / Oct. 2002 / Bling47 ✦✦✦

Jay-Z (Shawn Carter)

b. Dec. 4, 1970, Brooklyn, NY
East Coast Rap

Jay-Z reigned over the New York rap scene throughout the late '90s and early 2000s and steadily built up the Roc-A-Fella Records dynasty in the process. The Brooklyn rapper made his splash debut in 1996 and cranked out album after album and hit after hit throughout the decade and into the next. Jay-Z became so successful that Roc-A-Fella, the record label he began with Damon Dash, became a marketable brand itself, spawning a lucrative clothing line (Roca Wear); a deep roster of talented rappers (Beanie Sigel, Cam'ron, M.O.P.) and producers (Just Blaze, Kayne West); a number of arena-packing cross-country tours; and even big-budget Hollywood films (*Paid in Full*, *State Property*). While such success is amazing, Jay-Z's musical achievements outweigh the commercial achievements of his franchise. Every one of his albums sold millions, and his endless parade of singles made him omnipresent on urban radio and more. Moreover, he retained a strongly devoted fan base— not only the suburban MTV crowd but also the street-level crowd as well— and challenged whatever rivals attempted to oust him from atop the rap industry, most notably Nas. As a result of his unchecked power, Jay-Z and his Roc-A-Fella clique greatly influenced the rap industry and established many of the trends pervaded during the late '90s and early 2000s. He worked with only the hottest producers of the moment (Clark Kent, DJ Premier, Teddy Riley, Trackmasters, Erick Sermon, Timbaland, Swizz Beatz) and if they weren't hot at the time, they surely would be afterward (Neptunes, Kayne West, Just Blaze). He similarly collaborated with the hottest rappers in the industry, everyone from East Coast rappers like the Notorious B.I.G. ("Brooklyn's Finest"), Ja Rule ("Can I Get A..."), and DMX ("Cash, Money, Hoes"), to the best rappers from the dirty South (Ludacris, Missy Elliott) and the West Coast (Snoop Dogg, Too Short).

Born and raised in the rough Marcy Projects of Brooklyn, NY, Jay-Z underwent some tough times after his father left his mother before the young rapper was even a teen. Without a man in the house, he became a self-supportive youth, turning to the streets, where he soon made a name for himself as a fledgling rapper. Known as "Jazzy" in his neighborhood, he soon shortened his nickname to Jay-Z and did all he could to break into the rap game. Of course, as he vividly discusses in his lyrics, Jay-Z also became a street hustler at this time, doing what needed to be done to make money. For a while, he ran around with Jaz-O, aka Big Jaz, a small-time New York

rapper with a record deal but few sales. From Jaz he learned how to navigate through the rap industry and what moves to make. He also participated in a forgotten group called Original Flavor for a short time. Jay-Z subsequently decided to make an untraditional decision and start his own label rather than sign with an established label like Jaz had done. Together with friends Damon Dash and Kareem "Biggs" Burke, he created Roc-A-Fella Records, a risky strategy for cutting out the middleman and making money for himself. Of course, he needed a quality distributor, and when he scored a deal with Priority Records (and then later Def Jam), Jay-Z finally had everything in place, including a debut album, *Reasonable Doubt* (1996).

Though *Reasonable Doubt* only reached number 23 on *Billboard*'s album chart, Jay-Z's debut became an undisputed classic among fans, many of whom consider it his crowning achievement. Led by the hit single "Ain't No Nigga," a duet featuring Foxy Brown, *Reasonable Doubt* slowly spread through New York; some listeners were drawn in because of big names like DJ Premier and the Notorious B.I.G., others by the gangsta motifs very much in style at the time. By the end of its steady run, *Reasonable Doubt* generated three more charting singles—"Can't Knock the Hustle," which featured Mary J. Blige on the hook; "Dead Presidents"; and "Feelin' It"—and set the stage for Jay-Z's follow-up, *In My Lifetime, Vol. 1* (1997).

Much more commercially successful than its predecessor, *In My Lifetime* peaked at number three on the *Billboard* album chart, quite a substantial improvement over the modest units *Reasonable Doubt* had sold. The album boasted numerous marketable contributors such as Puff Daddy and Teddy Riley, which no doubt helped sales, yet Jay-Z's decision to move in a more accessible direction for much of the album, trading gangsta rap for pop-rap, increased his audience twofold. Singles such as "Sunshine" and "The City Is Mine" confirmed this move toward pop-rap, both songs featuring radio-ready pop hooks and little of the grim introspection that had characterized *Reasonable Doubt*. *In My Lifetime* still had some dramatic moments, such as "Streets Is Watching" and "Rap Game/Crack Game," yet these moments were few and greatly eclipsed by the pop-rap.

Jay-Z's next album, *Vol. 2: Hard Knock Life* (1998), released a year after *In My Lifetime*, furthered the shift from gangsta rap to pop-rap. Though Jay-Z himself showed few signs of lightening up, particularly on brash songs like "Cash, Money, Hoes," his producers crafted infectious hooks and trend-setting beats. Thus, songs like "Can I Get A..." and "Hard Knock Life (Ghetto Anthem)" sounded both distinct and unforgettable, garnering enormous amounts of airplay. Again, as he had done on *In My Lifetime*, Jay-Z exchanged the autobiographical slant of his debut for a sampler platter of radio-ready singles; and again, he reached more listeners than ever, topping the album chart and generating a remarkable six singles: the three aforementioned songs as well as "Jigga What?," "It's Alright," and "Money Ain't a Thang."

Like clockwork, Jay-Z returned a year later with another album, *Vol. 3: Life and Times of S. Carter* (1999), which sold a staggering number of units and generated multiple singles. Here Jay-Z collaborated with yet more big names (nearly one guest vocalist/rapper on every song, not to mention the roll call of in-demand producers) and his most overblown work yet resulted. Jay-Z scaled back a bit for *The Dynasty Roc la Familia* (2000), his fifth album in as many years. The album showcased mostly Roc-A-Fella's in-house rappers: Beanie Sigel, Memphis Bleek, and Amil. Jay-Z also began working with several new producers: the Neptunes, Kayne West, and Just Blaze. The Neptunes-produced "I Just Wanna Love U (Give It 2 Me)" became a particularly huge hit single this go around.

Jay-Z's next album, *The Blueprint* (2001), solidified his position atop the New York rap scene upon its release in September. Prior to the album's release, the rapper had caused a stir in New York following his headlining performance at Hot 97's Summer Jam 2001, where he debuted the song "Takeover." The song features a harsh verse ridiculing Prodigy of Mobb Deep, and Jay-Z accentuated his verbal assault (including the lines "You's a ballerina/I seen ya") by showcasing gigantic photos of an adolescent Prodigy in a dance outfit. The version of "Takeover" that later appeared on *The Blueprint* also included a verse dissing Nas as well as Prodigy. As expected, the song ignited a sparring match with Nas, whom responded with "Ether." Jay-Z accordingly returned with a comeback, "Super Ugly," where he rapped over the beats to Nas' "Get Ur Self A" on the first verse and Dr. Dre's "Bad Intentions" on the second. The back-and-forth bout created massive publicity for both Jay-Z and Nas.

In addition to "Takeover," *The Blueprint* also featured "Izzo (H.O.V.A.)," one of the year's biggest hit songs, and the album topped many year-end best-of charts. For the most part, Jay-Z performs alone on all of the album's songs except an Eminem collaboration, "Renegade." The lack of guest rappers made *The Blueprint* Jay-Z's most personal album since *Reasonable Doubt*. Consequently, many began comparing the two, calling *The Blueprint* Jay-Z's best album since *Reasonable Doubt* or even going so far as calling *The Blueprint* his best album yet. Jay-Z capitalized on the album's lasting success by issuing two versions of the single "Girls, Girls, Girls" and also the song "Jigga That N****a" as yet another single. Furthermore, he collaborated with the Roots for the *Unplugged* album (2001) and with R. Kelly for *Best of Both Worlds* (2002). He then went on to record, over the course of the year, 40 or so new tracks, 25 of which appeared on his next record, the double album *The Blueprint²*: The Gift & the Curse *(2002). Though billed as a sequel, Blueprint*² was remarkably different from its predecessor. Where the first volume had been personal, considered, and focused, the second forsook those qualities and instead offered an unapologetically sprawling double-disc extravaganza showcasing remarkable scope. As usual, it spawned a stream of singles, led by his 2Pac cover "03 Bonnie & Clyde." —Jason Birchmeier

☆ **Reasonable Doubt** / Jun. 25, 1996 / Roc-A-Fella ◆◆◆◆◆
Before Jay-Z fashioned himself into hip-hop's most notorious capitalist, he was a street hustler from the projects who rapped about what he knew—and was very, very good at it. Skeptics who've never cared for Jigga's crossover efforts should turn to his debut, *Reasonable Doubt*, as the deserving source of his legend. *Reasonable Doubt* is often compared to another New York landmark, Nas' *Illmatic*. A hungry young MC with a substantial underground buzz drops an instant classic of a debut, detailing his experiences on the streets with disarming honesty, and writing some of the most acrobatic rhymes heard in quite some time. (Plus, neither artist has since approached the street cred of his debut, *The Blueprint* notwithstanding.) Parts of the persona that Jay-Z would ride to superstardom are already in place: he's cocky bordering on arrogant, but playful and witty, and exudes an effortless, unaffected cool throughout. And even if he's rapping about rising to the top instead of being there, his material obsessions are already apparent. Jay-Z the hustler isn't too different from Jay-Z the rapper: hustling is about living the high life and getting everything you can, not violence or tortured glamour or cheap thrills. In that sense, the album's defining cut might not be one of the better-known singles—"Can't Knock the Hustle," "Dead Presidents II," "Feelin' It," or the Foxy Brown duet, "Ain't No Nigga." It just might be the brief "22 Two's," which not only demonstrates Jay-Z's extraordinary talent as a pure freestyle rapper, but also preaches a subtle message through its club hostess: bad behavior gets in the way of making money. Perhaps that's why Jay-Z waxes reflective, not enthusiastic, about the darker side of the streets; songs like "D'Evils" and "Regrets" are some of the most personal and philosophical he's ever recorded. It's that depth that helps *Reasonable Doubt* rank as one of the finest albums of New York's hip-hop renaissance of the '90s. —Steve Huey

In My Lifetime, Vol. 1 / Nov. 4, 1997 / Roc-A-Fella ◆◆◆◆◆
After the death of friend and compatriot the Notorious B.I.G. in early 1997, Jay-Z made his claim for the title of best rapper on the East Coast (or anywhere) with his sophomore shot, *In My Lifetime, Vol. 1*. Though the productions are just a bit flashier and more commercial than on his debut, Jay-Z remained the tough street rapper, and even improved a bit on his flow, already one of the best in the world of hip-hop. Still showing his roots in the Marcy projects (he's surrounded by a group of kids in a picture on the back cover), Jay-Z struts the line between project poet and up-and-coming player, and manages to have it both ways. He slings some of the most cutting rhymes heard in hip-hop, brushing off a legion of rappers riding his coattails on "Imaginary Player." For "Streets Is Watching," high-tension background strings and vocal samples from the gangster film *Sleeper* emphasize the pitfalls of a rapper everyone's gunning for ("If I shoot you, I'm brainless/But if you shoot me, then you famous"). The song leads right into "Friend or Foe '98," the sequel to a track from *Reasonable Doubt* that only increases the sense of paranoia. But Jay-Z plays the ghetto celebrity equally well, and continues his slick, Cristal-sipping image with "I Know What Girls Like" (featuring Puff Daddy and Lil' Kim), "(Always Be My) Sunshine" (featuring Babyface and Foxy Brown), and "Lucky Me." Puff Daddy's Bad Boy stable is responsible for almost half the productions, and though they often verge far into pop territory, Jay-Z usually rescues them from a complete crossover. (Ironically, the most commercial production is actually from Teddy Riley on

"The City Is Mine," with an unfortunate interpolation of Glenn Frey's "You Belong to the City.") Having one of the toughest producers around (Premier) as well as one of the slickest (Puff Daddy) sometimes creates a disconnect between who Jay-Z really is and who he wants to become, but he balances both personas with the best rapping heard in the rap game since the deaths of 2Pac and Notorious B.I.G. —John Bush

Vol. 2: Hard Knock Life / Sep. 29, 1998 / Def Jam ◆◆◆
Coming on the heels of two strong records which revealed the extent of Jay-Z's talents, *Vol. 2: Hard Knock Life* (it may be titled *Vol. 2*, but it's his third album, arguably his fourth if you count the *Streets Is Watching* soundtrack) is a little bit of a relative disappointment. Jay-Z had established himself as a savvy, street-smart rapper on those two records, but with *Hard Knock Life* he decided to shoot for crossover territory, for better and for worse. At his best, he shows no fear—witness how the title track shamelessly works a Broadway showstopper from *Annie* into a raging ghetto cry, yet keeps it smooth enough for radio. It's a stunning single, but unfortunately, it promises more than the rest of the album can deliver. Jay-Z remains a first-rate lyricist and MC, but too often his subjects are tired, especially since he winds up with no new revelations. Unfortunately, the same could be said for his music. For every "Hard Knock Life," there are a couple of standard post-gangsta jams that don't catch hold—and that's really too bad, because the best moments (including several tracks produced by such stars as Timbaland, Kid Capri, and Jermaine Dupri) are state of the art, R&B-inflected mainstream hip-hop. And that's the problem—before, Jay-Z wasn't trying to play by the rules of the mainstream, but here he's trying to coopt them. At times he does, but the times that fall flat have less strength or integrity than their predecessors, and that's what makes the entire record not quite as effective, despite its numerous high points. —Stephen Thomas Erlewine

Vol. 3: Life and Times of S. Carter / Dec. 28, 1999 / Def Jam ◆◆◆
After the crossover success of 1998's *Vol. 2: Hard Knock Life* (complete with highly publicized samples from *Annie*), Jay-Z returned to the streets on his fourth proper album overall, 1999's *Vol. 3: Life and Times of S. Carter*. A set of hard-hitting tracks with some of the best rhymes of Jay-Z's career, the album is much more invigorating than its predecessor, and almost as consistently entertaining as his best album, *In My Lifetime, Vol. 1*. As good as his rapping has become, the production here plays a large part as well. Befitting his superstar status, Jay-Z boasts the cream of hip-hop producers: Timbaland (four tracks total), DJ Premier, Swizz Beatz, and Rockwilder. DJ Premier's "So Ghetto," Timbaland's "Snoopy Track" (with Juvenile), and DJ Clue's "Pop 4 Roc" are innovative tracks that push the rhymes along but never intrude too much on Jay-Z's own flow. If this album doesn't quite make it up to Jay-Z's best, though, it's the fault of a few overblown productions, like "Dope Man" and "Things That U Do" (with Mariah Carey). —John Bush

The Dynasty Roc la Familia / Oct. 31, 2000 / Roc-A-Fella ◆◆◆
At the time of *The Dynasty Roc la Familia*'s release, Jay-Z had already established himself as a towering figure in the rap world. His previous two albums— *Vol. 2: Hard Knock Life* and *Vol. 3: Life and Times of S. Carter*— spawned numerous gigantic hits and were filled the brim with the biggest hitmakers in rap: producers like Timbaland and Swizz Beatz; rappers like Juvenile and DMX. So rather than try to one-up these albums with yet more superproducers and big-name rappers, Jay-Z took a different approach on *The Dynasty*. He brought in a stable of up-and-coming producers—the Neptunes, Just Blaze, Kayne West—and handed the mic to his in-house roster of Roc-A-Fella rappers—Beanie Sigel, Memphis Bleek, Freeway—in hopes of recording a fresh album unlike his previous work while furthering his "dynasty" of young labelmates at the same time. The approach works well. *The Dynasty Roc la Familia* still sounds like a Jay-Z album, but it's different enough from his past work to make it exciting and unique. In particular, the production set Jigga apart from his peers in 2000, especially "I Just Wanna Love You (Give It 2 Me)" by the Neptunes, a fun, playful song miles away from the rugged Ruff Ryder beats Swizz Beatz had been offering Jay-Z a year earlier. In regard to rapping, the omnipresence of Beanie Sigel and Memphis Bleek spices up "Parking Lot Pimpin'," another album highlight, but you tire of them as the album lumbers on toward its long-winded conclusion. Guest appearances by Snoop Dogg and Scarface are much more welcome, two of only three non-Roc-A-Fella guests invited along. Thus in the end *The Dynasty* plays like a Roc-A-Fella showcase rather than a Jay-Z album. This, of course, means you have to endure a lot of promotional posse tracks, particularly

toward the end of the album. Still, the few standout tracks here are career highlights and well worth wading through the filler to find. —*Jason Birchmeier*

★ **The Blueprint** / Sep. 18, 2001 / Uptown/Universal ✦✦✦✦✦

When Jay-Z dropped "The City Is Mine" in 1997 and claimed New York's hip-hop throne upon the Notorious B.I.G.'s demise, many smirked and some even snickered. Four years later in 2001, when he released *The Blueprint*, no one was smirking and no one dared snicker. At this point in time, nobody in New York could match Jay-Z rhyme for rhyme and nobody in New York had fresher beats—and many would argue that Jigga's reign was not just confined to New York but was, in fact, national. Yes, Jay-Z had risen to the top of the rap game in the late '90s and solidified his position with gigantic hits like "Big Pimpin'" and "I Just Wanna Love You (Give It 2 Me)." Furthermore, *The Blueprint's* leadoff single, "Izzo (H.O.V.A.)," dominated urban radio numerous weeks before the album hit the streets, generating so much demand that Def Jam had to push up the album's street date because it was being so heavily bootlegged. So when Jay-Z opens *The Blueprint* dropping rhymes about "runnin' this rap shit," it's not so much arrogance as it is a matter of fact. And by the time he brutally dismisses two of his most formidable opponents, Mobb Deep and Nas, less than ten minutes into the album, there's little doubt that Jay-Z's status as the top MC in the game is justified. But that's just one song. There are 12 other songs on *The Blueprint*—and they're all stunning, to the point where the album seems almost flawless. Besides rhymes that challenge those on *Reasonable Doubt* as the most crafted of Jay-Z's career to date in terms of not only lyrics but also flow and delivery, *The Blueprint* also boasts some of his most extravagant beats, courtesy of impressive newcomers Kayne West and Just Blaze. Moreover, if the rhymes and beats alone don't make *The Blueprint* a career highlight for Jay-Z, the minimal guest appearances surely do. For once, listeners get exactly what they want: Jay-Z and nothing but Jay-Z, over beats so loaded with marvelously flipped samples the songs don't even need big vocal hooks. Besides, when you're already the top MC in the game, there's no need for crossover attempts. Half-satisfying albums like *Hard Knock Life* were the crossover attempts, and now that Jay-Z is "runnin' this rap shit," a fully realized masterpiece like *The Blueprint* is the glorious result. —*Jason Birchmeier*

Unplugged / Dec. 18, 2001 / Def Jam ✦✦✦✦

Following the success of *The Blueprint*, Jay-Z took a break from the studio productions of Timbaland and Just Blaze and stepped into acoustic surroundings for a taped edition of MTV's long-running *Unplugged* series. With the talents of the Roots as his backing band, Jay-Z fails to miss a step and feels just as comfortable in the unplugged arena as he does with drum machines and a mixing desk in front of him. The skills of Roots drummer Ahmir Thompson emulate even the slightest nuance from the originally programmed electronic beats, and Jay-Z fails to take this for granted, gently shifting from one song to the next in medley form with ease. With a strong track listing spanning his entire career of chart-topping hits, this album is the perfect introduction to Jay-Z's prolific catalog and a fun listen for the most dedicated of fans. —*Rob Theakston*

The Blueprint²: The Gift & the Curse / Nov. 12, 2002 / Def Jam ✦✦✦

Jay-Z kept *The Blueprint* incredibly tight, focusing on a single sound and letting nothing interfere with some of the best raps of his career. *The Blueprint²: The Gift & the Curse* is a radically different record, with the most respected rapper in the business trying on a range of styles, collaborating with a lot of guests (from Rakim to Lenny Kravitz to Scarface to Beyoncé Knowles), and working with an army of producers (Neptunes, Dr. Dre, Timbaland, Heavy D, Kanye West). No one else in hip-hop possesses enough power of personality to carry a 110-minute double album, and if Jay-Z can't quite manage it either, he certainly delivers some solid material in the process. The discs are split into "The Gift" and "The Curse," though there's no concept in view, just a loose collection of tracks ranging from unapologetically sexed-up party joints to theatrical epics and even taking in a dirty South feature for Outkast's Big Boi. It's clear Jay-Z's in control even here, and though his raps can't compete with the concentrated burst on *The Blueprint*, there's at least as many great tracks on tap, if only listeners have enough time to find them. Good choices for highlights include the Neptunes' bounce track "Excuse Me Miss," the horn-driven blast of "The Watcher 2" produced by Dr. Dre (featuring Truth Hurts), and "I Did It My Way," which balances the trad-pop singalong of "Hard Knock Life" with the digital drumrolls of "The Takeover." —*John Bush*

Jayo Felony

Hip-Hop, Gangsta Rap, Hardcore Rap, West Coast Rap

San Diego-based rapper Jayo Felony (aka Bullet Loco or Peer Pressure) turned to music after spending his teen years in a gang, a decision that ultimately resulted in a stint in prison; after recording a handful of underground tapes he issued the single "Piss on Your Tombstone," selling it on consignment at local record stores. The single brought him to the attention of Run-D.M.C.'s Jam Master Jay, who signed Felony to his JMJ label to release 1995's *Take a Ride*; after the disc quickly disappeared from sight, it took four years for the rapper to resurface with his sophomore effort, the Def Jam release *Whatcha Gonna Do? Underground* followed in 1999. —*Jason Ankeny*

● **Take a Ride** / May 30, 1995 / JMJ/RAL ✦✦✦

This San Diego rapper tells inner-city tales of death and crime, but shows no solutions to the problems he explains. Jam Master Jay helps with the production. —*John Bush*

Crip Hop / Oct. 23, 2001 / American Music ✦✦✦

Fans of *The X-Files* ought to snap up this long-awaited disc from San Diego rapper Jayo Felony, since he's got a conspiracy theory to explain every obstacle he's faced in his career. Originally signed to Def Jam, Jayo's parting with the label was somewhat less than amicable, and he's been mad ever since. The main targets of his ire on *Crip Hop* (named in honor of his gang affiliation) are Jay-Z and Snoop Dogg, each (dis)honored with a separate track, but there's plenty of beef to go around. Which is too bad, really, because while his hot air is sometimes entertaining, Jayo's enemies list overshadows a legitimate talent. Over a series of musical, G-funk-influenced tracks, he offers personality to spare, with a powerful delivery that makes up for some of the routine gangbangin' themes. And he shows he has an ear for the all-important hook, in off-kilter but ear-catching concoctions like the loopily chanted "Swing," as well as the impressive crossover move "She Loves Me" (which features a guest appearance by pint-sized Young Nube, all of seven years old). The biggest problem facing Jayo could be what will happen if he ever runs out of foes—but a quick flip through the detailed liner notes to *Crip Hop* makes that seem like an unlikely prospect indeed. —*Dan LeRoy*

Jazzyfatnastees

Group / Alternative Rap, Underground Rap

Vocalists Tracey Moore and Mercedes Martinez make up Jazzyfatnastees. In 1993, they were part of a vocal quartet that had landed a deal with Tommy Boy. But by 1995, the deal had fallen through. After drifting for a few years, Moore and Martinez found themselves in Philadelphia, their quartet reduced to a duo by departures. The two had known the guys in the Roots for a few years, having opened shows for them in the past. For their debut album as Jazzyfatnastees, Moore and Martinez signed with Motive Records, the Roots' imprint at MCA. *The Once and Future*, their self-written and self-produced debut album, arrived in 1999. Filled with sunny harmonies and laid-back grooves, the album was ahead of its time, or at least ahead of the neo-soul movement, which would peak a few years later with the arrival of songbirds like Macy Gray and India.Arie. Nevertheless, the Jazzys persevered. They founded Black Lily, a showcase for artists of the very noncategories—neo-funk and neo-soul, organic hip-hop—in which they found themselves. They also began work on their sophomore effort, which arrived in September of 2002. *The Tortoise & the Hare*, released through the duo's new deal with Coolhunter/Ryko distribution, continued to hone Moore and Martinez's soulful, modern, and definitely groovy sound. With the rest of the music world having caught up to their sound, Jazzyfatnastees planned a third album for 2003. —*Johnny Loftus*

● **The Once and Future** / Aug. 31, 1999 / MCA ✦✦✦

The soulful duo of Mercedes Martinez and Tracey Moore, nurtured with a record contract, production expertise, and backup playing by the Roots, contribute a solid record of hip-hop soul that simultaneously looks to the past as well as the future. The grooves are chunky and well fed by the Roots' experienced players, while Martinez and Moore trade vocals and raps on standout tracks like "The Wound." —*Keith Farley*

The Tortoise & the Hare / Sep. 3, 2002 / Cool Hunter ✦✦✦

JCD & the Dawg LB.

Group / Hip-Hop, Hardcore Rap

Early examples of between-coasts hardcore rap, JCD & the Dawg LB. came out of St. Louis with their 1992 debut, *A Day in the Life*. Their lone single, "Get Naked," wasn't a success, and Profile dropped them before a second album could be recorded. Producer Erich "Hypsta" Krause also worked with Luke. —*John Bush*

● **A Day in the Life** / 1992 / Profile ◆◆◆

Unlike New York, L.A., Philadelphia, Oakland, Atlanta, and Miami, St. Louis wasn't considered a major city for rap in the 1980s or 1990s. This isn't to say that St. Louis didn't have its share of rappers, but not many of them recorded for well-known labels or enjoyed anything more than local or regional success. One rap act that came out of St. Louis in the early '90s was JCD & the Dawg LB., whose *A Day in the Life* is a likable, if uneven, hardcore rap outing. Rapper JCD and his associates don't bring any unique, distinctive, or groundbreaking perspectives to hip-hop—for the most part, they rap about their sexual misadventures and how rough the streets of St. Louis' inner-city areas are. But tunes like "St. Louis Niggas," "Over Pussy," and "Kibbles and Bits" are catchy enough, and some of their reflections on urban life are rather funny in a twisted, dark-humored sort of way. Like many blues and country artists, rappers such as JCD have a way of laughing at the dark side of life (Everlast wasn't off base when he called Johnny Cash a "b-boy"). *A Day in the Life* is far from a hip-hop masterpiece, but this obscure CD isn't without its pleasures. —*Alex Henderson*

Wyclef Jean

b. Oct. 17, 1972, Croix-des-Bouquets, Haiti

Producer, Vocals, Guitar / Hip-Hop, Urban, Alternative Rap, East Coast Rap, Contemporary R&B

Lead Fugees rapper and sometime guitarist Wyclef Jean was the first member of his group to embark on a solo career, and he proved even more ambitious and eclectic on his own. As the Fugees hung in limbo, Wyclef also became hip-hop's unofficial multicultural conscience; a seemingly omnipresent activist, he assembled or participated in numerous high-profile charity benefit shows for a variety of causes, including aid for his native Haiti. The utopian one-world sensibility that fueled Wyclef's political consciousness also informed his recordings, which fused hip-hop with as many different styles of music as he could get his hands on (though, given his Caribbean roots, reggae was a particular favorite). In addition to his niche as hip-hop's foremost global citizen, Clef was also a noted producer and remixer who worked with an impressive array of pop, R&B, and hip-hop talent, including Whitney Houston, Santana, and Destiny's Child, among many others.

The son of a minister, Nelust Wyclef Jean was born in Croix-des-Bouquets, Haiti, on October 17, 1972. When he was nine, his family moved to the Marlborough projects in Brooklyn, NY; by his teenage years, Jean had moved to New Jersey, taken up the guitar, and begun studying jazz through his high school's music department. In 1987 he also joined a rap group with his cousin Prakazrel Michel (aka Pras) and Michel's high-school classmate Lauryn Hill. Initially calling themselves the Tranzlator Crew, they evolved into the Fugees, a name taken from slang for Haitian refugees. The trio signed with Ruffhouse Records in 1993 and released their debut album, *Blunted on Reality*, the following year; it attracted little notice, thanks to an inappropriate hardcore stance that the group wore like an ill-fitting suit. But the Fugees hit their stride on the follow-up *The Score*, ignoring popular trends and crafting an eclectic, bohemian masterpiece that sounded like nothing else on the hip-hop landscape in 1996. Thanks to hit singles like "Fu-Gee-La" and "Killing Me Softly," *The Score* became a chart-topping phenomenon; in fact, with sales of over six million copies, it still ranks as one of the biggest-selling rap albums of all time.

Wyclef Jean was the first Fugee to declare plans for a solo project, setting to work soon after the group completed its supporting tours. Released in the summer of 1997, *The Carnival* (full title: *Wyclef Jean Presents the Carnival Featuring the Refugee Allstars*) was even more musically ambitious than *The Score*. Its roster of guests included not only the remainder of the Fugees but also Jean's siblings (who performed together in the duo Melky Sedeck), Cuban legend Celia Cruz, New Orleans funk mainstays the Neville Brothers, and Bob Marley's female backing vocalists the I Threes. The breadth of his ambition was further in evidence on the album's two hit singles; "We Trying

to Stay Alive" recast the Bee Gees' signature disco tune as a ghetto empowerment anthem, and the Grammy-nominated "Gone Till November" was recorded with part of the New York Philharmonic Orchestra. Those two songs helped push *The Carnival* into a Top 20, triple-platinum showing, and most reviews were naturally quite positive.

In the wake of *The Carnival*, Wyclef stepped up his outside work for other artists; over the next few years, he collaborated as a producer, songwriter, and/or remixer with a typically diverse list of artists: Destiny's Child ("No No No"), Sublime, Simply Red, Whitney Houston (the title track of her *My Love Is Your Love* album), dancehall reggae star Bounty Killer, Cypress Hill, Michael Jackson, Eric Benet, Mya, Santana ("Maria Maria"), Tevin Campbell, the Black Eyed Peas, Kimberly Scott, Sinéad O'Connor, Mick Jagger, and Canibus. Clef also served as Canibus' manager for a short time in 1998; prior to their split, a report surfaced that Wyclef had pulled a gun on *Blaze* editor Jesse Washington over a negative Canibus review the magazine was slated to run (Wyclef vehemently denied the accusation, and no charges were filed). By the time Wyclef began work on his second solo album, rumors were flying about tension between individual Fugees, and despite their denials, the fact that no follow-up to *The Score* was in sight seemed to lend credence to all the speculation.

Although Wyclef had previously announced he would put off his sophomore effort until after the next Fugees album, he was well into the project by early 2000, giving an early release the anti-police brutality track "Diallo" (with guest vocals from Senegalese superstar Youssou N'Dour) via the Internet. The full album, titled *The Ecleftic: 2 Sides II a Book*, was released toward the end of the summer and entered the charts at number nine. Besides N'Dour, guests this time around included Mary J. Blige (on the Grammy-nominated duet "911"), Earth, Wind & Fire, Kenny Rogers, and even wrestling star the Rock ("It Doesn't Matter"); Clef also threw in a left-field cover of Pink Floyd's "Wish You Were Here." This time around, some critics suggested that Wyclef's sprawling ambitions were growing messy, but the record went platinum nonetheless. Shortly after its release, he also started up his own record label, Yclef.

With no Fugees reunion in sight, Wyclef began preparing his third solo album, *Masquerade*, in 2001; he also appeared in the Jamaican gangster flick *Shottas* and, sadly, suffered the death of his father in a home accident. *Masquerade* was released in the summer of 2002, and in addition to the usual worldbeat fusions, it found Wyclef reworking songs by Bob Dylan and Frankie Valli, and featured guest shots from Tom Jones and Israeli violinist Miri Ben-Ari. *Masquerade* entered the charts at number six, proving that Wyclef's freewheeling approach still held quite a bit of appeal. —*Steve Huey*

● **Presents the Carnival Featuring the Refugee Allstars** / Jun. 24, 1997 / Columbia ◆◆◆◆

The Score was one of those rare hip-hop albums that came out of nowhere and rewrote the rules. In the aftermath of its success, many pundits predicted that rap would move away from gangsta and toward a richer, more varied existence. Given such heady praise, perhaps it was reasonable that Wyclef Jean, the guitarist and male rapper for the Fugees, decided to follow *The Score* with a solo project. However, *The Carnival* comes across like Jean presenting his case that he is the *true* genius in the Fugees. And he's partially right. He has the ambition and drive common to many great artists, but he lacks the skills to fulfill his vision. Of course, the very fact that he has an original vision makes Jean one of the more compelling figures of late-'90s hip-hop. Not content to rely solely on hip-hop, Jean adds all manners of influences to his music. You can hear reggae, soul, disco, Caribbean rhythms, worldbeat, and opera scattered throughout *The Carnival*, giving the record the riotous atmosphere of its title. Even so, Jean occasionally tries too hard, forcing disparate genres to mix and spending more time on production than songwriting. But even with all its faults, *The Carnival* delivers great thrills when operating at full strength, demonstrating that Jean is at least half a genius. —*Leo Stanley*

The Ecleftic: 2 Sides II a Book / Jul. 25, 2000 / Columbia ◆◆◆◆

Wyclef Jean serves up another slice of his music and remixing creativity with his latest, *The Ecleftic: 2 Sides II a Book*. Loaded with pop-culture commentary and often directly naming social names, *The Ecleftic* is sure to stir up some emotions from not only the famous but from the general public as well. The purest example is "Diallo," named after the man who was shot 41 times by patrolling night officers when he reached for his wallet, not a gun as the police had thought. With this, Wyclef shows his refugee camp roots, acting as a 21st-century Bob Marley. As much as it is loaded with serious urban observations, Wyclef also serves up a good party and even some love songs. In the beginning, *The Ecleftic*, is loaded with classic and catchy samples, such as the song about his undying love for a stripper paying her way through college entitled "Red Light District." Though older listeners will probably cringe at the thought of Kenny Rogers singing of turntables, this move is no surprise from a man who introduced the Bee Gees to the hip-hop generation with the sample of "Staying Alive" on his album *The Carnival*. On *Ecleftic*, Wyclef comes full fisted with commentary on the police system, urban ills, and stereotypes. Though some are merited, after the first dozen they lose their impact and are swallowed by catchy beats. Overall, another commentary and playfully meticulous production by Wyclef Jean who has struggled to separate himself from the Fugees. It is clear, with a good retrospective listen, how much Jean's production style was a large part of the praised trio. With *The Ecleftic: Two Sides II a Book*, Jean takes another strong step toward solidifying his own identity. —*Diana Potts*

Masquerade / Jun. 18, 2002 / Columbia ◆◆◆
Wyclef Jean prides himself on having a vision, which he does. Few of his peers are as determined to appeal to as broad an audience as a possible, dabbling in everything from raggae to sugary pop, tying it all together as a self-conscious "big statement." His ambition has been clear since *The Score*, if not the Fugees' debut, and with each of his post-Fugees solo projects, he's worked with the same basic template—a lot of pop, a lot of hip-hop, reggae, and world-beat touches, lots of social consciousness, a little does of party anthems, all produced with enough gloss and melody to reach a wide audience, yet with enough NPR sensibility to bring in the serious-minded progressives, no matter their age. If anything, he perhaps tipped a little bit too close to the pop last time around, letting Kenny Rogers in for a new version of "The Gambler," so the first part of his third album, *Masquerade*, feels like a bit of an over-correction, as he toughens up the beats, brings in the hard(er) rappers, and aims to the street. Then, after the point has been made, it settles into a Marley-esque reggae groove, before easing into pop for awhile, then winding up back in Marley territory with "War No More." Throughout it all, Jean's musical skill is impressive and most of this long, 20-track album is quite pleasurable, but his skills as a recordmaker waver on occasion. The primary problem is that Wyclef wants to be everything to all people, so he'll hit too hard on the hip-hop, then back *way* up and invite Tom Jones into the studio for a new, not very good, version of "What's New, Pussycat," while rewriting Frankie Valli ("Oh What a Night") and Dylan ("Knocking on Heaven's Door," which now contains shout-outs "to Biggie Smalls and Tupac…to my people in the twin towers") with equal abandon. He pushes too hard on sermonizing, no matter if pompous pleas to the ghettos or heartfelt laments (a spoken tribute to his recently passed father, "War No More," a "Redemption Song"-styled protest song with the unforgettable line, "this looks like a scene from the movie *Star Wars*"), which offsets the lighter tracks. Instead of sounding generous and open-hearted, it's a bit muddled and confusing, especially when taken all at once—but when isolated in parts, or heard in passing, it's an enjoyable record. —*Stephen Thomas Erlewine*

Jeep Beat Collective

Group / Turntablism, Hip-Hop, Big Beat
Prolific British DJ the Ruf began his Jeep Beat Collective project in 1994, one of his many aliases alongside Mindbomb and Godfather of Weird. The Jeep Beat project deals in instrumental hip-hop with booming bass and ample, but not overbearing, scratching. Along with many releases for his own Ruf Beats label, Jeep Beat Collective tracks have appeared on mixes from Andy Smith (Portishead), DJ Food, and the turntablist compilation *Return of the DJ*. —*Wade Kergan*

● **Technics Chainsaw Massacre** / Dec. 15, 1998 / Bomb Hip Hop ◆◆◆◆
This England turntable collective is primarily made up of one man, the Ruf. *Technics Chainsaw Massacre*, named for a popular brand of turntable, offers a double album of record-spinning wizardry. It satisfies hip-hop purists by utilizing samples and frequent scratches that more than manage to keep the beat ("Attack of the Wildstyle Beatfreak"). But more importantly, the Ruf doesn't just make you groove, he makes you think. Case in point is the superb and utterly original "The Stroboscope Syndrome." With poignant snippets from Run-D.M.C. ("People judging other people by the color of skin") and KRS-One ("Are you ready for peace and equality?"), the hip-hop color line is thoroughly examined. —*Craig Robert Smith*

Rodney Jerkins

b. New Jersey
Producer / Hip-Hop, Urban, Club/Dance
Prolific producer Rodney Jerkins' credits include hits by Mary J. Blige, Whitney Houston, Brandy, Monica, Joe, Kenneth "Babyface" Edmonds, Jennifer Lopez's number-one single "If You Had My Love," Tatyana Ali, Britney Spears, Will Smith, Toni Braxton, and Blackstreet, among many others. What's even more amazing is that Jerkins amassed this enviable resumé in just a few years.

Born the youngest son of a minister and choir director mother in a small town in New Jersey, Jerkins began taking classical music lessons on the piano as a small child and combining that with the gospel music he heard in church. As he grew, he added R&B and jazz to his repertoire. He worked obsessively on music, recording rap demos for local talent. By his teens, he wanted to become a record producer and began making demos, one of which caught the attention of Teddy Riley. His first professional writing and producing job came in 1994 for an artist named Casserine, and at 15, he wrote and produced his own gospel rap album, *On the Move*, with his brother Fred Jerkins III.

In 1997 Jerkins cowrote, arranged, and produced five songs for Mary J. Blige's four million-selling *Share My World* album, including the hit single "I Can Love You." He was named one of the hottest R&B producers in the country, and during 1999 he started his own label, Darkchild Records. The first two artists signed were So Plush and Rhona Bennet. —*Ed Hogan*

Jeru the Damaja (Kendrick Jeru Davis)

b. Brooklyn, NY
Lyricist, Producer / Hip-Hop, East Coast Rap, Hardcore Rap
Speaking out against what he saw as a decline in rap during the mid-'90s, Jeru the Damaja came to the fore as a self-proclaimed prophet and the savior of hip-hop, much as KRS-One had done almost ten years before. Jeru first appeared as a guest on Gang Starr's *Daily Operations* album, and his own deal with Payday/ffrr appeared soon after, resulting in 1994's *The Sun Rises in the East*. Though he made few friends in the rap world—given his outspoken criticism of such popular figures as the Fugees and Sean "Puffy" Combs—he proved a vital force in the emergence of the new rap consciousness of the late '90s.

Raised Kendrick Jeru Davis in Brooklyn, the Damaja began writing rhymes at the age of ten. At high school, he met Guru and DJ Premier of Gang Starr, and first guested on Gang Starr's "I'm the Man," from the 1992 album *Daily Operation*. Jeru toured with the group during 1993 and released his solo debut, *Come Clean*, for Gang Starr's Illkids label. The single became an underground sensation and led to his contract with Payday Records. He recorded *The Sun Rises in the East* with DJ Premier producing, and released the album in 1994. Though the album was well received, Jeru got some flak for the song "Da Bichez"—though he explicitly stated that most girls did not fit into the category. During 1994 he appeared on Digable Planets' second album (*Blowout Comb*) and recorded his follow-up, *Wrath of the Math*, with DJ Premier and Guru once again helping out with production. The independent record *Heroz4hire* followed in 1999, and his protégé, Afu-Ra, debuted in 2000 with *Body of the Life Force*. Jeru kept a surprisingly low profile thereafter, though he did appear on a stellar track from Groove Armada's *Goodbye Country (Hello Nightclub)*. —*John Bush*

★ **The Sun Rises in the East** / May 24, 1994 / Payday ◆◆◆◆◆
DJ Premier's first album-length production outside of Gang Starr was his best by far. Where Premier's productions hadn't shone underneath the cracking, overearnest vocals of Guru, with a superior stylist like Jeru these tracks became brilliant musical investigations with odd hooks (often detuned bells, keys, or vibes), perfectly scratched upchoruses, and the grittiest, funkiest Brooklynese beats pounding away in the background. Of course, the star of the show was Jeru, a cocksure young rapper who brought the dozens from the streets to a metaphysical battleground where he did battle with all manner of foe—the guy around the corner on "D. Original" or an allegorical parade of hip-hop evils on "You Can't Stop the Prophet." The commentary about inner-city plagues arising from spiritual ignorance only continued on "Ain't the Devil Happy," with Jeru preaching knowledge of self as the only rescue from greed and violence. Jeru also courted some controversy with "Da Bichez," at first explaining, "I'm not talkin' 'bout the queens…not the sisters …not the young ladies," but later admitting his thoughts ("most chicks want minks, diamonds, or Benz"). His flow and delivery were natural, his themes

were impressive, and he was able to make funky rhymes out of intellectual hyperbole like: "Written on these pages is the ageless wisdom of the sages/ Ignorance is contagious." It lacks a landmark track, but *The Sun Rises in the East* stands alongside Nas' *Illmatic* (released the same year, and also boasting the work of Premier) as one of the quintessential East Coast records. *—John Bush*

Wrath of the Math / Oct. 15, 1996 / Payday ♦♦♦♦♦
Jeru reunited with DJ Premier for this slightly sprawling second record, though fans must have been delirious with joy to find it was similar to—and usually just as strong as—his debut. Though it's clear Jeru isn't as hungry a rapper as he was two years earlier, he has just as much to say, and he's just as angry with the state of hip-hop and black life in general. Jeru goes into metaphysical drama once again with "One Day," wherein commercial rappers (including Puff Daddy and Foxy Brown) kidnap hip-hop, and continues his comic-book battles with the evils of rap amidst the backdrop of the Big Apple on "Revenge of the Prophet (Part 5)." Jeru also spends plenty of time directly addressing real-life issues, dissecting the crass, money-hungry hip-hop scene on "Scientifical Madness," running a sequel to "Da Bichez" called "Me or the Papes," and preaching more knowledge on "Ya Playin' Yaself." His version of the classic braggadocio track comes with "Not the Average" and "Whatever," where he uses knowledge as well as immense skills to foil anyone who's testing him. Though *Wrath of the Math* did sound similar to Jeru's debut, Premier was even more wide ranging for his backing tracks, ranging from the comparatively atmospheric ("Invasion") to a succession of momentary samples from out of nowhere ("Physical Stamina"). Unfortunately, it was their last time together; perhaps a bit jealous of Premier's sizable profile, Jeru began producing himself with his next record, *Heroz4hire*. *—John Bush*

Heroz4hire / Sep. 7, 1999 / Knowsavage ♦♦♦
Jeru the Damaja returned from a three-year absence with *Heroz4hire*, an independent album released on his own Knowsavage label, featuring both production and mixing by Jeru himself. His rapping style, as dense and inventive as ever, entails listening to the album at least three or four times to understand the tongue-twisting rhymes. From his last album, Jeru continues his interrogation of women with more than love on their mind on "Bitchez Wit Dikz," and contributes an apocalyptic production to the historical saga "Renegade Slave." Jeru is surprisingly good as a producer, weaving scratchy, repetitious samples around tough, lo-fi beats—similar to DJ Premier's work on the first two Jeru LPs. Though the hooks here aren't quite as catchy as Premier's, the incredibly raw production suits the independent status of *Heroz4hire*. Jeru also shares the mic and the credits on several tracks; female rapper Mizmarvel appears on "Verbal Battle" and "Anotha Victim." Highlights include the hilarious New York exposé "Seinfeld" and the paternity case "Blue Jean (Safe Sex)." *—John Bush*

Jigmastas

f. Brooklyn NY
Group / Hardcore Rap, Underground Rap
A Brooklyn-based act that took plenty of time to make an official album debut, hip-hop duo Jigmastas were nevertheless fairly well known by the time they released their first full-length outing early in 2001. That was partly due to the pair's much-hyped appearances in their native Big Apple, and owed even more to the production work of DJ Spinna, who was renowned throughout the '90s for his cut creating and remixing abilities, and had the hot client list (Mary J. Blige, Eminem, Mos Def, De La Soul, Les Nubians, and a host of others) to prove it. Spinna had been friends with MC Kriminul since the mid-'80s, and the two struck up an official partnership a decade later in between Spinna's outside jobs. Jigmastas debuted on wax with the single "Beyond Real" in 1996; besides becoming an underground hip-hop hit, it also provided the name for the duo's newly formed record label. However, it would still be half a decade before an album appeared, as the duo tried to appease their growing fan base with singles like "Last Will and Testimony" (released on the Tommy Boy Black Label) and the EP *Grass Roots: Lyrical Fluctuations* in 2000. Finally, the long-awaited *Infectious* saw the light of day in May of the following year, containing several textbook examples of Spinna's cut-and-paste wizardry, as well as cameos from ex-Living Colour guitarist Vernon Reid (on the police brutality-themed "Hollar") and Brand Nubian's Sadat X, who lent his voice to "Don't Get It Twisted." *—Dan LeRoy*

● **Infectious** / May 22, 2001 / Landspeed ♦♦♦
After marking time in the underground for a decade, Brooklyn hip-hop duo Jigmastas finally released their long-awaited debut album in 2001. And *Infectious* was worth the wait, primarily because of the platform it provides for DJ Spinna—one of the most creative producers in the game. A passionate advocate of finding and sampling rare beats and breaks, Spinna builds his intriguing soundscapes the old-fashioned way: around a snippet of drums or a snatch of vocal, out of which he coaxes hidden possibilities. "Don't Get It Twisted" is the best example here, getting over on little more than a tap-danced rhythm and a woman's disembodied voice, while the spacey "C.S.S." has a sped-up vocal sample as its disorienting hook. Of course, there are plenty of more conventional grooves, too, most notably on the bass-popping first single, "Till the Day." But Spinna's skills are so dominant that they often overshadow his partner, Kriminul, a solid MC who rises to the challenge occasionally (check the rapid-fire rhyming of "Vent") but also wastes time on run-of-the-mill beefs like the police brutality complaint "Hollar" (which also squanders a guitar cameo from Vernon Reid). Still, the music's so consistently captivating that *Infectious* more than lives up to its title. *—Dan LeRoy*

Bobby Jimmy & the Critters

f. Los Angeles, CA
Group / Old School Rap, Comedy Rap
Bobby Jimmy (born Russ Parr) formed the Los Angeles comedy rap group Bobby Jimmy & the Critters in the late '80s. One of the Critters was the Arabian Prince. His 1986 Macola album spent one week at the very bottom of the LP charts. *—Ron Wynn*

Roaches: In the Beginning / 1986 / Macola ♦♦♦
This album included the tasteless "We Like Ugly Women" and "Big Butt," which wasn't as humorous or clever as Jimmy Castor's "Bertha Butt." Other songs included "New York Rapper," a decent swipe at East Coast macho posturing, and "Bag Bobby Jimmy Jam," the one number that had the charm and outrageousness necessary for a good novelty tune. *—Ron Wynn*

Hip-Hop Prankster / Feb. 12, 1990 / Priority ♦♦
Described as "The Weird Al Yankovic of Rap," Bobby Jimmy is a cult figure specializing in parodies of rap and R&B hits. Jimmy (who was actually urban contemporary radio DJ Russ Parr) recorded for various small L.A. labels before signing with Priority in the late 1980s and recording the goofy *Hip-Hop Prankster*, his first album for the company. *Prankster's* first single was the insanely funny "Hair or Weave," a parody of Today's "Him or Me" making fun of women with hair weaves. N.W.A's "Gangsta Gangsta" becomes the clever "Prankster Prankster," while MC Hammer's "Let's Get It Started" is transformed into the silly "Somebody Farted." Highly entertaining, this CD was Jimmy's finest hour. *—Alex Henderson*

● **Bobby Jimmy, You a Fool (The Best of Bobby Jimmy & the Critters)** / Jul. 23, 1990 / K-Tel ♦♦♦♦♦

Erotic Psychotic / Jul. 11, 1991 / Priority ♦♦♦
Russ Parr was prominent on urban contemporary radio when he slipped into his Bobby Jimmy character once again and recorded the five-song EP *Erotic Psychotic*. Jimmy's wild sense of humor serves him well on everything from the title song (an account of being stalked by a "psychobabe") to "Rapper Rapper," which parodies Public Enemy, MC Hammer, Vanilla Ice, Snap, and other hip-hoppers who were popular in the early 1990s. "Minute Man Man" finds Jimmy portraying a man who suffers from premature ejaculation, while "Radio Radio" takes a humorous yet pointed jab at his industry and his bread and butter—commercial radio. Though novices would be better off starting out with *Hip-Hop Prankster*, Jimmy's cult following shouldn't overlook this release. *—Alex Henderson*

J.J. Fad

f. 1988, **db.** 1992
Group / Hip-Hop, Club/Dance, Pop-Rap, Electro
J.J. Fad (Just Jammin' Fresh and Def) made history in 1988 when they became the first female rap group to be nominated for a Grammy for their pop-rap hit "Supersonic." The L.A. trio—MC J.B. (Juana Burns), Baby D (Dania Birks), and Sassy C (Michelle Franklin)—were a stark contrast to their Ruthless labelmates and producers, N.W.A. Their 1988 debut, *Supersonic*, went platinum and stayed on the *Billboard* charts for over four months. A second

album, *Not Just a Fad*, was released in 1991, but didn't fare well on the charts or with rap fans; the group disbanded the following year. —*Wade Kergan*

Supersonic / 1988 / Ruthless ♦♦

A female pop-rap act that was the Kris Kross of its day. J.J. Fad's bubblegum raps tried at times to strike an air of street toughness, but were so light that no one took them seriously. They did land some chart hits, but were too firmly rooted in novelty charm and trendiness that they soon disappeared from the hip-hop spotlight. —*Ron Wynn*

● **Not Just a Fad** / 1991 / Ruthless ♦♦♦

In the late '80s, J.J. Fad was one of the pop-rap acts that hip-hop's hardcore loved to hate—the same hardcore rappers who complained about MC Hammer, Vanilla Ice, and L'Trimm were every bit as critical of J.J. Fad. But then, the female trio wasn't supposed to be a hardcore rap group; J.J. Fad made music for people who liked their rap laced with a lot of dance-pop and R&B. *Not Just a Fad* is a rather ironic title for the L.A. residents' second and final album; by the time this CD came out in 1990, the dance-pop and urban contemporary fans who bought 1988's *Supersonic: The Album* had seemingly lost interest in the threesome. J.J. Fad's 15 minutes of fame had passed, which doesn't mean that *Not Just a Fad* is terrible. Although uneven and inconsistent, this sophomore effort (which the Arabian Prince produced with N.W.A's DJ Yella) has its moments. The Angelinos are at their best when they find the right dance groove—"It's Da Fad" and "We in the House," just to give two examples, aren't remarkable but are catchy rap/house numbers. However, J.J. Fad doesn't fare as well when, on occasion, the trio tries to be more hardcore. "We Want It All" finds the pop-rappers delivering some tough—or rather, pseudo-tough—street talk and lambasting rival Roxanne Shanté. Not surprisingly, the results are clumsy and awkward; J.J. Fad's members were simply too girlish sounding to be convincing as hardcore street rappers. So it's just as well that 90 percent of this release is devoted to bubblegum pop-rap. Although *Supersonic* remains the group's most famous and noteworthy album, *Not Just a Fad* isn't without its pleasures—as long as you apply dance-pop or urban contemporary standards and aren't expecting an album of pure, undiluted hip-hop. —*Alex Henderson*

Joeski Love

Producer / Urban, Hip-Hop

Best known for his platinum-selling 1986 single "Pee Wee's Dance," whose trademark hook has been sampled numerous times, Joeski Love was originally part of a rap group that was signed by Vince Davis to his Elektra-backed Vintertainment label. After the group disbanded, Love stayed on with Davis, who produced "Pee Wee's Dance" as well as another single, "Say Joe." A chance meeting with producer Hank Shocklee caused Love to team up with Salt-N-Pepa producer Hurby "Luv Bug" Azor, who aided Love with his 1991 debut effort for Columbia Records, *Joe Cool*. —*Steve Kurutz*

● **Joe Cool** / 1991 / Columbia ♦♦♦

The Jonzun Crew

f. 1981, Boston, MA

Group / Urban, Electro

The Jonzun Crew was an electro group who carried their spin on Parliament/Funkadelic's loopy sci-fi themes throughout the '80s and early '90s for a handful of albums, which included singles like "Pack Jam (Look Out for the OVC)," "Space Is the Place," "Space Cowboy," and "We Are the Jonzun Crew." Florida-born brothers Michael, Soni, and Larry Johnson (better known as Maurice Starr) formed Jonzun Crew in Boston in 1981, with Gordy Worthy and Steve Thorpe filling out the lineup for different stretches of the group's existence. Starr and Michael would gain further notoriety for helping to bring New Edition and New Kids on the Block to the world; Michael (who continued using Jonzun as his last name) also went solo for a brief period on A&M, in addition to working on several other artists' releases. —*Andy Kellman*

We Are the Jonzun Crew [Single] / 1983 / Tommy Boy ♦♦♦

Straight out of Boston, the Jonzun Crew shot themselves out into the furthest reaches of the electro universe. Funny, irrelevant sci-fi-influenced lyrics compounded with brilliant production, their trademarks, are all in evidence here. This group manifesto, "We Are the Jonzun Crew," is replete with vocoder vocals and sweet low-end production. In keeping with their Beethoven-derived stage personae, the track features classically influenced multi-instrument layers that build to a freak-out crescendo. A funky instrumental version fills out the B side. —*Brian Whitener*

● **Lost in Space** / Nov. 1983 / Tommy Boy ♦♦♦

Despite including most of Jonzun Crew's best tracks, their debut album, *Lost in Space*, wasn't a successful LP. The Boston group with roots in funk were lousy songwriters at this point (more was to come from Maurice Starr), and what's worse, they insisted on writing songs instead of sticking with solid electro party jams like their singles classics "Pack Jam" and "Space Is the Place." Admittedly, the process did pay minor commercial dividends; "Space Cowboy" became a moderate R&B hit, though its electric interpolation of the trademark whistle from "The Good, the Bad & the Ugly" was hardly the stuff of legend. They sounded appropriately cool on the opener "We Are the Jonzun Crew," but the rest of the nonsingles material was stiff and formulaic. Far better to find Jonzun Crew's two landmarks on an old school/electro compilation. A 2001 reissue on Tommy Boy enticed consumers with two bonus tracks, one of which was Grooverider's drum'n'bass update of "Pack Jam (Look out for the OVC)." —*John Bush*

Cosmic Love / 1990 / Critique ♦♦

The Jonzun Crew's long-awaited fourth album, *Cosmic Love*, was released on the BMG-distributed Critique label in 1990. Michael Jonzun had—and still has—vast archives of songs recorded during this period. Like so many, the very excellent "Baby I Surrender" is not on this collection, but that doesn't stop *Cosmic Love* from being an important and highly listenable part of the Jonzun Brothers' history. A band that should have released at least a dozen discs by this point in time, Mission Control Studios owner Michael Jonzun crafted his album over many years, and the precision and care he put into *Cosmic Love* is obvious from start to finish. The controlled insanity of the band's earlier success is absent, replaced by smooth soul, studied R&B, and no-nonsense funk-rock. The title track shimmers with the vibrations found on the best records by the Commodores, while "Write Me Off" sounds like a direction Stevie Wonder could have chosen. Why the New Kids on the Block weren't brought in to promote this music in TV ads is perplexing—NKOTB were huge at the time and core fans of Jonzun Crew couldn't wait for their next release. There are ten songs here bookended by a prologue and epilogue, perfectly produced epics culminating in the superb "Wall of Fame." The general public had no idea that this was the coproducer of two hugely popular groups, along with hit recordings by Peter Wolf, and this album drifted into obscurity as one of the best-kept secrets in Boston rock & roll. La Vern Baker producer Barry Marshall shows up on guitar, as does Phil Greene from the '70s band Swallow—there are lots of Boston "underground" names on the disc, yet the band was never embraced by the Boston "critics" and few understood the depth of Jonzun's artistry. "Living in This World" is a nice ballad, while "Playhouse" is powerful dance-funk. The telling moment on the disc, though, the potential hit that never got the attention that it deserved is, as mentioned, the final song, "Wall of Fame." This one tune contains all the finest elements of the Jonzun Crew's best work, and that it didn't take the charts by storm is a sin. "Ordinary Man," "I Do Love You," "Spotlight," "This Time (Let's Talk It Over)" could all hit for artists smart enough to seek this material out, but it is at its best when performed by Michael Jonzun. Though *Cosmic Love* may have a few too many love songs and ballads for fans of the group's earlier hits, "Space Cowboy" and "Pac Jam," it still is an impressive artistic statement, and a beautiful work that deserves a better place in music history. —*Joe Viglione*

Down to Earth / Jul. 1, 1991 / Tommy Boy ♦♦♦♦

Down to Earth by the Jonzun Crew was originally released on the Tommy Boy label, re-released by A&M, and is now back on Tommy Boy. All confusion aside, this funk/rock/techno album by Michael Jonzun, his former wife Princess Loria, and brothers Soni Jonzun and Maurice Starr is a highly listenable important cornerstone of Boston area music history. "Tonight's the Night" is as melodic as Falco's "Rock Me Amadeus," and as commercial, but Jonzun's work came at least two years prior to Falco. The JC cover the spectrum; "We're Going All the Way" is reshuffled Motown—the Temptations about to turn into New Kids on the Block. Just a few years after the release of this disc, Starr and Jonzun would unleash NKOTB, the production evolution of their prior discovery, New Edition, with different faces. Here is the sound that was the formula for success. Although Michael Jonzun plays it tongue in cheek, this is serious R&B/pop. It's a shame that they did not have the opportunity that a Motown or even A&M afforded other acts. Jonzun is every bit as prolific as Prince, and a phenomenal stage performer. "You Got the Lovin'" is crossover pop with jangly guitar and keyboards that crackle. But the vocal work by the Jonzun Crew is truly what set the table for NKOTB, and that vocal work makes the songs come to life. Where Private Lightning on A&M a few years earlier suffered from a less-than-adequate production of a great band—and could have benefited from Michael Jonzun's skills (just look what he did for Peter Wolf), all the elements for a smash are here. Both record labels involved in *Down to Earth* had a real masterpiece on their hands, an album that works as a cohesive piece of art, but touches upon many genres. Three tracks, "Redd Hott Mama," "Lovin'," and "Skool Daze" were not on the original Tommy Boy release. "Lovin'" is exquisite R&B: an incessant bed of keys and percussion, with Jonzun's perfect voice gliding over it all. Catchy and smooth. "Mechanism" takes the band into the Kraftwerk world of industrial/dance/techno. For those who wondered why such talented guys would generate the bubblegum that Bobby Brown and the New Edition spawned, all one has to do is look at a record industry that failed to give this essential group the flexibility it deserved, and earned. Billy Loosigian of Atlantic's the Joneses and MCA's Willie Alexander & the Boom Boom Band adds guitar to "Lovin'," "You Got the Lovin'," "We're Going All the Way," and the rocking "Tonight." "Mechanism" should be blasting on classic hits radio to bring that format some much-needed flavor. This record is just waiting for a new audience to discover it. —*Joe Viglione*

Montell Jordan

b. Los Angeles, CA
Vocals, Producer / Urban, Contemporary R&B, Pop-Rap
Montell Jordan began singing in his hometown of Los Angeles in talent shows, church choirs, and, later, nightclubs. After graduating from Pepperdine University, he spent seven years looking for a record deal, finally getting an opportunity through Paul Stewart, the president of PMP Records. Jordan and Stewart flew to New York, where Jordan sang for Russell Simmons and was promptly signed to a contract. For his first album, Jordan heavily sampled B.B. King tracks (the first to do so), and took his lyrical inspiration from the more positive side of life in his native South Central L.A. in an attempt to balance the negative pictures coming out of most SoCal gangsta rap. Jordan was rewarded with a massive number-one smash in the party anthem "This Is How We Do It," which sold over one million copies; *More . . .* followed in 1996. Although it didn't match the success of *This Is How We Do It*, it was nevertheless a hit. In the spring of 1998, Jordan released his third album, *Let's Ride*; *Get It on . . . Tonite* followed a year later. —*Steve Huey*

● **This Is How We Do It** / Apr. 4, 1995 / PMP/RAL ✦✦✦✦
Montell Jordan was blessed with a strong set of producers for his debut album, *This Is How We Do It*. Working with material that is essentially subpar, the production team turns in a seamless performances, creating hooks and melodies from the deep bass and beats. Jordan's skills as a rapper are fine— he does nothing particularly noteworthy, yet he certainly does not ruin the tracks. It was just the sort of competent R&B that hits the chart, and it did hit the charts, becoming a number-one R&B album. —*Stephen Thomas Erlewine*

More . . . / Aug. 27, 1996 / Def Jam ✦✦✦
Montell Jordan's second album *More . . .* unfortunately doesn't quite live up to the promise of its title, despite a handful of excellent tracks. Jordan hasn't backed away from the hip-hop soul that brought *This Is How We Do It* to the top of the charts, and he delivers it as well as he did his first time around, but he just doesn't have as many strong songs as he did the last time out. "Falling" is an entrancing ballad and "Bounce Ta This" is a good up-tempo cut, yet they aren't enough to maintain interest over the course of the entire album. —*Leo Stanley*

Let's Ride / Mar. 31, 1998 / Def Jam ✦✦✦
When a debut single is as strong as Montell Jordan's "This Is How We Do It," it's hard to ever match or exceed the single's reputation—or at least, the perception that the single was the peak of the artist's career. As his third album, *Let's Ride*, proves, he has more to offer than just "This Is How We Do It," but it's still hard to shake that song from your head while listening to the album. The main problem is that, despite his sultry voice, Jordan has yet to establish a clear identity for himself and his material tends to have even less character. There are moments on *Let's Ride* that are quite enjoyable—after all, Jordan has a knack for classy, seductive contemporary grooves—but it never adds up to much of anything. Few of the songs make a lasting impression outside the title track, and the album essentially follows the same formula as his first two records, but with diminishing returns.

There are enough good grooves to make it interesting to fans, but *Let's Ride* suggests that Jordan will have to learn a few new tricks soon if he wants to keep cruising. —*Leo Stanley*

Get It On . . . Tonite / Oct. 26, 1999 / Def Jam ✦✦✦
Montell Jordan's fourth album *Get It On . . . Tonite* is a mixed bag of intelligently written songs and overbearing clichés. Jordan established himself in the mid-1990s as a surprisingly consistent R&B star with several successful albums, each featuring at least one major hit single. He also established himself as a top-notch songwriter, especially after penning Deborah Cox's unforgettable monster smash "Nobody's Supposed to Be Here." Those reasons make it all the more frustrating when, on his fourth album, Jordan relies so heavily on R&B loverman clichés, with tired "between the sheets" lyrics such as "your body layin' next to mine," "scream and moan," and "kisses down below" permeating way too much of his music ("Can't Get Enough" is beyond tacky). The album, which is divided into two halves (the first being "for those who like it fast," the second being "for those who need it slow,") does include several great tracks, including the irresistible leadoff single "Get It On . . . Tonite" (the single version featured LL Cool J, while the album version is just Jordan), the wonderful story song "Once Upon a Time" (which is also included as a surprisingly well-pronounced Spanish-language bonus track), the fun and hyphy disco party jam "Come Home," and the Latin/Asian-influenced "Maybe She Will." Jordan also employs plenty of female vocalists (á la Luther Vandross) to incredibly pleasing results, and there's no denying his talent in crafting a catchy pop song. If Jordan would lay off the clichés, and concentrate on well-written songs like "Once Upon a Time" then the sky is the limit, but his overbearing reliance on tired lothario lyrics is frustrating for those listeners who are well aware of his potential. As a final note, Jordan includes an adequate cover of Phil Collins' 1984 hit "Against All Odds." —*Jose F. Promis*

Montell Jordan / Feb. 26, 2002 / Def Soul ✦✦✦✦
Throughout the seven years following Montell Jordan's gigantic breakthrough with "This Is How We Do It" in 1995, the sultry vocalist never had a problem garnering commercial success. Every one of his first four albums had at least one hit song. However, despite the commercial success, Jordan did have somewhat of a problem garnering respect, never being able to escape the towering shadow of "This Is How We Do It." No matter how successful successive singles such as "Let's Ride" or "Get It On . . . Tonite" were, they never equaled the success of his debut single. Plus, it didn't help that most of Jordan's first four albums were weighed down by too much commercial schlock—the sort of by-the-numbers urban ballads streamlined for optimal radio play—not to mention all the filler. For his fifth album, a self-titled effort, Jordan finally made an album for himself rather than for his fans, an issue he addresses in the liner notes: "This is the 1st MONTELL JORDAN album. I have made party albums, street albums, Jeep albums, strip-club anthems, bedroom albums, and a bunch of other things that I thought YOU wanted to hear. This time, there was no one to look at but ME . . . sure, there is some 'ear candy' on this album, but a TRUE listener will come away from this album able to say that they finally know who Montell Jordan is, where he is at, and will hopefully appreciate and understand what I bring to the game." And, yes, this is a more introspective and sincere album than Jordan's past few efforts, justifying its eponymous title and worthy of the respect the vocalist hasn't been able to earn throughout his career. There aren't any big-name collaborations, and Jordan thankfully doesn't delve into pop-rap like he did on past albums in an effort to score crossover success. In a way, this was his least-commercial effort at the time of its release. Jordan works almost exclusively with producers Steven Estiverne and Focus, and gets very deep toward the conclusion of the album, not ashamed to express his spirituality. Yet as personal and uncompromising as this album is, it's still very accessible, particularly the radio-ready moments like "You're the Right One," "You Must Have Been," and "Mine Mine Mine." —*Jason Birchmeier*

Journalist (Rafiek George)

b. Philadelphia, PA
Hardcore Rap, East Coast Rap
Philadelphia rapper Journalist, whose real name is Rafiek George, gives much of the credit for his success to his mother, who supported her five sons and provided a strong example of what it means to be determined and to work hard. By his middle-school years, his dreams were sharply divided between careers in music or the NBA. In 1995, with his high school diploma

in hand, he made his choice and set out to snag a recording contract. Until opportunity came knocking, he supported himself with jobs as a public speaker and youth counselor. While employed by Children's Hospital in Philadelphia, he took part in a number of talent shows. Two years after graduating from high school, the rapper earned his first paycheck from performing when he triumphed in a talent search held at New Jersey's Stardust Ballroom. By 1999, with Julius Erving Jr. as his manager, Journalist auditioned for Charles Suitt, a vice president of Universal Records. Soon he was a member of the company's stable that also included young artists like Nelly and Juvenile. Unfortunately, his career did not take off as expected and the rapper moved to Motown. *Scribes of Life*, his debut Motown release, featured Journalist's version of the Patti LaBelle hit "On My Own." —*Linda Seida*

- **Scribes of Life** / May 7, 2002 / Motown ◆◆
A rangy young rapper from Philadelphia, Journalist did well with a first single ("Extended Family"), and dropped his debut album in 2002. As you'd guess from his *nom de plume*, *Scribes of Life* marks the genesis of an intelligent rapper; influenced by Rakim, Kool G Rap, and Nas, Journalist finds the hard truths about urban living and often works them into his rhymes, as on "Getting the Games Confused" and "Throwing It All Away." The single "Extended Family" is the highlight, with the M.O.P. duo trading rhymes over tough beats. Still, while it's clear he's using his imagination, Journalist's rapping isn't strong enough to carry an album mostly by himself, and his lyrics don't impress any more than any other 50 rappers already recording. —*John Bush*

JT the Bigga Figga

West Coast Rap, Underground Rap
San Francisco-based rapper JT the Bigga Figga became the subject of considerable underground buzz thanks to the success of his self-released 1993 LP *Playaz n' the Game*; a major-label bidding war ensued, and he ultimately signed with Priority to issue 1995's *Dwellin' in the Labb. Don't Stop Til We Major* followed a year later, and in 1997 JT returned with *Game Tight. Game for Sale* was issued in early 2001. —*Jason Ankeny*

Kick the Funk / 1991 / East West ◆◆
One MC who showed some promise in the early '90s was JT, whose *Kick the Funk* isn't extraordinary, but indicated that he had a lot of potential. Despite the R&B and dance music appeal some of the songs have, JT is essentially a hardcore rapper. The rapper is at his best on sociopolitical material. "Streets O Hardcore," "Priority," and "One Nation" are especially strong, while many of the boasting songs are average and not overly memorable. Unfortunately, JT remained obscure and never had a chance to develop. —*Alex Henderson*

Playaz n' the Game / 1994 / Get Low ◆◆◆
Bay Area trailblazer JT the Bigga Figga entered the independent label business early on, launching both Get Low Records and his prolific solo career in 1994. *Playaz n' the Game*, the debut for both Get Low and JT, certainly made its mark, as the rapper considerably differed from his many other West Coast colleagues at the time. Unlike the masses of gangstas down in Los Angeles, JT came hard, yet he emphasized creativity as much as delivery, associating himself with the burgeoning West Coast alternative rap scene of the time as much as with N.W.A. This album is his blueprint, and though its quality leaves room for improvement, its impact is just as important to consider, if not more so. San Quinn also makes his debut here. —*Jason Birchmeier*

Dwellin' in the Labb / Oct. 10, 1995 / Priority ◆◆◆
Dwellin' in the Labb makes JT the Bigga Figga's previous album, *Playaz n' the Game*, sound like a demo tape. Not only do the San Francisco rapper's rhymes improve but this album also finds better songwriting and better backing music. Sure, JT still may not be on the level of the best West Coast rappers—Ice Cube, Too Short, Eazy-E, and Latyrx—but he does manage to handle his words with flowing ease. Guest appearances by the GLP bring variety to the album and are almost on par with JT's rhymes. This album's better songwriting also makes it a more listenable record, integrating some catchy choruses for listeners to cling to. Finally, the production also moves forward on *Dwellin' in the Labb* with some bouncy beats, more than enough G-funk synths, and a dark aura. By the end of the album, one cannot stress how much JT and his crew have improved with just one album. —*Jason Birchmeier*

Don't Stop Til We Major / Sep. 9, 1996 / Priority ◆◆◆

Game Tight / Oct. 28, 1997 / Get Low ◆◆◆
On *Game Tight*, JT the Bigga Figga continues to polish his rhymes with quicker flow and more to say but still struggles to craft a solid album. Anyone already owning his *Dwellin' in the Labb* album will be frustrated to find that quite a few songs from that album reappear on this album along with some songs from the *Playaz n' the Game*. This mix of old and new presents some major consistency problems, mostly because JT has changed his style considerably since these early albums. For the first time, he shows a melodic R&B flavor on the new songs, integrating background soul vocalists and a smoother style of production. The appearance of Snoop Dogg on "Game Tight" and "Father Figga" also presents some problems. Snoop can lay down some tight rhymes, but his style doesn't exactly fit in with that of the other rappers on this album, especially on "Father Figga," a song he practically handles by himself with little assistance. It's sad to see that just as JT begins to master his rhymes and hook up with premium guest stars such as Snoop, he moves toward R&B and thinks that it will work on an album filled with many of his older songs with a strong gangsta flavor. —*Jason Birchmeier*

- **Operation Takeover** / Jun. 27, 2000 / Get Low ◆◆◆
Just one of the JT the Bigga Figga albums that flooded the market in 2000— thanks to several re-releases—*Operation Takeover* features a mild gangsta tone to a further degree than any previous albums by the California rapper. On this album, JT doesn't get lonely, being accompanied by a broad roster of fellow underground West Coast rappers. The many voices actually strengthens the album, making it more of a collaborative effort as if it were a GLP album. Unfortunately, it doesn't do much for JT's canon of work, which now seems even more confusing to navigate. So while this is a mild gangsta album with strong charisma and little cliché, one cannot attribute much of it to JT. Still, a good album is a good album; just don't expect this to be much like his previous albums. —*Jason Birchmeier*

Puttin' It on the Map / Jun. 27, 2000 / Get Low ◆◆◆
Just as JT the Bigga Figga began to build a name for himself after years of catering to a mostly cult audience of West Coast underground rap lovers, he took the time to put together *Puttin' It on the Map*, an album of old material polished up for his growing legion of fans. While this is far from his best album, it is a fairly fascinating listen, especially when one considers the fact that JT was only a teen when he busted these rhymes. On the song "History Class," he explains the story behind the album and introduces "Dank or Dope," the song that first established him as a respectable rapper. Even as a teen, JT's rhymes flow lucidly and quickly though often suffering from a lack of intriguing content. Still, one cannot deny this San Francisco area rapper's talent with a mic; unfortunately, though, he doesn't get the tight beats he deserves on most of these cuts, which often consist of little more than a bass synth and some looped percussion with the occasional Dr. Dre-like synth tones. Nothing here should win new fans for JT. The album works for what it is, a rarities collection, and should interest anyone who has followed the rapper throughout his prolific career. —*Jason Birchmeier*

Juggaknots

Group / Underground Rap, East Coast Rap
Juggaknots first gained underground renown for their appearances on Columbia University's The Stretch Armstrong & Bobbito radio program. When a record deal with Elektra went south, Bobbito Garcia issued the vinyl-only *Clear Blue Skies* on his Fondle 'Em label in 1996. Like almost all of the releases on the label, the record was out of print before most people got a chance to hear what all the fuss was about. Born and raised in the Bronx, brothers Buddy Slim—who also acts as group producer under the name Fever the Kid—and Breezly Brewin kept busy with outside projects. A Juggaknots collaboration with Company Flow and J-Treds appeared in 1998 under the name Indelable MC's and was featured on the *Lyricist Lounge* comp. The following year, Breezly worked with Prince Paul on his *Prince Among Thieves* album. *Clear Blue Skies* was reissued on CD in 2003 and the group added a third member, Queen Heroine. —*Wade Kergan*

Clear Blue Skies / 1996 / Fondle 'Em ◆◆◆
Juggaknots released their debut album on the ultra-independent, New York City label Fondle 'Em in 1996. Pressed only on vinyl and now difficult to find, the album is a mishmash of styles and themes. On the stunning title track, "Clear Blue Skies," the duo of Breeze and Buddy Slim detail the wrenching conversation between white father and son as they argue over the son's black

girlfriend. Juggaknots adopt a more apocalyptic tone on the churning "Loosifa." Unfortunately, most of the other tracks are a mess of noisy threats and boasts. Like a lot of underground hip-hop releases, the album suffers from low production values and has a muddy, dull sound. —*Christopher Witt*

Juicy J (Jordan Houston)

b. Memphis, TN

Producer, Engineer, Vocals / Hardcore Rap, Southern Rap

Together with production partner DJ Paul, Juicy J played an important role in the South's rise to prominence within the once East and West Coast-dominated rap industry. Behind the duo's leadership, Three 6 Mafia rose from an underground phenomenon in Memphis to a nationally recognized rap empire, spinning off numerous solo albums for the collective's many members in the mid- to late '90s. Like his production partner, Juicy J specialized in dark, eerie tracks driven by bass-heavy beats and haunting sounds. He also raps as a member of Three 6 Mafia and contributes rhymes to most of the albums he produces for such artists as his brother Project Pat, Gangsta Boo, La Chat, and Tear da Club Up Thugs. Moreover, Juicy J ventured into filmmaking with *Choices* (2001), a straight-to-video film starring most of the Three 6 Mafia collective.

Juicy J (born Jordan Houston) and DJ Paul (Paul Beauregard) first came together at the dawn of the '90s, when they worked as DJs in the Memphis area. The two soon began producing their own tracks and invited numerous Memphis rappers to rap over the beats. They released the resulting tracks locally as Triple 6 Mafia; years later these recordings would resurface as re-releases. In 1995 the loose collective changed its name to Three 6 Mafia and self-released its debut album, *Mystic Stylez*. The album became an underground success, and Three 6 Mafia, in turn, signed a distribution deal with Relativity for its Hypnotized Minds imprint. Throughout the late '90s, Juicy J and DJ Paul produced numerous albums a year for Hypnotized Minds and capitalized on the lucrative distribution deal. By the end of the decade, the two producers were at the helm of an empire, having extended their brand to alarming lengths, culminating with their commercial breakthrough album, *When the Smoke Clears* (2000), which debuted at number six on *Billboard*'s album chart. —*Jason Birchmeier*

Chronicles of the Juice Man: Underground Album / Jul. 2, 2002 / North-North Records ◆◆◆

During a break in Three 6 Mafia's usually busy recording schedule, group co-leader/rapper/producer Juicy J put together *Chronicles of the Juice Man*, which he bills as an underground release because of its anticommercial slant. Because the album isn't intended for mass consumption, it tends to be a little more authentic than one of Three 6's normal nationally released albums, and there's some great sampling here that would have had to have been cleared had this been a commercial release. Juicy spends a lot of mic time here venting about the recent incarceration of his brother, fellow Three 6 associate Project Pat. The particularly personal rhymes on *Chronicles of the Juice Man* should interest longtime Three 6 fans who want to learn what's on the mind of the group's co-mastermind, and it should similarly interest fans who favor the group's underground releases rather than their more commercial ones. —*Jason Birchmeier*

Jungle Brothers

f. 1986, New York, NY

Group / Golden Age, Political Rap, Alternative Rap, Jazz-Rap, Hip-Hop

Although they predated the jazz-rap innovations of De La Soul, A Tribe Called Quest, and Digable Planets, the Jungle Brothers were never able to score with either rap fans or mainstream audiences, perhaps due to their embrace of a range of styles—including house music, Afro-centric philosophy, a James Brown fixation, and of course the use of jazz samples—each of which has been the sole basis for the start-up of a rap act. Signed to a major label for 1989's *Done By the Forces of Nature*, JB failed to connect on that album—hailed by some as an ignored classic—or the follow-up, *J. Beez Wit the Remedy*.

Mike Gee (born Michael Small; Harlem, NY), DJ Sammy B (born Sammy Burwell; Harlem, NY), and Baby Bam (born Nathaniel Hall; Brooklyn, NY) came together as the Jungle Brothers in the mid-'80s and began their recording career at the dance label Idler. The result of the sessions, *Straight Out the Jungle*, was released in early 1988. The album's Afro-centric slant gained the

Jungle Brothers entry into the Native Tongue Posse, a loose collective formed by hip-hop legend Afrikaa Bambaataa, including Queen Latifah (and, later, De La Soul and A Tribe Called Quest). The album's most far-out cut was "I'll House You," a collaboration with house producer Todd Terry and an early experiment in what later became known as hip-house.

Though *Straight Out the Jungle* had not sold in large quantities, Warner Bros. signed the trio in 1989 and released a second album, *Done By the Forces of Nature*, that same year. Though it was issued around the time of De La Soul's groundbreaking *3 Feet High and Rising* LP and gained just as many positive reviews, the album was overlooked by most listeners. The Jungle Brothers' chances of mainstream acceptance weren't helped at all by a four-year absence after the release of *Done By the Forces of Nature*, inspired mostly by Warner Bros.' marketing strategies. Finally, in the summer of 1993, *J. Beez Wit the Remedy* appeared, complete with a sizeable push from Warner Bros.; unfortunately, the large amount of promotion failed to carry the album. Obviously not learning from their earlier mistakes, Warner Bros. also delayed the release of the group's fourth album, *Raw Deluxe*, until mid-1997. *V.I.P.* followed in early 2000, and *All That We Do* was released in 2002. —*John Bush*

★ **Straight Out the Jungle** / 1988 / Warlock ◆◆◆◆◆

The landmark opening salvo from the Jungle Brothers, *Straight Out the Jungle* was also the very first album from the Native Tongues posse, which would utterly transform hip-hop over the next few years. That alone would be enough to make it a groundbreaking release, but *Straight Out the Jungle* also contains the musical seeds for a number of soon-to-be-dominant trends. Their taste for jazzy horn samples helped kick-start the entire jazz-rap movement, and their concurrent James Brown fixation was one of the first to follow Eric B. & Rakim's lead. Plus, the group's groundbreaking collaboration with legendary house producer Todd Terry, "I'll House You," is also here; it paved the way for numerous hip-house hybrids that shot up the dance and pop charts over the next few years. The lyrics were often as cerebral as the music was adventurous and eclectic, appealing to the mind rather than the gut—and the fact that rap didn't necessarily have to sound as though it were straight off the streets was fairly revelatory at the time. "Black Is Black" and the title cut are some of the first flowerings of Afro-centric hip-hop, but the group isn't always so serious; "I'm Gonna Do You," "Behind the Bush," and the sly classic "Jimbrowski" are all playfully sexy without descending into misogyny. To modern ears, *Straight Out the Jungle* will likely sound somewhat dated—the raw, basement-level production is pretty rudimentary even compared to their second album, and makes the jazz-rap innovations a bit difficult to fully comprehend, plus, the album ends on several throwaways. But it is possible to hear the roots of hip-hop's intellectual wing, not to mention a sense of fun and positivity that hearkened back to the music's earliest Sugarhill days—and that's why *Straight Out the Jungle* ultimately holds up. —*Steve Huey*

Done By the Forces of Nature / Nov. 1989 / Warner Brothers ◆◆◆◆◆

The follow-up to their groundbreaking debut, *Done By the Forces of Nature* is the point where the Jungle Brothers' production catches up to their musical ambition. There's still a ruddy, lo-fi edge to the record, but the samples are more abundant and intricately woven, and there's an altogether fuller sound that gives the group a greater presence. Moreover, the group's nonmusical ideas come into greater focus as well. The Native Tongues' Afro-centric philosophy gets a more extensive airing here than on the debut, filling the record with positive consciousness raising, both cultural ("Acknowledge Your Own History," "Black Woman," "Beyond This World") and spiritual (the title cut, "In Dayz 2 Come"); there are even the occasional lyrical asides concerning good dietary habits. All of this makes *Done By the Forces of Nature* one of the most intellectual hip-hop albums released up to that point, but as before, the group tempered their cerebral bent with a healthy sense of humor and fun. Thanks to the improved production, the J. Beez are able to take it to the dancefloor better than ever before, and toss in some pure, good-time, booty-shaking grooves in the hits "What U Waitin' For" and "U Make Me Sweat." There's also "Belly Dancin' Dina," a narrative that echoes the playful come-ons of the debut, and proves that progressive thinking and respect for women don't necessarily have to cool the libido. Late in the album, the posse cut "Doin' Our Own Dang" offers the chance to hear most of the Native Tongues—Tribe, De La, and Latifah—dropping rhymes all in one place. Through it all, the J. Beez construct an eclectic musical backdrop borrowed from jazz, early R&B, funk, African music, and more. Even if *Straight Out the*

Jungle was the historical landmark, *Done By the Forces of Nature* feels more realized in many respects, and is arguably the more satisfying listen. —*Steve Huey*

J. Beez Wit the Remedy / Jun. 22, 1993 / Warner Brothers ✦✦✦
Willfully difficult, ceaselessly sarcastic and playful, Jungle Brothers had more talent than virtually all of their contemporaries in alternative rap, but often squandered it taking detours that did little to endear them to hip-hop fans. Four long years after their Native Tongues family had emerged with the success of De La Soul's *3 Feet High and Rising*, Jungle Brothers finally returned with their third record. Expectations were very high, from fans and their label (Warner Bros.), but if JB didn't exactly bring the remedy with this one, they still featured an obtuse playfulness sorely lacking in hip-hop. Mike Gee and Baby Bam didn't have as much to say as A Tribe Called Quest or even De La Soul; most of the songs here are loved-up sex raps or weed fantasies, and the group deliberately blurs the lines between the two, getting dangerously close to objectifying a woman on "Spark a New Flame," but speaking lovingly of marijuana on "I'm in Love With Indica." The chorus on the hilariously titled satire "My Jimmy Weighs a Ton" (a clear Public Enemy reference) skates back and forth between a sweet diva and a hardcore jam. The productions, virtually all of them by Jungle Brothers alone, are freewheeling and unpredictable, but vary in quality from intriguing to downright misguided. —*John Bush*

Raw Deluxe / Jun. 3, 1997 / Gee Street ✦✦✦
The Jungle Brothers' career was plagued with delays and setbacks, which resulted in each of their albums being released several years after they were officially due. Their fourth effort, *Raw Deluxe*, is no different. The Jungle Brothers remain one of hip-hop's most inventive crews, crafting remarkably sophisticated, jazzy beats and rhyming with skill and intelligence, but they sound more as if they were aligned with late-'80s trends, not the styles of the late '90s. This isn't a bad thing, since they are musically and lyrically gifted, but it also makes *Raw Deluxe* sound more like an artifact than a blazing comeback. —*Stephen Thomas Erlewine*

V.I.P. / Jan. 4, 2000 / V2 ✦✦✦✦
By the time the Jungle Brothers signed with Gee Street, there was a full decade between them and the days of artistic freedom and respect from critics and discerning hip-hop fans. Seeking a creative rebirth, they hooked up with British producer Alex Gifford of big beat dance group the Propellerheads—who'd actually sought out the J. Beez first to appear on their own album. The Jungle Brothers had embraced contemporary dance music right from the start, and their groundbreaking collaboration with Todd Terry, "I'll House You," gave them a lasting credibility in dance circles. The result of the team-up, *V.I.P.*, pretty much gives up on appealing to the masses or the purists, instead setting their sights on dance-music fans who enjoy hip-hop as well. And if you aren't expecting a return to the sounds and attitudes of the J.Beez's glory years, *V.I.P.* is fun, funky, and infectious—a party record where everyone sounds like they're having a blast. They try a little of everything, making for a pretty eclectic mix: the slamming big beat title track, a straight-up house groove on "Get Down," the blues pastiche of "Playing for Keeps," gonzo experiments in "Party Goin' On" and "JBeez Rock the Dancehall," and some cheerfully over-the-top loverman schtick on "Sexy Body" and "Freakin' You." Plus, there are a few reminiscences of hip-hop back in the day and hints of techno and drum'n'bass sprinkled throughout. Truth be told, the Jungle Brothers were never the most virtuosic MCs in the Native Tongues, and their rhymes can sound a little simplistic here—not just because it's 2000, but they also tend to lay back when Gifford's grooves take over the show. Plus, a few cuts are a little too long, making *V.I.P.* a qualified success. But even so, it's still pretty difficult to resist. —*Steve Huey*

All That We Do / Oct. 29, 2002 / Jungle Brothers ✦✦✦
Fifteen years after they formed, barnstorming hip-hop mainstays Jungle Brothers kept struggling for a degree of respect and recognition, releasing their third straight album for a different label (this one is basically self-released). For a producer, the duo made an odd choice: veteran house legend Todd Terry, who had rarely worked in hip-hop before but boasted a long pedigree in New York's club scene (he'd also produced the Jungle Brothers' club crossover "I'll House You" more than a dozen years earlier). Except for a few odd tracks where Terry and JB attempt to duplicate the pimp roll of the dirty South, his broad talents are a perfect fit for the rangy Jungle Brothers, who move easily from smooth, summer-day soul ("Candy") to stark electro-bass

("You in My Hut Now," "What's the Five O") to energetic old school party music ("Do Your Thing," "Buggin'"). The raps and tracks rarely vary, but Mike G and Afrika's sexed-up tales are hilarious and display a Neptunes-style weirdness that puts them right back into the hip-hop mainstream. —*John Bush*

Junior M.A.F.I.A.

Group / Hip-Hop, Gangsta Rap, East Coast Rap, Hardcore Rap
Junior Masters at Finding Intelligent Attitudes, or Junior M.A.F.I.A., were able to grab instant notoriety with two hit singles, "Get Money" and "Player's Anthem," thanks to their childhood crony and producer, the Notorious B.I.G. Their gold-certified debut album, *Conspiracy* (Undeas/Big Beat), was also released on Biggie's Undeas label in 1995. Hailing from Bedford-Stuyvesant, NY, the group was comprised of four separate acts: the 6s (Little Caesar, Chico, and Nino Brown), the Snakes (cousins Larceny and Trife), MC Klepto, and 47 MC Lil' Kim. Their rhymes mostly conveyed scenarios involving guns, money, and sex. The single "Get Money" was popular enough to help one of the group's members start a solo career. Lil' Kim, "the lieutenant" of Junior M.A.F.I.A., presented her own agenda and promiscuous persona, which some public figures protested, but fans concentrated on her skills as a rap artist. Her album *Hard Core* was released in 1996 and featured the hit singles "Crush on You," "Queen B@#$H," and "No Time" (which became a number-one rap single). Biggie, Sean "Puffy" Combs, and Little Caesar contributed to the album as well. Soon after, Kim's popularity paved the way for guest raps on songs by artists such as Missy Elliott, Mary J. Blige, and Sean "Puffy" Combs and appearances on the movie soundtracks *Money Talks* and *High School High*. —*Lynda Lane*

● **Conspiracy** / Aug. 29, 1995 / Undeas/Big Beat ✦✦✦
Under the guidance of the Notorious B.I.G., Junior M.A.F.I.A. released their first single, "Player's Anthem," in the summer of 1995, with the full-length *Conspiracy*. Not surprisingly, the group's music resembles that of the Notorious B.I.G.'s *Ready to Die*, complete with an opening sound collage. Considering *Ready to Die* was one of the seminal hip-hop releases of the early '90s, *Conspiracy* could have been an inspired, enjoyable sequel; instead, it's a fitfully successful replication of the earlier record's strengths. The major problem is Junior M.A.F.I.A. doesn't have enough personality to distinguish themselves from the B.I.G., who appears on four of the album's songs. Lil' Kim, the group's only female, does bring things to life on occasion, but it isn't quite enough to save the entire album. Nevertheless, the Clark Kent-produced "Player's Anthem" is a classic single, riding on its rubbery bass and surprisingly warm sentiments. Although the Notorious B.I.G. contributes some killer rhymes to the song, he doesn't dominate; he fits into the overall sound of the single. Instead, the true personalities of Junior M.A.F.I.A. shine through and they are impressive. —*Stephen Thomas Erlewine*

Jurassic 5

f. 1993, Los Angeles, CA
Group / Hip-Hop, Underground Rap, Alternative Rap, Turntablism
Though there's actually six of them, Jurassic 5 got everything else right on their self-titled debut EP. Part of the new rap underground of the late '90s (along with Company Flow, Mos Def, Doctor Octagon, and Sir Menelik), the sextet—rappers Marc 7even, Chali 2na, Zaakir, and Akil, plus producers Cut Chemist and DJ Nu-Mark—came together in 1993 at the Los Angeles cafe/venue named the Good Life. The six members were part of two different crews, Rebels of Rhythm and Unity Committee; after collaborating on a track, they combined into Jurassic 5 and debuted in 1995 with the "Unified Rebellion" single for TVT Records. At the tail end of 1997, the *Jurassic 5 EP* appeared and was hailed by critics as one of the freshest debuts of the year (if not the decade). Both Cut Chemist and Chali 2na are also part of the Latin-hop collective Ozomatli, while Chemist himself recorded several mix tapes plus the wide-issue album *Future Primitive Soundsession* (with Shortkut from Invisibl Skratch Piklz). The year 2000 found the group on tour with Fiona Apple and on the Warped Festival, just in time for the release of *Quality Control* that summer. Live work continued during 2000-2001, and a second record (*Power in Numbers*) appeared by the end of 2002. —*John Bush*

Jurassic 5 EP / Oct. 13, 1997 / Rumble/Pickininny ✦✦✦✦✦
Clocking in at just about one-third the running time of your average rap album circa 1997, Jurassic 5's debut was the most refreshing hip-hop release

of the year, and not just because it abandoned the epic-length concepts of the rap mainstream. With old school vibes to spare, excellent rhythmatic raps, and the production genius of Cut Chemist and DJ Nu-Mark, *EP* finally delivered on all the diverse talents promised by the growing hip-hop underground. "Jayou" is a flute-loop classic, and "Concrete Schoolyard" has that nostalgic "can it all be so simple" vibe so rarely heard from hip-hop. —*John Bush*

★ **Quality Control** / Jun. 6, 2000 / Interscope ✦✦✦✦✦
In June 2000, almost seven years after their formation, underground rap's most lauded crew finally hit with a full-length. Great expectations aside, *Quality Control* hits all the same highs as Jurassic 5's excellent EP of three years earlier, stretching out their resumé to nearly an hour with a few turntablist jaunts from resident beat jugglers DJ Nu-Mark and Cut Chemist. The formula is very similar to the EP, with the group usually going through a couple of lines of five-man harmonics before splitting off for tongue-twister solos from Zaakir, Chali 2na, Akil, and Mark 7even. As expected, there are plenty of nods to old school rap, from "Lausd," with its brief tribute to hip-hop classic "The Bridge" by MC Shan, to "Monkey Bars," where the group claim inspiration (yet just a bit of distance) from their heroes: "Now you know us but it's not the Cold Crush, four MC's so it ain't the Furious/Not the Force MCs or the three from Treacherous, it's a blast from the past from the moment we bust." Where *Quality Control* really laps previous Jurassic 5 material is not only the lyrical material, though, but the themes and focus of the message tracks "Lausd," "World of Entertainment (Woe Is Me)," and "Contribution." The four-man crew take on major media and the responsibilities of adulthood with a degree of authority, eloquence, and compassion never before heard in rap music. (Just check out the lyrics to any of the above three at an online archive like www.ohhla.com.) Though critics and uptight rap purists might fault them for not pushing the progression angle enough, Jurassic 5's rhymes are so devastating and the productions (by Nu-Mark and Cut Chemist) follow the raps so closely that it certainly doesn't matter whether the group are old school or not. —*John Bush*

Power in Numbers / Oct. 8, 2002 / Interscope ✦✦✦✦
Like a few other notable sophomore records from hip-hop acts (*De La Soul Is Dead, The Low End Theory*), Jurassic 5's *Power in Numbers* is darker than their first full-length; not as fresh and exuberant, but much more mature and intelligent. Granted, fans may not be happy to hear they've changed the formula so soon, or that the production doesn't play a starring role as it did on *Quality Control*. Instead, DJ Nu-Mark and Cut Chemist play it close to the vest, setting off the rhymes with a few well-placed beats and split-second samples (as well as the usual flute loops). Of course, allowing more room to hear four of the best rappers in hip-hop twisting tongues and telling tales has to be welcomed, and Jurassic 5 prove up to the added responsibility. Displaying a focus and intensity basically unseen in rap music during the past decade, the group practically bursts with message tracks; the skeletal first single "Freedom" finds Chali 2na and Akil delving into the concept as it relates to everything from Third World poverty to the American penitentiary system. "Remember His Name" and "Thin Line" (the latter with Nelly Furtado) are dark tales of urban passions, and they're a step forward in that it's not just the raps that are intricate, but the storytelling also requires a few listens to understand. The group still has plenty of time for a few old school anthems like "What's Golden" and "A Day at the Races," with Big Daddy Kane bringing his alliterative ammo to the track. And the instrumental jam "Acetate Prophets" shows DJ Nu-Mark and Cut Chemist refining their skill for merging turntablism and excellent productions. Perhaps the best statement of Jurassic 5's purpose comes from the group itself, on "If You Only Knew": "What we do is try to give you what you ain't used to." —*John Bush*

Just-Ice (Joseph Williams Jr.)

Vocals, Producer / Hip-Hop, Gangsta Rap, Hardcore Rap

A former bouncer at punk clubs, Joseph Williams Jr. was the first of the New York rappers to embrace gangsta rap, and when he burst out of Ft. Greene, Brooklyn as Just-Ice, he gained instant notoriety. Muscle bound, tattooed, aggressive—he resembled Mike Tyson in more than just looks—and with a mouthful of gold teeth, he certainly stood out. His debut album *Back to the Old School* proved he was more than just a pretty face. It came out on the independent New York label Sleeping Bag, and certainly sounded like no other hip-hop album, thanks to his fast, forceful rhymes and DMX's human beatbox as well as the distinctive production of Mantronix's Kurtis Mantronik.

When he was held by Washington, D.C., police regarding the murder of a drug dealer in 1987 ("Murder, Drugs, and the Rap Star" read a *Washington Post* headline), it gave him even greater notoriety (he was never charged with the murder). Declaring war on D.C.'s go-go scene and loudly criticizing Run-D.M.C. (then the ruling New York rap outfit), Just-Ice set a pattern for many a future hip-hop feud. Little could halt Just-Ice's ascension to hip-hop stardom, though the departure of Mantronik from Sleeping Bag was a bad omen. KRS-One stepped in to produce 1987's *Kool & Deadly*, an album that swapped Mantronik's hi-tech skills for raw, elemental beats and rhymes. The British and New York public that had so enthusiastically embraced *Back to the Old School* were diffident about this one, and 1989's *The Desolate One* (with KRS-One back in the producer's seat) was no great improvement. By 1990, both Just-Ice and Sleeping Bag appeared to be quickly fading as a new generation of rappers and labels overtook them. He continued to release albums at intervals across the 1990s, but they were on tiny independent labels and were rarely noticed. Just-Ice was a member of hip-hop super session, the Stop the Violence All Stars, who released one single ("Self Destruction") in 1990. The revival of interest in old school rap in the late '90s created fresh demand for *Back to the Old School*, but Just-Ice appeared unwilling or unable to capitalize on the renewed interest. —*Garth Cartwright*

● **Back to the Old School** / 1986 / Sleeping Bag ✦✦✦✦✦
It's impossible to describe how fresh this album sounded when first released—producer Kurtis Mantronik utilizes the Roland 606 drum machine more potently than any producer before and as its huge beats kick holes beneath Just-Ice's gold-toothed mumble of rhymes, curses, boasts, and yelps, the party gets underway. Back in 1986, this album burned eardrums and if now it sounds less revolutionary it remains a classic early hip-hop album, one that appeared as radical back then as the RZA's production of Wu-Tang Clan did in the late '90s. Neither Mantronik nor Just-Ice were to match it in their subsequent and separate solo work—it's worth reflecting on what might have been created if their partnership had endured. Opening track "Cold Gettin' Dumb" remains one of the most exhilarating tracks from an era when hip-hop was inventing itself day by day. The chauvinistic "Latoya" booms with block-rockin' beats. "Gangster of Hip Hop" and "Little Bad Johnny" lay the seeds for many an ominous rapper to come. —*Garth Cartwright*

Kool & Deadly / 1987 / Sleeping Bag ✦✦✦
Subtitled "Justicizms," this album boasts one of the ugliest covers ever—a close-up of Just-Ice's snarling gold dental work—and the sounds included are equally harsh. Producer KRS-One does not try to emulate Kurtis Mantronic's high-tech polyrhythms and samples, instead he strips the sound right back and keeps things very raw: at times there's little more here than Just-Ice's gruff vocals and the sound of a wheezing drum machine. Some old school fans rate this as the best album by the artist simply because it is so remorseless and raw. Perhaps the trick for newcomers is to check this album first and, if it interests you, then go to *Back to the Old School* for desert. Fans of KRS-One will want to own the record simply to hear him and Just-Ice trading rhymes on "Moshitup." The standout track is "Going Way Back," where Just-Ice rasps one of the first hip-hop history lessons and dares you to disagree that Brooklyn is where it all began. Ruff stuff. —*Garth Cartwright*

The Desolate One / 1989 / Fresh ✦✦✦
KRS-One is back at the controls and appears uninterested in changing the stark production formula he employed for *Kool & Deadly*. Of more interest are Just-Ice's rhymes, which have taken on a more detailed and darker worldview—on "Welfare Recipient" he delivers savage ghetto prose of a kind perhaps only the Geto Boys and Ghost Face Killah have matched. He's also been listening to Jamaican dancehall records—at the time in New York there appeared to be a real crossover between the two genres—and he chats in an effective raggamuffin style on "Sleng Teng" and "Na Touch Da Just." Not a bad record by any means but the limitations of Just-Ice's rhyming style and KRS-One's inability to develop his musical soundscape beyond elemental posed real problems for both of them as 1990 dawned and West Coast G-funk was about to sweep all before it. —*Garth Cartwright*

Masterpiece / 1990 / Sleeping Bag ✦✦
Sorry, Ice, but this ain't no masterpiece. It's not even a minor piece. On his last Sleeping Bag album, Just-Ice summons up as much bravado and boasts as is possible, but he's obviously aware that he's been relegated to the hip-hop retirement home. Without even KRS-One in his corner any longer, the muscle man of hip-hop sounds weak and alone and *Masterpiece* rarely finds him

putting his mouth to the right beat or smart rhyme. Around the time of this album, Just-Ice received his highest media profile since his 1987 tabloid exposure (on a trumped-up murder charge) due to his involvement with hip-hop supersession (Eazy-E, Chuck D, and Tone-Loc were among the heavyweights involved), the Stop the Violence All Stars, who released one single, "Self Destruction," in 1990. Perhaps this accounts for this album's rushed feel—Sleeping Bag was hoping that a public reacquainted with Just-Ice's name might buy the album. It didn't happen, and rapper and label parted company, both having their best days behind them. —*Garth Cartwright*

Gun Talk / 1993 / Savage ♦♦

With gangsta rap becoming the biggest business in hip-hop, Just-Ice tried to prove he could boast about guns and bitches like all the Cali' kids. He sure could—tracks such as "Gun Talk" sound like he knows how to handle a lethal weapon—but his problem is a similar one to that of his Philadelphia alterego Schoolly D: he lacks a producer with the necessary vision and skills to make him sound as relevant as the Snoop Doggs' of the West Coast. And after three years of silence you think he could come up with a few more imaginative rhymes than the static taunts and threats he hands out here. For those that like their hip-hop nasty, brutish, and short, this may be of interest, but otherwise there's nothing here that adds to Just-Ice's Sleeping Bag product. —*Garth Cartwright*

Kill the Rhythms (Like a Homicide) / Nov. 21, 1995 / IAM ♦♦

Considering the close brush with prison Just-Ice encountered when he was briefly held by Washington D.C. police regarding a homicide in 1987, you might be forgiven for thinking that he would possess some insight into murder and its repercussions. Uh-uh. Here he appears intent on showing how he can still rap harder, faster, and nastier than the multiplatinum gangstas who were still in short pants when he first grabbed a mic, but you get the feeling he's straining to impress rather than leading by example. Again, the record company's inability to match Just-Ice with a producer who can bring his voice and personality forward means listening to this album quickly becomes hard work. His old pal KRS-One drops in to trade some rhymes, but, compared to their efforts on *Kool & Deadly*, they both sound uninspired. —*Garth Cartwright*

VII / Apr. 7, 1998 / Warlock ♦♦

This is the last recorded effort of Just-Ice (although he appears to take around three years between albums). Still, it's nothing to get excited about—Just-Ice is still full of piss and swagger but he's never developed into a storyteller or rhyme cruncher of real interest and the hardcore raps on offer here come from a man who helped invent the gangsta style but now sounds desperately out of time. As ever, he's backed by beats-by-numbers and his label obviously didn't want to spend money on samples, as the music here is, for the most part, colorless. Considering that Just-Ice's former producer Kurtis Mantronic also appears to be on the unemployment line these days, perhaps someone could engineer a reunion. It's worked for old rockers, so why not old rappers? —*Garth Cartwright*

Justice System

f. 1992

Group / Hip-Hop, Urban, Acid Jazz, Jazz-Rap

Justice System's brand of up-tempo jazz-rap is especially fresh and invigorating since it's the creation of a real band, similar to the Roots. Members play guitar, bass, tenor sax, Rhodes piano, and drums. Their debut album, *Rooftop Soundcheck*, appeared in 1994 on MCA. Despite good word of mouth and constant live shows, the label dropped them. The group returned eight years later with *Uncharted Terrain*, on Ill River. —*John Bush*

● **Rooftop Soundcheck** / 1994 / MCA ♦♦♦

Another hip-hop band with a jazzy feel, Justice System uses live musicians to create the backing for their raps, including tributes to Afrika Bambaataa and Santana. Unfortunately, the album is a bit overproduced; unlike the group's frenetic live shows, *Rooftop Soundcheck* lacks the excitement and raw intensity that kindles great jazz-rap. —*John Bush*

Uncharted Terrain / Jul. 2, 2002 / Ill River ♦♦♦

Juvenile (Terius Gray)

b. New Orleans, LA

Southern Rap, Dirty South

New Orleans-based gangsta rapper Juvenile was born Terius Gray. After beginning his performing career while in his teens, he released a 1995 album on Warlock titled *Being Myself*. He eventually crossed paths with Cash Money

label owners Ronald "Suga Slim" and Brian "Baby" Williams, who issued 1996's *Solja Rags*; the album became a major underground hit, and set the stage for the release of 1998's *400 Degreez*. In 1999, with Juvenile's popularity growing, *Solja Rags* was reissued nationally, and Warlock jumped on the bandwagon with a remixed version of *Being Myself*. The year ended with the release of a new studio effort, *Tha G-Code*, followed by *Project English* two years later in 2001. —*Jason Ankeny*

Being Myself / Feb. 7, 1995 / Warlock ♦♦

Juvenile's debut album, recorded for Warlock, features the New Orleans rapper working through his distinctive bounce music with emphasis on club grooves and MC chatter. Though the sound is similar to Master P.'s No Limit posse, *Being Myself* fulfills the promise in the title for the most part, especially on tracks like "G-ing Men" and "U Can't C Me." —*Keith Farley*

Solja Rags / May 13, 1997 / Cash Money ♦♦

There's a bit of tongue-in-cheek humor to Juvenile's street-level raps on *Solja Rags*, and that's just about all that's salvageable from this Cash Money release. Guests include Magnolia Shorty, the Hot Boys, Big Moe, and the Big Tymers. —*Keith Farley*

● **400 Degreez** / Jun. 9, 1998 / Uptown/Universal ♦♦♦♦♦

Among the flurry of Cash Money releases during the late '90s, *400 Degreez* certainly stands out, and not just as Juvenile's shining moment but also as the album that forced everyone to suddenly take this dirty South collective very seriously. Before *400 Degreez*, Cash Money had been operating relatively well, securing a distribution deal with Universal and broadening its audience with every successive release. But nothing prepared anyone for the success of *400 Degreez*, particularly its two anthemic singles, the tongue-twisting "Ha" and the booty-calling "Back That Azz Up." These two songs alone make *400 Degreez* noteworthy. They're absolutely two of the best songs to come out of the late-'90s dirty South boom, and for years to come they established prototypes for countless subsequent hits. Moreover, two remixes of "Ha" come late on the album, one with the Hot Boys, the other with Jay-Z. These four highlights—"Ha," "Back That Azz Up," and the "Ha" remixes—break up the album, somewhat concealing the filler. And, yes, there is filler here, as with any Cash Money album, but even it is worthwhile, either because of Juvenile's carefully structured rhyming or producer Mannie Fresh's seemingly bottomless well of hot beats. Among the singles and the filler here, there are also a few great album tracks as well. In particular, "Flossin Season" features some incredibly brash boasts from the Big Tymers, and "Rich Niggaz" features an absolutely frantic beat that ricochets on for five breathtaking minutes. All of this, along with perfect timing, dropping just as the dirty South broke into the mainstream, made *400 Degreez* a phenomenal release for Cash Money, quite arguably the label's crowning achievement. This album, of course, made Juvenile a superstar and, in turn, towered over him for years as the achievement by which he would always be measured. —*Jason Birchmeier*

Tha G-Code / Dec. 7, 1999 / Cash Money ♦♦♦

Released in the wake of Juvenile's remarkable breakthrough success with *400 Degreez* and "Back That Azz Up" a year earlier, *Tha G-Code* seems a bit lackluster, no doubt overshadowed by the heights the rapper had previously attained. It doesn't help, though, that *Tha G-Code* plays precisely like a sequel, lead single "U Understand" reprising the rhyming style of "Ha" and follow-up single "I Got That Fire," likewise, recycling the formula that had made "Back That Azz Up" so appealing. These two singles, unfortunately, aren't nearly as spirited as their predecessors, and that's more because of Juvenile, who seems disinterested throughout this often rote album, than because of workhorse producer Mannie Fresh, who seems nobly determined to conjure some of the good-time spirit that had made *400 Degreez* so much fun, though you can sense here that he's understandably running out of ideas by this point. Even so, it's the production here that's most interesting, as omens of Juvenile's quick descent from momentary success tend to taint his performance. —*Jason Birchmeier*

Playaz of da Game / Sep. 26, 2000 / D3 ♦

Released in the wake of Juvenile's coast-to-coast success with "Back That Azz Up" and its accompanying album, *400 Degreez* (1999), *Playaz of da Game* repackages old, early recordings by the artist and tries to pass them off as new recordings. The Juvenile of this album, who dates from the early '90s and raps in the local bounce style of New Orleans, bears little resemblance to the Juvenile that recorded for Cash Money Records in the late '90s. Consequently, *Playaz of da Game* should mainly interest die-hard Juvenile fans curious about the rapper's early beginnings as well as fans of early-'90s bounce music. Everyone else should probably stick with Juvenile's Cash Money releases first, as they're far superior to this misleading repackaging of long-forgotten early recordings that were initially forgotten for a reason. —*Jason Birchmeier*

Project English / Jan. 30, 2001 / Uptown/Universal ♦♦♦

Many in the rap community were ready to write off Juvenile when *Project English* hit the streets. He'd been out of the spotlight for a good two years or so after becoming one of the biggest rap success stories of 1999 with "Ha" and "Back That Azz Up." His 1999 album, *Tha G-Code*, underwhelmed many, and set the stage for Juvenile's year-and-a-half sabbatical. During this year-and-a-half period, growing criticism mounted—many in the rap community had grown tired of the Cash Money Millionaires and their market-saturating approach, not to mention their flamboyance. Perhaps it was this criticism that resulted in *Project English*'s delayed release. Moreover, rumors spread about strife plaguing the Cash Money camp. In the end, *Project English* proves slightly revealing. First of all, it's not the calculated sequel that *Tha G-Code* was. Producer Mannie Fresh makes a conscious effort to deliver a fresh sound, even though you can tell he'd exhausted his techniques with the myriad Cash Money albums flooding the streets in 1999 and 2000. Secondly, Juvenile doesn't depart too far from what garnered him popularity in the first place. He doesn't get deep here and emphasizes his flow rather than his admittedly shallow lyrics. It's the album's trunk-shaking lead single, "Set It Off," that makes *Project English* more than just another Cash Money album. The song embodies everything that's special about the Cash Money style—a truly shining moment. But it's just one song, and some of the other songs do sound a bit generic. As a result, *Project English* ends up being a satisfying release yet nothing to get too excited about outside of the standout single. —*Jason Birchmeier*

JVC Force

f. Long Island, NY

Group / East Coast Rap, Hip-Hop, Jazz-Rap

Long Island's JVC Force, a rap group whose name stands for "Justified by Virtue of Creativity for All Reasons Concerning Entertainment" (that would actually make them "JVC Farce," but whatever) was a trio consisting of DJ Curt Cazal and MCs AJ Rok and MC B-Luv. Signed to B Boy, the group broke out with an underground hit single in the form of "Strong Island." The song would become the group's signature moment, and though a few successive tracks came close to rivaling the song's greatness, the group was never able to top it. The group left two albums in its wake, 1988's *Doin' Damage* and 1990's *Force Field.* —*Andy Kellman*

Doin' Damage / 1988 / B Boy ♦♦

● **Force Field** / 1990 / Warlock ♦♦

JVC Force's second and final album doesn't improve much on *Doin' Damage*, though there are a couple moments where the trio comes up with material that ranks close to—but doesn't quite surpass—their breakthrough "Strong Island" single from two years prior. "It's a Force Thing" was one of the better hip-house tracks released that year, and the imaginative sampling on "Trivial Pursuit" makes for another impressive cut. The biggest problem with the album is that JVC Force aren't talented enough MCs to sustain 18 tracks that play out at over an hour. They definitely should receive some credit for sampling Buffalo Springfield's "Stop" years before Public Enemy; ironically, the group also samples Isaac Hayes' "Hyperbolic"—the backbone of PE's "Black Steel in the Hour of Chaos," which was released a couple years before this. —*Andy Kellman*

K-Ci & JoJo

f. 1997, Charlotte, NC

Group / Urban, Hip-Hop, Contemporary R&B

Cedric and Joel Hailey comprise the romantic R&B duo K-Ci & JoJo, who were one of two pairs of brothers that made up the chart-topping '90s group Jodeci. The Haileys grew up singing in church choirs in Charlotte, NC, and toured the South with their father's gospel group. When they met the DeGrate brothers, Dalvin and "DeVante Swing," they decided to switch to secular music and formed Jodeci. After signing with Uptown, the quartet released three platinum albums over 1991-1995, with DeVante Swing writing and producing the vast majority of the material. The first rumblings of independence came when K-Ci recorded a solo single, a cover of Bobby Womack's "If You Think You're Lonely Now," for the soundtrack of the 1994 film *Jason's Lyric*. In 1996, a year after Jodeci's third album *The Show, The After Party, The Hotel*, K-Ci & JoJo officially teamed up to record "How Could You" for the soundtrack of the Damon Wayans/Adam Sandler comedy *Bulletproof*; they also supplied backing vocals on 2Pac's smash "How Do U Want It."

The brothers made their side project into a full-fledged collaboration with the release of their debut album, *Love Always*, in 1997. The lead single "You Bring Me Up" was a Top Ten R&B hit, and the follow-up "Last Night's Letter" was also successful. But the single that really broke them big was the sweet ballad "All My Life," which went all the way to number one on both the pop and R&B charts in early 1998. *Love Always* went on to sell over four million copies, and Jodeci went on an unofficial, indefinite hiatus (though they never broke up). K-Ci & JoJo assembled a follow-up album, *It's Real*, which stuck closely to the sound of its predecessor. It was another Top Ten, platinum-selling hit, and produced another smash single in "Tell Me It's Real," which topped out at number two on both the pop and R&B charts. The Haileys celebrated ten years in the recording industry with 2000's *X*, their third straight platinum album, which spun off the near-Top Ten pop hit "Crazy."

Shortly after the release of *X*, K-Ci & JoJo were invited to perform at the KIIS-FM Jingle Ball 2000 concert in Los Angeles. Despite the promoters' assurances that the show was safe for families, K-Ci allegedly fondled and exposed his erect penis during their performance, and was charged with indecent exposure and lewd conduct based on videotape evidence. He pleaded no contest and was fined and placed on probation. The duo's prolific recording pace subsequently slowed a bit, during which time they worked on material for a long-rumored Jodeci reunion album. They also released their fourth album, *Emotional*, in late 2002, but initial sales returns failed to duplicate the success of its predecessors. — *Steve Huey*

● **Love Always** / Jun. 17, 1997 / MCA ✦✦✦

After becoming two of the best-known R&B singers of the 1990s as half of Jodeci, brothers K-Ci & JoJo Hailey formed a cohesive duo for *Love Always*. A definite surprise to Jodeci fans, the CD contains few traces of new jack swing and lacks the type of suggestive, R-rated lyrics the foursome had become known for. It was clear that the great soul music of the 1970s was very much on K-Ci & JoJo's minds when they made this album, an unpretentious collection of ballads and slow jams that isn't mind blowing but is definitely above average. In contrast to the homogenized nature of so much '90s R&B, things are refreshingly organic on such cuts as "Now and Forever," "Still Waiting," and "Baby Come Back." And an impressive cover of L.T.D.'s 1976 hit "Love Ballad" may very well be the best thing the Hailey brothers have ever done—inside or outside of Jodeci. — *Alex Henderson*

It's Real / Jun. 22, 1999 / MCA ✦✦✦

K-Ci & JoJo's first album *Love Always* established the Jodeci refugees as fine R&B vocalists, blending classic soul traditions with contemporary urban

production and technique. Blessed with strong sales and good reviews, *Love Always* became a hit, setting up high expectations for the duo's second album, *It's Real*. For those expecting a flat-out masterpiece, *It's Real* will disappoint, primarily because it doesn't so much as expand on past glories as it simply replicates them. Since they're good singers with generally good material, this isn't a problem, even if it makes it all seem a little too pat and predictable. Occasionally, the Hailey brothers decide to rely a little bit too much on their impressive vocal technique, taking off on soaring glissanados that ultimately distract as much as they impress. That, combined with the stylistic similarity of the material, makes *It's Real* bog down a little bit, but the very best moments—"Makin' Me Say Goodbye," "I Wanna Get to Know You," "How Long Must I Cry," "Hello Darlin'," among others—are contemporary urban romantic soul at its finest, which is reason enough to hear the disc. — *Stephen Thomas Erlewine*

X / Dec. 5, 2000 / MCA ✦✦✦

X is the Roman numeral for ten, and this late-2000 release is titled *X* because it marks Cedric "K-Ci" Hailey and Joel "JoJo" Hailey's tenth anniversary in the recording business—first as two-thirds of the trio Jodeci, then as the duo K-Ci & JoJo. *X*, the duo's third album, isn't a radical departure from its two previous albums; like 1997's *Love Always* and 1999's double-platinum *It's Real*, this CD emphasizes romantic material and combines a high-tech urban contemporary production style with an appreciation of classic soul. K-Ci & JoJo were never a carbon copy of Jodeci, and *X* won't be mistaken for *Diary of a Mad Band*. Though *X* contains a few hip-hop-minded, up-tempo selections (including "Game Face" and "Thug N U Thug N Me"), romantic ballads and slow jams are dominant. A few of the tunes are retro-soul gems—especially "Wanna Do You Right" and the Bobby Womack-influenced "I Can't Find the Words"—although most of the time, *X* is merely decent urban contemporary. One thing that's never in doubt is the Hailey brothers' skills as vocalists; while a lot of urban contemporary artists get over on image alone, K-Ci & JoJo really do have impressive vocal ranges. *X* isn't a masterpiece, but unlike all of the urban artists who have nothing more than image and attitude going for them, the Hailey siblings bring some genuine talent to this generally pleasant, if predictable, CD. — *Alex Henderson*

Emotional / Nov. 26, 2002 / MCA ✦✦✦

Perhaps compensating for the negativity rampant in the rap world, K-Ci & JoJo's fourth record *Emotional* is not only unrepentently sincere and soulful but also one of the duo's first to completely ignore the influence of hip-hop altogether. Such a level of devotion to R&B is impressive considering the success of so many rap crossovers on the charts; it's a testament to the Hailey brothers' deep respect for the smooth love jams they grew up with. There's only one problem with *Emotional*, but unfortunately it's a big one. K-Ci & JoJo's amazing vocals and sincere performances simply aren't enough to compensate for the bland songs and formulaic arrangements. The single "This Very Moment" is a deeply felt performance of an uplifting song, a perfect selection for any contemporary wedding ceremony, but one that simply floats by the listener (like it floated by the charts) without a single element to distinguish it from hundreds of songs in the past. "Special" and "Down for Life" are also relationship songs with a power to melt the heart of any female in range, but nothing else to recommend them. The duo are fighting against a tide (and most of the rap/R&B crossovers feature a male rapper with a female R&B singer anyway), and *Emotional* simply isn't strong enough to resist. — *John Bush*

K-Os (Kheaven Brereton)

Vocals, Piano, Guitar (Acoustic) / Hip-Hop, Trip-Hop

Raised by Jehovah's Witness parents and having lived in locales as disparate as Toronto and Trinidad, it's no surprise that Kheaven Brereton, aka K-Os (pronounced: chaos), is a bit different than your average MC. A singer as well as an MC, and a producer to boot, K-Os proved on his debut album, Exit (Astralwerks), that being preachy didn't have to mean being boring. Arriving in early 2003, the LP was dramatically different, with lush, instrument-driven arrangements to go with the traditional hip-hop elements of drum programming, samples, and the like. Acoustic guitar and piano marked the single "Heaven Only Knows"; dub and reggae influences tinged "Freeze." Many of the tracks found the rapper singing, so much so that an argument could be raised about the genre to which K-Os in fact belonged. And that was just the way he liked it. A tour to support Exit stretched from late 2002 through summer 2003; the dates saw K-Os performing with such hip-hop luminaries as India.Arie and Floetry. In addition to the original version of *Exit*, Astralwerks released an extended version featuring three bonus tracks. —*Johnny Loftus*

● **Exit** / Jan. 28, 2003 / Astralwerks ◆◆◆◆

The spelling of Kheaven Brereton's first name is not coincidental: Brereton, aka K-Os, brings a heavy dose of spirituality to his debut hip-hop album, and a healthy dose of positivity as well. It's not the only aspect that deviates from the turn of the millennium hip-hop formula, though; it's also an eclectic mix of musical styles, incorporating everything from standard hip-hop beats to reggae, soul, and even flamenco. K-Os' mission is to defy expectations in the music and the message—rather than talking about standard themes like bucks and booty, it's about self-discovery. (For illustration, a snippet from the liner notes reads, "It seems that we all fear the ending of our 'selves,' but in reality we fear losing all the things we 'know,' especially who we THINK we are.") There's always a danger with albums like this that they may come across as preachy or, even worse, as novelties. Thankfully, *Exit* is neither. The music is always substantial, and K-Os is every bit as good a singer as an MC. Even more importantly, when it comes to the words, K-Os only guides, never demands. —*Sean Carruthers*

K-Otix

Group / Underground Rap

Presenting the lighter side of Houston rap, K-Otix forgoes gangsta clichés, strip-club antics, and DJ Screw intoxicants in favor of traditional hip-hop simplicity. More apt to remind listeners of A Tribe Called Quest than the Geto Boys, K-Otix provides beats and rhymes of classic design. With their producer Russel "the Are" Gonzalez having received much inspiration and some actual training from Gang Starr legend and ex-Texan DJ Premier, their music clearly expresses the reconstructive nature of the hip-hop aesthetic. As first and foremost an avid fan, diligent record collector, and student of jazz, soul, and funk music, the Are only then allows himself to become a crafty composer of original pieces. His knack for unearthing just the right samples and drum cadences to move crowds is of course greatly enhanced by the presence of Damien Randle and Micah Nickerson on microphones. Their aggressive manner of lyricism, characterized by blunt insights and percussive inflections, completes the K-Otix formula for dynamic rap music.

Quickly after the group's formation in 1992, K-Otix established itself as a formidable live act, extensively touring throughout Texas and even winning an award at the 1995 Gavin Convention in New Orleans. By the time their first official release surfaced in 1997, the *Spontaneity* EP, an already sizable fan base, teased for years by dirtily reproduced demo tapes, collectively jumped at the chance to purchase their finished material. Indeed, the high quality of the independently released record, as well as the buzz that it created, was enough to initiate a collaboration with legendary Philadelphia DJ Cash Money called "Do You Wanna Be an MC." On top of that, K-Otix also landed a major distribution deal by signing to Bronx Science. A series of singles put out by the New York-based label garnered much excitement surrounding K-Otix as songs such as "Mind Over Matter" and "World Renown" entered radio play lists across the country. With the release of their first full-length album, titled *Universal*, in 2001, K-Otix had truly become an international draw. Within the next year or so, tours of Japan and Europe were mingled amongst single collaborations with the Lone Catalysts and Dallas radio personality Head Krack. Refueling with a new series of recordings released on their own K-Otix imprint, both *Hustler's Theme* and *The Black Album* were unleashed in 2002. While the former presents the Are working with a cast of MCs that includes Count Bass D, Truth Enola, D-Ology, and K

of Example, the latter features Damien and Mic rhyming over their own production. —*Robert Gabriel*

● **Universal** / Oct. 9, 2001 / Bronx Science ◆◆◆

These boom-bap purists deep in the heart of Texas provide only classic hip-hop productions. A series of well-received singles comprises the meat of *Universal*, K-Otix's debut album. From the jangly funk of "Mind Over Matter" to the majestic strumming of "World Renown," from the motivating echoes of "U Know the Name" to the sliding cadence of "Take a Breather," K-Otix quickly established itself as a DJ favorite on the underground circuit. The group's biggest asset may in fact be its producer, the Are, who has an impeccable ear for effective samples. With tried and true MCs Damien and Mic fronting his refined creations, *Universal* is as polished as K-Otix is learned. —*Robert Gabriel*

K7 (Louis Sharpe)

Vocals, Producer / Hip-Hop, Freestyle, Club/Dance

New York City native K7 had success in the mid-'90s with his fusion of rap, dancehall, and dance. His 1994 album, *Swing Batta Swing*, spawned the pop hit "Come Baby Come" and a club favorite, "Zunga Zeng." Prior to his solo success as K7, Louis "Kayel" Sharpe was one-third of Latin freestyle group TKA. Both K7 and TKA remained quiet throughout the rest of the '90s before each re-emerged with new albums in 2001. — *Wade Kergan*

● **Swing Batta Swing** / 1994 / Tommy Boy ◆◆◆◆

K7's debut album *Swing Batta Swing* breaks loose with a rare style of rap verging on club or dance music, along with a bit of swing, before Gap commercials made it "hip" again. Everything in the album involves high-speed vocals, usually with high-speed backing beats to accompany. K7 adds in a tiny touch of a Latin flavor with some of the lyrics as well, which can aid in the speed factor that he seems to enjoy. To boot, he throws in some call and response working in absolutely every track. The final component of the album is sexuality, coming forth on "Body Rock," "I'll Make You Feel Good," "Hotel Motel," and "Beep Me." A pair of commercial hits are also on the album, "Come Baby Come" and "Move It Like This," both of which involve a good deal of those call and response patterns, but at a higher speed than most of the tracks, very danceworthy for a club (at least in 1994). Finally, there are a few reworkings of songs from other genres, infused with K7's vision. "Hi De Ho" is an overhaul of Cab Calloway's "Minnie the Moocher" made into a street-tough rap ballad. "Zunga Zeng" is presumably some sort of evolutionary step for Yellowman's "Zungguzungguguzungguzeng." Finally, "A Little Help From My Friends" takes a tiny bit away from the Beatles, again with K7's personal infusion. Overall, the album is noteworthy for the quality of the rap. The only gripe with the album is the similarity of the songs, though that's part of what makes it a good dance album. —*Adam Greenberg*

Love, Sex, Money / Apr. 9, 2002 / Select ◆◆◆

Years after the runaway success of "Come Baby Come," K7 had sort of disappeared. His contract with Tommy Boy had soured, and it wasn't until 2001 that he resurfaced on the indie label Select with the album *Love, Sex, Money*. The album also featured Ty Bless, an unknown artist at the time. Together, the two functioned well as a duo; however, the lack of a major-label budget—not to mention a major-label distribution deal and marketing push—really prevents *Love, Sex, Money* from sounding as great as it should. Both K7 and Ty Bless perform well, but they don't have the production they need to back them up. Nonetheless, anyone who missed K7 following his departure from the music industry for several years will no doubt find this album refreshing at the least, even if it's nowhere near as exciting as his greatest accomplishment, the *Swing Batta Swing* album on Tommy Boy. —*Jason Birchmeier*

K-Solo (Kevin Madison)

b. Central Islip, NY

Hip-Hop, East Coast Rap

K-Solo, aka Kevin Self Organization Left Others, is a New York MC best known for a style of rhyming that involves spelling out words. Originally from Central Islip, NY, K-Solo (born Kevin Madison) grew up with EPMD's Parrish Smith and—along with Redman and Das EFX—was part of the Hit Squad family. He had a guest spot on EPMD's *Unfinished Business* in 1989 and released his first solo album, *Tell the World My Name*, on Atlantic in 1990. *Time's Up* followed two years later, and signaled the end of the rapper's association with the now-defunct Hit Squad and EPMD. K then moved to the West Coast and signed with Death Row, recording an album in 1996 that was never released amid the label's considerable legal troubles. — *Wade Kergan*

Tell the World My Name / 1990 / Atlantic ✦✦✦

● **Time's Up** / 1992 / Atlantic ✦✦✦
Because K-Solo was a longtime friend of EPMD's Parrish Smith, some people assumed that his Atlantic releases would favor an EPMD-like flow. But in fact, *Time's Up* doesn't emulate EPMD, although Smith serves as executive producer. While Smith and Erick Sermon (the other half of EPMD) were known for a deadpan, relaxed style of rapping, K-Solo tends to be a lot more aggressive. Arguably, K-Solo's rapping style is closer to LL Cool J or Big Daddy Kane than EPMD. The thing that K-Solo has in common with Smith and Sermon is an unmistakably East Coast approach; in 1992 no one would have mistaken K-Solo for a Southern or West Coast rapper. And the production is as East Coast sounding as K-Solo's flow. The producers (who include Sam Anderson and Sermon, among others) favor the minimalist, sample-heavy format that was big in the northeastern U.S. in the early '90s—none of the producers show any awareness of either the sleek, keyboard-heavy G-funk sound that Dr. Dre popularized on the West Coast or the hyper bass music that was coming out of Florida. Lyrically, *Time's Up* is fairly diverse. While EPMD spent much of their time attacking "sucker MCs," K-Solo raps about everything from prison life ("Premonition of a Black Prisoner") to black-on-black crime ("Who's Killin' Who"). Although K-Solo isn't afraid to discuss the harsh realities of urban life, he doesn't get into gangsta rap at all—when he raps about black-on-black crime, the New Yorker is speaking out against thug life. *Time's Up* falls short of remarkable, but it's a solid, enjoyable outing from an EPMD ally who was a talented MC in his own right. — *Alex Henderson*

Ka'Nut

f. Flint, MI
Group / Hardcore Rap
A native of Flint, MI, who grew up in Oakland but returned to his hometown to jump start his career, Ka'Nut hooked up with trackmasters from both locales for his debut album, 1998's *Look at 'Em Now*. His cousin, Steve Pitts (who has worked with Flint's Dayton Family), and Bay Area producer E-A-Ski both helped out on the LP, and Dayton Family regulars Eric and Ira Dorsey make appearances as well. — *John Bush*

● **Look at 'Em Now** / Jun. 23, 1998 / Relativity ✦✦✦
Flint, Michigan rapper Ka'Nut comes out with a hard-hitting debut with *Look at 'Em Now*. The music falls halfway between Californian gangsta and Midwest hip-hop. While Ka'Nut occasionally falls prey to gangsta clichés, both lyrically and musically, he tempers them with soul influences—witness the vocals of Ready for the World's Melvin Riley on "50 G's"—and a fleeting sense of compassion. *Look at 'Em Now* can sound isolated on occasion, but it's nevertheless a good showcase for a promising rapper. — *Leo Stanley*

Kabir

b. London, England
Jazz-Rap, Underground Rap
Rapper Kabir was born in London, although at an early age he moved to Boston looking to make his name in hip-hop. After working with the funk/jazz group Uncle Trouble, he finally released his solo album, *Cultural Confusion*, in 2001. He continued to work with Uncle Trouble as well as another group called the Miracle Orchestra. — *Bradley Torreano*

● **Cultural Confusion** / 2001 / Landspeed ✦✦✦
Kabir raises the bar for lyrical prowess on his debut album, *Cultural Confusion*. While other rappers pride themselves on the bling of their ice, the figures of their women, or the diameters of their rims, Kabir prides himself on the depth of his lyrics, which are printed in this album's CD booklet. Similarly lyrically inclined rappers Mr. Lif, Virtuoso, and Esoteric join Kabir on "Deficiency Disease," "Democracy!" and "Run Out of Words?" respectively. Kabir produces many of the album's beats himself, though producers Dan Berkson, Nils Van Otterloo, and Solomon Grunge contribute beats as well. Overall, you can tell that Kabir's Boston locale influences his lyrics; he's one of the more academic MCs in the game, no doubt a result of the city's myriad academic institutions. — *Jason Birchmeier*

Kam

West Coast Rap, Hardcore Rap
With its overt sociopolitical stance, somewhat rare for a West Coast rapper, Kam's angst-ridden hardcore rap went largely unappreciated throughout the '90s, despite an early affiliation with Ice Cube. His releases appeared sporadically, debuting first on the *Boyz N the 'Hood* soundtrack, then releasing his first solo album, *Neva Again* (1993, Eastwest), followed by a largely ignored sophomore release, *Made in America* (1995, Eastwest). He then took some time off in the late '90s to pursue other interests before returning in 2001 on the indie Hard Tyme Records with *Kamnesia*, an ambitious comeback that found him bringing a slight club-friendly appeal to his hardcore rhymes. —*Jason Birchmeier*

Neva Again / 1993 / Eastwest ✦✦✦

Made in America / 1995 / Eastwest ✦✦✦

● **Kamnesia** / Mar. 20, 2001 / Hard Tyme ✦✦✦
Veteran L.A. rapper Kam has decided that he has been ignored for too long. After garnering acclaim for his underground work, Kam hits listeners with *Kamnesia*, a calculated attempt to reach a mass audience that is surprisingly successful. On *Kamnesia*, Kam changes his musical approach, providing club-friendly tracks such as "Where I Come From" and "Bang Bang," a remake of Sister Nancy's dancehall classic "Bam Bam." Although the sound may have changed, Kam's militant lyrics remain true to his underground roots. Kam's mix of politically charged lyrics with banging beats makes *Kamnesia* difficult to forget. —*Jon Azpiri*

Kane & Abel

Group / Dirty South, Gangsta Rap
Originally from New York, the hip-hop duo Kane & Abel moved to New Orleans as teenagers. When they arrived in New Orleans, they met Mia X, who eventually hooked the duo up with Master P, who helped Kane & Abel land a deal with No Limit Records. Their first album, 1996's *7 Sins*, was produced by KLC and Mo B. Dick, who formerly worked with Down South Hustlers and Tru. *Am I My Brother's Keeper* followed in 1998.

The next year, the duo broke from No Limit, starting their own label, Most Wanted, which was distributed through EastWest. Their first effort for the label was *Rise to Power*, which was released in the fall of 1999. Preceding the release, the twin brothers were arrested in May 1999 for conspiring to distribute cocaine with a convicted drug dealer named Richard Pena. This served as good publicity for their album, particularly as they argued that the bust was a conspiracy that was ultimately aimed at getting the two to testify against Master P. In the end, they plea bargained and released *Most Wanted* in late 2000. The album featured "Shake It Like a Dog," a popular club hit that eventually became such a success for the underground Southern duo that they re-released the album in summer 2001. The re-release of *Most Wanted* featured four new bonus tracks, including "Show Dat Work (Shake It Like a Dog, Pt. 2)" featuring Mystikal. — *Stephen Thomas Erlewine*

7 Sins / Oct. 8, 1996 / No Limit ✦✦
New Orleans-based rap duo Kane & Abel's debut album *7 Sins* reworks the same bass-driven gangsta rap as their mentors—Master P, KLC and Mo B. Dick. Which means that the music is fairly rote and predictable, so the album's success depends on the skills of Kane & Abel. For the most part, their verbal dexterity is engaging, yet their reliance on gangsta clichés grows rather tiresome. — *Leo Stanley*

● **Am I My Brother's Keeper** / Jul. 7, 1998 / No Limit ✦✦✦
Like every other No Limit release, Kane & Abel's second album, *Am I My Brother's Keeper*, is cookie-cutter gangsta with pretenses of being "underground." If underground means an album littered with profanity, violence, and drugs, *Am I My Brother's Keeper* fills the bill, but if it means moving the music forward, then it fails miserably. Not that it's a terrible album—it's just bland. A handful of cuts have slamming production and engaging rhymes, but for the most part, it just finds the No Limit production crew Beats by the Pound and the predictable host of guest rappers going through the motions. And those motions just happen to be the same motions that every No Limit soldier goes through—namely, loping bass, lazy beats, photocopied songs, and clichéd rhymes. It's the kind of record that sounds good if you're a fanatic or are unfamiliar with all the other albums in this style. Kane & Abel are competent rappers, but it makes no difference either way—these backing

tracks could have been used by anybody on No Limit, and since there are so many guest spots, almost every cut sounds like it could be on any No Limit album. It's an utterly anonymous, faceless record that is interchangeable with everything on the label...but that's what No Limit fans have come to expect. —*Stephen Thomas Erlewine*

Rise to Power / Sep. 21, 1999 / Most Wanted ✦✦✦
Give Kane & Abel credit for breaking from No Limit records, perhaps realizing that if they were one of the many soldiers in the No Limit army, there was no way they could ever distinguish themselves. Unfortunately, *Rise to Power*—their first effort for their own label Most Wanted, which is just a subsidiary of Eastwest—might as well have been released on No Limit, since it follows the same basic structure, sound, and style of a No Limit release. True, they try to mix it up a little, including a Spanish version of "Get Cha Mind Right" at the end (it might just be an alternate version, but the intention is noble), but the fact is, the music is generic dirty South and the rappers aren't distinguished. They happen to turn out a couple of good cuts, such as "Straight Thuggin'," but they will only be of interest to afficionados of this genre—much like most No Limit albums. Kane & Abel may have been able to leave Master P's stable, but they by no means escaped. —*Stephen Thomas Erlewine*

Most Wanted / Sep. 26, 2000 / Most Wanted ✦✦✦
Struggling to cut through the suddenly cluttered myriad of dirty South albums getting substantial distribution in late 2000, Kane & Abel's second post-No Limit album on their blossoming indie label finds them moving forward. *Most Wanted* bases a substantial amount of its content on the duo's drug bust, trying to turn this unfortunate incident into a positive one. As exploitative as this may be, it at least allows them to break away from strict cliché regurgitation. Yet for the most part, Kane & Abel stick to what got them to this point: gangsta posturing backed by thick, dirty South drum machine percussive rhythms. Despite the familiar feel of the production—a blend of No Limit's and Cash Money's sounds—there are few moment when the two Louisiana twins prove that their songs aren't merely generic, such as on the heavy metal guitar-sounding "Somebody Gotta Pay" or on the bounce sound of "Snakes" and "Lemme Get Up in Ya." The duo even contribute yet another entry into 2000's collection of booty anthems; "Shake It Like a Dog" isn't much of a departure from "Back That Azz Up" or "Wobble Wobble," surely Kane & Abel's attempt at commercial breakthrough. Still, even though this album rates above the majority of generic dirty South rap circa 2000, it's still highly derivative. Had this album hit the streets a year or two earlier, it would have been an exciting album, but in late 2000 they come off sounding a bit like laggards, despite the album's appeal. Most importantly, though, this is a positive step forward for the duo, who inch even closer toward being noteworthy rap artists. —*Jason Birchmeier*

The Last Ones Left / Oct. 15, 2002 / Entertainment Solutions ✦✦
Dropped from MCA and resurfacing on Baton Rouge's Entertainment Solutions, Kane & Abel delivered a rough and ready album that featured much more finesse in the lyrics than the spare, shoddy productions would seem to indicate. The producers work the same pimp roll through much of the album, and Kane & Abel haven't altered their purely paranoid themes, evidenced by tracks like "Whatcha Looking @," "Voices," and "Mind Playing Tricks." There's a lot of room for the duo's dense flow, but Kane & Abel have to keep listeners very interested to compensate for the lack of production expertise. In the end, they can't quite do it. —*John Bush*

The Kangol Kid

b. Brooklyn, NY
Vocals, Producer / Old School Rap, Electro
Brooklyn's Kangol Kid was a central member of U.T.F.O., the group best known for "Roxanne, Roxanne"—the song that provoked countless response songs. Like his fellow group member Doctor Ice, he broke into music as a dancer for Whodini. Though he took a step back from performing after the group's split, he never left the music industry—he got into songwriting, production, and management. This included taking the group No Curfew—made up of three of his sons—under his wing, in addition to writing jingles and music segments for New York's Hot 97 radio station. The Kangol Kid also became a frequent keynote speaker and panelist at music conferences. —*Andy Kellman*

Kankick

f. Oxnard, CA
Producer / West Coast Rap
Kankick is a hip-hop producer from Oxnard, CA. He was once a member of Lootpack, but has gone on to work with Declaime, tha Alkaholiks, and DJ Babu, among others. His first album is entitled *From Artz Unknown* and was released in 2001. —*Brad Mills*

● **From Artz Unknown** / Aug. 28, 2001 / Meanstreet ✦✦✦✦
This is an intriguing and surprisingly deep first album from West Coast producer Kankick. Responsible for the beats on the album, the instrumentals between tracks work magically, creating a good mix between beats and lyrics for an album intended to showcase his production skills. There are lots of jazzy compositions here, complete with trumpets, classical guitars, flutes, organs, rolling bass lines, and some classy MCs. The Visionaries, Krondon, Planet Asia, Declaime, Phil da Agony, Dr. Oop, and Wildchild from Lootpack all drop verses. Overall, this album was well thought out and put together, an enticing combination. —*Brad Mills*

Karlow the Great

Urban, Hip-Hop, Contemporary R&B, Pop/Rock, Pop-Rap
KaZaZZ Records recording artist Karlow the Great blurs the traditional lines between soul, rap, R&B, and rock. As a result, he sounded quite unlike any popular artist in late 2001 when KaZaZZ released *Attitude Adjustment*, his debut album. Karlow incorporates much of his "greatness" into his lyrics, which address "the Game," "the Times," and "the Life" (to quote his album). *Attitude Adjustment* includes three separate sections, each a group of songs grouped under one of these themes. Unlike most popular urban artists who mostly emphasize "the game," Karlow isn't afraid to sing and rap about the sometimes harsh realities of life and the proper perspective necessary to cope with these realities. As his debut proved, Karlow is ambitious, particularly for an entertainer. In fact, he takes such initiative with his music that KaZaZZ went so far as to market his music as "neo-hip-hop," an all-inclusive term symbolizing Karlow's broad scope and limitless approach to music making. —*Jason Birchmeier*

● **Attitude Adjustment** / Feb. 5, 2002 / KaZaZZ ✦✦✦✦
Attitude Adjustment seems far too thought out to be a debut album. Yet, as difficult as it may seem to consider Karlow the Great a rookie on this 2001 release by KaZaZZ Records, *Attitude Adjustment* is indeed his debut. And what a debut it is, encompassing three aspects of life: "the Game," "the Times," and "the Life," in that order. Karlow begins his album singing and rapping about the Game, which mostly centers around women. The album-opening "Girls" stands out as one of this album's highlights, a lively ode to what makes the Game such a sport for men like Karlow. After four more songs about the Game, the man known as the Great begins the most substantial section of this album, what he calls the Times. Here, Karlow explores a range of topics relevant to contemporary life, from songs about his male friends in the Game ("My Dogs") to himself ("Bald and Buff," "That's My Jam"). Finally, Karlow embarks on the most serious section of his debut album, the Life. Rather than emphasize the darker side of life—which can no doubt be harsh, even for someone as "great" as Karlow—the multitalented artist instead emphasizes the lighter side of life, first singing about "Havin' Fun" before getting quite personal on the album's two final songs, "Love My Life" and "Principles of Life." By the time you reach the conclusion of this album, you surely understand why Karlow is referred to as the Great—his world outlook is truly vast, and he articulates his outlook through songs that are as enjoyable as they are enriched with knowledge. Furthermore, you become so seduced by Karlow's themes that you often overlook the fact that he also produced this debut as well as wrote the entirety of it, yet another testament to his greatness. Considering *Attitude Adjustment* is only Karlow's debut, you can't help but wonder how much greater music is to come from such a unique and blessed artist. —*Jason Birchmeier*

KC Flightt

Alternative Rap, Hip-Hop, Jazz-Rap
KC Flightt is an MC, yes, but one more aligned with house than with hip-hop. Flight has at least one house classic in "Voices" from 1997. He's also part of saxophonist Bill Evans' acid jazz project, Push, which released two albums in 1994. —*Wade Kergan*

● **In Flightt** / 1989 / RCA ✦✦✦✦

Difficult to categorize and difficult to market, KC Flightt is a unique rapper who has remained in obscurity. Flightt, unlike most rappers, doesn't always rhyme, and can be quite angular and abstract. On his imaginative and visionary debut album, *In Flightt*, he draws on influences ranging from jazz to house music—and is considerably more musical and melodic than most rappers. Not terribly easy to absorb, this cerebral effort must be listened to several times in order to be fully appreciated. In the mid-'90s, Flightt resurfaced in the band of jazz saxophonist Bill Evans (who has been featuring rappers in much the same way jazz artists feature singers) but wasn't nearly as cerebral as he is on *In Flightt.* —*Alex Henderson*

Keak da Sneak

West Coast Rap, Hardcore Rap, Gangsta Rap

Keak da Sneak launched his career as one-third of 3X Krazy, a semisuccessful mid- to late-'90s hardcore rap trio from Oakland, and soon after embarked on a solo career in 1999. He signed to Moe Doe Records, who released his first three albums, *Sneakacydal* (1999), *Hi-Tek* (2001), and *The Appearances Of: Keak da Sneak* (2002), as well as a collaborative effort with former 3X Krazy colleague Agerman, *Dual Committee* (2000). Following this stint with Moe Doe, Keak moved on and continued to develop his career, beginning with the *Retaliation* album for the Sacramento-based hardcore rap label Black Market Records. —*Jason Birchmeier*

The Appearances Of: Keak da Sneak / 2002 / Moe Doe ✦✦✦

● **Retaliation** / Jan. 15, 2002 / Black Market ✦✦✦

Keak da Sneak joined the Black Market roster of West Coast hardcore rappers after some albums for Moe Doe for *Retaliation*. It's a logical partnership: Keak is about as hardcore as hardcore rappers get, and Black Market was the West Coast's premier hardcore rap label in 2002. Despite Black Market's large roster of affiliates, there are only a few guest appearances on the album—Scheem ("Squash Suckers"), Cilla Caine ("Shockn Niggaz"), Killa Tay ("Shockn Niggaz"), and Ager-Man ("Life Ain't Playin With You")—and three producers handle the majority of the beats: Lamont Blackshire, One Drop Scott, and KG. —*Jason Birchmeier*

R. Kelly (Steven Williams)

b. 1969, Chicago, IL

Producer, Vocals, Keyboards / Urban, New Jack Swing, Hip-Hop, Pop-Rap
Urban R&B producer/vocalist/multi-instrumentalist/songwriter R. Kelly and his supporting band Public Announcement began recording in 1992 at the tail end of the new jack swing era, yet he was able to keep much of its sound alive while remaining commercially successful. While he created a smooth, professional mixture of hip-hop beats, soulman crooning, and funk, the most distinctive element of Kelly's music is its explicit carnality. He was able to make songs like "Sex Me," "Bump n' Grind," "Your Body's Callin'," and "Feelin' on Yo Booty" into hits because his production was seductive enough to sell such blatant come-ons. As his crossover success broadened, Kelly also developed a flair for pop balladry that helped cement his status as one of the biggest-selling male artists of the '90s.

Kelly and Public Announcement released their debut album, *Born into the 90's*, at the beginning of 1992. It was an instant R&B smash, while earning a fair amount of pop airplay; "Honey Love" and "Slow Dance (Hey Mr. DJ)" were number-one R&B hits, while "Dedicated" was his biggest pop hit at number 31. *12 Play*, released in the fall of 1993, established Kelly as an R&B superstar, eventually selling over five million copies. The first single, "Sex Me, Pts. I & II," went gold, and the second, "Bump n' Grind," hit number one on both the pop and R&B charts in 1994; it stayed on top of the R&B charts for an astonishing 12 weeks, while logging four weeks at number one on the pop charts. The follow-up, "Your Body's Callin'," was another gold single, peaking at number 13 pop. Also in 1994, he produced *Age Ain't Nothing but a Number*, the hit debut album for then-15-year-old Detroit R&B singer Aaliyah. Late in the year, it was revealed that Kelly and Aaliyah had wed in August and gotten an annulment shortly thereafter. The news sparked a small storm of controversy in the media, yet it didn't hurt the careers of either singer. Kelly next wrote and coproduced "You Are Not Alone," the second single from Michael Jackson's *HIStory* album, which was released in the summer of 1995. Later that year, Kelly released a self-titled album which became his first to top the pop charts. *R. Kelly* sold four million copies and

produced three platinum singles—"You Remind Me of Something," "Down Low (Nobody Has to Know)," and "I Can't Sleep Baby (If I)"—all of which hit number one R&B and reached the pop Top Ten.

Kelly truly consolidated his crossover success with the 1996 single "I Believe I Can Fly," which he recorded for the Michael Jordan movie *Space Jam*. Transcending Kelly's prior sexed-up image, the song reached number two on the pop charts and won Grammy Awards for Best Male R&B Vocal Performance, Best R&B Song, and Best Song Written Specifically for a Motion Picture or for Television. Kelly remained in the public eye in 1997 with another Top Ten soundtrack tune, *Batman & Robin*'s "Gotham City." The ambitious two-disc *R.* followed in 1998, and even though it downplayed the explicit loverman routine that had made him a star, it became Kelly's biggest-selling album yet, going platinum seven times over. Its first single, a duet with Celine Dion titled "I'm Your Angel," became Kelly's second number-one pop hit with a six-week run on top. Even though subsequent singles "When a Woman's Fed Up" and "If I Could Turn Back the Hands of Time" were more successful on the R&B charts, Kelly was well on his way to landing more Top 40 hits in the '90s than any other male solo artist, and notched another with his guest appearance on Puff Daddy's R&B chart topper "Satisfy You." Moving his blockbuster success into a new decade, Kelly returned in 2000 with *TP-2.Com*, which spent three weeks at number one on the album charts and scaled back the ambition of *R.* to return to familiar lyrical themes. He scored two more R&B number ones with "I Wish" and "Fiesta" (the latter featuring guest Jay-Z), and had further hits with "Feelin' on Yo Booty" and "The World's Greatest," the latter from the soundtrack of the Will Smith film *Ali*.

In the wake of "Fiesta," Kelly and Jay-Z teamed up to record an entire album together. *The Best of Both Worlds* was heavily hyped and even more heavily bootlegged, but problems of a much more serious nature arose in February 2002, when *The Chicago Sun-Times* reported that it had been given a videotape showing Kelly having sex with a 14-year-old girl. When the scandal broke, other reports surfaced that Kelly had settled a civil suit in 1998 involving a sexual relationship with a then-underage girl, and that he was in the process of settling another suit brought by an Epic Records intern making similar allegations. Copies of the tape in question were sold as bootlegs and on the Internet, and while there was some question as to whether the man was really Kelly, and whether the girl really was underage, Kelly's past history seemed to lend credence to the charge. Some radio stations dropped him from their play lists, and anti-Kelly protests were staged in Chicago. Meanwhile, *The Best of Both Worlds* entered the charts at number two, but sold disappointingly; some blamed the scandal, others the extensive pre-release bootlegging, although the generally unfavorable reviews suggested that the record's overall quality might also have been to blame.

Following the initial sex-tape scandal, Kelly was dogged by numerous civil suits, including one from a girl who alleged that during her relationship with Kelly (which occurred while she was underage), she had become pregnant and gotten an abortion at the singer's urging. A variety of other sex videos purporting to feature Kelly appeared as bootlegs, and a onetime Kelly protégée, a singer called Sparkle, stepped forward to identify the girl on the original tape as her then-14-year-old niece. In June, Chicago police officially charged Kelly with 21 counts of child pornography-related offenses, all related to the original tape. Kelly pleaded not guilty and released a new song, "Heaven, I Need a Hug," which got extensive airplay for a brief period. Meanwhile, work on his next album, *Loveland*, stalled amid more heavy bootlegging. Kelly eventually scrapped some of the most pirated tracks, recorded some new songs, and reassembled the album as *Chocolate Factory* (which was slated to include a bonus disc with some of the deleted material). Released in advance of the album, lead single "Ignition" shot to number one on the R&B charts in late 2002. *Chocolate Factory* itself was released in early 2003. —*Stephen Thomas Erlewine and Steve Huey*

Born into the 90's / Jan. 14, 1992 / Jive ✦✦✦

One of the last popular new-jack groups, this East Coast unit had some smash singles in 1992 doing both conventional R&B/soul and hip-hop/new-jack tracks. They did both originals and covers, had an enthusiastic attitude, were well produced, and stayed on the urban contemporary outlets throughout the year. —*Ron Wynn*

● **12 Play** / Nov. 9, 1993 / Jive ✦✦✦✦✦

R. Kelly's debut album with Public Announcement from a year earlier, *Born into the 90's*, had been a fine new jack swing album, but it hardly foreshadowed the astonishing heights the all-around amazing producer/songwriter/singer summits on *12 Play*, a likewise all-around amazing album with a little bit of everything for everyone. There are a couple moments on *12 Play* that are reminiscent of *Born into the 90's*, specifically the sung/rapped ones: "Freak Dat Body" and "Back to the 'Hood of Things." These tend to be the least interesting of the 12 songs here, however, and their intermittent, mid-album sequencing is perhaps no coincidence. Rather, it's the swooning balladry of "Honey Love," a late-album gem from *Born into the 90's*, that Kelly reprises to great success throughout *12 Play*. The decision to do away with Public Announcement for the most part here is a wise one, as Kelly seems to have a real gift for late-night come-ons as well as elaborately produced musical accompaniment that's similarly alluring, as evidenced on the album-opening "Your Body's Callin'." This gentle song's inescapable pleading is then followed by another absolutely brilliant four minutes of tantalization, "Bump n' Grind," which eases in some throbbing beats to perhaps nudge up the intensity level a bit. From here, Kelly changes positions often, lightening up the mood a bit on songs like "It Seems Like You're Ready" and "For You" that seem intended for the slow to warm, while also getting a bit nasty on songs like "Freak Dat Body" and "Summer Bunnies" that seem intended for the fast and wild. He then returns to pure brilliance for the album's final climax: the breathless, 12-minute "Sex Me" and the lovely album-closing title track. What's most wonderful about *12 Play* isn't Kelly's mostly dreamy, occasionally dirty, always enrapturing rhetoric, nor his likewise arousing mood music; rather, it's his precise ability to tie them together so perfectly. This guy really is a genius, and no matter whether you find him fantastic or perverse, you have to marvel at his ability to do everything so masterfully. *—Jason Birchmeier*

R. Kelly / Nov. 14, 1995 / Jive ✦✦✦✦✦
With the salacious *12 Play*, R. Kelly established himself as one of the top R&B hitmakers of the mid-'90s, rivalled only by Babyface and Dr. Dre for overall consistency. *12 Play* was marred by occasionally slight tunes which were obscured by the explicit sexuality of the lyrics. *R. Kelly* isn't hampered by those flaws, although it isn't a perfect record by any means. Throughout the album, Kelly relies on melody and grooves instead of overtly carnal imagery. But that doesn't mean he has cleaned up—Kelly remains a sly, seductive crooner, and his sexiness is more effective when it is suggestive. Nevertheless, his lyrics and music are never subtle—even on the ballads that dominate this album—which can make *R. Kelly* tiresome if taken as a whole. Taken as individual songs, the album works better than anything he has recorded to date. *—Stephen Thomas Erlewine*

R. / Sep. 29, 1998 / Jive ✦✦✦
At the beginning of the '90s, R. Kelly was seen as a lewd, lascivious soulman. By the end of the decade, he had stripped those adjectives away and was seen as a contemporary equivalent of Marvin Gaye, thanks to the enormous success of "I Believe I Can Fly." Appropriately, *R.*, the double-disc album that followed "I Believe I Can Fly"'s parent album, finds Kelly trying to live up to that legacy. He may be talented, but he has neither the vision or the depth to match such classic soulmen as Al Green, Stevie Wonder, Prince, or Michael Jackson, all artists he emulates on *R.* Kelly's main strength is fusing contemporary material together into a slick, palatable, radio-ready record. Nobody else could have Jay-Z and Celine Dion on their album, and he's about the only one who could make it work, since he can work sensuous grooves as well as he can deliver a soaring ballad. To some, this may sound like nothing more than calculation—a big part of the reason why he doesn't instantly enter the hall of greats—because it's easy to see how he pieces it all together. When he's on, however, such calculation doesn't really matter, since it all flows, but such incidents only occur through about 40 percent of *R.* That's a major problem, considering the sheer length of the album. Clocking in at 29 long tracks, it takes real effort to sit through the record from beginning to end, especially since Kelly begins to repeat himself. If it was pruned a bit, the album would arguably be his best record. As it stands, *R.* is an admirable effort, one that is among his better records even with all of its faults. *—Stephen Thomas Erlewine*

TP-2.Com / Nov. 7, 2000 / Jive ✦✦✦
R. Kelly tames his ambitions a bit on *TP-2.Com*, assembling a simple sequel to his classic *12 Play* album from 1993 rather than another epic venture like his double-disc all-bases-covered *R.* album from 1998. The straightforwardness is somewhat of a welcome endeavor. As breath taking as had been *R.*—an album that straddled the huge gap between the sort of radio-

pop associated with Celine Dion as well as the street rap of Jay-Z and Nas—it also seemed too overblown at times, as if Kelly had something to prove during an era of double-disc epic rap albums. So to see him return to the simple singles approach of *12 Play* is refreshing, particularly since he has plenty of singles to work with here, just as he had with *TP-1*. Kelly furthermore unleashed his singles—"I Wish," a mass-appeal vocal pop number with an urban edge; "Fiesta," a Latin Invasion cash-in that aims for the dancefloor; and "Feelin' on Yo Booty," a whispery come-on for all the weak-kneed ladies and some of the mindful ones too—with tailor-made remixes to ensure himself broad airplay. Only one of those remixes is here, though, the "I Wish" one, so take heed. There's no Jay-Z-featuring remix of "Fiesta" and no up-tempo one of "Feelin' on Yo Booty," yet *TP-2.Com* is a strong album nonetheless, three steps ahead of practically every other non-rap urban album from 2000. It does seem like Kelly is coasting a bit here at times, though, particularly when you hold *TP-2.Com* up against its massive predecessor, but even when R.'s lounging, he's generally ahead of the pack. *—Jason Birchmeier*

The Best of Both Worlds / Mar. 26, 2002 / Universal ✦✦
Supergroups rarely fulfill their promise, particularly in pop music where the collaborations tend to be more about marketing than music. Thus it was unsurprising when Jay-Z and R. Kelly's much ballyhooed *Best of Both Worlds* collaboration fell a little short of the mark, commercially as well as artistically. Most were in agreement that the album was a bad idea to begin with, even though Jay-Z and R. Kelly were indeed some of the best urban music had to offer in 2002—the former sitting atop the rap game and still riding high on the success of his *Blueprint* album, which had won numerous year-end accolades; the latter a sure-shot crooner who had mesmerized masses of women who sought out his thuggish passion. The idea here is to cross-market one another—introduce Jay-Z to all the women buying Kelly's music; convince all the big ballers repping Jigga that Kelly isn't a sissy. However, rather than actually collaborate, the two give a halfhearted effort here, reportedly never even sharing the same studio and recording the album in a matter of weeks. The approach seems quite obvious: have the Trackmasters lay down a beat, have Kelly sing a catchy hook, and have Jay-Z rap on the verses—most likely in that order. And quite frankly, this album sounds like a weekend project for the artists; Jay-Z could have written these rhymes in his sleep, and Kelly simply recycles many of the same sort of hooks he'd been crooning for a decade. Chances are that more time was devoted to this album's marketing plan than its actual production. Nonetheless, even a halfhearted effort by these two often proves amazing, particularly the album's singles, "Get This Money" and "Take You Home With Me." The problem, though, is that every other song on the album tends to fall into one of these two categories: a song about getting paid or a song about getting laid—or, quite often, a synthesis of the two, getting both paid and laid. These themes can get a little trite after an hour or so, especially when delivered so brazenly. Overall, Jay-Z and Kelly had little to gain with this album—a few more crossover fans at most—but unfortunately much to lose. The urban audience, particularly the hip-hop crowd who had crowned Jay-Z king of New York, is finicky when it comes to integrity, and that's something obviously lacking here, eclipsed by greed and egotism. *—Jason Birchmeier*

Chocolate Factory / Feb. 18, 2003 / Jive ✦✦✦
R. Kelly was hardly a stranger to controversy in the early 2000s. In addition to being hit with 21 counts of child pornography in Chicago and 12 more in Polk County, FL, the beleaguered singer/producer faced various sex-related civil suits. All those scandals have, at times, overshadowed his music, which is regrettable because *Chocolate Factory* has a lot going for it. Emphasizing romantic slow jams, and not as ambitious or risk taking as 1998's *R.*—which is arguably Kelly's best, most essential release despite its own imperfections—*Chocolate Factory*, like 2000's *TP-2.Com*, tends to play it safe. But that doesn't mean *Chocolate Factory* is without merit; what it lacks in ambition it makes up for in terms of quality and craftsmanship. Many of the influences that have served Kelly well on previous efforts continue to serve him well on this 2003 release; influences that range from the Isley Brothers, Marvin Gaye, Al Green, Michael Jackson, and Stevie Wonder to Prince, Babyface, and hip-hop. All of those influences were noticeable on Kelly's '90s albums, and they are still noticeable on *Chocolate Factory*. Nonetheless, Kelly has always been his own man; that is especially obvious when he features Ronald Isley on "Showdown" (not to be confused with the Isley Brothers' 1978 recording). Hearing Kelly and Isley side by side, listeners can easily see how Kelly is able to draw

on Isley's influence while projecting a firm, recognizable identity of his own. One hopes that in the future, Kelly will come out with some more albums that are as challenging as *R.*; even so, *Chocolate Factory* will go down in history as a solid and pleasing, if somewhat predictable, addition to the Chicagoan's catalog. —*Alex Henderson*

K.F. Klik

Group / West Coast Rap, Gangsta Rap, G-Funk

Despite the popular decline of gangsta rap over the latter portion of the 1990s, the style remained vital in pockets of the West Coast into the 21st century. Of course, the environment that influenced gangsta's original emergence never went away. But the consistent marketability of the genre was also a significant factor in the second and third wave of gangsta MCs who were active on the West Coast long after G-funk pioneers such as Dr. Dre, Snoop Dogg, and Warren G had moved on. Los Angeles MCs Gee the Street Gamer and Mr. Wunderful (aka Mr. 1) first appeared as the Funkytown Professionals in late-'90s Los Angeles. Their lone release, *Reaching a Level of Assassination*, was hailed by indie Finest Entertainment as having been one of 2Pac's favorite albums when the slain icon was still active. In 1997, Gee and Wun altered their moniker to the unassuming Kali's Finest and released *Stay Ahead of the Game*. Another slice of gangsta chest bumping, the album also included in its lyrics a series of dos and don'ts for surviving in the rap game. The self-explanatory G-funk of *Spread Ya Hustle* followed in 1999; it featured such prominent guests as K-Ci & JoJo, MC Eiht, and Yo-Yo. Re-emerging in 2002 as the K.F. Klik, Gee and Mr. Wunderful released *Gangsta Khemistry* through the Finest Entertainment imprint. While the album was another recycling of the familiar gangsta/G-funk ethos, it nevertheless was an entertaining one, proving that the gangsta genre still had legs moving forward into another decade. *Gangsta Khemistry* also boasted guest shots from K-Ci & JoJo, as well as Bizzy Bone and the Eastsidaz MC Tray Deee, a protégé of Snoop Dogg. —*Johnny Loftus*

● **Gangsta Khemistry** / Oct. 15, 2002 / Finest Entertainment ◆◆◆
These days, rap has as many regional variations as the blues had in the '40s, '50s, and '60s. Back then, there were many local blues styles—Mississippi Delta blues, Chicago blues, Texas blues, Louisiana swamp blues, Piedmont blues, and so on. And similarly, contemporary rapping could be anything from a dirty South approach to a Philadelphia flow to Italian-language rapping in Milan. When *Gangsta Khemistry* starts playing, it doesn't take long to realize that K.F. Klik is a Los Angeles group—from the production style to the rappers' diction, this CD usually says South Central L.A. in no uncertain terms. One of the tunes on this 2002 release is titled "Represent Ya Hood," and there is little doubt that K.F. Klik is representing South Central. Most of the material is right out of the Dr. Dre/Snoop Dogg/Warren G school of L.A. gangsta rap and G-funk; anyone who has listened to those artists extensively won't find *Gangsta Khemistry* to be the least bit groundbreaking—certainly not by early-2002 standards. But if K.F. Klik is recycling gangsta beats and gangsta rhymes of the past, at least they're doing it well. While jams like "Represent Your Hood" (which borrows the melody from Rufus & Chaka Khan's 1974 hit "Tell Me Something Good"), "American Pimps," and "L.A." don't take West Coast rap in any new directions, the songs do get credit for being enjoyably funky. When *Gangsta Khemistry* came out in October 2002, K.F. Klik was hardly the only L.A. group with a strong Dre/Snoop/Warren G influence—in 2002, countless L.A. rappers were still milking the G-funk sound for all it was worth. Some did it badly, but K.F. Klik does it relatively well on these catchy, if derivative, grooves. —*Alex Henderson*

Kid Capri (David Anthony Love)

b. Bronx, NY
Producer, DJ, Vocals / Hip-Hop, Pop-Rap

DJ Kid Capri was born David Anthony Love in the Bronx, NY; he began scratching records as early as age eight, and was already an accomplished turntablist by his teens, later spinning records at the famed nightclub Studio 54 and earning a grass-roots following by selling mix tapes of his nightly sets. As his reputation grew, Kid Capri eventually signed to Warner Bros., where he produced sessions for everyone from Heavy D to Boogie Down Productions to Quincy Jones; he also spent seven seasons as the DJ for cable's *Russell Simmons' Def Comedy Jam*. Capri's first official solo release, *The*

Tape, appeared in 1991; the all-star *Soundtrack to the Streets* followed seven years later. —*Jason Ankeny*

● **The Tape** / Feb. 19, 1991 / Cold Chillin' ◆◆◆◆
This is an interesting, entertaining, erratic melange of rap, hip-hop, pop, funk, R&B, and dance looped, edited, and stitched together. You can hear every recent development in studio technology, plus bits and pieces of great songs, cleverly meshed together through fantastic production and editing. The performances are rather generic, but it really doesn't matter; the arrangements and the studio are the stars. —*Ron Wynn*

Soundtrack to the Streets / Nov. 3, 1998 / Track Masters/Columbia ◆◆◆

Kid Koala (Eric San)

b. 1975, Vancouver, British Columbia, Canada
DJ, Producer / Hip-Hop, Electronica, Underground Rap, Turntablism

Chinese-Canadian turntablist Kid Koala was born Eric San in Vancouver, British Columbia, in 1975. Classically trained on the piano, San instead put his fingers to work on a pair of Technics 1200s starting in the late '80s. He was a college pub DJ and bedroom turntable manipulator for nearly a decade before landing a recording deal with U.K. experimental hip-hop duo Coldcut's Ninja Tune imprint in 1997. San's eclectic approach to sound collage is actually closer to the latter's far-flung beat experiments than the old school New York and L.A. references which most often form the canon of the scratch DJ's art. It's also a circle closer of sorts: San's nascent mixing aesthetic was influenced early on by classic Coldcut records such as "(Hey Kids) What Time Is It?" and the "7 Minutes of Madness" massacre of Eric B. & Rakim's "Paid in Full." In fact, the coincidence of Koala signing to his heroes' label (despite the fact that it's based thousands of miles away and home mostly to instrumental trip-hop and computer-funk producers) was less a coincidence than it would at first appear; San managed to arrange an "inadvertent" car ride with the group when their label's Stealth tour passed through Montreal in 1996, making sure his mix tape, "Scratchappyland," was in the car stereo well beforehand. Excerpts from that tape doubled as Kid Koala's identically titled solo debut when Ninja Tune, duly impressed, released it as a 10" in July of 1997. Koala also appeared on the second volume of The Bomb's *Return of the DJ* compilation with his track "Static's Waltz," another excerpt from his mix tape. Subsequent Ninja Tune releases included Kid Koala remixes of DJ Food's "Scratch Yer Head" and (fittingly) Coldcut's classic "Beats and Pieces," plus the 2000 full-length *Carpal Tunnel Syndrome*. —*Sean Cooper*

Scratchappyland [Single] / 1997 / Ninja Tune ◆◆◆◆
Eric "Kid Koala" San's Ninja Tune debut was an identically named segment from his "Scratchappyland" mix tape. Located somewhere between the goofier moments of turntable groups such as the Invisible Skratch Piklz and the Beat Junkies and the schizophrenic sound collage of Coldcut and Steinski, the record is littered with obscure references culled from children's records and dust-caked dime-store novelties. Extremely rare but worth tracking down. —*Sean Cooper*

★ **Carpal Tunnel Syndrome** / Feb. 22, 2000 / Ninja Tune ◆◆◆◆◆
Unless you're a DJ or a student of electronic music making, turntablism can be something of an esoteric art form—everyone knows it's the foundation of hip-hop, but its techniques aren't as widely understood or appreciated as those of a traditional instrumentalist. The turntablist revival of the '90s produced some major talents (the Invisibl Skratch Piklz, the Beat Junkies, the X-Ecutioners), but the nuances of their skills were often lost on casual observers, and only sometimes translated to recordings. That's why Kid Koala's full-length debut, *Carpal Tunnel Syndrome*, is so important: it's capable of making turntablism engaging to a wider audience. It isn't that Kid Koala is necessarily the greatest DJ spinning, although he's clearly in the top tier. It's that he's able to bring so much personality and entertainment value to his work, which makes *Carpal Tunnel Syndrome* arguably the most appealing turntablist album yet released. Unlike many of his peers, Koala makes heavy use of dialogue snippets from movies and TV shows, instructional records, and other obscure sources. They provide a running commentary on the action, and Koala also assembles them into mini-skits, or makes wry jokes about the lack of respect afforded DJs as musicians. Elsewhere, there are aural jokes wholly dependent on Koala's DJ skill—"Drunk Trumpet," for example, is a cut-up jazz solo played on the crossfader. But all of this isn't to say that *Carpal Tunnel Syndrome* is a novelty item. Koala makes it easy for listeners to follow the transformation of his source material into totally

different creations, and builds some deceptively dense, layered tracks; plus, his explosive scratching (best heard on "A Night at the Nufonia") is the equivalent of a guitar shredder soloing. His infectious sense of fun is simply a gateway to *Carpal Tunnel Syndrome*'s readily apparent musical sophistication. All in all, a superb and accessible introduction to a specialist art form. —*Steve Huey*

Kid 'N Play

f. 1987, **db.** 1993
Group / Hip-Hop, Pop-Rap, Party Rap, Old School Rap

Among the first groups to tame rap's hardcore mentality into a positive, message-oriented music suitable for teens and mass audiences, Kid 'N Play debuted in 1988 with the platinum album *2 Hype*, which the duo later spun into a deal involving films and a Saturday-morning cartoon show, the first involving a rap act. Though their recording activity became limited during the gangsta-dominated '90s—1991's *Face the Nation* was their last album—the group managed two sequels to their original *House Party* film, as well as the 1991 teen flick *Class Act*.

Kid (born Christopher Reid; Bronx, NY) and Play (born Christopher Martin; Queens, NY) first met while performing in rival high school groups (the Turnout Brothers and the Super Lovers, respectively) and initially teamed up as Fresh Force. Play's former bandmate, Hurby "Luv Bug" Azor, became the duo's manager and signed Kid 'N Play to Select Records in 1987. Despite the predomination of James Brown samples during the mid-'80s, Azor gave *2 Hype* a production job more rooted in disco and pop; thanks to the near-Top Ten R&B hit "Rollin' With Kid 'N Play," the album eventually reached platinum status. Though many rappers were more successful at the time, Kid 'N Play became film stars due to their clean-cut image—Kid's six-inch "eraserhead" hairstyle, which seemed outrageous to white audiences, was vindicated by his honest, well-scrubbed face. The film *House Party* became a moderate success upon its release in 1990, and the duo even managed a proper LP that same year, *Funhouse*. During 1991, two Kid 'N Play films appeared: a sequel to *House Party* and *Class Act*. That same year, the album *Face the Nation* showed a growing reluctance to pander to pop audiences, but the duo was already entrenched in their style. A second sequel to *House Party* appeared in 1993, and little has been heard from them since. —*John Bush*

- **2 Hype** / 1988 / Select ✦✦✦✦✦

Kid 'N Play have been unfairly branded as pop sellouts over the years, despite the fact that they really never had a big crossover hit single. It was more their image that crossed over—they had their own unique sense of visual style, yet they were positive, nonthreatening, and, well, too gosh-darn *friendly* for the taste of street-level purists. Plus, they were young and clean-cut enough for middle-class teenage audiences to identify with. Accusations of being soft notwithstanding, those qualities are exactly what give their debut album, *2 Hype*, its refreshing charm. There isn't much on the duo's minds other than friendship, dancing, and dating, and everything stays pretty innocent—Kid even confesses to being shy around girls on "Undercover." If all of this seems safe and lightweight, it's also a tremendous amount of good, clean fun. Hurby "Luv Bug" Azor's production keeps things danceable and engaging throughout; the sound is fairly spare, with funky and occasionally club-friendly beats, catchy instrumental hooks behind the choruses, and basic DJ scratching. The whole album is pretty consistent, and the songs that were singles—"Rollin' With Kid 'N Play," "Gittin' Funky," and "2 Hype"—are nearly matched by some of the album tracks, particularly "Brother Man Get Hip," the story songs "Last Night" and "Undercover," and the explanation of the duo's signature dance move, "Do the Kid 'N Play Kick Step." Neither Kid nor Play is a master technician on the mic, but they're both quite respectable, in contrast to some of the would-be pop idols who followed in the years to come. And even if its sound and style are very much of their time, *2 Hype* still holds up surprisingly well, thanks to Kid 'N Play's winning personalities. —*Steve Huey*

House Party [Original Soundtrack] / 1990 / Motown ✦✦✦

For being the soundtrack to Kid 'N Play's breakout movie hit, *House Party* features surprisingly little Kid 'N Play: only the brand-new single "Funhouse" and "Kid vs. Play (The Battle)," the climactic sequence of the movie. As a matter of fact, *House Party* is pretty skimpy overall, containing only nine songs. The title cut is a showcase for co-stars Full Force and an array of their associates, including Lisa Lisa & Cult Jam, U.T.F.O., and Cheryl Pepsii Riley, among others. The Force M.D.'s, LL Cool J, and Flavor Flav ("I Can't Do

Nothing for You Man") are the other big names here, and the rest is fairly generic. The best few songs, however, do make it worthwhile for fans of the movie. —*Steve Huey*

Kid 'N Play's Funhouse / 1990 / Select ✦✦✦✦

Named after the duo's single from their hit film *House Party*, Kid 'N Play's *Funhouse* has more of the genial dance-rap that made Kid 'N Play's debut album a platinum-selling hit. This time out, the production is fuller and funkier, and the raps are correspondingly more ambitious in terms of tempo and flow—particularly Kid's, which makes sense since he was essentially the focal point. The lyrics are still chiefly about their partnership, their love of rap, and their love of dancing, but there's a distinct battle-MC tone present as well, which seems to indicate that the duo hopes to be taken more seriously as a mature hip-hop act. Individually, both rappers broaden their images based on the characters they played in *House Party*—Kid the reluctant star, Play the ladies' man—yet they're still wholesome at bottom. Their viewpoint crystallizes in "Back to Basics," a lament about hip-hop culture losing its innocent sense of fun and turning violent; it's a more self-aware stance that acknowledges their place in the spectrum. There's also an entertaining guest spot from Salt-N-Pepa on the Play-centered track "I Don't Know," in which Play comes out on the winning end of a love triangle. If *Kid 'N Play's Funhouse* doesn't have quite the same youthful charm as *2 Hype*, it's nonetheless a worthy successor that finds the duo progressing. —*Steve Huey*

Face the Nation / Sep. 24, 1991 / Select ✦✦

Kid 'N Play's final album, *Face the Nation*, simply doesn't feel as effervescent as *2 Hype* or *Funhouse*. That's partly because the duo tries to get more serious and substantive in their lyrical content, much as *House Party 2* suddenly developed a social conscience that left fans scratching their heads. Despite its admirable intentions, *Face the Nation* gets a little preachy at times. The title cut takes on issues like drugs, crime, and education, and "Slippin'" is a cautionary tale about a street hustler who falls victim to drugs and violence. "Next Question" disses the 2 Live Crew for having nothing positive to base a career on once their schtick wears off (and they were right, even in spite of the points made on the J.T. Money answer record, "Pussy Ass Kid and Hoe Ass Play"). The other problem with *Face the Nation* is that the dance tracks don't feel as effortless as before, possibly because the duo's heart isn't in them. A few make reference to being young and rich, which starts to dispel their rappers-next-door appeal, and the chorus of "Back on Wax" makes rather painful references to their movies, kick-step dance move, and cartoon (no rap group should ever call themselves "the ones that made Saturday morning fun"). In the end, Kid 'N Play might have lost their audience anyway, but *Face the Nation* only hastened the process. —*Steve Huey*

Kid Rock (Robert James Ritchie)

b. Jan. 17, 1971, Romeo, MI
Hard Rock, Heavy Metal, Rap-Metal, Rap-Rock, Alternative Metal

One of the unlikeliest success stories in rock at the turn of the millennium, Detroit rap-rocker Kid Rock shot to superstardom with his fourth full-length album, 1998's *Devil Without a Cause*. What made it so shocking was that Rock had recorded his first demo a full decade before, been booted off major label Jive following his Beastie Boys-ish 1990 debut *Grits Sandwiches for Breakfast*, and toiled for most of the decade in obscurity, releasing albums to a small, devoted, mostly local fan base while earning his fair share of ridicule around his home state. Nevertheless, Rock persevered, and by the time rap-metal had begun to attract a substantial audience, he had perfected the outlandish, over-the-top, white-trash persona that gave *Devil Without a Cause* such a distinctive personality and made it such an infectious party record. Bob "Kid Rock" Ritchie (born Robert James Ritchie, Jan. 17, 1971) grew up in Romeo, Michigan, a small rural town north of the Detroit metro area. Finding small-town life stiflingly dull, Ritchie immersed himself in rap music, learned to breakdance, and began making the talent-show rounds in Detroit. Inspired by the Beastie Boys' *Licensed to Ill*—white performers fusing rap and hard guitar rock—Kid Rock recorded his first demos in 1988, and eventually scored an opening slot at a Boogie Down Productions gig. That performance, in turn, led to a contract with Jive Records, which issued Kid Rock's debut album, *Grits Sandwiches for Breakfast*, in 1990. Produced by Kid Rock, Too Short, and D-Nice, the album was *heavily* derivative of *Licensed to Ill*. Rock briefly became notorious when a New York college radio station aired the album's profanity-laced ode to oral sex, "Yodelin' in the Valley," and was fined over $20,000 (a judgment later rescinded). However, despite a tour with Too Short and Ice Cube, Jive didn't see much of a future for Kid Rock and dropped him from their roster.

Moving to Brooklyn, Rock hooked up with the small Continuum label, and moved his brand of rap further into hard rock with *The Polyfuze Method*, released in 1993. Reviews were mixed, with some critics praising the record's humor and eclecticism while others dismissed it as awkward and forced. The EP *Fire It Up* followed in 1994, appearing on Rock's own Top Dog imprint (which was still distributed by Continuum). Rock eventually returned to the Detroit area and began work on another album; recorded on a shoestring budget, *Early Mornin' Stoned Pimp* was released in 1996. Although sometimes forced to sell bootleg dubs of his own records to pay the rent, Rock set about forming a full-fledged backing band, which he dubbed Twisted Brown Trucker. While its membership fluctuated early on, rapper Joe C. (born Joseph Calleja) was one of the first to join; a longtime fan and frequent concert attendee, Calleja caught Rock's eye in 1994, partly because of his diminutive stature (due to a digestive condition known as celiac disease, which required both dialysis and extensive medication) and partly because of his encyclopedic knowledge of Rock's song lyrics. The rest of the lineup settled around mostly Detroit-area musicians: guitarists Kenny Olson and Jason Krause, keyboardist Jimmy Bones (born Jimmy Trombly, he handles the bass lines himself), drummer Stefanie Eulinberg, DJ/turntablist Uncle Kracker (born Matt Shafer, who had been with Rock since the early '90s), and backing vocalists Misty Love and Shirly Hayden.

As rap-metal acts like Korn, Limp Bizkit, and Rage Against the Machine began to dominate the hard rock landscape, Atlantic Records decided to take a chance on signing Rock. *Devil Without a Cause* didn't do much upon its initial release in August 1998, but a big promotional push from the label and MTV helped make the album's second single and video, "Bawitdaba," a nationwide smash. The follow-up, "Cowboy," achieved similar success, and suddenly, after a decade of trying, Kid Rock was a superstar with a Top Five, seven-times-platinum album and a gig at Woodstock '99. While pondering how to follow up *Devil*, Rock acquired the rights to his indie-label recordings and remixed or re-recorded the best material for *The History of Rock*, which was released in the summer of 2000 and featured some new songs as well. Sadly, after being forced to take a break from touring a year earlier by his medical difficulties, Joe C. passed away in his sleep on November 16, 2000.

Even with a tragedy like this in his life, Rock continued work on his follow-up to *Devil Without a Cause*. The media focused more on his relationship with actress Pamela Anderson than his musical career, which many magazines were beginning to ridicule. His DJ, Uncle Kracker, had a successful solo career during the spring and summer of 2001, leaving Rock without one of his most frequent collaborators. Still, by the winter of that year he had completed work on *Cocky* and had released "Forever" to success on rock radio. *—Steve Huey*

Grits Sandwiches for Breakfast / 1990 / Jive ✦✦

When *Devil Without a Cause* exploded onto the scene in 1998, Kid Rock was suddenly everywhere, seemingly out of nowhere. But underneath that fedora was the mind of an individual whose white-trash Grandmaster Flash persona had been conceived of, constructed, and refined over almost ten years of dogged determination. As a teenager growing up in Romeo, MI, Rock immersed himself in hip-hop culture. He learned to breakdance, grew in a high-top fade, and began rapping in a style similar to the Beastie Boys' *License to Ill*. A series of demo recordings led to a gig opening for Boogie Down Productions; that led in turn to a recording contract with Jive Records. The result was 1990's *Grits Sandwiches for Breakfast*. While its similarity to *License to Ill* borders on tribute range, *Grits Sandwiches* nevertheless contains a few elements of the Bob Seger-loving, turntable-scratching, dirt-ass pimp character who would later emerge as the American Bad Ass. "Genuine Article" is an early version of Rock's distinctive first-person boast-speak; the track even includes a raw guitar sample in its verses. The riff from the Doobie Brothers' "China Grove" lights up the chorus of the otherwise tepid "With a One Two," though at this point in Rock's career, the reference was more likely an attempt to emulate the Beastie Boys' freewheeling use of rock samples over traditional beats than any nod to his later genre-mixing dirt-track irony. For despite Kid's distinct, hard-edged flow and references to the building blocks that would later make his career, *Grits Sandwiches for Breakfast* is a mostly laughable recording that apes not only the Beasties but also LL Cool J's

"Going Back to Cali" ("Yo-Da-a-Lin in the Valley") and Rob Base ("The Upside"), two other hip-hop heavyweights of the era. *Grits Sandwiches'* best track is likely "Super Rhyme Maker," which references the Rock's high-top fade (immortalized in cartoon form in the album's cover art), and rhymes "gave a hoot" with "knock the boots." *—Johnny Loftus*

The Polyfuze Method / 1993 / Continuum ✦✦✦

In 1990, Kid Rock landed a $100,000 record deal with Jive, only to be unceremoniously kicked to the curb when *Grits Sandwiches for Breakfast*, his corny debut, was much less than a blockbuster. Displaying the pluck that would contribute to his eventual stardom, Rock was undeterred by the chilly reception. He moved to New York City, signed on with indie label Continuum, and in 1993 released *The Polyfuze Method*. While it isn't much better than its predecessor, the album doesn't swipe as shamelessly from established hip-hop acts, and represents a significant leap forward not only in the development of Kid Rock's unlikely mixture of classic rock, hip-hop, and country influences but also his own trailer-park pimp-daddy persona.

While the 2 Live Crew-style bass workouts of *Grits Sandwiches* aren't as prominent, *The Polyfuze Method* does borrow liberally from the militant, congested sound of Public Enemy, as well as N.W.A. However, Rock isn't even in the same lyrical universe as Chuck D, so the influence doesn't seem like blatant theft. If anything, *Polyfuze Method*'s beefed-up production is a plus, as it strengthens Kid's occasionally weak raps by shouldering some of the centralizing pressure. "Killin' Brain Cells" features big percussion and a funky guitar sample underneath lines like: "People wanna know what I'm thinkin'/But I don't care/So I keep my thoughts in a bottle of Cuervo." The song foreshadowed the confluence of blind bravado, hard liquor, and rocking beats that would become such a successful formula with 1998's *Devil Without a Cause*. "Prodigal Son," "The Cramper," and "Fuck You Blind" feature similar sounds and themes; the latter's live guitar and percussion was a definite break from the prevailing hip-hop sound in 1993. Unfortunately, these relatively promising tracks can't save *The Polyfuze Method*. The album's second half is plenty raunchy, but songs like "Balls in Your Mouth" can't get by with lurid porn samples alone. The unfortunate slow jam "My Oedipus Complex" isn't good for anyone, either. The Rock himself may have delivered the final verdict on *The Polyfuze Method*. Many of its better songs were later re-released on the post-*Devil Without a Cause* retrospective *The History of Rock*. However, they were also re-recorded or largely reworked by Kid and his new band, Twisted Brown Trucker. Despite its strong suggestion of what was to come, *Polyfuze Method* doesn't really go anywhere. *—Johnny Loftus*

Early Mornin' Stoned Pimp / Jan. 9, 1996 / Top Dog ✦✦✦

● Devil Without a Cause / Aug. 18, 1998 / Lava ✦✦✦✦✦

I don't suspect that even Kid Rock believed he had an album as good as *Devil Without a Cause* in him. Nobody else believed it, that's for sure. But he didn't just find the perfect extention of his Beastie and Diamond Dave infatuations here; he came up with the great hard rock album of the late '90s—a fearlessly funny, bone-crunching record that manages to sustain its strength, not just until the end of its long running time, but through repeated plays. The key to its sucesss is that it's never trying to be a hip-hop record. It's simply a monster rock album, as Twisted Brown Trucker turns out thunderous, funky noise—and that's funky not just in the classic sense, but also in a Southern-fried, white-trash sense, as he gives this as much foundation in country as he does hip-hop. But what really reigns supreme on *Devil Without a Cause* is a love of piledriving, classic hard rock, not just that of hometown hero Bob Seger, but Lynyrd Skynyrd, Van Halen, and faceless arena rock ballads. The Kid makes it all shine with rhymes so clever and irresistible that it's impossible not to quote them. For all its modernity—Rock's rapping, the titanic metallic guitars, Joe C's sideshow sidekick, the plea to "get in the pit and try to love someone"—this is firmly in the tradition of classic hard rock, and it's the best good-time hard rock album in years (certainly the best of the last three years of the '90s). *—Stephen Thomas Erlewine*

The History of Rock / May 30, 2000 / Lava ✦✦✦✦

Devil Without a Cause was so good it caused everybody to reevaluate Kid Rock, including Rock himself. As he prepped a follow-up, he unleashed *The History of Rock*, a hodgepodge of new songs, unreleased tunes, demos, old cuts, and re-recordings. This not only bought the Kid time, it gave him a chance to revamp a past that was bordering on the seriously lame. According to *The History*, Rock always knew what he was doing. Anyone that's heard *The Polyfuze Method* knows that's not the case, but that's the beauty of *The*

History, since the early stuff now sounds of a piece with *Devil*. It isn't nearly as good, but it has some of the same thrills since his band hits harder and funkier than any of its rap-rock peers and Rock now has a fully cultivated persona. Still, the songs just aren't here. Apart from the "Get out of Denver" rewrite "Born 2 B a Hick," "Early Mornin' Stoned Pimp," "3 Sheets to the Wind," and maybe the Skynyrd-aping "Prodigal Son," the older recordings are still clumsy, something the new song "American Bad Ass" is not. A shameless slab of self-mythology where the former Bob Ritchie calls out tag lines from *Devil* and places himself in the company of Seger, the Beasties, and No-Show Jones, all to a sample of Metallica's "Sad But True," it's cool, more or less, but not as monumental as "Bawitdaba," which had true wit, original riffs, and a sense of purpose. But, once you've worn out *Devil* and you need a new fix, you're not going to find it on the older Kid Rock albums—you're going to find it here. It's not a great listen, but its swagger and white-trash style make it the second-best record in his catalog. —*Stephen Thomas Erlewine*

Cocky / Nov. 20, 2001 / Lava ♦♦♦♦
Great title. Pretty good album. Perhaps it shouldn't be a surprise that Kid Rock decided to follow his *Devil Without a Cause* blueprint for its follow-up, since that was the record where he figured out how to mix "the hard rock/Southern rock with the hip-hop," creating a towering, powerful original blend of country-fried metal, heartland rock, knowing arena rock posturing, old school rap, and classic American hard rock. It was what he planned to do from the outset, so why should he give it up now that he could finally do what he always wanted? Still, there's no denying that a sequel simply does not pack the punch and the surprise of the original, no matter how well it's constructed, and that's why it initially is easy to view *Cocky* as a bit of a disappointment, since it not only offers nothing new, it seems considerably tamer than its predecessor. How could it not? Not only does Kid have nothing to prove this time around—he not only went platinum, he did it ten times-plus and then landed Sheryl Crow and Pam Anderson—he no longer has his midget sidekick, Joe C., around to enhance the Midwestern carnival atmosphere of his entourage. That wild, white-trash Fellini-esque vibe is missed, as is the overwhelmingly great songwriting of *Devil*, but if not viewed as direct competition with its predecessor—which is, after all, *the* great hard rock album of the late '90s, filled with great sounds and songwriting—*Cocky* is a pretty good sequel. One that roots itself deeper in classic rock than in hip-hop and one that isn't as gonzo or as funny, but is still much, much funnier and looser than any of its competitors. If the songs aren't classics or if it tends to drift instead of staying focused like *Devil*, it still is better than anything else in Kid's catalog and anything else from his rap-metal competitors (he makes all of them sound like rank amateurs), and it has better riffs and earthier rhythms than any hard rock artist since 38 Special, while retaining a true Michigan flavor. That might not make it the equal of *Devil Without a Cause*, but unpretentious, blue-collar hard rock hasn't sounded this good in nearly 20 years, and that's reason enough to celebrate. —*Stephen Thomas Erlewine*

Killah Priest

b. Brooklyn, NY
East Coast Rap, Hardcore Rap
Killah Priest is a tangential associate of the Wu-Tang Clan. The Brooklyn native made his first recorded appearances on records by such Wu side projects and solo albums as the Gravediggaz, Ol' Dirty Bastard's *Return to the 36 Chambers*, and, most importantly, Genius/GZA's seminal *Liquid Swords*. His contributions became legendary and paved the way for the release of his acclaimed debut album, *Heavy Mental*, in the spring of 1998.

Born in Brooklyn and raised in Bedford-Stuyvesant and Brownsville, Killah Priest became infatuated with hip-hop as a child, listening to old school and new school acts like Eric B. & Rakim alike. He also was influenced by local rappers, like Genius and Onyx's Suave, who would often play local parties. Killah Priest began working on his rhyming and eventually earned a considerable reputation in Brooklyn, but instead of pursuing his musical career further, he took a sabbatical in order to educate himself, primarily about religion and history.

Killah Priest returned to rapping in 1995, appearing on several Wu projects. All of his cameos were noteworthy, but his role on *Liquid Swords* earned special attention. By the end of 1996, he formed his own side project, the Sunz of Man. In 1997, GZA suggested to Geffen that they sign Killah Priest,

and the label took his advice. Killah worked on the album with True Master and 4th Disciple, two producers associated with the Clan. The resulting album, *Heavy Mental*, was dense with religious imagery and filled with evocative sounds. It received excellent reviews upon its March 1998 release and was a respectable commercial success, debuting at number 24 on the pop charts. Killah Priest issued his second album, *View From Masada*, in the spring of 2000, further bolstering his status as one of the most compelling solo artists in the Wu-Tang stable. —*Stephen Thomas Erlewine*

● **Heavy Mental** / Mar. 10, 1998 / Geffen ♦♦♦♦
As one of the late-arriving members of the Wu-Tang Clan, perhaps it isn't surprising that Killah Priest doesn't follow the RZA blueprint as strictly as his peers. His debut record, *Heavy Mental*, uses the signature Wu sound as a foundation, stretching out RZA's impressionistic soundscapes with weird samples and drum loops. Nevertheless, Killah Priest isn't strictly about sound—he's about the entire picture, and his lyrics are decidedly stranger and more ambitious than the average late-'90s rapper. *Heavy Mental* is filled with weird religious imagery, unpredictable symbolism, and strange allegories, all of which are married to production that is the aural equivalent of his verbal surrealism. As a result, *Heavy Mental* is a welcome surprise—the rare late-'90s record that not only has ambitions, but also fulfills them. —*Stephen Thomas Erlewine*

View From Masada / May 9, 2000 / MCA ♦♦♦
With his 1998 debut, *Heavy Mental*, Killah Priest dropped so much knowledge that it literally seemed as if this metaphysical brother from the planet of Brooklyn was on another mental plan. Yet, even though his spacy production and spiritually enlightening wordplay went over the heads of many, at the very least it made for an interesting listening session. After a two-year hiatus the street preacher re-emerges, but in a distinctly less profound fashion, as his sophomore effort, *View From Masada* is neither a natural nor cohesive progression. While KP's narrative abilities are evident on the title track, his frequent and disorienting shifts between scholar ("Hard Times") and thug ("Gotta Eat") are ripe with contrast and hard to swallow. If *Masada* proves anything, it simply reiterates just how prevalent commercialism has become in the hip-hop culture, as no one is safe from its lure—not even a Priest. —*Matt Conaway*

Priesthood / Jul. 10, 2001 / Proverbs ♦♦♦♦
One of the most slept-on MCs in hip-hop, Killah Priest has dealt with more than his fair share of industry problems. Though he denies rumors of a beef with his mentors in Wu-Tang Clan, the rapper was noticeably absent from their disappointing *The W*. And despite solid sales and critical acclaim for his previous solo albums, Killah Priest was dropped from his major-label deal with MCA. But as one of hip-hop's finest lyricists, Killah was not about to be held down, and the self-released *Priesthood* is a razor-sharp statement of purpose that finds the underground MC in peak form. Songs like "Madness" match a profound, sociopolitically charged consciousness with an uncanny eye for urban detail, with Nicrocist's atmospheric production supporting Priest's dense rhymes. The irresistibly catchy "My Hood" is even more potent, with spiritually charged lyrics bemoaning the state of the streets backed by a funky, guitar-laden riff and singalong chorus. But the all-star appeal of "Horsemen Talk" makes it the album's most remarkable cut. A preface to the 4 Horsemen's eagerly anticipated debut, the song features Priest, Canibus, Kurupt, and Ras Kass—arguably the most underrated MCs in rap—trading vicious rhymes that will make weak MCs sit up and take notice. This underground manifesto may not break any sales records, but without major-label money or the big-name producers it usually affords, Killah Priest has released one of the year's most powerful hip-hop albums. —*Bret Love*

Killarmy

Group / Hip-Hop, Hardcore Rap
Part of the large family of groups based around the Wu-Tang Clan, Killarmy consists of Killa Sin, Shogun Assassin, 9th Prince (aka North Star, Madman), Baretta 9, Islord, and Dom Pachino. Predominantly produced by 4th Disciple—who has also worked with Shabazz the Disciple as well as Wu-Tang—Killarmy released two singles through Wu-Tang/Priority in 1997, "Camouflage Ninjas" and "Wu-Renegades," before releasing their debut album, *Silent Weapons for Quiet Wars*, in August of that year. *Dirty Weaponry* followed in 1998. —*John Bush*

Silent Weapons for Quiet Wars / Aug. 5, 1997 / Priority ◆◆◆

The fact that Killarmy's debut *Silent Weapons for Quiet Wars* was coreleased on Wu-Tang Records suggests that the hardcore crew is part of the Wu-Tang Clan. In reality, the group has more in common with Master P's legion of rip-off artists on No Limit, the label that coreleased *Silent Weapons*. Killarmy is a low-rent Wu-Tang, approximating some of the spare, haunting menace of RZA's productions, but without the tough, clever raps that make Wu-Tang so distinctive. Unlike many imitations, Killarmy is actually enjoyable—several of the tracks have catchy, noisy hooks and beats, and the group's rhymes have potential. *Silent Weapons for Quiet Wars* is too long to make a large impact—especially since they repeat many of their best ideas over the course of the record—but when its consumed in small doses, it's quite enjoyable. —*Leo Stanley*

● **Dirty Weaponry** / Aug. 11, 1998 / Priority ◆◆◆◆

With their second album, *Dirty Weaponry*, Killarmy makes great strides toward distinguishing themselves as an individual crew, not just a third-generation Wu-Tang relative. There are still traces of RZA and the Wu, to be sure, but the 4th Disciple's production has begun to develop its own identity, particularly in that his beats are fleshier and funkier. None of the six rappers have developed a lyrical style as distinctive as Ol' Dirty Bastard or Raekwon, but they're coming close, with the 9th Prince and Killa Sin standing out from the pack. That combination of better music and lyrical flow makes it more compelling than the debut, and its best moments qualify as some of the best Wu-family music of 1998. —*Leo Stanley*

Fear, Love & War / Aug. 7, 2001 / Relativity ◆◆◆

Every empire needs a military. The Wu-Tang empire has Killarmy, a group of roughnecks that create songs drenched with warfare imagery. Its third album is titled *Fear, Love & War* and while there is plenty of fear and war, love seems hard to find. Most of the album deals with topics the crew dealt with in its first two albums. "Monster" is a powerful call to arms while "Street Monopoly" benefits from a particularly haunting arrangement. Some love does sneak in on the album thanks to "Lady Sings the Blues" and it is a welcome respite from the bleak images on the rest of the album. It's clear that 4th Disciple has been trained well by Wu-Tang wizard RZA as his production captures the essence of Wu-Tang's dark, dank sound. Lyrically, the music suffers from repetition as too many of the songs deal with the same militaristic themes. After three albums, it seems that Killarmy needs to find a new battle to fight. —*Jon Azpiri*

Kinfusion

f. Detroit, MI

Group / Hip-Hop, Gangsta Rap, Underground Rap

A duo of James "Flip" Griffin and his cousin Lake "Dolla" Bates, Kinfusion was one of the few rap acts to break out of Detroit during the mid-'90s. Griffin and Bates formed the group while still in high school, and played various clubs and house parties around the area during the mid-'90s. After recording a three-track demo with local producer Art Forest, the pair took a bus to New York City armed only with 50 cassettes. After hooking up with Touchwood Records, Kinfusion signed a contract. The first single, "Crooked Green Papers"—taken from the demo tape—sold 15,000 copies through limited distribution. Debut album *Da Unhatched Breed* appeared in October 1997. —*John Bush*

● **Da Unhatched Breed** / Oct. 14, 1997 / Touchwood ◆◆◆◆

Full of haunting, eerie keyboards, *Da Unhatched Breed* is a perfect example of just how musical many of the rap albums of 1997 were. Play this CD (a commercial breakthrough for rap duo Kinfusion) next to some of the amelodic, highly abrasive recordings that Run-D.M.C. and LL Cool J made in the mid-1980s, and Kinfusion's tracks seem much more melodic by comparison. While those artists favored a bombastic musical assault, Kinfusion and other MCs who emerged in the mid-1990s preferred to groove and groove. The Detroit duo's boasting lyrics are fairly routine, and its observations on inner-city life on "Crooked Green Papers" and "Thug Dreams" aren't all that memorable. They certainly aren't saying anything that countless other rappers haven't already said. But musically, *Da Unhatched Breed* is a CD that commands attention. —*Alex Henderson*

Da King & I

Group / Hip-Hop, Bass Music, East Coast Rap, Party Rap

This jazz and dancehall-influenced Brooklyn duo consisting of Izzy the MC and Majesty the DJ made some rumblings in 1993 with their one and only

LP, *Contemporary Jeep Music*, primarily on the strength of two singles, "Flip Da Script" and "Tears." Conceived and produced by Atlanta hip-hop mogul Dallas Austin, the duo's sound is jazzy East Coast hip-hop with a slight southern twang. Although slightly reminiscent of Pete Rock & C.L. Smooth, their sound is relatively distinct. Izzy's voice and lyrical ability are quite superb and the album still sounds smooth and fairly fresh today. Unfortunately, the duo was unable to carve out their own niche in the early '90s between the hardcore pillars of Onyx and Naughty By Nature, and nary a peep has been heard from them since. —*Michael Di Bella*

● **Contemporary Jeep Music** / Jul. 13, 1993 / Rowdy ◆◆◆◆

Da King & I's one and only album is mostly a laid-back jazz-hip-hop exploration. The title of the album is slightly misleading because this is not the deep thundering bass of Jeep music but rather a smoothed out soulful journey. The debut single "Flip Da Script" was an East Coast hit and the follow-up single, "Tears," is an excellent hip-hop love lost/breakup record in the vein of the Pharcyde's "Passin' Me By." The album is filled with mostly lighthearted storytelling with a New York edge. The use of the horn sample was in vogue at the time and nearly every track is horn fueled. Most of the tracks are down to earth and accessible, reflecting a kinder, gentler hip-hop age. Although drawing comparisons to another DJ/MC duo, Pete Rock & C.L. Smooth, Da King & I have a unique style. This mellow album was largely slept on and the duo would never recover. —*Michael Di Bella*

King Tee

b. Los Angeles, CA

Concept, Voices, Producer / Hip-Hop, West Coast Rap

One of the West Coast's pioneering rappers, King Tee (later known as King T) released a number of commercially unsuccessful albums in the late '80s and early '90s before eventually being dropped by his label by the mid-'90s. Though these albums indeed sound dated to contemporary ears, his work alongside two of the West Coast's premier producers of the time—DJ Pooh and E-Swift—makes them historically important and no doubt influential. Yet even if King Tee's career never saw him cross over into national consciousness like many of his Los Angeles peers, he collaborated with most of the West Coast's rappers and producers throughout the '90s, including Ant Banks, Too Short, Rappin' 4-Tay, B-Legit, Xzibit, Ice Cube, and Ice-T, among others. He eventually became a loose affiliate of tha Alkaholiks posse and, even more importantly, was taken under Dr. Dre's golden wings. Dre tried to relaunch Tee's career during the inaugural era of his Aftermath label, but a slight appearance on the *Dr. Dre Presents the Aftermath* compilation and a poorly received solo album featuring some Dre production, *Thy Kingdom Come*, didn't do much to reestablish him. Yet the veteran rapper continued to align himself with Dre's camp in hopes of success, making cameo appearances on the *2001* album and also on Xzibit's *Restless*. —*Jason Birchmeier*

● **Act a Fool** / Nov. 16, 1988 / Capitol ◆◆◆◆◆

Defiant, angry, confrontational, and bemused raps from King Tee on this late-'80s rap release. While there's some blustering and macho/sexual posturing, there are also many moments where Tee's comments deserve close scrutiny. The production isn't as relentless in the number of fragments, samples, and snippets, or as intricately edited as many other recent hip-hop releases. —*Ron Wynn*

At Your Own Risk / Sep. 24, 1990 / Capitol ◆◆◆◆◆

Compton rapper King Tee's second album again blended humorous jibes, novelty cuts, and some messages, but it was far different from most of what was coming from Compton by 1990. Such songs as "Do Your thing," "Jay Fay Dray" and "On The Dance Tip" were light years away from N.W.A-style gangsta rap. Even the more serious cuts, like "At Your Own Risk," were more reflective than combative or prophetic, and Tee's rapping was a mix of clowning, taunting, and mocking, rather than declaring and challenging. —*Ron Wynn*

Tha Triflin' Album / 1993 / Capitol ◆◆

Sometimes titles can be quite accurate, and this one reflected the general attitude the hip-hop audience took toward King Tee's third CD. He had never been in the spotlight that much, and his rhymes and lighter rap approach now sounded dated and far off the mark. —*Ron Wynn*

IV Life / Mar. 28, 1995 / MCA ◆◆◆◆

King Tee has many things to be thanked for, from his humorous yet often very serious music to his early support of the now legendary Alkaholiks crew.

IV Life has many a classic track for you to ride to in your car, like "Super Nigga," "Down Ass Loc," or the obvious "Let's Go Dippin." This album is more with the times than his past work, but the King still maintains that slow methodical delivery he's been known for. While it may not reach the respect levels that his previous albums had among his fans, this is definitely one of his better albums. —*Brad Mills*

Ruff Rhymes: Greatest Hits Collection / Nov. 3, 1998 / Capitol ✦✦✦✦

Dee Dee King (Douglas Colvin)

b. Sep. 18, 1952, Fort Lee, VA, d. Jun. 5, 2002
Bass, Lyricist, Producer, Vocals / Punk, Old School Rap
Rapper Dee Dee King is actually rocker Dee Dee Ramone going through a whopping identity crisis in the late '80s. As Ramones drummer Marky Ramone put it, "Dee Dee isn't a rap artist, he's a rock artist. I thought it was sort of unusual. One day he started wearing Mercedes Benz chains around his neck and gold rings. It was crazy. You know, I really think he lost his mind."

After leaving the Ramones in 1989, Dee Dee also spent the '90s writing Ramones songs (including six tracks on the Ramones' 1995 *Adios Amigos*), doing some production work, recording a solo rock 45 with a new band called the Chinese Dragons, and releasing a pair of solo rock LPs. —*Matt Carlson*

Standing in the Spotlight / Jul. 1988 / Red Eye ✦
Dee Dee Ramone's "Standing in the Spotlight" will go down in the annals of pop culture as one of the worst recordings of all time. Which, of course, makes it one hell of a great collector's item. Dee Dee plumbs the depths of stupidity for this record, musically (hip-hop done in some sort of off-rhythm samba beat) and lyrically. To give some credit, "Poor Little Rich Girl" and "Emergency" sound like the same overproduced pop-punk the Ramones were putting out in the mid-'80s, while "The Crusher" was redone much more aggressively on the Ramones' 1995 *Adios Amigos*. Also, Debbie Harry sings backup on two tracks. —*Matt Carlson*

KJ-52 (Jonah Sorrentino)

Vocals, Producer, Drum Programming / Underground Rap, Hardcore Rap
Raised in a rough-and-tumble suburb of Tampa, FL, KJ-52 (real name: Jonah Sorrentino) was the product of a broken home, and eventually found himself mixed up in drugs, drinking, and chasing skirts. At 15 a family member challenged him to take up Christ, and being born again gave him the strength to move on. But rather than give up hip-hop and its tacit endorsement of sin, KJ poured his faith into his hip-hop. Even his name was devotional: "KJ" was an abbreviation of his old rap name, but "52" (pronounced "five-two") represented the miracle of the five loaves and two fish. KJ-52 believed he was spreading the word of the Lord in much the same way Jesus shared the food in the story. But his road to Christian hip-hop heaven wasn't easy. While still a teenager, KJ began working in youth ministry at a Florida inner-city church. He also recorded a demo, but it was largely ignored. Christian or not, getting your music noticed is tough. It wasn't until KJ met a young, likeminded rapper named Golden Child that things began to move forward. The two young men formed Sons of Intellect and began performing throughout Florida. Soon Golden Child moved on and the Sons dissolved. But that brief bit of success in the Christian rap game had whet KJ's appetite, and in the summer of 1998 he stepped down from his youth minister position to pursue his Christian rap dream full time.

A relationship with Gotee Records' Todd Collins led to a deal with Nashville CCM label Essential, and the label released the debut KJ-52 full-length, *Seventh Avenue*, in April of 2000. The LP featured collaborations with such Christian heavyweights as Cross Movement and Knowdaverbs. Extensive touring followed the release, and KJ-52 found he'd finally established himself as the Christian rapper he always felt he could be. In 2002, KJ-52 dropped *Collaborations*. The album's title referred to the numerous contributions made to the album by guest artists, including Ill Harmonics, Pillar, and Thousand Foot Krutch. The most interesting track on *Collaborations* was "Dear Slim." The track presented an open letter to Eminem, taking issue with Em's own song, "Stan," and some of the more extreme opinions expressed in the Detroit star's lyrics. A battle rap of sorts (albeit a warm fuzzy version), the song nicely encapsulated KJ-52's conversational rapping style, his intricate wordplay, and his devotion to the man upstairs. —*Johnny Loftus*

● **Collaborations** / Jul. 16, 2002 / Bec Recordings ✦✦✦✦
East Coast hardcore rap artist KJ-52 assumes the role of cool ringmaster over myriad coconspirators as he deftly deals sleek pop hooks, funky dance beats, and sharp-witted, streetwise wordplay on *Collaborations*. As the title implies, KJ-52 teams with various mixers, melding humor and aggression with musical and lyrical analogies that are entertaining and heartfelt. "5th Element," which details the five essential components of hip-hop from the first-person perspective of a shell-toe Adidas, a microphone, a turntable, and a spray can, is ingenious and infectious. An a cappella diatribe, "Industry" takes dead aim at the conflicts between art and commerce, pointing fingers at fellow rappers and record company executives with equal venom. "ABC's and 1, 2, 3's" evokes the amiable nature of television/film superstar Will Smith with a series of tongue-in-cheek lessons in life. "Where Were You" is the pure late-'60s sound of Motown via lush harmonies, slick choruses, and serious social and interpersonal consciousness. And "Dear Slim" is a nifty "Stan"-type open letter to bad-boy brother in arms Eminem. *Collaborations* reaches out to a wide audience with confidence and conviction. —*Tom Semioli*

K.M.D.

Group / Hardcore Rap, Hip-Hop
The crew known as K.M.D. first came to be known in 1989 as affiliates of Def Jam Recordings' highly talented trio Third Bass, an affiliation that would one day prove its irony. K.M.D. member Zevlove X contributed the concept and a compelling verse on the classic Third Bass jam, "The Gas Face." The crew composed primarily of Zevlove and DJ Sub-Roc kept close ties with emerging talents Third Bass for a couple of years, then went on to record their debut *Mr. Hood* on Elektra Records in 1991. On *Mr. Hood*, K.M.D. combined lighthearted humor with divisive political rhetoric, but the overall sentiment was one of youthful positivity. The album featured production from the Stimulated Dummies and a guest spot from Brand Nubian. "Peach Fuzz," a tale of young romance, rippled momentarily, but the crew could not capitalize on their connections to 3rd Bass (even with a "Gas Face" reprise entitled "The Gasface Refill").

The lightheartedness prevalent on *Mr. Hood* was transformed into something slightly more militant on the second K.M.D. album, *Black Bastards*. Originally planned for release in 1994, the album was shelved by Elektra due to its dark mood and controversial cover art depicting a cartoon-ish Sambo-like character hanging from a gallows. As disappointing as this censorship was, it pales in comparison to the larger tragedy in store for the group. In the midst of K.M.D.'s major label woes, Sub-Roc was fatally injured in a car accident. His death spelled the end of K.M.D. and put the fate of their album in limbo. The album was bootlegged quite heavily and many of the tracks were given legitimate (albeit limited) issue in the late '90s by New York indie Fondle 'Em, but it wasn't until 2001 that *Black Bastards* was issued as K.M.D. had intended. Met with high critical praise, *Black Bastards* is now considered a minor classic of the golden age of rap. Zevlove disappeared temporarily from hip-hop radar, returning in the late-'90s under an ever-growing series of aliases, most notably MF Doom. —*Michael Di Bella and Wade Kergan*

Mr. Hood / 1991 / Elektra ✦✦
● **Black Bastards** / May 15, 2001 / Sub Verse ✦✦✦
Originally scheduled for release back in 1994 but scrapped due to controversial cover art, K.M.D.'s follow-up to their debut *Mr. Hood* was considered to be one of the Holy Grail records in the annals of hip-hop history. The death of group member Sub-Roc in a car accident squashed the future of K.M.D. shortly after it was recorded. Employing ideals and samples from the album *The Blue Guerilla* by Kain of the Last Poets, the tone of this record was to be dramatically different than their first, which was lighthearted and playful while still spreading a message about racial stereotypes. Volatile yet poignant tracks like "What a Nigga Know" and "Black Bastards!" are hip-hop fireballs. Subjects like alcoholism ("Sweet Premium Wine"), drug use ("Smokin' That S*#%"), and women ("Plumskinzz") were all touched upon with incendiary tones. The sound of the record is very raw and sounds unfinished due to Elektra shelving the project, but it doesn't take away from the magic that would have made this a suitable follow-up. —*Douglas Siwek*

Suge Knight (Marion Knight)

b. Apr. 19, 1965, Los Angeles, CA
Executive Producer / Gangsta Rap, West Coast Rap, Hardcore Rap
The rap world is no stranger to controversy, but the vast majority involves its recording artists, and perhaps an occasional outbreak of violence at a show.

Yet, few industry figures ever attracted the kind of notoriety that Death Row Records label head Marion "Suge" Knight did. A particularly flamboyant and visible executive, Knight built Death Row into the biggest hip-hop label of the early '90s, thanks to a stable of talent that included Dr. Dre, Snoop Doggy Dogg, and 2Pac. Death Row brought gangsta rap to the top of the pop charts, and made the West Coast into the epicenter of '90s hip-hop. But along the way, Knight acquired a reputation for using threats of violence as a business tactic, and made little attempt to hide his gang connections. His public feuds with rivals and occasional run-ins with the law seemed to lend credence to his legend, and he was suspected by some of involvement in the murders of Tupac Shakur and the Notorious B.I.G.; though no allegations were ever proven, elaborate conspiracy theories swirled in the wake of police failure in both investigations. By that time, Knight was already serving hard time for a parole violation, which effectively crippled Death Row. He returned to the music industry upon his release, though it remains to be seen if he will ever enjoy a similar level of success.

Marion Knight was born April 19, 1966, in the tough Compton area of Los Angeles; his trademark nickname was short for "Sugar Bear." As a youth, he was involved with the Mob Piru Bloods street gang, and during his later years was frequently seen wearing their colors. However, he remained an excellent student and athlete, so much so that he won a football scholarship to UNLV, where he also made the dean's list. After school, he played professionally for the Los Angeles Rams for a short time, but couldn't quite make the grade. Instead, he found work as a concert promoter and a bodyguard for celebrities including Bobby Brown. Knight first ran afoul of the law in 1987, when he faced auto theft, concealed weapon, and attempted murder charges, but got off simply with probation. Two years later, he formed his own music-publishing company, and allegedly made his first big money in the business by coercing Vanilla Ice into signing over royalties from his smash album *To the Extreme*, owing to material that he supposedly sampled from one of Knight's company creations. (The apocryphal story holds that Knight held Ice by his ankles off of a 20th-floor balcony, though in Ice's version, the threat was more implied.)

Knight next formed an artist management company and signed prominent West Coast figures the D.O.C. and DJ Quik. Through the former, he met several members of the seminal gangsta rap group N.W.A, most notably budding superproducer Dr. Dre. Jumping into the royalty disputes between N.W.A and their label, Ruthless, Knight negotiated a contract release for Dre that, according to N.W.A's Eazy-E and manager Jerry Heller, involved Knight and his henchmen threatening the two with pipes and baseball bats. Whatever the methods actually were, Dre cofounded Death Row Records in 1991 with Knight, who famously vowed to make it "the Motown of the '90s." For a time, Knight made good on his ambitions: he secured a distribution deal with Interscope, and Dre's solo debut, *The Chronic*, became one of the biggest-selling and most influential rap albums of all time. It also made a star of Dre's protégé, Snoop Doggy Dogg, whose debut album, *Doggystyle*, was another smash hit. As Dre's signature G-funk production style took over hip-hop, Death Row became a reliable brand name for gangsta fans, and even its lesser releases sold consistently well.

However, Knight was already courting controversy. During the 1992 sessions for *The Chronic*, he was arrested for assaulting two aspiring rappers who allegedly used a phone without his permission, and placed on several years' probation. Meanwhile, Death Row had begun a public feud with Miami rapper Luke (2 Live Crew's Luther Campbell), and when Knight traveled to Miami for a hip-hop convention in 1993, he was allegedly seen openly carrying a gun. The following year, he opened a nightclub in Las Vegas called Club 662, so named because the numbers spelled out "MOB"—his gang affiliation—on telephone keypads; he also pleaded no contest to firearms trafficking charges, and was sentenced yet again to probation. In 1995 he ran afoul of activist C. Delores Tucker, whose criticism of Death Row's glamorization of the gangsta lifestyle helped scuttle a lucrative deal with Time Warner. Additionally, Knight's feud with East Coast impresario Sean "Puffy" Combs took a nasty turn when Knight insulted the Bad Boy label honcho on the air at an awards show. However, the year was partially redeemed when Knight offered to post a hefty bail for Tupac Shakur if the troubled rapper agreed to sign with Death Row. Shakur agreed, setting the stage for 1996's blockbuster double album *All Eyez on Me* and the smash hits "California Love" and "How Do U Want It."

2Pac temporarily helped Death Row stay on top of a marketplace that was already shifting back toward the East Coast, which had devised its own distinct brand of hardcore rap. However, the label suffered a major blow when Dr. Dre, frustrated with the company's increasingly thuggish reputation, decided to leave and form his own label. A stream of Dre-dissing records followed, but things turned tragic later in 1996, when Tupac Shakur was murdered in a drive-by shooting—a passenger in a car driven by Knight. When Shakur's East Coast rival, the Notorious B.I.G., was murdered in a similar fashion in early 1997, speculation immediately arose that Knight was somehow involved, that the killing was revenge. To date, both murders remain unsolved, but the investigations exposed a web of connections between Death Row Records, gang members who worked there, and L.A.P.D. officers who sometimes worked security for the label and its artists during their off hours. Moreover, Knight's story in the aftermath of Shakur's death was questionable: Medical reports contradicted Knight's claim that a bullet from the attack had lodged in his skull, and he also said in an interview that even if he knew who murdered Shakur, he wouldn't rat anyone out to the police.

Videotape at the Las Vegas hotel where Knight and Shakur had been watching a boxing match prior to the murder showed an altercation with Crips gang member Orlando Anderson, who some believe was the eventual triggerman. Knight's involvement in the fight violated the terms of his probation. Moreover, it was revealed that Knight's light sentence may have involved a conflict of interest on the part of prosecutor Lawrence Longo, who rented out a Malibu home to Knight and even had his teenage daughter sign a recording contract with Death Row. Knight was sentenced to nine years in prison, which effectively spelled the end of his Death Row empire. During his time in prison, Knight's home was burglarized, and police seized a vehicle at the Death Row offices thought to be the getaway vehicle in the Biggie Smalls murder. He was released in August 2001 after serving around five years, and immediately went back to work, retooling his label as Tha Row and searching for new talent. (Lisa "Left Eye" Lopes actually signed a contract shortly before her tragic death in a car accident.) In late 2002, police raided Tha Row's record offices and several of Knight's homes looking for evidence in two gang slayings. Only Knight's associates were implicated in the crimes, but consorting with gang members was another parole violation and Knight was briefly jailed again; he was eventually sentenced to 200 hours of anti-gang community service. *—Steve Huey*

Knightowl

Vocals, Producer / Gangsta Rap, Hardcore Rap, West Coast Rap, Latin Rap
Long considered one of the West Coast's top Chicano gangsta rappers, Knightowl forcefully made himself known with his 1995 self-titled debut. With every subsequent album, his status grew not only in terms of record sales but also in terms of prestige. *—Jason Birchmeier*

● **Shot Caller** / Aug. 24, 1999 / Familia ♦♦♦
Knightowl's third album, recorded for the Familia label, is a solid addition to the California rapper's discography. Though he doesn't use quite as many Latino phrases or accents as other rappers like Capone, and concentrates more on West Coast G-funk similar to Warren G. The productions are just interesting enough to sustain interest in what Knightowl has to say, and even though he seems a bit hung up on violence ("I Murder Mutha Fuckas," "Taking All You Bitches Out," "Still Bangin'," "Fools Yell for Mercy," "You Best Not Double Cross Me"), he's a good rapper. *—Keith Farley*

Knowdaverbs (Michael Boyer II)

b. Phoenix, AZ
Christian Rap, Underground Rap
One of the smoothest Christian rappers out there, Knowdaverbs has recorded for the Gotee label, home to Grits and affiliated with dc Talk. He started rapping at an early age, and spent time dancing with Grits during the mid-'90s. His debut, *Syllabus*, was released in 1999. *The Action Figure* followed one year later, and Knowdaverbs (his name a combination of "knowledge" and "verbalize") began hosting the Christian video show *Planet Hip-Hop* (on the Sky Angel satellite network). The release of his third album, *Unlocked* (the first where he was billed as Verbs), was delayed slightly when he spent six months in South Africa on a mission with his home church in Nashville. *—John Bush*

Syllabus / Feb. 9, 1999 / Gotee ♦♦♦

● **The Action Figure** / Aug. 15, 2000 / Gotee ♦♦♦♦
Rap fans shouldn't dismiss Knowdaverbs as a Christian rapper, since his rhymes are smooth and clever, his productions tight and inventive, and his

themes nearly universal (a rarity among the inbred CCM community). The first single, "God Is Big," makes a good point but belabors the message a bit; far better is "If I Were Mayor," a swinging track with Knowdaverbs taking commercial rappers to task for their negativity and telling his audience what it'd be like if he ruled the hip-hop game. The title track preaches the world-wide mission of the gospel, but he admits in the very next track ("Plane Scared") how anxious he is about traveling. Traits like modesty and forth-rightness certainly aren't the norm for the rap world, but his lyrical skills and great flow make him that rare thing: a talented gospel rapper. The produc-tion, by Incorporated Elements, is as good as their work on the Grits LP from the same year (*The Art of Translation*). — *John Bush*

Kokane

b. Los Angeles, CA
West Coast Rap, Gangsta Rap, G-Funk
Though Kokane had been involved with the West Coast rap scene since the dawn of gangsta rap, he was never able to secure any substantial success for himself until 2000 when he played a major role in the success of Snoop Dogg's *Tha Last Meal*. His eccentric vocal approach is half fluid rapping and half weird P-funk-influenced singing. This balance made Kokane a perfect choice to lay down the vocal hooks for Snoop's album, as he appeared on eight of the album's 19 tracks.

The son of Motown staff composer Jerry Long ("Ball of Confusion," "Just My Imagination," "Still Waters Run Deep"), Kokane's life has always included music, though it is the old school funk of the '70s that most influences his style. He began his career as a vocalist in the mid-'80s as rap was first appearing in his native Los Angeles before eventually signing to Eazy-E's Ruthless Records label in 1991. In addition to cowriting "Appetite for Destruction" for N.W.A's *Niggaz4life*, Kokane also contributed to other West Coast gangsta rap albums such as Above the Law's *Black Mafia Life*. His first solo single, "Nickel Slick Nigga," appeared on the *Deep Cover* soundtrack as well as his debut album for Ruthless, *Who Am I*. His second album for Ruthless, *Funk Upon a Rhyme*, appeared in 1994 but didn't sell many copies, dooming Kokane to a frustrating sabbatical period where he made the occa-sional cameo. He reappeared in late 1999 with a solo album on Eureka Records, *They Call Me Mr. Kane*, yet this album never escaped the under-ground. Ironically, it was on the L.A. posse track found on Dr. Dre's *2001* al-bum, "Some L.A. Niggaz," that Kokane scored big; this encounter with Dre's camp led to his relationship with Snoop, who signed him to Dogghouse Records, bringing a renewed sense of promise to Kokane's long-running career. — *Jason Birchmeier*

● **Funk Upon a Rhyme** / 1994 / Ruthless ✦✦✦

They Call Me Mr. Kane / Nov. 16, 1999 / Eureka ✦✦✦

Kool DJ Herc

DJ / Hip-Hop, Old School Rap
Kool DJ Herc is the originator of breakbeat DJing, essentially the essence of hip-hop. By isolating and repeating the "breaks," or most danceable parts, of funk records by Mandrill, James Brown, and the Jimmy Castor Bunch, Herc created the prototype for modern-day hip-hop. Though others such as Grandmaster Flash perfected and elevated the technique, it was Herc who is credited for its creation.

Beginning his DJing career in the early '70s at a time when disco was king, Herc immediately distinguished himself by spinning late-'60s funk records of James Brown and Mandrill and isolating their breaks. Among other things, Herc was notorious for throwing all-night parties and invari-ably present at a Kool Herc party during mid-'70s were usually young dancers (called b-boys) who were early incarnations of the breakdancers of the '80s. Another Kool Herc attraction was his mammoth sound system which was capable of overtaking a party-goer's body, making them literally feel the music.

Herc's career was sidelined, however, when he was stabbed at one of his parties, causing the DJ to curb his activities for several years. Though he was occasionally acknowledged during the '90s—appearing at the Source Awards to talk about hip-hop's early days as well as on the 1994 release *Super Bad* by Public Enemy DJ Terminator X—Herc drifted away from the hip-hop community and ceased to be a key player in the same way he was in the early to mid-'70s. — *Steve Kurutz*

Kool G Rap (Nathaniel Wilson)

b. Jul. 20, 1968, Elmhurst, Queens, NY
Vocals, Producer / Hardcore Rap, East Coast Rap
Kool G Rap never rose to superstar status during his late-'80s reign as a lead-ing member of Marley Marl's Juice Crew, but the Queens-bred hardcore rap-per endured for over a decade, eventually enjoying a renaissance in the early 2000s. Throughout his tour of duty, G Rap maintained a reverent following, mainly among his original late-'80s/early-'90s fan base and the subsequent wave of golden age revivalists. Cold Chillin' furthermore repackaged his key recordings with DJ Polo periodically over the years, so G Rap remained visible even as his productivity slowed considerably. While countless other golden age rappers thus fell by the wayside, G Rap quietly ascended to legendary status, perhaps as recognized in the early 2000s as he had been during his late-'80s prime.

The "Kool Genius of Rap" began life as Nathaniel Wilson in a rough sec-tion of Queens, where he first met Eric Barrier and Polo, two friends with a mutual interest in hip-hop. While Barrier went onto a short-lived yet suc-cessful career as the less-acknowledged half of Eric B. & Rakim, Polo and G Rap collaborated and released the "It's a Demo/I'm Fly" on Cold Chillin' in 1986. This legendary single was the first of several, "Streets of New York," "Poison," and "Road to the Riches" also being noteworthy singles. G Rap also graced Marl's "The Symphony," a performance that promised him legendary status in itself. By 1989 he was making LPs rather than 12" singles, signaling G Rap's rise from the underground to mainstream recognition. Yet while Juice Crew peers such as Big Daddy Kane and Biz Markie scored crossover singles, had big-selling LPs, and soon found themselves on MTV, G Rap strug-gled with his sudden position on the uncomfortable brink of crossing over. Sure, his LPs had their share of highlights such as "Road to the Riches" and "Erase Racism," in addition to the aforementioned singles, but his albums with Polo never achieved what many had hoped for in terms of popularity.

By the mid-'90s, G Rap parted ways with his longtime partner and at-tempted a solo career with *4,5,6* (1995) on Cold Chillin', followed by *Rated XXX* (1996) and *Roots of Evil* (1998). None of these albums garnered too much attention, commercial or critical, and it seemed as though G Rap was bound to suffer old school status like most of his '80s peers. As G Rap's name became less and less acknowledged among contemporary rap listeners in the late '90s, the stalwart MC simultaneously began channeling his efforts toward guest appearances. Collaborating with the likes of Fat Joe, Big Pun, M.O.P., Mobb Deep, Nas, RZA, Big L, and Talib Kweli—along with a surpris-ing appearance on U.N.K.L.E.'s high-profile *Psyence Fiction* album as well as the *Lyricist Lounge 2* compilation—G Rap gained substantial momentum. Once joining forces with Rawkus, the rapper's renaissance officially began as the label began promoting his comeback album months before its proposed 2001 release. The album, *The Giancana Story*, unfortunately wouldn't street until late 2002, as Rawkus became increasingly entangled in major-label affiliations. Though some of the anticipation simmered during the long delay, the album nonetheless impressed many and forcibly signaled another of G Rap's periodic returns. — *Jason Birchmeier*

4, 5, 6 / Sep. 12, 1995 / Cold Chillin' ✦✦
After a three-album run with DJ Polo that stacked up favorably to any other rap act, Kool G Rap went solo with 1995's *4, 5, 6*, and it's the only time he sounded as if he was running out of steam. Though "Ghetto Knows," "Take 'Em to War," and "Money on My Brain" (featuring a slick sample of Herbie Hancock's "Chameleon") are far from missteps, they have little on G Rap's legacy with DJ Polo. Furthermore, there are telltale signs that he either needs to gain new inspirations or take a break. "Blowin Up in the World"'s lyrics could've been written by just about any MC, and the lazy chorus is particu-larly dull by his standards. The production from Buckwild and T Ray is merely passable and lacks the unique spark that masters like Marley Marl, Sir Jinx, and Large Professor were able to provide years earlier. It has to be stressed that few other MCs could release a record like this and have it con-sidered a failure; in fact, had this been a debut from a youngster, it would've doubtlessly created a stir of some sort. Thankfully, G Rap went on a very necessary hiatus after this. — *Andy Kellman*

Roots of Evil / Nov. 10, 1998 / K-Tel ✦✦✦
Since his last album, Kool G Rap made two very critical life decisions that would greatly impact his career. First, he left the hustle and bustle of Queens behind and relocated to the blistering desert heat of Arizona. Second, tiring

of major-label hassles and poor promotion, he severed all ties with Cold Chillin' and started his own label, Ill Street. After a four-year hiatus, it was finally time for the self-professed Godfather of Street Rap to unleash his ferocious appetite for rhyme upon his unsuspecting prey. Sounding reinvigorated after a lengthy layoff, his skills remain completely intact, blazing verse after verse in grand fashion. Standout cuts include the eerie, bass-heavy "One Dark Night," and G Rap lyrically drenches the wavering keyboard of "Mobstas." Also, "Let the Games Begin" and the well-executed "Mafioso" stand out. One of this album's crown jewels, "Thugs Life Story (Chapter I, II, III)," is a nine-minute excursion into the underworld, finding G Rap at unparalleled echelons. Though rarely diverting from his usual topic matter of money, murder, and mayhem, there is a definitive method to his madness. G Rap's intricate storytelling ability and keen attention for detail enables him to flip futuristic tales of criminology in a totally unique fashion. However, just as the production failed to take his first solo album, *4,5,6*, to that next level, the same can be echoed here. It's abundantly clear that G Rap needs to map out a strategically stronger battle plan when searching for just the right tracks to compliment his flow, because that's the only thing holding him back on this album. —*Matt Conaway*

Greatest Hits / May 7, 2002 / Landspeed ✦✦✦✦
Despite the fact that only two of the 14 songs included on Landspeed's *Greatest Hits* were cut by Kool G Rap after he severed ties with partner DJ Polo, DJ Polo gets no billing whatsoever on this compilation, though he is included in the photos in the inner sleeve. This perplexing compilation once again covers the same general 1988-1992 territory already revisited four times previously. It follows 1994's *Killer Kuts*, 1996's *Rated XXX* (more a compilation of the duo's most sex-drenched output than a proper best-of), 2000's *The Best of Cold Chillin'*, and 2001's pairing of *Road to the Riches* and *Wanted: Dead or Alive* (which is confusingly subtitled "The Best of Cold Chillin'"). This particular disc is the way to go if the recent double-disc summations are too extensive and if you can't locate a copy of *Killer Kuts*, which has a better track selection. (A Kool G Rap & DJ Polo overview without "Operation CB" and "Wanted: Dead or Alive" is problematic.) The two decent tracks from Kool G Rap without Polo—"Fast Life" (featuring Nas) and "For da Brothaz"—are lifted from 1995's *4, 5, 6*, so *Roots of Evil* is completely unrepresented. Each Kool G Rap & DJ Polo compilation has its gripes, and this one is obviously no different in that respect. However, there's no denying that *Greatest Hits* is a good quick fix, stocked with greatness. —*Andy Kellman*

● **The Giancana Story** / Nov. 12, 2002 / Koch International ✦✦✦✦
Delayed for over a year while Rawkus sorted out its increasingly labyrinthine label affiliations (it was eventually licensed to a Koch subsidiary), *The Giancana Story* proves that time means nothing to one of the greatest rappers ever (though Rawkus took it too far when they declared "the game was named after him"). Don't call it a comeback because he never left—he recorded continually during the '90s—but Kool G's third solo record illustrates the rare case of the hip-hop world moving closer to a veteran than when he made his breakout. What sounded refreshing and genuinely unique in 1990—check out before-their-time shots like "Road to the Riches" or "Streets of New York"—was becoming nearly ubiquitous by the end of the millennium, and besides slipping in a few more words per line than he used to, the first real hardcore rapper hasn't changed his style a whit (or needed to). The opener "Thug for Life" is as clean a track as any classic golden age production, but with the type of mid-tempo roll that gets it closer to later hardcore. The single "My Life," with Capone-N-Noreaga, is the best track here, the only one with any crossover appeal (via a remix complete with talkbox and stuttered chorus). Everything else is pure hardcore, with all the dark intelligence and heavy venom hip-hop fans expect from a master. —*John Bush*

Kool G Rap & DJ Polo

f. 1987, New York, NY
Group / Golden Age, East Coast Rap, Hardcore Rap
Queens-based Kool G Rap & DJ Polo left one of the most impressive rap discographies in their wake. Though Kool G Rap's growth as an MC from their first single in 1986 to their final album in 1992 was considerable, the duo started off running and never looked back. The pair never had the large profile enjoyed by others in Marley Marl's extended family (including Big Daddy Kane, Biz Markie, and Roxanne Shanté), but aftershocks continue to

be felt throughout the East Coast, from the Notorious B.I.G. to Nas to Wu-Tang Clan to the underground scene.

When their first single, 1986's "It's a Demo"/"I'm Fly," was released on Cold Chillin', G Rap was already a formidable MC who could boast with the best of them. However, it would be narratives that he would become most known for, in addition to some of the raunchiest rhymes hip-hop has ever known. Throughout the years, Marley Marl, Large Professor, and Sir Jinx provided valuable production assistance. The duo released the formative "It's a Demo"/"I'm Fly" in 1986, but G Rap (born Nathaniel Wilson) truly broke out on the Juice Crew's "The Symphony," a group cut of great legend produced by Marley Marl that also included turns from Masta Ace, Craig G., and Big Daddy Kane. After a good deal of anticipation was built for the first Kool G Rap & DJ Polo album, *Road to the Riches* saw the light of day in 1989. Produced by Marl and released on his Cold Chillin' label, the album included a handful of timeless moments while alluding to greater potential. That potential was fulfilled with the following year's *Wanted: Dead or Alive*. Marley Marl remained partly responsible for the duo's sound, while Main Source's Large Professor and Eric B. also pitched in with production work. On this album, G Rap became an MC of top caliber; he expanded his range as a magnificent storyteller on tracks like "Streets of New York" (a number-three rap single) and "Wanted: Dead or Alive." Released in 1992, *Live and Let Die* landed the duo in a bit of hot water; its cover, depicting the duo feeding meat to rabid dogs in front of two restrained white men, gained a fair amount of attention in the press. The controversy played a role in shooting the album up to the Top 20 of the R&B/hip-hop albums chart, but the attention unfortunately waned. Just as accomplished as *Wanted: Dead or Alive* (if not more so), the album featured the sympathetic handiwork of Sir Jinx and Trakmasterz and helped bring G Rap's increasingly profane and vivid tales to extreme levels.

G Rap and Polo went their separate ways shortly after that. G Rap put out three albums between the mid-'90s and early 2000s, while Polo cut a single with Ice-T and porn star Ron Jeremy. Landspeed kept the duo's legacy alive through a low-key reissue campaign; in 2000 and 2001, separate releases combined the first two albums and anthologized their entire career together. —*Andy Kellman*

Road to the Riches / Mar. 14, 1989 / Cold Chillin' ✦✦✦✦
Kool G Rap & DJ Polo's *Road to the Riches* had been a long time coming when Cold Chillin' released it in 1989. It didn't disappoint. After some successful singles and G Rap's contributions to Marley Marl's Juice Crew, the duo arrived almost fully formed on its debut. Whether boasting (his greatest strength at this point) or spinning tales, G Rap's knife-edged rhymes—delivered with the hardest-sounding lisp in hip-hop—tear through Marley Marl's productions and DJ Polo's scratching with all the ferocity of a pit bull devouring a piece of meat. Though tracks like "Poison," "It's a Demo," and the title track won this record a lot of respect, there are several other moments that help make this a remarkable debut. On "Men at Work," lines like, "I drop rhymes on paper and then build a skyscraper/When I die scientists will preserve my brain/Donate it to science to answer the unexplained" whip by so fast that it's easy to overlook Marl and Polo's perfectly snarling, densely percussive backdrop. Marl's imaginative sampling gleans from all sorts of unexpected sources, like the harmonica from Area Code 615's "Stone Fox Chase," the odd phasings of Kraftwerk's "Trans-Europe Express" (no one used it like this), and the burbling synths from Gary Numan's "Cars" (remember, this was the late '80s). G Rap's occasional homophobic and woman-hating lyrics, along with some production nuances that haven't aged well, are the only hindrances. Aside from that, *Road to the Riches* showed promise while remaining jolting in its own right. —*Andy Kellman*

Wanted: Dead or Alive / Aug. 13, 1990 / Cold Chillin' ✦✦✦✦✦
Marley Marl remained on board, and Large Professor and Eric B. also hopped on to help produce Kool G Rap & DJ Polo's second album. With a wider range of sounds and the expansion of G Rap's lyrical range, *Wanted: Dead or Alive* is wholly deserving of classic status. The opening "Streets of New York" remains one of the most thrilling and unique rap singles released; the sparse rhythm, adorned with assured piano runs that complement the song to the point of almost making the song, falls somewhere between a gallop and a strut, and G Rap outlines more vivid scenes than one film could possibly contain. The track cemented Kool G Rap & DJ Polo's role as East Coast legends and showed Kool G Rap's talent as an adept storyteller like nothing before or

since. Likewise, "Talk Like Sex" is the nastiest, raunchiest thing he ever recorded, with "I'm pounding you down until your eyeballs pop out" acting as an exemplary claim—as well as one of the few that is printable—made in the song. The boasts, as ever, are in no short supply, but "Erase Racism" takes a break from the normal proceedings with guest spots from Big Daddy Kane and Biz Markie. It's both funny and sobering, with Biz Markie's Three Dog Night chorus providing comic relief after each verse. Adding yet another dimension to the album, DJ Polo throws in a hip-house instrumental that avoids coming off like a throwaway. This album is only part of a major swarm of brilliant rap records from 1990, but it will never be lost in it. —*Andy Kellman*

Live and Let Die / Nov. 24, 1992 / Cold Chillin' ✦✦✦✦✦
A strong case could be made for *Live and Let Die* as Kool G Rap & DJ Polo's crowning achievement. Who can really say for sure if the controversy surrounding the cover artwork—which shows the duo feeding steaks to a pair of rottweilers, in front of two noose-necked white men—clouded a proper consensus? With across-the-board stellar production help from Sir Jinx and Trakmasterz, G Rap (who also produces) thrives on his no-holds-barred narratives that peaked with *Wanted: Dead or Alive*'s "Streets of New York," but most everything on this album comes close to eclipsing that song. "Ill Street Blues" is practically a sequel to it, and it manages to use more swanky piano vamps and horn blurts without making for a desperate attempt at capitalizing on a past glory. Few tales of growing up in a life of crime hit harder than the title track, in which G Rap displays the traits—unforced frankness, that unmistakable voice, and a flow that drags you involuntarily along—that made him a legend. The album is one story after another that draws you in without fail, and they come at you from several angles. Whether pulling off a train heist, venting sexual frustration, analyzing his psychosis, or lording over the streets, G Rap is a pro at holding a captive audience. All die-hard East Coast rap fans, especially followers of the Notorious B.I.G., owe it to themselves to get really familiar with this album and the two that predated it. If you were to take this duo's best five songs away from them, they'd still be one of the top duos rap music has ever seen. —*Andy Kellman*

Killer Kuts / Mar. 29, 1994 / Cold Chillin' ✦✦✦✦✦
The unfortunate early-'90s bust-up between Kool G Rap & DJ Polo cleaved one of the finest rap duos of all time. Leaving behind a trio of fine LPs—the raw *Road to the Riches*, the refined *Wanted: Dead or Alive*, and the underrated *Live and Let Die* (the latter unfortunately gaining more notice for the provocative cover than the content)—the duo was nonetheless out before releasing a poor record or embarrassing themselves (i.e., they did not make a *Don't Sweat the Technique*). At the drop of a hat, Kool G Rap could shift gears from relaxed to vicious and from bawdy to philosophical, and DJ Polo's instrumental prowess could just as ably flit between fractured and grim to smooth and precious. The first disc commemorating their nearly decade-long run, *Killer Kuts* selects a handful of tracks from each of the three albums made for Cold Chillin'. It's a good introduction, hits all the crucial moments, and thankfully doesn't ignore *Live and Let Die*, an album that has gotten the short end of the stick since its release. This 1994 compilation would be trumped six years later by *The Best of Cold Chillin'*, a more extensive venture that also includes curiosities like the duo's first track ("I'm Fly") and another that had only appeared previously on the relatively disposable *Rated XXX* compilation. —*Andy Kellman*

Rated XXX / Jun. 4, 1996 / Cold Chillin' ✦✦✦
Doing a bit of a spin on themed anthologies that hone in on particular corners of an artist's catalog—like Smokey Robinson's *Ballads* or Aretha Franklin's *The Delta Meets Detroit: Aretha's Blues*—*Rated XXX* shines a light on Kool G Rap & DJ Polo's raunchier side, evidenced through titles like "Talk Like Sex," "Check the Bitch," and "Fuck U Man," a title that's meant to read like a superhero of sorts and not as a diss directed at another male (picture a big "F" emblazoned on Kool G Rap's chest). This disc hardly presents a full picture of the duo's output and does something of a disservice to Kool G Rap's versatility as a lyricist. Besides, Cold Chillin' wasn't able to find enough sex-crazed songs in their catalog to fill out the entire disc. "Rikers Island," for instance, hardly has anything to do with the theme. "Talk Like Sex," however, is the most exemplary of *Rated XXX*, containing lines such as this one: "Get a grip on your headboard and hold on to it/Or get sent right through it." (That's probably the tamest line, by the way.) At the time of its release, *Rated XXX* featured a couple of previously unavailable songs, but the early-2000s

overhaul given to the duo's catalog has eradicated the issue and makes this cash-in compilation all the more irrelevant. —*Andy Kellman*

★ **The Best of Cold Chillin'** / Oct. 17, 2000 / Landspeed ✦✦✦✦
One of the first in a long line of East Coast hardcore rappers, Kool G Rap was nevertheless overshadowed by premier players like Rakim, Chuck D, and his labelmate Big Daddy Kane. The Landspeed label rectified the matter somewhat with the release of the two-disc Kool G Rap & DJ Polo retrospective *The Best of Cold Chillin'*, which includes 19 tracks, all but one from the duo's prime of 1988 to 1992. Beginning with their first recording, 1984's "I'm Fly," the set begins with a disc including several rare tracks—"Rikers Island," and "Rhyme Tyme," previously released on the 1996 quasi-collection *Rated XXX*—and half a dozen tracks from their debut *Road to the Riches*, including raging tracks like "Men at Work" and the title track. Moving from tracks produced by Cold Chillin' boss Marley Marl to more finessed productions from Large Professor and Eric B., the second disc focuses on Kool G Rap & DJ Polo's sophomore *Wanted: Dead or Alive* with hardcore seminal cuts like "Streets of New York," "Money in the Bank," and the title track. —*John Bush*

Road to the Riches/Wanted: Dead or Alive / Jun. 26, 2001 / Landspeed ✦✦✦✦
Although this double-disc set is subtitled "The Best of Cold Chillin'," it shouldn't be confused with the rather different but overlap-prone compilation that is simply titled *The Best of Cold Chillin'*. This particular package is simply a pairing of Kool G Rap & DJ Polo's first two albums: 1989's *Road to the Riches* and 1990's *Wanted: Dead or Alive*. Without going into specifics about the side of the country the duo represented, what stylistic ground they covered, or their era of origin, there's no denying that these two albums are rap classics. Whether evidenced in the raunch of "Talk Like Sex" or the grit of "Streets of New York," Kool G Rap & DJ Polo were one of the most formidable duos of their time, perhaps just one notch below Eric B. & Rakim in terms of recorded legacy. The only problem with pairing these two records together is that it leaves their third and final record, 1992's underrated *Live and Let Die*, orphaned to an extent. As a result, *The Best of Cold Chillin'* (also a double-disc package) is the best place to get an overview. Not only does it touch upon *Live and Let Die*, but it includes pre-*Road to the Riches* material, nonalbum material, and it also offers more bang for the buck by leaving off the album filler that hamstrings this title a bit. —*Andy Kellman*

Kool Keith (Keith Thornton)

Vocals, Producer / Hip-Hop, Underground Rap
After single-handedly redefining "warped" as the mind and mouth behind the Bronx-based Ultramagnetic MCs, "Kool" Keith Thornton—aka Rhythm X, aka Dr. Octagon, aka Dr. Dooom, aka Mr. Gerbik—headed for the outer reaches of the stratosphere with a variety of solo projects. A onetime psychiatric patient at Bellevue, Keith's lyrical thematics remained as free-flowing here as they ever were with the NY trio, connecting up complex meters with fierce, layers-deep metaphors and veiled criticisms of those who "water down the sound that comes from the ghetto." His own debut single, "Earth People" by Dr. Octagon, was quietly released in late 1995 on the San Francisco-based Bulk Recordings, and the track spread like wildfire through the hip-hop underground, as did the subsequent self-titled full-length released the following year. Featuring internationally renowned DJ Q-Bert (also of the Invisible Skratch Picklz) on turntables, as well as the Automator and DJ Shadow behind the boards, *Dr. Octagon*'s left-field fusion of sound collage, fierce turntable work, and bizarre, impressionistic rapping found audiences in the most unlikely of places, from hardcore hip-hop heads to jaded rock critics. Although a somewhat sophomoric preoccupation with body parts and scatology tended to dominate the album, Keith's complex weave of associations and shifting references is quite often amazing in its intricacy. The record found its way to the U.K.-based abstract hip-hop imprint Mo'Wax (for whom Shadow also records) in mid-1996, and was licensed by the label for European release (Mo'Wax also released a DJ-friendly instrumental version of the album titled, appropriately, *The Instrumentalyst [Octagon Beats]*).

The widespread popularity of the album eventually landed Keith at Geffen splinter DreamWorks in 1997; the label gave *Dr. Octagon* (retitled *Dr. Octagonecologyst*) its third release mid-year, adding a number of bonus cuts. In early 1999, however, Keith's alterego Dr. Dooom unfortunately "killed off" Dr. Octagon on the opening track of *First Come, First Served* (released on

Thornton's own Funky Ass label). Kool Keith signed to Ruffhouse/MCA for his second album under *that* alias, 1999's *Black Elvis/Lost in Space*. Records released as Kool Keith followed in 2000 (*Matthew*) and 2001 (*Spankmaster*), while the 2002 collaboration *Gene* appeared as KHM (Kool Keith plus H-Bomb and Marc Live). —*Sean Cooper*

Sex Style / Feb. 3, 1997 / Funky Ass ✦✦✦
The first solo album released under Kool Keith's own name, *Sex Style* expands the dirtier parts of *Dr. Octagonecologyst* into a near-concept album. Sometimes a pimp, sometimes a pervert, Keith dubs his new approach "pornocore," cribbing dialogue from sex flicks to support astoundingly explicit raps that go places 2 Live Crew never had the capacity to imagine. Not only that, but when Keith turns his attention to inferior MCs, his disses are usually couched in elaborate sexual metaphors (a striking number of which involve water sports). Some songs do deviate from the theme, or at least tone it down a little, and while a few serve as a welcome respite, others simply don't have as much personality. The over-the-top raunch is Keith's main focus, and that's where the vast majority of the album's most imaginative rhymes come from. That makes *Sex Style* a polarizing entry in Keith's catalog. Musically, it's one of his most consistent solo outings, especially if you're just looking at the ones under his own name. It definitely benefits from production by KutMasta Kurt, who may not be as wildly inventive as Dan the Automator, but knows how to frame Keith's idiosyncratic flow with deep, funky beats. Thus, the album is borderline necessary for Keith fans; it really depends on your tolerance for the extremity of songs like "Sex Style," "Don't Crush It," "Make Up Your Mind," "Regular Girl," "Little Girls," or "Lovely Lady." But it is a chance to hear one of the freakiest rappers of all time at his freakiest. —*Steve Huey*

● **Black Elvis/Lost in Space** / Aug. 10, 1999 / Ruffhouse/MCA ✦✦✦✦
After killing off his Dr. Octagon alias and resurrecting himself as an intergalactic Little Richard named Black Elvis (coiffured appropriately), Kool Keith returned in 1999 with his much-anticipated debut for Ruffhouse. Compared to the scatological bombast sprayed all over his *First Come, First Served* LP (released as Dr. Dooom on his own Funky Ass label earlier that year), *Black Elvis/Lost in Space* is remarkably tame. And despite jettisoning cohorts the Automator and DJ Q-Bert, the results sound surprisingly similar to the *Dr. Octagon* album: sparse 808 beats, a few bizarre, faintly menacing organ lines for hooks, and a sample or two the likes of which have never been heard on a Dr. Dre record (like the odd banjo pickings on "Livin' Astro"). Also cropping up are a few of Keith's patented psychedelic nightmares (reminiscent of "Blue Flowers" and "Earth People"), including "Lost in Space," "Rockets on the Battlefield," and "I'm Seein' Robots." For "Supergalactic Lover," Keith injects a bit of stuttered Timbaland funk into the mix, though this tale of sexual prowess is appropriately schizoid. If *Black Elvis/Lost in Space* doesn't make quite the splash of 1996's *Dr. Octagon*, it's mostly because there's a distinct sense that Kool Keith is retreading familiar (through incredibly fun) territory. One thing's for sure, DJ Q-Bert's scratching is definitely missed. —*John Bush*

Matthew / Jul. 25, 2000 / Funky Ass ✦✦
There's a point when even the outrageous and bizarre becomes expected, even boring. With yet another LP of tuneless piano riffs and skeletal beats overlaid with his dense, paranoid raps, Kool Keith approaches the point of sounding like the same broken record he keeps sampling. True, he's just as original as on past masterpieces like *Dr. Octagon*, but the obtuse references and metaphors have grown just as tired as a Will Smith pop hit. He's also much more violent than on previous records, lashing out at the music industry as well as unnamed playas on "I Don't Believe You," "Operation Extortion," and "Lived in the Projects." The hilarious "Baddest MC" and "Extravagant Traveler" have the same self-effacing irony as "Supergalactic Lover" and "Master of the Game" (from 1999's *Black Elvis/Lost in Space*), but like Busta Rhymes—another notable super-freak rapper whose work grows less entertaining with each album—Kool Keith faces growing as predictable as a No Limit record. —*John Bush*

Spankmaster / Jun. 5, 2001 / TVT ✦✦✦
Kool Keith may not be one of the more popular MCs in the rap game, but he's surely proven himself to be one of the most creative. Particularly given the genre's commercial tendencies, Keith's limitless ability to engage with weird, perverse, and at times downright shocking music makes him stand out and merit special notice. Of course, anyone familiar with his past work—ranging

from his old school days fronting the Ultramagnetic MCs to his celebrated Dr. Octagon collaboration—knows that Keith is far from generic. Here, he joins forces with Detroit's Esham and Santos for *Spankmaster*, and heads even further toward insanity than his preceding trilogy of albums for Funky Ass foreshadowed. It's fairly safe to presume that Esham's psychotic reputation has inspired Keith to take his own music to unexplored extremes that challenge the boundaries of sleaze, antagonism, and eccentricity. In regard to the lo-fi yet impressive production, the Spankmaster himself actually crafted most of the 20 eclectic songs, with Esham and Santos taking the reins for the album's standout moments: "I Wanna Play," "Drugs," and "Spankmaster." The beats are nearly as untraditional as Keith's rhymes, culling their elements from a disparate concoction of sources, including quite a bit of live instrumentation. In the end, *Spankmaster* is no doubt an engaging listen, even if its budget quality level and lack of glitz and glimmer make it an album strictly for the underground. Recommended to the open-minded, particularly if you admire creativity, long for the uncanny, and secretly have a desire for perversity. Definitely not for the lighthearted. —*Jason Birchmeier*

Game / Nov. 19, 2002 / Number 6 ✦✦✦
The hip-hop triple-team of Kool Keith, H-Bomb, and Marc Live debuted with *Game*, a record that's par for the course of Kool Keith projects—but still eons away from the rap mainstream—complete with sub-basement productions and beats, left-field disses, dozens of paranoid ideas, and interstellar intelligence of all kinds. The threesome spend much of the album protecting the vagaries of underground rap from a devilish major-label executive attempting to steal Keith's style and persona (and even his wigs). There's plenty of room for commenting (probably) on issues of the day for "Copy What U Want" and "Rock Is Dead," and an indefensible conclusion on "Game," "game is game." As usual, Keith's entertainingly obscure, even going so far as to dis NBC News' (?) John Salley, who'd kept most of his commentary most recently to Fox Sports Network. Similar to Mark E. Smith of the Fall, he's able to keep the same distinctive, intriguing sound on each record, no matter who else appears on it—though H-Bomb and Marc Live each contribute a lot to what's heard. —*John Bush*

Kool Moe Dee (Mohandas Dewese)

b. 1963, Harlem, NY
Golden Age, Old School Rap, Pop-Rap, Party Rap
A member of one of the original hip-hop crews, Treacherous Three, Kool Moe Dee later became a solo star in his own right in 1986 by teaming with a teenaged Teddy Riley (later famed as the king of new jack swing) on the crossover hit "Go See the Doctor." The single earned him a contract with Jive Records, for which he recorded three successful late-'80s albums, dominated by his skillful speed raps. A long-running feud with LL Cool J—who stole his aggressive stance and rapping style, he claims—gained Kool Moe Dee headlines for awhile, but he began to fade by the early '90s.

Born Mohandas Dewese in 1963, Dee was an early hit at local block parties, performing with high school buddies L.A. Sunshine and Special K plus DJ Easy Lee as Treacherous Three. Introduced to longtime producer Bobby Robinson (Gladys Knight, the Orioles) by Spoonie Gee, Treacherous Three debuted on wax in 1980 with "The New Rap Language," released on Robinson's Enjoy Records. "Body Rock" and "Feel the Heartbeat" followed during 1980-1981 before Robinson sold the group's contract to Sugar Hill Records. Treacherous Three recorded several singles for Sugar Hill, but broke up by the mid-'80s.

Instead of climbing aboard the solo wagon after the breakup, Kool Moe Dee enrolled in college. After earning a communications degree from SUNY, he enlisted an unknown producer for his solo debut, "Go See the Doctor." The 17-year-old Teddy Riley more than vindicated himself, though, and the single became an underground hit. By 1986, Kool Moe Dee was signed to Jive Records, and his self-titled debut album appeared that same year.

With 1987's *How Ya Like Me Now*, Dee struck back at the brash young generation who had forsaken their forebears; the cover featured a red Kangol hat—the prominent trademark of LL Cool J—being crushed by the wheel of a Jeep. The album went platinum and was followed two years later by the gold-certified *Knowledge Is King*, for which Dee became the first rapper to perform at the Grammy Awards ceremonies. Also in 1989, Dee worked on two important projects: the single "Self-Destruction," recorded in conjunction with KRS-One's Stop the Violence Movement; and Quincy Jones' all-star *Back on the Block* LP, which united hip-hop stars with their musical forebears. Kool Moe Dee's fourth album, *Funke Funke Wisdom* was a bit of a disappointment when compared to his earlier successes, and Jive/RCA dropped him after releasing his *Greatest Hits* package in 1993. Hardly washed up, though, Dee recorded a Treacherous Three reunion album in 1993 and signed to DJ Easy Lee's label for the 1994 album *Interlude*. The title wasn't quite prophetic, however, it being his last album. —*John Bush*

I'm Kool Moe Dee / 1986 / Jive ✦✦✦

By the time he recorded this self-titled debut solo album, Kool Moe Dee was considered a veteran by hip-hop standards. The graduate of the Treacherous Three made no secret of the fact that he was among the founders of rap's old school—a term used to describe Kurtis Blow, Grandmaster Flash & the Furious Five, the Sugarhill Gang, Spoonie Gee, and others who'd been rapping since the late '70s. This engaging album proved that Dee still had considerable technique, and could be a commanding storyteller. Lyrically, he is undeniably blunt, and this bluntness works to his advantage on such gems as "Little John," a reflection on inner-city youth's life of crime; the anticocaine number "Monster Crack"; and the commentary on venereal disease "Go See the Doctor." Kool Moe Dee's infectious hit "Do You Know What Time It Is" was accused of being sexist, but such knee-jerk reactions to the song missed its point—the Harlem native was attacking materialistic women, not women in general. One of this album's producers is Teddy Riley, who went on to enjoy quite a bit of recognition a few years later as a member of the highly influential new jack swing outfit Guy. —*Alex Henderson*

How Ya Like Me Now / 1987 / Jive ✦✦✦✦✦

Kool Moe Dee resented the fact that in the mid- to late '80s, most of rap's founding fathers were enjoying little attention. But Dee himself was one of the few exceptions, and the old school survivor had a major hit with his sophomore effort, *How Ya Like Me Now*. He would have done better to devote more time to storytelling and less time to boasting, but he definitely brings plenty of soul and spirit (as well as technique) to this material. Though not as strong as his first album, it definitely has its share of classics, including "Wild Wild West," a reflection on the nitty-gritty environment that surrounded rap during its early years; his denunciation of materialism "No Respect"; and the infectious title song, which was clearly inspired by Dee's feud with LL Cool J. A few years later, much of the rap world was sick to death of hearing about the feud, but in 1987, it was a major topic of conversation in hip-hop. —*Alex Henderson*

Knowledge Is King / May 1989 / Jive ✦✦✦

What was true of *How Ya Like Me Now* is certainly true of Kool Moe Dee's third solo album, *Knowledge Is King*—the hardcore rapper spends too much time boasting and doesn't devote enough time to his real strength: meaningful storytelling. Nonetheless, his soulful spirit and considerable technique make this effort worthwhile—not remarkable, but certainly engaging. The CD's strongest offerings include "Pump Your Fist," an angry denunciation of social injustice; "The Avenue," a description of a day in the 'hood; and the controversial attack on materialistic women "They Want Money." The latter was accused of being sexist, but Dee rightly countered that criticizing women who judge men by the size of their wallets rather than the size of their hearts or their brains isn't sexist—it's honest. —*Alex Henderson*

Funke, Funke Wisdom / Jun. 4, 1991 / Jive/RCA ✦✦✦

Kool Moe Dee's popularity had faded considerably by 1991, when Jive/RCA released *Funke Funke Wisdom*. This is hardly his finest hour. Featuring sociopolitical commentators Chuck D (Public Enemy's leader) and KRS-One, the inspiring "Rise N' Shine" is a gem. But most of the album falls short of that song's excellence, and Dee often sounds like he's coasting on his talent. This isn't a terrible album by any means, but Dee is capable of much more. Though it's hard to miss just how much technique he has, it doesn't serve as well this time. And his boasting lyrics are sound very routine. Dee overdoes it with James Brown samples, which by 1991, had long since become a very tired cliché in hip-hop. —*Alex Henderson*

★ Greatest Hits / 1993 / Jive ✦✦✦✦✦

With a history dating back to the early days of Sugar Hill Records, Kool Moe Dee was able to reinvent himself as a solo artist during the latter half of the '80s, and in the process helped rap transform from an underground party music into a cultural phenomenon. *Greatest Hits* collects 14 of the most essential items from this seminal figure, kicking off with his two best-known

songs—the catchy "Wild Wild West" and the influential safe-sex rap "Go See the Doctor." His flow is most definitely old school—nearly every couplet is squared off at the end—but his technique was in the top of its class for its pregolden age time period ("Look at Me Now" is impressive by any standard). His chief rival was LL Cool J, and not just in the abstract sense—their on-record feud was the most legendary in early hip-hop, and it's chronicled here on "Let's Go," "Death Blow," and "How Ya Like Me Now." His MC boasts are among the best of their time, but he was also ambitious enough to tackle socially conscious material; apart from the aforementioned "Go See the Doctor," there's "No Respect," a cautionary tale of a street hustler who lost everything, and the Chuck D/KRS-One team-up "Rise 'n' Shine." His production is often heavy on the synths and drum machines, though there are also some James Brown-type samples; a few tracks are produced by new jack swing legend Teddy Riley, and those constitute some of the earliest work in his career. All in all, *Greatest Hits* is an essential look back at one of the greatest talents the old school ever produced. —*Steve Huey*

Interlude / Nov. 8, 1994 / Wrap ✦✦

The Jive Collection, Vol. 2 / Jun. 27, 1995 / Jive ✦✦✦✦✦

As a member of the influential act the Treacherous Three, Kool Moe Dee quickly asserted himself as a common-sense rapper in a genre often filled with party boys and up-and-coming gangsters. The unapologetic "Go See the Doctor" sums him up and then some. With his delivery—half stentorian, half wise guy—Moe Dee was the perfect component in producer Teddy Riley's new jack swing. Instant classics "Wild, Wild West" and the perfect "How You Like Me Now" had more heft than the synth-based R&B of the time. Tracks like "Funke Wisdom" and "Let's Go" profited from harsher production values mixed with old school R&B underpinnings. Despite the highs on *The Jive Collection, Vol. 2*, some of the tracks do present Moe Dee this side of tedious. "The Avenue" and "Look at Me Now" might have his direct-as-a-jackhammer rapper style a little too tough to take in large doses. While this doesn't have the bigger picture of his regular releases, this compilation captures early new jack swing and Moe Dee's best work. —*Jason Elias*

Krayzie Bone

Vocals, Producer / Gangsta Rap, Hip-Hop, Urban, G-Funk, Pop-Rap, Contemporary R&B

A member of Bone Thugs-N-Harmony, rapper Krayzie Bone was born Anthony Henderson in Cleveland, OH; also known as Leatherface, the Sawed-Off Gangsta, he joined Bone Thugs in 1993, debuting a year later with the EP *Creepin on Ah Come Up*. Subsequent LPs, including 1995's *E 1999 Eternal* and 1997's *The Art of War*, launched the group to rap superstardom, and as the decade drew to its close Krayzie Bone issued his solo debut, *Thug Mentality 1999*. —*Jason Ankeny*

Thug Mentality 1999 / Mar. 30, 1999 / Relativity ✦✦✦

Theoretically, an epic hip-hop album could be compelling, but almost of all of the sweepstake entries are tedious, serving to diminish the artist's music instead of enhancing it. Nowhere was that more true than Bone Thugs-N-Harmony's overwrought third album, *The Art of War* and, unfortunately, that same sense of hubris characterizes *Thug Mentality 1999*, the ridiculously inflated debut solo album from Krayzie Bone. Freed from the group setting but not necessarily the members—who fill some of the obligatory guest slots, along with Bone family members such as Relay—Krayzie doesn't hesitate to accentuate the already smooth surfaces of his music. Some of these cuts are positively smoove, which stands in direct contrast to the gangstafied lyrics, but that's always been a part of the Bone trademark. In fact, other than the occasional cut that veers toward urban territory, there isn't a whole lot to differentiate this from the average Bone release—there's just more of it. A lot more of it: 38 tracks, to be precise. Breadth does not necessarily mean depth. Even though there is more depth than there was on *The Art of War*, there's a whole lot of filler cluttering these two discs, including several tracks that feel as if they're designed to launch developing artists. Krayzie tries to keep it interesting by varying the flow, never putting too many similar tracks next to each other, but who the hell can make it through 38 tracks of this without a breather, even if some cuts are skits? It may be a cliché to say that this double record would have been much more potent if it was trimmed to a single disc, but that doesn't make it less true, especially since there are enough songs to make a very good record, possibly one of the best things Krayzie has been involved with. It's just hard to discern that for certain in this guise. —*Stephen Thomas Erlewine*

● **Thug on da Line** / Aug. 28, 2001 / Loud ✦✦✦

After listening to Krayzie Bone on his second solo album, *Thug on da Line*, you get the sense that he is dealing with some personal demons. After years of personal and professional strife, Krayzie raps about his frustration with thug life in his patented singsong style on tracks like "Can't Hustle 4 Ever" and "Talk to Myself." There is some room for positivity, however, as he demonstrates on the sunny track "I Don't Know What" and "Rollin' Up Some Mo,'" a playful ode to reefer that remakes Lou Bega's inconsequential hit "Mambo #5." Despite all of Krayzie's introspection about the thug life, he must not be too tired of it considering that nearly one-third of the tracks on the album have the word "thug" in the title. It seems that he's torn between celebrating thug life and wanting to escape from it. That conflict makes *Thug on da Line* a compelling listen. —*Jon Azpiri*

Kreators

f. Boston, MA
Group / East Coast Rap, Hip-Hop
The Boston rap crew Kreators comprised G Squared, Jayson, Big Juan, and XL; their debut album, *No Contest*, appeared on the Bomb Hip Hop label in mid-1999. —*Jason Ankeny*

● **No Contest** / Jul. 6, 1999 / Bomb Hip Hop ✦✦✦
The underground rap group known as Kreators surfaced for the first time with their debut album, *No Contest*. Rappers G Squared, Jayson, XL, and Big Juan have an ineffable rapping style that balances old school smarts and new school toughness with aplomb. The breakout single "Foreign Lands" is one of the more exciting tracks from the new hip-hop underground led by labels including Rawkus and Bomb. Ed O.G. makes a guest appearance. —*Keith Farley*

Kris Kross

f. 1991
Group / Hip-Hop, Pop-Rap
Thirteen-year-old rappers Chris "Daddy Mack" Smith and Chris "Mack Daddy" Kelly became the pop sensations of 1992 as Kris Kross. The two were discovered at an Atlanta mall in 1991 by then-19-year-old producer Jermaine Dupri, who took them under his wing and came up with the gimmick of having the duo wear all of their clothing backwards, lending more significance to their name. Thanks in part to savvy marketing, "Jump," which sampled the Jackson 5's "I Want You Back," became the fastest-selling single in 15 years, staying at number one for eight weeks on the *Billboard* charts and pushing the sales of their debut album, *Totally Krossed Out*, past four million. Another gold single followed in "Warm It Up," and Kris Kross toured Europe with Michael Jackson and appeared on innumerable teen-oriented TV shows.

By the time of their follow-up album, 1993's *Da Bomb*, the boys had hit puberty, and their voices were noticeably deeper; they tried to affect a tougher, more hardcore sound and image, with less success. "Alright" was their third single to go gold or better, but *Da Bomb* failed to even go platinum by the end of the year. Kris Kross took some time off and returned in 1996 with *Young, Rich and Dangerous*, which featured the gold-selling rap ballad "Tonite's tha Night." —*Steve Huey*

● **Totally Krossed Out** / Mar. 17, 1992 / Ruffhouse ✦✦✦✦
Totally Krossed Out, the debut album by kiddie-rap sensations Kris Kross, is so tailored to a particular audience in a particular time period that it's nearly impossible to judge by any objective standard. So let's try anyway. Producer Jermaine Dupri—still a teenager himself—wrote all the songs here, and he delivers a catchy, pop-friendly batch of tracks that manage to stay pretty consistently engaging (perhaps in part because they are short). The album's interview intro disses playground rivals Another Bad Creation (that would have been a *great* hip-hop feud) before segueing into the irresistible smash "Jump" (oh, just try and listen to it without smiling, you heartless grinch). Actually, the miggeda-miggeda-mack bit proves they're not bad rappers, if they're able to borrow technique from Das EFX—though they don't keep it up, if for no other reason than that kids want to understand the words to songs they like. And "Warm It Up" is nearly as good. Some of the album tracks are lyrically generic, but the story song "Party" finds Chris and Chris trying to sneak into a club to meet girlies. There are some surprisingly serious notes struck on "Lil' Boys in da Hood" and "A Real Bad Dream," which paint the duo as knowing street kids who are all too aware of the dangers they could easily fall into.

There's nothing terribly frightening, but it's more realistic than the innocent bubblegum you might expect. Of course, then there's the self-explanatory "I Missed the Bus." But overall, *Totally Krossed Out* isn't nearly as obnoxious or cutesy as adults might fear—even if the lads' MC boasts just make you want to pat them on the head. —*Steve Huey*

Da Bomb / Aug. 3, 1993 / Ruffhouse ✦✦✦

Young, Rich and Dangerous / Jan. 1996 / Ruffhouse/Columbia ✦✦✦
Ever since their first massive hit single "Jump," Kriss Kross has had a difficult time shaking the novelty tag bestowed upon them. They have literally grown up in public—the Kriss Kross of 1996 is a lot different than the Kriss Kross of 1992. For starters, the group is tougher and harder, flirting with gangsta rap and G-funk, and they have become more imaginative, fluent rappers. That doesn't necessarily mean *Young, Rich and Dangerous*, the duo's third album, is more enjoyable than their previous releases—it just means they're trying harder. Parts of the album click, but much of the music sounds generic or underdeveloped, which makes *Young, Rich and Dangerous* nothing more than an admirable, but failed, effort. —*Stephen Thomas Erlewine*

The Best of Kriss Kross Remixed: 92 94 96 EP / Nov. 26, 1996 / Ruffhouse/ Columbia ✦✦✦
This collection of lackluster remixes fails to improve on the greatness of the duo's classic "Jump" or lesser hits like "Da Bomb," "Allright," "Tonite's tha Night," "Live and Die for Hip Hop"; one track, "Raide," is previously unreleased. —*Jason Ankeny*

KRS-One (Laurence Krisna Parker)

b. Aug. 20, 1965
Political Rap, Hip-Hop, East Coast Rap, Hardcore Rap
KRS-One (born Laurence Krisna Parker) was the leader of Boogie Down Productions, one of the most influential hardcore hip-hop outfits of the '80s. At the height of his career—roughly 1987-1990—KRS-One was known for his furiously political and socially conscious raps, which is the source of his nickname, the Teacher. Around the time of 1990's *Edutainment*, BDP's audience began to slip as many fans thought his raps were becoming preachy. As a reaction, KRS-One began to reestablish his street credibility with harder, sparer beats and raps. BDP's 1992's *Sex and Violence* was the first sign that he was taking a harder approach, one that wasn't nearly as concerned with teaching. KRS-One's first solo album, 1993's *Return of the Boom Bap*, was an extension of the more direct approach of *Sex and Violence*, yet it didn't halt his commercial decline. Still, he forged on with a high-quality self-titled 1995 effort and 1996's *Battle for Rap Supremacy*, a joint effort with his old rival MC Shan. After 1997's *I Got Next*, he put his solo career on hiatus for several years, finally returning in early 2001 with *The Sneak Attack*. The following year brought two full releases: the gospel effort *Spiritually Minded* and *The Mix Tape*, the latter including a single ("Ova Here") that stood as a response to Nellie, only the latest hip-hop figure to feud with the Blastmaster. —*Stephen Thomas Erlewine*

Return of the Boom Bap / Sep. 28, 1993 / Jive ✦✦
Boogie Down Productions leader KRS-One's reputation began to slip in the early '90s, as he spent more time educating than performing. He hit back at his critics with the slamming *Return of the Boom Bap*, his first official solo release. Leaving behind the detailed production of the last BDP album *Sex and Violence*, *Boom Bap* returns the MC to the spare, gritty territory of *Criminal Minded*. KRS-One sounds reinvigorated, as well, spitting out his rhymes with fury and intelligence. Although the record isn't as didatic as *Edutainment* or *Sex and Violence*, KRS-One hasn't made his lyrics simplistic, nor has he abandoned his cutting, intelligent social commentary. The combination of hard, basic beats and exciting rhymes makes *Return of the Boom Bap* a genuine comeback for KRS-One, one of the founding figures of modern hip-hop. —*Stephen Thomas Erlewine*

● **KRS-One** / Nov. 7, 1995 / Jive ✦✦✦✦
For his second solo album, KRS-One worked with a variety of younger hip-hop talents, perhaps in an attempt to resuscitate his street credibility and his commercial standing. Featuring appearances by Das EFX, Mad Lion, Fat Joe, and Channel Live, *KRS-One* is loaded with fresh talent of the first rank and they help spark the Teacher into giving an inspired performance. The album also showcases a bit fuller production than *Return of the Boom Bap*, but that doesn't mean he has sold it out—it just means he's continuing to experiment,

which is one of the reasons KRS-One remained a vital artist nearly a decade after his first record. —*Stephen Thomas Erlewine*

I Got Next / May 20, 1997 / Jive ✦✦✦✦
Again working with a variety of collaborators, including DJ Muggs, Redman, and Rich Nice, KRS-One turns in a hard-hitting, vital set of street-level hip-hop with *I Got Next*. By working consistently and keeping his ambitions modest, KRS-One has turned into the most consistent rapper of his generation, turning out a series of remarkably strong records. *I Got Next* doesn't offer anything new for the rapper, but it's a well-constructed set that is thoroughly compelling, both musically and lyrically. It proves that it's possible to age gracefully within hip-hop. —*Stephen Thomas Erlewine*

A Retrospective / Aug. 22, 2000 / Jive ✦✦✦✦
It didn't take long after the emergence of rap at the turn of the 1980s for artists to begin tackling social and political topics, but it was midway through the decade before such lyrics could match or even overshadow the simple party anthems and posturing that remain at the form's core even today. While his phrasing may seem badly outdated and his beats perhaps tame by today's standards, KRS-One and the late DJ Scott La Rock were a head of their time with tracks as diverse as "My Philosophy," a track critical of then current hip-hop culture, and "Sound of Da Police," which pointed the direction West Coast rap in particular would take over the next few years. Throughout his heyday, KRS warned against emerging rappers going for the quick buck ("Love is Gonna Get'Cha") taught them to avoid trendy gimmicks ("I'm Still #1"). By the turn of the 1990s, however, rap had taken a turn that even the Teacher couldn't predict. Violence and misogyny sold far more records than lectures about knowledge and vegetarianism. That being said, *A Retrospective* works best as a solid history lesson of raps first great transitional period, and most importantly, of the man who led it, proving it was possible to be intelligent, literate, and insightfully critical of the emergent hip-hop culture while still remaining true to its roots. —*John Duffy*

The Sneak Attack / Mar. 27, 2001 / Koch ✦✦✦
With *The Sneak Attack*, KRS-One, the self-proclaimed "God" of hip-hop, has returned after a four-year sabbatical to reclaim his spot as hip-hop's moral conscience. It's evident that KRS' cocky swagger has not suffered during his prolonged hiatus. He remains the staunchest advocate of his lyrical skills, as illustrated by the boastful barbs of the MC-bashing "Hot," as well as "Attendance," where KRS gleefully details his list of accomplishments ("I'm the teacher, but you still can't see/Cause while you respected Tupac, Tupac respected me"). KRS' passion still resonates and his philosophies remain cutting edge. The musical accompaniment of "Sneak Attack," spearheaded largely by KRS' brother, Kenny Parker, lacks the unrelenting boom-bap that previous collaborators DJ Premier and Showbiz supplied on earlier solo endeavors. However, the Blastmaster's knowledge still reigns supreme, as the socially conscious sermons he delivers on "I Will Make It" and "Why" still leave an indelible mark. Though KRS' lyrical attacks are less enthralling than his "My Philosophy" heyday, he is still passionate about the culture of hip-hop, and his self-affirming messages convey that. Trying to reprogram—or simply reach—America's youth is a daunting task, but at least there are still a handful of MCs around, like KRS-One, who are still willing to try. Class is still in session! —*Matt Conaway*

Spiritual Minded / Jan. 22, 2002 / Koch ✦✦✦
In the late '80s he supplanted Public Enemy's Chuck D as the angriest man in hip-hop. In 2002 he released a surprisingly gospel-centric album, one that proved time had not dulled the sharp edge of KRS-One's rhymes. And the Blastmaster never does things by half-steps; *Spiritual Minded* isn't a gospel crossover record at all, it actually *is* a gospel record. Although his messages on tracks like "Come to the Temple," "Lord Live Within My Heart," and "Take It to God" are strictly uplifting and even rooted in doctrine, there's no tempering his aggressive delivery and skeletal productions. The highlight, "Take Your Tyme," features KRS talking directly to young women about the pitfalls of premarital sex; it's easily one of the most encouraging hip-hop tracks heard in several years. As for weaknesses, *Spiritual Minded* certainly doesn't have the gloss of most major-label rap albums, and occasionally the production and hooks are sacrificed for the message in the material. Still, it's intriguing to hear one of the best rappers in history turning out a gospel album; contemporary gospel, including Christian hip-hop, is actually much more artistic than most would give it credit for. Though much of his new audience

may not even recognize one of the most famous names in rap history, it's likely they'll enjoy hearing this level of talent. —*John Bush*

The Mix Tape / Aug. 27, 2002 / Koch ✦✦✦
KRS-One found himself in a war of words in 2002, as the young prince of mainstream hip-hop Nelly sought out a battle of epic proportions; little did he know what he had gotten himself into. Although KRS-One has built a reputation for releasing quality, reggae-tinged hip-hop over the last decade, on *The Mix Tape* he allows his thoughts to be shared with the masses, including the sensational retaliation on "Ova Here." While the album is 13 tracks long, there is very little material actually offered up, as more or less the intended goal was to release the lead single as soon as possible and let KRS-One's opinions be aired. Even with his scathing assessment of the current rap scene, this respected MC handles himself with dignity and class, using his intelligence to spark the war of words instead of his ego. As of such, *The Mix Tape* is a great, albeit brief, trip through the mind of KRS-One, and a thoroughly enjoyable listen. —*Jason D. Taylor*

Kurious

f. New York, NY
Club/Dance
Latino-American rapper Kurious Jorge hailed from the Uptown section of Manhattan known as Spanish Harlem. His brazen talents landed him a guest spot on the Prime Minister Pete Nice and Daddy Rich cut "Three Blind Mice" from their album *Dust II Dust* in early 1993. Having forged an allegiance with the former Third Bass rapper, Kurious dropped his own single "Walk Like a Duck" later that year with a little help from Pete Nice. The gifted lyricist with a Latino twang released his debut album *A Constipated Monkey* on Hoppoh Records in early 1994. Applauded by fans of the New York underground scene, the album's Spanglish tone called to mind the work of Queens' Latin rap trio the Beatnuts. Kurious' joint was slightly less vulgar than the Nuts' EP *Intoxicated Demons* and featured a spicy array of musical influences ranging from salsa to rock & roll. The singles and subsequent videos for "Uptown Shit" and "I'm Kurious" gave the album some longevity on DJ play lists and car stereos. *Constipated Monkey* afforded Kurious with healthy respect among hip-hop's die-hards, but Kurious never translated this success commercially and never returned with a sophomore effort. —*Michael Di Bella*

● **A Constipated Monkey** / Jan. 18, 1994 / Columbia ✦✦✦
Banking on the underground success of his singles "Walk Like a Duck" and "Uptown Shit," Kurious Jorge (the rapper, not the monkey from children's books) released his debut album in early 1994. The album's subtle mix of underground vigor and flavorful party anthems pleased many of hip-hop's discerning aficionados. A guest list that included The Hieroglyphics' Casual and DJ Lord Sear on the mic and a back-from-the-dead Bosco Money from Downtown Science, The Beatnuts and Pete Nice and Daddy Rich on production gave the album a session feel. The album's wide range of samples, from The Black Byrds to Fifth Dimension, made for a quirky overall musical effect. Kurious does well to play up the strength of his style, a concise and careful delivery without sacrificing wit. In the end, the catchy single "I'm Kurious" may be the album's only true watermark, but cuts like "Top Notch" and the B-side "Mansion and a Yacht" featuring Sadat X from Brand Nubian are also bona fide mid-'90s hip-hop jams. —*Michael Di Bella*

Kurupt (Ricardo Brown)

b. 1972, Philadelphia, PA
West Coast Rap, Gangsta Rap, Hardcore Rap
Kurupt began his winding career with Death Row Records and rose to momentary fame alongside Dr. Dre and Snoop Dogg, but struggled to establish himself as a successful solo artist. Born Ricardo Brown in Philadelphia in 1972, he moved to Hawthorne, CA, as a teen, where he befriended Snoop and joined the roster of Death Row. He debuted on Dre's *Chronic* album (1992) and continued to contribute guest appearances to successive Death Row releases, most notably Snoop's *Doggystyle* (1993). He ultimately debuted as one-half of tha Dogg Pound, a partnership with rapper/producer Daz Dillinger spun off from Snoop's enormous success at that time. Together with Daz and Snoop, Kurupt enjoyed sizable success with *Dogg Food* (1995) and its hit singles: "Let's Play House" and "New York, New York." Three years later the then-A&M-affiliated Antra Records released *Kuruption!* (1998), the

rapper's ambitious double-disc solo debut. The album met modest success but did not make much of a commercial impact, nor did its tighter, more traditional follow-up, *Tha Streetz Is a Mutha* (1999). Kurupt's next release, *Space Boogie: Smoke Oddessey* (2001), aimed for crossover success, incorporating pop-rap elements as well as unlikely big-name guests like Fred Durst and Everlast, but again made little impact beyond the rapper's limited following. Meanwhile, Kurupt teamed with Daz for another Dogg Pound album, *Dillinger & Young Gotti* (2001), which presented a much more underground sound, released independently by D.P.G. Recordz. Meanwhile, Death Row released *2002* (2001), a collection of leftovers from tha Dogg Pound's mid-'90s era. In the wake of these many releases and little accompanying commercial success, Kurupt returned to the long-quiet Death Row label in 2002 and helped Suge Knight revive the infamous label. —*Jason Birchmeier*

Kuruption! / Sep. 1, 1998 / A&M ✦✦✦
Kurupt is an example of a hardcore rapper who has one foot on the East Coast and the other on the West Coast. The MC grew up in North Philadelphia, but after moving to L.A., he became associated with Death Row Records and worked with the Dr. Dre/Snoop Doggy Dogg/Warren G crowd. When Death Row fell apart and Death Row's infamous Suge Knight was serving hard time in prison, Kurupt resurfaced with his A&M-distributed Antra label. The first Antra release was *Kuruption!*, a two-CD set that contains a "West Coast Disc" and an "East Coast Disc." While the West Coast disc has more of a G-funk flavor, it isn't devoid of East Coast influences. Kurupt may have been influenced by the California rappers he hung out with, but he never abandoned the type of tongue-twisting complexity that has often characterized New York rappers. The East Coast disc, meanwhile, lives up to its title—tunes like "No Feelings," "Light Shit Up," and "The Life" emphasize verbal technique and provide tongue-twister after tongue-twister. Kurupt's rapping skills are strong, but in terms of subject matter, he's rather limited and unfocused. Most of the time, he's content to simply boast about his rapping skills and hurl profanity at other MCs. The end result is a release that is uneven and not remarkable, but does have its moments. —*Alex Henderson*

Tha Streetz Iz a Mutha / Nov. 2, 1999 / Antra ✦✦✦
The Philly native and Southern California transplant's second solo venture minus Daz Dillinger (though Daz supplies production and makes a few lyrical appearances) is hardcore West Coast rap dripping with funk and violence. Kurupt, a truly talented and versatile lyricist who appeared on Pete Rock's *Soul Survivor*, prefers to downplay his wordplay in favor of confrontational flows on *Streetz Iz a Mutha*. This is an angry and somewhat controversial record, mainly on the strength of the damning "Calling Out Names." *Streetz* represents true new-wave SoCal gangsta rap. Daz drops a few LBC funk tracks, namely "Your Gyrlfriend" and the title cut. Dr. Dre provides a signature track and guest MCs on the laid-back "Ho's a Housewife." A philharmonic track provided by Bink Dawg lights up "Trylogy," and Kurupt teams up with the legendary Blastmaster KRS to show his more abstract side on "Live on the Mic." Production is slack in places, and those looking for anything but hardcore may be a little disappointed. This is a very listenable joint, swelling with an updated G-funk sound, but the lyrical content is not for the faint of heart. A veritable who's who of West Coast rappers make guest appearances, including Jayo Felony, Snoop Dogg, Nate Dogg, Xzibit, Warren G, Dr. Dre, T-Mo from Goodie Mob, and KRS-One. Fans of tha Dogg Pound and L.A. hardcore will definitely dig this. Unspectacular but solid, this was part of a late-1999 West Coast revival. —*Michael Di Bella*

Space Boogie: Smoke Oddessey / Jul. 10, 2001 / Antra ✦✦✦
Following his career-establishing debut on Dr. Dre's *The Chronic* in 1992, Kurupt quickly proved that he wasn't your standard West Coast gangsta rapper. No, Kurupt is much more than that—he has brash charisma and more than enough attitude. He doesn't shy away from drama and isn't afraid to speak his mind. Yet character only goes so far—even in rap. On *Space Boogie: Smoke Oddessey*, Kurupt finally brings some substantial creativity to that sense of character. This was what prevented *Streetz Is a Mutha* from being a great album—he had rhymes and beats but couldn't bring it all together into a satisfying album. He does that here, to an extent. Yes, Kurupt finally manages to bring a sense of songcraft to his rhymes on *Space Boogie*. Every song here seems to capture a different motif: some take a feel-good Cali-sunshine approach, others a theatrical gangsta approach. In addition, Kurupt employs a number of talented West Coast guests (Snoop Dogg, Xzibit, Nate Dogg), which brings a sense of variety, and employs primarily one top West

Coast producer (Fredwreck), which brings a sense of cohesion. So when you break the album down to its elements, *Space Boogie* has all the makings of a perfect rap album. But it ultimately falls a bit short. More than anything, Kurupt's songcraft goes a little too far as he seems willing to try everything from hardcore rap ("The Hardest…") to pop-rap ("It's Over"). And by sadly inviting along Fred Durst and DJ Lethal from Limp Bizkit, in addition to Everlast, Kurupt's ill-fated crossover ambitions seem a little too overt. Still, even if *Space Boogie* doesn't quite realize its ambitions by overreaching, it shows that Kurupt's on a steady path to superstardom. —*Jason Birchmeier*

Illya Kuryaki and the Valderramas

Group / Latin Pop, Club/Dance, Latin Rap, Latin Dance
Latin hardcore/rap Illya Kuryaki and the Valderramas was formed by ex-Pechugo Emmanuel Horvilleur and Argentine rock icon Luis Alberto Spinetta's son Dante Spinetta, making their debut with the release of *Fabrico Cuero* in 1991, being voted Revelation of the Year by local newspaper *Clarín*. 1993's *Horno Para Calentar Los Mares* was followed by *Chaco* in 1995. A year later, Illya Kuryaki and the Valderramas moved to the U.S. to make an MTV Unplugged, released under the name of *Ninja Mental*, later, successfully performing that same show at Buenos Aires' Opera Theater. In 1997 the Latin rappers recorded *Versus*, followed by 1999's *Leche*. —*Drago Bonacich*

● **Leche** / Aug. 24, 1999 / Universal ✦✦✦✦
Illya Kuryaki and the Valderamas return with their sixth album *Leche*, another example of the Argentinean group's fusion of rap and rock. Their psychedelic side emerges on tracks like "DJ Droga" and "Apocalipsis Wow!" while "Latin Geisha," "Robot," and "Guerrilla Sexual" demonstrate the fluidity of their rapping. Ballads like "Jennifer Del Estero" make *Leche* another diverse and entertaining release from one of Argentina's most inventive bands. —*Heather Phares*

Unplugged: Ninja Mental / May 1, 2001 / Polygram International ✦✦✦
After the international success of *Chaco*, Illya Kuryaki and the Valderramas did a logical step and recorded in March 1996 its own MTV Unplugged. All the hits from that album are acoustically reworked here, like "Abarajame," "Jaguar House," and "Chaco." Although most of the material belongs to that album, there are also a couple of songs from the sophomore *Horno Para Calentar Los Mares* and two new songs that were recorded in studio: "Lo Primal del Viento" (which is among the band's finest works ever) and "Ninja Mental." This is not their best effort, but it shows the band at its artistically and popularity peak. The duo was having fun at that time and that's well shown in that album. Enjoyable, though not earth shattering. —*Iván Adaime*

KutMasta Kurt (Kurt Matlin)

Producer, DJ / Underground Rap
One of the more underrated producers and DJs in the West Coast underground, KutMasta Kurt initially made his name working with Kool Keith, during which time he first donned his trademark Mexican wrestling mask. Kurt (born Kurt Matlin) had been DJing in the Bay Area since the mid-'80s, getting his start as a teenager on a Santa Cruz community radio station. In 1988 he moved on to the Stanford University college station, and also mixed live at parties around the University of California-Santa Cruz campus. As his reputation grew, local MCs began to approach him about producing tracks, and he bought some basic studio equipment and taught himself to use it. After a few remixes and small independent releases, Kurt's friendship with the groundbreaking, underappreciated Ultramagnetic MC's paid off when, in 1994, ex-leader Kool Keith tapped Kurt to handle DJ and production duties for his new solo career. Kurt produced a couple of tracks on Keith's landmark Dr. Octagon album, but their first full project together was 1997's *Sex Style*, the first album released under Keith's own name. Kurt also helmed Keith's album as Dr. Dooom, 1999's *First Come, First Served*, and 2000's *Matthew*.

By the time *Matthew* was released, Kurt had begun to build his own career apart from Keith. He provided remixes for the likes of the Beastie Boys, Planet Asia, Rasco, DJ Spooky, Luscious Jackson, Buffalo Daughter, and Blackalicious, among others. He also formed his own label, Threshold, and in 2000 released the full-length album *KutMasta Kurt Presents: Masters of Illusion*, a collaborative project that featured Kool Keith and underground MC Motion Man. His relationship with Keith was fraying, however, partly because of a false rumor that Keith was missing gigs because he'd been institutionalized. Keith eventually fired him, but Kurt's career stayed in good shape thanks to his production on Dilated Peoples' 2000 breakthrough single, *Work the Angles*. He soon went on to work with Hieroglyphics members Souls of Mischief and Pep Love, and did a high-profile remix of nu-metal band Linkin Park's single *In the End* in 2001. That same year, he also produced Motion Man's well-received solo debut, *Clearing the Field*. —*Steve Huey*

● **KutMasta Kurt Presents: Masters of Illusion EP** / Jun. 21, 1999 / Copasetik ✦✦✦✦

San Francisco's KutMasta Kurt is most renowned for being the sound provider for Kool Keith's numerous aliases, Dr. Octagon, Dr. Doom, and Black Elvis. However, if his stock was measured solely by the amount of requests for remixes that he receives, then Kurt's NASDAQ rating would make any Fortune 500 company blush (his portfolio includes the Beastie Boys and Dilated Peoples, among many others). For his debut, *KutMasta Kurt Presents: Masters of Illusion*, Kurt does not stray far for lyrical reinforcement, plucking dysfunctional associates Kool Keith and independent circuit vet Motion Man. While many will not subscribe to their misogynistic, bugged-out rhetoric, the backpacking element this triumvirate caters to will undoubtedly become smitten with the guilty pleasures they provide. Kurt saturates *KutMasta Kurt Presents: Masters of Illusion* with a host of minimalist grooves, exemplified by the tribal drums of "Urban Legends" and the oriental-flavored "We All Over." Yet, it is Kurt's array of sinister keyboard stabs ("Masters of Illusion") and sublime organ samples ("Partna's Confused"), in turn spliced and juggled by DJ Revolution, that exhibit the true depth of his diverse production. Though the producer-based compilation has become hip-hop's latest rage (Pete Rock, DJ Muggs, Prince Paul, Easy Mo Bee, and Dame Grease), this underground supergroup's well-formed chemistry distinguishes *KutMasta Kurt Presents: Masters of Illusion* from the accessories in an overcrowded format. —*Matt Conaway*

Kwamé

Vocals, Producer, Arranger / Alternative Rap

In contrast to many '90s rappers, Kwamé fashioned a good-natured, humorous, somewhat intellectual persona for himself and is one of the few rappers to utilize a live band (A New Beginning) both live and in the studio. Born Kwamé Holland, he grew up in New York City's jazz scene, receiving his first set of drums from Lionel Hampton and hanging out with Stevie Wonder as a child. Kwamé's 1989 debut, *Kwamé the Boy Genius: Featuring a New Beginning*, was produced by Hurby "Luv Bug" Azor (Salt-N-Pepa) and showcased his mix of old school and daisy-age styles. The follow-up, *A Day in the Life: A Pokadelick Adventure*, was a concept album about exactly what the title said: an ordinary day in Kwamé's life as a high schooler. 1991's *Nastee* wasn't as successful as his two previous releases, and he moved from Atlantic to Wrap/Ichiban. He released a new album, *Incognito*, in 1994 with partners DJ Tat Money and A-Sharp. —*Steve Huey*

Kwamé the Boy Genius: Featuring a New Beginning / 1989 / Atlantic ✦✦✦✦✦

Kwamé's debut album, *Kwamé the Boy Genius: Featuring a New Beginning*, is an all-too-brief affair, clocking in at just over half an hour. Although it makes no explicit connection, it's a perfect fit with the daisy-age revolution being spearheaded by De La Soul around the same time. Positive vibes and offbeat humor abound, and even if producer Hurby "Luv Bug" Azor is no Prince Paul, the music is bright, appealing, and funky. Despite a load of goofy boasts and disses, and an occasional reference to his Islamic faith, Kwamé doesn't take himself too seriously, and he keeps things upbeat and genial the whole way through. The album's centerpiece is the freewheeling narrative "The Man We All Know and Love," which quotes songs from *Sesame Street*, Louis Jordan, and Minnie Riperton (among others) as Kwamé seduces one of his mother's friends and then thinks better of it. It's proof that Kwamé is a sorely neglected figure today, even among fans of playful, intellectual hip-hop. —*Steve Huey*

● **A Day in the Life: A Pokadelick Adventure** / 1990 / Atlantic ✦✦✦✦✦

Nastee / 1991 / Atlantic ✦✦✦

Despite some strong moments, Kwamé's third album, *Nastee*, didn't go over quite as well with his cult fan base as its two predecessors. Part of the reason is likely that the production is more polished than the bright funk of his previous two albums, and the studio sound is just a bit tinny. Another part of the reason might be that as he got older, Kwamé also got a little more sexual and a little more profane, which is understandable but seemed to contradict the happy-go-lucky boy-genius persona fans had come to expect. Even hints of

hardness don't suit Kwamé all that well, but although his lyrical perspective is less consistent, *Nastee* still has some good moments. The opening exhortation to, "wake up! scratch yo' butt!" gives way to a fine dance track in "Dontmatta," and a few of the lines in "Ding Dong" will sound awfully familiar to anyone who's heard Busta Rhymes' "Dangerous." "Can U Feel It!?" hits the clever lyrical heights of old, and the title track is one of his better story songs. And even when he rhymes about weed on "Don't Wanna B Your Love Thang," it's couched in a clever metaphor. On the whole, *Nastee* isn't as underrated as Kwamé's first two albums, but it's still worth tracking down for aficionados. —*Steve Huey*

Talib Kweli (Talib Greene)

b. Brooklyn, NY

Hip-Hop, East Coast Rap, Alternative Rap

Toward the close of the '90s, Rawkus Records initiated a golden age hip-hop revival with a roster of righteous rappers led by Talib Kweli, who maintained close ties with Mos Def and Hi-Tek, two of the label's other leading artists. Kweli's thoughtful and heartfelt rhymes provided a welcome alternative to mainstream East Coast rap of the time (Jay-Z, Nas, Puff Daddy, Mobb Deep, Wu-Tang), and a large audience of golden age rap revivalists embraced his music, as did the alternative rap scene and most critics. Though Kweli didn't top the charts like many of his New York contemporaries, he did enjoy widespread respect and also loyal support from Rawkus, who supported his many endeavors.

Born in Brooklyn to a literate family with a proud taste for African culture, Kweli's first name, Talib, is an Arabian name meaning "the seeker or student" while his last name is a Ghanaian name meaning "of truth or knowledge." His ascent into hip-hop began after he met Hi-Tek during a trip to Cincinnati, where the DJ resided, in 1994; and then Mos Def during a stint at NYU, where the two studied theater in 1995. Kweli and Hi-Tek initially formed the MC/DJ duo Reflection Eternal and later added Mos Def to the mix and changed their name to Black Star. Rawkus Records began releasing their recordings: 12" singles, compilation appearances (*Soundbombing* [1997], *Lyricist Lounge* [1998]), and a self-titled Black Star full-length (1998). The recordings won enormous acclaim and acceptance, and subsequently the three members embarked on similarly successful solo careers. Kweli first revived his previous MC/DJ partnership with Hi-Tek for the *Reflection Eternal* album (2000) and then collaborated with several producers for his second, *Quality* (2002). —*Jason Birchmeier*

● **Reflection Eternal** / Oct. 17, 2000 / Priority ✦✦✦✦✦

After releasing a handful of essential 12"s on various Rawkus Records projects in the late '90s, Talib Kweli and DJ Hi-Tek were on the verge of becoming one of hip-hop's best-kept secrets. Yet their original incarnation as a duo expanded into a triumvirate with the inclusion of Mos Def and transformed their eventual manifestation into Black Star, thwarting their initial bid for acclaim. While Kweli's stardom may have been initially eclipsed by his more charismatic cohort, Mos Def, *Reflection Eternal* houses enough merit to establish Talib as one of this generation's most poetic MCs. Kweli is a rare MC, as his lyricism resounds with a knowledge that transcends his still tender age. He does not aspire to reprogram the masses with this album, just rehabilitate them, as he laments on "The Blast": "They ask me what I'm writing for/I'm writing to show you what we fighting for." In an effort to celebrate life, Kweli breaks down hip-hop's obsession with death on "Good Mourning" and "Too Late." But it is his varied lyrical content that is most inspiring, effortlessly transitioning from the poignant circle-of-life epic "For Women" to the rugged "Some Kind of Wonderful" and "Down for the Count," featuring Rah Digga and Xzibit. While the unassuming, largely minimalist grooves that Hi-Tek supplied on Black Star's debut longed for a dramatic flair, he displays a remarkable maturation on *Reflection Eternal*. In fact, Tek's loping keyboard wails, soulful staccato claps, and shimmering piano loops are often sublime in their arrangement and outcome. Though Kweli and Hi-Tek's debut harbors overambitious tendencies, clocking in at over 70 minutes in length, they are a duo that will undoubtedly stain their memory into hip-hop's collective memory with this noteworthy debut. Welcome to the new generation of Native Tongue speaking. —*Matt Conaway*

Quality / Nov. 19, 2002 / MCA ✦✦✦✦✦

While his erstwhile Black Star mate Mos Def concentrated on his acting career, Talib Kweli set about crafting a truly solo follow-up to his acclaimed debut, *Reflection Eternal*, this time with a variety of producers in place of partner DJ Hi-Tek. The excellent *Quality* only ups the ante, building on its predecessor's clear-minded focus with greater scope and a more colorful musical palette. Right off the bat, it's apparent that Kweli has traded his old school minimalism for a warmer, richer sound—complete with some live instrumentation—that's immediately inviting and accessible. The opening trio of songs—"Rush," "Get By," and "Shock Body"—ranks among the most exciting music he's recorded, and the album only branches out from there. Kweli can pull off genial, good-time hip-hop like lead single "Waitin' for the DJ" and the DJ Quik-produced "Put It in the Air," and follow it with the blistering (and incisive) political fury of "The Proud." He reflects on his image as a so-called conscious rapper on "Good to You," and pushes its boundaries on the Cocoa Brovaz collaboration "Gun Music," where he twists the lyrical conventions of dancehall reggae to his own ends. Pharoahe Monch and the Roots' Black Thought put in exciting guest spots on "Guerrilla Monsoon Rap," and Mos Def appears on "Joy," where Kweli manages to describe the births of his two children without getting self-indulgent. A couple of the mellow R&B jams do get a little *too* mellow for their own good, drifting along and slowing the album's otherwise consistent momentum. Nonetheless, nearly everything Kweli tries works, and the array of producers keeps things unpredictable. *Quality* is proof that intelligent hip-hop need not lack excitement, soul, or genuine emotion; it's one of the best rap albums of a year with no shortage of winners. —*Steve Huey*

Kwest tha Madd Ladd

b. Brooklyn, NY
Hip-Hop, Alternative Pop/Rock, Hardcore Rap
Kwest 'tha Madd Ladd, a pure freestyler from Queens who was inspired as a youth by hometown heroes LL Cool J and Run-D.M.C., began writing rhymes while in junior high. He graduated from high school at the top of his class and entered New York State University at Syracuse. After he met Don Charnas in 1992, the two began working together on several demos. Kwest left school to work on music full time, and his first single, "Lubrication," did well on rap radio. He then signed to American Recordings, which released *This Is My First Album* in August 1996. —*John Bush*

● **This Is My First Album** / Apr. 9, 1996 / American ✦✦✦
It's no coincidence that this artist's name is Kwest. Like obvious stylistic influence A Tribe Called Quest, *This Is My First Album* features jazzy samples, respectable lyrical prowess, and a unique flavor that lends itself to the "alternative rap" tag. But that's where the similarities end, as this jokester is more interested in sex, spliffs, and serious silliness than progressive social consciousness. It's an approach that suits his style well, establishing Kwest as a consummate entertainer who'll go to almost any length to get attention.

Though at times his earnest eagerness to win the listener's affections can grow mildly annoying, the rapper's charm, wit, and keen sense of the absurd makes his style ultimately ingratiating. —*Bret Love*

Kyper (Randall S. Kyper)

b. Baton Rouge, LA
Producer / Club/Dance, Electro, Pop-Rap, Party Rap, Dance-Pop
Kyper was born Randall S. Kiper in Baton Rouge, LA, in the early '70s. His self-written "Tic-Tac-Toe" amazingly became a hit in 1990. Equally as astounding, the pop smash did nothing on the R&B charts. The song was a pop-disco-rap mix dominated by electronic drums and was popular in clubs. Though Kyper wrote all his songs, he borrowed heavily from Midnight Star, and "Tic Tac Toe" ripped off the guitar riff from Yes' "Owner of a Lonely Heart." After his one-hit wonder, he remained active in the music business but never charted again.

Kyper's parents say he starting hamming at an early age, singing and dancing for family and friends in Baton Rouge. By his preteenage years, his dance act was opening shows for funk and hip-hop acts—including Zapp, World Class Wreckin' Cru, L.A. Dream Team, Irma Thomas—and he began DJing and producing as well with a local group named Reality. His parents were educators and demanded that he graduate from college with distinction. He postponed college, though, when one of his demos got him signed to Atlantic, who gave him a shot at stardom. In September 1990, his single "Tic-Tac-Toe" went to number 14 pop, and sparked a pair of albums, 1990's *Tic-Tac-Toe* and 1992's *Countdown to the Year 2000*. After he was dropped by Atlantic, several collections of past mixes and remixes appeared on the Tip Top label. —*Andrew Hamilton*

● **Tic-Tac-Toe** / 1990 / Atlantic ✦✦✦
In 1990, Kyper made a significant contribution to the history of electro, a style that peaked in popularity five years earlier but remained a seminal force in dance music (if not rap). Dominated by synthesizers, it had obvious roots in Kraftwerk and Giorgio Moroder, as well as Afrika Bambaataa's seminal "Planet Rock." The entirely electronic *Tic-Tac-Toe* isn't unlike the Egyptian Lover's and the World Class Wreckin' Cru's mid-'80s recordings, and unsurprisingly, Kyper appealed to dance clubs rather than hardcore hip-hoppers. Though jams like "Satisfaction," "Work It," and "Dangerous" are catchy enough, the song that stands out the most is the sobering "What Is This World Comin' To," which takes a look at the problems of the world and makes us wish Kyper did more political songs. Had Kyper made variety a higher priority, this CD might have been great instead of merely decent. —*Alex Henderson*

Countdown to the Year 2000 / 1992 / Atlantic ✦✦

L-Burna

Hardcore Rap

Rapper L-Burna first came to prominence as a member of the Cleveland out-fit Bone Thugs-N-Harmony, back then known as Layzie Bone. Bone Thugs hit the big time shortly after signing with Eazy-E's Ruthless label and issuing such hit albums as 1995's *E 1999 Eternal* (and its double-platinum smash single "Tha Crossroads"), 1997's *The Art of War*, and 2000's *BTNHResurrection*. In the wake of their success, the group formed their own label, Mo Thugs Records, with L-Burna named CEO of the company. Layzie soon began going under the new moniker L-Burna after he boasted that he would "burn" the competition after his first solo album was released. 2001 saw the release of L-Burna's first solo outing, entitled *Thug By Nature*. —*Greg Prato*

● **Thug By Nature** / Mar. 20, 2001 / Ruthless ✦✦✦
As a member of Bone Thugs-N-Harmony, Layzie Bone helped create a unique, singsong vocal delivery that became the group's trademark. Now under the new moniker L-Burna, he gives exactly what's expected from the Bone Thugs-N-Harmony family, and not much more. Most of the tracks on *Thug By Nature* are right out of the Bone Thugs playbook: introspective, thoughtful lyrics about street life delivered in rapid-fire fashion. Most of the time, however, L-Burna's good intentions fall flat. Songs like "Deadly Musicals" and "How Long Will It Last?" do little to draw the listener's attention. Only when L-Burna breaks from his usual form does he get any results. The unique horn loops on "Make My Day" and "Battlefield" help break the monotony and provide an all-too-brief glimpse of what might have been if L-Burna had been willing to take more chances. —*Jon Azpiri*

L'Trimm

f. 1987
Group / Old School Rap

Miami-based female rappers Tigra and Bunny D were 18 years old when they scored a mild hit, "Cars With the Boom," in 1988. For a brief period their CD, *Grab It!*, stayed on the charts after Atlantic leased it from Time-X, but they were unable to get another single to maintain the momentum, and kiddie pop gradually lost its audience. —*Ron Wynn*

● **Grab It!** / 1988 / Hot Productions ✦✦✦✦
L'Trimm was the sort of pop-rap group that hip-hop's hardcore loves to hate. Tigra and Bunny D weren't great rappers, and their detractors argued that they made a mockery of rap with their cutesy, girlish image and their frivolous, often silly lyrics. But then, the Miami-based duo wasn't trying to be the female equivalent of Run-D.M.C.—its albums were aimed at dance-pop audiences, and L'Trimm didn't expect to impress fans of hardcore rap any more than Poison expected to be compared to Metallica. *Grab It!*, L'Trimm's debut album, must be taken for what it is: silly, goofy, escapist fun. From "Sexy" and "Better Yet L'Trimm" to the hit "Cars With the Boom," L'Trimm's very pop-minded, club-oriented songs are infectious and entertaining despite the group's obvious limitations. No one who's seriously into hip-hop would think for a minute that Tigra or Bunny have great rapping skills, but for this type of crossover album, you don't need them. You need the right hooks and beats, and this 1988 release succeeds on that level. L'Trimm went on to record a few more albums, but *Grab It!* remains its most consistent and appealing effort. —*Alex Henderson*

Drop That Bottom / 1989 / Atlantic ✦✦
From their giggly, cutesy bimbo image to their hook-laden, club-oriented sound, South Florida's L'Trimm is exactly the type of pop-rap for which hardcore hip-hoppers have nothing but contempt. Be that as it may, the adolescent female duo's second album, *Drop That Bottom*, is an often entertaining and enjoyable effort that works quite well as club music. Like L'Trimm's 1988 debut, the album must be taken for exactly what it is: pure, unapologetic, mindless fun. True, rappers Tigra and Bunny D hardly possess the rapping skills of Queen Latifah or MC Lyte—far from it—but their sense of fun brings to life such infectious fare as "My Heart Went Boom," "Double Trouble," and a remix of *Grab It!*'s hit title song. L'Trimm may get no respect in the 'hood, but on the dancefloor, *Drop That Bottom* definitely has its place. —*Alex Henderson*

Groovy / 1991 / Atlantic ✦✦
Despite its sophomoric inclinations and the limitations of its sound, female duo L'Trimm can usually be counted on to deliver club-oriented pop-rap that is hardly remarkable, but likeable enough. With this album, Tigra and Bunny D attempt to evolve and pretty much move away from the Miami-bass sound for which they've been known. Though not quite as appealing as *Grab It!* or *Drop That Bottom*, *Groovy* isn't without its pleasures—including the rap/house number "Glamour Girls," a remake of the Archies' 1960s' pop hit "Sugar Sugar" and the new-jack-swing-inspired title song. Meanwhile, the influence of groups like C&C Music Factory and Snap is hard to miss on "Jungle," "Snap, Crackle, Pop," and "Get Loose." L'Trimm's popularity in club circles proved to be short lived, and by the mid-'90s, the duo was barely a footnote in rap and dance music history. —*Alex Henderson*

La' Chat

b. Memphis, TN
Hardcore Rap, Dirty South

Where most female artists in the rap game often boast more impressive looks than MC skills, La' Chat represented a new style of female rapper—the female thug rapper. Following the precedent set by fellow female thug rappers from the South—Mia X and Gangsta Boo—Chat broke through as a member of an established clique (Three 6 Mafia) and represented a feminine point of view. Yet Chat didn't rap about Prada like Foxy Brown, never resorted to overt sleaze like Lil' Kim, and wouldn't even bother with crossover tactics like Eve. No, Chat represented the ghetto with pride. She raps about street politics, drug dealing, casual sex, and staying true to the thug life. Her breakthrough came on Project Pat's "Chickenhead," one of the first Three 6 Mafia-produced songs to get national airplay. She then reprised her role as the feminine foil on Three 6 Mafia's "Baby Mama" from the *Baby Boy* soundtrack. These two impressive performances set the stage for her debut album, *Murder She Spoke*, which appeared in late 2001. —*Jason Birchmeier*

● **Murder She Spoke** / Oct. 23, 2001 / Koch International ✦✦✦
On her debut LP, *Murder She Spoke*, La' Chat quickly establishes the fact that she's more than just a Gangsta Boo soundalike. Like Boo, Chat represented the feminine side of the Three 6 Mafia sound—a ghetto thug bitch from Memphis not afraid to get lewd and tell you how it is. Indeed, the Three 6 camp plays a major role in this album's sound, with Juicy J and DJ Paul dropping their trademark beats, and the myriad Three 6 rappers making cameos throughout the album, often as foils to Chat's tough-girl stance. Unfortunately, it sounds like either J and Paul are saving their best beats for their own albums or, perhaps, that the duo is running a little short on ideas—their production work here is surprisingly subpar. Yet, as typically Three 6 as the beats sound on *Murder She Spoke*, Chat's performance more than compensates. Once again like Boo, she could be one of the best MCs in the Three 6 stable. She exudes a harsh attitude and delivers her rhymes with a liquid flow. Plus, she's not afraid to get exploitative, best exemplified on her interpolations of longtime Three 6 motifs: two examples being "Slob on My Cat" (interpolating "Slob on My Knob") and "Luv 2 Get High" (interpolating "Now I'm Hi").

Yet Chat never resorts solely to sleaze to engage her audience; most of her lyrics are street smart and center on street credibility and politics. More than anything, though, it's refreshing to see a female effectively represent her side of the thug life. So even if *Murder She Spoke* suffers from many of the same problems plaguing other Three 6 solo albums—namely, not enough fresh ideas and too much filler—it's still one of the better Three 6-affiliated releases to date and is indeed an impressive debut for Chat. —*Jason Birchmeier*

L.A. Dream Team

Group / Old School Rap, West Coast Rap, Hip-Hop

Rudy Pardee, a Cleveland native, and Los Angeles' Chris Wilson formed the L.A. Dream Team in the early '80s. The times were rife with experimentation and the dance-rap hybrid of electro was still a new form—not yet firmly aligned with dance, with dance itself still capable of embracing hip-hop. Enterprising and resourceful, the duo formed their own label, Dream Team Records, that would go on to issue not only Dream Team records but other early California rap as well, including the first single from J.J. Fad. The group's electro classics include "The Dream Team Is in the House" and "Rockberry Jam." In 1986 the group signed with MCA and recorded two albums with the label. Electro was fading from its brief mainstream popularity, however, and neither of the records sold well enough to sustain the group. L.A. Dream Team surfaced in 1993 as DTP to issue a few singles, including an update of one of their old hits, "Rockberry Revisited." Chris Wilson went on to pursue video and music production, while Rudy Pardee died tragically in a scuba-diving accident in 1998. —*Wade Kergan*

• **Kings of the West Coast** / 1986 / MCA ✦✦✦

Rudy Pardee and Chris Wilson didn't become kings or even princes of the West Coast. They came a lot closer to enjoying court jester status, as their 1986 debut contained only one mildly entertaining number, "Dream Team Is in the House." —*Ron Wynn*

Bad to the Bone / 1987 / MCA ✦✦✦

The second LP by West Coast rappers L.A. Dream Team tried to be both controversial ("What's a Skeezer") and cute ("Rudy and Snake," "She Only Rocks and Rolls"), but instead ended up being quickly forgotten. —*Ron Wynn*

L.A. Star

Gangsta Rap

In 1990, L.A. Star provided a woman's perspective on the gangsta life at a time when there weren't many female rappers willing to operate in that arena. At the same time, she also included some material with a romantic side, though she couldn't afford to juxtapose vulnerability too close to combativeness. *Poetess* was a decent debut on Profile, but there wasn't a follow-up. —*Ron Wynn*

• **Poetess** / Apr. 3, 1990 / Profile ✦✦✦✦✦

If Crystal Waters were a full-time rapper instead of a singer, she might sound something like L.A. Star, who also has a rather nasal, dry voice. Given the East Coast/West Coast rap rivalry that was taking place in some hip-hop circles, it was surprising that a New York rapper like Star would dare to have L.A. in her name (even if it did stand for Lisa Ali instead of Los Angeles). Star claimed N.W.A as a main influence, but in fact, *Poetess* is far from gangsta rap. While "Wondrous Dream," "Fade to Black," "Once Upon a Time," and other songs on the CD paint a troubling picture of urban life, Star has a lot more in common with MC Lyte than the gangsta rappers of the West Coast. Although decent, *Poetess* wasn't a big seller. And as much potential as Star showed on this album, she never recorded a follow-up. —*Alex Henderson*

Mike Ladd

b. Cambridge, MA

Producer, Vocals / Underground Rap, Hip-Hop, Alternative Rap

Mike Ladd is an iconoclast hip-hop figure, a producer with studio smarts and an intelligent MC as well, but a man with a wide-ranging set of aims that occasionally interfere with his music. The Bronx-based Ladd, whose roots lie in poetry and performance, has close ties to largely spoken-word artists like Saul Williams or Carl Hancock Rux as well as underground rap maestros like El-P or New Flesh. Born in Cambridge, MA, Ladd played bass or drums in varying types of garage bands while in high school and gathered a diverse set of influences, ranging from Funkadelic to King Tubby to Minor Threat to the work of Chess staff arranger Charles Stepney. He stayed close to home

for college, and spent time as a graduate student in English literature at Boston University. He gained favor in spoken poetry circles, winning the Nuyorican Poets Café Slam and also having his writing published in the 1996 protest tome *In Defense of Mumia*. He'd also begun producing and rapping, and released his first album, *Easy Listening 4 Armageddon*, in 1997 on Scratchie/Mercury. Critical praise led to a deal between his Likemadd label and Ozone Music for 2000's *Welcome to the Afterfuture* and the following year's *Vernacular Homicide EP*. Ladd had already recorded a 1998 single for top British underground label Big Dada, and he returned there for his third full-length, 2000's *Gun Hill Road*. The first in a trilogy of underground full-lengths staging a battle between the forces of good and evil (in hip-hop), it appeared as the Infesticons and earned the highest profile of any of his releases. The second in the trilogy, *Beauty Party* (recorded as the Majesticons), followed in 2003. —*John Bush*

Easy Listening 4 Armageddon / Jun. 10, 1997 / Mercury ✦✦✦✦

Gil Scott-Heron's name is tossed around every time some young hip-hopper aspires beyond the usual rhymes, but for all the invocations, there have been precious few rhymers worthy of carrying on his poetic legacy. One who is, however, is Mike Ladd, who offered an auspicious debut with *Easy Listening 4 Armegeddon*. Ladd makes comparison with Scott-Heron sensible in large part due to his lyrics, which don't forget the humor ("I'm Building a Bodacious Bodega for the Race War") even as they tackle serious aspects of racism and politics. But Ladd remembers something else that many would-be poets who followed Scott-Heron have forgotten: as compelling and evocative as his words can be, it's the music that gives them their staying power. And through a series of lo-fi beats and loops that make stunning use of a few choice samples, Ladd creates an eerie soundscape that perfectly matches his muttered musings. From the twilight jazz of "The Tragic Mulatto Is Neither" and "Bush League Junkie" to the alt-rock-flavored "Kissin' Kecia" to the stark, hypnotic backdrop of Ladd's seven-minute take on "Blade Runner," the tunes would be worth hearing on their own merits. In tandem with Ladd's poetry, the resulting hybrid is superb. —*Dan LeRoy*

• **Welcome to the Afterfuture** / Mar. 7, 2000 / Ozone ✦✦✦✦

After a decade of underground recognition, New York-based producer/lyricist Mike Ladd has emerged since 1998 as the hip-hop scene's prime genius. *Easy Listening 4 Armageddon* put him on the map, the all-star Infesticons album put him over, and *Welcome to the Afterfuture* is the articulation of a musical vision. Whether it will pan out in the real future is another matter, but at least it stands a chance. *Welcome to the Afterfuture* is a blender of sounds and styles and epitomizes the search that is leading cutting-edge hip-hop further into avant-garde and non-Western musical traditions. "Airwave Hysteria" has a sweet bollywood sample with a tight chorus broken up by some hypnotic scratching. The ring mod and time-stretched vocals on "Planet 10" are reminiscent of a Kid 606 album. There's a number of good tracks, but a few stand out, particularly "5000 Miles," where Ladd gets to display his lyrical skills ("I'm 5000 miles west/Of my future/Where's my floating car/My utopia") against fuzzed bass and organ figures. He gets props for entering the sci-fi realm without sounding like another Kool Keith carbon, although you might argue that it's simply more futurist than sci-fi per se. The most out track is "I Feel Like 100 Dollars"; it would be difficult to create more chaos at a slower tempo, for sure. There's some nice Air-esque jamming on "To the Moon's Contractor," and the title track features a crunked funk dissection of contemporary ills via *Nova Express*. Not so successful is the cut "No. 1 St.," which falls into all the pitfalls of trying too hard, with self-important rhyming. It's not often that album reviews name check Ezra Pound, Mogwai, and Run-D.M.C., so buy this album. If hip-hop should have a tradition, then this is it—experimentation. —*Brian Whitener*

Gun Hill Road / May 30, 2000 / Big Dada ✦✦

The cream of the underground hip-hop crop—a gaggle of lost gangstas and a Beastie Boy collaborator—constitute the wild and should-be-wonderful mob collectively know as the Infesticons, spearheaded by the inimitable Mike Ladd. It should be wonderful, but it isn't: *Gun Hill Road* suffers mightily from blurred vision, splintered beats, tuneless loops, too much noise, and a low rap standard. The sound is pure NYC underground and stellar moments abound, but the overall impact is scattershot. A stunning wealth and breadth of talent, anti-playa attitude, and derangement are on display here, but the feeling is showy and spotty. Highlights have to be Saul Williams' reassuringly nutcase "Monkey Theme," Rob Smith's waveless proto-rap "Chase Theme," and

Dana & Majesticon 69's transsexual/freak/funk show "Shampoo Theme." There are some reverential moments to Funkadelia and many of Smith and Majesticon's movements are often sheer labyrinths of voicescapes in the most ambitious of the rap traditions. —*Becky Byrkit*

Vernacular Homicide [EP] / Mar. 6, 2001 / Ozone ◆◆◆
Vernacular Homicide, a typically ambitious mini-album from rap raconteur Mike Ladd, charts his obsession with everyone from De La Soul to Jimi Hendrix. Over basement beats and a kitchen-sink production aesthetic, Ladd earns his freak credentials many times over. The highlight? "Northampton," featuring what sounds like a miniature chipmunk rapping over a Bruce Haack production. —*John Bush*

Beauty Party / Feb. 25, 2003 / Big Dada ◆◆◆
There's a party going on during *Beauty Party*, Mike Ladd's second full-length in a trilogy (begun as the Infesticons and projected to be completed as the Trusticons), and it's a record as smooth and self-satisfied as the Infesticons' *Gun Hill Road* was abstract and gritty. Ladd hasn't sold out, though; he's merely assumed the guise of the Majesticons, a hip-hop crew more obsessed with money than music, defeated by the Infesticons at the end of *Gun Hill Road* but making their comeback here. This "ultimate post-jiggy experience" is *The Empire Strikes Back* of underground rap, and Ladd pulls no punches in making a slick record that apes commercial rap ("Piranha Party," "Game Party") at its most asinine. Boasting a host of fictitious rappers like Ivy League, Disasterous, and Cheeta Chinchilla (all played by Ladd associates), the Majesticons strut their way through a hilariously lame Pet Shop Boys rip-off on "Brains Party" ("I've got the brains, you've got the looks/Let's make lots of money!"), go all No Limit on "Platinum Blaque Party" ("I've got so much assets to access/words cannot describe my success"), and touch on rolling G-funk for "Majestwest Party." Fortunately, as with the best Parliament records, the eternal struggle of funky vs. unfunky doesn't get in the way of some excellent music, like the swinging digital club tune "Prom Night Party" or the down-tempo R&B "Luv Thief Party." In the end, though, Ladd's *too* good at producing a realistic commercial rap record; *Beauty Party* falls prey to the same faults, and the occasionally bland material never rises above its satirical value. —*John Bush*

Lady of Rage

b. Farmville, VA
Voices, Producer / G-Funk, West Coast Rap, Gangsta Rap
Though she had made more than a dozen appearances on soundtracks as well as albums from her Death Row Records cohorts, the Lady of Rage didn't release an album until 1997. A native of Farmville, VA, she was discovered by Death Row's Dr. Dre and cut several vocals for the L.A. Posse's 1991 album *They Come in All Colors*. Her 1994 single for Death Row "Afro Puffs" (from the *Above the Rim* soundtrack) placed on both R&B and the pop charts, featuring Dre on production and backing vocals by Snoop Dogg. She was also featured on several Death Row albums, including Snoop's *Tha Doggfather*. Her own album, *Necessary Roughness*, hit the Top 40 upon release in June 1997. —*John Bush*

Afro Puffs EP / Sep. 6, 1994 / Interscope ◆◆◆
● **Necessary Roughness** / Jun. 24, 1997 / Interscope ◆◆◆
Lady of Rage was Death Row's attempt to reach the female market, but there isn't that much difference between her 1997 debut, *Necessary Roughness*, and the bulk of latter-day Death Row releases. Like many other later-period Death Row records, the form is more important than the content. *Necessary Roughness* is filled with minimally produced, bass-heavy productions that emphasize a fat, rolling groove. While there isn't anything particularly special about the rhythms, they are well produced and occasionally catchy, and they often show more care than the lyrics, which tend be simple gangsta clichés. For hardcore gangsta fans, there's enough going on in the beats to make *Necessary Roughness* worth a listen or two, but for casual fans of the genre, it may seem a little too generic. —*Leo Stanley*

Laquan

Hip-Hop, Gangsta Rap, Hardcore Rap
Sixteen-year-old rapper Laquan (born Kenneth Green), a native of Los Angeles, recorded one intelligent, mature, and musical album, *Notes of a Native Son*, in 1990. The LP featured a live band and backing singers on

every track and was produced by Bell Biv DeVoe collaborators Richard Wolf and Bret Mazur. —*Steve Huey*

● **Notes of a Native Son** / Sep. 10, 1990 / 4th & Broadway ◆◆
This is a spirited protest, sociopolitical and sometimes offensive gangsta rap, that didn't get widespread attention because it came out on a small label. Laquan told just as strong a story about inner-city injustices, horrors, and brutality as Ice-T, Public Enemy, Boogie Down Productions, or Scarface, and without as much sexism or vulgarity. —*Ron Wynn*

Large Professor (William Paul Mitchell)

b. Mar. 21, 1973
Producer / East Coast Rap, Hip-Hop, Underground Rap
Widely known initially for his work as a producer and MC with the rap group Main Source, Large Professor soon after became a full-time producer working with such acts as Big Daddy Kane and A Tribe Called Quest. Professor originally became involved in rap when he won a tryout held by Main Source members K-Cut and Sir Scratch in 1989. Contributing significantly to the creative direction of the group, Professor eventually broke with Main Source over creative differences . He then lent his hand to albums by some of rap's biggest names, including Eric B. & Rakim, Nas, and Pete Rock & C.L. Smooth. For his full-length solo debut, 2002's *1st Class*, Large Professor called in favors from friends including Nas, Q-Tip, and Busta Rhymes. —*Steve Kurutz*

1st Class / Oct. 8, 2002 / Matador ◆◆
He was programming beats and producing records for hip-hop legends while still a teenager, but Large Professor waited nearly a decade to put out his own album. If *1st Class* isn't as exciting as any of his outside productions (which are simply begging for a greatest-shots collection), it's because LP tries to handle nearly everything himself. The album's five tracks are in before we finally hear a guest, and it's a long wait—Large Professor doesn't have much to say on a track like "Brand New Sound" (with his beats *or* his rhymes), and he repeats the title enough to make it sound more like desperation than defiance. A three-track spate of features finds him trading some tough rhymes with Nas, Akinyele, and Q-Tip, though here Q-Tip is basically reduced to freestyling over the choruses. Large Professor gets back to boasting with "Born to Ball," but he doesn't prove up to the task. Either more space for guests or a little more time in the studio would've resulted in a better effort than this half-baked record. —*John Bush*

The Last Emperor

Political Rap, East Coast Rap
Taking his moniker from the Bernardo Bertolucci film epic of the same name, this West Philadelphia native has been an underground hip-hop mover and shaker since the mid-'90s. Having attended Overbrook High, Philadelphia's own hip-hop high, which saw the likes of Cool C, Steady B, and the Fresh Prince pass through its hallowed halls, Last Emp became a b-boy by osmosis in addition to being a wizard in the classroom. After graduating from the nation's first historically black college (Lincoln University), Emp took his act to New York, where he caught on with storied Lyricist Lounge. Emperor's first on-wax experience was a significant one, appearing alongside KRS-One and Rage Against the Machine's Zach de la Rocha on the cut "C.I.A." from 1998's *Lyricist Lounge, Vol. 1*. Having served notice to his scholastic street skill, Emperor hit the road to polish up his on-stage performance, occasionally popping up on mix tapes and 12"s from time to time. Having stirred the underground into a frenzy with rumors of a debut album, in early 2000 official word came that Emp had signed with independent kingpin label Rawkus. Distribution problems, however, kept the record off the racks. —*M.F. Di Bella*

● **Echo Leader/Charlie/Rap Tyranny [Single]** / 1999 / Hi-rise ◆◆◆◆
All three songs are different, but the Last Emperor pulls it off. "Echo Leader" has some hard guitar riffs that you rarely hear in hip-hop. While "Charlie" is a story-rap about a kid named Charlie, and "Rap Tyranny" is a little bit more of a upbeat party song. All in all, a solid release from the Last Emperor. —*Dan Gizzi*

Latyrx

f. 1992, Davis, CA
Group / Underground Rap, Hip-Hop, Alternative Rap
Members of the prodigiously talented SoleSides/Quannum collective, Latyrx went sorely underrecognized for their restlessly experimental brand of

hip-hop. Their lone album was far too eccentric for the masses, but even in underground circles, it fell prey to poor distribution (it went out of print twice) and poor timing (Quannum mates DJ Shadow and Blackalicious hadn't yet secured their status with hip-hop fans). The name Latyrx was a combination of its members' performing monikers, Lateef the Truth Speaker (born Lateef Daumont) and Lyrics Born (born Tom Shimura). The roots of their partnership lay in the formation of the SoleSides collective at the University of California-Davis. The crew's charter members—which also included DJ Shadow and the future Blackalicious team—were all involved in student radio and shared a progressive-minded approach to hip-hop. Lateef and Lyrics Born initially recorded as solo artists; under the name Asia Born, the latter released the first single on the SoleSides label, "Send Them," in early 1993.

The first proper Latyrx release came in 1996, and was actually the B side of Lateef's solo single "The Wreckoning." For the track in question, also called "Latyrx," both MCs recorded completely different raps that were played back simultaneously. Coupled with DJ Shadow's trippy production, the effect was mind bending and started to build an underground buzz for the duo. More solo sides followed that year—Lateef cut "The Quickening (The Wreckoning, Pt. II)" with Shadow on the boards, and Lyrics Born produced his own 12" release, "Balcony Beach" b/w "Burnt Pride." Most of these solo sides, along with a raft of new material, appeared on the duo's debut LP, *The Album*, which was released in 1997. DJ Shadow produced a total of four tracks, and Chief Xcel (later of Blackalicious) helmed two, while Lyrics Born handled the rest himself.

The Album earned rave reviews for its adventurous, electronic-flavored production and the distinctive flows of both rappers. It was followed closely by the *Muzapper's Mixes* EP, which contained the boundary-pushing single "Lady Don't Tek No." *Muzapper's Remixes* appeared in 1998, but unfortunately, *The Album* didn't stay in print much longer; it was reissued briefly in 1999 before disappearing again. Meanwhile, SoleSides was reconfigured into a new label, Quannum Projects, and the collective officially changed its name to Quannum as well.

Latyrx didn't record much following their brief reign as an underground sensation. They guested on "8 Point Agenda," a 1999 single by the Herbaliser, and also contributed new material to the *Quannum Spectrum* compilation that year. Meanwhile, *The Album* became something of a Holy Grail to the West Coast underground, with used copies selling for exorbitant sums. Quannum Projects finally reissued it in 2002, allowing it to take its place alongside the new crop of experimental hip-hop that included El-P's Def Jux crew, Antipop Consortium, and Anticon. By that time, both Lateef and Lyrics Born were reportedly working on solo projects, the former with Blackalicious' Chief Xcel. *—Steve Huey*

● **The Album** / Aug. 25, 1997 / SoleSides ✦✦✦✦✦
Latyrx's first full-length release, *The Album*, was as sonically inventive as it was overlooked—which makes sense, since it was hardly ever in print during its first five years of existence. Enough people heard the record to make it something of an underground legend, but its potential influence wound up unfortunately limited, especially given how forward looking the music on *The Album* is. It represents a major step for the SoleSides (later Quannum) collective in replacing the Hieroglyphics as the Bay Area's most adventurous underground crew. Mates DJ Shadow and Blackalicious' Chief Xcel both produce several tracks on *The Album*, with Shadow helming the groundbreaking experiment "Latyrx" (which also provided the catalyst for an album release). Both MCs recorded individual raps, which were then laid on top of one another in separate audio channels. Since both are heard simultaneously, and aren't interacting, it's almost impossible to follow either Lateef or Lyrics Born's individual flows, but it makes for a startling cumulative effect—it's vocal hip-hop as pure sonic texture. Nothing else is quite as avant-garde as "Latyrx," but there's a lot of highly progressive use made of electronics; the most attention-grabbing productions are built on spacy trip-hop beats, ambient synth textures, or burbling, minimal computer funk (with a couple of jazz-funk and dancehall-style cuts thrown in for good measure). Actually, despite the big-name backup, Lyrics Born produces the majority of the tracks on the album, and is just as responsible for its musical direction; he's also the more distinctive MC, growling, muttering, skanking like a reggae toaster, and half-singing his lines at times. Excellent early solo singles by both MCs ("The Quickening," "Balcony Beach," "Burnt Pride") sit alongside a few new

offerings—disappointingly few, actually, since it takes live cuts, freestyles, and interludes just to pad *The Album* past 45 minutes. Still, its key tracks are nothing short of visionary, making it an essential listen. *—Steve Huey*

Muzapper's Remixes / 1998 / SoleSides ✦✦✦
Although some versions of the songs on *Muzapper's Remixes* occasionally make Latyrx sound a bit more standard than the originals did, it's overall a welcome addition to the duo's slim discography. *—Steve Huey*

Lavar

Pop-Rap
It's ironic that Lavar's single, "The Vanilla Melt" was an angry attack on Vanilla Ice, for Lavar's rapping style was quite similar to Vanilla's. Like Vanilla, Lavar was a white rapper who took a very pop-minded, commercial approach, and like Vanilla, he was the type of rapper who was considered lightweight by hip-hop's hardcore. Lavar signed with Epic in 1991, when "The Vanilla Melt" was released and the tune "Girlz 'N the Room" was added to the single as a secondary track. The single didn't do much, and after Lavar was dropped by Epic, the pop-rapper never recorded for another label. *—Alex Henderson*

The Vanilla Melt [Single] / May 23, 1991 / Epic ✦

Leaders of the New School

f. 1989, Uniondale, NY
Group / Golden Age, Hip-Hop, East Coast Rap
Uniondale, NY, rappers MC Charlie Brown, MC Dinco D, MC Busta Rhymes, and Cut Monitor Milo issued *A Future Without a Past . . .* for Elektra in 1991 as Leaders of the New School. They combined Afro-centric message tracks with novelty throwaways, and got a little attention for "Teachers, Don't Teach Us Nonsense." They followed it with *T.I.M.E.* in 1993. *—Ron Wynn*

★ **A Future Without a Past . . .** / 1991 / Elektra ✦✦✦✦✦
Even in the vibrant early-'90s hip-hop scene, *A Future Without a Past . . .* emerged as a breath of fresh air, simultaneously presenting a throwback to the old school rhyme trade-offs and call-and-response rapping styles of crews like the Furious Five and the Funky Four Plus One, and vaulting rap headlong into its future. Brash and full of youthful energy and exuberance, Leaders of the New School was the perfect meshing of three distinctly different but entirely complementary personalities whose flows flew in the face of conventional MC etiquette, from Dinco D's straightforward, intellectual tongue-twisting to Charlie Brown's zany shrieks to Busta Rhymes' viscous, reggae-inspired toasting—skirting the line between seriousness and humor—which, only a few years later, would help him to his commercial pay dirt as a solo artist. That's not even to mention the DJ and sometime reggae-tinged MC, DJ Cut Monitor Milo. The result is one of the most infectious rap albums ever created. The songs are, first and foremost, meant to be fun and humorous, and they are certainly that, particularly on Charlie Brown's nonsensical "What's the Pinocchio's Theory," the insistent "Trains, Planes and Automobiles" and "My Ding-A-Ling," and Busta Rhymes' jovial ode to full-figured women, "Feminine Fatt." The cut-and-paste production is expert throughout, packed with fresh samples, thanks to Bomb Squad member Eric "Vietnam" Sadler, the Stimulated Dummies crew, and the Vibe Chemist Backspin, and the group also show themselves to be quite capable with a sampler, particularly Milo's incredible work on "Case of the P.T.A." and "My Ding-A-Ling." But it would be wrong to simply peg this album as a foray into kinder, gentler, more lighthearted and innocent hip-hop. First, the album has the feel and scope of a loose concept album and is separated into three sections—the first two set in school, the final one following the members after school lets out—and that alone points to a group of young men, mostly still teenagers, trying to move rap into new dimensions. Second, the ambience of New York permeates *A Future Without a Past . . .*, but it is simply presented from a younger and far less jaded perspective. Songs such as "Just When You Thought It Was Safe" and "Sound of the Zeekers @#^ ☆*?!," if not exactly hard edged and political, offer far more than throwaway sentiment, and lyrically L.O.N.S. never descend into naïveté. The album portrays a group of young men who are fully emerged in the sometimes less-than-innocent urban life that characterizes hip-hop culture, but are also able to transcend the inherent limits and pitfalls to which that life can lead. In that sense, it is a celebration of all the best aspects of hip-hop culture and youth. *—Stanton Swihart*

T.I.M.E. / Oct. 12, 1993 / Elektra ✦✦✦

Far be it for anyone to claim that Leaders of the New School lacked ambition during their fascinating, far too short lived career, which culminated on this follow-up to their exciting debut album. With *T.I.M.E.* the barely adult-aged members check in with their second loose concept album, this time delving into a sort of urban sci-fi mysticism. Obviously, the group doesn't entirely pull off this concept, and ther point understandably becomes murky or downright opaque. The ambition itself, however, is intriguing in practice, and the album is an endlessly interesting listen. Upon its release, many saw *T.I.M.E.* as a dramatic fall-off from the manic, happy-go-lucky charm and vitality of the unit's first album, which had simply combusted in the hop-hop community when it was released two years earlier. In hindsight, *T.I.M.E.* is a much more mature work, both musically and lyrically, pushing forward into territories never hinted at in the first; as a whole, it's also arguably a more interesting album. In its own way, the production here is just as strong as that on the first album. It's far less loopy and idiosyncratic (and less novel) this time around, often just building off a dense beat and an ominous bassline, as on the hypnotic "Syntax Era," instead of pasting together all manner of samples. This approach gives the album much more sonic cohesion and intellectual heft, however. Easily, this is a much more hard-edged venture into the hip-hop underground aesthetic. The entire first half of the album is a dazzling sequence of songs, any of which, regardless of the concept, could have been brilliant singles. Songs such as "Classic Material" (with an unforgettable horn hook), "Daily Reminder," and "Connections" relentlessly pound their way into your head, and in "A Quarter to Cutthroat," L.O.N.S. comes up with a sensational, gritty New York City and hip-hop anthem. A couple of the pieces on the record's second half don't maintain the same lofty heights as the first—the album is probably ten minutes or so too long—occasionally sounding redundant or flat. They are never complete missteps, however, and the posse cut "Spontaneous (13 MC's Deep)" gives the album its centerpiece. Alas, Busta Rhymes, having already fully reached his distinctive style, seemed a bit confined in the group dynamic here; not long after the album's release, he broke up the group and went solo. —*Stanton Swihart*

Archie Lee

Dirty South, Hardcore Rap

Texas rapper Archie Lee began his career with Swisha House, one of the Houston scene's leading labels, and moved on shortly afterward. His debut album, *Da Mista Masta* (2000), didn't make much of an impact outside of the South despite its Swisha House affiliation. Even so, Lee continued on with *8100%* (2001), retaining his small yet cultish following. —*Jason Birchmeier*

Da Mista Masta / Sep. 12, 2000 / Swisha House ✦✦✦

Archie Lee flaunts his down-South dialect quite extensively throughout *Da Mista Masta*, his debut album for Swisha House. He's far from the first rapper to proliferate a Lone Star lexicon and drawling flow, but he's certainly one of the most flamboyant Texans out there, self-describingly "swangin' wide wid a throwd swagger when not grippin' some grain while ballin.'" His colorful rhetoric is accentuated by a host of fellow Swisha House rappers—Big Tiger, Slim Thug, Blyndcyde, Big Pic, Lil' Ron, and more—and the sorta screwed-up post-G-funk so often associated with Houston at the turn of the century. The standout tracks here, like "Hopes and Dreams," tend to feature melodic, sung hooks that perfectly offset the lively rhythms that make *Da Mista Masta* as much of an album to bump at the club as one to thump in your trunk. In short, prime-era Swisha House. —*Jason Birchmeier*

LEN

f. 1991

Group / Hip-Hop, Alternative Dance

The alternative pop/dance group LEN was formed in Toronto in 1991 by Marc "The Burger Pimp" Costanzo and his sister Sharon, initially to perform punk pop-style music. However, an outside interest in hip-hop gradually crept into the group's style over the course of the EP and two full-length independent albums they issued from 1992 to 1996 (including 1996's *Get Your Legs Broke*). As time passed, LEN picked up new members, including D Rock, DJ Moves, and Planet Pea. National exposure of the bright, laid-back pop single "Steal My Sunshine" on the soundtrack of the 1999 film *Go* set the stage for LEN's debut album, *You Can't Stop the Bum Rush*, later that year. —*Steve Huey*

● **You Can't Stop the Bum Rush** / May 25, 1999 / Work ✦✦✦✦

The debut by the Canadian four-piece LEN is a set of old school tracks indebted to Sugar Hill Records and Afrika Bambaataa as well as more recent indie-rap agitators like the Beastie Boys. While the rapping is a bit stilted, the production is excellent and best heard on the first track, the monster hit "Steal My Sunshine," a bright slice of indie-pop with an old school guitar loop and a suitably bumping bassline. For all of the great tracks here, it's difficult to escape the feeling that *You Can't Stop the Bum Rush* is a low-rent version of the Beastie Boys' 1998 album *Hello Nasty*—Biz Markie has a few appearances as he did with the Beasties, and master turntablist Mr. Dibbs takes the role of Mix Master Mike with major contributions to one (very short) track. Still, the album's few derivative qualities never really get in the way of an enjoyable listen. —*John Bush*

Da Lench Mob

f. 1990

Group / Gangsta Rap, Hardcore Rap

An ardently political rap trio from the West Coast, Da Lench Mob earned notice for their breakout debut *Guerillas in tha Mist*. Formed by Shorty, J-Dee, and T Bone, the group debuted in 1990 on Ice Cube's *AmeriKKKa's Most Wanted* album. With Cube as executive producer, Da Lench Mob released *Guerillas in tha Mist* in 1992. Led by an incendiary video for the title track (based on the movie *Predator*), the album became popular within hip-hop circles, with confrontational tracks like "Freedom Got an A.K." and "Lost in tha System" almost as outspoken as Ice Cube himself. Though *Planet of da Apes* followed in 1994, Da Lench Mob disbanded soon after. —*John Bush*

● **Guerillas in tha Mist** / 1992 / Street Knowledge/Atco ✦✦✦✦✦

Looking like a cross between the Black Panthers and the Zapatistas on the album cover, Da Lench Mob fully embrace an urban revolutionary rhetoric consistent with their image. Unrepentantly political music of any sort can be difficult to listen to—particularly when it is almost blindly angry and coming from an inherently (though understandably) biased point of view, and also when it sidesteps some of the subtleties of the issues it raises. *Guerillas in tha Mist*, the group's debut album, is guilty of all those things, and yet it is an often brilliant, always invigorating, sometimes infuriating scowl of an album. The album is a relentless onslaught of attitude, but it is not misplaced vehemence or finger wagging. The final song on the album is titled "Inside tha Head of a Black Man," and that is exactly the psychic and psychological space that *Guerillas in tha Mist* occupies: confused, chaotic, complex, righteous, angry, and turbulent, but also permeated with a sense of braggadocio and looseness. Just because they have trouble on their mind doesn't mean they can't swing, too, and Ice Cube's production does just that, especially on tunes such as "All on My Nut Sac," "Freedom Got an A.K.," and the title track. He loads the songs with rolling fatback bass and funky keyboard riffs, and fills in every empty space with some sort of noise, generally a horn or siren or whistle. When listening to *Guerillas in tha Mist*, it is virtually impossible to catch your breath; in fact, it is so powerfully urgent that it feels as if you've just been punched in the gut. But when experiencing something this significant and consequential, you shouldn't want the blow to be pulled just to increase your comfort level. —*Stanton Swihart*

Planet of da Apes / 1994 / Priority ✦✦✦

Music's best political propaganda—which ranges from Merle Haggard on the right to Joan Baez, Public Enemy, Bob Marley, and U2 on the left—offers more than just rhetoric. It makes its case with coherent, well-reasoned arguments. Whether you agree or disagree with Haggard's stridently conservative "The Fighting Side of Me" or Marley's left-leaning Rastafarian manifesto "Get Up, Stand Up," those songs are political masterpieces. *Planet of da Apes*, Da Lench Mob's second album, is a fiercely political effort that doesn't contain any masterpieces. Combining a strong Public Enemy influence with West Coast gangsta rap, Ice Cube's L.A. colleagues provide a lot of inflammatory, militant rhetoric, but don't provide any lyrics that you could call brilliant. None of the tunes are in a class with Ice-T's "Colors," Public Enemy's "Night of the Living Baseheads," Boogie Down Productions' "South Bronx," or Grandmaster Flash's "New York, New York"; those sociopolitical rap classics are nothing short of brilliant, whereas *Planet of da Apes* is merely an exercise in angry rhetoric for the sake of angry rhetoric. Da Lench Mob often mines the same black nationalist waters as Public Enemy and BDP, but without being as coherent or as lucid—agree or disagree with them, Chuck D and

KRS-One have provided some of the most memorable political rhymes in the history of hip-hop (just as Haggard has provided some of the most memorable Republican propaganda in the history of country music). But despite its shortcomings, *Planet of da Apes* is an enjoyable, if limited, effort. The beats are often infectious, and, like Rage Against the Machine, Da Lench Mob can pull you in with its grooves and its passion even though its lyrics are too clichéd and rhetorical for their own good. —*Alex Henderson*

Lexicon

f. California

Group / Hip-Hop, Hardcore Rap, West Coast Rap

Brothers Nick (Nick Fury) and Gideon (Big Oak) Black are the rap duo known as Lexicon. The Southern California natives formed in the early '90s and worked with the Library Crew before making a name for themselves in the Los Angeles underground. Fueled by the brothers' exuberance and undeniable chemistry, Lexicon started turning heads with the release of a pair of 12"s and the EP *Antiquity* on Mums the World. It was during these sessions that Lexicon hooked up with DJ Cheapshot, a collaboration that would prove quit fruitful. After producing the single "Keep on Moving," Cheapshot signed the duo to his growing Spy-Tech label. Lexicon released their full-length debut, *It's the L!*, in the fall of 2001. Featuring production by DJ Cheapshot and Vin Skully (Styles of Beyond), the album scored an underground hit with "Nikehead" and quickly established Lexicon at the forefront of Los Angeles' independent hip-hop scene. —*Martin Woodside*

● **Antiquity EP** / Aug. 31, 1999 / Concentrated ✦✦✦
This relatively unknown duo from Los Angeles turned some heads with the EP *Antiquity*. They do a good job of combining some very different tracks, and have gathered a few guests for the show, including Iriscience of Dilated Peoples, 2Mex, and LMNO. They are part of a large underground movement from the L.A. hip-hop scene, including the Freestyle Fellowship, Living Legends, Hobo Junction, and Hieroglyphics. These groups have been doing a whole lot of trendsetting and discarding a big part of the hip-hop norm in doing so, and for the open-minded fans that love lyrics from the heart it really works. This EP isn't without it's flaws, though, and there are quite a few slow spots that will need polishing if they decide to release a full LP. Overall, this is a very well done record with tight production and conscious lyrics. —*Brad Mills*

It's the L! / 2001 / Spy-Tech ✦✦✦

Lighter Shade of Brown

f. 1990

Group / Hip-Hop, Alternative Rap, Latin Rap

Part of the early-'90s explosion of Latin rap, Lighter Shade of Brown (LSOB) was formed in Riverside, CA, in 1990, when the teenage ODM (One Dope Mexican, born Robert Gutierrez) was introduced to DTTX (Don't Try to Xerox, born Bobby Ramirez). The duo began cutting demos and secured a record deal within the year; they debuted with 1990's *Brown & Proud* for Quality Records hip-hop subsidiary Pump. Though they didn't break out on the level of Cypress Hill, the group garnered some positive reviews and established themselves as one of the better Latin rap outfits around. The follow-up, *Hip Hop Locos*, was released in 1992, and helped LSOB land a major-label shot with Mercury, where they contributed to the soundtracks of the Latino-oriented films *Mi Vida Loca* and *I Like It Like That*. 1994's full-length *Layin' in the Cut* proved disappointing, however, and the disillusioned partners took a temporary break from the music business. They returned in 1997 on Oakland's much smaller Thump Records (in partnership with the Greenside label), issuing a self-titled album with guests including Rappin' 4-Tay and Tony! Toni! Toné!'s Dwayne Wiggins. Thump released a greatest hits' collection in 1999, and their fifth album, *If You Could See Inside Me*, followed, producing a minor hit single in "Sunny Day." In late 1999, Gutierrez became a radio DJ in the Los Angeles area. —*Steve Huey*

Brown & Proud / 1990 / Pump ✦✦✦✦
Latino rappers have ranged from pop-oriented (Gerardo) to hardcore (Cypress Hill, Tha Mexikinz). Debuting with *Brown & Proud*, Lighter Shade of Brown made it clear that they fell into the latter category. The title says it all—the L.A. group wears its Mexican-American heritage like a badge of honor on this promising CD, and in doing so, is usually quite substantial. Most of the material is superb, including "El Varrio" (a no-nonsense description of

how tough life can be in L.A.'s working-class Hispanic neighborhoods), "T.J. Nights," and "Pancho Villa" (which salutes the Mexican rebel). *Brown & Proud* wasn't as commercially successful as some of Brown's subsequent work, but in Chicano rap circles, the group commanded some well-deserved respect. —*Alex Henderson*

Hip Hop Locos / 1992 / Quality ✦✦✦

Layin' in the Cut / 1994 / Mercury ✦✦✦

Lighter Shade of Brown / Nov. 18, 1997 / Thump ✦✦✦
By the time Lighter Shade of Brown released their eponymous album in late 1997, they had run out of momentum and their music no longer had the freshness that it did on *Brown & Proud*. That said, the group was still capable of cutting some supremely engaging fusions of Latin rhythms and hip-hop, and there are a few tracks on the album—including the Rappin' 4-Tay duet "World Famous"—that kick like their old stuff, and that's what makes *Lighter Shade of Brown* worthwhile for longtime followers. —*Leo Stanley*

● **Greatest Hits** / Oct. 19, 1999 / Thump ✦✦✦✦
Lighter Shade of Brown released an album every other year in the '90s, so for fans trying to catch up with the innovative Latin duo, Thump's *Greatest Hits* is a godsend. It wisely focuses on their raw debut *Brown & Proud* and the follow-up *Hip Hop Locos*, but also gives weight to later material. As could be expected, there are many highlights but "Brown & Proud," "Latin Active," and "On a Sunday Afternoon" are especially worthy of the compilation. —*John Bush*

Lil' Blunt

Hardcore Rap, Southern Rap

Lil' Blunt began his career alongside fellow Memphis rapper Indo G and went solo in the late '90s, releasing albums for a number of independent labels. Indo G & Lil' Blunt signed with Luke Records in the mid-'90s, making them one of the first Memphis acts to make an impact outside of Tennessee. Following two albums (*The Antidote* [1994] and *Up in Smoke* [1995]) and a regional hit ("Blame It on the Funk" [1994], later compiled on the *Ringmaster* soundtrack [1999]), Lil' Blunt maintained a low profile. He made his return with *A Higher Level* (1999) and released several other drug-themed albums, among them *A Higher Level* (1999), *Parafenalia* (2000), *Bluntnatized* (2001), and *Pure Dope* (2002). —*Jason Birchmeier*

A Higher Level / Jun. 22, 1999 / DownSouth 4 Life/Forty Street ✦✦
From the cover and a quick scan at the titles ("Swanging on the Block," "Movin' Tha Hitz," "What They Hittin' For"), it should hardly come as a surprise to either interested or disinterested listeners that *A Higher Level* by Lil' Blunt features 12 of the same old No Limit-styled street rollers. There are a few scant highlights, including "40 Thieves," but for the most part *A Higher Level* is a tired, played-out album. —*Keith Farley*

● **Bluntnatized** / May 22, 2001 / Fi ✦✦
If you've ever heard any of the Southern-style rappers from the No Limit or Cash Money cliques, chances are you've already heard a million records like this. After all, there was a time when Master P and his ilk were cranking out what seemed to be a new record every week. Problem was, no matter whose name appeared on the label, most of those records sounded the same, and even fans of the dirty South sound had difficulty telling the artists apart. Lil' Blunt, part of Atlanta's Fi-Clique rap quartet, isn't really bringing anything new to the table, either. The usual tales about living on the streets, thug life, drugs, guns, and bitches abound, backed by the same generic jeep beats you've heard ad nauseam. With its played-out lyrical themes (making money, putting "hoes" in their place, etc.), the album is notable only for an appearance by Too Short, who must have lost some sort of bet to lower himself to this. —*Bret Love*

Lil' Bow Wow

b. Columbus, OH

Pop-Rap, Dirty South

Columbus, OH, native Lil' Bow Wow, known simply as Shad to his friends, began rapping when he was only six years old. When he threw out his stylings to the audience on the Chronic Tour, one of those most impressed was Snoop Dogg, who quickly nicknamed the young talent Lil' Bow Wow. Things moved fast for Lil' Bow Wow, and by the age of 13 he had a long list of impressive credits by his name. He has worked on soundtracks for movies like the *Wild Wild West* and *Big Momma's House*, providing upbeat tracks like "Bounce with Me." He has been featured in a number of magazines, including *Esquire*, *Vibe*, and *People*. His photo has even been spread on millions of free book covers that Dr. Pepper produced for schools. In 2000, Lil' Bow Wow recorded a debut album, *Beware of Dog*, for the So So Def label. Under the guidance of executive producer Jermaine Dupri, the young artist reached multiplatinum success and delivered a hit follow-up, *Doggy Bag*, in late 2001. One year later, he starred in his first feature film, *Like Mike*. —*Charlotte Dillon*

● **Beware of Dog** / Sep. 26, 2000 / So So Def ✦✦✦
You have to wonder who's the real star of *Beware of Dog*: Lil' Bow Wow, the sensational teen rapper from Ohio who miraculously raps better than most MCs in the industry despite his youth, or Jermaine Dupri, the sly producer from Atlanta who somehow continues to strike gold every few years with a teenage pop-rapper. Alone, neither Bow Wow or Dupri are very impressive. Sure, the kid can rap circles around most of his adult peers and swoon all the girls while he's at it. But it takes more than talent and cuteness to succeed in the rap industry, especially when you're only a kid. Similarly, Dupri can produce hit songs in his sleep and defy whatever sort of trends risk his reign on the charts. But he's definitely not superstar material himself. Together, however, these two seem like the perfect pair: the prodigy and the sage. *Beware of Dog* certainly showcases why these two work so well together. Over the relatively brief course of the album, Dupri and coproducer Brian Michael Cox deliver sure-fire pop-rap: "Bounce With Me" is the sort of feel-good song destined to be a summer anthem; "Bow Wow (That's My Name)" is the sort of respect-demanding introduction perfect for name recognition; and "Ghetto Girls" is the sort of good-guy ballad sure to infect the hearts of innumerable teenage girls. Somehow, Bow Wow and Dupri managed to deliver just what rap needed in 2000—pure fun without all the bling-blingin' and ass shakin', without any swearing or sex—and did so in a way that didn't seem too obvious or derivative. Talk all you want about duos like Dre and Snoop or Puffy and Biggie; Bow Wow and Dupri are just as complementary, if not more so. —*Jason Birchmeier*

Doggy Bag / Dec. 18, 2001 / So So Def ✦✦✦
Nobody expected Lil' Bow Wow to go multiplatinum with his first album, *Beware of Dog*. His success was quite simply unprecedented, and that's perhaps why his follow-up album, *Doggy Bag*, feels awfully familiar. There are only nine songs here if you don't count the intro and the interludes, incredibly brief for a rap album in 2001. Furthermore, most of the nine songs are either interpolations of proven songs, such as New Edition's "Candy Girl" on "All I Know," or partially rehashed songs, such as DMX's "Party Up (Up in Here)" on "Up in Here." It seems as if Dupri, who coproduces and cowrites every song, is relying on either what worked well on the first Bow Wow album or else what has worked well in the past for other artists. But this shouldn't be much of a surprise; it's the nature of pop-rap and Dupri certainly knows how to craft it in a catchy way that you can't deny. He does so by sticking with the familiar, and that's precisely how *Doggy Bag* sounds. Everyone who loved songs like "Bounce With Me" and "Bow Wow (That's My Name)" will find much to savor here. As mentioned, Dupri mines the vaults of pop music for his hooks, as do the Neptunes on their hit contribution, "Take Ya Home." This isn't kids' music; it's music that appeals to everyone, kids and adults alike. —*Jason Birchmeier*

Lil' Cease (James Lloyd Jr.)

b. Brooklyn, NY
East Coast Rap, Pop-Rap
Rapper Lil' Cease was born and raised in Brooklyn's Bedford-Stuyvesant area, at age 15 becoming a protégé of the Notorious B.I.G. With his distinctive lisping style, he made his recorded debut in 1994 as a member of the Junior M.A.F.I.A., issuing the single "Players Anthem"; the full-length *Conspiracy* followed in 1995, and that same year Lil' Cease scored a hit with the Lil' Kim duet "Crush on You." On March 9, 1997, he and the Notorious B.I.G. were driving away from a party in Los Angeles when Biggie was shot and killed; Lil' Cease continued as a solo artist, signing to Lil' Kim's Queen Bee label and issuing *The Wonderful World of Cease A Leo* in mid-1999. —*Jason Ankeny*

● **The Wonderful World of Cease A Leo** / Jul. 13, 1999 / Atlantic ✦✦✦
Brooklyn-bred Lil' Cease burst out of Junior M.A.F.I.A. and into his own solo joint with 1999's *The Wonderful World of Cease A Leo*, a hardcore journey

that never lacks on bass, beats, or party jams. The single "Play Around" is an obvious highlight, though Lil' Cease hits hard throughout the album. Guests include Busta Rhymes, Lil' Kim, Jay-Z, Redman, and Puff Daddy on "Get Out of Our Way." —*Keith Farley*

Lil 1/2 Dead

Hip-Hop, Gangsta Rap, Hardcore Rap
Long Beach, CA's Lil' 1/2 Dead toured America on Dr. Dre's 1993 *Chronic* tour. His debut solo album, *The Dead Has Arisen*, has a similar sound to Dre's and Snoop's G-funk. —*John Bush*

● **The Dead Has Arisen** / 1994 / Priority ✦✦✦
Lil 1/2 Dead had been a member of tha Dogg Pound (Snoop Doggy Dogg's outfit) when, in 1994, the L.A. rapper came out with his first solo album, *The Dead Has Arisen*. The most obvious comparison on this CD is D.J. Quik—like Quik, 1/2 Dead is a gangsta rapper who has a relaxed, laid-back type of flow and tells it like it is without going out of his way to inundate the listener with violent lyrics. *The Dead Has Arisen* isn't nearly as violent or as graphic as N.W.A's *Straight Outta Compton* or Ice Cube's *AmeriKKKa's Most Wanted*—essentially, this is an R-rated party album along the lines of Dr. Dre's *The Chronic*, Warren G's *Regulate…G Funk Era*, or Quik's *Quik Is the Name*. A big part of this album's appeal is the smooth and melodic producing of Tracy Kendrick, Courtney "Tha Commander" Branch and others; though their Dre-influenced tracks aren't as imaginative as Dre's, they see to it that this is a nice-sounding CD. Rapping about sex, marijuana, and life as a "playa," 1/2 Dead doesn't bring any groundbreaking or earth-shattering insights to his album. But he manages to come up with his share of catchy rhymes and hooks, and when you combine them with the appealing production, you've got a party album that's decent, if conventional. —*Alex Henderson*

Steel on a Mission / May 21, 1996 / Priority ✦✦✦

Lil' J

Pop-Rap, Teen Pop
At a very young age, Lil' J never failed to impress with not only his ability to drop rhymes but also his ambition. By age seven he was rhyming outside of the local K-Mart with a tip jar, collecting money for his first demo tape. Years later in his early teens, J was still rhyming and still hustling his way into the rap game. In 1999, when he was just 14, J came to the attention of Trans Continental Records, best known for an affiliation with the hottest teen pop groups of the time, including the Backstreet Boys, O-Town, and LFO. They recognized J's talent and it wasn't long before the teen MC inked a record deal with Hollywood Records. In 2002 he made his major-label debut with *All About J*, a surprisingly slick LP featuring some of the industry's best producers from all coasts: Jermaine Dupri, L.E.S., and L.T. Hutton being just three of the more prominent. Futhermore, not content resting on his laurels, J toured and set his sights on Hollywood. —*Jason Birchmeier*

● **All About J** / Apr. 22, 2002 / Hollywood ✦✦✦
Arriving quickly on the heels of Lil' Bow Wow's and Lil' Romeo's commercial success in the rap game, Lil' J couldn't help but appear as an imitator. It happened when Kris Kross first broke through and had been happening for decades in the pop world—with one teen success comes a wave of imitators. Yet it's a disservice to call Lil' J an imitator, even if that's ultimately what he is in the eyes of the public and his record label. The kid has skills. That's the bottom line and what you'll realize if you actually give his debut album a chance. He may be barely a teen, but he sure can rap, and while his subject matter usually sticks to juvenilia, that's partly the beauty of it. If the rap game is short on anything, it's innocence and good-hearted fun. This is exactly what Lil' J brings to the table, particularly on songs like the lead single "It's the Weekend." What makes *All About J* even better, however, is the plethora of talented producers. You get Clark Kent and L.E.S. representing NYC, Jermaine Dupri representing the Southern sound, and L.T. Hutton bringing a little West Coast flavor to the album—essentially the sort of variety Lil' J needs if he hopes to cross over from coast to coast and everywhere in between. Of course, with any teen rapper, you really can't expect too much lyrical virtuosity or much naughtiness—two of rap's best qualities—but the innocence is a nice change of pace. So even if Lil' J isn't quite on par with Lil' Bow Wow and even if he can't help but seem to be riding on Bow Wow's coattails, Lil' J is definitely worth investigating if you enjoy the Will Smith-style of PG-rated rap. —*Jason Birchmeier*

Lil Jon & the East Side Boyz

f. Atlanta, GA

Group / Party Rap, Dirty South

Atlanta and the surrounding area had always been a hotbed for party rap and bass music throughout the '90s, and more than anyone else, Lil Jon & the East Side Boyz took these styles to the masses with a cutting-edge dirty South attitude perfect for the burgeoning club scene of the time. The Atlanta-based rapper/producer began as a club DJ before Jermaine Dupri invited him in 1993 to come work for So So Def Records, where Jon served as the executive vice president of A&R. In the meantime, Jon hosted a radio show at V103 and began producing and remixing tracks for such major Atlanta-area artists as Too Short, Xscape, Total, and Usher. After making a name for himself, Jon then debuted his East Side Boyz (Big Sam and Lil Bo) on *Get Crunk, Who U Wit: Da Album* (1997) and scored a club anthem, "Who You Wit?" For the next five years, Jon remained an underground phenomenon, mainly confined to regional success, until he broke into the national market with "Bia', Bia'," his second massive hit, this one featuring Ludacris, Too Short, and Chyna Whyte, and from *Put Yo Hood Up* (2001). Jon & the East Side Boyz returned quickly with another album, *Kings of Crunk* (2002), and with it yet another massive hit, "I Don't Give A..." —*Jason Birchmeier*

Get Crunk, Who U Wit: Da Album / Oct. 21, 1997 / Mirror Image ◆◆◆

● **Put Yo Hood Up** / May 22, 2001 / TVT ◆◆◆

For *Put Yo Hood Up*, Lil Jon moves further in the direction he experienced substantial success with on the late-'90s Southern club anthem "Who You Wit." The dirty South beats keep the subwoofers thumping, and the countless call-and-response vocal hooks ensure this album's place in the clubs. In fact, Jon almost sticks to his formula too well here. Thanks to his years as a DJ and also working for So So Def, the Atlanta-based artist knows how to get the club crunk, and he never steers too far from the sort of rowdy, energetic music that has become such a Southern staple. The big tracks on this album are "Bia', Bia'," which features a can't-miss lineup of superstar guests—Ludacris, Too Short, Chyna Whyte, and Big Kap—and also the title track, a bona fide "represent yo hood"-themed successor to "Who You Wit." The collaboration with Eightball & MJG, "Can't Stop Pimpin," isn't a far departure from that duo's more club-oriented offerings, while "Heads Off (My Ni**as)" is quite a departure for Jon, as he recruits New York rappers M.O.P., a truly unlikely pairing that is interesting if not effective. Furthermore, the album also features guest appearances by Three 6 Mafia, Gangsta Boo, and Khujo of Goodie Mob. As always, Jon crafts his own beats and gives his East Side Boyz plenty of time to shine on the mic. Overall, there aren't many surprises; Jon knows how to tear the club up and he sticks to what he knows best here. Far from a chill-out record, *Put Yo Hood Up* may be a bit too exhausting for some listeners with its exuberance, but should surely please anyone with a taste for the sort of club-oriented call-and-response anthems the South is known for. —*Jason Birchmeier*

Kings of Crunk / Oct. 8, 2002 / TVT ◆◆◆

There was a time when Southern rappers felt marginalized. That was before the rise of 2 Live Crew and their bass colleagues in the late '80s; Southern rap has long since become a huge industry, and dirty South MCs who hit big in cities like New Orleans, Memphis, and Miami can easily sell a ton of CDs in the South alone. While some dirty South rappers have a gangsta/thug life agenda and some are into serious sociopolitical messages, Atlanta rapper Lil Jon and his two East Side Boyz (Lil Bo and Big Sam) have tended to favor rowdy, in-your-face, profanity-filled party music. *Kings of Crunk*, like the trio's previous releases, is full of the sort of hook-filled, call-and-response jams that Southern hip-hop clubs are known for. The list of guests reads like a who's who of dirty South rapping—Mystikal, Petey Pablo, Trick Daddy, and Pastor Troy all have cameos—and Jon's trio works the crunk formula to death on relentlessly energetic tunes such as "Knockin' Heads Off," "Throw It Up," and the single "I Don't Give A ...." At times, the group sounds like it is recycling hits from previous albums, but one is inclined to be forgiving because even the CD's most formulaic tracks are infectious—the Atlanta residents do have a way with a hook. And to their credit, not every track is formulaic crunk. *Kings of Crunk* detours into more of a Texas-type sound when Jon features U.G.K. on the rock-influenced "Diamonds," and those who find that Jon's up-tempo material can be exhausting will be surprised at how much his group chills out on "Nothin's Free" and a few other smooth, R&B-drenched

items. Arguably the trio's most well-rounded album, *Kings of Crunk* will keep crunk fans happy, but has enough variety to keep listeners from calling them one-dimensional. —*Alex Henderson*

Lil' Keke

b. Houston, TX

Southern Rap, Dirty South, Underground Rap, Gangsta Rap

A member of the loosely organized Houston-based rap collective known as the Screwed Up Click, Lil' Keke quickly proved himself to be one of the collective's strongest artists, strongly aligning himself with the city's underground rap don DJ Screw. By not only appearing on countless "Screwed" DJ mixes but also a seemingly endless number of other albums to come out of the South, Keke also became one of Houston's most visible rappers, releasing solo albums for Jam Down Records. His debut album, *Don't Mess Wit Texas* (1997), affirmed his talent as a rapper, proving that he could hold down an album's worth of tracks. His follow-up, *Commission* (1998), similarly found him again showcasing his lucid flow. By the time of *It Was All a Dream* (1999), Keke had become one of the hottest young rappers in Houston and continued to record albums annually. —*Jason Birchmeier*

Don't Mess Wit Texas / Jun. 17, 1997 / Jam Down ◆◆◆

Lil' Keke's debut album, *Don't Mess Wit Texas*, is an entertaining, bass-heavy gangsta record. Like most of his Southern-based contemporaries, Lil' Keke spends more time working a groove than with his lyrics, which makes *Don't Mess Wit Texas* sound like a party record, not a hardcore mission statement. And that's not a bad thing, since he has more rhyming skill and personality than many of his bass-devoted peers, two attributes that mark him as a promising rapper well worth watching. —*Leo Stanley*

Commission / Mar. 24, 1998 / Breakaway ◆◆◆

Big ballin' Lil' Keke announces his dominant position atop the Houston rap scene on *Commission* and comes out of the gate fittingly with "Southside," his biggest runaway down-South anthem yet. DJ Screw makes a notable appearance here too, screwing "Still Pimpin Pens," Keke's big hit from his previous album, *Don't Mess Wit Texas*. —*Jason Birchmeier*

It Was All a Dream / Jul. 13, 1999 / Jam Down ◆◆◆

A year after his breakthrough dirty South anthem "Southside" ravished the Third Coast and crept beyond, Lil' Keke returned with more of the same, namely a hot remix featuring the biggest down-South baller of all, Eightball. The song leads off *It Was All a Dream*, Keke's third album in three years, all of them underground. This one also features the Hot Boys ("Make Em Break It"), who were on fire at this point in the game, and also Cali Bay Area underground veteran B-Legit. Certainly on a par with Keke's comparable previous albums, *It Was All a Dream* is likewise hampered a bit from shoddy production that's a step below major-label quality, yet such is the nature of underground rap like this, so it's not much of an issue. —*Jason Birchmeier*

● **Platinum in da Ghetto** / Nov. 6, 2001 / Koch ◆◆◆◆

Lil' Keke may not have moved as many units as Ludacris or Mystikal, but make no mistake: he's one of the most talented rappers in the late-'90s/early-2000s dirty South scene, arguably the best MC in Houston, TX. And Keke indeed goes out of his way to let you know this on *Platinum in da Ghetto*—the title itself commenting on his cult status. Yet as impressive as Keke's rhymes and posturing are on his early albums, his beats and his songwriting were admittedly lacking. Finally, Keke seems to have remedied these weaknesses on this album, his first for Koch and first since DJ Skrew's untimely yet highly publicized death. Keke seems to have realized his own trademark style of beats here, eschewing generic Mannie Fresh-meets-Timbaland dirty South beats in favor of a different sound that never resorts to cliché or emulation. And it doesn't hurt, either, that these beats sound polished. In addition to the fresh beats, Keke also brings some much improved songwriting to the table for this album. Every song here has a catchy hook, and many feature soulful female vocals—in other words, the sort of accessible singalong choruses crossover audiences require. Yet before you holler "sellout," it's important to note that Keke never strays far from his Texas roots. There are a hearty number of guests here, all from the South, and Keke's lyrical themes are very Dirty South-centric, best showcased on songs like "Cowgirl" and "Where da South At?" Overall, *Platinum in da Ghetto* is one of the best dirty South albums of 2001, not quite as commercial as efforts by Ludicris and Missy but surely ranking right up there with the bigger artists from the South. And surely Keke's most impressive album to date. —*Jason Birchmeier*

Lil' Kim (Kimberly Jones)

b. Jul. 11, 1975

East Coast Rap, Dirty Rap, Hardcore Rap

After making her presence known on Junior M.A.F.I.A.'s debut album, *Conspiracy*, Lil' Kim launched a solo career in 1996 with the release of her first record, *Hard Core*. As the album's title implies, Lil' Kim was a rarity among female rappers—one that not only concentrated on edgy, hardcore rap but also explicit sexuality, two territories that had long been the province of male rappers. Of course, Lil' Kim's near-pornographic sexuality and hard-edged rhythms made her an anomaly within hip-hop, but *Hard Core* proved that she was no novelty, as it garnered positive reviews and strong sales.

A native of Bedford-Stuyvesant, Brooklyn, Lil' Kim was raised by her parents until they split up when she was nine years old. Following their separation, she lived with her father, yet he threw her out of the house when she was a teenager. As a teen, she lived with her friends and, occasionally, on the streets. Eventually, she and her rhyming skills came to the attention of Biggie Smalls, who helped her cultivate her career. Smalls helped her become a member of Junior M.A.F.I.A., and Lil' Kim was a key part of the group's hit debut single, "Player's Anthem." Lil' Kim also made a big impression on the remainder of Junior M.A.F.I.A.'s 1995 debut album, *Conspiracy*.

Following the release of *Conspiracy*, Lil' Kim appeared on records by Mona Lisa, the Isley Brothers, Total, and Skin Deep. For her debut album, she worked with a variety of producers, including Sean "Puffy" Combs, High Class, Jermaine Dupri, and SKI. The result, entitled *Hard Core*, was released in late 1996. Lil' Kim's marketing campaign for the album was quite provocative—she was dressed in a skimpy bikini and furs in the advertisements, as well as the album covers—but instead of resulting in a backlash, the album became a hit, debuting at number 11 on the pop charts. The first single from the album, "No Time," a duet with Sean "Puffy" Combs, became a number-one rap single. The long-awaited *Notorious K.I.M.* followed in 2000. *—Stephen Thomas Erlewine*

● **Hard Core** / Nov. 12, 1996 / Undeas/Big Beat ✦✦✦✦✦

Lil' Kim certainly lives up to her provocative billing on *Hard Core*. Just a notch or two below other mid-'90s East Coast hardcore rap classics like the Notorious B.I.G.'s *Ready to Die* and Jay-Z's *Reasonable Doubt*, *Hard Core* emulates much of the gangsta attitude that had characterized the West Coast rap of the time yet retains an East Coast production style that is built upon sampling rather than G-funk. There's plenty of substance here as well as style, though, as the Queen Bitch herself gives it to you raw and salaciously like you'd expect, yet also quite wittily and nimbly. It's her wit and nimbleness that truly set her apart from her peers, as few and far between as they may be. After all, there's no shortage of porno rap out there, but few of the niche style's practitioners can earn your respect while still tickling your fancy. Kim is one of those very few, and she showcases her talents throughout *Hard Core*, beginning with "Big Momma Thang," her album-opening duet with Jigga. Elsewhere, she flosses with Puff Daddy on "No Time" ("Yeah, I Momma, Miss Ivana/Usually rock the Prada, sometimes Gabbana/Stick you for your cream and your riches/Zsa Zsa Gabor, Demi Moore, Prince Diane, and all them rich bitches"); imposes her gangstressness Biggie-style on "Queen Bitch" ("Hit hard like sledge hammers, bitch with that platinum grammar/I am a diamond-cluster hustler/Queen bitch, supreme bitch/Kill a nigga for my nigga by any means bitch"); and puts all the fellas in their proper place on the empowering "Not Tonight" ("The moral of the story is this/You ain't lickin' this, you ain't stickin' this/And I got witnesses, ask any nigga I been with/They ain't hit shit till they stuck they tongue in this…I don't want dick tonight/Eat my pussy right"). The relentless sexuality can be a bit much, even for the most ardent fans of hardcore rap. Even so, it's hard to think of such a categorically dirty rap album that's this accomplished, and it's furthermore refreshing to hear a woman turn the tables for once, particularly so cleverly with such a venerable supporting cast. *—Jason Birchmeier*

Notorious K.I.M. / Jun. 27, 2000 / Atlantic ✦✦✦

A long four years after making her big, salacious splash on *Hard Core*, Lil' Kim returns as a very different rapper on *Notorious K.I.M.*, and not necessarily for the better. For one, her close friend and collaborator the Notorious B.I.G. had been killed during the interim. The sad passing heavily informs this glitzy yet underlyingly somber album, not only the title but many of the lyrics too. Biggie had played a large role in the success of *Hard Core*, and his

absence here is gaping. For two, the Queen Bitch invites along a host of collaborators to fill the gap left behind by her departed former executive producer. Puff Daddy fills Biggie's very large shoes and unfortunately gives the album the same sort of gaudiness that had marred his round of releases from the year before on Bad Boy Records, namely his own *Forever* and Mase's *Double Up*. Like on those albums, nearly every track here on *Notorious K.I.M.* offers a different producer, many a different guest, and most some sort of pop-crossover concession. Sometimes the pop-rap tactics pay off, particularly on "Custom Made (Give It to You)," where the orgasmic moans of Lil' Louis' house classic "French Kiss" are looped ad infinitum to much effect, and on "How Many Licks?," where "Thong Song"-era Sisqó trades off one come-on after another in with Kim. But amid the other tracks—and there are many of them—the highlights are few and far between. The net sum is thus an overblown effort that's far too Puffy for its own good, as the onetime queen of porno rap goes pop. *—Jason Birchmeier*

Lil' Mo

Contemporary R&B, Neo-Soul, Hip-Hop

Lil' Mo is short in stature, not even hitting five feet in height, but there's nothing little about her drive, heart, or talent. Born Cynthia Loving, she was raised on Long Island but suffered frequent moves as the family followed her dad through the course of his military career transfers. The lack of permanent roots didn't keep her from knowing exactly where she wanted to end up: Manhattan. She wanted to make her mark there by becoming an entertainer, and she set her course for a way to get what she wanted. Wherever the family happened to be living, she competed in talent competitions. Later, with a contract in hand, she had to stand her ground when record company executives wanted to force a certain look on her, rather than allow her to sport the rainbow braids that have become something of a trademark for the singer. Once that particular battle was fought and won, she endured two years of anxiety as she waited for her debut to be released. The waiting was perhaps the hardest, and it brought Lil' Mo to the point where she was considering a switch to simply songwriting, rather than singing and performing.

Thanks to the intervention of heavyweights such as Snoop Dogg and Jay-Z, however, she stuck it out. The welcome she received from the public and the community of music artists made the long wait worth her while. Lil' Mo's 2001 debut album, *Based on a True Story*, was a success. The singer penned every track but one, "Time After Time," which was originally recorded by another rainbow-haired crooner, Cyndi Lauper. Lil' Mo has collaborated on "Hot Boyz" with Missy Elliott, and Elliott subsequently became a trusted advisor and friend. Lil' Mo also collaborated with Ja Rule on his "Put It on Me," and is featured on "Parking Lot Pimping" by Jay-Z. She has performed with, or written songs for, a long list of artists that includes Blackstreet, Next, Lil' Bow Wow, Keith Sweat, 3LW, and ODB.

Unfortunately, not everyone was as thrilled with Lil' Mo's success as she and her friends and collaborators were. Just before her debut was set to hit record store shelves in the summer of 2001, a man attacked the singer in San Francisco just outside the Warfield, a theater where she had just finished a performance. He used a champagne bottle to club the singer's head, and Lil' Mo ended up with almost two dozen stitches. A majority of the publicity appearances scheduled for the following month, which had been specially timed to coincide with the release of her debut, had to be canceled until she regained her health. Despite the aftereffects she suffered, the singer persevered and continued to sing and write. Months later, Lil' Mo started working on air at Baltimore's radio station WXYV, where she remained until leaving in June of 2002 to devote more time to her career. The next year, Lil' Mo prepped for the release of *Meet the Girl Next Door*. She wrote every song on the album except for one; the first single, a duet with rapper Fabolous, "4Ever" was a springtime smash. *—Linda Seida*

● **Based on a True Story** / Apr. 24, 2001 / Elektra ✦✦✦

On her long-awaited debut, Lil' Mo shows why stars like Jay-Z, Ja Rule, and Keith Sweat were so anxious to feature her on their own albums. The Big Apple rapper and singer is a protégée of Missy Elliot, but where Elliot's game is cutting lines and cutting-edge hip-hop, Lil' Mo is a lil' more subtle, preferring to tap into her roots in old-fashioned gospel and R&B. That's not to say this album lacks the requisite up-tempo club thumpers—"Gangsta" and "Superwoman, Pt. 2" certainly fill that bill. It's just that when things mellow out a bit, Mo really shines—on sweet slow jams like "How Many Times," or on the stunning, bitter kiss-off, "Ta Da." Probably the best reference point for Lil' Mo's winning blend of street smarts and classic soul divaship is Mary J. Blige, and *Based on a True Story* suggests that Blige could have some serious competition in the years to come. —*Dan LeRoy*

Lil Raskull

b. Nov. 24, 1972, Houston, TX

Christian Rap

Christian rapper Lil Raskull (aka Delbert Harris) grew up in Trinity Garden, a ghetto on the north side of Houston, TX. He began performing in 1993 and released his first single, "Luv Ya Groove," the following year on Deadgame Records. By 1995, Lil Raskull devoted himself to Christianity, founding Golgotha Missionaries and combining his faith with his music. The result was 1996's *Controverse All-Star, Crossbearing* followed three years later on Grapetree Records, and in early 2000 Lil Raskull returned with *The Day After.* —*Heather Phares*

Gory 2 Glory / Aug. 10, 1999 / Grapetree ♦♦♦

● **The Day After** / Feb. 29, 2000 / Grapetree ♦♦♦

Lil Raskull's third album for Grapetree shows the Christian rapper staying steady with positive-minded raps, no less tight for his religious stature. Though the productions seem to be following a bit behind mainstream rap, they're done well overall and highlight Lil Raskull's rhymes. —*John Bush*

Lil' Romeo

Dirty South, Teen Pop

One of the more curious entries into the early-2000s teen pop explosion, Lil' Romeo shot straight to the top of the *Billboard* charts with his first single at the unheard-of age of only 11. Alongside Lil' Bow Wow, Romeo proved that a substantial market existed for clean-cut preteen rappers with cute looks and PG-rated rhymes. Many of his biggest hits interpolated popular songs from the past in the grand tradition of the most unabashed pop-rap. Of course, the young rapper didn't break into the rap game alone. Just as Jermaine Dupri had masterminded Bow Wow's success, Romeo owed much to his father, notorious rap mogul Master P. Given his father's reputation as a savvy businessman, it was perhaps no surprise when a substantial buzz surrounded the youngster before his debut single, "My Baby," even hit the airwaves. When it did hit, it hit big, topping the Hot 100 chart. In a strange twist of fate, Romeo's success helped revive his father's career, which had soured. The two became inseparable, often wearing the same outfits and even getting their own television show on Nickelodeon.

With a father and two uncles—Silkk the Shocker and C-Murder—who were all superstars during No Limit's mid- to late-'90s reign over the hardcore rap scene, Romeo grew up surrounded by rap. It wasn't until 2000 though that Master P seriously considered catapulting his son into the spotlight. Around this time, No Limit had quickly crumbled; not only had most of the label's roster been dismissed, but sales were undeniably dismal. It was clear that Master P needed a new direction, even if that meant moving away from the gangsta motifs that had initially made his label famous. At this same moment in time, a young preteen rapper by the name of Lil' Bow Wow was monopolizing the airwaves with his innocent raps and cute looks. Master P did what he has always done best: find what sells, create a generic version, release it, and market the hell out of it.

Though many, no doubt, scoffed at Master P's questionable choice to propel his son into the spotlight, it worked better than anyone could have predicted. First came the expected media-targeted hyperbole, with Master P comparing Romeo to Michael Jackson. Next came the lead single, "My Baby," a song that took no shame with its overt interpolation of the Jackson 5's "I Want You Back." Then came the results: the song quickly rose to the top of the *Billboard* Hot 100 before the album even hit the streets. Suddenly, Master P seemed relevant once again, thanks to his son, with an album that didn't even warrant a parental advisory sticker; once again proving that even if the Southern entrepreneur's reputation had been built through exploitation rather than aesthetics, he was surely one of rap's craftiest businessmen. —*Jason Birchmeier*

● **Lil' Romeo** / Jul. 3, 2001 / Priority ♦♦♦

Better known for his savvy schemes and industry knowhow than for his rapping, Master P introduced the world to his son, Lil' Romeo, in 2001. Furthermore, he did so with one of the year's surprise hits, "My Baby." The song not

only made Romeo an overnight sensation but also revived Master P's struggling career. Suddenly, the rapper with the "Ice Cream Man" tattoo on his arm was better known for his fatherly ways than for saying "ugh" in a thuggish way. It's quite a dramatic story for sure. But even if you put aside the thug rapper-turned-loving-father story, Romeo's self-titled debut is still worthy of its success. Master P gives his son some great pop-rap productions to work with here. Some of the interpolations may be pretty obvious (the "I Want You Back" interpolation so central to "My Baby"'s success being a perfect example), but such is the nature of pop-rap, and Master P understands this perhaps better than anyone. He mined the past for hooks of his own, albeit never this well, and he does so to a further extent for his son's debut. If anything, give Master P credit for producing an album for his son that's more engaging than most of his own. —*Jason Birchmeier*

Game Time / Dec. 17, 2002 / No Limit ♦♦♦

Like just about every other album on the new (or old, for that matter) No Limit, *Game Time* is overly long and musically undernourished, its best songs built on samples threadbare from frequent use. But it also reminds you that label head Master P didn't make his millions by accident, because his 12-year-old son Lil' Romeo is the embodiment of his true genius: marketing. While nearly every other pint-sized rapper is chomping at the bit to be treated like a grown-up, Romeo sounds perfectly content on his sophomore outing to be a kid. (And so does his dad, shrewdly recognizing the potential audience for a G-rated young MC who nevertheless has some street cred, thanks to his bloodlines.) The competition would be trying to rhyme an older woman like Solange Knowles into the sack, but when she shows up as Romeo's duet partner on "True Love," he's respectful in way guaranteed to warm the hearts of frazzled parents. Despite the obvious image tinkering behind the scenes, though, his fresh-faced appeal is very real—the sort of charisma that once made Stevie Wonder and Michael Jackson national sweethearts. Romeo certainly isn't in that weight class, and his verses don't suggest an incredible musical future, either. Yet his charm gives a spark to even tired creations like "2 Way," built on the familiar strains of "It Takes Two," and suggests his true destiny—like that of another clean-talking young rapper, Will Smith—probably lies in front of the camera, instead of behind the mic. —*Dan LeRoy*

Lil Soldiers

Group / Southern Rap

Lil Soldiers were the youngest act signed to the No Limit label; sibling rappers Ikeim and Freequon were just nine and seven respectively when their debut, *Boot Camp*, was released on the label in 1999. —*Jason Ankeny*

● **Boot Camp** / Apr. 27, 1999 / No Limit ♦♦

Lil Soldiers stands as testimony to the marketing savvy of Master P—but what No Limit record doesn't? Master P knows what his audience wants, so much so that he can even anticipate needs they might not know they have—such as Lil Soldiers, a duo of hardcore youngstas who aren't even out of elementary school. A bizarre proposition, to be sure, and their debut album, *Boot Camp*, is every bit as weird as its description promises. True, the Lil Soldiers never swear anywhere on the record, but everything else on the record is 100 percent No Limit hardcore—production by Beats by the Pound, recycled hooks, tales of ghetto life, advertisements in the liner notes, and so on. Sonically, the album works well—it's one of Beats by the Pound's better pieces of work in a while, since it keeps a laid-back, scratchy funk groove rolling throughout the entire album—but it's disconcerting to hear thin, prepubescent voices rapping over these tracks. It's not that it's disturbing to hear the kids talk about gangsta violence (which may be offensive to some listeners)—it's that their flyweight voices don't have the gravity for these rhythm tracks, and their tag-team vocals are never, ever in synch with each other. At first, this is amusing, but about a quarter of the way into *Boot Camp*, the whole thing just becomes tiring—the music is acceptable, but not exceptional, and there's not enough camp value to hold interest. Which means that, despite their age, Lil Soldiers aren't really that different from the rest of the No Limit soldiers. —*Stephen Thomas Erlewine*

Lil' Troy

b. Houston, TX

Vocals, Producer, Mixing, Executive Producer / Dirty South

Lil' Troy managed to break out of Houston's thriving rap scene in the late '90s with "Wanna Be a Baller," one of the few Houston-based songs to reach national audiences. The song propelled his debut album, *Sittin' Fat Down South*, to respectable success, particularly for a Houston artist. Released in 1998, Universal picked up the album, re-released it in 1999, and helped "Wanna Be a Baller" spread from city to city. That was about all the success Troy had for a while, though. As the late '90s became the early 2000s, "Wanna Be a Baller" still garnered play, but Troy couldn't deliver a strong follow-up single, instead watching his moment of opportunity diminish. —*Jason Birchmeier*

● **Sittin' Fat Down South** / Jun. 23, 1998 / Uptown/Universal ✦✦✦
With its singsong chorus, melodic synth, and reverb-laden 808, "Wanna Be a Baller" became a regional hit in Texas, the South, and the Midwest. This track exemplifies the best aspects of *Sittin' Fat Down South*: heartfelt flows, crisp production influenced by classic Houston rap and Oaktown funk, and a slew of guest appearances. These elements make *Sittin' Fat* a commendable effort, but the release lacks lyrically. None of the cast ever step beyond retread gangsta themes; the sincerity with which they rhyme makes this palatable at first but cannot pull the listener through all 14 tracks. Additionally, Lil' Troy and crew are missing that almost intangible factor that takes rappers like Too Short and 2pac, of whom the Short Stop camp are conclusively fans, to that other level. This "X Factor" probably has something to do with where charisma, technical skill, and creativity meet. *Sittin' Fat Down South* still shows potential, though, and at many points is prone to get the head noddin'. As a note to Geto Boys fans, both Scarface and Willie D. represent with appearances. —*Matthew Kantor*

Back to Ballin / Sep. 11, 2001 / Koch International ✦✦✦
"Wanna Be a Baller" became a breakout hit for Lil' Troy in 1999, making him one of the few rappers in the gigantic Houston rap scene to score a national hit. But it was just one song. Granted, it was a great dirty South anthem with a catchy singalong chorus and a relevant message rap listeners on every coast could relate to. But, again, it was just one song. Troy hadn't had much success outside of the song, and it's tempting to call "Wanna Be a Baller" a fluke success. *Back to Ballin* certainly gives credence to this claim—nothing here comes close to matching "Wanna Be a Baller." In fact, the album's best song is an eight-minute, screwed version of "Wanna Be a Baller." *Back to Ballin* plays like your average Houston rap album: lots of materialistic and hedonistic ideology, along with a repressed sense of hopelessness, accentuated by lots of drum machine beats and singalong hooks. Unfortunately, like most average Houston rap albums, these qualities leave you a little disappointed. Troy's philosophy is shallow and somewhat depressing if you're not "ballin'" like he is. Even worse, the beats just don't connect—despite the numerous producers—and the hooks are more monotonous than catchy. One standout moment is "We Gon Lean," a collaboration with Lil' Flip that is successful mostly because of Flip. So, even if Troy is "back to ballin'," he needs to head back to the drawing board. This album comes nowhere close to delivering on the promise "Wanna Be a Baller" alluded to. —*Jason Birchmeier*

Lil' Wayne

Vocals, Producer / Southern Rap, Dirty South
Initially known best as the youngest Hot Boy, Lil' Wayne grew up quickly and enjoyed a steady stream of hits in the process. The New Orleans rapper began his long stint with Cash Money as part of the Hot Boys, a popular late-'90s supergroup also comprised of Juvenile, Turk, and B.G. that set the stage for respective solo careers. Juvenile and B.G. made their solo debuts first in 1999 and racked up a pair of simultaneous big hits, "Back That Azz Up" and "Bling-Bling," respectively. Lil' Wayne made his solo debut later that year and similarly came out of the gate with a huge hit, the title track of his album, *Tha Block Is Hot* (1999). Following this wave of astounding success in 1999, the Cash Money frenzy simmered a little bit thereafter. During the two years between Lil' Wayne's second album, *Lights Out* (2000), and his third, *500 Degreez* (2002), Cash Money consequently purged itself of Hot Boys, dropping Juvenile, B.G., and Turk while retaining only Lil' Wayne. The label's loyalty paid off, as *500 Degreez* sold massively, driven by the single "Way of Life." —*Jason Birchmeier*

Tha Block Is Hot / Nov. 2, 1999 / Cash Money ✦✦✦
Shortly after establishing himself as a prominent member of the Hot Boys, Lil' Wayne entered the solo realm with *Tha Block Is Hot*. From beginning to end, the teen rapper gets plenty of assistance from his former groupmates (Juvenile, B.G., and Turk), who back him on just over half of the album's 17 songs. In addition, the Big Tymers (Brian "Baby" Williams and Mannie Fresh)

make several appearances as well, and Fresh produces the entire album. Considering all this, *Tha Block Is Hot* isn't much different from other late-'90s Cash Money releases like *400 Degreez, Chopper City in the Ghetto*, and *How You Luv That?* Like those albums, *Tha Block Is Hot* is essentially a group effort despite Lil' Wayne's solo billing. Even so, he still gets plenty of time to shine here, particularly on the fiery album-opening title track, which proved to be one of Cash Money's biggest hits to date. The remainder of the album is as solid as late-'90s Cash Money albums get—a few standouts here and there, mostly because of Fresh's beats, with lots of filler toward the latter half of the album. Taken as a whole, *Tha Block Is Hot* surely has its moments, though Lil' Wayne still seems a little green here. Thankfully, the Cash Money posse comes to his aid often, resulting in an excellent debut for the youngster, highlighted by the undeniable title track. —*Jason Birchmeier*

Lights Out / Dec. 5, 2000 / Cash Money ✦✦✦
Lil' Wayne may still be a youngster on his second album, *Lights Out*, but he shows substantial growth, dropping serious lyrics over some of Mannie Fresh's wildest production to date. More than anything, the serious tone and the wild beats come as somewhat of a surprise. Up until this point, the Cash Money camp had churned out a staggering number of releases during the late '90s. These releases were anything but serious or wild, instead prototypically dirty South with their big, bass-heavy bounce beats and brash, bling-bling boastful banter. *Lights Out* retains plenty of this but is notably ambitious. Wayne is out to prove himself as more than a teen phenomenon, showcasing a socially conscious side largely absent on his debut, and Fresh is out to prove himself as a versatile producer, crafting a sonically adventurous sound denser than his past work. This ambition is somewhat fascinating, particularly for anyone who has followed Cash Money's evolution to here; however, it's also a bit overreaching. Wayne is deep on heartfelt songs like "Everything" and "Grown Man," and he is street smart on insightful songs like "Lil One" and "Get off the Corner." He's much more effective, though, when he lightens up his lyrics and has fun, as on "Shine," "Let's Go," and "Hit U Up," three album highlights. Similarly, Mannie Fresh misfires here and there on *Lights Out*, like on the oddly bluesy "Fuck Wit Me Now," but for the most part has never been more creative. His stuttering beats on "Tha Blues" are breathtaking, as are the Eastern-style ones on "Hit U Up," and the album opener, "Get off the Corner," sounds absolutely massive. The only problem with all of these is that you have to find them among the whopping 19 songs on *Lights Out*, making it somewhat of a frustrating album despite its several highlights. —*Jason Birchmeier*

● **500 Degreez** / Jul. 5, 2002 / Cash Money ✦✦✦✦
Following Big Tymers' *Hood Rich* up the charts, Lil' Wayne's third album tries to trump the big Cash Money hit by ex-labelmate Juvenile (*400 Degreez*). With the smooth, laid-back productions of Mannie Fresh leading the way for Wayne's drawling delivery, *500 Degreez* does just that. Yes, it's a little top-heavy, but the highlights come quickly, with the leadoff (after the intro) "Look at Me" sporting a freakfest vibe along with Fresh's top-flight beats. The whole album's powered by the infectious party hit "Way of Life," building on the rocksteady rhythm of Eric B. & Rakim's "Paid in Full." Even better is "Gangsta S****," a synth-heavy roller with Petey Pablo besting even Wayne himself on the mic. —*John Bush*

Link (Lincoln Browder)

b. Dallas, TX
Hip-Hop, Urban
Hip-hop soulster Link gained a contract with Relativity Records after he wrote the Top Five hit "My Body" for LSG, the R&B supergroup formed by Gerald Levert, Keith Sweat, and Johnny Gill. Born Lincoln Browder in Dallas, Link was active in gospel choirs and formed his own a cappella group while still a teenager. He was later recruited by R&B impresario Darrell "Delite" Allamby for a quartet named Protégé; when the group split up, Link kept working with Allamby. The duo wrote several songs with collaborator Antoinette Roberson, including "My Body," and when LSG began searching for a lead single, they looked no further. The track became a sizable hit, and soon enough, Link debuted with his own recording, 1998's *Sex Down*. He also wrote tracks for Silk and Kut Klose, plus Levert and Gill's solo careers. —*John Bush*

● **Sex Down** / Jun. 23, 1998 / Relativity ✦✦✦
Like many rappers and singers before him, Link realizes that songs about sex sell—and, like Luther Campbell and R. Kelly, he knows that explicitness is

bankable in the '90s. Taking his cue from those two trailblazers, Link pushes carnality to the forefront on his debut disc, *Sex Down*. There's no denying that Link has skills; positioning himself somewhere between hip-hop and smooth urban soul, he cleverly sells his tales of flesh by cloaking them with radio-ready hooks. *Sex Down* is pure ear candy—beneath those slick surfaces, there's not much there (apart from some dirty talk). Link only occasionally reaches the songwriting heights of his first single "Whatcha Gone Do" or "My Body," the hit he cowrote for LSG; when he has mediocre material, he makes it go down easy by creating alluring productions and slamming beats. So, *Sex Down* is frustrating—on one hand it shows considerable promise, on the other it shows that he relies on clichés and sex talk to cover up for his occasional lack of direction. There's certainly enough good stuff to make it worth a listen, but only a handful of cuts truly deliver on Link's promise. —*Stephen Thomas Erlewine*

Live Human

f. 1996, San Francisco, CA
Group / Underground Rap, Turntablism, Hip-Hop
San Francisco's experimental turntablist trio Live Human formed in 1996, when turntablist DJ Quest (aka Carlos Aguilar), drummer/percussionist Albert Mathias, and bassist Andrew Kushin united their diverse musical experiences to create spontaneous, constantly mutating instrumental hip-hop. Among their other credits, Aguilar worked with DJ Shadow on tracks for Quannum and Handsome Boy Modeling School, helped found the DJ crew Space Travelers, and collaborated on 1992's *Hamster Breaks*, one of the first breakbeat records tailored to the needs of scratch DJs; multi-percussionist Mathias maintains a solo recording career and tours and performs at universities and dance festivals as a teacher, composer, and accompanist; and Kushin performs in Closer to Carbon, an experimental string ensemble, and cofounded the label Out of Round Records. Kushin and Mathias also performed together in the similarly progressive collective Contraband and Thread, saxophonist Charles Sharp's free jazz trio. Live Human debuted their hybrid of sampling and live improvisation on 1997's *Live Human Featuring DJ Quest*, which was released by Cosmic Records in a limited-edition vinyl pressing of 1,000 copies. Later that year, London's Fat Cat label licensed four of the album's songs for release in Europe and the U.K. as the EP *Live Human: Improvisessions*. Fat Cat also released 1999's "Orange Bush Monkey Flower" single, which preceded Live Human's second full-length, *Monostereosis: The New Victrola Method*. The album was re-released in the U.S. by Hip Hop Slam in early 2000, just a few months before the group made their Matador debut with *Elefish Jellyphant*. —*Heather Phares*

● **Monostereosis: The New Victrola Method** / Jan. 17, 2000 / Hip Hop Slam
✦✦✦✦✦

The three-man turntablist rhythm section Live Human debuted with *Monostereosis*, an LP originally recorded for Britain's Fat Cat Records but later reissued on the American Hip Hop Slam label. With drummer Albert Mathias and Andrew Kushin laying down bedrock rhythms, DJ Quest gets plenty of space to stretch out on his turntables. As you'd expect from a live crew, the emphasis here isn't so much an old school rap redux as it is an attempt to exploit the infinitely expressive turntable as a true instrument. Even while he's scratching and sampling to his heart's delight, Quest ranges quite far for his samples, from the squawking horn-section blasts on the opener "Onetwothree" to a sitar and jaw harp "Grasshopper." The intense old school funk of "Orangebushmonkeyflower" leads right into reverb territory with "Percodan," while "The E Pod" is an excellent skate anthem in waiting. A record posed somewhere between Booker T. & the MG's and Invisibl Skratch Piklz, *Monostereosis* is one of the freshest turntablist items down the pipe in several years. —*John Bush*

Elefish Jellyphant / Jul. 11, 2000 / Matador ✦✦✦✦
With a sound that resides somewhere near the intersection where jazz, hip-hop, and ultra-experimental electronic music come together, this San Francisco trio draws on familiar musical elements, but can't be accurately compared to any one band. The opening track, "Prelude to a Jellyfish," features trippy sounds that wouldn't be out of place on a Radiohead album, while "Lesson #7" sounds more like Medeski Martin & Wood doing a jazz instrumental cover of a Beastie Boys tune. Combining hip-hop influences with improvisation and live instrumentation with sampling and turntable scratches, Livehuman makes studio-oriented music that genuinely sounds all the way

live. Perhaps the most apt comparison is introduced via a sample on "Lost World," which borrows sounds from the Art of Noise songbook to create an ambient feel that combines spacey, ethereal textures, jazzy bass riffs, and exotic percussion. I'm not sure how the eclectic smorgasbord of sounds the aptly named group creates on *Elefish Jellyphant* is supposed to find its audience—it's too funky for jazz fans, too weird for hip-hop heads, and not quite danceable enough for techno fiends. But if you enjoy visiting the intersection where jazz, hip-hop, and ultra-experimental electronic music come together, you'll love Livehuman's distinctive fusionary approach. —*Bret Love*

The Living Legends

Group / Hardcore Rap, Underground Rap
The Living Legends, a loose collective of MCs and DJs from the Oakland/San Francisco Bay Area, Los Angeles, Japan, and Europe, are unique for both their down-to-earth songs and approach to the music business. Following in the footsteps of California artists like Too Short who made a name selling tapes out of car trunks, the Legends also chose to stay independent from record labels. They took the street hustling mentality even further with world tours, an in-depth website, tireless self-promotion, and an organized business plan, which made their slogan "Control Destiny" ring very true. Living Legends served as an inspiration for other Bay Area heavyweight crews like Hieroglyphics and Hobo Junction, who along with hip-hoppers nationwide in the late '90s decided they could live without major labels.

Mystik Journeymen, a duo composed of BFAP and PSC, formed in 1992 and became legendary for their underground tapes and parties in East Oakland. The founding nucleus of the Living Legends, the two met the Grouch in 1995 and soon after embarked on the first of a long series of self-funded tours abroad, this time only to Europe. Upon their return, they met up with a trio called 3MG or Three Melancholy Gypsies (MURS, Eligh, and Scarub) who had broken off from their Los Angeles-based group Log Cabin and reunited in Oakland. The sextet officially formed Living Legends in 1996 (along with Aesop, Elusive, and Bizarro) and gained national renown with appearances on 1997's *Beats and Lyrics* compilation and 1998's *Rules of the Game*. As the Internet and their website www.LLcrew.com developed, the Legends were able to reach a huge new audience worldwide.

As their fame grew, the Legends tirelessly visited Europe, Asia, and Australia, a total of eight world tours in two years. Their membership also grew to international proportions after they linked up with Japan's Arata and DJ Quietstorm and Belgium's Krewcial. While home in California, they released a continuous stream of albums and tapes through their imprints Outhouse Records and Revenge Entertainment, produced their own magazine, *Unsigned and Hella Broke*, and put on annual Broke Ass Summer Jams. In 1999, Living Legends moved their base of operations to Los Angeles and added Basik as another member. —*Luke Forrest*

● **UHB, Vol. 3: Against All Odds** / 1997 / Outhouse ✦✦✦✦
As usual, this album takes you on an adventure in a way that few rap groups can do. From start to finish, the beats are crisp and inventive, lyrics on point, and their flows are simply unmatched. With so many guys in the crew it's difficult to tire of their albums, and the more you hear them, the more you want to see them live. There are a good number of welcome instrumental tracks found here, as well as plenty of beats starting and continuing longer than the verses, allowing the listener to savor their tasty beats. Some of the members appearing here are BFAP, PSC, Sunspot Jonz, Eligh, Mystik Journeymen, Murs, Beatdie, and Delite. —*Brad Mills*

The Underworld / 1999 / Outhouse ✦✦✦
Originally only available on cassette, *The Underworld* is a collection of songs recorded in 1995 and 1996 on a four track, and it's easily evident while listening. But great hip-hop has lived on plenty of cheap tapes that have been dubbed over way too many times, and it's a pleasure to see the Legends putting this onto the market for their fans to hear. There are tons of Bay Area rappers appearing, from the Mystik Journeymen to Bas-1, Dusty Black to DJ MF, plus the Legends regulars Arata, Grouch, and PSC, among others. As previously mentioned, the music is very raw and unmastered, but still the quality is much better than some other bootleggish freestyles and live shows out there. The quality of the MCs can't be diminished by poor equipment, and their energy and charisma shine through. A must for die-hard Legends fans. Four track is king. —*Brad Mills*

Livio

b. Eritrea, Africa

West Coast Rap, G-Funk, Gangsta Rap

Though the rap game was overpopulated with run-of-the-mill artists in the early 2000s—conveniently divided into one of three coasts and their respective styles—Livio impressed many in the underground scene with his unique twist on the standard West Coast style. Coming from the unlikely home base of Seattle, Livio aligned himself with the vibrant Cali scene, in particular working with experienced West Coast producer Funk Daddy (E-40, B-Legit, Sir Mix-A-Lot, C-Bo). The respected producer laid down all the beats on Livio's debut release for Pak Pros, *My Life, Vol. 1*. Moreover, despite being on an indie label and being from Seattle, Livio attracted an impressive roster of guests for his album, including D-12, Tray Deee, Noreaga, and Spice 1 among others. —*Jason Birchmeier*

● **My Life, Vol. 1** / 2002 / Pak Pros ♦♦♦

Livio's 2001 release for Pak Pros, *My Life, Vol. 1*, surprised many in the underground scene. Despite being on an indie label and being from Seattle, Livio attracted an impressive roster of guests for his album, including D-12, Tray Deee, Noreaga, and Spice 1, among others. Moreover, Livio worked with respected producer Funk Daddy (E-40, B-Legit, Sir Mix-A-Lot, C-Bo), who lays down all the beats on the album. Livio definitely reps the West Coast, but his flow and rhyming style are somewhat reminiscent of an East Coast MC, no doubt a testament to his abilities—he reps like a West Coast gangsta yet rhymes like an East Coast b-boy. Rarely do underground rap releases sound this polished and professional; if you didn't know otherwise, you'd assume this was a major-label release. —*Jason Birchmeier*

LL Cool J (James Todd Smith)

b. Jan. 14, 1968, Bayshore, Long Island, NY

Hip-Hop, East Coast Rap, Pop-Rap, Golden Age

Hip-hop is notorious for short-lived careers, but LL Cool J is the inevitable exception that proves the rule. Releasing his first hit, "I Can't Live Without My Radio," in 1985 when he was just 17 years old, LL initially was a hard-hitting, streetwise b-boy with spare beats and ballistic rhymes. He quickly developed an alternate style, a romantic—and occasionally sappy—lover's rap epitomized by his mainstream breakthrough single, "I Need Love." LL's first two albums, *Radio* and *Bigger and Deffer*, made him a star, but he strived for pop stardom a little too much on 1989's *Walking With a Panther*. By 1990, his audience had declined somewhat, since his ballads and party raps were the opposite of the chaotic, edgy political hip-hop of Public Enemy or the gangsta rap of N.W.A, but he shot back to the top of the charts with *Mama Said Knock You Out*, which established him as one of hip-hop's genuine superstars. By the mid-'90s, he had starred in his own television sitcom, *In the House*, appeared in several films, and had racked up two of his biggest singles with "Hey Lover" and "Doin' It." In short, he had proven that rappers could have long-term careers.

Of course, that didn't seem likely when he came storming out of Queens, NY, when he was 16 years old. LL Cool J (born James Todd Smith; his stage name is an acronym for "Ladies Love Cool James") had already been rapping since the age of nine. Two years later, his grandfather—he had been living with his grandparents since his parents divorced when he was four—gave him a DJ system and he began making tapes at home. Eventually, he sent these demo tapes to record companies, attracting the interest of Def Jam, a fledgling label run by New York University students Russell Simmons and Rick Rubin. Def Jam signed LL and released his debut, "I Need a Beat," as their first single in 1984. The record sold over 100,000 copies, establishing both the label and the rapper.

LL dropped out of high school and recorded his debut album, *Radio*. Released in 1985, *Radio* was a major hit and it earned considerable praise for how it shaped raps into recognizable pop-song structures. On the strength of "I Can't Live Without My Radio" and "Rock the Bells," the album went platinum in 1986. The following year, his second album, *Bigger and Deffer*, shot to number three due to the ballad "I Need Love," which became one of the first pop-rap crossover hits.

LL's knack for making hip-hop as accessible as pop was one of his greatest talents, yet it was also a weakness, since it opened him up to accusations of him being a sellout. Taken from the *Less Than Zero* soundtrack, 1988's "Goin' Back to Cali" walked the line with ease, but 1989's *Walking With a*

Panther was not greeted warmly by most hip-hop fans. Although it was a Top Ten hit and spawned the gold single "I'm That Type of Guy," the album was perceived as a pop sellout effort, and on a supporting concert at the Apollo, he was booed. LL didn't take the criticism lying down—he struck back with 1990's *Mama Said Knock You Out*, the hardest record he ever made. LL supported the album with a legendary, live acoustic performance on *MTV Unplugged*, and on the strength of the Top Ten R&B singles "The Boomin' System" and "Around the Way Girl" (number nine, pop) as well as the hit title track, *Mama Said Knock You Out* became his biggest-selling album, establishing him as a pop star in addition to a rap superstar. He soon landed roles in the films *The Hard Way* (1991) and *Toys* (1992), and he also performed at Bill Clinton's presidential inauguration in 1993. *Mama Said Knock You Out* kept him so busy that he didn't deliver the follow-up, *14 Shots to the Dome*, until 1993. Boasting a harder, gangsta-rap edge, *14 Shots* initially sold well, debuting in the Top Ten, but it was an unfocused effort that generated no significant hit singles. Consequently, it stalled at gold status and hurt his reputation considerably.

Following the failure of *14 Shots to the Dome*, LL began starring in the NBC sitcom *In the House*. He returned to recording in 1995, releasing *Mr. Smith* toward the end of the year. Unexpectedly, *Mr. Smith* became a huge hit, going double platinum and launching two of his biggest hits with the Boyz II Men duet "Hey Lover" and "Doin' It." At the end of 1996, he released the greatest-hits album, *All World*, while *Phenomenon* appeared one year later. *G.O.A.T. Featuring James T. Smith: The Greatest of All Time*, released in 2000, reached the top of the album charts, and 2002's *10* featured one of his biggest hits in years, "Luv U Better." —*Stephen Thomas Erlewine*

☆ **Radio** / 1985 / Def Jam ♦♦♦♦♦

Run-D.M.C. was the first rap act to produce cohesive, fully realized albums, and LL Cool J was the first to follow in their footsteps. LL was a mere 17 years old when he recorded his classic debut album *Radio*, a brash, exuberant celebration of booming beats and b-boy attitude that launched not only the longest career in hip-hop but also Rick Rubin's seminal Def Jam label. Rubin's back-cover credit ("Reduced by Rick Rubin") is an entirely apt description of his bare-bones production style. *Radio* is just as stripped down and boisterously aggressive as any Run-D.M.C. album, sometimes even more so; the instrumentation is basically just a cranked-up beatbox, punctuated by DJ scratching. There are occasional brief samples, but few do anything more than emphasize a downbeat. The result is rap at its most skeletal, with a hard-hitting, street-level aggression that perfectly matches LL's cocksure teenage energy. Even the two ballads barely sound like ballads, since they're driven by the same slamming beats. Though they might sound a little squared off to modern ears, LL's deft lyrics set new standards for MCs at the time; his clever disses and outrageous but playful boasts still hold up poetically. Although even LL himself would go on to more intricate rhyming, it isn't really necessary on such a loud, thumping adrenaline rush of a record. *Radio* was both an expansion of rap's artistic possibilities and a commercial success (for its time), helping to attract new multiracial audiences to the music. While it may take a few listens for modern ears to adjust to the minimalist production, the fact that it hews so closely to rap's basic musical foundation means that it still possesses a surprisingly fresh energy, and isn't nearly as dated as many other efforts that followed it (including, ironically, some of LL's own). —*Steve Huey*

Bigger and Deffer / 1987 / Def Jam ♦♦

LL Cool J rocketed atop the hip-hop world in 1985 with *Radio*, his astonishing debut, but he quickly lost his footing when he returned two years later with *Bigger and Deffer*, his disappointing follow-up. Yet, as much as the album itself doesn't measure up to *Radio*, its two big hits, "I'm Bad" and "I Need Love," certainly weren't disappointing at the time. The former begins the album with a bang ("No rapper can rap quite like I can!") as LL fires off one of the most ferocious lyrical displays of his entire career, and the latter gave the Queens rapper his first crossover hit as he showcases his vulnerable loverman side for all the ladies out there. Unfortunately, the rest of *Bigger and Deffer* lacks creativity. The beats are skeletal, typical of Def Jam's sound at the time, and LL struggles to find interesting subject matter, returning to many of the same themes he'd rapped about on *Radio*. Soon enough, rival rappers such as Kool Moe Dee called out LL for slipping here on *Bigger and Deffer*. When Cool J returned two years later in 1989 with

Walking With a Panther, he thankfully updated his style and sounded fresh once again. —*Jason Birchmeier*

Walking With a Panther / 1989 / Def Jam ✦✦✦✦

Released at a time when hip-hop's anxieties about crossover success were at a fever pitch, *Walking With a Panther* found LL Cool J trying to reinvent his sound while building on the commercial breakthrough of *Bigger and Deffer*. Even though the album succeeded on both counts, it did so in a way that didn't sit well with hip-hop purists, who began to call LL's credibility into question. Their fears about commercialism diluting the art form found a focal point in LL, the man who pioneered the rap ballad—and there are in fact three ballads here, all of them pretty saccharine (and, tellingly, none of them singles). Apart from that, some of the concerns now seem like much ado about nothing, and there are numerous fine moments (and a few great singles) to be found on the album. It is true, though, that *Walking With a Panther* does end up slightly less than the sum of its parts. For one thing, it's simply too long; moreover, the force of his early recordings is missing, and there's occasionally a sense that his once-peerless technique on the mic is falling behind the times. Nonetheless, *Walking With a Panther* is still a fine outing on which LL proves himself a more-than-capable self-producer. The fuller, more fleshed-out sound helps keep his familiar b-boy boasts sounding fresh, and force or no force, he was in definite need of an update. On the singles—"Going Back to Cali," "I'm That Type of Guy" (inexplicably left off *All World*), "Jingling Baby," and "Big Ole Butt"—LL exudes an effortless cool; he's sly, assured, and in full command of a newfound sexual presence on record. So despite its flaws, *Walking With a Panther* still ranks as one of LL's stronger albums—strong enough to make the weak moments all the more frustrating. —*Steve Huey*

☆ Mama Said Knock You Out / Aug. 1990 / Def Jam ✦✦✦✦✦

Increasingly dismissed by hip-hop fans as an old school relic and a slick pop sellout, LL Cool J rang in the '90s with *Mama Said Knock You Out*, a hard-edged artistic renaissance that became his biggest-selling album ever. Part of the credit is due to producer Marley Marl, whose thumping, bass-heavy sound helps LL reclaim the aggression of his early days. *Mama Said Knock You Out* isn't quite as hard as *Radio*, instead striking a balance between attitude and accessibility. But its greater variety and more layered arrangements make it LL's most listenable album, as well as keeping it in line with more contemporary sensibilities. Marl's productions on the slower tracks are smooth and soulful, but still funky; as a result, the ladies-man side of LL's persona is the most convincing it's ever been, and his ballads don't feel sappy for arguably the first time on record. Even apart from the sympathetic musical settings, LL is at his most lyrically acrobatic, and the testosterone-fueled anthems are delivered with a force not often heard since his debut. The album's hits are a microcosm of its range—"The Boomin' System" is a nod to bass-loving b-boys with car stereos; "Around the Way Girl" is a lush, winning ballad; and the title cut is one of the most blistering statements of purpose in hip-hop. It leaves no doubt that *Mama Said Knock You Out* was intended to be a tour de force, to regain LL Cool J's credibility while proving that he was still one of rap's most singular talents. It succeeded mightily, making him an across-the-board superstar and cementing his status as a rap icon beyond any doubt. —*Steve Huey*

14 Shots to the Dome / Jun. 1, 1993 / Def Jam ✦✦

It's not the tour de force of *Mama Said Knock You Out*, but *14 Shots to the Dome* is a solid effort finding LL Cool J maturing gracefully and strongly, without selling out. *14 Shots* may not have sold as well as *Mama* either, but at least half of the album ranks with his best work. —*Stephen Thomas Erlewine*

Mr. Smith / Nov. 21, 1995 / Def Jam ✦✦✦

On the strength of the slow-burning Boyz II Men duet "Hey Lover," LL Cool J returned to the top of the charts with *Mr. Smith*, meaning the album is somewhat of a comeback for the veteran rapper. LL Cool J's skills had never deserted him, but his previous album, *14 Shots to the Dome*, was an exercise in hardcore that only worked in fits and spurts. There are a couple of hard moments on *Mr. Smith*, but the album is at its most successful when he concentrates on his seductive, romantic side. LL has gotten a bit dirtier since the teenage days of "I Need Love," but he never steps over into the explicit, lewd come-ons of R. Kelly, preferring to suggest everything with a series of double entendres, metaphors, and analogies. *Mr. Smith* isn't a perfect record—there are too many slack moments for it to qualify as one of

his best—but it proves that LL Cool J remains vital a decade after his debut. —*Stephen Thomas Erlewine*

★ All World: Greatest Hits / Nov. 5, 1996 / Def Jam ✦✦✦✦✦

All World: Greatest Hits is an excellent compilation of LL Cool J's greatest hits, featuring 16 of his biggest and best singles, including "I Can't Live Without My Radio," "Rock the Bells," "I'm Bad," "I Need Love," "Going Back to Cali," "Jingling Baby," "The Boomin' System," "Mama Said Knock You Out," "Around the Way Girl," and "Hey Lover." It's the definitive retrospective of one of the greatest rappers to ever record, and if you doubt that statement's true, just take a listen to this collection. —*Stephen Thomas Erlewine*

Phenomenon / Sep. 23, 1997 / Def Jam ✦✦✦

Mr. Smith was the third comeback for LL Cool J, the third time he returned to commercial and creative strengths after being written off by many critics and fans. So, it shouldn't come as a surprise that its follow-up, *Phenomenon*, finds LL coasting—after all, after his two previous comeback albums, he allowed himself to slacken the pace a little bit and ride on his credentials. Fortunately, *Phenomenon* isn't nearly as weak as *14 Shots to the Dome* or *Bigger and Deffer*, but it simply doesn't have the power of masterpieces like *Radio* and *Mama Said Knock You Out*. Essentially, it's a retread of *Mr. Smith*, offering the same laid-back soul jams and rolling party beats. There's a couple of killer singles, a few dogs, and a lot of filler—more so than on *Mr. Smith*, in fact. Still, *Phenomenon* sounds good when it's playing and even if it doesn't leave a lasting impression, it's a solid, professional effort that illustrates why LL is still in the game, 12 years after his first record. —*Stephen Thomas Erlewine*

G.O.A.T. Featuring James T. Smith: The Greatest of All Time / Sep. 12, 2000 / Def Jam ✦✦✦

With his first release in the mid-'80s, LL Cool J hit the rap scene with a unique sense for freestyle lyrics. He kept it up over the years with hits like "I'm That Type of Guy," "Going Back to Cali," and "Mama Said Knock You Out." As artists age, there seems to be a natural progression in the production and lyrics that take place. With acts like Tribe Called Quest, we watched as Q-tip went from rapping about young ladies with long legs and long hair to wanting a woman with a more spiritual flair—to quote the man loosely. Despite marriage and children, this hasn't happened with LL, in fact it's the same lyrics, just with a different album cover. In addition, the raps of urban ills from a man who boasts publicly about his diamonds, riches, and furs (he often sports his fur coats in public during New York summer heat waves) are hard to believe. Once again, with the September 12, 2000, release of *G.O.A.T. Featuring James T. Smith*, LL Cool J disappoints. The first single off the album, "Imagine That," puts LL in a school setting where he's the teacher and he needs to teach his "naughty" student a couple bad things. The theme of LL as the older seducer who is better than the current man of a girlish temptress has been common through LL's albums ("Doin It Well," "Around the Way Girl"). It's like listening to the confessions of a horny 14-year-old teenage boy in the girls locker room. Even with the help of popular rap acts like DMX and Redman, LL Cool J has made the same album he did once before, with no new twists. —*Diana Potts*

10 / Oct. 15, 2002 / Def Jam ✦✦✦

No, "10" isn't the rating of LL Cool J's flexed biceps or his bare chest; it's the number of albums he's recorded for Def Jam—and the title of his latest. As on his last couple, LL moves back and forth between lovers rock and a few hardcore tracks. He sounds more comfortable singing to the ladies, though, with a little pleading and a lot of telling how it's going to be, balancing his usual gravelly delivery with plenty of sweet, female-lead choruses. Surprisingly, despite a strong roster of producers (Tone & Poke, the Neptunes, Ron "Amen-Ra" Lawrence), *10* isn't much of a head turner. Only the DJ S&S production "Fa Ha" lets LL Cool J relax into a solid hardcore groove. Just like on the cover, there's a lot of posturing going on here, but very little substance. —*John Bush*

Lone Catalysts

Group / Underground Rap, Hip-Hop

Columbus native J. Rawls started to make fans for himself in the hip-hop community as a producer when his tracks "Yo, Yeah" and "Brown Skin Lady" (the latter eventually something of a headphone classic) were featured on Mos Def and Talib Kweli's successful *Black Star* collaboration. Unbeknownst to a lot of those new fans, though, his duo Lone Catalysts, with Pittsburgh rapper J. Sands, had been knocking around the periphery of the scene since the mid-'90s. The team began to make its own ripples in the last few years of the decade by dropping a number of well-received 12" singles and appearing on a few popular compilation series (*Superappin', Hip Hop Independents Day*) as well as putting out the six-song EP *The Beginning*, before finally tackling *Hip Hop*, their debut 2000 full-length for their own nascent independent label B.U.K.A. Entertainment. *The Catalysts Files* followed in 2002, also on B.U.K.A.. —*Stanton Swihart*

● **Hip Hop** / 2000 / B.U.K.A. ◆◆◆◆
If there was a given going into Lone Catalysts' debut for their own label, it was the expert beatmaking capabilities of J. Rawls, and he did not disappoint on *Hip Hop*. Tight, metronomic rhythms and stark, head-nodding beats collide with an undertow of foggy, palliative jazz samples ("The Pro's," "Settle the Score," the speculative indie hit "If Hip Hop Was a Crime," and the cool "Due Process" with Kweli and Rubix), so the music goes down smoothly, but it keeps kicking once it's down. More of an unknown were J. Sands's skills on the microphone, and, if his technique wasn't particularly distinctive, the MC made up for a vaguely prosaic rhyme style with the poise and self-assurance of his rhymes. His lyrics concentrate almost entirely on the hip-hop lifestyle, so while the dexterity of his words refused to be slept on, their self-referential nature ensured that the album would remain an underground sleeper. As the title indicates, the duo comes from the no frills, straight-to-the-essence true-school of rap, so there is nothing flashy or exceptional about *Hip Hop*; but it is a rock-solid first effort on which its pair of lone catalysts mix an obvious sense of love for the game with a laid-back but perceptible prod against the staid predispositions of rap. —*Stanton Swihart*

The Catalysts Files / Mar. 19, 2002 / B.U.K.A. ◆◆◆

Lone Star Ridaz

Group / Southern Rap, Latin Rap
The Lone Star Ridaz features many of the rappers affiliated with Dope House Records, a Houston-based rap label, as well as producer Happy Perez, a prolific producer also from H-Town. The Texas supergroup debuted in 1999 with a self-titled album and returned quickly afterward with two follow-ups, *Wanted* (2001) and *40 Dayz/40 Nightz* (2002), both of which arrived with accompanying chopped and screwed versions, just as the group's debut had. —*Jason Birchmeier*

Wanted / Feb. 27, 2001 / Dope House ◆◆◆
The Lone Star Ridaz, a predominantly Chicano rap supergroup from Texas, team up with producer Happy Perez for *Wanted*. The variety of rappers here is most interesting, as each has his own distinct flow and dialect, perhaps none more distinct than that of South Park Mexican. He raps on the somber album highlight, "Drunk Man Talkin'," where Perez straightforwardly recreates the hook from Bobby Bland's "Ain't No Love in the Heart of the City." —*Jason Birchmeier*

● **40 Dayz/40 Nightz** / Feb. 5, 2002 / Dope House ◆◆◆◆◆
Superproducer Happy Perez rounded up the Lone Star Ridaz for another album in late 2001, *40 Dayz/40 Nightz*. Released a few months later in early 2002, the album found Perez furthering his already polished production style—making it even more trademark, more Texas; in other words, putting it on the same artistic level as Timbaland and Dr. Dre, though obviously not nearly as commercially successful. Featured MCs on the album include Grimm, Max Minelli, Merciless, Low G, Baby Beesh, Javi Picasso, Rasheed, South Park Mexican (SPM), Russ Lee, and a special appearance by Fat Joe. Most of the songs on the album will feature two or three of the MCs, along with the occasional vocalist on the hook. In addition, there are two posse songs, both album highlights: "City of Houston" and "Count Your Blessingz"—the former featuring an interpolation of the Red Hot Chili Peppers' "Under the Bridge" for its hook; the latter a ballad that acknowledges the tragic mood in post-September 11, 2001, America. Another album highlight is "South Park/South Bronx," which teams up SPM and Fat Joe, quite an unlikely pairing that's a pleasant surprise, particularly when you consider the two artists' Latin American roots. Then there's the "Screwed" version of "City of Houston" that closes the album. More than any one song, however, it's Perez's production that makes this such an amazing album, arguably one of the best albums to ever come out of Houston's Mexian-American rap scene—and surely evidence that Houston had become one of

America's rap meccas by the early 2000s, alongside New York, Los Angeles, and the Bay Area. —*Jason Birchmeier*

Lootpack

f. 1990, Oxnard, CA
Group / Underground Rap, Hip-Hop
The Lootpack was one of several old school revivalist crews to come out of Southern California during the '90s, and recorded some of the most underappreciated music on the revitalized West Coast underground scene. The group was formed in 1990 in Oxnard, CA (a smaller beach town about a hour outside of Los Angeles) by longtime friends Madlib (producer, MC, b. Otis Jackson Jr.), Wildchild (MC, b. Jack Brown), and DJ Romes (scratching, b. Romeo Jimenez). The trio members had been trying their hand at hip-hop since junior high, and formed an official group while in college. Their demo tape caught the attention of King Tee and Tash of tha Alkaholiks, and soon the Lootpack joined the related collective the Likwit Crew; they also produced two tracks on tha Alkaholiks' 1994 debut, *21 & Over*, and appeared on the follow-ups *Coast II Coast* and *Likwidation*. In the meantime, the Lootpack found it difficult to land a satisfying deal of their own. Their only recorded output for a time was the 1996 EP *Psyche Move*, which was funded by Madlib's father, soul singer Otis Jackson Sr. *Psyche Move* attracted the attention of Bay Area DJ Peanut Butter Wolf, who eventually signed the group to his Stones Throw label.

The Lootpack's first Stones Throw release was the 12" single "The Anthem" in 1998. Two more singles, "Whenimondamic" and "Questions," preceded the Lootpack's first full-length album, *Soundpieces: Da Antidote*, which was finally issued in 1999. While it wasn't massively popular, the record caused a stir in underground hip-hop circles, winning high praise from the musicians and critics who managed to discover it. It spun off another 12" in "Weededed," and marked Madlib as a producer to watch in the new millennium. In fact, several of his side projects—most notably the bizarre double-identity Quasimoto and the jazz-funk group Yesterday's New Quintet—consumed his attention in the immediate wake of *Soundpieces*. Though the Lootpack were largely silent on record, they continued to tour over the next few years, and DJ Romes released his own breakbeat record, *Hamburger Hater Breaks*, in 2001; also that year, the group assembled its own documentary film, *Da Packumentary*. The single "On Point" appeared in 2002, and a new Lootpack album was tentatively projected for the following year. —*Steve Huey*

● **Soundpieces: Da Antidote!** / Jun. 29, 1999 / Stones Throw ◆◆◆◆◆
The Lootpack's debut album, *Soundpieces: Da Antidote!*, ushered in a string of excellent releases on Peanut Butter Wolf's Stones Throw label, and helped serve notice that the West Coast underground scene was becoming one of tremendous creative vitality. Much of the album's success is due to fantastic production by Madlib, who takes his place as one of the West Coast's most imaginative trackmasters, underground or otherwise. His style is subtly otherworldly, drawing bits and pieces from countless obscure sources; every listen reveals new, unexpected sounds layered into the mix. With 24 tracks over the course of a full CD, *Soundpieces* does feel a bit excessive, but most of the tracks are thankfully focused and concise, and a few clock in at around a minute or less. The exception is the multisectioned suite "Episodes," an impressive b-boy bouillabaisse that showcases Madlib's fragmented genius. The rapping, by Madlib and Wildchild plus a guest roster of West Coast scenesters, is consistently high quality, and the album is studded with great singles: "Questions," "Whenimondamic," the eerie-sounding "The Anthem," and "Weededed," the latter an attack on MCs who rely on marijuana to enhance their rhymes (though not on the drug itself). Among the many guests, Dilated Peoples and Lootpack mentors tha Alkaholiks shine brightest on "Long Awaited" and "Likwit Fusion," respectively. The Lootpack are vulnerable to the same criticism that's been leveled at Dilated Peoples, namely that in returning to hip-hop's basics, they've substantially limited their lyrical content by focusing almost entirely on battle rhymes. They're clever and well-crafted battle rhymes, to be sure, and the group's microphone technique is impressive, but in 1999, it was hard not to want them to pay attention to something besides wack MCs. That's especially true given the imagination of Madlib's subsequent projects (Quasimoto in particular), not to mention his production here. Still, that isn't enough to keep *Soundpieces: Da Antidote!* from being a resounding success. —*Steve Huey*

Lord Finesse

Vocals, Mixing, Producer / Golden Age, Hip-Hop, Underground Rap, Club/Dance

Making sure the parental advisory sticker will never become obsolete, Lord Finesse broke into the rap game as yet another hardcore rapper. After gaining a following in his native New York, Finesse cut *Funky Technician*, an excellent debut for Wild Pitch Records. He then signed a management deal with Ice-T's Rhyme Syndicate Management and recorded his 1991 major-label debut, *Return of the Funky Man*, for Giant. When his rapping career didn't explode, Finesse began producing and has since become a competent studio player, producing albums by Notorious B.I.G. and Noreaga. —*Steve Kurutz*

● **Funky Technician** / 1990 / Wild Pitch ◆◆◆◆◆

It's a simple formula: bring together one of the East Coast's finest rappers with some of the most clever trackmasters in hip-hop, then add in a stellar DJ, and the results are bound to be exciting. *Funky Technician* was just that, an excellent LP of battle rap with Lord Finesse simultaneously claiming *and* proving his immense skills over a set of funky backing tracks that used the familiar James Brown blueprint but delivered it with unobtrusive class and innumerable displays of deft turntable wizardry. DJ Premier, Diamond D, Showbiz, and DJ Mike Smooth himself all contribute classic tracks; surprisingly, though Premier would soon forge a unique style and become one of the most respected producers in rap, it's Diamond D who gets in the best one (the title track), and that with the same sound that Premier would later make his own. Meanwhile, Lord Finesse is dropping rhymes to rank with Rakim and Kane, starting out on "Just a Little Something" with a raft of prize-winning multisyllables: "Now I'm the constabulary, great in vocabulary/I'm no joke, when up against any adversary." Finesse is fresh and imaginative on nearly every line, and invites AG (aka Andre the Giant) for a guest spot on "Back to Back Rhyming." There were a lot of great rap records coming out of New York around the turn of the decade, though, and *Funky Technician* never got the attention it deserved. —*John Bush*

Return of the Funky Man / 1991 / Giant ◆◆◆

Return of the Funky Man was Lord Finesse's first real record for a major label, with himself as the main producer and performer, though he got a little help on production from his crew in the form of Diamond D and Showbiz of Show & A.G. Not much has changed since Finesse's first album; the same rugged rapping flow and metaphorical supremacy are evident throughout. The first bit of the album gets a tad slow at times, but altogether this is a nice addition to the Lord Finesse library. —*Brad Mills*

Awakening / Feb. 20, 1996 / Penalty ◆◆◆◆

With his third album, Lord Finesse representing D.I.T.C. (Diggin' in the Crates crew) brought together some of the finest rappers of the moment for an album almost entirely produced by Finesse himself. Known as a producer first and rapper a close second, Finesse is gifted in metaphorical rhyming like other well-known MCs such as Big L or Chino XL, and again produces a great record deserving of any rap fan's archive. Guests like Akinyele, KRS-One, MC Lyte, O.C., A.G., Diamond D, and Kid Capri make up the all-star cast. Topping it all off are verses by Large Professor, Grand Puba, and Sadat X on arguably one of hip-hop's finest tracks ever, entitled "Actual Facts." With so much going for it, if you like you rap music there's really no reason you shouldn't own this album. As a side note for DJs out there, there is apparently a limited-edition instrumental version of this released on vinyl, so look for that floating around somewhere. —*Brad Mills*

Lord Tariq & Peter Gunz

Group / Hip-Hop, East Coast Rap, Hardcore Rap

The rap duo of Lord Tariq and Peter Gunz first emerged from the Bronx under the name the Gunrunners; additionally, both enjoyed concurrent solo careers, with Gunz signing to Shaquille O'Neal's T.W.is.M. label and Tariq—also a member of the Money Boss Players—appearing on tracks by the Notorious B.I.G., Jay-Z, Nas, and Mobb Deep. Upon forming their own label, the Columbia subsidiary Codeine, Tariq and Gunz debuted in 1998 with the LP *Make It Reign*, which launched the smash party anthem "Deja Vu (Uptown Baby)." —*Jason Ankeny*

● **Make It Reign** / Jun. 2, 1998 / Columbia ◆◆◆◆

You could compare the debut release from the rap team of Lord Tariq & Peter Gunz, *Make It Reign*, to the party rap albums of such hip-pop stars as Mase,

Puff Daddy, and the LOX, and you wouldn't be missing the mark by much. *Make It Reign* is an album tightly produced and packed together so that it rolls and flows from one end to the next with jiggy beats and braggart raps. On *Make It Reign*, Lord Tariq & Peter Gunz continue the trend of hip-hop's heavily danceable and materialistic reputation. They lace their ballin' beats with raps of mic supremacy, sexual prowess, Bronx shout-outs, and accounts of their extensive wealth, as witnessed on the album's first single, "Déjà Vu (Uptown Baby)." You won't find anything very innovative or original on this album, a fact the two readily admit in one of the many racy interludes when they remark that their party raps are designed for airplay and quick money, and not necessarily for "keeping it real." One refreshing aspect of *Make It Reign*, though, are the raw, hardcore raps that the two bluntly unload on occasion. Tariq and Gunz don't flow with vocals and hooks as catchy as those of their present-day counterparts in the rap game, but they make up for it with resolutely opinionated quips and boasts. —*Aric Laurence Allen*

Lords of the Underground

f. 1990, Raleigh, NC

Group / Golden Age, East Coast Rap, Hardcore Rap, Hip-Hop, Club/Dance

Though their name might imply violent gangsta rap, Lords of the Underground match socially conscious raps with hard-hitting beats. Newark, NJ's Doitall and Mr. Funke met Cleveland-native DJ Lord Jazz at Shaw University in NC; since the two were looking for a DJ, they hooked up with Jazz. A friend of Doitall's introduced the group to legendary producer Marley Marl, who invited them to record at his studio with help from K-Def. Before their debut album (*Here Come the Lords*) even appeared, the Lords placed three hit singles ("Psycho," "Funky Child," "Chief Rocka") on the rap charts. By the end of 1993, the Lords had received an award from BET as best rap group of the year. *Keepers of the Funk*, released in 1994, failed to keep the momentum going, and there was a five-year wait before third album *Resurrection* dropped in 1999. —*John Bush*

● **Here Come the Lords** / 1993 / Pendulum ◆◆◆◆

Lords of the Underground rattled off five great singles in a row between 1992 and 1994, all of which helped make *Here Come the Lords* one of the best rap debuts of 1993. "Psycho," "Chief Rocka," "Flow On," "Here Come the Lords," and "Funky Child" (with that wildly searing horn line) feature spare productions with crisp drum breaks and bone-rattling bass lines, most of which glean from the catalogs of Blue Note and James Brown. "Flow On" boasts the inimitable touch of Marley Marl and assistant K-Def, and yet it's hardly the most infectious of the batch. There's nothing lacking about the actual production—it's just that MCs Dupre "Doitall" Kelly and Mr. Funke are on top of their game when they're at their most uninhibited, as heard on "Funky Child." And who could forget the image of a diapered Doitall and a ridiculously afro'd Mr. Funke in that song's video (which played a big role in the album's success)? The remainder of the album has its share of middling moments, but the five singles and some other scattered flashes of greatness are more than enough to make for a record that stands alongside many of the other hallowed rap albums from the era. —*Andy Kellman*

Keepers of the Funk / 1994 / Pendulum ◆◆◆

After EPMD and the rest of the Hit Squad, Lords of the Underground was the East Coast crew who most frequently utilized the thickest vintage funk samples (look no further than the Parliament/Funkadelic title track, with a cameo by George Clinton himself) and pasted them into the most menacing and bare bones of contexts. As with the trio's freshman outing, *Keepers of the Funk* features production handiwork straight from the crates of the legendary Marley Marl and his protégé, Kevin "K-Def" Hansford, and again the pair developed backdrops as dense and absorbing—the gritty, rock-solid, low-end grooves, dug six-feet deep, and the crunching tempos—as they are disorienting and foreboding with their queasy swirl of keyboards and horn loops, but with a few additional nods to jazz this time around. On top of the music, Mr. Funke and Doitall bring it as terse and raw as ever, craftily trading off verses between gruff, crowd-shouted choruses, a fine approximation of what you might hear in the bowels of the New York/New Jersey underground but given just enough of a spit shine to bring it street level. *Keepers* is less consistent on the whole, and less catchy, than the sensational *Here Come the Lords*, but its high points are right up there on the same shelf: the exhilarating late-night chant "Tic Toc," with its Spartan, vibraphone-pocked track; the cool and collected cash grab "What I'm After"; an unexpected expression of "Faith"; and "Frustrated," another of the Lords' characteristic mental, free-form flows. —*Stanton Swihart*

Resurrection / Apr. 6, 1999 / Jersey Kidz ✦✦✦✦
After a break of almost five years, Newark, NJ's Lords of the Underground returned in 1999 with *Resurrection*, recorded for Queen Latifah's Jersey Kidz imprint. Right away, MCs Doitall and Mr. Funke and DJ Lord Jazz make clear their position with an introduction decrying hip-hop's loss of its own roots. Together with the first full track, "Retaliate," the intro establishes LOTU as a crew that's come back from the dead to help hip-hop do the same. While a bit of the gangsta posing that typified its early work still remains, this leaner and meaner version of the crew relies mostly on biting wit, verbose lyricism, and the swirling beats of Lord Jazz, instead of any played-out clichés. The descending piano line of "Take Dat" makes the song's martial beat queasy, while "Earth, Wind, & Fire" (featuring Joya) features smooth, mournful strings that match the song's street-level morality tale perfectly. Da Brat stops by for the old school rap of "One Day," while Funke and Doitall reassert their credentials on "Excuse Me." The two parts of "Hennessey," while featuring inventive arrangements courtesy of Lord Jazz, nonetheless sound a bit forced, as if LOTU is trying to force contemporary relevance. This is a mistake, since *Resurrection* is strongest when it relies on the classic tenets of hip-hop and its MCs' own talent, instead of grafting the latest trend onto an existing formula. —*Johnny Loftus*

The Lost Boyz

f. 1993, Queens, NY
Group / Hip-Hop, East Coast Rap
The Lost Boyz included Freaky Tah, Mr. Cheeks, Pretty Lou, and Spigg Nice. The rap quartet's first single—"Lifestyles of the Rich and Shameless"—earned them a contract with Uptown Records, which released their second single, "Jeeps, Lex Coups, Bimaz & Benz," later in 1995. After the "Renee" single (recorded for the *Don't Be a Menace to South Central While You're Drinking Your Juice in the 'Hood* soundtrack), the Lost Boyz released their debut album, *Legal Drug Money*. The LP hit the charts and was certified gold. *Love, Peace & Nappiness* followed in 1997. Freaky Tah was murdered on March 28, 1999; *LB IV Life* appeared that autumn. —*John Bush*

● **Legal Drug Money** / 1995 / Uptown/Universal ✦✦✦✦
Legal Drug Money covers the same themes that so many other hip-hop artists were covering in the mid-'90s. They rap about getting high, being rich, and other topics typical of the genre. The best track on this album is easily "Renee," a song about a woman who fell in love with an MC, but who gets killed. It's a really good piece; unfortunately, the rest of the album isn't as good. One might opt for Smif-n-Wessun's *Dah Shinin* or Heltah Skeltah's *Nocturnal* instead of this recording, as both are similar in style to *Legal Drug Money* but much better albums. —*Dan Gizzi*

Love, Peace & Nappiness / Jun. 17, 1997 / Uptown/Universal ✦✦✦
The Lost Boyz' second album, *Love, Peace & Nappiness*, finds the group adding touches of reggae and ragga to their hard-edged hip-hop. The deeper production—thick bass, echoing beats, and keyboards—makes *Love, Peace & Nappiness* more sonically intriguing than the average rap album, but the Lost Boyz occasionally struggle for material, leaving the record a fitfully enjoyable listen. —*Leo Stanley*

LB IV Life / Sep. 28, 1999 / Uptown/Universal ✦✦✦
The Lost Boyz third manifestation *LB IV Life* completes a tumultuous year for the Jamaica, Queens triumvirate—a year in which they lost not only a member of their core unit but also a family member with the tragic shooting death of hypeman Freaky Tah (which obviously casts an ominously somber ambience over this release). Still, the Lost Boyz' prosperity still depends heavily upon the effectiveness of frontman Mr. Cheeks. Relying on charisma, rather than content, Cheeks' strongest attribute remains firmly entrenched in the hook department. While not majestic in nature, there is a simple yet irresistible quality attached to his gravelly voice, and there is no escaping the urge to murmur his catch phrases aloud. Cheeks and company sound convincing over the fevered strings of "Take a Hike" and the Queens rock & roll number "Plug Me In." Their alluring lead single "Ghetto Jiggy" is destined for heavy rotation and fully illustrates the Lost Boyz's good-time brand of hip-hop. The second half of this disc, however, finds the Lost Boyz falling prey to previous Achilles' heels such as drab production, and crossover casualties suffocate the LP's continuity. Ultimately *LB IV Life* encompasses both the best

and worst of what the Lost Boyz have to offer hip-hop's masses, with little variance in between. —*Matt Conaway*

Lovage

Group / Lounge, Trip-Hop
Lovage is the name Nathaniel Merriweather, aka Dan the Automator, gave to the group he formed for his 2001 album *Music to Make Love to Your Old Lady By*. He was assisted by a variety of other performers, including Mike Patton (of Faith No More and Fantomas), Kid Koala, Damon Albarn (of Blur), Prince Paul, Jennifer Charles (of Elysian Fields), and others. *Music to Make Love to Your Old Lady By* was their first release. —*Blake Butler*

Music to Make Love to Your Old Lady By [Instrumental] / Nov. 6, 2001 / 75 Ark ✦✦✦
Hip-everything producer Dan "the Automator" Nakamura (acting here as Handsome Boy Nathaniel Merriweather) continues his tradition of releasing instrumental albums alongside his official releases (*The Instrumentalyst: Octagon Beats, Tron 3030: The Instrumentals*). The main complaint of the official *Music to Make Love to Your Old Lady By* was that the vocals from Mike Patton and Jennifer Charles were either too bizarrely aggressive or too faux-sensual (depending on who you ask), so these stripped-down instrumentals sound instantly more appealing. Unfortunately, six and a half minutes of the same vamp seems to run a little long on "Sex (I'm A)," and "Stroker Ace"'s repeated hook isn't really enough to hold even five minutes' worth of attention in the MTV age. Luckily the Kid Koala tracks exude the same ferocious wit and freshness that made his *Carpal Tunnel Syndrome* one of the landmark turntablist recordings. "Koala's Lament" and "Everyone Has a Summer," which round out the album, stand out as high points, with their self-help found sounds and movie clips. While this album may not be an all-engrossing listen, it is perfectly ideal for when the party is down to just four or five people and you don't really care if they leave or just crash on the floor. —*Zac Johnson*

● **Music to Make Love to Your Old Lady By** / Nov. 6, 2001 / 75 Ark ✦✦✦
Another art-hop incarnation from eccentric beat magician Dan "the Automator" Nakamura; the Automator's groundbreaking work appeared previously on such projects as Dr. Octagon's *Dr. Octagonecologyst*, Handsome Boy Modeling School, Deltron 3030, and the Gorillaz's self-titled album. For this affair, Nakamura returns as sonic paramour Nathaniel Merriweather (previously materializing as this character on the superb Handsome Boy joint) on a brooding but often darkly humorous journey through the dark side of the love life. The label 75 Ark's given definition for "lovage" is "an herb that is said to be a benefit for relieving abdominal pains due to gastrointestinal gas . . . also touted to reduce flatulence when consumed as a tea." This satirical bent on the album at first seems to be a gentle mock on the quiet storm genre that overromanticizes and almost trivializes the act of lovemaking. However, as Nakamura's ostensibly sensual beats begin to invade the listener's mind-frame, the music renders a feeling more of the painful nausea of a bad trip or a love hangover. While Nakamura is quite possibly one of the most accomplished beat processors in the realm of art hip-hop/electronica, his strict-composer approach on this project is occasionally inaccessible and at times unlistenable. Adding to the confusion is the erratic Neanderthal stylings of former Faith No More frontman Mike Patton and the sultry but often irritating vocals of Jennifer Charles (Elysian Fields). This duo represents the bulk of lyrical montage presented here and the results are often quite nightmarish sonically. Guest appearances from Afrikka Bambaata, Charmelle Carmel (Maseo of De La Soul), Chest Rockwell (Prince Paul), Damien Thorn VII of Deltron fame (Damon Albarn of Blur), and minimalist DJ Kid Koala lavish the project with texture and splotches of black humor. In the end, the Automator seems to have proposed something a bit too far flung to be enjoyable: exposing the act of love as a carnal and alienating endeavor. Too artsy and too much of a bitter herb to swallow. —*M.F. Di Bella*

Low Profile

f. Los Angeles, CA
Group / Hip-Hop, West Coast Rap
This short-lived group featuring DJ Aladdin and WC helped originate the West Coast rap sound in the late '80s. They only released one album, *We're in This Thing Together*, but both Aladdin and WC continued to make an

impact once they parted ways—Aladdin working with Ice-T, WC forming WC and the Maad Circle. —*Jason Birchmeier*

● **We're in This Thing Together** / Jan. 25, 1990 / Priority ◆◆◆
One of the best hip-hop DJs to come out of Los Angeles in the 1980s, DJ Aladdin teamed up with rapper WC at the end of that decade and formed the short-lived but noteworthy Low Profile. The duo showed some potential on its first and only album, the decent if uneven *We're in This Thing Together*. Especially riveting are "How Ya Livin'" (a commentary on urban violence) and "That's Why They Do It," which explains why some youths resort to drug dealing in the inner city. "Pay Ya Dues" makes a meaningful statement about rappers who get ahead without paying dues, but is marred by a homophobic reference. Though most songs fall under the heading of decent but not outstanding, the CD offers plenty of proof of Aladdin's impressive technique on the turntables. *We're in This Thing Together* wasn't a big hit, and after Low Profile broke up, WC went on to form WC & the Maad Circle a few years later. —*Alex Henderson*

LOX

f. 1996
Group / East Coast Rap, Pop-Rap
The LOX—an acronym for Living Off Experience—was a Yonkers, NY-based rap trio who worked their way up through the Bad Boy training camp; writing and rapping on hits by the likes of Puff Daddy, the Notorious B.I.G., Mary J. Blige, and Mariah Carey before releasing their debut album in early 1998. Sheek (Shawn Jacobs), Jadakiss (Jayson Phillips), and Styles (David Styles) began rapping together in their childhood. By the time they reached their late teens, they had settled on the name LOX. Eventually, they met Mary J. Blige. Impressed by their demo tape, Blige forwarded the tape to Sean "Puffy" Combs, who hired the trio as writers. Between 1996 and 1997, the group wrote and performed on a number of Combs' productions, including his own "It's All About the Benjamins" and "I Got the Power," Mase's "24 Hrs. to Live," Mariah Carey's "Honey," the Notorious B.I.G.'s "Last Day," Mary J. Blige's "Can't Get You Off My Mind," and Zhané's "Saturday Night." LOX received an unexpected boost in the summer of 1997, when their tribute to the late Biggie Smalls, "We'll Always Love Big Poppa," was picked as the B side of Puff Daddy's international number-one hit, "I'll Be Missing You." The single was the biggest hit of 1997, setting the stage for the January 1998 release of LOX's debut *Money, Power & Respect*, which went as high as number three on the pop album charts. After a switch to the Ruff Ryders label camp, *We Are the Streets* followed in early 2000. —*Stephen Thomas Erlewine*

Money, Power & Respect / Jan. 13, 1998 / Bad Boy ◆◆◆
LOX are some of the better rappers on the Bad Boy roster, more dexterous, clever, and hook conscious than their mentor, Puff Daddy. That doesn't necessarily mean that their debut *Money, Power & Respect* is better than Puff's record, but it does mean that it's frequently exciting and invigorating. Like most late-'90s hip-hop records, the album runs way too long and is bogged down by filler, but the very best moments on the album equal anything that has been released by Bad Boy, and in many cases even surpasses it in terms of lyrical skills and energy. —*Stephen Thomas Erlewine*

● **We Are the Streets** / Jan. 25, 2000 / Ruff Ryders ◆◆◆◆
LOX's (Jadakiss, Sheek, Styles) highly publicized and drawn-out defection from Puffy's Bad Boy Records to DMX's Ruff Ryders camp was imperative. Not only because Puffy's glossy sound openly clashed with the group's thug mentality, but the change of scenery also furnished LOX with an opportunity to assert their own identity. While LOX as a unit do not offer much in terms of topical dexterity, Jadakiss is one of the industry's most underappreciated lyricists, which he clearly reiterates on his solo cut "Blood Pressure." Ruff Ryders in-house producer Swizz Beatz handles most of the production duties, and although his syncopated production can become repetitive, DJ Premier ("Recognize") and Timbaland ("Ryde or Die Bitch," featuring Eve and Drag-On) provide some much-needed diversity with their signature sounds. The rowdy lead single "Wild Out" is an obvious reworking of Jay-Z's "Jigga My Nigga," but it was a hit on rap radio. —*Matt Conaway*

Lucas (Lucas Secon)

Vocals, Mixing, Producer / Hip-Hop, Pop-Rap, Club/Dance
Born to Danish painter Berta Moltke and songwriter and *Billboard* music editor Paul Sécon, rapper Lucas began his musical career inauspiciously

with the 1990 Uptown album *To Rap My World Around You*. Unsatisfied with the label's marketing of his music as teen-idol fare for adolescent girls and unwelcome after Uptown turned its attention to producing R&B aimed at the teen market, Lucas left the label and studied philosophy and creative writing at New York University and traveled in Europe to expose himself to other cultures. He eventually settled in London and in 1992 signed with Big Beat/Atlantic, for whom he recorded 1994's *Lucacentric*. The album incorporated elements of jazz and reggae, particularly the former, and featured the single "Lucas With the Lid Off." The accompanying video, which was shot in one continuous take while moving between several sets, garnered a fair amount of attention in England and soon America, and pushed the single onto the charts. —*Steve Huey*

To Rap My World Around You / 1991 / MCA ◆◆
● **Lucacentric** / 1994 / Big Beat ◆◆◆
"Lucas With the Lid Off" is an irresistible single, full of intoxicating beats, great horn loops, and a supremely confident boast by Lucas. Unfortunately, the rest of the rapper's debut album, *Lucacentric*, fails to ignite, but there are some tracks that will spark the interest of fans of the hit single. —*Stephen Thomas Erlewine*

Lucy Pearl

Group / Neo-Soul, Hip-Hop, Contemporary R&B
Hip-hop/urban soul supergroup Lucy Pearl was formed in the summer of 1999 as the brainchild of Tony! Toni! Toné! multi-instrumentalist and vocalist Raphael Saadiq (formerly known as Raphael Wiggins), who left the band he cofounded with his brother D'Wayne in 1998. Saadiq first contacted DJ Ali Shaheed Muhammad of A Tribe Called Quest, which had disbanded after their 1998 LP *The Love Movement*, and then ex-En Vogue member Dawn Robinson, who had originally departed that group for a solo career in 1997 but jumped at the chance to work with Saadiq and Muhammad. Relying a great deal on live instrumentation in addition to samples and turntable work (Muhammad even plays bass and guitar), Lucy Pearl issued its self-titled debut album in the spring of 2000. —*Steve Huey*

● **Lucy Pearl** / May 23, 2000 / Beyond ◆◆◆
For many years, there has been a glut of slick, soulless R&B and hip-hop where talent is obscured by the canned packaging. Members of three bands who broke from that stale scene—En Vogue, Tony! Toni! Toné!, and A Tribe Called Quest—have formed the alterego Lucy Pearl. With rock star makeovers gracing the cover and good press, you'd expect some crossbred, innovative results. But the new hip-hop, soul, rock, and R&B adventures are buried in the last third of the album. Until then, Dawn Robinson's rock-hard vocals, Raphael Saadiq's melodic and guitar talents, and Ali Shaheed Muhammad's knack for intricate beats seem lost in a gloss of overproduction, forgettable lyrics, and cookie-cutter melodies, despite some trippy jazz beats and the witty "I Can't Stand Your Mother." The groove finally gets hot with the Chic-inspired "Don't Mess With My Man" and blasts into the scathing music biz attack "Hollywood"—is this the real Lucy Pearl? Drawing samples from Albert Collins and the Notorious B.I.G., the trio mixes up a superloose feel, acoustic guitars, old school machine beats, and guest raps from Snoop Dogg and Q-Tip. The inventive, witty "Lucy Pearl Tells" looks back on college and growing up in the '80s, even calling up the Alabama A&M Marching Band covering the first Lucy Pearl single "Dance Tonight." —*Theresa E. LaVeck*

Ludacris

Southern Rap, Dirty South, Pop-Rap, Hardcore Rap
Ludacris rode the early-2000s dirty South explosion to widespread popularity, as his songs enjoyed an enormous embrace, mainly by urban media outlets but also MTV and pop radio. The Atlanta-based rapper went from local sensation to household name after Def Jam signed him to its Def Jam South subsidiary in 2000. In addition to connecting him with superproducers like Timbaland, the Neptunes, and Organized Noize, Def Jam gave Ludacris remarkable marketing push. Ludacris thus quickly became one of the rap industry's most in-demand rappers, guesting on hits for everyone from Missy Elliott ("One Minute Man") to Jermaine Dupri ("Welcome to Atlanta") when he wasn't dominating the urban market with his own hits, most notably "What's Your Fantasy?," "Southern Hospitality," "Area Codes," and "Rollout (My Business)."

Before he became the dirty South's most successful rapper, Ludacris DJed at an Atlanta radio station. He used the opportunity to hone his craft on the mic, learn about the industry, and make a name for himself throughout the Atlanta area, which had become the South's rap mecca starting in the mid-'90s. Eventually, he began aspiring toward a career as a rapper rather than as a radio jock, and after working with Timbaland—appearing on the superproducer's *Tim's Bio* album (the original version of "Fat Rabbit") in 1998—Ludacris began taking his rap career seriously. He recorded an album, *Incognegro* (2000), and released it on his independently released Disturbing tha Peace label. Ludacris primarily worked with producer Shondrae for the album, though also with Organized Noize to a lesser extent. *Incognegro* sold impressively in Atlanta, where Ludacris was well known for his radio work. Soon after *Incognegro* became the talk of Atlanta and "What's Your Fantasy?" became a regional hit, Scarface came knocking. Def Jam had given the veteran rapper the go-ahead to scout for talent in the South, since the dirty South movement was gaining steam at the time and Def Jam wanted to start a Def Jam South subsidiary. Ludacris became Scarface's first signing, and Def Jam repackaged the tracks from *Incognegro*, along with a few new productions: a U.G.K. collaboration ("Stick 'Em Up"), a Neptunes production ("Southern Hospitality"), and a remix of his previously released song with Timbaland (retitled "Phat Rabbit"). Def Jam then gave the resulting album, *Back for the First Time* (2000), substantial marketing push, choosing "What's Your Fantasy?" (an explicit duet about sexual fantasies from both the male and female perspective) as the first single. Though some radio stations were hesitant to air such a provocative song, "What's Your Fantasy?" became an enormous success—as did, to a lesser extent, its even more provocative remix featuring Foxy Brown and Trina—opening the door for countless other truly "dirty" dirty South songs that would soon become the norm rather than the exception.

Following his initial breakthrough with "What's Your Fantasy?," Ludacris remained ubiquitous. He toured the States with OutKast and released a flurry of successive hit singles: the Neptunes-produced "Southern Hospitality," the Timbaland-produced "Phat Rabbit," the Nate Dogg collaboration "Area Codes," the Timbaland-produced "Rollout (My Business)," the Organized Noize-produced "Saturday (Oooh Oooh!)," the KLC-produced "Move Bitch." His second album for Def Jam, *Word of Mouf* (2001), peaked at number three on the *Billboard* album chart in October and hovered at the top of the charts for a long time. Furthermore, he contributed to hits for other artists during this same time, most notably Missy Elliott's "One Minute Man" and Jermaine Dupri's "Welcome to Atlanta," and also released another album, *Golden Grain* (2002), which featured his Disturbing tha Peace posse. —*Jason Birchmeier*

Incognegro / May 16, 2000 / Disturbing tha Peace ✦✦
Ludacris began his quick ascendance toward superstardom with *Incognegro*, his independently released debut album, which Def Jam eventually enhanced and repackaged as *Back for the First Time*. *Incognegro* thus features most of the songs from *Back for the First Time*, including the breakthrough hits "What's Your Fantasy?" as well as the Organized Noize-produced "Game Got Switched" and the Pastor Troy-featuring "Get Off Me." Though surely impressive as is, *Incognegro* unfortunately lacks the three noteworthy songs Def Jam would later add: the Neptunes-produced hit single "Southern Hospitality," the previously released Timbaland-produced "Phat Rabbit," and the U.G.K.-featuring "Stick 'Em Up." So, there's really little reason to both with *Incognegro* since *Back for the First Time* is essentially an enhanced version of this same album, though fans may wish to track this rare release down for historical reasons. —*Jason Birchmeier*

Back for the First Time / Oct. 17, 2000 / Def Jam ✦✦✦
When Def Jam signed Ludacris in 2000, the Atlanta rapper had already released a regionally successful independent release (*Incognegro*) with a hot single ("What's Your Fantasy"), so all the powerhouse label did was repackage the album, re-release the single nationally, and throw in four big-name collaborations. It was a wise decision, as *Incognegro* certainly sounds like a major-label release, produced largely by talented newcomer Shondrae and to a lesser extent by top Southern rap producers Organized Noize. Plus, the four new tracks—the Neptunes-produced club banger "Southern Hospitality," the previously released Timbaland-produced "Phat Rabbit," the rowdy U.G.K.-featuring "Stick 'Em Up," and the provocative Trina- and Foxy Brown-featuring "What's Your Fantasy" remix—are album highlights, the sort of good-time collaborations that would become Ludacris' specialty hereafter. Elsewhere, though, *Back for the First Time* is a major-label album with an underground aesthetic. Producer Shondrae crafts dirty South-style beats with

a unique touch that resembles no other major-label producer circa 2000, and the sporadic guests—I-20, Fat Wilson, Shawna, Pastor Troy, and 4-Ize—are hungry underground rappers from the Atlanta scene. This array of Def Jam-payrolled big-name collaborations and previously released underground tracks ensures that *Back for the First Time* appeals to all, from the already-down-South scene to the lucrative national mass market, and also makes it a little edgier at times than later efforts, which are sometimes marred by their pop-crossover ambitions. —*Jason Birchmeier*

● **Word of Mouf** / Nov. 6, 2001 / Def Jam ✦✦✦✦
Ludacris' second album for Def Jam, *Word of Mouf*, is a superstar affair that aims for mass appeal with a broad array of different styles. Nearly every track features some sort of collaborator, either hitmaking producers like Timbaland and Organized Noize, big-name rappers like Mystikal and Twista, hook-singing crooners like Nate Dogg and Jagged Edge, or fellow Disturbing tha Peace group members I-20, Shawnna, Lil' Fate, and Tity Boi—and sometimes a combinations of these various ingredients. The resulting album is surely impressive, propelled by lively production, colorful guests, and an omnipresent touch of humor. Though the first two qualities are surely welcome, it's the lightheartedness that's most impressive. More hilarious than before, Ludacris lightens his lyrical style here, leaving behind much of thuggishness that had characterized his previous album, *Back for the First Time*, in favor of witty puns and sly innuendoes. A particularly humorous highlight is the previously released (on the *Rush Hour 2* soundtrack) single "Area Codes," where Ludacris twists the word "hoe" myriad ways, usually to amusing results, over a sunny, good-spirited Jazze Pha production. Less humorous though likewise astounding is the lead single, "Rollout (My Business)," a rallying Timbaland production with a seemingly simple yet inescapable hook. Other highlights include the Organized Noize-produced booty-shaker "Saturday (Oooh Oooh!)," the Jagged Edge-sung come-on "Freaky Thangs," and the Beats by the Pound-esque posse track "Move Bitch." There's also a hidden bonus track here that's likewise an explosive collaboration, the Jermaine Dupri-led "Welcome to Atlanta." All of this obviously means there are a lot of highlights here, and that's certainly true; however, amid all of these various team-ups you do lose a little bit of the sincere, personal edge that had characterized much of Ludacris' debut. Even so, it's overall a worthy exchange, since there's something here on *Word of Mouf* for everyone, signaling Ludacris' leap from the dirty South underground to the pop-rap mass market. —*Jason Birchmeier*

Luke (Luther Campbell)

Producer, Engineer / Dirty Rap, Bass Music, Party Rap, Southern Rap
Otherwise known as Luther Campbell, the entrepreneur and head of 2 Live Crew since its inception in the mid-'80s, Luke is a solo project for Campbell apart from his group's releases. The first release as Luke, 1993's *In the Nude*, was followed by an X-rated Christmas album and a greatest-hits LP before the project signed a contract with Island for 1997's *Changin' the Game*. Luke's *Freak Fest 2000* followed three years later; *Somethin' Nasty* appeared in spring 2001. —*John Bush*

● **Banned in the U.S.A.** / 1990 / Luke ✦✦✦✦✦
A decent parody of Bruce Springsteen's "Born in the U.S.A." helped turn the debut by 2 Live Crew founder Luther Campbell into a mini-event. Campbell didn't show any great rapping or rhyming skills on the microphone, but did speak frankly about those he considered fake "gangstas" in between the constant sexual innuendoes, invitations, admonitions, and declarations. —*Ron Wynn*

I Got Shit on My Mind / 1992 / Luke ✦✦✦
When Florida attorney Jack Thompson declared war on Luther Campbell, 2 Live Crew, and Luke Records (formerly Luke Skyywalker Records) in 1989 and claimed that their X-rated rhymes were in violation of American obscenity laws, he didn't put them out of business. All he succeeded in doing was making Campbell a poster child for the First Amendment and helping him sell even more albums and singles. When Campbell launched his solo career with *I Got Shit on My Mind* in 1992, it was obvious that he wasn't about to clean up his act—this CD is every bit as rude, crude, and X-rated as anything that he had done with 2 Live Crew. On raunchy, sexually explicit offerings like "Head Head and More Head" and "Menage a Trois," Campbell seems to be thumbing his nose at his adversaries by being as offensive as possible. And those adversaries not only include Thompson and various

Francis M (Francis Magalona)

Vocals / Foreign Rap

Francis M is widely respected as a pioneer in the field of Philippine rap. Born Francis Magalona, he's also known for incorporating aspects of his Philippine patriotism (stretching centuries into the past) in his music. The music of Francis M is adventurous and well performed and, though quite different from American rap, does achieve international standards. Though his recordings have never received Western distribution, he's been releasing popular records in his homeland since his debut on the OctoArts label in the early '90s. He came to regional prominence with his stint for BMG Philippines during the late '90s. His best wrap-up is a greatest-hits collection released in 2002 by Musiko. —*David Gozales*

Francis M: OPM Timeless Collection / 1997 / OctoArts/EMI ✦✦✦✦

In 1997 the Philippine record company OctoArts/EMI released *Francis M: OPM Timeless Collection*, a collection of songs recorded by Philippine male rapper Francis M for the label on three albums released between 1990 and 1993. Known for his patriotism, he uses the album opener "Mga Kababayan" (My Fellow Countrymen) as an entreat to Filipinos to be proud of their country and to refrain from doing anything that harms it. His rapping is often tempered by a soulful sound, as heard in the sung chorus to "My Only One." He incorporates a snappy horn section into "Tayo'y Mga Pinoy" (We Are Filipinos) and "Bahay Yugyugan" (Jam House). Another highlight is the hard-edged, guitar-driven "I Don't Like Being in the Dark," a song about the nationwide electricity shortages that plagued the Philippines in the early '90s. —*David Gonzales*

● **The Best of Francis M.** / 2002 / Musiko ✦✦✦✦

Philippine rap owes a debt of gratitude to local rapper Francis M, who, along with Andrew E., helped introduce rap music to the populace. After recording for local label OctoArts between 1990 and 1993, he recorded a number of albums for BMG Records Philippines between 1995 and 2000. One hopes 2002's *Best of Francis M.* doesn't signal the end of his career, for he is truly one of the Philippines' most talented musical artists, rap or otherwise. In contrast to Andrew E. and other rappers who rely on jokes and silly double entendre, Francis M plays it straight and makes music that attains international standards. Francis M is a versatile performer, and his music can have a hard-edged, rock/metal ambience, as heard in the blistering "Pintados" (no translation); "Baw-waw-waw" (Bark of a dog); and "Kabataan Para sa Kinabukasan" (Youth for the Future), on which he also sings a pretty chorus. He can also impart a soulful, almost tender touch, as heard on "Girl Be Mine," "Friends," and "Kaleidoscope World." He is known for his patriotism, and the hard-edged, "3 Stars & a Sun," the title of which describes the field of the Philippine flag, bursts with patriotism; "1-800-Ninety Six" describes events in the year 1896, during which an important uprising against Spanish rule took place. The searing guitar work on both songs is incisive. The cadences of Francis M's raps are well executed and often mesmerizing, and the accompanying instrumentation is always sterling and attitude driven. It's a wonder his albums didn't reach an audience beyond Philippine shores, and one hopes his career isn't over. —*David Gonzales*

Mac Dre

Vocals, Producer, Mixing / West Coast Rap, Gangsta Rap

From Vallejo, CA (also the home of the Click), gangsta rapper Mac Dre moved to the Romp label in 1996 after two small releases on the Strictly Business label. *Mac Dre Presents the Rompalation* made the R&B charts near the end of 1996; a sequel followed in 1999. *Turf Buccaneers* and *Mac Dre Is the Name* were issued in early 2001. —*John Bush*

● **The Best of Mac Dre** / May 31, 1993 / Thizz ✦✦✦✦✦

Within the span of a decade, Mac Dre released a plethora of albums, not only full-lengths under his own name but also multiple volumes in the *Rompilation* series. When his best-of finally appeared in 2002, it was about time a collection of this underground West Coast Bay Area rapper's music was compiled. *Tha Best of Mac Dre* goes back all the way to the early '90s, when Dre was recording albums for Strictly Business, compiling several songs from his *Young Black Brotha* (1993) album. There are a total of 32 songs on this best-of, spanning the distance of two discs. This is undoubtedly the place in Dre's huge discography to begin if you're new to his music. —*Jason Birchmeier*

Stupid Doo Doo Dumb / Apr. 28, 1998 / Romp ✦✦✦✦

Due to various legal troubles, Mac Dre didn't have the opportunity to deliver a full-fledged follow-up to his second album, *Young Black Brotha*, until 1998—five years after *YBB* was released. The resulting record, *Stupid Doo Doo Dumb*, doesn't quite live up to its predecessor, mainly because it's missing the production of Khayree. His replacements, K Lou, Funk Daddy, and Johnny Z, are all fine, but lack his distinctive spark. Nevertheless, they provide Mac Dre with a serviceable backdrop for his coolly funky West Coast hardcore hip-hop. Dre doesn't stray from the typical topics, but he has a good, stylish lyrical flow that makes *Stupid Doo Doo Dumb* relatively fresh in these gangsta-saturated, *fin de siècle* days. —*Leo Stanley*

Mac Mall

Group / Hip-Hop, Gangsta Rap, West Coast Rap

Along with better-known rappers like E-40 and 2Pac, Mac Mall was one of several who helped put the Bay Area on the map in the mid- to late '90s as a hot spot in the rap game. He collaborated with many of the Bay Area's best producers—Ant Banks, Khayree, Michael Mosley, and Rick Rock—and helped to define the scene's identity, particularly with his most successful album, *Untouchable* (1996), which featured perhaps his best-known song, "Get Right." His career simmered out quickly, however. He returned in 1999 after a three-year absence and few listeners seemed to notice. Mall was no longer on a major label and the Bay Area scene was no longer the hot spot it had been a few years earlier. Given his brief moment in the spotlight and his sudden decline, it was perhaps no surprise when Mall changed his style in 2001, incorporating a surprising amount of spirituality on his *Immaculate* album. —*Jason Birchmeier*

Illegal Business? / Jul. 12, 1993 / Young Black Brotha ✦✦✦

Mac Mall's first album, released locally in California on his own indie label, Young Black Brotha, is a refreshing entry in the West Coast gangsta rap genre for 1993. With Khayree's deep, bassy, funky beats accenentuating Mac's energetic and smooth style of rapping, what's produced is a thick album with plenty of differing styles and themes. Khayree has also produced beats for Tupac, Mac Dre, Ray Luv, Young Lay, and Master P, among others. The most notable songs on the album are "Sic Wit Tis," "Don't Wanna See Me," and the slow-grooving "Ghetto Theme." A music video for "Ghetto Theme" was released shortly after the album, and is the debut of Tupac Shakur as a video director. —*Brad Mills*

● **Untouchable** / Apr. 1996 / Relativity ✦✦✦✦

Immaculate / Feb. 20, 2001 / Sessed Out ✦✦

Mac Mall is one of many rappers who have attempted to incorporate religion into their music. More often than not, mixing faith with hip-hop is a very tricky proposition. *Immaculate* is Mac Mall's fourth album, and he has yet to find the right balance. Many tracks on the album, such as "Mac-nificient" and "Immaculate," feature typical hip-hop braggadocio while other tracks like

"Bossin' Up" and "Monster" paint clichéd portraits of street life. At times, however, Mac Mall hits the mark as in "War on Drugs," a searing clever indictment of America's drug policy. Aside from the few obligatory hip-hop clichés, much of Mac Mall's focus is on spirituality, and it doesn't really work. Mac Mall tries to have it both ways: he wants to be spiritual while still coming off as a gangster. He uses phrases like "Mac Jesus" and "God's gift to macking" that would be considered inappropriate by people of all faiths. Religion and spirituality are important topics that deserve serious discussion. Unfortunately, Mac Mall isn't able to provide it. —*Jon Azpiri*

Mack 10 (D'Mon Rolison)

b. Aug. 9, 1971, Inglewood, CA
Gangsta Rap, West Coast Rap, G-Funk
When the West Coast first rose atop the rap industry in the mid-'90s, Mack 10 emerged as one of the coast's most promising talents alongside his longtime associate Ice Cube. The two Los Angeles rappers cowrote "Foe Life," Mack 10's 1995 breakthrough hit, and united a year later with WC to form the trio Westside Connection, a West Coast gangsta rap supergroup. The Westside Connection album became a sizable hit, rocketing to number two on the *Billboard* album chart and boasting the anthemic "Bow Down." Mack 10 continued his affiliation with Ice Cube on each successive album while at the same time launching a label of his own, Hoo Bangin' Records. As the '90s came to a close, the rapper's popularity dipped a bit, and he signed with leading dirty South label Cash Money Records in 2001, where his career underwent some unlikely twists.

Born D'Mon Rolison in 1971, throughout his career Mack 10 perpetually represented Inglewood, the Los Angeles neighborhood he called home. His professional rap career began in 1995 when he signed with Priority, the premier label for West Coast rap at the time, and released his self-titled album. The West Coast gangsta rap movement was peaking around this time, and Mack 10 capitalized on the trend with "Foe Life," a song he wrote with Ice Cube, one of the West Coast's reigning talents. The partnership struck gold, and the song became a coastal anthem, opening the door for a successive single, "On Them Thangs." Mack 10 then partnered with Ice Cube again a year later to form the West Coast supergroup Westside Connection along with another Los Angeles rapper, WC. The three had united for a standout song on Mack 10's debut album, "Westside Slaughterhouse," and hoped to reprise their camaraderie for the Westside Connection album. They certainly did so, recording the boastful lead single "Bow Down," which taunted the East Coast, along with several other songs discussing the East-West tension that dominated rap at the time.

Mack 10 followed the number-two-charting Westside Connection album with his second album, *Based on a True Story*, and its lead single, "Backyard Boogie," in 1997. The album became his most successful, peaking at number 14 on the *Billboard* album chart, and confirmed his quick ascendance to fame. Moreover, the album is generally considered Mack 10's career highlight: it features a modest number of guests (Snoop Dogg, E-40, Ice Cube), top-notch G-funk-era producers (Ant Banks, Soopafly), and little of the filler that would begin to populate his successive releases. Mack 10 returned a year later with another Top 20 album, *Recipe*, which is notable for its abundance of guests. In fact, only one song featured Mack 10 alone; every other song featured at least one guest, if not more; everyone from Master P and Mystikal to Jermaine Dupri and Ol' Dirty Bastard. Following the extravagancies of *Recipe* in 1997, Mack 10's career began to slowly spiral downward, much like the West Coast gangsta rap scene he rode to fame. His only release in 1998 was *Hoo Bangin': Mix Tape*, more of a showcase for the many up-and-coming rappers on his Hoo Bangin' label than for himself, and listeners weren't very interested. When Mack 10 finally did return with another full-length of his own, *The Paper Route*, in 2000, two years after *Recipe*, listeners similarly weren't very interested.

The relative disappointment of *The Paper Route* brought Mack 10's souring relationship with Priority Records to an end, and along came Cash Money Records, who happily signed the rapper to a contract. The partnership seemed somewhat unlikely. Cash Money was a leading dirty South label with a small roster of in-house rappers such as Juvenile and Lil' Wayne; however, the label was looking to expand its roster as well as its reach, and Mack 10 offered it a great opportunity to unite the West Coast and dirty South. The resulting album, *Bang or Ball* (2001), neither topped the charts nor garnered substantial attention despite boasting "Hate in Yo Eyes," a Dr. Dre production that interpolated the Bee Gees' "Stayin' Alive." The album nonetheless

signaled a new direction for Mack 10, who sounded surprisingly comfortable working with one of the dirty South's premier producers, Manny Fresh. Less than a year later in summer 2002 came *Mack 10 Presents da Hood*, a Hoo Bangin' release prominently featuring numerous up-and-coming West Coast rappers: K-Mac, Deviossi, Skoop, Cousteau, and Techniec. More importantly, though, the album featured "L.A. for Ya," an anthemic song that was customized for the West Coast's leading radio stations as well as for Lakers and Clippers home games. The customized versions worked, and the song garnered quite a bit of airplay on the West Coast, making it one of Mack 10's biggest hits in years. —*Jason Birchmeier*

Mack 10 / 1995 / Priority ✦✦✦
Mack 10 doesn't come across as an original on his self-titled debut; he comes across as a follower. Over a standard G-funk backdrop, complete with deep bass and whining synths, Mack 10 dishes out a multitude of clichéd gangsta lyrics—he simply lacks personality. The only time *Mack 10* comes alive is when his mentor Ice Cube appears on "West Side Slaughter House." Cube adds fire and rage to an album that desperately needs more passion. —*Stephen Thomas Erlewine*

● **Based on a True Story** / Sep. 16, 1997 / Priority ✦✦✦✦
When Mack 10 returned in 1997 with his second album, *Based on a True Story*, the West Coast gangsta movement had begun to simmer in the aftermath of Death Row's dissolution, 2Pac's death, Too Short's retirement, Dr. Dre's confusion, and Ice Cube's move to Hollywood. Mack gladly fills the void with a spirited album that's proudly Cali and proudly gangsta, and he brings along a few select guests—Cube, Snoop, and producer Ant Banks—who further rally the remaining West Coast fan base. Perhaps most importantly, though, Mack maintains a lighthearted attitude here that emphasizes good times and sunny, loping G-funk rhythms rather than the sort of menacing, hardest-of-the-hardcore one that so many of his West Coast peers had turned toward in the post-2Pac era. This lighthearted attitude is evident throughout, particularly on the album's highlights: the early-album party starter "Backyard Boogie," the Ant Banks-laced E-40 duet "Can't Stop," and the Snoop-Cube-Mack team-up "Only in California." Mack furthermore throws in a trio of especially fun interpolations: "Mack 10, Mack 10" (U.T.F.O.'s "Roxanne, Roxanne"), "Inglewood Swingin'" (Kool & the Gang's "Hollywood Swinging"), and "Dopeman" (N.W.A's "Dopeman"). Amid all of these standouts, Mack throws in a few skits and guests along with some fine if unexceptional filler, keeping the album overall quite lean at just under 50 minutes. *Based on a True Story*, then, is one of the best West Coast gangsta rap albums of 1997, an otherwise lackluster year for the style, and should please anyone who misses Cali's former kingpins. —*Jason Birchmeier*

Recipe / Oct. 6, 1998 / Priority ✦✦✦
It became commonplace during the mid- to late '90s for rappers to litter their albums with a small nation's worth of guest stars, both for commercial purposes and for all-important sonic variety. At its worst, this tactic can lead to albums where the ostensible star ends up sounding like a guest at their own party. But at its best, the more-the-merrier formula can result in stellar albums like Mack 10's *Recipe*, an unambitious but enormously satisfying slice of pop-savvy late-'90s gangsta rap that features a slew of the hottest names in hip-hop, from Eazy-E to Master P to ODB and many, many more. Mack 10 got his big break from mentor/gangsta rap pioneer Ice Cube, who not surprisingly lends his gruff presence to two of the album's standout tracks: "Should I Stay or Should I Go," a borderline sacrilegious but effective reworking of the Clash classic, and "Ghetto Horror Show," a similarly cheesy but enjoyable slice of gangsta rap gothic featuring a scene-stealing turn by the underrated Jayo Felony. Snoop Dogg trades verses with the laconic but authoritative Mack 10 on another of the album's highlights, "LBC and the ING," driven by a familiar but undeniably infectious sample of "Heartbeat," one of the greatest and most-used loops in the history of hip-hop. "Money's Just a Touch Away," the album's Gerald Levert-assisted first single, is a too-slick attempt at radio-friendly crossover success, but Mack 10's sole solo showcase, "The Letter," is a surprisingly eloquent and well-reasoned defense of gangsta rap. *Recipe* probably won't convert many nonbelievers, but for fans of straightforward, late-'90s gangsta rap, it's about as good as it gets. —*Nathan Rabin*

The Paper Route / Sep. 5, 2000 / Priority ✦✦✦
When Mack 10 enthusiastically claims on the album-opening "From the Streetz," "I'm back to that O.G. gangsta fo' life gritty shit" and "Tell 'um where

I'm from!," his stance seems almost a bit too earnest to be taken seriously. Yet rather than question the rapper on his credibility, this album works best when you simply kick back, nod your head to the G-funk beats, and revel in this extended gangsta-flossing exercise, even if it's admittedly contrived. On songs such as "Nobody," featuring Ice Cube and WC along with the ever-innovative production of Timbaland, Mack once again showcases his gangsta fantasies: "Who go mo' money than us?" Once again, don't take this stuff too seriously; this song, along with others such as "Tha Weekend" (also with Cube) and "Pimp or Die" (with Too Short), are little more than male fantasies laid out on wax with the typical laid-back West Coast attitude. Yet, in the end, more than Mack's firm gangsta stance, the thick funk-filled beats make all this work—even with a stable of non-superstar producers—as the raps sound so much better with a bit of bounce to them. This isn't *The Chronic* or *AmeriKKKa's Most Wanted*, but *The Paper Route* is one of the better albums to argue that '90s West Coast gangsta rap didn't end with 2Pac's death. —*Jason Birchmeier*

Bang or Ball / Dec. 4, 2001 / Universal ✦✦✦

It wasn't easy being a West Coast gangsta rapper at the end of the '90s. Mack 10 will tell you that. Around 1996, the time "Foe Life" and "Backyard Boogie" were blowing up and Mack was putting it down for Cali with Ice Cube and WC on the Westside Connection album, everything was great—Mack was on top of the game. But his career simmered out—like nearly every other West Coast rapper's career—following the Death Row empire's demise. Suddenly, around 1999/2000, the rap community seemed to view Mack with indifference. His *Paper Route* album (2000) was his least successful and his record deal with Priority had gone sour. Then, along comes Cash Money Records, looking to extend its empire from the South to the West Coast—much like No Limit had done unsuccessfully with Snoop Dogg a few years earlier. The resulting album, *Bang or Ball*, features Mack rapping alongside the Cash Money Millionaires over Mannie Fresh productions. It's somewhat of a strange pairing—West Coast gangsta rap and the dirty South. The synthesis works surprisingly well—certainly better than Snoop's No Limit collaborations. Mack sounds comfortable dropping rhymes over Fresh's beats and sounds at home alongside the Big Tymers, in particular, rapping about the usual gangsta topics: sex, cars, drugs, money, player haters, boasting, and so on. "Hate in Yo Eyes," a Dr. Dre and Scott Storch track that interpolates "Stayin' Alive" for the hook, really helps *Bang or Ball*. It's one of Dre and Storch's best efforts and really starts the album off with plenty of club-ready energy. "Connected for Life," featuring Ice Cube, WC, and Butch Cassidy, is another obvious highlight. But the abundance of Fresh productions doesn't help *Bang or Ball*. Most of the in-house Cash Money producer's beats are admittedly great—not really West Coast and definitely not dirty South, but are instead somewhere between the two. However, a few more outside productions like the Dre track would bring some more diversity to this album. And that's really what's lacking here. By the time you hit the halfway mark, the album begins to sound a bit monotonous. Still, *Bang or Ball* is an engaging listen, especially the first time through. Even by the time this album came out in 2001, there hadn't been many collaborations between the West Coast and the South, and surely none this ambitious and this high profile. Give both Mack and the Cash Money Millionaires credit for taking a chance. —*Jason Birchmeier*

Mack 10 Presents da Hood / Jul. 23, 2002 / Riviera ✦✦✦

Following his first release for Cash Money Records, West Coast rap legend Mack 10 steps into the role of executive on *Mack 10 Presents da Hood*. The album features Cali rappers K Mac, Deviossi, Skoop, Cousteau, and Techniec, all of whom are part of Mack's Hoo Bangin' roster. Other rappers who make appearances include Lil Jon, Ice Cube, the Cash Money Millionaires, and more. Among the album's many songs, the anthemic "L.A. fo Ya" stands out, as does "Hittin Switches." With all the guests, Mack doesn't give himself as much time on the mic as you might expect. It's therefore best to view *Mack 10 Presents da Hood* as a stopgap posse spotlight rather than a traditional solo album. —*Jason Birchmeier*

Craig Mack

Vocals, Producer / Hip-Hop, East Coast Rap, Pop-Rap

An above-average rapper blessed with a bit of luck and connections as well as talent, Craig Mack practically *made* Puff Daddy's Bad Boy label with a remix of his 1994 hit "Flava in Ya Ear." Based in Brentwood, Long Island,

Mack cut his first single while still a teenager, though nothing came of it. He was working as a go-fer for hometown heroes EPMD when he hooked up with Sean "Puffy" Combs, who offered him a spot on a Mary J. Blige remix in 1992. Impressed, Combs offered him a contract on his Bad Boy label, distributed through Arista. What really sold the LP, however, was a platinum remix of the top single "Flava in Ya Ear." Featuring a parade of East Coast talent—the Notorious B.I.G., Rampage, LL Cool J, and Busta Rhymes—it ranked as one of the first posse tracks to go overground in a big way; a Top Ten pop hit, and number one on the rap and dance charts. Mack returned in 1997 (after having severed relations with Combs) with *Operation: Get Down*, an executive production of longtime East Coast head Eric B. The album didn't even make the Top 40, and Mack struggled for a contract during the rest of the decade. After recording a few white labels, he returned to Bad Boy with an appearance on Combs' *We Invented the Remix* LP ("Special Delivery" featuring Ghostface Killah and Keith Murray) and announced plans for a new Bad Boy LP. —*John Bush*

● **Project: Funk da World** / 1994 / Bad Boy ✦✦✦✦

The first hit album released on Sean "Puffy" Combs' Bad Boy label, Craig Mack's *Project: Funk da World* lacks the hardcore edge of Bad Boy's next breakout artist, the Notorious B.I.G., instead gunning for the dancefloor with a slight hint of street attitude. The beats are laid-back, mid-tempo, and effortlessly funky, influenced by the vibe of Dr. Dre's G-funk sound but not slavishly derivative at all. Mack isn't the most skillful rapper who ever lived, but he's game on most of these tracks, with a low, raspy voice and a loose, casual style that's hard to resist when he's on. When he isn't, he strays a little too far off the beat, or lacks enough variety in his flow and surprises in his rhymes to hold the listener's interest. But he's good enough to work a groove, and sometimes that's all you need for a great dance record. The formula gets repetitive over the course of an entire album, especially on the tracks with too many choruses, but there are some definite high points, most notably the smash hits "Flava in Ya Ear," "Get Down," and "Funk Wit da Style." There's also a clever sample of the *Days of Our Lives* theme song on "Real Raw." In the end, *Project: Funk da World* isn't a bad party record at all, though it's less engaging as a self-contained listen. —*Steve Huey*

Operation: Get Down / Jun. 24, 1997 / Street Life ✦✦✦

Rap audiences can be a fickle lot. In 1994, Craig Mack was riding high on the success of his debut album, *Project: Funk da World*, and a hit single, "Flava in Ya Ear." Three years later, his *Operation: Get Down* follow-up would have been more appropriately titled Operation: Fell Off. So what happened? Two things: First, Mack was backed by a rising Sean "Puffy" Combs on his debut, a relationship that was strained by the meteoric rise of the Notorious B.I.G.—who incidentally had his debut on the ear-popping remix of "Flava in Ya Ear." Second, three years is a long time in the pop world. If *Operation: Get Down* had appeared sooner, it's possible that "Drugs, Guns and Thugs" could have broken out as a single and Mack would never have had to write "Jockin' My Style"—a song attacking all the MCs who had taken on his style during the long absence. —*Wade Kergan*

Mad Flava

f. Dallas, TX

Group / Hip-Hop, Gangsta Rap, Hardcore Rap, Underground Rap

The four-man Dallas crew Mad Flava were brief players in the mid-'90s "weed-hop" scene that followed the breakout success of Cypress Hill. Comprised of MCs Cold Chris the Soulman (real name: Chris Parker) and Don Kasaan, DJ Baby G the Cut Selectah, and producer/MC Erich "Hype Dawg" Krause, Mad Flava procured a deal with Priority Records after upping their profile with support gigs throughout Texas for established artists like KRS-One, A Tribe Called Quest, and Cypress Hill themselves. Concurrent to the popular explosion of Cypress Hill was the House of Pain phenomenon of 1992-1993. The Muggs-produced "Jump Around" had popularized the notion of a Caucasian MC, and Mad Flava's main man, Cold Chris, was white *and* he and his group smoked prodigious amounts of marijuana. Everything pointed to Priority having a hit on its hands in *From tha Ground Unda*, the Flava's debut album. But litigation over sample licensing and distribution problems hung up its release, and by the time *Ground* finally arrived in late 1993, the Flava's brief window of opportunity had closed. A halfhearted promotional campaign from Priority did little to drive interest in the group, and soon Mad

Flava faded back into the Dallas underground, casualties of a fickle hip-hop market. —*Johnny Loftus*

From Tha Ground Unda / 1994 / Priority ✦✦

In hip-hop parlance, "flow" is a term that refers to a rapper's delivery or rhyming technique—what a musician calls "chops," a hip-hopper calls a "flow." On *From the Ground Unda*, Mad Flava emphasizes flow, flow, and more flow. While other rap CDs might concern themselves with telling some type of story or pulling the listener in with hooks or beats, the main purpose of this CD is showing off Mad Flava's flows. To be sure, the members of Mad Flava (an obscure group from Dallas) have strong technique, but unfortunately, hearing them do nothing but show it off wears thin after awhile. At first, the group's rhyming skills are admirable, but the approach seems limited after being inundated with nothing but technique for over an hour. When Mad Flava does nothing but boast on song after song, you find yourself wishing they would bring some much-needed variety to their lyrics. *From the Ground Unda* fell through the cracks, and when the 1990s were coming to an end, Flava had yet to come out with a second album. —*Alex Henderson*

Mad Lion

Producer, Vocals / Hip-Hop, Dancehall, Fusion, Club/Dance

Weaving a seamless blend of reggae and hip-hop, Mad Lion (born Oswald Priest) created one of the most influential sounds of the past two decades. The recipient of the 1994 *Source* award as Reggae Artist of the Year, Mad Lion has inspired similar-sounding recordings by such artists as Ini Kamoze, Capleton, and Rayvon.

A native of London, Mad Lion was raised in Jamaica. Shortly after moving to Brooklyn, NY, he met reggae performer Super Cat at Super Power Records. At Super Cat's suggestion, he adopted his professional name, an acronym for Musical Assassin Delivering Lyrical Intelligence Over Nations. Mad Lion's earliest success came in the mid-'80s when he applied his hip-hop rhythms to Shabba Ranks' hit single "Jam." He later appeared, along with Queen Latifah, on Salt-N-Pepper's 1997 album *Brand New.*

Launching his own label, Spinners Choice, Mad Lion was working on his debut album when he met and convinced producer KRS-One to work with him. The collaboration proved fruitful as Mad Lion's single, "Shoot to Kill," sold more than 100,000 copies. His next single, "Take It Easy," did even better, exceeding the 300,000 sale mark.

After releasing an album, *Real Ting,* in 1993, Mad Lion made countless guest appearances on such albums as *The New Jersey Drive* and *D&D Project,* compilations, and produced a tune for Born Jamericans. His second album, *Ghetto Gold & Platinum Respect,* was released in 1997. Four years later, his third album, *Predatah or Prey,* which also included an interactive game, arrived. —*Craig Harris*

● **Real Ting** / 1995 / Weeded ✦✦✦
KRS-One's production gives the beats on this album a precision that contrasts with Mad Lion's gravelly raggae vocals. The lyrics are typical dancehall material. —*John Bush*

Ghetto Gold & Platinum Respect / Jun. 24, 1997 / Weeded/Nervous ✦✦✦

Predatah or Prey / Jan. 30, 2001 / Killahpride ✦✦✦

Mad Skillz

Mixing, Producer / Hip-Hop, Gangsta Rap, Hardcore Rap, Club/Dance

With a second-place finish (behind Midwest rapper Supernatural) in the freestyle competition at the nation's most prestigious MC seminar in 1995, this aptly named Virginia native demonstrated his limitless verbal potential. The first salvo fired from Skillz was the single "The Nod Factor" of which a lengthy stanza appeared as a memorable Hip Hop Quotable in *The Source.* Skillz reigned supreme with his brand of harshly wicked witticisms, uncorking the type of sinister rhymes that would make a freestyle foe hang his head in shame. The consummate lyricist, Skillz mastered the unique art of double entendre with rhymes like: "put your clothes on backwards if you feel like frontin'." The lampooning onslaught came to a head with Skillz' debut in 1996, *From Where???,* which called attention to the virtually untapped talent within his home state. The album featured a few gems on production from Large Professor and Buckwild and a guest appearance from Q-Tip on "Extra Abstract Skillz." Many heads were checking for this album, although the same heads also clamored for more decisive production that would match the Mad one's singular lyrical gift. Mad Skillz reappeared in 1999 on Rawkus'

Soundbombing, Vol. 2 on "B-Boy Document" which also featured Mos Def. In 2000 he released his own single on Rawkus, "Ghost Writer" produced by fellow Virginian Timabaland. —*Michael Di Bella*

● **From Where???** / 1995 / Big Beat ✦✦✦✦

Throughout his debut album *From Where???* Mad Skillz proves that his name is well deserved. Simply put, Mad Skillz has incredible verbal skills, in terms of both speed and vocabulary. He weaves long, dense lines full of humor and messages. His freestyle rhyming is so hypnotizing that it's easy to forgive the pedestrian backing tracks, which rarely match the power of his raps. —*Stephen Thomas Erlewine*

The Madd Rapper (Deric "D-Dot" Angelettie)

Hip-Hop, East Coast Rap

The Madd Rapper was the alias of Brooklyn-born MC/producer Deric "D-Dot" Angelettie, who first rose to prominence as one half of the conscious rap duo 2 Kings in a Cipher, which scored an underground hit with "For the Brothers Who Ain't Here." From there, Angelettie went to work as intern with Bad Boy Entertainment, where over time he rose to the position of A&R Director before Sean "Puffy" Combs tapped him as a staff producer; credited as D-Dot, he helmed the hit singles "Been Around the World" and "All About the Benjamins," additionally serving as executive producer on projects from Mase (*Harlem World*), the LOX (*Money, Power & Respect*), Faith Evans (*Keep the Faith*), and Black Rob (*Life Story*). Angelettie invented the Madd Rapper persona as a satiric skit character for the Notorious B.I.G's *Life After Death* album, but it proved so popular with listeners that a solo album was announced; originally the Madd Rapper's identity was a closely guarded secret, but in November of 1998 Angelettie made headlines for an alleged attack on then-*Blaze* editor-in-chief Jesse Washington after the magazine published photos disclosing the character's true name. The 1999 single "D-Dot vs. the Madd Rapper" preceded the release of the full-length *Tell 'Em Why U Madd.* —*Jason Ankeny*

● **Tell 'Em Why U Madd** / Sep. 21, 1999 / Crazy Cat/Columbia ✦✦✦

What started as a Bad Boy Records skit to pull the cards of player-hating rap artists who had criticized the camp on wax for turning the rap game into a materialistic free-for-all ironically turned into a record deal for Bad Boy impresario Deric "D-Dot" Angelettie, the man behind the Madd Rapper. D-Dot, mainly known for his production credits (most notably "All About the Benjamins") does double-duty on his debut album. *Tell 'Em Why U Madd* is star-studded, self-serving hip-hop with hard-hitting beats tinged with outlandish street humor. Not trying to shake up the game or prove anything but that cash rules everything around us, this album serves as a showcase for up-and-coming talent on Crazy Cat Records, namely Fierce and Picasso Black. "Bongo Break," featuring Busta Rhymes, is premium high octane hip-hop and is arguably the best cut. However, the most significant cut was "How to Rob," featuring the clever lyrical stick-ups of 50 Cent, that while meant facetiously were taken to heart by some of the numerous rap artists mentioned in the cut, resulting in hard feelings. Keeping with the Madd Rapper theme, 50 shows to what lengths a rap artist would go to get paid. This album is the essence of jiggy hip-hop: heavy on anger and gun boasting, tempered slightly by tongue-in-cheek humor. Putting the gangsterism and money first, the art form of hip-hop a distant second, doesn't purport to be anything else but potentially offensive to hip-hop purists. Overall, this is a fairly entertaining album on the strength of the beats and the mix of guest appearances ranging from Eminem to the Beatnuts, but certainly nothing earth shattering. —*Michael Di Bella*

Madlib (Otis Jackson Jr.)

b. Oxnard, CA.

Producer, Vocals / Hip-Hop, Soul-Jazz, Fusion

From the unlikely beach town of Oxnard, 40 miles north of Los Angeles, the multidimensional Madlib quickly rose to prominence as one of the most interesting figures in late-'90s hip-hop. With his childhood buddies in the Lootpack, Madlib quickly made a name for himself as a rapper, producer, and DJ. In particular, his expansive style and deft touch for composition made him one of hip-hop's most sought-after producers. An enthusiastic crate digger, with a deep reverence for jazz and soul, Madlib branched out into a number of ambitious, engaging solo projects. Along with DJ Romes and Wild Child, Madlib formed the Lootpack in their hometown of Oxnard. The trio made their debut on tha Alkaholiks' *21 and Over* in 1993. They continued doing work for tha Alkaholiks and other artists before releasing their full-length *Soundpieces: Da Antidote* six years later. The album earned solid reviews but went largely unnoticed. Madlib did not, however. After hooking up with Los Angeles DJ Peanut Butter Wolf, Madlib did a lot of production for Wolf's Stones Throw label. In 1999 the label released Quasimoto's astonishing *The Unseen* LP. Doubling as himself and his alterego Quasimoto, Madlib handled vocals and production duties on the album, a huge critical success. Not resting on his laurels, Madlib followed *The Unseen* a year later with his Yesterday's New Quintet project. Madlib played all the instruments himself, infusing his exploration of jazz with both style and substance. Another stylistic detour followed in late 2002, when he released *Blunted in the Bomb Shelter Mix*, a spin through the vault of the classic dub/reggae label Trojan. —*Martin Woodside*

● **Blunted in the Bomb Shelter Mix** / Nov. 4, 2002 / Antidote ✦✦✦
Trojan sent most of their catalog over to Madlib's bomb shelter (the name given to his basement studio in California) and asked him to put together a mix CD of his favorite dub reggae joints. So after some time passed and he hadn't delivered the record yet Trojan began politely harassing him. The result is this attention-span-disorder delight put together in a single afternoon. Madlib moves abruptly through 45 Trojan sides with occasional interludes hosted by a computer voice and some of his beat arrangements (which smoothly transfer back to the subject at hand). Nothing is rocked for over a minute or two, and nothing picked for this continuous mix is short of excellent. Classics ranging from Lee Perry and the Upsetters' "Jingle Lion," King Tubby's "A Better Version," and the Skatalites' "Guns of Navorone" are here, but so are plenty of hidden favorites. Perfect for sunny afternoon lounging or bedroom headphone perusal, *Blunted in the Bomb Shelter Mix* doesn't disappoint. —*Jack LV Isles*

Madrok

Group / West Coast Rap, Golden Age
The West Coast rapper Madrok released just one LP, 1992's *Knowledge to Noise*, for AVC. Despite a few solid singles, it wasn't a success and he never released another full-length. —*John Bush*

● **Knowledge to Noise** / 1992 / AVC ✦✦✦
Although Madrok came out of the Southern California rap scene of the late '80s, it would have been easy to mistake his debut album, *Knowledge to Noise*, for the work of an East Coast rapper. Like so many MCs coming out of New York and Philadelphia at the time, Madrok favors a complex, cerebral style of rapping and places a lot of emphasis on technique. The impressive flow that he brings to tunes like "The Dopesmith," "Crazy Mental," "Fruit of Diligence," and "Checkmate!" reminds one of Public Enemy's Chuck D, and yet, it's clear that Madrok is very much his own man. The CD had a gem of a single in "Skin Tight," a hip-hop remake of the Ohio Players' 1974 hit that features some of the Players themselves. On the whole, *Knowledge to Noise* is very much a hardcore rap effort and offers little in the way of R&B or pop embellishments, but "Skin Tight" had considerable R&B appeal and should have been warmly embraced by radio. It was certainly one of 1992's best rap singles, but unfortunately it fell through the cracks, as did the album itself. —*Alex Henderson*

El Maestro

b. North York, Ontario
Latin Rap, Hip-Hop
Latino rapper El Maestro released just one record, 1995's *Going Insane*, for Explicit/Sunset Blvd. —*John Bush*

● **Going Insane** / Feb. 27, 1995 / Explicit/Sunset Blvd. ✦✦✦
El Maestro is among the Latino rappers who were active in Los Angeles in the 1990s. The thing that separates him from other L.A.-based Latino MCs is the fact that his heritage is Puerto Rican, not Mexican. While East Coast cities like New York, Philadelphia, and Boston are full of Puerto Rican rappers, the majority of L.A.'s Latino hip-hoppers were of Mexican descent. El Maestro's bilingual rapping on *Going Insane* is quite different from the bilingual rapping of Mexican-American or Chicano artists such as Kid Frost, tha Mexakinz, or Lighter Share of Brown. His approach is, in some respects, closer to the "nuyorican" rapping you'd hear in parts of the Bronx or Philly. The fact that dancehall reggae has been such a strong influence on El Maestro

makes this CD all the more interesting. So on *Going Insane*, you've got a Puerto Rican MC from L.A. who is heavily influenced by dancehall toasters from Jamaica, and who raps in both English and Spanish. Not a masterpiece, but as a chance-taking and unorthodox project, *Going Insane* is worth looking for. —*Alex Henderson*

Maggotron

f. Miami, FL
Group / Bass Music, Party Rap, Hip-Hop
Maggotron have the distinction of being one of the very first groups to recognize the developing Miami bass scene and use its growing popularity to launch an underground movement. Beginning with the classic *The Bass That Ate Miami*, the group would go on to release countless more compilations and full albums for a variety of labels. They used a variety of names, from Sonarphonic to the Maggotron Crushing Crew, but remained the same group of likeminded musicians. Their battles with the Pandisc label made their recordings hard to find around the turn of the century, but they persisted with making music despite having one of their chief outlets taken from them. —*Bradley Torreano*

● **The Best of Maggotron: Early Maggots** / 1990 / Hot Productions ✦✦✦✦

Main Source

f. 1989
Group / Golden Age, Hip-Hop, Alternative Rap, East Coast Rap, Jazz-Rap
Extremely significant for 1991's *Breaking Atoms* alone, Main Source's effect on hip-hop is nearly impossible to gauge, especially when considering Large Professor and K-Cut's contributions outside of the group. Consisting of MC/producer Large Professor (born Paul Mitchell) and twin DJs/producers K-Cut (born Kevin McKenzie) and Sir Scratch, the New York group came together in 1989 and debuted on Wild Pitch with Breaking Atoms—an undeniably classic album, regardless of its field—two years later. The group's production work, combined with Large Professor's masterful wordplay (from the brilliant baseball analogies drawn throughout the police brutality-themed "Just a Friendly Game of Baseball," to the disheartening romantic strife depicted in "Looking at the Front Door"), set a standard. While Gang Starr's DJ Premier is commonly heralded as a groundbreaking sampler and beatmaker, it was Large Professor and K-Cut who schooled him on how to master the SP1200. Not only that, but *Breaking Atoms*' "Live at the Barbeque" helped establish the careers of both Akinyele and Nas.

Large Professor left the group due to financial issues and began to concentrate on production work. K-Cut and Sir Scratch continued the group and installed MC Mikey D. for 1994's *F*ck What You Think*. Though it hardly holds a candle to *Breaking Atoms* (to be fair, it would've been tough to build on that record, even with Large Professor's presence), the album was hardly an artistic failure, but it came and went without much notice. Without their greatest weapon, the group's second go around wasn't given much of a chance. It didn't help that it took three years to reach fruition. Meanwhile, Large Professor was racking up production credits for Eric B. & Rakim, Akinyele, Mobb Deep, Nas, and Pete Rock & C.L. Smooth. He didn't make his proper solo debut until 2002, with the disappointing *1st Class*. —*Andy Kellman*

★ **Breaking Atoms** / 1991 / Wild Pitch ✦✦✦✦✦
Main Source's debut album, *Breaking Atoms*, is one of the quintessential cult classics in hip-hop history. Underappreciated compared to peers like A Tribe Called Quest, Gang Starr, or even Brand Nubian, the album probably doesn't get wider acclaim because it was recorded for the ill-fated Wild Pitch label, and thus remained out of print for much of the time its reputation was spreading. Group focal point the Large Professor is a fine rapper, but the album's legend rests more on his production—he debuts one of the most influential styles in hip-hop here, popularizing a number of now widely imitated techniques. Luckily, you don't have to know how to operate an SP1200 or exactly what panning, chopping, and filtered bass lines are, to appreciate the vibrant-sounding results. His intricately constructed tracks are filled with jazz and soul samples, layered percussion, off-kilter sampling effects, and an overall sonic richness. That's doubtlessly enhanced by the presence of two DJs in the group, who contribute lively scratching to the proceedings as well. The album is rather brief, clocking in at around 45 minutes even with a bonus remix, but there's also no wasted space whatsoever. The brightly soulful "Lookin' at the Front Door" is perhaps the best-known single, but there are

plenty of other highlights. "Just a Friendly Game of Baseball" is anything but, with its moody backing track and extended lyrical metaphor about police brutality and racial profiling. Meanwhile, "Live at the Barbeque" is one of the most legendary posse cuts ever recorded, featuring guests Joe Fatal, Akinyele, and Nas (the latter two make their recorded debuts here). Aficionados hype *Breaking Atoms* as one of the greatest hip-hop albums of all time, and at least musically speaking, they're not far off. (A Wild Pitch reissue program was underway in the new millennium, but despite rumors, *Breaking Atoms* still hasn't been a beneficiary.) —*Steve Huey*

F*ck What You Think / Mar. 22, 1994 / Wild Pitch ✦✦✦
Even if Main Source's lineup had remained the same for the follow-up to *Breaking Atoms*, the group would've had trouble following it up. That's not all the group had working against it. Most significantly, in a very gutsy move, K-Cut and Sir Scratch opted to keep Main Source running after the departure of Large Professor, easily their greatest asset as both an MC and a producer. They replaced him with the rougher-sounding Mikey D. and didn't return with *F*ck What You Think* until a full three years after *Breaking Atoms* impacted the hip-hop world. Needless to say, the group is much less of a force without their original member; while the in-house production isn't lacking by any stretch, it simply doesn't have the same degree of liveliness as *Breaking Atoms*, and there's nothing that makes Mikey D. a distinctive MC. Perhaps it's unfair to judge this record against a landmark that has such a different element to it; if this had been a debut by a new group, it probably would've gone down better. But, by retaining the name Main Source, K-Cut and Sir Scratch left themselves completely open. Regardless of the circumstances, *F*ck What You Think* does not sound like the work of a group; it sounds like the work of two remaining group members struggling to maintain completely lost momentum for all the wrong reasons. —*Andy Kellman*

Mangu

b. Dominican Republic
Hip-Hop, Dance-Pop, Latin Pop, Club/Dance, Latin Rap
Mangu was born in the Dominican Republic and raised in the Bronx, but he moved to Miami Beach to begin recording what he called fonquette, a Latin-based hip-hop style with some modern rap influences (including A Tribe Called Quest and KRS-One). His debut single, "La Playa," was produced by Joe Galdo and Cesar Sogbe; it featured the montuno piano-playing of Cuban Paquito Hechevarria. "La Playa" appeared in 1994, but Mangu didn't deliver his full-length debut until the spring of 1998, when *Calle Luna Calle Sol* was released by Island Records. —*John Bush*

● **Mangu** / Mar. 10, 1998 / Island ✦✦✦✦
Mangu's long-delayed eponymous debut album may not have been worth a four-year wait, yet it's still an impressive record. Mixing hip-hop, salsa, Miami bass, reggae, jazz, Latin pop, and Caribbean music, he has an infectious multicultural style, rapping in both English and Spanish. He also has the good sense to draft a number of cameos, including guest appearances from Beenie Man, Betty Wright, Johnny Pacheco, Carlton Coffie, and Mother Superia, which helps give the album a richer sense of tradition. Mangu's primary talent is for working a good groove, and if few songs have the lyrical or melodic weight of "La Playa" or his cover of the Latin standard "Calle Luna, Calle Sol," the album breezes by on sunny, danceable rhythms that are quite ingratiating. —*Stephen Thomas Erlewine*

Calle Luna Calle Sol / Apr. 21, 1998 / Polygram ✦✦✦

Kurtis Mantronik (Kurtis El Khaleel)

b. Sep. 4, 1965, Jamaica
Producer / Hip-Hop, Electronica, Big Beat
One of the most influential hip-hop producers of the 1980s, Kurtis Mantronik returned in the mid-'90s with a solo career that showed him fitting in well with the legion of big beat artists he had inspired. As the nominal leader of Mantronix, he produced a good half-dozen early rap classics, including "Basslines," "Ladies," and "King of the Beats." By the late '80s however, Mantronix had moved into R&B and house; after Mantronix disintegrated in 1991, he spent several years working on production, then left music altogether. He returned in the mid-'90s with the mini-LP *Burn the Elastic* and his first full-length, *I Sing the Body Electro*. Praise for the album spurred him to reform Mantronix and begin recording a new LP. —*John Bush*

● **I Sing the Body Electro** / Sep. 1, 1998 / Oxygen Music Works ✦✦✦✦✦
I Sing the Body Electro is that rare exception to the rule that influential artists should never attempt a ten-years-later comeback trying the same style their current inheritors have made commercial. Mantronik's production methods are completely up to date (and then some), resulting in an album that perfectly balances old school sampladelic hip-hop with the breakbeat-energized dance music of the late '90s. "King of the Beatbox V 3.0," "Bass Machine Re-Tuned," and "On the Beatbox" are stunning returns to the glory days of Mantronix, while vocal tracks like "Mad," "Push Yer Hands Up," and "One Time, Feel Fine" show that Mantronik's trackmaster skills could easily light up the world of mainstream rap, just as they did almost 15 years earlier. —*John Bush*

Mantronix

f. 1984, New York, NY **db.** 1991
Group / Golden Age, Hip-Hop, House, Club/Dance, Electro, Old School Rap
Over and above their standing as one of the best and most innovative groups from hip-hop's golden age, Mantronix provided rap music with its first man-machine, Kurtis Mantronik. A turntable master who incorporated synthesizers and samplers into the rhythmic mix instead of succumbing to the popular use of samples simply as pop hooks, Mantronik exploited technology with a quintessentially old school attitude which had little use for instruction manuals and accepted use. After the hip-hop world began to catch up with Mantronik's developments, he moved from hardcore rap to skirt the leading edge of club music, from electro to raggae, techno, and house. And though he never found a rapper worthy of his immense production talents, Mantronik inspired dozens of DJs and beatmeisters around the world during the next decade—in hip-hop, mainstream dance music, and the new electronica—even while his records were practically impossible to find (many snapped up, no doubt, by those same aspiring DJs).

Mantronik was born Kurtis El Khaleel in Jamaica, though his family soon moved to Canada and ended up in New York by the late '70s. Mantronik soon began DJing around the city and was working behind the decks at Manhattan's Downtown Records when he met MC Tee (born Touré Embden). After the duo had assembled a demo tape, they gave it to William Socolov, president of Sleeping Bag Records. He signed Mantronix soon after hearing it, and released their debut single, "Fresh Is the Word." The track lit up New York's streets and clubs during 1985, and brought the full-length *Mantronix: The Album* that year. Two new singles, "Ladies" and "Basslines," became big street hits as well and even crossed over to join the first wave of hip-hop chartmakers in Britain.

By that time, Mantronik had also begun working on A&R at Sleeping Bag, where he signed EPMD, produced KRS-One's first credit ("Success Is the Word" by 12:41), and helmed other intense tracks by Tricky Tee, Just-Ice, and T la Rock. The second Mantronix LP, *Music Madness*, continued to keep the duo fresh in the clubs. The increasing popularity of hip-hop gave Mantronix a chance at a major-label contract, and by 1987 the duo had signed with Capitol. *In Full Effect* emerged the following year, and portrayed Mantronik jettisoning many his more hardcore inclinations in favor of a fusion of dance and R&B, an early precursor to hip-house. The production excursion "Do You Like…Mantronik?" proved that Mantronik's ear for clever beats remained, however. And Mantronix's success in England prompted several of the first sampladelic hits, like "Pump Up the Volume" by M.A.R.R.S. and "Theme from S'Express" by S'Express.

Soon after *In Full Effect*, MC Tee left to join the Air Force. Mantronik replaced him with Bryce Luvah (the cousin of LL Cool J) and DJ Dee (Mantronik's own cousin). With 1990's *This Should Move Ya*, Mantronik made the move from hip-hop into more straight-ahead house. With vocalist Wondress in tow, a pair of Mantronix singles stormed the British Top 20, including the Top Five "Got to Have Your Love." He still used the rappers, but continued to work in dance within 1991's *The Incredible Sound Machine*. As a group entity, Mantronix disappeared at that point. Mantronik began producing other acts—mostly female vocalists or freestyle acts—and later exited music altogether. He returned in the mid-'90s as a breakbeat elder statesman, recording as Kurtis Mantronik and providing remixes for EPMD, Future Sound of London, and Dr. Octagon. A Mantronix respective and several album reissues began filtering out in 1999, and Mantronik began recording a new group album later that year. —*John Bush*

★ **Mantronix: The Album** / 1985 / Warlock ✦✦✦✦✦

Kurtis "Mantronik" Khaleel was often quoted as saying that his mission was to "take rap a step beyond the streets," and the innovative producer/mixmaster accomplished that goal on Mantronix's debut album, *Mantronix: The Album*. This excellent 1985 LP was way ahead of its time; while the rapping of Mantronix's partner MC Tee is pure mid-'80s New York hip-hop, the production is anything but conventional. On gems like "Needle to the Groove," "Bassline," and the hit "Fresh Is the Word," you can hear the parallels between Tee's rhyming and the East Coast b-boy rhymes that Run-D.M.C., LL Cool J, and the Fat Boys were providing in 1985. But *Mantronix: The Album*'s high-tech, futuristic production sets it apart from other New York hip-hop of the mid-'80s, and even though one of the LP's tracks is titled "Hardcore Hip-Hop," Mantronix had a hard time appealing to hip-hop's hardcore. *Mantronix: The Album* actually fared better in dance music, electro-funk, and club circles than it did among hardcore b-boys. But this is definitely a hip-hop record, and it is also Mantronix's most essential release. —*Alex Henderson*

Music Madness / 1986 / Sleeping Bag ✦✦✦✦✦

Many Mantronix fans will tell you that the group provided its best and most essential work when it was signed to the small Sleeping Bag label and MC Tee was still on board. Listening to *Music Madness*, it's hard to argue with that. This 1986 LP, which was Mantronix's second album and its last album before leaving Sleeping Bag for Capitol, is proof of how fresh sounding and creative Mantronix was in the beginning. The futuristic outlook that defines "Scream," the single "Who Is It," and other tracks sets *Music Madness* apart from other hip-hop albums that came from New York in 1986; Tee's rapping is very much in the 1980s b-boy tradition, but the club-minded producing and mixing of Kurtis "Mantronik" Khaleel is unlike anything you would have heard on a Run-D.M.C. or LL Cool J album back then. And that fact wasn't lost on hip-hop's hardcore, which felt that *Music Madness* wasn't street enough. Mantronik was fond of saying that his goal was to "take rap a step beyond the streets," and this album tended to attract dance music and electro-funk lovers and club hounds more than hardcore hip-hoppers. *The Album* remains Mantronix's best album, but this excellent LP runs a close second. —*Alex Henderson*

In Full Effect / 1988 / Capitol ✦✦✦

The Capitol debut for Mantronix, and the final album featuring rapper MC Tee, this album skirted the lower regions of the pop charts and had a less abrasive, smoother sound, although the patented dance/hip-hop/urban contemporary fusion hadn't been affected. But overall, it wasn't quite as risky or spirited as their Sleeping Bag records, despite Mantronik's continuing production excellence. —*Ron Wynn*

This Should Move Ya / 1990 / Capitol ✦✦✦

Mantronix switched labels in the late '80s, moving from the independent Sleeping Bag to the major label Capitol. This was their second Capitol album, and it worked out fine. Although the lineup had now changed, with Bryce Luvah and D.J.D. on board rather than MC Tee, the group had another strong single in "Got To Have Your Love," and Capitol was providing Kurtis "Mantronik" Kahleel with a bigger push and sharper production and sound. But the underground spirit that permeated Mantronix's Sleeping Bag albums was missing, as was the quirky air that marked their past singles. —*Ron Wynn*

The Incredible Sound Machine / Mar. 18, 1991 / Capitol ✦✦

Mantronix's high-tech and futuristic approach fared better in clubs and dance music circles than among b-boys and hip-hoppers, but make no mistake: the New York group created some of the most memorable rap of the mid-'80s. Unfortunately, things began unraveling for Mantronix artistically when it left the small (and now defunct) Sleeping Bag Records for Capitol. A pedestrian effort that surprisingly favors R&B, new jack swing, and house music over rap, *The Incredible Sound Machine* contains nothing that's even a fraction as imaginative as Mantronix's Sleeping Bag recordings. Rapper MC Tee is gone, and leader/producer Kurtis "Mantronik" Khaleel is joined by singer Jade Trini, among others. Trini's singing isn't bad—it's the material that's so forgettable and generic. —*Alex Henderson*

The Best of Mantronix 1985-1999 / Mar. 15, 1999 / Virgin ✦✦✦✦✦

A solid Mantronix compilation (though U.K. only) for all those unable to find the out of print originals, *The Best of Mantronix 1985-1999* includes undeniable hip-hop classics like "Bassline," "Ladies," and "King of the Beats"

as well as a new single, "Push Yer Hands Up" (which had first appeared on Mantronix's 1998 solo album). —*John Bush*

That's My Beat / 2002 / Soul Jazz ✦✦✦✦

As record store bins began to collapse under the weight of a baffling bumper crop of various-artist compilations put together by everyday artists, free of mixing ("I've never heard of this fellow but I absolutely need two songs on here"), it was pleasantly surprising that room was left for an innovator like Kurtis Mantronik to take his own turn at the game. *That's My Beat* goes way back to the time when Mantronik was coming up as a young buck (most of these tracks were originally released prior to his debut, 1985's *Mantronix: The Album*), and it exemplifies the mixed bag of electro, disco, and rap that helped form the sound of New York during the early '80s. This might as well be the fifth volume of Tommy Boy's phenomenal *Perfect Beats* series. For a record to become popular with party people during this era, it didn't matter who made it and it didn't matter if it was slow or fast—as long as it moved bodies, it got played. On this disc, a rather happy medium is found between scene standards (Yellow Magic Orchestra's kitschy but ever spectacular "Computer Games," the Art of Noise's concrete-bustin' "Beatbox," Funky Four Plus One's undeniably classic "That's the Joint") and less-popular but inspired choices (Machine's "There but for the Grace of God," Unlimited Touch's "I Hear the Music in the Streets," and Suzy-Q's "Get on up and Do It Again" are underground disco gems). While it's true that old jocks and younger trainspotters might groan at the availability of most of these tracks, those who are returning to this music or are finding it for the first time are in for a real good time. —*Andy Kellman*

Christian Marclay

b. 1955, San Rafael, CA

DJ, Producer / Experimental, Turntablism, Conceptual Art, Avant-Garde, Free Improvisation

Christian Marclay was the first non-rap DJ to make an art form out of the turntable, treating the instrument as a means to rip songs apart, not bridge them together. A longtime associate of Downtown improv figures John Zorn, Elliott Sharp, and Butch Morris as well as the Kronos Quartet, Marclay was inspired artistically by Joseph Beuys and musically by John Cage and the Fluxus group after a period studying at the Massachusetts College of Art. He noted the experimental applications made possible by using the turntable in ways hardly recommended by owners manuals and began performing as early as 1979. Marclay's methods included standard scratching, playback on damaged turntables, the actual destruction (and reassembly) of vinyl to record the results, and creating musical juxtapositions by mixing together a variety of radically different artists. His 1985 installation *Footsteps* included a gallery floor lined with thousands of records for people to walk over (the results were packaged and sold). His 1988 LP *More Encores* featured tributes to a variety of musical figures, including "John Cage" (recorded by gluing together pieces of several records to create one) and "Louis Armstrong" (using a hand-cranked gramophone to alter the pitch). Though he recorded much more sparingly in the 1990s, Marclay continued to appear on Zorn projects, including several editions of his *Filmworks* series. The Atavistic label has released the retrospective *Records 1981-1989. Moving Parts* was released in 2000. —*John Bush*

More Encores: Christian Marclay Plays With the Records Of . . . / 1988 / ReR ✦✦✦

Christian Marclay may be the unwitting inventor of turntablism. This disc is a stellar example of why. The music here is by such unlikely compatriots as Johann Strauss, John Zorn, John Cage, Serge Gainsbourg and Jane Birkin, Ferrante and Teicher, Louis Armstrong, Martin Denny, Maria Callas, Jimi Hendrix, and Frederic Chopin. Basically, Marclay terrorizes the listener with his turntable manipulations of music by these artists. Each of the pieces here is dedicated to an artist whose records were used to create it. In the case of the Cage composition, Marclay cut slices from several records and pasted them back together on a single disc. On everything else, the records were mixed together via several turntables simultaneously, then recorded and overdubbed in analog. So what does it sound like? It's a mess, pure and simple. But in many cases, it's a compelling mess. The Cage piece is one example where the deep cracks in the records are audible as pieces of music from "Works for Prepared Piano," the string quartets and "Atlas Eclipticalis," among others, were used. The Chopin piece is like mad circus music, careening like an organ grinder's monkey got hold of the instrument. The Louis Armstrong track was recorded using a hand-crank gramophone and therefore its non-sampled charm is everywhere present. Also, the Gainsbourg/Birkin track in some ways tracks better than their own songs. Ultimately, though, all the speed changes become irritating throughout. Given that this was the ultimate use of a turntable back in 1988, and was a different take on sampling, it's an interesting disc. (Originally issued as a 10" vinyl record, *More Encores* was reissued on CD by Chris Cutler's Recommended label in 1996.) — *Thom Jurek*

Black Stucco/In "Imaginary Landscapes" / 1989 / Elektra/Nonesuch ◆◆◆◆
Marclay plays turntables—using the clicks of vinyl discs, by scratching, back-and-forth manual rotation, mixing, varispeed, etc.—using recordings as artifacts of society. He has also created art objects with the same records; "Footsteps" is a one-sided record containing the sounds of footsteps. 3,500 copies were spread on the floor of the Shedhalle galleries in Zurich and people were invited to walk on them over the course of six weeks, and 1,000 of the records with dirt and scratches were made available by Gelbe Musik. He has also made a "record without grooves" with a gold label housed in a black velour cover with golden writing, signed and numbered. — *"Blue" Gene Tyranny*

Live Improvisations / 1994 / For 4 Ears ◆◆◆◆
All live improvisations should be this much fun! This live date between turntablist and electronic weirdmeister Christian Marclay and percussionist and electronics tinkerer Günter Müller is what the art of improvisation is supposed to be: fun, continually compelling textually, and inspired. While many intellectuals have made wild pronouncements about Marclay and his art—and it is art, make no mistake—writing all sorts of blather about how he strips the adult century bare by his cutting up of vinyl records and pasting them together with parts from other vinyl records, they never seem to mention that these sound collages of his are charming, very human, and quite often intentionally hilarious. When Marclay is paired with a mischievous percussionist like Müller, anything can happen and always does. Here, swathes of "beautiful music" from the likes of the Bert Kamephert Singers and Orchestra are layered against throbbing drum machines and slamming garbage can lids. There are snippets from the *Wizard of Oz* recordings, laid in swathes against thundering tom toms and shimmering cymbals, and then scratched against backward recordings of "Diddy Wah Diddy" done by a bubblegum teen choir as sheets of glass shatter and the sounds of John Wayne movie gunshots punctuate the mix. Yeah, yeah. Marclay and Müller may sift through the detritus of dead cultural artifacts to make something new, but it's not to make a political statement—it's because it sounds cool as hell. — *Thom Jurek*

● **Records 1981-1989** / Jun. 10, 1997 / Atavistic ◆◆◆◆◆
Records 1981-1989 is a fascinating collection of Marclay's work during the 1980s, the results of hours of home recordings—using up to eight turntables and various other instruments of his own making—plus many live performances (one track comes from a nationally televised appearance on the David Sanborn/Hal Willner program *Night Music*). Marclay did much more than just scratching and sampling for these tracks; "One Thousand Cycles" uses an increasing variety of repeated samples and clicks to create a complex rhythm of its own, while "Pandora's Box" varies the speed on its array of plunderphonics. (Though the latter sounds like an easy contemporary of late-'90s major-label turntablist LPs, it was originally released on a 1984 avant-indie compilation from Sweden that also featured Sonic Youth and Live Skull.) — *John Bush*

High Noon / 2000 / Intakt ◆◆◆◆◆
This duo of tone manipulator and distorter Christian Marclay and electric guitarist and synthesizer whiz Elliott Sharp pushes the limits with twisted sounds galore. Like a painting by Dali, there is a surreal feel to it all, a dreamlike trance interrupted repeatedly by never-ending nightmares. Pops, clicks, warbles, bangs, and dizzying bubblegum-like twists are interspersed with clanking metal to produce collages of some of the weirdest stuff on disk. Marclay is so seldom heard from that each of his recordings is a treasure, and this one is no exception. He takes Sharp's already disfigured lines and manages to mangle them further so that they are barely recognizable in their sliced- and-diced, transformed evolutionary state. It is hard to identify all of Sharp's instruments, but there is touch of what sounds like bass clarinet, shriveled by Marclay's deconstruction. The results are highly disturbing, but

gloriously so. Unadulterated noise/music, there is a clear "take no prisoners" approach, one which is sure to delight or incite. — *Steven Loewy*

Fuck Shit Up / Jan. 1, 2000 / Victo ◆◆◆
May 24, 1999: Sonic Youth members perform at the Festival International de Musique Actuelle de Victoriaville for the third time in four years. This time around, guitarists Thurston Moore and Lee Ranaldo flank experimental turntablist Christian Marclay. An audience member shouts, "F*ck sh*t up" just before they start playing—an album title delivered for free. And then they dived, playing a 63-minute set, followed by a nine-minute encore, bringing the festival to an end. Marclay weaves a backdrop of sounds—strange snippets of music, needle skipping, and surface noise—while Moore and Ranaldo produce huge waves of feedback and walls of electric guitar sounds. The piece aims at being organic, but it just doesn't quite reach that state. Was it communication problems? But the performers were mostly working each in their own corner. They produced a nice gust of sound, but it hardly came together and connected—fact is, the set almost collapsed halfway through. The encore finds Marclay delivering the performance of the night, blending noise rock with Dixie and Elvis Presley while Ranaldo accompanies him on what must be one of the last crackleboxes still around: the highlight of the album. The album was mixed down from two recordings of the show, one made in the venue itself, the other from Radio-Canada. — *François Couture*

Moving Parts / Aug. 8, 2000 / Asphodel ◆◆◆
Performer, sculptor, and sound artist Christian Marclay has been experimenting with phonograph records and turntables, applying the constructs of hip-hop to avant-garde sound art deconstruction since 1979. Having teamed up with Japanese turntablist and guitar player Otomo Yoshihide for their collaboration *Moving Parts*, the two continue in their ongoing quest to evolve music and sound far beyond anything that is even remotely accessible to a mainstream audience. *Moving Parts* is a ravenous bricolage of plunderphonics, pulling sounds from cut-up and reassembled records and the turntable itself. Even with all the noise, *Moving Parts* succeeds on a heady plane of association where, as Marshall McLuhan would definitely state, "The medium is the message." Juxtaposing Hawaiian guitars, gas being released from valves, faint carnival noises, and double-bass pluckings, Marclay and Yoshihide assemble these harsh noises with the elegance of impressionist painters. And that is truly how they might imagine themselves, painting subtle pictures that change with each viewing depending on the angle and distance with which they are seen. *Moving Parts* toys with the endless possibility of chance and takes the greatest pleasure in knowing that listeners will either passionately love or actively hate listening to this record. — *Ken Taylor*

Acoustiphobia, Vol. 1 / 2001 / Sublingual ◆◆◆◆
This two-disc set is actually two separate albums. The first is a live recording made by an ad hoc trio consisting of turntablist Christian Marclay, percussionist Ikue Mori (on drum machines), and guitarist/saxophonist Elliott Sharp, all of them mainstays of New York's downtown avant-garde scene. The second is a compilation of 20 compositions by students at the Boston Museum of Fine Arts' Sonic Arts program, where Sharp, Marclay, and Mori have all been visiting artists. Both discs are rewarding, each in a different way. The first disc is a treasure simply because new material by any one of these three artists is always worth hearing; improvising together, they create soundscapes that are by turns eerie, amusing, dense, and pointillistic. Sharp's approach to his instruments is completely unbounded by any traditional considerations, and the noises he produces are otherworldly; Marclay is a pioneering virtuoso of turntable manipulation, skilled at using the decks to take familiar sounds and twist them beyond recognition; and Mori spends at least as much time using her drum machines to produce pitches and textures as to produce beats. Somebody needs to get the three of them into a studio, and more than once. The student pieces on disc two are, understandably, a bit less consistent, but there are several distinct high points, such as Luke Walker's very lovely "Selma" and David Matorin's ingenious and beautiful "Clock Phase." These are highlights, but everything on the second disc is worth hearing. This one is highly recommended. — *Rick Anderson*

Marky Mark & the Funky Bunch

f. 1990, Boston, MA
Group / Pop-Rap, Club/Dance
It's almost hard to believe given the commercial and critical success later enjoyed by Mark Wahlberg as a screen actor that he was once the laughingstock

of the hip-hop nation—under the guise of Funky Bunch leader Marky Mark, Wahlberg was a pretty-boy pariah within the rap community, although he did score a chart-topping pop smash with the single "Good Vibrations." Wahlberg was born in Dorchester, MA, on June 5, 1971; at 13, he and older brother Donnie were recruited by teen pop svengali Maurice Starr to join the producer's latest project, New Kids on the Block. After just three months Mark left the group, although Donnie stayed on; the New Kids went on to emerge as one of the most commercially successful pop acts of the decade, earning untold millions on recordings and merchandise that appealed almost exclusively to teenage girls. In the meantime, Mark ran afoul of the law—in 1986 he was charged with racial harassment of a group of African-American students, and two years later he spent 45 days in prison after attacking a Vietnamese man. (Both incidents were detailed on the fan site www.markrobertwahlberg.com as part of a time line with the subhead "Mark Wahlberg—the loser.") Donnie agreed to help his troubled sibling restart his music career if he cleaned up his act, and after adopting the stage name Marky Mark, in 1990 Wahlberg formed the Funky Bunch with dancers/rappers Scott Ross (aka Scottie Gee), Hector Barros (Hector the Booty Inspector), Anthony Thomas (Ashley Ace), and Terry Yancey (DJ-T).

Donnie Wahlberg not only agreed to produce his brother's music, but also landed the Funky Bunch a slot opening for New Kids on the Block; the group's debut LP, *Music for the People*, followed in 1991, topping the pop charts on the strength of its lead single, "Good Vibrations," which also hit number one. Rap purists were appalled by Wahlberg's mediocre lyrical skills, lame samples, and tired beats, but the same teenage constituency that embraced the New Kids bought the record in droves—he also earned the approval of some older fans based on a series of revealing Calvin Klein underwear ads, even enjoying a rumored affair with Madonna. *You Gotta Believe* followed in 1992, but in the wake of Nirvana's landmark *Nevermind*, audiences had forsaken fluffy teen pop for grunge, and the record failed badly in its attempts to recapture the success of its predecessor. The Funky Bunch never formally disbanded, but in 1993 Wahlberg made his film debut in the direct-to-video effort *The Substitute*, and then earned surprisingly strong critical notices for his work in 1994's *Renaissance Man* and the following year's *The Basketball Diaries*. He earned his first starring role with 1996's *Fear*, and in 1997 rocketed onto Hollywood's A list with his starmaking turn as well-endowed porn star Dirk Diggler in Paul Thomas Anderson's much-acclaimed *Boogie Nights*. Solid work in films including *Three Kings* and *The Perfect Storm* further rehabilitated Wahlberg's image, and as the new millennium dawned he was firmly ensconced as a leading man, headlining projects including 2001's remake of *Planet of the Apes* and the following year's *The Truth About Charlie*. Theologians still maintain there is a special place in Hell reserved for Wahlberg in return for the pain he inflicted during his mercifully brief career as a rapper. —*Jason Ankeny*

● **Music for the People** / 1991 / Interscope ✦✦✦
On the strength of the number-one hit "Good Vibrations" and the Top Ten follow-up "Wildside," Marky Mark & the Funky Bunch's first album became a pop sensation. Unfortunately, the rest of the album couldn't match the catchy, pop-oriented rap of the singles, making the entire record a hit-or-miss affair. —*Stephen Thomas Erlewine*

You Gotta Believe / 1992 / Interscope ✦✦✦
Marky Mark tried to keep riding the wave he had enjoyed with *Music for the People*, but failed to score any pop or R&B hit, finding that it's much tougher to find another hit to scavenge or maintain a gimmick the second time around. He eventually enjoyed moderate success with "You Gotta Believe," but a combination of some ill-timed homophobic remarks in an interview and rather limp material like "Bout Time I Funk You" and "I Run Rhymes" extinguished whatever fires Marky Mark had previously lit. —*Ron Wynn*

Marley Marl (Marlon Williams)

b. Sep. 30, 1962, Queens, NY
Producer, DJ / Golden Age, Hip-Hop, Old School Rap, Pop-Rap
One of hip-hop's first (and finest) superproducers, Marley Marl was an early innovator in the art of sampling, developing new techniques that resulted in some of the sharpest beats and hooks in rap's golden age. As the founder of Cold Chillin' Records, Marl assembled a roster filled with some of the finest hip-hop talent in New York: MC Shan, Big Daddy Kane, Biz Markie, Roxanne Shanté, Kool G Rap & DJ Polo, and Masta Ace. His production work for those

and many other artists generally boasted a bright, booming, and robust sound that—along with his ear for a catchy sample—helped move street-level hip-hop's sonic blueprint into more accessible territory. Most important, though, were his skills as a beatmaker; Marl was among the first to mine James Brown records for grooves and also learned how to craft his own drum loops through sampling, which decreased hip-hop's reliance on tinny-sounding drum machines and gave his '80s productions a fresh, modern flavor.

Marley Marl was born Marlon Williams on September 30, 1962, and grew up in the Queensbridge housing project in Queens, NY. He became interested in music through local talent shows and neighborhood parties and became an accomplished DJ during rap's early days. He did mixing work on a number of singles for the old school hip-hop/electro label Tuff City and started up his own Cold Chillin' label, which he initially ran out of his sister's apartment in Queensbridge. Marl set about recruiting for what became one of rap's first talent collectives, the Juice Crew. He caught his first big break in 1984 when he produced Roxanne Shanté's "Roxanne's Revenge," one of many answer singles inspired by U.T.F.O.'s underground smash "Roxanne, Roxanne"; luckily, "Roxanne's Revenge" was the biggest and it put artist, label, and producer on the map. Marl trumped it by helming "The Bridge," an ode to Queensbridge by his cousin MC Shan that became the unofficial Queens rap anthem and inspired a spirited feud with Bronx native KRS-One. With Marl's success came the opportunity to produce artists outside the Cold Chillin' stable, which he did with the monumental Eric B. & Rakim single "Eric B. Is President," as well as full-length albums by Heavy D & the Boyz.

The end of the '80s is often referred to as hip-hop's golden age, a time when the form's creativity was expanding by leaps and bounds. Marl's Juice Crew was an important force in ushering in this era thanks to its advances in lyrical technique and the distinctive personalities of emerging stars like Biz Markie and Big Daddy Kane. With business at Cold Chillin' booming, Marl put out the first full-length release under his own name in 1988 (he'd previously recorded the single "DJ Cuttin'" in 1985 with the alias NYC Cutter). *In Control, Vol. 1* was mostly a showcase for various Juice Crew affiliates to strut their stuff, most thrillingly on the legendary, larger-than-life posse cut "The Symphony." Marl scored his greatest crossover success in 1990 by helming LL Cool J's *Mama Said Knock You Out*; bolstered by Marl's state-of-the-art production, the album restored LL's street credibility while becoming his biggest seller ever, making Marl an in-demand remixer. 1991 brought the release of *In Control, Vol. 2*, which unfortunately displayed signs that the Cold Chillin' talent pool was being depleted.

After working with TLC on their 1992 debut, Marl remained mostly quiet for a few years; 1995 brought the release of *House of Hits*, an excellent retrospective of his best productions over the years. Splitting off from Cold Chillin', Marl spent several years in a legal battle over money and ownership rights that, in 1998, finally resulted in his being awarded control of all the songs he'd produced for the label. In the late '90s, Marl's status as a high-profile producer was restored thanks to his work with artists like Rakim, Queensbridge's own Capone-N-Noreaga, and Fat Joe. In 2001, Marl put together another compilation of original productions with guest rappers for the British BBE label, titled *Re-Entry*. —*Steve Huey*

In Control, Vol. 1 / 1988 / Cold Chillin' ✦✦✦✦✦
In Control, Vol. 1 is a greatest-hits package (of a sort) featuring singles Marley Marl produced for his stable of artists on the Cold Chillin' label. Mostly, though, the album serves to show exactly how important Marley Marl was to the advancement of hip-hop. Before him, hip-hop relied mostly on primitive, artificial sounding 808 drum machine beats. He transformed the genre completely with his stock of drum loops, most lifted from James Brown records. His crisp beats enlivened hip-hop and set the tone for the sample madness that would eventually consume producers. *In Control, Vol. 1* includes some of the best moments from the producer's hip-hop revolution. Rap heavyweights Biz Markie and Heavy D try their hand at a Barry Manilow impression on their transformation of "We Write the Songs." Masta Ace and Action attempt some hip-hop upliftment on "Keep Your Eyes on the Prize," and Master Ace, Craig G., Kool G Rap, and Big Daddy Kane join forces for one of the best posse cuts in hip-hop history, "The Symphony." While some of these rappers, most notably Heavy D and Big Daddy Kane, would go on to further success, none ever would sound this tight again. Marley Marl's groundbreaking production and the strength of the various MCs showcased on *In Control, Vol. 1* make the album a must for anyone even remotely interested in hip-hop's history. —*Christopher Witt*

In Control, Vol. 2 / 1991 / Cold Chillin' ◆◆◆
By the time of the release of Marley Marl's *In Control, Vol. 2*, three years after the release of volume 1, hip-hop had changed paths. In 1988, Marley Marl's repertoire of drum loops and James Brown samples were revolutionary, but in 1991 they were anything but fresh. Even worse, Big Daddy Kane, Biz Markie, and most of the other artists who made *In Control, Vol. 1* such a success had parted ways with Marley Marl. On *In Control, Vol. 2*, the producer relies on a new set of artists. Unknowns such as MC Amazing, MC Cash, and Kevy Kev try their best, but they can't summon the energy of the original roster. A couple of unfortunate R&B songs and an excursion into reggae do nothing to lift the album. —*Christopher Witt*

★ **House of Hits** / Jun. 11, 1995 / Cold Chillin' ◆◆◆◆◆
Cold Chillin' certainly deserved the title *House of Hits* during the late '80s, with dozens of the best rappers recording classic tracks that placed high on urban play lists, if not the pop charts themselves. Marley Marl was blessed with a stable boasting immense talents, ranging from hardcore rhymers Big Daddy Kane and Kool G Rap to freewheeling talents Biz Markie and Masta Ace. As the classic *House of Hits* compilation ably proves over 15 tracks, Marley Marl was a master of tailoring productions to the talents of his varying rappers—from the hardcore intensity of Kool G Rap & DJ Polo on "Poison" to the quick-paced vocal dexterity of Big Daddy Kane on "Set It Off" to the all-in-one classic posse track "Symphony, Vol. 1" (with Masta Ace, Craig G., Kool G Rap, and Big Daddy Kane). Even the same artist could get wildly different tracks; Biz Markie played up the clown prince on "Make the Music With Your Mouth, Biz," but also indulged in some humdrum cynicism for "Vapors" over a production to match. Fans of Cold Chillin' will want to dig deeper with separate volumes on most of the artists here, but few rap compilations match *House of Hits* at illustrating a standard unmatched by any label save Def Jam and Sugar Hill. —*John Bush*

The Best of Cold Chillin': In Control, Vols. 1-2 / Oct. 9, 2001 / Landspeed ◆◆◆◆◆

Re-Entry / Oct. 23, 2001 / Beat Generation ◆◆◆
At 39 years of age, veteran rap producer Marley Marl's return to recording came as part of the London-based BBE (Barely Breaking Even) label's *Beat Generation* series. The series was an attempt to reclaim hip-hop from the clutches of overexposure. While Marl hadn't really recorded a true full-length album since his *In Control, Vol. 2* in 1991, he remained a fixture in the hip-hop community (and influence on producers like Pete Rock and Jay Dee), producing tracks throughout the '90s for artists such as Capone-N-Noreaga, Rakim, and K Def & Larry O. Marl was directly responsible for putting together the Juice Crew, one of hip-hop's all-time elite teams that included the likes of Roxanne Shanté, MC Shan, Big Daddy Kane, Masta Ace, and Biz Markie. The Juice Crew's late-'80s battle for rap supremacy with KRS-One and Boogie Down Productions remains one of the most compelling legends of rap lore. *Re-Entry*'s against-the-grain format just might have won over a few young undergrounders, but it is not extraordinary by any stretch. One would have thought that a superproducer of Marl's caliber would fetch a number of big-name MCs; this is unfortunately not the case, with the exception of Big Daddy Kane, Capone, and a couple of talented undergrounders. Some of the old Marl magic does resurface on the thuggish "What U Hold Down," and the maestro even branches out on the jazz-funk exploration "Hummin'," which features hip-hop forefather Roy Ayers. Many of the cuts here are just instrumentals that surely smack of filler, but *Re-Entry* certainly has its moments—moments that might just have some listeners reminiscing back to the Juice Crew era. —*M.F. Di Bella*

Marquis

Vocals, Producer, DJ / Underground Rap
Marquis may not be the most well-known member of Detroit's thriving underground rap scene, but he may be one of the hardest-working up-and-coming rappers in the city's scene. Raised in the Hamtramck area of the Motor City, Marquis first began contributing to the city's rap scene in 1995 when he formed a collective known as Internal Affairs. Following this move, he then began appearing at every imaginable venue in the Detroit area, including notables such as St. Andrews Hall and the Blind Pig. In addition, Marquis also managed to secure the opening slot on many of the hip-hop tours that swept through his city, opening for artists such as the

Hieroglyphics and the GZA, while also performing alongside Detroit's finest talents such as Slum Village and Eminem. His first record, "All About Me!," appeared in 1996 and instantly won him the respect of his peers, many of whom he began collaborating with. Then after years of steady improvement and patience, Marquis reached his largest audience yet with the release of his "Rock tha Beat/Feel the Vibe" 12" on local techno label Intuit-Solar's DTW rap sublabel as he worked on his first full-length album. —*Jason Birchmeier*

Rock tha Beat/Feel the Vibe EP / 2000 / Intuit-Solar ◆◆◆◆
Underground rapper Marquis lets his liquid smooth rhymes flow with a sense of Detroit-centric attitude on the two tracks found on this Intuit-Solar 12" EP. Detroit hip-hop may be primarily associated with psychotic artists such as Eminem, Kid Rock, Esham, and ICP, but Marquis comes from the city's thriving underground scene filled with other rap artists such as Slum Village, Paradime, Da Ruckas, and Hush. Like these latter artists, Marquis doesn't turn to the glamorized clichés of bud, bitches, and bank rolls that Detroit's superstar rappers represent to varying degrees. Furthermore, Marquis retains a good-mannered sense of self-pride as emanated in his feel-good rhymes that seem truly sincere and void of characterization or posing. "Rock the Beat" features the Detroit rapper laying down lyrics about having a good time in his hometown without focusing on ghetto themes but rather optimistic motifs that envision a laid-back city to chill in. On the flip side of the EP, Marquis drops a fun party tune that should incite plenty of joy in listeners and will work well in any festive context. Both songs and their accompanying instrumental versions are only strengthened by some soulful production that looks back to the heart-bleeding aural sentiment of Motown and to the clean, upbeat production found on the albums of East Coast artists such as A Tribe Called Quest and De La Soul, as well as Detroit producer Jay Dee. The lack of decadent themes and major-label backing may not ever propel this single outside of Detroit, but anyone favoring the optimistic rhymes and let's-make-hip-hop-a-feel-good-music-again attitude should absolutely love this EP. —*Jason Birchmeier*

Angie Martinez

Hip-Hop, East Coast Rap, Latin Rap, Hardcore Rap
Part of the New York City hip-hop scene, Angie Martinez got her start working in radio. Raised in Brooklyn, Martinez was first introduced to music via her mother's diverse (who was a program director for a jazz radio station) musical tastes. Eventually Martinez discovered hip-hop, and after a short stint at a Miami radio station working the phones, she moved back to NYC and began working at the popular dance station Hot 97 FM. Rapper KRS-One encouraged Martinez to give hip-hop a shot herself, impressed by Martinez's improvisational rapping skills. This led to a successful collaboration with Redman, "Heart Beat," as well as working with Mary J. Blige and performing on the Grammy-nominated single "Ladies Night," alongside Missy Elliot, Lil' Kim, Left Eye, and Da Brat. Martinez was signed shortly thereafter to Elektra, issuing her debut album, *Up Close and Personal*, in 2001. —*Greg Prato*

● **Up Close and Personal** / Apr. 17, 2001 / Elektra ◆◆◆◆
It doesn't hurt to have friends like Wyclef Jean, Snoop Dogg, and Mary J. Blige. But Angie Martinez stands her ground when rapping alongside mega-rap stars like these on her debut album, *Up Close and Personal* (Elektra Records). The Hot 97 FM DJ is no stranger to the scene; she's been fraternizing with hip-hop and rap stars and establishing friendships with many of them, including the artists that appear on the album. Martinez shines on tracks like "Gutter to tha Fancy Ish," on which she flaunts her quick-tongued rap technique and a tough-girl attitude while alternating verses with none other than Busta Rhymes. Speaking about hangin' with her girls, Martinez lays the truth down on the line when she says, "Underestimate me is to not know me/Analyze every situation/And I rise to any occasion." On the funky, bass-driven track "New York, New York," Martinez raps with Prodigy and DJ Clue. The album features mostly heavy, bass-driven rap tracks, but Martinez's playfulness trickles in through a pair of brief interludes—recordings of phone conversations with her rapper pals. Martinez then slips smoothly into hip-hop mode with the laid-back track "No Playaz," which showcases Martinez's singing ability and some backup verse from rappers Lil' Mo and Sunshine. "Live at Jimmy's" is by far the most energetic and fun song on the album. Mary J. Blige and La India come on board for the rap track "Breathe," which

could double as a pop tune with its breathy chorus and melodic beats. And Martinez proves that she's no lightweight on the fast-paced, aggressive track "Go!" On her first time around, Martinez has delivered a well-rounded album that features solid raps, Latin grooves, and a few lighter, melodic tunes. In between rapping with some of rap and hip-hop's heaviest hitters, Martinez slips in a mention of HBO's *Sex and the City* on one of the songs. Now, there's a girl you gotta respect. —*Kerry L. Smith*

Animal House / Aug. 20, 2002 / Elektra ♦♦
Martinez's day job is as a DJ at a NYC hip-hop station, and her second album is reason enough for her not to quit. Devoid of style and anything to say, Martinez merely recites her rhymes over flaccid beats, hoping to hook on to something. She falls into nearly all of hip-hop's traps (thankfully, she keeps *Animal House* at a reasonable 45 minutes): overwrought R&B choruses, lame-ass skits, and "featured" turns by guest-rapping B listers. She spins records better than she spins tales, most of which are concerned with giving mad props to herself. Only "If I Could Go" has a discernible hook, and it's a vaguely familiar one at that (same goes for the cut that sounds like it was cribbed from Jay-Z's *Blueprint* reel). Clearly, Martinez fancies herself a baby sis to Missy Elliott (who cameos) and Eve. But it's tough trekking when the beats are this sparse and the rhymes this ho-hum. Maybe she can get her pals at the radio station to play it. —*Michael Gallucci*

Marvaless

Group / Hardcore Rap, West Coast Rap, Gangsta Rap
Sacramento, CA-based hardcore rapper Marvaless debuted in 1994 with *Ghetto Blues*; in addition to successive solo releases including 1995's *Just Marvaless* and 1996's *Wiccked*, she also made a series of guest appearances on records by acts including 2Pac, Conscious Daughters, Mac Mall, Master P's *West Coast Bad Boyz*, and such Awol label mates as Lunasicc and C-Bo. *Fearless* followed in 1998. *Ghetto Blues 2001* appeared three years later. —*Jason Ankeny*

Just Marvaless / Jan. 24, 1995 / Awol ♦♦

Wiccked / Aug. 6, 1996 / Awol ♦♦♦

● **Fearless** / Apr. 21, 1998 / Awol ♦♦♦
Although Marvaless refuses to abandon her hardline hardcore hip-hop stance, the years have treated her well, if her fourth album *Fearless* is anything to go by. She's still spinning gangsta tales, with all the violence, sex and dope clichés that entails, but her music is tougher and catchier than before, and her lyrical flow is the best it has ever been. *Fearless* also boasts an impressive series of cameos—including spots from Lil' Bruce, Killa Tay, 4-C, Lunasicc, Steady Mobbin, Laroo, One Drop Scott, Ric Rok, and C-Bo—that helps make it Marvaless' strongest album to date. —*Leo Stanley*

Mase

b. Aug. 27, 1977, Jacksonville, FL
East Coast Rap, Hip-Hop
Best known as Puff Daddy's favorite sidekick, Mase secured his place as a Bad Boy label favorite through a series of guest appearances on hit singles by other artists. By the time he issued his debut album, the Bad Boy promotional machine had effectively already made him a star. His flow was slow and relaxed, and his raps often unabashedly simple, which helped make him especially popular with the younger segment of Puff Daddy's pop-rap audience (they could understand him and rap along). Of course, he was never much of a critical favorite for exactly the same reason, but that became a moot point when, just before the release of his second album, he announced his retirement from rap to pursue a career in the ministry.

Mase was born Mason Durrell Betha in Jacksonville, FL, on August 27, 1977. His family moved to Harlem when he was five, but at age 13, he was sent back to Florida amid concerns that he was falling in with the wrong crowd. He returned to New York two years later, and began rapping to entertain the other members of his school basketball team. He was a good enough basketball player to win a scholarship to SUNY, but hip-hop soon grew to be more important; under the name Mase Murder, he joined a rap group called Children of the Corn, which disbanded when one of its members died in a car accident. Mase went solo and started making connections around New York's hip-hop club scene. In 1996 he traveled to Atlanta for a music conference, hoping to hook up with Jermaine Dupri; instead, he met Sean "Puffy" Combs, who signed him to Bad Boy after hearing him rap.

Mase debuted on Combs' remix of the 112 single "Only You," and quickly became a near-ubiquitous guest rapper on Bad Boy releases and other Combs-related projects. He was a credited featured guest on the Puff Daddy smashes "Can't Nobody Hold Me Down" and "It's All About the Benjamins," handled the first verse of the Notorious B.I.G.'s number-one hit "Mo' Money, Mo' Problems," and made prominent appearances on Mariah Carey's "Honey," Brian McKnight's "You Should Be Mine (Don't Waste My Time)," Junior M.A.F.I.A.'s "Young Casanova," and Busta Rhymes' "The Body Rock," among others. By showcasing Mase in such high-profile settings, not to mention spotlighting him in several videos as well, Combs ensured that by the time Mase actually released his own album, every hip-hop fan in America would already know who he was.

Thus, when Mase's debut album *Harlem World* appeared in late 1997, it was an instant smash, spending its first two weeks of release on top of the *Billboard* album charts. It was a star-studded affair, naturally featuring Combs (both rapping and producing) and a galaxy of guests: Busta Rhymes, Jay-Z, DMX, Lil' Kim, Monifah, 112, the LOX, Eightball & MJG, Black Rob, and Lil' Cease, not to mention additional production by the Hitmen, Jermaine Dupri, and the Neptunes, among others. Reviews of the record were mixed; some critics praised Mase's unique rapping style, but others were far more harsh (this writer is fairly sure it was Ira Robbins who called Mase "the luckiest no-talent sidekick since Ed McMahon"). Nonetheless, *Harlem World* was a smash hit, eventually going platinum four times over; its first single, "Feels So Good" (which also appeared on the soundtrack of *Money Talks*), was a Top Five pop hit, and the follow-up "What You Want" was a fast-selling success as well.

In the meantime, Mase's string of guest spots continued unabated, with appearances on Brandy's "Top of the World," Puff Daddy's "Lookin' at Me," Cam'ron's "Horse and Carriage," 112's "Love Me," and the *Rugrats* soundtrack collaboration with Blackstreet and Mya, "Take Me There." In April 1998, Mase made headlines with his arrest in New York on disorderly conduct charges (he had initially been accused of soliciting a prostitute, which he denied). But the controversy was short lived, and by year's end Mase had put together his own group of protégés, also dubbed Harlem World, who issued their debut album, *The Movement*, in early 1999. With Puffy's Bad Boy empire still riding high, Mase's second album, *Double Up*, looked to be another blockbuster. But shortly after it was completed (and before it was released), Mase stunned close associates and observers alike by announcing his immediate retirement from the music business, calling it incompatible with his new calling to the ministry (he'd experienced a vision of himself leading people into Hell). He refused to promote *Double Up* with any live performances, although he did give interviews on its behalf. Perhaps it was the lack of promotional support, or perhaps audiences gave up their investment in him, but *Double Up* made a disappointing chart debut at number 11 upon its summer 1999 release, and only reached gold sales status. Despite what some initially thought, Mase's retirement has stuck; in the years since, he has worked extensively with inner-city youth, become an in-demand inspirational speaker on the religious circuit, and published a memoir titled *Revelations: There's a Light After the Lime*. —*Steve Huey*

● **Harlem World** / Oct. 28, 1997 / Bad Boy ♦♦♦♦
It's a little ironic that Mase, who made his reputation as a guest rapper on records by Puff Daddy and the Notorious B.I.G., almost seems like a guest himself on his debut album, *Harlem World*. Like many big-budget hip-hop records, *Harlem World* is nearly a various-artists collection, featuring an array of different producers and guest rappers that often obscure Mase himself. Still, all that talent guarantees that the record will be well crafted, and that certainly is true. With Sean "Puffy" Combs and Jermaine Dupri behind the decks for much of the album, *Harlem World* has a dense, funky sound that is up-tempo party-rap at its best. Like any late-'90s hip-hop record, it's a little too long for its own good, but the singles, such as the bouncy "Feel So Good," make it worthwhile. It still would have been nice to hear more of Mase on his own album, though. —*Leo Stanley*

Double Up / Jun. 15, 1999 / Bad Boy ♦♦♦♦
Shortly after he completed his second album, *Double Up*, Mase announced his retirement from hip-hop. He chose to follow the path of the Lord, which didn't just mean that he could no longer rap—he no longer had the desire to do so. Frustratingly, the album finds Mase continuing to improve, but falling short of delivering a stunning farewell that could stand as his last testament.

Double Up pretty much recycles the same hooktastic pop-rap formulas as *Harlem World*, following Puff Daddy's design of borrowing the best, regardless of the source (for example, Gary Numan provides the basis for one cut), and turning it into radio-ready party music. While this is pleasing to the ear, it tends to be a little monotonous and too predictable, especially when compared to Mase's raps. True, he still favors a flat, slow delivery, but there's a growing undercurrent of distaste for hip-hop clichés, a feeling that ultimately led to Mase throwing in the towel and turning to God. Certainly, this gives *Double Up* more lyrical drama than the average hip-hop album, and it's often enough to keep it compelling when the music flatlines. Still, there's still the sneaking suspicion that *Double Up* could have been more—either an excellent pop-rap record with no flab, or a convincing statement of purpose, evidence of why Mase had to leave hip-hop behind. As it stands, it's simply a good sequel to a promising debut. Which, of course, is all that it needed to be, but in light of Mase's retirement, it's hard not to want more. —*Stephen Thomas Erlewine*

Mass 187

Group / Southern Rap, Dirty South, Gangsta Rap
Mass 187 began promisingly enough with the 1996 hit single "Gangsta Strut" yet never bettered this initial success, quickly being overshadowed by countless other Texas-based rappers following their initial lead. The group debuted in 1996 with *Real Trues Paying Dues*, which made them one of the first Texas rap acts to approach national impact. Even so, Mass 187 never did attain national impact and instead fell into obscurity for a while, resurfacing years later in 2000 with *One Eighty Seven Thugs*. —*Jason Birchmeier*

● **Real Trues Paying Dues** / Aug. 27, 1996 / ffrr ♦♦♦
Despite their best efforts, the trio of Mass 187 turns in a standard gangsta rap record with their debut *Real Trues Paying Dues*. Mass 187 fancies themselves social commentors—gangsta reporters, if you will—so their songs should, in theory, be more incisive and insightful than their gangbanging brethren. You could assume that would be the case, but you would be wrong. Mass 187 is by-the-book gangsta—after all, their first single is "Gangsta Strut," which is hardly an indictment of the pimp lifestyle, is it? Sure, the Houston-based trio can rhyme with dexterity and they know the G-funk when they hear it, but if you just want to hear some beats, there are better places to go. —*Leo Stanley*

One Eighty Seven Thugs / Jul. 11, 2000 / Knock Solid Entertainment ♦♦

Massive Attack

f. 1987, Bristol, England
Group / Alternative Pop/Rock, Club/Dance, Trip-Hop, Alternative Dance, Electronica
The pioneering force behind the rise of trip-hop, Massive Attack were among the most innovative and influential groups of their generation; their hypnotic sound—a darkly sensual and cinematic fusion of hip-hop rhythms, soulful melodies, dub grooves, and choice samples—set the pace for much of the dance music to emerge throughout the 1990s, paving the way for such acclaimed artists as Portishead, Sneaker Pimps, Beth Orton, and Tricky, himself a Massive Attack alumnus. Their history dates back to 1983 and the formation of the Wild Bunch, one of the earliest and most successful soundsystem/DJ collectives to arrive on the U.K. music scene; renowned for their seamless integration of a wide range of musical styles, from punk to reggae to R&B, the group's parties quickly became can't-miss events for the Bristol club crowd, and at the peak of their popularity they drew crowds so enormous that the local live music scene essentially ground to a halt.

When the Wild Bunch folded during the mid-'80s, two of its members—Andrew "Mushroom" Vowles and Grant "Daddy G" Marshall—teamed with local graffiti artist 3D (born Robert Del Naja) to form Massive Attack in 1987; another Wild Bunch alum, Nellee Hooper, split his time between the new group and his other project, Soul II Soul. The group's first single, "Daydreaming," appeared in 1990; it featured the sultry vocals of singer Shara Nelson and raps by Tricky, another onetime Wild Bunch collaborator. The classic "Unfinished Sympathy" followed, as did another compelling effort, "Safe From Harm." Finally, in 1991 Massive Attack issued their debut LP, *Blue Lines*; while by no means a huge commercial success, the record was met with major critical praise, and was dubbed an instant classic in many quarters. Nelson, featured on many of the album's most memorable tracks, exited for a solo career soon after, and the group then

confusingly changed their name to simply "Massive" to avoid any implication of approval for the U.N.'s policy toward Iraq; in the wake of the disastrous U.S. tour that followed, many were quick to write the band off right then and there.

After a three-year layoff, Massive Attack—their full name now properly reinstated—resurfaced with *Protection*; again working with Hooper and Tricky, they also brought into the fold vocalist Nicolette, as well as Everything but the Girl's Tracey Thorn. Three singles—"Karmacoma," "Sly," and the title track—were released from the LP, which was also remixed in its entirety by Mad Professor and issued as *No Protection*. A lengthy tour followed, and over the next several years, Massive Attack's solo work was primarily confined to remixes for artists including Garbage; they also worked with Madonna on a track for a Marvin Gaye tribute album. Finally, to promote their appearance at the annual Glastonbury music festival, the group issued a new EP, *Risingson*, during the summer of 1997. The third full-length Massive Attack effort, *Mezzanine*, appeared in 1998; in addition to reggae singer Horace Andy, making his third consecutive LP appearance with the group, vocal chores were handled by the Cocteau Twins' Elizabeth Fraser and newcomer Sara Jay. *Mezzanine* became a cult hit among critics, clubs, and the college crowds, spinning successful singles such as "Teardrop" and "Inertia Creeps." A tour of America and Europe followed, but Vowles left the band after disagreeing with the artistic direction of *Mezzanine*. Del Naja and Marshall continued as a duo, later working with the likes of David Bowie and the Dandy Warhols, but Marshall later took a leave of absence to raise his family; producer Neil Davidge took up the slack. In February 2003, after a five-year wait, Massive Attack released their fourth album, *100th Window*, including collaborations with mainstay Horace Andy as well as Sinéad O'Connor. —*Jason Ankeny*

★ **Blue Lines** / Aug. 6, 1991 / Virgin ♦♦♦♦♦
The first masterpiece of what was only termed trip-hop much later, *Blue Lines* filtered American hip-hop through the lens of British club culture, a stylish, nocturnal sense of scene that encompassed music from rare groove to dub to dance. The album balances dark, diva-led club jams along the lines of Soul II Soul with some of the best British rap (vocals and production) heard up to that point, occasionally on the same track. The opener "Safe From Harm" is the best example, with diva vocalist Shara Nelson trading off lines with the group's own monotone (yet effective) rapping. Even more than hip-hop or dance, however, dub is the big touchstone on *Blue Lines*. Most of the productions aren't quite as earthy as you'd expect, but the influence is palpable in the atmospherics of the songs, like the faraway electric piano on "One Love" (with beautiful vocals from the near-legendary Horace Andy). One track, "Five Man Army," makes the dub inspiration explicit, with a clattering percussion line, moderate reverb on the guitar and drums, and Andy's exquisite falsetto flitting over the chorus. *Blue Lines* isn't all darkness, either—"Be Thankful for What You've Got" is quite close to the smooth soul tune conjured by its title, and "Unfinished Sympathy"—the group's first classic production—is a tremendously moving fusion of up-tempo hip-hop and dancefloor jam with slow-moving, syrupy strings. Flaunting both their range and their tremendously evocative productions, Massive Attack recorded one of the best dance albums of all time. —*John Bush*

Protection / 1994 / Virgin ♦♦♦♦
Massive Attack's sophomore effort could never be as stunning as *Blue Lines*, and a slight drop in production and songwriting quality made the comparisons easy. Still, from the first two songs *Protection* sounds worthy of their debut. The opening title track is pure excellence, with melancholy keyboards, throbbing acid lines, and fragmented beats perfectly complementing the transcendent vocals of Tracey Thorn (an inspired choice to replace the departed Shara Nelson as their muse). Tricky, another soon-to-be solo performer, makes his breakout on this record, with blunted performances on "Karmacoma," another highlight, as well as "Eurochild." But even though the production is just as intriguing as on *Blue Lines*, there's a bit lacking here—Massive Attack doesn't summon quite the emotional power they did previously. Guest Craig Armstrong's piano work on the aimless tracks "Weather Storm" and "Heat Miser" leans uncomfortably close to Muzak, and his arrangement and conducting for "Sly" isn't much better (vocals by Nicolette save the track somewhat). Though it's still miles ahead of the growing raft of trip-hop making the rounds in the mid-'90s, *Protection* is rather a disappointment. —*John Bush*

No Protection: Massive Attack Vs. Mad Professor / 1995 / Gyroscope
✦✦✦✦

Protection was widely considered a disappointing follow-up to Massive Attack's groundbreaking debut, *Blue Lines*. Where their debut bent all of the conventional hip-hop, dub reggae, and soul rules, *Protection* essentially delivered more of the same. Perhaps that's the reason why Mad Professor's remix of the album, *No Protection*, was welcomed with open arms by both Massive Attack fans and critics. Mad Professor has returned the group to their experimental, cut-and-paste dub reggae and hip-hop roots. He has gutted the songs—twisting and reassembling the vocal tracks, giving the songs deeper, fuller grooves and an eerily seductive atmosphere. In other words, he has made *Protection* into a more daring and fulfilling album with his remixes. —*Stephen Thomas Erlewine*

☆ **Mezzanine** / Apr. 27, 1998 / Virgin ✦✦✦✦✦
Increasingly ignored amidst the exploding trip-hop scene, Massive Attack finally returned in 1998 with *Mezzanine*, a record immediately announcing not only that the group was back but also that they'd recorded a set of songs just as singular and revelatory as on their debut, almost a decade old. It all begins with a stunning one-two-three-four punch: "Angel," "Risingson," "Teardrop," and "Inertia Creeps." Augmenting their samples and keyboards with a studio band, Massive Attack open with "Angel," a stark production featuring pointed beats and a distorted bass line that frames the vocal (by group regular Horace Andy) and a two-minute flame-out with raging guitars. "Risingson" is a dense, dark feature for Massive Attack themselves (on production as well as vocals), with a kitchen sink's worth of dubby effects and reverb. "Teardrop" introduces another genius collaboration—with Elizabeth Fraser from Cocteau Twins—from a production unit with a knack for recruiting gifted performers. The blend of earthy with ethereal shouldn't work at all, but Massive Attack pulls it off in fine fashion. "Inertia Creeps" could well be the highlight, another feature for just the core threesome. With eerie atmospherics, fuzz-tone guitars, and a wealth of effects, the song could well be the best production from the best team of producers the electronic world had ever seen. Obviously, the rest of the album can't compete, but there's certainly no sign of the side-two slump heard on *Protection*, as both Andy and Fraser return for excellent, mid-tempo tracks ("Man Next Door" and "Black Milk," respectively). —*John Bush*

100th Window / Feb. 11, 2003 / Virgin ✦✦✦✦
A new album from Massive Attack is an event, even if only one-third of the original group is present for the festivities. Just the group's fourth album in more than a dozen years, *100th Window* marked the departure of Mushroom (permanently, after artistic differences) and Daddy G (temporarily, to raise a family), leaving only one founding member, 3D (Robert Del Naja), to muddle along with arranger/producer Neil Davidge (who made his Massive Attack debut on 1998's *Mezzanine*). Though Del Naja is mostly successful giving the people what they want—a follow-up to *Mezzanine*, one of the most compulsive listens of '90s electronica—it unfortunately comes as a sacrifice to the very thing that made Massive Attack so crucial to dance music: their never-ending progression to a radically different sound with each release. For better or worse, *100th Window* has the same crushingly oppressive productions, dark, spiraling bass lines, and pile-driving beats instantly familiar to fans of *Mezzanine*. Fortunately, it also has the same depth and point-perfect attention to detail, making for fascinating listening no matter whether the focus is the songs, the effects, or even the percussion lines. Jamaican crooner Horace Andy is back for a pair of tracks ("Everywhen," "Name Taken") that nearly equal his features on the last record, while Sinéad O'Connor makes her debut with three vocal features. Unlike Liz Fraser or Tracey Thorn (two Massive Attack muses from the past), O'Connor's voice lacks resonance and doesn't reward the close inspection that a Massive Attack production demands. Still, her songwriting is far superior and the slight quaver in her voice adds a much-needed personality to these songs. "A Prayer for England" is a political protest that aligns itself perfectly with the group that coined its name as a satirical nod to military aggression. Another feature for O'Connor, "What Your Soul Sings," is the only song here that compares to the best Massive Attack has to offer, beginning with a harsh, claustrophobic atmosphere, but soon blossoming like a flower into a beautiful song led by her tremulous voice. In comparison, the four songs for 3D (the only MA member who ever sang) are average at best, mere recyclings of the same ideas heard years

earlier. That's satisfaction enough for those who kept *Mezzanine* near their stereo for years on end, but a disappointment to those expecting another masterpiece. —*John Bush*

Masta Ace (Duval Clear)

b. Brooklyn, NY
Vocals, Mixing, Executive Producer / East Coast Rap, Hip-Hop, Golden Age
With an impressive resume in rap that includes membership in the legendary Juice Crew (along with Marley Marl, MC Shan, Big Daddy Kane, Biz Markie, Roxanne Shanté, and Craig G) and a verse on the 1988 classic posse cut "The Symphony," Brooklyn's Masta Ace is truly an underappreciated rap veteran and underground luminary. Two years after "The Symphony," Ace released his debut album *Take a Look Around* on rap's version of the Motown label, Cold Chillin' Records. While not a huge commercial success, the album spawned a hit single and video for "Me and the Biz" which popped up on many popular rap video shows in the late '90s for nostalgia's sake. The album has Marley Marl's keen production aura all over it and also features a guest appearance from the Biz himself. After three years on the hush, Ace returned to the fold in 1993 this time with his crew as Masta Ace Incorporated (Lord Digga and Paula Perry) and dropped *SlaughtaHouse*. The album broke new ground by taking the synthesized West Coast sound and filtering it through an East Coast mentality. The memorable "Born to Roll," with its tweaked Moog/Kraftwerk bass line, brought Ace some serious commercial attention. In 2000 De La Soul used this classic beat on a remix of "All Good" featuring Chaka Khan. The album also produced a few hits for undergrounders including "Jeep Ass Niguhz" and "Style Wars." The album is highly notable for its cross-coast compatibility. In 1995 Masta Ace Incorporated dropped *Sittin' on Chrome*, a continuation of the themes on *SlaughtaHouse* and owning an even slicker sound. Using the Isley Brothers' much-sampled "For the Love of You" for the track "I.N.C. Ride" may have offended some of Ace's loyal fans, but the song's catchy vibe made it a hit. *Sittin' on Chrome* is another album chock full of Jeep beats that doesn't relinquish its standing with underground tastes. "B Side" and "4 the Mind" featuring the Cella Dwellas are also crucial jams. Ace has been known to release sleeper singles that cannot be found on his albums; one of the rarest, 1996's "Ya Hardcore," is a bumping indictment of studio gangsters and thug rap neophytes. The talented survivor in the rap game released a variety of singles in 2000 including "Hellbound," a duet with Eminem, giving him over twelve years of experience in the rap biz. —*Michael Di Bella*

Take a Look Around / Jul. 24, 1990 / Cold Chillin' ✦✦✦✦✦
Take a Look Around, Masta Ace's throbbing, Marley Marl-produced debut, mixed the loopy humor of Biz Markie (who shares a cut here, on "Me and the Biz") with the urgency of the best LL Cool J. The best cut by far is "Music Man," but nearly every track is up to a high caliber, including "Can't Stop the Bum Rush," "I Got Ta," and "Letter to the Better." —*John Floyd*

SlaughtaHouse / May 4, 1993 / Delicious Vinyl ✦✦✦✦✦
Five years after making his name as a member in Marley Marl's legendary Juice Crew (he was one of the featured MCs on the classic 1988 posse cut "The Symphony" from Marl's *In Control, Vol. 1*) and three years after recording his buoyant, artistically on-point (though commercially stillborn) debut album *Take a Look Around*, with its memorable hit duet with Biz Markie "Me and the Biz," the battle-scarred Brooklyn underground star returned for his second album with a newly tweaked name and his own supporting crew (Masta Ace Incorporated), a new sound and sharply honed style, and a cynical new outlook on the entire rap game. In fact, a disgusted new outlook might be a more appropriate characterization, as a controlled abhorrence oozes from every pore of *SlaughtaHouse*, lashing out not only at easy outside targets (bigoted police, for instance) but also at those shady characters inside the "Slaughtahouse" whose violence is enacted physically (Ace himself places the part of a mugger on "Who U Jackin?") rather than lyrically, bringing the entire community down in the process. A loose concept album, it is at once an intense exposé and a roughneck paean to the hip-hop lifestyle that broke new ground by merging the grimy lyrical sensibility, scalpel-precise technique, and kitchen-sink beats of East Coast rap with the funk-dripping, anchor-thick low-end of West Coast producers. The classic "Jeep Ass Nigguh" was one of the quintessential cruising singles of the summer of 1993. Its unlisted remix "Born to Roll," with its supersonic gangsta bass, is an equally thumping highlight, and (with its sample borrowed from N.W.A's "Real Niggas Don't Die") can be seen as the most explicit bridge between East and West. But

other hectic, relentless tracks like "The Big East," "Rollin' Wit Umdadda," and "Saturday Nite Live" are just as excellent, and Ace's crew—particularly Bluez Brothas Lord Digga and Witchdoc—really shine. —*Stanton Swihart*

Sittin' on Chrome / May 2, 1995 / Delicious Vinyl ✦✦✦
Although it suffers from the same lack of imagination and uneven songwriting that plagued *SlaughtaHouse*, Masta Ace's second album, *Sittin' on Chrome*, is a stronger effort than his debut. The best tracks show that Masta Ace Incorporated can turn out by-the-books gangsta rap with flair, but it's a little distressing that the best song, "Born to Roll," was initially featured as a bonus track on *SlaughtaHouse*. —*Stephen Thomas Erlewine*

● **The Best of Cold Chillin'** / May 22, 2001 / Cold Chillin' ✦✦✦✦✦
Masta Ace has always seemed to remain on the edges of hip-hop, leaving long periods between albums, often leaving fans wondering if there will even be another album. One thing is for sure though, Ace has had his share of neighborhood hits, most notably "Music Man," "Can't Stop the Bumrush," and his duo with old school rapper Biz Markie, "Me and the Biz." This compilation is an assortment of Masta Ace's work from his days on the Cold Chillin' record label that housed such legendary artists as MC Shan, Marley Marl, Roxanne Shanté, Kool G Rap, Big Daddy Kane, Wu-Tang Clan's Genius, and KRS-One. —*Brad Mills*

Disposable Arts / Oct. 18, 2001 / JCOR ✦✦✦✦
After a six-year period of disillusionment with the rap game, onetime Juice Crew member Masta Ace returned with this supposed sayonara album that reads like a bittersweet memoir. Though Ace had been active in the underground scene since the release of 1995's *Sittin' on Chrome*, appearing on a number of singles and contributing memorable verses to various collaborations, the artist's disdain for the industry and disgust with his contemporaries kept him out of the studio for lengthy recording sessions. Feeling that rap's heyday had passed with the deaths of rappers like 2Pac and Biggie, and seeing a media- and market-influenced, watered-down product, *Disposable Arts* broods with anger, cynicism, and satire for the modern rapper bent purely on trend capitalizing. The paradox here is that Ace himself seems to seek and feels worthy of the same multimillion that he accuses his contemporaries of securing through less-than-artistic means. The burden of underground respect that nets only underground sales seems to be the primary source of Ace's frustration. While smacking of classic player hate, Ace's response for the Cash Money Millionaires and Roc-A-Fellas of hip-hop is: "The rap game's a book and I read mad chapters/And if you ask me, it ain't enough Madd Rappers." Ace enlists a healthy balance of true schoolers (King T and Greg Nice) and eccentric up-and-comers (Punch, Words, and the delightfully weird MC Paul Barman) for the project. Musically, the album offers anything but the disposable; highlights include the eerie narrative "Take a Walk," the fierce dis record "Acknowledge," and the ingenious "Alphabet Soup," where Ace runs through the alphabet with some witty old school rhymes. More four-alarm flames light up "Something's Wrong," the psychedelic "Dear Diary," and the thumping homage to the West Coast, "P.T.A." A knockout punchliner with an airtight flow and delivery, Ace, in the face of everything he hates about hip-hop, turns in his most expansively satisfying work. With 24 strong tracks and only faint signs of misstep, *Disposable Arts* is tightly wrought thematically, musically, and lyrically, not to mention one heck of a parting shot. Most hip-hop albums of the modern era are lucky to cover even one of these areas. —*M.F. Di Bella*

Masta Plann

f. Philippines
Group / G-Funk, East Coast Rap
The Philippine hip-hop duo Masta Plann is comprised of Johnny "Tha Nontypical One" Luna and Butch "Supa Flip" Velez, who has also been known as Tracer One in the past. The duo has also been affiliated with DJ M.O.D. (real name: Noel Macanoya). The crew first appeared with 1992's *Masta Plann*. Released through Universal Philippines, the album established the crew as boasters of the highest order, content to emulate the chest thumping and territory marking of U.S. West Coast rap, while keeping the beats decidedly less extreme. *Way of the Plann* followed in 1994, and Masta Plann returned to the Philippine hip-hop scene in 2000 with *MastaPlann.Com*. Of course, the album was bursting at the seams with boastful rhetoric from Tha Nontypical and Supa Flip—the two MCs did so much bragging that they even alienated some fans who took issue with their hiatus, as well as their album's title, which some labeled a cheap shot at legitimacy in the age of the Internet.

Musically, the album broke no new ground. Masta Plann did score a hit, however, with "Crowd Pleazer," a rousing anthem based on a sample from Jean Knight's "Mr. Big Stuff." Lyrically, the song described—wait for it—the incredible greatness of Masta Plann. Nontypical One and Supa Flip—humble to the end. —*Johnny Loftus*

● **MastaPlann.Com** / 2000 / Musiko ✦✦✦
Philippine rap band Masta Plann believes they're masters of rap, and on 2000's *MastaPlann.Com*, they never let you forget it. Right away, on the opening "Reel Thang," Masta Plann declares their rapping supremacy, and ridicules other efforts as well: "I dis your krew/I'll dis your relatives/I stay competitive/You rap like you took a sedative/I'm way ahead…You must have slept/While I took a steady vigil/To stay original." In fact, the group spends so much time bragging that they mostly forget to explore other topics. Nonetheless, it doesn't hurt to have confidence, and when it comes to the music and the polished delivery of the raps, the album is an accomplished outing. The group excites musically on "Gett Down," as the rappers weave rousing lines telling how great they are over a funky guitar/keyboard line, rimmed by turntable scratching. The overall sound of this song is very professional and ranks with international standards. Another fine outing musically is the spirited "Crowd Pleazer," which uses the guitar lick from Jean Knight's 1970s hit "Mr. Big Stuff," over which the group raps about—you guessed it—how great Masta Plann thinks they are. The band is good, but they're not that good, and they need better lyrics, too. —*David Gonzales*

Mastamind (Gary Reed)

b. Detroit MI
Hardcore Rap, Underground Rap
For nearly a decade, Mastamind existed exclusively as a member of the Detroit acid rap group Natas before releasing his first solo album in 2000, proving that he was more than group leader Esham's righthand man. Ten years earlier while attending Osborne High School in Detroit, MI, Mastamind (born Gary Reed) passed a three-song demo tape to fellow student Esham. At the time, Esham had already released a full-length debut, *Boomin' Words From Hell*, along with a handful of EPs, making him a substantial superstar among his teenaged peers. Esham liked what he heard and decided to form a group with Mastamind and a friend named TNT. Together, the trio decided on the name Natas as a symbol of their disposition at the time and released their first album, *Life After Death*, on Esham's Reel Life Productions label in 1992. Subsequent years brought a number of follow-ups. In 1995, Mastamind's solo debut appeared, a five-song EP titled *Lickkuidrano*, but it wasn't until 2000 that his first solo LP appeared, *Themindzi*. With this release came critical acclaim among the hardcore rap underground, as *Murder Dog* magazine's readers voted Mastamind 2000's "most slept on" rapper while also praising his album. The rapper then went on the road in 2001, touring nationally for the first time and winning legions of new fans in the process. —*Jason Birchmeier*

Lickkuidrano EP / Jan. 17, 1995 / Reel Life ✦✦
This short EP impressively foreshadowed a promising solo career for Natas member Mastamind that unfortunately took several years to evolve. The few tracks here are on par with anything Esham or Natas were putting out at the time, particularly "Bitcheshate," a posse track featuring Esham and Dice, another hardcore Detroit rapper affiliated with the Reel Life camp at the time. This track is obviously the EP's centerpiece, as the other five tracks are all rather brief—still, they're impressive tracks even if they are short. As mentioned, Mastamind's follow-up to this debut didn't appear until late 2000, *Themindzi*, a quality album that found the rapper having changed his style substantially, which is understandable considering the time lapse. If you're into Esham's mid-'90s nihilist rap, then this EP fits that template perfectly and is worth hunting down. —*Jason Birchmeier*

● **Themindzi** / Oct. 24, 2000 / TVT ✦✦✦
Years after Mastamind debuted on Natas' initial album in 1992 and saw his solo debut on the impressive *Lickkuidrano* EP in 1995, he finally returned with his first full-length, *Themindzi*, a surprising album that moves away from the rapper's work in Natas. This departure isn't necessarily a bad thing, though; in fact, it's somewhat of a pleasant surprise. Had he returned with an album similar to his work on *Lickkuidrano*, it would sound quite outdated, since Esham wore that style out with his numerous 1990s albums. (Granted,

die-hard fans nostalgic for the original acid rap sound would probably savor the style's return.) Instead, on *Themindzi* Mastamind carves out a unique style all his own—just as hardcore as Natas and just as eerie as *Lickkuidrano*, yet also quite original. The production varies from bare piano-driven beats ("RLP") to near-techno-styled beats ("Reckless") to everything in between. In fact, it owes little to any conventional style—not the drum machine-ridden and synth-heavy dirty South sounds; not the sampladelic, clean-cut New York hip-hop sounds; not the poppin'-collar G-funk Cali sounds; and not the rock-sample-laced early-'90s Esham sounds. This fresh approach makes it an intriguing listen, even if some of the rhymes and some of the beats admittedly aren't that effective. Just being able to sit back and listen to Mastamind craft his own unique style with confidence is engaging enough to make this a worthwhile album. Similar to how Natas' *WWW.Com* album successfully headed into new territory, *Themindzi* foreshadows a sound soon to be co-opted by biting producers and MCs. —*Jason Birchmeier*

Master P (Percy Miller)

b. Apr. 29, 1970, New Orleans, LA
Vocals, Producer / Hip-Hop, Gangsta Rap, Southern Rap, Hardcore Rap
Master P created a hip-hop empire without registering on any mainstream radar. For several years, he operated solely in the rap underground, eventually surfacing in the mid-'90s as a recording artist and producer who knew exactly what his audience wanted. And what they wanted was gangsta rap. With his independent label No Limit, Master P gave them gangsta rap at its most basic—violent, vulgar lyrics, hard-edged beats, whiny synthesizers, and blunted bass. He wasn't a great rapper, nor was anyone on No Limit; occasionally, the No Limit rappers were even talentless and clumsy. But in a time when major labels were running away from the controversy that gangsta rap caused and Dr. Dre, the father of the genre, was proclaiming it dead, Master P stayed on course, delivering album after album of unadulterated gangsta. It was recorded cheaply and packaged cheaply, and almost all of the records on No Limit were interchangeable, but that didn't matter, because Master P kept making money and getting paid.

Appropriately for someone who operated outside of conventional hip-hop circles, Master P (born Percy Miller, 1970) didn't come from such traditional rap cities as New York or California. Master P was based in New Orleans, a city with a rich musical tradition that nevertheless had an underdeveloped hip-hop scene. It also had an unspoken violent side that affected Master P as a teenager. After his parents' divorce, he moved between the homes of his father's mother in New Orleans and his mother in Richmond, CA. During his teens, he was on the outside of the drug and hustling culture, but he also pursued a love of basketball. He won a sports scholarship at the University of Houston, but he left the school and moved to Richmond, where he studied business at Oakland's Merritt Junior College. His grandfather died and left him ten thousand dollars in the late '80s, which Master P invested in No Limit Records. Originally, No Limit was a store, not a label.

While working at No Limit, Master P learned that there was a rap audience who loved funky, street-level beats that the major labels weren't providing. Using this knowledge, he decided to turn No Limit into a record label in 1990. The following year, he debuted with *Get Away Clean* and later had an underground hit with *The Ghetto's Tryin to Kill Me!* in 1994. Around this same time, the compilation *West Coast Bad Boyz*, which featured rappers Rappin' 4-Tay and E-40 before they were nationally known, was released and spent over half a year on the charts. These latter two albums were significant underground hits and confirmed what Master P suspected—there was an audience for straight-ahead, unapologetic, funky hardcore rap. He soon moved No Limit to New Orleans and began concentrating on making records.

By the mid-'90s, No Limit had developed its own production team, Beats by the Pound (comprised of Craig B., KLC, and Mo B. Dick), which worked on every one of the label's releases. And there were many releases, hitting a rate of nearly ten a year, all masterminded by Master P and Beats by the Pound. They crafted the sound, often stealing songs outright from contemporary hits. They designed album covers, which had the cheap, garishly colorful and tasteless look of straight-to-video exploitation films. And they worked fast, recording and releasing entire albums in as quickly as two weeks.

Included in that production schedule were Master P's own albums. *99 Ways to Die* was released in 1995, and *Ice Cream Man* appeared the following year. By the time *Ghetto Dope* was released in the late summer of 1997,

Master P had turned No Limit into a mini-empire. He had no exposure on radio or MTV, but No Limit's records sold very well, and Tru—a group he formed with his younger brothers Silkk the Shocker and C-Murder—had Top Ten R&B hit albums. His success in the recording industry inspired him to make *I'm Bout It*, an autobiographical comedy-drama titled after Tru's breakthrough hit. Master P financed the production himself, and when he found no distributor, it went straight to video in the summer of 1997. His next film, *I Got the Hook Up*, appeared in theaters during the summer of 1998, concurrent with the release of his album *MP Da Last Don*. In between flirtations with the sports world—including a tryout with the NBA's Toronto Raptors and negotiating the NFL contract of Heisman Trophy winner Ricky Williams—Master P recorded 1999's *Only God Can Judge Me*. *Ghetto Postage* and *Game Face* followed. —*Stephen Thomas Erlewine*

Get Away Clean / 1991 / In-A-Minute/No Limit ♦♦
Master P's earliest release (serial number NLR 1001), *Get Away Clean* documents the era when No Limit was based in Richmond, CA, rather than down South. A few of the songs here feature Master P's group, Tru, and a few other rappers make appearances, most notable among them a very young Silkk the Shocker. *Get Away Clean* certainly doesn't boast very impressive production values, but it does boast a lawless attitude very much influenced by N.W.A and the other early West Coast gangsta rap acts of the time like Too Short and E-40. Undoubtedly a rare novelty item—particularly the original release rather than the 1998 re-release—*Get Away Clean* should interest only the most fanatical No Limit fans. —*Jason Birchmeier*

Mama's Bad Boy / 1992 / In-A-Minute/No Limit ♦♦
Released shortly after No Limit's debut release (Master P's *Get Away Clean*), *Mama's Bad Boy* signals a small step forward for the then-Cali-based store-turned-label. Here Master P unveils the earliest lineup of his so-called No Limit Mafia: Calli G, Markest Bank, Daniel Fry, Silk (later Silkk the Shocker), Sonya C, King George, C-Murder, Fonzo, and Big Ed. Most of these rappers would fall off the No Limit bandwagon quickly, yet it's fascinating to hear Master P emphasize a revolving roster of disposable rappers even at this early date. And that's about the primary value of *Mama's Bad Boy*—the insight it provides about the seldom documented beginnings of No Limit. The album certainly suffers from low production values as well as creatively challenged rapping, yet that's beside the point here. Rather, it's all about how savvily Master P follows in the footsteps of N.W.A, crafting a prototypical gangsta rap album that was surely trendy for its day—undoubtedly a perfect product for his store. As with the other Cali-era No Limit releases, *Mama's Bad Boy* is mainly for completists and historians, if even them, yet even the most casual No Limit fans should give one of these albums a listen sometime, as they're quite curious. —*Jason Birchmeier*

The Ghetto's Tryin to Kill Me! / Jul. 15, 1994 / No Limit ♦♦♦
Master P's early-'90s underground ventures blossomed on *The Ghetto's Tryin to Kill Me!*, a wonderfully exploitative album driven by lo-fi G-funk beats and gutter-mentality gangsta rhymes. The album itself doesn't sound too much different from Master P's other early releases, still marred by spare-change quality production; however, it's the execution that makes *The Ghetto's Tryin to Kill Me!* such an impressive step forward for the aspiring kingpin. Rather than simply emulate West Coast gangsta rappers like N.W.A and Above the Law as he had on previous releases, Master P begins to carve out a niche of his own here. The dirty South motifs still aren't quite yet apparent, but the griminess of the later releases certainly is, as nearly every song here references drug dealing and murder, particularly the standout title track. In fact, like all the other pre-*Ghetto D* albums, Master P is at his rawest here, willing to exploit whatever hardcore motifs he could in order to get a rise from his listeners. He's joined on practically every song by his Cali-era No Limit colleagues, including King George, C-Murder, Big Ed, Cali G, Sonya C, and Silkk the Shocker. Fellow Bay Area hardcore rappers JT the Bigga Figga and San Quinn join the festivities on "Playa Haterz." If you want to hear Master P at his most unapologetically exploitative, this is where to go—if you can find it, that is. (No Limit re-released and repackaged *The Ghetto's Tryin to Kill Me!* in 1997 after scoring its distribution deal with Priority. The original version from 1994 is significally different than the re-release, as Master P unfortunately cut the exceptional "Reverend Do Wrong" because of his beef with then-No Limit soldier King George and added two bonus tracks: the latter-day "Always Look a Man in the Eyes," which features Mystikal and Silkk the Shocker, and "Robbery," which is a C-Murder solo track. The "limited

collector's edition" re-release also altered the sequencing and cover art and billed the album misleadingly as "Master P's first underground rap album.")
—*Jason Birchmeier*

99 Ways to Die / Feb. 7, 1995 / No Limit ✦✦✦
Master P's career continued to evolve with *99 Ways to Die*, another of his several underground releases. Not much really sets this one apart from *Ghetto's Tryin to Kill Me!*, its closest companion, and it's not quite on the level of *Ice Cream Man*, though it is a big step up from *Get Away Clean* and *Mama's Bad Boy*, Master P's earliest two albums. All of these albums are mainly novelties best intended for completists and die-hard fans, and *99 Ways to Die* is certainly no different. —*Jason Birchmeier*

Ice Cream Man / Apr. 16, 1996 / No Limit ✦✦✦✦
After some underground recognition and a freshly inked deal with Priority, Master P wasn't exactly unknown by the time *Ice Cream Man* hit the streets, proven when the album debuted at number three on *Billboard*'s R&B chart with little to no press or airplay. This confidence reflects rather evidently as the rapper tries to make this album a bit thematic, casting himself as "Mr. Ice Cream Man." It's actually a rather witty analogy, as ice cream here represents crack. Furthermore, this album also represents what can be arguably seen as the final West Coast-sounding Master P album; the beats hit at a rather low-tempo with plenty of slow, flute-like synth melodies, bringing an ominous sound to the crack-dealing lyrical themes. As a rapper, Master P isn't any more talented here than he ever was, or ever would be, but he does perform effectively as a cinematic storyteller, entertaining listeners with his ghetto knowledge about drug dealing, making money, and keeping it real. The attempt at making this a thematic concept album instantly differentiates it from his previous albums, yet also stands as the album's weakness—Master P isn't as cinematic as he would like to think he is here. Even so, the rapper is only a step away from fully realizing his potential as a mass-producing dealer of the musical equivalent of crack: it's cheap, dirty, available, unsatisfactory, yet ultimately potent. —*Jason Birchmeier*

● **Ghetto D** / Sep. 2, 1997 / No Limit ✦✦✦✦✦
On the surface, *Ghetto D* may look like another piece of product from Master P's No Limit empire, and there's a certain amount of truth to that. Master P is a master marketer and he knows how to create demand for his product, which means informing the public that it is out there. He spreads the word about future No Limit releases throughout *Ghetto D*: artwork for forthcoming albums forms 90 percent of the album's artwork, and No Limit artists rap on the record as much as Master P himself. As a result, *Ghetto D* plays much like one of the *West Coast Bad Boyz* discs—it sounds like a various-artists sampler. It also sounds like a virtual catalog of '90s rap styles, from wimpy Bone Thugs-N-Harmony ballads ("I Miss My Homies") to Wu-Tang craziness ("Let's Get 'Em") to G-funk ("Weed & Money"). Master P is a consummate rip-off artist, capable of copying any number of popular records and styles with flair. He's done this on almost all of No Limit's records, but what makes *Ghetto D* different is the ease of the whole thing. Master P is using better equipment this time around, which helps him make better, more seamless records, thereby making his facsimiles sound similar to the originals. The shameless rip-offs make *Ghetto D* an entertaining listen—it's fun to guess who the No Limit crew is ripping off now—yet it's hampered by its ridiculous 80-minute running time. Theoretically, it gives you more bang for your buck, but by the ninth song, "Captain Kirk," the album seems endless. However, that overindulgence is a hallmark of Master P and No Limit, and that's what makes *Ghetto D* his definitive statement. —*Stephen Thomas Erlewine*

MP Da Last Don / Jun. 2, 1998 / No Limit ✦✦✦
The double-CD set that No Limit godfather Master P envisioned as his final solo album, *MP Da Last Don* was greeted with reams of press clippings by the media and open arms by the public, who sent it to 112 on the charts, the week *before* it was scheduled to be released. All this means is that Master P's master business plan worked—he was able to position himself as the leader of the underground just to sell records. And there's no other way to view *MP Da Last Don*; it's nothing but product, albeit well-made product. Spanning two CDs and 29 songs, the album is more of an advertisement for upcoming No Limit releases than a last will and testament. All of the No Limit roster appears somewhere on the disc, and info about upcoming releases (some of which have been in development for a year and a half) litters the liner notes. Master P himself makes his presence felt only because the formula *MP Da Last Don* follows is one he invented. If you've ever heard a No Limit record,

you'll know what to expect—cribbed hooks, predictable bass grooves, and drum loops, the standard gangsta lyrical clichés. The law of averages dictates that there will be a few passable tracks on an album this size, but there is no variety here at all—you could start the album at any point and feel like you've heard it all before. So, *Da Last Don* isn't a grand final statement from Master P, though its crass commercialism and blatant hucksterism offers as accurate a summation of Master P's career as anyone could hope. —*Stephen Thomas Erlewine*

No Tomorrow / 1999 / Ventura Distribution/No Limit ✦
Branching off from a successful rap career, Master P followed the lead of fellow rap stars Ice-T, Ice Cube, and LL Cool J by getting into the acting business, taking on basic tough-guy roles in films such as *Lockdown* and *No Tomorrow*. Not content with acting, however, he has also extended his efforts into producing and directing—the latter on this formula action flick. While there are some rough edges and the storyline sometimes fails to make sense, the picture is, on the whole, reasonably well done, with a good part for Pam Grier and a routine bad-guy part for Gary Busey. P himself takes a smaller, pivotal bad-guy role. Master P keeps the MTV styling down in favor of a more nuts-and-bolts approach, though this work is peppered with periodic big bangs and frantic (and sometimes confusing) shootouts, not to mention a nicely done plane crash. The DVD edition includes trailers, a video, and a Master P trivia quiz. —*Steven McDonald*

Only God Can Judge Me / Oct. 26, 1999 / No Limit ✦✦
Anyone hoping that Master P would return to the level of quality that he achieved on his 1997 breakthrough album, *Ghetto D*, will only find themselves even more disappointed with *Only God Can Judge Me*. *MP Da Last Don* had supposedly been Master P's final album, so when he decided to return after his very brief retirement, most thought it was to redeem himself after the immense criticism heaped onto him in 1998. Unfortunately, *Only God Can Judge Me* merely reaffirms that harsh criticism and actually warranted even *more* scathing words (as if there already weren't enough No Limit haters). After only a few minutes into the album it becomes obvious that Master P feels rather bitter about his critics and actually does make a sincere effort to make this a diverse album. This comes with the glut of somber songs such as "Ghetto in the Sky" and "Where Do We Go From Here" that retread the territory previously explored on radio-friendly songs such as "I Miss My Homies." Of course, there are a few moments when he sticks to proven formulas such as on "Step to This," a rather rousing song much in the spirit of "Make 'Em Say Uhh!" Yet for as sincerely as this album attempts to improve upon the dullness of *MP Da Last Don* by crafting a well-balanced album that alternates between bumpin' dirty South bounce tracks and sentimental life-is-rough-as-a-thug ballads, it's some of the clumsiest moments in Master P's career. —*Jason Birchmeier*

Ghetto Postage / Nov. 28, 2000 / No Limit ✦✦✦✦
It's hard to attribute musical quality to Master P's success in the late '90s, but primarily based upon the quality of *Ghetto Postage* rather than marketing gimmicks or musical trends, the rapper has come close to rivaling his best album of the 1990s, *Ghetto D*. Like that breakthrough album, *Ghetto Postage* is a simplistic *tour de force* through myriad proven gangsta rap motifs. Beginning with the standard "I'm Bout It" variation, this time titled "Bout Dat," Master P and his post-Beats by the Pound production team—primarily Carlos Stephens, XL, Ke-Noe, Myke Diesel, and Suga Bear—move through the motifs without making them seem too clichéd and, more importantly, performing with an aura of confidence and poise, two attributes sorely lacking on *Only God Can Judge Me*, this album's clumsy predecessor. So while *Ghetto Postage* doesn't win any awards for finesse or craft, even if it is one of the best No Limit albums, it does deserve acclaim for not surrendering to the trite stunnin'-bling-bling-flossfest clichés littering rap at the end of 2000 and for at least being a blatant motif exercise with integrity—thug farce or not, Master P is actually a rather *likable* guy here. And more than anything, he does what he does best: he gives his fans exactly what they want—ultra-simple, call-and-response gangsta rap with charisma—without any self-serving, egocentric attempts to be an "artist." —*Jason Birchmeier*

Game Face / Dec. 18, 2001 / No Limit ✦✦✦
Master P wore his "game face" in 2001 because he'd become somewhat of a joke in some circles. No one joked when he was selling millions of albums every week during the late '90s, but the game changed in the early 2000s. Master P's No Limit empire had indeed finally reached its limit. After

increasingly sluggish sales, all that remained was family—Silkk the Shocker, C-Murder, Lil' Romeo, and Master P himself. Yet just when it looked as if Master P was ready to become another has-been rapper, he put on his game face and went to work. This album represents Master P's new direction. He's not so much the hardcore gangsta rapper of old—the "Ice Cream Man" you once knew him as—but rather a serious, business-minded man on a mission. Perhaps having learned a lesson from the spectacular success of his son, Lil' Romeo, Master P isn't afraid to take the pop-rap approach, interpolating hits from the past—big hits, like Funkadelic's "One Nation Under a Groove," Kurtis Blow's "The Breaks," and the Bee Gees' "More Than a Woman," just to name a few. In fact, nearly every song here recycles a proven hit. And the ones that don't, like the album's big single, "Ooohhhwee," hark back to the sort of songs that had always proven successful for No Limit—in this case, the "Wobble Wobble"-style club track that's as much for the ladies as for the thugs. But just because Master P is more determined to get "back on top," as he raps about here with his brothers, that doesn't necessarily mean he has improved his music. *Game Face* isn't any more impressive than any of his past few albums since *Ghetto D*. However, it is a much more accessible album because of the pop approach. Plus, it's nice to see Master P get away from the excessive number of guests and the thuggish posturing that had so characterized his previous work. —*Jason Birchmeier*

Masterminds

Group / Hip-Hop, Urban, Underground Rap
Masterminds is a New York rhyme team, comprised of Oracle, Kimani, and Epod, a trio of rappers who met as students at Wesleyan University in 1994. They are a throwback to the late-'80s hip-hop era, but at the same time they offer a futuristic lyrical presentation that is quite refreshing. Masterminds released *The Underground Railroad*, their debut album, in 2000, followed two years later by *Stone Planet*. —*Nick Pfeiffer*

● **The Underground Railroad** / Jun. 13, 2000 / Ground Control ♦♦
The Masterminds' debut album, *The Underground Railroad*, isn't as good as some of their previous singles, but it suffices as an indie release. The reason the album falls short is the fact that the Masterminds tried to please everyone with this album. In other words, they tried to remain true to their underground roots, although some of the production on *The Underground Railroad* is extremely "jiggy" or pop sounding. One particular area the Masterminds excel in pertains to production; their producers have an aptitude for being able to incorporate samples from other MCs into their tracks (see "Hot Shit #12" and "Bring it Back"). All in all, I would have expected better from the Masterminds, but I have a feeling that this young group will come to maturity at some point. —*Nick Pfeiffer*

Mayhemm

Group / West Coast Rap, Gangsta Rap, Hardcore Rap
Briefly coming out of the West Coast rap scene in the late '90s, Mayhemm released only one record in its short existence. Featuring sexist raps, gangsta posing, and production from local celebrities like MC Eiht and DJ Slip, *Global Mayhem* was released by Native Records in 1997. Although the album appealed to fans of straight-ahead hardcore rap, it was only a regional success and the group disappeared soon after. —*Bradley Torreano*

● **Global Mayhem** / Mar. 25, 1997 / Native ♦♦
The extra "m" in Mayhemm could be for misery, which loves company, and plenty of record companies loved misery right back. That was the rationale behind West Coast gangsta rap: the darker the narrative, the more compelling the product, and the more likely that music fans would tune in to live the gangster life vicariously. At its best, gangsta rap is poetry borne from pain, delivered with a braggadocio that resonates with the invincible youth it's aimed at. At its not so best, you get bands like Mayhemm, who try to get by on heart rather than art and instead end up selling the medium short. *Global Mayhem* has its moments, striding large down dangerous streets for tracks like "Mr. Failure," "Deadliest Brothas," and "Psychos With Clips." But this music works best when the "rep" precedes the rap—remember, even the earliest outlaws like Jesse James and Billy the Kid owed their national reputations to the media. Mayhemm did at least get some good producers behind them, including MC Eiht, Prodeje, DJ Slip, and Ant Banks. And the disc starts out good, setting the horror-show stage with the eerie "Mayhemm Introduction," similar to the video-game-gone-bad soundtrack that Bushwick Bill

favored, which reappears on "Menace 2 the Neighborhood." For all the smart production, however, the raps rarely rise to the occasion. Graphic accounts of gangsta life can hide weak rhymes and good raps can replace the need for shock-value imagery, but if both those cylinders are firing on half strength (as they are here), the result can seem mean and mediocre. "Raw on delivery" is a fine motto if you're selling sushi, but not if you're selling music. Unless you're a hardcore fan of the West Coast scene, you can skip over *Global Mayhem* as a regional curiosity. —*Dave Connolly*

MC Brains (James De Shannon)

b. Cleveland, OH
Pop-Rap, Golden Age
Michael Bivins discovered Cleveland-born MC Brains (born James De Shannon) in 1992. With Bivins assistance and encouragement, MC Brains debuted on Motown with *Lovers Lane*. The single "Oochie Coochie" just missed the pop Top 20, while "Brainstorming" was a respectable follow-up. MC Brains style was pop crossover rather than hard or gangsta, but he showed enough potential the first time out to indicate a second release would be justified. —*Ron Wynn*

● **Lovers Lane** / 1992 / Motown ♦♦♦♦♦
MC Brains was discovered by former New Edition and current Bell Biv Devoe member Michael Bivins. He was 17 years old when this was released. Thus, it seemed appropriate that the teen angst/new-jack number "Oochie Coochie" would be the lone hit, peaking at number 21 on the pop charts. There was nothing confrontational or angry about this one, the MC moniker notwithstanding. If there were any questions about MC Brains' (and Bivins') intentions, they were thoroughly answered by tracks like "Strawberry Lane" and "G-String." —*Ron Wynn*

MC Breed (Eric Breed)

b. Flint, MI
Vocals, Producer / Hip-Hop, Dirty South, Gangsta Rap
One of the first rappers to come out the Midwest in the early '90s, MC Breed experienced modest success while based in Flint, MI, before leaving the Midwest to work with D.O.C. in L.A. and Too Short in Atlanta. Breed's debut album, *MC Breed & DFC*, was released on the tiny independent label SDEG (4103) and pictures Breed and da Flint Crew (DFC) in their b-boy stances, donning gaudy Detroit Tigers apparel. The album merged the East and West Coast sounds of the time, being both lyrical and funky; it also spawned a successful single, "Ain't No Future in Yo' Frontin'," which was later sampled for Ice Cube's "Wicked," and helped keep the album on *Billboard*'s R&B chart for a whopping 52 weeks. Following this initial success, unprecedented at the time for a Midwestern rap act, Breed adopted more of a West Coast gangsta sound like many success-hungry rappers of the time. He began working with D.O.C., who helped write and produce some of the songs on Breed's third album, *The New Breed*.

By this point, the Flint native had left the Midwest and DFC behind and was networking on all coasts. His efforts proved successful when his fourth album, *Funkafied*, peaked at number nine on the *Billboard* R&B chart in summer 1994. However, Breed would never match the success of that album, and subsequent releases throughout the '90s—many of them featuring Too Short, who Breed became close with when the two relocated to Atlanta—didn't chart nearly as well, partly because Breed never signed a major-label contract. Nonetheless, he remained prolific as an underground rapper, releasing generally an album a year and aligning himself with the dirty South movement. —*Jason Birchmeier*

MC Breed & DFC / 1991 / Warlock ♦♦♦
Few outside of the Midwest took notice back in 1991 when MC Breed debuted with da Flint Crew (DFC). At the time he was mostly a local phenomenon, stressing the word "phenomenon" because the Midwest didn't have many rappers to call its own at the time, let alone any as talented as Breed. Furthermore, few Midwest rappers had hits as big as "Ain't No Future in Yo' Frontin'," the song that put Breed on the map for years to follow and kept this album on the *Billboard* R&B charts for a year. With time, however, the Flint, MI, native would become one of the more impressive rappers to emerge in the '90s, eventually moving first to L.A. to hook up with D.O.C. and then Atlanta to hook up with Too Short. And it's those later efforts with D.O.C. and Too Short that generally garner the most attention among those who have

familiarized themselves with Breed's funk-laced rap. However, it's a shame that so many listeners overlook Breed's debut, which eventually went out of print for many years before finally being remastered and re-released by Warlock in 2002. Yes, it's a relatively lo-fi effort, an independently released album during a time when few rap albums were. But there is a certain sense of novelty that makes *MC Breed & DFC* sound even more special with time. As mentioned, it's one of the first rap albums to come out of the Midwest, merging the then-opposing East and West Coast sounds of the time. For example, "Ain't No Future in Yo' Frontin'" samples Flavor Flav's trademark "to the beat ch'all" for its intro, Zapp's "More Bounce to the Ounce" for its bass line, and uses the whining synth melodies Dr. Dre made famous a year later on his *The Chronic* for its hook (and a snippet of this synth hook would be sampled a year later for Ice Cube's "Wicked"). Breed drew equally from East and West for his sound, being as much influenced by Too Short and MC Eiht as Chuck D and EPMD. His later albums are no doubt more polished, but none of them are as pure as this, one of the few albums to vividly document the embryonic Midwest rap scene of the time. —*Jason Birchmeier*

20 Below / 1992 / Wrap ♦♦

Following an unexpectedly successful debut album, driven by the hit single "Ain't No Future in Yo' Frontin'," that made him one of the—if not *the*—Midwest's first rap superstars, MC Breed went gangsta for his second album. Blame N.W.A and the rest of the West Coast, which was on the rise in a major way at the time, if you want, but Breed definitely abandoned much of the open-minded, East-crossed-with-West style that characterized his unique debut album and adopted an Ice Cube-like posture for *20 Below*. Gone were the Public Enemy samples of his debut album and in were more of the P-funk-influenced motifs that made "Ain't No Future in Yo' Frontin'" such a popular song. Many of his fans were disappointed, and rightfully so. Where Breed had been quite socially conscious in a positive way on his debut, showing more than a little Chuck D influence, he is socially conscious in a negative way here, being more exploitative than passionate. Many, particularly his Midwest and East Coast fans, saw through his facade and accused him of trying to cash in on the West Coast trend that had been ignited a year before largely by N.W.A's *Niggaz4life* and Ice Cube's *Death Certificate*, two extremely successful albums that hit number one and number two, respectively, on *Billboard*'s pop charts. It's perhaps no surprise that *20 Below* would subsequently become Breed's least-remembered album; however, a year later he would more successfully cash in on the West Coast trend sweeping the rap world with his *The New Breed* album, where he worked with songwriter/ producer D.O.C. and had a hit single with 2Pac, "Gotta Get Mine." —*Jason Birchmeier*

The New Breed / 1993 / Wrap ♦♦♦♦

MC Breed may have synthesized East and West Coast styles on his debut album, partly explaining why it sounded so novel for its time, but by the time his third album, *The New Breed*, hit the streets in 1993 it was apparent: the Midwestern native had adopted the West Coast sound, which was at its zenith of popularity at the time. Dr. Dre's *The Chronic* was bumping everywhere in 1993, even on the East Coast, so it isn't too surprising that Breed, an artist who's never too far behind the latest trends, headed West and hooked up with D.O.C., the writer/producer who had quietly helped make Dre's *The Chronic* the success that it was. Furthermore, Breed also hooked up with Warren G, who produced some of this album, and a young and delightfully unthuggish 2Pac, who helped make "Gotta Get Mine," this album's hit single, a career highlight for the former Midwestern and soon-to-be dirty South rapper. In fact, Breed's decision to head West for this album proved to be a wise decision. His next album, *Funkafied*, peaked at number nine on *Billboard*'s R&B chart without little to no commercial airplay, a testament to just how impressed the public was by this album. —*Jason Birchmeier*

Funkafied / Jun. 7, 1994 / Wrap ♦♦♦♦

MC Breed's most successful album, *Funkafied*, an album that astonishingly peaked in the Top Ten of *Billboard*'s R&B chart, is also his most unique and arguably the turning point in his dynamic career. Breed's previous album, *The New Breed* (1993), featured the former Midwestern rapper adopting a West Coast sound, collaborating with such big-name Cali artists as D.O.C., Warren G, and a young 2Pac. Then, the album Breed would follow up *Funkafied* with, *Big Baller* (1995), would find him heading south to Atlanta to hook up with Too Short and begin a new era for the always-on-the-move rapper. *Funkafied* fits somewhere between these two albums. It doesn't feature any of the West Coast figures who helped make *The New Breed* such

a breakthrough album for him, and it doesn't feature Too Short or any of the Atlanta posse he would begin working with in successive years. Instead, it features no one particularly noteworthy besides one big name: George Clinton. And you shouldn't overlook that fact if you want an idea of what *Funkafied* sounds like. Just as the album title and cover art might lead you to presume, this is Breed's excursion into seriously funky territory. He isn't just rapping over funk samples like he did on previous efforts; he's submersing himself in funk—live funk—attributed largely to keyboardist Gerald Jackson and bassist Shorty B, who are both given special recognition for their efforts on the album's back cover. This is a dazzling album, for sure; however, many of the thousands who bought it during its first week of release didn't pick up Breed's next album, *Big Baller*. And that's not necessarily because this is a disappointing album; rather, it's because they were expecting *The New Breed, Pt. 2*, which this clearly isn't. Commend Breed for making such a creative album as this. It's undoubtedly the most idiosyncratic, and funky, release in his mammoth catalog. From here out, he would represent the dirty South, for better or worse. —*Jason Birchmeier*

Big Baller / Jun. 20, 1995 / Wrap ♦♦♦

MC Breed had a lot of momentum going into *Big Baller*, his fifth album in five years. A year before, in 1994, his *Funkafied* album reached *Billboard*'s R&B Top Ten, and a year before that, in 1993, he scored a big hit with 2Pac, "Gotta Get Mine." However, things started to go downhill for Breed here. First of all, he began moving toward the Southern sound that would evolve into dirty South by the end of the decade. That's fine and everything, particularly since he was able to get Too Short on his album, but his fans were left more than a little frustrated. After all, he began as a Midwestern rapper who synthesized East and West styles, then adopted a West Coast style, and here he is leaving that behind for a prototypical dirty South sound. And keep in mind that this all occurred within five years! Second, *Big Baller* didn't have any hits like "Ain't No Future in Yo' Frontin'" or "Gotta Get Mine." With little to no airplay and no major-label marketing budget, this album dropped and disappeared quietly. Last, his label at the time, the Atlanta-based Wrap, dropped a greatest-hits album only three months after *Big Baller* hit the streets, eclipsing sales and seeming like overkill to many. Nonetheless, even if *Big Baller* broke the momentum Breed had going into the album, the album still broke into *Billboard*'s R&B Top 20. —*Jason Birchmeier*

The Best of MC Breed / Oct. 3, 1995 / Wrap ♦♦♦♦♦

Released only a few months after MC Breed's *Big Baller* album in 1995, *The Best of MC Breed* compiled a few of the best tracks from each of his five albums released at the time. All of Breed's best-known songs are here: from *MC Breed & DFC* (1991) you get "Ain't No Future in Yo' Frontin'" and "Just Kickin' It"; from *The New Breed* (1993) "Gotta Get Mine," "Everyday Ho," and "Tight"; from *Funkafied* (1994) "Seven Years" and "Late Nite Creep (Booty Call)"; and from *Big Baller* (1995) "Game for Life" and "Real MC." There are also a few tracks exclusive to this compilation: "Aquapussy," "Well Alright," a remix of "Teach My Kids," and unreleased versions of "This Is How We Do It" and "Ain't Too Much Worried." Breed's second album, *20 Below*, is practically ignored here, unless you count the unreleased version of "Ain't Too Much Worried," which appeared on that album in its normal version; however, since *20 Below* is perhaps the artist's least remembered and most forgettable album, it really shouldn't be a major concern. After all, everything you really need is here, including the big hits like "Ain't No Future in Yo' Frontin'" and "Gotta Get Mine," plus a few exclusive tracks as a bonus. Overall, this is a perfect distillation of Breed's first half-decade of work. (Originally released in late 1995, *The Best of MC Breed* was re-released in late 2001 in the wake of Breed's biggest hit in years, "Let's Go to the Club.") —*Jason Birchmeier*

To Da Beat Ch'all / May 14, 1996 / Wrap ♦♦♦

If MC Breed's album from a year before, *Big Baller* (1995), found him trying to switch from a West Coast sound to a Southern sound, *To Da Beat Ch'all* finds him finalizing that switch. He wasn't working with D.O.C. or other West Coast artists like Warren G or 2Pac any longer, like he had only a couple years before on *The New Breed* (1993) (though D.O.C. does contribute some vocals). No, he had moved to Atlanta, just as Too Short had, and began working with Atlanta artists, most notably Jazze Pha and Hurricane, as well as Eric Sermon, who spent some time in Atlanta at the time. As a result, this is a fresh album for Breed, a firm step in a new direction. And it's also a formative album for the then-embryonic Southern rap scene. Unfortunately, just as *Big Baller* had, it left many of Breed's fans scratching their heads in dizzying confusion: first he was Midwest, then he was West Coast gangsta rap, and now he's a down-South baller. Commercial success aside, this is a solid album from Breed, who usually takes an album or two to successfully change styles. For instance, just as *The New Breed* bettered the West Coast style Breed struggled to adopt on *20 Below*, this album betters the down-South style he struggled to adopt on *Big Baller*. Plus, it's a really slick album with great production from Pha and Sermon, two producers who never cease to amaze. —*Jason Birchmeier*

Flatline / Sep. 16, 1997 / Wrap ✦✦✦✦
It took a year or two for MC Breed to make the transition from his early-'90s West Coast style to his late-'90s down South style, but by the time *Flatline* hit the streets in 1997, he had the *Southernplayalisticadillacmuzik*/pimpin'/ baller thing down to a science. Just as he had done a year before on the solid *To Da Beat Ch'all* album, he works mostly with producer Jazze Pha here, a soon-to-be big-name dirty South producer who really comes into his own on these late-'90s Breed albums. Furthermore, Breed teams up with Bay Area and longtime Too $hort producer Ant Banks for a few tracks, including the excellent lead single, "Dreamin'." In addition to Pha and Banks, Erotic D and D.O.C. help out on this album, which is just as solid as—if not a step up from—*To Da Beat Ch'all*. Breed's late-'90s albums may have not been as commercially successful as his early-'90s efforts, but they're surely more polished. At this point, Breed's a veteran, and it shows. —*Jason Birchmeier*

It's All Good / Feb. 9, 1999 / Roadrunner ✦✦
MC Breed's relationship with Wrap Records came to an end with 1997's *Flatline*, which ironically happened to be one of his best albums, featuring big-name producers like Ant Banks and Jazze Pha. When Breed returned in 1999 on Power Records (based in Atlanta and distributed for a while by Roadrunner), things were different. First of all, the label didn't have the budget that Wrap did, meaning that there weren't going to be any more big-name producers on Breed's albums. Second, the label didn't have nearly the marketing push that the artist was used to having, meaning that after nearly a decade of moderate success, the Atlanta-by-way-of-Michigan rapper was suddenly an underground rapper. Third, the dirty South movement was in full bloom by 1999, with labels like No Limit and Cash Money having changed the game, flooding record stores with more down-South rap than stores could handle. As a result, Breed was in an awkward situation on this album, though he tries to dismiss the pressures he faced by titling his album *It's All Good*. Well, Breed can call his album what he likes, but all surely wasn't good for the rapper, and he was entering a frustrating era that would find him falling off the map for a few years, working with a limited budget, and trying to adapt to overnight trends. As the No Limit/Cash Money circa 1999-looking album cover may lead you to presume, Breed unfortunately jumps on the bling-bling/thug trend of the time. You can tell he's uncomfortable trying to adapt to the sound of the time, but he was in a dire situation. For instance, when Breed opens the album with a remix of his five-year-old pre-Death Row 2Pac collaboration, "Gotta Get Mine," you know he's trying too hard. The aura of desperation that underlies the "it's all good" facade makes this an awkward album and one to avoid in favor of Breed's many better, and much more sincere, albums. —*Jason Birchmeier*

2 for the Show / Nov. 23, 1999 / Roadrunner ✦✦
Nearly all of MC Breed's albums for Power Records in the late '90s had something exploitative about them, and *2 for the Show* is arguably the most gimmicky of them all. The concept here is that Breed collaborates with other MCs on each of the tracks, with such high-profile guests as 2Pac, Eightball, Too $hort, Big Mike, and more. However, some of these songs, most notably the 2Pac song, "Gotta Get Mine," are previously released and readily available. Like the other Breed albums released by Power, you're best off avoiding these exploitative efforts in favor of Breed's much better work for Wrap in the early to late '90s and his post-Power work that begins with his return to sincerity, *The Fharmacist* (2001). —*Jason Birchmeier*

The Thugz, Vol. 1 / Jan. 18, 2000 / Power ✦✦
The Thugs, Vol. 1 is yet another of Power Records' exploitative MC Breed albums released at the height of the late-'90s/early-2000s dirty South feeding frenzy. Here the gimmick is that Breed "presents" a roster of thug rappers over the course of the album. It may have seemed attractive to the legions of listeners who bought all those thuggish late-'90s No Limit albums with all of their guest appearances, but much like all of those myriad interchangeable albums, this is an incredibly inconsistent album that sounds like it came off

an assembly line, made in about a week with a shoestring budget, more money being spent on the glossy cover art than the production. None of the beats come close to being as memorable as the ones Jazze Pha had blessed Breed with in 1996/1997, and none of these "thugz" are on a par with the "presenter," who unfortunately isn't as ubiquitous on this album as the big picture of him on the cover might lead you to believe. Overall, there are just way too many excellent Breed albums out there to even consider bothering with this cash-in-on-the-trend-of-the-moment album. —*Jason Birchmeier*

Rare Breed / Feb. 8, 2000 / Albatross ✦✦
This low-budget album of so-called rare MC Breed tracks released in 2000 by Albatross Records (distributed and marketed by R&D, based in Houston, TX) is yet another don't-bother-with album from the veteran rapper released during the dirty South feeding frenzy of 2000. Much like his albums for Power Records during this same time, it's sad to see such a great rapper sink to such exploitative levels in an effort to pay the bills. Raid his back catalog, particularly his albums for Wrap or his subsequent work for Fharmacy Records.
—*Jason Birchmeier*

The Fharmacist / May 8, 2001 / Fharmacy ✦✦✦
After a few years of embarrassingly exploitative attempts to cash in on the dirty South feeding frenzy of the late '90s, MC Breed somewhat returned to his roots in the Midwest. He had begun his career in Flint, MI, less than an hour's drive north on I-75 from Detroit, before criss-crossing the States during the '90s, heading first out west to work with D.O.C. and then to Atlanta to work with Jazze Pha and Too $hort. But in 2001, ten years after he'd broken through with "Ain't No Future in Yo' Frontin'," Breed returned to Detroit to work with the upstart Fharmacy Records and up-and-coming Midwest producer Gee Pierce. Since Breed's never been one to miss a trend—jumping first on the West Coast gangsta bandwagon and then cashing in on the dirty South trend—it's perhaps not surprising that he headed back to Detroit. By 2001, the city more identified with soul and techno than rap was experiencing something of a boom: following the initial success of Eminem, a number of other Detroit rappers broke out of the underground, the more noteworthy being D-12, Royce the 5'9", Drunken Master, E-Dub, Slum Village (which features producer Jay Dee), and more exploitative stuff like the Dayton Family and Esham. Overall, Breed's moving-up-north gamble seemed to work. The dirty South movement lost some of its steam in 2001, and Breed scored his biggest hit in years, "Let's Go to the Club," a remake of a song from his *It's All Good* album. The remake features production and rapping by Jazze Pha, and the song became a gigantic hit in Detroit—definitely a high-rollin', blunt-smokin', Stacey Adams-wearin', we-be-clubbin' city—where the song was ubiquitous on the radio for months. In addition to the hit single, the album finds Breed returning to sincerity after a few years of exploitation. He raps from the heart and looks back on his prolific decade in the rap game. In addition, it's nice to see Breed writing with D.O.C. again, and Pierce showcases why he was hailed as such a promising beatmaking talent. —*Jason Birchmeier*

MC Ciccone

Hardcore Rap, Party Rap, Political Rap
Few stories in the music world are as bitter and unusual as the creation of MC Ciccone, the alterego of Martin Ciccone. The older brother of megastar Madonna, Ciccone is a hard-partying bad boy who found himself getting in progressively bad situations as his habits began getting out of control. After an embarrassing cameo in Madonna's *Truth or Dare* documentary in 1991, Ciccone began to publicly speak about his bitterness toward his sister, claiming he lived in her shadow. The singer failed to respond to his comments, but when she refused his requests for bail money after a 1994 arrest, the situation grew from bad to worse. Ciccone, who had been experimenting with a rap recording at a studio in Inkster, MI, decided to publicly attack his sister with a tense and bitter track on his debut album. Graphically boasting the apparent rape he experienced (or possibly fabricated) during his three-month jail stay, dishing out love advice, and endorsing the Gulf War a full three years too late, *Judgment Day* was a huge flop financially and critically. Another unfortunate result of its release was a rift in his family that kept him out of contact with his sister for several years.

Delving deeper into his personal problems, Ciccone popped up occasionally in drug- and alcohol-related news bits as his sister monitored his situation through her family. When she had finally had enough, she contacted him in 1999 and continually begged him to get help until he agreed to meet her in May of that year. Entering rehab at her request, Ciccone retired the MC Ciccone moniker and kept out of the public's eye for a bit. After publicly admitting he hadn't been invited to her wedding (although, to her credit, he was in a rehab program at the time that she was paying for), he seemed to be done with discrediting his sister and started a restaurant in Los Angeles in 2000. *—Bradley Torreano*

● **Judgment Day** / 1994 / Razor Cut ♦♦

Some people get a lot of enjoyment over watching a potentially interesting idea fall flat on its face. Those same people will probably love MC Ciccone, the bitter and talentless brother of megastar Madonna. His only album, 1994's *Judgment Day*, is possibly one of the funniest rap albums ever made, but none of the humor is intentional. Ciccone cannot rap, so he speaks over the cheesy keyboard tracks with a goofy lounge lizard voice that lends no authenticity to his boasts. "MC Ciccone" is his biggest ego rant, where he makes several bold, ridiculous claims that are blatantly not true. Elsewhere, he gives his modest love advice ("Love the One You're With"), gets angry with greed ("People and Money"), and gives a belated endorsement for the Gulf War ("Kickin' It"). The "highlight" of the album is when fellow "rapper" Tri-Force helps him with his anti-Madonna track "Judgment Day." Among other things, he blames his sister for his jail time and brags about being raped in prison. Another bizarre touch is that, although Tri-Force is obviously just one rapper, on the inside cover it shows three people under that name. The entire album is hilarious from beginning to end, and highly recommended for those who find humor in really bad music. Anyone looking to listen to this album for any other reason should avoid it at all costs, as this really is a terrible album. *—Bradley Torreano*

MC Eiht (Aaron Tyler)

b. Compton, CA

Vocals, Keyboards, Mixing, Producer / Gangsta Rap, West Coast Rap, G-Funk
Veteran West Coast gangsta rapper MC Eiht dedicated much of his life to rap, beginning his seminal career with Compton's Most Wanted (CMW) while only a teenager. Despite his youth, Eiht's contributions helped catapult CMW to national fame in 1990 with *It's a Compton Thang.* The group followed the lead of fellow Compton gangsta rappers N.W.A, but were a bit less controversial and, in turn, much less popular. CMW released two more albums—*Straight Checkn'em* (1991) and *Music to Driveby* (1992)—before Eiht began his solo career in 1993 with the group's producer, DJ Slip, in tow and "Streiht Up Menace" as his solo debut single. His debut solo album, *We Come Strapped,* topped *Billboard's* R&B album chart a year later. Eiht's sales' numbers unfortunately went downhill from there, though he retained a cult audience over the years and remained loyal to longtime affiliates Slip and Mack 10.

Born Aaron Tyler in Compton, Eiht began his career as part of CMW while still a teenager. After the song "Rhymes Too Funky" became a local hit, the group signed to Orpheus, who released three albums by the group: *It's a Compton Thang* (1990), *Straight Checkn'em* (1991), and *Music to Driveby* (1992). These albums offered several singles for the group, but none measured up to Eiht's solo debut, "Streiht Up Menace," in 1993. The Slip-produced ballad came from the *Menace II Society* soundtrack, a popular film Eiht had acted in. Following the success of this single, Eiht signed to Sony's Epic Street division and entered the studio with Slip to record his full-length solo debut, *We Come Strapped.* Billed as "MC Eiht Featuring CMW," the album didn't really feature anyone from CMW except the rapper and producer. Nonetheless, the album debuted atop *Billboard's* R&B album chart despite lacking an omnipresent lead single and reached the Top Five of the pop album chart. The album also garnered headlines for featuring, not one, but two parental advisory stickers (Sony claimed no responsibility for the lyrical content).

None of Eiht's successive albums were as successful as *We Come Strapped,* though some were arguably better. Following his initial success in 1994, the rapper returned in 1996 with *Death Threatz* and 1997 with *Last Man Standing.* Both albums featured production by Slip and were arguably better albums than Eiht's chart-topping debut, yet Epic remained unimpressed and parted ways with the Compton gangsta rapper. It didn't take long for Eiht to return, though. He signed to Mack 10's Priority-distributed Hoo Bangin' label and recorded *Section 8* (1999), his most diverse album to date, if not his best. In successive years, Eiht recorded albums on an annual basis: *"N" My Neighborhood* (2000), *Tha8t'z Gangsta* (2001), and *Underground Hero* (2002), all

but *Tha8t'z Gangsta* for Hoo Bangin'. None of these albums topped the charts, but Eiht continued to move his career forward. For instance, he appeared alongside Ice Cube and Mack 10 in the 1999 film *Thicker Than Water* and even reunited with Compton's Most Wanted in 2000 for *Represent.* *—Jason Birchmeier*

● **We Come Strapped** / Jul. 19, 1994 / Epic Street ♦♦♦♦

Fresh from his small role in the 1993 film *Menace II Society,* MC Eiht followed "Streiht up Menace," his breakthrough hit single from the film's soundtrack, with *We Come Strapped.* The album may be his full-length solo debut, but Eiht is no rookie here. He had come of age as a member of Compton's Most Wanted, a semisuccessful gangsta rap group, and brought along the defunct group's producer, DJ Slip, to join him. And that's pretty much all there is to this album, Eiht and Slip. Make no mistake: *We Come Strapped* is a sparse and straightforward album, just Eiht's ghetto rhymes and Slip's showering keyboards. And that's it: no extensive guest appearances, no P-Funk interpolations, no lavish extravagances, just Eiht's rhymes and Slip's keyboards. It all seems incredibly unlikely now, especially when you consider that this album debuted atop *Billboard's* R&B album chart, but sometimes simplicity can be a beautiful thing, and that's definitely the case here. Take, for instance, "All for Money," the album highlight. Here Eiht rhymes gently about doing whatever it takes to get paid while Slip's keyboards hover alongside some smooth, jazzy guitar and "la la"s in the distance. It's simple, for sure, but it's distinct and evocative. This can be said for much of *We Come Strapped,* a distinctly West Coast album that evokes the glamorous-yet-grimy, sunny-yet-seedy streets of Compton as well as, if not better than, any other album from the golden era of G-funk. On successive albums, Eiht and Slip developed their sound and ironically met dwindling success. This is because *We Come Strapped* is very much of its era, a time when West Coast gangsta rap was both new and dangerous—in sum, exciting. Few albums from this era were more seminal than *We Come Strapped. —Jason Birchmeier*

Last Man Standing / Nov. 11, 1997 / Epic Street ♦♦

MC Eiht's *Last Man Standing,* occasionally gets monotonous, falling into standard hardcore hip-hop clichés, but the best tracks illustrate that he has a knack for deep bass grooves and slamming beats. He's a solid, if unexceptional rhymer, but he knows how to accentuate his gifts, even if he relies too much on the usual sex, drugs, crime, and money gangsta lyrics. The best moments, however, are first-rate hardcore hip-hop—too bad there just aren't enough of them. *—Leo Stanley*

Section 8 / Jun. 8, 1999 / Priority ♦♦♦

By the time MC Eiht released *Section 8* in 1999, he was five years removed from the success of his chart-topping *We Come Strapped* album and struggling to revive that success. *Section 8,* then, is certainly a pleasant surprise following the rote *We Come Strapped* follow-ups, *Death Threatz* (1996) and *Last Man Standing* (1997), particularly when Eiht makes a sincere effort to conjure the same laid-back summer-evening vibe of his big hit "All for Money" on "My Life," a similar gangsta ballad built around sampled '70s soul motifs. This song stands among Eiht's career highlights, but the same unfortunately cannot be said for much else on *Section 8.* Amid the many by-the-numbers West Coast gangsta rap tracks here, two other songs stand out: "Automatic," which boasts a remarkable Fredwreck Nassar production, and "Days of 89," a heartfelt collaboration with longtime producer DJ Slip. The spotty nature of *Section 8* can be frustrating, particularly the guest-laden second half. Even so, it should be a worthwhile listen for fans, even if only for the few highlights. *—Jason Birchmeier*

"N" My Neighborhood / Jun. 20, 2000 / Priority ♦♦♦

It's been nearly a decade since MC Eiht came to the attention of the world with "Streiht Up Menace." Since then, MC Eiht has built up a fledgling acting career and released several albums of West Coast G-funk. *"N" My Neighborhood* is more of the same. On "Hood Rats." he rhymes about girls from around the way on a track underpinned by a smooth bass line and '70s guitar. "Hood Is Mine" is a typical piece of West Coast hip-hop, with wave upon wave of synths and thugged-out rhymes provided by MC Eiht and Mack 10. "So Ruff" offers a pulsing, Zapp-influenced electronic beat and some of the best rhymes on the disc. For fans of West Coast hip-hop, there isn't much to complain about on *"N" My Neighborhood.* Still, after eight albums into the game, it's hard not to think that MC Eiht should be able to provide a bit more insight into street life. *—Jon Azpiri*

Underground Hero / Jul. 2, 2002 / Priority ✦✦✦

By the time he recorded *Underground Hero*, MC Eiht was no longer topping the charts like he had back in the mid-'90s. He had indeed become "underground"—like most of his many other '90s gangsta peers like Spice 1 and Mack 10—making his albums for a small cult following rather than for the masses. But Eiht seems indifferent about his status. In fact, he almost seems to savor being underground because he no longer has to worry about chart-topping hits or haters like he did back in 1994. Throughout *Underground Hero*, he works with a tight circle of producers—Nic & Tone, the Platinum Brothers, Young Trey, Daven the Mad Hatter, Big Resse—and never departs too far from his usual style of street rapping. He still drops his trademark "ch-yas" several times per song and he still name-drops Compton quite often. In sum, little has changed for Eiht despite the passing of time. —*Jason Birchmeier*

MC Ge Gee

b. Bronx, NY
Christian Rap

The first female in Christian rap music, MC Ge Gee was born in the Bronx and raised in Dallas, where her parents ran an inner-city youth outreach that was the subject of the film *The Cross and the Switchblade*. In the middle of the rap fray, she wasn't a hard rapper, nor a pop one. She picked up the serious, issue-oriented street-poetry legacy of her late brother, D-Boy Rodriguez. Her two albums, 1990's *I'm for Real* and the following year's *And Now the Mission Continues*, appeared on Frontline. —*Bil Carpenter*

I'm for Real / 1990 / Frontline ✦✦✦

● **And Now the Mission Continues** / 1991 / Frontline ✦✦✦✦

A Tim Miner production of midrange rap that's not too hard and not too pop, the style is urban funk with spare sampling. Most of the album is message oriented, such as "I Caught the Mike," a pickup of D-Boy's "I Dropped the Mike," which speaks to the continuance of his ministry to youth by Ge Gee. —*Bil Carpenter*

MC Hammer (Stanley Kirk Burrell)

b. Mar. 30, 1962, Oakland, CA
New Jack Swing, Hip-Hop, West Coast Rap, Pop-Rap, Party Rap

There had been hit rap singles and albums before him, but MC Hammer was the man who truly brought rap music to a mass pop audience. Armed with a flamboyant wardrobe (particularly his trademark baggy parachute pants) and a raft of sampled hooks lifted straight from their sources, Hammer's talents as a dancer and showman far exceeded his technique as an MC. Still, he had an ear for catchy source material, and that helped his second album, *Please Hammer Don't Hurt 'Em*, become the best-selling rap album of all time. Even if he was never able to duplicate that level of success, and even if his street credibility was virtually nonexistent, Hammer still broke down numerous doors for rap music in the mainstream, demonstrating that hip-hop had the potential for blockbuster success in the marketplace.

MC Hammer was born Stanley Kirk Burrell in Oakland, CA, on March 30, 1962. A member of a strongly religious family, he landed a job as a bat/ball boy for the Oakland Athletics baseball team, where he entertained fans by dancing during breaks in the game, and earned the nickname "Hammer" for his resemblance to all-time home run leader "Hammerin'" Hank Aaron. An aspiring ballplayer himself, he failed to catch on with a professional organization following high school, and enlisted in the Navy for three years. Long a fan of funk and soul, he became interested in hip-hop upon returning to civilian life, and began performing in local clubs; with the financial help of several Athletics players, he also started his own record label, Bust It, and recorded a couple of popular local singles. With ex-Con Funk Shun mastermind Felton Pilate producing, Hammer recorded an album titled *Feel My Power* in 1987. After impressing a Capitol Records executive with his already elaborate live show, he was signed to a multi-album deal, the first of which was a revamped version of *Feel My Power* retitled *Let's Get It Started*. Producing an R&B hit in "Turn This Mutha Out," *Let's Get It Started* went double platinum.

Still, nothing could have foreshadowed the phenomenon of *Please Hammer Don't Hurt 'Em*, the 1990-released follow-up. Its first single, "U Can't Touch This," blatantly copped most of its hooks from Rick James' funk classic "Super Freak," yet Hammer's added catch phrases (and young listeners' unfamiliarity with the original song) helped make it a smash. "U Can't Touch This" dominated radio and MTV during 1990 in a way few rap singles ever

had, and won two Grammys (Best R&B Song, Best Solo Rap Performance); save for a quirk in its release format—it was only available as a 12″, which cut down on its sales—it would easily have been the first rap single to top the *Billboard* pop chart. The next two singles, "Have You Seen Her" (a flat-out cover of the Chi-Lites' '70s soul ballad) and "Pray" (built on the keyboard hook from Prince's "When Doves Cry"), followed "U Can't Touch This" into the Top Ten, eventually pushing sales of *Please Hammer Don't Hurt 'Em* past the ten-million mark and making it the number-one album of the year. Still, a backlash was growing against Hammer's frequent borrowing (some said theft) of classic hooks for his own hits; hip-hop purists also railed about his often simplistic, repetitive lyrics (indeed, "Pray" set a new record for the number of times its title was repeated during the song, at well over 100). The charges of rank commercialism weren't lessened by the merchandising machine that soon kicked in: endorsement deals, MC Hammer dolls, even a Saturday morning cartoon show.

Seeking to counteract the criticism, Hammer dropped the "MC" from his name and used more live instrumentation on his 1991 follow-up album, *Too Legit to Quit*. While it sold very well (over three million copies) and produced a sizable hit in the title track, Hammer's stage show had become as lavish as his lifestyle; loaded with singers, dancers, and backup musicians, the supporting concert tour was too expensive for the album's sales to finance, and it was canceled partway through. Hammer scored his last big hit with "Addams Groove," the theme to the film version of *The Addams Family*, and then paused to reconsider his approach. In 1994, he returned with *The Funky Headhunter*, a harder-edged, more aggressive record that went gold, but failed to win him a new audience among hardcore hip-hop fans. On 1995's *Inside Out*, Hammer seemed unsure of whether he wanted to appeal to pop or rap audiences; the album flopped, and Hammer was let out of his contract. In 1996, Hammer filed for bankruptcy, his taste for luxury having gotten the better of his dwindling income; his mansion was sold at a fraction of its cost. The crisis prompted a religious reawakening, and he began to write new material with an emphasis on spirituality and family. The album *Family Affair* was slated for release on Hammer's own Oaktown 3.5.7. label, but plans were aborted at the last minute; only 1000 copies were pressed, and were never distributed nationally, save for limited Internet downloads. Several projects were rumored to be in the works, including another album (*War Chest: Turn of the Century*) and a soundtrack to the film *Return to Glory: The Powerful Stirring of the Black Man*, but none ever appeared. Finally, Hammer released a new album, the patriotic-themed *Active Duty*, through his own WorldHit label in late 2001. —*Steve Huey*

Let's Get It Started / 1988 / Capitol ✦✦✦

MC Hammer's double-platinum debut album, *Let's Get It Started*, made him a star in the R&B world even before he crossed over to the pop charts. It isn't as immediately hooky a record as *Please Hammer Don't Hurt 'Em*, in part because Hammer hasn't developed his signature sampling chutzpah. Sure, the hit single "Turn This Mutha Out" samples its title from Parliament's biggest hit, and "That's What I Said" borrows the bass line of "Freddie's Dead," but these aren't the wholesale appropriations that would take Hammer to the top. The main appeal of *Let's Get It Started* is simply that it's well produced, funky, and danceable, regardless of the quality of the raps. Consider this: by 1988, advancements in lyrical technique were beginning to render even superstars Run-D.M.C. a little outmoded. Just starting out, Hammer sounds slower and less forceful than those old school legends, and his rhymes are even more squared off and less fluid in their relationship to the beat. Still, he hollers his simple lyrics with energy and enthusiasm throughout the album, and he does have more power in his delivery here than on *Please Hammer Don't Hurt 'Em*. Plus, this style wasn't *totally* outdated in hip-hop's mainstream quite yet. Still, it isn't what makes the best cuts work. "Turn This Mutha Out" gets by more on its distinctive keyboard riff, and tracks like "They Put Me in the Mix" and "Pump It Up (Here's the News)" are designed more for the dancefloor than the street. —*Steve Huey*

Please Hammer Don't Hurt 'Em / Jan. 1990 / Capitol ✦✦✦

Still the biggest-selling rap album of all time at ten million copies (though the Beastie Boys' *Licensed to Ill* is gaining rapidly), *Please Hammer Don't Hurt 'Em* proved that rap music was no longer just a specialty niche genre, but had the crossover potential to be a commercial juggernaut. But in an art form so conscious of preserving its integrity, this wasn't the way to go about it—at least not from a creative standpoint. Hammer builds the majority of the songs here on obvious samples from easily recognizable soul and funk hits of the past, relying on the original hooks without twisting them into anything new (or, by implication, his own). That approach confirmed the worst fears of hip-hop purists about how the music might hit the mainstream. Taken on its own terms, *Please Hammer Don't Hurt 'Em* is a pretty slick—if unsubtle—pop confection. Hammer certainly has good taste in source material, if nothing else; the hits "U Can't Touch This" and "Pray" crib from Rick James' "Super Freak" and Prince's "When Doves Cry," respectively, and the ballad "Have You Seen Her" is a flat-out cover of the Chi-Lites' hit (with some updated lyrics). Other tracks sample Marvin Gaye; Earth, Wind & Fire; and the Jackson 5. Throughout the record, choruses are repeated ad infinitum for maximum memorability, which either makes it irresistible or irritating, depending on your taste. Hammer *has* improved as a rapper—his delivery is often more subtle, and he even attempts a little bit of verbal flash here and there. He still isn't technically on a par with the average MC of the time—he's a little too stiff, flowing awkwardly around the beat. Of course, his simple style also makes him easy to understand, and coupled with the highly danceable production and a great set of borrowed hooks, it's easy to see why *Please Hammer Don't Hurt 'Em* was so popular—and why it now functions chiefly as a nostalgia piece. —*Steve Huey*

Too Legit to Quit / Oct. 21, 1991 / Capitol ♦♦♦
With his third album, *Too Legit to Quit*, Hammer dropped the "MC" from his name, but didn't undergo any major changes musically. Indeed, *Legit* provided a heavy dose of the thing that made *Please Hammer Don't Hurt 'Em* so successful: likeable, fun pop-rap that appealed to mainstream Top 40 audiences more than the 'hood. For a few years, Hammer almost seemed to be the Michael Jackson of rap. Although it fell short of *Please Hammer's* artistic and commercial success, *Legit* definitely had its share of inviting hits, including "This Is the Way We Roll" and the title song. While Hammer hasn't always been the most challenging artist in the world, the Oakland native has some noteworthy social commentary in "Living in a World Like This" and "Brothers Hang On"—both of which are disturbing commentaries on the harsh realities of ghetto life. —*Alex Henderson*

The Funky Headhunter / Mar. 1, 1994 / Giant ♦♦♦
The former MC Hammer resurfaced with a new musical identity and rap approach on this 1994 album. Getting help from new school producers and debuting a video on *The Arsenio Hall Show*, Hammer's sound was leaner, his rapping tougher and more fluid, and his subject matter harder and less humorous. The results seemed to have worked; *The Funky Headhunter* peaked at number two on the R&B list, went gold, and remained in the Top 30 midway through the year. —*Ron Wynn*

Inside Out / Sep. 12, 1995 / Giant ♦♦
On *V Inside Out*, MC Hammer returned to his old moniker, as well as moving back to the more pop-oriented sound of *Please Hammer Don't Hurt 'Em*. Although the album initially fared well on the R&B charts, it didn't have much staying power, which could be due to the inconsistent quality of the record. MC Hammer seems unsure of himself throughout the album, attempting to gain some street credibility and a mass audience simultaneously. The result is a record that has a few good isolated moments, but never delivers a knockout punch, let alone a memorable hook or groove. —*Stephen Thomas Erlewine*

● **Greatest Hits** / Oct. 1, 1996 / Capitol ♦♦♦♦♦
Despite being one of the best-selling rappers of all time, none of MC Hammer's albums were very consistent—the singles stood out like a sore thumb among the filler on each record, which is why *Greatest Hits* is such a good bargain. *Greatest Hits* compiles 12 of Hammer's biggest hits for Capitol Records, including "U Can't Touch This," "Pump It Up," "Turn This Mutha Out," "They Put Me in the Mix," "Have You Seen Her," "Pray," "Here Comes the Hammer," "2 Legit 2 Quit," "Do Not Pass Me By," and "Addams Groove." It's not only an excellent introduction to MC Hammer, it's the best album in his entire catalog. —*Stephen Thomas Erlewine*

Back to Back Hits / Apr. 10, 1998 / Cema Special Markets ♦♦♦
MC Hammer and Vanilla Ice are a great pairing for a *Back 2 Back Hits* disc. Both artists were the personification of pop-rap in the late '80s/early '90s, and they unexpectedly became million-selling artists on the strength of just a handful of singles. MC Hammer's five songs do an excellent job of gathering his best material, as all of his biggest hits—"U Can't Touch This," "Addams Groove," "2 Legit 2 Quit," "Pray," "Have You Seen Her"—are included. Vanilla

Ice's half, on the other hand, is imperfect, to say the least. "Ice Ice Baby" is here, of course, as is his minor final single, "Cool As Ice (Everybody Get Loose)," which featured Naomi Campbell. However, "Play That Funky Music" and "I Love You" are taken from his lame live album, not *To the Extreme*, which is where the original hit versions are. That alone makes the value of his five songs negligible, but the Hammer section is so good, this disc is still recommended to budget-minded pop-rap fans. —*Stephen Thomas Erlewine*

The Hits / Dec. 12, 2000 / Disky ♦♦♦♦
It may not be a very popular idea anymore, but the fact is that MC Hammer made some of the biggest and catchiest rap music ever to break into the mainstream. His hard-edged delivery was really one of the first to break out of the slow and deliberate pattern that previous successes like Run-D.M.C. and LL Cool J had utilized. Along with Public Enemy, N.W.A, and a few others, he took the old school style of rap and updated it slightly without taking it to the next step à la A Tribe Called Quest. Instead, he took what was a hot formula at the time, found some excellent beats and tracks, and crafted the intense juggernaut *Please Hammer Don't Hurt 'Em*. The tracks off that album that made it to *The Hits* are blatantly the best songs on the whole album. From the emotional "Pray" to the classic "U Can't Touch This," MC Hammer was one of the guiding forces of the new jack swing movement in the early '90s. "2 Legit 2 Quit" couldn't be longer, going on for what seems like 700 hours as the same repetitive phrase drives itself into the listener's brain like a rusty dentist's drill. The tracks from that album (with the exception of the bouncy "This Is the Way We Roll") are so hideously bad that it's hard to imagine how he could have taken such a dramatic downswing after his unprecedented success. Of course, having a cartoon series based on your shoes after three years in the business must do something terrible to someone's mind, so maybe it was that instant mainstream acceptance that made it such a terrible record. The few songs that made it from *Let's Get It Started* are quite good, proving that before his rise to the top he genuinely had a talent for his craft. That is the cut-off point for this collection, ignoring the underrated experiment with gangsta rap (*Funky Headhunter*) and the Christian-influenced follow-ups (*Inside Out*, *Active Duty*) that he would unsuccessfully support throughout the '90s. MC Hammer was never great, but his rise and fall was one of the most extreme in the history of pop music, and this collection points out why his one successful album is really the only one in his career that could have had anywhere near the impact that it did at the time. —*Bradley Torreano*

MC Lyte

b. Oct. 11, 1971, Brooklyn, NY
Club/Dance, East Coast Rap, Pop-Rap
MC Lyte was one of the first female rappers to point out the sexism and misogyny that often runs rampant in hip-hop, often taking the subject head on lyrically in her songs and helping open the door for such future artists as Queen Latifah and Missy Elliott. Born and raised in Brooklyn, NY, Lyte began rhyming at the age of 12, which eventually led to a single, "I Cram to Understand U," which led to a recording contract with the First Priority label. MC Lyte's full-length debut, *Lyte as a Rock*, surfaced in 1988, while a follow-up, *Eyes on This*, followed a year later. Both discs are considered the finest of the rapper's career, especially her sophomore effort, which spawned the hit single "Cha Cha Cha" (peaking at number one on the rap charts) and the anti-violence track "Cappucino." Lyte turned to Bell Biv DeVoe's writers and producers Wolf & Epic for her third release overall, 1991's *Act Like You Know*, a more soul-music-based work than its predecessors and in 1993, issued *Ain't No Other* (the album's popular single, "Ruffneck," earned a Grammy nomination for Best Rap Single and turned out to be the first gold single ever achieved by a female rap artist).

By the mid-'90s, Lyte had relocated to a new record label, Elektra/Asylum, issuing such further releases as 1996's *Bad As I Wanna B*, which featured a duet with Missy Elliott on the track "Cold Rock a Party," and 1998's *Seven & Seven*, which included further guest appearances by Elliott, as well as Giovanni Salah and LL Cool J, the latter of which produced the track "Play Girls Play." In addition to her own albums, MC Lyte has teamed with other artists from time to time, including Atlanta's Xscape on the Soul Train Award-winning "Keep on Keepin' On" (a track that also appeared on the *Sunset Park* soundtrack and became Lyte's second gold single), and has tried acting, appearing on several TV shows, including such comedies as *Moesha* and *In the*

House, plus the crime drama *New York Undercover*. Lyte has also put aside time to become active in several social projects/organizations, including anti-violence campaigns, Rock the Vote, and AIDS benefits. In 2001, Rhino Records issued the 16-track career overview *The Very Best of MC Lyte*. Lyte then mounted a comeback in 2003 with *Da Undaground Heat, Vol. 1.* —*Greg Prato*

● **Lyte as a Rock** / 1988 / First Priority ✦✦✦✦✦
In the earliest years of the hip-hop game, women were quite frequently overlooked until a new breed of female lyricist came along and gave the proverbial middle finger to a male-dominated game. MC Lyte's debut ushered in the era of the female MC—confident, brazen, and not afraid to put male MCs in their misogynist place without flinching. The album starts off with a rather slow introduction before kicking things into high gear with the now-classic title track, which put Lyte in the center of a media frenzy. With Lyte reasserting her femininity over and over again without compromising production quality or lyric delivery, *Lyte as a Rock* has aged better than most records that came out during hip-hop's formative years, although at certain moments it has become dated since its release. But what has aged is more than compensated by the classic tunes and the disc's potent historical impact on a generation of women MCs. A classic. —*Rob Theakston*

Eyes on This / 1989 / First Priority ✦✦✦✦
A rapper with considerable technique and a fine sense of humor, Lyte was one of the most highly regarded female MCs of the late '80s and early '90s—especially on the East Coast. *Eyes on This*, the Brooklyn native's second album, tends to be one-dimensional lyrically—she spends too much time bragging about how superior her rapping skills are and how inept sucker MCs are. Though it's hard not to admire the technique and strong chops she displays on such boasting fare as "Shut the Eff Up! (Hoe)"—an attack on Lyte's nemesis Antoinette—and "Slave 2 the Rhythm," she's at her best when telling some type of meaningful story. Undeniably, the CD's standout track is "Cappucino," an imaginative gem in which Lyte stops by a Manhattan cafe and gets caught in the crossfire of rival drug dealers. In the afterlife, she asks herself: "Why, oh why, did I need cappucino?" Were everything on the album in a class with "Cappucino," it would have been an outstanding album instead of simply a good one. —*Alex Henderson*

Act Like You Know / Sep. 17, 1991 / First Priority ✦✦✦
Though highly respected in rap's hardcore, MC Lyte was never a platinum seller. Atlantic Records no doubt encouraged her to be more commercial on her third album, *Act like You Know*—a generally softer, more melodic and often R&B-ish effort than either of her first two LPs. But even so, the album is far from a sellout—Lyte's music still has plenty of bite, substance, and integrity. Like before, she's at her best when telling some type of story instead of simply boasting about her rapping skills. Especially riveting are "Eyes Are the Soul," a poignant reflection on the destruction caused by crack cocaine, "Lola at the Copa," a warning about how a one-night stand can lead to AIDS; and "Poor Georgie," which describes a young man's life and death in the fast lane. Lyte's change of direction proved to be short-lived—with her next album, *Ain't No Other*, she returned to hardcore rap in a big way. —*Alex Henderson*

Ain't No Other / 1993 / First Priority ✦✦✦
Whenever a hardcore rapper becomes more commercial, hip-hop's hardcore is likely to cry "sellout." That's exactly what happened to MC Lyte when she increased her R&B/pop appeal with 1991's *Act Like You Know*. The album wasn't without grit or integrity and even had some strong sociopolitical numbers, but hip-hop purists can be every bit as rigid as jazz purists—and they tend to be wary of any attempt to cross over. So in 1993, Lyte ditched the pop elements and emphasized hardcore rap on *Ain't No Other*. The song that did the most to define the album was "Ruffneck," a catchy, inspired single that found Lyte expressing her preference for raggamuffin street kids from the inner city. "Ruffneck" expressed Lyte's allegiance to hip-hop's hardcore, and she's equally rugged and hard edged on tunes like "Fuck that Motherfucking Bullshit," "Hard Copy," and "Brooklyn." As a bonus track, First Priority includes a remix of "I Cram to Understand U," the song that put Lyte on the map in 1987. Not earth shattering but generally decent, *Ain't No Other* will appeal to those who prefer Lyte's more hardcore side. —*Alex Henderson*

Bad As I Wanna B / Aug. 27, 1996 / EastWest ✦✦✦
MC Lyte's *Bad As I Wanna B* suffers from stilted production, conventional musical ideas, and overreaching lyrics. It is clear that MC Lyte wants to

restore the luster to her career, but she is not sure how. So, she surrounds herself with top-flight producers, who such away the passion from her music. Sure, there's a couple of good hooks and funky beats on *Bad As I Wanna B*, but for the most part, it's lacking in soul. —*Leo Stanley*

Seven & Seven / Aug. 18, 1998 / EastWest ✦✦✦
Ten years after releasing her first album, MC Lyte delivered *Seven & Seven*, her sixth album. During that time, Lyte remained remarkably unchanged, and *Seven & Seven* proves to be startlingly similar to the slick, R&B-influenced hip-hop she's been turning out since *Lyte as a Rock*. At times, that's not too bad, but the album's exhausting 77-minute running length makes the similarity of the material a little numbing. There are good songs buried in the album, to be sure—it just takes too much time to dig them out. —*Leo Stanley*

● **The Very Best of MC Lyte** / Sep. 4, 2001 / Rhino ✦✦✦✦
Rhino's 2001 collection *The Very Best of MC Lyte* is an excellent summary of MC Lyte's recordings for Atlantic records. The collection balances her career quite nimbly, with four tracks from her 1988 debut *Lyte as a Rock*, five from 1989's *Eyes on This*, three from 1991's *Act Like You Know*, two from *Ain't No Other*, and one from *Bad As I Wanna B*, with her guest appearance on Foster/McElroy's "Dr. Soul," and the Bad Boy remix "Cold Rock a Party" rounding out the compilation for good measure. The decreasing returns from each subsequent album signals that MC Lyte's material did dip as the '90s wore on, but this does contain credible highlights from those records, while her hardcore golden age recordings—"10% Dis," "I Cram to Understand U," "Kickin' 4 Brooklyn," "Cha Cha Cha," "I Am the Lyte," "Shut the Eff Up! (Hoe)"—still stand as fresh, powerful hip-hop. The first two records still hold their own, but this is a very good sampler and introduction in its own right. —*Stephen Thomas Erlewine*

MC 900 Ft. Jesus (Mark Griffin)

b. Dallas, TX
Producer, Vocals / Hip-Hop, Alternative Rap, Alternative Dance
Taking the name MC 900 Ft. Jesus from an Oral Roberts' sermon, the Dallas native Mark Griffin began recording in the late '80s. MC 900 Ft. Jesus' first records were bracing fusions of hip-hop, industrial, and spoken word, with hints of jazz. He became a favorite on college radio with his 1990 debut, *Hell With the Lid Off*, and 1991's *Welcome to My Dream*, yet he never established much more than a cult following. Laying low for a couple years, MC 900 Ft. Jesus returned with his most popular record to date in 1994, *One Step Ahead of the Spider*. Featuring the hit single "If I Only Had a Brain," the record was calmer than his earlier work, incorporating more elements of jazz and funk; it was a hit on both alternative radio and MTV. —*Stephen Thomas Erlewine*

Hell With the Lid Off / 1990 / Nettwerk ✦✦✦✦
Aligned more with a rap-informed industrial scene that included Consolidated and Meat Beat Manifesto than with rap itself, MC 900 Ft. Jesus did rhyme, but his delivery was closer to Kerouac's beat poetry than the hardcore poetry of KRS-One. Excellent scratching courtesy of DJ Zero complements the eclectic productions that range from the chop-happy jazz of "Truth Is Out of Style" to the techno-goth funk of "Real Black Angel." The affected irony of his delivery can be distracting, but *Hell With the Lid Off* remains a highly compelling recording, if only for its brash flirtation with so many styles—techno, funk, cool jazz, house—and its refusal to settle for any of them. —*Wade Kergan*

● **Welcome to My Dream** / 1991 / Nettwerk ✦✦✦✦
The follow-up to *Hell With the Lid Off* is darker, less cartoonish, and far more influenced by funk and jazz than before (if it weren't for the slightly whiny vocals over top of the opening cut, you might mistake the backing track for something from Miles Davis' fusion period). In a lot of ways, *Welcome to My Dream* was a precursor to trip-hop, layering hip-hop beats over jazzy breaks and dreamlike instrumentation. The problem is tracks like "Killer Inside Me" and "Adventures in Failure": the backing tracks are killer and the delivery of the rhymes are top notch, but they're ultimately a bit silly, which makes it a bit hard to take the rest of the album seriously. That's a shame because there are some great tracks here, like "The City Sleeps'" and "Falling Elevators." As before, DJ Zero scratches with aplomb. —*Sean Carruthers*

One Step Ahead of the Spider / Jun. 28, 1994 / American ✦✦✦✦
With a tamboura drone and an insistent bass ostinato, *One Step Ahead of the Spider* opens with a sound reminiscent of Mahavishnu John McLaughlin's *My Goals Beyond*, but the spoken-word narration that commences soon

afterward (mostly courtesy of singer/guitarist Mark Griffin) places this record in completely different territory. The vocals on this record are often quite entertaining, as in "Tiptoe Through the Inferno" (sample lyric: "Do not make the mistake of believing that I am the person who is speaking to you now/I am not; that is to say N-O-T/This is an indisputable fact that has been scientifically proven"), but sometimes the drawled delivery and shaky pitch don't work. A good example of this is the band's cover of Curtis Mayfield's "Stare and Stare," where the presence of guitar virtuoso Vernon Reid helps to liven up the slightly awkward vocal performance by Griffin. However, the emphasis on *One Step Ahead of the Spider* is most definitely the groove and, with drummer Earl Harvin Jr. assisted by Mike Dillon and Nikhil Pandya (on congas and tablas, respectively), the vibe is somewhere in between *Bitches Brew* and a neo-hippie drum circle, with a little '70s funk thrown into the mix for good measure. The Miles Davis connection really becomes obvious on "Bill's Dream," which sounds for all the world like an outtake from *In a Silent Way*. The almost-ambient album closer "Rhubarb" is a strong, enchanting song, with vocals that sound like they were recorded on a boom box. The cryptic conversation heard on this track closes the album out with a mysterious vibe, mirroring the haunting opener, "New Moon." *One Step Ahead of the Spider* is an eclectic mix of serious and humorous elements, of hipper-than-thou narration and funk-trance instrumentation, making for a unique sound. It's not a bad album by any means, but there is a bit of a dearth of really strong ideas to go with the creative concept. Worth searching out. —*Daniel Gioffre*

MC Peaches

Golden Age, East Coast Rap, Hip-Hop
Brooklyn rapper MC Peaches released just one album, 1991's *More Than Just a Pretty Face*, on EastWest, featuring productions from Audio Two and El Bravador. —*John Bush*

More Than Just a Pretty Face / 1991 / EastWest ♦♦

A female hip-hopper from New York, MC Peaches had decent rapping skills. But her chops don't prevent *More Than Just a Pretty Face* from being mediocre and forgettable. Even the input of the King of Chill and Brooklyn's Audio Two (both of whom were highly regarded in Big Apple hip-hop circles of the late '80s and early '90s and were known for their work with MC Lyte) as producers and mixers doesn't help—there's just no getting around the fact that "Dope Is How It's Done," "I'mma Let You Know," and other boasting numbers are routine and unimaginative. Peaches' interpretations of pop-rock hits like the Police's "Every Breath You Take" and John Waite's "Missing You" are as mundane as her more hardcore offerings. Among the few worthwhile songs on the CD are the angry "Keep It In Your Pants, Tucked Away," which urges young women not to sleep with men who disrespect them, and the infectious, jazzy "Good Thing." But on the whole, *More Than Just a Pretty Face* isn't anything to get excited about. —*Alex Henderson*

MC Ren (Lorenzo Patterson)

b. Jun. 14, 1969
Gangsta Rap, Hardcore Rap, West Coast Rap
MC Ren had a much less celebrated solo career than most of his former bandmates in N.W.A, despite enjoying some commercial success. Born Lorenzo Patterson on June 14, 1969, Ren was recruited to join N.W.A in 1988 while still attending high school. He was a strong presence on the group's landmark *Straight Outta Compton* later that year, and also wrote several tracks for Eazy-E's solo debut, *Eazy-Duz-It*. Following 1991's *Niggaz4Life*, N.W.A disbanded acrimoniously, and Ren stuck with Ruthless Records, kicking off his solo career with the six-song EP *Kizz My Black Azz* in 1992. It sold well, making the Top Ten on the R&B chart and nearly doing the same on the pop side. Ren subsequently converted to the Nation of Islam, which helped out relations with the remainder of N.W.A; he patched up his differences with Ice Cube, and remained neutral in the heated feud between Dr. Dre and Eazy-E. Meanwhile, he released his first full-length album, *Shock of the Hour*, in 1993 (the original title, "Life Sentence," was changed following his conversion). It hit number one on the R&B charts and sold quite well for a brief window of time. Shaken by Eazy-E's death from AIDS, Ren returned in 1996 with *Da Villain in Black*, which found him working with a G-funk blueprint with help from Above the Law. It, too, made the R&B Top Ten, and sold respectably well without much airplay support. Ren further updated his sound on 1998's *Ruthless for Life*, which briefly made the R&B Top 20. —*Steve Huey*

Kizz My Black Azz EP / Jun. 30, 1992 / Priority ♦♦♦

It would be easier to dismiss MC Ren's obsessively violent and sexist lyrics if his music wasn't so tight and menacing. Taken on purely musical terms, *Kizz My Black Azz* is thrilling; when it's analyzed more deeply, the simplistic, disturbing lyrics unravel the achievements of the music. However, the production and beats are so deeply funky that they almost lift Ren's debut solo EP out of the swamp of violent, misogynist gangstas. Almost. —*Stephen Thomas Erlewine*

● Shock of the Hour / 1993 / Ruthless ♦♦♦♦

MC Ren's debut LP is uneven, but it at least presents a lyrical vision when it's not spewing out familiar, tired, sexist clichés about women. Ren highlights American hyprocisy with a vengeance, and the title track foresees the nation's fiery end in an apocalyptic fury enabling black people to finally achieve justice. Both this tune and "Attack On Babylon" come closest to presenting a coherent, effective philosophy. Another provocative track is "Same Old S," a song that strips away any pretense of glamour around the gangsta lifestyle and outlines the brutality, paranoia, and violence at its core. These tracks display MC Ren's potential as a hip-hop theorist; the others just fill out the CD. —*Ron Wynn*

Da Villain in Black / Apr. 9, 1996 / Relativity ♦♦

MC Ren's solo career has suffered from an overreliance on gangsta rap clichés, and his second full-length album, *Da Villain in Black*, is no exception. Working with Above the Law's Cold 187um, Ren has constructed an album that doesn't deviate from clichéd G-funk grooves. Furthermore, Ren hasn't come up with lyrics to match his first two solo records, let alone Dre, Ice Cube, or Eazy-E. Relying on profanity instead of insight, the halfhearted raps sadly fit the unimaginative music perfectly. —*Stephen Thomas Erlewine*

Ruthless for Life / Jun. 30, 1998 / Ruthless ♦♦♦♦

Working with a new producer and enlisting an impressive roster of guest artists (including Snoop Doggy Dogg, Ice Cube, Eightball & MJG, and RBX), MC Ren reconfigures himself as a latter-day gangsta rapper, complete with stoned beatas and loping bass lines. It's sort of disconcerting to hear a former N.W.A rapper trying to position himself as a member of the No Limit posse, but Ren does this fairly well. There's a few weak tracks on *Ruthless for Life* and all of his ideas are a little shopworn, but it does sound better than another collection of hardcore post-N.W.A hip-hop would have. So, *Ruthless for Life* does revitalize Ren—it gives the opportunity to sound like a contemporary, not a washed-up veteran. And that, in a way, makes it one of his better solo records. —*Stephen Thomas Erlewine*

MC Serch (Michael Berrin)

b. May 6, 1967, Queens, NY
Golden Age, East Coast Rap, Alternative Rap
Widely recognized as one of the most respected white rappers, MC Serch (born Michael Berrin) made up one-third of 3rd Bass. After three full-lengths with Pete Nice and DJ Richie Rich—two studio albums and a remix collection—Serch went solo with 1992's *Return of the Product*. Like the 3rd Bass releases, it came out on Def Jam. One of the singles from the album, an extension of Main Source's "Back to the Grill," featured a rare rap performance from Nas and hit the top of the *Billboard* rap chart; Serch also primed Nas for stardom by tapping his "Halftime" for the *Zebrahead* soundtrack and working with him on *Illmatic*, both of which he executive produced. Once Serch receded from the MC spotlight, he ran a promotions company and also became a radio host. In 2002 he took over WJLB Detroit's morning program—he became the first non-black DJ at the station since Casey Kasem's run in the '50s. —*Andy Kellman*

● Return of the Product / 1992 / Def Jam ♦♦♦

MC Serch's first album after the breakup of 3rd Bass was a stripped-down, surprisingly melodic album that suffers from a lack of sharp production. Even so, Serch's skillful rhymes overcome most of the weaknesses of the record. —*Stephen Thomas Erlewine*

MC Shan (Shawn Moltke)

Producer, Mixing, Voices / Golden Age, Old School Rap, Hip-Hop
According to legend, MC Shan (born Shawn Moltke) got his big break in 1983 when the future boss of Cold Chillin' Records caught Shan trying to steal his car. Although the fact that old school superproducer Marley Marl was Shan's cousin probably didn't hurt either, Shan took advantage of the opportunity to become a member of Marl's Juice Crew All-Stars. After several

singles (including the old school classic "The Bridge"), his 1987 album debut *Down By Law* established a b-boy persona over tracks produced by his cousin. The same held for the 1988 follow-up, *Born to Be Wild*; on 1990's *Play It Again, Shan*, he opted for a more mature outlook and a new producer, but it proved to be his final effort. Though he moved into production work, he made a return on "Da Bridge 2001," from *Queensbridge's Finest*, a 2000 LP released by Nas. — *Steve Huey*

Down By Law / 1987 / Cold Chillin' ✦✦✦

MC Shan's album debut wasn't a success, despite the presence of one justifiable rap classic and several other interesting ideas for songs. Most of the problem lay in Marley Marl's productions, which took the sound of MC Shan no farther than his massive hit, "The Bridge," and seemed to merely duplicate the process with every track. Shan opened with a pair of intriguing project stories, one about a solid student turned junkie ("Jane, Stop This Crazy Thing") and the other about an easy girl ("Project 'Ho"). Admittedly, these tracks weren't quite as exciting as they were compelling, but Marley Marl's constant focus on stuttered-sampling madness soon lapsed into mildness and then simple frustration. Shan got a bit more hardcore on "Kill That Noise," responding again to KRS-One and Boogie Down Productions, and finally returned to the astounding energy level of "The Bridge" with a pair of later tracks, "Down By Law" and "Living in the World of Hip Hop." — *John Bush*

Born to Be Wild / Jul. 1988 / Cold Chillin' ✦✦✦

What once might have sounded rebellious seemed tame by contemporary standards on MC Shan's *Born to Be Wild*. When contrasted with the ranks of gun-toting, confrontational gangsta types, this seemed meek and unassuming by comparison, even though Shan's rhymes were often quite amusing and clever. — *Ron Wynn*

Play It Again, Shan / Jun. 1990 / Cold Chillin' ✦✦✦

Along with Big Daddy Kane, Biz Markie, and Roxanne Shanté, MC Shan was one of the rappers who put Cold Chillin' Records on the map. The New Yorker never had a multiplatinum seller, but he was an entertaining and often clever MC whose solid rhyming skills earned him a medium-sized following in the mid- to late '80s (especially on the East Coast). While *Play It Again, Shan* isn't outstanding, the CD has quite a few strong points, including "It Don't Mean a Thing," which draws on the Duke Ellington classic, "Death Was Quite a Surprise," an account of a youth who gets sick of working for minimum wage, becomes a drug dealer, and pays with his life; and the anti-drug commentary "Rock Stuff." The only weak offering is "I Want to Thank You," a clichéd Latin freestyle tune that aims for the TKA/Stevie B crowd and proves that Shan should stick to rap. — *Alex Henderson*

● Best of Cold Chillin' / May 22, 2001 / Cold Chillin' ✦✦✦✦

If they were completely honest, the compilers of MC Shan's career wrap-up *The Best of Cold Chillin'* would've either retitled the disc or made it a 12"/CD-5, combining his massive "The Bridge" with "Down by Law" or "Living in the World of Hip Hop." Still, the author of one undeniable hip-hop classic did record some other interesting tracks, incisive storytelling raps like "Jane, Stop This Crazy Thing," "Project 'Ho," and "Cocaine" (here in a live version) as well as a few solid battle raps ("Kill That Noise," "Beat Biter") and an LL Cool J loverman track called "Left Me Lonely." Marley Marl's productions only began varying with his latter-day material, making many of these tracks production soundalikes, but *The Best of Cold Chillin'* certainly doesn't miss anything from one of the Juice Crew's best. — *John Bush*

MC Shy D (Peter Jones)

b. Bronx, NY

Hip-Hop, Southern Rap, Party Rap

MC Shy D (born Peter Jones) is the Bronx-born cousin of Afrika Bambaataa. He began on Luther Campbell's label in 1987 with *Got to Be Tough* and *Comin' Correct in '88*. After one more record (1989's *Don't Sweat Me*), he went through a lean period but rebounded in 1993 with *The Comeback*. It was a more artistically ambitious release, with more contemporary production and a lean, refined rapping style. Another long hiatus preceded the appearance of *Recordnize*, featuring DJ Smurf. — *Ron Wynn*

● Got to Be Tough / 1987 / Luke ✦✦✦

Most of the rappers who recorded for Luther Campbell's Luke Skyywalker Records (which later became Luke Records) in the late '80s fell into the Miami bass category. But Peter Jones, aka MC Shy D, was an exception.

Originally from the Bronx, Shy D moved to the Atlanta area but never forgot his New York roots. Although the MC's debut album, *Got to Be Tough*, was recorded in Ft. Lauderdale, FL, and lists Campbell as its executive producer, none of the material is Florida sounding. In fact, this 1987 LP is consistently New York minded. Shy D's rapping style is right out of the Run-D.M.C./LL Cool J school of 1980s New York hip-hop, and his raw, hard-edged producing (which consists mainly of a drum machine, scratching, and samples) leaves no doubt that he was a major admirer of New York turntable wizards like Jam Master Jay and Cut Creator. When this LP came out, other Atlanta-based MCs were opting to project overtly Southern identities. Some were into the sort of fast, hyper bass music and X-rated booty rhymes that Campbell and his Florida colleagues were putting on the map —others favored a sound that was slower than bass but still very Southern sounding. Shy D, however, was never a Southern-style rapper. He was a native New Yorker who made Atlanta his adopted home, and *Got to Be Tough* sounds like it could have been recorded in Queens, Brooklyn, or the Bronx instead of the South. Occasionally, Shy D gets into social issues; "Paula's on Crack" is a blunt, hard-hitting tune about a young woman who has turned to prostitution to support her crack cocaine addiction. But most of the time, Shy D sticks to boasting lyrics on this LP, which falls short of remarkable but is still an enjoyable and decent slice of 1980s b-boy rhyming. — *Alex Henderson*

Comin' Correct in '88 / 1988 / Luke ✦✦✦

Don't Sweat Me / 1989 / On Top ✦✦

MC Skat Kat and the Stray Mob

Group / Pop-Rap

MC Skat Kat was a cartoon character created by Michael Patterson and Candace Reckinger for Paula Abdul's video "Opposites Attract." The Stray Mob was comprised of Fatz, Taboo, Leo, Micetro, Katleen, and Silk. *The Adventures of MC Skat Kat and the Stray Mob* flopped quickly after being issued in 1991 on Captive. — *Ron Wynn*

The Adventures of MC Skat Kat and the Stray Mob / 1988 / Captive ✦

Hip-hop's hardcore tends to take a very dim view of commercialism in rap. As many hardcore rappers see it, Middle America already made a mockery of rock, blues, and jazz and has equally dishonorable intentions where rap is concerned. So when an artist as commercial and mainstream as Paula Abdul served as an executive producer on this pop-rap effort, rap's hardcore responded with anger and resentment. But instead of condemning *The Adventures of Skat Kat* because it isn't a Public Enemy or Tupac Shakur album, it's best to take it for what it is: a cute, often amusing novelty item. The tunes are delivered from the perspective of the animated feline rapper known as MC Skat Kat, whose amusing song titles include "I Ain't No Kitty," "No Dogs Allowed," and "New Kat Swing." This is rap that's drenched with pop, urban contemporary, and dance music, and the rapping has little in common with Chuck D, Kool Moe Dee, or Ice-T but has everything in common with MC Hammer and Marky Mark. This CD isn't a masterpiece, but most of the songs are catchy as well as entertaining. — *Alex Henderson*

MC Solaar (Claude M'Barali)

b. Senegal

Hip-Hop, Jazz-Rap, Foreign Rap

The best and most popular French rapper, MC Solaar found success in America among fans of acid jazz and jazz-rap (if not the larger hip-hop community) after guesting on Guru's acclaimed *Jazzmatazz* project. His fluid phrasing makes up for his lack of English, and the production on his solo work (by DJ Jimmy Jay and Boom Bass of La Funk Mob) surpasses that of most of his hip-hop contemporaries.

Born Claude M'Barali in Senegal, Solaar later moved to Paris and released his first single, "Bouge de La," in 1990. Two later tracks became French hits, prompting the release of his first album, *Qui Seme le Vent Recolte le Tempo*, in 1991. Introduced to the U.S. by way of two compilations (Tommy Boy's *Planet Rap* and Island's *The Rebirth of Cool*), MC Solaar recorded "Le Bien, Le Mal" for 1993's *Jazzmatazz* LP. His second album, *Prose Combat*, earned an American release on Cohiba by 1994. *Paradisiaque* followed in 1997, and Solaar returned a year later with a self-titled effort. *La Tour de la Question* appeared in 1998. — *John Bush*

Qui Seme le Vent Recolte le Tempo / 1991 / Polygram ✦✦✦

● **Prose Combat** / 1994 / Cohiba ✦✦✦✦

After his high-profile duet with Guru on the first *Jazzmatazz* project, French rapper MC Solaar proved himself a major contender for international rap stardom with his U.S. debut. With the rapid-fire rhyme flow of Souls of Mischief and the smooth delivery of Q-Tip, the young MC conveys more moods in French than most rappers can in English. The extremely subtle grooves supplied by DJ/producer Jimmy Jay provide velvety smooth cushions that wrap around Solaar's warm voice tighter than O.J Simpson's glove, with jazzy, funky samples that prove perfectly suited for the fluid rhymes. One of the few bright spots in a year when the rap scene was largely devoid of originality, MC Solaar came across as refreshing as a cool Parisian breeze. —*Bret Love*

Paradisiaque / Jul. 8, 1997 / Polydor ✦✦✦

Returning after three years of silence with *Paradisiaque*, MC Solaar attempts to recarve a niche for himself in the ever-changing worlds of acid-house, hip-hop, and dance. At the time of his departure, he had earned some respect as one of the few French rappers to actually attempt original music, crafting a pretty interesting blend of hip-hop and acid jazz. However, *Paradisiaque* finds him following trends more than ever, working slow, stoned beats that are reminiscent of anything from trip-hop to G-funk. Solaar is entirely suited for this style, but his good sense of melody turns the best moments of the album into fine pop-rap that is entertaining even if you don't understand French. —*Leo Stanley*

Le Tour de la Question / 1998 / Eastwest ✦✦✦✦

Though he had never strayed too far, *Le Tour de la Question* returns Solaar to his roots in jazz-rap. Similar to his classic *Prose Combat*, it's a set of funky hip-hop with just the right amount of samples and Solaar's complementary rapping style, which always takes into account the production. It's a relief that he appears to have little concern for what's hitting the charts in America, since so many American rappers (and labels) follow whatever is hot when they're recording. He just keeps on making great hip-hop with a bit of jazz and a bit of old school flavor. Available in limited quantities, a special two-disc set of *Le Tour de la Question* includes deluxe packaging and a book. —*John Bush*

MC Solaar / Jul. 21, 1998 / Polydor ✦✦✦✦

French rapper MC Solaar spends his self-titled album showcasing exactly why he was instantly championed by the hip-hop community as an international talent. From the jazzy, trip-hop-like beats courtesy of producers Zdar, Boom Bass, and Evil D to Solaar's lucid flow, this is quality hip-hop without any major flaws. Of course, it's a bit of a frustrating listen if you don't know French, since you'll have no clue about what he's rapping about, but the way Solaar's words slide off his tongue makes it enjoyable nonetheless. On par with his best work of the '90s, this self-titled album may arguably be his most impressive, as it's uniform laid-back feel makes it a consistent and sutured listen. Few producers in the American hip-hop scene can parallel this album's mellow qualities. —*Jason Birchmeier*

Cinquieme As: Fifth Ace / Mar. 13, 2001 / Fifth Ace ✦✦

Of all the hip-hop that broke through from Europe in the early '90s, it was Parisian MC Solaar (aka Claude M'Barali) who stole the show with his debut. The aptly titled *Qui Seme le Vent Recolte le Tempo*, a play on the proverb "Whoever wants the wind receives a thunderstorm," was the first rap album to achieve platinum sales in France and broke him as an artist to watch worldwide. Rather than continue with the same formula, Solaar has continued to test himself with this, his fifth long player, elaborating on the rich strings of his eponymous 1998 effort with a prevalence of orchestration but shifting the production style closer to that of *Prose Combat*. For those concerned with their own sketchy knowledge of the language, Solaar's deft delivery papers the cracks, with the lyrics taking on the role of melody over meaning and not detracting at all from the listening experience. —*Kingsley Marshall*

MC Trouble (LaTasha Sheron Rogers)

b. 1972 **d.** 1991

East Coast Rap, Hip-Hop

Motown's first female rapper, MC Trouble seemed headed for a promising career until she died of an epileptic seizure in 1991. Born LaTasha Sheron Rogers, she hit the charts soon after her signing, with "(I Wanna) Make You

Mine" becoming a hit in 1990. Her lone full-length, *Gotta Get a Grip*, featured Full Force, among others. Her passing made a deep impact on the burgeoning hip-hop scene, and she earned shoutouts from A Tribe Called Quest's Q-Tip and Nefertiti (the latter's "Trouble in Paradise" was dedicated to her). —*John Bush*

● **Gotta Get a Grip** / 1990 / Motown ✦✦✦

MC Trouble's story is one of the most heartbreaking in the history of rap. Although not in a class with Queen Latifah or MC Lyte, she showed some promise on her debut album, *Gotta Get a Grip*. Trouble seemed to have a strong supporter in Motown Records, a label that had been weak in the area of rap and looked to her to change that. But MC Trouble never had a chance to develop or record a second album—she died during an epileptic seizure. Whether embracing hardcore rap or more commercial R&B-ish material, the aggressive rapper leaves no doubt that she has solid rhyming skills. Much of the time, she takes a fun, escapist approach focusing on such matters as the type of behinds she admires on a man; but when she does become sociopolitical on "Black Line" and the title song, she articulates quite effectively the need for social change in the inner city. —*Alex Henderson*

McGruff

b. Harlem, NY

Hip-Hop, East Coast Rap, Hardcore Rap

Rapper McGruff debuted in 1995 on Big L's *Lifestylez ov da Poor & Dangerous* and also appeared with Heavy D on Monifah's "I Miss You." Signed to his own contract, for Uptown/Universal, the Harlem rapper dropped his debut single, "Before We Start," in early 1998. The album *Destined to Be* followed in June, with appearances from Heavy D, the LOX, and Mase. —*John Bush*

● **Destined to Be** / Jun. 16, 1998 / Uptown/Universal ✦✦✦

While it occasionally suffers from clichéd songwriting and undistinguished production, McGruff's debut album *Destined to Be* is nevertheless a promising effort from the young rapper. McGruff is a little more pop oriented than many of his peers, as evidenced by his association with Heavy D, but he retains a slightly gritty edge, thanks in part to cameos by the likes of Cam'ron, Big L, and the LOX. When he can harness street-smart rhythms with slick hooks, as on the single "Before We Start," McGruff hits hard and there are just enough of these moments to make *Destined to Be* a promising debut. —*Stephen Thomas Erlewine*

MCJX

Political Rap, East Coast Rap

Based in New York, Islamic rapper MCJX released just one record, 1990's *Black in Time*, and faded away soon after. —*John Bush*

Black in Time / 1990 / Latin Sound NW ✦✦✦

Angrily sociopolitical, MCJX is among the Islamic rappers who came out of New York in the late '80s and claimed to be on the "positive tip." To be sure, some of what he has to say on *Black in Time* (an uneven CD, but one that has its moments) is positive. MCJX vehemently speaks out against drugs, black-on-black crime, and sexism, and on "Music Industry," he rightly protests the way black artists have so often been ripped off and exploited by labels. But there's nothing even remotely positive about MCJX's vicious gay bashing and his overtly homophobic lyrics. A supporter of Minister Louis Farrakhan and the Nation of Islam who also went by the name Jason X, he comes across as a racial separatist, and his "white man this" and "white man that" rhetoric gives the impression that he opposes whites in general and wouldn't make a distinction between civil rights activist Morris Dees and Klansman J.B. Stoner. *Black in Time* didn't sell, and MCJX faded into even greater obscurity. —*Alex Henderson*

Me Phi Me

f. 1988, Chicago, IL

Group / Alternative Rap, Hip-Hop, Jazz-Rap

An early alternative to hardcore and pop-rap, the positive, message-oriented rap group Me Phi Me formed in Chicago in 1988 around the duo Cee Cee Tee (Chris Cuben-Tatum) and Falasz (John Michael Falasz). Signed to RCA by the turn of the decade, Me Phi Me released a few singles, one of which ("Sad New Day") was a surprise entry on the singles charts. The group's full-length debut, *One*, was unfortunately their only album. —*John Bush*

● **One** / Feb. 1992 / RCA ✦✦✦

One, Mi Phi Me's first (and only) album, established the rapper group as a unique figure in hip-hop. Instead of relying on funk, soul, R&B, and rap, Mi Phi Me uses folk and pop as a musical foundation, creating a new-age hip-hop that has more in common with hippies than b-boys. It's an intriguing concept—few rappers have attempted a folk-rap fusion, especially one's with neo-psychedelic overtones—but their songwriting isn't always capable of conveying their ideas. When Mi Phi Me comes up with a song that combines his ambitions with a melody, like the single "Sad New Day," the result is a sweeping, atmospheric, catchy sound that has more in common with well-constructed pop than gritty R&B. When it doesn't work, the rappers seem like the '90s edition of overly precious progressive rockers. *—Stephen Thomas Erlewine*

Meanest Man Contest

Group / Underground Rap, Alternative Rap

Before Meanest Man Contest, Quarterbar (aka guitarist Noah Blumberg of Oakland, CA, indie rock outfit Jim Yoshii Pile-Up) and MC Eriksolo had been together in mic.edu; however, that project dissolved when fellow rapper A-Twice passed away unexpectedly. MMC emerged from the verdant Oakland underground with the 7" "Contaminated Dance Step"/"Feelin' Pretty Psyched (About Love)," released on MC Eriksolo's own Weapon-Shaped label. As Eriksolo laid down organic, vaguely Latyrx-esque raps, DJ/producer Quarterbar conducted the beat alchemy on the bottom end. The duo's smoky, abstract music made an immediate splash in the alternative hip-hop community, and paved the way for their full-length release. *Merit*, issued by Plug Research in February of 2003, was the sound of ghosts falling down stairs, or freestyling in the Fortress of Solitude. It marked a new direction for the always-vibrant Oakland/Bay Area underground sound, and put Meanest Man Contest on the map. *—Johnny Loftus*

● **Merit** / Feb. 11, 2003 / Plug Research ✦✦✦✦

Oakland's Meanest Man Contest is like Boards of Canada doing hip-hop. On "Sorry," the opening track of the duo's album *Merit*, Quarterbar's beats stumble and wobble beautifully. While Eriksolo's jazzy West Coast flow is both smart and grooving, it's the scratchy edges that make Meanest Man Contest so unique: the mellow strings and ambient textures on "Not Sorry"; the heavy, simple beats and guitar bits on "Carpal Twist"; and the creaking organs in the Serge Gainsbourg-ian café jazz noir of "Don't Die on Christmas." Largely down-tempo and psychedelic, Meanest Man Contest masterfully crosses bucolic and pastoral electro-acoustic music with the urban edge of smoky downstairs bars. Simply an unassuming and brilliant hip-hop record that quietly shifts the parameters of the genre. *—Charles Spano*

Mellow Man Ace (Ulpiano Sergio Reyez)

b. Apr. 12, 1967, Havana, Cuba

Golden Age, Latin Rap, Hip-Hop

A Hispanic rapper born in Cuba, Mellow Man Ace focused on lovers rap with occasional bilingual delivery and a heady gift for novelty rhymes. Born Ulpiano Sergio Reyez in 1967, he left Cuba with his family at the age of four and resettled in Los Angeles. With production from the Dust Brothers and Def Jef, Mellow Man Ace recorded his debut album, *Escape from Havana*, releasing it in 1989 on Capitol. Almost one year later, the single "Mentirosa" became a Top 20 hit with Ace rapping over a crafty hook from Santana's "Evil Ways." Also a part of the Latin Alliance project (and the brother of Cypress Hill's Sen Dog), Mellow Man Ace recorded one additional album, *The Brother With Two Tongues*, then virtually retired from the field, but 2000 brought forth the release *From the Darkness Into the Light. —John Bush*

● **Escape From Havana** / Aug. 30, 1989 / Capitol ✦✦✦✦✦

Cypress Hill, the Mexikinz, Kid Frost, and Afro-Rican are among the Latinos who have made valuable contributions to rap—a genre historically dominated by black males. Like those MCs, the distinctive Mellow Man Ace has used his experiences as a Latino to his artistic advantage when rapping. On his debut album, *Escape From Havana*, the L.A.-based Cuban-American fluctuates between aggressive hardcore rap and more melodic and commercial fare. Ace, who raps in both English and Spanish, had a major hit in "Mentirosa"—an infectious, salsa-influenced gem sampling Santana's "Evil Way." That song and the ballads "B-Boy in Love" and "If You Were Mine" show

that even at his most commercial, he still has integrity—while "Rap Guanco," "Mas Pignon," and "River Cubano" demonstrate how hard and forceful he can get. Ace, like a lot of rappers, spends too much time boasting about his microphone skills. Nonetheless, *Escape From Havana* is an individualistic, risk-taking work that's well worth hearing. *—Alex Henderson*

The Brother With Two Tongues / May 25, 1992 / Capitol ✦✦✦✦

Cuban-American/Latino rapper Mellow Man Ace's second Capitol release continued his merger of hip-hop and Afro-Latin musical, linguistic, and political elements. Unfortunately, he didn't create anything quite as commercially viable as "Mentirosa," but his beats and rhymes ranged from average to intriguing, while his rap style was again inspirational in its appeal to a multicultural audience. *—Ron Wynn*

From the Darkness Into the Light / Jul. 18, 2000 / X-Ray ✦✦✦✦✦

The history of hip-hop is full of MCs who had their 15 minutes of fame but didn't enjoy the longevity they hoped for. Mellow Man Ace scored a major crossover hit with 1989's "Mentirosa," but by 1993, the Havana-born rapper was without a record deal. Released in 2000, *From the Darkness Into the Light* was his first album since 1992's *The Brother With Two Tongues*. Eight years is a long time for an MC to go without a new album—especially when you consider how much hip-hop trends can change from one year to the next. But Ace, who was 33 when this CD came out, has no problem changing with the times and delivering an excellent album that is mindful of 2000's rap tastes. A revitalized Ace divides the disc into a Dark Side and a Light Side, which might lead one to assume that he is dividing his time between hardcore rap and pop-rap like he did in the past. But that isn't the case. Enlisting such producers as DJ Muggs (of Cypress Hill and 7A3 fame) and Tony G., Ace avoids pop-rap—this release doesn't offer anything as commercial as "Mentirosa"—and sticks to hardcore rap. Truth be told, the Dark Side and Light Side are equally hard hitting. The album has a consistently serious tone; Ace tackles a lot of social issues (everything from urban violence to child pornography), and he speaks candidly and openly about the fact that he went from fame to obscurity. Regrettably, *From the Darkness Into the Light* wasn't the major commercial comeback he was no doubt hoping for—the album received very little attention. But that doesn't make it any less compelling. *—Alex Henderson*

Memphis Bleek

Gangsta Rap, East Coast Rap

Rapper Memphis Bleek was raised in Brooklyn, NY's Marcy Projects housing community, making his recorded debut in 1996 on Jay-Z's *Reasonable Doubt*. A member of the Roc-A-Fella Records stable, Bleek made his solo debut in 1999 with *Coming of Age*. While his debut did warrant plenty of attention, he wasn't able to capitalize on the hype surrounding his debut, resulting in a questionable collection of songs—powered primarily by its Swizz Beatz-produced lead single—that didn't live up to the lofty expectations many had. In late 2000, his sophomore album, *The Understanding*, appeared alongside Bleek's high-profile appearance with Jay-Z in the "Hey Papi" single from the *Nutty Professor II* soundtrack and its Hype Williams-directed video (featuring a cameo appearance by Pamela Anderson). In addition to this eye-catching promotional ploy, the lead single from *The Understanding*, "Mind Right," soon followed. *—Jason Ankeny*

Coming of Age / Aug. 3, 1999 / Roc-A-Fella ✦✦✦

A collaborator on many of Jay-Z's albums (and a fellow native of Brooklyn's Marcy Projects), Memphis Bleek debuted his own solo career with the album *Coming of Age*, released on his mentor's Roc-A-Fella label, a subsidiary of Def Jam. Bleek's rapping style is a bit more street level than Jay-Z's, making for a distinctive album that comes as a bit of a surprise given the large amount of samey records that often come from the same hip-hop labels. Besides the obvious cameos—from Jay-Z, fellow Roc-A-Fella rappers Ja Rule and Beanie Sigel, plus Noreaga and Da Ranjahz—Memphis Bleek sounds good throughout. For the spotlight single "Memphis Bleek Is…," the rapper recruited Swizz Beatz, the hottest producer in hip-hop. The move pays off too, as the track is a solid DMX-style shouter, with the obvious catchline in the title. Many of the productions were recorded by Roc-A-Fella comrades, and the highlights ("What Do You Think of That," "Murda 4 Life," "You a Thug Nigga") have the same emphasis on bruising urban funk as most Jay-Z material. Still, *Coming of Age* is a fine debut that shows Memphis Bleek already leaps and bounds ahead of most rappers. *—Keith Farley*

● **The Understanding** / Oct. 10, 2000 / Roc-A-Fella ✦✦✦
For his second album, Jay-Z protégé Memphis Bleek makes small strides forward from his debut album, *Coming of Age*. Yet like *Coming of Age*, the tracks on *The Understanding* may be a level above most rap, but still aren't in the same category as Jay-Z or the other superstars from New York's hardcore school of rap: Nas, Ja Rule, Mobb Deep, and Raekwon. Ironically, Bleek just doesn't seem to have the understanding that he blatantly alludes to in the title of his album, writing shallow songs that come across as overtly juvenile, despite his ambitions to evolve into a respected rapper. Songs such as "All Types of Shit," "Hustlers," "Bounce Bitch," and "Is That Your Bitch" just come off sounding clichéd and too full of overblown male ego; sure, this album isn't anywhere near as vane as a lot of the West Coast gangsta rap, but one expects a bit more philosophical street knowledge from a New York rapper. Yet when one overlooks the standards placed upon up-and-coming New York rappers, Bleek does stand above most rappers on their second album. One can only hope that he continues to evolve with succeeding albums, eventually integrating a bit more earnest ambitions, rather than being so shallow. —*Jason Birchmeier*

Mercedes (Raquel Miller)

b. 1978, Louisiana
Southern Rap, Dirty South
One of the few female artists in Master P's No Limit stable, R&B/hip-hop singer Mercedes was born Raequel Miller in Louisiana in 1978 and grew up in Detroit, attending the city's High School for the Fine and Performing Arts and participating in the spiritually oriented Brazeal Dennard Youth Chorale. While studying music at Xavier University in New Orleans, she came to the attention of Master P at a talent show, and was signed immediately and christened Mercedes. After debuting on the *I'm 'Bout It* soundtrack, Mercedes issued her debut album, *Rear End*, in 1999, and reportedly retired from the music business shortly thereafter to attend law school. —*Steve Huey*

● **Rear End** / Jun. 29, 1999 / Priority ✦✦✦
In a promotional interview for her debut album *Rear End*, Mercedes claimed that it took just two weeks to cut the record—which is interesting, since the album was being advertised in No Limit discs well over a year before its release. That confirms the sneaking suspicion that No Limit readies its artwork before the artist even enters the studio, and gives the impression that *Rear End* is another piece of No Limit product, as faceless and interchangeable as the last. But even though there are sections as plodding as the average Beats by the Pound production, and familiar catch phrases scattered throughout the record, there's more sonic variety on *Rear End* than most No Limit albums. Beats by the Pound occasionally smooth things out, borrow slightly from Timbaland's skittering productions, or add a soulful groove. There's even an urban ballad with "Pony Ride," and a new-jack slow jam with "Candlelight & Champagne." Change-ups like this are welcome, as are productions by Dez & Charles, since the album is tedious when it trots out typical No Limit clichés—namely, guest rappers, recycled hooks, skits, and endless profanity. Since *Rear End* clocks in at 70 minutes—apparently, any hip-hop record less than hour long isn't perceived as a bargain—it could have used a little trimming, and these would have been prime candidates. That is, with the notable exception of "Do You Wanna Ride." It lifts the chorus from Pebbles' "Mercedes Boy" and the verse from Vanity's "Nasty Girl," and the end result is the best shameless recycling No Limit has come up with in quite some time. Whenever a label turns out product at such a rapid rate, it is a welcome surprise whenever a record is slightly different and better than its predecessors. —*Stephen Thomas Erlewine*

Merlin

f. Brixton
Group / Hip-Hop
The United Kingdom was an unlikely spot to find rappers in the late '80s. Merlin (of Jamaican descent) was born and raised in South London's Brixton. At 11, he sang and played in a funky church that used drum machines and synthesizers to augment the traditional organ and piano. With musical bloodlines—reggae star Smiley Culture is his uncle—Merlin formed the Juveniles to play at school dances. At 14, he started hanging with local rappers, befriending MC Blade. The teens won a big rap contest, and DJ Master Mix quickly whisked Merlin away to sign a solo deal with Rhythm King

Records. The British label released *Born Free*, and Merlin successfully collaborated with local rappers including Bomb and S'Express for many chart hits. His discography includes "Who's in the House" from 1989, and the LPs *Merlin* (1989) and *The New Rap Messiah* (1992). A six-month prison sentence for stealing checks from Mute Records stopped everything. He resumed rapping when released, but his glory days were over and his career ended before his 21st birthday. —*Andrew Hamilton*

● **Merlin** / 1989 / Sire ✦✦
The New Rap Messiah / Jun. 15, 1992 / Reprise ✦✦

Mesanjarz of Funk

f. Bronx, NY
Group / Latin Rap, Hip-Hop
A little-known group of Puerto Rican rappers, the New York-based Mesanjarz of Funk released just one 1993 self-titled full-length, on Atlantic. Based around Jose Moronta and Donald Powells, the group found little success with a pair of singles, "Keep It Flowin'" and "Funk in da Trunk." —*John Bush*

● **Mesanjarz of Funk** / 1993 / Atlantic ✦✦✦
The Latino rappers of the 1980s and 1990s often brought a strong regional flavor to their music. While Cypress Hill, A Lighter Shade of Brown, Kid Frost, and tha Mexakinz were very much a product of L.A.'s Mexican-American or Chicano experience, Mesanjarz of Funk favored a strong "Nuyorican" approach to hardcore rap on this enjoyable, if a bit uneven, debut album. These Latinos from the Bronx are instantly recognizable as New York rappers—they have sizable technique, and they aren't shy about showing it off and providing a lot of tricky tongue-twisters. The thing that separates Mesanjarz of Funk from New York's non-Latino MCs is their bilingual outlook. While most of the lyrics are English, Mesanjarz inject a fair amount of Spanish rapping on exhilarating numbers like "Keep it Flowin'," "Spanish Flavor," and "Buckwild Boricua." Hearing Mesangarz rap is a lot of like listening to a talented jazz virtuoso who is putting too much emphasis on showing off his or her chops—you know that the artist is overdoing it with technique, but you have to admire that technique nonetheless. Unfortunately, this CD fell through the cracks and turned out to be Mesanjarz' only Atlantic album. —*Alex Henderson*

Metabass 'N Breath

Group / Hip-Hop, Underground Rap
Sydney, Australia hip-hop crew MetaBass (aka MetaBass 'n' Breath) was formed by rappers Morganics, Baba, and Elf Transporter; subsequent additions to the lineup include DJ Nic Toth, keyboardist Sloth, bassist Jason, and drummer Brother Love. The group issued its debut EP, *Seek*, in 1997; the full-length *The Life and Times of a Beatboxer* followed two years later. —*Jason Ankeny*

● **The Life and Times of a Beatboxer** / Aug. 17, 1999 / Bomb Hip Hop ✦✦✦✦
The turntablist occupation of beatboxing is the equivalent of sparring, except with two turntables and an arsenal of scratching and spinbacks instead of jabs and fakes. The five-man Australian hip-hop group known as Metabass come on very similar to their comrades in the Northern Hemisphere, possessing a similar style to the Roots but with more emphasis on raggae and turntablist skills. Highlighted by the single "Possession," *The Life and Times of a Beatboxer* is a solid album of left-field hip-hop and a positive departure for the increasingly turntablist Bomb Hip Hop label. —*Keith Farley*

Metabolics

f. 1999
Group / Underground Rap, Alternative Rap
Metabolics came together in 1999 when horror film makeup aficionado and MC Mr. Dead and his menacing sidekick, Big Pat, met WordSound kingpin Spectre at the Prince Paul video shoot where Dead was doing makeup. Being at the helm of a label well known as a haven for the weird, Spectre was taken in by Metabolics' cocktail of grisly horror imagery, bizarre references, and straight-up East Coast-style rapping. *The M-Virus*, their WordSound debut, featured production and contributions from New Kingdom's Scott Harding, Prince Paul, and Spectre himself. Dead and Pat were immediately accepted by the larger hip-hop community as two more soldiers in the WordSound war against sucka MCs—specifically, purveyors of the pop/hip-hop sound that dominated the radio and music television. Despite critical acclaim, however,

The M-Virus was virtually ignored. Nevertheless, Mr. Dead persevered. In 2001, *Metabolics, Vol. 2: Dawn of the Dead* appeared. While billed as a Dead solo effort, the record was essentially a logical step forward in Metabolics' progression, focusing the duo's sound on the whirring crazy dynamo inside Dead's head. *Vol. 2* even featured Big Pat on numerous tracks, along with knob twirling from likeminded miscreants Dan the Automator, Scotty Hard, and M. Sayyid of Antipop Consortium. —*Johnny Loftus*

● **The M-Virus** / Jan. 5, 1999 / WordSound ◆◆◆
A trippy hip-hop duo coming straight outta Crooklyn, MCs Mr. Dead and Big Pat find inspiration in subject matter fueled in no small part by a variety of illicit chemical substances. Similarities to early-'90s rap duo New Kingdom abound, from the distinctively bizarre lyrical approach to the production of former New Kingdom knob twiddler Scott Harding (aka Scotty Hard) on the furiously freaky "Create and Divide." The production by BIMOS on the majority of the album's tracks is a little too underground (i.e., muddy and repetitive) to hit the big time, but the duo's sharp rhymes and unique lyrical flows show enormous potential. —*Bret Love*

Method Man (Clifford Smith)

b. Apr. 2, 1971, Long Island, NY
East Coast Rap, Hardcore Rap, Hip-Hop
Method Man was the first—and biggest—solo star to emerge from the groundbreaking Wu-Tang Clan. His mush-mouthed, sandpaper-rough bellow (at times recalling EPMD's Erick Sermon) and imaginative rhymes easily made him one of the most recognizable, unpredictable MCs in the group, yet his flow was more deliberate and laid-back than the Wu's resident loose cannon, Ol' Dirty Bastard. On his solo records, Method Man developed a persona that swung from offhand, understated menace to raucous stoner humor. Toward the end of the '90s, his frequent team-ups with Redman produced not only a terrific musical chemistry but also an eventual big-screen comedy team as well.

Method Man was born Clifford Smith on April 1, 1971, in Long Island, NY; he split his childhood between his father's Long Island residence and his mother's Staten Island home. It was the latter locale where he met his future Wu-Tang cohorts RZA, Genius/GZA, and Ol' Dirty Bastard; when they set about forming a hip-hop collective in the early '90s, Method Man was one of the first to sign on. Meth was heavily featured on the group's classic late-1993 debut *Enter the Wu-Tang (36 Chambers)*, even getting his own showcase track with "Method Man," which certainly put him out front in terms of name recognition. Thanks to the Wu's innovative contract—which allowed individual members to sign solo deals with whatever label they chose—Method Man inked a contract with Def Jam and in 1994, approximately one year after *Enter the Wu-Tang*'s release, he became the first Wu member to release a solo album with *Tical*. Highly anticipated, the album entered the charts at number four and quickly went platinum, while singles like "Bring the Pain" (which just missed the pop Top 40) and "Release Yo' Delf" made him an even bigger name in the hip-hop community. He began making numerous guest appearances on other artists' records and in the summer of 1995, his one-off single with Mary J. Blige, "I'll Be There for You/You're All I Need to Get By," soared into the pop Top Five, giving Meth his first major mainstream exposure. Shortly thereafter, another duet—this time with Def Jam labelmate Redman—on the compilation track "How High" climbed into the pop Top 20.

Wu-Tang Clan reconvened in 1997 for the double album *Wu-Tang Forever* and about a year later, another round of solo projects commenced. Method Man issued his sophomore effort *Tical 2000: Judgement Day* (ironically) in late 1998 and took a more expansive approach this time out, filling the album with between-song skits and a variety of guest rappers and producers. *Tical 2000* was another hit, entering the charts at number two. Meanwhile, in addition to recording the album, Meth had spent much of 1998 getting his acting career off the ground; after landing a few bit parts, he made his first prominent big-screen appearance in Hype Williams' *Belly*. In 1999 Meth partnered up with Redman to form a duo act that hit the road with Jay-Z's *Hard Knock Life* tour; they also entered the studio together to record the collaborative album *Blackout!*, which entered the charts at number three that fall and received highly complimentary reviews.

The Wu returned in late 2000 with the lower-profile *The W.* After completing the record, Meth refocused his acting career; in early 2001 he put in a month's worth of appearances portraying a young gangster on HBO's

gritty prison drama *Oz*, and teamed up with Redman for the Cheech & Chong-styled stoner comedy *How High*, which hit theaters toward the end of the year, around the same time as the fourth Wu-Tang album *Iron Flag.* —*Steve Huey*

● **Tical** / 1994 / Def Jam ◆◆◆◆◆
The first Wu-Tang Clan solo album to follow the seismic impact of *Enter the Wu-Tang*, Method Man's *Tical* similarly delivers an other-worldly wallop, one that instantly sets the madcap MC apart from his clansmen as the collective's shining star. Not only is Meth madcap, both in terms of mentality and delivery, he's also incredibly witty and wordy. Here he inspires hilarity as well as astonishment, and the way that he fires off his rhymes with such seemingly spontaneous ease compounds this sense of wonder. Just as Meth is quite clearly leagues above practically every other rapper in 1994 sans a small handful, if that, so is his producer, Wu-Tang abbot RZA, who produces the entirety of *Tical*: from the antiquated flutes and kung-fu flick samples that open the album, to the pulse-accelerating beats of "Bring the Pain" and the fist-pumping ones of "All I Need" (the b-boy version rather than the radio-geared one featuring Mary J. Blige), to the rallying, warlike horns of "Release Yo' Delf." Despite a few outside contributions, most notably from Raekwon on the rowdy spar fest "Meth vs. Clef," *Tical* is strictly a two-man show, Meth bringing da ruckus and RZA the swarming soundscapes, and that's precisely what further makes this album such a treasure amid the many Wu-Tang gems. Where most of Meth's clansmen delivered guest-laden albums that sounded more like group efforts than solo ones, *Tical* strictly spotlights the group's two stars and does so with refreshingly straightforward flair. There's none of the epic overreaching that mars so many rap albums of the era; rather, there's just over a dozen tracks here, and they're filled to the brim with rhymes and beats and little else—no pop-crossover concessions nor any heady experimentation for the sake of experimentation, just good ol'-fashioned hip-hop, albeit with a dark, dark, deranged twist. —*Jason Birchmeier*

Tical 2000: Judgement Day / Nov. 10, 1998 / Def Jam ◆◆◆
Unlike Method Man's straightforward debut, *Tical*, which was a simple yet brilliant MC/producer collaboration, and a classic one at that, his follow-up, *Tical 2000*, is an ambitious undertaking, involving a long list of collaborators and a conceptual scope. In many ways, it's a much more interesting album than its predecessor because of its ambitions. There are 28 tracks in total here, most of them featuring some sort of guest, mainly fellow East Coast hardcore rappers like Redman and Mobb Deep but also surprise guests like Chris Rock and Janet Jackson. The 28 tracks furthermore feature an abundance of producers rather than just RZA like last time. Some of the more notable contributors include Rockwilder, Erick Sermon, Prince Paul, Havoc, and the Trackmasters as well as in-house Wu-Tang beatmakers RZA and True Master. This large cast navigates its way through a loose narrative about a so-called Judgement Day that seems to liberally take its inspiration from the film *Terminator 2: Judgment Day.* All of this makes *Tical 2000* a daunting venture that is occasionally entertaining (the many skits), intermittently brilliant ("Dangerous Grounds" and the climactic title track), but unfortunately too often ill conceived (the overly calculated "All I Need, Pt. 2" ballad "Break Ups 2 Make Ups" featuring D'Angelo this time rather than Mary J. Blige) and also tiresome (again, the many skits). Rarely have such ambitious undertakings as this worked well for rap artists, and *Tical 2000* exemplifies this, as did many of the myriad other epic, often double-disc albums released during the late '90s that were heavy on collaborators but light on consistency. Hand it to Meth, though, for embarking on such a visionary engagement, for its final completion winded him so much that he'd take a few years off before even considering another solo endeavor. —*Jason Birchmeier*

Blackout! / Sep. 28, 1999 / Def Jam ◆◆◆◆
Hip-hop fans have known for years that Method Man and Redman are two of the top MCs in the field, and their tour together not only proved the fact but also showed they rap incredibly well together. Their deliveries are similar and the flow never falters, but the hint of gravel in Meth's voice makes them easily distinguishable. Now, with *Blackout!*, the duo's first album together (though both guested on each other's 1998 LPs), listeners have the proof on wax. Skating on top of spare, hard-hitting productions by Erick Sermon, Wu-Tang's RZA, Mathematics, and Redman himself—under his Reggie Noble alias—Meth and Redman trade off on hardcore rhymes and freestyle over each other. There's barely room for breath, but the rhymes are tight and inventive throughout. There are only two guest appearances

(for Ja Rule & LL Cool J on "4 Seasons" and Ghostface and Street on the hilarious *Blair Witch Project* send-off "Run 4 Cover"), and the focus on just Meth and Redman makes for an even tighter, more combustible LP. Even with the high expectations that come along with a project of this magnitude, *Blackout!* rarely disappoints. —*John Bush*

Tha Mexakinz

f. Long Beach, CA

Group / Hip-Hop, Hardcore Rap, Latin Rap, Club/Dance

Latin rap duo tha Mexakinz were formed in Long Beach, CA, by MCs I-Man and Sinful. Their fluid bilingual rhymes on such albums as 1994's *Zig Zag* and 1996's *Tha Mexakinz* garnered them an underground following among both hip-hop and alternative rock fans. 1998's *Crossing All Borders* began to reflect the influence of the latter genre while remaining grounded in the former. —*Steve Huey*

Zig Zag / May 17, 1994 / Wild West ✦✦✦

Verbal skills are in ample supply on tha Mexakinz' full-length debut, *Zig Zag*, which builds on the work of other Latin-American rappers (Cypress Hill, the Beatnuts) without blatantly imitating them. —*Steve Huey*

Tha Mexakinz / Aug. 13, 1996 / Wild West ✦✦✦

● **Crossing All Borders** / Oct. 13, 1998 / Wild West ✦✦✦✦

With *Crossing All Borders*, tha Mexakinz begin to expand their sound beyond the parameters of hip-hop, incorporating elements of alternative rock and SoCal ska-punk with intriguing results. Marshall Goodman (Sublime) cowrote the album's first single, "Rain on Your Parade," while the second single, "Lose My Cool," has a jazzy feel courtesy of Ozomatli trumpeter Asdru Sierra. —*Steve Huey*

Mexicano 777

Group / West Coast Rap, Underground Rap, Latin Rap

Puerto Rican Mexicano 777 became involved in the Latin hip-hop scene during the 1990s, achieving a local award for Rap Artist of the Year after issuing a song called "Se Testigo," making his international debut with "Razor Sharp," and releasing his debut album called *Entre El Bien y El Mal* in September 1998, which featured the hit single "Hagan Ruido Las Pistolas." Singing in both Spanish and English, Mexicano 777's following record, *God's Assasins*, was released in 2001. —*Drago Bonacich*

● **God's Assassins** / Mar. 13, 2001 / Sma ✦✦✦

If hip-hop is the opiate of the masses, this is a pup tent filled with crack cocaine. Puerto Rican rapper Mexicano 777 likes to keep control over the occupational side of things—albums released independently, videos shot by himself—and somehow finds time to demolish nagging inhibitions when it comes to the creatively nullifying atmospherics of the recording studio. Grab a bilingual Busta Rhymes, immerse him in bagpipe, rapid-fire raggae, and step away as KRS-One and Mad Lion help him find the narcotic side of free-diving into a big, raspy, hip-hop salsa sunsplash and you're halfway there. This is a raunchy rap assault on the senses that's as abject and insufferable as any self-respecting full-throttle wakeup call has every right to be. —*Dean Carlson*

MF Doom

f. New York, NY

Group / Gangsta Rap, Hardcore Rap, Underground Rap

Patterning his persona and logo after the Marvel Comics supervillain Dr. Doom, the man behind MF (Metal Face) Doom's iron mask is actually Daniel Dumile, aka Zev Love X, a member of former Big Apple hip-hoppers KMD. First featured on the 3rd Bass single "The Gas Face," the London-born, Long Island-raised Zev made his debut with KMD a couple of years later, along with his younger brother and musical partner DJ Subroc. The 1991 album *Mr. Hood*, released on Elektra Records, was part of a short-lived trend of Islamic Five Percent Nation hip-hop outings, along with efforts by groups like Poor Righteous Teachers and KMD's labelmates Brand Nubian. However, Subroc was fatally injured in 1993 when he was struck by a car, and when Zev and KMD returned the next year, it was with the even more serious and militant *Bl_ck B_st_rds*, an album whose cover art alone (featuring a Little Black Sambo-ish cartoon character being hanged) spelled the end of the group's contract with Elektra. With the album in limbo, Zev went underground for five years, "recovering from his wounds" and swearing revenge

"against the industry that so badly deformed him," according to his official bio, a reworking of Dr. Doom's origin. Meanwhile, *Bl_ck B_st_rds* was heavily bootlegged and Zev Love's legend grew, but few knew at first that the rapper who began showing up at the Nuyorican Poets Café in 1998, freestyling with a stocking covering his face, was actually Zev. The imaginative MC finally ended the mystery in 1999, resurfacing in his new identity as MF Doom and making up for lost time with a critically praised new album, *Operation: Doomsday*, on indie label Fondle 'Em Records. The following year saw the long-awaited official release of *Bl_ck B_st_rds* (complete with Sambo-style cover art), as well as several singles and an EP with fellow rhymer MF Grimm. In 2001, SubVerse re-released *Operation: Doomsday* and *Bl_ck B_st_rds*. —*Dan LeRoy*

● **Operation: Doomsday** / 1999 / Fondle 'Em ✦✦

MF Doom was known as Zev Love X of the group KMD. After KMD, he took on a new personality as MF Doom and came out with *Operation: Doomsday*, his first album. The project doesn't really work. For the most part, the problem lies in the beats that MF Doom raps over—most of them aren't that good. The record has more than its share of songs that don't work. On "Tick, Tick," for example, he and MF Grimm take turns rapping over a beat that slows down to a crawl, then snaps back to normal speed, then slows to a crawl again. The track follows this pattern throughout, and the end result is an awkward rhythm. Another example is "Red and Gold"; it offers a beat which amounts essentially to elevator music and doesn't mesh well with his flow. Such mistakes are expected when you try new things; sometimes it works and sometimes it doesn't. Where it does work you find the album's bright spots, such as "Hey!" and "Doomsday." MF Doom does a good job on the mic during these. "Doomsday" has a nice rhythm, and "Hey!"'s beat is from the cartoon *Scooby-Doo*. It's unlikely that many people would think that using the music to *Scooby-Doo* would make a good beat, but MF Doom did and it works. That's not the only cartoon sampled on this album; throughout the album are skits, and the main source for them is the cartoon *Fantastic Four* (because one of the enemies in the cartoon is named Doom). Although this album has a few high points, overall it misses the mark. —*Dan Gizzi*

Mia X

b. New Orleans, LA

Hip-Hop, Gangsta Rap, Hardcore Rap, Southern Rap

The first female rapper on Master P's No Limit label, Mia X was born in New Orleans, but her first rapping experience came in Queens, where the old school group New York Incorporated rocked a few block parties but called it quits after four years. She moved back down South and became affiliated with hometown hero Master P and his growing label empire, No Limit Records. Through Priority Records, No Limit released *Good Girl Gone Bad* in 1995. Her album *Unlady Like*, released a year and a half later, hit the Top 20 album charts. —*John Bush*

Good Girl Gone Bad / Nov. 21, 1995 / No Limit ✦✦✦

● **Unlady Like** / Jun. 24, 1997 / No Limit ✦✦✦✦

Mia X's second album, *Unlady Like*, finds the hardcore rapper following the footsteps of Lil' Kim and Foxy Brown, as she makes her music sexier and more profane than before. The results are somewht mixed, mainly because the music isn't always catchy or well produced—like many No Limit records, it suffers from cheap production and borrowed ideas that aren't restated particularly well. Still, Mia X has personality and can occasionally toss out a funny line, and there are a few cuts where it all gels; that's where *Unlady Like* becomes highly entertaining, sub-gangsta hardcore hip-hop. —*Leo Stanley*

Mama Drama / Oct. 27, 1998 / No Limit ✦✦✦

It's hard to view Mia X as anything other than No Limit's answer to Foxy Brown and Lil' Kim. That may be because she's marketed that way, but the fact is, her music sounds like the No Limit variation of Foxy and Kim—it's cheap, street-level music that panders to gangsta sensibilies. Mia X is a fairly talented rapper—more talented than the average No Limit rapper—but her gifts are obscured by the utterly flat production. Still, she and several of her collaborators, such as C-Murder, Fat Joe, and Silkk the Shocker, are able to make a couple of the tracks work through sheer force, and those cuts ("Bring it On," "What's Ya Point," "Don't Blame Me," "Six Ed.," "Play Wit Pussy") are reason enough for diehard No Limit heads to check this out, even if it won't convince any doubters. —*Stephen Thomas Erlewine*

Mic Geronimo

b. 1973, Flushing, NY

Hip-Hop, East Coast Rap, Pop-Rap, Club/Dance

A Queens rapper with a streetwise attitude as well as a few ties to Puff Daddy's pop-rap empire of the late '90s, Mic Geronimo grew up listening to LL Cool J and Big Daddy Kane, plus soul acts like Stevie Wonder and Prince. Discovered by producer Irv Gotti (DJ Irv) at a talent show, Mic Geronimo signed to Blunt/TVT and debuted with the 1995 LP *The Natural*. TVT wasn't exactly the most respected label in hip-hop, and the album made few waves despite the presence of several hard-hitting early singles, "Shit's Real" and "Masta I.C." The 1997 album *Vendetta* saw him with a higher profile, working with Puff Daddy-related acts, the LOX, and the producer himself on the single "Nothin' Move but the Money." —*John Bush*

The Natural / Nov. 28, 1995 / TVT ✦✦✦✦

● **Vendetta** / Oct. 28, 1997 / TVT ✦✦✦✦
With his second album, *Vendetta*, Mic Geronimo proves that his hard-hitting debut was no fluke. Geronimo may flirt a little too heavily with the crossover—Puff Daddy's production on "Nothin' Move But the Money" is a little too smooth, and the blatant materialism doesn't suit him well—but the fact of the matter is, even when he tries his hand at the pop game, Geronimo has more lyrical skills than many of his peers. Musically, he needs to toughen up a little and find his own sensibility, but there's no denying that his rhyming is strong and that the R&B-flavored productions are appealing, and that all makes the album a *Vendetta* worth pursuing. —*Leo Stanley*

Michie Mee

b. Canada

Dancehall, Raggae, Hip-Hop

Michie Mee has performed as a hip-hop artist in real life, and portrayed one on television. The Canadian rapper has recorded a few tunes, and appeared as the opening act for major stars such as Judy Mowatt, Salt-'N-Pepa, Queen Latifah, and Dream Warriors. Mee also landed acting parts in movies like *The Jimi Hendrix Story* and *In Too Deep*, and the television series *Drop the Beat*, *La Femme Nikita*, and *Traders*.

Canadian native Michie Mee was only 14 years old when she began performing professionally. Her talents soon landed her larger gigs, and with time brought her a recording contract that allowed her popularity to cross the border over into the United States. Her first album, *Jamaican Funk: Canadian Style*, hit the market in 1991. Some of the tracks from the debut are "Get It Together," "All Night Stand," "You're Feisty," "Kotch," and "If Only They Knew." Through the '90s, Mee toured and opened for other acts, but turned a lot of her attention toward putting down roots for an acting career. She did a lot of guest spots before auditioning in the late summer of 1998 for a role in a new series called *Drop the Beat*. Mee landed that role, and became the co-star of the show, playing the part of a hip-hop queen known as Divine. During this time, after a long break from recording, Michie Mee finally began working on a sophomore full-length offering, *The First Cut Is the Deepest*. The songs on this second album carry a smooth mixture of reggae and hip-hop. —*Charlotte Dillon*

● **Jamaican Funk: Canadian Style** / 1991 / First Priority ✦✦
Canadian rapper Michie Mee juggles hip-hop and reggae on her debut album, mixing them together on the title track and on a duet with dancehall tenor Finchers. By and large, though, Mee and her DJ L.A. Luv keep the rap and the reggae separate, with the last half of the record focusing exclusively on old school-flavored raps. —*Jason Ankeny*

Midwkid

f. Indiana

Group / Hip-Hop, Hardcore Rap

Offering a Midwest version of the bouncing beats and gruff vocals of the dirty South scene, Midwikid came out of Indiana in 2002 to drop their first record. Consisting of rappers M.A.G. and B12, the group came out of Michigan City, IN, at the turn of the century with a set of stark rhymes that reflected their small-town origins. Their demo ended up at Arista Records at the end of 2001, and by the next year they had signed to the label and were releasing their debut in the spring. Titled *Something Wikid This Way Comes*, the record included beats from L.A. Reid and Kay Gee, but mostly featured producer Eric "Rated X" Phillips, another homegrown Indiana talent. —*Bradley Torreano*

● **Something Wikid This Way Comes** / May 7, 2002 / Arista ✦✦✦
With hip-hop's inexorable spread into every nook and cranny of the fruited plain, rappers like Midwikid continue to get flushed from small-town obscurity and into the limelight. This duo sounds ready for that type of success, which is the best thing about their debut; their hunger to escape the drab Midwestern landscape of their songs can lend their verses a visceral kick. Just check out the first proper cut, "We Live," which finds M.A.G. (who sounds like a very raw Scarface) and B12 circling a lean, ping-ponging beat like caged lions in need of meat. That tune should have provided the blueprint for the rest of *Something Wikid*, but instead the pair try on a variety of other styles, from incongrously mellow R&B on "Balled" to squiggly synth funk on "Get It Off in the Club." Most are skillfully produced by the group's associate, Eric "Rated X" Phillips, yet the diversity robs Midwikid of developing a sound and lingo to truly call their own—a dirtier Midwestern counterpart to the fun and games of Nelly, perhaps. Coupled with occasional lapses into Gangsta 101 boilerplate, the overall impression is less than it could have been, given the obvious potential displayed. But tighter focus on the best parts of this album could make Midwikid wikidly good. —*Dan LeRoy*

The Mighty Bop (Christophe Le Friant)

Producer, DJ / Acid Jazz, Trip-Hop, Club/Dance

The man behind such productions as the Mighty Bop (down-tempo hip-hop), Bob Sinclar (house), and Réminiscence Quartet (acid jazz) is Chris the French Kiss (aka Christophe Le Friant), a Parisian DJ and head of the crucial French label Yellow Productions as well as a producer. Le Friant began DJing in 1987 while still a teenager, and formed Yellow Productions in 1993 with Alain Ho. Several of the first releases on Yellow were by Le Friant: the Mighty Bop's "Messe Pour le Temps Present," Réminiscence Quartet's "Roda Mundo," and his first LP, the French hip-hop summit *The Mighty Bop Meet DJ Cam et La Funk Mob*. Alongside releases from a parade of excellent French sources, including DJ companions Dimitri from Paris and Kid Loco, Yellow also hosted two more Mighty Bop LPs during 1996-1997, *La Vague Sensorielles* and *Autres Voix, Autres Blues*.

Eager to inject some fun into the burgeoning French house underground, Le Friant borrowed the name Bob Sinclar (from a character in the well-known French film *Le Magnifique*) and in 1997 produced his first Sinclar EP, *A Space Funk Project*. Soon enough, he had an entire Bob Sinclar LP ready to go, and *Paradise* appeared on Yellow just in time for summer 1998. One of the album's tracks, "Gym Tonic," began getting some club play in France thanks to its bouncy house vibe and incessant singalong chorus (lifted from a Jane Fonda workout record). A huge anthem during the summer season in Ibiza, "Gym Tonic" looked ready to explode on the charts until Fonda sought legal action for the illegal sample. Perhaps wary of overly burdensome commercial success, the song's coproducer—Daft Punk's Thomas Bangalter, who'd just recorded his own breezy house delight, Stardust's "Music Sounds Better With You"—refused to have even a remixed version released as a single. Nevertheless, assorted bootlegs cropped up and by October a mysterious artist named Spacedust—probably just a major-label-fronted cash-in attempt—hit the top of the charts in Britain with an almost identical remix of the Sinclar-Bangalter original, entitled "Gym and Tonic" (another crass Spacedust move, covering Bangalter's solo hit with the slimly disguised title "Music Feels Good With You," dropped like a rock).

With all the offending samples removed, Sinclar's *Paradise* LP was re-released worldwide in 1999. He also worked on remixes, providing tracks by Bangalter himself, Ian Pooley, Second Crusade, and the Yellow project Tom & Joyce with additional production. Le Friant returned to the Mighty Bop alias in 2000 with the retrospective mix collection *Spin My Hits*. (See also Bob Sinclar.) —*John Bush*

Meet DJ Cam Et La Funk Mob / 1995 / Yellow ✦✦✦

● **Spin My Hits** / 2000 / Yellow ✦✦✦✦
Down-tempo hip-hop at its most nocturnal and statuesque, the Mighty Bop's influences come from a variety of sources. Start with rap's golden age (for the beats), early New York and Chicago house (for the atmospheric synth), and a liberal dose of jazz and R&B (for the instrumentation and overall vibes). The French turntablist covers Bricusse/Newley's "Feeling Good," and even titles

one of his tracks "Moody's Mood" (though resemblances to the James Moody standard are slight). Elsewhere, "Freestyle Liguistique" is a solid minor-key hip-hop track with rapping by EJM, and the album hits another down-tempo high with "Sea, Sex & Fleurs," a sultry beat piece featuring vocals by Louise Vertigo. Overall, *Spin My Hits* is a delightful mix trip through the Mighty Bop back catalog. *—John Bush*

Miilkbone (Thomas Wlodarczyka)

Hip-Hop, Party Rap, Club/Dance

One of a long line of white rappers, Miilkbone acts as a link between early Caucasian rappers such as 3rd Bass and later artists such as Eminem. Born Thomas Wlodarczyka, Miilkbone grew up in the Delaney Projects of Perth Amboy, NJ, a rough-and-tumble neighborhood that influenced much of his work.

Miilk had some success with his debut single "Keep It Real" as well as "Where Da Party At?," which featured a cameo by Notorious B.I.G. His debut album *Miilkcrate*, however, was a commercial disappointment. Miilkbone laid low for nearly six years and did some work on Death Row's *Chronic 2000* album. In 2001, Miilkbone released his sophomore album *U Got Miilk?* *—Jon Azpiri*

● **Da Miilkcrate** / Jun. 20, 1995 / Capitol ◆◆◆

From Perth Amboy, Miilkbone's rapid delivery and pumping jams recall fellow New Jersey-ites Naughty By Nature. His lyrics deal with living an inner-city lifestyle, especially on "Ghettobiz." *—John Bush*

U Got Miilk? / Apr. 17, 2001 / Lightyear ◆◆

Just what the world needs, another white rapper. That's what many listeners will no doubt think when they hear Miilkbone's second album, *U Got Miilk?* Despite the fact that Miilkbone's career predates Eminem and rap-rock acts like Kid Rock, Miilkbone can't help but be perceived as another Caucasian rapper trying to cash in on hip-hop's legions of angry white fans. Miilkbone knows comparisons to Eminem are inevitable, and he confronts Slim Shady head-on in the track "Dear Slim," a venomous diatribe against Eminem where he sounds a bit like the deranged fan in Eminem's hit "Stan." Instead of focusing on his rivalry with Eminem, Miilkbone should have spent more time focusing on the rest of the album. Although Miilkbone had some success in the early '90s, there's little in *U Got Miilk?* that demonstrates he has evolved or matured as an artist. *—Jon Azpiri*

Mikah 9

East Coast Rap, Political Rap

Mikah 9 is a core player in the Freestyle Fellowship, a legendary yet still underground hip-hop group from California. His first solo project comes in the form of a performance compilation of sorts, with previously unreleased live show appearances from the early '90s, radio freestyles, and even some skat. *—Brad Mills*

● **Timetable** / Oct. 9, 2001 / Meanstreet ◆◆◆

Jazz-inspired music-scapes camouflaged as hip-hop beats grace the new productions on this album, while the old school live performances inject some microphone energy. Mikah 9 moves from thought to thought extremely quickly, but the beat follows him, and it gives the listener more than a few inspiring listens. Traditional Freestyle Fellowship fans will feel right at home here with his older work, and should enjoy his new tracks as well. This is also a great release for someone new to this experienced underground rhyme slayer. *—Brad Mills*

Militia

Group / Hip-Hop, Hardcore Rap

Militia, a production duo who met at the Mike Tyson bout where Tupac Shakur was shot and killed, began working together with the intention of uniting the fractured East and West Coast communities by recording tracks that combined the raw hardcore of New York with the funky bounce So-Cal is known for. Before meeting producer Emanuel Dean, Shawn "FMB" Billups had worked with the Luniz, while Dean worked production on Snoop Doggy Dogg's "Gin & Juice" and "What's My Name" as well as hits by tha Dogg Pound and Korrupt. After the two were introduced by rapper Smooth 7, they recruited several rappers for the recording of their debut album, including Devious and Diz, who appeared on the first single "Burn." Militia's self-titled debut appeared on Red Ant in February 1998. *—John Bush*

● **Militia** / Feb. 24, 1998 / Red Ant ◆◆◆◆

Militia's eponymous debut album is a skillful fusion of hardcore East Coast hip-hop and funky West Coast gangsta rap that manages to be distinctive. From time to time, they fall back on both lyrical and musical clichés, but that happens only occasionally. More frequently, the Bay Area crew pulls everything together. The members of the crew come from all areas of the country, which helps give Militia an integrated sound. There's no stereotyping here—there's West Coast funk, East Coast skills, and Southern grooves. The innovation of the best moments makes the whole thing worthwhile. *—Stephen Thomas Erlewine*

Minamina Goodsong

f. Atlanta, GA

Group / Underground Rap, Hip-Hop

Atlanta hip-hoppers Minamina Goodsong are definitely sillier than your average crew. But that doesn't mean Pgnut Prehistoric (Brandon Odum), Adahma AD (Evan Wix), and DJ T'Challa, aka the Teacher (Cedric Dodd) aren't serious about what they do. Pals since middle school, the trio cut their hip-hop teeth on classic releases of the late '80s and early '90s from De La Soul, the Beastie Boys, and New York's Native Tongues collective. Before Minamina, Pgnut himself contributed his skills to Kaleidoscope, which featured notable Atlanta underground star My Cousin Troy. AD built a reputation in Atlanta, with appearances on pH Balance crew member Captain Mudfish Starbolt's "Most Don't Know" as well as the *Perforated* EP from Psyche Origami. Emerging in 2001 with their own vehicle in *Time for Breakfast* (Royal Fuzz), Minamina Goodsong displayed a penchant for pop-culture-heavy rhymes shot through with towel-slapping humor about girls, sex, TV, and bodily functions. But despite their gift of goof on the mike, Pgnut and AD displayed true ability with their interwoven style, and T'Challa's beats were at once quirky and tight on the bottom end. The album featured collaborations from numerous members of the Kaleidoscope crew, as well as denizens of the local Plainzwalkers collective. Minamina followed up with their sophomore effort, 2003's *Snatch Grab I Love You*. The album expanded on some of the ideas put forth on their debut, but didn't lose the refreshing humor or unpredictable rhymes and samples that defined the group. In support of their material, Minamina Goodsong appeared with such acts as Dres tha Beatnik, Black Eyed Peas, Blackalicious, I Am the World Trade Center, and Antipop Consortium throughout 2002 and 2003. *—Johnny Loftus*

● **Time for Breakfast** / 2001 / Royal Fuzz ◆◆◆◆

With a distinctive hip-hop sound that deftly balances underground appeal with mainstream accessibility, Minamina (pronounced Ma-nuh ma-nuh) Goodsong is proof that white rappers don't have to be shocking á la Eminem or Insane Clown Posse to entertain. Songs like "Wow" and "Golden" boast memorable hooks that lodge themselves into your consciousness on first listen, while "Ghostman" matches a human beatbox with an off-kilter beat as the duo trades nimble rhymes that place them firmly in the alternative rap category. With a polished sound and style to spare, these cats are ready for the big time. *—Bret Love*

Miracle

Hip-Hop, Hardcore Rap, Southern Rap

Southern hardcore rapper Miracle hails from Augusta, GA, where he was discovered while working as a street rep promoting fellow Augusta native Pastor Troy. Miracle signed with the Sound of Atlanta label and issued his debut single, "Bounce," at the very end of 1999. It became a regional hit in the South, setting the stage for the release of his self-titled debut album in the spring of 2000. *—Steve Huey*

Miracle / May 9, 2000 / Uptown/Universal ◆◆

This Atlanta sound is the latest in a long string of Southern areas to take their crunk sound nationwide. Miracle's distinct, high-pitched voice often overpowers some of the lyrics on his self-titled debut. Production wise, many of the tracks have a typical Southern-fried sound, filled with pumped-up, fast-paced beats you'd expect from an artist from Atlanta. Some tracks do stand out, particularly the fierce "Huntin' Season" and the intricately designed rhythms of "If the Sun Don't Shine." Like many of his Southern counterparts, Miracle's tracks often trail into monotony, with every track paced at the same high tempo. If he finds a way to mix it up, his music will definitely find an audience outside of the dirty South. *—Jon Azpiri*

● **Keep It Country** / Nov. 13, 2001 / Universal ✦✦✦

Considering the dirty South movement's overnight success in the early 2000s when rappers like Nelly and Ludicris came out of nowhere to go multiplatinum, it's perhaps no surprise to see newcomers like Miracle get the glossy, major-label treatment. And, indeed, Miracle's debut album on Universal is no doubt glossy and radio ready. The rapper not only sounds strikingly similar to Nelly but also happens to call Atlanta, GA, home, like Ludicris. In sum, Miracle has the makings of an overnight sensation—from his style and his locale to his tattoos and producers. He's essentially Universal's attempt to break into the suddenly lucrative dirty South market. All of this isn't meant to discount Miracle's ability, of course. As *Keep It Country* illustrates, the young rapper no doubt has ample charisma and character, along with a lightning-quick delivery and the necessary manic tendencies. Furthermore, he has an ace production team in Gene Griffin and Paul Wright, aka Sound of Atlanta. These two produce the entire album and know the trademark dirty South production style inside out: drum machine pitter-patter, slamming bass beats, exuberant synth riffs, and so on. In fact, from top to bottom, *Keep It Country* plays like a dirty South album should. Yet, ironically, this ends up being the album's most glaring flaw—it's a very calculated approach, far too obvious. By late 2001, much of what Miracle offers on this album had descended from being unique to being clichéd. Whether he's rapping about representing the country, bouncing "dat ass," getting "da club krunk," or himself, you've heard all this before. And, quite frankly, it all sounded better the first time around. Albums like this are a bad omen for the dirty South's staying power—the floodgates need to close. —*Jason Birchmeier*

Miss Jones

Hip-Hop, Urban

Singer and rapper Miss Jones first earned attention during the mid-'90s, lending her skills to recordings from the likes of Biz Markie, Busta Rhymes, and DJ Red Alert. In 1994 she scored a pair of solo hits with the singles "Where I Wanna Be Boy" and "Don't Front"; however, Jones then left performing to assume an on-air job at station WQHT in New York. Finally, in 1998 she issued her debut LP, *The Other Woman*. —*Jason Ankeny*

● **The Other Woman** / Jun. 16, 1998 / Motown ✦✦✦

The Other Woman may run a little too long, but it demonstrates that Miss Jones is an ambitious performer, blending hip-hop and urban R&B in intriguing ways. She doesn't quite break from formula, choosing to build on Mary J. Blige's groundbreaking sound instead of creating her own, but the end results are often sexy, melodic, and danceable—which is enough to make it a fine debut. —*Stephen Thomas Erlewine*

Missin' Linx

Group / Hardcore Rap, West Coast Rap

The underground hip-hop group Missin' Linx is led by Al Tariq (formerly the Beatnuts' Fashion) and also includes Linx, Black Attack, and Problemz, among its core ranks. Their debut EP, *Exhibit A*, also featured appearances from Mobb Deep's Prodigy, Freddie Foxx, and the Beatnuts' JuJu, among others. —*Heather Phares*

● **Exhibit A** / Mar. 21, 2000 / Red Urban ✦✦

Missin' Linx like to take things slowly. After releasing their first single, "MIA," in 1998, the group did exactly that and wasn't heard from for two years. In 2000 they returned with the release of their EP *Exhibit A*. The six-song compilation highlights the skills of the group's leader, Al Tariq, formerly known as Fashion from the Beatnuts. Current Beatnut Juju even stops by to help out on the album, and he isn't the only one. Missin' Linx uses a host of producers working on the EP, such as Necro, Adam12, DJ EMZ, V.I.C., and the Alchemist. Despite all their efforts, few of the tracks on the EP come close to "MIA." There are, however, some good moments, most of which come from the interplay between MCs Al Tariq, Black Attack, and Problemz. Missin' Linx certainly show enough potential to have fans looking forward to the day when they release a full album, if they ever get around to it. —*Jon Azpiri*

Mista Sinista

Turntablism

New York-based turntablist Mista Sinista was introduced to DJing by his father, who would spin breaks in the family's basement while Sinista was still a little boy. He started spinning on his father's turntables at age 6, and by 14 earned his own pair, with which he began spinning at parties. He honed his craft throughout the '90s with the help of friends and fellow DJs Dr. Butcher and Rob Swift. In 1997 he joined the acclaimed DJ crew the X-Men, soon rechristened the X-Ecutioners. Along with appearing on the group's singles and their full-length album, *X-Pressions*, Sinista also collaborated with Common, the Beatnuts, Al Tariq, and Princess Superstar, among others. 2000 was a busy year for Sinista, with both a solo single and the X-Ecutioners' major-label debut arriving, as well as new collaborations with Cella Dwellas, Dead Prez and Common. He left the X-Ecutioners by 2002, just before the release of the LP *Built From Scratch*, to pursue other projects. —*Heather Phares*

Mr. Cheeks (Terrance Kelly)

b. Queens, NY

East Coast Rap, Hip-Hop

Before establishing himself as a solo artist in the early 2000s, Mr. Cheeks made a name for himself as a member of the Lost Boyz in the mid- to late '90s. Cheeks and the other members of the Lost Boyz practiced a sincere, literate, nonsensational style of New York hip-hop. As a result, they never attained substantial commercial success, yet garnered substantial critical acclaim and were underground favorites. But when Freaky Tah met an unfortunate demise, the Lost Boyz soon broke ranks and remained quiet. Cheeks resurfaced in late 2001, though, and he came with a more mature outlook on life that informed his rhymes with a greater sense of knowledge and truth than before. His debut solo album, *John P. Kelly*, featured the massive hit single "Lights, Camera, Action!" as well as production by a broad roster of producers including Stephen Marley, Bink!, and Easy Mo Bee. —*Jason Birchmeier*

● **John P. Kelly** / Oct. 16, 2001 / Uptown/Universal ✦✦✦

Mr. Cheeks' solo debut finds him having grown substantially since his days fronting the Lost Boyz. Where he used to rap about "Jeeps, Lex Coups, Bimaz & Benz" back in 1995 to much success, he takes a disparaging view of materialism and sensationalism here. It's a refreshing change, particularly given the glamorous state of hip-hop in 2001. Yet as wonderful as it is to hear Cheeks speak knowledge, express passion, and represent mind over materialism, he could really use some new producers. Granted, there are some amazing tracks here courtesy of Bink!, Stephen Marley, and Easy Mo Bee, but this trio only handles a fraction of the tracks here. The other tracks aren't nearly as effective, and it's not because of Cheeks—he's stellar throughout—but rather because of the producers. It's tough to take a disparaging view of *John P. Kelly* because Cheeks obviously has invested substantial emotion and effort into this record, and he truly shines. You just wish Bink!, Marley, and Mo Bee would have handled the entire album rather than just a song or two apiece. Despite the musical shortcomings, though, Cheeks' solo debut still impresses more than it disappoints, and it's a definite step forward from his days in the Lost Boyz—a step in the right direction. —*Jason Birchmeier*

● **Lights, Camera, Action! [Single]** / Feb. 12, 2002 / Universal ✦✦✦

When "Lights, Camera, Action!" became a much larger hit than probably anyone expected in early 2002—not only garnering tons of urban radio play but also storming up the *Billboard* singles chart, breaking into the Hot 100 chart's Top 25—Universal commissioned a remix featuring Missy Elliott and P. Diddy, two of East Coast urban radio's biggest artists at the time. Producer Bink! didn't alter his track too much for the remix and that's fortunate, since it was his beats more than Cheeks' rapping that make the song such a surprise success. You should also note that there are different remixes for "Lights, Camera, Action!": the "Club Mix" features Missy Elliott and P. Diddy, while the "Remix" features Petey Pablo in addition to the other two aforementioned artists, and the "Remix Instrumental," of course, features just Bink!'s track, albeit in a chopped-up version that's even more amazing than the original. —*Jason Birchmeier*

● **Back Again!** / Mar. 18, 2003 / Universal ✦✦✦✦

Mr. Cheeks hyped this album long and hard in the press during 2002, proclaiming to whomever was in earshot that he was making "the best damn rap album period," an obvious play on the successful sports talk show. While show hosts Tom Arnold and John Salley are nowhere within earshot of this record, Mr. Cheeks come forward with easily his most accomplished record since his days in the Lost Boyz. Thematically, Cheeks uses *Back Again!* as therapy; it features raw and unapologetic confessionals about life, covering the usual base of topics you'd expect to hear. The production is clean and tight throughout, with "Crush on You," a duet with Mario Winans, being the album's masterpiece. The cast of guest artists (Pete Rock, C.L. Smooth, Floetry, etc.) is top notch and highlights Cheeks' versatility in rapping over harder-edged street beats as well as the smoother R&B tunes. Thankfully absent of self-indulgent skits, obligatory shout-out intros, and other filler common in hip-hop records, there's nothing particularly innovative about *Back Again!*, but it's a solid party album worth your hard-earned dough. —*Rob Theakston*

Mr. Complex

Ambient Techno, Electronica, Underground Rap

Queens, NY-based rapper Mr. Complex has been showing up on DJ mix tapes since around 1995 with his own singles and appearing with others. His intelligent yet clear vocals have attracted some fans, and the year 2000 saw the release of his debut LP, *Complex Catalog*, closely followed by *Hold This Down* in 2001. —*Brad Mills*

Complex Catalog / 2000 / Corerecords ✦✦✦

● **Hold This Down** / Oct. 2, 2001 / 7 Heads ✦✦✦
To too many people this might as well be Mr. Complex's first LP, as the first was rather slept on and uncirculated. His connection with 7 Heads Records has definitely boosted his street credibility, with people like El Da Sensei of the Artifacts on their management team and up-and-coming artists such as J-Live and the Unspoken Heard in their lineup. The album is tight from the opening track to the inspired live performance in Belgium, Germany at the end. Complex is just that—a complex metaphorical rapper, intelligent enough to know there's more to rap about than guns, girls, and drugs. Admittedly, he's a lot easier to follow and understand than other metaphorical rhymers such as Aesop Rock or Chino XL, but still brings a fresh flow that sounds very loosely like Pharoahe Monch. This is a good album throughout, and surely worth its purchase price. —*Brad Mills*

Mr. Dead (C. Davis)

f. Brooklyn, NY

Group / East Coast Rap, Alternative Rap

Mr. Dead is an underground hip-hop artist hailing from Brooklyn, NY. Born C. Davis, the passionate horror movie fan worked as an accomplished makeup artist not only on B horror films but also on music videos, including some by rap act Gravediggaz. While doing makeup at a Prince Paul video shoot, he was introduced to WordSound, New York's underground hip-hop and illbient label. Dead teamed up with Big Pat to form the duo Metabolics, who released their first album, *The M-Virus*, on WordSound in 1999. In 2001 he released his first full-fledged solo effort, a continuation of the Metabolics project called *Metabolics, Vol. 2: Dawn of the Dead*. The album featured various guest artists, most notably Prince Paul, Dan the Automator, Sensational, M. Sayyid (of Antipop Consortium), Big Pat, and WordSound head Spectre, plus some unknown MCs, such as Herc Boogie and the Vandal. While Dead's voice is gruff and his pieces are dark, with horror movie samples and eerie effects, his music is less abstract than that of many of his labelmates. Unfortunately, even though both albums earned critical praise, they were barely noticed by the record-buying public. Apart from his own albums, Mr. Dead has also made guest appearances on other WordSound albums, most notably on Spectre's *The End* (2000) and volumes 2 and 3 of the compilation series *The Ill St. Presents Subterranean Hitz* (1998 and 2000, respectively). —*Chris Genzel*

● **Metabolics, Vol. 2: Dawn of the Dead** / Jan. 23, 2001 / WordSound ✦✦✦
Though it barely registered a blip on the radar, Mr. Dead's first LP, *M-Virus* (released under the name Metabolics with MC Big Pat), delivered a potent dose of raw, underground NYC hip-hop. Undeterred, Mr. Dead enlisted some of alternative rap's finest producers, including Prince Paul, Dan the Automator, and Scotty Hard, to create a deep, dark manifesto that rages against the trappings of mainstream hip-hop. Songs like "End of Days" and "Longevity" are fierce lyrical throwdowns that show off lethal mic skills while taking a strong philosophical stand, while the Prince Paul-produced title track is a less serious old school throwback that injects a welcome sense of lightheartedness into the proceedings. It may pose no threat to Eminem or Jay-Z for pop chart dominance, but with solid contributions from left-of-center MCs like Paul Barman, Sensational, and newcomer Herc Boogie, *Dawn of the Dead* should be popular with the underground set. —*Bret Love*

Mr. Dibbs

DJ, Producer / Turntablism, Hip-Hop, Club/Dance

Cincinnati DJ Mr. Dibbs is part of 1200 Hobos, a turntablist crew known for their mix tapes, considered more compositional and less-overtly dexterous than those of other DJs. Influenced by the first wave of rap and hip-hop culture, Dibbs' decision to become a DJ was cemented by seeing Grandmixer D.ST perform "Rockit" with Herbie Hancock. His mix style is informed by the hectic song cuts of Midwest radio DJs like Cleveland's Mixmaster Quick and Jeff "the Wizard" Mills from Detroit. Mr. Dibbs also organizes Skribble Fest, Cincinnati's annual festival heralding the cornerstones of hip-hop: breakdancing, graffiti, rapping, and DJing. —*Wade Kergan*

Bomb Beats / 1997 / Bomb Hip Hop ✦✦✦
First spotlighted on the Bomb Records compilation *Return of the DJ, Vol. 2*, Mr. Dibbs teams up with STS for one side each of this LP. While Mr. Dibbs' side is a bit too spare for most listeners, STS tightens up with a set of chunkier beats and loops. —*John Bush*

Primitive Tracks, Soundtrack to Photosynthesis / Oct. 17, 2000 / Habitat ✦✦✦
With the help of famous mixers like Kid Koala and Q-Bert, turntablism and its history, intertwined with hip-hop, has come into its own, and in some respects, also digressed. When turntablism started, it was more of an artform of piecing tracks together with skill and tact. Mr. Dibbs returns turntablism to its roots with *Primitive Tracks, Soundtrack to Photosynthesis*. An amazing cut-and-paste collage of hip-hop tracks and soundbytes, the record even features Dibbs playfully throwing in some Rage Against the Machine and classic rock. This album is best played in its entirety and is a trackspotter's challenge. Without the proper skills needed, an album this eclectic could have been a disaster. However, with Dibbs behind the decks, the album is a success. —*Diana Potts*

Live in Memphis / Oct. 31, 2000 / Stereo Type Records ✦✦✦
Comprised of two tracks from a live set by the Cincinnati DJ along with three studio tracks, *Live in Memphis* is not a groundbreaking turntablist recording—which isn't to say that it's not enjoyable. Mr. Dibbs may rely on too many well-known samples, but his beats and transitions are strong and he keeps the live set moving. The three studio tracks are throwaways, two of which already appeared on other compilations. As a result, they sound more like experiments (or, if you're not feeling kind, jokes) than actual songs. *Live in Memphis* is not an essential release, but worth keeping for some nice live breaks. —*Kurt Edwards*

● **The 30th Song** / 2003 / Rhymesayers ✦✦✦✦
A more concise work than many of his earlier mix tapes, *The 30th Song* is definitely one of Mr. Dibbs' producer records, a mostly instrumental journey through moods and grooves with (slightly) less emphasis on the sprawling grandeur of one of the Midwest's best turntablists. Instead of the usual flashy moves, Dibbs plays around with other techniques, using clever pauses and drop-outs to good effect for "I Hate Greg" and great transformer work for a screeching guitar solo on "Outreach 5" (with Fat Jon). The nine-minute live epic "Omega Prophecy" features Tommy Davidson and the Guinness-record-holding drummer Boo Boo McAfee (he once played the drums for a month straight). "231 Ways to Fry an Egg" samples another solo studio wizard (Paul McCartney), and the standout "Delta Bound" borrows from a pair of blues legends: the plaintive wail of Robert Johnson (from "Hellhound on My Trail") over the Chicago bump and grind of Muddy Waters ("I'm a Man"). The result is a turntable jam that's nearly as raw and effective as a blues. Poised halfway between the grandiose sonic austerity of DJ Shadow and the turntable madness of most turntablists, Mr. Dibbs shows how it's able to age gracefully in hip-hop. (Of course, as proved on the closer, "Porntablist," he's still able to have plenty of fun.) —*John Bush*

Mr. Len

Group / Alternative Rap, East Coast Rap, Old School Rap

Pursuing new boundaries for hip-hop, Mr. Len brought forth a new vision for old school rap. One of the founders of the independent hip-hop trio Company Flow, Mr. Len remained with the crew for more than six years. By 1999, however, following its disbanding, Len decided to begin working on his own. After two years of constant work, including the single "This Morning," created with the Juggaknots, and "What the Fuck?," with Mr. Live, Mr. Len finally released his debut full-length album. *Pity the Fool: Experiments in Therapy Behind the Mask of Music While Handing Out Dummys*, issued in 2001, featured guest appearances by Jean Grae, Juggaknots, and Mass Influence. —*Mario Mesquita Borges*

● **Pity the Fool: Experiments in Therapy Behind the Mask of Music While Handing Out Dummys** / Oct. 23, 2001 / Matador ♦♦♦
Mr. Len's solo debut is as intriguing and convoluted as its title. The ex-Company Flow DJ is all over the place here, teaming with an eclectic roster of guest MCs to create a sound that is certainly his own. Racing from the funky "Get Loose" to the unsettling "Taco Day," Mr. Len attacks with reckless abandon and leaves no stone unturned. *Pity the Fool* is incredibly ambitious; it almost seems as if Mr. Len is trying to condense any and everything a DJ can do into one not-so-tidy package. While some of it works and some of it doesn't, Mr. Len's formidable skills are never in question. It's a wild ride, but *Pity the Fool* maintains a playful tone throughout, offering plenty of fine moments along the way. —*Martin Woodside*

Mr. Lif (Jeffrey Haynes)

Alternative Rap, Underground Rap, Hip-Hop
When Mr. Lif began releasing singles in the late '90s, party rap was the dominant style most MCs favored, but Lif's lyrical agenda was a political and socially conscious one that recalled the rap stars of the previous decade—Public Enemy, Gang Starr, and Boogie Down Productions. Born Jeffrey Haynes, Mr. Lif grew up in the Boston, MA, suburb of Brighton, attending college for two years before focusing on a music career. He released his first single, "Elektro," in 1998, attracting the attention of labels Grand Royal and Def Jux. Working closely with producer and Def Jux label head El-P, Lif released a series of critically acclaimed singles and EPs, starting with *Enters the Colossus* in 2000. Touring kept him busy for the next year, but he still found time to release the "Cro-Magnon" single and a live CD. His most ambitious work to date followed in 2002 with a pair of concept releases. The *Emergency Rations* EP bookends collaborations with Edan and Akrobatik in an MC abduction scenario, while the *I Phantom* full-length contains a saga that leads from birth to apocalypse. —*Wade Kergan*

Live at the Middle East / Jan. 22, 2002 / Ozone ♦♦♦♦
Live at the Middle East is possibly the most unusual hip-hop album ever released. The idea of an artist essentially subjecting a paying audience to previously unreleased material (some of which is being improvised live on stage) is considered esoteric, the province of jazz and jam bands. By hip-hop standards, it's unheard of. Mr. Lif, however, is not your typical hip-hop artist, which renders *Live at the Middle East* a fascinating experiment. Not only is Lif a skilled MC and articulate lyricist, he has a quirky, original sense of humor, so in addition to one entire track dedicated to how Lif beat his DJ at Nintendo, there's also a spontaneous three-song cycle dramatizing an MC who starts off as an underground rapper, scores a major-label deal, and realizes he can never write a meaningful rhyme again. In addition to unveiling some material he recorded but did not release (such as the witty work-sucks diatribe "Live From the Plantation"), Lif invites his DJ Akbar and fellow rapper Akrobatic in an extended freestyle session, including a clever rhyme improvised when the record skips. Whether rapping about nuclear war in "Earthcrusher" or reminiscing about his past hairstyles in "Dreafro," Lif is simply one of the smartest, most original rappers around, and the range of his humor and skills makes *Live at the Middle East* a superb release to please any fan of smart, well-crafted hip-hop. —*Victor W. Valdivia*

Emergency Rations EP / Jun. 25, 2002 / Def Jux ♦♦♦♦
Boston rapper Mr. Lif has made a name for himself as a thoughtful, often incendiary lyricist. On the *Emergency Rations* EP, Lif plays the latter part of that equation to the hilt. This is a concept album, the premise being that Mr. Lif has been kidnapped—in the middle of a live performance—by unidentified (read: government) agents and is now missing. What made the diminutive MC so dangerous? The eight tracks quickly set out to answer that question, showcasing Lif's direct, uncompromising attacks on civil rights, censorship, and especially—in the wake of September 11, 2001—U.S. foreign policy. El-P and Akrobatik contribute haunting, dissonant production that helps set the mood with strong undercurrents of alienation and paranoia, and the rest is left in Mr. Lif's capable hands. The lyrics are as thoughtful as they are confrontational, and *Emergency Rations* is a provocative, well-crafted album that proves hard to ignore. —*Martin Woodside*

● **I Phantom** / Sep. 17, 2002 / Def Jux ♦♦♦♦
Mr. Lif, the hard-working Bostonian MC, drops a debut LP that playfully discloses in lyrical fashion his inner battle of whether or not to return to his nine-to-five job, but the long-overdue record practically guarantees he'll no longer need a day job. One of the working-class heroes signed to hip-hop indie Def Jux, Liffy enjoyed a busy 2002, releasing the *Emergency Rations* EP and appearing on several releases from the Jux camp. *I Phantom* is slightly less politically aggressive than the EP in overall aesthetic, with blue-collar rhymes over hype, funky tracks with great production by Fakts One, DJ Hype, Edan, and Lif himself. The guest appearances on the mic by Akrobatik, a fellow fledgling Bostonion, Edan, Aesop Rock, El-P, and Jean Grae make all the tracks quality and seal the deal on Lif's breakthrough set. —*Nic Kincaid*

Mr. Magic

DJ, Producer / Hip-Hop, East Coast Rap
An important figure in the world of hip-hop radio, Mr. Magic debuted in 1983 on WBLS-FM in New York City with the first exclusive rap radio show to be aired on a major station. Billing itself as Rap Attack, Magic's show featured Marley Marl as the DJ and Tyrone "Fly Ty" Williams as the show's coproducer. Magic's reign on the New York City airwaves lasted six years and was instrumental in broadening the scope and validity of hip-hop music. Magic also spent time as a producer, working on the Force MD's "Let Me Love You" and "Forgive Me Girl," as well as releasing a series of compilation albums from his radio show titled *Mr. Magic's Rap Attack*. Nearly 20 years after his radio debut, Mr. Magic made the transition to the digital realm and helmed Wildstyle, the rap channel for the new millennium's hottest video game, Grand Theft Auto: Vice City. —*Steve Kurutz*

● **Mr. Magic's Rap Attack** / 1985 / Profile ♦♦♦
Mr. Magic's Rap Attack, Vol. 2 / 1987 / Profile ♦♦♦

Mr. Marcelo (Carlos Marcelo)

Hardcore Rap, Southern Rap, Dirty South
Naming himself after the infamous don of the Dixie Mafia, Carlos Marcelo, this young rapper from the dirty South paid his dues in the underground scene before hooking up with Master P's No Limit empire. His autonomy with the tight-knit No Limit camp differentiates Mr. Marcelo from the countless other Southern rappers that were acquired by the label's swelling stable of artists. Rather than being an official No Limit soldier, Marcelo remains true to his own label, Tuff Guys, but enjoys the mass distribution and promotion that comes from an affiliation with No Limit and its parent label, Priority. As a result of this partnership with Master P's label, Marcelo's eyebrow-raising *Brick Livin'* album found itself on the shelves of most record stores in America and getting play in more than a few clubs.

Though still young, Marcelo wasn't new to the rap game when Master P sent him to the studio to record *Brick Livin'*. He had originally released an underground record with one of the pioneering Southern bounce producers, Devious D, titled *P' Poppa*. Following the local success of this record, Marcelo left for New York and performed some shows at the Apollo before eventually returning to the South just as the area began to become a hotbed for up-and-coming rap labels such as No Limit, Cash Money, and Suave House. Like every other ambitious rapper in the South at this time, Marcelo quickly started his own label with his business partner, Doe Doe, and released the first Tuff Guys compilation independently.

Eventually, this record fell into the hands of Master P, who liked what he heard and signed Marcelo to No Limit. One must keep in mind that this took place around the same time that No Limit began to struggle in the face of immense competition from other labels such as Cash Money that were eclipsing the unprecedented success of Master P's label. This mutually beneficial collaboration between the two resulted in *Brick Livin'*, an album that once again drew attention toward No Limit. The album brought together Marcelo's Tuff Guys camp with some of the No Limit camp, along with some of the South's best producers, resulting in a fresh update of traditional Southern rap motifs: booty shakin' anthems, get-crunk club tracks, odes to the ghetto, songs to blaze to, hard gangsta posing, and even a sentimental thug love song. —*Jason Birchmeier*

● **Brick Livin'** / Jul. 25, 2000 / Priority ♦♦♦♦
By stamping the No Limit logo on Mr. Marcelo's *Brick Livin'* album, Master P has breathed some life into his struggling label. In the late '90s, No Limit had thrived as the global outpost for dirty South thug anthems: songs about

living in the ghetto, being true to the game, getting high, being hard, and living the thug lifestyle. By the end of the '90s, No Limit had recycled these clichés one too many times, causing successive albums to sound far too similar to their predecessors. The fact that No Limit had flooded the market and diluted their stable of producers didn't help either, resulting in lackluster beats for the increasingly generic rhymes. But for as much as *Brick Livin'* stays true to these same motifs and uses these same producers, it succeeds where other albums from the same time such as C-Murder's *Trapped in Crime* suffered. What differentiates Marcelo from his other peers on No Limit is a strong sense of enthusiasm. After all, he isn't actually a No Limit soldier but rather the kingpin of his own label, Tuff Guys. He's essentially just using the No Limit logo as a means for mass distribution and major-label backing, just as Master P is using Marcelo to spice up his tired label. In terms of mandatory Southern rap motifs, *Brick Livin'* covers all the bases: booty shakin' anthems ("How U Like It"), "get crunk" tracks ("Somet'in"), hard gangsta posing ("Ha Brah"), representing the ghetto ("Brick Livin'"), being true to the game ("Soldiers for Life"), tracks to bounce to ("Southern Funk"), and even a sentimental thug love song ("Me & My Girl"). Sure, listeners aren't going to find anything new on this record; as good as this record is relative to other No Limit releases, it surely isn't on par with classic thug albums such as 2Pac's *All Eyez on Me* or Juvenile's *400 Degreez.* What listeners will find is a refreshing approach to increasingly generic motifs that could be the most enthusiastic record to bear the No Limit stamp since Master P's breakthrough album, *Ghetto D. —Jason Birchmeier*

Mr. Nitro (Derek Booker)

Vocals, Producer / Hardcore Rap, West Coast Rap, Party Rap, Hip-Hop
Mr. Nitro (born Derek Booker) started his career in 1994 producing beats with Queen Latifah's Flavor Unit imprint, under the name Daddy D. After a spell of disillusionment with labels MCA and Elektra Records (who couldn't comprehend his musical concept), he ventured out on his own with Nitro Entertainment, exposing the burgeoning talent in his hometown of Oklahoma City. His 2000 compilation CD, *Hustlin' Pays,* is a project that showed off Oklahoma's brightest stars. — *Trent Fitzgerald*

● **Hustlin' Pays** / May 23, 2000 / Columbia ✦✦✦
If you don't live in the Midwest, you've probably never heard of Mr. Nitro. But this ambitious MC-turned-producer is trying to build a reputation as an A&R for his hometown of Oklahoma City, a place not often considered for its rap music. The fruits of his ambitions can be found on his 2000 CD *Hustlin' Pays* (Columbia Records), an infomercial for Mr. Nitro's budding empire: Nitro Entertainment. The disc features up-and-coming artists like Young Fool, Lady Ace, Boy Dogg, Buccet Loc, MOB Playas, Z Real, C.A.P., NFamous, Pypa, and Mista Mase. What's surprising about this CD is that it doesn't sound contemporary. After 1999, the year we saw Master P, Juvenile, and Lil' Wayne rule hip-hop with their up-tempo electro-funk sound, Mr. Nitro seems content with rehashing old soundscapes like whining synthesizers, 808 drum beats, and bad sexual politics. As the music gets more into gangsta rap redux, the lyrics get more predictable. For example, Mr. Nitro and his crew decide to do an eight-minute remake of N.W.A's mid-'80s classic "Boyz-N-The Hood," which embodies much of the gangsta rap motif. It's a huge stretch, and four minutes too long and Nitro pulls it off by staying faithful to the gangsta rap classic. Funky tracks like the posse-cut "Millionaires," "Boy Damn," "Hennessey," and "Do the Damn Thang!" are recyclable dance tracks that will hype any house party. "Hustlin' Pays" has an infectious P-funk shuffle and whining synthesizers. Mr. Nitro even tries his hand at R&B in "Tangueray" (with NFamous). Time must be standing still in Oklahoma City because every track here sounds like mid-'80s proto-gangsta rap. Nevertheless, it's not a bad introduction to the Midwest's burgeoning talent. — *Trent Fitzgerald*

Mr. Pookie

Dirty South, Underground Rap, Southern Rap, Hardcore Rap
Mr. Pookie debuted nationally in 1999 with *Tha Rippla* and continued to extend his reach beyond Texas with successive releases, some of which were collaborative. —*Jason Birchmeier*

● **Tha Rippla** / Nov. 30, 1999 / Icon ✦✦
A fine if not exceptional album, Mr. Pookie's debut effort, *Tha Rippla,* ushers the Dallas rapper into the increasingly crowded dirty South scene with the usual Southern flair. A small stable of similar rappers join him—K-Roc,

Mr. Lucci, Remontis, C-Pone, Juiell, and Solo—while Kevin A. handles the production, engineering, and mixing. —*Jason Birchmeier*

Mr. Quikk

DJ, Producer / Hip-Hop, Hardcore Rap
Mr. Quikk has been putting out dirty South DJ mixes since the mid-'90s on the Dirty Harry Productions record label. Not only does he scratch and mix, but he usually remixes most of the latest mainstream party rap tracks for his albums. —*Brad Mills*

69 Wayz / Oct. 20, 1998 / Priority ✦✦✦

● **Murda Murda** / Jun. 12, 2001 / Dirty Harry ✦✦✦
Not just your typical mix tape, there's a fair amount of scratching, blending, remixing, and cutting throughout this full-length LP. For the casual listener who just wants the hottest tracks from down South, this is a nice little package. Included are tracks from Juvenile, OutKast, Ludacris, Dr. Dre, Snoop, Shyne, Big Tymers, and more. Pretty straightforward, no annoying yelling or skits, quality tracks, plus an experienced DJ putting his spin on things. —*Brad Mills*

Mr. Serv-On

Gangsta Rap, Hardcore Rap, Southern Rap
Another cog in Master P's No Limit Records machine, Mr. Serv-On went to high school with Master P (as well as most of the other members of No Limit) and signed to the label on the cusp of Master P's breakout into the mainstream. Around the time Master P's *Ghetto D* hit number one on the album charts, Serv-On's *Life Insurance* (using the No Limit production machine known as Beats by the Pound) reached number 23, in September 1997. *War Is Me, Pt. 1: Battle Decisions* followed three years later, and was his first release away from the No Limit imprint. Serv-On would continue to go through label strife before finally finding a home on D3 Entertainment and releasing *No More Questions* in early 2003. —*John Bush*

Life Insurance / Aug. 12, 1997 / Priority ✦✦✦✦
One of the better albums on No Limit Records, Mr. Serv-On's debut album, *Life Insurance,* isn't all that different from its fellow No Limit travelers. Like anyone else in Master P's stable, Mr. Serv-On churns out gangsta rap that panders to the lowest common denominator. In the case of *Life Insurance,* that isn't particularly bad, since Mr. Serv-On is a fine rapper and the production cleverly coopts a number of different styles, ranging from West Coast gangsta to Southern bass funk. Even though the album runs too long, there's a little here to appeal to any dedicated fan of hardcore rap, and it suggests that No Limit may have another star in the form of Mr. Serv-On. —*Leo Stanley*

● **Da Next Level** / Feb. 16, 1999 / Priority ✦✦✦✦
The phrase "taking it to the next level" is one of the perennial rap clichés, nearly as ubiquitous as "throw your hands in the air" or calling out for everyone in the house to say "yo." That alone would make an album called *Da Next Level* something of a joke, but it seems especially funny coming from a No Limit soldier, since Master P's posse is all about conformity, clichés, and possibly even market research. As it turns out, Mr. Serv-On turns the joke around on his and No Limit's detractors with *Da Next Level.* Yes, it follows the patented No Limit formula of tinny synths, cheap beats, and borrowed hooks, but there's a difference—there's more care in the craft and songs than on the usual No Limit platter. Sure, it is bloated at a whopping 75 minutes, but the best cuts on the record are tighter than the average album from the label. Plus, Mr. Serv-On shows a desire to improve his own craft, finding new ways of saying the same old thing and concentrating on his flow. These little differences certainly elevate *Da Next Level* to a level above the average No Limit release. —*Stephen Thomas Erlewine*

No More Questions / Mar. 18, 2003 / Riviera ✦✦✦✦
Former No Limit soldier Mr. Serv-On followed suit with several of No Limit's top recording artists (Mystikal, Snoop Dogg, 504 Boyz) and quietly left the label, finding refuge in several other labels before finding a home on D3 Records. Unsurprisingly, he retains the grit and raw vocal delivery of his earlier releases, as well as the sleek production gracing early No Limit releases. His ability to keep referring to himself as a "soldier" harks back to his days at No Limit, and the opening track gives off a feeling that it's an old outtake from those days. Apparently nothing else thematically has changed from release to release either, as his obsessions with blunts, women, hustlin', and

New Orleans remain at all-time high levels. Perhaps this is one of the reasons many of the No Limit soldiers were honorably discharged, as there's a lack of topics to cover and only so many artists to push them who will induce sales. But whatever the case, Serv-On delivers another chunk of the dirty South goods. The enhanced CD features bonus audio and video footage guaranteed to make you feel the Louisiana heat while listening in. —*Rob Theakston*

Mr. Short Khop

West Coast Rap

West Coast rapper Mr. Short Khop got his big break in a 7-Eleven, of all places. It was at the convenience store that Mr. Short Khop had a chance meeting with West Coast hip-hop legend Ice Cube. The two eventually struck up a business relationship with Short Khop making guest appearances on Ice Cube's album *War and Peace (Part 1)*. Ice Cube returned the favor by appearing on Mr. Short Khop's 2001 debut album, *Da Khop Shop*. —*Jon Azpiri*

● **Da Khop Shop** / Mar. 20, 2001 / TVT ♦♦
West Coast rapper Mr. Short Khop has made a name for himself for his various cameos on Ice Cube's records. In 2001, Short Khop breaks out with his first solo album and Cube's influence can be felt throughout. The best parts of the album are tracks, such as "Short Khop & Da Brain," that feature cameos by Ice Cube. Equally impressive is the single "Dollaz, Drank & Dank," a classic piece of West Coast G-funk. After those tracks, however, there is little to recommend. Instead of trying to come up with anything remotely original, Short Khop relies on the same tired clichés that have weighed down West Coast hip-hop for too long. "Kingpin & the Kockhound" and "Ya Trippin" leave the listener with little to do except keep count of how often the words "bitch" and "ho" are used in a single verse. If you want to hear where West Coast hip-hop is going, you should check out Dr. Dre's *2001*. If you want take a trip to the West Coast's all-too-familiar past, then you can settle for *Da Khop Shop*. —*Jon Azpiri*

Mr. 3-2

Hardcore Rap, Dirty South, Southern Rap

Mr. 3-2 broke into the flourishing Texas rap scene of the early 2000s with *The Governor* (2001), his debut effort for N Yo Face Records. —*Jason Birchmeier*

● **The Governor** / Sep. 11, 2001 / N Yo Face ♦♦
If there's one Mecca for the dirty South movement that swept the rap game by storm in the late '90s, it's probably Houston, TX. More rappers came out of Houston during the dirty South's popular peak than any other city down South—more than Memphis, more than Atlanta, more than New Orleans. So when you assign Mr. 3-2 the disparaging tag of "another Houston rapper," it's not so much a stab at the guy but simply a matter of fact. That's too bad, particularly because 3-2 really does showcase some obvious flair for MCing on *The Governor*, along with some charisma. But an appealing sense of character only goes so far—especially when you have lo-fi, rudimentary beats to rhyme over. And because the dirty South aesthetic is so reliant on its bass-heavy beats and tear-the-club-up rhythms—much more so than its admittedly shallow and predictable lyrical motifs—*The Governor* ends up being, unfortunately, a bland album. Mr. 3-2's rhymes can carry the album for only so long, something that becomes overly apparent as this lengthy album crosses the halfway point. Still, lackluster beats or not, 3-2 surely proves himself a talented Houston rapper with potential here. You just wish he had better producers and a label like Rap-A-Lot with clout to help him out. —*Jason Birchmeier*

Mix Master Mike (Michael Schwartz)

b. 1970

DJ / Hip-Hop, Underground Rap, Turntablism, Alternative Rap

Mix Master Mike (born Michael Schwartz in 1970) first attracted attention as a member of the Invisibl Skratch Piklz, one of the most acclaimed DJ collectives of their era—three-time winners of the annual world scratching competition, they were eventually barred from entering as a result of a lack of any solid competition. Debuting in 1996 with *Michristmasterpiece Muziks Worst Nightmare*, Mike's skills eventually brought him to the attention of the Beastie Boys, who recruited him to serve as the DJ on their 1998 LP, *Hello Nasty*, and on tour; his second solo record, *Anti-Theft Device*, appeared that same summer. —*Jason Ankeny*

Michristmasterpiece Muzik's Worst Nightmare / Nov. 5, 1996 / Down to Earth ♦♦♦

● **Anti-Theft Device** / Jul. 21, 1998 / Asphodel ♦♦♦♦♦
The first widely released LP from the Serial Wax Killer is a one-hour turntablist journey, balancing samples of staid military men with soul shouters and dire science-fiction warnings with instructional LPs, all of them overlaid with dozens of funky breaks and Mike's furious scratching. As consistently fresh and funky as *Anti-Theft Device* sounds, if this one lacks the energy of his mix tapes (to say nothing of his live appearances), the answer could lie in Asphodel's understandable wish to not get sued over the use of copyrighted material. —*John Bush*

Eye of the Cyklops EP / Mar. 21, 2000 / Asphodel ♦♦♦
Following up his full-length debut, *Anti-Theft Device*, armed with two turntables equipped with needles that shoot out audio laser beams, Mix Master Mike enters battle on this efficient, four-part suite containing 11 tracks. The music is centered around an attack by extra-terrestrial beings; the first suite, "Eye of the Cyclops," is the preparation for intergalactic warfare featuring alien-sounding gurgles, attack sirens, and the approach of the invading enemies. Suite two, "Agent Scanner 12," puts defenders of the musical universe into the fray with commanding force. The sonic counterattack that follows fires some of the funkiest breaks ever created in the history of turntable music. The audio war rages on in the two final suites, "Catapilla Spit" and "Solar Planet," complete with the sounds of combat exchange, retreat, and triumphant warfare. With *Eye of the Cyclops*, Mix Master Mike expands the realm of possibilities of this musical medium rather than simply push vinyl back and forth across the stylus. This is a 23-minute space adventure, futuristic war and victory not only for the galaxy but also for the universe between the listener's ears. —*Douglas Siwek*

Spin Psycle / Sep. 11, 2001 / Moonshine Music ♦♦♦♦♦
Mix Master Mike, the three-time DMC world champion, the guy who attracted Beastie Boys, and the same man who helped found the Invisibl Skratch Piklz (a group of the most talented turntablists the world knows) is back and surprising the world with something he's never done before—at least commercially. This is Mike's first hip-hop mixed CD, attracting exactly who he wanted on the album, including: Freddie Foxxx, Guru of Gangstarr, Binary Star, Fat Lip (ex-Pharcyde), Deltron 3030, Large Professor, KRS-One, Cali Agents, El the Sensei, and others. Anyone who can round up all those guys for some exclusive material and have it cut up by one of the world's best DJs is bound to create something beautiful, and that's exactly what this is. —*Brad Mills*

Return of the Cyklops / Aug. 27, 2002 / Asphodel ♦♦♦
The third full-length from Invisibl Skratch Piklz member Mix Master Mike is a compilation of three previously released EPs, *Eye of the Cyklops*, *Valuemeal*, and *Surprize Packidge*. It's mostly a showcase for his scratching ability, and Mix Master Mike most definitely has skills. He fires off snippets of songs and sounds at the listener, but isn't interested in creating his own songs and rarely spends more than a minute or even 30 seconds on one groove. The material he uses is mostly unfamiliar; he has scanned far and wide for original records and beats to screw with. However, there are some old school snippets chucked into the mix every so often. Since nobody could really dance to this record and there's no rapping or anything approaching real songs, it will probably be chiefly of interest to other DJs and true scratch fanatics. —*Adam Bregman*

MJG (Marlon Jermaine Goodwin)

b. Memphis, TN

Vocals, Producer / Southern Rap, Dirty South, Hip-Hop, Hardcore Rap, Gangsta Rap

As a member of the popular Eightball & MJG duo, the rapper born as Marlon Jermaine Goodwin is widely seen as one of the South's pioneers. His first solo album, *No More Glory*, appeared in 1997. —*Jason Birchmeier*

● **No More Glory** / Nov. 18, 1997 / Uptown/Universal ♦♦♦♦
MJG's solo debut *No More Glory* is a harder, more political record than anything he made with his regular partner, Eightball. While it has a few rough patches and it runs a little long, *No More Glory* is nevertheless an impressive display from MJG, revealing that he has greater lyrical insight and deeper musical gifts than previously suspected. The music is still Southern hardcore, with deep bass and hard-hitting rhythms, but the production is more textured than before, illustrating that the genre isn't as mindless as many critics claim.

The album could have used a little more of the light funk that makes the single "That Girl" so irresistable, but even so, *No More Glory* is a terrific first step forward from MJG. —*Stephen Thomas Erlewine*

Mo Cheda Mobstaz

Group / Dirty South, Hardcore Rap, Party Rap
Underground hip-hop producer DJ Squeeky began the Mo Cheda label in 2001 to release albums by himself and his friends. During various recording sessions, he got the various artists on his label to record an album with one another, 2002's *Mo Cheda Mobstas*. Boasting hardcore gangsta rhymes and dirty South beats, the album was a showcase not only for his talents but also for the talents of the various rappers he had helped along through the years. It also served to give his clique a nickname, something necessary in the scene-intensive rap world of 2002. —*Bradley Torreano*

● **Mo Cheda Mobstas** / May 21, 2002 / Warlock ♦♦
Reefer, booze, hoes, guns, and parties—are there any other topics more generic in the rap world than these five things? Yet it continues to sell, which results in albums like the eponymous debut from the Mo Cheda Mobstaz. Mo Cheda Records is a subsidiary of Warlock Records, and this collection represents the collaborative efforts of its various artists. The guru of these tracks is producer DJ Squeeky, whose tense beats are typical of the dirty South sound. He keeps things quite simple, relying on the usual gangsta fantasies to fill in the lyrics, while the beats maintain a contagious bounce. If these MCs had the imagination of a Dr. Dre or a Jay-Z, they might be able to survive on these elements alone. But they are more comparable to post-Dre Eazy-E, bragging about their lifestyles with rhymes so generic that they barely count as rapping ("Y'know a nigga got down on the hoe, of course/I pulled her over, got her name and her number, oh boy!") With artists like OutKast and Ludacris upping the stakes in the dirty South genre, crews like the Mo Cheda Mobstaz don't have much of a chance of moving beyond minor indie success without some twist to help them stand apart. Until these DJs and MCs find what that is, all they have are bland albums like this one to appeal to an increasingly demanding rap audience. —*Bradley Torreano*

Mo Thugs Family

Group / Hip-Hop, Urban, Gangsta Rap, Pop-Rap
Mo Thugs Family is an all-star project featuring Bone Thugs-N-Harmony along with a variety of acts signed to the group's Mo Thugs Records. Besides Bone Thugs members Layzie Bone, Krayzie Bone, Wish Bone, and Flesh-n-Bone, the Mo Thugs Family includes II Tru, Poetic Hustla'z, MT5, and Felecia. The supergroup debuted in March 1997 with *Mo Thugs Family Scriptures*, which hit number two on the charts and easily made platinum. The second Mo Thugs LP, *Chapter II: Family Reunion*, was released one year later; *Mo Thugs III: The Mothership* followed in 2000. —*John Bush*

Mo Thugs Family Scriptures / Mar. 13, 1997 / Mo Thugs ♦♦♦

● **Chapter II: Family Reunion** / May 26, 1998 / Relativity ♦♦♦
Mo Thugs Family isn't really an offshoot of Bone Thugs-N-Harmony—it's more of a collection of protégés with some of the Bones producing some of the tracks. Therefore, *Chapter II: Family Reunion* is much like its predecessor, featuring some veterans from the first record and a lot of new cuts from new rappers. While there are some really fine moments here, most of them are due to the terrific rapper Souljah Boy, who announces himself as a genuine find. Unfortunately, most of the new rappers and singers aren't quite as enthralling as Souljah Boy, and the album collapses on its own weight after a while. Still, there are enough interesting moments to make it a worthy follow-up to its popular predecessor, even if it doesn't quite gel into a cohesive album. —*Leo Stanley*

Mo Thugs III: The Mothership / Jun. 13, 2000 / Koch/State Street/Mo Thugs ♦♦
Like previous Mo Thugs volumes, *The Mothership* presents an array of Bone Thugs-N-Harmony affiliates, none of them too novel. Like the greater Bone enterprise, the Mo Thugs Family was unraveling around this point, desperate for a hit the mishmash coalition couldn't seem to score. —*Jason Birchmeier*

Mobb Deep

f. 1992, Queensbridge, NY
Group / East Coast Rap, Hardcore Rap, Gangsta Rap, Hip-Hop
Amid the burgeoning mid-'90s hardcore rap scene, Queensbridge duo Mobb Deep towered above their peers, instantly canonized for their influential,

trendsetting *The Infamous* album. The duo, comprised of Prodigy and Havoc, initially began as just another hardcore rap act, a role the two youths actually typecast themselves as on their rudimentary debut album, *Juvenile Hell* (1993), and their breakthrough album, *The Infamous* (1995). The startling latter became a touchstone album among the hardcore rap community, driven by the song "Shook Ones, Pt. 2," a time-tested anthem. Mobb Deep became widely known from coast to coast for its hellishly lyrical depiction of New York street life in Queensbridge, the rough housing project the duo called home. Mobb Deep's production style also became widely known, driven by haunting melodies and hard-hitting beats, the bleak aural equivalent of the duo's sullen rhymes. By the end of the decade, Mobb Deep's *Murda Muzik* debuted at number three on the *Billboard* album chart, exemplifying exactly how far the duo had come without compromising their harsh approach. Soon after attaining this commercial zenith, Mobb Deep's street credibility suffered a blow by Jay-Z in 2001 on the song "Takeover." Yet Prodigy and Havoc bounced back, not by retaliating as Nas had, but by scoring their biggest crossover hit yet, "Hey Luv (Anything)."

Mutually residing in Queens and sharing a passion for hip-hop, Mobb Deep members Prodigy and Havoc originally met while both attending the prestigious Graphic Arts High School in Manhattan. Still in their late teens, the duo released their debut album in 1993, *Juvenile Hell*, on the 4th & Broadway label. Though the album wasn't that successful from either a financial or critical standpoint, it did serve as a fitting platform for the duo to launch its career. Not only did Mobb Deep produce its own beats, it also crafted its own style of beat making: a street-smart poetic approach centering on the surrounding ghetto lifestyle. Prodigy and Havoc's brutally honest reality rapping and complementary melancholy beats landed them a deal in 1995 with the up-and-coming Loud label, who released *The Infamous*, Mobb Deep's breakthrough album.

The Infamous became a touchstone for mid-'90s East Coast hardcore rap beside such similar classics as *Reasonable Doubt*, *Enter the Wu-Tang*, and *Ready to Die*. Partially propelled to awareness by fellow Queensbridge rapper Nas, who lyrically took a similar approach on his championed *Illmatic* album in 1994, and partially by a successful single, "Shook Ones, Pt. 2," Mobb Deep suddenly found itself with a huge cult following. A year later in 1996, Prodigy and Havoc released *Hell on Earth*; debuting at number six on the *Billboard* album chart, the album found the duo further realizing its approach, dropping both evocative beats and cinematic rhymes that communicated the dark side of New York's urban landscape. And thanks to a grim video for "Hell on Earth (Front Lines)" and theatrical *Scarface*-like photos inside the CD booklet picturing the duo with guns and a mound of cocaine, Mobb Deep had created an elaborate image for themselves that took hardcore gangsta rap to a new level that the East Coast had yet fostered. It was then no surprise when fans heavily bootlegged Mobb Deep's successive release, *Murda Muzik*, while it was still in its demo stage, leaking rough versions of the nearly 30 songs the duo had recorded onto the streets and the Internet.

Months after the bootlegs first leaked and after several pushed-back street dates, *Murda Muzik* finally dropped in early 1999. It debuted at number three on *Billboard* and quickly went platinum on the strength of "Quiet Storm," a song epitomizing the signature Mobb Deep style. In late 2000, Prodigy finally released his long-rumored solo album, *H.N.I.C.*, which saw the more outspoken member of the group collaborating with outside producers such as Alchemist and Rockwilder on tracks similar to the trademark Mobb Deep style. On *H.N.I.C.* and later in an interview with *The Source*, Prodigy referenced his bout with illness during the time following *Murda Muzik*. During this same time, Jay-Z spoke out against Mobb Deep, and Prodigy in particular. The street-credibility challenging incident led to some publicity for Mobb Deep, who were then unwillingly thrown into the spotlight with New York's biggest rappers at the time, Jay-Z and Nas.

Mobb Deep overcame its hurdles with the release of *Infamy* at the tail end of 2001. The duo didn't challenge Jay-Z as Nas had. Instead, Mobb Deep veered notably toward pop-rap for the first time in its career, bringing in outside producers and vocalists. The crossover success of "Hey Luv (Anything)" resulted, upsetting some longtime fans who wanted to see the duo remain strictly hardcore. Yet for every fan that jumped ship, two climbed aboard, shuffling the composition of Mobb Deep's audience a bit. The duo were unfazed, however. Prodigy in particular noted that his bout with illness and Jay-Z had changed his outlook. —*Jason Birchmeier*

Juvenile Hell / Apr. 13, 1993 / 4th & Broadway ♦♦♦

On their debut, Havoc and Prodigy tell the listener in all sorts of overconfident manners that there are few people out there who can mess with Mobb Deep. In fact, they do so in 14 different ways on *Juvenile Hell*. Mostly produced by Mobb Deep themselves, this album is rawness at an unrelenting pace, with an undeniable, relentless, and often irrational energy. The intro cut sets the mood as a warning, set to a "Queens brand" production. The tempo is kind of fast, but the bass line rolls to easily facilitate a strong headnod. The sampled horn stabs help to remind you that after all, it's still music. Over this beat Prodigy cautions: "it's called *Juvenile Hell*, you won't survive long." In the first few songs, Mobb acquaints the listener with the life of a "frustrated and confused young juvenile" living in Queens. *Juvenile Hell* is hardcore, but not void of musical or creative effort and accomplishment; it's really cool, serious, and 100-percent hip-hop. Highlights include "Flavor for the Non Believes," "Peer Pressure," "Stomp Em Out" (featuring Big Noid), and "Hold Down the Fort." When *Juvenile Hell* was initially released, it didn't do so well in the stores. Perhaps it was the excess of threats and proclamations making up *Juvenile Hell* that kept buyers away in 1993, or maybe it was the label's inability to market this virulent project correctly. In any event, it's an album worthy of historical note. —*Qa'id Jacobs*

★ **The Infamous** / Apr. 25, 1995 / Loud ♦♦♦♦♦

One of the cornerstones of the New York hardcore movement, *The Infamous* is Mobb Deep's masterpiece, a relentlessly bleak song cycle that's been hailed by hardcore rap fans as one of the most realistic gangsta albums ever recorded. Given Mobb Deep's youthful age and art-school background, it's highly unlikely that *The Infamous* is drawn strictly from real-life experience, yet it's utterly convincing, because it has all the foreboding atmosphere and thematic sweep of an epic crime drama. That's partly because of the cinematic vision behind the duo's detailed narratives, but it's also a tribute to how well the raw, grimy production evokes the world that Mobb Deep is depicting. The group produced the vast majority of the album itself, with help on a few tracks from the Abstract (better known as Q-Tip), and establishes a spare, throbbing, no-frills style indebted to the Wu-Tang Clan. This is hard underground hip-hop that demands to be met on its own terms, with few melodic hooks to draw the listener in. Similarly, there's little pleasure or relief offered in the picture of the streets Mobb Deep paints here: they inhabit a war zone where crime and paranoia hang constantly in the air. Gangs are bound together by a code of fierce loyalty, relying wholly on one another for survival in a hopeless environment. Hostile forces—cops, rivals, neighborhood snitches—are potentially everywhere, and one slip around the wrong person can mean prison or death. There's hardly any mention of women, and the violence is grim, serious business, never hedonistic. Pretty much everything on the album contributes to this picture, but standouts among the consistency include "Survival of the Fittest," "Eye for a Eye," "Temperature's Rising," "Cradle to the Grave," and the classic "Shook Ones, Pt. 2." The product of an uncommon artistic vision, *The Infamous* stands as an all-time gangsta/hardcore classic. —*Steve Huey*

Hell on Earth / Nov. 19, 1996 / Loud ♦♦♦♦♦

Mobb Deep became a street-level sensation with its second album, *The Infamous*, and the duo saw no reason to tamper with its signature style on the follow-up, *Hell on Earth*. The first words on the record announce "You know how we did on the *Infamous* album, right? All right, well, we gon' do it again," and that's exactly what they do. *Hell on Earth* refines the Mobb Deep formula, amplifying much of what made *The Infamous* a success. The bleak street narratives are even more violent and extreme, and the production is even grittier and creepier. It's still indebted to—but more dramatic than—the RZA's work with the Wu-Tang Clan: eerie strings and bits of piano, underpinned by deep, echoing beats. Although the overall flavor is pretty much the same as before, it's a bit more sophisticated and cinematic. For those reasons, some Mobb fans actually prefer *Hell on Earth* over *The Infamous*, although it's missing some of the thematic unity and clearly emphasized details that made the world of *The Infamous* so cohesive. *Hell on Earth* also lacks some of the freshness, but even if Mobb Deep is repeating itself, it's doing so very effectively. The album is superbly moody and haunting, with the swirling horror-film atmospherics of "G.O.D., Pt. III" and the hypnotic "Hell on Earth (Front Lines)" standing out in particular. "Drop a Gem on 'Em" is another highlight, an answer song in the 2Pac beef that happened to appear not long before the rapper's

murder. Special guests Method Man, Raekwon, and fellow Queensbridge native Nas all put in worthy appearances. Even if it isn't quite the landmark that *The Infamous* was, *Hell on Earth* is nearly its equal in many other respects. —*Steve Huey*

Murda Muzik / Apr. 27, 1999 / Loud ♦♦♦♦

After a three-year hiatus and numerous release date pushbacks, Mobb Deep got on their job once again with the punishing release of *Murda Muzik*. The duo, well known for their lethal realism both in their infinitely dark yet moving beats and their stark and ruthless crime-rhyme lyrics, continued their grim odyssey with this, their fourth effort. Released amidst so much watered-down product, *Murda Muzik* is an arguable masterpiece in the Puffy and Master P era. Mobb Deep once described their music as the sound of hypnotic thug life. An accurate description, for their music is more than just guns and herb smoking, it taps into the collective sense of fear and horror, the evil in men's hearts, and the struggle for good in the gardens of waste. Mobb music can make you cry, can make you scared, can amplify your inner rage; its depth allows for the gamut of emotional reactions. On this album, primary producer Havoc reached a high level of mastery in his production efforts, a truly signature style of deep bass grooves, piercing organs, ice-cold snare pops, melodic samples, and haunting orchestral snippets. Each song creates its own mood whether it be a call to stop the violence on "Spread Love" or a call for full throttle livin' on "I'm Goin' Out." Guest appearances by Raekwon, Lil' Kim, Lil Cease, Cormega, Kool G Rap, Eightball, and Infamous Mobb add texture to already bangin' tracks. The album overall can best be described as pure ear- and mind-twisting pleasure and pain. The album will affect you, get under your skin, make you rash up, and then salve you. *Murda Muzik* is a complete album and a renewal of the truly hardcore movement. —*Michael Di Bella*

Infamy / Dec. 11, 2001 / Loud ♦♦♦

Long considered New York's most rugged and hardcore rap group of the '90s to ever make it big, Mobb Deep finally softened up a bit on *Infamy*. The album is a turning point for Prodigy and Havoc—and a timely one indeed. Shortly before *Infamy* hit the streets, Jay-Z had blasted Mobb Deep—as well as Nas—on "Takeover," berating Prodigy in particular for being fake. Nas fired back on his *Stillmatic* album with the cutting song "Ether"; Mobb Deep didn't. Instead, the Queensbridge duo went about its business and released *Infamy*, its most accessible album yet—the sort of album many fans never would have expected. Granted, Mobb Deep still repped the street life here, as songs such as "Kill That Nigga," "My Gats Spitting," and "Hurt Niggas" no doubt illustrate. However, songs such as "Pray for Me," "Hey Luv (Anything)," and "There I Go Again" sent quite a different message; the first featured Lil' Mo, the second 112, and the third Ron Isley—each there to smooth out Mobb Deep's rough sound for the masses. And it worked, particularly in the case of the ballad "Hey Luv (Anything)," which garnered the most exposure the duo had yet experienced and introduced Mobb Deep to a new audience of thug passion-seeking women. So there's little debating the fact: Mobb Deep did the unthinkable on *Infamy*, softening its sound a bit. But you really can't complain. This is Mobb Deep's most well rounded album to date, though unfortunately a bit out of character. After all, you have to wonder: are Prodigy and Havoc selling out or softening with age? The answer is unclear at this point, and it's safe to wager that longtime fans were left scratching their heads in wonder—and surely some in dismay. Nonetheless, Mobb Deep needed a change of direction at this point. Jay-Z had berated Prodigy on the most talked-about rap song of the year, and the duo's previous album, *Murda Muzik*, had sounded tired relative to *Hell on Earth*. So for the time being, *Infamy* made Mobb Deep relevant again, albeit for a more mainstream audience. —*Jason Birchmeier*

Moka Only

b. Vancouver, Canada

Hip-Hop, Underground Rap

One of Canada's busiest b-boys, Moka Only is an incredibly prolific artist. Since he appeared on the hip-hop scene in the in early '90s, the Vancouver-based MC and producer self-released more than a dozen full-length cassettes of his material. However, it took several years for him to attract widespread attention, through a collaboration with fellow Canadian Len and his own official debut album. Teamed with partner in rhyme Prevail, Moka Only began freestyling at house parties as a teenager, before heading to San Diego in 1994 and hooking up with such likeminded hip-hoppers as Mr. Brady. Returning to Vancouver the next year, Moka and Prevail formed Swollen Members crew with another local MC, Madchild. However, Moka also began putting out his own solo material on cassettes he distributed, finally leading to his appearance on the multiplatinum-selling *You Can't Stop the Bum Rush*, the 1999 debut album from the Beastie Boys–style Toronto hip-hop outfit Len. Two years later, Moka was ready to drop some new tracks of his own, and released *Lime Green* on Battleaxe Records, the label he'd helped found. His long-awaited official debut, a set of thoughtful, sometimes abstract rhymes set to melodic, jazzy backing similar to De La Soul or A Tribe Called Quest, showed that despite his prodigious output of the past, Moka had plenty of good new material as well. —*Dan LeRoy*

● **Lime Green** / Apr. 3, 2001 / Battleaxe ✦✦✦

"Am I really crazy?" Moka Only asks himself on "Magnitude." The answer appears to be no. This Vancouver native's lyrics may be introspective, but they're not particularly dark or disturbing, and his loose, self-assured, seemingly effortless flow seems better suited to a summer barbecue than an asylum. This self-assurance may be the result of his extensive experience in the West Coast (of Canada) scene, including both solo projects and work with artists such as Prevail (with whom he formed the duo Split Sphere) and Len (a guest spot on *Can't Stop the Bum Rush*). Lime Green, his first full-length release with worldwide distribution, features a classic underground hip-hop feel that may appeal to fans of De La Soul, Freestyle Fellowship, and Common. Moka, who produced most of the album himself, is comfortable with a smooth melodic groove; the songs are catchy and appealing although the jazzy piano, cheesy synths, bouncy bass lines, and two-part harmonies may be too sugary for some listeners. The guest appearances by Sun Spot Jonz, Abstract Rude, Perfect Strangers, LMNO, and Swollen Members add some rigor to his sound, but their styles don't quite mesh with the beats and their presence doesn't quite fit the personal tone of this project. Despite its flaws, however, this album is an appealing introduction to a talented performer. —*Todd Kristel*

Pharoahe Monch

Vocals, Producer / Hip-Hop, Alternative Rap, Underground Rap, East Coast Rap

While a member of the New York City duo Organized Konfusion, Pharoahe Monch developed a reputation as one of underground hip-hop's preeminent lyricists, crafting intricate and intelligent raps with partner Prince Poetry. After recording three albums together from 1991 to 1997, the two split up amicably, and Monch pursued a more aggressive solo style with the terrific independent label Rawkus. He made guest appearances on other artists' records and contributed tracks to the Rawkus compilation *Soundbombing II*, which raised expectations for his solo debut. The single/video "Simon Says" was released in the summer of 1999 and became a massive hit among rap and club audiences, setting the stage for a surprising debut—just short of the Top 40—for the full-length *Internal Affairs* upon its release several months later. —*Steve Huey*

● **Internal Affairs** / Oct. 19, 1999 / Rawkus ✦✦✦✦✦

After three cultishly revered albums with Organized Konfusion, underground legend Pharoahe Monch cut a solo deal with Rawkus and delivered his debut, *Internal Affairs*, in late 1999. Both Monch and Rawkus seemed to want to push their music farther above ground, and some longtime followers were shocked to hear a harder, angrier, more profane Monch, who seemed to be courting a more thugged-out audience. But it's a reinvention that doesn't compromise his high lyrical standards, making *Internal Affairs* a success on its own terms. Sounding like it was sampled from a monster-movie soundtrack, the club smash "Simon Says" sets the tone for the album; Monch delivers rapid-fire, intricately rhymed lines in between shouts of "get the fuck up!" and "girls, rub on your titties!" It proved to be the most successful crossover bid of Monch's career, and much of the rest of *Internal Affairs* manages to straddle the underground/mainstream divide surprisingly well. Even when he's just giving shout-outs to Queens, or enlisting guests like Canibus and M.O.P. to help pummel a track into submission, Monch lives up to his reputation as one of hip-hop's most technically skilled MCs. Nowhere is this balancing act more evident than on "Rape," a rather disquieting extended metaphor for his mastery of hip-hop (other MCs just "ain't fuckin' it right").

A more benign theme track is "Official," whose carefully constructed barrage of sports references demonstrates the cleverness that made Monch a cult legend. Not everything sits well together—the sophomoric "The Ass" is an odd way to lead into the love song "The Light," the Organized Konfusion reunion "God Send," and the reflective "The Truth," which features guest appearances by Common and Talib Kweli. But in terms of bringing an underappreciated hip-hop great to a (somewhat) wider audience, *Internal Affairs* generally gets it right. —*Steve Huey*

Money Mark (Mark Ramos-Nishita)

b. Detroit, MI

Keyboards, Producer / Soul-Jazz, Trip-Hop, Indie Rock, Electronica, Indie Pop

Money Mark is the alias of Mark Ramos-Nishita, a keyboardist whose funky, retro-flavored riffs earned him the unofficial title of the fourth Beastie Boy. Born in Detroit to a Japanese-Hawaiian father and a Chicano mother, Nishita moved to the West Coast when he was six; some years later, he hooked up with the Dust Brothers production team, and began overdubbing keyboards for the Delicious Vinyl label. While working as a handyman, Nishita accepted a job repairing the Beastie Boys' Silverlake, CA, home; soon he became a pivotal member of the group's Grand Royal posse, and performed on both 1992's *Check Your Head* and 1994's *Ill Communication*.

Recorded at his home studio, Money Mark's solo debut, *Mark's Keyboard Repair*—a loose, infectious collection of fuzzy organ noodlings performed on vintage equipment—appeared in 1995 as a set of three 10" records issued on the Los Angeles-based label Love Kit. Although the small pressing sold out almost instantly, the first record in the series found its way to Britain and the offices of Mo'Wax founder James Lavelle, who quickly flew to L.A. to meet with Nishita; a deal was struck, and *Mark's Keyboard Repair* was reissued in late 1995. *Push the Button* followed in 1998. —*Jason Ankeny*

● **Mark's Keyboard Repair** / 1995 / Mo' Wax ✦✦✦✦

Money Mark was the keyboardist on the Beastie Boys' *Check Your Head* and *Ill Communication*. Both albums demonstrated his influence, with his thick, funky organ appearing all over the place. On his own, Money Mark creates music that is quite similar to the instrumental tracks on the two Beastie albums, but his music is grittier and jazzier. *Mark's Keyboard Repair* sounds like a lo-fi, indie rock variation of '60s soul-jazz, particularly the records of Jimmy Smith and John Patton. Mark's attention span is extremely short— some of the songs don't last a minute—but the songs keep the same laid-back groove flowing throughout the album. *Mark's Keyboard Repair* features a full 30 songs on its American release—the original English version clocked in with 20—but it is rarely boring. Only the groove is important on the album, and Money Mark never lets it stop. —*Stephen Thomas Erlewine*

Push the Button / May 4, 1998 / Grand Royal ✦✦✦✦

Lacking the kaleidoscopic ambience of *Mark's Keyboard Repair*, Money Mark's second album, *Push the Button*, is a more cohesive affair than its predecessor. That doesn't mean it sticks to one style, either. Mark tries his hand at jazz, soul, funk, pop, and even ballads over the course of *Push the Button*, but where the sheer brevity of the numerous songs on *Keyboard Repair* made it seem like a colorful sketchbook, the songs here form a greater work. Not only has he taken the time to connect the songs, he also has decided to sing, adding further depth and color to his funky palette. While his vocals are a little flat, they fit the laid-back vibe of the record, and on occasion they really connect. Propelled by a relaxed shuffle and jazzy organ, "Hand In Your Head" is a gem of a summer single, and "Rock in the Rain" and "Maybe I'm Dead" aren't far behind, either. It may be removed from the lo-fi soul-jazz miniatures of *Keyboard Repair*, but *Push the Button* has a real soulful charm of its own—one that's equally seductive. —*Stephen Thomas Erlewine*

Change Is Coming / Sep. 18, 2001 / Emperor Norton ✦✦✦

For listeners expecting another collection of Money Mark's curiously endearing pop songs, *Change Is Coming* delivers only half of the package. Like his debut, *Mark's Keyboard Repair*, *Change* is an instrumental album, recorded in the same spirit of stylistic change-ups heard on easy-listening records (especially compared to the indie pop of *Push the Button*). Despite the lack of vocals, though, *Change* is a pleasant listen; Mark spins through genres with the greatest of ease—he translates Afro-beat into "People's Party (Red Alert)," turns to early-'80s funk (straight out of the *Sanford & Son* bag) for "Soul Drive Six Avenue," and toys with salsa for "Information

Contraband." There's also a nice summer samba named "Use Your Head," with Money Mark summoning the spirit of Brazilian organ heavyweight Walter Wanderley. The downside is that, much like his earliest material, *Change Is Coming* has a light feel that's undeniably enjoyable but also a bit tossed off. —*John Bush*

JT Money

Producer / Southern Rap, Dirty Rap

The former leader of the hip-hop group Poison Clan, JT Money has always been about creating music you can dance to. JT Money was discovered in a Miami talent show by 2 Live Crew founder Luther Campbell. He then went on to record three albums with Poison Clan on Campbell's label Skyywalker Records, but the group eventually disbanded after a dispute with Campbell. JT Money took some of the lessons he learned from his years with Campbell and used them on his first solo album, *Pimpin' on Wax*. The album featured the type of dancefloor-friendly hip-hop that Campbell helped popularize. JT Money's 2001 album, *Blood Sweat & Years*, brings listeners more of the same, proving that he is a performer that can produce club-friendly hip-hop on a consistent basis. *Return of the B-Izer* offered more of the same the following year. —*Jon Azpiri*

Pimpin' on Wax / May 25, 1999 / Priority ♦♦♦

JT Money's debut album, *Pimpin' on Wax*, sounds a little out of place in 1999. True, hardcore rap still ruled the hip-hop marketplace, but most hardcore rappers broadened their sound with late-'70s/early-'80s funk and smooth grooves. While he occasionally dips into that territory, JT Money pretty much keeps to hardcore California rap, with no apologies. He does this stuff pretty well, but his pimp style (heavily influenced by Too Short, a featured guest on the album)—as epitomized by "Playa Ass Shit," "Rap Ass Nigga," "On Da Grind," "Somethin' About Pimpin'," and "Ho Problems"—sounds tired, especially since the 14 cuts run a very long time. Ultimately, the success of *Pimpin' on Wax* depends on your tastes—if you can't get enough of the playas-pimps-n-hustlas scene, this will be a welcome debut, but to more discriminating tastes, this will sound a little rote. —*Stephen Thomas Erlewine*

● **Blood Sweat & Years** / Apr. 3, 2001 / Priority ♦♦♦

JT Money has only one thing on his mind—moving bodies on the dancefloor. The veteran rapper has been creating booty-bumpin' hip-hop tracks since his first solo album *Pimpin' on Wax*, and *Blood Sweat & Years* is more of the same. Tracks such as "Where My Thugs At" and "Hi-Lo" are all engineered with club DJs in mind. When JT Money is at his best, his lyrical flow can keep up with the music's blistering pace, but too often his rhymes lag behind, especially on tracks like "Superbitch" and the bilingual, Spanglish number "Sosa on That Chocha." JT Money will never be mistaken for a lyrical giant like Rakim, but the fact that his lyrics are subpar will mean little to clubgoers who will appreciate the album for exactly what it is—an invitation to get on the dancefloor. —*Jon Azpiri*

Monie Love (Simone Wilson)

b. London, England

Urban, Pop-Rap, British Rap, Club/Dance

London-born Simone Wilson, aka Monie Love, was featured on Queen Latifah's single "Ladies First" while still a teen. Her CDs as a leader have been erratic, often suggesting much more than they delivered, though they've usually contained at least one strong single. After *Down to Earth*, Love issued *In a Word or 2* in 1993. —*Ron Wynn*

Down to Earth / Oct. 30, 1990 / Warner Brothers ♦♦♦

Few British rappers have enjoyed much recognition among American hip-hop audiences. Perhaps the British MC who has received the most attention in the U.S. is the highly talented Monie Love, whose *Down to Earth* is one of the few British rap efforts released by a major label. With *Earth*, she managed to convert some American hip-hoppers while maintaining the strong respect she enjoyed in British rap circles. If a comparison to Love's American counterparts is needed, she has more in common with Queen Latifah than MC Lyte—Love is aggressive and outspoken, but not quite as hard as Lyte. There are some definite classics here, including "It's a Shame (My Sister)" and the wildly infectious "Monie in the Middle." But like so many American rappers, Love spends too much time boasting and not enough time telling meaningful stories. Nonetheless, her strong and interesting technique and

her overall musicality make this album enjoyable, though not outstanding. —*Alex Henderson*

● **In a Word or 2** / Mar. 23, 1993 / Warner Brothers ♦♦♦♦

After the sparkling debut of *Down to Earth*, Monie Love's *In a Word or 2*, arriving three years later in 1993, was hotly anticipated. But despite production and cowriting from Marley Marl, as well as the production contributions of Prince on "Born 2 B.R.E.E.D." and the title track, *In a Word or 2* never seems to go anywhere. Love's musical voice and singsong delivery are still in effect, but her raps are decidedly more aggressive, lacking the playful air of her first record. Where *Down to Earth* was open and honest about its issues, it didn't hit the listener over the head with a giant bat called "FEMINISM." *In a Word or 2* doesn't either necessarily; however, its rattling, crashing beats and aggressive delivery become disorienting after only a few songs. "Full Term Love" just isn't the phrase to build a song around, and the low-key soul of "In a Word or 2" is lost in reverb and not strong enough to break up the dissonance of the rest of the material. The jazzy horns and bass line of "4 da Children" make the song another potential strong point, but it's lost at the very end of the album. Most successful is the sunny "Born 2 B.R.E.E.D." ("Build Relationships where Education and Enlightenment Dominate"), with its funky guitar and ascending chorus. It lets Love's mostly engaging delivery shine, unfettered by the clattering beats that dominate the rest of the album. (A "Hip-Hop Mix" of "Born 2 B.R.E.E.D." is included as a bonus at the end of *In a Word or 2*; it replaces the warm vibe of the original with—no surprise here—clattering, shuffling beats.) —*Johnny Loftus*

Moochie Mack

b. Atlanta, GA

Vocals, DJ / Dirty South

Former Atlanta radio DJ Moochie Mack scored a large regional hit in 2000 with "Dirty South Is in da House," which led to an opportunity to record a full-length, 2001's *Broke Pimpin'*. Powered by the aforementioned Southern anthem and the singles "Ghetto Bounce" and "We Be on Dat," the album featured production by Street Flava, Lil Jon, DJ Herb, and Salam Wreck. —*Jason Birchmeier*

● **Broke Pimpin'** / Jun. 26, 2001 / Koch International ♦♦

The best parts of *Broke Pimpin'* feature the kind of raw energy found on Outkast albums mixed with the trademark bounce of the Hot Boyz. Moochie Mack clearly has a knack for clever rhymes and storytelling. "Jack N Da Jacker" amply displays Moochie's sense of humor while tracks like "Ummmh Ha" and "Ghetto Bounce" mix everything from gospel and blues with good old Southern bounce. As a former radio DJ, Moochie Mack knows how to keep an audience interested, but the listless production on many of the tracks on *Broke Pimpin'* fail to match Moochie Mack's buoyant enthusiasm, making for an uneven debut. —*Jon Azpiri*

M.O.P.

Group / Hip-Hop, East Coast Rap, Hardcore Rap

Lil Fame and Billy Danzenie formed hardcore rap act M.O.P. The duo's debut single, "How About Some Hardcore," became popular and led to the release of their first album, *To the Death*, in the spring of 1994. Two years later, they delivered *Firing Squad*. Third record *First Family 4 Life* was released in March of 1998; *Warriorz* followed two years later. —*Stephen Thomas Erlewine*

To the Death / Apr. 7, 1994 / Select ♦♦♦♦

On the success of their first single "How About Some Hardcore," the duo of Lil Fame and Billy Danzenie followed up with their first full-length album, which may as well be called "How About a Lot More Hardcore." The Mash Out Posse bring a level of intensity and energy to the microphone that has to be heard to appreciate. Of course, if you're not into that whole guns, thugs, and killing people kind of thing, this isn't for you; as they say on one of the skits on the album, where an interviewer asks them "Can you truly say your music promotes positive outlooks among its listeners?," "Next question!" But, for the gangsta rap aficionado, this album is not to be missed. —*Brad Mills*

Firing Squad / Oct. 22, 1996 / Relativity ♦♦♦♦

M.O.P. has succeeded in doing what few hardcore rap groups have been able to do, by increasing the quality of production on their album and still keeping that same raw, rough feel that typically disappears as money enters the equation. While the album is solid from start to finish, "Anticipation" stands out, partly inspired by KRS-One's "MC's Act Like They Don't Know." The title track, "Firing Squad," is a slow, rumbling tune with some low-end piano riffs helping to keep it moving along. DJ Premier of Gangstarr makes an appearance on "Downtown Swinga ('96)," providing a funky bass line for the duo to scream over. This is what you've waited for. —*Brad Mills*

● **First Family 4 Life** / Mar. 24, 1998 / Relativity ◆◆◆◆
Mash Out Posse returns with another dose of that strictly underground NY flavor. M.O.P. relies on no gimmicks as Lil Fame and Billy Danzenie continue to lick shots upside your head with reckless abandon. Sticking to their guns, M.O.P. refuses to soften their product in search of platinum plates. DJ Premier executive-produced this album and chipped in five slamming, standout tracks. With Primo behind the boards, the results are usually splendid, and M.O.P. takes full advantage of his presence. On "Breakin the Rules," M.O.P. breaks down the inner workings of the game, chastising those who don't follow proper procedures. M.O.P. and Bumpy Knucks (aka Freddie Foxxx) put it down for NY on "I Luv." Primo continues to bless M.O.P. with "Downtown Swinga 98," the third installment of this trilogy. With "Salute 98," Guru lends his voice to help M.O.P. take things one step further over the best of Primo's tracks found here (which is saying something). Also check out "Down 4 Whateva," featuring an always-on-point OC, and "Brooklyn/Jersey Get Wild" with an invigorated Treach. "Blood, Sweat, Tears," along with "What the Future Holds," are a nice change of pace and show M.O.P.'s maturity from previous efforts. One of the few missteps the duo takes is with "4 Alarm Blaze," as Teflon and Jay-Z (along with M.O.P.) deliver strong lyrics, but the track is less than riveting. Furthermore, "Ride Wit Us" and "New York Salute" become stagnated and do nothing to distinguish themselves. Primo's contribution helped M.O.P. take a step that was very much needed. His resounding, sharp drum kicks mesh perfectly with M.O.P.'s gritty sandpaper flow. When Lil' Fame and Billy speak, you can hear the pain, anger, anguish, and passion resonate from inside. —*Matt Conaway*

Warriorz / Aug. 29, 2000 / Loud ◆◆◆◆
The rabble-rousing Brownsville, Brooklyn, crew's fourth release is a heavy machete cutting through the forest of clones of the hip-hop field. A Molotov cocktail of an album featuring M.O.P.'s brand of harmonious high-energy thuggery. The Mash Out Posse deals strictly with street life themes and is not for the weak of heart or ear, but the musical element is always varied and flavorful. DJ Premier has always supported these underground soldiers and on this album he exercises his darker side on five tracks. While his influence and sound run throughout, for his own tracks Primo digs deep in his trick bag, deftly looping a swatch from Hendrix's "Burning of the Midnight Lamp" on "Follow Instructions," and testing out new sequencing patterns on "Everyday" and "On the Front Line." Billy Dance and Lil' Fame (Fizzy Womack) have never strayed from their military mind state and rhyme format, and *Warriorz* recapitulates the staples of their hardcore sound. Fizzy also applies his well-trained ear in the sound booth on tracks like the gangster jitterbug "Niggotiate" or lifting a segment from Foreigner's "Cold As Ice" for a track of the same title. Though the tone rarely changes and the lyrical content gets repetitive, musically the album hits enough high notes to make this a nice release. —*M.F. Di Bella*

10 Years and Gunnin' / Apr. 1, 2003 / Sony ◆◆◆◆
10 Years and Gunnin' is a completely thorough survey of M.O.P.'s career. Starting off with the legendary East Coast anthem "How About Some Hardcore," M.O.P.'s consistent delivery is relentless, and while some East Coast rappers pride themselves on revisiting such topics as their net income, their collection of automobiles, and other material things, M.O.P. keeps it underground. A fine collection for new listeners and a testament to the potency of the group over the preceding decade. —*Rob Theakston*

Mos Def (Dante Smith)

b. Dec. 11, 1973, Brooklyn, NY
Underground Rap, Political Rap, Hip-Hop, East Coast Rap
Initially regarded as one of hip-hop's most promising newcomers in the late '90s, Mos Def expanded his reach in the years to come, establishing himself as a serious actor and also making a bid to reshape the rap-rock genre. His artistic career began in the late '80s as a television actor, a profession he began directly out of high school. By the mid-'90s, though, Mos Def turned to

rap music as his new profession, frustrated by how little acting paid relative to rapping. Based in Brooklyn, he began affiliating himself with the local hip-hop scene, appearing on tracks by such esteemed groups as De La Soul and da Bush Babees. Following these guest appearances and some singles for Royalty (most notably "Universal Magnetic"), Mos Def began recording for the upstart Rawkus label. His first full-length album, *Black Star* (1998), a collaboration with Talib Kweli and DJ Hi-Tek, shook the hip-hop community, which embraced the album and spoke of a Native Tongue revival. His solo debut, *Black on Both Sides* (1999), did much the same a year later. For the most part, though, Mos Def maintained a low profile in successive years, rediscovering his passion for acting and forming the rap-rock supergroup Black Jack Johnson.

Born in Brooklyn, Mos Def pursued the arts at a young age, excelling as a performer. After high school, he began acting in a variety of television roles, most notably appearing on a short-lived Bill Cosby series in 1994, *The Cosby Mysteries*. He soon grew frustrated with life as an actor and switched to rapping. Appearances on songs by De La Soul ("Big Brother Beat") and da Bush Babees ("S.O.S.")—both released in 1996—began Mos Def's rap career with much propulsion. A year later, he released a single of his own for Royalty Records, "Universal Magnetic," and it created quite a stir. Soon he moved to Rawkus Records, which was just getting off the ground at the time, and began working on a full-length album with likeminded rapper Talib Kweli and beatmaker DJ Hi-Tek. The resulting album, *Black Star* (1998), became one of the most discussed rap albums of its time. A year later came Mos Def's solo album, *Black on Both Sides*, and it inspired further attention and praise.

Rap groups such as De La Soul, A Tribe Called Quest, and Brand Nubian—loosely known as the Native Tongue collective—had set a precedent years earlier for socially conscious, thoughtful rap music more likely to celebrate Afrocentricity than gangsta culture. Yet these artists had fallen out of favor by the late '90s as they aged. Mos Def, on the other hand, was young and charismatic, an apparently capable and willing heir. Thus, listeners, critics, and everyone else who had heard Mos Def's work for Rawkus championed him as a sort of savior, a genuine, important MC in an age of flossin' gangstas and angry thugs. And Mos Def certainly fit the role as newly crowned king of the new school Native Tongue artists such as Common and Kweli. However, for whatever reason—the hype, the pressure, the attention—he shied away from the recording studio after *Black on Both Sides* and began pursuing other interests.

During the early 2000s, he acted in several films (*Monster's Ball*, *Bamboozled*) and even spent some time on Broadway (the Pulitzer Prize-winning *Topdog/Underdog*). He simultaneously worked on the Black Jack Johnson project with several iconic black musicians: keyboardist Bernie Worrell (Parliament/Funkadelic), guitarist Dr. Know (Bad Brains), drummer Will Calhoun (Living Colour), and bassist Doug Wimbish (the Sugarhill Gang, Grandmaster Flash, Living Colour). This project aimed to reclaim rock music, especially the rap-rock hybrid, from such artists as Limp Bizkit frontman Fred Durst, who Mos Def openly despised. What made Black Jack Johnson so anticipated, though, was not so much the supergroup roster of musicians or even Mos Def himself, but rather the lack of black rock bands. Following the demise of Living Colour, there were few, if any, that had attained substantial success. Mos Def hoped to infuse the rock world with his all-black band and, during the early 2000s, he performed several small shows with his band around the New York area. —*Jason Birchmeier*

★ **Black Star** / Aug. 26, 1998 / Rawkus ◆◆◆◆◆
While Puff Daddy and his followers continued to dictate the direction hip-hop would take into the millennium, Mos Def and Talib Kweli surfaced from the underground to pull the sounds in the opposite direction. Their 13 rhyme-fests on this superior debut show that old school rap still sounds surprisingly fresh in the sea of overblown vanity productions. There's no slack evident in the tight wordplays of Def and Kweli as they twist and turn through sparse, jazz-rooted rhythms calling out for awareness and freedom of the mind. Their viewpoints stem directly from the teachings of Marcus Garvey, the legendary activist who fought for the rights of blacks all around the world in the first half of the 20th century. Def and Kweli's ideals are sure lofty; not only are they out to preach Garvey's words, but they also hope to purge rap music of its negativity and violence. For the most part, it works. Their wisdom-first philosophy hits hard when played off their lyrical intensity, a bass-first production and stellar scratching. While these MCs don't have all of the vocal

pizzazz of A Tribe Called Quest's Phife and Q-Tip at their best, flawless tracks like the cool bop of "K.O.S. (Determination)" and "Definition" hint that *Black Star* is only the first of many brilliantly executed positive statements for these two street poets. —*Jason Kaufman*

Black on Both Sides / Oct. 12, 1999 / Rawkus ✦✦✦✦✦
Mos Def's partnership with Talib Kweli produced one of the most important hip-hop albums of the late '90s, 1997's brilliant *Black Star*. Consciously designed as a return to rap's musical foundations and a manifesto for reclaiming the art form from gangsta/playa domination, it succeeded mightily on both counts, raising expectations sky high for Mos Def's solo debut. He met them all with *Black on Both Sides*, a record every bit as dazzling and visionary as *Black Star*. *Black on Both Sides* strives to not only refine but also expand the scope of Mos Def's talents, turning the solo spotlight on his intricate wordplay and nimble rhythmic skills—but also his increasing eclecticism. The main reference points are pretty much the same—old school rap, which allows for a sense of playfulness as well as history, and the Native Tongues posse's fascination with jazz, both for its sophistication and cultural heritage. But they're supported by a rich depth that comes from forays into reggae (as well as its aura of spiritual conscience), pop, soul, funk, and even hardcore punk (that on the album's centerpiece, "Rock N Roll," a dissection of white America's history of appropriating black musical innovations). In keeping with his goal of restoring hip-hop's sociopolitical consciousness, Def's lyrics are as intelligent and thoughtfully crafted as one would expect, but he doesn't stop there—he sings quite passably on several tracks, plays live instruments on others (including bass, drums, congas, vibraphone, and keyboards), and even collaborates on a string arrangement. In short, *Black on Both Sides* is a *tour de force* by an artist out to prove he can do it all. Its ambition and execution rank it as one of the best albums of 1999, and it consolidates Mos Def's position as one of hip-hop's brightest hopes entering the 21st century. —*Steve Huey*

Mosko

b. Compton, CA
Latin Rap, West Coast Rap, Gangsta Rap
Based in Compton, CA, Chicano rapper Mosko (R. Rodriguez) released his first album, *Enter the Game*, on the Fleezie label in 2002. —*John Bush*

● **Enter the Game** / Sep. 24, 2002 / Fleezie ✦✦✦
When the New York-based Mean Machine put a Puerto Rican spin on hip-hop with 1981's "Disco Dreams," West Coast Chicanos weren't far behind— a few years later, Mexican-American rappers were popping up all over the West Coast. Over the years, Chicano MCs have ranged from pop-rappers to hardcore rappers like tha Mexakinz, Lighter Shade of Brown, and Cypress Hill; on his debut album, *Enter the Game*, Mosko demonstrates that he identifies with the grittier, more hardcore side of West Coast rap. The Mexican-American rapper is from Compton, CA, the infamous area of Los Angeles County that gave listeners N.W.A, DJ Quik, and Compton's Most Wanted (among others). But instead of flowing exactly like African-American MCs, Mosko proudly acknowledges his Latino heritage and occasionally raps in Spanish (specifically, Chicano slang). What Mosko does on this 2002 release is hardly unprecedented—Mexican-Americans have been providing hardcore rap since the '80s. But while *Enter the Game* isn't groundbreaking, it is well executed; most of the time, Mosko's hard-hitting accounts of urban life are solid. It is important to note that even though Mosko is bilingual, English lyrics dominate this CD—at least 95 percent of the lyrics are in English rather than Spanish. Why doesn't Mosko rap in Spanish more often? Perhaps he doesn't want to risk scaring away non-Spanish-speaking listeners. Of course, there are plenty of MCs in Latin America and Spain who rap in Spanish exclusively. But those artists, unlike Mosko, are catering to listeners who speak Spanish as their primary language. And unlike a hip-hopper who might be representing Mexico City, Madrid, or Buenos Aires, Mosko is representing Compton on this decent, noteworthy debut. —*Alex Henderson*

Motion Man (Paul K. Laster)

Underground Rap
A rapper since the '80s, Motion Man has dozens of highlight features, though few of them have appeared on his own records. While Kool Keith fans know him for his tracks on three of Keith's LPs (*Black Elvis*, *Sex Style*, *First Come,*

First Served) and fans of *The Wake up Show* would recognize his rhymes in a flash, his best-known track of all, "The Terrorist," was done under the heading of Russian mixer/producer DJ Vadim. He also guested for several tracks on the KutMasta Kurt record *Masters of Illusion*, and was invited by Kurt to appear on a high-profile remix for Linkin Park ("In the End"). Motion Man, a self-professed fan of football and malt liquor, debuted on wax back in 1993—under his own name, no less—with the King Tech production "Mo' Like Flows On." His debut full-length, 2001's *Clearing the Field*, found him calling in favors from over a decade of rapping, with features from E-40 and Busta Rhymes as well as the expected Kool Keith and KutMasta Kurt. —*John Bush*

● **Clearing the Field** / Jan. 1, 2001 / Threshold ✦✦✦✦✦
Bay Area underground rap hero Motion Man, known as a regular on the *Wake up Show* and as a rhyming partner of Kool Keith, delivers an album of grand proportions with *Clearing the Field*. With a refreshing and wholly original style on the mic, Motion Man proves that uniqueness in rap can still be obtained without veering into other genres. Beats provided by KutMasta Kurt are presented from the perspective of a seasoned DJ, with especially hard drum kicks and frequent sample stabs leading the charge. His use of the opening line from Don Drummond's ska classic "Man in the Streets" to enhance "Hold Up," a song that also features the antics of Biz Markie, is very characteristic of KutMasta Kurt's in-your-face production style. Other guest appearances by the likes of Kool Keith and LC on "We Work Styles," Planet Asia on "Face 2 Face," and E-40 on "Reason 2 Panic" really help elevate the album into the realm of an overlooked classic. Indeed, hearing E-40 effectively spit lyrics over what many would consider a traditional backpacker beat is something that should surprise many of his naysayers. But lest you forget the extreme talents of Motion Man, an artist with so much personality that he should be dubbed the black Eminem. Tracks such as "Straight Flowin' on Em," "Clearing the Field," "Loose Cannon," and "Come on Y'all" are so filled with clever wordplay and punchlines that Motion Man could easily be considered a comedian as well as an MC. On his Too Short appreciation track called "Beotches," he even does an impressive job rhyming in Spanglish. And, unlike those found on so many other rap albums, his skits and interludes are actually hilarious. All in all, *Clearing the Field* presents everything that is right about West Coast hip-hop. —*Robert Gabriel*

Movement Ex

f. Los Angeles, CA
Group / Political Rap, West Coast Rap
Los Angeles' Movement Ex lasted long enough to release one powerful album of Five Percent Nation-inspired themes. The self-titled album, recorded while both members were teens and released in 1990 on Columbia, failed to make much of an impact on the hip-hop world, but it held its own when compared to other confrontational and politically charged albums from Paris, X-Clan, and Lakim Shabazz. The duo consisted of MC Lord Mustafa Hasan Ma'd and DJ King Born Khaaliq. They apparently parted ways after that. —*Andy Kellman*

● **Movement Ex** / 1990 / Columbia ✦✦✦✦
Movement Ex's 1990 debut was a forthright Islamic/Afro-centric outing, with tight studio production support. —*Ron Wynn*

Ms. Dynamite (Niomi McLean-Daley)

Contemporary R&B, Urban, 2-Step/British Garage
Ms. Dynamite (aka Niomi McLean-Daley) grew up in North London listening to reggae and turning into hip-hop at the age of 12. Even when she wanted to become a primary school teacher or a social worker, her passion for music was stronger. After starting out in a pirate radio station called RAW FM, Ms. Dynamite met Richard Forbes (aka Sticky) in a West End club. The two began working on her debut single, "Boo!," licensed from DJ Jason Kaye's Social Circles label to London Records.

Punch, Salaam Remi, Tony Kelly, and Dave Kelly produced her first full-length record in Miami, New York, and Jamaica. *A Little Deeper* featured the hit singles "Dy-Na-Mi-Tee" and "It Takes More." In September 2002, Ms. Dynamite became the first black female artist achieving a Mercury Music Prize, beating favorites the Streets, the Coral, and even music legend David Bowie. —*Drago Bonacich*

- **A Little Deeper** / Jul. 2, 2002 / Polydor ✦✦✦✦

She didn't get much respect as a member of the chart-running, violence-generating So Solid Crew, but that all changed when Ms. Dynamite released her solo debut, *A Little Deeper*. And with nary a two-step beat in sight, it would appear Ms. Dynamite has made a clean break from her garage past to embrace a form of British raggae/R&B that makes her one of the few evoking references to Roots Manuva and Lauryn Hill. She has as much personality and strength of delivery as either of them (high praise, that), and carries the album as much as the tight production. Another name to think of is Craig David; like the only two-step figure to make any impression on American R&B fans, *A Little Deeper* has a few concessions to commercial radio (i.e., the musically unadventurous). The Santana guitar lines on "Put Him Out" and the single "It Takes More" would fit perfectly on radio. Sure, the album's a bit more edgy than any of her American contemporaries ("Krazy Krush" is a great head-twisting track), but it's still not too far from Hill and other neo-soul figures. That may make her more palatable to a worldwide audience, but it also makes for a more diluted sound that doesn't impress quite like it could have. —*John Bush*

Ms. Jade (Chevon Young)

b. Philadelphia, PA
East Coast Rap, Pop-Rap

When no one believes in your dreams but you, it can get pretty lonely. Some people give up eventually, tired of the struggle. Others, like Ms. Jade, stick to their guns, stick it out, and triumph. These days she's on top with a recording contract and lots of people are listening to her music. Not too long ago, however, she had to decide whether she would listen to the dream inside her or to the criticism that came from outside sources. Those who didn't believe in her dream advised her to give it up and find "a regular job," such as working for the city of Philadelphia, where she was born and raised in the Nicetown section. Or, they suggested, maybe she should use that certificate she had earned from a Center City beauty school. Neither option appealed to the would-be rapper. Things were looking bleak when she stumbled upon India.Arie's *Acoustic Soul*. On a friend's recommendation, she took note of one song especially, "Strength, Courage, and Wisdom." The song sparked one of those lightbulb moments, electrifying the aspiring artist with a renewed sense of purpose.

Until that moment, things looked bleak. When she tried to get a foot in the door of the music world, the only thing she found was more negativity. Being from Philly, she heard the inevitable comparisons to another hometown girl who had made good in the music business, Eve. Why, she was asked, would they need another Philly girl? Ms. Jade knew Eve was good, but she felt that she could be too, in her own way. She kept chasing her elusive dream until she finally found someone who was willing to give her a chance. That someone was 215 Entertainment's Terrance Glasgow. He brought her to Missy Elliott in Manhattan, where she demonstrated what she could do. Impressed, Elliott picked up the phone and got Timbaland in on the act. Soon Philly's Chevon Young was renamed Ms. Jade, and she had a contract with Timbaland's Beat Club Records.

During her childhood, Ms. Jade liked the rock songs put out by Pat Benatar. Before turning ten, however, she had discovered Janet Jackson's *Control*. She committed all of the songs to memory and went on to perform them in talent competitions at her school. Before she'd hit her teens, she discovered the work of Queen Latifah and MC Lyte. Later, Ms. Jade took top honors in a high school talent competition with "How Could You Call Her Baby," a number that had been featured in the film *Waiting to Exhale*. Before she took home her diploma in 1997, she had become a fan of the Notorious B.I.G., Foxy Brown, Lil' Kim, and Mase. For a time, she earned cash by peddling knock-offs of designer handbags. —*Linda Seida*

- **Girl Interrupted** / Nov. 5, 2002 / Interscope ✦✦✦

Philadelphian Ms. Jade is closely associated with Timbaland, who produced nine tracks on her debut record, *Girl Interrupted*, and put it out on his Beat Club label, which is affiliated with Interscope. Ms. Jade definitely benefits from Timbaland's signature, laid-back beats. She also has plenty of rap's heavyhitters making appearances, including Jay-Z, Missy Elliott, and Nate Dogg. But Ms. Jade lacks a strong voice all her own. In fact, one can barely tell the difference between her voice and many other current women rappers on the radio, such as Eve. Perhaps the only difference in style is that Ms. Jade doesn't get nasty à la Lil' Kim or Foxy Brown. But thanks to Timbaland's

skills, there are some good songs here, including "Really Don't Want My Love," where Ms. Jade sounds at least a little bit inspired when tearing up an ex-boyfriend (though, there is a song like this on every single record by a female rapper), "Big Head," a fun, danceable tune with a silly chorus, and "Dead Wrong," where Nate Dogg steals the spotlight as usual with his soulful vocals, which seem to make for instant radio hits. But overall, Ms. Jade's rapping doesn't stand out. —*Adam Bregman*

Ms. Melodie (Ramona Parker)

b. Brooklyn, NY
East Coast Rap, Hip-Hop

A former member of the Boogie Down Productions family and the ex-wife of that group's KRS-One, Ms. Melodie—born Ramona Parker in Flatbush, Brooklyn—only stepped out for one solo record, but the formidable rapper made memorable appearances on BDP's records, and she was also part of the Stop the Violence Movement's "Self Destruction," as well as H.E.A.L.'s (Human Education Against Lies) releases (all of which were projects instigated by KRS-One). Her lone solo album, 1989's *Diva* (Jive), featured production from her aforementioned ex-husband, the Awesome 2, and Sam Sever. She also appeared briefly in Keenan Ivory Wayans' *I'm Gonna Git You Sucka*. —*Andy Kellman*

- **Diva** / 1989 / Jive ✦✦✦✦

Ms. Melodie turned some heads in the hip-hop nation with this excellent debut, featuring the aggressive single "The Hype According to Ms. Melodie." —*Ron Wynn*

Ms. Toi (Toikeon Parham)

b. Chicago, IL
Urban, Hip-Hop, Club/Dance

After struggling for ten years trying to break into the rap game—never an easy task for a female—Ms. Toi's big break came when Ice Cube and Mack 10 asked her to appear on their big club hit "You Can Do It," setting the stage for a major-label deal and a debut album that dropped a year later. Toi's impressive ability to drop rhymes like the most seasoned MCs while simultaneously being able to sing diva style when the situation calls for it made her a hot property in the urban music community. Her debut album for Universal, *That Girl*, featured a number of big-name guests from the West Coast, including E-40 and MC Ren, along with others like Nelly and producer Dame Grease.

Born in Chicago as Toikeon Parham, Toi's family moved to Inglewood, CA, when she was just 11. Upon graduating from high school, she began pursuing an interest in rapping, eventually leading to an opportunity to appear on a remix of Militia's "Burn." Her big break came, though, when she hooked up with Ice Cube and Mack 10 for "You Can Do It." The song became a huge club hit in 2000 and the video received ample airplay on BET. In addition, she was then invited to join the Up in Smoke tour in 2000 and saw her debut album released a year later, led by the singles "Handclap" and "Can't None Y'All." —*Jason Birchmeier*

- **That Girl** / Jun. 26, 2001 / Universal ✦✦

Best known for her cameos on Ice Cube records, Ms. Toi offers her first solo album with *That Girl*. The lead single, "Handclap," is a horn-filled confection that sounds like a pale reworking of Eve's "Who's That Girl?" Several tracks on the album, such as "Handclap" and the title track, "That Girl," suffer from subpar lyrics. Various cameos bring some energy to the project: the unmistakable slanguistics of Oakland rapper E-40 boosts "Work a Twist," and "Be Like Me" features the handiwork of St. Lunatics Nelly, Ali, and Murphy Lee. While *That Girl* is a respectable solo effort, Ms. Toi relies too heavily on other artists to provide her music with any lyrical punch. —*Jon Azpiri*

Muggs (Lawrence Muggerud)

b. Jan. 28, 1968
Producer, DJ / Hip-Hop, Trip-Hop, Hardcore Rap

Muggs never dabbled too much with hitmaking but remained a formidable and recognized rap producer because of his work with Cypress Hill and his series of collaborative solo albums. Fame came quickly for the California-by-way-of-New York producer, as he scored runaway hits right off the bat with House of Pain ("Jump Around") and Ice Cube ("Check Yo Self"), as well as with his group, Cypress Hill. As the mid-'90s transitioned to the late '90s, Muggs maintained a fairly low profile and didn't score any more big hits.

Cypress Hill's initial impact faded a bit, and the producer felt compelled to try something new. He then emerged with *Muggs Presents the Soul Assassins, Chapter I* (1997), an album laden with many various major-label rappers, including Goodie Mob, KRS-One, Mobb Deep, and RZA and GZA of the Wu-Tang Clan. The album spawned an MTV-aired single, "Puppet Master" (featuring Dr. Dre and B Real), and sold relatively well but did no chart topping. Muggs returned three years later with *Chapter II*, another guest-laden album featuring several big names, but after the disappointing sales of *Chapter I* Muggs was dropped from his record label, Columbia and released *Chapter II* on his own Rufflife label. He then signed to Anti, an independent label distributed by Epitaph. His debut Anti release, *Dust*, bore little resemblance to his past work, which had been dark hip-hop, instead veering toward trip-hop à la Massive Attack and Tricky. He meanwhile continued to work with Cypress Hill, who had begun integrating rock into their music and experienced periodic success as a result. —*Jason Birchmeier*

Muggs Presents the Soul Assassins, Chapter I / Mar. 4, 1997 / Columbia ✦✦✦✦

For the debut album of Cypress Hill DJ and House of Pain producer DJ Muggs, an excellent cast of MCs were assembled, including most of the best in hip-hop. It's hard to expect anything but uniform excellence from an album that includes Dr. Dre, Wu-Tang Clan's RZA and GZA/Genius, KRS-One, Mobb Deep, the Fugees' Wyclef Jean, Cypress Hill, and MC Eiht, and though the diversity might appear a bit daunting, Muggs' mostly uniform production style ties the album together well. Most collaboration albums end up being spoiled by the number of cooks, but *Soul Assassins* is that rare exception. Among the many highlights are "Puppet Master" by Dr. Dre & B Real, "Third World" by RZA/GZA, and "Move Ahead" by KRS-One. —*John Bush*

Muggs Presents the Soul Assassins, Chapter II / Oct. 3, 2000 / Rufflife ✦✦✦
Few hip-hop producers can craft such evocative soundscapes as Muggs. He doesn't just drop beats but rather reveals cinematic realms of sound with the uncanny ability to clearly communicate his smoky visions. Little more than halfway through *Muggs Presents the Soul Assassins, Chapter II*'s elegant opening track, "Real Life," the languid tempo that his laconic string of beats bounce at perfectly accentuates the song's drifting synth ambience and the similarly swaying sound of a haunting female voice. Every one of these 13 tracks serve as the sound of a ghostly world filled with somber melancholia, the lifted soul of Muggs conveyed through music. Yet in the hip-hop world, great beats aren't enough; not only is the MC equally important, but he often eclipses great beats, for better or for worse. On certain songs, the many guest rappers featured on this album make the beats even better, such as when GZA, Xzibit, Goodie Mob, or Kool G Rap step up to the mic. A few of the guest rappers do detract from the dark beauty of Muggs' poetry, as by no means is this a consistent album, but with such a broad roster of MCs from all coasts, you really can't expect that. *Muggs Presents the Soul Assassins, Chapter II* isn't quite as blessed with MC talent as the first *Soul Assassins* album, yet it's still a noble accomplishment by Muggs, lengths ahead of most hip-hop producers' work. —*Jason Birchmeier*

● **Dust** / Mar. 11, 2003 / Anti ✦✦✦✦✦
Assembling an intimate set of collaborators from the rock community, Muggs breaks from his usual hip-hop projects and takes a second stab at electronica on *Dust*. His first attempt was with 1999's *Juxtapose*, an uneven pairing with Tricky that was dominated by the British rapper's paranoid, druggy sound. *Dust* is more focused, with Muggs delivering a frequently brilliant collection of dense yet lovely soundscapes. The producer crafts each track with meticulous detail, mixing electronic beats, live instruments, and bizarre samples into epic down-tempo pop. Most impressive is "Rain," a majestic ballad that blends a shuffling beat, orchestral strings, acoustic guitars, and the fragile voice of Buckcherry's Josh Todd into a melancholy gem. "Tears" is a far more menacing highlight, boasting a tense mixture of ghostly female vocals and pounding dance beats. A collaboration with Greg Dulli results in "Cloudy Days," a gritty drug ballad that recalls the menacing soul of the Afghan Whigs' *1965*; while the throbbing "Morta" is a seductive, slow-burning vamp revolving around moody orchestral flourishes and a lazy tribal drumbeat. "Far Away" finishes the record with a sweeping dream pop coda, slowly devolving from a haze of chiming guitars and buried vocals into a blend of lush synths and chanting. The album's subtle build from bleak electronica to ethereal alternative rock is a stunning accomplishment; his productions haven't maintained this kind of flow since the first *Soul Assassins*

disc. Muggs has made a phenomenal journey back into trip-hop, delivering a brooding masterpiece of cinematic beats and late-night atmosphere. —*Bradley Torreano*

The Murderers
. . . .
Group / Hardcore Rap
Originally, the Murderers were slated to be an East Coast hardcore hip-hop supergroup consisting of Ja Rule, Jay-Z, and DMX. Although the trio received a fair amount of publicity concerning its imminent collaboration, very few actual recording sessions materialized. Ja Rule and producer Irv Gotti subsequently turned the Murderers into a showcase for their stable of up-and-coming talent, recording enough material to complete an album. That album, *Irv Gotti Presents: The Murderers*, was finally released in early 2000, heavily featuring Ja Rule, Tah Murdah, Black Child, and Vita, with brief appearances from Jay-Z, DMX, and Busta Rhymes. —*Steve Huey*

● **Irv Gotti Presents: The Murderers** / Feb. 15, 2000 / Polygram ✦✦✦
The Murderers project was initially a well-hyped supergroup which would have united Jay-Z, DMX, and Ja Rule. But amidst all of the posturing, the would-be platinum-plated collaboration never came to fruition, bogging down in the preliminary planning stages. Pressing on, burgeoning producer Irv Gotti and the hyperkinetic Ja Rule still found an outlet for their brainchild, turning Murder Inc. into an outlet to introduce their new stable of hungry MCs (Black Child, Tah Murder, O-1, Ronnie Bumps, and Vida). There is nothing new to the formula that Irv and Ja implement, using the name of one proven commodity (Ja Rule) in order to package a group of lesser-known artists. After all, 2Pac did it with the Outlawz, Snoop has his Eastsidaz, and the recently retired Mase introduced Harlem World, all with varying degrees of success. Yet, unlike Busta Rhymes' Flipmode Squad and DMX's Ruff Ryders, Irv and Ja's crew lacks the same depth. Besides Ja Rule, there is not one individual in the Murderers click that possesses star power, or any lasting redeeming qualities. While there are a few tracks that stand out, such as "Don't Give a Fuck," it is mostly due to Gotti's production, which is the LP's only consistent facet. —*Matt Conaway*

Keith Murray
. . . .
b. Long Island, NY
Vocals, Producer / Hip-Hop, Urban, Pop-Rap, Club/Dance
A native of Long Island, Keith Murray first hooked up with Erick Sermon (of EPMD) in 1994. The two worked together to produce Murray's debut single, "The Most Beautifullest Thing in This World," and the song became a hit by the end of the year. After an appearance on Sermon's album, *Double or Nothing*, Keith Murray released his first album in 1994, and titled it after his hit single. The album was certified gold, and Murray delivered his second set near the end of 1996. *It's a Beautiful Thing* followed in 1999. —*John Bush*

The Most Beautifullest Thing in This World / Nov. 8, 1994 / Jive ✦✦✦✦
Before he managed to get himself locked up for a brief bid later in the decade on an assault charge, Keith Murray was assaulting microphones and thesauruses alike with his ill "Sychosymatic" lyrical skills. Introduced to the rap world at the end of 1993 via a guest spot on the song "Hostile" off Erick Sermon's first solo album *Double or Nothing*, Murray stepped out on his own at the beginning of the next year with the mellow Sermon-produced hit single "The Most Beautifullest Thing in This World," then backed it up with a full-length debut by the same title. There is nothing new in Sermon's loping music that you couldn't get on EPMD albums or from other recordings by members of the Def Squad, although he did continue to bring the funk hot and viscous as always. The main attraction on *The Most Beautifullest Thing in This World*, then, is Murray's raw, emotionally charged flow and droll (though not as funny as Redman), articulate rhymes, straight out of the battle-rap school of hip-hop. His lyrics, in other words, are often tasty going down (particularly on "How's That" with Sermon and Redman and "Bom Bom Zee" with Paul Hightower and Hurricane Gee) but won't necessarily stick around to quell any sort of hunger. Still, the album went gold and is easily recommended for fans of *Double or Nothing* or *Whut? Thee Album*. —*Stanton Swihart*

Enigma / Nov. 26, 1996 / Jive ✦✦✦✦
With his second album, *Enigma*, Keith Murray continues to improve his rhythmic skills, as demonstrated by the deft lyrical gymnastics he performs throughout the record. Murray's style of production is defiantly East Coast

with its spare rhythms and emphasis on lyrical rhymes. This can make the record a little monotonous to some listeners, but his kinetic verbal energy keeps *Enigma* exciting and fresh. —*Leo Stanley*

It's a Beautiful Thing / 1999 / Jive ◆◆◆

Keith Murray may have a distinctive rapping style, but that doesn't necessarily make for distinctive albums if his third album, *It's a Beautiful Thing,* is any indication. It's no coincidence that the title recalls Murray's high-water mark, "The Most Beautifullest Thing in the World"—the entire album is a self-conscious attempt to return to those glory days, which is ironic because he's never really changed his style over the years. Still, name association means a lot, and that may be the reason why there do seem to be several highlights on *It's a Beautiful Thing,* since there are no real musical or lyrical breakthroughs anywhere on the album. Instead, it's by-the-books Murray, which will undoubtedly satisfy some long-term fans, who only need new songs to keep their interest. The rest of the audience will find the album a bit uneven, despite his obvious flair for lyrical gymnastics (or maybe because of them, since many of his rhymes don't make sense, even in the absurdist sense)—the sounds aren't really new and only a handful of songs catch hold. There's enough to make *It's a Beautiful Thing* a reasonably entertaining listen, even if they aren't enough to make it memorable. —*Stephen Thomas Erlewine*

- ### The Most Beautifullest Hits / Aug. 10, 1999 / Jive ◆◆◆◆◆

All of Keith Murray's strengths—his distinctive delivery, unique rhymes, and, best of all, his incredibly smooth flow—tended to suffer from excessive repetition on his individual solo albums. Each of his three LPs to date have paired a couple of incredible tracks with many more that try the same things and often fail simply because they'd already been tried. Given that, a best-of collection hitting on all of Murray's strongest tracks is a natural fit. Also important is the teaming of Murray with producer Erick Sermon (on 11 of the 14 tracks here). It has to rank as one of the best combos in hip-hop's history, and the duo has combined for tight, innovative tracks time and time again on Murray's albums. And thanks to fraternal licensing agreements, *The Most Beautifullest Hits* also includes Murray's best appearances on other rapper's records, back to his breakout on 1993's "Hostile" from *No Pressure* by Erick Sermon to the remix of LL Cool J's "I Shot Ya" (also featuring Foxy Brown, Fat Joe, and Prodigy) to his appearance on the soundtrack to 1997's *Dangerous Ground.* Taken in sum, the album is well compiled and skips over Murray's weaker joints to embrace all of his best. —*John Bush*

Murs

Underground Rap, Hip-Hop, Alternative Rap

A longtime friend of Def Jux leader El-P, rapper Murs came out in the spring of 2003 after nearly a decade of working with various groups in the underground. Based in Los Angeles, his first single was released in 1993, a self-released album from his first group, 3 Melancholy Gypsies. The track barely made a dent, but it did catch the attention of indie hip-hop fans in the area. Through indie the group became friends with Mystik Journeymen, who asked 3MG (their shortened name) to join him when he started the Living Legends collective in 1996. Between both 3MG and the Living Legends, Murs rapped on several influential indie rap albums, appearing on more than 20 records, EPs, and singles within a seven-year period. When El-P started to pull together his Def Jux label, Murs contacted the producer and told him he would release his solo record for the company once he had the opportunity. His commitments to both the Legends and 3MG often kept him from working on the album, but after a few years of slowly putting together tracks, Murs finally delivered *The End of the Beginning* in 2003. Featuring flashier production than his group projects, the album was more in tune with a mainstream hip-hop record, though a project with Anticon rapper Slug released at the same time under the name Felt unveiled his weird, experimental side. —*Bradley Torreano*

- ### The End of the Beginning / Feb. 25, 2003 / Def Jux ◆◆◆◆◆

A ten-year hip-hop veteran, Murs doesn't want to be called an up-and-comer anymore, and he proves his maturity with one of the most refreshing rap records in years, an excellent debut for Def Jux named *The End of the Beginning.* Murs has an old school flow that recalls Ice Cube, and unlike many in underground rap, he's got not only a clever delivery but also a lot to say. What immediately impresses about the album are the ample variety of moods and material: "The Night Before..." is a streets-is-watching nightmare

with a vicious chorus ("Last night I almost got shot on my block/Not the block where I live at/The block where I chill at"), but a few tracks later, Murs is inviting Digital Underground's Shock-G over to his pad for "Risky Business," and looking on in disbelief as Shock's alterego, Humpty Hump, wreaks more carnage than The Cat in the Hat (sample: "Yo, is your Dad's Rolls blue/Cuz I got bad news..."). "Transitions az a Ridah" has him remembering good times on a skateboard and ordering a moment of silence for all his favorite spots, while Aesop Rock stops by for the deliriously stoned "Happy Pillz." Whether he's ordering past-their-prime rappers off the mic ("Please Leave") or stressing over how much his favorite action figures cost ("BT$"), Murs is the most entertaining, down-to-earth rapper since Biz Markie, and with the skills of Ice Cube it's clear he's no novelty act. As usual, he says it best, on "The Night Before...": "Now some claim gangsta rap's to see an end of the streets, but its use is an excuse to pretend over beats/So I'm-a lend my speech to all within my reach to tell what *really* goes on, from sales to the streets." —*John Bush*

Mystic

b. Oakland, CA

Hip-Hop, Contemporary R&B

Originating from Oakland, CA, hip-hop singer Mystic merges literate rhymes charged with poetry and a lush singing voice beaming with a sense of soul. Signed to the Goodvibe roster–also including Slum Village and Bahamadia–she worked with a cast of respected underground hip-hop producers for her 2001 debut album, *Cuts for Luck and Scars for Freedom.* She participated in the summer 2001 Tree of Life tour with her labelmates to promote the album. Her debut was reissued the following year on Dreamworks with two new songs appended to the release. —*Jason Birchmeier*

- ### Cuts for Luck and Scars for Freedom / Jun. 19, 2001 / JCOR ◆◆◆◆

Even with Lauryn Hill taking an extended sabbatical, no one has stepped up in her absence to carry the hip-hop/songbird flame. That was, until Mystic. With her debut, *Cuts for Luck and Scars for Freedom,* Mystic seamlessly bridges the gap between soulful harmonizing and introspective lyricism; and no one since Hill bridged this gap so effectively. "Cuts for Life" is a soulful blend of spoken word poetry and introspective lyricism. Mystic effortlessly manages to implement her vocal and lyrical chops on the sublime "Neptune's Jewels" and the A+-produced, breakout single "The Life." Unlike other songbirds, Mystic rarely gets boxed in, or fixated on one style, as she ably floats between repping the West Coast's virtues with fellow Cali up-and-comer Planet Asia on "W") and questioning hip-hop's image-conscious nature with "The Gotta's." Mystic's voice contains a natural duality; as it can be gentle ("Forever and a Day") and pessimistic ("You Say I Say") at any given moment. Similarly, her vocals unfold with an emotional warmth that only a woman can provide, as it conveys a deep, motherly understanding, offering that tender shoulder to cry on ("Fallen Angels") but at the same time demanding respect for herself and her fellow sistas ("Girlfriend Sistagirl"). The extremely vivid "Fatherless Child" is a sympathetic and scolding account of her father's losing battle with drug addiction. While Foxy Brown and Lil' Kim push the envelope with their uninhibited brand of punany power, Mystic's socially relevant and personally revealing topic matter is just as uninhibited. Yet, while Mystic features the same voluptuous package (check the artwork for verification) as the aforementioned, instead of augmenting her breast size, Mystic's artsy *Cuts for Luck and Scars for Freedom* augments the mind—ladies first indeed! —*Matt Conaway*

Mystik Journeymen

f. 1992, Oakland, CA

Group / Underground Rap, West Coast Rap

Founders of the East Oakland underground collective Living Legends, PSC and BFAP formed as Mystik Journeymen in 1992. Southern Californian PSC hooked up with BFAP in Oakland while visiting a girlfriend, and later moved to join the group (at the time, it included a few other rappers who later drifted away). The pair became local legends by 1994, throwing parties (*Underground Surivivors*) and selling mix tapes. One year later, the Grouch began contributing and, after hitting the road doing shows as far away as Europe, Mystik Journeymen formed the Living Legends crew with new recruits including 3 Melancholy Gypsys (aka Murs, Eligh, and Scarub), Moonrocks (aka Bicasso and Nebulus), Aesop, and Arata. The duo's label, LLCrew, had begun releasing records by 1995, and Mystik Journeymen released a parade of LPs during the next few years, highlighted by 1995's *4001: The Stolen Legacy* and 1996's *Pressed 4 Time*. (They'd also expanded their touring base to include the Far East and Australia.) By 1999, the crew had moved from the Bay Area to Los Angeles and, with *The Black Sands ov Eternia*, began releasing records through Outhouse/Revenge. In 2002 Mystik Journeymen finally released a glimpse of their justly praised concert show with the LP *Living Legends: Live*, and their ninth album, *Magic*, followed late that year. —*John Bush*

4001: The Stolen Legacy / 1995 / LLCrew ♦♦

Pressed 4 Time / 1996 / LLCrew ♦♦

● **The Black Sands ov Eternia** / Jun. 22, 1999 / Outhouse ♦♦♦
The Black Sands ov Eternia is trippy, blunted stuff, full of lazy beats and philosophical rhymes. Lovers of mind-bending hip-hop will be intrigued but probably unsatisfied; "Mercury Rising" is far out, to be sure, but maybe too far out—it feels ragged and unfocused. Many of the tracks are short, experimental snippets; others go on at excessive length. Though the record is thoughtful and sincere, and pleasant enough to listen to—in particular boasting some very skilled drum programming—it simply lacks the distinct flavor that would lift it above the pack. —*Bill Cassel*

Magic / May 28, 2002 / Outhouse/Revenge ♦♦♦

Mystikal (Michael Tyler)

b. New Orleans, LA
Dirty South, Southern Rap
Originally one of the leading rappers on Master P's No Limit record label, Mystikal quickly evolved beyond the label's clichéd thug trappings and found himself one of the dirty South's most recognized rappers, alongside Juvenile. Like No Limit itself, Mystikal is a New Orleans native. He released an eponymous debut on the independent label Big Boy in 1995. It earned the attention of Jive Records, who signed him later that year. His official, major-label debut, *Mind of Mystikal*, was released early in 1996 and became a major hit in the rap underground, falling just short of going gold. He then hooked up with Master P and No Limit; the union produced *Unpredictable*, which was released in the fall of 1997 and helped the rapper build a substantial following. *Ghetto Fabulous* followed late in 1998, falling just short of debuting at number one on the album charts. Consolidating his status as a hot property, Mystikal wasted no time in issuing a follow-up; *Let's Get Ready* appeared in the fall of 2000, eclipsing his preceding releases in sales terms, as expected. Driven by the James Brown-like "Shake Ya Ass" as a lead single—an MTV staple before the album even hit the streets—it had become increasingly difficult to trace Mystikal's roots back to the trademark sound and motifs of the thuggish No Limit camp. *Let's Get Ready* demonstrated the wide-reaching ambitions that had only been hinted at in successive releases, eliminating the No Limit stigma and finally making his unique rhyme delivery accessible enough to cross over to the masses. In 2001, Mystikal's bombastic rap stylings came together for a fifth album, *Tarantula*. "Bouncin' Back (Bumpin' Me Against the Wall)" was one of 2002's hottest singles; the next year Mystikal garnered two Grammy nods for Best Male Rap Solo Performance and Best Rap Album. —*Stephen Thomas Erlewine*

Mystikal / Jun. 20, 1995 / Big Boy ♦♦
Before Mystikal enlisted in Master P's No Limit army, he recorded for Big Boy, another New Orleans label and one that foreshadowed the dirty South explosion that was about to take place in the late '90s. Mystikal delivers his rhymes with frenzied finesse here, not quite as aggressively as he would later but certainly as fluidly. This self-titled effort doesn't come close to matching Mystikal's later work, not even his No Limit albums, as the production is of budget quality and the songwriting similarly lacking. Even so, the stronger moments like "Ya'll Ain't Ready Yet" and "Not That Nigga" impressed Jive Records, who re-released this a year later in 1996 as *Mind of Mystikal*. That re-release is the one to get, since it appends "Here I Go," an amazing song that blows away anything here and one that quickly became a dirty South anthem. —*Jason Birchmeier*

Mind of Mystikal / Feb. 1996 / Big Boy ♦♦♦
Like many hip-hop albums of the mid-'90s, Mystikal's *Mind of Mystikal* is rooted in Dr. Dre's G-funk. While nothing in the production is particularly original, Mystikal's rapping is distinctive. Where many G-funk rappers are laid-back, Mystikal is hyper, zipping between obscure pop-culture refrences

and standard gangsta boasting. No matter how good his verbal skills are, he can't help the fact that his backing tracks are flat-out boring and that is what sinks his record. —*Stephen Thomas Erlewine*

Unpredictable / Nov. 11, 1997 / No Limit ♦♦♦
Mystikal's debut album, *Mind of Mystikal*, was an uneven collection of street-oriented G-funk, hampered equally by unimaginative songs and cheap production, courtesy of the No Limit team. Between that record and its follow-up, *Unpredictable*, both Mystikal and No Limit improved exponentially, resulting in a record that was considerably stronger than its predecessor, even if it was far from perfect. Like *Mind of Mystikal*, *Unpredictable* is essentially bare-bones, hard-hitting, vulgar gangsta rap. There's nothing new in the beats or in Mystikal's rhymes, but the execution is much better than before. Even though the album runs much longer than it should, dedicated hardcore hip-hop fans will be able to find enough highlights to make wading through the murk a worthwhile task. —*Stephen Thomas Erlewine*

Ghetto Fabulous / Nov. 10, 1998 / Jive ♦♦♦
With *Unpredictable*, Mystikal showed signs of breaking away from the No Limit murk of gangstas, guns, and money. Instead of continuing in this direction with its follow-up, *Ghetto Fabulous*, he decided to stick with No Limit's directionless recycling of beats, ideas, and themes. Like any of the label's 1998 offerings, there are glimmers of promise buried amid all the repetition, but what stands out is the monotony of the music and the lyrics. Since Mystikal is a better rapper than many of his No Limit cohorts, *Ghetto Fabulous* is more listenable than the average record the label puts out, but the music never challenges him to reach new heights. Consequently, the record feels flat, despite a few moments where Mystikal is able to truly show us what he's made of. —*Stephen Thomas Erlewine*

● **Let's Get Ready** / Sep. 26, 2000 / Jive ♦♦♦♦
Mystikal distances himself even further from his past with Master P's No Limit camp on *Let's Get Ready* than he had done on his previous album, *Ghetto Fabulous*. And perhaps not surprisingly, the further Mystikal distances himself, the more impressive his work becomes, as here he becomes the 21st century ghetto James Brown, exploding with more exuberance and energy than humans are supposed to have. This album's blazing lead single, "Shake Ya Ass," draws the connection between Mystikal and Brown well, illustrating the wild rapper's knack for hollering out seemingly spontaneous signature howls and other odd sounds that just sound straight-up funky: "whatcha self," "show me whatcha workin' wit," "here I go," and so on. Besides the limitless charisma that seeps out of Mystikal's loud, rude rapping-meets-shouting style of vocal delivery, the album also benefits from the production and songwriting variety that No Limit was never able to accomplish—with the sparse funk of the Neptunes-produced "Shake Ya Ass" again functioning as a perfect example. This variety also appears on songs such as "Come See About Me," when the album's superstar spars with his female equivalent, Da Brat. It's an engaging rhyme battle, particularly when Mystikal shouts out his little taglines such as "What's up whodi!" The album-closing "Neck uv da Woods" is another highlight, this one essentially an OutKast track featuring Mystikal rather than the other way around. The rambunctious rapper had always been No Limit's most impressive rapper, and here on *Let's Get Ready* Mystikal shows you precisely what he's capable of if given the opportunity to shine, as he sheds the trappings of Master P's budget-quality confines and loudly establishes himself as one of the dirty South's best. —*Jason Birchmeier*

Tarantula / Dec. 18, 2001 / Jive ♦♦♦♦
The coast-to-coast success of "Shake Ya Ass" thankfully didn't tame Mystikal too much. On *Tarantula*, Mystikal's first album in the wake of his commercial breakthrough in 2000, he's just as wild as ever—a blunt-smokin', big truck-drivin', ass-slappin' James Brown for his generation with no apologies and few pretensions. One thing has changed with Mystikal over the years, though: with each successive album, he's been graced with continuously improved production. Longtime collaborator KLC continues to improve here, crafting many of this album's liveliest moments, songs like "Pᵒᵒᵗᵉy Crook" and "Big Truck Driver" that find Mystikal at his least mannered. The Neptunes return with three excellent productions, one of them, "Bouncin' Back (Bumpin' Me Against the Wall)," attempting to duplicate the energy and appeal of the last song the duo produced for Mystikal, "Shake Ya Ass." Elsewhere, two of the industry's hottest producers of the moment, Rockwilder and Scott Storch, contribute some excellent tracks. Mystikal really couldn't ask for better production, overall—all the tracks have bouncy,

ass-shakin', club-ready beats, and nearly all have quite catchy hooks. And since Mystikal rises to the occasion, delivering rhymes that are just as rousing as the beats, he has recorded his second great album in a row. Like *Let's Get Ready, Tarantula* realizes the potential Mystikal's early work for *No Limit* promised—the potential to be one of the most successful and unique, yet still unrefined and uncompromising, rappers in the game. In fact, this album seems so fully realized, it's difficult to imagine Mystikal taking his music to yet another level without changing his style. —*Jason Birchmeier*

N2Deep

f. 1992

Group / West Coast Rap, Latin Rap, Gangsta Rap

Pioneering Chicano gangsta rappers N2Deep signed to Profile Records in the early '90s and remained an underground presence in Southern California for the remainder of the decade. Comprised of James Trujillo (Jay Tee) and Timothy Lyons (TL), the duo debuted with *Back to the Hotel* (1992) but left the fledging Profile afterward. N2Deep's successive efforts never quite lived up to their initial promise with Profile; however, the duo continued to release underground albums that fans appreciated, much of the better material distilled for a pair of competing best-of collections, one compiled by Soul Town (1999), the other by 40 Ounce (2002). —*Jason Birchmeier*

● **The Best of N2Deep** / 2002 / 40 Ounce ✦✦✦✦✦

Practically identical to the same-titled but quickly out-of-print *Best of N2Deep* by Soul Town in 1999, the 40 Ounce collection rounds up all of N2Deep's best moments from the 1990s. The Cali duo from Vallejo specialized in party rap, and that's mostly what's compiled here, particularly on "Back to the Hotel," "California Hot Tubs," and "All Night," probably N2Deep's three most recognized songs. There are plenty more highlights here, though, specifically "Toss Up," "V-Town," "Threesome," "Parkin' Lot Pimpin'," "Cali Lifestyles," and "1st We Drink." Actually, there aren't any flat-out weak moments here, as every song is a standout on its respective album. A few fellow Cali Bay Area guests pop up here and there, including B-Legit, E-40, Mac Lee, P.S.D., Dru Down, and the one and only Roger Troutman. Given the handful of N2Deep albums released during the '90s and also their questionable availability, 40 Ounce's *The Best of N2Deep* is surely the ideal place to begin, though the harder-to-find Soul Town collection should serve you just as well considering its practically identical track selection. —*Jason Birchmeier*

NAAM Brigade

Group / Hardcore Rap, Underground Rap

Formerly known as Task Force, NAAM Brigade was a hardcore rap outfit that came out of Philadelphia in the '90s. NAAM has several full-time members, including Sonni Blak, Eyse da SupaStar, Rambo, and Meek Millz; but like New Jersey's Wu-Tang Clan, NAAM has had an extended family of MCs and allies. In fact, there are some parallels between NAAM's thugged-out rhymes and comparable East Coast outfits like Wu-Tang and Queens, NY's Mobb Deep. But NAAM tends to be more dark humored, and unlike Wu-Tang, it doesn't get into martial arts imagery.

The members of NAAM grew up in a rough, impoverished ghetto neighborhood of Southwest Philly, where they formed a clique and often engaged in microphone battles with rival MCs. Not all sections of Southwest Philly are dangerous high-crime areas, but where NAAM's members lived, poverty, drugs, and violent crime were harsh realities. In those days—when NAAM was still going by Task Force—the outfit's core members were Sonni, Eyse, Rambo, and the late Q-Don, although there were plenty of neighborhood rappers who were down with their clique and helped them battle on the microphone. After selling mix tapes in their neighborhood for a few years, the crew signed with Elektra in 1998 as Task Force. But just when the hip-hoppers thought they were on the verge of national success, they hit a major bump in the road.

When an altercation broke out in a Philly nightclub, Q-Don was killed by a stray bullet that was meant for someone else; he was in the wrong place at the wrong time. So the Philadelphians parted company with Elektra and briefly took a break from music. But the former Task Force soon re-emerged as NAAM Brigade with a new lineup that included Sonni, Eyse, Rambo, and newcomer

Meek Millz (whose name is rather ironic because NAAM's odes to inner-city thug life are anything but meek). As NAAM, the group recorded a new mix tape titled *NAAM Brigade Mixtape, Vol. 2*, which is said to have sold about 20,000 copies in Philly. One of the tunes caught the attention of Power 99 FM (a major urban contemporary station in Philly) and became the theme of a popular mix show. *NAAM Brigade Mixtape, Vol. 2* also caught the attention of the Los Angeles-based ARTISTdirect Records, which signed the rappers in the early 2000s. *Early in the Game*, NAAM's debut album, was given an September 2002 release date. The album's title track, which features Jay-Z protégé Freeway, was released as its first single. —*Alex Henderson*

● **Early in the Game** / Sep. 24, 2002 / ARTISTdirect ✦✦✦

Regrouping after the retiring of the Task Force moniker subsequent to the shooting death of leader Q-Don took a few years, but the fruits of their labor came to fruition with a deal with Artist Direct and the *Early in the Game* debut. The disc has a few decent tracks, most notably the guitar-augmented, slamming "We Live It" and "Can't Let It Go," which incorporates Sting's "Shape of My Heart" and female vocal accompaniment of labelmate Sharli McQueen in a tale regaling the tough Philly streets. However, NAAM Brigade lacks a distinctive voice among the four MCs that make up the troupe, the production rarely stands out as anything special, and most of the lyrics don't expand much beyond the usual thugs-and-bitches musings, though the worst offender, "What You Doin' Wit Dat" (which features guest rapper Juvenile), is undeniably clever. —*Brian O'Neill*

Nadanuf

f. Cincinnatti, OH

Group / Pop-Rap

Nadanuf is a Cincinnati-based female pop-rap duo comprised of Skwert and Phor-One-One. The pair were discovered in their hometown by Aaron "Babyboy" Griffin, who helped secure them a contract with Reprise Records. Griffin was one of several producers—including Howie Tee, Soul G, Michael "Doc" Little, Def Jef, and H&H Productions—who worked on Nadanuf's debut album, *Worldwide*, which was released in late 1997. —*Stephen Thomas Erlewine*

● **Worldwide** / Nov. 11, 1997 / Reprise ✦✦✦✦

Nadanuf's debut album, *Worldwide*, is an engaging collection of crossover pop-rap despite a couple of weak moments. Skwert and Phor-One-One are competent rappers, but their primary appeal is their charisma, which helps enliven the group's predictably pop-savvy urban grooves. At their best, such as on "Caravan Ride" or their duet with Kurtis Blow on a cover of his seminal "The Breaks," Nadanuf creates fun, funky hip-hop, and at their worst, they're simply pedestrian, working the same grooves and rhyming the same rhymes as their peers. Still, there are enough moments on *Worldwide* to suggest that the duo can rise above their weakness and create a thoroughly winning record next time around. —*Leo Stanley*

Nappy Roots

f. 1995, Bowling Green, OH

Group / Southern Rap, Dirty South

Country and proud of it, Nappy Roots formed in 1995 around a sextet of students attending Western Kentucky University in Bowling Green. Four members of the group were Kentucky natives (Skinny DeVille, B. Stille, Ron Clutch, Big V.), bolstered by a pair of Oakland-born transplants (R. Prophet and Milledgeville). Nappy Roots began making music together at a local record shop cum studio named ET's Music, and released their full-length debut, *Country Fried Cess*, in 1998. Drawn to the group's distinctive twist on

Southern bounce, the major labels began flocking, and they eventually signed to Atlantic. Their label debut, *Watermelon, Chicken and Gritz*, was released in 2002. —*John Bush*

● **Watermelon, Chicken and Gritz** / Feb. 26, 2002 / Atlantic ◆◆◆◆
Nappy Roots' major-label debut is a fast-moving affair, stock-full of sweet pop hooks and loaded down with an easy, good-time feeling. *Watermelon, Chicken and Gritz* is a party album of a different sort, splitting the difference between the fat beats of the West Coast and the dirty South's gritty funk to carve out their own distinctive, high-octane jams. The group's six members met at Western Kentucky University—four are Kentucky natives—and make little secret of their Southern roots. With all six members taking turns on the mic, Nappy Roots keeps a rapid pace up, swerving through the 17 tracks here with effortless energy. Southern twang and drawl stand out on tracks like "Kentucky Mud" and the hit single "Awnaw," giving *Watermelon, Chicken and Gritz* a pleasant, down-home feeling. While the sound here is refreshing, the lyrics rarely stand out and after a while some of the tracks tend to blur together. Still, this is fun—perfect for rolling down the road on a sunny day and guaranteed to get the party started. —*Martin Woodside*

Nas (Nasir Jones)

b. Long Island, NY

Vocals, Executive Producer, Producer / Hip-Hop, East Coast Rap, Gangsta Rap

Heralded instantly as one of New York's leading rap voices, Nas expressed an outspoken, self-empowered swagger that rallied the streets his city and elsewhere. Whether proclaiming himself "Nasty Nas" or "Nas Escobar" or "Nastradamus" or "God's Son," the self-anointed king of New York battled numerous adversaries for his position atop the epicenter of rap; none more noteworthy than Jay-Z, who vied with Nas for the vacated throne left in the wake of Notorious B.I.G.'s 1997 assassination. Such headline-worthy drama informed Nas' provocative rhymes, which he delivered with both a masterful flow and a wise perspective over breathtaking beats by amazing producers: legends like DJ Premier, Large Professor, and Pete Rock; hitmakers like Trackmasters, Timbaland, and Dr. Dre; hometown favorites like Swizz Beatz, Megahertz, and the Alchemist; and personal favorites of his like L.E.S., Salaam Remi, and Chucky Thompson. Nas likewise collaborated with some of the industry's leading video directors like Hype Williams and Chris Robinson, presenting singles like "Hate Me Now," "One Mic," and "I Can" with dramatic flair. Throughout all the ups (acclaim, popularity, and success) and all the downs (pressure, adversaries, and overreaching), Nas continually matured as an artist, evolving from a young street disciple to a vain, all-knowing sage to a humbled godly teacher. Such growth made every album release an event and thus prolonged the rapper's increasingly storied career to epic proportions.

Born Nasir Jones, son of jazz musician Olu Dara, Nas dropped out of school in the eighth grade, trading classrooms for the streets of the rough Queensbridge projects, long fabled as the former stomping ground of Marley Marl and his Juice Crew as immortalized in "The Bridge." Despite dropping out of school, Nas developed a high degree of literacy that would later characterize his rhymes. At the same time, though, he delved into street culture and flirted with danger, such experiences similarly characterizing his rhymes. His synthesis of well-crafted rhetoric and street-glamorous imagery blossomed in 1991 when he connected with Main Source and laid down a fiery verse on "Live at the Barbeque" that earned him instant respect among the East Coast rap scene. Not long afterward, MC Serch of 3rd Bass approached Nas about contributing a track to the *Zebrahead* soundtrack. Serch was the soundtrack's executive producer and, like much of New York, had been impressed by "Live at the Barbeque." Nas submitted "Halftime," and the song so stunned Serch that he made it the soundtrack's leadoff track.

Columbia Records meanwhile signed Nas to a major-label contract, and many of New York's finest producers sought to work with him. DJ Premier, Large Professor, and Pete Rock ultimately entered the studio with the young rapper and began work on *Illmatic*. When Columbia finally released the album in April 1994, it faced high expectations; *Illmatic* regardless proved just as astounding as it had been billed. It sold very well, spawned multiple hits, and earned unanimous acclaim, followed soon after by classic status. The two years leading up to Nas' follow-up, *It Was Written* (1996), thus brought another wave of enormous anticipation. The ambitious rapper, who had begun working closely with industry heavyweight Steve Stoute, responded with a

significantly different approach than he had taken with *Illmatic*. Where that album had been a straightforward hip-hop album with few pop concessions, the largely Trackmaster-produced *It Was Written* made numerous concessions to the pop crossover market, most notably on the two hit singles, "Street Dreams" and "If I Ruled the World (Imagine That)." These singles—both of which drew from well-known songs, Eurythmics' "Sweet Dreams (Are Made of This)" and Kurtis Blow's "If I Ruled the World," respectively—broadened Nas' appeal greatly and awarded him the MTV-sanctioned crossover success he sought. This same crossover success, however, undermined some of his hip-hop credibility while his subsequent albums—*I Am...* and *Nastradamus* (both 1999)—and their crossover tendencies did so to an even further extent.

Around this point in the late '90s, Nas nonetheless reigned atop the New York rap scene alongside few contemporaries in the wake of the Notorious B.I.G.'s assassination. In addition to his endless stream of hits by the industry's most successful producers—"If I Ruled the World" (produced by the Trackmasters), "Hate Me Now" (Puff Daddy), "Nas Is Like" (DJ Premier), and "You Owe Me" (Timbaland), among others—he popularly co-starred in the Hype Williams-directed film *Belly* (1998) alongside DMX and contributed to the soundtrack. Furthermore, he led a short-lived supergroup of New York rappers known as the Firm (also comprised of rappers Foxy Brown, AZ, and Nature and also producers Dr. Dre and the Trackmasters) and assembled a broad coalition of fellow Queensbridge rappers for the *QB Finest* compilation (2000). Amid all of this publicity, though, criticism began to mount. For every crossover fan Nas won with his dramatic endlessly MTV-aired videos, he lost support in the streets, where many initial supporters felt he had sold out and abandoned hip-hop ideals in favor of commercial success. Nas' sales reflected this fading support, as each subsequent album sold less than its predecessor despite the consistent hitmaking.

A series of incidents in 2001 provided a key turning point for Nas' declining career. The rapper's personal life became increasingly conflicted, as his mother began suffering from cancer and his woman betrayed him. To make matters worse, longtime rival Jay-Z pointedly dissed Nas on "Takeover," the much-discussed lead song from his universally acclaimed *Blueprint* album (2001). Jay-Z called out Nas for not having put out a "hot" album since *Illmatic*, among other reasons, and also made demeaning comments about Nas' woman. And it didn't help that Jay-Z had indeed rose atop the New York rap scene, giving him ample justification to call out Nas, who had fallen from favor and receded from the public eye while he dealt with his personal issues. Following a much-circulated underground freestyle over the beat to "Paid in Full," Nas responded strikingly in December 2001 with *Stillmatic*, the title a reference to his one undeniable masterpiece, *Illmatic*, which had been released nearly a decade earlier. Most notably, *Stillmatic* opened with the song "Ether," a very direct response (featuring the chants "f**** Jay-Z" and "I will not lose"), followed by perhaps Nas' most aggressive single ever, "Get Ur Self A...." These two songs in particular rallied the streets while the moving video for "One Mic" received heavy support from MTV. Throughout 2002, Nas continued his comeback with a number of guest appearances, among them Brandy's "What About Us?," J-Lo's "I'm Gonna Be Alright," and Ja Rule's "The Pledge," as well as yet more headline-worthy controversy, this time involving his no-show at popular radio station Hot 97's annual Summer Jam.

Amid all of the drama, Nas managed to salvage his esteemed reputation and reclaim his lofty status atop the New York scene as well. *Stillmatic* earned immediate wide acclaim from fans and critics alike and sold impressively, and Columbia furthered the comeback fervor with two archival releases, one of remixes (*From Illmatic to Stillmatic* [2002]), the other of outtakes (*The Lost Tapes* [2002]). Then at the end of the year Columbia rush-released a new studio album, the personally themed *God's Son*, to combat bootlegging, and Nas once again basked in universal acclaim as the album sold well, spawned sizable hits ("Thugz Mansion," "Made You Look," "I Can"), and received rampant media support. —*Jason Birchmeier*

★ **Illmatic** / Apr. 19, 1994 / Columbia ◆◆◆◆◆
Often cited as one of the best hip-hop albums of the '90s, *Illmatic* is the undisputed classic upon which Nas' reputation rests. It helped spearhead the artistic renaissance of New York hip-hop in the post-*Chronic* era, leading a return to street aesthetics. Yet even if *Illmatic* marks the beginning of a shift away from Native Tongues-inspired alternative rap, it's strongly rooted in that sensibility. For one, Nas employs some of the most sophisticated jazz-rap producers around: Q-Tip, Pete Rock, DJ Premier, and Large Professor, who

underpin their intricate loops with appropriately tough beats. But more importantly, Nas takes his place as one of hip-hop's greatest street poets—his rhymes are highly literate and his raps superbly fluid, regardless of the size of his vocabulary. He's able to evoke the bleak reality of ghetto life without losing hope or forgetting the good times, which become all the more precious when any day could be your last. As a narrator, he doesn't get too caught up in the darker side of life—he's simply describing what he sees in the world around him, and trying to live it up while he can. He's thoughtful but ambitious, announcing on "N.Y. State of Mind" that "I never sleep, 'cause sleep is the cousin of death," and that he's "out for dead presidents to represent me" on "The World Is Yours." Elsewhere, he flexes his storytelling muscles on the classic cuts "Life's a Bitch" and "One Love," the latter a detailed report to a close friend in prison about how allegiances within their group have shifted. Hip-hop fans accustomed to 73-minute opuses sometimes complain about *Illmatic*'s brevity, but even if it leaves you wanting more, it's also one of the few '90s rap albums with absolutely no wasted space. Nas is a great lyricist, in top form, meeting great production, and *Illmatic* remains a perennial favorite among serious hip-hop fans. *— Steve Huey*

It Was Written / Jul. 2, 1996 / Columbia ✦✦✦✦
For his second album, *It Was Written*, Nas hired a bunch of hip-hop's biggest producers—including Dr. Dre, DJ Premier, Stretch, and Trackmasters—to help him create the musical bed for his daring, groundbreaking rhymes. Although that rhyme style isn't as startling on *It Was Written* as it was on his debut, *Illmatic*, Nas has deepened his talents, creating a complex series of rhymes that not only flow but also manage to tell coherent stories as well. Furthermore, Nas often concentrates on creating vignettes about life in the ghetto that never are apolitical or ambivalent. This time around, the production is more detailed and elaborate, which gives the music a wider appeal. Sometimes this is a detriment—Nas sounds better when he tries to keep it at street level—but usually Nas' lyrical force cuts through the commercial sheen. Combined with the spare but deep grooves, his rhymes have a resonance unmatched by most of his mid-'90s contemporaries. Because, no matter how deep his lyrics are, his grooves are just as deep and that bottomless funk and spare beats is what makes *It Was Written* so compulsively listenable. *— Leo Stanley*

I Am ... The Autobiography / Apr. 6, 1999 / Columbia ✦✦✦
I Am... is the third album and fourth stage in the evolution of Queensbridge's living legend Nasir Jones, from Nasty Nas to Nas to Nas Escobar to Nastradamus, the soothsaying megathug poet. This third installment is an introspective work from one of hip-hop's made men. Always billed as a hip-hop messiah, Nas rose through the ranks of hip-hop on the strength of powerful poetry. Contrary to the album's title, the scope of the work extends beyond the autobiography as Nas takes on politics, the state of hip-hop, Y2K, race, and religion with his own unique perspective. While *Illmatic* was Nas at his rawest and *It Was Written* was Nas' attempt to reconcile his underground leanings with his newfound fame, acclaim, and wealth, the Nas of *I Am...* is honest about his elevated status yet still feels the tension of no longer being ravenous on the mic. Musically, *I Am...* is somewhat unimaginative by Nas' stratospheric standards. Tried and true producers, the Trackmasters stamp the album with their signature catchy grooves and samples, but some of these tracks lack the sonic depth to do justice to the prophecies of the pharaoh, Nas. Superproducer Premier comes to save the day on two outstanding tracks: "NY State of Mind, Pt. II" and "Nas Is Like." These two cuts are nothing short of *Illmatic* perfection. "Nas Is Like"'s symphonic composition is the perfect complement for an MC of Nas' supreme vocal quality and precise lyrics. Despite some of the blandness on the production end, Nas still shines as the old-soul storyteller and crime rhyme chronicler on cuts like "We Will Survive," a dirge for fallen rappers. Nas also experiments stylistically on "Big Things," sporting a Midwest cadence, and on "You Won't See Me Tonight," a Timbaland-produced duet with R&B songstress Aaliyah. *— Michael Di Bella*

Nastradamus / Nov. 23, 1999 / Columbia ✦✦✦
From boy to man to king to prophet, Nas re-emerged six months after his third album with *Nastradamus*, a pre-millennial statement touching on the future, spirituality, and family—issues that Nas has broached before, though never with this much devotion. It could have been an intriguing concept album, but *Nastradamus* is continually compromised by tracks that don't contribute to the theme. For every emotional track like "Some of Us Have

Angels" or "God Love Us," there are the same old street-life anthems you'd expect to hear, like "Shoot 'em Up," "Come Get Me," "You Owe Me." They sound OK (thanks to production from L.E.S., DJ Premier, and Timbaland), but the result is yet another drawn-out hip-hop album that wanders aimlessly and never really says anything. Nas' rapping is superb as usual, but for the most part it's a wasted effort. *—Keith Farley*

QB Finest / Nov. 21, 2000 / Sony ✦✦
On the celebratory posse-cut "Da Bridge 2001," Nas laments, "We from the largest project/Yo the biggest on earth/Queens know the history/Left y'all cursed." While Nas' salvo may at first appear to be nothing more then your typical, MC 'hood-rappin rhetoric, there is truth to his manifesto. After all, the infamous borough of Queens has churned out a distinguished list of influential MCs and producers. While Nas offers *QB Finest* as the first project for his newly birthed record label Ill Will, this enigmatic compilation only hints at the talent residing in the bridge, as it comprises strictly the thug element of Queens' storied existence. *QB Finest* scores points for resurrecting the career of the bridge's first lady, Roxanne Shanté, who makes a triumphant comeback on "We Live This" featuring Havoc and Noyd. Yet, excluding the more notable individuals (Run-D.M.C., Rakim, Kool G Rap, and LL) who helped carve out QB's reputation, lends an unpolitically correct stigma to this unfulfilling gathering. Though Nas is a very active participant in a few underdeveloped cuts, the "Nasty" side of his personality surfaces on the introspective solo cut "Find Ya Wealth." Achieving an *Illmatic* lyrical intensity, the track's dusty soul sample mirrors the wisdom and pain Nas is so capable of conveying with his rhymes. Yet, minus a few crucial momentum boosters—Prodigy's heavily peddled, mix-tape banger "Pile Raps" and Nature's conversational "Fire"—there is very little left to cling to with *QB's Finest*. *—Matt Conaway*

Stillmatic / Dec. 18, 2001 / Ill Will ✦✦✦
Back on the hardcore block and with plenty to prove after two years without a record under his own name, Nas designed *Stillmatic* as a response: to the rap cognoscenti who thought he'd become a relic, and most of all to Jay-Z, the East Coast kingpin who wounded his pride and largely replaced him as the best rapper in hip-hop. The saga started back in the summer of 2001 with the mix tape "Stillmatic," Nas' answer track to an on-stage dis by Jay-Z. A few months after Jay-Z countered with the devastating "Takeover," Nas dropped the comeback single "Ether" and the full album *Stillmatic*; tellingly, Jay-Z had already released his response to "Ether" (titled "Super Ugly") before *Stillmatic* even came out. Dropping many of the mainstream hooks and featured performers in order to focus his rapping, Nas proves he's still a world-class rhymer, but he does sound out of touch in the process of defending his honor. "Ether" relies on a deep-throat vocal repeating the phrase "f*ck Jay-Z," while "You're da Man" hits the heights of arrogance with a looped vocal sample repeating the title over and over. "Destroy & Rebuild" is a solid defense of his Queensbridge home, and "Got Ur Self A..." is an outstanding track, the best here, complete with a chantalong chorus. Despite the many highlights, a few of these tracks (most were produced by either Large Professor or Nas himself) just end up weighing him down: "Smokin'," one of the worst, is an odd G-funk track that would've sounded dated years before its release. *Stillmatic* certainly isn't as commercial as past Nas output, but it places him squarely behind the times. Facts are facts: he's not the best rapper in the business anymore. *—John Bush*

From Illmatic to Stillmatic: The Remixes EP / Jul. 2, 2002 / Columbia ✦✦✦
Released in summer 2002, just in time to capitalize on Nas' *Stillmatic* resurgence, *From Illmatic to Stillmatic* compiles a few previously released remixes from the mid-'90s alongside a new remix of "One Mic." The previously released remixes come from *Illmatic* (1994)—"Life's a Bitch," "One Love," "It Ain't Hard to Tell"—and *It Was Written* (1996): "Street Dreams" and "Affirmative Action." The three *Illmatic* remixes aren't huge departures from the original versions, featuring the same vocals but different productions. Conversely, the two *It Was Written* remixes are huge departures, featuring both different vocal tracks and productions. In fact, these could just as well be brand-new songs: the "Street Dreams" remix by the Trackmasters is quite mellow with R. Kelly on the hook, most likely intended originally as a crossover single, and the "Affirmative Action" remix has the original the Firm ensemble—Nas, Foxy Brown, and AZ (the Cormega verse is notably missing)—rapping over an interpolation of Marley Marl's "The Symphony." The "One Mic" remix concluding this EP is the real gem, however. It's not

really much different from the original version, which was still getting substantial airplay at the time of this EP's release. The subtle difference lies within the production, which interpolates Mtume's oft-sampled "Juicy Fruit." It would have been nice, overall, to see more new mixes rather than strictly previously released ones. For instance, a remix of Nas' other big hit from *Stillmatic*, "Got Ur Self A...," would have been timely. Even so, *From Illmatic to Stillmatic* is a welcome addition to the Nas catalog, perfect for anyone looking to dig a little deeper without much effort or cost. —*Jason Birchmeier*

The Lost Tapes / Sep. 3, 2002 / Columbia ✦✦✦
Leading up to the release of *God's Son*, the second new Nas album in less than a year, Nas' Columbia-distributed label Ill Will dropped a collection of "lost recordings"—basically, tracks recorded for *I Am* and *Stillmatic* that just didn't make it. Though the liners are stretching it in parts ("these songs are famous for never having been officially released"), they definitely got it right when they said, "No cameos. No hype. No bullsh°t." From a few listens, it's clear most of these weren't bumped because they were low quality; "Doo Rags," "No Idea's Original," and "Black Zombie" stand up to anything Nas has recorded since the original *Illmatic*. In fact, they have more in common with his early recordings; there's more of a back-in-the-day, wasn't-it-all-so-simple-then sound to "Doo Rags" and "Poppa Was a Playa," two tracks that definitely wouldn't have fit on the raging *Stillmatic*. That's certainly no reason not to pick up this one, not just for Nas fans but also for hip-hop fans who want to hear some great rhyming with no added features. —*John Bush*

God's Son / Dec. 17, 2002 / Columbia ✦✦✦✦
God's Son is an emotional album, imbued with recent experiences in Nas' personal life, particularly his recent bout with Jay-Z and the unfortunate death of his mother, Ann Jones. These experiences had challenged the self-reappointed King of New York, attacking both his street status and his heart, and he in turn looked within, embracing both his craft and his spirit. Brazenly declaring himself God's Son, in tribute partly to his mother's legacy as well as his own increasingly Jesus-like one, Nas emerged from his experiences wiser, stronger, and holier than ever, less engaged by the material world than the inner one, less interested in flossing than teaching, and less obsessed with his riches than his soul. And his soul he bares nakedly; profusely personal, Nas' lyrical divulgence is sometimes even startling: "Last Real Nigga Alive" name-drops Biggie, Jay-Z, Wu-Tang Clan, and other '90s-era rappers; "Hey Nas" reflects on recent failed relationships with women; "Dance" is an ode to his mother; and "Heaven" questions spirituality. As usual, there's a street-rallying leadoff single here, "Made You Look," that announces Nas' periodic return with fury and bombast. Salaam Remi produces the Marley Marl-fashioned track and lays down similarly inventive beats on four others. He's joined by many of the other producers who had worked on *Stillmatic* a year earlier: Chucky Thompson, Ron Browz, and the Alchemist, all of whom deliver harsh tracks without pop gimmickry. In addition, *God's Son* includes three noteworthy collaborations: Nas and 2Pac trade gentle verses on "Thugz Mansion," Alicia Keys contributes the production and hook to "Warrior Song," and Eminem produces "The Cross." Throughout it all, *God's Son* plays like an album. The playing time is reasonable, clocking under an hour; the song selection is diverse, no two tracks resembling one another; and the themes are interwoven, giving the album a narrative sense. *God's Son* isn't quite the masterpiece is could be—mostly because Nas is *so* self-involved, sometimes seemingly intoxicated by his kingliness—but it's surely one of the most remarkable albums of the Queensbridge rapper's highlight-filled career, just a notch or so below *Illmatic* and *Stillmatic*. —*Jason Birchmeier*

Natas

f. Detroit, MI
Group / Hardcore Rap, Rap-Rock
Along with group leader Esham's numerous '90s solo albums, Natas' work during this same decade trailblazed a path through uncharted territory, defining a dark style of hardcore rap characterized by decadent motifs and heavy-metal-like aggression. Taking considerable influence from *Niggaz4life*-era N.W.A, the Detroit, MI, trio consisting of Esham, Mastamind, and TNT came hard on their 1992 debut album, *Life After Death*, to the point where their anger-exuding music alienated all but a small cult audience fascinated with their anarchic disposition and their self-termed style of acid rap. On this album they rapped about the most disturbing and shocking themes

imaginable, capturing the darkest corners of their burnt-out city's most horrible ghettos with their lyrics in an attempt to be as hardcore as possible. To further the impact of these lyrics, Esham self-produced the album, laying down gritty beats and making effective use of rock samples to give the album a harsher tone. Successive albums found the trio improving their rapping and their production, as they slowly matured, moving progressively away from mere exploitation. By the end of the '90s, their music had considerably evolved in terms of not only lyrical content and delivery but also production, resulting in an innovative realization of their original intent that finally blossomed on *WWW.Com (Wicket World Wide)*.

Before forming Natas, group leader Esham had already established himself as a solo artist, debuting at the end of the '80s with *Boomin' Words From Hell*, followed by a few EPs. At this time, Esham was a student at Osborne High School in Detroit, where he eventually crossed paths with Mastamind in the tenth grade. After listening to a three-song demo tape given to him by Mastamind, Esham decided to form a group with the promising rapper and TNT, a longtime friend. The three got together and decided to spell Satan backwards and call themselves Natas as a symbol of their anarchic, evil disposition at the time, being mere teenagers. In 1992, Esham released Natas' debut album, *Life After Death*, on his Reel Life Productions label (later re-issued by TVT). Two years later he released a similar follow-up album, *Blaz4me*, an album nearly as twisted and disturbing as its predecessor. Then came the dark *Doubelievengod* album in 1995, which found the trio moving forward artistically as well as ideologically.

When Natas released *Multikillionaire: The Devil's Contract* in 1997, it became clear that the group had reached a turning point. Along with Esham's accompanying *Bruce Wayne: Gotham City 1987* album from the same year, *Multikillionaire* broadened Natas' scope, aiming for conceptualism while abandoning the exploitative elements of previous works. Natas resurfaced in 1999 with *WWW.Com (Wicket World Wide)*, claiming that their name was an acronym for "nation ahead of time and space" rather than Satan spelled backwards in hopes of changing their image. The album improved upon *Mulitkillionaire*'s flaws and represented a more mature representation of the group's ambitions. Featuring live instruments where Esham used to place samples, the album's production was considerably innovative for its time, marrying a rock attitude with a rap aesthetic and garnering considerable acclaim from the underground. Following this release, both Esham and Mastamind took time off to work on solo albums in the wake of the album's success, and the Detroit rap scene's sudden evolution to a substantial hot spot for up-and-coming talent. —*Jason Birchmeier*

Life After Death / 1992 / TVT ✦✦
The first Natas album, *Life After Death*, introduces Esham's group, featuring TNT and Mastamind, and their merger of a N.W.A-style gang mentality, a 2 Live Crew-style attitude toward women, and the same sort of morbidity that Esham showcased on his solo albums. So while the synthesis of these three characteristics—violence, sex, and death—is no doubt potent, it comes off as far too contrived. The trio's attempt to be as hardcore as possible pushes their efforts from shocking to clichéd satire. Furthermore, in addition to the clichéd subject matter, the accompanying music isn't nearly as evocative as that found on Esham's solo albums. The group's later albums would eventually integrate a further sense of sincerity and fewer theatrics as well as a stronger musical soundtrack; this debut finds them simply trying to make a splash by being as insane as possible. Unfortunately, they take things too far for their own good. —*Jason Birchmeier*

Blaz4me / Jan. 8, 1994 / TVT ✦✦
The second Natas release finds the hardcore Detroit trio again trying to be as controversial as possible, and once again their ambition to be shocking results in an overly theatrical album. There are a few songs here with some noteworthy production, such as the guitar riff-driven beats of "I'm Bout 2 Do Sum Dirt" and the interpolation of "One Nation Under a Groove" on "Stay True to Your City," but it's somewhat sad when one realizes that the best moments on *Blaz4me* result from heavy sampling. So even if Esham, TNT, and Mastamind do stumble onto some interesting ideas quite unlike what anyone else was doing in hip-hop circa 1994, these great moments owe almost as much to Prince and George Clinton (two of the many artists sampled for the album). In fact, the uncredited sampling may be the most interesting aspect of the exploitative *Blaz4me*; like the Bomb Squad's collage-like approach on *It Takes a Nation to Hold Us Back* and Dr. Dre's neo-P-funk sound on *The*

Chronic, Esham crafts a particular aesthetic by endlessly raiding his record collection in classic postmodern fashion. Still, even if he unethically creates an innovative-for-its-time sound that merges Funkadelic guitar distortion with hard mid-'80s Def Jam-like beats, the often ridiculous lyrics ruin whatever validity the music may have. One doesn't need to look any further than the track listing—"He Raped Me," "Get My Dick out Yo Mouth," "Hands on My Nut Sac"—to see how juvenile this album's mentality is. Thankfully, Natas eventually grew as songwriters; unfortunately, this album doesn't showcase anything but ridiculous lyrical content. [*Blaz4me* was eventually re-released in 2000 with distribution by TVT Records.] —*Jason Birchmeier*

Doubelievengod / 1995 / Reel Life ✦✦✦✦
After two grimy albums of lo-fi production driven by P-funk and classic rock samples, Natas returned with *Doubelievengod*, a much more mature album in terms of both production and rapping. Most obviously, the platter of samples is gone; for whatever reasons, the emphasis is now on synth-driven beats (similar to post-*Closed Casket* Esham albums). The move toward eerie synth actually works in this album's favor, given its malevolent slant and ominous tone—it's not a rocking album but rather a haunting album. Group members Esham, Mastamind, and TNT further this aura by laying down some horror-themed raps that effectively emulate the album's tone. In the end, this beginning-to-end emphasis on darkness has made this a fan favorite, making the Esham/Natas camp's last sincerely horrifying album as they drifted increasingly toward self-conscious theatrics in an attempt to extend their reach beyond a tiny cult audience. Subsequent Natas albums are of higher quality than this, but *Doubelievengod* holds a special place in the Esham legacy alongside the *Judgement Day* albums as the summit of not necessarily his talent but rather his wickedness. —*Jason Birchmeier*

Multikillionaire: The Devil's Contract / Oct. 1997 / TVT ✦✦✦
With each album in the 1990s, Natas moved their music forward both as MCs and in terms of production, evolving from a juvenile exploitation group into an earnest group serious about changing the rap game with their increasingly realized rap style, a potent merger of Funkadelic guitar funk and Def Jam-era Rick Rubin-influenced beats. The less exploitative subject matter stands as the most noteworthy aspect of the group's growth with *Multikillionaire: The Devil's Contract*; the group doesn't rely so much on perverse sex, morbid obsessions, or heretical talk but rather attitude here to make their music interesting. This album isn't as realized as *WWW.Com*, but it's closer than any preceding Natas album. —*Jason Birchmeier*

● **WWW.Com (Wicket World Wide)** / Oct. 26, 1999 / TVT ✦✦✦✦✦
Natas' *WWW.Com* album finds the trio finally having abandoned their locker room mentality toward women and constant urge to provoke their audience in favor of less exploitative subject matter. Some may be disappointed with this, but most will agree that it's a change for the better. Furthermore, the album doesn't rely on samples as much as the early to mid-'90s Esham and Natas material, instead using live instrumentation, resulting in a potent collage of gritty hip-hop beats with an aggressive rock tone. It may have taken Esham nearly a decade to guide his group to this point, but the slow evolution and persistence on his part finally pays off: this is an important album, even if it didn't sell many copies. Sure, Esham's earlier work still retains a certain sense of importance, particularly as the prototype for rap-rock stars such as Kid Rock and Limp Bizkit. It's just far too hard to stomach his group's blatant theatrics of old—raunchy sex, Satanic baiting, unnecessary morbidity, an overall sense of utter irresponsibility, violent gang mentality—even if you take it lightly, making musically intriguing albums such as *Blaz4me* nearly intolerable. This album is arguably the first that you can actually take seriously from a lyrical standpoint as well as from a musical one. It's a bit unfortunate, though, that his album never crossed over with either rock, rap, or metal audiences, once again penetrating only Esham's firmly established niche. —*Jason Birchmeier*

Natural Selection

f. 1989
Group / Urban, Hip-Hop, Pop-Rap
Natural Selection was a duo that blended touches of hip-hop with R&B for a couple of successful singles and a self-titled album released in 1991. Elliot Erickson and Frederick Thomas formed the group in 1989; after their first recording, "Do Anything," caught on at the radio station Erickson was employed at, East West picked them up and gave the song a national release

in 1991. It hit the top of the R&B chart. An album and a pair of singles in support of it followed, but a planned follow-up never reached fruition; Erickson and Thomas parted in 1992. Thomas kept the Natural Selection name alive informally, with John Swan and early Shaun Ware brought into the group. A deal was sealed with SBK, but the label and, subsequently, the group fell apart. Several years later, the three came back together and recorded again. They independently released an eight-song recording titled *Infinity*, which didn't stray far from the group's initial recordings. —*Andy Kellman*

● **Natural Selection** / 1991 / East West ✦✦✦
Combine Prince's influence with traces of the System and a dose of hip-hop, and you've got Natural Selection, a male duo that consisted of Elliot Erickson and Frederick Thomas and showed some promise on this self-titled effort. Although the CD is rather uneven and doesn't fall into the essential category, the group's R&B/pop hooks can be catchy. Unlike so many of the urban contemporary songs recorded in the early 1990s, likable numbers like "Hearts Don't Think (They Feel)," "Bum Rush (Your Heart)," and "Do Anything" are the work of a group that was striving for originality, as opposed to being content to sound like the product of a musical assembly line. Despite its shortcomings, Selection had more heart and integrity than most of the urban contemporary acts that debuted in 1991. But regrettably, the obscure group fell through the cracks and disappeared without getting a chance to develop. —*Alex Henderson*

Nature (Jermaine Baxter)

b. Long Island, NY
Hip-Hop
Jermaine Baxter, known by fans as Nature, went to school with rapper Nasir "Nas" Jones. In fact, it was Nas who first took notice of Baxter's strong rhyming style, a style that seemed to come to the young hip-hop artist effortlessly.

Nature skipped the normal course of demo tapes and moved ahead to intros on recordings for other artists. The 1997 group the Firm was his next step to fame. Other members of this East Coast hardcore rap crew were AZ, Foxy Brown, and friend Nas. The foursome recorded an album, titled *The Album*, which quickly climbed to platinum and brought the guys plenty of attention.

In 2000, three long years after stepping away from the Firm crew, Nature at last finished a solo album, *For All Seasons*. It was recorded under the major label Columbia Records. Urban-life reality tracks like "We Ain't Friends," "Young Love," "Nature Shine," and "The Ultimate High" fill this 13-track first offering. The album carries explicit lyrics, but there is an edited version for younger fans. —*Charlotte Dillon*

● **For All Seasons** / Aug. 15, 2000 / Columbia ✦✦✦✦
With his laboriously delayed debut, *For All Seasons*, Nature is hoping to make up for lost time. Why? It was three years (an eternity in hip-hop) since Nature parted ways with the Firm, and in that time Nat has watched the anticipation for his debut slowly dissipate. His inaccessibility hasn't been lost on a fickle hip-hop populace that demands immediate gratification, as his once-prospective fan base has made stars out of thugs who were more readily available—Ja Rule, Beanie Sigel, and Black Rob. While Nat may have failed to capitalize on his window of opportunity, *For All Seasons* affirms that quality work can never be dated. Though his lyrics are recited strictly in a tempered, conversational manner, he is an exceptionally flamboyant and charismatic MC, which is evident on the braggadocios "Ultimate High" featuring Nas. But Nature is most intriguing when he eschews the typical thug banter and delves into the storytelling aspect of his repertoire; he weaves a fatal love triangle with "Young Love," and paints visceral montages of street life with "I Remember" and the sublime "It's a Man's World." Though Nature delivers a compelling debut, there are stretches of outdated productions that kept the record from joining the ranks of classic debuts from his borough's now-luminary figures (Run-D.M.C., Rakim, LL Cool J, and Nas). —*Matt Conaway*

Naughty By Nature

f. 1986, East Orange, NJ
Group / Golden Age, East Coast Rap, Hardcore Rap, Pop-Rap
Naughty By Nature pulled off the neat trick of landing big, instantly catchy anthems on the pop charts while maintaining their street-level credibility among the hardcore rap faithful; one of the first groups to successfully perform such a balancing act. The group was formed in East Orange, NJ, in

1986, while all three members—MCs Treach (born Anthony Criss) and Vinnie (born Vincent Brown), and DJ Kay Gee (born Keir Gist)—were attending the same high school. Initially called New Style, they began performing at talent shows and were discovered by Queen Latifah a few years later; she signed the group to her management company and helped them land a deal with Tommy Boy Records. Naughty By Nature's self-titled debut was released in 1991 and produced an inescapable Top Ten hit in "O.P.P." (which supposedly stood for "other people's property," though a close listen to the lyrics revealed that the second P represented male or female genitals). "O.P.P." made Naughty By Nature crossover stars, yet their ghetto sensibility and gritty street funk (not to mention Treach's nimble rhyming technique) made them popular in the hip-hop underground as well. Treach began a secondary acting career in 1992, appearing in *Juice*; he would go on to supporting roles in *The Meteor Man*, *Who's the Man?*, and *Jason's Lyric*, among others.

Naughty By Nature repeated their success with the 1993 follow-up album, *19 Naughty III*, which produced another ubiquitous crossover smash in the "hey! ho!" chant of "Hip Hop Hooray"; the album hit the Top Five and, like its predecessor, went platinum. 1995's *Poverty's Paradise* was the group's final album for Tommy Boy; though it didn't spawn any major hits, it went on to win a Grammy for Best Rap Album. A recording hiatus of several years followed; during that time, Treach pursued his acting career, most notably landing a recurring role on the HBO prison drama *Oz*; and Kay Gee greatly expanded his outside production work, helming records for Zhané, Aaliyah, Krayzie Bone, and Next, among others. Even outside of music, the group made headlines; in 1997, both Treach and Vinnie were arrested in Harlem for illegal weapons possession, and, in 1999, Treach married Pepa, of Salt-N-Pepa (a union that would dissolve two years later). Also in 1999, Naughty By Nature finally returned with a new album on Arista, titled *19 Naughty Nine: Nature's Fury*. "Jamboree," featuring Zhané, was a sizable hit, but though the group looked to be back on track, Kay Gee departed to concentrate full time on his production career. Treach and Vinnie struck a deal with TVT, and the first Naughty By Nature album as a duo, *IIcons*, was released in early 2002. —*Steve Huey*

Naughty By Nature / Sep. 3, 1991 / Tommy Boy ✦✦✦✦✦

There was not a bigger, more contagious crossover radio smash in the autumn of 1991 than Naughty By Nature's "O.P.P.," a song that somehow managed the trick of being both audaciously catchy and subversively coy at the same time. Its irrepressible appeal—the Jackson 5 sample, the saucy subject matter, the huge anthemic chorus, Treach's phat rat-a-tat flow—was so widespread, in fact, that it played just as well to the hardcore heads in the 'hood as it did to the hip-hop dabblers in the suburbs. The beauty of the trio's self-titled full-length debut is that it is every bit as musically accomplished, and every bit as ghetto-fabulous, in its entirety as that watershed first single. *Naughty By Nature* is both a pop and a rap classic that chews up stylistic real estate by the block, easily shifting from an old school rhyme-off between Treach and Vinnie ("Pin the Tail on the Donkey"), the unflappable "Louie Louie" Vega-produced posse cut "1, 2, 3" (with verses from Flavor Unit compadres Lakim Shabazz and Apache), and the teeth-clinching combative dirge "Guard Your Grill," all of which very much come out swinging from the streets, to the more measured, emotionally developed "Ghetto Bastard," which brings an upbeat but nail-tough point of view to a grim tale of parental and societal deprivation without ever asking for an ounce of sympathy. With the assistance of Queen Latifah's makeshift patois, the trio even brought something of the Caribbean to East Orange with "Wickedest Man Alive." All the tracks are as street as they are club astute, trimming the funk loops with live keyboards and saxophone and sanguine, soulful melodies. This is a must-have album for fans of East Coast rap. —*Stanton Swihart*

19 Naughty III / Feb. 23, 1993 / Tommy Boy ✦✦✦✦

Despite an excellent debut album, Naughty By Nature was pegged as a one-hit wonder by some observers—after all, they'd never duplicate the inescapably catchy "O.P.P.," would they? *19 Naughty III*'s lead single, "Hip Hop Hooray," proved that they could, and the album confirmed that Naughty By Nature were indeed highly underrated in terms of consistency. It's a shade less consistent than the debut but has all the same strengths: head-nodding beats, Treach's bouncy flow, and a difficult balance between street attitude and accessibility. Naughty By Nature clearly comes from the streets, and have all the aggression of the streets, but they don't glamorize the streets; sure, they'll take care of themselves in a harsh environment, but ultimately they prefer to steer

clear of trouble, cops, and jail. It's a refreshingly grounded and realistic perspective, best heard on "Daddy Was a Street Corner," "The Hood Comes First," and "The Only Ones." There are also energized guest appearances from Heavy D ("Ready for Dem") and Queen Latifah ("Sleeping on Jersey"). Kay Gee again shows himself a sorely underappreciated producer, with one foot in the clubs and the other one on the street corner, and that's true of the group as a whole. A few slower moments don't prevent *19 Naughty III* from ranking as Naughty By Nature's second straight triumph. —*Steve Huey*

Poverty's Paradise / May 2, 1995 / Tommy Boy ✦✦✦

For their third album, Naughty By Nature do little to truly change their style. Some of the beats are little slower and funkier, some of the rhymes are more dexterous, some of the rhythms are a little more complex—yet nothing distinguishes *Poverty's Paradise* from the group's two previous, and superior, records. —*Stephen Thomas Erlewine*

● Nature's Finest: Naughty By Nature's Greatest Hits / Mar. 9, 1999 / Tommy Boy ✦✦✦✦✦

Right from the get-go, Naughty By Nature's greatest-hits compilation reminds people that before there was the invasion of P. Diddy and the bling-blingers, there was a group who perfectly balanced the strength of street knowledge with accessible pop tunes that even had suburban mothers espousing the virtues of "O.P.P." *Nature's Finest: Naughty By Nature's Greatest Hits* is an amazing balance of their anthems and lesser-known tunes that had longevity in the clubs. But what set Naughty by Nature apart from many of their peers was their unwillingness to sacrifice the sound they developed over the years for commercial success, and some of their most brilliant efforts failed to reach the pop charts. Which isn't necessarily a bad thing either, as it lets fans rediscover classics and orient themselves to songs they might have overlooked. An essential piece of hip-hop history, this album is a treasure trove of greatest hits by one of the most consistently wonderful rap groups of the early '90s. —*Rob Theakston*

19 Naughty Nine: Nature's Fury / Apr. 27, 1999 / Arista ✦✦✦

Longevity is a rare for hip-hop artists, since audiences place a priority on new sounds. It's difficult for veteran acts to continue to cultivate new sounds, and many have fallen by the wayside as they've tried to keep up with the times—but not Naughty By Nature. They've never really changed their core sound, which is an alluring fusion of hardcore sentiments, pop hooks, and funky rhythms. But by not changing, they've managed to retain an audience, since they're reliable—each Naughty By Nature record sounds essentially the same, but it's a satisfying sound that balances catchy hooks and clever, literate rhymes. Few artists are ever able to establish a track record like that, and it's amazing that *19 Naughty Nine: Nature's Fury*—the group's fourth album and first for Arista Records—maintains the high quality. True, some listeners may wish NBN tried out different sounds and styles, but for the most part, the album delivers what any fan of the group could want: several killer party jams, a couple of slow numbers, and a handful of amiable filler. Nothing stands out as an outright classic in the vein of "O.P.P." or "Hip Hop Hooray," but there's genuine grit to the rhythms and rhymes, and the music remains accessible and catchy—in short, the best of *Nature's Fury* proves that it's possible to be melodic and hardcore at the same time, to have both hooks and substance. It might not break new ground, but the album proves that Vinnie and Treach have developed their own signature sound and have found ways to keep it fresh and exciting nearly a decade into their career. —*Stephen Thomas Erlewine*

IIcons / Mar. 5, 2002 / TVT ✦✦✦✦

Hip-hop does not look kindly on its veteran artists apart from anything other than lip service—names are dropped all the time, but it's hard to sustain a career into a second decade for many rappers. Naughty By Nature acknowledge that situation with a wink on their fifth album, titling it *IIcons* and offering a definition of the word on the cover, thereby setting themselves up as icons, as titans of their genre. Which, in many ways, they are, as this rock-solid record proves. They might never have been innovators on the level of Public Enemy or Ice Cube, but they were always strong, forceful MCs and good songwriters who made strong records. *IIcons* is firmly within that tradition. There are a few things that make it feel modern—some guest MC appearance, a production that is on the whole kind of spare, a stellar duet with Pink—but the overall aesthetic is from the early '90s, when the group was at their popular peak. This doesn't mean it sounds outdated; it means that the group still crafts dynamic, varied albums, where the singles aren't the only songs that are memorable. Sure, it's a bit traditionalist, but in the best possible sense—it keeps what's best about the form, giving the album a strong foundation, and builds on it, resulting a record that feels fresh and classic and thereby proving that it is possible to sustain a career in hip-hop without a loss of musical quality. Maybe these guys deserve to be called icons after all. —*Stephen Thomas Erlewine*

Necro

Vocals, Producer / Hardcore Rap

Brooklyn-based hardcore rapper Necro raised the bar for perversity in the late '90s and early 2000s with his music and films. Influenced by drugs, gore, pornography, and violence, Necro set out to incorporate these themes into his rapping. He effectively did so on his full-length debut, *I Need Drugs* (2000). The album featured drug songs (the title track, which is an interpolation of LL Cool J's "I Need Love"), gore songs ("Your Fucking Head Split"), porn songs ("Get on Your Knees"), and violent songs ("The Most Sadistic"). Moreover, Necro directed a video for "I Need Drugs" that featured people shooting up heroin and smoking crack while he rapped, and he also included lots of bizarre photos in the album's booklet.

Necro began his own label, Psycho+Logical Records, and created a website, www.necrohiphop.com, to market his music and movies. Following his debut album, Necro released a series of albums compiling random recordings of his from the '90s (mostly radio-aired freestyle performances and home demos) and followed up *I Need Drugs* with *Gory Days* (2001), a similarly exploitative effort. His films—*187 Reasons Y* (1997), *The Devil Made Me Do It* (1998)—are just as perverse, if not more, modeled after old school gore films as well as snuff and porn. Unsurprisingly, Necro aligned himself with various pornographers and began marketing their goods on his website as well, extending his brand name as far as he could. —*Jason Birchmeier*

I Need Drugs / Nov. 7, 2000 / Psycho+Logical ♦♦
By his own admission, Necro's music is sickening. The rapper tries to out-Eminem Eminem by unleashing a tirade of songs that are a putrid wash of music, drugs, sex, and bodily fluids. For a project filled with so much bile, the production is remarkably bland. A couple of tracks on *I Need Drugs*, namely "Get on Your Knees" and "I'm Sick of You," have some musical punch, but Necro's homemade production is mostly an afterthought. *I Need Drugs* seems to have no other point than to try and offend its listener. While he tries to be part LL Cool J and part GG Allin, he comes off as a 12-year-old trying to get the attention of the kids on the playground by telling dirty jokes. Ultimately, the album's unwavering desire to shock us is what makes it so boring. —*Jon Azpiri*

Gory Days / 2001 / Psycho+Logical ♦♦
Ultra-hardcore rapper Necro delivers his second ridiculously perverse album in a row, *Gory Days*. The album succeeds *I Need Drugs*, probably the most exploitative album the rap music industry had ever produced. The mothers of America would cry if they ever found their children listening to such an album. The lyrics are one thing, but the full-color booklet of crazy photos— filled with drugs, guns, violence, and women—makes the album more than just music. Like *I Need Drugs*, *Gory Days* goes beyond just music, again featuring a shocking booklet filled with crazy photos. Musically, the album isn't nearly as memorable as the photos. Though it's an easy comparison—perhaps even an obvious one—you can't help thinking it: Necro sounds exactly like Eminem. Or better yet, Necro sounds exactly like a more perverse Eminem— more perverse than Eminem would ever allow himself to be. Of course, the initial shock of hearing Necro wears thin quickly, leaving you to confront the facts, namely, that Necro isn't an impressive rapper. He may be perverse, but he's also lacking wit and has little to offer. Sadly, Necro offers, at best, a feeling of horror with *Gory Days*. And while that feeling may initially be pleasureful, it's a guilty pleasure that flees quickly. —*Jason Birchmeier*

Nefertiti

f. 1973, Chicago, IL
Political Rap, Hardcore Rap

Nefertiti's lone solo album, 1993's *L.I.F.E: Living in Fear of Extinction*, fared better critically than commercially. Despite production from Guru and DJ Pooh, along with guest spots from King Tee, DJ Premier, and MC Lyte, it failed to gather steam. The rapper's Islamic beliefs were instilled through her parents, who were both employed by Nation of Islam founder Elijah

Muhammad. Born in Chicago and transplanted to Los Angeles, Nefertiti was also a political activist, assisting Jim Brown's Amer-I-Can program and lecturing frequently within her community. —*Andy Kellman*

● **L.I.F.E.: Living in Fear of Extinction** / Oct. 19, 1993 / Mercury ♦♦♦
Nefertiti was a product of the Los Angeles rap scene of the early '90s, but *L.I.F.E.: Living in Fear of Extinction* didn't fit any of the convenient stereotypes of L.A. rappers who emerged during that period. Nefertiti was far from a gangsta rapper, and she stayed away from commercial pop-rap. Sounding like a cross between Queen Latifah and MC Lyte, Nefertiti showed some promise on this decent and often inspired, if a bit uneven, CD. The rapper's tough, hard-edged delivery suggests Lyte, but the positive-sister vibe she brings to sociopolitical rhymes like "I Don't Drink the Water," "Family Tree," and "Mecca to Watts" brings to mind Latifah. One of the best things on the album is "Trouble in Paradise," a poignant ode to the late MC Trouble. (You could say that Trouble's story is one of the most heartbreaking in the history of the rap—signed to Motown, the female rapper seemed to have a promising career ahead of her when an epileptic seizure claimed her life in 1990.) This album received generally favorable reviews from the hip-hop press, although commercial success would elude the underexposed Nefertiti. —*Alex Henderson*

Nelly (Cornell Haynes Jr.)

b. Austin, TX
Southern Rap, Pop-Rap

When Nelly first debuted nationally in summer 2000, he seemed like a novelty, but it quickly became apparent that he was, in fact, an exceptional artist, a rapper with truly universal appeal. He wasn't from the East or West Coast, and wasn't really from the dirty South, either. Rather, Nelly was from St. Louis, a Midwestern city halfway between Minneapolis and New Orleans. His locale certainly informed his rapping style, which was as much country as urban, and his dialect as well, which was, similarly, as much Southern drawl as Midwestern twang. Plus, Nelly never shied away from a pop-rap approach, embracing a singalong vocal style that made his hooks incredibly catchy. As a result, Nelly became an exceptional rapper capable of crossing all boundaries, from the dirty South to the *TRL* crowd and everything in between. His first hit, "Country Grammar (Hot ...)," became a summer anthem, and many more hits followed. In particular, his popularity peaked in summer 2002, when he topped seemingly every *Billboard* chart possible with his *Nellyville* album and its lead single, "Hot in Herre."

Nelly was born Cornell Haynes Jr. in Austin, TX, but moved frequently in his early years before ending up in St. Louis, MO, where he encountered the street temptations so synonymous with rap artists. And like so many of his contemporaries, a change in circumstance at a pivotal time in his life may have changed the course of Nelly's life. In his case, when he was a teenager, Nelly was taken away from those streets when his mother moved to nearby suburban University City. It was there that he shifted his attention to playing baseball, storytelling, and writing rhymes. With some high school friends, Nelly formed the St. Lunatics, who scored a regional hit in 1996 with a self-produced single, "Gimmie What You Got." Frustrated with failed attempts to land a record deal as a group, they collectively decided that Nelly would have a better chance as a single act, confident that his stage presence and rhyming skills would win through. The rest of the group could follow with solo albums of their own.

The gamble paid off, and soon Nelly caught the attention of Universal, who released his debut album, *Country Grammar*, in 2000. What distinguished Nelly's take on rap from others was his laid-back delivery, deliberately reflecting the distinctive language and Southern tone of the Midwest. The album featured contributions from the St. Lunatics as well the Teamsters, Lil' Wayne, and Cedric the Entertainer, and spent seven weeks on top of the U.S. album charts. All along, Nelly's goal was to put his hometown of St. Louis and the St. Lunatics on the hip-hop map. Though Nelly had become a star as a solo artist as planned, he said that he is and always will be a member of the St. Lunatics, a collective that also includes Big Lee, Kyjuan, Murphy Lee, and City Spud. Nelly fulfilled his promise in 2001 with the release of *Free City*, the debut St. Lunatics album featuring the hit single "Midwest Swing."

The following summer Nelly returned with his second album, *Nellyville*, and lived up to his self-proclaimed "number one" billing. The album topped the *Billboard* album chart while the Neptunes-produced lead single, "Hot in Herre," remained atop the singles chart. In all, Nelly impressively held the number one spot on ten different *Billboard* charts the week of *Nellyville's* release. Few Rap artists could boast such numbers, and Nelly surely savored his number-one status, particularly after being dismissed as a novelty two summers earlier when he debuted. You could call him a pop-rapper if you liked, but you surely couldn't challenge his number-one status. —*Jason Birchmeier and Ed Nimmervoll*

● **Country Grammar** / Jun. 6, 2000 / Universal ✦✦✦
With little precedent, Nelly emerged from St. Louis with *Country Grammar's* incredibly catchy title track as his lead single and had legions of listeners singing along within weeks. In particular, the song's tongue-twisting chorus is downright infectious: "I'm goin down down baby, yo' street in a Range Rover/Street sweeper baby, cocked ready to let it go/Shimmy shimmy cocoa what? listen to it pound/Light it up and take a puff, pass it to me now"—or something like that. There are, of course, many more singalong moments like this on *Country Grammar*, such as "Ride Wit Me" and "E.I.," that similarly stick with you despite being so tongue-twisting and puzzling. More than anything, Nelly's knack for writing, and singing, such infectious hooks makes *Country Grammar* such an exceptional album for its time. You get all the dirty South motifs here, both lyrical and musical; however, you also get lots of polished singalong hooks that seem more prevalent in pop music than rap. But this is precisely why *Country Grammar* is so successful despite being admittedly derived and spotty, not to mention lacking consistently engaging production. Nelly would thankfully iron out these weaknesses on his follow-up, *Nellyville* (2002), yet even if he seems like a wannabe thug here at times, such as on "Greed, Hate, Envy," this posturing doesn't spoil anything. *Country Grammar* made a huge splash in summer 2000, and did so for a reason. It's an exceptional album, one that breaks all the rap industry's unwritten rules. Who would have anticipated, after all, that a Midwestern rapper who sang somewhat nonsensical hooks would make such a huge splash? Not many, for sure. —*Jason Birchmeier*

Nellyville / Jul. 25, 2002 / Universal ✦✦✦
When it came time for Nelly to follow up his enormously popular debut album, the pop-rapper faced a particular challenge: how to do so without alienating his millions of fans. It wasn't so much about bringing in *more* fans; he already had a gigantic, widespread fan base that stretched coast to coast. It was more about giving all those millions of listeners more of what they liked about his debut, *Country Grammar* (2000), namely, bouncy rap songs with catchy singalong hooks. What made doing so difficult was the simple fact that *Country Grammar* had been a unique album, somewhat of an anomaly. The album didn't feature sure-fire producers like Timbaland, but rather Jason "Jay E" Epperson, a relatively unknown producer at the time who produced practically the entirety of *Country Grammar*. Plus, there was Nelly himself, a talented pop-rapper who tried to cast himself as a street-smart thug. So, when it came time for this follow-up album, Nelly had to make the calls: stick with Epperson or go with big-money producers and, also, stick with his thuggish posturing or accept his teen pop-esque status? Well, for the most part, he decided to stick with Epperson's bouncy beats (though he did bring in the Neptunes for "Hot in Herre") and he also decided to stick with his tough-guy front (though he does bring in Justin Timberlake for "Work It"). In other words, he didn't take any unnecessary risks—after all, the formula proved successful the first time around—and that's partly why *Nellyville* isn't as exciting as it perhaps could be. When Nelly joins the Roc-A-Fella clique and producer Just Blaze on the "Rock the Mic" remix placed late on the album, you see what could have been. Yet there's no reason to bicker because *Nellyville* is on a par with, if not a notch above, *Country Grammar*. In fact, it's essentially interchangeable, which means it should satisfy millions of listeners, if not impress them. —*Jason Birchmeier*

Nemesis
. . . .
f. Dallas, TX

Group / Bass Music, Southern Rap, Party Rap
An anomaly in its time, Nemesis stood out in the late '80s/early '90s as a Texas-based rap group with big-label connections during a time when nearly all rap came from either Los Angeles or New York. Featuring Big Al, the Snake, and MC Azimv, Nemesis didn't have much commercial success and weren't incredibly influential, but they do function as an omen of what was to come. The group synthesized a number of different rap styles from the era: New York MCing, Miami bass beats, and West Coast gangsta attitude. More

than any of these attributes, it was their beats that garnered the most attention, perhaps illustrated best by the group's bass-orientated album titles. The group debuted on Profile Records in 1989 with *To Hell and Back*, followed by *Munchies for Your Bass* in 1991. Generally viewed as the group's crowning achievement, *Munchies for Your Bass* found Nemesis discarding some of the New York school of MCing influence that had been so prevalent in favor of more Southern-style party rap. However, with successive albums, Nemesis' party-orientated lyrics became increasingly commonplace and clichéd, and the group fell into obscurity. Curiously, the group staged a comeback in late 2000 with *Munchies for Your Bass, Da Return*, an indie release with a No Limit-style album cover. Few noticed, however, confirming the fact that Nemesis' moment in the spotlight had come and gone with little notice and even less of a resulting legacy. —*Jason Birchmeier*

To Hell and Back / 1989 / Profile ✦✦✦
In 1979 and 1980, Dallas was the last place anyone expected to find a rap group; back then, the vast majority of MCs lived in and around New York. But when Nemesis' first album, *To Hell and Back*, came out in 1989, things were a lot different. An abundance of platinum-selling rappers were coming from the West Coast and the South, so why shouldn't a Dallas group like Nemesis do their thing? *To Hell and Back* makes no attempt to hide the MCs' Texas background—from quite open about the fact that they are representing Dallas (the city that gave listeners the D.O.C.). One hears a combination of influences on this CD. Big Al, the Snake, and MC Azim have been influenced by New York groups like Run-D.M.C. and the Fat Boys, but their sound also owes something to the West Coast and the bass artists who were coming out of Florida in the late '80s. However, no one would mistake *To Hell and Back* for a 2 Live Crew album. Some of the beats are bass influenced, but this CD doesn't inundate listeners with the type of X-rated booty rhymes that 2 Live Crew and their fellow Floridians are known for. The members of Nemesis insisted that they were Muslims, and their lyrics are uplifting, if a bit preachy, on conscious tracks like "Greet 'Em With Peace," "Pusherman," and the title track. However, the album also has plenty of fun, escapist material. This CD is uneven; some of the tunes hold up better than others. But more often than not, *To Hell and Back* paints an attractive picture of the Dallas group. —*Alex Henderson*

● **Munchies for Your Bass** / 1991 / Profile ✦✦✦
Nemesis' second album, *Munchies for Your Bass*, was a surprising departure from their 1989 debut, *To Hell and Back*. While that CD was full of conscious lyrics à la Brand Nubian, this sophomore effort is more of a party album—one with plenty of R-rated, sexploitive lyrics. Some hip-hoppers denounced *Munchies for Your Bass* as a sellout, arguing that when the conscious approach didn't result in multiplatinum sales for Nemesis, the Dallas group decided to take the easy way out and exploit sex. But even if this 1991 release was motivated by a desire to sell more CDs and seems less sincere than *To Hell and Back*, it's still an enjoyable party album. For those who are into R-rated fun, it isn't hard to move to infectious numbers like "Dallas We Come From," "S.O.U.L," and the single "I Want Your Sex" (which boasts a sleek, R&B-ish groove that recalls Steve Arrington's work with Slave in the late '70s and early '80s). A party atmosphere prevails on the urban contemporary-minded offerings, and it also prevails on the rock-influenced "Let's Have a Good Time" (which samples Led Zeppelin's "Whole Lotta Love"). One track that made some hip-hoppers question Nemesis' commitment to the Islamic faith is "Ali English and the 40 Oz. Thieves," a humorous, Beastie Boys-influenced number that celebrates the pleasures of malt liquor. Here's the thing: alcohol consumption is strictly forbidden in most sects of Islam, and in 1991 there were those who saw a major contradiction between Nemesis asserting "all praise due to Allah" only to turn around and encourage inebriation. But for those who can live with the group's contradictions, *Munchies for Your Bass* is arguably their strongest effort. —*Alex Henderson*

Temple of Boom / 1993 / Profile ✦✦✦
Nemesis was never a group that catered to bass purists; its brand of hardcore rap isn't pure bass in the sense that the 2 Live Crew, Afro-Rican, 95 South, and Tag Team are bass. Nonetheless, the Dallas combo was influenced by the bass music that came out of Florida and Georgia, and it tried to cash in on its popularity with album titles like *Munchies for Your Bass*, *Temple of Boom*, and *Tha People Want Bass*. Released in 1993, *Temple of Boom* was Nemesis' third album, and reunited the group with the Too Short-influenced Ron C.

This CD is quite similar to *Munchies for Your Bass*; like that 1991 release, this is an R-rated party album that is full of sleek R&B-influenced grooves. The conscious raps of Nemesis' first album, *To Hell and Back*, are long gone. Instead, this CD's concerns include sex, women in tight dresses, and malt liquor. Not surprisingly, some of the hip-hoppers who remembered the "all praise due to Allah" outlook that defined parts of *To Hell and Back* felt that Nemesis had sold out by becoming more sexually exploitive and questioned this album's sincerity. Regardless, this isn't without its pleasures. It isn't as consistent as *Munchies for Your Bass*, which is arguably the group's best album, but this CD does have its share of infectious grooves—most notably, "Cloud 7," "The Big, Bad, The Bass," and "Nemesis on the Premises." Although not the best album in the Nemesis catalog, *Temple of Boom* is good for some cheap thrills here and there. —*Alex Henderson*

Tha People Want Bass / 1995 / Profile ♦♦♦

Florida-style bass music never received much respect from hip-hoppers who lived in Northeastern cities like New York, Philadelphia, and Boston. As they saw it, bass was a lowest-common-denominator approach to rap. But all over the South, the Midwest, and the West Coast, bass was huge in the late '80s and '90s. Even though bass might have been a dirty word in the inner-city neighborhoods of North Philly and the Boogie Down Bronx, it was synonymous with commercial success in most parts of the U.S.—which is why Dallas residents Nemesis tried to cash in on bass' popularity with album titles like *Munchies for Your Bass* and *Tha People Want Bass*. For the most part, *Tha People Want Bass* isn't true bass; however, this album's hardcore rap incorporates elements of bass as well as West Coast rap. The CD's most Florida-sounding track is the hyper "Drop tha Bottom," which wouldn't have been out of place on an Afro-Rican album. Although uneven, *Tha People Want Bass* has its assets. The beats are infectious more often than not, and Nemesis' R-rated, sexually exploitive rhymes are entertaining for those who have a taste for off-color lyrics. Not surprisingly, there were those who questioned the group's motives—when MCs start out providing conscious raps à la Brand Nubian only to end up exploiting sex, some people are bound to call them sellouts. Regardless, *Tha People Want Bass* is generally entertaining—unless, of course, listeners find sexploitive lyrics offensive. *Tha People Want Bass* isn't Nemesis' best album—that honor goes to 1991's *Munchies for Your Bass*. But while this CD isn't a masterpiece, it has more strengths than weaknesses. —*Alex Henderson*

The Neptunes

f. Virginia Beach, VA
Group / Hip-Hop, Pop-Rap

The Neptunes quietly emerged from Virginia Beach at the turn of the century and quickly became the hottest producers within the rap industry, then the entire pop music industry. The peerless duo began their ascandance in the late '90s with a few party-themed hits: Ol' Dirty Bastard's "Got My Money" (1999), Mystikal's "Shake Ya Ass" (2000), and Jay-Z's "I Wanna Love U" (2001). The Neptunes crossed over from rap to pop in 2001 and began producing tracks for the likes of Britney Spears ("I'm a Slave 4 U"), *NSync ("Girlfriend"), and Usher ("U Don't Have to Call"). In addition to these pop stars, the duo continued producing hits for the biggest names in rap, working with everyone from LL Cool J ("Luv U Better") and Busta Rhymes ("Pass the Courvoisier") to Bow Wow ("Take Ya Home") and Nelly ("Hot in Herre"). Furthermore, the Neptunes began their own rap group, N.E.R.D., and introduced another one, the Clipse. By this point, the duo—Pharrell Williams and Chad Hugo—had become the pop-rap industry's most demanded producers, on a par with other big-name producers like Dr. Dre and Timbaland, if not perhaps even supplanting them. —*Jason Birchmeier*

N.E.R.D.

Group / Alternative Rap, Hip-Hop, Neo-Soul

One of the most respected production teams in the hip-hop community, Pharrell Williams and Chad Hugo (aka the Neptunes) propelled the talents of a number of artists since 1997, their punctuating beats and syncopated rhythms fueling a unique sonic aesthetic. N.E.R.D., which stands for No One Ever Really Dies, is their side project, and the debut album *In Search Of...* mixed everything from hard hip-hop beats to black psychedelic pop to classic rock to new wave, bringing a beguiling new sound to the pop landscape. —*Paul Clifford*

● **In Search Of . . .** / Mar. 12, 2002 / Virgin ♦♦♦♦

N.E.R.D. is nothing if they're not clever, and they brilliantly constructed a back-story to accompany their debut album, *In Search Of....* As every rock critic in the Western world has said in their review of the album, they originally released the record in Europe, then decided it was crap, withdrew it, re-recorded it with a live band, and then released it worldwide. Now, this story is probably true—as the first album by the band driven by the powerhouse production team the Neptunes (though these are *not* interchangeable terms, as they went to great lengths to make clear in the promo interviews), there was a lot riding on this record, so it had better be right—but it certainly helped them get valuable press, elevating this record to a near-event level. So, is *In Search Of...* worth the hoopla? Well, pretty much. Musically, it's a lively affair, breaking free of the signature Neptunes-approximated Prince beats, as they borrow heavily from classic soul, breakbeat aesthetics, and postmodern alt-culture, tying it together with live beats. It pretty much deliberately does everything that most modern rap does *not* do, and it's hard not to embrace it for that very fact. Alas, there are flaws, mainly in the raps, which are hardly as nimble as the music; actually, they're rather clumsy and embarrassing, especially since they attempt to cover "socially relevant" issues (i.e., politicians are equated with strippers). Choruses that croon, "She needs me/Because I'm the shit" are hard to stomach, no matter how supple the music is (or how ironic the delivery), but if you can ignore that, *In Search Of...* does provide genuine musical thrills. Although, be forewarned—it's easy to overrate this record simply because it deviates from the norm at a time when nobody deviates from the norm or has deviated from the norm in years. With better lyrics and a little less smirking hipsterism, it could have been the record it was intended to be, but as it stands it's still a pretty terrific listen and one of the most adventurous, intriguing hip-hop albums in a long, long time. —*Stephen Thomas Erlewine*

New Breed

f. California
Group / Christian Rap, Latin Rap

New Breed is a brother-sister Christian hip-hop duo out of the Puerto Rican streets of Boston, MA. Co-MCs Macho and Elsie Ortega first appeared as part of the Tunnel Rats, the underground Christian hip-hop collective based in California. Macho and Elsie rapped throughout tracks on that group's breakthrough 2001 release, *Tunnel Vision*, paving the way for their own full-length. *Stop the Music* was issued by Christian hip-hop upstart Uprok in early 2002; it included contributions from the Rats' Raphi as well as CCM underground heavyweights LPG. *Stop the Music* showcased Macho and Elsie's bold rhymes and decidedly Latin flavor. It didn't preach their gospel with so much fervor as to drive away secular audiences; nor did it shy away from a positive message. To that end, New Breed followed a trend in CCM—both in rock and hip-hop—to endorse a Christian lifestyle through music without having to recite "Footprints" for lyrics. This trend was followed by labels like Uprok, Tooth & Nail, and Essential, and included artists such as KJ-52 and Jeremy Camp. —*Johnny Loftus*

● **Stop the Music** / Feb. 12, 2002 / Uprok ♦♦♦

New Breed flaunts their Puerto Rican heritage and streetwise culture on *Stop The Music*, a powerful debut disc of poetry, imagery, and melody. Using sound blasts in the same manner that a rock guitarist would employ power chords, or an R&B band would punctuate a cut with horn arrangements, New Breed tethers rhythms and harmonic motifs with funky bass samples and an in-the-pocket backbeat that echoes reggae and disco. "Verse of the City" and "Stand" profess pride in Macho and Elsie Ortega's ghetto savvy and learning mores while the title track details the political and social climate that affects the underclass, then unexpectedly turns inward toward fellow rappers. "Song Speaks" declares the spiritual importance of rap via jazzy piano riffs, scat singing, and thought-provoking stream of conscious dialogue ("we're pros with prose"). The chant "stop the music" emerges in several instances, but the theme on this collection clearly affirms the opposite. —*Tom Semioli*

New Flesh

f. 1990
Group / Underground Rap, British Rap, Hip-Hop

Around since 1990, New Flesh took ten years to release an LP but quickly became dons of the British rap scene, as original and cutting edge as their much-hyped Big Dada labelmate Roots Manuva. When originally formed (as New Flesh for Old), the group included York native and graffiti sprayer Part 2 (aka Keith Hopewell) along with rappers Toastie Tailor (a native of Grenada), Horny Baker, and Out of Order. They did a few shows during the early '90s, and debuted with a 1995 single ("This Is the Space Age") on their own New Flesh Music. "Mesopotamia" followed a year later, and earned critical praise as well as a spot on DJ Vadim's *Organised Sound* compilation. Now consisting of Part 2 and Toastie Tailor plus newcomer Juice Aleem (a Birmingham native), the act started recording for Britain's Big Dada label with 1997's *Electronic Bombardment* EP. The full-length *Equilibriums* followed in 1999, while a second LP (2002's *Understanding*) displayed their increased standing in the hip-hop community via a series of high-profile collaborations—with Big Dada's own Roots Manuva and Ty, plus Blackalicious' Gift of Gab, Antipop's Beans, and hip-hop pioneer Rammellzee. —*John Bush*

Electronic Bombardment EP / Sep. 30, 1997 / Big Dada ◆◆◆
On their 1997 EP *Electronic Bombardment*, New Flesh for Old show an affinity for quirky, rhythmically complex late-'90s hip-hop. Part 2 especially recalls Dr. Octagon, while Toastie Tailor's choppy, ragga-inflected delivery is somewhat reminiscent of Busta Rhymes. New Flesh's lyrical obsessions are also intriguing, covering science fiction and ancient Egypt, among other topics. —*Steve Huey*

Equilibriums / Sep. 21, 1999 / Big Dada ◆◆◆◆◆
The debut LP for the three-piece British crew New Flesh for Old certainly qualified as foreign rap but, from the sound of it, hardly even sounded like it was created on this world. Tracks featured a nearly hoarse ragga shouter (Toastie Tailor) trading rhymes with a metaphysical dramatist (Juice Aleem) over a barrage of tough tech effects and cellar-level beats that sounded as though lifted from outer space. *Equilibriums* certainly owed few debts, whether to diggin'-in-the-crates hip-hop or digital rap of the Timbaland variety. It had the rough-edged reverb of ragga, effects with the sound of rusty pipes. Of any in the rap world, their style was closest to Company Flow; it had the same cold, alien production sense (harsh in a completely different way than DMX or Eminem), but was remarkably focused, rarely sounding as deliberately difficult as El-P and crew. Toastie Tailor shone on nearly indecipherable yet immensely powerful tracks like "Invisible Ink" and "186000 Miles," while Juice Aleem matched the lyrical and verbal skills of Gift of Gab (from Blackalicious) on his standout, "Adoration of Kings." Meanwhile, Part 2 programmed cold, funky beats and filled in all the gaps with ominous, paranoid samples from a variety of sources. One of the best, most distinctive debuts in the brief history of British rap. —*John Bush*

● **Understanding** / Feb. 5, 2002 / Big Dada ◆◆◆◆◆
New Flesh's futuristic second full-length features an all-star cast of underground MCs, including Roots Manuva, Ty, Beans (Antipop Consortium), and Gift of Gab (Blackalicious) backing up über producer Part 2 (aka Keith Hopewell) and lyricists Toastie Tailor and Juice Aleem. Well representing the freshness emerging from the often-underpraised U.K. hip-hop scene, the ever-progressive Big Dada label once again backs up its reputation as a supporter of innovators and leads the British invasion of the hip-hop movement back over the Atlantic with cosmopolitan renovations made. With an anything-goes attitude toward musical styles employed, *Understanding* uses drum'n'bass, hip-hop, dancehall, U.K. garage, soul, and R&B to create a mainstream-sounding experimental record, a paradoxical musical conquest comparable to the plight of Outkast over the last few outings. Part 2's production here is worth the price of admission alone, a job-performance record that led to remix work for Saul Williams and Roots Manuva. —*Nic Kincaid*

New Kingdom

f. 1987, New York, NY
Group / Alternative Pop/Rock, Funk Metal, Rap-Metal
Nosaj and Sebastian formed New Kingdom after meeting at a New York City clothing store where they both worked. Though both are fans of hip-hop, Sebastian spent some time in hardcore punk bands, while Nosaj was primarily influenced by Curtis Mayfield. They started recording '70s-influenced rap in 1987 but couldn't afford to continue making records. Later, however, engineer Scott Harding heard some demos and introduced the duo to Gee Street Records. After two years on a demo deal, they were officially signed in 1992. *Heavy Load* appeared one year later, while *Paradise Don't Come Cheap* surfaced in 1996. —*John Bush*

Heavy Load / 1993 / Gee Street ◆◆◆
One of the dozens of hip-hop groups signed in the early-'90s alternative rap feeding frenzy, this little-known duo is probably most notable for its seminal work with producer Scott Harding (aka Scotty Hard), who went on to work with artists like the Gravediggaz and Prince Paul. The first two tracks start their debut album off rather clumsily, with an in-your-face Beastie Boys-meets-Onyx vibe that falls a little flat. But by the time "Frontman" rolls around, with its relaxed Cypress Hill-influenced stoner vibe, they seem to have settled into a more comfortable groove. Songs like "Mad Mad World" and "Mighty Maverick" work especially well, with Sebastien's trippy spoken-word poetry matching the psychedelic musical backgrounds to create the drugged-out feel the band seems to strive for. And the freaky, funky effects of "Are You Alive" and the extremely goofy "Calico Cats" are so damn effective, you wonder why they bothered with the grating shtick of some of the earlier songs in the first place. Ultimately, *Heavy Load* shows an awful lot of promise, but all too often New Kingdom fails to deliver. —*Bret Love*

● **Paradise Don't Come Cheap** / Aug. 7, 1996 / Gee Street ◆◆◆◆
New Kingdom's second album of twisted, slow, and dirty queasy-psychedelia funk-blues hip-hop arguably beats out the fine debut *Heavy Load*—there's something even more belligerent, raunchy, and fiery about Furlow and Laws this time out. In light of later years where any number of acts wore their swampy roots heritage with pride, *Paradise Don't Come Cheap* seems even more prescient, at points suggesting a Goodie Mob/Bubba Sparxx collaboration produced by the RZA—or, say, Eminem's "Square Dance" completely gone to hell—well before its time. Indeed, with a song title like "Kickin' Like Bruce Lee" as a perhaps fortuitous sign, the Wu-Tang Clan probably could be the only easy comparison to New Kingdom at this point, the duo exhibiting the same confrontational attitude and attack on the verses as the larger collective. There's a less immediately desperate sound, though—the delivery throughout, as songs like the low-speed brawl of "Terror Mad Visionary" and the absolutely mind-blowing "Co Pilot" and "Suspended in Air" easily show, flows with the beat rather than fights against it. Still, the generous echo on top of the rough-voiced sass of the two often turns particularly claustrophobic and oppressive, especially on the brief singing turns here and there—the result is often disturbingly threatening, a slow-motion nightmare. The Lumberjacks' production, with the sharp help of folks like Scott Harding on guitar and, on a couple of cuts, the assistance of John Medeski from Medeski, Martin & Wood (his amazing organ performance on "Unicorns Were Horses" is a clear standout), makes for a clattering, woozy flow that more than once suggests what a Tom Waits—or a Foetus!—hip-hop album might sound like. Consider the haunted, off-kilter cabaret blues and breaks of "Infested" or the muted but snarling brass section on the title track—or even the brief "Half Asleep," which touches on everything from James Brown to Arabic music in under a minute. —*Ned Raggett*

Newcleus

f. 1979, Brooklyn, NY
Group / Electro, Old School Rap
Although they recorded only two albums, Newcleus contributed one true electro classic in "Jam on Revenge (The Wikki-Wikki Song)," which has been immortalized on hundreds of hip-hop mix tapes and often included in even techno DJs' sets. The origins of Newcleus lay in a 1977 Brooklyn DJ collective known as Jam-On Productions, including Ben "Cozmo D" Cenac, his cousin Monique Angevin, and her brother Pete (all teenagers and still in high school). Many members—MCs as well as DJs—came and went as the group played block parties all over the borough, and by 1979, the group centered around Cenac; his future wife, Yvette "Lady E" Cook; Monique Angevin; and *her* future husband, Bob "Chilly B" Crafton. (The foursome named their group Newcleus as a result of the coming together of their families.)

By this time, Cenac had begun to accumulate a collection of electronic recording equipment, and the quartet recorded a demo tape of material. With several minutes left at the end of the tape, Newcleus recorded a favorite from their block parties, with each member's vocals sped up to resemble the Chipmunks. The track, "Jam-On's Revenge," impressed producer Joe Webb more than the other Newcleus material, and it became the group's first single, released in 1983 on Mayhew Records. A huge street success, the track became known unofficially as "the Wikki-Wikki song" (after the refrain); when it was re-released later that year on Sunnyview Records, it had become "Jam on Revenge (The Wikki-Wikki Song)."

The single hit Top 40 on the R&B charts in 1983, and its follow-up, "Jam on It," did well on even the pop charts. "Computer Age (Push the Button)" was a more mature single, with accomplished rapping and better synthesizer effects, and it also hit the R&B Top 40. The first Newcleus LP, *Jam on Revenge*, was a bit of a disappointment, and their second album, *Space Is the Place*, did even more poorly upon release in 1985. Without a single as noteworthy as "Jam on Revenge" or "Computer Age," and with the advent of Run-D.M.C.'s organic, rock-influenced approach to rap music, Newcleus faded quickly. Though the Cenacs and the Craftons continued to record sporadically until 1989, they didn't hit the R&B charts after 1986. —*John Bush*

Jam on Revenge / 1984 / Sunnyview ✦✦✦

Space Is the Place / 1985 / Sunnyview ✦✦✦

● **Jam on This!: The Best of Newcleus** / Jul. 22, 1997 / Rhino ✦✦✦
Newcleus deserve mention in any history of electro/hip-hop of the early '80s because of two certifiable classics: "Jam on Revenge (The Wikki-Wikki Song)" and "Computer Age (Push the Button)." Two tracks hardly fill a major compilation album, and at first glance, the group wouldn't appear to deserve their own best-of set; however, the compilers at Rhino did a good job of selecting tracks from the group's two albums, 1984's *Jam on Revenge* and the following year's *Space Is the Place* (a reference to jazz mystic Sun Ra). Other than the obvious hits, great album tracks include "Auto-Man," "I Wanna Be a B-Boy," and "Let's Jam." —*John Bush*

Nice & Smooth

f. New York, NY
Group / Golden Age, Hip-Hop, Pop-Rap
New York City rap duo Gregg Nice (born Gregg Mays) and Smooth Bee (born Daryl Barnes) had an underrated 1991 debut release *Ain't a Damn Thing Changed.* It included the biting, nicely written, and bitterly performed "Sometimes I Rhyme Slow," which was a sizable hit in the R&B and hip-hop circuit. —*Ron Wynn*

Nice & Smooth / 1989 / Sleeping Bag ✦✦✦

● **Ain't a Damn Thing Changed** / Sep. 3, 1991 / Ral ✦✦✦✦✦
Nice & Smooth returned for a second album that injected a much-needed and entirely welcome sense of the absurd into the generally far too austere and sincere New York City underground hip-hop community, which has traditionally sacrificed humor for hardcore technique when it comes to rhyming. Greg Nice and Smooth Bee, however, are often downright silly and goofball on *Ain't a Damn Thing Changed.* Despite the conscientious-sounding title, there is very little on the album that is concerned with anything other than, first, rocking the microphone, and second, timing the punch line perfectly. There are certainly serious themes tossed out from time to time. The major hit "Sometimes I Rhyme Slow"—which is simply the track of Tracy Chapman's sober, solemn "Fast Car" matched with the duo's superimposed rhyming—makes references to guns, violence, and drug abuse, and several of the other songs contain similar allusions. But far more frequently, the album is characterized by a reckless old school (think Audio Two) sense of fun, with loony, stream-of-consciousness lyrics that are most interested in dropping the other shoe, shouted singalong choruses ("Sex, Sex, Sex," "Paranoia"), insanely catchy vocal hooks ("Sometimes," "One, Two and One More Makes Three"), and production filled with bouncy beats and cartoonish, electronic keyboards. The ubiquitous presence of fully harmonized (and occasionally out-of-tune) background vocals is another characteristic that gives the album a jarringly whimsical quality that most rap crews at the time would never have come within earshot of. A Partridge Family sample even plays a substantial role in "Hip Hop Junkies," and the theme song to *Sanford & Son* is the basic track of "Step by Step." Perhaps their sense of humor, to a certain extent, obscures the straight-up rhyming skills that the duo possesses. Greg Nice's abrupt, roughneck dramatics juxtaposed against Smooth Bee's serene, butter-slick delivery strikes the perfect vocal balance, and the posse cut, "Down the Line," which includes Gang Starr's Guru (perhaps the preeminent underground rapper), proves that they can bring it rugged and raw when they so decide. But because the duo is willing to poke fun at themselves and their craft so unsparingly, the album is completely addictive, in the same way that sugar is, because it is an energy boost and instantly brings into relief an entirely different side of rap: one that doesn't take itself so seriously. —*Stanton Swihart*

Jewel of the Nile / Jun. 28, 1994 / Ral ✦✦✦
Years before Puff Daddy found multiplatinum success sampling David Bowie and the Police, Nice & Smooth were perfecting their own unique style of guilty pleasure hip-pop, scoring big hits with the infectious singles "Hip Hop Junkies" and "Sometimes I Rhyme Slow," which sampled the Partridge Family and Tracy Chapman, respectively. The underrated duo's knack for irresistible pop hooks continues on their forth album, beginning with "Return of the Hip Hop Freaks," a jazzy leadoff track so insistently, irritatingly catchy—its chorus is the kind that sticks in your head for weeks at a time—that it makes "Hip Hop Junkies" sound like a tuneless dirge. A mere 11 songs long, including a CD-only remix of "No Bones," *Jewel of the Nile* is an unfairly ignored treasure of nineties hip-pop at its most ingratiatingly mainstream, a nearly perfect little album that proves that hip-pop needn't be a pejorative label. Never the world's greatest lyricists, Greg Nice and Smooth Bee instead excelled at left-field but enormously effective samples (*Jewel of the Nile*'s "Do Watcha Gotta" skillfully jacks the snake-charmer groove from Jefferson Airplane's "White Rabbit"), undeniable chemistry and remarkable pop savvy. Whether mixing it up with a pre-*Whitey Ford* Everlast over crunchy rock & roll guitars on "Save the Children" or holding their own alongside hip-hop royalty Slick Rick, Nice & Smooth are at their infectious, upbeat best throughout *Jewel of the Nile*, one of the most underrated and unfairly overlooked hip-hop albums of the '90s. —*Nathan Rabin*

Blazing Hot, Vol. 4 / Oct. 28, 1997 / Scotti Bros. ✦✦✦✦
Rappers Nice & Smooth have made a career out of making a little go a very long way. Never the world's best rappers, the duo more than made up for what they lacked in lyrical skill with their strong ear for hooks and melodies, winning chemistry and infectious enthusiasm. But by the time the time they got around to releasing their forth album, 1997's *Blazing Hot, Vol. 4*, their winning formula was starting to fade. *Blazing Hot* at least gets off to a strong start, with the title track nicely illustrating their still-potent knack for catchy choruses, and the second track, "Boogie Down Bronx/BK Connection" engagingly matching the singsongy flows of Nice and Smooth Bee with the butter-smooth production of superproducer Easy Mo Bee. But while the marriage of R&B and hip-hop works well early on, it falters soon after, undone by wildly uneven production and forgettable rhymes. And without memorable production and ridiculously catchy choruses, the remedial lyrics of Smooth Bee and Greg Nice are pushed to the forefront, a fatal error for a duo that's always succeeded in spite of their lyrics, not because of them. With only nine new songs, padded with two worthless intros and a listless live version of "Dwyck" minus Gang Starr, of course, *Blazing Hot* is both too short and too uneven to make much of an impression, resulting in an album that's easily the lyrically challenged duo's weakest to date. —*Nathan Rabin*

Rich Nice

Producer, Vocals / Golden Age, Hip-Hop
A producer and multi-instrumentalist, Rich Nice has worked on records by LL Cool J, KRS-One, Ice Cube, Nas, Foxy Brown, and Mary J. Blige. Long before he became a force in the studio as a behind-the-scenes player, he was signed to Motown as a solo artist. *Information to Raise a Nation*, his first and only full-length album, was released to little notice in 1990. —*Andy Kellman*

● **Information to Raise a Nation** / 1990 / Motown ✦✦✦
Rich Nice is a rapper with something of the awareness of a good beat poet, as well as the simplicity and directness of a street rhymer. He has also allowed himself to be encased in a solid production that sticks to original things, rather than swiping samples from every direction—here, the sampling is confined to sound bites, usually to snappy, intelligent, effect. While sometimes a little too fond of his own name on the inevitable brag numbers (Nice seems uncomfortable with these), Nice seems aware of what he's doing to a greater extent than most rappers. The messages here are delivered with a clear-eyed and intelligent directness over fresh, clear, beats. Yes, the man falls down once in a while—"Outstanding" is yet another dull rap ballad, while the sexual braggadocio of "So What You Gotta Man" falls flat even in spite of the perky beats. But there are elements of many things tied up in here—religion, the Third World, prophecy, ideas, intelligence. "Dead to the Knowledge", with its huge sinister backing track, is a sociohistorical rap that pleads the case of self-awareness and referring to history for clues on the present and future. "Information to Raise a Nation" fits neatly with that. It's not all so stentorian, though—the album opens up with the up-tempo fun of "The Rhythm, The

Feeling" and later kicks in with "It's Time to Get Hype." It's only with "Desperado" that things start to get a little serious, and even then there's "Trouble Man," a very odd "better rapper than anybody" number. This album has managed quite a feat—Rich Nice would have been somebody to keep an eye on in the future. Alas, he seems to have settled for behind-the-scenes work. —*Steven McDonald*

Nick Nack (Nick Malkiewicz)

b. Austin, TX
Turntablist, Producer, DJ / Hip-Hop, Turntablism
Nick "Nick Nack" Malkiewicz is a practicing proponent of true hip-hop. Combining the sensibilities of a DJ with that of a cultural visionary, he has been quite productive in his home state of Texas as both a creator of original music and a provider of opportunities for fellow artists. His masterwork to date, 2001's *Re: Construction*, features a wide array of Lone Star MCs and turntablists. Beginning his career as a battle DJ, Nick Nack first made a name for himself in 1995 by placing second in a Soundwars competition held in Dallas. As a student at the University of Texas, he hosted a radio program on Austin's KVRX and spearheaded a collaboration between Prince Poetry of Organized Konfusion and an MC named QB that culminated in a single titled "Long Distance" on Five Finger Records. He also began producing, and started up his own record label. Between 1999 and 2000, he recorded a beats tape (*In the Nick of Time*) and a Soundscape single, both released on his own Crowd Control label. Teaming up with Austin freestyle champion Bavu Blakes to comprise Soundscape, the duo scored an underground hit with "Listeners." His 2001 full-length, *Re: Construction* featured appearances from the likes of Environment, Head Krack, Tray God, Disgruntled Seeds, Lyrik, Enfoe, and Poetree, as well as Bavu Blakes and K-Otix. Nick Nack continued his search for challenges by joining a jazz ensemble called Blaze. —*Robert Gabriel*

● **Re: Construction** / 2001 / Crowd Control ◆◆◆
Nick Nack, a DJ and producer, put together this compilation album in an effort to "reconstruct" any negative perceptions of Southern hip-hop. Hailing from Austin, Texas, Nick Nack is part of an often-overlooked network of underground artists in the region who just so happen to deviate from the stereotypical norm. More comfortable expressing themselves with turntables and mics rather than with table dances and pipes, their natural ability to transcend dirty-dirty cliché only further legitimizes their status as true, down-to-earth Texans. Led by the success of K-Otix and the production techniques of the Are, Nick Nack provides beats and cuts for an impressive cast of MCs, including Damien and Mic of K-Otix, Bavu Blakes of Soundscape, Head Krack, Tray God, Poetree, Lyrik, Disgruntled Seeds, and Environment. Delivering the boom-bap on tracks such as "Reconstruct," "The Better," and "Show You How," Nick Nack propels his guests into supreme battle mode. Meanwhile introspective approaches are adapted on songs including "Lock Dee" and "Real Life." The two tracks that feature G-Smoove of Environment, "Greg Scott" and "Scarred Soul," almost sound as if they are on a 2Pac tangent, and they work that way. Crafty drum programming abounds as Nick Nack shows how extensive DJ experience translates to the studio. Indeed, the jewel of the album is a turntablist track titled "In Too Deep" that features Nick Nack and Enfoe practically matching the Invisibl Skratch Piklz lick for lick. A well-rounded album that certainly enhances the credibility of Texas hip-hop, *Re: Construction* is a sleeper in definite need of a wakeup call. —*Robert Gabriel*

Nicole (Nicole Wray)

b. Salinas, CA
Vocals / Urban, Hip-Hop
As Missy Elliott's first signing to her Gold Mind label, R&B singer Nicole became the subject of much criticism when her debut album heavily featured Elliott. Born in Salinas, CA, Nicole (born Nicole Wray) moved to Portsmouth, VA, as a child, where she met members of Elliott's family in her neighborhood. Nicole became one of her church's star choir members, and even began to model in local fashion shows. When one of Elliott's cousins introduced Missy to Nicole, the up-and-coming rapper/singer was impressed by the teenage singer's skills. Once her mainstream success allowed Elliott to start her own label, she signed the 17-year-old Nicole first, immediately going to work on her debut album. With producer Timbaland producing the beats while Elliott wrote the majority of the songs, Nicole finished and released the

record in 1998. Despite a star-filled video for the first single, "Make It Hot," the album's sales were only average, while critics were harsh on the record for Elliott's overwhelming presence. Still, Nicole wasn't phased by the reaction, continuing to work with her mentor on 2001's "I'm Lookin'" single as well as the material for her second album. —*Bradley Torreano*

● **Make It Hot** / Aug. 25, 1998 / East West ◆◆◆
The debut album from Missy Elliott disciple Nicole is virtually a textbook primer on Elliott's stylistic touch and influence on end-of-the-millennium hip-hop (she raps on, writes songs for, produces and executive produces *Make It Hot*—and it's on her custom label). Along with pal Timbaland, Elliott transforms young Nicole's somewhat standard bow into a stuttering slab of post-rap R&B that's as sleekly modern as it is customarily cold. Little of Nicole actually peeks through on *Make It Hot*, however, essentially making the album, and Nicole herself, an Elliott pet project. Some of it does work—the title tune featuring Elliott and Mocha is slippery-sexy, as is the solid "I Can't See"—but too often the artist herself gets buried beneath the overwhelming splendor of her ubiquitous mentor. —*Michael Gallucci*

Nightmares on Wax

f. 1988, Yorkshire, England
Group / Club/Dance, Trip-Hop, Electronica, Techno, IDM
The combined project of George Evelyn and Kevin Harper, Nightmares on Wax were one of the brightest spots on the post-rave British techno map of the early '90s. Although the group was later pared back to just Evelyn and a handful of contributors, N.O.W.'s debut album, *A Word of Science*, was—along with early tracks by LFO, Tuff Little Unit, and Tricky Disco—a crucial bridge between the competing influences of New York house and electro, Detroit techno and soul, London rave and acid, and the burgeoning eclecticism of the years to come. Forming in the late '80s in West Yorkshire as an extension of Evelyn and company's b-boy crew the Soul City Rockers, N.O.W.'s first singles, "Dextrous" and "Aftermath," were both highly regarded, and the latter shot into the pop singles Top 40. The subsequent album laid a good deal of the groundwork for the down-tempo experimental hip-hop/electro-funk worked over by Mike Paradinas, Luke Vibert, Spacer, and others, and earned the group a secure spot among techno's select crew of next-step innovators.

The group nonetheless disbanded following *Science*'s release, with Harper leaving to pursue a DJ career and Evelyn turning out a smattering of house tracks on Warp's Nucleus subsidiary before settling into bedroom woodshed mode. Following a four-year hiatus, Evelyn resurfaced with a track on the Mo'Wax *Headz* compilation and, soon after, *Smoker's Delight*, basically an instrumental hip-hop album with a distinctively British eclecticism. Still involved with the same sorts of genre-spanning sampler-and-sequencer experiments, *Smoker's Delight* is also less obvious, suited more to repeat listenings than previous material. The same was also true for 1999's *Carboot Soul*, Evelyn's first album as part of a deal with American indie label Matador for domestic distribution. In 2000, N.O.W. produced the first new material by De La Soul in several years, included on an EP (*The Sound of N.O.W.*) featuring the rap pioneers. Following hot on its heels was a volume in the Studio K7 mix series *DJ Kicks*. Two years later, Evelyn delivered his fourth LP, *Mind Elevation*. —*Sean Cooper*

A Word of Science / Sep. 16, 1991 / Warp ◆◆◆◆

Smoker's Delight / 1995 / Warp ◆◆◆◆
Evelyn's solo step is a whole delightfully unreducible to its parts, which, as with earlier releases, is largely electro, hip-hop, and soul, with bits of Latin percussion and down-tempo funk thrown in. The album spawned a pair of somewhat forgettable remix EPs, and was reissued by TVT immediately upon release. —*Sean Cooper*

● **Carboot Soul** / Apr. 12, 1999 / Matador ◆◆◆◆◆
Four years on from *Smoker's Delight* and, fortunately, little has changed for Evelyn's Nightmares on Wax project. While he could've easily been forgiven for following the nu-beat crowd and inserting a few prescient big beats into the blunted trip-hop formula, it's all clear from the opener "Les Nuits" (a N.O.W. theme of sorts, repeated from *Smoker's Delight*) that we have on hand a return to form, not a turn away from the trip-hop style that took such a beating during the late '90s. The lazy-day soul samples driving tracks like "Morse" and "Finer" are perfect examples that instrumental hip-hop doesn't have to resort to the usual producer's bag of tricks to make for music leagues beyond the average. There's also a focus here lacking from previous material;

fewer interludes make for a more concentrated listening experience. All in all, *Carboot Soul* is one of the best arguments yet for the continuing development of trip-hop beyond mere coffee table fare. —*John Bush*

DJ Kicks / Sep. 26, 2000 / K7 ✦✦✦✦
George Evelyn, one of the best production ears in trip-hop, came a bit late to the mix-album field (his volume in the series had actually been planned since 1995), but definitely came correct anyway. *DJ Kicks* spins through a raft of nu-school hip-hop (Aim, Blackalicious, Freddy Fresh, Syrup, Type), classic old school producers from A Tribe Called Quest ("Award Tour") to Kenny Dope ("Get on Down," "Superkat"), and tosses in a few of his own N.O.W. tracks to boot. Just as supremely chilled as the best Nightmares on Wax material. —*John Bush*

Mind Elevation / Sep. 3, 2002 / Warp ✦✦✦
George Evelyn, the Nightmares on Wax producer who provided the template for 2000-2001's downbeat movement almost a decade before it became the bane of mix album fans, returned just in time with another LP of supremely chilled beats. Unfortunately, though, *Mind Elevation* isn't the unqualified triumph of *Carboot Soul* or *Smoker's Delight*, with Evelyn substituting a couple of vocal tracks for the trance-state trip-hop of his previous work. Admittedly, the acid jazz groover "Date With Destiny" and the breezy dub track "70s 80s" prove that Evelyn is surprisingly proficient at crafting a good production for use under a vocal, combining a bare few elements (like the good acid-house producer he is) yet weaving them together well. And he can still stop time merely by repeating the right sample and manipulating the bass (as he does perfectly on "Humble" and "Say-Say"). Still, the N.O.W. blueprint of skeletal productions and a clever eye to detail appears to fail him in several places. The faux classical "Bleu My Mind" doesn't even rise to the level of *Classical Chillout*, and far too many tracks don't even rise above the quality of fair to middling downbeat. Ironically, the fact that there are so many vocals really saves *Mind Elevation* from being the first bland record by Nightmares on Wax; as it is, there's something to focus on for those few tracks where the old production genius just doesn't seem to be there anymore. —*John Bush*

Nigo

Producer, Organ, Synthesizer, Vocals / Electronica, Hip-Hop, Trip-Hop, Punk Revival
The trendy Japanese artist Nigo began his career drumming but used his later success as a clothing designer to catapult his music career forward, resulting in a prestigious opportunity to record for James Lavelle's Mo'Wax label. In addition to being the drummer for the Japanese punk band Toyko Sex Pistols, Nigo worked with fashion shoots where he would both DJ and occasionally style the shoots. During this same period, Nigo contributed to a trendsetting Japanese magazine called *Last Orgy 2* that enabled him to further make a name for himself within the exclusive world of fashion. Soon, he began his own clothing line, Bathing Ape, and began to throw parties in celebration of his fashions that would draw a collective of Japanese artists such as Cornelius along with others from around the world, namely, Lavelle (an advocate of Bathing Ape clothing). Inspired by Nigo's approach to fashion and his overall aesthetic, Lavelle became close acquaintances with the Japanese artist, presenting him with the opportunity to make a record for Mo'Wax. The resulting album, *Ape Sounds*, closely resembles Lavelle's own project as U.N.K.L.E., both overseen by an artist collaborating with a large stable of other talented artists. *Ape Sounds* drew heavily from hip-hop and punk for its general aesthetic, with a high-tech production style to help bring an overall motif to the many assembled takes on the two somewhat opposing genres, along with hints of modern sound collage in the style of DJ Shadow. —*Jason Birchmeier*

● **Ape Sounds** / Sep. 19, 2000 / Mo'Wax ✦✦✦✦
Orchestrated by Japanese clothing entrepreneur, DJ, and general tastemaker Nigo, this collection of hip electronic eclecticism reflects the varied influences of the posse that the Tokyo-based auteur has surrounded himself with. By roping in Mo'Wax label founder James Lavelle for a *Planet of the Apes* sample fest ("March of the General") and Beastie Boys keyboardist Money Mark for the laid-back Cornershop-like groove of "A Simple Song," Nigo proves his deft ability to canvas talent and extract exceptional product. No better example of his astute solicitations exists here than the space rock vibe of "Freediving," featuring Australian wunderkind Ben Lee. The only time that the formula collapses slightly is during "Kung Fu Fightin," when the awkward rapping exposes Nigo's modus operandi a bit too clearly. Nigo, like many Western

culture hawks from the East, illustrates here that his work is largely not about homegrown aesthetics as it about keen acquisition. —*Joe Silva*

Nilo MC (Nilo Castillo)

b. Havana, Cuba
Latin Rap
Along with Los Orishas, Nilo MC is one of the leaders in Cuban hip-hop, an unsanctioned music so deeply underground that only expatriates have much of a chance of being heard. Born Nilo Castillo in the rough Marianao district of Havana, he grew up in an artistic family (his mother danced at the Tropicana cabaret) and initially made his living as a painter. He listened to Cuban music growing up, but was galvanized by an encounter with Public Enemy's *Fear of a Black Planet* album, and began composing his own raps in 1989. In 1992, armed with a letter of recommendation from an art gallery, Castillo traveled to Ecuador, where he recorded an album called *Hora Cero* in 1995. Never officially released, it remains available only as a bootleg cassette circulating in Havana's musical underground. Castillo later went to Germany, where he hooked up with producer Bernd Kunz (of trip-hop act A Forest Mighty Black). The two went to Madrid in early 1998 and recorded the demo album *Coconuts* (which, again, was not officially released). Splitting time between Madrid and Berlin, Castillo worked part time as a DJ in the latter city, and made some connections in the former's hip-hop scene, including producer Juanjo Valmarisco. With Valmarisco at the helm, Castillo finally released his first official album as Nilo MC, *Guajiro del Asfalto*, on Virgin subsidiary Chewaka in early 2002; it was nominated for Best Rap/Hip-Hop Album at the third Latin Grammy Awards. —*Steve Huey*

Guajiro del Asfalto / 2002 / Chewaka ✦✦✦

Nine

f. Bronx, NY
Hip-Hop, East Coast Rap
The portrait of a starving MC, Bronx-native Nine got his big break in late 1993 as a featured guest on Funkmaster Flex and the Ghetto Celebs' "Six Million Ways to Die." The verse showcased Nine's harsh, gravelly flow and the artist was signed a deal with the now-defunct Profile Records. Nine's debut album, *Nine Livez*, appeared in early 1995 on the strength of the up-tempo single "Whatchu Want." While the album did not make a big splash, it spawned a slew of underground hits including "Redrum," "Everybody Won Heaven," and "Any Emcee," which tastefully borrowed from the Spinners' "I'll Be Around." Nine's signature black lung vocal tone drew some comparisons to the over-the-top antics of Busta Rhymes. Nine followed up with *Cloud Nine* in 1996, then mostly fell off hip-hop radar screens when Profile closed up shop. During his hiatus, Nine popped up on the TV series *NY Undercover* landing a bit part as a thug. In late 2000 the Bronx MC hinted at a comeback, releasing the single "It's Ugly." —*Micheal Di Bella*

● **Nine Livez** / 1995 / Profile ✦✦✦
With legendary NYC DJ Funkmaster Flex in his corner, the raspy-voiced Bronx MC Nine released his debut album in 1995. The self-proclaimed straight-out-the-gutter MC tattoos his rabid delivery and distinctly salacious lyrical bravado all over the album. The song that got the buzz going for this alley cat was "Whatchu Want," a slick radio-friendly joint despite its street mentality; the rest of the album belies the crossover appeal of this track. Nine's lyrics scratch, thrash, and claw on tracks like "Redrum" and "Everybody Won Heaven." The infectious, uneven groove supplied on "Redrum" is the artist at his grimy, low-down best. The Spinners' classic '70s soul tune "I'll Be Around" is the driving impetus behind arguably the best track on the album, "Any Emcee." It's smooth ruggedness pays homage to the b-boy tradition by featuring a superb lyrical sample from the legendary Rakim. Nine's throaty, expressive vocal tone gives this album a distinctively rugged slant. While far from a classic, *Nine Livez* is an underappreciated album from an underrated artist. —*Micheal Di Bella*

Cloud 9 / Aug. 7, 1996 / Profile ✦✦✦
Nine is one of those artists who's always around but doesn't really make a huge impact on the charts or in the hip-hop community. Much like his first album, *Cloud 9* hasn't seen much attention, yet it's solid from start to finish. Nine's raspy, deep catchy voice is ever present, and, with really simple beats complemented by hard bass lines, it's easy to throw this back in for another round. Smoothe da Hustler makes a welcome appearance on "Make or Take," while every other track on the album bangs just as hard. —*Brad Mills*

9.17 Family

Group / Southern Rap

Hank Shocklee, known for his quintessentially East Coast productions (Public Enemy, Slick Rick, LL Cool J) ventured down South to produce the Atlanta collective 9.17 Family. Formed by three groups (Bonafide, Kin, Backhome) plus a pair of solo artists (Yagaboo, Zoe), the crew debuted with a 2001 record (*Southern Empire*) that merged reggae with Southern bounce. —*John Bush*

Southern Empire / Apr. 24, 2001 / Motown ♦♦

Public Enemy producer Hank Shocklee is behind this Atlanta quintet, but those searching for the vet's inventive and impressive skills will be disappointed by the sameness and lameness of this generic slice of hip-hop. None of the rappers break from the pack, and the Southern bounce of most of the tracks has become rote. This is by-the-numbers hip-hop that offers nothing to the genre. —*Michael Gallucci*

95 South

Group / Club/Dance, Bass Music, Southern Rap

Before producers C.C. Lemonhead and Jayski McGowan went on to produce "Tootsee Roll" for the 69 Boyz and "C'Mon N' Ride It (The Train)" for the Quad City DJ's, the duo had a similarly big hit with 95 South's "Whoot, There It Is" in early 1993. The song was the first bass track to cross over to mainstream success (curiously followed, and one-upped, by Tag Team's "Whoop! [There It Is]" a month later). The full-length LP *Quad City Knock* reached *Billboard's* Top 20 R&B around the same time the single peaked at number seven R&B in April/May 1993. However, following the success of "Whoot, There It Is," Lemonhead and McGowan parted ways with 95 South to find more success producing, first the 69 Boyz ("Tootsee Roll") in 1994 and then Quad City DJ's ("C'Mon N' Ride It [The Train]") in 1996. The remaining members of 95 South didn't do so well in subsequent years. Albums like *One Mo' Gen* were overlooked and only the occasional single ("Rodeo") garnered attention. For the most part, 95 South has been and will continue to be remembered by "Whoot, There It Is," and also as the launching pad for Lemonhead's and McGowan's careers. —*Jason Birchmeier*

Quad City Knock / Apr. 15, 1993 / Wrap ♦♦♦

95 South's debut album is an enjoyable but generic collection of gangsta rap that shows some promise but doesn't have anything particularly noteworthy. —*Stephen Thomas Erlewine*

One Mo' Gen / 1995 / Rip-It ♦♦♦

Tightwork 3000 / Sep. 12, 2000 / RCA ♦♦

As one may imagine, innovation or creativity isn't exactly high on 95 South's agenda, as they once again focus on doing whatever it takes to get asses shakin' with their boomin'bass, electro rhythms, and sleazy rapping. There are a few tracks here that could send any dancefloor into a freaking, jigglin' frenzy—"Ms. Got Dat Booty," "Wet-N-Wild," "Hooked"—and a lot of tracks that just recycle all the clichés one would expect to find here. Surprisingly, there are a few straight-up gangsta tracks such as "Wrong Place, Wrong Time" that totally ruin the let's-get-freaky-and-get-naked vibes in favor of nihilism. Still, it's doubtful many will pick up this album expecting it to be anymore than something to bump to in the car or at parties; it's surely no *The Chronic, It Takes a Nation of Millions to Hold Us Back*, or even a *Nasty As They Wanna Be*. Think of it more as a disposable aural aphrodisiac with quickly diminishing returns. —*Jason Birchmeier*

Nivea

Vocals / Hip-Hop, Contemporary R&B, Dance-Pop, Urban

Nivea made waves in the rap community when she joined Mystikal for his smash hit "Danger." Nivea's sultry R&B grooves were hot and the new millennium was her time to shine. Nivea's self-titled debut appeared on Jive in 2001; however, it was reissued the following year thanks to the success of "Danger" and Nivea's debut single, "Don't Mess With the Radio." This particular cut joined Nivea and Organized Noize (of TLC's "Waterfalls" fame) at the production board and Jagged Edge's Brian and Brandon Casey on guest vocals; second single "Ya Ya Ya" was produced by R. Kelly and debuted in November 2002. In early 2003, "Don't Mess With My Man" earned a Grammy nod for Best R&B Performance by a Duo or Group with Vocal. —*MacKenzie Wilson*

● **Nivea** / Sep. 25, 2001 / Jive ♦♦♦

Back in the '80s—when rap was the new kid on the block—there were plenty of urban contemporary stations and R&B singers who wanted nothing to do with hip-hop. But times have changed, and these days rap and urban contemporary are joined at the hip. Just as an electric blues/classic soul mixture works well at a blues festival, an urban station might play Destiny's Child one minute and Jay-Z the next. Nivea's self-titled debut album is a perfect example of how hip-hop drenched R&B has become; from the production to the lyrics, this CD frequently underscores hip-hop's influence on modern R&B. Nivea doesn't get heavily into the neo-soul trend à la Mary J. Blige, Jaguar Wright, Alicia Keyes, or Jill Scott, although one does hear some '70s sweet soul influence on the slow jam "Laundromat" (which R. Kelly wrote and produced). Nivea is much more girlish than the neo-soul divas, which isn't to say that her material lacks bite. In fact, Nivea provides a likable blend of girlishness and grit on catchy, hip-hop-minded offerings like "Ya Ya Ya" (another Kelly contribution) and the single "Don't Mess With My Man" (which was produced by Bryan-Michael Cox). Nivea can be teen friendly, although not in a bubblegum way; in Nivea's case, "teen friendly" doesn't mean teen pop. Like a lot of younger urban contemporary artists who record for major labels, Nivea works with different producers and songwriters on different songs—and of course, she is at their mercy. Most of them serve her well, especially Kelly and Cox. There are, however, a few weak tracks. But if Nivea's debut is slightly uneven, it still has more ups than downs and is—thanks to the more on-the-ball producers and writers—worth the price of admission. —*Alex Henderson*

No Face

Group / Political Rap, Party Rap, Dirty Rap

A bizarre hip-hop duo that merged social-commentary hardcore with explicit party rap, No Face released only one record, 1990's *Wake Your Daughter Up*, for Ral/Columbia. Multi-instrumentalists Mark Sexx and the Shah had a lot to do with their lone hit, "Half," which nearly broke into the rap Top 40. —*John Bush*

● **Wake Your Daughter Up** / Aug. 21, 1990 / Ral/Columbia ♦♦♦♦♦

A hardcore rap group that dabbled in new jack swing, No Face had an underground hit in 1990 with *Wake Your Daughter Up*. In contrast to social and political commentators like Ice-T, Public Enemy, and KRS-One, No Face set out, not to educate or inform, but strictly to entertain. There's nothing groundbreaking or innovative about the group's sexually explicit lyrics—some blues artists had been offering raunchy lyrics 60 years earlier. But strictly as a party album, it succeeds. While the X-rated lyrics brought to mind the 2 Live Crew—which joins forces with No Face on "Fake Hair Wearin' Bitch"—the group's slower style of rapping and R&B approach to production are very much its own. No Face switches from rappers to singers on the engaging new jack swing number "Half," a commentary on being financially assaulted after a divorce. —*Alex Henderson*

No Good

Group / Hip-Hop, Southern Rap

Starting their collaboration in 1992, rappers Derrick Hill and Tracy Lattimer found themselves working with Luther Campbell as hype men and dancers. The two realized their talents and after spending time together in a dance troupe called No Good No Good they cut off half the name and transformed it into a rap group. Still maintaining their wild dancing skills, they began tearing up Miami nightclubs until they scored a record deal. Their first release, *Game Day, PBB*, was released in 2002 on Artist Direct Records. —*Bradley Torreano*

● **Lizard Lizard** / Sep. 1, 1998 / RCA ♦♦

As is to be expected from a Luther Campbell project, this debut album from a trio of guys who let Luke pretty much run the show is filled with plenty of sex rhymes and street talk. None of it is particularly interesting, and Campbell's Miami-based production tricks are pretty stale by this point. And he's not even capable of being shocking anymore, thereby quashing his relevance. The crime here isn't the rampant misogyny or sexism; it's the fact that it's all so dull. —*Michael Gallucci*

Game Day, PBB / May 21, 2002 / Artist Direct ♦♦

No Good's *Game Day, PBB* is one of the many dirty South albums to be released around the turn of the century. The key to this genre of music is the fluid style of rapping and lack of empty space in the tracks, something that No Good does a very good job of. However, that's about where the compliments end, as the album is one of the most generic examples of the genre to come along in quite a while. By repeating the exact same phrases countless times, they spend a good portion of the album avoiding any new verses. They continually chant the same stuff but change just one word each time, giving the illusion of new lyrics when they're just filling time. And when they do just throw out normal verses, they add horribly childish lyrics (example: "I'll be sweet 'til you're sleepy/Let y'all girls suck on my pee pee") that take the wind out of their better songs. They have some nifty production ideas, and many of the choruses are quite memorable, but that is a credit to their primal simplicity more than their ability to write interesting songs. With silly skits, bad lyrics, and a low-brow approach, No Good lives up to their name on this poorly executed album. —*Bradley Torreano*

Non Phixion

Group / Underground Rap

Discovered by Third Bass' MC Serch, during the heyday of Wild Pitch Records, Non Phixion quickly generated a lot of hype—and went through a number of labels—before their long-awaited debut was finally released. Composed of MCs Ill Bill, Goretex Medinah, and Sabac Red, along with DJ Eclipse, Non Phixion mixed graphic, unsettling lyrics over dirty, gritty beats—often composed by Ill Bill's brother, the even more controversial Necro. After dropping their debut single, "Legacy," on Fat Beats, Non Phixion was quickly snatched up by Geffen. The incendiary content of songs like "I Shot Reagan," 1998, may have been a bit much for the major label, and the group soon moved to the more independent Matador. Non Phixion's *The Future Is Now* was basically complete and the album was hotly anticipated by this point. After releasing the *Black Helicopters* 12", though, Non Phixion abruptly left Matador. The buzz around the band continued to grow as Non Phixion released more singles and several collaborations, often involving Necro and his emergent Psycho-Logical Records. Finally, in 2001, Non Phixion landed at Warner Bros. and *The Future Is Now* finally appeared set for release. That was not to be, however, for whatever reason the release was delayed and when it did arrive in the spring of 2002, it was on the Landspeed label. —*Martin Woodside*

● **The Future Is Now** / Mar. 26, 2002 / Landspeed ✦✦✦✦✦
Utilizing beats that would do Dr. Octagon-era Dan "the Automator" proud and rhyming schemes that bring to mind early Wu-Tang Clan or mid-'90s Gang Starr, Non Phixion exposes the sound of true underground hip-hop. This is music that reflects the sound and attitude of countless rappers selling their albums out of the back of their cars or in booths on the street, cutting together dirty and disjointed sounds with a confidence and quality that is unique to this particular genre. This would all be for nothing if it wasn't for the excellent raps from Ill Bill, Goretex, and Sabac Red, a trio of rappers who have a Tribe Called Quest-like chemistry. Their clever lyrics, respectable skills, and rough voices make this an intense and dark landmark in alternative rap. The ugly funk anthem "There Is No Future" is an egotistical boast that takes the exact opposite approach of most likeminded artists, bringing up everything from atheism to mosh pits with a thoughtful twist. "Drug Music" is a bright view of drugs and music that takes a few detours but ultimately leaves the listener with a skewed view of their opinions. DJ Premier's awesome production on "Rock Stars" is matched only by his unbelievable scratching on the same track, but Pete Rock's work on "If You Got Love" is almost as impressive. But the best track here might be "Say Goodbye to Yesterday," a reflection of their lifestyle that takes a look at how it has affected them throughout the years and how they feel looking back at their actions. Outside of a few key exceptions, this sort of thoughtfulness is almost unheard of on these types of songs, which usually just brag about how bad the MCs had it before they became rich. With beats that are both packed with tension and enjoyably sparse, a futuristic theme that fuels their intelligent lyrics, and a clever Voivod reference on the front cover, Non Phixion lives up to their fanfare and delivers a ramshackle collection of intelligent, literate rap tracks that points toward the future of hip-hop. —*Bradley Torreano*

The Nonce

Group / Hip-Hop, Club/Dance

Los Angeles rappers Nouka Base and Yusef Afloat—collectively known as the Nonce—mixed old school stylings with the jazzy vibe of crews like A Tribe Called Quest and Digable Planets. Their debut album, *World Ultimate*, was released in 1995. *Turning It Out* followed four years later. —*Steve Huey*

● **World Ultimate** / Feb. 28, 1995 / Wild West ✦✦✦
Combining old school b-boy rhymes with easygoing, jazzy beats, the Nonce manage to recall LL Cool J as well as the Pharcyde and A Tribe Called Quest on their debut album, *World Ultimate*. Occasionally, the duo can get a little too relaxed, but on the whole it's an engaging alternative to the standard West Coast gangsta fare. —*Steve Huey*

Turning It Out / Mar. 9, 1999 / Wild West ✦✦✦

Nonchalant

b. Washington, DC

Rap / Underground Rap, East Coast Rap

Nonchalant had a smooth, laid-back style delivering intelligent lyrics that fit her chosen name. The Washington, D.C., native released one album in 1996, *Until the Day*, in which she delivered intelligent lyrics over R&B-laced productions. It received critical acclaim at the time, but was not as well received commercially. —*Wade Kergan*

● **Until the Day** / Mar. 26, 1996 / MCA ✦✦✦✦
As excellent a rapper as Nonchalant is, she wasn't without her critics in the 1990s. Some hip-hop hardliners felt that the sleek, melodic tracks she rapped to (many of which would have been at home on a Dr. Dre or Too Short album) were too R&B minded, and others found some of her more sociopolitical lyrics preachy. But those critics can say what they will; *Until the Day* is an album that, for the most part, is as solid lyrically as it is musically and rhythmically. The R&B-drenched tracks are consistently appealing, and Nonchalant's lyrics are memorable whether she's rapping about relationships or addressing sociopolitical concerns on "Lights N' Sirens," "Crab Rappers," and her hit "Five O'Clock." The latter pulls no punches when it comes to the subject of black-on-black crime, which, she asserts, poses as great a threat to inner-city residents as racism. Like LL Cool J's "Illegal Search," "Lights N' Sirens" is a fairly reasonable commentary on police who she feels are pulling over young black motorists at random. The song could have done without Nonchalant's crack about cops spending too much time in doughnut shops—anyone whose job description includes possibly getting shot and killed is entitled to the occasional visit to Dunkin Donuts—but even so, Nonchalant avoids condemning law enforcement in general a la N.W.A's "Fuck Tha Police." It's ironic that the MC calls herself Nonchalant, for on this album, she comes across as someone who cares a lot. —*Alex Henderson*

Noreaga (Victor Santiago)

b. Queens, NY

Rap, Vocals, Mixing, Producer / Hip-Hop, Gangsta Rap, East Coast Rap, Hardcore Rap

One-half of the Queens hardcore rap duo Capone-N-Noreaga, Victor "Noreaga" Santiago met Kiam "Capone" Holley in 1992 while both were serving prison sentences. Signed to Penalty Records in 1996, the pair released a hard-hitting debut (*The War Report*) in June 1997, but after Holley was thrown back in jail on a parole violation, Santiago began recording a solo album (though Capone-N-Noreaga have never parted ways). His solo debut *N.O.R.E.*—an acronym for "Niggas on the Run Eating"—was an all-star affair, with contributions from Foxy Brown, Nas, Busta Rhymes, and Jay-Z, among others. *Melvin Flynt—Da Hustler* followed in 1999. —*John Bush*

N.O.R.E. / Jun. 16, 1998 / Penalty ✦✦✦✦
With his colleague Capone, Noreaga released an exciting debut album, *The War Report*, in 1997. Shortly after its release, Capone was sent to jail, leaving Noreaga to fend for himself on the follow-up. *N.O.R.E.* doesn't quite live up to the expectations set by *The War Report*, mainly because Capone is absent, but it often hits head-spinning high notes. Noreaga lined up an impressive team of guest rappers—Nas, Mase, Kool G Rap, Cam'ron, Big Punisher, and Busta Rhymes, among others, are all present, and most contribute some great, hard-hitting raps. Still, the whole thing adds up to the less than the sum of its parts. Maybe the thrilling interplay and fresh beats on *The War Report* raised hopes too high, but *N.O.R.E.* doesn't transcend expectations like you may anticipate. Instead, it simply delivers the goods. That does make for some great listening, but it's hard not to think that Noreaga is capable of greatness, not just merely good work. —*Stephen Thomas Erlewine*

Melvin Flynt—Da Hustler / Aug. 24, 1999 / Penalty ♦♦♦

In the grand tradition of rappers from Ice Cube to Nas, Noreaga's second album comes complete with an alternate identity, Melvin Flynt. As the cover portrays, Noreaga is struggling between himself and what the music industry wants him to become to sell more records. The record begins with a death that creates his alternate identity, and the rapper does in fact seem reborn on street-level tracks like "Gangsta's Watch," "Da Hustla" and "Wethuggedout." It's more than just an easy way to revel in gangsta imagery and themes without having to worry about criticism; *Melvin Flynt—Da Hustler* works because Noreaga puts feeling into the tracks. Though the production is a bit off compared to 1998's *N.O.R.E.*, the album is an interesting addition to gangsta lore. —*Keith Farley*

God's Favorite / Jul. 2, 2002 / Def Jam ♦♦♦♦

For Noreaga's long-awaited and oft-delayed third album, *God's Favorite*, the thuggish New York rapper returns with many of the same producers who contributed to his previous album, *Melvin Flynt—Da Hustler* (1999), namely, Ez Elpee, the Neptunes, and Swizz Beatz. Unlike on the often sparsely populated *Melvin Flynt*, though, numerous rappers join Noreaga on *God's Favorite*; in fact, nearly every song here features at least one guest, if not more. Despite all the assistance, the best songs are the few solo moments stacked near the album's beginning: "Nothin'," "Grimey," and "Nahmeanuheard." Despite all the comparisons to *Melvin Flynt*, which was a slight disappointment among Noreaga fans, *God's Favorite* is an improvement for the rapper, mostly because of the excellent production. The Neptunes contribute several bangers here, nearly one-third of the album, in fact. In addition, Swizz Beatz's contributions may be minimal in comparison ("Nahmeanuheard," "Wanna Be Like Him," "Nahmeanuheard Remix"), but they're some of the album's key moments. Furthermore, it's worth noting that Irv Gotti and Ja Rule collaborate with Noreaga on "Live My Life." If you're familiar with these producers, all of whom have very impressive track records and esteemed reputations, you know what to expect. On the other hand, given the patented sound of these producers, *God's Favorite* often sounds a bit more familiar than it probably should. Yet that seems to be the point. After falling off a bit since the late '90s, Noreaga needed a rock-solid return, and that's precisely what *God's Favorite* is, a straightforward album powered by sure-fire producers and colorful guests. —*Jason Birchmeier*

The Notorious B.I.G. (Christopher Wallace)

b. May 21, 1972 **d.** Mar. 9, 1997

Hip-Hop, Club/Dance, Gangsta Rap, East Coast Rap, Hardcore Rap, Pop-Rap

In just a few short years, the Notorious B.I.G. went from a Brooklyn street hustler to the savior of East Coast hip-hop to a tragic victim of the culture of violence he depicted so realistically on his records. His all-too-brief odyssey almost immediately took on mythic proportions, especially since his murder followed the shooting of rival Tupac Shakur by only six months. In death, the man also known as Biggie Smalls became a symbol of the senseless violence that plagued inner-city America in the waning years of the 20th century. Whether or not his death was really the result of a much-publicized feud between the East and West Coast hip-hop scenes, it did mark the point where both sides stepped back from a rivalry that had gone too far. Hip-hop's self-image would never be quite the same, and neither would public perception. The aura of martyrdom that surrounds the Notorious B.I.G. sometimes threatens to overshadow his musical legacy, which was actually quite significant. Helped by Sean "Puffy" Combs' radio-friendly sensibility, Biggie reestablished East Coast rap's viability by leading it into the post-Dr. Dre gangsta age. Where fellow East Coasters the Wu-Tang Clan slowly built an underground following, Biggie crashed onto the charts and became a star right out of the box. In the process, he helped Combs' Bad Boy label supplant Death Row as the biggest hip-hop imprint in America, and also paved the way to popular success for other East Coast talents like Jay-Z and Nas. Biggie was a gifted storyteller with a sense of humor and an eye for detail, and his narratives about the often-violent life of the streets were rarely romanticized; instead, they were told with a gritty, objective realism that won him enormous respect and credibility. The general consensus in the rap community was that when his life was cut short, sadly, Biggie was just getting started.

The Notorious B.I.G. was born Christopher Wallace on May 21, 1972, and grew up in Brooklyn's Bedford-Stuyvesant neighborhood. He was interested in rap from a young age, performing with local groups like the Old Gold Brothers and the Techniques, the latter of which brought the teenage Wallace his first trip to a recording studio. He had already adopted the name Biggie Smalls at this point, a reference to his ample frame, which would grow to be over six feet tall and nearly 400 pounds. Although he was a good student, he dropped out of high school at age 17 to live his life on the streets. Attracted by the money and flashy style of local drug dealers, he started selling crack for a living. He got busted on a trip to North Carolina and spent nine months in jail, and upon his release, he made some demo recordings on a friend's four-track. The resulting tape fell into the hands of Mister Cee, a DJ working with Big Daddy Kane; Cee in turn passed the tape on to hip-hop magazine *The Source*, which gave Biggie a positive write-up in a regular feature on unsigned artists. Thanks to the publicity, Biggie caught the attention of Uptown Records producer Sean "Puffy" Combs, who signed him immediately. With his new daughter in need of immediate financial support, Biggie kept dealing drugs for a short time until Combs found out and laid down the law. Not long after Biggie's signing, Combs split from Uptown to form his own label, Bad Boy, and took Biggie with him.

Changing his primary stage name from Biggie Smalls to the Notorious B.I.G., the newly committed rapper made his recording debut on a 1993 remix of Mary J. Blige's single "Real Love." He soon guested on another Blige remix, "What's the 411?," and contributed his first solo cut, "Party and Bullshit," to the soundtrack of the film *Who's the Man?* Now with a considerable underground buzz behind him, the Notorious B.I.G. delivered his debut album, *Ready to Die*, in September 1994. Its lead single, "Juicy," went gold, and the follow-up smash, "Big Poppa," achieved platinum sales and went Top Ten on the pop and R&B charts. Biggie's third single, "One More Chance," tied Michael Jackson's "Scream" for the highest debut ever on the pop charts; it entered at number five en route to an eventual peak at number two, and went all the way to number one on the R&B side. By the time the dust settled, *Ready to Die* had sold over four million copies and turned the Notorious B.I.G. into a hip-hop sensation—the first major star the East Coast had produced since the rise of Dr. Dre's West Coast G-funk.

Not long after *Ready to Die* was released, Biggie married R&B singer and Bad Boy labelmate Faith Evans. In November 1994, West Coast gangsta star Tupac Shakur was shot several times in the lobby of a New York recording studio and robbed of thousands of dollars in jewelry. Shakur survived and accused Combs and his onetime friend Biggie of planning the attack, a charge both of them fervently denied. The ill will gradually snowballed into a heated rivalry between West and East Coast camps, with upstart Bad Boy now challenging Suge Knight's Death Row empire for hip-hop supremacy. Meanwhile, Biggie turned his energies elsewhere. He shepherded the career of Junior M.A.F.I.A., a group consisting of some of his childhood rap partners, and guested on their singles "Player's Anthem" and "Get Money." He also boosted several singles by his labelmates, such as Total's "Can't You See" and 112's "Only You," and worked with superstars like Michael Jackson (*HIStory*) and R. Kelly ("[You to Be] Happy," from *R. Kelly*). With the singles from *Ready to Die* still burning up the airwaves as well, Biggie ended 1995 as not only the top-selling rap artist but also the biggest solo male act on both the pop and R&B charts. He also ran into trouble with the law on more than one occasion. A concert promoter accused Biggie and members of his entourage of assaulting him when he refused to pay the promised fee after a concert cancellation. Later in the year, Biggie pled guilty to criminal mischief after attacking two harassing autograph seekers with a baseball bat.

The year 1996 proved to be even more tumultuous. More legal problems ensued after police found marijuana and weapons in a raid on Biggie's home in Teaneck, NJ. Meanwhile, Junior M.A.F.I.A. member Lil' Kim released her first solo album under Biggie's direction, and the two made little effort to disguise their concurrent love affair. 2Pac, still nursing a grudge against Biggie and Combs, recorded a vicious slam on the East Coast scene called "Hit 'Em Up," in which he taunted Biggie about having slept with Faith Evans (who was by now estranged from her husband). What was more, during the recording sessions for Biggie's second album, he suffered rather serious injuries in a car accident and was confined to a wheelchair for a time. Finally, in September 1996, 2Pac was murdered in a drive-by shooting on the Las Vegas strip. Given their very public feud, it didn't take long for rumors of Biggie's involvement to start swirling, although none were substantiated. Biggie was also criticized for not attending an antiviolence hip-hop summit held in Harlem in the wake of Shakur's death.

Observers hoped that Shakur's murder would serve as a wake-up call for gangsta rap in general, that on-record boasting had gotten out of hand and spilled into reality. Sadly, it would take another tragedy to drive that point home. In the early morning hours of March 9, 1997, the Notorious B.I.G. was leaving a party at the Petersen Automotive Museum in Los Angeles, thrown by *Vibe* magazine in celebration of the Soul Train Music Awards. He sat in the passenger side of his SUV, with his bodyguard in the driver's seat and Junior M.A.F.I.A. member Lil' Cease in the back. According to most witnesses, another vehicle pulled up on the right side of the SUV while it was stopped at a red light, and 6-10 shots were fired. Biggie's bodyguard rushed him to the nearby Cedars-Sinai Medical Center, but it was already too late. As much as Shakur was mourned, Biggie's death was perhaps even more shocking; it meant that Shakur's death was not an isolated incident, and that hip-hop's highest-profile talents might be caught in the middle of an escalating war. Naturally, speculation ran rampant that Biggie's killers were retaliating for Shakur's death, and since the case remains unsolved, the world may never know for sure.

In the aftermath of the tragedy, the release of the Notorious B.I.G.'s second album went ahead as planned at the end of March. The eerily titled *Life After Death* was a sprawling, guest-laden double-disc set that seemed designed to compete with 2Pac's *All Eyez on Me* in terms of ambition and epic scope. Unsurprisingly, it entered the charts at number one, selling nearly 700,000 copies in its first week of release and spending a total of four weeks on top. The first single, "Hypnotize," went platinum and hit number one on the pop charts, and its follow-up, "Mo Money Mo Problems," duplicated both feats, making the Notorious B.I.G. the first artist ever to score two posthumous number-one hits. A third single, "Sky's the Limit," went gold, and *Life After Death* was certified ten times platinum approximately two years after its release. Plus, Combs—now rechristened Puff Daddy—and Faith Evans scored one of 1997's biggest singles with their tribute, "I'll Be Missing You." In 1999 an album of previously unreleased B.I.G. material, *Born Again*, was released and entered the charts at number one. It eventually went double platinum, but thus far it's been the only posthumous collection in Biggie's discography (unlike the cottage industry surrounding 2Pac).

In the years following Christopher Wallace's death, little official progress was made in the L.A.P.D.'s murder investigation, and it began to look as if the responsible parties would never be brought to justice. The 2Pac retaliation theory still holds sway in many quarters, and it has also been speculated that members of the Crips gang murdered Wallace in a dispute over money owed for security services. In an article for *Rolling Stone*, and later a full book titled *Labyrinth*, journalist Randall Sullivan argued that Suge Knight hired onetime L.A.P.D. officer David Mack—a convicted bank robber with ties to the Bloods—to arrange a hit on Wallace, and that the gunman was a hitman and mortgage broker named Amir Muhammad. Sullivan further argued that when it became clear how many corrupt L.A.P.D. officers were involved with Death Row Records, the department hushed up as much as it could and all but abandoned detective Russell Poole's investigation recommendations. Documentary filmmaker Nick Broomfield used *Labyrinth* as a basis for 2002's *Biggie and Tupac*, which featured interviews with Poole and Knight, among others. In April 2002, Faith Evans and Voletta Wallace (Biggie's mother) filed a civil suit against the L.A.P.D. alleging wrongful death, among other charges. In September of that year, the *L.A. Times* published a report alleging that the Notorious B.I.G. had paid members of the Crips gang $1 million to murder 2Pac, and even supplied the gun used. Several of Biggie's relatives and friends stepped forward to say that the rapper had been recording in New Jersey, not masterminding a hit in Las Vegas; the report was also roundly criticized in the hip-hop community, which was anxious to avoid reopening old wounds. —*Steve Huey*

★ **Ready to Die** / Sep. 13, 1994 / Bad Boy ✦✦✦✦✦
The album that reinvented East Coast rap for the gangsta age, *Ready to Die* made the Notorious B.I.G. a star, and vaulted Sean "Puffy" Combs' Bad Boy label into the spotlight as well. Today it's recognized as one of the greatest hardcore rap albums ever recorded, and that's mostly due to Biggie's skill as a storyteller. His raps are easy to understand, but his skills are hardly lacking—he has a loose, easy flow and a talent for piling multiple rhymes on top of one another in quick succession. He's blessed with a flair for the dramatic, and slips in and out of different contradictory characters with ease. Yet, no matter how much he heightens things for effect, it's always easy to see elements of Biggie in his narrators and of his own experience in the details; everything is firmly rooted in reality, but plays like scenes from a movie. A sense of doom pervades his most involved stories: fierce bandits ("Gimme the

Loot"), a hustler's beloved girlfriend ("Me & My Bitch"), and robbers out for Biggie's newfound riches ("Warning") all die in hails of gunfire. The album is also sprinkled with reflections on the soul-draining bleakness of the streets—"Things Done Changed," "Ready to Die," and "Everyday Struggle" are powerfully affecting in their confusion and despair. Not everything is so dark, though; Combs' production collaborations result in some upbeat, commercial moments, and typically cop from recognizable hits: the Jackson 5's "I Want You Back" on the graphic sex rap "One More Chance," Mtume's "Juicy Fruit" on the rags-to-riches chronicle "Juicy," and the Isley Brothers' "Between the Sheets" on the overweight-lover anthem "Big Poppa." Producer Easy Mo Bee's deliberate beats do get a little samey, but it hardly matters: this is Biggie's show, and by the time "Suicidal Thoughts" closes the album on a heartbreaking note, it's clear why he was so revered even prior to his death. —*Steve Huey*

Life After Death / Mar. 25, 1997 / Bad Boy ✦✦✦✦
It may have taken the Notorious B.I.G. a few years to follow up his milestone debut, *Ready to Die* (1994), with another album, but when he did return with *Life After Death* in 1997, he did so in a huge way. The ambitious album, intended as somewhat of a sequel to *Ready to Die*, picking up where its predecessor left off, sprawled across the span of two discs, each filled with music, 24 songs in all. You'd expect any album this sprawling to include some lackluster filler. That's not really the case with *Life After Death*, however. Like 2Pac's *All Eyez on Me* from a year before, an obvious influence, Biggie's album made extensive use of various producers—DJ Premier, Easy Mo Bee, Clark Kent, RZA, and more of New York's finest—resulting in a diverse, eclectic array of songs. Plus, Biggie similarly brought in various guest rappers—Jay-Z, Lil' Kim, Bone Thugs, Too Short, L.O.X., Mase—a few vocalists—R. Kelly, Angela Winbush, 112—and, of course, Puff Daddy, who is much more omnipresent here than on *Ready to Die*, where he mostly remained on the sidelines. It's perhaps Puffy himself to thank for this album's biggest hits: "Mo Money Mo Problems," "Hypnotize," "Sky's the Limit," three songs that definitely owe much to his pop touch. There's still plenty of the gangsta tales on *Life After Death* that won Biggie so much admiration on the streets, but it's the pop-laced songs that stand out as highlights. In hindsight, Biggie couldn't have ended his career with a more fitting album than *Life After Death*. Over the course of only two albums, he achieved every success imaginable, perhaps none greater than this unabashedly overreaching success. *Ready to Die* is a milestone album, for sure, but it's nowhere near as extravagant or epic as *Life After Death*. —*Jason Birchmeier*

Born Again / Dec. 7, 1999 / Bad Boy ✦✦✦
Considering it was released almost three years after his death, it'd be easy to dismiss the Notorious B.I.G.'s third album as a cash-in or merely a tribute album, similar to Puff Daddy's *No Way Out*. Fact is, *Born Again* includes a lot of previously unheard material from Biggie, and guest spots from Busta Rhymes, Redman & Method Man, Missy Elliott, Ice Cube, and Snoop Dogg work better than could be expected. It's difficult to say where all this material came from, but it's probable that the productions were simply arranged around old rhymes from Biggie himself. On most tracks, he takes a spotlight and then the guest rapper comes in. Thanks to executive producer Puff Daddy, it'd be easy to fool those not into hip-hop that the Notorious B.I.G. was still alive. The outro, a spoken-word reminiscence by Voletta Wallace (his mother) is a bit touching but also a bit ghoulish. For B.I.G. fans, this is another must-have, but for anyone who thinks the rap industry routinely goes too far in pursuit of the almighty dollar, *Born Again* is yet further proof. —*Keith Farley*

N.W.A

f. 1986, Los Angeles, CA **db.** 1991
Group / Golden Age, Gangsta Rap, West Coast Rap, Hardcore Rap
N.W.A, the unapologetically violent and sexist pioneers of gangsta rap, are in many ways the most notorious group in the history of rap. Emerging in the late '80s, when Public Enemy had rewritten the rules of hardcore rap by proving that it could be intelligent, revolutionary, and socially aware, N.W.A capitalized on PE's sonic breakthroughs while ignoring their message. Instead, the five-piece crew celebrated the violence and hedonism of the criminal life, capturing it all in blunt, harsh language. Initially, the group's relentless attack appeared to be serious, vital commentary, and it even provoked the FBI to caution N.W.A's record company, but following Ice Cube's departure in late

1989, the group began to turn to self-parody. With his high-pitched whine, Eazy-E's urban nightmares now seemed like comic book fantasies, but ones that fulfilled the fantasies of the teenage white suburbanites who had become their core audience, and the group became more popular than ever. Nevertheless, clashing egos prevented the band from recording a third album, and they fell apart once producer Dr. Dre left for a solo career in 1992. Although the group was no longer active, their influence—from their funky, bass-driven beats to their exaggerated lyrics—was evident throughout the '90s.

Ironically, in their original incarnation N.W.A were hardly revolutionary. Eazy-E (born Eric Wright), a former drug dealer who started Ruthless Records with money he earned by pushing, was attempting to start a rap empire by building a roster of successful rap artists. However, he wasn't having much success until Dr. Dre (born Andre Young)—a member of the World Class Wreckin' Cru—and Ice Cube (born O'Shea Jackson) began writing songs for Ruthless. Eazy tried to give one of the duo's songs, "Boyz-N-the Hood," to Ruthless signees HBO, and when the group refused, Eazy formed N.W.A—an acronym for Niggaz With Attitude—with Dre and Cube, adding World Class Wreckin' Cru member DJ Yella (born Antoine Carraby), the Arabian Prince, and the D.O.C. to the group.

N.W.A's first album, N.W.A. and the Posse, was a party-oriented jam record that largely went ignored upon its 1987 release. In the following year, the group added MC Ren (born Lorenzo Patterson) and revamped their sound, bringing in many of the noisy, extreme sonic innovations of Public Enemy and adopting a self-consciously violent and dangerous lyrical stance. Late in 1988, N.W.A delivered Straight Outta Compton, a vicious hardcore record that became an underground hit with virtually no support from radio, the press, or MTV. N.W.A became notorious for their hardcore lyrics, especially those of "Fuck tha Police," which resulted in the FBI sending a warning letter to Ruthless and its parent company, Priority, suggesting that the group should watch their step.

Most of the group's political threat left with Cube when he departed in late 1989 amid many financial disagreements. A nasty feud between N.W.A and the departed rapper began that would culminate with Cube's "No Vaseline," an attack on the group's management released on his 1991 Death Certificate album. By the time the song was released, N.W.A, for all intents and purposes, was finished.

In the two years between Cube's departure and the group's dissolution, N.W.A was dominated by Eazy's near-parodic lyrics and Dre's increasingly subtle and complex productions. The group quickly released an EP, 100 Miles and Runnin', in 1990 before following it up early the next year with Niggaz4life (spelled backwards on the cover as Efil4zaggin). Niggaz4life was teeming with dense, funky soundscapes and ridiculously violent and misogynist lyrics. Naturally, the lyrics provoked outrage from many critics and conservative watchdogs, but that only increased the group's predominately male, white suburban audience. Even though the group was at the peak of their popularity, Dre began to make efforts to leave the crew, due to conflicting egos and what he perceived as an unfair record deal.

Dre left the group to form Death Row Records with Suge Knight in early 1992. According to legend, Knight threatened to kill N.W.A's manager Jerry Heller if he refused to let Dre out of his contract. Over the next few years, Dre and Eazy engaged in a highly publicized feud, which included both of the rappers attacking each other on their respective solo albums. Ren and Yella both released solo albums, which were largely ignored, and Eazy continued to record albums that turned him into a complete self-parody until his tragic death from AIDS in March 1995. Before he died, Dre and Cube both made amends with Eazy. With his first solo album, 1992's The Chronic, Dre established himself as the premier hip-hop producer of the mid-'90s, setting the pace for much of hardcore rap with its elastic bass and deep, rolling grooves. Gangsta rap established itself as the most popular form of hip-hop during the '90s—in other words, N.W.A's amoralistic, hedonistic stance temporarily triumphed over the socially conscious, self-aware hip-hop of Public Enemy, and it completely rewrote the rules of hip-hop for the '90s. —Stephen Thomas Erlewine

N.W.A. and the Posse / 1987 / Ruthless ♦♦

Hip-hop was still very much dominated by New York in 1987, when Macola Records (a company that distributed numerous L.A. rap labels in the 1980s, including Eazy-E's Ruthless Records) distributed N.W.A's groundbreaking debut album N.W.A. and the Posse. Ice-T was among the few West Coast rappers enjoying national exposure, and gangsta rap was far from the phenomenon

it would become a few years later. A number of the songs—including the brutally honest "Dopeman"—would be reissued on Straight Outta Compton, while Eazy-E's first single, "Boyz-N-the Hood" would be included on his 1988 solo album, Eazy-Duz-It. And the entire album would be reissued by Priority in 1989. This CD ranges from those early and seminal examples of gangster rap to songs that are pure, unapologetic fun—such as the outrageously humorous "Fat Girl" and N.W.A associates the Fila Fresh Crew's "Drink It Up," an infectious ode to booze employing the melody from the Isley Brothers' "Twist and Shout." One of the Crew's members was the D.O.C., who Dr. Dre and Eazy-E took to the top of the charts in 1989. Though not quite on a par with Straight Outta Compton, this is an engaging and historically important CD that's well worth acquiring. —Alex Henderson

★ **Straight Outta Compton** / 1988 / Ruthless ♦♦♦♦

Straight Outta Compton wasn't quite the first gangsta rap album, but it was the first one to find a popular audience, and its sensibility virtually defined the genre from its 1988 release on. It established gangsta rap—and, moreover, West Coast rap in general—as a commercial force, going platinum with no airplay and crossing over with shock-hungry white teenagers. Unlike Ice-T, there's little social criticism or reflection on the gangsta lifestyle; most of the record is about raising hell—harassing women, driving drunk, shooting it out with cops and partygoers. All of that directionless rebellion and rage produces some of the most frightening, visceral moments in all of rap, especially the amazing opening trio of songs, which threaten to dwarf everything that follows. Given the album's sheer force, the production is surprisingly spare, even a little low budget—mostly DJ scratches and a drum machine, plus a few sampled horn blasts and bits of funk guitar. Although they were as much a reaction against pop-friendly rap, Straight Outta Compton's insistent claims of reality ring a little hollow today, since it hardly ever depicts consequences. But despite all the romanticized invincibility, the force and detail of Ice Cube's writing makes the exaggerations resonate. Although Cube wrote some of his bandmates' raps, including nearly all of Eazy-E's, each member has a distinct delivery and character, and the energy of their individual personalities puts their generic imitators to shame. But although Straight Outta Compton has its own share of posturing, it still sounds refreshingly uncalculated because of its irreverent, gonzo sense of humor, still unfortunately rare in hardcore rap. There are several undistinguished misfires during the second half, but they aren't nearly enough to detract from the overall magnitude. It's impossible to overstate the enduring impact of Straight Outta Compton; as polarizing as its outlook may be, it remains an essential landmark, one of hip-hop's all-time greatest. —Steve Huey

100 Miles and Runnin' EP / Aug. 1990 / Ruthless ♦♦♦

Released almost two years after the seminal Straight Outta Compton and a little less than a year before the flawed Niggaz4life, 100 Miles and Runnin' effectively accomplishes what an EP should. It both built upon the lingering hype that had surrounded Straight Outta Compton and foreshadowed the Niggaz4life-era N.W.A, a group that had grown increasingly dissident yet also much wiser after experiencing seemingly endless controversy. This EP's title track remains one of the group's best moments, and with the MTV-aired video picturing them fleeing from police, it was a fitting song for N.W.A to release at the time; furthermore, the song's thick, heavy production showcases rather brilliantly the fact that Dr. Dre had furthered his production talents immensely. Though perhaps hard to stomach for some, "Just Don't Bite It" is anything but forgettable, with Eazy-E and MC Ren's prerogatives transcending farce and heading into much more potent territory, making this the group's most amusing (in a sense) yet also its most effectively disturbing venture into misogynistic porno rap. The next song, "Sa Prize, Pt. 2," functions as a sequel to "Fuck the Police" while "Real Niggaz" then provides a sample of the racial belligerence that would fill the first half of Niggaz4life and "Kamurshol" promotes the upcoming album over a foreboding beat. Poignantly employing a heavy use of cinematic skits in addition to the songs themselves, 100 Miles and Runnin' showcases N.W.A's strengths succinctly, balancing them perfectly across just five songs, each representing different aspects of the group's tainted ideology. Any more is almost too much—as would arguably be the case with Niggaz4life. —Jason Birchmeier

Niggaz4life / May 30, 1991 / Ruthless ♦♦♦

It couldn't have been easy for N.W.A to succeed Straight Outta Compton, an indisputable landmark moment in rap history. So after three years of enormous controversy, inner strife, and anticipation, it wasn't exactly a surprise when the group's follow-up, *Niggaz4life*, found N.W.A a much different group. The departure of Ice Cube, the group's primary and most talented lyricist, surely made a difference, but there was more. Dr. Dre, Eazy-E, MC Ren, and prolific ghostwriter the D.O.C. weren't out to rouse people anymore à la "Fuck the Police"; they were out to shock. By mostly devoting the first half of this album to racial belligerence and the second half to merciless misogyny, N.W.A successfully made a truly disturbing, if not horrifying, album. Unfortunately, in its effort to create one of the most shocking albums ever, the group forsook some of its talent. For instance, some of Dre's most ominous productions ever often lie buried beneath nearly inaccessible lyrics. Occasionally, such as in "Automobile" or "I'd Rather Fuck You," Eazy manages to at least integrate some farce, but not everyone will share his twisted sense of humor. Taken as a whole, *Niggaz4life* exemplifies just how distraught the group members were with each other and also why their collaborations would quickly come to an end. They had taken their music as far as it could go with this album—too far for its own good, perhaps—yet there's a certain vicarious pleasure here if you view *Niggaz4life* as anti-establishment exploitation rather than sincerity. N.W.A pushed the limits of social acceptability here in every way imaginable in hopes of offending everyone. You may not agree with the shocking result, nor advocate it, but you can't help but admire the rebellious (and perhaps even self-parodying) intent, particularly when you keep in mind that this album amazingly debuted atop the *Billboard* album chart. —*Jason Birchmeier*

Greatest Hits / Jul. 2, 1996 / Ruthless ♦♦♦♦♦

N.W.A's career isn't necessarily one that lends itself well to anthologies. Though they had important singles, especially in the underground hip-hop community in the late '80s, they never received any support from radio or MTV, which meant they never had any official "hits." Instead, their albums were more important, popular, and influential than singles, even if individual tracks—"Fuck the Police," "Straight Outta Compton," "Gangsta Gangsta," "Express Yourself"—became the focus of attention. And, if you notice, all those songs were from *Straight Outta Compton*, the only good album the group ever made. *Greatest Hits* does include all of the high points from that album (the title track is present in a previously unavailable remix), plus a

scatter-shot sampling of raw early singles and the highlights from *100 Miles and Runnin'* and *Niggaz4life*. It's nice to have the good tracks isolated from the group's latter-day efforts, but *Greatest Hits* is unnecessary—all you need is *Straight Outta Compton*. —*Stephen Thomas Erlewine*

The N.W.A. Legacy, Vol. 1: 1988-1998 / Mar. 22, 1999 / Ruthless ♦♦♦♦

The N.W.A. Legacy, Vol. 1: 1988-1998 is a compilation of the best tracks from the family tree spawned by Ice Cube, Eazy-E, Dr. Dre, MC Ren, and Yella. There are only three tracks by the original group (including "Straight Outta Compton" and "███████ the Police"), but the solo tracks include "It Was a Good Day (Remix)" and "Dead Homiez" from Ice Cube, "Boyz-N-the Hood (Remix)" and "We Want Eazy" by Eazy-E, "California Love," "Natural Born Killaz" and "Let Me Ride" by Dr. Dre, plus tracks from Above the Law, Daz Dillinger, da Lench Mob, Mack 10, and Westside Connection. There are still a few great tracks missing from this set, but for the most part the selections are admirable and the collection is excellent. —*Keith Farley*

The N.W.A Legacy, Vol. 2 / Aug. 27, 2002 / Ruthless ♦♦♦

Despite the name, *The N.W.A. Legacy, Vol. 2* isn't an N.W.A release per se, but a compilation of tracks from the pioneering hip-hop group's members and various associates. Snoop Dogg, for instance, shows up five times (in various permutations), while N.W.A is only represented by three tracks, including album cut "Appetite for Destruction." The other two numbers, however, weren't featured on either 1988's *Straight Outta Compton* or 1991's *Niggaz4life*: "Hello," from Ice Cube's *War & Peace, Vol. 2*, and "Chin Check," from 1999's *Next Friday* soundtrack (and in which Snoop Dogg shows up a sixth time, filling in for Eazy-E, who passed away in 1995). This 78-minute release is a follow-up to 1999's well-received two-disc set *The N.W.A. Legacy, Vol. 1: 1988-1998*. If the lineup of artists isn't identical—2Pac and N.W.A's DJ Yella, for instance, don't make repeat appearances—it's quite similar (Mack 10 and D.O.C. do). Highlights include the two non-LP N.W.A tracks and the Westside Connection's Ice Cube-penned "Gangsters Make the World Go Round," a humorously ironic take on the Stylistics' 1971 hit, "People Make the World Go Round." You could say that volume 2 is more of a taster for the N.W.A fan—or soon-to-be fan—than a full-course meal, as Priority would re-release digitally remastered versions of *Compton*, *Niggaz4life*, and Eazy-E's *Eazy-Duz-It* only a few weeks later. —*Kathleen C. Fennessy*

Rodney-O & Joe Cooley

f. 1988

Group / Bass Music, Old School Rap, West Coast Rap

This Los Angeles rap trio was formed by Rodney Oliver and Joe Cooley with "General" Jeff Page, and debuted in 1989 with *Me & Joe*. Though not a sales hit, they scored enough underground attention with such singles as "Everlasting Bass" and "Cooley High" to land a deal with Atlantic. Their label debut was *Three the Hard Way* in 1990, but it didn't do much better. They also issued a Nastymix album *Get Ready to Roll.* —*Ron Wynn*

Me & Joe / 1989 / Egyptian Empire ◆◆◆◆

When Rodney-O & Joe Cooley's first full-length album, *Me & Joe*, came out in 1989, many hip-hoppers were reevaluating the Los Angeles rap scene. In the early to mid-'80s, L.A. wasn't famous for hardcore rap; many people associated Southern California with the high-tech, synthesizer-driven electro-hop sounds of the Egyptian Lover, the Arabian Prince, Uncle Jam's Army, and the World Class Wreckin' Cru (the group that Dr. Dre belonged to before N.W.A). But in 1987 and 1988, the disturbing gangsta rap of Ice-T and N.W.A was giving people a different impression of L.A. rap—and all of a sudden, hip-hoppers were expecting hardcore rap to come from Southern California. Although Rodney and Cooley both had electro-hop credentials, *Me & Joe* is essentially a hardcore rap effort. The LP isn't gangsta rap—Rodney doesn't rap in the first person about gang fights or drive-by shootings—but even so, it sent out a message that South Central L.A. could provide aggressive hip-hop (as opposed to crossover stuff). While some of Cooley's scratching shows an awareness of New York DJs like Jam Master Jay and Cut Creator, *Me & Joe* doesn't sound like it was recorded in the Big Apple. Rodney flows like a West Coast rapper—he doesn't sound like he's from Brooklyn, Queens, or the Boogie Down Bronx—and the production tends to be cleaner than what many New York hip-hoppers were favoring at the time. *Me & Joe* isn't a masterpiece; as far as L.A. rap goes, it isn't as important or as challenging a record as Ice-T's *Power* or N.W.A's *Straight Outta Compton*. But it's a decent and often catchy, if slightly uneven, footnote in the history of West Coast hip-hop. —*Alex Henderson*

Three the Hard Way / 1990 / Atlantic ◆◆◆

Moving from Egyptian Empire to Atlantic, Rodney-O & Joe Cooley tried again for hip-hop stardom with this 1990 album. It again mostly avoided gangsta-style music, although "Three the Hard Way" did try to tap into the 'hood ethic. But the problem wasn't so much the production as the fact that cuts like "Party" and "See Ya" weren't very interesting. —*Ron Wynn*

Get Ready to Roll / 1991 / Nastymix ◆◆

Rodney-O & Joe Cooley made some noteworthy contributions to L.A.'s rap scene in the 1980s, when they embraced hardcore rap as well as high-tech, dance-oriented sounds influenced by Afrika Bambaataa's "Planet Rock." When hardcore rappers on the West Coast starting selling millions of albums, the duo gave up tech-rap and went hardcore all the way. Recorded for Seattle's Nastymix label in 1991, *Get Ready to Roll* was their hardest album up to that point. This CD wasn't the big commercial breakthrough they were hoping for, although most of the material is decent. "Of Funky Stories" provides some anecdotes about life in the inner city, while "Nutty Block" is a sobering commentary on gang violence in South Central L.A. (Nutty Block, in fact, was the name of an L.A. gang faction). After *Get Ready to Roll*, Rodney & Cooley continued to focus on hardcore rap, and commercial success continued to elude them. —*Alex Henderson*

● **Greatest Hits** / Apr. 10, 2001 / Thump ◆◆◆◆◆

Oaktown's 357

db. 1992

Group / Pop-Rap, West Coast Rap

While riding high on his domination of commercial rap in the late '80s and early '90s, MC Hammer branched his empire further by bringing two of his seemingly endless entourage of dancers/stage-hanger-ons into the studio. The result was Oaktown's 357, a female duo some perceived as Hammer's answer to another highly successful female rap team, Salt-N-Pepa. Riding high on Hammer's ever-so-marketable name, the group released *Wild & Loose* to some commercial success, with "Juicy Gotcha Krazy" and "We Like It" both receiving heavy radio rotation. But like all good empires in history, this too has an unhappy ending. As Hammer's popularity slid, so did the rest of his entourage. And while the duo released two more records (1991's *Fully Loaded* and 1992's *Fila Treatment*), they were never quite able to match the success of the first, and quietly disbanded in 1992. —*Rob Theakston*

● **Wild & Loose** / 1989 / Capitol ◆◆◆

Wild & Loose, the debut from the MC Hammer-related project Oaktown's 357, featured a few good moments, like the singles ("Juicy Gotcha Krazy," "We Like It," "Yeah, Yeah, Yeah"), but overall was overly erratic and more than just a touch rambling. —*Ron Wynn*

Fully Loaded / Jul. 29, 1991 / Bust It ◆◆◆

Female rappers Oaktown's 357 began as a support ensemble and trio to MC Hammer. This follow-up to their debut was predominantly innuendo-laden pop fodder, with no compelling, catchy, or even interesting single to give the album a base or momentum. —*Ron Wynn*

Fila Treatment / 1992 / Bust It ◆◆

O.C. (Omar Credle)

b. 1973, Brooklyn, NY

Pop-Rap, Underground Rap, Hip-Hop

An early friend and collaborator with the boys from Organized Konfusion, O.C. appeared on the video for the duo's 1991 single "Fudge Pudge" and gained a record deal for his smooth, intelligent raps. Born in Brooklyn in 1973, Omar Credle moved to Queens when he was 11, moving into a house across the street from Pharoahe Monch. When Monch formed Organized Konfusion with Prince Poetry, O.C. kept in contact with the group and contributed a rap to "Fudge Pudge" from their self-titled debut. By 1994, O.C. had a deal of his own, though Wild Pitch Records had little money to promote his album debut, *Word…Life*. He refused to record again for the label and was dropped. He appeared on Organized Konfusion's second LP, *Stress: The Extinction Agenda*, and the *Crooklyn* soundtrack, but it was almost two years before O.C. was signed again, this time by the much more viable Payday Records (a subsidiary of PolyGram/EMI). O.C.'s second album, *Jewelz*, was released in August 1997. *Bon Appetit* appeared four years later. —*John Bush*

● **Word…Life** / 1994 / Wild Pitch ◆◆◆◆

O.C.'s auspicious debut announced the arrival of one of modern rap's more gifted storytelling lyricists. The artist dropped his thesis on "Time's Up" a '90s rap benchmark track that served to separate rap's true school from its ever-expanding species of frauds. On that track, O.C. takes umbrage with money-grubbing fake MC's over a combined droning bass guitar and well-plucked sample from Slick Rick's "Hey Young World." The album is drenched in classic, hardcore East Coast b-boyism, but O.C. puts the boasts on the shelf to take up more existential subject matter. On "Born to Live" he spins wistful fables from his childhood in order to discuss life's bittersweet fragility: "Born to live/A life to die/Life's so damn short and I wonder why." The soulful composition lifts a tasteful snippet from Keni Burke's "Keep Rising to the Top." O.C.'s connections to Organized Konfusion shine through on his debut, showcasing a thought-provoking intellectual diversity rarely seen on rap albums. Organized's Pharoah Monche sits in on the album, as do producers Buckwild and Lord Finesse. *Word … Life* saw little commercial success due, in part, to the drained coffers of the failed endeavor that was Wild Pitch Records, but one would be hardpressed to find a hardcore hip-hop fan without this recording somewhere in their collection—*Micheal Di Bella*

Jewelz / Aug. 19, 1997 / Payday ✦✦✦✦
D.I.T.C. cohort O.C. returned in 1997 with his second full-length LP, titled *Jewelz*, and that is exactly what it is. Even though his 1995 debut was well-received within the hip-hop community, the same adulation did not correlate to sales success. Instead of succumbing to mainstream pressure, O.C. kept his music street based, and the listeners reap the benefits of that high quality. With a production roster of top-flight NY producers (Premier, Buckwild, Da Beatminerz, Showbiz, Lord Finesse, and Ogee) your ears never get a rest. "My World" sets it off and of the four cuts Primo contributed, this shines brightest: "My skills ill and all of that above/Confidence I'm not worried about a street buzz/I'm O.C. who you I never heard a ya/Get out my face before I turn into a mother*uckin murderer/I want the green like endo/A mansion a car/A wife who's never been a bimbo/Too much to ask well to me that's simple/Wanna retire on a yacht called 'the S.S. Minnow'." "Win the G" teams O.C. with Freddie Foxx (one of the two tracks the pair collaborate on) over yet another Primo track. "Dangerous" is a party-type cut with O.C. and Big L flipping verses back and forth over a Beatminerz track. O.C. is truly one of the most skilled MCs in the business, and if he dropped a few cuts catered to radio we would probably hear more from him—but here's hoping he never goes that route. Like O.C. said in his classic single, "Time's Up": "I'd rather be broke and have a whole lot of respect." —*Matt Conaway*

Bon Appetit / Apr. 24, 2001 / JCOR ✦✦✦
Brooklyn/Queens rapper O.C. (Omar Credle)'s third release is a far cry from the underground rapper's groundbreaking mid-'90s work. The member of the D.I.T.C. family is an abundantly gifted lyricist with the kind of dynamic persona equaled by very few in the rap game. However, for an artist who delivered a definitively timeless blow against money-grubbing studio thug MCs with his 1994 classic cut "Time's Up" ("those who pose lyrical and really ain't true I feel … their time's limited hard rocks too"), O.C. effects a diametric shift in tone and character on *Bon Appetit*. While it is hard to fault a long-suffering artist for making a bid at financial freedom, there is something altogether distasteful about this project. O.C. serves up a full-course meal of corrupted ideals, thereby tarnishing his credibility as one of hip-hop's pillars of purity. While the occasional D.I.T.C. stamp helps this album from submerging irrevocably in mainstream iced-out production and concepts (Lord Finesse's gurgling beat on "Dr. Know" and a guest appearance from the gifted AG on "Weed and Drinks"), O.C. gorges himself on aimless rhymes and tired tales of decadence and arrogance. While O.C.'s robust storylines do pop up on an inspired ode to the late Big L ("Psalm 23") and even bend toward a lesson on the solid "Doin' Dirt," of the album's 13 cuts, only a few hint at the quality of his prior two efforts. Some of the blame rests on the shoulders of O.C.'s in-house producer Buckwild, who seems to be doing his best Jermaine Dupri impression throughout. While all is not lost for O.C., it's safe to say that the goals and mainstream market power of hip-hop have claimed another victim. This repast might just make a few hip-hop heads lose their lunch. —*M.F. Di Bella*

Kardinal Offishall (Jason Harrow)

Vocals, Producer / Hip-Hop, Trip-Hop, Ambient Breakbeat, Turntablism
Canadian rapper Kardinal Offishall is arguably the best-kept secret in Canadian hip-hop, a genre that is in itself the best-kept secret in hip-hop. The 6'4" rapper is also known as one of the best producers in Canada, having helped produce albums for other Toronto artists. Born Jason Harrow, Kardinal Offishall started rapping early and was winning competitions when he was 12. Signed to a publishing deal with Warner/Chappell Music Canada at the age of 20, Offishall blends soul, dancehall, reggae, hip-hop, and a wholly inventive approach to beats on his 21-track debut album *Eye & I*. Offishall earned a name for his work with other artists, including the Rascalz hit single "Northern Touch," along with Canadian rappers Choclair, Checkmate,

and Thrust. He also produced much of Choclair's album *Ice Cold* and played several instruments on the tracks, including the catchy piano hook in Choclair's hit single, "Let's Ride." With the success of Choclair, Kardinal released his 12" "Husslin," which quickly became an underground favorite and shows that the lanky rapper has the potential to reach audiences on both sides of the border. —*Jon Azpiri*

● **Quest for Fire: Firestarter, Vol. 1** / May 22, 2001 / MCA ✦✦✦
While there are a slew of Canadian MCs (Saukrates, Choclair, Rascalz, and Swollen Members) who appear ready to reverse the stigma of the up-north rapper, as of yet, none have been able to elude the novelty label. On "Bakardi Slang," the anthemic lead single to his *Quest for Fire: Firestarter, Vol. 1* major-label debut, Toronto's Kardinal Offishal declares "Kardinal gonna show you how the T-Dot rolls." Yet Kardinal, much like his fellow Circle member Choclair, displays only flashes of promise here. *Firestarter* takes on many identities: the insightful consciousness of "Man By Choice" (which explores the origin of the "N" word and all of its nasty connotations), the underground delight of the Saukrates-featured "Gotta Get It," and "Husslin." Yet, there is also a commercial element at work here, as a slew of tracks (e.g., "Powerful" and "Quest for Fire") are undermined by flimsy R&B hooks, which actually make you appreciate Lil' Mo. Granted, Kardinal does attempt to showcase some versatility with *Firestarter*, whether through the low-budget musing of "U R Ghetto 2002" or by soaking *Firestarter* with his tropically enhancing West Indian heritage, which is a major influence here. *Firestarter* has enough Jamaican dancehall riddims to make the average Bounty Killer fan say, "Bwoy," but at 73 minutes and change, it's also enough to make the average b-boy say, "Bo-ring." —*Matt Conaway*

Ol' Dirty Bastard (Russell Tyrone Jones)

b. 1969, Brooklyn, NY
Vocals, Mixing, Producer / East Coast Rap, Hip-Hop, Hardcore Rap
One of the founding members of the Wu-Tang Clan, who recorded some of the most influential hip-hop of the '90s, Ol' Dirty Bastard was the loose cannon of the group, both on record and off. Delivering his outrageously profane, free-associative rhymes in a distinctive half-rapped, half-sung style, ODB came across as a mix of gonzo comic relief and not-quite-stable menace. Unfortunately, after launching a successful solo career, his personal life began to exhibit those same qualities. ODB spent much of 1998 and 1999 getting arrested with ridiculous, comical frequency, building up a rap sheet that now reads not so much like a soap opera as an epic Russian novel. At first, his difficulties with the law made him a larger-than-life figure, the ringmaster of rap's most cartoonish sideshow. Sadly, his life inevitably slipped out of control, and the possibility that his continued antics were at least partly the result of conscious image making disappeared as time wore on. It was difficult for observers to tell whether ODB's wildly erratic behavior was the result of serious drug problems or genuine mental instability; bad luck certainly played a role in his downfall, but so did his own undeniably poor judgment. Despite being sentenced to prison on drug charges in 2001, it's worth noting that while he was running amuck, Ol' Dirty's offenses were largely nonviolent; the saddest part of his story is that, in the end, the only person he truly harmed was himself.

Ol' Dirty Bastard was born Russell Tyrone Jones in Brooklyn in 1969, and grew up in the neighborhood of Fort Green as a welfare child. As he got older, he started hanging out more and more with his cousins Robert Diggs and Gary Grice; they all shared a taste for rap music and kung-fu movies. The trio parlayed their obsessions into founding the Wu-Tang Clan, renaming themselves Ol' Dirty Bastard (since there was no father to his style), the RZA, and the Genius, respectively. The Wu grew into an innovatively structured hip-hop collective designed to hit big and then spin off as many solo careers for its members as possible. Buoyed by the RZA's production genius and a number of strong personalities, the Wu-Tang Clan's first album, *Enter the Wu-Tang (36 Chambers)*, was released at the end of 1993 and became one of the most influential rap albums of the decade. Earlier in the year, Ol' Dirty had been convicted of second-degree assault in New York, the only violent offense ever proven against him; trouble continued to stalk him in 1994, when he was shot in the stomach by another rapper in the Bedford-Stuyvesant section of Brooklyn following a street argument.

Luckily, the injuries weren't serious, and Dirty became the second Wu-Tang member to launch a solo career (after Method Man) when he signed with Elektra and released the RZA-produced *Return to the 36 Chambers: The Dirty Version* in early 1995. The stellar singles "Brooklyn Zoo" and "Shimmy Shimmy Ya" both became hits, making the album a gold-selling success. Additionally, his guest spot on a remix of Mariah Carey's "Fantasy" produced one of the year's most unlikeliest hitmaking teams. With the concurrent success of the other Wu solo projects, anticipation for the group's second album ran high, and when the double-disc *Wu-Tang Forever* came out in the summer of 1997, it sold over 600,000 copies in its first week of release. Included on the second disc was "Dog Shit," two and a half minutes of perhaps the most bizarre, scatological ODB ranting that had yet appeared on record. And then, the saga began.

In November 1997, Ol' Dirty Bastard was arrested for failing to pay nearly a year's worth of child support—around $35,000—for the three children he had with his wife, Icelene Jones (by this point, he'd fathered a total of 13 children, beginning in his teenage years). Things picked up in February 1998: he started his own clothing line, dubbed My Dirty Wear, and along with several protégés, he rushed out of a New York recording studio to help save a four-year-old girl who had been hit by a car and lay trapped underneath. The very next day, at the Grammy Awards (where the Wu had been nominated for Best Rap Album), there followed the incident that truly established the Ol' Dirty legend. During Shawn Colvin's acceptance speech for her Song of the Year award, ODB rushed the stage seemingly out of nowhere, clad in a bright red suit. He took over the microphone and launched into a rambling complaint about buying an expensive new outfit but losing the Grammy to Puff Daddy, whom he described as "good" but not as good as his own group, because "Wu-Tang is for the children." Hustled off stage after this puzzling, oddly timed outburst, ODB was the talk of the next day's news reports, and many mainstream outlets had to find ways of avoiding the "bastard" portion of his name. He further confounded the public by announcing in April that he was scrapping his Ol' Dirty Bastard alias (which headed up a long list that included Osirus [sic], Joe Bannanas [sic], Dirt McGirt, Dirt Dog, and Unique Ason) and calling himself Big Baby Jesus. None of his explanations in interviews even verged on coherence, and the press never took the switch all that seriously; even the erstwhile Big Baby Jesus himself seemed to forget about the idea after a short time.

The rest of 1998 was a slow downward spiral. In April he pled guilty to a charge of attempted assault on Icelene Jones, resulting in a protection order against him; the following month, a bench warrant was issued for his arrest after he missed two court dates concerning his child support payments (he finally did show up and signed an agreement to pay off the debts). In late June, ODB was shot in a robbery attempt in Brownsville, Brooklyn; two assailants pushed their way into ODB's girlfriend's apartment, stole some money and jewelry from the rapper, and shot him once. The bullet entered his back and went through his arm before exiting his body, but luckily the wounds were superficial, and several hours after receiving emergency-room treatment, ODB ignored the hospital's request for overnight observation and simply walked out. Only one week later, ODB was arrested in Virginia Beach for shoplifting, after walking out of a shoe store wearing a pair of $50 sneakers. Adding insult to injury, his SUV was stolen from outside a New York recording studio a couple weeks later. Undaunted, Dirty went ahead with his plans to tour, set up his own Osirus Entertainment label, and recorded with a group of protégés called D.R.U.G. (Dirty Rotten Underground Grimies). As a result, he missed several court dates concerning his Virginia Beach shoplifting charge, resulting in an order for his arrest.

That difficulty seemed to matter less when, in September, ODB was arrested in Los Angeles for making terrorist threats. He'd been attending a concert by R&B singer Des'ree at the House of Blues in West Hollywood, and refused to be escorted outside by security who'd grown tired of his drunken rowdiness; after he was kicked out, he returned and threatened to shoot the security staff—a felony in California, punishable by up to three years in jail. Not two weeks after posting bail, ODB was kicked out of a hotel in Berlin, Germany, for lounging on his balcony in the nude (no charges were filed). He later returned to California, where he was arrested once again in November on *more* charges of making terrorist threats—this time allegedly threatening to kill an ex-girlfriend (and mother of one of his children). ODB pled not guilty in both "terrorist" cases, and returned to New York in January. At this point, it was still difficult to view ODB as a genuine criminal—not that his conduct had been exemplary by any means, but there was a possibility that he was simply misunderstood, or that the California criminal justice system was essentially criminalizing the act of being a blowhard.

Shortly after ODB's return to New York, he was pulled over for a traffic violation while driving with his cousin. What happened next was never fully clarified. The officers claimed that ODB got out of his vehicle and started shooting at them; he was arrested and charged with attempted murder and criminal weapon possession. However, the police were never able to produce a matching weapon, ammunition, or empty ammo shells to support their claims, and there were a multitude of conflicting stories reported from their side as to the exact details of the incident. In February a grand jury decided there was not enough evidence and dismissed the case, after which an outraged ODB filed suit against the arresting officers. Just a couple of weeks later, ODB once again fell victim to the vagaries of the California legal system. After citing him for double parking his car in Hollywood, police discovered that he was driving without a license, and when they searched him, they found that he was wearing a bulletproof vest. This was understandable, given his recent experience in New York, but California had recently passed a law making it illegal for convicted violent felons to wear body armor—and because of his 1993 second-degree assault conviction, ODB fell under that category (in fact, his arrest was one of the very first under the law). In March, now back in New York, ODB was pulled over for *another* traffic violation (this time driving without license plates), and police found a small amount of crack cocaine in his SUV, leading to misdemeanor drug possession charges. Five days later, ODB was pulled over and cited *again* for driving without license plates, as well as driving with a suspended license. In the face of this impossible legal maze, April brought one small bit of good news—the terrorist-threat charges involving his ex-girlfriend were dismissed due to lack of evidence. What was more, former O.J. Simpson defense attorney Robert Shapiro signed on as ODB's legal representative.

Still, ODB's run of ill luck continued. At the end of July, he was jailed in California for failing to pay a portion of his bail from the House of Blues case (in a recent court hearing, he'd acknowledged financial difficulties stemming from his legal bills). He was able to post the money and was released; however, just days later, he was arrested in New York after running a red light. He was *still* driving on a suspended license, but what was more serious, officers discovered not only marijuana but also 20 vials of crack cocaine. He was able to post bail, but didn't return to Los Angeles for a hearing in the body-armor case, and his bail there was revoked and a bench warrant issued for his arrest. In mid-August ODB checked himself into a rehab center in upstate New York, hoping to address his escalating problem with hard drugs; he soon transferred to a different center in California.

Somehow, in the middle of his incredible, headline-dominating run as a bi-coastal outlaw, ODB had found time to record a new album under the auspices of several different producers, including the RZA and the Neptunes. Released in September 1999, *Nigga Please* entered the charts at number ten, aided by his position as the undisputed king of hip-hop bad boys; it also spawned a minor hit single in "Got Your Money." In November, ODB received more good news, of a sort: his sentencing in the two pending California cases (the body armor and the House of Blues) came out to one year in drug rehabilitation and three years' probation, with no prison time. Despite the fact that a resolution was in sight, ODB complained during the sentencing hearing that he felt police had been targeting him excessively. That sense of persecution manifested itself in a January 2000 hearing in New York, related to his drug charges; apparently exasperated by all the chaos, a sullen ODB ignored the presiding judge, talked dirty to a female DA (in typically bizarre fashion, he reportedly called her a "sperm donor"), and actually took a nap, thereby erasing any inclinations the prosecution had toward leniency. Afterward, he apparently got drunk, violating the terms of his rehab program and probation conditions; upon returning to California, he was kicked out of rehab and transferred to jail. Although he could have faced prison time for breaking probation, ODB received a more lenient sentence of six months in rehab.

Up until this point, ODB had managed to avoid prison time, since he was clearly a drug addict in need of help. Yet at the same time, his apparent unwillingness to be helped meant that, for better or for worse, he was running out of chances. While he'd suffered some terrible luck in his run-ins with the law, the last straw was entirely of his own making: in October 2000, with just two more months in rehab to go, ODB made a run for it. He spent the next month as a fugitive from the law, making his way across the country and secretly recording some new material with the RZA. ODB turned up in a very public fashion at the November record-release party for the new Wu-Tang

Clan album, *The W* (which had been dedicated to him, and featured his vocals on one track, "Conditioner"; other contributions had been deemed too bizarre for release). He took the stage in the Hammerstein Ballroom in front of hundreds of incredulous, wildly cheering fans, and only added to his mystique by managing to leave the facility without getting arrested, despite the large police presence outside. After a few more days on the lam, ODB was captured in a McDonald's parking lot in Philadelphia while signing autographs for a large crowd of fans; in fact, the crowd was so large that the restaurant manager had called police, not knowing what was going on. ODB was extradited to New York, where he stood trial on not only his prior drug charges but also the various traffic violations and a charge that he violated the protection order on Icelene Jones in 1998. After several trial postponements, in April 2001 ODB accepted a deal from prosecutors that essentially wiped out his other offenses in New York in exchange for a guilty plea to the cocaine possession charges. He received the minimum sentence of two to four years in state prison, and received credit for the eight months he'd already served; moreover, he was allowed to serve the jail time he owed the state of California concurrently. Still, the daunting prospect of state prison was nearly too much for ODB to bear; in July he had to be put on suicide watch pending a psychiatric evaluation, and reports surfaced that he'd suffered a broken leg after being assaulted in a holding facility.

It remained to be seen how ODB would hold up under the harsh environment of prison, and whether he would ever resolve his legal problems to the point where he could once again enjoy a productive recording career. Accordingly, Elektra issued the best-of compilation *The Dirty Story: The Best of Ol' Dirty Bastard* in 2001, despite the fact that he'd only released two albums. In early 2002, some of the material he'd recorded during his fugitive days surfaced on the new album *The Trials and Tribulations of Russell Jones*, put out by the small D3 label. With a dearth of actual ODB material to rely on, the album was padded out by a number of guest rappers and handled by unknown producers (even the RZA steered clear of the affair), and ODB himself went on record as knowing virtually nothing about the release. The reviews were almost uniformly scathing, calling *Trials and Tribulations* a shoddy piece of exploitation. —*Steve Huey*

● **Return to the 36 Chambers** / Mar. 28, 1995 / Elektra ✦✦✦✦✦
As a member of the Wu-Tang Clan, Ol' Dirty Bastard's bizarre, freeform rants added both comic relief and a dangerous unpredictability to the group's chemistry. ODB's RZA-produced solo debut *Return to the 36 Chambers* stretches his schtick over a full album, which if anything makes him sound even more unbalanced. Long before the album ends, it's clear that ODB has emptied his bag of tricks—loose, off-the-beat raps that sometimes don't even rhyme, unbelievably graphic vulgarity, gonzo off-key warbling (which sounds a little like Biz Markie as a mental patient), and general goofing off. Yet within that role as hardcore rap's clown prince of psychosis, ODB is pretty damned entertaining. His leaps in association are often as disturbing as they are funny, whether they're couched in scatological detail or not; they certainly don't make his widely publicized erratic behavior seem at all surprising. And, despite the unstructured feel dominating most of the album, there are a fair share of hooks, and two absolutely killer singles in "Shimmy Shimmy Ya" and "Brooklyn Zoo." Certainly, there's no reason for the album to be as long as it is, considering the dull filler toward the end. But, even though *Return to the 36 Chambers* might not be the most earth-shattering piece of the Wu-Tang puzzle, it's an infectious party record which proves that, despite his limitations, Ol' Dirty Bastard has the charisma to carry an album on his own. —*Steve Huey*

Nigga Please / Sep. 14, 1999 / Elektra ✦✦✦✦
Hollywood may have Austin Powers, but hip-hop has its own international man of mystery; his name is Ol' Dirty Bastard. ODB lives and suffers with the adage that any publicity is good publicity, since he hasn't spent the greater part of the last two years gaining widespread notoriety for the music he makes. Rather, he has spent a majority of that time turning up on local crime blotters from coast to coast, trying to raise bail money, recuperating from gunshot wounds, rescuing a kid who was struck by a car, and hijacking the 1998 Grammy awards. With that in mind, it should be obvious by now that personalities of ODB's magnitude come around once in a lifetime. And even though he is repetitiously contradictory with his neurotic ramblings, who cares? That's half of his appeal, as there is an irrefutable attraction to ODB's carefree and inebriated outlook on life. With rhymes frequently so garbled

that they are barely decipherable, calling ODB a quintessential lyricist would surely insult the intelligence of any hip-hop purist. Yet the dirt dog is indubitably a distinguished MC and a uniquely abrasive one at that, as he turns an array of voice-cracking/blood-curdling hooks into grisly masterpieces. Examples include the nonsensical crooning of his Rick James interpolations "Cold Blooded" and "You Don't Want to Fuck With Me," and the ridiculously addictive "Rollin Wit You." Despite that ODB's production chores are handled admirably by the Neptunes, Irv Gotti, and RZA, the backing acoustics are hardly needed; ODB rarely stays on beat and there is little, or no structure to his rhyme sequences. Safely nestled away in his own little world, there is no containing ODB's freespirited outlook on life. His is a world that is heavy on shock value, yet undeniably entertaining. —*Matt Conaway*

The Dirty Story: The Best of Ol' Dirty Bastard / Aug. 28, 2001 / Elektra ✦✦✦✦✦
Usually a two-album career doesn't warrant a best-of collection but then again, Ol' Dirty Bastard isn't your usual artist. *The Dirty Story* hit the streets in 2001, just as Ol' Dirty was in the headlines yet again for ongoing drug/legal problems. It's not exactly a mandatory addition to the troubled rapper's catalog, and feels more like an exploitative attempt to bank on the news headlines. You get the better moments from Ol' Dirty's debut, *Return to the 36 Chambers*—"Shimmy Shimmy Ya," "Brooklyn Zoo," "Raw Hide," "Proteck Ya Neck II in the Zoo"—and a few of the highlights from *Nigga Please:* "I Can't Wait," the Neptunes-produced tracks "Got Your Money" and "Recognize," and Ol' Dirty's Rick James cover, "Cold Blooded." Furthermore, since this album only features 11 songs and no interludes, it's a pleasant listen—no lulls, no filler, and refreshingly brief. Of course, anyone with one or more of Ol' Dirty's albums will find little justification for buying this. In essence, *The Dirty Story* is a distillation of two albums with the Mariah Carey collaboration "Fantasy" thrown in as a bonus. As such, *The Best of Ol' Dirty Bastard* is the perfect one-stop listen for anyone curious about the Ol' Dirty story, particularly those who don't already have the otherwise excellent *Return to the 36 Chambers* album. —*Jason Birchmeier*

The Trials and Tribulations of Russell Jones / Mar. 19, 2002 / D3 ✦✦
When he wasn't busy running from the authorities in late 2000, Ol' Dirty Bastard haphazardly recorded vocals for his third album after escaping a court-ordered drug rehab program in Los Angeles. ODB's record label at the time, Elektra, didn't want anything to do with the rapper; in fact, when the infamous Wu-Tang Clan member was convicted of possessing 20 vials of crack-cocaine a few months following his notorious escape from rehab, Elektra released a best-of collection, despite there only being a grand total of only two albums in the ODB catalog. This crafty decision by Elektra partly intended to capitalize on ODB's legal problems while simultaneously ending the label's relationship with the obviously troubled rapper. However, given the lucrative parade of posthumous 2Pac albums in the early 2000s, it wasn't surprising when the crass D3 label began assembling ODB's third album by any means necessary. First of all, D3 gathered all the miscellaneous vocals ODB had recorded as a fugitive. Second of all, since there weren't many vocals to work with, let alone many quality vocals, D3 hired a cast of guests to fill out the album and make the songs more palatable: C-Murder, Mack 10, E-40, Big Syke, Too Short, and more. Last of all, the label brought in the Insane Clown Posse for the album's lead single, "Dirty and Stinkin'," and recorded a hard rock version of the track as well. What all of this adds up to is *The Trials and Tribulations of Russell Jones*, a shallow album that substitutes exploitation for substance. Producers like RZA and the Neptunes made ODB's past work successful; not ODB himself. Unfortunately, the producers on this album aren't nearly as talented and don't have as much to work with here. ODB's rhymes are sloppier and more incomprehensible than ever, and the guests do most of the rapping. Furthermore, the 2Pac-esque "Trials and Tribulations" frame is nothing more than a frame; sure, there are many skits where ODB rambles illogically, but you're more likely to hear him narrate defecation—which, believe it or not, actually takes place late in the album—than speak rationally. In the end, it was perhaps smart of D3 to bring in the Insane Clown Posse, since that's precisely the level that ODB has sunken to on this album—juvenile exploitation for disenchanted suburban white boys. For years, ODB seemed funny, but here the laughter is nowhere to be found, replaced instead by the disheartening reality that the most outlandish member of the Wu-Tang Clan had fallen victim to America's drug war and, subsequently, to crass commercialism. —*Jason Birchmeier*

112

Group / Urban, Hip-Hop

Equally rooted in gospel, soul and hip-hop, 112 was the first and most successful urban vocal group to emerge from Sean "Puffy" Combs' Bad Boy Records roster. Not only was the group's eponymous 1996 debut popular, but the group could be heard on records by such Bad Boy artists as Puff Daddy. Unlike most artists on Bad Boy, 112's image was clean, pure, and wholesome, which helped the group cross over to a more mainstream audience.

The four members of 112—Marvin, Daron, Q, and Mike—met each other while attending high school in Atlanta, Georgia. The quartet began to play talent shows at school and local churches, eventually gaining the attention of Courtney Sills and Kevin Wales, who soon became the group's managers. Sills and Wales brought 112 to the attention of Sean "Puffy" Combs at Bad Boy Records. Combs signed on as the executive producer of 112's eponymous debut album, which featured songs the group cowrote with such professional songwriters as Stevie J, Wayna Morris of Boyz II Men, and Combs himself. "Only You," the group's debut single, was released in the summer of 1996 and climbed to number three on the R&B charts, peaking at number 13 on the pop charts. *112* was released in late 1996, and it steadily worked its way to gold status as the group's second single, "Come Seem Me," reached number 15 on the R&B charts. *Room 112* followed in 1998 and *Part III* was issued three years later. *—Stephen Thomas Erlewine*

● **112** / 1996 / Bad Boy ✦✦✦✦

As the first romantic soul group on Puff Daddy's Bad Boy label, 112 at least has the appearance of originality. However, their eponymous debut demonstrates that this is only an appearance—in reality, they are much like a Boyz II Men clone. That's not necessarily bad, actually. 112 have strong voices, and their smooth harmonies are quite seductive, making the lack of originality in their music easy to overlook. A little more variety on *112* would have been nice—the album consists almost entirely of ballads—but the group's sound and Puffy's professional production make it a pleasurable record nevertheless. *—Leo Stanley*

Room 112 / Oct. 20, 1998 / Bad Boy ✦✦

112, Puffy Daddy's four-man crew of smooth-crooning R&B loverboys, come on so aggressively sticky and heart-on-sleeve earnest throughout their second album, *Room 112*, that it's often difficult to wade through the torrent of molasses pouring down and through each of the songs. Combining old school doo wop harmonies with '90s hip-hop trappings—robotic beats, mechanic vocals, half-baked ideas—112 do very little to distinguish themselves from the pack. And because this is a Puffy project, the occasional heavy-handed sample creeps in for an unwelcome visit (the biggest offender here is the use of Shawn Colvin's "Sunny Came Home" during one particularly uninspired tune). The best cut here is "Love Me (Feat. Mase)," a bit of new-jack breakdown that swings and hammers with convincing verve and groove, something prominently absent from the rest of the dreary *Room 112*. *—Michael Gallucci*

Part III / Mar. 20, 2001 / Bad Boy ✦✦✦

112 have proven themselves as one of the most successful and enduring acts to emerge from the 1990s urban music explosion, and continue to prove their longevity on their third set, *Part III*. Their second album, *Room 112*, despite the hits "Love Me" and "Anywhere," failed to hint at any artistic progress for the group, but the third effort is a different story. A lot of the sappy ballads that impaired their previous outings are abandoned in favor of edgier, techno-flavored jams, resulting in a more modern and forward-sounding effort. The album's first single, "It's Over Now," is an aching slice of melodrama that proved to be the group's biggest hit to date, and one of the best singles of the year. Other cuts on the album pick up where that one left off, utilizing cutting beats and electronic sounds, such as the album's dance-flavored opener "Dance With Me," the second single "Peaches & Cream," and "All I Want Is You," which is augmented with rock guitars to fine effect. And as always, the group's vocals are nothing short of stellar. Despite some clichéd lyrics (case in point—"Don't Hate Me") and sagging ballads toward the middle of the album (although the ballad "Missing You" is a well-crafted slice of true soul), this set is definitely a step in the right direction for a hard-working group one can happily classify as having evolved. *—Jose Promis*

Shaquille O'Neal

b. Mar. 6, 1972, Newark, New Jersey

Hip-Hop, Club/Dance, Pop-Rap

With a little help from his friends (production came from Fu-Schnickens, Ali from A Tribe Called Quest, Def Jef, and Erick Sermon), basketball's brightest star of the early '90s, Shaquille O'Neal, released *Shaq Diesel*, a 1993 album showcasing his moderate rapping talents. The following year, he released *Shaq-Fu: Da Return*. In 1996, O'Neal released *The Best of Shaquille O'Neal* in November, followed a week later by his third album, *You Can't Stop the Reign*. He returned in 1998 with *Respect*. *—John Bush*

Shaq Diesel / Oct. 26, 1993 / Jive ✦✦✦

Shaq-Fu: Da Return / Nov. 8, 1994 / Jive ✦✦✦

Shaquille O'Neal's third album, *Shaq-Fu: Da Return*, is a solid (but not outstanding) rap CD that takes another step forward in that no-man's land between legitimacy and novelty act. Shaq's skills are in collaborating with A-list talent, and *Da Return* has its share with efforts by Warren G and Keith Murray, among others. This CD by the basketball great is notable for its more personal songs, including "Biological Didn't Bother," a testament to his stepfather whom he credits for much of his success. *The Best of Shaquille O'Neal* may be Shaq's best collection of songs, but *Shaq-Fu: Da Return* is the album where the artist first finds something to say. *—JT Griffith*

● **The Best of Shaquille O'Neal** / Nov. 12, 1996 / Jive ✦✦✦✦

The Best of Shaquille O'Neal is premature, to say the least. Compiling highlights from two albums that were only moderate hits, *The Best of* does contain all of the rapper's hits—including "What's Up Doc? (Can We Rock?)," "(I Know I Got) Skillz," "I'm Outstanding," "Biological Didn't Bother," and "No Hook"—making it the most consistent record in his catalog, but its quick appearance still makes the album feel like it's a quick cash-in instead of a genuine retrospective. *—Stephen Thomas Erlewine*

Respect / Sep. 15, 1998 / A&M ✦✦✦

Shaquille O'Neal's career as a rapper is a little puzzling, if you look at it closely. Unlike many athletes who dabble in music, Shaq didn't just release one album and move on—he carved out an alternate career, keeping up a regular schedule of releasing an album every two years. Each album was a little different, thanks to new sets of collaborators and a conscious eye to commercial trends, but they were all essentially the same: good natured, mildly entertaining, but ultimately pedestrian records by one charming man. His fourth album, *Respect*, is no different in that respect. It's a well-constructed album that isn't devoid of good moments, such as a cover of Above the Law's "Blaq Supaman," but it's also not particularly distinctive, either in the context of Shaq's career or from the multitudes of mainstream pop-rap albums that are released. As background party music, it works fairly well, but close listening doesn't reap any dividends. Then again, it wasn't meant to—*Respect*, like any Shaquille O'Neal album, sounds like it was meant to be simply a good time. The problem is, the musicians who made the record probably had a better time than the listeners at home. *—Stephen Thomas Erlewine*

Shaquille O'Neal Presents His Superfriends, Vol. 1 / Oct. 9, 2001 / Trauma ✦✦✦✦

It is unlikely that Shaq will ever dominate the charts as he does the backboard. His fifth album is as close to relevant to the mainstream pop world as any Shaq album may get. *Shaquille O'Neal Presents His Superfriends, Vol. 1* continues the center's pattern of regularly releasing new music and also in progressing as a rapper in small steps, not leaps and bounds. The music and rhymes sound more contemporary and less cliché. Shaquille O'Neal's raps are more street, melodic, and adult. Shaq actually no longer seems confused about his target audience; gone is the *Kazaam* zaniness and in its place is a more mature tone. ("Do It Faster," a duet with Twista and Trina, is a randy ode to love and sexual satisfaction.) The most common theme of *Shaquille O'Neal Presents His Superfriends, Vol. 1* is defensive boasting. Shaq hardly claims to be a victim, but these collected songs state that he is number one, has earned all his successes, and can bed any woman he wants. O'Neal and his superfriends lay out enough chronic rhymes to make this sexy, funny, and bold album slam with the dominant authority of a Shaq dunk. A video for "Connected" features W.C. and Nate Dogg in a full-out bling-bling party mode (similar to the real-life celebrations following the Lakers' second championship). A single for "In the Sun," with Common and Black Thought, received solid airplay on urban radio. If there is an essential Shaq track, it is

"I Don't Care" (with Next's RL), the first song in which he seems to have a uncontainable desire to say something. The track is an incendiary attack on those who criticize his free-throwing problems (including a Chick Hern sample). Such is a Shaq album, personal but not political. It is hard to criticize the big fella for pursuing his musical dreams, and while he will likely never release an essential rap album, Shaq will always be able to mobilize the best talent available and crank out a well-produced, fun album. *Shaquille O'Neal Presents His Superfriends, Vol. 1* includes guest vocals from Ludacris, Snoop Dogg, Nate Dogg, Mos Def, George Clinton, Angie Stone, Joi (Lucy Pearl), and others. The CD's producers have worked with Snoop Dogg, 2Pac, Jay-Z, Lauren Hill, and Santana. Music may be Shaq's hobby, but he doesn't mess around. *Shaquille O'Neal Presents His Superfriends, Vol. 1* likely won't appeal to any new fans, but those who have been along for the ride will be rewarded with his new CD. Maybe the best praise for Shaq is that, on the court and on wax, he is no Allen Iverson. A decidedly adult effort. —*JT Griffith*

Onyx

f. 1990, Queens, NY

Group / Hip-Hop, East Coast Rap, Hardcore Rap

Onyx's shouting, in-your-face brand of high-volume rapping proved to be more at home in the slam pit than on the dancefloor and brought the rap quartet instant chart success. Originally formed in Queens, NY, during 1990, the members of Onyx (Fredro Starr, Sticky Fingaz, Big DS, and DJ Suave Sonny Caeser) met while working as barbers. The band honed their rhyming skills and act by performing at local clubs, which eventually gained the attention of Run-D.M.C.'s Jam Master Jay, who signed the group to his label, JMJ Records, and even helped produce Onyx's debut full-length, *Bacdafucup*, in 1993. The album turned out to be a platinum-certified smash, spurred on by the runaway success of the hit single "Slam," which went on to become one of the year's biggest rap hits. The group confirmed that they were just as content attracting a heavy metal audience by a pair of collaborations with the NYC hardcore metal outfit Biohazard (a remix of "Slam" credited to Bionyx, and the title track to the motion picture *Judgment Night*). The album even beat out such stiff competition as Dr. Dre's rap classic *The Chronic* at the Soul Train Awards for Best Rap Album that year. But Onyx was unable to continue their commercial success as such subsequent albums as 1995's *All We Got Iz Us* and 1998's *Shut 'Em Down* came and went without much fanfare. The late '90s saw members Sticky and Fredro try their hand at acting, landing spots on HBO's *Strapped*, Spike Lee's *Clockers*, the Rhea Pearlman/Danny De Vito-directed *Sunset Park*, and Brandy's hit TV show *Moesha*. The various members tried to launch solo careers, but the records never connected with audiences. With the rap genre's continuous changes and shifts, they decided to try a comeback and reappeared with 2002's *Bacdafucup, Pt. II. —Greg Prato*

● **Bacdafucup** / 1993 / JMJ ♦♦♦♦

At the time that *Bacdafucup* hit the record racks and airwaves, Onyx seemed to be inventing a genre all their own: heavy metal rap. Of course, on closer inspection, it is not at all surprising stylistically, given their link to Def Jam and Run-D.M.C., the record company and crew that introduced heavy guitar riffs into hip-hop. Onyx, though, seemed far more threateningly hardcore than Run-D.M.C. ever were, and each song on their debut album seems like a quick-triggered, menacing chip set squarely on the shoulders of MCs Big DS, Suave, Fredro, and Sticky Fingaz. That the entire album from beginning to end circumvents almost any backlash by being so brilliantly catchy as well, is a sterling tribute to how strong a quartet Onyx truly is on this first effort. The group gives the impression that they wanted to spotlight the sort of cartoonish, directionless anger that existed in a lot of hardcore rap, and then funnel that sort of energy into songs full of singalong choruses and joyous, chanted hooks that lend a certain feeling of camaraderie to the whole album. The release is mostly coproduced by Run-D.M.C.'s Jam Master Jay and newcomer Chyskillz, and its music has a tense, wired edge that amplifies the vividness of the threatening lyrics. Sonically, it has a hardcore East Coast/New York City cast, full of throbbing bass and screeching siren-like effects. The grimy urban vibe is matched by Onyx's narrative thuggery, discharged straight from the streets like pumped-up news dispatches and predating the roughneck rap trend by several years. It's hard to imagine, given the gritty content of the album, that Onyx was aiming for airplay with

Bacdafucup; nevertheless, almost in spite of itself, it was so good that it earned just that. —*Stanton Swihart*

All We Got Iz Us / Nov. 1995 / Def Jam ♦♦♦

The second offering from Queens' Onyx is another fix of dark and psychotic microphone marauding. Unlike their debut album *Bacdafucup*, the trio's 1995 sophomore project contains no MTV-friendly cuts like "Slam." Rather, *All We Got Iz Us* is strictly the dark side, espousing basically one emotion: rage. This is a primal album of raucous wailing over sparse, rumbling beats. It is the sound of what slithers under the streets of New York. Sticky Fingaz asserts himself as the lyricist of the crew, sounding off like a powder keg ready to blow while Fredro Starr provides the solid but simplistic beats. Onyx cares little about solutions to the problems that have riled them up, they're simply reacting to them by letting out a guttural roar of anger and violence. Perhaps the forerunners of hardcore artists such as DMX, they in many ways authored the grimy, lowdown flow. In spite of their talents, without the benefit of airplay *All We Got Iz Us* fizzled. Regardless, Onyx maintained their "right to remain violent" and for what they do, they do it very well on this album. The standout cuts include "Last Dayz," "Live Niguz," "Walk In New York," "Shout," and "Geto Mentalitee," featuring All City. —*Michael Di Bella*

Shut 'Em Down / Jun. 2, 1998 / Def Jam ♦♦♦

Shut 'Em Down is officially the follow-up to *All We Got Iz Us*, but since that second album was largely forgotten, the record might as well have been a follow-up to *Bacdafucup*, the debut that briefly made Onyx a hip-hop sensation. Onyx haven't changed that much since then; their hardcore rhythms still hit hard, their lyrics are still profane, and they still shout their lyrics as often as they rap. In short, they still make the oversized, near-parodic hardcore rap that made "Slam" a smash hit. Unfortunately, there isn't anything on *Shut 'Em Down* nearly as good as "Slam." There's nothing that's flat-out bad, on the other hand, but there's no denying that the horrorcore schtick wears a bit thin. At first, it sounds good to have Onyx back, but it soon becomes clear that they need to develop a new sonic direction, otherwise they will have shut themselves down. —*Stephen Thomas Erlewine*

Bacdafucup, Pt. II / Jun. 11, 2002 / Koch ♦♦♦

Onyx burst onto the scene with *Bacdafucup*, a volatile rap album that embraced everything about thug life and told the world to slam. Unfortunately, later releases failed to live up to the lofty heights of *Bacdafucup*, and Onyx faded back as members evacuated and/or opted to experiment with acting and solo careers. After four years, a re-formed Onyx returned with *Bacdafucup, Pt. II*, an album that looks to once again grasp the hardcore rap title they helped invent. Fredro and Sticky Fingaz sound as dirty as ever as they boast grandiose flows concerning the game, the relevance of the bald legacy, and life over the group's tumultuous career. The question is, does *Bacdafucup, Pt. II* live up to its title? While this is not as revolutionary or edgy as its predecessor, this is surely Onyx's triumphant return. They have conformed to many of the expected trends of hip-hop, including Dr. Dre-like beats and DMX-esque rants, yet there is no mistaking the openly hostile intentions of one of rap's most cutting-edge trios. There is much here to recall Onyx's early days, including two of the album's best tracks, "Bring 'Em out Dead" and "Slam Harder," which may appear to be last-ditch retreads of past hits but are their own entities entirely. The group even treads into waters one wouldn't expect, referring to the 9/11 tragedy with more daring terms then some may like, yet the powerful thoughts delivered on "Feel Me" prove that Onyx is very serious about their terrorist opinions. Onyx may not be as offensive or aggressive as they once were, but *Bacdafucup, Pt. II* is easily the group's best outing since their hip-hop debut. —*Jason D. Taylor*

Organized Konfusion

f. 1990, Queens, NY

Group / Hip-Hop, East Coast Rap, Pop-Rap

Organized Konfusion are a Queens-based duo who specialize in intelligent rhymes, to the detriment of their usually lackluster production. Formed by neighborhood friends Prince Poetry and Pharoahe Monch, who began rhyming as Simply 2 Positive, Organized Konfusion began working with producer Paul C and scored a deal with Hollywood Records for their 1991 self-titled debut album. Three years later, the duo returned with *Stress: The Extinction Agenda*, their last album for the label. Organized Konfusion moved to the more rap-conscious Priority label for 1997's *The Equinox*, a song cycle following the life and times of two inner-city teens. —*John Bush*

★ **Organized Konfusion** / 1991 / Hollywood ✦✦✦✦✦

The inspired debut album from the duo of Prince Poetry and Pharoahe Monch was arguably *the* underground rap album of the 1990s, at a time when "underground," aside from Ultramagnetic MC's, didn't really yet exist in the coherent manner that it would later in the decade. It most definitely represented an alternative and ran perpendicular to much of what passed for mainstream hip-hop in 1991, with the possible exception of the Native Tongue family, with which Organized Konfusion shared a maverick, sometimes playful, sensibility if not an identifiable sound. The MCs trade rhymes and intertwining, singsong choruses like a pair of old school pros, but their lyrical flows and topical themes were decidedly progressive for the era, and even still manage to sound almost futuristic. Poetry is no slouch as a rapper and, in fact, probably would have been the headliner in almost any other group, but Monch is obviously the breakout star here. His vocal presence is looming and imposing, to an almost apocalyptic degree at times ("Prisoners of War," the title song), as he throws out a relentless jet stream of complex verbiage and knotty images. But each is constantly surprising throughout *Organized Konfusion*, the reason it felt like such a cobweb clearer upon its release, and still feels so today. The duo also handled most of the production chores itself, creating a dense, visceral tapestry of strangely organic sounds, from the syrupy smooth and viscous tones of "Fudge Pudge" and "Audience Pleasers" to "Releasing Hypnotical Gases," all gurgling, alien internal processes, to the first whimsical single, "Who Stole My Last Piece of Chicken?," presented here in its strikingly disparate original and remix versions. *Organized Konfusion* may be, alongside Main Source's *Breaking Atoms*, the quintessential cult hip-hop album from a decade full of forward-looking efforts. —*Stanton Swihart*

Stress: The Extinction Agenda / 1994 / Hollywood ✦✦✦✦✦

Like a number of ambitious rap artists and groups of the era, Organized Konfusion chose to up the ante on its sophomore effort and use the music as a springboard to explore some associated motifs and collect them together under a loose conceptual frame. Unlike the majority of those artists, OK made it work, and work exceptionally well, by keeping the concepts themselves vague while adding an extra fine-edged intricacy to its verbal licks. Pharoahe Monch and Prince Poetry are even more commanding as lyricists on *Stress*, spinning out stories much closer to the nuts and bolts of the street than on their debut. But in typical fashion for such gifted artists, they probe the psychological implications of urban life rather than merely relay its superficial qualities. In response, the album's sound is less eccentric without losing any of its innovation. In fact, the duo consistently draped its words in adroit and vibrant sound amalgams, frequently employing electric jazz samples to that end, especially on the Herbie Hancock-sampled "Extinction Agenda" and Buckwild-produced "Why," which brilliantly ties together various strains of the genre. The MCs also plumbed a darker periphery on the portentous "Bring It On," where each raised the level of the lyrical game to unusual heights. Those who prefer the funky-weird Organized of the first album still have plenty to enjoy as well, particularly "3-2-1" and "Let's Organize," a party cut that also bounced off guests Q-Tip and O.C. What *Stress* might have lost in freshness and mirth from its predecessor, though, it gained in cohesiveness, consciousness, resonance, and, most strikingly, vision. —*Stanton Swihart*

The Equinox / Sep. 23, 1997 / Priority ✦✦✦✦

Quite possibly one of the most underrated East Coast rap groups, Organized Konfusion's Prince Poetry and Pharoahe Monch deliver an album full of stimulating lyrics and well-arranged instrumentation on *The Equinox*, the group's third full-length project. Poetry and Monch extended their artistic reach by producing five of the 14 songs; each of the self-productions is serious in atmosphere, moderate in tempo, and dominated by lower-frequency tone colors. For example, "They Don't Want It" serves as a cautionary declaration to any competitors, chanted over a sequence with saturated kick drums and synthesizer tones reminiscent of a pair of old church bells deeply tolling on a rainy fall morning. "They Don't Want It" is followed by the first in a series of skits that tends to interrupt the musical flow from song to song, but makes listening to the album like a watching a movie. Other producers featured include Diamond D, Raheed, and Buckwild. Continuing in a pattern of rhymes that pull the listener in and allows them to be absorbed through involved lyrics and intriguing content, *The Equinox* features well-structured material that won't disappoint any listeners with high standards. —*Qa'id Jacobs*

Organized Noize

f. Atlanta, Georgia

Group / Hip-Hop, Southern Rap, Alternative Rap, Funk, Dirty South

The Atlanta-based production team Organized Noize first helped define and then represent the elegant side of late-'90s Southern rap, by producing many of the area's most esteemed artists. Consisting of Rico Wade, Ray Murray, and Pat "Sleepy" Brown, Organized Noize first made a name for themselves after producing TLC's mammoth hit song "Waterfalls" in 1994. Following this brush with amazing commercial success, the trio went on to produce two of the South's most progressive rap groups, Outkast and Goodie Mob; with Organized Noize producing the bulk of their 1990s albums, these two rap groups rose to prominence, establishing the South as a vital breeding ground for stylish hip-hop and also standing as effective alternatives to the glut of Master P-inspired gangsta rap that became synonymous with the South. Organized Noize also signed a distribution deal with Interscope in 1996 after their early success and started their own label; unfortunately, by 1999 the partnership had ended, as the label's roster—Kilo, Cool Breeze, Witchdoctor—had failed to score any substantial commercial success. Yet despite this disappointment, the group continued to produce critically acclaimed albums such as Outkast's *Stankonia*, along with a growing number of soundtrack affiliations such as *Shaft* and *Set It Off*. —*Jason Birchmeier*

Original Flavor

Group / Hip-Hop, Pop-Rap, Old School Rap, Club/Dance

One of rap's middle school crews headed by Ski, an MC/producer, Original Flavor dropped their inauspicious debut *This Is How It Is* in 1992. Although Ski worked with legendary New York DJ Clark Kent for the project, the album fizzled unceremoniously. For their follow-up, producer-in-training Ski enlisted the aid of a few more MCs including T-Strong, Chubby Chub, and a young Brooklynite with some experience in the rap field, Jay-Z. Jay-Z had worked with fellow Brooklynite Big Jaz on the track "Hawaiian Sophie" and the two were commonly referred to as Jaz and Jay-Z. Original Flavor was Jay-Z's training ground and served as a catapult for his future endeavors. Flavor's sophomore release *Beyond Flavor* was released in 1993 to a mostly unenthusiastic audience. However, the lead single "Can I Get Open" features Jay-Z in impeccable pre-Jayhova form, with a decidedly less edgy rhyme format. Jay-Z's skills far surpassed those of the rest of the crew and his solo career would begin soon after the release of *Beyond*. Jay Peso went on to guest MC on the classic Big Daddy Kane posse cut "Show & Prove" (among others), then released a number of singles on his own including "In My Lifetime." It was at this time that Jay-Z turned to Jigga and adopted the Tony Montana-styled persona. Jay-Z would continue to work with his Original Flavor partner Ski after the group disbanded, making him a member of his Roc-A-Fella staff. Ski produced four tracks on Jay's solo debut *Reasonable Doubt* in 1996 and two on 1997's *In My Lifetime, Volume One*. —*Michael Di Bella*

This Is How It Is / 1992 / Atlantic ✦✦✦

In 1993, just in time to record their second album, *Beyond Flavor*, Damon Dash would add a buddy of his—a young Brooklyn rapper known around the way for his superlative rhyming skills—to the lineup of Original Flavor, one of the two groups (the other being the excellent the Future Sound) he had under contract at the time. The MC's name? Jay-Z. Only an average album, the sky was nevertheless the limit for him from there on out. The verdict was less rosy for Original Flavor as a unit, and today, if the group is remembered at all, it is only because of that early association with the Jigga man. In actuality, the primary catalyst behind the crew was producer Ski, who later would go on to contribute a half-dozen strong tracks to Jay-Z's first two albums, and *This Is How It Is* turns out to be almost entirely his show. Although it is not on the whole a great outing, it definitely does have flashes. Much of the production, in fact, is quite accomplished—terrific, even. Scratch that: on a musical level, *This Is How It Is* frequently verges on the magnificent, with an impressive array of clever and uncommon samples and ingenious cut-and-paste breakbeats. It will certainly surprise no one who listens to the music to know that Ski would go on to become a highly successful hired gun. He is too often let down, however, by lackluster vocal support (including his own) on *This Is How It Is*. It is no wonder that Dash would try to bolster the MC side of Original Flavor after the album's release. As a result, the only completely quibble-free song on which everything clicks is "Way Wit Words," breezy lyrical froth on top of an asymmetrical chunk of bop piano that is very reminiscent of the Future Sound. Otherwise listeners get such innocuous fare as "Gumdrops," or battle boastfulness that doesn't even really sound convinced by itself, all of which tends to drain the color from the songs by the time they come to a close. Rap fans drawn more to production than lyrical skills, though, will have much to enjoy if they're able to scare up a copy of the album. —*Stanton Swihart*

● **Beyond Flavor** / 1993 / Atlantic ✦✦✦

Veteran jazz drummer Max Roach has often compared rap to bebop, and for all the differences between jazz and rap, there are, in fact, some parallels—especially on the East Coast. Like the beboppers of the 1940s and 1950s, many New York, Philadelphia, and Boston rappers have been obsessed with technique. Anyone who has attended a hip-hop competition in any of those cities knows how technique obsessed East Coast MCs can be; like bop icon Sonny Stitt, they view music as a form of sportsmanship and want to make sure you know how impressive their chops are. That obsession with technique is impossible to miss on 1993's *Beyond Flavor*, the second album by Original Flavor. This New York group is about flow, flow, and more flow, which is a different mindset from the gangsta rap mind-set of many West Coast rappers. If, in 1993, you asked a hip-hop expert what the main differences between East Coast and West Coast rappers were, he/she would have responded that while the West Coast was about beats, hooks, and storytelling, the East Coast was about rhyming technique. There were many exceptions to that generalization, but *Beyond Flavor* does fit that stereotypical view of New York rap; Original Flavor and its allies (including a young, pre-solo career Jay-Z) spend most of this CD bragging about their rapping skills and showing off their considerable technique. When MCs have this much technique, the flow-for-the-sake-of-flow approach can be exhilarating—even if it does wear thin after awhile. Listening to *Beyond Flavor* is a lot of like hearing a group of East Coast hard boppers showing you how fast they can play standards; although chops for the sake of chops has its limitations, you still find yourself admiring and enjoying the display of virtuosity. —*Alex Henderson*

Originoo Gunn Clappaz

f. 1995
Group / Hip-Hop

Including three members from the Fabulous Five ("Leflaur Leflah Eshkoshka"), Originoo Gunn Clappaz worked with the Beatminerz, OG, E-Swift, and Lord Jamar on their debut album *Da Storm*, released in October 1996. It hit the R&B Top Ten, and its single ("No Fear") reached the Top 15. By the time of their second, 1999's *M-Pire Shrikez Back*, the trio had renamed themselves O.G.C. —*John Bush*

Da Storm / Oct. 29, 1996 / Priority ✦✦✦

Originoo Gunn Clappaz's debut album *Da Storm* is an inventive fusion of streetwise rhythms and soul- and jazz-laced hip-hop, highlighted by the trio's clever rhymes, as well as the dense production, which has a number of unusual and delightful samples. —*Leo Stanley*

● **M-Pire Shrikez Back** / Aug. 17, 1999 / Priority ✦✦✦✦

Pinning their hopes of rejuvenation on a core of upstart producers, O.G.C. bids farewell to the ritualistic Boot Camp Click sound that encompasses their discordant debut *Da Storm*. Experiencing an epiphany of sorts, O.G.C. (Starang Wondah, Louieville, and Top Dog) warm up to a realm of organic instrumentation and orchestral arrangements. Lyrically, the standard BCC curriculum of getting weeded and pursuing honeys gets monotonous for stretches. O.G.C. is strikingly more appealing when they expand on their predictable topic matter. However, the distinctive/varying production supplied by Gray-Boy, Black-Market, and Justin Trugman manages to slightly mask that oversight, stepping up when most needed. Starang and Louieville continue to grow, and their two-man lyrical tag-team exhibition is augmented by Top Dog's high-spirited repartees. O.G.C.'s maturity is evident, and restructuring their sound did wonders for the group's chemistry, as they begin to show signs of blossoming on their brisk follow-up. —*Matt Conaway*

Orishas

Group / Latin Rap, Hip-Hop

Four-piece rap act Orishas was formed in the late '90s from ex-Amenaza known as Ruzzo and Youtel who moved from Havana to Paris as part of a school exchange program. Their collective name is based on divine beings worshipped by Yorubas from West Africa, later combined with Native Americans and

European Spiritualists. The Orishas remained in religious rituals in Cuba and Brazil. Orishas released *A Lo Cubano* in the year 2000, mixing Afro-Cuban music and universal rap beats and rhyme. —*Drago Bonacich*

A Lo Cubano / Oct. 3, 2000 / Universal Latino ✦✦✦✦

The debut from expatriate Havana rap quartet Orishas (named for the gods worshipped by Yoruba tribesmen), who met in Paris during a student exchange program, is solid evidence that finally the Americans labels are looking beyond their own borders for quality hip-hop. It's a good thing, too, since the gringo scene has suffered such a dearth of creativity since 1998. These cats take the House of Pain approach and cover their territory with "raise your hands and shout your 'hood" chants, while keeping the scratch mix direct and in the pocket. The rhythm tracks are layered against solid, traditional Cuban song and merengue. Lyrically, the set is completely free from the trappings that plague most Yankee hip-hop: there is no sexism, no violence, and no idle MC boasting. Instead, Orishas, in "Represent," "1.9.9.9," and "537 C.U.B.A.," take an approach that deals with issues like returning home, the struggle of Cuba, self-determination while living in the shadow of the beast 100 miles away, and the quest for freedom (both political and spiritual). But despite the heavy messages—and the intense Santeria influence—Orishas is among the most musically refreshing quartets hip-hop has ever produced. With music every bit as sophisticated and catchy as the Buena Vista Social Club and three times as tough, the Afro-Cuban rhythms and folk-song forms are married effortlessly to a seamless loop, scratch, and bass mix. This is the down groove on the steamy humid tip. It's also a historical, sociological, and musicological lesson that can be partied to. What else can you ask for? —*Thom Jurek*

● **Emigrante** / Jun. 11, 2002 / Surco ✦✦✦✦

Cuban hip-hoppers Orishas made a splash with their debut, *A Lo Cubano*. For their sophomore effort, there are no radical changes, just a refinement of style. Singing remains as important as rapping, in a manner true to their Cuban heritage, and though there's plenty of booty-shaking bass in the mix, the beats are spiced up by liberal doses of real percussion, bringing a complexity and springiness to the music that's rarely seen in hip-hop. The approach here is far more confident—they know what they want to do and how to achieve it—and they're not afraid of allowing guest stars, like salsa idol Yuri Buenaventura, to strut their stuff. The closest they come to experimenting with the sound is on "Que Bola?," with its psychedelic backward loops and phasing. And while there's nothing as immediately arresting as "537 C.U.B.A." on this disc, each cut builds with repeated listenings to make a more satisfying experience. Orishas speaks with the tongue of the gods. —*Chris Nickson*

Da Outfit

Group / Jazz-Rap, Hip-Hop

Da Outfit is comprised of MCs Hemp da Pimp and Crack da Mack. Though Hemp was from San Antonio and Crack hailed from South Central L.A., their collaboration was born in the jazz cabarets of Sarajevo, where the two friends would freestyle over the vibes of local Bosnian jazz combos. Eventually, a group was formed called Da Heineken Twins, which in turn became the Brews Brothers. Finally, Da Outfit solidified. Given their unlikely genesis, Da Outfit knew that their beats could not simply be bought at the corner store. After experimenting with instrumentals from outside producers, Da Outfit decided to do it themselves. Supa Tree Productions was created in a room at Hemp's house, and soon the duo had assembled enough beats and rhymes to enter a studio. Bosnian electronica producer Adi Lukovac and his band Ornamenti were enlisted as coproducers and sound engineers; *Lost Underground*, Da Outfit's debut, arrived in 2002 from Supa Tree Records. A collaboration not only of sound but also of cultures, *Lost Underground* became a document of what's possible when unlikely talents collide. —*Johnny Loftus*

● **Lost Underground** / Jun. 4, 2002 / Supa Tree ✦✦✦

Lost Underground is a very distinctive record, compared to the one-note rap mainstream, as well as the increasingly getting-in-line underground. Da Outfit, a duo of Crack da Mack and Hemp da Pimp, verge on the hardcore with tough lyrics and a volatile flow, though the production—heavy with echoey samples, noise, and skeletal drum machines—is *very* interesting. The leftfield lyrics match the sonic finesse on tap, too, especially on highlights like "E.M.C.E.E." and the title track. All in all, *Lost Underground* is a superb release from the group's Supa Tree label and the admirably independent Music Services Unlimited distribution. —*John Bush*

OutKast

f. 1992, Atlanta, GA

Group / Alternative Rap, Southern Rap, Dirty South, Hip-Hop

OutKast's blend of gritty Southern soul, fluid raps, and the rolling G-funk of their Organized Noize production crew epitomized the Atlanta wing of hip-hop's rising force, the dirty South, during the late '90s. Along with Goodie Mob, OutKast took Southern hip-hop in bold, innovative new directions: less reliance on aggression, more positivity and melody, thicker arrangements, and intricate lyrics. After Dre and Big Boi hit number one on the rap charts with their first single, "Player's Ball," the duo embarked on a run of platinum albums spiked with several hit singles, enjoying numerous critical accolades in addition to their commercial success.

Andre Benjamin (Dre) and Antwan Patton (Big Boi) attended the same high school in the Atlanta borough of East Point, and several lyrical battles made each gain respect for the other's skills. They formed OutKast, and were pursued by Organized Noize Productions, hitmakers for TLC and Xscape. Signed to the local LaFace label just after high school, OutKast recorded and released *Player's Ball*, then watched the single rise to number one on the rap charts. It slipped from the top spot only after six weeks, was certified gold, and created a buzz for a full-length release. That album, *Southernplayalisticadillacmuzik*, hit the Top 20 in 1994 and was certified platinum by the end of the year. Dre and Big Boi also won Best New Rap Group of the Year at the 1995 *Source* Awards. OutKast returned with a new album in 1996, releasing *ATLiens* that August; it hit number two and went platinum with help from the gold-selling single "Elevators (Me & You)" (number 12 pop, number one rap), as well as the Top 40 title track. *Aquemini* followed in 1998, also hitting number two and going double platinum. There were no huge hit singles this time around, but critics lavishly praised the album's unified, progressive vision, hailing it as a great leap forward and including it on many year-end polls. Unfortunately, in a somewhat bizarre turn of events, OutKast was sued over the album's lead single "Rosa Parks" by none other than the civil rights pioneer herself, who claimed that the group had unlawfully appropriated her name to promote their music, also objecting to some of the song's language. The initial court decision dismissed the suit in late 1999. Dre modified his name to Andre 3000 before the group issued its hotly anticipated fourth album, *Stankonia*, in late 2000. Riding the momentum of uniformly excellent reviews and the stellar singles "B.O.B." and "Ms. Jackson," *Stankonia* debuted at number two and went triple platinum in just a few months; meanwhile, "Ms. Jackson" became their first number-one pop single the following February. —*John Bush*

Southernplayalisticadillacmuzik / Apr. 26, 1994 / LaFace ✦✦✦✦

It is on OutKast's debut album that the fledgling production team Organized Noize began forging one of the most distinctive production sounds in popular music in the '90s: part hip-hop; part live, Southern-fried guitar licks and booty-thick bass runs; and part lazy, early-'70s soul. The album was not only artistically successful but also thrived commercially, leaping into the Top 20 album chart on the back of the outstanding hit single "Player's Ball" and eventually going platinum. Although a little bit too dependent on overly simplistic and programmed snare beats, the music is unconditionally excellent, with languid, mellow melodies sliding atop rapid, mechanical drums. Organized Noize already had their distinguishing sound figured out, down to the last twanged, wah-wahed note. But what makes *Southernplayalisticadillacmuzik* such a wonderful album has even more to do with the presence of its rappers, Dre and Big Boi. No one sounded like OutKast in 1994—a mixture of lyrical acuity, goofball humor, Southern drawl, funky timing, and legitimate offbeat personalities. Few rappers of the '90s have displayed such an inventive sense of rhyme flow either, and few rap artists in general have ears as attuned to creating such catchy melodic and vocal hooks. Almost every song has some sort of tuneful chant or repetitive hook that marks it as instantly memorable. There are occasional dull and mediocre spots, such as "Call of Da Wild" and the overlong "Funky Ride," that can't even be elevated by a head-nodding bass line or a tricky rhyme. Such low points, however, are far outshined by the brilliant moments. Already an extremely strong showing, OutKast would continue to develop into one of the finest, most consistently challenging (not to mention booty-shaking) rap groups of the decade. —*Stanton Swihart*

ATLiens / Aug. 27, 1996 / LaFace ✦✦✦✦✦

Though they were likely lost on casual hip-hop fans, *Southernplayalisticadillacmuzik* was full of subtle indications that OutKast were a lot more inventive than your average Southern playas. Their idiosyncrasies bubbled to the surface on their sophomore effort, *ATLiens*, an album of spacy sci-fi funk performed on live instruments. Largely abandoning the hard-partying playa characters of their debut, Dre and Big Boi develop a startlingly fresh, original sound to go along with their futuristic new personas. George Clinton's space obsessions might seem to make P-funk obvious musical source material, but *ATLiens* ignores the hard funk in favor of a smooth, laid-back vibe that perfectly suits the duo's sense of melody. The album's chief musical foundation is still soul, especially the early-'70s variety, but other influences begin to pop up as well. Some tracks have a spiritual, almost gospel feel (though only in tone, not lyrical content), and the Organized Noize production team frequently employs the spacious mixes and echo effects of dub reggae in creating the album's alien soundscapes. In addition to the striking musical leap forward, Dre and Big Boi continue to grow as rappers; their flows are getting more tongue-twistingly complex, and their lyrics more free-associative. Despite a couple of overly sleepy moments during the second half, *ATLiens* is overall a smashing success thanks to its highly distinctive style, and stands as probably OutKast's most focused work (though it isn't as wildly varied as subsequent efforts). The album may have alienated (pun recognized, but not intended) the more conservative wing of the group's fans, but it broke new ground for Southern hip-hop and marked OutKast as one of the most creatively restless and ambitious hip-hop groups of the '90s. —*Steve Huey*

☆ **Aquemini** / Sep. 29, 1998 / LaFace ✦✦✦✦✦

Even compared to their already excellent and forward-looking catalog, OutKast's sprawling third album *Aquemini* was a stroke of brilliance. The chilled-out space-funk of *ATLiens* had already thrown some fans for a loop, and *Aquemini* made it clear that its predecessor was no detour, but a stepping stone for even greater ambitions. Some of *ATLiens'* ethereal futurism is still present, but more often *Aquemini* plants its feet on the ground for a surprisingly downhome flavor. The music draws from a vastly eclectic palette of sources, and the live instrumentation is fuller sounding than *ATLiens*. Most importantly, producers Organized Noize imbue their tracks with a Southern earthiness and simultaneous spirituality that come across regardless of what Dre and Big Boi are rapping about. Not that they shy away from rougher subject matter, but their perspective is grounded and responsible, intentionally avoiding hardcore clichés. Their distinctive vocal deliveries are now fully mature, with a recognizably Southern rhythmic bounce but loads more technique than their territorial peers. Those flows grace some of the richest and most inventive hip-hop tracks of the decade. The airy lead single "Rosa Parks" juxtaposes porch-front acoustic guitar with DJ scratches and a stomping harmonica break that could have come from nowhere but the South. Unexpected touches like that are all over the record: the live orchestra on "Return of the 'G,'" the electronic, George Clinton-guested "Synthesizer," the reggae horns and dub-style echo of "SpottieOttieDopaliscious," the hard-rocking wah-wah guitar of "Chonkyfire," and on and on. What's most impressive is the way everything comes together to justify the full-CD running time, something few hip-hop epics of this scope ever accomplish. After a few listens, not even the meditative jams on the second half of the album feel all that excessive. *Aquemini* fulfills all its ambitions, covering more than enough territory to qualify it as a virtuosic masterpiece, and a landmark hip-hop album of the late '90s. —*Steve Huey*

★ **Stankonia** / Oct. 31, 2000 / LaFace ✦✦✦✦✦

Stankonia was OutKast's second straight masterstroke, an album just as ambitious, just as all-over-the-map, and even hookier than its predecessor. With producers Organized Noize playing a diminished role, *Stankonia* reclaims the duo's futuristic bent. Keyboardist/producer Earthtone III helms most of the backing tracks, and while the live-performance approach is still present, there's more reliance on programmed percussion, otherworldly synthesizers, and surreal sound effects. Yet the results are surprisingly warm and soulful, a trippy sort of techno-psychedelic funk. Every repeat listen seems to uncover some new element in the mix, but most of the songs have such memorable hooks that it's easy to stay diverted. The immediate dividends include two of 2000's best singles: "B.O.B." is the fastest of several tracks built on jittery drum'n'bass rhythms, but Andre and Big Boi keep up with awe-inspiring effortlessness. "Ms. Jackson," meanwhile, is an anguished plea directed at the mother of the mother of an out-of-wedlock child, tinged with regret, bitterness, and affection. Its sensitivity and social awareness are echoed in varying proportions elsewhere, from the Public Enemy-style rant "Gasoline Dreams" to the heartbreaking suicide tale "Toilet Tisha." But the group also returns to its roots for some of the most testosterone-drenched material since their debut. Then again, OutKast doesn't take its posturing too seriously, which is why they can portray women holding their own, or make bizarre boasts about being "So Fresh, So Clean." Given the variety of moods, it helps that the album is broken up by brief, usually humorous interludes, which serve as a sort of reset button. It takes a few listens to pull everything together, but given the immense scope, it's striking how few weak tracks there are. It's no wonder *Stankonia* consolidated OutKast's status as critics' darlings, and began attracting broad new audiences: its across-the-board appeal and ambition overshadowed nearly every other pop album released in 2000. —*Steve Huey*

Big Boi and Dre Present ... Outkast / Dec. 4, 2001 / LaFace ✦✦✦✦✦

OutKast's first hits compilation comes at the perfect time; after gaining millions of new fans (more of a whole different demographic) with the crossover hit *Stankonia*, Dre and Big Boi delivered a tight summation of their decade-long career for listeners whose familiarity grows hazy before the duo hit with "Ms. Jackson" and "B.O.B." OutKast has been doing great work since their fully formed debut with 1993's "Player's Ball," and their singles hold up well. Those looking for positivity and emotion on the level of "Ms. Jackson" will find it (wrapped in great productions) on "Rosa Parks" and "Git up, Git Out." The down-tempo "Elevators (Me & You)" is an OutKast history in miniature, while two excellent tracks from their debut—"Ain't No Thang" and "Southernplayalisticadillacmuzik"—introduced the group's formula of syrupy G-funk and intricate, slang-heavy rapping. Also included are three new tracks: the brass-heavy "Funkin' Around," a P-funk pastiche named "The Whole World," and the jazz-club jam "Movin' Cool (The After Party)." —*John Bush*

Outlawz

Group / West Coast Rap, Gangsta Rap, Hardcore Rap
West Coast rappers Outlawz are known primarily for their affiliation with 2Pac. It was on 2Pac's Makaveli album that Outlawz first came to the greater rap community's notice, appearing on a few songs. In 1999 they were co-billed on the posthumous 2Pac album *Still I Rise*, granting them even more recognition and furthering their short-lived affiliation. It wasn't until late 2000, though, that they finally got the go-ahead to release their debut album, *Ride Wit Us or Collide Wit Us*. Featuring a cover that placed 2Pac's image in the foreground, along with numerous references to the deceased legend, this debut made the most of Outlawz' reputation for being 2Pac's supposed protégés. Unfortunately, the album didn't prove to be much of a success, and neither did the group's follow-up album a year later, *Novakane*, also released on the group's Outlaw Recordz label (distributed by Koch). While the group no doubt retained 2Pac's West Coast thug/gangsta style, they unfortunately were fairly average rappers in terms of skills, too often fell back on their 2Pac affiliation, and far too often descended into generic thug motifs. And it didn't help that they weren't aligned with any of the West Coast's better producers. In fact, Outlawz weren't really aligned with anyone on the West Coast—not Snoop Dogg and his Dogghouse clique, or the Bay Area scene centered around E-40 and Spice 1. Ultimately, the group never lived up to the expectations they heaped upon themselves by forever comparing themselves to 2Pac. —*Jason Birchmeier*

● **Ride Wit Us or Collide Wit Us** / Nov. 7, 2000 / Outlaw ✦✦✦
About all anyone could say about the Outlawz when they dropped their debut album in late 2000 was that they used to be down with 2Pac. Of course, lots of people were down with 2Pac—though the legend's career ultimately ended prematurely, he'd collaborated with much of the West Coast, particularly on *All Eyez on Me*, which featured nearly every significant West Coast rapper and producer. But more than any of 2Pac's collaborators, the Outlawz went out of their way to make a career out of their affiliation with 2Pac, even going so far as to feature his image on the cover of their debut album. And perhaps the Outlawz really can't be blamed. After all, excluding their affiliation with 2Pac, they really didn't have much going for them. In fact, it took nearly five years before they even so much as released their own album. It took that long for a reason, though: they aren't that impressive of a group, to be quite frank. And *Ride Wit Us or Collide Wit Us* makes that fairly evident. They managed to score producer Mike Dean of Geto Boys fame for some beats, but even that can't save this album. Ultimately, the Outlawz are little more than standard-at-best West Coast hardcore rappers. They act all gangsta like 2Pac and forever claim that they keep it real and that they're thugs and

that you shouldn't f*ck with them and that they're keeping 2Pac's legacy going and so on and so on. In sum, they spout unending hyperbole and they don't spout it particularly well. But ardent 2Pac admirers who don't mind the fact that this is second-rate, if not third-rate, West Coast thug rap modeled largely after 2Pac's work should by all means give these guys a chance. Their intentions seem in place, at the least. They're loyal to 2Pac's legacy and go out of their way to keep things hard, even if they don't really offer anything overly enticing and are derivative at best. —*Jason Birchmeier*

Novakane / Oct. 23, 2001 / Outlaw ✦✦✦

Novakane doesn't really depart far from what the Outlawz accomplished a year earlier on their debut album, *Ride Wit Us or Collide Wit Us*. And that may please listeners, but more likely it should dishearten them. After all, despite their career-establishing affiliation with 2Pac, the Outlawz never really proved to be the protégés they should have been. 2Pac had gone out of his way to establish the group just before his untimely death, yet the Outlawz never really lived up to expectations. This became glaringly evident on *Ride Wit Us*, when the best they could really do was imitate 2Pac and carry on this legacy through derivative means—and they didn't even do that well. But to their credit, the Outlawz do keep their music street and maintain a hardcore thug approach, something which should no doubt appeal to fans of underground West Coast hardcore rap. So, as mentioned, *Novakane* doesn't really depart from the group's debut album. They're still going to lengths to impress listeners with their gangsta-isms, still trying to confront listeners with their street-level lifestyle, and still mentioning 2Pac's name more than they probably should. Unfortunately, the beats aren't quite on par here with their debut album—one possible saving grace gone sour. So if these things are added up—derivative rhymes that rarely depart from clichéd clichés delivered with lackluster skills over generic-at-best beats—one can come to the saddening conclusion that despite how many times the Outlawz tell listeners that they were down with 2Pac, little separates them from the standard subpar West Coast gangsta rappers. After two albums it's safe to say, like many other individuals in the rap industry, the Outlawz have exploited 2Pac's lucrative legacy for their own benefit. Don't believe the hype—the 2Pac affiliation is all that separates these guys from the pack, or so it seems at this point. —*Jason Birchmeier*

Outsidaz

f. 1991, Newark, NJ
Group / Hip-Hop, Hardcore Rap, East Coast Rap
When former Ruffhouse Records leader Chris Schwartz launched his Ruff-Nation Records in 1999, the first release he put out on RuffNation's Ruff Life label was by Outsidaz, a hardcore rap outfit from northern New Jersey. Outsidaz' first Ruff Life single, "The Rah Rah," was released in December 1999, followed by its six-song EP *Night Life* in January 2000. But the origins of the group (whose members include Young Zee, Pace Won, Slang Ton, Yah Ya, Ax, D.U., Az-Izz, Leun One, NawShis, DJ Muhammed, and Denton) actually go back to the early '90s. At first, Young Zee and Pace were rival MCs; Pace had a group called PNS, while Zee headed the group Skitzo. When PNS and Skitzo had a lengthly microphone battle in Newark, NJ, in 1991, Zee and Pace felt that neither group won the competition—it was a tie—and decided to unite into one group as Outsidaz. Around 1995, Outsidaz came to the attention of the Fugees, who went on to employ them on their song "Cowboys." Eventually, the group signed with Ruffhouse/Columbia, but when Schwartz left Ruffhouse, they went with him and ended up on Ruff Life. —*Alex Henderson*

Night Life / Jan. 18, 2000 / Ruff Life ✦✦✦

Ever since rap's beginnings in the late '70s, battle lyrics have been a major part of hip-hop culture. In fact, rap has had some of the most competitive artists since bebop—just as bop was famous for its saxophone battles of the 1940s and 1950s (Dexter Gordon vs. Wardell Gray, Phil Woods vs. Gene Quill, Sonny Stitt vs. Gene Ammons), hip-hop has been full of artists who spent much of their time rapping about their microphone prowess and dissing rival MCs. Of course, not all rap is about battling. Some MCs consider battle lyrics limited (which they are) and would rather rap about social and political issues, male-female relationships, or why they love or hate malt liquor. Regardless, battle lyrics will always be a part of hip-hop culture, and they're the main focus of *Night Life*. On this EP, New Jersey's Outsidaz finds countless ways to brag about their rapping skills and explain why they consider rival MCs inferior. While *Night Life* underscores the limitations of battle rhymes, you have to give the group credit for their technique and their often clever lyrics. These artists are saying the same thing that countless battle-minded rappers before them said—that they're the best in their field and put the sucker MCs to shame—but Outsidaz often find clever and amusing ways to say it. Ultimately, the storyteller approach to hip-hop holds one's attention longer than battle rhymes, which can wear thin after awhile. As *Night Life* demonstrates, however, microphone warfare is an art that, despite its limitations, isn't without its pleasures. —*Alex Henderson*

● **The Bricks** / May 22, 2001 / Rufflife ◆◆◆
Some of New Jersey's finest hardcore lyricists make up this underground unit known as the Outsidaz (Young Zee, Pace Won, Az Izz, Slang Ton, et al.). Members of the Outs gained some notoriety in 1996 after dropping verses for the track "Cowboys" on the Fugees' breakthrough album *The Score*. The crew went on to release the undernoticed EP *Night Life* in 2000. The posse's outlandish frontman, Young Zee, has the kind of voice and brash wit that can light up a record, and *The Bricks* definitely contains its share of flammable material. While many underground records warble and drone on account of dull, amateurish production, *The Bricks* economizes with swift Jersey-laced funk and multilayered noise. The textured musical component is anomalous for the style as most thug/battle MCs often stick to stripped beats. Megaproducer Rockwilder, who long since went the way of producing made-for-MTV tracks (including the hideous "Moulin Rouge," for example) manages to bring back a little green funk for "Keep On," but the rest of the beats truly scald the skin like a pit full of hot coals. DJ Twinz drops a funkadelic banger for "Who You Be," which features rap's version of Simon and Simon, Method Man, and Redman. Also, tracks like the fluttering, flute-powered "State to State" and the drug hijinx track "Rehab" are further clever postulations from these raw-dog hip-hoppers. While the Outs serve notice to their reputation for lyrical savagery throughout, in the end the album bogs down a bit after the crew seemingly runs out of ways to do tracks about afterparties, drugs, and punk-MC bullying. This type of release could never truly shake up the rap game, but it does supersede a large majority of modern rap records and even calls to mind some of the better efforts from years past. —*M.F. Di Bella*

Petey Pablo

b. Greenville, NC

Dirty South, Southern Rap

One of the more versatile rappers who came out of the dirty South school of hip-hop in the early 2000s, North Carolina native Petey Pablo is capable of being raunchy one minute and poignant the next. The gruff-voiced MC gets the Pablo part of his name from a close friend who was killed at a young age. Born and raised in Greenville, NC, Pablo is best known for his 2001 single "Raise Up"—an insistent, anthemic number that finds him paying tribute to his home state. While other dirty South rappers have represented New Orleans (Master P, Mannie Fresh), Atlanta (Outkast, Goodie Mob, Rehab), Texas (UGK), or Miami (Trick Daddy), "Raise Up" made it abundantly clear that Pablo was proud to be from North Carolina. Consequently, the single became an anthem among hip-hoppers in the Carolinas in much the same way that Boogie Down Productions' "South Bronx" became an anthem for the Bronx back in 1987.

The very fact that Pablo would loudly proclaim his allegiance to the Carolinas—or anywhere in the South, for that matter—shows how much rap has evolved since its early years. In the late '70s and early to mid-'80s, the vast majority of well-known rappers were from New York City and its suburbs. But in the late '80s, 2 Live Crew and their Miami colleagues put bass music and booty rhymes on the map; and in the 1990s, the dirty South explosion saw the rise of major MCs from all over the Southern states. One of them was New Orleans native Mystikal, who has been among Pablo's ardent supporters.

After rapping locally in North Carolina in the 1990s, Pablo landed a deal with Jive Records in 2000 and started to enjoy a lot of national attention when "Raise Up" became a hit in 2001. It was in November 2001 that Jive released Pablo's debut album, *Diary of a Sinner: 1st Entry*, a diverse effort that ranges from stereotypical dirty South decadence to poignant, autobiographical tunes that reflect on the challenges and hardships he experienced growing up poor in the deep South. —*Alex Henderson*

● **Diary of a Sinner: 1st Entry** / Nov. 6, 2001 / Jive ✦✦✦
Just as they'd done a decade earlier with West Coast gangsta rap, the major labels funneled millions of dollars into the early-2000s dirty South boom, catapulting previously unknown artists like Petey Pablo to overnight superstar status. Like Ludacris and Nelly, Pablo had a major label (Jive) with enough clout to guarantee national exposure and a lead single with a great video ("Raise Up") to drive album sales. And, like what happened with Ludacris and Nelly—and many others—Jive proved that they could manufacture a multiplatinum rap superstar overnight with its industry clout. But, as disheartening as the industry politics may be, particularly to all the myriad other dirty South rappers with no chance at similar success, you can't slight Pablo—he proves himself worthy of big-league success on his debut album, *Diary of a Sinner*. First of all, and most obviously, there's the gigantic lead single, "Raise Up." Jive went out of its way to hook up Pablo with Timbaland for a few songs, and the results are surely worth the hefty tab. Sure, "I" and "I Told Y'All" are album highlights, but it's "Raise Up" that once again showcases precisely why Timbaland is the best of the best. In addition to the trademark shuffling, bass-heavy rhythm, and the catchy, singalong hook, Timbaland throws in some swirling guitar and violin sounds for a frenzied feeling that makes "Raise Up" one of the rowdiest dirty South anthems of the decade. The remainder of the album isn't nearly as riveting as "Raise Up," but it's still worth listening to. Pablo shows that he's something of a Southern DMX—a gruff, thuggish man among boys who is thoughtful and lyrical as well as spiritual and moral. Plus, though he's not afraid to boast, he never raps about money, cars, women, drugs, or anything remotely associated with

"ballin.'" It's this emphasis on the inner self rather than materialism that makes Pablo so refreshing. And it doesn't hurt that he handles all the rhymes on his album. So, even if many will be disappointed to find that nothing else on *Diary of a Sinner* comes close to "Raise Up," it's still one of the better dirty South albums of the early 2000s, and surely one of the more sincere efforts. —*Jason Birchmeier*

Pacewon

Vocals, Producer / East Coast Rap, Hip-Hop

As a founding member of the Outsidaz, Pacewon was one of the many MCs to gain a solo career after his group's appearance on the Fugees' successful *The Score*. With a smooth voice and a sly, clever tone, his raps were often relaxed and thoughtful amidst the large hip-hop crew's various styles. Despite the early solo attempts by many of his bandmates, Pacewon waited until they had released their debut, *Night Life*, on Chris Schwartz's Rough Life Records. That, as well as guest appearances on records from Redman and Rah Digga, was enough to convince Schwartz to ask the MC for a solo record in 2002. With help from Wyclef Jean, Kurupt, and fellow Outsidaz member Young Zee, he put together *Won*, a collection of funky tracks courtesy of Jay-Z producer SKI that revolved around his charismatic voice and boastful rhymes. Later in the year, he collaborated with U.K. trip-hop act Morcheeba, who included the rapper on the title track of *Charango*. —*Bradley Torreano*

● **Won** / Mar. 5, 2002 / Ruff Life ✦✦
One of the founding members of New Jersey's eight-man crew Outsidaz steps outside *The Bricks* for his debut solo album. Having previously been floated on promo as *The Pacewon Effect*, it's a surprise to see both "Oriental" and "Secret" cut from this release, with the resultant selection offering little more than a barrage of thug talk. The pumps, cheeba, and general miscreant blinged braggadocio become a little overbearing over 21 tracks, though there is enough production quirk from Jay-Z deskman SKI to keep iterant ears from wandering too far. Further vocals are injected by Kurupt, Rah Digga, and fellow Outsida Young Zee as well as Wyclef Jean, who returns the favor of Pace's contribution to the Fugees' multiplatinum *Score*. —*Kingsley Marshall*

Paradime

b. Livonia, MI

Drum Programming, Vocals, Vocals (Background), Producer / Hip-Hop

Detroit underground mainstay Freddie Beauragard, aka Paradime, toiled in the up-and-coming Detroit hip-hop scene throughout the '90s. Upon the overwhelming commercial success of Detroit's own Slim Shady (Eminem) in 1999-2000, some focus in the rap game shifted to the Motor City, seen as hip-hop's next hotbed. Paradime benefited from this exposure and his 1999 debut LP *Paragraphs* was well received in the Midwest and on underground college radio shows across the country. The gifted wordsmith caught the ear of another Detroit *nouveau riche*, Kid Rock, who signed Paradime to his label Top Dog in 2000. —*Michael Di Bella*

● **Paragraphs** / 1999 / Silent/Beats-At-Will ✦✦✦✦
The polished full-length from Paradime, aka the Chubby Jon B, out of the dirty depths of Detroit, is further claim to the wealth of hip-hop talent from the Great Lakes State. This gruff, self-proclaimed boorish boozer brings a fierce gargling flow to the mic coupled with the signature Detroit twisted wit. Dime's lyrics and concepts are wickedly clever backed by a kaleidoscope of beats and compositions provided by the Beats-At-Will production squad. Paradime represents Detroit with a brash and unique sound by combining the abstract with just plain rowdiness. Tracks like "Fire and Ice" outline Dime's schizo niceness on the microphone, while cuts like "The Shining,"

"Gimme Mine," and the hip-hop drinking anthem "Ode to Guinness" feature tight lyrics over well-crafted beats. This one is more entertaining and innovative than 75 percent of major-label material. —*Michael Di Bella*

Vices / Oct. 23, 2001 / Beats-At-Will ✦✦✦✦
Paradime seems to be tugging on Eminem's coattails a bit here. Not because they're both from Detroit. Not because they both work with D-12. It's just that the angry-kid-metaphor-gone-way-too-far thing has been done before. Still, it hasn't been done to death, and the Eminem comparison is just inevitable. That said, Paradime really puts together a good album here. Plenty of the tracks are pleasant surprises, from the self-centered "Sultan of Slang" to the remake of the Temptations' funk classic "Papa Was a Rolling Stone" called "Rollin Dope" that's sure to catch some parents' ears. All of the MCs are lyrically proficient throughout, the production is busy and effective, and, as a whole, the album is amusing and playful while staying dead serious. —*Brad Mills*

Parental Advisory

Group / Hip-Hop, Gangsta Rap, Hardcore Rap
The cleverly named rap trio Parental Advisory (P.A.) consists of K.P., Mello, and Big Reese who have worked on albums with artists such as TLC, Pink, Mystikal, Rehab, Usher, Outkast, and Goodie Mobb. The Atlanta-based group debuted in 1993 with *Ghetto Street Funk* and signed to DreamWorks Records for their 1998 self-produced follow-up, *Straight No Chase.* Two years later they delivered *My Life, Your Entertainment*, which featured guest appearances by Noreaga, Eightball, C-Lo, Khujo, and Jim Crowe, among other hip-hop stars. —*Heather Phares*

Ghetto Street Funk / 1993 / MCA ✦✦✦

Straight No Chase / Jul. 14, 1998 / DreamWorks ✦✦✦✦
It was a long time between Parental Advisory's first album, *Ghetto Street Funk*, and their second, *Straight No Chase.* In between those two records, they shortened their name to P.A. and decided to pursue a live rap sound. The makeover was a success—*Straight No Chase* is a brilliantly funky, unpredictable record that veers between street hip-hop, soul, rock, and funk. It's a little chaotic, a little all over the place, but that's its charm—P.A. attempts a lot of different styles and pulls nearly all of them off, which is quite a remarkable feat. —*Stephen Thomas Erlewine*

● **My Life, Your Entertainment** / Aug. 1, 2000 / DreamWorks ✦✦✦✦✦
Members of Parental Advisory have been notable producers in the South since the early '90s, but rarely have they kicked it on the microphone to their tracks. They appear on every track of this release and prove they aren't slouches in the lyrical department either, demonstrating they can hold down from both ends like so few people have been able to do over the years, putting themselves in the same producer/MC category as Mobb Deep, Pete Rock, or Diamond D. The thing about this album that really stands out is the wide range of topics and styles covered throughout. From the bouncy and inspiring "They Come Thru" to the gangsta vibe of "My Life, Your Entertainment" to the melodramatic "My Time 2 Go" over to the slow heavy rock sounds of "Playaz Do" and, of course, the chillin-out funky rollin' in the car track "Sundown" with featured artist Eightball. Any fan of the dirty South should definitely pick up this album; there are just too many good songs to pass up. Overall it's a complete album, with tons of guest appearances and great replay value. —*Brad Mills*

Paris (Oscar Jackson Jr.)

b. Oct. 29, 1967, Illinois
Vocals, Engineer, Producer / Political Rap, Hip-Hop, Hardcore Rap
One of hip-hop's most militantly Afro-centric radicals, Paris struggled for most of his career to find acceptance for his fiercely political music, which drew from the provocative intelligence of Public Enemy and the gut-level rage of early Ice Cube. Born Oscar Jackson Jr. in Illinois on October 29, 1967, Paris earned a degree in economics from the University of California-Davis (near the San Francisco Bay Area); but hip-hop appealed to him more, and he founded his own record label, Scarface. He recorded a single, but found he lacked the resources to promote it properly, and wound up landing a deal with Tommy Boy Records. His debut album, *The Devil Made Me Do It*, was released in 1990, and attracted some attention (and praise) for the single "The Hate That Hate Made," as well as the title track, whose video was banned by MTV. Paris completed the follow-up album *Sleeping With the Enemy* in 1992; however, in the wake of the controversy over Ice-T's "Cop Killer," Tommy Boy

refused to release it, citing the anti-George Bush track "Bush Killa." Eventually, they decided the whole album was far too strident and inflammatory, and bought out Paris' contract. After distribution agreements with Polygram and Def American fell through for similar reasons, Paris resurrected Scarface (helped by the Tommy Boy settlement money) and finally put the album out himself. It was acclaimed as a major statement in some quarters, but failed to find a wide audience in the midst of the gangsta rap revolution. 1994's *Guerrilla Funk* met with a similar fate, slipping largely under the radar, and Paris spent four years away from the studio. When he returned with *Unleashed* in 1998, he'd largely abandoned his trademark political fury in favor of watered-down G-funk and gangsta clichés. He retired from hip-hop not long after and put his economics degree to use as a successful stockbroker. —*Steve Huey*

The Devil Made Me Do It / Oct. 9, 1990 / Tommy Boy ✦✦✦✦✦
One listen to *The Devil Made Me Do It* makes one wonder if Paris recorded the album in a cloistered, cold bunker—or at least the kind of abandoned warehouse he and his crew marched through during his videos. As with early Public Enemy (a primary inspiration) and the two X-Clan records, the best moments of Paris' debut work on two levels: Plenty of these tracks have dark, sleek grooves beneath them, built on expert beat programming and vicious claws instead of hooks. In addition to this, there are Paris' scholarly, tightly wound rhymes, which are crammed with pro-black themes—odds are Eldridge Cleaver's *Soul on Ice* and Bobby Seale's *Seize the Time* were committed to memory long before they were written. In a sea of early-'90s Afro-centric rappers, Paris was one of the most unique and most talented in his field, his angered voice cutting and tense enough to make any listener squirm in her or his seat. As often as these tracks are peppered with samples of Chuck D, Black Panthers, and Malcolm X, Paris is never outshined. Poignant tracks like "Break the Grip of Shame," "The Hate That Hate Made," "The Devil Made Me Do It," and "Wretched" ("Mindless music for the masses makes ya think less of the one that hates ya") make for a joyless listen, but it's just as riveting as the most provocative and hedonistic gangsta record. —*Andy Kellman*

● **Sleeping With the Enemy** / 1992 / Scarface ✦✦✦✦✦
The Devil Made Me Do It established Paris as a pro-black radical, a firebrand. The follow-up, 1992's *Sleeping With the Enemy*, saw the MC unleash his most provocative rhymes to such an extent that WEA, Tommy Boy's distributor at the time, opted to have no part in it. This forced Paris to reactivate his Scarface imprint; it delayed the album's release, but attention from the press helped take it to the Top 25 of the top R&B/hip-hop album chart. While Paris spent much of his debut relating his distrust of authority, two inflammatory songs—"Bush Killa" and "Coffee, Donuts & Death"—took that anger into revenge-fantasy territory. The former, formed on a grinding guitar riff and an "Atomic Dog"-based groove, goes into detail about his anger over the then-president's neglect of the inner city. Though it opens with a mock assassination and features graphic lyrical content, the rationale for Paris' last-resort approach is revealed thusly: "'Cause when I'm violent is the only time the devils hear it." This goes directly into "Coffee, Donuts & Death," in which Paris avenges racist policemen who rape females and abuse power in his community. Lost in all the controversy were some of Paris' most somber and compelling tracks, including "Thinka 'Bout It," "The Days of Old," and "Assata's Song." Worlds apart from the menacing tones of his best-known work, these are introspective, pensive, and frankly beautiful songs that look at the way blacks hurt their own and the value and resilience of black women. The album's production honestly comes close to rivaling the Bomb Squad, with samples—from a young DJ Shadow—and a tense, chaotic mix swirling throughout the more agitated tracks. The only true gripe is the number of lengthy interludes. —*Andy Kellman*

Guerrilla Funk / Oct. 4, 1994 / Priority ✦✦✦✦
Guerrila Funk wasn't quite as scathing as the previous *Sleeping With the Enemy*, but that's only a relative term. Paris hasn't tempered his rage at all, he's just expanded his range, adding more societal issues to his hit list. In addition, the music hasn't lost any of its potency, making *Guerrilla Funk* a worthy match for one of the most incendiary hip-hop albums of the '90s. —*Stephen Thomas Erlewine*

Unleashed / Feb. 24, 1998 / Whirling Record/Coconut Grove ✦✦✦
One of the most underrated artists in hip-hop, throughout his career Paris has struggled to find an audience for his righteously angry brand of overtly

political hip-hop. But where earlier albums attempted to mask the stridently noncommercial nature of Paris' lyrical content with accessible, commercial-minded productions, 1998's *Unleashed* finds Paris damn near giving up on trying to reach his audience politically, instead hopping on the West Coast gangsta rap bandwagon with dispiriting gusto. Paris' gruff baritone remains as powerful and commanding as ever, but it's depressing to hear someone whose work once resonated with conviction and idealism spit gangsta rap clichés like some sort of lost Suge Knight flunky. Where Paris' lyrics once took dead aim at the racist white power structure, *Unleashed* finds Paris and his unpromising protégés venting their nihilistic anger at anyone and everyone, from women to wack rappers to dishonest record labels. Bitterness and disillusionment seep into nearly every track, as Paris takes oral revenge on a world that never really accepted him or his music. Sonically, *Unleashed* is steeped in the sinister, low-riding West Coast G-funk pioneered by Dr. Dre, full of accessible, professional, but not particularly distinctive grooves and laid-back samples. If *Unleashed* was the work of an up-and-coming West Coast rapper, it would be a lot easier to forgive the bleak nihilism of its lyrics or the familiarity of its production. Coming from an artist of Paris' stature, however, it's a tremendous disappointment, and easily his worst album to date. Given the consistent air of desperation and hopelessness that pervades *Unleashed*, it's not surprising that Paris retired from the rap game shortly after its release, giving up the hip-hop lifestyle to become, of all things, a wealthy and successful stockbroker. —*Nathan Rabin*

Park-Like Setting

Group / Hip-Hop, Alternative Rap, Turntablism
Put together by Peanuts & Corn labelheads John Smith and Mcenroe, Park-Like Setting was a conceptual project that included fellow Vancouver resident DJ Hunnicutt on turntables. Based around the idea of a college curriculum presented in hip-hop form, the album's songs had titles like "Political Science" and "Extracurricular Activities," with lyrics that play off of the idea that Smith and Mcenroe are the unofficial "teachers" in the group. Releasing *School Day 2, Garbage Day 4* in 2001, it would be the only release from the trio. —*Bradley Torreano*

● **School Day 2, Garbage Day 4** / 2001 / Peanuts & Corn ✦✦✦✦
A Peanuts & Corn supergroup of sorts, Park-Like Setting brings together Mcenroe, DJ Hunnicutt, and John Smith for a 22-track distance education course, plus extracurricular activities. As with other projects from the label, Mcenroe handles all the production and shares MCing duties with Smith. The members have proved on past projects that they're not particularly interested in hip-hop's more traditional subject matter, instead covering consumerism, high school politics, and the inner workings of the music industry. The earnestness of some of the subject material is offset by the sense of humor of the participants—the samples are well chosen and often funny, and none of the members can resist digs at themselves when things start to get too heavy (funniest of all is Hunnicutt's lecture to the kids about how to be a good promoter, but guest Pip Skid's answering machine messages come close). —*Sean Carruthers*

Man Parrish (Manny Parrish)

Producer, Keyboards, Associate Producer / Club/Dance, Electro, Hip-Hop, Disco
Although he produced only a handful of tracks of renown and disappeared into obscurity almost as quickly as he had emerged from it, Manny Parrish is nonetheless one of the most important and influential figures in American electronic dance music. Helping to lay the foundation of electro, hip-hop, freestyle, and techno, as well as the dozens of subgenres to splinter off from those, Parrish introduced the aesthetic of European electronic pop to the American club scene by combining the plugged-in disco-funk of Giorgio Moroder and the man-machine music of Kraftwerk with the beefed-up rhythms and cut'n'mix approach of nascent hip-hop. As a result, tracks like "Hip-Hop Be Bop (Don't Stop)" and "Boogie Down Bronx" were period-defining works that provided the basic genetic material for everyone from Run-D.M.C. and the Beastie Boys to Autechre and Andrea Parker—and they remain undisputed classics of early hip-hop and electro to this day. A native New Yorker, Parrish was a member of the extended family of glam chasers and freakazoids that converged nightly at Studio 54. His nickname, Man, first appeared in Andy Warhol's *Interview* magazine, and his early live shows at

Bronx hip-hop clubs were spectacles of lights, glitter, and pyrotechnics that drew as much from the Warhol mystique as from the Cold Crush Brothers.

Influenced by the electronic experiments of Klaus Nomi and Brian Eno as well as by Kraftwerk, Parrish together with Raúl Rodríguez recorded their best-known work in a tiny studio sometimes shared with Afrika Bambaataa, whose own sessions with Arthur Baker and John Robie produced a number of classics equal to Parrish's own, including "Wildstyle," "Looking for the Perfect Beat," and the famous "Planet Rock." What distinguished "Hip-Hop Be Bop," however, was its lack of vocals and the extremely wide spectrum of popularity it gained in the club scene, from ghetto breakdance halls to uptown clubs like Danceteria and the Funhouse. After he discovered a pirated copy of his music being played by a local DJ, Parrish found his way to the offices of the Importe label (a subsidiary of popular dance imprint Sugarscoop), with whom he inked his first deal. He released his self-titled LP shortly after, and the album went on to sell over two million copies worldwide. Following a period of burnout, Parrish recorded and remixed tracks for Michael Jackson, Boy George, Gloria Gaynor, and Hi-NRG group Man 2 Man, among others, and served as road manager for the Village People. While Parrish's subsequent material achieved nowhere near the success or creative pitch of his earlier work, he continued to record from his Brooklyn studio and has been a frequent DJ at New York S&M clubs. His second LP, *Dreamtime*, appeared on Strictly Rhythm in 1997. —*Sean Cooper*

Man Parrish / 1982 / Polydor ✦✦✦✦
While most of Man Parrish's first LP hasn't stood up very well, it's almost impossible to hear "Hip-Hop Be Bop (Don't Stop)" too many times, and "Man Made" is a lost classic nearly the equally of Parrish's best-known work. Parrish's disco roots are apparent in the tracks "Street Clap" and "Heatstroke," the latter of which first appeared on the soundtrack to a porno movie. —*Sean Cooper*

2 / Apr. 2, 1996 / Hot ✦✦✦

● **The Best of Man Parrish: Heatstroke** / Dec. 24, 1996 / Hot ✦✦✦✦
Man Parrish, cloaked wizard of the synthesizer, made the artificial appear irresistibly funky. *The Best of Man Parrish: Heatstroke* includes 14 of his best productions, from the seminal electro classics "Hip Hop Be Bop (Don't Stop)" (a John Robie coproduction) and "Boogie Down Bronx" (a feature for JVC Force) to his more exploratory dance collages like "Six Simple Synthesizers" and "Techno Trax." Similar to avant-turntablist Christian Marclay, Parrish was a figure with more relevance to the disco avant-garde than the hip-hop scene—certainly his collaborators Klaus Nomi and Bowie acolyte Cherry Vanilla wouldn't have shown up on Sugarhill. Parrish's experimental nature makes for a rocky ride through a "hits" compilation, which takes in mainstream dance ("Heatstroke"), ruddy vocoder electro ("Man Made"), and the type of robot pop that would've made even cut-up popsters Perrey-Kingsley cringe. Still, barring the random old school/electro compilation that includes a Man Parrish cut, this is the only place to hear what made him stand out. —*John Bush*

Part 2 (Keith Hopewell)

b. York, England
Producer / Hip-Hop, Club/Dance, Ambient Breakbeat, Ambient Techno, Electronica
Though he's recorded as a solo act for DJ Vadim's Jazz Fudge label, most of Part 2's excellent production work has come for New Flesh, the group he formed in the mid-'90s with Toastie Tailor and Juice Aleem. Born Keith Hopewell in York, he got into hip-hop via a successful graffiti career, which saw him move into actual legal venues, where he was displayed alongside artists including notorious part-time writers like Req and Goldie. He began producing as well, and formed New Flesh for Old early in the '90s. After recruiting Toastie Tailor and Juice Aleem, the group recorded a few self-released singles and then LPs for London independent Big Dada. Part 2's own recordings have appeared on Jazz Fudge (*Prelude to Cycle 6*) as well as Big Dada (a single with Juice Aleem). —*John Bush*

● **Prelude to Cycle 6** / Jun. 2, 1997 / Jazz Fudge ✦✦✦✦
Although he's known more as a graffiti artist than a recording artist, Part 2's album debut proves he's comfortable in either world. Released on DJ Vadim's Jazz Fudge Records, *Prelude to Cycle 6* highlights the abstract hip-hop Vadim is known for, but with a bit more energy than most; Part 2's use of what sounds like vintage synth gear pushes the album, and DJ Vadim's remix of "Automator" includes a rap by Toastie Taylor. —*John Bush*

Pastor Troy (Micah LeVar Troy)

b. College Park, GA
Vocals, Producer, Executive Producer, Drum Programming / Southern Rap, Hardcore Rap, Dirty South

By integrating self-consciousness and sincerity into his otherwise prototypical dirty South style of rap, Pastor Troy stood out among the masses of up-and-coming Southern MCs trying to break nationally in the early 2000s. Perhaps more than anything, Troy's deeply religious youth shapes his ideology, which also features the usual dirty South themes of getting crunk, living large, representing the South, and garnering respect. He's fairly open about his faith, juxtaposing this earnest quality with his sometimes reckless mentality. In addition to his MCing, Troy also proved himself to be a capable producer, crafting trunk-banging, 808-laden tracks for his albums.

As a youth, Micah LeVar Troy grew up in the well-known College Park area of Atlanta, where he was exposed to the street life at an early age. His father, a former drill sergeant turned pastor, made sure Troy was exposed to the church life as well, though. These two often contrasting lifestyles presented a constant dilemma for Troy: he was drawn to street culture and, in particular, his Geto Boys and N.W.A albums, but his father wouldn't allow the music to be played in the family's home. Eventually, Troy began attending Payne College in hopes of becoming a history teacher. There, free of his father's influence, he began devoting himself to rap, and before long he was making his own beats and writing his own rhymes.

It didn't take long before Troy put college behind him and funneled his efforts into the rap game. He organized a clique of friends called the Down South Georgia Boys (D.S.G.B.) and went about recording his debut album, *We Ready—I Declare War* (1999). Peddled out of the trunk, the album became a local success and eventually a regional success without any radio play or national distribution. Next, a much-publicized, drawn-out feud with Master P didn't hurt, and soon Universal Records came knocking and offered Troy a record deal. Led by the single "This tha City," the resulting album, *Face Off* (2001), did well but enjoyed mostly regional success. Troy's next album, *Universal Soldier* (2002), extended his reach beyond the South a bit, propelled by the Timbaland-produced lead single, "Are We Cuttin'." —*Jason Birchmeier*

Face Off / May 22, 2001 / Uptown/Universal ✦✦✦
Atlanta-based rapper Pastor Troy is probably best known for his long-standing feud with rapper Master P. While Master P went on to sell millions, Pastor Troy became a favorite of underground hip-hop fans. *Face Off* features several songs that were previously released on his independent albums. Most of the songs, such as "Rhonda" and "Eternal Yard Dash," feature lyrics drenched with thug imagery that, while familiar, still has an impact on the listener. Troy's lyrical flow is powerful and offsets the often lackluster production. Despite the fact that many of the tracks are up to two years old, the weight of Pastor Troy's voice and lyrics make them still sound fresh. —*Jon Azpiri*

● **Universal Soldier** / Sep. 24, 2002 / Universal ✦✦✦
Pastor Troy's second attempt at a breakthrough album only furthers the frustration that many expressed with 2001's *Face Off.* The record tries to throw around Troy's beliefs and opinions without direction, which leads to songs that shoot off into tangents that have little to do with the subject matter. The fantasy thug anthems where he threatens his enemies are typical of the dirty South genre, but often he'll contradict those threats with lyrics about his righteous devotion to Christianity. He tries to come off as a pious voice of reason on most of the tracks here, but this tactic fails when the next moment he's talking about his sexual exploits and marijuana intake. This spotty approach to lyrics really hurts certain tracks, as his religious beliefs are in direct opposition to almost everything else he raps about. His other negatives are related to the production work, as few of the producers here, outside of Lil Jon and Timbaland, do anything very interesting beyond the generic crawl of dirty South. Still, when he reins in these bad habits, Pastor Troy can be a fascinating lyricist. "Bless America" quotes "Real American," Rick Derringer's ode to Hulk Hogan, while blasting terrorism, which already makes it seem ridiculous from the outset. But Troy meditates over the effect that bombings have on victim's families and the psyche of the American public, giving the chorus a depth that is hard to fathom without hearing it. The lush throb of Lil Jon's "Who, What, When, Where" is another highlight, as Troy proudly claims Georgia as his home with a clever defensiveness that never strays from the

topic. And when he simply leaves Jesus out of songs, like in Timbaland's awesome club anthem "Are We Cuttin'," Troy can be downright fun. It isn't that Christianity is what makes this album so uneven, it's Troy's poor judgment of when to discuss the topic. When Pastor Troy is focused, he's on top of the dirty South genre. But the sloppy way *Universal Soldier* is put together reveals more of his faults than his positives, making it another average record from a rapper who shows so much potential. —*Bradley Torreano*

Sean Paul (Sean Paul Henriques)

b. Jan. 8, 1973
DJ, Producer / Dancehall, Hip-Hop, Alternative Rap

Dancehall DJ Sean Paul began scoring hit singles in Jamaica starting in 1996, and has since attracted American attention with his appearance on the soundtrack of Hype Williams' *Belly* (with Mr. Vegas and DMX) and his 1999 hit "Hot Gal Today." Born Sean Paul Henriques on January 8, 1973, the multi-ethnic Paul (his parents had Portuguese, Chinese, and Jamaican blood) grew up comfortably in St. Andrew, Jamaica, his mother a renowned painter. He was a skilled athlete, excelling in swimming and especially water polo, playing for the Jamaican national team in the latter. Although his education was enough to land a prosperous career, dancehall music remained Paul's first love, particularly crafting rhythm tracks. He became a DJ after he began writing his own songs, patterning his style largely after Super Cat and finding a mentor in Don Yute; he also found contacts in several members of the reggae-pop band Third World in 1993, which helped open up business connections. Sean Paul released his debut single, "Baby Girl," with producer Jeremy Harding in 1996; it proved a significant success, leading to further Jamaican hits like "Nah Get No Bly (One More Try)," "Deport Them," "Excite Me," "Infiltrate," and "Hackle Mi."

In 1999, Sean Paul started to make inroads to American audiences; he was first commissioned to collaborate with fellow dancehall hitmaker Mr. Vegas on a production for rapper DMX; titled "Here Comes the Boom," the song was included in director Hype Williams' film *Belly*. Also that year, Paul scored a Top Ten hit on the *Billboard* rap charts with "Hot Gal Today," which quickly became his signature tune. Unfortunately, Paul had a very public falling out with Mr. Vegas over the packaging of the latter's remix of "Hot Gal Today"; still, it didn't slow Paul's career momentum, as he played the Summer Jam 2000 in New York City, the center of his American popularity. That fall, Paul released his first album on VP Records; the sprawling *Stage One* collected many of Paul's previous hit singles and compilation cuts, plus a few brand-new tracks. —*Steve Huey*

Stage One / Mar. 21, 2000 / VP ✦✦✦
This extra long CD showcases popular dancehall "riddims" overlaid with DJ Sean Paul's rather pedestrian "toasting." Since he possesses neither an unusual voice nor outstanding skill, this CD can become rather tiresome after awhile, especially after one too many skits on a 25-track album. Still, there are some enjoyable tunes here, namely, the hit single, "Infiltrate," which burned up dance halls with its pumping beat, and "Hot Gal Today," a duet with ultrahot DJ Mr. Vegas, which displays an interesting blend of Sean Paul's hard voice with Vegas' smoother vocals. "Faded," a take on Shania Twain's "Looks Like We Made It," also illustrates clever treatment. —*Rosalind Cummings-Yeates*

● **Dutty Rock** / Sep. 24, 2002 / VP ✦✦✦✦
Sean Paul's *Dutty Rock* is an infectious record, bursting with hooks and filled with energy; it is a surprise U.S. hit. Paul's mix of dancehall and modern R&B and hip-hop is lightweight and easy to dance to. It slows down near the end as some filler creeps in, but at its best, *Dutty Rock* is almost revolutionary. Paul utilizes big-name producers like Sly & Robbie, Steely & Clevie, Jeremy Harding, and the ubiquitous Neptunes, whose sexy "Bubble" is one of the highlights of the record. The best track, the stuttering, can't-get-it-out-of-your-head, catchy "Get Busy," is produced by Steven "Lenky" Marsden and features his staggeringly popular diwali rhythm and a great vocal by Paul. Other tracks, like the hit single "Gimme the Light" and the "Louie Louie"-influenced "Like Glue," are almost as good. Paul has a good ear for melody and his flat, distinctive voice is perfect for his sing-jay style (sing-jay being a blend of DJ and singing). Paul also ropes in Busta Rhymes for an amped-up remix of "Gimme the Light" and Rahzel of the Roots to provide rapping and silly noises on "Top of the Game." This is such a good record that even the skits are pretty good. "Police Skit" may even provide a few chuckles. Sean

Paul's blend of dancehall and hip-hop brings out the best of each genre, and *Dutty Rock* should be booming out of your Jeep if you are a fan of either. *—Tim Sendra*

Pazdat

Group / Gangsta Rap, West Coast Rap, Underground Rap

West Coast gangsta rappers Pazdat debuted in 2002 with *Family Jewels, Vol. 1*. The quartet self-released the album on Pazdat Records and collaborated with producer Big Shade Dawg. *—Jason Birchmeier*

● **Family Jewels, Vol. 1** / May 21, 2002 / Pazdat ◆◆◆

Los Angeles' rap scene has come a long way since the early to mid-'80s. Back then, L.A. rappers felt marginalized, and most of hip-hop's million-selling MCs lived in or around New York—in those days, many hip-hop heads wondered if an L.A.-based rapper could ever sell as many records as Run-D.M.C., the Fat Boys, LL Cool J, or Whodini. But when Ice-T and N.W.A hit big in the late '80s, L.A. rap became a huge industry—and these days, the field is incredibly crowded. Pazdat's *Family Jewels, Vol. 1* was among the countless gangsta rap releases that came from Los Angeles County in 2002, and the all-male group was up against an insanely long list of competitors—in 2002, countless gangsta rap releases were coming out every week. So how does Pazdat compare to the competition? Overall, *Family Jewels, Vol. 1* is above average. The group's lyrics aren't revolutionary by early-2000s standards; their thugged-out gangsta rhymes employ the usual playa/baller/hustler imagery that numerous other West Coast rappers have employed over the years. But while Pazdat's lyrics are far from groundbreaking, its beats, grooves, and hooks do make for enjoyably funky listening. Pazdat has a way with a hook, and Big Shade Dawg's funk-loving production quickly grabs a listener's attention. Dawg doesn't have as elaborate a production style as the influential Dr. Dre; his tracks tend to be more spare. But like Dre, he loves '70s funk and shows his appreciation of classic funksters like Parliament/Funkadelic and Rick James. *Family Jewels, Vol. 1* isn't innovative or groundbreaking, but all things considered, this CD is among the more noteworthy and likable gangsta rap releases that came out of L.A. in 2002. *—Alex Henderson*

Peaches (Merrill Nisker)

Experimental Techno, Electro-Techno

Peaches (Merrill Nisker) burst into transcontinental favor with her very particular brand of cock-sure rapping and spurting groovebox beats. Indeed, this vulgar Canadian temptress may have come from an underground womb of acoustic folk (Mermaid Café), avant-jazz (Fancypants Hoodlum), and deconstructed noise swarms (the Shit), but it wasn't until 2000's new guise that her fearless, apolitical gender-play truly raised heads. European trawls unearthed new admirers, and collaborations with the equally lewd Chilly Gonzales certainly fueled the fire for her first solo effort. By the time she signed onto Berlin's Kitty-Yo label and unleashed *The Teaches of Peaches*, her niche had already been carved out. Peaches simultaneously sounded like a *Penthouse* Forum and Grandmaster Flash, Shirley Manson, and Charles Manson—or just Justine Frischmann hitting her sexual peak. *—Dean Carlson*

● **The Teaches of Peaches** / Sep. 5, 2000 / Kitty-Yo ◆◆◆◆◆

Originally released by the German label Kitty-Yo in 2000, *The Teaches of Peaches* is a crash course in Peaches' (aka Merrill Nisker) punk-disco burlesque. "Sucking on my titties like you wanna be callin' me all the time like Blondie/Check out my Chrissie be-Hynde it's fine all of the time" she sings on the opening manifesto "Fuck the Pain Away," which crystallizes her sound and approach—her music is equal parts sex, humor, rock, and dance, with her frank, and often frankly hilarious, lyrics riding atop stark drumbeats, throbbing bass lines, and repetitive but undeniably rockin' guitar riffs. Trashy, energetic tracks like "Rock Show" and "Lovertits"—which is strangely reminiscent of the Stones' disco period, à la "Emotional Rescue"—put the "rude" back in rudimentary; it's the kind of cleverly stupid music that's made by pretty bright people. Indeed, it's quite possible to read all sorts of women's studies theories into Peaches' music; she's unrepentantly, triumphantly sexual and turns the tables by objectifying guys (particularly on "AA XXX," where she sings, "I like the innocent type/Deer in the headlights," and on the funny, kinky "Hot Rod," where she demands "Huh? What? Show me whatcha got/Rub it against my thigh"), but the fact that her sexually explicit music

isn't presented as a bravely feminist act is, paradoxically, exactly what's so liberating about it. Things start to falter on *The Teaches of Peaches* when the tempo slows down and the electronic elements are emphasized, as on "Diddle My Skittle," "Suck and Let Go," and "Felix Partz," which feel a little draggy compared to the album's high-octane first half but do have a hypnotic pull that's worth noting. However, the flirty, disco-inspired "Set It Off" and bitchy breakup song "Cum Undun" express her punk attitude and dance ambitions much more naturally. And even though songs like "Sucker" sound a bit warmed over, it's fairly remarkable for an artist with such a brash, distinctive style that she doesn't start repeating herself until the very end of the album. Funny, sexy, outrageous, and danceable (not to mention endlessly quotable) all at once, *The Teaches of Peaches* is a great introduction to a unique artist who defines herself by gleefully blurring boundaries. The 2002 reissue on Beggars/XL includes a bonus disc of covers and remixes that map out Peaches' influences and contemporaries, including her versions of Jeans Team's "Keine Melodien" and Berlin's "Sex (I'm A)," a new version of "Felix Partz" featuring Gonzales, Kid 606's remix of "Fuck the Pain Away," and a mix of "Set It Off" by Tobi Neuman. *—Heather Phares*

Peanut Butter Wolf (Chris Manak)

b. San Mateo, CA

DJ, Producer / Hip-Hop, Underground Rap, Turntablism, Electronica

Among the true talents in the late-'90s new school of old school hip-hop, Peanut Butter Wolf began DJing as a teenager and became quite an entrepreneur at his San Jose, CA, high school, selling mix tapes of his turntable work. He debuted on wax in 1989 with "You Can't Swing This" on All Good Vinyl, recorded with a smooth MC named Lyrical Prophecy. By the end of the year, PBW began working with MC Charizma, and the two gelled quickly, perfecting their skills at block parties and shows with the likes of the Pharcyde, House of Pain, and Nas. Just after the duo gained a record deal with Hollywood Basic in 1992, Charizma was shot and killed.

Unsure of where to turn without the talents of his MC, Peanut Butter Wolf began issuing strictly instrumental work, including his first release, *Peanut Butter Breaks* on Heyday Records. Tracks followed for the Bomb label (on the excellent *Return of the DJ* compilation) as well as Om Records. Though the MC had ruled the world of hip-hop since the mid-'80s, selected DJ crews began to get exposure in the dance underground by the late '90s, including DJ Shadow, the Invisibl Skratch Piklz, and the X Men (whose name was later changed to the X-Ecutioners, for copyright reasons). Peanut Butter Wolf joined the elite as well, recording for dance labels 2 Kool (the *Lunar Props* EP) and Ninja Tune (remixing the Herbaliser) as well as contributing production work for fellow old schooler Kool Keith. With the foundation of his Stone's Throw label, PBW began developing tracks recorded earlier with MC Charizma and released work by another Bay Area crew, Fanatik. His debut production LP, *My Vinyl Weighs a Ton*, appeared in 1999. The year 2002 brought two excellent compilations, *The Best of Peanut Butter Wolf* and the Stone's Throw 7" collection *Jukebox 45's*. *—John Bush*

● **My Vinyl Weighs a Ton** / Jan. 18, 1999 / Copasetik ◆◆◆◆◆

Digger of crates, master of tracks, Peanut Butter Wolf has an influences list that stretches into the hundreds (nearly all of them are actually listed in the credits, broken down by year) and a working knowledge of beats and samples that must number in the thousands. There aren't quite that many on his first production album, but he winnowed it down to a cool 75 or 100 to create one of the grooviest, funkiest underground records of the '90s. Unlike fellow NoCal mixer/producer DJ Shadow, PBW has plenty of space for collaborations, with nearly a dozen different rappers stopping by, along with nearly *every* top turntablist of the era: Babu, Q-Bert, Rob Swift, Cut Chemist, Kid Koala, Z-Trip, Shortkut, and A-Trak (granted, quite a few of them all show up for one gigantic posse track, "Tale of Five Cities"). *My Vinyl Weighs a Ton* boasts deep beats and choice samples, all of them working brilliantly together, and enough great cutting to keep each track raw and full of energy. Obviously learning a few lessons about sequencing and pacing from classic mix tapes (of his and of others), PBW sprinkles the rappers throughout this record and only recruits the best. Vocal highlights come with Planet Asia's mid-tempo grind "In Your Area," Pablo's feature on "Rock Unorthodox," and a two-part soundclash for the excellent Lootpack crew on "Styles Crew Flows Beats." He name-checked Wild Man Fischer along with Erick & Parrish; got recommendations from rare-groove heroes like Reuben Wilson, Galt

MacDermot, and Fred Wesley; and delivered an excellent record that offered just as much to fans of rare grooves, great rappers, and deft DJs. —*John Bush*

The Best of Peanut Butter Wolf / Feb. 12, 2002 / Copasetik ◆◆◆
The Best of Peanut Butter Wolf is a slightly premature release—the turntable master, despite having released singles for over a decade, had only made one previous full-length album, 1999's *My Vinyl Weighs a Ton*, and a good chunk of that album is reprised here, occasionally remixed and even retitled—but it's a solid overview of the skills of one of the best DJs in underground hip-hop. If anything, the album focuses too much on his work with various MCs (most notably *My Vinyl Weighs a Ton*'s Rasco, who appears on half a dozen tracks) and not enough on the wiggy breakbeats and cerebral crosscutting that are Peanut Butter Wolf's true strengths. It's wild cutting contests like the nine-minute "Tale of Five Cities" and the self-explanatory "Styles, Crews, Flows, Beats" that really shine, but the album as a whole, with its brief inter-track examples of Peanut Butter Wolf's turntable skills, is a fine introduction. —*Stewart Mason*

Jukebox 45's / Sep. 3, 2002 / Stones Throw ◆◆◆◆
Self-confessed 7" obsessive Peanut Butter Wolf has almost every hip-hop 45 ever recorded, and by 1998, he began issuing new ones as well, on his own Stones Throw label. Drafting a host of friends—including Madlib, Karizma, Breakestra, and A-Trak—plus a few original rare grooves from the '70s, his series got the CD compilation treatment here, and it's one of the tightest, most invigorating breakbeat releases of the year, literally packed with excellent productions, hilarious one-offs, and truly obscure funk. Madlib has some of the best tracks (under various guises), like a remix of Quasimoto's "Microphone Mathematics"—basically a freestyle treatment over a cut-up De La Soul sample—and a dark track called "The Ox (Fantastic Four)." For another big highlight, "My 2600," Jeff Jank's Captain Funkaho project, turns in the meanest groove ever tied to an Atari tribute, calling off cartridges like Debbie Harry name-checks Fab 5 Freddie in "Rapture." The five tracks of older material are excellent as well, including a spaced-out children's record called "Rocket Ship," performed by the Stark Reality and apparently produced by Hoagy Carmichael Jr. Old and new, funk and hip-hop and acid rock, it all flows together perfectly on this collection of rare grooves, with more attitude than *Big in Wigan* and better productions than a dozen Irv Gottis. —*John Bush*

Penthouse Players Clique

Group / West Coast Rap, Gangsta Rap
Signed to Ruthless Records and produced by DJ Quik and Eazy-E, the Penthouse Players Clique began promisingly enough. Comprised of Playa Hamm and Tweed Cadillac, the short-lived West Coast gangsta duo debuted in 1992 with a full-length album (*Paid the Cost*), a pair of singles ("Explanation of a Playa" and "P.S. Phuk U 2"), and an appearance on the *Trespass* soundtrack ("I'm a Playa"). That was it, though. Years later, Cadillac resurfaced with the Mackadelics on *Exposed to the Game* (1996) while Hamm embarked on a solo career, beginning with *Layin' Hands* (2001). —*Jason Birchmeier*

● **Paid the Cost** / 1992 / Priority ◆◆
The Penthouse Players Clique wasn't a full-time group; rather, they were a studio project boasting such well-known gangsta rappers as DJ Quik, AMG, and the late Eazy-E. Unlike N.W.A's *Straight Outta Compton*, Ice Cube's *Death Certificate*, or Ice-T's *Power*, *Paid the Cost* doesn't have a cohesive sociopolitical message. The goal of the Penthouse Players was simply to have some profane, over-the-top fun, and they do so with uneven and unfocused but sometimes entertaining results. While the lyrics aren't all that violent, they are rude, crude, and sexually explicit. In fact, tunes like "Pimp Lane" and "Trust No Bitch" make a point of being as vulgar and offensive as possible. Intellectuals in the hip-hop press generally trashed *Paid the Cost*, calling it a lowest-common-denominator release and denouncing much of it as a pointless exercise in sexism for the sake of sexism. But then, the Penthouse Players didn't record this album to please hip-hop's intelligentsia. *Paid the Cost* isn't remarkable, although it's sometimes amusing and fun if you have a taste for off-color humor. —*Alex Henderson*

People Under the Stairs

Group / Club/Dance, Underground Rap
The underground hip-hop outfit People Under the Stairs were formed by Mike Turner (Double K) and Chris Portugal (Thes One), who met on the

fringe of L.A.'s late-'90s hip-hop underground. The duo, devoted to jazzy samples, danceable beats, intricate rhyming skills, and laid-back humor, debuted in 1999 with the acclaimed *The Next Step* and followed it up in 2000 with *Question in the Form of an Answer*. Gathering heavy praise and touring with De La Soul, the group took their road experiences and brought them to the studio to record their next album. The final results appeared in the summer of 2002 under the name *O.S.T.* —*Steve Huey*

The Next Step / Mar. 23, 1999 / PUTS ◆◆◆
Before finding a home further north on San Francisco's Om label, People Under the Stairs released this debut set of understated productions and steady rhymes via their own PUTS imprint. The subject matter on display is hardly unusual, taking in the requisite MC boasting ("Ten Tough Guys"), three tales of hip-hop love gone sour ("The Turndown"), inebriation out on the town ("Mid-City Fiesta"), and odes to the group's birthplace ("Los Angeles Daze") and their adopted home ("San Francisco Knights"). Unfortunately, the duo fails to follow up on the promise of "Death of a Salesman," a gem of dizzying storytelling that arrives early on. Elsewhere, though the train of thought is more easily followed, the two MCs remain well above par, applying the same agile wordplay to almost everything in sight. Stark outlines of rugged, organic beats are tastefully fleshed out by anonymous walking bass lines, horn traces, and ominous keyboard chords from deep record crates. These samples set the stage without dominating it as *The Next Step* manages to dodge most of the jazz-rap pitfalls. Ultimately however, the album falls under the category of promising debut. PUTS' independent philosophy and their "true school" tag created high expectations during a time when the hip-hop underground was attempting to establish the music's role as "art not income" ("Wannabes") and "developing a new system" ("Intro/4 Everybody"). Yet, rather than "developing a new system," *The Next Step* finds People Under the Stairs performing quite well within the boundaries of old. —*Nathan Bush*

Question in the Form of an Answer / Jun. 6, 2000 / Om ◆◆◆
The People Under the Stairs' Thes One and Double K have not succumbed to "sophomore jinx" with their second album *Question in the Form of an Answer*. In fact, they come with a very solid hip-hop album from top to bottom, the rhymes are creative and the beats are very on point. Refusing to use any keyboards (a rarity in the modern hip-hop era), the duo constructs their music completely from the funky records they dig up; Pete Rock would love these guys and their pure hip-hop aesthetic. Although I like the fact that the album has over 20 solid tracks, PUTS could have used an A&R here to cut out a few of the lesser tracks and up the ante on the more solid tracks, making them even more banging. But overall, PUTS really establishes a solid record with this release. —*Nick Pfeiffer*

American Men Vol. 1 / May 1, 2001 / PUTS ◆◆◆
This appears to be a compilation put out by the People Under the Stairs on their own record label, although it's been difficult finding out any more information about the album. It's composed of approximately 60 minutes of previously unreleased material in typical PUTS fashion: tight, jazzy beats littered with classic samples. Unlike some of the duo's other work, there seems to be some keyboard/synthesizer used in the production. Lyrically, the duo remains on point with an often humorous and laid-back approach on the mic, frequently sounding almost old school in the style of delivery. Not as inspiring, creative, or complete as their first two records, but that's to be expected in a compilation effort. Fellow rappers Murs, Scarub, Sam Spade, and a few others also make welcome appearances. —*Brad Mills*

● **O.S.T. (Original Soundtrack)** / Jun. 4, 2002 / Om ◆◆◆◆
It's hard not to appreciate what People Under the Stairs are trying to accomplish with their third full-length. Fortunately, the attempt (i.e., the finished product) works just as well in practice as in theory. Although there could be a little more variety from track to track, this is one fun and funky record. There's a democratic, stylistic purity to *O.S.T.*—hence the title—that is wholly consistent with its predecessors. As Thes One explains in the liner notes, it's "an album that is made up of old records and personal experiences"—no more, no less. Both One and Double K serve as MCs and DJs and think of themselves more as b-boys than artists or musicians. They eschew live instrumentation (with the exception of the bass on "The Breakdown") and rely instead on their distinctive, loose-limbed raps; deep, diverse record collections; and mad turntable skills. Consequently, the Los Angeles duo has been compared more often to the underground hip-hop combos of the 1980s and 1990s, like the Pharcyde and Freestyle Fellowship, than to their

contemporaries of the 2000s. The best example of their no-frills approach comes to fruition on the horn-blasted party anthem "Hang Loose," a cross between Grandmaster Flash & the Furious Five and Poor Righteous Teachers (and in which they compare themselves to Kool & the Gang). Laid-back grooves and shout-outs to 1970s TV shows (like *Scooby Doo*), cold beverages (Long Island iced teas), and tasty treats (fish and chips) make *O.S.T.* one of the more enjoyable hip-hop releases of 2002. *—Kathleen C. Fennessy*

Pep Love

Underground Rap, West Coast Rap

Pep Love, aka PL, an often-slept-on member of East Oakland, CA's Hieroglyphics family labored as an MC for many years, earning only shout-outs and the occasional guest verse on Hieroglyphics projects. While lending a creative hand on Souls of Mischief's debut *'93 Til Infinity* and even getting background lyrical credits on two tracks ("When Ya Lost" and "Batting Practice"), Love's first shot at an actual verse came on the B-side "Undisputed Champs" alongside Del tha Funkee Homosapien and Q-Tip. After appearing on Casual's debut album, *Fear Itself,* on the track "Who's It On" and Extra Prolific's "Like It Should Be," Pep Love would vanish as Souls of Mischief and the Hiero crew went on a relative sabbatical for a couple of years. PL finally resurfaced in 1998 on the Hiero compilation album *Third Eye Vision;* his verse on "After Dark" again serving notice to this underrated giant, making listeners do an auditory double-take in the process. During his years as a Hiero understudy, Pep Love formed a close alliance with fellow Hiero member and producer Jay Biz. A human thesaurus with a knack for high-speed wordbending, Love's metaphysical talent would finally be unleashed in full panoply on his debut solo album, *Ascension,* in 2001 (with his pal Jay Biz doing most of the production). *Ascension* was released on the Hiero Imperium label maintaining loyalty to the crew that originally put him on the map. *—M.F. Di Bella*

● **Ascension** / Jul. 24, 2001 / Hiero Imperium ◆◆◆◆
If the Hieroglyphics crews' wildly inconsistent discography proves anything, it's that you can count on them to deliver one thing—dope debuts. However, from being too experimental (Del's *Both Sides of the Brain*), missing in action (Casual), or just woefully inept (Souls' *Trilogy*), Oaktown's finest have seen their stock as individual artists, and as a crew, plummet. With history on his side, though, the last Boy Scout of Hieroglyphics, Pep Love, has finally stepped out of the shadows with his rejuvenating debut *Ascension.* For those who yearn for uplifting and positive hip-hop, then Love is your kind of MC, as *Ascension* yearns to inspire. Eschewing material greed and trivial matters, Love seeks to reach higher levels of consciousness, and wants you to join him on this self-help trek. Yet, what separates Love from other pulpit prophesiers is that he drops knowledge ("Grime and Grit" and "U.S.") without sounding overly preachy. Likewise, Love's pleas for responsibility ("What You Are," "A+") and the ode to young love, "T.A.M.I.," in an otherwise irresponsible genre are utterly refreshing. While *Ascension* is a notch below the classic debuts delivered by Love's more established teammates, it is a critical building block, as it generates renewed faith in the Hiero collective. As "Act-Phenom" reiterates, *Ascension* "is a ritual you will enjoy." *—Matt Conaway*

Perfec

b. North Long Beach, CA

West Coast Rap

Perfec is a California rap artist from Long Beach, but not the typical gangsta rapper often seen from the area. His creativity shows through on his full-length debut, *Best Kept Secret* on the Ark 21 record label, released in 2001. *—Brad Mills*

● **Best Kept Secret** / Apr. 3, 2001 / Ark 21 ◆◆◆
The first thing to say is that Perfec is not perfect, and his debut album is far from the best-kept secret in hip-hop. Although he stands out among some of the other hardcore rappers from California, he just can't compete lyrically on a level like many of the better lyricists from the East. At only 21 years old, he still has plenty of time to prove himself. That said, what listeners have here is an album of mixed quality. Perfec aims at being a storyteller on a good number of the tracks. On a few, he succeeds at weaving an interesting tale, but doesn't manage to keep things going throughout a whole song. Other offerings see him rapping about his lifestyle in sunny California and the

typical rap topics—girls, money, drugs, and guns. When the dust clears, *Best Kept Secret* should probably remain one. *—Brad Mills*

The Pharcyde

f. 1990, Los Angeles, CA

Group / Political Rap, Hip-Hop, Alternative Rap, West Coast Rap, Underground Rap

An influential alternative rap quartet from South Central Los Angeles, the Pharcyde was formed by MCs/producers Tre "Slimkid" Hardson, Derrick "Fatlip" Stewart, Imani Wilcox, and Romye "Booty Brown" Robinson. Hardson, Wilcox, and Robinson were all dancers and choreographers who met on the L.A. underground club circuit in the late '80s, worked together for a while, and served a stint as dancers on *In Living Color.* Stewart, meanwhile, performed at local clubs and eventually hooked up with the others in 1990. Under the tutelage of Reggie Andrews, a local high school music teacher, the group learned about the music industry and the process of recording an album. They landed a deal with Delicious Vinyl in 1991, and a year later released their eccentric debut album, *Bizarre Ride II the Pharcyde,* which went gold. After support slots for De La Soul and A Tribe Called Quest as well as a successful spot on Lollapalooza's second stage in 1994, the group released its second album, *Labcabincalifornia,* which was calmer than their first but no less warped. After a five-year break, which saw little action except for the debut of Stewart as a solo rapper (his single "What's Up Fatlip" became an underground hit), the Pharcyde returned in late 2000 with their third album, *Plain Rap. —Steve Huey*

★ **Bizarre Ride II the Pharcyde** / 1992 / Delicious Vinyl/Rhino ◆◆◆◆◆
The cover shot of a Fat Albert-ized Pharcyde roller coasting their way into a funhouse makes perfect sense, as the L.A.-based quartet introduced listeners to an uproarious vision of earthy hip-hop informed by P-funk silliness and an everybody-on-the-mic street-corner atmosphere that highlights the incredible rapping skills of each member. With multiple voices freestyling over hilarious story songs like "Oh Shit," "Soul Flower," the dozens contest "Ya Mama," and even a half-serious driving-while-black critique named "Officer," *Bizarre Ride II the Pharcyde* proved daisy-age philosophy akin to De La Soul and A Tribe Called Quest wasn't purely an East Coast phenomenon. Skits and interludes with live backing (usually just drums and piano) only enhance the freeform nature of the proceedings, and the group even succeeds when not reliant on humor, as proved by the excellent heartbreak tale "Passing Me By." The production, by J-Sw!ft and the group, is easily some of the tightest and most inventive of any hip-hop record of the era. Though *Bizarre Ride II the Pharcyde* could have used a few more musical hooks to draw in listeners before they begin to appreciate the amazing rapping and gifted productions, the lack of compromise reveals far greater rewards down the line. *—John Bush*

Labcabincalifornia / Nov. 14, 1995 / Delicious Vinyl/Rhino ◆◆◆
Labcabincalifornia is a more mature record than the Pharcyde's debut. That's not necessarily a good thing, as the group's playful attitude and comic raps were much of what made them so irresistible. True, age has enlightened the Pharcyde on "Moment in Time" and the single "Runnin'," the former a salute to the past and the latter a description of their flight from South Central's Pharcyde Manor to the Hollywood Hills. But the music is much of the problem here. Though the raps are solid, tempos never vary from the usual midtempo jam. The keyboard-driven melodies are good—some better than others—but a little variety is needed. The last three tracks ("The Hustle," "Devil Music," "The E.N.D.") do evoke the spirit of the debut, but by that time it's too late—the sophomore jinx has hit. *—John Bush*

Plain Rap / Nov. 7, 2000 / Edeltone ◆◆◆◆
In late 2000, the Pharcyde resurfaced for their first major release since 1995. Having lost the lazy-flowed Fatlip to a solo career, the original trio of Slim Kid Tre, Imani, and Booty Brown were left to carry the torch. The L.A. underground artists put forth a classic album with their debut *Bizarre Ride* in 1992 and followed up with the superbly crafted but somewhat maligned *Labcabincalifornia* in 1995. While the various pitfalls of the industry claimed the quartet's unity, the core three came back with a bittersweet vengeance, lamenting past failures and frustrations but looking ahead positively as only the Pharcyde can. The album offers 11 one-word-titled tracks, sort of a rap version of Miles Davis' *Aura,* each track creating a specifically colorful mood. "Trust" testifies to the crew's resilient style, unwavering in theme and quality: "When it seems there's no one trust/You can always count on Pharcyde to

bust." "Somethin" and "Misery" feature the subtle stylings of Slimkid Tre and both Imani and Booty Brown employ strong spoken-word-influenced poetics throughout. While the heft of the Pharcyde sound is diminished slightly by their broken circle, this is an emotionally tangible album that combines delicate content with tight production. The Pharcyde attempts to bring a ray of California sunshine to dark times. —*Michael Di Bella*

Cydeways: The Best of the Pharcyde / Jan. 16, 2001 / Rhino ✦✦✦✦
If rap music has taught people anything, it's that even the annoying shimmer of a Mercedes Benz and a pool of high-price hookers can't overshadow true talent. Surprisingly enough, it became clear that the Pharcyde is one of hip-hop's few modern ensembles that stares down modern-day rap and challenges it to a fight. Crafty and cool, *Cydeways* isn't necessarily genius. Its offbeat and stylistic rhythms and rhymes are an acquired taste at best. But the album still carries innovation that hasn't been touched in years: rap music thriving on a genuine mix of fact, fiction, humor, and memory. "Runnin," "Ya Mama," and "Oh Shit" are creative excerpts from a diary that these boys have carefully crafted. It becomes a kind of coming-of-age story, from making jokes about each other's mother to getting their ass kicked in school. Its undeniable soul is what makes the Pharcyde an underappreciated addition to hip-hop's overplayed and overrated existence in the coming century. So if you still believe in hip-hop, but have become intimidated by its current barrage of smut, simplicity, and stupidity, fear not, friends—the Pharcyde's got your back. —*Darren Ratner*

Phife Dawg (Malik Taylor)

b. Apr. 20, 1970, Brooklyn, NY
Alternative Rap, East Coast Rap, Underground Rap
As part of the pioneering rap group A Tribe Called Quest and its extended Native Tongues family, Phife Dawg helped to usher in a whole new style of intelligent hip-hop. Born Malik Taylor, Phife grew up in Queens, NY, where he spent his childhood writing poetry and eventually rapping at school and in his neighborhood whenever the opportunity was available. Along with high school classmates Q-Tip (Jonathan Davis) and Ali Shaheed Muhammad, Phife founded ATCQ, whose legendary decade-long career ended in 1998 with *The Love Movement*. The Atlanta-based Phife began flexing his new freedom in 1999 with *Bend Ova*, the first single with his new U.K.-based label, Groove Attack. A full-length titled *Ventilation: Da LP*, including appearances from Phife's alterego, Mutty Ranks, was released the following year. —*Wade Kergan*

● **Ventilation: Da LP** / Sep. 26, 2000 / Groove Attack ✦✦✦
After A Tribe Called Quest culminated a decade of influence with *The Love Movement*, the group's loyalists immediately shifted gears, turning their attention to frontman Q-Tip's solo debut, *Amplified*, and delegating the group's oft-neglected member, Phife Dawg, back into a role he has become very accustomed to: second fiddle. Eager to step out of Q-Tip's shadow, Phife's solo debut, *Ventilation*, reveals not only his true musical ambitions but also the feelings he has repressed since the legendary group disassembled. Though the group's split was deemed amicable, "Flawless" suggests otherwise. Sending tremors through Tribe's sacred foundation, Phife spares the rod on the third group member, Ali, but questions his former partner's new "jiggy" image on "Flawless": "FUBU suit with Steve Madden boots make me wanna puke/Phat Farm shorts with a garter belt looking like a whore/Or a purple bandana cuz it matches your shaw." Though Phife's frivolous lyrical banter becomes monotonous for stretches, an esteemed production squad—Hi-Tek, Pete Rock, and Jay Dee—keeps *Ventilation* musically stimulating throughout. Phife sparks the most immediate chemistry with Hi-Tek on "D.R.U.G.S." and "Alphabet Soup," as his unassuming voice flourishes over the producer's minimal grooves. What Phife's solo debut lacks in execution, though, is compensated with intrigue. Other than a few aimless party cuts, such as "The Club Hoppa," Phife steers *Ventilation* on a fairly consistent course. One thing's for certain: after hearing *Ventilation*, Q-Tip will be wondering who let the Dawg off his leash. —*Matt Conaway*

Philly's Most Wanted

Group / East Coast Rap, Party Rap
Helmed by the Neptunes just as the production duo had begun overtaking the entire rap industry, Philly's Most Wanted's debut album, *Get Down or Lay Down* (2001), made a huge, albeit momentary, impact upon its release.

Comprised of Mr. Man and Boo-Bonic, the duo didn't have many credentials at the time, so the Neptunes affiliation helped them garner national radio support for "Cross the Border" and "Please Don't Mind." —*Jason Birchmeier*

● **Get Down or Lay Down** / Aug. 7, 2001 / Atlantic ✦✦
Technically, Philly's Most Wanted is comprised of rappers Mr. Man and Boo-Bonic, but the real star of the show are the Neptunes, the hot production team that has worked with everyone from Jay-Z to Mystikal to Britney Spears. Their trademark sound is felt throughout *Get Down or Lay Down*, and the slick style works best on their single "Cross the Border," which mixes slick rhythms with a splash of Latin guitar and horns. Although this is far from their best work, the Neptunes provide enough danceable hip-hop to get the job done. The same can't be said about Mr. Man and Boo-Bonic, who fail to bring anything to the table. Their rhymes are utterly pedestrian, rhyming about the usual thug scenarios without a hint of originality. The duo better hope that the Neptunes are willing to work with them again, because, without their musical wizardry, Philly's Most Wanted may never be heard from again. —*Jon Azpiri*

Phoenix Orion

b. Brooklyn, NY
Hip-Hop, Underground Rap, East Coast Rap
Born and raised in Brooklyn, Phoenix Orion first turned heads at local clubs in NYC—most notably at the legendary Giant Step—as a guest MC. Eventually, he produced a demo that surfaced on both coasts and led to an underground following, thanks to his dark, apocalyptic view of the future and the intergalactic beats that accompanied it. PO's dystopic perspectives were further explored on his 1999 full-length debut, *Zimulated Experiencez*, which included collaborators Hive, Daddy Kev, Hermes, and DJ Rhettmatic (of Beat Junkies fame). He returned in late 2001 with *Secret Wars*, recorded for the Meanstreet label. —*Mike DaRonco*

● **Zimulated Experiencez** / Mar. 2, 1999 / Celestial ✦✦✦
Phoenix Orion doesn't have a positive outlook beyond the year 2000. In marked contrast to the utopian visions of *The Jetsons*, Phoenix raps about the apocalyptic second coming of the "Cyber Christ Clone." Other bleak visions of the future can be heard on the intergalactic sounds of *Zimulated Experiencez*, which also gives evidence of this MC being a fan of William Gibson writings and *The X Files*. There are enough mind-warping sci-fi references to spin heads at a *Star Trek* convention, but don't associate the word "geek" with Phoenix Onion; "dystopic" is more fitting. Hive, Daddy Kev, and Hermes can also be found here, with scratching provided by DJ Rhettmatic, spreading the warnings of our eventual cultural ruin. Not the most positive outlook on how the future turns out, but maybe Phoenix Orion knows something we don't. —*Mike DaRonco*

Phunké Assfalt

Group / Hip-Hop, Gangsta Rap, Hardcore Rap, West Coast Rap
Consisting of rapper Novacain (formerly MC Casanova) and DJ/producer World, Phunké Assfalt was a talented, though underexposed, hip-hop duo that was active in Los Angeles in the 1990s. Their gritty, R&B-minded music was hardcore rap, but the duo steered clear of the type of violent gangsta rap that was prevalent on the West Coast at the time. Novacain and World met in 1987 at California State University, Fullerton, where World had been DJing at campus parties on weekends and invited Novacain to rap with him after hearing the MC's parody of a U.T.F.O. song. The two soon formed a group called the Kold Krush Krew (not to be confused with the Cold Crush Brothers, one of hip-hop's pioneering New York groups of the late '70s and early '80s), and they would participate in various projects before recording as Phunké Assfalt in 1994. In 1991-1992, Novacain led a funk-rock band called Roxanne (not to be confused with Roxanne Shanté, the Real Roxanne, or pop-rockers Roxette), and after that, he spent a year rapping for the hip-hop/jazz group Bare Bones. Then, in 1994, Novacain and World teamed up as Phunké Assfalt and recorded *Tales From the Crib* for A-Street. The CD, which included the sexy single "Indonesha," didn't receive as much attention as it deserved—and the duo didn't record another album in the 1990s. —*Alex Henderson*

● **Tales From the Crib** / Jan. 17, 1995 / A-Street ✦✦✦
The terms "gangsta rap" and "California rap" were often used interchangeably in the late '80s and '90s, but not every rap act that came from the West

Coast during that time was into gangsta-style lyrics. In fact, one could easily compile a long list of non-gangsta MCs who were California based back then—that includes everyone from the Pharcyde, Digital Underground, and MC Hammer to Young MC, Too Short, and Tone-Loc. Another California rap act that rejected gangsta rap was the L.A.-based duo Phunké Assfalt. Their 1995 album *Tales From the Crib* is heavily influenced by 1970s soul and funk, and it combines samples with an abundance of real instruments. You won't hear rapper Novacane—who, along with producer World, composes Phunké Assfalt—giving any first-person accounts of drive-by shootings. *Tales From the Crib* is primarily a party album, and samples of 1970s classics like the Ohio Players' "Pain" and the Roberta Flack/Donny Hathaway duet "Back Together Again" help keep the R&B-minded party alive. World doesn't shy away from technology, although he also uses real musicians to provide real horns, real drums, real bass, and real guitar. On "Pinocchio," Freddie Fox's electric guitar solo draws on such funk-rock influences as Funkadelic and Ernie Isley. A few of the tunes have a sociopolitical focus, including "Brother's Keeper" and "Mo Time Than Money," which takes a humorous look at the challenges of searching for a job; but on the whole, this CD favors escapism and does so with fun and infectious results. —*Alex Henderson*

Richy Pitch

Hip-Hop
Producer and DJ Richy Pitch is a rare British name signed to an independent American hip-hop label. Born in Hertfordshire, he studied education at the nearby University of London, and began organizing his first parties around the same time. Influenced by old school hip-hop, he received spinning dates for Gilles Peterson (Talkin' Loud) and Soul II Soul, and moved to full-fledged promoting with a British tour by the American 7 Heads collective. The relationship led to a contract, and Pitch's first record, *Live at Home*, was released in 2002. —*John Bush*

● **Live at Home** / May 28, 2002 / 7 Heads ✦✦✦
Despite Adam Fenton having proven that U.K. hip-hop production has much to offer via his all-star *Kaos* project, it still comes as something of a surprise to see a U.K. school teacher skimming his beats across the Atlantic from the comfort of the home counties north of London and into the Brooklyn offices of Wes Jackson's respected U.S. independent, 7 Heads. Like Fenton, Pitch—real name Parker—prefers the studio desk to the microphone, drafting in an array of collaborators to an album that charts the day in the life of a b-boy, replete with the occasional time check and scene setting. Great vocal contributions from the likes of El Da Sensei, Apani B, J-Live, and Mr. Complex accompany unusually full arrangements and turntablisms from notable deck technicians Mr. Thing, First Rate, and the Nextmen's Dom Search; classic themes attach themselves to a happy-go-lucky musical agenda that is nothing if not endearing. Richy Pitch is one to watch. —*Kingsley Marshall*

Planet Asia (Jason Green)

Underground Rap, West Coast Rap
Planet Asia rose from the uncharted hip-hop territory of Fresno, CA, to become one of the stars of the West Coast "true school" generation which emerged in late '90s. After breaking on the national scene in 1998, he quickly gained a reputation for his crisp, intense rhyme delivery, his versatile lyrical content, and his consistent productivity. Green moved from Fresno to the San Francisco Bay Area in 1998 at the age of 22 and met up with producer Fanatik, whose sparse relaxed beats provided an interesting backdrop to Planet Asia's battle-tested flow. The two appeared together on Tripek Records' *Rules of the Game* compilation alongside veterans like Living Legends and the Coup, creating instant national buzz. Planet Asia released his self-titled debut soon after and never looked back, appearing on over 20 releases in the next two years and working with countless artists, big and small. He and Fanatik parted ways as Asia's sound evolved and he found more up-tempo, New York-influenced beats to his liking. Collaborations with Rasco showcased a special chemistry, and the two formed a group, Cali Agents, and released a full-length, *How the West Was One* in 2000. After releasing his second solo EP, *The Last Stand*, Planet Asia scored a deal with Interscope Records. —*Luke Forrest*

● **The Last Stand** / Oct. 3, 2000 / Mona ✦✦✦
One of the rising stars in West Coast's underground hip-hop scene in the late '90s, Planet Asia has proven talent as a lyricist. His signature aggressive flow and unique voice have been highlights of many compilations and posse jam

cuts, but like fellow Californians Ras Kass and Xzibit, he often seems to be better in a team than as a soloist. Following closely on the heels of the wonderful Cali Agents LP *The Last Stand* is a slight disappointment. Without a partner in rhyme, Planet Asia's songs are plagued by a lack of direction and mediocre choruses. Although "You Can't Miss" and "Holdin' the Crown" have solid beats (provided by Amp Live and 427, respectively) and rhymes, they lack the firepower of Asia's work with Rasco, Talib Kweli, and others. It's telling that the album's best two songs feature guests. Planet Asia and the appropriately named Punchline (part of the duo Punch & Words) trade verses with vigor to lay their claim as "Head Honchos" of rap's new generation, and the vastly underrated 427 and King Koncepts guest on "Takin' Ova." The remainder of *The Last Stand* is similar to Asia's self-titled solo debut EP—quality listening but unexceptional. What it reveals is an MC struggling to find his sound as a solo artist and fulfill his enormous potential. —*Luke Forrest*

P.M. Dawn

f. 1988
Group / Urban, Alternative Rap, Pop-Rap
Comprised of brothers Prince Be (Attrell Cordes) and DJ Minute Mix (Jarrett Cordes), the early-'90s group P.M. Dawn straddled the gap between hip-hop and smooth '70s-style soul, creating an innovative urban R&B that owed as much to pop as it did to rhythm and blues. The brothers recorded their debut single, "Ode to a Forgetful Mind," in 1988, but P.M. Dawn didn't release a full-length album until 1991. The record, *Of the Heart, of the Soul and of the Cross: The Utopian Experience*, was an immediate hit, thanks to the single "Set Adrift on Memory Bliss," which sampled Spandau Ballet's new-wave hit "True." Both the album and the single received glowing reviews, as did the 1993 follow-up, *The Bliss Album . . . ?*, which featured the hit singles "I'd Die Without You" and "Looking Through Patient Eyes." In 1995, P.M. Dawn returned with *Jesus Wept*, which received strong reviews but weak sales. *Dearest Christian, I'm So Very Sorry for Bringing You Here. Love, Dad* followed in 1998; by this time, the group had virtually dropped out of sight as a commercial force, even though most corners continued to praise the artistic quality of their work. A greatest-hits compilation, *The Best of P.M. Dawn*, appeared in the summer of 2000. —*Stephen Thomas Erlewine*

★ **Of the Heart, of the Soul and of the Cross: The Utopian Experience** / Aug. 6, 1991 / Gee Street ✦✦✦✦✦
It may not have been embraced by the entire hip-hop community, but P.M. Dawn's ponderously titled debut *Of the Heart, of the Soul and of the Cross: The Utopian Experience* was a startling reimagination of the music's possibilities. In the post-De La Soul age, hip-hop seemed open to all sorts of eccentrics, but P.M. Dawn was still difficult for purists to accept: they were unabashed hippies whose sound and sensibility held very little street appeal, if any. *Of the Heart . . .* is soaked in new-age spirituality and philosophical introspection, and a song title like "To Serenade a Rainbow" is likely to raise eyebrows among more than just skeptical b-boys. It's true that there's some occasional sappiness and navel-gazing, but it's also true that the group's outlook is an indispensable part of its musical aesthetic, and that's where *Of the Heart . . .* pushes into the realm of transcendence. It still sounds revolutionary today, although you'd have to call it a Velvet revolution: it's soft and airy, with ethereal vocal harmonies layered over lush backing tracks and danceable beats. The shimmering ballads "Set Adrift on Memory Bliss" (built on an unlikely sample of Spandau Ballet's "True") and "Paper Doll" were the hits, but they aren't quite representative of the album as a whole. Some tracks, like "Comatose" and "A Watcher's Point of View (Don't 'Cha Think)," are surprisingly funky and driving, and there's also an even more explicit nod to the dancefloor in the Todd Terry hip-house collaboration, "Shake." The more reflective raps ("Reality Used to Be a Friend of Mine," "Even After I Die," "In the Presence of Mirrors") strike a fascinating balance between those sensibilities, and there's still little else like them. In the end, *Of the Heart . . .* is enormously daring in its own way, proving that pop, R&B, and hip-hop could come together for creative, not necessarily commercial, reasons. —*Steve Huey*

The Bliss Album . . . ? / Mar. 23, 1993 / Gee Street ✦✦✦✦✦
After the breakout pop success of their debut album, P.M. Dawn played up the lush, soothing urban-soul qualities of their sound on the follow-up, *The Bliss Album . . . ?* For all of hardcore rap's hysteria over the duo's gentle demeanor and pop influences, *Of the Heart, of the Soul and of the Cross*

had been a predominantly rap-oriented album. That changes on *The Bliss Album . . . ?*, which downplays Prince Be's rapping (only on about a third of the tracks) in favor of dreamy melodies throughout the songs, not just on the choruses. It's a logical move, since P.M. Dawn's most unique moments were often also their most reflective, and they had an obvious knack for crafting original hooks. *The Bliss Album . . . ?*'s approach also provides more opportunities for the ethereal, layered vocal overdubs that had become one of the duo's signatures. While the results don't quite reenvision hip-hop the way the debut did, they're still tremendously inventive, playing to P.M. Dawn's strengths. The musical landscapes are even more lushly arranged, and the pop numbers positively shimmer, thanks to the duo's increasing sense of craft. A couple of the more aggressive rap tracks break up the mood a little, as with "Plastic," a sly rebuttal of the charges leveled by the group's macho detractors. It seems unnecessary, though, since P.M. Dawn's cosmic mysticism and vastly different influences clearly aren't competing on the same turf. Luckily, *The Bliss Album . . . ?* refuses to acknowledge any artificially imposed purist boundaries, continuing to chart new sonic territory and expanding the possibilities in P.M. Dawn's music. —*Steve Huey*

Jesus Wept / Oct. 3, 1995 / Gee Street ◆◆◆◆
With their third album, *Jesus Wept*, P.M. Dawn doesn't necessarily make a great leap forward. Instead, they make some great refinements. Prince Be's lyrics are just as trippy and cryptic as ever, but they appear more focused, offering a poetic, spiritual worldview that is supported by the lovely, layered music. Using artists like Prince, Stevie Wonder, Marvin Gaye, and the Beatles as starting points, Prince Be creates a unique world assembled equally from soul, pop, hip-hop, and psychedelia. As individual pieces, the songs might not always make much sense, but taken as a whole, they create a singular world that is rich in lush melodies and sumptuous arrangements. Occasionally, P.M. Dawn's ambition gets the best of them and the results sound self-indulgent, not transcendent. However, those moments are few and far between on *Jesus Wept*, the group's best album. —*Stephen Thomas Erlewine*

Dearest Christian, I'm So Very Sorry for Bringing You Here. Love, Dad / Sep. 29, 1998 / Gee Street ◆◆◆
By the time of P.M. Dawn's fourth album, the formerly chart-topping act had become a cult favorite, exploring its own brand of psychedelic soul while hip-hop continued evolving relentlessly into other realms. But then again, so did P.M. Dawn—having almost thoroughly eschewed MC work for singing on *Jesus Wept*, Prince Be continued in that vein, invoking the heavens with his lovely voice right from the start while only occasionally returning to his earlier vocal approach. Musically, the duo's ear for a wide range of bands and styles serves it as well as before with the opening, "Music for Carnivores," touching on everything from gentle gospel singing and big-band samples to ambient cascades (the concluding "Untitled" is even more of a quietly wild collage, not to mention being one fine late-Beatles tribute). Occasional nods to the technology-heavy styles of late-'90s hip-hop and R&B turn up (check the beginning of "Misery in Utero"), but, generally speaking, *Dearest Christian* relies on calmer keyboard melodies and textures and exquisite backing vocal overdubs to make its point. The downside is that a fair amount of the album's songs often blend into each other, with stretches often sounding like variations on a similar melody or tune. However, that makes the subtle touches in each—the low-key shuffles and beats in "Yang: As Private I's," the listing of modern cultural complaints in "Hale-Bopp Regurgitations"—all the more fun. Perhaps the best songs, like "Music for Carnivores," strike a truly individual note, such as the vocal and acoustic guitar combination on the gorgeously sad "Screaming at Me" or the lovers rock reggae lope of "No Further Damage." *Dearest Christian* contains beauty, ambition, good songs, rich production, and more, enough to justify its existence when so many of the band's peers had run themselves into the ground. —*Ned Raggett*

The Video Collection / Oct. 27, 1998 / V2 ◆◆◆
Island released P.M. Dawn's *The Video Collection* a few years too late when this set hit the shelves in 1998. By that time, the band had sadly disappeared from the pop landscape. However, the collection does showcase some great videos. The collection, thus, serves as a remembrance of a band whose talent was significant and whose influence was truncated. Appropriately, it starts with its breakthrough hit, "Set Adrift on Memory Bliss," which is a very good psychedelic music video that you will not see on MTV anytime soon. "Paper Doll," also from its debut album, is a stunning visual accompaniment to a standout track. At 13 tracks, P.M. Dawn's *The Video Collection* clocks in at a

substantial 53-minute tour but is missing "Norwegian Wood," "Hale Bop Regurgitations," and "Gotta Be . . . Movin on Up," none of which are as essential as what is included. Nonetheless, this collection is a good way to rediscover P.M. Dawn. —*JT Griffith*

The Best of P.M. Dawn / Jun. 20, 2000 / V2 ◆◆◆◆◆
Compiled from P.M. Dawn's four albums and the *Senseless* soundtrack *The Best of P.M. Dawn* not only plays like an audio time capsule of slick, tuneful, '90s urban pop, it's a remarkably coherent listening experience. The New Jersey duo's sweet combination of classic silky soul, trip-hop, psychedelia, and pop was one of the most groundbreaking sounds of the decade and influenced countless bands tremendously. All the usual suspects are present and accounted for, beginning with the band's first number-one single "Set Adrift on Memory Bliss," an amazingly mature debut tune, and moves forward with two tracks from 1998's relatively obscure Dearest Christian, *I'm So Very Sorry for Bringing You Here, Love, Dad*. A remix of "A Watcher's Point of View" and the rare 7" versions of "Reality Used to Be a Friend of Mine" as well as "The Ways of the Wind" are also here. The latter track's single and album versions are included; though they're significantly different, it's a bit redundant. The edgy hip-hop of "A Watcher's . . .," "Reality . . .," and "Gotta' Be . . . Movin' on Up," a track from the *Senseless* soundtrack, break up P.M. Dawn's otherwise lush, glossy sound on this hour-long, 14-track disc. Any band that samples Deep Purple, George Michael, and Joni Mitchell has an astonishingly diverse set of influences, but what made P.M. Dawn special is how they incorporated them into music that was uniquely their own. Despite nonexistent liner notes and a few omissions, what is here flows smoothly, especially considering the songs were recorded from 1991 to 1999. Like most timeless music, *The Best of P.M. Dawn*'s songs remain fresh, innovative, and enduring. —*Hal Horowitz*

Poison Clan

f. Miami, FL
Group / Hardcore Rap, Southern Rap, Dirty Rap, Bass Music
One of the few successful rap groups from the South in the early '90s, Poison Clan played an important role in the development of the dirty South movement that would arise late in the decade. The group began as a 2 Live Crew-sponsored group on Luke Records and came to an end when the group's driving force, J.T. Money, went on to a more successful solo career after a business-related dispute with Luke. In retrospect, though Poison Clan struggled to gain notoriety outside of Miami in the '90s, the group's style of sleazy, club-orientated, bass-driven rap provided the template for the late-'90s dirty South movement.

Originally, Poison Clan was a duo featuring Debonaire and J.T. Money as featured on *2 Low Life Muthas* (1990). The two Miami rappers had impressed Luke enough for him to sign them to his then-fledging label, Luke Records, and have Mr. Mixx, 2 Live Crew's DJ, produce the album. *2 Low Life Muthas* became a modest sensation in the South with its blend of dirty rap, gangsta rap, and Miami bass. It was Poison Clan's second album, *Poisonous Mentality* (1992), and its big hit, "Shake Whatcha Mama Gave Ya," that expanded the group's reach outside of the South. Furthermore, *Poisonous Mentality* found J.T. Money taking over as Poison Clan's driving force—though Poison Clan paraded itself as a collective, it was actually more of a solo project. Successive albums—*Ruff Town Behavior* (1993) and *Strait Zooism* (1995)—had moderate success, but none had songs that were as popular with national audiences as "Shake Whatcha Mama Gave Ya." By this point in the mid-'90s, 2 Live Crew and, in particular, Luke, had fallen off the map, resulting in tensions between Luke and J.T. Money, allegedly over unpaid royalties—as the story so often goes. And it wasn't a surprise, then, when J.T. Money parted ways with Luke and embarked on a solo career that got off to a great start in 1999 with "Who Dat." That same year, Luke released *The Best of J.T. Money & Poison Clan*, which collected the best moments from Poison Clan's five-year run. —*Jason Birchmeier*

2 Low Life Muthas / 1990 / Effect/Luke ◆◆◆
Discovered by Luther Campbell, Poison Clan was initially molded similarly to 2 Live Crew, as evidenced by *2 Low Life Muthas*' production—executed by Campbell and 2 Live Crew producer Mr. Mixx—and its mostly lighthearted but occasionally raunchy themes of womanizing, partying, and goofing around. J.T. Money and Debonaire broke out with this album's booming, "Shaft"-sampling "Dance All Night." Not terribly dissimilar from 2 Live Crew

tracks like "Move Somethin'," it's one of the few clean songs Poison Clan released—it's easily their most accessible, and it's also one of the best dance-rap singles of the early '90s; some rotation of the video on *Yo! MTV Raps* helped give the group some notice, but the remainder of the album didn't do a great deal to build on its success. The duo proves to be competent on the mic, but they don't go much beyond that, and Mr. Mixx's production work rarely hits the level of his best work for 2 Live Crew. J.T. Money briefly hits on the gangsta themes that would saturate the remaining PC records; on "Bad Influence," he shows he's most comfortable with hard-edged rhymes. This decent debut comes off as 2 Live lite, an issue that would be rectified right after this. —*Andy Kellman*

- **Poisonous Mentality** / 1992 / Effect/Luke ✦✦✦✦
Poisonous Mentality goes to show that J.T. Money wasn't truly in his element on *2 Low Life Muthas*. The departure of his partner, Debonaire, to Home Team ("Pick It Up") brought about a radical shift (a look at the album's cover, depicting J.T. and his droogs escaping with a bag of loot, indicates this) from relatively lighthearted material to harder production and an endless flurry of expletives. Whether relating crude and often cruel sexual exploits or tales of criminal dirty work—often within the same song—it's plain to see that the album has much less to do with J.T.'s desire to keep up with the times, and all to do with him coming into his own. The only full-on nod to the party crowd is "Shake Whatcha Mama Gave Ya"—featuring one of Luther Campbell's delivered-while-on-the-can guest choruses—and it just happens to be one of the best of its kind. This is one of the toughest, meanest records to have come from the South, from one of the most sick-minded and hilarious MCs of the era. The fact that the album was an anomaly when compared to most of the others coming from Florida at the time has a lot to do with why it isn't widely recognized as such. —*Andy Kellman*

Ruff Town Behavior / 1993 / Luke ✦✦✦
Poison Clan's most popular singles—"Dance All Night," "Shake Whatcha Mama Gave Ya"—and their affiliations with Luther Campbell have often left them pegged as Miami bass, a notion that would've been blown apart if more attention had been paid to the albums and the vast majority of songs not featuring group call-and-response vocals. *Ruff Town Behavior*, J.T. Money and company's third album for Campbell's label, is no exception. Released a year after *Poisonous Mentality*, the album is little more than a continuation of its predecessor and isn't nearly as exciting. It's not that J.T. seems tired, but it's definitely apparent that he's spreading himself too thin by putting out too much material. Few tracks have the bite of *Poisonous Mentality*'s middling moments, and the fact that it's formatted almost exactly like that album (one or two full songs broken up by minute-long jokes and interludes, for over an hour) makes it all but impossible to be compared to it. Even "Put Shit Pass No Ho," the album's top highlight, jacks the beat from Ice Cube's "The Nigga Ya Love to Hate"; J.T.'s flow on the track even resembles Ice Cube's, showing the album's shortage of new ideas. This is a holding-pattern record, plain and simple. —*Andy Kellman*

Strait Zooism / Nov. 7, 1995 / Warlock ✦✦✦
After hitting the brick wall of *Ruff Town Behavior*, J.T. Money severed his ties with Luther Campbell, citing shady business practices and promotional neglect. So he took his anything-but-PC Poison Clan over to Warlock and released *Strait Zooism* in 1995. J.T. had yet to leave Miami completely behind (that would come a few years later), as he continued to work with producer Mike "Fresh" McCray. However, the production on this album is downright crisp sounding when compared to earlier Poison Clan albums, and on most of the tracks, J.T. delivers his lyrics in an uncharacteristically gruff, raspy manner (if anything, it could've been a record from the West Coast—right on down to the Funkadelic swipe in "Something About Them Bitches"). At times, he sounds as if he's more concerned with breaking from his past than anything else, but this really isn't a problem if you keep his previous records out of the context. J.T.'s new but temporary situation seems to have fostered an album with more life to it than its mediocre predecessor, but it still seems like just another Poison Clan record. Thankfully, J.T. would revitalize himself after heading to Atlanta and going solo in name. —*Andy Kellman*

- **The Best of J.T. Money & Poison Clan** / Jun. 29, 1999 / Luke ✦✦✦✦
The best tracks from Poison Clan as well as former frontman J.T. Money, this collection includes "Faking Like Gangsta's," "Shake Watcha Mama Gave Ya," "Dance All Night," "Check Out the Ave. Pt. 1 & 2," and "Action" (featuring Likkle Wicked). —*Keith Farley*

Polyrhythm Addicts

f. New York, NY

Group / East Coast Rap, Hip-Hop, Underground Rap

Put together by Nervous Records after a successful single featuring the participants, the Polyrhythm Addicts were a one-album group that united several talented New York City rappers for a collaborative project. It began when Mr. Complex put together his "Not Your Ordinary" single, which included producer DJ Spinna and MCs Shabaam Sahdeeq and Apani B Fly Emcee. They decided to release it as the Polyrhythm Addicts, and it became a big hit with the New York City underground rap scene. When Nervous saw the response, they asked for a full album from the foursome. Cut over the spring of 1999, the record was an inspired collaboration, with Spinna's old school beats mixing well with the individual approaches of the other participants. The group didn't intend on promoting the record, so when Nervous started booking them shows following its 1999 release, the Polyrhythm Addicts disbanded. —*Bradley Torreano*

- **Rhyme Related** / Jun. 8, 1999 / Nervous ✦✦✦✦
Once in a blue moon there is a group that seemingly emerges out of nowhere to raise the stakes. Polyrhythm Addicts (DJ Spinna, Shabaam Sahdeeq, Apani B, and Mr. Complex) do just that, delivering an LP old school purists can sink their teeth into. "Motion 2000" bottles up what is still right about underground NY hip-hop. Apani B, Mr.Complex, and Shabaam all treat us to a verbal massage, adding their own unique stamp to DJ Spinna's spacey and addictive drum loop. Old school aesthetics take center stage on the mellow "Take Me Home" f/ Pharoah Monch on the hook. Mr. Complex display's his versatility dropping off and on cadences over the jazzy "Not Your Ordinary." Similarly, "Big Phat Boom" is an odyssey into space, augmented by twinkling chimes and a dazzling verse from Apani B. The sonically constructed "Nervous Breakdown" is intricately arranged serving as theme music for the countdown to Armageddon. It's obvious DJ Spinna spent many nights burning the midnight oil digging thru dusty 12", as he provides production crafted with care, and nurtured with love. While not a household name on the mainstream circuit, his work has not gone unnoticed by underground fans. Each of Polyrhythm's MCs brings different styles, but nevertheless mesh them cohesively to fit a group environment. Shabaam is your quintessential NY battle rapper, full of confidence and skills. Mr. Complex switches personalities and flows mid-verse, and his witty repartees add another dimension to the group's diverse chemistry. Apani B is the X-factor, a polished female MC who hands out lyrical beatdowns. Her flavor speaks volumes, as her verses are devoid of sexual overtones, or the materialistic references many of her fellow female counterparts partake in. Polyrhythm Addicts catapult us back in time when creativity and innovation prevailed; even though this EP contains a sparse track listing (ten cuts), it hardly matters, because the tracks included are saturated with quality from top to bottom. —*Matt Conaway*

Poor Righteous Teachers

f. 1989

Group / Political Rap, Golden Age, Hip-Hop, Jazz-Rap

Part of the growing contingent of Islamic-oriented message rappers, Poor Righteous Teachers formed in Trenton, NJ, when teenage friends Culture Freedom and Wise Intelligent (songwriting credits are listed as S. Phillips and T. Grimes) decided to form a more positive rap group as an alternative to the gangsta style (which they vehemently defend). Joined by DJ and producer Father Shaheed, the group recorded two albums (1990's *Holy Intellect* and 1991's *Pure Poverty*) stressing their religious beliefs and philosophy; in spite of sometimes neglecting their music for their message, the albums sold respectably well. *Black Business* (1993) proved to be their most musically satisfying outing, drawing praise for Wise's ability to use the style and intonation of a reggae/dancehall toaster; however, it was also criticized for its liberal sprinkling of homophobia. *New World Order* followed in 1996. —*Steve Huey*

- **Holy Intellect** / 1990 / Profile ✦✦✦✦✦
Holy Intellect is a sharp session, squarely in an Afro-centric groove, featuring dozens of intelligent lyrics on tracks like "Time to Say Peace," "Holy Intellect," and "Word From the Wise." Poor Righeous Teachers also illustrated they were capable of moving a party as well with "Rock Dis Funky Joint." —*Ron Wynn*

Pure Poverty / 1991 / Profile ✦✦✦✦
Rappers who take a strong moral stance were beginning to proliferate when the second Poor Righteous Teachers album came out, but this young trio had been "teaching the righteous way" since the beginning, combining hard, funky beats with culture-conscious didacticism. With stage names like Wise Intelligent, Culture Freedom and Father Shaheed, the three may have come across as a bit pretentious, but they really were quite serious; their stated goal was to "teach the blind, deaf, and dumb who the real living God is." Okay, maybe a lot pretentious. And if it weren't for the spare, airtight beats and the dexterous samples, their lyrics of cultural awareness, self-sufficiency, and religious discipline would probably have fallen flat. But those beats are there and so is the flow—Wise Intelligent's lilting, reggae-influenced speed rap is especially fine, especially on the dancehall-inflected "Easy Star" and "I'm Comin' Again," an a cappella rap. There are occasional moments of self-contradiction, maybe even hypocrisy: though they solemnly preach respect for "the black woman," they apparently see nothing wrong with using her orgasmic moans and groans to spice up a track or two. But the album's still a winner overall. —*Rick Anderson*

Black Business / 1993 / Profile ✦✦✦✦
The Poor Righteous Teachers offered more Islamic and Afro-centric raps on this album, sometimes becoming overly pedantic, but also keeping the raps and rhymes flowing and the beats moving. Their material's propagandistic tone was offset to some extent by the use of reggae and funk influences, but few groups are more open about their religious and political affiliations and beliefs. —*Ron Wynn*

New World Order / Oct. 1, 1996 / Profile ✦✦✦✦

Porn Theatre Ushers

f. 1997
Group / East Coast Rap, Hip-Hop
Influenced by production denizens DJ Premier and Large Professor as well as funky offbeat lyricists such as Ultramagnetic MC's, De La Soul, and Organized Konfusion, the white duo Porn Theatre Ushers exploded out of the vibrant late-1990s Boston underground hip-hop scene passionate about the music but disappointed in its growing lack of humor. With that in mind, they set out to bring the fun back to rap music, marrying wittily irreverent and clever lyrics with idiosyncratic, frequently whimsical production.

Nabo Rawk and Mister Jason first met in 1997 when fellow Boston rapper Esoteric introduced the two. Both were already involved in the local scene, but as it so happened, Nabo was looking for a DJ and Mister Jason for someone to produce for. They immediately struck up a friendship, and soon thereafter a partnership. Their break came the following year when Nabo Rawk tied for first in the Biscuithead Battle, a freestyle event, and DJ Bruno offered to put out a 12″ single on his Biscuithead Recordings, a fledgling local label. Over the next couple years, the duo released singles like "Me & Him" and "My Imagination" to underground acclaim and created a small buzz in the rap community, while Mister Jason became an in-demand producer for other local MCs as well. The duo finally released their first definitive statement in 2000 with the nearly LP-length EP *Sloppy Seconds*, which included their earlier singles and collaborations with Cage and K-No Supreme as well as new recordings. —*Stanton Swihart*

● **Sloppy Seconds EP** / 2000 / Biscuithead ✦✦✦✦
Eminem may have been crowned the commercial Caucasian face of hip-hop by critics and commentators, but he was hardly the only (or necessarily even the best) white kid to excel in the form as the millennium was turning over. Underground heads like El-P from Company Flow, High & Mighty, Sage Francis, and Mister Jason and Nabo Rawk—who collectively make up the Boston duo Porn Theatre Ushers—were equal or greater forces of rap creativity, yet worked well beneath the radar of mainstream success. After generating significant waves in the underground hip-hop community with the outstanding "Me & Him/My Imagination/Catnip" single in the waning moments of the 1990s, Porn Theatre Ushers finally put together their first full-length statement with *Sloppy Seconds*. Not quite an official long player but more than an EP (the vinyl release was called a double-12″ EP), the album may not have been the wealth of extraordinary new material that fans had been hoping for ever since the single dropped, but since it does at least collect all the duo's material up to that point in one convenient place, it is a perfect introduction to their wonderful mayhem. Almost half of the material had already shown up elsewhere in official or unofficial form, but that does

nothing to obscure the luster of the album. The album partly hearkens back, much like the work of contemporaries Jurassic 5, to an era when kids used to trade playful verses on street corners or in clubs for fun and a sense of one-upmanship, less competitive than communal, more artistic than economic. Nabo Rawk drops a series of connected non sequiturs that range effortlessly from sarcastic to humorous and self-deprecating sentiments, and he carries the story more with attitude than through any sort of coherent narrative. His style variously recalls Nas, MC Serch, and De La Soul, but the overall tone is Nice & Smooth, tough when need be but more often jocular. Even when he does talk smack or go roughneck, he seems to do so with the slyest of grins. Mister Jason's production is expert throughout, keeping one foot in hardcore urban reality with edgy, syncopated beats and one in the world of whimsy, with samples that are sometimes ridiculously goofy and fun, sometimes deeply tongue in cheek, and occasionally spacy or mystical, like the sitar intro that opens "Catnip" and the '50s sci-fi siren that runs throughout the rest of the song. The highlight of the album is the incredibly swinging "Me & Him," but virtually every track is supreme, with "Balloon Knots" featuring Cage, the hilarious joke posing of "Girls Sweat Me," and the steely "Bug Men" featuring K-No Supreme being the standout moments. All in all, this is a bracing debut that deserves more attention. —*Stanton Swihart*

Positive Black Soul

f. 1989, Senegal
Group / Foreign Rap, Hip-Hop, Golden Age
One of the first rap and hip-hop groups in Senegal, Positive Black Soul represents a collaboration between Didier Sourou Awadi, formerly with Didier Awadi's Syndicate, and Doug E. Tee (born: Amadou Barry), formerly with the King MCs. Accompanied by the rhythmic onslaught of traditional Senegealese instruments—including percussion, kora, and balafon—the two inspire each other with heavily political rhyming and DJ-like toasting, mostly in the Wolof language. Forsaking traditional outfits and folklore, the group takes an ultramodern approach to their performances.

The year 1992 proved to be a pivotal one for Positive Black Soul. After stirring excitement with their performance at the Dakar French Cultural Center's music festival, Dakar 92: Mbalax, Jazz, and Rap, the group was invited to be the opening act for the Dakar debut of French rap star MC Solaar in October. Solaar was so impressed by the group's performance that he asked them to continue opening shows for him in France. Positive Black Soul released a self-produced cassette album in 1993, with the project underwritten by the French Cultural Center in Dakar. The following year, the group toured England, Switzerland, and France.

Returning to Senegal, the members of Positive Black Soul were invited to improvise with a traditional chorus on one tune, "Swing Yela," on Baaba Maal's album, *Firin' in Fouta*. They recorded their debut album, *Salaam*, shortly afterward with several tracks produced by Boom Bass of La Funk Mob and the remaining tracks produced by Raw Stylus. During 1997 they performed 130 shows in Europe and North America. —*Craig Harris*

Salaam / 1996 / Mango ✦✦✦

Positive K

b. Bronx, NY
East Coast Rap
Positive K scored a major rap hit with 1992's "I Got a Man." Leading up to that, the Bronx-born rapper cut a few underground compilation appearances, including one—"I'm Not Havin' It," a duet with MC Lyte—that upped his profile significantly. A guest spot on Grand Puba's debut album, along with a self-released, Big Daddy Kane-produced single ("Nightshift"), set the stage for *The Skills Dat Pay da Bills*. His full-length debut, released on Island subsidiary 4th & Broadway, balanced Nation of Islam themes with gangsta-isms and more pop-based moments. Meanwhile, he kept his Creative Control label in operation, signing and cultivating new talent. —*Andy Kellman*

● **The Skills Dat Pay Da Bills** / Nov. 3, 1992 / 4th & Broadway ✦✦✦✦
A duet with MC Lyte on "I'm Not Havin' It" and some underground compilation appearances led to Positive K's 1992 debut for 4th & Broadway, and it features another song where Positive K has female troubles. "I Got a Man" hit the top of the rap singles chart in 1993 and even reached number 14 on the pop chart, giving him the most success he'd ever enjoy. The remainder of the album has more of a hard edge to it, with the Big Daddy Kane-produced

"Nightshift" and the downright raw "Carhoppers" and "One 2 the Head" adding dimensions to the album. There's much more to this album than a fluke hit. —*Andy Kellman*

Pras (Prakazrel Michel)

Vocals, Drum Programming, Engineer, Mixing, Producer / Hip-Hop, Alternative Rap, East Coast Rap, Pop-Rap

A member of the seminal '90s rap trio the Fugees, Pras' solo career hasn't risen to the same heights as those of his colleagues Wyclef Jean and Lauryn Hill, in part because he's concentrated more on acting than music. Of Haitian descent (like his cousin Wyclef), Pras was born Prakazrel Michel in New Jersey. Along with his high school classmate Lauryn Hill, he cofounded the rap group Tranzlator Crew in 1987; cousin Wyclef, who'd been hanging out with Pras quite a bit since moving to the United States, joined a short time later. Eventually, the trio renamed themselves the Fugees, after an expression for Haitian refugees, and signed with Ruffhouse Records in 1993. Their 1994 debut, *Blunted on Reality*, was aimed at the hardcore crowd, which didn't really fit the group's own sensibilities, but with their all-inclusive groundbreaking sophomore effort *The Score*, the Fugees created one of the biggest-selling rap albums of all time, adored by critics and record buyers alike.

Pras was the last of the Fugees to release a solo album, although he did cut his first solo track in 1997, covering Eddy Grant's '80s smash "Electric Avenue" for the soundtrack of the Chris Tucker flick *Money Talks*. In 1998, Pras contributed "Ghetto Supastar (That Is What You Are)" to the soundtrack of Warren Beatty's *Bulworth*. With appearances from Ol' Dirty Bastard and Mya, "Ghetto Supastar" became a substantial hit, climbing to number three pop and number one R&B. Pras immediately rushed to put together his first solo album, solving the problem of coordinating guest appearances by inviting celebrities to leave him answering-machine messages. *Ghetto Supastar* the album didn't fare nearly as well as the single, spending only two weeks in the Top 100 upon its release in late 1998. Undaunted, Pras turned some of the narratives from *Ghetto Supastar* songs into a novel—also naturally titled *Ghetto Supastar*—in early 1999. He also struck a deal with Madonna's new film production company to turn *Ghetto Supastar* into a movie, starring himself.

First, though, Pras made his feature film debut in the 1999 Ben Stiller superhero comedy *Mystery Men*, playing a supporting villain. He then set to work on *Ghetto Supastar* the movie, whose title was eventually changed to *Turn It Up* (perhaps for variety's sake). *Turn It Up* hit theaters in the summer of 2000 (two years after Pras' initial hit single), and it too performed disappointingly. Still, Pras was slated to appear in the films *Higher Ed* and *Full Contact*, and began work on a new album in late 2000, which to date has not been released. —*Steve Huey*

● **Ghetto Supastar** / Oct. 6, 1998 / Columbia ✦✦✦

Pras' single, "Ghetto Supastar," was omnipresent in 1998 on radio, on MTV and blasting from car stereos, and with good reason; it's an absolutely irresistible combination of funky bass and drums, excellent rapping from Pras and ODB and angelic singing by Mya. He apparently was under a lot of pressure to produce the full-length follow-up, and the result is a scattershot, throw-in-the-kitchen-sink approach. You get the single, 11 more songs, versions of "Hallelujah" and "Amazing Grace," and a whole bunch of Pras' answering-machine messages (four tracks totaling 12 minutes—a bit much). That said, *Ghetto Supastar* isn't half-bad. Aside from the title track, highlights include "Can't Stop the Shining," featuring reverb-heavy guitar from Lenny Kravitz, the tense, minimalist "For the Love of This" and the trippy "Murder Dem," with its stuttering rhythm and strange sound effects floating through the mix. Pras' cause is furthered throughout by crisp, clear production with an emphasis on the low end. With a little editing, *Ghetto Supastar* could've been a killer; as is, it's an entertaining slice of R&B-oriented hip-hop. Some versions of *Ghetto Supastar* include a four-track bonus disc credited to the "Refugee Camp Navy SEALS"; this is pretty forgettable stuff and not worth going out of your way to find. —*Bill Cassel*

Prime Minister Pete Nice & Daddy Rich

f. 1992

Group / Hip-Hop, Alternative Rap, East Coast Rap, Pop-Rap

The original lineup for the rap ensemble 3rd Bass featured rappers Pete Nice (born Pete Nash), MC Serch, and DJ Richie Rich (born Richard Lawson), the group's lone African American. When Serch split in 1992, Nice and Rich tried

it as a duo. Their 1993 debut *Dust to Dust* failed to equal the success of 3rd Bass. —*Ron Wynn*

● **Dust to Dust** / Apr. 27, 1993 / Def Jam ✦✦✦

The breakup of 3rd Bass proved ill-fated for perhaps the more talented member, Pete Nice, and the group's DJ/producer Daddy Rich. While MC Serch made a little noise with his solo effort, *Return of the Product*, and went on to become a record label executive, Pete Nice's solo record flopped unceremoniously. Sounding somewhat confused and less confident without the aid of his more charismatic former partner, Pete Nice's erudite degenerate persona got lost in the cloudy mess of production on *Dust to Dust*. Despite some inventive samples from the likes of the Velvet Underground, Iron Butterfly, and Albert King and offbeat humor reminiscent of *Derelicts of Dialect*, the album is without a sonic pulse. Even most of the illbeat craftsmen the Beatnuts' tracks are imperfect and muddled. The only marginal hit, "Kick the Bobo," featured some memorable rhymes, including "Never steer you wrong/Beats fatter than the fat kid from P.M Dawn," but vanished from the rap charts soon after its release. The Beatnuts-produced "Outta My Way Baby" is also worthy of note. —*Michael Di Bella*

Prime Suspects

Group / Dirty South, Southern Rap, Gangsta Rap

During the late-'90s golden era of No Limit Records, Prime Suspects released only one album of their own, *Guilty Til Proven Innocent* (1998), yet contributed heavily to those of their colleagues: Master P's *Ghetto D* (1997), C-Murder's *Life or Death* (1998), and Soulja Slim's *Give It 2 'Em Raw* (1998), among others. Furthermore, the trio (comprised of E, Skinew, and Gangsta T) appeared on some of No Limit's various-artist collections, namely, the *I'm Bout It* (1997) and *I Got the Hook Up* (1998) soundtracks and the *Mean Green: Major Players* compilation (1998). —*Jason Birchmeier*

● **Guilty Til Proven Innocent** / Oct. 6, 1998 / No Limit ✦✦✦✦

Master P stocked his No Limit Records with a stable of artists who, collectively, read like rap's answer to Stan Lee's superheroes. You've got the gangsta, the gun moll, the playboy, the tight-knit group of homies, and various permutations of those stereotypes (e.g., the tight-knit group of playboys). If it all seems contrived to move product, it also all comes down to the quality of the product, which is diamond solid on *Guilty Til Proven Innocent*. Twenty tracks total, this is really two Prime Suspects albums for the price of one: an all-star set of ten songs showcasing their No Limit labelmates (Snoop Dogg, Mystikal, Silkk the Shocker, etc.) and ten songs on their own. With so many guest rappers dropping by, and five different producers for the sessions (Master P is credited as executive producer), *Guilty Til Proven Innocent* is a wild and varied ride. Although it wouldn't be fair to call any one song a highlight (the disc is too high too often), standout moments include Silkk the Shocker spitting bullets on "Money Makes…," Fiend and Snoop Dogg pushing the voodoo vibe of "My Old Lady" into ecstasy, Prime Suspect's own superhero theme song on "Ride Wit My Heat," and the horror-show setting of "Last Days." In between are rhymes that pay off in stuttered rhythms like the soundtrack to a bad dream, grooves that go down as smooth as kahlua and creme (especially those from DJ KLC), and some poignant moments that resonate with hard-earned life experience ("Of All Da Hustlers"). And yet, in such auspicious company, Prime Suspects fail to carve out the unique vocal niche that make a Snoop Dogg or Mystikal special. The trio of E, Skinew, and Gangsta T stand tall when their turn comes to deliver good rhymes, but only by standing on the shoulders of the No Limit label do they deliver gangsta rap this righteous. —*Dave Connolly*

Prince Markie Dee (Mark Morales)

East Coast Rap, Pop-Rap, Urban

Mark Morales, best known as Prince Markie Dee and one-third of the Fat Boys, went solo during the '90s with a pair of albums. 1992's *Free*, billed to Prince Markie Dee & the Soul Convention, combined R&B with rap and was serious as often as it was humorous; though not a solid album by any stretch, the single "Typical Reasons (Swing My Way)" topped *Billboard*'s rap chart, and "Trippin' Out" peaked at number ten. The follow-up to the debut, *Love Daddy*, didn't come until 1995. The gap between releases proved to be detrimental, since the album stalled at number 91 on the R&B/hip-hop albums chart. During this period, Morales was also honing his skills as a producer; throughout the '90s and into the early 2000s, he racked up an impressive number of credits, working with the likes of Mary J. Blige, Craig Mack, Shabba Ranks, Mariah Carey, Destiny's Child, and Lisa Stansfield. —*Andy Kellman*

Free / Aug. 11, 1992 / Columbia ♦♦

Onetime Fat Boys member Prince Markie Dee and the Soul Convention tried to mix vintage soul with hip-hop production, novelty raps, and some quasi-romantic material. The results were an uneven and unsuccessful effort that didn't remind anyone of either the Fat Boys or anything that was very interesting. —*Ron Wynn*

Prince Paul (Paul Huston)

b. Apr. 2, 1967

Producer / Hip-Hop, Alternative Rap, Underground Rap

Beginning his career as a DJ for Stetsasonic, rapper and producer Prince Paul has lent his skills to albums by Boogie Down Productions, Gravediggaz, MC Lyte, Big Daddy Kane, and 3rd Bass, among others. Paul's big break came when he produced De La Soul's *3 Feet High and Rising* album. Shattering the acknowledged rules of hip-hop production, he sampled not only funk, but all types of music to create fresh and original backing tracks. By throwing in comedy sketches as well, Prince Paul and De La Soul completely ushered in a new era for hip-hop. In 1994, Paul returned to rapping, joining RZA and Stetsasonic member Frukwan in Gravediggaz, a side project that debuted with *6 Feet Deep*. He also began working with the new elite in underground rap, recruiting the Automator, New Kingdom's Scott Harding, and Spectre for his debut solo album, 1997's *Psychoanalysis: What Is It? A Prince Among Thieves* followed in 1999, and later that year Paul formed Handsome Boy Modeling School with the Automator to release the album *So...How's Your Girl?* —*Steve Kurutz*

Psychoanalysis: What Is It? / Oct. 21, 1997 / Tommy Boy ♦♦♦

From George Clinton and De La Soul to Ornette Coleman and Frank Zappa, a lot of great artists haven't hesitated to be self-indulgent. It's a question of *how* self-indulgent an artist chooses to be, and on *Psychoanalysis: What Is It?* Prince Paul is much too self-indulgent for his own good. Known for his membership in the group Stetsasonic and for producing De La Soul, Queen Latifah, and others, Paul has an impressive resumé. But this unfocused, incoherent CD wasn't his finest hour. Though it contains a few worthwhile rap tunes (including "Psycho Linguistics" and "J.O.B.—Das What Dey Is"), *Psychoanalysis* isn't a rap album so much as a collection of soundbites, samples, and dialogue played over tracks. Overall, the album is pointless and serves no purpose other than Paul's desire to amuse and entertain himself. He may have gotten a few laughs out of it, but listeners will be left out in the cold and find themselves asking if there is a point to all this. —*Alex Henderson*

● **A Prince Among Thieves** / Feb. 23, 1999 / Tommy Boy ♦♦♦♦♦

The concept album has been something of a rare beast in hip-hop. There have been plenty of rap albums with a cinematic feel, but very few actually tie things together with a coherent narrative throughout. Leave it to Prince Paul, long one of hip-hop's most imaginative producers, to assemble the first successful rap opera in *A Prince Among Thieves*. Not only does it maintain a coherent storyline via skits that actually *aren't* filler, it manages to stay musically compelling and focused throughout. And that's no mean feat, considering the array of guest stars and the huge range of styles Prince Paul employs for the characters' supporting tracks. Perhaps the most daring aspect of the record is that it frames the story as fiction, with no pretense of the realism (or illusion thereof) that hardcore prides itself on. The story concerns a young rapper named Tariq (played by the Juggaknots' Breeze), who needs $1,000 to complete a demo tape for a pending record deal. For quick cash, he turns to his friend True (Sha), once his mentor in the rap game but now a drug dealer who secretly resents Tariq's good fortune. As True immerses Tariq in the underworld, a tragedy of cinematic proportions unfolds. The star-studded cast features Kool Keith as a weapons dealer, Big Daddy Kane as a pimp, Chubb Rock as a gang kingpin, Chris Rock and De La Soul as crack addicts, Everlast as a crooked cop, and Sadat X and Xzibit as prison inmates. Yet the much lesser known Sha and Breeze shine even in this select company, which is part of the reason the album works. The main reason, however, is that Prince Paul sounds like he can do anything, and do it well. *A Prince Among Thieves* touches on every sound he's ever tried on record, and it's conceptually airtight; in both senses, it's his magnum opus, and the crown jewel of a brilliant career. —*Steve Huey*

Princess Superstar (Concetta Kirshner)

Hip-Hop, Underground Rap

With her long blond hair, wrap-around shades, and style tips taken straight from Debbie Harry, Concetta Kirshner would seem the least likely person to make her name in the world of alternative hip-hop, where authenticity—especially in Kirshner's native New York City—means nearly as much as the music. Nevertheless, in 1994, with dreams of giving the music world something innovative, Kirshner named herself Princess Superstar and made her first demo, armed only with a four-track and two tape decks. The demo was called *Mitch Better Get My Bunny*, a play on words from a popular urban catch phrase (and a rap song by AMG) at the time. The response to demo was immediate and gained her a write-up in *CMJ* magazine's "Futures" section that described Princess Superstar's eclectic mixture of hip-hop, punk rock, and outrageous humor. She signed with 5th Beetle Records and recruited a backup band consisting of Kirsten "Pro" Jansen on drums, Doug Pressman on bass, and Art "F" Lavis on guitar. 5th Beetle released *Strictly Platinum* in 1996. *CMJ* called the music "super sly hip-hop with jaw droppingly clever lyrics and inventive sampling"; *A.P.* went even further with its praise: "If you yearn for the days when a rap record was both exciting and innovative, as well as fun, *Strictly Platinum* has got your name scrawled across it...in neon peach lipstick." The rest of the press response was similarly overwhelming.

Following the buzz, Kirshner moved from her Clinton Street place to Avenue A, where she was christened "The Queen of Avenue A" by *CMJ*. *Strictly Platinum* gained momentum, even shooting to the number-one spot on some college radio stations in New York and Los Angeles, while also gaining airplay throughout the U.S. and Canada. The band played live shows all over the East Coast and Canada. *Strictly Platinum*'s "Theme Song" and "Flavis Special" were even used on NBC's *NBA Roundup* and MTV's *Slam and Jam*. Kirshner took steps toward musical autonomy by the end of 1996 by founding her own record label, the tongue-in-cheek-named A Big Rich Major Label, and vowing never to sign with a "real" major label again. She also assembled a new band: Ski Love Ski on bass, Mike Linn on drums, and DJ Science Center spinning records live. The group recorded the second Princess Superstar album, *CEO*, which was released in 1997. The album again garnered national acclaim.

Following the album's release, Princess Superstar booked the Hostile Takeover Tour '98, a six-week tour through the U.S. and Canada, which included playing to a packed house at the South by Southwest music conference. Playing the Transmusicales de Rennes festival in France with Nashville Pussy followed in December of 1999, as did a mini-jaunt in London. Kirshner also spent the beginning of 1999 working on her third Princess Superstar album, *Last of the Great 20th Century Composers*, having again assembled a new backing band (Money Mike Linn on drums, DJ Cutless Supreme manning the turntables and playing guitar, and Walter Sipser holding down bass duties). Kirshner also chose to rename A Big Rich Major Label, opting instead for The Corrupt Conglomerate for the release of the third album. By the new millennium, Kirshner hooked up with Curtis Curtis for a fourth album. *Princess Superstar Is*, which was issued in early 2002, featured collaborations with Kool Keith, the X-Ecutioners' Mista Sinista, Beth Orton, and others. —*Stanton Swihart*

● **CEO** / Nov. 25, 1997 / Big Rich Major ♦♦♦♦

Is it possible for an album to be too get-down funky? That's a rhetorical question, of course, because *CEO* is about as funky as it gets, and it is a nearly perfect album. Greasy, glittery, electric funky, and great, the modus operandi here is hip-hop. The vehicle is Princess Superstar, the alias of the irrepressible Concetta Kirshner. On *CEO* she is joined by new bandmates Ski Love Ski (bass), Mike Linn (drums) and DJ Science Center, and if you think the names are supersonic, you should hear their chops. The record—the first release on Kirshner's own slyly christened A Big Rich Major Label—is actually a concept album parodying and skewering the starchy, disingenuous world of big business (Kirshner has vowed never to sign with a "real" major label). The clever, referential lyrics—full of pop-cultural references and inspired wordplay—must, by law, be compared to those of the Beastie Boys (Princess Superstar would, in fact, be unthinkable without them). The brilliant musical gumbo of the album is equally ambitious, pulling wildly inventive samples out of left field like the Dust Brothers and Prince Paul, ensuring that Princess Superstar sounds like no one else before them. Some of the music is reminiscent of early Luscious Jackson, though the Luscious ladies only wish they were this funky. Casio noodling, blaxploitation riffs, and fat-bottom bass run head-on into each other, making for a wide-ranging and distinctive mix. "The Little Freakazoid that Could" is robotic funk over jazzy drumming, while the ubiquitous "yeahs" that open "I Got to Get Aloan with You" sound like they come out of a *School House Rock* commercial. There is also a distinctive punk rock/early New York new wave (think Blondie) vibe to *CEO*, especially on songs such as "Get My Sh'Off" and the title track. Everything is gloriously sifted through a hip-hop filter and a sound framework that verges on musical blasphemy. Who else would think of sampling Taco's "Puttin' on the Ritz" or Tommy Roe's "Dizzy" at all, let alone on the same record? *CEO* is simply phenomenal. Why Princess Superstar is not famous is beyond comprehension. —*Stanton Swihart*

● **Last of the Great 20th Century Composers** / Apr. 25, 2000 / Corrupt ✦✦✦✦✦

Last of the Great 20th Century Composers comes with a fascinating backstory. In the "Porn Wars of 2113," New York City is destroyed. Centuries later archaeologists discover beneath the rubble and ruin a mysterious cylindrical artifact containing recordings from an artist known only as Princess Superstar. The archaeologists carbon date the recordings to the end of the 20th millennium, and thus the artist thenceforth mythically comes to be considered "the last of the great twentieth century composers." As such a wildly creative premise suggests, Princess Superstar literally sweats urban creativity, and never more so than on her third full-length. As on her previous efforts, the album knows no bounds and uncoils in every conceivable direction, down every dark alley and into every nightscape the city has to offer. The brilliant syncopated electro-rock of "Do It Like a Robot" is the best kind of mechanical rump shaking. Jon Spencer later turns the same song into deconstructed avant-rock sludge-boogie via a remix, and it almost sounds like a different song, but it also gives one clue as to the limitless range and skill of Concetta Kirshner. The Beastie Boys-like hardcore punk workout "Sex (I Like)" takes that skill to one extreme, and "I Hope I Sell a Lot of Records at Christmastime"—the best hip-hop holiday cut since Run-D.M.C.'s "Christmas in Hollis" and maybe the most relevant spin on modern Christmas season sensibilities yet—pushes it to the other. Besides being sharp eyed and tart tongued, Kirshner is terribly intelligent, twisting every conceivable sonic touchstone, personal insight, play on words, double entendre, and pop cultural reference into brilliantly fun concept-hop-urban music of the most progressive type. "Meet You Halfway (Keep It on the Alright)" is aeronautically funky abstract hip-hop that is a good three or four steps ahead of everyone else in the underground hip-hop community, with the exception of visionaries such as Prince Paul and Kool Keith (who both, tellingly, contribute to the album, the latter on "Kool Keith's Ass"). And yet it is also completely grounded in the call-and-response quality of old school crews. Kirshner's offbeat flow on songs such as the hyper party-funk house of "NYC Cunt" and the grimy, low-down groove of "Year Two Thousand" is light years more interesting than conventional beat rocking. A healthy portion of the album is crass and occasionally tasteless (the porn-hop of "Come up to My Room," featuring Baron Ricks, for instance), but that is half of the fun, and Kirshner is such a clever and inventive lyricist that the stream of potty-mouthed diatribes that emanate from her imagination are easy to swallow and even easier to love. *Last of the Great 20th Century Composers* is, in a few simple words, pure warped genius. —*Stanton Swihart*

Princess Superstar Is / Jan. 29, 2002 / Rapster ✦✦✦✦

A hip-hop album of pure, silly fun with zero pretensions, Princess Superstar's *Is*, her fourth record, should have a wide appeal, as it is mostly about sex, and though there are a zillion hip-hop albums about sex (especially from women rappers), few are this clever. One of the few white gal rappers out there (try to come up with another one off the top of your head), Princess Superstar is an oddity on the rap scene not unlike Jewish hip-hopper MC Paul Barman, on whose album she appeared. (Both caught Prince Paul's attention who has produced their songs.) Unlike other gal rappers Lil' Kim and Foxy Brown, Princess Superstar doesn't have a voice made for rap. Her vocals are higher and her flow less smooth, but what she does have, which, say Foxy Brown doesn't, is skillfully written rhymes that aren't about building on rap stereotypes. For instance, Foxy for all her sass has never come up with a song as zany and unique as "Bad Babysitter," where Princess Superstar raps about inviting her boyfriend over and humping him on the couch while babysitting and getting paid six bucks an hour. Also, there's the ultra-silly "Keith 'N Me"

featuring Kool Keith, with the ridiculous repeated chorus, "Baby, you can feel my love/I've got my shorts on/And I'm takin' 'em off." Mostly, though, the album is Princess Superstar rapping about how horny she is in various witty scenarios. Funny throughout, *Is* should mark her arrival. —*Adam Bregman*

Prodigy

East Coast Rap, Hardcore Rap

Acknowledged as the more skilled member of the duo Mobb Deep on the mic, Prodigy spent years making a name for himself alongside partner Havoc on acclaimed albums such as *Hell on Earth* (1996) and *Murda Muzik* (1999) before releasing his first solo album, *H.N.I.C.*, on Loud Records in late 2000. With this album, Prodigy teamed up with a roster of outside producers such as the Alchemist and Rockwilder, trying to prove his own without Havoc's production to carry him. And even though Havoc did appear on two tracks, Prodigy undoubtedly proved himself to be a visionary solo artist, even going as far as to produce a couple songs himself. Though the album didn't elevate him to the superstar status of Jay-Z or DMX, Prodigy did win the hearts of both critics and fans alike as he had with his work in Mobb Deep, dropping harsh reality-based rhymes about the darker side of urban life with an unbalanced and sedate flow.

Mobb Deep members Prodigy and Havoc originally met while both attending the prestigious Graphic Arts High School in Manhattan as teenagers, thanks to their mutual residence in Queens along with their mutual passion for hip-hop. Still in their late teens, the duo released their debut album in 1993, *Juvenile Hell*, on the 4th & Broadway label. Though the album wasn't that successful from either a financial or critical standpoint, it did serve as a fitting platform for the duo to launch their careers; not only did the duo produce their own beats, but they also crafted their own style: a street-smart poetic approach centering on the ghetto lifestyle surrounding them. Their brutally honest reality rapping and complimentary melancholy beats landed them a deal with the up-and-coming Loud label in 1995, resulting in their first major-label release, *The Infamous*.

Propelled to awareness partially by fellow Queens rapper Nas, who took a similar approach lyrically on his championed *Illmatic* album from 1994, as well as with the aid of a successful single, "Shook Ones," Mobb Deep suddenly found themselves developing a quickly growing cult following. A year later in 1996, Prodigy and Havoc released *Hell on Earth*; debuting at number six on *Soundscan*, the album found them fully realizing their approach, dropping both evocative beats and cinematic rhymes that communicated the dark side of New York's urban landscape. And thanks to a grim video for "Hell on Earth (Front Lines)" and theatrical *Scarface*-like photos inside the CD booklet picturing the duo with guns and a mound of cocaine, Mobb Deep had created an elaborate image for themselves that took hardcore gangsta rap to a new level that the East Coast had yet fostered. It was then no surprise that their succeeding release, *Murda Muzik*, was heavily bootlegged while it was still in its demo stage, leaking rough versions of the nearly 30 songs the duo had recorded onto the streets and over the Internet.

Months after the bootlegs first leaked and after several pushed-back street dates, *Murda Muzik* finally dropped, debuting at number three on *Soundscan* and quickly going platinum on the strength of "Quiet Storm," a song that epitomized the signature Mobb Deep style. Not surprisingly, the album was welcomed by critics, who again applauded the group's lucid cinematics, driven primarily by Havoc's inimitable production. In late 2000, Prodigy finally released his long-rumored solo album, *H.N.I.C.*, which saw the more lyrically gifted member of the group collaborating with outside producers such as the Alchemist and Rockwilder on tracks that didn't depart far from the trademark sullen Mobb Deep style. —*Jason Birchmeier*

● **H.N.I.C.** / Nov. 14, 2000 / Loud ✦✦✦

The vitriolic Queensbridge MC, one-half of the enduring kings of reality core Mobb Deep released his first solo album in late 2000. P's grave lyrics chronicle an insular, nightmarish urban world, but the MC paints such precise, chilling pictures that he opens up this world of horror to all listeners. This is a corrosive album with a cinematic bent, a veritable *Shining* on wax. Some of the production is a bit slack considering that the tracks P dusts tend to be classics. Prodigy's Mobb Deep partner Havoc usually supplies these classic haunting beats, but he is mostly absent here. Regardless, the album creeps up on you, like a movie you get into despite the fact it makes your flesh crawl. The lyrics are venomous, a product of P's dark and armored intellect. On tracks like the piano-heavy "Keep It Thoro," "Trials of Love," and the dirge-like "Veterans' Memorial," the production perfectly complements P's deadpan style. The most outstanding cut may be "Never Feel My Pain," where P gives heartfelt voice to being afflicted with sickle-cell anemia. Although nihilistic, overall this is a poignant and visceral album detracted only slightly by its unpolished feel musically. —*M.F. Di Bella*

Professor Griff (Richard Griffin)

Vocals, Producer / Political Rap

Professor Griff (born Richard Griffin) was the minister of information for Public Enemy until June of 1989. He gave a controversial interview to *The Washington Post* that included comments deemed anti-Semitic by many. In the ensuing furor, Chuck D eventually fired him from Public Enemy and even briefly disbanded the group, only to reform them. Griff formed his own band, the Asiatic Disciples. The results were mixed, the slant predictably Islamic and Afro-centric on efforts like 1998's *Blood of the Profit.* —*Ron Wynn*

Pawns in the Game / 1990 / Luke ✦✦✦

Kao's II Wiz-7-Dome / Jul. 23, 1991 / Luke ✦✦✦

Professor Griff tried again with this 1991 release on Luther Campbell's Luke label. But like his previous effort, Griff failed to realize that advocacy alone, regardless of the justness of his message, couldn't overcome pedestrian production, unconvincing rhymes and a stiff, leaden rap style. Rather than threatening, the net effect was boring. —*Ron Wynn*

Blood of the Profit / Aug. 18, 1998 / Blackheart ✦✦✦

And the Word Became Flesh / Sep. 11, 2001 / Right Stuff ✦✦

Former Public Enemy controversy starter Professor Griff decided that rap music was wholly bereft of misguided political conjecture, something that he amply provides with this September 2001 recording. Many will remember Griff as Public Enemy's troubled minister of information who supposedly made various anti-Semitic remarks in an interview with *The Washington Post* in 1989, remarks that eventually led to his expulsion from the group. While Griff's left-wing black nationalism and conspiracy theories hearken back to the heyday of Public Enemy and X Clan, and Griff manages to raise some interesting sociopolitical quandaries, it is tough to distinguish whether his political poetry comes as result of careful research or a combination of propaganda and angry pedantry. Also, Griff's musings are not tied together by a lucid overarching philosophy, and his mixture of gangsta rap posturing and potty-mouth spoken word come off sounding like a cross between a second-rate Eazy-E and a Gil Scott-Heron rip-off. Some legitimacy is lent to the album by an appearance from Last Poet Umar Bin Hassan on "European on Me," and even some genuine attempts at revolutionary rap (virtually unheard) are commendable. However, the erratic philosophies presented amount to "The Hate That Hate Made" and no thoughtful solutions are offered. Griff's railing against the establishment would be better served by less-chaotic production and sloppily constructed poems. Chuck D also appears on the album. —*M.F. Di Bella*

Professor X

Vocals, Producer / Hip-Hop, Hardcore Rap

After leaving the militant X-Clan, Professor X made a series of equally strong political records in the early '90s. —*Stephen Thomas Erlewine*

● **Years of the 9, On the Blackhand Side** / 1991 / 4th & Broadway ✦✦✦✦✦

A New York-based hip-hopper who preached a black nationalist philosophy, Professor X was the founder of the black Muslim organization known as the Blackwatch Committee and the leader of the group X-Clan. X's debut solo album, *Years of the 9, On the Blackhand Side*, contrasted sharply with the type of graphic, profane gangster rap that had become incredibly popular. You won't find any gratuitous violence or sexually exploitive material on tunes like "Vanglorious Crib," "The Sleeper Has Awakened," and "Reality," which encourage black pride, self-respect, and cultural awareness. But while some hip-hop writers were quick to praise the Professor's positivity (especially on the East Coast), this enjoyable CD wasn't nearly as big a seller as many of the gangsta rap recordings the West Coast provided in 1991. —*Alex Henderson*

Puss 'N Boots (The Struggle Continues . . .) / Jun. 22, 1993 / Polydor ✦✦✦

The second Professor X album was even more unrelenting in its Islamic and Afro-centric slant than the first. There was little thematic variety, and the

production was very much a background prop to the propaganda, which was quite heavy. —*Ron Wynn*

Project Pat (Patrick Houston)

b. Memphis, TN

Hardcore Rap, Dirty South

Of the many hardcore rappers to emerge from Memphis during the late '90s, Project Pat certainly stood above his peers. His affiliation with the Three 6 Mafia collective introduced him to many listeners, especially after he guested on the group's hit song "Sippin' on Some Syrup" in 2000. Yet Project Pat (born Patrick Houston, brother to Three 6 Mafia founder Juicy J) made his mark on much of America with a hit song of his own a year later, "Chickenhead." The song—which features production by Juicy J and DJ Paul along with vocals by La Chat—became a dirty South anthem in 2001 and propelled Pat's third album, *Mista Don't Play: Everythangs Workin*, into the Top Five, an amazing feat for such a hardcore artist.

Rap music had long been a part of Pat's life before he soared to national fame in the early 2000s. His brother, Juicy J, cofounded influential Memphis hardcore rap group Three 6 Mafia during the early '90s. Though never an official member of the group, Pat affiliated himself with the Mafia, appearing on such albums as *Crazyndalazdayz* (1998) and Indo G's *Angel Dust* (1998). A year later, Pat recorded a solo album of his own for Hypnotize Minds/Loud, *Ghetty Green.* Though the solo debut didn't propel Pat to superstar status, it did establish him within the growing dirty South scene, and his follow-up album, *Murderers & Robbers* (2000), did much the same; though this second album was independently released rather than through Loud.

Next came Pat's high-profile appearance on Three 6 Mafia's "Sippin' on Some Syrup," and when that song became a huge hit, the stage was set for one of his own. That hit would be "Chickenhead," a song also featuring La Chat, the successor to Gangsta Boo's position as the token female member of Three 6 Mafia. The song pitted the two against one another in typical dirty South style: La Chat talking badly about Pat, him calling her a "chickenhead." Such indigenous slang had long been a staple of the Memphis scene, yet "Chickenhead" became an unprecedented success, extending its reach far beyond the South and taking its vernacular with it.

Just as his career had reached exciting heights, Pat's longtime legal skirmishes began to catch up with him. During the interim period following the success of "Chickenhead," Pat struggled with legal problems stemming from a January 2001 parole violation, when police pulled him over for speeding and discovered two revolvers. On March 13th of that same year, a federal jury found him guilty of two counts of being a felon in possession of a firearm. (He had been on parole for aggravated robbery.) Perhaps because of these legal matters, or for whatever reason, Loud continually pushed back the release date for Pat's fourth album, *Layin' da Smack Down.* —*Jason Birchmeier*

Ghetty Green / Jun. 29, 1999 / Loud ✦✦✦✦

Then known almost exclusively for his affiliation with Three 6 Mafia, Project Pat introduced his large self to the world on *Ghetty Green*, the solo debut album he recorded with producers DJ Paul and Juicy J. Like most other Hypnotized Minds releases during the late '90s, *Ghetty Green* raised the bar for hardcore rap. While Three 6 Mafia had always come hard on its albums, Project Pat isn't a collective like the Mafia but rather one man—a very large man with a large temper and large presence. Thus, his debut was a big one, and although *Ghetty Green* doesn't have a widely known song like "Chickenhead," it does offer several appearances by the Cash Money Millionaires, who were similarly making a name for themselves in the South at the time. If you want to hear the roots of Memphis hardcore rap, you need to hear this album. It's a landmark. —*Jason Birchmeier*

● **Murderers & Robbers** / Jul. 25, 2000 / Project ✦✦✦✦✦

When visiting Memphis, out-of-towners will inevitably head toward Graceland to commune with the ghost of Elvis Presley, maybe tour the legendary Sun Studios, and later take a stroll down historic Beale Street. Few tourists venture close to the north side of the Bluff City, though, and after listening to the haunting "North, North," the defining track of Project Pat's "underground album," *Murderers & Robbers*, even most natives would be scared to death to take a ride on Pat's turf. An affiliate of Memphis rap pioneers Three 6 Mafia, Project Pat (born Patrick Houston) grew up on the north side of the city, a hard-luck area cratered by poverty where crime is casual and violence is frequent. This is the world outlined lyrically by Pat on his independently released second album, *Murderers & Robbers*. The brutal lyrics of the nightmarish "This Ain't No Game" are enforced by a sparse, dark-hued instrumental track. The chilling "Bitch Smackin Killa" is a tale of betrayal and violence, a crime where the police will respond too late to do much more than pull a body bag out of the trunk. The title track uses the chant of "murderer" like a hard rock guitarist will use a recurring riff, while the dead-end tale of woe, "Easily Executed," provides an antique feel, sounding like a slightly scratchy record in the background while Pat slings rhymes. Although no producer is listed on *Murderers & Robbers*—the CD packaging looks for all the world like an illicit bootleg—the songs were most likely shaped by Three 6 Mafia masterminds Juicy J (Pat's brother) and DJ Paul. The production is deft and imaginative, heightening the paranoia and claustrophobic nature of Pat's rhymes, making *Murderers & Robbers* a solid representative of the dirty South sound, heavily influenced by the hardcore style of Houston's Geto Boys. If the pornographic sex, random violence, and hard-edged lyrics of *Murderers & Robbers* seem too exaggerated to be real, a look at the newspaper headlines will remind listeners otherwise. Only in Project Pat's Memphis could gang members confined to the county jail hold gladiatorial battles between inmates, brutal clashes that left many participants crippled for life. Gangsta rap doesn't get any more starkly realistic than *Murderers & Robbers*. —*Rev. Keith A. Gordon*

Mista Don't Play: Everythangs Workin / Feb. 13, 2001 / Relativity ♦♦

A charter member of Memphis' Hypnotize Camp Posse (along with Gangsta Boo and Three 6 Mafia), Project Pat is a skilled demonstrator of mid-South baller hip-hop. The Hypnotize Camp tends to market its releases in the manner of Master P's No Limit label and the Cash Money Millionaires but with much less gloss. With menacing beats (courtesy of DJ Paul and Juicy J) consisting of heavy, repetitive drum kicks and sinister high-hat snares, Pat takes drug-hustling rap into the same deranged dimension as his Memphis cohorts, Three 6 Mafia. This third release (second on a major label) is solid in places, but for anyone other than hardcore fans of the Memphis scene, the album only stretches so far musically and lyrically. The often inaccessible vibe is probably how Pat and his North Memphis boys want it, for to truly understand the music would be to understand the complicated, seamy drug underworld that produces it. Southern pimp slang from rap's underbelly mixed with eerie low-end synth grooves is the way of the walk here. Strictly gangsta, Pat's unique flow combines a rapid Midwest cadence with a singsong Southern format. In the end with its sprawling number of tracks, it's best to hone in on a few of the standouts: "Life We Live," "If You Ain't From My Hood," "Break Da Law 2001," and "So High." —*Michael Di Bella*

Layin' da Smack Down / Aug. 6, 2002 / Loud/Columbia ♦♦

There's nothing like an arrest record to bolster a rapper's street credibility, and at the time of the long-delayed 2002 release of Project Pat's fourth album, *Layin' da Smack Down*, the Memphis gangsta was facing parole violation charges due to a weapons arrest. Although his imprisonment might have limited promotional opportunities for the album, the Three 6 Mafia affiliate's notoriety certainly didn't hurt *Layin' da Smack Down* as much as Project Pat's own limited abilities. The home of Elvis Presley and Graceland, Stax Records and Sun Studios, Memphis also has some of the meanest streets in the Southeast, easily the equal of L.A.'s Compton or Houston's infamous projects. It's from the dangerous Memphis that surrounds the shellshocked Hollywood Avenue neighborhood that produced Project Pat (aka Patrick Houston) and Three 6 Mafia, and it's from this crime-plagued area of the Bluff City that Project Pat draws his lyrical inspiration. Whereas Project Pat's previous albums, such as *Mista Don't Play* and *Ghetty Green*, offered their fair share of misogynist rhymes, *Layin' da Smack Down* revels in demeaning, pornographic sex. When not concentrating on his own carnal pleasures, Project Pat offers the usual lyrical litany of drugs, crime, and random violence that dominate hardcore rap, the rapper obviously running out of fresh perspectives on the subject matter. Although producers Juicy J (Pat's brother) and DJ Paul bring a bouncy and bright sound to *Layin' da Smack Down*, Pat's material lacks the mix of intelligence, humor, and menace that fuels the best Three 6 Mafia songs. *Layin' da Smack Down* shows Project Pat to be a less charismatic, more thuggish alternative to other dirty South artists such as Eightball or OutKast, one of the slighter talents in the Three 6 Mafia stable. —*Rev. Keith A. Gordon*

Promatic

f. 2002, Detroit, MI
Group / Hardcore Rap

Detroit rappers Proof and Dogmatic came together in 2002 to record one song and ended up recording an entire album as Promatic. The two rappers had been longtime members of the Detroit rap scene—Proof as a member of D-12 and Dogmatic as a solo artist—and found they had much in common. They worked with the Sicknotes production crew for their self-titled *Promatic* album and supported its release on the Contra Music label by joining Eminem's Anger Management tour in summer 2002. —*Jason Birchmeier*

● **Promatic** / Aug. 27, 2002 / Contra Music ♦♦♦

Promatic is a hip-hop amalgamation of lower-class superstars, and their full-length debut is an interesting ride through pure ghetto rap. MCs Proof (who also happens to be a member of the infamous D-12) and underground rapper Dogmatic have evident skills, although they in no way compare with such legends as Rakim or Chuck D, and their humorous thug-life tales make this self-titled debut an enjoyable listen. As these two MCs rap about Detroit life, the feminine body, oral sex, drugs, and the other expected topics, one finds it hard not to like the slick rap flow rolling from the speakers. Fellow D-12 member Bizarre makes a comical guest appearance on "Ecstasy," which helps thrust this song into the spotlight, yet although Promatic has made an entertaining album, it is nothing more than generic hip-hop, and explores no new ground. —*Jason D. Taylor*

Prophet Posse

f. Memphis, TN
Group / Hardcore Rap, Southern Rap

A Three 6 Mafia offshoot, Prophet Posse features members of that Memphis, TN, group—Gangsta Boo, Indo G, Koopsta Knicca—along with many of their Southern and Midwest peers. Masterminds Juicy J and DJ Paul play a large role in the group, both because of their musical contributions and also because the group is named after their Prophet label. Their 1998 debut, *Body Parts*, emphasized gory violence and featured contributions by the Dayton Family. —*Jason Birchmeier*

● **Body Parts** / 1998 / Prophet ♦♦

Body Parts features Prophet Posse's large amalgam of rappers laying down horrifying rhymes over Three 6 Mafia-like beats. It's quite a provocative album, not just in terms of the terrifying lyrics but also in terms of production; these beats are about as hardcore as hardcore rap gets, rivaling Three 6 Mafia's most rousing moments. Given these characteristics, this album probably won't appeal to most rap listeners' tastes, except for the most perverse hardcore rap fanatics. Three 6 Mafia, the Kaze, Indo G, and M-Child, in addition to several others, play a large role in the album; furthermore, abrasive Flint, MI, hardcore rap group the Dayton Family guests, bringing yet more aggression to an already malevolent album. If you can stomach the horror themes and the testosterone, this is actually a rather effective album; the coupling of the hard beats and the angry rapping really evokes a striking, riot-starting aura. Yet, this isn't a phenomenal album by a long shot; there are just too many rappers for a consistent feel, and the emphasis often tends to be on shocking exploitation rather than skills. —*Jason Birchmeier*

PSK-13

Gangsta Rap

Coming off of the Wreckless Klan's only release, PSK-13 started a solo career after Klan members Ice Lord and .38 were jailed and murdered, respectively. Starting with 1997's *Born Bad?*, PSK-13 crafted a somewhat typical hardcore sound, offering brief glimmers of regret between tracks that celebrated the gangsta lifestyle. After starting his own Black Monopoly Records, PSK-13 released *Pay Like You Weigh*, a compilation of singles and new tracks that were mostly produced by himself and Jo Traxx. The same year he also dropped *Flagrant: The Hustle Game Project, Vol. 1*, featuring all new songs and guest appearances from his former bandmates Ice Lord and Point Blank. He also began to associate with other Texas rappers and producers, including the South Park Mexican and DJ Screw, the latter who introduced PSK-13 to his "screwed" production style. This involved slowing down tracks to half their speed or more, complimenting the mind-altering drugs that were also popular in the scene. Adapting to the new production style, PSK became one of the main artists to release albums this way, with most of his releases after

Flagrant slowed down and warped to compliment his new approach. This includes the *Somethin' to Lean To* series, albums that feature himself as well as associates like the Nightshift Hustlas performing in this way. *—Bradley Torreano*

● **Born Bad?** / Oct. 21, 1997 / Priority ✦✦✦

From the Wreckless Klan, PSK-13's *Born Bad?* features guest spots by Ice-T, UGK, and Ghetto Twinz. Although the album isn't quite as distinctive as the Wreckless Klan's *Blowin' Up Tha Scene* (much of the rapping and production emulates Master P), it features several good jams, including "Play for Keeps," "Go for Whatchu Know," and "Headed Fo' My Trunk (Remix)." *—John Bush*

The Psycho Realm

Group / Hip-Hop, Alternative Rap, West Coast Rap, Latin Rap, Rap-Rock
A hip-hop trio related to Cypress Hill and signed to their Ruffhouse label, the Psycho Realm was formed by Jacken and Duke. The duo's performances impressed Cypress Hill's B Real so much he decided to join the group on the recording, since Cypress Hill had recently broken up (they actually returned in mid-1998). With a Wu-Tang production style provided by the Psycho Ward—actually B Real, Jacken, and Duke, plus Cypress Hill percussion expert Bobo—they released their self-titled debut album in October 1997. *—John Bush*

● **The Psycho Realm** / Oct. 28, 1997 / Ruffhouse/Columbia ✦✦✦✦

Psycho Realm's eponymous debut album is an impressive collection of hardcore West Coast gangsta rap. Led by B Real, one of the masterminds behind Cypress Hill, the trio is a dark hardcore outfit—there's genuine menace in their rhymes and music, which is why it hits so hard. Where other crews deal with cartoonish violence, Psycho Realm's surrealistic imagery and impressionistic music—which is still grittily funky—creates genuine tension. It's not a perfect record—it runs on a little too long, which has the unfortunate side effect of dulling their message—but it tries more things than the average hip-hop record, and that alone makes it worth a listen. *—Stephen Thomas Erlewine*

A War Story / Oct. 3, 2000 / Meanstreet ✦✦

Mostly recognized as a side project for Cypress Hill's B Real and Bobo, the Psycho Realm seems like a good idea: a lyrically focused hip-hop group featuring a trio of vocalists going off about harsh social issues over melancholy beats. The group's eponymous debut reflected these concepts effectively; unfortunately, *A War Story* never comes close to approaching a utopian execution of this idea. The beats are just way too sparse and simple to hold one's attention, and to make them worse, the sound quality is unbearably poor, on a par with a home-produced four-track recording (which can perhaps be attributed to the fact that the group was dropped from their major label). Furthermore, the vocals courtesy of Bobo, Jacken, and B Real are sorely lacking any sort of aesthetically pleasing flow; if not for the lyric sheet, they would be indecipherable, sounding like murky mumbling. A positive note involves the tone of the music; it may not necessarily sound great, but it does possess a strong emotive feel to it, embodying feels of desperation. But that's about all this album has going for it. Not even the biggest Cypress Hill fans should find much value here. *—Jason Birchmeier*

Public Enemy

f. 1982, Long Island, NY
Group / Golden Age, Political Rap, Hip-Hop, East Coast Rap, Hardcore Rap
Public Enemy rewrote the rules of hip-hop, becoming the most influential and controversial rap group of the late '80s and, for many, the definitive rap group of all time. Building from Run-D.M.C.'s street-oriented beats and Boogie Down Productions' proto-gangsta rhyming, Public Enemy pioneered a variation of hardcore rap that was musically and politically revolutionary. With his powerful, authoritative baritone, lead rapper Chuck D rhymed about all kinds of social problems, particularly those plaguing the black community, often condoning revolutionary tactics and social activism. In the process, he directed hip-hop toward an explicitly self-aware, pro-black consciousness that became the culture's signature throughout the next decade. Musically, Public Enemy were just as revolutionary as their production team, the Bomb Squad, created dense soundscapes that relied on avant-garde cut-and-paste techniques, unrecognizable samples, piercing sirens, relentless beats, and deep funk. It was chaotic and invigorating music, made all the more intoxicating by Chuck D's forceful vocals and the absurdist raps of his

comic foil Flavor Flav. With his comic sunglasses and an oversized clock hanging from his neck, Flav became the group's visual focal point, but he never obscured the music. While rap and rock critics embraced the group's late-'80s and early-'90s records, Public Enemy frequently ran into controversy with their militant stance and lyrics, especially after their 1988 album, *It Takes a Nation of Millions to Hold Us Back*, made them into celebrities. After all the controversy settled in the early '90s, once the group entered a hiatus, it became clear that Public Enemy were the most influential and radical band of their time.

Chuck D (born Carlton Ridenhour, August 1, 1960) formed Public Enemy in 1982, as he was studying graphic design at Adelphi University on Long Island. He had been DJing at the student radio station WBAU, where he met Hank Shocklee and Bill Stephney. All three shared a love of hip-hop and politics, which made them close friends. Shocklee had been assembling hip-hop demo tapes, and Ridenhour rapped over one song, "Public Enemy No. 1," around the same time he began appearing on Stephney's radio show under the Chuckie D pseudonym. Def Jam cofounder and producer Rick Rubin heard a tape of "Public Enemy No. 1" and immediately courted Ridenhour in hopes of signing him to his fledgling label. Chuck D initially was reluctant, but he eventually developed a concept for a literally revolutionary hip-hop group—one that would be driven by sonically extreme productions and socially revolutionary politics. Enlisting Shocklee as his chief producer and Stephney as a publicist, Chuck D formed a crew with DJ Terminator X (born Norman Lee Rogers, August 25, 1966) and fellow Nation of Islam member Professor Griff (born Richard Griffin) as the choreographer of the group's backup dancers, the Security of the First World, whom performed homages to old Stax and Motown dancers with their martial moves and fake Uzis. He also asked his old friend William Drayton (born March 16, 1959) to join as a fellow rapper. Drayton developed an alterego called Flavor Flav, who functioned as a court jester to Chuck D's booming voice and somber rhymes in Public Enemy.

Public Enemy's debut album, *Yo! Bum Rush the Show*, was released on Def Jam Records in 1987. Its spare beats and powerful rhetoric were acclaimed by hip-hop critics and aficionados, but the record was ignored by the rock and R&B mainstream. However, their second album, *It Takes a Nation of Millions to Hold Us Back*, was impossible to ignore. Under Shocklee's direction, PE's production team, the Bomb Squad, developed a dense, chaotic mix that relied as much on found sounds and avant-garde noise as it did on old school funk. Similarly, Chuck D's rhetoric gained focus and Flavor Flav's raps were wilder and funnier. *A Nation of Millions* was hailed as revolutionary by both rap and rock critics, and it was—hip-hop had suddenly became a force for social change. As Public Enemy's profile was raised, they opened themselves up to controversy. In a notorious statement, Chuck D claimed that rap was "the black CNN," relating what was happening in the inner city in a way that mainstream media could not project. Public Enemy's lyrics were naturally dissected in the wake of such a statement, and many critics were uncomfortable with the positive endorsement of black Muslim leader Louis Farrakhan on "Bring the Noise." "Fight the Power," Public Enemy's theme for Spike Lee's controversial 1989 film *Do the Right Thing*, also caused an uproar for its attacks on Elvis Presley and John Wayne, but that was considerably overshadowed by an interview Professor Griff gave *The Washington Post* that summer. Griff had previously said anti-Semitic remarks on stage, but his quotation that Jews were responsible for "the majority of the wickedness that goes on across the globe" was greeted with shock and outrage, especially by white critics who previously embraced the group. Faced with a major crisis, Chuck D faltered. First he fired Griff, then brought him back, then broke up the group entirely. Griff gave one more interview where he attacked Chuck D and PE, which led to his permanent departure from the group.

Public Enemy spent the remainder of 1989 preparing their third album, releasing "Welcome to the Terrordome" as its first single in early 1990. Again, the hit single caused controversy as its lyrics "still they got me like Jesus" were labeled anti-Semitic by some quarters. Despite all the controversy, *Fear of a Black Planet* was released to enthusiastic reviews in the spring of 1990, and it shot into the pop Top Ten as the singles "911 Is a Joke," "Brothers Gonna Work It Out," and "Can't Do Nuttin' for Ya Man" became Top 40 R&B hits. For their next album, 1991's *Apocalypse 91... The Enemy Strikes Black*, the group re-recorded "Bring the Noise" with thrash metal band Anthrax, the first sign that the group was trying to consolidate their white audience. *Apocalypse 91* was greeted with overwhelmingly positive reviews upon its fall release, and it debuted at number four on the pop charts, but the band began to lose momentum in 1992 as they toured with the second leg of U2's Zoo TV tour and Flavor Flav was repeatedly in trouble with the law. In the fall of 1992, they released the remix collection *Greatest Misses* as an attempt to keep their name viable, but it was greeted to nasty reviews.

Public Enemy was on hiatus during 1993, as Flav attempted to wean himself off drugs, returning in the summer of 1994 with *Muse Sick-n-Hour Mess Age.* Prior to its release, it was subjected to exceedingly negative reviews in *Rolling Stone* and *The Source*, which affected the perception of the album considerably. *Muse Sick* debuted at number 14, but it quickly fell off the charts as it failed to generate any singles. Chuck D retired Public Enemy from touring in 1995 as he severed ties with Def Jam, developed his own record label and publishing company, and attempted to rethink Public Enemy. In 1996 he released his first debut album, *The Autobiography of Mistachuck.* As it was released in the fall, he announced that he planned to record a new Public Enemy album the following year.

Before that record was made, Chuck D published an autobiography in the fall of 1997. During 1997, Chuck D reassembled the original Bomb Squad and began work on three albums. In the spring of 1998, Public Enemy kicked off their major comeback with their soundtrack to Spike Lee's *He Got Game*, which was played more like a proper album than a soundtrack. Upon its April 1998 release, the record received the strongest reviews of any Public Enemy album since *Apocalypse 91: The Enemy Strikes Black.* After Def Jam refused to help Chuck D's attempts to bring PE's music straight to the masses via the Internet, he signed the group to the web-savvy independent Atomic Pop. Before the retail release of Public Enemy's seventh LP, *There's a Poison Goin' On...*, the label made MP3 files of the album available on the Internet. It finally appeared in stores in July 1999. After a three-year break from recording and a switch to the In the Paint label, Public Enemy released *Revolverlution*, a mix of new tracks, remixes, and live cuts. *—Stephen Thomas Erlewine*

Yo! Bum Rush the Show / 1987 / Def Jam ♦♦♦♦♦

Sometimes, debut albums present an artist in full bloom, with an assured grasp on their sound and message. Sometimes, debut albums are nothing but promise, pointing toward what the artist could do. Public Enemy's gripping first album, *Yo! Bum Rush the Show*, manages to fill both categories: it's an expert, fully realized record of extraordinary power, but it pales in comparison with what came merely a year later. This is very much a Rick Rubin-directed production, kicking heavy guitars toward the front, honing the loops, rhythms, and samples into a roar with as much in common with rock as rap. The Bomb Squad are apparent, but they're in nascent stage—certain sounds and ideas that would later become trademarks bubble underneath the surface. And the same thing could be said for Chuck D, whose searing, structured rhymes and revolutionary ideas are still being formed. This is still the sound of a group comfortable rocking the neighborhood, but not yet ready to enter the larger national stage. But, damn if they don't sound like they've already conquered the world! Already, there is a tangible, physical excitement to the music, something that hits the gut with relentless force, as the mind races to keep up with Chuck's relentless rhymes or Flavor Flav's spastic outbursts. And if there doesn't seem to be as many classics here—"You're Gonna Get Yours," "Miuzi Weighs a Ton," "Public Enemy No. 1"—that's only in comparison to what came later, since by any other artist an album this furious, visceral, and exciting would unquestionably be heralded as a classic. From Public Enemy, this is simply a shade under classic status. *—Stephen Thomas Erlewine*

★ It Takes a Nation of Millions to Hold Us Back / Apr. 1988 / Def Jam ♦♦♦♦♦

Yo! Bum Rush the Show was an invigorating record, but it looks like child's play compared to its monumental sequel, *It Takes a Nation of Millions to Hold Us Back*, a record that rewrote the rules of what hip-hop could do. That's not to say the album is without precedent, since what's particularly ingenious about the album is how it reconfigures things that came before into a startling, fresh, modern sound. Public Enemy used the template Run-D.M.C. created of a rap crew as a rock band, then brought in elements of free jazz, hard funk, even musique concrète, via their producing team, the Bomb Squad, creating a dense, ferocious sound unlike anything that came before. This coincided with a breakthrough in Chuck D's writing, both in his themes and lyrics. It's not that Chuck D was smarter or more ambitious than his contemporaries—certainly, KRS-One tackled many similar sociopolitical tracts,

while Rakim had a greater flow—but he marshaled considerable revolutionary force, clear vision, and a boundless vocabulary to create galvanizing, logical arguments that were undeniable in their strength. They only gained strength from Flavor Flav's frenzied jokes, which provided a needed contrast. What's amazing is how the words and music become intertwined, gaining strength from each other. Though this music is certainly a representation of its time, it hasn't dated at all. It set a standard that few could touch then, and even fewer have attempted to meet since. *—Stephen Thomas Erlewine*

☆ Fear of a Black Planet / Mar. 20, 1990 / Def Jam ♦♦♦♦♦

At the time of its release in March 1990—just a mere two years after *It Takes a Nation of Millions*—nearly all of the attention spent on Public Enemy's third album, *Fear of a Black Planet*, was concentrated on the dying controversy over Professor Griff's anti-Semitic statements of 1989, and how leader Chuck D bungled the public relations regarding his dismissal. References to the controversy are scattered throughout the album—and it fueled the incendiary lead single, "Welcome to the Terrordome"—but three years later, after the furor has died down, what remains is a remarkable piece of modern art, a record that ushered in the '90s in a hail of multiculturalism and kaleidoscopic confusion. It also easily stands as the Bomb Squad's finest musical moment. Where *Millions* was all about aggression—layered aggression, but aggression nonetheless—*Fear of a Black Planet* encompasses everything, touching on seductive grooves, relentless beats, hard funk, and dub reggae without blinking an eye. All the more impressive is that this is one of the records made during the golden age of sampling, before legal limits were set on sampling, so this is a wild, endlessly layered record filled with familiar sounds you can't place; it's nearly as heady as the Beastie Boys' magnum opus *Paul's Boutique* in how it pulls from anonymous and familiar sources to create something totally original and modern. While the Bomb Squad was casting a wider net, Chuck D's writing was tighter than ever, with each track tackling a specific topic (apart from the aforementioned "Welcome to the Terrordome," whose careening rhymes and paranoid confusion are all the more effective when surrounded by such detailed arguments), a sentiment that spills over to Flavor Flav, who delivers the pungent black humor of "911 Is a Joke," perhaps the best-known song here. Chuck gets himself into trouble here and there—most notoriously on "Meet the G That Killed Me," where he skirts with anti-homophobia—but by and large, he's never been as eloquent, angry, or persuasive as he is here. This isn't as revolutionary or as potent as *Millions*, but it holds together better, and as a piece of music, this is the best hip-hop has ever had to offer. *—Stephen Thomas Erlewine*

☆ Apocalypse 91 ... The Enemy Strikes Black / Oct. 1, 1991 / Def Jam ♦♦♦♦♦

Coming down after the twin high-water marks of *It Takes a Nation of Millions* and *Fear of a Black Planet*, Public Enemy shifted strategy a bit for their fourth album, *Apocalypse 91 ... The Enemy Strikes Black.* By and large, they abandon the rich, dense musicality of *Planet*, shifting toward a sleek, relentless, aggressive attack—*Yo! Bum Rush the Show* by way of the lessons learned from *Millions.* This is surely a partial reaction to their status as the Great Black Hope of rock & roll; they had been embraced by a white audience almost in greater numbers than black, leading toward rap-rock crossovers epitomized by this album's leaden, pointless remake of "Bring the Noise" as a duet with thrash metallurgists Anthrax. It also signals the biggest change here—the transition of the Bomb Squad to executive-producer status, leaving a great majority of the production to their disciples, the Imperial Grand Ministers of Funk. This isn't a great change, since the Public Enemy sound has firmly been established, giving the new producers a template to work with, but it is a notable change, one that results in a record with a similar sound but a different feel: a harder, angrier, *determined* sound, one that takes its cues from the furious anger surging through Chuck D's sociopolitical screeds. And this is surely PE's most political effort, surpassing *Millions* through the use of focused, targeted anger, a tactic evident on *Planet.* Yet it was buried there, due to the seductiveness of the music. Here, everything is on the surface, with the bluntness of the music hammering home the message. Arriving after two records where the words and music were equally labyrinthine, folding back on each other in dizzying, intoxicating ways, it is a bit of a letdown to have *Apocalypse* be so direct, but there is no denying that the end result is still thrilling and satisfying, and remains one of the great records of the golden age of hip-hop. *—Stephen Thomas Erlewine*

Greatest Misses / Sep. 15, 1992 / Def Jam ✦✦✦

It would be unfair to say that 1992's *Greatest Misses* is where it all began to go wrong for Public Enemy, but it wouldn't be entirely inaccurate. Following *Apocalypse 91* by a little less than a year, the album is a jumble of six new songs and six remixes, with a live cut added as a bonus track—a sure sign that the group was either finding a way to buy time or didn't quite have the energy to finish a full album. The resulting record doesn't indicate which answer is better, which is part of the problem: it never quite comes into focus, which is a startling change in course from a crew who, prior to this, never took an unsure step with their recordings. That lack of direction is what really hurts the record, since it seeps into not just the superfluous remixes (many waterlogged with introductory hot-button talk-show samples) but also the new material. Here, the Bomb Squad and their legions of coproducers—most prominently the Imperial Grand Ministers of Funk, but also Dr. Treble and Mr. Bass—sound restrained as they try to move PE away from their signature sonic assault and into newer, soulful territory. To a certain extent, it works on "Hit da Road Jack," but when the Parliament allusions are hauled out on this album's obligatory Flavor Flav showcase, "Gett off My Back," for the first time Public Enemy sound like followers, not leaders. This trouble is compounded by the fact that the tracks where they sound the most comfortable—"Tie Goes to the Runner," the basketball saga "Air Hoodlum," and the record's best track, "Hazy Shade of Criminal"—are the ones that sound closest to the band's classic sound, which at that point was beginning to sound outdated as hip-hop became ensconced in gangsta. In retrospect, it sounds better—still not among their best material, but solid genre material nonetheless, with the aforementioned songs (apart from "Gett off My Back") all being satisfying within the sound that PE has developed, even if it's not among their best work. So, *Greatest Misses* is not the outright disaster that it seemed at the time, but neither is it a lost treasure, since it's just too damn diffuse to be something worthwhile for anyone outside of the dedicated. —*Stephen Thomas Erlewine*

Muse Sick-n-Hour Mess Age / Aug. 23, 1994 / Def Jam ✦✦✦

If *Greatest Misses* was viewed as a temporary stumble upon its release in 1992, *Muse Sick-n-Hour Mess Age* was viewed as proof positive that Public Enemy was creatively bankrupt and washed up when it appeared in 1994. By and large, it was savaged in the press, most notably in a two-star pan by Touré in *Rolling Stone*, whose review still irked PE leader Chuck D years later. In retrospect, it's hard not to agree with Chuck's anger, since *Muse Sick* is hardly the disaster it was painted at the time. In fact, it's a thoroughly enjoyable, powerful album, one that is certainly not as visionary as the group's first four records but is as musically satisfying. Its greatest crime is that it arrived at a time when so few were interested in, not just Public Enemy, but what the group represents—namely, aggressive, uncompromising, noisy political rap that's unafraid and places as much emphasis on soundscape as it does on groove. In 1994, hip-hop was immersed in gangsta murk (the Wu-Tang Clan's visionary 1993 debut, *Enter the Wu-Tang*, was only beginning to break the stranglehold of G-funk) and nobody cared to hear Public Enemy's unapologetic music, particularly since it made no concessions to the fads and trends of the times. Based solely on the sound, *Muse Sick*, in fact, could have appeared in 1991 as the sequel to *Fear of a Black Planet*, and even if it doesn't have the glorious highs of *Apocalypse 91*, it is arguably a more cohesive listen, with a greater sense of purpose and more consistent material than that record. But, timing *does* count for something, and *Apocalypse* did arrive when the group was not just at the peak of their powers, but at the peak of their hold on the public imagination, two things that cannot be discounted when considering the impact of an album. This record, in contrast, stands outside of the time, sounding better as the years have passed, because when it's separated from fashion and trends, it's revealed as a damn good Public Enemy record. True, it doesn't offer anything new, but it offers a uniformly satisfying listen and it has stood the test of time better than many records that elbowed it off the charts and out of public consciousness during that bleak summer of 1994. —*Stephen Thomas Erlewine*

Bring the Noise 2000, Vol. 1 / Mar. 17, 1998 / Chronicles ✦✦✦

After spending nearly four years in semi-retirement, Public Enemy planned 1998 as the year they would come back strong, but to some fans, it was a little disconcerting that the first record they released was a megamix album entitled *Bring the Noise 2000, Vol. 1*. Boasting hits, album tracks, B sides, Terminator X solo cuts, and previously unreleased tracks, the disc runs through

27 truncated tracks in a fury. Fortunately, the mixes are inventive and invigorating—anything less would be sacrilege to the Bomb Squad, the most creative production team in hip-hop history. Even so, *Bring the Noise 2000* isn't for every Public Enemy fan—its sonic deluge will primarily be of interest to fans who are into the claustrophobic sampling and scratching of their best records, not the raging rhymes of Chuck D, which are considerably downplayed here. And while it isn't a triumphant comeback, it's strong enough to set the stage for the *He Got Game* and *Resurrection* albums, which appeared a month later. —*Stephen Thomas Erlewine*

He Got Game / Apr. 21, 1998 / Def Jam ✦✦✦✦

Nominally a soundtrack to Spike Lee's basketball drama, but in reality more of an individual album, *He Got Game* appeared in 1998, just the second Public Enemy album since 1991's *Apocalypse 91*. Even though Chuck D was pushing 40, the late '90s were friendlier to PE's noisy, claustrophobic hip-hop than the mid-'90s, largely because hip-hop terrorists like the Wu-Tang Clan, Jeru the Damaja, and DJ Shadow were bringing the music back to its roots. PE followed in their path, stripping away the sonic blitzkrieg that was the Bomb Squad's trademark and leaving behind skeletal rhythm tracks, simple loops, and bass lines. Taking on the Wu at their own game—and, if you think about it, Puff Daddy as well, since the simple, repetitive loop of Buffalo Springfield's "For What It's Worth" on the title track was nothing more than a brazenly successful one-upmanship of Puff's shameless thievery—didn't hurt the group's credibility, since they did it *well*. Listen to the circular, menacing synth lines of the opening "Resurrection" or the scratching strings on "Unstoppable" and it's clear that Public Enemy could compete with the most innovative artists in the younger generation, while "Is Your God a Dog" and "Politics of the Sneaker Pimps" proved that they could draw their own rules. That said, *He Got Game* simply lacked the excitement and thrill of prime period PE—Chuck D, Terminator X, and the Bomb Squad were seasoned, experienced craftsmen, and it showed, for better and worse. They could craft a solid comeback like *He Got Game*, but no matter how enjoyable and even thought provoking the album was, that doesn't mean it's where you'll turn when you want to hear Public Enemy. —*Stephen Thomas Erlewine*

There's a Poison Goin' On . . . / Jul. 20, 1999 / Play It Again Sam ✦✦✦

Opening with a sonic collage straight out of *Fear of a Black Planet*, *There's a Poison Goin' On...* comes out of the gates sounding like classic Public Enemy, which is exactly what Public Enemy intended, since their slight sonic change-up on *He Got Game* didn't result in a hit. In a way, PE's feud with Def Jam over downloadable MP3 music was a good thing, since it brought them media attention, which is rare for a veteran hip-hop band. Such increased exposure also brought a minor controversy over "Swindlers Lust," which some perceived as anti-Semitic, but this outrage was isolated because Public Enemy was now at the margins of hip-hop. They were no longer considered cutting edge, and younger kids never picked up their records, so the only place for this controversy to reside was among the rock critics and aging fans who remembered when *It Takes a Nation of Millions* changed the world ten years prior. Chuck D must have known that they would be the only ones paying attention to the album, since it consciously copies PE's past and never really breaks from that blueprint. In some respects, that's a disappointment, since *He Got Game* showed that PE could subtly incorporate modern hip-hop and do it better than some modern acts. But *There's a Poison Goin' On . . .* is nevertheless a strong album, even if it is doggedly classicist. It's also dogmatic, with Chuck preaching to the converted about the evils of the record industry and conformity in hip-hop, which does become a little trying by the end of the record. But he delivers lyrically and PE delivers musically, in a manner that's entirely familiar to fans of Public Enemy, offering a solid continuation of *Apocalypse 91*. Ultimately, it's their most satisfying record in several years—which is a subtle difference that only the converted will notice. —*Stephen Thomas Erlewine*

20th Century Masters—The Millennium Collection: The Best of Public Enemy / Jun. 19, 2001 / Def Jam ✦✦✦✦

In a way, Public Enemy is a band that defies compilations because each of their records is so perfectly crafted, such an ideal statement, that they can't seem to exist in any other way. But, like any great band, the individual songs stand on their own merits, and if they're put together in the right order, the end result would be nothing less than phenomenal. *20th Century Masters* is not phenomenal. It's not even executed particularly well, missing some absolutely essential songs (how the hell do you put out a PE comp without

"Rebel Without a Pause" and "Black Steel in the Hour of Chaos"?) and sequenced in a halting fashion. So, it's not perfect, but some Public Enemy is better than none, especially if "Welcome to the Terrordome," "Bring the Noise," "Don't Believe the Hype," "Fight the Power," and "Night of the Living Baseheads" constitute half the album. The rest of the record is pretty damn good, too—only the Anthrax-assisted re-recording of "Bring tha Noize" is execrable, yet "By the Time I Get to Arizona," "Shut 'Em Down," and "Nighttrain" make up for its presence—but there's so much missing that it's hard to give this a ringing endorsement. Some haphazard compilations wind up quenching your thirst, others leave you wanting more; this is one that leaves you thirsty, especially if you get positively weak from hearing Chuck D's voice—the way that some quake at the sound of Coltrane's saxophone, Miles' trumpet, Clapton's guitar. There's no other instrument quite as overwhelming as this, and it's damn irresistible. —*Stephen Thomas Erlewine*

Revolverlution / Jul. 23, 2002 / Koch ◆◆◆

They may go in and out of fashion, fall out of critical favor, have comebacks and slumps, but even at their worst, the truly great artists have flashes where their brilliance shines through. Public Enemy is one of those bands. When they released *Revolverlution* in 2002, they had been out of favor for a full decade, and throughout that time in the wilderness, the band fluctuated between brilliance (*He Got Game*) and unfocused meandering (*Muse Sick*), but the one constant remained—even when they were bad, it was a thrill to *hear* them, especially Chuck D, whose voice is one of those intangible, transcendent thrills in all of popular music; it's as magical and undefinable as John Coltrane's sheets of sound, Jeff Beck's head-spinning guitar, Duke Ellington's piano, Frank Sinatra or Hank Williams' singing, Keith Richards' open-G chords—no matter the quality of the material at hand, it's worth listening just to hear him rap. That was true when the Bomb Squad was producing PE, but as subsequent recordings have proved, Chuck and PE could still sound shatteringly good without them. True, they built on that sound, but they did find ways to expand it, and, unlike their peers and many new artists, they were restless, not afraid of falling on their face by trying something new. Indeed, Chuck D made a point of trying something new, as he says in the liner notes for *Revolverlution*. Given the state of the industry and hip-hop, he's decided that there's no reason for Public Enemy to release a new album unless it covered uncharted territory. Unlike many veteran artists, he's acutely aware that new product directly competes with the band's classic albums, and that the new audience has changed, looking for individual tracks instead of full-fledged, cohesive albums—and that might mean that they want killer new songs, live tracks, contemporary remixes, old remixes, whatever sounds good. So, *Revolverlution* is an attempt to craft a record along those lines. Cohesion has been thrown out the window in favor of new tunes, live tracks from 1992, new remixes by fans, remixes of songs *debuted* on this album, PSAs, and interviews—the kind of album you'd burn if you spent some time on a really good artist's MP3 site. There's a bunch of good stuff here, whether it's new stuff ("Gotta Give the Peeps What They Need," the title track, the fiercely political "Son of a Bush," and "Get Your Sh*t Together"), remixes or archival material (great live versions of "Fight the Power" and "Welcome to the Terrordome"), along with collector-bait interview snippets that don't amount to much. But, there's a lot to be said for old-fashioned, cohesive albums—they keep a consistent tone and message, delivering an album that felt unified, and thereby easier to listen to at length. This is deliberately the opposite of that kind of record, which is an admirable artistic move, but it does make the album feel like a bewildering hodge-podge, even after you understand the intent behind the entire thing. Even so, it's a worthwhile listen because, no matter what, it *is* still a thrill to hear Public Enemy. They might not be hip, they're not as innovative as they used to be, but they still make very good, even great music, and that's evident on *Revolverlution*. If only it were presented better. —*Stephen Thomas Erlewine*

Puff Daddy (Sean Combs)

b. Nov. 4, 1970, Harlem, NY

Producer, Vocals / Hip-Hop, Urban, East Coast Rap, Pop-Rap

The biggest hip-hop impresario of the mid-'90s, Sean "Puffy" Combs—alternately known as Puff Daddy or P. Diddy—created a multimillion dollar industry around Bad Boy Entertainment, with recordings by the Notorious B.I.G., Craig Mack, Faith Evans, 112, and Total, all produced and masterminded by Combs himself. Responsible for over 100 million dollars in total

record sales and named ASCAP's 1996 Songwriter of the Year, Combs was, on the other hand, criticized by many in the hip-hop community for watering down the sound of the underground and also for a perceived overreliance on samples as practically the sole basis for many of his hits. A very successful A&R executive at Uptown Records during the early '90s responsible for sizeable hit records by Father MC, Mary J. Blige, and Jodeci, Combs formed his own Bad Boy label; signed Notorious B.I.G., Evans, and Craig Mack; and earned enough hits to cement an alliance with Arista Records. A highly publicized feud with Death Row Records (in which Tupac Shakur and labelhead Suge Knight served as West Coast/Dark Side equivalents to the Notorious B.I.G. and Combs) was summarily ended in late 1996, when Shakur was murdered and Knight jailed. Six months later, Notorious B.I.G. was dead as well and after Combs mourned his friend's death, he hit the pop charts in a big way during his biggest year, 1997.

Born in Harlem in 1970, Sean Combs spent much of his childhood in nearby Mt. Vernon, NY. Already a shrewd businessman through his two paper routes, Combs applied to Howard University in Washington, D.C., and while attending, convinced childhood friend Heavy D to sign him up as an intern at the label he recorded for, Uptown Records. Several months later, he was an A&R executive with his sights set on the vice presidency, serving as the executive producer for Father MC's 1990 album *Father's Day*, which became a hit. Successful albums followed for Mary J. Blige (*What's the 411?*) and Heavy D & the Boyz (*Blue Funk*) during 1992, though Combs was fired from Uptown by the following year (probably because he was a bit *too* ambitious). He worked as a remixer during 1993 and set up Bad Boy Entertainment as his own venture, running the label out of his apartment during long hours with only several employees. After more than a year of hard work, he finally signed two hit artists, former EPMD roadie Craig Mack and the Notorious B.I.G. Mack hit the big time in mid-1994, when a remix of his "Flava in Ya Ear" single (featuring LL Cool J, Busta Rhymes, Rampage, and Notorious B.I.G.) hit the Top Ten and became the first platinum record for Bad Boy. B.I.G. notched the second at the beginning of 1995, when his own second hit "Big Poppa" reached number six on the pop charts. Mack's album *Project: Funk Da World* eventually went gold and Notorious B.I.G.'s *Ready to Die* was certified double-platinum.

Sean "Puffy" Combs began branching out Bad Boy during 1995, adding platinum R&B acts Faith Evans and Total (both of whom were connected to B.I.G., Evans as his wife and Total as his former backing vocal group) plus another platinum seller, 112, in 1996. He also produced for many outside artists (including Aretha Franklin, Boyz II Men, Mariah Carey, TLC, SWV, and Lil' Kim) and added two straight-ahead hip-hop acts, Mase and the LOX. By that time, however, Combs and B.I.G. were embroiled in a feud with Death Row Records' head Suge Knight and star Tupac Shakur. Shakur accused Combs of involvement in his 1994 shooting, mocked B.I.G. by saying he had slept with Faith Evans, and threatened the two in the lyrics to his hit song "Hit 'Em Up." (The video for the track featured two characters, P.I.G. and Buffy, who are humiliated in various ways.) In September 1996, however, Shakur was shot and killed by unknown assailants; just six months later, in March of 1997, B.I.G. himself was killed in the same fashion. Just three weeks later, his second album debuted at number one and was eventually certified six times platinum. The single "Hypnotize" also hit number one, and stayed on the charts for months after B.I.G. was killed. Though Combs had been preparing his own solo debut, under the name Puff Daddy, he quit working for several months out of grief for his longtime friend. When he returned in mid-1997, it was with a vengeance, as the single "Can't Nobody Hold Me Down" held the top spot on the singles charts for almost two months. Following quickly behind was another monster number-one hit, "I'll Be Missing You," a tender tribute to Notorious B.I.G. with Faith Evans providing background vocals. Combs' subsequent LP as Puff Daddy, *No Way Out*, shot straight to number one and was certified platinum several times over; in 1998 it won the Grammy Award for Best Rap Album and "I'll Be Missing You" won the award for Best Rap Performance by a Duo or Group.

Forever followed in 1999, but the rushed release and lack of any new ideas disappointed fans and dampened sales. On top of that, on April 15 of that year, he was accused of severely beating Interscope Records exec Steve Stoute and was brought to court for the incident. Puffy managed to get his sentence trimmed down to second-degree harassment when he finally reached the courts in September, much to his detractors' dismay.

More controversy started brewing when his relationship with singer/actress Jennifer Lopez was made public around the same time. Engagement rumors haunted them for a few months, but the real problems began when they were present at a shooting in a New York City club that December. The couple was brought in for questioning, and eventually both faced charges for illegal possession of a firearm. Meanwhile, rapper Shyne was indicted for the incident, but Puffy was not dismissed because of the weapons charge. His trial date for the club shooting was finally set, while October found two new lawsuits facing the rapper. First, his driver sued for $3 million due to personal injury and stress, followed by a $1.8 million suit from the club owner stemming from poor business following the shooting. Though Lopez initially supported Puffy, she broke off their relationship on Valentine's Day 2001.

A planned gospel album was pushed back to a summer release during the mess, but by March some good news finally hit the Bad Boy camp. Puffy was acquitted of all charges stemming from the club incident, which also snuffed out the civil suits also revolving around his involvement in the club situation. In a move sure to spark comparisons with Prince (and not the good kind of comparisons), he announced that he was changing his professional name to P. Diddy at the end of the month, and also predicted a new direction for himself and his label. By the summer, he had released his gospel album, *Thank You*, as well as a new solo album, *The Saga Continues*. "Bad Boy for Life" became his biggest hit in years late in the summer, and a collaboration with David Bowie appeared on the *Training Day* movie soundtrack. He took a serious blow in the spring of 2002 when Arista Records stopped distributing Bad Boy Records and took Faith Evans with them. 112 attempted to also jump ship to Def Jam, but Puffy filed a restraining order before the group could make a clean break. —*John Bush and Bradley Torreano*

● **No Way Out** / Jul. 1, 1997 / Bad Boy ◆◆◆◆
Before releasing his first solo album, Puff Daddy (aka Sean "Puffy" Combs) was famous as the producer of the Notorious B.I.G., Junior M.A.F.I.A., Craig Mack, Lil' Kim, and many other rappers. As he was making his solo debut, the Notorious B.I.G. was murdered, and that loss weighs heavily on Puff's mind throughout *No Way Out*. Even though the album has some funky party jams scattered throughout the record, the bulk of the album is filled with fear, sorrow, and anger, and it's evident not only on the tribute "I'll Be Missing You" (a d'uet with Faith Evans and 112 that is based on the Police's "Every Breath You Take") but also on gangsta anthems like "It's All About the Benjamins." That sense of loss makes *No Way Out* a more substantial album than most mid-'90s hip-hop releases, and even if it has flaws—there's a bit too much filler and it runs a little long—it is nevertheless a compelling, harrowing album that establishes Puff Daddy as a vital rapper in his own right. —*Leo Stanley*

Forever / Aug. 24, 1999 / Bad Boy ◆◆◆
It was never much of a contest, but with his second solo album, Puff Daddy retains his crown as the biggest ego in hip-hop, if not popular music. It's an arrogance that asserts itself in the over 20 pictures included in the album booklet (all with different poses and outfits) and in the opening track—"Forever (Intro)"—that updates listeners with all the sordid details of Puffy's personal life. With all this ego strutting around, Puffy's sizable production talents have consistently been underrated. The truth is, he's been one of the best hip-hop producers of the '90s, creator of countless solid party jams, heavy on the groove and quite creative for their crossover potential. Though most of the tracks on *Forever* are coproductions with young lieutenants from his Bad Boy organization, Puffy's productions shine through. And he's downplayed sampling obvious pop hits for the main groove of his songs, perhaps a response to the constant criticism of hip-hop fans. Puffy's also a better rapper than he used to be, almost up to the level of the MC superstars guesting here. There are no tracks as propulsive as the hits from *No Way Out* ("It's All About the Benjamins," "Been Around the World"), and the ballad track "Best Friend," which samples Christopher Cross' "Sailing," is a lame rehash of the Biggie tribute "I'll Be Missing You." The final track (and first single), the Public Enemy-sampling "P.E. 2000," is an apt metaphor for Puff Daddy's second

album; it's a solid production, not quite as exciting as it should be, informed by a mindset that uses hip-hop as a ladder to pop success and wealth. —*Keith Farley*

The Saga Continues / Jun. 19, 2001 / Bad Boy ◆◆◆
A lot happened to Sean Combs during the two-year gap between *Forever* and *The Saga Continues*. Besides the obvious name change to P. Diddy and his daily appearances in the news, the overdramatic rap artist saw his popularity drop considerably during those two years—a serious issue for someone as attention hungry as Combs. *The Saga Continues*, then, signals to everyone that his Bad Boy empire is in fact still an empire. "Bad Boy for Life," the album's big, opening anthem, perhaps sums up the situation best: "We ain't going nowhere/We can't be stopped." It's a fairly simple claim, but this pretension towers largely over every single second of this album. Combs isn't just trying to make great music anymore; he's trying to reclaim his credibility. In his mission to do so, he has recruited the latest roster of Bad Boy talent, anchored by two stellar rappers, Black Rob and G. Dep, who are to be viewed as the successors to the departed Biggie Smalls and Shyne. Combs gives these two plenty of time in the spotlight here—as much as himself—and they definitely showcase their talent commendably, as do many of the other family members. It's nice to see Combs stay in house for this album rather than assemble a disparate best-of-the-best roster like he did on *Forever*. This decision helps give the album more of a cohesive feel, as these family members, and also the often daring production, make this an impressive album at times. It's Combs himself, though, who mars what could be a solid album with his rhetorical swagger. When he's surrounded by his crew, he's fine, though you wish he could rap as well as he can present the talent of others. Rather, it's when Combs steps into the spotlight, particularly during the numerous interludes, that his swaggering often goes too far, teetering on the fine line between self-assurance and farce. —*Jason Birchmeier*

Thank You / Aug. 7, 2001 / Bad Boy ◆◆◆
Featuring the production expertise of Sean "P. Diddy" Combs and Hezekiah Walker, *Thank You* combines talent from Combs' Bad Boy label (Faith Evans, 112, Carl Thomas) with a number of proven gospel artists (Fred Hammond, Mary Mary, Kim Burrell) and a few big-name urban artists (Brandy, Joe, Brian McKnight). It's clear to see that there's plenty of talent here, and it's this mass-market potential that sets *Thank You* apart from your typical gospel album. The album's single, "You," is an ensemble performance, featuring Evans, 112, Walker, and several others. The remaining songs are mostly solo showcases, offering plenty of variety. —*Jason Birchmeier*

We Invented the Remix / May 14, 2002 / Bad Boy ◆◆◆◆
Sean "P. Diddy" Combs isn't your standard remixer. He doesn't just alter the beats of his songs; he rewrites his songs—new beats, new vocalists, new lyrics, new everything. Of course, Combs doesn't actually do this himself. Rather, he outsources the work to his roster of producers (the Hit Men) and some of the biggest names in urban music. So, even if you question Combs' artistry, it's difficult to question his hitmaking ability. Money doesn't seem to be an issue for Combs. He wants to make hit songs, and he's willing to do whatever it takes to do so, whether that means bringing in superstars like Usher or hiring sure-fire producers like Irv Gotti. And he indeed offers many songs on *We Invented the Remix* that are chart-topping quality, in particular the two versions of "I Need a Girl" and the Ashanti/Notorious B.I.G. duet "Unfoolish." In fact, in many ways, *We Invented the Remix* is better than Combs' previous album, *The Saga Continues*. Most every song here was—or became—a hit, and the abundance of guests spare you *We Invented the Remix*'s weakest characteristic, Combs himself. He seems much more reserved here than he had on *The Saga Continues*, and since this album is of a modest length at only 12 songs, there isn't much space for filler. As a result, *We Invented the Remix* confirms Combs' return to the top of the urban music world after a few years of struggle. —*Jason Birchmeier*

Q-Tip (Jonathan Davis)

b. Nov. 20, 1970, Brooklyn, NY

Hip-Hop, Alternative Rap, East Coast Rap

The longtime MC with pioneering alternative hip-hop trio A Tribe Called Quest, rapper Q-Tip was born Jonathan Davis in New York City on November 20, 1970. While a student at the Murray Bergtraum High School for Business Careers, he cofounded A Tribe Called Quest with fellow students Ali Shaheed Muhammad and Phife (Malik Taylor) in 1988; the following year, Q-Tip guested on De La Soul's groundbreaking *3 Feet High and Rising* LP, with the two groups forever linked through their association with the Native Tongues collective. Tribe's debut single, "Description of a Fool," appeared in the summer of 1989, and after signing to Jive Records, the trio issued their debut LP, *People's Instinctive Travels and the Paths of Rhythm*, a year later. With their fiercely intelligent, socially progressive lyrics and brilliant fusion of rap and jazz, the group emerged as one of the most popular and influential in all of hip-hop, producing such classic LPs as 1991's *The Low End Theory* and 1993's *Midnight Marauders* before disbanding in 1998. Q-Tip then mounted a solo career with the 1999 release of *Amplified*. —*Jason Ankeny*

● **Amplified** / Nov. 23, 1999 / Arista ◆◆◆◆◆

Just over a year after A Tribe Called Quest issued its final album, the group's nominal frontman Q-Tip issued his debut solo album, *Amplified*. For Tribe fans able to get over the fact that Q-Tip isn't trading off on rhymes with Phife Dog and Ali as usual, *Amplified* is an excellent work, almost up to the same level as the group's underrated final Jive album, *The Love Movement*. The sound here is *very* similar to *The Love Movement*, obviously no coincidence since production credits throughout go to Jay Dee and Q-Tip for the Ummah, the same combo that produced most of A Tribe Called Quest's material. It's a style that emphasizes deep grooves and clipped beats with a polished sheen that takes Tribe's jazz-rap into the age of quiet storm and fusion. Q-Tip's rapping is as smooth and inventive as ever, though it's a mild surprise that he doesn't include any message tracks (most Tribe albums have at least one or two). The band's breakup was a blow to hip-hop fans all over the world, but *Amplified* will make everyone feel much better. —*John Bush*

Kamaal the Abstract [Not Released] / Apr. 23, 2002 / Arista ◆◆◆◆

A personal, unique project compared to *Amplified* (Q-Tip's first under his own name), *Kamaal the Abstract* fittingly sounds more like a solo album; whereas *Amplified* merely built on the digital soul of the last Tribe Called Quest album (*The Love Movement*), this one is wide ranging and diverse, a relaxed, loose-limbed date. Q-Tip lays way back on these cuts, rapping in a quick, low monotone for the opener, "Feelin'," even while the song breaks into some restrained guitar grind on the choruses. Guitars, in fact, crop up all over this record. Setting aside comparisons to the contemporary record by N.E.R.D. (the rock side project of hip-hop superproducers Neptunes), Q-Tip crafted a record that pays homage to the last gasp of organically produced mainstream pop in the '70s and '80s, paying a large compliment to Prince and Stevie Wonder, even as he proves himself far more talented than D'Angelo (if not quite as soulful). The beats are pointed and clipped, to be expected on a Q-Tip record, but he allows plenty of space for the arrangements to speak, like the trim trumpet lines pacing "Even if It Is So" or allowing plenty of room for extended blowing from a flute on the warm, pastoral "Do You Dig You." The former is one of the best tracks here, Q-Tip introducing his story song with a fluid, ten-second speed rap that says more about the plight of the single mother he adores than any other rapper could with an entire album. This wasn't the kind of record that lights up the charts—which could account for the reason it didn't appear on the shelves in late April 2002, as expected—but in many ways it's superior to the released *Amplified*. —*John Bush*

Quad City DJ's

f. 1995

Group / Hip-Hop, Dance-Pop, Club/Dance, Southern Rap, Party Rap

The production team of C.C. Lemonhead (Nathaniel Orange) and Jay Ski (Johnny McGowan) met as high school pals in Jacksonville, FL. Interested in the bottom-heavy sound of Miami bass, the pair began producing and worked with Icy J and Three Grand before creating the most popular bass anthem of all time, "Whoot (There It Is)." Recorded as 95 South, the single went platinum three times over in 1993 and led to work with Dis-n-Dat ("Freak Me Baby") and for 69 Boyz, the double-platinum single "Tootsee Roll." As producers of "Tootsee Roll" and the subsequent album by 69 Boyz (*199Quad*), C.C. and Jay Ski picked up an award for *Billboard*'s Best Rap Single of 1994 and placed in the top ten producers of that year. In 1995, the duo united as Quad City DJ's and produced another platinum hit—"C'mon n' Ride It (The Train)." The following album, *Get on up and Dance*, hit the Top 40 and was certified gold. —*John Bush*

● **Get on up and Dance** / Jun. 25, 1996 / Quadrasound/Big Beat ◆◆◆

If the majority of bass music producers were even half as talented as C.C. Lemonhead and Jay Ski, the genre might have become more than a hokey cul-de-sac off hip-hop road. The Jacksonville, FL, production team of Lemonhead and Ski not only were responsible for the anthems "Whoot (There It Is)" and "Tootsie Roll" (as 95 South and 69 Boyz, respectively), but they also struck platinum with Quad City DJ's' "C'mon n' Ride It (The Train)." One of the biggest singles of 1996, the song was a relentlessly catchy workout full of witty, shoutable lyrical couplets. Just as the duo's previous triumphs had, "C'mon n' Ride It" extricated the raunch from bass music, but retained and even expanded on the booty-shaking rhythms, almost to cartoonish proportions. While "C'mon n' Ride It" was a success as a single, applying its formula to a bankable album was a trickier prospect. Lemonhead and Ski didn't necessarily succeed with *Get on up and Dance*—it suffers from repetition, and nothing is as undeniably catchy as the single. But as nothing more than a party record, *Get on up* is a harmless, humorous, and entertaining diversion. "Work Baby Work (The Prep)" is almost a dub plate of "C'mon n' Ride It," "Summer Jam" reinterprets the summery piano line of Sister Sledge's "We Are Family" over a rap that cops the meter of "Tootsie Roll," and "Hey DJ" steals Ready for the World's "Love You Down" (just as INOJ later would for her So So Def-affiliated single "Love You Down"). Hovering at an average of 132 beats per minute, *Get on up and Dance* also never makes the mistake of including a ballad or an unfunny skit. It's all about dancing, all the time. Two "C'mon n' Ride It" remixes close out the party on a familiar and fun note. —*Johnny Loftus*

Quadrant Six

Group / Electro, Old School Rap

Just like Soul Sonic Force's "Planet Rock," Planet Patrol's "Play at Your Own Risk," C-Bank's "One More Shot," and Jonzun Crew's "Space Is the Place," Quadrant Six's "Body Mechanic" was, in part, the work of Arthur Baker associate John Robie (the writing credits on the release also go to the lesser-known E. Innocenti). Quadrant Six only produced the one 12"; released in 1982 on Atlantic, it peaked at number 25 on the clubplay chart and has since become one of the better-known electro singles. "Body Mechanic" has been included on numerous retrospectives since its release, including the fourth volume of Tommy Boy's 1995 *Perfect Beats* series. —*Andy Kellman*

Quannum

Group / Underground Rap, Hip-Hop

Both a label (Quannum Projects) and a collaborative concern, Quannum brought together the brightest talents from the former SoleSides label: Lyrics

Born and Lateef the Truth Speaker (from Latyrx), Chief Xcel and Gift of Gab (from Blackalicious), and DJ Shadow. An artist-run label, SoleSides was founded in 1992 at KDVS, the college radio station for the University of California-Davis, with most of the above artists involved, plus mentor DJ Zen (Jeff Chang). Its first release, DJ Shadow's 1993 slab "Entropy," gained a worldwide profile after tastemaker James Lavelle released it on his Mo'Wax label. SoleSides hit with further releases like Blackalicious' *Melodica* EP (also licensed to Mo'Wax) and the self-titled debut single by Latyrx. By 1997, SoleSides had become Quannum Projects, and the label debuted in 1999 with a masterstroke, the brilliant collaborative *Quannum Spectrum*, including a bounty of West Coast underground talent—Jurassic 5, Divine Styler, Souls of Mischief, and Poets of Rhythm. Quannum Projects continued releasing records, including full-lengths for Blackalicious (*NIA*) and Poets of Rhythm (*Discern/Define*), a single by *Spectrum* contributor Joyo Velarde, and most rewarding of all, the two-disc history lesson *SoleSides Greatest Bumps*. —*John Bush*

● **Quannum Spectrum** / Jul. 27, 1999 / Mo'Wax ✦✦✦✦
A label-compilation project showcasing the varied and growing talents of the rejuvenated SoleSides crew, now known as Quannum, *Quannum Spectrum* represents the unparalleled ambition of one of underground rap's most respected collectives. Though the critics have given DJ Shadow most of the attention, *Quannum Spectrum* boasts excellent productions and intricate rapping from a half-dozen important figures, including Chief Xcel and Gift of Gab (from Blackalicious), Lateef the Truth Speaker and Lyrics Born (from Latyrx), plus—for one track—guest producer El-P. Opening with the groovy Quannum/Jurassic 5 soundclash "Concentration," *Quannum Spectrum* works through over a dozen wildly diverse tracks, subtly reinforcing the concept of a freeform late-night radio show (it's occasionally broken up by spoken-word meanderings by "host" Mack B. Dog). Though "Storm Warning" and "Divine Intervention" provide a one-two punch early on, the album really never lets up; midway, an irresistible groove number ("People Like Me" by Joyo Velarde) fades into a great Lyrics Born number ("I Changed My Mind") that plays more like blues-rock than hip-hop. It's easily one of the most effective statements of purpose ever produced in hip-hop, much less the underground rap scene. —*John Bush*

Spectrum Instrumental / Aug. 30, 1999 / Mo'Wax ✦✦✦✦

Quasimoto (Otis Jackson Jr.)

Producer, Drum Programming, Vocals, Sequencing, Rhythm Arrangements / Hip-Hop, Underground Rap, Alternative Rap, Jazz-Rap
Quasimoto is the utterly bizarre alterego of production wizard/MC Madlib (born Otis Jackson Jr.), one of the leading underground producers on the West Coast hip-hop scene. Madlib got his start with the Oxnard, CA-based Lootpack, which recorded an acclaimed album, *Soundpieces: Da Antidote*, for Peanut Butter Wolf's Stones Throw label in 1999. At Peanut Butter Wolf's urging, the initially reluctant Madlib subsequently began to concentrate on his Quasimoto side project, with which he'd been experimenting since 1996. Quasimoto's music had a decidedly different flavor: free-associative raps sped up during the recording process to sound like their creator had been inhaling helium, backed by liquid-flowing jazz loops and a heavy stoner atmosphere. Madlib debuted the Quasimoto voice on Peanut Butter Wolf's *My Vinyl Weighs a Ton* in 1999, and also used it sparingly on the Lootpack album. The first Quasimoto single, *Hittin' Hooks*, appeared later in 1999, and the *Microphone Mathematics* 12" began to make Madlib's mysterious "protégé" an underground favorite. A second 12", *Come on Feet*, was released in 2000, and the first Quasimoto full-length, *The Unseen*, followed on its heels. *The Unseen* was greeted with generally glowing reviews (and some confusion as well), earning comparisons to legendary hip-hop eccentrics like Prince Paul and Kool Keith; some critics went so far as to call it a left-field masterpiece. An instrumental version of the album followed later, and as its reputation continued to spread, Quasimoto returned in 2002 with the three-song, vinyl-only EP *Astronaut*. —*Steve Huey*

● **The Unseen** / Jun. 13, 2000 / Stones Throw ✦✦✦✦✦
Quasimoto's *The Unseen* is one of the most imaginative albums of the new West Coast underground, a puzzling, psychedelic jazz-rap gem riddled with warped humor and fractured musical genius. Producer Madlib actually outdoes his inventive work on the Lootpack's debut album, *Soundpieces: Da Antidote!*, crafting deep, dreamy jazz loops littered with found sounds and

wiggy vocal samples. Quasimoto's helium-huffing voice is actually Madlib's, electronically altered for an effect not unlike Prince's abandoned *Camille* project. It might put some listeners off as gimmicky, and it's really a shame if it does, because it isn't really the focal point of *The Unseen*'s left-field brilliance. It's more of an added textural element for Madlib's off-kilter soundscapes and a vehicle for the cartoonish humor hinted at in his choice of samples. The lyrics are highly free-associative (that is to say, stoned beyond belief), and by turns paranoid, threatening, or hallucinatory. But it all melts into the warm, druggy haze of the music; unlike, say, the Wu-Tang Clan or Dr. Octagon, this dream isn't supposed to be a nightmare. Quas' scattershot flow isn't what you'd call technically accomplished, but that's by design—he's supposed to be fragmented, not quite all there. The song structures are similarly loose, with rhymes coming from nowhere and disappearing just as quickly; the tracks are short (all under four minutes) and end abruptly, as though Quas is too blunted to think of anything else to say. (Madlib does appear as himself on occasion, and usually sounds just as noncommittal as his "collaborator.") Highlights are plentiful, and include the brilliant singles "Microphone Mathematics" and "Come on Feet," the bizarre trash talking of "Bad Character" and "Put a Curse on You," and the joy-of-music cuts "Return of the Loop Digga" and "Jazz Cats, Pt. 1," which recount Madlib's obsession with record collecting and name-check his favorites. It takes some time to assimilate, but *The Unseen* gradually reveals itself as one of the most unique and rewarding albums of its era. —*Steve Huey*

The Unseen [Instrumentals] / Feb. 13, 2001 / Stones Throw ✦✦✦
For those taken aback by the straight-up production genius of Quasimoto's *The Unseen*, it would seem like the instrumental version of that record would be endlessly fascinating. While it does provide for some interest and maybe some DJ tools, it ends up feeling flat and missing something…like the vocals. But aside from that, it's totally lacking in the actual narrative and concept that makes *The Unseen* amazing. It's still good, and in actuality, it's not intended to surpass the original—so it's no slight to say that it feels like an average sibling compared to its accelerated relative. —*Jack LV Isles*

Astronaut [Single] / 2002 / Antidote ✦✦✦
Lord Quas returns for a short spell on this 12" single released by Antidote. As one of the more interesting alter-personalities of scientist and producer Madlib, Quasimoto drops some great tracks here. Particularly, the nontitle tracks—"Am I Confused" and the instrumental "Lonely Piano"—each provide some food for those hungry for a follow-up to *The Unseen*. —*Jack LV Isles*

Queen Latifah (Dana Owens)

b. Mar. 18, 1970, Newark, NJ
Vocals, Producer / Hip-Hop, Pop-Rap, Alternative Rap, Golden Age
Queen Latifah was certainly not the first female rapper, but she was the first one to become a bona fide star. She had more charisma than her predecessors, and her strong, intelligent, no-nonsense persona made her arguably the first MC who could properly be described as feminist. Her third album, *Black Reign*, was the first album by a female MC ever to go gold, a commercial breakthrough that paved the way for a talented crew of women rappers to make their own way onto the charts as the '90s progressed. Latifah herself soon branched out into other media, appearing in movies and sitcoms and even hosting her own talk show. Yet even with all the time she spent away from recording, she remained perhaps the most recognizable woman in hip-hop, with a level of respect that bordered on iconic status.

Queen Latifah was born Dana Owens in Newark, NJ, on March 18, 1970; her Muslim cousin gave her the nickname Latifah—an Arabic word meaning "delicate" or "sensitive"—when she was eight. As a youngster, she starred in her high school's production of *The Wiz*, and began rapping in high school with a group called Ladies Fresh, in which she also served as a human beatbox. In college, she adopted the name Queen Latifah and hooked up with Afrika Bambaataa's Native Tongues collective, which sought to bring a more positive, Afro-centric consciousness to hip-hop. She recorded a demo that landed her a record deal with Tommy Boy, and released her first single, "Wrath of My Madness," in 1988; it was followed by "Dance for Me." In 1989, Latifah's full-length debut, *All Hail the Queen*, was released to strongly favorable reviews, and the classic single "Ladies First" broke her to the hip-hop audience. In addition to tough-minded hip-hop, the album also found Latifah dabbling in R&B, reggae, and house, and duetting with KRS-One and De La Soul. It sold very well, climbing into the Top Ten of the R&B album charts.

Latifah quickly started a management company, Flavor Unit Entertainment, and was responsible for discovering Naughty By Nature. Her 1991 sophomore album, the lighter *Nature of a Sista*, wasn't quite as popular, and when her contract with Tommy Boy was up, the label elected not to re-sign her. Unfortunately, things got worse from there—she was the victim of a carjacking, and her brother Lance perished in a motorcycle accident.

Latifah emerged with a new sense of purpose and secured a deal with Motown, which issued *Black Reign* in 1993. Dedicated to her brother, it became her most popular album, eventually going gold; it also featured her biggest hit single, "U.N.I.T.Y.," which hit the R&B Top Ten and won a Grammy for Best Solo Rap Performance. By this point, Latifah had already begun her acting career, appearing in *Jungle Fever, House Party 2*, and *Juice*, as well as the TV series *The Fresh Prince of Bel Air*. In 1993, she was tabbed to co-star in the Fox comedy series *Living Single*, which ran until 1997; during that period, acting was her primary focus, and she also co-starred as a bank robber in the 1996 film *Set It Off*. That same year, Latifah was pulled over for speeding and was arrested when a loaded gun and marijuana were discovered in her vehicle; she pled guilty to the charges and was fined.

After *Living Single* was canceled in 1997, Latifah returned to the recording studio and finally began work on her fourth album. *Order in the Court* was released in 1998 and found her playing up the R&B elements of her sound in a manner that led some critics to draw comparisons to Missy Elliott; she took more sung vocals, and also duetted with Faith Evans and the Fugees' Pras. The album sold respectably well on the strength of the singles "Bananas (Who You Gonna Call?)" and "Paper." The same year, she appeared in the films *Sphere* and *Living Out Loud*, singing several jazz standards in the latter. *The Queen Latifah Show*, a daytime talk show, debuted in 1999 and ran in syndication until 2001. In November 2002, Latifah ran afoul of the law again; she was pulled over by police and failed a sobriety test, and was placed on three years' probation after pleading guilty to DUI charges. However, this mishap was somewhat overshadowed by her performance in the acclaimed movie musical *Chicago*, which garnered her Best Supporting Actress nominations from both the Screen Actors Guild and the Golden Globes. —*Steve Huey*

All Hail the Queen / Nov. 1989 / Tommy Boy ♦♦♦♦♦
As strong a buzz as Queen Latifah created with her debut single of 1988, "Wrath of My Madness" and its reggae-influenced B-side "Princess of the Posse," one would have expected the North Jersey rapper/actress' first album, *All Hail the Queen*, to be much stronger. Though not a bad album by any means, it doesn't live up to Latifah's enormous potential. The CD's strongest material includes "Evil That Men Do," a hard-hitting duet with KRS-One addressing black-on-black crime and other social ills; the infectious hip-house number "Come Into My House"; the rap/reggae duet with Stetsasonic's Daddy-O "The Pros"; and the aforementioned songs. Unfortunately, boasting numbers like "A King and Queen Creation" and "Queen of Royal Badness" aren't terribly memorable. Especially disappointing is "Mama Gave Birth to the Soul Children," a duet with De La Soul that, surprisingly, is both musically and lyrically generic. To be sure, Latifah's rapping skills are top notch—which is why *All Hail the Queen* should have been consistently excellent instead of merely good. —*Alex Henderson*

Nature of a Sista / Sep. 3, 1991 / Tommy Boy ♦♦♦
Nature of a Sista isn't the outstanding album Queen Latifah is quite capable of recording. But even so, it's a decent sophomore effort that has more strengths than weaknesses. The North Jersey native tends to spend too much time boasting about her microphone skills—something that can wear thin in a hurry—but there's no denying the fact that she has considerable technique. As on her first album, Latifah indicates that she could hold her own in a battle with just about any rapper, male or female. And the positive image she projects is certainly commendable. But as likeable as much of this album is, it's obvious that she is capable of a lot more. Artistically, Latifah is selling herself short. —*Alex Henderson*

Black Reign / Nov. 16, 1993 / Motown ♦♦♦♦
Black Reign marked Latifah's move to Motown, and was also a return to the tough-talking, lyrically frank, frequently controversial material that established her as arguably the finest female rapper. "Coochie Bang" and "Weekend Love" were harsh and explicit attacks on would-be hit-and-run lovers, while "Just Another Day" and "I Can't Understand" examined the continuing inequities plaguing inner-city youth, and "Superstar" took a

pointedly unglamorous view of her situation and the perils of hip-hop supremacy. —*Ron Wynn*

Order in the Court / Jun. 16, 1998 / Motown ♦♦♦
Queen Latifah opens up her sound on *Order in the Court* by adding old school R&B and contemporary soul flourishes to her trademark hip-hop. Of course, she has never been reluctant to experiment—even on her first album, she aligned herself with the Native Tongues instead of running with hardcore rappers like Public Enemy. The difference with *Order in the Court* is that she's trying to fit into the fuzzy post-Fugees world where the lines between hip-hop and urban are nearly invisible. She performs duets with Pras and Faith Evans, letting them bring her closer to the urban-hip-hop fusion that she envisions. It's an intriguing blend that's occasionally successful, but it's hard not to yearn for the harder-edged Latifah that dominated her early albums. There are some good moments on *Order in the Court*, like the hard-hitting "Bananas" or the smooth "Paper," but they're a double-edged sword—they're good but they reveal that she's capable of delivering something better than *Order in the Court* ultimately turns out to be. —*Stephen Thomas Erlewine*

● **She's a Queen: A Collection of Hits** / Sep. 17, 2002 / Universal ♦♦♦♦♦
Even though she'd been a household name in the music and film world for nearly 15 years, by 2002 Queen Latifah still didn't have a compilation of her own. Then again, since she'd spent so much time in the world of television and film, Latifah had only released one album since 1993's *Black Reign*. Finally Motown gave her the career treatment with *She's a Queen: A Collection of Hits*, a brief collection that has most of her best performances but can't escape its perfunctory air—there are no liner notes, only one fuzzy picture, and an overall lack of design quality. Motown did make a small gesture, though, by licensing three tracks from her first two albums (originally on Tommy Boy), including two of her most powerful performances: "Ladies First" and "Latifah's Had It up 2 Here." The compilation skips over the delightful De La Soul feature "Mama Gave Birth to the Soul Children," but does provide the best of her strong material from the early '90s like "U.N.I.T.Y." and "Just Another Day…," plus "Paper," her intriguing 1998 redo of "I Heard It Through the Grapevine," produced by Pras. The new tracks, however, won't join the Queen Latifah pantheon like the rest already have; "Go Head" finds her aping Missy Elliott in both sound and delivery, and there isn't much to recommend the others, either. With just a little more effort, Motown could've made this Queen Latifah collection a brilliant summation of her career; just as it had for almost 40 years, the label seemed more interested in reaching the charts than giving proper due to the artists who've already had success. —*John Bush*

Queen Mother Rage

Political Rap, Hip-Hop
Queen Mother Rage was a member of the Blackwatch Committee, a collective consisting of activists, writers, and musicians led by X-Clan frontman Professor X. After contributing to several X-related albums in a small capacity, she released a solo record in 1991 entitled *Vanglorious Law*. Although her positive Afro-centric lyrics and smooth production (courtesy of fellow Blackwatch member Paradise) predated similar work from Arrested Development, the record quickly disappeared from the charts. She geared up to record a second album in 1992, but when her record label folded, she abandoned the project and left the rap industry. —*Bradley Torreano*

● **Vanglorious Law** / 1991 / Cardiac ♦♦
An obscure East Coast rapper of the early '90s, Queen Mother Rage was an associate of Professor X, who led the group X-Clan and founded the Blackwatch Committee (a black Islamic organization). The Professor has quite a few spots on *Vanglorious Law*, a likable CD that is definitely on the "positive tip." At a time when countless West Coast gangsta rappers were making a point of being as graphic, sexually explicit, and profane as possible, songs like "Key Testimony," "Vibrations of Blackness," and "Emphasis on a Sister" preach black pride, black unity, and clean living. Though *Vanglorious Law* received some favorable reviews from the rap press, it was far from a big seller. And when Cardiac folded in 1992, Rage became even more obscure. —*Alex Henderson*

Queen Pen (Lynise Walters)

Pop-Rap
A protégé of artist/producer Teddy Riley, rapper Queen Pen first surfaced to deliver a memorable rap on the chart-topping BLACKstreet smash "No

Diggity." Signed to Riley's Lil' Man label, she made her solo debut with 1997's *My Melody*, which Riley also produced. —*Jason Ankeny*

● **My Melody** / Dec. 16, 1997 / Lil' Man/Interscope ✦✦✦
Queen Pen is obviously a talented songwriter and rapper from the range of themes on her debut album, *My Melody*. One problem however, is that the album was produced by Terry Riley, who doesn't really know how to write songs in the vein of Foxy Brown or Lil' Kim, whom Queen Pen appears to be styled after. The result is an album produced with a pop/R&B diva in mind, though she is neither pop nor a diva. —*John Bush*

Conversations With Queen / May 22, 2001 / Uptown/Universal ✦✦
Pen's second album is aggressive, tuneful, and fluid. Unfortunately, you have to sift through several tracks to get all this (not one song features all these estimable qualities). Teddy Riley jacks up the album's best cut, "I Got Cha," while the see-sawing "Baby Daddy" is more representative of *Conversations'* tone and style. This is a solid, if unremarkable, sophomore showing. —*Michael Gallucci*

Questionmark Asylum

Group / Hip-Hop
Washington, D.C., hasn't produced any breakthrough rap stars, which is why Questionmark Asylum remains unheard by most hip-hop fans. The four members—Mistafiss (Kenny Jones), Rosta Swan (Marcell Gadson), Digge Dom (Dominick Warren), and Ding-Ding (Douglas Francis)—lasted long enough to release *The Album* on RCA before fading away. —*Wade Kergan*

● **The Album** / 1995 / RCA ✦✦✦✦
Nine out of ten rap fans surveyed could not tell Questionmark Asylum from the Pharcyde in a blind taste test. After all, the D.C.-based quartet possesses mad dance skills, has a uniquely tripped-out rhyme style, and sticks to a primarily positive alternative rap approach. Thankfully, all four MCs have their own unique lyrical flows, and *The Album* ultimately defies easy comparisons. On "Curse of the Q," which laments the loss of their original major-label record deal, they reveal distinct personalities that make the catchy hook and freaky vocal melody even more memorable, with Mistafiss and Digge Dom assuming drum and keyboard duties, respectively, as sidemen Kevin "KC" Campbell and Jesse "Twin" Blanks add guitar and bass to the ultra-funky

mix. On "Love, Peace, Soul," go-go music legend Chuck Brown adds distinctive flavor to the acid jazzy mix, while "Get With You" samples Bootsy Collins' classic "I'd Rather Be With You" for a funky reinvention. *The Album* is an impressive debut from unfairly overlooked hip-hop shoulda-beens. —*Bret Love*

?uestlove (Ahmir Khalib Thompson)

b. Philadelphia, PA
Drums, DJ / Hip-Hop, Jazz-Rap
Drummer for the original all-live, all-the-time hip-hop band the Roots, ?uestlove was also arranging and producing Roots tracks from their 1993 recording debut. He also appeared on or produced for Common, Dilated Peoples, and Nikka Costa, though his first record under his own name, *Babies Makin' Babies*, was a mix tape of smooth soul instead of his own productions. —*John Bush*

● **Babies Makin' Babies** / 2002 / Urban Theory ✦✦✦✦
Social historians curious about the origins of the echo boom need look no further than the smooth soul being pumped out during the late '70s. For several years, soul veterans ranging from Barry White to Curtis Mayfield to Earth, Wind & Fire recorded dozens of soft and sultry love anthems even while disco and, later, Muzaky quiet storm stole some of their thunder. Though his birth predated any possible lovemaking session prompted by any of these songs, ?uestlove from the Roots displays a great affinity while compiling *Babies Makin' Babies*, a lengthy collection of stone grooves by some of the most sensual soul artists of the late '70s: Minnie Riperton, Bill Withers, Smokey Robinson, Deniece Williams, Rufus featuring Chaka Khan, Patrice Rushen, the Isley Brothers, Roy Ayers, and more. Listeners who haven't heard this much soul this smooth may be surprised at the gorgeous, genuinely inventive production sense behind these tracks. Beginning with Smokey Robinson's "Quiet Storm," one of the most luscious songs of the era, ?uestlove shows a fine sense for putting a mix tape together, dropping hot tracks like Minnie Riperton's "Inside My Love," Bill Withers' "Can We Pretend," and even the occasional surprise ("The Wheels of Life" by Gino Vannelli works very well in context). During an era rife with hardcore rappers, *Babies Makin' Babies* is an expressive reminder of what soulful music should be. —*John Bush*

R

Ra Desperidos

Group / Hardcore Rap

Following a frustrating affiliation with the Mo Thugs Family, Ra Desperidos embarked on a solo career. The group debuted in 2002 with *Tired of Strugglin'* on Koch Records. Mr. T N Tee leads the group, which also features Gold and Menenski. These hardcore rappers spoke harshly of the Mo Thugs Family despite the onetime affiliation, using this hostility to fuel its debut album. Even with the seemingly contrived drama, the album unfortunately reached few listeners, being more talked about than listened to. —*Jason Birchmeier*

● **Tired of Strugglin'** / Dec. 31, 2001 / Koch ✦✦✦

Few knew who Ra Desperidos were when Koch Records released *Tired of Strugglin'* in 2002. The hardcore rap group's only claim to fame had been an appearance on the third Mo Thugs Family album, but that really wasn't much of a claim to fame since the Mo Thugs Family's albums had sold poorly. Furthermore, in 2002 no one cared about the Mo Thugs Family—or, for that matter, Bone, the rap group at the core of the Mo Thugs Family. Bone's onetime success in the mid-'90s had long since dissipated, and every Bone-related album released in the early 2000s had proven disappointing. Thus, Ra Desperidos really don't have much of a claim to fame and, worse, their music isn't going to attract much notice. In general, Ra Desperidos are a standard hardcore rap trio; they follow the style's conventions and at best are run of the mill. And while that's wonderful for followers of the style, the glut of hardcore rap albums flooding the streets in 2002 prevents this album from being anything more than "just another hardcore rap album." Notably, Ra Desperidos antagonize the Mo Thugs Family in the liner notes: "Mr. T N Tee would like to say f*ck Mo Thugs as a label comany [sic] and what it sands [sic] for f*ck Steven Layzie Bone Howse for being the fakest buster in the rap game. F*ck Bone as a whole for being stupid as f*ck and not business minded enough to get the f*ck away from Tomeka before yall carer [sic] went from sugar to sh*t." While it's always disheartening to witness such antagonistic claims, particularly in rap where these sort of squabbles often get out of hand, these ugly liner notes happen to be the most engaging aspect of this album. Without this sort of drama, *Tired of Strugglin'* really doesn't have much to offer. —*Jason Birchmeier*

Racionais MC's

f. Brazil

Group / Hip-Hop, Foreign Rap

Racionais MC's are one of the most important Brazilian rap and hip-hop groups. Deeply involved in a movement of awareness of the marginalized Negro population in the working-class boroughs of the big cities, the group has criticized the press and the phonographic market (they refuse invitations by big networks) as being part of the capitalist system they combat because, in their view, it promotes drug trafficking, misery, and violence. Their aggressive lyrics and stage persona try to awaken the population out of its state of, as described by them, humiliation. Nevertheless, their success brought them to a major audience and as a result, they were awarded by the mainstream nationwide broadcasting TV station MTV.

The group was formed in 1990 in São Paulo, attracting attention for its first recording effort: the songs "Pânico na Zona Sul" and "Tempos Difíceis," included in the collection *Consciência Black* (Zimbabwe). Their first LP, *Holocausto Urbano* (Zimbabwe, 1992), sold 50,000 copies. After many shows during the years of 1990 and 1991 (when they opened for Public Enemy at the Ibirapuera Stadium), the Racionais started to develop community work doing lectures in schools on drugs, police violence (one of their preferred themes),

and racism. "Voz Ativa" ("Active Voice") and "Negro Limitado" ("Limited Negro"), from their second LP (1992), yielded them increased popularity and they were the main attraction in the rap concert that took place in late 1992 at the Vale do Anhangabaú (São Paulo). The CD *Raio X do Brasil* was a decisive step toward success, with Mano Brown winning the Prêmio Sharp award with his song "Homem na Estrada." In late 1994, though, another show at the Vale do Anhangabaú ended in a riot when the group's members were arrested by the police under the accusation of inciting violence. The confusion delayed the release of their third album and led them to leave their recording company and create their own label, Cosa Nostra. They ended up releasing *Sobrevivendo no Inferno* through it, the album representing the concretization of their success on a broad scale: 500,000 copies sold. With the music videos "Diário de um Detento" and "Mágico de Oz" (1998), they won the Vídeo Music Brasil (promoted by MTV Brasil), and were awarded with the prizes for Best Rap Group and Audience's Choice. —*Alvaro Neder*

● **Racionais MC's** / Sep. 5, 2000 / Zimbabwe ✦✦✦✦✦

Radioinactive (Kamal Humphrey)

Underground Rap

Part of the talented and often hilarious Dirty Loop collective, Radioinactive debuted on the West Coast rap scene in the mid-'90s by appearing with Log Cabin (aka 7 Imaginary Gypsys: Murs, Eligh, Scarub) and recorded a pair of well-received EPs (by the hip-hop underground at least), "Fotractor" and "Balance." Born Kamal Humphrey, he's appeared on plenty of records by his Dirty Loop/Mush companions, including the cobilled Busdriver/Radioinactive LP *The Weather* and the various-artists compilations *Ropeladder 12* and *Beneath the Surface.* He released his proper debut, *Pyramidi,* in 2001 for Mush. —*John Bush*

● **Pyramidi** / Nov. 27, 2001 / Mush ✦✦✦

With the Dirty Loop collective having defined itself as a purveyor of the most twisted of hip-hop beats, it comes as little surprise to find the 30 tracks which make up Radioinactive's full-length debut behemoth as messed up as anything they have released to date. The lo-fi production values prove the only effective counter to the schizophrenic delivery of lyricist Radio, but even with the beats simple, they still find themselves flustered by the endless stream of crazed verbals—with the collapse of the eight-track on "Bop Nightmare," the inevitable mechanical option for the overworked machinery, lone trumpeter Todd Simon is left to hustle the depths of his improvisational resources to throw together some melodics before the track is chewed into chaos. The resultant aural complexity amounts to one of the tougher listening experiences to be found in the Mush catalog, but will offer endless joy to those in search of something advanced. —*Kingsley Marshall*

Raekwon (Corey Woods)

b. Jan. 12, 1968

East Coast Rap, Hardcore Rap

Raekwon may not have achieved the solo stardom of his fellow Wu-Tang Clan mates Method Man or Ol' Dirty Bastard, but along with Genius/GZA and frequent partner Ghostface Killah, he's done some of the most inventive, critically acclaimed work outside the confines of the group. Born Corey Woods and also nicknamed the Chef (because he's "cookin' up some marvelous shit to get your mouth watering"), Raekwon joined the Staten Island, NY-based Wu-Tang collective in the early '90s and played an important role on their groundbreaking late-1993 debut album *Enter the Wu-Tang (36 Chambers).* Although the group's contract allowed its individual members to sign with whatever label they chose, Raekwon stayed with Loud when the first round of Wu-related solo projects began to appear. Following his 1994 debut single, "Heaven and Hell," his own solo debut, *Only Built 4 Cuban Linx*, appeared in 1995; while it didn't sell on the level of Method Man's *Tical*, singles like "Ice Cream" and "Criminology" earned him a reputation in the hip-hop underground. Moreover, the album received near-unanimous critical praise for its evocative, image-rich storytelling and cinematic Mafia obsession (on some tracks, he adopted the guise of gangster Lex Diamonds). Also notable was Raekwon's crackling chemistry with heavily featured collaborator Ghostface Killah, who enjoyed something of a coming-out party with all the exposure (he hadn't been nearly as much of a presence on *Enter the Wu-Tang*).

Raekwon returned to the Wu-Tang fold for the group's 1997 sophomore effort *Wu-Tang Forever*. That LP was followed by a second round of solo albums and Raekwon's *Immobility* was released in late 1999, this time on RCA. This time around, neither RZA nor Ghostface Killah contributed to the album at all, and perhaps as a result, reviews were more mixed. Raekwon recorded with the Wu on their subsequent albums *The W* (2000) and *Iron Flag* (2001), and announced plans to reteam with Ghostface Killah for a sequel to *Cuban Linx*. — *Steve Huey*

★ **Only Built 4 Cuban Linx** / 1995 / Loud ✦✦✦✦✦
A serious contender for the title of best Wu-Tang solo album (rivaled only by the Genius' *Liquid Swords*), *Only Built 4 Cuban Linx* is also perhaps the most influential, thanks to Raekwon's cinematic imagination. If the Genius is the Wu's best overall lyricist, Raekwon is arguably their best storyteller, and here he translates the epic themes and narratives of a Mafia movie into a startlingly accomplished hip-hop album. Raekwon wasn't the first to make the connection between gangsta rap and the Cosa Nostra (Kool G Rap pioneered that idea), but he was the one who popularized the trend. *Cuban Linx's* portraits of big-money drug deals and black underworld kingpins living in luxury had an enormous influence on the New York hardcore scene, especially Mobb Deep and Nas, the latter of whom appears here on the much-revered duet "Verbal Intercourse." The fellow Clan members who show up as guests are recast under gangster aliases, and Ghostface Killah makes himself an indispensable foil, appearing on the vast majority of the tracks and enjoying his first truly extensive exposure on record. Behind them, RZA contributes some of the strongest production work of his career, indulging his taste for cinematic soundscapes in support of the album's tone; his tracks are appropriately dark and melancholy, shifting moods like different scenes in a film. *Cuban Linx's* first-person narratives are filled with paranoia, ambition, excess, and betrayal, fast rises and faster falls. There are plenty of highlights along the way—the singles "Criminology" and "Ice Cream," the gentle "Rainy Dayz," the influential posse cut "Wu-Gambinos"—and everything culminates in "Heaven & Hell" and its longing for redemption. Like the Genius' *Liquid Swords*, *Only Built 4 Cuban Linx* takes a few listens to reveal the full scope of its lyrical complexities, but it's immensely rewarding in the end, and it stands as a landmark in the new breed of gangsta rap. — *Steve Huey*

Immobility / Nov. 16, 1999 / Loud/RCA ✦✦✦
It's a rare Wu-Tang solo album that doesn't bear the stamp of the collective's production mastermind, RZA, to some extent, and Raekwon's second full-length is no different. Except for the fact that RZA doesn't actually *appear* on *Immobility*, the paranoid synth strings and soundtrack feel he pioneered on Wu-Tang's *Enter the Wu-Tang* (*36 Chambers*) and *Forever* are all over this album. The producers, including Raekwon's American Cream Team, Infinite Arkatechz, and Six July Productions, give *Immobility* the same sounds RZA gave to Raekwon's first album, *Only Built 4 Cuban Linx*. Though few rappers are more entitled to the sound than Raekwon, most of these songs just don't contribute to the lyrical concerns or delivery (a notable exception is "Sneakers," the only track produced by Pete Rock). And since the album's success depends wholly on Raekwon himself, it's almost impossible for him to trump the excellence of his first album. — *Keith Farley*

Rah Digga

b. New Jersey
East Coast Rap, Hardcore Rap, Hip-Hop, Gangsta Rap, Alternative Rap, Pop-Rap, Underground Rap

As the female member of hip-hop's Flipmode Squad (which also counts Busta Rhymes, Rampage, and Lord Have Mercy among its ranks), Rah Digga is one of rap's most prominent women MCs. Though her rapping is hard hitting,

Digga's background is surprisingly stable. Born in New Jersey, she attended a private school in Maryland and studied electrical engineering at the New Jersey Institute of Technology. She started rapping with Twice the Flavor and was the only woman in Jersey's Da Outsidaz clique. When A Tribe Called Quest's Q-Tip discovered her at a performance at New York's Lyricist Lounge, he introduced her to Busta Rhymes, who invited her to join the Flipmode Squad. As a part of that hip-hop clique, she appeared on Rhymes' 1997 album *When Disaster Strikes* and the Flipmode Squad's *The Imperial Album* from 1998. She also appeared on the Fugees' "Cowboys" and dueted with Bahamadia on "Be Ok" from *Lyricist Lounge, Vol. 1*. Her full-length solo debut, *Dirty Harriet*, arrived in 2000 and featured cameos from Rhymes and the Ruff Ryders' Eve. — *Heather Phares*

● **Dirty Harriet** / 2000 / Elektra/Asylum ✦✦✦✦
In the hip-hop arena, female MCs have usually been overshadowed by their predominantly male counterparts. While it has taken a decade for Queen Latifah, MC Lyte, and Lauryn Hill to earn respect, the wave of scantily clad MCs that followed in their footsteps have transgressed, as these leading ladies are more renowned for their curvaceous figures then their lyrical endowments. Leading Busta Rhymes' Flipmode Squad into a new millennium, Rah Digga's debut, *Dirty Harriet*, proves why she is an exception to the rule. While Digga's verses are replete with an endless array of colorful metaphors, she proves to be more than a punchline MC, showing diversity over the signature horn loops of Pete Rock on "What They Call Me" and the choppy Premier-laced "Lessons of Today." Regardless of gender, what is most intriguing about Digga's debut lays in her ability to transcend genres, as "Tight" and "Imperial" (with Busta Rhymes) are both commercially viable records that any bedroom DJ would actually admit to spinning. — *Matt Conaway*

Raheem

Vocals / Hip-Hop, Gangsta Rap, Hardcore Rap, Southern Rap

Raheem, a member of the Geto Boys' crew back as early as 1986, began recording two years later with *The Vigilante*. Showcasing production and lyrical themes that echoed the Geto Boys' own, it was followed four years later by *The Invincible*. Raheem moved to Solar Records by the mid-'90s, releasing *Down South Comin' Up* and *Tight 2 Def* during 1995-1996. His *Greatest Hits 1986-1997* compilation was released in mid-1997. In the spring of 1998, he released *Tight 4 Life*. — *John Bush*

The Vigilante / 1988 / A&M ✦✦✦
Raheem Bashawn, formerly of the Geto Boys, was only 17 when, in 1988, he recorded his first solo album, *The Vigilante*. Because the infamous, highly controversial Geto Boys are best known for gangsta rap, some people might assume that *The Vigilante* is a gangsta rap album. But it isn't. Although *The Vigilante* is definitely hardcore rap, it doesn't contain any first-person accounts of drive-by shootings, gang bangs, or carjackings. Raheem actually spends most of the album attacking rival MCs and articulating why he believes he's superior; so lyrically, *The Vigilante* is much closer to LL Cool J, Run-D.M.C., or Big Daddy Kane than N.W.A, Ice-T, or the Geto Boys. When Raheem raps about getting out the shotgun, it's merely a figure of speech—he's saying that his rhyming skills have the power to make "sucker MCs" get out of hip-hop and find another line of work. A few of the tracks tackle social issues (including "Say No" and "Peace"), but most of the material is apolitical. But while *The Vigilante* is dominated by fairly conventional lyrics, the production of Karl Stephenson and James Smith sets it apart from many of the rap albums that came out in 1988. At the time, a lot of hip-hop producers (especially on the East Coast) went for the drum machine/scratching/sampling formula favored by East Coast residents like Marley Marl. But *The Vigilante* is more musical, and Stephenson uses synthesizers to play real melodies: pop/rock melodies, funk melodies, and reggae melodies. Musically, this LP is impressive, and like a lot of Dr. Dre's work with N.W.A, Snoop Doggy Dogg, and others, it demonstrates that hip-hop can be hardcore and musical at the same time. — *Alex Henderson*

The Invincible / 1992 / Priority ✦✦✦

● **Greatest Hits 1986-1997** / May 13, 1997 / Tight 2 Def ✦✦✦✦
Drawing from *The Vigilante* (1988), *The Invincible* (1992), and *Tight 2 Def* (1996), and adding several non-LP singles as well, *Greatest Hits 1986-1997* is the definitive retrospective of Raheem's career, featuring all of the hardcore rapper's best-known songs and biggest hits. — *Leo Stanley*

Tight 4 Life / Apr. 7, 1998 / Breakaway ✦✦✦

Anchored by the infectious single "Most Beautiful Girl," *Tight 4 Life* finds Raheem exploring a middle ground between bass music and hardcore hip-hop. Usually the mix is successful, but there's also a number of songs that don't have any truly memorable hooks, beats, or rhymes. So, *Tight 4 Life* is an uneven affair, but the best moments are almost strong enough to make the weaknesses forgivable. —*Leo Stanley*

Rahzel (Rahzel M. Brown)

Beatbox / Hip-Hop, Underground Rap

Probably best known in the semi-mainstream world as a member of the Roots, Rahzel is an MC that specializes in the "fifth element" of hip-hop culture—beatboxing (which comes after graffiti spraying, DJing, MCing, and breakdancing). He actively discourages classification of his sound, attempting to remain on the eclectic edge of the commercial music. According to the artist, his influences include Biz Markie, Doug E. Fresh, Buffy of the Fat Boys, Bobby McFerrin, and Al Jarreau. His goal is to gain respect for beatboxing as a true art form on its own merits. Growing up, Rahzel looked up to his cousin Rahim of the Furious Five, and went to Grandmaster Flash's shows regularly. He later became a roadie for the Ultramagnetic MC's. Rahzel has in fact mastered the art of beatboxing, able to recreate full songs, with accompaniment by himself without instrumentation, able to sing a chorus and provide a backing beat simultaneously, able to invoke impressions of singers and rappers on a whim. Any fan of hip-hop should definitely invest in his *Make the Music 2000* album. —*Adam Greenberg*

● **Make the Music 2000** / Jun. 22, 1999 / MCA ✦✦✦✦✦

Spinbacks, rewinds, incredibly deft scratching, playing the old school hits for an in-the-know audience—these are the skills that have put hip-hop DJs from Grandmaster Flash to Q-Bert above their contemporaries. Welcome to the ranks one of the most unique talents hip-hop has ever seen: the human turntable known as Rahzel, the Godfather of Noyze. There've been several great human beatboxes in the world of hip-hop (Doug E. Fresh is the most famous), but Rahzel's techniques at recreating a DJ on the turntables are close to unbelievable. On several tracks (taken from live performances), he even recreates specific hip-hop classics—LL Cool J's "Rock the Bells" and Wu-Tang Clan's "Wu-Tang Clan Ain't Nothing to F***** With"—with surprising accuracy. And for those with the impression Rahzel is a novelty who can't hold up over the course of a full-length, *Make the Music 2000* proves that he's a great lyricist and straight-ahead rapper as well. The production is uniformly excellent, including trackmasters Marley Marl (on the spotlight title track), Pete Rock, Scott Storch, and Bob Power, as well as Rahzel himself on a few tracks—including one of the best, "Bubblin' Bubblin' (Pina Colada)." And the man also vaults a hurdle with the album's guest rappers. While incredibly passé on most rap albums circa 1999, appearing here are excellent names like Q-Tip, Branford Marsalis, Slick Rick, and Erykah Badu. It's not only one of the most fun hip-hop albums of the year, it's one of the best. —*John Bush*

Rakim (William Griffin Jr.)

b. Jan. 28, 1968, Wyandanch, NY

Hip-Hop, East Coast Rap, Hardcore Rap

Although he never became a household name, Rakim is near-universally acknowledged as one of the greatest MCs—perhaps *the* greatest—of all time within the hip-hop community. It isn't necessarily the substance of what he says that's helped him win numerous polls among rap fans in the know; the majority of his lyrics concern his own skills and his Islamic faith. But in terms of how he says it, Rakim is virtually unparalleled. His flow is smooth and liquid, inflected with jazz rhythms and carried off with an effortless cool that makes it sound as though he's not even breaking a sweat. He raised the bar for MC technique higher than it had ever been, helping to pioneer the use of internal rhymes—i.e., rhymes that occurred in the middle of lines, rather than just at the end. Where many MCs of the time developed their technique through improvisational battles, Rakim was among the first to demonstrate the possibilities of sitting down and writing intricately crafted lyrics packed with clever word choices and metaphors (of course, he also had the delivery to articulate them). Even after his innovations were worshipfully absorbed and expanded upon by countless MCs who followed, Rakim's early work still sounds startlingly fresh, and his comeback recordings (beginning in the late '90s) only added to his legend.

Rakim was born William Griffin Jr. on January 28, 1968, in the Long Island suburb of Wyandanch. The nephew of '50s R&B legend Ruth Brown, Griffin was surrounded by music from day one, and was interested in rap almost from its inception. At age 16, he converted to Islam, adopting the Muslim name Rakim Allah. In 1985, he met Queens DJ Eric B., whose intricately constructed soundscapes made an excellent match for Rakim's more cerebral presence on the mic. With the release of their debut single, "Eric B. Is President," in 1986, Eric B. & Rakim became a sensation in the hip-hop community, and their reputation kept growing as they issued classic tracks like "I Ain't No Joke" and "Paid in Full." Their first two full-length albums, 1987's *Paid in Full* and 1988's *Follow the Leader*, are still regarded as all-time hip-hop classics; Rakim's work set out a blueprint for other, similarly progressive-minded MCs to follow, and helped ensure that even after the rise of other fertile scenes around the country, East Coast rap would maintain a reputation as the center of innovative lyrical technique. The last two Eric B. & Rakim albums, 1990's *Let the Rhythm Hit 'Em* and 1992's *Don't Sweat the Technique*, weren't quite as consistent as their predecessors, but still had plenty of fine moments.

Unfortunately, their legacy stopped at four albums. Both Eric B. and Rakim expressed interest in recording solo albums to one another, but the former, fearful of being abandoned by his partner when their contract was up, refused to sign the release. That led to their breakup in 1992, and Rakim spent a substantial amount of time in the courts, handling the legal fallout between himself, his ex-partner, and their ex-label, MCA. His only solo output for a number of years was the track "Heat It Up," featured on the 1993 soundtrack to the Mario Van Peebles film *Gunmen*. Moreover, a reshuffling at MCA effectively shut down production on Rakim's solo debut, after he'd recorded some preliminary demos. Finally, Rakim got a new contract with Universal, and toward the end of 1997 he released his first solo record, *The 18th Letter* (early editions contained the bonus disc *Book of Life*, a fine Eric B. & Rakim retrospective). Anticipation for *The 18th Letter* turned out to be surprisingly high, especially for a veteran rapper whose roots extended so far back into hip-hop history; yet thanks to Rakim's legendary reputation, it entered the album charts at number four, and received mostly complimentary reviews. His follow-up, *The Master*, was released in 1999 and failed to duplicate its predecessor's commercial success, barely debuting in the Top 75. Moreover, while *The Master* received positive reviews in some quarters, others seemed disappointed that Rakim's comeback material wasn't reinventing the wheel the way his early work had, and bemoaned the lack of unity among his array of different producers. Seeking to rectify the latter situation, Rakim signed with Dr. Dre's Aftermath label in 2001, and the two began recording a new album early the next year, to be titled *Oh My God*. In the meantime, to help heighten anticipation for the summit between two legends, Rakim guested on the single "Addictive" by female R&B singer and Aftermath labelmate Truth Hurts; "Addictive" hit the Top Ten in the summer of 2002, marking the first time Rakim had visited that territory since he and Eric B. appeared on Jody Watley's "Friends" in 1989. —*Steve Huey*

The 18th Letter / Nov. 4, 1997 / Uptown/Universal ✦✦✦✦

It took Rakim five years to begin his solo careeer, but the wait was worth it—*The 18th Letter* is one of the strongest records a veteran rapper has released in the late '90s. Working with a variety of producers (Pete Rock, Clark Kent, Father Shaheed, DJ Premier), Rakim sounds sharp, focused, and strong, rapping with a force unheard of on his classic albums with Eric B. He still retains his knack for rolling, laid-back rhymes, but what's impressive is how he can switch between that style and a more aggressive technique. There are a few slow spots on the record, but in general, few latter-day albums by '80s rappers sound as powerful and vital as *The 18th Letter*. —*Leo Stanley*

The 18th Letter/Book of Life / Nov. 4, 1997 / Universal ✦✦✦✦✦

This two-disc set is an excellent collection of material that succinctly outlines the career of this well-known, highly respected, and deft lyricist. The first disc, also released alone as *The 18th Letter*, was released in late 1997 after a four-year period of inactivity and features 12 tracks of previously unreleased material. The collection of producers on this album show Rakim's ability to change his lyrical and vocal style so as not to bore the listener, but at the same time maintain a consistent and dependable level of creativity and ingenuity. The two R&B-tinged tracks, "Stay a While" and "Show Me Love," represent two instances where R&B and hip-hop successfully merge without too much sugarcoating or hazy outlines. "The Mystery (Who Is God?)" is a serious lyrical synopsis of Rakim's spiritual beliefs and social commentary; still in the relaxed but intense style of delivery that Rakim is known for are "Guess Who's Back" and "New York (Ya' Out There)," among other songs. No track on *The 18th Letter* stands out more than another because each is strong in content and rhythmically powerful. The second disc in this set is a collection of popular songs from the four albums Rakim had released as one-half of a rapper-DJ duo with DJ Eric B.: *Paid In Full, Follow the Leader, Let the Rhythm Hit 'Em,* and *Don't Sweat the Technique.* Also included in the songs on this disc is "Know the Ledge," an edgy, up-tempo declaration of rhyming skill from the *Juice* soundtrack that provided a brief dose of Rakim during his hiatus after *Let the Rhythm Hit 'Em.* Including titles such as "I Know You Got Soul," "Microphone Fiend," "My Melody," "Move the Crowd," "Mahogany," and "Paid In Full," the second disc (known as *The Book of Life*) is an ideal introduction to the impressive past of Rakim as a lyricist. —*Qa'id Jacobs*

- **The Master** / Nov. 30, 1999 / Universal ✦✦✦✦✦
When you've been named the best rapper ever in countless readers' and critics' polls, it must be easy to get a bit complacent. And as a veteran who's been on the mic since 1985 (yes, there are several rappers who weren't even on the earth back then), it also must be easy to make a few concessions to all the rappers and delivery styles that have come since Kangols were all the rage—the first time, that is. Thankfully, Rakim's second solo album shows hip-hop's best rapper outdoing himself yet again, and not conceding a whit to '90s rap. Rakim has always been known for his laid-back flow and, accordingly, he never pushes himself here; his flow is smooth as syrup, and will undoubtedly make hip-hop fans realize just what rhythm is after merely a few tracks. He plays with internal rhymes (one of his trademarks) and constructs the most dense lyrics heard in hip-hop for years. *The Master* also benefits from its stellar cast of producers—Clark Kent, DJ Premier, Ron "Amen-Ra" Lawrence, The 45 King, and even Rakim himself. The productions are tough and catchy (no strings here, thankfully), but they never outshine the rhymes. Rakim praises himself on quite a few tracks ("Flow Forever," "When I B on the Mic," "I Know," "It's the R"), but after a listen or two, listeners will likely agree with every boast he makes. After one album (*The 18th Letter*) to get back into things, Rakim is arguably doing the best work of his career. —*John Bush*

Ram Squad

f. Philadelphia, PA
Group / Hardcore Rap, East Coast Rap, Hip-Hop
Coming out of the projects of North Philadelphia, Ram Squad has gone from local heroes to national players on the hip-hop scene. The group is composed of Boy Backs, Tommy Hill, Six 9, and Suave, four young rappers who grew up in the Richard Allen Project and formed Ram Squad (which stands for Richard Allen Mob). Prior to getting into music, Boy Backs and Tommy Hill were drug dealers and Hill spent time in prison for theft.
The personal histories of some of the group's members formed the foundation of the group's hardcore sound. Influenced by artists such as Kurupt and Notorious B.I.G., Ram Squad got some local attention and they released several independent records such as 1996's *Operation Lock the City,* 1997's *Thee Album Regardless,* and *Ram Squad Raw,* which all sold over 30,000 copies in Philadelphia alone.
The year 2001 saw Ram Squad's first release on a major label with *R.andom A.ccess M.oney,* an unrelentingly raw debut album aimed straight at the heart of hardcore hip-hop fans. —*Jon Azpiri*

Thee Album Regardless / 1997 / Bank ✦✦✦

- **R.andom A.ccess M.oney** / Jun. 19, 2001 / JCOR ✦✦✦
Ram Squad's major-label debut is a moderately effective portrait of life in North Philly's Richard Allen projects. While the group has earned fame in its hometown for its gritty lyrics, it is the album's solid production that gives it its shine. Tracks like the anthemic "Ballers (Up in Here)" and the Wu-Tang Clan-inspired "Snake Sh*t" boast strong hooks and bumping rhythm tracks. Despite the group's street credibility, some of the tracks come off as overkill. Various songs feature wild boasts that fail to ring true with listeners and fall into cliché. Tracks with overly self-explanatory titles such as "Sex Sex Money Money Thug Thug" and "Shootout" fail to pack any narrative punch. Still, there are enough good moments in *R.andom A.ccess M.oney* to make it a solid, if unspectacular, debut. —*Jon Azpiri*

Rammellzee

Hip-Hop
Rammellzee was an important player in the initial crossover of hip-hop culture to the mainstream. He participated in hip-hop's earliest phases, though the bizarre edge his aggressively fanciful inventions brought to the original hip-hop style has been somewhat blunted by the dominance of the gangsta pose and its supposed "reality." Though he performed and recorded as an MC, Rammellzee achieved greater fame as a visual artist, with exhibitions in fine art venues of both North America and Europe. He began his art career "bombing" New York City subway trains, but the subway system influenced more than his artwork. Dynamite D, a conductor who rhymed boasts of the superior condition of his superclean D-train over the train's intercom, is named by Rammellzee as an early rap inspiration. Partnered with MCs Shock Dell and Jamal, Rammellzee participated in early hip-hop sound system battles, where he developed the "W.C. Fields" and "Gangsta Duck" voices originated by Jamal. Rammellzee employed the "Gangsta Duck" on "Beat Bop," a dense dialogue with K-Rob, nominally produced by the late painter Jean Michel Basquiat, and released on Profile Records. "Beat Bop" was the result of some improvised role playing, with Rammellzee playing a pimp and K-Rob in the character of a schoolboy. The resulting rap is the best and most sustained example on record of Rammellzee's flights of wordplay, fantasy, and street surrealism. He also appeared in the film *Wildstyle* and can be heard on the soundtrack LP of the movie. Though mostly concentrating on his visual art, he has collaborated on several progressive hip-hop projects, most often with Bill Laswell. —*Richard Pierson*

Rampage

b. 1975
Hardcore Rap, Hip-Hop
A childhood friend of Busta Rhymes while the two were growing up in Brooklyn, Rampage again hooked up with his old pal in the Flipmode Squad, the loose collective of rappers (also including Spliff Star, Lord Have Mercy, Rah Digga, and Serious) centered around Busta Rhymes for his first solo album, 1996's *The Coming.* When the album proved a hit, Rampage earned his own solo deal the following year. The two had begun playing music together while listening to Rampage's musician father, and though Busta later moved out to Long Island and formed Leaders of the New School, the pair remained friends. Rampage gained his own record deal with Rowdy Records in 1994, releasing his debut album, *Ramp Sack,* but later leaving the label for their lack of hip-hop how-to. Later that year, both Rampage and Busta Rhymes contributed to the legendary 1994 remix of Craig Mack's "Flava in Ya Ear" (which broke the Notorious B.I.G. and relaunched LL Cool J), also appearing together on four tracks from Busta's *The Coming.* After signing with Elektra/Asylum, Rampage released *Scouts Honor...By Way of Blood,* in July 1997, with several tracks including the Flipmode Squad. —*John Bush*

Priority One / Feb. 1996 / Almo Sounds ✦✦✦
As the cousin of Busta Rhymes, Rampage had a bit to prove on his debut album, *Priority One.* Fortunately, he acquits himself well on the record, proving that he is nearly the equal of Busta's insane rhyming and dense musical production. Working with DJ Scratch, DJ Backspin, and Rashad Smith, Rampage creates funky, menacing soundscapes that are perfectly suited to his wild, careening rhymes. While he's not as inventive or freaky as Busta, he has his own style—one that's harder and more controlled—and that makes *Priority One* a hardcore hip-hop debut of the first order. —*Leo Stanley*

- **Scouts Honor...By Way of Blood** / Jul. 29, 1997 / Elektra/Asylum ✦✦✦
Busta Rhymes certainly found a legitimate member for his Flipmode Squad in cousin Rampage, as he shows on his 1997 album release. Music from Lord Have Mercy, Rampage, Spliff Star, and of course Busta himself set them up to be a major player among the top crews in hip-hop, such as the Wu-Tang Clan, Boot Camp Clik, and D.I.T.C. On this album, a young Rampage is presented with some of the best production work done so far by Flipmode, and his flow works well with the beats. Lyrically, he has a simplified style of rapping without much wordplay, standing out more on the tracks where he's telling a story. The hypnotic piano on "Wild for the Night" easily makes for the best track on the album, but "Conquer Da World" and "Get the Money and Dip" are definite bangers. —*Brad Mills*

Raphi (Raphi Henly)

Underground Rap, Hip-Hop
Underground MC Raphi spent years with the Los Angeles crew known as the Tunnel Rats before breaking out on his own to release an album. Joining the band in 1993, Raphi (last name Henly) went under the name Shame for a time while he cemented his reputation as the pugnacious youngest member. Part of his aggressive behavior stemmed from his upbringing in an artistic household, where his mother (a Broadway actress) and father (manager for Debby Boone) taught their son to reach his goal however necessary. Luckily, his reputation began to disappear as his talents began to overshadow his behavior in his professional and personal lives. He began guest appearing on other rapper's albums as well, as he began to become a live attraction in L.A.'s hot rap scene. After almost ten years in the business, he decided to use his talents for smooth flow and thoughtful lyrics for a solo album. Stepping into the studio in the spring of 2002, the resulting *Cali Quake* arrived in early fall of the same year. —*Bradley Torreano*

● **Cali Quake** / Jul. 30, 2002 / Uprok ◆◆◆
On his debut album, *Cali Quake*, rapper Raphi splashes into the underground with an impressive set of skills. Offering a tight rhyming style that brings to mind the mid-'90s work of Nas, Raphi manages to constantly impress when it comes to his actual abilities. The only problem is that he hasn't managed to find an effective production style to compliment his skills, which leads to a fairly dull album altogether. A lot of the songs rely on repetitive beats that never change up, pasting sounds and mildly melodic tones over flat beats without a sense of change or dynamics applied to any of it. Although it can be quite hard for underground rappers to get decent producers to handle their material, it would have been nice to hear what someone like Peanut Butter Wolf or Dan the Automator could have done with his talents. As it is, this sounds very much like a demo tape: filled with all sorts of promise but not delivering a satisfying finished product. Raphi is obviously quite talented, but his clever rhymes and effective lyrics are rendered weak by the bland and uninspired beats that are found here. —*Bradley Torreano*

Rappin' 4-Tay (Anthony Forté)

Gangsta Rap, West Coast Rap, Hardcore Rap
San Francisco-based Rappin' 4-Tay (aka Anthony Forté) was fresh out of high school when he debuted on Too Short's "Don't Fight the Feelin'" (from *Life Is...Too Short*). A conviction for selling marijuana landed him in prison for ten months, but he returned in 1991, forming Rag Top Records with friends Franky J and Fly. In January 1992 they released his debut, *Rappin' 4-Tay Is Back!!!*. His second album, *Don't Fight the Feelin'*, made him a local favorite, due to his hardcore style, which didn't romanticize the ghetto. After 1995's *I'll Be Around*, 4-Tay returned a year later with the celebratory *Off Parole*. *4 Tha Hard Way* followed in 1997, and he resurfaced two years later with *Introduction to Mackin'*. —*John Bush*

Rappin' 4-Tay Is Back!!! / 1992 / Rag Top ◆◆◆

● **Don't Fight the Feelin'** / Sep. 13, 1994 / Chrysalis ◆◆◆◆◆
After a strong debut on his own label, Rappin' 4-Tay's second record only increased the profile of the strongest rapper in the second wave of Bay Area hip-hop. 4-Tay sounded equally smooth and confident on laid-back party jams (the rolling "Playaz Club," one of his best tracks, and "Dank Season"), but really raised it up a notch with his tougher gangsta material ("I'll Be Around," "Keep One in the Chamba"). Franky J's productions contributed a lot as well, syrupy and flowing like most of the West Coast G-funk tracks, but much more dynamic than the usual. Guest rhymers included JT the Bigga Figga, Fly, and Sef the Gaffla, with beats coming from RBL Posse's Black C and J-Mack, among others. On his future material, Rappin' 4-Tay would return to the same types of tracks he did here, but he never did better than "Playaz Club" and "I'll Be Around." —*John Bush*

Off Parole / Mar. 19, 1996 / Get Low ◆◆◆
On his second album, *Off Parole*, Rappin 4-Tay plays it a little too safe. Occasionally, he lets it rip—the title track and a duet with Too Short, "Never Talk Down," are lean, funky workouts—but for the most part, he rolls along on a lazy Californian groove that never really catches fire. *Off Parole* isn't a bad record, but it isn't a noteworthy one, either—it delivers safe G-funk thrills that only sound good while it's playing. There's not much that stays around after the record is finished. —*Stephen Thomas Erlewine*

4 Tha Hard Way / Oct. 21, 1997 / Virgin ◆◆◆
A product of the San Francisco Bay Area rap scene, Rappin' 4-Tay is known for his associations with Too Short and the late Tupac Shakur, and sadly, he's also known for serving prison and jail terms on Various charges, some drug related. In fact, 4-Tay had been locked up in San Quentin Prison when *Off Parole* came out in 1996 and sold over 300,000 units. A positive and congenial tone defines 4-Tay's fourth album, *4 Tha Hard Way*, which favors melodic, R&B-flavored tracks. "Lay Ya Gunz Down" and "Element of Surprize" lament the type of crime and violence he'd seen too much of among young black men, and on the thoughtful "Ain't Nobody Coachin'," 4-Tay urges hip-hoppers to do everything they can to coach and help younger rappers. This decent but not remarkable CD made listeners hope that 4-Tay would heed his own advice and stay out of trouble. —*Alex Henderson*

Introduction to Mackin' / Oct. 26, 1999 / Celeb ◆◆◆◆
Though given Rappin' 4-Tay's decade in the rap game, fans hardly need an *Introduction to Mackin'*, the album turns out to be one of his best yet. Part of the reason is the great cast of guest appearances—Snoop Dogg, Kurupt, Daz, Frost, Jayo Felony—but it's also due to 4-Tay himself, who provides a focus for each track, lends his production skills to the music making, and wraps his rhymes around quite a few compelling grooves. It's nowhere near perfect, but *Introduction to Mackin'* is more than just another played-out gangsta fairytale. —*Keith Farley*

RaRa

Vocals / Alternative Rap, Hip-Hop, R&B, Urban
Los Angeles-based rapper RaRa introduced his party jam style with his debut album, *Holla at Me*, which was released by MCA Records in summer 2000 and featured work with Immature and Randy Jackson. —*Heather Phares*

● **Holla at Me** / Jun. 13, 2000 / MCA ◆◆◆
When a rap CD is coproduced by Chris Stokes (known for his work with Shanice Wilson and Bell Biv DeVoe, among others), features members of IMx (formerly Immature), and lists Randy Jackson as one of its executive producers, you tend to assume that it's a rap CD with a lot of R&B/pop appeal. And, to be sure, Los Angeles rapper RaRa's debut album, *Holla at Me*, does make R&B/pop elements a high priority. Although RaRa's rapping dominates the tunes, urban contemporary singing is often used as an embellishment. But for all its slickness and R&B/pop appeal, *Holla at Me* is far from lightweight. RaRa has solid rhyming skills, and his rapid-fire performances on tracks like "Feel RaRa" and "Playaz & Hustlaz" make it clear that the Angelino has a lot of technique. The guests that RaRa features range from the members of IMx to female rapper Mila J, who was only 16 when this album came out in 2000 and demonstrates that she has a knack for quirky tongue-twisters. None of the material is fantastic, but all of it is catchy and competent and lets you know that RaRa has potential. —*Alex Henderson*

Ras Kass (John Austin)

f. Watts, CA
Hip-Hop
Rapper Ras Kass was born John Austin in Watts, CA; a voracious reader throughout his youth, he adopted his stage name in honor of the African king Ras Rass. After releasing a pair of independent singles, Ras Kass emerged as one of the most highly regarded new rappers in some time, winning particular acclaim for his skills as a lyricist (in the space of six months, he twice earned *Rap Pages* magazine's Rhyme of the Month award as well as *The Source*'s Hip Hop Quotable honor); his long-awaited debut LP, *Soul on Ice*, finally appeared on Priority Records in 1996. *Rasassination* followed two years later. —*Jason Ankeny*

● **Rasassination** / Sep. 22, 1998 / Priority ◆◆◆◆
The knock on Ras Kass has always been that he's a great MC who has never made a truly great album, thanks to substandard production from beatsmiths whose work fails to do justice to his dense, multilayered lyrics and cocky delivery. But while the beatwork on Kass' albums has seldom been as bad as critics have charged—check out the swaggering, ornate gangsta waltz that powers "Ghetto Fabulous"—lackluster production does seem to be the Achilles' heel keeping the Watts, CA, native from receiving the critical and commercial acclaim he deserves. A rapper's rapper, Kass has a flair for pitch-black humor, elaborate metaphors, and ambitious song concepts, as

illustrated by "Interview With a Vampire," a lyrical and intellectual *tour de force* that finds Kass rapping from the perspective of God, himself, and Lucifer. But Kass' God complex doesn't end there. A legend in his own mind whose arrogance belies his paltry album sales, Kass spits delectably misanthropic, comically conceited verses throughout *Rassassination*, claiming on "The End," for example, that "When it's all over I'm a retire to an Island in the Caymans/Enslaving Caucasians/Living off your mama's life savings." *Rassassination* is full of such smart, polysyllabic hip-hop quotables, but not even guest appearances from the high-powered likes of Xzibit, RZA, and Dr. Dre could place the album on the mainstream hip-hop radar. *Rassassination* isn't quite a great album—the production flounders at times and it's far too long and uneven—but its many transcendent moments suggest that a great Ras Kass album is not only highly possible, but pretty much inevitable. *—Nathan Rabin*

Van Gogh / Oct. 23, 2001 / Priority ◆◆◆
Like his previous releases, Ras Kass' third album, *Van Gogh*, showcases both his talents and his pretensions. He's surely one of the West Coast's most literate and thoughtful MCs, favoring creative wordplay and witty humor rather than the gangsta clichés that so often characterize West Coast rap music. However, though his talent is highly evident, so is Kass' pretension. Take, for example, this album's title, a vain allusion to popular painter Vincent Van Gogh, an undeniable master of his craft who—perhaps like Kass—wasn't appreciated during his years of activity. How much you appreciate this album depends, first of all, on whether you savor Kass' literate approach to rhyming and, second of all, on whether you can either accept or overlook his pretensions. *—Jason Birchmeier*

Rascalz

f. Vancouver, British Columbia, Canada
Group / Underground Rap
This quintet from Vancouver, Canada, prides itself on representing every aspect of hip-hop culture: MCing, DJing, graffiti, and breakdancing. The Vancouver quintet made up of MCs Red 1 and Misfit, DJ Kemo, who is also an accomplished graffiti artist, and breakers Zebroc and Dedos has achieved remarkable success by becoming Canada's best-selling hip-hop group ever. The group from Canada's West Coast have been instrumental in uniting Canada's nascent hip-hop scene. Their 1997 anthemic single "Northern Touch" was a collaboration with other Canadian artists such as Choclair, Checkmate, Kardinal Offishall, and Thrust. The single earned the Rascalz a Canadian Juno Award, but the group caused a stir in the Canadian music scene after refusing to accept their Juno as a protest for the lack of support for urban music by both the Junos and the Canadian music establishment. The group formed on the east side of Vancouver, where they competed as breakdancers. They released an independent effort in 1991. Their 1997 album *Cash Crop* became one of the few Canadian hip-hop albums to reach gold status. With the release of their 1999 album *Global Warming*, the group was poised for commercial success while still staying true to hip-hop's roots. *—Jon Azpiri*

● **Cash Crop** / 1997 / Figure IV ◆◆◆◆
The Vancouver quintet pride themselves on their dedication to all elements of hip-hop while mixing Caribbean and rock influences, and *Cash Crop* shows the group at its best. The highlight of the album is "Northern Touch," a pounding hip-hop track that has become the unofficial anthem of Canadian hip-hop. The track features Canadian rappers Choclair, Kardinal Offishall, Thrust, and Checkmate rapping over the same B.T. Express sample that fueled DMX's hit single "Get at Me Dog." Many of the other tracks reflect the group's Caribbean heritage, including the fluid reggae track "Dreaded Fist" and the heavy funk of "FitnRedi." On "Solitaire," the producer uses a haunting strings sample and pounding bass to offset the lyrical dexterity of MCs Red 1 and Misfit. Guided by the steady hand of the group's DJ Kemo, *Cash Crop* is an album that lets everyone know that Canadian hip-hop is a force to be reckoned with. *—Jon Azpiri*

Global Warning / 1999 / Figure IV ◆◆◆◆
Rascalz' second album is a compelling follow-up to their impressive album, *Cash Crop*. In an attempt to reach out to a wider audience, Rascalz employ a variety of guest stars that range from Canadian rappers K-Os, Muzion, and Choclair to American MCs KRS-One and Beatnuts. Throw in more cameos by dancehall legend Barrington Levy, Canadian rocker Esthero, and

professional wrestler Bret "The Hitman" Hart and you have a wildly diverse assembly of artists that only enhance the rhymes of Rascalz' MCs Red 1 and Misfit. The highlight is the album's second single, "Top of the World," where Rascalz' let their dancehall roots shine. The track features a guest appearance by dancehall legend Barrington Levy whose trademark riffing and yodeling lay over a tight guitar and string track. "Priceless" mixes a Tchaikovsky melody with a mellow sax loop and a haunting vocal by Esthero, and "As It Is" makes effective use of a harpsichord sample underlying a guest appearance by Choclair. "Population Control," a plea for greater community involvement, shows Rascalz' lyrical maturity. The album's biggest disappointment is the album's first single, "Sharpshooter," a misguided rap/rock hybrid that features pro wrestler Bret "The Hitman" Hart. More impressive is the guitar-based "Can't Relate," a slamming track featuring Psycho Les and Juju from Beatnuts. On the whole, the album highlights the band's impressive production by Kemo, who has an uncanny ability to mix genres, demonstrating that Rascalz are capable of producing a wide variety of music while still staying true to their roots. *—Jon Azpiri*

Rasco

b. San Mateo, CA
Underground Rap
San Mateo native Rasco worked as a member of the West Coast hip-hop group Various Blends and also has released solo works for Stones Throw. His deep voice and straight-ahead rap style came to the public's attention with his 1997 12", "The Unassisted," and has earned him several honors including number one on the Bay Area Hip Hop Coalition chart, number one on the independent hip-hop chart in *Hits* magazine, and number one on Sway & King Tech's nationally syndicated *Wake Up Show* for four weeks straight. His debut album *Time Waits for No Man* was released in 1998, and the follow-up EP *The Birth* arrived in 1999. His production team includes many underground rap artists, among them Kut Masta Kurt of the King Tech *Wake Up Show*, Paul Nice, Peanut Butter Wolf, and Evidence of the group Dialated Peoples. *—Zac Johnson*

Time Waits for No Man / Jul. 21, 1998 / Stones Throw ◆◆◆◆
Rasco wastes not a second of his debut solo LP, *Time Waits for No Man*. The Solefather's commanding rhyme style is unleashed with the precision of a drill sergeant. And although he represents the West Coast, there is a distinct East Coast vibe prevalent throughout. Rasco showcases his nasty mic prowess over floating piano riffs and booming drum loops, while even resurrecting the forgotten art of scratching. With the standout title cut, Rasco divides mic duties with fellow West Coast underground phenom Encore over an imposing track from up-and-coming producer Paul Nice. On "Bits & Pieces," Rasco crowns himself "the first-year rookie that be killing the pros." In addition, "Major League" is a West Coast cipher killer featuring guest vocals from Likwit crew family members Defari and Dilated Peoples. With "View to a Kill," Rasco flaunts his narrative abilities. "Hip Hop Essentials" is a state of emergency inquisition that addresses hip hop's studio gangsta mafioso mentality with brutal honesty. With no major label throwing huge promotion dollars anywhere near his vicinity, Rasco is forced to do things the old-fashioned way: word of mouth. His engaging debut runs rings around the consistently hyped, big-budget cats whose faces are plastered over every magazine imaginable. *—Matt Conaway*

The Birth / Jul. 12, 1999 / Copasetik ◆◆◆
After delivering one of 1998's strongest underground releases, Rasco returns with a teasing six-track EP—*The Birth* is not only the name of Rasco's latest brainchild but also the birth of his creative independence and the first release of his newly founded label. Unleashing his rhymes with the precision of a drill-sergeant commando, "Back on the Scene" and "Return of the MC" reestablish Rasco's insatiable quest to rid the planet of spineless MCs. But this EP's most fruitful moments come courtesy of the Cali Agents (Rasco and Planet Asia). Asia's complicated rhyme schemes and Rasco's braggadocio lyrics are a combustible and well-rounded combination. Rasco is, in every sense of the word, a throwback—a no-frills, all-skills battle rhymer—and his personality is compelling enough to keep his limited topic matter from wearing thin. While his methodical formula is unspectacular, it is sufficient enough to keep listeners entertained. *—Matt Conaway*

20,000 Leagues Under the Street / Oct. 17, 2000 / Pockets Linted ◆◆◆
Rasco caught some attention from people who knew what was going on in underground hip-hop in 1998, and has continued to represent the Bay Area

since. This is a compilation with underground heroes such as Phil da Agony, the Grouch, Saafir, Planet Asia, Zion 1, Cali Agents, and more. The selection of guest appearances is a great blend of styles and influences, and they work well together from track to track throughout the album. Diverse production is done mainly by Rasco himself with a bit of help on a few tracks from Grouch and DJ Cue (from *Cue's Hip Hop Shop* fame). Fans of Bay Area rap will appreciate and most likely already own this album. *—Brad Mills*

● **Hostile Environment** / Aug. 14, 2001 / Copasetik ✦✦✦✦✦
No one will ever accuse Rasco of being humble. The Bay Area rapper has built a career on braggadocio. Several of his early underground releases are almost entirely about extolling his own virtues while putting down every punk MC that gets in his way. With *Hostile Environment*, however, Rasco seems to have broadened his scope, finding a way to talk about everything from the perils of street life ("Gunz Still Hot Remix") to drinking and driving ("Message From the Bottle") to the responsibilities of fatherhood ("Sunshine [Ayanna]"). Along with Rasco's no-nonsense lyrical flow, much of the album's success should be credited to the producers, such as Khalil and J. Rawls, who help create a swirling collage of pianos and strings. With thoughtful lyrics and innovative beats, Rasco finally has something to brag about. *—Jon Azpiri*

Rasheeda

Dirty South
Motown hip-hop artist Rasheeda released her debut album *Dirty South* in October 2000. *Dirty South* features collaborations with Kurupt, Kool Ace, and chart-topping rapper Nelly. *—MacKenzie Wilson*

Dirty South / Oct. 10, 2000 / Uptown/Universal ✦✦
More Southern-fried hip-hop from another trash-talkin' female MC. Rasheeda has neither the chops nor skill to even approach Missy or Lil' Kim territory, and her album crew of producers and guest rappers rarely assist her the way they should (everyone here seems to be concerned only with promoting themselves). Unless this is your type of thing, there's no need to invest any time here. *—Michael Gallucci*

Raw Fusion

Group / West Coast Rap
Raw Fusion was a low-key Digital Underground side project driven by that group's Money-B. 1991's *Live From the Styleetron*, the group's first album, featured cameos from 2Pac, Shock-G, and Saafir, and it broke away from Digital Underground's proclivity for Parliament/Funkadelic-derived goofiness with production values that were closer to the Jungle Brothers/A Tribe Called Quest end of the spectrum, with liberal dashes of reggae shadings (dub, dancehall, roots). Featuring cuts like "Don't Test" and the jhericurl send-up "Ah Nah Go Drip," the album stayed in the underground but proved to be a strong full-length. Three years passed before the follow-up, *Hoochiefied Funk*. The project presumably ended after that, with Money-B delivering a various-artists comp and a solo album before the end of the '90s. *—Andy Kellman*

● **Live From the Styleetron** / Nov. 12, 1991 / Hollywood ✦✦✦✦
When Money-B came out with his side project Raw Fusion, it was clear that the Digital Underground member wasn't trying to duplicate Underground's sound. Parts of *Live From Styleetron* are as quirky and eccentric as Underground, but while Underground was heavily influenced by the 1970s funk grooves of George Clinton and Parliament/Funkadelic, Fusion had more in common with jazzy alternative rappers like A Tribe Called Quest, De La Soul, and the Jungle Brothers. The production is interesting, and Raw Fusion keeps things unpredictable by sampling everything from jazz and funk to reggae. Humor is an important element of cuts like "Traffic Jam," "Nappy Headed Ninja," and "Ah Nah Go Drip," which pokes fun at the jheri-curl hairstyle that was popular in the 1980s. But the CD takes a more serious turn with "Wild Francis," the tale of an inner-city woman who grows up to be a Marxist revolutionary and is killed in a confrontation with the police. Some of Money's associates from the Underground are on board, including Shock-G and Humpty Hump, but again, no one's going to mistake *Styleetron* for an Underground album. With *Styleetron*, Money saw to it that Raw Fusion was a strong rap act in its own right. *—Alex Henderson*

Hoochiefied Funk / Apr. 26, 1994 / Hollywood ✦✦
Digital Underground's Money-B and DJ Fuze surprisingly returned with their second album as Raw Fusion in 1994. Released three years after their good

if patchy debut, *Hoochiefied Funk* doesn't show that much growth has occurred with the duo. "Freaky Note" is an uncharacteristically lewd track by Money-B's standards; his rhymes fail to touch any buttons, and the production is an uninvolving garden-variety slinky beat that seems to last twice as long as it actually does. It's only three songs in, and yet, by the time it's over, it feels as if you're wading through the latter half of the album's second side. Nothing is as fun as the average Digital Underground song, and the duo unfortunately opted to shed most of the reggae splashes that helped color *Live from the Styleetron*. If anything, this album proves that Money-B's light, boyish rasp is best suited for a supporting role. *—Andy Kellman*

J. Rawls

Hip-Hop
Known throughout the world of independent rap for his production skills, J. Rawls has built tracks for Mos Def and Talib Kweli and El da Sensei plus his day job, Lone Catalysts, with J. Sands. *The Essence of J. Rawls*, his first solo album, featured guests J-Live, dose one, and Asheru, among many others. *—John Bush*

● **The Essence of J. Rawls** / May 8, 2001 / Landspeed ✦✦✦✦
While J. Rawls may be better known for his contributions to Mos Def and Talib Kweli's Black Star project, he is also the beatmaking half of the underground Cincinnati duo Lone Catalysts (which also includes lyricist J. Sands).

With his jazzy mood music in tow, J. Rawls stepped out with his first solo project, *The Essence of J. Rawls*. This compilation is an underground gathering of like souls, which includes J-Live's storytelling expertise on "Great Live Caper," the African terminology of Unspoken Heard's Asheru on "Nommo," J. Sands and Grap Luva's "Check the Clock," and Rawls' whimsical solo cut "They Can't See Me." While Rawls' laid-back compositions (with their piano samples and minimalist guitar riffs) are both provocative and passionate, pretentious hip-hop fans seem likely to overlook his keen musical sensibility, largely because it is neither abrasive nor mind altering. *—Matt Conaway*

Ray J

b. Jan. 17, 1981, McComb, MS
Contemporary R&B, Pop-Rap, Hip-Hop
Arriving on the heels of big sister/R&B star Brandy, rapper Ray J parlayed his success on television into a music career at the age of 14. Born in McComb, MS, Ray J's family moved to Carson, CA, when he was still a toddler, landing him in the center of the entertainment industry. He started auditioning for commercials at age eight, scoring several gigs until he caught the eye of comedian Sinbad, who was casting children for his upcoming TV show. Ray J got the role playing Sinbad's foster son until the show was canceled in 1993. From there, he began acting in movies, appearing in the films *Steel* and *Mars Attacks!* in minor roles. At the same time, he was also itching to try his hand at the music industry, inspired by Brandy's early successes. He signed with Elektra in 1995, recording *Everything You Want* the following year with a set of superstar songwriters and producers behind him. In 1997 he performed in a television special with his sister, but despite the mainstream attention, he was dropped by Elektra soon after.

His easygoing image and boyish looks appealed to the producers of Brandy's television show, *Moesha*, scoring him a role on the popular UPN series starting in 1999. He also started producing, putting together the music for several commercials and a few of the demos for his second record. Still, when he stepped back into the studio he called on the Neptunes, Rodney Jerkins, Brycyn "Juvie" Evans, and several other hitmaking producers to help him compile *This Ain't a Game*, a pop-oriented record that featured more of his singing than his debut. The album dropped in 2001, but despite a strong promotional push from new label Atlantic Records, it wasn't the breakthrough success it seemed designed to be. *—Bradley Torreano*

● **This Ain't a Game** / Jun. 19, 2001 / Atlantic ✦✦
Ray J may be the brother of R&B singer Brandy, but his music has little relation to her squeaky-clean brand of R&B. That's not necessarily a good thing, as *This Ain't a Game* is full of macho posturing that is more than a little tedious. The best of the tracks on the album feature production from the Neptunes. "Formal Invite" offers suave Spanish guitars and Ray J's typical sexual braggadocio. The lead single, "Wait a Minute," features a half-hearted cameo by Lil' Kim where she utters the line, "Hey, wait a minute. Ain't that Brandy's

brother?" Since *This Ain't a Game* has so little to offer, that line is what listeners will remember most about Ray J. —*Jon Azpiri*

Ray Luv

b. San Francisco, CA
Vocals / Hip-Hop, Gangsta Rap, Hardcore Rap
Bay Area rapper Ray Luv debuted in 1992 with the album *Who Can Be Trusted?* Aside from a handful of compilation tracks and cameo appearances, he was silent before resurfacing on Atlantic in 1995 with *Forever Hustlin'*; *Coup d'Etat* followed four years later. —*Jason Ankeny*

Who Can Be Trusted? / 1992 / Strictly Business ✦✦✦

● **Forever Hustlin'** / Aug. 1, 1995 / Atlantic ✦✦✦
In the tradition of classic Bay Area rap, following the lineage of artists such as the Mack, Mac Dre, and Mac Mall, Ray Luv delivers funked-out "tales of triple beams and ice cream." With a lyrical style similar to that of 2Pac (during the late '80s the two MCs were in a group together called Strictly Dope), Ray Luv chronicles his participation in the game with a flair that's much respected throughout Northern Cali and beyond. With Khayree, the genius behind Mac Mall's *Illegal Business*, providing his trademarked production and beat changes, *Forever Hustlin'* practically serves as a blueprint for Bay Area playa rap. In 1995 the album indeed battled with the Luniz' *Operation Stackola* for regional supremacy. Sporting heavy, heavy bass and Dr. Dre-influenced synths, songs such as "The Factor" and "Keep Ya Mask On" present mobbin' music at its finest. Frenzied collaborations with Ant D.O.G. and Young Grinn on "Definition of Ah Hustla'" and "What U in It 4" up the ante even further, yet Ray Luv also shows his smoother side on tracks including "I'd Rather Be a Pimp" and "We Do This Everyday." Very well rounded for a gangsta rap album, *Forever Hustlin'* has earned underground classic status for good reason. —*Robert Gabriel*

Coup d'Etat / Jun. 8, 1999 / Big Eddie ✦✦✦

RBL Posse

f. San Francisco, CA
Group / Gangsta Rap, Hardcore Rap, West Coast Rap, Hip-Hop
A Bay Area rap duo formed at the beginning of the 1990s, RBL Posse (short for Ruthless By Law) was originally founded by Black C and Mr. Cee. The pair began producing tracks at Black C's studio and emerged in 1991 with the underground hit "Don't Give Me No Bammer." Thanks solely to their own independent distribution through In-A-Minute Records, RBL sold almost half a million copies of their first two albums, *A Lesson to Be Learned* and *Ruthless By Law*. Following the 1995 side project *Solo Creep*, the duo was ready to hit the big time with a major-label contract through Atlantic; tragedy struck, however, when Mr. Cee was murdered in a street killing. Black C soldiered on, recruiting producers Mike Mosely, Rick Rock, and Barr 9 plus MC Eiht for the 1997 LP *An Eye for an Eye*. *H2O, Vol. 1* followed in 1999, and *Hostile Takeover* appeared two years later. —*John Bush*

● **Ruthless By Law** / Oct. 25, 1994 / In-A-Minute ✦✦✦✦
With fist-pumping beats, the Posse (RBL stands for Ruthless By Law) raps about the gangsta life with more of a kidding pose ("Niggas on the Jock," "Pass the ZigZags") than the straitlaced genre usually allows. "Bounce to This" and "FunkDaFied" are solid G-funk jams, and though the album isn't quite a revolution in sound, it does make for a lot of fun. —*John Bush*

Solo Creep / Oct. 30, 1995 / Right Way ✦✦✦

An Eye for an Eye / Sep. 30, 1997 / Big Beat ✦✦✦

Bootlegs & Bay Shit: The Resume / Sep. 26, 2000 / Right Way ✦✦
The broad scope of *Bootlegs & Bay Shit* assembles an excellent sample of RBL Posse's varied output from the 1990s, going as far back as their debut album, 1992's *A Lesson to Be Learned*. The fact that this double-disc assembles mostly obscure tracks from many random compilations makes it a perfect addition to the Bay Area group's small canon of albums; unfortunately, there aren't that many remarkable moments here. Most of these tracks were unreleased or left to compilations for a reason: they aren't the group's best work. Furthermore, anyone new to the group's music will find this album a perfect sampler but undoubtedly far from the best representation of the group's potential. The few tracks culled from the group's albums, such as the classic "G's By the 1,2,3's" from the group's debut album, provide perspective, illustrating why this group developed such a cult following; however, most of

the songs here aren't nearly as good. This album will be best appreciated by existing fans familiar with the group's albums. Newcomers should start elsewhere; this album is just far too shoddy to provide a positive perspective on this underrated gangsta group. —*Jason Birchmeier*

RBX

Gangsta Rap, Hardcore Rap, West Coast Rap
A cousin of Snoop Doggy Dogg, RBX ("Reality Born Unknown") got his start as a member of Dr. Dre's Death Row Records stable, contributing to both Dre's *The Chronic* and Snoop Doggy Dogg's *Doggy Style*. An in-house controversy ensued when the release of RBX's solo project, *The RBX Files*, was delayed indefinitely by Dre. RBX claimed that it was simple unfairness on Dre's part, also charging that he had not been paid for his work on the aforementioned albums, and appealed to Death Row CEO Suge Knight to intervene. His album was eventually released in 1995, and the first single, "A.W.O.L.," ripped both Dre and Snoop for RBX's troubles. However, most of his subject matter concentrates on positive messages reflecting his Islamic faith. By 1996, RBX had reconciled with Dre and appeared on his *The Aftermath* album; still, nothing much was heard from RBX for a time, save for his contribution to the *Fakin' the Funk* soundtrack. Finally, in 1999, RBX resurfaced with a new album titled *No Mercy No Remorse*. —*Steve Huey*

● **The RBX Files** / Sep. 26, 1995 / Premeditated ✦✦✦
Many of the hip-hoppers who heard RBX's cameos on Dr. Dre's *The Chronic* and Snoop Dogg's *Doggy Style* recognized the L.A. rapper's potential and asked, "When will this guy have an album of his own out?" But regrettably, RBX's first solo album, *The RBX Files*, ended up being delayed a few years because of the MC's problems with Dre and Snoop, both of whom he vehemently attacks on the single "A.W.O.L." Accusing Dre and Death Row Records of exploiting Warren G and others, RBX makes no attempt to conceal the anger he felt for the influential producer/rapper at the time. But RBX's attacks on Dre and Snoop aren't the main things that make *The RBX Files* noteworthy—the thing that brings the CD to life is RBX's distinctive rapping style. With influences ranging from West Coast gangsta rap and East Coast Afro-centric rap (especially Professor X and the X-Clan) to Jamaican dancehall, RBX has an impressive technique—and that technique serves him well on this interesting, if uneven, debut. —*Alex Henderson*

No Mercy, No Remorse/The X-Factor / Jun. 29, 1999 / Street Solid ✦✦✦
Four years after his debut album, *The RBX Files*, RBX resurfaced on Street Solid with his sophomore effort, *No Mercy, No Remorse/The X-Factor*. While a four-year wait between albums wouldn't be as big of a deal in jazz, blues, pop, or country, it's an eternity in hip-hop—a genre in which trends and tastes can change radically in the course of a few years. And when you consider that the release of *The RBX Files* was delayed a few years because of RBX's problems with Dr. Dre in the early 1990s, you're really talking *more* than a four-year gap between albums. But delays and all, RBX's rapping style still sounds quite fresh on this 1999 CD. Quirky and hardcore at the same time, RBX is a very recognizable rapper—he came out of the Dr. Dre/Snoop Dogg school of Los Angeles gangsta rap, but RBX reminds listeners that he's very much his own man on tunes like "Ambush & Torture," "Oh, No," and "Make My Day," which features Treach of Naughty By Nature. Taken as a whole, the album doesn't make a single, cohesive statement—essentially, it serves as a vehicle for RBX's interesting rhyming technique. With Solid Entertainment founder Jay Warsinske serving as executive producer, *No Mercy, No Remorse/The X-Factor* is a respectable, long overdue follow-up from an MC who should have recorded a lot more often in the 1990s. —*Alex Henderson*

Real Live

Group / Hip-Hop, East Coast Rap
Preferring the roles of hip-hop insiders rather than recording artists, DJ/producer K-Def and vocalist Larry O kept a low profile in the game for a number of years. K-Def lent production work to artists such as Da Youngstas while Larry O honed his microphone skills at open mics and freestyle competitions throughout New York and New Jersey. In 1996, having paid their dues and made a name for themselves in the business, the duo decided to release an album aptly titled, *The Turnaround: A Long Awaited Drama* under the moniker Real Live. The duo's complementary styles were applauded by fans and critics alike, but without much ballyhoo the duo faded into the fog soon after their album ran its course. —*Michael Di Bella*

- **The Turnaround: A Long Awaited Drama** / Oct. 1, 1996 / Big Beat ◆◆◆
Illuminated by K-Def's slick production skills and with a little help from friend and big-time superproducer Marley Marl, *Turnaround: A Long Awaited Drama* had a fresh sound and became an underground success. The album, recorded at Marley Marl's legendary House of Hits studio, was a showcase for amplified crime rhyme. The hit single "Real Live S**t" benefited from a prodigious timpani drum track laid down by Marl, and the album also featured an all-star remix of the track with appearances from Ghostface Killah and Cappadonna from the Wu-Tang family. K-Def's production inflated the album with thick, heavy drum kicks and subtle strings, while Larry O's raw and unpretentious lyrics revolved around drug trafficking and its many perils. —*Michael Di Bella*

The Real Roxanne (Adelaida Martinez)

Golden Age, Old School Rap, Hip-Hop
Following the massive success of U.T.F.O.'s "Roxanne, Roxanne" single in late 1984 and early 1985, over 100 answer records appeared, and several female rappers adopted the Roxanne alias; the Real Roxanne (born Adelaida Martinez) was perhaps the most talented of the bunch and really only had to contend with Roxanne Shanté for the title. It took her until 1988 to release an album, by which time the Roxanne fad had run its course; still, the self-titled release packed a wallop thanks to producers Jam Master Jay, Howie Tee, and Full Force, plus the Real Roxanne's own forceful, sassy personality. She attempted a comeback in 1992 with *Go Down (But Don't Bite It)* without much success. —*Steve Huey*

- **The Real Roxanne** / 1988 / Select ◆◆◆◆
With the aid of Jam Master Jay, Howie Tee, and Full Force, this Puerto Rican whipped up a stunning debut that highlighted her inimitable skills as a rapper and lyricist, as well as her band's way with the funk. Highlights include "Bang Zoom," "Respect," and "Roxanne's on a Roll." —*John Floyd*

Go Down (But Don't Bite It) / 1992 / Select ◆◆◆

Frank Real

Hardcore Rap, Southern Rap
Atlanta is home to some of the biggest names in Southern hip-hop, most notably Goodie Mob and OutKast. Both have been around since the mid-'90s and have pretty much owned the Atlanta scene. Witchdoctor released *A.S.W.A.T. Healin' Ritual* in 1997, Cool Breeze came with *East Point's Greatest Hits* in 1999, while 2000 saw Frank Real's self-titled debut LP go on sale. Real is also from East Point, and although not as commercially popular as his peers, he trusts his music will speak for itself. —*Brad Mills*

- **Frank Real** / Nov. 14, 2000 / Dee Money ◆◆◆◆
This is an impressive debut from a relatively unknown artist from Atlanta, GA. The opening song, "My Afterlife," opens with a very young girl asking her father to "come back and play with us daddy," and is a chilling introspective where Frank Real carries on a conversation with God about the life he just lost. On the track he delves into life's devils, killing a priest, and burning a church along the way. The song works well and sets the mood for both a brutal and brutally honest album mainly about Frank, his thoughts, and his life. As musically appealing as it is intelligent and thought provoking, there are welcome appearances from Cee-Lo of Goodie Mob, Bun B of UGK, Yung Wun of Rough Riders, Boo the Boss Playa, Wall St, and Spade. Overall, this is still a hardcore gangsta rap album, and easily one of the better Southern rap records of 2000. —*Brad Mills*

Rebel MC (Michael West)

b. 1965, London, England
Vocals, Producer / Club/Dance, Jungle/Drum 'N Bass
The '80s popster turned proto-jungle revolutionary was born Michael West in 1965 in London. He formed Double Trouble in the early '80s with Michael Menson and Leigh Guest, releasing the ska-pop hit "Street Tuff." Rebel MC later gained fame in England as a pop-rapper, but by 1991 he had released *Black Meaning Good*, an album that presaged jungle with hardcore techno married to dub bass lines and raggae toasters such as Barrington Levy and P.P. Arnold. His 1992 singles "Rich Ah Getting Richer" and "Humanity" also showed the new direction. "Code Red"—released as Conquering Lion— became an outright jungle smash in 1994, bringing the jungle movement to the British masses. —*John Bush*

- **Rebel Music** / 1990 / Desire ◆◆◆
Before Michael West began recording on his own as Rebel MC, he was half of the Cockney rap duo Double Trouble; afterward, he went on to become a prime mover in the development of London's jungle movement of the early to mid-'90s. As Rebel MC, he made two not terribly distinguished albums of music that seemed to lack definition; this was the first of them. Where some artists intentionally borrow from multiple dance music genres and make a virtue of eclecticism, on *Rebel Music* Rebel MC just sounds confused, unable to decide whether he wants to stick with house music, reggae, or hip-hop. He tries to resolve the confusion in part by recycling previously successful songs, such as Double Trouble's hit "Street Tuff" (offered here in a remixed version), and in part by recycling tunes from within the album itself ("Better World" is presented in no fewer than three different mixes). Most of the material is rhythmically and melodically pedestrian, though the scintillating "Cockney Rhythm" and a nice funky reggae remix of "Better World" both stand out. This one's worth keeping an eye out for in the bargain bins, but not necessarily something you should make a concerted effort to acquire. —*Rick Anderson*

Redhead Kingpin and the F.B.I.

Group / Hip-Hop, Pop-Rap
This carrot-topped b-boy scored numerous hits with his teen-geared raps, which were sometimes vulgar and sometimes amusing. "Pump It Hottee" was his finest moment, appearing on his 1989 debut for Virgin, *A Shade of Red*. Two years later, *The Album With No Name* was released on Virgin, but he gained his last hit in 1992. —*John Floyd*

- **A Shade of Red** / Jul. 24, 1989 / Virgin ◆◆◆
Shade of Red, the album debut for Redhead Kingpin and the F.B.I., was a set of entertaining rap tracks that are icy and confrontational at times. The lead singles "Pump It Hottee," "Do the Right Thing," and "We Rock the Mic Right" were hits on the R&B charts as well as the dance side. —*Ron Wynn*

The Album With No Name / Apr. 2, 1991 / Virgin ◆◆◆

Redman (Reggie Noble)

b. Newark, NJ
Vocals, Producer / Hip-Hop, East Coast Rap, Hardcore Rap
New Jersey rapper Redman made his initial impact with *Whut? Thee Album* in 1992. He blended reggae and funk influences with topical commentary and displayed a terse though fluid rap style that was sometimes satirical, sometimes tough, and sometimes silly. Redman returned in 1994 with his second album, *Dare Iz a Darkside*, which was a harder album than his debut. *Muddy Waters*, Redman's third album, followed in 1996; he returned two years later with *Doc's Da Name 2000*. —*Ron Wynn*

- **Whut? Thee Album** / Sep. 22, 1992 / Def Jam ◆◆◆◆◆
Whut? Thee Album is a terrific debut that established Redman as one of the top MCs on the East Coast. His aggressive delivery is more than hardcore enough for the streets, but *Whut?* is first and foremost a party record. Redman's subject matter centers around his love of funk and his equal love of pot, with some sex and violence thrown in for good measure. He's able to carry it all off with a singular sense of style, thanks to a wild sense of humor that results in some outlandish boasts, surreal threats, and hilarious left-field jokes. In "Blow Your Mind," for example, he announces, "Watch me freak it in Korean!," stumbles through part of a verse, and mutters, "Ah, forget it"; another great moment is "Redman Meets Reggie Noble," a brief duet between himself and his own alterego in the great Slick Rick tradition. Other offbeat highlights include the genuinely useful instructional track "How to Roll a Blunt" and the hilarious sexcapade story song "A Day With Sooperman Lover." Credit for the album's infectious vibe also has to go to producer Erick Sermon, who fills *Whut?* with deep, loose-limbed beats cribbed from P-Funk and Zapp. Slamming party jams like "Time 4 Sum Aksion," "Rated R," and "Watch Yo Nuggets" are the real meat and potatoes of the record, and Redman's driving, forceful rhyme style makes them all the more invigorating. Still the strongest, most consistent outing in his catalog, *Whut? Thee Album* clearly heralds the arrival of a major talent. —*Steve Huey*

Dare Iz a Darkside / Nov. 22, 1994 / Def Jam ◆◆◆
Redman may have become a household name among the rap community by the end of the '90s, but there was a time when he garnered little more than

a cult following. Why? Well, *Dare Iz a Darkside* illustrates this better than any of his other '90s albums—nowhere else has Redman ever been this odd, to be quite frank. It's fairly evident here that he'd been listening to his George Clinton records and that he wasn't fronting when he alluded to "A Million and 1 Buddah Spots" that he'd visited. In fact, this album often divides his fans. Many admire it for its eccentricities, while others deride it for being quite simply too inaccessible. It's almost as if Redman is trying to puzzle listeners on *Dare Iz a Darkside* with his continually morphing persona. In fact, there's actually little questioning his motives—it's a matter of fact that Redman's trying to be as crazy as he can without alienating *too* many of those who first knew him for his affiliation with EPMD. And while that affiliation does aid this album, since Erick Sermon plays a large role in production, it's not quite enough. If this album has one unforgivable flaw besides the debatable quirks in Redman's persona, it's the production. Sermon isn't up to his usual standards here, unfortunately, and the album could really use some of his trademark funk. But the reason most fans either feel devotion or disdain for this album isn't the beats, but rather Redman's antics. If you appreciate his wacky sense of insane humor, this album is a gold mine. If you're more into his latter-day Method Man-style rhymes, then this album probably isn't one you want to bother with. After all, though Redman became a household name by the end of the '90s, it surely wasn't because of albums like this. —*Jason Birchmeier*

Muddy Waters / Dec. 10, 1996 / Def Jam ✦✦✦✦
Despite a heavy dose of Redman's eccentric humor, *Dare Iz a Darkside* often threatened to disappear in a haze of blunt smoke, so for his third album, he and producer Erick Sermon backed off the muddled sonics of *Darkside* and returned to the hard funk of his debut set. There isn't as blatant a P-Funk/Zapp influence on *Muddy Waters*; the beats are more indebted to the New York hardcore movement, and the tracks themselves are sparer and more bass driven. Lyrically, Redman is as strong as ever, and if his subject matter hasn't changed all that much, he's still coming up with clever metaphors and loose, elastic rhyme flows. He projects more energy than Method Man (who appears on "Do What Ya Feel"), but isn't quite at the madman level of Busta Rhymes. The numerous skits tend to drag the album's momentum down a little, but overall, *Muddy Waters* solidifies Redman's growing reputation as one of the most consistent rappers of the '90s—even when the music is unspectacular, he manages to deliver the goods on the microphone. —*Steve Huey*

Doc's Da Name 2000 / Nov. 24, 1998 / Def Jam ✦✦✦✦
The sound Redman achieves on this album is characteristic of his previous albums. With production credits going mostly to Erick Sermon, the bass-intensive and melodic beats on *Doc's Da Name 2000* allow Redman to deliver the raw Newark, NJ, flow for which he's known and liked. Redman himself produced a few of the songs on this album, including "Jersey Yo!" A mildly funny skit that describes the attitude of a certain Little Bricks resident precedes this selection. There are actually five skits on the album, which, like most skits on an often-played album, become very unfunny after a few repetitions. On "Jersey Yo!," Redman uses a slow and funky guitar sound over tight drums and a fluid bass line. Redman is also responsible for the production of "Da Goodness," a song that features Busta Rhymes. The instrumentation in this song has a futuristic, almost minimal, sound that mimics a lot of the music Busta Rhymes frequently flows over. Not stopping there, Redman spits lyrics in "Da Goodness" with what could be identified as Busta's lyrical style—and he does it well. The result is an entertaining song that exemplifies Redman's skill as a talented lyricist and producer. "Beet Drop," another cut produced by Redman, is a brief but funny cover of the Beastie Boys' "It's the New Style." —*Qa'id Jacobs*

Malpractice / May 22, 2001 / Def Jam ✦✦✦
During the three-year gap separating Redman's previous album, *Doc's Da Name 2000* (1998), from *Malpractice*, the crazed New Jersey rapper became a bona fide superstar thanks to his collaboration with the ubiquitous and ridiculously recognized Method Man. It now seems that the same sort of excessively brash attitude that somewhat burdens Method Man's superstar ego has become a staple of Redman's as well. That sort of lazy overconfidence often leads to effortless redundancy—this is a problem that creeps into *Malpractice*. After nearly a decade, Redman's countless skits and his ever-wacky but still-the-same antics just don't seem as fresh and amusing as they once were. Furthermore, with his newfound Method Man-like arrogance, his

old tricks seem even tougher to stomach. It'd be different if Redman took a Missy Elliott-like approach to *Malpractice* and made an effort to continually flip styles and keep things fresh with each album. That's not the case, though. Rather, he turns in a repeat performance of his last few solo albums. Erick Sermon again crafts a number of the beats, and Redman returns to many of the same lyrical motifs that fueled his past work. So, in a sense, you can commend Redman for his consistency; after all, his rhymes are always a grin and he even produces a good chunk of *Malpractice*. Unfortunately, if you've heard his previous albums, this is going to feel very familiar. It's guests like George Clinton and the aforementioned Missy Elliott who keep things fresh, and there's no shortage of guests here, but even they can't salvage the record's déjà vu feeling. It's not easy criticizing *Malpractice*, since it is a relatively strong album with some nice moments such as the lead single, "Let's Get Dirty." But being Redman's fifth solo album, you expect a little more growth; instead you get what feels like a repeat performance. —*Jason Birchmeier*

Reflection Eternal

Group / Hip-Hop, Alternative Rap, East Coast Rap
Lyrical prodigy Talib Kweli and extraordinary underground hip-hop producer DJ Hi-Tek constitute Reflection Eternal. Kweli—whose name literally means "seeker of truth"—also owns a small bookstore in Brooklyn and is more than just an average MC, being also a key to the Mos Def collaborational LP *Black Star*. He first met Hi-Tek in 1994 while visiting Cincinnati, and appeared on a track from Hi-Tek's group Mood After Reflection Eternal's inception in 1997, the pair were signed to indie powerhouse Rawkus Records, where they released their first single "Fortified Live" b/w the indie sensation "2000 Seasons." The best way to describe Talib Kweli is as an erudite wordsmith prodigy; he incorporates political issues, complex metaphors, vivid imagery, a braggadocio rhyme style, and an overall charisma into his precise lyrical presentation. Although Reflection Eternal is an "underground" hip-hop group in principal, the relevance of Kweli's lyrics and the resonance of Hi-Tek's production propelled them to the forefront of quality hip-hop. Reflection Eternal was also featured on Mos Def's album *Black on Both Sides*, as well as the anti-establishment opus album entitled *The Unbound Project*. The duo's self-titled debut LP was actually filed under the name of Talib Kweli & DJ Hi-Tek. —*Nick Pfeiffer*

Rehab

Group / Hardcore Rap, Southern Rap
The southern hip-hop duo called Rehab is literally a product of their namesake. Danny Boone and Brooks, both recovering alcoholics and drug addicts, met at a local rehab facility and connected over their love of music. Songwriting is also their cathartic way of dealing with personal criticism and social conformists. Rehab released their debut *Southern Discomfort* on Epic in fall 2000. —*MacKenzie Wilson*

● **Southern Discomfort** / Oct. 24, 2000 / Epic ✦✦✦✦✦
From Ice-T and Schoolly D to Eminem, hip-hop has been full of dark, twisted humor. And there is no shortage of it on *Southern Discomfort*—this first Epic release by the Atlanta-based hip-hop duo Rehab is an impressive effort full of dark-humored references to drug and alcohol abuse. Anyone who finds Eminem's Slim Shady character entertaining will find in-your-face items like "My Addiction" (based on Run-D.M.C.'s "My Adidas") and "Crazy People" equally entertaining. But here's the tragic part: Danny Boone and Brooks—the white rappers who constitute Rehab—have firsthand knowledge of the type of things they rap about. The MCs really *did* meet in rehab, and the dark humor that is a big part of *Southern Discomfort* is their way of confronting their own history of drug addiction and alcohol abuse. So even though some of Rehab's lyrics are hilarious (if you appreciate warped humor), they are no doubt cathartic for Boone and Brooks. Much of the time, this CD is a perfect example of laughing to keep from crying, which isn't unusual for hip-hop—like the blues and country, hip-hop has a history of using humor to cope with things that are tragic. Rehab's lyrics have a way of jumping out at the listener, and the same can be said about the tracks the duo raps to. Musically, *Southern Discomfort* is fairly diverse; depending on their mood, Boone and Brooks will rap to anything from funk and soul to hard rock and pop/rock. Both lyrically and musically, *Southern Discomfort* is among 2000's most memorable hip-hop releases. —*Alex Henderson*

The Representativz

f. 1994, Brooklyn, NY
Group / Hip-Hop
After spending a majority of their life growing up in Brooklyn, NY, MCs Lidu Rock and Supreme had a lot to get off of their chests upon forming the Representativz in 1994. With the angst of urban blight remaining as the lyrical topic, the duo had the chance to record with Heltah Skeltah, O.G.C., and on the compilation *For the People*, all which appeared on Duck Down Records. *Angels of Death* followed in 1999. —*Mike DaRonco*

● **Angels of Death** / Oct. 19, 1999 / Duck Down ✦✦✦
After a rash of disappointing releases (excluding *O.G.C.*) it is now time for the BCC's elder statesman to momentarily step aside and let some new blood attempt to plug their ever-widening holes. Debuts have always been Duck-Down's strong point, and it is the Brownsville duo of Supreme and Lidu Rock (Rock of Heltah Skeltah's little brother) who are next in line to carry on that tradition. The Reps take a step in the right direction production wise, moving away from the camp's decomposing griminess for a more subtle organic sound (isolated guitar riffs, mandolins, streaming pianos). While the Reps' debut contains no immediate concept, the duo is much more engaging when they're broadening their anticipated topic matter, as on "The Ritch" (Tek), "Tell Me," and "Stand or Fall." —*Matt Conaway*

Req

Producer / Trip-Hop, Ambient Breakbeat, Electronica
Brighton graffiti artist/producer Req in some respects embodies the clichés of British underground club music: no formal musical training whatsoever; a youth spent tagging, DJing, and breakdancing in the wake of the first wave of hip-hop culture to hit the U.K.; a knack for pushing received artistic sensibilities to their breaking point and coming up with exciting new directions in the offing. Req's music, however, is hardly clichéd, combining a warped, abstract approach to sampled breaks with a knack for extracting a haunting moodiness out of even the most minimal of electronic and sampledelic soundscapes.

One of the U.K.'s most respected graffiti artists, Req began writing in 1984, after the Beat Street tour hyped his senses to the basic tenets of hip-hop. Although he only began making music by the time he was into his late twenties, Req's years spent bedroom DJing refined his instinct for effective composition, a skill that tends to compensate for his music's somewhat limited sonic palette. Req's debut for esoteric beathead imprint Skint (home also to Fatboy Slim and Bentley Rhythm Ace) was his *Garden* EP, four tracks of breathy down-tempo hip-hop similar to the breakbeat abstractions of DJ Krush and DJ Cam. With stated influences spanning from early Detroit techno and old school hip-hop to the Black Dog, Req's tracks are more stylistically rooted in the Mo'Wax/Cup of Tea camp, stripping hip-hop of its extraneous elements and focusing on the bass, the beats, and the atmosphere around them. *Req: One*, his debut Skint full-length (with a wraparound cover displaying a mural of his artwork), was released in 1997, and was praised highly by everyone from Coldcut to *The Wire*. —*Sean Cooper*

Req: One / Mar. 3, 1997 / Skint ✦✦✦
Req takes the opportunity of the long-form format to spread his sound out a bit, resulting in an alternating collection of rooted, downtempo beat music and floaty, meandering ambience. Req's stated intention with *Req: One* was for the music to "hint at a direction" without ever actually settling down into one, an interesting approach one would expect to prompt self-righteous cries of "MUSO!," but for the fact that Req's inspired amateurism is too honest and freeflowing to warrant it. Overall, pretty samey-sounding, but a good listen. —*Sean Cooper*

● **Frequency Jams** / Feb. 16, 1998 / Skint ✦✦✦✦
Like its predecessor, the undersung *One*, Req's *Frequency Jams* is a blurry, choppy assemblage of fractured rhythms and lo-fi Tascam experimentalism. And as with his debut, Req more than makes up in concept what he lacks in craft, dragging a for-all-intents *purist's* hip-hop into some of the most interesting, inventive corners of instrumental beats. Highlights include the heavy-on-the-attack old school rhythms of "I (Linn Mix)" and Req's haunting, fuzzy, lonesome tribute to the African finger piano, "Mbira." —*Sean Cooper*

Sketchbook / Mar. 5, 2002 / Warp ✦✦✦
Req resurfaced on the left-leaning Warp after two LPs recorded for big beat boutique Skint, and the results put to shame any notions of underground rap

practiced by Rawkus or Def Jux. Though his sub-basement sound aesthetic won't win him any crossover converts, *Sketchbook* makes a good listen out of downtempo beatbox musings, similar to DJ Vadim's earliest work. The beats have an absence of sound quality, reminiscent of tape decks dusty with age, and there's really not much else happening: a few odd keys, melodica, bells, and occasionally some light scratching far away in the background. Those looking for label context will find much to enjoy, since Warp's notion of avant-beat listening music makes far more sense for a producer like Req than the go-go party music of Skint. —*John Bush*

RES

b. Philadelphia, PA
Hip-Hop, Contemporary R&B
Res (pronounced Reese) released her debut album, *How I Do*, in 2001. The mixture of hip-hop, rock, and soul (the hip-hop influence being the most prominent) was largely produced by Doc, who had worked on Esthero's 1998 release, *Breath From Another*. Prior to this debut, RES, born and raised in Philadelphia's suburbs, sang on GZA's *Beneath the Surface* and performed guest vocals for Talib Kweli & Hi Tek's *Reflection Eternal*. —*Richie Unterberger*

● **How I Do** / Jun. 26, 2001 / MCA ✦✦✦
RES' first album is a competent and accomplished, and not great, crossover of soul, pop, rock, and some hip-hop-type beats. The songs sometimes go into more ambitious and meaningful territory than many such efforts, addressing the shallowness of media images in "Golden Boys." Mostly it's about relationships, however, though there's more ambiguity to keep the interest aroused than is the norm for contemporary R&B. Her voice is likably cocky, and the production diverse and inventive, keeping a pop base even on the tracks most soaked in beats and rhythm, and using a good amount of funky guitars. The closer, "Say It Anyway" (not listed on the sleeve), is far more rock oriented than anything else on the disc; with its buzzing guitars and hook-riddled chorus, it sounds (unlike the rest of the CD) made to order for modern-rock radio airplay. —*Richie Unterberger*

Restiform Bodies

Group / Alternative Rap, Underground Rap
A mysterious and highly experimental hip-hop group, Restiform Bodies deconstruct rap with the same approach that bands like Sonic Youth and Swans took toward punk in the early '80s. Often harsh, moody, and quite bizarre, the troupe is made up of producers the Bomarr Monk and Agent Six and rappers Passage and Telephone Jim Jesus. Inspired by electronica, ghetto-tech, progressive rock, and vintage R&B, the group took an aggressively inspired view of the genre, taking alternative rap beyond the fringes already established by Kool Keith and Cannibal Ox. Often sounding more like Stereolab than any other point of reference, the group's unique sound and image led to a deal with Anticon Records (a collective that Passage belongs to), who released their 2002 eponymous debut. —*Bradley Torreano*

● **Restiform Bodies** / Apr. 9, 2002 / 6 Months ✦✦✦✦✦
Shattering the expectations of modern hip-hop and presenting a jagged, oddball debut, the Restiform Bodies are one of the most distinct voices in the genre. No other rap albums in 2002 presented a dreamy avant-garde synth instrumental and then traveled through a dense landscape of fuzzy noises and old school percussion just to change gears and embrace the corpse of early-'80s new wave. And certainly none of them had the gall to do it all within the first six minutes. But the Restiform Bodies are far more Sonic Youth than Eminem, unafraid of experimentation and change in a genre dictated by a small set of mainstream producers. This is music that welcomes innovation and abstract thought, from the unbelievable production to the thin-voiced beat poetry of rappers Passage and Telephone Jim Jesus. Their raps create an icy distance from the listener via creative wordplay and weird subject matter, but their complicated rhymes are an excellent counterpart to the production from the Bomarr Monk and Agent Six. Their approach to the tracks is comparable to Dan the Automator being set loose in a Sam Goody with a handful of psychedelics, with just about any genre that can be twisted into a beat being successfully drafted into the mix. Not everything works, but so much of it does that it's easy to forgive the moments that don't quite gel. Besides, no one outside of the Anticon collective is even close to matching the

Restiform Bodies' experimental spirit and unique sound. These guys work very hard, and it results in an awesome debut that spits in the face of tradition and presents one of the true classics in the indie hip-hop scene. —*Bradley Torreano*

Rha Goddess

b. Brooklyn, NY
Spoken Word, Vocals / Gangsta Rap, Hardcore Rap, Hip-Hop
Brooklyn native Rha Goddess has spent her career trying to bridge the gap between hip-hop, spoken word, and political activism. A former spokesperson for KRS-One's Zulu Nation, Rha Goddess has also worked tirelessly as a community activist and a university lecturer, and has worked alongside KRS-One in creating the Temple of Hip-hop.

On top of her commitment to social consciousness, Rha Goddess has also carved out a respectable music career. She has worked alongside rappers, such as Chuck D, as well as spoken word artists such as the Last Poets. Rha Goddess also coined the term "floetry," which she defines as a fusion of poetry and music. —*Jon Azpiri*

● **Soulah Vibe** / Mar. 14, 2000 / Divine Dime ✦✦✦✦✦
Rha Goddess' style is so unique that she invented her own word for it: floetry. By her definition, "floetry" is a blending of rhythm, poetry, hip-hop, and politics. Hearing an artist proudly declare her work be to so original that a new word needs to be created to describe it may be considered a tad pretentious, but Rha's natural talent and forceful voice back up all of her claims. *Soulah Vibe* is Rha's debut album, although she is hardly a newcomer. She has long been associated with KRS-One's Zulu Nation and has performed with rappers such as Chuck D, as well as spoken-word performers such as the Last Poets. *Soulah Vibe* is a polished effort, and Rha has a natural presence and a remarkably rich, emotive voice. On "Elements," she makes a connection between the four elements of nature and the four elements of hip-hop, while "Soulah Vibe" acts a spiritual manifesto. Just when you think Rha is about to get a little too heavy handed with the spirituality, she proves she can throw down some funk on "Can't Touch This" and "My Pen (Remix)." Rha's style and versatility have been compared to that of Lauryn Hill's and such high praise is certainly warranted. Like Hill, Rha Goddess has a fresh take on hip-hop that is both politically astute and deeply personal. —*Jon Azpiri*

Richie Rich

b. Oakland, CA
Gangsta Rap, West Coast Rap
His rapping style an influence on Snoop Doggy Dogg (by Snoop's own admission), Richie Rich first entered music in the late '80s with the Oakland-based group 415. With D-Loc, DJ Darryl, and JED, Rich crafted a Bay Area classic called *41Fivin'*, which sold well around the region and spawned a Richie Rich solo album, *Don't Do It*. As the group was ready to sign a major-label contract with Priority in 1990, however, Richie Rich was arrested for possession of cocaine. 415 released its next album and faded from the scene soon after, while Rich sat in jail; he was released a year later, and began appearing on tracks by the Luniz and 2Pac before forming his own label Oakland Hills 41510 and releasing *1/2 Thang*. By 1995, Richie Rich had become the first Bay Area rapper to sign with New York's Def Jam Records, and his major-label solo debut, *Seasoned Veteran*, was released in late 1996. His long-awaited sophomore effort, *The Game*, was issued four years later. —*John Bush*

Don't Do It / 1990 / Big League ✦✦✦

Seasoned Veteran / Nov. 5, 1996 / Def Jam ✦✦✦
Seasoned Veteran was the album to make Richie Rich into a star, but the album just falls short of its mark. Richie Rich is a good rapper, but he's not a great one, which means that the production has to be impeccable for the record to really take hold. Unfortunately, only a handful of songs—"It's On," "Let's Ride," "Real Pimp," and the 2Pac duet "Niggas Done Changed"—make much of an impression, which leaves *Seasoned Veteran* a frustrating listen, especially in light of Richie Rich's long and underappreciated legacy in Californian rap. —*Leo Stanley*

● **Greatest Hits** / Apr. 25, 2000 / Big League ✦✦✦✦

Stone Rivers

b. Bronx, NY
East Coast Rap
Rapper Stone Rivers released a 2001 record (*All My Life*) on Serchlite, a division of Warlock run by 3rd Bass' MC Serch. —*John Bush*

● **All My Life** / Apr. 24, 2001 / Warlock ✦✦✦
The debut album from Stone Rivers is a remarkably thoughtful album. While Rivers uses many of the same thug scenarios that so many rappers do, he struggles to find a deeper meaning in songs like "What's Going On" and "I Cry." He also manages to create convincing up-tempo tracks like "The Song Is You" and "I'm You." While his lyrics often don't match the high production value, Rivers makes up for it with his sincerity and unique rhyming style. *It's My Life* manages to be equally aggressive and introspective. —*Jon Azpiri*

RJD2

b. May 27, 1976, Eugene, OR
Producer / Alternative Rap, Hip-Hop
RJD2's music is a collage of cut-and-paste hip-hop that combines disparate elements to make for soulful, moody portraits of the world. Born in Eugene, OR, on May 27, 1976, he moved to Columbus, OH, a few years later and was raised there. He first busted out onto the hip-hop scene in 1998—a time when producers were emerging from the shadows to seize the spotlight—as the DJ/producer for the Columbus-based group Megahertz. MHz had two 12" singles released on Bobbito Garcia's Fondle 'Em Records and the group was mentioned in *Vibe* magazine's "History of Hip Hop."

In 2000, RJD2 produced Copywrite's debut single, "Holier Than Thou," on Rawkus Records. In the spring of 2001, he made his first formal appearance as a solo artist on the *Def Jux Presents...* compilation, proving he could hold his own alongside such luminaries as Company Flow, El-P, Cannibal Ox, and Aesop Rock. RJD2's debut album, *Dead Ringer*, followed on Def Jux in 2002. One of the best underground hip-hop releases of the year, it melded dirty samples and a classic approach to song structure for an end result that gave DJ Shadow, DJ Spooky, and Moby a run for their money. —*Charles Spano*

Your Face or Your Kneecaps / 2001 / Bustown Pride ✦✦✦✦
Before he hit the big (or at least moderately sized) time as a solo artist with the release of his official debut, *Dead Ringer*, on El-P's Def Jux label, RJD2 put together the extremely limited-edition *Your Face or Your Kneecaps* more or less as a promotional item. Irregardless of its semi-legitimate status, the album managed to get the producer noticed by *Rolling Stone* magazine, and it is definitely worth tracking down. It is conspicuous as the rawer blueprint for what *Dead Ringer* would eventually succeed fully at becoming: self-contained instrumental hip-hop of the highest order. *Your Face or Your Kneecaps* is of a much rougher finish—it is a self-described "mix CD," after all, and lacks the glossy veneer of a studio product—but it also has spontaneity and a ragged bedroom soul in spades. The album's main course is "Poorboy Lover Megamix," a virtuoso display of the art of the sampler. The song's 37 snippets (the majority of them cherry-picked out of the 1960s and '70s) mostly run no longer than 30 or 40 seconds apiece, but the whole 39-minute collage comes together like the greatest obscure, freeform funk 'n' jive live jam you've never heard. Both "Rain" and "Find You Out" have the same sort of effect, but on a much smaller scale. While they feel more rooted in the earth, they are just as haunting as the mystical landscapes of DJ Shadow. And they help make the album more than simply a warm-up from an extraordinary artist. —*Stanton Swihart*

● **Dead Ringer** / Jul. 23, 2002 / Def Jux ✦✦✦✦
His debut LP for Def Jux, DJ/producer RJD2's *Dead Ringer* is a deeply creative and musically poignant hip-hop record for summer 2002. Creating a raging underground listenership from a series of 45s and white labels and being the only non-MC signed to Def Jux, RJD2's talent as a DJ and as producer, to match beats and lay cult/pop gems over dusty soul tracks, is paralleled only by people like DJ Shadow and Z-Trip. However, his ability to record and marry MCs to his primarily instrumental and sample-based style is evidenced in outstanding tracks with Copywrite and Blueprint as well as his legacy with the MHz crew; at the end of day that puts our man from Ohio ahead of his primarily one-dimensional peer group. This set will stand out as monumental for Def Jux, who with their first record outside of the New York MC box continues to stride toward really being definitive in their roster and catalog of independent hip-hop. —*Nic Kincaid*

Roc Raida

DJ, Producer, Turntables / Hip-Hop, Underground Rap, Turntablism
Roc Raida started DJing hip-hop at the age of ten with his father's help. From there he's gone on to found one of the most prolific turntablist crews the world has yet to see, with partners Mista Sinista, Rob Swift, and Total Eclipse. Collecting championship titles and awards across the world, he's brought an art form back that may well have been slowly motioned to obscurity, creating excitement by injecting pure passion into his mixes. —*Brad Mills*

● **Crossfaderz** / Jul. 11, 2000 / Moonshine ◆◆◆◆
A founding member of the New York City battle DJ crew the X-Ecutioners (formerly known as the X-Men), Raida pulls off a great compilation with an underlying radio-show theme with *Crossfaderz*. This is a collection of late-'90s rap hits with a bit of an emphasis on NY's Diggin' in the Crates crew (D.I.T.C.) featuring Showbiz, AG, Fat Joe, and Big L. There's even a play on Big L's first album, *Lifestyles of the Poor and Dangerous*, with a skit entitled "Lifestyles of the Rich and Dangerous." The cutting and scratching on this album is top notch, as Raida is considered one of the world's best turntablists. There's also a welcome appearance by Q-Bert and D-Styles of the Invisibl Skratch Pikklz DJ crew from San Francisco. DJ Q-Bert was the DMC World Turntablist Champion three years in a row in the mid-'90s. —*Brad Mills*

Rock Master Scott & the Dynamic Three

Group / Old School Rap
Rock Master Scott & the Dynamic Three were responsible for "The Roof Is on Fire"—one of the most memorable old school party jams—a number-five dance hit from 1985. The flipside of the release was "Request Line," which also enjoyed chart success by reaching number 21 on the Hot R&B/hip-hop singles chart. Both tracks have appeared on numerous various-artist compilations throughout the years. —*Andy Kellman*

The Roof Is on Fire [Single] / 1984 / Reality ◆◆◆
Rock Master Scott & the Dynamic Three's "The Roof Is on Fire" didn't even crack the Top 40 of the R&B/hip-hop singles chart when it was released in 1985. The fact that the group's "Request Line" fared much better (it nearly cracked the Top 20) is all the more odd when considering that it didn't provide the hip-hop world with an endlessly repeated phrase. "The roof! The roof! The roof is on fire!" and its following lines continued to be recalled and reused decades after it first appeared on wax. The crew's instrumental backing is little more than a beat and a synthetic handclap track, but like so many other old school rap singles, it proved that a song didn't need many elements to be catchy and exciting. —*Andy Kellman*

The Rock Steady Crew

f. 1977, South Bronx, NY
Group / Old School Rap
Active since its 1977 formation in the South Bronx, the Rock Steady Crew is both a breakdancing collective and occasional recording outlet that has spread its membership to include chapters in Japan, Italy, and Great Britain. Initiated by Jojo and Jimmy D., the crew has continually mutated throughout its existence; members have left the fold over the years, and those who join must first battle an existing member and win in order to be included. A 1982 show with Afrika Bambaataa earned enough respect from the pioneer that he allowed them to join the Zulu Nation. Members Ken Swift, Crazy Legs, Frosty Freeze, and Mr. Freeze briefly appeared in *Flashdance* in 1983, and by 1984, the Rock Steady Crew had a recording contract with Virgin. The single "Hey You (The Rock Steady Crew)" hit number 38 on the dance chart in the U.S.; it fared even better in the U.K., where sales exceeded a million copies. The full-length *Ready for Battle* followed shortly after that, but legal issues prevented the group from performing for a long stretch. Despite this, the RSC remained an entity throughout the early 2000s. A single for Backspin was released in 2000. —*Andy Kellman*

Pete Rock (Peter Phillips)

Producer, Vocals / Hip-Hop, Jazz-House, G-Funk, Jazz-Rap
Rapper, DJ, and producer Pete Rock first emerged in 1991 as half of a duo with C.L. Smooth, debuting with the *All Souled Out* EP; the hit LP *Mecca and the Soul Brother* followed before the two went their separate ways in the wake of 1994's *The Main Ingredient*, with Rock remaining a prolific studio presence

prior to the release of his solo debut, *Soul Survivor*, four years later. BBE issued the hip-hop-centric *PeteStrumentals* in spring 2001. —*Jason Ankeny*

Soul Survivor / Nov. 10, 1998 / RCA ◆◆◆
With partner C.L. Smooth, Pete Rock made one hip-hop milestone, 1992's "They Reminisce over You (T.R.O.Y.)," before going his own way in the mid-'90s. On his debut solo album, *Soul Survivor*, Rock enlists pals Method Man, Raekwon, Kool G Rap, Black Thought, MC Eiht, and Heavy D, among many others, to shape his ideas and ideals into a solid sound structure that's part post-Wu-Tang bombast, part old school classicism. And like its title implies, *Soul Survivor* is a funky fresh affair, one that ties '70s soul with slick '90s hip-hop. Rock tosses in R&B elements more readily than most of his contemporaries, and his smooth flow (as well as those of his guest rappers) slip around the grooves with a mellow grace. The biggest problem is its length: 74 minutes is too much time for Rock's otherwise-slim approach, allowing some filler to creep into the project. —*Michael Gallucci*

Funk Spectrum III: Real Funk for Real People / Feb. 20, 2001 / BBE ◆◆◆◆◆
British DJ and beatminer extraordinaire Keb Darge has made a name for himself by finding long-forgotten funk and soul tracks and packaging them to a modern audience. *Funk Spectrum III: Real Funk for Real People* is the continuation of his very successul series for BBE Records, and this time he gets a little help from legendary hip-hop producer Pete Rock. As with any Keb Darge disc, there is little to criticize. Too often, compilations of obscure oldies appeal only to collectors, but Darge has an uncanny knack for finding old tracks that appeal to anyone. Highlights include tracks by long-forgotten tracks like the Chosen Few's twangy anthem "We Are the Chosen Few" and "Nothin But a Party (Part 1)" by the Blenders. Pete Rock contributes a few obscure tracks from well-known artists like the wonderfully moody "Chains & Things" by BB King and the surprisingly funky "Nothing Is the Same" by '70s rockers Grand Funk Railroad. Also included is the Motown-influenced "Hey Joyce" by Lou Courtney. None of the tracks on *Funk Spectrum III: Real Funk for Real People* could be considered essential to anyone's collection. One could get a full sense of the funk genre without ever hearing music from groups with unintentionally hilarious names like Mad Dog & the Pups and Charles Pryor & Power of Love. But that's beside the point. The real joy comes from rediscovering something that might have been lost forever. As usual, Keb Darge has done all the footwork by unearthing these lost classics, leaving you with nothing to do but sit back and enjoy. —*Jon Azpiri*

● **PeteStrumentals** / May 1, 2001 / BBE ◆◆◆◆◆
PeteStrumentals follows Jay Dee's *Welcome 2 Detroit* as the second offering in BBE's producer spotlight "Beat Generation" series. If you approach Pete Rock's joint as a song-oriented pop album, you may feel disappointed. Only two tracks ("Cake" and "Nothin' Lesser—Jamie's Mix") feature MCs, and the repetitive, consistently mid-tempo beats get somewhat monotonous by the end of most tracks. If you approach the album as a radical work of sonic architecture, you may also feel disappointed, since Rock's relatively old school sensibility isn't likely to make you hear music in a completely new way. But if you approach *PeteStrumentals* on its own terms—as a laid-back collection of atmospheric beats ideal for late-night chilling or freestyling over—then you may enjoy Pete Rock's soulful funk-jazz grooves, which are first rate for this type of recording. The deep bass and whispered "play back" vocal sample on "For the People," jazzy piano loop on "Hip Hopcrisy," big-band sax on "Smooth Sailing," layered horns and vibes on "Pete's Jazz," and strings on "Give It to Y'all" (as well as the scratching that starts about two minutes into the song) all fit together to form a first-rate instrumental joint. The MC tracks with Rock Marciano, Divine, Godfree, and Laku are located near the end of the album; this makes them seem almost like bonus tracks, or perhaps a late attempt to ensure that the listener hasn't nodded off, but they still fit fine in the overall flow of *PeteStrumentals*. —*Todd Kristel*

Pete Rock & C.L. Smooth

f. 1990, Mt. Vernon, NY **db.** 1995
Group / Golden Age, Hip-Hop, East Coast Rap, Jazz-Rap
Mt. Vernon, New Yorkers Pete Rock (a producer/DJ) and rapper C.L. Smooth emerged in 1992 as both a powerhouse performance duo and as prolific producers. Their 1992 album *Mecca and the Soul Brother* was a hip-hop classic with great cuts including "They Reminisce Over You (T.R.O.Y.)" and "Straighten It Out." They later collaborated with Mary J. Blige for a remix of

her song "Reminisce" that effectively merged the two tracks in a re-edited hit. Their next album, *The Main Ingredient*, appeared in 1994, but they split for solo careers one year later. They also recorded many productions for both hip-hop acts and urban contemporary artists like Johnny Gill. —*Ron Wynn*

All Souled Out EP / 1991 / Elektra ✦✦✦✦✦

This six-song EP officially introduced Pete Rock & C.L. Smooth to the hip-hop listening community, and it is hard to imagine a stronger or more confident introduction. Pete Rock's unmatched production sound is already in place, fully formed, and drenched in obscure soul music samples and rumbling, cavernous bass. Characterized by his trademark sonic signature, muted and phased trumpet, and flute loops, the songs sound regal with endless depth (with the exception, perhaps, of his own enjoyably buoyant rhyming vehicle, "The Creator"). Of course, C.L. Smooth's lyrics have just as much to do with that regal quality. His vocals are so laid-back and understated—even soothing—that they can be deceptive and difficult to grasp. Once the listener finds a way in, however, there is much to be found in his words; bypassing the normal rap self-involvements, Smooth instead opts to make moral arguments and ask intellectual questions of the urban community, in essence holding a mirror up to that community without ever devolving into didacticism or soapbox judgment. He is decidedly tough minded but also sympathetic. Standouts include both versions of "Good Life," the irresistible "Go With the Flow," and the anthemic title track, with rapid-fire rhyming from Smooth and a perfectly funky organ riff, but the whole EP is essential. —*Stanton Swihart*

★ Mecca and the Soul Brother / 1992 / Elektra/Asylum ✦✦✦✦✦

It would have been hard to match the artistic success of their debut EP on a full-length recording, but Pete Rock & C.L. Smooth did just that on *Mecca and the Soul Brother*, and they did so in the most unlikely way of all after the succinctness of *All Souled Out*—by coming up with a sprawling, nearly 80-minute-long album on which not a single song or interlude is a throwaway or a superfluous piece. Granted, 80 minutes is a long stretch of time for sustained listening, but the music is completely worthy of that time, allowing the duo to stretch out in ways that their EP rendered impossible. Again, the primary star is Pete Rock's production acumen, and he ups the ante of rock-solid drums, steady cymbal beats, smooth-rolling bass, and fatback organ, not to mention his signature horn loops. C.L. Smooth is the perfect vocal match for the music. He is maybe one of the few MCs capable of rapping a fairly credible love song, as he does on "Lots of Lovin.'" "They Reminisce Over You (T.R.O.Y.)," a tribute to friend and Heavy D dancer Trouble T-Roy, who was accidentally killed, packs a poignant emotional weight, but it is Smooth's more direct and conscientious—and frequently autobiographical—side which ultimately carries the album lyrically. The songs are connected and the album is propelled forward by Rock's quick, soul-tight interludes; these are usually bits of old R&B and soul tunes, but sometimes they're spoken pieces or spontaneous, freestyle sessions. These interludes provide a sort of dense spiritual tone and resonance in the album that is not religiously based at all, but fully hip-hop based, emerging from the urban altars that are the basements and rooftops of the city. —*Stanton Swihart*

The Main Ingredient / 1994 / Elektra ✦✦✦

On their third release overall and second full-length, Pete Rock & C.L. Smooth scaled back on the expansive scope of their sprawling first opus, *Mecca and the Soul Brother*, indeed opting to magnify the main ingredients of their sound: Pete Rock's brilliant production chops and C.L Smooth's complex lyrical delivery. The result is an album that is far more focused, with all the ragged edges and loose threads tied up. It is also just as good as the first record, perhaps an even more satisfying single listen. *The Main Ingredient* is full of rich, resonant, hypnotic songs—the production being among some of the most seductive in hip-hop—that subtly, but absolutely, swing with their lock-step precision. In characteristic Pete Rock fashion, all of the sharp edges have been sanded down, leaving a vibrant and completely lush musical backdrop that seems to have a dreamy nostalgia about it. Old '60s and '70s soul, soul-jazz, and funk samples abound, and the music is dotted with gauzy keyboard washes, hugely echoed bass-drum kicks, milky bass lines, and muted horn loops, almost sounding like they are emanating out of water. All of the songs feel immediate, yet they are infused with the sort of roomy ambience that lends to each the impression of a classic tune, evocative of an earlier era, but not one that can be described exactly, and not one to which you can definitively point. As usual, C.L. Smooth is lyrically on point, spitting out intellectual rhymes and narratives that are just as

propulsive and engaging as the music. The only negative aspect about the album, then, is that it ended one of the finest hip-hop duos of the first half of the 1990s. —*Stanton Swihart*

Rare Tracks / Feb. 23, 1999 / East West ✦✦✦

Be prepared to shell out a hefty sum for Pete Rock & C.L. Smooth's *Rare Tracks*. Precisely what the title says it is—a collection of remixes and alternate versions of many of the duo's best-known and loved songs, all of them either previously unavailable or difficult to come by in America—the compilation was only made available through East West Japan. So, the $30-to-$35 question: is it worth the cost it takes to track down? The admittedly noncommittal answer: yes and no. It is an emphatic "yes" for committed enthusiasts or collectors of the duo's music. *Rare Tracks* has in abundance everything that we've come to expect from Pete and C.L., and like all their domestically released music, every song is marked by high-quality craftsmanship. Rock, too, has always been just as important a remixer as producer, so even his rare mixes are first rate. The answer is probably "no," on the other hand, if you approach the album expecting illumination. All the songs on *Rare Tracks* had already come out in some form or another, and while the versions here feature sometimes significant differences from the originals (a particularly robust "Lots of Lovin,'" a keyed-up "Mecca and the Soul Brother" that is outstanding), the new glosses don't really add any revealing insights into the songs or the group itself. It is still fantastic, though, to have them available and laying around the house. —*Stanton Swihart*

La Mala Rodríguez (María Rodríguez)

Latin Rap

Spanish rap performer La Mala Rodríguez, previously known as La Mala María, got involved in the local hip-hop scene by the end of the '90s. After recording "Yo Marco El Minuto" and "Tengo Un Trato," singles released by local Super Ego-Yo Gano, Mala Rodríguez made her debut album, called *Lujo Ibérico*. —*Drago Bonacich*

● Lujo Ibérico / Jun. 4, 2002 / Universal Latino ✦✦✦

With J. Lo fast becoming just a latter-day Olivia Newton-John, the task fell to a new generation of Latinas to stand up for themselves. Spanish rapper La Mala Rodríguez may not have the same crossover potential (at least, not until she starts rapping in English), but her debut, *Lujo Ibérico*, is an intriguing record, and not a mainstream one in the least. First, she's a great rapper with a solid delivery that owes much more to low, monotonal rappers like DMX or Eve than most foreign rappers. The production—by Supernafamacho and Jota Mayúscula—is hard hitting and mostly minimalist, the tracks driven by little more than sample riffs and drumbreaks, with little bass. There's some imaginative scratching on "Con Diez o Con Veinte," but for the most part, these are backgrounds for Rodríguez's rapping. It's understandably difficult, however, to get hooked by a rap album when you don't know the language, and that takes a lot away from *Lujo Ibérico* for non-Spanish speakers. —*John Bush*

The Roots

f. 1989, Philadelphia, PA
Group / Hip-Hop, Alternative Rap, Jazz-Rap
Though popular success has largely eluded the Roots, the Philadelphia group showed the way for live rap, building on Stetsasonic's "hip-hop band" philosophy of the mid-'80s by focusing on live instrumentation at their concerts and in the studio. Though their album works have been inconsistent affairs, more intent on building grooves than pushing songs, the Roots' live shows are among the best in the business.

The Roots' focus on live music began back in 1987 when rapper Black Thought (Tariq Trotter) and drummer ?uestlove (Ahmir Khalib Thompson) became friends at the Philadelphia High School for Creative Performing Arts. Since the duo had no money for the DJ essentials—two turntables and a microphone, plus a mixer and plenty of vinyl—they re-created classic hip-hop tracks with ?uestlove's drum kit backing Black Thought's rhymes. Playing around school, on the sidewalk, and later at talent shows, the pair began to earn money and hooked up with bassist Hub (Leon Hubbard) and rapper Malik B. Moving from the street to local clubs, the Roots became a highly tipped underground act around Philadelphia and New York. When the group was invited to represent stateside hip-hop at a concert in Germany, they recorded an album to sell at shows; the result, *Organix*, was released in 1993 on Remedy Records. With a music-industry buzz surrounding their activities, the Roots entertained offers from several labels before signing with DGC that same year.

The Roots' first major-label album, *Do You Want More?!!!??!*, was released in January 1995; forsaking usual hip-hop protocol, the album was produced without any samples or previously recorded material. It peaked just outside the Top 100, but was mostly ignored by fans of hip-hop. Instead, *Do You Want More?!!!??!* made more tracks in alternative circles, partly due to the Roots playing the second stage at Lollapalooza that summer. The band also journeyed to the Montreux Jazz Festival in Switzerland. Two of the guests on the album who had toured around with the band, human beatbox Rahzel the Godfather of Noyze—previously a performer with Grandmaster Flash and LL Cool J—and Scott Storch (later Kamal) became permanent members of the group.

Early in 1996, the Roots released *Clones*, the trailer single for their second album. It hit the rap Top Five, and created a good buzz for the album. The following September, *Illadelph Halflife* appeared and made number 21 on the album charts. Much like its predecessor, though, the Roots' second LP was a difficult listen. It made several very small concessions to mainstream rap—the band sampled material they had recorded earlier at jam sessions—but failed to make a hit of their unique sound. The Roots' third album, 1999's *Things Fall Apart*, was easily their biggest critical and commercial success; *The Roots Come Alive* followed later that year. The long-awaited *Phrenology* was released in late November 2002 admist rumors of the Roots losing interest in their label arrangements with MCA. —*John Bush*

Organix / 1993 / Remedy ✦✦✦

The Roots' low-profile debut set out many of the themes they would employ over the course of their successful career. An intro, "The Roots Is Comin'," is barely over a minute long, yet long enough to exemplify the band's funky bass line (here played by Leonard Hubbard), their dreamy and emotional organ chords (thanks to Scott Storch), and their ferociously swift yet clear rhymes from the group's focal MC Black Thought. The song that follows, "Pass the Popcorn," would have been called a posse cut in 1993. Everyone could've used a little more practice before stepping up to the mic on this song, but the spirit of the song is not lost in the amateurishness. The creative venture "Writers Block" is an example of just the opposite, as Black Thought flows with spoken word, comically and creatively expressing the experience of a day in the life of a Philadelphian using mass transit. The instrumentation is appropriately frantic and punctuated by [cymbal] crashes (like any mass transit system). Fans of *Do You Want More*, the Roots album released immediately following *Organix*, will recognize the music of "I'm Out Deah," "Leonard I-V," and "Essawhamah?" Another track to note is "The Session (Longest Posse Cut in History),"—no false claim at 12 minutes and 43 seconds. This album should be a part of any Roots fan's collection—not so much because it is an example of their artistry at its best, but because it allows you to see where they came from and how fruitful of a journey it's been. —*Qa'id Jacobs*

Do You Want More?!!!??! / Jan. 17, 1995 / DGC ✦✦✦✦

Because the Roots were pioneering a new style during the early '90s, the band was forced to draw its own blueprints for its major-label debut album. It's not surprising then, that *Do You Want More?!!!??!* sounds more like a document of old school hip-hop than contemporary rap. The album is based on loose grooves and laid-back improvisation, and where most hip-hoppers use samples to draw songs together and provide a chorus, the Roots just keep on jamming. The problem is that the Roots' jams begin to take the place of true songs, leaving most tracks with only that groove to speak for them. The notable exceptions—"Mellow My Man" and "Datskat," among others—use different strategies to command attention: the sounds of a human beatbox , the great keyboard work of Scott Storch, and contributions from several jazz players (trombonist Joshua Roseman, saxophonist Steve Coleman, and vocalist Cassandra Wilson). By the close of the album, those tracks are what the listener remembers, not the lightweight grooves. —*John Bush*

Illadelph Halflife / Sep. 24, 1996 / DGC ✦✦✦✦

The Roots always had ambition, which theoretically placed them ahead of many of their mid-'90s hip-hop contemporaries. Where many of their peers settled for gangsta clichés, tedious displays of lyrical skills, alternative hip-hop, or half-hearted jazz-rap fusions, the Roots decided to take an entirely different route by merging street-level rhythms with jazz and old school

technique, and performing everything on live instruments. While their approach works well in theory, it doesn't always work in practice. Though it is decidedly tougher and more adventurous than the group's debut, *Illadelph Halflife* just misses the mark. Part of the problem with the record is the fact that it doesn't capture the relentless energy of their live show; without the reckless, rampaging momentum of their live show, the record is only sporadically engaging. Still, the best moments of *Illadelph Halflife* demonstrate that the Roots are an exciting, inventive band with great potential—they just haven't quite fulfilled it yet. —*Leo Stanley*

● Things Fall Apart / Feb. 23, 1999 / MCA ✦✦✦✦✦

One of the cornerstone albums of alternative rap's second wave, *Things Fall Apart* was the point where the Roots' tremendous potential finally coalesced into a structured album that maintained its focus from top to bottom. If the group sacrifices a little of the unpredictability of its jam sessions, the resulting consistency more than makes up for it, since the record flows from track to track so effortlessly. Taking its title from the Chinua Achebe novel credited with revitalizing African fiction, *Things Fall Apart* announces its ambition right upfront, and reinforces it in the opening sound collage. Dialogue sampled from Spike Lee's *Mo' Better Blues* implies a comparison to abstract modern jazz that lost its audience, and there's another quote about hip-hop records being treated as disposable, that they aren't maximized as product or as art. That's the framework in which the album operates, and while there's a definite unity counteracting the second observation, the artistic ambition actually helped gain the Roots a whole new audience ("coffeehouse chicks and white dudes," as Common puts it in the liner notes). The backing tracks are jazzy and reflective, filled with subtly unpredictable instrumental lines, and the band also shows a strong affinity for the neo-soul movement, which they actually had a hand in kick-starting via their supporting work on Erykah Badu's *Baduizm*. Badu returns the favor by guesting on the album's breakthrough single, "You Got Me," an involved love story that also features a rap from Eve, cowriting from Jill Scott, and an unexpected drum'n'bass breakbeat in the outro. Other notables include Mos Def on the playful old school rhymefest "Double Trouble," Slum Village superproducer Jay Dee on "Dynamite!," and Philly native DJ Jazzy Jeff on "The Next Movement." But the real stars are Black Thought and Malik B, who drop such consistently nimble rhymes throughout the record that picking highlights is extremely difficult. Along with works by Lauryn Hill, Common, and Black Star, *Things Fall Apart* is essential listening for anyone interested in the new breed of mainstream conscious rap. —*Steve Huey*

The Roots Come Alive / Nov. 2, 1999 / MCA ✦✦✦✦

Releasing an album recorded live in concert makes more sense for the Roots than any other hip-hop artist, considering they've always concentrated on live prowess over their skills on the mic or in the production booth. The standard guitar/drums/bass/keyboards lineup of most rock bands is a reality for this group, and after years of requests from rabid fans, the Roots acquiesced with a document of their live experience, titled *The Roots Come Alive*. Recorded at two venues in New York and one in Paris, the album distills exactly what the Roots bring to the hip-hop world—a live experience built on call-and-response vocals that bring the show to the audience like few other artists. The sound is fantastic, especially on early keyboard-driven tracks like "Proceed," "Essaywhuman?!???!!!," and "Mellow My Man." Though the raps themselves often suffer from the live setting, the rhythms are crisper than in the studio, and the bass-driven grooves are much beefier. The Roots' resident turntablist, Scratch, takes a large role as well, as does human beatbox Rahzel the Godfather of Noyze (though the latter only appears on about half of the album). This is a live album that not only satisfies fans but also offers neophytes more entertainment than any of the Roots' studio efforts. It's difficult to make any live album a first pick, but *Come Alive* displays the group doing exactly what it does best. —*John Bush*

Phrenology / Nov. 26, 2002 / MCA ✦✦✦✦✦

The easy-flowing *Things Fall Apart* made the Roots one of the most popular artists of alternative rap's second wave. Anticipated nearly as much as it was delayed, the proper studio follow-up, *Phrenology*, finally appeared in late 2002, after much perfectionist tinkering by the band—so much that the liner notes include recording dates (covering a span of two years) and, sometimes, histories for the individual tracks. Coffeehouse music programmers beware: *Phrenology* is not *Things Fall Apart* redux; it's a challenging, hugely ambitious opus that's by turns brilliant and bewildering, as it strains to push the very sound of hip-hop into the future. Despite a few gentler tracks (like the

Nelly Furtado and Jill Scott guest spots), *Phrenology* is the hardest-hitting Roots album to date, partly because it's their most successful attempt to re-create their concert punch in the studio. ?uestlove's drums positively boom out of the speakers on the Talib Kweli duet, "Rolling With Heat"; the fantastic, lean guitar groover "The Seed (2.0)" (with neo-soul auteur Cody ChesnuTT); and the opening section of "Water." The ten-minute "Water" is the album's centerpiece, a powerful look at former Roots MC Malik B's drug problems that morphs into a downright avant-garde sound collage. Similarly, lead single "Break You Off," a neo-soul duet with Musiq, winds up in a melange of drum'n'bass programming and live strings. If moves like those, or the speed-blur Bad Brains punk of "!!!!!!," or the drum'n'bass backdrop of poet Amiri Baraka's "Something in the Way of Things (In Town)" can seem self-consciously eclectic, it's also true that *Phrenology* is one of those albums where the indulgences and far-out experiments make it that much more fascinating, whether they work or not. Plus, slamming grooves like "Rock You," "Thought @ Work," and the aforementioned "The Seed (2.0)" keep things exciting and vital. If this really is the future of hip-hop, then the sky is the limit. (The two hidden bonus tracks are "Rhymes and Ammo," the Talib Kweli collaboration that appeared on *Soundbombing, Vol. 3*, and "Something to See," another techno-inflected jam.) —*Steve Huey*

Roots Manuva (Rodney Smith)

Vocals, Producer, Remixing / Hip-Hop, British Rap, Dub, Dancehall

British rapper/producer Rodney Smith established himself as Roots Manuva in the late '90s and released several albums through Big Dada/Ninja Tune. Smith's work spanned the music spectrum, firmly rooted in raggae but also incorporating much of the trip-hop style often associated with Ninja Tune. He debuted in 1999 with *Brand New Second Hand*, a promising album that garnered a sizable amount of attention from the international hip-hop crowd. Beginning in late 1999, shortly after the release of his first album, Smith returned to the studio to begin work on *Run Come Save Me*, his follow-up. He completed the album and released it on Big Dada/Ninja Tune; however, he also had about 15 songs that didn't make the album. He began tweaking these remaining songs for a dub album, *Dub Come Save Me*, which he then released in 2002. —*Jason Birchmeier*

Brand New Second Hand / Mar. 23, 1999 / Big Dada ✦✦✦✦

A bright moment for British rap, the debut album from Roots Manuva introduced a hip-hop chameleon boasting dark productions and a distinct style, plus much more to say than most rappers. Both his raps and his productions rely on ragga as a bed, but instead of leading the party, Roots Manuva used it to reflect on the world ("Strange Behaviour") and his religious background ("Baptism"), as well as play the usual game of the dozens ("Dem Phonies"). Also of interest is the devastating "Clockwork," originally released on the Ninja Tune label compilation *Funkungfusion*. If anything, these low-key, bass-heavy productions (some by the rapper himself) aren't able to convey Roots Manuva's lyrical finesse and thematic complexity. —*John Bush*

● **Run Come Save Me** / Jan. 1, 2001 / Big Dada ✦✦✦✦✦

Just when the British hip-hop community seemed on its last legs, the victim of an overpowerful American marketing machine, Roots Manuva hit the stratosphere with his second record, the nearly *Mercury* prize-winning *Run Come Save Me*. A stunning record, it balanced the stark digital soul of British raggae with lurching beats and Rodney Smith's star-making delivery and wide-ranging repertoire. "Witness (1 Hope)" earned its place as the best British rap single since Tricky's "Aftermath," while "Bashment Boogie," "Hol' It Up," and "Artical" were distinctive, hard-hitting, surprisingly groovy performances. As on his LP debut, *Brand New Second Hand*, Smith also spent time reflecting on his religious upbringing, with a distinctly unhumorous track ("Sinny Sin Sins," never mind the title) that dealt with his heavily disciplinarian father. And where his debut featured tracks produced by Mr. Manuva himself or Wayne Bennett, for *Run Come Save Me* he stuck to the professionals: Bennett and the astonishing Lord Gosh, whose Blow's Yard Studio quickly took its place next to New York's legendary D&D Studios as a home to distinctive underground rap. Roots Manuva handled every type of song with flowing confidence and a bemused air, whether it was a club jam or a message track. —*John Bush*

Dub Come Save Me / Jul. 23, 2002 / Big Dada ✦✦✦✦✦

The perfect candidates for a dub album, rapper Roots Manuva and producer Lord Gosh prove they've got plenty of incredible productions up their sleeves,

barely a year after *Run Come Save Me* earned plaudits as the best British LP of the year. *Dub Come Save Me* balances remixes of tracks from the album with altogether new songs, leading off with "Man Fi Cool," a glittering electro dub that's as impressive as anything he's done in the past. Shortly after comes "Revolution 5," yet another track it's hard to believe was ever left behind, the supernatural pairing of Roots Manuva with another of the deepest rhythmatic rappers in the business, Chali 2na from Jurassic 5. The dub versions are just as incredible, with a parade of speaker-rattling Lord Gosh productions ("Highest Grade," "Styles") and a rubbery remix of "Dreamy Days" by another top British iconoclast, Super Furry Animals. Lord Gosh comes roaring back, though, with a synth monster named "The Lynch," the perfect bed for another great Roots Manuva performance. Fans of the single "Witness (1 Hope)" can rest assured that it's present here as well, in a suitably deconstructed dub that closes out the album. It's the rare dub/remix album that even comes close to the original; *Dub Come Save Me* nearly trumps the last one. —*John Bush*

Badmeaningood, Vol. 2 / Nov. 5, 2002 / Ultimate Dilemma ✦✦✦

Rough House Survivors

Group / Hip-Hop, Hardcore Rap

Rough House Survivors released one album, *Straight From the Soul*, in 1992. DJ Swinn and MCs Dread One, Kev, and Roberto made up the quartet, who were lucky enough to deliver their rhymes on top of some of Tony Dofat's (Mary J. Blige's *What's the 411*, Monifah's *Mo'hogany*, Heavy D's *Blue Funk*) best production work. Although its stature was bolstered somewhat with appearances from Brand Nubian's Grand Puba and Sadat X, as well as C.L. Smooth—not to mention singles like "Check da Back Pack" and "You Got It"—*Straight From the Soul* slipped through the cracks and never went beyond cult status as a great golden age-era album. —*Andy Kellman*

● **Straight From the Soul** / Nov. 17, 1992 / Relativity ✦✦✦✦

One might surmise that an album produced by Tony Dofat and including guest appearances from C.L. Smooth, Sadat X, and Grand Puba Maxwell, all at the height of their rapping powers, would be a solid hit waiting to happen. Such was not the case with the Rough House Survivors' sole record, *Straight From the Soul*, but it is not for lack of appeal. Indeed, the album disappeared without leaving any vestiges, despite the fact that it was incredibly catchy and artistically successful. The work of Pete Rock seems to have exerted quite an influence on Dofat's strong production, especially in the rock-steady drum and cymbal patterns, mellow Saturday-afternoon organ, creamy bass lines, and the goofball shouts and horn loops that percolate disorientedly beneath the music on stellar cuts such as "Take a Trip," "Can U Dig It?," "We Come to Get Wreck," and the straight burner "Once Again." Although this almost plays as a lost Rock production, the music deviates enough from the template to develop its own alternately upbeat and mellow, distinctly New York City vibe, and *Straight From the Soul* further distances itself through the loose, insouciant flows of rappers Kev, Roberto, and Dread One (DJ Swinn being the fourth member of the crew). They borrow the give-and-take rhyming of Leaders of New School and the buoyant, all-for-one lyrical energy of Brand Nubian's first album; then they step on the accelerator just slightly and blend it all into an incessantly contagious and singular style. Only the group's foray into raggamuffin reggae ("Rough House") doesn't quite come off. But in the freestyle-like session of "Check Da Back Pack" and the legitimately swinging "So! Survivors We Can Rhyme," Rough House Survivors create a duo of songs that can easily stand with anything from the era in hip-hop, and the rest of the songs aren't far behind. Unfortunately, only a few people ever seemed to find out that. —*Stanton Swihart*

Royal Flush

Vocals / East Coast Rap

East Coast rapper Royal Flush made a solid yet ultimately unsuccessful bid for a mainstream breakthrough in 1997 with an album (*Ghetto Millionaire*) and a pair of singles ("World Wide" and "Iced Down Medallions"), none of which made much impact. Originally affiliated with Mic Geronimo, the Queens rapper recorded for Blunt Recordings, which TVT Records distributed briefly, and collaborated with some established producers, most notably EZ Elpee, Hi-Tek, and L.E.S. —*Jason Birchmeier*

● **Ghetto Millionaire** / Aug. 19, 1997 / TVT ✦✦✦

Royal Flush's debut album, *Ghetto Millionaire*, is a pedestrian set of hardcore gangsta rap that occasionally catches fire. Lyrically, Royal Flush's rhymes have potential, yet their music is too conventional and predictable to be of much interest to anyone outside of gangsta fetishists. —*Leo Stanley*

Royce da 5'9"

Underground Rap, Hardcore Rap

Whenever anyone mentions the name of Detroit rapper Royce Da 5'9", a whole list of other names surround it. First, people mention his passing resemblance to LL Cool J. Others might know him as the guy who teamed up with teen singer Willa Ford on her 2001 hit "I Wanna Be Bad." He is also known as the rapper who got a major boost from legendary producer DJ Premier, who produced his 2000 hit, "Boom." Mostly, though, people associate him with Eminem. The pair have rolled together since their early days in Detroit and have worked together on several occasions. With the release of his 2002 album, *Rock City*, Royce Da 5'9" hopes to finally make a name for himself. —*Jon Azpiri*

● **Rock City [Version 2.0]** / Nov. 26, 2002 / Game ◆◆◆◆
Finally arriving with a full-length after appearing on records with Eminem, Dr. Dre, Method Man, DJ Premier, and even Willa Ford, Royce da 5'9" makes the most of his growing exposure on *Rock City [Version 2.0]*. The disc was meant for release in 2000, but after label intervention and multiple problems with the final product, it took a massive overhaul of the tracks and production to arrive at the final version of *Rock City*, hence the subtitle [Version 2.0]. But the wait was worth it, as Eminem's old hype-man steps out of his friend's shadow on the awesome tracks here. Boasting a voice like vintage LL Cool J but without the grit, Royce tells intriguing tales of self-reflection that have become a staple of Detroit MCs. His smooth delivery is complemented by the liquid funk production, carrying his vocals over a bed of bouncing beats and sensual synths courtesy of DJ Premier and the Neptunes, among others. The rollicking hometown anthem "Rock City" includes Eminem on the snappy chorus, but the verses are pure Royce as he waxes philosophical his role in the Motor City scene. The funky "Mr. Baller" brings the Clipse and Pharrell Williams into the picture, and Royce holds his own and more against the production mastermind and his protégés. And "Boom" was fantastic as a single, but the new album version reveals what a multilayered masterpiece DJ Premier put together for the Detroit MC. But most tracks don't necessarily stand out on *Rock City*; instead they act more as a pieces of a complete picture of an MC that is still actively connected to the underground. From the beats to his rhyming style, Royce rarely attempts to do anything that resembles commercial rap. The awesome "Take His Life" is a perfect example; the harsh beat and sparse piano samples carry Royce's thoughtful defense of his murder fantasies with an eerie clarity, but despite being one of the best songs on the album, it could never survive as a single. This is rarely a detriment, although a few tracks suffer from being indistinct because of his attitude toward hooks and poppy touches. But when the songs are as powerful as "Soldier's Story," it's hard to argue with his method. Royce had been unfairly labeled as an Eminem creation in the past, but *Rock City [Version 2.0]* reveals an exciting voice that has little in common with his former running buddy. Instead, he brings the underground to the mainstream and crafts an album that isn't perfect but is an endearingly gruff, dense, and promising debut. —*Bradley Torreano*

Ruff Ryders

f. 1999

Group / East Coast Rap, Hardcore Rap

The all-star hip-hop collective/production team Ruff Ryders included CEOs Chivon, Dee, and Waah Dean, producers Swizz Beatz, DJ Shok, and P.K., and gold and platinum-selling rappers DMX, Eve, Drag-On, and the LOX (Shawn "Sheek" Jacobs, Jayson Phillips, and David Styles). This incarnation of the Ruff Ryders crafted 1999's *Ryde Or Die Compilation, Vol. 1*, which also featured appearances from Big Pun, Mase, Jay-Z, and Jermaine Dupri. Parle, Yung Wun, and Cross & Infa-Red also appeared on Ruff Ryders tracks, with *Ryde or Die, Vol. 2* hitting the streets in 2000. —*Heather Phares*

Ryde or Die Compilation, Vol. 1 / Apr. 13, 1999 / Ruff Ryders ◆◆◆
Ruff Ryders, the production team behind DMX's first two platinum-plus albums, made their bid for superstardom with *Ryde or Die Compilation, Vol. 1*. The trio appeared to be following the blueprint of No Limit's Master P: they've formed their own label, assembled a cast of wide-ranging acts under its umbrella, and surrounded them with a variety of productions by

Ruff Ryders associates like Swizz Beatz and DJ Clue. *Ryde or Die, Vol. 1* features tracks from established names like the LOX, Jay-Z, Jermaine Dupri, Big Pun, Mase, and DMX himself plus new signees to the label like Eve and Drag-On. Though several of the track productions are excellent (including the New Orleans horns of "Down Bottom" featuring native-born Juvenile and the salsa rhythms on "What Ya Want"), the album suffers elsewhere by trying to be everything to everyone. It's got a few hardcore tracks, a few bounce tracks, and a few mid-tempo R&B tracks, but it's far too scattershot and never jells as it should (two complaints often lodged against No Limit albums). The team saves their best productions for DMX spotlights: the minute-long "Bugout" and the title track. —*John Bush*

● **Ryde or Die, Vol. 2** / Apr. 25, 2000 / Interscope ◆◆◆
Though the stable of rappers on the second *Ryde or Die* volume make it a diverse album of many rapping styles, the patented Ruff Ryders-style of production makes it a surprisingly consistent listen. Once again, producer Swizz Beatz steals the spotlight with his garish synth-powered rhythms, while the other producers—Swizz Beats, P. Killer Trackz, Teflon, and Mahogany—do their best to emulate his signature style. There are moments when the music overshadows the rappers, reaffirming the reasons why Swizz Beatz became such a renowned producer ("Holiday" and "2 Tears in a Bucket," in particular, come to mind), and there are moments when his fellow producers lay down equally stunning soundscapes, particularly "Weed, Hoes, Dough" and "Got It All" by Teflon and "Go Head" by Swizz Beatz. Yet there are also moments when Beatz' music almost goes too far with its excessive synth use; the same sort of prominent synth stab riff that propelled "Party Up" from DMX's *And Then There Was X* album to club anthem status appears on "WWIII" and "Friday Night," balancing the fine line between genius and gaudiness. In addition to the noteworthy production on the album, there is also some stunning rapping by the album's superstars—Method Man ("2 Years in a Bucket"), Snoop Dogg ("WWIII"), and Busta Rhymes ("Friday Night") along with some impressive performances by up-and-coming rappers in the Ruff Ryders stable—Drag-On's "Weed, Hoes, Dough" and Jadakiss' "My Name is Kiss." There are a few disappointing moments such as DMX's mediocre "The Great," the awkward chorus in "Friday Night," and the questionable synth gaudiness, but these moments are rare, making this a well-rounded collection of talented rappers backed by some of the most ambitious rap productions of 2000. —*Jason Birchmeier*

Ryde or Die, Vol. 3: In the "R" We Trust / Dec. 4, 2001 / Ruff Ryders ◆◆◆
Expanding their reach beyond their East Coast locale, the Ruff Ryders collective features a number of rappers from the South on their third *Ryde or Die* volume along with an array of new producers. Songs such as "Some South Shit" (featuring Ludacris, Fiend, and Young Wun) and "They Ain't Ready" (featuring Bubba Sparxxx alongside Jadakiss over a Timbaland production) will probably surprise those accustomed to preceding Ruff Ryders releases, which tend to feature exclusively East Coast artists. These songs are deliberate attempts to appeal to the growing legions of listeners championing the dirty South movement. Elsewhere, "Eastside Ryders" features tha Eastsidaz alongside Styles, functioning as the album's West Coast track. Besides these West- and South Coast-targeting tracks, the remaining songs are what you've come to expect from the Ruff Ryders camp. Eve offers one of her best moments yet on "U, Me & She," one of the album's singles, produced by Ja Rule collaborator Irv Gotti. There's also the obligatory DMX track, "Friend of Mine," and several songs featuring members of the LOX. Furthermore, there are several new producers on this volume in addition to staple Ruff Ryder producers Swizz Beatz and P.K. These newcomers remain consistent with the trademark synth-heavy Ruff Ryder sound but do bring a fresh approach to the album that was somewhat missing on the preceding volume. Chances are, if you enjoyed the previous volumes—or if you simply enjoy the sound of commercial rap circa 2001—you'll find much to savor here. There's enough variety here to offer something for everyone, even if that means no one will enjoy everything. —*Jason Birchmeier*

Run-D.M.C.

f. 1982, Queens, NY **db.** Nov. 6, 2002

Group / Golden Age, Hip-Hop, East Coast Rap, Hardcore Rap

More than any other hip-hop group, Run-D.M.C. are responsible for the sound and style of the music. As the first hardcore rap outfit, the trio set the sound and style for the next decade of rap. With their spare beats and excursions into heavy metal samples, the trio were tougher and more menacing than their predecessors Grandmaster Flash and Whodini. In the process, they opened the door for both the politicized rap of Public Enemy and Boogie Down Productions, as well as the hedonistic gangsta fantasies of N.W.A. At the same time, Run-D.M.C. helped move rap from a singles-oriented genre to an album-oriented one—they were the first hip-hop artist to construct full-fledged albums, not just collections with two singles and a bunch of filler. By the end of the '80s, Run-D.M.C. had been overtaken by the groups they had spawned, but they continued to perform to a dedicated following well into the '90s.

All three members of Run-D.M.C. were natives of the middle-class New York borough Hollis, Queens. Run (born Joseph Simmons, November 14, 1964) was the brother of Russell Simmons, who formed the hip-hop management company Rush Productions in the early '80s; by the mid-'80s, Russell had formed the pioneering record label Def Jam with Rick Rubin. Russell encouraged his brother Joey and his friend Darryl McDaniels (born May 31, 1964) to form a rap duo. The pair of friends did just that, adopting the names Run and D.M.C., respectively. After they graduated from high school in 1982, the pair enlisted their friend Jason Mizell (born January 21, 1965) to scratch turntables; Mizell adopted the stage name Jam Master Jay.

In 1983, Run-D.M.C. released their first single, "It's Like That"/"Sucker M.C.'s," on Profile Records. The single sounded like no other rap at the time—it was spare, blunt, and skillful, with hard beats and powerful, literate, daring vocals, where Run's and D.M.C.'s vocals overlapped, as they finished each other's lines. It was the first "new school" hip-hop recording. "It's Like That" became a Top 20 R&B hit, as did the group's second single, "Hard Times"/ "Jam Master Jay." Two other hit R&B singles followed in early 1984—"Rock Box" and "30 Days"—before the group's eponymous debut appeared.

By the time of their second album, 1985's *King of Rock*, Run-D.M.C. had become the most popular and influential rappers in America, already spawning a number of imitators. As the *King of Rock* title suggests, the group were breaking down the barriers between rock & roll and rap, rapping over heavy metal records and thick, dense drum loops. Besides releasing the *King of Rock* album and scoring the R&B hits "King of Rock," "You Talk Too Much," and "Can You Rock It Like This" in 1985, the group also appeared in the rap movie *Krush Groove*, which also featured Kurtis Blow, the Beastie Boys, and the Fat Boys.

Run-D.M.C.'s fusion of rock and rap broke into the mainstream with their third album, 1986's *Raising Hell*. The album was preceded by the Top Ten R&B single "My Adidas," which set the stage for the group's biggest hit single, a cover of Aerosmith's "Walk This Way." Recorded with Aerosmith's Steven Tyler and Joe Perry, "Walk This Way" was the first hip-hop record to appeal to both rockers and rappers, as evidenced by its peak position of number four on the pop charts. In the wake of the success of "Walk This Way," *Raising Hell* became the first rap album to reach number one on the R&B charts, to chart in the pop Top Ten, and to go platinum, and Run-D.M.C. were the first rap act to received airplay on MTV—they were the first rappers to cross over into the pop mainstream. *Raising Hell* also spawned the hit singles "You Be Illin'" and "It's Tricky."

Run-D.M.C. spent most of 1987 recording *Tougher Than Leather*, their follow-up to *Raising Hell*. *Tougher Than Leather* was accompanied by a movie of the same name. Starring Run-D.M.C., the film was an affectionate parody of '70s blaxploitation films. Although Run-D.M.C. had been at the height of their popularity when they were recording and filming *Tougher Than Leather*, by the time the project was released, the rap world had changed. Most of the hip-hop audience wanted to hear hardcore political rappers like Public Enemy, not crossover artists like Run-D.M.C. Consequently, the film bombed and the album only went platinum, failing to spawn any significant hit singles.

Two years after *Tougher Than Leather*, Run-D.M.C. returned with *Back From Hell*, which became their first album not to go platinum. Following its release, both Run and D.M.C. suffered personal problems as McDaniels suffered a bout of alcoholism and Simmons was accused of rape. After McDaniels sobered up and the charges against Simmons were dismissed, both of the rappers became born-again Christians, touting their religious conversion on the 1993 album *Down With the King*. Featuring guest appearances and production assistance from artists as diverse as Public Enemy, EPMD, Naughty By Nature, A Tribe Called Quest, Neneh Cherry, Pete Rock, and KRS-One, *Down With the King* became the comeback Run-D.M.C. needed.

The title track became a Top Ten R&B hit and the album went gold, peaking at number 21. Although they were no longer hip-hop innovators, the success of *Down With the King* proved that Run-D.M.C. were still respected pioneers.

After a long studio hiatus, the trio returned in late 1999 with *Crown Royal*. The album did little to add to their ailing record sales, but the following promotional efforts saw them join Aerosmith and Kid Rock for a blockbuster performance on MTV. By 2002, the release of two greatest-hits albums prompted a tour with Aerosmith that saw them travel the U.S., always performing "Walk This Way" to transition between their sets. Sadly, only weeks after the end of the tour, Jam Master Jay was senselessly murdered in a studio session in Queens. Only 37 years old, the news of his passing spread quick and hip-hop luminaries like Big Daddy Kane and Funkmaster Flex took the time to pay tribute to him on New York radio stations. Possibly the most visible DJ in the history of hip-hop, his death was truly the end of an era and unfortunately perpetuated the cycle of violence that has haunted the genre since the late '80s. —*Stephen Thomas Erlewine*

☆ **Run-D.M.C.** / 1984 / Profile ✦✦✦✦

Years after the release of Run-D.M.C.'s eponymous 1984 debut, the group generally were acknowledged to be hip-hop's Beatles—a sentiment that makes a lot of sense, even if *Run-D.M.C.* isn't quite the equivalent of a rap *Please Please Me*. Run-D.M.C. were the Beatles for rap because they signaled a cultural and musical change for the music, ushering it into its accepted form; neither group originated the music, but they gave it the shape known today. But, no matter how true and useful the comparison is, it is also a little misleading, because it implies that Run-D.M.C. also were a melodic, accessible group, bringing in elements from all different strands of popular music. No, Run-D.M.C. expanded their music by making it tough and spare, primarily by adapting the sound and attitude of hard rock to hip-hop. Prior to this, rap felt like a block party—the beats were funky and elastic, all about the groove. *Run-D.M.C.* hit *hard*. The production is tough and minimal, built on relentless drum machines and Jam Master Jay's furious scratching, mixing in a guitar riff or a keyboard hit on occasion. It is brutal urban music, and Run's and D.M.C.'s forceful, muscual rhymes match the music. Where other MCs sounded cheerful, Runs and D.M.C. prowl and taunt the listener, sounding as if they were a street gang. And while much of the record is devoted to braggadocio, boasting, and block parties, Run-D.M.C. also addressed grittier realities of urban life, giving this record both context and thematic weight. All of this—the music, the attitude, the words, the themes—marked a turning point for rap, and it's impossible to calculate Run-D.M.C.'s influence on all that came afterward. Years later, some of the production may sound a bit of its time, but the music itself does not because music this powerful and original always retains its impact and force as music. —*Stephen Thomas Erlewine*

☆ **King of Rock** / 1985 / Profile ✦✦✦✦

Take the title of Run-D.M.C.'s *King of Rock* somewhat literally. True, the trailblazing rap crew hardly abandoned hip-hop on their second album, but they did follow through on the blueprint of their debut, emphasizing the rock leanings that formed the subtext of *Run-D.M.C.* Nearly every cut surges forward on thundering drum machines and simple power chords, with the tempos picked up a notch and the production hitting like a punch to the stomach. If the debut suggested hard rock, this *feels* like hard rock—overamplified, brutal, and intoxicating in its sheer sonic force. What really makes *King of Rock* work is that it sounds tougher and is smarter than almost all of the rock and metal records of its time. There is an urgency to the music unheard in the hard rock of the '80s—a sense of inevitability to the riffs and rhythms, balanced by the justified boasting of Run and D.M.C. Most of their rhymes are devoted to party jams or bragging, but nobody was sharper, funnier, or as clever as this duo, nor was there a DJ better than Jam Master Jay, who not just forms the backbone of their music, but also has two great showcases in "Jam-Master Jammin'" and "Darryl and Joe" (the latter one of two exceptions to the rock rules of the album, the other being the genre-pushing "Roots, Rap, Reggae," one of the first rap tracks to make explicit the links between hip-hop and reggae). Even if there is a pronounced rock influence throughout *King of Rock*, what makes it so remarkable is that it never sounds like a concession in order to win a larger audience. No matter how many metallic guitar riffs are on the record, this music is as raw and street level as the debut. It manages to be just as dynamic, exciting, and timeless as that album, as it expands the definition of what both Run-D.M.C. and rap could do. —*Stephen Thomas Erlewine*

★ **Raising Hell** / 1986 / Profile ✦✦✦✦✦

By their third album, Run-D.M.C. were primed for a breakthrough into the mainstream, but nobody was prepared for a blockbuster on the level of *Raising Hell*. Run-D.M.C. and *King of Rock* had established the crew's fusion of hip-hop and hard rock, but that sound didn't blossom until *Raising Hell*, partially due to the presence of Rick Rubin as producer. Rubin loved metal and rap in equal measures and he knew how to play to the strengths of both, while slipping in commercial concessions that seemed sly even when they borrowed from songs as familiar as "My Sharona" (heard on "It's Tricky"). Along with longtime Run-D.M.C. producer Russell Simmons, Rubin blew down the doors of what hip-hop could do with *Raising Hell* because it reached beyond rap/rock and found all sorts of sounds outside of it. Sonically, there is simply more going on in this album than any previous rap record—more hooks, more drum loops (courtesy of ace drum programmer Sam Sever), more scratching, more riffs, more of everything. Where other rap records, including Run-D.M.C.'s, were all about the rhythm, this is layered with sounds and ideas, giving the music a tangible *flow*. But the brilliance of this record is that even with this increased musical depth, it still rocks as hard as hell, and in a manner that brought in a new audience. Of course, the cover of Aerosmith's "Walk This Way," complete with that band's Steven Tyler and Joe Perry, helped matters considerably, since it gave an audience unfamiliar with rap an entry point, but if it was just a novelty record, a one-shot fusion of rap and rock, *Raising Hell* would never have sold three million copies. No, the music was fully realized and thoroughly invigorating, rocking harder and better than any of its rock or rap peers in 1986, and years later, that sense of excitement is still palpable on this towering success story for rap in general and Run-D.M.C. in specific. —*Stephen Thomas Erlewine*

Tougher than Leather / 1988 / Profile ✦✦✦✦

At the end of 1986, *Raising Hell* was rap's best-selling album up to that point, though it would soon be outsold by the Beastie Boys' *Licensed to Ill*. Profile Records hoped that Run-D.M.C.'s fourth album, *Tougher than Leather*, would exceed the Beastie Boys' quintuple-platinum status, but unfortunately the group's popularity had decreased by 1988. One of Run-D.M.C.'s strong points—its love of rock & roll—was also its undoing in hip-hop circles. Any type of crossover success tends to be viewed suspiciously in the 'hood, and hardcore hip-hoppers weren't overly receptive to "Miss Elaine," "Papa Crazy," "Mary, Mary," and other rap/rock delights found on the album. Thanks largely to rock fans, this album did go platinum for sales exceeding one million copies—which, ironically, Profile considered a disappointment. But the fact is that while *Tougher than Leather* isn't quite as strong as Run-D.M.C.'s first three albums, it was one of 1988's best rap releases. (*Tougher than Leather* was remastered and reissued in 1999.) —*Alex Henderson*

Back From Hell / 1990 / Profile ✦✦✦

Longevity isn't a realistic goal for most rappers, who are lucky if they aren't considered played out by their third or fourth album. By 1990, Run-D.M.C.'s popularity had decreased dramatically, and the Queens residents had lost a lot of ground to both West Coast gangster rappers like Ice Cube, Ice-T, and Compton's Most Wanted. With its fifth album, *Back From Hell*, Run-D.M.C. set out to regain the support of the hardcore rap audience and pretty much abandoned rock-influenced material in favor of stripped-down, minimalist, and consistently street-oriented sounds. Not outstanding but certainly enjoyable, such gritty reflections on urban life as "Livin' in the City," "The Ave.," and "Faces" made it clear that Run-D.M.C. was still well worth hearing. (*Back From Hell* was remastered and reissued in 1999.) —*Alex Henderson*

★ **Together Forever: Greatest Hits 1983-1991** / Nov. 6, 1991 / Profile ✦✦✦✦✦

For the most part, all of Run-D.M.C.'s most important singles and biggest hits are included on *Together Forever: Greatest Hits 1983-1991*. That alone makes the compilation a necessary purchase. However, that doesn't mean that it is a perfectly assembled collection. Instead of presenting the singles in chronological order, the sequencing skips back and forth—for example, it opens with "Sucker M.C.'s," jumps ahead to "Walk This Way," jumps further ahead to "Together Forever," then slams back to "King of Rock." Still, *Together Forever* has 18 of the groundbreaking group's absolutely essential items, from "It's Like That" and "Hard Times" to "It's Tricky" and "Run's House," which makes it an ideal introduction and an enjoyable retrospective. It's just not the definitive collection it could have been. —*Stephen Thomas Erlewine*

Down With the King / May 4, 1993 / Profile ✦✦✦

After 1990's lackluster *Back From Hell*, most hip-hop fans thought that Run-D.M.C. was no longer capable of delivering a solid record. *Down With the King* proved those doubters wrong. Although it didn't burn up the charts like *Raising Hell* and wasn't as innovative as their first album, *Down With the King* showed that they remained strong and talented; it also didn't hurt that the production was provided by several of the 1990s' most talented artists, including Public Enemy, Pete Rock, Naughty By Nature, and Q-Tip. —*Stephen Thomas Erlewine*

Crown Royal / Oct. 12, 1999 / Arista ✦✦

Being one of the most beloved hip-hop groups ever assembled has certainly become a double-edged sword for Run-D.M.C. As one of the culture's most influential groups, the names of Run, D.M.C., and Jam Master Jay immediately garner a certain degree of well-earned respect. Conversely, it has also put the trio under an incredibly intense microscope, a dissection that will become more exacerbated with the shameful *Crown Royal*. With virtually no input from D.M.C. (he appears on a sparse three tracks) *Crown Royal* spirals so recklessly into contrasting segments that it's easy to forget you are even listening to a Run-D.M.C. record. Lacking any discernible sense of direction or continuity, the once cutting-edge trio has seemingly lost touch with its original fan base. They miserably play the role of alternative genre rockers on "Rock Show" (featuring Stephan Jenkins) and "Here We Go" (featuring Sugar Ray). And though tracks with Limp Bizkit's Fred Durst ("Them Girls") and Kid Rock ("The School of Old") may eventually strike a chord with *TRL* fanatics, the groupings lack ingenuity and conviction. So what's left for the fan who was weaned on Run-D.M.C.? Not much! Sure, they throw the hip-hop populace a few bones on "It's Over" (featuring JD), "Queens Day" (featuring Nas and Prodigy), and "Simmons Incorporated" (featuring Method Man). But even these mediocre offerings are not nearly enough to satisfy any of their loyal supporters. If hip-hop has proven anything since its inception, it's that few MCs or groups age gracefully. Hopefully, with its legacy still somewhat intact, Run-D.M.C. will now trade in the shell-toed Adidas, fat gold chains, and leather pants for a long overdue and deserved bow. —*Matt Conaway*

☆ **Greatest Hits** / Sep. 10, 2002 / Arista ✦✦✦✦✦

Supplanting the 1991 collection *Together Forever*, BMG Heritage's 2002 *Greatest Hits* also runs 18 tracks and shares ten of the same songs—namely, all the big hits and usual suspects. Of the eight tracks left behind, there are some big ones—no "Peter Piper" or "My Adidas"—and the sequencing, while flowing much better than its predecessor, is still not chronological, which robs the narrative of some power even if the music retains all of it. So, that means we're still waiting for the perfect Run-D.M.C. collection, but until that arrives, this is an excellent listen and works well as both a summary and introduction to one of the greatest bands of the '80s. —*Stephen Thomas Erlewine*

Rysque

b. Dallas, TX

Dirty Rap, Dirty South

Like most female rappers from the South, Rysque made a name for herself with sexual allure, no doubt living up to her name. After starting her own label, Archive Records, in Houston, TX, she released her debut album, *Peep Show*. As the album's title may lead you to presume, *Peep Show* dealt with sexual subject matter quite explicitly, as well as other dirty South topics like ballin' and smokin'.

Born in Dallas, TX, as Dauwnn McGhee, Rysque participated in many creative activities as a child, including drama, dance, writing, and acting. After obtaining a master's degree in liberal arts and business management affairs, she started Archive Entertainment Corporation, the parent company of her two record labels, Archive and Archdian Records. —*Jason Birchmeier*

RZA (Robert Diggs)

Producer, Vocals / East Coast Rap, Hardcore Rap, Alternative Rap

The Wu-Tang Clan's chief producer, RZA (aka the Abbott, Prince Rakeem, the Rzarector, and Bobby Steels) was born Robert Diggs; he first surfaced during the early '90s as a member of the rap unit All in Together Now, a group which also featured fellow Wu-Tang members the Genius (aka GZA) and Ol' Dirty Bastard. Following All in Together Now's dissolution, he signed to Tommy

Boy under the name Prince Rakeem, issuing the 1991 EP *Ooh We Love You Rakeem* before joining the Wu-Tang; the group's 1993 debut, *Enter the Wu-Tang (36 Chambers)*, was one of the most influential hip-hop records of the era, with RZA's lean, menacing production work much imitated throughout the rap community in the years to follow. In addition to remaining a member of the loose-knit Wu-Tang family and producing many of the group members' solo efforts, RZA also joined the Gravediggaz, helming their 1995 debut *6 Feet Deep*; his first full-length solo LP, *RZA as Bobby Digital in Stereo*, followed in 1998. In 1999, *The RZA Hits*, a compilation of some of the Wu-Tang family's best-known tracks, from both group and solo projects, was released under RZA's name. —*Jason Ankeny*

RZA as Bobby Digital in Stereo / Nov. 16, 1998 / Gee Street ✦✦✦✦
RZA's first solo album, the soundtrack to a film involving experimental self-transformation, has many of the same fractured strings and crisp, staccato beats he made trademarks on Wu-Tang Clan recordings. In fact, this could well *be* a Wu-Tang album, even more so than the legion of other related albums. The only contributors to the project are Wu members (Method Man, Ol' Dirty Bastard, Ghostface Killah, U-God, Inspectah Deck) or relatives (Killarmy, Masta Killa, Sunz of Man). *Bobby Digital in Stereo* is also a more focused work than the last Wu-Tang Clan album (*Forever*), and just a bit more diverse. Though the hooks aren't as big and the raps aren't as upfront, this is a producers album, designed to showcase RZA's talents in the control room, not in front of the mic. —*Keith Farley*

★ **The RZA Hits** / Jun. 22, 1999 / Epic ✦✦✦✦✦
Perhaps the best overall introduction to the dauntingly large Wu-Tang universe, *The RZA Hits* is an excellent singles compilation covering the first round of Wu projects—their debut *Enter the Wu-Tang (36 Chambers)* and the five solo albums recorded in its wake. The material here traces the Wu's rise from underground heroes to full-fledged stardom in hip-hop's mainstream, and arguably no other album captures their offbeat menace and outsized personalities with such stunning consistency. All 13 singles collected here were produced by RZA, giving a primer on his eerie, cinematic style; moreover, these songs were all highlights of their respective albums, from the era when the Wu's quality control was at its highest. Every album represented here is at least an entertaining listen, and three—the group debut, the Genius' *Liquid Swords*, and Raekwon's *Only Built 4 Cuban Linx*—are undisputed classics. Which means that this is only a starting point, but the material is so consistently terrific that it makes *RZA Hits* one of the richest listens in '90s hip-hop. Sure, you can do without the RZA's between-track narrations, or the "bonus track" "Wu Wear, The Garment Renaissance," a lengthy plug for the group's clothing line. But this is the absolute cream of the crop, gathering tremendous singles by Method Man, Ol' Dirty Bastard, the Genius, Raekwon, and Ghostface Killah. Anyone wondering why the Wu-Tang Clan is acknowledged as one of the greatest rap groups of all time need look no further than this collection. —*Steve Huey*

Ghost Dog: The Way of the Samurai / Apr. 11, 2000 / Razor Sharp ✦✦✦
For a movie steeped in hip-hop and an Eastern philosophical aesthetic (an aesthetic largely informed by director Jim Jarmusch's collaboration with Wu-Tang high priest and producer of the soundtrack, RZA), the soundtrack itself is largely banal when detached from the visuals of the film. On the basis of the film's eerie, seamless score, one would expect a soundtrack that would underscore the film's shadowy mood and artistry. However, RZA (or the label) stingily held back some of the musical gems from the film and the result is, on the whole, unsatisfying. RZA, the consummate other-galaxy sound craftsman, appears to be suffering from an inspirational drought induced by his cinematic contributions musically and through his cameo in the film, relying heavily on recycled beats. The soundtrack is not a Wu project, it is an RZA project featuring Wu affiliates and a fragmented Clan. A few of the compositions do break new ground and hit like only RZA's beats can. One of the more expressive cuts is Wu songstress Tekeitha's "Walking Through the Darkness" backed by a lingering bass line and effortless guitar riff. Jeru the Damaja and Afu-Ra's brief "East New York Stamp" is poignant with Afu-Ra ripping the mic relentlessly. "Cakes," featuring Kool G Rap along with RZA; "Stay With Me" by Melodie and Twelve O'Clock; and the rag-tag Wu-Tang Clan's "Fast Shadow" are the only other noteworthy cuts. Quotes included from the film, while relevant, are out of sequence seemingly. Overall, the soundtrack fails to deliver the goods. The minimalism of the film is not resonated by a soundtrack of dark, ponderous, and thought-provoking soundscapes but rather by glancing snapshots that almost muddle the arch-cool and bizarre nature of the film. In the end, RZA's soundtrack amounts to only superficial speculation musically. The film gets an easy A, but the soundtrack barely makes the grade. —*Michael Di Bella*

Digital Bullet / Aug. 28, 2001 / Koch ✦✦✦✦
Digital Bullet is RZA's second album under his latest alias, as Bobby Digital. It's no shock that he brought Bobby back; the first Digital outing, *Bobby Digital in Stereo*, was a high mark in the Wu-Tang Clan producer's prolific career. What is a bit surprising is the sound of this effort, which frequently stretches all the way back to the mystical murk of the Clan's first album, *Enter the Wu-Tang*. The muffled beats and disorienting, late-night soundscapes of that hip-hop classic have been imitated countless times since its 1993 release, but nobody does 'em like the Rizza, and uneasy tracks like "Must Be Bobby" and "Domestic Violence Pt. 2" seem to bring him full circle—as does the presence of several Clan members, including the jailed ODB. Even the nods to the mainstream—"Glocko Pop" and the swaying single "La Rhumba"—seem, like RZA's best work, to have arrived from a slightly different dimension. Meanwhile, there is a storyline to this installment of the Digital story, but as on *In Stereo*, listeners have to use some imagination to fill it out; RZA's rhymes are often as evocative and opaque as the kung-fu flicks he loves. But as always, he creates tracks that are more about atmosphere than message—and when he's on his game, as he is here, it's hard to argue with that approach. —*Dan LeRoy*

Saafir

Hip-Hop
From the Bay Area, Saafir first appeared on Casual's *Fear Itself*, Digital Underground's *The Body-Hat Syndrome*, and the *Menace II Society* soundtrack. With a deal from Qwest Records, the rapper recruited the Hobo Junction production team (J Groove, Jay-Z, Rational, Big Nose, and Poke Marshall) for his freestyle debut, *Boxcar Sessions* (1994). He appeared in the film *Menace II Society* and recorded an album (*Trigonometry*) under the alias Mr. No No before returning as Saafir in 1999 for *The Hit List*. —*John Bush*

● **Boxcar Sessions** / 1994 / Qwest ♦♦♦
In the 1990s, the Bay Area rap scene was full of gangsta rappers and G-funksters. But not every rapper who came from Oakland or San Francisco in the 1990s was into gangsta rap; in fact, there were plenty of Bay Area MCs who had nothing to do with that style or G-funk. Take Saafir, for example. *Boxcar Sessions*, the Oakland rapper's first album, favors an abstract, jazz-influenced approach to hip-hop. In terms of complexity and abstraction, Saafir's angular rapping style (which involves a lot of freestyling) is right up there with Digable Planets, A Tribe Called Quest, the Pharcyde, and De La Soul. Saafir is as jazzy as any of those alternative rappers, and he doesn't go for simplicity. But unlike Digable Planets or the Pharcyde, Saafir doesn't embrace a neo-hippie vibe. Many of the lyrics on *Boxcar Sessions* (which was produced by the Hobo Junction crew) are venomous battle rhymes; Saafir spends much of the album attacking "sucker MCs" and "player haters" in an angry, aggressive fashion. The jazz-minded tracks and the complex, abstract nature of Saafir's rapping style might remind the listener of alternative rap, but the lyrics are not neo-hippie rhymes—*Boxcar Sessions* is, much of the time, a declaration of war on the rappers who Saafir places in the "sucker MC" and "player hater" categories. Obviously, battle rhymes were hardly something new in 1994; Kurtis Blow and other old school rappers were lambasting sucker MCs 15 years before this CD came out. But Saafir finds clever, interesting ways to boast about his rhyming skills and attack rival MCs. Between Saafir's rapping style and the jazzy production, *Boxcar Sessions* is fairly fresh sounding. —*Alex Henderson*

Trigonometry / Jan. 20, 1998 / Hobo ♦♦♦
Beyond a stint backing Digital Underground, an appearance in the film *Menace II Society*, a solo debut album titled *Boxcar Sessions*, and participation in an infamous Wake-Up Show battle, Saafir made paying tribute to his hometown of Oakland his next priority. So in 1997 on Hobo Records, under the moniker Mr. No No, he independently released *Trigonometry*, an album that thoroughly reeks of East Bay street funk. Known by some as mob music, Saafir gives the genre more of an abstracted treatment as compared to cohorts such as 3X Krazy and Mac Mall. With slump-worthy beats provided by J.Z. and Shock-G, Saafir effectively conjures images of late-night sideshows and other devilish escapades. Highlights include "Street Scene," "I'm Saafir," and "J.Z. Theme," as well as the inclusion of older tracks such as "Rock the Show" and "In a Vest." While not quite up to snuff when compared to the breadth of *Boxcar Sessions*, *Trigonometry* makes for a fine album to ride to. —*Robert Gabriel*

The Hit List / Oct. 26, 1999 / Qwest ♦♦♦
Out of the depths of Oakland's underground, Saafir returned late in 1999 with *The Hit List*, officially his sophomore release after a five-year hiatus. Claiming no affiliations to the now rag-tag Hieroglyphics crew and making no real mention of his former Hobo Junction allegiance, Saafir the lyrical heavyweight is one of hip-hop's starving artists. Refusing to bow down to label demands and the drain of the commercial industry, Saafir pleads for respect and paper but feels the tension of realizing what financial success inevitably costs. Saafir, of the penetrating voice and abstract lyrical concepts, is known for his prolific freestyling capabilities. *The Hit List* espouses this freestyle technique. Scoffing at crossovers that would call him a professor of "mad-rapperism," this off-center artist offered the masses *The Hit List*, a meandering album with sparse production and airtight lyrics. Despite its underground appeal and Saafir's superior lyricism, musically, *The Hit List* often misses the mark. The Bay Area underground is known for its compressed, dense sound, and the enigmatic left coast off-the-cuff rhymer who first found his way to the sound booth on Casual's *Fear Itself* is clearly coming out of left field. Even with Saafir's vocal stranglehold, something is missing here either from the artist or, more likely, from the hip-hop game itself. Best tracks here are the Carlos "Six July" Broady- (of late Wu-Tang Clan projects) produced "Six Digits" and "Mask-a-Raid" featuring SoCal's Jayo Felony. "Final Thrill," "Smart Bomb," and "25 ta Life" featuring flame thrower Chino Xl are also top shelf. —*Michael Di Bella*

Sadat X (Derek Murphy)

Vocals, Producer / East Coast Rap, Hip-Hop, Jazz-Rap
As a member of Brand Nubian, Sadat X (born Derek Murphy) was one of the key MCs who related messages inspired by the Five Percent Nation. Two years after Brand Nubian's third album, *Everything Is Everything*, he made his solo debut with *Wild Cowboys*, which built on his lyrical reputation on top of tough, jazz-inflected arrangements. The album, featuring production from Diamond D and Buckwild, was a solid solo debut that didn't quite scale the heights of his legacy with Brand Nubian. *No Better Way*, also released in 1996, improved on the debut and was produced by a cast that opened up to include Da Beatminerz and Pete Rock. Sadat teamed back up with Brand Nubian for 1998's *Foundation*, but he didn't appear again as a solo artist until *The State of New York Vs. Derek Murphy*, an EP released on Relativity in 2000. —*Andy Kellman*

No Better Way / 1996 / Light Records/Upper Room Records ♦♦♦

● **Wild Cowboys** / Jul. 15, 1996 / Loud ♦♦♦
With his first solo album, *Wild Cowboys*, Sadat X continues the jazz-hip-hop fusion that distinguished Brand Nubian's body of work. But the difference between *Wild Cowboys* and Nubian's latter-day records *Everything is Everything* and *In God We Trust* is the approach. As a solo artist, Sadat X is looser and more relaxed, letting the groove flow and casually demonstrating his verbal vacility. With a first-class prodcution crew—including Pete Rock, Beatminerz, Diamond D, Buckwild, and Alamo—Sadat X has created a fun, laid-back album in *Wild Cowboys* that nearly manages to equal the studied intensity of Brand Nubian with its nonchalant virtuosity. —*Leo Stanley*

The State of New York Vs. Derek Murphy / Sep. 19, 2000 / Relativity ♦♦♦
After reuniting in 1998 with his Brand Nubian brothers on the underappreciated *Foundation*, Sadat X resurfaced with two collaborative gems, "1-9-9-9" featuring Common, and the previously vaulted "Come On," which was one of the few highlights from Biggie's disappointing posthumous release. While his solo debut, *Wild Cowboys*, failed to strike a chord with the masses, Sadat shows signs that he may yet establish himself as a solo vocalist with *The State of New York Vs. Derek Murphy*. He enlists a few familiar contributors (Diamond D, Minnesota) and some new ones as well (A Kid Called Roots, Dart La) to update his sound; a revision that is gratuitously bouncy but light in substance. He basks in the glow of Diamond's sublime guitar riffs on the divine "You Can't Deny." But it is the lesser of their two groupings that supplies Sadat with a taste of the commercial success that has alluded him

with the Funk Flex-endorsed "X-Man." While *The State* is remarkably short winded (six tracks), this EP setting is more conducive to his unorthodox style, as it manages to evade the monotonous feel his solo debut conveyed. —*Matt Conaway*

St. Lunatics

f. 1993, St. Louis, MO
Group / Underground Rap

Hailing from St. Louis, MO, the five-piece rap outfit St. Lunatics formed in 1993 and includes members Ali, Nelly, City Spud, Kyjuan, and Murphy Lee. In 1996 the group recorded their debut single, "Gimme What You Got," which turned into a regional hit—selling 8,000 copies and receiving frequent airings on the St. Louis FM station 103 the Beat. Two years later, St. Lunatics met up with the owner of Fo' Reel Entertainment (and Mase's former manager), Cudda Love, who took the rappers under his wing. He landed the band not only a deal with Universal Records but also solo deals for each individual member. June 2001 saw the release of St. Lunatics' debut album, *Free City*. —*Greg Prato*

● **Free City** / Jun. 5, 2001 / Uptown/Universal ◆◆◆
If you're looking for protest rap with socially conscious lyrics and dense soundscapes unlike anything you've heard before, then you've come to the wrong place. But if you're looking for songs about cars and girls with singsong rhymes and bouncy, big-bottom beats, then you may want to hold your party here. As the deliberately off-key, drawling vocals on "Midwest Swing" suggest, these down-to-earth rappers aren't at great risk of taking themselves too seriously; they're more interested in shout-outs to St. Louis and having a good time in general. Fans of Nelly will probably enjoy his work on this album, but it should be noted that St. Lunatics is a group and not just a Nelly side project. Murphy Lee's rougher, faster, and higher-pitched mic style complements Nelly's highly recognizable voice, while Ali, Kyjuan, and City Spud (whose incarceration inspired the album's title) also contribute to this album. Unfortunately, their rhymes and deliveries are often fairly unremarkable, so Nelly remains the dominant voice on *Free City*, even though he shares time with his peeps. It's producer Jason "Jay E" Epperson, however, who's the album's MVP; he keeps the music interesting even when the raps aren't particularly memorable. There are relatively few guest stars here, but Brian McKnight sings joyfully on the lovers' track "Groovin' Tonight," which features an interesting light jazz loop, and Penelope shows plenty of attitude on "Jan a Lang." Overall, this album isn't quite as catchy as *Country Grammar*, but it's still a relatively affable party album. —*Todd Kristel*

Salt-N-Pepa

f. 1985
Group / Hip-Hop, Pop-Rap, Urban

By the late '80s, hip-hop was on its way to becoming a male-dominated art form, which is what made the emergence of Salt-N-Pepa so significant. As the first all-female rap crew (even their DJs were women) of importance, the group broke down a number of doors for women in hip-hop. They were also one of the first rap artists to cross over into the pop mainstream, laying the groundwork for the music's widespread acceptance in the early '90s. Salt-N-Pepa were more pop oriented than many of their contemporaries, since their songs were primarily party and love anthems, driven by big beats and interlaced with vaguely pro-feminist lyrics that seemed more powerful when delivered by the charismatic and sexy trio. While songs like "Push It" and "Shake Your Thang" made the group appear to be a one-hit pop group during the late '80s, Salt-N-Pepa defied expectations and became one of the few hip-hop artists to develop a long-term career. Along with LL Cool J, the trio had major hits in both the '80s and '90s, and, if anything, they hit the height of their popularity in 1994, when "Shoop" and "Whatta Man" drove their third album, *Very Necessary*, into the Top Ten.

Cheryl "Salt" James and Sandy "Pepa" Denton were working at a Sears store in Queens, New York, when their coworker and Salt's boyfriend, Hurby "Luv Bug" Azor, asked the duo to rap on a song he was producing for his audio production class at New York City's Center for Media Arts. The trio wrote an answer to Doug E. Fresh and Slick Rick's "The Show," entitling it "The Show Stopper." The song was released as a single under the name "Super Nature" in the summer of 1985, and it became an underground hit, peaking

at number 46 on the national R&B charts. Based on its success, the duo, who were now named Salt-N-Pepa after a line in "The Show Stopper," signed with the national indie label Next Plateau. Azor, who had become their manager, produced their 1986 debut *Hot, Cool & Vicious*, which also featured DJ Pamela Green. He also took songwriting credit for the album, despite the duo's claims that they wrote many of its lyrics.

Three singles from *Hot, Cool & Vicious*—"My Mike Sounds Nice," "Tramp," "Chick on the Side"—became moderate hits in 1987 before Cameron Paul, a DJ at a San Francisco radio station, remixed "Push It," the B side of "Tramp," and it became a local hit. "Push It" was soon released nationally and it became a massive hit, climbing to number 19 on the pop charts; the single became one of the first rap records to be nominated for a Grammy. Salt-N-Pepa jettisoned Greene and added rapper and DJ Spinderella (born Deidre "Dee Dee" Roper) before recording their second album, *A Salt With a Deadly Pepa*. Though the album featured the Top Ten R&B hit "Shake Your Thang," which was recorded with the go-go band E.U., it received mixed reviews and was only a minor hit.

The remix album *A Blitz of Salt-N-Pepa Hits* was released in 1989 as the group prepared their third album, *Blacks' Magic*. Upon its spring 1990 release, *Blacks' Magic* was greeted with strong reviews and sales. The album was embraced strongly by the hip-hop community, whose more strident members accused the band of trying too hard to cross over to the pop market. "Expression" spent eight weeks at the top of the rap charts and went gold before it even cracked the pop charts, where it would later peak at 26. Another single from the album, "Let's Talk About Sex," became their biggest pop hit to date, climbing to number 13. They later rerecorded the song as a safe-sex rap, "Let's Talk About AIDS."

Before they recorded their fourth album, Salt-N-Pepa separated from Azor, who had already stopped seeing Salt several years ago. Signing with London/Polygram, the group released *Very Necessary* in 1993. The album was catchy and sexy without being a sellout, and the group's new, sophisticated sound quickly became a monster hit. "Shoop" reached number four on the pop charts, which led the album to the same position as well. "Whatta Man," a duet with the vocal group En Vogue, reached number three on both the pop and R&B charts in 1994. A final single from the album, "None of Your Business," was a lesser hit, but it won the Grammy for Best Rap Performance in 1995. Since the release of *Very Necessary*, Salt-N-Pepa have been quiet, spending some time on beginning acting careers. Both had already appeared in the 1993 comedy *Who's the Man? —Stephen Thomas Erlewine*

Hot, Cool & Vicious / 1986 / Next Plateau ◆◆◆
One of the first albums to be released by an all-female rap group, *Hot, Cool & Vicious* is paced by its opening track, "Push It," one of the first rap songs to hit number one on the dance singles charts. Considering how little Salt-N-Pepa actually rap on "Push It," which is all about its instrumental hook, they maintain a surprisingly strong presence over most of *Hot, Cool & Vicious*. No, they aren't technical virtuosos on the mic, but their fairly basic raps are carried off with brash confidence and enthusiasm. Some of the other key tracks borrow ideas from outside sources: the single "Tramp" is a rap remake of the Otis & Carla soul classic, and "The Show Stopper" is an answer record to Doug E. Fresh's "The Show." The duo's sass comes across very well on "My Mic Sounds Nice" and "I'll Take Your Man," and they're equally assertive on "Chick on the Side." In the end, the album needs a little more weight to really come across well, but it's fun and danceable all the same. —*Steve Huey*

A Salt With a Deadly Pepa / 1988 / London ◆◆◆
Attempting to follow up the crossover success of "Push It," Salt-N-Pepa hastily recorded *A Salt With a Deadly Pepa*, which essentially tries to replicate the charms of their debut without expanding on them very much. It doesn't end up quite as engaging, and the duo's limitations start to show themselves on the more underdeveloped material here. There are some good moments, but the album's centerpieces are once again borrowed ideas. "Shake Your Thang" is another hip-hop remake in the vein of "Tramp," this time of the Isley Brothers' "It's Your Thing"; there's also a less-satisfying Isleys cover from a different era in "Twist and Shout" (which lifts the beat of Toni Basil's "Mickey"), plus a rap take on Joe Tex's "I Gotcha." Elsewhere, "I Like It Like That" recycles the beat and brash shout-outs of "Push It." Thankfully, the next time out, Salt-N-Pepa would rethink their music and assume much greater creative control. —*Steve Huey*

● **Blacks' Magic** / Mar. 19, 1990 / London/Next Plateau ✦✦✦✦✦
Prior to the release of their third album, *Blacks' Magic,* Salt-N-Pepa were
viewed as little more than pop crossover artists. Most of their singles had
been rap remakes of old R&B songs, and they hadn't even rapped all that
much on their biggest hit, "Push It," which got by on its catchy synth hook.
But *Blacks' Magic* was where Salt-N-Pepa came into their own. It wasn't that
their crossover appeal diminished, but this time they worked from a funkier
R&B base that brought them more credibility among hip-hop and urban
audiences. More importantly, they displayed a stronger group identity than
ever before, projecting a mix of sassy, self-confident feminism and aggres-
sive but responsible sexuality. The album's trio of hit singles—"Expression,"
"Do You Want Me," and the playful safe-sex anthem "Let's Talk About
Sex"—summed up this new attitude and got the group plastered all over
MTV. But there was more to the album than just the singles—track for track,
Blacks' Magic was the strongest record Salt-N-Pepa ever released. Even if
there's still a bit of filler here and there, *Blacks' Magic* successfully remade
Salt-N-Pepa as their own women, and pointed the way to the even more
commercially successful R&B/pop/hip-hop fusions of *Very Necessary.*
—*Steve Huey*

Very Necessary / Oct. 12, 1993 / London ✦✦✦✦
While Salt-N-Pepa definitely took their time releasing albums during their career, they returned from a three-year sabbatical in 1993 with *Very Necessary,*
a smart album that furthers the progressive femininity that had worked so
well for them on *Blacks' Magic.* As a whole, *Very Necessary* isn't quite as
strong of an album as *Blacks' Magic,* but the female rappers do come prepared with a pair of potent singles capable of carrying the album, "Shoop"
and "Whatta Man." Given the success of "Let's Talk About Sex" three years
earlier, it's unsurprising that Salt-N-Pepa instill that song's progressive feminine stance into both "Shoop" and "Whatta Man." Like "Let's Talk About Sex,"
these two songs aren't overly serious—employing a safe, club-friendly hip-
hop rhythm and catchy, radio-friendly vocal hooks—but they do manage to
effectively communicate their message of feminine pride and a social norm-
challenging view of female sexuality without sacrificing any sense of fun.
Besides these two obviously contrived singles, there aren't too many other
major highlights here, with the exception of "None of Your Business," another
song laden with subtle social commentary regarding femininity. Elsewhere,
a few songs such as "I've Got AIDS" and "Sexy Noises Turn Me On" are interesting from an ideological standpoint but just aren't that impressive in
terms of rapping or production. This can be said for much of the remaining
album as well. When you benchmark the best moments here against the
lesser moments, you get the sense that Salt-N-Pepa are more interested in
crafting the obligatory crossover singles rather than a solid album from beginning to end. *Very Necessary* nonetheless stands as one of the strongest albums of Salt-N-Pepa's 15-year career and is thus a worthwhile, if not very necessary, listen if you're a fan. —*Jason Birchmeier*

Brand New / Oct. 21, 1997 / London ✦✦✦
The four years separating Salt-N-Pepa's latter-day blockbuster *Very Necessary*
and its successor, *Brand New,* is an eternity in hip-hop. During that time,
styles and fashions change rapidly, leaving many artists behind. Salt-N-Pepa
suffer from being out of the spotlight for so long. They don't sound in tune
with the times; they sound like they're stuck in 1993. However, that isn't necessarily a bad thing, since the group does this kind of thing very well. There
isn't anything that stands out like "Whatta Man" or "Shoop," but there are
enough strong moments to make it worthwhile for long-time fans. —*Stephen
Thomas Erlewine*

The Best of Salt 'n Pepa / Jan. 25, 2000 / FFRR ✦✦✦✦
The Best of Salt 'n Pepa is an excellent 15-track overview of the groundbreaking female rap group's career, featuring all their big hits from the early
days up through their platinum success in the '90s. The main problem is that
it hasn't been released in the U.S., and it's also the only good Salt-N-Pepa compilation on the market to date—so if you want it, you'll have to pay an excessive import price for it. That's a shame, because it's an excellent summary
of their career. There are a few alternate mixes included, like the video version of "Whatta Man" and two different versions of "Push It," but there are
no glaring omissions or substitutions. It might have been nice if the tracks
were ordered chronologically, so that the group's development from cover-
happy dance rappers to sexy crossover hitmakers could be traced more readily. But their assertive self-confidence and underlying feminism hold every-

thing together, and the best singles here rank as influential hip-hop classics.
If only there were a domestic compilation.... —*Steve Huey*

Deion Sanders

Hip-Hop, Party Rap
One of the few professional athletes to make a bid for rap success, Deion
Sanders recorded an album (*Prime Time*) and a pair of singles ("Must Be the
Money" and "Prime Time Keeps on Tickin'") in 1995 for Bust It Records. The
recordings didn't make much impact, and Sanders continued on with his fa-
mous sports career, where he became the only athlete ever to play in both the
World Series (1992) and Super Bowl (1995 and 1996). —*Jason Birchmeier*

Prime Time / 1995 / Bust It ✦✦
That dual-sport superstar Deion Sanders didn't bring the same game to the
recording studio as he did to the playing field hardly qualified as a surprise.
The only real intrigue of *Prime Time,* as with most celebrity albums, is how
the star managed to defeat his high-profile friends' attempts to make him interesting. In this case, it wasn't difficult for Sanders to short-circuit contributions from pals like Too Short, Dallas Austin, and Ant Banks: his nasal rapping and inability to offer any references beyond his own rags-to-riches
sports biography make this one a yawner almost from the outset. Not that
the G-funk that surrounds Deion's rhymes is much to get excited about. In
fact, the only thing that might keep a listener awake is his overwhelming ego.
Of course, it's definitely time for a snooze when said ego leads the barely able
to rhyme Deion to indulge himself in a little crooning, defacing Austin's bass-
popping "Must Be the Money," one of the few decent tracks. The others bite
from obvious sources ("Too Hot" on "Y U NV Me?" and "We Will Rock You"
on "It Ain't Over") making *Prime Time* competent at best. At worst, it's not
just for sports fans—it's not for anyone. —*Dan LeRoy*

Sauce Money

*East Coast Rap, Hardcore Rap, Hip-Hop, Gangsta Rap, Alternative Rap,
   Underground Rap*
Rapper Sauce Money emerged from Brooklyn's Marcy Projects as a member
of Jay-Z's Roc-A-Fella clique, making a number of appearances on sound-
tracks and mix tapes (as well as scoring a writing Grammy for his work on
Puff Daddy's blockbuster "I'll Be Missing You") before issuing his solo debut,
Middle Finger U, on Priority in 1999. —*Jason Ankeny*

● **Middle Finger U** / Nov. 2, 1999 / Priority ✦✦✦
Even though Sauce Money is most acclaimed for turning the art of ghost writing into a lucrative and highly compensated occupation, by penning Puffy's
haunting, Grammy Award-winning tribute to B.I.G., "I'll Be Missing You," he
is no new jack to discerning hip-hop heads. While "I'll Be Missing You" garnished Sauce widespread recognition, this MC from the infamous Marcy
Projects had already begun to solidify his spot in underground circles with
appearances on Jay-Z's first two LPs and the blazing DJ Premier produced
"Against the Grain" from the *Soul in the Hole* soundtrack. Sauce does not attempt to re-create the wheel with his debut, *Middle Finger U,* as it is a loose
unregimented project that contains little in the form of concept. Yet, what
holds this project together is Sauce's gift of gab, as his slick street bravado
and witty punchlines are most arousing on "Pregame" featuring Jay-Z,
"What's My Name," and his reunion with Premier, "Intruder Alert." While
Sauce's facetious vocals and verbal flair abound with crossover possibilities,
his debut sorely lacks one prerequisite—consistent production. Although
Middle Finger U fails to meet expectations, Sauce Money need not fret, after
all, Puffy will always need another hit. —*Matt Conaway*

Saukrates

b. 1977
Producer, Vocals / Hip-Hop, Underground Rap
A Toronto-based rapper with an ear for music (classically trained in the
violin and cello) and a head for business, Saukrates was fed on the mid-'80s
rap styles of De La Soul, Special Ed, and the Native Tongue rap movement.
He freestyled rhymes on the fly, basing his lyrics on personal experiences
and dreams, just as other rappers before him. Once he started putting his
rhymes to paper in 1989, the young MC began to seriously fine-tune his
skills. Saukrates hit pay dirt with his first single, "Hate Runs Deep," released
in late 1994. It won top prize at an MC contest and, at 18, he followed with
"Brick House" on Slammin' Records. In 1997, a mix-tape release hit the

streets and Saukrates became well known in college radio circles for the rap jams "Father Time" and "Play Dis." Just when success was all but guaranteed, his then-label Warner Bros. essentially shut down its rap music division, leaving Saukrates with recorded material but no mode of distribution. Joining creative and financial forces with his manager, Chase Parsons, he created Capital Hill Music and in early summer 1999 they released *The Underground Tapes* in the United States under the Serious Entertainment label. Later that same summer, *The Underground Tapes* was re-released in Canada on Capital Hill Music/ILL Vibe with six additional tracks. *—Roxanne Blanford*

● **The Underground Tapes** / 1999 / Capital Hill ✦✦✦
Prepare yourself for a Canadian offensive, because Saukrates is only one of a few accomplished Maple Leaf artists ready to infiltrate U.S. soil. Influenced by the quintessential New York sound of old, Saukrates' self-produced jazzy synthesizers and organic string sections permeate with a Native Tongues vibe. But it's lyrically where Saukrates distinguishes himself, as his flow and domineering habitation on the mic are utterly hypnotic. Many of Sauk's finest moments come courtesy of expansive collaborations, as guests include Pharoe Monch on "Innovations," Common on "Play Dis (99 Sox Remix)," and Xzibit on "Keep It Moving." *—Matt Conaway*

Scaramanga

Producer / Underground Rap
Scaramanga gained experience from being part of Kool Keith's production front in the early '90s. With Kool Keith, Scaramanga helped create the Dr. Octagon concept, cowrote and produced tracks, and toured with the group. Upon his return to New York, he took on the alias Sir Menelik and teamed with Rawkus for a series of singles and appearances on the MTV show *Lyricist Lounge*. The Rawkus album was delayed endlessly and Scaramanga went solo, with the end product being 2001's full-length, *Seven Eyes Seven Horns*. The album hosted a large handful of New York MCs and producers including DJ Spinna and Goldfinghaz of the Wu-Tang Clan. *—Diana Potts*

● **Seven Eyes Seven Horns** / Feb. 2, 1999 / Sun Large ✦✦✦
Scaramanga's debut, *Seven Eyes Seven Horns*, features the Brooklyn MC better known as Sir Menelik spinning big-player fantasies over sparse beats. He and coconspirator Scholarwise go back and forth spitting rhyming nonsequiturs. The names of clothing brand, mathematical formulas, and general tough guy talk all find their way into their verses. On "Special Efx" featuring Godfather Don, and "Strip Club Bait," in which the dialing of a cellular phone forms the basis of the beat, this weird amalgamation works. On others, Scaramanga just loses himself in his own nonsensical fantasies. *—Christopher Witt*

Scarface (Brad Jordan)

Vocals, Producer / Gangsta Rap, Hardcore Rap, Southern Rap
Scarface quickly became the South's most admired rapper and remained so throughout the '90s after breaking away from the Geto Boys to launch his solo career in 1991. Even if he never scored any national hits or stormed up the *Billboard* charts with any of his numerous albums throughout the '90s, no one could question his clout throughout the South. He essentially defined what it meant to be a Southern thug rapper years before anyone even coined the term "dirty South". This became glaringly evident in the late '90s when a massive wave of young MCs arose from Houston, New Orleans, and Memphis emulating his style of hard-boiled, ghetto-bred, straight-up hardcore rapping. Besides serving as the father of Southern thug rap, it seemed as if every hardcore rapper wanted to align himself with Scarface during the '90s— everyone from Ice Cube and Dr. Dre to 2Pac and Master P collaborated with the former Geto Boy—all in an attempt to foster credibility among the loyal Southern rap audience. Yet despite his unquestionable influence, Scarface never crossed over to mainstream acceptance. His albums were often plagued with half-hearted filler, his lyrics were simply too harsh for radio, and his uncompromising devotion to producer Mike Dean led to a stagnant, albeit trademark, sound. Still, likely *because* Scarface never crossed over and remained aligned to the streets, his influence never waned, making him one of the few veterans able to sustain in the here-today, gone-tomorrow rap game. In the early 2000s, Def Jam Records rewarded his staying power with a lucrative contract, a wealth of industry connections, and a powerful marketing push. Scarface consequently enjoyed the most successful album of his career,

The Fix (2002), and a revival of interest in his back catalog, which his former label, Rap-A-Lot, repackaged that same year on *Greatest Hits*.

Before Brad Jordan became known as Scarface, he called himself Akshen. As such, he began his rap career first as a solo artist in his native Houston during the mid-'80s for James Smith's then-fledging Rap-A-Lot label. Smith was trying to launch a group he tagged the Geto Boys, and eventually asked Akshen to join the group in the late '80s. The Geto Boys' debut album—*Grip It! On That Other Level* (1990), later repackaged and re-released that same year simply as *The Geto Boys*—shocked many with its vivid depictions of violence and its overall extreme nature. This album featured the song "Scarface," which introduced Akshen's alterego, a title he would keep from that point onward. The ensuing controversy surrounding the group's debut put the Geto Boys on the map and set the stage for the impressive *We Can't Be Stopped* (1991). In the wake of the group's national success came solo albums, one of which being Scarface's debut, *Mr. Scarface Is Back* (1991). The album made it evident who the group's most talented member was, and the acclaim showered on Scarface resulted in bitter tensions among his fellow Geto Boys, Bushwick Bill and Willie D.

By the time Scarface returned with his follow-up album, *The World Is Yours* (1993), his reputation overshadowed that of his group's. Willie D consequently departed, and the the Geto Boys never again rivaled *We Can't Be Stopped*, releasing half-hearted, albeit popular, efforts with a new lineup before later reuniting in the late '90s. In the meantime, Scarface continued to funnel his efforts into additional solo efforts: *The Diary* (1994) and *Untouchable* (1997). He then released the double-disc *My Homies* (1998), a bloated effort laden with guests, many of the South's leading rappers. It wasn't until 2000, though, that Scarface won substantial admiration from the greater rap community with *Last of a Dying Breed*, his most personal and focused album in years. As a result, he was awarded Lyricist of the Year at the 2001 *Source* awards and was offered a promising deal with Def Jam Records. The powerhouse East Coast label wanted Scarface to helm its Def Jam South subsidiary division, and the rapper obliged, first signing Ludacris, who became an overnight superstar, and then releasing his own album, *The Fix* (2002). Led by a Kanye West-produced collaboration with Jay-Z, "Guess Who's Back," it spawned a popular single, "My Block," and attracted widespread embrace. Rap-A-Lot furthered Scarface's newfound coast-to-coast acceptance with the rapper's first best-of collection, *Greatest Hits* (2002). *—Jason Birchmeier*

● **Mr. Scarface Is Back** / Oct. 3, 1991 / Rap-A-Lot ✦✦✦✦
Fresh from the brilliant success of "Mind Playing Tricks on Me," his breakthrough hit with the Geto Boys, Scarface continues his streak of excellence with his exceptionally creative solo debut, *Mr. Scarface Is Back*. One of the first genuine masterpieces of the gangsta era, the album draws heavily from the densely layered samplescapes of the Bomb Squad and the provocative ghetto storytelling of Ice Cube. What sets Scarface apart from his New York and Compton peers, though, is his deep-Texas Houston locale, where coke and crime are daily operations. Scarface exploits this reality shockingly and cinematically throughout *Mr. Scarface Is Back*, beginning with the album-opening Al Pacino samples ("All I have in this world…"). From there, Scarface makes an explosive entry ("Ahh yeah, hah/Mr. Scarface is back in the motherfuckin' house once again!") and tremors through one rhyme after another about the ins and outs of the gangsta life in a loose narrative sequence: drug dealing gone well ("Mr. Scarface"), the joy of recreational sex ("The Pimp"), heedless murder ("Born Killer"), mental unsoundness ("Murder by Reason of Insanity"), further mental unsoundness ("Diary of a Madman"), intoxicating heights of street superiority ("Money and the Power"), drug dealing gone awry ("Good Girl Gone Bad"), and the consequential last hurrah ("A Minute to Pray and a Second to Die"). The narrative format of *Mr. Scarface Is Back* flows from beginning to end with engaging fluidity, though the album is just as enjoyable in bits and pieces, particularly the ferocious "Mr. Scarface," the remorseful "A Minute to Pray and a Second to Die," and the extensive sampling (Marvin Gaye's "What's Going On," War's "Four Cornered Room," and more, less-obvious source material). Scarface had always been the standout Geto Boy, and he's finally given ample space for his trademark street narratives on *Mr. Scarface Is Back*, one of the first gangsta rap albums to offer as much imagination as it does exploitation. *—Jason Birchmeier*

The World Is Yours / Aug. 17, 1993 / Rap-A-Lot ✦✦✦
Scarface once again quickly follows a Geto Boys album, *Till Death Do Us Part*, with a solo release, *The World Is Yours*, just as he'd done two years

earlier with his brilliant solo debut, *Mr. Scarface Is Back*. The circumstances are otherwise quite different, though. Scarface had been on a roll in 1991: fresh off the breakthrough success of "Mind Playing Tricks on Me" and its similarly well-received Geto Boys album, *We Can't Be Stopped*, he unveiled a cinematic, somewhat conceptual solo debut that made him a bona fide national superstar. Furthermore, much changed within the rap world between 1991 and 1993, specifically the end of free-for-all sampling and the widespread proliferation of gangsta rap. Scarface thus delivers a follow-up that's a huge leap forward from his debut, both in terms of production and rhetoric. He works here mostly with producer N.O. Joe, who crafts a G-funk style distinctly modeled after the West Coast sounds of the moment à la *The Chronic*, and he favors personally introspective rhymes rather than his heedful narratives of the past. The heartfelt seven-and-a-half-minute "Now I Feel Ya" showcases this new lyrical approach best, as Scarface rhymes at one point about his new son and how in turn he's had to alter his lifestyle. The significant changes Scarface has made here on *The World Is Yours* showcase his unwillingness to revel in the past, as glorious as his past may have been, yet they at the same time may frustrate fans of his early work, as his new style moves him further into the gangsta rap mainstream. —*Jason Birchmeier*

The Diary / Oct. 18, 1994 / Rap-A-Lot ✦✦✦✦
With the dissolution of the Geto Boys far behind him, Scarface follows the epic overreaching of *The World Is Yours* with *The Diary*, a refreshingly modest album with a few really strong moments and little filler. Never short on ideas, Scarface had nonetheless gone a little too far with the 70-minute *The World Is Yours*. There was plenty of brilliance there, including the stunning "Now I Feel Ya," but you had to do some sifting to find it. That's less the case with the 43-minute *Diary*, which doesn't overextend its ambitions. Scarface here once again offers a laid-back gangsta ballad, "I Seen a Man Die," that's as thoughtful and somber as the style gets and also perhaps the album highlight. Elsewhere, he teams up with fellow gangsta veteran Ice Cube on "Hand of the Dead Body" and reprises his best-known song, "Mind Playin' Tricks 94." Not counting the interludes, there are only ten songs here, and they're nearly all produced by the team of N.O. Joe and Mike Dean. It may make the album a short listen, yet it also makes *The Diary* one of Scarface's most solid efforts, one where you rarely, if ever, feel inclined to skip a song. And that's something you can't say about the work of most rappers, particularly ones as creative as Scarface. —*Jason Birchmeier*

Untouchable / Mar. 11, 1997 / Rap-A-Lot ✦✦✦
Scarface's fourth album, *Untouchable*, is yet another collection of hardcore gangsta rap, this time spiked with a G-funk influence—both Dr. Dre ("Game Over") and 2Pac ("Smile") appear on the record, lending their rhyming skills to the deep bass grooves. While the production is impeccable, Scarface offers nothing distinctive on the album, and the record runs way too long to stay interesting. A handful of cuts, including those with Dre and 2Pac, are worthwhile, but *Untouchable* is his weakest effort yet. —*Leo Stanley*

My Homies / Feb. 24, 1998 / Rap-A-Lot ✦✦✦
Scarface was never one of the more consistent hardcore rappers, falling prey to a tendecy for cartoonish violence and comic-book gangsta fantasies. As long as his music hit hard, such traits were forgivable, but he began to slip in the mid-'90s, relying on familiar styles, samples, beats, and grooves. All of these factors are reasons why his double-disc opus, *My Homies*, was not the greatest of ideas. Scarface simply doesn't have enough ideas to sustain an album of this gargantuan size, especially since it follows *Untouchable* by just a year. He recycles beats and bass lines, and he repeats themes over and over again. The moments that do work, such as the dynamic Master P collaboration "Homies & Thuggs," only put the weakness of the remaining album in sharper relief. *My Homies* would have been tiring if it had been a single 70-minute disc, but at this bloated double length, it's plain exhausting. —*Stephen Thomas Erlewine*

Last of a Dying Breed / Oct. 3, 2000 / Rap-A-Lot ✦✦✦
The sixth album from Scarface doesn't stray too far from his usual subjects: pain, murder, mayhem, and vengeance are all well represented on this sort-of concept album involving a life in turmoil. It's certainly Scarface's most personal album, with the rapper taking more responsibility for his actions and accounting for his words (and actually providing some well-deserved introspection on a few tracks). But this is still a street album, and Scarface still

often takes a lazy street stance. Nonetheless, it's a good representation of a gangsta's development into conscientiousness. —*Michael Gallucci*

● **Greatest Hits** / Jul. 16, 2002 / Rap-A-Lot ✦✦✦✦✦
The prototype for the dirty South thug image that came years after his debut, Scarface is a harsh and gritty MC who never broke into the mainstream because he had little desire to cross over. On *Greatest Hits*, Scarface collects most of his singles and well-known album tracks in a collection that has the tiniest thread of chronological order (most of his older songs are found toward the beginning), but maintains a variety that keeps it interesting. What emerges is an image of Scarface the innovator, as he continually evolves his funky gangsta rap without latching onto popular sounds or trends. Growing from a tight and somewhat-dated new jack swing sound to an eerie liquid funk through the years, Scarface maintained an originality that kept him a vital force in the underground. His loyalty to producer Mike Dean is the main reason, giving his body of work a common thread that most MCs rarely bother with. His unique delivery predates the gruff dirty South sound with a harsh and immediate approach, but his often-overlooked lyrics are some of the most personal in the genre. None of his awesome Geto Boys tracks are included, but his simplistic early solo work transitions into his complex and thoughtful later years quite well. Scarface isn't afraid to look at both sides of his raps, and he often injects harsh truths into songs that would be nothing more than childish fantasies in the hands of lesser lyricists. Almost like a sequel to the Geto Boys' excellent *Uncut Dope* collection, *Greatest Hits* documents the solo years of one of the genre's most respected voices. It may be an acquired taste, but Scarface is a chilling realist in a music style known for its consequence-free boasts. —*Bradley Torreano*

The Fix / Aug. 6, 2002 / Def Jam ✦✦✦
Brad Jordan, head of A&R for Def Jam South, was a big success after just a few months on the job; his signing of Ludacris in 2000 paid off in triple platinum after less than a year. It's not every A&R man who's rewarded for great work with an album of his own, but then again, not every A&R man is also one of the most influential voices in the history of hip-hop. After defining the down-South gangsta during the late '80s with Geto Boys, Scarface began a solo career that earned him a couple of gold albums and saw some of the biggest names in rap (2Pac, Ice Cube, Kurupt, Too Short) angling to work with him—this back when posse tracks were rarities. Scarface fans will recognize quite a few of the usual themes throughout *The Fix*, like the good-times-and-bad territory anthem "My Block" (complete with an old school production, '70s style) and "In Cold Blood," a first-person journal entry from a gang banger. The highlights, though, find Scarface morphing back into Jordan the bottom-line businessman, banking on the familiar names: "Guess Who's Back" is more a Jay-Z track with a little room for Scarface than the other way around, and the same goes for the Nas feature, "In Between Us." And Pharrell from Neptunes takes over "Someday," with Faith Evans adding a little sugar to the chorus to make up for the patented Scarface growl on the verses. Though *The Fix* has him reaching for the charts as well as focusing on the personal, the inimitable Scarface balances the competing concerns well. —*John Bush*

Schoolly D (Jesse B. Weaver Jr.)

b. Philadelphia, PA
Golden Age, Gangsta Rap, East Coast Rap, Hardcore Rap
Opinion has been widely mixed about the merits of Philadelphia rapper Jesse B. Weaver Jr. aka Schoolly D. Long before the debate about gangsta rap lyrics became an easy way to get national newsprint, there was outrage over Schoolly D's explicit and undiluted narratives on inner city strife. *Saturday Night! The Album* in 1987 and *Smoke Some Kill* in 1988 had city officials openly endorsing removal of the albums from record stores. He has continued in the same vein with 1989's *Am I Black Enough for You?* and 1996's *A Gangster's Story: 1984-1996*. Schoolly D's rather lackluster rapping style and repetitive material don't place him in the forefront of hip-hop creators, but he does merit mention (or blame, depending on your perspective) for being an early gangsta proponent. His career got a bit of a boost after the Chemical Brothers sampled him on their 1997 *Dig Your Own Hole* album, creating a bit of interest in a rapper few of the late-'90s youth were familiar with. Furthermore, Schoolly D's relationship with esteemed film director Abel Ferrara gave him the opportunity to collaborate on the soundtracks to several of the director's films such as *The Addiction* and *Kings of New York*.

In late 2000, the rapper released his *Funk 'N Pussy* album, trying to reignite his faltering career. —*Ron Wynn*

Schoolly D / 1986 / Jive ✦✦✦
It was unclear on this self-titled LP whether Schoolly D wanted to be a comic or a poet, a philosopher or a storyteller, and whether he wanted to concentrate on topical issues or lighter material. Perhaps it was a reflection of the uncertainty in his raps and the muddiness of his rhymes, because no clear vision or direction emerged on this record. —*Ron Wynn*

The Adventures of Schoolly D / 1987 / Rykodisc ✦✦✦✦
Gangster rap is associated primarily with the West Coast, but one of its earliest figures was Philadelphia's Schoolly-D who sent shock waves through hip-hop circles with "Saturday Night," "P.S.K. What Does It Mean?," and other hard-hitting tales of inner-city crime and violence included on this 1987 compilation. Instead of simply examining social problems in the third person, he made things especially jolting by rapping in the first person about life as he knew it growing up in West Philly. Unfortunately, the underrated Schoolly never enjoyed the sales or recognition of Ice-T, Dr. Dre, or Ice Cube. But listening to "P.S.K."'s shocking imagery, it becomes clear just how seminal a figure he was. Though Schoolly isn't nearly as graphic as some of his West Coast counterparts would be, there's no denying his influence. For those interested in hearing some of the earliest examples of gangster rap, *The Adventures of Schoolly D* is essential listening. —*Alex Henderson*

Saturday Night! The Album / 1987 / Jive ✦✦✦✦
Philadelphia rapper Schoolly D functions better as an absurdist commentator exploring the netherworld of inner-city chaos than as a political philosopher or Afro-centric advocate. This 1987 album was among his best, precisely because he chose to be bizarre rather than prophetic and kept things freewheeling instead of didactic. —*Ron Wynn*

Smoke Some Kill / 1988 / Jive ✦✦
Philadelphia rapper Schoolly D was among the earliest gangstas to generate censorship threats. This 1988 LP included lewd descriptions of genitalia, vivid commentary on drug use and its impact, plus "Gangster Boogie II" and "Black Man." Schoolly D's rapping was erratic and often seemed disjointed, while his rhymes hardly flowed. It was more chaotic than creative, but did manage to generate considerable East Coast controversy among more sedate types. —*Ron Wynn*

Am I Black Enough for You? / Jul. 27, 1989 / Jive ✦✦✦
While Schoolly D's attempts to present Afro-centric philosophy and call for self-determination were commendable, he failed to present them in either a musically satisfying or lyrically convincing manner. This 1989 album did little beyond rip white society for its ills and injustices in a fashion merging the worst excesses of rambling propaganda and irrational nationalism. —*Ron Wynn*

How a Blackman Feels / Oct. 14, 1991 / Capitol ✦✦✦
Although one of the founders of gangster rap, Schoolly D never enjoyed the gold or platinum success of the many gangster rappers who reached the top of the charts in the late '80s and early to mid-'90s. The Philadelphian had recorded four albums for Jive/RCA when he resurfaced on Capitol with the uneven and erratic *How a Blackman Feels*. This isn't a bad album, but it isn't one of Schoolly's stronger efforts either. The CD's most engaging offerings include "Die Nigger Die" and "King of New York," both of which are chilling, first-person depictions of a drug dealer's violent world. The album will be of interest primarily to Schoolly's more devoted fans, while those investigating his music for the first time would do better to acquire *Saturday Night! The Album* or *Smoke Some Kill*. —*Alex Henderson*

Welcome to America / Feb. 1, 1994 / Ruffhouse ✦✦✦✦
Schoolly D returns with a spare, dark attempt to recapture the gangsta audience he helped create back in the 1980s; it helps that the record contains the best music he has ever recorded, although the best moments can't hide the fact that Schoolly D doesn't have the lyrical grace of the rappers that followed in his footsteps. —*Stephen Thomas Erlewine*

Reservoir Dog / Apr. 16, 1995 / PSK ✦✦✦
Nobody should be shocked at how influential George Clinton was to his '80s-and '90s-era hip-hop brethren; Philadelphia's Scholly D is among the many hip-hoppers acknowledging Clinton's impact—down to the '70s-era cartoon character's exclamation ("Damn, bopped again"). The sound on *Reservoir Dog* is as dense as previous albums, but Schoolly doesn't skimp on the

groove. Unlike other artists who produce themselves, he appreciates the virtue of simplicity and does all the keyboards, leaving the rhythm work to a small supporting cast. (Long-time DJ Code Money is present, but mixed less prominently than prior albums.) The organic approach stays largely sample free, resulting in a sparse but uncluttered sound. Rhyming-wise, Schoolly remains focused on the foibles and follies of urban America. The standout track is "Nigger Entertainment," which satirizes the banality of urban violence taken for granted—a drift abundantly mined on "Hustler Life" and "Gotta Hustle to Survive." (The latter track is one of several featuring Tamika Vines's forceful vocal presence.) Other tracks draw loose inspiration from today's *film noir* malaise—notably "Date With Death" and "Eternity" (which credits its inspiration to director Abel Ferrara, who's used several Schoolly tracks in movies). But Schoolly hasn't checked his fun at the door, either, as the bumptious bass work on "Ghettofunkstylistic" and "Welcome to Funkadelica" makes clear. In many ways, Schoolly's vision hasn't moved terribly far from dark-humored classics like "I Know You Want to Kill Me," and he's hardly the deftest lyricist that picked up a microphone (rhyming "drunk" and "little punk" may well be grounds for calling out the cringe police). But the fans who've followed him this long probably couldn't care less, because his entertainment quotient is proudly intact; sometimes, that's good enough. —*Ralph Heibutzki*

The Jive Collection, Vol. 3 / Jun. 27, 1995 / Jive ✦✦✦✦✦
According to the charts, Schoolly D never had any official hits, but a number of singles were underground sensations during the early '80s. *The Jive Collection, Vol. 3* compiles the bulk of these singles and throws in a handful of album tracks and lesser-known singles for good measure. The result is not only an ideal introduction to his music but also a definitive retrospective of his glory days, when he was still a respected rapper within the hip-hop community. —*Stephen Thomas Erlewine*

A Gangster's Story: 1984-1996 / Aug. 6, 1996 / CTRA ✦✦✦✦
Gangster's Story functions as an excellent introduction to Schoolly D, one of the first gangsta rappers of the '80s. Although the production on the album has aged-poorly and some of the songs sound tame compared to what came later, *Gangster's Story* showcases what Schoolly D was all about, both for better and for worse. It's not the kind of disc that will convert listeners to gangsta rap, but historians and aficionados will find it a useful collection. —*Stephen Thomas Erlewine*

Funk 'N Pussy / Oct. 24, 2000 / Chord ✦✦✦
Without a major release in several years and with little mainstream success over the course of the 1990s, Schoolly D quietly released *Funk 'N Pussy* in late 2000 to an indifferent public. Though the Philadelphia rapper relied more on exploitation than talent to first make a name for himself in the late '80s, this album suggests that Schoolly may have found some substantial inspiration in the late '90s. First of all, he deserves accolades for producing this album by himself, an accomplishment few rappers can claim and a feat he performs in a rather stunning manner. Granted, Schoolly's murky and collage-like beats aren't going have the rap industry knocking on his door, but they do sound quite inventive with their messy chaos. Second, the chaotic production serves another worthwhile purpose by slightly eclipsing his rapping. With his vocals buried in the thick mix—well below the samples, beats, and other assorted sounds—it becomes less apparent that Schoolly is a mediocre rapper at best. When the vocals do manage to come across intelligibly, it's clear that the pioneering gangsta rapper still claims to be "hardcore to the motherfuckin' bone," which should make his small cult audience happy. In the end, this album comes across as an admittedly interesting listen, not so much because of its innovation or craft but rather because of its uniqueness—Schoolly's indifference about the norms of rap production proves him well. Yet beneath this novelty, he's still an old school rapper, not an engaging quality by any means in an age chock full of mind-blowing MCs. *Funk 'N Pussy* isn't fascinating enough to resurrect Schoolly's sunken career, but it's interesting enough to warrant a listen if you're a dedicated fan of his unique approach. —*Jason Birchmeier*

● **The Best of Schoolly D** / Feb. 18, 2003 / Jive ✦✦✦✦✦
If *The Best of Schoolly D* looks similar to another compilation that was released a few years prior to this one, it's because it *is* that compilation. *The Best of Schoolly D* simply is *The Jive Collection, Vol. 3* with a different title. It features the same 12 tracks, but the sound quality is slightly improved here. The disc is a decent mix of underground hit singles and album cuts, like

"Smoke Some Kill," "P.S.K. What Does It Mean?," "Saturday Night," "Gucci Time," and "Fat Gold Chain." Schoolly D did put out some solid albums during the latter half of the '80s, but this is a fine place to start. —*Andy Kellman*

Scientific Universal Noncommercial (S.U.N.)
(Santonio Hughbanks)

b. Ypsilanti, MI
Vocals / Underground Rap, Hip-Hop
Scientific Universal Noncommercial (Santonio Hughbanks) is no stranger to the wide world of hip-hop. Rhyming from the early age of a 16, S.U.N.'s earliest incarnation as half of the group UBU gave hip-hop heads everywhere their first taste of the spiritual nature and consciousness in content that would come to define S.U.N.'s contribution and artistic integrity as an MC. UBU partnered S.U.N. and Brother Browne in a musical alliance that allowed them to pose lyrical musings on subjects of cultural and ethereal significance while establishing credibility as serious verbalists. Backing these abstract inspirations with unquestionably tight beats gave the duo two successful independent releases, "Deep Space" and "Radical Spiritual Progression." Even though UBU was enjoying local success and rave critical reviews, S.U.N.'s desire to put forth a solo album became a defining force in his career. In 1997 S.U.N. was finally offered the chance to do exactly that as he crafted his debut release, "Shining Underground."

With featured flows from Paradime, Invincible, Browne, Bizarre, and Mr. Sinns, Scientific Universal Noncommercial laid down eight full tracks with production by newcomer Tink Thomas. The guest spots not only beefed up his tracks with the verbal sparring but also established the fact that he was unafraid of the neighboring schools of hip-hop. Especially in the case of Bizarre, whose misogynist and purposefully offensive rhymes would make any elevated soul cringe, S.U.N. lets his talent speak for itself. The contrast of their rhyming styles does manage to make a perfect playground for each to do their thing without detracting from or lessening either's credibility.

Shining Underground produced the single "T.H.U.G. (True Heart Underground)" and few other shining tracks that brought the Ypsilanti, MI, native some well-deserved respect. While S.U.N. was busy supporting his first solo effort, a foundation was being laid for his next studio joint, *School of Thought*. If "Shining Underground" is an introduction of S.U.N. as a solo artist, then *School of Thought* is his manifesto as a hip-hop warrior. His 2000 release is a confident and daring collection of cerebral metaphors, powerhouse tracks, and ingenious MC collaborations. S.U.N.'s sophomore effort not only one-ups his own achievements but also raises the bar on what true self-expression should sound like. —*Emilie Litzell*

● **School of Thought** / 2000 / Black Soul On Vinyl ◆◆◆◆
Scientific Universal Noncommercial (Santonio Hughbanks) has had a long time running in the hip-hop game. Perfecting his own blend of spirituality, truth, and metaphoric wordplay has proven to be no small feat, but *School of Thought* might have him doing exactly that. S.U.N.'s 2000 release is a manifesto of intelligent rhymeplay, laced-over sci-fi beats, and some truly classic hip-hop vibes to boot. While S.U.N. served as the executive producer over the entire joint, Houseshoes, OPM, and Jeff Baraka all bring in solid beats and distinctive grooves. The truly remarkable trait this album offers is the diversity S.U.N. puts out in the tracks all the while maintaining lyrical consistency. "Deadly Toxins" comes through with a heavy drop-down beat, "Cosmic Consciousness" is right on the tail of it with a down-tempo groove, and synth-happy vocals on the hook. From one song to the next, the beats vary just enough to keep you interested, but without sacrificing the art, skill, or content S.U.N. provides as an MC. One of the unquestionable highpoints of this album is the collaboration between S.U.N. and the 16 other artists featured on various tracks. Whether it's the laid-back Jeff Baraka beat of "Radiate" with the quick flowing verses traded between S.U.N., O Type Star, and Juice, or the classic hip-hop presented on "Writings" with One Man Army, the feature spots are perfectly planned on the rest of the album. "Radiate" and "Writings" may leave you with some decidedly chill sensations, but before you get to comfortable in that vibe, S.U.N. hits you with "Different Forces." Chemical, Nate the Great, Combat, Mr. Sinns, and Paradime join forces with the Scientific One for a true down-and-dirty Detroit vibe. All three tracks have one thing in common: not a rhyme out of place, not a beat wasted, and every track offers up its own sound. As for the MC himself, the rhymes are on point from start to finish. S.U.N.'s delivery

can only be defined as masterful. His voice comes at you with a relaxed tone and down-tempo pace with raw intensity seething just under the surface. When S.U.N. drops his verses, the shining begins. This album is nothing more than an audio testament to that. —*Emilie Litzell*

Scienz of Life

Group / Hip-Hop, Jazz-Rap, Underground Rap
Making it a point to fight negativity and hatred through their uplifting rhymes, Scienz of Life is one of the lesser-known jazz/hip-hop fusion acts in the rap genre. Formed by MCs I D-4 Windz, Inspectah Willabe, and Lil Scienz, the crew first started to get a buzz in New York City, where their laid-back grooves and positive message were warmly received by the local underground hip-hop scene. Hooking up with Bobbito the Barber's Fondle 'Em Records, the "Powers of the Nine Ether" single dropped in the late '90s to an enthusiastic reception. Sub Verse Music was quick to catch on to their popularity, offering to release their full-length debut, *Coming Out By Day*, in 2000. Based on an Egyptian-themed concept and filled with heady productions that combined a harsh set of beats to jazzy bass lines and horns, the record was well received in the underground but made only a minor impression in the mainstream. Still, their sound was unique enough to warrant an invitation to the 2001 Montreux Jazz Festival, making them one of the few rap groups to receive such an honor from the organizers. A year later, *Project Overground: The Scienz Experiment* was released, a smooth sophomore album that added more live instrumentation and had a more varied production style overall. —*Bradley Torreano*

● **Coming Out By Day: The Book of the Dead** / May 2, 2000 / Sub Verse ◆◆◆◆◆
Scienz of Life's one long player shows the chops that won them a spot at the Montreux Jazz Festival in July 2001. With A Tribe Called Quest and Digable Planets overdue for tributes, here's more positive-thinking jazz/hip-hop fusion that will irritate hip-hop fans who must have clarity and brutality. The best sample floats Billie Holiday in a nice little compote of alto sax and strummed piano strings on a cut called "Strange Fruit." "Afro DZ Act 1" samples kalimba keys so tiny they must have cut Maurice White's fingers. The recessive beats of *Coming Out By Day: The Book of the Dead* don't fail to focus—they defy focus, moving as if crunching peanut shells and pizza crusts into the carpet of a den. And talk about recessive: the ruminative raps by I D-4 Windz, Inspectah Willabe, and L'il Sci are less "I'm-tellin'-you" and more "you-tell-me," which probably comes easy to guys who've been friends since 1993. But these murk slingers frame a great late-night listening party, kindly ignoring the carpet to fill overflowing ears with one more saxophone riff ("God-Core") or flute chorale from minor artists; it's too deep in the night to keep track of the keyboards, which noodle around like Herbie Hancock's on Miles Davis' *Water Babies*. And among many indecipherable pronouncements, "USA (Undaground Starvin Artist)" stands out because it runs one insight on repeat: "Negativity sells/But positivity dwells/In the mind/Of the illest rhymer." That's a charitable dissection of the will to sell in the minds of the grimmest rappers; it shows that Scienz of Life is on to their illin' sojourners. Every now and then, charity is preferable to clarity. This is also available on vinyl. —*John Young*

Screwball

f. Queensbridge, NY
Group / Hip-Hop, Hardcore Rap
Screwball is a foursome of frenetic, energetic, and poetic hardcore rappers from the public housing projects of Queensbridge, NY, and go by the stage names, Poet, Solo, KL, and Hostyle. They performed and recorded, individually and together, throughout the late '80s with Poet appearing as half of the duo PHD, and Solo and KL as Kamakazee. Their first release under the guise of Screwball was *Set It*, which was recorded in 1993 and produced by Poet. Screwball went on to make several guest appearances on underground and independent recordings before releasing their major-label debut, *Y2K*, in 1999. *Loyalty* appeared two years later. —*Roxanne Blanford*

● **Y2K** / Oct. 19, 1999 / Tommy Boy ◆◆◆◆
Controversy sells—it's a well-known fact in the recording industry—and the group Screwball learned this lesson quickly. This inner-city quartet first gained notoriety when they released the somewhat disturbing single "Who Shot Rudy?" (concerning the fictional shooting of New York City mayor Rudy

Giuliani). With the debut of their full-length CD, *Y2K*, Screwball continued to illustrate harrowing tales of coming of age in New York, specifically in the Queensbridge section of the Bronx. Their style is immediate and unrelenting; their stories are vivid and graphic. Guest stars on this record include life-long acquaintances Mobb Deep, MC Shan, Noyd, and Comega. With the DJ Premier-produced track *"F.A.Y.B.A.N."* and some solo cuts that permit individual members to shine and show their rhyming skills, *Y2K* cleverly positions itself as one of the definitive rap releases of 1999. —*Roxanne Blanford*

Screwed Up Click

f. Houston, TX

Group / Hip-Hop, Southern Rap, Underground Rap, Dirty South, Gangsta Rap, Hardcore Rap

Centering on the efforts of the infamous DJ Screw, the Screwed Up Click loosely comprises a wide-ranging roster of Houston, TX, rappers, of which Lil' Keke and Yungstar are the most well known. Other significant members include Big Pokey, Fat Pat, and Botany Boys. In 1999 they released the *Blockbleeders* compilation. In addition to this recording, the numerous members have all played a significant role in the hundreds of DJ Screw mix tapes to filter out of Houston during the 1990s. —*Jason Birchmeier*

● **Blockbleeders** / May 18, 1999 / Straight Profit ✦✦✦
The *Blockbleeders* album features various members of the Houston, TX, Screwed Up Click laying down rhymes and some Southern-flavored beats, making it an excellent introduction to the scene's unique style. —*Jason Birchmeier*

2nd II None

Group / Hip-Hop, Pop-Rap

Los Angeles cousins Tha D and KK attended high school in Compton with DJ Quik before landing a record deal with Profile. Their debut *2nd II None* had two strong compositions: "Be True to Yourself" and "If You Want It," both of which did respectably. The album was re-released in 1999 as a precursor to a brand-new full-length, *Classic 220*. —*Ron Wynn*

● **2nd II None** / Sep. 6, 1991 / Profile ✦✦✦✦✦
Tha D and KK once confessed publicly that they were not capable of freestyling in the grand tradition of rap, so it would be quite reasonable if *2nd II None* were not the most groundbreaking album in terms of its concepts and rhymes. And it is, in fact, lacking to some extent in those departments. On this debut album, the duo tended toward conventional gangsta braggadocio and, unfortunately also typical of the form, a rather blatant strain of misogyny. Crews like N.W.A and the Geto Boys, while similarly inclined, had nonetheless found ways to undercut or at least give context to the more repugnant, offensive, and sexist themes running through their songs in the way of a trenchant ghetto philosophy that spoke to harrowing issues of the inner-city experience. 2nd II None had little of that insight or ability to tweak gangsta rap clichés. What they did have was their own Dr. Dre sitting behind the boards in the person of DJ Quik, their skilled labelmate, and as a result the album does not lack in the least in the vitality of its sound, a deep, organic funk. His skilled way with a sampler and, frequently, live instruments makes it entirely possible to listen to wonderful tracks like "Underground Terror" and the smoked-out blaxploitation porno of "Mystic" without noticing the trite words at all. Still, Tha D and KK deserve credit for breaking gangsta rap out of its aversion to the more melodic aspects of urban music. The duo had a tendency to slip into smooth R&B crooning during choruses, a novel technique at the time, previously seen as an affront to street authenticity but since quite commonplace in hip-hop. It helped the album break into the mainstream, and the singles "Be True to Yourself" and the horny "If You Want It" remain minor old school classics by consequence. —*Stanton Swihart*

Classic 220 / Sep. 14, 1999 / Arista ✦✦✦
Thanks to the success of Arista's hip-hop reissue compilation *Profilin' the Hits*, the duo 2nd II None earned a contract with the label and recorded a second album, eight full years after their debut. Produced by long-time friend DJ Quik as well as 2nd II None themselves, *Classic 220* keeps the vibe old school. Even though the production and beats are updated for the hip-hop world of the late '90s, KK and D focus on simply moving crowds as they did with classic early singles like "Be True to Yourself" and "If You Want It." The classic in waiting here is "Up 'N Da Club," an irresistible party anthem that grows better with each listen. Though *Classic 220* doesn't peak as many

times as 2nd II None's debut did, it's an intriguing return to form for a hip-hop crew that never made as many records as they should have. —*John Bush*

Baba Sehgal

b. Lucknow, India

Hip-Hop, Foreign Rap, Indian Pop, Club/Dance

In India, one performer dominates the rap scene: the Lucknow, India-born Baba Sehgal. Baba Sehgal's rap is far removed from the sting and grit of Public Enemy, Ice-T, or, to take an example of rap transplanted into another language, French wit MC Solaar. Sehgal's safe, inoffensive pop-rap employs a cutesy-pie image with cheeky Hindi lyrics about hobnobbing with Madonna on the telephone. Interjections of a Hinglish nature (a relative of Japlish, the seemingly dyslexic or random plucking of English words in advertisements or on bomber jackets or baseball caps in Japan), like "Five star hotel," "James Bond," "Madonna is a very good friend of mine," abound. Superstardom is his self-professed goal. Despite the transparency of his aims, his is a rare instance of non-film success in India. —*Ken Hunt*

● **Thanda Thanda Pani & Other Hits** / 1992 / Magnasound/OMI ✦✦✦✦✦
The compilation includes the smash hit song "Thanda Thanda Pani" (of "Five star hotel" fame) which launched him in style—in the wake of which sales of his previous albums *Dilruba* and *Alibaba* (respectively released in 1990 and 1991) picked up tremendously. Instant transitoriness, instant, as he might say, lyrical tapori-ness (nonsense). —*Ken Hunt*

Self Scientific

Group / Underground Rap

Before recording as Self Scientific, the duo of Chance Infinite (Aaron Johnson) and DJ Khalil (Khalil Abdul-Rahman) had recorded as the Numbskulls. They met at a basketball camp, and recorded demos at Ice-T's studio in 1994 that got them signed to Loud. The deal fell through, however, and they re-formed as Self Scientific a few years later. The pair began recording on an independent basis, selling mix tapes on the cheap and recording singles for self-release. A pair of 1997-1998 singles, "Run the Depth" and "Return," became big favorites with DJs regionally—and, eventually, worldwide. Self Scientific's later work began appearing on their own label, S.O.L. Music Works, though it was Tommy Boy who gave them their first big shot, with a track on the 1999 compilation *The Black Label*. By early 2001, the duo had released their full-length debut, *The Self Science*, through S.O.L. Music Works and Landspeed. —*John Bush*

● **The Self Science** / Feb. 20, 2001 / S.O.L. ✦✦✦
After emerging from Cali's thriving underground scene in 1998 with "Return" (a celebratory ode that lauded hip-hop's humbler beginnings), Self Scientific's (Chance Infinite and DJ Khalil) debut, *The Self Science*, offers more of that romanticism, as it is an intriguing mixture of old and new school philosophy. Like so many of the great left-coast underground collectives, Self Scientific's musical platform emanates with a very distinguishable East Coast vibe. Though it's evident both members were weaned during hip-hop's most progressive stage (early '90s), *Self Science* is a mixed collective of that glorious period. Chance Infinite's Islamic beliefs and self-mastering ideologies play a major role in his lyrical inflections ("Love Allah" featuring Krondon and "Self Science"). While Infinite's Five Percent Nation references are refreshing, the righteous path he conveys frequently clashes with the unflattering portrait he depicts of women on "You Can't Fall" and "The Best Part," where Infinite passes on the swine but freely advocates sexual promiscuity. While MCs have long overshadowed the DJ, Self Scientific is an exception to that rule. Serving as the group's backbone, DJ Khalil delivers a slew of diverse aural selections, ranging from the plush violins and heavenly string backdrop of "The Covenant" to the spine-tingling instrumental "Opus," which is augmented by a melodious acoustic guitar sample and angelic chanting. Self Scientific delivers an impressive debut. Yet, it is one that is marked largely by the group's earlier material, as their latest batch of work fails to resonate like the end-to-end burners ("Return") contained in their previously released 12" catalog. —*Matt Conaway*

Sensational

Hip-Hop, Illbient

Also known as Torture, Sensational was a member of the Jungle Brothers on their album 1993 *J. Beez Wit Da Remedy*. He released his self-produced solo debut, *Loaded With Power*, in 1997. The follow-up, *Corner the Market*, appeared two years later and *Heavyweighter* was issued in fall 2000; *Get on My Page* followed a year later. —*Steve Huey*

● **Loaded With Power** / Nov. 18, 1997 / WordSound ✦✦✦
Sensational's self-produced solo debut, *Loaded With Power*, is an inventive, if not high-tech, series of soundscapes featuring the MC's offbeat vocals, reminiscent of Ol' Dirty Bastard or Busta Rhymes. Most of the sounds were played by Sensational himself, giving the music a raw, immediate feel. —*Steve Huey*

Corner the Market / Apr. 20, 1999 / WordSound ✦✦✦
Sensational's sophomore effort, *Corner the Market* boasts clearer production values—and thus, more intelligible lyrics—than its predecessor, although the hazy, lo-fi futuristic style is still very much in evidence, as is the (intentional?) sloppiness. Sensational's own chaotic flow adds to the record's odd, disturbing, and paranoid vibe, maintaining his position as a rapper who—love him or hate him—sounds like very few others. —*Steve Huey*

Heavyweighter / Sep. 19, 2000 / WordSound ✦✦✦
Even by underground hip-hop standards, Sensational is a truly unusual artist. It's not just his raspy, unmelodic voice, which he makes even more unnerving by running it through echo chambers and recording it in what appears to be a cardboard box. Nor is it his beats, which are utterly devoid of melody or, when a melody is provided, without exception creepy and ominous (such as in "The Best" or "Sittin' On Top"). It's that even with his quirky experimentalism, several of his songs still cover standard hip-hop concerns, what with boasting about his record sales in "The Best," bragging about his income in "Extravaganza," and proclaiming himself the king of hip-hop in "Sittin' On Top." All of which begs the question: who is this album meant for? Underground hip-hop fans will be puzzled by the lyrics, which aren't too different from the standard bling-bling of mainstream hip-hop (like Jay-Z) while mainstream hip-hop fans will be alienated by the defiantly unmelodic and spare music. Sensational is too talented an MC (and producer) to ignore, but with its idiosyncratic beats seemingly mismatched with out-of-place lyrics, *Heavyweighter* is really an acquired taste. —*Victor W. Valdivia*

Get on My Page / Jun. 12, 2001 / Ipecac ✦✦✦
For the fourth release from the onetime Jungle Brother, Sensational again cultivates an anti-rhythmic freeform persona for his discordant brand of hip-hop. Sounding like a hybrid of the rugged minimalism of old school rapper Schoolly D, the loopy abstraction of Saafir's Hobo Junction days, and the off-the-wall style of Milk D, at times Sensational hits the mark with his anti-industry format. Hailing from Brooklyn, NY, Sensational takes his styles way beyond Gotham, from the Bay Area to the dirty South and back east to square one. While the granular texture of his self-blueprinted white-noise beats matches perfectly with his effects-driven vocal tone, the album is best handled in small dosages. Thematically, *Get on My Page* is mostly vacant, sticking to drug topics and bombast almost exclusively. However, the release seems more an exercise in style and an experimental excursion into ambient electronica and hip-hop than anything else. Certainly not for all tastes or moods, but those who celebrate anomalies in hip-hop may dig this one. —*M.F. Di Bella*

The Sequence

f. Columbia, SC
Group / Urban, Old School Rap, Electro
The Sequence hailed from Columbia, SC, and consisted of Angela Brown Stone, Cheryl Cook, and Gwendolyn Chisolm. Recording for Joe & Sylvia Robinson's Sugarhill Records label, they hit with "Funk You Up" in early 1980; "Funky Sound (Tear the Roof Off)," a remake of Parliament's 1976 gold single "Tear the Roof Off the Sucker" in summer 1981; and "I Don't Need Your Love (Part One)" from spring 1982. Their two charting LPs were the similarly titled *Sugarhill Presents the Sequence* (1980) and *The Sequence* (1982). Angie Stone sang lead on Vertical Hold's 1993 Top 20 R&B hit "Seems You're Much Too Busy" and had a gold single with "There's No More Rain in This Cloud" from her 1999 gold album *Black Diamond.* —*Ed Hogan*

Sugarhill Presents the Sequence / 1980 / Sugar Hill ✦✦✦
No doubt, Salt-N-Pepa emulated the Sequence, who preceded them as tough rap divas. The lineups and attitudes are similar, and none of the curvy rappers comes off as passive, unliberated women. Gwendolyn (Blondie) Chisolm,

Cheryl (Cheryl the Pearl) Cook, and Angela (Angie B) Brown Stone, bka Sequence were street wise, gritty, and butter bred. "Simon Says" has a contagious, comical beat that's made for disco. Showing they do more than rap, they break off in "The Times When We're Alone," a slow and sensual winner. The nursery-rhyme raps on "We Don't Rap the Rap," with its energetic beats, are like dancing pills. *Sesame Street*-like sounds continue, lyrically anyway, on "Funk a Doodle Rock Jam"; infants must have loved this one, they could pronounce some lyrics, particularly "doodle." Heavy beats and well-spaced horns, married with Sequence's three-part harmonies and leads, keep you rocking until the end. The group borrowed from Parliament's "Give Up the Funk" and came up with "Funky Sound" where Blondie, Angie B, and Cheryl the Pearl take turns busting bodacious raps. —*Andrew Hamilton*

The Sequence / 1982 / Sugar Hill ✦✦✦✦
The Sequence's second album contains all of the same funky, soulful grooves they busted on *Sugarhill Presents the Sequence.* It's almost an even split between the ballads and hip-hop numbers: "I Don't Need Your Love," a wailing beauty, pulled up lame at number 40 on *Billboard*'s R&B chart in May of 1982, a poor showing for one of their best performances; "Love Changes," led by Angie B, is seven-plus minutes of gut-wrenching soul searching; "Unaddressed Letter" is an unexpected piece of traditional soul that works like a charm; James Brown's "Cold Sweat" gets a makeover and a new feel; and finally, "Funk That (You Mothers)" and "Get It Together" are hip-hoppers accented with hot raps. —*Andrew Hamilton*

● **The Best of the Sequence** / Dec. 17, 1996 / Deep Beats ✦✦✦✦
Many aren't aware of neo-soul singer Angie Stone's roots in the Sequence, a versatile female trio that recorded for Sugarhill during the early '80s. The Sequence cut only two albums, but they made enough impact to inspire the likes of Salt-N-Pepa, who obviously took a thing or two from this group and became much more popular in the process. Put together by Sequel's Deep Beats offshoot, *The Best of the Sequence* culls a dozen tracks from 1980's *Sugarhill Presents the Sequence* and 1982's *The Sequence*, and includes their three Top 40 black singles: "Funky Sound (Tear the Roof Off)," "I Don't Need Your Love," and "Funk You Up." Though it seems like it might've been preferable to simply combine the group's two albums on one disc, this anthology does an admirable job of leaving off the filler from those albums and concentrating on highlights. This lean disc also demonstrates the group's ability to gracefully switch gears from funk to soul to rap. —*Andy Kellman*

Erick Sermon

b. Nov. 25, 1968, Bayshore, NY
Vocals, Producer / Hip-Hop, East Coast Rap, Hardcore Rap
One-half of the legendary hip-hop duo EPMD, Erick Sermon was also among the genre's most prominent producers, deservedly earning the alias "Funklord" with his trademark raw, bass-heavy grooves. Born in Bayshore, NY, on November 25, 1968, Sermon—aka E Double, the Green Eyed Bandit, and MC Grand Royal—teamed with rapper Parrish Smith in 1986 to form EPMD, an acronym for "Erick and Parrish Making Dollars"; signing to the tiny Sleeping Bag label, they soon released their debut 12", "It's My Thing," which went on to sell an astounding 500,000 copies. In the years to follow, EPMD emerged as one of rap's most vital acts, their hard-edged beats and Sermon's mumbled, monotone delivery becoming a great influence on the burgeoning gangsta movement. In addition to producing their own material, the duo also helmed records for the extended family of performers dubbed the Hit Squad, whose ranks included Redman, K Solo, and Das EFX. In early 1993, EPMD disbanded, and Sermon soon resurfaced with his solo debut, *No Pressure*; he also became a sought-after producer and remixer, working with everyone from En Vogue to Blackstreet to Shaquille O'Neal. After a second solo effort, 1995's *Double or Nothing*, he and Smith re-formed EPMD in 1997, releasing the LP *Back in Business.* —*Jason Ankeny*

● **No Pressure** / 1993 / Def Jam ✦✦✦✦
When EPMD finally unravelled after months of rumors and internal turmoil, Erick Sermon wasted no time grabbing the mike. He's quite obsessed with proving he can cut it alone, although *No Pressure* didn't move far from EPMD's trademarks: fat, crunching bass lines, neatly inserted samples lifted mainly from Zapp, tight vocal edits, and Sermon's mush-mouthed, deadpan raps. His targets included condoms, sexual warfare, hip-hop groupies, and would-be rap challengers. While this contains the obligatory "bitches" and "niggas" references, there's not as much gun worship as you might expect.

No Pressure is as much, if not more, EPMD's final release as Erick Sermon's debut. —*Ron Wynn*

Double or Nothing / Nov. 7, 1995 / Def Jam ✦✦✦✦
Erick Sermon is one-half of the influential East Coast hip-hop duo EPMD (the other half being Parrish Smith). *Double or Nothing* is his second solo album. Every song isn't great, but there are no bad ones either. This is an album that you might listen to from beginning to end, free of the impulse to fast forward. Of course, Erick Sermon's signature funky sound is here, along with the influences of fellow Def Squad members Redman and Keith Murray. The three team up on the aggressive "Sound Off," sounding nice together, as usual. Redman appears on quite a few tracks, bringing the punchlines and bold attitude that work so well for him. —*Dan Gizzi*

Music / Sep. 25, 2001 / J Records ✦✦✦✦
Perhaps because EPMD is so ingrained into listeners' psyches, Erick Sermon has never been given a fair shake as a solo artist. While he has exerted every bit of his energy to carve out his own separate identity outside of the EPMD spectrum, it has really been to no avail. That is why the breakout hit "Music" could not have appeared at a more needed time for Sermon. After innocently fiddling around with some old, unreleased Marvin Gaye lyrics, Sermon ended up fashioning a perfect marriage of sampling with "Music," which ultimately spawned a renewed interest in the Green Eyed Bandit and led to his subsequent deal with J Records. Sermon's *Music* sounds like he realizes that he has only one life left (Lil' Kim's sparse appearance on "Come Thru" is included merely for name recognition only). Recalling his influential past, Sermon waxes longingly about his fame on "Genius E Dub" featuring Olivia (which includes another uninspired recycling of the Tom Tom Club's "Genius of Love"). Yet, the script is then flipped on the gospel-tinged "The Sermon" (featuring R. Kelly), on which Sermon relays a feeling of abandonment and discloses how the phone stopped ringing when the hits dried up, though Sermon was sent stumbling to his corner for an eight count after the Erick Onassis debacle. Thanks to *Music*, this batch of music is the smelling salt that will enable this brother from the boondocks to make it out of his corner for another round. —*Matt Conaway*

React / Nov. 26, 2002 / J Records ✦✦✦
Erick Sermon, one of the few dedicated artists in hip-hop with a steady hand on both the mic *and* the mixing board, delivered a hardcore follow-up to his 2001 crossover hit *Music*. With Sermon spitting rough, raw raps and sequencing the tracks to match, *React* is much closer to the dark tone of his main concern, EPMD, than on his J Records debut. The hit here is the title track, with Sermon and guest Redman locking into a killer groove, helped along by an Indian film loop. "To tha Girlz" proves that Sermon's better telling off the guys than talking to the ladies, but it's one of the few missteps here. For fans of hardcore hip-hop with no concessions to R&B or any type of crossover, Sermon's fourth album is a breath of fresh air. —*John Bush*

7L & Esoteric

f. 1992, Boston, MA
Group / Underground Rap
7L & Esoteric first came together in 1992 after 7L heard Esoteric DJing at a local college radio station in Boston, MA. Esoteric's sets were mostly hip-hop based, but on occasion he would fuse his own material into his playlists. After hearing Esoteric's material, 7L contacted him in the hopes of forming an artistic collaboration. And collaborate they did. Reverting back to the standard hip-hop formula for success—one DJ, one MC—they immediately started to build on a common love for hip-hop born of 1986-1989. The pair headlined shows in smaller venues throughout Boston, New York, and Philadelphia as well as opened for some hip-hop heavyweights like Bahamadia, Rakim, Redman, and Company Flow.

The duo released their first single under the name God Complex in 1996. The single was immediately dubbed one of the best rap singles of the year, receiving huge responses from Los Angeles, New York, Canada, and Overseas markets. Soon after, the *Rebel Alliance* LP was released. Calling together their fellow MCs and DJs from their hometown, (including Virtuoso, Mr. Lif, Tony Infamous, and Force Five) *Rebel Alliance* was a compilation showcasing the talent and skills held in the scene that raised them. As soon as Rebel Alliance was in the stores, 7L & Esoteric followed up with an 7L & Esoteric 12" featuring the tracks "Be Alert," "Protocol," and yet another collaboration with Virtuoso, "Touch the Mic." While "Be Alert" received mad attention to

the ingenious sampling of the Transformers cartoon show, "Protocol" was garnering intense recognition for Esoteric's nonstop lyricism. *The Source* magazine even went so far as to label "Protocol" one of the five best hip-hop tracks of the '90s. Their next single, released on Direct Records, earned 7L & Esoteric praise from coast to coast. "Def Rhymes" was exactly what the title implied, while "Headswell" brought back the now-expected pairing of Esoteric and Virtuoso.

Consistently winning critical acclaim and underground credibility is apparently a no-brainer for Boston's dream team. With a partnership spanning over nine years, the singles and guest spots speak for themselves. —*Emilie Litzell*

● **Soul Purpose** / Jul. 10, 2001 / Landspeed ✦✦✦✦✦
Since 1996, when this duo dropped its first single, many people have been awaiting a full-fledged album release. Five years later it finally arrived, and *Soul Purpose* is definitely worth the wait. The production on the album is top notch, with quality cutting and sampling that works well for the overall sound. The beats produced by 7L are space odyssey-ish, with a bit of Deltron 3030 and a futuristic feel, with xylophones, brass instruments, and strange throbbing sounds. The beats match with Esoteric's strong, slow, plodding delivery found on just about every track. His rhymes seem to stand out more when there's another MC on the track, such as with Mr. Lif on "Operating Correctly" or with Apathy and Reks on "Public Execution." There's an interesting circus-sounding beat on "Guest List" that should be checked out, too. A good album overall, with depth and great length at 20 tracks, *Soul Purpose* is evidence of what these guys are capable of. Definitely look forward to more good things from these two. —*Brad Mills*

7 Notas 7 Colores

Group / Hip-Hop, Latin Rap
Spanish hip-hop act 7 Notas 7 Colores was formed by ex-Los Poetas Violentos Dive Dibosso and MC Mucho Muchacho (born Oliver Gallego). Known by their twisting lyrics and powerful performances, this rap act founded their own label, Madre, releasing a few singles and 7 Notas 7 Colores' debut album, called *Hecho, Es Simple*. After being discovered by producer Juan Brujo in 1998, Dive Dibosso and MC Mucho Muchacho signed up to Kool Arrow, issuing their album in the U.S. In addition, La Madre released *77* in 1999. —*Drago Bonacich*

Hecho, Es Simple / Nov. 16, 1999 / Kool Arrow ✦✦✦

71 North

f. Cleveland, OH
Group / Party Rap, Underground Rap
71 North emerged from the Midwest in 2002 with a fun novelty single, "Cleveland Shuffle," a line-dance song driven by the famous opening bars of Michael Jackson's "Billie Jean." The Cleveland group had earlier made waves with its "Boodie Bounce" single, which was later re-released, along with two mixes of "Cleveland Shuffle," on their debut album, *Watch Us Roll* (2002). Warlock Records also released a more economical maxi-single that year that included two mixes of "Cleveland Shuffle," two mixes of "Boodie Bounce," and "Watch Us Roll." —*Jason Birchmeier*

● **Cleveland Shuffle [Single]** / Apr. 23, 2002 / Warlock ✦✦✦
Forget 71 North's full-length album, *Watch Us Roll*. The group's "Cleveland Shuffle" maxi-single is all you need. It has the singles—"Cleveland Shuffle" and "Boodie Bounce"—as well as the album's title track without any filler. —*Jason Birchmeier*

Watch Us Roll / Aug. 27, 2002 / Warlock ✦✦
Combining the fast-paced bounce of the classic Miami bass scene with a taste of the infamous dirty South sound, 71 North delivers a hard and exuberant blend on *Watch Us Roll*. This full-length debut was inspired by the success of the club hits "Cleveland Shuffle" and "Boodie Bounce," so the group attempts to replicate their dance anthem magic throughout the rest of the record. But much like efforts from previous club crossovers the Outhere Brothers, the repetitive nature of the genre dooms their album's success. There are definitely several catchy and fun club anthems to be found here, but when heard back to back it begins to become a serious detriment to the overall record. The usual throbbing bass beats and anxious percussion accompanies the simplistic booty chants, but with no change of pace the album renders itself boring by the fourth track. There are a few decent singles

hidden within, but mostly this is the sound of a group that hasn't moved beyond a formula that was played out seven years earlier. —*Bradley Torreano*

Shabazz

b. San Jose, California

West Coast Rap

After growing up in the California Bay Area, Shabazz moved to Atlanta, where he launched his rap career with the *Baysickinstinct* album. The album features production by Studio Ton, one of the Bay Area's more prolific producers during the '90s (E-40, B-Legit, Celly Cel, Kurupt, Snoop Dogg). In addition to Studio Ton, the album also boasts Shabazz's thoughtful lyrics and his seasoned rap flow, two qualities that set him apart from his many peers trying to break into the industry. —*Jason Birchmeier*

● **Baysickinstinct** / Apr. 2, 2002 / Sura ◆◆◆

Over the course of his debut album for Sura, *Baysickinstinct*, Shabazz showcases his broad outlook, rapping about everything from finances ("Can't Stop the Money") and religion ("Stressed Out") to gossip ("My Git Down") and partying ("Steady Ballin & Top Billin"). Accomplished West Coast rap producer Studio Ton contributes the beats. His experience helps make *Baysickinstinct* sound like the work of a veteran rather than a debut release. —*Jason Birchmeier*

Lakim Shabazz (Larry Welsh)

b. New Jersey

Golden Age, East Coast Rap, Political Rap, Hip-Hop

Affiliated throughout his career with DJ Mark "the 45 King," New Jersey's Lakim Shabazz—a Five Percenter born Larry Welsh—came up in the mid- to late '80s as a member of the 45 King's Flavor Unit, a crew that included Queen Latifah and Apache within its membership. Shabazz took part in the 45 King's notorious *900 Number* EP, the Tuff City release that elevated the status of everyone involved, especially that of the 45 King. Signed with Tuff City himself, Shabazz released a pair of 45 King-produced LPs, 1988's *Pure Righteousness* and 1990's *Lost Tribe of Shabazz*—both filled with Afrocentric and politically conscious rhymes that incorporated the Five Percent Nation's doctrine. The former included "Black Is Back," one of the truly great underground rap classics of the late '80s. Shabazz, who developed production skills of his own, has produced some of his own tracks, in addition to lending his talents to Diamond D & the Psychotic Neurotics' *Stunts, Blunts, and Hip Hop*. —*Andy Kellman*

● **Pure Righteousness** / 1988 / Tuff City ◆◆◆◆

Lost Tribe of Shabazz / 1990 / Tuff City ◆◆◆

Shade Sheist

b. Los Angeles, CA

Hardcore Rap, West Coast Rap

From his flow to the beats that he rhymes over, everything about hardcore rapper Shade Sheist screams West Coast in no uncertain terms. Sheist has, on occasion, worked with some East Coast rappers—including Ja Rule and Naughty By Nature member Kay Gee—but even so, Sheist is very much a product of the Southern California rap scene. Heavily influenced by West Coast gangsta rappers such as Snoop Doggy Dogg, DJ Quik, Warren G, Dr. Dre, and the late N.W.A. agitator Eazy-E, Sheist was born and raised in the Los Angeles area. Anyone who forgets how long rap has been around need only think about how long Sheist has been alive; the Southern Californian was born in the early '80s, which means that he was only a baby when trailblazing old school East Coast rappers like Kurtis Blow, Grandmaster Flash & the Furious Five, the Sugarhill Gang (as in "Rappers Delight"), and the Treacherous Three were at the height of their popularity. It also means that he was only two or three years old when Ice-T—the seminal father of West Coast gangsta rap—started recording in 1983.

Growing up in Inglewood, CA (home of the Inglewood Forum) and South Central L.A., Sheist was raised on rap. He was hip to what MCs from the East Coast and the deep South were doing, but ultimately, it was the West Coast that had the greatest impact on his lyrics and his flow. Growing up in the 'hood in the '80s and '90s, Sheist was well aware of the gang violence and the infamous Crips/Bloods rivalry that plagued South Central L.A.; however, he has been quoted as saying that he was wise enough to avoid getting caught up in the gang scene. It was in 2000 that Sheist started to get some breaks as

a rapper; that year, he was featured on "If You Were My Bitch," one of the tunes that Irv Gotti produced for the CD *Irv Gotti Presents: The Murderers*. The Murderers' project was where Sheist met East Coast hardcore rapper Ja Rule, who invited him to be a guest on his Def Jam album *Rule 3:36* (which went triple platinum). It was also in 2000 that Sheist met the L.A.-based producer Damizza, who was serving as a senior director of artist relations for L.A.'s urban contemporary station Power 106 and had a production company/label called Baby Ree Entertainment. Damizza went on to feature Sheist on the 2000 single "Where I Wanna Be," which appears on the compilation *Damizza Presents: Where I Wanna Be*. In September 2002, MCA released Sheist's first full-length solo album, *Informal Introduction*; the disc's producers include Damizza as well as DJ Quik and Naughty By Nature's Kay Gee (who brings an East Coast background to what is usually a very West Coast-sounding album). —*Alex Henderson*

● **Informal Introduction** / Sep. 10, 2002 / MCA ◆◆◆

Back in the '60s and '70s, soul music had plenty of regional sounds. Memphis had a distinctive sound, as did Chicago, Philadelphia, and Detroit. And in the 21st century, hip-hop can be every bit as regional as R&B was back in the day. New York and Philly MCs tend to have their own way of flowing; rappers from the South and the West Coast also have their regional rapping styles. If one heard *Informal Introduction*—Shade Sheist's first full-length solo album—without knowing anything about the rapper, it would be easy to assume that he was from the West Coast. And sure enough, Sheist was born and raised in the Los Angeles area. This 2002 release is unmistakably West Coast—Sheist's rapping style is right out of Snoop Dogg, Warren G, DJ Quik, and Eazy-E, and the sleek, R&B-drenched grooves (some of which have a strong George Clinton/P-funk influence) owe a lot to the influential Dr. Dre. Because of that heavy Snoop/Quik/Dre/Warren G influence, Sheist will inevitably be categorized as a gangsta rapper. But lyrically, *Informal Introduction* isn't all that violent. Although Sheist uses plenty of profanity and employs a lot of playa/baller/hustler/pimpin' imagery, this CD is more entertaining than threatening—essentially, *Informal Introduction* is an R-rated party album. By 21st century standards, Sheist is hardly groundbreaking; no one who has listened to Snoop, Dre, Warren, and Quik extensively in the '90s will find *Informal Introduction* to be the least bit innovative. But the grooves are generally likable, and tunes like "Thug Luv" and "Stop...And Think About It" are fairly catchy—highly derivative, certainly, but catchy nonetheless. *Informal Introduction* won't go down in history as one of West Coast rap's definitive releases, but it's a decent, if slightly uneven, effort that does have its moments. —*Alex Henderson*

Shades of Culture

f. Montreal, Quebec, Canada

Group / Hip-Hop, Alternative Rap

Part of a relatively unknown yet growing cadre of Canadian hip-hop performers, Montreal's Shades of Culture are considered pioneers of the genre by many in the region. This trio from Notre-Dame-de-Grâce, consisting of DJ Shade, Revolution and DJ Storm labored steadily throughout the '80s and '90s to perfect their considerable rap skills. The result was *Mindstate*, a full-length CD on 2112 Records. By early 1999, Shades of Culture had formed their own label, Windmill Records. —*Roxanne Blanford*

● **Mindstate** / May 1998 / 2112 ◆◆◆◆◆

Taking a thematic cue from rapper KRS-One, Canada's Shades of Culture made their debut with *Mindstate*, a concept album emphasizing cultural unity and the power of knowledge over defeatism. Stunning verbal dexterity and penetrating beats on tracks such as the cautionary "Think Twice," and the motivational "Main Objective" present an antithesis to popular gangsta rap. On the whole, this makes for an uplifting, lyrically vibrant offering that employs turntable scratching and human beatbox techniques laid over a foundation of rich instrumentation. *Mindstate* conforms to all the traditions of old school rap while simultaneously making a successful appeal to the more progressive branch of the genre. —*Roxanne Blanford*

Roxanne Shanté (Lolita Gooden)

b. Long Island, NY

Golden Age, Old School Rap

Roxanne Shanté (born Lolita Gooden) was walking outside a New York housing project called Queensbridge when she heard three men talking about how the trio U.T.F.O. had canceled their appearance at a show they were promoting. Gooden offered to make a rap record that would get back at U.T.F.O., who'd previously recorded "Roxanne, Roxanne," a song about a woman too stuck up to notice them. The three—Tyrone Williams, DJ Mister Magic, and producer Marley Marl—took her up on the idea, with Marl producing "Roxanne's Revenge." The song was confrontational, sneering, boastful, and even borderline obscene, and it spawned 102 additional answer records. Eventually U.T.F.O. threatened to sue Shanté for using their B side as the musical foundation. She settled with them and recut the song with a different, though related, track. Shanté's fortunes were thin shortly after the heyday of "Roxanne, Roxanne," though she did share a number-one R&B and a Top Ten pop hit with Rick James in 1986, "Loosey's Rap."

Shanté retired when she was 25 to focus her attention on obtaining a higher education. She went on to receive a Ph.D. in psychology, eventually running her own practice and raising a family in New York. She stayed involved with the entertainment industry by being a mentor to young, female rappers and taking part in a series of Sprite commercials that highlighted freestyling hip-hop artists. —*Ron Wynn and Diana Potts*

Roxanne / 1988 / Columbia ✦✦✦

Bad Sister / Oct. 20, 1989 / Cold Chillin' ✦✦✦

Greatest Hits / Sep. 12, 1995 / Cold Chillin' ✦✦✦

● **The Best of Cold Chillin'** / Oct. 9, 2001 / Landspeed ✦✦✦✦
Most hip-hop fans wouldn't recognize a single track from Roxanne Shanté *other* than "Roxanne's Revenge," making some wonder whether *The Best of Cold Chillin'* is worth it when compared to all the great compilations that include her lone rap classic. There's a case to be made, though, since "Roxanne's Revenge" was her first single and she greatly improved over five years of recording. She found her niche quite soon, as evidenced by tough, nonsense beats-and-rhymes tracks like "Bite This" and "The Payback." Also, Shanté's "Def Fresh Crew" featured a lovable human beatbox named Biz Markie, and the future commercial king of Cold Chillin' makes a great appearance on "Def Fresh Crew." (Another all-time rapper, Kool G Rap, stops by for "Deadly Rhymes.") Listeners might be surprised at the quality of material here, but all in all *The Best of Cold Chillin'* definitely works best for golden age fans who want to get back in the mood with a few period tracks they haven't heard before. —*John Bush*

Shinehead (Edmund Carl Aiken)

b. Kent, England
East Coast Rap, Dancehall, Raggae
The fact that Shinehead split his time growing up between Jamaica and America was reflected in his recordings; the Kent, England-born vocalist (born Edmund Carl Aiken) released several albums between the late '80s and early '90s that blended dancehall and raggae with hip-hop. Whether Shinehead was toasting or crooning or flat-out rapping, he always balanced his material between the positive and socially conscious with more lighthearted sentiments. He got involved with music by performing at New York sound systems in the early '80s and began releasing singles as early as 1984, including a cover of Michael Jackson's "Billie Jean," which truly got his career rolling. His recording schedule slowed down during the latter half of the '90s, but he returned in 1999 with *Praises*, an album that consisted mostly of covers. —*Andy Kellman*

Unity / 1988 / Elektra ✦✦✦
Shinehead's unique fusion of dancehall and hip-hop might've had something to do with why it failed to make much of a dent in any of the *Billboard* charts. While reggae's influence on hip-hop was made known at the time with MCs like KRS-One, no one was truly blending the two styles like Shinehead. *Unity* is a little too reggae to be considered straight hip-hop, and it's a little too hip-hop to be considered straight reggae. Plus, *Unity* was too lighthearted and positive to catch the ears of hip-hop heads who were beginning to lean on harsher sounds that were developing. Still, it's a fun and accomplished start for the MC. Davy D. and Jam Master Jay lend production skills throughout. —*Andy Kellman*

● **The Real Rock** / Jun. 21, 1990 / Elektra ✦✦✦✦
In the late 1980s and early '90s, New Yorkers ranging from Boogie Down Productions to Heavy D were combining rap with dancehall reggae. Another key player in this rap/reggae experimentation was Shinehead, who keeps things

very positive and uplifting on his sophomore effort *The Real Rock*. However, much of the CD isn't reggae influenced, and the East Coast resident wisely avoids being predictable. Ranging from such fun, lighthearted material as "World of the Video Game" and "Musical Madness" to the more serious messages of "Family Affair" (which draws on the Sly Stone classic and stresses the importance of a cohesive family unit), the anti-smoking tune "Cigarette Breath" and the spiritual title song, *The Real Rock* was one of the best rap releases of 1990. It's unfortunate that Shinehead's popularity was so short lived. —*Alex Henderson*

Sidewalk University / Oct. 12, 1992 / Elektra ✦✦
Shinehead's third Elektra CD was a disappointment. Where he was once in the hip-hop/reggae vanguard, his music now sounded dry and muddy. There was neither the passion of roots reggae nor the bawdy intensity of contemporary dancehall in his compositions, while his rap style was rote and his rhymes forgettable. —*Ron Wynn*

Praises / Jun. 1, 1999 / VP ✦✦✦
A versatile artist who croons and DJ with equal skill, Shinehead can take any hit and put his silky stamp on it. *Praises* is a showcase for this talent, as he delves into '70s and '80s pop and R&B classics and transforms them. The opening track, "Never Make a Promise," is a sizzling take on Dru Hill's 1997 R&B hit, accented with a killer rhythm by the Roots Radics. It's followed by interpretations of Seals & Crofts '70s classic "Summer Breeze," changed into "Collie Weed" in the essential ode to marijuana; the Whispers' '80s hit, "Olivia," topped with a spicy bass rhythm; and Roberta Flack's "The First Time Ever I Saw Your Face," perked up with Shinehead's bongo playing. The covers don't always work, however, as witnessed by lackluster treatment of Heatwave's "Mind Blowing Decisions" and the Beatles "My Love." Ironically, the original tune "Pay Me" and the politically aware "Their Plan" shine the most. —*Rosalind Cummings-Yeates*

Sh'Killa

Gangsta Rap, West Coast Rap
Along with Suga T and Lady of Rage, Sh'Killa stood as one of the few female rappers amid the '90s West Coast gangsta scene. She recorded an album, *Gangstrez From Da Bay* (1996), for GWK Records that fellow West Coast gangstas Havoc & Prodeje produced. *Gangstrez From Da Bay* benefited from the wide distribution of Priority Records, who where the prime movers of West Coast gangsta rap at the time, but the album never found much commercial success. —*Jason Birchmeier*

● **Gangstrez From Da Bay** / Mar. 26, 1996 / GWK ✦✦✦
Some listeners might wonder if the Havoc & Prodeje who do their share of producing on Sh'Killa's *Gangstrez From Da Bay* is the same duo that formed Mobb Deep in Queens in the early '90s, but in fact, they're two entirely different duos. Gary "Havoc" Calvin and Austin "Prodeje" Patterson—the Havoc & Prodeje heard on this CD—are an obscure gangsta rap duo from South Central L.A., while the Havoc & Prodigy of Mobb Deep were key players in the Queens scene that also gave us Capone-N-Noreaga. Sh'Killa, meanwhile, is easily recognizable as a West Coast MC, and her other guests on this album include such West Coast gangsta rappers as Spice 1 and Gripsta. The Dr. Dre/Snoop Doggy Dogg/Warren G school of L.A. gangsta rap is a major influence on this melodic, R&B-drenched effort, which isn't remarkable or innovative but has its share of catchy hooks and infectious beats. Sh'Killa isn't one to emphasize flow or technique—while artists like MC Lyte and Queen Latifah are interested in letting you know just how much technique they have, Sh'Killa's style of rapping isn't nearly as complex. Much of *Gangstrez* favors the usual Dre/Snoop type of shock value, but the album takes a poignant turn with the Tupac Shakur-ish "Ghetto Tears." Though not a gem, *Gangstrez* is a fairly entertaining, if derivative, footnote in 1990s gangsta rap. —*Alex Henderson*

Shoestring

b. Flint, MI
Hardcore Rap, Gangsta Rap
After helping form the Dayton Family with Bootleg, Shoestring played a primary role in the group's quick success within the Midwestern hardcore rap underground. Unfortunately, the group's quick success came to an end following their second album, *F.B.I.*, when the group encountered numerous problems with the law. Despite these obstacles, Shoestring went on to sign

with Tommy Boy and released his solo debut, *Representin' Till the World Ends*, in 1999. Yet when the album didn't meet Tommy Boy's high expectations, the Flint, MI, rapper soon found himself without a label deal. In early 2001, he signed with Detroit rapper Esham's Overcore label and released his second album, *Cross Addicted*, an album that found him returning to his street-level roots. —*Jason Birchmeier*

Representin' Till the World Ends / Aug. 10, 1999 / Tommy Boy ✦✦✦
Shoestring's debut solo album mines much of the same territory as his previous work with the Dayton Family, both in terms of rapping and production. He's still representing his hardcore delivery and harsh lyrics, along with the unique experiences he's had living in Flint, MI, a city with none of the glamour of California or New York. Furthermore, he never raps about material possessions such as cars or jewelry. He seems content surviving in a rough city and occasionally getting high. It's a simple and rather untraditional ideology, but admittedly more sincere than the "ghetto fabulous" mentality of most rappers. The album's production does the job and that's about it. So, in the end, the most enticing aspect of this album is Shoestring's tough ideology; it's very realistic and quite refreshing. Unfortunately, there isn't anything very commercial about this album or the artist. His mentality is to be respected, as is his rapping, but there isn't anything too glitzy about this. —*Jason Birchmeier*

● **Cross Addicted** / Apr. 3, 2001 / Overcore ✦✦✦
Following an unsuccessful one-album stint with Tommy Boy, Midwestern hardcore rapper Shoestring returned to his indie roots, joining forces with the Detroit-based Overcore label. While the major-label, glossy sound of his Tommy Boy album was indeed a pleasure, the gritty, lo-fi sound of *Cross Addicted* is more fitting for Shoestring, an artist far too harsh for the majors (one wonders what Tommy Boy was even thinking!). Besides the street-quality production—featuring quite a bit of live instrumentation and a modestly unique approach—Shoestring brings some menacing rhymes to the table, along with some catchy hooks, dropping lyrics about everything from cars and drugs to hoes and parties to cops and killing. With 20 songs, there's plenty of ground to cover, and a steady degree of variety from one track to the next. It's perhaps most impressive how Shoestring doesn't rely on guest rappers for the sense of variety, instead relying on the production, his subject matter, and his songwriting. Overall, the Flint, MI, rapper doesn't compromise his agenda for anybody here, giving all the thugs and ruffnecks what they're looking for—an album of rugged tracks about the *real* street lifestyle, meaning no money flashin' or collar poppin', just representin'. An improvement over his debut, *Cross Addicted* also shows Shoestring's growth as an artist. —*Jason Birchmeier*

Shortee (Shannon Burke)

DJ / Hip-Hop, Alternative Rap, Turntablism
Hailing from the D.C. area, Shortee (born Shannon Burke) was the most successful female turntablist of the late '90s. With a style that ranged from hard house, swing, hip-hop, and drum'n'bass to dub, she was a strong force in both group and solo efforts. Shortee brought nearly two decades of percussion/drum playing to her DJ work, and it showed in tight, complex rhythms that used what had been accomplished before by other turntablists as a mere jumping-off point. She was a quick study to the DJ style: only three months after learning how to maneuver turntables, she issued her first tape, the aptly named *Its in My Nature*. In 1997 she issued her second mix tape, *No Shortcuts*, which showed off the skills that helped her win the 1997 Fever/Buzz Battle of the DJs, the largest techno/house/jungle mixing competition in the U.S. A series of projects with DJ Faust (born Bobby Bruno), who was romantically as well as musically linked to her, provided some of her first formal record releases. She appeared on Faust's 1998 album *Man or Myth*, which featured a kind of turntablist tribute to musicians whom she and Faust admired, from the Steve Miller Band to Public Enemy.

Faust's next effort, 1999's *Inward Journeys*, displayed a greater sense of creativity as she and Faust manipulated the samples that they used so that their sources were indistinguishable and the records that they used became more like tones and textures than recognizable pieces of music. She was a founding member of the Citizenz (with Faust and T-Rock), and also worked with the Space Kadets Collective and recorded a limited-edition vinyl EP in 1999 called *Fathomless* (with Faust and Craze). Her first solo album, *The Dreamer*, was the first DJ/turntablist album ever released by a female

performer on an established label. Beyond that, the album was original and inventive with a fascinating concept: Shortee created songs that were supposed to characterize the transformation of a person's brain patterns as they dreamed, with the dreams being transformed into sound. The result was beautiful, surprising, and a great hint of the things that were yet to come. —*Stacia Proefrock*

● **The Dreamer** / Oct. 12, 1999 / Bomb Hip Hop ✦✦✦✦✦
Part of Atlanta's the Citizenz DJ crew with her fiancé, DJ Faust, this petite turntable wizard is helping to put both women and the South on the turntablist map. Her inventive debut is a conceptual piece of sorts, with floating, trans-cendental tracks that flow seamlessly from one into the other like a dream. The esoteric liner notes help interpret the concept, telling the tale of a dreamer who learns through sleep research how to harness the creative energy of her subconscious mind. The story captures *The Dreamer's* hypnotic feel perfectly, as it moves effortlessly from ethereal, ambient passages to deep dub reggae to slammin' hip-hop grooves. It's a beautiful piece, devoid of the flashy showiness that plagues too many turntablist records while showcasing Shortee's skills and knowledge of music as a whole. —*Bret Love*

Shorty Mac (Robert Leonard Wood)

Vocals / Hip-Hop, Gangsta Rap, Hardcore Rap
Robert Leonard Wood at 14 was one of the most sobering gangsta rappers to arrive when his mean-spirited, grizzled Shorty Mac persona released a harrowing album of street stories in 1996. How much of his life was fictionalized is a point of contention, but Wood's rhymes were world-weary views into the ghetto from the eyes of a teenager. When his debut was released on VTX Records in 1996, Shorty Mac was the most brutal and menacing child rapper to date, but he never followed up the record, instead joining DJ Screw's Texas-based clique for a series of guest appearances. In March of 2002, he was arrested for cocaine distribution and sentenced to ten years in prison. —*Bradley Torreano*

● **Shorty Mac** / Feb. 27, 1996 / VTX ✦✦✦
At 14 years of age, Shorty Mac sure has been around the block a couple times. Throughout his self-titled debut, he spins tales of crime and violence with a world-weary eye well beyond his years. Unfortunately, this doesn't mean he comes up with new insights. Shorty Mac spits out the same gangsta clichés, but since he's only a child, that is excusable. Every now and then he has a couple of rhymes that suggest he might eventually evolve into something original and distinctive. For now, he's strictly pedestrian. —*Stephen Thomas Erlewine*

Showbiz & AG

Group / Pop-Rap, Hip-Hop
The rebirth of hip-hop's originating borough the Bronx can be credited in part to this two-man crew. While late-'80s/early-'90s hip-hop had gotten to be mostly party oriented and at times downright corny, this duo brought back some swagger and soul. Show and AG were the first out the box from the superb Diggin' in the Crates crew, an elite team of MCs and producers who can claim much clout and influence on genuine East Coast hip-hop. The spirit of rap's forefathers can be felt in the gritty weight of this duo's pioneering sound. Learning from their cohort Lord Finesse, the two started an underground buzz by street promoting their demos then selling the tapes out of the trunks of their cars. The street sales helped them polish their debut single "Soul Clap" b/w "Party Groove," a cut that banged dance clubs and got love on Yo! MTV Raps for many a week, a self-titled EP was released in March of 1992. Their debut album, *Runaway Slave*, followed in the fall and is seen as an early-'90s hip-hop essential. The album brought a bouncing hardcore sound of crisp, jazzy horns, stiff drum kicks, and snapping snares that could get a party hopping but could also satisfy the nondancing purist nodding his head in the back of the club. The album truly is a D.I.T.C. family affair and introduced such legendary names as the late Big L, Fat Joe, and Diamond D, whose classic debut solo album *Stunts, Blunts, and Hip Hop* dropped the same week in 1992.

The albatross of making unadulterated rap music is that it sometimes costs a crew acclaim, for Show and AG are some of rap's disturbingly underrated. The sequel to their raw, stripped sound came in 1995 with the underappreciated *Good Fellas* and the two were major contributors to D.I.T.C.'s eponymous debut album in 2000. —*Micheal Di Bella*

Showbiz & AG EP / Mar. 17, 1992 / Payday ✦✦✦✦
In the late '70s and early '80s, the majority of well-known rappers came from Harlem and the South Bronx. But by the mid-'80s, Queens and Brooklyn were major players in hip-hop—and in the late '80s, the popularity of West Coast gangsta rap and Florida bass made it clear that an MC didn't have to come from any of New York's five boroughs to sell millions of albums. However, many Big Apple MCs remained unaffected by rap trends in the deep South or on the West Coast. Representing the Boogie Down Bronx, the duo Showbiz & AG show no awareness of non-New York styles on this self-titled EP from 1992. The material, all of it enjoyable, is straight-up New York. Favoring a jazzy approach along the lines of Gang Starr and the Jungle Brothers, Showbiz & AG are instantly recognizable as an East Coast group. The beats are consistently New York sounding, and the same goes for the rapping—back in 1992, no one would have mistaken Showbiz & AG for Southern or West Coast MCs. They always flow like New Yorkers, just as Snoop Doggy Dogg, Too Short, and Warren G always flow like California rappers. While this EP was not a huge seller, it did help Showbiz & AG acquire a small cult following—especially in New York, Philadelphia, and other areas of the U.S.' Northeastern corridor. And it demonstrated that the Bronx should not be overlooked in the early '90s. —*Alex Henderson*

● **Runaway Slave** / Sep. 22, 1992 / PolyGram ✦✦✦✦
A product of the tight-knit Bronx underground posse D.I.T.C., *Runaway Slave* is a cornerstone album of hip-hop's middle school phase. Building on and borrowing from the layered, jazz-influenced sound of such contemporaries as Gang Starr and Pete Rock & C.L. Smooth, Showbiz & AG affixed a gangster mentality to grainy, fortified beats, etching their own unique style. While the crossover "Soul Clap" and "Party Groove" are club cuts, the rest of the album is more densely expressive. Showbiz and his talented peer Diamond shape their beats around simple, deep drum tracks—but add subtle loops of chaotic horns, loose strings, or abrupt piano notes to create concise and hard-hitting overtures. Tasteful flute swatches light up "Silence of the Lambs," an ear-ringing saxophone buzzes on "Still Diggin'," and the motor-mouthed late legend Big L introduced himself on the classic down-the-line jam "Represent," pulling such punchlines as "MCs be braggin' about cash they collect/But them chumps is like Ray Charles 'cause they ain't seen no money yet." The young AG (aka Andre the Giant) flows effortlessly throughout this album, an MC whose skill and unique voice would only mature in the future. While some of the import of this album is muted by modern-day technological sound booth advancements, Showbiz & AG did it raw and undiluted and the resulting sound was fresh, innovative, and most of all satisfying for hip-hop heads. —*Micheal Di Bella*

Good Fellas / May 30, 1995 / Ffrr ✦✦✦
The second shot fired from D.I.T.C.'s charter members Show & AG is a shade darker than their debut. While 1992's *Runaway Slave* was definitely no new jack swing affair, *Good Fellas* is decidedly more grimy and a lot less playful, both on the production and the lyrical ends. The lead single, "Next Level," also remixed exceptionally on the album by DJ Premier, was the only track that made any above-ground noise. Arguably the best cut on the album, the track is a manifesto of real hip-hop over a melodic guitar sample. Much of the album rumbles along to the tune of low bass grooves and noisy ambient loops of a jazzy variety. From bouncy xylophones to the standard Showbiz horns and kick drums, the production here is tightly constructed. At the time of its release (mid-1995), East Coast hip-hop was cruising along in a rugged gangster mode. All the while an ugly coastal battle was brewing that would conspire to darken hip-hop forevermore. This album steers clear of the coast bashing despite its unmistakable East Coast stamp and appeal. A few tracks do lack a distinct flavor, but overall the methodical, unassuming D.I.T.C. sound here has since been grafted but never duplicated. Show & AG affirm that the road to respect-worthy hip-hop status is, not through releasing an album every six months, but by letting things marinate for a few years and then proving you're still on top of your game. —*Micheal Di Bella*

Shyheim

b. Staten Island, NY
Vocals / Hip-Hop, Alternative Rap, Underground Rap, Club/Dance
The youngest member of the Wu-Tang Clan, Shyheim entered with his debut album at the ripe young age of 14. Lyrically he impressed rappers with a skill level that would make any hip-hop fan forget about his age altogether. A native of Staten Island, NY, Shyheim even spent time living with Wu-Tang member Ghostface Killah. Shyheim released *The Lost Generation* in 1996, while the acclaimed *Manchild* followed in 1999. —*Brad Mills*

Shyheim a/k/a the Rugged Child / Feb. 22, 1994 / Virgin America ✦✦✦
Shyheim's age of 14 can be easily recognized in his voice on this, his debut album, but lyrically it's difficult to believe this young rapper is already so skilled. What really makes him different than other young rappers is that he's where he is, not just because of his youth. The sound works well, with funky, lively beats, and Shyheim's hardcore violence-heavy lyrics combining for some great tracks. Only time will tell how this artist will develop, but if this is any indication of what we can expect from him in the years to come, the Rugged Child will surely not disappoint. —*Brad Mills*

The Lost Generation / May 28, 1996 / Noo Trybe ✦✦

Manchild / Jun. 22, 1999 / Priority ✦✦✦
At the ripe age of 14, Shyheim (the youngest affiliate of the Wu-Tang Clan) released his debut, *a/k/a the Rugged Child*, which made it abundantly clear that he was genetically predisposed to rock a mic. However, the prodigy's next effort, *The Lost Generation*, was less momentous, coming and going without the same fanfare or critical adulation. Even though Shyheim has spent the last four years fashioning his talents to the silver screen, the prolonged lay-off has done little to diminish his God-given abilities. Successfully transitioning from adolescent thug to astute street philosopher, Shyheim broadens his lyrical horizons on *Manchild*, exposing a vulnerability that his earlier work did not allude to; a good example is his search for innocence lost on the introspective title track. While Shyheim loses focus on "Spectacular" and the extremely misogynistic "Cease Fire (Wildflower 2000)," he reaps the benefit of two posthumous appearances from underground icon Big L, who adds his verbal flamboyance on "Furious Anger" and his production flare on "Trust It's On." Shyheim's most heart-wrenching ode, "Unconditional Love," reflects on his mother's struggles with chemical dependency. But, in what becomes a recurring theme, this emotional roller coaster clashes rudely with the jubilant pop production that accompanies it. —*Matt Conaway*

Shyne (Jamal Barrow)

b. 1979
Gangsta Rap, East Coast Rap, Hardcore Rap
Puff Daddy had intended Shyne to replace the deceased Notorious B.I.G., as the two sounded remarkably similar, but the young soundalike barely had a chance before he was imprisoned during Puffy's headline-grabbing scuffle with the law in early 2001. Shyne had originally been indicted on attempted murder charges on January 5, 2000, yet managed during the course of the year to complete his self-titled debut album, which Bad Boy released in September with much hoopla. The album spawned a few radio singles ("Bad Boyz" and "That's Gangsta") but didn't swoon too many fans. —*Jason Birchmeier*

● **Shyne** / Sep. 26, 2000 / Bad Boy ✦✦
The long-awaited debut by Notorious B.I.G.'s successor on Puff Daddy's Bad Boy label follows through on its promise to present a thuggish, hardcore equivalent to the seemingly irreplaceable, deceased gangsta superstar. The album unfortunately comes across as far too contrived, seeming staged and overly theatrical, even compared to the traditionally postural norms of gangsta rap in general. From the opening monologue ("Dear America, I'm only what you made me/Young, black, and f*cking crazy/Maybe if all you niggas were building schools instead of prisons, I'd stop living the way I'm living/Probably not/I'm so used to serving rocks and burning blocks"), there's little denying that Shyne is trying to be what his audience wants him to be: the hardest rapper yet, harder than 2Pac, Biggie, and DMX. His efforts here are indeed commendable, particularly considering the precedent he's following, but ultimately this is a rather forgettable album, on a par with other here-today, gone-tomorrow post-Biggie Bad Boy releases like Black Rob's *Life Story* (1999) and G. Dep's *Child of the Ghetto* (2001). —*Jason Birchmeier*

Beanie Sigel (Dwight Grant)

b. Philadelphia, PA
East Coast Rap, Hardcore Rap, Hip-Hop, Gangsta Rap
Philadelphian rapper Beanie Sigel had a rapidly rising career, beginning with his appearance on one of underground rapper/producer DJ Clue's mix tapes, to his cameos on Jay-Z's *Vol. 2: Hard Knock Life*, to a consequent solo deal

with Roc-A-Fella Records. His distinctive, slightly drawling delivery and his clever but hard-hitting rhymes were showcased on his debut album, 2000's *The Truth*, which featured contributions from Jay-Z, Memphis Bleek, Eve, and Scarface, and production by the Ruff Ryders' Swizz Beatz and Suave House's Tony Draper. His second album, *The Reason*, hit the streets in summer 2001, led by the single "Beanie (Mack B*****)." —*Heather Phares*

● **The Truth** / 2000 / Def Jam ✦✦✦✦
In 1998, Philadelphia native Beanie Sigel was just another hungry voice in the crowd. However, after an impromptu verse on the Roots' *Adrenaline*, he caught the attention of Jay-Z, who quickly inked the young MC to a deal with his Roc-A-Fella empire. While the momentum of a few dazzling collaborations catapulted his meteoric rise up the hip-hop ranks, more importantly it showed an MC who was on the cusp of greatness. Beanie's debut, *The Truth*, is the culmination of that promise. While Beanie's monosyllabic flow is methodical and offers little variation, his lyrics are remarkably detailed. "What Ya Life Like" is such a frightening depiction of incarceration that it warrants inclusion in any *Scared Straight* documentary. Also, Beanie ingeniously parallels the life of a drug dealer to that of video game characters on "Mac Man." Although Beanie is not ready to supplant his esteemed mentor, Jay-Z, he is one of the most intriguing lyricists to emerge in the post-2Pac era. —*Matt Conaway*

The Reason / Jun. 26, 2001 / Roc-A-Fella ✦✦✦
Arguably the hottest thing to come outta Philly since the Roots, Beanie Sigel had hip-hop heads from coast to coast bobbing along to the infectious beats and dark inner-city tales of his impressive debut, *The Truth*. But while emotional songs like "Mom Praying" make *The Reason* a solid enough follow-up, it essentially boils down to more of the same ol', same ol'. Sigel's familiar streetwise persona shines through on cuts that are more concerned with hustling and hanging out than glitz and glamour, but the repetitive tales of thug life and gangsterisms grow a bit redundant by album's end. The production is consistently banging, and songs like "Tales of a Hustla" and "Think It's a Game" (featuring Jay-Z) more than live up to the promise first glimpsed on *The Truth*. But ultimately, Sigel's sophomore effort isn't so much an artistic step forward as it is a step sideways. —*Bret Love*

Silkk the Shocker (Vyshonne Miller)

b. Feb. 22, 1980, New Orleans, LA
Gangsta Rap, Hardcore Rap, Dirty South
Next to Master P (and maybe C-Murder), Silkk the Shocker (born Vyshonne Miller) was the preeminent rapper on No Limit Records, the underground hip-hop label that became a sensation in the late '90s. Since he is the brother of Master P, the founder of the label, you'd expect nothing less, actually. As a member of Tru, as a guest rapper, and as a solo artist, Silkk the Shocker appeared on most of No Limit's most successful records. His omnipresence says more about the way No Limit was run than it does about his skills. No Limit aggressively marketed each of their artists, so they appeared to be superstars before they ever released an album; Silkk was no different. A modestly gifted rapper, Silkk never wanted to break boundaries, only to work within the confines of gangsta rap, and that's exactly what he did, turning out a series of records that celebrated all the clichés gangsta critics dismissed. Obviously, that's what his audience wanted, since his first two records went platinum without support from radio, MTV, or the music industry at large.

Like his brothers Master P and C-Murder, Silkk the Shocker was born and raised in New Orleans. He began rapping as a teenager, joining a number of gangsta crews including the Down South Hustlers. He also joined Master P's group Tru, which also featured C-Murder. Before he launched his solo career, he had appeared on albums by the Down South Hustlers, the West Coast Bad Boyz, and Tru. In 1996, Silkk released his debut, *The Shocker*, on No Limit Records. Shortly after its release, he appended "The Shocker" as a surname. *The Shocker* slowly became an underground success, largely based on strong word of mouth. Throughout the course of 1997, Silkk the Shocker was all over No Limit releases, appearing on the *I'm Bout It* soundtrack, Tru's *Tru 2 Da Game*, Mia-X's *Unlady Like*, Mystikal's *Unpredictable*, and Master P's *Ghetto D*. His long-awaited second album, *Charge It 2 Da Game*, finally appeared in February 1998, after being promoted by No Limit for nearly eight months. *My World, My Way* was released three years later. —*Stephen Thomas Erlewine*

The Shocker / Aug. 20, 1996 / No Limit ✦
Silkk had worked with a number of gangsta rappers—including Down South Hustlers, Tru, West Coast Bad Boys, and Master P—before releasing his debut

album, *The Shocker*. Perhaps he should have continued his apprenticeship a little longer, because *The Shocker* is an unfocused, uncaring slice of West Coast gangsta rap. Sure, there are a handful of strong backing tracks and Silkk is a competent rapper, even if he isn't particularly distinctive. But his calculated violence and his rampant misogyny ("Hoes Ain't Nothin' But Hoes" just about sums it up) make *The Shocker* nearly unlistenable. If he had something special to say or a unique way of saying it, Silkk's various shortcomings would be acceptable, but as it stands, his average music and his desire to exploit all the commonplace gangsta themes make him nearly intolerable. —*Leo Stanley*

● **Charge It 2 Da Game** / Feb. 17, 1998 / No Limit ✦✦✦
Although it certainly wasn't planned that way, *Charge It 2 Da Game* was No Limit's first major release since the breakthrough success of Master P's *Ghetto D*. Like any No Limit album, *Charge It 2 Da Game* is primarily notable for the way it coopts current trends. Granted, it doesn't sound as derivative as *Ghetto D*, possibly because Snoop Doggy Dogg, Ice Cube, and Eightball & MJG make guest appearances, along with the usual cast of No Limit refugees. Silkk himself is a fine rapper, but he's not particularly distinctive, and neither are the backing tracks. It's an improvement from the scattershot violence 'n' misogyny of his debut *The Shocker*, and it's better than many of its No Limit peers, but *Charge It 2 Da Game* is by and large just an average gangsta album. —*Stephen Thomas Erlewine*

Made Mann / Jan. 19, 1999 / No Limit ✦✦✦
Once No Limit was thrust into the spotlight, the label began to churn out albums even faster than they did before Master P was a superstar—which is really saying something, since the soldiers usually took about a year to ready a new record. The new cycle apparently dictated that a year was the maximum between albums, if the rapid appearance of Silkk the Shocker's third album *Made Mann* is any indication. Released less than a year after *Charge It 2 Da Game*—which in itself was one of the No Limit classics (of course, that's on the No Limit scale, not a hip-hop scale)—*Made Mann* illustrates the perils of such an approach. No Limit records are notorious for their recycling, cheapness, and tedium, and the shorter release cycle accentuates these shortcomings. It follows the formula exactly, piling on the cameos, photocopied bass lines, and appropriated rhythms, all in an attempt to approximate the sound of the streets. To a certain extent it works, since it never takes chances and delivers what the audience wants, but naysayers will wonder if even the hardcore fans aren't getting sick of all No Limit albums sounding identical by now. —*Stephen Thomas Erlewine*

My World, My Way / Feb. 27, 2001 / No Limit ✦✦✦
Despite selling an impressive number of albums with *Charge It 2 Da Game* (1998) and *Made Mann* (1999), and also scoring a gigantic hit single with "It Ain't My Fault, Pt. 2," Silkk the Shocker's first album in two years, *My World, My Way*, shows that the young No Limit rapper hasn't grown much as an artist. For the most part, this album is what you'd expect; Silkk doesn't take any chances here as a rapper and the No Limit production team still proves itself more inclined to imitate than innovate. Fans of Silkk's preceding work should find *My World, My Way* a comforting listen, though a close listen does reveal that Master P's youngest brother has indeed done a lot of growing up since *Made Mann*. Still, his maturity never shines through like it probably should; Silkk's still catering to his young wannabe thug audience, a demographic more into idealistic clichés than heartfelt sincerity. So if you can look past this theatrical approach and treat the album as simply a stylistic exercise, there are indeed some enjoyable moments here, the most notable one being "He Did That," one of the more impressive No Limit songs of the early 2000s. There's really not too much else to say about this album that hasn't been said about every other No Limit album. Seasoned listeners may be left wondering how long No Limit can keep churning this stuff out before making some changes—how many variations on the same formula can one person stomach? —*Jason Birchmeier*

Russell Simmons

Producer, Executive Producer / East Coast Rap, Hip-Hop
Russell Simmons is the most important businessman in the history of rap music. As cofounder of the Def Jam label, Simmons' street-friendly taste and marketing savvy helped bring hip-hop crashing into the mainstream of American culture and mass media. He's often been compared to Motown impresario Berry Gordy, but there's one important difference: where Gordy

strove to make assimilationist R&B that would be considered respectable by pop audiences, Simmons ensured that his artists remained as uncompromisingly rebellious as possible. That attitude made hip-hop a music of choice for a generation of teenagers simply by staying true to its roots; it was a multi-cultural phenomenon that succeeded—more or less—on its own terms. Simmons was the entrepreneur who shepherded rap music into big business, gradually building his own communications company into the largest black-owned enterprise in the industry. By the time he sold Def Jam for $100 million in 1999, he was one of the most respected figures in the rap business, and continued to take an active interest in shaping the culture's future direction.

Russell "Rush" Simmons grew up in the Hollis area of Queens, NY, and spent some of his teen years as a street hustler. He later enrolled at CCNY-Harlem to study sociology, and in 1978, he began using his spare time to promote early hip-hop block parties and club shows around Harlem and Queens, often in tandem with his friend Curtis Walker. A rapper in his own right, Walker adopted the name Kurtis Blow, and Simmons became his manager, also cowriting his 1979 single "Christmas Rappin'." By this time, he'd quit school to pursue artist management full time, forming his own Rush Productions company. In 1982 he took on his younger brother Joseph's group as clients, christening them Run-D.M.C. and helping to guide their meteoric rise to stardom over the next few years. In the meantime, Simmons met a producer and punk rock fan named Rick Rubin, who shared his taste for raw, aggressive, street-level hip-hop. Putting up a few thousand dollars apiece, Simmons and Rubin founded the Def Jam record label in 1984, and secured a distribution deal with CBS after some early success with LL Cool J (who recorded Def Jam's first-ever single, "I Need a Beat").

Over the next few years, Def Jam grew into one of the most popular and creatively vital labels in hip-hop history. In addition to LL Cool J, the label also released acclaimed and influential recordings by Slick Rick, Public Enemy, the Beastie Boys, EPMD, 3rd Bass, Onyx, and many others. Simmons had already turned the story of Def Jam's founding into the fictionalized film *Krush Groove* (1985), which starred Blair Underwood as Simmons and also featured Rubin and Run-D.M.C. as themselves. Critically panned as a plotless vehicle for musical performances, the film was nonetheless a smash hit with hip-hop fans (for pretty much the same reason). Rubin left Def Jam in 1988, leaving Simmons the sole head of the company. Another film, the Run-D.M.C. vehicle *Tougher Than Leather*, followed that year. It was a sign that Simmons was beginning to build a full-fledged entertainment empire, with hip-hop as the foundation but not the sole focus. In 1991 he began producing the groundbreaking HBO series *Russell Simmons' Def Comedy Jam*, a forum for black standup comedians to perform their uncensored routines for a wider audience; among the talents showcased over the series' seven seasons were Martin Lawrence, Chris Rock, Jamie Foxx, Bernie Mac, Cedric the Entertainer, Steve Harvey, D.L. Hughley, and Chris Tucker.

Simmons continued to branch out into other business ventures. In 1992, he launched Phat Farm, a successful men's clothing line; it later spawned a female companion, Baby Phat, which was overseen by onetime supermodel Kimora Lee (who eventually married Simmons in 1999). He returned to films in 1995 with the hip-hop documentary *The Show*, and the following year produced Eddie Murphy's comeback hit *The Nutty Professor*. 1996 also saw the launch of a hip-hop lifestyle magazine, *One World*, which spun off a syndicated TV show hosted by Lee. Further film ventures included 1997's *Gridlock'd* and *How to Be a Player*. Meanwhile, after a downturn during the West Coast G-funk era, Def Jam kept going strong through the '90s with hard, street-level artists like Redman, Method Man, DMX, and Ja Rule, among others.

In 1999, Simmons sold the remainder of his 40-percent share of Def Jam to Universal Music Group for a reported $100 million, staying on as a nominal chairman. In the intervening years, he's kept up his other business ventures, and returned to HBO in 2001 with the spoken-word show *Russell Simmons' Def Poetry Jam*, hosted by Mos Def. He's also devoted ample attention to the Hip-Hop Summit Action Network, among other philanthropic concerns. The Action Network was a nonprofit outgrowth of a 2001 meeting among label heads, artists, and other key figures to discuss responsible directions in image and marketing for hip-hop to take in the new millennium. It made headlines in early 2003 when Simmons called for a boycott of Pepsi, based on the company's decision to jettison rapper Ludacris as its spokesman after Fox news anchor Bill O'Reilly objected to his lyrical content

(Pepsi went on to hire equally profane rocker Ozzy Osbourne in his stead). The company admitted handling the situation poorly, and agreed to donate $5 million to Ludacris' charity foundation. —*Steve Huey*

Simply Jeff (Jeff Adachi)

b. 1966, Sacramento, CA

DJ, Producer / Club/Dance, Funky Breaks, Turntablism, House

West Coast DJ Simply Jeff, previously known as DJ Spinn during the mid-'80s while working at Los Angeles radio hot spots like KROQ and MARS-FM, is the head of Dr. Freecloud's Mixing Lab and Fund Da-Fried Therapeutics, a progressive-leaning club night that allows him to spin everything from chunky trip-hop and down-tempo to trance and rave on the same night. He debuted early in the '90s with tracks recorded for Moonshine as X-Calibur (with Brian Scott). After forming his own Orbit Transmission label, Jeff released more material during 1995-1996, as X-Calibur and the DJ's Project (with Scott, DJ Dan, and Scratchmaster DJ Rectangle). By 1997, Jeff had released his first full-length, *Funk Da-Fried*. The follow-up appeared one year later, and in the spring of 2000, Jeff returned with *Funky Instrumentalist*. —*John Bush*

● **Funk-Da-Fried** / Jun. 10, 1997 / City of Angels ✦✦✦✦
Like the similarly L.A.-based DJ Cut Chemist, Simply Jeff is much better at igniting crowds than the more exhibitionist, philosophical squads up in San Francisco like Invisibl Skratch Piklz. On his first major mix album, Jeff does just that, with a trio of his own tracks, two cuts from the big-beat extraordinaires at Britain's Skint Records and the balance provided by West Coast breakbeat artists of all kinds, from Freaky Chakra to Liquitek Pimps. Moving from old school through acid disco and house, Simply Jeff lets the partyhearty beats and great psychedelic grooves lead the way, and it's an enjoyable journey. —*John Bush*

Funky Instrumentalist / Apr. 18, 2000 / BML ✦✦✦
For Simply Jeff's third major mix album, the veteran SoCal DJ culled tracks from a variety of big-beat, techno, trance, and hip-hop producers. What these tracks have in common is an irresistible funk attitude that's perfect for the dancefloor no matter the origin of the producer, from the chilled British drum'n'bass act E-Z Rollers, to New York's hyper techno DJ Frankie Bones, to master trance remixer Rennie Pilgrem. Though his mix isn't quite as hands-on as the volumes in his *Funk-Da-Fried* series, there are some great tracks here, like the great Zapp tribute "Ride the Funky" by World of Crime, "Shutdown" by Speed Freaks, Jeff's own "Break It Down," and "Hot Stop" by DJ Icey. —*John Bush*

Breakbeat Massive / Mar. 12, 2002 / Moonshine Music ✦✦✦
Los Angeles breaks figurehead Simply Jeff is no stranger to the mix-CD market. *Breakbeat Massive*, his fourth major CD release, opens with his own deconstruction of the all-time breakbeat classic, Afrika Bambaataa's "Planet Rock." But unlike Jeff's previous mixes, its not all hit-the-deck bass drops and insane asylum samples. At least, not throughout the entire CD. The first half of the mix emphasizes the nu breaks movement, with its subtler blending of breaks'n'bass with techier explorations. Experimental breaks guru T. Power is represented, along with several newer artists. But just before the CD becomes just another nu breaks bore-fest, Jeff kicks it up fifth gear with West Coast big-beat pioneer Überzone working with U.K. trance breaks leader Rennie Pilgrem. From there on out, it is the classic-L.A. raver breaks that made Simply Jeff a name. So while he may have settled down slightly in energy, Jeff still knows how to rock a party in your living room. Just give him a moment to get to it. —*Joshua Glazer*

Sindicato Argentino del Hip Hop

f. 1992, Argentina

Group / Hip-Hop, Latin Rap

A Latin rap group from Argentina, Sindicato Argentino del Hip Hop was formed in 1992 by 12 local musicians, making their debut on the first Argentinean hip-hop compilation, *Nacion Hip Hop*, which featured "Del Barrio" and "Pide Mas." Soon, they were participating in *MTV Lingo* along with Control Machete and Illya Kuryaki and the Valderramas, among other similar artists. In 1999, Sindicato Argentino del Hip Hop became a five-piece act, recording 2001's *Un Paso a la Eternidad*, which featured a rap version of the Los Abuelos de la Nada classic "Mil Horas." A year later, Smoler, Derek,

Frost, Huexo, and DJ Fabry were nominated for a Latin Grammy Award for Best Rap/Hip Hop album. —*Drago Bonacich*

● **Un Paso a la Eternidad** / Dec. 11, 2001 / Universal ◆◆◆◆
Sindicato Argentino del Hip Hop's *Un Paso a la Eternidad* garnered international attention after being awarded the Hip-Hop Album of the Year at the 2001 Latin Grammys. The group features a number of different MCs, including Smoler, Frost, Huexo, and Derek, along with DJ/percussionist Fabry. Though no doubt influenced by the stateside hip-hop tradition firmly rooted in New York, these Argentineans draw more heavily from Latin music styles than funk, disco, or soul like their stateside contemporaries. They're also not afraid to feature vocalists on their hooks, such as in "Del Barrio, Pt. 2," though they stick to MCing for the most part. Though this album probably won't convert many monolingual stateside listeners, it's no doubt a dazzling accomplishment for these artists, who don't have such a rich hip-hop tradition to draw from like their New York contemporaries. —*Jason Birchmeier*

Sir Dyno

West Coast Rap, Gangsta Rap, Hardcore Rap, Latin Rap
DarkRoom Familia affiliate Sir Dyno became one of the first Chicano hardcore rappers to make an impact on the West Coast. He debuted in 1996 alongside the Chicano supergroup DarkRoom Familia (*Barrio Love*) and as a solo artist (*Interview With a Chicano*). He continued collaborating with the Familia and recording solo albums through the decade and became widely known for his introspective view of barrio life in California, particularly the dark side with its drugs and violence and its emphasis on survival. In 2002, Brown Power released a pair of Sir Dyno albums, *Engrave These Words on My Stone* and the *Good Times, Bad Times* best-of collection. —*Jason Birchmeier*

Interview With a Chicano / Oct. 15, 1996 / Explicit ◆◆

Chicano Chronicles / Jun. 29, 1999 / Dogday ◆◆
Sir Dyno's second album of harsh Hispanic rap also includes members of his full-time group DarkRoom Familia. —*Keith Farley*

● **Greatest Hits: Good Times, Bad Times** / Jul. 9, 2002 / Brown Power ◆◆◆◆
Greatest Hits: Good Times, Bad Times compiles the highlights from Cali Chicano rapper/producer Sir Dyno's first three albums—*Interview With a Chicano* (1996), *Chicano Chronicles* (1999), and *What Have I Become?* (2000)—as well as a couple stray soundtrack contributions. With a grand total of 20 tracks, there's plenty of variety here, some tracks leaning toward rabble-rousing hardcore rap (presumably the good times) while others toward sullen gangsta balladry (the bad times). Dyno's albums feature a lot of worthwhile moments not compiled here, but *Good Times, Bad Times* indeed rounds up the best of the best and is thus the best place within his discography for newcomers to begin. —*Jason Birchmeier*

Sir Mix-A-Lot (Anthony Ray)

b. Aug. 12, 1963
West Coast Rap, Pop-Rap
Sir Mix-A-Lot put Seattle on the rap map in the late '80s with catchy, comedic dramas drenched in b-boy culture and punctuated by his whiny vocals. Sir Mix-A-Lot vaulted into the spotlight and into controversy with the single "Baby Got Back." Not only was it an enormous pop and R&B hit, it triggered a backlash against what was widely viewed as both sexist and racist lyrics from Mix-A-Lot, in his celebration of rear ends and put-down of women who lacked them. It helped make the *Mack Daddy* album one of 1992's biggest, although 1994's *Chief Boot Knocka* and 1996's *Return of the Bumpasaurus* failed to match its success. In 2000, Rhino released an 18-track best-of titled *Beepers, Benzos & Booty: The Best of Sir Mix-A-Lot.* —*John Floyd*

Swass / 1988 / American ◆◆◆
Sir Mix-A-Lot is one of greatest ironies in the history of rap. His occasional sociopolitical statements show he can be every bit as intelligent a commentator as KRS-One or Chuck D, but Mix's forte has always been the type of fun, escapist, even goofy fare that dominates his debut album, *Swass*. Though forceful and aggressive at times, the distinctive Seattle native never considered himself a hardcore rapper and is quick to point out that his influences range from quirky new waver Gary Numan to metal bands to George Clinton. Ranging from aggressive rap-metal like "Hip-Hop Soldier" and an

inspired interpretation of Black Sabbath's "Iron Man" (which employs headbangers Metal Church) to his enjoyably silly impression of hillbillies on "Square Dance Rap" and "Buttermilk Biscuits," *Swass* set the tone for Mix's career by appealing to pop fans more than hardcore rap listeners. His strongest sociopolitical raps (including "Society's Creation" and "Jack Back") would come later. —*Alex Henderson*

Seminar / 1989 / American ◆◆◆
With his second album, Sir Mix-A-Lot continued focusing primarily on the type of material that made his first reach gold status: escapist, lighthearted pop-rap that fared well among pop, R&B and dance-music circles, but generally wasn't well received in the 'hood. What few sociopolitical songs the CD does contain are first rate, including "The (Peek-A-Boo) Game" (which uses Siouxsie & the Banshees as a reference point) and "National Anthem." An angry number addressing the Iran-contra scandal, the drug plague, and the plight of Vietnam vets, the latter is as powerful as anything Public Enemy, KRS-One, or Ice-T has done. Nonetheless, what made *Seminar* a hit weren't those gems, but odes to cars, gold chains, and "fly girls." As enjoyable as such escapist fare as "My Hooptie" and "Beepers" is, Mix sells himself short by not including more message songs. —*Alex Henderson*

Mack Daddy / 1992 / American ◆◆◆
The massive success of "Baby Got Back" may have earned Sir Mix-A-Lot the dreaded "one-hit wonder" label, as well as an appearance on VH-1's "Where Are They Now?," but the Seattle native has always been a much more interesting and important figure than his reputation would suggest. One of the first rappers outside of New York and L.A. to score significant chart success, Mix-A-Lot's music is generally a lot more irreverent and tongue-in-cheek than people give him credit for, the work of a chubby studio geek living out his most ridiculous playboy fantasies on wax. "Baby Got Back" may be the song that put Sir Mix-A-Lot on the map, but it's actually one of the album's weaker tracks. Far better is *Mack Daddy*'s first single, "One Time's Got No Case," a song that finds Mix-A-Lot addressing standard hip-hop subject matter in a novel fashion, striking out against racist police officers, not through gunplay or violence, but by handing the guilty parties a righteous legal smackdown in a court of law. The rest of *Mack Daddy* charts a similarly cheeky cruise through the not-so-mean streets of Seattle, with Mix-A-Lot addressing such vital subject matters as the nefarious proprietors of fake designer merchandise at swap meets ("Swap Meet Louie") and the importance of not getting whipped by opportunistic females ("Sprung on the Cat"). It's all extremely silly stuff, made even more so by Mix-A-Lot's nasal flow and knack for ridiculous double entendres: "Yo baby, I got a big snake, all you gotta do is make it dance" is a typically subtle Mix-A-Lot come-on. But damn if isn't infectious, funky, and downright fun, making *Mack Daddy* one of the premiere hip-hop guilty pleasures of the '90s. —*Nathan Rabin*

Chief Boot Knocka / Jul. 19, 1994 / American ◆◆◆
Anyone who has had the pleasure of interviewing Sir Mix-A-Lot can tell you that he's extremely intelligent. The Seattle rapper can spend hours talking about political and social issues, and his best sociopolitical offerings are in a class with anything that Public Enemy, KRS-One, and Ice-T have done. But Mix was never marketed as a hip-hop intellectual or a hardcore rapper; listeners usually think of him as the quirky, goofy pop-rapper who gave us "Baby Got Back" and "Posse's on Broadway," and Mix gladly went with the flow because fun, escapist tunes are what earned him the big bucks. *Chief Boot Knocka*, Mix's second album for American and fourth album overall, doesn't pretend to be a Public Enemy release—this is pop-rap that must be judged by pop-rap standards instead of hardcore rap standards. And when those standards are applied, the album is a winner. While fun, frivolous numbers like "Let It Beaounce" and the hit "Put 'Em on the Glass" didn't get much respect from hip-hop's hardcore, there is no denying how infectious they are. The fact is that there is good pop-rap and bad pop-rap; like Salt-N-Pepa and Young MC, Mix knows how to provide material that is commercial but still has some bite. The Seattle resident does get into serious topics on "Take My Stash" (which was inspired by his problems with the IRS) and "Don't Call Me Da Da," but overall this is very much a party album. Is it regrettable that someone who is capable of writing sociopolitical gems like "National Anthem" and "Society's Creation" has neglected his more hard-hitting side? Absolutely. But that doesn't make *Chief Boot Knocka* any less effective as party music. —*Alex Henderson*

Return of the Bumpasaurus / Aug. 27, 1996 / American ✦✦✦
Having been quite visible in the R&B and pop markets thanks to such hits as "Baby Got Back," "Beepers," and the erotic "Put 'Em on the Glass," Sir Mix-A-Lot had his share of detractors in hardcore rap circles—which can be every bit as rigid and dogmatic as jazz purism. The Seattleite gives his detractors a vehement tongue lashing on his fifth album, *Return of the Bumpasaurus*, which is essentially a fun and escapist party album despite all the anger it expresses. True to form, the distinctive Mix effectively combines the hard hitting, the gritty, and the intense with healthy pop quirkiness. Once again, he makes a mistake by not including more social or political commentary—one of his strong points. But when it comes to party songs, he still delivers the goods. —*Alex Henderson*

● **Beepers, Benzos & Booty: The Best of Sir Mix-A-Lot** / Jun. 20, 2000 / Rhino ✦✦✦✦✦
Rhino's *Beepers, Benzos & Booty: The Best of Sir Mix-A-Lot* collects the Seattle rapper's definitive tracks, including the infamous "Baby Got Back," "My Hooptie," "Society's Creation," "Just Da Pimpin' In Me," "Posse On Broadway," and "Square Dance Rap." This is a compilation of one of rap's most consistently funny artists. —*Heather Phares*

Sisqó (Mark Andrews)

b. Baltimore, MD
Urban, Pop-Rap
Even before Sisqó became an overnight superstar in summer 2000 with the infamous "Thong Song," he was no stranger to success. Not many may have recognized his name, but his voice was no doubt familiar, since he was a member of the massively successful '90s R&B group Dru Hill. In 2000, though, Sisqó finally became a household name thanks to his debut solo album, *Unleash the Dragon*. "Thong Song" and its scandalous yet ubiquitous video on MTV propelled the album to the top of the charts, followed by another huge hit, "Incomplete." By the end of 2000, Sisqó was not only a music star but also a teen phenomenon because of his youthful looks, toned body, trendy clothing, and stylish hair—and his omnipresence on MTV obviously didn't hurt. A year after "Thong Song" first blew up, Sisqó returned with his second album, *Return of Dragon*, and also had lined up a startling number of acting opportunities, reaffirming his superstar status.

Long before Sisqó dyed his hair and tattooed his body, he was born Mark Andrews in Baltimore, MD. He cofounded the group Dru Hill in 1995 with high school friends Jazz, Nokio, and Woody and saw their debut album released in 1996, instantly notable for Keith Sweat's production work. But Dru Hill quickly became noteworthy themselves with "Tell Me," a huge R&B hit. Two years later in 1998, Sisqó again graced the airwaves with the second Dru Hill album, *Enter the Dru*. After the success of this album, it didn't take long for the prolific young artist to bounce back the following fall with his solo album, *Unleash the Dragon*. The album's hit singles propelled it to multiplatinum success, setting the stage for Sisqó's forays into acting. He first appeared in the teen comedy *Get Over It*, before signing a development deal with NBC television and a five-picture deal with Miramax.

Following commercially successful guest appearances on DMX's "What These B⬛⬛⬛⬛s Want" and Lil' Kim's "How Many Licks" that kept him in the spotlight while he spent time in the studio, Sisqó re-emerged in the summer of 2001 with *Return of Dragon*, his attempt to prove that "Thong Song" wasn't just a novelty success. Featuring production by Teddy Riley on the lead single, "Can I Live," the album certainly seemed positioned for mammoth success. And if the music wasn't potent enough, Def Soul's marketing barrage, again featuring tons of MTV exposure and an aggressive targeting of the teen audience, ensured the album's success. —*Jason Birchmeier*

● **Unleash the Dragon** / Nov. 30, 1999 / Def Soul ✦✦✦
By the end of his debut solo album, Dru Hill's finest singer Sisqó has beaten the same rhythmic pattern, which is churned in and out of nearly every song, into the ground. Loaded with whispered bedroom moans, which have become late-'90s R&B clichés, *Unleash the Dragon* is short on any real songs to justify the pointless replay of these familiar grooves. Only when he actually unleashes his inner dragon, like on the club thumper "Thong Song," does Sisqó sound at all like the ferocious soulman he fancies himself to be. There's also little distinction among the guest spots here (though Make It Hot's turn on the jittery "Got to Get It" offers some sparks). And once the beats—which borrow heavily from the contemporary R&B playbook—are programmed,

there's little for Sisqó to do but coast along the grooves, with all the conviction and commitment of a soul robot. —*Michael Gallucci*

Return of Dragon / Jun. 19, 2001 / Def Soul ✦✦✦
Sisqó's second solo album, *Return of Dragon*, follows up a debut that unexpectedly shot to the top of the charts a year earlier and remained there, week after week. That debut album, *Unleash the Dragon*, was almost solely powered by an omnipresent summer anthem in "Thong Song"—a difficult feat to duplicate, an even more difficult feat to top. But even if *Return of Dragon* doesn't have a sure-fire novelty hit like "Thong Song" on it, it still has enough firepower to carry Sisqó back to the top of the charts. It's a safe record, no doubt, offering only ten full-length songs and an ensemble cast of songwriters and producers. But regardless of how few risks Sisqó takes on this album, the result is commendable, an energetic, slick, and stylish album with plenty of subtle sex and overt gloss—everything early-2000s pop listeners demand in their superstars. To be honest, though, pop fans aren't looking for well-crafted albums but rather dynamite singles. And this album has its fair share. In fact, somewhere around half of these ten songs could function as hit singles in 2001, with "Can I Live," "Dance for Me," and "Close Your Eyes" being the most obvious choices. In particular, "Can I Live" stands out on the album mostly because of its over-the-top execution; here, the timeless Teddy Riley takes the reigns with songwriting partner D'Wayne Jones, crafting a jittery Timbaland-style beat and working various members of Sisqó's new affiliates, the Dragon Family, into the song. Yet while "Can I Live" stands out as a step in a new direction for Sisqó, "Dance for Me" takes a look back to "Thong Song," resulting in a similarly sexy dancefloor anthem that is just dying for a sleazy, near-naked-dancers-everywhere MTV treatment. In short, Sisqó gives you exactly what you want—assuming you liked his debut album—offering a can't-miss collection of should-be hits and even more of his ceaseless crooning. —*Jason Birchmeier*

Sister Souljah

Political Rap, Hip-Hop, Hardcore Rap
Then-presidential candidate Bill Clinton helped turn the little-known rapper Sister Souljah briefly into a celebrity when he attacked her album *360 Degrees of Power*. During an interview, Souljah called for African Americans to stop destroying their own property and turn their efforts on the white power brokers instead. Clinton accused her of appealing to hatred and urging blacks to randomly target and kill whites. The resulting controversy didn't sell many copies of her record, but did get her onto numerous talk shows and into many general interest magazines. She was eventually dropped by Epic when the record bombed. —*Ron Wynn*

360 Degrees of Power / Jan. 1992 / Epic ✦✦
Seldom has something so mundane generated more controversy. Candidate Bill Clinton garnered some cheap positive publicity when he attacked Sister Souljah for allegedly encouraging African Americans to blindly strike against whites. If he had actually heard the CD, he would have known that Sister Souljah's raps and rhymes were so unappealing and delivered so flatly that few hip-hoppers, let alone any adults, would be paying much attention after the first few minutes. —*Ron Wynn*

6 Shot (Jermaine Tucker)

b. New Orleans, LA
Vocals / Underground Rap, Southern Rap
6 Shot is a relatively unknown rapper from New Orleans, LA. Not nationally known, his first LP was called *The Actual Meaning*. Born Jermaine Tucker, he took his name from his fondness for revolvers. Ironically, a few years after selecting his name, he was actually shot six times and lived. —*Brad Mills*

● **The Actual Meaning** / Oct. 23, 2001 / Street Level ✦✦✦✦
Although it's the work of a lyrically skilled rapper, this album will be remembered more for its inventive beats than 6 Shot's lyrical prowess. The music almost seems like a ride through a comic book most of the time, like a funky city adventure. Simply put, it's hard to make a hip-hop album living in New Orleans. In an area that has Cash Money Records and No Limit Records, plus the 504 Boyz, Skull Duggery, Tec-9, and more, it's just tough to compete and not get killed trying. Fortunately, this is a quality album and should put 6 Shot on the map, at least in the South. This could probably really sell well

in places like New York and California, too, with its funky, jazzy beats and catchy hooks making it a truly complete album. —*Brad Mills*

69 Boyz

f. Jacksonville, FL

Group / Hip-Hop, Bass Music, Southern Rap, Party Rap, Club/Dance

69 Boyz is one of the half-dozen bass-music production efforts headed by C.C. Lemonhead and Jay Ski (of Quad City DJ's and 95 South). The actual group, rappers Van "Thrill da Playa" Bryant, Fast, Slow, and Rottweiler "Mike Mike," came together in Jacksonville, FL. After Lemonhead and Jay Ski hit triple platinum with 1993's "Whoot (There It Is)" as 95 South, they formed their own CeeJai Productions company and wrote and produced the single "Tootsee Roll" for 69 Boyz. The track hit the Top Ten of the R&B charts, and went double platinum. The album *199Quad* followed later that year, and also hit platinum. Second album *The Wait Is Over* followed in 1998 and *2069* arrived two years later. —*John Bush*

199Quad / 1994 / Rip-It ✦✦✦✦

The Wait Is Over / Jul. 14, 1998 / Big Beat ✦✦✦

The 69 Boyz don't change their tune on *The Wait Is Over*, the follow-up to their third debut, *199Quad*. That's both a good and bad thing. It's good, since lead boy Van "Thrill da Playa" Bryant can craft an incredible bass track, keeping the party rolling from beginning to end. It's bad because it shows no artistic progression, nor any sign that Bryant will continue to develop his sound. That, however, turns out to be a minor point, because "art" is the furthest thing from anyone's mind when *The Wait is Over* is playing. Every cut on the album has a deep, bass-heavy groove, and while some are more memorable than others, it all adds up to a good time. —*Stephen Thomas Erlewine*

● **Greatest Hits** / Sep. 11, 2001 / D3 ✦✦✦✦

It is quite easy to step back and laugh at this album; one would not think that 69 Boyz would warrant a *Greatest Hits* album. But oddly enough, this group is perfect for this type of retrospective. Featuring huge hits like "Tootsee Roll," "Kitty Kitty," "C'mon N' Ride It (The Train)," "Space Jams," and countless others, this is a very complete collection. Of course, the main problem with this genre has been sustaining interest over an entire album. 69 Boyz may be the most famous booty group of the '90s, but there still is not an entire album's worth of material here. Instead, there are some massively huge hits mixed in with some typical filler. The most interesting inclusion is "Whoop (There It Is)," a minor hit that capitalized on the success of "Whoop (There It Is)" by changing one letter. The fact that this song was a success goes to show how simple it can be to make money in this industry, something that this entire compilation proves. Anyone who needs these songs on a CD should invest in this. Otherwise, do not expect this album to be an exciting retrospective of an artist's career—it really is not. —*Bradley Torreano*

Skee-Lo

b. Poughkeepsie, NY

Hip-Hop, Pop-Rap

Skee-Lo was an anomaly in the rap world of the '90s: instead of spinning violent gangsta tales or extolling the virtues of marijuana, Skee's songs were profanity-free, good-time stories with a self-deprecating sense of humor. Skee-Lo was born in Poughkeepsie, NY, and moved to Riverside, CA, at age nine. He was turned on to rap by Kurtis Blow records, admiring their down-to-earth quality. His *I Wish* single, with a video that parodied *Forrest Gump*, became a huge hit on radio and MTV during the summer of 1995, and his identically titled debut album was released shortly thereafter. Five years later, Skee-Lo resurfaced to issue his long-awaited follow-up *I Can't Stop*. —*Steve Huey*

● **I Wish** / Jun. 27, 1995 / Volcano ✦✦✦✦

"I Wish" was an irresistible piece of pop-rap, featuring a slinky, funky beat and a sunny hook that rang in your head for days. It's undeniably the highlight of Skee-Lo's debut album, but he has enough charm and self-deprecating wit to make the rest of the record enjoyable, even if none of the songs have beats, lyrics, or hooks quite as intoxicating as the title track. —*Stephen Thomas Erlewine*

Tom Skeemask

b. Memphis, TN

Dirty South, Hardcore Rap, Underground Rap

As the leading figure in DJ Squeeky's Mo Cheda camp, Tom Skeemask spent years as a legend in the Memphis, TN, rap scene before extending his reach

to a national audience. His first big release, *2 Wild for the World*, became a modest success in the South without the help of airplay, and in 2001, Skeemask returned with a follow-up album, *You Can't Hold Me Back*, both of which featured production by Squeeky. —*Jason Birchmeier*

● **2 Wild for the World** / Feb. 24, 1998 / Relativity ✦✦✦

Before his debut album *2 Wild for the World*, Tom Skeemask was known as an underground bass producer, working on such records as *Young Southern Playaz, Taylor Boyz,* and *Money Butt Naked*, plus hits from Eightball & MJG. Not surprisingly, *2 Wild for the World* sounds very similar to those records, complete with the bottomless bass and loping grooves. However, Skeemask is simply a better producer than many of his peers, with a better grasp of how to make a good record. That shows throughout his official debut—even though a couple of songs sound a little generic, it's by and large a killer bass party record that keeps the action moving whenever it's on and it's loud. —*Leo Stanley*

Skinny Boys

Group / Old School Rap, Comedy Rap, Hip-Hop

Known for a few old school classics, the Skinny Boys made a lasting impression. The trio features Jock Box (Jacque Harrison), Shockin' Shaun (Shaun Harrison), and Super Jay (James Harrison), and had a record deal with Jive. Though they aren't often cited as being one of the more influential old school rap groups, their 12"s remained popular with hip-hop DJs, "Rip the Cut" and "Skinny & Proud" being two of their more popular tracks. —*Jason Birchmeier*

Weightless / 1986 / Warlock ✦✦

They Can't Get Enough / 1988 / Jive ✦✦

The second album for erstwhile rappers/urban contemporary artists the Skinny Boys had a few comic nuggets, but was otherwise a dreary collection of fashionable clichés, samples, snippets, and beats. Their performances, whether vocals or raps, ran out of steam about ten minutes into the album and were sorely flagging by the end. —*Ron Wynn*

Skull Duggrey

Hip-Hop, Southern Rap, Dirty South, Hardcore Rap, Gangsta Rap

New Orleans rapper Skull Duggrey fell in love with hip-hop as a child and began hanging out with the Nature Boys, a locally popular dance and rap crew. Skull's longtime friend, Master P, put him on the gold-selling *Down South Hustlers* compilation, and his reputation grew from there. Two years later, his debut album appeared, and No Limit and Penalty Records co-released the follow-up *These Wicked Streets. 3rd Ward Stepper* arrived in 2000 on the Hoodlum Entertainment imprint. —*Heather Phares*

Hoodlum Fo' Life / Oct. 1, 1996 / Priority ✦✦✦

● **These Wicked Streets** / Sep. 8, 1998 / Penalty/No Limit ✦✦✦

Basically, anyone purchasing a No Limit record in the fall of 1998 knows what to expect from Skull Duggrey's *These Wicked Streets*—the standard post-gangsta record, complete with predictable samples and loops, by-the-book rhymes, endless guest appearances, and utterly predictable grooves, all packaged in an album that runs way too long. That's exactly what *These Wicked Streets* delivers. To some, this may be really frustrating, since No Limit simply repeats its formula over and over again, without offering any variations. Nevertheless, there are many listeners who have become addicted to what No Limit offers, and anything new from the label is worth their time—even if it sounds like the producers and the rappers not only didn't care about the final product, but that they weren't even in the same studio much of the time. That's the No Limit way, and if you like it, by all means add this to your collection. —*Stephen Thomas Erlewine*

Sleepy's Theme

Group / Hip-Hop

Organized Noize was the primary architect behind virtually the entire "Hotlanta" sound of the 1990s. As the mainstay of the production group, Pat "Sleepy" Brown (whose father was a member of '70s funk band Brick) could lay claim to being one of the most influential behind-the-boards men in music. Along with fellow multi-instrumentalists Rico Wade and Ray Murray, Brown was responsible for hit singles from TLC ("Waterfalls") and En Vogue ("Don't Let Go (Love)"), arguably the two most influential female R&B groups of the decade; and, on the rap side of the divide, he called the shots in the control booth during the creation of the landmark '90s albums of Goodie Mob and OutKast, alongside Organized Noize, two of the key cogs in the mammoth Dungeon Family collective. It was Brown's somnolent falsetto, in fact, that could be heard oozing from OutKast's premier hit "Player's Ball" in 1994.

It was no surprise, then, when Brown, Wade, and Murray sought an outlet on the side to record their original music. They first stepped out on their own as three-fifths of Society of Soul, which released a solid 1995 album, *Brainchild*, that, only partly successfully, attempted to bring the '60s and '70s urban milieu into a '90s context. More successful was their second attempt under the moniker Sleepy's Theme. Released on micro-indie Bang Ii in 1998, *The Vinyl Room* added a sleek and pimped-out new chapter to the funk-and-soul storybook that previously had been written by such loose-limbed, mood-driven stalwarts as Isaac Hayes, Barry White, Curtis Mayfield, the Isley Brothers, the Commodores, Earth, Wind & Fire, and the Gap Band. Among the finest soul albums of the year, *The Vinyl Room* unfortunately was accorded little promotional push, and as a result failed to find much airplay even inside urban markets. — *Stanton Swihart*

● **The Vinyl Room** / Jul. 14, 1998 / Bang Ii ✦✦✦
This particular vinyl room must be filled with every imaginable urban soul 45 and LP that was released between 1968 and 1977, because that is exactly the atmosphere this debut album from Sleepy's Theme, part of Organized Noize's Atlanta cadre, creates. Right from the get-go of *The Vinyl Room*, the vision of huge floppy hats, bell bottoms, fur coats, afros, old Lincolns and Cadillacs, hustlers, and players, is irrevocably evoked, albeit through a hazy late-'90s light. Sleepy's Theme is not at all interested in kowtowing to '90s soul and R&B etiquette or following the conventions of those formulas. Their rulebook was instead written by the Impressions, Isaac Hayes, Barry White, Donny Hathaway, the O'Jays, and any number of more obscure, delectable funky-soul treats from the '70s. There are no sterilized beats or vocal histrionics within earshot of *The Vinyl Room*. As funky as their chops are, the band never seems to be going exactly retro or copying their influences (emulating, perhaps). If anything, Organized Noize's production sounds even more '70s-ish than did the soul music that emanated from that period, which theoretically could turn the music more into a parody than homage. And yet by marrying their trademark production touches—beautifully dreamy, lazy melodies, ingratiating synthesizer textures, stately bits of orchestration and brass, crisp drumming, and wayward drum-machine beats—with the sonic touchstones of that era and filtering it through the organic instrumentation from Sleepy's Theme, Organized Noize arrives at a sound that, while it eschews trends, is nevertheless wholly contemporary and grounded in the sampladelic spirit of hip-hop. It is what made their sound one of the most acclaimed and recognizable of the '90s. Within that context, though, every song lopes along at a weed-stoned pace, with Curtis Mayfield-like falsetto leads, noir-ish spoken-word raps, and testifying, honey-coated female background vocals that coil around the music like vines. And the music is so mackadociously somnolent and sweet—full of creamy bass grooves, paper-soft cymbal pats, raindrop-drowsy keyboards, and sly, country-fried guitar runs, with bad-mother (shut your mouth!) wah-wah licks all over the place—that you feel magically transported to an episode of *Starsky and Hutch* or *Mod Squad* and half expect to pan down and find yourself decked out in a silk shirt and scarf, polyester flares, Italian loafers, and a feathered hat. That, of course, is a high compliment. Only someone irredeemably jaded could dismiss flawlessly mood-driven songs such as "Choked Out Saturday Night," "Still Smokin,'" "Private Party," and "Menage A Trois"—the titles of which impart all the information that a listener really needs to know—without at least a bit of guilty pleasure. — *Stanton Swihart*

Slick Rick (Richard Walters)

b. Jan. 14, 1965, London, England
Golden Age, Hip-Hop, Hardcore Rap
Slick Rick foreshadowed and epitomized the pimpster attitude of many rappers during the late '80s and early '90s, with gold chains, his trademark eye-patch, and recordings that were no less misogynistic—"Treat Her Like a Prostitute," for example, became an underground hit in 1988, though it was justly criticized for its view of women. His 1988 album, *The Great Adventures of Slick Rick*, was a certified-platinum classic, but before he could record a follow-up, Slick Rick was arrested for attempted murder. Out on bail thanks

to Def Jam Records' labelhead Russell Simmons, Rick recorded *The Ruler's Back* in three weeks and released the album in 1991. After his release from prison two years later, he recorded *Behind Bars* for a 1994 release.

Born to Jamaican parents in South Wimbledon, London, on January 14, 1965, Ricky Walters was blinded by broken glass as an infant and took to wearing an eyepatch from an early age. He emigrated with his family to the Bronx in the late '70s and attended the La Guardia High School of Music & Art, where he became friends with future rapper Dana Dane. The two formed the Kangol Crew, and began performing in hip-hop battles around the city. At one 1984 battle in the Bronx, Rick met Doug E. Fresh, and began playing with his Get Fresh Crew (which also included Chill Will and Barry Bee). Fresh's number-four R&B hit, "The Show," exploded just one year later, and MC Ricky D—as Rick was then known—leaped to a solo contract two years later, after an acquaintance with Russell Simmons led to his signing to Def Jam Records, the biggest label in hip-hop at the time.

Slick Rick recorded his debut record, *The Great Adventures of Slick Rick*, and released the album in 1988. "Treat Her Like a Prostitute" became a sensation on the streets, but R&B radio stations were understandably reluctant to play the track; instead, they pushed his duet with Al B. Sure!, "If I'm Not Your Lover," and it made number two in 1989. "Children's Story" hit the R&B Top Five that same year, but early in 1990, Slick Rick was arrested after shooting at his cousin—who allegedly harassed Rick's mother—and leading police on a high-speed chase. Before his sentencing, 21 songs were recorded and hastily released as *The Ruler's Back*. The album failed to move at all, though Rick's confession track "I Shouldn't Have Done It" scraped the R&B charts later in 1991. Featured in the rap documentary *The Show* (released in 1995)—in a segment where Russell Simmons actually visits the prison—Slick Rick was released on a work program in 1996, although his *Behind Bars* album appeared in 1994. *The Art of Storytelling* was issued in 1999, an artistically successful comeback that paired him with MCs like Outkast and Snoop Dogg but did more to emphasize his talents as a solo artist.

While performing live on a Florida cruise ship in the summer of 2002, INS officials seized the rapper and brought him to prison. Although the organization had unsuccessfully been trying to deport Rick since 1991, they finally appealed enough times to get the Board of Immigration Appeals to make a ruling in favor of sending him back to England. Although his wife, children, and parents are all American citizens, the fact that Rick was born in England is enough of a technicality to warrant his deportation. The situation was even more frustrating because of the INS' insistance on deporting the rapper, spending more than ten years trying to send him back despite the ridiculous circumstances surrounding the situation. His parents had lived in London because of their job situation, and moved him back to the United States at the age of 11. He had never bothered to change his citizenship because of the young age at which he had been relocated. Held in prison through the end of the year, famous friends like Russell Simmons and Will Smith attempted to help his cause, but he was continually refused bail. — *John Bush*

★ **The Great Adventures of Slick Rick** / 1988 / Def Jam ✦✦✦✦✦
Slick Rick's reputation as hip-hop's greatest storyteller hangs on his classic debut *The Great Adventures of Slick Rick*, one of the most influential rap records of the late '80s—for better and worse. Most of the production is standard early Def Jam, but Rick's style on the mic is like no one else's. His half-British accent and odd, singsong cadences often overshadow the smoothness of his delivery, but there's no overlooking the cleverness of his lyrics. His carefully constructed narratives are filled with vivid detail and witty asides, and his cartoonish sense of humor influenced countless other rappers. He'll adopt a high voice for his female characters, and even duets with his old alterego MC Ricky D on "Mona Lisa." But there's also a dark side to *The Great Adventures*—namely its vulgarity and offhanded misogyny. No MC had ever dared go as far on record as Rick, and the tracks in question haven't really lost much of their power to offend, or at least raise eyebrows. The notorious "Treat Her Like a Prostitute" is the prime suspect, undermining well-intentioned advice (don't trust too quickly) with cynical, often degrading portrayals of women. "Indian Girl (Adult Story)," meanwhile, is an X-rated yarn with a barely comprehensible payoff. Yet this material is as much a part of Rick's legacy as his more admirable traits, and he was far from the last MC to put seemingly contradictory sides of his personality on the same record. And it's worth noting that most of his *Great Adventures*, no matter how dubious, end up as cautionary tales with definite consequences. That's especially true on

the tragic "Children's Story," in which a teenage robber's increasingly desperate blunders lead to his destruction. In the end, *Great Adventures* is simply too good not to deserve the countless samples and homages by everyone from Snoop Dogg to Black Star. — *Steve Huey*

The Ruler's Back / Jul. 2, 1991 / Def Jam ♦♦♦♦

It was easy to dismiss *The Ruler's Back* before it was even released, or to assume that there was no way it could live up to *The Great Adventures of Slick Rick*. Of course, it did not attain the same level of artistic success as that debut, and it certainly did not equal that album's commercial success, in fact seemingly passing beneath the radar of the whole hip-hop community, for the most part. At the time of its release, the album received mixed reviews and indifferent reactions even from fans of Slick Rick. That's another unfortunate, ill-fated aspect of *The Ruler's Back*, because, in truth, it is a strong, albeit uneven, progression from the debut and occasionally strikes a flawless note. To think of the album as anything other than a confused, transitional effort would be inaccurate, but it does not follow that it isn't an intriguing record. The messiness of its execution perfectly encapsulates the sort of turmoil Slick Rick was experiencing in his life at the time, and the music pulls the listener into that sort of tangled experience. Both Vance Wright's production and Slick Rick's rapping sound pressed for time, and they rush through the songs with a whip-lashing intensity. It can be a disorienting listen, but it is also a pure adrenaline rush. Slick Rick was going through a time of hurtling change, and the hurried breathlessness of the music captures that. *The Ruler's Back* is all over the map, lacking the thematic focus that held the first album together, but its frayed-threads, seams-showing immediacy is part of what makes it such an underrated album in the hip-hop canon. — *Stanton Swihart*

Behind Bars / Nov. 22, 1994 / Def Jam ♦♦

Within hip-hop, Slick Rick is arguably the most acclaimed MC of them all. Snoop Dogg, for one, owes a huge debt to his detached, effortless delivery on the microphone. At his best, Slick Rick was always coolness personified. The London-born artist's troubles, however, have been well documented. They are further addressed by the man himself on the title track to this recording, completed during a work release program with the help of veteran hip-hop producer Prince Paul (Rick was in jail for the 1990 shooting of an innocent bystander while attempting to chase down a bodyguard). Before Ol' Dirty Bastard cornered the market, Slick Rick was rap's bad-boy-in-chief. On this uneven record, he pays witness to the events that shaped him, rather than detail his current incarceration. Regardless, there are times when the listener might wish for a more reflective and less violently female-baiting narrator; absolution and regret aren't particularly high on his agenda when he proclaims "bitches ain't no good." — *Alex Ogg*

The Art of Storytelling / May 25, 1999 / Def Jam ♦♦♦♦

If there's one thing Slick Rick has mastered, it is *The Art of Storytelling*. Ever since his debut, *The Great Adventures of Slick Rick*, he has been known for his literate, winding narratives, but his career was marred by legal troubles that kept him in prison for much of the '90s. Consequently, *The Art of Storytelling* is only his fourth album, but it's the first to rank as a worthy sequel to his classic debut. *The Ruler's Back* came close to capturing the feel of *The Great Adventures*, but *The Art* has a continually stunning set of stories and tales, and the presence of guest artists—even rappers as talented as Outkast, Nas, Raekwon, and Snoop Dogg—only emphasizes what a singular talent Rick is. The smooth production may be a little bit mired in contemporary rap clichés, but it's all enjoyable. Besides, Rick is about the lyrics, not the music, and he has written a stellar set of songs here, songs that are continually surprising and thought provoking. It's a masterful set from one of the true lyrical masters of hip-hop. — *Stephen Thomas Erlewine*

Slum Village

f. Detroit, MI

Group / Hip-Hop, Underground Rap

Rising from the rugged streets and rich musical tapestry of Detroit, MI, Slum Village is poised to carry on the old school, funk, and soul-filled hip-hop torch of genre pioneers A Tribe Called Quest, De La Soul, and the Pharcyde. Growing up in the Conant Garden neighborhood of Detroit and forming together during their high school days at Detroit's Pershing High School, MCs Baatin, Jay Dee, and T3 quickly garnered praise and recognition in the local underground scene. In the mid-'90s, Jay Dee became part of the hip-hop elite as a

member of the Ummah, the production team responsible for multiple hits by Q-Tip, A Tribe Called Quest, D'Angelo, the Pharcyde, De La Soul, and Common, as well as remixes for Janet Jackson and Brand New Heavies. In 1998, Slum Village gained further recognition as an opening act for A Tribe Called Quest's farewell tour. Two years later, after some record-industry politics, the group released *Fantastic, Vol. 2*, an album featuring appearances from D'Angelo, Q-Tip, and DJ Jazzy Jeff. For fans with an ear to the underground and a few questions concerning the whereabouts of *Fantastic, Vol. 1*, the trio assumed an alias (J-88) to release *Best Kept Secret*.

Two more years went by before the group was heard from, but "Tainted" broke their silence in the summer of 2002 to become a growing hit on MTV2. The album that followed, *Trinity (Past, Present and Future)*, boasted fewer guest appearances and a well-rounded combination of the first album's rough-and-tumble productions with the second album's soulful vibe. The record also featured Jay Dee in a reduced role, with new member Elzhi picking up the slack. — *Brian Musich*

● **Fantastic, Vol. 2** / Jun. 13, 2000 / Goodvibe ♦♦♦♦

After being released by their previous label, the debut from Slum Village (Jay Dee, T3, and Baatin) had been collecting dust for over a year. The trio of Detroit natives witnessed a renaissance for the album in underground hip-hop circles, as critical praise of the LP (*Fantastic, Vol. 1*) by the Roots and D'Angelo paved the way for it to become one of the most heavily bootlegged albums in recent years. Even though *Fantastic* has been given the seal of approval by those highly influential artists, the man most responsible for this LP's resurrection is group member Jay Dee. Due to his work with A Tribe Called Quest, Common, Macy Gray, and a solo Q-Tip, Jay's stock has risen considerably, and he has become one of this industry's most sought-after beat technicians. With *Fantastic*, Jay consistently demonstrates what all of the fuss is about, as his hypnotic instrumentals range from the straight soul of "Tell Me" featuring D'Angelo to the sublime keyboard grooves of "Fall in Love" and the quirky "Hold Tight," which features a pouty Q-Tip. Yet, even with all of Jay's wonderfully melodious production, *Fantastic* is more of an enigma then it is a triumph. While Jay exudes diversity behind the boards, he and the rest of his Slum Village mates are trivial MCs, slapping together a host of inept rhymes ripe with misogynistic overtones. — *Matt Conaway*

Dirty District / Jun. 25, 2002 / Sequence ♦♦♦

Community activists on a level that gives them few rivals in hip-hop, the Slum Village trio dedicated *Dirty District*, their 2002 mix tape for Sequence, to breaking over a dozen fellow Detroit MCs. Boasting a darker, dirtier sound than the group's 2000 debut, most every track on *Dirty District* was recorded at one studio, with Slum Village compatriots RJ Rice and T3 overseeing the production. After T3's own intro and a fresh track from Slum Village ("One"), *Dirty District* gets into it with dense tracks and excellent rapping by Lo Louis ("Throw That 'D'") and Elzhi & Mu ("Me and Mu"). Ironically, the best track was one of the few *not* recorded in Detroit: the Alchemist's production of Twin's "Big Twinz." — *John Bush*

Trinity (Past, Present and Future) / Aug. 13, 2002 / Barak ♦♦♦

With a young, new rapper (Elzhi) taking the place of a mostly departed producer and mentor (Jay Dee), it'd be easy to expect a letdown from the second full Slum Village LP. Despite a bloated track listing and a mostly overblown concept, though, *Trinity (Past, Present and Future)* is an excellent statement from one of the most mature groups in the rap underground. Yes, Jay Dee's three productions are among the best of the lot, though the others—quite a few of them by Slum Village's own T3 and one each from the Roots' Scott Storch and Hi Tek—both recall and push forward Jay Dee's blueprint for point-perfect groove. The single "Tainted" is one of the best on tap here, while the laid-back dancefloor anthem "Disco" finds Slum Village so ambitious they plan on getting played in barbershops and beauty salons as well as the clubs. Twenty-three tracks, though, are just too much to try and wrap your head around, and the theatrical concept is a touch too far. (Each track relates either to the past, present, or the future; "Star" concerns the present, while "Hoes" and "Insane" apparently represent the future of the group.) — *John Bush*

Slumplordz

f. 1997, Oakland, CA

Group / Underground Rap

With Oakland, CA, serving as their backdrop, Slumplordz formed as a rap group in 1997. Comprised of individual members Hard Rard, Moon, J. Jonah,

Gravanaught, and Irahktherigor, the collective also breaks down into sub-groups, including Sunnmoonsekt, the Yakuza, and the Original Raw Elements. Slumplordz' initial release on Knock Factor Records in 1999 came in the form of *Sunnmoonsekt*, which primarily featured Hard Rard and Moon. The cassette version of the album made enough waves in the underground for Slumplordz to be picked up by Stray Records, a subsidiary of Dogday. In 2000, the Oakland-based label released a Slumplordz single called "Slump," followed by an album titled *The Yakuza In: Don't Worry About the Caliber*. In 2001, Stray Records re-released the *Sunnmoonsekt* album. Slumplordz are rooted in a unique production style, indigenous to the Bay Area. Merging the tenets of classic mob rap from the likes of Khayree and RBL Posse with the minimalist sensibilities of electronica, the "slump" sound takes shape. The Roland TR-808 is heavily relied upon as insane drum claps urge each musical endeavor. Their MCing is somewhat of an acquired taste, but for anyone schooled in the ways of Too Short, Digital Underground, and Del, Slumplordz are far from a stretch and close to an extension. —*Robert Gabriel*

The Yakuza In: Don't Worry About the Caliber / Oct. 17, 2000 / Stray ♦♦

● **Sunnmoonsekt** / Feb. 20, 2001 / Stray ♦♦♦♦
Sunnmoonsekt delivers nothing less than East Bay funk for the space age. Building upon the traditions of Too Short, Mac Mall, Hobo Junction, and Zion I, Slumplordz have updated the Oakland rap sound for the new millennium. With heavy bass in tow, their Moog applications and electro accents refresh their "status on the microphone, raw apparatus." Hard Rard and Moon are more than ample MCs, especially when they approach controversial topics such as conspiracy theories and tax revolt. Very much a consistent album, *Sunnmoonsekt* is as entertaining as it is time honored. So while typical misogyny is expected, so too is an uplifting experience, reminiscent of a MacArthur Boulevard sideshow frequented by spaceships. Stray Records strikes again. —*Robert Gabriel*

Smif-n-Wessun

f. 1993, Brooklyn, NY
Group / Hip-Hop, East Coast Rap, Hardcore Rap
Part of Brooklyn's talented Boot Camp Clique, this powerful tandem got their start on Black Moon's classic debut, *Enta Da Stage*, in 1993. Rudeboy MCs Tek and Steele made their presence felt on the cuts "U Da Man" and "Black Smif-n-Wessun." In early 1994, the crew scored a massive underground hit with "Bucktown," a reference to their violence-plagued Bedford-Stuyvesant stomping grounds and "home of the original gun clappas." Their debut LP, *Dah Shinin'*, followed soon thereafter, unleashing more heavy artillery from the military-minded BCC. With a canvas of dark, gluttonous beats provided by the gifted Beatminerz production squad, the duo expanded the limits of harsh-sounding, neck-snapping hip-hop by adding a melodic element. The crew released their album during the heyday of one of the '90s most influential independent hip-hop labels, Wreck Records, which many other indies (Rawkus) have patterned themselves around. Their name alone implies violence, but the weaponry they deploy is also of the verbal variety. Tek and Steele both possess signature flows, the former a bit more straight-laced while the latter showcases West Indian influences. *Dah Shinin'* was a focused album with a sharp compacted sound that still contained depth, albeit strictly from the dark side.

Forced to reincarnate themselves after a legal battle with the Smith and Wesson firearm company, the duo resurfaced in 1997 as the Cocoa Brovaz, a reference to their heritage and also to their marijuana fixation. Their second album (and first as the Cocoa Bs), 1998's *The Rude Awakening*, was a more sprawling and chaotic venture, as well as being a shade more frighteningly dark. Since 1998, the two partners have released a few singles, including "Super Brooklyn," which features a superbly innovative use of a sample from the old Super Mario Bros. Nintendo game. —*Michael Di Bella*

● **Dah Shinin'** / Jan. 10, 1995 / Wreck ♦♦♦♦♦
Upon its release in 1995, Smif-n-Wessun's *Dah Shinin'* was unfortunately swept aside by the popular onslaught of the Notorious B.I.G. and the Wu-Tang Clan. That's too bad, the group's album is a masterpiece of New York City crime rap. The stars of the album aren't really the two MCs, Tek and Steele, but the Beatminerz production team. They were responsible for the ground-breaking tracks on Black Moon's *Enta Da Stage*, the album on which Smif-n-Wessun made its debut, and they continue their strong track record

on *Dah Shinin'.* The Beatminerz craft their songs with deep, fluid bass lines and moody jazz samples. On Smif-n-Wessun's debut, they create a series of hazy soundscapes perfect for the group's brand of lyrical mayhem. Tek and Steele don't break any new ground, but they bring enough joyful abandon to their tales of guns, drugs, and thugs to keep things interesting. Their smoked-out rhymes match the beats perfectly. Indeed, few hip-hop albums offer such a unified coherent effort. *Dah Shinin'* is certainly Smif-n-Wessun's strongest album to date, and it represents the Beatminer'z high point as well. —*Christopher Witt*

DJ Andy Smith

b. Jan. 23, 1967, Thornbury, England
DJ / Club/Dance, Trip-Hop, Electronica
Portishead's DJ Andy Smith first met group frontman Geoff Barrow while the two were at school; he eventually joined Barrow's touring band as support DJ. He also appeared with the Fugees, Republica, and Prophets of the City, and released his debut mix album, *The Document*, in 1998. —*John Bush*

● **The Document** / May 19, 1998 / Polygram ♦♦♦♦
As the DJ for Portishead, Andy Smith wasn't necessarily one of the better-known mixers in electronic music. After all, most of the music the band made was credited to Geoff Barrow, the mastermind of Portishead's albums. Perhaps that's why Smith went ahead and released *The Document*, a continuous-mix, various-artists collection that comes close to capturing his opening sets for Portishead. It's an unpredictable, surprising disc, one where Jeru the Damaja, the James Gang, Peggy Lee, Barry White, Grandmaster Flash, and the Spencer Davis Group all occupy the same space. Surprisingly, the album works, as Smith's juxtapositions are both revealing and entertaining. It's not necessarily an album you'd return to frequently, but *The Document* is quite enjoyable as it's playing. —*Stephen Thomas Erlewine*

Will Smith (William Smith III)

b. Sep. 25, 1968, West Philadelphia, PA
Hip-Hop, Urban, Pop-Rap
Beginning his career during the mid-'80s under the name the Fresh Prince, by the following decade rapper Will Smith was one of the biggest superstars of his time—not only a pop music sensation, he also conquered television and eventually feature films, starring in a string of box-office megahits. Born September 25, 1968, in Philadelphia, he was 16 when he met aspiring DJ Jeff Townes; joining forces as DJ Jazzy Jeff & the Fresh Prince, the duo immediately became local favorites, but their continued existence was threatened when Smith graduated high school and was offered a scholarship to MIT. Ultimately, he chose to pursue a career in music, and in 1987 he and Townes issued their debut record, *Rock the House*, scoring a hit with the single "Girls Ain't Nothing but Trouble."

Propelled by the smash "Parents Just Don't Understand," DJ Jazzy Jeff & the Fresh Prince broke into the mainstream a year later with *He's the DJ, I'm the Rapper*, one of the first hip-hop LPs to achieve double-platinum status. Clean-cut, witty, and easygoing, the duo's bubblegum approach was a stark contrast to the dominant, harder-edged rap sound of the period; viewed as a non-threatening alternative to their peers, they received the parental seal of approval, and their appeal spread across racial lines as well. *And in This Corner…* followed in 1989, and soon Hollywood began taking notice of Smith's success; in 1990 he was tapped to star in *The Fresh Prince of Bel-Air*, a sitcom for NBC. An immediate hit, it made Smith a household name and continued in production through 1996.

Smith also continued his music career, and in 1991 DJ Jazzy Jeff & the Fresh Prince scored their biggest chart hit to date with the excellent "Summertime," from the album *Homebase*. The year following, he made his feature film debut in the drama *Where the Day Takes You*; in 1993 his supporting turn in *Six Degrees of Separation* was the subject of much critical acclaim. That same year, the final Jazzy Jeff/Fresh Prince record, the disappointing *Code Red*, was released. In 1995, Smith co-starred in the action film *Bad Boys*, a major box-office hit; it set the stage for his leading role in 1996's *Independence Day*, the summer's biggest smash. A year later, he starred in *Men in Black*, again the box-office champ of the summer season; recording for the first time under his given name, he also scored a smash with the movie's rap theme. Smith's debut solo LP, *Big Willie Style*, also appeared in 1997, notching the hits "Gettin' Jiggy Wit It," "Just the Two of Us," and

"Miami." Shortly on the heels of his first box-office disappointment, 1999's *Wild Wild West*, he returned with the album *Willennium*. —*Jason Ankeny*

Big Willie Style / Nov. 25, 1997 / Columbia ✦✦✦✦

Will Smith wisely decided not to change his style too much on *Big Willie Style*, the first record he released since becoming a major movie star with appearances on *Independence Day* and *Men in Black*. Instead of trying to toughen his image, Smith continued with the friendly, humorous pop-rap that has been his trademark since *He's the DJ, I'm the Rapper*. Of course, he gives the music a glossy modern sheen (ironically based on early-'80s funk) to prove that he's still hip—and it works. Sure, there's filler scattered all the way the through the album, but the best moments—the disco-thumping "Gettin' Jiggy Wit It," the Larry Blackmon duet "Candy," the ballad "I Loved You," and the riotous "Men in Black"—rank among his best singles. —*Stephen Thomas Erlewine*

Willennium / Nov. 16, 1999 / Columbia ✦✦✦✦

By the time Will Smith released *Willennium* in November 1999, it was fashionable to put him down, especially since he was recovering from his first major stumble, the overblown *Wild Wild West*. Probably just the fact that he was everywhere made certain spoilsports long to take him down a notch, but *Wild Wild West* wasn't a mess because of him; in fact, he provided the only glimmers of fun in the whole misguided mess, through sheer star power. And that star power drives *Willennium*, turning it into a bold, brassy delight. Smith just doesn't care what anyone thinks; he knows he's a superstar, and he revels in his status. He likes to make fun music, and he likes to make it on a grand scale. Furthermore, he has no shame about entertaining. Consequently, *Willennium* is a gonzo pleasure in the way only a handful of big-budget pop albums can be: gaudy, giddy, infectiously silly, and proudly over the top. Case in point, its de facto title track, "Will 2K." Smith and his producers picked the Clash's "Rock the Casbah" as the foundation for an end-of-the-century party jam, a move so mind-bogglingly unpredictable that it's hard not to smile. And that spirit carries throughout the album, as Smith drops lyrical and musical allusions that are at once well known and totally out of left field. All of this is done to bright, joyful party music that celebrates its big beats and big hooks. Smith isn't quite as convincing when it comes to slow jams, but still his charm shines through. The heart of the album lies in the up-tempo dance numbers, since they're what make *Willennium* irresistible. And this is one of the rare times that an abundance of cameos enhances the spirit of an album, making *Willennium* feel like a Y2K blowout where everyone is invited. —*Stephen Thomas Erlewine*

Born to Reign / Jun. 25, 2002 / Columbia ✦✦✦✦

It'd be inaccurate to call Will Smith's third album the musical equivalent of *Ali*—a bid for artistic credibility from an artist so assured and smooth, it's been easy to pigeonhole him as merely a pop artist—but given the range and harder edge on *Born to Reign*, it's hard not to think of it at first. Make no mistake, this is *not* as serious as *Ali*; nor is it a record whose first intent is to enlighten and educate (this is not a KRS-One or Wyclef Jean project). It's a fun, pop-leaning record, much like his first two records, and never is it afraid to return to the sounds and styles that brought the former Fresh Prince (deserved) big hits, but among comfortably familiar jams, Smith stretches his legs. Some of the hip-hop hits harder; there's a touch of reggae; he even appropriates a bit of a Ricky Martin vibe on "I Can't Stop." It's a small but significant change, and while it doesn't result in a record that flows as effortlessly, or giddily, as *Willennium*, it's easy to appreciate the effort to stretch, because even if all the experiments aren't necessarily successful (sometimes the idea is better than the execution), it does reinvigorate the Smith signature pop-rap sound (apart, oddly, from the theme for *Men in Black 2*, "Black Suits Comin'," the only cut in this vein to fall flat), and results in another solid record from Smith. Maybe not as consistent as its predecessors, but still enjoyable in its familiar turf, while provoking admiration for its ambition, even when it's not always satisfying. Not a bad way to stretch. (This is a copy-protected disc, which on the average computer doesn't mean that you simply can't copy the disc—it means that it will freeze your computer if you just want to listen to it via your CD-Rom. Not realizing this, I lost work when trying to write and listen at the same time, so buyer beware.) —*Stephen Thomas Erlewine*

• **Greatest Hits** / Nov. 26, 2002 / Columbia ✦✦✦✦✦

In retrospect, the point at which Will Smith went too far was with 1999's "Freakin' It," on which, over samples from "Love Hangover" and "Rapper's

Delight," he boasted of his movie earnings, defended himself against charges of being a "soft" rapper, and criticized his peers. It was hard to dispute any of his arguments (though the citation of the American Music Awards as an example of his superiority seemed a bit of a stretch), but the song also emphasized—in the wrong way, as far as fans were concerned—how far Smith had come from Philadelphia, and it flopped. After that, his movies and records had to struggle more for attention. All careers go through peaks and troughs, however, and this collection of Smith's musical high points makes the case for his popularity, dating back to the late-'80s days of DJ Jazzy Jeff & the Fresh Prince, whose work is licensed from Jive Records for one-third of the tracks here. Not all of the early duo's hits are included, but the signature ones, particularly the breakout "Parents Just Don't Understand," are. In a sense, this is Smith at his most appealing, using rap to create novelty records that reveal the comic sense that later would light up movie screens. He remains engaging through solo hits like "Men in Black" and "Getting' Jiggy Wit It," even if he already seems to be starting to believe his press clips. By this point, the musical career has become an appendage of the movie career, and movie stardom begins to inform the raps, culminating in the defensiveness of "Freakin' It." Along the way, however, there is some clever writing, always put across by Smith's expansive personality, which enabled him to swim against the current of contemporary rap, at least for a time. —*William Ruhlmann*

Tim Smooth

Dirty South, Gangsta Rap

Appearing in the early '90s on Priority Records, rapper Tim Smooth has made the transition from a basic G-funk-style rapper to one of the first artists to be recognized in the dirty South movement. Releasing his debut, *Straight up Drive 'Em*, in 1994, his music was heavily influenced by the West Coast artists of the time, resulting in a competent but unmemorable record that almost succeeded on the strength of his hilarious lyrics and effortless flow. Released from the label soon after, Smooth kicked around the rap underground, ghostwriting for rappers on Big Boy Records under the name Playboy Sha-Burnke. It was during this period that he hooked up with Mobo Records, a New Orleans label that was instrumental in the growing dirty South scene. Smooth's debut was highly respected by many of the rappers associated with the label, so when he recorded *Da Franchise Playa* in 1998, he had support from artists like HWA, Bushwick Bill, and a young Mystikal. Released that summer, the album's liquid funk production and gruffer vocal style made it a hit in the area, making Smooth one of the dirty South's premier vocalists upon its arrival. Unfortunately, national radio didn't catch on to his new style, and soon artists like Mystikal and Juvenile were eclipsing him in sales and public recognition. Smooth chose not to follow up on the album immediately, instead sporadically guest appearing on other rapper's songs while trying to put together a group, the Pimptations, which never seemed to come together. —*Bradley Torreano*

Straight up Drive 'Em / Apr. 26, 1994 / Priority ✦✦✦

• **Da Franchise Playa** / Jul. 21, 1998 / Mobo ✦✦✦

If you've heard this album, you definitely know that Tim Smooth is quite heterosexual. On this album he talks for almost an hour about his crazy sex life and not a whole lot else. The beats are funky and he's got one of the most dramatic rapping styles in all of rap music, as he's definitely put a lot of effort and criticism in how his delivery works with the beat. The result is a blend of long, deep bass lines, languid gangsta raps, and a few complementary appearances from Mystikal, G-Slimm, Nas-T, and Rated X. Most surprisingly, there is yet another remix of 1985's "La Di Da Di" by Slick Rick and legendary beatboxer Doug E. Fresh. Snoop Dogg did his own rendition of the song in 1994 on *Doggystyle*, and Tim Smooth's track is a somewhat blatant rip-off of Snoop's version—perhaps an unneccesary addition at the end of a pretty good album. —*Brad Mills*

Smut Peddlers

Group / East Coast Rap, Hardcore Rap, Underground Rap

Long before Eminem, the Smut Peddlers were pushing the boundaries of good taste. In the early '90s, the Smut Peddlers' frontman Cage rapped about violence and drug use. In 1999 the group hit it big with their release *Home Field Advantage*. Cage started a rivalry with Eminem, claiming that the platinum-haired rapper had ripped off much of his act. The two were at odds for quite awhile, continually dissing each other on their records. Eminem had the upper hand in terms of sales and mainstream acceptance, but by sticking to their underground roots, the Smut Peddlers hoped to have the last laugh. —*Jon Azpiri*

● **Porn Again** / Feb. 13, 2001 / Priority ✦✦✦

Mr. Eon's incarnation as Dick Starbuck (porno detective) on Hi & Mighty's debut, *B-Boy Document*, may have ushered in the Smut Peddlers' (Eon, Cage, and producer Mighty Mi) regime. However, the trio's debut, *Porn Again*, takes hip-hop's skinz fetish to new extremes, as it is a collection based solely on the joys of crushing. Though outlandish, the album is not blazing any new ground conceptually—Too Short and Kool Keith (among many) have been doing this for years. Yet, these ill reputes are an entirely different virus. Mr. Eon and Cage are the offspring of two twisted minds, as they commingle the straight sleaze of Larry Flynt with the unpolitically correct humor of Howard Stern. Though the two offer a slew of highly quotable material, their lyrical exchanges are largely ephemeral. While their volatile chemistry pays dividends on "Medicated Minutes" and Eon's solo cut "Diseases," their limited topic matter becomes predictably insipid over extended listens. While Mighty Mi's sparse arrangements (thick bass grooves, and up-tempo drum beats) manages to adequately highlight Eon and Cage's insatiable sexual appetite. His stark minimalist boardwork here offers few surprises, as it is largely unassuming and untypically reserved. The Smut Peddlers do deliver a few less gratuitous offerings; RA the Rugged Man makes an impressive cameo on the cellar-dwelling "Bottom Feeders," and "One By One (Revamped)" picks up where Hi & Mighty left off. Yet, *Porn Again* is not unlike any other guilty pleasure we habitually engage in; one that supplies momentary bouts of bliss but with the accompanying dreaded morning-after side effects. Romance truly is dead! —*Matt Conaway*

Snoop Dogg (Calvin Broadus)

b. Oct. 20, 1972, Long Beach, CA
G-Funk, West Coast Rap, Gangsta Rap

As the embodiment of '90s gangsta rap, Snoop Dogg blurred the lines between reality and fiction. Introduced to the world through Dr. Dre's *The Chronic*, Snoop quickly became the most famous star in rap, partially because of his drawled, laconic rhyming and partially because the violence that his lyrics implied seemed real, especially after he was arrested on charges of being a murder accomplice. The arrest certainly strengthened his myth, and it helped his debut album, 1993's *Doggystyle*, become the first debut album to enter the charts at number one, but in the long run, it hurt his career. Snoop had to fight charges throughout 1994 and 1995, and while he was eventually cleared, it hurt his momentum. *Tha Doggfather*, his second album, wasn't released until November 1996, and by that time, pop and hip-hop had burned itself out on gangsta rap. *Tha Doggfather* sold half as well as its predecessor, which meant that Snoop remained a star, but he no longer had the influence he had just two years before.

Nicknamed Snoop by his mother because of his appearance, Calvin Broadus (born October 20, 1972) was raised in Long Beach, CA, where he frequently ran into trouble with the law. Not long after his high school graduation, he was arrested for possession of cocaine, beginning a period of three years where he was often imprisoned. He found escape from a life of crime through music. Snoop began recording homemade tapes with his friend Warren G, who happened to be the stepbrother of N.W.A.'s Dr. Dre. Warren G gave a tape to Dre, who was considerably impressed with Snoop's style and began collaborating with the rapper.

When Dre decided to make his tentative first stab at a solo career in 1992 with the theme song for the film *Deep Cover*, he had Snoop rap with him. "Deep Cover" started a buzz about Snoop that escalated into full-fledged mania when Dre released his own debut album, *The Chronic*, on Death Row Records late in 1992. Snoop rapped on *The Chronic* as much as Dre, and his drawled vocals were as important to the record's success as its P-funk bass grooves. Dre's singles "Nuthin' but a 'G' Thang" and "Dre Day," which prominently featured Snoop, became Top Ten pop crossover hits in the spring of 1993, setting the stage for Snoop's much-anticipated debut album, *Doggystyle*. While he was recording the album with Dre in August, Snoop was arrested in connection with the drive-by shooting death of Phillip Woldermarian. According to the charges, the rapper's bodyguard, McKinley Lee, shot Woldermarian as Snoop drove the vehicle; the rapper claimed it

was self-defense, alleging that the victim was stalking Snoop. Following a performance at the MTV Music Awards in September 1993, he turned himself to authorities.

After many delays, *Doggystyle* was finally released on Death Row in November 1993, and it became the first debut album to enter the charts at number one. Despite reviews that claimed the album was a carbon copy of *The Chronic*, the Top Ten singles "What's My Name?" and "Gin & Juice" kept *Doggystyle* at the top of the charts during early 1994, as did the considerable controversy over Snoop's arrest and his lyrics, which were accused of being exceedingly violent and sexist. During an English tour in the spring of 1994, tabloids and a Tory minister pleaded for the government to kick the rapper out of the country, largely based on his arrest. Snoop exploited his impending trial by shooting a short film based on the *Doggystyle* song "Murder Was the Case" and releasing an accompanying soundtrack, which debuted at number one in 1994. By that time, *Doggystyle* had gone quadruple platinum.

Snoop spent much of 1995 preparing for the case, which finally went to trial in late 1995. In February of 1996, he was cleared of all charges and began working on his second album, this time without Dre as producer. Nevertheless, when *Tha Doggfather* was finally released in November 1996, it bore all the evidence of a Dre-produced, G-funk record. The album was greeted with mixed reviews, and it initially sold well, but it failed to produce a hit along the lines of "What's My Name?" and "Gin & Juice." Part of the reason of the moderate success of *Tha Doggfather* was the decline of gangsta rap. 2Pac, who had become a friend of Snoop during 1996, died weeks before the release of *Tha Doggfather*, and Dre had left Death Row to his partner Suge Knight, who was indicted on racketeering charges by the end of 1996. Consequently, Snoop's second album got lost in the shuffle, stalling at sales of two million, which was disappointing for a superstar.

Perhaps sensing something was wrong, Snoop began to revamp his public image, moving away from his gangsta roots toward a calmer lyrical aesthetic. He also began making gestures toward the rock community, signing up to tour with Lollapalooza 1997 and talking about two separate collaborations with Beck and Marilyn Manson. The solo *Da Game Is to Be Sold Not to Be Told*, Snoop's first effort for No Limit, followed in 1998; *No Limit Top Dogg* appeared a year later and *Dead Man Walkin'* the year after that. *Tha Last Meal* followed in December of that same year. The heavy release schedule resulted in varying musical quality from album to album, but by the turn of the century, Snoop had become such a cultural phenomenon that his albums almost became secondary to the personality behind them. An autobiography appeared in 2001, followed by a stream of movie roles in several high-profile pictures. Late in 2002, Snoop released his first album for Priority, *Paid tha Cost to Be da Bo$$.* —*Stephen Thomas Erlewine*

★ **Doggystyle** / Nov. 23, 1993 / Death Row ✦✦✦✦✦

If Snoop Dogg's debut, *Doggystyle*, doesn't *seem* like a debut, it's because in many ways it's not. Snoop had already debuted as a featured rapper on Dr. Dre's 1992 album, *The Chronic*, rapping on half of the 16 tracks, including all the hit singles, so it wasn't like he was an unknown force when *Doggystyle* was released in late 1993. If anything, he was the biggest star in hip-hop, with legions of fans anxiously awaiting new material, and they were the ones who snapped up the album, making it the first debut album to enter the *Billboard* charts at number one. It wasn't like they were buying an unknown quantity. They knew that the album would essentially be the de facto sequel to *The Chronic*, providing another round of P-funk-inspired grooves and languid gangsta and ganja tales, just like Dre's album. Which is exactly what *Doggystyle* is—a continuation of *The Chronic*, with the same production, same aesthetic and themes, and same reliance on guest rappers. The miracle is, it's as good as that record. There are two keys to its success, one belonging to Dre, the other to Snoop. Dre realized that it wasn't time to push the limits of G-funk, and instead decided to deepen it musically, creating easy-rolling productions that have more layers than they appear. They're laid-back funky, continuing to resonate after many listens, but their greatest strength is that they never overshadow the laconic drawl of Snoop, who confirms that he's one of hip-hop's greatest vocal stylists with this record. Other gangsta rappers were all about aggression and anger—even Dre, as a rapper, is as blunt as a thug—but Snoop takes his time, playing with the flow of his words, giving his rhymes a nearly melodic eloquence. Compare his delivery to many guest rappers here: Nate Dogg, Kurupt, and Dat Nigga Daz are all good rappers, but they're good in a conventional sense, where Snoop is something special, with unpredictable turns of phrase, evocative imagery, and a distinctive, addictive flow. If *Doggystyle* doesn't surprise or offer anything that wasn't already on *The Chronic*, it nevertheless is the best showcase for Snoop's prodigious talents, not just because he's given the room to run wild, but because he knows what to do with that freedom and Dre presents it all with imagination and a narrative thrust. If it doesn't have the shock of the new, the way that *The Chronic* did, so be it. Over the years, the pervasive influence of that record and its countless rip-offs have dulled its innovations, so it doesn't have the shock of the new either. Now, *Doggystyle* and *The Chronic* stand proudly together as the twin pinnacles of West Coast G-funk hip-hop of the early '90s. —*Stephen Thomas Erlewine*

Tha Doggfather / Nov. 12, 1996 / Death Row ✦✦✦
A lot happened to Snoop Doggy Dogg between his debut *Doggystyle* and his second album, *Tha Doggfather*. During those three years, he became the most notorious figure in hip-hop through a much-publicized murder trial, where he was found not guilty, and he also became a father. Musically, the most important thing to happen to Snoop was the parting of ways between his mentor Dr. Dre and his record label, Death Row. Dre's departure from Death Row meant that Snoop had to handle the production duties on *Tha Doggfather* himself, and the differences between the two records are immediately apparent. Though it works the same G-funk territory, the bass is less elastic and there is considerably less sonic detail. In essence, all of the music on *Tha Doggfather* reworks the funk and soul of the late '70s and early '80s, without updating it too much—there's not that much difference between "Snoop's Upside Ya Head" and "Oops Up Side Your Head." Though the music isn't original, and the lyrics break no new territory, the execution is strong— Snoop's rapping and rhyming continue to improve, while the bass-heavy funk is often intoxicating. At over 70 minutes, *Tha Doggfather* runs too long to not have several filler tracks, but if you ignore those cuts, the album is a fine follow-up to one of the most successful hip-hop albums in history. —*Stephen Thomas Erlewine*

Da Game Is to Be Sold Not to Be Told / Aug. 4, 1998 / No Limit ✦✦
As the Death Row ship was sinking, Snoop Dogg bailed, heading over to the new bastion of street cred, No Limit Records. Master P worked his way to the top of the charts by giving the people what they wanted—straight-up gangsta, with no frills, creativity, or substance. It was all a little rawer (actually, just cheaper) than Death Row's productions, but there was no denying that they knew what sold, and it seemed as if Snoop was making No Limit legitimate in the eyes of the mainstream world. Master P is a master marketer, and he knows how to reshape everyone on his roster into good No Limit soldiers. And that's precisely what Snoop Dogg is on *Da Game Is to Be Sold, Not to Be Told*, his third album proper and first for No Limit. There are a few concessions to G-funk scattered throughout the record, but by and large, Beats By the Pound and P give Snoop a set of standard No Limit backing tracks and have him do the No Limit dance—record a long-winded, monotonous album, filled with "interpolations" of '80s soul and rap songs, and loaded with No Limit cameos. But there's one crucial difference: unlike most of Master P's grunts, Snoop has style, miles and miles of style. His loose, languid delivery is positively enthralling, which makes it all the more frustrating when No Limit hacks interrupt the flow. That happens on almost all of the tracks—only a handful are Snoop alone, and those illustrate that he can, on occasion, turn bland music into something interesting. Still, they can't excuse the banality of *Da Game Is to Be Sold, Not to Be Told*. Signing to No Limit might have preserved Snoop Dogg's street cred, but it ruined his creativity. —*Stephen Thomas Erlewine*

No Limit Top Dogg / May 11, 1999 / No Limit ✦✦✦
As time keeps on slipping into the future, it becomes apparent that Master P's greatest gift is marketing, particularly when his advertising masquerades as liner notes. Witness P's work for Snoop Dogg, once considered the brightest rapper of the '90s but now merely a general in the No Limit army. The Master began plugging *Top Dogg*, Snoop's second No Limit release, in the liners for his label debut, even mentioning a release date only months away. Clearly, Snoop had indeed been placed on the No Limit production line, and there was every indication that from now on, Snoop would churn out moderately enjoyable, dirty South-lite records crammed with cameos and appropriated hooks. Turns out he had a trick up his sleeve, because *Top Dogg* is about as individualized an album as possible under the No Limit precepts. Since the outset of his career, Snoop has shown a fondness for early-'80s

synth funk, and for the first time, he lets that form the basis of an album. And while there may be a bit too much recycling for some tastes, the end result isn't just the freshest-sounding Snoop album since his debut, it's easily the freshest-sounding No Limit album. Unfortunately, it's still a No Limit album, which means it runs way too long and is filled with superfluous, even irritating, cameos, and also that Snoop is content to haul out low-rent gangsta clichés. Since he's a gifted rapper, he makes the dope 'n' crimes, sex 'n' violence rhymes go down easily (compare his delivery to some of his guests if you have any doubts), but his lyrics just aren't as clever as they were five years earlier. But records don't have to be deep; they can be appreciated as a pure sonic experience, and taken on that level, *Top Dogg* satisfies. —*Stephen Thomas Erlewine*

Dead Man Walkin' / Oct. 31, 2000 / D3 ✦✦✦
As he'd done with 2Pac's leftovers, Suge Knight dug up some of Snoop Doggy Dogg's (remember he was still a "doggy dog" back then). He then dressed them up with ample production and released them on Death Row Records under the guise of newness, perhaps not coincidently just as No Limit Records was marketing their final, much-awaited Snoop release, *Tha Last Meal*. And again like he'd done with 2Pac's leftovers, Suge repackages Snoop's in a halfhearted manner, presenting you with a mishmash to sift through. If you're a Snoop fan, or a Death Row one for that matter, it may indeed be a worthwhile venture, since there are some gems here worth digging for. Some, like the Daz-produced "Tommy Boy," sound like outtakes from Snoop's final album for Death Row, *Tha Doggfather*, while others, like "Change Gone Come" and "May I," sound like a cappella vocal tracks dressed up by Death Row's in-house staff. This two-sidedness makes for a somewhat uneven listening experience, but it's not the production that's particularly interesting here anyhow. Rather, it's Snoop himself, who rattles off some topnotch rhymes—in addition to a fair share of throwaways, of course. So, you're left feeling a little conflicted by the end, wishing that Suge had put a little more care into this compilation, but you're at least thankful to have these leftovers served in the first place. —*Jason Birchmeier*

Tha Last Meal / Dec. 5, 2000 / No Limit ✦✦✦✦
Snoop Dogg leaves much of his gangbanging past behind him in favor of preened pimp posturing on his final album for No Limit Records, *Tha Last Meal*. Snoop's increasingly old school pose suits his gracefully aging self well. Despite his former affiliation with Death Row Records and his much publicized murder trial, Snoop never seemed like much of a thug, which is partly why hostile albums like *Tha Doggfather* (1996) and *Da Game Is to Be Sold Not to Be Told* (1998) seemed a bit forced. Contrarily, it seems more natural for him to rap about the pampered pimp life, as he does here on *Tha Last Meal*—tall glasses of Hennesey, glistening pairs of Stacey Adams, overcast clouds of chronic smoke, hungry hordes of so-called bitches—over truck-rattling G-funk bass lines that lope along at a languid tempo. These impressive beats come courtesy of a similarly impressive roster of producers: second-wave g-funksters Meech Wells, Battlecat, Jelly Roll, and Soopafly, and brand-name hitmakers Dr. Dre, Scott Storch, and Timbaland. Among this roster, Timbaland certainly stands out, as do his contributions, "Snoop Dogg (What's My Name, Pt. 2)" and "Set It Off," which place Snoop in an uncharacteristically energetic context. He handles himself well on these bouncy songs regardless, yet seems more at home on Dre's smoother contributions, "Hennesey n Buddah" and "Lay Low." Beyond these four tracks, the remaining 15 are a mixed bag, most of them Crip walking along at a stoned tempo, featuring soulful P-funk hooks by Kokane, and offering laid-back respite while this lengthy album moves leisurely toward its throwback album capper, "Y'all Gone Miss Me." Following this misty-eyed finale, you're left with the thankful sense that Snoop has finally taken control of his career after succumbing to the oppressive fancy of Suge Knight and Master P ever since parting ways with Dr. Dre following *Doggystyle* (1993). —*Jason Birchmeier*

Death Row's Snoop Doggy Dogg Greatest Hits / Oct. 23, 2001 / Death Row ✦✦✦✦
When it came time for the cash-strapped Death Row Records to repackage Snoop Dogg's Doggy Dogg era, this time to coincide with a string of the rapper-turned-actor's Hollywood ventures, Suge Knight and Co. decided to mix a few classics with a sizable serving of leftovers and market it as a best-of. The long-titled *Death Row's Snoop Doggy Dogg Greatest Hits* compilation thus aims to please all, though risks pleasing none as a result. As you'd expect from a greatest-hits compilation, it offers most of the essentials:

"Nuthin' but a 'G' Thang," "Gin & Juice," "Murder Was the Case," "Doggy Dogg World," and "Who Am I (What's My Name)." But unlike you'd expect from a greatest-hits compilation, it also offers a half-album's worth of rarely heard vault recordings and also a pair of remixes: a Timbaland remake of "Doggfather" and a rock/rap one of "Snoop Bounce." The vault recordings aren't poor at all; in fact, they're worthwhile listening for all Doggy Dogg-era Snoop fans. But they're certainly not on a par with "Nuthin' but a 'G' Thang" or "Gin & Juice," and that makes this randomly sequenced compilation rather uneven. All griping aside, this is a welcome release on behalf of Death Row, at least until a true Snoop best-of surfaces. After all, the label had only two Snoop albums to choose from—*Doggystyle* (1993) and *Tha Doggfather* (1996)—yet also a lot of leftovers to repackage, so this compilation makes sense. And it also makes sense from a marketing perspective, because it's a disc all Snoop fans will want, both casual ones and diehards. —*Jason Birchmeier*

Paid tha Cost to Be da Bo$$ / Nov. 26, 2002 / Priority ✦✦✦✦
Though Snoop Dogg never slipped from the charts, *Paid tha Cost to Be da Bo$$* smacks of a comeback, and it's a great one. After finally being released from No Limit (he's still distributed by Priority), Snoop Dogg drafted a set of great producers for his sixth album, as well as a varied cast of featured guests capable of drawing in just about every segment of the hip-hop audience. Still one of the smoothest rappers around and the bemused observer of all around him, he slips on the tried-and-true pimp and godfather personas, but also has the nerve to feature an X-rated sex romp ("Lollipop," with Jay-Z and Nate Dogg) directly after a tender anthem to love and marriage ("I Believe in You")—and he sounds extremely convincing with both. The pair of tracks produced by the Neptunes ("From tha Chuuuch to da Palace" and "Beautiful") are the highlights, two of the best they've done since their commercial breakout. Hardcore fans of rap, though, will want to skip ahead to "The One and Only" for a perfect meld of West Coast and East Coast—the first meeting of Snoop and DJ Premier on wax. (Premier also turns in a hilariously cartoonish production for "Batman & Robin.") Yes, there are a few missteps: the G-funk roll on a few tracks sounds a little dated, and Bootsy Collins impersonator Mr. Kane makes a few embarrassing appearances ("Stoplight" is a bland, unnecessary update of Parliament's "Flashlight"). And two other remakes sound OK but won't have a long shelf life. The first is virtually a cover of Eric B. & Rakim's "Paid in Full" called "Paper'd Up," and it's immediately followed by a redo of Robert Palmer's Jam & Lewis anthem "I Didn't Mean to Turn You On" ("Wasn't Your Fault"). You've got to be a strong figure to keep together an album this long and this rangy, but Snoop Dogg is up to the task. —*John Bush*

Snow (Darrin O'Brien)

b. Oct. 30, 1969, North York, Ontario, Canada
Hip-Hop, Dance-Pop, Urban, Dancehall, Club/Dance, Ragga, Pop-Rap, Reggae-Pop, Contemporary Reggae
Canadian rapper Snow scored one of 1993's biggest hits with his single "The Informer." His patois-laced song soared up the pop and R&B charts, even though only hardcore reggae listeners could understand it without a lyric translation sheet. The album *12 Inches of Snow* also did well, with the second single, "Girl I've Been Hurt," becoming a hit. —*Ron Wynn*

● **12 Inches of Snow** / 1993 / East West ✦✦✦✦
Canadian dancehall rapper Snow became a celebrity when his patois-laced single "Informer" soared to the top of the charts in 1993. The song shattered the myth that pop audiences wouldn't embrace any tune whose lyrics weren't in pristine English; when his video was released, it included a rolling translation at the bottom. Unfortunately, the rest of this album was mildly pleasant, instantly forgettable pop/reggae delivered in a manner that made Shabba Ranks sound like U-Roy. —*Ron Wynn*

Murder Love / 1995 / East West ✦✦✦
Snow's follow-up to his multimillion-selling debut isn't a departure from his pop-oriented dancehall, yet he doesn't have the songs to pull off another crossover hit. —*Stephen Thomas Erlewine*

Justuss / Jan. 14, 1997 / East West ✦✦
The lackluster follow-up to Snow's debut follows in the vein of his earlier, hip hop-inspired reggae. In addition to the single "If This World Were Mine," the album features a remix of the cut "Anything for You," which includes cameos

from Buju Banton, Beenie Man, Nadine Sutherland, and Terror Fabulous. —*Jason Ankeny*

● **The Greatest Hits of Snow** / Oct. 21, 1997 / Elektra/Asylum ✦✦✦✦✦
Considering that Snow's career crashed around the release of his second album, *Murder Love*, a record that didn't even chart, it might seem that the release of a greatest hits album is a little misleading. After all, he had only one album, *12 Inches of Snow*, that produced any hit singles, of which there was a grand total of exactly two: "Informer" and "Girl, I've Been Hurt." Naturally, those two songs are included on *The Greatest Hits of Snow*, along with an assortment of 11 other songs that range from album tracks to failed singles like "Sexy Girl." Anyone with any interest in Snow—whether they're a long-term fan or a casual listener who liked the mock raggae of "Informer"—will probably be equally satisfied by *The Greatest Hits of Snow* or *12 Inches of Snow*, since they contain the same hits surrounded by similar filler, and both illustrate why Snow couldn't successfully follow those two catchy hits. —*Stephen Thomas Erlewine*

Snypaz

f. 1993, Chicago, IL
Group / Hardcore Rap
Formed in the mid-'90s in Chicago, IL, Snypaz consists of members 2/4, Chilla, R-O-B, and Sic Wic. The quartet issued a tape in 1995, *Ridin' High*, and a year later released the six-track EP *My Life as a Snypa* (the latter selling 80,000 copies). The quartet then relocated to Houston, TX, to record tracks with Do or Die (1998's *Headz or Tailz*), and through that association hooked up with Scarface (appearing on his 1998 album *My Homies*). Not much was heard from Snypaz until 2001, when they signed with Virgin Records and issued their major-label debut, *Livin' in the Scope*. —*Greg Prato*

● **Livin' in the Scope** / May 22, 2001 / Virgin ✦✦✦
Given Chicago's Midwestern locale somewhere between the West, the South, and the East, it's perhaps no surprise that Snypaz draws inspiration from all three coasts' rap scenes. The first characteristic that stands out about the Windy City-based group is its hardcore attitude, an approach that is just as much indebted to the Geto Boys' legacy as N.W.A.'s and Mobb Deep's. In fact, the group's name itself is a representative indication of how these four guys look at the world—this isn't carefree, feel-good music by any means. Secondly, their hard beats also hark back to the early-'90s work by the first two aforementioned gangsta rap pioneers, the sort of clenched-fist beats that go well with angst-ridden lyrics. In the end, you're left wondering if these guys are merely paying homage to their disparate influences, which can be traced just as easily to the South as to the West, or if they're actually synthesizing these influences into a commendable new sound. Judging by this album, the former approach is probably the more accurate viewpoint, though there's enough promise on this album to suggest that their follow-up may warrant the latter approach. —*Jason Birchmeier*

So Solid Crew

Group / 2-Step/British Garage, Garage/House, Club/Dance
The genesis for this group was MC Megaman and MC Romeo, both of whom were promoting various British garage club shows as well as other parties. The parties, named So Solid as part of the promotions, grew in popularity. In 1998, while meeting at the Killer Watt Carnival Soundsystem, the group was created. In December 2000, the band released its first single, "Oh No," which reached the British charts. In August 2001, the band hit number one in the singles charts with "21 Seconds." This was followed by a MOBO Award for Best British Act and also a British Award for Best Video. Unfortunately, though, controversy surrounded the band. In October 2001, two men were shot at one of the group's concerts in London. The publicity meant a canceled British tour. In November 2001 the band released its debut album, *They Don't Know*, on Independiente Records. —*Jason MacNeil*

● **They Don't Know** / 2001 / Independiente ✦✦✦
An army of producers/rappers/chatters/vocalists capable of overwhelming Roni Size's Reprazent or Wu-Tang Clan with little difficulty, So Solid Crew can't quite translate their numerical superiority and energetic sound into a solid album. The group splashed onto the British charts with a slate of uptempo garage nuggets featuring plenty of braggadocio plus some irresistible production work. Those tracks—"Oh No," "21 Seconds," the title track—are here, obviously, with the rhythmic hailstorm "Oh No" featuring So Solid

trading off tough British raps with diva vocals. A few album tracks ("If It Was Me," "Deeper") get it right too, with all the garage staples—hit-'em-low tech bass lines, stuttered rhythms, tongue-twisting chatting, and falsetto harmonies cribbed from American R&B. The rest suffer from lack of songwriting, new ideas, even a good groove at times. A few too many weak rhymes on the half-lines, a few too many faux-dramatic symphonic synthesizer lines, a few too many tracks *altogether* (there are 20 in all). From this, their debut full-length, it's clear So Solid Crew are better heard on the handful of essential British garage mixes than their own hour-long production. —*John Bush*

Society of Soul

Group / Hip-Hop

Coming out of the Atlanta hip-hop scene that also includes OutKast, the Goodie Mob, and producers Organized Noize, the Society of Soul is composed of singers Espraronza and Sleepy Brown (whose father was a member of Brick), plus Big Rube, producer Rico, and Ray. Strongly influenced by '70s funk, the group also combines elements of rap and gospel, the latter courtesy of Espraronza. The group's 1995 debut, *Brainchild*, was partially recorded at Curtis Mayfield's CurTom studios. —*Steve Huey*

● **Brainchild** / Sep. 26, 1995 / La Face ✦✦✦

Brainchild, Society of Soul's debut album, has a smooth, organic flow to its grooves that makes the group's lapses into didactic preaching tolerable. The group mixes light hip-hop rhythms with the sly funk of '70s soul, particularly in the form of Stevie Wonder and Curtis Mayfield. Society of Soul can work a groove with ease and dexterity, but they have a bit of trouble shaping their rhythms into full-fledged songs. Then again, with beats as liquid as these, that's only a minor problem, at least when the record is playing. After it's finished, only a handful of tracks have enough weight to make an impact. —*Stephen Thomas Erlewine*

Son of Bazerk

Vocals / Hardcore Rap, Golden Age, East Coast Rap

The sharply dressed Son of Bazerk and his equally dapper cohorts—Cassandra (aka MC Halfpint), Almighty Jahwell, Daddy Rawe, and Sandman, collectively dubbed No Self Control—delivered the remarkably explosive *Bazerk Bazerk Bazerk* for MCA in 1991. Produced by the Bomb Squad and boasting the turntable skills of Public Enemy's Terminator X, the album featured the dizzying James Brown-inspired "Change the Style," one of the best singles released during rap's golden age. Two other singles—"Bang (Get Down, Get Down)" and "What Could Be Better Bitch"—didn't catch on as well as "Change the Style," but the album as a whole stands proud next to the Bomb Squad's other classic productions. —*Andy Kellman*

● **Bazerk Bazerk Bazerk** / May 14, 1991 / Soul ✦✦✦✦✦

The first release on the Bomb Squad's short-lived MCA imprint SOUL Records was the controversial debut album from Young Black Teenagers. The second was this strange, uncategorizable (soul rap?), one-of-a-kind effort from the aptly monikered five-piece Son of Bazerk (which, incidentally, took its name from its gruff frontman). In the dozen or so years prior to 1991, James Brown's landmark R&B had literally served as the mother's milk for hip-hop DJs and producers. *Bazerk Bazerk Bazerk*, on the other hand, seems to imagine what the Godfather of Soul might have sounded like had he and the JBs actually been sired and suckled, rather than merely recycled, by the rap community. With virtually no pauses between songs, the music is so mercilessly nonstop that it knocks your ears for a loop before they have a chance to cry "uncle." Hank and Keith Shocklee's studied chaos is every bit as brilliant on *Bazerk Bazerk Bazerk* as it was on Public Enemy's *Fear of a Black Planet*, and even more combatively piled with samples, loops, sound effects, keyboards, and criss-crossing rock guitars. The headache-inducing tempos and relentlessly turbulent rivers of sound that result detonate, when matched to the Son's gargled-glass toasting (and his quartet of idiosyncratic backup vocalists Almighty Jahwell, Daddy Rawe, Sandman, and MC Halfpint), into donnybrooks of noise. Occasionally things unravel and spin out of control, and the offhanded chauvinism that creeps into some of the lyrics ("Sex, Sex & More Sex," the otherwise fantastic "What Could Be Better Bitch") might help to fan a few flames. But whenever the group harnesses the clatter and hits on a groove, the music is thrillingly, primitively muscular and impulsive, spontaneous and recklessly authoritative in all the right ways. Luckily, that

amounts to significant swaths of the record, from piston-pumping sonic trains like "The Band Gets Swivey on the Wheels," "Part One," and "One Time for the Rebel" to the sly, uncharacteristically stripped-down posse cut "N-41" and sinister ghetto dispatch "Lifestyles of the Blacks in the Brick." Even with its faults, *Bazerk Bazerk Bazerk* is an exceptional slab of guts, aggression, and punk soul. —*Stanton Swihart*

Sonrise Sunset

Group / Urban, Pop-Rap

Rap duo Sonrise Sunset bridged the stylistic and geographic gap separating the East and West Coasts by teaming New York MC Squint Lo with California native One Pizzie. Their debut album, *Turn of the Century*, appeared in 1999. —*Jason Ankeny*

● **Turn of the Century** / Sep. 21, 1999 / Lightyear ✦✦✦

Sonrise Sunset attempts to move mainstream hip-hop forward by blending elements of East and West Coast together. Their intentions may be very good, but the end result often sounds a bit like a parody, especially with songs like "Havana Trump," "Hawaii 5-0," and "Nitty Gritty Bang Bang." Still, there are points where the duo pulls it off, combining the funkiness of Cali with the swift street rhymes of New York. They do it often enough to keep *Turn of the Century* an interesting listen and promising debut. —*Stephen Thomas Erlewine*

Sottotono

Group / Foreign Rap

The Italian rap duo Sottotono (Undertone) first appeared in 1994 on the hip-hop compilation *Nati Per Rapppare* (Born for Rap), where the laid-back raps of MCs Fish and Tormento were a hit with the burgeoning Italian hip-hop audience. Their debut LP, *Sopratutto Sotto*, appeared that year; *Sotto Efetto Stono* followed in 1996. By now, Sottotono's mixture of Warren G-style West Coast flow with soul-inflected grooves reminiscent of Bone Thugs-N-Harmony was well established. They shook things up a bit with 1999's *Sotto Lo Stesso Effetto*, dabbling in the aggressive drum'n'bass that was in vogue at the time. Tormento also began to unveil a talent for singing that had not previously been apparent. The duo remained active in the Italian hip-hop scene, collaborating with likeminded MCs like Leftside and Lyricalz. In February of 2003, Sottotono released *Vendesi*, a best-of collection that featured one previously unreleased track, "(Sei Tu) Che Mi Dai." —*Johnny Loftus*

Sotto Effetto Stono / 1996 / WEA ✦✦✦

● **Sotto Lo Stesso Effetto** / 1999 / Wea International ✦✦✦

Sotto Lo Stesso Effetto features Italian rap duo Sottotono. Many of the duo's tracks on this album are produced by Da Fish for Area Cronica Sound Designs, including such songs as "Buone Motivazioni?!?," "La Vita Dei Gaggi," "Quei Bravi Ragazzi, Pt. 2," and "Nel Jet Set del Rap," in addition to many others. —*Jason Birchmeier*

Soulism

f. Macon, GA

Group / Southern Rap

Around the same time Southern rap began embodying artists like OutKast, Goodie Mob, and Eightball & MJG rather than the bass music of years prior, Soulism made their bid for success. The Macon, GA-based group united with Wall Street Records in 1996 for a self-titled album and an accompanying single ("Taste the Flava"). The releases didn't find much success nationally, as the South hadn't yet become as marketable as it would a few years later during the dirty South boom. —*Jason Birchmeier*

● **Soulism** / Aug. 27, 1996 / Wall Street ✦✦✦

In rap circles, the Southeastern U.S. (especially Florida, but parts of Georgia as well) is best known for "bass music"—fasttempo, hyper acts like the 2 Live Crew and Luther Campbell, 95 South and Afro-Rican. But it's important to stress that the Southeast has given us quite a few rappers who don't fall in the bass category, and in 1996, Macon, GA, group Soulism showed no bass influence whatsoever on this decent CD. Soulism favors slow tempos, and their melodic, sleek, and very R&B-minded tracks aren't unlike those of West Coast MCs. Some of the boasting songs are pretty routine, but most of the material is impressive. When Soulism reminisces about childhood on "Turn Back the Clock," describe the challenges of poverty on "Flat Broke," and examines the crime plaguing their Macon neighborhood on "That's How It Be," it's clear that they can be very substantial lyricists. —*Alex Henderson*

Soulja Slim

Gangsta Rap, Hardcore Rap, Dirty South
Another of Master P's No Limit soldiers, rapper Soulja Slim made his solo debut in 1998 with *Give It 2 'Em Raw. The Streets Made Me* appeared three years later, and after a move to Cut Throat Committy, *Years Later* followed in late 2002. —*Jason Ankeny*

Give It 2 'Em Raw / May 19, 1998 / No Limit ✦✦✦

● **The Streets Made Me** / Jul. 24, 2001 / No Limit ✦✦✦✦
Another new release from Master P's label, No Limit Records, *The Streets Made Me* is the second album by Southern rapper Soulja Slim. As is the case with many of Master P's releases, the real star of the album is the production. Handled mainly by production wizard Beats by the Pound, the album has an original style that manages to shake the cobwebs off of No Limit's trademark sound. His technical mastery makes cliché-riddled tracks, like the playful "That's My Hoe" and "Ya Heard Me," sound fresh. On "Straight to the Dance Floor," he manages to get away with sampling Michael Jackson's "Don't Stop Till You Get Enough" and make it his own. As for Soulja Slim, he doesn't just come along for the ride—he adds his own unique style to the mix. While he spends plenty of time rapping about thug life in tracks like "I'm a Fool" and "What You Came Fo'," he also seems to have grown a bit of a conscience on "Soulja for Life." It would be nice to see Soulja Slim explore that consciousness. *The Streets Made Me* provides everything a No Limit soldier could ask for. —*Jon Azpiri*

Souls of Mischief

f. Oakland, CA

Group / Hip-Hop, Underground Rap, Alternative Rap, Hardcore Rap, West Coast Rap
The East Oakland backpacker crew are members of the loose underground hip-hop consortium known as Hieroglyphics. The group consists of four erudite but hardcore MCs: A+, Phesto, Opio, and Tajai. Their debut album in 1993, *'93 'Til Infinity,* produced an early-'90s anthem of the same name and spawned a movement toward bohemian yet rugged hip-hop. The crew drew comparisons to De La Soul and A Tribe Called Quest for their abstract, whimsical style of storytelling. *'93 'Til* was a youthfully impressionistic album echoing jazz and funk influences combined with precocious lyrical gestures. Such tracks as "That's When Ya Lost" and "Never No More" were memorable for their lyrics and feel alike. Two years later, SOM shucked off their reputation for their sophomore release, *No Man's Land,* a derisive and brash departure from *'93 'Til.* While the crew lost some fans who were looking for a '95 'Til, they managed to cultivate a loyal fan base who respected their out-on-a-limb artistic development. Rather than stick to the formula that made them popular with the college hip-hop set, they chose to shatter their image similar to De La Soul's second album *De La Soul Is Dead.* Their Northern California mindset combines chaos, danger, and the avant-garde, all from a very intellectual b-boy perspective. The crew dropped the virtually invisible *Focus* strictly for web heads in 1999, then returned with *Trilogy: Conflict, Climax, Resolution,* another dark, trippy, and brooding exploration, in 2000. —*Michael Di Bella*

★ **'93 'Til Infinity** / Sep. 6, 1993 / Jive ✦✦✦✦✦
One of hip-hop's great lost masterpieces, *'93 'Til Infinity* is the best single album to come out of Oakland's Hieroglyphics camp, and ranks as a seminal early classic of the West Coast underground. The Souls of Mischief weren't even out of their teens when they completely redefined the art of lyrical technique for the West Coast, along with fellow standard bearers Freestyle Fellowship, the Pharcyde, and Hiero founder Del tha Funkee Homosapien. The Souls come off as four brash young MCs who are too smart for their own good, yet they're so full of youthful exuberance that it's impossible to dislike them for it. They're also excellent storytellers, punctuating their tales with a wry wit and clever asides; still, they're able to take on the grittier subjects of violence and death with a worldliness beyond their years. The production—all by various core Hieroglyphics members—is just as good as the raps, driven by complex beats, unpredictable bass lines, and samples drawn from spacy fusion records and East Coast jazz-rap crews. Main Source and Gang Starr both provide track foundations here, and it's possible to hear the intricately constructed loops of the former and the lean attack of the latter (circa *Step in the Arena*) in the record's overall style. A better comparison, though, would be to the effortless flow and telepathic trade-offs of A Tribe

Called Quest. In fact, *'93 'Til Infinity* seems to actively aspire to the fluidity of the best Tribe albums; tracks often segue directly into one another without pause—and the transitions are seamless. Although the title cut is an underappreciated classic, *'93 'Til Infinity* makes its greatest impression through its stunning consistency, not individual highlights. Put it all together, and you've got one of the most slept-on records of the '90s. —*Steve Huey*

No Man's Land / Oct. 10, 1995 / Jive ✦✦✦
After the critical and underground success of the Souls of Mischief's debut, *'93 'Til Infinity,* expectations were high for the group's sophomore release. The release of *No Man's Land* in 1995 revealed a greatly changed Souls of Mischief, and fans and critics alike turned their backs on the group. Gone is the youthful giddiness of the debut, in its place is confrontation. Instead of detailing their youthful misadventures with drink and around-the-way girls, Souls of Mischief contemplates groupies, overzealous hip-hop heads, and success or the lack of it. *No Man's Land* is laced with touches of anger and bitterness. The change in production style is even more shocking than the change in attitude. The golden funk of *'93 'Til Infinity* has been replaced with muddier, harsher beats. While the complex layering of drum breaks and jazz samples is still there, the effect is one of paranoia rather than of wild extroversion. Once the surprise wears off, *No Man's Land* reveals itself to be a solid hip-hop album, despite the cool welcome it first received. While Souls of Mischief's second album is certainly a notch below *'93 'Til Infinity,* it deserves more attention and respect than it has been accorded. —*Chris Witt*

Focus / 1999 / Hieroglyphics Imperium ✦✦
The first two Souls of Mischief albums made nary a commercial ripple at the times of their release (though the debut, *'93 'Til Infinity,* has since been given its due acclaim in cult circles). So on their third collection, *Focus,* Souls have gone the self-release route, peddling their cassette-only music via the Hieroglyphics web site (at www.hieroglyphics.com), which ensures two things: one, that the band will move modest numbers of the cassette; yet, two, those who buy it will be hardcore, loyal fans. Souls seem, at this point in their career, uninterested in, or at least unconcerned with, expanding their fan base. They are satisfied with making music for the heads that they know will appreciate it. That, in many cases, can make for cloistered, self-interested art, something that you have to be inside to value and enjoy. Souls of Mischief, however, bend backwards to avoid that dangerous knife edge as if to confirm the characteristic that has always been a primary element of the Hieroglyphics crew: pure syntactical skill and interplay. The expressive joy of old shines through on a couple cuts, but by and large, *Focus* is an exercise in bluntness and, well, focus. Unlike prior releases, the album mostly avoids good-time anthems (other than the out-of-place "Step Off") for piercing commentary. Millennial-like noir ("Way 2 Cold," "Make Way") coexists with more trenchant analyses with Souls directing their lyrical scalpel mainly at the music business ("Pay Due") and fly-by-night MCs ("Shooting Stars"). Uncharacteristically, however, Souls of Mischief have bypassed the inventive, left-field samples, viscous bass lines, and jaunty beats of their early songs for a more brittle and paranoid production that seems to draw mostly from East Coast underground hip-hop, specifically Rza's work, and the results are much gloomier and stifling. Granted, they overshadow nearly every group working similar musical ground, and they are still virtually peerless in terms of lyrical ability alone (at one point in "Big Shit," "effervescent" is rhymed with "epileptic"), but it is a slight disappointment and certainly perplexing to hear Souls inching back down toward the status quo rather than making others elevate their game just to approach the Hiero stable. —*Stanton Swihart*

Trilogy: Conflict, Climax, Resolution / Oct. 24, 2000 / Red Urban ✦✦✦
Souls of Mischief's groundbreaking 1993 debut, *'93 'Til Infinity,* introduced the underground sound of Oakland, a city known more for its deep bass and the funky pimpery of Too Short than for backpacker hip-hop. Precocious and innovative, each member of the crew brought a unique flow and formidable lyrical weaponry to the table. Their follow-up release, *No Man's Land* in 1995, was a much more dark and brooding work, more scholarly gangster than whimsical. Released in 2000, *Trilogy: Conflict, Climax, Resolution* is a further exploration of their darker side, a murky album of edgy decadence. Gone are the Souls' funky youthful misadventures, replaced now by fully grown sharp attitudes and emotions; however, their focus on bookish word bending remains the same. The tracks are moody and stripped down to their raw essence, the depth provided purely by the lyrical content, while the droning atonal music almost gets in the way. The album has a twisted

visceral feel reflecting the more chaotic mental states of the four restless Souls. In fact, the compressed vibe of *Trilogy* may isolate all but the Souls' die-hard listeners. While the Souls of old were able to satisfy nouveau hippies and heads alike with their debut, their focus is much more implicit here. Here they enter the mouth of madness, tapping into the primordial rivers of rage and anger. The result is an album of dense, demonic Oaktown funk that defies a true groove but astounds with its rawness and blithe yet still expansive lyrical content. The frenzied and frightful "Interrogation" featuring other Hieroglyphics enlistees Casual and Pep Love is the purest example of their developing sound. The Souls then dig deep into Webster's for astute hardcore tracks like "That Ain't Life," "Acupuncture," and "Enemy Minds." There are more Digital Underground, 2 Pac, and Too Short influences here to go along with the group's characteristic encyclopedic style. An introverted album that reveals more with each subsequent listen, *Trilogy* still makes it evident that the inner sanctum of the Souls remains impenetrable. —*M.F. Di Bella*

Soundmaster T

Producer / Party Rap, Bass Music, Dirty Rap
Bass music producer Soundmaster T made a significant contribution to the short-lived booty music craze with "2 Much Booty (In Da Pants)," a hugely successful dance single that appeared in the summer of 1997. Catching on in Southern clubs before making a transition to urban radio, the track's bouncing beat and simple, dirty lyrics made it his biggest hit by far. Although future collaborations with Jah Rista and the minor club success "Hit It From da Back" would follow, the track remains the one single he would be remembered by. —*Bradley Torreano*

2 Much Booty (In Da Pants) / Jun. 17, 1997 / Wrap ✦✦✦✦✦

Source of Labor

f. 1992, Seattle, WA
Group / Underground Rap, Hip-Hop
The Seattle-based crew Source of Labor have been an integral part of the overlooked Pacific Northwest hip-hop scene since 1992. Having opened for a diverse range of acts—including Gil Scott-Heron, Goodie Mob, Nas, De La Soul, the Pharcyde, and Ice Cube—SoL has gained their share of underground respect. The group was formed by rapper Wordsayer along with producers Negus I and Vitamin D. Wordsayer and Negus I are brothers born in Seattle but raised at Atlanta; they returned to the Northwest in the early '90s and founded the group. They also started up a label, Jasiri Media Group, and are heavily involved in the community (Wordsayer as a creative writing teacher at Seattle's Franklin High School, Negus I as the director of an after-school program). The trio began concentrating on Source of Labor recordings by the turn of the millennium, issuing the *Full Circle* EP as well as their debut full-length, *Stolen Lives*. —*M.F. Di Bella and John Bush*

Full Circle EP / May 15, 2001 / Sub Verse ✦✦✦

● **Stolen Lives** / Aug. 21, 2001 / Sub Verse ✦✦✦
Stolen Lives is the sophomore project from Source of Labor, released on the heels of *Full Circle*, an EP that received some critical acclaim. From the start, it's impossible to separate the SoL style from their obvious influence, the Roots. The problem here is that SoL attempts to effect the live-instrument production feel almost entirely through synthetic measures (most glaring is the pervasive, billowy effects-ridden keyboard that is a clear homage to the Roots crew). Head MC Wordsayer's (who also moonlights as a high school creative-writing teacher in inner-city Seattle) well-constructed, politically tinged lyrics often mesh well with the swampy production of Negus I and Vitamin D, but the Roots formula is followed so precisely that there is even an Ursula Rucker soundalike on the spoken-word-styled track "Invaded Lands." While SoL's sentiments and attempt at hip-hop reclamation are worthwhile and undeniably authentic, their stylistic employ comes off sounding rather unoriginal. In the end, if you're looking for something exceptional from hip-hop's "Wetlands," you're simply S.O.L. —*M.F. Di Bella*

South Central Cartel

Group / Gangsta Rap, Hardcore Rap, West Coast Rap
As one of the original early-'90s West Coast gangsta collectives to follow N.W.A's lead, South Central Cartel first appeared with their debut album *South Central Madness* in early 1992 before releasing a succession of albums throughout the remainder of the decade. After their follow-up, 1994's *N Gatz*

We Truss, generated a sizable amount of attention in the gangsta rap underground, Def Jam signed the group, eventually resulting in their most realized album, 1997's *All Day Everyday*. During this same era, group leaders Havoc and Prodeje released a string of albums on Quality Records as well, helping to garner a small yet healthy cult audience. Unfortunately, Def Jam dropped the group in the late '90s, and they ended up releasing the relatively disappointing *Concrete Jungle, Vol. 1* on an indie label, which signaled their plummet into oblivion. Despite their lack of commercial success, the group does stand alongside fellow early-'90s West Coast collectives such as N.W.A, Compton's Most Wanted, and Above the Law as gangsta rap pioneers. —*Jason Birchmeier*

South Central Madness / Jan. 22, 1992 / Pump ✦✦

N Gatz We Truss / May 10, 1994 / G.W.K./RAL ✦✦✦

● **All Day Everyday** / Jun. 3, 1997 / Def Jam ✦✦✦✦
South Central Cartel's much-delayed third album *All Day Everyday* may recycle gangsta clichés, but it does so with so much skill that it may be hard to argue the point. Certainly, there are the standard lyrical themes of guns, sex, and crime, but the Cartel can fashion these warhorses into killer pieces of G-funk. Just as often, however, they wallow in *both* lyrical and musical clichés, but there are enough instances where they break free from their straitjacket to make *All Day Everyday* worthwhile for gangsta diehards. —*Stephen Thomas Erlewine*

Concrete Jungle, Vol. 1 / Aug. 10, 1999 / Mouthpiece ✦✦✦
When gangsta rap first became popular in the late '80s, it was cutting edge and compelling. N.W.A.'s *Straight Outta Compton* and Ice-T's *Power* were hip-hop masterpieces that brilliantly articulated the pain and desperation of ghetto life in South Central Los Angeles. But gangsta rap became increasingly cliché ridden in the 1990s, when a lot of it lacked the freshness that had characterized the innovations of Ice-T, N.W.A., Schoolly D, and the Geto Boys in the 1980s. Released in 1999, *Concrete Jungle, Vol. 1* breaks no new ground for the South Central Cartel or gangsta rap in general. The CD is full of the usual gangsta clichés about thug life in the 'hood, but Cartel leaders Gary "Havoc" Calvin and Austin "Prodeje" Patterson (who shouldn't be confused with the Havoc and Prodigy of Queens' Mobb Deep) are so skillful that you end up liking the material despite all its clichés. The rapping is solid—none of the various West Coast MCs who join Havoc and Prodeje have any problem flowing—and Prodeje's production is consistently attractive. Jams like "What You Waitin' 4" and "Thug Disease" aren't innovative or groundbreaking; the Cartel doesn't tell you anything that Ice Cube and Ice-T didn't tell you in 1988. But they're infectious, and *Concrete Jungle, Vol. 1* ends up being an enjoyable, if limited, exercise in foot-pattin' G-funk. —*Alex Henderson*

South Park Mexican (Carlos Coy)

b. 1971, Houston, TX
Hardcore Rap, Southern Rap, Latin Rap, Gangsta Rap
Originating in the Southern rap mecca Houston, South Park Mexican (SPM) slowly built up his own personally run record label, Dope House Records, for years before eventually signing a distribution deal with Universal Records. With the promising deal in place, SPM stood on the verge of extending his reach outside of the South and becoming one of the first Mexican-American rappers to attain national success. He unfortunately never fulfilled his promise. First, his releases for Universal failed to top the charts during the early 2000s, and then he went to prison in June 2002 after a Houston jury convicted him of sexually assaulting a nine-year-old girl.

Before he became South Park Mexican, Carlos Coy spent years in the dope game. Born in Houston's predominantly Hispanic South Park neighborhood, Coy scored his first felony at the tender age of ten and continued on a path of crime, eventually getting involved with drugs by his teens. After several years of hustling on the streets, he finally got out of the dope game after a deal went bad. Around the same time, his daughter was born, causing him to reexamine his priorities. It was at this time in 1994 that Coy turned to a new hustle—the rap game. Even though he had never really rapped much before in his life, he started his own record label and began honing his rhymes. At first he did what he could, hustling tapes for five dollars a piece in his neighborhood, and by the late '90s, he was putting out his own CDs on his label. His two 1998 albums—*Hustle Town* and *Power Moves*—established him in the South as an up-and-coming rapper and his rigorous touring throughout Texas won even more fans.

Coy won a deal with Universal following releases in 1999 and 2000—*3rd Wish to Rock the World* and *SPM: The Purity Album*, respectively—and had his *Time Is Money* album on the streets by the end of 2000. The following year, he returned with his second album for Universal, *Never Change*. Though Universal heavily marketed the album, like it had done with *Time Is Money*, the results were similar—no crossover. Big marketing budget or not, Coy's hardcore rapping proved to be too harsh for the masses. His 2002 release, *Reveille Park*, a collection of freestyles, proved no different, especially since Universal chose not to release it. Finally, Coy met his unfortunate fate on May 18th, when a Houston jury convicted him for aggravated sexual assault of a child; in June the same jury sentenced him to 45 years in prison. Coy testified that he did not assault the nine-year-old girl, who had spent the night at his house with his daughter. However, Coy did admit to having sex in 1993 with a 13-year-old girl who had a son, which didn't help his case with the jury. —*Jason Birchmeier*

Hustle Town / Mar. 3, 1998 / Dope House ♦♦
South Park Mexican's first major album and a document of life in Houston's ghettos, *Hustle Town* is the Mexican American's most rugged album, full of hunger and ambition, even if it is a bit lacking in terms of both production and polished rapping. Subsequent SPM albums improve on these areas yet, unfortunately, also lose a bit of this album's enthusiasm. This is a cult favorite. —*Jason Birchmeier*

● **Power Moves** / Dec. 22, 1998 / Dope House ♦♦♦♦
The album that broke South Park Mexican out of the South, *Power Moves* features a number of his best-known songs: "Holla at Cha Later," "Illegal Amigos," and "West Coast, Gulf Coast, East Coast." It's definitely a more polished and crafted work that his preceding *Hustle Town* and proves that rap artists can thrive without major-label support. In sum, this is arguably the best place to start when investigating SPM. His later albums are often on a par with *Power Moves* in terms of both rhymes and beats, but none capture the essence of what makes this particular artist so alluring to his cult audience as this breakthrough album. Later albums such as *3rd Wish to Rock the World* often go out of their way to feature lackluster guest rappers as well. As a bonus, *Power Moves* also comes with a second disc that features screwed and chopped versions of many of the album's best songs, as well as his first big hit, "Mary-Go-Round," originally featured on *Hustle Town*. —*Jason Birchmeier*

3rd Wish to Rock the World / Nov. 23, 1999 / Dope House ♦♦♦
Rapper SPM acknowledges a past as a drug dealer, and that former occupation continues to inform his approach to his current career, from the name of his record label, Dope House, to the subject matter of his raps. His is a world of crime and retribution, expressed in language laced with the usual epithets and expletives. The raps are slower and more deliberate, the music more melodic than most other rap, and there are occasional surprises. "Land of the Lost" is a melodramatic narrative that looks back with regret, while "Miss Perfect" is a love rap, an unabashed tribute to SPM's wife. Like other rap label heads, the artist uses his own albums to introduce other rappers on his label. In fact, the album is basically a label sampler, featuring 23 rappers and groups in addition to SPM himself and containing tracks from upcoming Dope House releases. Four of the 16 tracks don't even feature the artist. Nevertheless, he remains the most distinctive presence on the album, and his perspective, while including much of the standard-issue opinions and expressions of the genre, is individual enough to be distinctive. —*William Ruhlmann*

SPM: The Purity Album / Aug. 15, 2000 / Dope House/Universal ♦♦
This album seems more like a compilation than an SPM solo album, with an ensemble cast of Dope House Records MCs guesting on almost every track here. Shadow Ramirez and Happy Perez' beats are on a par with the previous album, *3rd Wish to Rock the World*, still bass heavy and fueled by drum machines much in the spirit of Beats by the Pound and Three 6 Mafia. Unfortunately, the excessive guests really hamper the album's continuity. Skip this album unless you're a completist or a big Dope House Records fan. —*Jason Birchmeier*

Time Is Money / Dec. 12, 2000 / Uptown/Universal ♦♦♦
Houston native South Park Mexican is a cult hero in his home state of Texas with his old school rhyming style and beats influenced by old school legends N.W.A. The Texan was hoping to break out of the Lone Star State with his fourth album, *Time Is Money*, but the 16-track effort is unlikely to catch on. Lyrically, South Park Mexican fails to break any new ground. Tracks like

"Hillwood Hustlaz III" and "Throw Away Gats" cover the same territory that Eazy-E did a decade before. On the production side, the songs lack distinction. Tracks on the album fail to sound different not only from other artists but also from each other. While there is nothing wrong with being down with the old school, South Park Mexican fails to bring anything new to the table that is worthy of national attention. —*Jon Azpiri*

Never Change / Nov. 6, 2001 / Universal ♦♦♦
South Park Mexican (SPM) continues to polish his sound with *Never Change*, his most crafted album yet. The Houston, TX, rapper/producer does almost everything on this album with the exception of a few outside producers and some vocalists on the album's many hooks. It's the outside vocalists who characterize this album more than anything. SPM hasn't changed much as either a producer or a rapper—his trademark snail-paced, low-toned idiom and his mid-tempo, sparse tracks are highly evident. What has changed, though, is the way SPM emphasizes the vocal hooks—they anchor each of his songs, with Ayana handling most of the hooks. Overall, *Never Change* sounds great. SPM's music has never been this crafted. However, it's also just as formulaic as it is crafted. Sure, SPM has perfected his craft, but he's also fallen victim to its confines. He seldom ventures into new territory and seems overly content polishing up his trademark sound. And that's unfortunate because as crafted as these songs are, they're also a bit too routine. Nonetheless, even if many of the hooks are as catchy as hooks are intended to be, it's worth repeating that this album sounds great. Songs like "I Must Be High" are among SPM's best, and the inclusion of a few screwed songs is also nice, particularly since they're distributed throughout the album and since they fit into the album's sedate tone. —*Jason Birchmeier*

Reveille Park / Apr. 30, 2002 / Dope House ♦♦♦
The South Park Mexican is one of the more unique rappers in the gangsta rap genre; his smooth rhymes and excellent sense of rhythm have made his previous releases minor gems. *Reveille Park* is his tribute to his Latino roots. The album was released on the fifth of May (Cinco de Mayo, a traditional Mexican celebration) and consists of nothing but freestyles. Of course, the album is well designed and produced, making it fairly obvious that there is more than just freestyles featured here. But it does seem like a large portion of this has been improved, and that sort of lyrical skill is quite impressive. Several of the songs are slow enough to see how it might not be that hard to freestyle over them, but many of the tracks are fast enough to really unveil an incredible rapping skill. The songs go a little long, and the lyrical content can be quite empty at moments. This is due to the general lack of subject matter, but the South Park Mexican does his best to connect the rhymes he spouts. Plus, there are some very obvious moments that are predetermined, and that may help the music move in the right direction. Overall, this is a very interesting and fun album that may not be up to par with his usual material, but still features a wonderfully executed gimmick and some interesting production ideas. —*Bradley Torreano*

Southside Playaz
Group / Dirty South
The Southside Playaz bore DJ Screw's and the Screwed Up Click's stamp of approval during the late '90s. The trio recorded for Laf Tex Records and debuted with *You Gottus Fuxxed Up* (1998), followed by *Street Game* (2000). —*Jason Birchmeier*

● **Street Game** / Aug. 1, 2000 / Laf Tex ♦♦
One of the better offerings from Texas' burgeoning underground rap scene, Southside Playaz' *Street Game* features some near-cinematic charisma as the trio flosses while still keeping a hard stance. Songs such as "What's Going On," which relax a bit from gangsta posturing to lay into a mellow R&B feel with calm, melodic choruses. Yet even during calm moments such as this, the Southside Playaz still represent the gangsta life, never showing a soft or sentimental side, even when they emote. With their slick production and fine stable of fellow underground Texas gangsta rappers guesting, they seem to understand the formula for quality rap music. —*Jason Birchmeier*

Southside Posse
f. Kansas City, MO
Group / Underground Rap, Southern Rap, Hardcore Rap
The first underground rap group from Kansas City, MO, to make much headway beyond the local scene, the Southside Posse brought together a large

circle of hardcore rappers in the late '90s for a debut album, *Ghetto Soldiers* (1996). The album made ripples throughout the Midwest as well as the South, and the Playaz returned a few years later with *Anticipation of Death* (2000). —*Jason Birchmeier*

Anticipation of Death / Jul. 4, 2000 / Southside Production ♦♦♦
A few years after debuting in 1996 with *Ghetto Soldiers*, the Southside Posse dropped *Anticipation of Death* and reflected on the loss of former possemate D-Man. The album is rather sullen as a result, as the fiery group seems a little sobered after a death within their ranks. Even so, standout rappers Mon-E-G and Badger Kaine keep things hella bangin', as do the Boogieman's skeletal beats. You wonder what the Southside Posse would sound like with a major-label gloss, but their enthusiastic performance more than compensates for whatever the lo-fi *Anticipation of Death* lacks in sound quality. —*Jason Birchmeier*

Spearhead

f. 1994
Group / Political Rap, Hip-Hop, Alternative Rap, Jazz-Rap
Michael Franti released only one album as half of the Disposable Heroes of Hiphoprisy but was praised for his insightful raps and Public Enemy-influenced beats. After disappearing for two years, Franti resurfaced in 1994 with Spearhead, a band more rooted in '70s funk; their debut, *Home*, was followed in 1997 by *Chocolate Supa Highway*. —*John Bush*

● **Home** / Sep. 20, 1994 / Capitol ♦♦♦♦♦
Former Disposable Hero of Hiphoprisy Michael Franti takes his ideas even further with his debut record, covering a wide range of topics addressing the social conditions relevant not only to the African-American community but also to society in general. Immediate comparisons to other artists such as A Tribe Called Quest and Arrested Development are inevitable. They were all socially conscious and chose to have a message in their music, an angle decidedly different from the other two avenues of hip-hop of the time that focused on either gangster material or good-time, mindless commercial fodder. With a dark, brooding voice that could easily place him as the heir to Isaac Hayes or Barry White, *Home* greatly stressed consciousness and social thought over material value, but not at the expense of cheapening any other aspect of production. The whole vibe brought forth by employing a live band and backing singers easily paved the way for many nu-soul artists who continue to seek this path of influence. In the annals of hip-hop history, *Home* is an essential cornerstone to bringing socially conscious soul music and hip-hop close together. —*Rob Theakston*

Chocolate Supa Highway / Mar. 25, 1997 / Capitol ♦♦♦♦
What sets *Chocolate Supa Highway* immediately apart from Spearhead's previous album, *Home*, is its sound—boasting a murky, bass-heavy atmosphere clearly influenced by the rise of trip-hop, the album lends Michael Franti's politically charged raps a cinematic distinction missing from his previous efforts. Spanning from R&B-textured urban grooves to jagged rap anthems, *Chocolate Supa Highway* is no less challenging or confrontational than its predecessor, but for part most part Franti's music bears an importance equal to his message. —*Jason Ankeny*

Special Ed

b. 1973
Hip-Hop
In 1989, this 16-year-old released a technically dazzling debut album that highlighted his rapid-fire delivery and the ace production of hip-hop mastermind Howie "Hitman" Tee. —*John Floyd*

● **Youngest in Charge** / 1989 / Profile ♦♦♦♦♦
In 1989, at the tender age of 16, Brooklynite Special Ed burst on the scene with enough talent and swagger to stake his claim among hip-hop's big boys. For Special Ed, M.C. stands for master of cleverness, and *Youngest in Charge* is replete with it. The gifted manchild boasts a versatile repertoire, using various lyrical styles and rhymes spiked with punchlines and metaphors that indicate wisdom beyond his 16 years. The meat of the album lies in its first three tracks. The opening cut, "Taxing," is Ed's coming-out party as he kicks entertaining verses over a slickly produced, squealing-guitar-riff-laced track produced by Howie Tee. The following track is a masterpiece, Ed's claim to hip-hop immortality, "I Got It Made." It's four-plus minutes of artful arrogance, an instant hip-hop classic and anthem for all precocious hip-hop-heads

of the era. To round out the trio, "I'm the Magnificent" is a continuation of Ed's bragging rights over a sample from "Shantytown" (off Jimmy Cliff's *The Harder They Come* soundtrack). Because the first three tracks are so stellar, the rest of the album seems to be something of an afterthought; however, the remainder of the album does contain a few jewels. "The Bush," Ed's ode to his stomping grounds of Flatbush, features a sample of Al Green's "Love and Happiness," while "Think About It" is Ed's warning to those who wish to test his supremacy on the mic. On "Heds and Dreds," Ed flips a dancehall cadence to show his West Indian heritage. *Youngest in Charge* is a delightful release from a young hip-hop pioneer, a demonstration of the Edenic age of hip-hop when youthful exuberance and expression were highly valued. —*Michael Di Bella*

Legal / 1990 / Profile ♦♦♦
If you asked most hip-hoppers of the late '80s or early '90s what main the difference between East Coast and West Coast rappers was, they would have explained that while West Coast rappers were primarily concerned with beats and lyrics, the top priority of East Coast rappers was their rapping technique. Having interesting lyrics a la Ice-T and Ice Cube or impressive tracks *a la* Dr. Dre would get you respect in L.A., San Diego or Oakland, but if you were an aspiring MC in Queens, Philadelphia or Atlantic City, the best way to earn the respect of your homeboys and homegirls was showing off your flow or rhyming technique. Around 1989-1991, Special Ed was among the East Coast's most respected rappers, and the thing that earned him so much respect was the type of excellent technique he brings to his second album, *Legal* (so named because he had turned 18). Produced by Hitman Howie Tee, the main purpose of this CD is showing off Ed's rapping skills—and, to be sure, they're quite solid. That said, the album's best moments come when he tells some type of story instead of simply boasting and displaying his technique. "Livin' Like a Star" and "The Mission" demonstrate that the Flatbush, Brooklyn native can be a funny and clever storyteller when he puts his mind to it; the problem is that he doesn't do nearly enough storytelling. This is a generally likable effort, although it certainly isn't without its limitations. —*Alex Henderson*

Revelations / Jun. 27, 1995 / Profile ♦♦♦
Five years passed between Special Ed's sophomore effort, *Legal*, and his third album, *Revelation*. The Brooklyn native was 23 when this CD came out, and the hip-hop landscape had gone through its share of changes since Ed's emergence as a teenager in the late 1980s. So the rapper adjusted his flow to appeal to 1995 tastes, but he was still quite recognizable as Special Ed—and he was still a technique-oriented boasting rapper first and foremost. Boasting, in fact, is about all he does on *Revelations*. But as clever as many of his boasts are, hearing nothing but bragging can wear thin after awhile. A few songs into the album, you're admiring Ed's flow but wishing he would talk about something other than how great a rapper he is and how inferior rival MCs are. And after over an hour of hearing nothing but boasting and nothing but technique, you're painfully aware of how limited this approach can be. *Revelation* isn't a bad album by any means, but it could have used some variety. —*Alex Henderson*

Spectre

Vocals, Producer / Trip-Hop, Underground Rap, Experimental Ambient, Illbient
An appropriately shadowy entity with several albums for WordSound and production spots for Prince Paul and Techno Animal, Spectre is the Nosferatu of underground horrorcore, channeling the more isolated tones of industrial-dub and illbient into hip-hop productions of an intensely paranoid nature. Inspired by the rich legacy of horror films and dark industrial pioneers like Skinny Puppy as well as the old school of hip-hop, the rapper/producer debuted by hosting *The Ill Saint Presents Subterranean Hitz*, a seminal illbient compilation released on WordSound in 1996.

Spectre's first album, *The Illness*, dropped later that year (sample track title: "Spectre Meets the Psycho Priest in the Temple of Smoke"), also on WordSound. Between LPs he kept quite busy, making appearances on Prince Paul's *Psychoanalysis* LP, the second volume in Virgin's *Macro Dub Infection* series, Techno Animal's remix album *Vs. Reality*, and Unitone Hi-Fi's *Rewound & Rerubbed*. Spectre also released *RuffKutz*, a 90-minute mix tape spotlighting his new label, Black Hoodz, with tracks by Dr. Israel, Sensational, Mr. Dead, and the Jungle Brothers. Sophomore LP *The Second*

Coming was released in late 1998; *The End* followed in early 2000. —*John Bush*

● **The Illness** / Jan. 1, 1996 / WordSound ✦✦✦✦
Fusing hip-hop mysticism more than worthy of Wu-Tang with an approach to music-making allied to Lee "Scratch" Perry, Spectre's debut album is an excellent entry in the continuing branch of horrorcore rap operating from deep underground the streets of Brooklyn. The beats are solid, the production is basement-level, and the effects are deep, making tracks like "Mayday/Nightstalker" and "Spectre Meets the Psycho Priest in the Temple of Smoke" chilling pieces of hip-hop noir. —*John Bush*

The Second Coming / Jan. 6, 1998 / WordSound ✦✦✦
Second Coming fuses trip-hop, dub, drum'n'bass, and hip-hop, with guest vocals by Sensational and Mr. Dead. Spectre utilizes a great deal of live instruments to a sinister, atmospheric effect. —*Steve Huey*

Psychic Wars / 2002 / WordSound ✦✦✦
Spectre is back with his fourth album of new material, and this time his trademark dark, brooding atmosphere is leavened a bit by more energetic beats and lively interpolations of exotic foreign musical elements. After a pair of brief and unnecessary introductory tracks, *Psychic Wars* gets down to serious business with "Valour," which nicely fuses a sort of hip-hop/trip-hop beat to North African instrumental samples, to very nice effect. "Rolling Force" takes a similar approach, using sampled orchestral strings. One of the album's highlights is "Secrets," a dubbed-up hip-hop number that benefits greatly from the presence of vocalist Honeychild (heard previously as part of Raz Mesinai's Badawi project) and from the mixing genius of Pere Ubu alumnus Tony Maimone. Things bog down a bit after that; the cameo appearances by Sensational are both less than inspired, but "Remembrance" raises the temperature again. Overall, this album is just further proof that Brooklyn is, indeed, the world capital of experimental and progressive hip-hop and general off-kilter beat wizardry. Recommended. —*Rick Anderson*

Speech (Todd Thomas)

b. Oct. 25, 1968, Milwaukee, WI
Vocals, Producer / Alternative Rap, Hip-Hop
Speech rose to success in the early '90s as the leader of the groundbreaking alternative rap group Arrested Development. Born Todd Thomas in Milwaukee, WI, on October 25, 1968, he was raised primarily in Ripley, TN, before relocating to Georgia in 1987 to attend the Art Institute of Atlanta. There he met fellow student Tim Barnwell, and together they laid the foundations for Arrested Development's 1988 formation; adopting the stage name Speech, Thomas' lyrics reflected a positive, socially conscious, and deeply spiritual world-view far removed from the negative stereotypes of the burgeoning gangsta rap movement, while the group's music served up a rootsy, organic fusion of hip-hop, soul, funk, and blues. Arrested Development's 1992 debut, *3 Years, 5 Months & 2 Days in the Life of…*, was among the year's most critically and commercially well-received efforts, launching the hits "Tennessee" and "Everyday People," earning several Grammys and topping a number of year-end music-writers' polls. After 1994's *Zingalamaduni* fell victim to the sophomore slump, however, Speech disbanded Arrested Development and mounted a solo career, debuting in 1996 with a self-titled LP on Capitol; *Hoopla*, his first release for new label TVT, followed three years later. A period of rest gave Speech the opportunity to become a father and get back in touch with his family, allowing him to take time to reflect on his life and prepare for his next album. The result of this downtime was *Spiritual People*, a record filled with positive messages and a sense of unity that brought to mind his days with Arrested Development. —*Jason Ankeny*

Speech / Jan. 23, 1996 / Chrysalis ✦✦
Speech disbanded Arrested Development after the failure of *Zingalamaduni*, the band's second album, embarking on a solo career. As it turned out, it wasn't dissimilar from his former band at all. *Speech*, his eponymous 1996 debut, followed the same peaceful, soulful vibe that informed Arrested Development's two studio albums in a more tempered fashion. Where his former group sounded rootsy and gritty even at their most laid-back, Speech's record sounds slick, generally lacking in funk or dirt. *Speech* is not as immediate or infectious as *3 Years*, but it certainly more focused than *Zingalamaduni*. That sense of direction is a welcome relief after the confused mess of Arrested Development's farewell but Speech needs to write more shots of energy like "Ghetto Sex" in order to win back his audience. —*Stephen Thomas Erlewine*

Hoopla / Aug. 3, 1999 / TVT ✦✦✦
Three years in the making, Speech's second album finds the former Arrested Development frontman still working through his roots-centric vision of hip-hop. More Stevie Wonder than Silkk the Shocker, *Hoopla* incorporates much laid-back session material and even a few live-and-onstage jam sessions, right in line with hip-hop's growing affection for building songs from the groove up with live musicians. Thankfully, his relaxed rapping style shows little influence from any recent developments in the rap world, and it's always right in line with the material he's performing. It could have been a remarkable comeback record, but *Hoopla* suffers from several bizarre miscues. Speech remakes the consistently annoying 4 Non Blondes hit "What's Up" for his own track, titled "The Hey Song." To give him credit, Speech rebuilds the song with a female R&B chorus instead of just sampling the original, but that hardly makes it any less grating. The deep grooves and Speech's considerable production skills make for several intriguing tracks ("Movin' On," "Clocks in Sync with Mine," "Our Image"), but *Hoopla* isn't exactly worthy of celebration. —*Keith Farley*

● **Spiritual People** / Sep. 10, 2002 / Vagabond ✦✦✦✦✦
Speech's third album, an ambitious knockout of sprawling, invigorating music influenced by hip-hop, soul, raggae, alternative, and folk, was released in Asia just one year after 1999's *Hoopla* (though it waited two years for a bulked-up American release). It begins with a vigorous polemic on the state of music (from what sounds like a sampled Baptist sermon), but *Spiritual People* is no less enjoyable for the scattered "message" songs present. "Brought to You By…(Music & Life)" offers a few apologies for his extravagant lifestyle (still no match for Tommy Lee no doubt), then delivers a fantastic hook that deserves a slot in the Top Ten at least. "Cruisin' in My Super Beetle" is a super pop throwaway oddly reminiscent of Matchbox 20 (though it, too, offers a few hints about the fine line between relaxation and taking things for granted). Unsurprisingly, Arrested Development fans will find a lot to love here, much more than on his previous solo albums: excellent songs with clear, positive messages like "The Simple Love of Life" and "Always in Love," the latter an earnest, string-laden anthem with the lyric "I really love you, I want children with you/be with you always, always in love." "Livin' in the Real World" is postmodern folk with an alternative bent, while "Jungle Man" and "Y-O" meet jazzy hip-hop halfway to A Tribe Called Quest. "Burning Rage Inside," a halfway apologetic anthem to jealousy, has a smooth AOR production sounding like latter-day Steely Dan, even while Speech lets it all hang out. Fortunately, the songwriting's tough enough to stand up to such a varied sound, while Speech's delivery and musical personality prove so strong that he ties it all together easily. Just like Stevie Wonder, one of his prime influences, the subtleties of Speech's music don't suffer when tied to universal themes, the type of songs most contemporary artists wouldn't touch. —*John Bush*

Spice 1

b. Byron, TX
Gangsta Rap, Hardcore Rap, West Coast Rap
Too Short discovered rapper Spice 1, who'd been born in Texas before moving to California. His self-titled debut was as vivid and fatalistic a gangsta album as possible, and his hard-edged, angry, and pessimistic rapping style and tone only added to the despair emanating from the disc. He followed it with an even more bitter and nihilistic release, *187 He Wrote* in 1993, complete with simulated gunfire. Other releases included 1995's *1990 Sick* and 1997's *Black Bossalini (aka Dr. Bomb From Da Bay)*. *Immortalized* followed two years later, and in the spring of 2000 Spice 1 returned with *Last Dance* and *Playa Rich Project*. A sequel to the latter brought him into 2002, while the *Spiceberg Slim* album came out that summer. Unlike many rappers in his position, Spice 1 did not suffer a critical backlash from such a high volume of releases in such a short amount of time. He continued to change with the times, and that reflected on his consistant sales and unwavering fanbase. —*Ron Wynn*

Let It Be Known / 1988 / Triad ✦✦

Spice 1 / May 12, 1992 / Jive ✦✦✦
The sheer vulgarity, anger, coarseness, sexism and horror unveiled, celebrated and presented on Oakland rapper Spice 1's debut release can be frustrating and saddening. But more importantly, it should not be ignored. Spice 1 has done what "gangsta" rap's detractors should want; he's stripped

away even the slightest veneer of glamour around the atmosphere of casual violence, sexual exploitation and drug selling he examines. His style, an appropriate mix of irony, disdain, acceptance and confusion, never succumbs to the situation or seeks to justify or downplay the sense of impending doom. *—Ron Wynn*

187 He Wrote / Sep. 28, 1993 / Jive ✦✦✦✦
Spice 1 continues his bleak, stripped-down version of gangsta rap with *187 He Wrote*, an album that can be harrowing and appalling. Throughout the record, the spare, funky production keeps the music engaging, making the disturbing lyrics cut even deeper. *—Stephen Thomas Erlewine*

AmeriKKKa's Nightmare / Nov. 22, 1994 / Jive ✦✦✦
Numerous gangsta rappers came out of the Oakland rap scene of the late 1980s and 1990s, many of whom were faceless and interchangeable. One of the city's more noteworthy gangsta rappers was Spice 1, whose third album *AmeriKKKa's Nightmare* appealed to hip-hoppers who had been savoring Dr. Dre's *The Chronic* in 1994. Spice doesn't bring any new insights to gangsta rap—tunes like "Face of a Desperate Man," "Jealous Got Me Strapped" (featuring the late Tupac Shakur), "You Done Fucked Up," and "Murder Ain't Crazy" don't say anything that Ice Cube, N.W.A, the Geto Boys, or Ice-T hadn't said already. But the CD manages to hold attention thanks to Spice's appealing flow (his rhyming skills are solid, to be sure) and the very Dre-ish tracks produced by Blackjack, DJ Slip of Compton's Most Wanted fame, Ant Banks, and Spice himself. Dre's influence is impossible to miss on this album; like him, the producers favor a sleek, highly melodic approach that combines hip-hop beats with a strong appreciation of George Clinton's P-Funk innovations. Though *AmeriKKKa's Nightmare* falls short of the excellence of *The Chronic*, this is an enjoyable, if derivative, release that fans of the Dre/Snoop Doggy Dogg/Warren G school of 1990s gangsta rap will treasure. *—Alex Henderson*

1990-Sick / Dec. 5, 1995 / Jive ✦✦✦✦
Spice-1 doesn't change his style much on *1990-Sick*, his third album. Building from a solid West Coast hip-hop base, Spice-1 adds raggamuffin and dancehall flourishes, which makes him distinctive as an MC. Much of the record suffers from unimaginative production and standard musical ideas, but Spice-1 is an engaging rapper—he's talented enough to disguise the weaknesses in the music with his verbal skills. *—Stephen Thomas Erlewine*

The Black Bossalini (aka Dr. Bomb from Da Bay) / Oct. 28, 1997 / Jive ✦✦✦
Although the cover looks like a 2Pac bootleg, *Black Bossalini (AKA Dr. Bomb From Da Bay)* doesn't find Spice 1 changing his formula that much. There are a couple of Southern Californian flourishes here and there, but this is pretty much straight-ahead Bay Area hip-hop, highlighted by guest appearances from Ice-T, MC Breed and Mack 10. It isn't very different from his early albums, and it's a little disheartening to think that he hasn't progressed at all in ten years, but it's a solid record that should appeal to his legions of fans. *—Stephen Thomas Erlewine*

● **Hits** / Nov. 10, 1998 / Jive ✦✦✦✦

Immortalized / Sep. 14, 1999 / Jive ✦✦✦
One of the grimmest, most fatalistic rappers ever since his debut ten years before, Spice 1 only continued what he's known for on *Immortalized*. Track titles like "F**** the World," "Ride Fo' Mine," "Killerfornia," and "What the F****" tell most of the story, though Spice's rhymes are tight and inventive throughout. The production, by Rick Rock on most tracks, is classic California G-funk with a more high-tech edge, excellent on the first few tracks though the quality bottoms out midway through. The highlight, "Suckas Do What They Can (Real Playaz)," includes not only Yukmouth from the Luniz and Spice's mentor Too Short, but also features one of the last appearances by Zapp's Roger Troutman before his death. For listeners able to handle so much negativity on one full-length, *Immortalized* offers a few quality tracks but becomes a cohesive album. *—John Bush*

The Playa Rich Project / Nov. 21, 2000 / Mobb Status ✦✦✦
Spice 1 continues his reign of terror on the Bay Area, bringing a compilation together, sporting some of the rugged, hardcore gangsta rappers we expect. Artists include the Hot Boys, Mr. Serv On, Three Six Mafia, B-Legit, C-Bo, Tray Dee, Outlaws, and, of course, Spice 1 himself. The formula hasn't changed much over the years; it's still the same gangsta tales laid on staccato funk grooves that has made Spice 1 so famous on the West Coast gangsta rap scene. *—Brad Mills*

Hits, Vol. 2: Ganked & Gaffled / Feb. 20, 2001 / Mobb Status ✦✦✦
Spice 1's first of two greatest-hits collections in two years, *Hits, Vol. 2* compiles a modest number of the notorious West Coast hardcore rapper's performances. The 16 songs featured on this best-of come from a variety of obscure sources, and it's very questionable whether or not these songs were really so-called "hits" since Spice 1 had few, if any, hits since the mid-'90s. Furthermore, you'd probably presume that a greatest-hits collection such as this would encompass Spice 1's numerous albums for Jive during the '90s—like the excellent *Hits* collection had—but that is not the case here. As mentioned, the 16 songs on *Hits, Vol. 2* are obscure recordings most fans probably have never heard. Thus, you should think of this best-of album as a rarities collection, since that would be a more accurate description. Unfortunately, Thug World Entertainment assumed titling this collection as a hits rather than rarities collection would no doubt sell better, even if listeners were misled in the process. Regardless, many guests appear over the course of this album—Too Short, Eightball, 2Pac, E-40, Roger Troutman, Big Mike—and that may be reason enough for many to seek out this collection. *—Jason Birchmeier*

The Playa Rich Project, Vol. 2 / Jan. 22, 2002 / LGB ✦✦✦
Spice-1's *Playa Rich Project, Vol. 2* is a mix of rappers from both the mainstream and the underground. Featuring big names like himself, E-40, and Kurupt, this album mostly serves to showcase some of the lesser-known rappers in the business, including Captain Save 'Em, Lil' Keke, and Serv-On. *—Bradley Torreano*

Hits, Vol. 3 / Apr. 9, 2002 / Thug World ✦✦✦
Spice 1's second of two greatest-hits collections in two years, *Hits, Vol. 3* compiles a modest number of the notorious West Coast hardcore rapper's performances. The dozen songs featured on this best-of come from a variety of obscure sources, and it's very questionable whether or not these songs were really so-called "hits" since Spice 1 had few, if any, hits since the mid-'90s. Furthermore, though you'd probably presume that a greatest-hits collection such as this would encompass Spice 1's numerous albums for Jive during the '90s—like the excellent *Hits* collection had—that is not the case here. As mentioned, the dozen songs on *Hits, Vol. 3* are obscure recordings most fans probably have never heard. Thus, you should think of this best-of album as a rarities collection since it's the more accurate description. Unfortunately, Thug World Entertainment assumed titling this collection as a hits rather than rarities collection would no doubt sell better, even if listeners were misled in the process. Regardless, many guests appear over the course of this album—Too Short, Rappin' 4-Tay, MJG, Three 6 Mafia, Jayo Felony, Tray Deee—and that may be reason enough for many to seek out this collection. *—Jason Birchmeier*

Spiceberg Slim / Jun. 11, 2002 / Riviera ✦✦✦
At this point in Spice 1's career, you begin to wonder what more he has to offer. He's released more albums than most independent labels ever survive long enough to release, and he's old enough to have fathered most of his fans. For these reasons and more, his popularity waned with each successive release beginning in the late '90s. Despite his waning popularity, which was inevitable after so many releases, Spice 1 continues to deliver heartfelt, meaningful music with *Spiceberg Slim*. The album is rather straightforward: minimal guests (Rappin 4-Tay, Jay-O Felony, the Outlawz, Tray Deee, Kokane, Spade), two producers (Wino, Tone Tovin), only 13 songs (none of them skits), and nothing fancy. Granted, such a straightforward album isn't going to revive Spice 1's career, and it's not going to ignite some sort of second phase for him either. What it will do, though, is satisfy his fans and, in turn, retain them. If you've ever been fond of Spice 1's street-smart rhymes, you'll find much to enjoy here. *Spiceberg Slim* is for the longtime fans, the listeners who respect Spice 1 for staying true to the underground for so long without ever selling out or dropping off. *—Jason Birchmeier*

Jimmy Spicer

Old School Rap
Jimmy Spicer released a number of old school rap singles during the late '70s and early '80s, including the epic "Adventures of Super Rhymes" (Dazz, 1979), "The Bubble Bunch" (Mercury, 1982), "Money (Dollar Bill Y'all)" (Spring, 1983), and the Rick Rubin-produced "Beat the Clock" (Def Jam, 1985). "The Bubble Bunch" is also noteworthy for the fact that it featured Jellybean Benitez's first remix. *—Andy Kellman*

Spontaneous

b. Chicago, IL

Vocals / Hardcore Rap

Though he originally hails from Chicago, rapper Spontaneous paid his dues in L.A.'s underground hip-hop scene. He released his 1998 debut single "Waterproof" on the local rap label Goodvibe Recordings, which also released singles like 1999's "Next School MCs" and 2000's "Reprezen'n," as well as his full-length debut *Spur of the Moment Musik.* —*Heather Phares*

● **Spur of the Moment Musik** / Jan. 25, 2000 / Goodvibe ◆◆◆◆
The title may be *Spur of the Moment Musik,* but its clear that the beats weren't just thrown together; they are very diverse, from "The Spontaneous Anthem," which has a classical music sound, to the thumping drums in "Next School MC's." There's also variety in the guests on the album, with West Coast MCs Tash (of the Alkaholiks) and Xzibit, and East Coast MCs Rock (of Heltah Skeltah) and Bahamadia, among others. Although he gets help from such topnotch guests, the ever energetic Spontaneous shows that he can hold his own on the mic in songs like "Spur of the Moment" and "Disco Technology." This is an impressive debut album, especially considering that Spontaneous also produced all of the songs. —*Dan Gizzi*

Spooks

Group / Pop-Rap, Hip-Hop, Alternative Rap

Inspired by the rap/R&B success of the Fugees, Spooks came together in the late '90s with a similar message and group structure, but a much different musical approach. Consisting of vocalist Ming Xia and MCs Mr. Booka-T, Vengeance, Water Water, and Hypno, the group's male-female dynamic brought comparisons to the Fugees almost immediately. The difference lies in the production, which referenced trip-hop and jungle and rarely stuck to a typical hip-hop structure. Boasting this unique approach, the group recorded *S.I.O.S.O.S., Vol. 1* in 2000 for Artemis Records. The album was a huge success in Europe, where it turned gold in France, Belgium, Sweden, and Germany, but hardly made a dent in American markets. They re-released the record and put together a live band for their live shows in an attempt to woo U.S. audiences, but the single for "Things I've Seen" did catch on and the group quietly disappeared soon after. —*Bradley Torreano*

● **S.I.O.S.O.S., Vol. 1** / May 23, 2000 / Antra ◆◆
S.I.O.S.O.S. (Spooks Is on Some Other Shit) is an eclectic mix of jazz, reggae, hip-hop, and neo-soul, and it's also not that good. Spooks are comprised of four gruff, male MCs and female singer Ming Xia, but five is truly a crowd and often the arrangements are so cluttered that the vocalists trip over themselves and interrupt each other like overeager grade-schoolers. The first single, "Things I've Seen," does have a nice hook propelled by the jazzy vocals of Xia, but overall the record attempts to take on too much and suffers for it. —*Steve Kurutz*

Spoonie Gee (Gabriel Jackson)

Hip-Hop, Old School Rap

Spoonie Gee was the nephew of veteran R&B producer Bobby Robinson and one of the earliest rap artists. He was known as the "love rapper," an image that was established by his first record, "Love Rap," released on his uncle's Enjoy label as the flip side of the Treacherous Three's "The New Rap Language." The bulk of early rap records reproduced an MC's party routine with a loose sequence of narrative, boasting, and call and response. Spoonie's initial outing, however, organized a hip-hop styled record around a romantic theme, coming closer to the lyrical norms of pop music. The intimate "Love Rap" was accompanied only by drum set and congas, and Spoonie's next record continued in a similarly minimalist vein. The voice-over on 1979's "Spoonin' Rap" stuck to more conventional old school boasting but looks forward to the gangsta attitude in its jailhouse references. "Spoonin' Rap" was also prophetic in its use of flexatone and heavily echoed voice, suggesting the Jamaican connection that was denied in early interviews by some of the rap originators. In 1980, Spoonie collaborated with Sequence on a classic single, "Monster Jam," probably the last word on the series of "Good Times"/"Another One Bites the Dust" variations, and a classic in the Sugarhill vein, complete with a bone-crushing bass line and ecstatic crowd noises. —*Richard Pierson*

● **The Godfather ... Rap** / 1987 / Tuff City ◆◆◆◆◆
Spoonie Gee was among the earliest old school rappers, performing in a coarse, terse style over funk beats. He was never a great rapper, but he was

an effective one, and this album showcased his functional approach on material ranging from straight come-ons to microphone challenges and message cuts. —*Ron Wynn*

Godfather of Hip Hop / Jun. 18, 1996 / Ol Skool Flava ◆◆◆

Sporty Thievz

Group / Hip-Hop, Hardcore Rap

The hip-hop trio Sporty Thievz comprised former Wrecking Crew members King Kirk (aka Thieven Stealberg) and Big Dubez (aka Safecracker) in collaboration with Marlon Brando (aka Robin Hood); signing to the Ruffhouse label, the group debuted in 1998 with *Street Cinema.* —*Jason Ankeny*

● **Street Cinema** / Aug. 18, 1998 / Roc-A-Blok ◆◆◆
The very name Sporty Thievz leaves little doubt that the Yonkers trio are straight-up, stylish gangstas. And, since this is New York, not L.A., that means an emphasis on lyrical gymnastics and hard-hitting beats. And since their debut *Street Cinema* was produced by Ski, a collegue of Jay-Z, it does contain some irresistible beats and grooves, designed to keep the party jumping. And it would keep the party jumping, if *Street Cinema* wasn't conceived as an audio movie, necessitating the appearance of sketches and dialogue between songs. Telling a story with an album ain't that easy—the Who couldn't do it with *Tommy,* Genesis couldn't do it with *The Lamb Lies Down on Broadway*—and the worst of it is, *Street Cinema* doesn't even really want to tell a story; it just wants the appearance of a narrative, so the album might stand out from the rest of the pack. A narrative would also hopefully make people ignore the crew's cribbing of various lyrical styles. A little stealing, though, doesn't matter (especially when you declare yourselves to be Sporty Thievz), since the group can turn out good street-level hip-hop. They just don't do it often enough on the record, and when they do, there's too much junk floating around the album to make the good stuff instantly recognizable. Still, that handful of good cuts makes the entire enterprise worth investigating once, even if you find that you won't return to this *Street Cinema* that often. —*Stephen Thomas Erlewine*

Fredro Starr (Fredro Scruggs)

b. Queens, NY

Hardcore Rap, Hip-Hop, East Coast Rap

Rapper Fredro Starr has a lot on his plate. The Queens, NY, native balances both an acting and a music career. Starr began his rapping career when he founded the hardcore rap/hip hop group Onyx in 1991 with rap compatriots Sticky Fingaz and Sonee Seeza. The group's first album (*Bacdafucup,* 1993, UNI/Def Jam Records) went platinum, but since the breakup of Onyx after their 1998 album, *Shut 'Em Down* (Def Jam), Starr (born Fredro Scruggs) ventured out on his own to start his solo career. Starr has also built a solid acting resumé (he has had no formal training), starring in numerous television shows and several movies. He starred in the 2000 Paramount/ MTV film *Save the Last Dance* and appeared as Brandy's love interest Quentin on the WB's television show *Moesha.* The ambitious actor/rapper has had roles in *NYPD Blue* and such films as *Light It Up,* Spike Lee's *Clockers,* and HBO's *Strapped.* Starr's solo rap debut, *Firestarr* released in January of 2001. On the track "Soldierz," Starr teamed up with Onyx partner Sticky Fingaz. One of Starr's cuts, "Theme From Save the Last Dance," is featured on the movie's soundtrack song, "Shining Through." In addition, Starr also runs his multi-faceted entertainment entity, OPM (Other People's Money). —*Kerry Smith*

● **Firestarr** / Jan. 23, 2001 / Koch International ◆◆◆
With his signature rapping style, former Onyx frontman Fredro Starr creates an impressive solo album that features enough party tracks to keep Onyx fans happy while also offering some deeper tracks that will appeal to a new audience. After appearing in several films and the television series *Moesha,* many have questioned Starr's street credibility, and he replies capably with hard tracks like "Thug Warz." Starr also shows a more pensive side on "What If." Unfortunately, the album is weighed down by too many guest appearances by unseasoned rappers like Mieva. Still, *Firestarr* is a solid reply to his critics and proof that, if given the chance, Fredro Starr can still shine. —*Jon Azpiri*

Lovebug Starski

b. The Bronx, NY

Producer / Old School Rap

With a career that began in the early '70s, Lovebug Starski has performed in nearly every hip-hop club throughout the New York area. Born in the Bronx, Starski began his career as a record boy in 1971. After years on the scene,

Starski became the house DJ at the famed club Disco Fever in 1978. Soon thereafter, he began DJing at Club Harlem World and the Renaissance. Branching out to vinyl, Starski recorded his first single, "Positive Life," on Tayster Records. Soon after, he recorded the soundtrack to the 1986 film *Rappin'* on Atlantic Records before recording his first LP, *House Rock*, on Epic. A five-year jail sentence curtailed Starski's activities throughout the late '80s, but in the '90s he began DJing again with old pal DJ Hollywood. —*Steve Kurutz*

Steady B (Warren McGlone)

b. Philadelphia, PA
Hip-Hop, Gangsta Rap, Pop-Rap
Along with Schoolly D and the Fresh Prince (now better known as actor/rapper Will Smith), Steady B (born Warren McGlone) was one of the first wave of Philadelphia-area rappers to gain notoriety. With an appealing blend of battle raps and freestyle lyrics, Steady's style is an accurate representation of post-Run-D.M.C./pre-Public Enemy era hip-hop. At his best, Steady mixed well-written metaphors and wordplay with sparse yet catchy drum tracks. As was often the case in 1980s rap though, Steady just as frequently relied on gimmicky themes and corny yarns to fill out his albums. After releasing five albums with mixed success, Steady formed the hardcore group C.E.B. in an effort to update his style, and sales. The C.E.B. album failed, and Steady faded into obscurity. It would have been far better for Steady if he'd simply remained unheard from, but in 1996, Steady and his old C.E.B. partner Cool C were convicted of a botched armed robbery and murder. To avoid a possible death sentence, Steady confessed to the robbery and was sentenced to life without possibility of parole. —*Mtume Salaam*

● **Bring the Beat Back** / 1986 / Jive ✦✦✦
Half engaging freestyles and battle raps, and half album filler, *Bring the Beat Back* was 17-year-old Steady B's debut release. Standout tracks like "Get Physical," "Stupid Fresh" and, most notably, the title song itself, established Steady as an up-and-coming lyricist. But with its corny dance tunes ("Do the Fila") and lightweight novelty songs ("Yo Mutha" and "Cheatin' Girl"), *Bring the Beat Back* is a mixed bag. —*Mtume Salaam*

What's My Name / 1987 / Jive ✦✦✦
Steady B's second album continued in the style of his first—it was solid, if unexceptional, '80s-era hip-hop. Producer Lawrence Goodman and Steady's DJ Tat Money were becoming a little more adventurous, adding brief samples, scratched breaks and even a live drum or two to accent the straight-forward rhythm tracks. Less gimmick laden than the previous *Bring the Beat Back*, *What's My Name* was Steady's most satisfying album. —*Mtume Salaam*

Let the Hustlers Play / 1988 / Jive ✦✦✦
By 1988, hip-hop was changing, becoming increasingly politicized and topical. *Let the Hustler's Play* found Steady B struggling to keep up with the changes. With his delivery sounding, at times, strained and affected, Steady attempted to harden his style. Producer Lawrence Goodman again did an able job with the backing tracks, but only a few of these songs are memorable. Guest producer KRS One contributed three tracks and occasional vocal asides. A later KRS remix of a 12" single release landed Steady B on national video channels, but despite this exposure, Steady B's brand of good-natured hip-hop was fading out of vogue. —*Mtume Salaam*

Going Steady / 1989 / Jive ✦✦✦✦✦
This contained good, occasionally clever raps and rhymes in a mostly apolitical tone by Steady B. Hip-hop hadn't yet been overrun by gangstas, so lightweight party material and microphone challenges were still the dominant compositional terrain. —*Ron Wynn*

Steady B 5 / 1991 / Jive ✦✦
Things sounded played out for Steady B on this 1991 disc. Perhaps he had stayed around too long, lost track with hip-hop's vibe, or simply burned out, but this album didn't contain a single number that even the most die-hard fan would ever want to hear again. It's doubtful that they would get through several tracks the first time around. —*Ron Wynn*

Steady Mobb'n

f. New Orleans, LA
Group / Gangsta Rap, Southern Rap
Steady Mobb'n are a New Orleans-based gangsta rap outfit masterminded by Master P, the head of No Limit Records. Steady Mobb'n released their debut

album, *Pre-Meditated Drama*, on No Limit in the spring of 1997; *Black Mafia* followed a year later. —*Stephen Thomas Erlewine*

● **Pre-Meditated Drama** / May 6, 1997 / Priority ✦✦✦✦
Under the direction of Masta P and his No Limit production team, Steady Mobb'n turn in a predictable but satisfying gangsta rap collection with their debut, *Pre-Meditated Drama*. Although rappers Crooked Eyz and Billy Badd don't offer any lyrical insights—their rhyming skills aren't particularly distinctive, and they're often overshadowed by guest rappers like Mystikal and Richie Rich—the sound of the record is superb. The No Limit producers have created a tour de force of urban funk and streetwise rhythms that keeps *Pre-Meditated Drama* continually entertaining. Even if it offers nothing new or unexpected, it's a hell of a listen. —*Leo Stanley*

Black Mafia / Nov. 24, 1998 / Priority ✦✦✦✦
Black Mafia may look like the average No Limit album, but it differs in some important ways. The main difference is that it isn't nearly as flat musically as most No Limit records, exploring interesting sonic territory while retaining the deep, stoned, funky grooves that make the records popular. Furthermore, Steady Mobb'n are better rappers than the average No Limit MC, as the guest appearances illustrate. Sure, there are a few dull spots that pop up throughout the record, but it's not nearly as often as on the average No Limit record, and that alone makes *Black Mafia* kind of noteworthy. —*Stephen Thomas Erlewine*

Steinski (Steve Stein)

Producer, Turntables / Old School Rap
Forefather of all the zanier aspects of turntablism, Steinski created a succession of extra-legal works of studio art—"Lesson One: The Payoff Mix," "Lesson Two: The James Brown Mix," "Lesson 3: The History of Hip-Hop"—that quickly became DJ landmarks and some of the most valued bootlegs in rap history. Steinski, born Steve Stein, was a DJ and record collector when he wasn't working as an ad writer. After hearing in 1983 of a nationwide competition to remix G.L.O.B.E. & Whiz Kid's "Play That Beat Mr. DJ" sponsored by Tommy Boy Records (official title: "Hey Mr. DJ Play That Beat Down by Law Switch the Licks Mastermix Contest"), he hooked up with Double Dee (Douglas DiFranco, a studio engineer) to produce "Lesson One: The Payoff Mix," a track that sprinkled the usual funk breakbeats with a parade of samples from feature films and cartoons, including all manner of pop-culture references. A panel including Afrika Bambaataa, Arthur Baker, and Shep Pettibone awarded it first prize after one listen, and the remix gained even more airplay than the original. Soul Brother No. 1 was next on the docket, and "Lesson Two: The James Brown Mix" introduced Clint Eastwood, Bugs Bunny, and instructional LPs into the mix. By the time of "Lesson 3: The History of Hip-Hop," the third record released by Tommy Boy, offended sample victims began demanding its removal from retail shelves, and for most hip-hop fans, Double Dee & Steinski entered the realm of the legendary.

While DiFranco went back to his engineering job, Steinski continued recording with "The Motorcade Sped On," a JFK tribute featuring samples from radio broadcasts, Walter Cronkite, the killing of Lee Harvey Oswald, and JFK himself. Subsequent records provided commentary on television ("We'll Be Right Back") and the Gulf War ("It's Up to You"), and Steinski also remixed for Frankie Goes to Hollywood. He also spent considerable time with his day job, but the duo's enormous influence on sampladelic hip-hop finally convinced him to release another, produced for the London-based, Coldcut-affiliated *Solid Steel* program. That record, *Nothing to Fear: A Rough Mix*, appeared in 2002 on the Soul Ting label.

● **Nothing to Fear: A Rough Mix** / 2002 / Soul Ting ✦✦✦✦✦
Despite the title, there's nothing rough about this mix, a point-perfect ride through the world of hip-hop studded with so many perfectly timed samples (and split-second scratching) that the man should have the legal hounds of Hollywood at his heels (not to mention the greater music industry), if only they could track down the sources. Those who know Steinski only through his hefty influence on the British beat-obssessives at Ninja Tune—and not the succession of extra-legal, occasionally bootlegged twelves he recorded during the mid-'80s—will find themselves in very familiar territory, occupied by the man who connected all the dots between the what's-next aesthetic of party hip-hop and the type of pop-cultural cues later made famous by retro-culture. Produced for the BBC via the *Solid Steel* program ("the broadest beats in London"), *Nothing to Fear* comes from a person who describes himself as

"elderly," but despite the absence of 50 Cent or Ja Rule, Steinski sounds only as out of touch as Coldcut or David Holmes or any other celebrity soundtracker making hundreds of thousands from the silver screen. The occasional scratching (by the unheard-of F. Olding Munny and the Poolroom Loafer) adds an edge to the mix that nudges it closer to the mainstream, but Steinski is still the star here. No more than four or five of the 28 tracks are pure vocal cuts; all the better for him to drop in dozens of extended sample passages, each of which gets in where it fits in—perfectly. —*John Bush*

Stereo MC's

f. 1985, London, England
Group / House, Acid Jazz, Club/Dance, Trip-Hop, Hip-Hop

One of the most successful hip-hop acts to emerge from Great Britain, Stereo MC's formed in London in 1985, when rapper Rob B. (born Rob Birch) and DJ/producer the Head (Nick Hallam) formed the Gee Street label as a means of promoting their music. Gee Street soon signed a distribution deal with the New York-based 4th & Broadway label, and a series of singles followed before Stereo MC's' debut album, *33-45-78*, surfaced in 1989.

After the departure of founding member Cesare, the group—now consisting of Rob B., the Head, drummer Owen If (born Owen Rossiter), and vocalist Cath Coffey—issued the 1990 single "Elevate My Mind," which became the first British rap single ever to reach the U.S. pop charts. Following the release of the album *Supernatural*, Stereo MC's toured with the Happy Mondays and EMF before returning to the studio to record their 1992 breakthrough *Connected*, a sample-free album recorded completely with live instruments which spawned major hits like "Step It Up," "Creation," "Ground Level," and the title track. Throughout several years of production and remix work, the group's long-awaited (and oft-delayed) follow-up remained unreleased, though in 1997, Coffey did at least issue her debut solo single, "Wild World." For their 2000 mix album *DJ Kicks*, Stereo MC's recorded three new tracks, "Rhino, Pts. 1-3," and finally in 2001 issued a new album, *Deep Down & Dirty*, after a long nine-year hiatus. —*Jason Ankeny*

33-45-78 / Jul. 24, 1989 / ✦✦✦

Supernatural / 1990 / 4th & Broadway ✦✦✦✦

● **Connected** / 1992 / Gee Street ✦✦✦✦✦
Stereo MC's' American breakthrough is an energetic, club-oriented collection of colorful, funky dance tracks—the raps almost seem like an afterthought, yet that doesn't distract from the sheer pleasure of their sound. —*AMG*

DJ Kicks / Mar. 28, 2000 / K7 ✦✦✦✦
Eight years on from their last LP, Stereo MC's returned not with a studio work but a mix album that shows their long career in a new light, as not just one-hit wonders but breakbeat renegades who've been searching for the perfect beat—both as recording artists and as label heads—for over 15 years. *DJ Kicks* trips back and forth between beat-heavy cinematic music from the '70s, rap from the old school to the new-skool, and trip-hop from producers who, just like Stereo MC's themselves, take the template of breakbeat music down new paths. Truth to tell, though, there'd been so many similar mix albums released in the previous few years that it wasn't difficult to believe the bottomless well of obscure, funky music was just about tapped. Fortunately, Rob H. and Nick come through with a lineup of widely varied artists and crucial tracks. Most of the instrumental highlights are obscurities like "Back to the Hip Hop" by the Troubleneck Brothers, "Do It Do It" by the Disco Four, "Moon Trek" by the Mike Theodore Orchestra, and a surprisingly chilling track by 101 Strings titled "Flameout." The rap tracks are solid too, including old school heroes like Kool G Rap & DJ Polo ("Road to the Riches") and Ultramagnetic MC's ("Poppa Large"), as well as more recent artists from the growing hip-hop underground like 57th Dynasty ("Pharoah Intellect") and Divine Styler ("Tongue of Labyrinth"). Another highlight is the new, three-part track "Rhino" produced by Stereo MC's. Fitting in well with the album itself, "Rhino" is an old school groove number with heavy drums and Hammond keys. It's easy to wonder if Stereo MC's even *have* any fans left from the days of *Connected*, but this mix album might gain them a few. —*John Bush*

Deep Down & Dirty / Jun. 12, 2001 / Island ✦✦✦✦
In 2001, several years after *any* listeners could've expected a follow-up to 1992's *Connected*, Stereo MC's finally delivered with *Deep Down & Dirty*. It's a tribute to how far ahead of the curve Stereo MC's were ten years earlier that

Deep Down & Dirty never strays far from the spirit of *Connected*, but still sounds perfectly up-to-date for 2001. It's clear the productions are more mature and more complex, but they still plumb the depths of deep-groove beatbox funk, with nods to soul-jazz and gospel. Still tossing out lines with the half-assed cool of Shaun Ryder or Ian Brown, frontman Rob Birch doesn't rap quite as much as he used to (that's a good thing), and the productions are a tad more down-tempo and dubby than when the band was at its most clubbed-up in the early '90s. The title-track opener sets things off in fine fashion, working a stuttered mid-tempo groove with split-second snippets from the horn section and a full-throttle vocal backing. In true soul tradition, the upfront mover "Graffiti, Pt. 1" segues into a bongo-led "Graffiti, Pt. 2." Birch even sends up his slacker-cool image on "Sofisticated," a groovy piano-and-beatbox number. Along with Birch, producer Nick Hallam (aka the Head) is the other key to what makes *Deep Down & Dirty* so much fun, packing his productions to the bursting point with dusty beats, lines from old Hammond organs, and samples of bygone soul shouters. Despite a few traditionalist, anthemic tracks ("We Belong in This World Together," "Running") which don't work as well as they would've in the heady days of 1993, *Deep Down & Dirty* is a solid record that reveals no trace of cobwebs from Stereo MC's long hiatus. —*John Bush*

Stetsasonic

f. 1981, Brooklyn, NY, **db.** 1992
Group / Hip-Hop, Golden Age

One of the first rap groups to use a live band, Brooklyn's Stetsasonic formed in 1981 and were also among the first to promote a positive black consciousness that found its ultimate expression in the so-called daisy-age sounds of De La Soul and the Jungle Brothers. The group consisted of DJs "Prince Paul" Huston and Leonard "Wise" Roman, keyboardist/drummer/DJ Marvin "DBC" Nemley, and rappers Glenn "Daddy O" Bolton, Martin "Delite" Wright, and Bobby "Frukwan" Simmons. Daddy O and Delite founded the group as the Stetson Brothers, after the hat company, and began performing in New York hip-hop clubs, picking up other members along the way. Their debut, *On Fire*, was released in 1986, but it was the follow-up, *In Full Gear*, that brought them critical acclaim and an R&B hit, "Sally." 1991's *Blood, Sweat & No Tears* was considered by many to be their best and most diverse album, but Daddy O decided that they had run out of ideas and broke up the band. He went on to work with Mary J. Blige, Queen Latifah, Big Daddy Kane, and the Red Hot Chili Peppers as a producer and remixer. Meanwhile, Prince Paul had already established himself as a producer for his work with De La Soul and Fine Young Cannibals, and later worked with Frukwan in the Gravediggaz. —*Steve Huey*

On Fire / 1986 / Tommy Boy ✦✦✦
There weren't many bands utilizing a hip-hop format in the mid-'80s, making Stetasonic quite unique on the pop front in 1986. While their subject matter was invariably light and their raps now hopelessly tame and effete, they were groundbreaking at the time and retain a certain charm. —*Ron Wynn*

★ **In Full Gear** / 1988 / Tommy Boy ✦✦✦✦✦
Stetsasonic's acknowledged classic, *In Full Gear* greatly expanded the musical approach of their debut, making full use of new sampling technology as well as their unique live-band format. It's an ambitious double-LP set that seemingly aims for nothing less than to encompass every stylistic branch of hip-hop circa 1988. Over the course of 17 tracks, the group runs through state-of-the-art street-level hip-hop, an R&B crossover ballad, human beatboxing, Afro-centric spoken-word poetry, Def Jam-style minimalism, DJ cuts, James Brown and Sly Stone samples, proto-Daisy Age sounds courtesy of Prince Paul, early jazz-rap, dancehall reggae, slamming Run-D.M.C.-style rap-rock, and Miami bass. It all makes for a staggering tour de force and a highly individual record that really doesn't sound quite like anything else—whether before, after, or during its time. The group makes no secret of its desire to help hip-hop push music forward, calling hip-hop "the most progressive form of music since jazz" in the liner notes, and launching a spirited defense of sampling as an art on the groundbreaking single "Talkin' All That Jazz." Yet no matter how progressive-minded things get, Stet keeps a warm, genial block-party vibe going throughout the record, which holds all the experimentation together. Prince Paul fans tracing his career backward might initially be disappointed that his warped humor isn't much in evidence here, since he was an equal member of a multi-talented six-man crew, and gets

(or shares) production credit on only six tracks. But, even if it isn't wholly a product of his vision, the vibrant eclecticism of *In Full Gear* is very much in keeping with his aesthetic anyway. This album doesn't always quite get its due, partly because of the flurry of hip-hop classics released around the same time, but it's certainly up near the head of the class of '88. —*Steve Huey*

Blood, Sweat & No Tears / Jul. 1, 1991 / Tommy Boy ◆◆◆◆
What turned out to be Stetsasonic's parting long-player, *Blood, Sweat & No Tears* may have disappointed those expecting another *In Full Gear*, but there was much to love here despite a long-winded, partially deflating running time. Starting out with a devastating instrumental, "The Hip Hop Band," Stetsa sounded fresher than ever on "No B.S. Allowed" and the funky groupie tribute, "Speaking of a Girl Named Suzy." "Go Brooklyn 3" sounded surprisingly reminiscent of West Coast hardcore, but the very next track, "Walkin' in the Rain," was a smooth ballad that sampled the 1972 Love Unlimited hit (and re-created the oh-so-sexy Barry White phone conversation). As a band, Stetsasonic still had plenty of ties to funk, dropping expressive party jams like "So Let the Fun Begin" and the P-Funk name-dropping "Don't Let Your Mouth Write a Check That Your Ass Can't Cash." Prince Paul, then coming off the success of De La Soul's *3 Feet High and Rising*, hardly dominated this record; Bobby Simmons and Daddy O each produced as many (or more) tracks as he did (most of them great), while DBC and Wise also contributed. If it lacks the classic status that *In Full Gear* instantly commanded, *Blood, Sweat & No Tears* was still a fitting last hurrah to one of the golden age's most diversely talented combos. —*John Bush*

Sticky Fingaz (Kirk Jones)

b. Brooklyn, NY
Hardcore Rap, East Coast Rap, Hip-Hop
Rapper Sticky Fingaz was the frontman of hardcore rap goup Onyx and is best known for his husky voice and brash rapping style that dragged the hip-hop sound into the mosh pit. The Brooklyn-born Kirk Jones spent much of his early life as a member of a notorious New York street gang. Jones began performing with his cousin Fredro Starr, and the pair was soon discovered by hip-hop legend Jam Master Jay. Soon after, they formed Onyx. In 1993, Onyx released their first album, *Bacdafucup*, which became a crossover hit thanks in large part to Sticky Fingaz' gritty style and raspy voice. The group produced two more records before Fingaz left the group to pursue solo projects. Jones also pursued a side career as a film actor. His first solo album, *Black Trash: The Autobiography of Kirk Jones*, which was released in 2000, is a conceptual album that is cinematic in scope that tells the story of Kirk Jones, a down-on-his-luck ex-con who finds himself wrapped up in the street life. The record stands as an impressive debut that blends Sticky Fingaz' two loves: film and hip-hop. —*Jon Azpiri*

● **Black Trash: The Autobiography of Kirk Jones** / Nov. 21, 2000 / Universal ◆◆◆
Sticky Fingaz' oft-delayed solo debut, *Black Trash: The Autobiography of Kirk Jones*, is a bold conceptual endeavor that loosely follows the same format Prince Paul implemented on his hip-opera *Prince Among Thieves*. Scripted to fit the silver screen, *Black Trash* chronicles the trials and tribulations of Kirk Jones, a down-on-his-luck knucklehead who always manages to find trouble. Playing out like a lyrical collage, *Black Trash* is an emotional roller coaster that tackles the quintessential tale of good vs. evil. Though highly imaginative, like most Hollywood blockbusters, *Black Trash* fights bouts of long-windedness (this is particularly evident toward the LP's conclusion), yet there is still plenty to chew on in between. Displaying a lyrical diversity that his stint with Onyx rarely suggested, Sticky serves up a slew of profound moral messages on the thought-provoking "Why" and "Oh My God," where in a maniacal state Sticky questions God's existence. Yet, his lyrical transformation is best exemplified on "Money Talks" (featuring Raekwon), where Sticky speaks in third-person, as a dollar bill, and vividly depicts how the material possessions people strive to own eventually end up owning them. While the dramatic ebb and flow of *Black Trash* is the LP's saving grace, as the running dialogue (contributed by Omar Epps) and frequent skits ingeniously captures the many complex intricacies that make up Sticky/Jones' conflicting personas. However, it is hard to feel sympathetic for the character, as he is a man who, through the course of this LP, shows little regard for human life, kills his best friend, beats his wife, and deserts his child. Yet, similar to James Gandolfini's portrayal of Tony Soprano, Sticky convincingly

brings Jones to life, and he is such an enigmatic character that you can't help but root for him, even though he doesn't deserve it. —*Matt Conaway*

Scott Storch

Keyboards, Producer, Piano / G-Funk, East Coast Rap, West Coast Rap
Scott Storch's knack for laying down dazzling keyboard lines led to a burgeoning career as a musically blessed producer by the early 2000s after aligning himself with production duties for high-profile rappers such as Snoop Dogg and Busta Rhymes. Long before Storch was crafting entire tracks for superstar rappers, he was a humble keyboardist. He contributed to mostly forgotten Philadelphia-area efforts such as Schoolly D's *Welcome to America* (1994) and G. Love & Special Sauce's self-titled debut (1994), yet his humble contributions to a then low-profile, indie-label debut album by another Philadelpha act ended up being his path to success. This particular album happened to be the Roots' *Organix* (1993), an album that led to a major label deal for the Roots, solidifying Storch's role as keyboardist for the group. Yet as the years passed and his reputation grew as the talented keyboardist in America's premier live hip-hop "band," Storch began extending his reach, taking on production opportunities. His big break came when his keyboard riff laced the mammoth lead single to Dr. Dre's comeback album, "Still D.R.E." Working alongside Dre obviously had its pluses, and soon Storch found himself co-producing the lead single to Xzibit's *Restless* album, "X," and getting the opportunity to produce three tracks for Snoop Dogg's *Tha Last Meal* ("Brake Fluid," "Ready 2 Ryde," "Y'all Gone Miss Me"). —*Jason Birchmeier*

Greg Street

Producer / Southern Rap
Greg Street, a fierce hip-hop DJ for radio station V-103 (WVEE) in Atlanta, was also tapped to host a Slip N Slide compilation of Southern rap. Aptly titled after the hour his show begins, *Six O'Clock, Vol. 1* was preceded with a single, Trina and Deuce Poppi's "Thug Like Me," in July 2001. Street shared the executive producer's hat with Ted Lucas. —*Eleanor Ditzel*

● **Six O'Clock, Vol. 1** / Oct. 16, 2001 / Atlantic ◆◆◆◆◆
Slip N Slide, using the ever-competent production skills of Greg Street, put together a 21-track compilation of Southern rap stars titled *Six O'Clock, Vol. 1* and released it in October 2001. *Six O'Clock, Vol. 1* provides nonstop rap by those who have proven they know how to rap and by newcomers to the arena who also have a talent. Jermaine Dupri, highly respected as a producer of R&B and rap, put his talents with Tigah to rap "Somebody Better Tell 'Em." Ludacris raps a one-minute version of "Beat Box"; Trina and Deuce Poppi (of Slip N Slide Records) come on with their single "Thug Like Me." Relying on the talents of Trick Daddy rapping in his version of ghetto slang from the street life of Miami's Liberty City to longtime favorites like Erick Sermon. Street also sandwiched in newer talents such as Big Bali and the Wreck Shop Krew, which featured Z-Ro, Big Mo, Ronnie Spencer, and D. Gotti. —*Eleanor Ditzel*

The Streets

f. Birmingham, England
Group / 2-Step/British Garage, Garage/House
Mike Skinner's recordings as the Streets marked the first attempt at adding a degree of social commentary to Britain's party-hearty garage/2-step movement. Skinner, a Birmingham native who only later ventured to the capital, was an outsider in the garage scene; though his initial recordings appeared on Locked On, the premiere source for speed garage and, later, 2-step from 1998 to the end of the millennium. He spent time growing up in north London as well as Birmingham, and listened first to hip-hop, then house and jungle. Skinner made his first tracks at the age of 15, and during the late '90s, tried to start a label and sent off his own tracks while he worked dead-end jobs in fast food. At the end of 2000, he earned his first release when the Locked On label—already famous for a succession of burning club tracks from Tuff Jam, the Artful Dodger featuring Craig David, Dem 2, and Doolally—signed him for the homemade "Has It Come to This?" By the following year, the single hit Britain's Top 20 and the inevitable full-length followed in early 2002. That album, *Original Pirate Material*, unlike most garage compilations and even the bare few production LPs, found a home with widely varying audiences, and correspondingly earned Skinner a bit of

enmity from the wider garage community. By the end of the year, it had been released in the States as well, through Vice. *—John Bush*

● **Original Pirate Material** / Mar. 25, 2002 / Locked On ✦✦✦✦✦
When Streets tracks first appeared in DJ sets and on garage mix albums circa 2000, they made for an interesting change of pace; instead of hyper-speed ragga chatting or candy-coated divas (or both), listeners heard banging tracks hosted by a strangely conversational bloke with a mock cockney accent and a half-singing, half-rapping delivery. It was Mike Skinner, producer *and* MC, the half-clued-up, half-clueless voice behind club hits "Has It Come to This?" and "Let's Push Things Forward." Facing an entire full-length of Streets tracks hardly sounded like a pleasant prospect, but Skinner's debut, *Original Pirate Material*, is an excellent listen—and almost as good as the heavy-handed hype would make you think. Unlike most garage LPs, it's certainly not a substitute for a night out; it's more a statement on modern-day British youth, complete with all the references to Playstations, Indian takeaway, and copious amounts of cannabis you'd expect. Skinner also has a refreshing way of writing songs, not tracks, that immediately distinguishes him from most in the garage scene. True, describing his delivery as rapping would be giving an undeserved compliment (you surely wouldn't hear any American rappers dropping bombs like this line: "I wholeheartedly agree with your viewpoint"). And a few songs, like "Geezers Need Excitement," don't wear their Wu-Tang Clan influences very well, while "It's Too Late" piles on the melodrama with the ins and outs of a relationship. Still, nearly every other song here succeeds wildly, first place (after the hits) going to "The Irony of It All," on which Skinner and a stereotypical British lout go back and forth "debating" the merits of weed and lager, respectively (Skinner's meek, agreeable commentary increasingly, and hilariously, causes "Terry" to go off the edge). The production is also excellent; "Let's Push Things Forward" is all lurching ragga flow, with a one-note organ line and drunken trumpets barely pushing the chorus forward. "Sharp Darts" and "Too Much Brandy" have short, brutal tech lines driving them, and really don't need any more for maximum impact. Though club-phobic listeners may find it difficult placing Skinner as just the latest dot along a line connecting quintessentially British musicians/humorists/social critics Noël Coward, the Kinks, Ian Dury, the Jam, the Specials, and Happy Mondays, *Original Pirate Material* is a rare garage album: that is, one with a shelf life beyond six months. *—John Bush*

Str8 Young Gangstaz

Group / Christian Rap, Gangsta Rap
Among the many Christian gangsta rap artists that popped up in the late '90s, Str8 Young Gangstaz came out of South Central with a sound that was heavily reminiscent of Dr. Dre's early-'90s work for Death Row Records. Put together by rapper Big Tone for his G-Like Records, Str8 Young Gangstaz was born out of Tone's conversion to Christianity in the spring of 1991. It was in church that he met many of his future collaborators, who also came out of South Central looking for an alternative to the murder- and money-oriented lyrics of their nationally infamous rap scene. As his associates began to start groups in the area, Tone turned to rappers Low-Key and Duv Mac to help him spread his message. Purposefully aping Dre's production style in order to appeal to fans of the genre, Str8 Young Gangstaz released *Tha Movement* in the fall of 1999, followed by a string of appearances at Christian music festivals over the next few years. *—Bradley Torreano*

● **Tha Movement** / Nov. 2, 1999 / Grapetree ✦✦✦
The concept of "God's gangstas" might seem bizarre to some, but that's exactly what you'll find on *Tha Movement*, the second album by the South Central L.A. Christian rap group Str8 Young Gangstaz. The album follows the common Christian-music approach of aping popular secular styles and simply substituting Christian lyrical content. This approach makes for a juxtaposition that's even stranger than usual when you consider the subject matter of 2Pac and the Dr. Dre-era Death Row Records stable, two influences on the S.Y.G.z' sound so dominant as to make the G-funk grooves, George Clinton samples, and vocal deliveries sound like slavish imitations. That's perfect if you're a Christian listener who greatly enjoys the West Coast rap *sound*, but can't stomach the hard-edged, sometimes amoral hedonism of the artists who pioneered it; it also might appeal to some secular rap fans who like the sound more than the lyrical content (although it's more difficult to imagine that to be true for this style of music than it would be for other

genres). Outsiders may find the album further confirmation of most Christian music's essentially reactionary nature—calculatedly packaging the message in pre-existing popular sounds and making sure to incorporate "insider" themes and language for credibility, rather than creating new forms of expression *a la* classic African-American gospel—but this music isn't aimed at that audience, so it doesn't really matter in the end. *—Steve Huey*

Strings

Vocals / Hip-Hop, Hardcore Rap
Chicago-based female rapper Strings appeared on Keith Sweat's single "I'm Not Ready" and R. Kelly's "Gotham City for the Ghetto" and performed in the videos for each before releasing singles like "Pu$$y/Kitty," "Raise It Up," and "Tongue Song," which was the answer to Sisqó's hit "Thong Song." Her debut album, *The Black Widow*, arrived in mid-2000 and featured collaborations with producers and hip-hop artists such as Swizz Beatz, Mannie Fresh, the Infamous Syndicate, and Juvenile & the Hot Boyz. *—Heather Phares*

● **The Black Widow** / May 30, 2000 / Epic ✦✦✦
Somebody should have told Strings that the role of hip-hop vixen is already being occupied by the likes of Lil' Kim, Foxy Brown, Eve, and Gangsta Boo, among others. New vixens need not apply. Listening to *Black Widow*, it's hard not to be a little cynical. Strings, a former exotic dancer, is not afraid to use her sexuality to get attention. But beneath all that sexual bravura lies a modicum of rhyming skills. Strings rhymes at length about her former profession on tracks like "Table Dance," which tells the story of a female murder suspect, and the stripper's performance is more interesting lyrically than one would think. "Hey Ya" features cameos by Juvenile and the Hot Boys, and features a solid beat and slinky guitar that is a cut above the usual Cash Money track. "The Tongue Song" is a memorable X-rated reply to Sisqó's "Thong Song" that is sure to garner some attention. Eventually, however, the listener becomes desensitized to Strings' sexed-up lyrics, and the album becomes monotonous. If she doesn't bring more to the table than a table dance, her act will be played out pretty fast. *—Jon Azpiri*

Styles

Hardcore Rap, East Coast Rap
For years known primarily because of his membership in the L.O.X., Styles broke away from his groupmates in 2002 with his debut solo album and its hit single, "Good Times." Up until the album's release, Styles may have not been well-known on his own yet was certainly no stranger to success. He united with childhood friends Jadakiss and Sheek to form the L.O.X. and signed with Bad Boy in the late '90s. The trio appeared on numerous Bad Boy-affiliated songs as guests and even released an album of its own, *Money, Power & Respect* (1998), which yielded a hit single of the same name. The L.O.X. left Bad Boy soon after to join the Ruff Ryder camp, where the trio's style of hardcore rap fit better alongside other rugged rappers such as DMX and Eve. There, the L.O.X. released its second album, *We Are the Streets* (2000), followed by solo albums for each of the members. Styles' solo debut, *A Gangsta and a Gentleman*, came in summer 2002, led by the Swizz Beatz-produced hit single "Good Times." *—Jason Birchmeier*

● **A Gangster and a Gentleman** / Jun. 25, 2002 / Ruff Ryders ✦✦✦
As one-third of the intrepid street rap trio L.O.X., Styles Paniro had seen hip-hop go through a number of awkward phases since the death of friend and mentor the Notorious B.I.G.. Biggie Smalls and Sean "Puffy" Combs were the first to recognize the talents of Styles and fellow Yonkers natives Jadakiss and Sheek Luciano. After Biggie's passing, L.O.X. released their debut, *Money, Power & Respect*, in 1998, and Styles was always the MC who listeners looked forward to hearing on the track. After L.O.X. became fed up with Puff Daddy's glammed-out approach to the rap game, they rediscovered their gully roots and resurfaced with DMX, Swizz Beats, and the Ruff Ryder camp in early 2000, releasing the far-more-edgy *We Are the Streets* later that same year. After fellow L.O.X. member Jadakiss found solo success with his summer 2001 release *Kiss the Game Goodbye*, it was only a matter of time before Styles, every bit as talented a lyricist as Jada but perhaps a little less marketable, came forth with a solo venture. The buzz for this album was spurred by two singles in particular: the soulful memoir "My Life," featuring Pharoah Monche (originally released on Rawkus' *Soundbombing III*), and the herbalist's anthem "Good Times." But this album is more than just a two-track wonder, as Styles divides equal time between his bipolar persona. On

the gangster side, Styles offers thuggish joints like the kettle-drum-laced "Styles," the stirring "Lick Shots" featuring the L.O.X. crew, and the party banger "Soul Clap," which loops a snippet from the classic Native Tongues remix of "Scenario." Styles shows a more humanist side on the laid-back "Black Magic" featuring Angie Stone and expends heartfelt lamentation on the death of his older brother on "My Brother." The album's haphazard track sequencing detracts from its overall quality, as the songs do not transition well from one to the next. Also, despite Styles' made-man, one-foot-in-the-spirit realm approach, the MC fails to carry a couple of tracks (which may be the result of some spotty, soulless production). These minor glitches aside, Styles' debut hits hard like a double shot of Glenlivet or a haymaker to the thorax. —*M.F. DiBella*

Styles of Beyond

f. 1995, Woodland Hills, CA
Group / Hip-Hop, Alternative Rap, Underground Rap

Consisting of MCs Ryu and Takbir, Styles of Beyond take their inventive Los Angeles-based hip-hop to the millennium and try to propel the form into uncharted territory. The group came together in 1995 when the two aspiring MCs met and freestyled together while on a break from class at Pierce Community College in Woodland Hills, CA. They were instantly impressed with each other's off-the-cuff wordplay and decided to start Styles of Beyond, a name Takbir was already using along with DJ Cheapshot. SOB released their first single, "Killer Instinct," independently on Bilawn Records in 1997. The song was video game-based and featured hip-hop cult legend the Divine Styler, a longtime family friend of Takbir whose older brother Bilal Bashir has produced for Ice-T, Everlast, and Divine Styler, in addition to helping out Styles of Beyond, including the title track of 2000 Fold. "Killer Instinct" was able to start a small buzz in the hip-hop community, especially in hip-hop mix shows and with critics. Styles of Beyond was even named Best New Artist of 1997 by the Wake Up Show, a highly respected hip-hop radio program. SOB released *2000 Fold* in the summer of 1998 to satiate a demand in the underground hip-hop community. The group signed to the Dust Brothers' Hi-Ho Records at the beginning of 1999, and *2000 Fold* was re-released by the label. —*Stanton Swihart*

● **2000 Fold** / Aug. 18, 1998 / Bilawn ✦✦✦✦

Styles of Beyond keep one foot firmly planted in the hip-hop underground, while the other one jets forward into wholly uncharted territory on its debut album *2000 Fold*. Despite their sometimes bizarre lyrical flights of fancy, Ryu and Takbir opt to maintain the menacing delivery of most hardcore and street MCs, but that does not render the message at odds with the medium. Instead, it fits the idea of the increasingly burdensome millennium that is a primary theme on the album, and the duo's inventiveness does, indeed, move the music forward, challenging hip-hop convention with experimental and wide-ranging lyrical ideas and themes. They still indulge in boastfulness and occasional dark imagery, but it is done in a much more playful (though not at all lighthearted) way and is interspersed among ideas that reach far beyond hardcore posturing. On the suspense mystery "Spies Like Us," the duo spy on hip-hop, plotting and preparing to take it over, while they extend an invitation to alien life forms to come on down and show themselves in "Gollaxowelcome." Musically, Ryu and Takbir maintain a dedication to the foundations of hip-hop by featuring a host of turntablists as part of their soundscape. DJ Revolution, DJ Rhettmatic (of the Beat Junkies) and DJ Cheapshot all supply production and scratching on the album, and *2000 Fold* also features production from their most frequent collaborator, Vin Skully, as well as Divine Styler and Bilal Bashir. There is something distinctly sparse and futuristic about the musical underpinning of *2000 Fold*, like a hip-hop version of *Black Hole*. RZA seems to be a primary production influence; bits of film noir strings ("Winnetka Exit") are employed, as are short, eerie piano loops, repeated spaghetti-Western guitar figures and sharp, metallic-sounding beats. "Muuvon," however, veers much closer to the Daisy Age (a sample of Q-Tip on "Easy Back It Up" solidifies the connection)—Styles have professed and display an appreciation for that early-'90s mindset—with cleverly used electro-funk samples and rapid rhyming tradeoffs between Ryu and Takbir. Styles of Beyond may not yet be light years ahead of the rest of the rap industry, but it is not trailing far behind the coattails of, say, Prince Paul or Kool Keith. —*Stanton Swihart*

The Sucka MCs

f. Iowa City, IA
Group / Underground Rap, Alternative Rap

Representing Iowa City—a small urban center tucked deep in the middle of the Midwest, about as far away from the coasts as you can get—the Sucka MCs make rap music that is fittingly about as far away from traditional rap as you can get. The collective of Midwestern white boys with goofy names like Coolzey, Dr. Don, the Warden, the Worm, and DJ Damn Them Balls Are Tasty make hip-hop music, but they take a much different approach than most hip-hop artists, emphasizing light-hearted comedy above all. The collective debuted in 1997 with their *Steppin' in Shit* album, which didn't break out of the Midwest. Five years later, the Sucka MCs returned with another album (*Da Album*), a record deal with Ace Fu, and a publicity deal with Midnight Feeding in Brooklyn. —*Jason Birchmeier*

Steppin' in Shit / 1997 / ✦✦✦

The Sucka MCs debuted in 1997 with *Steppin' in Shit*, a collection of insane hip-hop tracks that are more funny than tough or stylish. The Iowa City-based collective are no doubt influenced by another group of white boys, the Beastie Boys—and, in particular, that group's riotous 1986 classic debut album, *Licensed to Ill*, the benchmark for all insane white-boy rap groups. Another album didn't appear until 2002, when the Sucka MCs returned with *Da Album*, a much more ambitious release than *Steppin' in Shit*. —*Jason Birchmeier*

● **Da Album** / Mar. 2002 / Ace Fu ✦✦✦

Five years after debuting modestly with *Steppin' in Shit*, the Sucka MCs returned in 2002 with *Da Album*, a more satisfying collection of the Iowan hip-hop collective's goofy rhyming. There are ten songs on *Da Album* and one skit, all of which feature numerous group members, each being quite charismatic, taking strange names like Coolzey, Dr. Don, the Warden, the Worm, the Sunshine Kid, DJ Damn Them Balls Are Salty, and Egg Nog. Though this sounds quite unlike traditional hip-hop because of the geeky white-boy humor, the Sucka MCs are really straightforward b-boys at heart, particularly when it comes to beatmaking. If you strip away the humor, the songs on *Da Album* are rather straightforward hip-hop, albeit underground hip-hop with a noticeably lo-fi aesthetic. And in terms of rhyming, the Sucka MCs are quite dexterous, not what you'd expect from a bunch of white boys from Iowa. However, it's the constant onslaught of humor and antics that make the Sucka MCs seem so uncanny. Sure, Biz Markie and the Beastie Boys were goofy at times, but none were this relentlessly comic—and not comic in a funny, ha-ha-ha way but rather in a downright silly, wierdo way. If you like this sort of "smart" humor and you like underground hip-hop, there's a good chance you'll like this album. —*Jason Birchmeier*

Suga Free

b. Los Angeles, CA
Hip-Hop, Gangsta Rap, G-Funk, Hardcore Rap

This West Coast gangsta rapper's career got off to a slow start despite a promising debut album for Polygram produced by acclaimed producer/rapper DJ Quik—1997's *Street Gospel*—that ultimately proved disappointing. In 2000, Suga Free returned to the spotlight with high-profile guest appearances on Xzibit's *Restless* and Snoop Dogg's *Tha Last Meal*. —*Jason Birchmeier*

● **Street Gospel** / May 20, 1997 / Laid Black ✦✦✦✦

Suga Free's debut album *Street Gospel* is a competent collection of street-level, hardcore G-funk, highlighted by DJ Quik's savvy production. Although Suga Free is a strong rapper, he isn't particularly distinctive, and he's often given pedestrian backing music, which makes the album a little tedious. Still, he's charismatic enough to make the best songs, like the single "If You Stay Ready," powerful and that nearly makes the album worthwhile. —*Leo Stanley*

The Sugarhill Gang

f. 1979, New York, NY, **db.** 1985
Group / Old School Rap

Though the Sugarhill Gang inaugurated the history of recorded hip-hop with their single "Rapper's Delight," a multi-platinum seller and radio hit in 1979, the group was cooked up to cash in on a supposed novelty item. Music-industry producer and label-owner Sylvia Robinson had become aware of the massive hip-hop block parties occurring around the New York area during the late '70s, so she gathered three local rappers (Master Gee, Wonder Mike, and Big Bank Hank) to record a single. Infectious and catchy, "Rapper's Delight" borrowed the break from Chic's "Good Times" and became a worldwide hit, eventually selling more than eight million copies. Most industry people figured rap for a short-lived trend, and though they were dead wrong, the Sugarhill Gang certainly didn't carry the torch; despite several modest hits ("8th Wonder," "Apache") the trio faded quickly and was gone by the mid-'80s, only returning in 1999 with *Jump on It*, a rap album for children. *—John Bush*

The Sugarhill Gang / 1980 / Sugar Hill ✦✦✦✦

Although the Sugarhill Gang didn't invent hip-hop, it was the first rap act to have a huge international hit. Released in 1979, "Rapper's Delight" was millions of listeners' first exposure to hip-hop—before that, very few people outside of New York even knew what hip-hop was. The Sugarhill Gang was also among the first rap acts to record a full-length LP; when this self-titled debut album came out in 1980, the vast majority of old school MCs were only providing 12" singles. So *The Sugarhill Gang* is a historically important album even though it is a bit uneven. While "Rapper's Delight" and "Rapper's Reprise" (which features the Sequence, hip-hop's first all-female group) are excellent, most of the material is merely decent. And the ironic thing is that half of the songs aren't even rap. "Bad News Don't Bother Me" and "Here I Am," both of which find the Sugarhill Gang singing instead of rapping, are romantic R&B slow jams- and "Sugarhill Groove" is a sleek disco-funk number that hints at Roy Ayers. So this LP can hardly be called the work of hip-hop purists; in 1980, Sugarhill Records leader Sylvia Robinson (herself a veteran R&B singer) evidently felt that putting out an all-rap album would be risky. But, while *The Sugarhill Gang* isn't a masterpiece, it's still an album that hip-hop historians will find interesting. *—Alex Henderson*

8th Wonder / 1982 / Sugar Hill ✦✦✦

While they didn't garner the critical praise of their label cohorts, Grandmaster Flash & the Furious Five, the Sugarhill Gang still produced their share of memorable slices of early hip-hop. Helping to bring Sylvia Robinson's Sugar Hill Records into the limelight, the label's namesake group erred more on the funk side of the hip-hop equation, plying a steamy, all-night mix of go-go grooves, straight funk singing, and rapping. *8th Wonder* features the hits "Apache" and the title track, as well as such slick funk burners as "Hot Hot Summer Day" and the incredible bit of uptown dance alchemy "Funk Box" (shades of Prince here). *8th Wonder* may not be as good a starting point for newcomers as roundups on Rhino and Sequel, but it certainly will be one fans won't want to miss. *—Stephen Cook*

● The Best of Sugarhill Gang / Jul. 16, 1996 / Rhino ✦✦✦✦✦

Sugarhill Gang's biggest hits are collected on this single-disc compilation. In addition to "Rapper's Delight"—the first rap single to reach the pop Top Ten—the group's seven other R&B hits are included on the disc, plus three other singles that never made the charts. All of the songs are presented in their original 12" versions. Not all of the material is first-rate—in retrospective, the group's old school groove tended to be a little simplistic, monotonous, and too polished, while their rhymes were frequently stilted and sometimes just outright silly—but this music, especially "Rapper's Delight," is important historically. Most casual fans of old school hip-hop will be content with purchasing "Rapper's Delight" on a various artists collection, but for those wanting to dig deeper into the trio's history, *The Best of Sugarhill Gang* is a definitive retrospective. *—Stephen Thomas Erlewine*

Showdown: Sugarhill Gang Vs. Grandmaster Flash / Feb. 2, 1999 / Rhino ✦✦✦✦

On paper, *The Showdown: The Sugarhill Gang vs. Grandmaster Flash and the Furious Five* seems like a good idea. Take two of the greatest old school hip-hop groups, pair off six of their best tracks each, offer commentary and insight from Chuck D and Ice-T, and then see who wins. It's a cute, clever idea, but halfway through the album, it becomes tiring—you no longer find the "boxing match" amusing, you just want to hear the music, especially since the music is so good. Of course, it's possible to program around the sketches, and then you'll just have a really good collection (including a previously unreleased cut from the Sugarhill Gang, "One for the $") but most listeners will be happier with collections devoted to either artist. *—Stephen Thomas Erlewine*

Jump on It! / Apr. 6, 1999 / Rhino ✦✦✦

The long-time reissue label Rhino Records made a transition from faithful historian to active participant in the world of modern music with *Jump on It!*,

the first new album by the Sugarhill Gang in more than 15 years. Combining their recent emphasis on old school rap and children's records, label executives brought Big Bank Hank, Master G and Wonder Mike back together to record an album of updated *Schoolhouse Rock*-type raps. Each of the ten songs are message tracks, beginning with the title track, a shout-out to kids that they're never too young to start reaching for their dreams. Other tracks focus on either specific educational subjects ("ABC's," "The Vowels," "Last Day of School") or on subjects more generally beneficial for kids' well-being ("Fireworks," "Sugar Hill Groove," "My Little Playmate"). As fun and educational as *Jump on It!* is for kids, though, this album is a non-starter for hip-hop fans. The trio's raps haven't progressed beyond (and may have even fallen back from) "Rapper's Delight," and from the sounds of it, *Jump on It!* was recorded in much the same way as all the classic material from Sugar Hill Records—the music credits go to the Sugar Hill House Band, though individual members aren't listed. It's a much better tack than trying to update the Sugarhill Gang for the late-'90s hip-hop world, but this children's album doesn't make any kind of transition to adult audiences. *—Keith Farley*

Sunz of Man

Group / Hip-Hop, Hardcore Rap, Underground Rap
Another of the many outgrowths of the Wu-Tang Clan, rappers the Sunz of Man comprised 60 Second Assassin, Killah Priest, Prodigal Sunn, and Hell Razah. Their debut LP, *The Last Shall Be First*, appeared in 1998 on Red Ant. *Saviorz Day* followed in 2002 for Riviera. *—Jason Ankeny*

● The Last Shall Be First / Jul. 21, 1998 / Red Ant ✦✦✦✦

To the ever-expanding Wu-Tang family comes the Sunz of Man, comprised of Hell Razah, 60 Second Assassin, Prodigal Sunn and Killah Priest, the only member with a full-fledged solo career. Like many latter-day Wu projects, there's a certain familiarity about the album that works against it—though each member has their own distinct lyrical style, the music itself becomes a little similar. Sunz of Man realize that this is a problem and have hired outside producers like Wyclef Jean to add a different dimension to their sound. It works to a certain extent, but *The Last Shall Be First* doesn't quite offer a new dimension to the Wu formula. Of course, that doesn't mean it's a bad album. The Wu family remains the most consistent and adventurous outfit in all of hip-hop, and there are certainly a number of rhymes and sonic textures that are quite intriguing, but *The Last Shall Be First* isn't essential for anyone outside hardcore Wu fans. *—Stephen Thomas Erlewine*

Saviorz Day / Sep. 3, 2002 / Riviera ✦✦✦

It's good to see Sunz of Man still making albums. Their songs have never been too popular on the radio, and they've never really tried to appeal to the mainstream either, even while being part of the Wu-Tang Clan. Ghostface Killah makes his presence felt on this album on a couple of tracks, a nice addition, and although there isn't a whole lot new here, their music still has that grimy and gritty feel that it's always had. Still, even the Sunz of Man have made the evolution from strictly street talk to the money game, as seen on their track "Banksta'z." Many parts of the album have a slow-moving, methodical style; the beats are almost too slow to bob your head to. RZA comes through with a verse, Ghostface collaborates on a few tracks, Madam D does as well, and there's a really surprising guest verse by West Coast rapper MC Eiht. Method Man shows up for the outro and doesn't drop a verse, which won't make sense to more than a few listeners. Still, the record has a complete feel with RZA and Fatal Son on production, and is a worthy addition to the Wu-Tang family of records. *—Brad Mills*

Supreme NTM

f. 1991, France
Group / Foreign Rap, Hardcore Rap
The hard-hitting, frequently polemical French hip-hop group Supreme NTM was formed in 1989 by Dee Nasty, Joeystarr, and Koolshen with their DJ, Détonateur S. They debuted one year later with a track on the compilation *Rappattitude* and their first single, "Le Monde de Demain." *Authentik*, the Supreme NTM debut full-length, appeared in 1991, and the group made their American live debut later that year. The album was followed two years later by *1993... J'appuis Sur la Gâchette*, which brought them to the attention of the French gendarmes (a la N.W.A and Ice-T/Body Count) with a song named "Police." The group's third album, 1995's *Paris Sous Les Bombes*, became their most successful, but also earned them a fresh bout of controversy. The song

"Plus Jamais Ça" was an anti-National Front (the fascist/anti-immigrant movement led by Jean Marie Le Pen) broadside that got Supreme NTM six-month prison sentences for playing it at a concert in a city in southern France with a just-elected National Front mayor (shades of Public Enemy). *Suprême NTM* followed in 1998, eclipsing its predecessor in sales and earning raves for its inclusion of a new generation of French rappers (like Lord Kossity). —*John Bush*

● **Paris Sous les Bombes** / Mar. 1995 / Epic ✦✦✦

On 1996's *Paris Sous Les Bombes*, Supreme NTM continued their vision of sonic terrorism with their third album, *Paris Sous les Bombes*. The controversial "Plus Jamais Ça"—which got Supreme NTM six-month prison sentences for playing it—doesn't *sound* that provocative or wild musically (outside of the repeated sax wail sample as a hook), but Public Enemy's sound collage technique is the main model here. It's a gentler collage since French hip-hop is generally smoother, with acid jazz touches that reflect the French language tones that main rappers Kool Shen and Joeystarr fit into an effective flow. Both "Tout N'est Pas Si Facile," a longing look at the true-believers-only early days of French hip-hop, and "La Reve" are very mellow and nicely acid jazzy. With its bass riff pumping hard, "Nouvelle Ecole" is a throwback to the funky good-time, old school flavor that marked the *J'appuis* album. Only the title track matches it for forcefulness with its bomb-shelter vocals almost whispered beneath a scratched voices and noise mix. But the groove to "Pass Pas Le Oinj"—a mix of scratchy vintage vinyl samples, turntable scratches, acid jazz keyboard touches and mellow bass—kicks off a strong closing rush. Until then, *Paris Sous Les Bombes* suffers from a problem common to international hip-hop artists with listeners outside the native tongue. If you can't catch the drift of the lyrics and the music is subtle and not built on familiar dancefloor models, the verbal flow of the raps is about the only thing left to plug into. This is a good disc, valuable for anyone interested in the global spread of hip-hop, but the more musically immediate and physical *1993…J'appuis Sur la Gâchette* may be a better introduction to Supreme NTM for non-French speakers. —*Don Snowden*

Survival Soundz

f. New York

Group / Hip-Hop, Soul, Urban, Fusion, Alternative Rap, Jazz-Rap

The eclectic New York City band Survival Soundz—once described as an ultra-Black Talking Heads—fused a wide range of Afro-centric musical influences into an enticing urban brew that found a devoted following in the '90s urban underground scene. The band initially started out as the brainchild of two Caribbean transplants, bassist Jomo 'Itembe' Jones and drummer Jamaki Knight, who had moved from their native St. Croix to New York in the late '80s to attend The New School as undergraduates. In 1989, they discovered sampling and formed the hip-hop duo Rude Kulcha, recording an album, *Freedom Boots*, with the help of featured musicians such as Afrika Baby Bam of the Jungle Brothers, Bernie Worrell, and Warren Hayes of the Allman Brothers Band. Songs such as "Revolution Cries," "Soul Skanking," and "Rag-gaDelic Moisture" earned substantial underground airplay and acclaim and set the groundwork for the self-coined concept, RootzBOP, a term used to describe the underlying oneness of all musical forms—the sound that manifests itself as an amalgamation of musical genres. Shortly thereafter, with the intention of moving beyond samplers and studio musicians, Jones and Knight set out to expand Rude Kulcha into a true live band. Guitarist Tesfa Zawdie had met Jones and Knight in 1990 while playing lead guitar with Watusi and rhythm guitar with Mau Mau. He joined them in early 1992, bringing a new band name, Survival Soundz. The following year Joshua Levitt (soprano & tenor saxophone, flutes, keyboards) was added to the lineup, as was alto saxophonist/clarinetist Andrew 'Groovie' Joseph, whom Levitt and Knight had met at the Warren Smith Composers Workshop and quickly asked to join the group. Survival Soundz played the New York City underground circuit throughout the early '90s at spots such as SOB's and Birdland, developing a strong reputation and honing both their RootzBOP concept and their sound. Lead vocalist Carla Gomez, formerly of the Atlanta band FA, rounded out the lineup in 1994 and completed the band's stylistic transformation to Survival Soundz. The group continued playing throughout New York for the next few years, developing original material, sharing bills with artists such as Public Enemy, Roy Ayers, Goodie Mob and Montell Jordan, and also acting as a backing unit for the likes of Dr. Octagon and the Last Poets. As 1997 rolled around, tired of doing the normal gigs around New York and at the Lyricist Lounge, Survival Soundz began their own forum, Avant Yard, a multimedia extravaganza promoted by the band on one Saturday every month at the TriBeCa gallery ThoughtForms, and featuring artwork, DJ sets, and live performances from Survival Soundz and whatever guest artists showed up, from Mos Def to Black Thought to spoken word poets Jessica Care Moore and Saul Williams. That same year, they contributed to the Mutant Sound System compilation, *Mutant Beatz*, as well as the first volume of *Land of Baboon*. The next year they composed the interludes that appeared between songs on *Lyricist Lounge, Vol. 1* and also recorded their debut longplayer, *RootzBOP Melodies*, produced and released by the band itself through their website, www.survivalsoundz.com. —*Stanton Swihart*

● **Rootz Bop Melodies** / 1998 / Survival ✦✦✦✦✦

Throughout the '90s, numerous artists were hailed as progenitors of a hip-hop/jazz amalgam, but Survival Soundz is the only artist to find a seamless nexus, not only developing their own distinctive mix in the process but also christening the sound "Rootzbop." Their first independently released album, *RootzBop Melodies*, is a representation of that sound, a textured blend of roots dub, hip-hop, sweet soul, and jazz, with additional hints of Caribbean and African music. Atmospherically, the band hearkens back to the wildly eclectic urban scene of the early '70s, while their sound is immersed in many of the sonic touchstones of the '90s. The music, however, is timeless, indebted to most urban-derived forms that came before it, but dependent on and encumbered by none of them. It results in a loose, sexy, in-the-pocket groove that is irresistibly seductive and honey-coated. It's easy to see why Survival Soundz felt compelled to give their sound its own designation (or as they put it themselves, create another branch on a very ancient tree); it resists and ultimately rejects any description forced on it. They move from genre to genre with effortlessness, making the different stylistic determinations sound like nothing so much as arbitrary niches created for convenience's sake. The album smelts music into a true liquid coalescence. The music itself is both the sunny warmth of day and the steely darkness of night, sonically but also thematically, with both motifs echoing throughout the record. It moves from the breezily upbeat "Wind" and "Mornin' Sunshine" to the late-night dub and jazz of "Blue Dub" and "Twilight," respectively. The heart of the music originates from the city, and would be unthinkable coming from any other context, but there is something inherently organic and earthy in its execution. *RootzBop Melodies* strikes a tricky balance between otherworldly new age sentiment, spiritual determination, and conscientious sociopolitical observations, as on the anthemic lesson in the history of slavery, "Peace a de Rock." On "Wind" vocalist C sings about a flower poking through the concrete of the ghetto, and that, it turns out, is exactly what Survival Soundz represents. [The album is available directly from the band at http://www.survivalsoundz.com.] —*Stanton Swihart*

Da Survivors

f. Memphis, TN

Group / Gangsta Rap, Hardcore Rap, Southern Rap

A small collective out of Memphis, Da Survivors debuted in 2000 with the album *Blood, Sweat and Tearz* on Dig Dat Records. The record featured work from Project Pimp, AYG, and G-Nutts, among others. —*Brad Mills*

● **Blood, Sweat and Tearz** / Jun. 13, 2000 / Dig Dat ✦✦✦

Hard beats, fast delivery, and appearances by some other more popular artists come together on this album. A relatively unknown group from Tennessee, Da Survivors manage to pull off a good first effort propelled mainly by the popularity of Southern rap music in 2000. Sounding like a morph between the distinct sounds of No Limit, Cash Money, and Outkast, there isn't much left in the way of an original sound. Artists featured on this album include Project Pimp, AYG, G-Nutts, Pistol and a few others. —*Brad Mills*

Sway & King Tech

Group / Hip-Hop, Hardcore Rap, Underground Rap, Turntablism, Club/Dance

The hosts of the nationally syndicated radio program *Wake Up Show*, the Bay Area-based duo of Sway and King Tech also enjoyed rap careers of their own; as Flynamic Force, they released a self-titled LP before rejecting the name in time for 1990's *Concrete Jungle*. Several volumes of *Wake Up Show*-related releases have been released on the 880 label. —*Jason Ankeny*

Concrete Jungle / 1990 / Giant ✦✦✦

Concrete Jungle is a good example of a very musical rap CD that isn't remarkable but grabs your attention with its attractive sound. King Tech is the one who can take credit for the album's appealing and high-tech sound—as half of the early-'90s duo Sway & King Tech, he handles all of the producing and arranging and programs all of the synthesizers and drum machines. Although Sway is a competent rapper, most of his lyrics are run-of-the-mill boasting fare; it's Tech's sleek production that makes you take notice of "Future Source," "Let Me See You Move" and "In Control." However, the Northern California duo does get into sociopolitical territory on "Time for Peace" and the title song. Tech isn't in a class with Dr. Dre or Mantronik, but the album makes it clear that he knows his way around a studio. *Concrete Jungle* should have made Tech well known as a hip-hop producer, but surprisingly, the disc was far from a big seller. —*Alex Henderson*

● **This or That** / Jun. 15, 1999 / Interscope ✦✦✦✦

Testing the waters of major-label mix-tape swapping is a natural progression for legendary West Coast radio show pioneers Sway and Tech. While Funkmaster Flex originated it and DJ Clue reinvented it, the Wake Up Show duo of Sway and Tech, up to this point, are the undisputed champs at it. The bi-coastal coalition "The Anthem" merges a bevy of lyrical assassins into one tightly knit assemblage of unity. The list of MCs assembled is enough to satisfy anybody as RZA, Eminem, Xzibit, Kool G Rap, KRS-One, Pharoe Monch, Jayo Felony, Chino XL, Tech 9ne, and Sway all play hot potato with the mic. Guru of Gang Starr uses his monotone vocals to rough up MCs on the enticing "NY Nigus." Bringing nothing but "Underground Tactics," Heltah Skeltah, Planet Asia, and Crooked Eye breathe life into one of Sway and Tech's crisp staccato tracks. Eminem was supplied with a less than stellar broken Casio keyboard track, but his neurotic deviant wordplay saves "Get You Mad." Ill Advised and Rasheed team up with the Roots, Black Thought, and Malik B for a Bomb Squad-like rendition of "1986." Jurassic 5's stock continues to rise, and their chemistry is exquisite on "Improvise." Juice Crew affiliates Big Daddy Kane and Kool G Rap team up with the MC that other MCs love to hate—Chino XL—on "Three to the Dome." A hungry and upstart Dirty Unit gives a rhyming-in-the-park element to "Clientele," which features a well-placed Nas voice sample. Digitized chants signal RZA's entrance on the sonic "Belly of the Beast," while the Dilated Peoples build with fellow Likwit crew member Defari on "Dilated Remix." Supervising the LP's ambiance, DJ Revolution admirably blends and cuts up sets of old school and contemporary favorites that would keep any dancefloor packed. Sway and Tech have little trouble getting the best out of their hired hands of proven vets and thirsty underground talent, keeping them one step ahead of their competition. —*Matt Conaway*

Wake Up Show: Freestyles, Vol. 1 / Aug. 21, 2001 / 880 ✦✦✦✦

Sweatshop Union

f. 2000, Vancouver, Canada

Group / Underground Rap

An MC collective based in Vancouver, Sweatshop Union was formed in 2000 by a trio of groups—Dirty Circus, I.B.S. (Innocent By Standers), and Creative Mindz—plus solo rapper Kyprios, who all wanted to cut costs and improve efficiency. They self-released their self-titled debut, then watched the buzz take over and earn the album a second release on Battle Axe, the label run by Mad Child from Swollen Members. —*John Bush*

● **Sweatshop Union** / Sep. 3, 2002 / Battle Axe ✦✦✦

This ensemble cast of Canadian rappers and hip-hop artists join forces on this interesting and sometimes exciting offering. Although the opening *Nothing Makes Sense* is more of a spoken word trip-hop tune that misses the mark, the Latin touches on *Union Dues* are far more pleasing. Resembling a contemporary Santana effort, the tune works quite well despite a mediocre chorus. The backdrop of Joe Cocker on "Feelin' Alright" results in Kyprios giving a quality performance. He also does a good job with a frantic track, "The Revolution." A mild and relaxing tempo is found on several songs, but occasionally the song suffers, especially on "The Humans' Race." Other tracks like "President's Choice," named after a Canadian "no-name" brand, are improved by subtle horns. "Don't Mind Us" is perhaps the worst of the dozen tracks, a lewd and generally dumb tune. The album's highlight is the up-tempo and funky "The Truth We Speak" by Dirty Circus. Artists like Buck 65 come to mind during "A Wrinkle in Time" by Innocent Bystanders, another selling point for the record. —*Jason MacNeil*

Sweet Cookie

b. Baltimore, MD

R&B

Born and raised in Baltimore, Sweet Cookie is an obscure female rapper who was active in the 1980s. Cookie never became well-known nationally, although she managed to attract some attention in her home town and nearby Washington, D.C. Favoring a feminine, sexy image rather than a tough, combative image à la MC Lyte, Cookie looked more like an R&B singer than a rapper—and in fact, her music did have a lot of R&B appeal. Comparable to Salt-N-Pepa and Whodini, Cookie's music was melodic, commercial, and R&B-minded but still have an edge. It was around 1983 that Cookie met her mentor Irving S. Lee Jr., a Baltimore-based producer/songwriter who wrote all of her material and brought her to the attention of the small Checkpoint label. In 1984, Checkpoint released Cookie's debut single, "Heartbreaker"; the record did OK locally, and Cookie became an opening act for major rappers like Run-D.M.C. and Whodini when they performed in Baltimore. Then, in 1987, Cookie signed with the Fantasy-distributed Danya Records, which was doing quite well with Doug E. Fresh at the time. "Mind Your Business," her first Danya single, became a small local hit, selling about 25,000 copies around Baltimore and Washington, D.C. Lee wrote and produced "Mind Your Business" as well as everything else on Cookie's debut album, *Do You Wanna Dance*, which Danya released in late 1987. The LP didn't do much outside of Baltimore and Washington, D.C., and Cookie never recorded a second album. —*Alex Henderson*

● **Do You Wanna Dance** / 1987 / Danya ✦✦✦

When Sweet Cookie's debut album, *Do You Wanna Dance*, came out in late 1987, many New York MCs were still insisting that the Big Apple would always be the capitol of hip-hop. But the success of rappers from Los Angeles (Ice-T, N.W.A), Oakland (Too Short), Philadelphia (Will Smith, aka the Fresh Prince) and Miami (2 Live Crew) made it clear that a successful MC didn't have to come from one of the five boroughs. So Baltimore resident Sweet Cookie figured that she had a shot as well. Outside of Baltimore and nearby Washington, D.C., *Do You Wanna Dance* received very little attention; nonetheless, it's a decent effort that is commercial without being toothless. This LP isn't hardcore rap á la MC Lyte or Roxanne Shante; sleek, R&B-drenched items like "The Other Woman" and "Want You Back" were obviously designed to cross over to urban contemporary audiences. But at the same time, *Do You Wanna Dance* isn't without grit. Though much of the material is fun and lighthearted, Cookie tackles social issues on the poignant "Ricky" and the angry "Chains on Me." The people that Cookie inspires comparisons to are Salt-N-Pepa and Whodini; like those New Yorkers, she demonstrates that a rapper can have a lot of R&B appeal and still be substantial. If, in 1987, you were the type of R&B fan who had only a casual interest in rap but appreciated Salt-N-Pepa and Whodini, there was no reason why you couldn't get into Sweet Cookie as well—that is, if you had a chance to hear her. Outside of Baltimore and nearby Washington D.C., the vast majority of rap fans didn't even know that this record existed. Nonetheless, *Do You Wanna Dance* is a pleasant footnote in the history of 1980s hip-hop. —*Alex Henderson*

Sweet Tee (Toi Jackson)

b. Queens, NY

Pop-Rap

Queens rapper Sweet Tee (born Toi Jackson) debuted with *It's Tee Time* in 1989. Hurby "Love Bug" Astor produced what was a strictly pop-oriented session that generated only brief response. —*Ron Wynn*

● **It's Tee Time** / 1989 / Profile ✦✦✦✦

It's Tee Time compiles Sweet Tee's initial pop-rap singles with some new material, all of it produced by Hurby Azor and the Invincibles. Tee's rapping style is an elastic one, comfortable in both the self-explanatory "On the Smooth Tip" to the more house-oriented "I Got Da Feelin." The record's flaw is the production, which simply lacks originality. —*Jason Ankeny*

Rob Swift

DJ, Scratching / Hip-Hop, Underground Rap, Turntablism, Illbient

Turntablist hero Rob Swift debuted with one of the top scratching groups of the '90s, the X-Men (later known as the X-Ecutioners). A mix-tape favorite, after one album with the group Swift released his own wide debut, *Soulful Fruit*, in 1997 on Stones Throw, followed by *The Ablist* in 1999. Thereafter, he released a succession of mixes for Triple Threat (*Airwave Invasion*), Tableturns (*Sound Event*), and Six Degrees (*Under the Influence*). —*John Bush*

● **Soulful Fruit** / May 13, 1997 / Stones Throw ✦✦✦✦
After hearing *Soulful Fruit*, it's hard to tell whether Rob Swift is a better composer or turntable wizard, because he's melded the two so well on his first solo album. A member of the X-Men, Swift is the kind of DJ who makes you wonder why the turntablist element is so often neglected on hip-hop albums. The turntable is undeniably at the very core of hip-hop, and with a skill set as refined as Swift's, it just doesn't make sense why more MCs aren't looking to talented DJs to help them produce that elusive classic album. This record extends itself to many forms of music, including hip-hop, jazz, funk, breaks, turntablism, and soul, and accomplishes what few artists have been able to do over a full album—create a solid musical balance. There is a 14-minute live battle between Swift and Rahzel (the now famous beatboxer from the Philadelphia-based Roots crew), pitting beatboxing against turntablism and thereby creating something truly exciting to listen to. —*Brad Mills*

The Ablist / Feb. 23, 1999 / Asphodel ✦✦✦✦
Directly influenced by Herbie Hancock's "Rockit," an early melding of jazz and hip-hop, *The Ablist* is Swift's attempt to introduce the turntable as a virtuosic instrument capable of being played with the same feeling and skill as any other instrument. He uses the turntable in various contexts, from solo scratching to full band. Much of the album is stellar jazz-inflected hip-hop, even if it falls somewhat short of the incredibly high goals of its composer, but those high goals are what make *The Ablist* such a thrilling listen. Many songs use the turntable in ways that have not been explored. On "What Would You Do?," Swift's scratches act as a sort of instrumental answer to the question posed. "Fusion Beats" shows that the turntable can be a jamming instrument as well, with some nice interplay with keyboards on what is actually some pretty straight jazz. Turntables are also brought into a full-band context on "Modern Day Music" and "All that Scratching Is Making Me Rich!" "Modern Day Music" features the band's three MCs and Swift's DJ Premier-like cutting up of words and phrases over a deep groove. Swift's spare style of cutting often recalls Premier, and his production skills are similar to Large Professor, emphasizing rolling bass and swinging but steady beats. Overall, Swift has crafted a strong personal statement. The album echoes old school skills without devolving into a pastiche of past hip-hop styles or following commercial rap trends. Instead, *The Ablist* suggests directions in which hip-hop can go to remain viable. The album doesn't entirely follow through on all its promises and Swift doesn't always reach his goals, which can make the album a frustrating listen at times. Overall, however, *The Ablist* redefines the turntable as a musical instrument that can bring new dimensions to both structured and improvised music, and it shows that Swift is capable of some incisive music that works outside the normal confines of turntablist music. —*Stanton Swihart*

Airwave Invasion / Jun. 8, 2001 / Triple Threat ✦✦✦✦
The mix-tape world always expects a little bit more from anyone in the X-Ecutioners camp, mainly because they haven't disappointed in the past. Rob Swift makes normal DJs embarrassed to hear themselves, but is an inspiration by his own example. He's the kind of DJ that can make an entirely new beat with two records, and is a true force behind where turntablism is and will be beyond 2001. Swift takes more of a funk and soul ride with this record, plus his usual breakbeats and skits. There's also some key appearances on the Future Flava radio show hosted by legendary producers Pete Rock and Marley Marl. Those that are looking for the latest, hottest hip-hop records cut and diced will have to look elsewhere, but with the number of those mixes floating around, that kind of thing won't be hard to find. What's found here is a fresh little break from the norm by a DJ whose name is synonymous with turntable skill. —*Brad Mills*

Sound Event / Oct. 2, 2002 / Tableturns ✦✦✦
Turntablist Rob Swift gets a little help and inspiration aplenty from his friends and heroes on *Sound Event*, an explosive and intelligent collection of wicked scratching, in-the-pocket beats, startling imagery, and whiz-kid wordplay. Recalling his first impressive encounter with stream-of-conscious rapper Supernatural, Swift passes the mic over to the freestyling MC to herald the second coming (i.e., Swift's second solo release), tethering the titles of each track into a poetic diatribe. "2 3 Break" incorporates kinetic free jazz riffing atop a hypnotic drum loop that resonates with the rattle of a loose snare. With Bob James, D-Styles, and Swift's mom, Clara Aguilar, onboard, "Salsa Scratch" tears down the barrier between Latino tradition and hip-hop. "The

Ghetto" introduces a Jimi Hendrix-like rhythm guitar motif punctuated by a legato horn solo as a canvass for a fierce dialogue detailing the hard truths of growing up on the wrong side of the tracks. Progressive and engaging, *Sound Event* is as important as its title suggests. —*Tom Semioli*

Under the Influence / Feb. 4, 2003 / Six Degrees ✦✦✦✦
The latest and best entry in the Six Degrees label's *Under the Influence* series is a DJ mix by the well-respected X-ecutioners alumnus and East Coast Turntable Champion Rob Swift, who has selected a brilliant program of rare vintage funk and soul recordings by such obscure masters of the genre as the Vibrettes, Chuck Carbo and the Explosions, along with more recent material by Davey DMX and DJ Quick and a couple of tracks from Afro-Cuban vocalist Bobi Céspedes. As with any good turntablist set, half the fun is the source material itself, all of which works together as a sort of historic kaleidoscope of funk, and half of it is in Swift's artful juxtapositions and virtuosic cutting and scratching. Swift is maybe just a bit too respectful and restrained in his approach to the really old school stuff, but he cuts loose (pun intended) with a vengeance on Davey DMX's "One for the Treble", Charlie Chase's "We're Gonna Need a Little Scratch" and, especially, the classic "Man Marley Marl". Toward the end, Swift gets busy with a Latin feel on his remix of Bobi Céspedes' "Lenu", which makes for a nice rhythmic and textural change-up. The best way to improve on this album would have been to make it last more than 45 minutes. —*Rick Anderson*

Swizz Beatz (Kasseem Dean)

b. The Bronx, NY
Producer, Vocals / East Coast Rap, Hardcore Rap
Swizz Beatz was born Kasseem Dean in the Bronx area of New York City. He relocated to Atlanta as a teenager, where he started to DJ parties. When his relatives became involved with the Ruff Ryders label, he began to produce tracks at the tender age of 16. Forgoing the practice of using samples, he used real instruments whenever possible and tried to accentuate the performance aspect of his music. He produced countless rap and R&B acts, from DMX to Eve, but he never really got much credit for his work. It wasn't until his first solo album, 2002's *G.H.E.T.T.O. Stories*, that he started to get notices for his production style and interesting ideas. —*Bradley Torreano*

● **Presents G.H.E.T.T.O. Stories** / Dec. 10, 2002 / DreamWorks ✦✦✦✦
The full-length debut for Ruff Ryders trackmaster Swizz Beatz is that rare thing in the rap world: a record with a single production style. Considering most mainstream rappers hire out two producers for every three tracks they release, hearing an entire LP with a uniform sound is as welcome as it is surprising. Still, Swizz Beatz' Kasseem Dean does vary his sound a bit, and experiments more than any you'd hear on a randomly selected 17 of his productions from other artists' albums. *G.H.E.T.T.O. Stories* finds him moving from quasi-acoustic soul (with the LL Cool J feature "Ghetto Love") to a few in the usual Ruff Ryders style (for Jadakiss on "Big Business" and Eve on "Island Spice") to a ragga track with Bounty Killer, but also introduces Ja Rule to Metallica for a heavy metal extravaganza called "We Did It Again." The highlight "Endalay" features Busta Rhymes livening up what would've been a comparatively bland production on its own, and Styles hits on all cylinders for "Good Times." Dean is actually a great rapper too, able to command the mic and the mixing board for three tracks here—he should've given himself more. As it is, despite the great sounds and great features, too much of *G.H.E.T.T.O. Stories* finds one of the hottest producers in hip-hop resting on his laurels. —*John Bush*

Swollen Members

f. Vancouver, Ontario, Canada
Group / Hip-Hop, Underground Rap, West Coast Rap
The meeting of two West Coast rappers fuelled this talented Canadian band. In 1996, Mad Child was a solo artist performing in San Francisco when he returned to his hometown of Vancouver. There he met Prevail, who was gaining attention for his energetic live shows and abilities. The two joined forces and headed to San Diego to perform at the annual B-Boy Summit. The group was initiated into the Rock Steady Crew, one of only three bands to do so. Following this, the group released three independent singles before releasing *Balance*, their debut effort in 1999 on Battle Axe Records. A world tour and hundreds of performances followed. In 2001, the band released its second album, *Bad Dreams*. The same year they received a Juno Award for Best Rap Recording for *Balance*. In 2002, the band performed with Nelly Furtado and won a second Juno Award for Best Rap Recording. Their music has been featured on

soundtracks, computer games, and other outlets. They've also worked with members of the Beat Junkies and Jurassic 5, among others. —*Jason MacNeil*

Balance / May 31, 1999 / Jazz Fudge ◆◆◆◆
Romancing the elements of nature, the witching-hour lyricism of the Swollen Members (Madchild and Prevail) delves deeply into topics that have yet to be captured or pontificated on wax. SM are shaman-like oddities in this game, and judging from their topic matter alone, they would seem to fit in more at a Renaissance festival than in hip-hop's machismo-filled atmosphere. Prevail and Madchild divulge their cloak-and-dagger lyrics in a highly animated manner, and their chemistry is very developed for a group embarking on their freshman effort. Western guitar riffs and staccato high hats augment the duo's mental gymnastics on "Out of Range," and the Alchemist leads a one-man symphony on the possessed "Horrified Nights." Swollen Members enlist a stellar supporting cast throughout, with Dilated Peoples ("Counterparts"), Evidence ("Bottle Rocket"), Everlast, Divine Styler, and Del's Hieroglyphics ambiance, prevalent on "Left Field" with Unicorn. The witchdoctors of hip-hop are definitely at the forefront of developing a new style, and after listening to the Swollen Member's debut, your view of hip-hop may never be the same. —*Matt Conaway*

● **Bad Dreams** / Nov. 13, 2001 / Battle Axe ◆◆◆◆◆
The second LP from L.A.-/Vancouver-based Swollen Members is a natural and overwhelmingly positive evolution from 1999's *Balance*. An 18-track movement with banner production, an incredible lineup, vital energy, and a quiet confidence rarely found in hip-hop, *Bad Dreams* is an inspired and unique set from front to back. With appearances from Jurassic 5's Chali 2Na, Evidence, DJ Babu, Planet Asia, DJ Revolution, Joey Chavez, Son Doobie, Moka Only, and other key members of the Battle Axe crew, the album both takes itself extremely seriously and throws a great party at the same time. The record's highlights are many, though the appearance of the highly acclaimed 2NA with Dilated Peoples' Evidence on "Full Contact" is easily the record's biggest asset in a paramount rap-along collaboration. "Take It Back" and "Total Package" feature music from the sensational DJ Revolution, who makes funk-hop sound groundbreaking all over again. And while their rotating DJs and producers make the whole set progressive and lively, it's the tag-team duo of Mad Child and Prevail who pull everything back into SM's familiar fold. —*Nic Kincaid*

Monsters in the Closet / Nov. 12, 2002 / Nettwerk ◆◆◆
This trawl through the vaults of the Vancouver-based hip-hop collective Swollen Members is unusual for a collection of B-sides and leftovers—in that it ends up being more forward- than backward-looking. That's because the underground stalwarts—Mad Child and Prevail, plus recent addition Moka Only—decided to record a few new songs to fill out the disc, which ends up pointing the way to possible commercial successes previously undreamed of. "Breath," with its hook from Nelly Furtado and a juicy R&B foundation, could slot comfortably between the latest Murder Inc. and P. Diddy hits on a mix tape, while the manic "Battle Axe Exclusive" rages along in true Eminem fashion. Such moments won't necessarily be a pleasant surprise for the Members' devoted fanbase, but the remainder of *Monsters in the Closet* provides a generous helping of the less-conventional musical ambition that has won the group comparisons to Jurassic 5, Dilated Peoples, and other old school revivalists. There's one true gem—"Long Way Down," a sensitive love song that samples Sarah McLachlan's "Ice Cream"—and many outtakes of better-than-average quality; though they aren't all monsters, they certainly deserve to come out of hiding. —*Dan LeRoy*

SX10

Group / Hip-Hop, Hard Rock, Alternative Pop/Rock, Alternative Metal, Rap-Metal
Cypress Hill's Sen Dog took note of his previous band to form the hip-hop rawness of SX-10. Composed of guitarists Jeremy Fleener and Andy

Zambrano, bassist Frank Mercurio, and drummer Glen Sobel, SX-10 was Sen Dog's dangerous outlet for creating music. He wanted wide-open funk incorporated with old school rhymes and Latin tinges, and that's the mold behind SX-10. Their debut *Goin' Crazy* was released on Elektra in 1999 and *Mad Dog American* followed a year later on Cleopatra. —*MacKenzie Wilson*

● **Mad Dog American** / Jun. 6, 2000 / EMI ◆◆◆
Gosh, you know how hard this band works to be threatening—just look at the wild graffiti art on the cover, check the lyrics, note the speedy rock/rap mixture. But nothing makes them sound tough. Just about any rapper, vet or kid, can rap edgier and impersonate insanity more insanely than Sen Dog of the Cypress Hill triune, even with Eric Bobo and DJ Muggs joining him. And this is a downright likable garage rap-metal album for all that; any two tracks would've fit nicely on the *Judgement Night* soundtrack. Sen Dog and his Caucasian/Latino band rock as fast and loose as a good old SST act. As a bonus, they brought in ten musicians from what might as well be other garages in the 'hood to add a garage organ and garage gospel background vocals to the whatta-relief anthem "I'm Not Jesus," as well as garage Latin percussion to "Tequila" and a few other tunes. And wouldn't you know it—this is part of Sen Dog's charm—no matter how loud he raps, the twang in his voice takes the edge off even his sharpest ranting. The band sounds like a stripped-down, unambitious Rage Against the Machine—and though this couldn't have been the intention, for better or worse, SX-10 is more enjoyable than most of the Cypress Hill you're likely to hear. —*John Young*

Sylk E Fyne

Hip-Hop, Urban, Hardcore Rap
Female rapper Sylk E. Fyne has been checking the rhymes since her early high school days, refraining from her rough west side neighborhood in South Central Los Angeles. Determined to make it real, Sylk E. Fyne beat the odds by earning a college degree and joining forces with some of hip-hop's biggest names. She cut lyrics for Too Short, Eazy-E, and Tupac Shakur, and toured with Bone, Thugs 'N Harmony. Thanks to such experience, her skills were perfectly honed in order for Sylk E. Fyne to mastermind her 1998 debut, *Raw Sylk*, on RCA. She may be cast in the middle of the bad boys of rap, but Fyne established the fact that she too is as nasty as she wants to be, and sultry too. She got dangerous once again on her sophomore effort, *Tha Cum Up*, which was released in mid-2000. —*MacKenzie Wilson*

● **Raw Sylk** / Mar. 24, 1998 / RCA ◆◆◆
As one of the stable of Grand Jury artists, Sylk-E. Fyne doesn't necessarily stand out from the pack that much. Essentially, she's the Grand Jury equivalent of Foxy Brown, only without the explicit, near-pornographic sex appeal. Musically, however, her debut album *Raw Sylk* is in the same vein. Working with producers Gerald Baillergeau and Victor Merritt, Sylk-E. has created a polished record that keeps one eye on the streets and one on the charts. There are hard-hitting gangsta tracks, including a duet with Too Short, but they're balanced by pop-oriented tracks designed for crossover airplay. As a result, *Raw Sylk* never quite forms its own identity, and it's loaded with filler, but the best moments—namely singles like "Romeo & Juliet"—are very good contemporary hip-hop, helping make the album a promising debut. —*Stephen Thomas Erlewine*

Tha Cum Up / Jul. 11, 2000 / Rufftown ◆◆
One of the few female rappers to come out of the West Coast scene, Sylk-E. Fyne comes straight out of Compton with her sophomore effort, *Tha Cum Up*. Sylk-E.'s lyrical work leaves much to be desired, especially on tracks like "Why Oh Why" and "Playazz Come Up," and the production on the album is not much better. The few highlights on the album come from guest appearances by Bizzy Bone and Snoop Dogg on "Ya Style." As a whole, *Tha Cum Up* is an undistinguished album that will be nothing more than an afterthought in the respective histories of women's hip-hop and West Coast rap. —*Jon Azpiri*

T la Rock

Vocals / Old School Rap, East Coast Rap
The older sibling of Treacherous Three's Special K, T la Rock's greatest contribution to hip-hop was "It's Yours," a 1984 single produced by Rick Rubin. Special K was originally set to record the song, which was written by both of the brothers, but he convinced his brother to do it instead. Although it's been said that it was the first Def Jam release, it actually wasn't—it was technically released by Partytime/Streetwise, and the sleeve design only featured an early Def Jam logo. T la Rock went on to record albums for Fresh and Sleeping Bag: 1987's *Lyrical King* was released on the former, and 1989's *On a Warpath* was released on the latter. Kurtis Mantronik helped out with production on the debut; Todd Terry leant a hand to the follow-up. —*Andy Kellman*

● **Lyrical King** / 1987 / Fresh ◆◆◆

Tag Team

f. Atlanta, GA
Group / Hip-Hop, Dance-Pop, Bass Music, Southern Rap, Party Rap
One of the most popular party rap/bass music duos of the early '90s, Atlanta's Tag Team—aka Steve RollN and DC the Brain Supreme—scored a massive hit with their 1993 single "Whoomp! There It Is," which sold over four million copies, making it one of the best-selling singles of all time. The song's booming bass and seemingly endless chant of "Whoomp! There It Is" made it instantly memorable and instantly popular; the group also turned out slight variations on the song, "Addams Family (Whoomp)" and "Bulls There It Is," that year, along with a full-length album named after their first success. But singles were Tag Team's forte, and over the next two years the duo released plenty of them, including "Here It Is, Bam!" "Whoomp! There It Went," "U Go Girl," "Pig Power," and "Funkey Situation," which was the title cut from their 1995 album. None of their efforts matched the success of "Whoomp! There It Is," however, though the single was immortalized on countless party rap and jock jams compilations; the group released a best-of album in early 2000. —*Heather Phares*

Whoomp! (There It Is) / Jul. 20, 1993 / Life ◆◆◆
Although "Whoomp! There It Is" is a wonderfully mindless single, it can't carry an entire album alone. Nothing else on Tag Team's debut album comes close to matching the delirious chanting and rolling beats of the single, making *Whoomp! (There It Is)* a pretty tedious affair. —*Stephen Thomas Erlewine*

Audio Entertainment / Aug. 4, 1995 / Life ◆◆◆

● **The Best of Tag Team** / Feb. 1, 2000 / Bellmark ◆◆◆◆
Since Tag Team are primarily a singles act, any singles collection on the market is the perfect way to acquire all of the production team's best moments. Obviously including their breakout single "Whoomp! (There It Is)," *The Best of Tag Team* also touches on their other dance hits: "Bobyahead," "Just Call Me DC," "What U Waitin' 4," and "Oweee." Tag Team never put out a better single than "Whoomp! There It Is," but the other tracks here are pretty solid, though definitely in the same vein. —*John Bush*

Tahir

Producer, Vocals / Hip-Hop
After producing hit singles for Dead Prez, Tahir suddenly appeared on the rap scene as an up-and-coming producer. Part of the People's Army, Tahir began preparing a solo album after doing some production work for Black Thought's solo album. Before releasing the album, though, Tahir released the *Holiday Pay/Plow Plow* 12". —*Jason Birchmeier*

● **Homecoming** / Oct. 30, 2001 / Raptivism ◆◆◆
This Tallahassee-born rapper tries to balance dirty South bounce with the political awareness of his Florida compatriots, Dead Prez, on his full-length debut. Sounding at times like a more refined and socially conscious No Limit release, *Homecoming* interweaves party tunes with calls for enlightenment. Unfortunately, Tahir doesn't really have anything new to say. The bass-heavy rhythms and call-and-response vocals are overly familiar, although this would be a forgivable limitation if Tahir came up with more songs as catchy as "Army Boys." The messages aren't particularly new either; you may find positive values in the statement of purpose at the beginning of "Army Boys" ("We the People Army, come together as a unit, so that we can all live better lives"), the call for family solidarity in "Never Alone," and the dedication to "all the political prisoners worldwide" in "Willpower," but ultimately the political awareness seems to boil down to the standard anti-establishment posturing of "f*ck the law, f*ck the cops" ("Raw and Treal"). Overall this isn't a bad album, but it isn't anything remarkable either. —*Todd Kristel*

Faouzi Tarkhani

b. France
Vocals / Foreign Rap, Worldbeat
One of the few hip-hop artists to escape the stranglehold of censhorship in Algeria, Faouzi Tarkhani recorded a surprisingly successful record in 1999, *Guerrier Pour la Paix*. —*John Bush*

● **Guerrier Pour la Paix** / Apr. 20, 1999 / Polydor ◆◆◆◆
French Algerians have been some of the most powerful forces in hip-hop music in France, but heavy censorship has kept them underground in their native country. Faouzi Tarkhani is one of the first Algerian hip-hop artists to release a commercially successful album. Entitled *Guerrier Pour la Paix* (Warrior for Peace), the Francophone album combines West Coast-style funk-influenced hip-hop with smooth R&B tracks. The sound borrows heavily from American music, but the lyrics, which are a mixture of love and political themes, seem straight from Tarkhani's heart. Slick production wraps it all up into a professional package, making this album likely to make a major impact on the French charts, as well as garnering interest elsewhere. —*Stacia Proefrock*

Tash (Rico Smith)

b. 1972, Columbus, OH
Gangsta Rap, Hardcore Rap
West Coast rapper Tash was born Rico Smith in Columbus, OH, in 1972, relocating to California at age 16; a protégé of King Tee and Ice-T, in 1992 he cofounded tha Alkaholiks, issuing their debut album, *21 & Over*, the following year. In the wake of the group's third album, 1997's *Likwidation*, Tash began working on his solo debut, 1999's *Rap Life*. —*Jason Ankeny*

● **Rap Life** / Nov. 2, 1999 / Loud ◆◆◆◆
As one-third of the California rap trio tha Alkaholiks, Tash has been responsible for some of the most raucous and rowdy lyrical gems ever laid down by any West Coast crew. But in 1999, Tash branched out on his own for a solo debut and committed his talents toward broadening the hip-hop audience with his own brand of smooth yet compelling beats packaged within the hardcore tradition. *Rap Life* delivers easy, bass-heavy compositions right alongside the requisite b-boy and club tracks. On "Castashtrophe Meets Kuruption," rapper Kurupt battles with Tash through a saucy stream of verbal punches and counterpunches, and on "Rap Life," Raekwon joins Tash to rap about life as an MC. Standout cuts "Falling On" and "Ricochet" allow Tash to freely exhibit his rap skills with masterful fluidity. Featuring appearances

from B Real, Big Boi, Carl Thomas, and Outkast, *Rap Life* represents the merging of West Coast and East Coast styles to deliver a record that is not only accessible but also more than likely to reach commercial success. —*Roxanne Blanford*

Tear Da Club Up Thugs

Group / Hardcore Rap, Southern Rap, Dirty South

Comprised primarily of Three 6 Mafia members Lord Infamous, Juicy J, and DJ Paul, Tear Da Club Up Thugs debuted with *Crazyndalazdayz* in late '98, just as Three 6 Mafia and the other Southern rappers appearing here began their rise to commercial success. The collective's name refers to Three 6 Mafia's 1997 anthem, "Tear da Club Up." The group's material tends to feature gangsta-themed lyrics. —*Jason Birchmeier*

● **Crazyndalazdayz** / Nov. 10, 1998 / Relativity ♦♦♦

Tear Da Club Up Thugs' debut album, *Crazyndalazdayz*, represents the rowdiest side of Three 6 Mafia, both in terms of beats as well as rhymes. Most of the songs have blatant references to riot-inciting violence, particularly songs such as "Get Buck, Get Wild" and "Elbow a Nigga." And when the rappers aren't trying to lyrically start fights, they're most likely spouting misogynist rants in songs such as "Slob on My Knob" and "All Dirty Hoes." So when you really sit down and think about it, this music appeals to the most primal male instincts. Furthermore, the up-tempo, hard-hitting beats only further evoke base feelings. So if you have a taste for rowdy music, this is about as rousing as music can get. In terms of cast, the album features a wide range of rappers, including everyone from the Three 6 Mafia camp, as well as guests such as Spice 1 and Too Short. Yet just as Prophet Posse focused almost exclusively on the horror side of Three 6 Mafia, Tear Da Club Up Thugs focuses almost exclusively on their violent side—making the two groups quite similar, in fact. Yet this one-dimensional slant proves limiting over the course of an entire album, a problem that plagued Prophet Posse's *Body Parts* album as well as this one. Where Three 6 Mafia's better albums present a wide range of variety in terms of both lyrical content as well as beats, this album is nothing but rowdy, up-tempo calls to violence. That's wonderful if that's all you're looking for, but for most this will prove a bit too redundant to be truly effective. —*Jason Birchmeier*

Tech N9ne (Aaron Yates)

Hardcore Rap, Underground Rap

Like many underground rappers in the Midwest, Tech N9ne specialized in bizarre hardcore rap and stood as one of the few recognized rappers based in Kansas City when he debuted in the late '90s. He made the major-label jump with *Anghellic* (2001), which JCOR Entertainment released with the backing of Interscope Records. The album didn't find a large audience, though, and Tech N9ne returned to the underground and prepared his next album, *Absolute Power* (2002). A year later Tech N9ne's new label, Strange Music, re-released *Anghellic*, which had gone out of print in the wake of JCOR's fallout with Interscope. —*Jason Birchmeier*

Straight From tha Ramp!! / 1995 / Cash Money ♦♦♦

Anghellic / Aug. 28, 2001 / JCOR ♦♦♦

● **Absolute Power** / Sep. 24, 2002 / Strange Music ♦♦♦♦

One of the most unique lyricists and performers in the underground rap universe, the enigmatic Tech N9ne (aka Aaron Yates) has put Kansas City on the hip-hop map both through his work with stars like 2Pac and Eminem and with a handful of his own hardcore solo efforts. Tired of getting ripped off by fly-by-night indie labels, Tech N9ne took matters into his own hands with *Absolute Power*, releasing the album on his Strange Music label. Expressing disdain for the music industry, its immoral business practices, and the de facto segregation of the radio airwaves, Tech N9ne opens *Absolute Power* with the powerful "The Industry Is Punks." The song is delivered with the rapper's trademark rapid-fire rhythm, hitting the listener like the business end of a sledgehammer and matched with an almost operatic chorus. "Here Comes Tecca Nine" is a shout-out to Kansas City; "Imma Tell" uses a strange repeating vocal sample that sounds like it was taken from an old Italian comedy film and thrown behind a tale of hometown high jinks. "Slacker" provides a new definition to the fabled lifestyle, while "Slither," based on N9ne's experiences in K.C.-area strip clubs, is a theatrical horror story complete with sexy vampires. Tech N9ne's self-professed insanity (crazy like a fox, actually) manifests itself in cuts like "Trapped in a Psycho's Body," the artist struggling with

personal demons, and on the Middle Eastern-flavored "She Devil" (with Detroit crew D-12), the song's protagonist yielding to temptation with disastrous results. The high point of *Absolute Power* is "Worst Enemy," N9ne's vocal gymnastics punctuated by anger and confusion as he reveals the shocking identity of his "enemy" at the song's conclusion. What sets Tech N9ne apart from his hip-hop counterparts is an unusual ability to change the flow of his rhymes, from scattershot, machine-gun styling to absurd, almost DJ Screw-like vocal molasses. Paired with his intelligent, cinematic-oriented poetry, Tech N9ne is a cerebral assassin using words as his weapon and music as his medium. An important and groundbreaking release, *Absolute Power* is as original in its delivery and all-encompassing in its scope as the early Public Enemy albums. A bonus DVD included with *Absolute Power* offers six previously unreleased songs and live performance and interview video footage. —*Rev. Keith A. Gordon*

Tela

b. Memphis, TN

Southern Rap, Dirty South, G-Funk

Hip-hopper Tela came busting out of Memphis in 1996 with a contract for the Suave House label (Eightball & MJG). First album *Piece of Mind* appeared in November of that year; *Now or Never* followed in late 1998, and *The World Ain't Enuff* in fall 2000. —*John Bush*

Piece of Mind / Nov. 5, 1996 / Suave House ♦♦♦

Tela's debut is an inconsistent but promising set of Southern rap, highlighted by cameos from Suave labelmates Eightball & MJG. Though he tries to push his hardcore side throughout the record, his true strength is in new-jack ballads, such as "Let It Rain," which bring the record to another level. There's not quite enough of them on *Piece of Mind*, but the bulk of the record is promising and entertaining enough to make it worth a listen. —*Leo Stanley*

● **The World Ain't Enuff** / Sep. 19, 2000 / Rap-A-Lot ♦♦♦

Four years after Tela collaborated with Eightball & MJG and Suave House Records on his breakthrough single, "Sho Nuff," the playboy rapper from Memphis recorded his second album for Rap-A-Lot, *The World Ain't Enuff.* The album bears little resemblance to the G-funk Tela had recorded for Suave House. He instead embraces a livelier, more contemporary dirty South style that's driven by bass-heavy dance beats rather than smoked-out *Chronic*-esque ones, and he boasts this new style on an up-tempo remake of his signature hit, "Sho Nuff." It's immediately followed by a likewise club-orientated Jazze Pha remix of "Table Dance," another of his previous hits. These back-to-back remakes come mid-album and showcase how far Tela had come during the late '90s stylistically. The glossy remakes also serve as a nice climax before Tela returns to his new songs, which include a few highlights, among them the album-closing title-track collaboration with the Rap-A-Lot don himself, Mr. Scarface. —*Jason Birchmeier*

Terminator X (Norman Rogers)

b. New York, NY

DJ, Producer / Hardcore Rap

Best known as the innovative DJ of Public Enemy, Terminator X (born Norman Rogers) also pursued a secondary solo career beginning in 1991. His debut, *Terminator X & the Valley of the Jeep Beets*, was not a radical departure from his work with PE and consisted largely of dance tracks, although there were some vocal contributions from Andrew 13 and Sister Souljah. Prior to the release of his second solo album in 1994, Terminator X suffered two broken legs in a motorcycle accident from which he recovered. *Super Bad* featured appearances by Grandmaster Flash, Kool Herc, and the Cold Crush Brothers. —*Steve Huey*

● **Terminator X & the Valley of the Jeep Beets** / May 7, 1991 / Def Jam ♦♦♦

For hardcore Public Enemy fans, the release of Terminator X's debut solo album, *Terminator X & the Valley of the Jeep Beets*, in 1991 was a major event. Terminator X, of course, is best known for his work as Public Enemy's DJ; his cutting and scratching added a lot to five-star albums like *Fear of a Black Planet* and *It Takes a Nation of Millions to Hold Us Back*, and he has a well-deserved reputation for being one of hip-hop's most creative turntable manipulators. When you're talking about great hip-hop DJs, Terminator's name deserves to be mentioned along with the likes of Grandmaster Flash, Jam Master Jay, Cut Creator, and the seminal Kool DJ Herc. Not surprisingly, Public Enemy's influence is quite strong on this album, and yet *Terminator X*

& the Valley of the Jeep Beets is hardly a carbon copy of PE's releases. Public Enemy leader Chuck D has a cameo on "Buck Whylin'," but ultimately this album is about Terminator's skills as a DJ/producer. Various rappers are featured—including Juvenile Delinquintz, Andreas 13, the Interrogators, and the controversial Sister Souljah—and the album detours into R&B singing when Section 8 is employed on "No Further." Overall, the raps are decent without being remarkable; most of the rapping isn't on a par with what Chuck D and Flavor Flav gave us on PE gems like "Fight the Power" and "Don't Believe the Hype." Terminator's turntable skills are what, more than anything, make this CD worth the price of admission. Even if a particular rap is merely adequate, Terminator maintains one's attention with his consistently imaginative DJing. Not perfect but generally enjoyable, *Terminator X & the Valley of the Jeep Beets* is worth checking out if you're an admirer of his work with Public Enemy. —*Alex Henderson*

Super Bad / Jun. 21, 1994 / Def Jam ♦♦

Terror Squad

Group / Hip-Hop, West Coast Rap, Latin Rap

A confederation of rappers led by Fat Joe and his protégé Big Punisher, the Terror Squad also comprised Cuban Link, Armageddon, Triple Seis, and Prospect. Their debut, *Terror Squad*, was released on Atlantic on 1999, generating the hit "Whatcha Gonna Do." —*Jason Ankeny*

● **Terror Squad** / Sep. 21, 1999 / Atlantic ♦♦♦

Terror Squad spends much of their eponymous debut trading in gangsta clichés—it only seems like there's been a hundred songs called "Pass the Glock"—but beneath those rehashed themes lay some clever rhymes and music. Fat Joe and Big Punisher lead the group, which contains such promising rappers as Prospect and Cuban Link. The two established rappers often take a back seat, letting the other four members showcase their talents. All six members are very talented and their skills are enhanced by the productions, which are not only funky but also show some imagination. It would have been nice if there was a little more imagination behind the lyrics, but the record itself is a good, solid effort that's better than many of hardcore rap efforts in recent memory. —*Stephen Thomas Erlewine*

3rd Bass

f. 1987, Queens, NY **db.** 1992

Group / Golden Age, Alternative Rap, East Coast Rap

3rd Bass was one of a still-small number of white hip-hop artists to achieve wide acceptance in the larger community. Along with the Beastie Boys, 3rd Bass proved that white hip-hop wasn't necessarily going to become a watered-down, commercially exploitative rip-off of the genuine article, as so many white interpretations of black musical forms had been in the past. Instead, they were possessed of a well-developed lyrical technique and were respectfully well versed in hip-hop culture and tradition. They helped set the tone for the way white rappers could credibly and intelligently approach the music, and despite staying together for only two albums, they managed to create a highly positive lasting impact.

3rd Bass was formed by Queens-born MC Serch (born Michael Berrin) and Brooklyn native Prime Minister Pete Nice (born Pete Nash), along with African-American DJ Richie Rich (born Richard Lawson). Nice had been an English major at Columbia University and hosted a short-lived hip-hop show on the radio station WKCR. Serch, meanwhile, had honed his skills battle-rapping at clubs and block parties and had previously released a solo single called "Hey Boy" on the small independent Idlers label. Both Serch and Nice were working as solo acts until producer Sam Sever convinced the two 20 year olds to join forces in 1987. Along with Prince Paul and the Bomb Squad, Sever produced their 1989 Def Jam debut *The Cactus Album* (aka *Cee/D*), which was greeted with enthusiastic reviews in most quarters. Clever, good-humored singles like "The Gas Face," "Steppin' to the A.M.," and "Brooklyn-Queens" helped make 3rd Bass's name in the hip-hop underground. They followed it in 1991 with *Derelicts of Dialect*, which featured one of the first recorded appearances by Nas and contained a viciously funny jab at Vanilla Ice called "Pop Goes the Weasel." Accompanied by an equally humorous video, "Pop Goes the Weasel" became 3rd Bass's biggest chart single and performed some much-needed damage control in the hip-hop community: not only did it prevent 3rd Bass from getting lumped in with Ice, but by extension, it also distanced at least some of the Caucasian

race from the whole phenomenon, opening doors for greater inclusiveness later on.

Despite their success, 3rd Bass disbanded in 1992 when MC Serch went solo. He issued *Return of the Product* later that year, and the remainder of the group, billed as Prime Minister Pete Nice & DJ Daddy Rich, teamed up for *Dust to Dust* in 1993. Neither was as successful or high profile as the two gold-selling 3rd Bass albums. Serch, interested in discovering new talent, became the head of A&R at the respected, now-defunct Wild Pitch label, and later founded his own label, Serchlight Productions. Nice, meanwhile, dropped out of the music business and opened a store in Cooperstown, NY, that sold baseball memorabilia. In 2000, 3rd Bass reunited for several concerts. —*Steve Huey*

★ **The Cactus Album** / Oct. 23, 1989 / Def Jam ♦♦♦♦♦

Besides the upper-middle-class frat-punks-in-rap-clothing shtick of the Beastie Boys and emissary/producer Rick Rubin, who both gained a legitimate, earned respect in the rap community, there were very few white kids in rap's first decade who spoke the poetry of the street with compassion and veneration for the form. That is, until *The Cactus Album*. Matching MC Serch's bombastic, goofy good nature and Prime Minister Pete Nice's gritty, English-trained wordsmithery (sounding like a young Don in training), 3rd Bass' debut album is revelatory in its way. For one, it is full of great songs, alternately upbeat rollers ("Sons of 3rd Bass"), casual-but-sincere disses ("The Gas Face"), razor-sharp street didacticism ("Triple Stage Darkness," "Wordz of Wizdom"), and sweaty city anthems ("Brooklyn Queens," "Steppin' to the A.M.," odes to day and night, respectively), with A+ production by heavy-weights Prince Paul and Bomb Squad, as well as the surprising, overshadowing work of Sam Sever. The duo may not have come from the streets, but their hearts were there, and it shows. The album embodies New York life. Not every single idea plays out successfully—Serch's Louis Armstrong impression on "Flippin' Off the Wall ..." is on the wrong side of the taste line, and "Desert Boots" is a puzzling Western-themed insertion—but they are at least interesting stretches that add to the dense, layered texture of the album. *The Cactus Album* was also important because it proved to the hip-hop heads that white kids could play along without appropriating or bastardizing the culture. It may not have completely integrated rap, but it was a precursor to a culture that became more inclusive and widespread after its arrival. —*Stanton Swihart*

Cactus Revisited / Sep. 7, 1990 / Def Jam ♦♦♦

A bit of a between-album attempt to keep the band in people's sights, *Cactus Revisited* takes most of the biggest hits from 3rd Bass' debut and hands them over to such respected mixers as Marley Marl, Dave Darrell, and Prince Paul for them to play with. It is a patchy diversion. Some remixes such as the more danceable version of "The Cactus" or Prince Paul's terrifically energized take on "Gas Face" are mighty entertaining, but others seem to just sit on their thumbs and lengthen the original tracks. "Wordz of Wisdom," for instance, is clearly the worst delinquent because despite an absolutely delightful use of Depeche Mode samples, it quickly staggers as it tries to stretch out into its eight-minute entirety. Plus, to make matters worse, the previously unreleased "3 Strikes 5000" quickly loses its collector gem value since it later appeared on the band's superb *Derelicts of Dialect* full-length. In any case, for those desperately looking for anything new from a band cut too short in their career, *Cactus Revisited* might still placate such woes, flaws and all. It's just unfortunate that while 3rd Bass might have been one of the most underappreciated hip-hop acts around, this patchy remix collection too frequently gives their detractors more than enough ammo to fire back at them. —*Dean Carlson*

Derelicts of Dialect / Jun. 18, 1991 / Def Jam ♦♦♦

Although 3rd Bass didn't fully realize their tremendous potential, the Queens, NY rappers offered enjoyable, if uneven, albums. Like the group's 1989 debut, their second and final album, *Derelicts of Dialect*, makes it clear that the MCs weren't aiming for the pop charts—and were loyal only to the hip-hop hardcore. When MC Serch and Pete Nice tear into such aggressive and forceful declarations as "Pop Goes the Weasel" (an inflammatory attack on Vanilla Ice), "Portrait of the Artist as a Hood," and "Ace in the Hole," it's clear why they were among the few white MCs who were successful in the young black community—someone who heard their rapping without seeing their picture could easily assume they were black. Although the goofy "Herbalz in Your Mouth" shows some De La Soul and A Tribe Called Quest influence, 3rd Bass doesn't allow itself to be nearly as lighthearted, and keeps things hardcore and intense. —*Alex Henderson*

Threat

b. California

Vocals / Hip-Hop, Gangsta Rap, Hardcore Rap

Californian rapper Threat earned his start on the track "Color Blind," dropping one of the more memorable verses of Ice Cube's 1991 *Death Certificate* album. He followed up with his debut solo album, *Sickinnahead*, featuring exceptional production by DJ Pooh. He then became a member of the group Black Menace, who released their first album, *Drama Time (x)*, in 1996. He followed with another solo album, *Drama Az Usual*, in 1997. —*Brad Mills*

● **Sickinnahead** / Jul. 20, 1993 / Polygram ♦♦♦♦

Threat's debut album hasn't seen much attention outside of his native California, but is one of the better albums from the West Coast in 1993. DJ Pooh provides some very intricate and detailed production work, with differing sounds and even tempo changes in the middle of the tracks. Properly used sampling and scratching are heard throughout, with funky horn and saxophone riffs used to accompany the deep bass lines. There are also a few guest producers on this album, including Suede and the legendary King Tee. Threat doesn't disrespect the beats either, bringing an energetic and often comedic spirit to what at its basic level is still a hardcore gangsta rap album. —*Brad Mills*

Three 6 Mafia

f. 1995, Memphis, TN

Group / Hardcore Rap, Southern Rap, Underground Rap

Without compromising their dark image as a malevolent rap group from the South, Three 6 Mafia quickly evolved from a humble underground rap collective to a commercially successful dynasty by retaining their raw qualities and releasing countless albums under a number of monikers. Representing Memphis, TN, the group's six core members—Crunchy Black, Gangsta Boo, Lord Infamous, Koopsta Knicca, Juicy J, DJ Paul—give the group its dark image, vividly rapping about drug use, violent aggression, pornographic sex, and anything else remotely evil. Furthermore, group leaders Juicy J and DJ Paul's cinematic production perfectly complements the group's theatrical rapping, causing many to call them the South's Wu-Tang Clan, as both groups are led by in-house production, feature a closed roster of rappers, and also release a glut of affiliated solo and compilation albums. After releasing their first official album in 1995 and their first major-label album in 1997, Three 6 Mafia soon found themselves on the verge of superstardom; once *When the Smoke Clears* debuted at number six on *Billboard*'s album charts in summer 2000, it became evident that Three 6 Mafia no longer were an underground group.

Before Three 6 Mafia became a sprawling slew of loosely connected side projects, DJ Paul began his musical career as a popular Memphis DJ around 1990, creating mix tapes at home with his brother, Lord Infamous. In 1991, DJ Paul met up with another hot local DJ, Juicy J, who was a fan of his mix tapes; the two began producing tapes with them rapping over beats and they eventually began integrating local MCs into their music. After Juicy J and DJ Paul honed their beats to the point where they had developed a trademark sound (later showcased on *Underground, Vol. 1*, a collection of their early recordings from 1991 to 1994), they began officially collaborating with local MCs; these resulted in their first underground release as Triple 6 Mafia, *Smoked out Loced Out*. After an enthusiastic response within the South, the group changed their name to Three 6 Mafia and put out their first official album in 1995, *Mystic Stylez*.

At this early point in their career, the early Three 6 Mafia camp prided themselves on being as raw as possible, rapping explicitly about sex, drugs, and violence. While these topics weren't exactly MTV material, they did garner a considerable cult following—quite similar to what Esham was doing in Detroit at the time—and the group used controversy to further fuel their growing popularity via the media by releasing an EP, *Live By Yo Rep (B.O.N.E. Dis)*, which took lyrical shots at Bone Thugs-N-Harmony. After following up their debut and EP with a second album, *Da End*, Three 6 Mafia signed to Relativity Records. Having released their early albums on the group's independently run Prophet Entertainment label, their first major-label release,

Chapter 2: World Domination, found the group polishing up their production and tweaking their image a bit. They also reprised "Tear da Club Up" from *Mystic Stylez* as "Tear da Club Up '97" and found themselves with a respectable anthem that made its way out of the South.

At this point in the group's evolution, having signed to a major label and having scored an admirable hit single, group leaders Juicy J and DJ Paul began extending their brand by releasing group member solo albums (Gangsta Boo, Koopsta Knicca), nongroup member solo albums (Project Pat, the Kaze), and also compilation-styled albums (Tear the Club Up Thugs, Hypnotize Camp Posse). Similar in approach to Master P's No Limit Records at the end of the '90s, a glut of Three 6 Mafia-affiliated albums soon flooded the market. Though even the most diehard fan couldn't possibly keep up with every release, these many albums did help bring increased awareness about what was going on in Memphis. This became evident in summer 2000 when the long-awaited "official" Three 6 Mafia follow-up to 1997's *Chapter 2* album, *When the Smoke Clears*, finally hit the streets. Aided immensely by the surprising national success of the lead single, "Sippin' on Some Syrup," in a few non-Southern markets, the album debuted at number six on *Billboard*'s album charts. Following the success of this album (which received no MTV and little national radio rotation), Three 6 Mafia began work on a direct-to-video film and on affiliated solo albums. —*Jason Birchmeier*

Mystic Stylez / May 25, 1995 / SOH ♦♦♦

Though Three 6 Mafia would later release their early recordings on the Smoked Out label as Triple 6 Mafia (their original name), *Mystic Stylez* stands as their first official album in the eyes of most fans. Furthermore, it has become a considerable cult favorite, undoubtedly the group's most eerie album, characterized by a sincerely fearful mentality. The album's terrifying tone is mostly in debt to producers Juicy J and DJ Paul, who craft a skilled blend of haunting synths with hard drum machine beats. Over top of the evocative production, the various group members lay down their rugged rhymes saturated with a malevolent ideology. "Tear da Club Up" is the album's highlight, a rowdy club anthem that the group would later reprise for their *Chapter 2: World Domination* album. In addition, "Now I'm Hi Pt. 3" and "Porno Movie" are also shocking tracks that prove just how provocative these Memphis rappers could be. Of course, the themes of violence, drugs, and sex would appear on every subsequent Three 6 Mafia album, but here they sound unbelievably raw. Part of this album's potency can be attributed to the album's poor production values. Ironically, the album's muddy sound actually complements the already hallucinogenic production. Though later albums such as *Chapter 2: World Domination* and *When the Smoke Clears* are undeniably much stronger albums with better rapping and better beats, this album has retained its uncanny allure over the years, making it a cult favorite among not only Three 6 Mafia fans but also fans of horror-styled rap music in general. —*Jason Birchmeier*

Live by Yo Rep / Dec. 5, 1995 / Prophet ♦♦

This short EP followed Three 6 Mafia's debut album, *Mystic Stylez*; driven by two versions of its title track, a Bone Thugs diss, the EP is a nice sampler of the Memphis, TN, hardcore rap group's rowdy style. While "Tear da Club Up (Da Real)" only affirms the group's aggressive tendencies, other tracks here (such as "Triple 6 Mafia," for example) showcase the group's eerie side, rounding out its overall malevolent personality. Since original versions of "Tear da Club Up" and "Live by Yo Rep" already appear on the excellent *Mystic Stylez* album, only die-hard fans who want to hear the other nonalbum tracks should have any dire need to acquire this EP. To be honest, the nonalbum tracks are quite effective and, furthermore, the "screwed" version of "Live by Yo Rep" is also a good listen—so this is probably worth finding for the fanatic. Casual fans are better off with the group's first album. —*Jason Birchmeier*

Da End / Dec. 3, 1996 / Prophet ♦♦

A respectable step forward from their muddy yet unbelievably eerie debut, *Da End* finds Three 6 Mafia further realizing their malevolent style of hardcore rap. Here the songs aren't quite as evil sounding but rather violent—the beats hit hard and often, and the group members spit their lyrics with enormous spite. It's a potent album, for sure. Songs such as "Gette'm Crunk" and "Body Parts" pick up where "Tear da Club Up" left off, functioning as uptempo anthems; similarly, songs such as "Late Night Tip" and "End" illustrate rather vividly just how evocative producers Juicy J and DJ Paul's beats can be. In a way, this is an album worth skipping for all but dedicated Three 6 Mafia fans. Sure, it has its share of strong moments; however, three of the best moments here—"Body Parts," "In 2 Deep," and "Late Night Tip"—appear on their subsequent album, *Chapter 2: World Domination*, an essential album in the group's canon. Furthermore, outside of the handful of standout songs here, there are quite a few lackluster songs. You're better off skipping this album and coming back to it later once you've heard their other albums. Where *Mystic Stylez* is as raw as the group would ever get, *Chapter 2* is their first fully realized album, and *When the Smoke Clears* is their first attempt to cross over to mainstream acceptance, *Da End* doesn't really have anything novel about it. In fact, it's no coincidence that the group reprised several songs from this album on *Chapter 2*; outside of those few songs, this is an album that's better left on the shelf. —*Jason Birchmeier*

● **Chapter 2: World Domination** / Oct. 7, 1997 / Relativity ✦✦✦✦
For Three 6 Mafia's first album distributed through Relativity, the hardcore rap group created their most varied and most cinematic album to date. Building on the horror motifs of their debut, *Mystic Stylez*, and the posse raps of their second album, *Da End*, *Chapter 2: World Domination* functions almost as a summation of their output to date, reprising a few songs from their preceding albums and featuring a large number of rousing new tracks. Of the old tracks that reappear here, "Tear da Club Up '97" is an obvious highlight, a clear anthem for the group. In addition, "Late Night Tip," "Bodyparts 2," and "In 2 Deep" are also all strong songs that stand out, even if they were previously available. But, for the most part, the album is composed of new material which is well-crafted and an obvious step forward for the group. "Hit a Muthafucka" stands right alongside "Tear da Club Up" as one of the group's trademark rowdy moments, and might just be the best song on the album. Furthermore, "Neighborhood Hoe" and "Weed Is Got Me High" bring some sex and drugs to the group's aggression, making for a potent blend of violence, sex, and drugs—exploitative rap at its best. Yet it's important to note that Three 6 Mafia aren't mere controversy rappers; Juicy J and DJ Paul's production is stunning here, lush with eerie synths and hard-hitting drum machine percussion, just as the group members' rapping has never sounded better. Though their past albums never really settled the debate whether Three 6 Mafia were more exploitation or talent, *Chapter 2: World Domination* wonderfully showcases not only the decadent ideology but also the group's often-overlooked credentials. —*Jason Birchmeier*

Three 6 Mafia Presents: Hypnotize Camp Posse / Jan. 25, 2000 / Loud ✦✦✦
Three 6 Mafia Presents: Hypnotize Camp Posse isn't so much a Three 6 Mafia album as it is a sampler of the many rappers loosely affiliated with the six-member group. Of the many who make appearances on this album, Project Pat is the most notable, with others such as Pastor Troy and T-Rock also proving their worth. Yet even with the large ensemble of rappers passing the mic to one another every 30 seconds or so for the entirety of the album, this still sounds like a Three 6 Mafia album, mostly because of Juicy J and DJ Paul's patented production style. Furthermore, most of the guest rappers sound awfully similar to the existing members, so it's often hard to tell who's on the mic at a given moment. Yet even though this sounds like a standard Three 6 Mafia album, it's not quite on par. There are just way too many artists here to give the album a unifying sound—if you had a hard time differentiating the six original members from one another, this album will drive you crazy! Furthermore, many of the nonaffiliated rappers just aren't that impressive. And while the production is pretty standard for the group, its mostly of the up-tempo variety; some down-tempo "Late Night Tip"- or "Sippin' on Some Syrup"-style beats would be very welcome here. Probably most similar to the Tear Da Club Up Thugs project, this compilation is fairly one-dimensional, characterized by aggressive posse songs. Granted, the Three 6 camp does this better than almost anyone in rap circa 2000, but this album gets pretty redundant fast, no matter how many guest rappers they pass the mic to. —*Jason Birchmeier*

When the Smoke Clears / Apr. 11, 2000 / Relativity ✦✦✦✦
As more and more underground rap groups get major-label distribution at the end of the '90s, the groups need a distinct yet appealing sound to cut through the clutter. For many of the rap groups from the Southern U.S. such as Cash Money in New Orleans, a regional sound and ideology that differs from the West and East Coast motifs have become not just an option but also a necessity. In the case of the Memphis, TN, collective Three 6 Mafia, the group focuses on its signature down-tempo, electro-influenced soundscapes filled with drum machine beats and melancholy piano melodies and also its

non-glamorous, survive-or-die ghetto Mafia attitude. A crystal clear production sound helps producers DJ Paul and Juicy J deliver their sparse, cinematic soundscapes reigning subtly in the songs' backgrounds, evoking a strong sense of mood that seldom eclipses the songs' lyrics. In addition, the group's rappers possess some impressive skills, delivering their rhymes with refreshing clarity. It's nice to actually hear what the collective has to say because they weave some truly decadent portrayals of their lives in Memphis. Over the course of 22 songs, they push drug use to dangerous extremes in "Take a Bump," with it's refrain of "Break out the dollar/And take a bump/Pick out the seeds/And spit the blunt," and also during "Sippin' on Some Syrup." Traditionally misogynous themes get interesting during songs such as "Tongue Ring" and "Barrin' You Bitches" when one of the group's best rappers, Gangsta Boo, presents her strong feminine point of view. These degenerate themes of drugs, sex, and the associated Mafia-like ghetto lifestyle have been covered before on countless gangsta rap albums, but Three 6 Mafia take it in new, darker directions away from violence toward sheer degenerateness. In "Take a Bump," they ask, "How high can you get sippin' gin and juice," commenting on their urge to take things further than the more glamorous, romanticized gangsta lifestyles of Snoop Dogg, 2Pac, and Notorious B.I.G. ever went. In fact, thanks in part to the eerie musical score underlying the lyrics, *When the Smoke Clears* ends up being a downright scary album. Its no-holds-barred attempt to epitomize the modern meaning of "ghetto Mafia thug" seems deathly sincere, making it a very intriguing yet ultimately perverse listen that may darkly taint your perception of inner-city ghetto life. —*Jason Birchmeier*

Three Times Dope

f. Philadelphia, PA
Group / Hip-Hop
Philadelphia rappers Duerwood Beale, Walter Griggs, and Robert Walker formed Three Times Dope and released their debut, *Original Stylin'*, in 1989. It was filled mainly with boasting, self-promoting narratives, and comic/novelty material, though the "What's Going On" medley attempted to address social issues. Their second release was *Live From Acknickulous Land* in 1990, which tried to be a more serious "concept" work. —*Ron Wynn*

● **Original Stylin'** / 1989 / Arista ✦✦✦✦✦
Three Times Dope made their debut with this record, which was still in an old school mode. They spent much of the album proclaiming their microphone superiority, although the "What's Going On" medley offered some good social commentary and "Once More You Hear The Dope Stuff" was a good boasting number. —*Ron Wynn*

Live From Acknickulous Land / 1990 / Arista ✦✦✦
Things weren't so dope for Philly rappers Three Times Dope on their second album. The implied fantasy concept translated into a rather lame reality as the trio came up short in the compositional, production, rapping, and rhyme departments. —*Ron Wynn*

Da Sequel / Mar. 10, 1998 / Cass ✦✦✦

3X Krazy

f. Oakland, CA
Group / Gangsta Rap, Hardcore Rap, Underground Rap, West Coast Rap
West Coast gangsta rap trio 3X Krazy rose from Oakland alongside a small wave of other similar-minded groups during the mid-'90s and retained its hardcore slant throughout the decade as its group members broke away for respective solo careers. Comprised of B.A., Agerman, and Keak da Sneak, 3X Krazy debuted in 1995 with the *Sick-O* EP, which depicted the members in straightjackets on the cover. Two years later, 3X Krazy returned with its full-length debut, *Stackin Chips* (1997), which featured big-name guests Yukmouth and E-40. Released by Noo Trybe, which had major-label affiliations with Virgin at the time, *Stackin Chips* won 3X Krazy a significant fan base on the West Coast, and the group responded with two more albums: *Immortalized* (1999) and *Real Talk 2000* (2000). At this point, the group members began breaking away for solo ventures, Keak da Sneak's being the most productive. In the meanwhile, two best-of collections appeared, *20th Century* (2000) and *Best of 3x Krazy, Vol. 2* (2002), both of which were spotty and non-comprehensive. —*Jason Birchmeier*

Immortalized / Jun. 22, 1999 / Big Block ✦✦✦

20th Century / Oct. 10, 2000 / Sneak ◆◆◆

20th Century compiles some of 3X Krazy's songs from the '90s, including songs from the albums *Sick-O* (1995), *Stackin Chips* (1997), and *Immortalized* (1999), yet it's far from a comprehensive best-of collection. In fact, it inexplainably doesn't include several of 3X Krazy's best moments, such as "Keep It on the Real." A second compilation, *Best of 3x Krazy, Vol. 2* (2002), isn't any better, though, so this double-disc collection still may be the most comprehensive offering available, even if it's indeed far from ideal. If you're not willing to wade through two discs of material, much of which is disposable, or simply want a solid album, you might want to instead go with *Stackin Chips*, 3X Krazy's strongest full-length. It's actually a stronger collection than this one, even if it doesn't span the group's career. —*Jason Birchmeier*

● **Best of 3X Krazy, Vol. 2** / Mar. 26, 2002 / Sneak ◆◆◆◆

Best of 3X Krazy, Vol. 2 compiles many of the same songs as 3X Krazy's previous best-of, *20th Century*. Like that double-disc collection from 2000, *Best of 3X Krazy, Vol. 2* features the West Coast hardcore rap group's career highlights: "Somethin' 4 Dat Ass," "Can't Fu#k With This," "Hit the Gas," and "Sick-O." There's one obvious problem, however: this best-of only features songs from 3X Krazy's first two albums—*Sick-O* and *Stackin Chips*—not including a single song from the group's third and fourth albums—*Immortalized* and *Block Report*. Whatever the reason, this is a serious issue: *Best of 3X Krazy, Vol. 2* isn't actually a best-of in the traditional sense since it only compiles songs from two of the group's albums. What makes this even more problematic is the group's previously released best-of, *20th Century*, which featured these same songs—along with songs from *Immortalized* (*Block Report* hadn't been released yet). In the end, you're left feeling confused—first of all, because there isn't a "Best of 3xKrazy, Vol. 1" (it's titled *20th Century* instead) and, second of all, because half of the group's catalog is ignored for this so-called best-of. —*Jason Birchmeier*

Thrill da Playa (Van Bryant)

Vocals, Producer / Southern Rap, Party Rap, Bass Music
The driving force behind one of the South's leading party rap groups, 69 Boyz, Thrill da Playa spun off a less successful solo career during the late '90s while still keeping the Boyz going strong. Born Van Bryant, the rapper/producer grew up in Jacksonville, FL, and spent a little time overseas in the Army. Upon returning from Germany, where he had been stationed, Thrill hooked up with producer C.C. Lemonhead, who knew Bryant from his days of high school football (where the artist originally earned his nickname). Thrill contributed to Lemonhead's solo album, *Bass to Another Level* (1993); and the producer best known for 95 South's "Whoot (There It Is)" returned the favor, overseeing the debut 69 Boyz album, *199Quad* (1994), and its enormously successful club hit, "Tootsee Roll." The song made an impact across the States, infiltrating even the pop mainstream as a novelty hit. The follow-up album, *The Wait Is Over* (1998), took several years to prepare, and by the time it did drop, the fervor over "Tootsee Roll" had subsided. Following *The Wait Is Over*, Thrill began his solo career with *The Best of Home Bass* (1999), which compiled some of his previous work for the underground label. After another 69 Boyz album, *2069* (2000), Thrill issued a pair of solo releases, *Dunks N D's* (2001) and *The Return of the Big Bronco* (2001). —*Jason Birchmeier*

● **Dunks N D's** / Sep. 25, 2001 / Thundershot ◆◆◆

69 Boyz leader Thrill da Playa invites a number of leading Southern party rap artists to his *Dunks N D's* album. Every song here features someone, and some of the more notable contributors include Tear Da Club Up Thugs ("Slob on My Knob"), JT Money ("How We Roll [Remix]"), Luke ("Strokin"), Jay Ski ("Roll It Up"), and the 69 Boyz ("Summa Dat"). The album thus plays more like a various-artists collection than a traditional album, showcasing some of the best rappers from the Florida area. Plus, there are a few surprises such as an appearance by Daz Dillinger, the West Coast gangsta rapper best known for his Dogg Pound work in the mid-'90s. Amid all of the guest appearances, though, you sometimes forget about Thrill, who seems content lingering in the background. —*Jason Birchmeier*

Thug Life

Group / Gangsta Rap, Hardcore Rap, West Coast Rap
Led by the late Tupac Shakur, the rap crew Thug Life also featured Big Syke, Macadoshis, Mopreme (Shakur's half-brother Komani), and Rated R; the group's lone album, *Volume 1*, appeared on Jive in 1994. —*Jason Ankeny*

● **Volume 1** / 1994 / Jive ◆◆◆

Socially conscious rappers Thug Life rap about inner-city happenings, but also address the problems that cause the hopeless feeling of many residents. Musically, they borrow aspects of G-funk and New York hip-hop. Though it's led by the rap hit "Cradle to the Grave," *Volume 1* has more to offer, like the ghetto lament "Pour out a Little Liquor" and the intriguingly reflective "How Long Will They Mourn Me?" featuring Nate Dogg. —*John Bush*

T.I.

b. Atlanta, GA
Vocals / Southern Rap
Southern rapper T.I. debuted with a 2001 full-length that earned moderate attention for its single "I'm Serious," featuring additional vocals from Beenie Man and production from the Neptunes. A Georgia native, he signed to Arista and delivered *I'm Serious* in October 2001. Though the album charted, the single failed to generate any action. —*John Bush*

● **I'm Serious** / Oct. 9, 2001 / Arista ◆◆◆

Atlanta rookie T.I. wants to be taken seriously, but after listening to the first couple of tracks on his debut album, it's hard to do that. The young rapper is filled with so much bluster and confidence that it's hard to take him at face value. *I'm Serious* is, after all, his first album, and he has the audacity to call himself the king of the South. Despite all the bravado, T.I. still has plenty of lyrical ability and uses it to chronicle his ability to get women ("The Hotel") and to dump women ("I Can't Be Your Man"). He also shows a more sensitive side on the track "I Still Ain't Forgave Myself." Production-wise, *I'm Serious* doles out plenty of typical Southern-fried funk, with the Neptunes producing one of the best tracks on the album with "What's Yo Name," as well as the title track, "I'm Serious." Unfortunately, too many of the other tracks sound the same and a few are blatant rip-offs, namely "Do It," which is a note-for-note remake of Juvenile's hit "Back That Azz Up." T.I. claims to be the king of the South, but on *I'm Serious* he fails to show and prove. He does, however, have potential. If his talent ever matches his confidence, he may be headed for stardom. —*Jon Azpiri*

Tim Dog (Tim Blair)

b. Bronx, NY
East Coast Rap
Bronx rapper Tim Dog (born Tim Blair) fired fresh shots in the long-simmering hip-hop coastal war with his 1991 album *Penicillin on Wax*. His single "F—- Compton" triggered answers and comebacks in West and East Coast circles, and helped his album become an underground sensation, though not a major hit. Tim Dog's alternately leering and fiery tone, confrontational diatribes, and cutting beats were even more vigorous on the follow-up, *Do or Die*, in 1993. —*Ron Wynn*

● **Penicillin on Wax** / Nov. 12, 1991 / Ruffhouse ◆◆◆◆

Bronx rapper Tim Dog informed the world what he thought of West Coast types with the single "F—- Compton." It was the definitive composition on his debut album, setting the stage for a series of angry, often vicious and sneering taunts, challenges, boasts, and putdowns. —*Ron Wynn*

Do or Die / 1993 / CBS ◆◆◆

Tim Dog fired more shots in the constant East vs. West Coast war. His second CD was just as defiant and disrespectful as his debut. Dog once more refused to moderate his chip-on-the-shoulder attitude, the results sometimes being mildly amusing and extremely offensive on other occasions. —*Ron Wynn*

Timbaland (Tim Mosley)

b. Mar. 10, 1971
Producer / East Coast Rap, Hip-Hop, Pop-Rap
Timbaland ascended to the top of the rap industry in the late '90s, remarkably balancing his in-demand hitmaking abilities with his outlandish production style. Few rap producers were capable of such a balance between commerce and craft. Timbaland produced an endless list of hits, primarily for a select group of affiliates (Missy Elliott, Aaliyah, Jay-Z, Ginuwine) though also for a number of other A-list artists (Ludacris, Snoop Dogg, Nas, Justin Timberlake). Yet even so, he always infused a remarkable sense of individuality and creativity into his productions. When you hear a Timbaland production there is no mistaking it for anyone else's work: stuttering bass-heavy bounce beats offset resounding high-end synth stabs, all of this often

complemented by his own signature quiet murmuring beneath the track; and no sampling.

In the late '90s, when Timbaland was still relatively new on the scene, the Virginia native worked extensively with Missy ("The Rain"), Aaliyah ("If Your Girl Only Knew"), and Ginuwine ("Pony"). Later, once he'd established himself with these three, he began working with the top rappers in the industry, namely Jay-Z ("Big Pimpin'"), Nas ("You Won't See Me Tonight"), Snoop Dogg ("Snoop Dogg [What's My Name, Pt. 2]"), and Ludacris ("Rollout [My Business]"). He also worked occasionally with lesser-known regional artists such as Petey Pablo ("Raise Up"), Pastor Troy ("Are We Cuttin'"), and Tweet ("Oops [Oh My]"). As a result of his exceptional success as a producer, Timbaland eventually established his own record label, Beat Club, and began unveiling his own stable of artists (Bubba Sparxxx, Ms. Jade). *—Jason Birchmeier*

● **Welcome to Our World** / Oct. 28, 1997 / Blackground ◆◆◆◆
Welcome to Our World was one of the better rap debuts of 1997, establishing Timbaland & Magoo as gifted hip-hop musicians in their own right. The pair had previously written or produced tracks for such stars as Missy Elliott and Ginuwine, and the spare, kinetic beats of "Supa Dupa Fly" and "Pony" are a good indication of what's available on *Welcome to Our World*. Without relying too heavily on samples, producer Timbaland has created a distinctive sound that is funky in an edgy, creative way—these beats are modern yet timeless, as the hit "Up Jumps Da' Boogie" illustrates. Furthermore, Timbaland is clever enough to keep shifting the tone of the album, balancing the up-tempo party numbers with ballads and menacing, mid-tempo crawls. Magoo is generally up to the challenge, delivering fluid freestyle raps and only occasionally lapsing into cliché. There are still a few slow spots on the record—like most modern-day hip-hop albums, it simply runs way too long—but at its best, *Welcome to Our World* is a welcome change of pace. *—Leo Stanley*

Tim's Bio / Nov. 24, 1998 / Blackground Enterprises ◆◆◆◆
Timbaland, the producer most responsible for the sound of hip-hop circa the late '90s, finally released his proper solo debut (after a 1997 LP recorded as Timbaland & Magoo) in late 1998. It's not quite the personal statement implied in the title, but it is full of excellent productions. He spoofs the hip-hop fad of sampling '80s pop by rewiring familiar themes, like those of *Spider-man* and *I Dream of Jeanie*, into barely recognizable forms. Timbaland regulars like Missy Elliott and Magoo contribute tracks, though the best songs here feature multi platinum rappers like Nas ("To My") and Jay-Z ("Lobster & Scrimp"). Though his trademark style of stuttered beats and obtuse samples is probably best witnessed on singles by Missy Elliott and Aaliyah, *Tim's Bio* is a solid introduction to the talents of hip-hop's best young producer of the late '90s. *—John Bush*

Indecent Proposal / Nov. 20, 2001 / Blackground ◆◆◆
It's easy to forgive Timbaland for putting his solo career on the back burner during the late '90s; after all, he'd been incredibly busy, lending his track-master skills to some of rap's biggest hitters: Ludacris, Bubba Sparxxx, Aaliyah, Jay-Z, Memphis Bleek, and Snoop Dogg, as well as old friend Missy Elliott. Three years after *Tim's Bio*, hip-hop's most distinctive producer finally returned with another project, cobbled with right-hand man Magoo. Though it finds him caught between providing an outlet for his more experimental productions and trying to hit on his own, *Indecent Proposal* still succeeds on most counts. True, it starts off with the uninventive "Drop," but then moves into a set of productions certainly stranger than anything else in the world of commercial rap. Timbaland airs out one of the oddest vocal treatments ever heard on the languorous "Love Me," gets in touch with his P-funk roots by replaying an early Funkadelic track ("I Got a Thing…") for "Baby Bubba," and pumps up the beats to match Jay-Z and Twista's excellent rhyme-trading on "Party People." "It's Your Night" and "Indian Carpet" both spin the Timbaland blueprint into new dimensions, the former with a quirky love jam and the latter with an infectious, inane chorus. Stuck at the end of the LP is the most eagerly awaited track—"I Am Music"—featuring one of the last performances from Timbaland protégé Aaliyah. (Alt-powerhouse Beck was originally slated to duet.) It's not an exciting track and comes as a bit of a letdown (the closest a conscientious producer would ever get to dripping the pop syrup of Puff Daddy), but it doesn't sink the album. Fans of the major-label rap game looking for more than scary strings and tedious rap celebrities will find it an intriguing diversion. *—John Bush*

Time Zone

f. 1983
Group / Electro, Hip-Hop, Alternative Dance
Taking the same approach to hip-hop that funk maverick George Clinton took to his own projects, Afrika Bambaataa created the Time Zone project in the early '80s as another outlet for his projects. Despite the different name, their singles were essentially just Bambaataa productions, with various collaborators like Bill Laswell and James Brown included on certain tracks. Their first release was "Wild Style," a breakdancing single that employed the futuristic synth lines and tight funk instrumentation that he had pioneered on the massive "Planet Rock" 12". Next came the six-part "Unity" single, in which James Brown delivered verses while Bambaataa, bassist Doug Wimbish, guitarist Skip McDonald, and drummer Keith LeBlanc put together one of the funkiest beats of his career. The last '80s Time Zone project was *World Destruction*, a rap/punk crossover that utilized Public Image Ltd.'s *Album* lineup—producer Bill Laswell, organist Bernie Worrell, guitarist Nicky Skopelitis, and drummer Aiyb Dieng—to deliver Bambaataa's angry duet with singer John Lydon. Although the track was a groundbreaking effort, Bambaataa retired the Time Zone name for almost ten years. In the fall of 1995, a number of Bambaataa's late-'80s/early-'90s singles and several new tracks were put together on *Warlocks and Witches, Computer Chips, Microchips and You*, a compilation credited to a new all-star version of Time Zone. Featuring many members of Bambaataa's Zulu Nation as well as several outside collaborators, it did share the same apocalyptic message and P-funk-inspired music that made the original Time Zone singles so powerful, but it had a hard time connecting with rap audiences and proved to be the last release to use the Time Zone moniker. *—Bradley Torreano*

● **Warlocks and Witches, Computer Chips, Microchips and You** / Oct. 31, 1995 / PRO ◆◆◆
A seeming repository for a number of Bambaataa's hit singles of the late '80s/early '90s, this album from Time Zone (one of the groups within the Zulu Nation collective) covers a bit of dancehall reggae, a bit of soul, and a whole pile of hip-hop. Singles represented therein include "Funky Beeper," a remix of "Unity" (with James Brown), "Throw Ya Fuckin' Hands Up," and "Zulu War Chant." Relatively apocalyptic in many respects lyrically, the album still isn't all that horrible in most respects. For fans of Bambaataa's music, it isn't too bad of an addition to the collection. Non-fans should look elsewhere. *—Adam Greenberg*

Tiro de Gracia

f. Chile
Group / Hip-Hop, Tropical
Chilean hip-hop/urban threesome Tiro de Gracia was formed in the mid-'80s by friends Juan Sativo and Lengua Dura, later joined by singer Zaturno, keyboardist Patricio Loaiza, and multi-instrumentalist Camilo Cintolesi. The band made its debut with the release of two independent records, *Arma Calibrada* and *Homosapiens*. After successfully performing at a local TV show and releasing *El Demo Final*, Tiro de Gracia signed up to EMI. They recorded *Ser Humano* in 1997, with contributions from well-known Chilean acts such as Chancho en Piedra, los Tetas, Joe Vasconcellos, and Matahari's Ema Pinto. Soon, the group hit the charts with "El Juego Verdadero." The following album, called *Decisión Final*, was recorded in the U.S. and released in 1999. In June of 2000, Zaturno left the act to join a new project called Tapia Rabia Jackson. *—Drago Bonacich*

● **Ser Humano** / 1997 / EMI ◆◆◆

TLC

f. 1991, Atlanta, GA
Group / Hip-Hop, Dance-Pop, Urban, Club/Dance
TLC was one of the biggest-selling female R&B groups of all time, riding a blend of pop, hip-hop, and urban soul to superstardom during the '90s. Tionne "T-Boz" Watkins, rapper Lisa "Left Eye" Lopes, and Rozonda "Chilli" Thomas managed to appeal equally to pop and R&B audiences, blending catchy hooks and bouncy funk with a sassy, sexy attitude. Initially, their image was equal parts style and spirit, bolstered by a flamboyant, outrageous wardrobe. As time passed, they became equally well known for their chaotic personal lives, leaving a trail of headlines that read like a soap opera plot: arson, rehab, bankruptcy, serious illness, high-profile romances, and countless

intragroup squabbles. After their star-making second album, *CrazySexyCool*, TLC fell into disarray, taking over four years to record the follow-up *FanMail*; even so, they returned more popular than ever, and the hits kept on coming. Unfortunately, tragedy struck in early 2002, when Lopes was killed in a car accident in Honduras.

TLC was formed in Atlanta, GA, in 1991, when Watkins and Lopes decided to split off from another all-female group. In short order, they met Thomas, locally based producer Dallas Austin, and '80s R&B singer Pebbles, who became their manager. They quickly scored a record deal with L.A. Reid and Babyface's new label, LaFace, and in 1992 issued their new-jack-styled debut album *Ooooooohhh...On the TLC Tip*. The video for the sexy, aggressive lead single "Ain't 2 Proud 2 Beg" established their quirky, colorful fashion sense, and true to her nickname, Lopes stirred some attention by wearing a condom over her left eye to promote safe sex. The song became a Top Ten hit, as did its follow-ups, the ballad "Baby-Baby-Baby" (a number-two hit) and "What About Your Friends." TLC was definitely a success, but they weren't quite stars yet, and it remained to be seen whether they could maintain their momentum over the long haul.

Not long before the release of their second album in late 1994, Lisa Lopes was arrested on arson charges. In an alcohol-fueled fit of rage, Lopes vented all the frustrations from her often-stormy relationship with NFL wide receiver Andre Rison, burning his Atlanta mansion to the ground and vandalizing several of his cars. Lopes' lawyers claimed that she had a drinking problem, and while Lopes herself wasn't happy with that defense, she avoided jail time with a sentence of five years' probation; she was also later admitted to an alcohol rehab program. All the publicity certainly didn't hurt *CrazySexyCool*, which became a blockbuster success, albeit for other reasons. Taking a cue from Salt-N-Pepa's makeover on *Very Necessary*, *CrazySexyCool* toned down the boisterousness of their first record in favor of a smoother, more mature presentation; they were still strong and sexual, but now fully adult as well, and were more involved (especially Lopes) in crafting their own material. The slinky lead single "Creep" became TLC's first number-one pop hit, topping the charts for four weeks. It was followed by three more Top Five singles: "Red Light Special," "Waterfalls" (which became their biggest hit ever, spending seven weeks at number one), and "Diggin' on You." TLC was a bona fide phenomenon, and their stylish videos and live performances kept upping the ante for outrageous fashion sense. *CrazySexyCool* eventually sold over 11 million copies in the U.S. alone, and won a Grammy for Best R&B Album.

All was not well, however. In 1995, TLC filed for bankruptcy, claiming debts of over $3.5 million, in part stemming from Lopes' insurance payments over the arson incident. They also claimed they hadn't seen their fair share of royalties from *CrazySexyCool*; LaFace countered that they were simply trying to get a bigger contract. TLC did wind up splitting from Pebbles' management company over the money issues (not helped by the fact that Pebbles' marriage to LaFace head L.A. Reid had gone through a nasty breakup). What was more, it was announced that for some time, Watkins had been battling sickle-cell anemia, which sapped her energy and often made performing difficult. TLC spent much of 1996 getting their financial affairs in order, and was set to reenter the studio in the summer of 1997. The sessions had trouble getting off the ground, though, thanks to the group's public spat with producer Dallas Austin, claiming that his fee was far too high; not only had Austin played a significant role in the creation of their music, but the split was all the more awkward because he and Thomas had just had a son together. It took until early 1998 to finally resolve the producer situation, and Austin wound up handling the vast majority of the record. Still, it took quite some time to put together; Lopes announced in the summer of 1998 that she was working on a solo record, and Watkins tried her hand at acting with an appearance in the Hype Williams-directed *Belly*. All the delays, tension, and side projects fueled rumors of the group's impending breakup.

TLC's third album was finally released at the beginning of 1999. The hotly anticipated *FanMail* debuted at number one, and its first single, "No Scrubs"—a dismissal of men who didn't measure up—topped the charts as well for four weeks. The critically acclaimed follow-up, "Unpretty," tackled unrealistic beauty standards, and spent three weeks at number one. *FanMail* wound up going six-times platinum, and won another Best R&B Album Grammy. As TLC prepared to tour in late 1999, tensions between the individual members spilled over into a public feud; Watkins and Thomas criticized Lopes for putting herself before the group, and Lopes responded by

blasting TLC's recent music and challenging her bandmates to record solo albums, so that fans could see who the real talent lay with. The blowup was only temporary, but rumors about TLC's future continued to swirl. Lopes continued to publicize her upcoming solo project, and Thomas eventually began working on her own album as well. Watkins married rapper Mack 10 in the summer of 2000, and had their first child not long after. Meanwhile, tabloid favorite Lopes continued to make headlines when she disappeared for over a week, missing a family function and a press conference (she turned out to be with a new boyfriend).

In 2001, TLC somehow managed to regroup and enter the studio together to work on material for a new album. That summer, a report surfaced that Lopes had postponed a wedding with, of all people, Andre Rison. Meanwhile, her solo debut, *Supernova*, was scheduled for release and then scrapped on several occasions; it eventually came out overseas, but domestically Arista pulled the plug. Meanwhile, TLC's recording halted while Watkins was hospitalized from complications with her anemia. At the beginning of 2002, Lopes announced that she had signed a solo deal with the infamous Suge Knight's new label Tha Row, for which she would begin recording a follow-up to the unreleased *Supernova* under the name N.I.N.A. (New Identity Non-Applicable). Sadly, she would never get the chance. Vacationing in her favorite getaway spot, Honduras, Lopes was driving a rented SUV with at least seven (possibly eight) passengers. Reportedly speeding, she lost control of the vehicle, which flipped over; she was the only member of the party to be seriously injured, and died from severe head trauma on April 25, 2002. The surviving members of TLC announced their intention to complete the album they'd begun, though without their most vibrant character, the group's long-term future remained in doubt. —*Steve Huey*

Ooooooohhh...On the TLC Tip / Feb. 25, 1992 / LaFace ✦✦✦

TLC's debut album, *Ooooooohhh...On the TLC Tip*, established the trio's image and unorthodox fashion sense, which at this point was based on baggy, brightly colored clothes and Lisa "Left Eye" Lopes' trademark condom. Some accused them of borrowing their look from Bell Biv DeVoe, and their female-positive, pro-safe-sex attitudes from Salt-N-Pepa, but TLC has the boundless enthusiasm to make it all convincingly their own. What they don't always have are the songs to pull off a consistent album. The most infectious songs are naturally the singles: "Ain't 2 Proud 2 Beg" is bouncy, catchy, and sexually assertive, and "What About Your Friends" is an equally danceable meditation on true friendship. The chart-topping ballad "Baby-Baby-Baby" is typically well-crafted Babyface, if a little by the numbers. Some of the album tracks keep the sense of fun going, but others fall flat—not that they're bad, they just aren't that memorable. On the plus side, Left Eye gets a lot of space for her distinctively nasal, girlish rapping, and the entire group drops rhymes on "Das da Way We Like 'Em." Although it's uneven, the best moments of *On the TLC Tip* deserved their popularity, and set the stage for the group's blockbuster success the next time out. —*Steve Huey*

★ CrazySexyCool / Nov. 15, 1994 / LaFace ✦✦✦✦✦

On their second album, TLC downplays their overt rap connections, recording a smooth, seductive collection of contemporary soul reminiscent of both Philly soul and Prince, powered by new-jack and hip-hop beats. Lisa Lopes contributes the occasional rap, but the majority of *CrazySexyCool* belongs to Tionne Watkins and Rozonda Thomas. While they aren't the most accomplished vocalists—they have a tendency to be just slightly off-key—the material they sing is consistently strong. As the cover of Prince's "If I Was Your Girlfriend" indicates, TLC favors erotic, mid-tempo funk. Yet the group removes any of the psychosexual complexities of Prince's songs, leaving a batch of sexy material that just sounds good, especially the hit singles. Both "Creep" and "Red Light Special" have a deep groove that accentuates the slinky hooks, but it's "Waterfalls," with its gently insistent horns and guitar lines and instantly memorable chorus, that ranks as one of the classic R&B songs of the '90s. —*Stephen Thomas Erlewine*

FanMail / Feb. 23, 1999 / LaFace ✦✦✦✦

CrazySexyCool was one of those records that defined an era. Few records before it combined hip-hop and classic soul songwriting quite as intoxicatingly or gracefully—the performances and productions were utterly seamless. It would have been difficult to top anyway, but TLC had it doubly bad, since a number of behind-the-scenes problems delayed a sequel for nearly five years. As with any eagerly anticipated record, that follow-up, *FanMail*, arrived with too many expectations. And initially, it may be disappointing to realize TLC doesn't forge new ground with *Fanmail*, but after a few spins, it settles in that nobody else makes urban soul quite as engaging as this. Not that it was easy to make this record, as the head-spinning list of collaborators indicates. Almost ten producers worked on the record, all trying to replicate the easy, appealing sound of *CrazySexyCool*. And "replicate" is the right word, since there are no new innovations on *Fanmail*, apart from a few lifts from the Timbaland book of tricks. Nevertheless, that may be for the best, since TLC and their army of producers have spent time crafting the songs and productions, turning *Fanmail* into a record that almost reaches the peaks of its predecessor. By the end of the record, it appears that they can do it all—funky, hip-hop-fueled dance-pop, seductive ballads, and mid-tempo jams—and they can do it all well. Other groups try to reach these heights, but they don't have the skills or the material to pull it off quite so well. True, the five-year wait felt interminable, and they're now standard-bearers instead of pioneers, but if it takes TLC as long to make a sequel to *Fanmail*, so be it—they have one of the best track records in '90s urban soul. —*Stephen Thomas Erlewine*

3D / Sep. 17, 2002 / La Face ✦✦✦

How good is TLC? So good that they survive the tragic, early death of a key member—Lisa "Left Eye" Lopes was killed in a car accident during the recording of *3D*—with grace and style, turning out a record that sits comfortably next to their modern classics, *CrazySexyCool* and *Fanmail*. Perhaps surviving members Chilli and T-Boz spend a little too much time in the lyrics paying tribute to their colleague, but it's easy to glide past that and just concentrate on the strong songwriting and stylish production. Like their previous albums, the particulars don't matter as much as the overall impression. No member of TLC has an astounding voice, but their skills are exploited to the hilt, since the material not only suits them, it's melodic, memorable, and grows in stature with each play. Best of all, the production plays to the strength of the song, balancing the group's character and abilities with the hooks and character of the song. Perhaps *3D* doesn't blaze trails like their other albums, but it never plays it safe and it always satisfies, and it's one of the best modern soul albums of 2002. A bittersweet triumph, perhaps, but it's better to go out on a positive note. —*Stephen Thomas Erlewine*

Tone-Loc (Anthony Smith)

b. Mar. 3, 1966, Los Angeles, CA

West Coast Rap, Pop-Rap

Tone-Loc (born Anthony Smith) soared from obscurity into pop stardom in 1989 when his hoarse voice and unmistakable delivery made the song "Wild Thing" (using a sample from Van Halen's "Jamie's Cryin'") a massive hit. The song was cowritten by Marvin Young, bka Young MC, as was the second single smash, "Funky Cold Medina." The album *Loc-ed After Dark* became the second rap release ever to top the pop charts. Tone-Loc expanded his horizons into acting in 1992 and 1993, appearing a few times on the Fox sitcom *Roc.* He was also in the films *Posse* and *Ace Ventura: Pet Detective*, and in 1991 returned to recording with *Cool Hand Loc.* —*Ron Wynn*

● **Loc-ed After Dark** / 1989 / Delicious Vinyl/Rhino ✦✦✦✦

A forgotten man in the rise of West Coast rap, Tone-Loc was effectively cut off from his hometown scene in Los Angeles by his unexpected pop success. Paced by the singles "Wild Thing" and "Funky Cold Medina"—both cowritten by a pre-fame Young MC, and some of the earliest productions by the legendary Dust Brothers—Loc's debut album, *Loc-ed After Dark*, became the second rap album to top the pop charts, following the Beastie Boys' *Licensed to Ill.* Loc's distinctively rough, raspy voice and easygoing delivery made him an appealing storyteller, but he was aiming for the streets more than the pop charts. So there's the occasional profanity, the stalker-tinged title track, and "Cheeba Cheeba," which made waves at the time as one of the earliest pro-marijuana raps on record (of course, this was before Cypress Hill, and Nancy Reagan's "Just Say No" campaign was still fresh in the public's mind). The minor singles "I Got It Goin' On" and "On Fire" (the latter the first record ever released on Delicious Vinyl) are both pretty good, but some of the album's momentum is wasted on some fairly standard MC boasts (Loc has much more personality than he does lyrical technique). Even if *Loc-ed After Dark* is erratic, though, it still deserves more respect than it's generally accorded. —*Steve Huey*

Cool Hand Loc / Nov. 19, 1991 / Delicious Vinyl/Rhino ✦✦✦

Aiming for credibility among hardcore hip-hoppers, Delicious Vinyl was careful not to include a lot of pop-influenced material on Tone-Loc's second

album, *Cool Hand Loc.* But sadly, the inventiveness he displayed on "Wild Thing" continued working against Loc among b-boys and hip-hop's hardcore, who still resented the success he'd enjoyed in the pop market. Though not quite as strong as the triple-platinum *Loc-ed After Dark*—either commercially or artistically—the album is a respectable and satisfying effort. The former L.A. gang member tends to overdo it with boasting lyrics—a problem he shares with quite a few other rappers—but his boasts are often quite clever. Sadly, Tone-Loc didn't have much longevity; after *Cool Hand Loc*, little was heard about him. —*Alex Henderson*

Too Short (Todd Shaw)

b. Apr. 28, 1966, Los Angeles, CA

Vocals / Dirty Rap, West Coast Rap, G-Funk, Dirty South, Golden Age

Born in Los Angeles, but an Oakland resident by the age of 14, Too Short was the first West Coast rap star, recording three albums on his own before he made his major-label debut with 1988's gold album *Born to Mack*; his next four all went platinum. Anticipating much of the later gangsta phenomenon, he restricted his lyrical themes to tales of sexual prowess and physical violence, with the occasional social-message track to mix things up. After the release of *Gettin' It (Album Number Ten)* in 1996, Too Short decided to retire, his status assured as one of the most successful solo rappers of the 1980s and early '90s, although that decision would prove short-lived.

Born Todd Shaw on April 28, 1966, Short grew up in L.A.'s South Central; soon after his family moved to Oakland in the early '80s, he began selling tapes out of the back of his car. Signed to the local label 75 Girls, he released his first proper album in 1983, *Don't Stop Rappin'*. Three albums followed in the next two years, after which Too Short formed his own Dangerous Music label with friend Freddy B. He recorded *Born to Mack* in 1988, and sold more than 50,000 copies just by riding around the region. New York's Jive Records picked up on the buzz from across the country, and provided a national deal for the album one year later. With virtually no radio airplay, *Born to Mack* went gold and its follow-up, *Life Is… Too Short*, achieved platinum sales by 1989.

The immense success of Too Short during 1988 and 1989 made him much more viable for radio airplay, and "The Ghetto"—from 1990's *Short Dog's in the House*—made number 12 on the R&B charts, even enjoying a brief stay just outside the pop Top 40. He continued his hit track record with 1992's *Shorty the Pimp* and 1993's *Get in Where You Fit In*, both of which went platinum. By the time of 1995's *Cocktails*, however, Too Short began to be drowned out by a glut of similar-sounding West Coasters, and though *Gettin' It (Album Number Ten)* became his fifth platinum album, by late 1996, he decided to retire. Just three years later, he returned with the aptly titled *Can't Stay Away*, which debuted in the Top Ten and went gold. *You Nasty* followed in the fall of 2000. —*John Bush*

Players / 1985 / 75 Girls ✦✦

Born to Mack / 1988 / Jive ✦✦✦

By the time Jive Records released *Born to Mack*, Too Short's major label debut, the young rapper was already a music industry veteran, having released several albums on the independent 75 Girls label. With *Born to Mack* Too Short continued the formula that had already made him a regional star—sexually explicit lyrics over sparse, bass-heavy rhythm tracks. What is missing from this album, though, is any levity, humor, or musical exploration. Without benefit of a lyrical wink or nod, and without any sign of his future head-nodding, funk workouts, Too Short's trademark "pimp" tales were stripped bare, revealing themselves too misogynist to be enjoyable. Even so, due to the success of the nearly ten-minute, underground smash, "Freaky Tales," *Born to Mack* expanded Too Short's fan base past his Oakland, CA hometown, eventually selling past gold status. Many of Short's later efforts, such as *Life Is… Too Short* and *Shorty the Pimp* were funnier, funkier, and plain better, but *Born to Mack* stands as most of the world's introduction to one of rap's most enduring, and best-selling, artists ever. —*Mtume Salaam*

★ **Life Is … Too Short** / 1988 / Jive ✦✦✦✦✦

Too Short never had the skills or technique of LL Cool J or Big Daddy Kane, but what the Oakland rapper lacks in technique, he's always more than made up for with irresistible, '70s-inspired funk grooves that simply won't quit. When Short—after enjoying a small cult following for a few years in Northern California—joined a major label with *Life Is… Too Short's* predecessor, *Born to Mack*, too many East Coast MCs were inundating hip-hop with clichéd tracks consisting of only James Brown samples and a drum machine. Too

Short, however, presented an attractive alternative with highly melodic, danceable tracks that made no secret of his love of '70s funk heroes like Parliament, the Ohio Players, and Cameo. This CD's X-rated, sexually explicit lyrics received their share of vehement criticism, and the MC responded that Too Short is an outrageous character who shouldn't be taken too seriously. Be that as it may, his commanding reflection on the drug plague, "City of Dope," underscores the fact that he's cheating himself artistically by not devoting more time to social commentary and less time to exploiting sex. —*Alex Henderson*

Short Dog's in the House / Aug. 1990 / Jive ✦✦✦✦

With *Short Dog's in the House*, Oakland's most sexually explicit MC gave his followers more of what he was known for—X-rated lyrics, a relaxed style of rapping and addictive, melodic tracks recalling the spelendor of '70s funk. R&B fans who complained that rap on the whole wasn't sufficiently melodic couldn't make that complaint about the distinctive Too Short. When his raunchy lyrics continued to come under fire, he maintained that he was simply portraying a character—and that he wasn't really the ghetto pimp he portrayed. As entertaining as his albums are, Short's inspired interpretation of Donny Hathaway's "The Ghetto" makes it crystal clear that he would do well to be more lyrically challenging more often. —*Alex Henderson*

Shorty the Pimp / Jul. 14, 1992 / Jive ✦✦✦✦

Shorty the Pimp was Too Short's seventh album. As one would expect from an entertainer with six albums behind him, Too Short had by now perfected his craft. Though his focus was still on womanizing and pimping, by 1992 the rest of the rap world had "caught up" with the Oakland rapper's explicit brand of boasting and bragging. Aware of this, Too Short had gradually begun adding battle rhymes ("In the Trunk"), social commentary ("I Want to Be Free"), and cautionary tales ("So You Want to Be a Gangster") to the mix. Never particularly gifted as a rapper, Too Short's proved himself a wily veteran in his ability to squeeze every bit of effect out of his relatively simple style. But what separated *Shorty the Pimp* from the rest of the now-crowded rap field was the music. Producer Ant Banks, multi-instrumentalist Shorty B, and Too Short himself created a satisfying blend of funk samples augmented by live drums and deftly played bass lines. Many of the backing tracks are composed well enough to be successful on their own. —*Mtume Salaam*

Get in Where You Fit In / Oct. 26, 1993 / Jive ✦✦

Greatest Hits, Vol. 1: The Player Years, 1983-1988 / Nov. 10, 1993 / In-A-Minute ✦✦✦✦✦

If you've never read the collected works of Chester Himes or Iceberg Slim, simply run through this Too Short anthology and you'll have the general idea. Although never an inventive rapper or clever composer of rhymes, Too Short was smart enough to find his niche and stick to it. Most people who continually mined the pimp arena quickly become merely tedious; Too Short became both tedious and profitable. —*Ron Wynn*

Cocktails / Jan. 24, 1995 / Jive ✦✦✦✦

CD number nine from Too Short carries on his tradition of lyrics about the joys of pimping, rapped moderately to groovy, funky, jazzy beats. Delete the raps from Too Short tales, and you still have a commercial product. Spacy Bootsy Collins-influenced vocals appeared on some cuts, giving the funk an eerie feel. Too Short likes naked, foxy ladies on his covers, and *Cocktails* is no exception; he picked a beauty pictured with a snake coiled around her curvaceous brown body. Homie Ant Banks appears on "Can I Get A B#tch," and 2Pac, MC Breed, and Father Dom join him on "We Do This"—some nice rappin' on this one. "Coming Up Short" catches Too Short at his pimpingest best, spitting out mack lyrics to a funky-azz beat like an ol' school Chicago pimp. A female vocalist changes the pace on "Things Changes," adding some emotive vocal runs; Baby D, who sounds like he's seven, appears like a regular and gets off a tight rap that belies his age. Too Short is all geeked on "Paystyle," a mini macking fable and his best rap on the set. On the last track, "Sample the Funk," he acknowledges the creators of funk, James Brown, George Clinton, Bootsy Collins, Johnny "Guitar" Watson, the Ohio Players... and so on. According to Too Short and his homies, pimping is an all-American game, and they praise the nefarious endeavor on every track. —*Andrew Hamilton*

Gettin' It (Album Number Ten) / Jun. 18, 1996 / Jive ✦✦✦

At the time of its release, Too Short claimed that *Gettin' It* was his retirement album. If that is indeed the case, he picked the perfect moment to drop out of the hip-hop business—as the album shows, he's already beginning to border

on self-parody. There are some good moments on the album, particularly the singles "Buy You Some" and "Gettin' It," which feature Erick Sermon and Parliament/Funkadelic, respectively. But too much of the album consists of tired boasts and worn-out beats. Furthermore, the album is padded with filler, making it more difficult to dig out the gems buried next to the dreck. TooShort may not have worn out his welcome with *Gettin' It*, but a string of albums similar to it would prove to be too much for even his dedicated fans. After *Gettin' It*, he either needs to make good on his promise of retiring, or he needs to find a new sound. —*Stephen Thomas Erlewine*

Can't Stay Away / Feb. 23, 1999 / Jive ✦✦✦

TooShort was 33 when *Can't Stay Away* came out in 1999, and for a rapper, that's old age. Many MCs have seen their fortunes decline considerably by the time they hit 30, although Short managed to have more longevity than most of his peers. The Oakland rapper had claimed that 1996's *Gettin' It* would be his last album, but obviously, he wasn't ready to give up rapping just yet. You won't find anything groundbreaking on this CD—Short continues to combine sexually explicit rhymes with a relaxed, laid-back style of rapping and melodic, sleek tracks that recall the funk and soul music of the 1970s. Many hip-hop writers argued that his formula had long since grown tiresome, and to be sure, Short is cheating himself creatively by being so predictable and not trying something different. Nonetheless, he still comes up with some infectious, catchy grooves here and there, and there are times when his off-color humor is still fairly amusing—"Invasion of the Flat Booty Bitches" and "More Freaky Tales" are definitely good for a few laughs. Much of the album finds Short featuring various rappers who were signed to his Too Short label; clearly, he was a smart enough businessman to reason that even if his own popularity faded, he could make money putting younger MCs to work. *Can't Stay Away* is far from Short's best album, but it has its moments—and it's an album that many of his diehard fans will probably want despite its limitations and shortcomings. —*Alex Henderson*

You Nasty / Sep. 12, 2000 / Jive ✦✦✦

On the appropriately titled *You Nasty*, the ever-pimpin' Too Short continues to do what he does best: drop commentary rhymes about relations between powerful men and desperate women over sparse beats, knee deep in '70s-flavored funk. There's little denying that he can rhyme with masterful finesse—this is his 12th album, after all—and that his beats are once again top-notch, but the real issue here involves how heedful his themes have increasingly become. A shadow of bitterness seems to have overcast his agenda, as his rhymes are generally cautionary here, much more so than before. They're nonetheless brilliantly witty, particularly "2 Bitches," throughout which Short colorfully narrates the sort of fantastic scenario he'd downright patented over the years, beginning most famously with "Freaky Tales." Other songs like the opening pair—"Anything Is Possible" and the title track—aren't quite as ideal, instead expressing the jaded bitterness that had begun creeping into his rhymes during the latter half of the '90s. Crème de la crème production by Ant Banks, Erick Sermon, and Jazze Pha certainly make Short's bitch-this, bitch-that rants as palatable as ever. If there's one thing sorely missing here, however, it's not the funk, nor the wit, nor the sleaze, but rather the fun—the sort of lighthearted fun that made classic songs like "Mack Attack" and "Cocktails" such a laugh. The cautionary tone of *You Nasty* certainly portrays Short's pimp wisdom. Chances are, though, that you're here for "2 Bitches"-style good times rather than heedful lectures about the evils that women do. —*Jason Birchmeier*

Chase the Cat / Nov. 20, 2001 / Jive ✦✦✦

Over a dozen albums into his career by the time *Chase the Cat* came out in 2001, Too Short had exhausted his ideas years before. However, just because Short doesn't have anything new to say doesn't mean he's not worth listening to. In fact, it's rather remarkable how Short was able to sustain his career, album after album with song after song about sexual politics—year after year after year. No matter how many times he hollers "bitch!" in his trademark dialect ("bee-atch!"), it never seems to lose its effect. And no matter how many times Short tells you his "Freaky Tales" and how to manage your relationships, you still feel like calling him Uncle Too Short—the wise old uncle who's experienced it all and is always glad to give you advice about certain kinds of women and life. The reason he's still effective, even a dozen albums into his career, is because little has changed since the days of *Born to Mack*—even then Short was a veteran, relating his firsthand experiences from the streets, and remains so on *Chase the Cat*. Here, he works with many of the same producers (SBX [Xavier Hargrove], Jazze Pha, Ant Banks) and rappers (E-40, B-Legit, MC Breed, Erick Sermon) that he worked throughout the latter end of the '90s. It shouldn't surprise you then when *Chase the Cat* sounds a lot like the preceding few albums: *You Nasty, Can't Stay Away,* and *Gettin' It.* Unfortunately, though, *Chase the Cat* isn't quite as inspired as those albums. Short often lets his guests do most of the work, and this approach works well on album highlights like "I Luv" (featuring Trick Daddy, Scarface, and Daz Dillinger) and "Domestic Violence" (featuring E-40). However, even if *Chase the Cat* is ultimately just another Too Short album, perhaps even one of his lesser albums, it should still satisfy longtime fans. —*Jason Birchmeier*

What's My Favorite Word? / Sep. 10, 2002 / Jive ✦✦
Ever since Too Short returned from his brief retirement in 1999 with *Can't Stay Away,* he's sounded increasingly comfy with letting his supporting cast flavor his albums, and *What's My Favorite Word?* is no different. Short invites his usual guests—longtime Cali standbys Ant Banks, E-40, and B-Legit; Atlanta rabble-rouser Lil Jon; and the one and only George Clinton—along with a few surprise ones: Twista, Petey Pablo, Big Gipp, and U.G.K. members Bun B and Pimp C. This lively cast of characters certainly colors the album and makes it more than just another Too Short album, even if that's precisely what *What's My Favorite Word?* is. The highlight here is Lil Jon's two-part "Quit Hatin'," which begins like your typical Eastside Boyz club-banger à la "Bia', Bia' " and "I Don't Give A…" and then transitions into a screwed-style interpretation given a further Texan feel when Pimp C steps up. Elsewhere, Short spits mostly pimp game as you'd expect, though perhaps a bit more laconically and with a bit more sung hooks than usual. *What's My Favorite Word?* isn't extraordinary relative to Short's dozen-plus other albums, yet it should still please his fans, particularly those who enjoy his usual post-*Gettin' It* supporting cast. —*Jason Birchmeier*

Top Quality

Vocals / East Coast Rap, Hardcore Rap
Out of all of EPMD's associates who broke out during the early '90s, Top Quality was one of the least successful, failing to attain the kind of popularity enjoyed by Keith Murray, Das EFX, Redman, and even K-Solo. *Magnum Opus,* his 1993 album for RCA, was produced by EPMD's Parrish "PMD" Smith and Charlie Marotta (EPMD, Das EFX, Redman). —*Andy Kellman*

● Magnum Opus / Nov. 14, 1993 / RCA ✦✦
For a short span of time during the early '90s, the offshoots of EPMD stylistically held the entire New York City rap scene on lockdown. While Erick Sermon's Def Squad scored early and often with Redman leading the charge, PMD's Hit Squad was left hoping to follow up the success of Das EFX with the release of *Magnum Opus* by Top Quality. Despite its obscurity and lackluster reception, the album reveals an uncanny panorama of East Coast hip-hop circa 1993. Complete with references to Philly blunts and "Buddha," formatted at times in pig Latin and abrasively delivered by a roughneck MC, the clichés on *Magnum Opus* are abundant. But Top Quality actually proves why such confrontational music became so overwhelmingly popular in the first place. With a lyrical versatility seldom expressed within a single rap album, Top Quality pulls out all of the stops in order to outwit his beats. Indeed, the title track has become somewhat famous as an exercise in creative sampling. Other highlights include the story of the "Graveyard Shift," along with a few moments of compelling production provided by Charlie Marotta. —*Robert Gabriel*

Total Devastation

f. 1988
Group / Hip-Hop, Dancehall
Sort of an underachiever version of Cypress Hill, Total Devastation began as a trio in 1988 with Rasta Redeye, Soopa Dupa, and DJ Tuf Cut Tim the Fat Beat Maker. The San Francisco group released a self-titled debut in 1993 that fused reggae and hip-hop in a single-minded dedication to the subject of marijuana. An underground hit single, "Many Clouds of Smoke," guaranteed that the group would issue a follow-up. Total Devastation was reduced to a duo of Rasta Redeye and Big Tone when their *highly* anticipated sophomore effort, *Stone Age,* appeared five years later. — *Wade Kergan*

Total Devastation / 1993 / PGA ✦✦
For those who can't get enough of Cypress Hill's *Black Sunday,* Total Devastation offers another stash of marijuana-based rap. Sporting a cartoon

cover of the band members toting a "Legalize It!" sign, *Total Devastation* credits the originator of that phrase by beginning with a snippet of the Peter Tosh classic. Yet despite similar touches throughout the album, it's obvious that the band's appreciation of Jamaican culture centers on ganja rather than reggae. Updating Cheech and Chong for the '90s, tracks like "Hemp Rally" and "Many Clouds of Smoke" contain amusing raps that cover topics ranging from marijuana legislation to then-President Bill Clinton's infamous "I didn't inhale" sound bite. The latter song also sums up the group's philosophy by declaring, "There's only three things in life that I need/Money, safe sex, and a whole lot of weed." Although not really a song in the traditional sense, "Hemp Hemp Hooray (Relegalize Today)" provides the most interesting diversion, as guest speaker Michael M. of H.E.M.P. educates listeners with a historical defense of the controversial plant. While *Black Sunday*'s liner notes contained a similar lesson in a written format, *Total Devastation*'s packaging goes one step further, encouraging grass-roots activism by including the addresses and phone numbers of cannabis-friendly organizations. Total Devastation might have been wise to expand on that angle instead of pursuing the sophomoric humor and gratuitous misogyny that sink to a nadir on the unforgivable "Fat Blunt Caper." Even when the lyrical content is tolerable, unimaginative samples from such overused sources as George Clinton's "Atomic Dog" often result in myopic mediocrity. *Total Devastation*'s best tracks suggest the group is capable of generating more than a weak, fading buzz, but the album as a whole indicates they're probably too stoned to care. — *Vince Ripol*

Tony Touch

DJ, Producer / Hip-Hop, Hardcore Rap, Turntablism
Brooklyn-based Puerto Rican freestyle DJ/producer Tony Touch has been an influential force in the mix-tape scene since 1991, crafting reggae, rap, house, R&B, and Latin underground tapes. Two of his tapes, "50 Emcess Parts 1 & 2," won Touch the annual Mixtape Awards' Best Freestyles award two years in a row. Touch has spun at clubs in New York, Miami, and Puerto Rico; has toured with Guru, the Roots, Fat Joe, and Big Punisher, among others; and produced songs by Flipmode Squad, Sunz of Man, and Cocoa Brovaz. As an MC, he has worked with P.F. Cuttin' and DJ Muggs on the *Rican-Struction* EP. Touch also records under the names Von Bo Bo, Mr. Coco Tosso, and Tony Toca, and has released over 60 mix tapes, including *Can't Sleep on the Streets* and *Power Cypha 3: The Grand Finale,* many of them on his own Touch Entertainment empire. In 1999 he signed to Tommy Boy and released *The Piece Maker* in spring 2000. —*Heather Phares*

● Power Cypha 3: The Grand Finale / 1999 / Touch/Tommy Boy ✦✦✦✦✦
Power Cypha 3: The Grand Finale (subtitled "Another Fifty MCs") is the 60th mix tape produced by Tony Touch; however, one should not expect tired beats, unoriginal tracks, or weak artists. Touch, who is known as the "Taino Turntable Terrorist," has established an amazing number of contacts throughout the rap industry, especially in New York City and Puerto Rico, during his eight years of producing mix tapes. These musical allies give Tony Touch the edge over both commercial and underground mix tapes. On this album alone, Common, Wyclef Jean, Q-Tip, Black Star, Eminem, and over 45 other artists contribute original material. The result is an incredible collection of hip-hop's best artists on two excellently mixed discs. *Power Cypha 3: The Grand Finale* is not perfect, though—a few of the tracks suffer from poor recording quality and raps are usually only a minute or two long—but this underground mix tape that is "For Promotional Uses Only" is still recommended. —*John Hinrichsen*

The Piece Maker / Apr. 18, 2000 / Tommy Boy ✦✦✦
DJ Touch has assembled an impressive list of guests (both rappers and fellow turntablists) on this sprawling disc of state-of-the-art hip-hop. Too bad some of it is marred by homophobic proclamations and played-out clichés (how many more Scarface interludes can the hip-hop community tolerate?). Still, appearances by Gang Starr, Wu-Tang Clan, De La Soul, and Mos Def rise above the muck and elevate Touch's skills above the pedestrian paths they sometimes take. —*Michael Gallucci*

Traffixx

b. Chicago, IL
Hardcore Rap
Though few if any commercially successful rappers came out of Chicago, Traffixx proved to be one of the Midwestern city's more promising artists. The

rapper worked closely with producer Snatcha Beatz on *Watch Me Now*, an album highlighted by the single "Throw It Up." Like most of his Chicago peers, Traffixx delivers his rhymes with force and slight aggression, repping his city despite its lowly status in the rap game. —*Jason Birchmeier*

● **Watch Me Now** / 2001 / Soulsound ✦✦✦

Highlighted by the high-energy "Throw It Up," *Watch Me Now* features rapper Traffixx on the mike and producer Snatcha Beatz on the boards. The Chicago duo—born Antoine Larkins and Erik Hammond, respectively—performs nearly the entire album, with the exception of only a few minor guest appearances. As mentioned, "Throw It Up" is the album's standout track, also appearing in remixed format as a bonus track. —*Jason Birchmeier*

Tre-8

b. Sep. 7, 1981, Detroit, MI
Producer, Vocals / Hardcore Rap, Hip-Hop, Dirty South
Producer/rapper Tre-8 is one of the many hip-hop artists to come out of Master P's No Limit Records during the mid-'90s, when P had one of the most exciting collections of young talent in the rap industry. Tre-8 was born in Detroit but had relocated to New Orleans, where he first began to explore his skills as a producer. He began to craft tracks that fit into the lazy drawl and stripped-down production of many other New Orleans rappers, and soon he caught the ear of local entrepreneur Master P. When the two met, they discovered that Tre-8's beats fit P's vision of no-frills, hardcore hip-hop, which made P enthusiastic about adding Tre to his stable of producers. He signed a distribution deal with the label, but wouldn't commit to a contract that would give P exclusive rights to his output, which created bad blood between the two. Despite the growing tension, he was still included on their next compilation, 1995's *Down South Hustlers*. His solo debut, *Ghetto Stories*, was also released through No Limit, but he continued to look for a major-label deal despite P's insistence that he sign. After contributing beats to Master P's *Ice Cream Man* and Mia X's *Good Girl Gone Bad*, he ended his relationship with the label, starting his own Smoke 1 Records for 1996's *Dey Scarred of Me*. This would turn out to be his biggest mistake, since No Limit's popularity grew during the next few years while Tre struggled to get distribution and found it hard to get his material heard in the competitive New Orleans scene. Still, he continued to release his own records, including 1998's *Nuttin' but Drama* and 2002's *2 Hot 4 TV*. —*Bradley Torreano*

● **Nuttin' But Drama** / 1998 / Smoke 1 ✦✦✦

Armageddon / Jun. 29, 1999 / Smoke 1 ✦✦

Treacherous Three

f. 1978, Harlem, NY
Group / Old School Rap, Hip-Hop
One of the first rap groups on record, Treacherous Three recorded for both of the major old school labels (Enjoy, Sugar Hill) and introduced a faster style of rapping (dubbed speed rapping) that influenced the later course of hip-hop. Formed by a trio of Harlem high school friends—Kool Moe Dee (Mohandas Dewese) and L.A. Sunshine (Lamar Hill), plus DJ Easy Lee (Theodore Moy'e)—the group picked up a formerly Bronx-based MC named Special K (Kevin Keaton) and became Treacherous Three. Just after the group began performing in 1978, they learned that another friend, Spoonie Gee, who'd recently recorded his first single, was about to record again for Bobby Robinson's Enjoy label. They practiced for months (with Kool Moe Dee especially spending time working on his speed raps) and recorded "The New Rap Language," which furnished the B side for Spoonie Gee's 1980 single "Love Rap." "The New Rap Language" upped the ante for all other active rappers, and sparked a pair of Enjoy classics: "The Body Rock" and "At the Party" (the latter slightly cribbed from Grandmaster Flash's "Birthday Party").

By 1981, Treacherous Three had moved to Sugar Hill, following fellow Enjoy act Grandmaster Flash & the Furious Five. The singles "Feel the Heart Beat" and "Whip It" were classic rap party jams, benefiting from Sugar Hill's crack-house band: bassist Doug Wimbish, guitarist Skip McDonald, and drummer Keith LeBlanc. One of their live jams with Funky Four Plus One appeared on a long-playing 12" titled *Live Convention '81* (Disco Wax), and the trio made the jump to the screen with 1984's *Beat Street*, in which they performed "Xmas Rap" with the debut of Doug E. Fresh, but broke up soon after. Kool Moe Dee initially attended college, but began a successful solo career by 1986, while Special K put out his own solo single in 1987, and

DJ Easy Lee did a little production work. Treacherous Three reunited in 1993 to record their first LP, *Old School Flava*. —*John Bush*

Old School Flava / Feb. 1994 / Wrap ✦✦

● **Turn It Up** / Jul. 11, 2000 / Sequel ✦✦✦✦✦

Sequel's winning wrap-up of one of the best old school crews does have a major miscue (not including their debut, "The New Rap Language"), but it certainly overwhelms all the other poor excuses for Treacherous Three compilations. From Kool Moe Dee's blistering speed rap to open "Whip It," Treacherous Three proved that hip-hop was soon going to transcend the block-party aesthetic to become a phenomenon focused on MCs testing each other in dramatic rap battles, more akin to jazz blowing contests. Still, for all the party jams and braggadocio exercises ("At the Party," "The Body Rock," the title track, "Bad Mutha"), *Turn It Up* also illustrates that these three were already looking to the emergence of message tracks; "Yes We Can Can" is an example of classic empowerment hip-hop years before it became popular, and "Dumb Dick" preaches (albeit rather crudely) about the benefits of staying in school and staying away from promiscuity—a prelude to Kool Moe Dee's own solo hit "Go See the Doctor." Though most of these had the sound of Sugar Hill in full effect ("Feel the Heartbeat" is the classic Treacherous Three track from the label), "Get Up" was an imaginative detour into electro, while Sequel wisely chose the rarer X-rated version of "Xmas Rap" (one that barely would've prompted a parental advisory 15 years later). —*John Bush*

A Tribe Called Quest

f. 1988, Queens, NY **db.** 1998
Group / Hip-Hop, Alternative Rap, East Coast Rap, Jazz-Rap
Without question the most intelligent, artistic rap group during the 1990s, A Tribe Called Quest jumpstarted and perfected the hip-hop alternative to hardcore and gangsta rap. In essence, they abandoned the macho posturing rap music had been constructed upon, and focused instead on abstract philosophy and message tracks. The "sucka MC" theme had never been completely ignored in hip-hop, but Tribe confronted numerous black issues—date rape, use of the word "nigger," the trials and tribulations of the rap industry—all of which overpowered the occasional game of the dozens. Just as powerful musically, Quest built upon De La Soul's jazz-rap revolution, basing tracks around laid-back samples instead of the played-out James Brown fests that many rappers had made a cottage industry by the late '80s. Comprised of Q-Tip, Ali Shaheed Muhammad, and Phife, A Tribe Called Quest debuted in 1989 and released their debut album one year later. Second album *The Low End Theory* was, quite simply, the most consistent and flowing hip-hop album ever recorded, though the trio moved closer to their harder contemporaries on 1993's *Midnight Marauders*. A spot on the 1994 Lollapalooza tour showed their influence with the alternative crowd—always a bedrock of A Tribe Called Quest's support—but the group kept it real on 1996's *Beats, Rhymes and Life*, a dedication to the streets and the hip-hop underground.

A Tribe Called Quest was formed in 1988, though both Q-Tip (born Jonathan Davis) and Phife (born Malik Taylor) had grown up together in Queens. Q-Tip met DJ Ali Shaheed Muhammad while at high school and, after being named by the Jungle Brothers (who attended the same school), the trio began performing. A Tribe Called Quest's recording debut came in August 1989, when their single, "Description of a Fool," appeared on a tiny area label (though Q-Tip had previously guested on several tracks from De La Soul's *3 Feet High and Rising* and later appeared on Deee-Lite's "Groove Is in the Heart").

Signed to Jive Records by 1989, A Tribe Called Quest released their first album, *People's Instinctive Travels and the Paths of Rhythm*, one year later. Much like De La Soul, Tribe looked more to jazz as well as '70s rock for their sample base—"Can I Kick It?" plundered Lou Reed's classic "Walk on the Wild Side" and made it viable in a hip-hop context. No matter how solid their debut was, second album *The Low End Theory* outdid all expectations and has held up as perhaps the best hip-hop LP of all time.

The Low End Theory had included several tracks with props to hip-hop friends, and A Tribe Called Quest cemented their support of the rap community with 1993's *Midnight Marauders*. The album cover and booklet insert included the faces of more than 50 rappers—including obvious choices such as De La Soul and the Jungle Brothers—as well as mild surprises like the Beastie Boys, Ice-T, and Heavy D. Though impossible to trump *Low End*'s brilliance, the LP offered several classics (including Tribe's most infectious single to date, "Award Tour") and a harder sound than the first two albums. During the summer of 1994, A Tribe Called Quest toured as the obligatory rap act on the Lollapalooza Festival lineup, and spent a quiet 1995, marked only by several production jobs for Q-Tip. Returning in 1996 with their fourth LP, *Beats, Rhymes and Life*, Tribe showed signs of wear; it was a good album, but proved less striking than *The Low End Theory* or *Midnight Marauders*. While touring in support of 1998's *The Love Movement*, the group announced their impending breakup. —*John Bush*

People's Instinctive Travels and the Paths of Rhythm / Apr. 17, 1990 / Jive ✦✦✦✦✦

One year after De La Soul re-drew the map for alternative rap, fellow Native Tongues brothers A Tribe Called Quest released their debut, the quiet beginning of a revolution in noncommercial hip-hop. *People's Instinctive Travels and the Paths of Rhythm* floated a few familiar hooks, but it wasn't a sampladelic record. Rappers Q-Tip and Phife Dawg dropped a few clunky rhymes, but their lyrics were packed with ideas, while their flow and interplay were among the most original in hip-hop. From the beginning, Tribe focused on intelligent-message tracks but rarely sounded overserious about them. With "Pubic Enemy," they put a humorous spin on the touchy subject of venereal disease (including a special award for the most inventive use of the classic "scratchin'" sample), and moved right into a love rap, "Bonita Applebum," which alternated a sitar sample with the type of jazzy keys often heard on later Tribe tracks. "Description of a Fool" took to task those with violent tendencies, while "Youthful Expression" spoke wisely of the power and growing responsibility of teenagers. Next to important message tracks with great productions, A Tribe Called Quest could also be deliciously playful (or frustratingly unserious, depending on your opinion). "I Left My Wallet in El Segundo" describes a vacation gone hilariously wrong, while "Ham 'n' Eggs" may be the oddest topic for a rap track ever heard up to that point ("I don't eat no ham and eggs, cuz they're high in cholesterol"). Hard to guess it from the titles, but the opener, "Push It Along," and "Rhythm (Dedicated to the Art of Moving Butts)" were fusions of atmospheric samples with tough beats, special attention being paid to a pair of later Tribe sample favorites, jazz guitar and '70s fusion synth. Restless and ceaselessly imaginative, Tribe perhaps experimented too much on their debut, but they succeeded at much of it, certainly enough to show much promise as a new decade dawned. —*John Bush*

★ The Low End Theory / Sep. 24, 1991 / Jive ✦✦✦✦✦

While most of the players in the jazz-rap movement never quite escaped the pasted-on qualities of their vintage samples, with *The Low End Theory*, A Tribe Called Quest created one of the closest and most brilliant fusions of jazz atmosphere and hip-hop attitude ever recorded. The rapping by Q-Tip and Phife Dawg could be the smoothest of any rap record ever heard; the pair are so in tune with each other, they sound like flip sides of the same personality, fluidly trading off on rhymes, with the former earning his nickname (the Abstract) and Phife concerning himself with the more concrete issues of being young, gifted, and black. The trio also takes on the rap game with a pair of hard-hitting tracks: "Rap Promoter" and "Show Business," the latter a lyrical soundclash with Q-Tip and Phife plus Brand Nubian's Diamond D, Lord Jamar, and Sadat X. The woman problem gets investigated as well, on two realistic yet sensitive tracks, "Butter" and "The Infamous Date Rape." The productions behind these tracks aren't quite skeletal, but they're certainly not complex. Instead, Tribe weaves little more than a standup bass (sampled or, on one track, jazz luminary Ron Carter) and crisp, live-sounding drum programs with a few deftly placed samples or electric keyboards. It's a tribute to their unerring production sense that, with just those few tools, Tribe produced one of the best hip-hop albums in history, a record that sounds better with each listen. *The Low End Theory* is an unqualified success, the perfect marriage of intelligent, flowing raps to nuanced, groove-centered productions. —*John Bush*

☆ Midnight Marauders / Nov. 9, 1993 / Jive ✦✦✦✦✦

Though the abstract rappers finally betrayed a few commercial ambitions for *Midnight Marauders*, the happy result was a smart, hooky record that may not have furthered the jazz-rap fusions of *The Low End Theory* but did merge Tribe-style intelligence and reflection with some of the most inviting grooves heard on any early-'90s rap record. The productions, more funky than jazzy, were tighter overall—but the big improvement, four years after their debut, came with Q-Tip's and Phife Dawg's raps. Focused yet funky, polished but raw, the duo was practically telepathic on "Steve Biko (Stir It Up)" and "The

Chase, Pt. 2," though the mammoth track here was the pop hit "Award Tour." A worldwide callout record with a killer riff and a great pair of individual raps from the pair, it assured that *Midnight Marauders* would become A Tribe Called Quest's biggest seller. The album didn't feature as many topical tracks as Tribe was known for, though the group did include an excellent, sympathetic commentary on the question of *that* word ("Sucka Nigga," with a key phrase: "being as we use it as a term of endearment"). Most of the time, A Tribe Called Quest was indulging in impeccably produced, next-generation games of the dozens ("We Can Get Down," "Oh My God," "Lyrics to Go"), but also took the time to illustrate sensitivity and spirituality ("God Lives Through"). A Tribe Called Quest's *Midnight Marauders* was commercially successful, artistically adept, and lyrically inventive; the album cemented their status as alternative rap's prime sound merchants, authors of the most original style since the Bomb Squad first exploded on wax. —*John Bush*

Revised Quest for the Seasoned Traveler / 1994 / Jive ✦✦✦

As the years go by, the number of obnoxious remix collections multiplies faster than a tribble. The dance contingent is the worst criminal of this exercise, whereas the farthest hip-hop groups usually stray is by releasing "instrumental" versions of their albums. Thankfully, *Revised Quest for the Seasoned Traveler* is a refreshing exception to both such workmanlike rules. Fans will notice something pleasant right off the bat: the majority of the remixes on this compilation are actually done by the band themselves. So you get the rather faithful retake of "Description of a Fool" by A Tribe Called Quest (and the Jungle Brothers), "Public Enemy" in a more club-friendly environment, and even the smiley "Bonita Applebum" turned into a fun piece of Top 40 cheese. It's most of the third-party perspectives that should be passed over (the simplistic house of Tom and Jerry's "Luck of Lucien" remix is as predictable as it sounds). Which means only a couple of these outsiders go much above and beyond the call of remix duty. The "Boilerhouse Mix" of "Can I Kick It?" adds a layer of dark solidity to the Lou Reed-sampling classic while Norman Cook (in his pre-Fatboy Slim days) does a fiesta, hornblaring reggae take on "I Left My Walled in El Segundo." Both of these are unique—and tasteful—remixes done of such Tribe favorites. So generally, the quality is quite high here compared to what one may expect from cobbledtogether remix albums. It's halfway personal, halfway engaging. *Revised Quest for the Seasoned Traveler* is a treat for both hardcore fans as well as those listeners curious enough as to how to properly compile a hip-hop remix collection. Especially without the tribble. —*Dean Carlson*

Beats, Rhymes and Life / Jul. 30, 1996 / Jive ✦✦✦

With each of its first three albums, A Tribe Called Quest seemed to be on its way to bigger and better things, artistically and commercially. *Beats, Rhymes and Life* promptly ended that streak and still ranks as the group's most disappointing listen. Amplifying the bare beats and bliss of *The Low End Theory* but erasing the hooks of *Midnight Marauders*, *Beats, Rhymes and Life* simply wasn't a compelling record. In fact, A Tribe Called Quest sounded bored through most of it—and, to put it bluntly, there wasn't much to get excited about. Previously so invigorating and idea driven, Q-Tip and Phife strutted through their verses, often sounding confused, hostile, and occasionally paranoid (check out the battle tracks, "Phony Rappers" and "Mind Power"). Meanwhile, the skeletal productions offered little incentive to decode the lyrics and messages, most of which were complex as expected. Though several other tracks had solid productions (like the spry, bass-driven backing to "Phony Rappers"), *Beats, Rhymes and Life* saw A Tribe Called Quest making its first (and only) significant misstep. (Constant touring off the success of *Midnight Marauders* may have been a factor.) Yes, they were still much better than the vast majority of alternative rappers, but it seemed they'd lost their power to excite. One of the few successes was a surprising R&B crossover called "1nce Again" (featuring Tammy Lucas). —*John Bush*

The Love Movement / Sep. 29, 1998 / Jive ✦✦✦✦

Continuing with the subdued, mature stylistic flow of *Beats, Rhymes and Life*, *The Love Movement*, the fifth album from A Tribe Called Quest, is the group's most subtle album yet—which may just be a polite way of saying it's a little monotonous. Throughout the record, Tribe mines the same jazz-flavored, R&B-fueled beats that were the hallmark of *Beats*. Although the "love" concept provides a thematic cohesion to the album—almost all of the songs are about love, in one way or another—the overall effect is quite similar to its immediate predecessor: the music is enthralling for a while, but soon it all sounds a little too familiar. Part of the problem is that Tribe functions on a cerebral level, a point made painfully clear by Busta Rhymes' and Redman's roaring, visceral cameos on "Steppin' It Up." On their own, Tribe favors craft over raw skills. That means there are plenty of pleasures to be had from careful listening, but they've reached a point where it's easier to admire Ummah's stylish production and the subtle rhymes of Q-Tip, Phife, and Shaheed than it is to outright love them, which is ironic for an album bearing the title *The Love Movement.* —*Stephen Thomas Erlewine*

Anthology / Oct. 26, 1999 / Jive ♦♦♦♦♦
For those who haven't discovered that A Tribe Called Quest made several of the best LPs in hip-hop history, *Anthology* is a perfect way to encapsulate the trio's decade-long career into one manageable portion. All of their best and biggest songs are here, from the early neglected joint "Luck of Lucien" to classic jazz-rap from *The Low End Theory* like "Jazz (We've Got)," and their 45-rpm peak with "Award Tour," all the way to their last big hit, "Find a Way," from 1998's *The Love Movement.* Yes, anyone who enjoys hip-hop needs to own at least *Midnight Marauders* and *The Low End Theory,* but *Anthology* succeeds in delivering all the highest points from a great hip-hop group's career. The collection also includes the first solo track from Q-Tip, 1999's "Vivrant Thing." —*John Bush*

Trick Daddy (Maurice Young)

b. Miami, FL
Dirty South, Hardcore Rap
One of the most thuggish rappers ever embraced by the mainstream, Trick Daddy broke out of the South in 2001 with "I'm a Thug" and established himself as an unlikely national superstar. Before his breakthrough, he scored a few regional hits here and there but remained largely an underground rapper. In particular, he became known for his club anthems, which were characterized by their rousing beats and his rowdy lyrics. "Nann Nigga" and "Shut Up" became his best-known early successes, each featuring a feisty young rapper named Trina, who would go on to her own success in subsequent years. When Trick Daddy finally did break into the mainstream in 2001 with the appropriately titled "I'm a Thug," it came as somewhat of a surprise. No one questioned his talent, but his image hardly matched that of other mainstream rappers. He certainly lived up to his thug billing, known as much for his rapping as his trademark omnipresent grimace, bald head, prickly whiskers, forearm tattoos, and gold grill. Nevertheless, thug or not, Trick Daddy became a national superstar, earning substantial mainstream airplay and climbing atop the *Billboard* charts.

Born Maurice Young in Miami, FL, the rapper originally known as Trick Daddy Dollars earned his stripes in 1996 as one of the lead rappers on Luke's "Scarred," the leadoff track from the former 2 Live Crew leader's *Uncle Luke* album. The song became a sizable hit among the booty crowd, and listeners were drawn to the remarkably fluid and quick flow of Trick Daddy Dollars. Among those drawn to him was Ted Lucas, a former concert promoter who signed the rapper to his newly formed Slip-N-Slide Records. The debut Trick Daddy Dollars album, *Based on a True Story,* came soon after, released in late 1997. The album sold well for an independent release, driven by some regional hits, but didn't impress too many people outside of the Miami area.

A year later everything changed with the release of *www.thug.com* (1998). Trick Daddy dropped the "Dollars" from his name and scored himself a breakout hit with "Nann Nigga," a club-banger that pitted him against a female nemesis, the then-unknown Trina. The hit spread throughout the South and even trickled out into the Midwest and Southwest, so much so that Atlantic Records took interest and signed Trick Daddy to a record deal. The first Atlantic release, *Book of Thugs: Chapter AK Verse 47* (2000), fulfilled its promise, setting the stage for the rapper's eventual commercial breakthrough. Driven by "Shut Up," a rowdy club hit similar to "Nann Nigga" and again featuring Trina, *Book of Thugs* extended Trick Daddy's reputation from coast to coast and established him as one of the dirty South's more promising talents.

The big payoff came a year later with the release of *Thugs Are Us* (2001), the album that catapulted Trick Daddy alongside Ludacris and Mystikal as one of the few nationally championed dirty South rappers; and it similarly catapulted him onto the playlist of every urban radio station in America, not to mention MTV. In particular, the album boasted "I'm a Thug," Trick Daddy's biggest hit yet and, more importantly, his most accessible. Despite his tattoos, gold grill, and overall thuggish aura, Trick Daddy earned mainstream airplay and climbed the *Billboard* charts. A year later he did so again with his fifth

album in six years, *Thug Holiday* (2002), and its lead single, "In da Wind," perhaps Trick Daddy's most inventive work yet. —*Jason Birchmeier*

www.thug.com / Sep. 22, 1998 / Warlock ♦♦

Book of Thugs: Chapter AK Verse 47 / Feb. 15, 2000 / Slip-N-Slide/Atlantic ♦♦♦
Trick Daddy takes his career to the next level on *Book of Thugs: Chapter AK Verse 47,* moving to a major label, Atlantic, and delivering his first coast-to-coast hit, "Shut Up." His previous two releases, *Based on a True Story* (1997) and *www.thug.com* (1998), had established him as one of the dirty South's most promising rappers, particularly after "Nann Nigga" became an underground hit, but these gritty releases never crossed the Mason-Dixon line nor the Mississippi River. On the contrary, *Book of Thugs* burst out of the South, thanks largely, if not entirely, to the financial backing of Atlantic. For the first time in his career, Trick Daddy had a sizable budget to work with, and the results are wonderfully evident. Both the beats and the vocals sound incredibly vibrant, on a par with anything coming out of New York or Los Angeles at the time; furthermore, two big-name guests, Mystikal and Twista, make notable appearances, finally giving Trick Daddy some impressive talent to tangle with. Above all, though, *Book of Thugs* boasts "Shut Up," his rowdiest club-banger yet, also notable for reprising the dynamic Trick Daddy-Trina collaboration that had made "Nann Nigga" such a success two years earlier. Elsewhere, *Book of Thugs* features a few other highlights ("Boy," "Get on Up," "Thug for Life"), but it's by no means a solid album. The excessive guests are a bit frustrating, tempting you to fast-forward through lackluster verses far too many times, and the production of Righteous Funk Boogie and Black Mob Group is spotty, sounding less impressive as the album creeps toward its distant end. *Book of Thugs* nonetheless raised the bar for Trick Daddy, elevating him to national status and setting the stage for his commercial breakthrough. —*Jason Birchmeier*

● **Thugs Are Us** / Mar. 20, 2001 / Slip-N-Slide ♦♦♦♦
With every subsequent album throughout the late-'90s, Trick Daddy had taken a step farther toward his long-awaited national breakthrough, and with *Thugs Are Us* he finally reached his elusive commercial summit, breaking out of the South and into heavy rotation on every urban radio station in America. "Shut Up," the club anthem from his previous album, *Book of Thugs* (2000), had almost broken him through, just as "Nann Nigga" had nearly done so even earlier. Yet neither of those hits compare to what Trick Daddy delivers on *Thugs Are Us.* This is by far the Miami rapper's most impressive work to date, in terms of not just lyrics and beats but also commercial sensibility. Trick Daddy and his Slip-N-Slide team pull it all together on *Thugs Are Us,* especially on the album's highlights: the club-banging "Take It to da House," the commercial-radio-serviced "I'm a Thug," and the dirty South-rallying "Can't F**k With the South." On these songs, and to a lesser extent the others, Trick Daddy retains his thuggish posture yet also manages to integrate just enough of a parodic wink to make *Thugs Are Us* as accessible to the inner-city thugs as it is to the suburban wannabe-thugs. This shift is subtle yet nevertheless noteworthy. Representative of the dirty South in all its tarnished grace yet accessible enough for the mainstream, Trick Daddy's tongue-in-cheek charm offsets his gold grill and tattoos, more so here than on any previous album. On the downside, like *Book of Thugs* before it, *Thugs Are Us* does frustratingly incorporate a plethora of guests, none of them superstars in their own right. Yet as it stands, unwanted hangers-on and all, *Thugs Are Us* places Trick Daddy alongside Mystikal and Ludacris among the elite class of nationally sanctioned dirty South rappers. —*Jason Birchmeier*

Thug Holiday / Aug. 6, 2002 / Slip-N-Slide ♦♦♦
Even after releasing more than an album each year since 1997, Trick Daddy kept up the quality control with 2002's *Thug Holiday.* The production's a bit amateurish and a bit skeletal in places, but the South's most consistent rapper still has a lot to offer, especially when he gets together with Cee-Lo from Goodie Mob and Big Boi from OutKast on "In da Wind." The title track is a bit too dramatic for such a usually enjoyable hip-hop name, but great party tracks like "Play No Games" and "All I Need" more than make up for a few half-baked message tracks. —*John Bush*

Tricky (Adrian Thaws)

b. 1964, Knowle West, Bristol, Avon, England
Producer, Vocals / Alternative Pop/Rock, Trip-Hop, Electronica
Originally, Tricky was a member of the Wild Bunch, a Bristol, England-based rap troupe that eventually metamorphosed into Massive Attack during the

early '90s. Tricky provided pivotal raps on Massive Attack's groundbreaking 1992 album, *Blue Lines*. The following year, he released his debut single, "Aftermath." Before he recorded "Aftermath," he met a teenage vocalist named Martina, who would become his full-time musical collaborator; all albums released under Tricky's name feature her contributions.

Tricky signed a contract with Island in 1994. The contract contained a clause that allowed him to release side projects under different names, in addition to regular Tricky releases. "Ponderosa" and "Overcome" were released over the course of 1994; that same year, he made a cameo on Massive Attack's second album, *Protection*. Tricky's debut album, *Maxinquaye*, appeared in the spring of 1995. Not only did the album receive overwhelmingly positive reviews when it was released, but it entered the U.K. charts at number two, despite the total lack of daytime radio airplay. Throughout 1995, Tricky was omnipresent in the U.K., collaborating with and remixing for a wide variety of artists, including Björk, Luscious Jackson, and Whale. In the fall of 1995, he released *Tricky Vs. the Gravediggaz*, a collaboration with the American hardcore rap group, as well as a single called "I Be the Prophet," which was released under the name Starving Souls. At the end of the year, *Maxinquaye* topped many year-end polls in Britain, including *Melody Maker* and *NME*.

In February of 1996, *Nearly God*—an album featuring Tricky's collaborations with artists as diverse as Terry Hall, Björk, Alison Moyet, and Neneh Cherry—was released, again to strong reviews; the album was released in the U.S. six months later. After completing the second full-fledged Tricky album, he relocated to New York City early in 1996, where he began working with underground rappers. An EP called *Grassroots* was released in the U.S. in September. Two months later, Tricky's official second album, *Pre-Millennium Tension*, was released. Again, Tricky received positive reviews, though there were a few dissenting opinions.

In addition to his three releases of 1996, he remixed artists as diverse as Elvis Costello, Garbage, Yoko Ono, and Bush. Tricky's next full-length solo effort, *Angels With Dirty Faces*, appeared in 1998, followed a year later by *Juxtapose*, a collaboration with Cypress Hill's DJ Muggs and DMX's Grease. In 2001, Tricky returned with the *Mission Accomplished* EP, which was released by Epitaph's subsidiary label Anti. *BlowBack*, his first for Hollywood Records, appeared later that June and included various collaborations with Hawkman, Live's Ed Kowalczyk, and Red Hot Chili Peppers' Anthony Kiedis and John Frusciante. —*Stephen Thomas Erlewine*

★ **Maxinquaye** / Apr. 18, 1995 / Island ◆◆◆◆◆

Tricky's debut, *Maxinquaye*, is an album of stunning sustained vision and imagination, a record that sounds like it has no precedent as it boldly predicts a new future. Of course, neither sentiment is true. Much of the music on *Maxinquaye* has its roots in the trip-hop pioneered by Massive Attack, which once featured Tricky, and after the success of this record, trip-hop became fashionable, turning into safe, comfortable music to be played at upscale dinner parties thrown by hip twenty- and thirty-somethings. Both of these sentiments are true, yet *Maxinquaye* still manages to retain its power; years later, it can still sound haunting, disturbing, and surprising after countless spins. It's an album that exists outside of time and outside of trends, a record whose clanking rhythms, tape haze, murmured vocals, shards of noise, reversed gender roles, alt-rock asides, and soul samplings create a ghostly netherworld fused with seductive menace and paranoia. It also shimmers with mystery, coming not just from Tricky—whose voice isn't even heard until the *second* song on the record—but also his vocalist, Martine, whose smoky singing lures listeners into the unrelenting darkness of the record. Once they're there, *Maxinquaye* offers untold treasures. There is the sheer pleasure of coasting by on the sound of the record, how it makes greater use of noise and experimental music than anything since the Bomb Squad and Public Enemy. Then there's the tip of the hat to PE with a surreal cover of "Black Steel in the Hour of Chaos," sung by Martine and never sounding like a postmodernist in-joke. Other references and samples register subconsciously—while Isaac Hayes' "Ike's Rap II" flows through "Hell Is Around the Corner" and the Smashing Pumpkins are even referenced in the title of "Pumpkin," Shakespeare's Sisters and the Chantels slip by, while Michael Jackson's "Bad" thrillingly bleeds into "Expressway to Your Heart" on "Brand New You're Retro." Lyrics flow in and out of consciousness, with lingering, whispered promises suddenly undercut by veiled threats and bursts of violence. Then there's how music that initially may seem like mood pieces slowly reveal their ingenious structure and arrangement and register as full-blown songs, or how the alternately languid and chaotic rhythms finally complement each other, turning this into a bracing sonic adventure that gains richness and resonance with each listen. After all, there's so much going on here—within the production, the songs, the words—it remains fascinating even after all of its many paths have been explored (which certainly can't be said of the trip-hop that followed, including records by Tricky). And that air of mystery that can be impenetrable upon the first listen certainly is something that keeps *Maxinquaye* tantalizing after it's become familiar, particularly because, like all good mysteries, there's no getting to the bottom of it, no matter how hard you try. —*Stephen Thomas Erlewine*

Nearly God / Apr. 29, 1996 / Island ◆◆◆◆◆

Nearly God is Tricky's unofficial second album—he calls it a collection of brilliant, incomplete demos. When Tricky signed his contract with Island, it allowed him to release an album a year under a different name. *Nearly God* is the first of these efforts. Tricky recorded the record with a diverse cast of collaborators—in addition to his partner Martina, there's Terry Hall, Björk, Neneh Cherry, Cath Coffey, Dedi Madden, and Alison Moyet (Damon Albarn pulled his track just before the album's release). Building on the ghostly, dark soundscapes of Tricky's debut, *Maxinquaye*, *Nearly God* narrows the focus of his first record by making the music slower, hazier, and more disturbing. It's not as coherent as *Maxinquaye*, but that's part of its appeal. *Nearly God* is a haunting, fractured, surreal nightmare that doesn't always make sense, but never fails to make an impact. Certain collaborators work better than others—Tricky understands the eeriness of Terry Hall's voice, but he does nothing to tame Alison Moyet's inappropriate bluesy shrieking—but the overall effect of the album is quietly devastating. It gets under your skin and stays there. It's a brilliantly evocative nightmare. —*Stephen Thomas Erlewine*

Pre-Millennium Tension / Nov. 11, 1996 / Island ◆◆◆◆

Maxinquaye was an unexpected hit in England, launching a wave of similar-sounding artists, who incorporated Tricky's innovations into safer pop territory. Tricky responded by traveling to Jamaica to record *Pre-Millennium Tension*, a nervy, claustrophobic record that thrives in its own paranoia. Scaling back the clattering hooks of *Maxinquaye* and slowing the beat down, Tricky has created a hallucinatory soundscape, where the rhythms, samples, and guitars intertwine into a crawling procession of menacing sounds and disembodied lyrical threats. Its tone is set by the backward guitar loops of "Vent," and continued through the shifting "Christiansands," and the tense, lyrically dense "Tricky Kid," easily Tricky's best straight rap to date. Occasionally, the gloom is broken, such as when the shimmering piano chords of "Makes Me Want to Die" ring out, but nearly as often, it becomes bogged down in its own murk, as in the long raggae rant "Ghetto Youth." While the lyrics are often quite effective in conveying dope-addled paranoia, what ties the album together are its layered rhythms and soundscapes. Though it might not sound that way immediately, *Pre-Millennium Tension* is as much Tricky reaching back to his hardcore rap roots as it is a sonic exploration. As such, it stands as a transition record for Tricky, but its overall effect is only slightly less powerful than *Maxinquaye* or *Nearly God*. —*Stephen Thomas Erlewine*

Angels With Dirty Faces / Jun. 2, 1998 / Island ◆◆◆

Perhaps *Maxinquaye* was such a startling, focused, brilliant debut that Tricky's subsequent albums would have paled in comparison, regardless of their quality. Nevertheless, his desire to distance himself from the coffeehouse trip-hop that appeared after *Maxinquaye* forced him into a dark, paranoid corner. Determined to strip away all of his fair-weather fans, he delivered the claustrophobic *Pre-Millennium Tension*, a paranoid record that its follow-up, *Angels With Dirty Faces*, mirrors. Since it builds upon *Pre-Millennium* instead of breaking new ground, *Angels* may strike some listeners as merely a retread, but it gradually reveals new layers on repeated listens. Tricky has been redefining his rhythms, adding skittering jungle loops and hardcore hip-hop beats to his trademark dub-warped trip-hop. On top of that, he's expanding his sonic palette, adding cheap synthesizers and avant-garde guitarists to create a nightmarish junk pile of hip-hop, dub, electronica, rock, and gospel. Again, Martina is on board and her stylish croon adds moments of relief to the enveloping dread, as does Polly Harvey on the odd gospel-tinged "Broken Homes." Specific tracks work well individually—"Mellow," "Singing the Blues," "Angels With Dirty Faces," and the absurd, bile-ridden "Record Companies," in particular—but on the whole *Angels With Dirty*

Faces is less than the sum of its parts. By being slightly different but essentially the same as *Pre-Millennium Tension*, *Angels With Dirty Faces* demands that listeners meet it on its own terms. Whether they'll want to is another matter entirely. —*Stephen Thomas Erlewine*

Juxtapose / Aug. 17, 1999 / Island ✦✦✦
Tricky's potential once seemed boundless, but by the time of his fifth album, *Juxtapose*, he hadn't expanded his trademark sound: a creeping, menacing blend of hip-hop, alternative rock, and raggae, all delivered with stoned paranoia. Perhaps Tricky realized that its rewards were smaller with each subsequent album, since he designed *Juxtapose* to be his most ambitious, eclectic album since *Maxinquaye*, and the one that finally broke him to the mainstream American hip-hop audience. So, he teamed up with DJ Muggs (the architect of Cypress Hill's sound, a clear precedent for Tricky's) and DMX's producer, Grease. The end result is hardly a collaboration—in fact, it feels truncated, weighing in at a mere 35 minutes—but it works in other ways, since Tricky often seems revitalized. That much is evident on the stellar opening cut, "For Real"; the music is spaced-out, sexy, melodic, and appealing, even when it gets foreboding. It's a terrific beginning, suggesting that this will be the first album to offer significant variations on Tricky's signature sound. And it does, but it may not go far enough for some tastes, since a good portion of this brief album is devoted to retreads, which reveal his weaknesses all too well. Tricky remains unduly infatuated with raggae, letting British toaster Mad Dog run wild; his frenetic delivery single-handedly breaks the spell of each track he's featured on. But elsewhere, Tricky pushes forward in inventive ways that add weight to *Juxtapose*—"Contradictive" is his best pop move to date, blessed by Spanish guitars and elongated strings; the paranoid drums of "She Said" successfully deepen the menace; and "Scrappy Love" is a haunting blend of soul and trip-hop, with eerie piano reminiscent of DJ Shadow. *Juxtapose* is a qualified success, but it is a success since the moments that work are his best in years. —*Stephen Thomas Erlewine*

BlowBack / Jun. 26, 2001 / Hollywood ✦✦✦
There are no new tricks on *BlowBack*, the star-studded 2001 comeback by Tricky, the pioneering trip-hopper that wandered his way into the wilderness. He wandered so far that nobody really cared anymore if he had anything to say—particularly because he wound up saying the same thing, slightly differently, over and over again. He doesn't escape from this problem here, yet he's found a map—and that map is craft. He knew this before, since the best moments of *Angels With Dirty Faces* and *Juxtapose* were when he knew how to spin his signatures just right, so they jelled into something brilliant. He has the same gift here, and he extends it throughout the record, so this is the first record that really plays smoothly from start to finish since *Pre-Millennium Tension*. That, of course, isn't the same thing as being as good, since he has ceased to innovate, and he has a couple of annoying flaws, including his tendency to create one mood and sustain it without developing it, plus his love of dancehall toasting. The thing is, for all of his genius, Tricky doesn't really have the greatest taste in the world. Yes, he's worked with Björk and PJ Harvey, but he's also brought Bush into the studio, and here Live's Ed Kowalczyk, three members of the Red Hot Chili Peppers, and Cyndi Lauper all contribute sonic coloring. The genius of Tricky is, he knows how to pull out the best in such unlikely collaborators, making it sound like a natural extension of his work. Then again, it could just be that John Frusciante and Flea know "Brand New You're Retro" so well, it's easy to turn it out again on "Wonder Woman." So, it's a mixed bag, but it plays sharper than his albums of late. Yes, there are some astonishing slips—the backing track of "Something in the Way" sounds great, but Hawkman, the raggae bane of this album, castrates it of its power—but, at this point, that's a given with Tricky. Once you get past that, once you stop expecting genius—or at least something that matches *Maxinquaye* (or even *Tension*)—it's much easier to enjoy *BlowBack*. —*Stephen Thomas Erlewine*

A Ruff Guide / May 7, 2002 / Island ✦✦✦✦
It's not sequenced in chronological order, but that's about the only flaw with Island's 2002 compilation, *A Ruff Guide*. Over the course of 17 tracks, the highlights from Tricky's Island albums unspool, hitting every single and many of the great album tracks (including cuts from the *Nearly God* album). Although this may seem like it'd be just for the fellow travelers—the kind of casual fan that just wants the hits—this is actually a very useful compilation for those that followed his career closely, since Tricky's albums after his brilliant debut *Maxinquaye* grew more erratic with each release. Therefore, this

collection works really well as a collection of the moments where Tricky flashed his brilliance on uneven albums ("Broken Homes," "Tricky Kid," "For Real," among them). Yes, *Maxinquaye* is the masterpiece—one of the great, defining albums of the '90s—but as a summary of his uneven career this is excellent. —*Stephen Thomas Erlewine*

Trina

b. Miami, FL
Dirty South, Hardcore Rap
Miami-based rapper Trina first gained notoriety in 1998 with her appearance on Trick Daddy's *www.thug.com* album. Her own debut album, *Da Baddest Bitch*, featured a cameo by Trick Daddy and was released in early 2000 on Slip-N-Slide and distributed by Atlantic. She spent the next two years honing her raw, raunchy style. She paired up with Missy Elliott for the recording of her second effort, 2002's *Diamond Princess*. —*Heather Phares*

Da Baddest Bitch / Mar. 7, 2000 / Slip-N-Slide ✦✦✦
Rapper Trina hopes to pick up where Lil' Kim, Da Brat, and a host of other potty-mouthed hardcore gals left off, rhyming about sex and her ability to go at it all night and her quest to find a man willing to do the same for her. By the end of her debut album, it all gets a bit monotonous. Only so many sleazy sex rhymes are tolerable before they become weary. *Da Baddest Bitch* is at its best when Trina steps out of the gutter and cops a Miami dancefloor than the bedroom. The title track and "Off Glass," as well as guest performances from Trick Daddy, Twista, and J-Shin, keep the momentum relatively steady. —*Michael Gallucci*

● **Diamond Princess** / Aug. 27, 2002 / Slip-N-Slide ✦✦✦✦
So many female rappers as attractive as Trina are there because of two things: first, they know someone; second, they're gorgeous. While Trina is definitely sexy and is in good with Trick Daddy, it was evident from her first album that she was making music for another reason—she's a formidable rapper. There hasn't been a ton of female rappers to emerge from the South, and Trina blends her southern style nicely with intelligible lyrics to give her some national appeal. She's like a new Roxanne Shanté or Lil' Kim, but from down South. Trina makes this album a worthy follow-up to her last LP by bringing some very talented help with her. Bathgate, Ludacris, Deuce Poppi, and Rick Ross from the Slip-N-Slide label, as well as Missy Elliott, all make guest appearances here (does a female rapper ever do an album without another female rapper on it?). Although this record differs a lot from her first, it's a step in the right direction and should provide her with fans from a much larger area. Trina is a dirty girl from the dirty South, and she proves her hardness in the Eazy-E remake of "No More Questions." If you liked her first album, this is a different-sounding record but arguably better. —*Brad Mills*

Triple M

Vocals / Hip-Hop, Pop-Rap
Triple M was around long enough as a pop-rap artist to release one 1991 album on A&M. Despite the release of a supporting single ("Prisoner of Passion"), the album failed to make much of a dent commercially. Triple M seemed to disappear after that, though he did make a guest appearance on To Be Continued's 1993 album *Free to Be*. —*Andy Kellman*

● **Triple M** / 1991 / A&M ✦✦
In the late '80s and early '90s, the success that MC Hammer, Vanilla Ice, Marky Mark, and Gerardo enjoyed in pop and dance circles inspired many major labels to sign pop-rappers. While none of those artists had much credibility among hip-hop's hardcore, their success in the pop market made the majors take notice. At A&M, one of 1991's pop-rap signings was Triple M, who doesn't have great rapping skills but occasionally comes up with some catchy grooves on this self-titled debut album. It is pointless to judge Triple M by hardcore rap standards because that isn't what he's going for; however, it is fair to compare him to other pop-rappers and explain what his flaws are. If one measures Triple M by Hammer's standards, they won't find this album terribly impressive. Hammer, regardless of what people may say, definitely has strong rapping skills—he might not be one's cup of tea for purists who only like hardcore rap, but no one can honestly claim that Hammer can't rap. Triple M, however, wouldn't last long in a microphone battle with Hammer (if pop-rappers were into mic battles). His rapping skills are limited, which is something one could forgive if this album had a lot of memorable grooves. But most of the material is pedestrian, although Triple M does, on occasion,

come up with something memorable; "Deep Game" and "Prisoner of Passion" are among the CD's catchier tracks. Triple M turned out to be a one-album wonder—he never recorded a second album, and this disc is only a small footnote in the history of pop-rap. —*Alex Henderson*

Triple 6 Mafia

f. Memphis, TN
Group / Hardcore Rap, Southern Rap, Dirty South
The Triple 6 Mafia rap crew consisted of Koopsta Knicca, Crunchy Black, Gangsta Boo, Lord Infamous, Juicy J, and DJ Paul. An ongoing media rivalry with Bone Thugs-N-Harmony raised the group's public visibility, and in 1995 they issued their debut album, *Mystic Stylez*; the success of the follow-up, *The End*, landed the Triple 6 a deal with Relativity, and after issuing *Live By Yo Rep (B.O.N.E. Dis)*, a limited-edition swipe at the Bone Thugs posse, they returned with the gold-selling *World Domination Chap. 2. Club Memphis Underground, Vol. 2* followed in 1999 and *Kings of Memphis: Underground, Vol. 3* was issued in fall 2000. —*Jason Ankeny*

Underground, Vol. 1: 1991-1994 / Mar. 2, 1999 / Smoked Out ✦✦✦

● **Club Memphis Underground, Vol. 2** / Aug. 24, 1999 / Smoked Out ✦✦✦
The second volume in Smoked Out's best-of series known as *Club Memphis Underground* includes tracks from solo projects by DJ Paul, Juicy J, Lord Infamous and Project Pat. Somewhere between horrorcore, Wu-Tang-styled string paranoia, and the lewd side of the dirty South, tracks like "Half on a Sack or Blow" and "Liquor and Dat Bud" are solid, though the incessant tagline on tracks like "Lick My N*tts" and "Suck a Nigga D**k" are going to be a bit too much for most listeners. —*Keith Farley*

Kings of Memphis: Underground, Vol. 3 / Oct. 31, 2000 / Smoked Out ✦✦✦

Tru

Group / Gangsta Rap, Hardcore Rap, Southern Rap, Dirty South, Hip-Hop
Tru is a three-piece gangsta rap group that No Limit mastermind Master P formed with his younger brothers, Silkk and C-Murder. Tru became the most popular act on No Limit with their 1995 debut album, *True*; it sold over 200,000 copies with little promotion or airplay, and helped establish No Limit as an underground hip-hop force. Tru released its second album, *Tru 2 Da Game*, early in 1997. Shortly afterward, No Limit exploded, making Master P into a superstar. Given his many duties at the label, along with his forays into filmmaking, basketball, and sports management, *plus* the burgeoning solo careers of Silkk and C-Murder, it wasn't a surprise that it took Tru two years—an eternity in No Limit time—to produce its third album, *Da Crime Family*. —*Stephen Thomas Erlewine*

True / Jul. 25, 1995 / No Limit ✦✦✦
This album is full of cliché themes and lyrics that talk about the gangster life. It was important to No Limit Records, however, because it contains the song "Bout It Bout It," which became a hit not only in the South but also on the East and West Coasts as well. It provided the break that No Limit needed. The company went on to become a very popular record label in the mid- to late '90s. —*Dan Gizzi*

● **Tru 2 Da Game** / Feb. 18, 1997 / No Limit ✦✦✦✦
Tru 2 Da Game is fairly standard hardcore gangsta rap, intercut with just a touch of deep, funky bass grooves. Tru doesn't have any particularly noteworthy rhyming skills, and the music is predictable, yet their workmanlike gangsta rap makes for a worthwhile set for aficionados. —*Leo Stanley*

Da Crime Family / Jun. 1, 1999 / No Limit ✦✦✦
When Tru released their second album, the cleverly titled *Tru 2 Da Game*, in early 1997, its mastermind, Master P, was on the verge of superstardom. Nobody knew it at the time, of course, he was just one of the biggest figures in the dirty South. That summer, Master P broke big, taking No Limit along with him. Of course, this was also good news for his fellow Tru colleagues, Silkk tha Shocker and C-Murder, who became stars in their own right. Of course, this built up expectations for *Da Crime Family*, Tru's third album and their first since stardom. But, as the saying goes, the more things change, the more they stay the same. Tru may be big stars now, but they haven't taken that as an opportunity to expand or develop their music—they simply made the same album anybody on No Limit (with the notable exception of Snoop Dogg) made in the two years following Master P's elevation to stardom. In other words, *Da Crime Family* feels identical to *Tru 2 Da Game*, with the

same sort of recycled beats, hooks, and lyrics that graced that record. At least that album had some grit and (maybe) some element of surprise. Here, the trio feels as if they're putting their gangsta suit on and going to work. Perhaps it shouldn't be a surprise that an album by a man who's more notorious for his business practices than his music sounds, but it's nevertheless amazing how rigid and formulaic this sounds. There are no surprises: the rhymes, rhythms, hooks, and skits all fall into place exactly where they should. To some, that may be a blessing, since that's all they're looking for from a No Limit record, but discerning listeners may start to wonder why they have a shelf full of discs that are all essentially the same. —*Stephen Thomas Erlewine*

True Mathematics

Group / Hip-Hop
True Mathematics was a mysterious rap act generally thought to be a collaboration between producers Hank Shocklee and Carl Ryder, with vocals generally credited to Eric Sadler. —*John Floyd*

● **Greatest Hits** / 1988 / Elektra ✦✦✦✦
This overlooked rap masterpiece is a collaboration between Hank Shocklee (Public Enemy), Eric Sadler, Carl Ryder, and someone credited as K. Houston. It leaps from pulsating, understated anthems ("For the Money") up to several black frat-party romps. —*John Floyd*

Tuff Crew

f. Pennsylvania
Group / Soul
Pennsylvania-based rappers Tuff Crew comprised Ice Dog, L.A. Kid, Monty G, Tone Love, and DJ Too Tuff, debuting in 1988 with the Warlock Records release *Danger Zone*. *Back to Wreck Shop* followed a year later, but in the wake of 1991's *Still Dangerous*, Tuff Crew dropped from sight. —*Jason Ankeny*

Danger Zone / 1988 / Warlock ✦✦✦
An uneven, but sometimes hilarious patchwork quilt of hip-hop and urban contemporary tracks, sociopolitical commentary, and sometimes inspired production and arrangments. The Tuff Crew were alternately delightful, confrontational, abrasive, or lewd, but never boring or mundane. Only the lack of a few standout singles kept this from being a bigger album. —*Ron Wynn*

Back to Wreck Shop / Jul. 10, 1989 / Warlock ✦✦

Still Dangerous / 1991 / Warlock ✦✦

The Tunnel Rats

f. 1993
Group / Underground Rap, West Coast Rap
Underground rap collective the Tunnel Rats formed in 1993 and challenged the conventions of commercial hip-hop throughout their career. The group's original approach to rhyming, beatmaking, and songwriting made it well-known on the West Coast, appearing on albums by artists such as Mars III, DJ Maj, Coalition, Deepspace 5, and the Grits, not to mention side projects such as LPG, New Breed, and Peace 586. In the early 2000s, the group hooked up with Uprok Records in Seattle for the *Tunnel Vision* full-length, which featured LPG, New Breed, Sev Statik, Raphi, Zane, and Dert. —*Jason Birchmeier*

● **Tunnel Vision** / Nov. 6, 2001 / Uprok ✦✦✦
Almost a decade into their existence, underground rap collective the Tunnel Rats hooked up with the Seattle-based Uprok Records in 2001 for the *Tunnel Vision* album, which features appearances by LPG, New Breed, Sev Statik, Raphi, Zane, and Dert. The album highlights the Tunnel Rats' anti-commercial approach to hip-hop, showcasing intelligent rhymes, creative beats, and original songwriting. —*Jason Birchmeier*

T.W.D.Y.

Group / G-Funk, West Coast Rap, Gangsta Rap
Led by prominent Oakland producer Ant Banks, T.W.D.Y. (The Whole Damn Yey) also features Dolla Will and Captain Save'm. This trio focuses on the hard, sleazy, gangsta style of rap Banks helped to define on his work for Too Short, Spice 1, and E-40 among others. Their first release, *Derty Werk*, appeared in 1999 after Banks had spent the better part of the decade making a name for himself as one of the West Coast's best producers and also with a handful of his own less-successful solo albums. The single "Players Holiday" catapulted

Derty Werk to moderate success in urban America and remained in rotation in many areas until the quick follow-up, *Lead the Way. —Jason Birchmeier*

Derty Werk / Apr. 20, 1999 / Thump ✦✦

● **Lead the Way** / Oct. 3, 2000 / Thump ✦✦✦✦
Excluding the phenomenal single "Players Holiday," the first T.W.D.Y. album *Derty Werk* never really met its full potential, with Ant Banks somewhat struggling to duplicate the sort of G-funk that made him such a renowned West Coast producer and an overall lack of quality rapping. But with *Lead the Way*, Banks seems to have finally brought his project to its full realization. His beats have never sounded better, harking back to his best work with Rappin' 4-Tay, Too Short, and Spice 1, and in addition to his impressive beats, a mind-blowing roster of the California Bay Area's best rappers make appearances on this album. So rather than just be a showcase for the trio that comprise T.W.D.Y.—Banks, Captain Save'm, and Dolla Will—the album functions almost as a platform for the entire Bay Area camp. Though these rappers—Too Short, E-40, Kurupt, MC Eiht, WC, C.J. Mac, B-Legit, Ice-T, and many others—often fall into tired gangsta clichés, they do it with charisma and skill, shining more in terms of delivery than content. *—Jason Birchmeier*

Tweet

Urban, Contemporary R&B, Hip-Hop, Neo-Soul
The successful duo of Missy Elliott and Timbaland presented Tweet in early 2002, a soulful vocalist with hip-hop savvy and unrestrained sexuality. Like Sparxxx's debut album, Tweet's debut, *Southern Hummingbird*, featured production by Timbaland and vocals by Elliott, most notably on the lead single, "Oops (Oh My)." The single became an overnight hit, and a remix for the song featuring Fabolous garnered even more spins on urban radio, helping her cross over to the rap audience and setting the stage for her album's awaited release date. Before debuting with "Oops (Oh My)," Tweet had appeared alongside Elliott on "Take Away" (a single also featuring Ginuwine from *Miss E... So Addictive*) and "X" (an album track from Ja Rule's *Pain Is Love*). *—Jason Birchmeier*

● **Southern Hummingbird** / Apr. 2, 2002 / Goldmind/Elektra ✦✦✦✦
Prior to her debut album, *Southern Hummingbird*, Tweet made her name as a protégée of Missy Elliott, appearing as a backing/guest vocalist on a few tracks with Elliott and, naturally, Elliott's producer, Timbaland. It should come as no surprise that those are the two dominant personalities on *Southern Hummingbird*, even if Tweet produces and cowrites several cuts here, since this whole axis has one sound that has served them well. Served them so well, it's given them critical and chart hits, along with a host of imitators, so there is no reason to abandon it now, even if the skeletal rhythms and endlessly looped riffs are beginning to wear a bit thin. This formula depends more on the overall sound of the track than the charisma of the singer—but, ironically enough, it works best when its fronted by somebody with personality, like Elliott. Tweet fades into the mix. She's attractive and is sweetly sexy, but isn't forceful. That works to her advantage on the lead single, "Oops (Oh My)," where she's so taken by a seduction she can barely speak, or even name who's taking her. Driven by a clever Casio-bass clarinet loop, it's the hottest thing on the record, punctured slightly by Elliott's disarming murmur, "I was feeling so good I had to touch myself," but it's good enough to withstand that. The rest of *Southern Hummingbird* sustains the essential feel of that track, occasionally forcing a *Sign 'O' the Times*-era Prince to the forefront (which is welcome), and it does have a few songs that distinguish themselves, such as "Smoking Cigarettes," but it all blends together a little bit too much to be distinctive and, as such, it has a faint feel of product, a slow seduction record for the Timbaland-worshiping hipster set. A feel that is only enhanced by the end of the record, when Tweet actually *records* her thank-you shout-outs as a full track, then, as a bonus, there are two uncredited Missy Elliott tracks that don't seem to have a trace of Tweet to them. Their inclusion is puzzling, unless you consider them the overdue payment of distinctive hip-hop for those hardcore fans who sat through the even-handed, stylish but samey urban soul that is *Southern Hummingbird. —Stephen Thomas Erlewine*

12th Tribe

f. 1985, California
Group / Christian Rap
The California duo of Dave Portillo and Eddie Sierra began rapping in 1985 under the name of Deity, later changing it to 12th Tribe. Influenced by soul and heavy metal, they liked the rap of Kool Moe Dee, Whodini, and the Fat Boys. They took their name from the 12th tribe of Israel—the Benjamites, mighty warriors—and released an album in 1991 for Frontline. They portrayed a tougher image than most Christian rap artists and had a comparatively hard street-rap sound. *—Bil Carpenter*

● **Knowledge Is the Tribe of Life** / 1991 / Frontline ✦✦✦✦✦
Knowledge Is the Tribe of Life, the 12th Tribe debut, was produced, engineered, and mixed by master urban dance musician Scott Blackwell, who easily moves into the hard, funky side of Christian rap here. There are 15 rhymes on war, peace, and knowing God. The sound is very black, very hard, with a few metal elements; a good set though not overly original outside of the gospel music industry. *—Bil Carpenter*

12 Gauge

b. Georgia
Hardcore Rap, Southern Rap, Dirty Rap, Club/Dance
Georgia native Isaiah Pinkney began as a DJ, but turned to rapping due to Miami rap, R&B, and 2 Live Crew inspirations. His debut album appeared in 1994 on Scotti Bros. Records and was followed in 1998 by *Freaky One. —John Bush*

● **12 Gauge** / 1995 / Scotti Bros. ✦✦✦✦
12 Gauge's debut album features his stupid, infectious bass-driven salute to short shorts, "Dunkie Butt." While the rest of the album has competent bass music workouts, he fails to come up with anything as funky and catchy as his hit, though fans of the genre might enjoy the remainder of the record. *—Stephen Thomas Erlewine*

Freaky One / Sep. 30, 1997 / Roadrunner ✦✦✦
12 Gauge has always been one of the most reliable Miami bass artists, but *Freaky One* doesn't quite live up to his standards. It's not that he tries new territory on the album—it's the same throbbing party music it always is—it's just that the grooves aren't quite as solid as they have been before. There are still a few cuts to satisfy hardcore bass-heads, but anyone who isn't already deep into the scene will find *Freaky One* a little repetitive. *—Leo Stanley*

Twilight 22

Group / Electro
The '80s electro outfit Twilight 22 was led by computer/synth wiz Gordon Bahary, but also featured contributions from lead singer and co-songwriter Joseph Saulter. Bahary got his start when he was invited to assist the great Stevie Wonder during the recording of his 1976 classic *Songs in the Key of Life* (Bahary was only 16 years old at the time). Wonder invited Bahary to help out on his next recording, 1979's *Journey Through the Secret of Plants*, for which the teenager produced and programmed synthesizers. It was around this time that Bahary met Saulter through a mutual acquaintance (Herbie Hancock), while Bahary was working on Hancock's *Feets Don't Fail Me Now*. Although Saulter was originally a drummer (playing in a Los Angeles-based outfit called Rhythm Ignition), it was his vocal skills that drew the most attention, leading to the formation of Twilight 22 in the early '80s. Their lone single, "Electric Kingdom," was one of the seminal moments for electro, but their 1984 self-titled full-length for Vanguard was their last label before splitting up shortly thereafter. Both Bahary and Saulter went on to play on other artist's records, as well as production. *—Greg Prato*

Twilight 22 / 1984 / Vanguard ✦✦✦

Twin Hype

f. New Jersey
Group / East Coast Rap, Golden Age
New Jersey's Twin Hype released a pair of albums during a short career that spawned one undeniably brilliant single in the form of "Do It to the Crowd." Twin brothers Sly (Glennis Brown) and Slick (Lennis Brown) were joined by DJ King Shameek (Jose Matos) for a self-titled 1989 album and *Double Barrel*, a 1991 follow-up—both of which were released on Profile. Each album had its fair share of filler, and neither Slick nor Sly were exemplary rappers, but singles like "Do It to the Crowd" and "Wrong Place, Wrong Time" provided thrills. The trio presumably split after the second album. *—Andy Kellman*

● **Twin Hype** / 1989 / Profile ✦✦✦
Twin Hype's self-titled debut LP from 1989 is filled with zesty, energetic raps, as on "Do It to the Crowd," their biggest hit single (and best moment).

Unfortunately, the themes on most of the other tracks were mundane, and the duo just couldn't keep up the energy level. —*Ron Wynn*

Double Barrel / 1991 / Profile ♦♦

For the recording of *Double Barrel*, their second album, New Jersey duo Twin Hype recruited the Hollywood Impact as producer. It resulted in a set of tracks with vastly improved studio and production techniques, but as before, the raps tended to wander. —*Ron Wynn*

Twinz

Group / West Coast Rap, G-Funk

In the wake of his "Regulate" success, G-funk producer/rapper Warren G helmed the short-lived career of the Twinz, a duo of West Coast rappers. The timing seemed right. G had scored a huge hit with "Regulate" and the successive release of his *Regulate... G Funk Era* album (1994); the entire G-funk movement itself, spearheaded by Death Row Records, had created a huge fan base; and the Twinz, comprised of actual twin brothers Deon and DeWayne Williams, had signed a distribution deal with G's label, Def Jam. The album, *Conversation* (1995), generated a few singles—"Round & Round," "Eastside LB," and "Jump ta This"—but none made much of an impact. The Twinz contributed to G's second album, *Take a Look Over Your Shoulder* (1997), but their effort did little to salvage their stint with Def Jam. The label consequently parted ways with the Twinz, as did G, who himself began to struggle. —*Jason Birchmeier*

● **Conversation** / Aug. 22, 1995 / G Funk/RAL ♦♦♦

Although they were immortalized in Warren G's Top Ten hit "This DJ," Twinz were an overlooked branch of the G-funk family tree who made good use of their connections to create the steady *Conversation* in 1995. Twin brothers Deon and DeWayne Williams wisely allow Warren G to dominate their album, and he skillfully wears the hats of producer, songwriter, additional percussionist, and background vocalist. Yet it's the female vocal support by Nanci Fletcher and Tracey Nelson that adds a shimmer to tracks like "Round and Round" and "Good Times." The enjoyably clichéd "Eastside LB" incorporates Deniece Williams' "Free" as deftly as Warren G "regulated" Michael McDonald's "I Keep Forgettin' (Every Time You're Near)." But unlike the latter, the Twinz' clever interpretation did not become a huge hit. In parallel fashion, *Conversation* makes good use of proven post-*Chronic* elements (funky '70s synthesizer samples, arresting diva vocals, loc'ed lyrics), but the Twinz were unable to catch the Dr. Dre wave, which swept many of their Long Beach peers to success. Lack of a distinctive identity contributed to their obscurity, since the brothers' party raps are overshadowed by the dominant female vocalists and striking production elements. Those familiar sounds and themes give *Conversation* a pleasantly familiar consistency which should appeal to Snoop and Nate Dogg fans who might have missed the Twinz during the '90s G-funk explosion. —*Vince Ripol*

Twista

b. Chicago, IL

Gangsta Rap, Hip-Hop

Chicago rapper Twista made his recording debut on "Po Pimp," a platinum single by his fellow Windy City rappers Do or Die. Following "Po Pimp," Twista signed with Big Beat/Atlantic and released his debut, *Adrenaline Rush*, in the summer of 1997. *Mobstability* followed a year later, and in 1999 Twista returned with *Legit Ballin'*. In fall 2002, Twista hooked up with Ludacris, Jay-Z, Bone Thugs-N-Harmony, and other rap moguls for the recording of his fourth album. *Kamikaze* was slated for an early 2003 release. —*Stephen Thomas Erlewine*

Adrenaline Rush / Jun. 24, 1997 / Big Beat/Atlantic ♦♦♦

Twista's *Adrenaline Rush* is an uneven debut, fluctuating between gritty hip-hop and party-ready rap. He has enough charisma and skill to make many of the pedestrian beats engaging, but it's only when he has a genuine song, like the first single "Emotions," that *Adrenaline Rush* truly lives up to its title. —*Leo Stanley*

● **Mobstability** / Oct. 6, 1998 / Creator's Way/Big Beat ♦♦♦

Twista lives up to his official title as the world's fastest rapper and Chicago-style rap ambassador on his 1998 release, *Mobstability*, with the Speedknot Mobstaz. After breaking out on Do or Die's platinum single, "Po Pimp," in 1996 and releasing his major-label solo debut, *Adrenaline Rush*, in 1997 for Atlantic's Big Beat imprint, this follow-up hit record stores in 1998. Joining

Twista are fellow MCs Mayz (whose smooth flow complements Twista's rapid-fire attack perfectly) and Liffy Stokes. Literal snapshots of street hustling and violence are sliced between musical tracks that are equally focused on lurid, violent, and macho imagery typical of '90s hip-hop. Highlights include the Bone Thugs-N-Harmony callout "Crook County" and the reworked West Coast groove of the single and title track. With some nice hooks and Twista's incessant, precise flow, there aren't too many Midwestern efforts of this era that are more impressive than *Mobstability*. —*Vincent Jeffries*

Twiztid

Group / Hardcore Rap, Rap-Rock

Protégés of the Insane Clown Posse, the Detroit-area Caucasian rap duo Twiztid based their act on a similarly theatrical, outrageous, makeup-heavy image and an obsession with serial-killer horror films. Jamie Madrox and the Monoxide Child cast themselves as psychotic axe murderers on their 1998 debut album, *Mostasteless*, which was reissued with new artwork and extra tracks a year later in the wake of ICP's rise to national notoriety. Twiztid's second album, *Freek Show*, was released on Halloween 2000 in conjunction with ICP's *Bizzar/Bizaar* sets; *Mirror Mirror* followed two years later. The duo toured extensively throughout the States in the early 2000s, developing a small cult following throughout the Midwest in particular. —*Steve Huey*

Mostasteless / Jun. 22, 1999 / Psychopathic ♦♦

To all but the hardcore juggalos (and I've discovered that there isn't any other kind), the thought of a group of Insane Clown Posse protégés isn't exactly inspiring, but Twiztid may take you by surprise. Trading in the same horror comic book schtick that has made ICP the most inexplicable cult phenomenon of the '90s, Twiztid is, if anything, even more ridiculously exaggerated than their mentors. That, of course, is their selling point, and the weird thing is, their debut album *Mostasteless* actually works better than most ICP records. Like *The Amazing Jeckle Brothers*, *Mostasteless* is focused and benefits greatly from the musicality of producer Mike E. Clark, who not only plays the great majority of the instruments but also mixes, programs, and engineers the album, along with writing the music for over half the record. Clark is clever and he helps Twiztid segue convincingly between '70s soul jams, thrash metal, and street jams. But that may give too much credit to Clark, since the duo wrote and played the two most convincing cuts on the record, "2nd Hand Smoke" and "Diemuthafuckadie!" (which contains an effective, surprising sample from Gentle Giant's "Spooky Boogie"). Also, Twiztid are better rappers than their mentors, and less cartoonish (except when paired with them on the freestyle-styled "$85 Bucks an Hour"). Of course, this is all a relative judgment—compared to almost any other rapper, including Detroit peers Eminem, Twiztid is a cartoon—but throughout *Mostasteless* Twiztid often is more convincing than their Dark Carnival colleagues. It has to be said, that if you don't buy into the whole comic-book horror schtick, *Mostastless* (which isn't nearly as offensive as it would like, simply because after years of horrorcore posturing, it's hard to find endless streams of profanity offensive) will be irritating, but if you've bought into it, you'll enjoy this record as much as, if not more than, most ICP albums. —*Stephen Thomas Erlewine*

Freek Show / Oct. 31, 2000 / Polygram ♦♦

● **Mirror Mirror** / Apr. 2, 2002 / Psychopathic ♦♦♦

Shock rappers Twiztid always had a bit of an advantage over their mentors, the Insane Clown Posse. Where the Posse is more about emphasizing their own importance and toughness, Twiztid comes off as a Marilyn Manson-inspired duo of angst-filled rappers who are more frustrated with their place in the world. Making music that is hopelessly offensive and immature, the duo still manages to touch on a few subjects that make them somewhat relevant. Songs like "CNT" are teenage anthems that actually have more than a passing similarity to the juggalos' hated foe, Eminem. Although they lack his insight and cleverness, they craft an equally unhappy and blunt image of disaffected youth, they just simplify it and make it more teen oriented. Despite the fact that few outside of the juggalo cult will give this a chance, this might be one of the most accurate portrayals of the mood of most unhappy young people in 2002. The last track, "Your the Reazon," is one of the few songs in the Psychopathic Records catalog that actually shows some sort of positive message toward their fans, emphasizing how little popularity and political correctness should matter in comparison to showing loyalty toward friends. To make such a mature statement on a record that contains one of the filthiest rap songs ever written ("Dirty Lil Girl") only goes to show why this music is so important to their hardcore fans. This is hard to recommend to anyone outside of that fan base, but to dedicated fans this is one of the best albums to ever spew forth from the Detroit label. —*Bradley Torreano*

2 Black 2 Strong

b. Harlem, NY

Political Rap, East Coast Rap

Harlem's confrontational 2 Black 2 Strong came with the backing of MMG, a collective that included members Mean Gene, Johnny Marrs, Warchild, C Dogg, and Dark Chocolate. *Doin' Hard Time on Planet Earth*, 2 Black 2 Strong's 1991 album, was prefaced the previous year with the *Burn Baby Burn* EP. The cover of the EP depicted a burning U.S. flag and tipped off the subject matter of the title track. When Relativity's In-Effect offshoot attempted to press promotional copies, its tape manufacturer refused to comply. Eventually, it was pressed up through another source. 2 Black 2 Strong's continued testing of freedom of speech was met with resistance, especially since "Burn Baby Burn" included the line, "Fuck the red, white and blue." His solid album also tackled issues like the war on drugs, police brutality, and other inner-city plights. —*Andy Kellman*

● **Doin' Hard Time on Planet Earth** / Jul. 1, 1991 / Clappers ✦✦✦✦

One of the strongest—and most unjustly neglected—rap releases of 1991 was 2 Black 2 Strong's *Doin' Hard Time on Planet Earth*. Though the Harlem MC can be excessively strident and overly inflammatory at times, the album is a riveting, gutsy work that makes its share of highly valid points when addressing social and political issues. "Skulls" decries the crack epidemic with frightening accuracy, while "War on Drugs" asserts that the civil rights violations occurring in response to the plague are as bad as the plague itself. "Iceman Cometh" tends to unfairly generalize about law enforcement, although its point about excessive force is well taken. Unfortunately, as the '90s progressed, 2 Black 2 Strong remained undeservedly obscure. —*Alex Henderson*

2 Deep

Group / East Coast Rap

2 Deep was the duo of MC Jay Supreme and Thomas "On Time." In 1989 they released their sole album, *Honey, That's Show Biz*, on Cold Chillin'. Aside from the single "I Didn't Do My Homework," the album didn't cause much of a ripple, and the duo split without recording a sophomore album. —*Andy Kellman*

Honey, That's Show Biz / Oct. 1989 / Cold Chillin' ✦

At its best, rap music is a vehicle for expressions of social anger and devastating humor. At its worst, it's dull, tedious, and doesn't have anything to say. 2 Deep's debut album, unfortunately, falls into the latter category, suffering from leaden rhythms and powerless rhymes that keep falling into brag numbers—there are no apparent targets for all the dissin' going on here, but that doesn't stop MC Jae Supreme, or even engineer Thomas "On Time" when he gets up there to rattle out "For Those Who Dissed Me." The one time this really works is with "Simply Done," which manages to blow through four different styles in one piece without losing its energy. Meanwhile, when not bragging or dissing, 2 Deep gets busy trying to throw in their soggy rap ballad, "Stay in My Life," in which you find out they can't sing worth a damn. After that queasy discovery, you get a deadly dull rap about Jae's girl deciding she wants to go off and be by herself. "All Alone," attacking the subject with a sense of humor and an interesting arrangement, tackles the same subject and comes up more of a winner. "I Didn't Do My Homework," the opening track and the first single from the album, is really sort of misleading. It's a "Kids Screw Up" number straight out of DJ Jazzy Jeff & the Fresh Prince. It's a good opener, but the entire album, after the instrumental "2 Deep Intro," goes off in another direction entirely. Sound-wise, the album has problems. Aside from the vinyl noise from the albums used as samples on "Groovy Thang" and "& Funky Sound," the mixes are terrible. An overall muddy quality mars the whole affair and the rappers themselves often end up too pushed far back in the mix. Sometimes, they're buried completely. The same vinyl noise of "Groovy Thang" drowns MC Jae Supreme out completely at several points. All told, this is not the most auspicious debut 2 Deep could have had, and it's not a good way to step out into a market that's by now approaching saturation point. —*Steven McDonald*

Two Kings in a Cipher

Group / Political Rap, East Coast Rap

Two Kings in a Cipher—a duo that consisted of D.O.P. (born Deric Angelettie) and the Noble Amen-Ra (born Ron Lawrence)—was one of the many Afro-centric rap groups who came out from the East Coast during the early '90s. *From Pyramids to Projects*, their debut album for RCA subsidiary Bahia, came out in 1991. Despite the album's failure to make much of an impact, Angelettie and Lawrence went on to extremely successful production careers. They worked together and separately, scoring credits on records by the likes of Puff Daddy, Faith Evans, Mary J. Blige, LL Cool J, the Notorious B.I.G., and Mase. —*Andy Kellman*

● **From Pyramids to Projects** / Aug. 1991 / RCA ✦✦

In the early '90s, an abundance of Afro-centric rappers came from the Northeastern corridor—the region of the U.S. that gave fans Brand Nubian, X-Clan, Professor X, Isis, Queen Mother Rage, and quite a few similar artists. These hip-hoppers showed no awareness of either the gangsta rap that was coming from the West Coast or the bass music and booty rhymes that were inescapable in the deep South; instead of rapping about thug life or being sexually explicit, Afro-centric MCs were more likely to talk about African history or the Islamic faith. One of the lesser-known acts that came out of hip-hop's Afro-centric school was the East Coast duo Two Kings in a Cipher, whose debut album, *From Pyramids to Projects*, is competent but not remarkable. The rappers had an intriguing name and an interesting image—D.O.P. dressed very b-boy and sported baseball caps, whereas the Noble Amen-Ra wore a fez and dressed like an Islamic scholar from Egypt or Morocco. But, unfortunately, the material isn't as interesting as the group's image. That isn't to say that *From Pyramids to Projects* is a bad album. D.O.P. and Amen-Ra are capable rappers, and their rhymes aren't weak—but they aren't mind blowing either. Most of the time, D.O.P. and Amen-Ra sound undeveloped; one hears their potential, but they settle for adequate instead of excelling. With the right guidance, support, and direction from a record company, perhaps Two Kings in a Cipher could have developed into a group that was exceptional instead of merely competent. But that's only speculation. The duo never recorded a second album, and this little-known CD is only a small footnote in the history of East Coast Afro-centric rap. —*Alex Henderson*

2 Live Crew

f. 1986, California

Group / Bass Music, Southern Rap, Dirty Rap, Party Rap, Hip-Hop

No rap group (save, perhaps, N.W.A.) has stirred more controversy or provoked more heated debate than the 2 Live Crew. The furor over the graphic sexual content of their X-rated party rhymes—specifically their 1989 album *As Nasty as They Wanna Be*—was a major catalyst in making rap music a flashpoint for controversy and an easily visible target for self-appointed moral guardians. The fierce attacks on the group's First Amendment rights put many of their defenders in an awkward position—passionately supporting their freedom of speech on the one hand, but often finding little artistic merit in their music. And they were indeed crude and coarse, and frequently misogynistic by most standards; even if they fit squarely into a tradition of raunchy, sexually explicit black comedy (Redd Foxx, Rudy Ray Moore, Blowfly, etc.), many critics and intellectuals found their view of sex repellently juvenile, even ugly (and if they found it funny, it was hard to say so publicly). Despite (or, more likely, because of) that fact, the 2 Live Crew was fairly popular even before all the uproar and benefited greatly at first from all the publicity, although later on the novelty perhaps wore off due to overexposure.

Regardless of whether one enjoys their sense of humor, to focus only on the controversy ignores the 2 Live Crew's musical contributions. They were responsible for popularizing the booming, hard-driving sound of Miami bass music, and they were the founding fathers of a populist, dance-oriented rap subgenre that relied on simple, explicit chants and up-tempo rump-shaking grooves, appropriately dubbed "booty rap."

Despite their inextricable link to Miami, the 2 Live Crew actually started out in California, with a membership of Fresh Kid Ice (born Chris Wong Won in Trinidad), DJ Mr. Mixx (born David Hobbs), and Amazing V. The trio released their debut single "Revelation" in 1985 and its popularity in Florida led the group—sans Amazing V—to move to Miami, and after second single "What I Like," they were joined by Brother Marquis (born Mark Ross). They scored a record deal with local impresario Luke Skyywalker (born Luther

Campbell in Miami), who initially served as their manager, and then joined the group as a performer and bandleader. With Campbell came a big part of the group's on-record taste for sleaze, and accordingly their 1986 debut album *The 2 Live Crew Is What We Are* featured songs like "We Want Some Pussy" and "Throw the D" (as in dick). It became a word-of-mouth success, eventually going gold. Even at this early stage, obscenity was an issue; in 1987, a Florida record store clerk was acquitted of felony charges after selling the album to a 14-year-old girl. Campbell hit upon the idea of selling "clean" and "dirty" versions of the group's albums so that younger fans would have a less explicit alternative. 1987's *Move Somethin'* was the first album released in this format, and it became an even bigger underground hit than its predecessor, thanks to notorious cuts like "One and One," an X-rated retelling of the Kinks' "All Day and All of the Night" (which established the Crew's penchant for blatantly copped samples). In 1988, a record store in Alabama was fined for selling a copy of *Move Somethin'* to an undercover cop (a conviction later overturned on appeal), setting the stage for the Crew's home state to declare war.

As Nasty as They Wanna Be was released in 1989 and became the group's biggest hit yet; the single "Me So Horny" even climbed into the Top 40 despite virtually nonexistent airplay. Word spread even farther about the group's unadulterated raunchiness, attracting the attention of the ultraconservative watchdog group the American Family Association, who weren't satisfied with the album's parental advisory warning sticker. AFA supporter Jack Thompson, a lawyer and religious activist, convinced Florida governor Bob Martinez to open an inquiry into whether *As Nasty as They Wanna Be* violated Florida obscenity laws. The state prosecutor determined that action had to be taken on the local, not state, level, and thus in early 1990 Broward County sheriff Nick Navarro obtained a copy of the album and secured a ruling from County Circuit Court Judge Mel Grossman that there was probable cause that the album was legally obscene. Navarro warned record stores around the county that selling the album might subject them to prosecution, and the 2 Live Crew filed suit alleging that Navarro had unconstitutionally overstepped his bounds. In June, District Court Judge Jose Gonzalez ruled that *As Nasty as They Wanna Be* was legally obscene, and therefore illegal to sell. Record retailer Charles Freeman was arrested two days later for selling the album to an undercover cop, and the three rapping members of the 2 Live Crew were arrested on obscenity charges for performing material from the record in a local club. They were acquitted a few months afterward, thanks in part to expert testimony from Duke professor Henry Louis Gates, and Freeman's conviction was later overturned on appeal.

Meanwhile, *As Nasty as They Wanna Be* had become the forbidden fruit of choice for teenage boys across the country, selling over two million copies. Several other incidents were reported around the country involving record store owners being arrested for selling the album. The publicity also attracted the attention of George Lucas, who successfully sued Campbell for trademark infringement over his stage and label name, Luke Skyywalker; he subsequently shortened both to Luke. Capitalizing on the media frenzy, Campbell struck a distribution deal with Atlantic and put together a semipolitical album called *Banned in the USA*, after securing rights for the title track from Bruce Springsteen; it was billed to Luke Featuring 2 Live Crew. It sold like hotcakes on first release, and the title single became the group's second Top 40 hit. In 1991, the group released the first full-length live rap album ever, *Live in Concert*, as well as the official follow-up to *Sports Weekend: As Nasty as They Wanna Be*, Pt. 2. They sold disappointingly, especially considering the group's recent notoriety, and proved to be the last albums they would record together as a quartet. To compound matters, Luke Records was successfully sued for $1.6 million in royalties by MC Shy D.

In 1992, the Court of Appeals in Atlanta overturned Jose Gonzalez' ruling that *As Nasty as They Wanna Be* was legally obscene. At issue was Gonzalez' refusal to heed expert testimony (he'd pronounced himself fit to judge community standards of decency, since he'd lived in the community for 30 years), as well as the fact that the burden of proof of obscenity should have rested with Sheriff Navarro, who submitted nothing besides a copy of the album as evidence. The appeals court's decision was later upheld by the Supreme Court. Meanwhile, the 2 Live Crew was drifting apart. Luke and Fresh Kid Ice both released solo albums (*I Got Shit on My Mind* and *The Chinaman*, respectively), and original Crew members Ice and Mr. Mixx teamed up as the Rock on Crew for *Deal With This*. Luke continued his solo career over the rest of the '90s.

In 1994, Luke, Fresh Kid Ice, and new rapper Verb (born Larry Dobson) regrouped as the New 2 Live Crew, issuing the album *Back at Your Ass for the*

Nine-4. The same year, the group found themselves back in court yet again, this time over a lawsuit by the publishers of Roy Orbison's "Oh, Pretty Woman." They charged 2 Live Crew with plagiarism for recording a parody of the song on *As Clean As They Wanna Be*, alleging that the reinterpretation tarnished the image of the original. The case went all the way to the Supreme Court, which ruled that parody constituted fair use and found in favor of the group. The New 2 Live Crew didn't last long, as Luke chose to concentrate on his solo career. In 1995, Luke Records filed for bankruptcy, as Campbell was beset by creditors and expenses; both he and the remaining 2 Live Crew wound up on Little Joe, a label founded by his ex-business partner Joe Weinberger. In 1996, Fresh Kid Ice, Brother Marquis, and Mr. Mixx re-formed the 2 Live Crew without Campbell and released *Shake a Lil' Somethin'*. Brother Marquis departed afterward, and down to the two original California members, the 2 Live Crew issued *The Real One* in 1998. Luke, meanwhile, continued to record steadily, as well as releasing several compilation albums showcasing new South Florida talent. —*Steve Huey*

Revelation [Single] / 1985 / Makola ◆◆◆

When people think of Luther Campbell and his infamous 2 Live Crew, they think of X-rated Miami bass music—raunchy, sexually explicit stuff that managed to offend everyone from the Jerry Falwell/Pat Robertson crowd on the far right to radical feminists on the far left. But 2 Live Crew didn't always specialize in X-rated booty rhymes. Released in 1985, "Revelation" is a little-known 12" single that is surprisingly different from the type of sexploitive tunes that put the group on the map a few years later. Those who associate 2 Live Crew with "We Want Some Pussy" and "Me So Horny" will be surprised to learn that "Revelation" is a sociopolitical number that examines a variety of issues (including poverty, unemployment, drugs, and black-on-black crime) and comes to the conclusion that all of these problems are part of biblical prophecy. Obviously, Biblical prophecy isn't what 2 Live Crew were rapping about on "We Want Some Pussy." But then, the group had yet to find their niche when they recorded this 12" single. It's also important to note that "Revelation" isn't Miami bass—the synth-driven production is closer to the West Coast electro sound that Egyptian Lover and World Class Wrecking Crew were known for at the time. Meanwhile, the single's more New York-sounding B side, "2 Live," is a mildly catchy, if unremarkable, tune that favors the sort of scratching/beatbox sound that East Coast MCs were famous for in 1985. As far as '80s message rap goes, "Revelation" isn't in a class with Grandmaster Flash's "New York, New York" or Run-D.M.C.'s "It's Like That." Nonetheless, this is a single that rap historians will find interesting if they can find a copy. —*Alex Henderson*

The 2 Live Crew Is What We Are / 1986 / Luke ◆◆◆◆

There was a time when many New York hip-hoppers refused to believe that rappers from Miami could record a gold or platinum album or give them any real competition. That was before 1986, when the 2 Live Crew's debut album, *The 2 Live Crew Is What We Are*, came out on Luther Campbell's Miami-based Luke Skyywalker Records (later renamed Luke Records). This LP did a lot to popularize Florida-style bass music, and like the gangsta rap that was coming from California, it demonstrated that rappers didn't have to be from New York to sell a lot of records. Musically, *The 2 Live Crew Is What We Are* was a definite departure from New York rap—the grooves are much faster—and lyrically, the album put booty rhymes on the map. The 2 Live Crew wasn't the first rap group to talk about sex, but this album did take sexually explicit rap lyrics to a new level of nastiness. With X-rated offerings like "Throw the D" and "We Want Some Pussy," Campbell and his colleagues popularized a style of rap that thrives on decadence for the sake of decadence. These tunes are as humorous as they are raunchy; Campbell has often compared the 2 Live Crew's booty rhymes to the off-color humor of Richard Pryor, Andrew Dice Clay, and Rudy Ray Moore—and, to be sure, there are some parallels. Like those comedians, the 2 Live Crew is genuinely funny—but only if you have a taste for X-rated humor. Anyone who finds Moore, Pryor, and Clay offensive should avoid the 2 Live Crew as well. But for those who do appreciate that type of humor, *The 2 Live Crew Is What We Are* is a classic of its kind. —*Alex Henderson*

Move Somethin' / 1987 / Luke ◆◆◆◆

Although the 2 Live Crew's debut album, *The 2 Live Crew Is What We Are*, went gold and sold more than 500,000 copies in the U.S., the LP wasn't without its detractors. Some New York hip-hoppers argued that Luther Campbell and his associates were pandering to the lowest common denominator, and everyone from church groups to feminists argued that their X-rated booty rhymes were nothing more than pornography with a beat. But the Crew's fans didn't care what their critics had to say, which is why their second album, *Move Somethin'*, was also a big seller. Anyone who found *The 2 Live Crew Is What We Are* offensive was unlikely to be converted by *Move Somethin'*; booty rhymes like "HBC," "One and One" (an X-rated interpretation of the Kinks' "All Day and All of the Night"), and "S&M" are as crude and sexually explicit as anything on the group's previous album. "S&M," as its title indicates, is an ode to kinky sex. The 2 Live Crew was hardly the first group to address the subject of bondage and sadomasochism—back in 1967, the Velvet Underground's "Venus in Furs" was among the kinkier rock songs of its day. Some of the Ohio Players' pre-Mercury album covers employed S&M/bondage imagery, and the 1980s heavy metal band Bitch had a female lead vocalist who loved to sing about the pleasures of being a whip-toting dominatrix. But kinky sex hasn't been a prominent subject in hip-hop, and "S&M" is unusually kinky for rap. Of course, the Crew didn't need to rap about whips and chains to offend people; even without "S&M," this LP would have been X-rated. *Move Somethin'* was trashed by the Crew's critics, but those who aren't offended by X-rated humor will find it to be a thoroughly entertaining sophomore effort. *—Alex Henderson*

☆ **As Nasty as They Wanna Be** / 1989 / Luke ✦✦✦✦✦

A year after N.W.A. and Too Short significantly raised the bar for sexually explicit rap in 1988 with *Straight Outta Compton* and *Born to Mack*, respectively, the 2 Live Crew go one step further, to outright pornography, with *As Nasty as They Wanna Be*. The Miami foursome are certainly no strangers to sexually explicit rap, as they'd already released a pair of albums, *The 2 Live Crew Is What We Are* (1986) and *Move Somethin'* (1987), with their fair share of dirty rhymes, particularly on songs like "Throw the 'D'," "Move Somethin'," and "Do Wah Ditty Ditty." The 2 Live Crew had been more humorous than literal then, though, whereas here on *As Nasty as They Wanna Be* they are precisely that—not so much humorous as nasty. You furthermore have to wonder who the group is referencing as "they." You'd presume Luke and company are referencing nasty women in general, though it's just as likely they're thinking of their fans, who had grown proportionately to the degree of evident nastiness. It's perhaps not coincidental, then, that for their third album the 2 Live Crew offer their most evidently nasty one to date, where the majority of the 18 songs are directly about recreational sex and the minority are about partying, rather than the other way around as on their previous albums. The album opener, "Me So Horny," perhaps summarizes the album's mood best, in title as much as in substance, and other songs like "D.K. Almighty" (aka "Dick Almighty"), "C'Mon Babe" ("…fuck me!"), and "If You Believe in Having Sex" ("…say hell yeah!") need little introduction. Elsewhere, the few nondirectly sexual songs like "Fraternity Record," "Mega Mixx III," and "Coolin'" highlight Mr. Mixx, the group's impressive DJ, but are nonetheless pushed to the end of the 18-song album and understandably less immediate. It'd be easy to brush aside *As Nasty as They Wanna Be* as commonplace exploitation (or pornography, depending on your attitude) if only it wasn't so masterfully conceived. Like them or not, the 2 Live Crew have pieced together a brilliant album that's as rich in sophomoric merriment, animalistic voyeurism, and sample-delic soundscapes as in good old-fashioned perversity. A million and one teenage boys (and perhaps a few lighthearted adults) will gawk at Luke's "Seven Bizzos" and giggle at his "Dirty Nursery Rhymes" for years to come, and while the novelty of hearing porno rhymes over "Voodoo Child (Slight Return)" samples may perhaps diminish with time, there's still something very special about *As Nasty as They Wanna Be* that goes far beyond guilty pleasure. *—Jason Birchmeier*

Banned in the USA / Jul. 13, 1990 / Little Joe ✦✦✦

When Florida attorney Jack Thompson did everything he could to have the X-rated music of 2 Live Crew outlawed, his assault on the First Amendment led many free-speech advocates to take up the group's cause. Thompson's actions inspired quite a bit of anger from both white liberals and African-American rappers, who saw something obscene about a prosperous lawyer declaring war on a young black entrepreneur who had avoided the pitfalls of Miami's Liberty City ghetto. Luke was under attack for doing the very thing Republicans consistently advocate—using free enterprise to pull himself up by the bootstraps. Ironically, many of those who defended his First Amendment rights had little or no use for his lyrics. *Banned in the USA*, the Crew's first album for a major label and its first after the battle with Thompson, is for many a guilty pleasure. Say what you will about Luke's high

school locker-room lyrics; the Crew's Miami bass rap can be quite catchy, infectious, and amusing. Many New York hip-hoppers were quick to critcize the fast tempos employed by Miami rappers like Luke, but the fact that they did it their own way instead of emulating Northeastern MCs is something to admire instead of lambast. *—Alex Henderson*

Sports Weekend: As Nasty as They Wanna Be, Pt. 2 / Oct. 8, 1991 / Luke ✦✦✦

As the proper follow-up to 2 Live Crew's infamous *As Nasty as They Wanna Be* album, *Sports Weekend* definitely delivered more of the same lewdness that had made its predecessor such a success. Unfortunately, though, by this point the joke had run its course, and it proved that 2 Live Crew was limited in their repertoire. You see, *As Nasty as They Wanna Be's* most successful attribute was its shock effect—the first listen or two were undeniably intriguing if nothing else. Yet if you were able to endure even chunks of *As Nasty as They Wanna Be*, nothing here will deliver the same initial shock of its predecessor. Sure, there are moments when the Miami rappers take their already excessively pornographic lyrics to new heights of profanity, but with the increased emphasis on pornographic extremity rather than humor or satire, this album isn't nearly as entertaining—where the original was an uneven mix of sex and humor, this album is just sex with little humor. This formula should appeal to those who take a juvenile interest in the profanity, but for most there just isn't much here worth bothering with. The production is again lackluster, and the songwriting seems almost nonexistent this time around. This is blatant proof that 2 Live Crew had evolved into exploitative pornographers rather than comedic, and admittedly perverse, artists. *—Jason Birchmeier*

● **2 Live Crew's Greatest Hits** / Sep. 29, 1992 / Luke ✦✦✦✦✦

Uncle Luke and company have made a career out of Miami bass/electro that's as raw, funky, and unforgivingly sexually explicit as humanly possible. This collection takes the highlights from four of their earliest and most controversial records, and puts them together for a very convenient and near-accurate survey of their classic and most recognizable hits. Completists will note the glaring absence of such 2 Live staples as "Do Wah Diddy," "One and One," and "Banned in the USA," but this shouldn't deter anyone other than the cult followers. This is still by far the most comprehensive collection of their work on the market, and is the ideal place to start filling freaky needs. *—Rob Theakston*

Back at Your Ass for the Nine-4 / Feb. 8, 1994 / Little Joe ✦✦

Goes to the Movies: Decade of Hits / Oct. 21, 1997 / Little Joe ✦✦✦

2 Live Crew has released enough compilations to choke a horse, so what is one more in the scheme of things? This showcases songs that were either on movie soundtracks or recorded to be on movie soundtracks. This explains the hilarious "Crew to Crüe," a duet with Mötley Crüe that was meant to capitalize on both groups' media exposure during 1989/1990. Slated for inclusion on the *Juice* soundtrack, the tensions between the two groups led to its disappearance. Hearing Vince Neil sing "Hanging with the homeboys/We're gonna have some fun tonight" is priceless, making for a wonderful camp moment to kick off the disc. From there it's a typical Luther Campbell collection, featuring his usual filthy sex rhymes ("We Want Some Pussy," "If You Believe in Having Sex") and a few genuinely good hit singles ("Me So Horny," "Yakety Yak"). Anyone looking for a little variety in their 2 Live Crew compilation can start here for the bad-yet-entertaining duet; otherwise, there are several more hits collections that are more complete and flow better. *—Bradley Torreano*

The Real One / Apr. 7, 1998 / Little Joe ✦✦

Although Luther Campbell is long gone, 2 Live Crew remain the same, turning out the same lewd rhymes and bass-heavy grooves as they did in the eight-six. Which means, of course, that *The Real One* may indeed satisfy some fans of the group, since it delivers what the Crew always delivers, yet some longtime listeners will have to admit that the porn/rap schtick ran out of steam long ago. Nevertheless, there's a handful of cuts that have a strong enough groove to satisfy the needs of hardcore fans who just want to hear some new material from their favorite groups. *—Stephen Thomas Erlewine*

2 Live Jews

Group / Novelty, Comedy Rap, Ethnic Comedy

Hot on the stiletto heels of 2 Live Crew's 1989 cultural firebomb *As Nasty as They Wanna Be* was the ethnic joke with a beat, 1990's *As Kosher as They*

Wanna Be. 2 Live Jews' debut album featured the rhyming skills of "Moisha MC" and "Easy Irving," two aged Jewish-American men who had ostensibly discovered a latent penchant for rocking the mike. In actuality, they were personas created in a studio by Eric Lambert (Moisha) and Joe Stone (Irving), who weren't even elderly. Featuring songs like "Shake Your Tuchas" and "Oui! It's So Humid" ("I was sweating like a mule/I was frying like a blintz"), *Kosher* was the comedy rap opposite of 2 Live Crew's *Nasty.* Chock-full of in-jokes and Jewish clichés, the album was also a goof on the emerging clichés of hip-hop itself—in this case, the chest-thumping bravado and canned bass music-backing beats of 2 Live Crew. "Shake Your Tuchas" found Moisha and Irving bragging in Yiddish slang over the synthesized cowbell beat common to early hip-hop. While Lambert and Stone were likely hoping only for a quick payday, *As Kosher as They Wanna Be* was a genius novelty record that functioned on numerous levels. But just as 2 Live Crew effectively blew their wad with "Me So Horny" and *Nasty,* "Shake Your Tuchas" and *Kosher* represented the creative apex of 2 Live Jews. The 1991 "Hebe-hop" reworking of *Fiddler on the Roof, Fiddling With Tradition,* may have been comedy rap's first concept piece, but it quickly faded. The self-explanatory *Disco Jews* appeared in 1994; *Christmas Jews* followed in 1998. The latter featured such hilarity as "Bagel Rock" (set to the tune of "Jingle Bell Rock") and "Christmas Wrap." The entire 2 Live Jews catalog eventually became featured fodder for Dr. Demento's late-night radio hijinks. *—Johnny Loftus*

● **As Kosher as They Wanna Be** / 1990 / Kosher ✦✦✦

A very cute novelty item, *As Kosher as They Wanna Be* would make Dr. Demento proud. "Novelty" is definitely the right word—2 Live Jews wasn't a real rap group, but rather a studio creation that was good for a few laughs. This goofy CD features the fictional characters Easy Irving and Moisha MC, two elderly Jewish-American men who took up rap in their old age. The brains behind this project were themselves Jewish, and one who hasn't spent a lot of time in a city with a large Jewish population may not fully appreciate the humor of "Oui! It's So Humid," "Shake Your Tuchas," or "The Matchmaka' Game." About the only time this CD becomes serious is on "Young Jews Be Proud," which brings to mind Run-D.M.C.'s "Proud to Be Black," except that it's reflecting on Jewish history instead of black. But for the most part, *Kosher's* main purpose is providing some comic relief. *—Alex Henderson*

Fiddling With Tradition / 1991 / Kosher ✦✦

Disco Jews / Nov. 8, 1994 / Hot Productions ✦✦

2Pac (Tupac Amaru Shakur)

b. Jun. 16, 1971, New York, NY **d.** Sep. 13, 1996, Las Vegas, NV
Vocals, Producer / Gangsta Rap, West Coast Rap, Hardcore Rap, G-Funk
2Pac became the unlikely martyr of gangsta rap, and a tragic symbol of the toll its lifestyle exacted on urban black America. At the outset of his career, it didn't appear that he would emerge as one of the definitive rappers of the '90s—he started out as a second-string rapper and dancer for Digital Underground, joining only after they had already landed their biggest hit. But in 1991, he delivered an acclaimed debut album, *2Pacalypse Now,* and quickly followed with a star-making performance in the urban drama *Juice.* Over the course of one year, his profile rose substantially, based as much on his run-ins with the law as on his music. By 1994, 2Pac rivaled Snoop Dogg as the most controversial figure in rap, spending as much time in prison as he did in the recording studio. His burgeoning outlaw mythology helped his 1995 album *Me Against the World* enter the charts at number one, and it also opened him up to charges of exploitation. Yet, as the single "Dear Mama" illustrated, he was capable of sensitivity as well as violence. Signing with Death Row Records in late 1995, 2Pac released the double-album *All Eyez on Me* in the spring of 1996, and the record, as well as its hit single "California Love," confirmed his superstar status. Unfortunately, the gangsta lifestyle he captured in his music soon overtook his own life. While his celebrity was at its peak, he publicly fought with his rival, the Notorious B.I.G., and there were tensions brewing at Death Row. Even with such conflicts, however, 2Pac's drive-by shooting in September 1996 came as an unexpected shock. On September 13, six days after the shooting, 2Pac passed away, leaving behind a legacy that was based as much on his lifestyle as on his music.

The son of two Black Panther members, Tupac Amaru Shakur was born in New York City. His parents had separated before he was born, and his mother moved him and his sister around the country for much of their childhood. Frequently, the family was at the poverty level, but Shakur managed to gain acceptance to the prestigious Baltimore School of the Arts as a teenager. While he was at the school, his creative side flourished, as he began writing raps and acting. Before he could graduate, his family moved to Marin City, CA, when he was 17 years old. Over the next few years, he lived on the streets and began hustling. Eventually, he met Shock-G, the leader of Digital Underground. The Oakland-based crew decided to hire him as a dancer and roadie, and as he toured with the group, he worked on his own material. 2Pac made his first recorded appearance on the group's spring 1991 record, *This Is an EP Release,* and he also appeared on their second album, *Sons of the P.* The following year, he released his own debut, *2Pacalypse Now.* The album became a word-of-mouth hit, as "Brenda's Got a Baby" reached the R&B Top 30 and the record went gold. However, its blunt and explicit lyrics earned criticisms for moral watchdogs, and then Vice President Dan Quayle attacked the album while he was campaigning for reelection that year.

Shakur's profile was raised considerably by his acclaimed role in the Ernest Dickerson film *Juice,* which led to a lead role in John Singleton's *Poetic Justice* the following year. By the time the film hit theaters, 2Pac had released his second album, *Strictly 4 My N.I.G.G.A.Z.,* which became a platinum album, peaking at number four on the R&B charts and launching the Top Ten R&B hit singles "I Get Around" and "Keep Ya Head Up," which peaked at number 11 and 12, respectively, on the pop charts. Late in 1993, he acted in the basketball movie *Above the Rim.* Although Shakur was selling records and earning praise for his music and acting, he began having serious altercations with the law; prior to becoming a recording artist, he had no police record. He was arrested in 1992 after he was involved in a fight that culminated with a stray bullet killing a six-year-old bystander; the charges were later dismissed. 2Pac was filming *Menace II Society* in the summer of 1993 when he assaulted director Allen Hughes; he was sentenced to 15 days in jail in early 1994. The sentence arrived after two other high-profile incidents. In October of 1993, he was charged with shooting two off-duty police officers in Atlanta. The charges were dismissed, but the following month, he and two members of his entourage were charged with sexually abusing a female fan. In 1994 he was found guilty of sexual assault. The day after the verdict was announced, he was shot by a pair of muggers while he was in the lobby of a New York City recordings studio. Shakur was sentenced to four and a half years in prison on February 7, 1995.

Later that month, Shakur began serving his sentence. He was in jail when his third album, *Me Against the World,* was released in March. The record entered the charts at number one, making 2Pac the first artist to enjoy a number-one record while serving a prison sentence. While he was in prison, he accused the Notorious B.I.G., Puffy Combs, Andre Harrell, and his own close friend Randy "Stretch" Walker of orchestrating his New York shooting. Shakur only served eight months of his sentence, as Suge Knight, the president of Death Row Records, arranged for parole and posted a $1.4 million bond for the rapper. By the end of the year, 2Pac was out of prison and working on his debut for Death Row. On November 30, 1995—the one-year anniversary of the New York shooting—Walker was killed in a gangland-styled murder in Queens.

2Pac's Death Row debut, *All Eyez on Me,* was the first double disc of original material in hip-hop history. It debuted at number one upon its February release, and would be certified quintuple platinum by the fall. Although he had a hit record and, with the Dr. Dre duet "California Love," a massive single on his hands, Shakur was beginning to tire of hip-hop and started to concentrate on acting. During the summer of 1996, he completed two films, the thriller *Bullet* and the dark comedy *Gridlock'd,* which also starred Tim Roth. He also made some recordings for Death Row, which was quickly disintegrating without Dre as the house producer, and as Knight became heavily involved in illegal activities.

At the time of his murder in September 1996, there were indications that Shakur was considering leaving Death Row, and maybe even rap, behind. None of those theories can ever be confirmed, just as the reasons behind his shooting remain mysterious. Shakur was shot on the Las Vegas strip as he was riding in the passenger seat of Knight's car. They had just seen the Mike Tyson-Bruce Seldon fight at the MGM Grand, and as they were leaving the hotel, 2Pac got into a fight with an unnamed young black man. It has been suggested that this was the cause of the drive-by shooting, and it has also been suggested that Knight's ties to the mob and to gangs were the reason; another theory is that the Notorious B.I.G. arranged the shooting as retaliation for 2Pac's comments that he slept with Biggie's wife, Faith Evans. Either way, Shakur was shot four times and was admitted to University of Nevada Medical Center. Six days later, he died from his wounds.

Hundreds of mourners appeared at the hospital upon news of his death, and the entire entertainment industry mourned his passing, especially since there were no leads in the case. Many believed his death would end the much-hyped East Coast-West Coast hip-hop rivalry and decrease black-on-black violence. Sadly, six months after his death, the Notorious B.I.G. was murdered under similar circumstances. As Shakur's notoriety only increased in the wake of his death, a series of posthumous releases followed, among them *Don Killuminati: The 7 Day Theory* (issued under the alias Makaveli in 1996), *R U Still Down? (Remember Me)* (1997), *Still I Rise* (1999), *Until the End of Time* (2001), and *Better Dayz* (2002). —*Stephen Thomas Erlewine*

2Pacalypse Now / Nov. 12, 1991 / Interscope ✦✦✦
Few expected former Digital Underground member Tupac Amaru Shakur to become hip-hop enemy number one when he made his solo debut with this 1991 album. Songs like "Crooked Ass Nigga" and "Tha' Lunatic" might have hinted that storm clouds were on the horizon, but there were also excellent advocacy numbers like "Words of Wisdom" and "Young Black Male." This didn't make him a celebrity, but it put Tupac Shakur on the road to stardom. —*Ron Wynn*

Strictly 4 My N.I.G.G.A.Z. / Feb. 16, 1993 / Jive ✦✦✦✦
Fulfilling much of the promise showcased on 2Pac's debut album, *Strictly 4 My N.I.G.G.A.Z.* offers a wealth of thoughtful moments such as "Keep Ya Head Up" yet still makes plenty of room for good-time celebrations such as "I Get Around." These two hits in particular make *Strictly 4 My N.I.G.G.A.Z.* a noteworthy, if sometimes overlooked, moment amid 2Pac's cluttered catalog. They also represent the two approaches 2Pac initially took with his music, emphasizing his thoughtfulness (another insightful highlight being "Papa'z Song") rather than the thuggishness so often associated with him, particularly in the wake of his death. A few notable West Coast rappers join the festivities here—Ice Cube and Ice-T on "Last Wordz" and Digital Underground on "I Get Around"—but 2Pac unfortunately doesn't have any notable producers to support him, as the quickly dated production stands as the album's only potential drawback. Not quite as remarkable as 2Pac's following two masterpieces, *Me Against the World* (1995) and *All Eyez on Me* (1996), *Strictly 4 My N.I.G.G.A.Z.* nonetheless merits acknowledgment, particularly in relation to the string of posthumously released Makaveli-era recordings littering his catalog. —*Jason Birchmeier*

☆ Me Against the World / Mar. 14, 1995 / Interscope ✦✦✦✦✦
Recorded following his near-fatal shooting in New York, and released while he was in prison, *Me Against the World* is the point where 2Pac really became a legendary figure. Having stared death in the face and survived, he was a changed man on record, displaying a new confessional bent and a consistent emotional depth. By and large, this isn't the sort of material that made him a gangsta icon; this is 2Pac the soul-baring *artist*, the foundation of the immense respect he commanded in the hip-hop community. It's his most thematically consistent, least-self-contradicting work, full of genuine reflection about how he's gotten where he is—and dread of the consequences. Even the more combative tracks ("Me Against the World," "Fuck the World") acknowledge the high-risk life he's living, and pause to wonder how things ever went this far. He battles occasional self-loathing, is haunted by the friends he's already lost to violence, and can't escape the desperate paranoia that his own death isn't far in the future. These tracks—most notably "So Many Tears," "Lord Knows," and "Death Around the Corner"—are all the more powerful in hindsight with the chilling knowledge that he was right. Even romance takes on a new meaning as an escape from the hellish pressure of everyday life ("Temptations," "Can U Get Away"), and when that's not available, getting high or drunk is almost a necessity. He longs for the innocence of childhood ("Young Niggaz," "Old School"), and remembers how quickly it disappeared, yet he still pays loving, clear-eyed tribute to his drug-addicted mother on the touching "Dear Mama." Overall, *Me Against the World* paints a bleak, nihilistic picture, but there's such an honest, self-revealing quality to it that it can't help conveying a certain hope simply through its humanity. It's the best place to go to understand why 2Pac is so revered; it may not be his definitive album, but it just might be his best. —*Steve Huey*

★ All Eyez on Me / Feb. 13, 1996 / Death Row ✦✦✦✦✦
Maybe it was his time in prison, or maybe it was simply his signing with Suge Knight's Death Row label. Whatever the case, 2Pac re-emerged hardened and

hungry with *All Eyez on Me*, the first double-disc album of original material in hip-hop history. With all the controversy surrounding him, 2Pac seemingly wanted to throw down a monumental epic whose sheer scope would make it an achievement of itself. But more than that, it's also an unabashed embrace of the gangsta lifestyle, backing off the sober self-recognition of *Me Against the World*. Sure, there are a few reflective numbers and dead-homiez tributes, but they're much more romanticized this time around. *All Eyez on Me* is 2Pac the thug icon in all his brazen excess, throwing off all self-control and letting it all hang out—even if some of it would have been better kept to himself. In that sense, it's an accurate depiction of what made him such a volatile and compelling personality, despite some undeniable filler. On the plus side, this is easily the best production he's ever had on record, handled mostly by Johnny J (notably on the smash "How Do U Want It") and Dat Nigga Daz; Dr. Dre also contributes another sure-fire single in "California Love" (which, unfortunately, is present only as a remix, not the original hit version). Both hits are on the front-loaded first disc, which would be a gangsta classic in itself; other highlights include the anthemic Snoop Dogg duet "2 of Amerikaz Most Wanted," "All About U" (with the required Nate Dogg-sung hook), and "I Ain't Mad at Cha," a tribute to old friends who've gotten off the streets. Despite some good moments, the second disc is slowed by filler and countless guest appearances, plus a few too many thug-lovin' divas crooning their loyalty. Erratic though it may be, *All Eyez on Me* is nonetheless carried off with the assurance of a legend in his own time, and it stands as 2Pac's magnum opus. —*Steve Huey*

Don Killuminati: The 7 Day Theory / Nov. 5, 1996 / Death Row ✦✦
Everything about *Don Killuminati: The 7 Day Theory* smacks of exploitation. Released only eight weeks after Tupac Shakur died from gunshot wounds, Death Row released this posthumous album under the name of Makaveli, a pseudonym derived from the Italian politician Niccolo Machiaveli, who faked his own death and reappeared seven days later to take revenge on his enemies. Naturally, the appearance of *Don Killuminati* so shortly after Tupac's death led many conspiracy theorists to surmise the rapper was still alive, but it was all part of a calculated marketing strategy by Death Row—the label needed something to sustain interest in the album, since the music on the album is so shoddy. *All Eyez on Me* proved that Tupac was continuing to grow as a musician and a human being, but *Don Killuminati* erases that image by concentrating on nothing but tired G-funk beats and tiring, back-biting East Coast-West Coast rivalries. Tupac himself sounds uninterested in the music, which makes the conventional, unimaginative music all the more listless. If he had survived to complete *Don Killuminati*, it is possible that the record could have become something worthwhile, but the overall quality of the material suggests that the album would have been a disappointment no matter what circumstances it appeared under. —*Stephen Thomas Erlewine*

Stop the Gunfight / Apr. 22, 1997 / Intersound ✦✦✦
Stop the Gunfight is a cheap attempt to capitalize on 2Pac's and the Notorious B.I.G.'s untimely murders by including a couple of tracks featuring the gangsta rappers. The theme of the album is to curb violence in our communities; it even includes a rap about the perils of drinking and driving. Thirteen of the 14 songs were written by Trapp, who also produced the LP. All well and good, but nothing here prompts repeated listens. The best song here is "Be a Realist," which features 2Pac and B.I.G. on a catchy but boring number; the repetitive beat gets quite tiresome, but 2Pac's rap makes the song. A rap rendition of the Commodores' "Brick House" compels for about 30 seconds, and then your mind starts wandering. Trapp and Chocolate Chip (whose raps fail to move) meant well, but only diehard 2Pac and B.I.G. collectors will find any pleasure here. —*Andrew Hamilton*

R U Still Down? (Remember Me) / Nov. 25, 1997 / Amaru/Jive ✦✦✦
Shortly after 2Pac died, there were rumors that hundreds of unreleased songs remained in the vaults; a mere two months after his death, the first posthumous record, *Don Killuminati: The 7 Day Theory*, appeared. Death Row released the record, and shortly afterward 2Pac's mother, Afeni Shakur, gained the rights to all of his unreleased recordings from both the Interscope and Death Row labels. She founded the Amaru label and released the double-disc *R U Still Down? (Remember Me)* in late 1997. Culled from 2Pac's unreleased Interscope recordings between 1992 and 1994, including several tracks that have had backing musical tracks "reconstructed," *R U Still Down?* doesn't have the aura of exploitation that haunts the Makaveli album, but it isn't much better, either. For the most part, Shakur sounds good, spinning out rhymes that are alternately clever or startling, but he eventually begins repeating

himself and running out of ideas. That's much better than the music itself, which is pretty much standard-issue gangsta rap that never deviates from the course. There are enough hidden gems to make it worthwhile for hardcore 2Pac fans, but it doesn't necessarily bode well for the Amaru label's series of unreleased recordings. If this mediocre mess is the top of the heap, they'll truly be hurting for strong material once they reach the bottom of the allegedly hundreds of unreleased 2Pac recordings. —*Stephen Thomas Erlewine*

1 in 21: The Tupac Shakur Story / Jan. 12, 1998 / Aim ♦♦

1 in 21 compiles 2Pac's early recordings as a member of Strictly Dope in 1990, as well as numerous versions of the song "Static," which was a 1991 collaboration with Force One Network. These songs have been anthologized on numerous bootlegs and semi-bootleg collections over the years, and none are really that enlightening or impressive. In fact, they're a bit underwhelming, even for the most ardent 2Pac fans. It wasn't until 2Pac began working with Digital Underground that he really blossomed as a rapper. Here he's still in primitive form. And it doesn't help that these songs sound pretty bad, characterized by rudimentary production quality. The Strictly Dope songs from 1990—"Panther Power," "Never Be Beat," "Case of the Misplace Mic," and "My Burnin' Heart"—also feature Ray Tyson, the other member of the short-lived duo. Most will be startled at how good natured and straight edged 2Pac sounds on these tracks. You would never assume that he'd be sporting a "thug life" tattoo a few years later and running around with the shady Death Row camp. The 1991 collaboration with Force One Network, "Static," is more impressive, though it's still not worth going out of your way to track down. It's featured here in numerous versions, including an "Extended Club Mix" that approaches ten minutes in length. These numerous remixes help make *1 in 21* seem like more of a collection than it really is. When you take away all the superfluous remixes, what this collection essentially boils down to is five songs—not much, particularly when they're this unimpressive. Sure, these songs shed light on 2Pac's earliest years as a rapper, but they're much more interesting than enjoyable—a novelty and not much more. A tiny footnote at best. —*Jason Birchmeier*

One Million Strong / Jun. 9, 1998 / Addictive ♦♦♦

Originally released on the Sound of Los Angeles record label in early 1995, just before 2Pac became a genuine superstar, *One Million Strong* is a solid collection of gangsta rap from a diverse selection of artists. 2Pac takes center stage with the title track, but Notorious B.I.G., Dr. Dre and the Wu-Tang Clan also make appearances—just a few short months later, such team-ups would only seem possible in a fantasy world. It's a little brief and a couple cuts fall flat, but *One Million Strong* remains a good snapshot of the state of gangsta rap circa 1995. —*Stephen Thomas Erlewine*

In His Own Words / Jul. 21, 1998 / Mecca ♦♦

It's marketed as if it were an official collection of unreleased Tupac Shakur music, but *In His Own Words* is far from being a legitimate collection of unreleased recordings. Instead, it's mainly an interview disc, culled from a session at the San Francisco radio station KMEL-FM, augmented by a handful of unreleased songs, including two songs recorded with the Notorious B.I.G. The source for these unreleased songs is questionable, and the entire record is more a sham than a success; only nondiscriminating fans need to seek it out. —*Stephen Thomas Erlewine*

• Greatest Hits / Nov. 24, 1998 / Death Row ♦♦♦♦♦

Greatest Hits is a strange release. Sure, Tupac Shakur had more than enough hits to make a terrific compilation, but its appearance in the fall of 1998 felt a bit like another opportunity to milk his catalog, simply because of the plethora of releases from previously unheard recordings to interview discs and bootlegs. Even with these misgivings taken into account, it has to be said that *Greatest Hits* does its job well. Given that it runs 25 tracks and two CDs, some may argue that it does its job a little too well, but the fact of the matter is, this contains all of his big hits, from "Keep Ya Head Up" and "Dear Mama" to "California Love" and "I Ain't Mad at Cha." Some may argue that it would have been more effective if it was sequenced in chronological order, but this remains the best place for casual listeners to get all the 2Pac they need. —*Stephen Thomas Erlewine*

1 in 21: The Remixes / Jun. 29, 1999 / Aim ♦♦

The "Remixes" version of *1 in 21* isn't particularly different from the normal version of the Australian import featuring early 2Pac recordings. Both albums feature different versions of the same songs: "Never Be Beat," "Panther

Power," "My Burning Heart," "Case of the Misplaced Mic," and "Static." None of these different versions are much different from one another, and none were especially distinct to begin with. The remixes are just as low budget as the original versions, and 2Pac's performance—which is what you're most interested in—doesn't change, just the beats. So, in sum, if you have one of the *1 in 21* collections, you probably don't need the other. And, unless you're a 2Pac fanatic, you probably don't want these albums in the first place; they're more novel than they are impressive. —*Jason Birchmeier*

Still I Rise / Dec. 14, 1999 / Interscope ♦♦♦

More than three years after his death, it's difficult to believe there's still unreleased 2Pac material out there, much less *quality* material. After no less than three posthumous albums built around what 2Pac produced when he was still alive (plus an assortment of bootlegs making the rounds), the well apparently still hasn't run dry, and *Still I Rise* is the inevitable result. As on the Notorious B.I.G. album released just weeks before, though, there are some pretty wide gaps on *Still I Rise* between rhymes actually delivered by 2Pac. There's also an undeniable—some would say obvious—impression that this album just doesn't bear the mark of 2Pac himself. Making up the difference in both categories is Outlawz, a quartet of rappers keeping the flow going between 2Pac fragments. As with 2Pac's other posthumous releases, *Still I Rise* comes with four or five solid tracks that may have survived the cuts on a *real* 2Pac album. The title track and "Letter to the President" are obvious winners, still reliant on the syrupy G-funk that 2Pac made famous, and (thankfully) not influenced by the increasing late-'90s insurgence of muzaky hip-hop productions. And "Baby Don't Cry (Keep Ya Head Up II)"—2Pac's self-produced follow-up to 1993's "Keep Ya Head Up"—is a surprisingly touching message track. For any of 2Pac's fans, it'll be so good to hear his voice again on new material that the cash-in nature of *Still I Rise* can easily be overlooked. It's just not the album 2Pac would have produced had he still been alive. —*John Bush*

The Lost Tapes / Apr. 18, 2000 / Herb 'n Soul Sounds ♦♦

One among several 2Pac collections presenting his 1989 recordings with Strictly Dope and producer Chopmaster J (some legal, some otherwise), *The Lost Tapes* compiles the rapper's earliest recorded rhymes. A few of these tracks—"Panther Power," "The Case of the Misplaced Mic," and "Static"—are more readily available than others: the truly rare "Let Knowledge Drop," "Never Be Beat," "A Day in the Life," "My Burnin' Heart," and "Minnie the Moocher." *The Lost Tapes* is thus one of the better collections of early 2Pac you're likely to come across; plus, it's one of the most legitimate, as Chopmaster J himself unearthed these recordings from his mother's basement and released them on Herb 'n Soul Sounds, which WEA distributed widely. As Chopmaster J explains on the back cover, "I thought that Tupac's fans would like to hear what his first recordings sounded like back when turntables, TR-808 and SP-12 drum machines and socially conscious themes ruled Hip-Hop." Though there's indeed little more here than skeletal drum-machine beats for production, it's 2Pac's rhymes that are most interesting. "Panther Power" is perhaps his most inspired moment here and an omen of the outspokenness that would eventually come to characterize 2Pac. The others are fairly conventional ventures about the usual golden age themes, though perhaps a bit more rudimentary that you're likely to expect. After all, keep in mind that 2Pac was still years away from his solo debut. He's inspired here, no doubt, but nonetheless a bit clumsy and imitative. Even so, these are incredibly insightful recordings that every die-hard fan should hear at least once, either here or on some other early-recordings collection, another good one being *1 in 21: The Tupac Shakur Story.* —*Jason Birchmeier*

The Rose That Grew From Concrete / Oct. 17, 2000 / Interscope ♦♦

This album features a large cast of hip-hop personalities reading 2Pac's poetry and writing, much in the spirit of a traditional spoken-word album. —*Jason Birchmeier*

Until the End of Time / Mar. 27, 2001 / Interscope ♦♦♦

Yet another album released in the wake of 2Pac's 1996 death, *Until the End of Time*, certainly offers plenty of music, two disc's worth to be precise, yet doesn't offer too many highlights, besides the chilling title track. As with many of 2Pac's posthumous recordings, the songs here seem overdone, too often dressed up with layers upon layers of production, choruses of background vocals, and a seemingly endless parade of guests. All of this overproduction obscures 2Pac's performances, which somehow remain remarkable no matter how deep into the vault Afeni Shakur and Suge Knight have dug. Songs like "Letter 2 My Unborn," "When Thugz Cry," and the title track are just as heartfelt as "Keep Ya Head Up," "Dear Mama," and "I Ain't Mad at Cha" had been but unfortunately are marred by radio-orientated production that's too glossy for such stark, literate lyrics. The title track is somewhat of an exception, though. It's one of 2Pac's most desperate, spirited performances ever—the voice of a man face to face with his own fate—and it's accompanied by an anxious yet lulling interpolation of Mr. Mister's 1985 pop hit "Broken Wings" that is far more affective than you'd imagine. Note, however, that there are two versions here of the title track (the best one being the original one, which features RL on the hook), as there are also two versions of a few other songs. These nearly interchangeable remixes function as little more than filler, particularly since the production throughout *Until the End of Time* is rarely noteworthy. What at first seems like an epic recording, offering 19 tracks in total, consequently seems as overdone as the production. Had this album been pared down to the length of a single disc, it could be an exhilarating listen; as it stands, though, *Until the End of Time* is a mishmash—too short on standouts like the title track and too loaded with dressed-up, guest-laden overproduction—that you'll find yourself fast-forwarding through far more often than you'd prefer. —*Jason Birchmeier*

Better Dayz / Nov. 26, 2002 / Interscope ♦♦♦♦
Though it was released on the eve of the busiest year in 2Pac's posthumous career, *Better Dayz* shouldn't be overlooked—and with the schedule including a feature documentary (with soundtrack), plus two books and another double album, it might be easy for this one to slip from the radar. A lengthy two-disc set, it benefits from a raft of still-compelling material by one of the two or three best rappers in history, as well as excellent compiling by executive producers Suge Knight and Afeni Shakur, 2Pac's mother. Organizing the set roughly into one disc of hardcore rap and one of R&B jams makes for an easier listen, and the R&B disc especially has some strong tracks, opening with a remix of 1995's "My Block" and including quintessentially 2Pac material—reflective, conflicted, occasionally anguished—like "Never Call U B✲✲✲✲ Again," "Better Dayz," "Fame," and "This Life I Lead." Most of the tracks are previously unreleased, the rest coming from scattered compilations like Knight's *Chronic 2000: Still Smokin'* or 1995's *The Show* soundtrack. It's 2Pac's best album since his death, and bodes well for future material by, and concerning, rap's most legendary figure. —*John Bush*

II Tru

f. Cleveland, OH
Group / Hip-Hop
A female rap duo signing from Bone Thugs-N-Harmony's hometown of Cleveland, OH, II Tru debuted on *Family Scriptures* by the all-star side

project Mo Thugs Family. The group began when Jhaz and Blaine founded Big Daddy Coalition, an informal rap project with two self-released cassettes, *The Dark Side* and *Welcome to Cleveland*. After meeting up with Brina, the trio began building a following in the city. After warming up the crowd at local appearances by Scarface and 2Pac, among others, II Tru were invited to join Mo Thugs Records, the home of Cleveland heroes Bone Thugs-N-Harmony. The trio guested on Mo Thugs' *Family Scriptures* in 1996, then released their proper debut, *A New Breed of Female*, in September 1997. —*John Bush*

A New Breed of Female / Sep. 9, 1997 / Relativity ♦♦

Ty

b. London, England
Underground Rap, British Rap
Mild-mannered British rapper Ty lacks the raggae flow and quick patois of most rappers from the Big Dada label; he's more the big brother, with clever, mature themes that commonly go far beyond the usual shot callers involved in rap music. Born in London to Nigerian immigrants, Ty began recording during the mid-'90s, and appeared on tracks produced by IG Culture's New Sector Movement, MC Mell 'O', DJ Shortee Blitz, and DJ Pogo. He also hosted a hip-hop night called *Lyrical Lounge*, and worked with the *Ghetto Grammar* poetry workshop. His Ty debut came on Big Dada in late 2000 with the single "Break the Lock." His first full-length, *Awkward*, appeared early the following year and earned kudos from dozens of musical sources. —*John Bush*

● **Awkward** / Feb. 6, 2001 / Big Dada ♦♦♦♦
British MC Ty's vocal delivery is smooth, soulful, and relaxed with clear diction, a self-deprecating sense of humor, and little indication of anger or braggadocio; the accompanying beats are tasteful, crisp, melodious, stylistically diverse, generally laid-back, and sometimes mixed to resemble funk more than typical hip-hop; the literate lyrics mention Brian Eno and address topics such as sexual politics without resorting to misogyny or mean-spiritedness; and Ty even recalls the school bully without fantasizing about violent revenge. In other words, *Awkward* is an early contender for politically correct hip-hop album of the year. That doesn't mean that it's a bad album, however, since there's no rule that an MC has to drop offensive lyrics to be good. Ty has enough technique to make it seem like he's rhyming even when he isn't, and while some may consider the album too mellow and perhaps even somewhat bland, it does have enough musical variety to keep it interesting, ranging from Eric Appapoulaye's rock guitar on songs such as "The Nonsense" to the guest French MC and African music influence on "Zaibo." —*Todd Kristel*

U-God (Lamont Hawkins)

Vocals / East Coast Rap, Hardcore Rap

One of the lesser-known MCs in the nine-member Wu-Tang Clan, U-God was born Lamont Hawkins, and also raps under the aliases Golden Arms, Lucky Hands, Baby U, and 4-Bar Killer. U-God missed out on the first round of Wu-Tang solo projects, which occurred in between the releases of the *Enter the Wu-Tang* (*36 Chambers*) and *Wu-Tang Forever* albums; however, he got his chance during the second go-round that followed. 1999's *Golden Arms Redemption* made him the eighth member of the group to record a solo album. —*Steve Huey*

● **Golden Arms Redemption** / Oct. 5, 1999 / Priority ◆◆◆

The eighth of nine core Wu-Tang members to get his own solo joint (leaving only Masta Killa out in the cold), U-God doesn't have the personality appeal of Wu-Tang's well-known names Method Man, Ol' Dirty Bastard, Raekwon, or even Ghostface Killah. He also doesn't have the rapping skills, though given the wealth of talent spread all over Wu-Tang, being the fourth or fifth best rapper in the crew is hardly the slam it may seem. His attempt at a trade-mark track, "Enter U-God," leads off *Golden Arms Redemption*, and gets the full production treatment from RZA. While the beats mine territory farther below terra firma than has ever been heard from RZA, U-God shows off his solid rhymes. If there's a problem here, though, it's his utter lack of emotion. In fact, when Method Man, Inspectah Deck, and Leatha Face make welcome guest appearances on "Rumble," the leap in energy is immediately recognizable. U-God's entry in the Wu-Tang solo canon isn't one of the best, but compared to much of the hip-hop being produced in the late '90s, it's a welcome addition. —*John Bush*

The U-Krew

f. Portland, OR

Group / Urban, Hip-Hop

The U-Krew (short for the Untouchable Krew) signed to Enigma and released one self-titled album before splitting. The Portland quintet was formed by programmer/producer Larry Bell and vocalist Kevin Morse in the mid-'80s, but their first and only album didn't come out until 1989. Supported by a trio of singles, only "If You Were Mine" managed to peak in the Top 30 of the pop chart ("Let Me Be Your Lover" and "Ugly" were the other singles), and the group presumably were no longer shortly after that. Like several groups of the time, the U-Krew blended hip-hop elements with R&B. —*Andy Kellman*

● **The U-Krew** / Oct. 5, 1989 / Enigma ◆◆

Portland rappers the U-Krew landed a Top 30 pop hit with their 1989 *The U-Krew*. "If U Were Mine" was among the last romantic/love-style singles to make much headway on the hip-hop scene, and a moderately successful follow-up single, "Let Me Be Your Lover," helped get the album onto the lower reaches of the pop chart. Of course, Kevin Morse's sentimental vocals probably had more to do with this than the raps or production. —*Ron Wynn*

UGK

f. 1990

Group / Southern Rap, Dirty South, Hardcore Rap

Southern gangsta rappers Pimp C and Bun B formed UGK (aka Underground Kingz) in the early '90s and signed to Jive Records for their debut album, 1992's *Too Hard to Swallow*. After second album *Super Tight...*, UGK hit the R&B charts with 1996's *Ridin' Dirty*, which ascended to the number-two spot. *Dirty Money* followed in late 2001. —*John Bush*

Super Tight... / Aug. 30, 1994 / Jive ◆◆◆

● **Ridin' Dirty** / Jul. 29, 1996 / Jive ◆◆◆◆◆

UGK's third album, *Ridin' Dirty*, is their first to be released by a major label, which gives you some sort of indication of how far the group has gone in four short years. In that span of time, UGK scaled to the top of the small but vicious hip-hop scene in the South, creating a distinctive gangsta hybrid in the process. UGK is just as hedonistic and materialistic as those rappers out on the West Coast, but they don't infuse their music with the deep funk of the Cali scene, nor do they revel in the buoyant bass of their Miami brethren. Instead, they take a more stripped-down approach, which is all the better to hear their celebratiosn of money, drugs, and women—all of the typical gangsta accessories. If UGK doesn't really have something new to say, at least they have come up with an engaging way to say it—the sound of their record is vibrant and direct, bringing you right into the thick of things. It's not exceptional gangsta rap, but it is entertaining. —*Leo Stanley*

Dirty Money / Nov. 13, 2001 / Jive ◆◆◆

Five years passed between 1996's *Ridin' Dirty* and 2001's *Dirty Money*, and in rap, that is an eternity. Rap tastes can easily change from one year to the next, which is why a lot of talented MCs have watched their popularity fade after only two or three albums. At any rate, *Dirty Money* has no problem picking up where *Ridin' Dirty* left off; UGK's lyrics are as decadent as ever. In the '90s, the Texas duo epitomized the dirty South school of rap, and this 2001 release indicates that Pimp C and his partner aren't about to tone down their off-color approach; UGK's music is still a totally unapologetic celebration of promiscuous sex, marijuana, money, and jewelry. In other words, it is exactly the type of album that critics of hardcore rap love to hate. None of the lyrics on *Dirty Money* are groundbreaking—the album's subject matter has been covered time and time again by West Coast gangsta rappers and G-funksters as well as UGK's Texas, Georgia, Tennessee, and Louisiana colleagues in the dirty South arena. But while UGK's themes were never innovative, the Texans have usually had interesting ways of getting their points across, and that holds true on *Dirty Money*. The Texans still have clever ways of delivering their sex/money/jewelry/drugs mantra. Another thing that makes the CD memorable is the production; UGK's sleek, keyboard-driven tracks are, for the most part, as interesting as their Texas-fried rapping style. *Dirty Money* falls short of superb, but those who aren't offended by explicit lyrics will find it to be an enjoyable, entertaining slice of dirty South rap that is good for some cheap thrills. —*Alex Henderson*

Ugly Duckling

f. Los Angeles, CA

Group / Hip-Hop, Alternative Rap, Jazz-Rap

Comparable to De La Soul, A Tribe Called Quest, the Pharcyde, the Jungle Brothers, and Digable Planets, Ugly Duckling is a quirky, jazz-influenced alternative rap trio who formed in the Los Angeles suburb of Long Beach in 1995. Group members Dizzy, Young Einstein, and Andycat started collaborating around 1995, and the hip-hoppers took the name Ugly Duckling because they felt like outcasts on the Southern California hip-hop scene of the mid-'90s. Gangsta rap was the West Coast's dominant hip-hop trend at the time, and Ugly Duckling's members had no interest in the type of macro posturing and violent, threatening lyrics that gangsta rap was known for. In 1998, the group put out "Fresh Mode," a single that sold more than 3,000 copies and seemed to get a buzz going. Later that year, Ugly Duckling was signed to 1500 Records and recorded their debut EP, which was also titled *Fresh Mode* and came out in 1999; *Journey to Anywhere* followed a year later. —*Alex Henderson*

Fresh Mode EP / Apr. 6, 1999 / 1500 Records ✦✦✦
Certain slang terms are so dated that you can't hear them without being transported back to another era. The word "swell" immediately brings to mind the swing era, while "groovy" makes one think of the hippie subculture of the 1960s. And in hip-hop, the term "fresh" takes you back to the 1980s, an era when Run-D.M.C., the Fat Boys, and Whodini were on top and breakdancers were all over the streets of Manhattan and Philly as well as Hollywood. In the 1990s, the term "fresh" sounded quite dated and was seldom heard on rap recordings anymore, but Ugly Duckling uses it repeatedly on its debut mini-album, *Fresh Mode*. The L.A. group made no secret of its dissatisfaction with much of the hardcore rap of the late 1990s, and by saying "fresh" repeatedly, Duckling was longing for what it saw as a more creative era in hip-hop. Comparable to alternative rappers like De La Soul, the Pharcyde, the Jungle Brothers, Digable Planets, and A Tribe Called Quest, Duckling favors a quirky, jazz-influenced approach on tunes like "Einstein's Takin' Off," "Now Who's Laughin'," and "Everything's Alright." The CD is full of references to 1980s and early-'90s rap hits, and Duckling pays homage to everyone from Run-D.M.C. and Biz Markie to Rob Base. The end result is a derivative and nostalgic effort, but an likable one nonetheless. —*Alex Henderson*

● **Journey to Anywhere** / Sep. 26, 2000 / 1500 ✦✦✦✦
It's easy to dismiss Ugly Duckling as just three white kids clowning around. Of course, the same could have been said about the Beastie Boys and they eventually turned into legitimate hip-hop artists. The trio has a scattershot comic approach, lampooning the excesses of modern hip-hop. In *Journey to Anywhere*, the trio attacks materialism in "A Little Samba" as well as hip-hop's obsession with sex in "Pickup Lines." Their antics could come off as pretentious if they weren't willing to poke fun at themselves, something that MCs Andycat and Dizzy are more than willing to do. While the MCs still have a lot to learn, the real star of the show is DJ Young Einstein who seems to have a knack for cleverly cutting up old school grooves. Although it's unlikely this trio will every reach the lofty heights of the Beasties, Ugly Duckling may someday prove to be good for more than just a few laughs. —*Jon Azpiri*

Ultra

Group / Underground Rap
Ultra was a teaming of Kool Keith, the offbeat onetime frontman of the Ultramagnetic MC's, and Tim Dog, best known for cutting one of the earliest East Coast-West Coast feud records, "Fuck Compton." Tim Dog had gotten his start as a peripheral member of Ultramagnetic, and when the group fell apart, he put his solo career on hold to rejoin Keith under the shortened moniker. Ultra recorded one album, *Big Time*, and released it on the tiny Our Turn Records in 1996. Once Kool Keith had blossomed into a leading underground rap figure, the ultra-rare Ultra album was given a somewhat wider reissue by the Threshold label. The duo reportedly made some recordings afterward, but no follow-up album appeared. —*Steve Huey*

Big Time / 1996 / Our Turn ✦✦✦✦
One of Kool Keith's first projects following the breakup of the Ultramagnetic MC's, Ultra teamed the legendary eccentric with MCs associate Tim Dog (by then the subject of cult adoration for his gonzo near-classic *Penicillin on Wax*) and up-and-coming producer/DJ Kutmasta Kurt. Their lone album to date, *Big Time* went woefully underexposed upon its release due to frankly awful distribution (its subsequent reissue has partly rectified the problem). It's become something of the Holy Grail of the Kool Keith catalog, owing mostly to its rarity. But the real reason to track it down is that it's pretty damn solid almost all the way through. Parts are as gleefully vulgar as you'd expect (and, perhaps, hope) from a Tim Dog/Kool Keith collaboration, although it's a little disappointing that the two don't interact all that much; in fact, there's a surprising number of basically solo tracks. But they actually hang together pretty well, not just because of both MCs' taste for the explicit but also because of their mutual frustration with the fakeness of the record business. It's an overarching theme for much of the album, and reaches its apex in the blistering "Industry Is Wak," which features (among other rants) Tim Dog's tough but fair perspective on the Dre/Snoop beef of years past. It's not all negative, though; the title cut is a G-funk-tinged player's anthem, while "Fat Lady" and "Bizarre" are back-to-back Keith cuts that out-crazy any Ol' Dirty Bastard sex rap. Plus, there's the album-closing "No Face," where Tim assumes one of the ghoulish characters pictured on the back-cover art. Keith fans will be pleased, but Tim is actually the revelation on *Big Time*—he sounds booming and

authoritative whenever he raps, and this is some of his most vital work in quite some time. This one's definitely worth hunting for. —*Steve Huey*

Ultramagnetic MC's

f. 1984, Bronx, NY **db.** 1993
Group / Golden Age, Hip-Hop, East Coast Rap, Underground Rap
Arising from the Boogie Down Bronx in the mid-'80s as a far-flung hip-hop trio with a heap of new ideas to try out, Ultramagnetic's Kool Keith, Ced Gee, and DJ Moe Love occupy something of a singular place in the old school pantheon. Combining funk-heavy tracks with jeep-rocking beats and obscure lyrical references, Ultramagnetic MC's have a list of firsts to their credit: the first group to employ a sampler as an instrument, the first to feature extensive use of live instrumentation…the first to feature a former psychiatric patient (Keith) on the mic. Early singles like "Something Else" and "Space Groove" were block-party staples and created waves in the underground, eventually landing the group on the disco-dominated Next Plateau label, where they released their underappreciated debut. The following years found the group shuffling from label to label, releasing albums on Mercury and Wild Pitch before splitting to pursue various projects. —*Sean Cooper*

★ **Critical Beatdown** / 1988 / Next Plateau ✦✦✦✦✦
Besides being an undeniable hip-hop classic, the first album by the cult crew Ultramagnetic MC's introduced to the world the larger-than-life, one-of-a-kind personality of Kool Keith. That alone would make this some sort of landmark recording, but it also happens to be one of the finest rap albums from the mid- to late-'80s new school in hip-hop that numbered among its contributors Run-D.M.C., Public Enemy, and Boogie Down Productions. *Critical Beatdown* easily stands with the classic recordings made by those giants, and it is, in some ways, more intriguing because of how short-lived Ultramagnetic turned out to be. It would be wrong to assume that the finest thing about the album is its lyrical invention. Lyrically the group is inspired, to be sure, but the production is equally forward looking. *Critical Beatdown* is full of the sort of gritty cuts that would define hip-hop's underground scene, with almost every song sounding like an instant classic. Although he turns in a brilliant performance, Kool Keith had not yet taken completely off into the stratosphere at this early point. He still has at least one foot planted on the street, and gives the album a viscerally real feel and accessibility that his later work sometimes lacks. His viewpoint is still uniquely and oddly individual, though, and he already shows signs of the freakish conceptualizing persona that would eventually surface fully under the guise of Dr. Octagon. If Kool Keith gives the album its progressive mentality and adrenaline rush, Ced Gee gives it its street-level heft, and is, in many ways, the album's core. Somewhere in the nexus between the two stylistic extremes, brilliant music emanated. *Critical Beatdown* maintains all its sharpness and every ounce of its power, and it has not aged one second since 1988. —*Stanton Swihart*

Funk Your Head Up / Mar. 17, 1992 / Mercury ✦✦✦
Four years in the making, the follow-up to *Critical Beatdown* was somewhat easy to ignore, overly crowded with half-thought ideas and water-treading glances back. Still, *Funk Your Head Up* did produce the radio hit "Poppa Large." —*Sean Cooper*

The Four Horsemen / Aug. 10, 1993 / Wild Pitch ✦✦✦
Ultramagnetic's final album featured the foursome trying to balance Kool Keith's bizarre battle raps with the kinds of beats and rhymes that would put them in company with other East Coast groups like Gang Starr or EPMD. Surprisingly, *The Four Horsemen* was largely a live album, with a studio band attempting to reconstruct the classic hip-hop structure. Unfortunately, most of the results were muddy productions with little more than a stray brass line or two over the drummer's pedestrian East Coast beats. Only the opener, an instant classic named "We Are the Horsemen," approached the eccentric but head-nodding genius of their early material, though a few other tracks did feature interesting ideas: "Saga of Dandy, the Devil & Day" took a look at black baseball. Most of the other tracks should've been delegated to demo territory, with Kool Keith often reduced to endless repetitions of banal, baffling lines like this gem: "See that man on the street?/Who's at the corner, yeah!" —*John Bush*

Basement Tapes: 1984-1990 / May 17, 1995 / Tuff City ✦✦✦
Basement Tapes: 1984-1990 compiles a selection of Ultramagnetic MC's outtakes, rarities, and demos. Considerably rougher than their official studio records, *Basement Tapes* has raw street vibe, and although it's clear why

some of these tracks were never widely released, it's an exciting record, proving that the Ultramagnetic MC's were sorely neglected while they were active. —*Stephen Thomas Erlewine*

New York What Is Funky / Apr. 4, 1996 / Ol Skool Flava ✦✦✦
One of several frequently available Ultramagnetic MC's wrap-ups, *New York What Is Funky* includes alternates, rough cuts, and a succession of bizarre studio experiments from Kool Keith, Ced Gee, and co. It's definitely an odds-and-sods collection, occasionally energizing ("Grip the Mic," the tribute track "Chuck Chillout") but often baffling as only Kool Keith can do it: "Biscuits and Eggs" features the jaw-dropping rhyme "Don't give me biscuits and eggs/I wanna marry you." —*John Bush*

B-Side Companion / Oct. 7, 1997 / Next Plateau ✦✦✦✦
The Ultramagnetic MC's belong in the groundbreaking rap category (along with the likes of Run-D.M.C., Grandmaster Flash, etc.). Formed in the mid-'80s, the group rejected the fun rap style popular at the time (i.e., the Fat Boys and early Beastie Boys) and set out to create their own serious, funky, and bass-heavy groove style. The group definitely succeeded, but like many early rap artists, they did not meet with the commercial success they deserved for their trailblazing efforts. Back in the '80s, the 12" single was the main format for rappers to show their stuff (few rappers were granted full-length albums). So the Ultramagnetic MC's made the most of the 12", releasing many before their 1988 full-length *Critical Beatdown* appeared. An abundance of B sides amassed after a while (with many as strong, if not better than, the featured A side), so Next Plateau Records compiled the crème de la crème of these hard-to-find tracks on *B-Side Companion*, remixing most to give them a more contemporary feel. Their first-ever release, "Ego Trippin'," is featured here as "Ego Trippin' 2000" and sets the tone for the rest of the album. You can't go wrong with tracks like "Watch Me Now," "MC's Ultra Part 2," and "Funky," all equally strong old school rap that deserves to be heard. The seeds for today's rap stars were planted on the tracks included on *B-Side Companion*. —*Greg Prato*

UMC's
f. New York, NY
Group / Alternative Rap, East Coast Rap, Hip-Hop
The UMC's was a short-lived New York-based rap duo, comprised of members Hass G and Kool Kim. The duo issued a pair of releases during their brief career—1991's debut *Fruits of Nature* and 1994's *Unleashed*—but their lighthearted subject matter seemed out of place during an era when gangster rap ruled the charts, leading the UMC's to split shortly thereafter. —*Greg Prato*

● **Fruits of Nature** / Oct. 14, 1991 / Wild Pitch ✦✦✦
On their debut album, *Fruits of Nature*, the UMC's—Hass G and Kool Kim—are endlessly imaginative, witty, and effervescent by disposition and lyrical flow, and always intelligent. When it came to the music, coproducers Hass G and RNS decked it out in vintage soul and old Blue Note-styled tracks, with reams of obscure, idiosyncratic vocal samples tossed in as hooks, breaks, and bridges. The resulting effort is yet another vastly underrated rap album out of those banner years in hip-hop, 1991 and 1992, when commercial and economic instincts had yet to turn the music formulaic. The ironic thing is that nearly everything on *Fruits of Nature* is singalong catchy and so ebullient that it would have sounded great bounding out of radios or from MTV. Unfortunately, it is also the sort of hip-hop that is too idiosyncratic and brainy to garner a widespread audience. Instead of alchemizing their jazz-tinged sensibility into a more earnest and reverent underground hip-hop extension of the jazz tradition, UMC's twist their jazzy inclinations into what are essentially pop songs that, even while generating a singular style all their own, cover the full range of the catchiness spectrum: ingratiating melodic tunes ("One to Grow On"), carbonated word/play ("Blue Cheese"), cleverly disguised boasts and straight rhyming ("Kraftworks," "Swing It to the Area," "Any Way the Wind Blows"), loping urban anthems ("You Got My Back," "Jive Talk"), and more serious-minded cuts ("Morals"). There's even an urban take on storybook tales ("Never Never Land") and a sort of ballad ("Feelings"). The commercial failure of the UMC's and groups like them opened up hip-hop to the same sort of Top 40-ready and cookie-cutter artistry in the latter part of the decade that had previously swallowed rock and pop music. For a brief couple years, though, rap as uniquely excellent as *Fruits of Nature* could be found around every urban corner. —*Stanton Swihart*

Unleashed / Jan. 25, 1994 / Wild Pitch ✦✦

Uncle Jamm's Army
f. Los Angeles, CA
Group / Hip-Hop, Electro, Old School Rap, West Coast Rap
Los Angeles was a key capital on the tiny corner of the early hip-hop map known as electro, and Uncle Jamm's Army were one of the primary reasons for that. An extended crew of producers, DJs, and vocalists including Ice-T, Egyptian Lover, the Unknown DJ, and Chris "The Glove" Taylor, Uncle Jamm's Army released a string of popular, influential electro cuts during 1984-1986, including "What's Your Sign," "Dial-a-Freak," and "Yes, Yes, Yes," all for the Freak Beat label. Notable for their all-around musicality; driving, effective rhythms; and uncompromising attitude, Uncle Jamm's Army remain one of the most important pieces in the old school electro puzzle and have influenced scores of new school electro producers, from Autechre to I-F. —*Sean Cooper*

Yes, Yes, Yes [Single] / 1984 / Freak Beat ✦✦✦
Though marred somewhat by muddy production, this vocoder-led party jam is typical L.A. electro—heavily syncopated beats, simple, minor key synth melodies, and only thinly veiled sexual nuances. —*Sean Cooper*

● **What's Your Sign? [Single]** / 1985 / Freak Beat ✦✦✦
This is a solid, driving mid-tempo electro cut that holds up surprisingly well more than a decade after it was released. Although this single's flip side, "Dial-A-Freak," is the track included on most compilations, "What's Your Sign?" is clearly superior. —*Sean Cooper*

Uncle Kracker (Matthew Shafer)
DJ, Vocals / Rap-Metal, Rap-Rock, Pop/Rock, American Trad Rock, Singer/Songwriter, Album Rock, Turntablism
Slicing and dicing for his hometown chum, the mainstream rap hero Kid Rock, Uncle Kracker (born Matt Shafer) stepped out from behind the turntables to release his debut solo album, *Double Wide*, on Kid Rock's own Top Dog/Atlantic/Lava label. Yet another Detroit combination of funky post-grunge rock and hip-hop aesthetic, Uncle Kracker makes his predecessor proud.

Kid Rock and Uncle Kracker are practically family. The two met in Clawson, MI, in 1987, where Rock was spinning in an all-ages DJ contest at a popular night spot called Daytona's. The two had similar musical tastes (The Commodores, Run-D.M.C., Lynyrd Skynyrd, and George Jones) and became fast friends. Kracker's first musical contribution was on Rock's 1991 debut, *Grits Sandwiches for Breakfast*, and he also cowrote and performed on Rock's multiplatinum *Devil Without A Cause*. It was just a matter of time for Kracker to do his own thing.

It's neither surprising that the media has tagged *Double Wide* as more radio friendly than *Devil Without A Cause*, nor that Rock and his band, Twisted Brown Trucker, come together to bang things up on *Double Wide*. Like his pal, Uncle Kracker wanted a maddening country growl woven into mainstream modern rock to create a mind-blowing rap excursion; *Double Wide* was just that, released in summer 2000. "Follow Me" was a popular single among radio and MTV's TRL. Two years later, Uncle Kracker returned with *No Stranger to Shame*. —*MacKenzie Wilson*

Double Wide / Jun. 13, 2000 / Lava ✦✦✦
With Kid Rock's "Only God Knows Why" playing in the background, Kid Rock's protégé Uncle Kracker poses his mentor a question: "What if I don't make it?" It's hard to believe that a musician would open his major-label debut CD with inspirational career advice from Kid Rock. But Kid Rock does know a thing or two about becoming a rock icon to legions of suburban teens and porn stars. As Kid Rock's self-proclaimed best friend/DJ/backup singer/multiplatinum cowriter/sidekick thug boy, Uncle Kracker has Kid Rock's MTV-ready charisma and raunchy rock/rap fur-lined coattails to thank for the existence of this album. Maybe there is something in his native waters of Detroit, but Uncle Kracker definitely takes full advantage of the opportunity and delivers an amusing, party-ready debut CD of country, rockabilly, and hip-hop-infused rock & roll that is guaranteed to please. Each song drips with Uncle Kracker's laid-back, white-trash, Detroit-worshiping, beer-swilling attitude. "Better Days" is a soulful, country-fried rock ode to drifting through life, ready-made for an afternoon of lawn chairs and sun. "What 'Chu Lookin' At?" is a declaration of moving on, dissing girls of the past, and partying on. "Heaven" is a memorial to the glory of Detroit that perfectly blends

the twanging country guitars of "If Heaven Ain't a Lot Like Dixie" with testosterone-drenched hard rock. It's male bravado, plain and simple. Your opinion of Uncle Kracker, however, is largely dependent on your opinion of Kid Rock. Kid Rock's fingerprints are left all over the album, which is understandable considering he produced and cowrote nearly every song. The album is even filled with samples from Kid Rock's breakthrough album, 1998's *Devil Without a Cause*. If you loved *Devil Without a Cause* and *History of Rock*, you'll find *Double Wide* a welcome third helping. It's more of the same; however, Uncle Kracker provides an added dose of melody to the Kid Rock formula with his gravelly, mellow, and rather soulful voice. It lacks the mosh-pit power of *Devil Without a Cause* but eclipses nearly everything on *History of Rock*. At times, the album does sound a bit recycled, but when you're having this much fun at a party, who really cares? Who knows how long the formula will remain fresh, but on *Double Wide*, Uncle Kracker hits like a full house of raucous dynamite. —*Brian Musich*

● **No Stranger to Shame** / Aug. 27, 2002 / Lava ✦✦✦
On his sophomore effort, Uncle Kracker (born Matthew Shafer) steps out from behind Kid Rock's turntable to prove he's a viable artist on his own. The album *No Stranger to Shame* is a collection of willowy jangle rock with Motown and rap influences thrown in. It kicks off with the Motown feel of "I Do" and continues through a journey of country on "Letter to My Daughters" and funky rap on "Keep It Comin'." *No Stranger to Shame* is vastly different from his rap-riddled debut, *Double Wide*. His full-time employer, Kid Rock, is only credited as executive producer, unlike *Double Wide*, on which the rap-rocker made multiple appearances. Uncle Kracker proves he can sing throughout *No Stranger to Shame*. His takes on "Drift Away," a duet with Dobie Gray, and "Baby Don't Cry" showcase Uncle Kracker's blues sensibility. *No Stranger to Shame* should keep radio busy for quite some time—most of the songs remain in the listener's mind long after the CD ends. —*Christina Fuoco*

Unity 2

f. New York, NY
Group / Dancehall, Raggae, Hip-Hop
Sean "Cavo" Dinsmore and Lionel "Nene" Bernard formed Unity 2 as a way to fuse Jamaican reggae toasting with its rap offshoot. Both were members of the Toasters, a New York City ska outfit, and their 1990 debut album, *What Is It, Yo?!*, covers ska, dub, hip-hop, and a good deal in between. —*Steve Huey*

● **What Is It, Yo?!** / Oct. 16, 1990 / Reprise ✦✦
When singers Lionel "Nene" Bernard and Sean "Cavo" Dinsmore left the Toasters, it was in answer to the call of the big time: a lucrative offer from Reprise Records, who thought that interracial reggae/hip-hop fusion was going to be the next big thing. Maybe it could have been, but not on the strength of this album, which bombed, and with good reason. There were several reasons, actually, but the two most important ones were an almost complete dearth of hooks and an abundance of excruciatingly bad lyrics (i.e., "Hey Cavo, that girl's so fly, she's got wings!") delivered in an amateurish flow by both rapper and singers. "Brooklyn Story" is Cavo's whining account of getting mugged on the D train, while "Interview," "What Is It, Yo?!," and "Funky Reggae Stylee" all address—with little musical interest—Cavo's and Nene's upbringing, genuine streetsmarts, musical prowess, and (big) plans for the future. "Funky Reggae Stylee" is both funky and hooky, but it is marred by Nene's awkward rap that doesn't rhyme; "Can You Feel It" is a surprisingly effective, if lightweight, soca workout. The album has one genuine success, the cute "Shirlee" (provided in two mixes), but it's nowhere near enough. Despite heartwarming band demographics and a full complement of ace studio musicians, this album and group both sink. —*Rick Anderson*

U.N.K.L.E.

f. 1994, London, England
Group / Trip-Hop, Alternative Rap, Ambient Techno, Ambient Breakbeat, Electronica, Alternative Dance
Experimental hip-hop outfit U.N.K.L.E. was one of the original artists releasing material through noted U.K. label Mo'Wax, which helped launch the instrumental mid-'90s downtempo breakbeat revival eventually termed trip-hop. Though hardly the label's highest profile group (at least until the long-delayed release of their debut LP in 1998), U.N.K.L.E. numbered among its members labelhead James Lavelle, who formed Mo'Wax while still in his teens as an antidote to the increasingly stale acid jazz/Northern soul scene.

Stripping the music down to its barest of essentials—bass, percussion, minimal samples, and heavy effects—the Mo'Wax sound (best exemplified by the second Mo'Wax label comp, *Headz*, as well as its sequel, the two-part *Headz 2*) quickly gained respectability and a large audience. Although not as prolific as other Mo'Wax artists such as DJs Shadow and Krush, Lavelle's group nonetheless played a crucial role in cementing Mo'Wax's early sound though their *The Time Has Come* double EP, the latter of which featured remixes of the title track by Plaid, Portishead, and U2 producer Howie B.

The group comprised the trio of Lavelle, Tim Goldsworthy—a mate of Lavelle's since childhood—and producer Kudo, of seminal Japanese label Major Force (and a member of the on-again, off-again psychedelic beat crew Skylab). Previous to his entree into production, Lavelle along with Goldsworthy was deep into New York hip-hop and electro, the emerging late-'80s Sheffield bleep scene, the English acid jazz scene (which he covered as a columnist for *Straight No Chaser* magazine), and of course the acid house and techno explosions that were redefining the English counterculture at the time. The pair hooked up with third-member Kudo through the growing rep of the latter's Love T.K.O. project, whose outbound interpretations of breakbeat and acid jazz drew Lavelle's ear. While Goldsworthy and Kudo remained more heavily involved in nuts'n'bolts production (especially given the success of Mo'Wax, with the penning on an expansive partial ownership deal with A&M Records in 1996), Lavelle is heavily involved in the conceptual and organizational end, crafting beats and laying out vague sketches his partners then expand into full-blown tracks. Despite the scarcity of released material, U.N.K.L.E. grew to wider acclaim during 1996 through remix projects for the Jon Spencer Blues Explosion and Tortoise. After Goldsworthy and Kudo were effectively replaced by Mo'Wax bill payer DJ Shadow, the all-star LP *Psyence Fiction* finally appeared in 1998. (See Also: DJ Shadow.) —*Sean Cooper*

The Time Has Come EP / 1995 / Mo' Wax ✦✦✦
With a subtitle referencing Sun Ra and a cover splashed with the bright, abstract figures of old school graffiti artist Futura 2000, U.N.K.L.E.'s *The Time Has Come EP* (closer to a mini-album at over a half-hour in length) is a sprawling bouillabaisse of influences, all impeccably arranged. Hip-hop, funk, and jazz are of course the most obvious, but the soundtracky deviations of ambient, as well as hitting electro-boogie and spy movie theme music (particularly on Portishead's remix) also figure in. Remixes from Plaid and Howie B. also make this one of the tastiest, most varied release in the Mo'Wax catalog. —*Sean Cooper*

Berry Meditation EP / Mar. 3, 1997 / Mo' Wax ✦✦✦
Berry Meditation sees Mo'Wax and U.N.K.L.E. leader James Lavelle exploring a circa "Nights Interlude" Nightmares on Wax vibe. Though "Berry Meditation" never matches the atmosphere or innovation of "Nights Interlude," the fact that this EP doesn't overstay its welcome through more than 20 minutes of the same general melody and tone is a good sign that Lavelle knew what he was doing in the studio. The original version, track one here, is the most compelling. The song consists of repeated high-pitched synth notes, throbbing bass, and various tweaked electronics. The "last ever mix" starts out lazy and slow, but turns into a shuffling, flanged drum'n'bass excursion. Lavelle piles on sci-fi sound effects, many of them seemingly originating in a plumbing pipe. The "darker the berry the sweeter the juice mix," a remix by Attica Blues wastes a minute on random ambient sounds before breaking down the original song into a minimalist form, punctuated by heavy drums and space station blippery. *Berry Meditation* might not be Mo'Wax's finest 20 minutes, but label leader James Lavelle takes tiny steps toward a credible music-making career of his own with the EP. —*Tim DiGravina*

● **Psyence Fiction** / Sep. 29, 1998 / Mo' Wax ✦✦✦
James Lavelle and DJ Shadow are unequal partners in U.N.K.L.E., with the former providing the concept and the latter providing music, which naturally overshadows the concept, since the only clear concept—apart from futuristic sound effects, video game samples, and merging trip-hop with rock—is collaborating with a variety of musicians, from superstars to cult favorites Kool G Rap, Alice Temple, and Mark Hollis (who provides uncredited piano on "Chaos"). Since DJ Shadow's prime gift is for instrumentals, the prospect of him collaborating with vocalists is more intriguing than enticing, and *Psyence Fiction* is appropriately divided between brilliance and failed experiments. Shadow and Lavelle aren't breaking new territory here—beneath the harder rock edge, full-fledged songs, and occasional melodicism, the album stays on the course *Endtroducing* set. Shadow isn't given room to run wild

with his soundscapes, and only a couple of cuts, such as the explosive opener "Guns Blazing," equal the sonic collages of his debut. Initially, that may be a disappointment, but U.N.K.L.E. gains momentum on repeated listens. Portions of the record still sound a little awkward—Mike D's contribution suffers primarily from recycled *Hello Nasty* rhyme schemes—yet those moments are overshadowed by Shadow's imagination and unpredictable highlights, such as Temple's chilly "Bloodstain" or Badly Drawn Boy's claustrophobic "Nursery Rhyme," as well as the masterstrokes fronted by Richard Ashcroft (a sweeping, neo-symphonic "Lonely Soul") and Thom Yorke (the moody "Rabbit in Your Headlights"). These moments might not add up to an overpowering record, but in some ways *Psyence Fiction* is something better—a superstar project that doesn't play it safe and actually has its share of rich, rewarding music. — *Stephen Thomas Erlewine*

The Unknown DJ (Andre Manuel)

b. Compton, CA
Producer / Old School Rap, Electro, Gangsta Rap, West Coast Rap
The Unknown DJ pioneered the mid-'80s style of electro popularized by the Egyptian Lover ("Egypt, Egypt") and the World Class Wreckin' Cru ("Surgery"), then went on to produce the trailblazing gangsta rap group Compton's Most Wanted at the end of the decade. Born Andre Manuel, the Unknown DJ recorded only a few 12" singles during the mid-'80s: "Beatronic" (1984), "808 Beats" (1985), "Let's Jam" (1985), "Basstronic" (1988), "Breakdown" (1988), "X-Men" (1988), and "Revenge of the X-Men" (1988), the latter two also produced by DJ Slip (Terry Allen). These few 12" singles didn't attain much commercial success, yet they proved highly influential, particularly among the techno bass scene that would later emerge in the 1990s (see the *Electro Boogie* series). Beginning in 1989, the Unknown DJ and Slip put aside the electro they had been producing and joined Compton's Most Wanted, a gangsta rap group that resembled N.W.A. As part of Compton's Most Wanted, the Unknown DJ enjoyed considerable success for a few years as he and Slip produced a trio of popular albums: *It's a Compton Thang* (1990), *Straight Checkn'em* (1991), and *Music to Driveby* (1992). Following these albums, CMW's lead rapper, MC Eiht, embarked on a long solo career and the group dissolved, and with it the Unknown DJ's decade-long stint as a producer. — *Jason Birchmeier*

● **X-Men [Single]** / 1988 / Magick Kuts ✦✦✦
It's ironic that, at this time, little is known about the Unknown DJ except his proper name, Andre Manuel, and that he was the producer of some classic late-'80s West Coast rap tracks and an early and influential exponent of bass music. This track, with DJ Slip, features the complex rhythmic sensibility and solid, deep bass grooves that mark the Unknown DJ's production. The flip side includes an instrumental version and a bonus remix of "X-Men," which significantly departs from the original track. — *Brian Whitener*

U.N.L.V.

f. New Orleans, LA
Group / Hip-Hop, Hard Bop
U.N.L.V. was the first group signed onto Cash Money Records, nationally more famous for artists such as the Hot Boyz, Juvenile, Baby Gangsta, Lil' Wayne, and more. Along with Pimp Daddy, U.N.L.V. helped pioneer a new sound and style of hip-hop in New Orleans, and paved the way for CMR's many later successes. Their first album, *6th & Baronne*, is considered a classic in Louisiana, although their major claim to fame is the track "Drag Em 'n' Tha River" from *Uptown 4 Life* where the group disses No Limit Records' rapper Mystikal through a lengthy song. — *Brad Mills*

Uptown 4 Life / Jul. 11, 1996 / Cash Money ✦✦✦

● **6th & Baronne** / Feb. 24, 1998 / Cash Money ✦✦✦✦
This album was first released locally in New Orleans in 1993, gaining tons of attention for Cash Money Records. It's been re-released now that Cash Money has a distribution deal and the rest of the nation can finally hear what started it all. Unpolished and raw with messy, cluttered beats and a bunch of Southern kids yelling into the microphone, this is about as real as it gets. Not surprisingly, it works really well for them on most of the tracks, although by the end of the album it's a bit tiresome. Most of the time they rap about their adeptness with girls, and truly it's hard to find them rapping about anything else here. Assuming "My 9" is about a gun proves to be only partially correct, as the track sees their entire weapons arsenal used for some

hardcore sex. This is a must-have record for collectors and one of U.N.L.V's better albums; those who are into the Cash Money label should check it out. — *Brad Mills*

Urban Dance Squad

f. 1986, Amsterdam, The Netherlands **db.** 1999
Group / Rap-Rock, Rap-Metal, Alternative Rap
The Amsterdam-based rock/rap collective Urban Dance Squad began in 1986, playing and jamming together on an informal basis. They played a gig at the Utrecht Festival and, surprised by the raves their performance drew, became a more serious project. The group gigged for two years, and with the proceeds released 1990's *Mental Floss for the Globe*. Urban Dance Squad's mix of rock, rap, funk, ska, folk, hip-hop, and soul signaled the trend toward genre bending that prevailed in '90s music. *Mental Floss* featured the single "Deeper Shade of Soul" which charted at number 21 in the U.S. on *Billboard*'s Hot 100.

The group spent another year touring constantly, and released their second album *Life 'n Perspective of a Genuine Crossover* in 1991. Unfortunately, it failed to match *Mental Floss*' critical or commercial success, as did 1994's *Persona Non Grata*. 1999 saw Urban Dance Squad release their fourth album, *Planet Ultra*, as well as re-release their earlier releases on the Triple X label. — *Heather Phares*

● **Mental Floss for the Globe** / Mar. 8, 1990 / Arista ✦✦✦✦
The 1990 debut of Urban Dance Squad revealed a band smashing the boundaries between rock, funk, punk, metal, and hip-hop. "Fast Lane" leads the program with a blistering groove powered by chugging guitar and sampled horns. Later, "Brainstorm on the UDS" alternates rap verses with a punky shoutalong chorus, while "The Devil" borrows a murky string bass line and greasy slide guitar from the Tom Waits bag. Rudeboy never really sings; rather he raps or, when the song demands it, sort of chants along in a singsong cadence. But for a nonsinger he has a great voice, one that comes from the chest but has a sharp enough edge to cut through the mix. Also notable are polymath guitarist Tres Manos and the unbelievably funky bass of Silly Sil. This reissue includes a bonus live disc that documents an alternately metallish and bluesy (!) Hollywood concert from 1990. — *Rick Anderson*

Life 'n Perspective of a Genuine Crossover / Oct. 1, 1991 / Arista ✦✦✦
The sophomore slump hit Urban Dance Squad rather hard, or maybe it just seemed that way based on the consistently high quality of their debut. *Life 'n Perspectives of a Genuine Crossover* sounds aimless where its predecessor came off as shrewdly eclectic. It's not that there aren't great moments: "Careless" is nice mid-tempo hip-hop with a blues base, and the strangely named "(Thru) the Gates of the Big Fruit" showcases some great turntable work from DJ DNA as well as countryish slide guitar from Tres Manos. But the four-part approach to "Life 'n Perspectives" is annoying and "Routine" goes nowhere. Somehow the high points aren't quite enough to carry the weight of the low ones. However, the live-in-Tokyo bonus disc that accompanies this reissue is more consistently rewarding. — *Rick Anderson*

Persona Non Grata / Apr. 1994 / Triple X ✦✦✦✦
The Urban Dance Squad's penultimate album was also its most heavy metal influenced. "Demagogue," the album's opener and centerpiece, is an utterly bracing concoction of raw-throated rap and spare, bright metal guitar, all underlaid with minimalist funk drums. That formula remains basically unaltered throughout the rest of the album—"Good Grief," "(Some) Chitchat," and "Selfstyled" all step to the same stripped-down hip-hop beat. It starts sounding pretty samey by the end, of course, but taken in measured doses, the funky beats are guaranteed to move your booty, while the roaring guitars clear your sinuses. It's too bad DJ DNA was no longer in the band by this point; his turntable scratching would have given a welcome additional dimension to the sound. Bonuses abound: like the original release, this one features two hidden tracks, one a remix and the other a live version of "Demagogue." This reissue also adds a bonus live disc. — *Rick Anderson*

Planet Ultra / Jan. 26, 1999 / Triple X ✦✦✦
The most recent Urban Dance Squad album is reissued here in a deluxe twofer that also includes a live recording from New York in 1997. Kudos to Triple X for the fine packaging and for having the good taste to give these Dutch metal/hip-hop-heads another shot at the U.S. market that ignored them, so inexplicably, during their seven-year career. It's not that Americans don't like the idea of rock/hip-hop fusion—witness the popularity of the Red Hot Chili

Peppers. But for some reason, the Urban Dance Squad never caught on the same way. That's our loss. *Planet Ultra* opens with the highly crunchy "Nonstarter" before sliding into the downright melodic "Temporarily Expendable." It then bounces back and forth from straight-ahead metal fare, like "Forgery," to the slow and deeply funky "Pass the Baton Right." DJ DNA was long gone by this point, but someone's playing pretty cool turntable on that last track. The live disc doesn't cohere quite as well, but it's worth hearing. —*Rick Anderson*

Artantica / May 9, 2000 / Triple X ♦♦♦♦
For those who think of rap-metal fusion as something invented by bands like Korn and Limp Bizkit, Urban Dance Squad is back to remind you that they've been doing it for ten years now—and from a home base in Holland. Led by a cheerful shouter named Rudeboy, this band has been shaking people's fillings loose with roaring guitar and funky drumming since Fred Durst was in junior high. Now, after an extended hiatus that saw the band's previous albums remastered and reissued as well as Rudeboy pursuing his techno/drum'n'bass muse as a member of Junkie XL, the UDS is back with what may be its most interesting and varied album since *Mental Floss for the Globe* and its most compelling one since *Persona Non Grata*. "Letter to da Better" nicely combines singing and rapping, "Craftmatic Adjustable Girl" makes extensive use of turntablist DNA under Rudeboy's jackhammer flow, and "Music Entertainment" marks perhaps the first time a theremin has been used on a hip-hop album. Nothing here has quite the raw power of "Demagogue," but everything on this album is worth hearing more than once. —*Rick Anderson*

Urban Flow

f. Philippines
Group / Foreign Rap
Rap trio Urban Flow hails from the Philippines, where rap became a thriving art form during the influx of American hip-hop culture throughout the '90s. Philippine rap pioneers like Francis M and Salbakuta picked up on this trend and furthered it with their own unique take on the genre, which in turn spawned many outfits in the late '90s, including Urban Flow. Unlike their influences, their sound was based more in live instrumentation, and their broader exploration of genres like jazz and funk made their sound more distinct to international audiences. The distributors at OctoArts heard Urban Flow's *Mass Comm* in 1999, and gave the group their only American release when they put out the record the same year. —*Bradley Torreano*

● **Mass Comm** / 1999 / OctoArts ♦♦♦♦
Don't let the loose vibe of Philippine rap group Urban Flow fool you—these guys know what they're doing. According to the album credits, Urban Flow has three members, but it's not specified whether or not they play instruments. Nonetheless, the musicianship is strong throughout the album, as is the rapping. The group mixes up its sound and the album doesn't get monotonous, as has occurred on some Philippine rap albums. "Sayang Lang" contains a jazzy, urban-styled piano lick and a soft, funky guitar line, over which Urban Flow lays down a loose, appealing rap, which leads to a mellifluous chorus sung by the group. The lyrics tell of a guy's disillusionment with women: a girl he loves returns to her former boyfriend because he now has a lot of money. "Somebody's Watching Me" contains fast rapping as well as singing to the chorus of the international song "Somebody's Watching Me." The melodic "Buhat" is mostly sung, and features a guest female singer. Urban Flow has a good, distinctive sound. —*David Gonzales*

Us3

f. 1991, London, England
Group / Hip-Hop, Club/Dance, Jazz-Rap
The jazz/hip-hop fusion collective Us3 scored a major hit in 1994 with "Cantaloop (Flip Fantasia)," a song that displayed the group's fondness for sampling classic recordings on the Blue Note label (in this case, Herbie Hancock's "Cantaloupe Island"). The group was founded in London in 1991 when concert promoter and jazz writer Geoff Wilkinson met Mel Simpson, who was writing music for television shows and ad jingles and had once played keyboards with John Mayall. The two produced an independent single, "Where Will We Be in the 21st Century?," which sold less than 250 copies. In 1992, their song "The Band That Played the Boogie" attracted the attention of Blue Note owner Capitol Records, which gave Simpson and Wilkinson free rein to

sample anything from the catalog. The two immediately went to work, hiring several musicians and rappers Kobie Powell and Rahsaan Kelly, with Tukka Yoot joining later. The sessions resulted in the hit "Cantaloop" and the album *Hand on the Torch*. The group toured Japan and Europe, gradually weaning itself away from using samples in a live setting, and played a well-received show at the 1993 Montreux Jazz Festival. *Hand on the Torch* was ignored by most jazz publications, but was chosen Album of the Year by Japan's *Swing Journal*, and the group were named Jazz Musicians of the Year by Britain's *The Independent*. After a nearly three-year delay, Us3 returned in 1997 with *Broadway & 52nd*, an album that received positive reviews but failed to generate a hit. —*Steve Huey*

● **Hand on the Torch** / Nov. 16, 1993 / Blue Note ♦♦♦♦
Hip-hop/jazzers Us3 have forged the most elaborate union between the styles since the early days of Gang Starr and A Tribe Called Quest. Blue Note's vast catalog gives them a huge advantage over several similar groups in terms of source material, and classic sounds by Art Blakey, Horace Silver, and Herbie Hancock provide zest and fiber to their narratives. Indeed, when things falter, it's because the raps aren't always that creative. They are serviceable and sometimes catchy, but too often delivered without the snazzy touches or distinctive skills that make Quest and Gang Starr's material top-notch. But when words and music mesh, as on "Cantaloop" or "The Darkside," Us3 show how effectively hip-hop and jazz can blend. —*Ron Wynn*

Broadway & 52nd / Apr. 8, 1997 / Blue Note ♦♦♦
Broadway & 52nd continues the breakthrough formula achieved by Us3 on *Hand on the Torch* of mixing classic jazz samples from the Blue Note library with hip-hop. As before, producer Geoff Wilkinson (joined by Jim Hawkins, replacing Mel Simpson) augments the samples with live performances from various soloists. The fusion itself works better on this record than on most jazz-rap hybrids, with every element coming together to form one coherent whole. Whatever else might be said about it, this record definitely does not sound like an unnatural combination the way some other crossover attempts have. However, there are weak points, the weakest point being the quality of the MCs. The raps are split by KCB and Shabaam Sahdeeq, and while Sahdeeq's contributions are competent, if uninteresting, KCB just sounds stiff and forced. However, even when the raps are boring or awkward, the songs are never derailed. The main reason for this is the fact that, for the most part, the arrangements are rather nicely split between the samples, the raps, and the live playing. But does any of it work especially well? That answer, unfortunately, is far from an enthusiastic yes. But as the sum of its parts, *Broadway & 52nd* is well worth a listen. —*Daniel Gioffre*

Flip Fantasia: Hits & Remixes / May 18, 1999 / Blue Note ♦♦♦
When hearing Us3's groundbreaking 1993 debut, *Hand on the Torch*, the first thing a knowledgeable listener does is identify every riff sampled from the enormous Blue Note catalog: "That's Freddie Hubbard" or "That's Herbie Hancock." *Hand on the Torch* was a pioneering release in the acid-jazz world, arguably the first album to make the jazz part of the equation as important as the hip-hop. However, listening to this rather unexpected 1999 hits and remixes compilation—the much-delayed follow-up, 1997's *Broadway & 52nd*, had all but disappeared upon release, and acid jazz was no longer as viable as it had been a half-decade before—it's telling to notice that listeners immediately latch onto the instantly recognizable jazz riffs, mostly because there's not a lot else going on here. London natives Geoff Wilkinson and Mel Simpson show excellent taste in jazz samples and a remarkable facility at turning them into hip-hop riffs, as with the lifts from Hancock's "Cantaloupe Island" on their excellent hit single "Cantaloop (Flip Fantasia)," probably the best acid jazz single ever. Unfortunately, their rappers are uniformly uninspired and forgettable, and the four remixes, including a Nellee Hooper mix of "Cantaloop" that pointlessly removes the best elements of the song, are unessential. You might as well go buy the original Blue Note records. —*Stewart Mason*

U.T.F.O.

f. 1983, Brooklyn, NY db. 1990
Group / Hip-Hop, Old School Rap
U.T.F.O. was a Brooklyn, NY-based rap group, comprised of the Kangol Kid, Doctor Ice, the Educated Rapper, and Mix Master Ice. The quartet first met as dancers for Whodini, before forming U.T.F.O. (which stood for "Untouchable Force Organization") in 1983. Early on, the group referred to themselves as

"the Village People of Rap," due to the fact that each member possessed a specific image (Doctor Ice was the "Hip-Hop Physician," Educated Rapper was a college student who wore a suit and tie, Mix Master Ice assumed the persona of a ninja since he would "cut things up" on the turntables, and Kangol Kid got his name due to his affinity for always wearing Kangol-brand hats). Signing to the Select label in 1984, U.T.F.O. scored a massive hit single right off the bat with "Roxanne, Roxanne," which struck such a chord with the burgeoning rap scene that it spawned countless "response" songs by other artists, including "Roxanne's Revenge," "The Real Roxanne," "Roxanne You're Through," "Roxanne's Mother," "Roxanne's Brother," "Roxanne's Doctor," and perhaps strangest of all, "Roxanne's a Man" (in addition, several female rappers adopted the "Roxanne" name themselves, including Roxanne Shanté and the Real Roxanne).

The year 1985 saw U.T.F.O. issue a self-titled full-length debut, which included their own "Roxanne, Roxanne" follow-up, "Calling Her a Crab (Roxanne Part 2)," which failed to match its predecessor's success; as the group toured alongside such fellow influential rap acts as Run-D.M.C., Kurtis Blow, the Fat Boys, and Newcleus, on a 30-city venue tour called the New York City Fresh Fest. For U.T.F.O.'s sophomore effort, 1986's *Skeezer Pleezer*, the Educated Rapper took a brief leave of absence, before returning for *Lethal* a year later; an album that was criticized by the group's original following due to its stylistic shift to more racy material (although the anti-drug title track featured a musical contribution from heavy metallists Anthrax, which predated Anthrax's more renowned collaboration with Public Enemy by several years). But after two more releases, 1989's *Doin' It!* and 1991's *Bag It & Bone It*, U.T.F.O. decided to call it a day. In the wake of their split, Doctor Ice issued several solo releases (including such titles as *Mic Stalker* and *Rely on Self*); while a 20-track hits collection surfaced in 1996, *The Best of U.T.F.O.*, and a two-for-one CD release of *Skeezer Pleezer/Lethal* was issued in 2000. — *Greg Prato*

U.T.F.O. / 1985 / Select ✦✦✦✦
The Brooklyn production/performance combo U.T.F.O. shot to fame in the mid-'80s with their "Roxanne, Roxanne." It generated a flood of answer songs, started the careers of both Roxanne Shanté and the Real Roxanne, and for a moment put U.T.F.O. in the thick of hip-hop and urban contemporary music. Unfortunately, they really weren't that gifted, as they showed on such singles as "Bite It," "Beats and Rhymes," and "Lisa Lips." They're now rightly regarded as novelty/one-hit wonders. — *Ron Wynn*

Skeezer Pleezer / 1986 / Select ✦✦✦
Reality began to set in for U.T.F.O. with their second album in 1986. They got a little buzz from the single "We Work Hard," but were essentially already in stylistic retreat as the gimmick tag they picked up for the success of "Roxanne, Roxanne" was proving difficult to shake. It didn't help that songs like "Bad Luck Barry" and "House Will Rock" didn't exactly inspire generations of aspiring rappers. — *Ron Wynn*

Lethal / 1987 / Select ✦✦
Everyone including Roxanne (the Real one and all stand-ins, substitutes, and replacements) had forgotten by the time of album number four that U.T.F.O. had once had an underground smash with "Roxanne, Roxanne." Instead, audiences had tuned out the group's novelty/comic fare, microphone challenges, sexual posturing, and anything else they tried. — *Ron Wynn*

Doin' It! / 1989 / Select ✦✦✦
Long after they'd peaked with "Roxanne Roxanne," U.T.F.O. attempted to consolidate their position as progenitors of the East Coast's exploding rap scene with *Doin' It!* Although it's solid by hip-hop standards, the group seemed uncomfortable fitting their loose-fit old school style onto a hardcore base. On the album's bright spots, U.T.F.O. simply relaxes and produces tracks closer in mood to their early-'80s peak. — *Keith Farley*

Bag It & Bone It / 1991 / Jive ✦✦
● **The Best of U.T.F.O.** / Dec. 10, 1996 / Select ✦✦✦✦✦
U.T.F.O. never had many hits. During the mid-'80s, the rap group released a series of singles, but only one stood out, and for good reason, because that song, "Roxanne, Roxanne," is one of the classic rap singles of all time. Though "Roxanne, Roxanne" only hit number ten on the R&B charts, it was far more popular than its chart position suggests, spawning a craze of answer records that ran for nearly two years. Unfortunately, U.T.F.O. never released anything else that quite matched the quality of "Roxanne, Roxanne," though their follow-up, "The Real Roxanne," was entertaining in its own right. Since the group had an uneven track record, *The Best of U.T.F.O.* is the best way to get acquainted with the group, even though it has a number of weak spots itself. Nevertheless, it has all the necessary items U.T.F.O. ever recorded, and "Roxanne, Roxanne" is a single that should be heard by all rap and hip-hop fans. — *Leo Stanley*

The Uzi Bros.

f. Los Angeles, CA
Group / Hip-Hop, West Coast Rap, Pop-Rap
When the Uzi Bros. came out of Los Angeles in the late '80s, some people assumed that they were a gangsta rap group. But in fact, their forte was above-average, R&B-drenched pop-rap. Their lyrics were generally positive, and they had a fairly unthreatening image. Although much of their music was commercial, they weren't afraid to address social and political issues such as gang violence, drugs, and the prison system. What the Uzi Bros. didn't have was a huge following. In 1989 they signed with music industry veteran Art Laboe's Original Sound label (best known for its *Oldies but Goodies* series) and seemed to have the potential for commercial success. But 1990's *Kick That Thang!*, their only album for Original Sound, didn't sell. After that, little was heard from the group. — *Alex Henderson*

● **Kick That Thang!** / 1990 / Original Sound ✦✦
A melodic effort with lots of soul and pop appeal, *Kick That Thang!* has a lot more in common with Young MC than Ice-T or Ice Cube. This isn't to say the CD is fluff; like Young, the Uzi Bros. demonstrated that commercial pop-rap could still have an edge. In fact, they successfully tackle social issues on "There's a Riot Jumpin' Off" (which takes a look at the prison system), "Nothin' But a Gangster," and an interpretation of the Stylistics' "People Make the World Go 'Round." Another high point of the album is a clever remake of Dyke and the Blazers' "We Got More Soul." While the original version paid tribute to 1960s soul icons like James Brown and Johnnie Taylor, the Uzis update the song by mentioning Ice-T, N.W.A, Public Enemy, and Anita Baker. This is a highly enjoyable album that should have done a lot better. — *Alex Henderson*

Vanilla Ice (Robert Van Winkle)

b. Oct. 31, 1968, Miami Lakes, FL
Hardcore Rap, Pop-Rap

With his hit single "Ice Ice Baby" and its accompanying album, *To the Extreme*, Vanilla Ice became the second white rapper to top the charts. Unlike the Beastie Boys, he didn't have any street credibility, so the Miami-born rapper decided to invent some of his own, claiming he had a seriously violent gangster past. Nevertheless, "Ice Ice Baby" became a number-one hit late in 1990, thanks to the pulsating bass riff from David Bowie and Queen's "Under Pressure." *To the Extreme* also went to the top of the charts, spending 16 weeks at number one and selling over seven million copies. Ice began filming a feature film, *Cool as Ice*, in the spring of 1990, but by the time the film came out in the fall, his star had fallen dramatically; *To the Extreme* was at number one longer than the soundtrack to *Cool as Ice* was on the charts. Sensing that his time had passed, Vanilla Ice took a couple years off, re-emerging in 1994 with *Mind Blowin'*. Dispensing with the pop-rap formula of his debut, the rapper adopted the lazy, rolling funk of Cypress Hill, as well as that trio's obsession with pot. The album was a commercial disaster, disappearing from sight immediately after its release. With 1998's *Hard to Swallow*, Ice attempted to reinvent himself as a hardcore, gangsta-styled rapper; again the public wanted no part of it. A similar attempt, 2001's *Bipolar*, tried to reinvent him as both rapper and rocker, much to the public's general disinterest. —*Stephen Thomas Erlewine*

● **To the Extreme** / 1990 / SBK ✦✦✦
An enormous hit in its time, with sales of over seven million copies, *To the Extreme* proved that a white rapper could be made into a mainstream pop idol. It also proved that traditional pop-idol marketing tactics wouldn't work for very long on rap audiences. Ice's undoing wasn't so much his actual music as it was his fabricated credibility—his wholly imaginary street-gang background, his ridiculous claims that "Ice Ice Baby" was not built on an obvious sample of Queen's and David Bowie's "Under Pressure." It's hard to listen to *To the Extreme* now and believe a word he's saying; the posturing just doesn't ring true at all. The odd thing is, not all of the record is as awful as it's cracked up to be. Ice's mic technique is actually stronger and more nimble than MC Hammer's, and he really tries earnestly to show off the skills he does have. Unfortunately, even if he can keep a mid-tempo pace, his flow is rhythmically stiff, and his voice has an odd timbre; plus, he never seems sure of the proper accent to adopt. He's able to overcome those flaws somewhat in isolated moments, but they become all too apparent over the course of an entire album. Outside of "Ice Ice Baby" and the not-as-good "Play That Funky Music" ("steppin' so hard like a German Nazi"???), there are some decent dance tracks and a few forgettable mediocrities. There are also a few inexcusable low points: the poorly rapped sexcapade "Life Is a Fantasy," the awkward reggae toasting of "Rosta Man" [sic], and "I Love You," a lyrically simplistic, overemoted ballad that makes LL Cool J's "I Need Love" sound like "Straight Outta Compton." Overall, *To the Extreme* might technically be better than *Please Hammer Don't Hurt 'Em*, but its hubris isn't quite as much fun. —*Steve Huey*

Extremely Live / Mar. 1991 / SBK ✦
Rushed out to get another piece of Vanilla Ice product on the market, *Extremely Live* eroded what little credibility he had left as a rapper and placed him squarely in teen idol town. Performance-wise, he stays on the beat just fine, but his breath control is amateurish at best, probably due in part to the demands placed on him as a dancer. He often sounds like he's overcompensating for his thin, oddly pitched voice, and sometimes—consciously or otherwise—adopts a more African-American accent, especially when he's

bantering with the crowd ("Awwwww yeeeeeah!"). The crowd noise sounds awfully tinny, and often it's hard to tell exactly why they're cheering at the lines they are. I'm not saying the crowd noise is augmented, because I don't know ... but it is odd how they're suddenly mixed way in the background of the single "Rollin' in My 5.0." But that's definitely the crowd rapping big chunks of "Ice Ice Baby," and it's highly debatable whether those teenage girls needed that much space on record. "Rollin'" is one of two new singles here, the other one being a rap remake of "Satisfaction" that's present in both live and studio versions. Ice tries to make the otherwise unaltered chorus into a call-and-response with the Stones, and it's horribly awkward; both singles flopped badly. But, as on *To the Extreme*, the lowest point is an unbearably smarmy version of "I Love You," which predictably sends the audience into a tizzy. Kitsch fans beware: it's not as much fun as you might hope, not so much awful as instantly forgettable. —*Steve Huey*

Cool as Ice (Original Soundtrack) / Oct. 8, 1991 / SBK ✦✦

Mind Blowin' / Mar. 22, 1994 / SBK ✦✦
Four years after *To the Extreme*, Vanilla Ice came back with a refashioned, modern sound, borrowing from the blunted Cypress Hill, the deep funk of Dr. Dre, the quick-tongued rapping of Das EFX—basically, anything that's been popular since his first album. While he spends an obscene amount of time dissing 3rd Bass, he counters all charges of being a sellout by stating that he has sold over 11 million records. There isn't a single moment that establishes a distinct musical identity, and the whole thing is rather embarrassing. Not surprisingly, the record dropped out of sight almost a month after its release. —*Stephen Thomas Erlewine*

Hard to Swallow / Oct. 20, 1998 / Republic ✦✦
To avoid kicking someone when they're down, jokes relating to the title of Vanilla Ice's third release should be reserved for another time and place. With every successive moment that has passed since *To the Extreme* ended a 16-week reign at the top of the album charts in 1990, Robert Van Winkle has simply continued to be exposed for the fraud it looks like he always was. Despite his success with infectious dance grooves, Vanilla Ice has tried, with no success, to keep his act fresh over the years. His second album was almost gangsta rap, and this one just reeks of heavy metal and rap fusion. Even the album art is reminiscent of Marilyn Manson. And the fact that the producer of *Hard to Swallow* has spent time with the likes of Limp Bizkit and Korn is not surprising in the least, because Vanilla Ice attempts to make the transition to that style with this incredibly poor album. You have to wonder how much more of a joke and footnote in American music history Vanilla Ice can make himself. The answer is—reserve judgment until the next embarrassing album hits stores. Who knows, maybe he'll start his own swing band. —*David M. Childers*

Bipolar / 2001 / Liquid ✦✦
Bipolar is the new album from critical whipping boy Vanilla Ice. Split into two sides, one filled with his rap-metal noodling and the other with his hip-hop, the album is wildly uneven and at times hilariously bad. It is easy to be needlessly cruel to Vanilla Ice—his rapid rise and fall is one of music's biggest jokes. But his reputation is not improved by the music he continues to release. Much like his *Hard to Swallow* album from 1998, the heavy metal half of the album is not only derivative of bigger acts like Korn and Deftones but also terribly generic. He tries to mix things up with a Godsmack-style delivery on songs like "Mudd Munster," but it comes off more as an imitation than a change of style. The rap side of his album is a complete switch after the numbing metal that litters the first half. The beats are surprisingly solid, inspired by both RZA and Dr. Dre. Unfortunately, the raps themselves are both boring and simplistic. And out of nowhere, Chuck D suddenly appears and

makes a guest appearance on "Elvis Killed Kennedy," instantly making it not only the best song on the album but also a sadly rare example of the talent that the former Public Enemy frontman still has. And then there are a series of answering-machine messages from wrestlers, friends, and even Vanilla Ice himself quoting *Cape Fear*. The message from former producer Ross Robinson is a good example of the needless filler that clogs up this album. A lot of people familiar with rap-metal know who Robinson is, but honestly does anyone care what he has to say about dirt biking on Vanilla Ice's answering machine? Vanilla Ice tries really hard to make quality music, but he seems far more concerned with the genre he's assimilating than the actual music, leaving listeners with an empty album that only the most curious listener should dare listen to. —*Bradley Torreano*

The Best of Vanilla Ice / Mar. 13, 2001 / EMI ◆◆◆
Vanilla Ice is one of those artists whose best moments are widely considered indefensible, and many listeners will be satisfied with having "Ice Ice Baby" on a various-artists compilation for the nostalgia and/or kitsch value. For those who want a bigger extract (ha!) of Vanilla's career, *The Best of Vanilla Ice* offers ten tracks that summarize things pretty effectively. There's one major selection drawback, namely, that the hit version of "Play That Funky Music" is replaced by a live performance, but if you want it badly enough to buy a Vanilla Ice album, there's always *To the Extreme*. So what's here that isn't on his one big album? Quite a bit, actually. You get "Ninja Rap," his oddly anthemic theme to one of the *Teenage Mutant Ninja Turtles* movies; a non-LP version of "Satisfaction," whose samples are typically obvious and straightforward; the theme to Ice's movie, "Cool as Ice (Everybody Get Loose)"; "Rollin' in My 5.0," the new track from *Extremely Live;* and "Roll 'Em Up," the calculated, Cypress Hill-style ode to marijuana from 1994's *Mind Blowin',* which failed to reinvent him for the hardcore set. So if *To the Extreme* captures Vanilla Ice the short-lived pop phenomenon, *The Best of Vanilla Ice* also covers the misfires that sped up his already-rapid decline and fall. —*Steve Huey*

Various Blends

f. 1991, San Fransisco, CA
Group / Hip-Hop, Dub, Club/Dance, Trip-Hop, Alternative Rap
Alternative rappers Various Blends were originally formed in the San Francisco Bay Area in 1991, and consisted of MCs/producers Friz-B and Eb.F (both friends from childhood) and MC Rasco. They grew out of a previous group called Children of One Destiny, which also included future solo artist Saafir. In 1995 the trio released a local 12" single, "Chill as I Flex," but went on hiatus when Rasco departed for a solo career the following year (he would go on to record for Peanut Butter Wolf's Stones Throw label). In the meantime, Eb.F DJed around the area under the name DJ Rasta Cue Tip, and he and Friz-B reconvened as Various Blends in 1999. With production by both group members, as well as Peanut Butter Wolf, and turntable contributions from DJ Serg, Various Blends finally issued their first full-length album, *Levitude,* on Baraka in late 1999. It gained favorable reviews for its inventive, trippy production, but not much exposure. Baraka also issued an instrumental version of the album in 2000. —*Steve Huey*

Levitude / Nov. 30, 1999 / Baraka ◆◆◆◆
MCs/producers Friz-B and Eb.F are Various Blends, an alternative rap outfit formed in 1991 and finally issuing their first full-length, *Levitude,* in 1999 (minus founding member MC Rasco). It's an impressive record, highlighting the duo's ample lyrical skills and skewed perspective, while featuring a number of mostly West Coast guests: Del tha Funkee Homosapien, Saafir, the Mystik Journeymen, Pizmo of Burnt Batch, Rashinel of Hobo Junction, and members of the Coup and Invisibl Skratch Piklz. —*Steve Huey*

Levitude: Instrumentals / Sep. 16, 2000 / Baraka ◆◆◆

Verbal Threat

f. Virginia
Group / Hip-Hop, East Coast Rap
Not to be confused with a similarly named West Coast rap group who've played shows with the Pharcyde, Verbal Threat was a Virginia-based hip-hop band who released 1996's *The Essence* for the Action Verbz label. —*John Bush*

● **The Essence** / 1996 / Action Verbz ◆◆
East Coast jazz-rap with a touch of funk, *The Essence* is a solid, consistent release from Virginia's Verbal Threat. The band's strengths lie mainly in the

rhythm section. Owens (drums) pops the skins in a tight, crisp manner reminiscent of Curtis Watts, drummer for Smokin Suckaz Wit Logic, another East Coast rap group. Owens is a standout on all cuts, "Eons" in particular. Bassist Kilgore lays down the groove on "Streetcorner Coliseum," and he and Lilliston (sax) provide the highlights on the jazz-laced "Systematiks," a relatively laid-back cut. In fact, Lilliston injects a jazz undertone throughout the project with his ethereal, floating sax, creeping in the background of the opener, "Living Dread," among others. The coupling and occasional juxtaposition of the vocalists is another plus on *The Essence,* although the lyrics are often difficult to discern. Of all these intelligent and aurally pleasing compositions, guitarist Carey surfaces only on the funky "Herban Souljah." —*David Ross Smith*

Vico-C (Luis Armando Lozada)

b. Sep. 8, 1971, Brooklyn, NY
Vocals, Producer / Latin Rap
Puerto Rican rapper Vico-C experienced wavering popular success throughout the '90s in the United States while remaining consistently popular in Latin America. Born Luis Armando Lozada on September 8, 1971, in Brooklyn, NY, Vico grew up surrounded by the rough streets of New York, where crime, violence, and drugs are often a part of life. He took an early interest in hip-hop when it first blossomed in the early '80s with such artists as Run-D.M.C. and, in turn, took the stage name Vico-C in a bid to become a rapper himself. In addition to his rapping ambitions, Vico also developed his production skills and launched his professional career at the end of the '80s. He produced hits for such Latin artists as Lisa M. ("El Pum Pum") and Francheska ("Menéalo") and began collaborating with Jossie Esteban on songs of his own in the early '90s. In particular, "La Recta Final" became a big hit for Vico, whose early-'90s work blended rap with merengue. Following a few early-'90s releases and much success in Puerto Rico as well as throughout Latin America, Vico suffered a life-threatening automobile accident that sidelined him for a substantial amount of time. He returned in 1998 with *Aquel Que Había Muerto,* an album that found him renouncing his past vices and proclaiming a renewed faith in God, and his level of success grew enormously. Several best-of albums flooded the market around this time in the late '90s and Vico spent successive years furthering his success as well as basking in it such as on the live album *Vivo* (2001). —*Jason Birchmeier*

● **Greatest Hits** / Nov. 22, 1994 / RCA ◆◆◆◆
Vico-C's *Greatest Hits* collection compiles several of the Spanish-language rapper's shining moments as of 1994. There are only ten songs here, two of which are megamixes, yet there's plenty of variety. The collection opens with two of Vico's relatively hardcore collaborations with DJ Negro, "La Recta Final" and "Viernes 13," and then moves on to a pair of lighter songs cowritten by Isaac Young: the Latin dance-styled "Mundo Artificial" and a gentle piano ballad, "Me Acuerdo," featuring a chorus sang by Irene Flores. The following pair of songs, "La Inglesa" and "Xplosión," likewise lean more toward Latin dance than hip-hop, though the next two, "Saboréalo" and "María," return to the golden age rap style of "La Recta Final," as both draw from popular English-language songs, the latter practically an interpolation of Kool G Rap & DJ Polo's "Poison." The collection then concludes with a pair of megamixes that are a fitting last hurrah for this brief yet overall diverse collection of Vico's early-career highlights. —*Jason Birchmeier*

Historia / Jan. 12, 1999 / RCA ◆◆◆◆

Historia, Vol. 2 / Mar. 23, 1999 / RCA ◆◆◆

Vivo / Jun. 5, 2001 / EMI ◆◆◆
After a career of 15 years, Puerto Rican Vico-C (born Luis Armando Lozada) delivers a collection of his greatest hits recorded live at Hato Rey's Luis Muñoz Marin Amphiteater. *Vivo* features "I Like/Baby Quiero Hacerlo," performed with Lissy Estrella, and the previously unreleased song "El Super Heroe," based on an imaginary hero who's coming to save the world. A comic book focused on that character has been included in the album. In addition, *Vivo* features a medley comprised of some of Vico-C's most popular hits: "El Filósofo," "La Calle," "En Coma," "Sin Pena," and "La Recta Final." —*Drago Bonacich*

Vinnie Vin

Pop-Rap, Hip-Hop, Comedy Rap
During the pop-rap boom of the late '80s/early '90s, Vinnie Vin had a brief run at the spotlight before dropping out of the music industry. Vin had a breezy

approach to hip-hop, rapping about girls and parents with a likable, profanity-free personality. After signing to Starway in 1990, he cut *The Show Must Go On* with producer Charles "Poogie" Bell. The record made little impact, and Vin dropped out of the hip-hop scene soon after. —*Bradley Torreano*

The Show Must Go On / Apr. 23, 1991 / Capitol ♦♦
Steering clear of profanity and violent lyrics, Vinnie Vin took a lighthearted approach to pop-rap on *The Show Must Go On.* The most obvious comparison on this decent yet obscure CD is DJ Jazzy Jeff & the Fresh Prince, who were described as "the Cosby Kids of Rap" because of their clean-cut image. Much like the Will "the Fresh Prince" Smith, Vinnie favors fun, unthreatening anecdotes on such tunes as "Oh, What a Night," "Have You Seen Her," and "One Night Stand." Vinnie doesn't have the Fresh Prince's technique or charisma, but he isn't a bad rapper either. Another thing the Brooklyn rapper didn't have was the Fresh Prince's high profile. Though generally decent, *The Show Must Go On* received very little attention. —*Alex Henderson*

Volume 10
....
West Coast Rap
Part of Los Angeles' Heavyweights Crew, which included Freestyle Fellowship, Medusa, and Ganjah K, Volume 10 was part of the West Coast's vibrant underground rap scene in the '90s. Like many Los Angeles MCs, Volume 10 honed his skills during battles at the Good Life Cafe, but set himself apart as an MC able to balance both thuggish violent imagery and skill-heavy open-mike styles. After a guest spot on Freestyle Fellowship's *Inner City*

Griots in 1993, he released his debut full-length, *Hip-Hopera.* The album spawned a hit single, "Pistolgrip-Pump," which would later be covered on Rage Against the Machine's *Renegades.* 10 also appeared on the *Project Blowed* compilation in 1995, considered by many to be one of the underground's defining moments. A second solo CD, *Psycho,* appeared in 2000 on 10's own Pump Productions. —*Wade Kergan*

● **Hip-Hopera** / Sep. 1994 / RCA ♦♦♦
With the release of "Pistolgrip-Pump" as his debut single in 1993, Volume 10 set quite an ambitious precedent for himself. As the song and its off-centered interpretation of "More Bounce to the Ounce" captured anthem status across the States, no one quite knew what to expect next from the self-proclaimed lyrical Heavyweight. When his full-length album *Hip-Hopera* hit stores in 1994 it sure enough put a schizophrenic spin on what was quickly becoming typical Los Angeles gangsta rap. As a product of the Goodlife open mic sessions, Volume 10 utilized psychedelic-tinged beats provided by the likes of the Baka Boyz, Fat Jack, and Bosco Kante to cover almost every topic under the South Central sun. While 'hood warfare gets the flamboyant treatment on tracks such as "Knockoutchaskull" and "Flow Wood," a more introspective approach is taken on "Where's the Sniper" and "First Born," which respectively tackle the topics of alcoholism and fatherhood. As a second single, "Sunbeams" didn't even come close to matching the reach of "Pistolgrip-Pump," but it did prove that a touch of nature could still be enjoyed among even the most tense of urban situations. —*Robert Gabriel*

Psycho / Oct. 3, 2000 / Pump ♦♦♦

Wagon Christ (Luke Vibert)

b. Cornwall, England

Producer, Remixing / Jungle/Drum 'N Bass, Trip-Hop, Ambient Techno, Ambient Breakbeat, Electronica, IDM

Luke Vibert is one of a new breed of European club music experimentalists whose work spans several genres simultaneously, and is one of a very few of that set to make any headway with U.S. audiences. A native of Cornwall, Vibert's work has been compared with other West Country bedroom denizens like Aphex Twin and μ-Ziq, although his output over the past few years has been far more eclectic than that connection would seem to imply. Beginning with tweaky post-techno and moving through ambient and experimental hip-hop as Wagon Christ and, more recently, experimental drum'n'bass as Plug, Vibert has explored the outer reaches of post-techno electronica without sounding hasty or swank. Although Vibert's first musical experience was in a Beastie Boys knockoff band called the Hate Brothers, he quickly moved into the low-cost environment of solo bedroom composition. Although he had no intention of ever releasing any of the work, his reputation as a creative young voice in stylistic cross-pollination has created an increasing demand for his pioneering, often left-field work.

Vibert became involved in electronic music through his passion for hip-hop (he has commented that hip-hop is the only music style he really keeps up with), as well as the environment of bedroom experimentalism associated with the swelling late-'80s U.K. dance scene. He released an album through the Rephlex label (a solo album nonetheless billed as *Vibert/Simmonds*) before coming to the attention of Caspar Pound's Rising High label. As a result of the growing exchange value of the style, RH commissioned an ambient album from Vibert, who, despite never having heard much ambient, delivered the well-received *Phat Lab Nightmare* under the Wagon Christ name in 1993. Silent (but for the quickie EP *At Atmos*) for nearly two years following its release, Vibert came back in late 1994 with *Throbbing Pouch*, a collection of minimal, funky, off-kilter hip-hop that had fans familiar with his earlier work scratching their heads. Though lumped in with the so-called trip-hop movement attributed to Portishead, Tricky, Massive Attack, and the Mo'Wax label, the album's upbeat, cheeky edge was anything but stony and laid-back. Following up with a number of remixes and a Mo'Wax EP under his own name, Vibert embarked on his next major mutation with his Plug project, releasing a trio of sample-laden, epileptic jungle EPs, as well as the *Drum'n'Bass for Papa* LP in 1996. Wagon Christ's *Tally Ho!* followed in 1998, and Vibert reverted to his own name for 2000's *Stop the Panic*. *Musipal* followed in early 2001. —*Sean Cooper*

Phat Lab Nightmare / 1993 / Rising High ♦♦♦

Twittering and at times noodly experimental ambient, Vibert's lack of familiarity with the genre's more formal properties is probably what makes this a worthwhile release. —*Sean Cooper*

● **Throbbing Pouch** / 1994 / Rising High ♦♦♦♦

Scattered with dime-store samples and goofy melodies, this is easy-listening instrumental hip-hop like Jay-Z or Premier would do it. Though the material is heavily sequenced, Vibert's arranging skills are in rare form, reordering elements and dropping tracks in and out with liquid, barely noticeable aplomb. (The original British CD version includes a bonus disc with the *At Atmos* EP included.) —*Sean Cooper*

Tally Ho! / Sep. 28, 1998 / Astralwerks ♦♦♦♦♦

Luke Vibert, one of Europe's more prolific electronic masterminds, slips into his Wagon Christ alterego once again and comes through with one of his more accessible efforts. *Tally Ho!* doesn't have the personality-driven energy of Prodigy or the Chemical Brothers' slam-bang theatrics, but that doesn't mean it's short on character by any means. Vibert paints himself as a sly mixmaster with music that contains a smokiness quite different from the dark, misty shadows associated with the most familiar electronic noir. Instead, bursts of color appear in these dense, loungey compostions. The songs here branch out in various directions, whether it's R&B beats giving way to classical piano flourishes or swelling bass lines embracing gurgling samples, robotic blips, and kabuki drums. Anyone lost in the thick, endless vines of drum'n'bass will be surprised by these crisp, controlled soundscapes (its hour-long running time is modest by today's DJ standards). It's Vibert's emphasis on the R&B vibe that gives *Tally Ho!* its definitive edge. Cool jazz piano and ricocheting drum tracks surface, which would sound ideal nestled below sultry hip-hop rhymes. If anything, Vibert, a confessed hip-hop fan, could really break barriers by bringing some of these otherworldly sounds to rap's universe. Sly grooves on "Fly Swat" and "Memory Towel" are ripe for swiping by sample-happy DJs. —*Jason Kaufman*

Musipal / Mar. 6, 2001 / Ninja Tune ♦♦♦♦

Luke Vibert's first LP for the fellow hip-hop obsessives at Ninja Tune is a back-to-basics record, recycling a few of the same ideas (and, occasionally, samples) of his Wagon Christ classic *Throbbing Pouch* from 1994. And though it's difficult to knock the pioneering flavor of *Throbbing Pouch*, *Musipal* may be an even better record—despite the dozens of hilarious samples that open the album on "The Premise," it's definitely a more mature album, with clearer ideas and a better production framework for them. Though "Thick Stew" uses some very familiar—at least to Wagon Christ fans—syrupy, distorted bass lines, it's arguably a better track than the *Throbbing Pouch* classic. Thankfully, there are only a few nods to the queasy-listening flavor of his wider-issue releases through Astralwerks, and plenty of only-for-the-smokers tracks like "Boney L" and "It Is Always Now, All of It Is Now." Throw in two drum'n'bass burners ("Natural Suction," "Perkission") and an interesting take on up-tempo live funk ("Receiver"), and listeners are left with a solid production LP that can't quite knock off a touchstone like *Throbbing Pouch*, but definitely makes its own statement. —*John Bush*

Justin Warfield

House, Hip-Hop

Rapper Justin Warfield was only 20 years old when his debut album, *My Field Trip to Planet 9*, was released to curious ears in 1993. Produced by Prince Paul, the album was a bizarre mix of psychedelic loops and unpredictable beats that was not a very large success, but established him as a young talent to watch for. Of course, he turned completely against his first album when *The Justin Warfield Supernaut* appeared in 1995. Comprised of a charming classic rock sound, it still did not make a difference in terms of sales but it did confound his fans. Even stranger was his sudden disappearance after the promotion of his sophomore effort, making sporadic guest appearances with bands like Placebo and Cornershop but staying away from releasing his own album. —*Bradley Torreano*

● **My Field Trip to Planet 9 By Justin Warfield** / Jul. 13, 1993 / Qwest ♦♦♦

The hip-hop debut of Justin Warfield is built around old school rhythms fleshed out with some intriguing samples, drawn largely from the canon of '60s psychedelic rock. Though "K Sera Sera" was a solid single, unfortunately it didn't include one of his best shots, 1991's "Season of the Vic." —*Jason Ankeny*

WC

Vocals / West Coast Rap, Gangsta Rap

A longtime staple of the gangsta rap scene, WC began his career with the groups Low Profile and the Maad Circle before forming Westside Connection with Ice Cube and Mack 10. His solo debut, *The Shadiest One*, followed in 1998, landing in the pop Top 20 in its first week of release. "Better Days" and "Just Clownin'" were moderate R&B hits, and his second record, 2002's *Ghetto Heisman*, entered the pop charts as well. —*Jason Ankeny*

● **The Shadiest One** / Mar. 17, 1998 / Payday/ffrr ◆◆◆

As his first solo release since Westside Connection's hit effort, *The Shadiest One* was positioned as WC's breakthrough to the major league of rap superstars. The hardcore edge that dominated his earlier releases with the Maad Circle has been tamed somewhat, so he can reach a wider audience. Of course, he still retains his gangsta image, relying on familiar lyrical and musical trappings, but everything's a bit more subdued than before, with mixed results. In the case of "Keep Hustlin'," the slight pop makeover works well, but other times it falls flat. And, like any of WC's albums, *The Shadiest One* runs too long. On several songs, the music simply meanders without any hooks to bring it back into focus. But that isn't a fatal flaw, especially since it's a familiar one, and the best moments on the record are as good as anything he's ever recorded, making *The Shadiest One* another solid entry in his catalog. —*Stephen Thomas Erlewine*

Ghetto Heisman / Nov. 12, 2002 / Def Jam ◆◆

Def Jam's forays into the world of West Coast gangstas haven't always gone well (remember the bitter parting with San Diego thug Jayo Felony), but the label nevertheless signed up Jayo's fellow Crip walker WC, late of Maad Circle and Westside Connection, giving the underrated Cailfornia rhymer the break many felt he'd long deserved. Yet he doesn't take full advantage of it on *Ghetto Heisman*, despite an impressive parade of guests that includes Snoop Dogg and even old pal Ice Cube, lured back to the rap game from his silver screen duties. The rich, Clinton-sampling G-funk sounds just as good here as it did in its early-'90s heyday, but WC's verses too often lapse into gangsta boilerplate; when he gives it a fleet-tongued twist on "Bellin," the results really are Heisman-worthy. But the most impressive and troubling moment comes with "Something 2 Live 4," a fantasy worthy of Eminem in sound and subject matter. The gory fantasy about the kidnapping of Dub's daughter won't shock anyone who's lived through Slim Shady's "Kim"—or the Geto Boys, Schoolly D, or a long list of other acts, hip-hop and otherwise. Using it to deliver a message about the important things in life, however, closes the album on an unnervingly twisted note. —*Dan LeRoy*

WC and the Maad Circle

Group / West Coast Rap, Gangsta Rap

Following the dissolution of Low Profile, a late-'80s West Coast MC/DJ partnership between WC and DJ Aladdin, the rapper formed WC and the Maad Circle and released a pair of albums, *Ain't a Damn Thang Changed* (1991) and *Curb Servin'* (1995). The albums spawned a few popular singles, notably "Dress Code" (1991), "West Up!" (1995), and "One" (1996). In addition to the former Ice-T affiliate WC, the talented group also included DJ Crazy Toones, longtime Ice Cube producer Sir Jinx, and future chart-topping pop-rapper Coolio. Because the latter two were so occupied with their own respective solo careers, the Maad Circle dissolved, and WC decided to form a new, better group, Westside Connection, which also featured Ice Cube and Mack 10. That supergroup didn't last long for similar reasons, though, and WC embarked on a promising solo career with the powerhouse Def Jam Records. —*Jason Birchmeier*

Ain't a Damn Thang Changed / Sep. 17, 1991 / Priority ◆◆◆

● **Curb Servin'** / Oct. 3, 1995 / Payday ◆◆◆

Musically, WC and the Maad Circle's *Curb Servin'* is by-the-books West Coast gangsta rap, with deep funk grooves and lazy, rolling beats. Coolio, who used to be a member of the crew in the early '90s, and Ice Cube make guest appearances, but what distinguishes it from others of the genre is the lyrical flair of WC, who spices up his rhymes with surreal, original imagery, even on the standard boasting tracks. —*Stephen Thomas Erlewine*

Wee Papa Girls

f. United Kingdom

Group / British Rap, Hip-Hop

A female British rap duo that existed during the late '80s and early '90s, Wee Papa Girls issued a pair of albums before going their separate ways: 1989's *The Beat, The Rhyme, The Noise* and 1990's *Be Aware*. Although the duo were completely forgotten, Wee Papa Girls helped pave the way for such subsequent, similarly styled, chart-topping acts as TLC. —*Greg Prato*

The Beat, The Rhyme, The Noise / 1989 / Jive ◆◆

The Beat, The Rhyme, The Noise, the full-length debut for Wee Papa Girls, featured some energetic, elastic performances (like the hit single "Heat It Up"), but nearly all of them were wasted on slight songs. —*Ron Wynn*

Be Aware / 1990 / Jive ◆◆

Westside Connection

f. 1996

Group / Hip-Hop, Gangsta Rap, Hardcore Rap, West Coast Rap

The rap supergroup Westside Connection came together in late 1996, comprising Ice Cube, Mack 10, and WC (of WC and the Madd Circle). The trio released the single "Bow Down" in September, and it reached number 21 on the singles charts. The subsequent album, also titled *Bow Down*, hit number two and quickly achieved gold status. Subsequent work, like 1998's *The Shadiest One*, appeared under WC's name. —*John Bush*

● **Bow Down** / Oct. 22, 1996 / Priority ◆◆◆◆

Following *Lethal Injection*, Ice Cube's career was beginning to sag slightly, both in terms of sales and critical respect. As a response, he formed Westside Connection with fellow West Coast gangsta rappers Mack 10 and WC—the first hip-hop supergroup ever formed. *Bow Down*, the trio's debut, is everything you would expect from this pedigree, for better and for worse. Musically, the record is fantastic, with tight, slamming production that alternates between driving hardcore rhythms and elastic booty funk. Similarly, all three rappers give brilliant performances, rhyming with fierce venom and grace. The problem is, the trio—who have all demonstrated exceptional observational skills and social commentary in the past—have decided to abandon their conscious for a spirited defense and celebration of gangsta rap. If anyone has represented the best gangsta has had to offer, it would be Ice Cube, Mack 10, and WC, but none of their lyrics here illustrate this; instead, they simply make halfhearted excuses for the violence and no political attacks at authority, which renders it nearly devoid of content. Nevertheless, *Bow Down* is filled with so much exceptional music that it ranks as one of the finest latter-day gangsta rap records. Listening to it, however, it's hard not to believe that it is an epitaph for the genre. —*Stephen Thomas Erlewine*

Whodini

f. 1981, New York, NY

Group / Golden Age, Hip-Hop, Old School Rap

Coming out of the fertile early-'80s New York rap scene, Whodini were one of the first rap groups to add a straight R&B twist to their music, thus laying the groundwork for the new jack swing movement. The group consisted of rappers Jalil Hutchins and John "Ecstasy" Fletcher, adding legendary DJ Drew "Grandmaster Dee" Carter, known for being able to scratch records with nearly every part of his body, in 1986. Whodini made its name with good-humored songs like "Magic's Wand" (the first rap song to feature an accompanying video), "The Haunted House of Rock" (a rewrite of "Monster Mash"), and "Freaks Come Out at Night," and their live shows were the first rap concerts to feature official dancers (U.T.F.O. members Doctor Ice and Kangol Kid). Following 1987's *Open Sesame*, Whodini went on hiatus due to problems with their record company, as well as to concentrate on new families. The group attempted a comeback in 1991 with *Bag-A-Trix* without much success, despite receiving their due as rap innovators. Five years later, Whodini returned with their sixth album, appropriately titled *Six*. The album disappeared shortly after its release. —*Steve Huey*

Whodini / 1983 / Jive ◆◆◆

More singers than straight rappers, Jalil Hutchins and Ecstasy made a successful conversion to hip-hop, scoring two hits on their debut with "Rap Attack" and "The Haunted House of Funk," a reworking of "The Monster Mash." —*Ron Wynn*

Escape / 1984 / Jive ✦✦✦✦✦

A vast improvement over the previous year's debut, *Escape* is the second album from the seminal no-nonsense New York rappers. Unlike many rappers, Whodini got their beats and musical backing from synthesizers. While this isn't a conceptual masterpiece and really is nothing more than sure-shot singles and soundalike single, "Five Minutes of Funk" was an instant classic. The just-as-good "Freaks Come Out at Night" has the guys talking about nocturnal freaks with vivid lyrics and a little too much inside information. Listening to *Escape*, one has to be struck with the minimalism offered here. On "Big Mouth" and "Friends," producer Larry Smith provides clutter-free tracks for the guys to rap over. In contrast, the fast-paced "Escape (I Need a Break)" brings in ambulance sounds and ends up being a great instance of unconsciously danceable rap. Better yet, the closer "We Are Whodini" distills the essence of the group more than the other groundbreaking tracks here, and still retains a sense of freshness. The real unsung hero on *Escape* is the DJ, Grandmaster Dee, who provides deft work. Recorded at Battery Studios in England, *Escape* has a countless amount of memorable lines and productions, and has held up over time better than the debut. —*Jason Elias*

Back in Black / 1986 / Jive ✦✦✦

As one of the first successful rap acts, Whodini albums quickly became standard bearers and necessary purchases for fans. The Brooklyn-raised trio of Jalil Hutchins, Ecstasy, and DJ Grandmaster Dee first came to national attention with the single "The Haunted House of Rock." Their third record, *Back in Black*, is the follow-up to a multiplatinum album, 1984's *Escape*. Those expecting a by-the-numbers sequel of sorts to that effort won't be too let down here. Although *Back in Black* does revisit lyrical and musical themes of previous efforts, it also offers a few new tricks or two. The first track (and a single release), "Funky Beat" features monster bass and drums, the one-two punch of Hutchins and Ecstasy, as well as a rare rap from Grandmaster Dee. The well-produced "One Love" has great synth signatures and the guys dispensing their brand of pithy and pragmatic advice. They seem to unlearn those lessons by the time the hilarious "I'm a Ho" rolls around. The slow, scratch-laden track has a boastful chorus ("I rock three different freaks after every show") and some great rhymes from Hutchins. Despite the group's best efforts, *Back in Black* does often seem to be style over substance. Luckily the producer Larry Smith knew how to keep things sonically interesting. On the lyrically foggy "Fugitive," the hard rock guitars and clanging cymbals mesh especially well with Ecstasy's droll and abrupt delivery. "Echo Scratch" is also all over the road, but it was a great chance for Grandmaster Dee to show off his turntable skills. Also recorded at Battery Studios in London (as was *Escape*), *Back in Black* wasn't as influential as its predecessor, but it's nearly as enjoyable. —*Jason Elias*

Open Sesame / 1987 / Jive ✦✦

Mille Jackson made a wonderful guest appearance on "Be Yourself," but not only was the handwriting on the wall, it was soon readable by everyone. —*Ron Wynn*

★ **Greatest Hits** / Jun. 1990 / Jive ✦✦✦✦✦

When funksters and soulsters who reached adulthood in the 1960s and '70s criticize rap, their number one complaint is usually that too much of it isn't melodic enough. But they seldom make that complaint about Whodini, which in the mid-'80s, enjoyed a lot more support from R&B fans than the more forceful and abrasive sounds of Run-D.M.C. or LL Cool J. While those artists rocked hard, Whodini grooved. Many of Whodini's early albums are well worth acquiring—including *Escape* and *Back in Black*—but for the more casual listener, *Greatest Hits* serves as a fine introduction. From the poignant rap ballad "One Love" to such addictive and highly danceable grooves as "Five Minutes of Funk" and "Freaks Come Out at Night," *Greatest Hits* makes it clear why Whodini was so successful in the mid-'80s. —*Alex Henderson*

Bag-A-Trix / Mar. 19, 1991 / MCA ✦✦

Whodini's popularity had decreased considerably by the 1990s, when the Brooklyn rappers left their longtime home of Jive/Arista Records for MCA. Though a decent effort, Whodini's first MCA release, *Bag-A-Trix*, wasn't strong enough to help Whodini return to the top of the charts. The group's approach—very danceable and melodic compared to a lot of rap, and drawing heavily on '70s soul and funk—hadn't changed much since the early '80s, and remained quite recognizable. While nothing on *Bag-A-Trix* is in a class with "Freaks Come Out at Night," "Five Minutes of Funk," or "One Love," this CD definitely has its strong points, including the invigorating "The

Party Don't Start," the erotic "Taste of Love," and an inspired remake of the Undisputed Truth's soul classic "Smiling Faces Sometimes." A better introduction to Whodini would be *Escape*, but for the most devoted fans, this is worth hearing. —*Alex Henderson*

The Jive Collection, Vol. 1 / Jun. 27, 1995 / Jive ✦✦✦✦✦

Jive Collection, Vol. 1 collects Whodini's greatest hits, as well as some lesser-known tracks and a few remixes. The groundbreaking group's synthesis of soul grooves and hip-hop texture is on display in the original recordings of hits like "Freaks Come Out at Night," "Five Minutes of Funk," and the poignant "Friends." "Haunted House of Rock" is corny yet appealing, an early example of humor's prominent role in hip-hop. The album cuts included here are drawn mainly from 1986's *Back in Black*, the follow-up to *Escape*. "Funky Beat"'s production is amazing, with a beat of its own that, while oddly unfunky, is nevertheless successful when matched with Jalil Hutchins and Ecstasy's earnest rhyming. "I'm a Ho" is at first off-putting, but eventually seems like an elaborate condemnation of other MCs' bravado. *Jive Collection* would already be a great purchase as an introduction to Whodini, but the inclusion of "Fugitive" makes acquiring the album crucial. A memorable mixture of enormous rock guitar with the group's synth-heavy sound, the song embodies the promise and pure potential that permeated the early days of hip-hop. The album's bonus tracks include a cool beatbox remix of "Big Mouth," as well as the seven-minute "Whodini Friends Mastermix." —*Johnny Loftus*

The WhoRidas

f. 1995, Oakland, CA

Group / Hip-Hop, Hardcore Rap, West Coast Rap

Coming out of Oakland during the mid-'90s, the WhoRidas represented a new generation of hip-hop: hard but intelligent, musical but still deeply funky. Cousins King Saan (Hasaan Mahmoud) and Mr. Taylor (Meikeo Taylor) began freestyling together, and after King Saan made an appearance on his older brother Saafir's 1994 debut album, *Boxcar Sessions*, the WhoRidas began recording. Their first single, "Shot Callin' & Big Ballin'," sold 15,000 copies out of the back of their car, and with the help of Saafir the pair signed to Delicious Vinyl. With the help of their production crew, Hobo Junction, the WhoRidas released their debut album, *Whoridin'*, in August 1997; the follow-up, *Hightimes*, appeared in 1999. —*John Bush*

● **Whoridin'** / Aug. 19, 1997 / Delicious Vinyl ✦✦✦

Despite the group's tendency to rely on gangsta lyrical clichés, the WhoRidas' debut album *Whoridin'* is a refreshingly funky West Coast hip-hop record. The group has a good rhythmic flow and terrific grooves that make it easy to overlook their shortcoming. After all, *Whoridin'* is a debut, and it's natural that there would be some flaws—it's the fact there's enough good stuff to make the flaws easy to ignore that makes *Whoridin'* a successful debut. —*Leo Stanley*

Hightimes / Jun. 29, 1999 / TVT ✦✦✦

The sophomore album from Choppa Saan and Mr. Taylor features the underground hit "Get Lifted" and the new single "Dock of the Bay" sprinkled amongst the duo's lyrical flow. Guests include Xzibit and Sondoobie. —*Keith Farley*

The Wild Pair

Group / Dirty South

The Wild Pair consists of Step-1 and Scotty, two thuggish hedonists from the dirty South who debuted with their *I Want It All* album, released by the Florida-based Dun Deal Productions label. The duo celebrates both materialism and hedonism, while also representing the South and getting buck. —*Jason Birchmeier*

● **I Want It All** / Oct. 23, 2001 / Dun Deal ✦✦✦

Wild Pair members Step-1 and Scotty celebrate materialism and hedonism on their debut album, *I Want It All*. The standout track here is the title track, with its singalong chorus that lists everything the duo treasures in this world: guns, drugs, sluts, clubs, shoes, and so on. If you can appreciate the iced-out, bling-blingin' mentality of the Hot Boys and the don't-give-a-crap thug attitude of Trick Daddy, then you'll find much to savor here. Unfortunately, the Wild Pair don't have the lyrical skills or the producers that the Hot Boys and Trick Daddy do. Theirs aren't nearly on that same level of quality, leaving much to be desired. —*Jason Birchmeier*

Wildchild

b. California

Underground Rap

As an MC for the indie hip-hop group Lootpack, Wildchild gained a lot of attention when they dropped their first record in 1999 for his verbose, articulate rhymes and positive message. This was quite an accomplishment for the rapper, a California native who had started rhyming with fellow Lootpack members DJ Romes and Madlib in college. After the group proved to be a hit on the West Coast live circuit, Stones Throw Records offered the trio a contract, which they signed in late 1998. The next year they got together with a number of producers, including Peanut Butter Wolf, and recorded *Soundpieces: Da Antidote* for the label. Although not a commercial success, the album proved to be popular with fans of underground hip-hop and drew favorable notices from critics. When Lootpack took a break after their debut, Wildchild started working on his solo record, which would incorporate more of his poetry and explore some different sides of his writing. Produced by Madlib and Oh No, he released *Secondary Protocol* on Stones Throw Records in the spring of 2003. *—Bradley Torreano*

Will.I.Am

Producer, Vocals / Underground Rap

Will.I.Am is a rapper and producer whose work in Black Eyed Peas helped make them one of the most intriguing acts in hip-hop. In 2001, following lauded projects from Jay Dee and Pete Rock, British beat obsessives BBE hired him to record his own production album, *Lost Change*. *—John Bush*

● **Lost Change** / Sep. 25, 2001 / Beat Generation ✦✦✦✦

Jay Dee and Pete Rock's extremely contrasting contributions to BBE's ambitious and rapidly unfolding beat-suite series has made it increasingly difficult to discern where the label's "true" musical vision lies. While Jay Dee's *Welcome to Detroit* was a more rhyme-orientated opus, Pete Rock's *Petestrumentals* was a distinctly jazzy, instrumental-based endeavor. Will.I.Am's *Lost Change* is a solid extension of this movement, as it cozily nestles itself in between these two releases, sprinkling in an equal assortment of both beats and rhymes. Though Will has taken the instrumental-based series and put his own stamp on it, that stamp still contains occasional hues of Black Eyed Peas' (of which Will is a member) organic stylings ("Ev Rebahdee" featuring Planet Asia). Yet, BBE's progressive format frees Will up to dabble in a menagerie of musical styles. And he is up to the challenge, as "Lost Change" fuses together aspects of jazz, electronica, funk, Caribbean, and trip-hop rhythms. While the straight-up rhyming tracks border on sublime ("I Am") to humdrum ("Money" featuring Huck Fynn, Oezlem, and Horn Dogs), it is the instrumental format where Will truly flourishes. Showing a true knack for experimentation, Will leisurely darts back and forth between the reggae-scented "Possessions," "Lost Change" (which coalesces jazzy horns with junkyard band riffing), and the hazy electronic fuzz of "Thai Arrive," which unfolds like a Radiohead track, minus the attitude. Similarly, "Lay Me Down" has the potential to be a breakout hit, as Will's infectious snare claps and blissful horn snippets provide a cooled-out platform for Terry Dexter's soulful vocal scatting. On "Control Tower" Will inserts a vocal clip that states, "I'm on the brink of a great achievement." Though "Lost Change" falls short of those expectations, Will does an admirable job of implementing a host of different styles, without losing the listener in the process, as "Lost Change" is a sophisticated, musically enthralling endeavor, which still manages to be accessible. *—Matt Conaway*

Hype Williams

b. Queens, NY

Video Director / Hip-Hop

The definitive video director for late-'90s rap music, Hype Williams worked with every major rapper of the era, from Nas and DMX to Missy Elliott and Puff Daddy, and even made the admirable leap to feature films as well. Born in the Hollis, Queens, neighborhood of New York to working-class parents, Williams grew up aspiring to become a painter like Basquiat or Keith Haring. Rather than take a traditional approach to art, he took the street approach, tagging graffiti throughout the city. "Hype" was his tag and, in turn, became his moniker of choice. In the late '80s he made the jump from graffiti to film. He attended Adelphi University, where he studied film, and subsequently joined Classic Concept Productions, where he swept floors on the sets of golden age rap video shoots. In 1993 he launched his own production company, Big Dog Films, and made his first major video in 1994, Wu-Tang Clan's "Can It Be All So Simple." Following the video's airing, offers began pouring in, and Williams took on as many as time allowed, directing numerous videos every year until the decade's end.

Within only a few years, Williams had become an award-winning director, taking home the 1996 *Billboard* Music Video Award for Best Director of the Year, the 1997 NAACP Image Award, and the 1998 MTV Video Music Award for Best Rap Video, among others. During this late-'90s run, he worked with every major rap artist imaginable, and earned a reputation for incredibly stylish videos characterized by fish-eye lens work and glitzy wardrobes. Williams made the leap to feature-film directing in 1998 with *Belly*. The Artisan-released film starring rappers DMX, Nas, and Method Man became a substantial cult hit among the urban audience. Around this same time, he also began directing commercials for major brands such as Nike, Fubu, and The Gap. Williams' output slowed a bit after the close of the '90s, yet he maintained his well-known status, releasing *Hype Williams: The Videos, Vol. 1* in 2002, a DVD featuring many of his most memorable works. *—Jason Birchmeier*

● **Hype Williams: The Videos, Vol. 1** / May 28, 2002 / Palm Pictures ✦✦✦✦

One of the most stylistically prominent music video directors of the '90s, Hype Williams' defined aesthetic was one of the most sought after in the genre—as it almost ensured heavy rotation on MTV, which in turn guaranteed large amounts of commercial success and sales. This DVD collection of videos handpicked by Williams himself is not necessarily a collection of his most-well-known videos, but a very accurate and tastefully compiled survey of landmark videos that very clearly show his evolution as a cinematographer/director. While there are some very glaring omissions (most notably absent are Missy Elliot's classic "The Rain [Supa Dupa Fly]" and the groundbreaking "What's It Gonna Be?" featuring Busta Rhymes and Janet Jackson), many of these videos will be all too familiar to MTV viewers and will bring back fond memories of first-time viewing. Some definitely outweigh the songs they are visually representing, which makes the urge to hit fast-forward on the remote very tempting. But overall the pluses definitely outweigh the minuses on this DVD, which is excellent viewing for anyone interested in watching the gradual evolution of one of music video's most gifted directors. *—Rob Theakston*

Witchdoctor

b. Georgia

Hip-Hop, Urban

Witchdoctor was an ambitious hip-hop artist from Georgia who blended Afro-centric spirituality, soul, rap, and urban R&B. His Organized Noize-produced debut album, *A S.W.A.T. Healin' Ritual*, was released by Interscope in 1997. *—Stephen Thomas Erlewine*

● **A S.W.A.T. Healin' Ritual** / 1997 / Interscope ✦✦✦

Produced by the Organized Noize team, Witchdoctor's debut album *A S.W.A.T. Healin' Ritual* is an intriguing blend of contemporary beats, Afro-centric spirituality, southern soul, and urban R&B. Witchdoctor's relaxed, rural delivery calls attention to itself, but Organized Noize's seamless production is what makes the album a compelling listen. *—Leo Stanley*

Won-G

b. Port-au-Prince, Haiti

Hip-Hop, Urban, Club/Dance, Alternative Rap, Hardcore Rap, Pop-Rap

Rapper Won-G spent the first 15 years of his life splitting time between Brooklyn and his native Port-au-Prince, Haiti, soaking up a legion of musical and linguistic contrasts. His family subsequently settled permanently in the U.S., where he began entering talent competitions. Success in this area led him to record a small-scale indie-label album, *Do It Do It*, in 1995 with the help of his father and brother. Won-G next founded his own label, Happy World, in partnership with a friend's parents, and caught the ear of Beyond Music, which picked up his 2000 album *The Royal Impression*. Produced by Won-G's brother Dubble M and featuring cameos from Layzie Bone, the Outlawz, Yukmouth, and Sylk E. Fine, *The Royal Impression* projected an upbeat, positive energy and a freewheeling, eclectic range of influences ranging from pop, dance, and urban to the sounds of the rapper's native Haiti. *—Steve Huey*

The Royal Impression / Sep. 26, 2000 / Beyond ✦✦✦
A truly odd album, *The Royal Impression* features Won-G, a self-acclaimed Haitian rapper with a poster-boy stance best illustrated on the text- and photo-heavy CD booklet. His rhymes flow quickly with surprising liquidity, and the beats bounce with esoteric flavor, making this an alluring yet uncanny album that doesn't seem to fit any established template, not even a niche rap style—a rare and undeniably remarkable attribute for the oft-derivative rap genre circa 2000. Though intriguing, something is just too out of place with Won-G's persona as illustrated on this album to ever make him an idolized rapper, unfortunately. This album functions best as a novelty oddity. —*Jason Birchmeier*

● **Explosion** / Apr. 9, 2002 / Town Sound ✦✦✦
Won-G continues his eclectic style of Haitian-flavored rap on *Explosion*, his follow-up to *The Royal Impression*. During the time span separating the two albums, Won-G released another album, *No Better Than This*; however, that album featured the same songs that would end up appearing on *Explosion*, its cover photo even appearing inside the CD booklet. Despite the odd circumstances characterizing *No Better Than This* (2001) and *Explosion* (2002)—for instance, both albums feature the same songs, yet in a different sequence—one of the two is all you need. Dubble M produces nearly every track on *Explosion*, giving the album a very consistent production style; DJ Quik contributes (and also raps on) "Nothing's Wrong" and L.T. Hutton contributes three tracks—"Do You Think I'm Scared," "I Love TNO," and "If You Wanna Ride" (the latter featuring Layzie Bone). —*Jason Birchmeier*

Woodie (Ryan Wood)

b. Antioch, CA
Vocals, Producer / West Coast Rap, Gangsta Rap, Underground Rap
Fed up with a life of gang-related violence and hopelessness, Woodie dedicated himself to rap music and quickly rose through the ranks of the Cali Bay Area's underground scene, eventually signing to Koch Records. Hailing from Antioch, CA, Woodie (born Ryan Wood) grew up in an environment filled with gangs, drugs, violence, and crime. Life was rough. For example, Woodie's friend, Carlos "Blackbird" Ramirez, was shot to death by local police; another close friend, Gabriel "Snoop" Robinson, was locked up in Folsom Prison for a crime he didn't commit; and Woodie himself had run-ins with the law, nearly charged with attempted murder. After all this drama, Woodie turned to the rap game, recording *Yoc Influenced*, his debut release. The record became a local sensation, selling thousands of copies throughout the Bay Area thanks to the Northern Cali anthem "Norte Sidin'." Woodie then returned to the studio with executive producer D-Small to record the East Co. compilation *Northern Expozure, Vol. 1*. The record showcased not only Woodie's lyrical skills but also his production talents. Soon, underground gangsta rap magazine *Murder Dog* was praising his work, introducing Woodie to a national audience. This underground success culminated with Woodie being offered a record deal with Koch, a large, nationally distributed label with plenty of money and clout. Woodie's first release for Koch, *Demonz N My Sleep* (2001), again showcased his skills as both an MC and as a producer—he produces all but three of the album's songs. —*Jason Birchmeier*

Yoc Influenced / Sep. 14, 1999 / East Co. ✦✦
Woodie debuted with *Yoc Influenced*, an EP that may have been brief but proved itself to be a succinct summation of the Northern California rapper's talents. This EP proved so successful, in fact, that Woodie found himself getting his next solo release, *Demonz N My Sleep*, distributed by Koch. —*Jason Birchmeier*

● **Demonz N My Sleep** / Aug. 28, 2001 / Koch ✦✦✦
The California Bay Area was flooded with underground gangsta rappers by the early 2000s, Woodie being one of the more impressive. Many of the Northern Cali rappers had skills but most were hampered by poor production quality. Not Woodie, however. He not only had the skills; he also had impressive production quality—a street-level indie rapper with major-label sound quality. Woodie self-produces most of the tracks on *Demonz N My Sleep*, and it's debatable which is more impressive, his tracks or his rhymes. He summons an impressive array of sounds out of his limited gear on this album, crafting a distinctly West Coast hardcore rap album—lots of synth flourishes, many of them eerie and creepy. In addition, his rhymes are distinctly Bay Area—gangsta, quick, lucid, and harsh. Overall, Woodie may not be your prototypical rap star and may have the cards stacked against him in the major-label-dominated rap game, but his skills are overly evident on *Demonz N*

My Sleep. Woodie is yet another Bay Area rapper who doesn't get the acclaim he probably should. —*Jason Birchmeier*

The World Class Wreckin' Cru

Group / Electro, Old School Rap, West Coast Rap
The World Class Wreckin' Cru recorded some solid West Coast electro with Dr. Dre in the production chair, hitting the pop charts with a smooth love jam named "Turn Off the Lights" during 1988, the same year Dre's N.W.A delivered the gangsta landmark *Straight Outta Compton*. The group was formed by Lonzo (Alonzo Williams), owner of the Compton club Eve After Dark, who recruited a pair of popular local DJs, Dr. Dre and DJ Yella, along with Dre's high school friend Cli-N-Tel. Early singles like "Surgery" and "Juice"—many of them recorded at a four-track studio that was part of the Eve After Dark complex—stood alongside work by the Egyptian Lover and L.A. Dream Team as stellar examples of the fast-moving fusion of old school rap and electro. But even as the World Class Wreckin' Cru became one of Southern California's most popular rap acts, Dr. Dre and DJ Yella were pursuing other production opportunities, one of which came from a new label (Ruthless) formed by Eazy-E. Along with Ice Cube, they wrote a single named "Boyz-n-the Hood" that was initially offered to the Ruthless act HBO, but later prompted the entire crew to form as N.W.A. After street-level singles like "Dopeman" and "8 Ball" became huge local hits, the World Class Wreckin' Cru became less of a priority for both Dr. Dre and Yella. Even after the loverman ballad "Turn Off the Lights" entered the R&B Top 40 in 1988, they continued with N.W.A *Phases in Life*, a World Class Wreckin' Cru LP released in 1990, was basically a solo release by Lonzo. —*John Bush*

Phases in Life / 1990 / Creative Funk ✦✦

Turn Off the Lights (Before the Attitude) / Mar. 5, 1991 / Creative Funk ✦✦

● **Turn Off the Lights: Greatest Hits Plus** / Nov. 13, 2001 / Thump ✦✦✦
Noted as the first group blessed with Dr. Dre's production expertise, the World Class Wreckin' Cru recorded some solid West Coast electro singles, more energetic than the style's other prime production act (Egyptian Lover), if not as revolutionary. Dre certainly rated with the prime electro producers across the nation—New York's Arthur Baker (Afrika Bambaataa) and Detroit's Juan Atkins (Cybotron)—and his best work ("Surgery," "Juice") was a big revelation on bass music as well as West Coast rap. *Turn Off the Lights: Greatest Hits Plus* has all of the best World Class Wreckin' Cru tracks, but there's still plenty of samey filler. The single "Turn Off the Lights" is bland enough to have sounded totally innocuous on the charts during 1988, while dance tracks like "Cabbage Patch" and "The Fly" are tired novelties. The only other interesting inclusions are a pair of tracks that point toward Dre's work in N.W.A—the surprisingly hardcore "Mission Possible" and "B.S." (the first a Public Enemy soundalike, but the last one completely original gangster fantasy). Still, unless you're very curious about Dr. Dre's origins in the Compton clubs, it's far better to seek out an old school compilation that includes "Surgery" or "House Calls." —*John Bush*

Wreckless Klan

f. Houston, TX
Group / Dirty South, Gangsta Rap
Wreckless Klan only recorded one album, *Blowin' Up tha Scene* (1996), because group members Point Blank, PSK-13, and Ice Lord maintained busy solo careers. Like the individual members, the Houston-based Klan recorded for Bigtyme Records. —*Jason Birchmeier*

● **Blowin' Up tha Scene** / Jun. 1996 / Bigtyme ✦✦✦
Wreckless Klan went through a number of trials and tribulations—including the death of one member, .38, and the jailing of another, Ice Lord—before they could release their first album, *Blowin' Up tha Scene*. Some of those painful experiences come through on the album, but for the most part, *Blowin' Up tha Scene* merely celebrates the gangsta lifestyle instead of examining it. Fortunately, the lyrical skills of Point Blank and PSK-13 make their sentiments somewhat forgiveable. Even so, the music on the album is far too predictable to make the album an impressive debut. —*Leo Stanley*

Wreckx-N-Effect

f. 1989
Group / Hip-Hop, New Jack Swing, Party Rap, Pop-Rap
Wreckx-N-Effect earned a huge crossover smash with the single "Rump Shaker" off their 1992 album *Hard or Smooth*. The accompanying video with

its array of shapely women following the directions of the lead singer generated nearly as much heat as Sir Mix-A-Lot's "Baby Got Back." It also helped the group secure a platinum certification, something it hardly seemed they'd earn from their Motown debut *Wrecks-N-Effect* in 1989. Markell Riley, brother of superproducer Teddy Riley, was part of the rap ensemble along with Aquil Davidson and Brandon Mitchell; Mitchell was killed in a 1990 shooting. Following the success of "Rump Shaker," the group resurfaced in 1996 with *Raps New Generation.* —*Ron Wynn*

● **Wrecks-N-Effect** / Sep. 1, 1989 / Motown ✦✦✦✦
While Keith Sweat was the soul loverman, Bobby Brown the R&B bad boy, and Guy the new jack of all trades, Wreckx-n-Effect was the rap contingent of Teddy Riley's new jack swing juggernaut. And before there was the monster crossover single "Rump Shaker" (with its immodestly fleshy video), there was the somewhat tamer (though still fairly lascivious) pleasures of *Wreckx-N-Effect.* Lyrically and thematically, this debut recording does not exactly get over on its ambition. Aside from fascinating deviations into hypnotic soul-rap ("Soul Man," with it chant-like overtones) and fusion (the drawn-out jazz keyboards of "Deep" and "V-Man"), the album mostly splits the difference between battle-style boasting ("Leave the Mike Smoking'," a showcase for Aqil Davidson, the trio's primary mic man), nods to quiet storm R&B (the cornball but somehow endearing, slow-mo sleaze of "Juicy"), and club workouts ("Club Head," "Wipe Your Sweat"). But then, Wreckx-N-Effect wasn't pretending to make anything but good, sweaty, slightly debauched fun, a goal it accomplishes quite wonderfully. This is party-starting and extending music. Still, with the insistent "New Jack Swing" (produced by Riley's brother, Markell), the trio also came up with a call to arms for the then-neophyte genre that was precisely midway between the squelchy funk of the Gap Band and old school rap. It remains arguably the most memorable thing they ever recorded. —*Stanton Swihart*

Hard or Smooth / 1992 / MCA ✦✦✦✦
Together with "Baby Got Back," Wreckx-N-Effect's "Rump Shaker" helped to blur the line between decency and debauchery that, in the early '90s at least, was allegedly still intact. But unlike Sir Mix-A-Lot, who capitalized on his 1991 monster hit with a seemingly endless cache of goofy double entendres, lurid song ideas, and bombastic productions, W-N-E was unable to reprocess the elements of its single into additional hits. Nothing on *Hard or Smooth* is as infectious as the single, mainly because Markell Riley and Aqil Davidson repeatedly exaggerate particular parts of that song without applying anything very interesting around the pieces. Davidson is appropriately jocular on "Knock-N-Boots," but the song's gang vocals are identical to those of "Rump Shaker," without its addictive beat. "Wreckx Shop" features effective production, but the lyrics are raunchy without being particularly inventive. Additionally, the album's irritating habit of naming songs after portions of the W-N-E moniker doesn't help matters any, either. Despite these faults, when its songs expand on the sonic and lyrical themes of its single, *Hard or Smooth* is able to make some progress. "New Jack Swing II" employs an overused sample, but Davidson and Riley's intertwining flow turns the song into a success. "My Cutie"'s lighter beat and hints of soul give the MCs some much-needed breathing room. But the album's dominating, insistent tempo returns with "Wreckx-N-Effect," and continues through the final three tracks. This gritty, grinding percussion definitely helps *Hard or Smooth* succeed as a party album. But it's also where it falls short, since the permeating beat and interwoven samples only suggest "Rump Shaker" without really complementing or bettering it. —*Johnny Loftus*

Raps New Generation / Sep. 24, 1996 / MCA ✦✦
Wreckx-N-Effect's fusion of party hip-hop and soulful urban R&B was a revelation on its first two albums, but it has grown tired and predictable on its belated third album *Raps New Generation.* Few of the tracks demonstrate any lyrical or musical imagination, and the good-time grooves all fall flat—in short, it sounds like a party you can't wait to leave. —*Leo Stanley*

Wu-Syndicate

f. Virginia Beach, VA
Group / Hardcore Rap, East Coast Rap
Unofficially considered the Southern representatives of Wu-Tang Clan, Wu-Syndicate wasn't always associated with the legendary New York crew. In fact, Joe Mafia, Myerlansky, and Napoleon were originally known as the Crime Syndicate, a Mafia-themed group who formed in Virginia Beach at the

beginning of the '90s. They became friends with Wu-Tang Clan soon after, when both were signed to the independent Slot Time Records. When Wu came to visit the label's headquarters in Virginia Beach, the two crews got along well and promised that they would support one another if either crew got leverage in the industry. The Wu had no idea they were so close to mainstream success, but within a few years they had built a huge fan base with their gritty, kung-fu-themed hip-hop. When they started their own label in the late '90s, one of the first acts they contacted was the Crime Syndicate. Their "Where Was Heaven" track was included on *The Swarm* compilation, but not without changing their name to the Wu-Syndicate. The name change wasn't an issue since the group needed the publicity, and the label equally benefited from their marketable gangster image. Wu-Syndicate's eponymous debut was released in 1999, but despite a good reception from Wu-Tang Clan's audience, the album was overshadowed by the stream of releases coming out on their collective. When money began disappearing, the group peacefully disassociated from the Wu-Tang Clan before the situation became too heated. Myerlansky and Napoleon both ended up going to prison soon after, so they spent the next few years waiting out their sentences, promising that they would return as a trio when all three could get back together again. —*Bradley Torreano*

● **Wu-Syndicate** / Apr. 20, 1999 / Priority ✦✦✦
Wu-Syndicate is a Wu-Tang-related album minus the production talents of main-man RZA (credited here as executive producer). Produced by newcomers DJ Devastator, Tata, Dred, and Mathematics, *Wu-Syndicate* is far from the worst Wu-Tang cash-in, in part because the productions occasionally transcend the trademarked Wu sound. While rappers Myerlansky and Joe Mafia are cartoonish gangsters closer in concept to the 1930s than the gangsta '90s (similar to No Limit's Gambino Family), tracks like "Pointin' Fingers," "Ghetto Syringe," and "Muzzle Toe" are well produced and even superior to several tracks from the latest "real" Wu-Tang Clan album, *Forever.* —*Keith Farley*

Wu-Tang Clan

f. 1992, Staten Island, NY
Group / Hip-Hop, East Coast Rap, Hardcore Rap
Emerging in 1993, when Dr. Dre's G-funk had overtaken the hip-hop world, the Staten Island, NY-based Wu-Tang Clan proved to be the most revolutionary rap group of the mid-'90s—and only partially because of their music. Turning the standard concept of a hip-hop crew inside out, the Wu-Tang Clan were assembled as a loose congregation of nine MCs, almost as a support group. Instead of releasing one album after another, the Clan was designed to overtake the record industry in as profitable a fashion as possible—the idea was to establish the Wu-Tang as a force with their debut album and then spin off into as many side projects as possible. In the process, the members would all become individual stars as well as receive individual royalty checks.

Surprisingly, the plan worked. All of the various Wu-Tang solo projects elaborated on the theme the group laid out on their 1993 debut, the spare, menacing *Enter the Wu-Tang (36 Chambers).* Taking their group name from a powerful, mythical kung-fu sword wielded by an invincible congregation of warriors, the crew is a loose collective of nine MCs. All nine members work under a number of pseudonyms, but they are best known as RZA (formerly Prince Rakeem; aka Rzarecta, Chief Abbot, and Bobby Steels; born Robert Diggs), Genius/GZA (aka Justice and Maxi Million; born Gary Grice), Ol' Dirty Bastard (aka Unique Ason, Joe Bannanas, Dirt McGirt, Dirt Dog, and Osirus; born Russell Jones), Method Man (aka Johnny Blaze, Ticallion Stallion, Shakwon, Methical, and MZA; born Clifford Smith), Raekwon the Chef (aka Shallah Raekwon and Lou Diamonds; born Corey Woods), Ghostface Killah (aka Tony Starks and Sun God; born Dennis Coles), U-God (aka Golden Arms, Lucky Hands, Baby U, and 4-Bar Killer; born Lamont Hawkins), Inspectah Deck (aka Rebel INS and Rollie Fingers; born Jason Hunter), and Masta Killa (aka Noodles; born Elgin Turner).

Although he wasn't one of the two founding members—Genius/GZA and Ol' Dirty Bastard were the first—the vision of the Wu-Tang Clan is undoubtedly due to the musical skills of RZA. Under his direction, the group—through its own efforts and the solo projects, all of which he produced or coproduced—created a hazy, surreal, and menacing soundscape out of hardcore beats, eerie piano riffs, and minimal samples. Over these surrealistic backing tracks, the MCs rapped hard, updating the old school attack with vicious violence, martial arts imagery, and a welcome warped humor. By 1995, the sound was one of the most instantly recognizable in hip-hop.

It wasn't always that way. Like most rappers, they began their careers trying to get ahead whatever way they could. For RZA, that meant releasing a silly single, "Ooh, I Love You Rakeem," on Tommy Boy Records in 1991. On the advice of his label and producers, he cut the humorous, loverman single that went absolutely nowhere. Neither did the follow-up single, "My Deadly Venom." The experience strengthened his resolve to subvert and attack record-industry conventions. He found partners in Genius and Ol' Dirty Bastard. Genius had also released a record in 1991, the full-length *Words From the Genius* on Cold Chillin', which was preceded by the single "Come Do Me." Both records were unsuccessful. After the failure of his album, Genius teamed with an old friend, Ol' Dirty Bastard, to form the crew that would evolve into the Wu-Tang Clan within a year.

RZA quickly became part of the crew, as did several other local MCs, including Method Man, Ghostface Killah, Raekwon, U-God, Inspectah Deck, and Masta Killa, who rarely raps. The nine rappers made a pact to a form an artistic and financial community—the Wu-Tang Clan wouldn't merely be a group, it would be its own industry. In order to do this, they decided to establish themselves through a group effort and then begin to spread the word through solo projects, picking up additional collaborators along the way and, in the process, becoming stronger and more influential.

The first Wu-Tang Clan single, the hard-hitting "Protect Ya Neck," appeared on their own independent label and became an underground hit. Soon, the record labels were offering them lucrative contracts. The group held out until they landed a deal that would allow each member to record solo albums for whatever label they chose—in essence, each rapper was a free agent. Loud/RCA agreed to the deal, and the band's debut album, *Enter the Wu-Tang (36 Chambers)*, appeared in November of 1993. *Enter the Wu-Tang (36 Chambers)* was both critically acclaimed and commercially successful; although its financial success wasn't immediate, it was the result of a slow build. "C.R.E.A.M.," released in early 1994, was the single that put them over the top and won them a devoted following. The group wasted no time in pursuing other projects, as a total of five of the members—Genius, RZA, Raekwon, Method Man, and Ol' Dirty Bastard—landed solo contracts as a result of the success of "C.R.E.A.M." RZA was the first to reenter the studio, this time as a member of the Gravediggaz, a group he founded; in addition to RZA, who was rechristened RZArecta, the group included De La Soul producer Prince Paul, Stetsasonic's Frukwan, and Brothers Grimm's Poetic. The Gravediggaz's album *6 Feet Deep* appeared in August 1994; it eventually would go gold. Labeled "horrorcore" by the group, it was an ultraviolent but comical *tour de force* that demonstrated RZA's production prowess. Shortly after its release, Raekwon released his first single, "Heaven and Hell," on the *Fresh* soundtrack; the song was produced by RZA and featured Ghostface Killah.

The first Wu-Tang member to become a major solo star was Method Man. In November 1994, he released *Tical*, the first official Wu-Tang solo album. Again, RZA produced the album, creating a dense, dirty sonic collage. *Tical* became a big hit in early 1995, as did Meth's duet with Mary J. Blige, "I'll Be There for You/You're All I Need to Get By." Ol' Dirty Bastard followed Method Man's breakthrough success with *Return to the 36 Chambers*, which appeared in March 1995 on Elektra Records. Thanks to the hits "Brooklyn Zoo" and "Shimmy Shimmy Ya," the record became a gold success. Out of all the solo albums, it was the one that sounded the most like *Enter the Wu-Tang*, although it did have a more pronounced comic bent, due to Ol' Dirty's maniacal vocals. *Tales From the 'Hood*, a movie soundtrack featuring Inspectah Deck's first solo track, appeared in May.

Later in 1995, the two most critically acclaimed Wu-Tang records appeared: Raekwon's *Only Built 4 Cuban Linx* and Genius/GZA's *Liquid Swords*. Raekwon released his album on Loud/RCA in August 1995; the record featured extensive contributions—a total of 12 songs—from Ghostface Killah, his greatest exposure yet. Genius' second solo album was released by Geffen Records in November 1995. In February of 1996, Ghostface Killah's first solo track, "Winter Warz," appeared on the *Don't Be a Menace to South Central While You're Drinking Your Juice in the 'Hood* soundtrack. Later that October, he released his own solo debut, the critically acclaimed, '70s soul-flavored *Ironman*; the record was the first released on RZA's new Epic subsidiary, Razor Sharp Records.

The Wu-Tang Clan finally reconvened and returned with their second album, the double-CD *Wu-Tang Forever*, in June of 1997. Hugely anticipated, the album entered the charts at number one—selling over 600,000 copies in its first week alone—and quickly spawned the hit single "Triumph." There were several contributions from guest associate Cappadonna (born Darryl Hill), who'd appeared on *Only Built 4 Cuban Linx* and *Ironman*, and would later become the tenth member of the Wu-Tang Clan. The group toured extensively in support of the album, getting into a few minor scuffles with the law along the way.

In the meantime, the next phase of the Wu-Tang plan started to take shape: unearthing new associates and spinning the resulting stable of talent into a brand-name franchise. A group of Wu protégés dubbed Killarmy released their debut album, *Silent Weapons for Quiet Wars*, on Priority Records in August 1997, drawing heavily upon the Clan's martial imagery. 1998, however, was truly the year for Wu-related side projects. In March, Cappadonna released his solo debut *The Pillage* on Columbia. The same month, Killah Priest—not an official part of the Clan, but a frequent guest and a member of another protégé group called the Sunz of Man—made his solo debut on Geffen Records with *Heavy Mental*, an acclaimed album filled with spiritual imagery that established him as one of the more distinctive solo artists in the Wu-Tang orbit. In July the Sunz of Man released their own debut album, *The Last Shall Be First*, on Red Ant, and yet another group of up-and-comers dubbed the Wu-Tang Killa Bees released their first album, *The Swarm, Vol. 1*, on Priority, featuring a number of guest appearances by Wu members and associates. In August, Killarmy issued their second album, *Dirty Weaponry*.

1998 was also the year Ol' Dirty Bastard began a long and bizarre saga of erratic behavior and run-ins with police that found him making headlines with alarming (and ridiculous) regularity. In February he interrupted Shawn Colvin's acceptance speech at the Grammy Awards to protest the Clan's loss in the Best Rap Album category; shortly thereafter, he announced he was changing his name to Big Baby Jesus, an idea that never picked up steam. This was only the beginning—over the next year and a half, ODB would be arrested for a litany of offenses that included assault, shoplifting, making terrorist threats, wearing body armor after being convicted of a felony, possessing cocaine, and missing countless court dates. Plus, in early 1999, the whole Clan fell under suspicion of masterminding a gun-running operation between Staten Island and Steubenville, OH, charges that were never proven to have any validity.

In the midst of this legal sideshow, the Clan kicked off a second round of solo projects in late 1998. This time around, RZA curtailed his activities somewhat, making appearances but often leaving the majority of the production duties to his protégés. Still, he released his own solo debut, the soundtrack-styled *RZA as Bobby Digital in Stereo*, in November of 1998 on V2; the same month, Method Man's second album, *Tical 2000: Judgement Day*, debuted at number two on the charts. June 1999 saw the release of an excellent singles compilation, *RZA Hits*, which covered the first Wu-Tang album and the first round of solo albums (1994-1995); the very next week, Genius/GZA's second album, *Beneath the Surface*, was released. September brought plenty of new Wu product: Ol' Dirty Bastard's *Nigga Please*, released while the rapper was in rehab; Method Man's acclaimed duo album with Redman, *Blackout!*; and the first-ever solo album by Inspectah Deck, *Uncontrolled Substance*, which appeared on Relativity. Another Wu member made his solo debut in October, when U-God issued *Golden Arms Redemption* on Priority; Raekwon returned the following month with *Immobilarity*. Finally, Ghostface Killah issued his well-received sophomore set, *Supreme Clientele*, in January 2000.

However, this second round of Wu-Tang solo albums didn't attract as much attention, either critically or commercially. True, Method Man remained a popular solo star (and, to a lesser degree, so did ODB), and reviews were highly positive for Ghostface Killah (and, to a lesser degree, Genius/GZA). But the Wu franchise was suffering from inconsistency, overexposure (they'd spawned a clothing line, a video game, a comic book, and more), and a flood of musical product that even diehards found difficult to keep up with. Their once-distinctive sound was becoming commonplace and diluted, not just through the collective's own releases but also RZA's many imitators; plus, by this time, Timbaland had taken over the mantle of hip-hop's most cutting-edge producer.

Indie filmmaker Jim Jarmusch commissioned RZA to compose a soundtrack for his acclaimed *Ghost Dog: The Way of the Samurai*, the results of which were unveiled in early 2000. Other than that, the Clan reconvened for a new album and was mostly quiet during much of 2000—aside from Ol' Dirty Bastard, who unfortunately continued to spiral out of control. He spent some time in a California jail for violating the terms of his probation, but appeared to be on the right track when suddenly, in October—with just two months of rehab to go—he escaped the California facility and spent a month on the run from the law. Fans were shocked when ODB turned up on stage at the New York record-release party for the Clan's new album, *The W*, which was released with considerably less fanfare in November 2000. A leaner, more focused collection, *The W* featured only one track from ODB and pictured Cappadonna as a full-fledged member of the group (though he remained unnamed on their official contract with Loud).

ODB managed to exit the club after his surprise performance but was soon captured by police in Philadelphia and extradited to New York to face charges of cocaine possession. In April 2001, he cut a deal with prosecutors that resulted in a sentence of two to four years in state prison, bringing his outlaw saga to a sad end. In August 2001, RZA issued his second Bobby Digital album, *Digital Bullet*; November brought solo albums from Ghostface Killah (*Bulletproof Wallets*) and Cappadonna (*The Yin and the Yang*). This time, though, there was no full round of solo projects in between Wu albums; the full group (minus ODB) assembled for their fourth album, *Iron Flag*, which was released in December 2001, just one year after its predecessor. —*Stephen Thomas Erlewine and Steve Huey*

★ **Enter the Wu-Tang (36 Chambers)** / Nov. 1993 / Loud ✦✦✦✦✦
Along with Dr. Dre's *The Chronic*, the Wu-Tang Clan's debut, *Enter the Wu-Tang (36 Chambers)*, was one of the most influential rap albums of the '90s. Its spare yet atmospheric production—courtesy of RZA—mapped out the sonic blueprint that countless other hardcore rappers would follow for years to come. It laid the groundwork for the rebirth of New York hip-hop in the hardcore age, paving the way for everybody from Biggie and Jay-Z to Nas and Mobb Deep. Moreover, it introduced a colorful cast of hugely talented MCs, some of whom ranked among the best and most unique individual rappers of the decade. Some were outsized, theatrical personalities, others were cerebral storytellers and lyrical technicians, but each had his own distinctive style, which made for an album of tremendous variety and consistency. Every track on *Enter the Wu-Tang* is packed with fresh, inventive rhymes, which are filled with martial arts metaphors, pop-culture references (everything from Voltron to Lucky Charms cereal commercials to Barbra Streisand's "The Way We Were"), bizarre threats of violence, and a truly twisted sense of humor. Their off-kilter menace is really brought to life, however, by the eerie, lo-fi production, which helped bring the raw sound of the underground into mainstream hip-hop. Starting with a foundation of hard, gritty beats and dialogue samples from kung-fu movies, RZA kept things minimalistic, but added just enough minor-key piano, strings, or muted horns to create a background ambience that works like the soundtrack to a surreal nightmare. There was nothing like it in the hip-hop world at the time, and even after years of imitation, *Enter the Wu-Tang* still sounds fresh and original. Subsequent group and solo projects would refine and deepen this template, but collectively, the Wu have never been quite this tight again. —*Steve Huey*

Wu-Tang Forever / Jun. 3, 1997 / Loud ✦✦✦✦
By the time the Wu-Tang Clan finished their first round of solo projects and reconvened for their second album as a group, the double-disc album had become the hip-hop fad of the moment. So why not give it a shot? With a main crew of nine MCs (plus new protégé Cappadonna), the Wu wouldn't have to depend heavily on guest appearances to flesh out two whole discs of material, as Biggie and 2Pac had. While the result, *Wu-Tang Forever*, is frequently brilliant, it's also sprawling and unfocused, losing its handle on the carefully controlled chaos of *Enter the Wu-Tang*. On the one hand, there's more social consciousness on *Wu-Tang Forever*, taking hard looks at ghetto life while finding pathos and offering encouragement and uplift ("A Better Tomorrow," "Impossible"). On the other hand, you also get some of the group's most explicit sex raps yet ("Maria," "The Projects," the utterly bizarre ODB solo track "Dog Shit"). In other words, the group is starting to go off in more individual directions here, making it harder to maintain an overall focus. Once you get past the rambling Five Percenter introduction, the first disc is pretty tight, partly because it was kept short to leave room for enhanced CD content. The second disc is far too long, diluting the impact of its better songs (the terrific single "Triumph") with an excess of lackluster material. *Wu-Tang Forever*

easily would have made a brilliant single CD; RZA's production is more polished than the debut, thanks to a bigger budget and better equipment, and leans heavily on soundtrack-style strings to underscore the album's cinematic scope. Some hailed *Wu-Tang Forever* as the best double-disc hip-hop album yet released, but others regarded it as a disappointment; despite its many high points, it's the first time the Wu didn't quite fulfill their ambitions. —*Steve Huey*

Wu-Chronicles / Mar. 23, 1999 / Wu-Tang ✦✦✦
The continuing marketing of Wu-Tang Clan product hit a new low with the release of *Wu-Chronicles*. Though the concept of a Wu-Tang compilation—in effect, spanning the dozen or so albums released by members and cutting away the dross—is perfect for the legion of fans who haven't been able to keep up with the collective's hectic release schedule, this disc stretches everything a bit thin, including tracks by fringe-of-the-fringe groups like Heltah Skeltah, Ras Kass, Killarmy, and some artist known as Wu-Syndicate. Yes, it's hard to argue with any album that features some great productions by RZA, and *Wu-Chronicles* does include some good collaborations—notably Ol' Dirty Bastard with tha Alkaholiks on "Hip Hop Drunkies" and Cocoa Brovaz (formerly Smif-n-Wessun) with Raekwon on "Black Trump"—but for the most part it's a wasted attempt at releasing an excellent collection. —*Keith Farley*

The W / Nov. 21, 2000 / Columbia ✦✦✦✦✦
After a host of disappointing solo albums and quickly diminishing celebrity (most of the latter devoted to the continuing extra-legal saga of Ol' Dirty Bastard), Wu-Tang Clan returned, very quietly, with 2000's *The W*. The lack of hype was fitting, for this is a very spartan work, especially compared to its predecessor, the sprawling and overblown *Wu-Tang Forever*. While the trademark sound is still much in force, group mastermind RZA jettisoned the elaborate beat symphonies and carefully placed strings of *Forever* in favor of tight productions with little more than scarred soul samples and tight, tough beats. The back-to-basics approach works well, not only because it rightly puts the focus back on the best cadre of rappers in the world of hip-hop but also because RZA's immense trackmaster talents can't help but shine through anyway. Paranoid kung-fu samples and bizarre found sounds drive the fantastic streets-is-watching nightmare "Careful (Click, Click)." Unfortunately, though, *The W* isn't quite the masterpiece it sounds like after the first few tracks. It falls prey to the same inconsistency as *Forever*, resulting in half-formed tracks like "Conditioner," with Snoop Dogg barely saving Ol' Dirty Bastard's lone appearance on the LP, a phoned-in vocal (in terms of sound *and* quality). When they're hitting on all cylinders, though, Wu-Tang Clan are nearly invincible; "Let My Niggas Live," a feature with Nas, isn't just claustrophobic and dense but positively strangling, and singles material like "Protect Ya Neck (The Jump Off)" and "Do You Really (Thang, Thang)" are punishing tracks. Paring down *Wu-Tang Forever*—nearly a two-hour set—to the 60-minute work found here was a good start, but the Wu could probably create another masterpiece worthy of their debut if they spent even more time in the editing room. —*John Bush*

Wu-Chronicles, Chapter 2 / Jul. 3, 2001 / Priority ✦✦✦
Not really a collection of rarities and not really a best-of either, the *Wu-Chronicles* series is actually more of a grab bag featuring some well-known songs and also some that even the most ardent Wu fanatic probably has never heard. This is what makes this second installment both stunning and frustrating at the same time. The stunning moments come on songs like "Left & Right" and "Rumble"—the former a D'Angelo song featuring Method Man, the latter from U-God's *Golden Arms Redemption*—excellent songs that may have been overlooked by fans given the Wu's prolific output. Other available, yet possibly overlooked, gems included on *Wu-Chronicles: Chapter 2* include Gang Starr's "Above the Clouds," which features Inspectah Deck over one of DJ Premier's finest beats; "N.Y.C. Everything," a simple yet standout moment from RZA's hit-and-miss *Bobby Digital* album; "Dangerous Mindz," a Gravediggaz classic; "Hard to Kill," a Spice 1 song featuring Method Man; and a few others, like DJ Spooky's "Catechism," great Wu-featuring songs that were probably missed by fans. So, sure, these songs all merit attention from Wu fanatics since they are undoubtedly great songs. The problem, though, is that most fans have at least a few of these songs in their collection—at least songs like "Hip Hop Fury" and "N.Y.C. Everything" that appear on the Wu solo albums. Fortunately, there are enough seldom-heard songs here, like Shyheim's "In Trouble," to

offer surprises for everyone—even the most fanatic Wu fans. This is what makes *Wu-Chronicles: Chapter 2* worth checking out—nearly everything here is high quality, and those who haven't heard it will probably want to. Of course, given the myriad Wu albums out there, this is far from essential, but something fanatic fans will surely want in their collection. —*Jason Birchmeier*

Iron Flag / Dec. 18, 2001 / Columbia ♦♦♦♦
Even when it seemed they were tearing apart from in-group miscommunication and a welter of baffling solo albums, the Wu-Tang Clan came together again like *Voltron* for another excellent full-length. Expanding on the strengths of their third album, *The W*, *Iron Flag* focuses squarely on the Wu's immense twin strengths: bringing together some of the best rappers in the business, and relying on the best production confederacy in hip-hop (led by RZA) to build raw, hard-hitting productions. Nothing brings a group together better than invasion from outside, and even though the flag they're raising on the cover is their own, Wu-Tang respond to the terrorist attacks of 9/11 with guns blazing—Ghostface Killah puts it simply, "Together we stand, divided we fall/Mr. Bush sit down, I'm in charge of the war!" The production is rough and ruddy, much more East Coast than their last two full-lengths (both of which were recorded in Los Angeles). Original East Coast head Flavor Flav even makes an appearance on "Soul Power (Black Jungle)," though he doesn't even attempt to trade rhymes with the heaviest crew in hip-hop. (Instead, RZA indulges him by running the tape on an extended reminiscence with Flav and Method Man talking about growing up on Long Island.) The singles "Uzi (Pinky Ring)," "In the 'Hood," and "Ya'll Been Warned" are all excellent tracks with excellent raps and, though the vaguely familiar horn samples driving most of them sure weren't tough to record, RZA deserves a lot of credit for keeping the production simple. Even while most rappers have turned R&B overnight, Wu-Tang are really the only ones left in the hardcore game who sound like they're in it for more than money or prestige. —*John Bush*

Wu-Tang Killa Bees

Group / Hip-Hop, East Coast Rap, Hardcore Rap
Another in the ongoing list of projects concerning rap's most visible congregation, Wu-Tang Killa Bees includes Wu-Tang members RZA, Method Man, Ghostface Killah, Raekwon, Inspectah Deck, and Masta Killa plus relatives Cappadonna, Killarmy, and Sunz of Man. Debut album *Swarm, Vol. 1* appeared in July 1998. —*John Bush*

● **The Swarm, Vol. 1** / Jul. 21, 1998 / Priority ♦♦♦
The Wu-Tang sword is double edged. On one side, there's no sense denying that the amorphous, ever-expanding crew has been responsible from some the best, most creative hip-hop in the '90s, yet it's also true that their impact has been diluted by a proliferation of side projects and solo albums. Even RZA's brilliant, menacingly minimalist production loses its bite through repetition, and that's what hurts the otherwise fine *The Swarm, Vol. 1*. The Wu-Tang Killa Bees are foot soldiers in the Shaolin army—they're not among the elite, they're newly adopted members of the Wu Family. Usually, the Wu-Tang name is enough to guarantee a hit, but to ensure sales, Ghostface Killah, Cappadonna, and Inspectah Deck were all brought in for a couple of tracks. As a result, *The Swarm* really feels no different than any of the Wu albums since Ghostface Killah's *Iron Man*—it's the same mix of dirty beats, skeletal strings, hackneyed martial arts metaphors, and B-movie samples. It sounds as good as it ever did, but it no longer has the element of surprise or ominous tension that made the first handful of Wu-Tang records so compelling. And that's not the fault of the Ruthless Bastards, A.I.G., Shyheim or any of the new members of the family—if it's anyone's fault, it's RZA's, since neither he nor his associates, D.B. Allah and Mathematics, have found a way to expand his signature sound. It still provides pleasure, but not surprises—unfortunately, one of the pleasures of the Wu-Tang Clan was its ability to surprise, and without that, they no longer seem quite as majestic as they once were. —*Stephen Thomas Erlewine*

X-Clan

f. Brooklyn, NY
Group / East Coast Rap, Hardcore Rap, Political Rap, Golden Age
A good number of Afro-centric, politically oriented rap groups put out records during the late '80s and early '90s. Very few of those groups were on the level of the hard-hitting X-Clan, a Brooklyn-based collective that released a pair of stellar albums—1990's *To the East, Blackwards*, and 1992's *Xodus*—before breaking up. The group's primary members were Grand Verbalizer Funkin Lesson "Brother J" (born Jason Hunter), Lumumba Professor X "The Overseer" (born Lumumba Carson, the son of prominent and influential activist Sonny Carson), the Rhythem Provider "Sugar Shaft" (born Anthony Hardin), and Grand Architect "Paradise" (born Claude Grey), and they were joined by a cast of associates, which included powerful MC Isis (aka Lin Que). X-Clan were activists outside of music as well; they were Blackwatch members and vocal supporters of several pro-black organizations. Unfortunately, the group's political stance and their bold red-black-green garb often gained more attention than their records, which featured Brother J's accomplished vocal skills and teacher-like lyricism over in-house productions that flipped the overused Parliament/Funkadelic sampling routine on its back as well as any other group. *To the East, Blackwards* and *Xodus* were almost equally strong, reflected in the fact that both albums peaked at number 11 on the Top R&B/hip-hop album chart. Before the group's split, both Professor X and Isis released spin-off solo albums. After the group's split, Brother J formed Dark Sun Riders, a project that released an album in 1996. The year before that, Sugar Shaft succumbed to AIDS-related causes. None of this prevented the group from re-forming at the end of the '90s; however, as of 2003, the group had yet to release anything commercially. —*Andy Kellman*

● **To the East, Blackwards** / Apr. 19, 1990 / 4th & Broadway ✦✦✦✦✦
The self-sufficient X-Clan should've made a bigger splash with *To the East, Blackwards*, the group's debut album for 4th & Broadway. Name-dropping Nat Turner and Marcus Garvey and dressing in red, black, and green instead of black and silver didn't exactly lend itself to marketability in 1990, but there's no evidence to the contrary that this Afro-centric group released one of the best rap records that year—which is saying a great deal. Yes, plenty of groups had already swiped liberally from Funkadelic, and true, "Grand Verbalizer"'s instrumental backdrop is nearly identical to "Microphone Fiend," but there's an infectious vigor with the way each track is fired off that makes those points moot. Brother J's bookish, caramel-smooth delivery is like no other, and Professor X's jolting appearances after nearly every verse ("This is protected by the red, the black, and the green—*with a key*! Sissy!") add even more character to the album. X-Clan relentlessly pushes its pro-black motives and beliefs, and though the points are vague at times, at no point does it ever grow tiring. This isn't just a testament to the skills of the MCs—it also stands as a testament to the group members as producers. Like the best work of BDP and PE, a thorough listen to *To the East, Blackwards* is more likely to provoke deep thought than an entire chapter of the average American school's history book. And history books simply don't provide this kind of electric charge. —*Andy Kellman*

Xodus / May 19, 1992 / Polydor ✦✦✦✦
More of the same is hardly a bad thing when considering X-Clan's second album. They're still jacking beats—from Special Ed, D-Nice, and Main Source, for instance—and they're still spreading their knowledge with righteous, if occasionally vague, verve. The most significant change in the group's sound is the decreased reliance upon Funkadelic and George Clinton samples. This serves them well and shows that they had more going for them than most people gave X-Clan credit for. Furthermore, expecting them to come out with some form of party jam or anything less serious than their typical material was just plain wrongheaded—they wouldn't have worn it well at all. And so, they stick to what they do best: railing against racism and the other issues that hold blacks down ("F.T.P.," which refers once again to Yusef Hawkins' 1989 beating at the hands of a white mob) and bolstering their doctrine with tight, detailed productions. The normally relaxed and somewhat reserved Brother J breaks from his usual playbook on "Rhythem of God" with a blitzing, forceful delivery. On "Cosmic Ark," he rhymes with such authority and momentum that the end of the track seems to make him stop prematurely; the track lasts five and a half minutes but could've gone on into double digits. Not quite as excellent as the debut, *Xodus* is nonetheless another album lacking dull moments. Unfortunately, the group split before it was able to make a third. —*Andy Kellman*

The X-Ecutioners

f. 1989, New York, NY
Group / Hip-Hop, Underground Rap, Turntablism
New York-based turntable group the X-Ecutioners were, along with San Francisco's Invisibl Skratch Piklz, among the first all-DJ outfits to sign a recording contract, and the first to release a full-length album focusing on the art of turntable tricknology. Formerly known as the X-Men (they changed their name, for copyright reasons, when they signed with the Asphodel label in 1997), the four-person group consists of Mista Sinista, Rob Swift, Total Eclipse, and Roc Raida; a world-renowned crew whose past credits include national and international titles for trick and battle DJing, as well as live and studio work with artists such as Organized Konfusion, Large Professor, the Beatnuts, and Artifacts. Originally formed in 1989 by Roc Raida with Steve D, Johnny Cash, and Sean Cee, the group adopted the name X-Men on the occasion of a battle with another New York crew, the Supermen (that battle never happened). They went to return the DJ to a position of prominence in hip-hop, a position largely usurped in the '80s and '90s by MCs and producers, as rap grew into one of the largest and most profitable genres in the American music industry. Making entirely new tracks from bits and pieces of other records manipulated by hand (rather than with a sampler and sequencer), the X-Ecutioners combine state-of-the-art scratching with the hip-hop DJ's bedrock of cutting, mixing, and beat juggling. The group play live often, and have performed in clubs, exhibitions, and competitions on four continents. —*Sean Cooper*

● **X-Pressions** / Sep. 23, 1997 / Asphodel ✦✦✦
X-Pressions is the first full-length release by the relatively new phenomenon of the turntable orchestra. Like the first efforts of other young genres such as trip-hop and drum'n'bass, the album tends to be overlong and lacking in variety. Restricting themselves to the sounds of hip-hop past (old school references and battle-wearied scratch noises dominate), the group nonetheless manages a sufficiently engaging full-length debut, switching between group and solo performances and even pulling a few rappers (strictly underground, no big names) in on the fun. —*Sean Cooper*

Built From Scratch / Jan. 29, 2002 / Relativity ✦✦✦
Though it's a clever play on words, the title of the second record from the X-Ecutioners is somewhat of an overstatement. The New York turntable crew reworks a few notable songs from rock and hip-hop's history (Tom Tom Club's "Genius of Love" being the best known), while including several familiar sounds and vocals from the genre's early days. Still, *Built From Scratch* is a sharp ode to old school hip-hop that focuses on the roll of the turntable rather than the vocals of an MC. That has been the group's intent since the early '90s, and *Built From Scratch* provides a great showcase for the quartet's

turntable skills. However, those skills are sometimes overshadowed by the many collaborations from big names such as Pharaoh Monch, Xzibit, Everlast, Inspectah Deck, and the seemingly out-of-place Linkin Park. That doesn't mean that these cuts are commercially friendly. These are nitty-gritty rap ventures that stay true to the X-Ecutioners' roots and are free of any deliberate pop hooks. (The disc was also released with a bonus remix courtesy of Lo Fidelity Allstars.) —*Kenyon Hopkin*

X-Raided (Anarae Jones)

f. Waco, TX

Group / Hip-Hop, Gangsta Rap, Hardcore Rap

Notorious gangsta rapper X-Raided was born Anarae Jones in Waco, TX, and was raised primarily in Sacramento, CA. Shortly after releasing his 1992 debut LP *Psycho Active*, he was convicted on murder charges—in fact, the album's violent lyrics were even cited as evidence at the trial. While languishing in prison, X-Raided managed to record another album entirely over the telephone, a painstaking process eventually yielding 1995's *Xorcist. Unforgiven* followed four years later and *Initiation* was issued in early 2001. —*Jason Ankeny*

Unforgiven / Apr. 20, 1999 / Black Market ◆◆◆
There's little question that X-Raided, unlike many of his gangsta peers, truly lives the life he preaches; he recorded his third album, *Unforgiven*, while incarcerated at a Sacramento prison. X-Raided recorded all the vocals while in jail, and the music was laid down in a local studio. At the very least, this makes the album unique, but it's hard to view it as anything other than a novelty, even though X-Raided isn't half bad as a rapper. However, the vocals (not surprisingly) sound strangely isolated from the music, and the cumulative effect of his lyrics is a little creepy. All of this makes it worth one listen, to be sure, but the music and rhyming aren't strong enough overall to reward subsequent plays. —*Stephen Thomas Erlewine*

Vengeance Is Mine / Oct. 11, 2000 / Black Market ◆◆◆◆
While many rappers make their living by making up stories about crime, X-Raided doesn't have to. Currently serving a 30-plus year prison sentence in California, he has plenty of his own stories to tell, and most of them aren't pretty. *Vengeance Is Mine* was recorded with an illegally acquired DAT recorder, and despite its lack of studio polish, it is a fascinating and challenging chronicle of prison life in America. "Write What I See" describes the drudgery life behind bars with painstaking detail. On "Hold On," X-Raided shows some perspective, looking back on the twisted road that led him to a jail cell. Although an artistic success, *Vengeance Is Mine* was created with more than a little controversy. The rapper is being sued by his victim's family under the "Son of Sam" law, and tougher prison regulations mean that this could be his last album. Wherever you stand on the legal issues surrounding his work, the fact remains that X-Raided's music is a creative success. *Vengeance Is Mine* is a brutally honest look at the consequences of a man's actions, as well as a stark depiction of a reality that most of us would rather ignore. —*Jon Azpiri*

● **X-Ology: The Best of X-Raided** / Aug. 14, 2001 / Black Market ◆◆◆◆

Xzibit (Alvin Nathaniel Joiner)

West Coast Rap, Hardcore Rap

West Coast heavyweight Xzibit expanded his following with a series of increasingly superstar-laced albums beginning in the late '90s, ultimately aligning himself with Cali kingpin Dr. Dre at the decade's end. Years before, Xzibit began as a member of the Likwit Crew, a loose collective of West Coast rappers including the Alkaholiks and King T. After touring with them in 1995, Loud Records released the feisty young rapper's debut album, *At the Speed of Life* (1996). The album became an underground hit, and when Xzibit released his follow-up, *40 Dayz & 40 Nightz* (1998), he was again heralded one of the West Coast's most promising talents.

Xzibit's big break came when he joined Snoop Dogg for the Dre-produced coast-to-coast hit "Bitch Please." Next, he appeared on the posse song "Some L.A. Niggaz" from Dre's *2001* (1999) album, yet another high-profile appearance. By this time, Dre had obviously recognized Xzibit's talent and invited the young rapper to criss-cross America during summer 2000 with the massive Up in Smoke tour, which featured Snoop, Eminem, and Ice Cube, among many others. That winter, Loud released Xzibit's biggest-budget album yet, the Dre-executive-produced *Restless* (2000), which boasted the single "X."

The song became the rapper's biggest hit yet but didn't top the charts or break him into heavy rotation at either urban radio or MTV.

Two years later, Xzibit returned with another big-budget superstar-laced album, *Man vs Machine* (2002), and yet again he fell a bit short of mainstream success. Even so, Xzibit remained as hardcore as ever and continued to collaborate with his closest West Coast colleagues, primarily Ras Kass, Saafir, and tha Liks, along with bigger names like Snoop and Eminem. His allegiance to the West Coast and those he came up with continued to win him much respect from his fans, who remained dedicated if not massive in number. —*Jason Birchmeier*

At the Speed of Life / Oct. 1, 1996 / Loud ◆◆◆
Xzibit's debut album *At the Speed of Life* is an excellent mixture of hardcore showcases for his lyrical virtuosity and ruminative, reflective hip-hop ballads. Though his rhyming skills are impeccable, the production from tha Alkaholiks' E-Swift, Muggs, and Diamond D gives the album the musical weight it needs to keep it interesting throughout the album. —*Leo Stanley*

40 Dayz & 40 Nightz / Aug. 25, 1998 / RCA ◆◆◆◆
The dysfunctional member of the Likwit Crew once again re-emerged to lyrically decapitate fake MCs. Xzibit's verbal asperity and rough, blunted diction is unmistakable. The sophomore jinx is null and void as Xzibit rips line after line over a grab bag of sizzling tracks. Sir Jinx and Xzibit combine production duties on the haunting "Torture Chamber," which incorporates elements of Ice Cube's "When Will They Shoot." The propensity at which Rass Kass, Saafir, and Xzibit drop bombs over "3 Card Molly" is sick, with each flipping an exceptional verse. Another gem is the marvelously crafted, Jesse West-produced "What U See Is What U Get" in which Xzibit touches all bases over a fluctuating piano and synthesizer track. On "Handle Your Business," Xzibit and Defari coalesce to show and prove for Cali over an expansive, well-constructed track from DJ Pen One. In addition, Xzibit gives you a survival guide for the City of Angels with "Los Angeles Times." When the Likwit Crew convenes on a cut, the results are usually splendid, and "Let It Rain" is no exemption to that rule. The Liks, King T, and Xzibit drench this E-Swift track, with Tash shining in grand fashion. A newcomer to the Likwit family, Montageone touches down on the flame-broiled "Recycled Assassins." Also, Xzibit brings the heat in ridiculous ways on "Focus" and "Deeper." *40 Dayz & 40 Nightz* is sure to whet your appetite with a nonstop accumulation of lyrics and a prolific variety of production. —*Matt Conaway*

● **Restless** / Dec. 12, 2000 / Loud ◆◆◆◆
It's only appropriate that Xzibit's highly anticipated, and often-delayed, *Restless* concluded hip-hop's millennial melting pot. After all, Xzibit's association with Dr. Dre and his Aftermath regime have attached very lofty expectations to *Restless;* X was publicly anointed as the next MC expected to blow up. Surely, with Dre as executive producer and guest shots from Eminem, Snoop Dogg, and Dre himself, Xzibit was virtually assured of acquiring the mainstream success that eluded him on previous efforts (*At the Speed of Life* and *40 Dayz & 40 Nightz*). Thanks largely to Dre's knob-twisting input, *Restless* became aural kin to Dre's own *2001* comeback vehicle, as the head-nod factor is immediately established on "Front to Back," and the heavenly synth stabs "X" and "Get Your Walk On." The main flaw in *Restless'* formula lies primarily with Xzibit's extensive list of guest collaborators. While contributions from Dre ("U Know"), Snoop ("D.N.A."), and Eminem ("Don't Approach Me") are all welcomed, appearances from DJ Quik and KRS-One, among many others, take the focus off Xzibit's formidable lyrical boasting, which precludes *Restless* from forming a desired level of cohesiveness. On "X," Xzibit pledges to "Rearrange the game with my rugged sound," and he periodically delivers on that promise. However, it would have taken nothing short of a masterpiece for Xzibit to appease hip-hop's finicky masses. And while *Restless* isn't the crowning achievement many predicted, it is X to the Z's most consistent effort to date. —*Matt Conaway*

Man vs Machine / Oct. 1, 2002 / Columbia ◆◆◆
Four albums deep, Xzibit's presence on the microphone rivals that of the better MCs of the latter day. However, on *Man vs Machine*, Xzibit seems to have lost some of the edge on his lyrical blade, which once tested in underground fires more than a half-decade before he hit the mainstream in 1999. The man who brought listeners "Paparazzi," "Foundation" (from his 1996 debut, *At the Speed of Life*), and "What U See Is What U Get" (from the 1998 release *40 Dayz & 40 Nightz*) managed to avoid the sophomore slump, but instead found the junior jinx with the disappointing 2000 release of *Restless*, even

with Dr. Dre in his corner. While X is still in cahoots with the good Dre here, unfortunately *Man vs Machine* is a continuation of his lackluster spiral rather than the masterpiece that X fans thought to be inevitable when he linked up with the likes of Dre, Snoop Dogg, and Eminem in the Y2K. Things start off with dark zest on the cleverly worded and sinisterly composed "Release Date," produced not by Dre but by East Coaster Rockwilder. Dre chimes in with lyrics for the awkward and clunky "Symphony in X Major" and beats for the delightfully raunchy "Choke Me, Spank Me" and the slightly above-workaday "Losin' Your Mind" featuring Snoop Dogg. Also, taking a somewhat shameful page out of P. Diddy's book, producer Jellyroll turns to early-'80s Toto ("Africa") for inspiration on the painfully inane "Heart of Man." Things pick up some on the Dre camp's retort to a Jermaine Dupri dis on the Eminem-produced "My Name" (featuring some patented Slim Shady punch-lines and a G-hook from Nate Dogg) and the cross-continental banger "BK to LA" featuring Brownsville Sluggers M.O.P. The heartfelt ode to his mother ("Missin' U") notwithstanding, after the floss and gloss of this release is peeled away, there's a lot more of Xzibit the MC caught in the machine of the hip-hop industry than there is of Xzibit the gifted man. —*M.F. DiBella*

Ya Kid K (Manuela Barbara Moasco Kamosi)

b. 1973, Zaire
Pop-Rap, Club/Dance

Ya Kid K was born Manuela Barbara Moasco Kamosi in Zaire, 1973. By the time she was 11, Kamosi had moved to Belgium. From there she traveled to Chicago, arriving in the Windy City just in time for the mid-'80s underground house music boom. Kamosi ingratiated herself into the scene, eventually taking the rap name Ya Kid K. After moving back to Antwerp, Ya Kid K started rapping with the local Fresh Beat Productions crew. (FBP were well known as one of the initial groups in the frit-hop scene, which was what rapping in Flemish came to be known as.) At the same time, would-be techno producer and transplanted American Jo Bogaert (real name: Thomas de Quincy) was shopping his demo of music that fused house rhythms with hip-hop vocals and attitude. It found its way to Ya Kid K and Welshman MC Eric (last name: Martin), and the two quickly united with Bogaert to form Technotronic. Technotronic's single "Pump up the Jam" was an international smash in 1989. Featuring Ya Kid's laconic, somewhat androgynous vocals over an insistent 4/4 beat and pulsating synths, the song was the embodiment of Bogaert's hip-house formula. But in a classic case of record-business tomfoolery, Ya Kid K was almost shut out of stardom. Despite K's lead rap on "Pump up the Jam," Bogaert had hired South African model Felly to appear on the cover of Technotronic's debut, as well as in the "Pump up the Jam" video, lip-synching raps in a language she did not speak. Controversy ensued, and both Ya Kid K and MC Eric were featured in the videos for the sound-alike follow-up singles "Get Up! (Before the Night Is Over)" and "Rockin' Over the Beat."

K went on to contribute a rap to Belgian rap crew Hi Tek 3's 1990 hit "Spin That Wheel." She also did what any newly minted celebrity would do: she contributed a song to the soundtrack for *Teenage Mutant Ninja Turtles II*. "Awesome" appeared in August of 1991 and led up to the release of her solo debut. In 1992, at the world-weary age of 19, Ya Kid K issued *One World Nation*. Led by the Technotronic cast-off single, "Move This," the album received a brief boost when the song was used in a wide-ranging campaign for Revlon cosmetics. But despite the popularity of similar dance acts like C+C Music Factory and Real McCoy, Technotronic and Ya Kid K were old news, and *One World Nation* failed to sell. There was, of course, the comeback album. 1995's hopefully titled *Recall* failed to help anyone remember the group, and once again Technotronic disbanded. Not much was heard from Ya Kid K until she resurfaced with a guest rap on *Life Transmission*, the 2001 album from Belgian avant-rockers DAAU. —*Johnny Loftus*

● **One World Nation** / Nov. 3, 1992 / SBK ✦✦✦✦
Ya Kid K rose to fame as the rapper and vocalist for Belgian house act Technotronic, and provided vocals for classic early-'90s hits such as "Pump up the Jam" (even though she wasn't featured in the video) and "Get Up! (Before the Night Is Over)." Two years after the Technotronic album cooled down, one of the album's tracks, "Move This," was used in a Revlon commercial, became a Top Ten pop hit, and was featured (in remixed form) as the premiere single for Ya Kid K's solo album, *One World Nation*. The album is an intoxicating mix of dance, house, hip-hop, and pop, although most of the tracks, such as "Let This Housebeat Drop" and "Jump It Out," lean more toward house, and "You Told Me Sex" echoes techno. The end result is a thoroughly well-produced set that showcases Ya Kid K not only as an engaging rapper but also as an effective singer with a sweet singing voice, evident on the sparse ballad "Come Back Home" and the soulful, irresistible standout "Risky Business." What is an enigma, however, is why this album, which is rife with socially and politically themed lyrics, failed to ignite the charts. The album's second single, "That Man," was arguably one of the funkiest and catchiest songs to

hit the airwaves in 1992, but completely failed to become the hit it should have been. Perhaps the reason is because grunge and gangsta rap took over around the time of this album's release, even though other dance acts—such as Haddaway, CeCe Peniston, and Real McCoy—managed to score massive pop/dance hits at around the same time. *One World Nation* is a surprisingly good album filled with intelligent dance, soul, and pop songs that pulls off its lofty ambitions. It is truly a mystery why this well-produced and engaging set failed to even slightly dent the charts or impact airwaves. —*Jose F. Promis*

Yaggfu Front

f. 1991, North Carolina
Group / Hip-Hop, Club/Dance

This funk and jazz-rap combo all grew up in North Carolina. Spin 4th, Jingle Bel, and D'Ranged & Damaged recorded their debut album, *Action Packed Adventure*, and it appeared on Mercury Records in 1994. —*John Bush*

● **Action Packed Adventure** / 1994 / Mercury ✦✦✦✦
This trio's debut album has turned a lot of heads in the underground hip-hop scene, with their strange lyrical style and funky breakbeats. The sound is something between Das EFX and the Pharcyde, yet something all their own too. Notable tracks are "Frontline," where the group talks about guys who use money and glamorous things as their front to attract women, and "Left Field," where each member takes the role of a different character, all speaking on their theories as to why they can't seem to get a girl. All in all, this is a great album, and probably even worth the import prices you'll have to pay to pick it up. —*Brad Mills*

Yankee B. (Joseph Hannam)

b. 1975, Waterhouse, Kingston, Jamaica
Raggae, East Coast Rap, Dancehall

Jamaican-born rapper Yankee B. emerged from New York City with a fresh raggae/rap sound that incorporated elements of dancehall, East Coast rap, and even jungle techno. Born Joseph Hannam in a subsection of Kingston, Jamaica, Yankee B. grew up during a period of turmoil and witnessed first-hand the violent feuding between political parties in his area. His parents moved to the Jamaica Queens region of New York City when he was in his teens, and in the process he was exposed to the exciting first efforts of the Native Tongues collective as well as upcoming rappers like Nasty Nas and the Wu-Tang Clan. This, combined with the dancehall and raggae he had heard in Kingston, inspired him to try his hand at rapping. After a few years he began to release demos, and soon his first single, "Send Threat," was being released through Jamaica's Stone Love label. He built enough of a fan base in New York to get the attention of DJ Bobby Konders, who began to spin Yankee's "Sexy for Sure" single on his radio show. The track was a success, and soon he was releasing singles regularly through Massive B Records and building a large local following.

A show with Beenie Man put him in contact with Gee Street Records, and by 1998 he had signed with the label and released his solo debut, *Mucho Dinero*. Collecting his Massive B singles as well as several new tracks, the record was a hit on the dancehall charts and even briefly made a dent on R&B radio with "That Feeling," a remake of Marvin Gaye's "Sexual Healing." Despite his success, he didn't follow with another album, but did keep active on a number of compilation tracks, including a memorable duet with Big Punisher on *The Year of the Backslap*. —*Bradley Torreano*

● **Mucho Dinero** / Jul. 28, 1998 / Gee Street ✦✦✦
New Yorker-via-Jamaica Yankee B.'s debut album, a stream of hip-hop-accented dancehall, doesn't bring anything particularly new to the genre (the

gruff toasting and boasting, classic street beats and rhythms, and a sense of historical awareness are all here), but with a sharp insight into the blending of the two not-so-disparate worlds, *Mucho Dinero* achieves a cultural bridge that plays the mainstream more forcefully than any of its contemporaries. Yankee B. parades guest MCs and rap riffs more readily than his peers, too, ultimately giving the album equal doses of R&B suavity and reggae roughness. It just all sounds a bit redundant, with one song title merely supplementing another as the tunes tread familiar ground. Check out the traditional sway of "Live By the Gun" and "That Feeling" (a rewrite of Marvin Gaye's "Sexual Healing"), though; these are late-'90s hip-hop/dancehall at its most swaggeringly potent.—*Michael Gallucci*

YB
b. Denmark
Vocals / Foreign Rap, Hip-Hop
He raps in English and if it wasn't for the occasional odd pronunciation, he could be from the Bronx, but YB is in fact Danish. He released one album of dance-friendly party rap in 1992, *I Am What I Am*. YB has also worked with a number of high-profile Danish producers, including Soulshock, Cutfather, and Mo'Wax veterans the Prunes. Some of his work has also appeared under the name Obi. —*Wade Kergan*

- **I Am What I Am** / Oct. 27, 1992 / Savage ✦✦✦
At the start of the 1980s, hip-hop was a New York phenomenon that was dominated by MCs from Harlem and the South Bronx—at the end of the 1980s, hip-hop was an international phenomenon that was as popular in Brazil as it was in Sweden. Many rappers from Europe and Latin America don't rap in English at all; a big part of hip-hop is being "down with the 'hood," and if your 'hood is in Milan, Italy, you're likely to rap in Italian. If your 'hood is in Rio de Janeiro, you're likely to rap in Portuguese. However, many Danish MCs have preferred to rap in English; Denmark's YB, in fact, raps in English exclusively on *I Am What I Am*. A lot of Danes learn to speak English fluently in Denmark's public school system, and YB (short for Youngblood) has no problem rhyming in perfect English on this solid alternative rap effort. If you didn't know better, you would assume he was from the U.S.; his rhyming style owes a lot to American alternative rappers like De La Soul, A Tribe Called Quest, and the Jungle Brothers. Like those MCs, YB is quite musical. Dance music (especially house) is an influence, and jazz is an even greater influence—Lee Morgan, Lou Donaldson, Grant Green, and Grover Washington Jr. are among the jazz greats he samples on this CD, which, for the most part, was produced by SoulShock & Cutfather. *I Am What I Am* wasn't a big seller in the U.S., although the album makes it clear that you don't have be American to have strong rapping skills. —*Alex Henderson*

Ying Yang Twins
f. Atlanta, GA
Group / Gangsta Rap, Southern Rap, Party Rap, Dirty South
Atlanta's party rap duo Ying Yang Twins scored a hit with the single "Whistle While You Twurk," which received nationwide airplay on urban and crossover radio stations. Their full-length debut album, *Thug Walkin'*, appeared later in 2000. —*Heather Phares*

- **Thug Walkin'** / Apr. 25, 2000 / Collipark ✦✦
Those looking for consciousness hip-hop should probably pass on *Thug Walkin'*. Ying Yang Twins rap about blunts and broads—and they aren't ashamed of it. Tracks like "Ballin' G" deal with sex, women, and drugs, while "The Dope Game" deals with drugs, sex, and women. The duo has nothing new to say, but they do say it cleverly at times. Unfortunately, the repetition of the same themes on *Thug Walkin'* quickly grows old. Ironically, the one thing that Ying Yang lacks is balance. —*Jon Azpiri*

Alley . . . Return of the Ying Yang Twins / Mar. 26, 2002 / Koch International ✦✦
Ying Yang Twins' sophomore feat finds the Atlanta duo playing it by the books, offering very little to inspire or impress. D-Roc and Kaine may word themselves in a way that could catch your attention, yet their rhymes very rarely amount to anything more then sex, drugs, and women. "Say I Yi Yi" follows in the footsteps of *Thug Walkin'*s hit single, "Whistle While You Twurk," rehashing vapid rhyme schemes and routine beats. *Alley . . . Return of the Ying Yang Twins* features several guest appearances, yet these special guests add nothing to the overall generic flavor Ying Yang Twins churn out.

Alley . . . Return of the Ying Yang Twins has about as much appeal as one could expect from the overprocessed majority of the Southern hip-hop scene, and its mediocre format and inept lyrical value prove that Ying Yang Twins have not grown at all since their 2000 debut. —*Jason D. Taylor*

Yo-Yo (Yolanda Whitaker)
b. Aug. 4, 1971
Hip-Hop, Hardcore Rap, West Coast Rap
Yo-Yo (born Yolanda Whitaker) has been among the most sophisticated and unpredictable female rappers around. She doesn't take an overtly feminist tack but urges young women to show sexual restraint and use their minds as well as their bodies. Yo-Yo came out less embracing and more confrontational on *You Better Ask Somebody*, her 1993 album. There was little compromise in her rapping, or the record's mood. Where before she'd sometimes seemed conciliatory, this time she was stark and combative, particularly in her demands for respect. In 1996, she returned with *Total Control*; *Ebony* followed two years later. —*Ron Wynn*

Make Way for the Motherlode / Mar. 19, 1991 / East West ✦✦✦✦✦
As positive as Queen Latifah but as abrasive in her delivery as MC Lyte, Yo-Yo showed some potential on her debut album, *Make Way for the Motherlode*. The decent, if uneven, CD (which Ice Cube produced with Sir Jinx and Del tha Funkee Homosapien) was more of a critical success than a commercial success. The hip-hop press was quick to praise Yo-Yo, who urges young women to practice responsible sexuality, respect themselves and demand respect from men. On "Girl, Don't Be No Fool," Yo-Yo stresses that women shouldn't allow men to physically abuse them under *any* circumstances—a message that definitely needed to be heard, although regrettably, the song doesn't distinguish between the "dogs" and "good guys." Cube has memorable cameos on "What Can I Do?" and "You Can't Play With My Yo-Yo," but his presence wasn't enough to make *Motherlode* anything more than a moderate hit. —*Alex Henderson*

- **Black Pearl** / Jun. 1992 / East West ✦✦✦✦✦
Led by "Home Girl Don't Play Dat" and the title track, the message on *Black Pearl* was so vital that this was onetime putting out a so-called clean version made some sense. —*Ron Wynn*

You Better Ask Somebody / Jun. 22, 1993 / East West ✦✦

Total Control / Oct. 29, 1996 / Elektra/Asylum ✦✦✦

Yoga Frog (Ritchie Desuasido)
b. 1974
Scratching / Turntablism
Yoga Frog was one of the lesser-known members of the world-renowned Bay Area DJ collective the Invisibl Skratch Piklz. He rarely performed with the group in public or on record, instead concentrating more on the collective's business affairs. Born Ritche Desuasido on September 26, 1974, he started scratching in a Daly City-based DJ crew called Second to None before hooking up with the Piklz in 1996. Yoga Frog mostly practiced with the more experienced DJs of the group, and though his official performing debut was promised sometime in 2000, his only public work with the Piklz was on one of the home videos periodically posted on the group's website as "Turntable TV." The Piklz officially disbanded in 2000, and Yoga Frog busied himself with Thud Rumble, the management/production/distribution company he co-founded with fellow Pikl DJ Q-Bert. —*Steve Huey*

Yohimbe Brothers
f. 2002
Group / Illbient, Turntablism
Naming themselves after the African root used to enhance male sexual performance, longtime collaborators Vernon Reid and DJ Logic united in 2002 as Yohimbe Brothers and released *Front End Lifter*, a dense album of guitar-fueled turntablism. The two New York-based artists first came together in the early '90s as founding members of the Black Rock Coalition. At the time, Reid led Living Colour, a short-lived yet enormously successful hard rock band driven largely by his guitar playing, and Logic participated in the band Eye & I. Following the demise of both Living Colour and Eye & I, the two artists partook in numerous projects, both mutually and independently, before finally making their partnership official in 2002 as Yohimbe Brothers with

the release of *Front End Lifter* on Ropeadope Records. A month-long cross-country tour followed in October. *—Jason Birchmeier*

● **Front End Lifter** / Sep. 10, 2002 / Ropeadope ✦✦✦✦✦
Though you get the sense *Front End Lifter* is simply a good-time side project for free-willed New York artists Vernon Reid and DJ Logic, the resulting album is so staggering you really wish the duo would get together more often. Over the course of 15 relatively brief, incredibly dense, and surprisingly varied compositions, the guitarist and turntablist showcase remarkable creativity, offering much more than the expected—guitar riffing over turntable scratching. In fact, there's very little, if any, of that; rather, the two compose what very well could be thought of as sound collages or free jazz-style illbience. The two invite along a long list of guests—bassists, drummers, vocalists, rappers, saxophonists, violinsts, and more—yet somehow make all of these musicians sound like little more than some of the many samples used to craft these chaotic soundscapes. And the duo does all this in a very silly kind of way, adopting a Handsome Boy Modeling School-style demeanor. From the album title to the song titles, not the mention the Yohimbe reference, everything here seems as though it's a double entendre. Thus what seems, musically, like a very heady project comes off as a good-time side project. And given the reputation of Reid and Logic, two prolific yet willingly nomadic artists of undeniable genius, *Front End Lifter* is no more than a one-off project. Even so, it's a marvelous one that transcends the usual contexts these guys work in. Reid will probably forever be known as the guy from the late-'80s hard rock band Living Colour, and Logic will probably remain known as the turntablist of choice among the New York avant jazz scene; however, *Front End Lifter* couldn't be more distant from either of those trappings, but are instead fun-spirited, sexploitative illbience in all its unlikely glory. *—Jason Birchmeier*

Yomo & Maulkie

f. 1991, Los Angeles, CA
Group / Hardcore Rap, Hip-Hop
A talented but little-known hardcore rap duo, Yomo & Maulkie were down with the members of N.W.A but had more in common with Public Enemy lyrically. Despite the N.W.A association, Yomo & Maulkie were far from gangsta rap. The MCs both came out of L.A., where they signed with Eazy-E's Ruthless label in the early '90s. In 1991, Eazy served as executive producer on their superb debut album, *Are U Xperienced?*, which was distributed by Atlantic and took its name from Jimi Hendrix's famous debut album. Unfortunately, the album fell through the cracks, and commercial success continued to elude Yomo & Maulkie. *—Alex Henderson*

● **Are U Xperienced?** / Sep. 17, 1991 / Ruthless ✦✦✦
Because *Are U Experienced?* was produced by N.W.A's DJ Yella and had Eazy-E for its executive producer, some listeners might have thought that Yomo & Maulkie were a gangsta rap duo. But in fact, this promising but underexposed CD is far from gangsta rap. The production may have an N.W.A-ish quality—Yella obviously learned a few things from Dr. Dre—but the lyrics and the rapping are closer to Public Enemy. Much like PE, Yomo & Maulkie bring an angry sociopolitical perspective to "Society's Relentless," "Mockingbird," "Watch Out Black Folks," and "Glory." But they also bring in some psychedelic imagery—*Are U Experienced?* was named after Jimi Hendrix's legendary debut album, and "Soul Psychedelic Side" underscores their appreciation of Sly Stone and early Funkadelic. Focused, intelligent, riveting, and risk taking, this CD should have been a huge hit. But sadly, the vast majority of hip-hoppers have never even heard of Yomo & Maulkie. *—Alex Henderson*

Young Black Teenagers

Group / Hip-Hop, Pop-Rap
Despite their name, the Young Black Teenagers (YBT) weren't ethnically black at all—four of them were white, and another of them Puerto Rican descent. The concept struck some in the hip-hop community as ridiculous and even offensive, but the group was sincerely attempting to pay tribute to the black culture they loved and identified with. What's more, they had the backing of Public Enemy and their production team, the Bomb Squad; in fact, YBT was the first act signed to Hank Shocklee's Sound of Urban Listeners label, founded in 1990. Young Black Teenagers were composed of MCs Kamron, Firstborn, ATA, and Tommy Never (the first three of whom all had DJ experience), plus full-time DJ Skribble. Kamron had previously worked as a live DJ alongside members of PE, which was instrumental in landing the group a record deal. They debuted in 1991 with an eponymous album, which spun off several singles, including "Nobody Knows Kelli" (a humorous tribute to *Married With Children*), "Proud to Be Black," and "To My Donna" (which roasted Madonna for lifting the PE track "Security of the First World" as the basis for "Justify My Love"). YBT next moved up to MCA and released their biggest hit, "Tap the Bottle," which appeared on their 1993 sophomore effort, *Dead Enz Kids Doin' Lifetime Bidz*. However, a falling out with the PE camp left the group in the lurch, and they eventually disbanded. DJ Skribble went on to greater fame in the late '90s as an MTV in-house DJ, appearing on a number of network productions while continuing to DJ at clubs around New York. *—Steve Huey*

Young Black Teenagers / Feb. 19, 1991 / Soul ✦✦✦✦✦
In the early 1990s, a rap group stirred some controversy by calling itself Young Black Teenagers. The name wouldn't have made a difference if they really were black, but in fact, the Teenagers were actually white. Some MCs were angry and resentful, while others realized that YBT was actually making a pro-black statement. Among the quintet's supporters were Public Enemy, and in fact, this impressive CD (which had a cover modeled after *Meet the Beatles*) was produced by the team that had been producing PE and Ice Cube, the Bomb Squad. Anyone who dismissed YBT as a mere novelty didn't seriously listen to "Punks, Lies & Videotape," "Mack Daddy Don of the Underworld," or "Daddy Called Me Niga Cause I Likeded to Rhyme," all of which prove that their rapping skills were quite strong. Like House of Pain and 3rd Bass, YBT was a white group that rejected pop-rap, and it is the hardcore approach that wins out on this rewarding and provocative disc. *—Alex Henderson*

Dead Enz Kidz Doin' Lifetime Bidz / Feb. 2, 1993 / MCA ✦✦✦

Young Bleed

b. Lousiana
Southern Rap, Gangsta Rap, Dirty South
Like many artists on No Limit, Young Bleed is a native of Louisiana. He was signed to the label after earning the attention of No Limit founder and CEO Master P, who had Young Bleed rap on the *I'm Bout It* soundtrack in early 1997. Around that time, his debut album, *My Balls & My Word*, was put on the No Limit schedule. It was finally released in January of 1998 and went gold within a month of its release, reaching the Top Ten on the pop album charts. *My Own* followed in late 1999 and didn't do as well commercially, released by Priority rather than No Limit. Young Bleed returned in 2002 as Young Bleed Carleone with *Vintage*, the inaugural release by Da'tention Home Records. *—Stephen Thomas Erlewine*

My Balls & My Word / Jan. 20, 1998 / Priority ✦✦✦
There are a few moments of inspiration on Young Bleed's debut *My Balls & My Word*, but by and large, it's a conventional late-'90s gangsta record, with blunted beats, deep bass, and endless tales of violence and sex, gangs, and guns. The main problem is that the rappers and the production blindly follow convention without second-guessing it or adding their own spin to the material. The rhymes are fine, but nothing special, and there are the occasional dope beats, but simply aren't enough of them to make the album of interest to anyone outside of hardcore rap fans. *—Stephen Thomas Erlewine*

● **My Own** / Oct. 19, 1999 / Priority ✦✦✦✦
Young Bleed finds a new sound for himself after leaving Master P's No Limit label, moving toward a smoother style of hip-hop that accentuates his lyrical delivery. This album's production, courtesy of Da' Crime Lab, looks back to the soul-drenched sound of classic '70s funk (Curtis Mayfield, Isaac Hayes) for its inspiration, laying down a sedate layer of beats with the subtle inclusion of quick, scattered electro-style beats. With music such as this to rap over, Young Bleed keeps his quick, Southern-accented lyrics flowing at a relentless pace in a hushed tone that emanates a sense of calmness. In a way, this album sounds like a Southern version of the West Coast G-funk featured on the albums of rappers such as Too Short, Warren G, and DJ Quik. Furthermore, Young Bleed raps on the majority of his album, resulting in a refreshing alternative to his guest rapper-polluted affair on No Limit. The Southern rapper is good enough on the mic in terms of delivery, lyrics, and personality to hold his own on this album, which stays succinct at only 12 strong songs rather than 20-some tracks that rehash the same motifs over and over. By 1999, most Southern hip-hop artists still sounded a bit

amateur, but *My Own* finds Young Bleed sounding like a veteran on some truly fresh beats. —*Jason Birchmeier*

Young Disciples

Group / Acid Jazz, Alternative Rap

One of the finer groups of the early-'90s acid jazz scene, the short-lived Young Disciples featured Carleen Anderson (vocals, keyboards), Marc Nelson (bass, guitar, organ), and Femi Williams (percussion, programming). Their debut single came in 1990 with "Get Yourself Together," which was followed in 1991 by the Top 20 U.K. hit "Apparently Nothin'." *Road to Freedom*, the group's lone album (aided by appearances from Masta Ace, Maceo Parker, Fred Wesley, and Pee Wee Ellis) was released on Talkin' Loud in the U.K., and was issued in the States through Polygram. After the group folded, Anderson went solo; both Nelson and Williams continued background studio work. —*Andy Kellman*

● **Road to Freedom** / Jan. 26, 1993 / Polygram ✦✦✦✦

On their impressive debut, *Road to Freedom*, the fiercely political Young Disciples offer muscular funk garnished with jazz, hip-hop, and R&B flourishes. The majority of vocals are handled by Carleen Anderson, whose low, smoky voice at times brings to mind the likes of Chaka Khan, Anita Baker, and Oleta Adams. The production is clever and unpredictable; gospel organs open "Get Yourself Together" and then fade into the oncoming beats, while airy guitars introduce "Talkin' What I Feel" before pulling a similar about-face when confronted with some surging hip-hop rhythms. —*Jason Ankeny*

Young MC (Marvin Young)

b. May 10, 1967, London, England

Hip-Hop, Pop-Rap, West Coast Rap

Intelligent and middle class, rapper Marvin Young earned a degree in economics from USC, where he met Michael Ross and Matt Dike, cofounders of the fledgling Delicious Vinyl rap label. He made his debut as Young MC on the single "I Let 'Em Know." In 1989, Young collaborated with Tone-Loc on "Wild Thing," the first Top Ten pop hit for a black rapper, and the follow-up smash "Funky Cold Medina." Young stepped out on his own later in the year with the Top Ten smash "Bust a Move," a good-natured examination of romantic successes and failures spiced by his sense of humor and quick-tongued rapping. The song won a Grammy for Best Rap Performance, and its strong pop appeal helped the attendant album, *Stone Cold Rhymin'*, go platinum. The follow-up, "Principal's Office," was a humorous, everyday high school tale resembling a Chuck Berry plot and also climbed into the Top 40.

Following Young's success, he split acrimoniously from Delicious Vinyl, citing restrictions on his work and unwanted tinkering with his album; the label sued him for breach of contract and eventually settled out of court. Young signed with Capitol and released *Brainstorm* in 1991, expanding into message tracks promoting personal responsibility. The album didn't fare as well, and by 1993, audience tastes had shifted toward harder-edged hip-hop, rendering *What's the Flavor?* a flop. In late 2000, he attempted a return with *Ain't Going Out Like That* on the indie label Young Man Moving. It didn't make much of an impression in the rap world, but Young tried again in 2002 with *Engage the Enzyme*. —*Steve Huey*

★ **Stone Cold Rhymin'** / 1989 / Delicious Vinyl/Rhino ✦✦✦✦✦

Young MC wasn't given props at the time and he wasn't respected in the years following the release of his debut *Stone Cold Rhymin'*, largely because he worked entirely in the pop-rap/crossover vein. All the same, that's what's great about his debut, since it's exceptionally clever and effective, a wonderful combination of deft rhymes and skillful production. And there's no discounting Matt Dike, Michael Ross, the Dust Brothers, and engineer Mario Caldato Jr. (the latter two names are members of the Beastie Boys' inner circle), who make this record easily accessible, without a trace of guilt, even if it does sample from familiar sources. And, really, Young MC is a gifted rapper, spinning out rhymes with a deft touch and turning out rhymes much more clever than they should be. Yes, *Stone Cold Rhymin'* is a product of its time, particularly in its sound and lyrical references, but divorced from the Bush era, it comes off as one of the catchiest, friendliest pop-rap records and it's still an infectious party record years after its release. —*Stephen Thomas Erlewine*

Brainstorm / Aug. 5, 1991 / Capitol ✦✦✦

In hardcore hip-hop circles, more commercial rappers generally aren't thought of as having a lot of technique—the consensus is that they're getting over on their pop or R&B appeal rather than their rapping skills. After "Bust a Move"

became a major hit in the R&B market, Young MC was viewed suspiciously by b-boys. But make no mistake: the clean-cut L.A. rapper has considerable technique and could no doubt hold his own in a microphone battle. While his second album wasn't the hit that *Stone Cold Rhymin'* was, it's a decent, enjoyable effort with strong hooks and definite dancefloor appeal. Such congenial, R&B-ish fare as "That's the Way Love Goes," "Listen to the Beat of the Music," and "After School" obviously wasn't aimed at hardcore rap audiences, but leaves no doubt that Young MC could flow with the best. —*Alex Henderson*

Return of the 1 Hit Wonder / Jul. 22, 1997 / Overall ✦✦✦

Ain't Going Out Like That / Oct. 24, 2000 / Young Man Moving ✦✦✦

Engage the Enzyme / Aug. 6, 2002 / Stimulus ✦✦✦

Once, Young MC was a more clever Fresh Prince, a guy whose pop hits tapped the same middle-class themes without all the smarminess. Things might have worked out better if Young MC (aka Marvin Young) had been insufferable instead: while Will Smith was plugging his latest blockbuster film, *Men in Black 2*, with an accompanying single, Young was releasing this comeback on a small independent label to little fanfare. However, time and circumstances haven't eroded Young MC's mic skills. Still one of the wittiest rhymers around, he sounds like he's back to his old chart-topping form on *Engage the Enzyme*, which is full of tunes that back his sly observations with sturdy hooks. Of course, Young MC knows the odds against scoring another hit; "Stress Test" details the music industry's disinterest in his kinder, gentler approach. But that doesn't diminish the simple pleasures of "Unsigned Diva," a tale of bootylicious wannabe singers, or "Heatseeker," where the star tries to score at a club and is advised, "Young MC is much thinner/And he's got more hair." The album's finest moment, however, is "Crucial"—which not only became hip-hop's best 9/11 song on its release but also easily bettered most of the attempts in any musical genre to capture that fateful day. Unencumbered by the conspiracy-theory paranoia of many of Young MC's peers, or the moral relativism of the rock world, "Crucial" is a straightforward recounting of the attacks and their aftermath that isn't afraid to blame the terrorists or display some authentic patriotism. "I never really been a big fan of war/But if we don't fight now, what will we fight for?" demands Young MC; the irony is that a belief shared by so many Americans could have so little chance of reaching them, as there was scant chance hip-hop radio would have any use for the song or its sentiments. Yet those who seek it out—along with the rest of *Engage the Enzyme*—will find it more than worth their trouble. —*Dan LeRoy*

Young Prodeje

Hip-Hop

After flexing his producing skills with the likes of Havoc & Prodeje and South Central Cartel (the latter being a project he got together in 1991), being featured on the Def Jam soundtrack for *The Show*, and collaborating with the Dogg Pound and Ice-T, among others, Young Prodeje has been around, to say the least. But after paying his dues, working with others, and always having to share the mic, he finally went on his own in 1999 with the album *Diablo Flame-On: Movie on Wax*. —*Mike DaRonco*

● **Diablo Flame-On: Movie on Wax** / Jul. 27, 1999 / Damian ✦✦✦

A member of South Central Cartel and the younger brother of Prodeje (also of SCC), Young Prodeje worked with Spice 1 and Ice-T before gaining his own solo album. Produced by his brother, *Diablo Flame-On* includes hardcore raps and street styles, from the cut-up single "Pass the Mic" to the ballad-of-sorts "Playground" (featuring LV). —*Keith Farley*

Young Zee

East Coast Rap, Hardcore Rap

With his charismatic yelp and brash personality, Young Zee is the best-recognized member of the Outsidaz, a large hip-hop crew that became the first act signed to Ruff Life Records. What he isn't always recognized for is his solo career, where he has produced several singles and even released a record in the mid-'90s. He first garnered notice in 1995, when his "Everybody Get" single became the first major release from the Outsidaz collective. Next was an appearance on the Fugees' "Cowboys," one of the tracks on their surprise hit record *The Score*. This appearance was enough to convince indie label Perspective to sign the rapper for an album, and by the end of the year he had dropped *Musical Meltdown*. Although the disc made little headway, the Outsidaz's reputation continued to grow in underground hip-hop until they had become one of the most sought-after groups in the East Coast scene. That's when Ruffhouse Records stepped in, signing the collective in 1999. Zee made an appearance on Rah Digga's first solo album around the same time, before discovering that labelhead Chris Schwartz had left Ruffhouse and started Ruff Life Records. Schwartz contacted the group about switching sides, and by the end of the year their contract had been bought out by the upstart label. The Outsidaz released *Night Life* in 2000, an angry EP that was heavy on bravado and featured battle tracks between one another. Zee began to increase his solo output as well, lending tracks to several compilations in 2001. The next year he reached his greatest exposure yet when his solo track, "That's My Nigga fo' Real," was included on the smash-hit soundtrack to Eminem's film *8 Mile.* —*Bradley Torreano*

● **Musical Meltdown** / 1995 / Perspective ✦✦✦
Young Zee attracted some attention through his appearance on the Fugees' "Cowboys," which didn't quite prepare his audience for the sound of his debut, *Musical Meltdown.* On the basis of the record, Young Zee has more in common with the stripped-down, minimalist funk of rappers like Redman, not the organic eclectic funk of the Fugees. Nevertheless, *Musical Meltdown* is refreshing. Young Zee consciously avoids many standard gangsta rap clichés—he openly dimisses them on several tracks, as a matter of fact— which gives the album a spark. That doesn't mean it's without flaws—he's an average rapper, without a particularly distinctive flair for rhymes or beats. Even so, he delivers the goods—just don't expect something revolutionary. —*Stephen Thomas Erlewine*

Youngbloodz

f. Atlanta, GA
Group / Hip-Hop, Southern Rap
At Atlanta's Miller Grove Middle School, two young wannabe rappers met up with each other, left their individual rap crews, and joined forces to become Youngbloodz. Sean Paul, who claims that rapping is second nature and easier than conversation, and J-Bo, the DJ of the two, were heavily tied in with the Atlanta rap/production posse known as the Attic. While they honed their skills and showcased their talent for various record labels, opening the door for the Attic crew to get noticed, it took only one meeting with LaFace A&R executive, PA, to sign the Youngbloodz duo. *Against Da Grain* is their full-length debut. —*Roxanne Blanford*

● **Against Da Grain** / Sep. 14, 1999 / LaFace ✦✦✦
Against Da Grain is a collection of danceclub-ready anthems packed with familiar ghetto boasts and party grooves. The Atlanta, GA-based duo Youngbloodz employs guitar-driven tracks layered with pulsing bass rhythms and laid-back beats to complement their easily plied Southern drawl rap attacks. The production crew on this release includes worthy contributions from the Attic and the Dungeon Family, conglomerates of local rappers and producers providing beats and backing rhymes. While this makes for a homegrown project certain to please fans of the Southern bounce sound, it also creates an abundance of soundalike tracks, making this debut relatively indistinguishable from other recordings out of the same region. —*Roxanne Blanford*

Da Youngsta's

f. Philadelphia, PA
Group / Pop-Rap, Hip-Hop
The precocious Philadelphia trio consisting of Tajj, Tarik, and Qu'ran may have been the most talented teen rappers ever to grace a hip-hop stage. However, the untimely release of their March 1992 debut *Something 4 Da Youngsta's* coincided with the preteen pop-rap phenomenon that was Kriss Kross. Da Youngsta's first release showed the trio's incredible promise, especially considering that they penned their own lyrics in stark contrast to the Mack Daddy and the Daddy Mack. The trio's amazingly advanced skills raised the eyebrows of many a hip-hop luminary and their sophomore release, *The Aftermath,* unleashed an angrier lyrical style combined with a variety of sparkling beats. The all-star production squad included the likes of DJ Premier, Pete Rock, C.L. Smooth, and the Beatnuts. The track "Wild Child" best represented Da Youngsta's newfound brasher leanings, but it was the rough, rhythmic "Crewz Pop" that rewarded the group with a respectful following. The strength of *The Aftermath* brought praise to Da Youngsta's from their much older peers. The trio recorded their third album in three years in 1994, this time on a larger label, East West (a subsidiary of Atlantic Records). For *No Mercy,* the Illy Philly threesome called upon the production talents of

Marley Marl and K-Def as they continued to develop their styles. The trio continued to paint grim pictures of urban life through clever wordplay and storytelling, but it was the smoothed-out "Hip Hop Ride," an ode to the hip-hop tradition, that turned out to be the most successful cut on the album. After collaborating with Mobb Deep for the single "Bloodshed and War" in 1995, Da Youngsta's mostly disappeared from hip-hop radar screens. —*Michael Di Bella*

Somethin 4 Da Youngsta's / 1992 / East West ✦✦
The Aftermath / Apr. 20, 1993 / East West ✦✦✦✦
With Mobb Deep and Illegal at one end of the spectrum (the more authentically streetwise one), Kris Kross and Chi-Ali on the (more commercially savvy) other, and Leaders of the New School occupying the eccentric, artistic center, the early '90s did not want for teen-aged rap artists. Philadelphia's Da Youngsta's was yet another trio of underage MCs who made a brief but fairly impressive splash on the hip-hop scene. Impressive enough, in fact, to draw the attention of some of the genre's major personalities. *The Aftermath* leans toward the street side of the divide, but has some of the artistic heft of L.O.N.S., mostly as a result of the production work of a quartet of heavyweights: the Beatnuts, Pete Rock, Marley Marl, and DJ Premier. Unlike the clear legitimacy that was immediately bestowed by the community upon Mobb Deep's Prodigy and Havoc, however, it is not always easy to take the relentlessly hardcore stance of Da Youngsta's seriously. First, though, it is somewhat superficial as a reason, the voice of at least one of the group's members was still stuck in puberty hell at the time the album was recorded. It is cartoonish, in a decidedly sinister way, to hear such a voice making physical threats and lyrical boasts. Second, Lawrence "L.G." Goodman, who oversees the proceedings (and comes up with some strong beats of his own), just happens to be father to two-thirds of the crew (the third member was a cousin). The fact that Da Youngsta's, in reality, were not exactly callous street urchins takes some of the wind and conviction out of their more menacing rhetoric. Those failings aside, the album still has a bevy of platinum moments, especially the Beatnuts track "Wild Child," Pete Rock's "Iz U Wit Me" and "Who's the Mic Wrecka," Premier's "Wake Em Up," and Goodman's own "Count It Off." —*Stanton Swihart*

● **No Mercy** / Sep. 20, 1994 / East West ✦✦✦✦✦
Some members of Da Youngsta's were so young during the making of *The Aftermath* that they were still waiting for their voices to fully change. It made for a few cringe-inducing moments—especially considering that the trio tried to talk tough for most of the album—on an otherwise tonal recording. Cracking voices posed no impediment to the group's sophomore effort, *No Mercy,* a considerably more mature album that takes them confidently beyond juvenilia. Gone for the most part are the exaggerated rebelliousness and hyperbole that marred the debut, and in their place is a welcome sense of realism. There is still some embellishment here and there, but on the whole, *No Mercy* is a great deal more genuine, mixing the few moments of impetuousness with celebrations of the city and the hip-hop lifestyle, and even a venture into ghetto romance ("Put Me On"). The album also has a more consistent sound, due to the less-cooks-in-the-kitchen approach. The legendary Marley Marl shares most of the production duties with Kevin "K-Def" Hansford, and although it is always a blow to lose the skills of a Pete Rock or DJ Premier, the two create an exquisite, jazz-slanted underground aesthetic that blends the gritty with the chill, a sound that lends itself to the more measured approach of Da Youngsta's this time around. The music is, ironically enough, less commercial as a result of this shift in tone and intent, but it makes for a better album in almost every way. —*Stanton Swihart*

Yukmouth

Vocals / West Coast Rap, Hardcore Rap, Gangsta Rap
Rapper Yukmouth first surfaced as one-half of the Oakland, CA-based duo the Luniz; debuting in 1995 with the album *Operation Stackola,* they launched a major hit with the single "I Got 5 on It." With the release of 1997's *Lunitik Musik,* Yukmouth rechristened himself Smoke-A-Lot, but took back his old name in time to make his solo debut a year later with *Thugged Out: The Albulation. Thug Lord: The New Testament* and *Block Shit* were issued in spring 2001. The following year, Yukmouth tried to further reconnect with his street roots with the ambitious *United Ghettos of America* album. —*Jason Ankeny*

● **Thugged Out: The Albulation** / Nov. 3, 1998 / Virgin ✦✦✦
Three years after splitting from the Luniz and partner Knumskull, West Coast rapper Yukmouth revealed himself to be a competent, thought-provoking

solo entertainer. His debut, *Thugged Out: The Albulation*, a double-CD, 28-track package, delivered straight-on, in-your-face rap narratives on urban warfare, sexual misadventure, reflections on parenting, and coming of age in his home town of Oakland, California. Yukmouth's rap lyrics range from the sentimental "Falling" and the expletive-laden "Stallion," to the comical. For the most part, he has kept pace with his gangsta rap contemporaries, essentially covering the same ground. Fortunately, groove-heavy bass lines, guest rappers MC Ren and Tech 9, as well as solid production redeemed this effort to make it actually listenable. — *Roxanne Blanford*

Thug Lord: The New Testament / Mar. 27, 2001 / Virgin ♦♦

The second album by Yukmouth is just a shadow of the rapper's previous work as a solo artist and with the group Luniz. Yukmouth spends most of his time on *Thug Lord* dissing other rappers rather than focusing on what he has to say. Tracks like "Regime Killers 2001" and "Oh! Boy" take aim at all the usual suspects: fake rappers and music execs who keep true rappers like himself down. There are a few highlights, however. "World's Most Wanted" cleverly interpolates the theme song from the soap opera *Young and the Restless*, and "Puffin' Lah" is a steel drum-filled ode to marijuana use. Despite the occasional bright spot, *Thug Lord* shows just how far Yukmouth has fallen since his days with Luniz. — *Jon Azpiri*

Yungstar

b. Houston, TX

Hip-Hop, Gangsta Rap, Hardcore Rap

Yungstar grew up on the west side of Houston and began rapping at age ten. In the early '90s, he began working with DenDen, CEO of Straight Profit Records. He first gained attention freestyling over tapes made by DJ Screw and emerged nationally with a guest appearance on Lil' Troy's "Wanna Be a Baller." Straight Profit released his debut album, *Throwed Yung Playa*, and it sold 40,000 copies before being picked up and re-released in a revised form by Epic Records in 2000. — *William Ruhlmann*

● **Throwed Yung Playa** / 2000 / Epic ♦♦♦

The practice of having guest rappers featured on recordings credited to others is well established and often serves as a means of introducing new talent. Indeed, Yungstar made his name as a featured rapper on Lil' Troy's "Wanna Be a Baller." But his debut album, initially released by Houston-based Straight Profit Records and reissued in this beefed-up version by Epic, takes the guest rapper trend to its logical absurdity: There are so many guests—no less than 22, with as many as six performing on a single track—that it's hard to hear much of the nominal headliner. The youthful-sounding Yungstar makes his most prominent appearance on "Knocking Pictures Off Da Wall" early on, but for the rest of the album Straight Profit CEO DenDen seems to be using the tracks to try out a succession of performers. They share several slang terms and an overall attitude of pride about their area, dubbed "The 3rd Coast" (i.e., the coast of the Gulf of Mexico). Refreshingly, they indulge in derogatory and obscene language and subject matter to only a limited extent; the album contains a parental advisory sticker, but it is far less offensive than much current rap. Still, it functions more as a various-artists sampler than as Yungstar's debut album, and the rappers come and go so quickly that none of them make a distinct impression. — *William Ruhlmann*

Throwed Yung Playa: Screwed / Jul. 20, 1999 / Straight Profit ♦♦

Throwed Yung Playas, Pt. 2 / Jun. 20, 2000 / Straight Profit ♦♦♦

Z

Zimbabwe Legit

Group / Alternative Rap, Hip-Hop

Though Zimbabwe Legit was the first African group to record hip-hop in America, it's not their vocal talents that cause their lone 12" to fetch hundreds of dollars when it's available for auction online. Produced by Mista Lawnge from Black Sheep (and engineered by Scotty Hard), it included a remix from DJ Shadow and was his first appearance on record, back when he was still making the transition from Hollywood Records studio maven to independent producer and cohead of SoleSides Records. Released on 12" as well as CD EP, *Zimbabwe Legit* didn't spend much time in print, though Shadow's mix appeared later on the 1996 Mo'Wax compilation, *Headz II.* The pair of rappers, Akim Ndlovu and his brother Dumisani, later performed under the name Of Unknown Origin. —*John Bush*

● **Zimbabwe Legit EP** / Mar. 10, 1992 / Hollywood ✦✦✦✦

The odds that a record of this type would work had to be pretty low; the whole project smacked of a novelty, and one that would probably result in an overly poppy crossover. Surprisingly, the only two tracks put out by Zimbabwe Legit prove that the Ndlovu brothers had skills right in line with some of the best alternative East Coasters working then. Over a hard-hitting, jazzy production, the rappers switch deftly between languages on "Doin' Damage in My Native Language," betraying little of a foreign account and indulging in rhymes much better than could be expected for *anyone's* debut. (Indeed, their profile was so low that Zimbabwe Legit could well have been an alias for a pair of American rappers.) Of the remixes, Mista Lawnge's is pretty solid, but DJ Shadow's is in another league altogether—one of the seminal productions in hip-hop history, his sprawling, six-minute "Legitimate Remix" remade the original into a late-night, back-to-Africa sample symphony. —*John Bush*

Zion I

Group / Hip-Hop, Urban, Club/Dance, Jungle/Drum 'N Bass, Trip-Hop, Underground Rap

This trio of genre-bender pride has made a name for itself on the Bay Area scene by successfully mixing spiritualism and hip-hop. Oakland's MC Zion and DJ/producer Amp Live blend hip-hop and trip-hop beats with lyrics focused on a message of unity, hope, and spiritual awareness. After a couple of indie hits, the trio slowly made inroads while opening for rap royalty like De La Soul, Rakim, and Run-D.M.C. Their debut album, *Mind Over Matter*, was released in May of 2000 and features collaborations with fellow Bay Area rappers Rasco, Planet Asia, and the Grouch. Although Zion I operates out of Berkeley, the group was originally formed in Atlanta, making their music difficult to classify as strictly West Coast hip-hop. Their musical style makes them even harder to define. With a style that borrows from hip-hop, trance, drum'n'bass, and reggae, Zion I's style is equally mystical and mystifying. —*Jon Azpiri*

● **Mind Over Matter** / May 30, 2000 / Ground Control ✦✦✦

This Bay Area trio's debut album is a loaded 22-track effort that dares you to try and classify it. Influenced equally by hip-hop and various forms of electronica, Zion I offers listeners a collage of new sounds mixed with ancient spiritualism. *Mind Over Matter*'s lead single, "Creation," is a track that combines choppy drum snares, razor-sharp scratches, and great interplay between Zion and Bay Area rapper Planet Asia, and should appeal to hip-hop fans who are down with abstract rappers such as Blackalicious and Digable Planets. Other songs such as "Metropolis," with its mellow keyboards, are bound to appeal to fans of trip-hop. On top of Amp Live's varying beats are Zion's mystical rhymes such as "Trippin'," which focus on spirituality and are a welcome relief from much of the materialism that permeates modern hip-hop. Many of the other tracks fall somewhere in between rap and trip-hop, and its lack of a center may mean that Zion I may struggle to find listeners. That's too bad, because, unlike so many other artists, this trio actually has something to say. —*Jon Azpiri*

Deepwater Slang, V2.0 / Feb. 18, 2003 / Raptivism ✦✦

This Berkeley-based (big ups, Cal Bears!) underground hip-hop duo's sophomore effort is chock full of their usual lyrical hooks and flows, but as with much product released by those looking to make their way in the bling-bling marketplace, it suffers somewhat in the production department. Not that the overly synthetic sounds—such as depthless keys, Casio-style hi-hat swipes, and denatured snare hits—aren't still hot when it comes to artists as varied (and/or lame) as Jay-Z and 50 Cent. On the contrary, hip-hop's musical register has moved farther and farther (some would argue backwards) away from noise and impact in favor of highlighting its vocal counterparts ("Here comes the drums!" this ain't). Truth is, as wordsmiths go, MC Zion is one of the more interesting talents flying underneath MTV and BET's radar. But *Deep Water Slang, V2.0* works best when the music matches him in skill, such as on the varied "Finger Paint" or in the poignant piano work found on "Flow," featuring the underground siren Goapele. Or when MC Zion gets some added wordplay from hip-hop all-stars like Aceyalone, whose turn on the homage to all things green, "Cheeba Cheeba," is this (ahem) joint's finest moment. Don't misunderstand, the music has its moments too, such as on the stellar "Kick Snare" (featuring some humorous German samples and an addictive beatbox complement from Killa Kela) or "Dune," a silky smooth trance dance track that closes out the album. Not to mention the hidden track, "One More Thing," which showcases some heartfelt guitar plucking. But *Deep Water Slang, V2.0* may leave those with a hip-hop memory that goes back farther than *The Chronic* wanting more meat and less vegetables. Dig? —*Scott Thill*

Various Artists

10th Anniversary Get Low / Sep. 18, 2001 / Get Low ◆◆◆◆
10th Anniversary Get Low is a rap compilation featuring several low-profile and underground rappers. Although both Juvenile and Method Man appear in the first ten minutes, their contributions are only a small part of what makes this album good. Mostly, it is the more unknown rappers that come off sounding more interesting and have the better songs. Highlights include JT, San Quinn, and Mississippi Mike on the catchy "Southern Exposure," and the vicious combination of Yukmouth, the Gamblaz, Dru Down, and Mac Mall on the up-tempo "Block Shit." This is a surprisingly good album and is recommended for those wondering what the brighter lights of the underground scene are. —*Bradley Torreano*

10th Anniversary: Rap-A-Lot Records / Feb. 1997 / Rap-A-Lot/Noo Trybe ◆◆◆
There are several great cuts from the Geto Boys on this Rap-A-Lot retrospective, though contributions from 5th Ward Boyz, Ganksta Nip, and DMG force the compilation a bit below par. —*Keith Farley*

110 Below / 1994 / Beechwood ◆◆◆◆
The first volume in *New Electronica*'s series of earthy beat excursions focuses on dub, setting a course for the style which has room for a variety of groups, from Tricky to Leftfield to Killing Joke to African Headcharge. —*Keith Farley*

110 Below, Vol. 2: Trip to the cHip sHop / 1995 / New Electronica ◆◆◆
The second volume in the series takes hip-hop as its template, then turns the music on its head with inclusions from Freddy Fresh, Howie B, U.N.K.L.E., DJ Krush, and Beck, as well as more straight-ahead breakbeat merchants like Ultramagnetic MC's. —*Keith Farley*

110 Below, Vol. 3: No Sleeve Notes Required / 1995 / Beechwood ◆◆◆◆
The third volume of this excellent trip-hop series in the New Electronica series focuses on more avant-garde explorers, including Brian Eno, Jah Wobble, Anton Fier, and Material. Other appearances include Urban Dance Squad, Muslimgauze, Harr/Airto/Purim, Thessalonians, Squid, and Planet Jazz. —*Keith Farley*

2 Nasty 4 Radio / Nov. 27, 1990 / Cold Chillin' ◆◆◆
Whether the Christian right wants to admit it or not, Luther Campbell is a shining example of many of the things that Republicans preach. Hard work, entrepreneurship, and pulling yourself up by the bootstraps are the sorts of things that Republicans espouse, and Campbell—who came from an inner-city background and used the capitalist system to overcome obstacles and make a fortune—definitely pulled himself up by the bootstraps. But Florida attorney Jack Thompson wasn't thinking about those things in 1990 when, declaring that the sexually explicit lyrics of Campbell and his 2 Live Crew violated American obscenity laws, he tried to put the group out of business. Thompson, however, only succeeded in making Campbell an unlikely poster child for the First Amendment—Democrats, Libertarians, and moderate Republicans all rushed to Campbell's defense. Thompson's actions also inspired various record companies to assemble hardcore rap compilations that were full of sexually explicit lyrics; those compilations were the labels' way of thumbing their noses at Thompson and his Christian right supporters. One such compilation was the 1990 Warner Bros. release *2 Nasty 4 Radio*. All of the X-rated and R-rated material on this CD was recorded for Warner Bros., Cold Chillin' (which Warner Bros. was distributing at the time), or Sire, and that includes Ice-T's "Girls, L.G.B.N.A.F" and Everlast's "Fuck Everyone" as well as Kool G Rap's "Talk Like Sex," Roxanne Shanté's "Brothers Ain't Shit," and the hilarious "Big Daddy Vs. Dolemite" (Big Daddy Kane's duet with comedian Rudy Ray Moore). *2 Nasty 4 Radio* is a compilation that Thompson would not approve of, which is why Warner Bros. put it out—that, and a

desire to make money. This compilation is far from the last word on raunchy rap in the late '80s and early '90s, but it is generally entertaining if you have a taste for that type of material. —*Alex Henderson*

8 Mile / Oct. 29, 2002 / Interscope ◆◆◆◆
This may be the soundtrack for Eminem's movie debut, but don't think of *8 Mile* of as an Eminem album, because it's not. It's a soundtrack and plays like a soundtrack, with many cuts from current stars and new artists (several associated with Eminem's fledgling Shady imprint), plus a couple of previously released tracks, most of it very high quality, whether it's a hard-hitting Jay-Z, a sultry Macy Gray, or Taryn Manning's Boomkat's sexy slow burn "Wasting My Time." Sure, there are a couple of tracks that fall flat—Young Zee and Obie Trice feel strained—but it all flows well, and it's all strong. But it's also overshadowed by four blindingly great new songs from Eminem (four and a half, if you count his show-stealing appearance on D-12's "Rap Game"), all illustrating a step forward from *The Eminem Show*, even if they work a familiar pseudo-biographical ground. What impresses is not just the wordplay and delivery but also the music itself—fuller, richer than anything on his previous records, appropriately cinematic in scope, and pushing Eminem toward new heights. The opening track and first single "Lose Yourself" is easily equaled by the title song with its layered pianos, while "Rabbit Run" is nearly as good. Hearing these, it's hard not to greedily hunger for a full album of this, but the soundtrack is excellent as is and these new Eminem cuts make it a necessary purchase. —*Stephen Thomas Erlewine*

The '80s: Hip Hop Hits / Feb. 22, 2000 / K-Tel ◆◆◆
Hip-hop wasn't born in the 1980s—the hip-hop culture was created in New York in the late 1970s, and early rap acts like Kurtis Blow, Grandmaster Flash & the Furious Five, and the Sugarhill Gang started recording before 1980. But it was in the 1980s that hip-hop went from having a small cult following on the East Coast to being a huge international phenomenon. It was during the 1980s that hip-hop not only became the music of choice for many young African Americans—it also influenced a lot of pop/rock and dance music and became so widespread that you could walk into a club in Berlin and hear young guys rapping in German. Just as many R&B historians have described the 1960s and 1970s as R&B's classic era, many hip-hop historians will tell you that the 1980s and early '90s were hip-hop's classic era. Released in 2000, this 12-song compilation spans 1984-1990 and makes East Coast rap its main focus. The only West Coast rapper K-Tel includes is Too Short, whose "Life Is Too Short" from 1988 is among the Oakland native's cleaner hits. *The '80s: Hip Hop Hits* doesn't get heavily into gangsta rap—although Philadelphia native Schoolly D's "P.S.K. What Does It Mean?" is considered one of the earliest gangsta rap classics—and it doesn't get into Florida bass music at all. But it paints an attractive picture of Northeastern Corridor MCs by including major hits by Run-D.M.C. ("It's Tricky"), Whodini ("Friends"), D.J. Jazzy Jeff & the Fresh Prince ("Parents Just Don't Understand"), Kool Moe Dee ("Go See the Doctor"), and others. Though alternative rap and hip-hop house aren't high priorities, the CD acknowledges alternative rap with A Tribe Called Quest's "I Left My Wallet in El Segundo" and touches on hip-house with the Jungle Brothers' "I'll House You." This collection is far from the last word on 1980s hip-hop, but all things considered, *The '80s: Hip Hop Hits* isn't a bad CD to have in your collection. —*Alex Henderson*

Above the Rim / Mar. 22, 1994 / Interscope ◆◆◆◆◆
The soundtrack *Above the Rim* is an example of how all soundtracks should sound. Coordinated by Dr. Dre, the record is a virtual catalog of the cutting edge of hip-hop and urban R&B in 1994, featuring stars as well as unknowns that wind up making a big impression. Every artist turns in a first-rate song, but the real attraction of the record is Warren G's hit single, "Regulate," which

straddles the line between rap and soul with grace and style. —*Stephen Thomas Erlewine*

Absolutely: The Very Best of Electro / May 6, 1997 / Deep Beats ✦✦✦✦

Three discs of electro cuts from the '80s includes several classics—Grandmaster Flash's "White Lines," Man Parrish's "Hip Hop Bee Bop (Don't Stop)," Shannon's "Let the Music Play"—and a handful of even rarer cuts, from the West Street Mob, Warp 9, Melle Mel, and Konk. Though the ratio of unknown to familiar tracks is a bit higher than Rhino's *Electric Funk* box, *Absolutely* includes a lot of classic material not found elsewhere; also, every track is an extended 12" mix, not a radio edit. —*John Bush*

Ack'n A Azz: Wreckshop / Dec. 4, 2001 / Priority ✦✦✦

Ack'n a Azz features songs from the Wreckshop label, an underground rap label from Houston, TX. The album features a variety of performers, including D Gotti, D Reck, Tyte Eyes, Dirty $$, Noke D, and UGK. Featured performances include the album-opening title track, "Power Up," "Look Into Our Eyes," "4s Recline Tops," and 14 others. Those who appreciate Houston-style Southern rap with an emphasis on the gangsta side of life should find this album delightful. —*Jason Birchmeier*

Africa Raps / Mar. 12, 2002 / Trikont ✦✦✦✦✦

For many Americans and Europeans, West African music means Youssou N'Dour and Baaba Maal; the existence of a vibrant Senegalese rap scene has generally escaped the notice of the rest of the musical world. This excellent compilation should help to remedy that. Culled from the cassette releases that drive the music business in West Africa, *Africa Raps* consists primarily of French-language material by Dakar legends like Positive Black Soul and Da Brains, but a fair number of the raps are delivered in other local languages (and, in at least one case, in what sounds like Arabic) by artists less well known, even in their native regions. For the most part, the music itself is fairly derivative of standard U.S. hip-hop (of the dark, slow-rolling variety), but there are notable exceptions, such as Gokh-Bi System's "Kaesal," which incorporates traditional Senegalese music into the mix, and the Malian crew Tata Pound, whose "Badala" is a thrilling combination of speed rap and local pop sounds. The album's high point is the absolutely brilliant "Libre Ego," a freestyle rap recorded live by Didier Awadi in collaboration with a bunch of his Dakar colleagues. Anyone with an interest in hip-hop in general and African hip-hop in particular should snatch this one up. —*Rick Anderson*

Alienated Individuals / Sep. 4, 2001 / Most Entertainment ✦✦

Alienated Individuals features a large cast of relatively unknown rappers affiliated with the Joemama Beats label. Some of the featured performers include the Gypcees, the Shiesty Individuals, the Lyrical Felonz, Doomzday, and Jimmy Finguz. Nothing here's particularly impressive, and the album's dizzying number of rappers makes it difficult to maintain a consistent level of attention. It's a fairly lo-fi album, characterized to a large degree by its grimy, rudimentary production. Don't bother with this unless you're into low-budget ghetto rap, and even then you may want to look elsewhere first—you can do better than this. —*Jason Birchmeier*

All About the Benjamins / Feb. 19, 2002 / New Line ✦✦✦

An initial glance at the track listing for this soundtrack isn't going to impress you. There aren't many big names here, and the big names that are here offer previously released songs: B.G.'s "Bling-Bling," the O'Jays' "For the Love of Money," and Puff Daddy's "It's All About the Benjamins." Furthermore, considering Ice Cube stars in this film, you'd think he'd contribute a song, but there isn't even a previously released song by him here. However, if you give this soundtrack a listen, you'll discover that there are actually quite a few quality songs here. First of all, the aforementioned previously released songs are undeniably great and certainly fit the film's theme. Furthermore, the Puff Daddy track appears here in a remixed version featuring a new verse by the Notorious B.I.G. and a few other new—and surprisingly welcome—modifications. Second of all, the soundtrack's leadoff track, Trina's "Told Y'All," may very well be the album's highlight, one of the best tracks to come out of the Florida-based Trick Daddy/Trina camp, on a par with "Da Baddest Bitch," "Nann Nigga," and "Take It to da House." Other songs by Petey Pablo and Mystic are also worth checking out. —*Jason Birchmeier*

And Then There Was Bass: Dis Bass Game Real / Apr. 29, 1997 / LaFace ✦✦✦✦

And Then There Was Bass compiles the best tracks from contemporary "bass" dance music (a bottom-heavy and ungodly marriage of disco and techno) artists circa 1997 into more than an hour of pounding rhythm tracks supporting little of any musical consequence. It's incomprehensible that the classy, genuinely talented Babyface graces this anthology (coproducing with Daryl Simmons a remix of "Have I Never" for 69 Boys & K-Nock). B-Rock & The Bizz pump up the volume on the first single, "MyBabyDaddy" (which loops the Emotions' "Best of My Love"), and dance diva Miss Dana lights into Shirley Murdock's torchy "As We Lay." Luke, already the proud progenitor of such platinum hits as "Me So Horny," proposes "Let's Ride," and Charles "Da Real One" Trahan transforms the Rupert Holmes hit single "Escape (The Pina Colada Song)" into "U Like Pina Colada." That ingenious title provides a pretty accurate indication of the level of creativity demonstrated on this album. —*Chris Slawecki*

ASR, Vol. 1: New York Hip-Hop Battles / Jan. 25, 2000 / Thump ✦✦✦

ASR 1: New York Hip-Hop Battles is a collection of material from authors, rappers, DJs, producers, singers, and performers who are known for their street-smart sassiness and stone-cold rhyming throughout the streets of New York. This 13-track compilation features cuts from Organized's Prince Po, Konfusion, Pearl Picasso, and Red Handed of LaFace, among others. —*MacKenzie Wilson*

Baby Boy / Jun. 19, 2001 / Uptown/Universal ✦✦✦✦✦

The rap songs from the *Baby Boy* soundtrack will no doubt garner the most attention, but for the most part, the numerous contemporary urban soul songs are what make this such a great album. Laid-back slow jams by D'Angelo, the Transitions, Raphael Saadiq, Felicia Adams, and a Anthony Hamilton/Macy Gray duet are all wonderful, lulling songs filling in the album's gaps. Furthermore, two classics—Bootsy Collins' "I'd Rather Be With You" and Marvin Gaye's "Just to Keep You Satisfied"—are welcome additions. Yet as commendable as these numerous soul songs may be for their mood-inducing effects, it's hard to miss the few big-time rap songs functioning as the soundtrack's selling points. In particular, "Just a Baby Boy"—featuring Snoop Dogg, Tyrese, and Mr. Tan over a Battlecat production—is yet another of Snoop's forays into R&B territory, with Mr. Tan doing the crooning; the onetime Doggfather seems to have found a new, more dynamic songwriting formula that makes his '90s work seem formative in comparison. Besides the Snoop track, Three 6 Mafia and La Chat's "Baby Mama" is essentially a rewrite of Project Pat's "Chicken Head," a sort of ghetto "Mrs. Jackson" that is a trademark Juicy J/DJ Paul production; B.G.'s "Thatshowegetdown" also stands out, featuring a welcome new sound for Cash Money producer Mannie Fresh; and then there are two more Battlecat productions featuring tha Eastsidaz and Lost Angels, which are both fairly forgettable. It must be stressed again, though, that the numerous slow jams make this album such a success. Sure, the rap artists have the name recognition, but the contemporary urban soul artists are just as talented, as they prove here, even if their names aren't as familiar. If you can appreciate rap as well as contemporary urban soul, this soundtrack should be a feast for you with its dynamic mix, alternating between interludes of film dialogue, big rap songs, and some smoking slow jams. —*Jason Birchmeier*

Bad Boy's Greatest Hits / Sep. 29, 1998 / Bad Boy ✦✦✦✦✦

Though albums by Bad Boy Records artists always sold incredibly well, the single productions of Sean "Puffy" Combs lit up the charts. Collected here is the essence of Bad Boy, including all of the label's best tracks: the remix of Craig Mack's "Flava in Ya Ear" that practically made the label, the Notorious B.I.G.'s "One More Chance/Stay With Me," Puff Daddy's "It's All About the Benjamins," and Mase's "Feel So Good." Unless you're a big fan, that's about all the Bad Boy you need. It's a bit of a shame that it doesn't include the B.I.G. tribute "I'll Be Missing You," but *Bad Boy's Greatest Hits* is still an excellent summation of the label's hit production. —*John Bush*

Bad Company / Jun. 4, 2002 / Hollywood ✦✦✦

The producers of the soundtrack to the Joel Schumacher-directed, Anthony Hopkins- and Chris Rock-starring action-thriller *Bad Company* did something smart. For their collection of music inspired by the movie—which is heavy on hip-hop, rap, and urban soul—they in general found songs with a dark, ominous, paranoid feeling appropriate for a film about a rogue nuclear bomb. True, this doesn't apply to every song on the collection, but even when Next serves up the smooth "Tonite," there's a nocturnal vibe that gives the record character that sustains it over some uneven patches. It's not enough to make the record transcend its genre, but it's quite good within its genre, thanks to such standout tracks as Tricky's "Excess," OutKast's "B.O.B. (Bombs

Over Baghdad)," and Gorillaz/D-12's "911," which also features Terry Hall. —*Stephen Thomas Erlewine*

Barbershop / Aug. 27, 2002 / Sony ✦✦✦
At the time of its release, the various artists collection containing music from the motion picture *Barbershop* boasted two tracks, Fabolous & P. Diddy featuring Jagged Edge's "Trade It All Part 2" and Ginuwine's "Stingy," that were rising on the R&B Top 40, which seemed to bode well for this collection of rhythmic urban music. Typically, not a note of Terence Blanchard's score to the film was included, but there were three tracks on the album, Best Man's "I See You," Jordan Brown's "Better to Leave," and Collin's "Baby, Baby, Baby," not actually featured in the film, and P. Diddy & the Family's "And We" was presented in a different version from the one contained in the film. That last track was one of several marred by awkward and not very deceptive "clean" edits that managed to mangle the songs' rhythms without actually obscuring the vulgar intent of the lyrics. Much of the album, however, consisted of romantic ballads, and the package concluded with two old school favorites, Marvin Gaye's "Got to Give It Up (Part 1)" and the Staple Singers' "I'll Take You There." The album opened and closed with dialogue excerpts from the film that suggested it was a comedy keyed to the questionable macho wisdom that might be overheard in an establishment largely frequented by men. —*William Ruhlmann*

Bass Mixx Party Club Classics / Sep. 7, 1999 / Little Joe ✦✦✦
For those who might be unfamiliar with which tracks to look for in a collection of bass classics, rest assured that *Bass Mixx Party Club Classics* does actually include quite a few classics of the style. It features work by 2 Live Crew ("Move Somethin," "Do the Damn Thing," "Hoochie Mama"), Poison Clan ("Shake Whatcha Mama Gave Ya," "Dance All Night"), Luke ("Breakdown," "Work It Out"), Bustdown ("Nasty B*tch"), and Lejuan Love ("Everybody Say Yeah"). —*Keith Farley*

Battle Axe Warriors Compilation / Nov. 14, 2000 / Battle Axe ✦✦✦
One of the most desirable things about underground hip-hop has been the diversity of places it originates from. Most (if not all) of the MCs on this compilation are from Vancouver, British Columbia, including artists such as Moka Only, LMNO, Buc Fifty, and the Swollen Members (a duo composed of MadChild and Prevail). The music's unique blend of breaks and jazzy background samples, with some of the best MCs to ever hail from Canada laying down the lyrics. Extra attention should be paid to MadChild's verses; his skill with words is exceptional. This is the second compilation like this from Battle Axe Records; the first was released in 1999 entitled *Defenders of the Underworld*. —*Brad Mills*

Bay Area's Greatest Hits, Vol. 1 / Jun. 30, 1998 / Virgin ✦✦✦
From Too Short to MC Hammer to Souls of Mischief, NoCali has often rivaled SoCal in hip-hop talent and exposure, and this Virgin compilation actually *does* include some of the best hip-hop to come out of Oakland and San Francisco. Among the stars are Digital Underground, MC Pooh, RBL Posse, E-40, the Luniz, and Dru Down. —*Keith Farley*

The Beat: Go-Go's Fusion of Funk and Hip Hop / Sep. 4, 2001 / Liason ✦✦✦✦
The Beat: Go-Go's Fusion of Funk and Hip Hop looks back to the early-'80s go-go era and handpicks 19 of the era's best moments. Primarily a Washington, D.C.-based movement, go-go didn't last too long. Bringing together hip-hop and funk music and performed by live bands rather than producers and samplers, go-go no doubt had its highlights. Some of the highlights featured on his two-disc collection include Chuck Brown's "Bustin' Loose," Trouble Funk's "Pump Me Up," Kurtis Blow's "Party Time," and E.U.'s "Da' Butt." Fun music, for sure. More than anything, however, this collection serves as an excellent showcase for this mostly forgotten movement. —*Jason Birchmeier*

Beats & Rhymes: Hip-Hop of the '90s, Vol. 1 / Oct. 28, 1997 / Rhino ✦✦✦
With the three-volume *Beats & Rhymes: Hip-Hop of the '90s*, Rhino attempts to sketch a history of rap in the early '90s, before gangsta rap dominated the marketplace. Hip-hop was thriving between 1990 and 1993, as both veteran artists like Boogie Down Productions and new crews like A Tribe Called Quest began pursuing adventurous territory, fusing hip-hop with jazz and pop, among other things. There aren't many big crossover hits on any of the three volumes, but there are big names and cuts that were important in the underground. Unfortunately, there's some mediocre stuff mixed in with the prime cuts, but the bulk of each disc is so strong and the set's budget-line

price is so attractive that the entire series functions as an excellent primer, especially when the liner notes by Harry Allen are added into the equation. Among the highlights on the 15-track *Beats & Rhymes: Hip-Hop of the '90s, Vol. 1* are cuts by A Tribe Called Quest ("Bonita Applebum"), the D.O.C. ("It's Funky Enough"), Main Source ("Looking at the Front Door"), Poor Righteous Teachers ("Rock Dis Funky Joint"), Big Daddy Kane ("I Get the Job Done"), and Jungle Brothers ("Doin' Our Own Dang"). —*Stephen Thomas Erlewine*

Beats & Rhymes: Hip-Hop of the '90s, Vol. 2 / Oct. 28, 1997 / Rhino ✦✦✦
Beats & Rhymes: Hip-Hop of the '90s, Vol. 2 picks up where its predecessor left off, running through a number of rap classics and underappreciated gems from the early '90s. Cut for cut, the 15-track *Vol. 2* isn't as consistent as its predecessor, but there are still plenty of terrific moments on the disc—including tracks by Leaders of the New School ("Case of the P.T.A."), A Tribe Called Quest ("Check the Rhyme"), Brand Nubian ("Slow Down"), Eric B. & Rakim ("What's On Your Mind"), DJ Jazzy Jeff & the Fresh Prince ("Summertime"), and the UMC's ("Blue Cheese")—that make it an essential history lesson. That said, there's still no reason why there are no less than three Chubb Rock cuts on this disc. —*Stephen Thomas Erlewine*

Beats & Rhymes: Hip-Hop of the '90s, Vol. 3 / Oct. 28, 1997 / Rhino ✦✦✦
The third and final volume of *Beats & Rhymes: Hip-Hop of the '90s* is as effective as its two predecessors, chronicling the period in the early '90s before gangsta rap became the dominant form of hip-hop. Several years after its original release, much of this music retains the excitement and spirit of adventure, and it shames much of the music that followed it in the mid-'90s. *Vol. 3* rivals *Vol. 1* for sheer consistency, boasting cuts by A Tribe Called Quest ("Hot Sex," "Scenario"), Grand Puba ("360 Degrees [What Goes Around]"), Main Source ("Fakin' the Funk"), Naughty By Nature ("Guard Your Grill"), the Pharcyde ("Ya Mama"), Fu-Schnickens ("La Schmoove"), Del tha Funkee Homosapien ("Mistadobalina"), and Digital Underground ("No Nose Job"). Not only does it capture the depth and range of the era, it's also an excellent listen. —*Stephen Thomas Erlewine*

Beneath the Surface / Jun. 22, 1999 / Celestial ✦✦✦✦
In the tradition of *To Whom It May Concern* and *Project Blowed*, the L.A. underground produced yet another rap compilation of extraordinary merit. Released in 1998, *Beneath the Surface* teamed a collection of over 25 Blowed MCs with O.D., a virtually unknown producer at the time. The result was cathartic, in that the album transcended the genre of hip-hop, moving fearlessly into the aesthetics of classic rock. Native American rhythms utilized in the opening track by Alien Nation, literary narratives delivered by Aceyalone and Self-Jupiter, the demented soliloquy executed by AWOL 1, the extreme antics of Otherwize, plus "Leaving Shire" samples aplenty provide rich texture. Countering Darkleaf's declaration that "it's absurd to think that the word could ever capture the pure elements," O.D. sonically paints the cosmos, making *Beneath the Surface* as compelling as it is innovative. —*Robert Gabriel*

Best of B-Boy Records / Jul. 9, 2002 / Landspeed ✦✦✦
B-Boy Records was one of the first rap labels started as the original wave of rap acts began to fade in the early '80s. They released a great many 12" singles by acts like Cold Crush Brothers, Jewel T, KC Work, Levi 167, and Spicey Ham—artists who haven't really stood the test of time but helped keep rap and hip-hop going strong at a time when many wondered if the genre would die out. One act that B-Boy discovered became legendary: Boogie Down Productions, whose KRS-One is still keeping it real today. This 15-track CD compiles the best B-Boy had to offer, and includes BDP's landmark cut, "Criminal Minded." A nice sampler for rap fans who want a history lesson. —*Tim Sendra*

The Best of Black Market Records, Vol. 1 / May 13, 1997 / Priority ✦✦✦
The Best of Black Market Records, Vol. 1 is a comprehensive, 20-track collection that contains a selection of highlights from the underground hip-hop label. There's only a handful of artists on the compilation—Brotha Lynch Hung, Mr. Doctor, X-Raided, Homicide, and Cold World Hustler feature the most prominently—but much of the record is good hardcore gangsta rap, even if none of it pushes the boundaries of the genre. —*Stephen Thomas Erlewine*

The Best of Electric Slide / 1991 / Creative Funk ✦✦✦✦✦
The Best of Electric Slide compiles old school hip-hop tracks that provide the best fit for rhythms of the popular dance. The artists are mostly obscure; the World Class Wreckin' Cru is the biggest name here (because member

Dr. Dre would go on to much greater fame). Still, *The Best of Electric Slide* includes a number of forgotten singles that are worth the trouble, such as Chill Rob G's original version of the Snap hit "The Power." —*Steve Huey*

The Best of Enjoy Records / 1989 / Hot Prod. ✦✦✦

The Best of Enjoy Records contains 11 tracks from the old school rap label's vaults, including the Furious Five's "Superappin'," Spoonie Gee's "Love Rap," Kool Moe Dee's "Body Rock," the Fearless Four's "It's Magic," the Disco Four's "Move with the Groove," Doug E. Fresh's "Just Having Fun," the Treacherous Three's "New Rap Language," and the Masterdon Committee's "Funk Box Party." —*Stephen Thomas Erlewine*

The Best of International Hip Hop / Aug. 8, 2000 / Hip-O ✦✦✦✦

The straightforwardly named, *The Best of International Hip-Hop* gathers rap from around the world, including "Agite (It's On!)" by Argentina's El Sindicato Argentino Del Hip Hop and "Helvetik Parc" by Switzerland's Sens Unik. Greenland's Nuuk Posse delivers "Uteqqippugut (Back in Business)," Japan's K-Dub Shine performs "Setsumei Fuyou (No Need to Explain)," and South African rappers Mr. Mann & Pointblank offer "The Bermuda Triangle." Hip-hop acts from Romania, Israel, France, Algeria, Portugal, Croatia, and Greece complete this diverse, fascinating look at the style's international reach. —*Heather Phares*

The Best of Sacramento / Dec. 15, 1998 / Black Market ✦✦✦✦

The Best of Sacramento features performances by most of the key gangsta rappers that have put the city on the map as one of the world's epicenters for nihilistic gangsta rap. In particular, the performances by C-Bo and Brotha Lynch Hung should attract some attention to this compilation, even if many of the featured rappers are fairly unknown. Furthermore, fans of Black Market recordings should adore this collection as it is focused primarily on that label. The capital of California, Sacramento isn't nearly the metropolis or major urban center that Los Angeles and San Francisco are, yet the city's gangsta rap scene rivals either of these cities. Unfortunately, there haven't been any Sacramento rappers that have yet broken out of the underground. The city's strictly underground status has not so much to do with talent but rather with accessibility; these rappers don't merely retread traditional gangsta themes, instead taking the genre into darker and more morbid terrain than it has yet ventured with the exception of crazed artists such as Esham or Three 6 Mafia. No record on the market better sums up the trademark style of malevolent gangsta rap that thrived in Sacramento in the '90s than this one. —*Jason Birchmeier*

The Best of Sugarhill Records / Oct. 6, 1998 / Rhino ✦✦✦✦✦

If Rhino's massive five-disc summation of the crucial old school label Sugarhill makes you cringe, this single-disc set is a much better distillation of the label (and the period) than much else out there. It covers the three tracks that are hands-down classics—"Rapper's Delight" by the Sugarhill Gang plus "The Message" and "White Lines" by Grandmaster Flash & the Furious Five. In addition, there are at least a half-dozen minor standouts like the Sugarhill Gang's "8th Wonder" and "Apache," the Funky Four Plus 1's "That's the Joint," Kevie Kev's "All Night Long (Waterbed)," and Grandmaster Flash's "Scorpio" and "New York New York." —*John Bush*

BET: Best of Rap City / Sep. 21, 1999 / Virgin ✦✦✦✦✦

BET: Best of Rap City is an excellent collection of some of the best and most popular hip-hop singles of 1998 and 1999, nicely summing up the state of contemporary mainstream rap while providing a consistently strong listen. Some of the biggest names present are Eminem ("My Name Is"), Busta Rhymes ("What's It Gonna Be?!" with Janet Jackson), Jay-Z ("Hard Knock Life"), Master P ("Make 'Em Say Uhh!"), Nas ("Nas Is Like"), and Tupac ("Changes"), among many others. It's a great way to pick up a lot of hit singles all at once, and it truly does play like a *Best of Rap City* episode. —*Steve Huey*

Big Phat Ones of Hip Hop, Vol. 1 / 1995 / BOXtunes ✦✦✦✦✦

Big Phat Ones of Hip Hop, Vol. 1 is a collection of big hip-hop hits from the mid '90s, as presented by The Box video network. It's one of the best collections of rap singles of its era, featuring hits by Coolio, Warren G, Salt-N-Pepa, Notorious B.I.G., and R. Kelly. —*Stephen Thomas Erlewine*

Big Phat Ones of Hip Hop, Vol. 2 / Nov. 25, 1997 / Polygram ✦✦✦

Big Phat Ones of Hip Hop, Vol. 2 is a strong collection of mid-'90s hip-hop hits from the likes of Junior M.A.F.I.A. ("Get Money"), E-40 ("Rappers Ball"), Goodie Mob ("Cell Therapy"), Dru Hill ("In My Bed [So So Def Mix]"), Camp Lo ("Luchini aka [This Is It]"), Tupac ("I Get Around"), Too Short ("Gettin' It"),

and Bone Thugs-N-Harmony. Most of these songs were designed to get the dancefloor moving, and although a handful sound anemic when separated from the dance club, there are several great singles here that make the sampler worthwhile. —*Stephen Thomas Erlewine*

Big Pimpin' / Jan. 30, 2001 / Flip Tha Switch ✦✦

Flip Tha Switch records' *Big Pimpin'* compilation rounds up an ensemble cast of underground hardcore rappers. The album is executive produced by Cadillac Todd, who also raps on the songs "Gorilla Pimpin'," "I Thought U Knew," and "If You U Fake, U Can't Go." Other rappers appearing on this album include Daz Dillinger, J.T. tha Bigga Figga, Baby Nucc Dogg, J-Loc, and Mr. Sinatra, in addition to countless other rappers who aren't quite as well known. Overall, though, there's no shortage of rappers featured on this collection, the quality is unfortunately low. None of the rappers put much effort into their rhymes, with the exception of Cadillac Todd, who obviously feels a sense of responsibility as the executive producer. —*Jason Birchmeier*

Big Pimpin' / Jul. 2, 2002 / Priority ✦✦✦✦

Priority's *Big Pimpin* isn't the first hip-hop compilation to be released under that name—Flip Tha Switch was behind the one from 2001—but it may be the best. Granted, it doesn't exactly come with an endorsement from N.O.W. ("Bitch has more ass than brains," "Bitch, I pimp your mama," etc.), but the title alone should make that clear. Many of the more popular self-proclaimed "pimps" of the rap world are present and accounted for: Too Short (represented by four tracks), Ice-T (two tracks, including the previously unreleased "Pimp or Die"), and Snoop Dogg (three tracks, including the previously unreleased "Back Up Ho"). Altogether, there are five previously unreleased tracks and at least one certifiable classic, Big Daddy Kane's "Pimpin' Ain't Easy." The strongest track just happens to be the first—also an unreleased one—Ant Banks' T.W.D.Y. featuring Captain Save-Em's laid-back "Super Pimpin'" with its slinky gangster lean chorus. Fans of Jay-Z are sure to notice that *Big Pimpin* doesn't include his hit single of the same name, but that may be because the focus is more on "the game" as it's played on the West Coast (and in the South) rather than the East. —*Kathleen C. Fennessy*

Black and White / Mar. 28, 2000 / Loud ✦✦

Black and White makes a good argument for rap music's ability to maintain the thread of a film's themes and play less the role of an MC-studded ticket-pusher. That's not to say the big guns featured on the album, like Raekwon, Prodigy, the late Big Pun, and Xzibit, don't command your attention. The record cleverly opens with the hum of a movie projector followed by the deadpan delivery of the line "Black and White? So, we movie-settin'?," which sets the pace for a fangs-bared montage of politically charged manifestoes aimed at jersey-wearing wannabes. It's the player haters and fakers that get the brunt of this 13-track beating. Queen Pen's "You'll Never Be Better Than Me" combines fierce rock-tinged guitar riffs with harsh words for those who'd try to accessorize the toughest elements of African-American culture, while the American Cream Team gives the "Middle Finger Attitude," recalling a confrontation in the movie between Italian mobsters moving in on the nightclub turf of rap gangsters. Prodigy of Mobb Deep keeps the peace with the laid-back tempo and swooping violins of "Don't Be a Follower," along with other more temperate tracks, such as the sampled harpsichord and sweet beats of *Black and White* costar Raekwon's "Wake Up" and Big Pun's "Dramacide" with Kool G Rap and turntablists the X-Ecutioners. —*Derrick Mathis*

Black Gangster / Jul. 13, 1999 / Lightyear ✦✦✦✦

The soundtrack for a film based on Donald Goines' blaxploitation novel (and commemorating the 25th anniversary of his tragic death), *Black Gangster* includes original tracks from a host of hip-hop superstars including Jay-Z, DMX, and Ghetto Mafia, as well as new names Ja Rule and Darcsyde. The spotlight track is "This Life Forever" by Jay-Z, a great rapping turn and, as it turns out, a production better than most heard on Jay-Z's *Hard Knock Life* album. Though DMX's "The Story" is the only other standout track, *Black Gangster* includes great songs by Mac Dre ("Give It Up"), Freddie Foxxx ("Pimpin' Ain't Easy"), and Kasual ("Money Tree"). —*John Bush*

Blade II / Mar. 19, 2002 / Virgin ✦✦✦

This soundtrack to the relatively large-budgeted, B-movie sequel starring Wesley Snipes is the third in a series of soundtrack records that Happy Walters of Immortal Records assembled. The first, for the movie *Judgement Night*, included hip-hop and rock acts pairing up for new songs, and the second was for *Spawn* and featured electronica and hard rock acts. For *Blade II*, it's hip-hop and electronica acts, and Walters has assembled many of the biggest names in both genres. Electronica can work perfectly with hip-hop, adding a lot of fancier beats and grooves and making the songs distinctive from the usual hip-hop soundtrack. But as with a lot of these sorts of projects, many of the big names are just making appearances, while only a few seem to be putting much effort into this. Among the best tracks is Eve and Fatboy Slim teaming up on "Cowboy" and even better is Ice Cube and Paul Oakenfold on "Right Here, Right Now," a song that's reminiscent of Cube's over-the-top performance on the huge single "We Be Clubbin'." Both of these tracks are catchy enough to be huge rap radio hits. Redman also adds plenty of character to his teaming with the Gorillaz, "Gorillaz on My Mind," a silly tune backed by some superfunky music and some smooth background vocals. But Mos Def sounds like he doesn't care about the lackluster "I Against I" with Massive Attack, and Cypress Hill, Bubba Sparxx, and Busta Rhymes' contributions are similarly forgettable. —*Adam Bregman*

Bomb Worldwide / Oct. 14, 1997 / Bomb Hip Hop ✦✦✦✦
The toast of the hip-hop underground, Bomb Records circled the globe to bring together the best international DJs, hailing from Australia, Germany, Japan, Canada, Britain, and of course America. Challenging tracks abound, though the names won't be familiar even to turntablist fans. Among the highlights are contributions from Mindbomb, Down 2 Earth, Cipher, Muro Feat, Gore Tex, and Funky DL. —*John Bush*

Bones / Oct. 9, 2001 / Priority ✦✦✦
The soundtrack to *Bones*—Ernest Dickerson's urban horror/blaxploitation homage starring Snoop Doggy Dogg—mixes rap and contemporary R&B from the likes of Kokane, D-12, and of course Snoop himself. His collaborations with MC Ren and RBX on "Legend of Jimmy Bones," Bad Azz, Chan, and Coniyac on "The Death of Snow White," Soopafly on "Jimmy's Revenge," and Outkast on "Endo" and "Fresh and Clean (Remix)" are among the collection's highlights. D-12's "These Drugs," Kurupt and Roscoe's "It's Jimmy," and FT's "F-It-Less" maintain the dark, hard-hitting vibe, while William DeVaughn's "Be Thankful" adds a retro-soul touch to the album. An appropriately streetsmart, eerie soundtrack. —*Heather Phares*

Boom Box Flava / Jul. 23, 2002 / Universal Special Products ✦✦✦✦
Rap collections are very hard to put together, no doubt because many of the varying styles that the genre has to offer are often not compatible. *Boom Box Flava*, one such collection, attempts to mix several different styles into one fairly consistent album. Jumping between eras from song to song, this reflects the genre's evolution from old school boasts (Kurtis Blow's "If I Ruled the World") to minimalist street anthems (Slick Rick's "Children's Story"), from poppy new-jack dance hits (Heavy D's "We Got Our Own Thang") to hardcore gangsta rap (Onyx's "Slam"). The addition of EPMD and Eric B. & Rakim to the album is a major plus, and almost every song is solid. The only exceptions are the tracks from Father MC and MC Brains, which haven't aged gracefully compared to the rest of the album. For anyone seeking a collection of old school rap that offers variety without sacrificing quality, *Boom Box Flava* is a fine place to start. —*Bradley Torreano*

Bootyz in Motion / Mar. 24, 1998 / Interscope ✦✦✦✦
Perhaps the ultimate booty music compilation, *Bootyz in Motion* features all the big booty hits like Sir Mix-A-Lot's "Baby Got Back" and 2 Live Crew's "Me So Horny," as well as some lesser-known booty tunes. For those unfamiliar with this fairly obscure subgenre of rap, booty music came out of the South and featured rapid disco beats and lyrics mostly about women's posteriors. It's pretty simple stuff, and it eventually mutated into the whole dirty South sound, though booty music is distinctive in that its subject matter pretty much stuck to girls and booties, and rarely went beyond that. It is fun music, though one can only stand so much of it. This fine compilation put together by DJ Magic Mike has all the hits, as well as a few songs that DJ Magic Mike has added beats to and turned into booty music, like Bone Thugs-N-Harmony's "Tha Crossroad." Fans of old school rap as well as disco fiends who somehow missed the booty music movement (as it didn't last very long) should check out this compilation. —*Adam Bregman*

Brazil 1: Escadinha Fazendo Justiça Com as Própria / 1999 / Zambia ✦✦✦
Brazil 1 features numerous Brazilian rap artists, all of whom pledge their allegiance to their people and their culture. This is meaningful music intended for contemplation; however, it's also very lively and energetic, so you find it

to be enjoyable as well as enlightening. The production is somewhat low-budget, but this ironically works in the music's favor, making it seem even more sincere rather than commercial. Some of the featured performances include X's "Encarcerado," Mv. Bill's "A Escolha É Sua," Xis' "A Fuga," Gog's "Um Simples José," and others. The CD booklet includes all the lyrics, which is a nice bonus given the political nature of the album. —*Jason Birchmeier*

Breaking Out: The Alcatraz Concert / Sep. 1, 1998 / Ventura ✦✦✦
In 1997, Image Entertainment made a video to educate inner-city youths about career opportunities in the entertainment industry. Framing the message of breaking out of poverty within the story of a jailbreak (!), over 20 hip-hop and rap acts performed a concert under the Golden Gate Bridge. Each performance is intercut with conversations with people working in the entertainment industry (even the crew on this video) and celebrities who urge kids to follow their dreams. The message is solid, but its delivery is a bit strange. There could have been more behind the scenes documentation of the making of the concert, for example. Good performances by Dru Hill, Usher, Run-D.M.C. (without D.M.C.), Da Brat, Naughty By Nature, and Kurtis Blow stand out among some now-obscure R&B groups. Breaking Out: The Alcatraz Concert was better as a three-day live event that entertained and educated thousands of at-risk youths than it is as a DVD. However, in spite of some appearances by groups that today's kids will not have heard of, the target audience will still appreciate the message. —*JT Griffith*

Bring in 'da Noise Bring in 'da Funk / Jul. 29, 1996 / RCA ✦✦✦✦✦
Savion Glover's smash Broadway hit *Bring in 'da Noise Bring in 'da Funk* took critics by storm, and this album is a live recording of a performance of the show. The album progresses through five main movements of black history and tap. "In 'da Beginning" pertains to the slave era. "Urbanization" portrays the Chicago black scene. "Where's the Beat" deals with the progression of dancing. "Street Corner Symphony" deals with the new urban era, and "Noise/Funk" is a demonstration of the prowess of Glover and his comrades in hittin', the new style of tap created by Glover, which involves less of the visual show associated with dance, and serves primarily to create music with the sounds of the tap shoes, as well as associates on various objects (paint buckets, chains, fencing, etc.). In truth, stripped of the costuming and visual effects, the album becomes a large work of poetry, sounding at times like *Stomp*, with orchestral accompaniment and vocalists. The work can seem like musique concrète at times, but retains a large musical interpretation of black culture, as well as some impressive percussion pieces, in the "Noise/Funk" section. The music is exceptional, but for the full power of the show, one really needs to see Savion Glover at work. —*Adam Greenberg*

Bring It On / Aug. 22, 2000 / Sony ✦✦✦
Suppose you had the responsibility for assembling music for a motion picture, and you were told that the film was a comedy set among high school students competing in a cheerleading contest, with a largely white squad pitted against a largely black one? Your approach would be obvious, wouldn't it? You would divide the tracks up between contemporary teen pop and contemporary R&B, and you would look for songs that borrowed from cheerleading chants, right? If so, you probably would come up with something that sounded a lot like *Bring It On*'s "music from the motion picture" album. (Actually, one track, 3LW's "Til I Say So," is not from the film.) Among the teen pop entries, the most prominent is B*witched's cover of the Toni Basil hit "Mickey," which recreates its cheerleader sound, while the obvious emphasis track among the R&B songs is Blaque's "As If," presented in two versions, one of them featuring Joey Fatone Jr. Ideally, these songs will march up their respective charts, to be followed by selections from such less-well-known peers as Sygnature ("2 Can Play") and sister2sister ("What's a Girl to Do"). That may occur, but the actual music supervisor of *Bring It On* never went beyond the obvious (and the available), and little of the album is distinguishable from current trends. The exception is Daphne & Celeste's "U.G.L.Y.," a cheerleader anthem derived from the kind of outrageous put-downs Bo Diddley used to put in his songs, which has a real spark and could be a novelty hit that could go down in high school history. —*William Ruhlmann*

The Brothers / Mar. 20, 2001 / Warner Brothers ✦✦✦
Another in the ever-lengthening series of African-American romantic comedies of the late '90s and early 2000s, *The Brothers* provides an excuse for a various-artists compilation of contemporary R&B music. "Featuring all new music," reads a note on the album cover, which also lists all the recording artists, who range from veterans like Maze featuring Frankie Beverly to more

recent acts such as Somethin' for the People featuring Fuzzy. An unusually large number of the tracks, five out of 16, are ringers, not actually heard in the film. Curiously, these songs, which include AB's "Happy," Dave Hollister's "Forever," and No Question's "Remember Us," seem to support the film's romantic theme particularly well. But so do many of the ones included, notably Eric Benét's "Love Don't Love Me," in which the singer confesses, "Fear of commitment is a hard habit to break." This is not entirely a collection of slow jams, however, with the likes of Snoop Dogg bringing a typically blunt, physical tone to his rap on "Hi 2 U." The producers don't seem to have decided how far to go in terms of the usual vulgarities. "Let It Go" by Jaheim featuring Castro has an obscenity edited out, but in the next track, "Two of a Kind" by Eddie Levert Sr. featuring Gerald Levert, a variant of the same word gets through. (The album is not stickered for explicit content.) Marcus Miller wrote the score for the film, but one gets only a taste of it in "The Love Theme," which concludes the album. Though no track really stands out, there would seem to be plenty of possibilities for singles from this collection, if properly promoted, which could make the soundtrack more memorable than the film from which (some of) it comes. — *William Ruhlmann*

Brown Sugar / Sep. 24, 2002 / MCA ✦✦✦✦

The soundtrack album to the 2002 film about a hip-hop-centered romance has 15 songs by a wide variety of the music's veterans and more recently emerged talents. Mary J. Blige, Erykah Badu, and Eric B. & Rakim are some of the better-known contributors on a compilation that mixes neo-soul and harder hip-hop styles. In the neo-soul bag, there's Jill Scott, whose romantic "Easy Conversation" is one of the better selections. Jazz/R&B crossover singer Cassandra Wilson covers Cyndi Lauper's "Time After Time," while the Roots offer some of the harder beats and scratching on the remix of "Act Too (Love of My Life)." On the whole it's an adequate sampler of some early 21st-century hip-hop sounds, leaning toward the more pop-accessible segment of the genre. — *Richie Unterberger*

Bullet Proof Love / Jun. 5, 2001 / Motown ✦✦

Bullet Proof Love, Vol. 1 was created to be introduction to a group of MCs signed to Henchmen Entertainment, an offshoot of Motown records. The album uses the tried-and-true method of mixing in new artists with more established stars such as Memphis Bleek and Prodigy. The new artists, such as Dangerr and Sharissa, are serviceable but are often bogged down by dull, derivative production. The braintrust at Henchmen did a good job of putting together a list of established stars for *Bullet Proof Love*. Unfortunately, they fail to achieve the album's real goal of showcasing their new talent, many of whom do not seem ready for the big time. — *Jon Azpiri*

Bussen Heads and Gettin' Paid / Aug. 24, 1999 / Smoked Out ✦✦✦

Featuring tracks by the Hot Boys, Big Tymers, and Mannie Fresh, this spotlight for Houston's Smoked Out Records doesn't look like much from the outside packaging and lack of track information. It's surprising, then, that the productions (most by Relley Rell) and raps are excellent. Halfway between Timbaland-style electro-funk and Master P's down South bounce, Relley Rell uses brief samples from even weirder sources than Timbaland has become known for, but never loses the groove. And though it's difficult to tell who's performing on each individual track, the raps are usually up to the production level. As a whole, *Bussen Heads and Gettin' Paid* is a very pleasant surprise. — *Keith Farley*

C-Style Presents 19th Street LBC Compilation / Mar. 10, 1998 / 19th Street/Noo Trybe ✦✦✦

Masterminded by producer Big C-Style, *C-Style Presents 19th Street LBC Compilation* is a 14-track collection of new and upcoming Long Beach rappers. All the songs on the album are interrelated, intending to tell the tale of a typical day on 19th Street in Long Beach. It's a good concept, and for the most part, it works well, even if some of the tracks are a little flat musically. Another problem is that there are too many rappers on each track, which means it's hard to tell who contributes what. Nevertheless, most of the record works—it's an excellent, compelling hardcore hip-hop album that happens to be one of the more inventive various-artists rap collections in some time. — *Leo Stanley*

Cali Connected / Apr. 8, 2003 / Priority ✦✦✦✦

The three Los Angeles rappers who comprised the West Coast supergroup Westside Connection in the late '90s—Ice Cube, Mack 10, and WC—are spotlighted on *Cali Connected*, a 12-track compilation from the Priority vaults

that includes many of their more notable individual songs from the '90s. Of the three, Ice Cube certainly had the most hits, though the ones compiled here ("You Know How We Do It," "Steady Mobbin'," "The Nigga Ya Love to Hate," and "My Summer Vacation") aren't necessarily his biggest ones. Even so, they're all excellent inclusions, and "You Know How We Do It" opens the compilation well with a laid-back Cali sunshine vibe. On the other hand, the Mack 10 and WC (the latter performing also as both WC and the Maad Circle and Low Profile) inclusions are indeed their biggest hits, including "Westside Slaughterhouse," which brings all three rappers together for a fine performance that initially set the stage for the subsequent Westside Connection album. It's curious that Priority didn't make a more overt reference to the Westside Connection association here on *Cali Connected*. The album's packaging makes it seem as though this is a compilation of various Los Angeles rappers, but that's certainly not the case, as the usual suspects like Snoop Dogg and Dr. Dre are nowhere to be found here. While most fans will probably already have many of these songs, as none of them are rare or exclusive, the collection itself is still worth seeking out, as it's sequenced and compiled well. If anything, *Cali Connected* is a bit brief relative to most rap albums, yet this is a minor issue and probably for the better in the end since the playing time doesn't drag on to tiring lengths. — *Jason Birchmeier*

★ Cash Money Records Platinum Hits, Vol. 1 / Nov. 19, 2002 / Universal ✦✦✦✦✦

Christmas on Death Row / Sep. 16, 1996 / Universal ✦✦✦

In theory, a holiday album by the most vulgar and violent rap label should be a wonderfully tasteless guilty pleasure, but *Christmas on Death Row* doesn't quite meet expectations. Part of the problem is that only a handful of cuts on the album are gangsta rap—the majority of the album is dedicated to fairly ordinary post-new-jack urban soul. Of course, the reason why G-funk is in such short demand on the album is the fact that producer Dr. Dre left the label several months before the album was recorded. Since he was the primary creative force on the label, particularly in terms of hardcore rap, the quality of their work isn't as strong as it was while he was with Death Row, which is painfully obvious on the cookie-cutter approach of most of the rap cuts. The urban tracks sound halfhearted as well, as if they are an attempt to keep pace with the ventures into soul that Dre was working on with his *The Aftermath* project. And that lack of vision means that *Christmas on Death Row*, which could have been crude and infectious, is merely plodding and predictable. A few tracks, such as Michel'le's "Silver Bells" and Snoop Dogg's "Santa Claus Goes to the Ghetto" are strong, but the entire project feels unnecessarily belabored. — *Stephen Thomas Erlewine*

Chronic Jointz: The Hitz, Vol. 1 / Apr. 9, 2002 / Koch ✦✦✦

According to compilation producer/former A&R guy Jonathan P. Fine's liner notes, "Marijuana heightens the appreciation of music. And no music is better to appreciate with a big blunt blazin' than hip-hop." This claim is no doubt debatable—many would argue that dub-reggae or perhaps ambient techno sounds better with the chronic; others, the Grateful Dead or, perhaps, Pink Floyd. Yet one thing is clear: a lot of rap artists write songs about smoking marijuana. And *Chronic Jointz* compiles many of those songs, beginning with Tone-Loc's "Cheeba-Cheeba," originally released in 1987 at a time when, according to Fine, "some rappers, like Grandmaster Flash & the Furious Five—'White Lines (Don't Don't Do It)'—were protesting the use of drugs." However, as Fine notably points out, "Of course, rap aficionados know pot's not a drug, so as time passed, and people became more educated, attitudes like Loc's became the norm." And indeed they did, as the following songs no doubt illustrate. Three of the most well known get-high-to songs follow: Cypress Hill's "Hits From the Bong," the Pharcyde's "Pack the Pipe," and the Luniz's "I Got 5 on It." From there, *Chronic Jointz* compiles a variety of chronic-smoking songs, though it's almost seems blasphemous to not have a Dr. Dre or Snoop Dogg song here; after all, they're the ones who made "chronic" a noun rather than an adjective. Regardless, *Chronic Jointz* is somewhat of a fun novelty, more noteworthy perhaps in concept than execution. — *Jason Birchmeier*

Chuck D Presents: Louder Than a Bomb / Aug. 31, 1999 / Rhino ✦✦✦

The idea behind *Chuck D Presents: Louder Than a Bomb* is sound. After all, Chuck D may not have invented socially and socially conscious rap, but he sure became the spokesman for it during the peak years of his groundbreaking outfit, Public Enemy. Therefore, he was the perfect choice to present this 17-track compilation, containing many of the greatest protest songs in hip-hop history, including Run-D.M.C.'s "Proud to Be Black," Boogie Down Productions' "You Must Learn" (available in a "Live From Caucus Mountains Remix [single edit]"), Grandmaster Flash & the Furious Five's "The Message," Ice-T's "Freedom of Speech," and Public Enemy's "Fight the Power." Most of this dates from hip-hop's golden age, which gives the album some sort of thematic consistency, but not all the tracks are right; for instance, Ice-T's "Freedom of Speech" is the Body Count rerecording with Jello Biafra, not the original from *The Iceberg*. Little differences like this, along with a somewhat tiring sequencing, means that *Louder Than a Bomb* falls short of its promise, but it's still an admirable effort to chronicle the best protest hip-hop in one collection and is thus worth a listen. —*Stephen Thomas Erlewine*

Clickalation / Jul. 24, 2001 / Street Sound ◆◆◆
Like most rap from the post-*Chronic* era of music, this compilation focuses on the deep funk and bass grooves made popular by West Coast rappers such as Dr. Dre and Warren G. Promoting the underground hip-hop of the moment, *Clickalation* focuses on four groups: Crimetimers, Telee, G-Whiz, and Mark C. Crimetimers have a good sound that is weighed down by the weak hooks and murky production. Still, they have good verbal skills and obviously have had little time in the industry as of this album. Telee is the best rapper here—his rhymes flow smoothly and naturally over the generic backing tracks. Again, the songs still sound amateurish and suffer from bad mixing. G-Whiz has the best overall sound on the album; his songs may be slightly generic, but his production and microphone skills are up to par with major-label rap releases. Mark C is the weakest of the four—his songs feature some good production ideas, but suffer from his poor cadence and unmemorable voice. This collection features several rappers who need to break away from the G-funk sound that has obviously been done better by artists who are far more well known. Otherwise, these tracks are mildly entertaining but easy to tire of. —*Bradley Torreano*

Clockers / 1995 / 40 Acres And A Mule ◆◆◆◆
The soundtrack to Spike Lee's adaptation of Richard Price's drug-dealer/murder drama *Clockers* is alive with first-rank hip-hop and soul artists, accurately reflecting the urban sounds of 1995. From the smooth soul of Seal, Des'ree, and Chaka Khan through the hip-hop/jazz fusions of Buckshot LeFonque to the intense Crooklyn Dodgers (Jeru The Damaja, Chubb Rock, O.C., and DJ Premier), the *Clockers* soundtrack offers a wide variety of style. Nothing on the soundtrack became a hit, but that doesn't mean the album isn't worthwhile. More than most soundtracks, it captures both the spirit of the movie while standing as its own, entirely listenable, entity. —*Stephen Thomas Erlewine*

Coast Ridas: Orlie's Lowriding Competition / Mar. 9, 1999 / World Movement ◆◆◆
In California, the term "low rider" refers to young Mexican Americans who cruise around in cars that they do a great deal of work on while listening to music that they carefully select. The low-rider subculture (which War saluted with its 1975 hit "Low Rider") has been passed down from one generation to the next. While the low riders of the '50s and '60s favored doo wop and soul, the post-Baby Boomer low riders of the '80s and '90s were seriously into rap. *Coast Ridas* is a 1999 rap compilation aimed at low riders. The CD's primary emphasis is on West Coast rappers, and World Movement has included likable selections by Latino MCs ranging from Lighter Shade of Brown (which has a R&B-flavored tune in "Whatever You Want") to the quirky, Cypress Hill-influenced Funkdoobiest ("Doobie Knows"). But the collection doesn't focus on Latino rappers exclusively—rather, its general theme is rap that would appeal to low riders, and that also includes material by DJ Quik, 2nd II None, tha Alkaholiks, and other black MCs. *Coast Ridas* isn't a great collection, but it's a decent one that has its moments. —*Alex Henderson*

Connected / Apr. 21, 1998 / 321 ◆◆
The strongest aspect of this album lies in its concept: a diverse collection of urban music, most selections pushing the margins of contemporary musical expectations. According to the liner notes, the music is "predominantly hip-hop and dub, with some soul, cut & scratch, old school, and some new flavor tracks"—overall, an accurate description. In addition, keeping with the progressive nature of this project, a portion of the proceeds received from the sales of this album will be donated to PAX, an anti-gun violence organization. The first track on this album, "Touch the Stars," is a rap performed by Bay Area MC Blackalicious. The instrumentation over which he rhymes is elemental; a four-count bass loop with diffused snare accents and a futuristic

sound effect that jumps in on the one beat. Channel Live (of the Boogie Down Productions crew) comes as hard as ever on "Red Rum (Sign O' the Times)." The instrumentation, produced by Tuffy, is eerie and begins with a deep and grating guitar lick. Consistent with the consciousness-raising and apocalyptic lyrics Channel Live is known for, "Red Rum" is on point. The Angel is credited with "Selector (On Tha Otha Side of Midnite)." Featuring Cokni O' Dire, this mostly instrumental, trip-hop-like track is slower in tempo with a dominant droning bass line. "Don't Stop the Reggae Music" is a dancehall cut performed by Spida (of the Refugee Camp) and features the Tarantula Crew. With a refrain inspired by Stevie Wonder's "Don't Stop the Music," this selection is without surprises. Well-known rap group Ultramagnetic MC's blesses this project with "It's All the Way Live." Produced by member Ced-G, this track uses a familiar sample over which Kool Keith and Ced-G deliver lyrics detailing their verbal capabilities. On the whole, this is a very interesting listen that can serve as a remedy for the monotony that tends to encrust popular urban music releases. —*Qa'id Jacobs*

Constant Elevation / Jun. 11, 2002 / Astralwerks ◆◆◆◆
Constant Elevation is loosely positioned as a sequel to 1997's *Deep Concentration*, a turntablist compilation that featured such well-known names as Prince Paul, Kid Koala, and Cut Chemist demonstrating the state of what was then an art in a period of renaissance. The hipness quotient of turntablism having peaked, anthologist Joseph Patel is back with a collection of cutting-edge progressive hip-hop, much of it instrumental, some of it showcasing the cutting and scratching talents of a handful of young DJs, but most tracks spending their energy exploring the outer boundaries of the genre in more adventurous ways. Sometimes innovation looks backward, as is demonstrated by Recloose on his charming "Chiqwanga," which combines old school beats with modern techno textures; sometimes it takes modern elements and juxtaposes them in new ways, as does Omid with "Schrödinger's Cat," a clever pastiche of prog rock organ and jungle breakbeats. And sometimes it falters, like on Freestyle Fellowship's goofy "Crazy." But the inspirational moments greatly outnumber the forgettable ones on this fine compilation. —*Rick Anderson*

Contents Under Pressure / Jul. 20, 1999 / Bomb Hip Hop ◆◆◆◆
From the hottest label in the world of underground rap comes a different kind of compilation. Instead of the beat-centric slant of previous releases like the *Return of the DJ* and *Revenge of the B-Boy* collections, *Contents Under Pressure* tilts the platters to the abstract side of hip-hop, along the lines of foreign DJs like Cam, Krush, and Vadim. None of these are participants, though, since Bomb Hip-Hop usually focuses on filling its compilations with good talent and quality tracks, not necessarily recognizable names. There are a few well known DJs here (notably T-Rock, Faust, and Grazzhoppa), but most of the best tracks come from newcomers like Wildstyle Bob Nimble ("80 Something Below"), Greedy Boy (the Jeru-driven "Scientifical Madness"), Pepe Deluxe ("D.O.A."), and the excellently blunted Hydroponic Sound System ("No Secret Something Spiritual"). The album's two highlights are both DJ T-Rock productions: "Abduction & Analysis" by T-Rock & DJ Faust, plus "Annihilator Robot" by the man himself. —*Keith Farley*

Cooley High Class of 2000 / May 2, 2000 / Motown ◆◆◆◆
Cooley High Class of 2000 an entertaining album that features songs by well-known artists such as Jay-Z, Mobb Deep, and Xzibit, but the best songs are done by some of the lesser known artists like Mass Hysteria, All Natural, and Juice. Besides the songs, the listener is treated to some nice mixing and scratching, compliments of DJ Presyce. Some of the standout songs are "I Get a Rush," "Concrete," and "Ill Advised." "I Get a Rush" by Mass Hysteria has a fresh beat, and MCs Mike Treese and G-Field do a good job on the mike. "Concrete," with its addictive beat, teams up Shabaam Sahdeeq and Xzibit. The best song may be "Ill Advised" by Chicago artists All Natural and Juice—Capital D of All Natural doesn't disappoint, and flows over a nice beat while telling all the MCs that Chicago MCs don't play. *Cooley High Class of 2000* has a good mix of songs from well-known and underground artists. —*Dan Gizzi*

Cradle 2 the Grave / Feb. 18, 2003 / Def Jam ◆◆◆
No matter his acting abilities, DMX was a natural for the silver screen. Ever since his album debut, *It's Dark and Hell Is Hot*, the former Earl Simmons has flaunted a flare for the dramatic, and his work ethic is one of the toughest in hip-hop. He must have been especially busy filming, since the soundtrack for *Cradle 2 the Grave*, his first starring turn (with Jet Li), has only three

features for DMX himself. Taking up the slack, fortunately, are some of the hottest rappers circa 2003: Eminem, with a track featuring DMX as well, plus 50 Cent, Foxy Brown, Clipse, and Drag-On. The leadoff track is DMX's own "X Gon' Give It to Ya," a typically grandiose contribution that compares pretty well to the rest of his work but doesn't sound too special. Eminem's self-produced "Go to Sleep" is an extremist (even for him) murder fantasy that goes down in a hail of screams and bullets, while "My Life (Cradle 2 the Grave)" finds Foxy Brown turning curiously reflective (and more than just a bit poignant). Surprisingly, amidst the raft of big names, DMX affiliate Drag-On steals one of the best tracks, "Fireman," an off-kilter track that blows through a pair of contrasting percussion lines, borrowing from "Papa Was a Rolling Stone" and "Pusherman," but sounds completely original nevertheless. —*John Bush*

Cronica 2013 / Nov. 13, 2001 / Lideres ◆◆

Cronica 2013 features a number of underground rappers affiliated with the Low Profile label teaming up for a bunch of gangsta-ish posse tracks. As the album title and cover (which both reference Dr. Dre's *2001* album) may lead you to presume, this album is mostly about blazing up the chronic, passing it to your homies, and getting as high as possible. Some of the featured rappers who advocate the sticky-icky on this smoked-out album are Royal T, Frank V, OG Spanish Fly, Silencer, Califa Thugs, Drowsy, Mr. Sancho, and a few others. Besides puffin' on the Cali greens, the "Low Pro gang" rap about "jackin' ballers" and "bumpin' the real," which they also refer to as "'hood music," at their "gangsta parties" that "don't stop." For the most part, though, these blunt-blazin' Cali thugs are mostly all about getting high on the chronic and providing listeners a soundtrack to do the same to. Sure, it's kind of humorous and admittedly kind of fun in a stoned kind of way, yet even if you are trippin' on some freshly harvested purple haze, an entire album of get-high-to-this songs can be a little monotonous, as this album most certainly does by the time you get to "Smells Like Weed" and "So High" around the album's halfway point. Much like when it comes to getting stoned, sometimes you can overdo it, something the Low Profile posse should have kept in mind. —*Jason Birchmeier*

Cuban Hip-Hop All Stars, Vol. 1 / Sep. 25, 2001 / Papaya ◆◆◆

Cuban Hip-Hop All Stars, Vol. 1 features a number of relatively unknown Cuban hip-hop performers. Far from a crossover album, this collection is much more rooted in the Cuban side of the equation than the hip-hop side. The songs are in Spanish, which should cause some problems for non-fluent listeners, not to mention the Cuban-centric references in the lyrics. More of a curiosity than anything. Some of the featured performers include Groupo Ache Lya, Reyes de las Calles, los Hermanos, Alto y Bajo, Bajo Mundo, and several others. —*Jason Birchmeier*

Cuddiez From the Crest, Vol. 1 / Sep. 25, 2001 / Triple Crown ◆◆◆

Cuddiez From the Crest, Vol. 1 is yet another hip-hop compilation featuring another underground rap scene. This particular scene is based around the Country Club Crest, a crew of rappers who include Da' Unda' Dogg, Mac Dre, and Tic Toc. The rapping is bland and generic, with none of the rappers really standing out or doing anything new. Despite some good production (especially on "Da Flizow"), nothing about this album makes it unique from the many similar compilations available. Fans of gangsta rap may find this interesting, and it is always nice to see a new scene put out an album, but this is strictly pedestrian and is not recommended for anyone but hardcore collectors. —*Bradley Torreano*

Cue's Hip Hop Shop, Vol. 1 / Nov. 10, 1998 / Dogday ◆◆◆

Cue's Hip Hop Shop, Vol. 1 compiles tracks by some of the most accomplished underground hip-hop artists on the West Coast. The collection is sponsored by Cue's, a popular record store in Daly City, CA, that specializes in underground hip-hop. In addition to West Coast artists such as Rasco, Kut Masta Kurt, Live Human, and Westside Chemical, there are a few East Coast artists featured here who also happen to be the collection's most well known performers: Rob Swift (Queens, NY), Roc Raida (Bronx, NY), and Mr. Dibbs (Cincinnati, OH). There's plenty of diversity here, with a particular emphasis on turntablism. —*Jason Birchmeier*

Cup of Tea: A Compilation / Jul. 22, 1996 / Cup of Tea ◆◆◆

The collection of tracks from the Bristol trip-hop label Cup of Tea charts the course of music seemingly more influenced by the Smiths than the Ultramagnetic MC's. Monk & Canatella's effete "I Can Water My Plants" is one

example, while acts like Statik Sound System and Purple Penguin contribute tracks a bit more in a danceable mold. Still, there are three Monk & Canatella tracks (plus a remix), making this one dance collection that fans of indie rock's dour side could enjoy as well. —*John Bush*

Da Undaground Sound, Vol. 1: East Side / Jun. 25, 1996 / Pryority ◆◆◆

Da Underground Sound: East is an excellent sampler of edgy New York rap, highlighted by the Wu-Tang Clan's classic "C.R.E.A.M.," Das EFX's "Mic Checka," Brand Nubian's "Punks Jump Up to Get Beat Down," and Redman's "Tonight's Da Night." It's a terrific portrait of the sound of the East Coast in the early and mid-'90s. —*Stephen Thomas Erlewine*

Da Undaground Sound, Vol. 2: West Side / Jun. 25, 1996 / Pryority ◆◆◆◆◆

Da Undaground Sound: West is an excellent collection of some of the best and most important Californian hip-hop acts the early and mid-'90s. Several classics—including Dr. Dre's "Let Me Ride" and "Deep Cover," Dre and Snoop Dogg's first track together—are included, among hits by Bone Thugs-N-Harmony, Ice Cube, Too Short, Coolio, and N.W.A. It's a terrific portrait of the sound of West Coast hip-hop circa 1994. —*Stephen Thomas Erlewine*

Da Undaground Sound, Vol. 3: East Meets West / Apr. 1, 1997 / Priority ◆◆◆

Da Undaground Sound, Vol. 3: East Meets West doesn't quite consist of nothing but underground hip-hop—after all, it's hard to call artists like Ice Cube, A Tribe Called Quest, and Junior M.A.F.I.A. (all of whom reached number one) underground—but it's still a good collection of hardcore hip-hop from the late '90s. Features such songs as Keith Murray's "Get Lifted," Junior M.A.F.I.A.'s "Realms of Junior M.A.F.I.A.," Bahamadiah's "Proceed III," Ice Cube's "Lil Ass Gee," WC and the Maad Circle's "One," BUMS' "Take a Look Around," Genius' "Labels," Mobb Deep's "Trife Life," and A Tribe Called Quest's "Glamour and Glitz." —*Stephen Thomas Erlewine*

Dangerous Minds / 1995 / MCA ◆◆◆◆◆

Thanks to Coolio's monolithic single "Gangsta's Paradise," the soundtrack to Michelle Pfieffer's urban high school drama tore up the charts. Even with a single as powerful as Coolio's masterpiece, the *Dangerous Minds* soundtrack wouldn't have stayed at the top of the charts, selling over three million copies, if there was only one good song on the album. Like many soundtracks of the mid-'90s, *Dangerous Minds* is an expertly crafted urban R&B/hip-hop collection, featuring stellar production and songwriting from a number of the best and most popular artists of 1995. Admittedly, "Gangsta's Paradise" remains the standout, but there's not much disappointing material on the rest of the disc. —*Stephen Thomas Erlewine*

Dark Angel / Apr. 23, 2002 / Artemis ◆◆◆

Dark Angel exceeds your expectations for a television show soundtrack. Many of the songs here are quite impressive, beginning with the album-opening "Dark Angel Theme," a collaboration between Public Enemy and MC Lyte. As the soundtrack progresses, you may not be dazzled by the superstar quotient, but you're likely to be wowed by such songs as Khia's "My Neck, My Back," Samantha Cole's "Bring It to Me" (including its appended remix), and Mystic's "The Life." The hip-hop tracks unfortunately don't quite measure up to the neo-soul tracks. This seems to be a female-orientated soundtrack, perhaps because of the show's female lead character. Yet the few hip-hop moments aren't disappointing by any means, just a bit lackluster in comparison. Finally, *Dark Angel* includes a couple of previously released songs, including "Candy," a sassy collaboration between Foxy Brown, Kelis, and the Neptunes. This catchy song—as fun and naughty as anything the Neptunes did in the early 2000s—adds even more value to this already impressive soundtrack. —*Jason Birchmeier*

Death Row Greatest Hits / Dec. 1996 / Death Row/Priority ◆◆◆◆

More than any other label, Death Row defined gangsta rap and hip-hop in the early '90s, and the double-disc *Death Row Greatest Hits* captures nearly all of the label's biggest hits from artists like Dr. Dre, Snoop Dogg, and Tupac. Although the disc bends some rules by including cuts that weren't released on Death Row and containing an abundance of previously unreleased songs, the compilation sums up the feeling of the early and mid-'90s. A single disc would have provided more consistent thrills—and it would have eliminated the annoying remixes on disc two—but the sprawl is also indicative of the self-indulgence of gangsta rap, which is essential to understanding the genre. And *Death Row Greatest Hits* has a string of great songs—"Let Me Ride," "What's My Name," "Gin and Juice," "Nothin' But a G Thang" (but no

"California Love")—making it an excellent summation of gangsta rap's glory days. —*Stephen Thomas Erlewine*

Deep: A Family Production / 2001 / Beat Kings ◆◆◆

Deep: A Family Production features a variety of rap artists from three independent labels: HooDDRocKK Records (Cali Bay Area), Chocolate Thunder Entertainment (Denver), PocTown/O.E.S. Mobb Entertainment (Central Coast of Cali). Given the number of artists contributing to this wide-ranging collection, there's no shortage of variety here. Many of the tracks are produced by DonzeLLi, and O.E.S. produces a handful of the tracks as well. Though none of these rappers or producers are relatively well known, they're all quite impressive, making this a similarly impressive collection that is full of pleasant surprises. —*Jason Birchmeier*

Def Beats, Vol. 1 / Music of Life ◆◆◆

A mediocre rap anthology released in the wake of Run D.M.C., so it's no surprise that several of the acts here sound suspiciously like them (although thumbs up to Microphone Prince for his revamping of Abbot and Costello for "Who's the Captain"). Released in the U.K. by Music of Life, most of the artists come from Profile and Powerplay, but sneakily, they have added Derek B, one of the first wave of British rappers—and not a particularly good one—under the banner "The hardest hip-hop in the world direct from New York City." The collection closes with a weak megamix by producer Simon Harris. —*Ted Mills*

Def Jam 1985-2001: History of Hip Hop, Vol. 1 / Feb. 27, 2001 / Universal ◆◆◆◆◆

A flawless compilation, *Def Jam 1985-2001: History of Hip Hop, Vol. 1* showcases just how powerful the New York-based record label was during the '80s and '90s. In fact, no label came close to challenging Def Jam's status as the premier rap label—not Death Row, not Jive, not Sugarhill, not Cold Chillin'; no label even came close. The early mid- to late-'80s hits that catapulted the label to recognition during the Russell Simmons/Rick Ruben era are here: LL Cool J's "I Can't Live Without My Radio," Beastie Boys' "Fight for Your Right," and Slick Rick's "Children's Story." So are plenty of the early-'90s hits that solidified Def Jam's status during a time when it finally had to fend off competitors and a fledging West Coast scene: Public Enemy's "Fight the Power," EPMD's "Crossover," and Onyx's "Slam." And there are also a handful of the late-'90s hits that redefined Def Jam's image once the label shed many of its veteran artists: Jay-Z's "Can I Get A...," DMX's "Party (Up in Here)," and Method Man's "I'll Be There/You're All I Need." While the *Def Jam Music Group—Ten Year Anniversary* box set is undeniably more thorough and informative, this convenient single-disc compilation features nothing but the big hits and also features the late-'90s artists that aren't found on that pricey box set. —*Jason Birchmeier*

☆ Def Jam Music Group Inc.: 10th Year Anniversary / 1995 / Def Jam ◆◆◆◆◆

In the '80s, Def Jam Records became the leading rap and hip-hop label in America. Featuring a roster filled with superstars—including Public Enemy, LL Cool J, the Beastie Boys, Slick Rick, and EPMD—Def Jam released many of the most innovative and groundbreaking records of the late '80s and, as the four-CD box *Ten Year Anniversary* proves, the music has lost none of its impact over the years. Over the course of the four discs, the set runs through a number of hip-hop classics, including "I Can't Live Without My Radio," "Fight the Power," "(You Gotta) Fight for Your Right (To Party)," "Slam," "Don't Believe the Hype," "Rock the Bells," "Regulate," "Crossover," and over 50 other tracks. The one (minor) drawback of the set is the fact that it isn't sequenced chronologically; nevertheless, each disc in the box is compulsively listenable. In sheer musical terms, *Ten Year Anniversary* is one of the best box sets ever compiled and is essential to any popular music collection. —*Stephen Thomas Erlewine*

Def Jam's Greatest Hits / Sep. 9, 1997 / Def Jam ◆◆◆◆

Although it doesn't follow any chronological order and doesn't always gel musically, *Def Jam Greatest Hits* is a good cross-section of the pioneering hip-hop label's biggest hits, featuring such classics as Onyx's "Slam," the Beastie Boys' "Brass Monkey," LL Cool J's "Around the Way Girl," 3rd Bass's "Gas Face," Domino's "Getto Jam," Slick Rick's "Children's Story," and Warren G's "Regulate." —*Stephen Thomas Erlewine*

Def Jam's Greatest Hits: Hardcore / Sep. 9, 1997 / Def Jam ◆◆◆◆

A companion piece to *Def Jam Greatest Hits*, *Def Jam Greatest Hits: Hardcore* is very similar to its predecessor in that it doesn't quite follow any specific

chronological order and combines the label's early hits with later hits, which doesn't always make musical sense. Also, there are as many hardcore songs on *Greatest Hits* as there are on *Hardcore*, so the musical difference between these two discs is negligible. Still, *Def Jam Greatest Hits: Hardcore* has a number of terrific singles, including Public Enemy's "Public Enemy #1," Method Man's "Method Man (Remix)," EPMD's "Gold Digger," LL Cool J's "I Need a Beat," Redman's "Blow Your Mind," and the Beastie Boys' "Paul Revere," which makes it a worthwhile purchase for casual rap fans. —*Stephen Thomas Erlewine*

Defenders of the Underworld / Oct. 5, 1999 / Battle Axe ◆◆◆

Hip-hop fans would be forgiven for quickly passing over this independent rap compilation; after all, the cover photo of a Norse god makes the album a natural for a death-metal compilation. For those who manage to find it, though, *Defenders of the Underworld* is a good compilation charting the breadth of the growing hip-hop underground, courtesy of a few unreleased tracks from notables like Kool Keith, Swollen Members, Divine Styler, Aceyalone, the Arsonists, and Dilated Peoples, plus plenty of new names contributing great tracks of their own. The vibes are dark and the grooves and rhymes are tight on excellent debuts from Defari ("Cookin' Up Your Brain"), Buc Fifty ("Worst Enemy"), Pycho Realm ("Pow Wow"), and Moka Only ("Variety")—the latter a real wonder in late-'90s hip-hop of any stripe, a great positive-minded track. From the familiar names, best is Kool Keith's "Get off My Elevator," a brilliant, hilarious moment of paranoid bliss with some of the best rhymes he's come up with in awhile. —*John Bush*

Def Jux Presents, Vol. 2 / 2002 / Def Jux ◆◆◆◆

Conjoined by forces as varied as lyrical progressiveness, underground status, New York, and the production/A&R resource that is label-chief El-P, the artists making up the Def Jux crew come together on this 2002 compilation *Def Jux Presents, Vol. 2*. Featuring tracks off their respective label releases, Aesop Rock, Mr. Lif, the Weathermen, RJD2, and El-P himself all drop tracks that through their fairly visible profile expose more unknown artists like Camu Tao, Rob Sonic, Masai Bey, Yak Balls, and Atoms Family to the judicious hip-hop listenership. In an industry climate too frugal and impatient for real label brands to develop, El Producto has managed to put together a stable of some of the most poignant and gifted musicians that are both similar enough for intermingling, while maintaining a collective movement boasting innovation, intelligence, and individuality. Highlights include cuts off the El-P full-length, RJD2's expansive beats on "I Really Like Your Def Jux Baby Tee," the Weathermen's "Same As It Never Was," and Mr. Lif & Murs' "Sneak Preview." The result is easily the most legitimate hip-hop compilation out in 2002 on the label most important to watch. —*Nic Kincaid*

Dexter's Laboratory: Homeboy Genius / Aug. 2002 / Rhino ◆◆◆◆◆

Mixing hip-hop with Cartoon Network fave *Dexter's Laboratory* sounds like a potentially unstable combination, but *Dexter's Laboratory: Homeboy Genius* is surprisingly successful because of the talent involved with it. When Coolio's goofy, dub-inspired "Dexter (What's His Name)" is one of the album's *weaker* tracks, you know you're listening to something special. All of the artists on this seven-song effort rose to the challenge of mixing their individual styles with different aspects of Dexter's world, crafting music that's fun and catchy, but not at all patronizing to kids or older listeners. Phife Dawg's "Love According to Dexter" and De La Soul's adorable "Sibling Rivalries" concentrate on Dexter's sometimes turbulent relationship with his sister DeeDee, while YZ's "Mandark's Plan" has sympathy for Dexter's nemesis (as well as a cool sample of the young evil genius' cackle looping in the background). Not surprisingly, though, the best tracks on *Dexter's Laboratory: Homeboy Genius* focus on Dexter the inventor: Will.I.Ams (from Black Eyed Peas) "Secret Formula" describes Dexter's lab with such mischievous glee that he may as well be talking about his studio; while Prince Paul's "Back to the Lab" takes an unsuccessful experiment in stride. Fortunately, *Dexter's Laboratory: Homeboy Genius* is a complete success; its only drawback is that it's too short. Still, all kids' albums—and hip-hop albums, for that matter—should be this much fun to listen to. —*Heather Phares*

Diggin' in the Crates for Beats Y'all / Apr. 9, 1996 / Hot Productions ◆◆◆◆

Hot Productions' collection of early-'80s electro goes beyond the average to include a few lesser-known tracks from the seminal era. Beside the easily available classics ("Planet Rock," "Jam on It," "Set It Off," "Electric Kingdom," "Hip Hop Bee Bop [Don't Stop]"), obscure acts like Quadrant 6, George Kranz (with the original "Din Daa Daa"), and Key-Matic (the hilarious "Breaking in Space") make *Diggin' in the Crates* more enjoyable than the average electro compilation. —*John Bush*

Diggin' in the Crates, Vol. 1: Profile Rap Classics / 1994 / Profile ◆◆◆◆
When hip-hop became huge in the early '80s, its popularity put quite a few independent labels on the map. One of the most important was Profile, which was founded in 1981 and went on to become one of the top indie labels in the U.S. Profile never recorded rap exclusively (the company also provided its share of dance classics), but it was hip-hop more than anything that brought attention to the label. In 1994, Profile looked back on its rap output of the early to mid-'80s with this gem-laden collection. The CD's oldest track is Dr. Jeckyll & Mr. Hyde's "Genius Rap"—a 1981 classic that finds the hip-hop pioneers rapping to the Tom Tom Club's "Genius of Love"—and its most recent is Dana Dane's quirky "Nightmares" from 1986. Gems like Run-D.M.C.'s "Sucker MCs," Pebblee-Poo's "A Fly Guy" (a female's response to the Boogie Boys' "A Fly Girl"), and Pumpkin's "Here Comes That Beat!" transport the listener back to a classic era in hip-hop—a time when New York still dominated the genre, breakdancers were doing their thing on the sidewalks of major American cities, gangsta rap had yet to become popular, and MCs used the term "fresh" to praise things that excited them. *Diggin' in the Crates* reminds us that Profile's contributions to rap were sizable. —*Alex Henderson*

Disco Juice, Vol. 2 / May 28, 2002 / Counterpoint ◆◆◆
The second volume of *Disco Juice* shows that the first volume, though stronger overall, hardly ransacked all the goods from the catalogs of the labels run by Patrick Adams and Peter Brown during the late '70s and early '80s. The prolific producers' quietly pioneering work largely went unrecognized in the reissue world until Counterpoint came along to release these crucial documents of underground dance music. However, referring to the lovingly assembled *Disco Juice* compilations as mere documents would be grossly limiting, as they offer plenty of disco, soul, and old school rap that—for the most part—sounds terrific decades after original release. Where the first volume of *Disco Juice* stuck primarily to disco, the second volume opens things up to incorporate soul (Florence Miller's "The Groove I'm In," Cloud One's "Dust to Dust") and rap (Margo's Kool out Crew's "Death Rap," Willie Wood & Willie Wood Crew's "Willie Rap," Super-jay's "Super-jay Love Theme"; as a side note, the latter two incorporate Johnson Products' "Johnson Jumpin'"). Hot disco isn't in short supply, either. "New York Moving" by Ahzz, "Roller Rink Funk" by Shift (a great roller jam that slightly resembles Michael Jackson's "Workin' Day and Night"), and "The Guardian Angel Is Watching Over Us" by Golden Flamingo Orchestra (a great cross between the Staple Singers and Sister Sledge) highlight the more floor-friendly selections. Despite their strength, the most astonishing aspect of the *Disco Juice* compilations is that they hardly exhaust the career highlights of the producers/labelheads they spotlight. Putting together retrospectives of their freelance work would be a monstrous task. —*Andy Kellman*

Down to Earth / Feb. 20, 2001 / Sony ◆◆◆◆
For the most part, the *Down to Earth* soundtrack provides a revealing look at the ever-trendy contemporary R&B landscape circa early 2001. The roster of featured artists won't astound you, though a few artists such as Monica, Genuwine, Jagged Edge, and Lauryn Hill obviously stand out as established artists. In addition to these artists, who all turn in impressive songs, some of the more surprising efforts actually come from less-established artists such as Jill Scott and Kelly Rowland (of Destiny's Child)—two artists deservedly on the brink of pop-crossover success at the time of this album's release. When you break these songs down and listen to them individually, this album is an incredible collection of contemporary R&B; however, a sporadic infusion of rap ruins the album from being a marvelously engaging listen from beginning to end. The album-opening Scott Storch-produced contribution from the Roots and Amel Larrieux, "Glitches," is a welcome addition to the album and fits in rather well with the successive songs by Monica and Ginuwine. Unfortunately, the other rap songs ruin the album's continuity: Sticky Fingaz and Eminem's "What If I Was White" comes across as incredibly distasteful and ill-conceived in its attempt to be comedic and without any memorable hooks to propel it beyond these flaws; similarly, Bone Thugs' "Thug Music Play On" isn't any better, even as it tries to assimilate its thug themes into the album's underlying sense of soulful motif with its employment of vocal harmony; finally, Snoop Dogg's "Gin and Juice" is at least a classic song, but still is obviously out of place. As mentioned previously, *for*

the most part, this soundtrack is a truly wonderful sample of well-written contemporary R&B songs, only plagued by its interruptive rap moments. —*Jason Birchmeier*

Dr. Dolittle 2 / Jun. 5, 2001 / J-records ◆◆◆◆
As a broad collection of contemporary urban R&B and pop-rap songs, with a few that fit somewhere between those two related styles, the *Dr. Dolittle 2* soundtrack has a little something for everybody. Granted, half of the 13 songs are undeniably in a class above the others, but even the filler here is commendable for its conventional execution at the same level. If you're a contemporary urban R&B fan, look toward Angie Stone and Raphael Saadiq's "Makin' Me Feel," O-Town's "We Fit Together," and Deborah Cox's "Absolutely Not," in particular, as highlights. If you're more of a rap fan, there aren't quite as many highlights, but Snoop Dogg and Battlecat's "Do U Wanna Roll (Dolittle Theme)" and Flipmode Squad and the Neptunes' "What It Is, Pt. 2" are arguably the best songs on the entire soundtrack, capable hit singles for sure. The former song—also featuring Lil' Kim representing the East Coast and R.L. crooning in the background—is pretty much a straight-up interpolation of Zapp's "Doo Wa Ditty (Blow That Thing)," a feel-good, PG-rated summer song with a catchy sung chorus courtesy of Snoop. The latter finds the Neptunes turning in yet another elastic, bottom-heavy, booty-shaking beat with an infectious chorus sung by Kelis. And if these highlights aren't enough, there are two other noteworthy songs: Next and Lil' Zane's "Lookin' for Love," a fine song illustrating an excellent synthesis of singing and rapping, and Jimmy Cozier's "Two Steps," an otherwise passable song featuring a trendy attempt by producer Soulshock to integrate a two-step rhythm in the chorus. Overall, though *Dr. Dolittle 2* isn't a beginning-to-end collection of standout songs, it has its moments and goes out of its way to offer something of quality for everybody, from the urban crowd to the rap crowd. —*Jason Birchmeier*

Drumline / Dec. 10, 2002 / Jive ◆◆◆
When rap was still the new kid on the block in the '80s, some of the older R&B singers refused to take it seriously. But times have changed, and these days, urban and rap are joined at the hip. Rappers incorporate R&B singing; urban and neo-soul singers incorporate hip-hop. Rap and urban R&B are certainly joined at the hip on the soundtrack for the movie *Drumline*, which finds producer Dallas Austin receiving the title "executive music producer." Under Austin's direction, this soundtrack stands on its own regardless of whether or not one has seen the movie. Some soundtracks are nothing more than souvenirs of the corresponding film, but the *Drumline* soundtrack has a life of its own—even if one never sees the movie, this is still a generally decent collection of urban and rap. And it is also an appealingly diverse collection; listeners are exposed to everything from neo-soul singing to dirty South rapping. Petey Pablo's "Club Banger" and Trick Daddy's "Let's Go" are right out of the dirty South school of hip-hop, while Syleena Johnson's "Faithful to You" and Alicia Keys' "Butterflyz" have a neo-soul outlook—that is, they combine urban/hip-hop beats with classic pre-'80s soul values. Johnson and Keys are rootsy enough to be called soul singers yet modern and high-tech enough to appeal to the urban contemporary market of the early 2000s. But while neo-soul is part of urban contemporary, not all urban singing is neo-soul; Monica's "Uh Oh" and Nivea's "What You Waitin' For" are among the urban tracks that don't have a neo-soul perspective. Overall, Austin does his job well on the *Drumline* soundtrack, which moves in different directions but still manages to have a certain continuity. —*Alex Henderson*

Duck Down Records Presents: The Album / Sep. 14, 1999 / Priority ◆◆◆
The Boot Camp Click (Black Moon, Heltah Skeltah, Cocoa Brovas, O.G.C., etc.) in their prime were a dynasty in the making and consorted with the elite of New York's underground hip-hop scene. Since their auspicious arrival, however, these talented MCs have been a shell of their former selves, suffering from a variety of growth-stunting ailments that have depleted their once-generous arsenal. Much like their first gathering, this project suffers from many of the same deficiencies: lack of direction and unregimented, Beatminerz-less production. This camp has always been regulated by their more established heavyweights, more specifically by their Napoleonic general Buckshot who continues his offensive with the Beatminerz, revitalizing his original crook style on the spunky "Jump Up." The BDI Thug also appears on the brutish, mix-tape-leaked "Eye of the Scorpio" with Rock, whose bone-jarring vocals steal the spotlight. Heltah Skeltah's lone group effort, the enticing "Ultimate Rush" features Canada's MC, Saukrates. However, in most compilations or soundtracks, there is no way around the requisite amount of

filler material or trivial collaborations, and this recording is by no means any different. —*Matt Conaway*

DV-10: A Decade of Delicious Vinyl / Oct. 26, 1999 / Delicious Vinyl ◆◆◆◆
Delicious Vinyl came busting out of the gates in the late '80s with huge hits by Tone-Loc ("Wild Thing," "Funky Cold Medina") and Young MC ("Bust A Move"), plus critically acclaimed records by the Pharcyde and Brand New Heavies. They never quite had another stretch like that, but that particular era was pretty terrific, as *DV-10: A Decade of Delicious Vinyl* proves. The 14-track collection concentrates on the late '80s and early '90s, when the label was at its peak. Some may complain that some latter-day cuts are missing, but the fact of the matter is, this results in a better, entertaining listen, and gives an accurate portrait of the label's strengths. —*Stephen Thomas Erlewine*

Eastern Conference All-Stars / Aug. 24, 1999 / Landspeed ◆◆◆
Eastern Conference is the record label started by High and Mighty members Mr. Eon and Mighty Mi. This album is essentially a collection of 12" releases put out by the label, such as "Cranial Lumps" and "The Meaning." There are a few new tunes like "E=MC2," but for the most part the songs here have already been released on vinyl. Another new song (to a degree) is "Hands On Experience Pt.II." It is available on the High and Mighty album *Home Field Advantage*, but the version on the *Eastern Conference All-Stars* release has the original beat, which works better than the *Home Field Advantage* version. Also on this album are two Smut Peddler pieces: "One by One" and "The Hole Repertoire." —*Dan Gizzi*

Eastern Conference All-Stars [DVD] / Sep. 17, 2002 / Music Video Distributors ◆◆
The 2002 DVD *Eastern Conference All-Stars* is a 122-minute showcase of a few artists on the Eastern Conference rap label. The majority of the video is comprised of promo video clips by such acts as High & Mighty, Kool G Rap, and the Smut Peddlers, the latter of which includes a cameo from the frequent Howard Stern guest (and DVD cover model) Beetlejuice. In addition to the promo clips, there are additional bonus features, such as Beetlejuice recording his vocal parts with the Smut Peddlers, among other bits. Although the Beetlejuice-related material is quite funny, it doesn't completely hide the fact that the majority of the artists on *Eastern Conference All-Stars* are neither original nor entirely memorable, which means that the DVD will probably only appeal to fans of the Stern show. —*Greg Prato*

Eastern Conference All-Stars, Vol. 3 / Nov. 12, 2002 / High Times ◆◆◆◆
The Eastern Conference imprint shored up its lineup on this full-fledged flavor free for all. Presented by Philly underground session heads High & Mighty and High Times Records, this is the first volume of the series not released on the failed venture that was Rawkus. Past volumes featured the handiwork of such underground venerables as Eminem (whom the label vehemently despises), Mad Skillz, Kool Keith, Pharoahe Monch, and Mos Def. Hip-hop hash and herb heads will find a variety of high grades on this compilation, as artists like Mr. Eon (of High & Mighty), Cage, Copywrite, Tame One (formerly of the Artifacts), R.A. the Rugged Man, and Kool G Rap push the East Coast's rugged brand of syllable flipping with a barrage of headspinning flows. Though psychotropic drugs and skullduggery seem to be this unit's main mantras, there's no denying the crew's ready wit and plentiful prowess in its practice of a dying art form. Virtually any cut measures up with the underground's best of the modern era; Tame One's "Dreamz," Copywrite's "Jeah," and Smut Peddlers' "Bart Blunt vs. Sherm Penn" are exceptional examples of the album's many guilty pleasures. The emergent skills of the Columbus, OH, native Copywrite truly stand out here, including such gut-busting filth as "Competitors are slain by this intelligent gunner/Quick to pop the trunk like an elephant hunter." Also of note, the album features an unreleased original version of High & Mighty's "Last Hit" featuring their nemesis, Slim Shady. —*M.F. DiBella*

Ego Trip's the Big Playback / Apr. 11, 2000 / Priority ◆◆◆◆◆
The soundtrack to *Ego Trip's Book of Rap Lists* salutes its namesake by offering a dozen classic tracks from the mid-'80s golden age of hip-hop. Still, rap fans may be a bit surprised at the track list; there's nobody here with the name recognition of the period's heroes (Eric B. & Rakim, Public Enemy, EPMD, LL Cool J) or even those with renewed underground cred during the late '90s (Ultramagnetic MC's, Kool G Rap & DJ Polo). Instead, this compilation focuses on *real* obscurities, not necessarily the best tracks of all time, but top-rate cuts that never got the attention they deserved. Obviously, it's re-

quired listening for readers of the book, the perfect way to actually *hear* some of the out-of-print classics mentioned in sections like "Quarter Pound of Underacknowledged Hip Hop Cuts" and "Disses You Might Have Missed." Even for fans who aren't interested in a book of rap lists, *Ego Trip's the Big Playback* is a stellar compilation, providing a couple of the original tracks whose samples might sound very familiar to '90s fans: "Holy War (Live)" by Divine Force (used by DJ Premier on a Jeru the Damaja cut) and "Get Retarded" by MC EZ & Troup (used by Dr. Dre on "Zoom" from the *Bulworth* soundtrack). Other highlights among these rarities include "Marly Marl Scratch," the first solo-billed track by Marly Marl, and "Get Down Grandmaster" by Grandmaster Caz, a great latter-day cut by the old school legend. —*John Bush*

8 Mile: More Music From / Nov. 26, 2002 / Interscope ◆◆◆◆◆
Though it's yet another in the long line of soundtrack sequels, from *More Dirty Dancing* to *Trainspotting 2*, *More Music From 8 Mile* is a distinctly different record than its predecessor, and in one sense, much better at placing the listener in the milieu of the movie. Unlike the original *8 Mile* soundtrack, which was much more along the lines of a modern soundtrack (with several high-profile features for the star and new offerings from everyone included), this one has only tracks from the mid-'90s or earlier. It's hard to imagine how the compilers could've done a better job of collecting the absolute best in hardcore hip-hop then, just a few years just before Biggie and Tupac were killed and the rap game became the biggest in the music business. The tracks come mostly from the hardcore East Coast, with all-timers like Mobb Deep's "Shook Ones, Pt. II," Notorious B.I.G.'s "Juicy," and Method Man's "Bring da Pain" leading the way. Tupac represents as well with "Gotta Get Mine," a feature on an MC Breed track. The burgeoning Wu-Tang axis gets the most shots, though, with four straight tracks featuring either the group itself—or solo shots like Ol' Dirty Bastard's legend-making "Shimmy Shimmy Ya." Two party jams, "Feel My Flow" by Naughty By Nature and "Player's Ball" by Outkast, lighten the mood just when it's needed, and "Runnin'" by the tremendously underrated Pharcyde makes for a great left-field choice. No, there are no tracks here from Eminem, and that's just the way it should be to evoke the time when he was just an obscure Detroit rapper, struggling to make it to the big time. —*John Bush*

Electric Funk, Vol. 1 / 1996 / Priority ◆◆◆
Electric Funk, Vol. 1 is a good collection of electro-funk and old school rap from the early '80s. It's not a comprehensive overview by any means, but it's still a good sampler, featuring cuts by Afrika Bambaataa & Soulsonic Force ("Planet Rock"), World Class Wreckin' Cru ("Juice"), Trinere's ("I Know You Love Me"), Freestyle's ("The Party Has Just Begun"), Uncle Jam's Army ("Dial-a-Freak"), Orbit ("The Beat Goes On"), Egyptian Lover ("Girls"), and Grandmaster Flash & the Furious Five ("The Scorpio"). —*Stephen Thomas Erlewine*

Escape From Death Row / Aug. 31, 1999 / Crash ◆◆◆
Escape From Death Row is a decent collection of hardcore hip-hop and gangsta rap coming from the neighborhoods of South Central. Featuring tha Dogg Pound orginators and rap mainstays such as Daz Dillinger, Soopafly, Kurupt, and RBX, this compilation also showcases cuts from Ruff Dogg, Silva Satin, Lil C-Style, Ebony-E, and more. —*MacKenzie Wilson*

Escena Alterlatina: The Future Sound in Español / Mar. 13, 2001 / Ark 21 ◆◆◆◆
Judging from most of the Latin music that makes it to the shores of North America, you'd think the Latin genre is filled either grinning pop artists like Ricky Martin or old school traditionalists like the Buena Vista Social Club. In fact, Latin America produces a wide range of music, some of it the best, most hard-hitting music out there. *Escena Alterlatina: The Future Sound in Español* is an attempt to compile the best of the rest of Spanish-language music. What is most surprising about the album is the range of music—L.A.'s Tres Delinquentes offers some Spanglish hip-hop with "Return of the Tres" while rockers Los Mocosos' "Caliente" offers some funk alongside members of the Tower of Power horns. Meanwhile, Panama's Los Rabanes play some fierce dancehall reggae with "My Commanding Wife." Covering such a wide variety of music, *Escena Alterlatina* suffers from a lack of focus, but most of the music has so much flavor that you're willing to forgive the album of its eccentricities. —*Jon Azpiri*

Essential Underground Hip Hop, Vol. 1 / Jun. 11, 2002 / Landspeed ◆◆◆
Boasting an array of hip-hop figures old and new school, *Essential Underground Hip Hop, Vol. 1* virtually proves the promise in the title. Making

appearances are veterans Guru, Masta Ace, Ed O.G., M.O.P., Phife Dawg, and Royce Da 5'9'', along with newer names like Planet Asia, J. Live, Jigmastas, Hi-Tek, Cormega, and Akrobatik. —*John Bush*

Excavation: Beat Alchemy / Jan. 5, 1999 / Innerhythmic ✦✦✦
A compilation of the experimental edge of dub hip-hop, *Excavation: Beat Alchemy* includes tracks by WordSound favorites like Spectre, Dr. Israel, Sensational, and Material as well as turntablists like DJ Disk. —*John Bush*

Exit Wounds / Mar. 20, 2001 / Virgin ✦✦✦✦
The *Exit Wounds* soundtrack may bounce around from smooth urban sounds to buck-wild dirty South to hardcore East Coast rap, but no matter the style, it maintains a stunning level of exceptional quality. In fact, it's difficult to narrow down the best moments, since there are so many. On the one hand, several of the gritty East Coast moments here—DMX's "No Sunshine," Drag-On's "Off da Chain Daddy," Lady Luck's "Hey Ladies," in particular—could garner substantial radio play. Similarly, the three dirty South moments featured—Trick Daddy and Trina's "We Got," Three 6 Mafia's "They Don't Fuck Wit U," Cash Money Millionaires' "Steady Grinding"—all stand as impressive songs driven by excellent production and a decadent air. And if that isn't enough to make this a notable soundtrack, the three sultry urban soul moments—Ideal's "It's on Me," Playa's "Incense Burning," Timbaland's "Hell Yeah (Remix)"—challenge the rap songs for the status of being album highlights. In sum, this album is filled to brim with amazing songs. Granted, a few songs such as Black Child and Ja Rule's "State to State" should be skipped over, and a few other artists who usually turn in quality music—Nas, Memphis Bleek, the Lox—turn in throwaways. For the most part, though, this album illustrates exactly how great soundtracks occasionally can be; not only does it have an ensemble of amazing songs, but it also offers a variety of styles—hardcore East Coast rap, dirty South, naughty urban soul—that should appeal to a number of audiences and make this album a commercial success. —*Jason Birchmeier*

Explicit Rap / 1990 / Priority ✦✦✦
In the early 1990s, Luther Campbell became an unlikely poster child for the First Amendment when Florida attorney Jack Thompson declared that the 2 Live Crew's lyrics violated obscenity laws and tried to shut him down. But Thompson's war against the U.S. Constitution failed, and a variety of free-speech advocates rushed to Campbell's defense—Democrats, Libertarians, even some moderate Republicans (who felt that parents, not the government, should monitor what kids listen to). In 1991, Priority stood up for Campbell—and hardcore rap in general—by assembling the compilation *Explicit Rap.* Priority's goal was to promote free speech (and make some money in the process) by putting together a compilation that hardcore rap's detractors would find offensive, and, sure enough, there is plenty to offend delicate ears. If you like your music clean-cut and wholesome, you won't appreciate explicit offerings like the 2 Live Crew's "Me So Horny," Ice-T's "Girls, L.G.B.N.A.F.," Too Short's "Cusswords," and N.W.A's "A Bitch Iz a Bitch." If Priority wanted to thumb its nose at critics of hardcore rap, this compilation does exactly that. Some people saw *Explicit Rap* as not only an attack on Thompson but also an attack on Tipper Gore and the Parents' Music Resource Center. Here's where things become ironic: some of the same music industry people who were lambasting the PMRC in the 1980s and early 1990s made generous contributions to Al Gore's presidential campaign in 2000. Perhaps they decided that Tipper Gore, unlike Thompson, wasn't trying to get anyone's music banned—she was only trying to help parents monitor what their kids were listening to. At any rate, *Explicit Rap* isn't the last word on hardcore rap in the late 1980s and early 1990s, but it's generally enjoyable if you like your rap on the raunchy side. —*Alex Henderson*

Extra Yard / Oct. 1, 2002 / Big Dada ✦✦✦✦✦
Far and away Britain's finest hip-hop label (and one of the finest in the world), Big Dada spent its first five years assembling a crucial stable of producers and rappers who forged a fresh style owing surprisingly little to rap music of the American variety. The Big Dada sound is a meld of digital raggae with hip-hop breakbeats and a distinctly British West Indies style of rapping—heavy on the flow *and* the verbiage. *Extra Yard*, the label's second compilation, is all unreleased and excellent from start to finish, the perfect way to sample the Big Dada style without risk of release overlap. Flagship rapper Roots Manuva gets no less than four tracks, two of them solid remixes ("Bashment Boogie," "Dreamy Days"), one a version of his massive track "Witness" rejuvenated with a posse of rappers, and the last a new track ("Born Again," with

new name Wildflower). Veteran Ty wins the best-track sweepstakes with "We Don't Care," driven by a deep, distorted bass line and his awesome vocal turn fading into a great group vocal on the chorus. Ace producer Part 2 makes a specialty out of excellent tracks, and all of the ones he directs here get the nod as well: "Life Without You" (a sleek R&B tune featuring LSK on vocals, with a bit of a two-step bounce to it) and two New Flesh songs, "Lie Low" and "Eat More Fruit," both studded with deep, stuttered beats. The raps are top-notch, the productions next level, and the whole package is mixed into a fine froth by DJ Excalibah, on loan from the Beeb. —*John Bush*

Fat Beats & Bra Straps: Battle Rhymes & Posse / Mar. 17, 1998 / Rhino ✦✦✦
The second volume of Rhino's female hip-hop series *Fat Beats & Bra Straps* spotlights *Battle Rhymes & Posse Cuts*—that is, cutting contests and songs recorded by a full group. Like its predecessor, the disc is a little light on actual classics—there's Roxanne & U.T.F.O.'s "The Rel Roxanne," plus LL Cool J's "Doin' It," which really stretches the limits of the "female" designation, since LeShaun is essentially used as window dressing—but the strength of the collection is that it rounds up a lot of rarities, obscure singles and forgotten album tracks that haven't been widely heard since their initial release. Among the more interesting cuts are De La Soul and Shortie No Mass' "In the Woods," Sparky D's "Sparky's Turn," Pebblee-Poo's "A Fly Guy," J.J. Fad's "Ya Goin' Down," the Coup's "This One's a Girl" and "The Show Stoppa (Is Stupid Fresh)" by Super Nature, which was an early incarnation of Salt-N-Pepa. Anyone serious about hip-hop will find cuts like these quite interesting, but listeners looking for a handful of hits should realize that this is more of an archival, historical release than a hits collection. —*Stephen Thomas Erlewine*

Fat Beats & Bra Straps: Hip Hop Classics / Mar. 17, 1998 / Rhino ✦✦✦✦
Despite the borderline-offensive title, *Fat Beats & Bra Straps* is a valuable collection of early rap and hip-hop from female rappers. The first installment of the three-volume series spotlights *Classic Hip-Hop*, featuring both classic songs and cult classics from a variety of female artists, including the Real Roxanne ("Romeo, Pts. 1 & 2," "Bang Zoom (Let's Go-Go)"), Roxanne Shanté ("Have a Nice Day," "Runaway"), Queen Latifah ("Inside Out," "Wrath of My Madness"), Ice Cream Tee ("Can't Hold Back"), Sweet Tee & Jazzy Joyce ("It's My Beat"), Dimples D. ("Sucker D.J.'s [I Will Survive]"), Sparky-D ("Throwdown"), 2 Much ("Wild Thang"), Hurby's Machine, featuring Antoinette ("I Got an Attitude"), and Oaktown's 3-5-7 ("Juicy Gotcha Krazy"). There are a handful of classic cuts, but most of this is primarily of interest to collectors and serious hip-hop fanatics, since many of these tracks are forgotten singles or album tracks that haven't been widely heard since their initial release. It does fulfill a valuable role, however, because it presents a real, convincing argument that females had a more vital role in the development of hip-hop than many histories have suggested. —*Stephen Thomas Erlewine*

Fat Beats & Bra Straps: New MCs / Mar. 17, 1998 / Rhino ✦✦✦
The third and final installment of Rhino's female hip-hop series *Fat Beats & Bra Straps* concentrates on *New MCs*—that is, '90s rappers that haven't quite gotten widespread exposure and remain unheard even by many serious hip-hop fans. Of all the volumes in *Fat Beats*, this is the most uneven because it lacks the historical perspective that make the first two discs so interesting, and several acts are included simply because the compilers needed to fill out the disc. Still, *New MCs* is a wildly diverse, frequently interesting collection of promising female rappers, featuring cuts by the Conscious Daughters, Suga T., Bahamadia, Makeba Mooncy, Love N' Props, Natural Resource, and the Herbaliser. —*Stephen Thomas Erlewine*

Fat Beats Compilation, Vol. 1 / May 22, 2001 / Koch ✦✦✦✦✦
Fat Beats is best known as a much-respected underground hip-hop store, with franchises in New York and Los Angeles (the latter of which has a strong connection to the Beat Junkies turntablist crew). In 2001, Fat Beats branched out into releases of their own with *Fat Beats Compilation, Vol. 1,* a mix of newly recorded tracks and underground joints from the last several years that had never before appeared on CD. Opening and closing with turntablist cuts from the X-Ecutioners and the Beat Junkies' DJ Babu, respectively, the compilation brings to light a generally excellent selection of singles that deserve to be heard by more than just dedicated crate diggers. Big-name veterans the RZA (as Bobby Digital), Grand Puba, and KRS-One all fit the underground-purist aesthetic quite well, but the real focus is on the lesser-knowns and new names. Bumpy Knuckles' raw style fits his politically incorrect references to a tee on the hugely entertaining "The Lah," which is immediately followed by "Legacy," the terrific first single by backpacker favorites Non-Phixion.

Elsewhere, Canadian MC Saukrates comes off well on the spare "Father Time"; the Juggaknots' "Clear Blue Skies" is a full-fledged drama on the subject of interracial romance; Pacewon's "Sunroof Top" has a brash appeal; Virginia's Supafriendz build their highly literate "Consequences and Repercussions" on a Beethoven sample; and female MC Helixx weighs in with the trip-hoppy "My Time." All in all, it's a wide-ranging cross-section of hip-hop's underground at the dawn of a new millennium, and the future looks bright indeed. With a little more publicity, *Fat Beats* could well take over the mantle of Rawkus' *Soundbombing* series as the top name in underground hip-hop compilations (and its re-release on the larger Koch label is a step in the right direction). — *Steve Huey*

FB Entertainment Presents: The Good Life / Sep. 11, 2001 / Universal ✦✦✦
Already a staple of the rap community as a popular fashion brand, Fubu extended its reach beyond fashion in late 2001, releasing its first compilation of rap music, *FB Entertainment Presents: The Good Life*. Released through Universal, Fubu's roster of performers includes a few big names—Nate Dogg, Nas, Ludacris, LL Cool J, Keith Murray, Beenie Man, Erick Sermon—and a lot of no-name artists. Yet, surprisingly, it's many of these no-name artists that offer the album highlights. In particular, Mr. Cheeks and Drunken Master steal the spotlight. Best known as a member of the Lost Boyz, Mr. Cheeks keeps the energy level jumpin' with "Lights, Camera, Action," a great club-ready track with a lively beat and a catchy hook. Barely known in his native Detroit, let alone to a national audience, Drunken Master delivers a creative, somewhat novelty performance on "50 Ni**** Deep," a song that defies standard categorization. Elsewhere, there are a lot of lackluster moments on this compilation once you get past the few highlights. You have to commend Fubu for going with lesser-known artists like Mr. Cheeks and Drunken Master rather than more sure-fire artists like Ludicris and Nate Dogg. Still, it's unfortunate that the album ultimately suffers because of this choice. — *Jason Birchmeier*

Fear of a Black Hat / Sep. 26, 2000 / Avatar ✦✦✦
Rusty Cundieff's satirical mockumentary *Fear of a Black Hat* was billed as rap's answer to *This Is Spinal Tap*, and while it didn't quite match that film's brilliance—partly because it was admittedly derivative, partly because it was less subtle and its dialogue less dense—its sendups of hip-hop clichés and personalities were deadly accurate and frequently hilarious. Nearly every song on the soundtrack was cowritten by Cundieff, and most parody specific songs or artists with wicked glee. What's just as impressive, however, is the attention paid to the variety of production styles among those artists. It's no mean feat to replicate sounds as diverse as those of Snoop Dogg, C+C Music Factory, PM Dawn, N.W.A, LL Cool J, Public Enemy, and *Licensed to Ill*-era Beastie Boys, but *Fear of a Black Hat* apes them all in elaborate detail. That's what sets it apart from the similarly conceived *CB4*, and that's what makes it such an entertaining listen even apart from the film. — *Steve Huey*

Finatic Compilation of Hip-Hop and R&B / Apr. 13, 1999 / Finatic ✦✦
This sampler showcases artists on the roster of Finatic Records, a Miami-based label concentrating mostly on urban contemporary R&B with touches of hip-hop. The more memorable tunes here tend to be the explicit, let's-get-it-on come-ons, with the backing music a perfect blend of smooth, romantic soul and raunchy bump'n'grind. Highlights include tracks from Trini ("I Need a Man," "In and Out"), Stephan ("Body Say Yes"), and A.R.P ("Whip Tip," "Baby Your Love"). — *Steve Huey*

First Generation Rap / Feb. 13, 2001 / Collectables ✦✦✦
At four discs and 40 songs, *First Generation Rap* may be a tad excessive for the casual fan. But to rap aficionados, there is quite a lot here to absorb. Featuring some of old school rap's true innovators, this collection shows some of the first examples of things that most people take for granted when listening to rap. One example is the hard street anthem "Ghetto Life," one of the very first reality-based rap songs from the little-known rapper Source. Virtually every rapper today writes the same sort of true life stories into their rhymes, but at the time there were few other musicians outside of Grandmaster Flash and Los Angeles punk rockers who would talk about what was really going on in the American ghetto. A very young Doug E. Fresh appears, performing one of the first songs to incorporate the human beatbox, "Get Fresh Doug and Do the Box Beat." Although it was a trend that eventually played itself out, rap first introduced the idea of the human beatbox, and musicians still reference it in samples at times. These are only examples of the sort of musical breakthroughs that appear on this compilation. These may not be the very

first instances of these trends, but to hear the framework for the future of hip-hop being built is still an important experience. Anyone curious to hear rap's origins should look to this album, as it is not only quite interesting but the music is still quite good. As on many of the vinyl singles of the time, instrumental versions of some of the original tracks are available on the album also. — *Bradley Torreano*

Flamin' B-Dawgs Come Better / Jan. 30, 1996 / TX ✦✦
More of a gimmick than an actual album, *Flamin'* consists of a number of tracks written, performed, DJed, and rapped by members of the Bloods street gang. The most notable artist on the compilation is Mike T., a former member of CIMW, so it should be clear that the disc is filled with mediocre or substandard artists. All of the cuts on *Flamin'* are standard, by-the-books hardcore gangsta rap, with bland instrumental tracks and raps by undistinguished MCs. If these rappers weren't members of the Bloods, it's unlikely they would ever have been recorded. — *Stephen Thomas Erlewine*

Flavor Unit 10th Anniversary, Vol. 1 / Mar. 7, 2000 / Flavor Unit ✦✦✦✦
A fine collection of music from the record label founded by Queen Latifah, this album shows off the stellar talent that she was able to attract. Songs by Naughty By Nature, OutKast, Zhane, and Chill Rob G, among others, highlight some of the best in hip-hop over the previous ten years, showing off not only the best work of the label but also of hip-hop itself. — *Stacia Proefrock*

Le Flow / Jun. 6, 2000 / Ultra ✦✦✦
The mainstream success of R&B-influenced artists Les Nubians turned many Americans on to the new R&B and rap music coming out of France. This collection brings together some of the hottest new musicians and DJs from the French scene. Combining American, African, Middle Eastern, and French influences, the music is truly intriguing, forceful, and graceful. — *Stacia Proefrock*

Foolish / Mar. 23, 1999 / Priority ✦✦✦
The soundtrack to Master P's 1999 film *Foolish* is a rather predictable No Limit all-star compilation including tracks from Master P himself, plus Silkk the Shocker, Snoop Dogg, Mia X, Mystikal, and C-Murder. — *Keith Farley*

Freestyle Explosion, Vols. 1-5 / May 2, 2000 / Thump ✦✦✦✦✦
Thump's *Freestyle Explosion* compilation series was an excellent, definitive overview of the Latin-influenced dance-pop style born and bred in the clubs of Miami. Thump repackaged all five volumes of the series into a limited-edition slipcased box set, giving devoted freestyle fans a handy way to pick them all up at once. While some of the artists here scored bigger pop-chart successes with ballads, these collections concentrate only on the dancefloor; some of those artists include Stevie B, TKA, Sweet Sensation, the Cover Girls, Exposé, Taylor Dayne, Sa-Fire, Lisette Melendez, Lisa Lisa & Cult Jam with Full Force, Dino, Will to Power, Nu Shooz, and Pretty Poison. — *Steve Huey*

Friday / 1995 / Priority ✦✦✦✦✦
By 1995, R&B and hip-hop artists expended some of their greatest creative energy on soundtracks, turning in compilation albums that frequently were more compulsively listenable and adventerous than solo artist collections. *Friday* was no exception. The soundtrack to a lightweight comedy cowritten by Ice Cube, the record conveys all the strengths of hit urban radio. Keeping all of the good elements of the format—including the G-funk of Dr. Dre, old school soul, contemporary R&B, and gangsta rap—the record sounds like a "Best of the '90s" collection. — *Stephen Thomas Erlewine*

Friday After Next / Nov. 19, 2002 / Hollywood ✦✦✦
Friday After Next, the soundtrack to Ice Cube's second sequel to the original *Friday*, balances new tracks by modern rappers with a few classics of the old school (from Donny Hathaway, the Temptations, Leon Haywood, and Slave). Cube's Westside Connection gets pride of place with the opener, "It's the Holidaze," a good Christmastime jam, while Busta Rhymes' Flipmode Squad and Nappy Roots hit the ground running with great jams. Hands down the highlight, though, is Krayzie Bone's "Wonderful World," an instant classic that works a holiday sample (and not much else) with one of the few tracks to have the same lazy-day atmosphere of the original *Friday*. — *John Bush*

● **The Funky Precedent** / Sep. 21, 1999 / Loose Groove ✦✦✦✦✦
There aren't many records that you can recommend with no hesitation whatsoever, but this one is them. For one thing, *The Funky Precedent*, a compilation featuring artists such as Dilated Peoples, Jurassic 5, Aceyalone, Ozomatli, Black Eyed Peas, and more, benefits music education at Fremont High School and Manchester Elementary School in Los Angeles and Mission

High School in San Francisco. In addition to supporting a good cause, however, *The Funky Precedent* is simply a damn fine record. Particular highlights include J5's triumphantly groovy "Concrete Schoolyard," Ugly Duckling's psychedelic travelog "Journey to Anywhere," and Divine Styler's "Make It Plain," which seamlessly melds hard-nosed 1999 rap with Stevie Wonder circa 1972. While concentrating mostly on L.A.-style hip-hop, *The Funky Precedent* extends its stylistic reach to old-fashioned soul ("Getcho Soul Together") and acoustic Malian-inflected balladry ("Building"). Almost every track is a winner, and the others are merely unspectacular, not actually awful (not many compilations can say the same). The only quibble worth mentioning is that Ozomatli's contribution, "Cumbia de los Muertos," is lifted from their self-titled album, not a new track as the CD's packaging implies. This is a minor point, especially since it is in any case a breathtaking song well worth hearing again. *The Funky Precedent* is one solid good vibe from beginning to end. —*Bill Cassel*

The Funky Precedent, Vol. 2 / Jul. 31, 2001 / Matador ✦✦✦✦✦
Narrowing the focus of the first volume from L.A. and San Fran to just the Bay Area, *The Funky Precedent, Vol. 2* is another crucial compilation of independent rappers, producers, DJs, and even a band. It kicks off with a stellar track (and ultratight production) by the underground supergroup Skhool Yard, and goes forth balancing rap tracks with some excellent turntablist joints, including Live Human's "Lagoona's Bliss Elephant Mix" and DJ Vinroc's "3ThaHardWay." *The Funky Precedent, Vol. 2* goes even farther than its predecessor to bring in all aspects of breakbeat hip-hop, and one of the most entertaining is a great live funk cut, "Fan Club" by Stymie and the Pimp Jones Love Orchestra. Though the contributors won't be as well known as on the original *Funky Precedent*, volume two once again proves that the best hip-hop of the late '90s and early 2000s was happening, not on the charts, but deep underground. —*John Bush*

Game Tight / Nov. 12, 2002 / Landspeed ✦✦✦
Game Tight, the first compilation documenting the artists of Game Recordings, is an uneven collection of artists that take the underground seriously but still maintain an appealing sound. The artist that appears the most is Detroit MC Royce da 5'9", a quick-witted rapper whose raps offer a personal reflection that Motor City rappers have become famous for. From his awesome duets with former partner Eminem to the incredible "Boom" (featuring a fantastic beat courtesy of DJ Premier), Royce is the obvious centerpiece of this compilation. Lord Digga's humorous "My Flow Is Tight" is another highlight, while Agallah's gruff funk anthem "Five Star Milas" recalls the clever lyrical explorations of vintage Ghostface Killah. But sadly, the label offers little else here, instead filling out the rest of the album with somewhat generic contributions that are mostly known for their appearance on the video game Grand Theft Auto III. Although nothing is outwardly bad, the other tracks are far below the standard set by the more innovative artists found here. Still, this makes for a nice sampler for anyone looking into the scene Game is trying to create, but be warned that it isn't a uniform compilation whatsoever. —*Bradley Torreano*

Gang Tapes / Aug. 27, 2002 / Activate ✦✦✦
Back in the '30s, '40s, and '50s, the Hollywood studios had in-house orchestras that provided instrumental background music for their movies. But these days, things are done differently in the film industry. A filmmaker can hire someone to program faceless background music on a computer, or he/she might want something more personal—in other words, real songs that could feature a singer (country, rock, blues, or R&B), a rapper (hip-hop), or an instrumentalist (jazz). Different types of films call for different types of songs; the 2002 film *Gang Tapes* deals with gang violence in South Central Los Angeles, and quite appropriately, its soundtrack is dominated by West Coast gangsta rap. Many films that have an inner-city focus favor a combination of rap and urban contemporary, but *Gang Tapes* offers hardcore rap exclusively—and most of the selections have an unmistakably California flavor. That includes Above the Law's "Smoke" and the South Central Cartel's "We Gonna Ride" as well as Sir Jinx's "My" and LV & Prodeje's "In the Mood" (which features Coolio). One doesn't have to be familiar with *Gang Tapes* to find its soundtrack meaningful; this CD can stand on its own whether or not one has seen the movie. The listener does, however, need a strong appreciation of West Coast gangsta rap, although a few of the tunes aren't by California rappers. "What You Got" by New Jersey's Chino XL and "Livin' ah Vida Loca" by New York's Kool Keith are straight-up East Coast. But they're

hardcore enough to fit right in, and when all is said and done, the listener has experienced a decent, satisfying hardcore rap compilation that spends most of its time in Southern California but makes some enjoyable East Coast detours on occasion. —*Alex Henderson*

Gangsters & Bosses / Sep. 25, 2001 / LGB ✦✦✦
Gangsters & Bosses rounds up a number of the dirty South's most well-known performers. While big-name rappers like Ludacris and Outkast are missing, there are a few popular names here like the Big Tymers ("Rally Up"), UGK ("I Wanna Be Free"), Lil' Keke ("Hoggin the Lane"), C-Bo ("Don't Play That Shit"), South Park Mexican ("Illegal Amigos"), and Three 6 Mafia ("Doin What We Do"). In addition, West Coast gangsta rappers Spice 1 and the Outlawz contribute one song ("Turn the Heat Up"). Given the emphasis on the dirty South and the number of well-known artists here, *Gangsters & Bosses* makes for a nice sampler of the dirty South's darker side circa 2001. —*Jason Birchmeier*

Genius of Rap / Jun. 30, 1982 / Castle ✦✦✦✦✦
When Island released this rap compilation in England in early 1982, people were still debating whether hip-hop was here to stay or was merely a passing fad. But hip-hop wasn't showing any signs of slowing down—it was only getting bigger and bigger, and those who insisted that it was here to stay were absolutely right. In those days, hip-hop was dominated by 12" singles; it wasn't until the rise of second-generation rappers like Run-D.M.C., Whodini, and the Fat Boys that hip-hop became known for its albums. So in early 1982, *Genius of Rap* was a hip-hop LP in a sea of hip-hop singles. This compilation is far from the last word on old school rap, but it does boast some of the most essential hip-hop classics of the late '70s and early '80s, including Afrika Bambaataa's "Jazzy Sensation" (which preceded 1982's influential "Planet Rock"), T-Ski's Valley's "Catch the Beat!," and Dr. Jeckyll & Mr. Hyde's "Genius Rap" (which finds the duo rapping over the Tom Tom Club's 1981 hit "Genius of Love"). The oldest track is Grandmaster Flash & the Furious Five's "Superappin'," which was among hip-hop's earliest singles and preceded the group's association with Sugarhill Records. The compilation also offers a track by a mainstream R&B act: Twennynine & Lenny White's "Twennynine (The Rap)," which isn't hardcore hip-hop but does illustrate rap's influence on funk in the early 1980s. An excellent compilation, *Genius of Rap* was required listening for hip-hop fans in 1982. —*Alex Henderson*

Get Crunk / Sep. 21, 1999 / Tommy Boy ✦✦✦
"Getting crunk" is the hip-hop equivalent of the alterna-kid's moshing. It's a communal thing, mostly fueled by Southern-fried beats and rhymes. *Get Crunk*, the album, is a collection of Southern-stewed hip-hop by such stalwart crunkers as Three 6 Mafia, Goodie Mob, Crooked Lettaz, Lil Ke Ke, and Skullduggery. Yet its newcomers LG's (Lyrical Giants) best represent this splintered hip-hop form by shifting from Miami bass to No Limit-style electrobeats with a playful aggression. But like a mosh punk's monotonous set list, crunk stylists tend to all sound the same. And the experience is diluted outside the clubs for which the music is made, rendering this compilation ineffective when removed from its environment. —*Michael Gallucci*

Get on the Bus / Oct. 8, 1996 / Interscope ✦✦✦
The soundtrack *Get on the Bus*, Spike Lee's tribute to the Million Man March of 1995, is comprised of new songs from soul and hip-hop arrists as diverse as Curtis Mayfield, D'Angelo, Stevie Wonder, Doug E. Fresh, Blackstreet, the Neville Brothers, Guru, and Earth, Wind & Fire. Nearly every song is loosely tied into the film's theme of black empowerment and social liberation. Even with an explicit political agenda on hand, the music rarely sinks into dogma, simply because these musicians are too talented for that. Much of the music here is first-rate, and the album holds together *because* of its diversity, not in spite of it. One complaint: though the advertisements mention it prominently, the song Michael Jackson wrote explicitly for *Get on the Bus* is left off the soundtrack, per the King of Pop's orders. —*Stephen Thomas Erlewine*

Get Your Ass in the Water and Swim Like Me! / 1998 / Rounder ✦✦✦✦✦
Here collected are "toasts" of the black American oral tradition. It is obvious that herein lies the roots of modern rap in its most nihilist of expressions. The bulk of these recordings were made in the most fertile breeding ground of this violent and graphic poetry: jails. Hell-bent characters like The Signifying Monkey, Stackolee, and 'Flicted Arm Pete suffer degradingly, take their revenge cruelly, and perform supernatural sexual feats in the common vocabulary of anal-genital idioms and vivid slang. Unlike most songs, these pieces

lack choruses, but elements of rhythm and rhyme aid the orators in accurate recitations from memory of this lively and adults-only entertainment. Pimps, hustlers, and way bad dudes perform legendary, heroic feats while mucking about in the slimiest depths of society. The impromptu deliveries of these jovial but hardened performers come across as whimsical and nostalgic, and not a single syllable is given with intent to be rude or insulting. Every line is charged with the unveiling of a secret and gritty world. The booklet contains complete texts of these base odes, including a Halloween-themed orgy called "Dance of the Freaks." The title, incidentally, refers to a timely inclusion of a tough, black Titanic survivor's tale. Any individual's royalties from this bawdy examination of jailhouse tradition are donated to Amnesty International. *—Tom Schulte*

Givin' Up Props: A Tribute to Run-D.M.C. / Nov. 16, 1999 / Illstyle ♦♦

Illstyle's *Givin' Up Props: Tribute to Run-D.M.C.* primarily features a group of bands raised on the terrible Anthrax/Public Enemy duet, who vaguely remember the Run-D.M.C./Aerosmith version of "Walk This Way"—which means it's a bunch of rap-metal bands that have heavy riffs and shouted chants. There are few deviations from that formula here, but pretty much this is the hardest-rocking rap band remade into a thudding metallic din. Clumsy and arrhythmic, this has no sense of pacing, nor style—the bands just plod around, twisting around the meanings of the songs and erasing whatever innovations Run-D.M.C. made. That's not much of a tribute. *—Stephen Thomas Erlewine*

Guesswhyld Presents Past, Present and Future / May 8, 2001 / Landspeed ♦♦♦

This album is reminiscent of a *Soundbombing* or *Lyricist Lounge* recording, in that it's a compilation that's as much fun and entertaining as it is quality music. Appearing are the now-standard New York underground artists such as Talib Kweli, Mos Def, Mike Zoot, Punchline, and Wordsworth, plus verses by Queensbridge native Nature, Street Smartz, Royal Flush, Agallah (formerly 8-Off the Assassin), and El Da Sensei, along with production by Tommy Tee, DJ Spinna, and Large Professor. The track by the Lone Catalysts featuring Talib Kweli is probably the most prolific track but, strangely enough, it's already been published on their own debut album. Matt Fingaz makes a big impact here, appearing on a few tracks and really having fun with his rhyming. That kind of positive natural energy really adds to his appeal as an upcoming artist, and it helps him to shine above the rest, especially on the "Cum Again" remix. Overall, there aren't many weak moments, except for the Labba solo track "Big Bklyn," which just doesn't seem to fit in. *—Brad Mills*

Hardest Hits: 10 Years in the Game 1992-2002 / Nov. 27, 2001 / 40 Ounce ♦♦♦♦

Hardest Hits: 10 Years in the Game 1992-2002 features some of the highlights from the West Coast rap label 40 Ounce Records. Every song here features Jay Tee (James Trujillo), if not as a rapper then as a producer. Most of the songs are performed by Jay Tee's group N2Deep ("Do tha Crew," "Gatha Roun," "Playa Jay Tee"), along with a few Latino Velvet songs (another Jay Tee group), a few Jay Tee solo tracks, and a song by So Cold (featuring Jay Tee). Given this album's broad scope, it's a great introduction to Jay Tee's work during the '90s, with an emphasis on his late-'90s work. *—Jason Birchmeier*

Headz / 1994 / Mo'Wax ♦♦♦♦

The first double-disc/triple-vinyl installment of the *Headz* trilogy is easily the least of the batch. Though it features some heavyweights, the compilation suffers from a series of lengthy tracks that are too simplistic for their own good. Monochromatic and sluggish in long stretches to the point of approximating aural wallpaper, no amount of outer stimulation can add life to half of the material. Even an uncharacteristic Autechre track is weak. Nonetheless, decency is offered by the likes of DJ Shadow's U2-sampling "Lost and Found" (also a culprit of unnecessary length), Patterson's "Freedom Now," and DJ Krush's remix of Olde Scottish's "Wildstyle." Other notable appearances include U.N.K.L.E, Palmskin Productions, and Howie B. *—Andy Kellman*

Headz II: Part A / Oct. 28, 1996 / Mo'Wax ♦♦♦♦♦

The first of two separately released double-disc sets that document the history of British trip-hop, *Headz II: Part A* includes Mo'Wax stalwarts—DJ Krush, U.N.K.L.E., Solo, RPM—with contributions from artists not directly linked to trip-hop, such as Tortoise, the Beastie Boys, Stereo MCs, and Folk Implosion. Other big names include DJ Food (aka Coldcut, PC, and Strictly Kev), Massive

Attack, Nightmares on Wax, and jungle hero Peshay, who contributes a down-tempo rendition of his jungle track, "The Real Thing." *—John Bush*

Headz II: Part B / Oct. 28, 1996 / Mo'Wax ♦♦♦♦

The second half of the Mo'Wax magnum opus compilation features the usual crew of label acts (DJ Krush, Attica Blues, U.N.K.L.E., Palmskin Productions) as well as significant detours through hip-hop (Jungle Brothers, Money Mark, the Dust Brothers, the Beastie Boys) and jungle (Roni Size, Peshay, DJ Krust, Source Direct, Special Forces aka Photek), and even British techno like As One, Black Dog Productions, and Max 404. The breadth of material threatens to overwhelm, but there are over 25 great tracks on this double-disc set. *—John Bush*

Heavy Loungin' / Sep. 26, 2000 / Fat City ♦♦♦

As the East Coast American underground hip-hop scene exponentially grew through the latter half of the 1990s, supply outgrew demand as there was more quality music than labels to support and release it. As an alternative, many artists turned to Western Europe and Japan, where fans and the press were more supportive and open minded, and there were record companies willing to financially back projects that weren't aiming for MTV domination. One offspring of these intercontinental relationships was an impressive bunch of quality compilations, primarily featuring American MCs but released abroad, including *Wide Angles*, the *Superrappin'* series, and *Heavy Loungin'*. Put together by U.K.-based Fat City Recordings but distributed by German imprint Grooveattack, *Heavy Loungin'* carries a true multinational flavor, including musical contributions from Canada, Japan, England, Germany, and the U.S. Reflecting the second half of the title, the songs here have a generally mellow flavor, and can be described as thinking people's hip-hop. The Aboriginals and Abyss sum up the attitude of all MCs present with the chorus of their collaborative effort, "Try These": "Kill kill kill, money money money, drugs and dealers, trigger-squeezing dummies/If you need something different, then try these." Other highlights include the funky drums and clever rhymes on "Can It," the jazz-club vibe "Renaissance" of Midwesterners All Natural and Lone Catalysts, and the Catalysts' revision of Boogie Down Productions' safe-sex classic "Jimmy Hats." Although few of the tracks will blow anyone away or ignite any parties, there genuinely isn't a bad song here—and for a various-artists compilation such as this one, that's an accomplishment in itself. *—Luke Forrest*

Hi Power Soldiers, Book 1 / Oct. 23, 2001 / Hi Power ♦♦♦

Hi Power Soldiers, Book 1 features several of the rappers affiliated with the Southern California Chicano rap label Hi Power, best known for launching the career of Mr. Capone-E. In addition to Capone-E, this compilation also features tracks by Scrappy Loco, Wicked Willie, Ms. Beautiful, Daffy, and Snapper. Though neither the rappers nor the producers are relatively exceptional or even impressive, they do represent the burgeoning California Chicano rap scene in the early 2000s. *Hi Power Soldiers, Book 1* functions as an excellent sampler for the label, showcasing several artists on Hi Power. *—Jason Birchmeier*

Hi Power Soldiers, Book 2 / 2002 / Hi Power ♦♦♦

Much like the first volume released a year earlier in 2001, *Hi Power Soldiers, Book 2* features several of the rappers affiliated with the Southern California Chicano rap label Hi Power, best known for launching the career of Mr. Capone-E. In addition to Capone-E, this compilation also features tracks by Malow, Mr. Criminal, Lil Dreamer, Snapper, Daffy, Payaso, Nfumis, Brown Boy, and Lucky. Though neither the rappers nor the producers are relatively exceptional or even impressive, they do represent the burgeoning California Chicano rap scene in the early 2000s. On a par with the first volume, *Hi Power Soldiers, Book 2* functions as an excellent sampler for the label, showcasing the artists on Hi Power. *—Jason Birchmeier*

High School High / Sep. 1996 / Big Beat ♦♦♦♦

Although the Jon Lovitz movie *High School High* was a juvenile, predictable low-brow parody of *Dangerous Minds* and other inner-city dramas, the soundtrack to the film is considerably sharper and more attractive. Assembled (and marketed) with the knowledge that the film would likely alienate its target audience of hip-hop and urban R&B fans, the soundtrack is a stellar sampler of mid-'90s musical styles, featuring everything from hardcore rap to smooth new jack balladry and alternative rap. Over the course of its 20 tracks (the sheer number of songs makes the album a worthwhile purchase), Faith Evans, the Braxtons, Quad City DJs, D'Angelo, De La Soul, A

Tribe Called Quest, Jodeci, Scarface & Facemob, Lil' Kim, the Braids (who cover Queen's "Bohemian Rhapsody"), Spice 1 with E-40 & the Click, and the Roots all deliver excellent cuts; there are also two Wu-Tang Clan cuts, including the first solo track from RZA (the song-as-commercial "Wu-Wear: The Garment Renaissance") and Inspectah Deck & U-God's collaboration with Street. Though its momentum sags in a couple of places, *High School High* remains a thoroughly enjoyable and surprisingly eclectic listen, and is easily one of the finest soundtracks of 1996. It's certainly more fun than the film it supports. —*Stephen Thomas Erlewine*

Hip Hop 24/7 / 2001 / Decadance ✦✦✦
The triple-disc *Hip Hop 24/7* box set released by Deca Dance in 2001 features a diverse and debatably illogical array of rap music. The featured songs are all featured in their original 12" mixes and date as far back as 1979 (Sugarhill Gang's "Rapper's Delight") with most being from the '90s. The first disc is mostly hardcore rap, characterized by four classics from the Death Row archives (Dr. Dre, Snoop Dogg, Tupac, Warren G) and some East Coast tracks (Public Enemy, KRS-One, Jeru the Damaja, Wu-Tang). The second disc is a mixed bag of mostly obscure songs, though there are a few bigger artists here (Notorious B.I.G., Method Man, A Tribe Called Quest, Wu-Tang); however, even the contributions from these big-name rappers are fairly obscure. The third disc features plenty of old school classics: the aforementioned "Rapper's Delight," Grandmaster Flash's "Adventures of Flash on the Wheels of Steel," Hashim's "Al-Naayfysh (The Soul)," and others that are a bit more obscure. Overall, this collection spans not only time and geography but also style—it's a haphazard history of rap, showcasing everything from old school electro to West Coast G-funk. And while many of these songs are undeniable classics, about half the collection is comprised of obscure songs by forgotten artists like Aim and Hijack. That this collection is of British origin may partly explain the questionable track selection, but you can't help but feel a little cheated by the filler and the overabundance of Death Row and Wu-Tang tracks. —*Jason Birchmeier*

Hip Hop Classics, Vol. 1 / May 23, 1996 / Priority ✦✦✦
Not everything on *Hip-Hop Classics, Vol. 1* lives up to its billing, but the 15-track collection contains enough great cuts—including Eric B. & Rakim's "Eric B. Is President," EPMD's "You're a Customer," MC Shane's "The Bridge," Doug E. Fresh's "Di Da Di," Biz Markie's "Make the Music with Your Mouth," Too Short's "Frekay Tales," Eazy-E's "Boyz-'n-the-Hood," Public Enemy's "Rebel without a Pause," N.W.A's "Straight Outta Compton," and Ice Cube's "Amerikkka's Most Wanted"—to make it worth its budget price. —*Stephen Thomas Erlewine*

Hip Hop Classics, Vol. 2 / May 23, 1996 / Priority ✦✦✦

Hip Hop for Respect / Apr. 25, 2000 / Rawkus Entertainment ✦✦✦✦
Inspired by the death of Amadou Diallo and organized by Mos Def and Talib Kweli, this EP brought together the cream of the hip-hop intelligentsia in protest against police brutality. The more well known and popular artists were featured on "One Four Love," a two-part song produced by Organized Noize, the team responsible for most of Goodie Mob's and Outkast's early albums. An intense, frantic, and bass-heavy beat laid the foundation like a Southern-fried version of Public Enemy's Bomb Squad while the artists each dropped their two cents and then chanted the chorus in unison, reminiscent of KRS-One's "Self-Destruction." This song was not the EP's only high point, though, as the lesser-known and independent artists on the other two tracks more than held their own. "A Tree Never Grown," produced by 88 Keys, featured a haunting chorus sung by Mos Def, and "Protective Custody," produced by Mr. Khaliyl (formerly Mr. Man of the Bush Babees), contained a clever homage to KRS-One, sampling his classic anti-police song "Who Protects Us From You?" So often collaborations with such high aspirations as this one are burdened down by their own weight, but this EP provided a combination of musical excellence and fierce political activism rarely seen in hip-hop since the early '90s. —*Luke Forrest*

Hip Hop High: Class of 1990-1991 / Aug. 13, 2002 / Capitol ✦✦✦
Each volume in Capitol's *Hip Hop High* series provides an accurate, unbiased snapshot of the rap world for the period being covered. However, each disc only contains a slim number of ten tracks (filling out roughly half the space a CD allows), and the range of styles presented on each volume unapologetically shoots from one end of the spectrum to the other—whether it's gangsta rap from the West Coast, jazz-rap from the East Coast, pop-rap from one-hit

wonders, or any point in between, these discs will only appeal to a select type of person who needs these songs and can appreciate every single flavor of rap music. The first volume covers 1990-1991 and features DJ Jazzy Jeff & the Fresh Prince's "Summertime," N.W.A's "100 Miles and Runnin'," Digital Underground's "The Humpty Dance," and MC Hammer's "U Can't Touch This." —*Andy Kellman*

Hip Hop High: Class of 1992-1993 / Aug. 13, 2002 / Capitol ✦✦✦
The second volume covers 1992-1993 and features Dr. Dre and Snoop Dogg's "Deep Cover," Ice Cube's "Check Yo Self," Kris Kross' "Jump," and Digable Planets' "Rebirth of Slick (Cool Like Dat)." —*Andy Kellman*

Hip Hop High: Class of 1994-1995 / Aug. 13, 2002 / Capitol ✦✦✦
The third volume covers 1994-1995 and features Craig Mack's "Flava in Ya Ear," Coolio's "Gangsta's Paradise," Wu-Tang Clan's "C.R.E.A.M.," and Bone's "Thuggish Ruggish Bone." —*Andy Kellman*

Hip Hop Most Wanted, Vol. 2 / Apr. 1, 1997 / Priority ✦✦✦
Hip Hop Most Wanted, Vol. 2 contains 13 hardcore hip-hop cuts from the '90s, many of which are culled from Priority Records. The quality of the music is a little uneven, but there are enough first-rate cuts—including Westside Connection's "Bow Down," Jay-Z's "Ain't No Nigga," Originoo Gunn Clappaz's "No Fear," Genius' "Shadowboxin'," Domino's "Physical Funk," Naughty By Nature's "Craziest," Too Short's "Gettin' It," and the Pharcyde's "Runnin'"—to make it a worthwhile collection. —*Stephen Thomas Erlewine*

Hip Hop Na Veia: So Sangue Bom / 2000 / Som Livre ✦✦✦✦✦
Hip Hop Na Veia: So Sangue Bom compiles a number of Brazil's most noteworthy hip-hop artists, making it a wonderful sampler for those interested in the burgeoning breakbeat culture developing in the South American country at the beginning of the 21st century. Much like how Brazilians began co-opting England's drum'n'bass culture in the late '90s, they had similarly began cooptting New York hip-hop during the same era. By the time of this compilation's release in 2000, there was a fully developed breakbeat culture in Brazil featuring both drum'n'bass and hip-hop. Though there isn't much drum'n'bass influence on this collection, there is a broad variety of approaches to the classic New York hip-hop sound as well as a few tracks that toy with the West Coast gangsta style (MV Bill's "Traficando Informação") and rap-metal (Jigaboo's "Corre-Corre" and Pavilhao 9's "Mandando Bronca," the latter featuring Max Cavalera of Sepultura fame). These occasional idiosyncratic moments help make *Hip Hop Na Veia: So Sangue Bom* even more interesting than it already is. Nonetheless, most of the songs feature some sort of turntablism, usually DJ scratching and samples, and most of the beats are breakbeats—two attributes forever associated with the classic Bronx-born hip-hop sound. Don't underestimate these Brazilian rap artists. They may have not grown up listening to DJ Red Alert or Funkmaster Flex on the radio, but they obviously understand the art of hip-hop and have crafted their own unique styles. And you can't help but feel this is just the beginning of what will eventually blossom into something much larger. —*Jason Birchmeier*

Hip Hop with R&B Flava / Mar. 30, 1998 / Rebound ✦✦✦
If you're confused by what *Hip Hop with R&B Flava* means, since "R&B" can mean oh so many different things, think of it as crossover hip-hop or pop-rap, because nearly every song on this 12-track (nine on cassette) budget-priced collection made its presence known on the pop charts. Of course, the mere mention of "crossover" implies that the song has less street credibility than most hip-hop, but that's simply not the case with a compilation that contains a song by Redman and two cuts by Method Man. The fact of the matter is, this compilation contains some of the greatest hip-hop singles of the '90s—Warren G's "Regulate," Montell Jordan's "This is How We Do It," Salt-N-Pepa's "Shoop," Digital Underground's "The Humpty Dance," Redman & Method Man's "How High," Method Man's "I'll Be There for You/You're All I Need to Get By." The rest of the compilation may not quite live up to those high standards, but it's all very, very good, making it a budget-priced disc that is certainly a bargain. —*Stephen Thomas Erlewine*

Hip-Ol' Skool / Sep. 9, 1997 / Hip-O ✦✦✦
In the Hip-O compilation tradition, this is a trawl through a musical genre (old school rap) without much rhyme, reason, or liner notes, although the music isn't bad. Stretching from 1980 to 1992, this includes the truly old, old school rap of Kurtis Blow's "The Breaks," Grandmaster Flash's "The Message," and Whodini's "Five Minutes of Funk," but generally concentrates much more on late-'80s cuts from Roxanne, Biz Markie, Debbie Deb, DJ Mark, and

others, as well as a couple of early-'90s tracks from Brotherhood Creed and Eric B. & Rakim. Even given the fact that there weren't many vintage rap compilations on the market at the time of this release, there are much better overviews of the style's first decade. —*Richie Unterberger*

House Party / Jul. 24, 2001 / Motown ◆◆◆

The bad news is that, with a few exceptions, it's an absolutely typical song score album—mostly a collection of banal, dull, boring, routine tracks that follow dull, boring, routine patterns. There are some good moments—Flavor Flav's "I Can't Do Nothing for You, Man!" is a mess as far as the sound quality is concerned, sounding remarkably as though it was recorded on a cassette unit. However, this house mix-propelled call-and-response rap possesses a considerable energy and dynamic that overcomes the sonic disadvantages, and gives the piece an edge. Kid 'N Play, the rap duo who stars in *House Party*, is here with two tracks, and they're both good stuff—rough, often raw, loping powerhouse raps with big, big beats behind them, and a Roadrunner sensibility and bozo energy that makes mincemeat of the fact that they tend to be strut raps. It's always nice to see rappers with a sense of humor. The rest of the album is filler, mostly nice enough. The big problem here is that several of the tracks start off promising a lot, and then, 30 seconds later, are limping along in an unconvinced and routine fashion—limp dweeb ballads, dancefloor numbers that lack energy completely. Full Force Family (Full Force and lots of friends) almost get it right with "House Party," which sounds like the result one might expect from a meeting of the minds and music of Parliament/Funkadelic and Art of Noise. As with almost everything else on the album, it proceeds to dwindle down to a bland groove and stay there. Major points for Kid 'N Play and Flavor Flav. As for the rest—snore. (The 2001 reissue takes "Surely" and "I Ain't Going Out Like That" and switches their order in the track sequence.) —*Steven McDonald*

How High / Dec. 11, 2001 / Def Jam ◆◆◆

Def Jam's *How High* soundtrack comes close to being another Method Man & Redman album, a follow-up to the blunt-smoking duo's successful *Blackout!* album from two years before. But it's not a proper follow-up, even though Def Jam markets it as if it was indeed another Meth & Red album. This becomes evident about halfway through *How High*, when the album segues into previously released Def Jam material such as DMX's "Party Up (Up in Here)" and Ludacris's "What's Your Fantasy." Up until this point, this album features mostly new Meth & Red songs. And they're not throwaways but instead songs recorded specifically for this soundtrack. Most noteworthy is "Part II," yet another version of the Meth & Red staple "How High." Erick Sermon produces this update, which prominently features Toni Braxton on the hook. It's a catchy song, one of the duo's better smoking anthems—which is saying a lot since smoking anthems are the duo's specialty. Elsewhere, Meth and Red hook up with Rockwilder and Cypress Hill for an update of War's "Cisco Kid." It's not much of a departure from the original—for example, the hook is practically untouched—but this is exactly why it's such a standout song: the original "Cisco Kid" is as fine as it is and makes for a great smoked-out hip-hop track. The other new Meth & Red songs aren't particularly novel, and you're left with lots of Def Jam's back catalog: the aforementioned DMX and Ludacris songs, in addition to previously released Meth & Red tracks like "Da Rockwilder," "How High Remix," and "How to Roll a Blunt." Overall, you can approach the *How High* soundtrack with different presumptions: it's both a Meth & Red album, yet it's also a compilation of previously released Def Jam songs. Either way, everything on the album is of high quality, what you've come to expect from not only Meth & Red, but also Def Jam. However, this doesn't prevent you from feeling a little cheated. After all, you're listening to this soundtrack for the new songs, not old songs like "Bring da Pain" or promotional guest spots like Saukrates' "Fine Line." And as great as the new songs are, there's not enough to leave you satisfied. Instead, you get just enough to tide you over until the next Meth & Red release. —*Jason Birchmeier*

Hurby's Machine: House That Rap Built / Next Plateau ◆◆◆

During the mid-to-late '80s, Hurby "Luv Bug" Azor was one of rap's most successful producers, crafting pop-oriented records for Kid 'N Play and Dana Dane. Seven of his discoveries are included here, chief among them Salt-N-Pepa; included are their "I'm Down" and a remix of their commercial breakthrough, "Push It." The remainder of the entries come from now-forgotten rappers like the Mau Mau Clan Overlords, Antoinette, and the Fabulous Two. —*Jason Ankeny*

I Got the Hook Up / Apr. 7, 1998 / Priority ◆◆◆

After conquering the music charts and releasing a successful video movie, Master P decided to concentrate on filmmaking with the cellular phone farce *I Got the Hook Up*. Knowing that you can't have a successful urban movie without a good soundtrack, he poured a lot of effort into *I Got the Hook Up*, making sure that it contained as many hot underground rappers and members of the No Limit posse as possible. Since Master P's main talent is marketing, not music, it's not entirely surprising that the album looks better on paper than it does in reality. The main problem is that the album doesn't deviate from the No Limit blueprint in the slightest, offering a collection of blunted hardcore rap and hip-hop-flavored urban R&B that is professionally produced but ultimately rather faceless. Certainly, the album will satisfy the needs of fans of Master P, Silkk the Shocker, C-Murder, the Gambino Family, etc., but it has no true standout tracks and, therefore, it's nearly interchangeable with any other No Limit release. —*Stephen Thomas Erlewine*

I'm Bout It / May 13, 1997 / Priority ◆◆◆◆

I'm Bout It, the soundtrack to Master P's self-produced and self-financed film of the same name, is a way to showcase P's production skills, as well as the roster of his No Limit label. The album illustrates No Limit's strengths and weaknesses in equal measures. It shows that they are quite adept at crafting solid G-funk and gangsta rap knockoffs, but they also fall prey to the genre's worst excesses, wallowing in cartoonish sex and violence. In that sense, *I'm Bout It* works well as an introduction to Master P and No Limit, but the fact is, if you're not already interested in this level of hardcore gangsta rap and bass party music, this silly, over-the-top collection won't change your mind. —*Leo Stanley*

In Tha Beginning . . . Tha Originals / Nov. 25, 1997 / Priority ◆◆◆

The *In Tha Beginning* project seems like a good idea in theory. Take some of the greatest hip-hop singles from the '80s, have some hot '90s stars record new versions, then release companion albums, one containing the originals, the other the covers. It's an excellent marketing scheme that has one major flaw—there's no way that the new versions could match the originals. After all, N.W.A's "Dopeman" and "Fuck tha Police," Ice-T's "6 in the Mornin'," Doug E. Fresh's "The Show," BDP's "I'm Still #1," Biz Markie's "Make the Music with Your Mouth," LL Cool J's "Big Ole Butt," EPMD's "Knick Knack Patty Wack," and Rock Master Scott's "The Roof Is On Fire" are all seminal singles in their own way, showcasing some of the greatest musical and lyrical talents of their time. Which means, of course, that *In Tha Beginning . . . Tha Originals* is a great listen, since it contains 12 timeless tunes. There are better hip-hop compilations, of course, but this is still a great primer in the roots of hardcore hip-hop. —*Stephen Thomas Erlewine*

In Tha Beginning . . . There Was Rap / Nov. 25, 1997 / Priority ◆◆◆

The idea behind *In tha Beginning . . . There Was Rap* looks good on paper: take several of the biggest rappers of the '90s and have them cover classics from the '80s. Unfortunately, it doesn't play nearly as well as it reads. The big problem is that many of the artists don't add anything new to the original—Puff Daddy's "Big Ole Butt" and Master P's "6 'n tha Mornin'" are prime examples of lazy rhythms and lazy rapping. Half of the album works fairly well—the Wu-Tang Clan's "Sucker M.C.'s," Coolio's "Money (Dollar Bill Y'all)," Cypress Hill's "I'm Still #1," Snoop Dogg's "Freaky Tales," and the Roots' "The Show"—but that's not enough to make such failures as Bone Thugs-N-Harmony's castration of "Fuck tha Police" acceptable. Some hardcore hip-hop fans might find it worthwhile to wade through the disc to find the good cuts, but they may find it a little exhausting as well. —*Stephen Thomas Erlewine*

Judgment Night / 1993 / Epic ◆◆◆

The gimmick here is that on each track a hard rock act has been combined with a rap act—Sonic Youth & Cypress Hill, Living Colour & Run-D.M.C., etc. The idea, as with Run-D.M.C.'s duet with Aerosmith on "Walk This Way," is to achieve musical synergy and commercial crossover, and at least the second goal was met when this album went gold while the movie it accompanied went into the dumper. But, as on any duet album, from Sinatra to Elton John, the concept has to be translated into appropriate pairings on good songs to really work. Sometimes, it has. Living Colour & Run-D.M.C. meld well on "Me, Myself & My Microphone," and Slayer & Ice-T make an angry thrash of "Disorder." But in both cases, the rappers are familiar with the style—Ice-T has a metal band of his own in Body Count. Elsewhere, neither the rappers nor the metal kids sound distinctive enough to make a striking impression beyond a faithfulness to a hard, angry approach. —*William Ruhlmann*

Kurtis Blow Presents the History of Rap, Vol. 1: The Genesis / Aug. 19, 1997 / Rhino ✦✦✦✦

The first volume of the three-part *Kurtis Blow Presents the History of Rap* is subtitled *The Genesis*, which means that it covers a period of time when rap was strictly a live art form and rarely made it to record. That means, of course, that the disc is filled with funk records—specifically ones with extended rhythm breaks and grooves that provided ideal instrumental backdrops for rappers. *The Genesis* leans toward the obscure, where even the most familiar names (James Brown, the Isley Brothers, Booker T. & the M.G.'s, the Jackson 5) are represented with unfamiliar songs, and the remainder of the compilation is filled with cult artists (Baby Huey, Michael Viner's Incredible Bongo Band, Black Heat, Rhythm Heritage). While many of these songs may be unfamiliar, there are beats and samples that have been popularized through sampling, which makes listening to the disc fascinating. Unfortunately, it never becomes truly intoxicating, since it's a historical recording that's designed for education, not entertainment, but anyone interested in the birth of hip-hop will find it necessary listening. —*Stephen Thomas Erlewine*

Kurtis Blow Presents the History of Rap, Vol. 2: The Birth of the Rap Record / Aug. 19, 1997 / Rhino ✦✦✦✦✦

As the second installment of *Kurtis Blow Presents the History of Rap, The Birth of the Rap Record* chronicles the moment that hip-hop entered the popular consciousness. The record that broke the doors down was "Rapper's Delight," which is represented here, like the ten other tracks on the compilation, in an extended version that allows both the beats and the rhymes to flourish. Where most early rap compilations focus on records that made an impact on the R&B charts, *The Birth of the Rap Record* is devoted to the underground. There are a number of familiar songs here—"The Breaks," "The Message"—but the majority of the disc is devoted to underappreciated artists like the Sequence, Spoonie Gee, "Love Bug" Starski, Davy DMX, and Funky Four Plus One More, or unfamiliar songs by artsits like Afrika Bambaataa and the Treacherous Three. Unlike its predecessor, *The Genesis, Vol. 2: The Birth of the Rap Record* plays smoothly, making it a rare historical release that is as entertaining as it is educational. —*Stephen Thomas Erlewine*

Kurtis Blow Presents the History of Rap, Vol. 3: The Golden Age / Aug. 19, 1997 / Rhino ✦✦✦✦✦

Where *Kurtis Blow Presents the History of Rap, Vol. 2: The Birth of the Rap Record* chronicled rap's first forays into the mainstream, *Vol. 3: The Golden Age* documents the point when hip-hop culture became an undeniable part of popular culture. There are more hits on *The Golden Age* than on any other disc in *The History of Rap*, featuring classics by such artists as Run-D.M.C. ("Rock Box"), Whodini ("Friends"), the Fat Boys ("Jail House Rap"), U.T.F.O. ("Roxanne, Roxanne"), Public Enemy ("Rebel Without a Pause"), Boogie Down Productions ("Criminal Minded"), Big Daddy Kane ("Raw"), Rob Base & DJ E-Z Rock ("It Takes Two"), and Biz Markie ("Vapors," "Just a Friend"). At that time, rap was becoming more diverse, boasting different rhyming and production styles—where early rap was similiar stylistically, there was a world of difference between the dizzying hardcore of Public Enemy and the comedy shenanigans on Biz Markie. The musical depth of rap is evident on *The Golden Age*—it certainly does not all sound the same—and while it does overlook some artists, it nevertheless is an invaluable sampler, capturing the essence of the era. —*Stephen Thomas Erlewine*

The Ladies of Gangster Rap / May 4, 1999 / Deff Trapp ✦✦

Deff Trapp's *The Ladies of Gangster Rap* shouldn't be seen as the definitive word on distaff gangsta, but it isn't a bad sampler, since it contains fine cuts from Foxy Brown ("Chyna Whyte"), MC Lyte ("For All the Years"), Lil' Kim ("Not Tonight"), Mia X ("What 'Cha Wanna Do"), and Gangster Boo ("Where Dem Dollars At"). The second half isn't as good as the first, since it contains three cuts from Cl'che and two from Trapp, and it all sounds a little monotonous. Nevertheless, the first half makes it worthwhile for listeners who are already fans of the genre. —*Stephen Thomas Erlewine*

Lake Entertainment Presents: The 41st Side / Sep. 11, 2001 / Landspeed ✦✦✦

The 41st Side features the extended Queensbridge rap family—Nas, Havoc, Prodigy, Cormega, Big Noyd, Nature, Tragedy Khadafi, Capone, Noreaga, and many more—dropping rhymes over the course of 21 tracks. Though there is an exorbitant amount of interludes here, there's still no shortage of songs. Yet even so, due to the endless list of rappers, no one gets more than a verse or

two. That's unfortunate because many of the better-known rappers here—Nas, Mobb Deep, Capone-N-Noreaga—are some of the best MCs in the rap game, whereas many of the no-names here are essentially amateurs. It's this wavering level of quality MCing, along with what seems like a halfhearted effort on everyone's part—rappers and producers—that makes *The 41st Side* less than noteworthy. The preceding year's *QB Finest* compilation featured most of these same rappers, yet managed to get a much better performance out of everyone, in addition to featuring some excellent production. *The 41st Side* feels awfully similar to *QB Finest*, though not nearly as effective. Go with *QB Finest* first, and if that really impresses you, then seek out *The 41st Side*—it's mostly recommended to Queensbridge fanatics. —*Jason Birchmeier*

Latin Hip Hop Flava / Feb. 22, 1996 / Priority ✦✦✦

Latin Hip-Hop Flava is a reasonably entertaining collection of Latin rap tracks from the '80s and '90s, featuring such tracks as Kid Frost's "La Raza," Mellow Man Ace's "Mentirosa," Too Down's "Oceanfront," Brotherhood Creed's "Helluva," and Hi-C's "Sitting in the Park." —*Stephen Thomas Erlewine*

Latino Gangster Rappers / May 4, 1999 / Deff Trapp ✦✦

Despite the fact that it plays fast and loose with the definition of "Latino"—Biggie Smalls and Makaveli (aka Tupac) were not Latin, nor is Detroit white boy Eminem—Deff Trapp's *Latino Gangster Rappers* is overall a pretty good sampling of hardcore Latin hip-hop, featuring cuts by Big Punisher ("Still Not a Player"), Fat Joe ("Bet Your Man Can't"), South Park Mexican ("Holla At Cha Later"), D'Linquent Habits ("Here Comes the Homies"), Frost ("Rock On"), and Cypress Hill ("Windows of My Room"). Although the featured songs aren't necessarily the artists' best, and although there's a noticeable lull in the second half, when three Trapp songs in a row follow each other, it's still a pretty enjoyable listen, both for fans of the genre and for the curious. —*Stephen Thomas Erlewine*

Legal Dope / Nov. 7, 1995 / Priority ✦✦✦

Legal Dope contains 16 tracks from mid-'90s underground rappers like JT the Bigga Figga, TRE-8, Brotha Lynch Hung, Young Murder Squad, TRU, San Quinn, and Master P, the only rapper here to go on to genuine stardom. All these rappers may be underground, but they don't take much pride in standing apart from the crowd—everything here sounds shockingly similar, with familiar drum loops, blunted bass lines, and lyrics about guns, money, drugs, and hos. A few cuts make an impression on their own, but only aficionados will sort the wheat from the chaff. —*Stephen Thomas Erlewine*

Let's Talk About Love / Jul. 20, 1992 / Dino ✦✦

Let's Talk About Love collects late-'80s and early-'90s dub, hip-hop, and R&B from the likes of Omar, Timmy Thomas, Bomb the Bass, and Beats International. As with almost any compilation, it's a mixed bag, offering as many seminal tracks as it does fair-to-middling ones. Massive Attack's "Unfinished Sympathy (Nellee Hooper 7" Mix)," Monie Love's "It's a Shame (My Sister)," and A Tribe Called Quest's "Can I Kick It?" are examples of the former, while M.C. Hammer's "Have You Seen Her" is chief among the latter. De La Soul's "Ring Ring Ring (Ha Ha Hey) (Party Line Edit)" and LL Cool J's "I Need Love" help make *Let's Talk About Love* an entertaining, if scattershot, collection. —*Heather Phares*

Like Mike / Jul. 2, 2002 / So So Def ✦✦✦

So So Def boss Jermaine Dupri rounds up a number of playful pop-rap songs for the *Like Mike* soundtrack, unsurprisingly including a number of Lil' Bow Wow performances. The 15-year-old rapper stars in the film so it's expected that his contributions will be significant, and indeed they are, beginning with "Basketball," the album's opening song. Here Bow Wow, Fabolous, and Dupri drop a verse each about their passion for the game, while Fundisha sings the hook. A little bit later in the album come the two standout Bow Wow songs, though: the Neptunes-produced "Take Ya Home" and Just Blaze-produced "Playin' the Game." Both songs feature top-notch production and incredibly catchy hooks, so much so that the former became one of Bow Wow's biggest hits yet. Elsewhere on *Like Mike*, Dupri includes so-so songs by TQ, Mario, and Solange, three artists likely to appeal to the same listeners who like Bow Wow. But the real surprise comes late in the album with Nas' "Rule" and TCP's "Hoop It Up," both much more adult than the preceding songs. The previously released Nas song, which interpolates Tears for Fears' "Everybody Wants to Rule the World," falls a bit short of being another "If I Ruled the World (Imagine That)" for the New York rapper, but it's still quite moving. And the TCP song is a fast-paced bass song that concludes the soundtrack perfectly, embodying the heart-racing nature of basketball. —*Jason Birchmeier*

Lockdown / Jun. 20, 2000 / Capitol ♦♦♦

During its early years, hip-hop was dominated by New York. But that changed in the late '80s, when an abundance of MCs from the South and the West Coast demonstrated that they were quite capable of going gold or platinum. By 1987 and 1988, it was obvious that a rapper didn't have to be from Manhattan, Queens, Brooklyn, Staten Island, or the Boogie Down Bronx to sell millions of albums. On the West Coast, the San Francisco Bay Area has been a major player in hip-hop, and rappers from Northern California are the focus of this 2000 collection. Produced by BIG Drawz—who favors a sleek, Dr. Dre-influenced production style, *Lockdown* emphasizes gangsta rap and spotlights some established rappers (including Rappin' 4 Tay and E-40) as well as some of the Bay Area's lesser-known talent. Not everything on *Lockdown* (which contains previously unreleased recordings) is about incarceration specifically; however, many of the CD's 20 tracks examine the sort of violent crime that can easily lead to it. Most of the material isn't mind blowing, but a lot of it is decent. Some of the more memorable contributions come from San Quinn and Willie Henn on "The Flossy Way," Deranged Lunatix on "Let's Mobb," Tabb Doe and Redd on "Misery," and Neva Legal on "Lawless." As far as West Coast hip-hop goes, *Lockdown* is far from essential. But it does have its moments. —*Alex Henderson*

Loud Records: The Early Daze / May 7, 2002 / RCA ♦♦♦♦

By pairing a couple of all-time Wu-Tang Clan tracks with classics from a host of other great rappers, *Loud Records: The Early Daze* becomes an excellent look at the state of East Coast hardcore through the '90s. Sprinkled among the big-timers—Wu-Tang's "Protect Ya Neck," "Method Man," and "C.R.E.A.M."; Mobb Deep's "Shook Ones, Pt. II"; Akinyele's "Put It in Your Mouth"; tha Alkaholiks' "Likwit"—are great one-shots from Cella Dwellas ("Perfect Match") and Mad Kap ("Proof Is in the Puddin'"). —*John Bush*

Loud Rocks / Sep. 5, 2000 / Sony ♦♦♦

Loud Rocks is a collection of songs by rap acts on the Loud label—most prominently the Wu-Tang Clan, but also tha Alkaholiks, Xzibit, Mobb Deep, Big Punisher, and Dead Prez—who've been paired up with popular hard rock and heavy metal artists à la the *Judgment Night* soundtrack. Most of the latter group comes from the alternative-metal world (System of a Down, Incubus, and Sevendust, most notably), but there are a few acts already fusing rap with rock (Shootyz Groove, Everlast), some veterans (Ozzy Osbourne, Tony Iommi, Sick of It All), and a poppier collaboration between tha Alkaholiks and Sugar Ray. Like most projects of this nature, not everything hits the mark—some pairings feel forced and a few lack that spark of collaborative interplay—but the overall quality of the Loud roster ensures that most of what's here is at least listenable. And a lot of it is much better than that, some tracks offering new interpretations of old songs, others presenting a surprising range of distinctive approaches to the rap/rock form. It isn't without flaws, but overall, *Loud Rocks* is pretty successful. —*Steve Huey*

Louder Than Ever, Vol. 1 / Apr. 11, 2000 / Relativity ♦♦♦

Louder Than Ever, Vol. 1 is a sampler of the Loud hip-hop label and several affiliates, most prominently Relativity; issued in early 2000, it features cuts from those labels' more recent releases around that time, plus a smattering of rarities. Since it's mostly a promotional tool designed to make consumers curious about hearing more, it doesn't quite capture any particular moment in hip-hop, but it is a fairly consistent sampler, all told. Artists present include the Beatnuts, Raekwon, Xzibit, Big Punisher, Inspectah Deck, Krayzie Bone, and Mobb Deep with Lil' Kim. —*Steve Huey*

Love and a Bullet / Jun. 11, 2002 / TVT ♦♦♦

Acting as the soundtrack to rapper Treach's (Naughty By Nature) acting vehicle, *Love and a Bullet* is a high-energy release that offers some harsh and unique hip-hop from the underground. Many of the artists included aren't necessary lyrical pioneers, but what makes their songs stand out is the powerful production that backs many of the tracks. Techniec's "Payback" offers a symphonic mesh that brings to mind classic blaxploitation scores, while Sixx John's use of a manic accordion sample provides a bizarre backbeat for the Jay-Z-style rap over the top of it. Many of the producers utilize classic-sounding instruments to drive the various songs along, which makes it seem much more like a uniform film score than a simple collection of songs. Sadly enough, one of the weakest entries is Naughty By Nature's "Rah Rah," which

is put to shame by the intensely creative offerings from the other inclusions here. Where most of the younger groups featured offer a distinct twist on their tracks, Naughty By Nature is stuck playing catch-up with their dated and unoriginal street anthem. It isn't like *Love and a Bullet* is strikingly different, but it contains several underground hip-hop acts that offer something more than the played-out thug anthems of their mainstream peers. The future of hip-hop has always belonged to the young, and several potential candidates for this honor get some well-deserved exposure here. —*Bradley Torreano*

Love Hip-Hop / May 16, 2000 / Hip-O ♦♦♦

Love Hip-Hop collects romantic rap songs like Blackstreet's "No Diggity," Heavy D's "Now That We Found Love," 3rd Bass' "Pop Goes the Weasel," and Tony! Toni! Tone!'s "If I Had No Loot." Though the compilation could use a few more contemporary tracks to balance its late-'80s, early-'90s focus, *Love Hip-Hop* is an entertaining album for hip-hop lovers. —*Heather Phares*

Lowrider Jams / Aug. 11, 1998 / Thump ♦♦♦♦♦

Lowrider Jams is a surprisingly solid compilation of low-frequency dance music of the 1980s, from electro to freestyle to bass and beyond. Besides pop anthems like "Wild Thing" by Tone-Loc and "Me So Horny" by 2 Live Crew, the album includes electro classics like "Al-NaaFiysh (The Soul)" by Hashim, "Don't Stop the Rock" and "It's Automatic" by Freestyle, "Electric Kingdom" by Twilight 22, "Egypt Egypt" by the Egyptian Lover, "Clear" by Cybotron, and "When I Hear Music" by Debbie Deb. —*Keith Farley*

Luke's Hall of Fame / Jan. 28, 1997 / Luke ♦♦♦

This collection of hits from the notorious Luke Records label includes 2 Live Crew's "Me So Horny," "Throw the 'D'," and "Banned in the U.S.A."; Luke's "I Wanna Rock" and "Work It Out"; and Poison Clan's "Shake Whatcha Mama Gave Ya." —*Jason Ankeny*

Luke's Hall of Fame, Vol. 2 / Oct. 21, 1997 / Little Joe ♦♦♦

Luke's Hall of Fame, Vol. 3 / Sep. 22, 1998 / Little Joe ♦♦

Luke's Peep Show / Sep. 30, 1997 / Priority ♦♦

Luke's Peep Show doesn't offer anything dramatically different from any other post-controversy Luther Campbell project—it's just a set of mind-bogglingly loud and deep bass music with nasty lyrics. Campbell lets other rappers have center stage, but they all mimic his aesthetic, so there really isn't much of a difference between this and a 2 Live Crew record, other than that this sounds fresher and more dynamic. It might be stupid party music, but it's pretty good stupid party music. —*Leo Stanley*

Lyricist Lounge, Vol. 1 / May 5, 1998 / Priority ♦♦♦♦

Lyricist Lounge, Vol. 1 is an excellent showcase of underground and alternative rappers, including Kool Keith, De La Soul, 88 Keys, Natural Elements, Talib Kweli, Bahamadia, Q-Tip, and Jurassic 5, among many, many others. It's a great way to hear a number of the most talented and underappreciated rappers of the late '90s. —*Leo Stanley*

Lyricist Lounge, Vol. 2 / Nov. 28, 2000 / Priority ♦♦♦♦

The second installment of *Lyricist Lounge* compilation takes on a decidedly different direction then its predecessor. While the first segment catered toward breaking new, less-familiar talent, names like Prime, Mike Zoot, and Sarah Jones have been phased out and replaced by Erick Sermon and (gasp) JT Money. Yet, the transition is a fairly smooth one, and considering that the Lyricist Lounge has expanded from its open mike night roots into a successful MTV comedy show, this revision is not entirely surprising. Though not without filler material, *LL 2* achieves what most compilations promise but never deliver—a satisfactory LP that will appease both the chest-beating backpacker and the bling-bling tunnel faction. The quest in trying to meet this goal is really half the fun, as some interesting collaborations unfold; fellow Detroit natives Royce 5'9" and Jay Dee hook up on the autobiographical "Let's Grow," and Talib Kweli and Dead Prez revitalize the pro-black ideology over Hi-Tek's spaghetti western guitar riffs on the eye-opening "Sharp Shooters." However, the closest example of what *LL 2* aspires to be is captured on Redman and Saukrates' "WKYA" (Will Kick Your Ass), as the easily accessible but fiery rhymes of Red and Sauk are truly universal in their flavor. Though *LL 2* may not portray the idealism or spirit that the Lyricist Lounge was initially founded on, it does successfully represent the differing tastes of all hip-hop fans. That in itself is this compilation's biggest accomplishment. —*Matt Conaway*

Mad Flavas: Beats for the Boulevard / Nov. 3, 1998 / Thump ◆◆◆
This compilation includes several stellar hip-hop tracks of the 1990s, including De La Soul's "Say No Go," Craig Mack's "Flava in Ya Ear," Erick Sermon's "Stay Real," and Coolio's "Too Hot." —*Keith Farley*

Mad Flavas: Beats for the Boulevard, Vol. 2 / Jul. 27, 1999 / Thump ◆◆◆◆
The second volume in the party-anthem series known as *Mad Flavas* includes classics like R. Kelly's "Your Body's Calling," Will Smith's "Summertime," Ice Cube's "You Know How We Do It," and Montell Jordan's "This Is How We Do It," plus other greats by Shaquille O'Neal, Wu-Tang Clan, SWV, Tevin Campbell, and Dr. Dre. —*Keith Farley*

Más Allá del Perreo / May 14, 2002 / Universal Latino ◆◆
A refreshing fusion of rap and Latin dance, the *Más Allá del Perreo* compilation boasts a dozen tracks by a community of likeminded artists, including Joel & Fernan, Melson, Menin Black, and Yamir & Delf. The production aesthetic is similar throughout, with heavy use of drum machines and spidery, synthesized strings reminiscent of dirty South hip-hop teams like Eightball & MJG. The rapping is pretty good, and the occasional singing is surprisingly melodic. Melson's contributions, including a self-titled dis called "M-E-L-S-O-N," are the only tracks that match the braggadocio of hardcore rap. Other good tracks come with the weekend anthem "Fin de Semana" by Yamir & Delf and "El Perro Baratito" by Menin Black. —*John Bush*

Master P Presents No Limit All Stars: Who U Wit? / May 25, 1999 / No Limit/Priority ◆◆◆
If anything is more predictable than a No Limit album, it's a No Limit various-artists collection. *Master P Presents No Limit All Stars: Who U Wit?* proves that it is true that all the artists on the label sound the same—this collection of hits, remixes, outtakes, and album tracks holds together because all of the featured artists (including Master P himself, No Limit's top dog Snoop Dogg, and C-Murder, among others) are given the same cookie-cutter dirty South production. Ironically, the formulaic production and multitude of artists just makes the comp sound like a proper No Limit album, which is filled with predictable productions and guest stars. Really, there's nothing on *Who U Wit?* that distinguishes itself from the legions of No Limit records. It's not particularly good, but it's not bad, either—if you like the sound and are searching for something new in the same vein, this will likely quench your thirst. —*Stephen Thomas Erlewine*

● **Masters of the 1 & 2: History's Greatest DJ's** / Jan. 25, 2000 / Priority ◆◆◆◆◆
MTV Masters of the 1 & 2: History's Greatest DJ's is a riveting set of hip-hop beats layered with urban grooves and gangsta rap. Featured artists include De La Soul, rap pioneer Grandmaster Flash, Gang Starr, Ozomatli, and more. —*MacKenzie Wilson*

Mean Green: Major Players Compilation / Sep. 29, 1998 / Priority ◆◆◆
A collection covering No Limit's deep roster of rappers and producers, *Major Players* includes tracks by Fiend, UGK, Too Short, Master P (who, appropriately, provides the title track), E-40, C-Murder, Gambino Family, Mystikal, Mr. Serv-On, B-Legit, Mack 10, and others. Considering that most individual albums by No Limit rappers include just as many different artists as this compilation does, *Major Players* doesn't really sound that different from any regular CD on No Limit. —*Keith Farley*

Memphis Drama / Sep. 18, 2001 / Family Biz ◆◆◆
Like hundreds of other scene-oriented rap compilations, *Memphis Drama* takes several unknown and underground rappers and showcases their homegrown talents. The Memphis sound is very similar to most other gangsta rap sounds, taking the click and pop beats made popular by Miami rappers like Master P and combining them with the deep funk that the West Coast rappers are known for. The fast rhyming and angry yelling cover up some of the weaker rappers, but only a few songs really stick out. Kingpin Skinny Pimp's "Catch a Case" has a good haunting backbeat that is similar to Dr. Dre's work on Snoop Dogg's solo albums, while "I'm the Nigga" is a better-than-average boast that features Al Kapone's charismatic yelp. But overall, there are few true gems to be found on this album, and this will probably appeal to Memphis fans and hardcore hip-hop collectors only. —*Bradley Torreano*

Miami Bass: Heat Mix '96 / 1996 / Cold Front/K-Tel ◆◆◆
Miami bass takes a lot of criticism from hip-hoppers in New York, Philadelphia, and Boston; many northeastern hip-hoppers see it as lowest-common-denominator music and argue that bass artists take the easy way out by exploiting sex for a quick buck. But there is no law stating all rappers have to be as intellectual as Chuck D or KRS-One—and while many bass artists may not have the most profound lyrics in the word, their beats are insanely infectious. Released in 1996, this bass compilation doesn't pretend to be intellectual—it's simply a great party album. *Miami Bass: Heat Mix '96*, which spans 1987-1993, contains some definitive examples of bass music, including the Dogs' "Do the Nasty Dance," Uncle Al's "Girls-N-Da-House," Viscious Bass' "Shake That Thang," and Half Pint's "Big Booty Girls." Most of the tunes are state-of-the-art bass—the tempos are ultrafast, and the lyrics are all about wild, trashy, decadent fun. However, Bass Patrol's high-tech "Rock This Planet" (1988) is really electro-hop rather than bass. The track was obviously influenced by Afrika Bambaataa's "Planet Rock," and it inspires comparisons to the World Class Wreckin' Cru (the group that Dr. Dre belonged to before he joined N.W.A and became a gangsta rapper) and the Egyptian Lover instead of the 2 Live Crew, Tag Team, or 95 South. Nonetheless, "Rock This Planet" does have a South Florida connection; so it makes sense that Cold Front/K-Tel would include the song. *Miami Bass: Heat Mix '96* isn't the last word on bass, but it's among the CDs to add to your collection if you're interested in exploring this wild and rowdy form of rap. —*Alex Henderson*

Miami Bass: Heat Mix, Vol. 2 / May 20, 1997 / Cold Front/K-Tel ◆◆◆
In the late 1980s and early to mid-1990s, the dominant rap style in the Southeastern U.S. was "bass music"—fast, hyper, very danceable party jams usually escapist in nature. Instead of favoring either the complex rapping styles of New York and Philly or the political commentary of L.A. and Oakland rappers, bass artists go for wild, rowdy fun. Fast tempos prevail on *Miami Bass: Heat Mix, Vol. 2*, a 1997 compilation offering the type of hyper, nervous sounds one might have heard at a black club in Miami, Orlando, or Jacksonville at the time. Half Pint's "Drop It Low," Exit 25's "Do the Hop Scotch," and Uncle Al's "Slip and Slide" sound nothing like the hip-hop coming out of New York and L.A. at the time, and that's exactly the point. Most of the artists on this disc had no interest in emulating non-Southern rap styles, and were quite happy to see Florida doing its own thing. For a taste of bass at its most club oriented, *Heat Mix, Vol. 2* wouldn't be a bad choice. —*Alex Henderson*

Microphone Fiends / Oct. 21, 1997 / Hip-O ◆◆◆
Hip-O's *Microphone Fiends* has an odd selection of old school cuts from the early '80s and classic rap from the late '80s. As a result, the album isn't necessarily coherent, but it does have some great singles—including Boogie Down Productions' "My Philosophy," De La Soul's "Jenifa Taught Me," N.W.A's "Express Yourself," EPMD's "Let the Funk Flow," Mantronix's "Gangster Boogie (Walk Like Sex, Talk Like Sex)," Ice-T's "6 in the Mornin'," and Eric B. & Rakim's title track. Those hits are reason enough to acquire the album, especially since a couple of songs aren't available on any other collection, but it's too brief and uneven to be considered an essential purchase. —*Stephen Thomas Erlewine*

Millennium Hip-Hop Party / May 5, 1999 / Rhino ◆◆◆◆◆
One of Rhino's main gifts as a record label is that they know a good gimmick when they see it, and there's no better gimmick than the millennium. Hence, their series of *Millennium Party* albums. None of the *Millennium* discs demonstrate much imagination, but they do make a good argument that sometimes it's better to stick to the basics. For instance, *Millennium Hip-Hop Party* contains 18 tracks, most of them hits from the Bush era, but also a couple of earlier singles ("White Lines [Don't Don't Do It]," "Walk This Way," "Parents Just Don't Understand") and latter-day G-funk ("What's My Name," "Nuthin' But a 'G' Thang"). There are no surprises among these 18 songs, but when the core of the album features some of the best crossover rap ever made—"Funky Cold Medina," "The Humpty Dance," "Bust a Move," "It Takes Two," "U Can't Touch This," "Around the Way Girl," "Set Adrift on Memory Bliss," "Tennessee," "Now That We Found Love," "Good Vibrations," "Baby Got Back," "Jump Around," "Hip Hop Hooray"—there really aren't any complaints to be made. In fact, few collections offer a better primer of big hip-hop hits than this, and it's not a bad addition to any rap collection. —*Stephen Thomas Erlewine*

Mission Control Presents Prehistoric Sounds / Nov. 7, 2000 / Mission Control ◆◆◆◆
An amazing compilation put together by the likes of Talib Kweli, *Prehistoric Sounds* brings together some of the best artists in underground hip-hop circa 2000. Not surprisingly, the veteran Talib Kweli provides the album's highlight with "Millionaires." Newcomers Mood and Elite Terrorist hold their own

amid a stirring sound collage that melds elements of trip-hop and hip-hop in a way that is as entrancing as RZA's stellar work on the soundtrack for *Ghost Dog: The Way of the Samurai*. Forget about the title, *Prehistoric Sounds* represents the future of hip-hop. —*Jon Azpiri*

Mixmasters / Jul. 23, 1991 / MCA ✦✦✦

The Mixmasters weren't a group per se; rather, this generally commercial rap CD was a project whose coordinators included Greg Mack (a radio DJ who had been a key figure at L.A. urban contemporary station KDAY-AM, which played more rap than any other station in the U.S. before abandoning its urban format in the early 1990s), DJ Romeo (one of the DJs who came out of the L.A. hip-hop scene of the 1980s), and the team of Wolf & Epic. This CD features four little-known rap acts: Kid Loose, Trick (a male solo artist), Imoni, and the female duo Motse Thabong. Of the four, Kid Loose is the hands-down winner and shows a lot of promise on the catchy "Hot Stuff" and "Neighborhood Nomad," a poignant reflection on the life of a homeless man. Female rapper Imoni, meanwhile, is featured on "Imoni's Time" and "Ain't We Funky," both of which are routine but let us know that Imoni is a competent rapper—what she needed was stronger material to work with. Trick's performance on the R&B-minded "In and Out" is mildly fun, if lightweight, while contributions by Motse Thabong (clearly the weakest of the four acts) on "He's a Daniel" and "Contact" are most unimpressive. The duo has little in the way of personality, and its rapping skills are minimal at best. Overall, this is far from a great CD, but it has its moments. —*Alex Henderson*

Mo'Wax First Chapter / 1995 / Mo'Wax ✦✦✦✦

The first collection of Mo'Wax tracks includes several label classics like DJ Shadow's "In/Flux," DJ Krush's "Slow Chase," La Funk Mob's "Motor Bass Get Phunked Up," and Palm Skin Productions' "Spock with a Beard." Though even Mo'Wax includes a few duds—tracks by Monday Michiru, Bubbatunes, Marden Hill—the majority of *Mo'Wax First Chapter* is quite solid. —*John Bush*

Mobbin' Thru the Bay, Vol. 1 / Oct. 8, 1996 / Swerve ✦✦✦

Mobbin' Thru the Bay, Vol. 1 is a compilation of San Francisco Bay-area hip-hop—nearly all of it gangsta rap—covering some of the area's top artists and a number of obscure and up-and-coming acts. The biggest names here are probably J.T. the Bigga Figga ("State Penn") and Dru Down with N2Deep (collaborating on "California Lifestyles"). It's pretty inconsistent, but some of the lesser-known acts do acquit themselves well. —*Steve Huey*

Monsters of Rap, Vol. 1 / Jul. 25, 2000 / Razor & Tie ✦✦✦

Monsters of Rap gathers hip-hop hits from the late '80s and early '90s, including A Tribe Called Quest's "Scenario," Run-D.M.C.'s "Walk This Way," Young MC's "Bust a Move," and Tone-Loc's "Wild Thing." Sir Mix-A-Lot's "Baby Got Back," Positive K's "I Got a Man," MC Hammer's "U Can't Touch This," and Vanilla Ice's "Ice Ice Baby" are some of the other emblematic rap singles included on the album, and tracks from Technotronic, C+C Music Factory, 3rd Bass, Snap, Onyx, and Wreckx-N-Effect round out this fun collection. —*Heather Phares*

Monsters of Rap, Vol. 2 / Mar. 19, 2002 / Razor & Tie ✦✦✦

MTV Presents: Hip-Hop Back in the Day / Feb. 17, 1998 / Priority ✦✦✦✦

Released to coincide with the first showing of MTV's program *This Is Music: Hip-Hop Back in the Day*, *MTV Presents: Hip-Hop Back in the Day* is an excellent collection of early rap hits. While a handful of the songs stretch past old school and into the late '80s (Boogie Down Productions' "South Bronx," LL Cool J's "Rock the Bells," Tone-Loc's "Funky Cold Medina," MC Shan's "The Bridge"), the majority of the collection is devoted to early- and mid-'80s hits like Kurtis Blow's "The Breaks," Grandmaster Flash's "The Message," Afrika Bambaataa's "Planet Rock," the Fat Boys' "Fat Boys," U.T.F.O.'s "Roxanne, Roxanne," Doug E. Fresh's "The Show," Whodini's "Freaks Come Out at Night," and Heavy D's "The Overweight Lover's In the House." Almost every one of these tracks was a hip-hop milestone, and this isn't a bad way to pick them up on one disc, even if the presence of the bonus 1998 remix of "The Message" leaves a bitter aftertaste. —*Stephen Thomas Erlewine*

MTV the First 1000 Years: Hip Hop / Nov. 2, 1999 / Rhino ✦✦✦✦

It may be hard to get beyond the title of Rhino's series *MTV the First 1000 Years*, which just may be the dumbest title in the first 1,000 years of the recording industry, but the actual discs aren't bad at all. For instance, the *Hip Hop* volume is a terrific collection of hip-hop staples from "The Message" to "Player's Ball." Most of these songs were regularly played on MTV, and not just on *Yo! MTV Raps* either. "Walk This Way," "Wild Thing," "The Humpty Dance," "Jump Around," "Tennessee," "What's My Name," "It Was a Good Day," "Nuthin' But a 'G' Thang," "Fantastic Voyage," and "California Love" were all some of the biggest hits of their era, and listening to them here—along with "Colors," "Express Yourself," and "Rebirth of Slick (Cool Like Dat)," which were never crossover hits—is an exhilarating journey through the past. There are a lot of hip-hop collections, but few are as consistently entertaining as this one. —*Stephen Thomas Erlewine*

Murder Was the Case / 1994 / Interscope ✦✦✦✦✦

The soundtrack to an 18-minute film inspired by Snoop Doggy Dogg's "Murder Was the Case" provides more thrills than the average hip-hop release. Again, Dre relies on his standard production tricks and crew, introducing a couple of new members to the mix. But the result sounds anything but stale—it ranks alongside *The Chronic, Doggystyle*, and *Above the Rim* in terms of quality. In fact, various artist compilations like *Murder Was the Case* are the ideal vehicle for Dr. Dre—they show his versatility. *Murder* has the harrowing title track from Snoop Dogg, as well as the smooth funk of Warren G and the chilling hardcore of "Natural Born Killaz," the first track from Dre's collaboration with Ice Cube. At some point, Dre will need to find some new tricks, but *Murder Was the Case* finds him at the top of his game. —*Stephen Thomas Erlewine*

Nervous Hip Hop / 1995 / Nervous ✦✦✦

Far more than a detour into rap territory, Nervous Records alternates breakbeat workouts by its artists (the Wreck All Stars led by Kenny "Dope" Gonzalez, Franki Feliciano's Groove Asylum, and Live & Die Reck) with tracks by acknowledged rap titans like Smif-n-Wessun, Funkmaster Flex, and even dancehall's Mad Lion. Most tracks are successes, though many of the recruited house producers interpret hip-hop through the medium of more subtle, danceable fare. —*John Bush*

New Beats From the Delta / Oct. 24, 2000 / Fat Possum ✦✦✦

Fat Possum Records continues to push the blues and rap envelope by releasing an entire disc mixing hip-hop with Delta blues. *New Beats From the Delta* sets the gritty blues of Junior Kimbrough, Johnny Farmer, and Cedell Davis to hip-hop beats incorporated by producers including Organized Noize and Camp Go Gittas. This hybrid was tried on R.L. Burnside's 1998 release *Come On In* with mixed reviews. Chances are, if you're a blues purist, you may want to pass on this, while listeners open to experimentation should check it out. —*Al Campbell*

New Jersey Drive, Vol. 1 / 1995 / Tommy Boy ✦✦✦

Just another case of a stellar soundtrack outshining a lackluster film. Volume 1 of this star-studded set of songs inspired by the ill-fated urban carjacking film highlights the movers and shakers of mid-'90s hip-hop. The Notorious B.I.G. lends a classic verse on Puff Daddy girl group Total's "Can't U See"; the song is fueled by a time-honored sample from James Brown's "The Big Payback." Other lesser-known gems include Newark, NJ, representer and one of Jacktown's finest, Redman, on the Cosmic Sloppy "Where Am I"; the country-fried automobile-lover's anthem "Benz or a Beamer" provided by Outkast; and "East Left," a cut from cold wildin' Long Island native Keith Murray. While some irritating filler is sprinkled in with the hits, there is also a strong West Coast flavor provided by the likes of MC Eiht and Young Lay, and a taste of dancehall stylings from Black Panta. This volume also features the classic dance hit "Before I Let Go" by Frankie Beverly and Maze. —*Michael Di Bella*

New Jersey Drive, Vol. 2 / 1995 / Tommy Boy ✦✦✦

Contrasting the 14 hit-or-miss tracks on *New Jersey Drive, Vol. 1* is the quality-packed volume 2. Condensed down to an extended play format, this second offering packs more of an underground wallop. The Boot Camp Clique mash up "Headz Ain't Ready" with enamoring verses from Buckshot, Smif-n-Wessun, and Ruck and Rock of Heltah Skeltah. The scathing anti-car theft jam "You Won't Go Far" by Organized Konfusion and O.C. is an icily realistic portrayal of the actual act of car jacking. Jeru the Damaja's "Invasion" thumps with a jumpy off-sequenced beat injected by DJ Premier and the unheralded and heretofore unheard from E. Bros. chime in with the jazzy "Funky Piano." Mad Lion delivers his punishing brand of dancehall on the up-tempo banger "Own Destiny." Biz Markie's classic old school jam "Nobody Beats the Biz" is also featured on the album and rounds out the consistently terrific volume 2. —*Michael Di Bella*

New Millennium Hip-Hop Party / Apr. 25, 2000 / Rhino ✦✦✦✦✦
The sequel to Rhino's terrifically entertaining *Millennium Hip-Hop Party* compilation, *New Millennium Hip-Hop Party* features more of rap's best crossover pop hits, dipping a little later into the mid-'90s than its predecessor (cuts from Coolio, the Notorious B.I.G., and the Wu-Tang Clan, which demonstrate the infiltration of gangsta themes into a greater variety of mainstream hip-hop). But for the most part, the collection still covers pop-rap's late-'80s/early-'90s heyday, when some of the most creative sounds in hip-hop were also among its most playful and accessible. There are cuts from some of the first alternative rappers (De La Soul's "Me Myself & I," A Tribe Called Quest's "Scenario," Arrested Development's "People Everyday"), plus flat-out great singles like Naughty By Nature's "O.P.P.," Run-D.M.C.'s "You Be Illin'," DJ Jazzy Jeff & the Fresh Prince's "Summertime," Rob Base & DJ E-Z Rock's "Joy and Pain," Mellow Man Ace's "Mentirosa," Tone-Loc's "Wild Thing," Grandmaster Flash & the Furious Five's "The Message," and even more. Like the first installment, *New Millennium Hip-Hop Party* is an excellent way to collect some of the most compulsively listenable hip-hop singles yet recorded. —*Steve Huey*

The Next Chapter: Strictly Underground / Oct. 31, 1995 / Immortal/Epic ✦✦✦
Too seldom do independent/underground artists get to showcase their talents on a major label without being signed to one. However, on Immortal/Epic Records' compilation *The Next Chapter*, the underground MCs get to reveal their skills via mainstream means. Given that there are only unsigned (at that point) artists on this album, there are going to be some lesser-quality songs; however, there are a few worth listening to. Defari's "Big Up," Phunky Dialect's "L.A.P.D.," and Dilated Peoples' "End of the Time" are all good tracks in their own right. It's worth seeking out this compilation, if not just to hear some artists who went on to obtain major record deals in their premature state (Defari and Dilated Peoples, to mention a few). —*Nick Pfeiffer*

Next Friday / Dec. 7, 1999 / Priority ✦✦✦
The sequel to Ice Cube's *Friday* includes music from the star himself plus a great roster of hip-hop superstars including Snoop Dogg, Wu-Tang Clan, Eminem, Dr. Dre, and Lil' Zane, plus tracks from Pharoahe Monch, Krayzie Bone, and Ron Isley. —*Keith Farley*

Next Up: Rap's New Generation / Jun. 13, 2000 / TVT ✦✦✦
Next Up: Rap's New Generation is a close look at hip-hop's millennial innovators. This collection of explicit rap tracks from TVT Records showcases the genre's significant and upcoming artists in gangsta rap and hardcore rap, which necessarily might not make it on MTV's *TRL*. Artists featured on *Next Up* include Da Wastlanz, Blackhand, Xzibit, and more. —*MacKenzie Wilson*

No Face Killaz / Jul. 28, 1998 / Black Market ✦✦
No Face Killaz is a sampler of the roster of the hardcore rap label Black Market, featuring artists like Brotha Lynch Hung, Locc 2 Da Brain, Cedsing, Mr. Doctor, Homicide, and many more. If you're looking for an introduction to the label, this isn't quite as good as *The Best of Black Market Records: Hounds of Tha Underground, Verse 1*; nonetheless, it is a decent sampler for fans of hardcore and gangsta rap. —*Steve Huey*

No Limit Soldiers Compilation: We Can't Be Stopped / Dec. 8, 1998 / No Limit/Priority ✦✦✦
No Limit Soldiers Compilation: We Can't Be Stopped offers a generous sampling of highlights from the No Limit vaults, which is a mixed blessing. Mixed because these songs—with the exception of three cuts—are all on previously released records, and the only people that may be interested in them are hardcore No Limit freaks, who probably won't need to buy these again. Then again, casual or curious listeners don't necessarily need this album, since it doesn't really capture the label at its best. It is representative, to be sure, but that's because *all* No Limit albums sound the same. So, it's a toss-up—either you want this as a sampler, and you don't care if there aren't many hits, or you're a collector who needs the exclusive tracks. Either way, it's not a great listen or bargain. —*Stephen Thomas Erlewine*

No More Prisons / Sep. 14, 1999 / Raptivism ✦✦✦✦✦
If hip-hop is supposed to be a voice of the urban masses bringing awareness to the injustices of everyday life, too many albums are released devoid of political messages. With that sentiment in mind, Raptivism Records' 1999 release *No More Prisons* is a gorgeous answer to a full-blown crisis. Uniting underground MCs from coast to coast, *No More Prisons* comes complete with 23 tracks of personal insight, reflection, and sociopolitical commentary on the national prison system and the hypocritical foundation those prisons stand on. If the cause wasn't enough motive to hear this album out, the hip-hop it offers certainly is. Apani B-Fly MC, El Battalion, Rubberoom, Lyric, Dead Prez, and so many more bring their styles to the table to create an impressive joint from start to finish. There truly is a little bit of everything here. From Apani B-Fly MC and L.I.F.E.'s down-tempo tirade on the circular trap of getting caught in the system ("Outa Site"), to the aggressive jump-up beats on "Where Ya At" (B.K.N.Y.), to the spoken-word musings of Lyric on "Let Us Go," the common thread is in the issue these tracks illuminate. There are too many shining stars on this joint to even begin to mention them all. DJ Shame, Hedrush, Steele, Kriminal Krash, and still more throw down beats to round out the entire affair. Rarely does an album come complete with an actual message, conscious content, above-the-board production values, and mad skills behind the mike. When all of those elements are seamlessly blended into a complete expression of unity, watch out. The bar's been raised. —*Emilie Litzell*

Non Stop Hip Hop / Jun. 19, 2001 / Razor & Tie ✦✦✦
There's definitely no shortage of hits on *Non Stop Hip Hop*, a compilation that looks back to mid-'80s hip-hop classics like Salt-N-Pepa's "Push It" and Rob Base and DJ EZ Rock's "It Takes Two" up to '90s party rap staples like Kris Kross' "Jump" and Tag Team's "Whoomp! There It Is." The emphasis seems to be on the lighter side of hip-hop with the inclusion of kid rappers like Another Bad Creation and Kris Kross and pop rappers like Will Smith and MC Hammer. The most provocative booty-style song here is probably "The Humpty Dance" and the closest this gets to gangsta territory is Warren G and Nate Dogg's "Regulate." This, of course, means that *Non Stop Hip Hop* aims its focus a bit at the younger crowd; casual hip-hop listeners should also find much to treasure. On the other hand, seasoned hip-hop listeners probably won't find much worth bothering with here. Granted, there are a lot of hits, but the nonstop mix is to be scoffed at, and a lot of these songs, classics or not, are quite frankly played out. —*Jason Birchmeier*

Nuthin' but a Gangsta Party / Jul. 4, 2000 / Priority ✦✦✦✦
Nuthin' but a Gangsta Party is a solid collection featuring tracks from some of rap's most popular artists and innovators such as Ice Cube, Tupac, Snoop Dogg, Krayzie Bone, Mack 10, Kurupt, Xzibit, and more. —*MacKenzie Wilson*

Nuthin' but a Gangsta Party, Vol. 2 / Jul. 3, 2001 / Priority ✦✦✦
The second volume in Priority's excellent *Nuthin' but a Gangsta Party* series again offers a roster of the West Coast's best gangsta rap artists and many of their most well-known songs. You get the obvious—rappers like Snoop Dogg, Ice Cube, and Kurupt; songs like "Nuthin' but a 'G' Thang," "Who Am I (What's My Name)," and "Hello"—and you also get the not so obvious: lesser-known artists like Suga Free and Ra the Rugged Man and a little No Limit flavor. Plus, there's Low Profile's "Funky Song," a long-forgotten song from 1989 that is a welcome inclusion for its historical significance—it gives one an idea of where West Coast rap began and how its sound has always owed a heavy debt to the P-funk. Overall, there's little to complain about. Even the lesser artists turn in excellent performances, and while it's tempting to dismiss the No Limit songs for being out of place on a West Coast rap collection, the two chosen songs—"Down for My N's" and "Got 'Em Fiending"—both have an obvious West Coast sound to them. So what you have is 19 standout songs from Priority's vaults that illustrate everything that's wonderful about the West Coast gangsta sound. And, finally, it's also important to note that this isn't the aggressive side of gangsta rap, but rather the funky side of gangsta rap. The fact that Priority includes a classic like "Funky Song" rather than something from N.W.A, for example, perfectly illustrates the sort of vibe they're going for here. —*Jason Birchmeier*

Nutty Professor II: The Klumps / Jun. 23, 2000 / Def Jam ✦✦✦
Four years after his eponymous *The Nutty Professor*, Eddie Murphy gets even more hilarious on the sequel *The Nutty Professor II: The Klumps*. The original soundtrack was brief enough to keep the fun around, especially with tracks from Warren G and Montell Jordan, but the second installment gets raunchy. Aside from the sweet upbeat R&B track from Janet Jackson ("It Doesn't Really Matter"), this album is heavy with gangsta rappers and their brash attitudes to boot. Songs from Jay-Z, DMX, and Eminem call for a rollicking good time, and female rappers such as Eve also keep the party rolling. But it's too harsh for the comedic aspect. More appropriately, LL Cool J keeps things clean on "Snippets." —*MacKenzie Wilson*

O.G. Funk: Locking, Vol. 1 / May 19, 1998 / VRL Muzik ✦✦✦✦

In 1998, brothers Thomas and Paul Guzman-Sanchez released their documentary *Underground Dance Masters: History of a Forgotten Era*, which took a look at the 1970s dance crazes known as "popping" and "locking." L.A.'s poppers and lockers of the 1970s have been compared to the breakdancers who subsequently came out of New York's hip-hop subculture. It was in 1998 that Thomas' label, VRL Muzik, released *O.G. Funk: Locking, Volumes 1 and 2* for its Underground Dance Masters Music Series. Boasting the 1970s funk classics that were heard in the film, the compilations contain the type of gems that poppers and lockers danced to. But while popping and locking were an underground phenomenon, most of the 1970s funk classics VRL chose for these compilations were far from underground. On *Locking, Vol. 1* (which spans 1971-1997), VRL offers well-known hits like Kool and the Gang's "Hollywood Swinging," Dennis Coffey's "Scorpio," Hamilton Bohannon's "Let's Start the Dance," and Rick James' "High On Your Love Suite." Most of the selections were played extensively on R&B stations, and some of them were played over and over on pop/Top 40 stations as well. Also included are some new funk/hip-hop recordings the Guzman-Sanchez brothers did themselves. But while those offerings aren't terribly memorable, the 1970s classics are excellent. Combine an abundance of funk pearls with attractive liner notes and good sound quality, and you've got a series that is well worth checking out. —*Alex Henderson*

O.G. Funk: Locking, Vol. 2 / May 19, 1998 / VRL Muzik ✦✦✦✦

When VRL included *O.G. Funk: Locking, Volumes 1 and 2* in its Underground Dance Masters Music Series, the L.A. label was using the word "underground" in reference to the urban dancers who got into "popping" and "locking" in the 1970s. But while poppers and lockers were certainly underground, most of the music they danced to wasn't. The majority of songs VRL includes on *O.G. Funk, Vol. 2* (which spans 1971-1997) are far from underground. The Average White Band's "Pick Up the Pieces," Aretha Franklin's "Rock Steady," War's "Me and Baby Brother," and other 1970s funk and soul classics heard on *Locking, Vol. 2* were major hits that soared to the top of the charts. Mass Production's "Groove Me" (1978) could be considered an underground classic (except for 1979's "Firecracker," MP was more of a club act than a radio act), but songs as famous as Kool and the Gang's "Open Sesame" and B.T. Express' "Express" hardly qualify as underground. Although most of VRL's choices are excellent, some 1997 hip-hop/funk recordings by the Guzman-Sanchez brothers are pretty routine. The abundance of 1970s pearls are what make this collection worth owning. —*Alex Henderson*

O.L.C.: Operation Left Coast / Nov. 13, 2001 / Rah Rah ✦✦✦✦

O.L.C.: Operation Left Coast features some of the West Coast's more prominent hip-hop artists. Don't expect the notorious gangsta style so often associated with Cali but rather the more straightforward and golden age-influenced hip-hop sound associated with Dilated Peoples and Jurassic 5. Some of the better-known artists here include the Beat Junkies, Freestyle Fellowship, Dafari, Tash, and Phil da Agony. Those who appreciate good-natured lyrics, deft rhyming, and flashy turntablism rather than blunts, bitches, and Benzes should have plenty to savor on *O.L.C.: Operation Left Coast*. —*Jason Birchmeier*

Old School Basic / 1995 / Sugar Hill/P-Vine ✦✦✦✦

An old school sampling of rap jams originally released by Sugar Hill Records featuring the Sugarhill Gang on their everlasting "Rappers Delight." Kevie Kev does the erotic (but tasteful according to today's standards) "All Night Long (Waterbed)" and the Funky Four Plus One light it up on "That's the Joint." Grandmaster Flash & the Furious Five deliver two heavyweights: "Freedom," an adaptation of a tune originally waxed by Jackson, MS, funk band Freedom, and their immortal "The Message." —*Andrew Hamilton*

Old School Funkin' Hip-Hop / Jun. 6, 2000 / Thump ✦✦✦✦

Thump Records' *Old School Funkin' Hip-Hop* collects rap from Mark Morrison, Father MC, the WhoRidas, and the Lost Boyz. Digital Underground's "Kiss You Back," Heavy D & the Boyz' "Overweight Lovers in the House," Arrested Development's "Mr. Wendall" and "Tennessee," and Luniz' "I Got 5 on It" are some of the highlights of this album, which also features tracks from Warren G and Westside Connection. This is an eclectic mix of hip-hop hits. —*Heather Phares*

Old School Jams / Jul. 28, 1998 / Thump ✦✦✦

The best of '80s funk and R&B, *Old School Jams* includes tracks by Average White Band, Tower of Power, Zapp, Planet Patrol, the Time, and Chaka Khan, among others. —*Keith Farley*

Old School Jams, Vol. 2 / Nov. 5, 1996 / SPG ✦✦✦

Old School Jams, Vol. 2 follows the precedent established by its predecessor and features a number of longtime dance favorites from the '70s and '80s. Though all of these songs retain much of their initial charm, with some even having grown more novel with age, this is a disparate collection, featuring a little bit of everything—from late-'70s disco-funk like Slave's "Just a Touch of Love" to early-'80s electro-funk like Man Parrish's "Boogie Down Bronx." However, every song does retain an emphasis on funk—some disco inflections, others more urban inflections. Other featured songs include Class Action's "Weekend," Loose Joints' "Is It All Over My Face?," and Lakeside's "Fantastic Voyage," in addition to several others. —*Jason Birchmeier*

Old School Jams, Vol. 3 / Nov. 13, 2001 / SPG ✦✦✦✦

Old School Jams, Vol. 3 expands upon preceding volumes, featuring not one but two discs of late-'70s to late-'80s urban dance classics. Furthermore, these aren't the widely known album or radio versions but rather the extended dance mixes, many of which are quite difficult to find. There's no shortage of classics here: Cameo's "Word Up," Rick James' "Super Freak," the Gap Band's "You Dropped a Bomb on Me," and Blondie's "Rapture" are just a sample of the many longtime favorites featured on this double-disc collection. This collection should appeal to not one but two different audiences, those looking for a one-stop collection of late-'70s to late-'80s urban dance favorites and those looking for the many hard-to-find extended mixes featured here. In fact, this volume is so impressive that you'll want to skip the first two volumes and head straight for this one. It's so loaded with great music that you may not even need to bother with the other volumes. —*Jason Birchmeier*

Old School Rap, Vol. 1 / Aug. 16, 1994 / Thump ✦✦✦✦

From the mid-'80s peak of old school rap come 14 classics, including "Give It All You Got" by Afro-Rican, "The Message" and "White Lines" by Grandmaster Flash, "The Breaks" by Kurtis Blow, "Roxanne Roxanne" by U.T.F.O., "Rappers Delight" by the Sugarhill Gang, and "The Freaks Come out at Night" by Whodini. —*Keith Farley*

Old School Rap, Vol. 2 / Oct. 3, 1995 / Thump ✦✦✦

The second in the series includes more classics, like "It's Like That" by Run-D.M.C., "The Show" by Doug E. Fresh, "Brass Monkey" by the Beastie Boys, and "Rockberry Jam" by the L.A. Dream Team. —*Keith Farley*

Old School Rap, Vol. 3 / 1996 / Thump ✦✦✦✦✦

Old School Rap, Vol. 3 is an entertaining budget-line collection of ten classic rap hits from the mid- and late '80s, including Young MC's "Bust A Move," and Eric B & Rakim's "Check Out My Melody," Boogie Down Productions' "My Philosophy," Doug E. Fresh's "La Di Da Di," Big Daddy Kane's "Ain't No Half Steppin'," Kool Moe Dee's "Go See the Doctor," and Tone-Loc's "Wild Thang." Though the album was thrown together without much consideration and isn't very comprehensive, it is a fun listen and wortwhile for casual rap fans. —*Leo Stanley*

Old School Rap, Vol. 4 / Jun. 29, 1999 / Thump ✦✦✦

Tracks like "Ice Ice Baby," "Funky Cold Medina," and "Elevate My Mind" by Stereo MCs may not be everyone's definition of old school rap, but this fourth volume in the series includes quite a few excellent back-in-the-day rap hits, including "P.S.K. What Does It Mean?" by Schoolly D, "Paid in Full" by Eric B. & Rakim, "My Adidas" by Run-D.M.C., and "Freaky Tales" by Too Short. —*John Bush*

On the Rap Tip / 1989 / Priority ✦✦✦

The ten-track mid-line collection *On the Rap Tip* is a little schizophrenic, bouncing between hardcore hip-hop and melodic crossover rap, but it's nevertheless an entertaining listen. There are some filler cuts that have been forgotten over the years, but there's also a number of terrific songs, including Tone-Loc's "Funky Cold Medina," De La Soul's "Me Myself and I," Slick Rick's "Teenage Love," Sir Mix-A-Lot's "Iron Man," EPMD's "So What Cha Sayin'," and N.W.A's epochal "Straight Outta Compton." —*Stephen Thomas Erlewine*

One Big Trip / Aug. 13, 2002 / Red Urban ✦✦✦✦

The soundtrack to a road movie (included as a seperate DVD disc), *One Big Trip* is an impressive collection of some of the finest underground hip-hop acts of the moment. The Hieroglyphics, the all-star crew that includes Del tha Funkee Homosapien, produced and compiled the album, and appear on four tracks, as well as a solo cut by Del. All are superb, showing much improvement over the sometimes uneven quality of the first Hieroglyphics album. Similarly, Jurassic 5's opener, "Verbal Gunfight," is first-rate. What's more, the album is impeccably sequenced, so Dan the Automator's instrumental dance cut flows seamlessly with the Dilated Peoples and Swollen Members contributions, which are much darker and use chilling piano loops and vocals. Even the more party-flavored cuts—such as Lootpack's "Movies 2 Groupies"—have first-rate production that allows them to fit in seamlessly with the more underground tracks. *One Big Trip* will please anyone looking for smart, well-crafted hip-hop. — *Victor W. Valdivia*

Oz / Jan. 9, 2001 / ✦✦✦

Featuring a broad ensemble of rap artists from all three coasts, the *Oz* soundtrack is far from consistent in terms of style. In fact, very few of the 17 tracks feature many similarities; one moment Snoop Dogg is getting funky to Meech Wells' West Coast beats, followed by Pharoahe Monch representing classic New York hip-hop and then Master P getting rowdy to patented No Limit-style beats courtesy of Carlos Stephens. What makes this uncanny blend of differing styles and ideologies works so well is everyone's focus on quality. Rather than contribute leftovers and throwaways, most artists here drop tracks representative of their better material. Furthermore, as opposed to most rap soundtracks, *Oz* featuring almost nothing but proven artists, some of the best from all coasts. With so many impressive artists and so much quality material, there are several highlights, of course, but perhaps the most noteworthy inclusions are Cypress Hill's "Can I Live" (top-notch production by Muggs), Three 6 Mafia's "War Wit Us" (what you'd expect from this underrated group), and Kurupt and Nate Dogg's "Behind the Walls" (two talented artists at their best). The same sense of variety that makes this album so engaging upon the initial listen ultimately ends up being the album's primary fault, though; not many rap listeners are going to enjoy all of the many offerings equally, making it an album that doesn't work well from beginning to end but rather as a wide-ranging sampler of rap music circa 2001. — *Jason Birchmeier*

Pass the Mic: The Posse Album / May 31, 1996 / Priority ✦✦✦

Pass the Mic: The Posse Album showcases 13 hip-hop tracks where a number of different rappers get a chance to rap. These are songs that sound like old block parties, where the microphone is passed to each rapper, who gets a chance to freestyle. Because of this, the album is a lyrical showcase, even though the rhythms themselves are quite good. It's not an essential album, but every cut is entertaining and some—including Gang Starr's "Dwyck," De La Soul's "Buddy," EPMD's "Knick Knack Patty Wack," Fu-Schnickens' "La Schmoove," Big Daddy Kane's "Just Rhymin' with Biz," and Monie Love's "Ladies First"—are excellent. — *Stephen Thomas Erlewine*

Pepsi World / Nov. 24, 1998 / Damian ✦✦✦

Pepsi World is a collection of generally pop-oriented urban R&B and hip-hop, with a little straight-ahead dance-pop thrown in. There's material from SWV, K-Ci and Jo-Jo, R. Kelly, Sylk-E. Fyne, Mary J. Blige, Coolio, Big Punisher, Salt-N-Pepa, the Backstreet Boys, Robyn, and the All Saints, among others. It's an engaging collection in spite of the blatant marketing tie-in, and fans of mainstream '90s urban pop probably won't mind that very much. — *Steve Huey*

Phat Blunts: Rap Unda Tha Influence / Jan. 23, 1996 / Priority ✦✦✦

Phat Blunts: Rap Unda Tha Influence has a bit of a cutesy concept—collect a bunch of hardcore songs about substances, from booze to the chronic—and it would be unbearable if the music itself wasn't good. Sure, there are some lame cuts here, but there are more than enough great moments—including N.W.A's "Dopeman," Too Short's "City of Dope," Ice Cube's "My Summer Vacation," Tone-Loc's "Cheeba Cheeba," Boogie Down Productions' "Illegal Business," tha Alkaholiks' "Mary Jane," and Dr. Dre's "Puffin' on Blunts and Drankin' Tanqueray"—to make it worth a listen. — *Stephen Thomas Erlewine*

Pimps, Players & Hustlers / Jun. 20, 2000 / Little Joe ✦✦✦✦

Pimps, Players and Hustlers is loaded with the Miami bass sound and bawdy lyrics popularized by the 2 Live Crew, which shows up here on several tracks (Luke also makes a couple of solo appearances). Freak Nasty's national hit "Da Dip" appears here as well; other than that, the artists won't be incredibly well known, though Verb effectively sums up the tone of the compilation in the title of "Weed, Money and Hoes." — *Steve Huey*

Pootie Tang / Jun. 26, 2001 / Hollywood ✦✦✦

If you have eclectic taste in music, some movie soundtracks can be a lot of fun. The Robert De Niro masterpiece *A Bronx Tale*, for example, called for material by everyone from John Coltrane to the Impressions to the Moody Blues. But other soundtracks, depending on the nature of the film, only

require certain styles of music. This isn't one of those soundtracks that jumps from industrial to Chicago blues to adult contemporary; the makers of the 2001 blaxploitation film *Pootie Tang* wanted urban and rap, and for the most part, its soundtrack caters to the urban/hip-hop scene of the early 2000s. There are exceptions; Zapp's "I Want to Be Your Man" goes back to the 1980s, and Bell Biv DeVoe's "Poison" was one of 1990's definitive new jack swing smashes. But overall, the uneven *Pootie Tang* soundtrack is early 2000s minded, which means providing rap by the likes of Master P ("Make Em Say Ugh"), Lil J ("You Know What?"), and Majic ("Dirty Dee") along with some hip-hop-flavored R&B by 702 ("Pootie Tangin'") and Erykah Badu ("Southern Girl"). The latter, which shouldn't be confused with Maze & Frankie Beverly's 1980 classic, is one of the best things on the CD—this very ironic gem finds Badu making fun of stereotypes of black women from the deep South. Those who don't pick up on the tune's ironic nature might think that Badu is promoting those stereotypes, but she's actually poking fun at them—sort of like Margaret Cho making fun of stereotypes of Asians. On the whole, this soundtrack isn't remarkable; but there are a few gems here and there, and most of the other tunes are at least decent or competent. —*Alex Henderson*

Price of Glory / Apr. 4, 2000 / New Line ✦✦✦✦✦

The soundtrack to the critically acclaimed Latino boxing drama *Price Of Glory* collects songs from Latin and Latino-American artists including Cypress Hill's "Jack U Back," Mano Negra's "King Kong Five," Aterciopelados' "Lado Oscuro," Ozomatli's "Dos Cosas Ciertas," and Los Lobos' "Cumbia Raza." The Texas Tornados' "Rueda De Fuego," Puya's "Keep It Simple," and King Chango's title track are some of the other highlights from this album, which also features songs from Le Boot, Pastilla, and Control Machete. A worthwhile companion to an equally strong and consciousness-raising film, *Price Of Glory* also stands on its own as a fine introduction to contemporary, Latin-based music. —*Heather Phares*

Profilin' the Hits / Jun. 15, 1999 / Profile/Arista ✦✦✦✦

Along with Sugarhill and Def Jam, Profile was one of the major rap labels for the music's early development, releasing countless hip-hop classics from Run-D.M.C., EPMD, Rob Base & DJ EZ Rock, DJ Quik, Dana Dane, Poor Righteous Teachers, Special Ed, and many more. And even after many labels had come and gone, Profile continued to release material by hot new artists including Camp Lo. The retrospective compilation *Profilin' the Hits* includes 11 of the best the label has to offer, making for a great (though short) compilation. Just kicking off with two of the most infectious hip-hop singles of all time, Rob Base's "It Takes Two" and Run-D.M.C.'s "It's Like That," is a pretty good guarantee of success. But *Profilin'* also includes quite a few less famous tracks, many of which were unjustifiably neglected. Camp Lo's "Luchini AKA This Is It" is a brilliant fusion of a brief, horn-driven sample and the duo's syrupy flow, while Dana Dane's "Cinderfella Dana Dane" is another classic. Even a novelty item like "Inspector Gadget" by the Kartoon Krew comes off with more than just a bit of quality. *Profilin'* is a solid compilation charting hip-hop's genesis in the 1980s and rise to the top the following decade. —*John Bush*

Project Blowed / 1995 / A-Team/Afterlife ✦✦✦✦

At a time when Tupac and Notorious B.I.G.'s tragically overhyped beef threatened to give hip-hop a black eye in the public consciousness, the ever-idealistic Aceyalone was attempting to unite the progressive wing of West Coast hip-hop through *Project Blowed*. Drawing inspiration from the titular open-mike night and label, *Project Blowed* maps out a bold new direction for the West Coast underground, bringing together wildly diverse acts whose common bond is a shared love and respect for hip-hop coupled with a desire to expand its musical, thematic, and lyrical horizons. A defiantly low-fi, low-budget compilation that makes even underground projects like Rawkus' *Lyricist Lounge* and *Soundbombing* series look like the collected lost singles of Puff Daddy, *Project Blowed* makes up for what it lacks in slickness with creativity, originality, and a strong sense of purpose. Guided by the progressive vision of A-Teamers Aceyalone and Abstract Rude, *Project Blowed* runs the gamut of far-left indie hip-hop, from the bizarrely literal pimp rap of Tray Loc's "Once Upon a Freak" to Figure Uv Speech's bluntly feminist and black nationalist "Don't Get It Twisted," a remarkably assured blend of jazz, poetry, spoken word, and hip-hop. Executive producer Aceyalone makes his presence felt throughout, reuniting with Freestyle Fellowship for the jazzy give and take of "Hot" and teaming with fellow A-Teamer Abstract Rude for "Maskaraid Part 1 & 2," a characteristically ambitious and conceptual track abstractly criticizing hip-hop's propensity for posturing and role playing. *Project Blowed*'s lo-fi aesthetic and willingness to experiment may alienate even fans of likeminded but far slicker underground acts like Mos Def, De La Soul, and Black Star. But for those tuned into Aceyalone and company's bohemian, progressive take on hip-hop, *Project Blowed* is coffeehouse hip-hop at its finest. —*Nathan Rabin*

Pump Ya Fist: Hip-Hop Inspired by the Black Panthers / Apr. 11, 1995 / Avatar ◆◆◆◆

This is a varied collection of hip-hop acts (such as Arrested Development, Yo-Yo, Chuck D, and KRS-One) that unites around pro-black themes for each song. It's a great release by some of the best acts in the rap world. —*John Bush*

Q.D. III Soundlab / 1991 / Qwest ◆◆◆◆

Hip-hop was at something of a crossroads when this album was released. On the one hand, pop-rappers like MC Hammer and Vanilla Ice were using it as a convenient vehicle to pop superstardom. At the other end of the spectrum, gangsta rappers like N.W.A and Ice-T were using harder beats and violent, frequently sexist imagery to corner the adolescent male market. These and others like them got all the press at the time. But there were other hip-hop figures around as well, ones who managed to create bruising beats and grown-up lyrics without talking incessantly about pimping and busting caps. You weren't reading much yet about artists like Justin Warfield or Kenyatta, but they were out there delivering intelligent rhymes and artful beats. Some of them assembled under the aegis of Q.D. III (the *nom de musique* of the son of famed producer Quincy Jones), whose production prowess contributes significantly to the success of this compilation. Highlights include the powerful rhymes of the tag team Poet Society and the positive messages of Kenyatta, but almost every track has something to recommend it. The only exception is the smarmy "Gigolo Lifestyle" by S.R.-One, a classic of self-centered machismo that is musically boring to boot. —*Rick Anderson*

A Rap Collection / Mar. 13, 2001 / Giant ◆◆◆

Although rap music has existed since the late '70s, it is a rather unforgiving and ahistorical genre in which yesterday's records and their performers tend to be discarded rapidly. And the music moved so fast in the late '90s and early 2000s that even the early '90s quickly came to seem "old school" from "back in the day." After all, that was before the deaths of Tupac and the Notorious B.I.G., which were ancient history by 2001. Giant Records was not known as a major player in rap, but, especially in its deal with Ice-T's Rhyme Syndicate organization, it had access to plenty of rap in the first half of the '90s (not that rappers have ever been hard to find). This compilation surveys the label's roster of 1991-1995, some of it popular stuff at the time (Hammer, Ahmad, Ice-T), plenty of it also-ran even then. What strikes you immediately is how much less sophisticated the percussion tracks are as compared with those common a decade later, then how straightforward the raps are, in part driven by those simple beats. What hasn't changed is the attitude, which remains vulgar and boasting, a tone that can seem hopeful in young rappers and challenging in current ones, but that seems pathetic coming from these has-beens and never-weres. *A Rap Collection* is given a deliberately unassuming title that suggests its contents are generic, and that's not far wrong, as long as you add the qualification "of the early '90s." —*William Ruhlmann*

Rap Declares War / 1992 / Rhino ◆◆◆◆

Conceptually, this is very strong. With the imprimatur of the remaining members of War and their longtime manager Jerry Goldstein, the group's tracks are used as samples and/or backing for some well-known and not-so-well-known rappers to pay homage to. For the most part it works, because the talent (e.g., The Beasties, Ice-T, Tupac, De La Soul) is there. However, tracks by those artists have been available on their earlier discs. And the lesser-known material, which also comes from previously released sources, is simply not as outstanding, ranging from the lackadaisical (Too Short) to the doggedly polemical (Brand Nubian). The title track is a new War number and does a great job of stating the band's significance. In fact, this entire disc is fairly remarkable in showing how influential War has remained as a source point for rap, both in groove and social consciousness... —*John Dougan*

Rap en Español / 1991 / Globo ◆◆◆

Over the years, hip-hoppers have rapped in a variety of languages, including German, Italian, French, Portuguese, Dutch, and even Japanese. But if hip-hop has an unofficial second language, it's Spanish. Many Puerto Ricans were down with the hip-hop culture when it emerged in New York in the late '70s, and the Mean Machine's bilingual 1981 single "Disco Dreams" contains the first recorded example of rapping in Spanish. Since then, many other Latinos have demonstrated that an MC can rap in both English and Spanish—everyone from Puerto Rican New Yorkers (Mesanjarz of Funk, Hurricane G) to Chicanos in Southern California (Cypress Hill, the Mexakinz, Lighter Shade of Brown, Kid Frost, Proper Dos). Various Latino rap compilations came out in the 1990s; while *Latin Hip-Hop Flava* on Priority and *Latin Lingo: Hip-Hop From the Raza* on Rhino went the bilingual route, *Rap en Español* is dominated by Spanish lyrics. Priority and Rhino didn't want to risk scaring away non-Spanish-speaking listeners, but this 1991 release came out on a Latin label (Globo) and was aimed at Latino audiences. *Rap en Español* spotlights five different Latino hip-hoppers: Vico C, Jelly D, Lisa (who shouldn't be confused with the early-'80s dance-pop singer who gave us "Sex Dance" and "Rocket to Your Heart"), Ruben D.J., and Pablo Diaz. Most of the material is commercial pop-rap, including Lisa's "Trampa" and Ruben D.J.'s "La Escuela." And Diaz's "Mi Ritmo House" is hip-house with Spanish lyrics. But things get more street on some of Vico's offerings, which include "La Recta Final" (a tune that was influenced by Ice-T's "Colors") and "Viernes 13, Part II." Viernes is the Spanish word for Friday, and the latter is based on the *Friday the 13th* series of horror flicks. Overall, this collection isn't fantastic. But it's generally decent, and it demonstrates that even though English is still hip-hop's primary language, it certainly isn't its only language. —*Alex Henderson*

Rap G Style / Jun. 1, 1995 / Priority ◆◆◆

Rap G Style contains a selection of hardcore hip-hop and Gangsta Rap, primarily from West Coast rappers like Ice Cube, Dr. Dre, Snoop Dogg, Spice 1, Eazy-E, Da Lench Mob, Paris, Ice-T, and Brotha Lynch Hung; there are also a few cuts from Southerners like Geto Boys and Scarface. The selection is a little uneven and the songs can sound a little samey, but *Rap G Style* remains a good budget-priced collection, thanks to cuts like "No Vaseline," "Nuthin' but a 'G' Thang," "Six Feet Dep," "Chocolate City," and "One Time fo Ya Mind." —*Stephen Thomas Erlewine*

Rap Mania: The Roots of Rap [DVD] / May 16, 2000 / Red Hill ◆◆◆

Rap Mania: The Roots of Rap begins with an interesting concept but never fully delivers on it. The album stems from a one-night concert celebrating the roots of the genre recorded at L.A.'s Palace and NYC's famous Apollo Theater. Recorded in 1990, *Rap Mania* was meant to be an East-meets-West, old school-meets-new school rap special event with a little "We Are the World" added to the mix. It was recorded before the gangsta craze and the true coastal rivalries began. Because it is pre-Snoop Dogg, Suge Knight, Notorious B.I.G., and Tupac, the two concerts have a decidedly dated feel. When Run-D.M.C. takes the Apollo stage, it is magical. Nothing in the DVD captures the electricity of seeing a dancing crowd enjoy a song by one of the most famous rap groups of all time. Unfortunately, many of the other acts get booed during their performances (the sound from the crowd is muted out of the DVD). Some of the performers like LL Cool J, Run-D.M.C., Grandmaster Flash, Slick Rick, and others have maintained their popularity or remained in high regard since this concert was filmed. But many more have faded to beyond the margins, like 3rd Bass. An early performance by Everlast before he joined up with House of Pain is included. (It's pretty weak.) The standout performance is Biz Markie's "Just a Friend." The flip side of the DVD contains "extras"—really only another 30 minutes of concert footage from the lesser-known acts on the bill, like Nefertiti, Whodini, and Prince Whipper Whip. The sound is poor and the performances worse on the flip side. There are some interview segments cut into the DVD version of what was a live satellite pay-per-view broadcast, and these are interesting conversations with Grandmaster Flash and others. The lack of other extras is a big loss. *Rap Mania: The Roots of Rap* is a fun DVD, but it is hardly the true retrospective the genre deserves. —*JT Griffith*

Rap's Greatest Disses / 1992 / Priority ◆◆◆

Contrary to what the title may lead you to believe, *Rap's Greatest Disses* does not consist of records that slam other rappers—it consists of records that slam either fictional characters or namells rappers. Once you get past that disappointment, the budget-priced collection is pretty entertaining, since these songs—including Ice Cube's "Jackin' for Beats," EPMD's "You're a Customer," MC Shan's "Bridge," LL Cool J's "To Da Break of Dawn," and the Beastie Boys' "She's Crafty"—contain some of the greatest lyrical trips of the '80s. The only problem is, like many Priority compilations, the disc is a little short, but it more than delivers considering its cheap price. —*Stephen Thomas Erlewine*

Rap's Greatest Hits, Vol. 1 / Jan. 23, 1997 / Priority ✦✦✦
Clocking in at only nine tracks, *Rap's Greatest Hits, Vol. 1* may be a little brief, but the collection isn't a bad sampler of old school cuts from the early '80s. There are a couple of weak cuts, but Kurtis Blow's "Basketball," D-Nice's "Call Me D-Nice," Rock Master Scott's "The Roof Is on Fire," Whodini's "Bigmouth," and U.T.F.O.'s "Roxanne, Roxanne" make the disc worth its budget price. —*Stephen Thomas Erlewine*

Rap's Greatest Hits, Vol. 2 / Jan. 23, 1997 / Priority ✦✦✦
Clocking in at only nine tracks, *Rap's Greatest Hits, Vol. 2* may be a little brief, but the collection isn't a bad sampler of crossover pop-rap hits from the late '80s. There are a couple of weak cuts, but Tone-Loc's "Wild Thing," Queen Latifah's "Dance for Me," Young MC's "Bust a Move," DJ Jazzy Jeff & the Fresh Prince's "Parents Just Don't Understand," Whodini's "Freaks Come out at Night," and Doug E. Fresh's "Lovin' Every Minute of It" make the disc worth its budget price. —*Stephen Thomas Erlewine*

Rap's Greatest Stories / 1992 / Priority ✦✦✦
Rap's Greatest Stories is a budget-priced compilation that contains nine narratives from '80s hip-hop artists. Some of these songs aren't really stories— why include the Beastie Boys' "Brass Monkey" and not "Paul Revere," which actually tells a story?—but it's a pretty enjoyable listen, thanks to such cuts as Ice Cube's "Gangsta's Fairytale," Slick Rick's "Children's Story," Biz Markie's "The Vapors," Kool Moe Dee's "Go See the Dotor," and DJ Jazzy Jeff's "Girls Ain't Nothing But Trouble." —*Stephen Thomas Erlewine*

Rapmasters, Vol. 1: Best of the Jam / Priority ✦✦✦✦
This is an ambitious and exhaustive historical survey of rap from the early days up to yesterday. The categorical divisions of each volume don't mean much, and each one contains at least four songs that are essential to any rap collection. Mix 'em, match 'em, or buy 'em all. —*John Floyd*

Rapmasters, Vol. 2: Best of the Rhyme / Priority ✦✦✦✦

Rapmasters, Vol. 3: Best of the Cut / Priority ✦✦✦✦

Rapmasters, Vol. 4: Best of Hip-Hop / Priority ✦✦✦✦

Rapmasters, Vol. 5: Best of the Word / Priority ✦✦✦✦

Rapmasters: From Tha Priority Vaults, Vol. 1 / Aug. 26, 1996 / Priority ✦✦✦
Rapmasters: From Tha Priority Vaults, Vol. 1 is an excellent budget-priced collection that spotlights hardcore hip-hop from Priority's rappers. The disc skillfully balances hits and strong album cuts, making it something more than the average budget-line rap collection—it's something that would interest aficionados as well as casual fans, simply because it reconfigures familiar cuts in an interesting way. Among the highlights are Ice Cube & K-Dee's "Make it Rff, Make it Smooth," Ice-T's "G Style," Paris' "Guerila Funk (Deep Fo' Real Mix)," Nice & Smooth's "Ooh Child," EPMD's "Let the Funk Flow," and N.W.A's "Express Yourself." —*Stephen Thomas Erlewine*

Rapmasters: From Tha Priority Vaults, Vol. 2 / Aug. 26, 1996 / Priority ✦✦✦

Rapmasters: From Tha Priority Vaults, Vol. 3 / Nov. 5, 1996 / Priority ✦✦✦

Rapmasters: From Tha Priority Vaults, Vol. 4 / Oct. 24, 1996 / Priority ✦✦✦

Rapper's Delight & Other Old School Favorites / Jan. 20, 1998 / Rhino Flashback ✦✦✦
Rapper's Delight & Other Old School Favorites presents ten classics from rap's golden age, including the title track by the Sugarhill Gang, Newcleus' "Jam on It," Sylvia's "It's Good to Be the Queen," and Trouble Funk's "Hey Fellas." Tracks from Grandmaster Melle Mel, the West Street Mob, Spoonie Gee, and Grandmaster Flash give the collection an undeniably solid track listing, but the short running time may make it more satisfying for casual hip-hop listeners than fans looking for an extensive collection of old school hits. —*Heather Phares*

Raza Unida: Hip Hop Decade / May 23, 2000 / Priority ✦✦✦
Since the Latin explosion in the late '90s, genre-specific musical molds have been able to successfully integrate into popular areas. In celebration of that comes the 15-track compilation *Raza Unida: Hip Hop Decade*. Featured artists include Big Punisher, Kid Capri, Junebug Slim, tha Mexakinz, Noreaga, and more. —*MacKenzie Wilson*

Return of the DJ, Vol. 1 / 1996 / Bomb Entertainment ✦✦✦✦✦
Although vocal rap has become all but synonymous with hip-hop, effectively displacing DJs as the prime movers in determining the music's distinctive aesthetic, a new generation of hip-hop DJs are going it alone, approaching

the turntable as a instrument in its own right. San Francisco promoter David Paul's brilliant *Return of the DJ* compilation charts this continuing evolution, with sturdy, mind-bogglingly complex turntable orchestration from such names as Q-Bert, Mixmaster Mike, DJ Disk, the Beat Junkies, New York's X-Men, Z-Trip, and DJ Ghetto, among others. Fluid beats, vast, layered instrumental passages, and tons of deft scratching loosely cement the notion of a restless, DJ-based hip-hop avant-garde craving only one thing: innovation. —*Sean Cooper*

Return of the DJ, Vol. 2 / 1997 / Bomb Hip Hop ✦✦✦✦
The Bomb's second guided tour through the bedrooms of hip-hop's new experimental underground draws this time from an international pool of beat junkies, with tracks checking in from London, New York, Finland, Montreal, Norway, Detroit, and Paris, among others, with names both familiar and unknown—Roc Raider, DJ EQ, Z-Trip, and Godfather, as well as Kid Koala, Tommy Tee, and Jimmie Jam. The follow-up to the Bomb's scorching debut double LP, *Return of the DJ, Vol. 2* features 16 tracks in all of consistently mind-blowing (if not quite as innovative) instrumental turntable experiments. —*Sean Cooper*

Return of the DJ, Vol. 3 / 1999 / Bomb Hip Hop ✦✦✦
Hear Faust and all of his Mephistophelean mixmasters on the sampler *Return of the DJ, Vol. 3*. Their samplers and turntables spill over with memorable snippets from speeches, video games, sports, and even the Egyptian Magician of Jerky Boys fame. This continuation of the series sees Z-Trip continue with funk drumming on "Rockstar II," but generally goes in the direction of samples over turntables. —*Tom Schulte*

Return of the DJ, Vol. 4 / Aug. 21, 2001 / Bomb Hip Hop ✦✦✦

Revenge of the B-Boy / Jul. 13, 1999 / Bomb Hip Hop ✦✦✦✦
Several years after Bomb Hip-Hop's *Return of the DJ* compilations did much to resurrect the lost art of turntablism, the label is back to attack with *Revenge of the B-Boy*, a collection of electro, old school, and breakbeat tracks designed expressly for body lockers and disco dancers. Including producers and DJs from all over the world (and many return appearances from the *Return of the DJ* discs), the album includes a standout track, "The All Out Kid" by DJs Faust and Shortee, plus tracks by Jeep Beat Collective, DJ Format, and relative newcomers like Hydroponic Sound System and Clockwork Voodoo Freaks. —*John Bush*

Ridin' Low: West Side Low Riders / Sep. 25, 2001 / Capitol ✦✦✦
Ridin' Low: West Side Low Riders features a number of West Coast gangsta rappers, with a particular emphasis on Latino rappers like Frost, Mellow Man Ace, and Latino Velvet. Other non-Latino rappers here notably include King T and Kurupt ("Outlaws") and E-40 ("Fo Sho"). Other performers include the G'Fellas, who contribute two songs to the collection. *West Side Low Riders* supplements other volumes in the *Ridin' Low* series, each with a different emphasis. —*Jason Birchmeier*

Roll Wit Tha Flava / Apr. 5, 1993 / Epic ✦✦✦
Roll Wit Tha Flava collects a diverse array of rap singles from Nikki D., Flavor Units MCs, Latee, and Cee/Leshaun. Queen Latifah's "L.A. Bring Tha Flava," Bigga Sistas' "Sounds of Fattness," Brooklyn Assault's "On the Bone Again," Naughty By Nature's "Bring It On," and Rottin Razkals' "Enough Is Enough" are among the highlights of the album, which also includes songs by Jhane, Apache, Groove Garden, and Freddie Foxxx. —*Heather Phares*

Roots of Rap, Vol. 1: 12 Inch Singles / 1984 / Celluloid ✦✦✦
This compilation was put together in 1984, when the art form was still young and still relied more on beatboxes than samplers, when vocoders were new and exotic, and the rhythms tended to be a bit more blocky and straightforward. The artists featured on this collection of 12" mixes are mostly names since consigned to the hip-hop history books—turntablist Grandmaster D.St is still active (now recording as D.X.T.), but Fab Five Freddy, Futura 2000, and Time Zone haven't been heard from in years. But while no one could call this music timeless—in light of later developments, much of it sounds fairly rudimentary and simplistic—it does have a certain enduring charm. The tag-team rapping on Grandmaster D.St's "Home of Hip Hop" celebrates the Bronx in charmingly chest-thumping style to the accompaniment of sparkling keyboards, minimalist machine beats, and shards of metal guitar. On "World Destruction," Time Zone is joined by John Lydon for a heartwarming dose of intercontinental musical insurrection, while the Clash

guests on Futura 2000's "Escapades of…." All of it will bring a smile to the face of anyone who was a teenager in the 1980s. *—Rick Anderson*

The Roots of Rap: Classic Recordings from the 1920's and 30's / 1996 / Yazoo ✦✦✦✦

This ambitious and thought-provoking project turns to early black-and-white, religious, and secular traditions for antecedents to modern rap styles. Drawing from the commercial recordings of the 1920s and '30s, *The Roots of Rap* provides a broad sampling of rural voices straddling the lines of speech and song against the rhythms of piano, banjo, and guitar. The roots of rap, this collection argues, existed in early black work songs and in the Southern pulpit; in the performances of singing street evangelists; and in black vocal traditions such as the "dozens." Early forms of rap emerged in the vaudeville routines of minstrel and medicine shows, arising also in the country humor and talking blues of many rural white performers. To illustrate its thesis, the album draws from some of the greatest performers of the period, including Blind Willie Johnson, Seven Foot Dilly, Butterbeans and Susie, and Memphis Minnie, whose extraordinarily funky "Frankie Jean" closes the set. Like the best of Yazoo's projects, this effort is carefully and intelligently constructed, as well as consistently entertaining. *—Burgin Mathews*

Ruffhouse Records Greatest Hits / May 4, 1999 / Ruffhouse/Columbia ✦✦✦✦

Although it never gained the notoriety of Def Jam, Death Row, or No Limit, Ruffhouse had its share of excellent artists during the '90s, most notably Cypress Hill, the Fugees, Lauryn Hill, Wyclef Jean, and Kris Kross. As a celebration of nearly ten years in the business—or at least as a way of celebrating the massive success of Hill's debut solo album—the label released *Ruffhouse Records Greatest Hits*, a generous compilation that contains 14 of their biggest hits, along with an interesting but superfluous Jason Nevins remix of "Insane in the Brain." Perhaps that mix was added as incentive to collectors, but the reason to pick up the compilation are the hits themselves; the best of these—"How I Could Just Kill a Man," "Fu-Gee-La," "Killing Me Softly With His Song," "Insane in the Brain," "Doo Wop (That Thing)," "Gone Till November," and "Jump"—sound like contemporary classics, while such lesser numbers as Tim Dog's silly, silly "Fuck Compton" are great nostalgia trips. It's not perfect, of course—although the Fugees and their side projects are rightly emphasized, it's at the expense of some good music by other artists—but it still is a first-class portrait of the label. *—Stephen Thomas Erlewine*

Rules of the Game / May 26, 1998 / Tripek ✦✦✦

Bay Area hip-hop, historically defined by artists such as Too Short, Digital Underground, Paris, Spice 1, Tupac, E-40, Mac Mall, and RBL Posse has long been known for its distinctive street sound. As the mid-'90s gave way to gangsta rap cliché, a new generation of Northern Californian MC emerged to help usher in a new millenium. *Rules of the Game* is a compilation album that represents a trend toward consciousness in Bay Area rap. Oakland residents Mystik Journeymen and Mystic, with So Musch Soul and OK…Alright each offer uplifting meditations on the value of educated youth. Meanwhile, Fillmore dwellers Bored Stiff, Equipto, and Andre Nickatina vigorously elaborate on "Conspiracy Theory" and "Blueprints of War." Planet Asia proves why he's become known as one of the most lethal MCs on the underground circuit with a series of blazing verses on "Basic Training." San Quinn and D-Moe team up to accurately "Strike First" at the establishment, and the Coup dutifully joins the fray like armed Panthers with a political fixation. Uniting lyrical soldiers under a common flag, *Rules of the Game* signifies the hip-hop revolution as well as any album out there. *—Robert Gabriel*

Rush Hour 2 / Jul. 31, 2001 / Def Jam ✦✦✦

Many things can be said about Def Jam's *Rush Hour 2* soundtrack, an album that is both impressive yet at the same time disappointing. The 17 songs here essentially function as a sampler, giving nearly every artist from Def Jam and Def Soul a moment in the spotlight. And given this approach, you can't help but be impressed by Def Jam's deep pool of talent: Ludacris, Method Man, Redman, Montell Jordan, Keith Murray, LL Cool J, Musiq, and just as many up-and-coming artists such as teen pop singer Christina Milian. Furthermore, Def Jam hires some of the industry's top producers—Swizz Beatz, Jazzy Pha, Teddy Riley, the Neptunes, Rodney Jerkins—and some other big-money artists such as Snoop Dogg, Scarface, Nate Dogg, and Macy Gray. Unfortunately, despite all the talent, there aren't many standout moments. Teddy Riley's two songs—"Party and Bullshit" and "Figadoh"—are probably the

biggest disappointments. The legendary producer tries to lay down some Neptunes-meet-Timbaland-crossed-with-Swizz-style beats, but you can't help feeling that he's desperately struggling to remain relevant. Similarly, LL Cool J sounds incredibly outdated rapping over a club-ready Swizz beat on "Crazy Girl." Still, there are two absolutely stunning moments here that arguably compensate: Ludacris and Nate Dogg's "Area Codes" and Hikaru Utada and Foxy Brown's "Blow My Whistle." The former seems almost effortless but is incredibly catchy—partly because of its simplicity, partly because of Nate Dogg, but mostly because of Jazzy Pha's inventive sampling of "Do It (Til You're Satisfied)." The latter is yet another can't-miss production by the Neptunes, featuring scorching rhymes by Brown and some wonderfully sung hooks courtesy of Utada. So even if most of this soundtrack ultimately results in disappointment, these two golden moments may be reason enough for many to seek this out. *—Jason Birchmeier*

The Killer Album / 1990 / EMI America ✦✦✦✦

U.K. hip-hop groups with the temerity to adopt a hardcore stance à la the U.S. gangsta crews were ridiculed, with good reason, for their mannered street-toughisms in the late '80s and early '90s. Of all those who tried to convey the black urban British experience, the only crew to get close were Manchester's Ruthless Rap Assassins, who achieved some notoriety when MC Kermit subsequently joined Shaun Ryder in Black Grape. *The Killer Album* stands out as a real watershed in U.K. rap development by dint of its one outstanding track, "Justice (Just Us)." Only one other composition comes close to matching its impact—the contrasting "Just Mellow," which advocated a return to old school hip-hop values long before this plea had become common currency. "Justice (Just Us)" conversely kicks off with a Bomb Squad-style martial beat and bleak scratch-DJing. Its carefully structured narrative works because it doesn't try to impersonate American vocabulary or diction. Instead, it challenges the listener with its insistent hookline: "There ain't no justice, just us." For a fleeting moment we had a British group worthy of citing Public Enemy's influence. *—Alex Ogg*

Ruthless Tenth Anniversary: Decade of Game / Mar. 24, 1998 / Ruthless ✦✦✦

Ruthless Tenth Anniversary: Decade of Game is a double-disc set celebrating a decade of gangsta rap from Ruthless. The compilation could have been a definitive look at the early days of gangsta rap, but the disc suffers from relying on too many obscurities and album tracks at the expense of hits. That's not a fatal flaw, but it makes the record less attractive to casual listeners who simply want a summary of Ruthless' highlights. What you get instead is a summary of Ruthless' sound. Over the course of two discs, most of the group's heavy hitters—N.W.A, the D.O.C., Eazy-E, Above the Law, Michel'le, MC Ren, JJ Fad, HWA—are heard (only Bone Thugs-N-Harmony is missing). Occasionally they're represented by their best songs, occasionally not, but they all have representative tracks, and that alone makes it interesting, if not entirely successful. Collectors should note that the disc contains two previously unreleased Eazy-E tracks, "24 Hours to Live" and "Black Nigga Killa," neither of which are particularly noteworthy. *—Stephen Thomas Erlewine*

S2PID LUV / 2002 / Viva ✦✦✦

The biggest radio hit in late 2001 to mid-2002 in the Philippines was "Stupid Love," by rap group Salbakuta, which uses for its foundation Barbra Streisand's "Evergreen." The rap tells of a guy's undying—but stupid—love for a woman who treats him like dirt, leading to the group singing the chorus from "Evergreen," over which at strategic pauses the rappers shout "Stupid!" It seems like everyone knew this song, from four-year-olds to grown-ups. So it's no surprise that a movie was made using the same title, although the spelling was changed somewhat to *S2PID LUV*. Keep in mind that Viva Films, which released the film, is a sister company of Viva Records, which released Salbakuta's album, as well as this soundtrack. *S2PID LUV* contains the original hit song by Salbakuta, as well as a new "all-star" version featuring esteemed male rappers Andrew E. and Blakdyak. While the premise for "Stupid Love" sounds ridiculous, after awhile the song grows on a listener. The rest of the soundtrack offers more than just filler material, much more in fact. "Body Language" starts on a metal-like chord progression, leading to an entertaining rap by Andrew E., now signed to Viva Records after a stint at Sony Music Philippines, who tells here of meeting a girl on a lucky night. Another good rap outing is "Hayzkool Life" (slang for High School Life), performed by rap group Cruzzada, which uses the tender and penetrating "High School Life," first sung by Sharon Cuneta, as the basis for a reflection on (good) days gone by in high school. This is a worthwhile, enjoyable album. —*David Gonzales*

Scratch / Feb. 12, 2002 / Transparent ✦✦✦✦
Scratch, the soundtrack to a turntablism documentary by Doug Pray, presents performances from some of the best DJs in history, all the way from Grand Wizard Theodore ("inventor" of the tweak scratch, who's heard explaining its origins during the intro) through to Young Turks like DJ Faust and DJ Disk. In between lie over 20 years of scientific madness, much of it (overly) informed by the soundtrack's compiler/constructor/producer, Bill Laswell, who's acted as turntablism's most important (or most connected) flag waver ever since his 1996 *Altered Beats* compilation brought together far-flung mixers from New York's Prince Paul to San Francisco's DJ Q-Bert to Japan's DJ Krush. Except for a few interview snippets throughout, *Scratch* focuses mostly on tracks from the very best in the business: MixMaster Mike, Q-Bert, DJ Disk, Rob Swift, and even the often overlooked Grandmixer DXT. Highlights include "Skin Cracked Canals," a duet freakout featuring DJ Disk with guitar menace Buckethead, and "Rockit 2.002," an all-star jam on the 1982 Herbie Hancock classic—and commercial genesis of scratching—featuring half a dozen current DJs (MixMaster Mike, Rob Swift, Q-Bert, Faust, Babu, Shortee) cutting up over the original. True to form, several tracks from Laswell-related projects are recycled here. Still, give Laswell credit for a tight, entertaining compilation: there's no dead air here and, as difficult as it is to sustain energy for a project like this over the course of 45 minutes, he accomplishes the mission. —*John Bush*

Seattle . . . The Dark Side / 1993 / American Rec/Rhyme Cartel ✦✦✦
When a music lover thinks of Seattle in the early 1990s, the word that immediately comes to mind is "grunge." It was Seattle, after all, that gave us Nirvana and Pearl Jam, the bands that did the most to make major labels realize that alternative rock could be commercially viable. But as important as grunge was, it was hardly the only worthwhile music coming out of Seattle at the time. The city also had a noteworthy rap scene; although it might not have been considered a major-league player in hip-hop á la New York, L.A., Oakland, or Philadelphia, it was noteworthy just the same. With Sir Mix-A-Lot (Seattle's most famous rapper), Rick Rubin, and Ricardo Frazer serving as executive producers, *Seattle…The Dark Side* takes an enjoyable look at some of the Seattle hip-hoppers and detours into urban contemporary and spoken word. The album's highlights range from Mix's infectious "Just Da Pimpin' in Me" and E-Dawg's groovin' "Drop Top" (which samples the Gap Band's "Outstanding") to Jay-Skee's gritty "12 Gauge" and Kid Sensation's catchy "Flava You Can Taste." R&B group 3rd Level has a likable slow jam in "Show You," but the album's strongest track is Jazz Lee Alston's "Love… Never That," a disturbing spoken-word account of a woman's relationship with a man who abuses her physically and emotionally. Generally decent and occasionally excellent, *Seattle…The Dark Side* is worth picking up if you come across a copy. —*Alex Henderson*

Seditious Jewels / Feb. 25, 2003 / Sub Verse ✦✦✦✦
Underground rap label Sub Verse Music's compilation of remixes and rarities *Seditious Jewels* lives up to both parts of its name. Sub Verse artists tend to prefer the political to the party-hard, and tracks like the Hemisphere's "Run Aways 2," a first-person narrative of a runaway slave's trek, are as sharp and pointed as any political rap of the era. (They're not without a sense of humor, though, as illuminated by the sly wit of "Yikes!!!" by Scienz of Life, who recall the silly/serious vibe of the Native Tongues movement.) However, unlike some political rappers, who either go for the Public Enemy style of sonic overload or else keep their beats so skeletal they're practically nonexistent, these 14 tracks use varied and interesting musical beds, from acid jazz piano riffs to MF Grimm's "I Hear Voices 2," which is built on what sounds like the sort of cheesy ARP synth riffs that were played over the introduction and end credits of '70s-vintage industrial safety films. Clever, committed, and musically rich, *Seditious Jewels* is the perfect antidote to bling-bling overload. —*Stewart Mason*

Set It Off / Sep. 24, 1996 / Elektra/Asylum ✦✦✦✦
The soundtrack to the black female gangsta movie *Set It Off* is surprisingly short on high-quality hardcore rap. Apart from a couple excellent tracks from the likes of Busta Rhymes, Goodie Mob, and Queen Latifah (who also stars in the film), the majority of the album consists of urban R&B and swingbeat balladry, often in degrees of varying quality. En Vogue's reunion's track "(Don't Let Go) Love" is a stellar contribution, proving that they haven't lost

any power, while the Chaka Kahn/Brandy/Tamia cut "Missing You" is surprisingly not disappointing. What is disappointing is the preponderance of cut-rate tracks from the likes of Seal, Bone Thugs-N-Harmony, and Simply Red, whose inclusion is simply baffling. In short, it's an average soundtrack, with enough good tracks to make it worth acquiring and enough mediocre material to make it frustrating. —*Leo Stanley*

Sex, Alcohol and Pistol Grips / Sep. 26, 2000 / Brown Man ✦✦✦
This collection of druggy, misogynist gangsta rap represents the West Coast Bay Area's underground scene. With its large roster of guest rappers and revolving cast of producers, there isn't much consistency here besides in terms of themes. Overall, though, this collection functions well as a compilation, supplying plenty of variety and a number of fairly impressive tracks relative to most West Coast gangsta rap collections. And if anything, *Sex, Alcohol and Pistol Grips* showcases just how burgeoning the Bay Area's underground gangsta scene had grown to a decade after N.W.A. —*Jason Birchmeier*

Sexy: Rap / Feb. 13, 2001 / Import ✦✦✦
Part of the Party Animal label's *Sexy* series of compilations, *Sexy: Rap* collects a dozen old school rap songs, including a couple classics. Contrary to what the album's title may lead you to presume, these songs aren't actually "sexy"—as difficult as that may be for contemporary rap listeners to imagine given the style's predominant emphasis on sex. There are a few bona fide classics here, most notably the Sugarhill Gang's "Rappers Delight" (widely considered the first rap song) and Grandmaster Flash's "The Message" (the first rap song to be taken seriously by critics because of its socially conscious lyrics). The other ten songs—by Grand Wizard Theodore, Whistle, the Real Roxanne, Chubb Rock, Heavy Load, Brick, Spoonie Gee, and the 45 King—aren't nearly as significant yet are still substantial entries in the old school rap canon. Though *Sexy: Rap*—much like the other *Sexy* compilations—isn't a definitive collection by any means, it showcases plenty of excellent old school rap, certainly enough to give you an accurate sample of the style. Most importantly, however, it features "Rappers Delight" and "The Message," two of the most important songs in the development of rap music. —*Jason Birchmeier*

Show Me the Money: Hip Hop Pays / May 29, 1997 / Priority ✦✦✦
Show Me the Money: Hip Hop Pays contains a selection of 12 hardcore hip-hop songs about, well, cash money. It's a cute concept, but it works, since the songs are, by and large, pretty entertaining. A few cuts fall flat, but songs like Jay-Z's "Dead Presidents," N.W.A's "Alwayz Into Somethin'," Kane & Abels' "Git'n Paid," Ice Cube's "What Can I Do?," Tru's "Another Day, Another Dollar," and Eazy-E's "Nobody Move" make it worthwhile. —*Stephen Thomas Erlewine*

Shreveport Wants In / Aug. 7, 2001 / Boot Style ✦✦✦
Since the mid-'80s, rap compilations featuring multiple artists from the same area have introduced some of the hotbeds of hip-hop to America. *Shreveport Wants In* introduces rappers from Louisiana trying to make their mark in the rap world. Producer Mojo Nicosia presents many young talents from the area, including Yeast, Lil' Lee, Lil' Dill, and Poppa. Most of these artists cultivate a similar sound, mixing the Southern drawl of Outkast with deep, G-funk beats. But it is actually Mojo himself who has the most original, memorable, clear-cut sound of the bunch. "It's So Hard" and "Do Your Thang (Slow Mix)" use sparse beats combined with haunting keyboards and deep bass to come up with a very distinct hip-hop voice. Nothing on the album is sonically challenging (something that hurts most independent rap collections), but perhaps most importantly, it presents a scene that has come into its own. —*Bradley Torreano*

Sick Wid It's Greatest Hits / Nov. 9, 1999 / Jive ✦✦✦✦
Sick Wid It never had any crossover hits, but their albums sold steadily throughout the gangsta-saturated '90s, mainly because the label offered straight-up West Coast gangsta with no muss, fuss, or apologies. Released in the waning months of the decade, *Sick Wid It's Greatest Hits* compiles the label's best-known singles and R&B/rap chart hits, which mainly breaks down to three songs from E-40, three songs from Click, three songs from B-Legit, two from D-Shot, two from Celly Cel, and one from Suga T. This is all pretty generic stuff, but it's not bad and certainly the cream of the Sick Wid It crop, which makes it a good choice for aficionados of the style or to anyone looking to dig a little deeper than Death Row and No Limit. —*Stephen Thomas Erlewine*

Slammin Ol Skool Trax / Jun. 25, 1996 / Scotti Bros. ✦✦✦

Slammin' Ol Skool Trax has a good cross-section of early '80s funk and mid-'80s hip-hop, featuring everyone from Parliament and Brick to Run-D.M.C. and Whodini. The selection is scattershot and the concept is underdeveloped, but it's a fun listen and it does contain some genuine classics, namely, Parliament's "Flashlight" and Run-D.M.C.'s "You Be Illin." —*Stephen Thomas Erlewine*

Sleeping Bag Records Greatest Rap Hits / May 22, 2001 / Warlock ✦✦✦✦✦

It may have taken a frustrating amount of time for this collection to appear, but it's been worth the wait. Nearly two decades after the original release of these songs, the defunct Sleeping Bag label's gold mine of old school rap classics finally sees a CD release. Featuring 15 classics by pioneers such as Mantronix, Just-Ice, Nice & Smooth, EPMD, and T La Rock, *Sleeping Bag Records Greatest Rap Hits* showcases the storied New York label's formative sound, a sound which shaped countless late-'80s and early-'90s East Coast MCs and producers. Granted, these songs no doubt sound dated and are a little stiff to contemporary ears, but their historical importance is undeniable. —*Jason Birchmeier*

Snoop Dogg Presents Doggy Style Allstars: Welcome to tha House, Vol. 1 / Aug. 13, 2002 / MCA ✦✦✦

Technically, *Welcome to tha House, Vol. 1* is a compilation. Different rappers—most of them from the West Coast—are heard on different tracks, and Snoop Dogg is only one of the many MCs who are featured. But for all intents and purposes, *Welcome to tha House, Vol. 1* is a Snoop album. Snoop's stamp is all over this 2002 release, which spotlights several rappers who signed with his Los Angeles-based Doggy Style Records (including Mr. Kane, E-White, and Soopafly) but also features various guests who weren't part of the Doggy Style roster—and those guests range from RBX to Lady of Rage to Special Ed. Although Snoop is featured on many of the tunes, he isn't featured on all of them. But whatever rapper gets on the mike, Snoop's influence usually comes through in a major way. This is true whether the distinctive gangsta rapper is teaming up with RBX and Mr. Kane on "The Strong Will Eat the Weak" or Soopafly and E-White on "Hey You." However, there are a few times when *Welcome to tha House, Vol. 1* gets away from its West Coast gangsta rap/G-funk orientation. Urban contemporary singer Latoiya Williams, a Doggy Style signing, is featured on "Fallen Star" and "It Feelz Good"—both of which have a neo-soul outlook and a strong Aretha Franklin influence. Although about 85 percent of this CD is West Coast gangsta rap, the other 15 percent is straight-up R&B—and that's where Williams and singer Vinnie Bernard (who is heard on the haunting "Trouble") come in. *Welcome to tha House, Vol. 1* is slightly uneven; some of the tunes are more memorable than others. But there are more ups than downs, and even though this 78-minute CD isn't essential, Snoop's hardcore fans will probably want a copy anyway. —*Alex Henderson*

So So Def: Definition of a Remix / Jul. 2, 2002 / Sony ✦✦✦

Jermaine Dupri's version of a remix album, *Definition of a Remix*, opens with a proper coast-to-coast redo of the So So Def anthem "Welcome to Atlanta" that moves from New York (P. Diddy) to St. Louis (Murphy Lee) to Los Angeles (Snoop Dogg). Of the seven tracks, three are of the R&B quartet Jagged Edge, including a remix of "Let's Get Married" that features Joseph "Run" Simmons freestyling over a sample of his own "It's Like That." Actually, the best track here isn't really a remix at all; the Neptunes production of Jermaine Dupri's "Let's Talk About It 2" is just the radio edit, but no less good for it. —*John Bush*

Soldiers United for Cash: The Soundtrack / May 15, 2001 / ✦✦✦✦

Soldiers United for Cash: The Soundtrack features members of the loosely knit Screwed Up Click, a Houston, Texas, underground rap collective led by DJ Screw. Of course, when Screw met an untimely death in 2001, the Click lost its leader, the man responsible for many of these rappers' careers. That's why many of the songs on this soundtrack are a bit solemn and mournful—they're odes to the infamous DJ who pioneered the practice of "chopping" and "screwing" rap tracks. The roster of performers on this collection is a who's who of the Houston scene: Lil' Flip, Lil' Keke, H.A.W.K., Big Pokey, Botany Boyz, Southside Playaz, Fat Pat, and many more. Moreover, most of the songs are produced by either T.J. Music or Slugger, two of the Houston scene's most prolific producers. Though most of the songs on *Soldiers United for Cash* are exclusive to this soundtrack, it's important to note that a few are licensed and therefore available elsewhere. Even so, this is an excellent sampler for anyone curious about the Houston Screwed Up Click; all the major artists are here in fine form. —*Jason Birchmeier*

Sole Beats One / 2002 / Sole ✦✦✦✦

Based in Glasgow, Sole Music refuses to place stylistic, geographical or ethnic limitations on it sources of funk, as is proven by the diversity of this compilation. And this is not your typical back catalog collection either. The proprietors of Sole Music went through the effort to license several tracks from a variety of labels including the trip-hop loops of Benny Blanko's "Listen" and Pablo's funky drummer disco on "Supersweet," just because they sat nicely next to their own releases, including Tony Free's "Do It Anyways" and the latin beat experimentation by the traditionally hip-hop producer DJ Spinna. Then you add in the Nu-Soul female rap of Silent Poets's "Someday," the space-age analog bass slap of Porn Theater Usher's "Me & Him," and the gospel-inspired interlude of "Emancipation" by UK black music scholars Black Science Orchestra, and you discover that this relatively brief, ten-song compilation has checked off an astounding spectrum of modern and classic soul nuances. So while *Sole Beats One* is competing with an overabundant market of down-tempo compilations, many from more well-known urban sources, it might have taken a couple of blokes from Scotland and their distant perspective to really gather an open-ended collection of what we call modern soul music. —*Joshua Glazer*

SoleSides Greatest Bumps / Oct. 31, 2000 / Quannum ✦✦✦✦✦

If you're down with progressive hip-hop and aren't hip to the sounds of the collective formerly known as SoleSides, you need to check out this two-CD retrospective. DJ Shadow, Chief Xcel, the Gift of Gab (aka Blackalicious), Mack B. Dog, Lateef, and Lyrics Born (aka Latyrx) are among the finest artists in Bay Area hip-hop, laying the groundwork that forms the foundation of the West Coast alternative rap scene. With a crate digger's attention to detail, you can hear Shadow's skills all the way back on 1993's "Entropy," while Blackalicious' dextrous lyrics on 1994's "Lyric Fathom" are evidence of the clique's trademark abstract expressionist rhyme style. For those who have followed the SoleSides crew's careers, there are plenty of unreleased cuts, rare B sides, and remixes here to make this a worthwhile investment. For those who haven't, freestyle throwdowns like "Lateef's Freestyle" and posse cuts like "Blue Flames" are ample evidence that this is one of the most potent crews in hip-hop. —*Bret Love*

SoleSides Greatest Bumps, Vol. 2 / 2000 / Quannum ✦✦✦✦✦

In 1992, the unlikely locale of Davis, CA, gave rise to SoleSides, a record label and musical collective that brought together a group of likeminded hip-hop fanatics. During their first six years together, members DJ Shadow, Gift of Gab, Chief Xcel, Lateef, and Lyrics Born released a series of singles and EPs that promised a virtual reinvention of rap music. By 1998, on the brink of new projects and wider recognition, the group adopted the Quannum banner. *SoleSides Greatest Bumps* is a fond look back at their formative years, gathering all of the groups finest moments. It begins where SoleSides began, with their first sessions at Dan the Automator's Glue Factory. Already, their unique fire is present in the eyes of Lyrics Born on "Asia's Verse," a performance oozing with cool confidence. In a genre built on self-aggrandizement, the SoleSides MCs managed to come up with ever more inventive ways to declare superiority on the mike. This reached its apex on "The Wreckoning." Over a haunting DJ Shadow backing, Lateef mercilessly destroys his opponent with his "lesson of perfection." He then proceeds to take the tale beyond your wildest imagination, detailing the death and decomposition of his challenger with true crime realism. As half of Latyrx, Lateef would play the hyper-intelligent older sibling to Lyrics Born's sly, more unruly misfit. The concept of "Latyrx" (the song from which the duo took their name) is baffling. On this a cappella excerpt, the two MCs rap like they inhabit separate, yet parallel, realities. Though cut from a more conventional hip-hop cloth, Gab and Xcel (Blackalicious) were a sure-fire rhyme-and-beat team that contributed SoleSides' minor hit "Swan Lake" from their stellar *Melodica* EP. Almost everything on *SoleSides Greatest Bumps* is now out of print and highly collectable. As Quannum, the collective have taken a subtle shift away from the more organic beats and jazz samples of SoleSides toward a sort of electro-soul sound. On later recordings like "Lady Don't Tek No" and "Blue Flames," the rapping was becoming similarly diluted. Consequently, listeners never hear the likes of SoleSides again. —*Nathan Bush*

Soul in the Hole / Jul. 29, 1997 / RCA ✦✦✦✦

The soundtrack album to a basketball documentary of the same name, this record serves as an ideal sampling of late-1990s hip-hop. The roster of primarily New York artists resemble a hoops all-star team with stellar contributions from artists like the Wu-Tang Clan, Big Punisher, Mobb Deep, Xzibit, and Common. It heartily satisfies with thick and funky tracks throughout, and when the Cocoa Brovas (formerly known as Smif-n-Wessun) deliver braggadocio-filled raps over a hypnotic, stabbing beat, you want to jump out on the court and join them. —*Craig Robert Smith*

Sound Ink: Colapsus / 2002 / Sound-Ink ✦✦✦✦✦
A refreshing compilation from a new label hoping to kick-start a new style, the astonishing *Sound Ink: Colapsus* definitely succeeds on all counts. Comprising a few familiar names (and many more obscure ones) in the growing fusion of junkyard hip-hop and heavily processed electronica, the compilation has the same sense of flow that made 1999's *Quannum Spectrum* sound more like a single-artist album. There's a devastatingly dark atmosphere to the proceedings and a take-no-prisoners air to the productions—cribbing from Indian music, '80s pop, post-punk, even IDM. Producer King Honey is responsible for two of the highlights: the opener "Motions" (with Mental) and "Monday Night at Fluid" (with MF Doom, Kurious, and King Ghidra). Another great track comes at the end, with a collaboration between techno producer John Tejada and rapper Divine Styler. All in all, it's one of the most important records for underground hip-hop since *Quannum Spectrum* or *The Cold Vein*. —*John Bush*

Soundbombing / Oct. 14, 1997 / Rawkus ✦✦✦✦
Hitting stores in 1997, *Soundbombing* arrived at a crucial juncture for rap music, just as the deaths of Tupac and Notorious B.I.G. forced hip-hop to reexamine its priorities, and the commercial dominance of Bad Boy necessitated a smart, socially conscious alternative to P. Diddy's blatantly commercial brand of karaoke hip-pop. A DJ Evil Dee-mixed collection of early Rawkus singles, many of them originally available only on vinyl (in keeping with the company's hip-hop purism), *Soundbombing* announces Rawkus as the anti-Bad Boy, taking its cues from hip-hop iconoclasts like Ultramagnetic MC's and Brand Nubian rather than the commercial kings of the day. The influence of Kool Keith is felt most heavily early on, with artists like Company Flow and the Indelible MCs paying tribute to Keith's unique brand of bizarre, stream-of-consciousness hip-hop before Keith himself pops up on "So Intelligent" alongside kindred spirit Sir Menelik. The second half of the disc is dominated by the soon-to-be-famous trio of Reflection Eternal (Talib Kweli and DJ Hi-Tek) and Mos Def, who would soon team up with Kweli to form Black Star. Early Def solo tracks like "If You Can Huhh" and "Universal Magnetic" find the future superstar rocking over uncharacteristically spare, Jay Dee-inspired grooves, while "Fortified Live" and "Freestyle" show off Def and Kweli's burgeoning chemistry. But *Soundbombing* doesn't really hit its peak until its final track, "2000 Seasons," a somber, melancholy, and unforgettable Reflection Eternal song that offers an early glimpse of the quiet, politically minded b-boy revolution Black Star, Reflection Eternal, Mos Def, and Rawkus would go on to lead over the course of the next few years. —*Nathan Rabin*

Soundbombing, Vol. 2 / Apr. 27, 1999 / Rawkus ✦✦✦✦
With their first *Soundbombing* collection, Rawkus introduced a ravenous stable of hungry underground MCs, but more importantly it also laid the preliminary groundwork for Mos Def and Talib Kweli's Black Star movement. Both play a large role in the development of *Soundbombing, Vol. 2* as well. Mos screens a preview from his impending solo LP, the high-tech "Next Universe," and divulges "Crosstown Beef" with his Medina Green outfit. Talib and Hi-Tek's manifestation as Reflection Eternal contributes two highly illuminant tracks: "On Mission" and the cultivated "Chaos" (featuring Bahamadia). Rawkus' latest coup, Pharoahe Monch, gets militaristic with Shabaam Shadeeq on "WW III" and the virulent "Mayor." Eminem works his magic over a cartoon-like Beatminerz track on the neurotic "Any Man." *Soundbombing, Vol. 2* contains an abundance of prolific collaborations, exemplified by Common and Sadat X's elegant "1999," Dilated Peoples and Tash's regal "Soundbombing," and Sir Menelik's "7XL" (featuring Sadat X and Grand Puba). One relatively minor blemish arises in the Beat Junkies' control of the LP's continuity—their cutting and blending methods are peculiarly ineffective, and oftentimes lack direction. User friendly for underground or mainstream fanatics, *SB 2* is the quintessential Rawkus project, and the label's finest moment to date. —*Matt Conaway*

Soundbombing, Vol. 3 / Jun. 4, 2002 / Rawkus ✦✦✦
Like soul music in the '60s and '70s, rap is full of regional styles. In classic soul, it is easy to tell a Memphis sound from a Philly or Detroit sound—similarly, rappers from the West Coast, the Northeast, and the South tend to

have different ways of flowing. Released in 2002, *Vol. 3* of Rawkus' rap-oriented *Soundbombing* series is heavily Northeastern—and yet, the compilation does acknowledge hip-hop styles from other parts of the United States. RA the Rugged Man's nostalgic "On the Block (Golden Era)" salutes New York rappers of the '80s and mentions many of that era's top MCs, although RA's rhyming style is quite contemporary (by early-2000s standards). And *Vol. 3* is equally Northeastern sounding on tracks by the Roots ("Rhymes and Ammo"), Q-Tip ("What Lies Beneath"), and Kool G Rap ("My Life"). The East Coast school of thinking-man's rap receives a fair amount of attention on this release, thanks to material by the Roots, Q-Tip, Mos Def, and Talib Kweli, who the Roots feature on "Rhymes and Ammo." And Chicago native Common, who Zap Mama employs on "Yelling Away," is to the Midwest what Q-Tip is to New York. Here's where things get especially interesting: on "Put It in the Air," Kweli performs a duet with DJ Quik. Hip-hoppers couldn't have asked for a more unlikely combination—while Kweli is often hailed as a thinking man's rapper, Compton, CA's DJ Quik is the essence of West Coast gangsta rap. But Kweli and Quik manage to find some common ground, and "Put It in the Air" turns out to be one of the album's best tracks. Usually decent and occasionally excellent, *Soundbombing, Vol. 3* is among 2002's more noteworthy rap compilations. —*Alex Henderson*

The Source Hip-Hop Music Awards 1999 / Aug. 17, 1999 / Def Jam ✦✦✦✦
For the few persons out there still unaware that rap music is an overground force and steadily growing faster than the rock industry, the album version of the television extravaganza known as *The Source Hip-Hop Music Awards* should dispel any ignorance. And given the wide sway of the mega-major-label group PolyGram/Universal—including under its corporate umbrella No Limit, Priority, Def Jam, Interscope, Roc-A-Fella, Payday, Cash Money, and MCA—it's a lock that this one should include some of the biggest hits of the year. From Jay-Z's "Can I Get A…," Eminem's "My Name Is," Silkk the Shocker's "It Ain't My Fault," and Juvenile's "Ha" to the Roots' "You Got Me," Busta Rhymes' "Party Is Goin' on Over Here," and Method Man's "Break Ups 2 Make Ups," *The Source Hip-Hop Music Awards* indeed features many of the most popular hip-hop acts of the year. It's definitely one of the best summations of hip-hop in 1999 brought out yet, though the big artists not included (DMX, Lauryn Hill, Missy Elliott) are missed in a big way. —*Keith Farley*

The Source Hip-Hop Music Awards 2000 / Aug. 15, 2000 / Def Jam ✦✦✦✦
As the title suggests, *The Source Hip-Hop Music Awards 2000* presents 16 of the year's best hip-hop singles, as chosen by *The Source* magazine. DMX's "What's My Name," Mos Def's "Ms. Fat Booty," Jay-Z's "Jigga My Nigga," Beanie Sigel's "The Truth," and Redman & Method Man's "Da Rockwilder" are some of the standout tracks from the album. The official soundtrack of *The Source's* annual Hip-Hop Awards show, it's also a good overview of contemporary hip-hop trends. —*Heather Phares*

The Source Hip-Hop Music Awards 2001 / Aug. 14, 2001 / Uptown/ Universal ✦✦✦✦✦
Like past volumes in the series, *The Source Hip-Hop Music Awards 2001* features many of the year's biggest rap hits, emphasizing quality as well as popularity. While the majority of these songs are from the East Coast, there are a few West Coast songs—Snoop Dogg's "Lay Low" and Xzibit's "X," both Dr. Dre productions—and quite a few dirty South songs: Ludacris' "Southern Hospitality," Trina's "Pull Over," Scarface's "Look Me in My Eyes," Nelly's "E.I.," and Mystikal's "Shake Ya Ass." There are a few songs here that weren't big chart toppers—Talib Kweli's "Blast," MOP's "Ante Up (Robbing-Hoodz Theory)," Poe Boy Family's "Making It," and the Mos Def, Pharoahe Monch, Nate Dogg collaboration, "Oh No"—yet thankfully made the album due to their quality. It's this offering of different styles and mix of chart toppers and critical favorites that make this *Source Hip-Hop Music Awards* a representative sample of rap in the year 2000, with a slight bias toward the East Coast. —*Jason Birchmeier*

The Source Presents: Hip Hop Hits / Dec. 16, 1997 / Polygram ✦✦✦✦

The Source Presents: Hip Hop Hits, Vol. 2 / Nov. 3, 1998 / Polygram ✦✦✦✦

The Source Presents: Hip Hop Hits, Vol. 3 / Nov. 30, 1999 / Def Jam ✦✦✦
The Source Presents Hip Hop Hits, Vol. 3 gathers tracks from some of the most popular hip-hop acts of 1998-1999, which means that it has pronounced leanings toward gangsta and hardcore rap, and not the underground's increasing emphasis on positive themes and more complex wordplay and

lyrical rhythms. But for those who want the most popular artists all in one place, this will be highly satisfying. Material is included from Snoop Dogg, Nas, DMX, Foxy Brown, Mobb Deep, Juvenile, Jay-Z, Lil' Troy, Tru, Ja Rule, Trick Daddy, JT Money, Redman with Busta Rhymes, and Q-Tip, among others. —*Steve Huey*

The Source Presents: Hip Hop Hits, Vol. 4 / Dec. 12, 2000 / Def Jam ✦✦✦

The Source Presents Hip Hop Hits, Vol. 4 doesn't have as many pop crossover hits as its predecessors, though many of these tracks will be familiar to the hip-hop faithful. Nelly's "Country Grammar," Eminem's "The Real Slim Shady," and Dr. Dre and Snoop Dogg's "The Next Episode" are likely already registered in the consciousness of most listeners, and even though the collection is a little erratic, there are some other great singles here as well. Some of the artists include Common, LL Cool J, De La Soul (featuring Redman), DMX, Shyne, Big Pun, and Lil' Kim. —*Steve Huey*

The Source Presents: Hip Hop Hits, Vol. 5 / Dec. 18, 2001 / Def Jam ✦✦✦✦

The fifth volume in *The Source*'s *Hip Hop Hits* series compiles many of the most popular rap songs of 2001, resulting in a convenient year-end summation for the holiday season. As expected, there's a little bit of everything here: East Coast rap (DMX's "We Right Here," P. Diddy's "Bad Boy for Life," and Jadakiss' "Put Ya Hands Up"), dirty South (Trick Daddy's "I'm a Thug," Ludacris' "Area Codes," and Missy Elliott's "Get Ur Freak On"), pop-rap (Ja Rule and J Lo's "I'm Real," Eve and Gwen Stefani's "Let Me Blow Ya Mind," and Nelly's "Ride Wit Me"), and West Coast rap (Xzibit's "Front 2 Back"). Unfortunately, while it's no doubt hard to please everyone, a few more West Coast tracks would have been nice, since Xzibit's contribution isn't really that spectacular and Snoop Dogg's appearance on a remix of Outkast's "So Fresh, So Clean" doesn't really count. Plus, you have to wonder why the Iconz' "Get F***ed Up" and Benzino's "Bang Ta Dis" are here, since they were minor hits at best. Nonetheless, you can't argue with most of the picks, particularly since the essentials—"I'm Real," "Let Me Blow Ya Mind," and "Get Ur Freak On"—are here. —*Jason Birchmeier*

The Source Presents: Hip Hop Hits, Vol. 6 / Dec. 10, 2002 / Def Jam ✦✦✦

South Coast Ballers / Jun. 1, 1999 / Big Baller/Epic ✦✦✦

Most of the artists on Big Baller/Epic's *South Coast Ballers* sampler are from South Florida, and everyone on the Big Baller label roster makes an appearance here; popping up most frequently—whether on their own cuts or as guests on someone else's—are the M.I.N.T. Squad, Live Luciano, Po Boy, and King James. It's mostly Southern gangsta rap with lower-budget production; nothing really stands out as original (the M.I.N.T. Squad in particular seem very influenced by Tupac), but Live Luciano and Lady Dice show some potential for the future. —*Steve Huey*

The South Will Rise Again / Sep. 19, 2000 / Swirl ✦

The South Will Rise Again results from the late-'90s revolution of Southern rap artists appearing out of nowhere on small independent labels, hoping for a No Limit-like path to success. Unfortunately, for as much as critics complain about the diluted quality of the No Limit camp circa 2000, many of the tracks on this compilation make Master P's soldiers sound like craftsman. Granted, there are a few noteworthy productions on this compilation that show exactly why those outside of the South began paying attention to this former niche in first place. In particular, Indo G and Gangsta Boo's "Remember Me Ballin'" and Goodie Mob's "Soul Food" represent the potential talent formerly ignored; however, these two tracks are by far the exception. For the most part, the other artists here merely derive their themes and sounds from already-proven Southern artists such as Mannie Fresh and his Cash Money Millionaires, Master P and his 504 Boyz, or Three 6 Mafia and their Hypnotize Camp Posse. —*Jason Birchmeier*

Southern Invasion / Jan. 26, 1999 / Strate Atcha ✦✦✦

Southern Invasion compiles a number of tracks by obscure and up-and-coming Southern rappers, and as such there's a heavy Master P influence on a lot of this material. Gangsta Pat is probably the biggest name here, and there are also selections from Krycez, Blackhaven, Mista Ian, and the Prophet Posse, to name a few. —*Steve Huey*

Southern Rollers: Big Gamin' / Apr. 27, 1999 / Simitar ✦✦✦

Southern Rollers: Big Gamin' is a definitive look at Southern rap, complete with 16 tracks of some of hip-hop's most raunchy players. It's a tough and raw collection, and songs from Kurupt, Goodie Mob, Xzibit, and Too Short bust out the shot callers just fine. —*MacKenzie Wilson*

Space Jam / Nov. 12, 1996 / Atlantic ✦✦✦

Like the movie it promotes, *Space Jam* is more of a marketing exercise than an artistic endeavor. Comprised entirely of urban R&B, light hip-hop, and mainstream pop, the album sounds expensive and slickly produced, complete with shimmering synth textures and gently insistent beats—despite the presence of LL Cool J, Q-Tip, and Salt-N-Pepa, there is no hardcore rap here. Instead, the album is designed for kids, who will like the party hip-hop of Coolio or Quad City DJs' theme song, and their parents, who will groove to Seal's cover of "Fly Like an Eagle." In other words, it's designed for maximum radio airplay, and a couple of cuts, like R. Kelly's over-the-top gospel-soul "I Believe I Can Fly," work well with repeated exposure, but most of the material just falls flat, which makes it hard to excuse the callous commercial aspirations of the entire *Space Jam* project. —*Stephen Thomas Erlewine*

State Property / Dec. 11, 2001 / Universal ✦✦✦

Roc-A-Fella Records co-CEOs Jay-Z and Damon Dash executive produced this soundtrack to the feature film of the same name. The film and soundtrack chronicle the lives of a tight-knit band of Philadelphia hustlers trying to come up in the rap game/drug game. While the territory of the soundtrack is well trodden, Roc-A-Fella heavyweight (and Philadelphia native) Beanie Sigel headlines the project, lending his bruising and dexterous lyrical styles throughout. The album also gives a good sneak peak at the Roc's on-deck project (and fellow Philadelphian), Freeway. Freeway, of the high-pitch pimp chatter, is on the next level of intelligent hoodlumism. Sigel and Freeway certainly carry this project, appearing on nine and six tracks respectively (the album boasts a total of 13 cuts). The production here is heavy and flossed out, but not without dashes of Philly soul à la the O'Jays/Harold Melvin & the Blue Notes; the catchy feel of the Philly soul era is rebuffed and transposed to mesh with the "hard-knock life" tone of the album. The album has tremendous crossover appeal, having been released in an era in which gangsta rap had fully reached the MTV masses. The single "Roc the Mic" was proof positive of this, as it became a smash hit with rap's diehard fans and weekend hip-hop listeners alike. —*M.F. Di Bella*

Stimulated, Vol. 1 / Oct. 2, 2001 / Stimulated/Loud ✦✦✦

Stimulated rounds up a number of rap artists from the Loud label's roster of talent for this impressive compilation. There aren't too many big names here. For the most part, these rappers are relatively little known to the general public—De La Soul, Xzibit, Everlast, Dilated Peoples, Camp Lo, Prodigy, and Rah Digga being the best known. Moreover, in general, the featured tracks are exclusive to this compilation. If you have a taste for alternative rap with an emphasis on the hip-hop ideology and sound, this should appeal to you. Even if these artists are fairly unknown to the general public, they're all talented and well respected in the underground. You do get the feeling, however, that the songs here are outtakes or some other form of throwaway—none are particularly impressive. —*Jason Birchmeier*

Stolen Moments: Red Hot + Cool / 1994 / GRP ✦✦✦✦✦

Stolen Moments: Red Hot + Cool is undoubtedly the most successful incarnation of the *Red Hot* albums whose proceeds go toward research in fighting the AIDS virus. Unlike fellow albums in this series, which generally reinterpret the work of several classic songwriters (Gershwin, Porter, Jobim, etc.), *Red Hot + Cool* is a collection of new material which aims musically to directly confront the AIDS epidemic, particularly how it affects the African-American community. With direct issue-oriented lyrics, apt liner notes with commentary by Professor Cornell West, and an assembly of musicians whose work has always bent toward political awareness, this musical explosion is an abridged lexicon of the evolutions in black music during the post-bop era. If forced to categorize this sprawling album, of course, the virtual catch-all "acid jazz" would apply, but this album goes far deeper—it's a history piece. Jazz masters like Ron Carter, Pharoah Sanders, and Donald Byrd join forces with jazz's new regime, Joshua Redman, Ronny Jordan, etc. The evolution of rap is traversed as the Pharcyde, Guru, Michael Franti, MC Solaar, and others trade tracks with the politics of hip-hop progenitors the Last Poets. Unfortunately, the bonus CD that accompanies the album proper takes away from its power. It includes tired reworkings of John Coltrane's "A Love Supreme," by Alice Coltrane and Branford Marsalis, and a botched sampling of tracks from Pharoah Sanders' breakthrough album, *Karma*. The best advice is to throw out this sidecar upon purchase of the two-disc set. —*Joshua David Shanker*

Str8 Up Loco / May 25, 1995 / Moola ✦✦✦

It didn't take Latinos very long to discover rap. Back in 1979, the Sugarhill Gang's "Rapper's Delight" sold a lot of copies in Latino neighborhoods, and New York's Mean Machine brought a "Nuyorkican" flavor to hip-hop when they recorded "Disco Dreams" in 1981. The thing that made many Latino MCs interesting in the '80s and '90s was their willingness to put their own spin on rap; instead of trying to sound exactly like African-American rappers, they celebrated their Latino heritage. This was true of Puerto Ricans and Cubans on the East Coast as well as Mexicans on the West Coast. Assembled in 1995, *Str8 Up Loco* is primarily a compilation of Chicano rap—the CD doesn't get into a lot of Puerto Rican MCs from New York and Philadelphia or Cuban rappers from Miami. The front cover, in fact, looks like an issue of *Lowrider* magazine, which is appropriate because many of the young Chicanos who were reading that publication in 1995 were the people Moola Records was going after with selections like tha Mexakinz' "Phonkie Melodia," Aztlan Nation's "Born 2 Play the Bad Guy," and the Main One's "Learn to Be a Man for Self." Most of the material is hardcore rap, although *Str8 Up Loco* detours into commercial pop-rap with the Unit's "(La La) Love" (which samples the Delfonics' "La La Means I Love You") and the Latin Alliance's interpretation of War's "Low Rider." The only track that is out of place is MC Breed's 1991 hit "Ain't No Future in Your Frontin'"; although enjoyable, the tune is inappropriate for this CD because Breed is from Michigan and wasn't part of California's Chicano rap scene. Nonetheless, *Str8 Up Loco* is a rewarding compilation that is highly recommended to anyone who is interested in Mexican-Americans' contributions to hip-hop. —*Alex Henderson*

Straight from da Streets, Vol. 1 / 1994 / Priority ✦✦✦✦

In the 1980s and 1990s, Priority was one of the top labels for rap compilations. Priority usually didn't provide the type of comprehensive, meticulously detailed liner notes you could expect from Rhino, but its rap compilations often contained their share of essential hits. Released in 1994, *Straight from da Streets, Vol. 1* isn't the last word on early-'90s hip-hop but nonetheless offers many of the classic rap hits from that period. Variety is the rule on this compilation, which ranges from the hyper Florida-style bass music of Tag Team's "Whoomp! (There It Is)" and Duice's "Dazzey Dukes" to the jazz-influenced alternative rap of Digable Planets' "Rebirth of Slick." Northeastern hardcore rap is represented by Public Enemy's "Can't Truss It" and Black Sheep's "The Choice Is Yours," while L.A. gangsta rap is represented by Dr. Dre's "Let Me Ride" and Ice Cube's "It Was A Good Day." And on "Baby Got Back," Sir Mix-A-Lot's ode to women with large derrieres, the Seattle rapper reminds us how distinctive and unique he is. Toward the end, the CD makes an infectious detour into P-funk with George Clinton's "Atomic Dog" and a rare live version of Funkadelic's "One Nation Under A Groove"—neither are hip-hop, but Priority probably reasoned that the songs deserved to be on a rap compilation because they've been sampled by so many MCs. Ranging from decent to superb, *Straight from da Streets* is recommended to listeners who are looking for a diverse survey of early-1990s rap styles. —*Alex Henderson*

Straight Outta Compton: N.W.A 10th Anniversary Tribute / Nov. 3, 1998 / Priority ✦✦✦

It's hard to imagine what rap music would be without N.W.A. And, luckily, Priority Records has found a way to let today's rap artists pay tribute to the pioneers of gangsta rap without completely disrespecting them in the process. While it certainly will never be even a partial replacement for the original, the tribute album *Straight Outta Compton* at least avoids embarrassment and frustration. Some of the better contemporary artists, including Bone Thugs-N-Harmony and Mack 10, put a little of their own spin on what is perhaps rap's single greatest album. Some of Master P's "No Limit Soldiers," including Silkk the Shocker and new arrival Snoop Doggy Dogg, also help keep the quality of the album relatively high. Some of the rewrites are questionable, but of course, some are unavoidable. Just looking at the gaping difference between the original album and the tribute speaks volumes about how far the genre has fallen since N.W.A defined it years ago. Rap may still be alive, but there was a time when it didn't need life support to stay there. —*David M. Childers*

Street Jams: Electric Funk, Vols. 1-4 / Jul. 16, 1996 / Rhino ✦✦✦✦✦

Available either as a box set or as individual discs, *Street Jams: Electric Funk, Vols. 1-4* is an excellent, comprehensive overview of the groundbreaking electro-funk of the early '80s. Over the course of four discs, most of the genre's major players, including Afrika Bambaataa and Grandmaster Flash, are rep-

resented by their biggest hits and best-known remixes; many of its one-hit wonders are here as well, adding depth and context. Much of this music is presented in 12" mixes, which gives a more accurate portrait of electro-funk and how it stretched and played with rhythms and electronics. For casual listeners, the sheer length of some of these songs may be intimidating—some push the ten-minute mark—but any serious collector or listener of hip-hop, urban R&B, electronica, or modern music should be familiar with many of these songs and mixes. —*Stephen Thomas Erlewine*

Street Jams: Hip-Hop from the Top, Vols. 1-4 / Aug. 20, 1996 / Rhino ✦✦✦✦

Available either as a box set or as four individual discs, *Street Jams: Hip-Hop from the Top, Vols. 1-4* is a superb collection of old school rap, featuring most of the major singles and artists from the genre's formative years. Over the course of the series, such classics as "Rapper's Delight," "The Breaks," "The Message," "It's Like That," "The Roof Is on Fire," "Roxanne, Roxanne," "The Real Roxanne," "The Show," "Freaks Come Out at Night," "Nightmares," and "La-Di-Da-Di" are presented, usually in their full-length 12" mix. It's comprehensive and surprisingly listenable, illustrating that even from the start, all hip-hop did not sound the same. It's an essential collection for any comprehensive urban, rap, or pop library. —*Stephen Thomas Erlewine*

Street Life in Zoo York: Hip Hop / May 11, 1999 / Mastertone ✦✦

Although Mastertone's *Hip Hop* boasts a generic name, the collection is anything but. The disc concentrates on New York hip-hop, focusing on forefathers like Erick Sermon and Marley Marl, plus newer artists and underground rappers like Beatnuts, Godfather Don, Mike Heron, and Mobb Deep. Although the featured selections aren't always representative, there's no filler on the disc, and it's one of the few contemporary hip-hop samplers that's listenable from beginning to end. —*Stephen Thomas Erlewine*

Streets Is Watching / May 5, 1998 / Def Jam ✦✦✦

Jay-Z decided to get into the process of myth making with *Streets Is Watching*, a documentary about his life. Unlike many hip-hop movies, the film purports to be about the real Jay-Z and how he keeps things on the street. While that matter is open to debate, it is true that the soundtrack is street-level hip-hop, both for better and for worse. Many of the artists on the collection are underground rappers—Jay-Z and Noreaga are the best-known names here—who all follow a similar style: hard-hitting beats and blunt (as well as blunted) freestyle raps. There are some really good moments here, enough to make it worthwhile for dedicated fans of the genre, but there's also enough repetition here to make it a little trying for casual listeners. —*Stephen Thomas Erlewine*

Streetsounds: The Best of Electro, Vol. 1 / 1995 / Beechwood ✦✦✦✦✦

Beechwood's mid-'80s series of hip-hop and electro compilations played an important role in introducing the sound of American urban electronic dance music to European audiences. *The Best of Electro, Vol. 1*, released in 1995, is a nice distillation of those earlier comps, with tracks by Man Parrish, Cybotron, Warp 9, Egyptian Lover, Hashim, West Street Mob, and the Russell Brothers filling out a good portion of early electro history (although the absence of Miami artists such as Freestyle and Tony Butler is somewhat curious). Released on CD and gatefold double-vinyl LP, this compilation is a sturdy, enduring necessity. —*Sean Cooper*

Strength Magazine Presents Subtext / Oct. 5, 1999 / Sire ✦✦✦

Sire's *Strength Magazine Presents Subtext* is an intriguing collection of hardcore and underground hip-hop from the late '90s. There are a few familiar names, at least to rap fans—Rob Swift and Del tha Funkee Homosapien have been around for a while—but the main strength of the compilation is that it introduces lesser-known names to a wider audience, including curious listeners that may have heard of the names, but not the specific recordings. There may be some things that don't work as well as others, but overall, there's quite a lot of very good stuff here and it's worth a listen. —*Stephen Thomas Erlewine*

Strictly B-Boy Breaks, Vol. 1 / Nov. 13, 2001 / Mzee ✦✦✦

Unfortunately, too many breakbeat/b-boy/funk mixes are recorded so poorly that they usually sound better on the ghetto blasters from which they were produced. *Strictly B-Boy Breaks, Vol. 1* is no different, though it does offer an amazing amount of great music and mixing sensibility. The incredible skill of the DJs is buried beneath paper-thin production quality, and little is done to EQ or master the recording. But certainly such mastering can be cost prohibitive for a small upstart label just trying to get their mixes out to the buying public. This collection, on Germany's Mzee Records, was compiled by Zeb.Roc.Ski and premixed by Def Cut and DJ Spitfire. Their first series of three tracks illustrates Spitfire's remarkable mixing and scratching skills and Zeb.Roc.Ski's overall taste for hard, sweet beats that look back to old school hip-hop and funk while incorporating a cool sense for Detroit and Chicago tech-house style. Zeb.Roc.Ski's own "Keep Prepared for the Battle" is a standout track that harks back to the battle MC and DJ days of Afrika Bambataa and Mantronix. As well, track contributions from Def Cut are among the best on the disc. The tighter the music gets, the harder it is to even notice the disc's amateur production values. This is a valiant effort that could've benefited from a little more time in the studio. —*Ken Taylor*

Strip Club Classics / Nov. 23, 1999 / Little Joe ✦✦✦

Strip Club Classics isn't the sort of "strip for your husband" orchestral music that enjoyed a brief kitsch revival with the '90s lounge music fad; rather, it's a set of mostly lewd, bass-heavy party rap dominated by material from 2 Live Crew ("Me So Horny," "Get It Girl," "Get Loose Now," "Take It Off," a medley of "C'Mon Babe" and "Doo Doo Brown," and, of course, "The Strip Club"). There are a few other artists fleshing out the collection, and there are some pretty catchy singles mixed in among the lot: Freak Nasty's "Da Dip," Bass Patrol's "The Dirty Bird," Poison Clan's "Shake Whatcha Mama Gave Ya," and Half Pint's "One Leg Up." All in all, if you enjoy Miami-style bass music, *Strip Club Classics* is a great party album thanks to the consistency of the grooves and the sexual subject matter. —*Steve Huey*

Strip Jointz: Hot Songs for Sexy Dancers / Nov. 12, 1996 / Robbins ✦✦✦✦✦

It may have a silly name, but *Strip Jointz: Hot Songs for Sexy Dancers* is an excellent collection of risqué and sexy funk, rap, dance and urban R&B. Instead of concentrating on one era, the album spans over two decades, running from Clarence Carter's "Strokin'," and Labelle's "Lady Marmalade," the Commodores' "Brick House" and Rick James' "Superfreak" to Wreckx-N-Effect's "Rump Shaker," R. Kelly's "Bump 'N Grind," 2 in a Room's "Wiggle It," H-Town's "Knockin' Da Boots," the Outhere Brothers' "Boom Boom Boom," 2 Live Crew's "Me So Horny," and Tone-Loc's "Wild Thing." *Strip Jointz* is an extremely fun, danceable compilation, with almost no weak tracks, making it a terrific party record. —*Stephen Thomas Erlewine*

Suave House Records: Off Da Chain, Vol. 1 / Mar. 21, 2000 / Suave House/Artemis ✦✦✦

Off Da Chain represents Suave House's attempt to market their roster of artists similar to how Ruff Ryders have done on their *Ryde or Die* albums and how Bone Thugs-N-Harmony have done on their *Mo Thugs* albums. Suave House's anchor, the proven duo of Eightball & MJG, make brief appearances on this album, with Eightball addressing the listeners during "Intro" and "We Got Them Things for You." Besides these two rappers, there is a wide range of rappers that represent different styles, from the gangsta flow of Gillie Da Kid to the tough female attitude of Toni Hickman to the impressive rhymes of Lil' Noah. Overall, the talent on this album competes with most any other team out there, including Dr. Dre's camp and any of Suave House's neighbors in the South. Sure, there are some similar voices here, such as the Tupac sound of Psychodrama and the Notorious B.I.G.'s wit crossed with Eminem's delivery of Lil' Noah, but what makes or breaks these songs is the beats. The sounds of Dre define Aftermath just as Mannie Fresh's soundscapes define the sounds of Cash Money and the Bomb Squad gave Public Enemy their classic sound. Unfortunately, Suave House doesn't have a sole producer, resulting in an inconsistent sound that sometimes moves into booty-shakin' Southern-beat territory, and other times moves into the stark eeriness of minimal piano notes and darks synths that Dre and his protégé, Mel Man, have become associated with. So no matter how good Suave House's rappers may be, it takes more than rhymes to make a great rap album. Had the camp stuck with one producer and crafted a unique sound, this would be an amazing release, but with its hit-and-miss sounds, occasionally weak rapping, and its tendency to fall into played-out clichés—"Money Sex & Drugs," "Do You Wanna Ride?," "Get Money," "Something to Bounce To"—the album becomes average. Pick up Eightball & MJG's *In Our Lifetime, Vol. 1* for a much more consistent, more impressive taste of this Southern label. —*Jason Birchmeier*

Subterranean Hitz, Vol. 1 / Jan. 7, 1997 / WordSound ✦✦✦

Illbient dub and abstract hip-hop appear in equal degree on WordSound's first compilation in the *Subterranean Hitz* series. Rob Swift, Prince Paul, Spectre, and Torture each make appearances. —*John Bush*

Subterranean Hitz, Vol. 2 / Jan. 6, 1998 / WordSound ✦✦✦

Compiled by Spectre, who also contributes a track, *Subterranean Hitz, Vol. 2* showcases off-kilter, dub-influenced hip-hop by the likes of the X-Ecutioners' Rob Swift, ex-Jungle Brother Africa "Baby Bam," Prince Paul, New Kingdom's Scotty Hard, and more. —*Steve Huey*

Sugar Hill Club Classics / Apr. 20, 1999 / Import ✦✦✦✦✦

Sequel's impressive *Sugar Hill Club Classics* collection focuses less on the label as a hip-hop pioneer and more on how Sugar Hill fit into the fraternal, interconnected club culture around New York City during the early '80s. After the disco era lost steam amidst a wave of commercial imitations, the dance scene splintered and went underground. At the same time, hip-hop began moving downtown from the South Bronx and gradually assimilated into all the other dance styles then current, from go-go to electro to R&B to funk to the last remnants of disco. Even though *Sugar Hill Club Classics* includes all the obvious hip-hop must-hears—"Rapper's Delight," "The Adventures of Grandmaster on the Wheels of Steel," "White Lines (Don't Do It)," "The Message," and "Monster Jam"—it also features a raft of more obscure, club-oriented cuts like the bomb-dropping "Spoon'nin Rap" by Spoonie Gee, "Pump Me Up" and "Drop the Bomb" by Trouble Funk, "Mosquito (aka Hobo Scratch)" by West Street Mob, and "We Got the Funk" by Positive Force (none of which appear on Rhino's massive five-disc box *The Sugar Hill Records Story*). —*John Bush*

★ The Sugar Hill Records Story / Feb. 4, 1997 / Rhino ✦✦✦✦✦

Sugar Hill Records was the first rap and hip-hop label, giving many listeners their first exposure to the urban rhyming and scratching that transformed pop music during the '80s. Like most indie labels, they had troubles with finances and distribution; eventually, that situation resulted in their records remaining out of print during the rise of the hip-hop during the late '80s and the '90s. The five-disc *Sugar Hill Records Story* remedies this situation by collecting all of the label's classic A sides, many in their full-length mixes, on one set. Tracks by the Sugarhill Gang, Grandmaster Flash, and the Treacherous Three are commonplace and remain excellent, but the true revelation of the box set is how strong largely forgotten cuts by Spoonie Gee, the Funky Four Plus One, Trouble Funk, the Sequence, Super-Wolf, and West Street Mob are—these are supremely funky, infectious, and inventive cuts, which have been made familiar through samples and quatations on modern rap records. Another surprise is how integrated this music is—male and female rappers trade lines without hesitation, and there is none of the misogyny or violence that characterized gangsta rap. But that doesn't mean the old school rap on *The Sugar Hill Records Story* sounds dated—much of this bright, elastic electro-funk has provided the foundation for '90s hits by the likes of the Beastie Boys and Dr. Dre. But the most surprising thing of all is how *The Sugar Hill Records Story* barely loses momentum over the course of five discs. There is the occasional dull spot or oddity (check out the bizarre B-52's rip-off "At the Ice Arcade" by the Chilly Kids) that interrupts the flow, but the music is consistently strong, even on the fifth disc. It was inevitable that *The Sugar Hill Records Story* would be an important historical document, but what makes it truly essential is how rich, diverse, and timeless the music actually is. —*Stephen Thomas Erlewine*

The Sugar Hill Story: To the Beat Y'All / 1994 / Sequel ✦✦✦✦✦

A welcome and definitive retrospective of the beginnings of commercial rap, the three-CD British import *The Sugar Hill Story: To the Beat Y'All* collects many of the most worthwhile tracks released by Sylvia Robinson's innovative, pioneering Sugar Hill Records label. Robinson and Sugar Hill took the novel brand of music heard booming from sound systems set up at inner-city block parties and clubs and not only made it palatable to the wider listening audience but also literally invented hip-hop culture as we know it. Musically, the collection focuses on Sugar Hill's brief but groundbreaking three-year run commenced by the Sugarhill Gang's classic (and commercially successful, selling eight million copies) "Rapper's Delight" in 1979 and ending in 1982 when Afrika Bambaataa's "Planet Rock" ushered in a new progressive era in hip-hop. It is unlikely rap music would have ever flourished without Sugar Hill Records and the singles that were released on the label; *To the Beat Y'all* is a perfect reminder of that. The taut, streamlined classic hits of Melle Mel, the Furious Five & Grandmaster Flash's groundbreaking and influential turntable masterpiece, "Adventures of Grand Master Flash on the Wheels of Steel" are here—as are hits by notable names such as Spoonie Gee, Funky Four Plus One, Busy Bee, Treacherous Three, and go-go band Trouble Funk.

Then too, there are also a great number of equally excellent surprises, one-hit wonders, and novelties: the female trio Sequence, the sensationally dance-worthy breakbeat-heavy "Break Dancin'-Electric" by West Street Mob; the lean funk groove of Wayne & Charlie's "Check It Out"; and Reggie Griffin's proto-electro cut "Mirda Rock." Most of these selections still resonate 20 years later with the same energy, freshness, and humor. It's amazing and occasionally shocking to hear, in their original contexts, all of the catchphrases, lines, and mottoes that have been subsequently sampled as hooks, referenced by countless MCs and DJs, and so absorbed and etched into the legacy and lore of hip-hop that they seem almost anonymous or part of the public domain. These songs are literally the bricks that built the foundation of rap music. —*Stanton Swihart*

Suge Knight Represents: Chronic 2000 / Apr. 27, 1999 / Priority ♦♦
The marketing event of the millennium (according to jail-bound executive producer Suge Knight), *Suge Knight Represents: Chronic 2000* is as much an album of its time as the original, Dr. Dre's 1993 masterpiece *The Chronic*. While the original introduced a new era of commercial gangsta crossover hip-hop, the follow-up signals everything that's wrong with the state of hip-hop circa the end of the millennium. It's not that the production is substandard; tracks like "Top Dogg Cindafella" (by Top Dogg) and the title track (by VK Featuring Treach) are solid productions that hold their own with many of their contemporaries in the world of chartbound hip-hop. The problem is, this is the same type of music that even Dr. Dre moved past several years ago, and the range of participants is an amalgam of post-gangsta crossover, veteran (Kurupt, Treach, DJ Quik, Daz Dillinger, even the long-gone Tupac) and rookie (Top Dogg, Doobie, Capricorne, Mac-Shawn). It doesn't just smack of a marketing scam—it's bad music making and should be avoided at any cost. —*Keith Farley*

Superstars of Bass / Oct. 20, 1998 / Max ♦♦♦
Superstars of Bass does include some of the best-selling artists and tracks in bass music, including "Kitty Kitty" by 69 Boyz, "Rodeo" by 95 South, "Girls" by DJ Smurf, "Too Much Booty in Da Pants" by Sound Master T, and "C U Ride" by the Knuckleheads. —*Keith Farley*

Superstars of Bass, Vol. 2 / Jul. 27, 1999 / Max ♦♦♦
The second volume in the classic bass series includes tracks from Luke, the Knuckleheads, DJ Laz, and Freaknasty plus a clutch of current chart hits like Chuck D's "Who Let the Dogs Out." —*Keith Farley*

Survival of the Illest: Live from 125 NYC / Oct. 27, 1998 / Def Jam ♦♦♦
The hardest of the hardcore each get several tracks on this Def Jam collection, including DMX ("Money, Power, Respect," "Get at Me Dog"), Onyx ("Throw Ya Gunz," "Shut 'Em Down"), Cormega ("Dead Man Walking," "Slow Down"), and Def Squad ("The Most Beautiful Thing in This World," "I Shot Ya"). —*Keith Farley*

Temple of Hiphop Kulture: Criminal-Justice from Darkness to Light / Nov. 9, 1999 / Warner Brothers ♦♦♦♦
A nonstop, excellent compilation of late-'90s hip-hop, *Temple of Hiphop Kulture: Criminal-Justice from Darkness to Light* includes a great variety of MCs and rappers, from the smooth, fast rush rapping of Thor-El to the dancehall delivery of Mad Lion, with several appearances by KRS-One. By no means for innocent ears, the lyrics deal with hardness, violence, and drugs (though not necessarily in a supportive light). "Dealing with live facts and effects, not the study of dead material," as the interlude explains, this release is intended to represent the body of hip-hop culture and is definitely recommended for rap and hip-hop fans. —*Joslyn Layne*

Tenth Anniversary Rap-A-Lot Records / Nov. 19, 1996 / Virgin ♦♦♦♦
Tenth Anniversary Rap-A-Lot Records is a retrospective of the first decade of the Texas-based hip-hop label, featuring hit singles by the Geto Boys, Scarface, Blac Monks, Raheem, 5th Ward Boyz, and Gangsta Nip, among many others. Though some of this material is simply straightforward gangsta rap, the very best moments here—particularly the Geto Boys' classic "Mind Playin' Tricks on Me"—rank among the best hardcore rap of the late '80s and early '90s, and any dedicated rap fan should explore what it has to offer. —*Stephen Thomas Erlewine*

THC: The Hip Hop Collection, Vol. 1 / Apr. 30, 2002 / Music Up ♦♦♦♦♦
Celebrating the unbridled love of marijuana that many hip-hop artists promote, *THC: The Hip Hop Collection, Vol. 1* is a tribute album to the drug. There are no notable differences among the tracks found here outside of the

beats and samples; otherwise, each song essentially says the same thing—weed is good. This message may have worked for four or five songs, but to dedicate an entire album to this idea without exploring the legal aspects or even tell some stories about being high seems rather ridiculous. The good tracks here are distinguished by the skills of the rappers and producers, as well as how they approach the singular message found here. Shabaam Sahdeeq and Steele deliver the most memorable track on the first half of the album, but their piano-driven "Roll Up" is really the only exceptional track out of the first nine songs. The album takes a dramatic shift for the better after these songs, featuring more avant-garde (for rap) artists who are willing to experiment more with their tracks. The Pharcyde don't do anything terribly spectacular, but their obvious mike talent allows them to still be above most of the album. Lootpack's "Take a Hit" is a laid-back track that uses the marijuana theme as only a small part of what is essentially a really well-produced brag-a-thon. RZA and Timbo King deliver an incredibly slow and deliberate tribute to being really high that perfectly captures the foggy mental situation and relaxed atmosphere that their scenario results in. And Ripshop has the best song of the bunch, an amiable track that promotes the community environment created by pot smoking and featuring a great backing track, smooth rapping, and clever lyrics. This album is nothing to write home about when viewed as a collection, but when picked apart there are several individual songs that are quite memorable. Although the album is uneven, anyone looking to support this cause or at least get a few good rap songs about weed should give this a shot. —*Bradley Torreano*

Thicker Than Water / Oct. 5, 1999 / Priority ♦♦♦
The double-disc soundtrack to rapper Mack 10's directorial debut, *Thicker Than Water* features additional contributions by such artists as Ice Cube, Big Pun, Fat Joe, MC Eiht, Children of Da Ghetto, CJ Mac, and Eightball & Big Duke, among others. Even employing this sampler approach, the difficulties of producing enough high-quality material to make a consistently engaging double-disc hip-hop set are apparent, as there's some obvious filler here. However, high points do appear often, and the coexistence of West Coast and East Coast elements is an encouraging sign of things to come. —*Steve Huey*

This Is for the Homies / Apr. 18, 2000 / Thump ♦♦♦♦
This Is for the Homies is an unusual hip-hop collection that pays tribute to Chicano rap pioneers and David Gonzalez's comic strip "Homies," which appeared in *Lowrider* magazine in the late '70s. Slow Pain's "Homies," Mr. Shadow's "Go Ahead," Cisco's "Just Like Mexico," and Lawless' "Here's to You" are some of the album's highlights. Also included are tracks by Frost, L.A.C., Beesh, Funky Aztecs, and A.L.T. Gonzalez's "Homies" characters fill the album's artwork and liner notes, adding another level of authenticity to this worthwhile compilation. —*Heather Phares*

This Is Hip Hop / Apr. 14, 1998 / This Is ♦♦♦
This three-disc set doesn't include many tracks, but they are some of the best hip-hop ever, including "Gangsta's Paradise" by Coolio, "Fight the Power" by Public Enemy, "Step into a World" by KRS-One, "Can't You See" by the Notorious B.I.G., and "Luchini AKA This Is It" by Camp Lo. The third CD is a bonus mix disc with tracks from the first two of the set. —*Keith Farley*

The Thong Song Album / Jul. 25, 2000 / Koch ♦♦♦
The Thong Song Album delivers a dozen classic and current booty hits, including a remake of Sisqó's title track by female rapper DJ Boo and two songs by the booty king, Luke: "Scarred" and "I Wanna Rock." Moochie Mack's "Shake That Thang," Split Personality's "Shake Junt Queen," and DJ Laz's "Mami el Negro" are some of the other standout tracks on this raunchy rap compilation. —*Heather Phares*

Thug Law: Thug Life Outlawz: Chapter 1 / Oct. 23, 2001 / D-3 Entertainment ♦♦♦
Thug Law rounds up a number of West Coast gangsta rappers like the Outlawz, Mack 10, Mac Mall, Krayzie Bone, and Above the Law. No one here is particularly popular outside of the insular West Coast gangsta scene, and quite a few rappers—Big Skye, EDI, Swerv, Sundae—make numerous appearances. Definitely rooted in the Tupac school of thug rap, *Thug Law* will probably appeal to anyone who considers him- or herself an admirer of this harsh music. —*Jason Birchmeier*

Thump'n Freestyle Quick Mixx / Aug. 20, 1996 / Thump ♦♦♦♦
The first volume in Thump Street's *Thump'n Freestyle Quick Mixx* series compiles many freestyle classics from the '80s, including songs by Exposé

("Point of No Return"), the Cover Girls ("Because of You"), and Stevie B. ("Spring Love"). Many of the artists featured on this collection aren't nearly as well known, yet their songs are just as impressive as those of the aforementioned pop stars, if not more impressive. *Thump'n Freestyle Quick Mixx* is intended more as a dance album than as a comprehensive freestyle best-of; however, it functions well as that too. —*Jason Birchmeier*

Thump's Hottest Hits / Aug. 1, 2000 / Thump ✦✦✦

Thump's Hottest Hits delivers just what the title promises: a collection of songs from the label's most popular artists, including TWDY's "Player's Holiday," Gemini's "Doctor Doctor (Party Mix)," Claudia Mia & Don Caligula's "Lingerie," and Katalina's "DJ Girl." Tracks by Chacho, Stevie B, Ambrosia, Laura Martinez, and Lighter Shade of Brown featuring Tony! Toni! Tone! complete this retrospective of Thump's hip-hop and club-based roster. —*Heather Phares*

Tommy Boy Essentials: Hip-Hop, Vol. 1 / Apr. 24, 2001 / Tommy Boy ✦✦✦✦✦

While released as part of Tommy Boy's 20th-anniversary reissue series, most tracks on *Tommy Boy Essentials* are culled from the label's peak years of 1988-1994. All tracks are 12" remixes, one-off singles, and promotional tracks, and most of them were never before issued on compact disc. Highlights include remixes of House of Pain's "Jump Around," Queen Latifah's "Wrath of My Madness," and Prince Rakeem's "Ooh I Love You Rakeem." (Rakeem is better known today as Wu-Tang Clan's RZA; the song included here was his first appearance on record.) Lost classics include Uptown's densely polyrhythmic "Dope On Plastic" and the rare and cryptically titled "Sh.Fe.MC's," a long-sought-after collaboration between De La Soul and A Tribe Called Quest that is worth the disc's asking price alone. While rap's long-overdue self-examination of its own past is crippled by the fact that artists and styles seem to have a sell-by date of about 18 months, most of the cuts on *Tommy Boy Essentials* were judiciously chosen for their longevity. A lack of any liner notes or artist information is disappointing, but to any serious beat hound or student of hip-hop's meteoric development, this CD is a must-have, plain and simple. —*John Duffy*

Tommy Boy's Greatest Beats 1981-1996 / Oct. 27, 1998 / Tommy Boy ✦✦✦✦

Only one label, Tommy Boy, spans hip-hop's entire recorded history with no loss of hits or perfect beats over the course of those ten years. The five-disc box released to commemorate the label's 15th anniversary includes a wealth of hip-hop classics, everything from "Planet Rock" to "Plug Tunin'" to "Humpty Dance" to "Jump Around" to "Play at Your Own Risk" to "Hip Hop Hooray" to "Gangsta's Paradise." The addition of a few dance cuts—from Information Society, Coldcut, and 808 State—don't work quite as well as they should, but on the whole *Tommy Boy's Greatest Beats 1981-1996* is an excellent collection that sums up hip-hop better than any other label could. The fifth disc includes nine Tommy Boy classics given the remix treatment, resulting in intriguing combinations like Grooverider with Jonzun Crew's "Pack Jam," Dimitri From Paris with Stetsasonic's "Talkin' All That Jazz," and DJ Premier with Queen Latifah's "Wrath of My Madness." —*Keith Farley*

Tommy Boy's Greatest Beats, Vol. 1 / Oct. 27, 1998 / Tommy Boy ✦✦✦✦

The first volume in Tommy Boy's 15th-anniversary reissue campaign includes label classics like "Planet Rock" by Afrika Bambaataa, "Plug Tunin'" by De La Soul, "Doowutchyalike" by Digital Underground, "Can't You See" by Total, and "Ladies First" by Queen Latifah. The disc is also available in the five-disc set *Tommy Boy's Greatest Beats 1981-1996.* —*Keith Farley*

Tommy Boy's Greatest Beats, Vol. 2 / Oct. 27, 1998 / Tommy Boy ✦✦✦✦

The second volume in Tommy Boy's 15th-anniversary reissue campaign includes label classics like House of Pain's "Jump Around," K7's "Come Baby Come," Digital Underground's "Humpty Dance," and Afrika Bambaataa's "Jazzy Sensation." The disc is also available in the five-disc set *Tommy Boy's Greatest Beats 1981-1996.* —*Keith Farley*

Tommy Boy's Greatest Beats, Vol. 3 / Oct. 27, 1998 / Tommy Boy ✦✦✦✦
Tommy Boy's Greatest Beats, Vol. 4 / Oct. 27, 1998 / Tommy Boy ✦✦✦✦
Too Gangsta for Radio / Sep. 26, 2000 / Death Row ✦✦

This overview of the 2000 Death Row roster—i.e., after Suge Knight's imprisonment and Dr. Dre's departure—features a few veterans, but mostly attempts to introduce new artists. There are a couple of Tupac cuts from the label's vault (it seems like the run of posthumous Tupac releases has long

since passed the point of exploitation), and there are also appearances by the likes of Ja Rule, Kurupt, Above the Law, Treach, Scarface, Ruff Ryders, and the LOX. That only accounts for a few of the tracks, however; much of the collection is devoted to new signings like Crooked I and Mac-Shawn. The newcomers generate a few good cuts, but too much of the album is nondescript and lackluster, following trends instead of setting them. Even if there are some good moments here, *Too Gangsta for Radio* doesn't exactly give Death Row fans a reason to get excited about the label's future. —*Steve Huey*

Too Short Mix Tapes, Vol. 1: Nationriders / Jul. 27, 1999 / Jive ✦✦✦

The aims of hip-hop mix tapes are to showcase the skills and knowledge of DJs involved and introduce listeners to the best material from a variety of different artists. Consequently, DJs from Funkmaster Flex to Clue get a chance to display their skills while they're enlightening their public on great jams coming their way. Too Short's version of a mix tape, however, includes only artists from his own label (plus a guest shot when he can get it). And even though it includes no less than four DJs mixing the album (don't ask how), the tracks just barely lead into each other and are never actually mixed into each other. Still, it's all about the music and *Nationriders* turns out to be a good compilation of West Coast bounce tracks. Naturally, Too Short leads off the affair with "Here We Go (Remix)" and "Tell the Feds" (the latter produced by Short Records' Quint Black). A few Short acts (Slink Capone, Murda One, Nation Riders) get three or four tracks each, while the others (Jezabell, Zu, Al Block, G-Side, Dolla Will) get just one. The production is funky but just a bit overdone, leaving *Nationriders* as a solid compilation that's best for those interested in Too Short but enjoyable for all kinds of hip-hop fans. —*Keith Farley*

Training Day / Sep. 11, 2001 / Priority ✦✦✦

Training Day, the film, follows a rookie cop through his first day as an L.A.P.D. narcotics officer. He comes to terms with the ugly truths of his job and the brutal realities of the city he's trying to protect. *Training Day*, the soundtrack, is just as ugly and brutal as the movie. Each track is a graphic portrait of city life, from the profiling style of street business to the kill-or-be-killed philosophy engrained in even the innocent. The soundtrack is graphic, but not gratuitous. Songs that may have otherwise been viewed as unnecessarily violent or sexual feel completely appropriate and are more effective in the context of the film. That may be why some of rap's most respected names, including Dr. Dre, P. Diddy, and Cypress Hill signed on for the project. Their veteran status is supported by the aggressive energy of rap newcomers like Nelly, Krubsnatcha, and Pharoahe Monch. David Bowie joins P. Diddy & the Bad Boy Family on "American Dream," but the collaboration feels forced and Bowie's unmistakable glam rock voice seems tragically out of place. It's really the only track that doesn't work, which is rare for a soundtrack. If this soundtrack lacks anything, it's variety. Songs about dirty cops, ruthless killings, and meaningless sex are followed by songs about meaningless killings, dirty sex, and ruthless cops. Few of the tracks stand out from the rest, but maybe that's the idea. Maybe its just like Napalm says and they're "all singing the same song." —*Brad Kohlenstein*

Trespass / 1992 / Sire ✦✦

This first soundtrack album from *Trespass* (there is also an album of Ry Cooder's score) contains "music from the motion picture" "plus bonus tracks." It is a gangsta rap sampler featuring Ice-T and Ice Cube, who star in the film, along with Public Enemy and others. In other words, there's a lot of rage, many threats of violence, and a generous helping of obscenities, all set to some busy rhythms. —*William Ruhlmann*

True School, Vol. 1 / Nov. 5, 1996 / K-Tel ✦✦✦

K-Tel's *True School* series contains a number of old school classics, making it a brief, but effective, introduction to the early days of rap. *Vol. 1* contains selections by Spoonie Gee ("Spoonin' Rap"), Funky Four Plus One ("Rappin' & Rockin' the House"), Grandmaster Flash ("Super Rappin'"), Kurtis Blow ("The Breaks"), and Treacherous Three ("New Rap Language"), among others. —*Leo Stanley*

True School, Vol. 2 / Nov. 5, 1996 / K-Tel ✦✦✦
True School, Vol. 3 / Nov. 5, 1996 / K-Tel ✦✦✦
Twista Presents New Testament 2K: Street Scriptures / Feb. 27, 2001 / Legit Ballin ✦✦✦✦

Not be confused as a Twista solo album, *Twista Presents New Testament 2K: Street Scriptures* is actually a sampler for the Chicago-based Legit Ballin' label. Though Twista is by far the album's standout artist—along with the undeniably seductive Ms. Kane—his labelmates are also impressive, as are producers Cayex and Toxic. What's perhaps most impressive about this album, though, is the surprising amount of diversity. The lead single, "Ball Wit Us," integrates some Latin rhythms and R&B singing, for example, while other songs go for a more traditional hardcore/gangsta vibe. As the label's name no doubt implies, these rappers aren't your typical crew, even if they still like to floss and represent their city. Underneath the pimp posturing is a subversive, good-hearted tone. Overall, Legit Ballin' proves itself to be a promising camp, and undoubtedly one of the top indie labels in the rap game circa 2001. Furthermore, their unique locale (Chicago) and their diverse range of sounds (both vocals and production) help them stand out as a crew to watch. *—Jason Birchmeier*

Uncle Luke Presents: Chipman and the Buckwheat Boy / Sep. 25, 2001 / Koch ♦♦♦

At the time of this album's release in late 2001, the onetime Luke Skyywalker was ten years removed from his popular days with the 2 Live Crew. His career had gone downhill ever since the controversy surrounding *As Nasty as They Want to Be* simmered. Perhaps that's why *Uncle Luke Presents: Chipman and the Buckwheat Boy* seems so much like a joke. To be frank, it's hard to take Uncle Luke seriously. It was hard enough to take him seriously in the early '90s when he was in the national spotlight, let alone in the early 2000s when he was still trying to bank off his controversial days with the 2 Live Crew. After all, the guy could barely keep his own career afloat, let alone "present" two new artists. You're better off steering clear of this unless you're a Luke loyalist. And even then, you might want to pass this one by. *—Jason Birchmeier*

Undercover Brother / May 21, 2002 / Hollywood ♦♦♦♦

The soundtrack to the amusing blaxploitation parody *Undercover Brother* wisely keeps it to the classics, adding only three new tracks—the excellent blaxploitation homage "Undercova Funk (Give Up the Funk)" by Snoop Dogg, the solid Lil' J cut "I Need Luv (2002)," and Stanley Clarke's absolutely brilliant "Theme From Undercover Brother"—to a set of 11 classic funk and soul songs from the '70s. There are a lot of familiar titles here—"Pick Up the Pieces," "Brick house," "Play That Funky Music (White Boy)," "Say It Loud (I'm Black and I'm Proud)," "Love Train," "Ladies Night," etc.—spiced by just a couple of smaller hits and cult favorites, but the music flows so well, it doesn't matter. This works well as a collection of classic funk and soul, and it offers a perfect aural souvenir of this movie, which makes it arguably the best soundtrack so far of the 2002 summer movie season. *—Stephen Thomas Erlewine*

Urban Jungle / Aug. 24, 1999 / Priority ♦♦♦

This mix collection presents some of the best tracks in an emerging crossover between the quintessentially British dance style (jungle or drum'n'bass) and the quintessential American dance style (hip-hop). A few of the tracks are simply jungle productions, though by rap-influenced producers like Aphrodite, Roni Size, Natural Born Chillers, and Urban Takeover. The best tracks here chart an intriguing fusion between the two styles, resulting in the Joker (from the Dream Team) remixing Ice Cube and Mack 10, Dillinja reworking the Jungle Brothers, and Aphrodite redoing N.W.A. Given the raft of jungle compilations out there, it's a pleasant surprise to find an album that gives a new slant on two increasingly commodified styles. *—John Bush*

Violator: The Album / Aug. 10, 1999 / Def Jam ♦♦♦

Featuring a who's who of rap stars from the late '90's, *Violator: The Album* saves you the trouble of purchasing individual releases in order to get a good sampling of hip-hop funk from its heyday. Contributions from Mobb Deep, Busta Rhymes, Missy Elliot, and LL Cool J serve to confirm their status at the top of hip-hop hierarchy, while Mysonne, Ja Rule, and Hot Boys establish themselves as more than just mere pretenders to the throne. A few missteps abound (in particular, the lazy title track, "Violators"), but for a rap compilation, this disc makes for a credible edition to the catalog of hip-hop must-haves. *—Roxanne Blanford*

Violator: The Album, Vol. 2 / Jul. 24, 2001 / Loud ♦♦♦

The second installment from rap overseer label Violator (distributed by Columbia sublabel Loud records) is modern rap at its most volatile and glossy. This compilation piece brings together some of rap's brightest, some of rap's neophytes, and some of rap's most thugged out. While the iced-out set gets plenty of bad press, their product continues to bring in top dollar,

proof positive that rap music is a stable investment for record companies. Even with the musical and marketing frosting, *Violator, Vol. 2* does contain some marvelous rough-cut hip-hop music. The irresistible "What It Is" is a powerful combination of an electronically rippling track from Virginia-bred mega-producers the Neptunes and the intergalactic verbal antics of Busta Rhymes. The Neptunes score again with the synthetically pounding "Grimey" by the lyrically vicious Noreaga. Soundbombing also abounds on tracks like the Havoc-produced "U Feel Me"; "Options," featuring Capone and Noyd; and "Come Thru," with Styles and Noreaga. The album sticks with this slick-gangster protocol throughout but falls off musically with tracks from crossover giants like Missy Elliot, Ja Rule, and Fabolous. Also, while much of the production is sharp and focused, there are five or so tracks that could have been left on the studio floor. Despite these diluted aspects, this is a worthwhile album with a fair amount of bang for your buck. *—M.F. Di Bella*

The Wash / Sep. 25, 2001 / Universal ♦♦♦

More than just another rap soundtrack, *The Wash* actually functions more as a Dr. Dre album. The West Coast don not only executive produces the album but also produces a few tracks and even raps on three. And the tracks that don't feature him no doubt reflect his influence—most of the producers here clearly studied at the Dr. Dre school of beatmaking. It's perhaps not a surprise, then, that *The Wash* sounds an awful lot like *Chronic 2001*. Dre and Snoop Dogg anchor the album and perform on the album's best songs, including the title track, which consciously references "Nuthin' but a 'G' Thang" with not only its lyrics but also its beats. Furthermore, like *Chronic 2001*, *The Wash* features a large cast of performers, most from the West Coast and several relatively unknown, big-name exceptions being D-12, Bilal, Xzibit, Busta Rhymes, and Bubba Sparxxx. Of the unknowns, two singers/rappers in particular get the spotlight: Shaunta and Knoc-Turn'al, both signed to Dre's Aftermath label and both making their debuts here. The soundtrack's highlight comes on "Bad Intentions," one of Dre's most club-oriented songs ever. Overall, *The Wash* could use a few more standout moments. The D-12 and Bubba Sparxxx songs are impressive but unfortunately out of place on such a West Coast-centric album. More than anything, though, it's worth giving this album a listen even if only to hear Dre's changing sound—his trademark production sound is all over this soundtrack. *—Jason Birchmeier*

Waxing Off: Delicious Vinyl's Greatest Hits / Jul. 3, 2001 / Rhino ♦♦♦♦

Delicious Vinyl was one of the great independent labels of the late '80s, cultivating a roster of quirky rap, hip-hop, and urban soul artists who proudly operated outside of the mainstream. That doesn't mean that they didn't hit the mainstream, of course, since their two biggest artists, Tone-Loc and Young MC, provided the label with their biggest hits ("Wild Thing," "Funky Cold Medina," and "Bust a Move," respectively) and helped break down the doors to the pop charts for hip-hop. Still, those were quirky, clever songs, given productions so funky and hooks so catchy that they couldn't help but be big hits. The rest of Delicious Vinyl was comprised of artists equally off kilter, and they ranged from the smooth acid jazz of the Brand New Heavies to the Latin rap of Masta Ace Incorporated and the Whoridas, to Born Jamericans and the incomparable delightful bizarreness of Pharcyde and Fatlip. Though Rhino's 15-track *Waxing Off: Delicious Vinyl's Greatest Hits* doesn't contain all of the label's biggest hits (Young MC's "Principal's Office" is conspicuously missing, for instance), it does provide an excellent overview of the label's peak years of the late '80s/early '90s, while touching often enough on highlights from the late '90s to illustrate that the label hadn't lost its touch—times simply had changed, and Delicious Vinyl's deliberately, cheerfully quirky vibe had seemed more underground than ever. This collection captures all of that, and while it's not perfect, its songs have more character and personality than much of the hip-hop of the '90s—just like the label itself. *—Stephen Thomas Erlewine*

We Came From Beyond / Oct. 9, 2001 / Razor & Tie ♦♦♦

Providing an alternative to the slick nonsense of contemporary rap radio, Mike N.'s *We Came From Beyond* radio show on college station KXLU in Los Angeles has been churning out an altogether different hip-hop groove for 13 years. Mike N.'s show is an MC-driven enterprise and among the finest guides to the vast universe of hip-hop that's ignored by commercial radio. But this compilation of unreleased, rare, and exclusive tracks isn't the best introduction to *We Came From Beyond*. There are a few dope tracks, but in general the record doesn't live up to the show's best moments, when Mike N. might drop six amazing songs in a row by artists no one has ever heard of. "Liquor-land" by Mighty Casey is a goofy, fun song, as is "Doo Doo (In the Pot)" by Fat Hed & DJ Fred C, while "Unified Rebelution" is an early Jurassic 5 tune showcasing the L.A. act's talents. Mike N. also drops a fine remix of the Beastie Boys' "Pass the Mic." But Dilated Peoples' "Weed Vs. Beer (You Make the Choice)" is not one of their best tunes, and selections from Eyedea, Pep Love, and Blackalicious are immediately forgettable. The feel of the record is totally underground hip-hop, though these aren't the best examples of that scene. —*Adam Bregman*

We're All in the Same Gang / Jun. 12, 1990 / Warner Brothers ✦✦✦
In 1988, violence at rap concerts and black-on-black crime inspired Boogie Down Productions leader KRS-One to found the Stop the Violence Movement and produce the all-star single "Self Destruction." That project was dominated by East Coast rappers, and some Californians wondered why more West Coast rappers hadn't been asked to participate. They reasoned that because black-on-black crime was as serious a problem in L.A. and Oakland as it was in New York, more West Coast MCs should have been part of Stop the Violence. So in 1990, some of California's top rappers formed the West Coast Rap All-Stars and recorded *We're All in the Same Gang*, which became California's equivalent of Stop the Violence. The list of participants is impressive—Dr. Dre, Quincy Jones III (son of the famous Quincy Jones), and Bilal Bashir are among the producers, and the rappers include Ice-T, Tone-Loc, MC Hammer, King Tee, Young MC, Def Jef, and members of N.W.A, Digital Underground, Oaktown's 357, and Above the Law. Though some of the material is fun and escapist, the CD's overriding theme is a sociopolitical one—inner-city residents are encouraged to unite and put an end to black-on-black crime. The most compelling tracks include the title song, the South Central Posse's "Livin' in South Central L.A.," and M.C. Supreme's "Black in America." Although generally enjoyable, the album on the whole isn't the all-out gem it could have been—some of the songs are excellent, while others are merely decent. But while *We're All in the Same Gang* isn't perfect, its historic value is undeniable. —*Alex Henderson*

Well Connected / May 11, 1999 / Soul Town ✦✦✦
Soul Town's *Well Connected* contains second-tier cuts and also-ran singles from such stars as Too Short, Luniz, C-Bo, Flesh N Bone, Richie Rich, B-Legit, and Snoop Dogg, plus tracks from such underground and unknown rappers as 3X Krazy, Black C, and Whoridas. There's some good material here, especially from the well-known artists, but on the whole, it's too uneven to be of interest to most listeners. —*Stephen Thomas Erlewine*

West Coast Bad Boyz, Vol. 1 / Jul. 22, 1997 / Priority ✦✦✦
West Coast Bad Boyz, Vol. 1 was the first significant shot from Master P, the mastermind behind the South's fiercely independent gangsta label No Limit. Master P was the executive producer of *West Coast Bad Boyz, Vol. 1*, organizing the entire project, reigning in big names like Too Short, finding unknown rappers and defining the sound, which is essentially cheaply produced G-funk. Nobody on the compilation is a particularly gifted rapper, nor is the music original or even interesting (it occasionally is terrible, as a matter of fact), but *West Coast Bad Boyz, Vol. 1*, along with its successor, illustrates what some hip-hoppers mean by "keeping it real"—i.e., keep turning out the same hardcore rap, without any musical or lyrical innovations. And, if you agree with that viewpoint, *West Coast Bad Boyz, Vol. 1* probably is a record for you. If not, it's a mighty rough ride. —*Leo Stanley*

West Coast Collection, Vol. 1 / Mar. 18, 1997 / Scotti Bros. ✦✦✦
West Coast Collection, Vol. 1 contains 12 sanitized versions of Californian hip-hop hits from the late '80s and early '90s, including classics by Tone-Loc ("Wild Thing") and Young MC ("Bust A Move"). Although the song selection is fairly uneven—there are cuts by stars like Kid Frost, E-40, and Spice 1, but also forgotten tracks by Rodney O & Joe Cooley and the Conscious Daughters—it's an entertaining listen, especially for casual fans who just want a couple of hits, not a comprehensive overview. —*Stephen Thomas Erlewine*

West Coast Gambinos / Oct. 26, 1999 / Celeb ✦✦✦
The *West Coast Gambinos* compilation practically lives up to its title, considering the wealth of rapping talent in assembly—B Real, Sen Dog, Frost, Mellow Man, Southpark Mexican, Latino Velvet, Jay Tee, Lawless Click, and several others. Tracks like "It Ain't Easy," "How We Ride," "Cuban Connection," and "Chicano Gambinos" are easy-rolling West Coast joints with plenty of attitude and great trading on rhymes from the cast. —*Keith Farley*

West Coast Kings / Nov. 28, 2000 / Eastside Smokes ✦✦
This is a compilation album of hardcore West Coast rap artists, including two tracks by the late Tupac and plenty of other appearances by people such as Triple J, Funky Aztecs, Assassin, Coolio Da Undadogg, Lil-One, and Prodeje. There are some decent cuts on this album, but quite a few slow spots and questionable deliveries. For those really into that West Coast gangsta vibe, this might be just what they're looking for, and at 72 minutes it's a lot of music. —*Brad Mills*

The West Coast Never Dies / 1999 / Deff Trapp ✦✦✦
An album of collaborations between producer Trapp (the head of Deff Trapp Records) and West Coast rappers including Mack 10, Kurupt, Too Short, Daz Dillinger, E-40, and Spice 1, *The West Coast Never Dies* is a solid album charting the coast's answer to Southern players and East Coast hardcore. Trapp's production is excellent, halfway between the slicker end of No Limit-style bounce and the laid-back end of West Coast G-funk (complete with liquid bass lines and mid-tempo hand claps) on the best tracks, "A Touch Away" by Mack 10, "Don't Go Back" by E-40, and "The Ghetto" by Bay Area veteran Too Short. There aren't many innovative techniques, but for rap fans looking for a return to the glory days of Dre and Snoop, *The West Coast Never Dies* is a great response. —*Keith Farley*

West Coast Rap: The First Dynasty, Vol. 1 / 1992 / Rhino ✦✦✦✦✦
Although it contains too many obscurities and novelties to make it absolutely essential for casual listeners, *West Coast Rap: The First Dynasty, Vol. 1* is an excellent compilation of early-'80s hip-hop from the likes of Ice-T ("The Coldest Rap"), Egyptian Lover ("Egypt, Egypt"), L.A. Dream Team ("Rockberry Jam"), World Class Wreckin' Cru ("Slice"), 2 Live Crew ("2 Live"), and Bobby Jimmy & the Critters ("We Like Ugly Women"). Only Timex Social Club's "Rumors" stands out as a stone-cold classic, but the rest of the record is first-rate old school rap, and worth the time of any serious hip-hop fan. —*Stephen Thomas Erlewine*

West Coast Rap: The First Dynasty, Vol. 2 / 1992 / Rhino ✦✦✦✦
Like its predecessor, *West Coast Rap: The First Dynasty, Vol. 2* is short on indisputable classics, yet the overall quality of the material is quite high. Over the course of 13 tracks, *West Coast Rap* runs through several funky old school highlights from the likes of Ice-T ("Body Rock"), D.J. Matrix ("Feel My Bass"), Kid Frost ("Rough Cut"), L.A. Dream Team ("Calling on the Dream Team"), Darkstar ("Sexybaby"), and Egyptian Lover ("Freak-A-Holic"). Most of this is simply party music, but it's good party music, and the collection is worthwhile for any devoted rap listener, even though its momentum occasionally sags. —*Stephen Thomas Erlewine*

☆ **West Coast Rap: The First Dynasty, Vol. 3** / 1992 / Rhino ✦✦✦✦✦
Like the other two collections of *West Coast Rap: The First Dynasty, Vol. 3* promises more than it delivers, since it is short on genuine classics and long on novelties. Despite its flaws, *Vol 3*, like the rest of the *West Coast Rap* series, remains one of the best old school hip-hop compilations on the market, since it was put together with some care and the overall quality of the music is quite high, even if certain names (Ice-T, Egyptian Lover, Kid Frost, 2 Live Crew, Bobby, Jimmy & the Critters) are a little too familiar from the disc's predecessors. Nevertheless, there are enough solid cuts to make this a strong addition to any comprehensive hip-hop collection. —*Stephen Thomas Erlewine*

What's Up? Rap Hits of the '90s / 1995 / Rhino ✦✦✦✦✦
Although Rhino was hardly the only label that was putting out rap compilations in the '90s, it's safe to say that no label put more thought into its rap collections than Rhino. Focusing primarily on major rap singles of the early '90s, *What's Up?* is impressive not only because of its abundance of excellent material but also because of its attractive packaging and comprehensive, detailed liner notes. If you didn't know a lot about the selections and the artists before acquiring the 1995 CD, you could learn a lot reading Shannita Williams' informative essay. Instead of focusing on underground rap, Rhino offers mostly songs that crossed over to R&B and pop audiences, including Monie Love's "It's a Shame (My Sister)," Marky Mark's "Wild Side," Digital Underground's "Kiss You Back" and Salt-N-Pepa's "Do You Want Me." You didn't have to be down with rap's hardcore to be aware of MC Brains' "Oochie Coochie" or Jazzy Jeff & the Fresh Prince's "Boom! Shake The Room." A few of the tunes that Rhino includes are inappropriate—Snap's "Rhythm is a Dancer" is dance music instead of rap, and TLC's "Ain't 2 Proud to Beg" and

Another Bad Creation's "Iesha" are essentially R&B (although R&B with a strong hip-hop influence). This isn't to say that those songs aren't enjoyable—they're just out of place on a rap compilation. Nonetheless, *What's Up?* is a pleasing collection that can serve as a nice introduction to early-'90s rap. —*Alex Henderson*

Wide Angles / Dec. 6, 1999 / Blindside ✦✦✦✦
Wide Angles is an excellent collection of mostly cerebral underground/alternative rap, showcasing a number of established and (predominantly) up-and-coming hip-hoppers who have obviously spent time honing and woodshedding their lyrical skills. De La Soul appears with Truth Enola, and there's a contribution from heavyweights Mos Def and Talib Kweli. For the most part, however, *Wide Angles* concentrates on lesser-knowns, and overall, they acquit themselves well. —*Steve Huey*

Wild Pitch Classics / Jul. 12, 1994 / Capitol ✦✦✦
Gang Starr is the biggest name to be found on '80s/'90s hip-hop label Wild Pitch's roster, but they had to move to a bigger home to do their best work. Instead, look to a handful of singles—Main Source's "Looking at the Front Door" and "Fakin the Funk" and UMC's "Blue Cheese" are good places to start—for the real deal on this patchy compilation. Not quite rap classics, but still pretty representative of the era's indie scene. —*Michael Gallucci*

Wild Style / Aug. 19, 1997 / Rhino ✦✦✦✦✦
Wild Style largely went unseen upon its 1983 release, but its soundtrack became one of the key records of early-'80s hip-hop, providing rappers a treasure trove of beats and rhymes. None of the cuts on *Wild Style* became crossover hits, but the songs became underground staples, inspiring new rappers and offering rhythms that were sampled over the years. Although much of this music now sounds dated, the rhymes and rhythms remain exciting, illustrating why *Wild Style* was one of the cornerstones of underground hip-hop in the '80s. —*Leo Stanley*

Wild Wild West / Jun. 15, 1999 / Interscope ✦✦✦
It's easy to complain about big-budget soundtracks to big-budget blockbusters, whining that they're as calculated as the film to reach a certain audience. That's always true—as much as it is true of the film itself—since whenever there's a lot of money involved, a certain amount of calculation is inevitable. The key is whether the artists behind the expensive machinations have enough charm and showbiz flair to make you forget the calculation and just smile, thrilled that you're being taken for a ride. That's the case with the soundtrack for the Barry Sonnenfeld-directed, Will Smith/Kevin Kline showcase *Wild Wild West*—it's shiny and commercial, but it has enough craft and humor to keep it entertaining, even during the slow spots. Like in the film itself, Smith takes the center stage, once again proving that he's an entertainer of enormous charm. His title track—which shamelessly borrows from Stevie Wonder and Kool Moe Dee (who also is on the cut, along with Dru Hill)—is giddy, irresistable summer fun that sets the pace for a record that feels breezy even though it clocks in at an hour. Sure, there are some slow moments on the record, but not enough to bog down the momentum set by such highlights as BLACKstreet's seductive "Confused," Enrique Iglesias' appealingly lightweight "Bailamos," Dr. Dre & Eminem's cartoonishly menacing "Bad Guys Always Die," Faith Evans' smooth "Mailman," and Slick Rick's typically stunning "I Sparkle." These may not rank as major moments for any of these artists, but they're all entertaining and elevate *Wild Wild West* to a fine summer party album. —*Stephen Thomas Erlewine*

Winners of the World's Worst Rap Competition / 1998 / Teach ✦✦✦
This 7" record swings in two different listening directions. For one thing, this is one of the funniest records since Robin Williams' *A Night at the Met*. On the other hand, this is the most painful listen from an act who couldn't even be loosely described as "hip-hop." Basically, this suburban hip-hop act called Black Tea recorded a demo tape on what sounds like a four-track recorder and released it only to have some wise guy bootleg it and re-release it under the title of *Winner of the World's Worst Rap Competition*. Indeed this is. If it isn't the choppy and blatantly stolen beats, it's the stuttering vocalist who takes himself way too seriously. This has to be heard to be believed. —*Mike DaRonco*

Xen Cuts / Sep. 19, 2000 / Ninja Tune ✦✦✦
Commemorating its tenth anniversary in similar fashion to the festivities at Warp during 1999, Ninja Tune Records celebrated with a three-disc compilation that spotlights, not necessarily the greatest, but definitely the most overlooked moments in the label's history. Founded in 1990 by Coldcut's Jonathan More and Matt Black in response to increasing frustration with major labels, Ninja Tune only earned notice after a few years of mediocre sampladelic records. When the enterprise really exploded in 1995, however, it soon spawned an excellent roster of artists from all sorts of beat-oriented camps: trip-hop (Funki Porcini, Up Bustle & Out), drum'n'bass (Amon Tobin, Animals on Wheels), and hip-hop (DJ Vadim, the Herbaliser, Kid Koala), as well as more ambient techno (Irresistible Force, Neotropic) via the Ntone sub-label. *Xen Cuts* presents almost 50 tracks spread over three hours, and the focus on previously unreleased (or unavailable on compact disc) material makes for a compilation of many pleasant surprises. Remixers provide many of the highlights, including Jimpster (Irresistible Force's "Nepalese Bliss"), Squarepusher (East Flatbush Project's "Tried by 12"), Roots Manuva (Amon Tobin's "Saboteur"), Fourtet (Cinematic Orchestra's "Channel 1 Suite"), and John McEntire (the label classic "More Beats & Pieces" by Coldcut). Anyone seeking an overview that hits every high will be disappointed—there's barely an original single to be found on this entire collection, despite the preponderance of B sides—but Ninja Tune exercised such remarkable quality control during the mid- to late '90s that it barely shows. —*John Bush*

Yo! MTV Raps!, Vol. 1 / May 25, 1989 / Jive ✦✦✦✦✦

Yo! MTV Raps!, Vol. 2 / 1991 / Jive ✦✦✦
This is the second collection of cuts culled from the television show. —*Ron Wynn*

Yo! MTV Raps: Hits / Jun. 24, 1997 / Def Jam ✦✦✦✦
Released shortly after MTV decided to pull the plug on the show, *Yo! MTV Raps: Hits* is a fine collection of some of the biggest hip-hop hits of the '90s. Concentrating on pop crossovers, but throwing in a couple of hip-hop hits like Lost Boyz' "Jeeps, Lex, Coups, Bimaz and Benz" for good measure, the album is an entertaining cross-section of mid-'90s rap, running the gamut from gangsta to jazz-rap. Not everything here is well known—the Method Man soundtrack obscurity "The Riddler" is here instead of "I'll Be There for You/You're All I Need To Get By," his number-one duet with Mary J. Blige—and there are a few dogs scattered throughout, but Wu-Tang Clan, A Tribe Called Quest, LL Cool J, Tupac, Lil' Kim, Junior M.A.F.I.A., Foxy Brown, and Outkast make *Yo! MTV Raps: Hits* a compilation worth acquiring. —*Stephen Thomas Erlewine*

Young Southern Playaz, Vol. 1 / Aug. 27, 1996 / Priority ✦✦✦
Young Southern Playaz, Vol. 1 collects a number of underground singles by developing gangsta rappers like DJ Screw ("Screwed Up Click"), Slicc & Ghetto Twinz ("Down and Out"), Alkatraz Syndicate ("Playa Hataz Lullabye"), Gangsta Pat ("Real Niggaz Tote Glocks"), and Young Lo, who has the only genuine radio hit with "Serious." For aficionados and the adventerous, *Young Southern Playaz, Vol. 1* is an interesting listen, but there aren't enough first-rate cuts to make it a worthwhile purchase for anyone else. —*Stephen Thomas Erlewine*

Young Southern Playaz, Vol. 2 / Oct. 7, 1997 / Priority ✦✦✦
Like its predecessor, *Young Southern Playaz, Vol. 2* collects 14 underground singles from developing gangsta rappers like DJ Squeeky ("Surrounded by Haters"), Juicy J ("Respect"), Boo Tha Boss Playa ("Check Out Time"), Bolo ("Ful-Feeling"), Crooked Eye "Q" ("Hustlers Don't Die"), Kaz'e ("Life or Death"), Lil' Milt ("Cash Flow"), and Tommy Wright III ("Hell on Earth"). The collection is primarily for listeners with a deep interest in Southern hip-hop, not for casual listeners, but for those aficionados, this may be an interesting journey. —*Stephen Thomas Erlewine*

Young Southern Playaz, Vol. 3 / Aug. 29, 2000 / Forty West ✦✦
Volume 3 in the series *Young Southern Playaz* features 14 tracks capturing hardcore highlights from the Southern gangsta rap underground, including Big Ed the Assassin's "We Represent," Point Blank's "Go Live," Al Kapone's "Innocent," Gangsta Pat's "Shootin' on Narcs," and Thugz From da Southside's "Whatcha Claimin'." While this compilation is bold, it's geared toward hardcore fans of the genre rather than casual listeners. —*Al Campbell*

Essays

Old School Rap

Old school rap is one of those terms that can mean different things to different people. In the 21st century, a hip-hopper who is in his/her teens or 20s might think of Run-D.M.C., the Fat Boys, and other MCs who were big in the mid-'80s as old school rappers—they certainly had a very different rhyming style from Eminem, Jay-Z, and other rap stars of the 2000s. But to hip-hop's founding fathers, old school rap isn't Run-D.M.C. or LL Cool J—those artists were part of hip-hop's second wave, and they didn't become popular until 1984 or 1985. To those who are old enough to remember hip-hop's first wave, old school rap means pre-Run-D.M.C. artists who emerged in the late '70s or very early '80s—artists like Kurtis Blow, Grandmaster Flash & the Furious Five, the Sugarhill Gang, the Treacherous Three, Afrika Bambaataa, and Kool DJ Herc. Those were hip-hop's founding fathers—the architects of early hip-hop—and they are the main focus of this essay on rap's old school.

Run-D.M.C. have often been described as the Beatles of Rap, and that is an excellent analogy because they took rap to another level just as the Beatles took rock & roll to another level (both commercially and creatively). With the rise of Run-D.M.C., the Fat Boys, Whodini, the Beastie Boys, LL Cool J, and other second-wave rappers, hip-hop went from having a small cult following (mostly on the East Coast) to being a huge international phenomenon. Those artists gave us a lot of reason to believe that rap was here to stay, much like Beatlemania made rock & roll even more popular and convinced a lot of people that it would be a permanent part of the musical landscape. If Run-D.M.C. were the Beatles of Rap, pre-Run-D.M.C. favorites like Flash, Blow, and Bambaataa were the hip-hop equivalent of Little Richard, Chuck Berry, Elvis Presley, Carl Perkins, Fats Domino, and Bill Haley & the Comets. Rap's old school era—roughly 1976-1982, give or take a year—was to rap what the 1954-1961 period was to rock & roll's pre-Beatlemania, pre-British Invasion era.

Rapping didn't start with hip-hop's old school; the Last Poets, Gil Scott-Heron, and the X-rated comedian Rudy Ray Moore were talking and rhyming over a beat in the early '70s. Although Scott-Heron was a singer first and foremost, he was rapping—not singing—when he recorded "No Knock" and "Whitey on the Moon" in the early '70s. There were times when, in the '40s, jazz legend Louis Armstrong (who was primarily a trumpeter/singer) introduced his band members in a rapping, rhyming style—and some classic country-rock had what was essentially rapping (Commander Cody's 1972 smash "Hot Rod Lincoln," for example). But when hip-hop got started in the late '70s, it was more than vocalists occasionally rapping instead of singing—it was a genre in which the vocalists did nothing but rap and the DJs provided the beats that they needed. Jazz and country had the occasional rapping vocal during the pre-hip-hop years, but with the hip-hop explosion of the late '70s, rappers were running the show.

According to Kurtis Blow, hip-hop got started around 1976, when he had his first club gigs; Grandmaster Flash & the Furious Five began working together the following year. And the birthplace of old school rap was New York City—specifically, Harlem (which is part of Uptown Manhattan) and the South Bronx. Those were the places that gave us hip-hop pioneers like Flash, Blow, Melle Mel, Kool DJ Herc, the Treacherous Three (which included Kool Moe Dee before he went solo), Afrika Bambaataa, the Funky Four Plus One, Grandmaster Caz, Dr. Jeckyll & Mr. Hyde, and Love Bug Starsky. During rap's second wave, Queens and Brooklyn became equally important—Queens with Run-D.M.C. and LL Cool J and Brooklyn with Whodini and the Fat Boys. But in the beginning, hip-hop was dominated by Harlem and the Boogie Down Bronx. However, one of old school rap's best-known groups, the Sugarhill

Gang, was from northern New Jersey just outside of the Big Apple. And for many radio listeners, the Sugarhill Gang was an introduction to rap. Released in 1979, the group's debut single, "Rappers Delight," was a huge national hit. The year 1979 also saw the release of Flash's "Superappin'" and Blow's first single, "Christmas Rapping." That year, Blow became the first rapper to sign with a major label (Mercury/PolyGram), and in 1980, he had a big hit with his second single "The Breaks" (which reached number four on *Billboard*'s R&B singles chart).

But unlike Blow, most old school MCs recorded for small independent labels. "Rappers Delight" was released by Sugarhill Records, a small indie that was as important to early hip-hop as Blue Note and Prestige were to jazz and Motown and Stax were to '60s soul. Not to be confused with a folk label that is also called Sugar Hill Records, the Sugarhill described in this essay was run by Sylvia Robinson—a veteran singer/producer who had her first taste of commercial success in the '50s, when she was half of the male/female duo Mickey & Sylvia (best known for their 1957 hit "Love Is Strange"). As a solo artist in the early '70s, Robinson favored a sleek, ultra-sexy style of Northern soul; her biggest hit from that period was the luscious "Pillow Talk." But by the late '70s, Robinson was more of a producer/A&R person than a singer, and she was among the first people to document old school hip-hop. In the late '70s and early '80s, hip-hop was Sugar Hill Records' bread and butter—several years before Russell Simmons was leading Def Jam Records with producer Rick Rubin, Robinson was overseeing Sugar Hill releases by Grandmaster Flash, Super Wolf, Spoonie Gee, and the Funky Four Plus One. Sugar Hill Records was also the home of the Sequence—hip-hop's first important all-female rap group—and Lady B, whose "To the Beat, Y'all" was the first rap single by a female solo artist. Unlike most of the artists who recorded for Sugar Hill, Lady B lived in Philadelphia, where she made a name for herself as a radio DJ—not a rapper. In various interviews with this journalist, Lady B has tended to put down "To the Beat, Y'all" and has insisted that she was never much of a rapper; nonetheless, "To the Beat, Y'all" was an important single for its time. And Lady B can honestly say that she was a female rapper before MC Lyte, Queen Latifah, Roxanne Shanté, or the Real Roxanne.

During rap's old school era, the lyrics tended to be fun and frivolous—even silly at times (much like disco). Hip-hoppers have always spent a lot of time boasting about their rhyming skills and attacking "sucker MCs" (rival rappers). But compared to many of today's gangsta rap and dirty South lyrics, the boasting and dissing of 1979, 1980, and 1981 seems relatively tame. There were microphone battles back then—historically, MCs have been very competitive and viewed rapping as a type of musical sportsmanship. But overall, rap's pre-1982 lyrics were fun and innocuous. The classic that did so much to push rap lyrics in a much more challenging direction was Grandmaster Flash & the Furious Five's 1982 hit "The Message," a disturbing, sobering piece of social commentary that vividly described the problems of the inner city. Before "The Message," old school rappers usually talked about sucker MCs, shaking your booty, and waving your hands in the air like you just don't care—"The Message" talked about "Rats in the front room/Roaches in the back/Junkies in the alley with a baseball bat." Thanks to "The Message," it became fashionable for MCs to write sociopolitical lyrics—that gem paved the way for the message raps that Run-D.M.C., Public Enemy, Boogie Down Productions, Ice-T, and numerous others subsequently provided. "The Message" was old school rap, but it had a major impact on rap's second wave.

The year 1982 was a year of transition for hip-hop—the old school era was reaching the end, and rap's second-wave was getting ready to take over. Whodini (one of the most popular second-wave rap groups) recorded their first album in 1982, and the success of Run-D.M.C., LL Cool J, and the Fat Boys was just around the corner. In 1985 and 1986, those artists were considered cutting edge, and pioneers like Flash and Kurtis Blow were considered old-fashioned. One of the few old school rappers who was still considered cutting edge in the mid- to late '80s was Kool Moe Dee, who went solo after the breakup of the Treacherous Three. But Kool was the exception instead of the rule; few old school rappers were still having major hits in 1988 and 1989.

In the 21st century, the old school rap recordings of the late '70s and early '80s sound very dated—for that matter, "Rappers Delight" and "Christmas Rapping" were sounding very dated in 1984. But "dated" doesn't mean that something lacks quality—only that it was obviously recorded during a particular era. Hip-hop has evolved considerably since its early years; it will no doubt continue to evolve in the future. And when one looks back on rap's history, it is important to remember that Blow, Flash, Bambaataa, and other old school pioneers were the ones who got the ball rolling.

Recommended Recordings:

Kurtis Blow, *Kurtis Blow* (Mercury)

Kurtis Blow, *The Best of Kurtis Blow* (Mercury)

Grandmaster Flash & the Furious Five, *Message From Beat Street: The Best of Grandmaster Flash* (Rhino)

Various Artists, *The Sugar Hill Records Story* (Rhino)

Various Artists, *Kurtis Blow Presents: The History of Rap, Vol. 2* (Rhino)

Various Artists, *Genius of Rap* (Island)

Various Artists, *Hip-Hop Heritage, Vol. 1* (Jive)

Various Artists, *Rapmasters: The Best of the Street* (Priority)

—Alex Henderson

Electro

Although a mere historical blip on the evolutionary map of urban dance-based music, electro sits at the apex of many of its most widespread and significant forms, including rap, techno, jungle, freestyle, and bass music. A curious fusion of '70s funk and disco, German and Japanese techno-pop, and everything from the futurism of Alvin Toffler to kung-fu movies, video games, and the Smurfs, electro has proven to be one of the most important and influential components of the ongoing development of dance-based experimental electronic music. As the first style of American breakbeat to utilize the drum machine as its central rhythmic component, electro has worked its influence into a staggering range of styles—from Run-D.M.C., Egyptian Lover, and Ice Cube to Madonna, Nine Inch Nails, the Black Dog, and Bochum Welt.

Electro's proper heyday was the period 1982-1988, following the explosion of early hip-hop culture in a number of American inner cities. Initially designed as breakdance music, with distinctive drum patterns modeled, in part, on the style of DJing developed by early hip-hop DJs such as Kool Herc and Grandmaster Flash (which involved the manual looping, using two turntables and a mixer, of drum breaks from funk, soul, jazz, and rock records), electro's immediate forebearers included Kraftwerk, Gary Numan, and Japan's Yellow Magic Orchestra. Kraftwerk's "Trans-Europe Express" was the blueprint for Soul Sonic Force's legendary first-blast "Planet Rock," and early cuts by Man Parrish, the Jonzun Crew, Grandmaster Flash in New York, and Juan Atkins and Rick Davis in Detroit (among others) set the tone for many of the records that would follow: a strong backbeat, often with sparse rapping (particularly through a vocoder or talk box), scratching, odd electronics, and frequent rhythm breaks.

Although electro began almost immediately to evolve into various other styles—rap (through Run-D.M.C., LL Cool J, Schoolly D, and Ice-T, among many others), techno (Atkins' Cybotron and Model 500 projects), Miami bass and freestyle (Maggotron, Freestyle Dynamix II, and Trinere), industrial (Front 242, Ministry)—the mid- to late '80s was probably the music's height of popularity. And while the increasing availability of samplers and MIDI-encoded devices (both of which offered a wider palette of sound and creative possibility) meant many grew bored with the relatively static musicality of electro's machine aesthetic, the style continued to grow and evolve, particularly in Florida and California, where artists as diverse as "Pretty" Tony Butler, Omar Santana, and Dynamix II in Miami and Ice-T, the Unknown DJ, and the Egyptian Lover in L.A. were taking the style in new directions. With Butler, Dynamix, and Santana, that involved an increasing emphasis on the low-end (Miami bass) and the marriage of electro with Latin rhythms, female vocals, and simple melodies (freestyle). L.A. artists such as Ice-T and the Egyptian Lover were exploring the lyrical potential of rap while remaining true to the

beatbox (a devotion that continues to inform the '90s G-funk styles of Dr. Dre, Tupac, Snoop Dogg, and Spice 1).

As rap took center stage in the latter '80s as the musical form of choice among inner-city (and suburban) youth, electro began dying out, carrying on in the bass and freestyle of Miami, New York, and L.A., but for the large part only of interest to historians and the odd collector. That's begun to change, however, as the innovations of U.K. and German experimental electronic artists have made their electro roots clear. Artists as diverse as the Jedi Knights (Tom Middleton and Mark Pritchard of Global Communication/ Link), Aphex Twin, Phil Klein, Autechre, Atom Heart, and Biochip C. have built on electro's legacy in their own contexts, taking the hitting machine breaks of the music's early years and combining it with a digital aesthetic and increasing musicality that have refired its relevance. American musicians, too—from Tupac to the Bass Kittens, "Mad" Mike, and Drexciya—are rediscovering the roots of techno and hip-hop in the electronic breakbeat, and have updated the sound for a '90s sensibility.

Although the history's still being written, a number of good introductions to electro's past and present exist. Rhino Records' *Street Jams: Electric Funk* is a four-CD box set covering many of the bases of the early electro sound; from New York and Miami to Detroit, L.A., and beyond. The U.K.-based Beechwood label (instrumental in bringing the American electro sound to British audiences as it was happening, through their Streetsounds compilations) released a best-of from their earlier compilations in 1995, titled *Streetsounds: The Best of Electro, Vol. 1*, which reaches even deeper into electro's early underground to unearth some truly hard-to-find material. In 1998, Tommy Boy released *The Perfect Beats*, an excellent four-volume set of electro/ dance classics that rescued many worthy obscurities from the vaults. On the new-style tip, Submerge's *Origins of a Sound* is a good introduction to the new-style Detroit electro promulgated by artists such as AUX 88, Drexciya, "Mad" Mike, and Will Web. Finally, the It label brought U.K. electro DJ Marco Arnaldi in to compile *It: Electro*, a CD and double LP combining early tracks with more up-to-the-minute material.

New York

The history of New York electro is intimately tied up with that city's role in the birth and evolution of hip-hop. Consequently, tracks by early Big Apple innovators such as the Jonzun Crew, Man Parrish, the Soul Sonic Force and Marley Marl are dominated by a vocal presence and a more party-oriented vibe. Still, the musicianship (many of these groups employed traditional instruments side by side with electronics, even playing live) is top notch and tracks such as "Hip-Hop Be-Bop (Don't Stop)" and "Boogie Down Bronx" by Man Parrish, "Space Is the Place" and "We Are the Jonzun Crew" by the Jonzun Crew, and "The Party Scene" by the Russell Brothers remain watermarks of the style.

Detroit

Like the Detroit techno into which it almost immediately evolved, early Detroit electro emphasized melody along with rhythm, with tight beats and bass lines and melancholic, minor key sweeps the dominant features on still-classic cuts such as "Clear," "Cosmic Cars," "Technicolor," and "R9." Although most of these tracks were the product of one person—Juan Atkins—the influence of peers and collaborators such as Derrick May, Rick Davis, and Kevin "Reese" Saunderson should not be underestimated.

Los Angeles

Like New York, the L.A. electro scene was party oriented, with cuts by Egyptian Lover, the Unknown DJ, the Wreckin' Crew, and Uncle Jamm's Army emphasizing skills on the cut, the mike, or the dancefloor in sparse, often electronic raps. B-boy boasting aside, however, the L.A. sound (neatly expressed in label names such as Freak Beat, Techno Hop, and Techno Kut) was most concerned with adapting new technology to the emerging hip-hop sound, and beat-jacking tracks such as "Jam the Box," "What's Your Sign" by UJA, "808 Beats" and "Tibetan Jam" by the Unknown DJ, and "Egypt, Egypt" and "Dance" by the Egyptian Lover are hard to match for rhythmic innovation.

Miami Bass/Freestyle

Freestyle and Miami Bass are two related styles with common roots in the mid-'80s tracks of Omar Santana, Dynamix II, and Tony Butler, the latter of whose Music Specialist label was the organizational center of Miami electro. Bass music, for its part, is as its name suggests: deep, resonant bass (the type of music heard booming from mini-trucks and tricked out low riders), backed by tight machine bass and not much else. Freestyle is Miami electro's dance

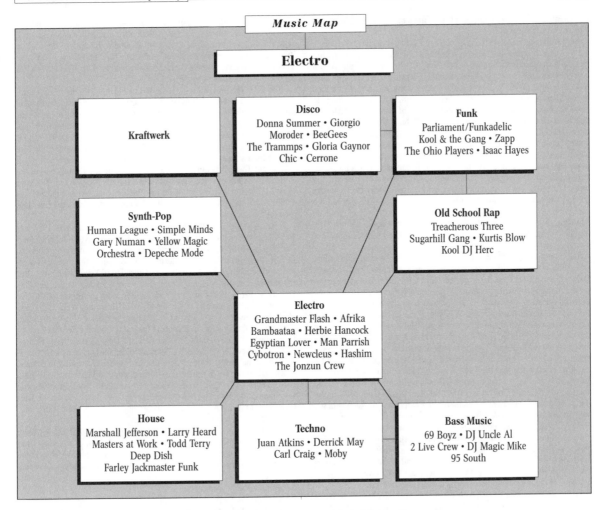

Music Map

Electro

Kraftwerk

Disco
Donna Summer • Giorgio
Moroder • BeeGees
The Trammps • Gloria Gaynor
Chic • Cerrone

Funk
Parliament/Funkadelic
Kool & the Gang • Zapp
The Ohio Players • Isaac Hayes

Synth-Pop
Human League • Simple Minds
Gary Numan • Yellow Magic
Orchestra • Depeche Mode

Old School Rap
Treacherous Three
Sugarhill Gang • Kurtis Blow
Kool DJ Herc

Electro
Grandmaster Flash • Afrika
Bambaataa • Herbie Hancock
Egyptian Lover • Man Parrish
Cybotron • Newcleus • Hashim
The Jonzun Crew

House
Marshall Jefferson • Larry Heard
Masters at Work • Todd Terry
Deep Dish
Farley Jackmaster Funk

Techno
Juan Atkins • Derrick May
Carl Craig • Moby

Bass Music
69 Boyz • DJ Uncle Al
2 Live Crew • DJ Magic Mike
95 South

music descendent, with Latin percussion, simple four-part melodies, and bubblegum vocals adding a pop dimension to the music's funky edge.

Techno Bass

Although electro never died out in Detroit's underground (Motor City block parties still rock "Technicolor" and "Get Some" to this day), by and large the musicians the city produced were primarily involved in the four-on-the-floor aesthetic of house and techno. Partly ideological, partly descriptive, techno bass was an attempt by a core of Detroit dance music artists to realign techno with its breakbeat roots, and was mostly the vision of the Direct Beat/430 West labels, whose artists include purveyors of the style such as AUX 88, Will Web, Posatronix, and DJ Dijital, although other prominent artists such as Drexciya and Underground Resistance have been just as active in reinvigorating electronic breaks.

Neo-Electro

Largely a product of the U.K. dance music media's more colonialist tendencies, neo-electro was coined in 1994 to signify the collective output of artists such as the Jedi Knights, Elecktroids, and Drexciya, and labels such as Clear, Evolution, and (aspects of) Warp. The tenuous connection of much of the music's actual stylistic attributes to electro notwithstanding, many of these artists were clearly inspired by the music's original machine aesthetic, with most of them having grown up listening to it. The real electro revival, however, largely took place through smaller, more obscure labels such as Dodge, Panic Trax, Immortal, Overexposed, Direct Beat, Transparent Sound, and the odd B side or 12-inch release on experimental techno staples such as Force Inc., Eidesche, Sahko, and Underground Resistance.

Recommended Recordings:
Various Artists, *Street Jams: Electric Funk, Vols. 1-4* (Rhino)
Various Artists, *The Perfect Beats, Vols. 1-4* (Tommy Boy)
Cybotron, *Clear* (Fantasy)
Freestyle, *Don't Stop the Rock* (Hot Productions)
Man Parrish, *The Best of Man Parrish: Heatstroke* (Hot Productions)
Dynamix II, *Electro Bass Megamix: 1985 to Present* (Joey Boy)
Various Artists, *Origins of a Sound* (Submerge)
Various Artists, *Techno Bass: The Mission* (Direct Beat)

—Sean Cooper

Bass Music

When rap fans think of Florida-style bass music, they think of sexually explicit lyrics and fast, hyper, ultra-energetic tracks—in other words, the main ingredients of a 2 Live Crew album. Bass music doesn't necessarily have to have X-rated lyrics; DJ Magic Mike, one of bass' founding fathers, isn't known for inundating audiences with raunchy lyrics (which are known as "booty rhymes" in the Southern United States). But whether the lyrics are sexually explicit, mildly risqué, or relatively clean (or even if a bass tune doesn't have any lyrics at all), bass is straight-up party music and takes dead aim at dance clubs—specifically, black dance clubs of the deep South, where bass has enjoyed its greatest popularity. And even though bass hasn't had much acceptance from hardcore hip-hoppers in Northeastern cities like New York,

Philadelphia, and Boston, millions of bass albums have been sold below the Mason-Dixon line.

Bass artists don't necessarily have to live in Florida; some have come from other Southern states like Georgia (especially Atlanta) and Alabama. But Florida is considered the capitol of bass, and it is the home of the Miami-based 2 Live Crew and the Orlando-based DJ Magic Mike (who was born Mike Hampton in 1967). However, the 2 Live Crew was actually formed in Los Angeles, where they recorded their debut single, "The Revelation," in 1985. Lyrically, the song was worlds apart from the X-rated booty rhymes that the 2 Live Crew would be known for only one year later. A very sociopolitical offering, "The Revelation" found the group addressing issues like poverty, unemployment, drugs and black-on-black crime and concluding that all of those problems were part of biblical prophecy. And musically, "The Revelation" was quite different from what was to come; the tune's high-tech, synthesizer-driven production was mindful of the West Coast electro-hop sound that artists like the Egyptian Lover, Uncle Jamm's Army, the Unknown DJ, and World Class Wreckin' Cru were known for at the time. Nor did the single's B side, "2 Live," have the Miami bass sound; "2 Live," with its scratching/beatbox approach, is very New York sounding. So neither "The Revelation" nor "2 Live" were typical of the 2 Live Crew's '80s output—not musically, not lyrically.

The album that put Florida-style booty rhymes on the map didn't come until 1986, when the 2 Live Crew recorded their first album, *2 Live Crew Is What We Are*. By that time, the group had left L.A. for Miami and given themselves a musical and lyrical makeover. The ultrafast, dance-oriented grooves were the essence of bass—Luther Campbell's version, anyway—and the lyrics were about sex, sex, and more sex. "We Want Some Pussy," the album's lead single, was certainly a major departure from "The Revelation"; so was the equally raunchy "Throw That D" (another major hit from that album). Rapper/producer/A&R man Campbell (who started out as the 2 Live Crew's manager before becoming an actual member) can take much of the credit for the sleazier approach that the 2 Live Crew decided to take after moving to Miami. He was a major fan of comedians like Rudy Ray Moore, Richard Pryor, and Redd Foxx, and *2 Live Crew Is What We Are* reflected Campbell's appreciation of their off-color humor. Commercially, Campbell's obsession with sex paid off; *2 Live Crew Is What We Are* went gold and made the 2 Live Crew's version of bass extremely popular in the South. Their relentlessly exuberant grooves influenced everyone from Afro-Rican (a Florida group) to Uncle Al to female pop-rappers L'Trimm (a delightfully silly group that was detested by hip-hop's hardcore but was still a lot of fun). Not all of the bass artists who came out of Florida in the late '80s were influenced by the 2 Live Crew's lyrics, but most of them were influenced by their beats and their tracks.

DJ Magic Mike, meanwhile, had his own version of bass in the late '80s—one that was influenced by the Ultramagnetic MC's and Mantronix (both New York acts) and didn't try to emulate the 2 Live Crew's tracks or lyrics. But like Campbell and the 2 Live Crew, Mike was very club friendly and acquired a devoted following in the South. Although Mike sold millions of albums in the '80s and '90s, he didn't receive as much publicity as the 2 Live Crew—and that stems from the fact that he wasn't nearly as controversial. Campbell and his associates received a lot of negative publicity in the late '80s and early '90s, which only made them sell more records.

In 1989, the 2 Live Crew's third album, *As Nasty as They Wanna Be* (which contained the hit "Me So Horny") came under attack from the Christian right. Jack Thompson, an attorney who was active in the Christian right movement, declared war on the 2 Live Crew and argued that their sexually explicit recordings were in violation of obscenity laws—Thompson even went so far as to assert that *As Nasty as They Wanna Be* should be banned and that retailers who sold the album should be arrested and jailed. By doing so, he made Campbell a poster child for the First Amendment. Many First Amendment advocates argued that banning *As Nasty as They Wanna Be* would be blatantly unconstitutional—that even though a tune like "Me So Horny" wasn't everyone's cup of tea, it didn't violate obscenity laws. The people who criticized Thompson came from both the left and the right; the attorney's critics ranged from ACLU members to some of the more libertarian Republicans (who reasoned that if conservatives are supposed to believe in small, limited government, Thompson was really an authoritarian instead of a true conservative).

The more Thompson railed against Campbell and his company Luke Records (originally known as Luke Skyywalker Records), the more *As Nasty*

as They Wanna Be sold; eventually, it went double platinum. And Campbell used all of the controversy to land a distribution deal with Atlantic Records, which distributed the 2 Live Crew's fourth album, *Banned in the USA*, in 1990. Unintentionally, Thompson not only gave the 2 Live Crew a boost—he gave bass music in general a boost. So in the final analysis, Thompson's war on the First Amendment backfired.

Banned in the USA was a big seller, but by the mid-'90s, the 2 Live Crew's popularity had decreased. However, bass music on the whole still had a lot of fans. Some of the major bass artists of the '90s included, among many others, 95 South, Uncle Al, the Get Funky Crew (who had a Southern hit with "Shake Them Titties"), Freak Nasty, the Quad City DJs, and the 69 Boyz. 95 South is best known for their 1993 hit "Whoot, There It Is," which shouldn't be confused with a similar bass tune by Tag Team (an Atlanta-based duo) called "Whoomp! There It Is." In 1993, the latter became the theme song of the Philadelphia Phillies when they battled the Toronto Blue Jays in the World Series. Phillies fans chanted the phrase "Whoomp, there it is" repeatedly at Phillies/Blue Jays games, although the chanting ended when the Blue Jays won the World Series that year.

Hearing people in Philly chanting the lyrics of a bass tune in 1993 was ironic because for the most part, bass music hasn't received a lot of support from rap fans in Philly, New York, or Boston. Some Northeastern hip-hoppers, in fact, have been downright hostile to bass, which they see as lowest common-denominator music and a bastardization of New York hip-hop. But the bass artists of the '80s and '90s didn't lose any sleep over the fact that they weren't as big in Philly or New York as they were in Atlanta, Miami, or Memphis—like the gangsta rappers of the West Coast, they realized that one could easily sell plenty of albums without the support of the Northeastern Corridor. Again, most of bass' support has come from the Southern states, where tunes like the 69 Boys' "Tootsee Roll," the Dogs' "Do the Nasty Dance," Duice's "Dazzey Duks," Uncle Al's "Slip and Slide," the Quad City DJs' "C'mon N' Ride It (The Train)," and Exit 25's "Do the Hop Scotch" were club hits and fared well among black fraternities. If you attended a black fraternity gathering in Florida, Georgia, Mississippi, or Alabama in the late '80s or '90s, you were bound to hear some bass jams. Bass has also done well on the West Coast—certainly much better than it has around the Northeastern Corridor—but overall, bass has been a Southern thing.

In the late '90s and early 2000s, bass' popularity in the South was seriously challenged by rap's dirty South school, which has given us everyone from New Orleans' Master P to Atlanta's Goodie Mob. Even so, no discussion of the history of Southern rap would be adequate without some mention of the bass phenomenon.

Recommended Recordings:
2 Live Crew, *As Nasty as They Wanna Be* (Luke)
2 Live Crew, *2 Live Crew Is What We Are* (Luke)
DJ Magic Mike, *This Is How It Should Be Done* (Cheetah)
DJ Magic Mike, *Represent* (Cheetah)
Various Artists, *Miami Bass: Heat Mix, Vol. 2* (Cold Front)
Various Artists, *Miami Bass: Heat Mix '96* (Cold Front)
Various Artists, *Bass Mix USA* (Cold Front)
95 South, *Quad City Knock* (Ichiban)
L'Trimm, *Grab It!* (Atlantic)

—Alex Henderson

West Coast Rap

If, in 1981 or 1982, you told a New Yorker that West Coast rappers would someday be selling as many units as East Coast rappers, you probably would have heard, "Yeah, in your dreams." Hip-hop was born in New York, and for a longtime, it was dominated by the East Coast. If hip-hop got started around 1976—when Kurtis Blow had his first gigs in Harlem clubs—it took West Coast rap about eleven years to make serious commercial inroads. But eventually, West Coast rappers did, in fact, give their East Coast counterparts a serious run for their money. The list of West Coast MCs who had gold or platinum albums in the late '80s and/or '90s is a long one—a list that includes, among many others, Ice-T, N.W.A, Dr. Dre, Ice Cube, Cypress Hill, Coolio, Tone-Loc, Snoop Dogg, Warren G, Young MC, DJ Quik, MC Hammer, Too Short, Sir Mix-A-Lot, and Digital Underground. And that list is especially impressive when you consider that for so long, many A&R people refused to take West Coast rappers seriously.

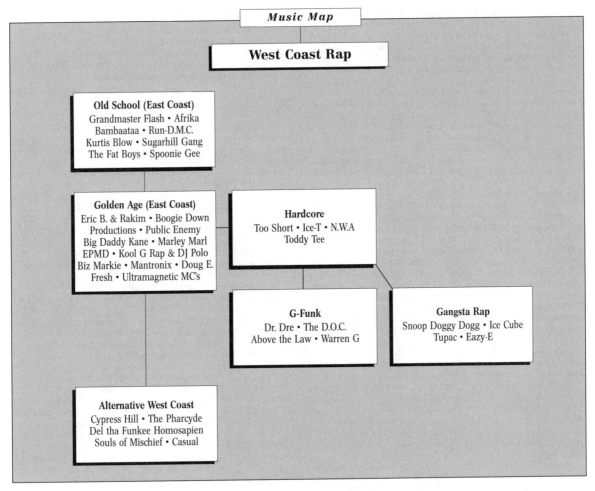

Music Map

West Coast Rap

Old School (East Coast)
Grandmaster Flash • Afrika
Bambaataa • Run-D.M.C.
Kurtis Blow • Sugarhill Gang
The Fat Boys • Spoonie Gee

Golden Age (East Coast)
Eric B. & Rakim • Boogie Down
Productions • Public Enemy
Big Daddy Kane • Marley Marl
EPMD • Kool G Rap & DJ Polo
Biz Markie • Mantronix • Doug E.
Fresh • Ultramagnetic MC's

Hardcore
Too Short • Ice-T • N.W.A
Toddy Tee

G-Funk
Dr. Dre • The D.O.C.
Above the Law • Warren G

Gangsta Rap
Snoop Doggy Dogg • Ice Cube
Tupac • Eazy-E

Alternative West Coast
Cypress Hill • The Pharcyde
Del tha Funkee Homosapien
Souls of Mischief • Casual

A few people on the West Coast were rapping as early as 1979, when they heard East Coast singles like the Sugarhill Gang's "Rappers Delight" and Kurtis Blow's "Christmas Rapping." At that point, rap wasn't nearly the phenomenon in Los Angeles or Oakland that it had been in New York. But a few Californians liked "Rappers Delight" and "Christmas Rapping" enough to try rapping themselves. The first rap recording by L.A. residents was Disco Daddy and Captain Rapp's 1981 single "Gigolo Rapp," which received very little attention on the East Coast but was a minor hit in L.A. and enjoyed some exposure on local urban contemporary station KGFJ-AM. Other West Coast rap singles followed, including the Rappers Rapp Group's "Rappin' Partee Groove" in 1982 and Ice-T's first single, "The Coldest Rap," in 1983. By 1983, hip-hop was huge on the West Coast—b-boys were breakdancing on Hollywood Boulevard and at Venice Beach, and Californians were spending plenty of dollars on New York rappers.

It was also in 1983 that Captain Rapp recorded "Bad Times (I Can't Stand It)," a sociopolitical classic that was heavily influenced by Grandmaster Flash and Melle Mel's message songs. And 1983 was a year in which electro-hop singles by Uncle Jam's Army (a collective of L.A.-based rappers, DJs, and producers) and the Egyptian Lover (who was part of that collective) hit the streets. Several years before the rise of gangsta rap in the late '80s, L.A.'s high-tech electro-hop style (which was heavily influenced by Afrika Bambaataa's 1982 hit "Planet Rock") had an underground cult following in Southern California. Electro-hop, however, wasn't hardcore rap—it was pop-rap for the dancefloor, and electro-hoppers like Uncle Jam's Army, the Egyptian Lover, the Arabian Prince, the World Class Wreckin' Cru (which included Dr. Dre in his pre-N.W.A days), and the Unknown DJ were never taken seriously on the

East Coast. For that matter, not all of Southern California's rap fans were into electro-hop—in 1984, 1985, and 1986, New York rappers like Run-D.M.C., the Fat Boys, and Whodini were selling a lot more records in South Central L.A. than the Egyptian Lover or the L.A. Dream Team. Nonetheless, L.A.'s rap scene was growing in the mid-'80s, and the city did have some hardcore rap—if you knew where to find it. Ice-T, King Tee, and Toddy Tee (best known for his 1985 single "Batter Ram") were providing hardcore rap in the mid-'80s, and so was Kid Frost (the first important Mexican-American rapper). But those artists were very underground back then; they had small cult followings, and the East Coast still dominated hip-hop. In the mid-'80s, most of rap's big names were New Yorkers.

In 1987, however, Ice-T went from being an underground cult figure to being a national star. That year, Sire/Warner Bros. released his first album, *Rhyme Pays*, which did a lot to popularize gangsta rap. N.W.A's *N.W.A and the Posse*, also from 1987, was another triumph for hardcore rap on the West Coast. And during the last few years of the decade, it became clear to a lot of A&R people that West Coast rap shouldn't be ignored. West Coast rappers started selling like hotcakes in the late '80s, a time that also saw the rise of everyone from the L.A.-based Young MC (who was actually a transplanted New Yorker) to Oakland's raunchy, X-rated Too Short to Seattle's Sir Mix-A-Lot. West Coast rap ran the gamut in the late '80s and early '90s—it was everything from the thugged-out gangsta rhymes of Ice-T, N.W.A, Compton's Most Wanted, Cypress Hill, and Above the Law to the commercial pop-rap of MC Hammer (whose second album, *Please Hammer, Don't Hurt'Em*, went multi-platinum), Oaktown's 357, and Mix-A-Lot (who was quite capable of providing hardcore sociopolitical rhymes but is best known for goofy, lighthearted crossover hits like "Baby Got Back"). L.A.'s Tone-Loc also had some major pop-rap smashes in the late '80s (including "Wild Thing" and "Funky Cold Medina"), but those who listened to his albums in their entirety realized that he recorded mostly hardcore rap and wasn't strictly a crossover artist.

In the early '90s, it was evident that West Coast rap had become a huge industry—which was quite a contrast to the years in which L.A. and Oakland MCs struggled for national recognition. At major labels, the same A&R people who were ignoring West Coast rappers in the mid-'80s were signing them left and right in the '90s. But not everyone was happy about the commercial success that West Coast rappers were enjoying. In some New York hip-hop circles, there was a lot of resentment—some New York b-boys (though certainly not all) felt that because the Big Apple had built hip-hop, the West Coast didn't deserve such a big piece of the pie. At first, the East Coast-West Coast rivalry in hip-hop was just a war of words—when Bronx rapper Tim Dog dissed Southern California rappers (especially N.W.A) on his 1991 single "Fuck Compton," no one shot him for it. But a few years later, hip-hop's East-West battle turned downright ugly.

Actually, hip-hop's East-West battle was basically a New York-L.A. battle; Philadelphia and Boston pretty much stayed out it, as did Seattle and Portland, OR. The rivalry was between two posses: (1) the L.A.-based Death Row Records, home of Dr. Dre, Snoop Dogg, and Tupac, and (2) producer Sean "Puffy" Combs' New York-based Bad Boy Entertainment, home of Brooklyn star the Notorious B.I.G. (also known as Biggie Smalls) and urban singer Faith Evans. Tupac Shakur and the Notorious B.I.G became bitter enemies, as did Combs (aka Puff Daddy or P. Diddy) and Death Row's infamous Suge Knight. In 1996, Shakur died from bullet wounds he received during a drive-by shooting in Las Vegas; the following year, a similar drive-by shooting in L.A. claimed the Notorious B.I.G.'s young life. Nothing was proven, although there was speculation that the Notorious B.I.G. was murdered in retaliation for Shakur's murder. Neither Shakur's killer nor B.I.G.'s was ever caught.

Of course, not all East Coast rappers resented the success of West Coast rappers. Chuck D featured Ice Cube on Public Enemy's "Burn Hollywood Burn", and KRS-One even equated N.W.A with the Black Panthers in an interview—he saw them as militant freedom fighters whose seminal *Straight Outta Compton* brought attention to a lot of important social issues. In a 1990 interview, members of New York's A Tribe Called Quest told this journalist that they were happy for the West Coast; as they saw it, the West Coast rap explosion was a healthy and inevitable part of hip-hop's evolution. And they gave the West Coast a shout-out with their eccentric single "I Left My Wallet in El Segundo," which acknowledges one of L.A.'s suburbs.

It is important to stress that even though gangsta rap has been an important part of West Coast rap in the '80s and '90s, not all West Coast rap is gangsta rap. Def Jeff, Madrok, Too Short, Kid Frost, Paris (a militantly sociopolitical MC from Oakland), Del tha Funkee Homosapien, and female rapper Yo-Yo were never gangsta rap—hardcore rap, but not gangsta rap. Nor was the Pharcyde, a jazz-influenced, L.A.-based alternative rap group along the lines of De La Soul, Digable Planets, and A Tribe Called Quest. The Pharcyde, in fact, has often been described as a West Coast group with an East Coast sound. And there was never anything gangsta about West Coast pop-rappers like MC Hammer, J.J. Fad, Oaktown's 357, or Young MC (who was arguably an L.A. equivalent of Philadelphia's Will Smith, aka the Fresh Prince).

When the 21st century arrived, West Coast rap wasn't turning out as many major stars as it had been in the late '80s and early to mid-'90s—the West Coast had lost some ground to other regions of the U.S., just as the Northeast had lost some ground to the West Coast and the South in the late '80s. Nonetheless, West Coast rap has often been an exciting and creative part of the hip-hop saga.

Recommended Recordings:
Tone-Loc, *Loc-ed After Dark* (Delicious Vinyl)
Ice-T, *Rhyme Pays* (Sire)
N.W.A, *N.W.A & the Posse* (Ruthless)
Eazy-E, *Eazy-Duz-It* (Ruthless)
Dr. Dre, *The Chronic* (Interscope)
Ice Cube, *AmeriKKKa's Most Wanted* (Priority)
Young MC, *Stone Cold Rhymin'* (Delicious Vinyl)
Sir Mix-A-Lot, *Beepers, Benzos & Booty: The Best of Sir Mix-A-Lot* (Rhino)
The Pharcyde, *Bizarre Ride II the Pharcyde* (Delicious Vinyl)
Too Short, *Life Is…Too Short* (Jive)
Digital Underground, *Sex Packets* (Tommy Boy)

MC Hammer, *Please Hammer, Don't Hurt 'Em* (Capitol)
Snoop Dogg, *Doggystyle* (Priority)
Coolio, *Gangsta's Paradise* (Tommy Boy)
Various Artists, *West Coast Rap: The First Dynasty, Vol. 1* (Rhino)
Various Artists, *West Coast Rap: The First Dynasty, Vol. 2* (Rhino)
Various Artists, *West Coast Rap: The First Dynasty, Vol. 3* (Rhino)
—Alex Henderson

Pop-Rap

Just about any genre of music—be it R&B, jazz, reggae, blues, country, or salsa—has its purists as well as crossover artists who have a more pop-friendly outlook. Rap is no different. Just as country has long had its hardcore honky tonkers (Dwight Yoakam, Buck Owens, George Jones) and its crossover stars (Willie Nelson, Garth Brooks, Crystal Gayle)—and just as jazz has had its hard boppers and its pop-jazz figures—there have always been hardcore rappers as well as pop-rappers. The difference between DMX and Will Smith, aka the Fresh Prince, is a lot like the difference between Phil Woods and David Sanborn—DMX and Smith are both rappers, but DMX is more likely to impress hip-hop purists just as jazz purists are likely to prefer Woods over the R&B-influenced Sanborn. That isn't to say that Smith lacks rapping skills; his technique is superb, in fact. But he does have a lot more pop appeal than a hardcore rapper like DMX (although by the late '90s, even the most hardcore rappers could attract largely white audiences and sell a ton of CDs in suburbia—including DMX).

Pop-influenced rap isn't something new. In the late '70s and early '80s, the Sugarhill Gang (for all their funkiness) had a somewhat poppier sound than Kurtis Blow, Grandmaster Flash & the Furious Five, or the Treacherous Three. Even Afrika Bambaataa, who was a hardcore rapper first and foremost, showed his appreciation of Kraftwerk (the seminal German group that wrote the book on synth-pop and electronica) on his 1982 hit "Planet Rock" (which became the basis for the West Coast electro-hop that Uncle Jam's Army, the Egyptian Lover, and others came out with in the '80s). But it was in the mid-to late '80s that we started to see an abundance of full-time pop-rappers. That was when the Northeast gave us Salt-N-Pepa, Kid 'n Play, Heavy D & the Boyz, DJ Jazzy Jeff and the Fresh Prince, and Sweet Cookie (an overlooked female MC), and when the West Coast gave us pop-rappers from Oakland (MC Hammer, Oaktown's 357), Seattle (Sir Mix-A-Lot), and Los Angeles (JJ Fad, the L.A. Dream Team). L.A. was also the home of Young MC, a major pop-rapper from that era; however, Young MC was actually a native New Yorker who had moved west. Miami, meanwhile, gave us the goofy female pop-rap duo L'Trimm, who are best remembered for their 1988 single "Cars with the Boom."

Those artists had no problem appealing to pop, dance, and urban contemporary audiences. Expose and Lisa Lisa fans could get into Salt-N-Pepa's "Push It" or JJ Fad's "Supersonic"; Michael Jackson fans were receptive to Kid 'n Play's "Rollin' with Kid 'n Play," Young MC's "Bust a Move," and Hammer's "U Can't Touch This." Hammer, like a lot of pop-rappers, became a frequent whipping boy of hip-hop's hardcore—as the purists saw it, he was watering rap down. But pop and R&B audiences adored him; Hammer's second album, *Please Hammer, Don't Hurt 'Em* (released by Capitol in 1990) sold an amazing ten million copies in the United States alone. The album, which was also a blockbuster smash all over Western Europe, managed to outsell the Beastie Boys' *Licensed to Ill* and Run-D.M.C.'s triple-platinum *Raising Hell*.

In terms of sales, the pop-rapper who gave Hammer the most competition in the early '90s was Vanilla Ice, whose 1990 release *To the Extreme* went multiplatinum and is basically a rap version of teen pop. Vanilla Ice never appealed to hip-hop's hardcore; his fans (many of them teenage girls) were likely to be Debbie Gibson, Tiffany, or New Kids on the Block fans. And Gerardo, a Latino pop-rapper who was born in Ecuador, also went after the teen pop crowd with his 1991 hit "Rico Suave." The person who produced Gerardo's debut album, *Mo' Ritmo*, was pop singer Michael Sembello, best known for his 1983 hit "Maniac" (from the movie *Flashdance*). No one expected an album that Sembello produced to contain hardcore rap, and *Mo' Ritmo* is far from hardcore—Gerardo was always a crossover act, pure and simple. So was Icy Blu, a white rapper whom Giant Records envisioned as a female version of Vanilla Ice. Giant reasoned that the teen pop aficionados who were buying Vanilla Ice and Gerardo in 1991 would also be receptive to the equally bubblegum Icy Blu, but her self-titled debut album fell through the cracks.

In the late '80s and early '90s, it became obvious to Europeans that pop-rap didn't have to be recorded in the United States. During that era, England gave us the Wee Papa Girls and the Cookie Crew—two female pop-rap groups that were a British equivalent of Oaktown's 357 or Salt-N-Pepa. Neither the Wee Papa Girls nor the Cookie Crew were big in the U.S., but they were stars in Great Britain and other parts of Europe. England was also the home of the half-Scottish, half-Malaysian female pop-rapper Betty Boo, whose clever 1990 debut, *Boomania*, didn't get much respect from hip-hop's hardcore but was a hit among British dance-pop audiences.

Not only does pop-rap not have to come from the U.S.; it doesn't even have to be in English. Mellow Man Ace, Gerardo, and other Latinos have rapped in English as well as Spanish, and the German group Die Fantastischen Vier (who are big in Europe but little known in the U.S.) have been described as a German-language equivalent of DJ Jazzy Jeff & the Fresh Prince.

Being a pop-rapper and a hardcore rapper aren't always mutually exclusive; there are some hardcore rappers who occasionally dabble in pop-rap. LL Cool J, for example, is primary a hardcore rapper, but he has made some pop-rap moves on hits that range from "I Need Love" in 1987 to "Around the Way Girl" in 1990. And Tone-Loc is really more of a hardcore rapper than a pop-rapper, but he is best remembered for crossover hits like "Wild Thing" and "Funky Cold Medina." Meanwhile, Seattle's Sir Mix-A-Lot is famous for fun, lighthearted pop-rap tunes such as "Baby Got Back" and "Posse's on Broadway," but anyone who has heard "Society's Creation," "National Anthem," or "The (Peek-A-Boo) Game" knows that Mix is also quite capable of providing angry, biting sociopolitical commentary. Those gems indicate that if Mix had played his cards differently, he could have gone down in history as a hardcore rapper instead of a pop-rapper. But then, being called a pop-rap or crossover artist isn't something that Mix is ashamed of—far from it. The Seattle native was always very upfront about the fact that he never considered himself a rap purist; Mix has cited '80s new-wave favorite Gary Numan as a major influence and has often asserted that he considers his audience a rock/dance-pop/urban contemporary audience rather than a hardcore rap audience.

Superstar producer/rapper Sean "Puffy" Combs, aka Puff Daddy or P. Diddy, is a perfect example of someone who can be either pop minded or hardcore, depending on the mood he's in. And Mellow Man Ace is another person who has recorded both hardcore rap and pop-rap. The Cuban-born MC is best known for his 1989 hit "Mentirosa"—which was a major crossover hit and enjoyed extensive airplay on Top 40 stations in the U.S.—but not everything Ace did was pop minded. The thing is that once a rapper has been labeled a crossover artist, he/she can have a hard time living down that reputation and winning over hip-hop's purists.

After his 15 minutes of fame, Ace never returned to the top of the charts. Similarly, the pop-rap group Kriss Kross had a major hit with 1992's "Jump" but didn't stay on top very long; Kriss Kross serves as a reminder of how fickle pop audiences can be.

Although hip-hop purists tend to dislike pop-rap on principle, the fact is that not all pop-rap is the same. Some pop-rap has been lightweight, but some of it has been gritty and soulful. The best pop-rappers of the '80s and '90s—Salt-N-Pepa, Sir Mix-A-Lot, Heavy D, Young MC, Kid 'n Play, the Fresh Prince, among others—could be quite creative. Young MC, Heavy D, and Kid 'n Play were never purists, but they definitely knew how to flow. And in some cases, pop-rap can even have an angry, in-your-face approach. Gillette, a Chicago-based pop-rapper and dance-pop singer, brought plenty of venom and aggression to her 1994 release *On the Attack*.

Every hip-hop era has had hardcore rappers as well as crossover stars, and the early 2000s are no different. The early 2000s saw the rise of St. Louis' Nelly, whose work has been commercial but not without integrity. Like the Fresh Prince, Salt-N-Pepa, Kid 'n Play, and Young MC before him, Nelly has demonstrated that pop-rap can have some soul and grit and doesn't have to be total fluff. Hardcore rap and pop-rap both have their place, and chances are that both of them will be a permanent part of the rap landscape.

Recommended Recordings:
MC Hammer, *Please Hammer, Don't Hurt 'Em* (Capitol)
Kid 'n Play, *2 Hype* (Select)
Sir Mix-A-Lot, *Seminar* (Nastymix)
Salt-N-Pepa, *Hot, Cool and Vicious* (Next Plateau)
Young MC, *Stone Cold Rhymin'* (Delicious Vinyl)
L'Trimm, *Grab It!* (Atlantic)

Mellow Man Ace, *Escape From Havana* (Delicious Vinyl)
DJ Jazzy Jeff & the Fresh Prince, *He's the DJ, I'm the Rapper* (Jive)
Nelly, *Nellyville* (Universal)

—Alex Henderson

Political Rap

Chuck D, founder and leader of Public Enemy, has often described rap as "the CNN of the streets," and he knows what he's talking about. Since the early '80s, rappers have addressed a wide variety of social and political topics—everything from gang violence, AIDS, drug addiction, racism, domestic violence, and prostitution to U.S. foreign policy in Latin America. And ironically, all of these sociopolitical lyrics have come from a genre that was best known for party songs in the beginning.

The first well-known example of sociopolitical rap came in 1982, when Grandmaster Flash & the Furious Five recorded "The Message"—a highly influential gem that inspired numerous rappers to address social and political subjects. Before "The Message," most rap lyrics were escapist in nature and shared disco's "let's party" outlook, including the singles that Flash's group recorded in 1979, 1980, and 1981. In those days, old school MCs typically spent their time boasting about their rapping skills, explaining why "sucker MCs" (rival rappers) were inferior and asking audiences to wave their hands in the air like they just don't care. "The Message" didn't eradicate boasting rhymes—which are still a major part of rap in the 21st century—but it did show numerous rappers that it was OK to write challenging, thought-provoking lyrics.

There were certain pre-1982 recordings—some rap, some R&B—that helped pave the way for "The Message." In the early '70s, the Last Poets (who were mainly a spoken-word group) wrote a lot of angrily sociopolitical lyrics and sometimes performed them in a rapping style. It was also in the early '70s that Gil Scott-Heron (who is primarily a jazz-influenced soul singer) experimented with pre-hip-hop rapping on sociopolitical scorchers like "Whitey on the Moon" and "No Knock" (which lambasted the FBI for going after the Black Panthers). Scott-Heron's best-known song from that period is "The Revolution Will Not Be Televised"; some have described that classic as early rap, although it's really spoken word. "Whitey on the Moon" and "No Knock," however, are closer to what came to be called rap—and there are certainly parallels between those tunes and the militant recordings that Public Enemy started providing about 17 years later.

The more sociopolitical soul recordings of the early '70s—gems like Marvin Gaye's "Inner City Blues," Curtis Mayfield's "Pusherman," and the O'Jays' "For the Love of Money"—also helped pave the way for sociopolitical rap. During the disco era of the mid- to late '70s, there weren't nearly as many message songs coming from R&B, and "The Message" reminded the music world that African-American music didn't always have to be about love, sex, partying, and dancing.

Hip-hop audiences got a slight taste of social commentary in 1980, when old school rapper Spoonie G recorded "Spoonin' Rap" for Sugar Hill Records (the same company that put out "The Message"). Although "Spoonin' Rap" was mostly a boasting/party tune, Spoonie did throw in some lyrics about life behind bars: "In jail, they got a game/They call it survival/They run it down to you on your first arrival." And those lyrics were borrowed in late 1982, when Grandmaster Melle Mel (of the Furious Five) used them on "Survival," a hard-hitting sequel to "The Message."

The year 1980 was also when Kurtis Blow rapped about the challenges of a recession on "Hard Times," one of the lesser-known gems on his self-titled debut album. If "Spoonin' Rap" and "Hard Times" offered some hints of what was to come, the gloves came all the way off with Flash's sobering "The Message," which talked about drugs, crime, violence, poverty, and other horrors of ghetto life. Back in 1982, "The Message" was such a jolt to the hip-hop world; after so many party-oriented lyrics, no one expected to hear Flash's colleagues rapping about "junkies in the alley with a baseball bat"—or about a young man going to prison for armed robbery and being gangraped repeatedly before being "found hung dead in the cell." Powerful stuff.

The popularity of "The Message" and "Survival" inspired Flash and Mel to come out with some equally hard-hitting gems in 1983, including "New York, New York" (which painted a troubling picture of life in the Big Apple) and "White Lines" (a song about cocaine abuse). And thanks to Flash's group, many other rappers were inspired to come out with sociopolitical gems in the

'80s—gems like Run-D.M.C.'s "It's Like That," Captain Rapp's "Bad Times (I Can't Stand It)," Dr. Jeckyll & Mr. Hyde's "Fast Life," and MC Shy-D's "Paula's on Crack."

Flash's message rhymes were a strong influence on Boogie Down Productions, one of the most intellectual rap groups of all time. Led by Blastmaster KRS-One, BDP has tackled a wide variety of issues, including crack cocaine, venereal disease, gang violence, racism, and inner-city violence. Sadly, urban violence is something that KRS has firsthand knowledge of; the rapper's partner Scott La Rock (whom he cofounded BDP with) was murdered in the Bronx after the group's 1987 debut *Criminal Minded.* When La Rock was killed, KRS considered discontinuing BDP, but thankfully, he decided to keep the group going. KRS' political/spiritual philosophy has been an interesting mixture of black nationalist, Hindu, and Rastafarian ideas—one may not always agree with his politics, but he's certainly been admirably thought provoking over the years.

No essay on political rap would be complete without some mention of Public Enemy, whose militant lyrics have influenced everyone from 2 Black 2 Strong (a Harlem rapper) and the Oakland-based Paris to rap-metal favorites Rage Against the Machine. Founded by rapper Chuck D, Public Enemy shares BDP's black nationalist outlook and has been heavily influenced by the politics of Malcolm X and the Black Panthers. In the late '80s and early '90s, PE were at the height of their popularity; the group was huge back then, and their lyrics were always interesting even if you didn't agree with everything they had to say. Not that Chuck D expected all of his fans to agree with all of his positions—for example, there were some diehard PE fans who disagreed with their endorsement of the controversial Nation of Islam leader Louis Farrakhan (just as not all of Merle Haggard's followers are in total agreement with the politically conservative ideas that the country legend expressed on "Okie from Muskogee" and "The Fighting Side of Me"). Ultimately, PE wasn't about indoctrination—like Haggard on the right or Joan Baez and Bob Dylan on the left; they were really about expressing a point of view and making people think.

Public Enemy became popular around the time that gangsta rap became popular. Although Chuck D has rapped about many of the same things as gangsta rappers—drugs, crime, racism, poverty—there is a huge difference between PE and gangsta rap. The thing that makes someone a gangsta rapper is a willingness to rap in the first person about thug life—Chuck D, Melle Mel, and Run-D.M.C. rapped in the third person about the actions of urban criminals, but they didn't actually portray criminals on their albums. Gangsta rappers Ice-T and N.W.A, on the other hand, became known for first-person accounts of life in the 'hood. In the late '80s, those Los Angeles residents wrote the book on gangsta rap; they portrayed thugs and gang members on their albums and gave listeners a guided tour of South Central L.A.'s troubled ghetto areas. In the '90s, gangsta rap started sounding like a formula—the market became saturated with gangsta rap. But in the beginning, gangsta rap was more educational than exploitive, and the best gangsta rap albums—which include N.W.A's *Straight Outta Compton,* Ice-T's *Power,* Ice Cube's *Death Certificate,* and the late Tupac's *Me Against the World*—are sociopolitical classics.

Ironically, some of the best sociopolitical rap of the late '80s and early '90s came from someone who is much better known for lighthearted, escapist lyrics: Sir Mix-A-Lot. When Mix's name is mentioned, most hip-hop heads immediately think of fun pop-rap like "Baby Got Back" (his biggest hit), "Posse's on Broadway," and "Beepers." But anyone who thinks of Mix as strictly a party animal should take a close listen to searing message raps like "National Anthem" (which addresses the Iran-Contra scandal and the plight of Vietnam veterans, among other things), "Society's Creation," and "The (Peek-A-Boo) Game." So why haven't more people acknowledged Mix's sociopolitical side? It really comes down to marketing; labels released his fun songs as singles and promoted them aggressively. Mix would include one or two political smokers on an album, but he was marketed as a party rapper and went with the flow.

In the 21st century, rap lyrics continue to run the gamut—they can be frivolous, or they can be serious. And whenever an MC tackles a social or political issue, he/she should be thankful that Grandmaster Flash and his colleagues opened the door back in 1982.

Recommended Recordings:

Public Enemy, *It Takes a Nation of Millions to Hold Us Back* (Def Jam)
Public Enemy, *Fear of a Black Planet* (Def Jam)

Grandmaster Flash & the Furious Five, *Message From Beat Street: The Best of Grandmaster Flash* (Rhino)
Boogie Down Productions, *By All Means Necessary* (Jive)
Ice-T, *Power* (Sire)
Ice-T, *O.G. Original Gangster* (Sire)
N.W.A, *Straight Outta Compton* (Priority)
2 Black 2 Strong, *Doing Hard Time on Planet Earth* (Combat)
Paris, *Sleeping with the Enemy* (Scarface)
Ice Cube, *Death Certificate* (Priority)
Tupac, *Me Against the World* (Interscope)

—Alex Henderson

Gangsta Rap

Ever since some gang-related violence occurred at a Run-D.M.C. concert in Long Beach, CA, in 1986, rap music has been controversial; hip-hop had its detractors in the '80s and still has plenty of them in the 21st century. And no form of rap has been more controversial than gangsta rap, which has been attacked by everyone from Tipper Gore to conservative talk-show host Bill O'Reilly. Why have so many people been critical of gangsta rap, including some of hip-hop's non-gangsta MCs? It all comes down to the first-person format; instead of rhyming in the third person about the problems of the inner city, gangsta rappers rhyme in the first person about the lives of thugs, felons, gang members, pimps, and crack dealers. Gangsta rappers portray the thugs they're rapping about, which is a lot different from what Grandmaster Flash & the Furious Five (one of rap's earliest groups) did on their 1982 classic "The Message." That gem found Flash and his New York colleagues rapping in the third person about the oppressive conditions of the inner-city ghetto, but they didn't actually portray criminals—gangsta rappers, however, give listeners the perspective of a gangbanger, a drug dealer, or someone who is serving hard time for armed robbery. And for that reason, gangsta rap has often been accused of glorifying—or even promoting—crime and violence. But many gangsta rappers have countered that portrayal should not be confused with advocacy; in other words, the fact that Ice-T, Snoop Dogg, and Dr. Dre have portrayed thugs on record doesn't mean that they're encouraging listeners to live the thug life. Ice-T would argue that when he gave first-person accounts of thug life on "6'N the Mornin'" and "Colors," it was comparable to Joe Pesci and Robert De Niro portraying hoodlums in *Casino* and *Goodfellas*—that he wasn't promoting thuggery any more than director Martin Scorsese's modern film noir.

Like any style of music that has generated gold and platinum sales, gangsta rap has been saturated with clone artists—people who reasoned that the easiest way to sell a lot of CDs was to emulate N.W.A or the late Tupac Shakur instead of developing something original. And in the hands of the clones, gangsta rap can seem like cheap exploitation and an endless stream of sexist, violent clichés. But the most compelling gangsta rappers—including Ice-T, N.W.A, Tupac, Schoolly D, Ice Cube, Dr. Dre, and the Geto Boys—weren't about shock value for the sake of shock value. The best gangsta rap has served as an audio-documentary on the problems of the inner city; at its best, gangsta rap is film noir with a beat.

Gangsta rap got started around 1986, when the seminal Ice-T wrote a disturbing tune called "6'N the Mornin'." Rapping in the first person, Ice-T took his audience on a guided tour through the world of a Los Angeles criminal. It wasn't the first time that a rapper examined the darker side of urban life; when Grandmaster Flash & the Furious Five recorded "The Message" in 1982 and "New York, New York" in 1983, they painted a very troubling and depressing picture of the inner city. And there were many other East Coast MCs who, in the early to mid-'80s, rapped about social problems, including Run-D.M.C. and Kurtis Blow. But they never rapped about thug life in the first person—if anything, they were complaining about the criminals who were making New York a dangerous place to live. "6'N the Mornin'," however, found the L.A.-based Ice-T portraying the sort of felon Flash and Run-D.M.C. were trying to avoid in their songs. And the first-person approach was effective on subsequent Ice-T offerings like "Drama," "Pain," "Colors," and "The Hunted Child," all of which were vehemently criticized by those who thought that he was glorifying crime and violence. But Ice-T often countered that his lyrics were being taken out of context—that if you listened closely, his lyrics were actually anti-crime. In fact, there were no happy endings for the pimps, players, and gangbangers in Ice-T's songs; they usually ended up dead or incarcerated, much like the thugs

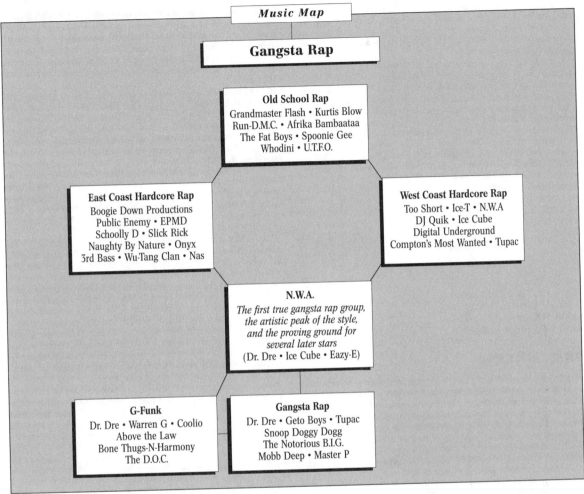

Music Map

Gangsta Rap

Old School Rap
Grandmaster Flash • Kurtis Blow
Run-D.M.C. • Afrika Bambaataa
The Fat Boys • Spoonie Gee
Whodini • U.T.F.O.

East Coast Hardcore Rap
Boogie Down Productions
Public Enemy • EPMD
Schoolly D • Slick Rick
Naughty By Nature • Onyx
3rd Bass • Wu-Tang Clan • Nas

West Coast Hardcore Rap
Too Short • Ice-T • N.W.A
DJ Quik • Ice Cube
Digital Underground
Compton's Most Wanted • Tupac

N.W.A.
*The first true gangsta rap group,
the artistic peak of the style,
and the proving ground for
several later stars*
(Dr. Dre • Ice Cube • Eazy-E)

G-Funk
Dr. Dre • Warren G • Coolio
Above the Law
Bone Thugs-N-Harmony
The D.O.C.

Gangsta Rap
Dr. Dre • Geto Boys • Tupac
Snoop Doggy Dogg
The Notorious B.I.G.
Mobb Deep • Master P

---

that James Cagney and Edward G. Robinson often portrayed in the '30s and '40s. In a subliminal way, Ice-T was telling his fans that crime doesn't pay; "The Hunted Child" and "Drama" paint as unattractive a picture of crime as Cagney's characters did in *White Heat* and *Public Enemy* (1931).

Although gangsta rap was dominated by the West Coast in the '80s, one of the early gangsta rappers was Philadelphia's Schoolly D. Lyrically, Schoolly wasn't as violent or as graphic as his West Coast counterparts; however, some of the first-person rhymes he came out with around 1985-1987 were more thuggish than anything else that the East Coast had to offer at the time. "PSK What Does It Mean?," "Saturday Night," and other singles that Schoolly provided during that period weren't as bloody as N.W.A or the Geto Boys, but they were still ahead of their time and deserve to be recognized as gangsta rap classics.

If gangsta rap's detractors found Ice-T and Schoolly D troubling, they were even more shocked when they heard N.W.A's influential *Straight Outta Compton.* Released in late 1988, that album turned out to be even more violent than Ice-T's work. N.W.A's members (Dr. Dre, Ice Cube, MC Ren, DJ Yella, and the late Eazy-E) covered a lot of the same ground as Ice-T—gang violence, drive-by shootings, drug dealing, etc.—and the L.A.-based rappers didn't think twice about being as inflammatory as possible. One of the songs on *Straight Outta Compton,* "Fuck tha Police," inspired the FBI to write an angry letter to Priority Records. But *Straight Outta Compton,* for all its graphic violence, was far from an example of cheap exploitation—it was really a cry for help, and the album told people all over the world just how dangerous life in Compton, CA, and South Central L.A. could be.

Other noteworthy gangsta rappers from the late '80s and early '90s ranged from the Houston-based Geto Boys to L.A.'s Cypress Hill, who brought some of the Chicano/Mexican-American influence to gangsta rap. Cypress Hill wasn't the first rap group with a Latino influence, but they were the first major group that brought a Latino perspective to West Coast gangsta rap. Meanwhile, the L.A.-based Boo-Yaa T.R.I.B.E. has demonstrated that Samoan Americans can be a part of gangsta rap.

As influential as N.W.A turned out to be, the group only lasted about four years. In 1991, N.W.A broke up, and Dr. Dre launched his solo career with 1992's *The Chronic* (which was among the best-selling gangsta rap albums of all time and put the distinctive Snoop Dogg on the map). Ice Cube, meanwhile, had been recording solo albums since 1990, when he left N.W.A and had a falling out with Dr. Dre and Eazy-E (who died of AIDS-related causes in 1995). Cube's solo output has always been extremely sociopolitical; if anyone has bridged the gap between the militant black nationalism of Public Enemy and the thuggery of gangsta rap, it's Ice Cube.

Most gangsta rappers have distanced themselves from the thug life that they rhyme about; a tragic exception was the late Tupac Shakur, who was all too familiar with the urban horrors that he describes on albums like 1995's compelling *Me Against the World.* There was plenty of violence on Shakur's recordings, but there was also plenty of remorse—Shakur, at times, expressed regret over having lived the thug life, and yet, he seemed addicted to it. The rapper had numerous run-ins with the law in the early to mid-'90s, and he made his share of enemies in the hip-hop world. Shakur was only 25 when, in September 1996, an unknown gunman shot him four times in Las Vegas;

on September 13, 1996 (six days after the attack), Shakur's bullet wounds ended his life. And only six months later, Shakur's East Coast rival the Notorious B.I.G. was also murdered by gunfire. There was speculation that whoever murdered the Notorious B.I.G. did so to avenge Shakur's death, but nothing has ever been proven.

If gangsta rap hadn't received enough negative publicity in the late '80s and early '90s, it received even more when Shakur was killed in 1996. Nonetheless, gangsta rap continued to be incredibly popular and was still going strong when the 21st century arrived. In 2001 and 2002, gangsta rap's critics weren't any less vocal than they had been 13 and 14 years earlier—if anything, they had become even more vocal. And even some of gangsta rap's defenders had grown tired of all the predictable artists who kept jumping on the gangsta bandwagon. But despite all those things, the best gangsta albums—gems like Shakur's *Me Against the World*, Ice-T's *Power*, and N.W.A's *Straight Outta Compton*—continue to hold up well and offer riveting descriptions of the tragic side of urban life.

Recommended Recordings:

Ice-T, *Power* (Sire)
Ice-T, *O.G. Original Gangster* (Sire)
N.W.A, *Straight Outta Compton* (Priority)
Schoolly D, *The Adventures of Schoolly D* (Rykodisc)
Dr. Dre, *The Chronic* (Death Row)
Geto Boys, *Geto Boys* (Def American)
Boo-Yaa T.R.I.B.E., *New Funky Nation* (4th & Broadway)
Ice Cube, *Death Certificate* (Priority)
Eazy-E, *Eazy-Duz-It* (Ruthless/Priority)
Tupac, *Me Against the World* (Interscope)
Cypress Hill, *Cypress Hill* (Ruffhouse)
Snoop Dogg, *Doggystyle* (Priority)

—*Alex Henderson*

Alternative Rap

Historically, the word "alternative" has been applied to styles of music that are outside of a genre's mainstream—alternative rock, alternative country, alternative metal, etc. These days, the term "alternative rock" is really just a figure of speech because alternative rock and alternative pop-rock have been very mainstream since the early '90s. Artists who are considered alternative rock or alternative pop-rock—which could be anyone from Pearl Jam to No Doubt to Garbage—are very much a part of rock's mainstream and have sold millions of albums in the '90s or 2000s. And alternative metal (which is part of alternative rock) now dominates the metal field.

But alternative rap, like alternative country, is another matter. Alternative rappers are still outside of hip-hop's mainstream—they aren't necessarily obscure or unknown, but they aren't expected to have as much commercial success as Eminem or Lil' Kim either. So one can argue, with some justification, that alternative rap really is an alternative to something. Just as the Blood Oranges and Frog Holler (two alternative country-rock/No Depression bands) are considered an alternative to Faith Hill, Shania Twain, and Garth Brooks— the big names of modern country radio—alternative rappers like the Roots, Blackalicious, and Common (formerly known as Common Sense) could be considered an alternative to Jay-Z or Snoop Dogg. Alternative rap is an alternative to hardcore rap, gangsta rap, and dirty South; it is also an alternative to commercial pop-rap.

Alternative rap isn't one particular sound but, rather, a variety of sounds— alternative rap could be anyone from De La Soul and their disciples to Gang Starr to the very sociopolitical Disposable Heroes of Hiphoprisy. Exactly when alternative rap got started is open to debate. Arguably, the first important alternative rap effort was De La Soul's adventurous debut album, *3 Feet High and Rising*, which Tommy Boy Records released in 1989. Incorporating everything from psychedelic rock to jazz, the Long Island group's first album was amazingly ambitious and went down in history as one of alternative rap's definitive releases. *3 Feet High and Rising* wasn't as pop-rap—certainly not in the way that Salt-N-Pepa, DJ Jazzy Jeff & the Fresh Prince, or MC Hammer were pop-rap. But at the same time, De La Soul didn't have the macho, hyper-masculine image that Run-D.M.C., Big Daddy Kane, and LL Cool J were known for—let alone the thug image that N.W.A, Ice-T, the Geto Boys, Schoolly D, and other gangsta rappers were projecting in the late '80s. Rather, De La Soul went for a hipster image, and *3 Feet High and Rising* appealed to

the alternative rock crowd as well as hip-hop audiences. But in some cases, alternative rappers have appealed to alternative rock audiences almost exclusively. The Disposable Heroes of Hiphoprisy, for example, had a lot more acceptance in alternative rock circles than they had from hip-hop's hardcore—and the fact that they reworked the Dead Kennedys' "California Uber Alles" (an early-'80s punk classic) certainly didn't hurt their credibility in rock circles.

3 Feet High and Rising proved to be quite influential—even seminal. The artists who De La Soul influenced in the late '80s or '90s included, among others, A Tribe Called Quest, Digable Planets, Common, and the Pharcyde. De La Soul was part of a larger East Coast posse known as the Native Tongues; other members of that alternative rap-minded posse included the Jungle Brothers and A Tribe Called Quest, whose 1990 debut *People's Instinctive Travels and the Paths of Rhythm* was every bit as eccentric, quirky, and experimental as *3 Feet High and Rising*. The Native Tongues were known for their eccentricity (among other things), and in alternative rap circles, eccentricity is a plus. Beck, one of the many alternative rockers who has been greatly influenced by hip-hop, obviously identifies with alternative rap's quirkiness and eccentricity—his 1996 smash "Where It's At" had alternative rap and the Native Tongues written all over it.

Alternative rap was never dominated by any one particular city. A lot of important alternative rappers have come from the New York area, including De La Soul, A Tribe Called Quest, the Jungle Brothers, and Gang Starr. But some of the most critically acclaimed alternative rappers have also come from Philadelphia (the Roots), Chicago (Common), Oakland (Digital Underground), and Los Angeles (the Pharcyde). And alternative rap doesn't necessarily have to come from the United States; MC Solaar, for example, is a French alterna-rapper who made a name for himself in the early '90s. Musically, there are parallels between Solaar and American alternative rappers like Digable Planets and Common, but Solaar's lyrics are in French—and the language barrier has prevented him from becoming well known among American hip-hop fans. However, Solaar is a major star in Europe, where people are likely to speak more than one language.

One of the things that alternative rappers have been known for is sampling jazz extensively. When other East Coast rappers were still sampling James Brown to death in the late '80s and early '90s, De La Soul and A Tribe Called Quest were sampling jazz recordings. There is no law stating that alternative rappers have to sample jazz, but the practice has been quite common. John Coltrane, Donald Byrd, Art Blakey, Horace Silver, Freddie Hubbard, and Herbie Hancock are among the countless jazz heavyweights who have been sampled by alternative rappers—check the credits of a Digable Planets or Tribe Called Quest CD, and you're bound to see some jazz samples listed. The members of Digable Planets were obviously Miles Davis fans; the title of their 1993 hit "Rebirth of Slick (Cool Like That)" was no doubt inspired by Davis' seminal *Birth of the Cool* sessions of the late '40s and early '50s (which wrote the book on cool jazz). In fact, a lot of veteran jazz artists have received royalty payments when their work was sampled by alternative rappers—that is, if they held onto their publishing. When this journalist interviewed the late soul-jazz/hard-bop organist Jack McDuff for some liner notes back in 1997, he pointed out that one of his fellow jazz veterans (a saxophonist) had received a royalty check for no less than $257,000, thanks to an alternative rapper who had sampled one of his old recordings. McDuff knew the saxophonist personally, and he took pleasure in knowing that a hip-hopper had enabled one of his colleagues to earn an additional $257,000 for something he had recorded decades ago. So in McDuff's mind, alternative rap was a very good thing for veteran jazz musicians who had kept their publishing.

As a rule, alternative rap has been marginalized in the hip-hop world; nonetheless, some alternative rappers have sold a lot of units, including De La Soul, A Tribe Called Quest, and the George Clinton-influenced Digital Underground. But in many cases, alternative rappers have underscored the fact that what music critics like and what rap audiences actually buy can be two very different things. The Roots, the Disposable Heroes of Hiphoprisy, Blackalicious, the Jurassic 5, and Common are five perfect examples of alternative rappers who have been adored by critics but have often received more support from alternative rock fans than from hip-hop's hardcore. Those artists have received more than their share of rave reviews—and they have had their share of devoted fans—but they haven't sold as many CDs as hip-hop's major superstars. The Roots aren't as big as Eminem or Nelly; Blackalicious and

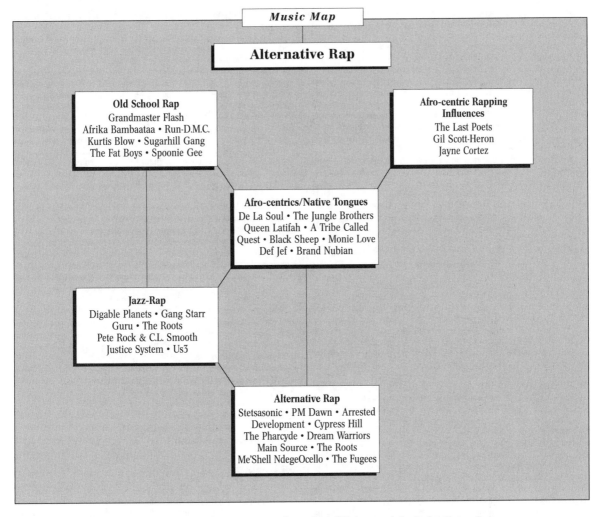

Alternative Rap

Old School Rap
Grandmaster Flash
Afrika Bambaataa • Run-D.M.C.
Kurtis Blow • Sugarhill Gang
The Fat Boys • Spoonie Gee

Afro-centric Rapping Influences
The Last Poets
Gil Scott-Heron
Jayne Cortez

Afro-centrics/Native Tongues
De La Soul • The Jungle Brothers
Queen Latifah • A Tribe Called
Quest • Black Sheep • Monie Love
Def Jef • Brand Nubian

Jazz-Rap
Digable Planets • Gang Starr
Guru • The Roots
Pete Rock & C.L. Smooth
Justice System • Us3

Alternative Rap
Stetsasonic • PM Dawn • Arrested
Development • Cypress Hill
The Pharcyde • Dream Warriors
Main Source • The Roots
Me'Shell NdegeOcello • The Fugees

Common haven't outsold DMX or Busta Rhymes. And it isn't uncommon for an alternative rapper to be a college radio favorite who has a hard time getting airplay on urban contemporary stations. But that doesn't necessarily worry alternative rappers—some of them thrive on their outsider status and don't stress over the fact that they're more popular among college radio and indie rock audiences than they are in the 'hood.

For the most part, alternative rap has been known for unthreatening, non-violent lyrics; De La Soul and their allies were never into the thug-life imagery of gangsta rap. But that isn't to say that alternative rap lyrics are fluff—far from it. The Disposable Heroes of Hiphoprisy, for example, were as fiercely sociopolitical a group as Public Enemy or Boogie Down Productions, and they rapped about issues like racism and sexism. But their rock-minded, industrial-friendly approach kept them from appealing to rap purists. Common, meanwhile, isn't as consistently sociopolitical as the Disposable Heroes of Hiphoprisy, although he questioned gangsta rap's excesses on his 1994 single, "I Used to Love H.E.R." (which led to a mini-feud with former N.W.A member Ice Cube).

It's unlikely that alternative rap will ever become rap's primary direction the way that alternative rock became rock's primary direction in the early '90s. Nonetheless, the music that is loosely defined as alternative rap has had an enthusiastic cult following and will probably continue to do so.
Recommended Recordings:
De La Soul, *3 Feet High and Rising* (Tommy Boy)
The Pharcyde, *Bizarre Ride II the Pharcyde* (Delicious Vinyl)

Digital Underground, *Sex Packets* (Tommy Boy)
A Tribe Called Quest, *People's Instinctive Travels and the Paths of Rhythm* (Jive)
Digable Planets, *Reachin' (A New Refutation of Time and Space)* (Pendulum)
The Roots, *Phrenology* (MCA)
Disposable Heroes of Hiphoprisy, *Hypocrisy Is the Greatest Luxury* (4th & Broadway)
Common, *Resurrection* (Relativity)
Blackalicious, *Blazing Arrow* (MCA)

—*Alex Henderson*

Hip-House

Just about any genre of music has its hardcore purists as well as those who are more liberal and broad minded in their outlook. That is true of everything from jazz to country to Afro-Cuban music, and it is certainly true of rap. Hip-hop purists have been very protective of their music and have been disdainful of rappers who make any type of crossover moves; they see pop-rap hits like Tone-Loc's "Wild Thing," Salt-N-Pepa's "Push It," and MC Hammer's "You Can't Touch This" as attempts to take hip-hop out of the 'hood, water it down, and make it safe for the suburbs and the shopping malls. And the purists who look down on pop-rap are no less critical of hip-house, a fusion of rap and house that reached its creative peak in the late '80s and early to mid-'90s. Telling a rap purist that hip-house has artistic merit is like trying to convince a jazz purist or a bop snob that fusion favorites like Return to Forever, Weather Report, Pat Metheny, and the Yellowjackets are a valid part of the jazz spectrum; rap purists, like jazz purists, are very set in their ways and have strong feelings about how things should be done.

If you judge hip-house by hardcore rap standards, it does indeed fall short—anyone who expects a hip-house act like Belgium's Technotronic to emulate Public Enemy, Ice-T, or Big Daddy Kane is bound to be disappointed. But here's the thing: hip-house shouldn't be judged by hardcore rap standards because it never claimed to be hardcore rap any more than Shania Twain claims to be Kitty Wells or David Sanborn claims to be a straight-ahead be-bopper. Hip-house should be judged by dance music standards because that's what it is—rapping for the dance floor. Hip-house is straight-up party music, pure and simple; it is a house groove that emphasizes rapping instead of singing. That isn't to say that hip-house excludes singing altogether; rapper Biscuit's 1993 song "My Music" (which came out on Los Angeles-based producer Jay Warsinske's AVC label) is a perfect example of a hip-house tune that used a female singer during the chorus and rapping during the verses. While hardcore rap caters to the 'hood, hip-house has always catered to the clubs. Hip-house came out of Chicago's dance-club culture, and it was equally popular among club hounds in New York and Europe. Hip-house has been around almost as long as house music itself—when house got started in Chicago in the early '80s, there were house records that incorporated rapping. And as rap got bigger and bigger in the '80s, hip-house became increasingly popular in the house world.

The list of artists who embraced hip-house in the '80s and/or '90s ranges from Technotronic, Snap! and the C&C Music Factory to Doug Lazy, a rapper who recorded one album for Atlantic: 1990's *Doug Lazy Gettin' Crazy*. Although Lazy had solid rapping skills, his Atlantic album didn't get much respect from hip-hop's hardcore. Nor did the recordings of Mr. Lee, an obscure Chicago-based rapper who made hip-house the main focus of his 1990 album *Get Busy* (a Jive release). Lee, like Lazy, was dismissed by hip-hop purists. Not that either Lazy or Lee were going after purists—they made albums for the clubs instead of the 'hood, and their audience was basically an Inner City/Black Box/Deee-Lite/Ten City audience instead of a Doug E. Fresh/Stetsasonic/Eric B. & Rakim audience (which isn't to say that some listeners aren't eclectic enough to enjoy hardcore rap one minute and dance-pop the next).

Not everyone who provided hip-house recordings in the '80s or '90s was consistently club oriented—there were plenty of rappers who occasionally dabbled in hip-house even though it was hardly their main focus. Queen Latifah, for example, acknowledged hip-house with her 1989 single "Come Into My House," which wasn't typical of the rapper/actress' work but fared well in clubs. Similarly, the Jungle Brothers (whose specialty was alternative rap) dabbled in hip-house when they teamed up with DJ Richie Rich on the 1988 single "I'll House You" (which was arranged by dance music icon Todd Terry). "I'll House You" wasn't typical of the Jungle Brothers' work any more than "Come Into My House" was typical of Queen Latifah, but club hounds ate the tune up in the late '80s. And JJ Fad, a female pop-rap group from Los Angeles, acknowledged hip-house on their 1990 recordings "It's Da Fad" and "We in the House" (both from their second Atlantic album *Not Just a Fad*). Hardcore rappers, as a rule, stayed away from hip-house because they didn't want to risk being labeled club/dance acts, but pop-rappers didn't have that worry because they were club friendly to begin with. So when LTrimm, another female pop-rap group, recorded a hip-house number titled "Glamour Girls" in 1991, they certainly didn't have anything to lose—in fact, embracing hip-house made a lot of sense commercially if, in the early '90s, you were a rapper who had pop or dance music leanings and didn't care about appealing to hip-hop purists.

Even Madonna made a few hip-house moves when she recorded her 1990 smash "Vogue." Granted, the tune was 90-percent singing, but "Vogue" (which was among the best-selling house singles of all time) did include a brief rap section. Although it would be inaccurate to describe "Vogue" as hip-house, it is safe to say that Madonna gave the hip-house trend some mainstream/Top 40 acknowledgment by throwing in a bit of rapping. The early '90s, in fact, found hip-house—and house music in general, for that matter—peaking in terms of exposure on pop/Top 40 stations. Back then, hip-house tunes like Technotronic's "Pump Up the Jam," Snap!'s "The Power," C + C Music Factory's "Gonna Make You Sweat (Everybody Dance Now)," and AB Logic's "The Hitman" were finding their way to pop stations. The pop stations that were receptive to singer-oriented house gems like Deee-Lite's "Groove Is in the Heart," Crystal Waters' "Gypsy Woman (She's Homeless)," and Black Box's

"Everybody Everybody" were also receptive to a handful of hip-house singles from that era.

Rap purists, not surprisingly, weren't the least bit happy about hearing Technotronic, C + C Music Factory (the brainchild of the Robert Clivillés/David Cole producing/songwriting team), Snap!, or AB Logic on the radio in the early '90s; they saw those artists as opportunists who were exploiting and ripping off the hip-hop culture that they cherished. But then, none of those artists ever pretended that they had anything to do with hardcore rap—they were totally open and honest about the fact that they specialized in club-minded dance music. Therefore, the standards that one applies to LL Cool J, MC Lyte, the Notorious B.I.G., or Ice Cube should not be applied to someone like Technotronic's Zairean-born Ya Kid K, who never pretended to be a hardcore rapper or a hip-hop purist. Complaining about Ya Kid K's lack of hip-hop purity is like complaining because Bon Jovi wasn't a carbon copy of Black Sabbath or because Grover Washington Jr. wasn't a replica of Dexter Gordon—in other words, an apple shouldn't be faulted for not tasting like an orange if it never claimed to be anything other than an apple. Technotronic, C + C Music Factory, Snap!, and AB Logic were great at what they did, and from a marketing standpoint, they were never guilty of false advertising.

Another C + C Music Factory smash from the early '90s was "Here We Go, Let's Rock & Roll," which successfully fused hip-house with rock and became a big radio hit. But for the most part, hip-house was more of a club phenomenon than a radio phenomenon; the hip-house recordings that enjoyed a lot of radio exposure were the exception rather than the rule. At least that was true in the United States, where both urban contemporary and pop/Top 40 radio formats can be quite rigid and conservative.

When the 21st century arrived, hip-house wasn't as popular or as prevalent as it had been in the '80s and early to mid-'90s. By that time, trance had replaced house as the world's leading form of dance music. But hip-house had a good run, and it went down in history as a fun part of '80s/'90s club culture.

Recommended Recordings:

Technotronic, *Pump Up the Jam: The Album* (SBK)

C + C Music Factory, *Gonna Make You Sweat* (Columbia)

Snap!, *Snap! Attack: The Best of Snap!* (Ariola)

Biscuit, *Biscuit's Back!* (AVC)

AB Logic, *AB Logic* (Interscope)

Doug Lazy, *Doug Lazy Gettin' Crazy* (Atlantic)

Stereo MCs, *Connected* (Gee Street)

—Alex Henderson

Jazz-Rap

For a generation of hip-hop artists who remembered Charlie Parker or John Coltrane LPs resting on their parents' turntables, and who had ready access to sampling technology during the 1980s and '90s, jazz-rap worked simultaneously as a salute and connection point to the music of their youth and forebears, an alternative to the increasingly hardcore aspects of rap music as well as a way to introduce the somewhat alien aspects of hip-hop to inexperienced listeners (and critics). While rap's artistic vision and commercial sales grew during the late '80s and early '90s, the sampler was often replaced or expanded on by jazz instrumentalists, from Branford Marsalis, Donald Byrd, and Herbie Hancock to Pharoah Sanders and Roy Ayers. For these jazz artists, the style functioned as an enjoyable holiday away from overanalytical critics and stuffy purists, as well as a chance to play to younger audiences unfamiliar with their vast bodies of work. For all involved, the style's shining moments reflected what each side could learn about another uniquely African-American cultural experience—the virtuoso playing and cerebral flair of jazz could add a new professionalism to the world of hip-hop, while the hard-hitting grooves and energetic free thought of rap's young lions could inject jazz with a renewed sense of purpose and vision.

The early pioneers of rap music were little concerned with jazz however, whether it was the DJs at South Bronx block parties of the mid-'70s, or the initial disco-inspired rap recording artists of the late '70s and early '80s. And when the use of samplers in rap became widespread during the mid-'80s, it was a heavy metal fanatic, Rick Rubin, who used the machine to push the singles of his artists (Run-D.M.C., LL Cool J, and the Beastie Boys) by adding guitar riffs from AC/DC and others. (Rubin did play around just a bit with jazz, sampling Bob James for the Run-D.M.C. track "Peter Piper" in 1986). The first glimpses of serious rappers and producers wishing to pursue their roots

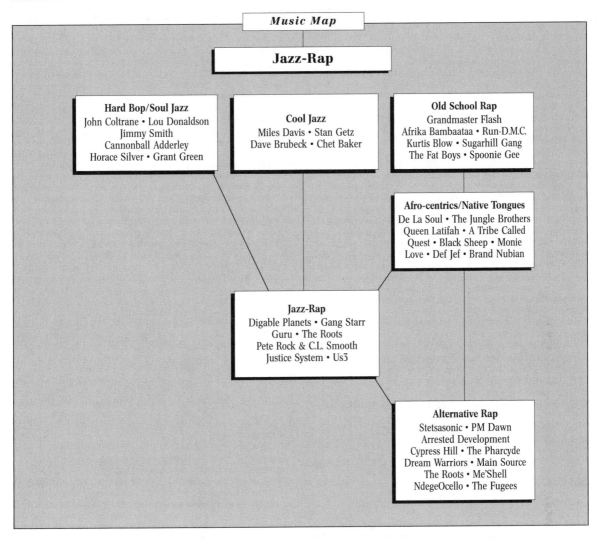

Music Map

Jazz-Rap

Hard Bop/Soul Jazz
John Coltrane • Lou Donaldson
Jimmy Smith
Cannonball Adderley
Horace Silver • Grant Green

Cool Jazz
Miles Davis • Stan Getz
Dave Brubeck • Chet Baker

Old School Rap
Grandmaster Flash
Afrika Bambaataa • Run-D.M.C.
Kurtis Blow • Sugarhill Gang
The Fat Boys • Spoonie Gee

Afro-centrics/Native Tongues
De La Soul • The Jungle Brothers
Queen Latifah • A Tribe Called
Quest • Black Sheep • Monie
Love • Def Jef • Brand Nubian

Jazz-Rap
Digable Planets • Gang Starr
Guru • The Roots
Pete Rock & C.L. Smooth
Justice System • Us3

Alternative Rap
Stetsasonic • PM Dawn
Arrested Development
Cypress Hill • The Pharcyde
Dream Warriors • Main Source
The Roots • Me'Shell
NdegeOcello • The Fugees

in the field of jazz emerged a few years later. In 1988, the hip-hop band Stetsasonic sampled Lonnie Liston-Smith for a track called "Talkin' All That Jazz," and Gang Starr issued their debut single, "Words I Manifest," with a Charlie Parker line used as the main melody. The group's debut album *No More Mr. Nice Guy*, released one year later, caught the ear of filmmaker Spike Lee, who tapped the duo to appear on the soundtrack to 1990's *Mo' Better Blues*. Alongside Branford Marsalis, Terence Blanchard, and Kenny Kirkland, the group appeared on the last cut, "Jazz Thing," with a spoken-word history of jazz (written by Lotis Eli) set to a hip-hop beat and rapping.

Enter the Native Tongues posse, a loose collective of Afro-centric artists inspired by hip hop pioneer Afrika Bambaataa and his Zulu Nation crew. Along with Queen Latifah and A Tribe Called Quest, the Jungle Brothers (whose Afrika Baby Bam gave the posse it's name) were founding members of the Native Tongues. The J. Beez debut, 1988's *Straight Out the Jungle*, was rife with jazzy textures. The following year, De La Soul released their own debut, *3 Feet High and Rising*. One of the most important albums in terms of rap's growing maturity in the 1980s, it was also the first to show the wide range of opportunities available to those with a large record collection and a sampler. The group's producer, Prince Paul, weaved the strains of whitebread pop groups like Hall & Oates, the Turtles, and Steely Dan alongside the trio's intelligent raps.

Though De La Soul's follow-ups to *3 Feet High and Rising* were never half as interesting as their debut, one other Native Tongues group picked up the

torch and took the artistic possibilities of jazz-rap to new heights. On their debut album, *People's Instinctive Travels and the Paths of Rhythm*, A Tribe Called Quest sounded much like their fellow Native Tongues, with an array of samples almost too eclectic for their own good, though their tough rapping style and ear for melody overcame many difficulties. A Tribe Called Quest's second album, *The Low End Theory*, was very nearly a perfect album, jazzy in mood and texture, though the only direct jazz ingredients were a Grant Green sample and a live appearance from bassist Ron Carter. No other group had made jazz-inspired hip-hop that actually enhanced the quality of the music, but on *The Low End Theory*, A Tribe Called Quest showed how smooth the style could sound.

The mellow innovations of De La Soul and A Tribe Called Quest proved quite influential and made them many fans (in the field of rap as well as alternative rock). Hence, the sound of jazz-rap gained significant exposure during 1992-1993. Just before his death, Miles Davis cut an album called *Doo-Bop*, where he incorporated hip-hop rhythms and rapping for the first time, though Davis' weakened condition and the relative anonymity of the hip-hop partakers decreased its appeal. The trio known as Digable Planets made the first significant singles-chart success with their Top 20 debut single "Rebirth of Slick (Cool Like Dat)," and sampled Eddie Harris, Sonny Rollins, Art Blakey, and the Crusaders (among others) on the accompanying album, *Reachin' (A New Refutation of Time and Space)*. A tour with live musicians failed to advance the cause of jazz-rap very far—the players just repeated short lines instead of truly soloing—but the group branched out on their second, *Blowout Comb*, with several solos and more live playing than sampling.

Up to this time, many samples by all but the most prominent groups had been obtained without permission, and both De La Soul and Biz Markie had lost notable cases over unauthorized sampling (significantly derailing their careers in the process). In mid-1993, however, Blue Note Records gave its stamp of approval to sampling by signing a British production duo named Us3 and giving them exclusive license to plunder the vaults for any samples they wished. With a couple of New York rappers in tow, Us3 hit the Top Ten in early 1994 with "Cantaloop (Flip Fantasia)," encompassing samples from Herbie Hancock's "Cantaloupe Island" and Pee Wee Marquette's introduction to an Art Blakey date at Birdland.

The most successful fusion of live jazz and rap, with little ground given to either, was a project begun by Gang Starr's rapper, Guru. Named *Jazzmatazz, Vol. 1* and released in mid-1993 (around the time of jazz-rap's greatest success on the charts), the album featured Roy Ayers, Courtney Pine, and Lonnie Liston Smith (among others), given much space to solo between the heady raps of Guru and others. In 1994, the AIDS benefit compilation series *Red Hot* introduced *Stolen Moments: Red Hot + Cool*, an album that paired jazz players with hip-hop acts, creating interesting combos like Me'Shell NdegeOcello with Herbie Hancock, Digable Planets with Lester Bowie and Wah Wah Watson, and the Roots with Roy Ayers. Standard groups that mixed live jazz playing with rapping and hip-hop beats included Branford Marsalis' Buckshot Lefonque project, an R&B group with equal inspirations from mainstream jazz and hip-hop, and the self-contained rap band the Roots. For the most part, though, by the late '90s most rap groups were less concerned with jazz-rap fusion, settling instead for occasional samples from the old masters.

Recommended Recordings:

The Jungle Brothers, *Straight Out the Jungle* (Warlock)
De La Soul, *3 Feet High and Rising* (Tommy Boy)
A Tribe Called Quest, *The Low End Theory* (Jive)
Gang Starr, *Daily Operation* (Chrysalis)
Guru, *Jazzmatazz, Vol. 1* (Chrysalis)
Digable Planets, *Reachin' (A New Refutation of Space and Time)*(Pendulum)
Us3, *Hand on the Torch* (Blue Note)
Various Artists, *Stolen Moments: Red Hot + Cool* (GRP)
Buckshot Lefonque, *Buckshot Lefonque* (Sony)
The Roots, *Do You Want More?!!!??!* (DGC)

—*John Bush*

Southern Rap

There was a time when southern MCs were very marginalized in the rap world. Back when New York still dominated hip-hop—the late '70s and early to mid-'80s—there weren't a lot of rap superstars who lived south of the Mason-Dixon line. But commercially, Southern rap has come a long way since then—first with bass, then with the dirty South school of hip-hop. "Dirty South," which got its name from a 1995 song by the Atlanta-based Goodie Mob, is an umbrella term that has been used to describe a wide variety of Southern rappers who emerged in the '90s or early 2000s. Dirty South isn't one particular sound but, rather, many different sounds from different parts of the Southern United States. Dirty South is New Orleans rapper Master P and his No Limit posse; dirty South is Atlanta-based artists like Ludacris, OutKast, Pastor Troy, Jugga the Bully, and the abovementioned Goodie Mob. Some dirty South rhymers have come from Memphis (Eightball & MJG, Three 6 Mafia, Gangsta Blac, Indo G) or Miami (Trick Daddy), and some have come from the Carolinas (including Greenville, NC's Petey Pablo and Charleston, SC's Infinity Tha Ghetto Child). Because hip-hop is constantly evolving and trends can easily change from one year to the next, it would be misleading to single out any city as the capitol of dirty South rhyming. Suffice it to say that Atlanta, New Orleans, and Memphis have all been major players in the dirty South field, although one certainly doesn't have to be from any of those cities to contribute to dirty South—every one of the Southern states has, since the '90s, made some type of dirty South contributions.

And if one thinks of Texas as a Southern state, Houston and Dallas should also be considered dirty South hotbeds. Someone from Georgia or North Carolina will tell you that Texas is really a Western state, not a Southern state. But people from the Northeastern Corridor tend to think of Texas as part of the South—at least it seems Southern if you're from Boston or Philadelphia, and a Texas group like UGK is essentially a part of the overall dirty South trend (just as British and Irish rappers are considered European rap even though the British Isles aren't right on the European continent).

Why do Southern rappers use the term "dirty South" to describe both their music and their region? Because so many of the southern MCs who emerged in the '90s and early 2000s have favored dirty lyrics—perhaps sexually explicit, perhaps violent, perhaps both. Dirty South can be as sexually explicit as Oakland's Too Short or as violent as the Los Angeles gangsta rap of N.W.A, Ice-T, and Above the Law. But dirty South doesn't necessarily have to be either of those things. Some dirty South is gangsta rap; some isn't. Some dirty South lyrics are X-rated; some are only mildly risqué. In other words, some dirty South lyrics are dirtier than others—it all depends on what a particular artist chooses to project. But as a rule, dirty South has been known for its abundance of decadent, hedonistic material.

To understand dirty South's roots, one has to go back to the late '80s. That was when producer/rapper Luther Campbell and the Miami-based 2 Live Crew (originally from Los Angeles) popularized a style known as bass, which favored ultrafast tempos and a hyper, extremely energetic approach. The 2 Live Crew were also known for their humorously X-rated, sexually explicit lyrics, which were influenced by comedians like Richard Pryor, Rudy Ray Moore, and Redd Foxx. Along with Orlando, FL's DJ Magic Mike, the 2 Live Crew put Florida-style bass music on the map and made Southern rap a huge industry. In the late '80s and early to mid-'90s, bass was the South's dominant rap style, but in the late '90s, dirty South became the dominant style (or styles) of Southern rap.

Lyrically, the 2 Live Crew and other bass artists were a major influence on dirty South, although dirty South is a lot different musically. Instead of emulating bass' ultrafast tempos, the dirty South artists who emerged in the late '90s and early 2000s were more likely to be influenced by the beats and grooves of West Coast gangsta rap—especially the G-funk sound of Dr. Dre's 1992 masterpiece *The Chronic*. That album was incredibly popular in the South, as were the '90s recordings of Dre's L.A.-based G-funk colleagues Snoop Dogg and Warren G And lyrically, gangsta rap also had a major impact on dirty South (although not all dirty South rappers are into rhyming about thug life—it varies from rapper to rapper). So, to summarize, bass influenced dirty South's lyrics; West Coast gangsta rap and G-funk influenced dirty South both musically and lyrically.

G-funk was a strong influence on New Orleans' entrepreneurial gangsta rapper Master P, whose No Limit Records became a dirty South empire in the '90s; tales of urban thug life were the bread and butter of Master P and his stable of artists (who included Silkk the Shocker, C-Murder, the Gambino Family, Ghetto Commission, Fiend, Soulja Slim, and many others). But again, not all dirty South is gangsta rap. Crunk, for example, is a popular form of dirty South rapping that functions as party music more than anything. The ingredients of crunk (a style associated with the Atlanta-based Lil Jon & the East Side Boyz) have included, among other things, a barking rap style and infectious call-and-response chants. Lil Jon has stated that he doesn't consider himself a true rapper—that what he does is really chanting, not rapping. Nonetheless, crunk is generally considered part of hip-hop's dirty South school.

One of the most intriguing groups in the dirty South field is Field Mob, who hail from Albany, GA, and have proudly described themselves as "country rappers"—not country as in country music, but country as in being from small-town America. Of course, Albany, GA, isn't really a small town; it's a medium-sized city. But it isn't a megametropolis like Chicago either, and Field Mob's Boondox Blax put it best when he described Albany as being "like a metropolitan area, but it's rural at the same time." The group's rural/urban perspective has been an interesting departure from most hip-hop, which thrives on big-city imagery and tales of life in the urban jungle.

The vast majority of dirty South rappers have been black; however, some white MCs have made significant dirty South contributions, including Georgia's Bubba Sparxxx (who has often been described as a redneck version of Eminem) and the Atlanta-based duo Rehab. The two members of Rehab, Danny Boone and Brooks, call themselves Rehab because they met in a drug rehab facility. Their Epic debut *Southern Discomfort* (a 2000 release) is full of clever, dark-humored references to drug and alcohol abuse—something that, sadly, the Georgia rappers have firsthand knowledge of. Throughout *Southern Discomfort*, Boone and Brooks use warped, twisted humor to

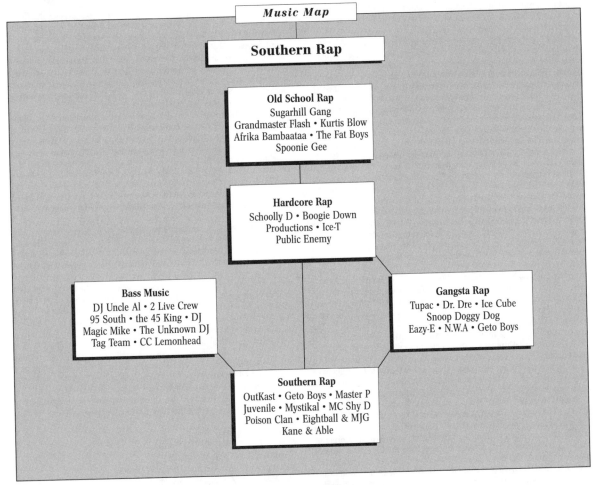

Music Map

Southern Rap

Old School Rap
Sugarhill Gang
Grandmaster Flash • Kurtis Blow
Afrika Bambaataa • The Fat Boys
Spoonie Gee

Hardcore Rap
Schoolly D • Boogie Down
Productions • Ice-T
Public Enemy

Bass Music
DJ Uncle Al • 2 Live Crew
95 South • the 45 King • DJ
Magic Mike • The Unknown DJ
Tag Team • CC Lemonhead

Gangsta Rap
Tupac • Dr. Dre • Ice Cube
Snoop Doggy Dog
Eazy-E • N.W.A • Geto Boys

Southern Rap
OutKast • Geto Boys • Master P
Juvenile • Mystikal • MC Shy D
Poison Clan • Eightball & MJG
Kane & Able

confront their demons—the disc is a perfect example of how rap artists, like blues and country artists, have often laughed to keep from crying. Rehab demonstrated that dirty South isn't always a celebration of decadence; the same goes for OutKast's 2000 hit "Mrs. Jackson," a poignant gem that finds a young father urging the mother of his child to give him a chance to be a responsible parent and take a proactive role in the kid's upbringing. "Mrs. Jackson" acknowledged the importance of fatherhood, and it was one of dirty South's finest moments.

Dirty South isn't as popular in the Northeastern U.S. as it is in the deep South or on the West Coast. Historically, rap fans from the Northeastern Corridor have tended to prefer MCs from their own part of the country, and dirty South rappers usually don't sell as many albums in New York, Philadelphia, Atlantic City, or Boston as they do in New Orleans or Memphis. But these days, a rapper certainly doesn't need Northeastern support to sell millions of CDs—Southern rappers can get rich from the South alone, and they become even more prosperous when you add support from the West Coast, the Midwest, and Europe (where dirty South—and hip-hop in general—is extremely popular).

Although Southern rap wasn't taken seriously in the late '70s and early to mid-'80s, those days are long gone. Southern rap has since become a huge industry, and the dirty South field has created a lot of wealthy individuals below the Mason-Dixon line.

Recommended Recordings:
Field Mob, *From Tha Roota to Tha Toota* (MCA)
Rehab, *Southern Discomfort* (Epic)
Bubba Sparxxx, *Dark Days, Bright Nights* (Interscope)

OutKast, *Stankonia* (LaFace)
Infinity Tha Ghetto Child, *Pain* (MCA)
Lil Jon & the Eastside Boyz, *Put Yo Hood Up* (TVT)
Petey Pablo, *Diary of a Sinner: 1st Entry* (Jive)
Master P, *Ghetto D* (No Limit)
Mystikal, *Let's Get Ready* (Jive)

—*Alex Henderson*

Latin Rap

Hip-hop was invented by African Americans, but it didn't take Latinos very long to get in on the action. In fact, Latinos have been strong supporters of the hip-hop culture since the late '70s, when the first Grandmaster Flash, Kurtis Blow, and Sugarhill Gang singles came out. What is Latin rap? In a nutshell, it's rap music by Latinos, and that can mean a wide variety of things. Latin rap can be Puerto Ricans from Brooklyn, Queens, or the Bronx; it could be Chicanos from East Los Angeles or Cubans from the Little Havana section of Miami. Latin rap can be in English or Spanish—many Latino MCs have been bilingual, although some have opted to rap in either English or Spanish exclusively. Latin rap can be as commercial and pop minded as Gerardo, or it can be the thugged-out gangsta rhymes of Cypress Hill, Funkdoobiest, and tha Mexakinz. The Latino rappers who are best known in North America—Cypress Hill, Mellow Man Ace, Gerardo, among others—have come from the United States. But a Latino rapper certainly doesn't have to be a United States citizen to have a career; hip-hop is huge all over Latin America as well as in Spain, and there have been many non-U.S.

rappers who catered to Spanish-speaking countries. An MC who is selling a lot of CDs in Spain, Argentina, or Mexico can easily turn a profit even if he/she ignores the U.S. market.

And for that matter, Latin rap doesn't have to be in either English or Spanish to be successful. In Brazil—which is the largest country in Latin America and a place where hip-hop is quite popular—the official language is Portuguese, and many Brazilian MCs have rapped in Portuguese exclusively. If English and Spanish are Latin rap's two primary languages, Portuguese is its unofficial third language. There have been rap scenes in all of Brazil's major cities, including Rio de Janeiro, São Paulo, and Salvador—and in all of those cities, Brazilian rappers have combined hip-hop with the samba beat. A good example of rap/samba fusion with Portuguese lyrics is "Salvador Astral," which was a hit for the group MD MC's in the early '90s and has the Afro-Brazilian sound that is popular in the Brazilian state of Bahia. "Salvador Astral," like most Brazilian rap recordings, is little known in North America. Brazilian rappers usually cater to the Brazilian market, and most of them aren't going to lose any sleep if they aren't hitting big in the U.S. (or for that matter, the Spanish-speaking countries of Latin America).

These days, hip-hop is a huge international phenomenon, and there are rap scenes in countries that range from Japan to Poland to Ireland. But in the beginning, hip-hop only had a small cult following—mostly in and around New York. The vast majority of early rappers were African American, and they included pioneers like Grandmaster Flash & the Furious Five, the Treacherous Three, Kurtis Blow, and Afrika Bambaataa. Most of the people who attended their late-'70s shows in Manhattan or the Bronx were black—most, but not all. A lot of Puerto Ricans and Dominicans live in the Big Apple's five boroughs, and young listeners in the Big Apple's Latino communities proved to be quite receptive to early rap singles like Blow's "Christmas Rapping" and the Sugarhill Gang's "Rappers Delight" (both from 1979). The first Latin rap recording came in 1981, when the Mean Machine recorded "Disco Dreams." That groundbreaking single contained lyrics in both English and Spanish—Puerto Rican-style Spanish, to be exact. Countless Puerto Rican rappers have come along since then, and the most noteworthy have ranged from the group Mesanjarz of Funk to the Real Roxanne (whose real name is Adelaida Martinez) to female Brooklyn native Hurricane G.

Those who haven't studied Spanish may have a hard time telling the many different Latino accents apart, but Spanish speakers know that their language is spoken many different ways. Just as the British way of speaking English is much different from the way English is spoken in Georgia or Alabama, a Mexican accent is much different from the Caribbean ways of speaking Spanish that one hears among Cubans, Puerto Ricans, and Dominicans. And Latin rap has reflected the diversity of the Latino world. While Mesanjarz of Funk and Hurricane G have brought a Nuyorkican perspective to hip-hop and used Puerto Rican slang, Southern California rappers like Kid Frost, tha Mexakinz, Lighter Shade of Brown, Proper Dos, Aztlan Nation, Hi-C, and Cypress Hill have brought a Mexican-American or Chicano flavor to the table. While the first Latino hip-hop heads were Puerto Rican or Dominican, Mexicans weren't far behind. L.A.'s Kid Frost, who is widely regarded as the first important Chicano MC, started rapping in the early '80s—and countless Chicano rappers have come along since then. On the West Coast, Chicano rap isn't just one sound but, rather, a variety of sounds. Chicano rappers have ranged from commercial bubblegum artists to thugged-out gangsta rappers like Cypress Hill, tha Mexakinz, E-Side Ghetto, and Lil' Blacky. But not all hardcore rap that has come from Chicano MCs is gangsta rap. For example, Kid Frost (whose real name is Arthur Molina Jr.) is a hardcore rapper but not a gangsta rapper.

The most famous Cuban rapper is the L.A.-based Mellow Man Ace, who is best known for his 1989 hit "Mentirosa" (which sampled Santana's "Evil Ways"). Ace, who was born Ulpiano Sergio Reyez in Cuba but moved to L.A. when he was only four, has rapped with an unmistakable Cuban accent—and the bilingual MC acknowledged his Cuban heritage by calling his first album *Escape from Havana*. Although "Mentirosa" was a smash, Ace's popularity didn't last very long. Rap audiences (much like urban and dance-pop audiences) can be extremely fickle, and by 1993, the Cubano was without a record deal. After an eight-year absence from the studio, Ace attempted a comeback in 2000 with the excellent *From the Darkness into the Light*—which, regrettably, didn't sell and received very little attention.

It is important to know the difference between Latino rappers and Latino dance-pop singers. In the '80s, the term "Latin hip-hop" was coined to describe the Latin-influenced dance-pop of artists like Expose, the Cover Girls, TKA, Nayobe, Nancy Martinez, and Sweet Sensation. A synonym for that style of music is "Latin freestyle" or simply "freestyle," and those terms are preferable to "Latin hip-hop" because Expose and their colleagues are not hip-hoppers or rappers in the true sense—rather, they are dance-pop singers with Latin and hip-hop influences. Latin freestyle, like Hi-NRG and deep house, is basically a form of post-'70s disco—and there is a major difference between singers like Expose and the Cover Girls and Latino rappers such as Kid Frost, Mellow Man Ace, and Hurricane G.

In the '90s, Latin rap became the focus of various compilations. One of the best was Rhino's 1995 release *Latin Lingo: Hip-Hop from the Raza*, which has a Mexican orientation. While Cuban rapper Mellow Man Ace's "Mentirosa" is included, Chicano MCs dominate the compilation (which contains some very insightful liner notes by journalist Gabriel Alvarez). Other noteworthy Latin rap compilations of the '90s include Priority's *Latin Hip-Hop Flava*, Moola's *Str8 Up Loco*, and Globo's *Rap En Español*; while *Latin Hip-Hop Flava* and *Str8 Up Loco* contain mostly English lyrics, the Globo compilation was aimed at the Latin-American market and spotlights rap recordings that are totally in Spanish.

One of the most famous Latino pop-rappers of all time is Gerardo, who was born in Ecuador. Best known for his early '90s hit "Rico Suave," Gerardo never received much respect from hip-hop's hardcore (which dismissed him as a Latino equivalent of Vanilla Ice). But then, Gerardo never claimed to be a hardcore rapper or a hip-hop purist—he was always a commercial pop-rapper and never pretended to be anything else. Gerardo always went after the pop market, and most of the people who bought "Rico Suave" were more likely to be New Kids on the Block fans or Debbie Gibson fans than Ice-T fans.

In the late '90s and early 2000s, there was considerable talk of a "Latin explosion" in the non-Latin media. By "Latin explosion," non-Latin publications were referring to the commercial success that pop singers Jennifer Lopez, Ricky Martin, Marc Anthony, and Shakira were enjoying among non-Latin listeners. But truth be told, Latin music was a huge market long before any non-Latin listeners bought Martin's "Livin' la Vida Loca" in 1999—and Latin rap has long been a viable part of the Latin market. Latinos—Mexican, Spanish, Puerto Rican, Cuban, Brazilian, or otherwise—have been rapping for a longtime, and it is a safe bet that they will keep rapping well into the 21st century.

Recommended Recordings:

Cypress Hill, *Cypress Hill* (Ruffhouse)
Hurricane G, *All Woman* (H.O.L.A.)
Mesanjarz of Funk, *Mesanjarz of Funk* (Atlantic)
Tha Mexakinz, *Zig Zag* (Mad Sounds)
Lighter Shade of Brown, *Brown and Proud* (Pump)
Mellow Man Ace, *From the Darkness into the Light* (X-Ray)
Various Artists, *Rap en Español* (Globo)
Various Artists, *Latin Lingo: Hip-Hop From the Raza* (Rhino)
Various Artists, *Latin Hip-Hop Flava* (Priority)
Various Artists, *Str8 Up Loco* (Moola)

—Alex Henderson

Turntablism

Born in New York's South Bronx in the mid-'70s, rap music became a worldwide cultural and musical phenomena. From LL Cool J to Eminem and on, stars have been born, their exploits well documented, their music topping the charts. But the history of rap music would never be complete without the parallel history of the DJ.

The modern hip-hop DJ first began to take shape with the innovations of Kool Herc. In 1967, Herc moved from Kingston, Jamaica, to the Bronx where he attempted to reestablish his sound system. He soon found that it was not the reggae dub plates he had been spinning back home that moved crowds, but the deep grooves of urban funk. He also noticed the crowd's appetite for the instrumental sections of isolated drums on the records he played. Accordingly, Herc began looping two copies of the same song on separate tables to maintain the energy. These "breakbeats" as they came to be known, became the building blocks for rap. The music's essential embellishment came in 1977 or 1978 when Grand Wizard Theodore stumbled upon the scratch (the sound created by manually moving the record back and forth under the stylus) during his bedroom experiments.

Hip-hop took its first steps in 1979 with the Fatback Band's "King Tim III" and the Sugarhill Gang's "Rapper's Delight." For DJs, however, the most astonishing development was the 12" recording "The Adventures of Grandmaster Flash on the Wheels of Steel" (1981). Capturing the public imagination with an entirely fresh musical language, "Adventures" outlined the DJ's methodology. Bringing together records as diverse as Queen's "Another One Bites the Dust" and a sampled children's story, Flash created a seven-minute sound collage laid down live in the studio. A great, early innovator, Flash would take Theodore's scratch invention to new heights. In 1983 Herbie Hancock's Bill Laswell production "Rockit" starred the scratch work of Grandmixer D.St. With its crossover success (surely a novelty to some) and heavy rotation on MTV, "Rockit" inspired a generation of DJs. As the backbone of the rap crew, the DJ would define a number of signature styles. Some, like Pete Rock and Gang Starr's DJ Premier, would become renowned producers as well. Rarely in the spotlight, however, DJs had to subsist on the occasional showcase track and the usual scratch work and sample stabs. With the rising profile of the MC, even these elements were in danger of extinction.

By the mid-'90s, there was a widening gap between what many felt was "real" hip-hop music/culture and its mainstream form. It became difficult to tell the difference between a hit rap record and a slice of watered-down R&B. Few outlets existed for those opposing this uniformity. Most labels weren't willing to put diverse product on the market. Radio and MTV were far too streamlined. It was a situation ripe for an underground uprising (the kind rock witnessed a decade earlier), and that's exactly what came about.

Having the hindsight of the first decade and a half of hip-hop history and innovations, a number of DJs and DJ groups emerged, determined to resurrect the music's spirit and carry it into the 21st century. Key players included Invisibl Skratch Piklz, the X-Ecutioners, and Beat Junkies, and DJs Kid Koala and Peanut Butter Wolf. DJ Babu, a member of Beat Junkies, dubbed his art turntablism. In 1995, San Francisco's Bomb Hip Hop released the genre's defining compilation, *Return of the DJ, Vol. 1*. This new generation took the arts of scratching and beat de/reconstruction to entirely new levels.

DJs have always had to overcome misconceptions about their craft. Many assume that they just spin other peoples records. While this may be true of club DJs who please crowds with their ability to seamlessly blend the latest hits (albeit with great skill), the turntablist creates something entirely new out of existing materials. Try decoding the Invisibl Skratch Piklz' mind-blowing "Invasion of the Octopus People," a record created by three DJs working six turntables. Others feel the DJ is not an authentic musician, yet crews like the Skratch Piklz have developed highly complex, entirely live, beat-juggling routines. Using two turntables, one DJ works a kick and snare like a live drummer while others add embellishments and scratch. Developing the skills and musicianship required to put it all together requires the time and creativity equal to almost any traditional instrument.

By the end of the century, both rock groups and jazz ensembles were sporting a DJ in their ranks. Such are the tonal possibilities of the record player that many felt the DJ's place in a conventional classical ensemble was inevitable. As former Skratch Pikl DJ Q-Bert proclaimed, the art of the turntablist had evolved beyond the DJ battles that were its lifeblood, into the realm of pure music. Recognizing it as such is perhaps the greatest honor.

Recommended Recordings:
Various Artists, *Return of the DJ, Vols. 1-4* (Bomb Hip Hop)
Various Artists, *Masters of the 1 & 2: History's Greatest DJ's* (Priority)
Christian Marclay, *Records 1981-1989* (Atavistic)
Invisibl Skratch Piklz, *The Shiggar Fraggar Show!, Vol. 1* (Hip Hop Slam)
DJ Q-Bert, *Wave Twisters, Episode 7 Million: Sonic Wars Within the Protons* (Galactic Butt Hair)
Beat Junkies, *The World Famous Beat Junkies, Vol. 1* (P.R.)
Cut Chemist/Shortkut, *Live at Future Primitive Sound Session* (Ubiquity)
Rob Swift, *The Ablist* (Asphodel)
Kid Koala, *Carpal Tunnel Syndrome* (Ninja Tune)

—Nathan Bush

Hip-Hop Producers

Just about any genre of music has its share of producers who are as famous (or almost as famous) as the artists themselves. That is true in rock, country, jazz, and R&B, and it is also true in rap. From Sylvia Robinson to Russell Simmons to Sean "Puffy" Combs, rap has had its share of famous producers

over the years. This essay takes a look at some of hip-hop's most important studio wizards—people who have been as important to hip-hop as Bob Ezrin and Jimmy Iovine are to rock, Orrin Keepnews is to jazz, and Kenny Gamble & Leon Huff are to Philadelphia soul.

During hip-hop's old school era of 1976-1982—old school as in pre-Run-D.M.C.—the most important producer was Sylvia Robinson of Sugar Hill Records (not to be confused with a folk label that has the same name). Robinson (b. Mar. 6, 1936) was a vocalist herself and had a resumé long before her involvement with early hip-hop; in the '50s, she was half of the male/female R&B duo Mickey & Sylvia (best known for their hit "Love Is Strange"). And in the early '70s, Robinson recorded as a solo artist and favored a sensuous, sexy approach to Northern soul; her biggest solo hit during that period was "Pillow Talk," although the single "Sweet Stuff" also enjoyed some radio airplay. In those days, Robinson was both a producer/A&R person (she worked with the Moments and other soulsters) and a vocalist. But by the late '70s, Robinson was putting most of her energy into A&R and producing. At Sugar Hill Records, she became one of the first people to document rap. The Sugarhill Gang's 1979 smash "Rappers Delight" put Sugar Hill Records on the map, and the company soon acquired a reputation for being the Motown or Stax of old school hip-hop. In fact, their roster was a who's who of pre-Run-D.M.C. rappers—a roster that included Grandmaster Flash & the Furious Five, the Sequence (rap's first all-female group), Lady B (the first female rapper to record as a solo artist), the Funky Four Plus One, Spoonie Gee, Super Wolf, and, of course, the Sugarhill Gang. Robinson worked with every one of those artists, and she would have been quite capable of working with Kurtis Blow if given the chance. But that famous old school rapper never recorded for Sugar Hill; instead, he signed with Polygram in 1979 and became the first rapper to record for a major label.

When Blow recorded his self-titled debut album in 1980, he was being managed by Russell Simmons (the older brother of Run-D.M.C.'s Joseph "Run" Simmons). That year, Russell Simmons had a fledgling company called Rush Productions. But several years later, Rush would be a lot more than just a small business. When hip-hop's old school era ended and the second-wave rappers (Run-D.M.C., LL Cool J, etc.) took over around 1983-1985, Simmons built a hip-hop empire—not only as a producer and the head of Rush Productions but also as the cofounder of Def Jam Records. The list of artists Simmons worked with in the '80s (as a producer, manager, or A&R person) included, among many others, Run-D.M.C., LL Cool J, Public Enemy, Davy D, and the Beastie Boys.

The person Simmons cofounded Def Jam with in 1984 was Rick Rubin, who is important as both a rap producer and a rock producer. For several years, Simmons and Rubin were quite a team. But in the late '80s, they parted company due to creative differences. Rubin shared Simmons' love of hip-hop; as a producer, he worked with Run-D.M.C., LL Cool J, Public Enemy, and the Beasties. But he also wanted to produce a lot of rock, whereas Simmons wanted to make hip-hop his main focus. So when Simmons and Rubin parted company and Simmons assumed full control of Def Jam, Rubin founded his own label Def American. At Def American, Rubin continued to produce rappers (including the Geto Boys and Sir Mix-A-Lot), but he also signed everyone from the Black Crowes to Danzig to the infamous death metal/thrash band Slayer.

While Def Jam is Simmons' baby, Cold Chillin' Records was the home of Marlon Williams, aka Marley Marl—one of the top rap producers of the late '80s and early '90s. At Cold Chillin', the Queens, NY, native fashioned a distinctive East Coast sound that combined drum machines with extensive sampling; Marl, in fact, did a lot to popularize the use of James Brown samples. All of the New Yorkers on the Cold Chillin' roster (who included Big Daddy Kane, Kool G Rap, Roxanne Shanté, Biz Markie, and MC Shan) had the Marley Marl sound, which influenced DJ Mark the 45 King, Audio Two, the King of Chill, and other East Coast rap producers of that period.

Marley Marl was known for a very raw, hard-edged, rugged type of sound, while fellow New York producer Hank Shocklee (who was part of the Bomb Squad) is famous for the dissonant, abrasive, noisy sounds that he helped Public Enemy bring to life in the late '80s. But out on the West Coast, Andre Young, aka Dr. Dre (b. Feb. 18, 1965), envisioned something totally different. Dre's style of producing, which came to be called G-funk, was much sleeker and smoother than what one expected from Marley Marl, DJ Mark the 45 King, or Shocklee. The Los Angeles-based Dr. Dre (not to be confused with New York's Doctor Dre, as in Doctor Dre & Ed Lover) started out as a member of the World Class Wreckin' Cru in the early '80s, but it was during his years with N.W.A (1987-1991) that he came to be recognized as a studio genius. During his N.W.A years, Dre not only produced N.W.A—he also worked with Dallas rapper the D.O.C., L.A. gangsta rappers Above the Law, female pop-rap group JJ Fad, and urban contemporary singer Michel'le. And Dre became even more famous as a producer when, in 1992, he launched his solo career with *The Chronic*. That album was amazingly influential; thanks to Dre, countless hip-hoppers embraced the G-funk sound (especially on the West Coast) and went for a combination of clean grooves and dirty lyrics. Whether Dre was working with Eminem, Snoop Dogg, or the late Eazy-E, his production style has always been distinctive and recognizable.

One of the many people *The Chronic* influenced was New Orleans gangsta rapper/producer Master P, a major player in the dirty South school of rap (which became popular in the '90s and was still going strong in the early 2000s). Not all dirty South is gangsta rap, but gangsta rap has been the main focus of Master P and his No Limit label. Not only did Dre influence the lyrics of Master P's No Limit artists—who have included Ghetto Commission, Silkk the Shocker, Fiend, the Gambino Family, Soulja Slim, and C-Murder—he also influenced Master P's production style.

The '90s also saw the rise of two major producers who had one foot in rap and the other in R&B: the New York-based Sean "Puffy" Combs, aka Puff Daddy or P. Diddy, and Timbaland. Puff Daddy (b. Nov. 4, 1970) heads Bad Boy Entertainment, and that company has been both a hip-hop outfit and an urban contemporary outfit. In the '90s, Bad Boy (which is both a label and a production company) was known for the Notorious B.I.G., but it was also known for R&B singer Faith Evans. Puff Daddy's work has often underscored the way R&B and rap became seriously joined at the hip in the '90s; all of the urban singers he has produced (who range from Evans to Mary J. Blige to Total) have been greatly influenced by hip-hop.

Similarly, Virginia native Tim Mosley, aka Timbaland, became known for both hip-hop and hip-hop-drenched R&B in the late '90s. Timbaland (b. Mar. 10, 1971) is famous for his work with Jay-Z, Nas, and other major rap stars, but he is just as famous for working with urban singers like Missy Elliott, Total, K-Ci & JoJo (of Jodeci fame), and the late Aaliyah. Timbaland (who heads the Beat Club label) has extensive dirty South credits; Ludacris, Petey Pablo, Bubba Sparxxx, Shade Sheist, and Pastor Troy are among the many Southern rappers he has produced. But Timbaland is just as likely to work with someone from another part of the U.S., such as L.A.'s Snoop Dogg, New York's Jay-Z, or Chicago's Da Brat.

Of course, Dre was producing hip-hop-drenched R&B before either Puff Daddy or Timbaland. In 1990, Dre's work with Michel'le showed listeners the possibilities of a hip-hop-minded style of neo-soul—and that album came two years before Mary J. Blige's first album, *What's the 411?* But rap has been Dre's primary focus, whereas Timbaland (like Puff Daddy) is as much of an R&B producer as he is a rap producer. And in the late '90s and early 2000s, it was impossible to listen to urban radio without coming across something that Timbaland produced.

There is no telling where hip-hop production styles will go in the future; in hip-hop, trends can come and go quickly. With R&B and rap having formed such a close alliance in the '90s, it's quite possible that there will be a lot more producers like Timbaland and Puff Daddy—that is, studio wizards who are both rap friendly and R&B friendly. Here's what we can say for certain: from the late '70s to early 2000s, hip-hop has been a very lucrative field for a lot of producers.

Recommended Recordings:
Various Artists, *The Sugar Hill Records Story* (Rhino)
Various Artists, *Def Jam Music Group Inc.: 10th Year Anniversary* (Def Jam)
Marley Marl, *House of Hits* (Cold Chillin')
Marley Marl, *In Control, Vol. 1* (Cold Chillin')
Public Enemy, Fear of a Black Planet (Def Jam)
Dr. Dre, *The Chronic* (Interscope)
Various Artists, *Bad Boy's Greatest Hits* (Bad Boy)
Timbaland, *Tim's Bio* (Atlantic)

—*Alex Henderson*

Guest Rappers

In 1981, the *Los Angeles Times* published an article on the rap phenomenon and interviewed several people to get some insights. Old school rapper

Kurtis Blow predicted that hip-hop, like rock and R&B, was here to stay—he was right, of course—while Gerry Thomas of the funk-oriented Fatback Band (which dabbled in rap with 1979's "King Tim III") told the *Times*: "I hope Kurtis and the Sugarhill Gang are saving their money because rapping is a thing of the past." In those pre-Run-D.M.C., pre-LL Cool J days, many R&B artists had their reservations about rap's durability—R&B's naysayers doubted that hip-hop would still be around in 1985, let alone 2003. But these days, you would be hard-pressed to find an R&B singer under 40 who doubts that hip-hop is a permanent part of the musical landscape. The urban contemporary world (like the alt-rock world) has long since embraced hip-hop in a big way, which is why so many R&B singers of the '90s and 2000s have featured guest rappers on their recordings. From Mariah Carey working with Snoop Dogg to Mary J. Blige featuring Lil' Kim, there have been countless examples of R&B singers using guest rappers. This is not only done for creative purposes—it is also done because urban singers and producers are well aware of hip-hop's commercial appeal and want to tap into that gold mine.

The use of guest rappers by singers is hardly limited to urban contemporary. The Jamaican reggae group Black Uhuru featured Ice-T on their song "Tip of the Iceberg" in 1991, and there have been numerous examples of rappers making guest appearances on rock recordings. Snoop Dogg and Lil' Kim, for example, were among the guest rappers who former Mötley Crüe drummer Tommy Lee employed on Methods of Mayhem's debut album in 1999. Two Public Enemy members (Chuck D and Flavor Flav) had a guest spot on Living Colour's "Funny Vibe" in 1988, and in 1998, Ice Cube was featured on Korn's "Children of the Korn." But the main focus of this essay is the use of guest rappers on urban contemporary recordings, and there have been many examples of that—especially in the '90s and 2000s. However, the practice goes back to the '80s.

It was in 1984 that Chaka Khan featured old school rapper Melle Mel (a member of Grandmaster Flash's Furious Five) on her smash remake of Prince's "I Feel for You." Prince's original 1979 version of "I Feel for You" was a lot more subtle and relaxed—Khan, however, envisioned something exuberant and up-tempo as well as something hip-hop minded, and Grandmaster Melle Mel fit right in. In fact, it's hard to imagine Khan's "I Feel for You" remake without him.

Khan's 1984 single wasn't the first example of a major R&B star featuring a well-known MC; in 1983, funkster Rick James featured Grandmaster Flash on a gem called "P.I.M.P. the S.I.M.P.," which decried the ways a pimp can abuse, mistreat, and exploit a prostitute. Flash had been coming out with a lot of sociopolitical songs (including "The Message" and "New York, New York"), and he was an excellent choice for a guest rapper when James wanted to tackle a social issue. Although "P.I.M.P. the S.I.M.P." (which is from James' *Cold Blooded* LP) was a great album track, it wasn't among the funkster's hits. Khan's version of "I Feel for You," however, was huge; the single soared to number one on *Billboard*'s R&B singles chart. And the success of "I Feel for You" sent an important message to the R&B world: that having a guest rapper on your single could, from a commercial and creative standpoint, be a very good thing.

Although hip-hop influenced a lot of R&B artists in the '80s—everyone from Lisa Lisa & Cult Jam to Bobby Brown to Cameo—it was during the '90s that R&B and rap formed an even closer alliance and became seriously joined at the hip. So many of the post-Baby Boomer R&B stars who emerged in the '90s—R. Kelly, Mary J. Blige, TLC, Lauryn Hill, among countless others—were more than hip-hop influenced; they were hip-hop *drenched*. They were obviously R&B singers who lived and breathed hip-hop. And because R&B had become so hip-hop obsessed, it stood to reason that more guest rappers would be turning up on R&B recordings.

In 1993, Janet Jackson featured Public Enemy's Chuck D on a sociopolitical item titled "The New Agenda." And Blige has always seen the wisdom of featuring rappers on her recordings; the list of rappers who have appeared on Blige's albums has included, among others, Lil' Kim, Ol' Dirty Bastard, Grand Puba, Eve, and Keith Murray.

Like Blige, R. Kelly has a long history of featuring guest rappers. So far, they have included the Notorious B.I.G. on 1995's *R. Kelly*; Jay-Z, Noreaga (of Capone-N-Noreaga fame), and Foxy Brown on 1998's *R.*; and Ja Rule on 2003's *Chocolate Factory*.

One of the things that has made the guest rappers phenomenon a success is the fact that some of the major rap producers who emerged in the '90s were also R&B producers. Timbaland is a perfect example; so is rapper/producer

Sean "Puffy" Combs, aka Puff Daddy or P. Diddy. Throughout his career, Combs has had one foot in rap and the other in R&B. Combs' Bad Boy Entertainment was the home of the Notorious B.I.G.—who did so much to revitalize hardcore rap on the East Coast in 1993—but Combs has also worked with Blige, Faith Evans, and other urban singers. And when producers like Timbaland and Combs are both R&B friendly and rap friendly, it is safe to assume that they are going to bring singers and MCs together.

Missy Elliott (who had a track record as a producer/songwriter before she recorded any albums as a vocalist) has always seen the wisdom of using guest rappers on her CDs. Da Brat, Busta Rhymes, and Lil' Kim all had guest spots on her debut album of 1997, *Supa Dupa Fly*, and Elliott's 1999 sophomore outing, *Da Real World*, employed several major rappers as guests (including Eminem, Lil' Kim, Juvenile, Redman, and OutKast's Big Boi). Then, in 2001, she worked with everyone from Eve to Method Man to dirty South favorite Ludacris on her third album, *Miss E... So Addictive*.

Even the very pop friendly Mariah Carey—who is as much of an adult contemporary star as an R&B star—has featured rappers on more than one occasion. The interesting thing is that she hasn't just worked with crossover pop-rappers; Carey has also joined forces with various hardcore rappers and gangsta rappers, including Snoop Dogg on "Crybaby" in 1999. You know that hardcore rap has become amazingly far reaching when someone as middle of the road as Carey is working with Snoop Dogg. And "Crybaby" was hardly Carey's last encounter with hardcore rappers; in 2001, Ja Rule, Ludacris, Da Brat, Mystikal, Busta Rhymes, and Nate Dogg were among the rappers who appeared on her *Glitter* album.

Carey is only one of the many singers who has employed Snoop Dogg as a guest. One expects Snoop to show up as a guest on rap albums—New Orleans gangsta rap entrepreneur Master P has featured him on more than one No Limit project—but the Los Angeles resident has also been a guest of several R&B singers (including Rick James, Babyface, Bootsy Collins, and Keith Sweat) as well as rock-oriented artists like Kid Rock and Darius Rucker (of Hootie & the Blowfish fame).

The sort of regional prejudices that one continues to find in hip-hop haven't had a tremendous impact on most R&B singers' relationships with the rap world. Historically, hip-hop has had its share of regional battles; things got downright nasty when L.A.'s Death Row Records and Puff Daddy's New York-based Bad Boy empire became bitter enemies in the mid-'90s. Some Northeastern hip-hop heads have been known to be unreceptive—even hostile—to rappers from other regions of the United States. But for the most part, this type of regionalism doesn't enter the consciousness of urban contemporary singers—which is why it isn't uncommon for R&B albums to feature guest rappers from different parts of the country. On *Glitter*, for example, Carey crossed paths with MCs from four regions of the U.S.: the Northeastern Corridor (Busta Rhymes, Ja Rule), the West Coast (Nate Dogg), the South (Mystikal, Ludacris), and the Midwest (Da Brat).

In 2002, urban singer Ashanti became famous for her encounters with rappers, including Ja Rule on "Always on Time" and Fat Joe on "What's Luv?" Ashanti is hardly the only female vocalist who has thrived on singer/rapper contrasts, but she has done it especially well. The thing that works for Ashanti is her use of the feminine/masculine juxtaposition; Ashanti, who has a sexy, very feminine voice, will typically join forces with a rugged sort of rapper.

And it is a safe bet that she isn't the only R&B singer who will be doing that sort of thing in the future. As long as rap and R&B maintain a close relationship, one can safely assume that the use of guest rappers will continue to be a common practice on urban contemporary recordings.

Recommended Recordings:

Mary J. Blige, *Share My World* (MCA)

R. Kelly, *R.* (Jive)

Ashanti, *Ashanti* (Universal)

Missy Elliott, *Supa Dupa Fly* (Elektra)

Janet Jackson, *Janet* (A&M)

Chaka Khan, *I Feel for You* (Warner Brothers)

—Alex Henderson

Posse Tracks

Throughout the history of jazz, there has been a system of mentoring. Established improvisers will hire lesser-known improvisers as sidemen and feature them prominently; a sideman receives valuable exposure and

guidance and eventually goes on to record as a leader. In the mid-'40s, Miles Davis was a Charlie Parker sideman before he started recording as a leader; similarly, John Coltrane was a sideman for Dizzy Gillespie in the early '50s and Miles Davis in the mid-'50s before he recorded any sessions of his own. And in the hip-hop world, a similar system exists—a system known as "posse tracks," "posse recordings," or "crew cuts." The idea is for a well-known rapper to feature a younger rapper (usually someone who has yet to become well known) on one of his/her recordings and help the MC make a name for himself/herself. One of the most famous examples of a posse track is Dr. Dre's 1992 smash "Nuthin' But a 'G' Thang," which featured fellow Los Angeles gangsta rapper Snoop Dogg and is from Dre's first solo album, *The Chronic*. When Snoop was hired to rap on "Nuthin' But a 'G' Thang" and other parts of *The Chronic*, he had yet to record any solo albums or become a major rap star—the goal was for the mentor (Dre) to make the protégé (Snoop) famous, and that goal was accomplished. Snoop's appearance on "Nuthin' But a 'G' Thang" made him well known and paved the way for the success of his first solo album, *Doggystyle*, in 1993. Just as Charlie "Bird" Parker had been Miles Davis' mentor back in 1945, Dre was Snoop's mentor in 1992—Dre saw Snoop's potential, just as Bird saw Davis'.

Back in the Wild Wild West of the 19th century, the word "posse" referred to a group of people who apprehended outlaws; someone who robbed a train in the Arizona or Texas of 1880 ran the risk of being confronted by a posse. But in hip-hop, the word "posse" has a very different connotation. To hip-hoppers, a posse, or "crew," is a large group of people with close ties. Ice-T's Rhyme Syndicate outfit is an example of a posse; so is Russell Simmons' Rush empire, Puff Daddy's Bad Boy Entertainment, and Master P's No Limit operation (a stable of Southern gangsta rappers that became huge in the '90s). Members of a hip-hop posse aren't necessarily rappers; they can also be producers, promoters, DJs, managers, A&R people, or even someone's secretary. If a hip-hop posse wants to be profitable, it makes sense to nurture younger rappers and make them well known; that's where posse tracks come in. Posse tracks are usually about marketing; when Dre produced *The Chronic*, he used his popularity to make Snoop a star. And Snoop wasn't the only rapper Dre showcased on *The Chronic*; if he wasn't featuring Snoop, Dre was featuring That Nigga Daz, RBX, Kurupt, or Rage. In fact, everything on *The Chronic* was a posse track of some sort—the posse was Death Row Records, and *The Chronic* established Death Row as one of the top rap labels of the '90s.

Posse tracks have been going on in hip-hop since the '80s. Back in 1987, one of the most famous posse tracks was DJ Jazzy Jeff & the Fresh Prince's "Guys Ain't Nothing But Trouble," which was a sequel to their hit "Girls Ain't Nothing But Trouble" and featured Philadelphia rapper Ice Cream Tee. Her guest appearance on "Guys Ain't Nothing But Trouble" should have paved the way for a long solo career; many listeners assumed that she would go on to become a major solo star. And Ice Cream (who was managed by female rapper and Philly radio personality Lady B) did, in fact, pursue a solo career. However, her first solo album, *Can't Hold Back* (released by Strong City/MCA in 1989), was a commercial disappointment—and she didn't provide any more solo albums after that.

But if Ice Cream Tee didn't live up to the commercial potential that she showed on a posse track, there were countless other rappers who did. Everyone from Lil' Kim to Ja Rule to Everlast has benefited from the posse system in some way. Everlast, for example, was part of Ice-T's Rhyme Syndicate posse in the late '80s and early '90s, and he was among the West Coast MCs Ice-T featured on the tune "What Ya Wanna Do?" in 1989. "What Ya Wanna Do?" was hardly the only posse track that Ice-T recorded during his commercial heyday; 1988's "The Syndicate" and 1989's "My Word Is Bond" (which featured Donald D and Bronx Style Bob) are two more examples of posse tracks that were designed to pump up Rhyme Syndicate Productions and promote Ice-T's allies. Everlast's spot on "What Ya Wanna Do?" didn't make him a huge name in rap; his first solo album, *Forever Everlasting* (released by Warner Bros. in 1990), wasn't a big hit, and it wasn't until Everlast recorded with the group House of Pain in 1992 that he became a major rap star. Nonetheless, Ice-T and Rhyme Syndicate Productions did their part to help Everlast build a resumé.

While Ice-T was a mentor to Everlast and Dr. Dre was a mentor to Snoop Dogg, the late Christopher Wallace, aka the Notorious B.I.G. or Biggie Smalls, was a mentor to Lil' Kim. In the mid-'90s, B.I.G. was the brains behind a Brooklyn, NY-based posse known as the Junior M.A.F.I.A., which included Lil' Kim. B.I.G. saw Kim's potential, and in 1995, she was among the various

Brooklyn rappers he featured on the M.A.F.I.A.'s gold album *Conspiracy* (which came out on B.I.G.'s Undeas label). Kim had yet to record as a solo artist when *Conspiracy* came out, but the hit single "Get Money" (which featured her) helped pave the way for a solo career—and the following year, Kim's solo debut, *Hard Core*, took the rap world by storm. *Conspiracy* did for Kim what *The Chronic* did for Snoop Dogg.

The posse system was also very kind to Ja Rule. Thanks to posse tracks by Jay-Z and Mic Geronimo, Ja Rule was well known by the time his first album, *Venni Vetti Vecci*, was released by Def Jam in 1999.

In the '90s, no East Coast posse had a smarter marketing plan than Staten Island's Wu-Tang Clan, a distinctive outfit that combined hardcore rap with martial arts imagery. Pretty much everything Wu-Tang has recorded since 1993 has been a posse track; Wu-Tang has always been designed to build solo careers, and many of its members have indeed gone on to become successful solo stars. That is true of founding members Genius/GZA and Ol' Dirty Bastard, and it is true of rapper/producer RZA (who wasn't a founding member but had become the posse's musical director by 1993). In fact, the success of Wu-Tang's first album, *Enter the Wu-Tang (36 Chambers)* (released on Loud/RCA in 1993) and the hit single "C.R.E.A.M." enabled at least five members to land record deals as solo artists: Genius/GZA, Ol' Dirty Bastard, RZA, Method Man, and Raekwon. Ghostface Killah, another Wu-Tang member, also went on to have a solo career.

Arguably, Wu-Tang was to East Coast hardcore rap what Art Blakey & the Jazz Messengers were to hard bop in the '50s, '60s, '70s and '80s: an outfit that was designed to feature fresh young talent and find the big names of tomorrow. Many of the people who passed through the Jazz Messengers came to be recognized as bop or post-bop heavyweights—people like Lee Morgan, Freddie Hubbard, Wayne Shorter, Cedar Walton, and Benny Golson—and similarly, the Wu-Tang Clan paved the way for many successful solo careers in the '90s.

Below the Mason-Dixon line, New Orleans gangsta rapper Master P has always been well aware of the posse tracks concept; posse tracks were often an important part of the albums that he released on his No Limit label in the '90s or early 2000s. Master P has his share of detractors, and some of No Limit's releases have been criticized for sounding formulaic and calculated. But no one will ever accuse him of lacking skills as a businessman; in the '90s, Master P turned No Limit Records into a Southern gangsta rap empire. Posse tracks have been a valuable element of Master P's marketing plan—if you bought one No Limit release, he wanted to make sure you knew who else was on the label and would buy their albums as well. A Master P album was never just about promoting Master P the solo artist; it was about promoting No Limit Records as a whole, and the company's overall business plan was evident whether the album was by Silkk the Shocker, Ghetto Commission, C-Murder, Soulja Slim, the Gambino Family, Mia X, or Fiend.

Inevitably, trends in hip-hop will change. But as long as labels are hoping to promote and establish new rap stars, we can safely assume that posse tracks will continue to be an effective marketing tool.

Recommended Recordings:
Dr. Dre, *The Chronic* (Death Row)
Snoop Dogg, *Doggystyle* (Priority)
Ice-T, *The Iceberg/Freedom of Speech...Just Watch What You Say* (Sire)
Wu-Tang Clan, *Enter the Wu-Tang (36 Chambers)* (Loud)
Junior M.A.F.I.A., *Conspiracy* (Undeas)
Jay-Z, *Vol. 2: Hard Knock Life* (Def Jam)

—Alex Henderson

Female Rap

Historically, rap has been a very male-dominated idiom—much more so than R&B, country, or dance-pop. That is true in the United States; it is true in Europe and Latin America, where women don't play nearly as prominent a role in rap as they do in Latin pop (a field that has given us countless female superstars). Nonetheless, female rappers have made some important and valuable contributions to hip-hop, which would have been a lot poorer without Queen Latifah, Salt-N-Pepa, MC Lyte, or, more recently, Eve. From rap's old school era (roughly 1976-1982, give or take a year) to the early 2000s, the same pattern has prevailed when it comes to gender: male rappers outnumber female rappers, but talented female rappers will inevitably break through commercially. Every hip-hop era has been male dominated but has also had

some important female rap stars—and they range from Queen Latifah, MC Lyte, and Salt-N-Pepa in the '80s to Foxy Brown, Nonchalant, Da Brat, and Lil' Kim in the '90s, and Eve in the early 2000s.

From the beginning, hip-hop has had a lot of testosterone; it has often functioned as a form of musical sportsmanship. The old school rappers who were active in Harlem or the South Bronx in the late '70s could be an extremely competitive bunch; microphone battles were quite common back then, and rappers spent a lot of time articulating why they thought they were the best and why "sucker MCs" (rival rappers) were inferior. Machismo was always a big part of hip-hop; talk-show host Bill Maher (who had everyone from Chuck D to Snoop Dogg to Lil' Kim on his *Politically Incorrect* show when it was on ABC in the late '90s and early 2000s) has often said he loves the fact that rap is the one form of American music in which a male point of view is celebrated instead of marginalized. That said, hip-hop hasn't necessarily excluded a feminist perspective either—the female rappers who have succeeded in their field have had a reputation for being assertive, take-charge women. No one could ever accuse MC Lyte, Roxanne Shanté, Queen Latifah, or Foxy Brown of projecting a wimpy image or coming across as shrinking violets; if anything, the fact that hip-hop (hardcore rap more than pop-rap) tends to be so competition minded forces female participants to have more of a feminist outlook.

The first example of a female rapper recording as a solo artist came in 1980, when the Philadelphia-based Lady B recorded her single "To the Beat, Y'all" for Sugar Hill Records. After that, Lady B didn't make rapping her main focus; she ultimately made her mark as a radio DJ in Philly. Nonetheless, she is a historically important figure, as are the members of the Sequence—an early female rap group that also recorded for Sugar Hill Records in the early '80s and was quite popular during hip-hop's old school era. Another noteworthy female MC from that period was Sha Rock, who was part of a mostly male group called the Funky Four Plus One.

Unfortunately, the female rappers who were popular during rap's old school era were unable to maintain their commercial success when hip-hop's second wave (Run-D.M.C. , LL Cool J, Whodini, the Fat Boys, among others) took over around 1983-1984. In rap, the turnover can be mind blowing—hip-hop has always had an "out with the old, in with the new" attitude, and MCs who stay on top as long as LL Cool J are the exception instead of the rule. By the mid-'80s, Sha Rock and the Sequence were considered old school, and there were plenty of younger hip-hop women to take their place (if you want to look at it that way). Roxanne Shanté, the Real Roxanne (a Puerto Rican MC), MC Lyte, Salt-N-Pepa (who were originally known as Super Nature), Queen Latifah, Antoinette, Sparky-D, Ice Cream Tee, Monie Love, Sweet Cookie, and Pebblee-Poo are among the female rappers who emerged in the mid- to late '80s. And that list of artists underscores the fact that female rappers are as diverse a bunch as male rappers. While Shanté and MC Lyte are essentially hardcore rappers and are famous for their battle rhymes, Salt-N-Pepa have had more of a pop-rap focus—the group has had no problem appealing to urban contemporary and dance-pop audiences.

When it came to female rappers, the term "pop-rap" could mean different things in the '80s. Salt-N-Pepa and Oaktown's 357 (who were MC Hammer protégées from Oakland, CA) had crossover appeal, but they weren't bubblegum—certainly not the way that J.J. Fad and L'Trimm (two female pop-rap groups of the late '80s/early '90s) could be bubblegum. The Miami-based L'Trimm (best known for their 1988 hit "Cars with the Boom") never received any respect from rap purists, who disliked their cutesy, girlish image and their frivolous lyrics. But L'Trimm's work should be enjoyed for what it is: goofy, silly, frivolous, escapist fun. Comparing L'Trimm to MC Lyte or the Real Roxanne would be like comparing Poison to Slayer—L'Trimm didn't pretend to be hardcore rap any more than Poison pretended to be death metal.

The early '90s saw the rise of a variety of female rappers, who ranged from Ice Cube associate Yo-Yo to the militantly sociopolitical (and downright controversial) Sista Souljah to some very sexually explicit groups: Chicago's HWA (Hoes with Attitude) and L.A.'s Bytches With Problems (BWP). Both of those groups came out with their debut albums in 1990, which was six years before the release of Lil' Kim's debut solo album, *Hard Core*. Like HWA and BWP before her, Kim has never been the least bit shy about having X-rated lyrics. Kim commands a large following, but she also has her detractors; some feminists have argued that her willingness to exploit sex promotes the objectification of women. But if anyone is being objectified on Kim's albums, it's men. Kim has always projected a take-charge image on her albums—if anything, Kim's releases have portrayed her as the dominatrix and men as the submissives who do her bidding. On the song "Not Tonight," for example, Kim bluntly states that she expects any man she is intimate with to perform oral sex on her—and that men who cannot pleasure her in that way shouldn't even bother wasting her time.

The list of other female rappers who started recording in the '90s is a long one. It's a list that includes, among many others, Nonchalant, Da Brat, Mia X, Foxy Brown, Bahamadia, LeShaun, the Conscious Daughters, Shorty No Mas, Heather B, Overweight Pooch, Tam Tam, and Queen Mother Rage. Gangsta rap was very male dominated in the '90s—like rap in general—but it did give us Sh'killa, a Bay Area rapper who set out to be the female equivalent of Dr. Dre, Snoop Dogg, or Warren G Sh'killa's *Gangstrez from da Bay* (released by Priority in 1995) was right out of the Dre/Snoop/Death Row Records school of West Coast G-funk.

The majority of female rappers have been black—at least in the United States. But some white female rappers have recorded albums over the years, and they have ranged from L.A.'s aggressive, in-your-face Tairrie B (who was very much a hardcore rapper) to pop-rapper Icy Blu (who Irving Azoff's Giant Records envisioned as a female version of Vanilla Ice). In 1990, Tairrie went after the hip-hop world with her debut album, *The Power of a Woman*, which didn't sell. And subsequently, she shifted her focus from hardcore rap to rap-metal and alternative rock as a vocalist for the band Manhole (more recently known as Tura Satana).

When the 21st century arrived, rap wasn't showing any signs of becoming less male dominated—the high level of testosterone that rap had in the late '70s and early '80s wasn't any weaker in 2000, 2001, or 2002. But if women were still a minority in rap, they were a commercially viable minority; Lil' Kim and Foxy Brown (just to give two examples) continued to command sizable followings, and the early 2000s were a great time for the Philadelphia-based Eve (whose first album came out in 1999). Again, every hip-hop era has had some major female stars, and there is no reason to believe that the future will be any different.

Recommended Recordings:
Queen Latifah, *She's a Queen: A Collection of Hits* (Universal)
MC Lyte, *Eyes on This* (First Priority)
Lil' Kim, *Hard Core* (Big Beat)
Roxanne Shanté, *Greatest Hits* (Cold Chillin')
Eve, *Scorpion* (Interscope)
The Sequence, *The Best of the Sequence* (Deep Beats)
Various Artists, *Fat Beats & Brastraps: Hip-Hop Classics* (Rhino)
Various Artists, *Fat Beats & Brastraps: Battle Rhymes & Posse Cuts* (Rhino)
Various Artists, *Fat Beats & Brastraps: New MCs* (Rhino)
Salt-N-Pepa, *The Best of Salt-N-Pepa* (WEA)
Bytches With Problems, *The Bytches* (Columbia)

—Alex Henderson

White Rappers

In the early 2000s, more than a few observers of pop culture found it incredibly ironic that the top rapper was white (Eminem) and the top golfer was black (Tiger Wood). Golf has a reputation for being a very white sport, and hip-hop has been dominated by black males—at least in the United States. But if an African American has the skills and the talent necessary to rise to the top of professional golf—and Tiger Wood obviously does—there is no reason why he shouldn't be praised. Similarly, Eminem's success in hardcore rap is well deserved; the bottom line is that Marshall Mathers is damn good at what he does.

To be sure, Eminem has his detractors, who see his success as yet another example of white America's refusal to embrace African-American culture unless it puts on a white face. The problem with that argument is that many of the white kids who buy Eminem's CDs have also been strong supporters of Jay-Z, DMX, Snoop Dogg, and Ja Rule—all of those hardcore rappers have attracted very integrated audiences, and deservedly so. Very few of the white (or black) kids who bought *The Slim Shady LP* in 1999 or *The Marshall Mathers LP* in 2000 honestly believed that hip-hop needed a white face to be legitimate—many of Eminem's white fans are people who had helped make Dr. Dre, Too Short, and Ice-T rich long before they had ever heard of Marshall Mathers.

Nonetheless, the subject of white rappers remains a controversial one. Just as the question "Can a white man really sing the blues?" has persisted over

the years, there are those who feel that white people (or Latinos and Asians, for that matter) shouldn't even try to rap. But over the years, the best white rappers—Eminem, 3rd Bass, Everlast, the Beastie Boys, among others—have demonstrated that some white artists can, in fact, make valuable contributions to hip-hop.

The first example of a white person rapping in a hip-hop-minded style came in 1980, when Blondie had a major hit with the historic "Rapture"—a gem that was way ahead of its time. Before that, various country artists had embraced a type of rapping—Commander Cody's "Hot Rod Lincoln" (1972) and C.W. McCall's "Convoy" (1975) are two examples of country hits that involved speaking in rhyme instead of singing. But Deborah Harry's vocal on "Rapture" was the first example of a major pop-rock singer doing some rapping in a hip-hop-minded fashion. Then, in 1981, white soul/urban singer Teena Marie did some rapping on her hit "Square Biz." But neither Harry nor Marie were ever full-time rappers—they were singers who wanted to offer some acknowledgment of hip-hop. The first example of white artists becoming full-time rappers came a few years later when the Beastie Boys decided to make hip-hop their main focus. The Beasties didn't start out as a rap group; formed in 1981, they were a punk band in the beginning. But by the time they recorded their 1984 single ("Rock Hard"), the Beasties had taken the hip-hop plunge. And two years later, in 1986, their first full-length album, *Licensed to Ill*, became a multiplatinum smash.

Though hip-hop continued to be dominated by African Americans—who invented the art form, after all—more white rappers recorded albums in the late '80s and early '90s, including 3rd Bass, Vanilla Ice, Everlast, and an obscure Southern group called the White Boys (who provided some enjoyable but little-known albums for Tin Pan Apple, home of the Fat Boys). In terms of styles, those artists ran the gamut. Everlast (who got his start with Ice-T's Rhyme Syndicate Productions) and 3rd Bass favored tough, gritty hardcore rap, as did the White Boys (who, like the Beastie Boys, had a strong rock influence). Vanilla Ice, however, was the epitome of bubblegum pop-rap; he appealed to a pop/Top 40 audience rather than hip-hop's hardcore. But he didn't appeal to either Everlast or the members of 3rd Bass, a Brooklyn group. As Everlast and 3rd Bass saw it, Vanilla Ice's rapping skills were limited at best—and they felt that he was making it even harder for white rappers to be taken seriously. In fact, 3rd Bass' 1991 song "Pop Goes the Weasel" was an angry attack on the multiplatinum pop-rapper.

But if one believes that Vanilla Ice's bubblegum work caused other white rappers to be viewed with suspicion, you wouldn't know it by looking at 3rd Bass or Everlast's sales figures. Both of them were respectable sellers, although Everlast didn't become a huge name until he joined the group House of Pain in the early '90s. Everlast's debut album, *Forever Everlasting* (released by Warner Bros. in 1990) wasn't a big seller, and his contributions to House of Pain's self-titled debut album of 1992 are what made him a major rap star. After recording two more albums with House of Pain, Everlast resumed his solo career with 1998's ambitious *Whitey Ford Sings the Blues.* That Tommy Boy release found Everlast singing as well as rapping and exploring everything from folk-rock and alternative metal to Memphis soul; *Whitey Ford Sings the Blues* isn't for rap purists, but that doesn't make the album any less impressive.

Although the majority of white rappers has been male, some white female rappers have occasionally been signed. One of the most noteworthy was L.A.'s totally in-your-face Tairrie B, who described herself as "the ruthless bitch you love to hate." Despite the presence of N.W.A's Eazy-E, Schoolly D (who produced two songs), and Ice-T associate Bilal Bashir, Tairrie's debut album, *The Power of a Woman* (released by MCA in 1990) didn't sell—in the early '90s, the hip-hop world obviously wasn't ready for a white female with such an angry, aggressive, in-your-face attitude. Nonetheless, Tairrie's album is historically important; *The Power of a Woman* marked the first time that a major label put out an album by a white female MC.

While Tairrie was very much a hardcore rapper, Icy Blu was the exact opposite; she was a bubblegum pop-rapper who Giant Records envisioned as a female equivalent of Vanilla Ice or a hip-hop version of Tiffany. Her self-titled debut album (which Giant released in 1991) was obviously aimed at the Tiffany/Debbie Gibson crowd—Giant no doubt figured that the teen-pop audiences who were listening to Gibson one minute and Vanilla Ice the next would be equally receptive to Icy Blu. But Icy's album turned out to be a commercial disappointment. U.K. resident Betty Boo, however, was a half-Scottish, half-Malaysian female pop-rapper who did well in the early '90s (in Europe more than in the U.S.). *Boomania*, her first solo album, went platinum in England.

Other noteworthy white rappers who were active in the '90s or early 2000s included Young Black Teenagers (who weren't really black—their name was meant to be ironic), Poverty, Tony D (whose 1991 release *Droppin' Funky Verses* was a solid but neglected outing), Stagga Lee, and Bubba Sparxxx (a Georgia native). Sparxxx is among the white rappers who have come from hip-hop's dirty South school, as are Tennessee's Haystak and the Atlanta-based duo Rehab, whose *Southern Discomfort* (released by Epic in 2000) was full of dark-humored references to substance abuse (a subject that, sadly, the duo's members had firsthand knowledge of).

No essay on white rappers would be complete without some mention of Kid Rock. Never a hip-hop purist, Rock is known for combining rap and alternative metal—a potent combination, and one that has earned him more recognition from the rock world than from hip-hop's hardcore.

Most of the white rappers who have been big in North America have been U.S. citizens. But there is a whole other rap world that most American hip-hop heads—black, white, Latino, or otherwise—know little or nothing about: the world of European rap. In Europe—where hip-hop has been very integrated since the '80s—there have been many famous white rappers, who have ranged from Italy's Articolo 31 to Germany's Die Fantastischen Vier. Although little known in the U.S., those groups are major hip-hop stars in Europe—a place where MCs don't necessarily rap in English. Rappers usually rhyme in English in England, Ireland, and Scotland, but in other parts of Western Europe, one is likely to hear white rappers getting busy in French, German, Italian, or Dutch. And in Eastern Europe (where hip-hop has become increasingly popular since the fall of communism), white rappers have been flowing in languages like Russian, Polish, and Czech. Not that black rappers have been marginalized in Europe—that isn't the case at all. However, it is safe to say that most of the European hip-hop audience has long since grown accustomed to hearing white artists rap and believes that rapping doesn't necessarily have to be done in English. An Italian rap fan in Milan or Florence, for example, might appreciate everyone from OutKast to Italy's angrily sociopolitical 99 Posse, who have been compared to Public Enemy (although Chuck D and Flavor Flav, unlike the 99 Posse, have never rapped in Italian). Stylistically, the white rappers of Europe (much like Europe's black rappers) are an extremely diverse bunch. They range from hardcore rappers like Ireland's Scaryéire to pop-rappers such as Die Fantastischen Vier, who have been described as a German-language equivalent of DJ Jazzy Jeff & the Fresh Prince or Young MC.

Hip-hop came out of African-American culture, and chances are that the majority of important rappers will continue to be black (in the U.S., anyway). Nonetheless, the best white rappers deserve a shout-out and should be applauded for their contributions to hip-hop.

Recommended Recordings:
Eminem, *The Marshall Mathers LP* (Interscope)
Rehab, *Southern Discomfort* (Epic)
House of Pain, *Same as It Ever Was* (Tommy Boy)
3rd Bass, *Derelicts of Dialect* (Def Jam)
Tairrie B, *The Power of a Woman* (MCA)
Everlast, *Whitey Ford Sings the Blues* (Tommy Boy)
Bubba Sparxxx, *Dark Days, Bright Nights* (Interscope)
Tony D, *Droppin' Funky Verses* (4th & Broadway)
Beastie Boys, *Licensed to Ill* (Def Jam)
Young Black Teenagers, *Young Black Teenagers* (MCA)

—*Alex Henderson*

Rap-Metal

Back in the '80s, many rock stations—like urban contemporary stations—offered little acknowledgment of rap. But times have changed. These days, the playlists of alternative rock stations are full of artists who have some type of hip-hop influence, and that could be anyone from the eclectic Beck to rap-metal favorites Korn. Not all rap-rock is rap-metal—Beck, for example, is a hip-hop-influenced alternative pop-rocker who has nothing whatsoever to do with rap-metal. But rap-metal is an important part of rap-rock, not to mention a very popular part. As its name indicates, rap-metal is a fusion of rap and heavy metal. In the '90s and 2000s, the big names in rap-metal have included, among others, Rage Against the Machine, Korn, Limp Bizkit, Kid

Rock, (hed) pe, the Insane Clown Posse, and Methods of Mayhem (a band that drummer Tommy Lee put together after he left Mötley Crüe and before he started recording as a solo artist). Rap-metal vocalists don't necessarily spend all of their time rapping; Limp Bizkit, (hed) pe, and Korn, for example, have actually included more singing than rapping on their albums. But rapping is still an important part of what those bands have done, and they tend to appeal to rockers who are also major hip-hop heads; quite often, a Korn or Limp Bizkit fan is the sort of listener who will get into Soundgarden one minute and Jay-Z the next—or the sort of listener who would play Tool and White Zombie on his/her way home from a Lil' Kim show. When gangsta rapper Ice Cube (formerly of the seminal N.W.A) went on tour with Korn in 1998, Korn's fans knew exactly who he was; some of them were probably Ice Cube and N.W.A fans before they were Korn fans.

Although the term "rap-metal" is usually associated with artists who emerged in the '90s or 2000s, the fusion of rap and heavy metal actually goes back to the '80s. It was in 1984 that two of the earliest rap-metal recordings came out: Run-D.M.C.'s "Rock Box" and the Beastie Boys' "Rock Hard." Those New York artists had different backgrounds; Run-D.M.C. were always rappers, whereas the Beastie Boys started out as a punk band but evolved into a rap group. The thing they had in common was an ability to find the common ground between rap and metal/hard rock, both of which are known for having a very rebellious spirit and an in-your-face attitude. For 1984, "Rock Box" and "Rock Hard" were quite revolutionary—back then, it came as a shock to hear MCs rapping over a crunching heavy metal guitar because so many pre-Run-D.M.C. rappers had been using funk and disco tracks. At the same time, the rap-metal combination made perfect sense when you thought about it—and Run-D.M.C. and the Beastie Boys obviously saw the parallels between the two. Nor were the parallels lost on the artists' fans; in 1984, more and more non-black rock fans were getting into hip-hop, and Run-D.M.C. was attracting very integrated audiences. "Rock Box" was only the first of many rap-metal recordings that came from Run-D.M.C., who were equally metal or hard rock minded on subsequent gems that included "You're Blind," "Kings of Rock" (the title track of their second Profile album), and a 1986 remake of Aerosmith's 1975 classic "Walk This Way" (which united Run-D.M.C. with Aerosmith members Steven Tyler and Joe Perry).

The Beasties, having started out as a punk band, appealed to rock audiences from the beginning—and when they made the transition from punk to rap, many of their fans were receptive. The metal/hard rock influence is impossible to miss on their debut album, *Licensed to Ill*, which Def Jam/Columbia released in 1986. It is no coincidence that Rick Rubin, who produced *Licensed to Ill*, has also produced metal and/or hard rock bands that include Slayer, Danzig, the Cult, and AC/DC.

After Run-D.M.C. and the Beastie Boys got the rap-metal ball rolling in 1984, many other '80s rappers provided rap-metal recordings—everyone from LL Cool J ("Go Cut Creator Go"), Whodini ("Fugitive"), Public Enemy ("Sophisticated Bitch"), the D.O.C. ("Beautiful But Deadly"), and the Fat Boys ("Rock-N-Roll") to the innovative gangsta rapper Ice-T (who sampled Black Sabbath's "War Pigs" on the title track of his debut album, *Rhyme Pays*, and sampled Heart's "Magic Man" on "Personal"). Like Run-D.M.C., Ice-T had more than a casual interest in rock—he was a serious headbanger who started a metal/punk band of his own, Body Count, in the early '90s. Another rapper who was also a metalhead was the Seattle-based Sir Mix-A-Lot, who joined forces with Northwestern headbangers Metal Church when he put a hip-hop spin on Black Sabbath's "Iron Man."

While Run-D.M.C., Ice-T, and many others brought metal and hard rock into rap in the '80s, Anthrax was among the first bands that brought rap into metal—thrash metal, to be specific. The madcap "I'm the Man," released in 1987, found Anthrax offering a quirky and very fresh sounding mixture of metal, rap, and punk, and the New York headbangers subsequently teamed up with Public Enemy for a 1991 remake of PE's "Bring the Noise." Hard rocker Joan Jett, meanwhile, acknowledged rap on her 1986 recording "Black Leather," and the bands that dabbled in rap-metal in the late '80s ranged from Faith No More and the Red Hot Chili Peppers to Living Colour and 24-7 Spyz.

If rap-metal started with Run-D.M.C. and the Beastie Boys in 1984, it evolved considerably in the '90s—a decade that found metal in general (or rock in general, for that matter) changing quite a bit. As a rule, the rap-metal favorites who emerged in the '90s weren't rapping over Black Sabbath or AC/DC songs; instead, bands like Rage Against the Machine, Korn, Limp Bizkit, and (hed)pe were firmly planted in post-'80s alternative metal. Their riffs weren't Judas Priest or Ronnie James Dio riffs; they were the sort of chugging, punk-minded riffs that alternative metal is known for.

But as much as metal in general changed in the '90s, it maintained one of the prime ingredients of '70s and '80s metal: testosterone. In the '90s rap-metal was full of testosterone-powered aggression—that's one of the things that Korn, Limp Bizkit, and Methods of Mayhem have in common with AC/DC, Van Halen, Kiss, and other metal/hard rock bands that were big in the '70s and '80s. In most cases, the angst-ridden rap-metal of the '90s wasn't sociopolitical—it was angrily rebellious, but not in a sociopolitical way. However, one rap-metal band that was extremely sociopolitical in the '90s and early 2000s was Southern California's Rage Against the Machine, which combined alt-metal's chugging guitars with a strong appreciation of Public Enemy. Without question, Rage Against the Machine was heavily influenced by Chuck D's outfit—both musically and lyrically. Rage Against the Machine, like Public Enemy, became known for having very radical, militant politics, and some of Rage's far-left positions were highly controversial (such as their endorsement of the Sendero Luminoso or Shining Path, a group of Maoist/Stalinist guerrillas who were trying to overthrow the government of Peru). But whether one agrees or disagrees with their politics, Rage was among the best-sounding rap-metal bands of the '90s and early 2000s.

No headbanger has been more willing to change with the times than drummer Tommy Lee, whose Methods of Mayhem project of 1999 was a radical departure from his former band Mötley Crüe. Methods of Mayhem's self-titled debut album of 1999 was full-fledged rap-metal in the Korn/Limp Bizkit vein, and it didn't sound anything like *Shout at the Devil* or *Theater of Pain* (which were among Mötley Crüe's famous '80s albums). Some of Lee's longtime fans were no doubt hoping for something more Crüe-minded, but Methods' album was well received in the rap-metal market—and the drummer's more-broad-minded fans admired his desire to forge ahead. In 2002, Lee continued to travel in an alternative-metal direction when he recorded his first solo project, *Never a Dull Moment*, for MCA. Few of the songs on that release were straight-up rap-metal, although many of them were hip-hop influenced in some way.

When the year 2000 arrived, rap-metal was still going strong; in fact, rap-metal was experiencing saturation at that point (just like any trend that becomes hot). And if one agrees that rap-metal started with Run-D.M.C. and the Beastie Boys in 1984, it could be argued that rap-metal celebrated its 19th birthday in 2003. One can only speculate on where rap-metal will go in the future, but it is a safe bet that hip-hop will continue to influence the alternative metal field.

Recommended Recordings:
Limp Bizkit, *Three Dollar Bill Y'All* (Interscope)
Korn, *Follow the Leader* (Immortal)
Rage Against the Machine, *The Battle of Los Angeles* (Epic)
Kid Rock, *Devil Without a Cause* (Lava)
Run-D.M.C., *Raising Hell* (Profile)
Run-D.M.C., *King of Rock* (Profile)
Beastie Boys, *Licensed to Ill* (Def Jam)
Methods of Mayhem, *Methods of Mayhem* (MCA)
Fat, *Fat* (A&M)
(hed)pe, *Broke* (Jive)
Anthrax, *I'm the Man* (Island)
Body Count, *Body Count* (Sire)

—Alex Henderson

European Rap

"Representing the 'hood" is a term that one frequently hears in hip-hop circles. Historically, rappers have been obsessed with telling you where they're from and why they're proud to be from a particular area. That's why Run-D.M.C. described themselves as "kings from Queens" (as in the Queens borough of New York City), and it's why N.W.A called their second album *Straight Outta Compton* (as in Compton, CA, the tough Los Angeles ghetto that N.W.A was from). It's also why hip-hoppers from Long Island, NY, affectionately call that area "Strong Island" and why many Southern MCs refer to their region as the dirty South (not dirty as in physically unclean—dirty as in having explicit lyrics). From Master P in New Orleans to the Roots in Philadelphia, rappers all over the United States have been representing the 'hood and

doing so in a very loud, vocal way—they want to make sure that listeners know exactly where they're from.

But the 'hood doesn't necessarily have to be in the United States or anywhere else in North America. Rap is huge in most parts of the world, and there are hip-hop scenes in places that range from Rio de Janeiro, Brazil, to Tokyo, Japan, to Johannesburg, South Africa. There are rappers in Mozambique; there are rappers in the Philippines and different parts of India (where numerous Indian pop singers have incorporated hip-hop elements). The main focus of this essay, however, is European rap, and that could be anything from an Irish MC in Dublin to a German rapper in Munich (which the English-language section of a German hip-hop website calls "Muthaphukkin' Money Makin' Munich"). When a European rapper talks about life in the 'hood, he/she could be talking about Venice, Italy—or perhaps the 'hood could be in Stockholm, Sweden, or Barcelona, Spain. From Scandinavia to Portugal, hip-hop has been huge in Europe since the '80s.

In terms of European geography, this essay does not take a purist approach and classifies British, Scottish, and Irish rap as part of the European hip-hop spectrum. Technically, the British Isles are not right on the European continent; one couldn't drive a car from London to Vienna or from Dublin to Geneva (unless the car could also function as a submarine—and those kind of cars only exist in sci-fi movies). Nonetheless, the countries of the British Isles (England, Ireland, and Scotland) are essentially part of the greater European community, and Americans tend to think of them as European countries—if your ancestors were from Ireland but you were born and raised in New Jersey, you're considered a Euro-American. And if you're busting a rhyme on the streets of Manchester, Dublin, or Glasgow, you're as much a part of European rap as someone from Paris, Copenhagen, or Berlin.

For the most part, European rap has received very little attention in the U.S.—and the language barrier has been a definite factor. To a hip-hop head from West Philly, East Oakland, or South Central L.A., it might sound strange to hear Germany's Die Fantastischen Vier rapping in German, Italy's Articolo 31 rapping in Italian, or France's MC Solaar rapping in French. But it isn't considered strange in Europe, where all of those artists are well known and have sold a lot of CDs. Europeans, for the most part, tend to be a lot more multilingual than Americans; it isn't uncommon for someone to graduate from a European high school speaking several languages fluently (including English). Consequently, European hip-hop heads are used to hearing MCs flowing in different languages—they speak enough English to understand most or all of Jay-Z's lyrics, but they're also quite comfortable hearing MC Solaar getting busy in French. Solaar (a jazz-influenced alternative rapper along the lines of De La Soul, A Tribe Called Quest, and the Jungle Brothers) is not only a major rap star in France; he's also sold a ton of CDs in other European countries. Solaar isn't nearly as well known in the U.S., but like other major European rappers, he has demonstrated that an MC can be a superstar by catering to the European market.

The fact that Europeans tend to be more multilingual than Americans not only explains why European rap fans are willing to hear rapping in different languages—it also explains why some rappers from countries where English isn't the official language have been able to rap in English exclusively (including Denmark's Bootfunk and Sweden's ADL). Again, becoming multilingual is encouraged in many of Europe's public school systems, and fluency in English is a goal of many European kids—they want to be able to understand the dialogue in a Martin Scorsese movie, the lyrics of a Lil' Kim tune, or the material on CNN's website. In terms of language, European MCs generally feel that different options are available; a Dutch rapper might feel perfectly comfortable flowing in English, or he/she might prefer to rap in Dutch. Hip-hop fans in Holland (where the popular rappers have ranged from DTF and 24K to the Osdorp Posse) are open to hearing local artists rapping in either Dutch or English—for that matter, Dutch rap fans are open to hearing rapping in French, German, Italian, or Spanish. MC Solaar and Die Fantastischen Vier (whose name is German for the Fantastic Five) have sold plenty of CDs in the Netherlands.

Because English is the primary language of the British Isles, it stands to reason that British, Irish and Scottish MCs have a greater chance of reaching the American market than someone who raps in Dutch, German, French, or Italian exclusively. And on rare occasions, British rappers have enjoyed exposure in the U.S.—Monie Love, who reached her commercial peak in the late '80s and early '90s, is the British MC who has enjoyed the greatest commercial success in North America. Other noteworthy British hip-hoppers have ranged from the London Posse, Derek B, and the Demon Boyz to the Wee Papa Girls and the Cookie Crew (two female pop-rap groups that have been described as a U.K. equivalent of Salt-N-Pepa). Linguists who take a close look at the hip-hop trends of the British Isles will hear the English language used in many different ways; British rap has, in some cases, sounded like a mixture of Cockney and African-American slang, whereas Irish and Scottish rappers have often combined a brogue with African-American slang. In fact, one can hear the parallels between House of Pain (the Irish-American rap group that made Everlast famous) and Scaryéire, a hardcore rap group from Ireland. Scaryéire is an intriguing example of multiculturalism—the Irish rappers love African-American culture, but instead of trying to sound exactly like black MCs from the U.S., they combine African-American and Irish/Celtic influences. Instead of rapping about growing up in the projects of North Philly—something they haven't experienced—Scaryéire's members are wise enough to rap about something they do have firsthand knowledge of: life in Ireland. Scaryéire has represented the 'hood, which is also what rappers have done in Italy (where noteworthy hip-hoppers have ranged from Nuovi Briganti to the militantly sociopolitical 99 Posse). Italian hip-hop heads will tell you that MCs from different parts of Italy rap with different accents—in Palermo, for example, one might encounter MCs with a Sicilian/Southern Italian way of rapping, whereas MCs from Milan have more of a Northern Italian flow. And there's a similar situation in Spain, where a rapper from Barcelona is likely to have a different accent than a Madrid-based rapper. It should be noted that Spanish-language rapping in Spain sounds a lot different from Spanish-language rapping in Latin America; similarly, Portuguese-language rapping in Portugal sounds a lot different from Portuguese-language rapping in Brazil (the only Latin American country where Spanish isn't the official language).

Although much of this essay has focused on Western Europe, hip-hop has been getting bigger and bigger in Eastern Europe. Back in the '80s—when Eastern Europe was still dominated by Soviet-style communist regimes—hip-hop was very underground in places like the Soviet Union, Poland, Czechoslovakia (now the Czech Republic), and Hungary. Rap, like rock, was especially frowned upon in Albania and Romania, both of which had brutally repressive, totally xenophobic Stalinist regimes. But after the fall of communism in Eastern Europe in the late '80s and early '90s, it became a lot easier to obtain rap CDs in that part of the world. Rappers from former communist countries have ranged from Poland's BZiK to the Czech Republic's Rapmasters.

Whether or not European rap artists will make inroads in the U.S. remains to be seen; obviously, Europeans who rap in English have a better shot than those who don't (although British, Irish, and Scottish rappers have tended to do much better in Europe than in North America). But then, plenty of European MCs have been selling a ton of CDs with little or no help from the U.S. market—and that trend will likely continue for some time.

Recommended Recordings:
Monie Love, *Down to Earth* (Warner Brothers)
MC Solaar, *Qui Seme le Vent Recolte le Tempo* (Polygram)
Die Fantastischen Vier, *4.99* (Columbia)
Articolo 31, *The Best of Articolo 31* (Best Sound)
Wee Papa Girls, *The Beat, the Rhyme, the Noise* (Jive)
Various Artists, *Planet Rap: A Sample of the World* (Tommy Boy)
—Alex Henderson

Label Descriptions

AMERICAN

It would be inaccurate to describe American Recordings (originally known as Def American Recordings) as a rap-oriented label because rap is only part of what the Los Angeles-based company has put out. Nonetheless, American deserves a big shout-out from the hip-hop world because its founder/owner is someone who has made valuable contributions to hip-hop over the years: producer Rick Rubin. The native New Yorker has a long history of aggressively supporting hip-hop, but Rubin is a true eclectic–he has worked with everyone from LL Cool J to Johnny Cash to Slayer—and American has inevitably reflected his desire to be both a rap producer and a rock producer. Rubin's involvement with hip-hop A&R goes back to 1984, when he cofounded Def Jam Records with producer/manager Russell Simmons. At Def Jam, Rubin played a major role in the success of LL Cool J, the Beastie Boys, and Public Enemy. But as much as Rubin loved hip-hop, he didn't want to produce it exclusively. So in the late '80s, Rubin and Simmons parted company. Simmons assumed full control of Def Jam, and Rubin founded American. Throughout the '90s, American reflected Rubin's diversity. It was the home of well-known rock acts like Slayer, the Black Crowes, and Danzig, but American also released albums by hip-hoppers who ranged from Houston's gangsta rap-oriented Geto Boys to Seattle pop-rapper Sir Mix-A-Lot. And American was where, in 1994, Rubin produced the folk-oriented American Recordings for country legend Johnny Cash. Again, how many producers can say that they have worked with LL Cool J and Johnny Cash and Slayer?

BAD BOY

Bad Boy Entertainment is to producer/rapper Sean "Puffy" Combs, aka Puff Daddy or P. Diddy, what Def Jam is to Russell Simmons and Ruthless was to the late Eazy-E–Bad Boy is Puff Daddy's baby, and in the '90s, the native New Yorker turned Bad Boy into a rap/R&B empire. Bad Boy, which has functioned as both a label and a production company, underscores the way hip-hop and R&B became joined at the hip in the '90s—at Bad Boy, Combs has often brought a strong hip-hop flavor to R&B projects and a strong R&B flavor to rap projects.

Born in 1970, Combs was only in his early 20s when he became an A&R executive for Uptown Records in the early '90s and worked with Mary J. Blige, Heavy D & the Boyz, and Father MC. When Uptown fired Combs—probably for political reasons, not because he didn't have a track record—he wasted no time starting Bad Boy. In 1994 and 1995, Bad Boy was huge, thanks to a roster that included major rappers like the Notorious B.I.G. and Craig Mack as well as R&B artists who included Faith Evans and Total. Sadly, things turned downright ugly when Bad Boy had a well-publicized East Coast/West Coast feud with Death Row Records (home of Tupac Shakur) in the mid-'90s. Combs and Death Row's infamous Suge Knight became bitter enemies, as did B.I.G. and Shakur (both of whom were killed by bullets they received in drive-by shootings—Shakur in 1996, B.I.G. in 1997). But despite that tragic side of Bad Boy's history—and despite Puff Daddy's various legal problems in the early 2000s—he continued to be a major name in both R&B and rap.

COLD CHILLIN'

One of the prime labels during rap's golden age, Cold Chillin' was not only the first to legitimize sampling but also the major recipient of the clampdown on unlicensed use. The label was the brainchild of entrepreneur Tyrone "Fly Ty" Williams and superproducer Marley Marl, with radio DJ Mr. Magic. During the early '80s, Williams was coproducing Mr. Magic's radio show *Rap Attack* on New York's WBLS when he met Marley Marl, a frequent DJ for the show; the trio began billing themselves as the Juice Crew in 1983, after Magic's

nickname Sir Juice. One year later, Marley began producing after his neighbor, Roxanne Shanté, approached him about delivering an answer rap to U.T.F.O.'s "Roxanne, Roxanne." The devastating single, "Roxanne's Revenge," earned massive airplay around New York (thanks initially to Mr. Magic), the first shot in an answer-record craze that eventually spawned more than 100 recordings.

Though Shanté recorded for the Pop Art label, she helped bring many other artists into the Juice Crew fold, including Biz Markie. Markie spawned the founding of Cold Chillin' in 1986 with a Marley Marl-produced EP released on Prism, run by Len Fichtelberg. With Marley's production finesse, Fichtelberg's capital, Williams' executive talents, and Mr. Magic's drawing power, Cold Chillin' was a success right off the bat. Thanks to a distribution deal with Warner Bros. in 1987, releases by Shanté, Markie, and MC Shan performed well even before Markie's "Just a Friend" hit the pop Top Ten in 1990. (Also helping matters was an ongoing feud with KRS-One and his South Bronx-based Boogie Down Productions, which resulted in promotion for both crews as well as two of the hottest singles in rap history: MC Shan's boast rap "The Bridge" and BDP's answer record, "The Bridge Is Over.")

During the late '80s and early '90s, Cold Chillin' was home to a large share of the best rappers in hip-hop, including Big Daddy Kane, Kool G Rap & DJ Polo, Craig G, and Masta Ace, as well as those mentioned above. In 1992, Marley launched a subsidiary label called Livin' Large that saw releases from YK and MC Shan. Three years later, distribution switched to Sony's Epic Street label, though Cold Chillin' hadn't recorded a hit in several years. Marley Marl later sued Cold Chillin' for $500,000 in back payments; the suit was settled out of court and Marley received ownership of all his productions for the label.

DEATH ROW

When N.W.A broke up in 1991, the group's ex-members concentrated on their solo careers. Ice Cube, who had left N.W.A in 1990, already had a solo career and stayed with Priority. MC Ren signed with Capitol, while Eazy-E (who died of AIDs in 1995) ran his Ruthless label. And Dr. Dre formed a partnership with the infamous Suge Knight and formed Death Row Records, which turned out to be one of the hottest, most influential gangsta rap labels of the '90s. It didn't take Death Row long to become a success; released in 1992, Dre's first solo album, *The Chronic*, went multiplatinum and introduced rap fans to the talents of Snoop Dogg (who was prominently featured on various tracks). Subsequent Death Row releases, including albums by Snoop and the late Tupac Shakur, were also huge. But sadly, Death Row's commercial success was often overshadowed by all of the negative publicity the company received.

In the mid-'90s, things turned downright nasty when Death Row had a major feud with producer/rapper Sean "Puffy" Combs' Bad Boy Entertainment. Knight and Combs became bitter enemies, as did Shakur and the Notorious B.I.G. (Bad Boy's top rapper at the time). In 1996, Shakur was killed by bullet wounds he sustained during a drive-by shooting; B.I.G. was killed the same way the following year, and there was speculation that B.I.G. was murdered in retaliation for Shakur's murder (although nothing was proved). Dre, who became fed up with Knight's strong-arm tactics, ended his partnership with him in 1996 and formed a new label called Aftermath. Knight, who went to prison on racketeering charges in 1997, ended up changing Death Row's name to The Row after his incarceration ended.

DEF JAM

Def Jam Records could be described as "the house that Russell built"—that is, Russell as in producer/manager Russell Simmons, who has been a part of hip-hop since the late '70s. Simmons (the older brother of Run-D.M.C.'s Joseph "Run" Simmons) made Def Jam a success with the help of fellow producer Rick Rubin, whom he cofounded the label with in 1984. For several years, the two of them made quite a team; together, they helped make LL Cool J, the Beastie Boys, Public Enemy, Slick Rick, and others successful. And Def Jam (which landed a distribution deal with Columbia in 1985 and moved to Polygram in 1994) was only part of the hip-hop empire that Simmons created in the '80s; he was also the head of Rush Productions, a management company that he founded in 1979 (when the native New Yorker started managing old school rapper Kurtis Blow). Rush went on to manage Run-D.M.C. (who recorded for Profile) as well as many of the artists who recorded for Def Jam in the '80s.

By the end of that decade, Simmons and Rubin had gone their separate ways. Rubin wanted to be both a rap producer and a rock producer, whereas Simmons was mainly interested in rap. So when they parted company, Simmons assumed full control of Def Jam and Rubin founded his own label: Def American Recordings. In the early '90s, Def American had a roster that ranged from rockers (including Slayer, Danzig, and the Black Crowes) to rappers (Sir Mix-A-Lot, the Geto Boys). Def Jam, meanwhile, maintained a hiphop-oriented direction in the '90s with LL Cool J, Public Enemy, and others. In the early 2000s, Def Jam was still going strong with a roster that ranged from Jay-Z and Beanie Sigel to the impressively durable LL.

DEF JUX

Until a more monolithic (and powerful) label "lost their sense of humor" (in the words of labelhead/producer/MC El-P), Def Jux was more commonly known as Def Jux to those on the street (technically, the label name has always legally been Def Jux…but was shortened by hip-hop audiences). Angry at the way the Rawkus label had treated his artistic visions, El-P formed the label as a vehicle for his group Company Flow and their eventual solo endeavours. However, since the dissolution of Company Flow, Def Jux has grown from its original role significantly; finding El-P alongside some of the most talented producers and MCs in underground hip hop, including Aesop Rock, Cannibal Ox, Mister Lif, and RJD2.

DELICIOUS VINYL

Delicious Vinyl Records is a label that started out with a hip-hop orientation before branching out into everything from retro-soul/funk (the Brand New Heavies) to rock (the Bogeymen, Spinout). In the beginning, hip-hop is the thing that put Delicious Vinyl on the map—specifically, hip-hop from the West Coast. Delicious Vinyl was founded in Los Angeles in 1987, a time when things were looking promising for West Coast rap. Ice-T was signed to Sire/Warner Bros., and N.W.A was creating a strong local buzz; so Delicious Vinyl concentrated on the ever-growing L.A. rap scene with a roster that included Tone-Loc, Young MC, Def Jef, and the female duo Body & Soul.

Delicious Vinyl, which landed a distribution deal with Island in 1988, had been in business about a year when the hits began to come in. Tone-Loc had major crossover hits with "Wild Thing" and "Funky Cold Medina," and "Bust a Move" was a smash for Young MC. Because of Young MC's and Tone-Loc's success, Delicious Vinyl became closely identified with West Coast rap. But in the early '90s, the company showed its diversity by signing various rockers as well as the Brand New Heavies, a British soul/funk band with a '70s-like sound and a strong appreciation of Tower of Power, Rufus & Chaka Khan, and the Average White Band. Not that Delicious Vinyl ever lost interest in rap—in the '90s, the company was also the home of the reggae-influenced Born Jamericans and the L.A.-based alternative rap group the Pharcyde. Delicious Vinyl is far from a rap-only label, but their reputation for being very rap friendly remains.

ENJOY

Barring only Sugar Hill, Enjoy was the most important rap label of the old school era. The label, founded back in 1963 by Harlem record store legend Bobby Robinson, was home to the debut recordings by Grandmaster Flash & the Furious Five, the Treacherous Tree, the Funky Four Plus One, and the Fearless Four. Robinson opened his first store in the mid-'40s; after a few years of giving advice to many independent labels concerning hot artists, he began recording doo wop and R&B himself by the early '50s—under many different banners, including Fury, Fire, Whirlin' Disc, Everlast, and Red Robin (most co-owned with his brother Danny).

Enjoy was formed in 1962, with sax-blower King Curtis the most frequent recipient of the label's few releases. Robinson recorded sparingly during the '70s, but got hipped to the nascent rap movement thanks to his nephew, Gabriel Jackson aka Spoonie Gee. In 1979, Robinson issued a pair of classics: Grandmaster Flash's first single, the epic "Superappin'," and Funky Four Plus One's "Rappin' and Rockin' the House." He followed up in 1980 with a devastating 1980 split single featuring Spoonie Gee's "Love Rap" b/w the Treacherous Three's "The New Rap Language." During the next few years, Enjoy released seminal rap singles by Fearless Four, Disco Four, and Dr. Ice, but also saw many of his acts moving to Sugar Hill for increased recognition. The year 1984 was the last for classic Enjoy material, with Doug E. Fresh's "Just Having Fun" and Masterdon Committee's "Paid the Cost to Be the Boss."

GRAND ROYAL

In the beginning, Grand Royal's biggest inspiration was Apple, the visionary label founded by the Beatles to support artists passed over or ignored by the record industry. But much like its inspiration, Grand Royal's idealism would eventually outpace its business acumen, and force its dissolution. Nevertheless, in its almost-ten-year existence, Grand Royal came to include a furiously creative, taste-making magazine; a respected, diverse roster of artists; and a popular, groundbreaking website.

The phrase "Grand Royal" and its distinctive cards-and-dice logo first appeared on the back of the Beasties' 1992 release *Check Your Head*, but the label didn't begin in earnest until later that year. Luscious Jackson's Jill Cunniff had asked Mike "Mike D" Diamond for help with releasing her band's demo. That spurred D and fellow Beastie Boys Adam "Ad-Rock" Horovitz, and Adam "MCA" Yauch to make their label idea official, and in late 1992 Luscious Jackson's *In Search of Manny* became Grand Royal's first release. It was followed by Beastie-related material like a reissue of their early hardcore material, the Ad-Rock side project Dead Fucking Last, and a DJ Hurricane solo effort. Inspired, the label began to sign artists who the Beasties (mostly Mike D) felt weren't getting their due. Early signees included Australian indie heartthrob Ben Lee and the Ween spin-off Moistboyz.

Grand Royal magazine debuted in 1993. From the beginning, the publication was like reading the crackling brainwaves of the Beastie Boys in print. With its hip-hop pedigree, street-level cool, and articles and interviews with rappers, rockers, and radicals, Grand Royal was a signifier of hip and an arbiter of cool. Unfortunately, its fuzzy release schedule made advertisers nervous, and after the first issue's initial print run of 50,000, subsequent appearances were spotty. Grand Royal got by on vapors until 1999, when funds finally ran dry and it switched its content to the Grand Royal team's website.

Meanwhile, the label side of the Beasties' vanity project seemed to be thriving, with releases from Buffalo Daughter, Sean Lennon, and Atari Teenage Riot, the shock unit founded by Alec Empire, kingfish of the short-lived "Digital Hardcore" movement. Luscious Jackson's 1996 full-length *Fever In Fever Out* was even certified gold. Obviously, what had started as a hobby or a fun idea had become a real live business.

Ultimately, this fact is what shut down the fun for good. A new regime was hired to effectively run the label, which diminished the hands-on involvement of Mike D. This led artists like Buffalo Daughter to look elsewhere for partners, since it was the artist-to-artist communication of Grand Royal's early days that had enticed them in the first place. Despite later successes like At the Drive-In's *Relationship of Command* (which sold over a million copies), Grand Royal ground to a halt in autumn 2001. "This is one of the most difficult decisions we've ever had to make," Mike D said in a statement posted on its website. "Our intentions were always simply to create a home for exciting music and the people who were passionate about it."

INTERSCOPE

There was a time when major record companies shied away from rap; obviously, those days are long gone, and Interscope is among the many large labels that have found rap to be extremely lucrative. It would be inaccurate to describe Interscope as strictly a hip-hop label—Interscope has, over the years, put out a lot more rock than rap, and rock fans associate the company with artists who have ranged from No Doubt to Marilyn Manson to Counting Crows. But it is definitely safe to say that Interscope has been very hip-hop friendly since the early '90s, when the label fared well in the teen pop market with Latino pop-rapper Gerardo (best known for his hit "Rico Suave"). Interscope, however, didn't ignore hardcore rap; when rapper/producer Dr. Dre (formerly of N.W.A) and the infamous Suge Knight formed the Los Angeles-based Death Row Records in 1992, Interscope became their distributor. That year, Dre's first solo album, *The Chronic*, established Death Row as a gangsta rap powerhouse and brought Interscope plenty of dollars. Death Row went on to enjoy more commercial success with albums by Snoop Dogg, the late Tupac and others.

In 1996, Dre became fed up with Knight's strong-arm tactics and ended their partnership. But that wasn't the end of Dre's association with Interscope; after leaving Death Row, Dre formed a new label called Aftermath—and Interscope became Aftermath's distributor just as it had been Death Row's distributor. From a rap standpoint, the late '90s and early 2000s were a great time for Interscope—not only because of Eminem (the top-selling rapper during that period) but also because of the Philadelphia-based female rapper Eve.

JIVE

A British label whose New York base paid major dividends during the '80s and '90s, Jive released records by nearly a dozen rap innovators before becoming a teen-pop powerhouse around the end of the millennium. Jive is one of the labels owned by Zomba Recordings (the gospel Verity and blues-based Silvertone are their other holdings), formed in London by native South Africans Clive Calder and Ralph Simon. A bassist and record scout for EMI while still living in Johannesburg, Calder formed a publishing and promotion company with Simon in 1971, and the duo founded Zomba in 1975 after they moved to London. Three years later, they had moved to New York, where they worked with pop artists ranging from Dire Straits to Billy Ocean to the Cars.

Jive entered the rap world in 1982 with the release of Whodini's "Magic's Wand," produced by new-wave wonder Thomas Dolby. After hiring Barry Weiss and Sean Carasov, and shifting distribution from Arista to RCA, the label hit the big time with releases by seminal artists including Boogie Down Productions, A Tribe Called Quest, Too Short, DJ Jazzy Jeff & the Fresh Prince, and R. Kelly. The label deftly stayed on the edge of commercial-leaning hip-hop that was recorded by highly artistic rappers, and became one of the most respected labels in rap music. Simon was bought out in 1991, and Calder and Weiss eventually engineered a transition to pop music that erased Jive's credibility but earned it pots of money and made it the largest independent label in the world. Thanks to a trio of heavyweight teen-pop artists—Backstreet Boys, Britney Spears, *NSYNC—Jive began selling hundreds of millions of records and earned a share of the American market in excess of 5 percent. By the dawn of the 21st century, Jive's roster included only a few straight-ahead rappers (E-40, Mystikal).

MO'WAX

Mo'Wax was formed in 1992 by James Lavelle, a columnist for the UK music magazine Straight No Chaser, nascent DJ, and hip-hop and electro head who'd become ingrained in England's wildly intersecting musical underground. Lavelle decided to start his own label after he watched the acid jazz scene in the North marginalize itself. He put out a call for demos in his column, and Mo'Wax was born.

Mo'Wax was never a straight-up hip-hop label, or even exclusively an electronic imprint. Instead, Lavelle sought out artists that blurred the lines between the genres. California's DJ Shadow was an early Mo'Wax participant who became one of its signature artists with his acclaimed, archivist's approach to instrumental, beat-driven hip-hop. It was the down-tempo fusions created by artists like Shadow and DJ Krush that led to the Mo'Wax sound being dubbed trip-hop by the English press. The tag wasn't entirely welcome, especially when lesser labels and artists began to coopt the term and elements of the original sound. After all, artists like Shadow viewed their work as a verbal progression of hip-hop, rather than a dangling participle. The label would not be pigeonholed. In 1995, Mo'Wax Excursions was launched, featuring five 12" singles in both hip-hop and techno styles. That year the label also signed a distribution deal with A&M; the agreement gave Mo'Wax a higher profile in the crucial American market, and gave wider exposure to its more prominent artists. Lavelle eventually left the label to pursue other interests.

Over the latter part of the 1990s, Mo'Wax established itself as the go-to brokerage house for adventurous music, bringing hip-hop, electronica, and numerous other styles and influences together. It released singles, compilations,

and LPs featuring the work of U.N.K.L.E., Money Mark, Howie B, and the Beastie Boys, to name only a few. It accessed and reassessed the role of graffiti in hip-hop through the cover artwork of New York graffiti artist Futura 2000. And despite its unwitting role in the fragmentation of hip-hop's sound into sub-genres like trip-hop, Mo'Wax was a landmark in the sometimes bewildering network of underground musical highways.

NO LIMIT

Eazy-E's Ruthless Records demonstrated that a fortune could be made from gangsta rap, and New Orleans gangsta rapper/producer Master P was well aware of that when he founded No Limit Records. In the '90s, Master P turned his No Limit label into a Southern gangsta rap empire. While Ruthless and Death Row Records paid especially close attention to artists from the West Coast, Master P realized that he didn't need to go to California to find gangsta rappers—there were plenty of them in the Southern part of the United States. And with New Orleans as his base, Master P oversaw a stable of Southern gangsta rappers who rhymed about thug life in Dixie.

Master P, who grew up in New Orleans, was living in the Bay Area when, in the late '80s, he started using the name No Limit Records. At first, No Limit was the name of a record store that Master P operated. But in 1990, he decided to turn No Limit into a record company. After moving back to his hometown, he went on to sign an abundance of Southern rappers—including Mystikal (who subsequently got away from a No Limit-type sound), C-Murder, Fiend, Ghetto Commission, Silkk the Shocker, Soulja Slim, and the Gambino Family. And No Limit never had to go far to find a producer: the company's releases were produced by its in-house production team Beats by the Pound. Along the way, No Limit landed a distribution deal with a company that knew a lot about gangsta rap: Priority Records, which had been the home of N.W.A in the late '80s and early '90s. No Limit has often been criticized for having a formulaic, assembly-line approach, but Master P's skills as a businessman/entrepreneur were never in doubt.

PRIORITY

Priority Records went down in history as the label that had the guts to sign N.W.A in the late '80s and let the controversial gangsta rappers say what they wanted—and make no mistake, that did take serious guts back then. The ironic thing is that Priority didn't set out to be a gangsta rap label—certainly not in the beginning. When Priority was founded in Los Angeles in 1985, the company wasn't modeled after Def Jam, Tommy Boy, or Profile, but rather K-Tel. In fact, Priority president Bryan Turner and his partners had previously been with K-Tel—and in the beginning, Priority did exactly what K-Tel was known for doing: they put out compilations of hit songs. But in 1988, Priority decided that instead of releasing compilations exclusively, they would branch out into what industry people call frontline recordings—that is, new recordings instead of previously released material that was licensed from other labels. Priority continued to put out non-frontline compilations of everything from rap to heavy metal to classic soul, but they released or distributed new frontline recordings by the Egyptian Lover, Big Lady K (an L.A.-based female rapper), and, of course, the controversial N.W.A—whose lyrics were even more violent and graphic than Ice-T's. Priority, much to its credit, didn't ask N.W.A to tone down their lyrics on their platinum *Straight Outta Compton* album or N.W.A member Eazy-E's platinum solo effort *Eazy-Duz-It*—Priority felt that N.W.A's members needed to tell their story the way they saw fit.

After N.W.A's 1991 breakup, Ice Cube continued to record for Priority as a solo artist. Priority had other rap (as well as rock and dance-pop) activities in the '90s, but the company's name would always be associated with the seminal gangsta rap of N.W.A and Eazy-E.

RAWKUS

The son of media powerhouse businessman Rupert Murdoch, James Murdoch started Rawkus after dropping out of Harvard in 1994. Determined to offer an antidote to the bling-bling saturation of rap and hip hop during of the early '90s, Rawkus delivered hard-hitting hip-hop classics that were the heir apparents to such conscious-minded groups as Public Enemy and Boogie Down Productions.

Beginning with the now-classic Company Flow Funcrusher Plus album, Rawkus developed a stable of talent that included Company Flow alongside Talib Kweli, Mos Def, Jurassic 5, Pharoahe Monch, and the Kweli-Mos Def collaboration Black Star. Rawkus enjoyed the luxury of being nearly unrivaled in the world of independent hip-hop; releasing one groundbreaking record after the next. The landmark *Lyricist Lounge* and *Soundbombing* compilations helped to cement their status, and *Soundbombing 2* featured nearly every major player on the East Coast hip-hop circuit (including a then-emerging MC from Detroit named Eminem).

However, their status as an independent changed when the junior Murdoch sold the majority of his share in the label to his father's NewsCorp conglomerate. While this caused a mild controversy and found a few artists quietly exiting the label, Rawkus continued to receive critical acclaim and found itself receiving Grammy nominations for several albums. The label also set a precedent by having the first vinyl-only release to hit number one on *Billboard*'s rap singles charts—the Mos Def, Pharoahe Monch, and Nate Dogg Grammy-nominated "Oh No."

RUTHLESS

Founded by the late N.W.A member Eric "Eazy-E" Wright (b. 1964, d. 1995), Ruthless Records was among the top West Coast rap labels of the late '80s and early '90s. Ruthless was best known for gangsta rap releases by N.W.A the group and Eazy-E the solo artist, but Ruthless wasn't strictly a gangsta rap label; Eazy's company also recorded everyone from bubblegum pop-rappers J.J. Fad and R&B singer Michel'le to The D.O.C., who was hardcore rap but not really gangsta rap.

N.W.A's most famous album was titled *Straight Outta Compton*, and Eazy was exactly that—the rapper grew up in Compton, CA, a tough, crime-ridden ghetto area of South Central Los Angeles. Compton was where Eazy met the other members of N.W.A, and where he had a successful career as a drug dealer in his pre-N.W.A, pre-Ruthless days. But Eazy realized that selling drugs could lead to incarceration or death, and he gave up drug dealing for good when he founded Ruthless in 1987. At first, Ruthless had a distribution deal with Macola, which distributed N.W.A's first album, *N.W.A and the Posse*, that year. But in 1988, Ruthless had a falling out with Macola and went to Priority for distribution; Eazy's first solo album, *Eazy-Duz-It*, and *Straight Outta Compton* (both of which went platinum) were marketed as Ruthless/Priority releases. But not all of Ruthless' post-Macola releases went through Priority for distribution; J.J. Fad, The D.O.C., and Michel'le were on Ruthless/Atlantic, while Above the Law were on Ruthless/Epic. When Eazy died of AIDS in 1995, Ruthless became the property of his widow, Tomica Wright (who was listed as executive producer on Ruthless releases by Bone Thugs-N-Harmony and MC Ren in the late '90s and L.A. gangsta rapper Baby S in 2002).

SLEEPING BAG

William Socolov and Arthur Russell started the Sleeping Bag label in 1982. Based in New York, the label was in the epicenter of the growth of hip-hop throughout the remainder of the '80s, though it became just as known for its contributions to left-field disco and early house music. Russell's own releases as Dinosaur L and Indian Ocean, along with later releases from house artists Todd Terry and Dhar Braxton, had a big impact on the dance community. The Fresh subsidiary was initiated in 1985 by Socolov. It was also that year that he signed a teenager named Curtis Khaleel, who had made a demo under the name Mantronix with MC Tee. The duo released the "Fresh Is the Word" 12", which set off a succession of singles and a pair of groundbreaking albums—1985's *Mantronix: The Album* and 1986's *Music Madness*. Khaleel, known professionally as Kurtis Mantronik, did production and A&R for the label; he brought in EPMD, Nice & Smooth, and a host of other artists who all helped make Sleeping Bag one of the most vital early rap independents. (He also worked on a number of the label's house releases.) EPMD's first two albums, along with singles from Stezo ("Freak the Funk"), T La Rock ("It's Yours"), Just-Ice ("Latoya"), and Cash Money ("Ugly People Be Quiet") only solidified the label's stature.

Sleeping Bag's hip-hop focus all but completely withered away when Mantronix defected to Capitol for 1988's *In Full Effect*. The label was no more by the early '90s.

SOLESIDES

SoleSides began around 1991, the outgrowth of friendships formed at the radio station of the University of California-Davis, KDVS. Lyrics Born (born Tom Shimura), Lateef the Truth Speaker (born Lateef Daumont), Chief Xcel

(born Xavier Mosley), Gift of Gab (born T.J. Parker), and DJ Shadow (born Josh Davis) united around a love of hip-hop and digging the crates. Originally, the MCs and DJs were all doing their own thing. Xcel and Gab, as Blackalicious, were shopping their demo to major labels; Shadow was DJing parties and making extended mixes. Eventually, mutual friend Jeff "DJ Zen" Chang suggested that the crew unite their energies. They knew about the dark side of the music business through their involvement with KDVS, and suddenly an independent label seemed like a better idea. SoleSides was officially born in 1993 with a split release, Lyrics Born's "Send Them" and "Entropy" from DJ Shadow. The raw, adventurous single made immediate waves in the hip-hop underground, and SoleSides was officially on the map.

Together with fellow California crews like Freestyle Fellowship and Hieroglyphics, as well as likeminded boutique labels like Mo'Wax in the U.K. (which licensed early singles by both Shadow and Blackalicious) the SoleSides collective helped establish an independent, underground hip-hop network. The label's success made it clear that a demo or contract with a major wasn't the only means an MC had to get the words out.

SoleSides found its greatest success with Latyrx, a collaboration between Lateef and Lyrics Born that grew out of a B-side single of the same name. Originally appearing as the flip to Lateef's single "The Wreckoning," the song "Latyrx" featured distinct raps from each MC played simultaneously over a spacey, looping DJ Shadow backing track. The song took the underground by storm, and led to a full-length LP in 1996, entitled *The Album*. By this point the SoleSides crew's prodigious talent, furious independence, and progressive approach to hip-hop were more well known than anyone had ever imagined, back there in the hallways of KDVS. SoleSides releases were being spun all over the world, and the label was thriving as an artist-run collective. One day in 1997, while on a retreat of sorts at Lateef's mother's mountain cabin, the decision was made to end the SoleSides label, but the SoleSides crew lived on. Reborn as Quannum, the crew established Quannum Projects, a logical, more varied progression from the previous label effort. In addition to its own releases, Quannum Projects reissued SoleSides material like Latyrx's *The Album*, and in 2000, the two-CD retrospective *SoleSides Greatest Bumps*.

STONES THROW

After being thrown around and eventually dropped from a major label, producer/DJ Peanut Butter Wolf formed Stones Throw in 1996. Dedicated to preserving the art of the 7" and hip-hop instrumentals, Stones Throw has a roster of artists at the forefront of cutting-edge hip-hop, including left-field producer Madlib (under the aliases Quasimoto and Yesterday's New Quintet), hip-hop live orchestra Breakestra, old school revivalists Lootpack, and legendary turntablists Cut Chemist and Rob Swift. The label achieved critical acclaim on a commercial scale when Peanut Butter Wolf's now-legendary *My Vinyl Weighs a Ton* assembled together a guest lineup that included virtually every well-known underground hip-hop producer and DJ on the West Coast scene. Much to the delight of beatheads and DJs everywhere, Wolf also commissioned a series of limited-edition 45s called the *Jukebox* series—highly sought after not only for their collectability but also for the quality of each release.

SUGAR HILL

Sugar Hill Records was the most important hip-hop label of rap's pre-Run-D.M.C. era; the company was as important to old school hip-hop as Stax was to Memphis soul and Chess was to Chicago blues. Cofounded by producer/singer Sylvia Robinson in 1979, Sugar Hill didn't necessarily document hip-hop from the very beginning—if one agrees that hip-hop started around 1976 (the year Kurtis Blow started rapping in Harlem clubs), then hip-hop had been around three years when Sugar Hill put out the Sugarhill Gang's "Rappers Delight." Nonetheless, Sugar Hill (not to be confused with a folk label that has the same name) was among the first labels to record old school hip-hop, and the company's late-'70s/early-'80s roster was a who's who of early rap—a roster that included not only the Sugarhill Gang but also Grandmaster Flash & the Furious Five, Spoonie Gee, the Sequence (rap's first all-female group), the Funky Four Plus One, Lady B, and Super Wolf.

Robinson had a long resumé when she cofounded Sugar Hill. She had been in the music business since the '50s, when she was half of the R&B duo Mickey & Sylvia (best known for their hit "Love Is Strange"). And in the early '70s, Robinson recorded as a solo artist and had a major soul hit with the sensuous "Pillow Talk." But at Sugar Hill, she emphasized rap, and many of the company's releases were truly historic. "Rappers Delight" was, for thousands of people, an introduction to hip-hop, while Lady B's "To the Beat, Y'all" (released in 1980) was the first rap single by a female solo artist. And Flash's 1982 gem "The Message" was the single that made sociopolitical rapping popular. By 1984, Sugar Hill's popularity had decreased. But the label's importance to pre-Run-D.M.C. rap cannot be denied.

TOMMY BOY

Tommy Boy Records has never been a rap-only label; the New York-based company has also put out plenty of dance-pop as well as some urban contemporary. But it is safe to say that Tommy Boy, which was founded by head honcho Tom Silverman in 1981, has always been extremely rap friendly. That was definitely the case back in 1982, when Tommy Boy signed old school rapper Afrika Bambaataa and released his Kraftwerk-influenced hit "Planet Rock"—a truly seminal record that became the basis for so much off the West Coast electro-hop that came from Angelinos like the Egyptian Lover and the World Class Wreckin' Cru. After Tommy Boy's success with Bambaataa, the label went on to sign other well-respected rappers in the '80s, including Stetsasonic, De La Soul, and Queen Latifah. The '80s also found Tommy Boy going after the dance-pop market with Latin freestyle group TKA and the urban contemporary market with the innovative Force MDs (who were providing a hip-hop-drenched style of neo-soul eight years before Mary J. Blige's first album came out).

For Tommy Boy, the '90s were a lot like the '80s—the label continued to fare well in the rap market, thanks to House of Pain, Digital Underground, and Apache (among others) in addition to putting out albums by Dutch singer Amber (best known for her 1996 hit "This Is Your Night") and other dance-pop artists. Tommy Boy is also where Everlast resumed his solo career after House of Pain's breakup and provided 1998's brilliantly eclectic *Whitey Ford Sings the Blues.* In 2001, Tommy Boy celebrated its 20th anniversary.

WILD PITCH

Wild Pitch amassed a discography during hip-hop's golden age that rivaled most others. The New York label was founded in 1985 by Stu Fine, who set about providing a platform for some of the era's most significant acts—Ultramagnetic MC's, Lord Finesse & DJ Mike Smooth, Main Source, the Coup, Gang Starr, and several others whose contributions were limited to one or two valued singles. Fine was partly responsible for the pairing of Gang Starr's DJ Premier and Guru; at the time, Guru had some 45 King- and Donald D.-produced material with Mike Dee under his belt, but Dee had moved to Boston, leaving him without a DJ. Fine had DJ Premier (then known as Waxmaster C) flown up to New York to meet Guru. Before long, the duo had 1989's "Words I Manifest" in shops, which ignited the career of one of the most revered rap duos. Subversive political group the Coup notched their first two albums on the label, but not before Main Source delivered what stands as one of rap's greatest with 1991's *Breaking Atoms.* Lord Finesse & DJ Mike Smooth's *Funky Technician,* released a year prior to that, was an underground conquest, featuring production from several of Finesse's Diggin' in the Crates running mates as well as DJ Premier. Plenty of singles, many of which were anthologized on 1994's *Wild Pitch Classics,* also continue to shine brightly. In addition to several from the above-mentioned figures, there was O.C.'s "Time's Up" and Chill Rob G's "Let the Words Flow," the latter of which was sampled for Snap!'s megahit "The Power."

After Wild Pitch went out of business in the mid-'90s, several of the releases gained momentum as hip-hop classics. JCOR obtained the catalog a few years later and began putting some of the most relevant releases back into circulation.

Essential Albums

Alternative Rap

Arrested Development, **3 Years, 5 Months & 2 Days in the Life Of...** (1992)
The Automator, **A Much Better Tomorrow** (2000)
Erykah Badu, **Baduizm** (1997)
Basehead, **Play With Toys** (1992)
Beastie Boys, **Paul's Boutique** (1989)
Beastie Boys, **Check Your Head** (1992)
Black Eyed Peas, **Behind the Front** (1998)
Black Sheep, **A Wolf in Sheep's Clothing** (1991)
Brand Nubian, **One for All** (1990)
Common, **One Day It'll All Make Sense** (1997)
Cypress Hill, **Cypress Hill** (1991)
De La Soul, **3 Feet High and Rising** (1989)
De La Soul, **De La Soul Is Dead** (1991)
De La Soul, **Buhloone Mindstate** (1993)
Del tha Funkee Homosapien, **I Wish My Brother George Was Here** (1991)
Digable Planets, **Reachin' (A New Refutation of Time and Space)** (1993)
Digital Underground, **No Nose Job: The Legend of Digital Underground** (2001)
The Disposable Heroes of Hiphoprisy, **Hypocrisy Is the Greatest Luxury** (1992)
Missy Elliott, **Supa Dupa Fly** (1997)
The Fugees, **The Score** (1996)
Handsome Boy Modeling School, **So...How's Your Girl?** (1999)
Jungle Brothers, **Straight out the Jungle** (1988)
OutKast, **Stankonia** (2000)
The Pharcyde, **Bizarre Ride II the Pharcyde** (1992)
P.M. Dawn, **Of the Heart, of the Soul and of the Cross: The Utopian Experience** (1991)
The Roots, **Do You Want More?!!!??!** (1995)
The Roots, **Things Fall Apart** (1999)
3rd Bass, **The Cactus Album** (1989)
A Tribe Called Quest, **The Low End Theory** (1991)
A Tribe Called Quest, **Midnight Marauders** (1993)

Bass Music

Bass Junkie, **Bass Junkie** (1998)
Bass Mekanik, **Sonic Overload** (1998)
DJ Magic Mike, **Bass Is the Name of the Game** (1988)
DJ Magic Mike, **Cheetah's Bassest Hit** (1993)
Dynamix II, **Electro Bass Megamix: 1985 to Present** (1997)
Gucci Crew II, **The Best of Gucci Crew II** (1994)
69 Boyz, **199Quad** (1994)
Tag Team, **The Best of Tag Team** (2000)
2 Live Crew, **As Nasty as They Wanna Be** (1989)
Various Artists, **Bass America: Collection One** (1996)
Various Artists, **Bass 4 Bassheadz, Vol. 1: 100% Bass Satisfaction** (1996)
Various Artists, **This Is Bass** (1989)

Christian Rap

dc Talk, **Free at Last** (1992)
dc Talk, **Jesus Freak** (1995)
Gospel Gangstaz, **I Can See Clearly Now** (1999)
M.C. Ge Gee, **And Now the Mission Continues** (1991)
Str8 Young Gangstaz, **Tha Movement** (1999)
12th Tribe, **Knowledge Is the Tribe of Life** (1991)

East Coast Rap

Various Artists, **Bad Boy's Greatest Hits** (1998)
Rob Base & DJ E-Z Rock, **It Takes Two** (1988)
Big Punisher, **Capital Punishment** (1998)
Boogie Down Productions, **Criminal Minded** (1987)
Boogie Down Productions, **By All Means Necessary** (1988)
Foxy Brown, **Ill Na Na** (1996)
Busta Rhymes, **The Coming** (1996)
Busta Rhymes, **When Disaster Strikes** (1997)
Das EFX, **Dead Serious** (1992)
EPMD, **Strictly Business** (1988)
EPMD, **Business Never Personal** (1992)
Eric B. & Rakim, **Paid in Full** (1987)
Eric B. & Rakim, **Follow the Leader** (1988)
The Fugees, **The Score** (1996)
Gang Starr, **Daily Operation** (1992)
Gang Starr, **Full Clip: A Decade of Gang Starr** (1999)
Ghost Face Killah, **Ironman** (1996)
Gravediggaz, **6 Feet Deep** (1994)
Genius/GZA, **Liquid Swords** (1995)
House of Pain, **House of Pain** (1992)
Jay-Z, **In My Lifetime, Vol. 1** (1997)
Jeru the Damaja, **The Sun Rises in the East** (1994)
Lil' Kim, **Hard Core** (1996)
LL Cool J, **Radio** (1985)
LL Cool J, **Mama Said Knock You Out** (1990)
Method Man, **Tical** (1994)
Nas, **Illmatic** (1994)
Nas, **It Was Written** (1996)
Naughty By Nature, **Naughty By Nature** (1991)
Naughty By Nature, **19 Naughty III** (1993)
Naughty By Nature, **Nature's Finest: Naughty By Nature's Greatest Hits** (1999)
The Notorious B.I.G., **Ready to Die** (1994)
The Notorious B.I.G., **Life After Death** (1997)
Ol' Dirty Bastard, **Return to the 36 Chambers** (1995)
Public Enemy, **Yo! Bum Rush the Show** (1987)
Public Enemy, **It Takes a Nation of Millions to Hold Us Back** (1988)
Public Enemy, **Fear of a Black Planet** (1990)
Public Enemy, **Apocalypse 91...The Enemy Strikes Black** (1991)
Puff Daddy, **No Way Out** (1997)
Raekwon, **Only Built 4 Cuban Linx** (1995)

Rakim, **The Master** (1999)
Redman, **Whut? Thee Album** (1992)
Pete Rock & C.L. Smooth, **Mecca and the Soul Brother** (1992)
Run-D.M.C., **Run-D.M.C.** (1984)
Run-D.M.C., **King of Rock** (1985)
Run-D.M.C., **Raising Hell** (1986)
Run-D.M.C., **Tougher than Leather** (1988)
3rd Bass, **The Cactus Album** (1989)
A Tribe Called Quest, **The Low End Theory** (1991)
A Tribe Called Quest, **Midnight Marauders** (1993)

G-Funk

Bone Thugs-N-Harmony, **The Collection, Vol. 1** (1998)
Compton's Most Wanted, **When We Wuz Bangin' 1989-1999: The Hitz** (2001)
Daz Dillinger, **Retaliation, Revenge & Get Back** (1998)
Dr. Dre, **The Chronic** (1992)
Warren G, **Regulate...G Funk Era** (1994)
Mack 10, **Based on a True Story** (1997)
Snoop Doggy Dogg, **Doggystyle** (1993)
Snoop Doggy Dogg, **Tha Doggfather** (1996)
Tupac, **Me Against the World** (1995)
Tupac, **All Eyez on Me** (1996)

Gangsta Rap

Above the Law, **Black Mafia Life** (1993)
Ant Banks, **The Best of Ant Banks** (1998)
Big Punisher, **Capital Punishment** (1998)
Bone Thugs-N-Harmony, **E 1999 Eternal** (1995)
Bone Thugs-N-Harmony, **The Collection, Vol. 1** (1998)
Boogie Down Productions, **Criminal Minded** (1987)
C-BO, **The Best of C-BO** (1995)
C-Murder, **Life or Death** (1998)
Compton's Most Wanted, **When We Wuz Bangin' 1989-1999: The Hitz** (2001)
Da Lench Mob, **Guerillas in tha Mist** (1992)
DJ Quik, **Quik Is the Name** (1991)
Dr. Dre, **The Chronic** (1992)
E-40, **Charlie Hustle: The Blueprint of a Self-Made Millionaire** (1999)
Fat Joe, **Jealous One's Envy** (1995)
Geto Boys, **Uncut Dope: Geto Boys' Best** (1992)
Ice Cube, **AmeriKKKa's Most Wanted** (1990)
Ice Cube, **Death Certificate** (1991)
Ice-T, **The Iceberg/Freedom of Speech...Just Watch What You Say** (1989)
Ice-T, **O.G. Original Gangster** (1991)
Junior M.A.F.I.A., **Conspiracy** (1995)
Kurupt, **Tha Streetz Iz a Mutha** (1999)
Mack 10, **Based on a True Story** (1997)
Master P, **Ghetto D** (1997)

MC Eiht Featuring CMW, **We Come Strapped** (1994)

MC Ren, **Shock of the Hour** (1993)

The Notorious B.I.G., **Ready to Die** (1994)

The Notorious B.I.G., **Life After Death** (1997)

N.W.A., **Straight Outta Compton** (1988)

N.W.A., **Niggaz4life** (1991)

Scarface, **Mr. Scarface Is Back** (1991)

Schoolly D, **The Jive Collection, Vol. 3** (1995)

Snoop Doggy Dogg, **Doggystyle** (1993)

Snoop Doggy Dogg, **Tha Doggfather** (1996)

Spice 1, **Hits** (1998)

Too Short, **Greatest Hits, Vol. 1: The Player Years, 1983-1988** (1993)

Tupac, **Me Against the World** (1995)

Tupac, **All Eyez on Me** (1996)

Westside Connection, **Bow Down** (1996)

Golden Age

Afros, **Kickin' Afrolistics** (1990)

Beastie Boys, **Licensed to Ill** (1986)

Beastie Boys, **Paul's Boutique** (1989)

Big Daddy Kane, **Long Live the Kane** (1988)

Big Daddy Kane, **The Very Best of Big Daddy Kane** (2001)

Biz Markie, **The Best of Cold Chillin'** (2000)

Boogie Down Productions, **Criminal Minded** (1987)

Boogie Down Productions, **By All Means Necessary** (1988)

Brand Nubian, **One for All** (1990)

EPMD, **Strictly Business** (1988)

EPMD, **Business Never Personal** (1992)

Eric B. & Rakim, **Paid in Full** (1987)

Eric B. & Rakim, **Follow the Leader** (1988)

Doug E. Fresh & the Get Fresh Crew, **The World's Greatest Entertainer** (1988)

Ice Cube, **AmeriKKKa's Most Wanted** (1990)

Jungle Brothers, **Straight out the Jungle** (1988)

Jungle Brothers, **Done By the Forces of Nature** (1989)

Kool G Rap & DJ Polo, **Road to the Riches** (1989)

Kool Moe Dee, **Greatest Hits** (1989)

LL Cool J, **Radio** (1985)

LL Cool J, **Mama Said Knock You Out** (1990)

Main Source, **Breaking Atoms** (1991)

Mantronix, **The Best of Mantronix 1985-1999** (1999)

Marley Marl, **House of Hits** (1995)

Masta Ace, **The Best of Cold Chillin'** (2001)

Naughty By Nature, **Nature's Finest: Naughty By Nature's Greatest Hits** (1999)

N.W.A., **Straight Outta Compton** (1988)

Public Enemy, **Yo! Bum Rush the Show** (1987)

Public Enemy, **It Takes a Nation of Millions to Hold Us Back** (1988)

Public Enemy, **Fear of a Black Planet** (1990)

Queen Latifah, **All Hail the Queen** (1989)

Pete Rock & C.L. Smooth, **Mecca and the Soul Brother** (1992)

Run-D.M.C., **King of Rock** (1985)

Run-D.M.C., **Raising Hell** (1986)

Run-D.M.C., **Tougher than Leather** (1988)

Schoolly D, **The Jive Collection, Vol. 3** (1995)

Slick Rick, **The Great Adventures of Slick Rick** (1988)

Stetsasonic, **In Full Gear** (1988)

3rd Bass, **The Cactus Album** (1989)

Too Short, **Life Is...Too Short** (1988)

Ultramagnetic MC's, **Critical Beatdown** (1988)

Whodini, **Greatest Hits** (1990)

Hardcore Rap

Big Daddy Kane, **Long Live the Kane** (1988)

Big Punisher, **Capital Punishment** (1998)

Boogie Down Productions, **Criminal Minded** (1987)

Boogie Down Productions, **By All Means Necessary** (1988)

DJ Quik, **Quik Is the Name** (1991)

DMX, **It's Dark and Hell Is Hot** (1998)

DMX, **...And Then There Was X** (1999)

Eminem, **The Slim Shady LP** (1999)

Eminem, **The Marshall Mathers LP** (2000)

EPMD, **Strictly Business** (1988)

Geto Boys, **Uncut Dope: Geto Boys' Best** (1992)

Ghost Face Killah, **Ironman** (1996)

Genius/GZA, **Liquid Swords** (1995)

Ice Cube, **AmeriKKKa's Most Wanted** (1990)

Ice Cube, **Death Certificate** (1991)

Jeru the Damaja, **The Sun Rises in the East** (1994)

Lords of the Underground, **Here Come the Lords** (1993)

Master P, **Ghetto D** (1997)

Method Man, **Tical** (1994)

Mobb Deep, **Hell on Earth** (1996)

Noreaga, **N.O.R.E.** (1998)

N.W.A., **Straight Outta Compton** (1988)

N.W.A., **Niggaz4life** (1991)

Onyx, **Bacdafucup** (1993)

Paris, **Sleeping With the Enemy** (1993)

Public Enemy, **Yo! Bum Rush the Show** (1987)

Public Enemy, **It Takes a Nation of Millions to Hold Us Back** (1988)

Public Enemy, **Fear of a Black Planet** (1990)

Redman, **Whut? Thee Album** (1992)

Redman, **Muddy Waters** (1996)

Spice 1, **Hits** (1998)

Tupac, **All Eyez on Me** (1996)

Wu-Tang Clan, **Enter the Wu-Tang (36 Chambers)** (1993)

Wu-Tang Clan, **Wu-Tang Forever** (1997)

Hip-Hop

Arrested Development, **3 Years, 5 Months & 2 Days in the Life Of...** (1992)

Afrika Bambaataa, **Looking for the Perfect Beat: 1980-1985** (2001)

Rob Base & DJ E-Z Rock, **It Takes Two** (1988)

Beastie Boys, **Paul's Boutique** (1989)

Big Daddy Kane, **Long Live the Kane** (1988)

Black Sheep, **A Wolf in Sheep's Clothing** (1991)

Mary J. Blige, **What's the 411?** (1992)

Kurtis Blow, **The Best of Kurtis Blow** (1994)

Boogie Down Productions, **Criminal Minded** (1987)

Busta Rhymes, **The Coming** (1996)

De La Soul, **3 Feet High and Rising** (1989)

Del tha Funkee Homosapien, **I Wish My Brother George Was Here** (1991)

Digital Underground, **Sex Packets** (1990)

Missy Elliott, **Supa Dupa Fly** (1997)

Eminem, **The Slim Shady LP** (1999)

Eric B. & Rakim, **Paid in Full** (1987)

Doug E. Fresh, **Greatest Hits, Vol. 1** (1996)

The Fugees (Refugee Camp), **The Score** (1996)

Gang Starr, **Daily Operation** (1992)

Genius/GZA, **Liquid Swords** (1995)

Grandmaster Flash, **Message From Beat Street: The Best of Grandmaster Flash, Melle Mel & the Furious Five** (1994)

Heavy D & The Boyz, **Heavy Hitz** (2000)

Jay-Z, **Reasonable Doubt** (1996)

Jungle Brothers, **Straight out the Jungle** (1988)

Jurassic 5, **Quality Control** (2000)

LL Cool J, **Radio** (1985)

LL Cool J, **Mama Said Knock You Out** (1990)

Main Source, **Breaking Atoms** (1991)

Mantronix, **Mantronix: The Album** (1985)

Marley Marl, **House of Hits** (1995)

Method Man, **Tical** (1994)

Nice & Smooth, **Ain't a Damn Thing Changed** (1991)

The Notorious B.I.G., **Ready to Die** (1994)

Ol' Dirty Bastard, **Return to the 36 Chambers** (1995)

OutKast, **Stankonia** (2000)

The Pharcyde, **Bizarre Ride II the Pharcyde** (1992)

Public Enemy, **It Takes a Nation of Millions to Hold Us Back** (1988)

Queen Latifah, **All Hail the Queen** (1989)

Rakim, **The Master** (1999)

Redman, **Whut? Thee Album** (1992)

Pete Rock & C.L. Smooth, **Mecca and the Soul Brother** (1992)

The Roots, **Do You Want More?!!!??!** (1995)

The Roots, **Things Fall Apart** (1999)

Run-D.M.C., **Run-D.M.C.** (1984)

Run-D.M.C., **King of Rock** (1985)

Run-D.M.C., **Raising Hell** (1986)

Salt-N-Pepa, **Blacks' Magic** (1990)

Slick Rick, **The Great Adventures of Slick Rick** (1988)

Stetsasonic, **In Full Gear** (1988)

TLC, **Crazysexycool** (1994)

A Tribe Called Quest, **The Low End Theory** (1991)

A Tribe Called Quest, **Midnight Marauders** (1993)

Ultramagnetic MC's, **Critical Beatdown** (1988)

Whodini, **Greatest Hits** (1990)

Wu-Tang Clan, **Enter the Wu-Tang (36 Chambers)** (1993)

Young MC, **Stone Cold Rhymin'** (1989)

Jazz-Rap

Brand Nubian, **One for All** (1990)

Brand Nubian, **In God We Trust** (1993)

Digable Planets, **Reachin' (A New Refutation of Time and Space)** (1993)

Digable Planets, **Blowout Comb** (1994)

Dream Warriors, **And Now, the Legacy Begins** (1991)

Dream Warriors, **Anthology: A Decade of Hits 1988-1998** (1999)

Gang Starr, **Step in the Arena** (1991)

Gang Starr, **Daily Operation** (1992)

Grand Puba, **Reel to Reel** (1992)

Guru, **Jazzmatazz, Vol. 1** (1993)

Jungle Brothers, **Straight out the Jungle** (1988)

Jungle Brothers, **Done By the Forces of Nature** (1989)

Main Source, **Breaking Atoms** (1991)

Poor Righteous Teachers, **Holy Intellect** (1990)

Pete Rock & C.L. Smooth, **Mecca and the Soul Brother** (1992)

The Roots, **Things Fall Apart** (1999)

A Tribe Called Quest, **People's Instinctive Travels and the Paths of Rhythm** (1990)

A Tribe Called Quest, **The Low End Theory** (1991)

Us3, **Hand on the Torch** (1993)

Latin Rap

The Beatnuts, **Street Level** (1994)

Cypress Hill, **Cypress Hill** (1991)

Various Artists, **East Side's Most Wanted, Vol. 1** (1999)

Mellow Man Ace, **Escape From Havana** (1989)

South Park Mexican, **Power Moves** (1998)

Tha Mexakinz, **Crossing All Borders** (1998)

Old School Rap

Various Artists, **The Best of Sugar Hill Records** (1998)

Kurtis Blow, **Kurtis Blow** (1980)

Kurtis Blow, **The Best of Kurtis Blow** (1994)

Cold Crush Brothers, **Fresh, Wild, Fly & Bold** (1996)

Various Artists, **Def Jam Music Group Inc.: 10th Year Anniversary** (1995)

The Egyptian Lover, **On the Nile** (1984)

The Fat Boys, **All Meat No Filler: The Best of Fat Boys** (1997)

Doug E. Fresh, **Greatest Hits, Vol. 1** (1996)

Full Force, **Full Force Get Ready 1 Time** (1986)

Grandmaster Flash, **Message from Beat Street: The Best of Grandmaster Flash, Melle Mel & the Furious Five** (1994)

Bobby Jimmy & the Critters, **Bobby Jimmy, You a Fool (The Best of Bobby Jimmy & the Critters)** (1990)

Various Artists, **Kurtis Blow Presents the History of Rap, Vol. 2: The Birth of the Rap Record** (1997)

Various Artists, **Kurtis Blow Presents the History of Rap, Vol. 3: The Golden Age** (1997)

Mantronix, **Mantronix: The Album** (1985)

Newcleus, **Jam on This!: The Best of Newcleus** (1997)

The Real Roxanne, **The Real Roxanne** (1988)

The Sequence, **Sugarhill Presents the Sequence** (1980)

Rozanne Shanté, **Greatest Hits** (1995)

Spoonie Gee, **The Godfather...Rap** (1987)

Various Artists, **The Sugar Hill Records Story** (1997)

The Sugarhill Gang, **The Best of Sugarhill Gang** (1996)

U.T.F.O., **The Best of U.T.F.O.** (1996)

Whodini, **Greatest Hits** (1990)

Party Rap

Freak Nasty, **Controversee...That's Life...And That's the Way It Is** (1996)

Gucci Crew II, **The Best of Gucci Crew II** (1994)

Ill Al Skratch, **Creep Wit' Me** (1994)

Luke, **Greatest Hits** (1996)

Marky Mark & The Funky Bunch, **Music for the People** (1991)

69 Boyz, **199Quad** (1994)

Tag Team, **The Best of Tag Team** (2000)

2 Live Crew, **2 Live Crew's Greatest Hits** (1992)

Political Rap

Arrested Development, **3 Years, 5 Months & 2 Days in the Life Of...** (1992)

Boogie Down Productions, **Criminal Minded** (1987)

Boogie Down Productions, **By All Means Necessary** (1988)

Boogie Down Productions, **Ghetto Music: The Blueprint of Hip Hop** (1989)

Boogie Down Productions, **Sex and Violence** (1992)

Common, **One Day It'll All Make Sense** (1997)

The Coup, **Steal This Double Album** (2002)

The Disposable Heroes of Hiphoprisy, **Hypocrisy Is the Greatest Luxury** (1992)

Freestyle Fellowship, **Inner City Griots** (1993)

Gang Starr, **Step in the Arena** (1991)

Intelligent Hoodlum, **Tragedy: Saga of a Hoodlum** (1993)

KRS-One, **KRS-One** (1995)

Mos Def & Talib Kweli, **Black Star** (1998)

Paris, **Sleeping With the Enemy** (1993)

Poor Righteous Teachers, **Holy Intellect** (1990)

Public Enemy, **Yo! Bum Rush the Show** (1987)

Public Enemy, **It Takes a Nation of Millions to Hold Us Back** (1988)

Public Enemy, **Fear of a Black Planet** (1990)

Public Enemy, **Apocalypse 91...The Enemy Strikes Black** (1991)

Spearhead, **Home** (1994)

Spearhead, **Chocolate Supa Highway** (1997)

X-Clan, **Xodus** (1992)

Pop-Rap

Various Artists, **Bad Boy's Greatest Hits** (1998)

Various Artists, **Def Jam Music Group Inc.: 10th Year Anniversary** (1995)

DJ Jazzy Jeff & the Fresh Prince, **He's the DJ, I'm the Rapper** (1988)

DJ Jazzy Jeff & the Fresh Prince, **Greatest Hits** (1998)

Father MC, **Close to You** (1992)

Heavy D & The Boyz, **Heavy Hitz** (2000)

Kriss Kross, **Totally Krossed Out** (1992)

Craig Mack, **Project: Funk da World** (1994)

Marky Mark & The Funky Bunch, **Music for the People** (1991)

MC Hammer, **Greatest Hits** (1996)

MC Lyte, **Eyes on This** (1989)

Keith Murray, **The Most Beautifullest Hits** (1999)

Puff Daddy, **No Way Out** (1997)

Will Smith, **Big Willie Style** (1997)

Snow, **12 Inches of Snow** (1993)

Tone-Loc, **Loc-ed After Dark** (1989)

Southern Rap

Boot Camp Clik, **Boot Camp Clik's Greatest Hits: Basic Training** (2000)

DJ Magic Mike, **Cheetah's Bassest Hit** (1993)

Eightball & MJG, **In Our Lifetime, Vol. 1** (1999)

Geto Boys, **We Can't Be Stopped** (1991)

Geto Boys, **Uncut Dope: Geto Boys' Best** (1992)

Goodie Mob, **Soul Food** (1995)

Goodie Mob, **Still Standing** (1998)

Juvenile, **400 Degreez** (1998)

Master P, **Ghetto D** (1997)

Mystikal, **Let's Get Ready** (2000)

Turntablism

The Beat Junkies, **The World Famous Beat Junkies, Vol. 2** (1998)

Cut Chemist/Shortkut, **Live at Future Primitive Sound Session** (1998)

DJ Faust, **Man or Myth?** (1998)

DJ Q-Bert, **Wave Twisters, Episode 7 Million: Sonic Wars Within the Protons** (1998)

DJ Rectangle, **Ill Rated** (1999)

DJ Spooky Vs. The Freight Elevator Quartet, **File Under Futurism** (1999)

Kid Koala, **Carpal Tunnel Syndrome** (2000)

Live Human, **Monostereosis: The New Victrola Method [US]** (2000)

Christian Marclay, **Records 1981-1989** (1997)

Mix Master Mike, **Anti-Theft Device** (1998)

Roc Raida, **Crossfaderz** (2000)

Shortee, **The Dreamer** (1999)

Rob Swift, **The Ablist** (1999)

Underground Rap

Antipop Consortium, **Tragic Epilogue** (2000)

The Automator, **A Much Better Tomorrow** (2000)

Blackalicious, **NIA** (2000)

Company Flow, **Funcrusher Plus** (1997)

The Coup, **Kill My Landlord** (1993)

The Coup, **Steal This Double Album** (2002)

Cut Chemist/Shortkut, **Live at Future Primitive Sound Session** (1998)

Dilated Peoples, **The Platform** (2000)

Dr. Octagon, **Dr. Octagonecologyst [Dr. Octagon]** (1996)

Esham, **Detroit Dog Shit** (1997)

Esham, **Bootleg: From the Lost Vault, Vol. 1** (2000)

Handsome Boy Modeling School, **So...How's Your Girl?** (1999)

Invisibl Skratch Piklz, **The Shiggar Fraggar Show!, Vol. 1** (1998)

Jurassic 5, **Quality Control** (2000)

Kool Keith, **Black Elvis/Lost in Space** (1999)

Talib Kweli & Hi Tek, **Reflection Eternal** (2000)

Mix Master Mike, **Anti-Theft Device** (1998)

Pharoahe Monch, **Internal Affairs** (1999)

Mos Def & Talib Kweli, **Black Star** (1998)

Prince Paul, **A Prince Among Thieves** (1999)

Slum Village, **Fantastic, Vol. 2** (2000)

The X-Ecutioners, **X-Pressions** (1997)

West Coast Rap

Above the Law, **Black Mafia Life** (1993)

Above the Law, **Time Will Reveal** (1996)

Ant Banks, **The Best of Ant Banks** (1998)

Compton's Most Wanted, **When We Wuz Bangin' 1989-1999: The Hitz** (2001)

Coolio, **Gangsta's Paradise** (1995)

Cypress Hill, **Cypress Hill** (1991)

Da Brat, **Funkdafied** (1994)

Digital Underground, **Sex Packets** (1990)

DJ Quik, **Quik Is the Name** (1991)

The D.O.C., **No One Can Do It Better** (1989)

Dr. Dre, **The Chronic** (1992)

Dru Down, **Can You Feel Me** (1996)

Eazy-E, **Eternal E** (1995)

Kid Frost, **Hispanic Causing Panic** (1990)

Funkdoobiest, **Which Doobie U B?** (1993)

Warren G, **Regulate...G Funk Era** (1994)

Ice Cube, **AmeriKKKa's Most Wanted** (1990)

Ice Cube, **Death Certificate** (1991)

Ice-T, **Power** (1988)

Ice-T, **O.G. Original Gangster** (1991)

Mack 10, **Based on a True Story** (1997)

N.W.A, **Straight Outta Compton** (1988)

N.W.A, **Niggaz4life** (1991)

The Pharcyde, **Bizarre Ride II the Pharcyde** (1992)

Sir Mix-A-Lot, **Beepers, Benzos & Booty: The Best of Sir Mix-A-Lot** (2000)

Snoop Doggy Dogg, **Doggystyle** (1993)

Snoop Doggy Dogg, **Tha Doggfather** (1996)

Spice 1, **Hits** (1998)

Tha Dogg Pound, **Dogg Food** (1995)

Tone-Loc, **Loc-ed After Dark** (1989)

Too Short, **Life Is...Too Short** (1988)

Too Short, **Greatest Hits, Vol. 1: The Player Years, 1983-1988** (1993)

Tupac, **Me Against the World** (1995)

Tupac, **All Eyez on Me** (1996)

Tupac, **Greatest Hits** (1998)

Various Artists, **West Coast Rap: The First Dynasty, Vol. 1** (1992)

Various Artists, **West Coast Rap: The Renegades** (1992)

World Class Wreckin' Cru, **Turn Off the Lights (Before the Attitude)** (1991)

Xzibit, **Restless** (2000)

Young MC, **Stone Cold Rhymin'** (1989)

Essential Songs

Alternative Rap

"Mr. Wendal," Arrested Development
"People Everyday," Arrested Development
"Tennessee," Arrested Development
"On & On," Erykah Badu
"Brand New Day," Basehead
"Not in Kansas," Basehead
"Hey Ladies," Beastie Boys
"Jimmy James," Beastie Boys
"So What'cha Want," Beastie Boys
"The Choice Is Yours," Black Sheep
"Retrospect for Life," Common
"Me, Myself and I," De La Soul
"Say No Go," De La Soul
"Mistadobalina," Del tha Funkee Homosapien
"Rebirth of Slick (Cool Like Dat)," Digable Planets
"The Humpty Dance," Digital Underground
"The Rain (Supa Dupa Fly)," Missy Elliott
"Fu-Gee-La," The Fugees
"Doo Wop (That Thing)," Lauryn Hill
"Doin' Our Own Dang," Jungle Brothers
"Jayou," Jurassic 5
"Looking at the Front Door," Main Source
"Simon Says," Pharoahe Monch
"B.O.B.," OutKast
"Soul Flower," The Pharcyde
"Ladies First," Queen Latifah
"Proceed," The Roots
"The Gas Face," 3rd Bass
"Award Tour," A Tribe Called Quest
"Check the Rhime," A Tribe Called Quest

Bass Music

"Drop the Bass," DJ Magic Mike
"Shake for Me," DJ Smurf
"Techno Bass," Dynamix II
"Banned in the U.S.A.," Luke
"Tootsee Roll," 69 Boyz
"Whoomp! (There It Is)," Tag Team
"Me So Horny," 2 Live Crew
"Move Somethin'," 2 Live Crew
"Basstronic," The Unknown DJ

East Coast Rap

"It Takes Two," Rob Base & DJ E-Z Rock
"Bridge Is Over," Boogie Down Productions
"My Philosophy," Boogie Down Productions
"Woo-Ha!! Got You All in Check," Busta Rhymes
"Mic Checka," Das EFX
"What's My Name?," DMX
"You Gots to Chill," EPMD
"I Know You Got Soul," Eric B. & Rakim
"Let the Rhythm Hit 'Em," Eric B. & Rakim
"Paid in Full," Eric B. & Rakim
"Words I Manifest," Gang Starr
"Can I Get A...," Jay-Z
"Can't Knock the Hustle," Jay-Z
"You Can't Stop the Prophet," Jeru the Damaja

"I Can't Live Without My Radio," LL Cool J
"Mama Said Knock You Out," LL Cool J
"Flava in Ya Ear," Craig Mack
"Bring the Pain," Method Man
"Hell on Earth (Front Lines)," Mobb Deep
"The World Is Yours," Nas
"Big Poppa," The Notorious B.I.G.
"Mo Money Mo Problems," The Notorious B.I.G.
"Shimmy Shimmy Ya," Ol' Dirty Bastard
"Bring the Noise," Public Enemy
"Fight the Power," Public Enemy
"Rebel Without a Pause," Public Enemy
"Incarcerated Scarfaces," Raekwon
"Blow Your Mind," Redman
"It's Like That," Run-D.M.C.
"Sucker M.C.'s (Krush-Groove 1)," Run-D.M.C.
"Scenario," A Tribe Called Quest

G-Funk

"Crossroad," Bone Thugs-N-Harmony
"Thuggish Ruggish Bone," Bone Thugs-N-Harmony
"In California," Daz Dillinger
"Fuck Wit Dre Day (And Everybody's Celebratin')," Dr. Dre
"Let Me Ride," Dr. Dre
"Nuthin' but a 'G' Thang," Dr. Dre
"Never Leave Me Alone," Nate Dogg
"Regulate," Warren G
"This D.J.," Warren G
"It Was a Good Day," Ice Cube
"Gin and Juice," Snoop Dogg
"Murder Was the Case," Snoop Dogg
"Who Am I (What's My Name)?," Snoop Dogg
"California Love (RMX)," Tupac

Gangsta Rap

"Money Don't Make a Man," Ant Banks
"Still Not a Player," Big Punisher
"Thuggish Ruggish Bone," Bone Thugs-N-Harmony
"Down for My N's," C-Murder
"Hood Took Me Under," Compton's Most Wanted
"Born and Raised in Compton," DJ Quik
"Get at Me Dog," DMX
"Fuck Wit Dre Day (And Everybody's Celebratin')," Dr. Dre
"Nuthin' but a 'G' Thang," Dr. Dre
"Boyz-n-the Hood (Remix)," Eazy-E
"Real Muthaphuckkin G's," Eazy-E
"Mr. Whomp Whomp," Fiend
"Damn It Feels Good to Be a Gangsta," Geto Boys
"Mind Playing Tricks on Me," Geto Boys
"Steady Mobbin'," Ice Cube
"New Jack Hustler," Ice-T
"O.G. Original Gangster," Ice-T

"Tha Streetz Iz a Mutha," Kurupt
"Guerillas in Tha Mist," Da Lench Mob
"Backyard Boogie," Mack 10
"Make Em Say Ugh," Master P
"Ruthless for Life," MC Ren
"Big Poppa," The Notorious B.I.G.
"Ready to Die," The Notorious B.I.G.
"Gangsta Gangsta," N.W.A
"Straight Outta Compton," N.W.A
"P.S.K. What Does It Mean?," Schoolly D
"Just Be Straight With Me," Silkk the Shocker
"Gin and Juice," Snoop Dogg
"Murder Was the Case," Snoop Dogg
"Who Am I (What's My Name)?," Snoop Dogg
"Trigga Gots No Heart," Spice 1
"The Ghetto," Too Short
"California Love (RMX)," Tupac
"Me Against the World," Tupac

Golden Age

"Raw," Big Daddy Kane
"Set It Off," Big Daddy Kane
"Just a Friend," Biz Markie
"Make the Music With Your Mouth," Biz Markie
"Bridge Is Over," Boogie Down Productions
"Stop the Violence," Boogie Down Productions
"They Want Efx," Das EFX
"Strictly Business," EPMD
"You Gots to Chill," EPMD
"Let the Rhythm Hit 'Em," Eric B. & Rakim
"Microphone Fiend," Eric B. & Rakim
"Paid in Full," Eric B. & Rakim
"The Show," Doug E. Fresh & the Get Fresh Crew
"360 Degrees (What Goes Around)," Grand Puba
"Doin' Our Own Dang," Jungle Brothers
"Jimbrowski," Jungle Brothers
"Wild Wild West," Kool Moe Dee
"Going Back to Cali," LL Cool J
"O.P.P.," Naughty By Nature
"Express Yourself," N.W.A
"Bring the Noise," Public Enemy
"Don't Believe the Hype," Public Enemy
"Fight the Power," Public Enemy
"Rebel Without a Pause," Public Enemy
"They Reminisce over You (T.R.O.Y.)," Pete Rock & C.L. Smooth
"It's Like That," Run-D.M.C.
"It's Tricky," Run-D.M.C.
"Walk This Way," Run-D.M.C.
"Steppin' to the A.M.," 3rd Bass
"Life Is...Too Short," Too Short
"Ego Trippin'," Ultramagnetic MC's
"Freaks Come out at Night," Whodini

Hardcore Rap

"Raw," Big Daddy Kane
"Set It Off," Big Daddy Kane

"Bridge Is Over," Boogie Down Productions
"What's My Name?," DMX
"My Name Is," Eminem
"Mind Playing Tricks on Me," Geto Boys
"Steady Mobbin'," Ice Cube
"You Can't Stop the Prophet," Jeru the Damaja
"Tha Streetz Iz a Mutha," Kurupt
"Bring the Pain," Method Man
"Hell on Earth (Front Lines)," Mobb Deep
"Straight Outta Compton," N.W.A
"Slam," Onyx
"Bring the Noise," Public Enemy
"Welcome to the Terrordome," Public Enemy
"Blow Your Mind," Redman
"Wu-Tang Clan Ain't Nuthing ta F' Wit,"
    Wu-Tang Clan

Hip-Hop

"Tennessee," Arrested Development
"Planet Rock," Afrika Bambaataa & Soulsonic
    Force
"It Takes Two," Rob Base & DJ E-Z Rock
"So What'cha Want," Beastie Boys
"The Choice Is Yours," Black Sheep
"No Diggity," Blackstreet
"You Bring Me Joy," Mary J. Blige
"The Breaks," Kurtis Blow
"Stop the Violence," Boogie Down Productions
"Woo-Ha!! Got You All in Check," Busta Rhymes
"Fantastic Voyage," Coolio
"Me, Myself and I," De La Soul
"Mistadobalina," Del tha Funkee Homosapien
"The Humpty Dance," Digital Underground
"Parents Just Don't Understand," DJ Jazzy Jeff &
    the Fresh Prince
"Let Me Clear My Throat," DJ Kool
"The Rain (Supa Dupa Fly)," Missy Elliott
"Let the Rhythm Hit 'Em," Eric B. & Rakim
"Paid in Full," Eric B. & Rakim
"Jail House Rap," The Fat Boys
"The Show," Doug E. Fresh & the Get Fresh
    Crew
"Fu-Gee-La," The Fugees
"Words I Manifest," Gang Starr
"The Message," Grandmaster Flash & the
    Furious Five
"White Lines (Don't Don't Do It)," Grandmaster
    Melle Mel
"Doo Wop (That Thing)," Lauryn Hill
"Jump Around," House of Pain
"Hard Knock Life (Ghetto Anthem)," Jay-Z
"Jayou," Jurassic 5
"I Can't Live Without My Radio," LL Cool J
"Rock the Bells," LL Cool J
"Flava in Ya Ear," Craig Mack
"Looking at the Front Door," Main Source
"King of the Beats," Mantronix
"Hell on Earth (Front Lines)," Mobb Deep
"Big Poppa," The Notorious B.I.G.
"Ms. Jackson," Outkast
"Fight the Power," Public Enemy
"Proceed," The Roots
"It's Like That," Run-D.M.C.
"Sucker M.C.'s (Krush-Groove 1)," Run-D.M.C.
"Push It," Salt-N-Pepa
"Creep," TLC
"Award Tour," A Tribe Called Quest
"C.R.E.A.M.," Wu-Tang Clan
"Bust a Move," Young MC

Jazz-Rap

"All for One," Brand Nubian
"Rebirth of Slick (Cool Like Dat)," Digable
    Planets
"My Definition of a Boombastic (Jazz Style),"
    Dream Warriors
"Words I Manifest," Gang Starr
"Loungin'," Guru
"Jimbrowski," Jungle Brothers
"Nouveau Western," MC Solaar
"Mellow My Man," The Roots
"Proceed," The Roots
"Check the Rhime," A Tribe Called Quest
"Cantaloop (Flip Fantasia)," Us3

Latin Rap

"Watch Out Now," The Beatnuts
"Insane in the Brain," Cypress Hill
"Brown and Proud," Lighter Shade of Brown
"Mentirosa," Mellow Man Ace
"Hillwood Hustlaz," South Park Mexican
"Illegal Amigos," South Park Mexican
"Rain on Your Parade," Tha Mexakinz
"U Don't Even Know Me," Tha Mexakinz

Old School Rap

"The Breaks," Kurtis Blow
"Fresh, Wild, Fly and Bold," Cold Crush
    Brothers
"Nightmares," Dana Dane
"One for the Treble," Davy DMX
"Egypt, Egypt," The Egyptian Lover
"Fat Boys," The Fat Boys
"The Show," Doug E. Fresh & the Get
    Fresh Crew
"The Adventures of Grandmaster Flash on the
    Wheels of Steel," Grandmaster Flash
"The Message," Grandmaster Flash & the
    Furious Five
"Scorpio," Grandmaster Flash & the Furious
    Five
"White Lines (Don't Don't Do It)," Grandmaster
    Melle Mel
"Bassline," Kurtis Mantronik
"The Bridge," MC Shan
"Jam on Revenge (The Wikki-Wikki Song),"
    Newcleus
"Roxanne's Revenge," Roxanne Shanté
"Love Rap," Spoonie Gee
"Monster Jam," Spoonie Gee
"8th Wonder," The Sugarhill Gang
"Rapper's Delight," The Sugarhill Gang
"Body Rock," Treacherous Three
"Roxanne, Roxanne," U.T.F.O.
"Freaks Come out at Night," Whodini
"Surgery," The World Class Wreckin' Cru

Party Rap

"Da' Dip," Freak Nasty
"I'll Take Her," Ill Al Skratch
"Good Vibrations," Marky Mark
"C'mon N' Ride It (The Train)," Quad City DJ's
"Tootsee Roll," 69 Boyz
"Whoomp! (There It Is)," Tag Team
"Me So Horny," 2 Live Crew
"Move Somethin'," 2 Live Crew

Political Rap

"People Everyday," Arrested Development
"My Philosophy," Boogie Down Productions
"Stop the Violence," Boogie Down Productions
"California Über Alles," The Disposable Heroes
    of Hiphoprisy
"Television, the Drug of the Nation," The
    Disposable Heroes of Hiphoprisy
"Arrest the President," Intelligent Hoodlum
"Sound of da Police," KRS-One
"Brown Skin Lady," Mos Def
"911 Is a Joke," Public Enemy
"Black Steel in the Hour of Chaos,"
    Public Enemy
"Fight the Power," Public Enemy
"Rebel Without a Pause," Public Enemy
"Welcome to the Terrordome," Public Enemy
"The Hate That Hate Produced," Sister Souljah
"People in tha Middle," Spearhead
"Heed the Word of the Brother," X-Clan

Pop-Rap

"Parents Just Don't Understand," DJ Jazzy Jeff &
    the Fresh Prince
"Summertime," DJ Jazzy Jeff & the Fresh Prince
"This Is How We Do It," Montell Jordan
"Jump," Kris Kross
"Around the Way Girl," LL Cool J
"Going Back to Cali," LL Cool J
"Pray," MC Hammer
"U Can't Touch This," MC Hammer
"Mo Money Mo Problems," The Notorious B.I.G.
"Ghetto Supastar That Is What You Are," Pras
"I'll Be Missing You," Puff Daddy
"It's All About the Benjamins," Puff Daddy
"Let's Talk About Sex," Salt-N-Pepa
"Push It," Salt-N-Pepa
"Baby Got Back," Sir Mix-A-Lot
"Gettin' Jiggy Wit It," Will Smith
"Funky Cold Medina," Tone-Loc
"Wild Thing," Tone-Loc

Southern Rap

"Damn It Feels Good to Be a Gangsta,"
    Geto Boys
"Mind Playing Tricks on Me," Geto Boys
"Black Ice," Goodie Mob
"Back That Azz Up," Juvenile
"I Miss My Homies," Master P
"Make Em Say Ugh," Master P
"Shake Ya Ass," Mystikal
"Just Be Straight With Me," Silkk the Shocker

Turntablism

"They Don't Understand," The Beat Junkies
"The Periodic Table," Cut Chemist
"Return of the DJ," DJ Faust
"Hot Stop," DJ Icey
"Turntable TV," DJ Q-Bert
"What Does Your Soul Look Like, Pt. 4," DJ
    Shadow
"Invasion of the Octopus People," Invisibl
    Skratch Piklz
"Like Irregular Chickens," Kid Koala
"Grasshopper," Live Human
"Suprize Packidge," Mix Master Mike
"The Chronicles (I Will Always Love H.E.R.),"
    Peanut Butter Wolf
"Turntablist Anthem," Rob Swift

"One Man Band," The X-Ecutioners
"Raida's Theme," The X-Ecutioners

Underground Rap

"Guaranteed," Dilated Peoples
"Work the Angles," Dilated Peoples
"Blue Flowers," Dr. Octagon
"Earth People," Dr. Octagon
"Invasion of the Octopus People," Invisibl
    Skratch Piklz
"Jayou," Jurassic 5
"Quality Control," Jurassic 5
"Rockets on the Battlefield," Kool Keith
"Lady Don't Tek No," Latyrx
"Simon Says," Pharoahe Monch

"Rock N Roll," Mos Def
"More Than U Know," Prince Paul
"Raida's Theme," The X-Ecutioners

West Coast Rap

"Fantastic Voyage," Coolio
"Gangsta's Paradise," Coolio
"Hand on the Pump," Cypress Hill
"How I Could Just Kill a Man," Cypress Hill
"Insane in the Brain," Cypress Hill
"Mistadobalina," Del tha Funkee Homosapien
"The Humpty Dance," Digital Underground
"Fuck Wit Dre Day (And Everybody's
    Celebratin')," Dr. Dre
"Let Me Ride," Dr. Dre

"Nuthin' but a 'G' Thang," Dr. Dre
"Boyz-n-the Hood (Remix)," Eazy-E
"Friday," Ice Cube
"It Was a Good Day," Ice Cube
"Colors," Ice-T
"New Jack Hustler," Ice-T
"O.G. Original Gangster," Ice-T
"Express Yourself," N.W.A
"Gangsta Gangsta," N.W.A
"Straight Outta Compton," N.W.A
"Gin and Juice," Snoop Dogg
"Who Am I (What's My Name)?," Snoop Dogg
"California Love (RMX)," Tupac
"Me Against the World," Tupac
"Bust a Move," Young MC

Non-Rap Artists Who Influenced Rap

Dennis Alcapone

b. Aug. 6, 1947, Clarendon, Jamaica

Vocals / DJ, Reggae

He wasn't the first—U-Roy wasn't nicknamed "the Originator" for nothing—but in Jamaica in the early '70s, Dennis Alcapone was part of a triumvirate of toasters, alongside U-Roy and Big Youth, who ruled the island. Crashing out of the sound systems and onto the airwaves like a tidal wave, this trio of talent was responsible for bringing the art of DJing to never before imagined heights. U-Roy was first off the starting block, releasing his debut single in 1969. But in his shadow, the young Dennis Smith was readying to follow suit. Born in Clarendon, Jamaica, on August 6, 1947, a move to Kingston and a name change were the first order of business. Then, with friends Lizzy and Samuel the First, Alcapone set up the El Paso Hi-Fi sound system in 1969. Its success was legendary, its popularity virtually unrivaled in its day. As the new decade dawned, the DJ recorded his first singles, both for Niney Holness and Rupie Edwards. Filling the platters with rhyming chatter—catchphrases, exuberant exclamations, bouncing off the original lyrics—while never losing step with the beats, Alcapone's unique singsong style immediately caught the public's attention.

Producer Clement "Coxsonne" Dodd quickly pounced. The Studio One label head was still smarting over losing U-Roy, who'd briefly DJed for Dodd's sound system, to his rival, Treasure Isle head Duke Reid. U-Roy was now sitting at the top of the Jamaican chart and Dodd was determined that Alcapone shoot him down. With the Studio One archives at his disposal, the DJ recorded a slew of seminal singles, and just as the producer intended, now seriously threatened U-Roy's own crown.

Versions of classic hits by Alton Ellis, Delroy Wilson, John Holt, the Heptones, and Carlton & the Shoes rained down. Alcapone's exhilarating "Forever Version" of the latter band's "Love Me Forever" titled his debut album, which compiled many of these hits. Of course, the title itself was yet another salvo in the battle with Reid, playing off U-Roy's own *Versions Galore* equally hits-heavy album.

But Alcapone was not recording exclusively for Dodd; he was doing equally spectacular singles for producer Keith Hudson. The DJ was already maturing and evolving, on "Spanish Amigo," a version of Ken Boothe's soulful "Old Fashioned Way," Alcapone manages to stuff the single not just with his expected catchphrases, but also engages in snatches of responses to the lyrics before running away with them entirely. Now, virtually every producer in town was knocking on the DJ's door and in 1971, much to Dodd's distress, Alcapone moved on to work with Bunny Lee for another clutch of hits. "Ripe Cherry," a version of "Cherry Oh Baby," "Horse and Buggy," a version of "Mule Train," and "Lorna Banana," a duet with fellow DJ Prince Jazzbo, all soared onto the charts. But none had the impact of "Guns Don't Argue"; a version of Eric Donaldson's "Love of the Common People," the song single-handedly introduced gunplay into the toaster's lyrical repertoire. Many of the singles cut with Lee were gathered up for 1971's *Guns Don't Argue*, which was later reissued by the Jamaica Gold label.

Leaving Lee behind, the DJ next settled down at Treasure Isle, where the hits just kept coming; the compilation *Soul to Soul: DJ's Choice*, released by Reid in 1973, features a number of these alongside cuts by fellow DJs U-Roy, Lizzy, and Little Youth. "The Great Woggie," a version of the Techniques' "You Don't Care," was arguably the best out of a fabulous batch Alcapone released in 1971, with "Teach the Children" taking the honors the following year. The latter's legacy has been the most enduring, even if Alcapone's version was actually the song's second (John Holt's "Sister Big Stuff" rhythm was itself a cover of Jean Knight's "Mister Big Stuff"). The DJ would turn it into the most

infectious spelling lesson of all time, and the chart-topping song was so popular that it has long been used by Jamaica's radio literacy shows.

And while Alcapone may have played the tough guy, especially on his album sleeves (*Forever Version*, for example, found him astride a cannon), in reality, it was his easygoing, personable style that drew the fans. On "DJ's Choice," he actually publicizes the competition, running down a list of top DJs and their catchphrases, with his own last, and encouraging listeners to "voice their choice." Fans could only infer that the congenial Alcapone didn't see the others as competition at all and loved their music as much as they did.

By 1972, the DJ's reputation had already crossed the Atlantic to Britain, and Alcapone now went off on his first British tour. He returned home in triumph and was awarded the Best DJ of the Year by *Swing* magazine. A second U.K. tour was even more successful than the first—while back home, he seemed to have the Midas touch.

In the three-year period running from his recorded debut in 1970 through to the end of 1973, Alcapone released over 130 singles. Working with virtually every name producer on the island and versioning classic after classic, the DJ's prolificacy is almost beyond belief. At an annual rate of almost 45 releases a year, what's truly stunning is just how good most of them are. From the scorching "This a Butter" produced by Phil Pratt, the rousting Byron Smith-produced "Out the Light," the witty "Go Johnny Go" produced by Byron Lee, the perfect banter of the Prince Tony-produced "Fine Style," the sermonizing "King of Kings," one of a clutch of classics cut with Alvin Ranglin, the wordplay on the Lee Perry-produced "Africa Stands," to his fabulous timing on "My Voice Is Insured for Half a Million Dollars," where Alcapone rides the beat like an equestrian champion, the list of spectacular releases could go on for pages. The Trojan label's *My Voice Is Insured for Half a Million Dollars* rounds up a bumper 25 tracks from this period, while Heartbeat has reissued *Forever Version* and *Guns Don't Argue*, available courtesy of Jamaica Gold.

In 1974, Alcapone followed his heart and relocated to London. Love may conquer all, but in the DJ's case, it conquered his seemingly unstoppable career. The lackluster *Belch It Off* album, produced by Sydney Crooks and released this same year, was a foreboding of things to come. Signing to the U.K. label Magnet, *King of the Track* also appeared this year and compiled older Bunny Lee-produced hits with four new tracks cut with Lee's associate Count Shelly. Any hopes Alcapone had of re-creating his Jamaican success in Britain swiftly faded with Magnet's own loss of interest. And back home, the DJ was quickly fading from memory, as a wave of new young guns swept into the scene and onto the charts. The man who once swamped the island with records was now reduced to cutting all of a half a dozen singles between 1975 and 1976.

A move to the Third World label offered a glimmer of hope. He recorded three albums for them—*Dread Capone*, *Six Million Dollar Man*, and the the Bunny Lee-produced set *Investigator Rock*—all before the end of 1977. However, none made much of an impression. The RAS label's *Universal Rockers* bundles up tracks from this era, a reminder that Alcapone hadn't lost his form so much as his following. There just wasn't large enough interest in the U.K. to sustain his stardom, while there wasn't enough output to keep him fresh back home. By the end of the decade, Alcapone had left music entirely—but not permanently.

In 1988, the DJ returned to the stage and the following year saw him take the *WOMAD* festival by storm. Alcapone returned to Jamaica in 1990 and began working again with Bunny Lee. Most of his releases since have been low profile and have had little impact on the current scene. In 1997, however, he cut the *21st Century Version* album with producer the Mad Professor, which received the most attention of this decade's output. Alcapone continues to record and appear live, but sadly, his glory days turned out to be far too brief. However, he led by example and his career and life can best be summed up by his own catchphrase, "Live it up." —*Jo-Ann Greene*

Forever Version / 1971 / Heartbeat ◆◆◆◆

A straight reissue of the original Studio One album from 1971, *Forever Version* includes material from Alcapone's prime early output and ably demonstrates why the young musical outlaw was on equal footing with the revered DJ innovator of the day, U-Roy. In addition to having his peer's toasting dexterity and lyrical wit, Alcapone found his own niche with a singing-talking combination and liberal doses of distinct whoops and high-pitched caws. The basic tracks Alcapon versions are vintage early reggae from Clement Dodd's vaults, including cuts by Alton Ellis, John Holt, the Heptones, Carlton & His Shoes, and Delroy Wilson. The stellar Sound Dimension band figures nicely into the mix, too, with contributions from organist Jackie Mittoo, tenor saxophonist Roland Alphonso, bassist Leroy Sibbles, and guitarist Ernest Ranglin, among others. Along with Trojan's equally impressive Alcapone disc, *My Voice Is Insured for Half a Million Dollars*, *Forever Version* counts as one of the best albums to emerge from the early days of Jamaican toasting. —*Stephen Cook*

● **Universal Rockers** / 1992 / RAS ◆◆◆◆◆

Dennis Alcapone had been one of Jamaica's most successful DJs, but by the time he signed to the British independent label Third World, his ranking had been seriously reduced by the rise of a new generation of toasters. He released two albums for the label in 1977, and it's these sets that *Universal Rockers* draws from. Both sank without a trace at the time, but their merits have become more evident with the passage of time. Producer Bunny Lee handed the DJ some of his best rhythms to toast over, all performed by his studio band the Aggrovators, with drummer Sly Dunbar enlisted for a number of the tracks here. The band laid down some of the most militant sounds around, and Lee further toughened them by focusing on their sizzling beats, honing them even sharper for the DJ. Lee created his own scintillating versions of current hits, including a clutch reprising singer Leroy Smart's recent hits, as well as reaching back into Jamaica's archives to resurrect rhythms from the past. Thus, the music is masterful—classic rockers from Jamaica's premier session band and a producer at his creative heights. Alcapone's exuberant toasting dovetails perfectly with the exhilarating rhythms. But at a time of thunderous preaching and serious reasoning, his very enthusiasm worked against the DJ. Yet it still remains inexplicable that classic cultural numbers like "Babylon Set Rasta Free" and "Natty Dread Walk With Love" failed to hit on the island, while such rave-ups as "Universal Rockers" and "Six Million Dollar Man" didn't strike home in the British reggae scene. But better late than never; now those who missed it all the first time around have a second chance. —*Jo-Ann Greene*

My Voice Is Insured for Half a Million Dollars / Aug. 29, 2000 / Trojan ◆◆◆◆

Consisting of tracks recorded between 1970 and 1973, when the young DJ was at the peak of his popularity, this album remains the single best summation of Dennis Alcapone's art. It's true that his style owed a deep debt to U Roy, but he managed to improve on his lyricism and melodic interest; although Alcapone was primarily a "chatter" in the established tradition, he frequently lapsed into singing and was also known for his strange whoops and yelps. *My Voice* has been reissued by Trojan before, but this issue ups the ante considerably by adding ten bonus tracks to the original program. Highlights are numerous and include the spectacular "Musical Alphabet," "Joe Frazier Round 2" (which continues a popular topic for DJs of the period), and most of all, his brilliant DJ cuts on the Ethiopians' classic "Selah" (titled "Rocking to Ethiopia") and Augustus Pablo's deathless instrumental "Java" ("Mava"). Of course, he's helped considerably by the consistently high quality of the rhythm tracks, which came to him courtesy of such top producers as Duke Reid, Winston "Niney" Holness, and Bunny Lee. This album should be considered an essential part of any serious reggae collection. —*Rick Anderson*

Beck (Beck Hansen)

b. Jul. 8, 1970, Los Angeles, CA

Vocals, Guitar / Alternative Dance, Indie Rock, Lo-Fi, Club/Dance, Alternative Pop/Rock, Singer/Songwriter

One of the most inventive and eclectic figures to emerge from the '90s alternative revolution, Beck was the epitome of postmodern chic in an era obsessed with junk culture. Drawing upon a kaleidoscope of influences—pop, folk, psychedelia, hip-hop, country, blues, R&B, funk, indie rock, noise-rock, experimental rock, jazz, lounge, Brazilian music—Beck created a body of work that was wildly unpredictable, vibrantly messy, and bursting with ideas. He was unquestionably a product of the media age—a synthesist whose concoctions were pasted together from bits of the past and present, in ways that could only occur to an overexposed pop-culture junkie. His surreal, free-associative lyrics were laced with warped imagery and a sardonic sense of humor that, while typical of the times, only rarely threatened the impact of his adventurous music. Beck appropriated freely from whatever genres he felt like, juxtaposing sounds that would never have coexisted organically (and his habitual irony made clear that he wasn't aiming for authenticity in the first place). If his musical style was impossible to pigeonhole, his true identity lay in that rootless, sprawling diversity, that determination to acknowledge no boundaries or conventions; everything he did bore the stamp of his distinctively skewed viewpoint. Beck caught his big break when the bizarre Delta blues/white-boy-rap pastiche "Loser" spawned a national catchphrase in early 1994. His debut album *Mellow Gold* became a hit, and the official follow-up, the Dust Brothers-produced *Odelay*, was widely acclaimed as one of the decade's landmark records. Beck followed those touchstones with genre exercises in folk and funk that still managed to dazzle with their variety, solidifying one of the most creatively vital oeuvres in alternative rock—or all of modern pop music, for that matter. —*Steve Huey*

☆ **Mellow Gold** / Mar. 1994 / DGC ◆◆◆◆

From its kaleidoscopic array of junk-culture musical styles to its assured, surrealistic wordplay, Beck's debut album *Mellow Gold* is a stunner. Throughout the record, Beck plays as if there are no divisions between musical genres, freely blending rock, rap, folk, psychedelia, and country. Although his inspired sense of humor occasionally plays like he's a smirking, irony-addled hipster, his music is never kitschy, and his wordplay is constantly inspired. Since *Mellow Gold* was pieced together from home-recorded tapes, it lacks a coherent production, functioning more as a stylistic sampler: there are the stoner raps of "Loser" and "Beercan," the urban folk of "Pay No Mind (Snoozer)," the mock-industrial onslaught of "Motherf—er," the garagey "F— in With My Head," the trancy acoustic "Blackhole," and the gently sardonic folk-rock of "Nitemare Hippy Girl." It's a dizzying demonstration of musical skills, yet it's all tied together by a simple yet clever sense of songcraft and a truly original lyrical viewpoint, one that's basic yet as colorful as free verse. By blending boundaries so thoroughly and intoxicatingly, *Mellow Gold* established a new vein of alternative rock, one that was fueled by ideas instead of attitude. —*Stephen Thomas Erlewine*

★ **Odelay** / Jun. 18, 1996 / DGC ◆◆◆◆◆

Beck's debut, *Mellow Gold*, was a glorious sampler of different musical styles, careening from lo-fi hip-hop to folk, moving back through garage rock and arty noise. It was an impressive album, but the parts didn't necessarily stick together. The two albums that followed within months of *Mellow Gold*—*Stereopathetic Soul Manure* and *One Foot in the Grave*—were specialist releases that disproved the idea that Beck was simply a one-hit wonder. But *Odelay*, the much-delayed proper follow-up to *Mellow Gold*, proves the depth and scope of his talents. *Odelay* fuses the disparate strands of Beck's music—folk, country, hip-hop, rock & roll, blues, jazz, easy listening, rap, pop—into one dense sonic collage. Songs frequently morph from one genre to another, seemingly unrelated genre—bursts of noise give way to country songs with hip-hop beats, easy listening melodies transform into a weird fusion of pop, jazz, and cinematic strings; it's genre-defying music that refuses to see boundaries. All of the songs on *Odelay* are rooted in simple forms—whether it's blues ("Devil's Haircut"), country ("Lord Only Knows," "Sissyneck"), soul ("Hotwax"), folk ("Ramshackle"), or rap ("High 5 (Rock the Catskills)," "Where It's At")—but they twist the conventions of the genre. "Where It's At" is peppered with soul, jazz, funk, and rap references, while "Novacane" slams from indie rock to funk and back to white noise. With the aid of the Dust Brothers, Beck has created a dense, endlessly intriguing album overflowing with ideas. Furthermore, it's an album that completely ignores the static, nihilistic trends of the American alternative/independent underground, creating a fluid, creative, and startlingly original work. —*Stephen Thomas Erlewine*

Midnite Vultures / Nov. 16, 1999 / DGC ◆◆◆

By calling the muted psychedelic folk-rock, blues, and tropicalia of *Mutations* a stopgap, Beck set expectations for *Midnight Vultures* unreasonably high.

Ironically, *Midnite Vultures* doesn't feel like a sequel to *Odelay*—it's a genre exercise, like *Mutations*. This time, Beck delves into soul, funk, and hip-hop, touching on everything from Stax/Volt to No Limit but using Prince as his home base. He's eschewed samples, more or less, but not the aesthetic. Even when a song is reminiscent of a particular style, it's assembled in strange, exciting ways. As it kicks off with "Sexx Laws," it's hard not to get caught up in the rush, and "Nicotine & Gravy" carries on the vibe expertly, as does the party jam "Mixed Bizness" and the full-on electro workout "Get Real Paid," an intoxicating number that sounds like a *Black Album* reject. So far, so good—the songs are tight, catchy, and memorable, the production dense. Then comes "Hollywood Freaks." The self-conscious gangsta goof is singularly irritating, not least because of Beck's affected voice. It's the first on *Midnite Vultures* to feel like a parody, and it's such an awkward, misguided shift in tone that it colors the rest of the album. Tributes now sound like send-ups, allusions that once seemed affectionate feel snide, and the whole thing comes off as a little jive. Musically, *Midnite Vultures* is filled with wonderful little quirks, but these are undercut by the sneaking suspicion that for all the ingenuity, it's just a hipster joke. Humor has always been a big part of Beck's music, but it was gloriously absurd, never elitist. Here, it's delivered with a smug smirk, undercutting whatever joy the music generates. —*Stephen Thomas Erlewine*

Big Youth (Manley Augustus Buchanan)

b. Apr. 19, 1949, Kingston, Jamaica
Vocals, Percussion / Contemporary Reggae, DJ

A man with a message, Big Youth arrived on the music scene in the wake of U-Roy, Dennis Alcapone, and I-Roy, but quickly established his own style, threatening to eclipse them all. The consummate cultural toaster, the DJ ruled the dance halls across the '70s, and although his career flagged in the next decade, he returned with a vengeance in the '90s, and continues to have an impact on both his own nation and beyond. Born in Kingston, Jamaica, on April 19, 1949, Manley Augustus Buchanan had his moniker long before he had picked up a mic. He was named Big Youth by his coworkers at the Kingston Sheraton hotel, where the tall teen was employed as a mechanic. Initially, he toasted to himself (the DJing equivalent of air guitar), but eventually he took the chance of picking up the mic at a few parties. The enthusiastic response he received prodded him to perform at dances, and by the late '60s, he had a small but avid following. This fan base swiftly grew and as the new decade arrived, Big Youth was now DJing regularly at Lord Tipperton's sound system, quickly becoming the top DJ for the outfit.

By this point, U-Roy, Alcapone, and I-Roy had already made their vinyl debuts, but Big Youth would wait another year, finally releasing his first single in January 1972. He cut "Movie Man" for African Museum, Errol Dunkley and Gregory Isaacs' label, and the song fittingly utilized the rhythm to Dunkley's own "Movie Star." Surprisingly, the single was barely noticed; other producers had no better luck. "The Best Big Youth" (aka "Black Cindy"), cut with Jimmy Radway, sank without a trace. Lee Perry did no better with "Moving," a version of the Wailers' "Keep on Moving." Producer Phil Pratt thought for sure his two cuts were chartward bound, but both "Tell It Black," a version of Dennis Brown's cover of "Black Magic Woman," and "Phil Pratt Thing," a sublime version of Derrick Harriott's "Riding for a Fall," followed its predecessors into oblivion. Even "Fire Bunn," produced by Niney Holness over his own smash "Blood & Fire" rhythm, failed to ignite the Jamaican buying public. The drought was finally broken by a young (just out of his teens) up-and-coming producer, Gussie Clarke. For "The Killer" single, he had the DJ toast over the rootsy Augustus Pablo number, and the result was magnificent. The pair followed it up with "Tippertone Rocking," another major hit. Big Youth was now in demand.

The ever-innovative producer Keith Hudson dragged a motorcycle into the studio to capture its revving engine for "S.90 Skank," a tribute to the popular Honda motorcycle, and roared Big Youth to the top of the Jamaican chart. Their follow-up, "Can You Keep a Secret," a duet between the toaster and his singing producer, did almost as well. In between times, Big Youth cut a pair of songs for Glen Brown, "Come Into My Parlour" and "Opportunity Rocks," the latter employing the popular "Dirty Harry" rhythm. Both were actually recorded the same day as "S.90 Skank." That same week, the DJ also cut a quartet of songs for Prince Buster: "Leggo Beast," "Cain and Abel," "Leave Your Skeng" (a version of "Get Ready"), and "Chi Chi Run" (cut over the rhythm of John Holt's "Rain From the Skies"). That latter track titled a

various-artists compilation that featured the DJ, a young acolyte Little Youth, a trio of top vocalists (Alton Ellis, John Holt, and Dennis Brown), all produced by Prince Buster.

Big Youth's own debut album, *Screaming Target*, arrived in 1973. Produced by Gussie Clarke, the album was stuffed with classic rhythms from the likes of Gregory Isaacs and Lloyd Parks, and filled with hits as well, including the magnificent title track. The DJ seemed to have now glued himself to the chart and during that year, four of his songs, including "Screaming Target" (a version of K.C. White's "No No No" and Buster's "Chi Chi Run"), the Derrick Harriott-produced "Cool Breeze," and the Joe Gibbs-produced "A So We Stay" (a version of Dennis Brown's "Money in My Pocket"), sat proudly on the Jamaican Top 20 for the entire year. Gibbs notched up a total of three hits with Big Youth in 1973; along with the aforementioned single, there was also "Chucky No Lucky" and the topical "Forman Versus Frazier."

From boxing bouts to the "Facts of Life," a hit cut for Sonia Pottinger, Big Youth was the tops on any topic. He'd matured swiftly, from a barely understandable mumbler who exhorted the crowds with typical U-Roy or Alcapone-sque exhortations, to a more relaxed, conversational style. And it was this very ease of delivery—relaxed, but so perfectly timed to the rhythms—that had entranced the nation. In 1974, Big Youth launched his own label, Negusa Nagast; it was later followed by a second, Augustus Buchanan. The former's name was particularly telling and is Amharic (the Ethiopian language) for king of kings. It announced a further shift in the DJ's performance toward a full-on cultural chanter/toaster. Negusa Nagast debuted with a quartet of the DJ's singles, "Hot Cross Bun," "Mr. Bunny," "Children Children," and, most spectacularly of all, "Streets in Africa." This latter was a cover of War's "The World Is a Ghetto," and features Dennis Brown backed by the equally sonorous tones of the Heptones. Big Youth released his second album this same year, *Reggae Phenomenon*, and it was as phenomenal as its title suggested. It featured new songs (all chartbound), remakes of earlier cuts, and smash hits like the title cut (another version of Dennis Brown's "Money in My Pocket"), "Dread Inna Babylon," and "Natty Dread No Jester," a version of the Paragons' "Only a Smile." And the DJ's phenomenal chart success continued with producer after producer. Glen Brown scored with "Dubbie Attack," Tony Robinson oversaw the mighty "House of Dreadlocks" and "Mammy Hot and Daddy Cold," Buddy Davidson produced "Johnny Dead," while Yabby You sat behind the desk for the most seminal of them all, "Yabby Youth," the first of several versions the DJ would cut over the "Conquering Lion" rhythm.

Big Youth would again pair up with Dennis Brown for the Harry J.-produced "Wild Goose Chase." Niney Holness liked what he heard and kept the duo together for his "Ride on Ride On." The two would go on to record a stunning version of Bob Marley's "Get up Stand Up." Marley's version wasn't alone; besides toasting over classic rock-steady rhythms, Big Youth was now increasingly utilizing heavier roots rhythms. Most notable was "I Pray Thee," a version of the Abyssinians' "Satta Amasa Gana," which was another seminal smash hit, and the DJ also cut a version of Burning Spear's classic "Marcus Garvey." Two more Wailers' versions also appeared around this time; Marley's "Craven Choke Puppy" and Bunny Wailer's "Bide Up" became, respectively, "Craven Version" and "Black on Black."

In 1975 the *Dreadlocks Dread* album appeared, a seminal album overseen by Prince Tony Robinson and split between Big Youth's toasts and instrumental dubs. Accompanied by Skin, Flesh & Bones Band, the album remains a masterpiece of dread roots and provocative cultural toasts.

Dreadlocks Dread had a massive impact on the U.K., where it was picked up by the Klik label and prompted Big Youth to tour there the following year. The year 1976 brought two albums in its wake, *Natty Cultural Dread* and *Hit the Road Jack*, both self-produced by a self-confident Big Youth at the peak of his power. Again the albums featured a clutch of Jamaican smashes—"Ten Against One" and "Wolf in Sheep's Clothing" amongst them—and new numbers equally biting at the chart bit. Interestingly enough, *Natty Cultural Dread* also boasts "Every Nigger Is a Star," backed by the I-Threes making their recording debut. Also featured are some of Big Youth's surprising covers. In the past, he'd versioned Motown hits, Gene Pitney, Al Green, and Otis Redding, "Dock of the Bay" of course. Now along with the title track, there was even "If I Had a Hammer." The year 1977 brought the masterful "Four Sevens," a clever version of Culture's "Two Sevens Clash." Produced by Niney Holness, the pair followed up with the provocative "Six Dead, 19 Gone to Jail."

Having now signed to the Frontline label in the U.K., Big Youth's debut album for the Virgin subsidiary was 1978's *Isaiah First Prophet of Old*, a fiercely roots record produced by D Russell. The DJ also had a cameo role in the movie *Rockers*. He's absolutely unmistakable, stepping out of a flash car and flashing a smile that shows off his front teeth embedded with red, yellow, and green jewels, as his long dreads whip around his face. But behind these eye-catching trappings was a thoughtful and thought-provoking DJ, as his records proved time and time again. The year 1978 also saw the release of the "Green Bay Killers" single, a fierce diatribe on the death of a group of Rastafarians at the hands of the Jamaican army. Perhaps Big Youth was now seen as too radical for Virgin, and the label chose not to release the DJ's next two albums, *Progress* and *Rock Holy*. Nor did they pick up on the former's dub companion, the excellent *Reggae Gi Dem Dub*, remixed by the up-and-coming master Sylvan Morris. However, the toaster's grip on Jamaica was also beginning to loosen, and a new generation of chatterers were beginning to come to the fore.

Big Youth continued to record, but no longer ruled the charts, and most of his singles were now self-produced and released through his own labels. The Heartbeat labels' *Some Great Big Youth* collects up many of this late-'70s/early-'80s material; the label's follow-up collection, *The Chanting Dread Inna Fine Style*, concentrates on earlier Negusa Negast singles.

The increasing violence in the dance halls prompted him back into the studio in 1982 for "No War in the Dance," cut for producer Lloyd Sparks. He proved his popularity wasn't totally gone, with a steaming, hits-filled set at *Reggae Sunsplash* before an adoring audience that summer, giving a repeat performance the following year, and again in 1987. In 1985, Big Youth released a surprising new album, *A Luta Continua*, where he transformed from toaster to singer and roots rasta to jazzman, accompanied by Jamaican jazz hero Herbie Miller. However, 1988's *Manifestation* found the DJ regaining his footing, for a roots-drenched set split between excellent toasting and sub-quality singing. Two years later, Niney Holness brought Big Youth back into the studio and cut the remarkable "Chanting." The DJ also contributed a fierce "Free South Africa" to the *One Man One Vote* artists' album. Big Youth later performed at the *Japansplash* festival in Osaka, with his powerful set caught on 1991's *Jamming in the House of Dread* album. He reappeared with a vengeance at *Reggae Sunsplash* the following summer.

With his profile now the highest it had been in years, Big Youth guest-starred on Capleton's *I Testament* album, Mutabaruka's *Gathering of the Spirits*, and Creation Rebel's *Feat of a Green Planet*. In 1995 the DJ released his own new album, *Higher Grounds*, overseen by Junior Reid; it was an intriguing mixture of R&B, reggae, and other styles. Another powerful set at *Reggae Sunsplash* was delivered the following year. The new millennium saw the release in the U.K. of the compilation *Tell It Black*, a two-CD set that rounds up 31 seminal songs from 1972 to 1975. But that pales next to *Natty Universal Dread*, released by the British Blood & Fire label that same year. Three albums and a total of 51 tracks brilliantly wrap up the best from 1973 to 1979 and include a clutch of Negusa Negast singles that have never been reissued. —*Jo-Ann Greene*

Screaming Target / 1973 / Trojan ◆◆◆◆◆
Achieving his first success on wax with "S 90 Skank" for producer Keith Hudson in 1972, Big Youth recorded *Screaming Target*, his debut full-length, one year later for Gussie Clarke. That album, along with a handful of 45s from the period, was largely responsible for bringing the DJ art form forward after U-Roy's innovations. Here, in place of hip, jive-derived phrases, listeners find Big Youth ruminating on themes that exemplified the new consciousness of the 1970s. The set-opening title track, for instance, finds the DJ promoting literacy and general positivity, Youth-style, over K.C. White's "No No No." Similarly, he chants down slavery and calls for equal pay for equal work on "Honesty." Elsewhere, "Tippertong Rock" is a misspelled reference to the sound system that the DJ got his start on, Lord Tippertone Hi-Fi. Many of roots reggae's most innovative releases emerged from the studios of young producers intent on rivaling established businessmen like Coxsone Dodd, Duke Reid, and Prince Buster, and *Screaming Target* is no exception. Clarke was but 18 when he began producing and 20 when he oversaw the sessions for this album. The rhythm selection is superb throughout, including Leroy Smart's "Pride and Ambition," Gregory Isaacs' "One One Coco Fill Basket," and Lloyd Parks' "Slaving," and Big Youth's toasts are a pure joy to listen to. Unfortunately, Trojan decided to separate the mix for the 1989 issue, sending Youth's toasts to the left channel and the rhythm track to the right, resulting in a rather unbalanced listening experience, depending upon your proximity

to the speakers. That aside, the music on this release is simultaneously a benchmark for reggae in general and the DJ form in particular—and a classic of recorded music, regardless of the genre. —*Nathan Bush*

The Chanting Dread Inna Fine Style / 1983 / Heartbeat ◆◆◆◆◆
Picking up where *Some Great Big Youth* left off, or more accurately left out, this compilation gathers up earlier cuts, and thus is a decided improvement over its predecessor. Once again, the set is culled from releases from Big Youth's own Negusa Negast label, all backed by guitarist Earl "Chinna" Smith's marvelous Soul Syndicate band. Big Youth toasts over many classic rhythms, although as was usual by now, most have been so stripped down that they can be difficult to recognize. The exuberantly bouncy "Skyjuice," for example, employs John Holt's "Sister Big Stuff," and was also used by Dennis Alcapone for his hit "Teach the Children." Another much recycled rhythm, the Paragons' "Only a Smile," here is re-created as "Dread Inna Babylon." U Roy versioned the song as well on "Flashing My Whip," but in this DJ clash, Big Youth's is far superior. "Mama Look" employs Dennis Brown's masterpiece, "Money in My Pocket," one of several versions Big Youth cut of that hit, and boasts a fabulously loose and relaxed toast, the DJ at his best. Brown's vocals have been stripped from that, but they do feature on "Streets in Africa," where he's backed by the Heptones. (The song itself is a cover of War's "The World Is a Ghetto.") Cool ruler Gregory Isaacs can also be found within this set. By this point in his career, Big Youth was at his toasting best when rapping about cultural themes, and *Chanting* is stuffed with these cuts. The Soul Syndicate provide a steaming, rootsy backing that meshes perfectly with the DJ's toasts. Chanting dread in a fine style indeed. —*Jo-Ann Greene*

★ **Tell It Black** / May 2, 2000 / Recall ◆◆◆◆◆
A spectacular two-CD compilation stuffed to the gills with hits, seminal early singles, and crucial cuts. *Tell It Black* rounds up 31 songs, all recorded between 1972 and 1975 for a variety of different producers, and showcases Big Youth at his undisputed height. Even two albums aren't enough to fit in all the chart-busters but, bar the inevitable omission of Prince Buster productions, it's an excellent overview. From such early singles as "Moving," "Fire Bunn," and the title track (produced respectively by Lee Perry, Niney Holness, and Phil Pratt), to his first hit, "The Killer," cut for Gussie Clarke, to his first Jamaican number one, the Keith Hudson-overseen "S.90 Skank," and on across a glittering string of further successes, this album has it all. The DJ cut singles for all the island's best producers, not just the aforementioned, but also the likes of Joe Gibbs, Sonia Pottinger, Tony Robinson, Glen Brown, and many more, and most are represented within. Working with nothing less than classic rhythms, once Big Youth conquered the chart, he then occupied it like an invading army. At one time the DJ had a staggering seven singles there at the same time, and his songs had longevity; in 1973, for example, four hung in the Top 20 for the entire year. Two of those, "Screaming Target" and "A So We Stay," are included. You'll also find such other fabulous songs as "Wolf in Sheep's Clothing," "Tippertone Rock," "Natty No Jester," and "Reggae Phenomenon." The latter versioned Dennis Brown's "Money in My Pocket" and the liner notes helpfully identify many of the original rhythms the DJ toasted over. Few had the ability to ride the rhythms like Big Youth, and his wonderful singsong vocals continue to enthrall. There are few better introductions to the DJ than this. —*Jo-Ann Greene*

Natty Universal Dread, 1973-1979 / Oct. 31, 2000 / Blood & Fire ◆◆◆◆◆
It should come as no surprise that the first collection to do full justice to the career of reggae DJ Big Youth was released by the Blood & Fire label, which has already distinguished itself with an exquisite catalog of reissues and collections designed to bring the music of reggae's classical period (the early to mid-'70s) back into the marketplace. This three-disc box set includes 51 tracks from Big Youth's most productive period, beginning with the early singles recorded for Joe Gibbs and on his own Negusa Nagast label (which included the charming "Hot Cross Bun" and "Hot Stock," a collaboration with Gregory Isaacs and Leroy Smart), and ending with the topical "Can't Take Wah Happen on a West" (written in the wake of the disastrous Westmoreland Flood of 1979) and the blistering "Political Confusion," which name-checks Margaret Thatcher and Jimmy Carter. This is also the period that found him releasing his bizarre and wonderful cover versions—"Hit the Road Jack," "Proud Mary" (titled "River Boat" here) and, best of all, "Sugar Sugar." As always, the digitally restored sound is exquisite, but this set does mark the first time that

Blood & Fire has messed up on packaging. It's beautiful and the booklet is jam-packed with rare photos and extensive liner notes, but the individual disc sleeves are equipped with annoying and self-destructing styrofoam spindles. Don't let that fact dissuade you from buying this marvelous collection, but be forewarned. —*Rick Anderson*

Black Grape

f. 1993, Manchester, England **db.** Jul. 1998
British Rap, Alternative Dance, Britpop, Alternative Pop/Rock
After the Happy Mondays disbanded in 1992, most observers would have guessed that the group's leader, vocalist Shaun Ryder, would succumb to the myriad drug addictions that hastened the breakup of the group. Instead of dying, Ryder recouped his strengths and came back with a new band, Black Grape, in the summer of 1995. Black Grape was embraced by both the British public and press, making Shaun Ryder one of the more unexpected comebacks in rock & roll history.

Ryder formed Black Grape in 1993, recruiting ex-Happy Monday Bez (dancing, percussion), rappers Kermit (born Paul Leveridge) and Jed from the Ruthless Rap Assassins, and ex-Paris Angels guitarist Wags. Black Grape began recording demos only weeks after the implosion of the Happy Mondays. Over the course of recording and writing *It's Great When You're Straight*, Ryder recruited a number of musicians, most notably producer and bassist Danny Saber, keyboardist/producer Stephen Lironi, and former Bluebells and Smiths guitarist Gary Gannon. Black Grape's debut album was recorded over a period of seven weeks in late 1994 and early 1995; after it was completed, the band signed with Radioactive Records. The group's first single, "Reverend Black Grape," entered the Top Ten upon its release. The group's debut album, *It's Great When You're Straight... Yeah*, was released in August of 1995. The album entered the U.K. charts at number one.

"In the Name of the Father" and "Kelly's Heroes" followed "Reverend Black Grape" into the Top 20 later in 1995. Toward the end of the year, Kermit suffered a severe case of septicemia, a form of blood poisoning caused by bad water he drank while in Mexico; although he came close to death—bits of his heart and liver were flaking off—he had recovered by the spring of 1996. Black Grape were prepared to head to America early in 1996 when the group were denied entry into the country due to their prior drug convictions. After a couple of months, the passports were cleared and the band was admitted into the U.S. Due to his illness, Kermit had to miss the tour, and his spot was filled by Psycho, who became a permanent member of the band after the completion of the tour. Before Black Grape launched their U.S. tour in spring of 1996, Bez left the band due to financial disagreements with the record company.

In May 1996, Black Grape returned with the single "Fat Neck," which entered the U.K. charts in the Top Ten; the song featured former Smiths member Johnny Marr on guitar. A month after the release of "Fat Neck," the group released their football anthem "England's Irie," which was recorded with Joe Strummer. Like "Fat Neck" before it, "England's Irie" became a Top Ten hit. *Stupid, Stupid, Stupid* followed in 1997. —*Stephen Thomas Erlewine*

● **It's Great When You're Straight . . . Yeah** / Oct. 10, 1995 / Radioactive ✦✦✦✦✦
When the Happy Mondays fell apart in 1992, most observers assumed that Shaun Ryder would never recover from his numerous drug addictions. No one could have ever predicted that he would return to the top of the charts three years later, relatively fit and healthy, with a new band that fulfilled all of the promises of his old group. Black Grape is what the Happy Mondays always were, only better. Leaving behind the stiff musicianship that plagued even the best Mondays records, Black Grape's debut *It's Great When You're Straight... Yeah* is a surreal, funky, profane, and perversely joyous album, overflowing with casual eclecticism and giddy humor. Working with a band that is looser and grittier than the Mondays, Ryder sounds reinvigorated, creating bizarre rhymes that tie together junk culture, drug lingo, literary references, and utter nonsense. Ryder's lyrics have always been free-wheelingly impenetrable, but now he's working with Kermit, a rapper that is the equal of his skills. Even better, the music has deep grooves and catchy pop hooks that come straight out of left field. From the blaring harmonica of the triumphant "Reverend Black Grape" and the trippy sitars of "In the Name of the Father" to the seedy, rolling "Shake Your Money" and the stinging guitars of "Tramazi Parti," *It's Great* is filled with music that goes in unconventional directions without ever sounding forced. Not only is *It's Great When You're*

Straight a triumphant return for Shaun Ryder and his sidekick Bez, it's the first album they have ever recorded that justifies all of the hype. —*Stephen Thomas Erlewine*

Blondie

f. Aug. 1974, New York, NY **db.** Oct. 1982
American Punk, New York Punk, Pop/Rock, Club/Dance, Pop/Rock, New Wave, Punk
Blondie was the most commercially successful band to emerge from the much-vaunted punk/new-wave movement of the late '70s. The group was formed in New York City in August 1974 by singer Deborah Harry (b. Jul. 1, 1945, Miami), formerly of Wind in the Willows, and guitarist Chris Stein (b. Jan. 5, 1950, Brooklyn) out of the remnants of Harry's previous group, the Stilettos. The lineup fluctuated over the next year. Drummer Clement Burke (b. Nov. 24, 1955, New York) joined in May 1975. Bassist Gary Valentine joined in August. In October, keyboard player James Destri (b. Apr. 13, 1954) joined, to complete the initial permanent lineup. They released their first album, *Blondie*, on Private Stock Records in December 1976. In July 1977, Valentine was replaced by Frank Infante.

In August, Chrysalis Records bought their contract from Private Stock and in October reissued *Blondie* and released the second album, *Plastic Letters*. Blondie expanded to a sextet in November with the addition of bassist Nigel Harrison (born in Princes Risborough, Buckinghamshire, England), as Infante switched to guitar. Blondie broke commercially in the U.K. in March 1978, when their cover of Randy and the Rainbows' 1963 hit "Denise," renamed "Denis," became a Top Ten hit, as did *Plastic Letters*, followed by a second U.K. Top Ten, "(I'm Always Touched By Your) Presence, Dear." Blondie turned to U.K. producer/songwriter Mike Chapman for their third album, *Parallel Lines*, which was released in September 1978 and eventually broke them worldwide. "Picture This" became a U.K. Top 40 hit, and "Hanging on the Telephone" made the U.K. Top Ten, but it was the album's third single, the disco-influenced "Heart of Glass," that took Blondie to number one in both the U.K. and the U.S. "Sunday Girl" hit number one in the U.K. in May, and "One Way or Another" hit the U.S. Top 40 in August. Blondie followed with their fourth album, *Eat to the Beat*, in October. Its first single, "Dreaming," went Top Ten in the U.K., Top 40 in the U.S. The second single, "Union City Blue," went Top 40 in the U.S. In March 1980, the third U.K. single from *Eat to the Beat*, "Atomic," became the group's third British number one. (It later made the U.S. Top 40.)

Meanwhile, Harry was collaborating with German disco producer Giorgio Moroder on "Call Me," the theme from the movie *American Gigolo*. It became Blondie's second transatlantic chart topper. Blondie's fifth album, *Autoamerican*, was released in November 1980, and its first single was the reggaeish tune "The Tide Is High," which went to number one in the U.S. and U.K. The second single was the rap-oriented "Rapture," which topped the U.S. pop charts and went Top Ten in the U.K. But the band's eclectic style reflected a diminished participation by its members—Infante sued, charging that he wasn't being used on the records, though he settled and stayed in the lineup. But in 1981, the members of Blondie worked on individual projects, notably Harry's gold-selling solo album, *KooKoo. The Best of Blondie* was released in the fall of the year. *The Hunter*, Blondie's sixth and last new album, was released in May 1982, preceded by the single "Island of Lost Souls," a Top 40 hit in the U.S. and U.K. "War Child" also became a Top 40 hit in the U.K., but *The Hunter* was a commercial disappointment. At the same time, Stein became seriously ill with the genetic disease pemphigus. As a result, Blondie broke up in October 1982, with Deborah Harry launching a part-time solo career while caring for Stein, who eventually recovered. In 1998 the original lineup of Harry, Stein, Destri, and Burke reunited to tour Europe, their first series of dates in 16 years; a new LP, *No Exit*, followed early the next year. —*William Ruhlmann*

Autoamerican / Nov. 1980 / Chrysalis ✦✦✦
The basic Blondie sextet was augmented, or replaced, by a dozen session musicians for the group's fifth album, *Autoamerican*, on which they continued to expand their stylistic range, with greater success, at least on certain tracks, than they had on *Eat to the Beat*. The rap pastiche "Rapture" and the Caribbean-flavored "The Tide Is High" both went to #1 on the singles charts, but they are the only memorable tracks on an album that leads off with a string-filled instrumental and also finds Deborah Harry crooning ersatz '20s pop on "Here's Looking at You" and tackling Broadway show music in a cover of "Follow Me" from *Camelot*. What a mess. —*William Ruhlmann*

★ **The Best of Blondie** / 1981 / Chrysalis ✦✦✦✦✦

Although Blondie made several first-rate albums, most of their best songs were released as singles, which makes *The Best of Blondie* an essential collection. *The Best of Blondie* glosses over their punk roots—very little from the first album, apart from the vicious "Rip Her to Shreds" and the seductive "In the Flesh"—but the band's pop hits are among the finest of their era and encapsulate all of the virtues of new wave. Apart from genuine chart hits like "Heart of Glass," "One Way or Another," "Dreaming," "Call Me," "Atomic," "The Tide Is High," and "Rapture," *Best of Blondie* picks up several of the group's best album tracks, like "(I'm Always Touched By Your) Presence, Dear" and "Hanging on the Telephone." *The Best of Blondie* isn't all you need to know, but it is an excellent introduction to one of the best new wave bands. [*Best of Blondie* is also available in an import release.] —*Stephen Thomas Erlewine*

Blowfly (Clarence Reid)

b. Feb. 14, 1945, Cochran, GA

Vocals / Blaxploitation, Funk, Comedy

Blowfly is the X-rated alterego of Clarence Reid, a songwriter/producer who had quite a bit of success under his own name in the '70s, writing and producing hits for Gwen MacRae, KC & the Sunshine Band, Betty Wright, and others while on the staff at the preeminent Florida disco label of the era, TK Records. It's as Blowfly that Reid is best remembered in certain circles, though. The Redd Foxx of the Southern soul circuit, Blowfly specializes in dirty parodies of current soul and pop hits; his over two dozen albums, almost all of them recorded live in the studio with the ambience of a liquor-fueled all-night party, are an entertaining mixture of filth and wit that are neither too disgusting to be funny nor too refined to be dirty.

Born in Cochran, GA, on Valentine's Day, 1946, Reid got his nickname in the early '60s when his grandmother caught the adolescent singing dirty lyrics to a popular hit and proclaimed that her grandchild was "nastier than a blowfly." Reid moved to the more dirty-word-friendly climes of Miami in the mid-'60s and hooked up with producer and label owner Henry Stone. Under his own name, Reid released several solid albums of straight R&B, and had several chart singles, starting with 1969's Top Ten soul hit "Nobody but You Babe," for Stone's Alston and TK imprints.

Reid never lost his knack for filthying up Top 40 hits, though, and after a few years of performing his parodies for friends and coworkers, Reid resurrected his adolescent nickname and went in the studio after hours with some studio musician buddies in 1970 and recorded Blowfly's debut album, *The Weird World of Blowfly*. Of course, Stone's labels couldn't touch the results, so Reid pressed the album on his own Weird World imprint, housing it in a bizarre homemade-looking sleeve featuring Reid standing on a trash can in a comically hideous monster mask, a pair of homemade wings, a blue sweater with "BF" printed on it in yellow, and a pair of tighty-whiteys and knee socks, holding a rubber chicken in one hand and clawing at two large-afro'ed nude women kneeling before him. A weird world indeed.

Sold on the same semi-underground circuit that traded in Rudy Ray Moore's Dolemite albums and other cultural oddities, the Blowfly records were massively popular. Although it was an open secret from the beginning that Blowfly was Clarence Reid, Reid always appeared in some sort of elaborate and/or strange costume on the record sleeves. His reticence to be publicly identified as Blowfly stemmed not only from his religious upbringing—despite his dirty mouth, Reid is a devout Christian who forswears liquor and cigarettes and has worked as a minister—but also from the criminal prosecution that Reid's latter-day buddies 2 Live Crew found out about the hard way. Stores have been prosecuted for carrying Blowfly albums in some communities, and Reid was sued by the then-president of ASCAP, Stanley Adams, after Blowfly parodied Adams' jazz standard "What a Difference a Day Makes" as "What a Difference a Lay Makes."

Reid released Blowfly records under a variety of label names through the '70s, '80s, and '90s, collaborating with likeminded folks like 2 Live Crew and even Flea from the Red Hot Chili Peppers. Blowfly is enough of a cultural icon that he even recorded his own holiday single in the mid-'70s. Of course, the songs were called "Jingle Fuckin' Bells" and "Queer for the New Year," but this is Blowfly we're talking about here, not Bing Crosby. Blowfly also starred in the low-budget documentary *The Twisted World of Blowfly* in 1991, and

several of his albums were reissued on CD through the '90s, capped by *The Best of Blowfly: Analthology* in 1996. —*Stewart Mason*

The Best of Blowfly: Analthology / Aug. 20, 1996 / Pandisc ✦✦✦

Reviewing a Blowfly album is a bit like discussing a porno film; you pretty much know what the dirty parts are going to be like at the outset, so the real question is: Does the work in question have any redeeming artistic merit? Clarence Reid, the semi-respectable creative mind behind the outrageously freaky persona of Blowfly, knows more than a little about making a solid R&B record, and once you get past the mega-filthy lyrics and titles like "Hole Man" and "Porno Freak," you can usually find some solid soul and funk grooves on the best Blowfly records. However, *The Best of Blowfly: Analthology* for the most part reflects the less-than-ideal state of old school R&B these days. While the original Blowfly albums on Weird World Records exuded the gloriously drunken ambience of an after-hours party gone nasty, *Analthology* consists of mid-'90s re-recordings of Blowfly's underground hits, with synthesizers and drum machines often replacing the live rhythm sections that conjured up the good groove behind Blowfly's classic albums (please remember "classic" is a relative term). Reid's performances are still enthusiastically filthy, and the jokes are just as funny as they've ever been (decide for yourself if that's good or bad), but the cleaner surfaces of the digital-friendly production make for a less-enjoyably dirty experience, sort of like the difference between a vintage adult movie shot on film and a modern porn quickie produced on videotape. Longtime Blowfly fans will be glad to hear the king of smut funk is still in solid form, but anyone looking for a real Blowfly greatest-hits disc ought to dig up *The Worst of Blowfly*, a collection of vintage Weird World material. —*Mark Deming*

● **The Worst of Blowfly** / Oct. 15, 1996 / Hot Productions ✦✦✦✦

The Worst of Blowfly is an aptly titled collection only if one thinks of the word "worst" in the sense of (to use one of the man's favorite words) "nastiest." This 1996 compilation, with tracks that stretch back over a quarter century to some of Clarence Reid's earliest recordings under his foulmouthed Blowfly persona, is for those who find Doug Clark & Hot Nuts too prim: these 20 songs are pure Southern gutbucket funk with absolutely filthy—and usually hilarious—lyrics. Titles like "Spearmy Night in Georgia" and "She Sucks on My Dick" say it all, yet there's a playfulness and good humor to these songs that keep them from being merely crude. Reid doesn't have a hateful bone in his body, and so there's no anger or spite in Blowfly's songs, just a schoolboy's glee in naughtiness for its own sake. It also helps that thanks to Reid's other career as a straight R&B singer, producer, and arranger, he has always been able to get ace musicians for his Blowfly sessions, with the result that songs like "Funky Party" work just as well as groove thangs. —*Stewart Mason*

The Brand New Heavies

f. 1985, London, England

Alternative Rap, Alternative Dance, Club/Dance, Acid Jazz, Urban, House, Hip-Hop

Pioneers of the London acid jazz scene, the Brand New Heavies translated their love for the funk grooves of the 1970s into a sophisticated sound that carried the torch for classic soul in an era dominated by hip-hop. Formed in 1985 by drummer/keyboardist Jan Kincaid, guitarist Simon Bartholomew, and bassist/keyboardist Andrew Levy—longtime school friends from the London suburb of Ealing—the Brand New Heavies were originally an instrumental unit inspired by the James Brown and Meters records its members heard while clubbing the rare groove scene in vogue at the moment. The trio soon began recording their own music, gaining enormous exposure when their demo tracks were spun at the influential Cat in the Hat Club.

Eventually adding a brass section, the Brand New Heavies built a cult following throughout the London club circuit, surviving the shift that saw the rare groove scene fade in the wake of acid house. After an earlier recording deal with Cooltempo yielded the single "Got to Give," the Heavies—now including vocalist Jay Ella Ruth—signed with the fledgling indie label Acid Jazz; recorded on a budget of just 8,000 pounds, the group's self-titled LP appeared in 1990 to strong critical acclaim, resulting in a licensing deal with the American company Delicious Vinyl. With Ruth now out of the band, Delicious Vinyl hand-picked N'dea Davenport as her successor, insisting the

Heavies re-record tracks from their debut for their first U.S. effort, also an eponymous release that appeared in 1992.

After scoring at home with "Dream Come True" and "Stay This Way," the single "Never Stop" soon landed on the American R&B charts, with the Heavies the first British group to accomplish such a feat with a debut single since Soul II Soul several years earlier; a subsequent New York performance augmented by rappers Q-Tip (A Tribe Called Quest) and MC Serch (3rd Bass) inspired the group to begin absorbing hip-hop, and that summer they cut *Heavy Rhyme Experience, Vol. 1*, an album including guest appearances by rappers including Main Source, Gang Starr, Grand Puba, and the Pharcyde. *Brother Sister* (1994), which went platinum in Britain, was Davenport's last recording with the Heavies before beginning a solo career; she was replaced by singer Siedah Garrett in time for 1997's *Shelter*. Two years later, the group reappeared with a British best-of album entitled *Trunk Funk: The Best of the Brand New Heavies*; the title was recycled the following year for an American compilation, *Trunk Funk Classics 1991-2000*, which featured a new song recorded with Davenport. —*Jason Ankeny*

Heavy Rhyme Experience, Vol. 1 / Aug. 3, 1992 / Delicious Vinyl ◆◆◆◆
"Brand New Heavies play the sh*t that/People used to listen to in '70s Chevys." With that succinct and flawless couplet from the awesome opening track, "Bonafide Funk," Large Professor helped to explain why there was a certain herd of influential rappers who were enthralled by the Brand New Heavies' sleek (some would say slick) and urbanely stylish Anglo take on classic American funk and soul after the quartet released its eponymous debut in 1991: They were pulling the very same vintage-groove LPs from their crates for inspiration. When the Heavies made their first trip to American shores, both Q-Tip and 3rd Bass' MC Serch were quick to show their respect by hopping on-stage with the band (likely the event that planted the seed for *Heavy Rhyme Experience*), and the latter rapper even predicted that *The Brand New Heavies* would be the source material for a decade's worth of loops and samples for rap producers. Serch's enthusiastic forecast never quite materialized, but it is hard to argue with his logic after you hear this landmark collaborative experiment. A live hip-hop band wasn't a complete novelty at the time—proto-rapper Gil Scott-Heron utilized jazz backing, Tackhead was the house band for Sugar Hill Records all the way back in the late '70s, and the self-proclaimed "world's one and only hip-hop band," Stetsasonic had been fully live for several years by that point—but never before had rap taken such an on-the-fly, jam-like approach. Spontaneous combustion resulted. Never before (and perhaps never since) had the Heavies managed to sound this deliciously in-the-pocket and playful, and the MCs beautifully follow their lead. Guru sounds looser and more whimsical on "It's Gettin Hectic" than on any Gang Starr track. Simon Bartholomew's teasing guitar lines poke holes in Grand Puba's swollen-tongued bluster on "Who Makes the Loot?" Kool G Rap is given the blaxploitation backing he had always deserved. And Ed. O.G. and Pharcyde do verbal gymnastics that must be heard. But every vocalist here blooms from the pairing. The only regret is that N'Dea Davenport was not included in some capacity, considering how much she added to the Heavies. Too bad, as well, that there was never a volume two. One wonders what sort of magic Posdnuos and Trugoy of De La Soul, the Leaders of the New School trio, Rakim, or Chuck D could have conjured had they been tapped as collaborators, or from the West Coast Ice Cube and Del tha Funkee Homosapien. Still, *Heavy Rhyme Experience, Vol. 1* is a match made in heaven. —*Stanton Swihart*

● **Trunk Funk Classics: 1991-2000** / Oct. 17, 2000 / Rhino ◆◆◆◆
Trunk Funk Classics: 1991-2000 is the first Brand New Heavies best-of available domestically in the U.S. Not to be confused with the similarly titled British release *Trunk Funk: Best of the Brand New Heavies*, the American version doesn't feature all of the group's U.K. chart singles ("Midnight at the Oasis" and "You Are the Universe" are missing), but it does give more airtime to the Heavies' collaborations with American rappers, including Main Source, the Pharcyde, Mos Def, and Q-Tip. There's also a newly recorded track, "Finish What You Started," which temporarily reunites the group with longtime vocalist N'Dea Davenport; wisely, it's also the 1991-1994 Davenport era that's most heavily drawn upon for the collection. It may not be *entirely* comprehensive, but *Trunk Funk Classics* does cover the essence of the Brand New Heavies, and just as importantly, it's a consistently infectious listen. —*Steve Huey*

Chuck Brown

b. Washington, D.C.
Vocals, Guitar / Go-Go, Soul
Washington, D.C., bandleader, performer, and songwriter Chuck Brown has been a prominent figure on the city's go-go scene since the late '70s. Brown & the Soul Searchers have also been one of the rare go-go acts to gain national attention, even though it was short-lived. The Soul Searchers included trombonist/keyboardist John "JB" Buchanan, trumpeter Donald Tillery, saxophonist/flutist Leroy Fleming, bassist Jerry Wilder, percussionist Gregory Gerran, organist Curtis Johnson, keyboardist Skip Fennell, drummer Ricardo Wellman, and guitarist LeRon Young. They vaulted into the spotlight with "Busting Loose," the top R&B single for four consecutive weeks at the end of 1978. Its fabulous arrangement; exuberant horn work; and arresting, terse vocals made the band momentary celebrities. But the follow-up, "Game Seven," flopped, and they were soon back on the go-go circuit. They had one more flirtation with the spotlight in 1984, as the single "We Need Some Money (Bout Money)" reached number 26 amid predictions that go-go was ready to explode into the mainstream. It didn't happen, but Brown remained active. He tried again in 1991 with *'90s Goin' Hard* for Goff. A documentary on the Washington, D.C., go-go scene appeared in 2002 and prominently featured Brown and his music. —*Ron Wynn*

● **Bustin' Loose** / 1979 / Valley Vue ◆◆◆◆◆
In the 1980s many of go-go's supporters insisted that it was going to become as big as rap. Regrettably, that never happened. Go-go was huge in Washington, D.C., where a Chuck Brown or Rare Essence show was as big a deal as a George Clinton concert, and a go-go release could be as impressive a seller as the latest Rick James record. But nationally, only a few go-go songs became major hits: E.U.'s "Da Butt" was huge in 1988, and Chuck Brown soared to the top of the R&B charts in 1978 with the insanely funky "Bustin' Loose." Brown and his band, the Soul Searchers, showed a great deal of promise on this debut album, which James Purdie produced at the famous Sigma Sound Studios in Philadelphia. The title song is one of go-go's all-time classics, and anyone with a taste for sweaty, hard-driving funk will also find a lot to love about "If It Ain't Funky" and "I Gotcha Now." But not everything on the album is aggressive. Even though Brown is best known for his gutbucket funk grooves, "Could It Be Love" and an inspired cover of the Jerry Butler/Gamble & Huff pearl "Never Gonna Give You Up" demonstrate that he has no problem handling romantic ballads and slow jams. It isn't surprising that the album's slower tracks are so heavily influenced by Philly soul. After all, Sigma Sound is where the O'Jays, the Intruders, Blue Magic, Teddy Pendergrass, the Stylistics, Billy Paul, and countless others recorded their biggest hits. Most of *Bustin' Loose*, however, isn't typical of recordings made at Sigma; the majority of the material is pure go-go, and *Bustin' Loose* went down in history as one of go-go's most essential releases. —*Alex Henderson*

Any Other Way to Go? / 1987 / Rhythm Attack ◆◆◆◆
Best known for their ferocious live gigging, Chuck Brown & the Soul Searchers' recorded catalog often falls by the wayside. But still, live shows aside, their albums remain one of the strongest and best chronicles of Washington, D.C.'s go-go sound. And *Any Other Way to Go?*, coming as the scene's spark was dying, is an excellent, tight masterpiece—easily as good as anything released in the frenzy of the genre's early days. Brown and his crew, alongside Trouble Funk and Rare Essence, constantly threatened to break the genre nationally during the 1980s without much luck. But, because this music and these songs fell so far below the radar at the time—they were never completely co-opted by mainstream music—they remain as vibrant as they ever were at the time of issue. And even at the end of go-go's party, the man who created the genre made sure this album was packed with goodies. Full of funk breaks, prominent drumbeats, and inspired raps, *Any Other Way to Go?* delivers. From the opening "Run Joe," an outstanding go-go-fied calypso, to "Go-Go Drug Free" and "Do That Stuff," Brown and the Searchers keep the groove moving. But Brown wasn't ready to stop there. He added a fresh trio of Sly Stone covers and put his own spin on them. The resulting "Stormy Monday," "Be Bumpin Fresh," and especially "Family Affair" are outstanding. Easily as good as their 1979 proto go-go smash *Bustin' Loose*, *Any Other Way to Go?* certainly capped a genre in ultimate style. Chuck Brown & the Soul Searchers are a vital, vibrant reminder of how good music could be in an era often remembered for such little substance. —*Amy Hanson*

Buckshot LeFonque

Fusion, Hip-Hop

When Branford Marsalis decided to stir up a little trouble in 1994 by juxtaposing and fusing mainstream jazz with hip-hop rhythms, rap, R&B, rock, reggae, and half a dozen other idioms, he chose to present his new music under the group name Buckshot LeFonque. This fanciful moniker is actually a resurrection of a pseudonym Cannonball Adderley used in the 1950s when moonlighting on a record label other than his own. The group's eponymous first album, a brilliant, playful, musically rich realization of this anything-goes fusion unfortunately drew a lot of fire from critics in every genre, a situation that Marsalis lamented on the group's equally eclectic yet less striking second album *Music Evolution*. Nevertheless, Marsalis was so enthused by his new group that he left his high-profile job as bandleader of the *Tonight Show* in part so that he could tour with Buckshot LeFonque in 1994-1995. The 1997 edition of Buckshot, as heard on *Music Evolution*, contains a nucleus of Marsalis (saxophones, keyboard, and drum programming), DJ Apollo ("wheels o' steel"), Frank McComb (vocals, keyboards), Carl Burnett (guitar), Russell Gunn (trumpet), Reginald Veal (bass), Rocky Bryant (drums), and 50 Styles: the Unknown Soldier (rap vocals). Of all of Marsalis' diverse pursuits, none project his unique combination of virtuosity and irreverence as completely as Buckshot LeFonque. —*Richard S. Ginell*

● **Buckshot LeFonque** / Aug. 2, 1994 / Columbia ✦✦✦✦

Lots of records are touted as breakthroughs by the hype machines and spin-masters, but this one really is—a marvelously playful and, above all, musical fusion of the old jazz verities and newer currents swirling around the 1990s. "Buckshot LeFonque" was a pseudonym for Cannonball Adderley in the 1950s, and you'll squint long and hard trying to find Branford's name on the jacket and cover except for the tiny note, "Produced by B. Marsalis." Maybe he was hedging his bets against the expected (and received) flak from the jazz purists, but the reality is that he has found a brilliant way to fuse hip-hop rhythms with mainstream jazz licks without compromising either idiom. The best number is a lovely setting of Maya Angelou's poem *"I Know Why the Caged Bird Sings,"* with absolutely gorgeous soprano by Marsalis, some great Miles-tinged muted trumpet from Roy Hargrove, and Angelou reciting her words against the big electronic backbeat. The free-thinking Branford also injects real funk into Elton John's "Mona Lisas (And Mad Hatters)"; throws in a little reggae, rap, and lots of sampling; gets down and dirty with Kevin Eubanks' slide guitar on the truckin' cut "Some Cow Fonque"; and unifies most of the package with a couple of recurring, catchy riffs and touches of horseplay. The only misfire is a totally incongruous, totally dull soul ballad called "Ain't It Funny" (sung by Tammy Townsend) that sounds as if someone suddenly switched CDs on your changer. Nevertheless, regardless of what the neo-boppers might say, this is a more imaginative record than any of Branford's estimable straight jazz projects—and a lot more fun. —*Richard S. Ginell*

Mariah Carey

b. Mar. 27, 1970, New York, NY

Vocals / Soft-Rock, Hip-Hop/Urban, Dance, Club/Dance, Adult Contemporary, Urban, Rock, Dance-Pop

The best-selling female performer of the 1990s, Mariah Carey rose to superstardom on the strength of her stunning five-octave voice; an elastic talent who moved easily from glossy ballads to hip-hop-inspired dance-pop, she earned frequent comparison to rivals Whitney Houston and Celine Dion, but did them both one better by composing all of her own material. Born in Long Island, NY, on March 27, 1970, Carey moved to New York City at the age of 17—just one day after graduating high school—to pursue a music career; there she befriended keyboardist Ben Margulies, with whom she began writing songs. Her big break came as a backing vocalist on a studio session with dance-pop singer Brenda K. Starr, who handed Carey's demo tape to Columbia Records head Tommy Mottola at a party. According to legend, Mottola listened to the tape in his limo while driving home that same evening, and was so immediately struck by Carey's talent that he doubled back to the party to track her down.

After signing to Columbia, Carey entered the studio to begin work on her 1990 self-titled debut LP; the heavily promoted album was a chart-topping smash, launching no less than four number-one singles: "Vision of Love," "Love Takes Time," "Someday," and "I Don't Wanna Cry." Her overnight success earned Grammy Awards as Best New Artist and Best Female Vocalist, and expectations were high for Carey's follow-up, 1991's *Emotions*. The album did not disappoint, as the title track reached number one—a record fifth consecutive chart topper—while both "Can't Let Go" and "Make It Happen" landed in the Top Five. Carey's next release was 1992's *MTV Unplugged* EP, which generated a number-one cover of the Jackson 5's "I'll Be There"; featured on the track was backup singer Trey Lorenz, whose appearance immediately helped him land a recording contract of his own.

In June 1993, Carey wed Mottola—some two decades her senior—in a headline-grabbing ceremony; months later she released her third full-length effort, *Music Box*, her best-selling record to date. Two more singles, "Dreamlover" and "Hero," reached the top spot on the charts. Carey's first tour followed and was widely panned by critics; undaunted, she resurfaced in 1994 with a holiday release titled *Merry Christmas*, scoring a seasonal smash with "All I Want for Christmas Is You." Released in 1995, *Daydream* reflected a new artistic maturity; the first single, "Fantasy," debuted at number one, making Carey the first female artist and just the second performer ever to accomplish the feat. The follow-up, "One Sweet Day"—a collaboration with Boyz II Men—repeated the trick, and remained lodged at the top of the charts for a record 16 weeks.

After separating from Mottola, Carey returned in 1997 with *Butterfly*, another staggering success and her most hip-hop-flavored recording to date. *#1's*—a collection featuring her 13 previous chart-topping singles as well as "The Prince of Egypt (When You Believe)," a duet with Whitney Houston effectively pairing the two most successful female recording artists in pop history—followed late the next year. With "Heartbreaker," the first single from her 1999 album *Rainbow*, Carey became the first artist to top the charts in each year of the 1990s; the record also pushed her ahead of the Beatles as the artist with the most cumulative weeks spent atop the Hot 100 singles chart.

However, the 2000s weren't as kind to Carey. After signing an $80 million deal with Virgin—the biggest record contract ever—in 2001 she experienced a very public personal and professional meltdown that included rambling, suicidal messages on her website; an appearance on *TRL* where, clad only in a T-shirt, she handed out Popsicles to the audience; and last but not least, the stupendously awful movie *Glitter* and its attendant soundtrack (which was also her Virgin Records debut). Both the film and the album did poorly, critically as well as commercially, with *Glitter* making just under $4 million in its total U.S. gross and the soundtrack struggling to make gold sales. Following these failures, Virgin and Carey parted ways early in 2002, with the label paying her $28 million. That spring, she found a new home with Island/Def Jam, where she set up her own label, MonarC Music. In December, she released her ninth album, *Charmbracelet*. —*Jason Ankeny*

● **#1's** / Nov. 17, 1998 / Columbia ✦✦✦✦✦

Protest as she may—and she does, claiming in the liner notes that *#1's* is "not a greatest hits album! It's too soon, I haven't been recording long enough for that!"—it's hard to view *#1's*, Mariah Carey's first compilation, as anything other than a greatest-hits album. Carey was fortunate enough to have nearly every single she released top the pop charts. Between 1990's "Vision of Love" and 1998's "My All," all but four commercially released singles ("Anytime You Need a Friend," "Can't Let Go," "Make It Happen," "Without You") hit number one, with only a handful of radio-only singles ("Butterfly," "Breakdown") making the airwaves, not the charts. That leaves 12 big hits on *#1's*, all number ones. Since Carey's singles always dominated her albums, it comes as no surprise that *#1's* is her best, most consistent album, filled with songs that represent state-of-the-art '90s adult contemporary and pop-oriented urban soul. That said, it isn't a perfect overview—a couple of good singles are missing because of the self-imposed "#1 rule"; plus, the Ol' Dirty Bastard mix of "Fantasy" is strong, but fans familiar with the radio single will be disappointed that the chorus is completely missing on this version. The album is also padded with a personal favorite (her Brian McKnight duet "Whenever You Call," taken from *Butterfly*) and three new songs—the Jermaine Dupri-produced "Sweetheart," the Whitney Houston duet "When You Believe" (taken from *The Prince of Egypt* soundtrack), and "I Still Believe," a remake of a Brenda K. Starr tune—which are all fine, but not particularly memorable. Still, that's hardly enough to bring down a thoroughly entertaining compilation that will stand as her best record until the "official" hits collection is released. —*Stephen Thomas Erlewine*

Neneh Cherry (Neneh Mariann Karlssson)

b. Mar. 10, 1964, Stockholm, Sweden

Vocals / Pop-Rap, Alternative Rap, Alternative Dance, Club/Dance, Urban, Dance-Pop

The stepdaughter of jazz trailblazer Don Cherry, vocalist Neneh Cherry forged her own groundbreaking blend of pop, dance, and hip-hop, which presaged the emergence of both alternative rap and trip-hop. She was born Neneh Mariann Karlssson on March 10, 1964, in Stockholm, Sweden, the daughter of West African percussionist Amadu Jah and artist Moki Cherry. Raised by her mother and her trumpeter stepfather in both Stockholm and New York City, Cherry dropped out of school at age 14, and in 1980 she relocated to London to sing with the punk group the Cherries.

Following brief flings with the Slits and the Nails, she joined the experimental funk outfit Rip Rig + Panic, and appeared on the group's albums *God* (1981), *I Am Cold* (1982), and *Attitude* (1983). When the band broke up, Cherry remained with one of the spin-off groups, Float Up CP, and led them through one album, 1986's *Kill Me in the Morning*. The band proved short-lived, however, and Cherry began rapping in a London club, where she earned the attention of a talent scout who signed her to a solo contract. Her first single, "Stop the War," railed against the invasion of the Falkland Islands.

After attracting some notice singing backup on the The's "Slow Train to Dawn" single, she became romantically and professionally involved with composer and musician Cameron McVey, who, under the alias Booga Bear, wrote much of the material that would comprise Cherry's 1989 debut LP *Raw Like Sushi*. One song McVey did not write was "Buffalo Stance," the album's breakthrough single; originally tossed off as a B side by the mid-'80s pop group Morgan McVey, Cherry's cover was an international smash that neatly summarized the album's eclectic fusion of pop smarts and hip-hop energy.

A pair of hits—the eerie "Manchild" and "Kisses on the Wind"—followed, but shortly after the record's release Cherry was sidelined with Lyme disease, and apart from a cover of Cole Porter's "I've Got You Under My Skin" for the 1990 *Red Hot + Blue* benefit album, she remained silent until 1992's *Homebrew*. A more subdued collection than *Raw Like Sushi*, it featured cameos from Gang Starr and R.E.M.'s Michael Stipe, as well as writing and production assistance from Geoff Barrow, who layered the track "Somedays" with the same distinct trip-hop glaze he later perfected as half of the duo Portishead. While the album was not as commercially successful as its predecessor, Cherry returned to the charts in 1994 duetting with Youssou N'Dour on the global hit "Seven Seconds." After another lengthy layoff spent raising her children, she resurfaced with the atmospheric *Man* in 1996. —*Jason Ankeny*

● **Raw Like Sushi** / May 1989 / Virgin ✦✦✦✦✦

Those arguing that the most individualistic R&B and dance music of the late '80s and early to mid-'90s came out of Britain could point to Neneh Cherry's unconventional *Raw Like Sushi* as a shining example. An unorthodox and brilliantly daring blend of R&B, rap, pop, and dance music, *Sushi* enjoyed little exposure on America's conservative, urban, contemporary radio formats, but was a definite underground hit. Full of personality, the singer/rapper is as thought-provoking as she is witty and humorous when addressing relationships and taking aim at less-than-kosher behavior of males and females alike. Macho homeboys and Casanovas take a pounding on "So Here I Come" and the hit "Buffalo Stance," while women who are shallow, cold-hearted, or materialistic get lambasted on "Phoney Ladies," "Heart," and "Inna City Mamma." Cherry's idealism comes through loud and clear on "The Next Generation," a plea to take responsibility for one's sexual actions and give children the respect and attention they deserve. —*Alex Henderson*

Homebrew / Oct. 27, 1992 / Virgin ✦✦✦✦✦

Neneh Cherry doesn't get into the studio nearly often enough. Three years passed before the British singer/rapper came out with a second album. Thankfully, she more than lived up to the tremendous promise of *Raw Like Sushi* on the equally magnificent and risk-taking *Homebrew*. Cherry shows no signs of the dreaded sophomore slump—everything on the CD is a gem. She triumphs with a seamless and unorthodox blend of hip-hop, R&B, dance music, and pop, and on "Money Love" and "Trout," the presence of R.E.M.'s Michael Stipe brings rock to the eclectic mix. As humorous as Cherry can be, her reflections on relationships and social issues are often quite pointed. While "Money Love" decries the evils of materialism, the moving "I Ain't

Gone Under Yet" describes an inner-city woman's determination not to be brought down by the poverty and drugs that surround her. And "Twisted" is about keeping yourself sane in a world gone insane. Unfortunately, *Homebrew* wasn't the commercial breakthrough Cherry was more than deserving of. —*Alex Henderson*

Cody ChesnuTT

Vocals / Neo-Soul, Contemporary R&B

The common life just wasn't enough for soul singer Cody ChesnuTT. In 1992, after working as a long-distance operator, he left his day job to make his dream in music come true. It would be another ten years until they were fully realized, but the trek made ChesnuTT the musician he is today.

ChesnuTT began tinkering with the guitar in his early teens in his native Atlanta. His father was a manager of several local bands. This, in turn, opened doors and by age 13 he was playing shows. By his late 20s, he founded the band Crosswalk and was a skillful guitar player. A major-label deal was in the works, but everything fell short for ChesnuTT. The new millennium, however, proved golden. He hibernated in his bedroom, a homemade studio he nicknamed the Sonic Promiseland, and began recording. What amassed from those personal sessions was a 36-track double disc entitled *The Headphone Masterpiece*. —*MacKenzie Wilson*

The Headphone Masterpiece / 2002 / Ready Set Go ✦✦✦✦✦

Cody ChesnuTT's debut album, *The Headphone Masterpiece*, is what all pop/rock-soul-R&B-hip-hop hybrids should be: good, raw, fun, and funky. ChesnuTT mixes '60s-style rock with '70s soul and '90s hip-hop and R&B in an eclectic celebration of sound. This lo-fi gem was recorded in his bedroom and sounds like it; it's essentially a 36-track musical diary. He sings testosterone-driven songs of passion and tender tales of mental anguish with equal abandon. When he whispers, "I know my breakdown is on the way," on "My Women, My Guitars," you feel his impending fall. He plays almost all of the instruments and sings most of the vocals, and he's often out of tune and off-key, but that only adds to the emotion and recklessness of the album. He holds everything together with a few polished and catchy tracks that are scattered throughout. On "Looks Good in Leather," he sounds like Terence Trent D'Arby or Ben Harper, but with a style that's all Cody ChesnuTT. "The World Is Coming to My Party" is a full-fledged dance anthem, complete with a rafter-shaking groove that Prince would be proud of. He just as easily channels Curtis Mayfield on the smooth "Serve This Royalty," which showcases ChesnuTT's soulful voice and may be the finest track, combining his great grasp of groove with clever lyrics like, "We can crown kings in Adidas." ChesnuTT is as comfortable in the hip-hop world as he is in the rock and soul spheres. He lays down a funky rap on "War Between the Sexes," and few hardcore gangstas can match his misogyny on "Bitch I'm Broke." While a few songs lack ChesnuTT's charm, the misses don't disturb the groove enough to hinder the overall effect: a masterpiece, with or without headphones. —*Michael Gowan*

Cibo Matto

f. 1994, New York, NY

Shibuya-Kei, Alternative Dance, Indie Rock, Trip-Hop, Alternative Pop/Rock

A Japanese-born duo relocated to New York and christened with an Italian band name, Cibo Matto's music mirrored the melting-pot aesthetics of their origins, resulting in a heady brew of funk samples, hip-hop rhythms, tape loops, and fractured pop melodies all topped off by surreal narratives sung in a combination of French and broken English. Cibo Matto comprised vocalist Miho Hatori and keyboardist/sampler Yuka Honda, a pair of expatriate Japanese women who arrived in the U.S. independently. Honda, a onetime member of Brooklyn Funk Essentials, settled in New York in 1987, and *Hatori*, an alum of the Tokyo rap unit Kimidori and a former club DJ, followed six years later. After meeting in 1994, they first teamed in the Boredoms-inspired noise outfit Leitoh Lychee (translated as "frozen lychee nut"); after that band's breakup, the duo formed Cibo Matto, Italian for "food madness" (their love of culinary delights quickly becoming the stuff of legend).

The group soon emerged as a sensation among the Lower Manhattan hipster elite, gaining fame for their incendiary live shows backed by guests including the Lounge Lizards' Dougie Bowne (Honda's ex-husband), Bernie Worrell, Masada's Dave Douglas, and Skeleton Key's Rick Lee. After a pair of acclaimed 1995 independent singles, "Birthday Cake" and "Know Your Chicken," Cibo Matto signed to Warner Bros., surfacing in 1996 with the

Mitchell Froom/Tchad Blake-produced *Viva! La Woman*, a delirious, stunningly inventive record celebrating love, food, and love of food. After touring with guest bassist Sean Lennon and Jon Spencer Blues Explosion drummer Russell Simins, the EP *Super Relax* followed in 1997. Lennon, percussionist Duma Love, and drummer Timo Ellis were installed as full-time members for the follow-up, 1999's *Stereo Type A. —Jason Ankeny*

- **Viva! La Woman** / Jan. 16, 1996 / Warner Brothers ✦✦✦✦✦
Fresh and funky, female and Japanese, the trip-hop/rap duo Cibo Matto has been the recipient of a lot of hype. Fortunately, it's well-founded; all trendiness aside, *Viva! La Woman* is an innovative and catchy mix of eclectic samples and stream-of-consciousness lyrics. The likes of Paul Weller, Ennio Morricone, and Duke Ellington combine with observations like "My weight is three hundred pounds/my favorite is beef jerky" (from "Beef Jerky") and "Shut up and eat! You know my love is sweet!" from ("Birthday Cake") in a fun and refreshing way. The tone of the album varies with each song; on tracks like "Sugar Water" and "Artichoke," Cibo Matto plays it spooky and ethereal, while "Birthday Cake" and the single "Know Your Chicken" find them as a couple of cryptic Beastie Girls, tossing off wacky non sequiturs over found soundscapes. Cibo Matto cooks up a tasty appetizer of their talent with *Viva! La Woman*. Like their tongue-in-cheek cover of "The Candy Man," Cibo Matto makes everything they bake satisfying and delicious. A diverse and entertaining album, *Viva! La Woman* leaves the listener hungry for more of their crazy food for thought. —*Heather Phares*

Stereo Type A / Jun. 8, 1999 / Warner Brothers ✦✦✦
Cibo Matto's eagerly anticipated second album, *Stereo Type A*, reflects growth and change in the band's lineup and sound. Joining the core duo of Yuka Honda and Miho Hatori are new band member Sean Lennon and guests like Arto Lindsay, Caetano Veloso, Sebastian Steinberg of Soul Coughing, and John Medeski and Billy Martin of Medeski, Martin & Wood. The new additions reflect the changing sound of Cibo Matto: Relying less on samples and more on their latent funk and jazz elements, *Stereotype A* sounds like summer in New York—eclectic, hot, and funky. Hatori's vocals are her most fluid and assured yet, and Honda's harmonies, particularly on "Moonchild," add a dreamy undercurrent to the sound. Though the hip-hop of "Sci-Fi Wasabi" and filmic quality of "Spoon" (which originally appeared on the *Super Relax* EP) hearken back to old school Cibo Matto, *Stereotype A*'s overall sound is more direct and less fanciful than of their debut album *Viva! La Woman*. Tracks like "Clouds" and "Morning" reflect a nice fusion of the group's old and new sounds, while the brassy "Speechless" and thrash metal of "Blue Train" round out a delightfully sunny collection from this diverse group. —*Heather Phares*

Imani Coppola

Vocals / Alternative Rap, Hip-Hop
While just a sophomore at the State University of New York (studying orchestra and later studio composition), Imani Coppola gained a record contract for her surrealistic, sample-laden pop vision of hip-hop, linked to Digable Planets as well as Neneh Cherry. While growing up, her entire family was musical, and Coppola began playing violin at the age of six. She began writing songs and practiced her vocals (although her recording career has featured her rapping more than singing). Her debut album, *Chupacabra*, featured the MTV hit "Legend of a Cowgirl." —*John Bush*

- **Chupacabra** / Oct. 14, 1997 / Columbia ✦✦✦✦
The debut album by Imani Coppola is a strong, confident pop album that never found its niche in the mainstream. Although boosted by the success of "Legend of a Cowgirl" and her exposure on Sarah McLachlan's *Lilith Fair* tour, the album was overlooked in a summer filled with successful female pop musicians. This is too bad because Coppola explodes with charm and talent on the 11 tracks that make up *Chupacabra*. The frantic rhythms mesh nicely with her rich voice on tracks like "I'm a Tree" and "Soon (I Like It)" while her personality shines through on the pleasantly egotistical "It's All About Me, Me, and Me" and on the Donovan-sampled "Legend of a Cowgirl." Even ballads like "Pigeon Penelope" are beautiful affairs that stay far away from the whispering acoustic affairs that her contemporaries are known for. Coppola left the recording industry after a failed attempt at a second album, making this even more of a lost treasure. Fans of funky, energetic female pop will want to find this album—they will not be disappointed. —*Bradley Torreano*

Corduroy

f. 1991, London, England
Club/Dance, Acid Jazz
The acid jazz outfit Corduroy assembled singer/keyboardist Scott Addison, his drummer brother Ben, guitarist Simon Nelson-Smith, and bassist Richard Searle (a former member of '80s one-hit wonders Doctor & the Medics). Formed from the ashes of the short-lived British pop group Boys Wonder, Corduroy played their first gig—a one-off New Year's Eve date—in 1991; the performance proved so successful that its members agreed to continue on full time, soon signing to the Acid Jazz label and issuing their debut LP, the largely instrumental *Dad Man Cat*, in 1992. *High Havoc*—the soundtrack to an imaginary film—followed a year later, launching the U.K. Top Ten hits "Something in My Eye," "The Frighteners," and "London, England." In the wake of 1994's *Out of Here*, however, Acid Jazz dropped Corduroy from its roster; after a long hiatus, the group finally landed on the Big Cat label, where they resurfaced in 1997 with *The New You! —Jason Ankeny*

- **The New You!** / Apr. 14, 1997 / Big Cat ✦✦✦✦✦
Corduroy isn't anything if they're not about style, and *The New You* is their finest creation to date. Working from the same acid jazz foundation that informed their previous records, the band has added slightly ironic flourishes of lounge music and movie soundtracks while beginning to develop a sophisticated sense of pop craft, largely modeled after Steely Dan. Portions of *The New You* sag under the group's own pretensions, but most of the record is endearingly kitschy, smooth and stylish. —*Stephen Thomas Erlewine*

Craig David (Craig Ashley David)

b. May 5, 1981, Southampton, England
Producer, Vocals / 2-Step/British Garage, Contemporary R&B, Garage/ House, Club/Dance, Urban
R&B sensation Craig David was barely out of his teens when he took a hold of the U.K. pop circuit, twisted it around, and threw it back on its bum during fall 2000. This fresh-faced native of Southampton, England, was merely playing into his love of funkadelic hip-hop and crooning urban stylings when he started writing songs as a teenager. His love for Terence Trent D'Arby, Sisqó, and Donnell Jones allowed him to put his creative love for art, culture, and history into a musical beat all his own. The new millennium belonged to him, and garage had been redefined.

Born Craig Ashley David on May 5, 1981, David was slicing and dicing raggae and R&B on the local station PCRS 106.5FM and found himself playing club gigs prior to rubbing elbows with some of music's finest. It was during this time he hooked with Artful Dodger's Mark Hill. After winning a national writing competition, Craig was more than ready to start producing with Hill. His big break came when he put his own additives on Damage's "I'm Ready," a B side to "Wonderful Tonight." Soon thereafter he remixed his own version of Human League's "Human" and started himself a regular spot in area clubs during the weekends. "Rewind" was another underground smash, specifically a definitive move for David. His respect for Stevie Wonder, Faith Evans, and R. Kelly was most apparent, however his own vocal talent was beginning to shine. His and Hill's specialty show on Capital Radio provided another outlet for David to shape his musical work of genius. "Fill Me In" proved yet another hit, shooting straight to number one in summer 2000. David was now the youngest British male solo artist to have a number-one single. He was 19 years old.

A deal with Wildstar Records in the U.K. sparked toward the end of the summer as "Re-Rewind" and "7 Days" gained praise in late November. A stateside agreement with Atlantic also led to more global hype. He had sold 3.5 million records worldwide, garage was finally becoming massive overseas, and it was David's debut *Born to Do It* that was at the head.

But not all were pulling for this R&B prodigy. Aside from winning three awards at the MOBO's in October, Craig David walked away empty handed at the 2000 Brit Awards in February 2001. He was up for six nominations, including Best British Male Solo Artist, Best British Newcomer, and Best British Single for "7 Days," but industry politics fell into operation. Many mainstream stars came to David's defense, artists such as Elton John, U2, and Robbie Williams, professing their disgust for the ill recognition for David and his musical efforts in the past year. Death threats soon followed for the superstar in spring 2001 as he took the stage in a show in London. An anonymous caller claimed a soldier would injure David with tear gas and hand grenades. Still, his record sales continued to soar in the U.K. with sales of *Born to Do It* increasing over 100 percent after his dismal beginning months of 2001. He bombarded American shores with a deal with Atlantic and released *Born to Do It* stateside in summer 2001. Mainstream radio flocked to him immediately. Missy Elliott, Beyoncé Knowles, and Usher called themselves fans.

The next year, things didn't simmer down for the now-international pop star. Craig David returned with a sophomore effort *Slicker Than Your Average* in November 2002. This particular album saw a much grittier side from David. His debut single, "What's Your Flava?," also became one of the year's hottest singles. —*MacKenzie Wilson*

● **Born to Do It** / Jul. 17, 2001 / Atlantic ✦✦✦✦
In his 2000 debut album, Craig David merges smooth-soul crooning with a cascade of glistening keyboards, circling guitars, and sophisticated rhythms. Displaying a healthy marriage of current R&B vocal stylings and U.K. club/dance fused beats, David's music skillfully evades feeling robotic and cold, while still sounding pristine and immaculate. As an artist who is in his late teens, he conjures up a personal and revealing work that delves into both his mature sound and youthful attitude. Co-writing and co-producing with Mark Hill of the British garage act the Artful Dodger, David wraps his scorching-cool vocals around a mellow attack of keyboards and drums, while distinctly focusing on romance, relationships, and clubbing. Guitars simmer on "7 Days," a day by day account of an adventurous first week with a woman he magically encounters while in a subway. In "Can't Be Messing 'Round," the performer's razor sharp vocals heat-seek while a keyboard hammers before being covered by a high-sounding whirlpool of strings. With the dance anthem "Time to Party," drums sting and a whispering guitar is faintly heard while he optimistically sings "Friday, payday/Ready to do the things we love." The lyrics do sometimes sound underdeveloped due to David's age, and the music can occasionally lack distinctiveness, yet those two factors do not hinder the celebratory power of *Born to Do It*. The album features an effortless presentation of limber and carefully articulated vocal talents by the singer that seamlessly glide through the polished collage of songs. —*Stephen Mercier*

Slicker Than Your Average / Nov. 19, 2002 / Atlantic ✦✦✦
The former British teen sensation kicked off his singing career with the stellar Grammy-nominated *Born to Do It*, which blended 2-step, R&B, and pop. With his second release, *Slicker Than Your Average*, Craig David shows a different side. While *Born to Do It* was filled with romantic lyrics, *Slicker Than Your Average* shares David's feelings about fame, with a small dose of his trademark love songs. On the title track, David takes a stab at those who criticize his "squeaky clean" image and musical style: "Now they're telling me that I'm too R&B/How I turned my back on the whole UK garage scene/Now they're stressing me when/I know there's so much more to see." Broken hearts and playing the field are prominent topics as well. Musically, *Slicker Than Your Average* is a collage of styles—dance ("What's Your Flava?," "Eenie Meenie," "Fast Cars") and 2-step ("2 Steps Back") as well as R&B/pop ballads ("World Filled With Love" and "Rise & Fall"). "Rise & Fall," a song featuring a guest vocal by Sting, is among the highlights on the album, as are "You Don't Miss Your Water ('Til the Well Runs Dry)," "What's Your Flava?," and the Beatlesque "World Filled With Love," which is filled with soaring harmonies. *Slicker Than Your Average* is stronger than the average sophomore effort, and it proves that Craig David's abilities are innate. —*Christina Fuoco*

Dubadelic

Illbient, Dub

The experimental dub ensemble Dubadelic, a WordSound label supergroup featuring Bill Laswell, ex-New Kingdom member Scotty Hard, and Spectre, among others, debuted in 1996 with *2000: A Bass Odyssey*. The follow-up, *Bass Invaders*, appeared two years later. —*Jason Ankeny*

● **2000: A Bass Odyssey** / Jan. 25, 1996 / Wordsound ✦✦✦✦
Despite its name, Dubadelic is not a reggae band. Instead, it's sort of a Brooklyn underground supergroup whose membership is never clearly defined, but which seems to consist of the Eye, Professor Shehab, the mighty Dr. Israel, Corporal Blossom, turntable wizard DXT and perhaps even Bill Laswell, among others. The noise that this crew makes draws equally on dub, old school hip hop and the dark, loping trip-hop that was just starting to

makes its way across the Atlantic from Brixton and Manchester, England at the time of this album's release. It's a pretty compelling sound: on "Johnny's Outta Jail," a compressed North African vocal sample drifts in and out of the mix as a Bootsy Collins-ish bass squelches along below and a bare-bones funk drum part stutters in between. "Dub of Justice" features an extremely low and minimal bassline and heavily altered drums, while "Psychobabble" lumbers along ponderously, powered by an elephantine drumbeat, weird vocal samples and outer-space keyboards. It's not really dance music; it's more like sit-down funk. —*Rick Anderson*

Elwood

Vocals / Alternative Rap, Hip-Hop

Elwood is the eclectic hip-hop/pop project of singer/songwriter/producer Prince Elwood Strickland III and coproducer and songwriter Brian Boland. Born and raised in North Carolina, Strickland grew up listening to rap, soul, country, folk, and pop and eventually became a recording engineer at Soho's Greene Street Recording Facility. During his decade-long stint there, he worked with artists like Tricky, Mos Def, De La Soul, the The, and Adam Yauch, and met Boland. The duo recorded a seven-song demo in Strickland's own studio, which led to a deal with the Palm Pictures imprint, and Elwood worked with acclaimed British producer Steve Lillywhite on tracks for their debut album *The Parlance Of Our Times*, which was coreleased in early 2000 by Palm Pictures and Lillywhite's label Gobstopper. —*Heather Phares*

The Parlance of Our Time / May 16, 2000 / Palm ✦✦✦
The alternative hip-hop slacker known as Elwood earned some radio airplay with an earthy cover of Gordon Lightfoot's anti-hip 1974 hit "Sundown." As with the debut by another folky hipster—namely, Beck—there's a bit more going on here than you'd suspect from the lightweight hit. Though the songs aren't uniformly solid, the productions are smart and catchy, from the jazzy brass on "Red Wagon" and "Picture of You" to the sitar on "Forty Five" and the jungle-fueled "Dive." Though a pair of songs—"Peaches" and the Donovan-sampling "Bush"—make him sound more like a horny frat boy than a hip singer/songwriter/rapper, *The Parlance of Our Time* is a creative, entertaining record. —*John Bush*

Fatback Band

f. 1970 db. 1985
Funk, Disco

A seminal funk ensemble, the Fatback Band made many great singles through the '70s and early '80s, ranging from humorous novelty tunes to energetic dance vehicles and even occasional political/message tracks. The original lineup featured drummer Bill Curtis, trumpeter George Williams, guitarist Johnny King, bassist Johnny Flippin, saxophonist Earl Shelton, and flutist George Adam. Synthesizer player Gerry Thomas, saxophonist Fred Demerey, and guitarist George Victory were integral parts of the group during their peak years. They began recording for Perception in the early '70s, and had moderate luck with "Street Dance" in 1973. They moved to Event in 1974, and while funk audiences loved such songs as "Wicki-Wacky" and "(Are You Ready) Do the Bus Stop," they didn't generate much sales action. Their first sizable hit was "Spanish Hustle" in 1976, which reached number 12 on the R&B charts. They shortened their name to Fatback in 1977, and landed their first Top Ten R&B hit with "I Like Girls" in 1978. Their 1979 single "King Tim III (Personality Jock)" is widely considered the first rap single in many circles. But their biggest year was 1980. They scored two Top Ten R&B hits with "Gotta Get My Hands on Some (Money)" and "Backstrokin'," their finest tune. Fatback kept going through the mid-'80s, landing one more Top 20 hit with "Take It Any Way You Can Want It" in 1981. They were backed by the female vocal trio Wild Sugar in 1981-1982, and Evelyn Thomas provided the lead vocal for "Spread Love" in 1985, their last song for Spring. Fatback also recorded a pair of LPs for Cotillion in 1984 and 1985. —*Ron Wynn*

XII / 1979 / Southbound ✦✦✦
Fatback maintained the same high standard of quality to produce another impressive slab of funk-tinged disco. *XII* is notable to hip-hop historians for the track "King Tim III (Personality Jock)," a song often tagged as the first rap song (it was released as a single shortly before the more popular "Rapper's Delight" by the Sugarhill Gang). "King Tim" remains a killer blast of hip-hop, seamlessly mixing a slick old school rap into the band's intensely funky blend of organ, energetic horn blasts, and a relentless walking bass line. However,

this isn't all there is to *XII*. The album's other tracks present a consistent mix of funky grit and disco slickness. Standout tracks include "Gimme That Sweet, Sweet Lovin,'" which layers a Bee Gees-style falsetto vocal with an addictive mid-tempo groove anchored by a synthesizer bass, and "Disco Bass," which blends a catchy chant-along chorus with the serpentine hook mentioned in the title. *XII* is also notable for the high quality of its sound, which filters the energy of their sound through a carefully crafted soundscape that brings out all the details of their sound: a good example is how the huge drum sounds that propel "You're My Candy Sweet" seem to leap out of the speakers. The only track that tends toward the filler that has marred past Fatback albums is "Disco Queen," but even it is redeemed by its punchy horn arrangement and some catchy background vocals. All in all, *XII* is one of Fatback's finest albums and a treat for anyone who likes their disco music especially funky. —*Donald A. Guarisco*

● **The Fattest of Fatback** / Mar. 18, 1997 / Rhino ✦✦✦✦✦
Those who fail to understand funk often complain about its use of repetition, but funk enthusiasts will tell you that repetition (as James Brown showed us) is something to be savored. A first-class party band, Fatback knew quite well that the secret to effective funk is finding a killer groove and working it to death. That's exactly what happens much of the time on *The Fattest of Fatback*, a 1997 CD that spans 1975-1983 and boasts many of the New York band's essential hits. From "I Like Girls" and "Gotta Get My Hands On Some (Money)" to "Backstrokin'" and "The Girl Is Fine (So Fine)," this CD shows us how exciting Fatback could be when it found the right groove. With 1979's "King Tim III," Fatback became one of the first R&B acts to acknowledge rap, and the pessimistic sociopolitical number "Is This the Future?" was among 1983's most vital and compelling rap singles. Though Fatback was best known for funk, "Can't You See" and "Angel" demonstrate that the band was quite capable of delivering excellent soul ballads. For those checking out Fatback for the first time, *The Fattest of Fatback* is definitely the best starting point. —*Alex Henderson*

Freestylers

f. 1996, London, England
Big Beat, Funky Breaks, Electronica, Trip-Hop
More old school hip-hop, electro, and raggae than big-beat techno (though they're often pigeonholed that way), the Freestylers were formed by the trio of Matt Cantor, Aston Harvey, and Andrew Galea. All three were British b-boys back in the day, and were heavily involved in Britain's dance scene by the late '80s, both as DJs and producers—Cantor recording as Cut'n'Paste, 2 Fat Buddhas, and Freska All Stars, among others; Harvey as Blapps! Posse (author of the 1990 breakbeat classic "Don't Hold Back"). Harvey had also worked with Rebel MC and Definition of Sound, but after meeting Galea, the pair began recording together as Sol Brothers and soon brought Cantor into the fold as well.
Taking the name Freestylers from their first sample (Freestyle's "Don't Stop the Rock"), the trio released their first single, "Drop the Boom (AK-48)" and formed their own Scratch City Records to release it. The track was a prime slice of vocoderized electro, and became an underground club classic as far afield as bass-driven Miami. The *Freestyle EP* followed late in 1996, and Freestylers also released singles on Freskanova (home of Cantor's many solo projects). The group even managed a chart hit (and *Top of the Pops* appearance) with 1998's "B-Boy Stance," a collaboration with vocalist Tenor Fly. A spate of remixing followed, for Audioweb, Afrika Bambaataa, and the Jungle Brothers (the latter a pair of the Freestylers' prime influences). The trio also helmed the big-beat compilation *FSUK 2* and contributed a Radio One Essential Mix (where Beenie Man, Public Enemy, the Fall, and Whodini all rubbed elbows). Live appearances at Glastonbury and around the European festival circuit met with much praise, and the Freestylers finally released their debut album, *We Rock Hard*, in 1999. The mix album *Electro Science* followed a year later. —*John Bush*

We Rock Hard / Jul. 14, 1998 / Mammoth ✦✦✦✦
Though it's more of a run through their back-catalogue than a proper debut, *We Rock Hard* comes through on the title's claim, with little of the push-button, big-dumb-techno aspects of most big-beat acts. Focusing on electro, ragga, breakbeat and a closing jungle workout ("Warning") with chatting by MC Navigator, the Freestylers up the ante for Britain's old school big-beat merchants. —*John Bush*

● **Pressure Point** / Jul. 31, 2001 / EMI ✦✦✦✦
Freestylers' second album follows much the same pattern as *We Rock Hard*, trading on varied Freestyler faves from ragga and rave to old school rap and electro. Still, this trio of seasoned producers hardly sounds bored by the same old sound, and relatively unseduced by any recent developments in British clublife. There's plenty of turntablist terror on the catchy intro, but also on what would've been just a standard R&B tune ("Told You So," with Petra Jean Phillipson). Freestylers again recruit chatters Tenor Fly and MC Navigator for multiple appearances, and find good ways to reuse everything from an old hip-hop standard (Black Sheep's "The Choice Is Yours") to an even older reggae standard (Willie Williams' "Armagideon Time"). One listen to "Bass Odyssey" and it's clear the trio also fondly remember the early-'90s heyday of rave. *Pressure Point* differs from *We Rock Hard* in that it doesn't emphasize the anthems/singles, but it's clearly a tighter, better listen. —*John Bush*

Freddy Fresh (Frederick Schmidt)

b. New York, NY
Producer, DJ / Trip-Hop, Electronica, Hip-Hop, Electro-Techno, Club/Dance, Techno
Freddy Fresh is among the most active and prolific American underground dance music artists, having released more than a hundred records on a dozen different labels in less than half a decade. Born and bred in New York, Fresh's name is more often associated with the Minneapolis scene, to which he relocated in the late '80s after kick-starting a passion for hip-hop and house music production. Fresh formed his longest-running record label, Analog Recordings, in Minneapolis, and his label empire has since grown to include a host of sublabels (first Butterbeat and EMF, then Socket and Boriqua), as well as Analog's U.K. arm. In addition to a growing stateside audience, Fresh is also one of the few contemporary non-Detroit techno/electro musicians to have a strong European following, and his records for Experimental, Harthouse, and Martin "Biochip C" Damm's Anodyne label have strengthened his international presence. Although Freddy's release history has included tracks in just about every style from hip-hop and house to techno and trance, his roots are most consistently pursued affectation lay in electro; his records thrive on buzzing modular analog noises and resolutely dirty production techniques, resulting in a distinct, instantly recognizable brand of funky, minimal, somewhat-experimental dance music.
Although Fresh grew up a gothic rock/new-wave junkie, a trip to the Boogie Down Bronx with his girlfriend (later his wife) in 1984 introduced him to the thriving NYC hip-hop scene. Instantly smitten, Fresh began collecting DJ tapes (Shep Pettibone, Jeff Mills, Frankie Bones, anything he could get his hands on) and, of course, records—everything from Jonzun Crew and Newcleus to Liquid Liquid and Cerrone, Bill Withers, and Cat Stevens—and his collection has since grown to over 10,000 strong (making his side gigs as a DJ a bit easier). Fresh's first work behind the boards came via Bronx legends Boogie Down Productions, with Fred remixing a track for a B-side release (although good luck finding it, and Fred recommends you don't try!). From there, Freddy began piecing together a studio, collecting many of the ancient analog synths that give his records their distinct, almost studio-jam feel (he mixes all his tracks live). In 1992, after releasing debut singles on Nu Groove and Silvo Tancredis' Experimental imprint, Fresh established his first label, Analog, to release his own tracks. The label and its offshoots have since attracted such weighty names as Thomas Heckman, Tim Taylor, Cari Lekebusch, DJ Slip, the Bassin Twins, and Biochip C. In 1995, Fresh inked a contract with noted German techno label Harthouse, and his second full-length, *Accidentally Classic*, was released by the label's U.K. arm in late 1996, with a Harthouse U.S. reissue following close behind. His third album, *The Last True Family Man*, followed on Harthouse Eye Q. Several singles and a mix album followed until the release of his next full-length, *Music for Swingers*, in 2001. Additionally, Fresh has released records through Wisconsin-based acid stronghold Drop Bass Network, Labworks, and noted German electro label Electrecord. —*Sean Cooper*

Fun Lovin' Criminals

f. 1993
Alternative Rap, Alternative Pop/Rock
Much like G. Love & Special Sauce, the New York trio known as Fun Lovin' Criminals hit the alternative airwaves with a blend of hip-hop beats,

alternative style, and bluesy rhythms. The group was formed in 1993 by bassist Fast and drummer Steve, who had met in Syracuse while going to school; the pair formed a techno group but later moved back to New York City, where they hooked up with vocalist/guitarist Huey. FLC played around the area, and released their self-titled debut album in 1995 on the Silver Spotlight label. Signed to Capitol the following year, the group gained an alternative radio hit with their single "Scooby Snacks," from *Come Find Yourself*. *100% Colombian* followed in 1998. —*John Bush*

Come Find Yourself / Feb. 20, 1996 / Capitol ♦♦♦
In some circles, the Fun Lovin' Criminals were touted as the heir apparent to the Beastie Boys. There were two problems, however, with this contention: the Beastie Boys weren't going away, and the Fun Lovin' Criminals certainly were not pushing anybody with this major-label debut. Aside from the radio hit "Scooby Snacks," nothing on the album had anywhere near enough staying power to distinguish the Criminals as anything more than a run-of-the-mill one-hit wonder. While the music of the Beastie Boys is eclectic, dynamic and laden with amusing pop-culture references, the music of the Fun Lovin' Criminals is predictable, unimaginative, and downright boring for the most part. While the band attempted to mix in some elements of the Beastie Boys and also tried to cash in on the same fusion of rock, rap, and punk, the results were decidedly inferior. —*David M. Childers*

100% Colombian / Nov. 17, 1998 / Virgin ♦♦♦♦
Fun Lovin' Criminals got a lot of mileage out of their Scorsese-meets-Beasties-meets-*Reservoir Dogs* schtick on their first-full length album, *Come Find Yourself*. Their stoned, funky grooves brought them an MTV hit in America and, inexplicably, critical acclaim in the U.K., where their New York attitude came across as…well, not genuine, but at least an authentic parody from a knowing source. Eventually, the British acclaim eclipsed the moderate U.S. success, so it shouldn't be surprising that they tailored their follow-up, *100% Colombian*, to the very things the British press loved—the tongue-in-cheek humor, the cartoonish gangsterism, the dope, the funk- and rap-inflected grooves, the cheeky pop culture references. It's a little jazzier, a little slower, a little more cinematic than its predecessor, which means it's more cohesive, as well as more sonically appealing. Of course, it's possible that the average listener—one who wasn't charmed or amused by *Come Find Yourself* and "Scooby Snacks"—will never discover this, since Huey's self-satisfied rapping and smug lyrics can be exceptionally grating if you're not smirking along with him. But if his '70s mob movie fetishism and ironic celebration of da streets uv Noo Yawk seem humorous, chances are *100% Colombian* will feel even better than *Come Find Yourself*. Everything's cool, everything's shmoove, put the money in the bag…—*Stephen Thomas Erlewine*

● **Mimosa** / Dec. 7, 1999 / EMI ♦♦♦♦
Smooth New York jazz rappers Fun Lovin' Criminals have quietly built their popularity stateside and particularly in Europe over the last six years by wrapping their tales of the Big Apple's underbelly with sweet grooves and live instrumentation akin to Cake, the Roots, and Luscious Jackson. The smoothness of their grooves and underground culture has always been just a stone's throw away from lounge-lizard heaven. With *Mimosa*, the band gives in to their Velveeta-smooth cheese urges and delivers a quirky collection of far-out covers and retoolings of their own songs.

It's an interesting collection, and works best when they stick to their own material. Reworked originals like "Scooby Snacks" and the excellent "I Can't Get With That" have a great, easy, witty feel not terribly far from the original recordings. Some tracks, like "The Summer Wind," with the surprising guest Ian McCullough, showcase the band's strong live performances. Others are just plain whacked out, like the ultra-wimpy '70s weepers "I'm Not In Love" and "Shining Star" (not the Earth, Wind & Fire song, another one). It seems like they might have taken a miscue from Cake, whose 1996 cover of "I Will Survive" is both hilarious but true to the spunk of the original. These covers lack the irony or campiness needed to make it interesting. —*Theresa E. LaVeck*

G. Love & Special Sauce
f. 1992, Philadelphia, PA
Alternative Rap, Post-Grunge, Indie Rock, Alternative
G. Love & Special Sauce are a trio from Philadelphia, PA. Their laid-back, sloppy blues sound is quite unique, as it encompasses the sound/production

of classic R&B and recent rap artists (the Beastie Boys, in particular). The group—G. Love (born Garrett Dutton) on guitar/vocals/harmonica, Jeff Clemens on drums, and Jim Prescott on upright bass—released their self-titled debut in 1994 on Okeh/Epic. It received enthusiastic reviews and nearly went gold on the strength of the MTV-spun video for "Cold Beverage." The group toured heavily, also landing a subsequent spot on the *H.O.R.D.E.* tour, and found a receptive young audience. They followed up this success with the more mature *Coast to Coast Motel* in 1995. Although it didn't sell as well as the debut, it was definitely a stronger album. On tour, the group nearly broke up due to bickering over finances. They decided to take a break from each other, while G. Love worked on a new album with three different bands (All Fellas Band, Philly Cartel, and King's Court) and special guest Dr. John. Soon, though, G. Love & Special Sauce made amends, and the next album featured Special Sauce plus combinations of the three other groups. *Yeah, It's That Easy* was released in October of 1997, and it turned out to be a soul-inflected effort, more similar to the debut than their second album. G. Love & Special Sauce soon embarked on another world tour, returning in 1999 with *Philadelphonic*. *Electric Mile*, issued in spring 2001, depicted another sultry and provocative mix from G. Love. —*Greg Prato*

G. Love & Special Sauce / May 10, 1994 / Epic ♦♦♦
Although this is G. Love & Special Sauce's most popular album (approaching gold status), it is not their best. Although there are quite a few musical surprises, the overall sound and quality of the compositions are neither as focused nor as rewarding as future releases would be. "Cold Beverage" became the band's signature tune and a fan favorite, featuring lighthearted jive lyrics and funky musical accompaniment, and its popular MTV video putting them on the map. "This Ain't Living" is a precursor to the comforting Philly soul style that would be explored more thoroughly on 1997's *Yeah, It's That Easy*. "Town to Town" adds variety to the album with its slow-as-molasses blues style. Most of the other tracks tend to blend into each other after awhile, because of their similar sound and feel ("Rhyme for the Summertime," "Shooting Hoops," etc.). Even with its mishaps, G. Love & Special Sauce's debut serves as the musical foundation on which the group would build their future sound. —*Greg Prato*

● **Coast to Coast Motel** / Sep. 19, 1995 / Epic ♦♦♦♦
Although not as commercially successful as their self-titled debut, *Coast to Coast Motel* is a definite improvement. The band keeps their hip-hop influence (much more prevalent on the debut) in check here, concentrating more on creating a mighty instrumental groove. It's also more of a traditional rock & roll approach for the band, with the results quite often being successful. The opening "Sweet Sugar Mama" is bass-driven and funky; other highlights include the smooth "Nancy," the uplifting "Chains #3," and the startling Led Zeppelin attack (musically, anyway) of "Small Fish." "Kiss and Tell" is an obvious attempt at a hit single, while some may consider the lyrics to "Soda Pop" a bit too foolish. As mentioned earlier, however, the group achieves some great, groovy interplay which can easily suck the listener in. Jimmy Prescott's upright bass playing and Jeff Clemens' drumming are tight and locked together, as G. Love adds his scratchy blues guitar on top. These guys have found the groove. —*Greg Prato*

The Best of G. Love and Special Sauce / Mar. 26, 2002 / Epic ♦♦♦♦
While major chart success has eluded G. Love for the length of his career, he has earned an impressive live following and even more impressive album sales with his uniquely 1990s blend of hip-hop, blues, and chill-out funk. Assembling a worthy career compilation should have been a no-brainer, though it seems the folks at Epic spent no more time than necessary putting *The Best of G. Love and Special Sauce* together. Favorites like the smooth, name-dropping exercise "Blues Music" and "I-76," the ultimate homage to the group's hometown of Philadelphia, are of course here, but at only 11 tracks, the disc kind of leaves you hanging. What, no extra bonus tracks, new cuts, or raving live performances could be found? A good sampler for initiates, but no doubt there are way better G. Love CD-R samplers in 1,000 college dorm rooms across the Northeast. —*John Duffy*

Genaside II
f. 1989, Brixton, London, England
Jungle/Drum 'N Bass, Club/Dance, Techno, Acid House
Creators of a seminal moment for drum'n'bass back in 1991, Genaside II returned more than five years later with their debut full-length, a piece of

high-powered, breakbeat futurism influenced by Manga animé. Basically a duo of Chilly Phatz and Koa Bonez (aka Kaos de Keeler) with engineer Charlie Meats, the crew were raised on the hard-life streets of Brixton and inspired by urban raggamuffins like Rebel MC and Ray Keith.

Debuting in 1989 with the cut-and-paste raggae terrorism of "Fire When Ready," Phatz and Bonez followed with the 1991 single "Narramine." Inter-splicing the sweet soulful vocals of Sharon Williams with blistering breakbeat raggae, the single became a major mover on the hardcore techno scene. Along with "Mr. Kirk" by 4hero, Genaside II defined the growing move toward darkness in hardcore, years before drum'n'bass emerged overground. Despite additional singles like "Hellraiser" (recorded with Ray Keith and featuring a beat later borrowed by Prodigy for "Firestarter"), personal problems kept the duo out of commission for several years.

By 1995, Phatz and Bonez had sorted things out and even signed to the major-label-connected Internal. After a live date with the New Power Generation, mutual friends introduced the duo to the Wu-Tang Clan while in America. As a result, Genaside II's 1996 debut album, *New Life 4 the Hunted*, featured Wu associate Cappadonna as well as Eek-a-Mouse and Rose Windross. *Ad Finite* followed in 1999. —*John Bush*

New Life 4 the Hunted / 1996 / Internal/London ✦✦✦
After almost a decade, Genaside II's debut LP shows the duo allied to contemporary acts (like Headrillaz) sitting on the divergence which separated breakbeat techno from full-fledged drum'n'bass. Obviously a pair of mature producers, Phatz and Bonez recruited vocalists Rose Windross (from Soul II Soul) for some classic house flavor, Eek-A-Mouse and Killerman Archer for ragga attitude, and Wu-Tang's Cappadonna for an interesting hip-hop/breakbeat collaboration. Though the album also includes a version of their 1991 classic "Narramine," it strays surprisingly close to a bland listen, with few full-fledged ideas holding together the many vocal tracks. —*John Bush*

● **Ad Finite** / Sep. 21, 1999 / Durban Poison ✦✦✦✦
Genaside II released their second full-length, *Ad Finite*, with an American distribution contract in hand, thanks to the patronage of Tricky (who was undoubtedly inspired by the group's acid-breakbeat terrorism from way back). The album improves on 1996's somewhat stillborn *New Life 4 the Hunted*, with better production and more of a focus on the music itself—the first album carried the art of vocal collaborations a bit too far. The pair obviously didn't spend much of their time trawling for beats; even middling old school fans will recognize just about every break used on *Ad Finite*, along with the sirens and effects from many a classic hip-hop record. It should be obvious, though, that what really counts is not the beats themselves, but what you do with them. Genaside II are among the best dance producers at layering their productions with interesting effects, and every break on *Ad Finite* you've heard before is used differently than you've ever heard it. The single "Mr. Maniac" and "50,000 Whats?" are invigorating darkside productions. The social critique inherent on Genaside II's earlier material is still being caned, from the opener—a British female paraphrases Gil Scott-Heron's "The Revolution Will Not Be Televised" for London circa 1999—to tracks like "Casualties of War," "Paranoid Thugism," and "Streets of San Fran Brixton." Still more tied to the aesthetic of 1989 than 1999 (that's a good thing), Genaside II make big beat serve their own ends, and the result is a raging political record miles away from the mindless dance of Fatboy Slim. —*John Bush*

Groove Collective

f. 1990, New York, NY
Club/Dance, Acid Jazz, Contemporary Jazz, Urban
The acid jazz outfit Groove Collective was formed in downtown New York City in 1990 by flutist Richard Worth, DJ Smash, and rapper Nappy G, all three staples of a nomadic dance club called Giant Step. In time, the trio was joined by keyboardist Itaal Shur, drummer Gengi Siraisi, and bassist Jonathan Maron, earning a growing cult following and eventually attracting the attention of Steely Dan vibist Bill Ware, who soon signed on along with saxophonist Jay Rodriguez, trombonist Josh Roseman, trumpeter Fabio Morgera, and percussionist Chris Theberge. Groove Collective's self-titled debut LP appeared on Reprise in 1993, followed three years later by the GRP label release *We the People*. The group resurfaced in 1998 with *Dance of the Drunken Master. It's All in Your Mind* was issued three years later. —*Jason Ankeny*

● **Declassified** / Jul. 20, 1999 / Shanachie ✦✦✦✦✦
Groove Collective's completely uninhibited, party-based jazz-funk is inspired by Sly Stone, acid jazz, hip-hop, salsa, Stevie Wonder, drum'n'bass, Parliament-Funkadelic, Fania—that is, anything or anyone from the late '60s on who knew how to get down. Their fourth album overall finds the congregation in a most jubilant mood, happy to simply stretch out on a series of infectious singalong jams, starting with the openers "Up All Night" (which trades honking sax solos with some great stuttered drum programming) and "Everything Is Changing" (a shuffling disco stomp). With no less than 14 pieces in the group, it's obvious that Groove Collective shouldn't have any trouble filling spaces, and truth to tell, just about every song on *Declassified* bristles with so many ideas, solos, and licks that listeners may get dizzy without a few listens under their belt. "On a Feeling," the spotlight for rapper Nappy G, isn't exactly the tightest hip-hop joint ever heard, but the sheer instrumental and musical prowess abundant all over this album makes it a joy for all to hear. —*John Bush*

Herbie Hancock

b. Apr. 12, 1940, Chicago, IL
Piano, Piano (Electric), Keyboards, Synthesizer / Hard Bop, Modal Music, Fusion, Jazz-Funk, Funk, Electro, Post-Bop
Herbie Hancock will always be one of the most revered and controversial figures in jazz—just as his employer/mentor Miles Davis was when he was alive. Unlike Miles, who pressed ahead relentlessly and never looked back until near the very end, Hancock has cut a zigzagging forward path, shuttling between almost every development in electronic and acoustic jazz and R&B over the last third of the 20th century. Though grounded in Bill Evans and able to absorb blues, funk, gospel, and even modern classical influences, Hancock's piano and keyboard voices are entirely his own, with their own urbane harmonic and complex, earthy rhythmic signatures—and young pianists cop his licks constantly. Having studied engineering and professing to love gadgets and buttons, Hancock was perfectly suited for the electronic age; he was one of the earliest champions of the Rhodes electric piano and Hohner clavinet and would field an ever-growing collection of synthesizers and computers on his electric dates. Yet his love for the grand piano never waned, and despite his peripatetic activities all around the musical map, his piano style continues to evolve into tougher, ever more complex forms. He is as much at home trading riffs with a smoking funk band as he is communing with a world-class post-bop rhythm section—and that drives purists on both sides of the fence up the wall.

Having taken up the piano at age seven, Hancock quickly became known as a prodigy, soloing in the first movement of a Mozart piano concerto with the Chicago Symphony at the age of 11. After studies at Grinnell College, Hancock was invited by Donald Byrd in 1961 to join his group in New York City, and before long, Blue Note offered him a solo contract. His debut album, *Takin' Off*, took off indeed after Mongo Santamaria covered one of the album's songs, "Watermelon Man." In May 1963, Miles Davis asked him to join his band in time for the *Seven Steps to Heaven* sessions, and he remained there for five years, greatly influencing Miles' evolving direction, loosening up his own style, and, upon Miles' suggestion, converting to the Rhodes electric piano. In that time span, Hancock's solo career also blossomed on Blue Note, pouring forth increasingly sophisticated compositions like "Maiden Voyage," "Cantaloupe Island," "Goodbye to Childhood," and the exquisite "Speak Like a Child." He also played on many East Coast recording sessions for producer Creed Taylor and provided a groundbreaking score to Michelangelo Antonioni's film *Blow Up*, which gradually led to further movie assignments.

Having left the Davis band in 1968, Hancock recorded an elegant funk album, *Fat Albert Rotunda*, and in 1969 formed a sextet that evolved into one of the most exciting, forward-looking jazz-rock groups of the era. Now deeply immersed in electronics, Hancock added the synthesizer of Patrick Gleeson to his Echoplexed, fuzz-wah-pedaled electric piano and clavinet, and the recordings became spacier and more complex rhythmically and structurally, creating its own corner of the avant-garde. By 1970, all of the musicians used both English and African names (Herbie's was Mwandishi). Alas, Hancock had to break up the band in 1973 when it ran out of money, and having studied Buddhism, he concluded that his ultimate goal should be to make his audiences happy.

The next step, then, was a terrific funk group whose first album, *Head Hunters*, with its Sly Stone-influenced hit single, "Chameleon," became the biggest-selling jazz LP up to that time. Now handling all of the synthesizers himself, Hancock's heavily rhythmic comping often became part of the rhythm section, leavened by interludes of the old urbane harmonies. Hancock recorded several electric albums of mostly superior quality in the '70s, followed by a wrong turn into disco around the decade's end. In the meantime, Hancock refused to abandon acoustic jazz. After a one-shot reunion of the 1965 Miles Davis Quintet (Hancock, Ron Carter, Tony Williams, Wayne Shorter, with Freddie Hubbard sitting in for Miles) at New York's 1976 Newport Jazz Festival, they went on tour the following year as V.S.O.P. The near-universal acclaim of the reunions proved that Hancock was still a whale of a pianist, that Miles' loose mid-'60s post-bop direction was far from spent, and that the time for a neo-traditional revival was near, finally bearing fruit in the '80s with Wynton Marsalis and his ilk. V.S.O.P. continued to hold sporadic reunions through 1992, though the death of the indispensable Williams in 1997 cast much doubt as to whether these gatherings would continue.

Hancock continued his chameleonic ways in the '80s: scoring an MTV hit in 1983 with the scratch-driven, proto-industrial single "Rockit" (accompanied by a striking video); launching an exciting partnership with Gambian kora virtuoso Foday Musa Suso that culminated in the swinging 1986 live album *Jazz Africa*; doing film scores; and playing festivals and tours with the Marsalis brothers, George Benson, Michael Brecker, and many others. After his 1988 techno-pop album, *Perfect Machine*, Hancock left Columbia (his label since 1973), signed a contract with Qwest that came to virtually nothing (save for *A Tribute to Miles* in 1992), and finally made a deal with PolyGram in 1994 to record jazz for Verve and release pop albums on Mercury. Now well into a youthful middle age, Hancock's curiosity, versatility, and capacity for growth have shown no signs of fading, and in 1998 he issued *Gershwin's World.* —*Richard S. Ginell*

Future Shock / 1983 / Columbia ◆◆◆

Herbie Hancock completely overhauled his sound and conquered MTV with his most radical step forward since the sextet days. He brought in Bill Laswell of Material as producer, along with Grand Mixer D.ST on turntables—and the immediate result was "Rockit," which makes quite a post-industrial metallic racket. Frankly, the whole record is an enigma; for all of its dehumanized, mechanized textures and rigid rhythms, it has a vitality and sense of humor that make it difficult to turn off. Moreover, Herbie can't help but inject a subversive funk element when he comps along to the techno beat—and yes, some real, honest-to-goodness jazz licks on a grand piano show up in the middle of "Auto Drive." —*Richard S. Ginell*

Sound-System / 1984 / Columbia ◆◆◆

In the grand tradition of sequels, *Sound-System* picks up from where *Future Shock* left off—if anything, even louder and more bleakly industrial than before (indeed, "Hardrock" is "Rockit" with a heavier rock edge). Yet Hancock's experiments with techno-pop were leading him in the general direction of Africa, explicitly so with the addition of the Gambian multi-instrumentalist Foday Musa Suso on half of the tracks. "Junku," written for the 1984 Olympic Games with Suso's electrified kora in the lead, is the transition track that stands halfway between "Rockit" and Hancock's mid-'80s Afro-jazz fusions. Also, "Karabali" features an old cohort, the squealing Wayne Shorter on soprano sax. Despite succumbing a bit to the overwhelming demand for more "Rockits," Hancock's electric music still retained its adventurous edge. —*Richard S. Ginell*

Perfect Machine / Oct. 1988 / Columbia ◆◆◆

Set upon recapturing the pop ground he had invaded with *Future Shock*, Hancock relies upon many of the former's ingredients for yet another go-'round on *Perfect Machine*. High-tech producer Bill Laswell is back, so is scratchmaster D. ST.—and armed with a warehouse of mostly digital keyboards, Hancock adds the distinctive bass of Bootsy Collins and the Ohio Players' vocalist Sugarfoot, who always sounds as if he had just swallowed something. The music is mostly thumping, funk-drenched techno-pop which still has some verve, particularly the designated single "Vibe Alive" and the "Maiden Voyage" interlude as heard through an electronic fun-house mirror. But this is not really an advance over Hancock's early-'80s pop projects. This would be Hancock's last album for at least seven years as he concentrated upon film projects and reunions with Miles Davis alumni (there was

also an aborted deal with the Qwest label). As such, *Perfect Machine* is an appropriate end to this chapter in his career. —*Richard S. Ginell*

Umar Bin Hassan

Vocals / Political Rap

In the early '70s, Umar Bin Hassan was a member of the street-poet godfathers of rap, the Last Poets. He joined the group in 1969 after seeing them perform in his native Ohio. With Hassan, the Poets released *The Last Poets*, *This Is Madness*, and *Last Poets at Last*. In mid-1993, he released his first solo album, *Be Bop or Be Dead*. Hassan combined rap, house, and jazz elements on the record, which was produced by Bill Laswell. —*John Bush*

Be Bop or Be Dead / Jul. 22, 1993 / Axiom ◆◆◆◆

Umar Bin Hassin was once part of the Last Poets, a group whose incendiary rhetoric was backed by African percussion and preceded the hip-hop generation's Afro-centric quips. Hassin now works solo, and his latest release has several updates/remakes of Last Poets staples, including two versions of "This Is Madness." Producer Bill Laswell recruited two Parliament/Funkadelic instrumentalists, bassist Bootsy Collins and keyboardist Bernie Worrell, plus many other fine players, and virtually recreated The Last Poets tapestry, except that this time there's an electronic overlay as well as a percussive one. Hassin's voice hasn't been dulled by the years and seems more enraged and angered at the nation's racial and social injustices. —*Ron Wynn*

● **To the Last** / Jul. 24, 2001 / Baraka Foundation ◆◆◆◆

The second solo record for Hassan, this time on the fittingly evolutionary Baraka Foundation label, *To the Last* is another collaboration with Bill Laswell and additionally features Ayib Dieng and Hamid Drake. In his fourth decade of educating and innovating with revolutionary cultural observations performed via a spoken word style that fathered modern hip-hop, this profound recording lays a bed of ambient, wide-mouthed drumming and slithery soundscapes underneath topics ranging from Harlem to the societal contributions of Miles Davis. Never has an artist taken a vocal delivery style so defined and made it sound as improvisational and fresh as Hassan's, who utilizes run-on phrasing like a jazz solo and teaches and inspires with his vocal trumpet—holding his tongue for no one and stopping at nothing in his communication of soul, beauty, and empowerment. While some jazz vocalists scat, and this particular work feels more like jazz than hip-hop, the power here is the decision to actually say something with music, and this is not a new decision for this New York-based artist. "And I hear the voice of nature whisper, 'the victory is yours if you want it,'" speaks Hassan in "A.M.," and truth be told that is the theme of the entire statement made within the crucial record. —*Nic Kincaid*

I-Roy (Roy Reid)

b. Jun. 28, 1949, Spanish Town, Jamaica d. Nov. 27, 1999, Spanish Town, Jamaica

Vocals / DJ, Dancehall

Along with U-Roy, Dennis Alcapone, and Big Youth, I-Roy was one of a quartet of DJs that reigned supreme over the Jamaican music scene during the early to mid-'70s. Of the four, I-Roy was the most eloquent, and his toasts were littered with references to pop culture, from movies to historical figures. He was also one of the most prolific, cutting scores upon scores of singles, and dozens of albums. Although the DJ's sun began to set at the end of the decade, I-Roy continued to record sporadically up to the '90s; by then, though, his life had taken a tragic turn.

The DJ was born on June 28, 1949, in St. Thomas, Jamaica. The young Roy Reid had no early dreams of becoming a sound system hero, and after graduating from Dinthill Technical College, he embarked on a civil service career, working as an accountant for the government. However, as the island's music scene blossomed during the '60s, other possibilities began to present themselves. Sound systems were flourishing and in 1968, Reid launched his own, Soul Bunny. Initially, the young man took advantage of the weekly early closing (a practice inherited from the British, who closed their businesses one afternoon a week). Thus, Reid set up his system on Wednesday afternoons down by the Victoria Pier. He made an immediate impact, and was soon offered a spot at Son's Junior system in Spanish Town. It was there he met producer Harry Mudie, who took the young Reid into the studio, christened him I-Roy (taking advantage of the success of U-Roy), and recorded four songs. Two paired him with Dennis Walks, "The Drifter" and "Heart Don't Leap";

the third with Ebony Sisters, "Let Me Tell You Boy"; while the fourth, "Musical Pleasure," became his solo debut. These songs were all hits, and I-Roy swiftly became in demand at the sound systems. He DJed for virtually all the outfits operating around Spanish Town, Stereo and Ruddy's Supreme included, and then spent some time with V-Rocket.

In contrast to his flirtations with the sound systems, I-Roy remained loyal to Mudie until 1971. By then, the DJ had developed a rabid following in Britain as well, and the pair fell out over the financial arrangements for a forthcoming European tour. With their partnership at an end, the DJ entered an amazingly prolific period, recording with virtually every major producer on the island. He cut "Hot Bomb" for Lloyd Campbell, "Mood for Love" with Winston Blake, and "Problems of Life" and "Musical Drum Sound" for Lloyd Daley. These singles were all big hits, and subsequently I-Roy was offered a slot at King Tubby's legendary Hi-Fi sound system. The year 1973 was a signature one; the hits came down like rain. Producer Bunny Lee oversaw three, the fabulous "Rose of Sharon," "Make Love," and "Who Cares." Derrick Harriott produced "Melinda," Jimmy Radway cut "Sound Education," and Keith Hudson produced "Silver Platter." Lee Perry took the DJ into the studio for "High Fashion" and "Space Flight," Ruddy Redwood was responsible for "Sidewalk Killer," Pete Weston oversaw the entertaining "Buck and the Preacher," Glen Brown was behind a trio of cuts including "Festive Season," while Byron Lee oversaw a tribute to the popular sci-fi show *Dr. Who*, there were others with Clive Chin, Rupie Edwards, and the list just continues. However, these many mighty cuts pale when compared to I-Roy's work with producer Gussie Clarke. The pair inaugurated their partnership with "Magnificent Seven," and followed it up with the equally impressive "High Jacking." In their sway came a flood of hits, and by the time the two men had completed work on I-Roy's debut album, *Presenting*, the record was already a virtual hits collection. The majority of the album is culled from Clarke cuts, with several of the best from Pete Weston also included. The centerpiece is the phenomenal "Blackman Time," which utilized the "Slaving" rhythm, while virtually everything else on it was nearly as strong. A second self-produced album, *Hell & Sorrow*, followed hot on its heels. A worthy successor to the DJ's debut, again it was hits heavy; "Buck and the Preacher" and "Monkey Fashion" are amongst the smashes included, and it was as big a success as its predecessor.

Britain was now paying serious attention and *Hell & Sorrow*, which had been domestically released via the Trojan label, had garnered nothing but acclaim. In response, I-Roy was off to the U.K., arriving in time to promote his next release, the excellent *The Many Moods Of*. He would be gone eight months, a lifetime in Jamaica's fast-changing music scene. I-Roy arrived home to discover that DJing had been declared dead, but he was having none of that and a battle brewed. With the rise of the DJs, Jamaican artists had taken a serious hit. The new genre was built around recycled rhythms (in Jamaican terms, the riddims, which is distinct from the actual rhythm— "riddim" refers specifically to the song's melody, not its actual rhythm, which was normally re-recorded with a reggae beat), initially using popular oldies from the rocksteady era. Producers would still need a rhythm section to re-record the songs with more modern beats, and as time went on more musicians were added to the brew, but singers were now virtually redundant. In response, the Jamaican Federation of Musicians, under their president, veteran jazzman Sonny Bradshaw, had fought long and hard to resurrect "real" music. This was the beginning of the shadowy conspiracy of veteran singers who now began unleashing a flood of vocal cuts onto the market. However, Jamaican fads are notorious for their short lives, and it's more likely that it was down to a normal cyclical change of taste, that saw the initial age of DJs fade away. But I-Roy hadn't admitted defeat yet, he was merely biding his time. In the interim, he took employment at Joe Gibbs and JoJo Hookim's brand new Channel One studio. Although he never held the title, and rarely received the credit, the former DJ became the studio's house producer, and was behind several of the studio's innovations.

Finally, in February 1975, I-Roy was ready to launch his attack. It began with "Black Bullet," on which the DJ paired with Jackie Brown. JoJo Hookim then oversaw a stream of I-Roy hits, "I Man Time," "Forward Yah!," "Roots Man," and the innuendo-laced masterpiece "Welding" amongst them. With Phil Pratt, the DJ cut "Ital Dish" and "Musical Air Raid," while Pete Weston oversaw "Natty Down Deh." That latter single was aimed directly at I-Roy's number-one enemy, Sonny Bradshaw (who's referred to as "Lockjaw" on the record), and the DJ couldn't help but gloat as the single sailed up the chart.

By the end of the year, I-Roy had sent a baker's dozen of cuts soaring up the chart, including "Fire Stick," "Dread in the West," "Padlock," "Teapot," and a pair of songs taking exception to fellow DJ Prince Jazzbo, one of a number of young toasters determined to knock I-Roy off his throne. Dissing the competition on record has a long and illustrious history in Jamaica, dating back to the early '60s and Prince Buster's feud with singer Derrick Morgan and producer Leslie Kong. That was personal; I-Roy's and Prince Jazzbo's musical battle was not, but that didn't stop the two from taking even more personal, and more hilarious, potshots at each other. I-Roy opened the account with "Straight to Jazzbo's Head," which prompted the victim to retort with "Straight to I-Roy's Head." Soon after, the younger DJ had a run-in with a bus, thankfully with only bruises resulting; the elder DJ utilized this incident for "Jazzbo Have Fe Run." As I-Roy had not suffered any misfortunes of his own, Jazzbo opted to question his manhood with "Gal Boy I-Roy." That received a sharp retort with "Padlock," wherein the DJ attempts to arouse the sleeping "Princess Jazzbo." And the sparring continued, much to audiences' delight, with other DJs jumping on the bandwagon to take their own potshots at the mighty I-Roy. Unlike earlier feuds, this one never resulted in clashes between supporters, and the two DJs remained friendly behind the scenes. Before this clash finally died out, it spawned a clash album, *Step Forward Youth*, which bundled up the pair's barrages onto one disc.

In 1990, the Ujama label would compile them up again on *Head to Head Clash*. The year 1975 also brought the release of I-Roy's fourth album, *Truth & Rights*, which was overseen by Pete Weston. Again the album was filled with recent hits, alongside some strong new material. In 1976, I-Roy inked a deal with the new Virgin subsidiary Front Line, and over the next three years they released a quite breathtaking nine albums by the DJ. In 1996 alone, I-Roy would release four albums. First up was *Can't Conquer Rasta*, a dub-filled masterpiece overseen by Bunny Lee. The two men had picked up again the year before, debuting with "Straight to Jazzbo's Head," and their relationship had continued across a string of other hits. His debut for Front Line (or more accurately Virgin, as Front Line wasn't quite up and running in time) was *Musical Shark Attack*, immediately followed by *Crisis Time*. Both records were slightly less ferocious than past efforts, probably keeping in mind the sensibilities of his overseas audiences, but do feature heavy roots and steaming toasts over a host of classic dread cuts. The Klik label also released *Dread Bald Head*. The following year, I-Roy joined forces with Niney Holness for a host of cuts, including "Zion Trip," "Point Blank," "Jah Come Here," and "Point Blank." He also went into the studio with Alvin Ranglin, emerging with *The Best of I-Roy* album. Contrary to its title, this is not a hits collection, but a record of new material, all recorded with the superb Revolutionaries. Although the rhythms are taken from Studio One classics, with the Heptones and Alton Ellis particularly favored, this is a laid-back, rootsy record, moodily atmospheric, and indeed remains one of the DJ's best. Equally good was *Ten Commandments*, also released this year. A brilliant concept album, musically the record is based on Bob Marley's *Exodus*, with each of the biblical commandments providing the theme for a single track.

After that, *Heart of a Lion* was going to pale somewhat, although Harry Johnson does nice work here. *The Godfather* paired I-Roy back with Bunny Lee and Roderick "Blackbeard" Sinclair, with the law (as compared to the commandments) and gangsters being the chattering themes of choice. *The General* sadly was of less note than its dub companion, *Spider's Web*. All of these albums arrived in 1977. Perhaps this very rash of records helped to suppress singles' sales, and the DJ was now no longer a constant on the chart. But the albums kept coming. The year 1978 brought *World on Fire*, again featuring Sly & Robbie's seminal rhythms. Joe Gibbs oversaw *African Herbsman*, and the DJ rejoined Harry J. for 1979's *Hotter Yatta*. That same year's *Cancer* must refer to I-Roy's zodiac sign, not the disease, while the topics revolve around movie stars and musical heroes. Intriguingly, 1980's *Whap'n Bap'n* was actually released under the DJ's real name, and paired him with the U.K. maverick producer Dennis Bovell, for a surprisingly subdued record.

I-Roy's Doctor Fish in 1981 was equally patchy, while 1983's *Outer Limits* found the DJ dipping into rap. Again there were a few highlights, but the majority of the set was lackluster, and it was becoming apparent that the DJ was beginning to lose his shine. Further albums seemed to confirm this fear, and sessions with Blackbeard in 1984 were so disappointing that the DJ's output now slowed to a trickle. Occasional records did appear; 1987 brought *We Chat You Rock*, on which the DJ paired with Jah Woosh; 1990 saw the arrival of *The Lyrics Man*, but none revived I-Roy's fortunes. By the '90s, the DJ was afflicted with a variety of health problems and his financial situation was so precarious that for stretches of time he found himself homeless.

By the end of his life, I-Roy had become financially reliant on his mentally retarded son. A second son was in prison and was killed there in October 1999. This terrible tragedy was perhaps the final blow for the weakened legend, and on November 27, 1999, the DJ died in a Spanish Town hospital from heart problems. An artist of I-Roy's stature would be best served by a multi-disc box set, but the copyright situation makes this difficult, as it does for most Jamaican stars, as I-Roy's recordings are spread across so many different producers. However, much of I-Roy's best work is still available, and there are a number of collections devoted exclusively to his recordings. The U.K. label Blood & Fire's *Don't Check Me With No Lightweight Stuff* is particularly noteworthy, and concentrates on his 1972-1975 heyday. *Crucial Cuts* (1983) culled the best from the Front Line material, while *Touting I Self*, released by Heartbeat in 2001, picked up the best of the DJ's work with Bunny Lee. I-Roy is also found showcased on compilations devoted to individual producers, as well as being featured on many DJ compilations. —*Jo-Ann Greene*

Presenting I-Roy / Apr. 1973 / Trojan ✦✦✦✦
In reality, by the time *Presenting I-Roy* arrived, the DJ needed no introduction—he was already one of the hottest toasters on the scene. This, his debut album, was virtually a hits collection, and any tracks that weren't hits would be soon enough. Initially seen as little more than copying his bigger brethren, I-Roy had swiftly developed into a mature and distinctive talent. His conversational style was far removed from his contemporaries, as his powerful toast on "Black Man's Time" perfectly illustrated. That song is the album's centerpiece, and was produced by Gussie Clarke. Built around the "Slaving" rhythm, it opened with a long spoken intro, unique at the time. "Red, Gold and Green" was equally cultural in nature, with "Peace" an exuberant demand for unity, while "Screw Face" takes a thoughtful look at solutions for Jamaica's endemic violence. However, I-Roy was just as effective chatting about less weighty matters, as on "Tripe Girl," while "Melinda" is just as charming, both excellently employing classic rocksteady rhythms, as does the wonderfully moody "Coxsonne Affair." On "Tourism Is My Business," meanwhile, the DJ exalts his island home, surely with tongue firmly in cheek. There are a dozen seminal cuts in all, and what better way to meet one of Jamaica's greatest DJs. —*Jo-Ann Greene*

Hell & Sorrow / Aug. 1973 / Trojan ✦✦✦✦✦
Picking up where *Presenting I-Roy* left off, *Hell & Sorrow* showcases another dozen crucial cuts, both new and old. Among the latter were two Jamaican smash hits, "Monkey Fashion" and "Buck and the Preacher." The former, produced by Roy Cousins, features a slow, intricate beat that the DJ adroitly skims along, the latter, a Pete Weston production, is a musical advertisement for the film of the same name, and just as entertaining as the movie itself. Notable among the new offerings is "Dr. Phibbs," another powerful version of the classic "Sidewalk Killer." The topics the DJ covers are diverse, running from the cultural themes found on "Black & Proud" and "African Descendent," to the religious, and on to the interpersonal discussions on "Deep and Heavy" and "Call on I." Often I-Roy would combine several themes within a single song, but a consistently uplifting message of unity and betterment shoots through most of his toasts, while still mashing up the dancefloor. More humorously, on "Medley Mood," the DJ begins with a cover of "Banana Boat Song" and then nimbly trips off across a toy chest's worth of nursery rhymes. "Learn to communicate, learn to appreciate, you can learn to elaborate," I-Roy advises on "John Lion Jungle," and certainly that was the secret of his success. Few DJs were able to equal I-Roy's ability to elaborate on a subject and communicate it with such panache to his listeners, while still appreciating the classic rhythms he was working. *Hell & Sorrow* showcases the master at his work. —*Jo-Ann Greene*

Truth & Rights / 1975 / Grounation ✦✦✦✦✦
Horns, organ, and a rhythm section by Sly & Robbie. Top-drawer toasting. —*Michael G. Nastos*

☆ Ten Commandments / 1978 / Frontline ✦✦✦✦✦
It was one of the most stunningly audacious concepts of all time. Versioning a song was one thing, and by 1977 an enormously popular one at that, but the idea of versioning an entire album was something no one had ever even considered, least of all versioning a masterpiece like Bob Marley & the Wailers' *Exodus*. But that's precisely what I-Roy did on *Ten Commandments*

(aka *Exodus Part II*). But the DJ didn't stop there, as the title makes clear; he hung the set around the Ten Commandments, with each track representing one of God's laws, beginning with I-Roy reciting, singing, or toasting about the commandment itself. Some provide the inspiration for his toast, as with "Commandment 6"'s "Thou shalt not kill," which is set to a sublime version of "Natural Mystic." Elsewhere, it's the actual song that sets the DJ rocking, as on "Commandment 5," where he sings along to "One Love," reminds listeners to "honor thy mother and father," and delivers up a romantically seductive toast to boot. On "Commandment 2," grave images get short shrift, as the DJ calls out warnings to the Wailers' "Heathen." Not all the songs are cultural in intent: "Commandment 7" confusingly starts off with I-Roy stating he's giving listeners "number six," but delivers up the seventh ("Thou shalt not commit adultery"); however, that's the only biblical reference, as the singer skanks off on a "Jamming" shock attack. The same is true with the jumping "Commandment 1," where I-Roy celebrates toasting itself. This number is the sole one not versioned from *Exodus* itself, and substitutes a punchy "Put It On" for the more downbeat "Turn Your Lights Down Low." Contrary to later legend, *Ten Commandments* does not version the original album itself, instead boasting spectacular recuts by the low-profile band Chalawa. It may be sacrilegious to suggest, but the versions here are arguably superior to the originals, and most are far rootsier than what the Wailers created on their record. "Exodus" (aka "Commandment 4") absolutely steams across the grooves, "Heathen" is positively ominous, "Natural Mystic" is stomach-dropping heavy, and even "Three Little Birds" have bulked up from fluttering sparrows to soaring eagles. Pete Weston's superb production emphasizes the dread auras the band creates, giving the record a dubby depth that shook sound systems around the world. An incredibly popular album in its day, it's beggars' belief that Frontline, who released the set in the U.K., let it fall from their catalog and has steadfastly refused to reissue it—a cultural crime if ever there was one. This album is a masterpiece that demands a new audience —*Jo-Ann Greene*

★ Don't Check Me With No Lightweight Stuff: 1972-1975) / Feb. 25, 1997 / Blood & Fire ✦✦✦✦✦
Like most Jamaican stars, I-Roy was prolific to the point of deluging the market with releases, but unlike many other artists, most of his work during the apex of his career was all of decidedly high caliber. A box set is desperately needed to round up the best of his work during the '70s, but as that's unlikely, *Don't Check Me With No Lightweight Stuff* is an excellent start. The title, incidentally, is taken from a spoken line in the intro to "Look a Boom," and is appropriate, as the set rounds up 16 heavy-hitting numbers. The collection draws exclusively from 1972-1975, the period between his breakthrough in Jamaica and his inking a deal with Virgin Records. Across this three-year period, I-Roy unleashed scores of singles, self-producing some while also cutting records for virtually every producer on the island. However, this is by no means a greatest-hits collection, as a number of the DJ's biggest smashes, "Black Man Time," "Monkey Fashion," and "Tripe Girl," are missing. However, you do get "Buck and the Preacher," an equal chart-buster, the seminal "Sidewalk Killer," and "Holy Satta," his Psalm-filled version of the Abyssinians' masterpiece, "Satta Massa Gana." One of I-Roy's many fortes was his thematic diversity, and his toasts ranged from Rasta-fired preaching inspired by the Psalms, strong societal messages, and chatty pieces on more popular concerns to sharp, rousing cuts aimed at firing up the crowds at the sound systems. This set showcases his versatility, his excitement at the latest black films ("Superfly" and the aforementioned "Buck and the Preacher"), keenness for literacy ("Sound Education"), condemnations of anti-social behavior ("Noisy Place" and "Hot Stuff"), and warnings to the wicked ("Double Warning" and "Hospital Trolley"). The DJ pays his respects to saxophonist Tommy McCook on "Sidewalk Killer," and offers comfort to a boxing great on the superb "Don't Get Weary Joe Frazier." Every one of the numbers boasts a superb musical accompaniment, all skillfully reworking rhythms into sizzling mixes that provide the perfect template for I-Roy's toasts. As one has come to gratefully expect from the Blood & Fire label, the album includes a sumptuous booklet, with a bio written from an interview with the late DJ, plus information on each track. By far, *Don't Check Me* is the best collection of the artist currently available. —*Jo-Ann Greene*

Deejay a-Menace Babylon / Apr. 1, 2003 / Burning Bush ✦✦✦✦
This collection of legendary and influential reggae DJ I-Roy's works is a gem. I-Roy toasts wicked and funny raps over rock-solid dub rhythms, sounding

like a cross between a carnival barker and a drunken poet. Each track is of the highest quality, roots reggae to the core. A large chunk of the tracks come from 1976's *Crisis Time*. *Deejay a-Menace Babylon* pulls ten songs from that landmark album, including the tough-as-nails "Equality and Justice" and the spacy "Moving on Strong." Six tracks come from I-Roy's late-'70s collaboration with Lee "Scratch" Perry (and were released by Burning Bush in 2002 on the *Sensimilla Showdown* disc). The other five come from parts unknown. Actually, the only way to find out where any of the tracks originated is to do research, since Burning Bush gives absolutely no information regarding sessions or albums or much of anything except for vague liner notes. Luckily, most people will just be able to enjoy the genius of I-Roy at the near-peak of his considerable powers. Anyone who requires documentation or wonders why they didn't add the other two tracks from *Crisis Time* and call the disc "Crisis Time Plus Bonus Tracks" should either skip buying *Deejay a-Menace Babylon* or chill out. —*Tim Sendra*

Linton Kwesi Johnson

b. Kingston, Jamaica
Vocals / Dub Poetry, Political Reggae
Although he has only released one album of new material in the last ten years, and has virtually retired from the live stage after his 1985 tour, Linton Kwesi Johnson remains a towering figure in reggae music. Born in Kingston, Jamaica, and raised in the Brixton section of London, Johnson invented dub poetry, a type of toasting descended from the DJ stylings of U-Roy and I-Roy. But whereas toasting tended to be hyperkinetic and given to fits of braggadocio, Johnson's poetry (which is what it was—he was a published poet and journalist before he performed with a band) was more scripted and delivered in a more languid, slangy, streetwise style. Johnson's grim realism and tales of racism in an England governed by Tories was scathingly critical. The Afro-Brits in Johnson's poems are neglected by the government and persecuted by the police. Johnson was also instrumental (with his friend Darcus Howe) in the publication of a socialist-oriented London-based newspaper, *Race Today*, that offered him and other likeminded Brits, both black and white, an outlet to discuss the racial issues that, under Margaret Thatcher's reign, seemed to be tearing the country apart. For one so outspoken in his politics, Johnson's recorded work, while politically explicit, is not simply a series of slogans or tuneful/danceable jeremiads. In fact, is was his second release, *Forces of Victory*, where his mix of politics and music united to stunning effect. Dennis Bovell and the Dub Band could swing (as in jazzy) more than many reggae bands, and guitarist John Kpiaye, the group's secret weapon, offered deftly played, dazzlingly melodic solos. But it was Johnson's moving poetry, galvanizing moments such as "Sonny's Lettah" and "Fite Dem Back," that made it obvious that he was a major talent.

Although he never intended to, Johnson became a star, in England anyway; in America he had a small yet devoted group of fans. But political activism was as important, perhaps more important, than churning out records and touring, and after the release of his third album, *Bass Culture*, in 1980, Johnson took time off from the music scene, turning his back on a lucrative contract from Island. He continued to perform, but it was in the form of poetry readings at universities, at festivals in the Caribbean, and for trade union workers in Trinidad. His organizing activities included the setting up the First International Book Fair of Radical Black and Third World Books, and greater involvement with the political organizations with which he had been long identified, namely, the Race Today Collective and the Alliance of the Black Parents Movement. In 1982, the BBC commissioned Johnson to create a series of radio programs on Jamaican popular music, a subject he'd been researching for years. The programs, entitled *From Mento to Lovers Rock*, were more than just musical history; Johnson contextualized Jamaican music socially and politically and offered a more nuanced and thorough examination of the popular music of his native and adopted countries.

Johnson returned to the pop music scene in 1984 with perhaps his best record, *Making History*. Again working with Dennis Bovell, Johnson's seething political anger suffuses this recording, but it is never undone by simple vituperation. Johnson is, if anything, a thoughtful radical, more analytical than simplistic, and that adds to the power of these seven songs. Unfortunately, this would be the last new music from Johnson until 1991's *Tings an' Times*, which proved yet again that regardless of how much time he takes off from music, when LKJ returns it's as if he's never missed a beat.

His most recent period of recording silence has been broken by the release of a music-less poetry album. —*John Dougan*

☆ **Dread Beat an' Blood** / 1978 / Caroline ♦♦♦♦♦
It's impossible to overestimate the impact that *Dread Beat an' Blood* had on the British scene. Its arrival had all the explosive power of a hydrogen bomb, detonating across the reggae, punk, and political scenes alike. By the time of its release in 1978, Linton Kwesi Johnson was already a major force within the West Indian community. A poet, with two books of collected poems to his credit, a respected journalist, and an ardent activist, Johnson had been involved in politics since his college days, and his words carried enormous power. Putting them to a musical backing only increased their potency, and brought them to a much wider audience. Johnson brought his journalistic eagle eye to *Dread Beat*, but viewed through a poetical prism, sharply etching real life situations with turns of phrases that deeply resonated, and imbuing them with his own impassioned political beliefs. The timing was also crucial, its release coming at a point of growing social conflict that was initially confined to immigrant areas, but was now spilling out of the punk scene and into the larger community's consciousness. Thus, even though six of the poems within this set were first published three years earlier in the book that shares the same title as the record, they equally described scenes taking place outside the West Indian community. "Five Nights of Bleeding" was set within a series of black concerts and shows, but punks were also experiencing the same police assaults on their own shows. "Doun di Road" is a smoldering look at intra-community violence, as well as the rise of the neo-Nazi National Front Party. The battles between punks and skins were equally fratricidal, while Front supporters were just as happy to give any stray punk they found alone on the street a good kicking as a lone black. And "Come Wi Goh Dung Deh" rings just as true for poor whites in England's poverty-ridden inner cities as for the immigrant ghettos Johnson was actually describing. Rock Against Racism had planted strong seeds of consciousness in growing segments of the white music scene, and *Dread Beat* provided the thunderstorm needed to help those crops flower. As poems, the words carried weight. With steaming, sizzling musical backings, their deep grooves and militant edges pulsing out of speakers, they echoed forth from clubs and sound systems across the U.K. and beyond. The two new poems, "It Dread Inna Inglan (For George Lindo)" and "Man Free (For Darcus Howe)," both powerfully addressed current events, adding an even more timely flavor to the set. However, it was arguably the older "All Wi Doin Is Defendin" that best encapsulated the passions of the day, a fervid rallying cry to the masses to choose their weapons and man the barricades. It was also prophetic, accurately predicting the riots that scorched the nation in 1981. One of the most militant and uncompromising albums ever released in Britain, a flaying of the nation, a political and musical masterpiece, no other record more vividly and passionately describes the state of the country in the late '70s. —*Jo-Ann Greene*

Forces of Victory / 1979 / Mango ♦♦♦♦♦
If *Dread Beat An' Blood* brought Johnson and initial flush of notoriety, then *Forces of Victory* was the record that cemented his growing reputation as a major talent. Bovell and the Dub Band swing hard on this set, especially on the album's opening track "Want Fi Goh Rave." This contains some of Johnson's most memorable songs/poems, such as the heartfelt prison saga "Sonny's Lettah" and the confrontational "Fite Dem Back," which he delivers in his trademark singsong Jamaican patois. Dramatic and intense to the point of claustrophobia, *Forces of Victory* is not simply one of the most important reggae records of its time, it's one of the most important reggae records ever recorded. —*John Dougan*

Bass Culture / 1980 / Mango ♦♦♦
I remember at the time of its release that many reviewers considered *Bass Culture* a slight disappointment because it didn't reach the highs of *Forces of Victory*. Granted, following up a record as great as *Forces of Victory* is no easy task, but all these years later I wonder what were people thinking. *Bass Culture* is tremendous, another successful collaboration between Johnson and Bovell with songs that are, at times, even more confrontational (e.g., "Inglan is a Bitch") than anything he had previously recorded. I will admit that the Dub Band sounds better on *Forces of Victory*, but Johnson is hitting his stride at the time of this release and experimenting with song structure and lyrics a little more (i.e., not everything is explicitly political here). Still, I defy anyone to come up with a reason to not own this record. An extra added bonus is John Kpiaye's great guitar playing. —*John Dougan*

★ **Independant Intavenshan: The Island Anthology** / Oct. 27, 1998 / Island
✦✦✦✦✦

Between 1979 and 1984, Linton Kwesi Johnson unleashed four seminal albums on the Island label—*Forces of Victory, Bass Culture, LKJ in Dub,* and *Making History.* This compilation draws crucial tracks from all four sets, as well songs off 12" singles. 1979's *Forces* and 1980's *Bass* are heavily represented, with their superb companion dubs appearing immediately after the vocal tracks. During these years Johnson's sound evolved, shifting from militant roots through an experimental period and finally toward a jazzier style, and with the set arranged in chronological order, listeners are able to note this musical transformation for themselves. Of course, there was a sizeable shift in sound between Johnson's debut album *Dread Beat an' Blood* and *Forces* with the inclusion of brass and fuller musical arrangements. *Dread* was one of the most militant albums ever to land on British shop shelves. *Forces* was equally radical, but Johnson's poems were now laced with irony and humor. "Fite dem Back" is so over the top one couldn't help but laugh, yet the words are so anthemic you're forced to shout along with its rousing refrain. "Independant Intavenshan" is as sarcastic as it is scathing. Even the album's masterpiece, "Sonny's Lettah (Anti-Sus Poem)," makes use of black humor to drive home its message, with the fight scene taking on a Tarantino-esque quality. There again, "It Noh Funny" isn't, while the ominous "Time Come" again predicts the riots that will sweep the nation in 1981, with Johnson's Cassandra-like warnings going unheeded. *Bass* continues down a similar thematic roads, but wanders along musical byways as well, from the Western-flavored "Street 66," to the joyous reggae of the aptly titled "Reggae fi Peach," through the almost Two Tone-esque "Di Black Petty Booshwah," and onto the jazzy lushness of "Loraine." That latter number is a perfect parody of a love song, the title track and "Reggae Sounds" are superb expostulations of the power of music, "Street" is a Western gunfight brought to an inner-city flat, "Booshwa" scathingly condemns that class, while "Inglan Is a Bitch" vividly describes the typical working-class hero the bourgeois where stepping on on their way up. "Peach" is an impassioned eulogy to Blair Peach, killed by the police during a protest at Southall Town Hall this same year. Two more tributes are included on this compilation, both from the *History* set. With "Reggae fi Radni," Johnson attempts to come to grips with the mysterious car bombing that killed the Guyanan author/activist Walter Rodney. "Reggae fi Dada" is a eulogy to the poet's late father, wherein the poet turns his scathing pen on Jamaica. Meanwhile, Johnson's prophesies have come to pass, and he celebrates with "Di Great Insohreckshan," a jubilant look at the Brixton riot. But *History*'s centerpiece is "New Crass Massahkah," the event that helped sparked the riots that swept England that year. Johnson's vivid description of this tragic fire powerfully conjure up this event, and so raw were people's emotions at the time that much of the piece is spoken word, with the band brought in only to create the atmosphere of the party where the fire took place itself. With this stunning piece, the compilation is brought to a close. All of these albums were masterpieces, and to have much of the best of them compiled onto two CDs is a welcome event. Excellent sleeve notes complete this stellar package, and this compilation can not be too highly recommended. —*Jo-Ann Greene*

Donell Jones

Producer, Vocals, Songwriter / Contemporary R&B, Urban

Beginning with his 1996 album *My Heart,* singer/songwriter/producer Donell Jones recorded a jazzy and soulful style of urban pop for LaFace Records and scored a few modest singles in the process. His first two singles—"In the Hood" and "Knocks Me Off My Feet"—established his reputation within the cluttered urban market. In particular, the latter song, originally a Stevie Wonder song from *Songs in the Key of Life* (1976), became a substantial hit for Jones, climbing to the upper reaches of the *Billboard* R&B chart and driving the album up the charts as well. In addition to his own music, he also wrote songs for other urban artists such as Usher ("Think of You") and 702 ("Get It Together"), among others.

Born the son of a gospel singer, Jones submersed himself in music at a young age. Later, he began to fall victim to the temptations of Chicago's Southside, where he grew up. At one point, after involving himself with gang culture, he decided to dedicate himself to music rather than the streets. He met Edward "Eddie F" Ferrell (former Heavy D & the Boyz member turned Untouchables Entertainment president), and the two formed a partnership with LaFace. Following the success of Usher's "Think of You" in 1994

(number eight R&B), a song which Jones wrote, LaFace executives L.A. Reid and Babyface gave the blossoming artist the go-ahead to begin work on his solo debut. Executive-produced by Ferrell, Reid, and Babyface, *My Heart,* peaked at number 30 on Billboard's R&B chart in 1996, propelled primarily by the success of "Knocks Me Off My Feet" as well as two other singles: "In the Hood" and "You Should Know."

When Jones returned three years later in 1999 with his second album, *Where I Wanna Be,* he had become known as an accomplished songwriter. He penned songs for 702 ("Get It Together," 1997) and Drea ("Not Gonna Letcha," 1998) and was well regarded within the industry as a result. Unsurprisingly, then, Jones attained impressive success with *Where I Wanna Be* and its singles: "U Know What's Up" and "Shorty (Got Her Eyes on Me)." Shortly after the album's release, Jones contributed a song to the *Shaft* soundtrack ("Do What I Gotta Do") and to Guru's *Streetsoul* album ("Hustlin' Daze," which he also contributed vocals to). Following some time off in 2001, Jones returned in 2002 with his third album, *Life Goes On.* —*Jason Birchmeier*

● **My Heart** / 1996 / La Face ✦✦✦✦
After working briefly for La Face Records as a songwriter (most notably Usher's "Think of You," a Top Ten R&B hit in 1994), L.A. Reid and Babyface gave Donell Jones the go-ahead to craft a solo debut. The resulting album, *My Heart,* introduced Jones to the masses with the help of "Knocks Me off My Feet," his lovely cover of a classic Stevie Wonder ballad. Not only does Jones write the songs and sing them on his debut album; he also produces the album and programs both the drums and keyboards. Thus, comparisons to Wonder are somewhat inevitable, especially because Jones sings with a similarly soothing tone of voice. His later albums show him growing as an artist, but here you see Jones first blossoming. In addition to "Knocks Me off My Feet," *My Heart* also features "In the Hood," Jones' smooth ode to street culture that appears here in two versions. —*Jason Birchmeier*

Life Goes On / Jun. 4, 2002 / La Face ✦✦✦✦
Donell Jones doesn't get as much credit as he deserves. Sure, he's had hits, as a solo artist and as a songwriter and producer, but his records never seem to break out to a wider audience, which is too bad, since they're consistently satisfying. *Life Goes On,* his third platter, keeps that streak going. The quiet storm streak that characterized its predecessor, *Where I Wanna Be,* has been toned down somewhat, and he's relying more on contemporary R&B sounds and production, but the end result is the same—a seduction record that is smooth, but also romantic. Perhaps it plays a little too much like lowlights mood music, with a few songs blending together, but that's hardly a fault, since the mood is sustained alluringly from start to finish (apart from "Freakin' U," a deliberate attempt to get an up-tempo change of pace in place—it works, but it interrupts the flow a little). Jones may not be as flashy as some of his modern soul peers—he's not a neo-soul artist, he's thoroughly modern, yet he never falls into the trap of putting his singing in front of the music, letting the mood take center stage—but that's what makes his records work, and what makes *Life Goes On* another fine addition to his catalog. [Note: As the sticker says on the cover, *Life Goes On* is a CD that "is protected against unauthorized copying. It is designed to play only on home audio CD players; it will not play on computers, some DVD players, or other devices." This statement is true—I slapped the CD into my computer as I was writing, not realizing the disclaimer; my system froze up, and I nearly lost my work. So, be careful out there.] —*Stephen Thomas Erlewine*

Bobby Konders

b. Philadelphia, PA

Producer, Engineer / Raggae, Club/Dance, Acid House, House

An incredibly respected figure of New York's dance-music underground since the mid-'80s, Brooklyn's Bobby Konders has been at the forefront of multiple movements, infamous parties, and radio programs that have kept house music alive and kicking. A selector, a label entrepreneur, a producer, a master of the airwaves, and a proponent of the breaking down of racial barriers, Konders' spot in the dance music Hall of Fame should be reserved well before any groundbreaking ceremony.

Konders first broke out as one of the higher-profile members of a collective that threw down at a series of parties called *Wild Pitch,* which helped fill the large shoes left empty by the unfortunate exit of *the Paradise Garage.* This DJ crew included Victor Rosado, Kenny Carpenter, Nicky Jones, John

Robinson, David Camacho, DJ Pierre, and Timmy Richardson—just to name a few (not to mention occasional appearances by legends Tony Humphries and Tee Scott). Just as Konders likes to point out that everyone bleeds red, he built his reputation as a DJ and producer on finding the common thread that runs throughout several styles of music: hip-hop, reggae, disco, house. During the late '80s and early '90s, Konders issued a series of productions on the Nu Groove label that went down well with the underground. At the height of house music's flirtation with mainstream appeal, Konders and his Massive Sounds crew landed on Polygram for a self-titled album. Unsurprisingly, the material proved to be too raw and not pop enough to cross over, so Konders and company happily remained outside of the general public's consciousness.

In the early '90s, Konders and partner Jabba formed Massive B Sound System, which has served as both a production outlet and as a formidable radio presence, bringing reggae of the dancehall variety to the listeners of New York's Hot 97.1 FM. Konders and Jabba have also taken their sound system to a number of other continents. In addition to cultivating talent for Massive B, Konders has remixed and produced for artists like Aswad, Shabba Ranks, Ziggy Marley, and Supercat. In 2002, Konders and Massive Sounds' back catalog of productions was anthologized with *A Lost Era in NYC 1987-1992*, a disc that focused on the man's trademark deep house/reggae hybrids. —*Andy Kellman*

- **A Lost Era in NYC 1987-1992** / 2002 / International DeeJay Gigolo ✦✦✦✦
While operating under several guises—House Rhythms, Jus Friends, Massive Sounds, Rydims, Dub Poets—during the late '80s and early '90s, Bobby Konders was making house history with a number of low-budget but high-quality tracks that blended love for house, reggae, and a number of less obvious forms with a production style that emphasized the dark and the deep amidst a mushroom cloud of ganja smoke. Virtually every bass line is remarkably pungent to an almost oppressive extent, casting an overriding dark or melancholic tone throughout each track. This doesn't mean that everything's doom and gloom, because there are some genuinely beautiful moments scattered across this long overdue compilation. Just through the addition of a prominent whistling flute, the "Flute Mix" of Massive Sounds' "Expressions" turns a typically haunting track into something full of beauty. "Blak and Whit" is even more emotional, with synth textures that are just as affecting as anything created by the first two waves of Detroit techno producers. At the other end, the most wicked track of all is the paranoiac nightmare of House Rhythms' "Nervous Acid." Konders' lone contribution to the acid house phenomenon, the track remains one of the heaviest in its field, placing an catapulting bass line and a clamping beat below a flurry of synth effects that sound as if a helicopter is hovering above. "Let There Be House" is a rush-inducing cousin to Marshall Jefferson's "Move Your Body," boasting repeated exclamations of "Let there be house!" over a jittering rhythm, warped synths, and tickling piano vamps. Konders' appeal and influence stretch far and wide, and though he eventually made the complete conversion to reggae as a DJ and producer, his presence continues to loom over house music. —*Andy Kellman*

The Last Poets

f. May 16, 1969, Harlem, NY
Political Rap, Poetry
With their politically charged raps, taut rhythms, and dedication to raising African-American consciousness, the Last Poets almost single-handedly laid the groundwork for the emergence of hip-hop. The group arose out of the prison experiences of Jalal Mansur Nuriddin, a U.S. Army paratrooper who chose jail as an alternative to fighting in Vietnam; while incarcerated, he converted to Islam, learned to "spiel" (an early form of rapping), and befriended fellow inmates Omar Ben Hassan and Abiodun Oyewole.

Upon the trio's release from prison, they returned to the impoverished ghettos of Harlem, where they joined the East Wind poetry workshop and began performing their fusion of spiels and musical backing on neighborhood street corners. On May 16, 1969—Malcolm X's birthday—they officially formed the Last Poets, adopting the name from the work of South African Little Willie Copaseely, who declared the era to be the last age of poets before the complete takeover of guns. After a performance on a local television program, the group was signed by jazz producer Alan Douglas, who helmed their eye-opening eponymous debut LP in 1970. A collection condemning both white oppression ("White Man's Got a God Complex") and black stasis ("Niggas Are Scared of Revolution"), *The Last Poets* reached the U.S. Top Ten

album charts, but before the group could mount a tour, Oyewole was sentenced to 14 years in prison after being found guilty of robbery and was replaced by percussionist Nilaja.

After the 1971 follow-up *This Is Madness* (which landed them on President Richard Nixon's Counter-Intelligence Programming lists), Hassan joined a Southern-based religious sect; Jalal recruited former jazz drummer Suliaman El Hadi for 1972's *Chastisement*, which incorporated jazz-funk structures to create a sound the group dubbed "jazzoetry." Following the 1973 Jalal solo concept album *Hustler's Convention* (recorded under the alias Lightnin' Rod), the Last Poets issued 1974's *At Last*, a foray into freeform jazz; after its release, Nilaja exited, and with the exception of 1977's *Delights of the Garden*, the group kept a conspicuously low profile for the remainder of the decade.

By the 1980s, however, the proliferation of rap—and the form's acknowledged debt to the Last Poets—made their early records sought-after collectors' items; finally, in 1984 the group resurfaced with the LP *Oh, My People*, followed in 1988 by *Freedom Express*. Another layoff ensued, during which time Hassan issued a solo LP, 1993's *Be Bop or Be Dead*, and Jalal mentored the British acid jazz unit Galliano. In 1995, two splinter groups simultaneously reclaimed the Last Poets name; while Jalal and El Hadi teamed for the single "Scatterrap," Hassan and Oyewole issued the LP *Holy Terror*. —*Jason Ankeny*

★ **The Last Poets** / 1970 / Metrotone ✦✦✦✦✦
Brutally honest and beautifully truthful, the Last Poets' eponymous 1970 debut would become one of proto-funk's most seminal sets. The album itself soared to the top of the R&B charts and reached respectably into the pop charts as well—an astonishing feat for such a politically-charged LP. The album's rise was made especially bittersweet as vocalist Abiodun Oyewole was sent to prison for robbery.

Pulling out the primal vocal essences that would later lie just in the background of any great funk song, and bringing them straight to the front, the Last Poets layered street poetry and manifesto over sparse instrumentation and tribal beats. But, in so doing, they created a unique landscape that reflected a pure passion for sound, for words, for the revolution of education. It was a formula to which rap would later owe an enormous debt. From beginning to end, it would be easy to label this album simply spoken word. But it is testament to the brilliance of the Last Poets that it also becomes so much more. This is perhaps best heard in the outstanding opener "Run, Nigger." As Oyewole laid his poetry across spare percussion, the stage was set for a vocal subtext which allowed poetry to become song as voices became instruments. This opener set the tone for the rest of the album, as the Last Poets utilized the same construction with subtle variations across other gems: "Niggers Are Scared of Revolution," "New York, New York," and "When the Revolution Comes." At no time does *The Last Poets* falter or fail to please. And perhaps, more importantly, it will always be as vital, alive, and fresh as it was the day it was recorded. —*Amy Hanson*

This Is Madness / 1971 / Get Back ✦✦✦✦✦
A legendary set featuring a group of extremely controversial street poets. The Last Poets used offensive language brilliantly, talked in graphic detail about America's social and racial failures, and helped expose a wider audience to the sentiments of the '70s black nationalists. They were the forerunners of today's Afro-centric rappers, and also showed the way to a jazz/rap union now being explored on both sides of the Atlantic. This has been reissued on CD. —*Ron Wynn*

Chastisement / 1972 / Charly ✦✦✦
Along with Gil Scott-Heron, the Last Poets' role in the creation of rap music cannot be overstated, although their 1972 album *Chastisement* also demonstrates that historical importance does not guarantee universal accessibility. Definitely not easy listening in any sense of the term, *Chastisement* presents lengthy diatribes set to stripped-down arrangements of conga, bass, and sax, creating a style which one song title dubs "Jazzoetry." The Last Poets' Afro-centric themes are often reverse-racist, but there's no denying the power and intelligence behind such material as "Before the White Man Came," which offers this closing glimpse of regretful culpability: "and now it's been 400 years since that eventful day/but if we had known what they had in mind/they all would have died in the bay/so now we are paying for our mistake/with only ourselves to blame/with memories of the good old years/before the white man came." "Black Soldier" assumes a similar position, merging a mock-marching chant with an anti-Vietnam tirade which

condemns black servicemen for indirectly assisting white oppressors back home in the ghetto. Alarmingly prophetic, "Black Soldier" simultaneously reviews past civil disturbances and foreshadows those of the future by proclaiming, "their law enforcement will not work/whatever they conspire/will only serve to make us strong/we will fight fire with fire/no that was not a riot/that they saw down in the slums/that was a dress rehearsal/for things that's yet to come." Far less angry, yet no less compelling, is the musical history lecture entitled "Bird's Word," which traces the development of blues and jazz while mentioning dozens of pioneers including Ma Rainey, Max Roach, Betty Carter, and Sun Ra. The inclusion of a lyric sheet might make *Chastisement* easier for some to digest by reading rather than listening, but such an education would be incomplete without experiencing the passion and fury of the Last Poets' seminal performances. — *Vince Ripol*

At Last / 1976 / Blue Thumb ✦✦✦
It was the combination of poetry with almost-frighteningly intense rhythm tracks, mostly done on hand drums, that helped create the Last Poets' reputation for being way ahead of the curve on the entire development of what would come to be called rap music. This album has the feel of an earlier, less-developed session, and the 1976 release date most likely indicates the interest certain record labels might have had in locating any and all projects by these musicians while their fire was blazing so hot. This sounds much more like the typical jazz and poetry project, meaning it is kind of bad—and that word is not used as a hipster might. The poets fall into the same kind of cadences that just about every poet performing with a jazz group has, which include a strained voice in order to be heard above the racket, a rushed sense of pacing trying to fit the words in somewhere between the arco bass doodles and honking sax, and an overall cadence that rises and falls as mechanically as one of Bob Dylan's most disembodied performances. That the poets have something significant to say and that they come up with amusing and even inspiring rhymes from time to time is a given, but there are much better examples of their recorded art. If this was truly recorded three years after the brilliant *This Is Madness*, it reveals the group's focus going fuzzy on them. —*Eugene Chadbourne*

Holy Terror / 1994 / Rykodisc ✦✦✦
With *Holy Terror*, the Last Poets lay their claim to be the originators of hip-hop. Containing some of the Poets' most trenchant political and social lyrics, *Holy Terror* shows the Last Poets, Umar Bin Hassan and Abiodun Oyewole, still as fiery and sharp as ever. "Homesick" and "Pelourinho" are descriptions of slavery that are as vivid and riveting as any movie. "Black Rage" paints a portrait of urban hell that will chill any listener to the bone. The album is also superbly produced, with a funk sound that supports the lyrics while never overshadowing them. Credit is due to seminal producer Bill Laswell, who, armed with a first-class band made up of P-Funk alumni George Clinton, Bootsy Collins, and Bernie Worrell, along with Grandmaster Melle Mel, constructs dense, intricate grooves that are simultaneously modern and traditional. For both fans of the classic Last Poets albums and newcomers interested in one of the missing links between classic funk and modern hip-hop, *Holy Terror* is worth a listen. — *Victor W. Valdivia*

Time Has Come / Apr. 15, 1997 / Mercury ✦✦✦✦
Picking up where *Holy Terror* and Umar Bin Hassan's solo album *Be Bop or Be Dead* left off, *The Time Has Come* is a scalding blend of avant-jazz, bebop and hip-hop, highlighted by cameos from Chuck D and Pharoah Sanders. These two guests may be impressive, but they don't steal the show—they merely demonstrate that the Last Poets are too diverse and way too smart to be pigeonholed into one particular category. Occasionally, the record may be a bit unfocused, and its relentless barrage of avant-poetry may be headache-inducing to some, but few records are as politically powerful and articulate as this. —*Leo Stanley*

Lightnin' Rod

Vocals / Blaxploitation, Old School Rap, Social Commentary, Funk
A former member of the Last Poets, Lightnin' Rod helped pioneer the spoken-rhyme style that would one day become rap. His most renowned album, *Hustler's Convention*, told the story of an ill-fated ghetto "player" and featured backing instrumentation by Kool & the Gang. —*Dan Heilman*

● **Hustler's Convention** / 1973 / Fuel 2000 ✦✦✦
With music by Kool & the Gang, Rod recites a rhyming story of gamblers, pimps, and players. —*Dan Heilman*

Liquid Liquid

f. 1980, New York, NY **db.** 1983
Electro, Post-Punk
The minimalistic funk of New York's Liquid Liquid consisted almost entirely of percussion grooves with a smattering of bass, plus congas, marimba, and the occasional vocal thrown in. The quartet consisted of Scott Hartley (drums, percussion, talking drum), Richard McGuire (bass, percussion, piano, guitar), Salvatore Principato (percussion, vocals), and Dennis Young (percussion, marimba, roto-toms). The band released three EPs during its existence— 1981's *Liquid Liquid* and *Successive Reflexes*, and 1983's *Optimo*. The latter contained the track "Cavern," which became the basis for Grandmaster Flash's "White Lines (Don't Do It)." In 1997, Grand Royal Records released a collection of those three EPs, plus a 1982 performance, *Live From Berkley Square*. —*Steve Huey*

● **Liquid Liquid** / Aug. 11, 1997 / Mo' Wax ✦✦✦✦✦
The angular, bass-propelled funk grooves of Liquid Liquid laid the groundwork for post-rock bands like Tortoise and Ui more than a decade before the fact—stripped of all excess and artifice, their hypnotically dub-like sound offered a starkly minimalist counterpoint to the prevailingly lush production of the concurrent disco movement, in the process impacting the development of everything from hip-hop to drum'n'bass. This superbly packaged 18-track retrospective collects the sum of Liquid Liquid's official output, recorded between 1981 and 1983, and all things considered, it's remarkable just how prescient and modern the group's music really was. Although only the standout, "Cavern" (the basis for the Grandmaster Flash rap classic "White Lines"), is even remotely familiar in any strict sense, the remaining material, with its thickly fluid bass lines and circular rhythms, will undoubtedly strike a chord of recognition in anyone versed in the sonic motifs of post-rock and electronica. Ui's Sasha Frere-Jones is thanked on the sleeve, but in truth he's the one owing the debt—for all intents and purposes, post-rock (and a whole lot more) starts here. —*Jason Ankeny*

L.V.

Vocals / Pop-Rap, Urban, Hip-Hop
Best known as the soulful vocalist assisting Coolio on the smash single "Gangsta's Paradise," L.V. (Large Variety) is perhaps even more remarkable for not only surviving being shot nine times at close range, spending eight months in the hospital and a year and a half in a wheelchair, but for recovering completely and being able to walk without a noticeable limp. L.V. grew up with a father who sang gospel music along with the radio every morning, and this helped to hook him on singing. He won a high school talent contest by performing L.T.D.'s "Concentrate on You," joined the Los Angeles City College choir, and contributed R&B vocals to a neighborhood rap group, the South Central Cartel. Following his success with "Gangsta's Paradise," L.V. landed a fat contract with Tommy Boy Records, which released his debut album, *I Am L.V.*, in late 1995. *How Long* followed five years later. —*Steve Huey*

● **How Long** / Aug. 29, 2000 / Relativity ✦✦✦
It's been years since L.V. brought his substantial vocal ability to Coolio's 1995 monster hit "Gangsta's Paradise." His menacing baritone was the highlight of that single, but on *How Long*, L.V. takes a decidedly smoother approach. While his name, L.V., stands for "large variety," one would think it stood for Luther Vandross after hearing him croon on track after track on *How Long*. The most successful song is the title track, "How Long," which features a catchy chorus and a sharp guitar line. On tracks like "Rain," he seems to try too hard, as he tests his vocal range beyond its limits and the results sound amateurish. As for how long *How Long* will be remembered, it is unlikely to linger in listeners' minds after a few listens, but it may be able to get them through a night or two. —*Jon Azpiri*

Mad Cobra (Ewart Everton Brown)

b. Mar. 31, 1968, Kingston, Jamaica
Vocals / Ragga, Dancehall, Reggae
Ragga DJ Mad Cobra was only 26 years old when he became the first reggae artist to score a number-one hit on the US. *Billboard* pop charts. He was the first dancehall artist to do so and only the second in all of reggae to have that distinction. Born Ewart Everton Brown in Kingston, Jamaica, he was raised in St. Mary's Parish until returning to Kingston in his teens. His nickname came from a character in the G.I. Joe comic books and was given to him by a

school teacher who noticed young Brown's tendency to doodle fearsome snakes all over his notebooks. He got his start with such sound systems as Mighty Ruler, Inner City, and Climax. It was his uncle Delroy "Spiderman" Thompson, an engineer at Tuff Gong, who produced his debut single "Respect Woman" in 1989. More local hits followed and Cobra was then produced by Banton Nelson and Captain Sinbad. In emulation of Ninjaman's dancehall success with gun talk, they steered Cobra toward such titles as "Shoot to Kill" and "Merciless Bad Boy." They soon garnered him a devoted following on the dancehall circuit and led him to sign to Donovan Germain's Penthouse studio, where he had even more hits with such Dave Kelly-produced singles as "Yush" and "Gunderlero." He teamed up with Beres Hammond to record "Feeling Lonely" and in 1991 had a major hit with the album *Bad Boy Talk*. During this time, the dancehall market was nearly flooded with Mad Cobra singles. He was a hardcore DJ at that time and was controversial for promoting gay bashing in such songs as "Crucifixion," long before Buju Banton and Shabba Ranks gained similar notoriety. Homophobic lyrics on the albums *Spotlight* and *Exclusive* led to their being pulled from the shelves in the U.S. By 1991, Cobra's popularity had spread to the U.K. and in one year he had five number-one hits on the country's reggae charts and at one time had nine Top 20 hits on the British charts. Cobra has frequently worked with other artists, including Bee Cat, Mafia & Fluxy, and Fashion. But though known for his hardcore lyrics, Cobra didn't have his big U.S. success until he softened up and recorded the buttery smooth "Flex," which he recorded over a Jamaican version of the Temptations' '60s hit "Just My Imagination." The song's success led him to sign with the U.S. label Columbia. His next single, "Legacy" (both songs appear on his Columbia album *Hard to Wet, Easy to Dry*), did little on the charts and he soon went back to the Jamaican dance halls, laying low until 1993, when he returned to energetic reggae music with such songs as "Mek Noise" and "Matie Haffi Move." —*Sandra Brennan*

Exclusive Decision / Jun. 1996 / VP ♦♦♦
Though it occasionally dips into political rhetoric, Mad Cobra's *Exclusive Decision* is more or less a party album, driven by his infectious toasting. Since it is a party album that means, of course, that there is a fair amount of chaff with the wheat, but the best tracks make the effort worthwhile. —*Leo Stanley*

Sexperience / Jul. 29, 1996 / Critique ♦♦♦♦
This slick dancehall reggae outing from Mad Cobra features the single "Wish You Were Here" as well as remakes of the club hits "Never Gonna Give You Up" and "Dirty Cash." —*Jason Ankeny*

Milkman / Sep. 17, 1996 / Capitol ♦♦♦
Joined by producers Salaam Remi, Tiny Dofat, Clifton "Specialist" Dillon and Dave Kelley, Mad Cobra continues in the explicit vein of his hit "Flex (Time to Have Sex)" on this banal light reggae outing, which includes "Big Long John" and "Sting Night," recorded with Ninja-Man. —*Jason Ankeny*

Methods of Mayhem

Rap-Metal, Alternative Metal, Heavy Metal, Hard Rock
Rap-metal combo Methods of Mayhem was formed by frontman Tommy Lee after quitting his drumming duties in Mötley Crüe. Born Thomas Lee Bass on October 3, 1962, in Athens, Greece, he grew up in Los Angeles, cofounding the band Christmas with bassist Nikki Sixx in 1981; with the subsequent additions of guitarist Mick Mars and singer Vince Neil, the group was renamed Mötley Crüe and immediately became a top attraction on the local hard rock scene. Signing to Elektra in 1983, the Crüe emerged as one of the best-selling and most notorious metal bands of the era, scoring a series of hit albums including 1985's *Theatre of Pain*, 1987's *Girls, Girls, Girls*, and 1989's *Dr. Feelgood*; famed for their glamorously excessive off-stage antics as much as their music itself, Lee in particular became steady tabloid fodder in 1986 with his marriage to *Dynasty* vixen Heather Locklear, a tumultuous relationship that ended in divorce eight years later.

Even as Mötley Crüe's fortunes waned, Lee remained in the limelight thanks to his 1995 marriage to pin-up Pamela Anderson, a union that produced two children as well as an infamous homemade sex video, which became a bestseller. Run-ins with the law were also common: in 1997, he and Sixx were arrested after encouraging fans to rush the stage during a concert stop in Phoenix, and a year later Lee was arraigned for assaulting a photographer. Most scandalously, in May 1998, he was sentenced to six months in jail for assaulting Anderson, although the two later reunited. He left Mötley Crüe in 1999, collaborating with rapper TiLo on Methods of

Mayhem, an all-star project featuring input from Limp Bizkit's Fred Durst, the Crystal Method, Kid Rock, Snoop Dogg, and Mix Master Mike. Signing to MCA, Methods of Mayhem issued their self-titled debut LP in late 1999. —*Jason Ankeny*

● **Methods of Mayhem** / Dec. 7, 1999 / MCA ♦♦♦
Tommy Lee's first project since leaving Mötley Crüe in mid-1999, Methods of Mayhem's self-titled debut album lands squarely in the rap-metal camp, an area the Crüe never ventured into even for all its stylistic shifting of the mid-to late-'90s. But while the sounds are different, the Crüe's party-hardy sensibility remains, albeit filtered through the adolescent humor of groups like Limp Bizkit. The record can't help but feel somewhat calculating in its contemporary production, as though Lee sometimes tries too hard to sound hip; that's further confirmed by the otherwise impressive array of guest stars, including Kid Rock, Snoop Dogg, the Crystal Method, Lil' Kim, Limp Bizkit's Fred Durst, George Clinton, and Beastie Boys collaborator Mixmaster Mike, plus production work from Rob Zombie. To be sure, these guests do enliven the proceedings, but it's also easy to see them as having been chosen for maximum popular appeal; moreover, it's difficult for Methods of Mayhem to carve out its own identity, opening up accusations of stylistic bandwagon-jumping. But to Lee's credit, he has made a commercially viable record, which isn't always the case when aging hard rockers try to update their sounds (witness the Scorpions' *Eye II Eye*). So even if the album is far from an unqualified success—it has its share of moments that feel stiff and forced—it's also an album that will find an audience thanks to its catchier tracks, like the lead single "Get Naked." —*Steve Huey*

Mutabaruka (Allan Hope)

b. Dec. 12, 1952, Rae Town, Jamaica
Vocals / Dub Poetry, Political Reggae
His poems have given voice to a nation and helped forge an entirely new genre of music, dub/rhythm poetry. Revolutionary, fiery, scathing, and stinging, Mutabaruka's words are as potent on paper as on CD, and so the literary community needed to create a new term just for his works—meta-dub. Born in Rae Town, Jamaica, on December 12, 1952, Allan Hope first realized the power of the word when he was in his teens. It was the '60s; the Black Power movement was at its height, and numerous radical leaders were putting their thoughts and histories in print. Malcolm X and Eldridge Cleaver formed the roots of Hope's own aspirations, although his initial career choice was far removed from their paths. Leaving school, the young man apprenticed as an electrician, and took a job at the Jamaican Telephone Company. Hope was already writing, however, and in 1971 he quit his job to pursue his craft full time. He moved away from the hustle and bustle of Kingston out to the quiet of the Potosi hills, in the parish of Saint James. Not long after, one of his poems was accepted by *Swing* magazine and from that point on, they would regularly publish his work.

In 1973, Hope formed the band Truth, his first attempt to combine his words with music. By now, the poet had converted to Rastafarianism and taken the name Mutabaruka. Not a word, but a phrase, "mutabaruka" comes from the Rwandan language and translates as "one who is always victorious." Even as roots was taking hold, Truth did not find a following. However, Mutabaruka was finding fans in the literary world after the publication of his collection, *Outcry*, in 1973. The following year brought further recognition with the poem *"Wailin',"* dedicated to Bob Marley, and written around Wailers song titles. Two years later, *Sun and Moon*, a shared volume of poetry with Faybiene, arrived to much acclaim. In 1977, Mutabaruka once again turned to the stage, and gave several live performances. Joined by the nyabinghi-fueled group Light of Saba, the poet recorded a version of his poem "Outcry" the next year, and found himself with a Jamaican hit. Meanwhile, guitarist Earl "Chinna" Smith had launched his own High Times label as a home for deep roots music, and swiftly signed the poet. Mutabaruka's star was rising, and his appearance at the National Stadium in Kingston this same year was a smashing success. Over the next few years, he cut a clutch of singles for High Times, and received even further literary acclaim in 1981 with a new volume of poems, *The Book: First Poems*. That same year, Mutabaruka had a hit with the single "Everytime a Ear De Soun," while their fiery debut at Reggae Sunsplash was captured for posterity for a live album released in 1982. It was this performance that brought Mutabaruka to international attention, and guaranteed his return appearance at the festival over the next two years.

His debut album, *Check It*, released in 1983, was a dubby classic with the poet accompanied by Smith's exquisitely rootsy guitar. The album was remastered and reissued by the RAS label in 2001. The year 1985 saw another successful return to Reggae Sunsplash and a project with the American Heartbeat label, overseeing the compilation of the dub poetry album *Work Sound 'Ave Power: Dub Poets and Dub*. A dub accompaniment followed, remixed by Scientist, along with a second dub poetry set, *Woman Talk: Caribbean Dub Poetry*, this time exclusively featuring women dub and rapso poets. Mutabaruka also struck a distribution deal with the American RAS label, and cemented the partnership with the ferocious *The Mystery Unfolds* album in 1986. Self-produced and featuring a host of guest musicians and vocalists, including Marcia Griffiths and Ini Kamoze, *Mystery* was totally uncompromising. Amidst a host of tough tracks like "Dis Poem," a number meant to puncture not only the listener's expectations but the poet's pretensions as well. One of Mutabaruka's most entertaining, yet thought-provoking poems, it would later be included in the definitive *The Routledge Reader in Caribbean Literature*.

Although neither 1987's *Outcry* nor 1989's *Any Which Way . . . Freedom* was quite as radically revolutionary as *Mystery*, Mutabaruka was quickly establishing himself as both a literary and musical giant, both in Jamaica and abroad. His Reggae Sunsplash appearances in 1987 and 1988 were highly anticipated, and did not disappoint. And while Mutabaruka continued to produce or coproduce his albums, he also occasionally cut singles for other producers, including the hard-hitting "Great Kings of Africa" for Gussie Clarke, which paired him with Dennis Brown. The *Blakk Wi Blak . . . K . . . K* album appeared in 1991, overseen jointly by the poet and Earl "Chinna" Smith, and featured a follow-up to "Kings," "Great Queens of Afrika," with guest vocalists Sharon Forrester and Ini Kamoze. It was a stellar album filled with tough talk, including the scathing "Ecology Poem" and the equally biting "People's Court." That latter number was followed up on Mutabaruka's equally excellent album, *Melanin Man*, which also boasted the stunning "Garvey." That arrived in 1994, by which time the poet had performed at three more Reggae Sunsplash festivals in 1991, 1993, and 1994; he'd return in both 1995 and 1996. The year 1994 also saw the launch of Mutabaruka's own Jamaican radio show on the IRIE-FM station. It was wildly popular, but ironically enough that station banned his song "People's Court" from the airwaves. Two years later, the poet scored a pair of Jamaican hits, both cut for the Exterminator label. "Wise Up" paired Mutabaruka with DJ Sugar Minott, while "Psalms 24" saw him in collaboration with the deeply religious DJ Luciano. The year 1996 also brought two albums in its wake, *Muta in Dub* and *Gathering of the Spirits*, the latter a spectacular recreation of the roots era, boasting a host of roots stars from the Mighty Diamonds, Sly & Robbie, Culture, and Marcia Griffiths amongst them. That same year, Mutabaruka toured Ethiopia with Tony Rebel, Yasus Afari, and Uton Green. *—Jo-Ann Greene*

● **The Ultimate Collection** / 1996 / Shanachie ◆◆◆◆
In 1996, Shanachie looked back on Mutabaruka's Shanachie output with *The Ultimate Collection*. The title is an exaggeration, and the CD is hardly the last word on Muta's work at Shanachie. In fact, some essential gems are missing—including "Blacks in America," "Angola Invasion" and *Outcry's* title song—so when these absences are taken into consideration, you realize just how lofty a title *The Ultimate Collection* is. All that said, this collection has a lot going for it. Drawing on *Melanin Man, Any Which Way Freedom, The Mystery Unfolds* and other albums, *The Ultimate Collection* contains such familiar gems as "Bun Dung Babylon," "Walking on Gravel" and "Witeman Country." But instead of offering the well-known studio version of "Witeman Country," Shanachie provides an exciting live version from 1989. The Ultimate Collection doesn't tell the whole story where Muta is concerned, but even so, it paints a compelling picture of the angrily socio-political dub poet. *—Alex Henderson*

Jason Nevins

b. 1970, New York, NY
Producer / Club/Dance, Hip-Hop
Cut-and-paste mixmaster Jason Nevins was born in New York City in 1970; he began DJing while working at his college radio station at Arizona State University, and upon returning to the East Coast began creating his first remixes. After producing a handful of compilation tracks, he issued his self-titled debut EP in 1994, followed in 1995 by the full-length *Green*. Remixes

for Janet Jackson and Lil' Kim followed before Nevins rocketed to international fame in 1997 with his mix of the Run-D.M.C. classic "It's Like That," which topped pop charts across Europe on its way to selling over three million copies. Much of Nevins' subsequent work also reflected his love for '80s hits, with reworkings of Run-D.M.C.'s "It's Tricky" and Rob Base's "It Takes Two" as well as Falco's "Der Kommissar" and Toni Basil's "Mickey" appearing soon after. *—Jason Ankeny*

Ozomatli

Rock en Español, Latin, Worldbeat
Brewing a vital concoction of Latin salsa, urban hip-hop, and jazz-funk, Ozomatli formed in Los Angeles in the mid-'90s with a lineup including Raúl "El Bully" Pacheco, Ulises Bella, Jiro Yamaguchi, Jose "Crunchy" Espinosa, Cut Chemist, Wil-Dog, William "Echo" Marrufo, Pablo Castorena, Justin "Niño" Porée, Asdru Sierra, and Chali 2na. After making their name on the local club circuit, the group made an appearance on the urban late-night talk show *Vibe!* and released their self-titled debut in June. Cut Chemist has also recorded as a solo act for Ubiquity. *—John Bush*

● **Ozomatli** / Jun. 16, 1998 / Almo Sounds ◆◆◆◆
Like many late '90s outfits, the Los Angeles-based Ozomatli is an eclectic conglomeration, fusing a wild variety of musics. At its core, the group is a dance band, blending funk, hip-hop, Latin rhythms, jazz, salsa, reggae, Tejano and worldbeat into its sound. It's a busy, heady mix and occasionally there's simply too much going on in the mix for it to be easy to digest. Nevertheless, it's easy to admire a group that challenges the listeners and Ozomatli certainly do that with their eponymous debut album. Not only is the music dense and exciting, but the lyrics are politically-charged and daring, adding substance to the infectious music. The result is an album that is both entertaining and rewarding—not a bad achievement for a debut. *—Stephen Thomas Erlewine*

Embrace the Chaos / Sep. 11, 2001 / Interscope ◆◆◆◆
Not many people heard Ozomatli's 1998 debut, but those who did loved its fearless blend of hip-hop, Latin rhythms, jazz, and rock. There was a long wait between that record and its 2001 successor, *Embrace the Chaos*, and while that prolonged gestation period may have not resulted in a radical new direction for the collective, it did give them time to grow. They're still working from the same basic template, but their results are richer and fuller than before, as their various influences come together seamlessly. In other words, they sound more themselves then ever, and while that still might bring them to a larger audience, those who do bother to seek this out—especially those who find classic Latin jazz as intoxicating as alternative hip-hop—will find this to be a thoroughly engaging, distinctive listen. *—Stephen Thomas Erlewine*

Shep Pettibone

DJ, Producer / House, Dance-Pop
Although best known for his work in association with Madonna, producer and remixer Shep Pettibone first emerged during the early '80s as a force in hip-hop; with Arthur Baker, he was responsible for Afrika Bambaataa and the Jazzy Five's influential "Jazzy Sensation," and concurrent with the rise of scratching and other turntable innovations created KISS-FM's "mastermixes." By the mid-'80s, Pettibone was in hot demand, producing and remixing tracks for such dance-pop innovators as the Pet Shop Boys and New Order; his most successful collaboration, however, was with Madonna, for whom he produced a series of hits, including "Vogue," "Causing a Commotion," and "Justify My Love." *—Jason Ankeny*

● **KISS-FM Presents Shep Pettibone's Mastermixes** / 1982 / Prelude ◆◆◆◆
If you lived in or around New York in the early '80s, one of the main reasons to listen to KISS-FM (a major urban contemporary station that shouldn't be confused with L.A.'s KIIS-FM) was Shep Pettibone, whose remixes of R&B, funk, hip-hop, and disco hits did their part to earn the station its high ratings. In fact, one could say that Pettibone was as important to KISS-FM as Frankie Crocker (one of New York's top R&B DJs in the 1970s and 1980s) was to WBLS-FM, KISS' main competitor in the New York market at the time. In 1982, Prelude sought to cash in on Pettibone's popularity by releasing *Mastermixes*, which boasts his dance remixes of such early-'80s hits as D-Train's "You're the One for Me," Unlimited Touch's "Searchin' to Find the One," Sharon Redd's "Can You Handle It," Jeanette "Lady" Day's "Come Let Me Love

You," and Secret Weapon's "Must Be the Music." This two-LP set enjoyed its greatest sales around the Northeastern Corridor, but one didn't have to be close to the Big Apple to appreciate hearing Pettibone do his thing on France Joli's "Gonna Get Over You," Gayle Adams' "Love Fever," or the Strikers' "Body Music." Unfortunately, *Mastermixes* has long been out of print, and Prelude won't be the label to reissue it on CD because the company folded in the 1980s. So if you come across a copy somewhere, grab it immediately. —*Alex Henderson*

Quarashi

f. Iceland

Rap-Rock, Alternative Metal

Though Icelandic rap-rock outfit Quarashi finally saw their U.S. debut released in early 2002, the band had been honing its music since the mid-'90s. Producer/drummer Sölvi Blondal and vocalists/rappers Hössi Olafsson, Steini Fjelsted (a former Icelandic skating champion as well as a graffiti artist), and Omar Swarez formed Quarashi (pronounced "kwa-ra'-she") in 1996. The band's name, a term meaning "supernatural," was adopted from a nickname given to Fjelsted. The quartet's full-length debut was recorded in October of 1997. In support of the album, the band opened for the Fugees and the Prodigy, while Blondal remixed the Prodigy's "Diesel Power." In 1999, Quarashi released *Xeneizes*, selling another 6,000 copies and earning them a second consecutive gold record in Iceland. *Jinx*, Quarashi's U.S. debut, was released in March 2002. The first single, "Stick 'Em Up," was included on the *Orange County* soundtrack. —*Kenyon Hopkin*

● **Jinx** / Mar. 12, 2002 / Columbia ♦♦♦

With cutting-edge artists such as Sigur Ros and Bjork coming out of Iceland, the last thing you'd expect from the remote country is a rap-rock band. Quarashi is straight from the Rage Against the Machine/Beastie Boys school of thought, though there is enough diversity on *Jinx* to keep things unpredictable. The quartet leans more toward three MCs and one DJ than a hard rock band with rappers and flogging guitars, while beats alternate between drum machine and live percussion. Only occasionally does the band embark into big metal riffs, like on the wild "Copycat." Elsewhere there are hints of reggae ("Weirdo") and even traces of the band's origin in Iceland ("Tarfur" is the only song with Icelandic vocals). For a band who programs most of its music, *Jinx* comes across sounding energetically organic. Definitely the kind of testosterone-fueled rock to which kids will want to wreck things. —*Kenyon Hopkin*

Rage Against the Machine

f. 1991

Rap-Metal, Alternative Metal, Heavy Metal, Alternative Pop/Rock

Rage Against the Machine earned acclaim from disenfranchised fans (and not insignificant derision from critics) for their bombastic, fiercely polemical music, which brewed sloganeering leftist rants against corporate America, cultural imperialism, and government oppression into a Molotov cocktail of punk, hip-hop, and thrash. Rage formed in Los Angeles in the early '90s out of the wreckage of a number of local groups: vocalist Zack de la Rocha (the son of Chicano political artist Beto) emerged from the bands Headstance, Farside, and Inside Out; guitarist Tom Morello (the nephew of Jomo Kenyatta, the first Kenyan president) originated in Lock Up; and drummer Brad Wilk played with future Pearl Jam frontman Eddie Vedder. Rounded out by bassist Tim Bob (aka Tim C., born Tim Commerford), a childhood friend of de la Rocha's, Rage debuted in 1992 with a self-released, self-titled 12-song cassette featuring the song "Bullet in the Head," which became a hit when reissued as a single later in the year.

The tape won the band a deal with Epic, and their leap to the majors did not go unnoticed by detractors, who questioned the revolutionary integrity of Rage Against the Machine's decision to align itself with the label's parent company, media behemoth Sony. Undeterred, the quartet emerged in late 1992 with their eponymous official debut, which scored the hits "Killing in the Name" and "Bombtrack." After touring with *Lollapalooza* and declaring their support of groups like FAIR (Fairness and Accuracy in Reporting), Rock for Choice, and Refuse & Resist, Rage spent a reportedly tumultuous four years working on their follow-up; despite rumors of a breakup, they returned in 1996 with *Evil Empire*, which entered the U.S. album charts at number one and scored a hit single with "Bulls on Parade." During 1997, the group joined

forces with hip-hop supergroup the Wu-Tang Clan for a summer tour and remained active in support of various leftist political causes, including a controversial 1999 benefit concert for death-row inmate Mumia Abu-Jamal. *The Battle of Los Angeles* followed later in 1999, also debuting at number one and going double platinum by the following summer. In early 2000, de la Rocha announced plans for a solo project, and the band performed an incendiary show outside the Democratic National Convention in August. The following month, bassist Commerford was arrested for disorderly conduct at MTV's Video Music Awards following his bizarre disruption of a Limp Bizkit acceptance speech, in which he climbed to the top of a 15-foot set piece and rocked back and forth. Plans for a live album were announced shortly thereafter, but in October, de la Rocha abruptly announced his departure from the band, citing breakdowns in communication and group decision making.

Surprised but not angry, the remainder of Rage announced plans to continue with a new vocalist, while de la Rocha refocused on his solo album, which was slated to include collaborations with acclaimed hip-hop artists including El-P of Company Flow. December 2000 saw the release of de la Rocha's final studio effort with the band, the Rick Rubin-produced *Renegades*; it featured nearly a dozen covers of hip-hop, rock, and punk artists like Afrika Bambaataa, Bruce Springsteen, Devo, the Rolling Stones, and more. —*Jason Ankeny*

● **Rage Against the Machine** / Nov. 3, 1992 / Epic ♦♦♦♦♦

The first album to successfully merge the amazingly disparate sounds of rap and heavy metal, Rage Against the Machine's self-titled debut was groundbreaking enough when it was released, and many would argue that its importance and influence remains unchallenged and unsurpassed to this day. The living embodiment of this culture clash, guitar wizard Tom Morello fuses his roots in '80s metal-style shredding with an unprecedented array of six-string acrobatics and rhythmic special effects, most of which no one has even tried to imitate. And from vocalist Zack de la Rocha, the group receives the meaningful rhymes and emotionally charged delivery that white-boy metal could never hope to achieve. Still, despite the unique elements upon which they are built, songs like "Bombtrack," "Take the Power Back," and "Know Your Enemy" are immediately memorable, surprisingly straightforward slabs of hard rock. And one need not look further than the main riff of the venomous "Wake Up"—lifted straight out of Zeppelin's "Kashmir"—for conclusive proof of Morello's influences. Even more impressive is the group's talent for injecting slowly mounting tension into such highlights as "Settle for Nothing" and "Bullet in the Head," both of which finally explode with awesome power and rage. In contrast, the band manages to convey their message with even more urgency through stubborn repetition, as seen on "Freedom" and their signature track, "Killing in the Name." With its relentlessly rebellious mantra of, "F*ck you, I won't do what you tell me," the song is a rallying cry of frightening proportions and the unequivocal climax of their vision. A stunning debut that remains absolutely essential. —*Ed Rivadavia*

Evil Empire / Apr. 1996 / Epic ♦♦♦♦

Rage Against the Machine spent four years making their second album, *Evil Empire*. As the title suggests, their rage and contempt for the "fascist" capitalist system in America hadn't declined in the nearly half-decade they were away. Their musical approach didn't change, either. Lead vocalist Zach de la Rocha is caught halfway between the militant raps of Chuck D and the fanatical ravings of a street preacher, shouting out his simplistic, libertarian slogans over the sonically dense assault of the band. Since the band didn't perform together much after 1993, there isn't a collective advance in their musicianship. Nevertheless, guitarist Tom Morello demonstrates an impressive palette of sound, creating new textures in heavy metal, which is quite difficult. Even with Morello's studied virtuosity, the band sounds leaden, lacking the dexterity to fully execute their metal/hip/hop fusion—they don't get into a groove; they simply pound. But that happens to fit the hysterical ravings of de la Rocha. Though his dedication to decidedly left-wing politics is admirable, his arhythmic phrasing and grating shouting cancel out any message he is trying to make. And that means *Evil Empire* succeeds only on the level of a sonic assault. —*Stephen Thomas Erlewine*

The Battle of Los Angeles / Nov. 2, 1999 / Epic ♦♦♦♦

Rage Against the Machine isn't really the only metal band that matters, but their aggressive social and political activism is refreshing, especially in an age of blind (or usually self-directed) rage due to groups like Limp Bizkit, Bush, or Nine Inch Nails. Recorded in less than a month, *The Battle of Los*

Angeles is the most focused album of the band's career, exploding from the gate and rarely letting go the whole way through. Like a few other famous revolution-in-the-head bands (most notably Minor Threat), Rage Against the Machine has always been blessed by the fact that the band is spewing just as much vitriol as its frontman. Any potential problems created here by Zack de la Rocha's one-note delivery and extremist polemics are smoothed over by songs and grooves that make it sound like the revolution really *is* here, from the single "Guerrilla Radio" to album highlights like "Mic Check," "Calm Like a Bomb," and "Born of a Broken Man." As on the previous two Rage Against the Machine albums, Tom Morello's roster of guitar effects and vicious riffs are nigh overpowering, and are as contagious as the band has ever been since their debut. De la Rocha is best when he has specific targets (like the government or the case against *Mumia Abu Jamal*), but when he attempts to cover more general societal problems, he falters. If anything less than one of the most talented and fiery bands in the music world were backing him, *The Battle of Los Angeles* wouldn't be nearly as high-rated as it is. —*John Bush*

Renegades / Dec. 5, 2000 / Epic ◆◆◆◆
Rush released after the late-2000 split between Zack de la Rocha and the rest of Rage Against the Machine, the covers album *Renegades* salutes the band's musical and philosophical roots, ranging from the old school Bronx to the hard-rockin' Motor City to protest-central Greenwich Village to gangsta-ridden L.A. As could be expected, the set works best when the group focuses on material from its most recent forebears: rappers and hardcore bands. Indeed, *Renegades* begins with a pair of powerful hip-hop covers—Eric B & Rakim's "Microphone Fiend" and Volume 10's "Pistol Grip Pump"—that spotlight Rage's immense strengths: Tom Morello's clean, heavy riffing and vocalist de la Rocha's finely tuned spray of vitriol, just this side of self-righteous. Another hip-hop blast (and the one closest to home), Cypress Hill's "How I Could Just Kill a Man," is even more devastating, an easy pick for the highlight of the album. Listeners familiar with the originals, however, may have trouble with Rage's covers of EPMD's "I'm Housin'," the Stones' "Street Fighting Man," and Dylan's "Maggie's Farm," a trio of original versions whose anger and emotion were conveyed more in the lyrics than the performances. Still, drummer Brad Wilk sets an appropriately frenetic hardcore tempo for the excellent version of Minor Threat's "In My Eyes," and de la Rocha stretches out well on the MC5's "Kick Out the Jams." With just a bare few excepions, *Renegades* works well, in part because Rage Against the Machine is both smart enough to change very little and talented enough to make the songs its own. —*John Bush*

Shabba Ranks (Rexton Rawlston Fernando Gordon)

b. Jan. 17, 1966, Sturgetown, Jamaica
Vocals / Raggae, Dancehall, Club/Dance
During the '90s, Shabba Ranks was the reigning king of reggae-rap, a combination of Jamaican dancehall and New York hip-hop filled with X-rated slack lyrics. As a performer, Shabba is known for his high energy hypersexual shows. With unabashed ambition to become a trendsetter, sex symbol, and innovator of Jamaican music, Shabba Ranks does not shy away from blatant commercialism in his music, and is more interested in providing listeners with a good time than raising their consciousness.

Born Rexton Rawlston Fernando Gordon in the hilly countryside of St. Ann's Parish, Shabba spent much of his youth growing up amidst the violence of West Kingston. Early inspirations included DJs such as Charlie Chaplin and Yellowman, but his idol was DJ Josey Wales. Blessed with a powerful baritone voice and a knack for rhyme, Shabba started out at age 14 during the early '80s. At first he performed under the name Co-Pilot, which appeared on his first single "Heat Under Sufferer's Feet." Later he chose Shabba after two gangsters with the same name died. Shabba did not begin to make a real name for himself until the mid-'80s after he began working with some of Jamaica's biggest producers. His unpredictable energy on and off stage made him a hit on the dancehall circuit and soon Shabba was in demand all over the West Indies. Soon he even eclipsed Yellowman, Ninjaman, and Johnny P as the biggest DJ around with such hits as "Roots and Culture," "Live Blanket," and his smash single, "Wicked inna Bed." Between 1989 and 1991, Shabba released 50 singles and has since toured Europe, Asia, and the U.S. He is particularly popular in Japan and in England where two of his albums, *Golden Touch* and *Rappin' with the Ladies*, earned him a six-figure income. In the early '90s, he made a three-album deal with Epic/Sony. He has

had considerable crossover success with three Top Ten R&B hits—"House Call (You Body Can't Lie to Me)," "Mr. Lover Man," and "Slow and Sexy"—as well as several other minor hits, the majority of them collected on the 1999 retrospective *Shabba and Friends*. —*Sandra Brennan*

Rappin' With the Ladies / 1988 / VP ◆◆◆◆
Shabba Ranks' career has focused on singles, including several on which he collaborated with other male DJs. *Rappin' With the Ladies*, in contrast, is a full album of songs by J.C. Lodge, Deborah Glasgow, and others reconceived as showcases for Shabba. The first track is "Telephone Love Deh Pon Mi Mind," a sequel to Lodge's "Telephone Love" constructed from the original. While this new version features studio remixing, the other new tracks rely on Shabba's presence alone to create a fresh sound. He comes through on "Mr. Loverman," a version of Glasgow's "Champion Lover." When Glasgow implores her lover "don't ease up tonight," Shabba answers her in a pulsating vocal delivery that heightens the power of the rhythm track. "Hardcore Loving" also makes good use of his presence to fill out the sound of Lodge's "Selfish Lover," and the remaining tracks follow this pattern. Shabba's sexual ability is the usual theme, of course, but the duet format forces a lyrical emphasis on intimacy and collaboration that is not typical in his solo work. That makes for a winning display of Shabba's talent, and with full-sounding production courtesy of Music Works, this disc offers consistent pleasures for dancehall fans throughout its generous length. —*John Gonsalves*

● **As Raw as Ever** / 1991 / Epic ◆◆◆◆◆
When dubwise (often described as reggae's equivalent of rap) evolved into dancehall in the 1980s, Shabba Ranks became one of the style's leaders. Most dancehall has come out on small independent labels, but in the early '90s, Epic saw how popular it had become and signed Ranks. Hard-edged, abrasive and tough, *As Raw as Ever* thrives on rhythm for its own sake. Listening to such cuts as "Gun Pon Me" and "Fist-A-Ris," one can hear the impact that classic dubwise artists like I-Roy, U-Roy, King Tubby and Big Youth had on dancehall. But while those greats could be very melodic, Ranks usually has little or no use for melody or harmony. Ranks is joined by artists ranging from rapper KRS-1 to reggae/pop singer Maxi Priest on this generally enjoyable, although limited, disc. —*Alex Henderson*

Rough & Ready, Vol. 1 / Jul. 14, 1992 / Epic ◆◆◆◆◆
Shabba Ranks kept the slack dancehall coming with this follow-up to *As Raw As Ever*. His thick, patois-laced delivery scored a pop hit with "Mr. Loverman," and a song that basically defined the CD. If you didn't get it the first time around, you sure understood it after hearing "Bad & Wicked," "Ca'an Dun," and "Gal Yuh' Good," among others. —*Ron Wynn*

X-tra Naked / Oct. 6, 1992 / Epic ◆◆◆◆◆
Shabba Ranks landed another pop hit on his third album to hit the charts over a two-year span. "Slow And Sexy" peaked at 33, providing ample momentum for another collection of sex cuts and come-ons. Ranks did include "Rude Boy" and "Two Breddrens," but otherwise, the focus stayed completely in the bedroom. —*Ron Wynn*

No Competition / 1993 / Critique ◆◆◆
DJ/toaster Shabba Ranks enrages reggae traditionalists and delights contemporary dancehall audiences with his fast-paced, sexually explicit commentary and quips. This 14-song set included not only Ranks but several other equally sassy dancehall stars such as Cocoa Tea, Laddy G, Deborah Glasgow, Cutty Ranks, Snagga, Krystal, E.T. and less suggestive veterans J.C. Lodge and the great Freddie McGregor. Ranks teamed with different performers on most cuts. Other than Cutty Ranks' hard-hitting "Wealth," there wasn't much sociopolitical material on this session. Instead, it was a showcase for dancehall, offering fans a primer of styles, sounds and themes. —*Ron Wynn*

Rough & Ready, Vol. 2 / 1993 / Epic ◆◆◆
Yet another sex-heavy dancehall collection from Shabba Ranks, whose superlewd material rivals the pedantic ramblings of X Clan and other Islamic/Afro-centric rappers in its utter lack of thematic variety. Not only were almost all the songs alike, but Ranks seemed like he was recycling the raps and beats as well. —*Ron Wynn*

A Mi Shabba / 1995 / Epic ◆◆◆
A nice mid-'90s release from Shabba Ranks, the defending champion of dancehall at the time. The fare is relatively standard, with some level of gun talk and slackness involved as a common motif. The more notable thing associated with Ranks is the re-elevation of the reggae DJ in the production

of sound. Relatively surprisingly, given the heavy levels of cameo appearances employed by his rivals, Ranks only makes use of three supporting vocalists, all from within the dancehall tradition. He enlisted some of the best as far as production is concerned as well, with the vast majority of the tracks produced (and played) by Sly and Robbie, and a couple of spare ones guest produced by Naughty By Nature and Puffy Combs (prior to his real dosage of fame). Not a bad dancehall album at all, heavily infused with hip-hop grooves here and there. For fans of contemporary dancehall (at a relatively low speed), this album should be worthwhile to listen to. —*Adam Greenberg*

● **Greatest Hits** / Aug. 7, 2001 / Epic/Legacy ◆◆◆◆◆
Sony Legacy dipped into the archives and pulled out a fistful of Ranks' most popular cuts for this compilation. Culled from the five albums the DJ recorded for Epic between 1991 and 1995, *Greatest Hits* is obviously aimed at American fans. There again, the label gave Ranks an incredibly long leash, allowing him to record in Jamaica with the island's hottest producers and rhythm teams, and the artist repaid the favor by refusing to compromise his rough and ready style one iota for an international audience. And thus his reputation remained unsullied at home and abroad. The 16 cuts featured here provide an excellent overview of Ranks' music, from his early raggamuffin days to his later conversion to more cultural concerns. The DJ's initial breakout came via a series of pairings with singers, including J.C. Lodge on her international smash "Telephone Love." A clutch of those collaborations appear here, notably with Mykal Rose on the hit "Shine Eye Gal," Maxi Priest on "Housecall," Chevell Franklin for "Mr. Loverman," and Cocoa Tea and DJ Home T on "Pirate Anthem." As the album is not chronological, it's difficult to chart Ranks' progress, but the varied lyrical themes signposts the way. From the conquesting hero of "Wicked in Bed" and "Bad and Wicked," albeit often with tongue in cheek, as on "Trailer Load a Girls," to the more thoughtful "Rough Life" and "Roots & Culture," on which he defends his toasts, the DJ connected with Jamaican dancehall crowds and eventually the world. This compilation shows precisely why. —*Jo-Ann Greene*

The Red Hot Chili Peppers

f. 1983

College Rock, Funk Metal, Alternative Pop/Rock
Few rock groups of the '80s broke down as many musical barriers and were as original as the Red Hot Chili Peppers. Creating an intoxicating new musical style by combining funk and punk rock together (with an explosive stage show, to boot), the Chili Peppers spawned a slew of imitators in their wake, but still managed to be the leaders of the pack by the dawn of the 21st century. The roots of the band lay in a friendship forged by three school chums, Anthony Kiedis, Michael Balzary, and Hillel Slovak, while they attended Fairfax High School in California back in the late '70s/early '80s. While Balzary and Slovak showed great musical promise (on trumpet and guitar, respectively), Kiedis focused on poetry and acting during his high school career. During this time, Slovak taught Balzary how to play bass, while the duo encouraged Kiedis to start putting his poetry to music, which he soon did. Influenced heavily by the burgeoning L.A. punk scene (the Germs, Black Flag, Fear, Minutemen, X, etc.) as well as funk (Parliament/Funkadelic, Sly & the Family Stone, etc.), the trio began to rehearse with another friend, drummer Jack Irons, leading to the formation of Tony Flow and the Miraculously Majestic Masters of Mayhem, a group that played strip bars along the Sunset Strip during the early '80s. It was during this time that the quartet honed their sound and live act (as they stumbled across a stage gimmick that would soon become their trademark—performing on stage completely naked, except for a tube sock covering a certain part of their anatomy). By 1983, Balzary had begun to go by the name Flea, and the group changed their name to the Red Hot Chili Peppers.

Word spread quickly about the up-and-coming band, resulting in a recording contract with EMI. But before the Chili Peppers could begin work on their debut, Flea and Kiedis were dealt a disappointing blow when both Slovak and Irons announced that they were leaving to focus more on another band they were in, What Is This. With replacement members Jack Sherman (guitar) and Cliff Martinez (bass) filling in, the Peppers released their self-titled debut in 1984. But the absence of the two original members showed, as the album failed to capture the excitement of their live show. While the album didn't set the world on fire sales-wise, the group began to build a dedicated underground following with college radio buffs. By 1985, *What Is This* was kaput (after issuing a single self-titled album), as Slovak

and Irons returned back to the Peppers, resulting in the George Clinton-produced *Freaky Styley*. While the album was an improvement over its predecessor, it still lacked the fire of the band's in-concert experience, a problem that would finally be solved with their next album, 1987's *The Uplift Mofo Party Plan*. The album was the group's first to make an impression on the charts, and they followed it up a year later with the stopgap five-track release, *The Abbey Road EP*, in 1988. But just as the world was warming up to the Peppers, tragedy struck when Slovak died from a heroin overdose on June 25, 1988.

In the wake of Slovak's death, Irons left the group for the second and final time, while Kiedis (who was also battling drug addiction at the time) and Flea decided to soldier on. After a new lineup consisting of former Parliament guitarist Blackbird McKnight and former Dead Kennedys drummer D.H. Peligro didn't work out, the duo found worthy replacements in newcomers John Frusciante and Chad Smith. The new-look Chili Peppers hit pay dirt straight away, as their first album together, 1989's *Mother's Milk*, became a surprise hit due to MTV's exposure of their videos for a cover of Stevie Wonder's "Higher Ground" and a song about their fallen friend Slovak, "Knock Me Down," as the album was certified gold by early 1990. The group knew that their next release would be the most important one of their career, so they moved into a mansion-turned-recording studio with producer Rick Rubin to work on what would become their most successful release yet, the stripped-down *Blood Sugar Sex Magik* (their first for the Warner Bros. label). The album became a monster hit upon its September 1991 release (going on to eventually sell a staggering seven million copies in the U.S. alone), as it spawned such hits as "Give It Away" and the group's first Top Ten single, "Under the Bridge."

But not all was well in the Chili Peppers camp. Like his predecessor, Frusciante had become addicted to hard drugs, and abruptly left the band mid-tour in early 1992. Undeterred, the band enlisted new member Arik Marshall, and headlined *Lollapalooza II* in the summer. When the band returned to the studio to work on their sixth release overall, it quickly became apparent that Marshall didn't fit in, so he was replaced by Jesse Tobias. But before Tobias could record a note with the group, he was handed his walking papers as well, and former Jane's Addiction guitarist Dave Navarro signed on. After a layoff of four years, the Peppers' much-delayed follow-up to *BSSM* was released in 1995, *One Hot Minute*. While the album was a sizeable hit, it failed to match the success and musical focus of its predecessor. It became apparent during the album's ensuing tour that Navarro wasn't fitting in as well as originally hoped, and he left the band in early 1998.

After Frusciante had left the group, he released a pair of obscure solo releases, 1995's *Niandra Ladies and Usually Just a T-Shirt* and 1997's *Smile From the Streets You Hold*, yet rumors circulated that the guitarist was homeless, penniless, and sickly with a death-defying drug habit. After checking himself into rehab and putting his demons behind him, Frusciante emerged once again refocused and reenergized, and promptly accepted an invitation to rejoin the Peppers once more. The group's reunion album, 1999's *Californication*, proved to be another monster success, reconfirming the Chili Peppers as one of alternative rock's top bands. The band put in a quick guest appearance on Fishbone's *Psychotic Friends Nuttwerx* before hitting the road to support the album. The following months found the band getting involved in bizarre situations and controversies. First, their refusal to play songs from *One Hot Minute* during the tour was an unpopular decision with some fans and a sore spot for Dave Navarro. Next, they reignited a personal feud between Kiedis and Mr. Bungle singer Mike Patton by refusing to play a series of European concerts with Bungle. Patton responded with a "tribute" show for the Peppers, where Bungle mocked their stage moves, faked shooting up heroin, and imitated Kiedis' comments about Patton. They also played the ill-fated *Woodstock '99* festival, where their headlining performance was met with piles of burning rubble and a full-scale riot. Tours with the Foo Fighters and Pearl Jam brought them into the next year without problems, but they stepped off the road after a planned stop in Israel was haulted due to security worries. They returned to the studio in November of 2001 and by the summer of 2002 they had a new album ready to drop, *By the Way*. —*Greg Prato*

Freaky Styley / 1985 / EMI ◆◆◆◆◆
Long before the Red Hot Chili Peppers became alternative rock darlings via tear-jerking ballads, they were firmly rooted in pure, uncut funk. Of course, their stint as a funk band extended for a very short time, from their inception

(showcased on their formative self-titled debut) to their more stylistically varied guitar-orientated efforts (hinted at on *Uplift Mofo* and fully realized on *Mother's Milk*). Of this short era before Anthony Kiedis decided to take a more poetic approach to songwriting, and before Hillel Slovak's unfortunate death, *Freaky Styley* stands as the group's masterpiece. Here, the Peppers seem fully in control of their vision to be accessible successors to '70s P-Funk, laying down a varied collection of quirky songs propelled by Flea's omnipresent bass riffs and Slovak's restrained efforts. Above all, though, much of this album's success from all angles goes to producer George Clinton, perhaps the most inspiring individual the Peppers could have worked with at this point in their career. *Freaky Styley* is the mid-'80s album that Clinton could never make on his own. Where Clinton's '80s albums seemed infused with the right ideas, he never had the seemingly limitless energy that the Peppers employ here. Above all, the Peppers' stunning rendition of Sly Stone's "If You Want Me to Stay" is a testament to just how funky the Peppers were at this point, even if it doesn't quite have the original's soul. Other notable moments include "Jungle Man" and "American Ghost Dance," two tight funk numbers with wonderful choruses. This album probably won't appeal to those weaned on "Under the Bridge" or "Scar Tissue," but it's undeniably a somewhat forgotten cult favorite, particularly to those infatuated with the group's short-lived Slovak era, the group's zenith in terms of quirkiness and funkiness. *—Jason Birchmeier*

Mother's Milk / Aug. 1989 / EMI ✦✦✦
The Chili Peppers' playing on *Mother's Milk* is more metallic than ever, thanks to newcomers Chad Smith (drums) and especially John Frusciante (guitar). Thanks to their presence, Kiedis and Flea sound reinvigorated in their performances, but the material is inconsistent, with too much of the second half in particular seeming like undeveloped, loud-fast-manic schtick. Still, there are more than enough quality tracks to make the filler worth sorting through, most obviously the heavy reworking of Stevie Wonder's "Higher Ground" and the cautionary, heartfelt "Knock Me Down," as well as several others scattered over the album. *—Steve Huey*

Blood Sugar Sex Magik / Sep. 1991 / Warner Brothers ✦✦✦✦✦
The Chili Peppers' best album, *Blood Sugar Sex Magik* benefits immensely from Rick Rubin's production—Frusciante's guitar is less overpoweringly noisy, leaving room for differing textures and clearer lines, while the band overall is more focused and less indulgent, even if some of the grooves drag on too long. Lyrically, Kiedis is as preoccupied with sex as ever, whether invoking it as his muse, begging for it, or boasting in great detail about his prowess, best showcased on the infectiously funky singles "Give It Away" and "Suck My Kiss." However, he tempers his testosterone with a more sensitive side, writing about the emotional side of failed relationships ("Breaking the Girl," "I Could Have Lied"), his drug addictions ("Under the Bridge" and an elegy for Hillel Slovak, "My Lovely Man"), and some hippie-ish calls for a peaceful utopia. Three of those last four songs (excluding "My Lovely Man") mark the band's first consistent embrace of lilting acoustic balladry, and while it's not what Kiedis does best as a vocalist, these are some of the album's finest moments, varying and expanding the group's musical and emotional range. Frusciante departed after the supporting tour, leaving *Blood Sugar Sex Magik* as probably the best album the Chili Peppers will ever make. *—Steve Huey*

● **What Hits!?** / Sep. 29, 1992 / EMI ✦✦✦✦✦
After the Red Hot Chili Peppers left EMI for Warner Bros. and hit the big time with "Under the Bridge," their former label gathered most of the best tracks from the group's first four albums for the compilation *What Hits!?* Since *Blood Sugar Sex Magik*, the Peppers' most popular album, was recorded for Warner, none of its songs are present—with the exception of "Under the Bridge," which was somehow licensed for use. *What Hits!?* does a pretty good job of sifting through the Peppers' uneven discography and picking out the best moments, making it a very useful sampler; it also contains "Show Me Your Soul," the band's contribution to the *Pretty Woman* soundtrack. *—Steve Huey*

Ursula Rucker

Vocals / Spoken Word, Jazz-Rap, Hip-Hop
Ursula Rucker isn't a funky diva—she's her own diva. Having collaborated with some of music's most sophisticated—the Silent Poets, King Britt, Josh Wink, the Roots—Rucker has honed her seductive spoken wordplay inside

Philly soul, hip-hop, and new jazz. She combines social awareness with womanhood, black culture, and love for something musically alluring. A graduate of Temple's journalism school, Rucker made her poetic debut in 1994 at Philly's celebrated *Zanzibar Blue*. From there, she proved her smart and sultry bravado without frills. The late '90s illustrated her abrasive poetic nature inside cuts like Josh Wink's "Sixth Sense" and 4 Hero's "Loveless." *Supa Sista*, Rucker's debut album showcasing a street-fighting spirit, was issued in September 2001 on K7. *—MacKenzie Wilson*

● **Supa Sista** / Sep. 4, 2001 / K7 ✦✦✦
Spoken word poetry is something of an acquired taste, and the debut from Philadelphia native Ursula Rucker, though promising, is unlikely to bring many new converts to the movement. The poetess has made quite a name for herself over the years, working with artists ranging from techno titans like King Britt and Josh Wink to hometown hip-hoppers the Roots and Bahamadia. On *Supa Sista*, she gets her turn in the spotlight, with a subdued speech pattern and sultry vocal cadences well-suited to the airy trip-hop grooves that back most of the tracks. Songs like "What???" and "One Million Ways to Burn" work wonderfully, the former matching aggressive lyrics about the state of black music today against 4 Hero's urgent rhythms, the latter pairing her sexy voice with a sensual funk groove from Jonah Sharp to create a perfect soundtrack for horizontal entwinement. But on some tracks, repetitive grooves or insistent chants prove irritating, taking the listener out of the mood the other tunes worked so hard to create. Still, all in all a fine debut. *—Bret Love*

Carl Hancock Rux

b. Harlem, NY
Vocals / Contemporary R&B, Vocals, Poetry, Urban, Spoken Word
Poet/spoken-word performer Carl Hancock Rux was born and raised in Harlem, NY; a product of the city's foster-care system, he later attended Columbia University. Named "One of 30 Artists Under the Age of 30 Most Likely to Influence Culture Over the Next 30 Years" in 1994 by *The New York Times*, over time Rux increasingly began incorporating elements of hip-hop, jazz, and R&B into his live poetry readings, and in 1999 he released his debut album, *Rux Revue*. *—Jason Ankeny*

● **Rux Revue** / Aug. 31, 1999 / Sony ✦✦✦
Move over Gil Scott-Heron and Michael Franti, there's another poet on the loose and he's got a mind to speak out: Enter lauded New York writer, the deep-voiced Carl Hancock Rux and his recording debut. Rux wastes no time cutting to the chase on the first track "Intro To (r)Evolution," while conjuring the spirit of the aforementioned musicians. His backing band is a dream roster who threaten to overshadow his message: Money Mark on keyboards, Joey Waronker on drums and the legendary Carol Kaye on bass, among others. They twist and turn the jazz, folk, hip-hop and rock rhythms inside out helping to complete Rux's thoughtful commentaries on ghetto-life and his place as a black male in the (art) world. In the end, Rux's soul power, delivered from various points of view wins-out, proving uneasy to ignore. *—Denise Sullivan*

Gil Scott-Heron

b. Apr. 1, 1949, Chicago, IL
Vocals, Piano, Guitar / Political Rap, Social Commentary, Fusion, Poetry
One of the most important progenitors of rap music, Gil Scott-Heron's aggressive, no-nonsense street poetry inspired a legion of intelligent rappers while his engaging songwriting skills placed him square in the R&B charts later in his career, backed by increasingly contemporary production courtesy of Malcolm Cecil and Nile Rodgers (of Chic). Born in Chicago but transplanted to Tennessee for his early years, Scott-Heron spent most of his high school years in the Bronx, where he learned firsthand many of the experiences which later made up his songwriting material. He had begun writing before reaching his teenage years, however, and completed his first volume of poetry at the age of 13. Though he attended college in Pennsylvania, he dropped out after one year to concentrate on his writing career and earned plaudits for his novel, *The Vulture*. Encouraged at the end of the '60s to begin recording by legendary jazz producer Bob Thiele—who had worked with every major jazz great, from Louis Armstrong to John Coltrane—Scott-Heron released his 1970 debut, *Small Talk at 125th and Lenox*, inspired by a volume of poetry of the same name. With Thiele's Flying Dutchman

Records until the mid-'70s, he signed to Arista soon after and found success on the R&B charts. Though his jazz-based work of the early '70s was tempered by a slicker disco-inspired production, Scott-Heron's message was as clear as ever on the Top 30 single "Johannesburg" and the number-15 hit "Angel Dust." Silent for almost a decade, after the release of his 1984 single "Re-Ron," the proto-rapper returned to recording in the mid-'90s with a message for the gangsta rappers who had come in his wake; Scott-Heron's 1994 album *Spirits* began with "Message to the Messengers," pointed squarely at the rappers whose influence—positive or negative—meant much to the children of the 1990s.

In a touching bit of irony which he himself was quick to joke about, Gil Scott-Heron was born on April Fool's Day 1949 in Chicago, the son of a Jamaican professional soccer player (who spent time playing for Glasgow Celtic) and a college-graduate mother who worked as a librarian. His parents divorced early in his life, and Scott-Heron was sent to live with his grandmother in Lincoln, TN. Learning musical and literary instruction from her, Scott-Heron also learned about prejudice firsthand, as he was one of three children picked to integrate an elementary school in nearby Jackson. The abuse proved too much to bear, however, and the eighth-grader was sent to New York to live with his mother, first in the Bronx and later in the Hispanic neighborhood of Chelsea.

Though Scott-Heron's experiences in Tennessee must have been difficult, they proved to be the seed of his writing career, as his first volume of poetry was written around that time. His education in the New York City school system also proved beneficial, introducing the youth to the work of Harlem Renaissance poet Langston Hughes as well as LeRoi Jones. After publishing a novel called *The Vulture* in 1968, Scott-Heron applied to Pennsylvania's Lincoln University. Though he spent less than one year there, it was enough time to meet Brian Jackson, a similarly minded musician who would later become a crucial collaborator and integral part of Scott-Heron's band. Given a bit of exposure—mostly in magazines like *Essence*, which called *The Vulture* "a strong start for a writer with important things to say"—Scott-Heron met up with Bob Thiele and was encouraged to begin a music career, reading selections from his book of poetry *Small Talk at 125th & Lennox* while Thiele recorded a collective of jazz and funk musicians, including bassist Ron Carter, drummer Bernard "Pretty" Purdie, Hubert Laws on flute and alto saxophone, and percussionists Eddie Knowles and Charlie Saunders; Scott-Heron also recruited Jackson to play on the record as pianist. Most important on the album was "The Revolution Will Not Be Televised," an aggressive polemic against the major media and white America's ignorance of increasingly deteriorating conditions in the inner cities. Scott-Heron's second LP, 1971's *Pieces of a Man*, expanded his range, featuring songs such as the title track and "Lady Day and John Coltrane" which offered a more straight-ahead approach to song structure (if not content).

The following year's *Free Will* was his last for Flying Dutchman, however; after a dispute with the label, Scott-Heron recorded *Winter in America* for Strata East, then moved to Arista Records in 1975. As the first artist signed to Clive Davis' new label, much was riding on Scott-Heron to deliver first-rate material with a chance at the charts. Thanks to Arista's more focused push on the charts, Scott-Heron's "Johannesburg" reached number 29 on the R&B charts in 1975. Important to Scott-Heron's success on his first two albums for Arista (*First Minute of a New Day* and *From South Africa to South Carolina*) was the influence of keyboardist and collaborator Brian Jackson, cobilled on both LPs and the de facto leader of Scott-Heron's Midnight Band.

Jackson left by 1978, though, leaving the musical direction of Scott-Heron's career in the capable hands of producer Malcolm Cecil, a veteran producer who had midwifed the funkier direction of the Isley Brothers and Stevie Wonder earlier in the decade. The first single recorded with Cecil, "The Bottle," became Scott-Heron's biggest hit yet, peaking at number 15 on the R&B charts, though he still made no waves on pop charts. Producer Nile Rodgers of Chic also helped on production during the 1980s, when Scott-Heron's political attack grew even more fervent with a new target, President Ronald Reagan. (Several singles, including the R&B hits "B Movie" and "Re-Ron," were specifically directed at the President's conservative policies.) By 1985, however, Scott-Heron was dropped by Arista, just after the release of *The Best of Gil Scott-Heron*. Though he continued to tour around the world, Scott-Heron chose to discontinue recording. He did return, however, in 1993 with a contract for TVT Records and the album *Spirits*. —*John Bush*

Small Talk at 125th and Lenox / 1970 / RCA ✦✦✦✦✦

Disregard the understated title; *Small Talk at 125th and Lenox* was a volcanic upheaval of intellectualism and social critique, recorded live in a New York nightclub with only bongos and conga to back the street poet. Here Scott-Heron introduced some of his most biting material, including the landmark "The Revolution Will Not Be Televised" as well as his single most polemical moment: the angry race warning "Enough." Still, he balances the tone and mood well, ranging from direct broadsides to clever satire. He introduces "Whitey on the Moon" with a bemused air ("wanting to give credit where credit is due"), then launches into a diatribe concerning living conditions for the neglected on earth while those racing to the moon receive millions of taxpayer dollars. On "Evolution (And Flashback)," Scott-Heron laments the setbacks of the civil rights movement and provides a capsule history of his race, ending sharply with these words: "In 1960, I was a negro, and then Malcolm came along/Yes, but some nigger shot Malcolm down, though the bitter truth lives on/Well, now I am a black man, and though I still go second class/Whereas once I wanted the white man's love, now he can kiss my ass." The only sour note comes on a brush with homophobia, "The Subject Was Faggots." —*John Bush*

Pieces of a Man / 1971 / RCA ✦✦✦✦

After decades of influencing everyone from jazz musicians to hip-hop stars, *Pieces of a Man* set a standard for vocal artistry and political awareness that few musicians will ever match. Scott-Heron's unique proto-rap style influenced a generation of hip-hop artists, and nowhere is his style more powerful than on the classic "The Revolution Will Not Be Televised." Even though the media—the very entity attacked in this song—has used, reused, and re-contextualized the song and its title so many times, its message is so strong that it has become almost impossible to co-opt. Musically, the track created a formula that modern hip-hop would follow for years to come: bare-bones arrangements featuring pounding bass lines and stripped-down drumbeats. Although the song features plenty of outdated references to everything from Spiro Agnew and Jim Webb to *The Beverly Hillbillies*, the force of Scott-Heron's well-directed anger makes the song timeless. More than just a spoken word poet, Scott-Heron was also a uniquely gifted vocalist. On tracks like the reflective "I Think I'll Call It Morning" and the title track, Scott-Heron's voice is complemented perfectly by the soulful keyboards of Brian Jackson. On "Lady Day and John Coltrane," he not only celebrates jazz legends of the past in his words but in his vocal performance, one that is filled with enough soul and innovation to make Coltrane and Billie Holiday nod their heads in approval. More than three decades after its release, *Pieces of a Man* is just as—if not more—powerful and influential today as it was the day it was released. —*Jon Azpiri*

Free Will / Aug. 1972 / RCA ✦✦✦

Gil Scott-Heron's third album is split down the middle, the first side being a purely musical experience with a full band (including flutist Hubert Laws and drummer Pretty Purdie), the second functioning more as a live rap session with collaborator Brian Jackson on flute and a few friends on percussion. For side one, although he's overly tentative on the ballad "The Middle of Your Day," Scott-Heron excels on the title track and the third song, "The Get Out of the Ghetto Blues," one of his best, best-known performances. The second side is more of an impromptu performance, with Scott-Heron often explaining his tracks by way of introduction ("No Knock" referred to a new police policy whereby knocking was no longer required before entering a house, "And Then He Wrote Meditations" being Scott-Heron's tribute to John Coltrane). His first exploration of pure music-making, *Free Will* functions as one of Scott-Heron's most visceral performance, displaying a maturing artist who still draws on the raw feeling of his youth. The Bluebird reissue from 2001 includes eight alternate takes, best being an alternate of the title track. —*John Bush*

Winter in America / Sep. 4, 1973+Oct. 11, 1973 / Strata East ✦✦✦

Gil Scott-Heron was at his most righteous and provocative on this album. The title cut was a moving, angry summation of the social injustices Scott-Heron felt had led the nation to a particularly dangerous period, while "The Bottle" was a great treatise on the dangers of alcohol abuse. He also offered his thoughts on Nixon's legacy with "The H2O Gate Blues," a classic oral narrative. Brian Jackson's capable keyboard, acoustic piano and arranging talents helped make this a first-rate release, one of several the duo issued during the 1970s. —*Ron Wynn*

● **The Revolution Will Not Be Televised** / 1974 / Bluebird ✦✦✦✦✦

Spanning 1970-1972, this superb collection takes us back to Gil Scott-Heron's early years, when he was working with jazz producer Bob Thiele—a man who had been in the studio with everyone from John Coltrane and Pharoah Sanders to Coleman Hawkins. But *The Revolution Will Not Be Televised* isn't a jazz collection per se; it's a collection of innovative R&B and spoken poetry that contains jazz influences and finds Scott-Heron employing such jazz musicians as flutist Hubert Laws and bassist Ron Carter. Like the Last Poets, Scott-Heron has been described as "one of the first rappers"—and while he was hardly the first person to speak in rhyme to music, there are definitely parallels between angry sociopolitical poems like "Whitey on the Moon," "No Knock," and "Brother" and hip-hop commentary from the 1980s. Poetry, however, doesn't dominate this album—most of the selections illustrate Scott-Heron's excellence as a singer, including "Home Is Where the Hatred Is," "Did You Hear What They Said?," and the poignant "Save the Children." One of the collection's less political tracks is "Lady Day and John Coltrane," an R&B classic that articulates how easily jazz can lift a person's spirits. *The Revolution Will Not Be Televised* isn't the last word on Scott-Heron's artistry—he recorded many more treasures after leaving Flying Dutchman for Arista in 1975. But it's one of the collections to acquire if you're exploring his artistry for the first time. —*Alex Henderson*

The First Minute of a New Day / Jun. 1975 / TVT ✦✦✦✦

This follow-up to the righteous and soulful *Winter In America* LP continues with the solid, decidedly left-of-center jazz-R&B that made him a cult figure throughout the '70s. This output, with the opening meditation of "Offering" and the right-on "Ain't No Such Thing as Superman," solidifies Heron's place in the pantheon of jazz poets. Dig the recited (possibly improvised) live take of "Pardon Our Analysis," a follow-up to his seminal "H2O Blues." And this reissue features four unreleased tracks, including a live medley of "The Bottle/Guan Guanco." —*Tim Sheridan*

From South Africa to South Carolina / Jan. 1976 / TVT ✦✦✦✦

The Gil Scott-Heron/Brian Jackson collaboration was now a formal one, as they were issuing albums as a team. This was their second duo project to make the pop charts, and it included anti-nuclear and anti-apartheid themes, plus less political, more autobiographical/reflective material like "Summer of '42," "Beginnings (The First Minute Of A New Day)" and "Fell Together." Scott-Heron was now a campus and movement hero, and Brian Jackson's production and arranging savvy helped make his albums as arresting musically as they were lyrically. —*Ron Wynn*

It's Your World / Nov. 1976 / TVT ✦✦✦✦✦

This Gil Scott-Heron double album, roughly two thirds of which was recorded live in Boston on July 2-4, 1976, makes the most of its Centennial-centric time frame. Between the American flag striped cover art and Heron's spoken word spiel on an 8-and-a-half minute poem/rant "Bicentennial Blues," the album loses little of its impact, regardless of how the years have mildewed once fresh political topics like Nixon, Agnew, and Watergate. Four of its songs are studio recordings ("It's Your World," "Possum Slim," "New York City," and "Sharing"), and even though they're up to Heron's usual jazz/blues/pop standards, the disc is most effective on the concert tracks. As he explains in the 2000 penned liner notes, The Midnight Band was a compelling live unit and one listen to the brisk, electrifying, 13-minute rendition of "The Bottle," one of Heron's most penetrating tracks, is all you'll need to understand why. More importantly, like the best protest music, these tunes have lost none of their lyrical edge or incisiveness throughout the years. Musically the band is taut and rehearsed down to the finest time change, yet loose enough to open up on the jams. The heavy Latin percussion/flute/piano—but remarkably guitar-less—sound is equal parts Santana and Mongo Santamaria with a strong jazz current throughout, especially on the John Coltrane tribute "Trane," featuring tenor hornman Bilal Sunni-Ali's fiery lead. Scott-Heron's deep, mellifluous voice is alternately soothing and cutting, infusing the music with heart and soul, while keeping the sound focused even during the longer improvisations. Only a dated '70s drum solo belies the year this was recorded. Chestnuts like "Home Is Where the Hatred Is" explode in extended live versions that become definitive readings of the tunes. Remastered for its reissue, *It's Your World* crackles with energy, presenting an accomplished band at their peak and placing the listener practically on stage for the live tracks with acoustics that are full, yet airy and spacious. One of Gil Scott-Heron's best albums as well as a compelling musical time capsule,

the disc is proof of the artist's musical and lyrical acuity and is a moving listening experience. —*Hal Horowitz*

Bridges / Dec. 1977 / Arista ✦✦✦✦

Gil Scott-Heron, Brian Jackson, and the Midnight Band take a slightly different approach with their 1977 effort, *Bridges*. With less of the gaping and world-infused sound prevalent on previous albums, the songs are more concise and Scott-Heron comes into his own as a singer depending less on his spoken word vocal style. This album may not be one of his better-known releases (the long out of print LP is slated to make it's CD debut in the fall of 2001), but the excellent songwriting exposes Scott-Heron at the height of his powers as a literary artist. The social, political, cultural, and historical themes are presented in a tight funk meets jazz meets blues meets rock sound that is buoyed by Jackson's characteristic keyboard playing and the Midnight Band's colorful arrangements. Scott-Heron's ability to make the personal universal is evident from the opening track, "Hello Sunday! Hello Road!," all the way through to the gorgeous "95 South (All of the Places We've Been)." The most popular cut on the album, "We Almost Lost Detroit," which shares its title with the John G. Fuller book published in 1975, recounts the story of the nuclear meltdown at the Fermi Atomic Power Plant near Monroe, MI, in 1966. This song was also contributed to the *No Nukes* concert and album in 1980. Along with the two records that would follow in the late '70s, *Bridges* stands as one of Scott-Heron's most enjoyable and durable albums. —*Jeff Schwachter*

1980 / Aug. 1979+Oct. 1979 / Arista ✦✦✦✦

1980 can be viewed as a precursor for the venomous rants Gil Scott-Heron would unleash on the eventual Reagan-led White House. Loaded with perceptive and poignant observations on the state of America as it advanced into a new and uncertain decade, *1980* is a powerful final album of the 1970s for Scott-Heron and his partner Brian Jackson. Amazingly, Scott-Heron's focus at the close of the decade is strikingly similar to his focus on his 1970 debut, *Small Talk at 125th and Lennox*; namely that social and political change has yet to come to many Americans, despite the advancements in technology and other seemingly less significant realms. The enemies are the same: nuclear power and big business ("Shut Um Down"), oppressive governments ("Shah Mot"), and racism ("Willing"). On the title track, Scott-Heron's gaze is set on the future with an eye on the past as well. When he sings, "Boogie-Woogie's somewhere in the lost and found," he's not only speaking of the changes in music, but also in popular culture. There is a hint of resentment on his part that this musical style, like other revolutionary African-American innovations, has been progressively stolen, mined, sterilized, and eventually discarded. This is not to say that the music throughout the album is marked by regret or sorrow. The spacey synthesizers, background vocals, and use of horns, along with Jackson's always-extraordinary arrangements, give the album a quality that matches the aura of the period without forgetting past musical styles. The descriptive "Alien (Hold on to Your Dreams)" is the album's most enduring song, vividly portraying the plight of Mexican illegal aliens living in Los Angeles and offering an uplifting refrain. Sadly, this album is hard to find in CD format, but vinyl versions turn up now and then in the "miscellaneous" sections of used record stores. —*Jeff Schwachter*

Real Eyes / Dec. 1980 / Arista ✦✦✦

In 1980, Gil Scott-Heron had a nice opportunity to promote his *Real Eyes* album when he became the opening act on Stevie Wonder's *Hotter Than July* tour. On his own, Scott-Heron usually played small clubs, but opening for Wonder gave him the chance to perform in front of thousands of Wonder fans in major stadiums and sports arenas. Many of Wonder's white fans seemed to be unfamiliar with Scott-Heron (who had never had a major pop hit), while a lot of Wonder's black fans at least knew him for "The Bottle" and "Angel Dust" even if they hadn't bought a lot of his albums. Opening for all those Wonder fans certainly didn't hurt Scott-Heron's career, but it didn't make him a superstar either. While it's possible that some Wonder fans enjoyed Scott-Heron's opening sets enough to go out and purchase *Real Eyes*, most of the people who acquired this LP were already confirmed Scott-Heron fans. Unfortunately, *Real Eyes* lacked a hit single, although the material is excellent nonetheless. As usual, Scott-Heron has a lot of sociopolitical things on his mind—"The Train From Washington" concludes that the working class can't depend on the U.S. government for anything, while "Not Needed" angrily points the finger at companies who consider longtime employees expendable. And the album's less sociopolitical songs are equally memorable. "Your

Daddy Loves You" is a touching ode to Scott-Heron's daughter Gia Louise (who was only a child in 1980), and the jazz-oriented "A Legend in His Own Mind" is a humorous, clever put-down of a wannabe "Casanova" who isn't nearly the ladies' man he brags about being. Scott-Heron's love of jazz serves him well on "A Legend in His Own Mind" and the smoky "Combinations," but make no mistake: *Real Eyes* is an R&B album more than anything. —*Alex Henderson*

Reflections / 1981 / Arista ♦♦♦
Although a major across-the-board hit always eluded the poet, singer, and activist Gil Scott-Heron, this album does contains one of his best-known songs. "B-Movie," an extended attack on Ronald "Ray-gun," unleashes 12 minutes of vitriol about the then recently elected president. Beginning with the declaration "Mandate, my ass," it's a laundry list of fears about Reagan, fantasizing that his election meant "we're all actors" in some surreal film. Delivered over a taut funk groove, parts of it are still funny. Elsewhere, Scott-Heron takes an early stab at endorsing firearm control on "Gun"; slows things down for "Morning Thoughts"; and explores reggae's rhythms and revolutionary power on "Storm Music," a direction he'd pursue more fully on his next album, *Moving Target*. The disc also includes a pair of covers that offer varying degrees of success: Bill Withers' "Grandma's Hands" is a natural for Scott-Heron's warm baritone and a bright soul-jazz arrangement from the Midnight Band, but the version of Marvin Gaye's "Inner City Blues," while it swings convincingly, has a lengthy spoken-word riff that fails to embellish on the pain implicit in the original. Overall, *Reflections* doesn't capture Scott-Heron at the peak of his game, though anyone who enjoyed the other works from his Arista period certainly won't be disappointed. —*Dan LeRoy*

Moving Target / Sep. 1982 / Arista ♦♦♦
Gil Scott-Heron's last proper album for more than a decade, *Moving Target* was recorded after a period of intense touring (hence the title) and, perhaps understandably, finds the Midnight Band playing a larger role than usual. It also may reflect the group's travels, as the typical, tastefully jazzy R&B and funk grooves—like set-opener "Fast Lane" and "Explanations"—are supplemented with more exotic sounds. Like Stevie Wonder, for whom he and the Midnight Band opened a tour in 1980, Scott-Heron and his bandmates were experimenting with reggae. "No Exit" has clear echoes of Bob Marley, while "Ready or Not" is a sultry island jam. Both tunes also had themes more personal than political, a shift noticeable elsewhere on the album (even "Washington D.C.," with its seemingly obvious subject, is as much about the resilient spirit of D.C.'s citizens as it's about the city's politicians). That's somewhat surprising, given that Scott-Heron had recently enjoyed success with "B-Movie," a pointed attack on then-president Ronald Reagan. But "Blue Collar" is a populist manifesto that gives shout-outs to working folks in a variety of professions across the fruited plain before concluding with the dispirited chorus, "There ain't no place we ain't been down," and "Black History/The World" offers nearly ten minutes of Afro-centric theorizing, beginning with a spoken introduction that hearkens back to Scott-Heron's sarcastic, poetic beginnings and ends with a simple—some would say simplistic—plea for peace and world change. —*Dan LeRoy*

The Best of Gil Scott-Heron / 1984 / Arista ♦♦♦♦
In 1975, Gil Scott-Heron became the first artist ever signed to Arista Records, but ten years later, he proved expendable when Clive Davis' company dropped him. It was sad to see Arista give Scott-Heron the boot in 1985, although it wasn't surprising—by the mid-'80s, Arista was only interested in superstars, and Scott-Heron was never a superstar. Though the singer commanded a loyal following, it was a small following. Scott-Heron was little-known among pop fans, and although R&B fans knew him for "The Bottle," "Angel Dust," and "Johannesburg," he was never a huge name in the R&B world. Not long before Arista dropped Scott-Heron, it released this LP, which offered one new song ("Re-Ron") but contains mostly previously released material. The only gem from Scott-Heron's pre-Arista years on Flying Dutchman is the 1970s incendiary "The Revolution Will Not Be Televised." Otherwise, *The Best of Gil Scott-Heron* (which spans 1970-1984) spotlights his Arista years and offers some of his most essential recordings for that label, which range from the singles "The Bottle" (a number 15 R&B hit), "Johannesburg" (which went to number 29 on the R&B singles charts), and "Angel Dust" to "Winter in America," "Shut 'Um Down," and "B Movie" (one of Scott-Heron's angry attacks on President Ronald Reagan). Even if you don't agree with all of Scott-Heron's politics, he was always thought-provoking and was certainly

an expressive, captivating R&B singer—it's too bad he ended up spending the second half of the 1980s without any type of label deal. For those who wanted an introductory overview of Scott-Heron's Arista output, this LP was, in the mid-'80s, a logical choice. —*Alex Henderson*

Spirits / Jul. 1994 / TVT ♦♦♦♦♦
With *Spirits*, Gil Scott-Heron made a triumphant return to the studio after a 12-year absence. Though the politically charged R&B singer's voice had deteriorated, much of his soulfulness comes through. His songwriting is consistently excellent, and songs ranging from "Message to the Messengers" (which advises young rap artists to use their power wisely) to "Work for Peace" leave no doubt that his sociopolitical observations are as sharp as ever. One of the most riveting cuts is "The Other Side," an extended remake of his early-'70s classic "Home Is Where the Hatred Is" (which describes a drug addict's struggle). The East Coaster had been battling addiction himself during his absence from recording, and this heartfelt song isn't for the squeamish. Scott-Heron had successfully dabbled in jazz over the years, and in fact, one of the CD's many strong points are the lyrics he adds to John Coltrane's "Spirits." One cannot help but wish Scott-Heron still had a great voice to go with this material, but even so, *Spirits* is powerful listening. —*Alex Henderson*

702

f. 1995
Urban, Hip-Hop
Discovered by Michael Bivins of New Edition, 702 is a teenage trio—Irish, Kameelah, and Lemisha—who made their recorded debut singing on Subway's hit single "This Lil' Game We Play." The group released their debut album, *No Doubt*, in the fall of 1996, preceded by the single "Steelo." Several other singles from the album followed in 1997, including the title track, "Get It Together," and "All I Want." The group returned in 1999 with a self-titled full-length as well as the single "Where My Girls At?" —*Stephen Thomas Erlewine*

No Doubt / Oct. 8, 1996 / Biv Ten ♦♦♦
702's debut album has a couple of fine moments—most notably the single "Steelo"—but their fusion of street-oriented rap and urban soul doesn't quite gel over the course of the album. —*Stephen Thomas Erlewine*

● **702** / Jun. 15, 1999 / Motown ♦♦♦
702 showed promise on their debut, but with their self-titled second effort, they're beginning to find their own voice. True, they need the help of some powerful collaborators and producers to get there—including Rick "Dutch" Cousin, SoulShock & Karlin and Missy Elliott, who clearly was an influence here—but the end result is a seamless, professional contemporary R&B album that is blessed with an appealing sound and some very good songs, such as "Where My Girls At?." Like many modern-day R&B records, it's padded a little bit with filler and runs a little bit too long, but there are a number of really good moments here that make it a true step forward for 702. —*Stephen Thomas Erlewine*

Star / Mar. 25, 2003 / Motown ♦♦♦
Over three years came and went between 702's second album and this one, and it continues in the group's tradition of being able to deliver a couple of solid singles surrounded by middling to fair album tracks. The biggest obstacle, beyond the trio's thin voices, is the fact that the title track, featuring an appearance from Clipse, is one of the Neptunes' weakest productions; it hardly rates with the best of 702's earlier singles. "I Still Love You" is so sparse and hollow—consisting of little more than a basic kick-drum pattern, drawn-out keyboard notes, and some hand claps—that it seems like the Neps spent about five minutes on it, but there's an awkward, spacious charm to it. Further production help from She'kspere, Buckwild, Mario Winans, and several others does little to bolster the album's appeal. And like a lot of records released during this era, *Star*'s impact could've been significantly increased with four or five of the weaker songs trimmed off. —*Andy Kellman*

Sneaker Pimps

f. 1995, Reading, England
Electronica, Alternative Dance, Adult Alternative Pop/Rock, Trip-Hop, Club/Dance
Sneaker Pimps are a trip-hop trio formed in Reading, England, in 1995, following the success of Portishead's *Dummy* and Tricky's *Maxinquaye*. Borrowing heavily from Portishead and Massive Attack, Sneaker Pimps

pursued a trancelike but edgy sound, highlighted by Kelli Dayton's soulful vocals. While Dayton was the focal point, Chris Corner (guitar) and Liam Howe (keyboards) are the band's leaders, writing all of the songs and producing the records. Howe and Corner had been playing in bands since the early '90s, to no success. After seeing Dayton sing with a pub band in 1995, they convinced her to join the fledgling Sneaker Pimps, who had taken their name from an article the Beastie Boys published in their *Grand Royale* magazine about a man they hired to track down classic sneakers.

Sneaker Pimps released their first single, "Tesko Suicide," in May of 1996, and it was greeted with positive reviews in the U.K. music press. *Becoming X*, the group's debut, was released in August and became a critical success, with *Q* magazine naming it one of the best albums of the year. However, the band failed to make an impact on the pop charts in the U.K. A remix album followed in early 1998, but by the time of the follow-up, *Splinter*, Dayton had left the group; most of the vocals were taken by Corner. Though *Splinter* wasn't released in America, 2002's *Bloodsport* earned a release on Tommy Boy. — *Stephen Thomas Erlewine*

● **Becoming X** / Aug. 19, 1996 / Clean Up ✦✦✦✦
Becoming X is one of the most engaging by-products of post-Portishead trip-hop. While the Sneaker Pimps don't have the doomed romanticism of Portishead, or the nasty experimental tendencies of Tricky, they have a cool sense of pop hooks and an edgier guitar attack than their predecessors. "Tesko Suicide" moves along with jagged guitars and rhythms, while "6 Underground" is cooly detached post-modern soul. *Becoming X* creates an airy, urban atmosphere, and while the record begins to unravel toward the end, it is an exciting, entrancing listen. — *Stephen Thomas Erlewine*

Total

f. New York, NY
New Jack Swing, Club/Dance, Urban, Hip-Hop
The "New Jill Flava" trio Total comprised singers Kima, Pam, and Keisha; signed to Sean "Puffy" Combs' Bad Boy Entertainment label, they first attracted attention backing the Notorious B.I.G. on his hits "One More Chance" and "Juicy," soon after scoring their own hit with the single "Can't You See" from the soundtrack to the film *New Jersey Drive*. Total's self-titled debut LP followed in 1996, launching the hits "No One Else," "Kissin' You," and "Do You Think About Us?" The single "Trippin'" preceded the release of Total's second LP, 1998's *Kima, Keisha & Pam*. — *Jason Ankeny*

● **Total** / Jan. 30, 1996 / Bad Boy ✦✦✦✦
Total first gained attention as the backup vocalists for the Notorious B.I.G., singing on his hits "One More Chance" and "Juicy." After releasing a hit single, "See," from the *New Jersey Drive* soundtrack, the girl group released their self-titled debut. While the album is simply too long to sustain the quality of "See" and "No One Else," most of the record is filled with deep, seductive funk that follows through on the group's promise. — *Stephen Thomas Erlewine*

Kima, Keisha & Pam / Oct. 27, 1998 / Bad Boy ✦✦✦
On their second album, these '90s soul sistas sex up their lives, and everything around them, quite a bit, turning their fairly standard take on the hip-hop girl group into a late-night bath of delight. But by inviting a who's-who roster into the tub with them (producers here include Missy Elliott, Sean "Puffy" Combs and Heavy D., among others), Total—the Kima, Keisha and Pam of the title—are barely heard. Brimming with the sounds of the world around it, *Kima, Keisha & Pam* is a studio-powered album that loses its individuality while trying desperately to be a part of the streets and scene. The best track, "Trippin'," is an Elliott-produced slice of robotic R&B that combines the gals' sweet harmonies with state-of-the-soul-art studio savvy. But an album's worth of the sexy same unveils Total's ultimate limitations. —*Michael Gallucci*

Trouble Funk

f. 1978, Washington, D.C. **db.** 1984
Go-Go, Disco, Funk
Miles off the radar of popular music during the early '80s, Trouble Funk energized their D.C. home with the sound of go-go music, an uproarious blend of swinging, up-tempo '70s funk and a '60s-style horn section. The band formed in 1978, and the lineup coalesced around drummer Emmet Nixon, percussionists Mack Carey and Timothius Davis, guitarist Chester Davis, bassist Tony Fisher, trombone players Gerald and Robert Reed, trumpeter

Taylor Reed, keyboard player James Avery, and saxophonist David Rudd. Trouble Funk earned a loyal fan base for their notoriously can't-miss live act, a raw, party-friendly version of dance and funk with few songs but plenty of extensive jams organized around audience-friendly vocal tags and callout hooks.

The first go-go record released *outside* of D.C., Trouble Funk's 1982 debut, *Drop the Bomb*, appeared on Sugar Hill, the same label then championing early hip-hop. (The two styles had very similar origins, in the breakbeat culture of urban block parties.) Though the band's second album, *In Times of Trouble*, appeared only on the local label D.E.T.T., Trouble Funk earned national distribution with a prescient concert record, 1985's *Saturday Night (Live from Washington, D.C.)*, released through Island. After taking the live act nationwide and even worldwide (they played the *1986 Montreux Jazz Festival*), Trouble Funk returned in 1987 with the boundary-breaking *Trouble Over Here, Trouble Over There*, featuring sympathetic heads like Bootsy Collins and Kurtis Blow. It was a bit of a stylistic misstep, however, and Island released the group from its contract. Undeterred, Trouble Funk kept on grooving around the city, playing often, even into the '90s, for nostalgic party goers as well as the musically curious. — *John Bush*

Live / 1981 / Infinite Zero ✦✦✦✦✦
There are no actual songs contained on Trouble Funk's *Live*; there are four near-15-minute jams, but they prove to be just as magical and rewarding as their compact songs (for Trouble Funk's more accessible tunes, check out the *Early Singles* compilation on Infinite Zero). Although the band never caught on nationally, for reasons unknown, they were huge in the Washington, D.C. area. And like other funk specialists (Graham Central Station, Funkadelic, etc.), Trouble Funk songs were infectious rave-ups that instantly created a party-like atmosphere. The group could really stretch out in concert, and although it may sound like a cliché, *Live* is the closest you can come to the Trouble Funk concert experience without actually attending one of their shows. Each of the four album sides twist, turn, bounce, groove, and breathe. There's lots of crowd chanting (done amazingly on cue), superb drumming/percussion (courtesy of Timothy David, Mack Carey, and Emmett Nixon), and rubbery synthesized sounds. The energy never dips, and the group is constantly inspired and at their peak. Also included are interesting liner notes from an unlikely Trouble Funk fanatic, Henry Rollins. — *Greg Prato*

Drop the Bomb / 1982 / Sequel ✦✦✦✦✦
Masters of Washington, D.C.'s '80s go-go craze, Trouble Funk brought early hip-hop (the group was part of Sugar Hill Records) to the dancefloor with deep bass, propulsive rhythms, and party lyrics. Being even more inspired by '70s funk bands like Chic, Cameo, and the Gap Band than either the Sugar Hill Gang or Grandmaster Flash, Trouble Funk and other go-go acts like EU and Chuck Brown used the MC to conduct party-time call-and-response sessions and not generally for street poetry raps à la Melle Mel and Kurtis Blow. A celebratory atmosphere certainly prevails on Sequel Records' fine Trouble Funk collection *Drop the Bomb*, with many of the band's prime dance hits like the title track, "Get on Up," and "Let's Get Hot" being featured in their extended versions. The band's nasty synth licks, up-front percussion, and sinewy funk guitar lines keep the music pumping throughout, while both the go-go/rap hybrid "Pump Me Up" and Barry White-inspired soul ballad "Don't Try to Use Me" show off the group's musical flexibility. It is then rounded out with the ten-minute, bring-the-house-down jam "Supergrit," which nicely incorporates the funk of Kool & the Gang and Earth Wind & Fire into the go-go mix. This is a great introduction to both Trouble Funk's music and the go-go sound. — *Stephen Cook*

Saturday Night (Live from Washington, D.C.) / 1985 / Island ✦✦✦
The Washington-based go-go sound never became the next big R&B thing, despite all the proclamations in the 1980s. The soulful style, with its '70s funk beats and '60s horn arrangements crafted onto an '80s sensibility, was swept aside in the hip-hop revolution. This mid-'80s album featuring Trouble Funk in a great live setting illuminates its charms. Those include nonstop energy, a swaggering attitude without misogyny or vulgarity, and an earthiness often missing from mainstream urban contemporary music. —*Ron Wynn*

● **Early Singles** / Mar. 11, 1997 / Infinite Zero/American ✦✦✦✦✦
While Chuck Brown & the Soul Searchers were longer lived and E.U. scored the biggest national hit, Trouble Funk was the best and most interesting group to come out of the Washington, D.C. go-go scene, and its relentless pursuit of the good groove, propelled by buoyant horn charts, P-Funk-inspired

keyboard lines, and tireless percussion jams, was a potent and satisfying reminder in the dying days of the disco era of just how joyous, muscular, and human good dance music could sound. This compilation (released by former D.C. resident and longtime fan Henry Rollins—yep, *that* Henry Rollins) features eight cuts from the band's early, self-released 12" singles, where Trouble Funk could stretch out its tracks to eight to ten minutes without outside influences urging the band to shoot for something more commercial or radio-friendly; this is go-go with enough grease for purists and enough groove to win converts, including the epochal "Supergrit," "So Early in the Morning," and an idiosyncratic reworking of Kraftwerk's "Trans Europe Express." A valuable archival release that will also give you enough fuel to set the dancefloor burning all night long. —*Mark Deming*

● **Droppin' Bombs: The Definitive Trouble Funk** / Aug. 25, 1998 / Harmless
✦✦✦✦✦

Believe the title—this two-CD best-of is the definitive collection by the most creative group to emerge from the Washington, D.C., go-go scene. Selected by the group itself, the songs don't sound like calls to party hearty as much as recorded parties with bassist Tony Fisher as the gruff-voiced but cordial host leading the rapped call-and-response chants over potent funk grooves. But Trouble Funk's real strength lies in its savvy command of dynamics and the creative variety the band melds with the percussive power of the cowbell and conga-laden go-go rhythm. "Drop the Bomb," "Let's Get Small," the convincing go-go adaptation of Kraftwerk's hit "Trans-Europe Express" on "Trouble Funk Express," the explosive opening to "Say What," and the monster horn riff driving "Hey Fellas" are just a few of the many highlights. Even two mediocre ballads can't derail the momentum of *Droppin' Bombs*, which clearly demonstrates how Trouble Funk and go-go were the mid-'80s missing link between George Clinton's Parliament-Funkadelic mob and the rap crews that flourished later in the decade. —*Don Snowden*

U-Roy (Ewart Beckford)

b. Sep. 21, 1942, Jones Town, Jamaica
Vocals / Contemporary Reggae, Roots Reggae, Dub, DJ
Known as the Originator, U-Roy wasn't the first DJ, nor even the first to cut a record, but he was the first to shake the nation and he originated a style so distinctly unique that he single-handedly changed his homeland's music scene forever. Born Ewart Beckford in Jones Town, Jamaica, in 1942, he received his famous moniker from a young family member unable to correctly pronounce Ewart and the nickname stuck.

U-Roy's rise to fame was slow, and took almost a decade. He began back in 1961, DJing at the Doctor Dickie's Dynamite sound system. Eventually, he moved onto the Sir Mike the Musical Thunderstorm outfit, and then in 1968 to the Sir George the Atomic sound system. The DJ was then lured away by Coxsone Dodd; however, soon tiring of playing second fiddle to longtime veteran King Stitt, he returned to Sir George. Around this same time, he met up with another royal figure, King Tubby, then working as a disc cutter at Duke Reid's studio. The mechanic was just beginning his musical experiments that eventually led him to develop dub, and at the moment he was giving his proto-dub experimental discs to a handful of his favorite DJs. The following year, King Tubby launched his own Hi-Fi sound system and brought in U-Roy as his top DJ. By then, the DJ had established himself as one of the premier talents of the sound system scene. Producer Keith Hudson was the first to recognize the possibilities and took U-Roy into the studio in late 1969 to cut the song "Dynamic Fashion Way." However, the tape lay in the studio while the producer went off on a trip to the U.S. and the DJ went off to try his luck elsewhere. Lee Perry paired U-Roy with Peter Tosh and recorded "Selassie," a version of Ras Michael & the Sons of Negus' "Ethiopian National Anthem." The single was originally credited to the Reggae Boys and on its subsequent reissue, under the title "(Earth's) Rightful Ruler," it was then credited to Peter Tosh and Hugh Roy, a spelling the DJ would adhere to for the next several years. U-Roy cut one more single with Perry ("O.K. Corral") then moved on to Keith Hudson, for whom he recorded "Dynamic Fashion Way," and Bunny Lee, with whom he cut "King of the Road." He next linked with producer Lloyd Daley for two singles, "Scandal" and "Sound of the Wise," which like their predecessors created a stir amongst the grassroots sound system crowds, but barely registered beyond them.

John Holt would change all that. One night early in 1970, he attended a sound system party and caught U-Roy DJing. The singer was blown away, not

least of all because the chatterer was exhorting the enthusiastic crowd over Holt's own hit "Wear You to the Ball." The next day the singer went around to see Duke Reid and adamantly stated that the producer must record the DJ. Reid was convinced and U-Roy was promptly put into the studio to cut two songs, over classic Treasure Isle singles, of course. The first release, "Wake the Town," did exactly that and an aroused Jamaica swiftly sent the single to the top of the charts. That song was a version of Alton Ellis' "Girl I've Got a Date"; the next, "Rule the Nation," was cut over the Techniques' "Love Is Not a Gamble," and that single was as prophetic as the first. It, too, slammed up the chart, as did its follow-up, "Wear You to the Ball." For a month and a half, all three singles boldly stood astride the top three spots on the Jamaican charts. U-Roy went on to cut another 29 songs with Reid, all versions of Treasure Isle's most beloved singles. The Frontline label's 1970 compilation *Version of Wisdom* bundled up much of the DJ's classic work for Reid, bringing together two previous albums: *Versions Galore*, initially released by Trojan in 1971, and Frontline's own 1979 compilation *With Words of Wisdom*. The British Attack label also sports a slew of this material on 1974's *U-Roy*, while Trojan's *Ace From Out of Space* grabs up 30 of them. The definitive collection comes from France's Esoldun label and *Super Boss* boasts all the classic cuts the DJ recorded for Reid. "Versions galore, you can hear them by the score," U-Roy exclaimed on "Versions Galore," and indeed you could.

Every producer in town was now vying to record DJs, pillaging through their back catalogs for appropriate rhythms. In U-Roy's wake came a flood of young hopefuls, Dennis Alcapone, I- Roy, Big Youth, Scotty, Lizzy, U-Roy Junior, and many, many others. Many of these early progenitors of the DJ scene, U-Roy included, can by found on the Trojan label compilation *With a Flick of My Musical Wrist*. U-Roy himself would never again place three singles at the top of the chart, but he continued to have smash hits and made his way happily around the studios. He recorded a number of notable songs for producer Alvin Ranglin, including "Way Down South" (a version of Billy Dyce's hit "Take Warning") and "Nana Banana." Working with Glen Brown, he cut "Number One in the World" over the much-versioned "Dirty Harry" rhythm, while also recording intriguing offerings for Niney Holness and Lloyd Daley. In 1975, U-Roy teamed up once again with Bunny Lee, cutting a number of songs with the producer. In 1983, the Vista Sounds label released remixes of these cuts as *DJ Masterpieces*, which also boasts tracks by other DJs, U-Roy amongst them, recorded for the producer. Now the reigning hero of the Jamaican DJ scene, U-Roy would come to international attention via a totally unexpected source. The American soul-lite duo Hall & Oates surprisingly enough recorded a cover of the DJ's hit "Soldiering" on their eponymous album. This prompted the Virgin label to sign him and, paired with producer Prince Tony Robinson, U-Roy recorded his debut album (*Dread Inna Babylon*), backed by the Skin, Flesh & Bones Band. The following year's *Natty Rebel*, again with Robinson at the helm, found the DJ now backed by the rootsy rhythms of Lloyd Parks and Sly Dunbar, and accompanied by a pair of singers.

U-Roy was now reaching the peak of his power. His toasts were utterly relaxed and conversational, yet always in perfect synchronicity with the rhythms. The DJ had now gained a significant following in the U.K. as well, and in August 1976 visited Britain for the first time. He performed at the London Lyceum, backed by the always excellent Revolutionaries, and the 1978 *Live* EP was drawn from this phenomenal show. Back in Jamaica, U-Roy began recording his new album, *Rasta Ambassador*, filling the studio with musicians and singers, 15 strong in all. The Gladiators provided particularly sonorous backing vocals, while the band, led by the rhythm team of Sly & Robbie, created a deep roots sound appropriate to the album's title and accentuated by Robinson's deeply dubby production.

Somehow, U-Roy found time in his busy schedule to launch his own sound system, Stur-Gav, that year. He also continued to run his own labels, Del-Ma and Mego-Ann, which the DJ had set up a few years back. The year 1978 brought a new album, *Jah Son of Africa*, arguably U- Roy's best. Again, a deeply rootsy outing; with a superb supporting cast (this time the Gladiators were joined by Ken Boothe), the album showcased the DJ at his cultural height. It was to be his final album for Virgin. In 1991, the label released the *Natty Rebel—Extra Version* album, which pulled tracks from both *Natty Rebel* and *Jah Son of Africa*, and also included the *Live* EP. A limited-edition three-CD box set *Three From the Frontline* appeared this same year, and bundled together *Version of Wisdom*, *Rasta Ambassador*, and *Natty Rebel—Extra Version*.

In the run-up to the 1980 election, Stur-Gav fell victim to the violence that swept Jamaica and the sound system was destroyed. Undeterred, U-Roy relaunched it the following year and brought in new DJs, including up-and-coming stars Josey Wales and Charlie Chaplin. U-Roy would collaborate with the former for the entertaining *Teacher Meets the Student*, whose tracks date from around this period. But perhaps the DJ was taking on too much between his sound system, labels, and live appearances, for his next album, *Love Is Not a Gamble* showed a sharp decline in standards. U-Roy seemed to recognize this and subsequently his recorded output slowed to a trickle of singles. He did, however, continue to perform live and on stage, and his power remained undiminished.

In 1982, he appeared at Reggae Sunsplash for the first time and a song from his powerful set can be heard on the *Best of Festival—Day One* compilation. In 1983, the DJ was behind the superb *King Stur-Gav Hi Fi Lee Unlimited* album, a live session recorded at his own sound system that featured a clutch of crucial DJs from Dillinger to the young Beenie Man, his two favorite protégés Charlie Chaplin and Josey Wales, as well as U-Roy himself. The follow-up, *King Stur-Gav Sounds Live at Clarendon J.A.*, amazingly doesn't feature U-Roy at all, except in the capacity of selector. The next year brought the excellent "Hustling" single, cut for producer Gussie Clarke; "Get Ready" recorded for Ossie Thomas; and a return engagement at Reggae Sunsplash that year, with a second appearance in 1985.

Silence followed for two years; then, as if to make up for lost time, in 1987 U-Roy jumped back into recording with a vengeance. He teamed up with Tappa Zukie for the *Line Up and Come* album, a stunning return to form that cruelly gained little notice. He also released *Music Addict*, overseen by Prince Jazzbo, that same year. However, halfway through that latter album, the DJ seems to run out of steam. Afterward, U-Roy once again lapsed into a lengthy silence, at least in the studio; he found his voice for Reggae Sunsplash the next summer, though, and kept it well exercised for another appearance in 1990. The following year found him back in London, on stage at London's Hammersmith Palais. But during all this time, the DJ continued steering clear of the recording studio. It was U.K. producer Mad Professor who coaxed him back in during 1991 for the *True Born African* album. Since then, U-Roy has continued recording under the Professor's aegis. *Smile Awhile* appeared in 1993 and featured a number of guest stars, including Yabby You, Aisha, Sandra Cross, and lovers rock heroine Susan Cadogan. Incidentally, the album's title was inspired by a line from the DJ's old hit "Flashing My Whip" ("smile awhile and give your face a rest"). Also in 1993, the DJ guested on Nolan Irie's album *Work So Hard*. In 1996, U-Roy joined Cadogan for a remake of her classic hit "Hurt So Good," which the DJ had previously versioned on *Smile Awhile*. U-Roy also released his own new album that year (*Babylon Kingdom Must Fall*). Four more years passed before its follow-up hit the shops. *Serious Matter* found the DJ toasting over an album's worth of classic songs, accompanied by a host of veteran vocalists, Dennis Brown, Gregory Isaacs, and Horace Andy amongst them. —*Jo-Ann Greene*

● **Dread in a Babylon** / 1975 / Frontline ✦✦✦✦✦

Even without the music, this album would still leap off the racks; its photo of U Roy exhaling a mushroom cloud of marijuana smoke from his ever-available pipe ranks among the all-time greatest covers, regardless of genre. However, U Roy doesn't have any trouble coming across as a distinctive presence; his scattershot repertoire of barks, chants, and screams is as critical or more important as the deft, unobtrusive backing woven behind him. U Roy imposes his own willful style, regardless of setting. Sometimes he pulls off a positively poppy veneer on tracks like "Runaway Girl" or "Silver Bird"; other times, he extemporizes slightly ahead of the beat on "Natty Don't Fear" or "The Great Psalms." His lyrics run the gamut of Rastafarian concerns, from facing adversity ("Dreadlocks Dread") to female troubles ("I Can't Love Another") and royalist run-ins ("Chalice in the Palace"). The uncredited musicians stay out of the way (although they get their own album-closing instrumental, "Trench Town Rock"). This album ranks among the '70s dub masterpieces, even if the odd lyrical clinker keeps it from perfection; "Runaway Girl"'s glistening skank can't paper over its sexism (which suggests the girl in question "may be nice/but you're not that smart"). Even so, sometimes an artist only needs charisma to get across, and U Roy handily wins on that score. —*Ralph Heibutzki*

Super Boss: The Best of U Roy / Jan. 29, 2002 / Nascente ✦✦✦✦✦

There have been many U-Roy collections since he burst on the Jamaican scene in 1970, but there are only two that are worth owning: The one on

Blood & Fire and this one. Super Boss collects 21 absolutely classic U-Roy tracks assembled by journalist Ian McCann of *Q* magazine in the U.K. with a strong emphasis on the collaborations. For instance, here is "You Keep On Running" with Delroy Wilson, "Rightful Ruler" with Peter Tosh, and "Tide Is High" with the Paragons. Other Jamaican stalwarts like Slim Smith, the Melodians, and Hopeton Lewis make appearances on various plates. But what is most prevalent is the U-Roy toasting style, the easy, slippery, laid-back groove over the dub. Check the dancehall hits like "Dynamic Fashion Way," "Behold," "Love I Bring," "Big Boy & Teacher," and "Tom Drunk." The groove is backbone slippery, the skank is righteous, and the shimmy in the hips comes from the flow of U-Roy's ultra-Rasta hipsterism. This is the real rap, kicking it back on the mic as the punters shimmy across the floor, crocked to the glory on their favorite mess. All of the tracks here were singles, as either the A- or B-sides, and all of them are vintage from 1970 to 1979, the true glory years of U-Roy. This is the wap'n'bap'n time dread jam in ultra cool sequence and righteous flow. —*Thom Jurek*

Usher (Usher Raymond)

b. 1979, Atlanta, GA

Vocals / Club/Dance, Urban, Hip-Hop

After being spotted by a LaFace Records executive at a talent show in his hometown of Atlanta, GA, it took no time for hip-hop crooner Usher Raymond's career to take off. The 14-year-old auditioned for LaFace Records co-founder L.A. Reid, who signed the gospel choir boy to a recording contract. Raymond was introduced to the world simply as "Usher," and released his debut album of the same name in 1994, which featured coexecutive producer Sean "Puffy" Combs. The first single, "Think of You," gained Usher notoriety and reached gold status. From that initial exposure, Usher was approached to do other projects. In 1995, he recorded a national holiday jingle for Coca-Cola. He also joined several top male R&B vocalists to form Black Men United for the single "You Will Know," featured on the *Jason's Lyric* soundtrack. He also teamed with teen singing sensation Monica for a duet remake of Latimore's "Let's Straighten It Out."

After graduating from high school, Usher graduated as well to his sophomore release, *My Way*, in 1997. In an attempt to display his maturity and songwriting abilities, Usher cowrote six of the nine songs and enlisted the help of producers Jermaine Dupri, Babyface, and, again, Sean "Puffy" Combs. The album's first single, "You Make Me Wanna," reestablished Usher as one of R&B's hottest artists, and also made him a crossover sensation; it topped the R&B charts for 11 weeks, hit number two pop, and eventually went double platinum. Both of the follow-up singles, "Nice & Slow" and "My Way," also went platinum; the former stayed at number one on the R&B charts for eight weeks and became his first number-one pop single. In the meantime, Usher launched an acting career, appearing in the 1998 horror spoof *The Faculty* and the 1999 urban high school drama *Light It Up*. To tide fans over, he issued a concert recording titled simply *Live* in 1999. Usher returned with his third proper album, *All About U*, toward the end of 2000. His third album, *8701* (2001), moved Usher from a teen pop star to a sultry R&B singer. —*Lynda Lane*

● **My Way** / Sep. 16, 1997 / La Face ✦✦✦✦

Usher proved that he had a strong, soulful voice with his self-titled debut, but he fulfilled his potential on his second record, *My Way*. What makes Usher distinctive from his urban loveman peers is the fact that he doesn't oversing; he simply delivers his songs soulfully. Unfortunately, he falls prey to uneven material, just like any of his peers, but there are more strong songs on *My Way* than many contemporary R&B albums from the late '80s. Both Jermaine Dupri and Babyface contribute seamless productions and fine songs; respectively, "You Make Me Wanna..." and "Bedtime" are their best ballad contributions. Even if the ballads are usually seductive and romantic, cuts like the funky "Just Like Me," which features a cameo from Lil' Kim, might make you wish Usher didn't play it cool all of the time. And while it's refreshing to hear a hip-hop/urban R&B album clock in at a reasonable running time, it would have been nice if the tenth track was something other than a remix of "You Make Me Wanna." Nevertheless, it's a strong second effort that showcases Usher at his best. —*Stephen Thomas Erlewine*

Live / Mar. 23, 1999 / La Face ✦✦

Usher broke big in 1997 with his second record, *My Way* and there was no looking back. After it rocketed up the charts, Usher capitalized on his good looks and sweet charms, attempting to break into movies and pushing his celebrity status. All of which meant, of course, that there was little time for him to concentrate on a sequel to *My Way*. Nevertheless, in pop music it's imperative to stay in the public eye, so *Live* was released a year and a half after *My Way*. Live albums often feel like a way to buy time while an artist figures out what to do, and there's no question that Usher's entry is part of that time-honored tradition, since there's no real reason for him to release a live album as his third record. And *Live* does feel like filler, since the only real evidence of his charismatic performances are the continual shrieks from the teenage audience. As a matter fact, he sounds tired and weary on many tracks, even his signature tunes "You Make Me Wanna" and "My Way." Hardcore fans will find his Bobby Brown medley of interest, since it doesn't appear on either studio record, and the live performances here all fall flat. The remixes that are tacked on to the end are better, especially Jermaine Dupri's reworking of "My Way," but they don't necessarily improve an unnecessary album. *—Stephen Thomas Erlewine*

8701 / Aug. 7, 2001 / Arista ✦✦✦
Usher has the reputation as a loverman, largely because he fits the bill so well. He looks good, his material is smooth and seductive, and he has a nice voice, even if he tends to favor miasma. This has been true throughout his career, and remains true on his third album, *8701*, a classy, seductive affair masterminded by Usher, Jermaine Dupri, and Antonio "L.A." Reid. There's not much new here, but Usher does move further in both directions—the ballads are lusher, the dance numbers hit a bit harder—but not so much so that it's really noticeable. Overall, the record is probably his strongest yet, but he still suffers from a lack of really memorable material (the singles usually are pretty good, but the album tracks are filler) and a tendency to oversing. Because of these two things, *8701* is more mood music than anything else, and while it does work fairly well on that level, it's not memorable outside of that mood. *—Stephen Thomas Erlewine*

Watts Prophets

f. 1967, Los Angeles, CA
Fusion, Poetry, Spoken Word
The West Coast's answer to the Last Poets, Watts Prophets didn't get quite the same recognition for their contributions to raising black consciousness and laying the foundations for rap. The group was formed at the Watts Writer's Workshop, an organization started by screenwriter Budd Schulberg designed to provide a creative outlet in the wake of the 1965 Watts riots. Father Amde Hamilton (an Ethiopian Orthodox priest, born Anthony Hamilton), Otis O'Solomon, and Richard Dedeaux met in the workshop circa 1967, and soon began performing together as Watts Prophets, setting their socially and politically conscious poetry to spare, often jazzy musical backing. They won second place in an inner-city talent show, which led to a residency at John Daniels' Maverick's Flat club in South Central L.A.; they also performed at fundraisers, in prisons, and around their community whenever possible. In 1969, Watts Prophets debuted with *The Black Voices: On the Streets in Watts*. Two years later, the group released *Rappin' Black in a White World* on ALA, with accompaniment by ex-Motown pianist DeeDee McNeil. The radical, incendiary tone of their work fit right in with the emerging black power movement, and attracted unfavorable notice from the government; the home of the Watts Writers Project was destroyed by fire in 1975 after having been infiltrated by an FBI informant. Record deals were hard to come by and were continually falling through (including one with Bob Marley's home, Tuff Gong, that evaporated with Marley's premature death). Still, Watts Prophets remained sporadically active as performers, and were rediscovered by the hip-hop generation as their records were sampled frequently; additionally, O'Solomon's "Hey World" was covered by Ziggy Marley. In 1997, Watts Prophets released an album of new material with pianist Horace Tapscott, *When the 90's Came*, on Payday/ffrr, which also reissued their two original LPs. The Prophets remain dedicated community activists today, promoting creative self-expression and the arts to young people around Southern California and beyond. *—Steve Huey*

The Black Voices: On the Streets in Watts / 1969 / ffrr ✦✦✦✦
The obvious comparison for this group is the Last Poets. Like those guys, the Prophets deliver politically charged poetry over African drums. Unlike them though, the mood here is a tad more relaxed, if the polemic certainly isn't. While each member steps to the mike to deliver his message, the others

can be heard in the background, adding a "right on" or "preach it" to the proceedings. Over most of the tracks a saxophone screeches and yowls, adding a nails-against-the-chalkboard tension to the proceedings. This caustic cup of tea isn't for every taste, but those hooked on the Last Poets will get a blast from the Left Coast side of things. Those into the movement, or the '60s in general, will find this a valuable document. *—Rob Ferrier*

Rappin' Black in a White World / 1971 / ffrr ✦✦✦
OK, so discs are distinct documents, especially a reissue like the second Watts Prophets record, linked to a specific place and time, but how about some consumer value, too? Why not pair this disc with the Afro-poetics quartet's debut from back in the day and have a historically valuable CD with a decent running length? *Rappin' Black in a White World* clocks in at under a half-hour, and it's disconcerting to look up after hearing what you think are two or three pieces and find you're already on track nine. It's totally a cappella, working off WordSound rhythms at first, with Dee Dee MaNail adding a female voice plus a piano and arco bass gradually fleshing out the later pieces. The bass enters on "Pain," and maybe not coincidentally, that's the first piece per se that's not just a quick hit of political self-affirmation. That's a big problem with the material here: the words are mostly about venting frustration, sloganeering, and raising consciousness, all of which may have been necessary and satisfying in the moment, but there's not much metaphor or insight that make you go hmm decades later. McNail's "What Is a Man" is a suite with the next tracks finding the three male Prophets offering different takes on the question. Richard Dedaux's "Tenements" is the best, throwing light on the internal head-trip frustrations of everyday life. "What It Is, Sisters" is kind of a surrealistic, first-generation Afro-centric "She Watches Channel Zero" that heaps ridicule on a Tom Jones-loving black woman (huh?). "There's a Difference Between a Black Man and a Nigger" flips gender on that proto-buppie front, offering a black female perspective on men and militancy that includes some sharp observations on those who prefer their women "Shine Eye Gal"-style. McNail's tracks are the most substantial—"The Prostitute" also takes you down inside to feelings and doubts. The pieces on *Rappin' Black in a White World* give very little sense of the times beyond the venting—it's a one-dimensional portrait of the era (again, not that it wasn't a necessary catharsis then) when you would expect poets like the Watts Prophets to provide deeper, more human/humane insights. And it's just too damn short. *—Don Snowden*

● **When the 90's Came** / Mar. 11, 1997 / ffrr ✦✦✦✦
Over a sort of trip-hop/acid jazzy groove broken by a "Superfly" strings bridge, the title track of *When the 90's Came* details Amde Hamilton's futile attempt to overcome his "negative social outlook" due to the same old, same old social problems persisting nearly 30 years after the Watts Prophets' first recording. But know what else happened when the '90s came? The Watts Prophets came back matured and fully grown into an elder/griot role for the hip-hop generation, their words now tempered and deepened by life-experience details, and *When the 90's Came* is an extremely convincing return. The sound collage mated to rhythm tracks technique developed in hip-hop turns out to be a perfect fit for the Prophets: the lead voice comfortably cuts through the arrangements throughout, and the counter commentaries are more creative. The varied lyrical themes are matched by a wider musical spectrum to draw from than was available 25-30 years ago: Horace Tapscott's piano brings back the jazz roots on several tracks, but "Hey World" tackles ecology over a moody keyboard bass, and the strong "Me Today, You Tomorrow" is reggae produced by Ras Michael. "Trippin'" rides the hip-hop tip over Rob Bacon's funky bass and producer DJ Quik's drums, and the addiction tale "Searchin'" is treated with a jungle drum machine and discordant piano and sax by producers Us3. "Everybody Watches" tackles apathy about African starvation and inner-city blues, and a "children today are raised like chickens" metaphor triggers an effective meditation on education with gentle Tapscott piano musings on "Breed What You Need." They use understated sarcasm, which can be as effective in bringing word as pissed-off anger, for the antiresignation message coursing through another nice trip-hop groove on "Nothin' New." Richard Dedeaux's "I Remember Watts" has a wonderful opener about other cities needing millions of watts to light up, but only one Watts was necessary to light up Los Angeles, and the lonely blues harmonica works on a lot of levels. The string of unaccompanied poems closing the disc doesn't lose the thread: Otis O'Solomon's "Public Enemy Number One" condemns the materialist basis of society, but "Hongry for Your Love" deals

on basic human need and "Vanity" looks at self-awareness. There's food for thought in them, not just youthful venting and flailing about, and a depth of experience that boils down to that old blues adage about paying your dues. The title track is reprised in their old school style, and you might add that when the '90s came, the Watts Prophets really found, and came into, their element as the griots/elders for the hip-hop youth they were looking for when they were coming up. —*Don Snowden*

Saul Williams

Vocals / Political Rap, Poetry, Hip-Hop

First establishing himself as an influential poet, and then as an award-winning screenwriter/actor, Saul Williams then went on to establish himself as an MC. His approach to MCing, though, wasn't exactly in line with the traditional school of hip-hop. His rhymes weren't really rhymes but rather his poetry delivered in a frenzied spoken-word manner that was more rhythmic than alliterate. His first major recording was a collaboration with KRS-One, "Ocean Within," which appeared on the soundtrack to *Slam*, the award-winning film he not only cowrote but also starred in. Around this same time in the late '90s, he began collaborating with other musicians, one of the more notable and impressive being the title track to drum'n'bass producer Krust's *Coded Language* album. These one-off performances, along with the attention that Williams garnered thanks to *Slam*, led to a deal with Rick Rubin's American Recordings. In late 2001, the long-awaited and much-hyped Williams solo debut album, *Amethyst Rock Star*, hit the streets. The album featured a full-scale band and Rubin's production, with Williams' manic vocals taking the fore. It wasn't a straight-ahead rap album, more rock/rap in the style of Rage Against the Machine than anything. Critical opinion wavered, though Williams indeed seemed to impress many; he not only was invited to the *2001 Detroit Electronic Music Festival* but also found himself a popular concert draw in Europe. —*Jason Birchmeier*

Amethyst Rock Star / May 8, 2001 / American ♦♦

The art of spoken word is a terribly delicate one. For every Jack Kerouac or Gil Scott-Heron—writers who were able to bring a melodicism and added dimension to the spoken word—there are a million bad poets who highjack open mic nights, making audiences cringe all across this great land. Saul Williams is a step above those hacks, but unless you've got a jones to get in touch with your inner Bobby Seale or have plenty of pent-up rage you'd like someone else to excise, this record is likely to make you scratch your head and ask "Huh?" Instead of giving his spoken poems a melody and rhythm, Williams prefers to use words as clubs, beating the listener over the head with abrasive, staccato runs while heavy hip-hop beats blast in the background. Some of the language is downright laughable (see the trite themes of "Fearless" for example) in any context, and the rest is mediocre at best. —*Steve Kurutz*

Zhané

f. 1993, Philadelphia, PA
Contemporary R&B, Club/Dance, Urban

Given a high-profile spot on the all-star compilation *Roll Wit tha Flava* as their first recording opportunity, Zhané lived up to the pressure and came away with one of the hip-hop party anthems of all time, "Hey, Mr. DJ." Jean Norris and Renee Neufville initially met while both were studying music at Philadelphia's Temple University (Norris is originally from Rhode Island, Neufville from Jamaica). After meeting Naughty By Nature Kay Gee, Zhané impressed the producer enough to go right into the studio to record for *Roll Wit tha Flava*. When "Hey, Mr. DJ" was released as a separate single as well, it hit number six on the pop charts and earned the group a contract with Motown in 1994. Their debut album, *Pronounced Jah-Nay*, produced two further Top 40 hits ("Groove Thang," "Sending My Love") and went gold by the end of the year. Zhané kept busy during 1995-1996 with spots on tracks by Busta Rhymes and De La Soul as well as new songs of their own on the *NFL Jams* and *NBA 50th Anniversary* compilations and the soundtracks to *Higher Learning* and *A Low Down Dirty Shame*—the latter, "Shame," became their fourth Top 40 hit. Norris and Neufville returned with a new LP in 1997, co-produced by Kay Gee, Eddie F., and themselves. It peaked just outside the Top 40. —*John Bush*

● **Pronounced Jah-Nay** / Feb. 15, 1994 / Motown ♦♦♦♦

In late 1993, the R&B vocal duo Zhané scored a Top Ten pop hit with the '70s Philly soul meets disco meets '90s hip-hop R&B smash "Hey Mr. DJ," a sleek slice of earthy, sophisticated soul that stands as one of the best R&B/pop hits of the '90s. Several months later the duo issued its highly anticipated debut, *Pronounced Jah-Nay*, on Motown, and the album yielded hit single after hit single for the better part of a year. Melding classic soul with honey-sweet vocals, hip-hop beats, jazz, disco, and pop, the duo stood out from the onslaught of manufactured R&B acts that dominated the airwaves and pop charts in the early to mid- '90s. The duo scored a Top 20 pop hit with its follow-up single, "Groove Thang," which, although still smooth and infectious, sounds like "Hey Mr. DJ" part two. Other singles included the glorious, elegant, and sleek "Sending My Love," which also managed to crack the pop Top 40, the funky R&B hit "Vibe," and the ballad "You're Sorry Now." The duo seems to shine brightest when tackling jazz ballads, such as the Sade-ish "La, La, La" and "Off My Mind," two songs that were never hits but easily rank as the album's overlooked treasures. *Pronounced Jah-Nay* is definitely one of the better R&B albums of the '90s—unfortunately, this album's success was never repeated, and that was most likely due to lousy marketing and single choices for the duo's sophomore outing, *Saturday Night*. —*Jose F. Promis*

Saturday Night / Apr. 22, 1997 / Motown ♦♦♦

More textured and funkier than their debut album, Zhane's second record *Saturday Night* is an infectious set of percolating funk, club beats, and new jack harmonies. The songs aren't always as strong as the performances, but Zhane's vocal charisma makes such shortcomings forgivable. —*Leo Stanley*

Index